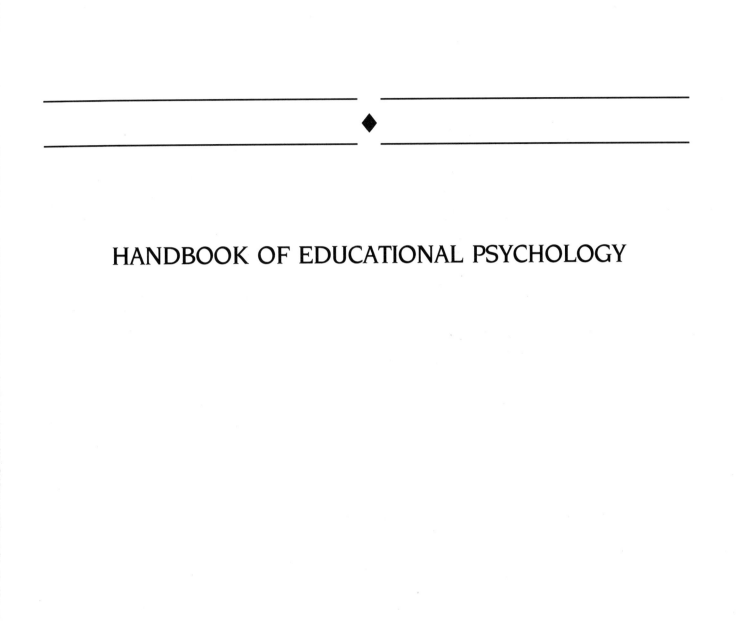

# HANDBOOK OF EDUCATIONAL PSYCHOLOGY

# HANDBOOK OF
# EDUCATIONAL PSYCHOLOGY

David C. Berliner
EDITOR

Robert C. Calfee
EDITOR

A Project of Division 15,
The Division of Educational
Psychology of the American
Psychological Association

**MACMILLAN LIBRARY REFERENCE USA**

Simon & Schuster Macmillan

New York

Prentice Hall International

London   Mexico City   New Delhi   Singapore   Sydney   Toronto

Macmillan Library Reference USA
Simon & Schuster Macmillan
1633 Broadway
New York, NY 10019

Library of Congress Catalog Card Number: 95-43348

Printed in the United States of America

Printing number
1   2   3   4   5   6   7   8   9   10

**Library of Congress Cataloging-in-Publication Data**

Handbook of educational psychology / David C. Berliner, editor, Robert
  C. Calfee, editor.
     p.   cm.
   Includes bibliographical references and index.
   ISBN 0-02-897089-6 (alk. paper)
   1. Educational psychology—Handbooks, manuals, etc.  I. Berliner.
David C.  II. Calfee, Robert C.
LB1051.H2354  1996
370.15—dc20                        95-43348
                                      CIP

# CONTENTS

## Part
## III

## SCHOOL CURRICULUM AND PSYCHOLOGY

## Part
# IV
## TEACHING AND INSTRUCTION

## Part
# V
## FOUNDATIONS OF THE DISCIPLINE

# REVIEWERS

Many reviewers provided invaluable suggestions that improved the quality of the manuscripts herein. Authors have expressed their thanks to those individuals personally as well as in the individual chapters. Here we wish to acknowledge the helpful considerations of a subset of those reviewers who were formally asked by the editors, on behalf of the Division of Educational Psychology, to help in the development of this reference work.

Donna Alvermann
University of Georgia, Athens

Richard C. Anderson
University of Illinois, Champaign

Ronald Berk
Johns Hopkins University

Jeffrey Bisanz
Michigan State University

Phyllis Blumenfeld
University of Michigan, Ann Arbor

Martin Booth
Cambridge University, England

Hilda Borko
University of Colorado, Boulder

Steven Bossert
Syracuse University

Henry Braun
Educational Testing Service

Susan Burgraff
Mount Holyoke College

Susan Carey
Harvard University

John B. Carroll
University of North Carolina, Chapel Hill

Robbie Case
Ontario Institute for Study of Education, Toronto

Susan Chipman
Office of Naval Research

Renée Clift
University of Illinois, Champaign

Michael Cole
University of California, San Diego

Lyn Corno
Teachers College, Columbia University

Martin Covington
University of California, Berkeley

Lee J. Cronbach
Stanford University

Edward Deci
University of Rochester

Andrea diSessa
University of California, Berkeley

Jacquelynne Eccles
University of Michigan, Ann Arbor

Robert H. Ennis
University of Illinois, Champaign

Noel Entwistle
University of Edinburgh, Scotland

Marshall Farr
Independent Consultant

Dexter Fletcher
Institute for Defense Analyses

Nathaniel Gage
Stanford University

Ronald Gallimore
University of California, Los Angeles

Frederick Genesee
McGill University, Montreal

Ronald Gentile
State University of New York at Buffalo

Pamela Grossman
University of Washington

Steven Guberman
University of Colorado, Boulder

Jan-Eric Gustafsson
University of Göteborg, Sweden

Giyoo Hatano
Dokko University, Japan

# ◆ 1 ◆

# INTRODUCTION TO A DYNAMIC AND RELEVANT
# EDUCATIONAL PSYCHOLOGY

### Robert C. Calfee
STANFORD UNIVERSITY

### David C. Berliner
ARIZONA STATE UNIVERSITY

Developing a handbook for a field of scholarship offers an unusual opportunity to examine what is known about the area. It allows scholars to reflect on present, past, and future. It provides a chance to examine the extant knowledge, to consider the current organization of that knowledge, and to propose new conceptions. It opens the way to explore fundamental and unresolved questions within the discipline. It offers scholars the opportunity to rethink the paradigms that undergird the discipline and to reexamine prevailing methodologies.

In every field of study, beliefs about what is essence and what is peripheral are not static but change over the decades, reflecting trends in scholarship both within and beyond the discipline. Disciplined inquiry in education has an additional feature. Transformations in the surrounding society are reflected in education, so that the very phenomena under investigation evolve into new forms. For all of these reasons a handbook of educational psychology presents a particular challenge, perched as it is between the discipline of scientific psychology, on the one hand, and the field of educational practice, on the other. The creation of this handbook has required authors to evaluate contributions to the knowledge, concepts, and methods in the discipline from which educational psychology springs as well as the field of practice that educational psychology aims to improve. Our tasks have been made more difficult because scientific psychology and educational practice are both undergoing enormous change. In both cases, the paradigms for interpretation are changing. This handbook has been designed to respond both to the challenges and to the opportunities that such turbulence produces.

We begin with a story, a fictional account of a day in the life of a teacher, a case study that we examine from the perspectives of educational psychology. Obviously, this is only one of the many stories that could be told to illustrate how educational psychology and educational practice relate. We rely on the narrative to introduce the volume because tales are more engaging than expositions, because a story places conceptual issues into an integrative context, and because qualitative methods are playing an increasingly important role in educational psychology.

---

## A TEACHER'S STORY

---

It is 7:32 in the morning as Andrea Cornbluth starts her day at the Melvin Klinger Middle School. Students will not arrive until 8:35, giving Andrea a chance to enter composition scores into the grade book. It had taken more time than she had expected to read the 120 essays the night before. Her math methods course had gone overtime, and it was 9:00 p.m. before she arrived home. She graded papers until 11:30 and fell asleep exhausted.

She took a moment to ruminate over this year's collection of students. Adolescence is a time of incredible change, full of trials for a middle-school faculty. Some youngsters have the physical characteristics of young adults, while others have yet to enter puberty. Some possess the maturity (and responsibilities) of an adult; others are still childlike. The Klinger students are typical of those in many contemporary schools. A large percentage of the youngsters come from poor families. Some families are intact, but many of the students live with a single parent or with relatives. Forty percent are of Hispanic origin; most speak English, but as a second language. The rest of the student body comprises roughly equal proportions of African-American, Anglo, and Asian youngsters.

Andrea, who grew up in a middle-class and largely white neighborhood, is fascinated by this variety, by the cacophony

---

We are grateful for the comments of N. L. Gage on drafts of this chapter.

of languages in Klinger's halls and school yards. She has been on the job for three years and is confident about her performance as a history teacher. Unfortunately, at year's beginning she was abruptly assigned also to teach a remedial math class. It has been a challenge. Most of the time she feels as though she is only a page or two ahead of her students.

Ten minutes before class, Ricardo Fuentes, Mary Douglas, and Harold Thu enter the room and Andrea's solitude is over. Today these students are to reenact for fellow seventh graders the speeches of the founding fathers at the outset of the Revolutionary War. The students have donned costumes and wigs. Andrea smiles at the sight, wondering why mathematics can't be as much fun as history.

As first period begins, Andrea worries about the benefits of this experience for her mainstreamed special education students. The presenters are using original documents, and many in the class have struggled with the archaic speech. A month ago she had led the class through a simulation on trade and tax agreements between England and the colonies. She prepared several lecture/discussion segments on economic issues, and twice brought in videos for discussion. Now the class will reenact the colonists' decisions: Should they declare themselves independent, or remain loyal to the King?

She hopes that the project will work out. What if students get the giggles? What will she do if—? Her thoughts are interrupted as Mr. DiMatteo suddenly drops in for an unscheduled observation. DiMatteo, the assistant principal for instruction, has offered numerous pointers since her arrival. His year-end evaluation will determine whether she receives tenure. "God," she thinks, "I really hope this goes OK—I hope they don't get the giggles!"

The class begins. Patrick Henry, played by Fuentes, a 4-foot-high firebrand who arrived 3 years earlier from El Salvador, opens by rousing the group to sedition. Thu, a Tory in dandy garb, begs the colonists to keep their contract with the King. Douglas, an impassioned Abigail Adams, reads a letter from her husband John, supporting independence. When she finishes, the class seems ready to take up arms. Well, most of the class. Andrea notices that Henry and Clarice are slumped in their seats, walled off from the performance. She wonders, not for the first time, how to get through to them.

After the speeches, cheers, boos, and wisecracks, Andrea separates the class into four teams. She allows each team 10 minutes for small-group work, and 15 minutes for individual writing: "If you were a colonist, would you remain loyal to the crown or become a rebel?" While the students are writing, Andrea wonders what they will remember of this lesson in years to come. How will any of this apply to their lives? She wonders, too, whether she asks for too much writing from a history class, and whether all the small-group work she does is as efficient as just telling them history, as so many of her teachers did when she was a student. The 50-minute period passes quickly, but she knows that DiMatteo is big on personal relevance, so this assignment should be a plus for her.

During the break before the remedial math class, she skims through a few essays. She is enthused by the sheer extent of the students' prose. A few months earlier it was a challenge to coax forth a paragraph, especially from students for whom English was a second language. Now most students can churn out page-long reports on brief notice. Except for Henry and Clarice. But on to the math class and fractions.

Reading the Revolutionary War essays later that evening, she reflects on the variety of students' responses. A Vietnamese girl describes the horror of war from her personal experiences. Three boys talk about the glory of battle. Some students see the speeches as dead documents, while others find inspiration for their own lives. During the small-group discussions that preceded their writing, several seemed to connect the assignment to their future rights and responsibilities as citizens, but others are still writing about "history."

All in all, the exercise came off quite well, and Andrea ponders again why mathematics cannot be taught more like history, using discussions and essays to develop student's mathematical thinking. She is not sure what and how much mathematics is learned from her daily routine of review, presentation, drill and practice, homework assignment. She wonders whether it would help to supplement her mathematics teaching with computer programs. But then she leaves the frustrations of math to return to the essays. Should she simply comment on the work or assign grades? Can she honestly assign grades to students' personal reactions? Can she fail a student who has made a genuine effort? What will DiMatteo think if she gives all students the same grade? Will students be motivated if there is no competition for grades? And what about Henry and Clarice? For the 10th time that day she returns to the question, "How can I reach them?" And for the second evening in a row, Andrea falls asleep exhausted.

## STORIES AND PROTOCOLS

Variations of the preceding story are spun out every day in millions of classrooms. This account of teaching in a multiethnic urban middle school contrasts with tales from a wealthy suburban high school, a military training program, or a Christian fundamentalist school. And teachers' stories differ from those of students, parents, and researchers. Common to all of these accounts, however, is the same underlying set of particulars—*someone* teaching *something* to *someone else* in some *setting*, a schema that Joseph Schwab (1978) laid out many years ago. The interplay among these "commonplaces" is at the heart of educational psychology's field of study. The someone (usually a teacher, but perhaps an aide, tutor, book, computer, or parent) acts to promote learning of something (reading or mathematics, but also tennis strokes or moral values) to someone else (usually a student, but sometimes friends, co-workers, or relatives) in some context (often a classroom, but as well in everyday, natural situations like playgrounds, homes, or offices). Recounting narratives of educational commonplaces—teaching and learning, teachers and learners—is the first step in the scientific enterprise of understanding and predicting.

Stories are a form of protocol, the fundamental record that is the basic stuff of research. Protocols may be in written, audio, or video formats, analyzed at a micro or macro level, captured as on-the-fly observations of playground activities or transcribed as the record of an intelligence test. In all these instances, the protocol—the record of what transpired—is the researcher's starting point. Protocols are the foundation for making categories, assigning numbers and testing hypotheses, for interpreting a statistical analysis and assessing a theoretical model:

The refinement of the protocol language—the language of what you "see"—is requisite to the nobler language of theory—the language of what you think you "see." (Mandler & Kesson, 1959, p. 169)

## THE ANALYSIS OF PROTOCOLS

How can Andrea's story be submitted to theoretical analysis? Sociology, anthropology, critical theory, and philosophy are among the many areas of scholarship with legitimate claims to this protocol. Each brings to bear a collection of analytic tools; each offers a particular perspective. But the concepts, theories, and methods of educational psychology provide a distinctive view of instructional situations, particularly those situated in classrooms and schools, a view in which the individual—student, teacher, administrator, aide, or parent—is the focus of attention. Educational psychologists have developed particular habits of mind that focus on behaviors, thoughts, and interindividual interactions. Some of those conceptions about schooling intersect with the dilemmas of practice that confront Andrea on a regular basis. We can use concepts and methods from the field of educational psychology to gain insight into Andrea's protocol: her concerns about learning, her worry about individual students, her anxieties about teaching math, her indecisions about grading.

### Educational Psychology, Learning, and Motivation

While teaching history, Andrea wondered what students would remember and be able to apply from her lesson, and by doing so she connected to two topics that are central to scientific psychology: learning and transfer. Contemporary views of these core topics are presented in two chapters of the *Handbook*. Chapter 2, by Greeno, Collins, and Resnick, is about cognition and learning, while chapter 3, by Mayer and Wittrock, covers transfer of learning. Because these are central topics in scientific psychology, they receive continuous attention by researchers, and hence undergo major changes from one generation of scholars to the next. The coverage of these topics in this *Handbook* is remarkably different from what would have been written in 1970 and what will be written in 2020.

Andrea prepared her students by engaging them with critical issues from the Revolutionary War. She then used a vivid history lesson with costumes and speeches, and had the students engage in group discussion to decide for themselves whether or not to join in the insurrection. In these ways, Andrea made the lesson and the topic more engaging, meaningful, and personal than if she had lectured on the topics. She increased her student's interest and attention as well as the memorability of the lesson and the topic for most students, though perhaps not for Henry and Clarice. Motivation, like learning, is also a central topic of scientific psychology. These issues are explored in chapter 4, by Graham and Weiner, who deal with theories and principles, and in chapter 5, by Stipek, who reviews research on instructional contexts. Learning and motivation, covered in the first section of this *Handbook,* are subjects of primary importance for educational psychologists and teachers alike.

### Educational Psychology and Individual Differences

Beyond the generalities of learning and motivation, educational psychology must deal with the fact that people differ. The physical and psychological development of the students at Klinger School is much on Andrea's mind because middle-school children, particularly, are undergoing profound changes in cognitive, physical, psychosocial, and psychosexual development. Educational and developmental psychology have long been linked in schools of education as foundation courses designed to help teachers understand the nature of individual differences, both the differences associated with development and those that arise from other sources.

The body of knowledge that informs Andrea as she addresses her students' developmental needs is treated in two *Handbook* chapters. Chapter 6, by Paris and Cunningham, describes the development of young children into middle-school students, roughly preschool age through adolescence. Chapter 7, by Wigfield, Eccles, and Pintrich, describes further development from early adolescence to adulthood.

But differences among Andrea's students reflect more than developmental factors. This is evident to Andrea as she scans her students' papers and sees differences in creativity, intelligence, motivation, language, and writing skill. Individual differences have fascinated and challenged parents and teachers throughout history and became a subject for educational psychologists after Sir Francis Galton's (1869) mid-19th century investigations. These topics permeate many *Handbook* chapters, two of which are devoted exclusively to the insights that contemporary educational psychology brings to these issues. Chapter 8, by Gustafsson and Undheim, reviews the issues surrounding cognitive functions; educational psychology's contributions to the concept of intelligence are included in this chapter. Over the 20th century much of the knowledge generated about intelligence—the established as well as the controversial—has come from educational psychologists as they have attempted to help policy makers, parents, and teachers such as Andrea make sense out of the often confusing claims made in this area. Chapter 9, by Snow, Corno, and Jackson, addresses individual differences in affective and conative functions—differences that affect students' ways of perceiving and acting on their environments.

Andrea also noted that several children in her class needed special help. Henry and Clarice simply were not involved in the instructional activities she had devised. Maybe they are learning disabled, or perhaps troubled by physical, emotional, or mental disabilities. Such children may be helped by school psychologists (a field of professional practice with close links to educational psychology; cf. Medway, 1992) and other professionals. National educational policy currently requires that all children be included in the regular classroom to the extent possible. Andrea is therefore expected to provide instruction for students across a broad range of special needs and talents. She could be helped in her task by the knowledge base on the psychology of exceptionality, presented in chapter 10, by Keogh and Macmillan.

But Clarice and Henry may be opting out of schooling for reasons that are societal rather than individual. The etiology of their withdrawal may reside in how children of poverty and of color are treated, and in how we socialize children. Insights from educational psychology about these issues appear in several places: in chapter 11, on the psychology of ethnicity, by Portes; in chapter 12, on gender roles, by Eisenberg, Martin, and Fabes; in Chapter 18, on bilingualism, by Hakuta and McLaughlin; and in chapter 19, on the informal curriculum, by McCaslin and Good. These chapters demonstrate the importance of a broad conception of educational psychology, one that reaches beyond the classroom walls, because what happens in the classroom cannot be separated from what is happening in the broader society in which education is embedded. Many of the challenging instructional and behavioral problems that emanate from the Henrys and Clarices in every teacher's class have their etiology in the ways that society responds to the inevitable differences associated with gender, race, ethnicity, and social conditions.

## Educational Psychology and School Subjects

Mathematics was not Andrea's strong suit, and she knew it. She had done all right in her math courses because she worked hard on assignments. But she lacked the pedagogical knowledge to be confident in teaching mathematics. Her task was all the more difficult because her students were struggling and discouraged by failure. Her mathematics methods class was helping her understand how children think about different kinds of math problems, how they construct their math knowledge, and how those constructions differ for various mathematical tasks, such as fractions, time-rate-distance problems, and so on. She now realized that students often use consistent and thoughtful, but incorrect, algorithms in approaching arithmetic. She was especially interested in strategies for enhancing the math performance of the girls in her classes. Too bad she hadn't benefited from such strategies! The psychology of mathematics and of women in science and mathematics is discussed in chapter 15, on teaching and learning science, by Linn, Songer, and Eylon; in chapter 16, on teaching and learning mathematics, by De Corte, Greer, and Verschaffel; and in chapter 12, on gender, by Eisenberg, Martin, and Fabes. The psychological investigations in these areas offer research findings, concepts, technologies, and theories that can help Andrea become a better math teacher—in time.

As Andrea muses about the differences between history and math, we see her nascent understanding of how subject matter influences teaching and learning, the subject of chapter 13, by Shulman and Quinlan, on the psychology of subject matters. This issue is also the subject of chapter 14, by Wineburg, on teaching and learning history, as well as chapter 16, by De Corte, Greer, and Verschaffel, on the teaching of mathematics. Fundamental psychological questions arise around issues like the representation of knowledge and the mastery of skills in different subject matter areas. How are different types of knowledge—mathematical symbols, geometric shapes, long division algorithms—coded and stored in memory? How are the routines and syntax of mathematics learned? In what ways might these be different from the learning of historical narrative? How can teachers support the storage and retrieval of these different forms of information?

Research on different types of knowledge—declarative, procedural, and episodic—can inform, though not necessarily prescribe, educational practice. Not only do subject matters differ in how knowledge is represented, they also differ in the structure, organization, and economy of their knowledge. We have learned a great deal about how knowledge gained in one context can transfer to other situations, as well as why learning often fails to transfer (Salomon & Perkins, 1989). It is rather amazing, for instance, that well-educated individuals think that seasonal changes result from shifts in the distance between the Earth and the sun, even though they have learned repeatedly in school that seasons are caused by the Earth's tilt. The general issues associated with this problem are discussed in part I, which deals with learning and transfer. The particulars of the concepts associated with different subject matters are discussed in the chapters of part III of this *Handbook*, all of which are about the psychology of different school subjects. Both old and new areas of research for educational psychologists, part III of the *Handbook* also includes chapters on the educational psychology of literacy, by Hiebert and Raphael, and the teaching and learning of second languages, by Hakuta and McLaughlin—subjects of critical importance to Andrea and her colleagues at Klinger Middle School.

## Educational Psychology and Assessment

Andrea enters grades into her record book, an easy task on the surface, but one requiring enormously complex judgments. Surveys show that while most teacher preparation programs include training on assessment methods, these are too short and scattered to influence classroom practice. Andrea, as is typical, had only a vague memory of the techniques that she had been taught for grading papers. She uses a "holistic primary-trait grading" method as a quick fix for the burden of dealing with 120 youngsters per day. Besides these brief readings, however, she selects several papers at random for detailed review. Her students know that she does more than browse their work. Her brief comments provide feedback and motivate the youngsters.

Educational psychology has a long history of theoretical work and practical advice about classroom assessment. The history begins with Thorndike's contributions at the turn of the 20th century. The advice of the experts in this field appears in the hundreds of educational psychology and measurement texts published since then. Measurement and assessment continues to be a fertile research area for educational psychologists, as Hambleton informs us in chapter 28.

Assessment typically focuses on cognitive and academic outcomes, but Andrea is also concerned about students' motivation under competitive and non-competitive systems of assessment. These and related issues are considered in chapter 4, by Graham and Weiner, and in chapter 5, by Stipek, each concerned with motivation; chapter 9, by Snow, Corno, and Jackson, also offers ideas about the assessment of affective and conative factors in teaching and learning.

## Educational Psychology and Professional Development

Andrea has passed the novice stage but is still learning her craft, even in teaching history. Her use of primary documents and dramatization demonstrates her growing confidence as a teacher, but she would be the first to admit rough spots. Time management is still difficult; she spends too much time with the class "getting ready" and too little time "doing it." She knows history but aspires to a better understanding of writing instruction. The processes of teacher growth and development are discussed in chapter 20, by Borko and Putnam, and Andrea's concerns about writing are explored in chapter 17, on literacy, by Hiebert and Raphael.

Andrea is in her third year as a teacher, and like teachers across the United States she will soon be evaluated for tenure. A casual visit by the assistant principal may affect her future and that of the thousands of students whom she might teach over the next few decades. In chapter 23 Dwyer and Stufflebeam offer a contemporary look at the assessment and evaluation of teachers throughout their professional development.

## Educational Psychology and Research on Teaching

Teaching mathematics for the first time has made Andrea appreciate the importance of instructional strategies and the delicate balance between science and art. In history she is willing to experiment with innovative group methods of instruction, topics discussed in chapter 26 by Webb and Palincsar. For mathematics she relies on a direct instruction model. Her inexperience and limited content knowledge leave her uneasy about departing from this tried-and-true approach, which so far is working reasonably well, although it lacks inspiration and challenge. In chapter 22 Shuell reviews the direct instructional model and findings from recent research programs that have attempted to relate particular kinds of teaching behavior to particular kinds of student achievement in classroom contexts. Such research influences educational psychology and teaching methods courses in teacher education institutions and it affects the choices of teaching methods and practices that Andrea and multitudes of other teachers make every day.

Although Andrea has used instructional technology (television) in her teaching and is looking into computers, she has little in the way of instructional-design theory to rely on and no mature understanding about what she may expect from technological adjuncts to her classroom teaching. Part of what Andrea needs to know is in chapter 24, by Derry and Lesgold, on instructional design and educational practice. More of what she needs to think about is in chapter 25, by Bransford, Goldman, and Hasselbring, of the Cognition and Technology Group at Vanderbilt University, which explores the uses of technology in education as psychologists currently understand it—a challenge in a field changing as rapidly as this one.

Thinking serious thoughts, acting on them, and reflecting on the complex, extemporaneous decisions she makes day after day, leaves Andrea near exhaustion. If you asked her to reflect on her brief career—What is her educational philosophy? What are her aspirations?—she would probably slump in despair. Like many competent and busy teachers, she is likely to answer such questions by saying, "I don't have time to think about such matters!" But researchers have overcome this resistance. Teachers' beliefs and thoughts have, indeed, been studied, and are discussed in chapter 21, by Calderhead. This chapter, in part IV of the *Handbook*, includes reviews of the psychological study of teaching, particularly the professional development of teachers, their thinking, their behavior in classroom contexts, and their evaluation.

## Foundations of Educational Psychology

Part V, the final section of the *Handbook* offers more to the academic educational psychologist than to the practitioner, concerned as it is with the foundations of the field, including methodology, philosophy, and history. The first four sections portray contemporary educational psychology as an academic discipline with profound relations to practice. But educational psychology is also a scientific enterprise, and the final section focuses on the technical underpinnings of the discipline. While Andrea Cornbluth may not give much thought to these matters, many of the principles that she learned during preservice preparation, as well as the work of others who design textbooks, tests, and other instructional materials, depend on foundational matters.

## EDUCATION AND PSYCHOLOGY

Everyone likes a story. Kidder's 1989 *Among School Children,* Freedman's 1990 *Small Victories,* Kozol's 1991 *Savage Inequalities,* and Sizer's 1984 *Horace's Compromise* all offer compelling stories about life in schools, and all became best sellers. Readers are engaged and informed by such writing. But beyond the telling of a commonplace educational story such as Andrea's is the need for understanding. We have already noted that the disciplinary knowledge in this first *Handbook of Educational Psychology* has relevance for the dilemmas and actions that confound her. To claim rights as one of the primary disciplines for analyzing a story like this, educational psychology must be able to interpret wisely Andrea's tale. What concepts explain her thoughts and actions? What principles are at work? How can educational psychology provide sensible advice as she juggles a tough job with limited resources and needy students?

Answers to these and related questions require x-ray vision, a capacity to look underneath the story scenes to the underlying scripts, to the basic systems that explain events that seem complex on the surface. For an analogy, think about the human body. To the novice it seems incredibly complicated and messy. In fact, physiologists have discovered a few systems (skeleton, muscles, nerves, glands, the circulatory system, and so on) that operate our bodies. As Simon (1981) noted, even the most complex entity can be decomposed into a few relatively separable substructures. In the human body, some substructures are obvious. We can see and feel our skeletal parts, for instance, and muscles stand out on some bodies. Blood vessels can be seen here and there, but the circulatory system took time to figure out. The nervous and glandular systems, much less obvious, were even more difficult discoveries.

How can we decompose Andrea's story? We can view the story through several disciplinary lenses: curricular, instructional, psychological, sociological, anthropological, even political and economic. In addition, lenses must also come from practice as well as science. Some lenses yield understanding, others guide action. Some lenses focus on details, others on the overall composition. And we must acknowledge that every time we decompose systems for analytic purposes we risk losing features of the whole that cannot be reconstructed from the parts.

Andrea's story is but one of many that we might have told.

The class could have been urban or rural, kindergarten or high school. The teacher could have been expert or novice, the students richer or poorer. The setting could have been a student's home or the principal's office, a school board meeting or a teacher team working on a science curriculum. Whatever the educational story, the scientific task remains the same, namely, to wrest meaning from the episode. This task requires analysis—the breaking of a whole into its constituent parts.

## Scientific Psychology

In situations like those sketched above and others that you can imagine, educational psychology unites the practice of education with the science of psychology. The practice of education encompasses the innumerable activities by which society transmits its cultural heritage to its young. The institution of schooling and the formal curriculum that it transmits are part of that process, but so are family and religious groups, popular culture and peer groups, work and citizenship. Anyone who aims to understand education is compelled to adopt a multidisciplinary perspective. As noted earlier, educational psychology is distinctive in its substance: *the systematic study of the individual in context*. Perception, memory, learning, problem solving, motivation, aptitude, and achievement—all mainstream areas of psychology—parallel the physiologist's skeletal, nervous, and other systems. These concepts provide the psychologist with the x-ray vision needed to study the substance. These concepts let us look beneath the surface behaviors of a teacher discussing quadratic equations in an algebra class, the student sketching notes for an expository essay on the Civil War, or a faculty meeting to select reading textbooks.

Although scientific psychology spotlights the individual, educational psychologists have come to recognize the importance of the interpersonal, social, institutional, and environmental contexts that shape thought and action. The psychological laboratory suffices for some purposes. Principles of fundamental importance have come from the study of eye movements during reading or the memorization of nonsense words by college sophomores. For educational psychologists, however, laboratory findings must meet additional standards of generalizability. Because educational psychologists are interested in practical applicability, they need data of established ecological validity more than does the laboratory psychologist. Because contexts vary enormously and interactions are common in real-world settings, educational psychologists face a tough scientific challenge in replicating their findings. The behavior of a new physics particle reported by a Swiss laboratory can be verified anywhere in the world in a reasonable time. Chemistry or physics experiments done at the turn of the 20th century still hold at the turn of the 21st century. But education is culture-specific, and so findings from different societies may vary. How does the level of reading among boys compare with that of girls? Educational psychologists can expect to find different answers and explanations for those answers in different countries. Studies of motivation and gender from the 1950s and 1960s are of questionable validity for the United States after the feminist revolution of the 1970s. The social scientist faces a greater challenge than the physical scientist because our work does not easily generalize from the laboratory to the school setting, nor does our scientific knowledge transfer easily across cultures

or over time. Ours is a contextual science, one of enormous complexity.

Educational psychologists confront a distinctive array of scientific problems, for which they have developed distinctive theories and methods. For this reason they do not consider their field to be simply an applied branch or subdiscipline of scientific psychology. This *Handbook* is primarily written by and features the work of educational psychologists, rather than psychologists interested in education. To view education merely as a site in which to practice psychology, an opportunity to apply scientific knowledge, misses at least two features of the discipline of educational psychology. First, over the past century educational psychologists have built a deep understanding of the nature of the educational enterprise. Second, educational psychologists have established collaborations with teachers and other educators that allow their discipline to benefit from the wisdom of practice. Becoming an educational psychologist means learning about life in schools. The connections with practice are essential in order for educational psychology's theoretical and methodological perspectives to be used sensibly and humanely in the service of those who work in school settings.

## Context and History

As noted above, educational psychology is inherently contextual. This *Handbook* describes education and psychology in developed nations where the institution of schooling is of paramount importance for educating the young. The *Handbook* is a project of a division of the American Psychological Association and so emphasizes the American perspective. To be sure, several authors and reviewers are from outside the United States, and the diversity that is characteristic of the United States is reflected in both topics and authors.

Nonetheless, the story in this book is largely an American story, one that begins just before the start of the 20th century, when several pioneers in general psychology founded the field of educational psychology (Berliner, 1993; Glover & Ronning, 1987; Hilgard, this volume). Harvard's William James, after launching American psychology in 1890 with his psychology textbook, followed soon after with a lecture series for teachers. In *Talks to Teachers,* James presented to educators what the psychology of that time had to offer (1899/1983). James's student, G. Stanley Hall, presided over the planning of the American Psychological Association and assumed office as its first president in 1892. His dissertation had investigated what children knew about the world. Teachers even helped him collect the data! He founded the child study movement that became so popular in the United States, and was regarded as a leader in promoting the scientific study of childhood and adolescence. One of Hall's students at Johns Hopkins was John Dewey, who subsequently gained renown as a psychologist and educator as well as becoming a preeminent philosopher of his time. While Dewey did not contribute to the empirical study of psychology, he was a driving force in the practical application of psychological principles. His founding of the Laboratory School at the University of Chicago was one of the most significant events in the history of progressive education in the United States.

James, Hall, and Dewey—three great *general* psychologists—were also major figures in the emerging field of *educational* psychology. They and their colleagues styled themselves as pragmatists, for whom general and educational psychology were virtually synonymous. Educational psychology, however, was given a more definite shape and mission, methodology and ideology, by another of James's students, Edward Lee Thorndike. E. L. Thorndike dominated educational psychology from the turn of the 20th century until the end of the Second World War. His 1903 *Educational Psychology* was the first college text of the new century to deal explicitly with the discipline, and in 1910 he helped establish the *Journal of Educational Psychology*, the flagship journal of the Division of Educational Psychology of the American Psychological Association.

With James, Hall, and Dewey as grandparents and Thorndike as parent, educational psychology rapidly became preeminent as a field of empirical inquiry for applying scientific methods to the study of education. The prestige of the field was such that it was characterized early in the 20th century by historian Ellwood Cubberley as "the master science of education" (Grinder, 1989).

At the outset, American psychology was pragmatic and functional; mainstream psychologists found schooling a natural setting for their knowledge and craft. The early focus on practical matters by persons of scientific eminence in general psychology lasted from about 1890 to 1920. The match was a happy one, because schools began to be viewed as businesses at the beginning of the 20th century. Administrators who were focused on efficiency found educational psychology a source of principled and rationalistic methods of inquiry and development, and came to rely on research for improving classroom instruction in areas like reading, spelling, and arithmetic.

But, partly as a result of Thorndike's influence, educational psychology moved away from the real world of students and teachers toward basic research on generalizable principles of learning and instruction. Investigations during the next period, roughly from 1930 to 1960, tended to depend on laboratory rather than field settings, a shift that had been argued against vehemently by both James and Hall (Berliner, 1993). Still, changes in research style appeared in response to changes in society as well as in psychology and education. By the 1950s, for reasons to be described below, the pragmatic emphasis had returned, and in recent decades the educational psychology community has shifted to the study of teaching and learning in real-world settings, and to research on a broad array of topics relevant to educational policy, such as teacher evaluation and certification, the design of curriculum frameworks, and school restructuring.

It was the Second World War that precipitated a dramatic shift in the work of American educational psychologists, whose contributions to the 1940s war effort included aptitude testing, personnel selection, and training. Their experience in these areas affected the research agenda for more than a decade after the war. As might be expected, the concerns of the discipline shifted to training more than education, adults more than children, and practical programs rather than theoretical ideas. In the late 1950s the launch of Sputnik spurred national concern about school productivity. The U.S. Office of Education allocated hitherto undreamed of funds for educational research and development. Although the federal government expected practical results, it also supported fundamental research in

learning theory and instructional design. Thus, around 1960, a new era began for the field of educational psychology.

Also in the early 1960s, an especially significant event took place in both general and educational psychology. That event was a shift from behaviorism, with its half-century-old concepts and methods, toward cognitive psychology, with its dramatically different concepts and methods. Educational psychology was at the forefront of significant advances in the study of language and thought, metacognition, discourse structures, strategic instruction, and teacher decision making. Studies of motivation moved from the effects of concrete rewards (and punishments) toward attribution, self-efficacy, and the wellsprings of achievement, matters directly related to school incentives and climates. The language of educational psychology today, at the end of the discipline's first century, differs strikingly from the language of the 1950s and 1960s, a period during which many of today's senior educational psychologists received their graduate preparation. There is now less talk of behavioral objectives, programmed instruction, stimulus control, operant level, contingency management, incentives, and other key concepts of a few decades ago. These shifts reflect more than a change in words; they mark dramatic changes in conceptual frameworks. And these changes occurred at a time of renewed interest in the role of context, both environmental and social, resulting in a broadening of scientific interest for the educational psychologist.

## Problems, Theories, and Methodologies

Educational psychology is remarkably eclectic and diverse (Ball, 1984; Berliner, 1993; Wittrock & Farley, 1989), making it hard at times to discern what is essence and what is ephemera. Nevertheless, the chapters in this *Handbook* reveal a discipline somewhat changed from its origins, but nonetheless possessing a remarkable coherence, given the range and diversity of interests of its members. Every discipline centers on a combination of *problems, theories,* and *methodologies*. These characteristics of educational psychology are all evident in this *Handbook*.

Educational psychology first found its origins in applied *problems,* and after many years of shunning such activities it has once again recognized the importance of the educational in the term "educational psychologist." *Theories* in educational psychology, however, have played a minor role until recently. Suppes (1974) bewailed the atheoretical empiricism of educational research while pointing out the opportunities for conceptual advances in support of pragmatic goals. We see in the *Handbook* remarkable progress toward strengthening the conceptual elements of the field. But the variety and complexity of educational issues place limits on theoretical possibilities. As Shulman (1987) has noted, the social sciences may be poorly served by any single paradigm, by a conceptual monotheism. Accordingly, readers will encounter throughout the *Handbook* a variety of minitheories that operate effectively within prescribed boundary limits. These limited-range theories may never coalesce into a grand unified theory, but they do offer stepping-stones to achieve practical goals with some degree of understanding. As Kurt Lewin (Lippitt, 1968) once noted, "Nothing is so practical as a good theory."

Views of *methodology* seem to have changed the most over the past century. The discipline adheres to the canons of scientific inquiry. Science depends on public scrutiny. Replication is critical: When a researcher presents evidence, he or she must describe how data were obtained and analyzed with sufficient clarity and detail to allow others to repeat the investigation. To be sure, some research cannot be replicated exactly (for example, the effects on community attitudes toward the public schools in Chicago after the decentralization of some decision-making and budgetary authority to the local schools). When researchers make claims they must provide supporting evidence and must convince others of the logic that connects the evidence to the claim. This is the basis for the researcher's warrant. Opinions and beliefs are not ruled out, but they have a different evidential status; they yield a weaker warrant.

For all these reasons, science depends on established methodologies. Some techniques in educational psychology are common in many other social sciences: attainment of control through appropriate designs, assurance that evidence is valid and consistent, care to avoid confoundings. Other procedures have been invented by the discipline: the alpha coefficient of reliability, generalizability theory, quasi-experimental design, meta-analysis, and methods for measuring learning.

Not too many years ago, methodology composed the core of advanced programs in educational psychology. Every graduate was familiar with psychometrics and multivariate statistics. Techniques for assessing reliability and validity were part of the tool kit, as were designs for experimental and quasi-experimental evaluation of instructional programs. The *substantive* content of doctoral programs was more variable; depending on the institution and student interests, a graduate might specialize in any of several topics found in the *Handbook*—and others not covered—with little appreciation of the discipline as a whole.

Methodology is no longer the tie that binds. Concepts of reliability and validity have moved from statistics toward the interpretation of evidence (e.g., Cronbach, 1988; Messick, 1989, 1994). The preeminence of psychologists in quantitative evaluation research has been challenged by innovative qualitative methods springing from anthropology and enthnography (Jaeger, 1988). Nor are these isolated examples. As education and educational research evolve, educational psychologists will confront new challenges and opportunities in finding the distinctiveness of their discipline in relation to a broad array of related disciplines with diverse perspectives. Future educational researchers will need to master a variety of theoretical orientations and research methods, and will need to develop the wisdom to discern the combinations that are useful for understanding a given situation.

A word of caution: The plethora of scientific and nonscientific approaches to educational research means that methodology has become more important, not less so. Within the editors' memories, methodology in educational psychology was a neat, albeit demanding, package. Not too many years ago, methodologists consulting on a research project were often persons without much substantive knowledge, valued primarily because they could structure questions in particular ways to allow a statistical analysis of quantitative data. The quantitative data provided answers to those questions structured in particular ways.

Today's methodologist needs substantive knowledge, for it is recognized that the substantive questions are the most important aspect of an inquiry, and appropriate methodology must fit the questions, not the other way around. In quantitative analysis, for example, researchers have learned that exploratory data analysis, not hypothesis testing, is often the more appropriate methodological choice. Moreover, investigators have learned that the methods chosen must be compatible with the social and physical context in which answers to questions are sought. High-quality problem formulations and data are always the primary goal. Today's methodological experts—in order to be more knowledgeable about the substantive issues in an area of research—must be more broadly read in social science and humanistic methods of inquiry than was true in past decades. Tomorrow's graduate in educational psychology will have access to a broader array of methodological techniques than ever before, many in the early stages of development and refinement, others undergoing fundamental rethinking and revision. Such choice requires greater methodological wisdom than ever before.

## Education as Schooling

If defining psychology poses a challenge, an even greater challenge is explaining the concept of education. Education represents a society's efforts to transmit its cultural heritage through institutions like the school (Jackson, 1990; Tyler, 1989). This position implies that education (and hence educational psychology) varies with place and time. Education in a democratic society entails different goals and approaches than education in a totalitarian state. And the meaning of a "democratic society" in the United States of the 21st century is greatly altered from its 18th-century origins. The concept of equal educational opportunity, for example, now embraces male and female, all religions and races, the poor as well as the rich, and extends to the mentally and physically disabled as well—ideas far more revolutionary than our forebears probably intended. In this *Handbook,* most authors have adopted a perspective on education that reflects contemporary conditions of schooling in the United States. But even this perspective covers a lot of territory: the prototypic suburban elementary school comes into view, but so do high schools and universities; stark buildings rising in urban ghettos along with schoolhouses in rural farmlands. Privatization dots the landscape with charter schools and home schooling. The sheer breadth of the educational enterprise makes its study inherently complex.

Societies rely on different institutions to support education. The main emphasis in the United States today is on formal schooling, but families and communities also play significant roles (Kellaghan, Sloane, Alvarez, & Bloom, 1993; McLaughlin, Irby, & Langman, 1994; Schoor, 1988). A few decades back, children typically lived with nuclear families in stable communities, supported by relatives, neighbors, shopkeepers, churches, clubs, and so on. The picture, while not always rosy, is a happier one than today's cacophony of poverty, homelessness, single parents, low-paying or no jobs, and faceless bureaucracies. The adversities of contemporary Western nations, including the United States, have led to educational challenges unimagined 30 years ago. Schooling now includes bilingual and multicultural instruction, drug-use prevention programs, programs for jobless and homeless youth and families, and so on, in what seems like an endless expansion of the role of schooling in society.

Given the changes in so many other familiar institutions, the school is beginning to look like the most trustworthy institution for supporting our children and their families. Tobias (1989) has proposed redesign of schools as sites for the integration of social services, where educational psychologists move their focus from research to direct involvement in school restructuring.

The promise and perils of major changes in schools in the United States and elsewhere are tantalizing topics, and the institution of schooling will be the primary focus in this *Handbook*. Whatever happens during the next few decades, schools will likely remain synonymous with education, and they will continue to serve as the chief policy instrument in most developed countries for achieving the transmission of societal artifacts. The *Handbook* does connect with the broader reaches of the educational enterprise, however. Educational psychology, like education itself, spans the spectrum from birth through the entire life span, from academic subject matters through the informal curriculum of social and personal responsibilities.

Education is an evolving social construction. Even if we limit discussion to the institution of formal schooling, we see enormous changes during the past century (Cuban, 1993; Tyack, Lowe, & Hansot, 1984). The image of the one-room schoolhouse run by the local schoolmarm is within the collective memory of the United States. The teacher, probably a high school graduate, ruled the roost. Books were scarce, standardized tests nonexistent. Instruction relied on the principle of "practice makes perfect." Curriculum was constrained; literacy meant 6 years of school attendance.

In mid-century, after the emergence of efficient and compulsory schooling, the buzzword became *management*—in particular, management by objectives. Mandated textbooks and tests were imposed by external administrators, a system that quickly undermined teachers' authority. The aim was to construct instructional approaches that were "teacherproof." Continuing trends from earlier in the century, schooling became large, hierarchical, complex, and depersonalized.

At the same time, and for different reasons, the United States began to take seriously its early commitment to the ideal of equal education. This commitment included the development of instructional programs that worked for all students, regardless of their family conditions. Education for the children of the poor, however, remains a major challenge in today's society. The achievement of minimal competency in basic skills turned out to be difficult and not worth the effort (Madaus, 1983). Policy makers at all levels have shifted their discussions from basic education to achievements sufficient for graduates to adapt to the changing worlds of the year 2000 and beyond. It has slowly become evident that fulfilling this aim depends on a system of education remarkably different from the one deemed appropriate at midcentury. The new vision of education relies on teachers more than on materials, on school experiences that are small, cooperative, focused, and personalized.

Central to this vision is a view of the teacher as a reflective practitioner, an adaptive expert, a participant in a community of inquiry (Calfee, 1992). Instruction has moved from transmittal of information to engagement in problem solving (Resnick, 1987). The social dimension of education has emerged as a significant mediating influence for cognitive achievement. The Russian psychologist Lev Vygotsky, whose writings from the 1930s and 1940s began to appear in English translations in the 1960s, has profoundly influenced contemporary educational psychology (Moll, 1990). Now Vygotsky's theoretical and practical contributions provide some of the substance to support some of Dewey's philosophical concepts for education that offer both quality and equality in a democratic society.

Assessment is also undergoing radical change in today's schools. Picking the right answer on a multiple-choice test still stands as the most frequent task used for judging educational outcomes. But assessment is rapidly shifting toward performance rather than testing, toward production rather than recognition (Wiggins, 1993). Nor is "doing" sufficient; today's students are asked to explain their work and to show that they can transfer learning to new situations.

All this indicates that schools are undergoing fundamental change. And as the character of schooling becomes even more complex and demanding in decades to come, so will the work of the educational psychologist. Some choices about what to investigate and how to investigate it will be shaped by substantive movements within education. Others will be guided by conceptual and methodological developments within the broader domains of scientific psychology (Cronbach & Suppes, 1969). Fads and fashion will also play a role; science resembles popular culture in some respects, although scientists are trained to be skeptics, and thus science is self-correcting. A seminal paper on transfer of learning or a novel approach to reliability can redirect research agendas for decades or more. The appearance of an innovative technique for teaching mathematics or a "cure" for dyslexia may attract substantial attention and funding for a time. The federal government also shapes the agenda for educational research by setting priorities for grant allocations, by establishing educational centers and laboratories, and by adding a political dimension to decision making in education (Wise, 1979). A successful political effort can direct massive amounts of educational resources to serve political ends. Such are the influences on the educational psychology of our times.

The design of this *Handbook* reflects the dynamic character of the discipline. We have not attempted to cover all areas of present-day scientific psychology or to review all areas of contemporary educational practice. Among the resources that do serve this purpose are other handbooks (Barr, Kamil, Mosenthal, & Pearson, 1991; Jackson, 1992; Linn, 1989; Pearson, 1984; Wittrock, 1986), all of which reflect substantial contributions from educational psychologists. Other sources include the *Review of Research in Education, Review of Educational Research, Educational Researcher,* and the yearbooks of the *National Society for the Study of Education,* as well as indexes like ERIC (the Educational Resources Information Center), *Current Index to Journals in Education* (CIJE), and *Resources in Education* (RIE).

As we have already noted, a handbook written 50 years ago would have been different from the present volume. When this project is redone a decade from now, we suspect that the assignment will be reconstruction rather than revision. By this comment we do not despair of general principles. Rather, we see the tasks of educational psychologists as like those confronting the crew of the spaceship *Enterprise*—an encounter with novel and unpredictable situations every week. Education and schooling may not metamorphose as swiftly and dramatically as *Star Trek* plots, but scholars and scientists who study education must search for constancies in the midst of complexity, change, and diversity (Calfee & Nelson-Barber, 1991).

## OVERVIEW OF THE HANDBOOK

In designing the *Handbook,* we balanced two features that characterize contemporary educational psychology: (a) the renewed engagement in issues of practice, and (b) the emergence of cognition as the prevailing theoretical framework. Cognitive psychology and its impact on conceptions of teaching, learning, and knowledge are featured throughout the volume. The *Handbook* focuses on the institution of schooling, with its starting point the commonplaces described by Schwab (1978) that we noted earlier—students, curriculum, teachers, and context—*"someone* teaching *something* to *someone else* in some *situation."* These four domains, therefore, provide the basic structure for organizing the *Handbook:*

*Students,* viewed psychologically, lead us to consider learning processes and learner characteristics. These issues are addressed in the sections covering learning and motivation, chapters 2–5; and in the sections covering development and individual differences, chapters 6–12.

*Curriculum,* viewed psychologically, leads us to consider the structure and use of knowledge, discussed in the sections on the psychology of school subjects, chapters 13–19.

*Teachers,* viewed psychologically, lead us to review teaching and instructional methods, taken up in chapters 20–26.

*Context,* viewed psychologically, leads us to discuss the social and institutional contexts of schooling, addressed throughout many of the chapters in the *Handbook.*

Part V, comprising chapters 27–32, provides a different look at the four previous sections. Scholars representing various foundational areas—measurement, research design, evaluation, history, philosophy—provide overviews of empirical findings, prevailing themes, recurring issues, grand successes, and continuing dilemmas in the previous chapters. The arrangement is admittedly unusual, in that methodological and foundational areas are usually presented at the beginning of a handbook. Following the advice of a member of the educational psychology community who responded to our initial planning survey, we decided that these reflections would be most appropriately placed at the end of the volume, which moves the substantive areas of the discipline to the foreground and the foundational areas of the discipline to the background.

All authors were asked to consider the following model in designing their chapters: a brief historical introduction to issues of theory, research, and practice; a description of pertinent methodology directly relevant to the topics of the chapter; the substance of the chapter, focused around a relatively few central issues and balancing conceptual and empirical substance; and a conclusion noting topics likely to receive attention in the future and connections with issues of educational practice and policy. Although our colleagues interpreted these guidelines in unexpectedly creative ways, we think that readers will be helped by a knowledge of the original design.

Finally, our aim has been to create a text that is readable more than exhaustive. Accordingly, we encouraged authors to select judiciously, write plainly, and keep it simple. But this is a technical volume, and readers must be prepared to wrestle with scholarly material. The *Handbook* is aimed toward a broad audience: practicing researchers, university teachers, and graduate students. As editors, we have been especially mindful of the last-mentioned group. We assume prior knowledge in the fields of education, psychology, and educational psychology, including familiarity with the "ways of thinking" that characterize our discipline. Above all, we assume an engagement in the systematic study of education, and a commitment to the improvement of educational institutions through the application of scientific methods and principles.

## *References*

Ball, S. (1984). Educational psychology as an academic chameleon: An editorial assessment after 75 years. *Journal of Educational Psychology, 76,* 993–999.

Barr, R., Kamil, M. L., Mosenthal, P., & Pearson, P. D. (Eds.). (1991). *Handbook of reading research: Vol. II.* New York: Longman.

Berliner, D. C. (1993). The 100-year journey of educational psychology: from interest, to disdain, to respect for practice. In T. K. Fagin & G. R. VandenBos (Eds.), *Exploring applied psychology: Origins and critical analyses* (pp. 39–78). Washington, DC: American Psychological Association.

Calfee, R. C. (1992). The inquiring school: Literacy for the year 2000. In C. Collins & J. N. Mangieri (Eds.), *Teaching thinking: An agenda for the twenty-first century* (pp. 147–166). Hillsdale, NJ: Lawrence Erlbaum Associates.

Calfee, R. C., & Nelson-Barber, S. (1991). Diversity and constancy in human thinking: Critical literacy as amplifier of intellect and experience. In E. Hiebert (Ed.), *Literacy for a diverse society: Perspectives, programs, and policies* (pp. 44–57). New York: Teachers College Press.

Cronbach, L. J. (1988). Five perspectives on validation argument. In H.

Weiner & H. Braun (Eds.), *Test validity* (pp. 3–17). Hillsdale, NJ: Lawrence Erlbaum Associates.

Cronbach, L. J., & Suppes, P. (1969). *Research for tomorrow's schools: Disciplined inquiry for education.* New York: Macmillan.

Cuban, L. (1993). *How teachers taught* (2nd ed.). New York: Teachers College Press.

Freedman, S. G. (1990). *Small victories: The real world of a teacher, her students, and their high school.* New York: Harper & Row.

Galton, F. (1869). *Hereditary genius: An inquiry into its laws and consequences.* London: Collins.

Glover, J. A., & Ronning, R. R. (Eds.). (1987). *Historical foundations of educational psychology.* New York: Plenum Press.

Grinder, R. E. (1989). Educational psychology: The master science. In M. C. Wittrock & F. Farley (Eds.), *The future of educational psychology* (pp. 3–18). Hillsdale, NJ: Lawrence Erlbaum Associates.

Jackson, P. W. (1990). *Life in classrooms.* New York: Teachers College Press.

Jackson, P. W. (Ed.). (1992). *Handbook of research on curriculum.* New York: Macmillan.

Jaeger, R. M. (1988). *Complementary methods for research in education*. Washington, DC: American Educational Research Association.

James, W. (1899/1983). *Talks to teachers on psychology and to students on some of life's ideals*. Cambridge, MA: Harvard University Press.

Kellaghan, T., Sloane, K., Alvarez, B., & Bloom, B. S. (1993). *The home environment and school learning*. San Francisco: Jossey-Bass.

Kidder, T. (1989). *Among school children*. Boston: Houghton Mifflin.

Kozol, J. (1991). *Savage inequalities*. New York: Crown.

Linn, R. L. (Ed.). (1989). *Educational measurement* (3rd ed.). New York: Macmillan.

Lippitt, R. (1968). Kurt Lewin. In D. L. Sills (Ed.). *International encyclopedia of the social sciences* (Vol. 19, pp. 266–271). New York: Macmillan and the Free Press.

Madaus, G. (Ed.). (1983). *The courts, validity, and minimum competency*. Boston, MA: Kluwer-Nijhoff.

Mandler, G., & Kessen, W. (1959). *The language of psychology*. New York: Wiley.

McLaughlin, M. W., Irby, M. A., & Langman, J. (1994). *Urban sanctuaries: Neighborhood organizations in the lives and futures of inner-city youth*. San Francisco: Jossey-Bass.

Medway, F. J. (1992). *School psychology*. Hillsdale, NJ: Lawrence Erlbaum Associates.

Messick, S. (1989). Validity. In R. L. Linn (Ed.), *Educational measurement* (3rd ed., pp. 13–103). New York: American Council on Education/Macmillan.

Messick, S. (1994). The interplay of evidence and consequences in the validation of performance assessments. *Educational Researcher, 23,* 13–23.

Moll, L. (Ed.). (1990). *Vygotsky and education: Instructional implications and applications of socio-historical psychology*. New York: Cambridge University Press.

Pearson, P. D. (Ed.). (1984). *Handbook of research in reading*. New York: Longman.

Resnick, L. B. (1987). *Education and learning to think*. Washington, DC: National Academy of Education.

Salomon, G., & Perkins, D. N. (1989). Rocky roads to transfer: Rethinking mechanisms of a neglected phenomenon. *Educational Psychologist, 24,* 113–142.

Schoor, L. B. (1988). *Within our reach*. New York: Anchor Press.

Schwab, J. J. (1978). The practical: Translation into curriculum. In I. Westbury & N. J. Wilkoff (Eds.), *Science curriculum and liberal education: Selected essays of Joseph J. Schwab* (chap. 12, pp. 365–383). Chicago: University of Chicago Press.

Shulman, L. S. (1987). Knowledge and teaching: Foundations of the new reform. *Harvard Educational Review, 57,* 1–22.

Simon, H. A. (1981). *The sciences of the artificial* (2nd ed.). Cambridge MA: MIT Press.

Sizer, T. R. (1984). *Horace's compromise*. Boston: Houghton Mifflin.

Sizer, T. R. (1992). *Horace's school*. Boston: Houghton Mifflin.

Suppes, P. (1974). The place of theory in educational research. *Educational Researcher, 3,* 3–10.

Thorndike, E. L. (1903). *Educational psychology*. New York: Science Press.

Tobias, S. (1989). New directions for educational psychologists. In M. C. Wittrock & F. Farley (Eds.), *The future of educational psychology*. Hillsdale, NJ: Lawrence Erlbaum Associates.

Tyack, D., Lowe, R., & Hansot, E. (1984). *Public schools in hard times: The Great Depression and recent years*. Cambridge MA: Harvard University Press.

Tyler, R. W. (1989). *Educational evaluation: Classic works of Ralph W. Tyler* (G. F. Madaus & D. L. Stufflebeam, Eds.). Boston: Kluwer.

Wiggins, G. P. (1993). *Assessing student performance*. San Francisco: Jossey-Bass.

Wise, A. (1979). *Legislated learning*. Berkeley: University of California Press.

Wittrock, M. (Ed.). (1986). *Handbook on research on teaching* (3rd ed.). New York: Macmillan.

Wittrock, M. C., & Farley, F. (Eds.). (1989). *The future of educational psychology*. Hillsdale, NJ: Lawrence Erlbaum Associates.

# COGNITION AND
# MOTIVATION

# ·2·

# COGNITION AND LEARNING

## James G. Greeno

STANFORD UNIVERSITY AND
THE INSTITUTE FOR RESEARCH ON LEARNING

## Allan M. Collins

BOLT, BERANEK AND NEWMAN, INC., CAMBRIDGE, MA, AND
NORTHWESTERN UNIVERSITY, EVANSTON

## Lauren B. Resnick

UNIVERSITY OF PITTSBURGH

## INTRODUCTION

Cognition and learning are central concepts in educational psychology. Research on these topics has been productive both for advancing fundamental scientific understanding and for informing educational practice. In this chapter, we review research accomplishments that have influenced the character of educational practice significantly. We also review research that has important practical implications but that has only begun to inform practices of education.

We believe that educational research is undergoing a major advance that will further deepen our theoretical understanding of fundamental processes of cognition, learning, and teaching and further strengthen our abilities to contribute to educational practice. This advance is leading toward a psychology of cognition and learning that includes individual, social, and environmental factors in a coherent theoretical and practical understanding. Accomplishing this change will require merging and extending concepts and methods that, until recently, have developed relatively separately in cognitive science, in ecological psychology, and in ethnographic anthropology and sociology.

The relationship between theoretical and practical understanding is one of the important aspects of our science that is currently in transition. One of the promising ideas is that research can provide more articulate and more valid principles that serve as assumptions of practice (A. L. Brown, 1994; A. L. Brown & Campione, 1994; J. S. Brown, 1991). To develop the principles of a practical theory, several groups of researchers

are conducting studies that we refer to as *design experiments* (A. L. Brown, 1992; Collins, 1992). In these studies, researchers and practitioners, particularly teachers, collaborate in the design, implementation, and analysis of changes in practice. Results provide case studies that can serve as instructive models about conditions that need to be satisfied for reforms of the same kind to be successful, and about conditions that impede success. Results also contribute to an accumulating body of theoretical principles about processes of cognition and learning in the social and material environments of schools and other settings.

There are distinct traditions in educational theories and practices that derive from differing perspectives on the phenomena of the domain. We organize our discussion with three general perspectives that have developed in psychological research. We recognize that other organizing principles could be chosen, and that many of our colleagues would characterize the field in different terms. Our version groups together many research contributions that could be distinguished in important ways. We have arrived at this grouping, however, in our own effort to understand broad trends and issues in educational research, and we hope that this characterization is helpful to readers in their efforts to grasp general characteristics of the field.

The perspectives correspond to three general views of knowing and learning in European and North American thought, which, generally following Case (1991, 1992) and Packer (1985), we refer to as *empiricist, rationalist,* and *pragmatist-sociohistoric*. For the third view, Case used the simpler label "sociohistoric," but we use the admittedly more cumber-

Preparation of this chapter was supported by National Science Foundation (NSF) grants No. MDR915400 and ESI9450522 to the Institute for Research on Learning (J.G.G.); by NSF grant No. MDR9053609 to Bolt, Beranek and Newman, Inc. (A.C.); by the National Research Center on Student Learning of the Learning Research and Development Center, University of Pittsburgh, with funds from the Office of Educational Research and Improvement, OERI Award No. R117G10003, United States Department of Education (L.B.R.); and by a grant from the Andrew W. Mellon Foundation (L.B.R.). We are grateful for comments by Robert Calfee, Robbie Case, and Richard Snow on drafts of this chapter, and for conversations with many colleagues, particularly with Giyoo Hatano, as we developed these ideas.

some term to emphasize the largely separate origins of the view in American thought. Packer's discussion, focused on the hermeneutic perspective, exemplified by Heidegger, provides background for the situative perspective (Winograd & Flores, 1986) described below. Empiricism, typified by Locke and Thorndike, emphasizes consistency of knowledge with experience. Rationalism, typified by Descartes and Piaget, emphasizes conceptual coherence and formal criteria of truth. Pragmatism, typified by Dewey and Mead, and sociohistoricism, typified by Vygotsky, emphasize that knowledge is constructed in practical activities of groups of people as they interact with each other and their material environments. Current manifestations of these three perspectives are the *behaviorist* perspective, the *cognitive* perspective, and the *situative* perspective.

All three of these perspectives have contributed, and continue to contribute, important insights to fundamental scientific knowledge and understanding of cognition and learning and have influenced educational practices significantly. While each perspective is valuable, they frame theoretical and practical issues in distinctive and complementary ways, somewhat in the way that physics, chemistry, and biology frame issues surrounding processes such as genetic replication in different but complementary ways. We hope, in this chapter, to convey the considerable strengths of all three of the perspectives and the value and importance of using their resources pluralistically in considering educational problems.

In the second section of this chapter we discuss theoretical developments within the three perspectives. The section is organized around three theoretical issues: the nature of knowing, the nature of learning and transfer, and the nature of motivation and engagement. We discuss research regarding each of these issues from the three perspectives.

In the third section we discuss ways in which the three perspectives contribute to understanding and carrying out educational practices. The section is organized around three practical issues: design of learning environments, analysis and formulation of curricula, and assessment, which we discuss from the three theoretical perspectives. We discuss these as examples of issues in educational practice in which recent and current design experiments have begun to develop a coherent body of principles in practice. Of course, these are a small subset of the practical issues that must be addressed and understood in the broad efforts to strengthen the educational system, and we discuss some additional issues briefly in the last section of this chapter (see CONCLUSIONS, p. 39).

## ISSUES OF THEORETICAL CONCEPTUALIZATION

This section considers three thematic issues in the theory of cognition and learning:

- the nature of knowing,
- the nature of learning and transfer, and
- the nature of motivation and engagement.

The three general perspectives, the behaviorist/empiricist view, the cognitive/rationalist view, and the situative/pragmatist-sociohistoric view, frame each of these issues in distinctive and complementary ways.

In the behaviorist/empiricist view, knowing is an organized accumulation of associations and components of skills. Learning is the process in which associations and skills are acquired, and transfer occurs to the extent that behaviors learned in one situation are utilized in another situation. Motivation is a state of the learner that favors formation of new associations and skills, primarily involving incentives for attending to relevant aspects of the situation and for responding appropriately. There are three traditions that we consider contributed to this view. *Associationism,* which goes back to Locke and Hume, viewed knowing as the associations between ideas and learning as building new associations. *Behaviorism* took the position that knowing could be characterized only in terms of observable connections between stimuli and responses and learning in terms of forming and strengthening or weakening and extinguishing those connections through reinforcement or nonreinforcement. *Connectionism* (or neural networks) treats knowledge as the pattern of connections between neuronlike elements and learning as the strengthening or weakening of those connections.

The cognitive/rationalist perspective on knowledge emphasizes understanding of concepts and theories in different subject matter domains and general cognitive abilities, such as reasoning, planning, solving problems, and comprehending language. There are three traditions of research that we consider to be branches of the cognitive perspective. The oldest of these is *Gestalt psychology,* which emphasized the structural nature of knowledge and the importance of insight in learning. A second tradition, *constructivism,* was originally developed by Piaget and is focused on characterizing the cognitive growth of children, especially their growth in conceptual understanding. The third tradition, *symbolic information processing,* was developed in American cognitive science by Chomsky, Simon, Newell, and others and is focused on characterizing processes of language understanding, reasoning, and problem solving. (Case (1992) classified symbolic information processing as an empiricist tradition because of its focus on knowledge as a set of associative networks and procedures. We locate it in the constructivist category because of its emphasis on the organization of information in cognitive structures and procedures. This is but one example of ways in which a classification has to include relatively arbitrary boundaries. Although there are significant differences of emphasis between these research traditions, they share important framing assumptions, especially the constructivist and information-processing traditions. All three traditions emphasize the importance of organized patterns in cognitive activity. The constructivist and information-processing traditions also focus on procedures and operations for representing and reasoning about information. Learning is understood as a constructive process of conceptual growth, often involving reorganization of concepts in the learner's understanding, and growth in general cognitive abilities such as problem-solving strategies and metacognitive processes. Discussions of motivation often emphasize that much learning apparently occurs without the need for extrinsic incentives, as in the case of learning one's first language, and instead focus on ways to foster the intrinsic interest of learners in ideas and concepts.

The situative/pragmatist-sociohistoric perspective views

knowledge as distributed among people and their environments, including the objects, artifacts, tools, books, and the communities of which they are a part. Analyses of activity in this perspective focus on processes of interaction of individuals with other people and with physical and technological systems. Indeed, the term *interactive* (Bickhard & Richie, 1983) is a close synonym for the term *situative*. Several research traditions have contributed to the situative perspective. The best established of these is *ethnography,* including the study of cultural practices and patterns of social interactions, as well as discourse analysis and conversation analysis in activity theory, sociolinguistics, anthropology, and sociology. Another research tradition is *ecological psychology,* which studies behaviors as physical interactions in which animals, including people, participate in physical and technological systems (e.g., Turvey, 1990, 1992). A third research tradition is *situation theory,* in logic and the philosophy of mind and language, which analyzes meaning and action as relational systems and is developing a reformulation of logic to support these relational analyses (e.g., Barwise & Perry, 1983; Devlin, 1991). Knowing, in this perspective, is both an attribute of groups that carry out cooperative activities and an attribute of individuals who participate in the communities of which they are members. A group or individual with knowledge is attuned to the regularities of activities, which include the constraints and affordances of social practices and of the material and technological systems of environments. Learning by a group or individual involves becoming attuned to constraints and affordances of material and social systems with which they interact. Discussions of motivation in this perspective often emphasize engagement of individuals with the functions and goals of the community, including interpersonal commitments and ways in which individuals' identities are enhanced or diminished by their participation.

## Views of Knowing

The main reason for schooling is that students should increase in what they know. But what is knowing? A major outcome of research in educational psychology is the development of theories, grounded in empirical evidence, that help us understand what knowing is, as well as how it develops in students' learning activities. Different beliefs about the nature of knowing underlie different priorities, values, technologies, and practices in educational activity.

*Knowing as Having Associations: The Behaviorist/Empiricst View.* A strong tradition in psychology seeks to characterize knowing as having an organized collection of connections among elementary mental or behavioral units. These units may be elementary sensory impressions that combine to form percepts and concepts, or stimulus-response associations, or abstract elements of parallel, distributed networks. This empiricist view emphasizes that what someone knows is often a reflection of that person's experience, and indeed, that coming to know something requires an experience in which that knowledge can be acquired.

Stimulus-Response Association Theory. A thoroughly developed version of the behaviorist view was accomplished beginning in the 1930s. Key figures in this development were Tolman (1932), Guthrie (1935), Skinner (1938), and Hull (1943), and the theoretical issues continue to be developed in current research (e.g., Rescorla & Wagner, 1972). All of these theories are framed by the assumption that behavior is to be understood as the responses of an organism to stimuli in the situation, and they make varying assumptions about the processes by which stimulus-response associations are strengthened and weakened in the events of an organism's activity and experience. Although most of the systematic theoretical development is based on the results of experiments on learning by animals, especially rats and pigeons, the theoretical ideas of stimulus-response associations were also developed in analyses of human learning, especially those involving rote memorization (e.g., Estes, 1959; Underwood & Schulz, 1960). A major influence of stimulus-response theory in education has been its support of a view of knowledge as an assembly of specific responses, a form of knowledge often expressed as detailed *behavioral objectives* in curricula and assessment.

An important general technique of *task analysis* has been built on the assumption of associative knowing. Associationist theories of learning called for analysis of school subjects into collections of stimulus-response connections (e.g., Thorndike, 1931). Under the influence of behaviorists such as Skinner (1958), a further proposal that the collections of specific associations be expressed as *behavioral objectives* was added, and Gagné (1965) developed an elaborate system of carrying out analyses of school tasks into discriminations, classifications, and response sequences. This approach has had an enormous influence on the design of curricula, where learning tasks are arranged in sequences based on their relative complexity according to a task analysis, with simpler components treated as prerequisites for more complex tasks in which the analysis indicates that the prerequisites are included as components (e.g., Gagné, 1968).

Parallel-Distributed Connectionism. The *parallel-distributed network* or *neural network* approach characterizes knowing in terms of patterns of activation of units that excite or inhibit each other (cf. Rumelhart, McClelland, & PDP Research Group, 1986). These networks differ from networks of associations in traditional behavior theory, which have units of stimuli and responses. They also differ from the structures and procedures of cognitive theory, which have units that receive and transmit symbols. In parallel-distributed connectionism, cognitive states are represented as patterns of activation in a network of elementary units. Each unit has only a level of activation and connections with other units that transmit either excitation or inhibition. In recognizing a pattern in the situation, the network settles into a characteristic pattern of active and inactive nodes that is relatively stable, and that is different from the activation pattern into which it settles under different stimulus conditions. In acting in the situation, a pattern of activation occurs that results in a specific pattern of movement. Different patterns that can be perceived, and different actions that can be performed, correspond to different patterns of activation involving the same units, rather than to different units.

Although connectionist theories have not yet been applied extensively to educational questions, the approach is potentially very significant. It suggests an analysis of knowledge in terms of attunement to regularities in the patterns of environmental events and activities rather than in terms of components, as in behavioristic task analyses.

***Knowing as Concepts and Cognitive Abilities: The Cognitive/ Rationalist View.*** A second view treats knowing as having structures of information and processes that recognize and construct patterns of symbols in order to understand concepts and to exhibit general abilities, such as reasoning, solving problems, and using and understanding language. This approach provides a basis for analyzing concepts and procedures of subject matter curricula in terms of information structures that have been specified in considerable detail. This has provided much stronger contact between cognitively oriented educational psychologists and educators concerned with the curricula and teaching of subject matter domains than there was with behavioristic educational psychologists.

Conceptual growth and the growth of reasoning have long been active research topics in developmental psychology, and these studies have provided characterizations of general abilities and understandings that change as children grow older. Information-processing theories have also provided ways to look at general cognitive abilities as general strategies for handling information and as metacognitive processes.

General Schemata for Understanding and Reasoning.   Piaget's extensive body of work on children's cognitive development was constructed over several decades, but became influential in American educational psychology in the 1960s. His early work (e.g., 1927/1972, 1929, 1932) had focused on the specific knowledge structures that children develop— knowledge about physical and social causality, about the origins of rules, laws, and moral obligation, about how machines work. Beginning in the 1940s, however, Piaget began to formulate a theory of the development of logical structures and, although he actively rejected notions of biological determinism in human development, he argued that the capacity to comprehend certain concepts was limited by the child's level of general *logicodeductive* development. Piaget's influence on educational practice has been considerable, especially in reinforcing and informing efforts to organize science learning in a way that involves students' discovery of principles and concepts.

Conceptual Understanding.   Research on children's understanding of general concepts continues to be a significant topic in developmental psychology. Recent research has focused on the growth of children's understanding in domains such as concepts of number (e.g., Gelman & Gallistel, 1978; L. B. Resnick, 1989), biological concepts about living and nonliving things (e.g., Carey, 1985; Hatano & Inagaki, 1987; Keil, 1989), and psychological concepts about mental functioning (e.g., J. Flavell, Green, & Flavell, 1986; Wellman, 1990). This research is developing accounts of the rich intuitive conceptual understanding that children have, and that undergoes significant change as they grow older. The research emphasizes that children's learning must be viewed as transforming significant understanding that they already have, rather than as simple acquisitions written on blank slates. The results suggest that children's understanding in the domain of concepts of a subject matter provides a more important guide for the organization of curricula and teaching than does the stage they have reached in developing their general operational abilities in reasoning. There is considerable evidence that as children grow, they are able to handle more complicated tasks (Case, 1985), but we doubt that educational practice needs to be guided very strongly by ideas about the development of general schemata of logico-deductive operations in children's reasoning.

Another line of research has examined conceptual understanding where people display conceptual misunderstandings that deviate from accepted scientific concepts. These alternative understandings have been characterized by some as "misconceptions" (e.g., McCloskey, 1983), and educators have been concerned to find ways to combat them. More recent analyses have characterized the results in terms of students' use of intuitive conceptions that need to be further refined to apply correctly in the situations that evoke misconceptions (e.g., Chi, Slotta, & de Leeuw, 1994; J. P. Smith, diSessa, & Roschelle, 1993/1994; see also chapter 15, this volume). This view suggests that intuitive understanding provides the basis for new understandings that develop and should be treated as an essential resource in students' learning.

Reading and Writing.   A major achievement of the information-processing approach to cognition has been the analysis of language abilities such as reading and writing. Reading has been analyzed as a combination of abilities to encode information from text into mental representations of letters and words, to recognize the words and activate representations of their meanings, to combine representations of words into the patterns of phrases and sentences and to form representations of propositions that they express, and to combine representations of propositions into coherent representations of information conveyed by texts (e.g., Just & Carpenter, 1980; Kintsch & van Dijk, 1978; A. M. Lesgold & Perfetti, 1978). The importance in these models of recognizing and representing relations among the components of a text has led to revised measures of text readability (Miller & Kintsch, 1980) and methods of systematically improving texts so they are easier to understand (Britten & Gülgöz, 1991; Chambliss & Calfee, 1996; Kintsch, 1994).

Problem Solving and Reasoning.   The cognitive theory developed in the 1970s and 1980s included information-processing models of problem solving and reasoning. Using concepts and programming methods from the theory of text comprehension (e.g., Kintsch & van Dijk, 1978) and problem solving (Newell & Simon, 1972), several analyses of understanding and solving text problems, especially in mathematics and science, have been developed (see Greeno & Simon, 1989; VanLehn, 1989, for reviews). The most popular programming format has been the production system, where each component of knowledge is represented as a condition–action pair in which the condition is a pattern of symbols and the action is another pattern of symbols that is constructed by the program if the pattern in the condition is matched in the situation. These models include simulations of text comprehension that construct representations of the given information of the problem using schemata for general patterns. Based on the question of the problem, a model simulates setting a goal to find that answer, and applies operators that transform information in the problem representation, setting subgoals if necessary, to construct a solution of the problem.

Researchers have also investigated reasoning and understanding that depends on mental representations, called *mental models,* that provide a kind of simulation of events rather than descriptions of events (Gentner & Stevens, 1983; Halford, 1993; Johnson-Laird, 1983). In reasoning with a descriptive representation, as Newell & Simon (1972) hypothesized, an operation is applied to an expression, such as an equation or a proposition, that describes a situation. The operation produces a new expression describing the situation. In reasoning with a mental simulation, a model represents properties of the system, and operating on the model changes some of those properties in ways that correspond to changes in properties of the system.

General and Specific Strategies and Competencies.    The idea of general problem-solving heuristics has also played an important role in the cognitive view of knowing and learning. Newell (1980) introduced the terms *weak methods* and *strong methods* as labels for the distinction between general skills and methods in specific domains. By *strong,* Newell meant that a person with a great deal of relevant, well-organized knowledge would be able to solve a new problem efficiently, in part by recognizing familiar patterns in the new situation, thus bypassing the need for tedious, step-by-step analysis. But strong methods require domain-specific knowledge, and everyone is likely to encounter problems for which they do not have the appropriate domain-specific knowledge. In those cases, they must rely on more general but weaker (more time-consuming, less reliable) general heuristics.

A specific theoretical version of weak problem-solving methods was expressed in the General Problem Solver (GPS), developed as a contribution to both artificial intelligence (Ernst & Newell, 1969) and cognitive psychology (Newell & Simon, 1972). The problem-solving method ("means–ends analysis") programmed in GPS is a general heuristic procedure that has to be combined with information in a specific domain to work on a problem.

General competencies for thinking have been studied and discussed extensively in developmental psychology (see our earlier discussion of Piaget), in the development of curricula for development of thinking skills (in part III), and in the psychology of individual differences (see chapters 8 and 9). In differential psychology, there is a long-standing debate over whether there is a significant factor of general intelligence (e.g., Spearman, 1904), or whether differences among individuals consist of multiple competencies in domains such as verbal, spatial, mechanical, and the use of formal symbols (Thurstone, 1938). The latter view has been developed in recent research and discussion by H. Gardner (1983).

Many writers concerned with learning in specific subjects have also emphasized the need for students to adopt general patterns of thinking and problem solving that are productive in those domains. A well-known example in mathematics is the work of Polya (e.g., 1945) who characterized heuristic methods for solving difficult problems in ways that can lead to enrichment of understanding. Schoenfeld (1985) has extended this line of thinking with systematic research on mathematical problem solving.

Recognition of the power of strong, knowledge-specific methods in problem solving was part of what has been called the *knowledge revolution* within cognitive science (Feigen-

baum, 1989). Cognitive research began to focus heavily on mapping the nature of the knowledge that supports strong problem solving and reasoning. In educational psychology, study after study showed that students' ability to understand texts, to solve mathematical problems, or to learn new concepts in the social or natural sciences depended heavily on what the students already knew (Glaser, 1984). People need organizing schemata in order to understand and use new information. The richer and more appropriate to the problem these schemata are, the faster and more effectively will people be able to solve the problem. We discuss research concerning general strategic aspects of knowing and the contents of subject matter domains further in the third section of this chapter, ISSUES OF PRACTICAL CONCEPTUALIZATION, p. 26.

Metacognitive Processes.    Another important theme in the cognitive view of knowing is the concept of *metacognition,* the capacity to reflect upon one's own thinking, and thereby to monitor and manage it. These strategies have been studied under many labels, all pointing to the importance of self-conscious management of one's own learning and thinking processes.

This theme was introduced by developmental psychologists (e.g., A. L. Brown, 1978; Flavell & Wellman, 1977), who noted that a reflective, self-monitoring capacity discriminated developmentally advanced children from their less advanced peers. For example, research with children who have special difficulty in reading has shown that they differ particularly from more able readers in being less likely to monitor their comprehension and actively generate expectations about the information in the passage (A. L. Brown & Campione, 1981).

Research comparing excellent adult learners with less capable ones also confirmed that the most successful learners elaborate what they read and construct explanations for themselves. Chi, Bassok, Lewis, Riemann, and Glaser (1989) provided a particularly clear demonstration in a study of physics students learning from worked-out example problems. Students were classified on the basis of their performance on a test given after they studied a chapter in a physics text, and of their activities during learning as they studied the example problems. The better students treated the examples quite differently, constructing explanations of solutions in terms of problem goals and physics principles discussed in the texts, rather than simply attending to the sequence of steps in solutions, as the poorer students tended to do. An assumption that learning is facilitated when students construct explanations of problem solutions is also supported by evidence provided by C. Lewis (1988), and is used in the tutoring systems that Anderson and his associates have developed for domains of high school geometry and algebra and LISP programming (Anderson, Boyle, & Reiser, 1985). A contrast like the one between Chi and colleagues' (1989) better and poorer students was also discussed by Marton, Hounsell, and Entwhistle (1984), who distinguished between deep and shallow strategic approaches to learning taken by different students.

Students' Epistemological Beliefs.    Students' learning activities are also influenced by their beliefs and understandings of the nature of knowing and learning. An example was observed by diSessa (1985), who contrasted the learning activities of two students in a college physics course. One student, who called himself a "results man," focused on acquiring the ability to solve problems correctly. The other student focused on understanding concepts and principles and their interrelations. DiSessa characterized these two students as having different naive epistemologies, that is, as basing their learning on different beliefs and understandings of what it means to know in the domain of physics. According to the "results man," knowing was constituted by the ability to solve problems correctly, but according to the other student, knowing involved conceptual understanding.

Dweck (1983; Dweck & Legett, 1988) studied how differences in students' epistemological beliefs and understandings interact with their engagement in tasks that involve difficult challenges and their persistence in the face of difficulties. She differentiated students as to whether they pursue performance goals (i.e., they want to do well) or learning goals (i.e., they want to become more capable). Those students who believe that intelligence is a fixed trait (you are either smart or not in some area) tend to adopt performance goals, while those who believe that intelligence is acquired tend to adopt learning goals. If students pursue learning goals, they seek challenges and show high persistence in the face of difficulties. But if they adopt performance goals, they will only seek challenges and persist when they are confident of their ability to accomplish the task. Surprisingly, adoption of performance versus learning goals does not correlate with intelligence. In fact, Dweck found that highly intelligent girls tend to adopt performance goals, whereas highly intelligent boys are more likely to adopt learning goals.

Research by Gilligan and her associates (e.g., Gilligan, Ward, Taylor, & Bardige, 1988) has shown that the experiences of many girls during adolescence have particularly debilitating effects on their beliefs and understandings of themselves as knowing agents. They attribute these effects to broad social influences, including strong social expectations that girls should not participate assertively in intellectual activities, at the risk of being perceived as unfeminine.

An extensive discussion of epistemological beliefs was provided by Belenky, Clinchy, Goldberger, and Tarule (1986), on the basis of interviews with women about their beliefs and understandings of their experiences and capabilities for learning. Belenky et al. distinguished several epistemological stances, including a belief that knowledge is received from authorities, and two varieties of constructivism, one in which knowledge is distinct from what is known, and one in which knowledge is a form of connection with the ideas, information, and people that one knows about.

***Knowing as Distributed in the World: The Situative/Pragmatist-Sociohistoric View.*** A third perspective on knowing focuses on the way knowledge is distributed in the world among individuals, the tools, artifacts, and books that they use, and the communities and practices in which they participate. The situative view of knowing, involving attunements to constraints and affordances of activity systems, suggests a fundamental change in the way that instructional tasks are analyzed. The change is away from analyses of component subtasks to analyses of the regularities of successful activity.

*Participation in Practices of Communities.* One form of knowing, from this point of view, is an attribute of groups that carry out cooperative activities. Groups are composed of individuals, of course, and considering knowing as abilities of groups in their practices (i.e., *collective knowing*) is complementary to considering knowing of individuals as their abilities to participate in those practices (i.e., *individual knowing*). The practices of a community provide facilitating and inhibiting patterns that organize the group's activities and the participation of individuals who are attuned to those regularities.

Cognitive research has begun to move out of the laboratory and toward a concern with more naturalistic learning environments. This research carries forward many elements of older traditions of human factors research, but it is much broader in scope and orientation, including ethnographic, ethnomethodological, and cultural psychology traditions. A theory of cognitive situations is beginning to emerge that takes the distributed nature of cognition as a starting point (J. S. Brown, Collins, & Duguid, 1989; L. B. Resnick, 1987b). In these theories, success in cognitive functions such as reasoning, remembering, and perceiving is understood as an achievement of a system, with contributions of the individuals who participate, along with tools and artifacts. This means that thinking is situated in a particular context of intentions, social partners, and tools (L. B. Resnick, Levine, & Teasley, 1991; J. M. Levine, Resnick, & Higgins, 1993).

The knowing of communities in their social practices has traditionally been studied more by anthropologists and sociologists than by psychologists (although see Cole, Gay, Glick, & Sharp, 1971), and recent analyses of cognitive performance in work settings continue that tradition (e.g., Hutchins, 1995; Workplace Project, 1991). Processes of discourse in social interaction have been studied for some time by sociolinguists and ethnomethodologists (e.g., Gumperz, 1982; Schegloff, 1991) and, more recently, by psycholinguists (e.g., Clark, 1992).

Everyday practices involving reasoning about quantities have been studied extensively, providing important information about reasoning capabilities that are not acquired in school (Lave, 1988; Nunes, Schliemann, & Carraher, 1993; Saxe, 1990). Practices of research communities have also been studied, for example, by Latour and Woolgar (1979/1986), Lynch (1993), and Ochs, Jacoby, and Gonzalez (1994). These studies have provided information about ways in which information is interpreted and portrayed in the construction of data and explanations in the literature of a field such as physics and biology.

Knowing how to participate in social practices plays a crucial role in all aspects of a student's learning in and out of school. Classroom activities are organized in various ways, and children participate in them more or less successfully. In typical patterns of classroom discourse described by Cazden (1986), Mehan (1979), and others, the teacher addresses questions to the class, receives an answer from someone he or she calls on, and evaluates the answer for the class's information. Different patterns of discourse in which small groups of students interact with each other (e.g., Cohen, 1986) or in which students in the class formulate questions and evaluate other students' presentations are possible and have been discussed (e.g., Cobb et al., 1991; Fawcett, 1938; Lampert, 1990; Schoenfeld, 1987). A major feature of these alternative patterns of discourse is the distribution of responsibility for proposing questions and explanations and for evaluating contributions made by students, with more of those functions in the hands of students than in traditional didactic instruction. Knowing how to participate in these discourse practices is an important aspect of ability to understand and inquire in subject matter disciplines, which includes ability to distinguish questions, arguments, and explanations that are taken as valid in the disciplines.

Abilities to Interact with Physical Environments.  Ecological psychology also redefines the nature of knowing, but the analysis focuses on relations between actions and the physical situation. Historically, a few psychologists have objected to the stimulus-response view of behavior, arguing that a more general, interactionist view of the relation between action and situations is appropriate (e.g., Dewey, 1896; Lashley, 1951). However, this interactionist view was not developed systematically until Gibson (1966) developed a theory of direct perception. Gibson focused on perception in the context of orienting and moving about in an environment and argued that perception should be understood as a process of picking up information as an aspect of the agent's activity, rather than as a process of constructing representations of the situation and operating on those representations. Gibson (1979/1986) also began to develop the concept of *affordances,* arguing that the psychologically significant information in environments specifies ways in which spatial settings and objects can contribute to our interactions with them. Recently, Turvey (1990, 1992) and others have been developing this interactionist view by working out specific analyses of activities, such as juggling, in which an agent and some physical objects interact, applying forces to each other and moving through space in a coordinated system. Norman (1988) has discussed principles in the design of artifacts that provide affordances—sometimes of a negative kind—for human interactions with them.

## Views of Learning and Transfer

Learning and transfer are critical issues for educational psychology. Learning is the process by which knowledge is increased or modified. Transfer is the process of applying knowledge in new situations. Educators want the knowledge that is acquired in school to apply generally in students' lives, rather than being limited to the situations of classrooms where it is acquired. That is to say, they want the knowledge to transfer. In this section, we summarize some of the contributions of psychological research to the understanding of learning and transfer and consider ways in which these contributions have been influenced by the views of knowing that we discussed in the previous section.

### Acquiring and Applying Associations: The Behaviorist/ Empiricist View

Learning.  When people's knowledge is viewed as their having associations between ideas or stimuli and responses, learning is the formation, strengthening, and adjustment of those associations. Processes that have been analyzed in research include (a) conditioning of reflexes, where a response to one situation comes to be associated with another situation; (b) reinforcement of stimulus-response associations, where particu-

lar connections are strengthened by feedback from the environment; and (c) forming associations among units of verbal items, as when people learn lists of words or digits.

The research on basic associative processes of learning has important implications for teaching and learning. One is the importance of individual students' having opportunities to give responses of the kind that they are to learn and of feedback that is contingent on the individual student's responses. For learning routine tasks, there are significant advantages of efficiency in individualizing instruction, so that each student responds actively to questions and problems and receives feedback for each response, feedback that the student can relate clearly to the response that he or she gave. This has informed the development of programmed instruction and computer programs that teach routine skills in mathematics, reading, and vocabulary. It has been found that students learn more effectively from such individualized instruction than from standard classroom instruction (e.g., Galanter, 1968; Suppes & Morningstar, 1972).

Researchers in behavioral conditioning also found that effective learning usually requires significant preparation, or *shaping,* in which the learner becomes oriented to the general conditions of activity in which learning will occur. This is especially important in *instrumental conditioning,* where the effect of instruction depends on being able to reinforce desired responses, which therefore must occur in order for the reinforcements to be provided. In conditioning experiments with animals, shaping involves a period in which the trainer attends carefully to the animal's activity in the learning environment, first providing reinforcement for being near the apparatus that the animal can respond to (e.g., a disk that a pigeon can peck), then for orienting toward the apparatus, then for touching it, and finally only for pecking it, the response that is desired. This kind of instruction-by-approximation has clear parallels in school learning, where skilled teachers attend to students' progress and provide encouragement for students' attention and efforts as they achieve better approximations to the patterns of behavior that they need in order to succeed.

Analysis of complex tasks into learning hierarchies (Gagné, 1968) has been used in designing instructional sequences and computer-based systems for learning routine skills. The hypothesis that smaller units of behavior need to be mastered as prerequisites for more complex units provides a basis for arranging sequences of instruction in which students are able to succeed by learning in small steps. This *decomposition hypothesis* is currently being questioned by many in the cognitive community (e.g., Resnick & Resnick, 1991), based on a concern that instruction limited to presentation of small-to-large components can result in mechanical knowledge without sufficient development of the usefulness or conceptual basis for procedures that are learned.

The phenomena of classical conditioning emphasize that important learning can occur that is unintended, called *incidental learning.* This is especially important regarding affective responses: Students' experiences of either pleasure and satisfaction or embarrassment and humiliation are likely to become conditioned to stimuli in the circumstances of their learning, thereby shaping students' future affective responses to the situations of school learning.

In the connectionist perspective, learning is viewed as developing a pattern of activity that is aligned better with the regularities of the environment and successful performance, rather than as additions of components to the learner's cognitive structure. Strengths of excitatory and inhibitory connections in the network are changed by presentation of feedback that allows the pattern of activation in the network to be compared with a desired pattern, and changes occur through a process of adjusting connections to increase the match between the actual pattern of activation and the desired pattern (e.g., Rumelhart, Hinton, & Williams, 1986).

Transfer.   In the view that knowing is having associations, learning in a new situation depends on how many, and which kinds of associations needed in the new situation have already been acquired in the previous situation. The idea of transfer in conditioning involves *gradients* of similarity along stimulus dimensions, so that a response learned as an association to one stimulus generalizes more strongly to other stimuli that are similar to it in all respects, and less strongly to stimuli that differ from it in one or more dimensions. Thorndike (1903) expressed this as a theory of transfer based on common elements. Later theories expressed parallel ideas, involving similarity between stimuli and responses (Osgood, 1949), and the numbers and kinds of condition–action production rules that are shared between procedures that are learned initially and procedures that are learned in a transfer situation (Singley & Anderson, 1989).

### Acquiring and Using Conceptual and Cognitive Structures: The Cognitive/Rationalist View

Conceptual Learning.   Most recent research on students' conceptual learning in subject matter domains has been organized by the framing assumption of *constructivism,* the assumption that understanding is gained by an active process of construction rather than by passive assimilation of information or rote memorization (Confrey, 1990). Constructivist research in the fields of subject matter teaching and learning has been strongly influenced by Piaget's ideas about cognitive development, particularly by the idea that conceptual abilities grow out of intellectual activity rather than by absorption of information (e.g., Steffe, Cobb, & von Glasersfeld, 1988).

Educational psychologists have contributed empirical and theoretical research to this constructivist program. Many of these studies have focused on use of concrete materials and other analogies that are manipulated in ways that illustrate conceptual principles (e.g., D. E. Brown & Clement, 1989; Brownell, 1935; L. B. Resnick & Omanson, 1987; Sayeki, Ueno, & Nagasaka, 1991; Wertheimer, 1945/1959). Several recent studies have shown ways in which conceptual understanding can be fostered in interactive computer environments (Kaput, 1989; Moore, 1993; Pea, 1993; Roschelle, 1992; Schwarz, Kohn, & Resnick, 1994; B. Y. White, 1993; Wiser & Kipman, 1988). These studies provide valuable information about conditions in which learning with understanding can occur.

Studies of cognitive development in subject matter domains also have contributed to the constructivist program. They show how significant conceptual growth in children's informal understanding of numerical, biological, and psychological concepts occurs over a period of years.

Another line of research emphasizes addressing students'

initial conceptual understandings by having them participate in conversations about the meanings of concepts, including formulating and evaluating questions, hypotheses, and arguments (Lampert, 1990; Minstrell, 1989; Yackel, Cobb, & Wood, 1991). The role of this discourse depends on the kind of knowledge that students have, and there are differing hypotheses about that, as we discussed in the previous section on p. 18. If one believes that students have an incorrect scientific theory or *misconception* in the domain, then it is appropriate to elicit their beliefs and confront them with contradictory evidence. On the other hand, if one believes that their understanding is based on intuitions that are valid in some circumstances, then a more exploratory kind of conversation is probably more effective. Then students can develop ways of talking and thinking about phenomena and gradually become more attuned to the ways in which properties in the domain are related (J. P. Smith, diSessa, & Roschelle, 1993/1994; B. White & Frederiksen, 1990).

Learning Problem-Solving Representations and Procedures.   Symbolic information-processing models of solving text problems characterize knowledge for solving problems in terms of procedures that represent problem information, set goals, and transform symbolic expressions to satisfy the main problem goal. Models of learning in this tradition simulate processes that add to and modify the learners' procedural knowledge (see VanLehn, 1989, for a review).

One example, the Soar program, developed by Newell (1990) and his associates, constructs new procedural knowledge using a combination of weak problem-solving methods (see p. 18) and a process of chunking that converts a trace of successful problem solving into new procedures. Soar works on a problem using whatever representations and procedures it already has. When it reaches an impasse that involves a subgoal for which it does not have adequate procedures, it constructs a problem space in which to find a solution to that subproblem using weak search methods. When it has found a way to achieve that subgoal it constructs a new procedure by a process of chunking.

Another example, by Anderson (1983), simulates three kinds of learning processes: proceduralization, tuning, and automatization. Anderson assumed that in an early stage of learning to solve a kind of problem, the student interprets information that is available in declarative form, such as written or spoken instructions or worked example problems. One hypothesis of the model is that procedural knowledge is constructed, in the form of condition–action production rules, that associate actions that are performed in interpreting the declarative information with goals and stimulus information that the student attends to. The conditions of production rules that are constructed are consistent with information in the specific situation in which they are formed, but those rules rarely have conditions that include just the features that are needed to provide correct performance. As learning proceeds, tuning of the production rules occurs in processes of discrimination and generalization, based on feedback that the student's responses are correct or in error. Finally, the model's procedures become more efficient by combining rules that occur together.

Some information-processing models of learning include hypotheses about roles of conceptual understanding in learning problem-solving procedures. One model, by VanLehn, Jones, and Chi (1992), simulates learning to solve physics text problems. Based on the finding of Chi et al. (1989) that better learners constructed explanations of problem steps in terms of problem goals and physics concepts, VanLehn et al. simulated the construction of explanations as a process of deriving the steps of solved examples and thereby adding problem-solving rules that are associated with relevant conditions of problems. The model also simulates learning of derivational knowledge by storing representations of its derivations in a form that allows their use as analogues to control search in later problem solving. Because of this latter feature, the model learns more effectively during its own problem solving, in addition to acquiring more useful rules while it studies examples.

Another example is in work by Ohlsson and Rees (1991), whose model hypothesizes knowledge of general principles in the form of constraints that are applied by the learning program or by a tutor to evaluate the results of applying the model's procedural knowledge as it works on problems. When a step in problem solving produces violation of a constraint, the model constructs new rules that take account of the conditions specified in the constraint.

Transfer.    Concepts and principles of a domain are designed to provide generality, and studies of learning and transfer in domains have often used tasks involving transfer to test whether students achieved understanding. In the cognitive perspective, transfer is assumed to depend on acquiring an abstract mental representation in the form of a schema that designates relations that compose a structure that is invariant across situations. In analyses of problem solving, there is evidence that the general schema has to be acquired in initial learning (Bassok & Holyoak, 1989; Gick & Holyoak, 1983), along with practice in applying the schema to examples (Holland, Holyoak, Nisbett, & Thagard, 1986), and that schemata that can be induced naturally as patterns of everyday experience are more easily taught than formal, syntactic rule systems (Nisbett, Fong, Lehman, & Cheng, 1987).

A large body of research has found that students often fail to transfer from learning that they have accomplished. A. L. Brown (1989) pointed out that in research about children's ability to transfer, the deck is stacked in favor of finding that transfer does not occur. Children are asked to solve a problem, then a new problem is presented, and the experimenter observes whether the new problem is solved in a way that uses the initial solution. Usually, experimenters do their best to hide the relation between the two problems when the second problem is presented, so that if children do transfer, we can be sure they did so spontaneously. More important, for Brown, the potential generality of the initial solution is not made clear. When Brown and Kane (1988) taught solutions of problems and asked children to explain why the solutions were examples of general themes, thus calling attention to their potential generality, the children in their experiments transferred much more successfully. (See also chapter 3.)

There is an important theoretical and educational principle in these results about transfer. The manner in which solutions of problems are presented can make a major difference for the generality of what is learned. If students understand the solution as an example of a general method, and if they understand the general features of the learning situation that are relevant to use of the method, the abilities they learn are more likely to

be applied generally. This idea is consistent with results of research that has studied educational programs that are designed to strengthen students' general strategies and schemata for thinking and reasoning. Two general conclusions of this research are (a) that productive learning of thinking practices occurs mainly in settings where subject matter content is involved, and (b) successful programs emphasize the social processes of explanation, formulation of problems and questions, and argumentation (L. B. Resnick, 1987a).

### Becoming Attuned to Constraints and Affordances Through Participation: The Situative/Pragmatist-Sociohistoric View

Learning.    When knowing is viewed as practices of communities and the abilities of individuals to participate in those practices, then learning is the strengthening of those practices and participatory abilities. Systems in which individuals learn to participate in social practices are very common and include apprenticeship and other forms of being initiated into the practices of a group. Lave and Wenger (1991) reviewed several studies of learning involving apprenticeship and concluded that a crucial factor in the success of such a system is that learners must be afforded legitimate peripheral participation, which involves access to the practices that they are expected to learn and genuine participation in the activities and concerns of the group. Lave and Wenger characterized learning of practices as processes of participation in which beginners are relatively peripheral in the activities of a community, and as they become more experienced and adept, their participation becomes more central. A crucial issue in the nature of learning is whether, and in what ways, the peripheral participation of beginners is legitimate. For an environment of apprenticeship to be a productive environment of learning, learners need to have opportunities to observe and practice activities in which their abilities will become stronger in ways that correspond to progress toward more central participation.

The view that learning of practices occurs through participation is at the root of the practices of apprenticeship, which occur in work environments where apprentices are guided and supervised by masters. In successful apprenticeship learning, masters teach by showing apprentices how to do a task (modeling), and then helping them as they try to do it on their own (coaching and fading). Lave and Wenger (1991) emphasized how an apprentice's identity derives from becoming part of the community of workers. They also noted that an apprenticeship relationship can be unproductive for learning. Productive apprenticeship depends on opportunities for the apprentice to participate legitimately, albeit peripherally, in the activities that he or she is learning. The motive for becoming a more central participant in a community of practice can provide a powerful motivation for learning. Of course, what is learned in apprenticeship may not easily generalize to other contexts. Collins, Brown, and Newman (1989) attempted to characterize how the modeling, coaching, and fading paradigm of apprenticeship might be applied to learning the cognitive subjects of school in an approach they called "cognitive apprenticeship."

Stein, Silver, and Smith (in press) have analyzed aspects of middle school mathematics teachers modifying their practices to involve students in more active meaning making and student-to-student communication from the perspective of their participation in a community of teachers working with shared goals for reform. Hutchins (1993) has given an account of how seamen learn the practices of navigating a large ship. The account includes discussion of an arrangement of tasks that the novice proceeds through in becoming competent and the importance of interaction with other, more experienced seamen in the situations in which the learning occurs.

A major goal of educational reform is to have students participate more actively in learning communities, including participation in formulating and evaluating questions and problems, and constructing and evaluating hypotheses, evidence, arguments, and conclusions. Abilities for participating in these activities have to be learned, and the research literature on that kind of learning is sparse. Several projects have focused on creating classroom practices of discussion and inquiry, and the investigators in those projects have discussed some aspects of the process of establishing norms and expectations by the students that support productive collaborative learning (Cobb, Wood, & Yackel, 1990; Cohen, 1986; Lampert, 1990; Slavin, 1983).

In ecological psychology, where learning involves attunement to constraints and affordances, progress in the learning of a skill can be measured by examining how the learner's performance corresponds to regularities that are important in coordinating the person's movements with relevant characteristics of the environmental system (Turvey, 1990).

Transfer.  In the view of learning as coming to participate in a community of practice, transfer becomes a problematic issue. The question is whether transfer applies to new practices within the community (e.g., for school communities this might mean working new problems or accomplishing new kinds of tasks) or to practices outside the community (e.g., for school communities these might be work environments). Many of the resources and supports that occur within a community of practice do not carry over to a different community, and so the problem of transfer becomes one of marshaling the resources needed to be successful in a new environment. This requires sophisticated social and information-processing skills: the kinds of skills that businesses think they will need in the future.

In the ecological view of learning as attunement to constraints and affordances of activity, performance and learning in a new situation depend on how the learner is attuned to the constraints of activity in that situation. To analyze the problem of transfer, we need to consider (a) constraints and affordances that support activity that is learned in the learning situation, (b) constraints and affordances that support successful activity in the transfer situation, and (c) the transformations that relate the learning and transfer situations, especially which constraints and affordances remain unchanged by the transformation from the learning situation to the transfer situation. For transfer to be possible, there must be some constraints and/or affordances that are invariant under the transformations that change the learning situation into the transfer situation. For transfer to occur, the learner must become attuned to those invariants in her or his initial learning. One of the ways to be attuned is to have an abstract representation that can apply in the new situation, but this is only one possible way for attunement to occur, and it may not be the typical way for many learned activities to generalize (Greeno, Smith, & Moore, 1993).

This approach to analyzing transfer is illustrated by classic experiments concerning transfer and conceptual understanding. Scholckow and Judd (Judd, 1908) and Hendrikson and Schroeder (1941) gave boys practice in hitting a target under water. Some of the boys received an explanation of refraction of light before their target practice, others did not. The boys who received the explanation did better in transferring their skill when the depth of the water was subsequently changed. Greeno et al. (1993) interpreted the finding as resulting from an effect on the boys' attention, due to instruction about refraction, to focus on more relational features of the situation of aiming at the targets, such as apparent angular displacements of the paths of objects as they entered the water. These relational features are invariant in the transformation of changing the depth of the water, whereas other features, such as the linear displacement to use to hit the target, change.

Another example is in the results of Sayeki and colleagues' (1991) instructional experiment involving areas of parallelograms. Children were given stacks of cards that could have the shape of a rectangle or, if the cards were slid, a parallelogram. The sliding corresponded to a shear transformation that left the area constant while changing the lengths of two of the sides. The base and height of the shape, as well as the area, were invariant under the transformation. Another device given to students was a box with fixed sides that could be bent at the corners to make parallelograms with different shapes. Although the lengths of the sides were constant, the area clearly changed. Experience with these materials supported students' understanding in a way that transferred to other problems, including writing equations for areas of parallelograms, triangles, and trapezoids. Greeno et al. (1993) interpreted this finding as an example in which learning experiences can result in attunements to constraints and affordances for reasoning that remain invariant across transformations of situations.

## Views of Motivation and Engagement

All of the psychological perspectives on learning school subjects assert that learning requires the active participation of students. Questions about this tend to be framed differently in the three broad perspectives, with an emphasis on *extrinsic motivation* in the behaviorist perspective, an emphasis on *intrinsic motivation* in the cognitive perspective, and an emphasis on *engaged participation* in the situative perspective.

***Extrinsic Motivation: The Behaviorist/Empiricist View.***  In the view that learning involves forming associations, engagement is assumed to occur mainly because of extrinsic motivations—rewards, punishments, and positive or negative incentives—that affect the individual's tendency to respond in the way that is needed for learning to occur. The motivations are extrinsic in the sense that they derive from outside the individual. But their effects depend on the internal goals and needs of the individual. A reward is only effective to the degree the person receiving it wants it, and a punishment to the degree the person wants to avoid it. Engagement in activities can also be considered as a decision based on expected utilities of outcomes of the engagement, which depend on the individual's subjective probabilities and utilities regarding outcomes of alternative participation in different ways in learning activities.

Behaviorists took a primarily biological view of motivation, believing that the needs of the organism for food, water, air, sleep, and so on, and the avoidance of pain were the fundamental motives for action. They hypothesized that other motives, such as attraction to social affiliation or interesting cognitive activity, or fear of other people or situations, developed through association of these stimuli with basic biological outcomes. For example, according to the behaviorists, a subject could become conditioned to anticipate negative reinforcement on presentation of a stimulus if that stimulus was associated with painful experiences. The range of basic biological factors in motivation was debated energetically. Harlow and Zimmerman (1958) argued that infant mammals need the comfort of contact with their mothers. Berlyne (1960) argued that mammals are inherently attracted to novel situations. R. W. White (1959) argued that humans, at least, are inherently motivated to achieve mastery of tasks that present behavioral challenges. All of these arguments were supported empirically and persuaded many psychologists that extrinsic motivational factors exist that are not based on individual short-term survival.

Decision-making theory is another expression of the idea that people do what they do because of extrinsically rewarding or punishing outcomes. A decision situation is one where there are alternative actions. The decision maker is assumed to choose an action on the basis of expectations of outcomes that could follow the various alternative actions. Each possible outcome of an action is assumed to have some positive or negative *utility* for the individual, as well as a degree of expectation or *subjective probability* of occurring if that action is chosen. The *subjectively expected utility* of an action is the average of the utilities for the outcomes, weighted by their subjective probabilities. This theory assumes that people make choices that are of greatest benefit to them in the long run.

School life is filled with many different kinds of extrinsic motivations. Rewards include high grades, extra credit, gold stars, positive comments on work done, chances to perform or to do enjoyable activities, smiles, pats on the head, and other affectionate or encouraging responses from the teacher. Punishments include low grades, doing work over again, detention, letters home to parents, negative comments, being removed from the classroom or the school, frowns, and corporal punishment.

Rewards and punishments are the traditional terms used in this view of motivation. Behaviorists introduced the terms *positive* and *negative reinforcement* to emphasize their view that rewards tend to strengthen particular response tendencies and punishments to weaken particular response tendencies, or to cause negative emotional states that interfere generally with performance. When an individual is motivated to respond correctly, according to some criterion, informational feedback— also called knowledge of results—provides positive reinforcement for accurate responding and negative reinforcement for inaccurate responding, along with information to guide an adjustment in the performance for future occasions. This idea of feedback fits the connectionist view in which information fed back to the system strengthens certain connections and weakens others.

Behaviorists generally emphasized motivational issues as central to learning. In their view, learning depends on reinforcements acting to strengthen or weaken stimulus-response bonds. They argued that it was critical that the reinforcements be di-

rectly tied to particular behaviors (e.g., be close in time) in order to be most effective.

Skinner (1953) believed that negative reinforcements are often harmful to learning, because they suppress responding and can discourage people from participating lest they be punished. So he developed an approach to learning, called programmed instruction, that emphasizes positive reinforcement (Skinner, 1958). In it, students carry out tasks that increase in difficulty in very small steps, so that almost everything they do is correct. Thus, they receive almost entirely positive reinforcements during learning. The trade-off with this approach is pacing: The instruction should not move so quickly that some students make mistakes and not move so slowly that other students are bored. Computers make it possible to adjust the increments in difficulty for each individual student.

Anderson et al. (1985), though cognitive researchers, have partially incorporated Skinner's theory of programmed instruction in their intelligent tutoring systems for teaching computer programming, geometry, and algebra. Students are given tasks of slowly increasing difficulty and they are prevented from making mistakes, so that they receive mostly positive reinforcement in working with these tutoring systems.

Connectionists also treat positive and negative reinforcements as critical to learning. Learning occurs in connectionist systems based on the match between expected outcomes and actual outcomes. Some connectionist experiments employ a "teacher" to reward certain outcomes and punish others (Rumelhart et al., 1986). But in either case, learning occurs by strengthening the connections that are active when a desired outcome occurs and weakening the connections that are active when an undesired outcome occurs.

***Intrinsic Motivation: The Cognitive/Rationalist View.*** When learning is viewed as the acquisition of knowledge and understanding of information, concepts, principles, and strategies, engagement is often considered to be a person's intrinsic interest in a domain of cognitive activity, such as music, athletics, or an academic subject. The cognitive view, with its emphasis on general concepts and methods, treats engagement in learning as an intrinsic property of the relation between individuals and the organization of information. Children are seen as naturally motivated to learn when their experience is inconsistent with their current understanding or when they experience regularities in information that are not yet represented by their schemata. This view is perhaps best exemplified in the theories of Piaget (1935,1969/1970) and Papert (1980). Unlike the behaviorist emphasis on manipulating rewards and punishments, the cognitive emphasis is on figuring out ways to foster students' natural tendencies to learn and understand.

Cognitive researchers have investigated the relations between intrinsic motivation and extrinsic motivation (Lepper & Greene, 1979). The major finding of this research has been that if people are rewarded for doing things they would choose to do for intrinsic reasons, they will no longer be willing to do them without the rewards (that is, for intrinsic reasons alone). Malone (1981) has developed a framework for intrinsic motivation in terms of three elements: challenge, fantasy, and curiosity. He attempted to characterize how to make learning environments more engaging in terms of ways to increase their challenge, fantasy, and curiosity for children. The cognitive goal is to develop learning activities that will engage students' participation in inquiry into the subject matter.

Students also differ in their participation in school learning activities based on their beliefs and understandings of themselves as knowing agents, and of what it means to know and understand. We discussed research that has characterized some of these differences in an earlier section (see p. 22).

*Engaged Participation: The Situative/Pragmatist-Sociohistoric View.* The view of learning as becoming more adept at participating in distributed cognitive systems focuses on engagement that maintains the person's interpersonal relations and identity in communities in which the person participates, or involves satisfying interactions with environments in which the individual has a significant personal investment. This view emphasizes how people's very identities derive from their participatory relationships in communities. According to this view, students can become engaged in learning by participating in communities where learning is valued.

An example of powerful learning of a social practice is learning one's native language in the contexts of communicating with other members of the family and community. Learning to read and write in our society is somewhat less automatic, but F. Smith (1988) argued that students will learn to read and write if they want to join the "literacy club." That is to say, if family and friends read and write, then children will want to learn to read and write. Smith noted that we all learn to speak and dress and present ourselves by our interactions with others—it is how we establish our identities. Yet our theories of school learning attempt to teach us in isolation from others by manipulating rewards and punishments, on the one hand, or by challenge and curiosity, on the other. Smith found it strange that we all believe that people learn by the company they keep, but that we have designed learning theories and environments that disregard the theory.

Lave and Wenger (1991) also treated the issue of identity as critical to their view of engagement in learning activities. An important characteristic of legitimate peripheral participation is genuine involvement in activities of the community, in which people can establish their identities in terms of functioning in the communities they join, and as they become more central to the functioning of a community, their sense of identity deriving from that community is enhanced. The motivation to learn the values and practices of the community then is tied up with establishing their identities as community members.

Educational innovations that have the goal of developing participation in social practices of inquiry and discourse can be organized to provide a community of learners to foster the engagement of students in those practices. A. L. Brown and Campione and their associates (e.g., A. L. Brown et al., 1993) organize communities of learners who collaborate on research and development of expository documents on significant academic topics, such as biology. Scardamalia and Bereiter (1991) organize communities in classes in which the members communicate concerning their discoveries and opinions about academic topics. Mathematics classrooms organized by the Algebra Project (Moses, Kamii, Swap, & Howard, 1989), Cobb et al. (1991), Lampert (1990), Schoenfeld (1987), and others are communities of practice in which students participate by thinking about mathematical topics and discussing their ideas. All these efforts emphasize creating communities where the students will develop identities as active learners with responsibility for what they learn.

Eckert (1989) focused on school culture and how different communities in American high schools (called "jocks" and "burnouts" by the students in the school Eckert studied) determine students' orientation toward school learning. The jocks adopted the school's values and hence they were engaged in ways that they recognized would result in achieving the various kinds of rewards that the school offered, such as participating in sports and performances, getting on the honor roll, and so forth. The burnouts, on the other hand, rejected the values that the school promulgated and developed a set of counterculture values and practices. Many students fell into neither of these groups, but the two communities formed an axis that was an important factor in the social organization of the school, an axis that had a major influence on students' engagement in academic learning activities, especially those involving mathematics and science education (Eckert, 1990), as well as other activities in the school.

Learning situations also present different opportunities for participation to different individuals. A teacher and other students may expect less understanding by members of a minority group or from girls than from majority students or boys, and therefore may provide fewer and less productive opportunities for them to participate in learning interactions. A provocative example was provided by McDermott (1993) in an article titled "The acquisition of a child by a learning disability," which described patterns of interaction in a classroom in which a child, the teacher, and the other children cooperated to define the child's role as one who was unlikely to understand, cooperate, or engage productively in learning activities.

Of course, effective learning involves being strongly engaged in activities that capture the learners' interests because of their intrinsic qualities as well as participation in communities. Individuals become strongly engaged in activities such as music, literature, chess, athletics, mathematics, science, computer games, and television programs, where they devote much time and energy, and their identities become invested in the growth and maintenance of abilities to participate productively in those environments. For some individuals, participation in these activities involves much group interaction; for others, it is primarily a solitary pursuit in which their social roles are defined significantly in terms of their extraordinary personal immersion in the domains of their special interests.

## ISSUES OF PRACTICAL CONCEPTUALIZATION

In this section we consider three issues of educational practice: designing learning environments, formulating curricula, and constructing assessments. We consider these issues from the point of view of design experiments (A. L. Brown, 1992; Collins, 1992), which combine the goals of improving some aspect of practice and of advancing theoretical understanding of fundamental principles. The principles that are investigated are assumptions of the practice, which A. L. Brown and Campione (1994; A. L. Brown, 1994) called *first principles*. Those principles may be largely implicit in the practice, and changes in them may be required for the desired changes in practice to occur. J. S. Brown (1991) argued that investigation of such principles should be a primary objective of research and reform, in which practitioners and researchers collaborate to identify assumptions that underlie current practices as well as assumptions of practices that they would prefer, both to contribute to general understanding of how practices are organized and to identify requirements for practical change.

The principles that we consider in relation to the practical issues of this section come from the three perspectives on the nature of knowing, learning and transfer, and motivation and engagement that we developed in the foregoing section. We discuss ways in which consideration of the practical issues differs depending on the theoretical perspective that is taken, and therefore, what some of the implications of those theoretical perspectives are for these aspects of educational practice. At the same time, consideration of these practical issues sheds further light on the theoretical issues.

As an overview, we present a summary statement of the set of design principles that we then consider more specifically in the subsections that follow. We arrange these principles here by the broad perspectives on cognition and learning that put them into focus. We index these with letters associated with the perspectives: b for behaviorist, c for cognitive, and s for situative.

## The Behaviorist/Empiricist View

In designing learning environments:

(b1) *Routines of activity for effective transmission of knowledge.* Learning activities can be organized to optimize acquisition of information and routine skill. In learning environments organized for these purposes, learning occurs most effectively if the teaching or learning program is well organized, with routines for classroom activity that students know and follow efficiently.

(b2) *Clear goals, feedback, and reinforcement.* For routine learning, it is advantageous to have explicit instructional goals, to present instructions that specify the procedures and information to be learned and the way that learning materials are organized, to ensure that students have learned prerequisites for each new component, to provide opportunities for students to respond correctly, to give detailed feedback to inform students which items they have learned and which they still need to work on, and to provide reinforcement for learning that satisfies students' motivations.

(b3) *Individualization with technologies.* Acquisition of basic information and routine skills can be facilitated by using technologies, including computer technology, that support individualized training and practice sequences.

In formulating curricula:

(b4) *Sequences of component-to-composite skills.* To facilitate learning of a complex but well-defined skill, the sequence of instruction should proceed from simpler components to the more complex component that they compose.

In constructing assessments:

(b5) *Assessment of knowledge components.* Tests of students' achievement in acquiring routine information and skill can be constructed by analyzing the procedures and information to be acquired and constructing items that assess students' knowledge of the components. Tests of elementary components of knowledge can be administered and scored fairly and efficiently, and can be evaluated rigorously regarding statistical properties of reliability and validity for predicting other performance that can be measured objectively.

## The Cognitive/Rationalist View

In designing learning environments:

(c1) *Interactive environments for construction of understanding.* Learning environments can be organized to foster students' constructing understanding of concepts and principles through problem solving and reasoning in activities that engage students' interests and use of their initial understandings and their general reasoning and problem-solving abilities.

In formulating curricula:

(c2) *Sequences of conceptual development.* Sequences of learning activities can proceed from issues and problems that are within reach of students' initial understanding and reasoning ability to issues and problems that require greater extensions of their intuitive capabilities, accomplishing conceptual growth by refining and extending their initial understandings.

(c3) *Explicit attention to generality.* The curriculum of a subject matter domain can be organized so that students come to understand the major unifying principles of the domain. Information and problem-solving methods can be presented and discussed in ways that make their general significance and usefulness salient.

In constructing assessments:

(c4) *Assessments of extended performance.* Assessments that evaluate students' work on extended projects, or performance for which they prepare over an extended period, can provide information about significant aspects of their intellectual abilities and growth that are not available in short-answer or simple-problem tests, and can focus educational efforts on these more significant aspects of learning.

(c5) *Crediting varieties of excellence.* Assessments of understanding and reasoning need to credit varieties of excellence, which can encourage students with diverse backgrounds and abilities to contribute to the community of learners and to have their successful contributions and achievements recognized.

## The Situative/Pragmatist-Sociohistoric View

In designing learning environments:

(s1) *Environments of participation in social practices of inquiry and learning.* Learning environments can be organized to foster students' learning to participate in practices of inquiry and learning and to support the development of students' personal identities as capable and confident learners and knowers. These activities include formulating and evaluating questions, problems, conjectures, arguments, explanations, and so forth, as aspects of the social practices of sense-making and learning, including abilities to use a rich variety of social and material resources for learning and to contribute to socially organized learning activities, as well as to engage in concentrated individual efforts.

(s2) *Support for development of positive epistemic identities.*

Learning environments can be organized to support the development of students' personal identities as capable and confident learners and knowers. This can include organizing learning activities in ways that complement and reinforce differences in patterns of social interaction and in expertise brought by students of differing cultural backgrounds.

In formulating curricula:

(s3) *Development of disciplinary practices of discourse and representation.* Sequences of learning activities can be organized with attention to students' progress in a variety of practices of learning, reasoning, cooperation, and communication, as well as to the subject matter contents that should be covered. Learning to participate in characteristic discourse in a domain and to use the representational systems and tools of the domain can be focused on the distinctive values and limitations of these practices, rather than on whether students correctly follow predetermined forms of discourse and representation.

(s4) *Practices of formulating and solving realistic problems.* Learning activities can focus on problematic situations that are meaningful in terms of students' experience and in which concepts and methods of subject matter disciplines are embedded. Substantial projects and long-term simulations of social activity systems can contribute to significant learning of practices of inquiry.

In constructing assessments:

(s5) *Assessing participation in inquiry and social practices of learning.* Assessments of students' abilities to participate in communities of practice require that observations of that participation should be included in the assessments of students' learning.

(s6) *Student participation in assessment.* Opportunities to participate in the formulation and conduct of assessment processes are an important aspect of fairness in assessment, and can facilitate students' development of mature judgment of and responsibility for their individual intellectual work and their contributions to the work of groups in which they participate.

(s7) *Design of assessment systems.* Assessments can be designed as systems that take into account the effects of assessment on the learning environments and teaching interactions of school activity, and that support the demanding requirements of human evaluation that are required for meaningful assessment of students' progress in learning.

## Designing Learning Environments

Many design experiments in education are focused on learning environments that are organized by a set of assumptions about the nature of knowing and learning and that provide information for evaluating the validity of those assumptions.

*Information Transmission and Training Environments: The Behaviorist/Empiricist View.* Traditional classroom learning environments are designed on the principles of the behaviorist view of knowing and learning. They are organized with the goal of students acquiring a maximum accumulation of organized information and procedural knowledge. They are designed to support interactions in which information can be efficiently transmitted to students by teachers, textbooks, and other information sources. Reading, attending to a teacher's presentations,

listening to radio broadcasts, and watching television, film, or videotape, are all forms of learning activity in environments that are organized to transmit information efficiently.

Traditional classrooms are also designed to support acquisition of routine skills. Correct procedures are displayed and opportunities are provided for rehearsal and practice, including practice that is done as homework, which may be checked and recorded during class sessions. The assumption that learning is the acquisition of associations supports arranging interactions in which components of information or procedures are presented systematically, taking into account what the students already know, and monitoring closely whether students have acquired the intended components before going ahead. Programmed instruction and computer-based drill-and-practice programs are designed to provide well-organized information and procedural training that is sensitive to individual students' progress through a prescribed course of study.

(b1) *Routines of activity for effective transmission of knowledge.* Across seven decades of theory and practical curriculum development, behaviorists have stressed the centrality of controlled practice on the elements of knowledge in the content domains. Research that has studied teaching and learning in didactic environments has confirmed the assumptions of behaviorist theory regarding conditions that favor learning of components of information and routine skills (see Brophy & Good, 1986, for a review). For behaviorists, it is the job of the curriculum and the teacher to organize the students' practice: to choose the materials students will use, schedule practice, and make sure appropriate rewards for practicing and learning are available. Students learn by carrying out the practice activities embodied in instructional materials and organized by teachers. Questioning by students or student efforts to organize learning activities for themselves play little role—except insofar as they motivate themselves and organize their time to practice in the ways laid out by teachers and materials.

(b2) *Clear goals, feedback, and reinforcement.* Behaviorist accounts stress the importance of rewarding correct responses to the practice items, although there have been rather heated debates about what constitutes reward. For example, feedback that informs students that a response was correct can function as a reward if the students are already motivated to learn that response, but not if they are indifferent to performing correctly. In general, effective use of reinforcement requires understanding of students' motivations and choosing reinforcers that are relevant to those motivations.

There have been differences of opinion over whether punishment of any kind is needed or appropriate. Skinner's behaviorism distinguished between punishment (a specific negative consequence) and extinction (no environmental reaction to an incorrect response), and psychologists working in the behaviorist tradition worked hard to arrange sequences of practice that would produce *errorless learning* (Terrace, 1966). The notion was that any practice of a wrong association would tend to strengthen it, even if there was some negative consequence. In addition, it was believed that punishment would produce negative reactions to, and thus avoidance of, the learning situation as a whole. The effort to avoid having students make errors was what gave programmed instruction its repetitive character.

Anderson et al. (1985; also see M. W. Lewis & Anderson, 1985), after testing the possibility of allowing students to explore incorrect sequences in solving a problem, found that their intelligent tutoring systems were more effective if students were required to follow one of the paths that the computer expert system could recognize—in effect, requiring practice of correct associations only. Anderson's tutors present students with graded sequences of whole proofs to build or equations to solve. They prevent student errors through the capacity of the intelligent computer program to detect errors "on-line," as the student works through the multiple steps of the problem.

Performance of correct responses is more likely if the situation does not include irrelevant stimuli that could distract the students. Behaviorist curricula, therefore, have presented the elements to be practiced in simple contexts, which do not have many of the features of everyday situations in which the responses could occur usefully. For example, the Thorndike (1917–1924) arithmetic textbooks, and the subsequent generations of texts and workbooks influenced by his theories, provide pages of drill on addition or multiplication without any problem or use contexts. The expectation in behaviorist curricula is that, once learned to a high standard of reliability, elements of knowledge can be called on in many different contexts. More complex contexts of practice make it harder to control the practice, and especially to avoid errors.

Research on information processing has provided additional results about learning environments that can support students' learning correctly. When the learning task is to assimilate information provided in texts, students are able to acquire that information better when they are given clear indications of the way the information is organized and are helped to learn how to use the organization of text information in their studying (Chambliss & Calfee, 1996). When the task is to learn how to solve routine problems, students are better able to learn problem-solving methods when strategic aspects of the method are presented explicitly in interactive computer environments (Anderson et al., 1985).

(b3) *Individualization with technologies.* If basic information and skills have functions in meaningful activities, we can expect many students to value opportunities to strengthen their abilities to perform them. Teachers can provide materials for transmitting and training basic information and skills with traditional work sheets and homework assignments. Alternative methods have become available, however. For symbolic skills such as arithmetic operations, manipulation of formulas, word problems, and proof exercises, computer-based systems for drill and practice (e.g., Suppes & Morningstar, 1972) can provide training in which exercises are chosen to be appropriate for individual students' level of skill and knowledge. Intelligent tutoring systems can diagnose and remedy specific kinds of errors and provide information that helps students understand the solutions of problems (Wenger, 1987).

A significant possibility exists for using computer systems in the way that practice rooms and training facilities are used in many learning environments. Computer systems for transmission and training can be valuable as resources to provide much of the routine training that currently occupies much of the time and effort of teachers.

*Problem-Solving and Exploratory Environments for Conceptual Understanding and Reasoning: The Cognitive/Rationalist View.* The views of knowing and learning as conceptual

understanding and general thinking abilities suggest that didactic learning environments can have unintended negative learning outcomes, even when they succeed in their functions of transmitting information and training procedural knowledge efficiently. Although basic information and skills are valuable and sometimes necessary for achieving expert levels of performance in significant activities of reasoning and problem solving, they are often taught as ends in themselves, rather than as resources for more meaningful activities. Wiggins (1989) likened this common practice to requiring prospective soccer players to practice dribbling, passing, and shooting without ever providing opportunities to play a game of soccer. Schoenfeld (1985) found that students develop distorted beliefs about the nature of mathematics, for example, that mathematical problems are typically solved within one or two minutes.

In the constructivist view, which emphasizes general conceptual understanding and thinking abilities, the reasons for disillusionment with didactic learning environments are mainly empirical. Considerable effort in didactic teaching is aimed at students' understanding of general concepts. The difficulty is that didactic teaching of concepts does not result, for most students, in general understanding. Most students who learn to recite definitions and formulas that express the meanings of concepts in general terms, or to carry out procedures with numbers or formulas, show limited proficiency in solving problems and understanding other situations in which those concepts or procedures could be used.

(c1) *Interactive environments for construction of understanding.* Behaviorist psychology recognizes the need for learners to be *active*—that is, to actively practice the bonds and associations laid out by experts. This is a very different meaning of active learner than we see in constructivist psychological theories. Constructivist learning environments are designed to provide students with opportunities to construct conceptual understandings and abilities in activities of problem solving and reasoning.

The activities of constructing understanding have two main aspects: interactions with material systems and concepts in the domain that understanding is about, such as interacting with concrete manipulative materials that exemplify mathematical concepts such as place value or fractional parts, and social interactions in which learners discuss their understanding of those systems and concepts. To be successful, a learning environment must be productive in both of these aspects. Most of the design experiments that have been done, however, have placed their primary emphasis on either the material aspect or the social aspect.

Several studies have focused on providing students with material systems, including physical materials and computational technologies. The designers of these systems have generally thought of them in terms of the constructivist idea of developing conceptual structures. On the other hand, they can also be considered from the point of view of ecological psychology in the situative perspective. In a situative view, understanding a concept is considered as being attuned to constraints of activity that a community treats as constituents of that concept (Greeno, 1995). The material and computational systems that we discuss here are designed with conceptual constraints built into the systems, so that by learning to interact successfully with the systems, students can become attuned to those constraints and thereby gain implicit understanding of the concepts.

Brownell's (e.g., 1935) studies of meaningful learning emphasized use of concrete materials to exemplify mathematical ideas, an approach that has been used extensively in elementary school mathematics teaching. Rods of lengths corresponding to numbers have been used to teach concepts of addition and subtraction (Gattegno, 1963). Sets of blocks or beads have been used to teach addition and subtraction of multidigit numbers (Dienes, 1966; Montessori, 1917/1964). Multiplication and division are explained using rectangles, and fractions are explained using regions, partitioned into equal subregions, with some number of the subregions distinctively colored. Many research studies have examined ways in which use of concrete, manipulative materials can enhance students' understanding and learning of correct procedures. The results of one study, by L. B. Resnick and Omanson (1987), suggested that an important role may be played by discussion of the meanings of manipulations of the concrete materials, rather than simply showing how the procedures work with the concrete materials and numerical symbols.

Materials such as place-value blocks and fraction circles are considered concrete because they have properties that correspond to mathematical ideas more directly than numerical symbols do. On the other hand, such materials are also abstract, in that they represent idealized objects that are designed to display mathematical properties much more directly than they appear in most situations. Nesher (1989) distinguished between *exemplifications* and *applications,* that is, between materials designed to display mathematical properties directly and situations in which mathematical principles and operations can be used to make inferences about realistic systems. Nesher argued for teaching concepts initially with exemplifications, in order for students to grasp the concepts clearly, and for teaching students to solve applications problems later.

A classic example of the use of concrete materials to learn a mathematics concept was given by Wertheimer (1945/1959). The example involved the concept of the area of a parallelogram. Wertheimer observed a class in which the teacher presented the formula for the area of a parallelogram, area = base × height, with directions for applying the formula to calculate the area of drawn parallelograms. Wertheimer discerned that this instruction may not have resulted in a kind of conceptual understanding that students might achieve; and he described, as an alternative, interactions he had with elementary students that began with a concept of area they already had, the number of square tiles that cover a rectangular shape. Wertheimer asked about the area of a parallelogram, and some students perceived the way in which a parallelogram can be transformed to a rectangle, providing understanding of the relation among the base, height, and area of a rectangle.

A different instructional activity for this concept was devised by Sayeki et al. (1991), who gave students stacks of paper that formed rectangular surfaces at the end of the stacks. The students experienced changes in the shapes of those end surfaces by sliding the papers to make different angles between the base and sides. This transformation does not change the area of the parallelogram at the end surface—it is composed of the same set of edges, just arranged differently—and it does not change the height, but it changes the lengths of the sides

of the parallelogram. Sayeki and colleagues' instruction can provide understanding by helping students become attuned to a constraint—the relation of height, base, and area of a parallelogram—that is invariant when a shear transformation is applied. They provided evidence of this understanding by asking students to construct formulas for the area of a parallelogram and other polygons, and many students succeeded in these tasks.

Interactive computer programs can support activities in which students construct understanding of concepts by manipulating and observing simulations. A learning environment for high school geometry is the Geometric Supposer (Schwartz, Yarushalmy, & Wilson, 1993), which has a computer interface that enables students to construct diagrams of geometric figures such as triangles or parallelograms. Numerical values of some of the quantitative properties of these figures are specified, and the program provides the numerical values of other properties. Students can change the values of some properties and observe whether other properties, or relations between properties, change or remain constant. Activities that use the interface are arranged to invite students to form conjectures about conditions in which some properties are invariant and to try to construct proofs that support those conjectures.

Simulations have been designed that allow students to control objects in a simulated Newtonian world without friction, and with gravity absent or in a controllable and inspectable form (diSessa, 1982; Roschelle, 1992; B. Y. White, 1983, 1993). Software used for investigating concepts in thermodynamics (Linn, 1992) uses a thermometer attached to a computer and graphs temperature as a function of time. The thermometer can be placed in a liquid that is being heated or cooled, and students can observe the graph of heating or cooling that occurs in different conditions. For example, two containers of liquid with different volumes can be heated to the same temperature, and the slower rate of cooling in the larger volume of liquid can be observed graphically, encouraging the understanding of cooling as a phenomenon of loss of heat, distinct from loss of temperature (Linn, Songer, Lewis, & Stern, 1993; see also chapter 15, this volume).

A simulation of heat exchange developed by Wiser and Kipman (1988) represents substances as collections of small particles that move more or less rapidly, depending on the temperature. Larger volumes of a substance have more particles, and therefore have greater amounts of motion at the same temperature than smaller volumes. The software simulates heat exchange by showing how a heat source changes the motion of particles near the source and the changes in the motion diffuse through the substance, taking longer if there is more of the substance to change.

Another example, developed by Pea and Goldman and their associates (Goldman, in press; Pea, Sipusic, & Allen, in press), emphasizes use of a standard scientific representational system in the domain of geometric optics. A graphical interface was developed that supports construction of ray diagrams, with light sources and objects that absorb, refract, or reflect light. Students use the interface to construct diagrams of situations in which they explore properties of light, such as shadows and the convergence of rays to form coherent images. Unlike standard instruction, in which construction of diagrams is a task that students need to learn to perform, this system presents diagrams as a resource for understanding phenomena and concepts in the domain. This provides opportunities for students to practice using the representations for inquiry.

In more complex settings, computer displays have been designed to provide visual support for the acquisition of mental models—that is, cognitive representations that support reasoning and understanding by simulating the behavior of systems in the world (e.g., Johnson-Laird, 1983). These simulations allow students to learn important knowledge and skills in contexts that they could never participate in naturally, to see features that are invisible in real environments (e.g., the center of mass, the inside of pipes), to control variables that are not possible to control in life, and to see these in action, unlike static text figures.

B. White and Frederiksen (1990) developed software that represents relations of electrical voltage, resistance, and current in a series of increasingly sophisticated mental models. In a training system for engineers who are learning to operate the power plant of a large ship, various components of the system, such as boilers, valves, pipes, and engines, are shown, with visual properties that represent relevant properties such as pressures and temperatures (Stevens & Roberts, 1983). The display simulates results of operating on the system in various ways, such as turning on a boiler. By interacting with the computational system, a learner can develop abilities to simulate the effects of operations in a model of the power plant.

Sherlock (A. Lesgold, Lajoie, Bunzo, & Eggan, 1988) is another system designed for learning mental models in training electronic maintenance technicians. Sherlock presents simulations of a complex electronic diagnostic system behaving with various malfunctions that learners have to diagnose. The learners apply tests and obtain information about readings that would be obtained. Learners' interactions with Sherlock are designed to facilitate their developing mental models of tests, including their functions in providing information relevant to the problem-solver's search in a large space of possible malfunctions and their symptoms (see chapter 24).

***Environments for Learning to Participate in Social Practices of Inquiry and Sense-Making: The Situative/Pragmatist-Sociohistoric View.*** We need to understand school learning environments in two ways: their effects on the subject matter knowledge and ability that students acquire, and their effects on the kinds of learners that students become. Students adapt to the practices of school learning positively or negatively. Those students who become engaged participants learn to participate in the activities that constitute their school's practices of learning.

Students acquire practices of learning by participating in classroom and homework activities, but the practices they acquire may not be those that are intended or valued by the teacher, the school, or the society. Practices are learned as individuals participate in activities of communities. They are not uniform—different members of communities act in different ways, and any individual acts differently in different circumstances. But significant aspects of activity that are recognized and valued in a community are learned by individuals as they interact with others, learning to coordinate what they do with others.

(s1) *Environments of participation in social practices of inquiry and learning.* Many educators and researchers are making efforts to develop and understand learning environments in which students' participation results in their learning to be more active in social processes of constructing understanding. The activities that students can learn to participate in include formulating and evaluating questions, problems, hypotheses, conjectures, and explanations, and proposing and evaluating evidence, examples, and arguments.

In this section we discuss studies that have focused mainly on aspects of learning environments involving social interaction, particularly discourse practices. In the situative view, an important part of learning the concepts of a domain is learning to participate in the discourse of a community in which those concepts are used. For example, an important part of understanding the mathematical concept of fraction is knowing how to talk about properties and relations of fractional quantities and how to use mathematical representations of fractions to communicate and reason. By participating in discourse in a domain, students should also become attuned to forms of explanation and argumentation that are standards of practice in the domain.

As we mentioned previously, both the social and the material aspects of learning environments are crucial for their support of conceptual growth. In the learning environments that we discuss now, material systems, including concrete exemplifications of mathematical concept, demonstrations of physical phenomena, and diagrams and other symbolic representations, play a critical role.

Learning environments for strengthening students' general skills in thinking, such as Philosophy for Children (Lipman, 1985, 1991) are organized as communication environments in which students learn practices of formulating questions and alternative positions on traditional philosophical issues, such as meaning, truth, aesthetics, reality and imagination, and ethics, that arise in the context of stories.

Students' classroom experiences differ in different subject-matter classes. For example, learning activities in many mathematics and science classes are more didactic and hierarchically authoritarian than are social studies classes or literature classes that the same students attend (e.g., Stodolsky, 1988). Schoenfeld (1988) identified beliefs that students derive from their experience in working on mathematics problems: for example, if the answer is not an integer, it is probably wrong; all the problems at the end of a chapter use the methods introduced in the chapter; if you cannot solve the problem in a couple of minutes, you probably do not know how to solve it; and so forth. Schoenfeld argued that most of these beliefs are counterproductive for learning to think mathematically as well as for problem solving in life, in addition to reflecting a grotesquely mistaken view of problem solving of the kinds that mathematicians engage in.

There have been several very successful examples of how effective group discussions can be as learning environments in classrooms. Classroom discourse can be organized so that students learn to explain their ideas and solutions to problems, rather than focusing entirely on whether answers are correct. In projects involving mathematics education, Cobb and his associates (e.g., Cobb et al., 1991) have worked with teachers in designing and working out classroom activities in first- and second-grade arithmetic. Much of the students' activity involves working in pairs, with the expectation that they will discuss how to solve problems and understand each others' ideas. Attention is given to norms of discourse, particularly involving respectful attention to others' opinions and efforts to reach mutual understanding. Results support the expectation that the quality of the students' explanations becomes more sophisticated and substantive as they engage in the practice.

In Lampert's (e.g., 1990) fifth-grade classroom, students offer proposed answers to questions that Lampert presents. Many of the questions are designed to elicit multiple answers and therefore to provide occasions for resolving different opinions. Lampert frequently asks the class to discuss one of the students' thinking about a problem, focusing on assumptions that may have led to a conclusion that other students did not reach. It is quite common, at the end of a discussion, for one or more of the students to say that they have "revised their thinking." Lampert works to establish that offering an opinion is helpful to the class discussion, whether or not it turns out to be correct, and that changing one's mind should be considered valuable, but that there should be mathematical reasons for changing one's mind, rather than just agreeing with someone else's view.

L. B. Resnick, Bill, Lesgold, and Leer (1991) developed an approach to teaching problem solving in arithmetic to "at-risk" elementary schoolchildren. The approach relies on encouraging children to use their own invented procedures, to bring problems from outside of school that they discuss in class, and to introduce formal notation and key mathematical structures as early as possible. Classroom activities have the form of discussions of problem situations, such as different ways to divide some cupcakes among the members of the class. As in the mathematics instruction that is standard in Japanese schools (Fernandez, Yoshida, & Stigler, 1992; Stigler & Perry, 1988), a considerable amount of time is spent developing understanding of one or a few problems, rather than focusing on skill in computational procedures. Although it might be thought that this shift would result in decreased learning of the standard computational material of the mathematics curriculum, the method led to dramatic increases (from the 30th to the 70th percentile) on California achievement tests, compared to students who were taught earlier by the same teacher using a more traditional approach.

A notable implementation of a discussion method in science education is the Itakura method (Hatano & Inagaki, 1991), in which students are asked to make different predictions about what will happen in an experiment. They then discuss and defend among themselves why they think their predictions are correct. After any revisions in their predictions, the experiment is performed and discussion ensues as to why the result came out the way it did.

The Jigsaw technique developed by Aronson (1978) provides a method of organizing school learning to facilitate communication activities among students. In it students break into groups, each of which learns about a different topic. Then the students regroup, so that there is one expert on each topic in each group, and the students then teach each other about all the topics. A. L. Brown and Campione and their associates (Brown et al., 1993) have developed a variant on the Jigsaw technique they call JIGSAW2. Groups of students research topics such as pollution or endangered species in order to prepare a booklet on each topic. Then, when they have written up their findings, they regroup to work with other students who are reading the booklets produced. The reading groups are run using the reciprocal teaching method (Palincsar & Brown, 1984), where the student who worked on each booklet acts as a teacher, getting other students to generate questions, summaries, clarifications, and predictions about the text.

The CSILE environment developed by Scardamalia and Bereiter (1991; Scardamalia, Bereiter, & Lamon, 1994) is a discussion environment where students communicate in writing over a computer network. They first formulate questions they want to investigate (e.g., "Why can humans speak when apes cannot?") and then each student in the group makes a conjecture about what he or she believes. Then they all start investigating the question, finding whatever relevant information they can from source materials and typing that into the system for others in the group to read. They also can receive commentaries written by an expert in the problem domain who monitors the notes that the students have written. Through written discussions they refine their theories for publication in the system to all the students in the class. Students frequently refer to their explanations with the phrase "my theory," and present arguments and questions for their own and other students' positions.

An environment that is organized to facilitate learning cognitive skills is the Fifth Dimension, developed by Cole and his colleagues (Laboratory of Comparative Human Cognition, 1982). Middle school students participate in an after-school club in an environment that has a rich variety of cognitively challenging activities, most of which are in gamelike formats. The students work with young adults—university students who do this as project work in a communications class—who provide general guidance and encouragement. They also communicate using electronic mail with a "wizard," who provides written advice and commentary. The progress that students make is recorded in terms of levels of skill they have achieved in the various activities they work on, and as they advance in skill, they hold tickets that permit them to engage in more advanced versions of the activities. The Fifth Dimension recruited students who were unsuccessful in standard school instruction, and many of them made remarkable progress in their cognitive capabilities through their participation.

Environments for remote discussion are becoming available in the form of electronic networks. During the past several generations, many friends and members of families have constructed learning environments by exchanging correspondence and conversing by telephone. Recently, remote conversational learning has expanded significantly for some people through electronic mail and fax machines. Several experiments now underway are exploring the potential for students in different locations to learn through exchanges of electronic messages (e.g., Reil & Levin, 1990).

(s2) *Support for development of positive epistemic identities.* Students in a classroom, like participants in any community, learn practices of participating in the activities of communities in the school setting. Some students learn to participate in ways that are recognized and valued by the teacher and the school. Some students learn to participate in ways that involve minimal engagement in activities that are officially recognized, but may have considerable value in the communities of their peers. These differences relate to ways in which individuals define their roles in the institution of learning, partly on the basis of the relations between those institutions and the communities in which they participate. These communities may be integrated well with the goals and practices of the institution or they may be antagonistic toward the institution, and this can create major differences in the ways that the various learners participate in the institutional learning activities.

An example was provided by Eckert (1989) in her ethnographic study of the social organization of a high school in which she identified well-defined groups that called themselves "jocks" and "burnouts." Differences between the groups included ways in which knowledge and information were understood and used. The jocks treated information as a commodity; to them, knowing something was a sign of success. Burnouts shared information, and contributing information to others was valued social participation. This difference in the social role of information was a significant factor, for example, in the courses that burnouts chose: Practically none of them elected courses in mathematics or science, where intellectual work is typically highly authoritarian, individualistic, and competitive (Eckert, 1990).

Families and communities in different cultural groups interact in different ways, and children from different cultural groups bring different resources of knowledge and custom to the situation of schooling. Learning activities in schools can be organized so that diverse styles and expertise are resources for enriching the learning experiences of all of the students. For example, Tharp (1989) discussed instructional methods adapted to children's different cultural styles, such as the use of a spoken story format with Hawaiian children and an emphasis on cooperative activity with Navaho children. Moll and his associates (Moll, Tapia, & Whitmore, 1993; Moll & Whitmore, 1993) studied a whole language bilingual classroom in which students and the teacher collaboratively chose themes for extensive study and in which students who differed in their familiarity with historical events contributed productively in discussions to their groups' understanding.

The Algebra Project (Moses et al., 1989) is an educational reform in mathematics organized around the central idea that all students should develop strong capabilities and strong identities as knowers of mathematics. Moses is particularly concerned about mathematics, which functions as a strong selection factor in U.S. society. The Algebra Project is organized to provide middle school students with opportunities to be prepared and confident in their abilities to take high school algebra. In its initial version, in Cambridge, Massachusetts, the Algebra Project emphasized community organization, an effort to establish a consensus including the school and the parents of students that all students should and could become able mathematics learners for whom high school algebra would be appropriate. The curriculum of the Algebra Project is focused on providing experiences that students share and that can be used as material for developing mathematical concepts and notations, as we discussed earlier.

Programs designed to assist selected groups of students can be informed by understanding of their different social practices of learning. An example involving university students was provided by Triesman (1990), in the Professional Development Program to assist African-American students at the University of California at Berkeley, particularly in their mathematics course work. Such programs often provide remedial instruction, assuming that minority students have not received adequate high school instruction in the subject matter. Such programs rarely do more than enable students to pass courses minimally, and Triesman had higher aspirations. He conducted a study in which he observed the learning activities of several African-American students, which he compared with the learning activities of several Asian-American students. He discovered that the African-American students almost always studied individually, while the Asian-American students spent much of their study time working in groups, where they shared understandings of course requirements and strategies of learning and taking tests, as well as understandings of course material. The Professional Development Program now encourages and facilitates African-American students in organizing groups of students who work together in their learning activities, as well as conducting sessions in which students work on problems that are among the hardest that will be included in course materials, rather than limiting their material to problems needed to succeed minimally.

## Formulating Curricula

A curriculum asserts a set of educational goals and a sequence of learning activities that are intended to promote development toward those goals.

***Curricula for Accumulating and Tuning Connections: The Behaviorist/Empiricist View.*** The leading theorists of empiricism throughout the 20th century have themselves applied their theories of knowledge and learning to the problem of the school curriculum. As a result of this direct engagement by leading research scientists, including Thorndike (1922), Skinner (1958), Gagné (1965), and Anderson (Anderson, Boyle, Corbett, & M. W. Lewis, 1990), empiricist theories have had a substantial and continuing influence on curriculum practice. Empiricist-inspired curricula span teaching technologies from the drill-and-practice workbook to the intelligent, computer-based tutor. In all of these examples, we can find similar types of activities, based on similar views of the relations between teacher, student, and instructional materials, and similar conceptions of how learning activities should be sequenced and participation controlled.

Empiricist theories of knowledge and learning assume that the task of the learner is to acquire the body of connections that an expert analysis of the subject matter reveals. Associationist and behaviorist psychologists have not, by and large, considered their science as capable of shedding light on the basic questions of what is worth knowing. Rather, they have accepted the school subjects as more or less established and have sought to show how they could be most efficiently acquired by students.

(b4) *Sequences of component-to-composite skills.* A major contribution of behavioral task analysis has been to support a successful technology of instructional design in which procedural and factual knowledge is divided into components that are arranged in a learnable sequence. Typical sequences of instruction begin with training in a procedure, facts, or vocabulary in a simplified context, followed by presentations of the material in somewhat more complicated settings. Standard mathematics textbooks are examples, in that procedures for calculating are presented and practiced, followed by word problems. Under the assumptions of this sequential learning scheme, it is important that students have mastered the simpler components to be ready to learn the more complex behaviors.

Empiricist-inspired curricula organize most practice as rehearsal of individual elements of knowledge or skill. In Anderson and colleagues' (1985) tutors, where rather complex sequences of proof or algebraic manipulations are being taught, evaluation of student responses proceeds on a step-by-step basis. After simpler components of vocabulary, facts, or procedures have been mastered, more complex units are presented. The mastery approach is a central feature of Gagné's (1968) and other learning hierarchy approaches to curriculum.

This method is widely used in the design of technical training and in corporations (see, e.g., Reigeluth, 1983) and its ideas are informally used in the design of some school curricula, especially in mathematics. A theoretical analysis by VanLehn (1990) used arithmetic subtraction as an example and developed a computational model of learning in which he showed that conditions such as adding only one subprocedure per lesson and showing the learner all relevant intermediate results are important enabling conditions to support learning of correct procedures.

### Curricula for Conceptual Understanding and General Abilities: The Cognitive/Rationalist View

(c2) *Sequences of conceptual development.* The theme of meaningful learning, where "meaningful" has tended to imply a focus on organizing concepts of a field of knowledge, has been a dominant counterweight to empiricist theories throughout the history of educational psychology. Although behaviorists have had significant influence on mainstream curriculum practice, including the organization of textbooks and testing, a stream of research in the 20th century has focused on identifying organizing themes and concepts and studying how students can best come to understand them. Gestalt psychologists (e.g., Katona, 1940) searched for organizing structures in human perception and thinking. Much of their work was focused on perceptual structures, often taken to be biologically determined ways in which individuals were attuned to the physical environment. A few Gestalt psychologists, most notably Max Wertheimer (1945/1959), proposed that there also exist organizing *conceptual* structures, and that these, rather than collections of specific associations, should become central in the school curriculum.

Research on conceptually meaningful learning has been most influential when psychologists have allied with subject matter specialists and have become deeply engaged in efforts to define curriculum in a particular subject, rather than concentrating on more generic theories of learning or instruction. Examples include the work of Brownell (e.g., 1935), who in the 1930s studied processes of meaningful learning in mathematics, stressing the role of understanding of concepts in promoting more stable computational performance, and Schwab's (1978) discussions of the structures of subject matter domains.

In the 1960s psychologists such as Bruner (1960) joined forces with a broad community of scientists and mathematicians in efforts to develop curricula grounded in the fundamental concepts of those disciplines. Central in Bruner's thinking was the question of how the complex concepts of scientific and

mathematical disciplines could be made accessible to children at different stages of cognitive development. Bruner's optimism about the possibilities—he argued that any concept could be taught in some intellectually honest form to children at any age—brought him into some theoretical conflict with Piaget, whose extensive body of work on children's cognitive development was, in the 1960s, just coming to the attention of American psychologists and educators (as discussed earlier in the second section, p. 18).

Piaget himself never wrote about curriculum as such. Indeed, his constructivist theory of knowledge—the theory that individuals do not absorb or copy ideas from the external world, but rather must construct their concepts through active observation and experimentation—led him to argue against direct teaching of disciplinary concepts (Piaget, 1935,1965/1970). What he was arguing against was direct teaching of the behaviorist bits-and-pieces variety, rather than the kinds of meaningful learning that psychologists such as Brownell and Bruner advocated. But Piaget's advocacy against direct teaching led many developmental psychologists to argue for a curriculum based almost entirely on children's construction of knowledge by direct interaction with elements of the physical environment (e.g., Ginsburg & Opper, 1969).

One educational result of Piaget's influence was that, for a considerable period of time, psychologists collaborated with science educators on an approach to curriculum that deliberately separated processes from content. Although Piagetians did not believe that specific science concepts could be directly taught, many, especially in America, believed that the processes of scientific reasoning could be. Curricula—such as *Science: A Process Approach*—were developed to teach children specific skills for observation, experimentation, data analysis, and the like, and avoided commitment to any specific knowledge.

Subject matter domains also contain general methods of reasoning and problem solving, which can be taught in ways that emphasize their general usefulness. An approach to general methods of reasoning and problem solving was encouraged by work in information processing, especially the characterization of general methods in programs such as the General Problem Solver (Ernst & Newell, 1969; Newell & Simon, 1972). In the spirit of the General Problem Solver and its claim that a limited set of strategies and heuristics could be applied successfully in all or most domains of knowledge, most programs for teaching problem-solving skills were initially "add-ons" to the standard subject matter curriculum. In educational terms, they belonged to the "study skills" strand of curriculum, embodied in special courses, often optional and often designed for students who were not performing at optimum levels, or for individuals interested in raising their own levels of performance (e.g., Hayes, 1981; M. Levine, 1988).

In the spirit of study skills courses, most thinking skills programs went beyond the cognitive strategies revealed by information-processing research to include a variety of self-management skills, including procedures for managing one's own time and motivation for study. These *metacognitive* abilities soon became an object of educational research and experimentation as well, especially in the field of reading comprehension. Two streams of curriculum thinking based on metacognition emerged. One was quite similar to the information-processing strategy programs. Children were taught about strategies for comprehending texts and the strategies themselves were the focus of practice, classroom conversation, and, quite often, tests. Most efforts to directly teach metacognitive skills and other deliberate learning strategies have been disappointing. The taught skills often are not retained, are not applied independently by students, or take a brittle form that does not seem to enhance other learning, even when the new strategies themselves are performed to specification. A repeated finding is that general strategies directly taught to students tend not to be spontaneously used under conditions different from those in which they were initially practiced (e.g., A. L. Brown & Campione, 1977).

On the other hand, there have been several demonstrations of successful instruction in strategic aspects of learning and problem solving when these were connected with the kinds of contents and activities that are contained in subject matter domains. An example was provided by Schoenfeld (1985), who developed an instructional approach designed to integrate the learning of general mathematical principles and their application to particular problems. His goal was to teach students general problem-solving heuristics, patterned after ideas of Polya (1945), such as constructing a simpler version of the problem and using analogies. He also taught metacognitive control strategies, such as considering alternative courses of action and monitoring to see whether you are making progress toward a solution. Finally, he emphasized teaching productive beliefs about problem solving. His teaching methods involved students solving many different kinds of problems, first as a whole class with him acting as facilitator, then in groups of three or four where he acted as a monitor, and finally alone as homework. Similar approaches to learning much earlier mathematics through problem solving, invention, and discussion are also being developed (e.g., Carpenter, Fennema, Peterson, Chiang, & Loef, 1989). (See p. 31).

An example of this approach in reading is reciprocal teaching (Palincsar & Brown, 1984). Reciprocal teaching maintains focus on the content of the texts but organizes special procedures to help children learn to monitor their comprehension by summarizing, asking questions, or predicting what might come next in the story.

Learning activities focused on strategic know-how also have been designed in writing and arithmetic. In learning to write, students often focus on the contents of their compositions, neglecting rhetorical factors that are crucial for their writing successfully. Bereiter and Scardamalia (1987) created an environment in which students commented on their own texts, choosing from a set of cards with statements such as "I need another example here," or "Even I seem to be confused about this," or "This is very clear." Computational environments for learning strategies were designed by J. S. Brown and Burton, including strategic aspects of playing a game to gain proficiency in arithmetic (Burton & Brown, 1982), and strategies of troubleshooting involved in choosing tests in electronic maintenance (J. S. Brown, Burton, & deKleer, 1982). These systems, like Bereiter and Scardamalia's cue cards, involve intervention in a student's work with strategic hints or requirements that they give strategic reasons for their actions.

These subject matter–based problem-solving programs represent an effort to resolve in curriculum terms the fundamental tension between what Newell (1980) called *weak* methods—

i.e., general skills—and *strong* methods—i.e., domain-specific procedures, as we discussed in a previous section. Many studies have shown that students' abilities to understand and learn new material depend strongly on what they already know (Glaser, 1984). Nevertheless, it appears that educators cannot build expertise by having their students memorize experts' knowledge. That kind of learning appears to produce "inert" knowledge (Whitehead, 1916), unlikely to be usable in complex performances. Instead, expert knowledge must be constructed through activity and experience. Knowledge construction, however, is time-consuming. The social and personal mental elaboration necessary for successful learning takes time—much more time than is typically allowed for the study of any topic in the school curriculum. This means that efforts to cover an extensive body of knowledge are bound to fail to produce significant learning. In response to this understanding, several leading thinkers have promoted a philosophy of "less is more" (e.g., Sizer, 1992; Whitehead, 1916)—that is, learning a few important ideas and concepts well is educationally more powerful than is a curriculum of extensive but superficial exposure. This has begun to engender a research agenda concerned with identifying powerful, generative concepts—the ones to include in the "less" curriculum—and with figuring out how to teach them so that they are, in fact, generative. This research on the generative curriculum is being pursued subject matter by subject matter, most often in collaborative teams that include cognitive researchers and subject matter experts.

The cognitive perspective brings psychologists into much more active contact with subject matter or disciplinary experts than has been the case for those working in the behaviorist perspective. Investigators using the cognitive approach did not initially raise questions about the content of the curriculum but gradually—partly through their own interest in the structure of information, and partly through the attraction of information-processing concepts and methods to some researchers in science and mathematics education—cognitive psychologists began to ally with subject matter specialists and with other branches of psychology that had long treated the structure of knowledge itself, and the ways in which people come to appreciate and use different knowledge structures as the central questions of the discipline.

Findings of research in which students are asked to explain phenomena that are theoretically problematic and in which their explanations have been interpreted as misconceptions (e.g., McCloskey, 1983) can be interpreted as raising problems for the constructive/rationalist assumption. Students may not have reached a sufficient operational stage to reason effectively, or their intuitions may be discrepant from expert understanding. On the other hand, our earlier discussion of research on children's conceptual growth (see p. 18) showed significant abilities to reason intuitively in conceptual domains, which suggests that classroom activities should build on the initial understandings of children. This can be achieved if the phenomena that we want students to understand can be presented in a way that affords students' understanding them in ways that can be extended toward expert understanding. To accomplish this, we need to find ways to activate versions of understanding that can serve as bases of the target understandings.

One example is a kind of lesson that Minstrell (1989) and A. L. Brown and Campione (1994) call a *benchmark lesson.*

Benchmark lessons are used to introduce conceptual problems that are known to present difficulties for students, and to elicit the students' understandings of situations in which the scientific concepts apply. Those phenomena then are used as foci of discussion for which alternative interpretations are developed, as extensions and transformations of the students' initial understandings. In another example, Roth (1986) reorganized the presentation of material in middle school biology texts to address students' initial understanding of plant nutrition as a process of ingestion, and related the idea of photosynthesis to the intuitive understanding that students have about manufacturing.

Students' initial understandings can also be brought to bear by using analogies in which the constraints of the system being studied are salient, as in D. E. Brown and Clement's (1989) use of a spring analogy to help students understand about normal forces. While it is counterintuitive for many students to think of a surface such as a table as exerting a force on a resting object, it is intuitive to think of a spring as exerting such a force. Then the system of a surface supporting an object can be thought of by analogy with the spring, by recognizing that there is a small compression of any surface when an object is resting on it. D. E. Brown and Clement hypothesized that in learning through analogies, students are able to develop mental models of systems that are attuned to the important causal constraints of the systems they are studying.

The principle of connecting instruction with students' understanding is also reflected in the activities involved in the learning environments that we discussed earlier (see pp. 29–33). When physical materials and computational environments are designed to represent conceptual structures, the representations are chosen to enable students' intuitive understandings to serve as a basis for developing their understanding of subject matter concepts. When classroom activities are organized to promote students' active construction of understanding through participation in discourse, problems and examples are used that evoke students' intuitive understandings, which are then appropriated for productive discussion and analysis in the class.

***Curricula for Learning Participation in Social Practices: The Situative/Sociohistoric View.*** According to the situative view, the curriculum should reflect a set of commitments about kinds of activities that students should learn to participate in, as well as the subject matter contents that they should learn about.

(s3) *Development of disciplinary practices of discourse and representation.* Subject matter disciplines have characteristic forms and styles of discourse, including ways in which questions, hypotheses, and conjectures are formulated and related to accepted knowledge and ways in which evidence, examples, and arguments are related to conclusions. They also have characteristic forms of representation that are used productively among practitioners. The curriculum of a subject matter domain can be organized to include students' coming to appreciate and learning to participate in these forms and styles of discourse and representation.

Formal arguments involving explicit definitions and postulates are concentrated in the high school geometry course. In typical instruction, students study proofs of theorems and learn to construct proofs in exercise problems. This gives them little or no experience in formulating the definitions and choosing postulates that the proofs depend on.

In a classic design experiment, Fawcett (1938) organized a high school geometry class around practices of deductive reasoning. The class engaged in discussion of alternative ways of defining terms and the necessity of stating assumptions explicitly for an argument to be formally valid. An important aspect of reasoning practices in mathematics is the attention given to explicit definitions and statements of assumptions. Fawcett led his class in discussions of alternative definitions, emphasizing relations between definitions of concepts and the uses of those concepts in constructing proofs. They also emphasized premises and conclusions of arguments, considering whether stated premises were sufficient to support claims as deductive consequences or whether additional assumptions were needed for some claims. Discussions included topics of geometry, where each student constructed a system of defined concepts and postulates that he or she used to prove a set of theorems. Discussions also included topics from everyday activity, which involved practices of examining definitions of concepts and validity of arguments from the point of view of mathematical rigor. For example, at the beginning of the term Fawcett noted that the school had decided to give an award to a "good citizen" at the end of the year, and his class discussed the problem of defining the concept of a "good citizen" sufficiently to support a decision of which student should be the winner.

The general point of Fawcett's example is that students learned practices of formulating mathematical definitions and arguments, learned how to judge the validity of mathematical claims, and learned to take responsibility for making and questioning mathematical assertions. For most students, learning these aspects of practice in a discipline requires a setting in which they can participate in the kinds of activities in which the discipline engages. Unless teachers organize the activities of learning to include participation in inquiry and discourse about concepts, claims, and arguments, with students having responsibility for their claims and questions, we cannot expect more than a few students to acquire these aspects of practice in subject matter disciplines.

Similarly, in Schoenfeld's (1987) course in problem solving, a major goal is for the students to develop standards of adequate argumentation. When they do so, they do not depend on the instructor to tell them whether a solution is correct or whether an argument they have developed is a valid proof.

In most instruction in behaviorist or cognitive approaches, technical representations are presented to students as systems they need to learn, and they need to learn to use those representations correctly. An alternative is to organize activities in which students will construct representational systems, thereby participating in discussions in which the meanings and functions of symbols are the results of their inquiry rather than simply a task for them to learn. In one example, diSessa, Hammer, and Sherin (1991) observed a teacher and a class develop several graphical representations that revealed students' intuitions about speeds of motion as a vehicle goes up a hill, stops, and rolls back down. A rich variety of graphical representations was developed in which students could learn to appreciate features such as continuity that characterize the standard system of graphing. In the Algebra Project (Moses et al., 1989), one of the ways that students have agency in their learning of mathematics is in developing their own symbols for mathematical relations such as the direction of a displacement in space, related to the sign of an integer.

The principle of introducing discourse practices of a discipline to students through their participation is reflected in all of the learning environments where students provide explanations of their opinions and arguments to support their conclusions.

(s4) *Practices of formulating and solving realistic problems.* In several design experiments, psychologists and educators are working to develop curriculum materials and activities in which students' learning experiences are focused on meaningful settings of activity in which the contents of subject matter disciplines are embedded. These activity structures engage students' interests and understandings, and support learning that extends their ability to reason with subject-matter concepts.

In one example, the Jasper project at Vanderbilt (Cognition and Technology Group at Vanderbilt, 1990, 1994; see also chapter 25) creates engaging videotape presentations of problem situations. One concerns someone finding an injured eagle in a location that can be reached only by helicopter, creating a problem that includes minimizing the time it will take to reach the site and transport the eagle to a place where it can receive care. The problems reflect the complex problem solving and planning that occurs in real life and provide opportunities for using mathematical methods to reason about significant aspects of a problem situation, rather than merely exercising mathematical procedures mechanically. Another example is the Middle-School Mathematics Through Applications Project at the Institute for Research on Learning in Palo Alto (Moschkovich, 1994), which creates computer-based learning environments in which students work on design problems, such as designing living and working space for a research team in Antarctica.

Projects are an attempt to bring research, design, and troubleshooting tasks from work environments into the school. For example, Dewey (Cuban, 1984) had students in his laboratory school build a clubhouse for the school, where they learned planning, mathematical, and construction skills. In Boston, Harel (1991) had fourth graders each develop a computer program to teach third graders about fractions. In Rochester, New York, eighth-grade students carried out research projects on the city of Rochester and on the life and times of George Eastman (Carver, 1990; Collins, Hawkins, & Carver, 1991) by interviewing adults and finding source materials. Their findings were produced as HyperCard stacks, which were displayed at the Rochester Museum and Science Center.

Project environments challenge the scope-and-sequence notion of curriculum because students typically need a wide variety of skills to carry out any project. These skills can be taught either before or during the project, and resources should be provided for students to learn how to do the things that are needed to proceed through their project work.

These projects are raising the fundamental issue of contents and cognitive processes in a strong form. Their activity settings are engaging and meaningful, and students participate actively in complex cognitive processes of problem formulation, understanding, and reasoning. These processes depend on principles of the subject matter disciplines, and students succeed and grow in their abilities. The subject matter concepts and principles, however, tend to be embedded in the contexts of their activity settings. It is a particular challenge to provide for students'

learning of systematic knowledge in subject matter domains when the curriculum is organized by realistic and extended projects.

A crucial topic for research, then, is to improve our understanding of relations between subject matter concepts and reasoning that relies on those concepts. An issue for curriculum analysis and formulation will be to develop learning agendas that give appropriate emphasis to both explicit and implicit understandings of subject matter concepts and principles that students can gain.

## Constructing Authentic Assessments

Assessment is integral to education in that it serves to guide the teaching and learning process and reports to parents and the public. The problems of assessment and testing have been central ones for educational psychology throughout its history. The development of theories and techniques for reliable and efficient testing is one of educational psychology's most important practical achievements. However, these theories and techniques have been developed almost entirely within only one of the three views of knowing and learning that we have discussed in this chapter, the behaviorist/empiricist view. This has led in recent years to calls for developing new approaches to assessment that are in better accord with the epistemological assumptions of the cognitive and situative views.

Whether an assessment of knowing and learning in a domain is authentic depends on whether it does what it claims to do—that is, to inform us about knowing and learning in that domain. Therefore, any evaluation of authenticity depends on the view of knowing and learning that the evaluation presupposes. The three views of knowing and learning that have organized our discussion support quite different views of assessment. The traditional behaviorist perspective supports a quantitative view of knowing and learning, in which assessment involves independent samples of knowledge or skill to estimate how much of the domain a student has acquired. The cognitive view of assessment emphasizes questions about whether students understand general principles in a domain and whether they use methods and strategies that are useful in solving problems in the domain. The situative view of assessment emphasizes questions about the quality of students' participation in activities of inquiry and sense-making, and considers assessment practices as integral components of the general systems of activity in which they occur.

### *Measuring Elements of Acquired Information and Skill: The Behaviorist/Empiricist View*

(b5) *Assessment of knowledge components.* In the behaviorist view, knowing in a domain is a collection of information and skills that a person has acquired. A mature technology supports the construction of achievement tests, which are used in assessments in many schools, states, nations, and international studies. The development of these tests relies on participation by knowledgeable experts in the subject matter disciplines of the test who provide authoritative judgments that the items in the test accurately represent knowledge in the discipline. A combination of expert judgment and empirical results is used to characterize the difficulty of items. The development of tests also is supported by the technology of analyzing tasks in the domain in terms of component procedures and prerequisites.

Technologies of psychological measurement arose from Binet's work in the early 20th century (1909). When Binet was asked to identify students who needed special help in school, he constructed a broad sample of items intended to measure ability. The tests that he developed, and that have been developed in the tradition of psychological measurement, consist of large sets of items, most of which can be answered quickly. This allows a broad sampling of intellectual activities of different kinds to be included in the test, but with little or no opportunity for sustained work on any complex problem or understanding any complex idea. Because intelligence has been viewed as an attribute of individual capability, primarily involving manipulation of symbols, tests do not include observation of an individual's interactions with other people or with complex mechanical or other environmental systems. Binet's test was designed for individual, clinical administration. Subsequently, considerable effort was devoted to creation of pencil-and-paper intelligence tests, made up of multiple short items, that could be administered to groups and scored mechanically.

Tests of multiple intellectual competencies (e.g., Guilford, 1967; Thurstone, 1938) have involved identifying factors of ability, such as spatial, verbal, or numerical ability. Such a test consists of a collection of items that relate to the ability that it is purported to measure, with the same properties of brevity and unambiguous scorability as characterize items on tests of general intelligence.

The techniques originally developed for intelligence tests were also applied to tests of knowledge and achievement in school subjects. *Standardized* achievement tests are typically based on large samples of small items that represent a broad range of content, but with tasks that do not include sustained work on complex problems, communication or collaboration with other people, or complex interactions with complex mechanical or other environmental technologies. The achievement tests in widest use in U.S. schools also use item selection techniques that are designed to compare students with each other in a process of *norm referencing,* rather than with an explicit standard of what students are expected to learn. A newer technology of *criterion referencing* (Glaser, 1994) has attempted to match test items to explicit learning expectations, but by and large it has maintained the atomistic nature of the individual test items.

Tests of ability or knowledge composed of atomistic items make sense if we assume that the question we need to answer is some version of "How much?"—that is, how much general intelligence does a student have? or how much ability of a more specific kind, such as spatial or verbal ability, does a student have? or how much does a student know in some domain such as mathematics, history, or biology? This method of measuring school achievement makes sense in the behaviorist perspective, which assumes that acquired knowledge consists of an accumulation of components of information and skill, and the question "How much has a student learned in this subject matter?" is answered meaningfully by scores on tests that sample the elements of that domain.

Measures of students' general intellectual abilities and background knowledge provide information that is used to predict their prospects for successful learning in traditional school and school-like settings. Entrants into the U.S. military, for example, take a test that measures several aspects of intellectual ability, and the results are used to assign inductees to training programs of various kinds. Most standardized achievement tests are constructed in the multiple-choice format, which supports both objectivity and efficiency in scoring. By the use of multiple-choice items and machine scoring, scores can be compared across the world, and tests can be judged against standards of statistical reliability and validity in predicting students' future performance in schools.

### Evaluating Growth in Reasoning and Understanding: The Cognitive/Rationalist View

(c4) *Assessments of extended performance.* When knowing is viewed as the ability to employ general reasoning schemata and strategies and understanding of general principles in domains, assessment emphasizes students' knowing and reasoning in accomplishing larger tasks. Short-answer tests can assess whether students can answer questions about general principles, but many people argue that to assess whether students can reason with and communicate about general principles, it is necessary to observe them in appropriate activities of reasoning and communication. Alternative assessments that are being developed include on-demand examination questions that take an hour or more of class time, projects that take several days or weeks, and portfolios of work that is accomplished throughout a term or year of study.

Psychologists working in the Piagetian tradition and educators studying learning in subject matter domains have developed assessments to evaluate children's levels of logicodeductive functioning and conceptual development, which have been used mainly in their research studies. These assessments typically use interview techniques and experimental methods that uncover children's conceptions and misconceptions in science and mathematics. (For example, see chapters in Carey & Gelman, 1991, or in M. Gardner, Greeno, Reif, Schoenfeld, diSessa, & Stage, 1990.) These approaches have not seen widespread use in school assessment, in large part because they are time-costly, relying on clinical interviewing or special experimental arrangements and individualized interpretation.

The argument for assessments based on more complex performances is essentially the same as that for assessing writing based on performance of students in writing tasks. Some years ago the English-language teaching community rebelled against short-answer items as a way to measure writing ability, based on the argument that it is impossible to assess writing ability without having students write. They developed several systematic scoring methods, in particular, holistic scoring, analytic scoring, and primary-trait scoring (Huot, 1990). Referees are systematically trained to make reliable judgments on a 4- to 6-point scale. It is possible to obtain very high interrater reliability in scoring (around 90%) with practice (Huot, 1990; Mullis, 1980). Similar techniques are used for Advanced Placement examinations and to assess portfolios for advanced placement in the arts.

These developments, having solved some of the problems of objectivity in scoring assessments based on extended performances, have begun to be used as the basis for developing new technologies of *performance assessment* in education (Mislevy,

1993; L. B. Resnick, 1994). Performance assessment provides a bridge between the cognitive and the situative perspectives on knowing and learning, because the extended performances needed to assess conceptual understanding and reasoning often also involve engagement with other people and with tools and artifacts that create natural, or "authentic," situations of activity.

An important example of this use of technology is the manner in which the introduction of video and computers into schools made it possible to consider assessing abilities that are not well captured in written performances (Collins, Hawkins, & Frederiksen, 1993). For example, videotape can record students' oral presentations, their work with other students, and their execution of hands-on activities. Computers can record information about students' problem solving in real-world contexts (e.g., playing the role of a bank teller), their responsiveness to hints and feedback, and their long-term learning in different task contexts. These two media make it possible to assess aspects of student performance that paper and pencil inherently cannot record.

(c5) *Crediting varieties of excellence.* An important contribution of psychologists working in the rationalist tradition has been a reformulation of the theory of multiple intellectual competencies with a focus on understanding and meaning (H. Gardner, 1983). An implication of this perspective is the importance of recognizing multiple approaches that students may use to solve problems and preferences that students may have for particular contents and styles of mental work. Understanding and reasoning occur in the contexts of activities that shape them and give them significance, and if they are addressed to a significant issue, there will always be multiple ways for an intellectual contribution to be productive.

The need to recognize multiple kinds of contributions means that evaluations of student work need to be made by individuals and groups of judges who are sensitive to the varieties of excellence that can occur. As psychologists and educators develop systems of evaluation and assessment, we can contribute to the valuing of diversity in the styles and methods of understanding and reasoning that develop within our society.

### Assessing Participation in Practices: The Situative/Pragmatist-Sociohistoric View

(s5) *Assessing participation in inquiry and social practices of learning.* When knowing in a domain is considered as ability to participate in the socially organized distributed practices of thinking and inquiry in the domain, assessment needs to be focused on evaluation of those abilities. Many of the proposals for alternative assessments, such as evaluation of projects and portfolios (e.g., Resnick & Resnick, 1991) are relevant to the assessment of participation in inquiry practices, because those materials are relatively direct products of inquiry. It is also valuable to base assessments on observation of work by individuals and groups in significant inquiry activities. These assessments can involve evaluations of the quality of activity of groups of students and their individual members in the course of their work on projects. It can also involve observation of students' work on problems that are presented for the purposes of assessment, sometimes called "on-demand" assessment.

(s6) *Student participation in assessment.* An important aspect of participation in a community involves being included in the community's processes of evaluation of its accomplishments and progress. The situative view of knowing and learning, therefore, supports the notion that students should participate meaningfully in the processes of assessment, not merely as people whose work is assessed, but also as contributors to the formulation of standards and judgments of quality of work. Participation in processes of assessing their own and other students' work can provide opportunities for them to develop their own standards, their abilities for intellectual judgment, and their sense of personal responsibility for their individual work and their contributions to the community's progress.

(s7) *Design of assessment systems.* The central issues around educational assessment concern its role in the overall system of schooling (Frederiksen & Collins, 1989). Many feel that it is the most powerful lever reformers have on the system and that if we can construct an assessment system that encourages thinking, then schools will change teaching practices (Resnick & Resnick, 1991). A contrasting view is that the educational system has evolved with assessment as one component, and that if assessment practices are changed independently of other components (curriculum, pedagogy, textbooks, etc.), then the system will force new assessment practices back toward current practice to fit with the other components (Cuban, 1984).

Human judgments of intellectual work play a crucial role in the kinds of evaluation of students' learning that are most significant. To accomplish the reforms that are needed in assessment of school learning, we need to develop systems of assessment practice in which the judgments that are produced can be interpreted and trusted. We believe that this requires development and support of communities of practice in assessment that will develop standards of evaluation as well as standards of quality in the work of students that they evaluate. This will be an important aspect of the professional work of teaching, and, like other aspects of teaching that are implied by the reforms of education, will have to be supported as an integral part of teachers' activity. As a part of this effort, research can be addressed to understanding the complex ways in which teachers and students generate and use information about the achievements and progress of students as inherent aspects of their everyday activities of classroom work (Hall, Knudsen, & Greeno, in press).

## CONCLUSIONS

We have presented our understanding of the current state of knowledge in educational psychology regarding the central issues of cognition and learning. We hope that we have conveyed both a sense of continuity in the development of research on these topics over the course of the 20th century and a sense of the transitional state that we believe the field is in at this time. We also hope that we have conveyed our belief that concepts developed in this research have both progressively enriched and deepened the scientific understanding of fundamental processes and significantly supported the understanding and improvement of educational practice. In this concluding section, we consider prospects for the continued development of the theoretical perspectives and research involving design experiments.

## Theoretical Issues

We have portrayed the theoretical state regarding cognition and learning as being organized by three general perspectives, all with long traditions, whose current versions we have called behaviorist, cognitive, and situative. These perspectives are not equally developed, of course. The behaviorist perspective was the main line of development in the psychology of learning for several decades. Development of the cognitive perspective became the major focus of psychological research on learning and thinking in the 1970s. And the situative perspective is still in an early stage of development as an organizing principle and set of work practices for psychological research.

We expect that in the next several years, one of the salient theoretical questions for this field will be the continuing clarification of relations among these three perspectives. In broad terms, there are at least two ways that this may develop.

One possibility is that the behaviorist, cognitive, and situative views analyze processes of cognition and learning at different levels of aggregation. A behaviorist analysis studies activities of individuals. A cognitive analysis is more detailed, studying individual activity at a level of its internal structures of information, including symbolic representations and processes that transform symbolic expressions. A situative analysis is more aggregated than a behaviorist analysis. A situative analysis studies activity systems in which individual agents participate as members of social groups and as components of larger systems in which they interact with material resources. Viewing the relation among these perspectives as focusing on different levels, we would expect theoretical developments that show how principles of activity at the level of groups and human resource systems can be understood as compositions of principles of individual behavior, along with principles of group and human resource interaction, and how principles of individual behavior are compositions of principles of information processing, along with other principles such as motivation and emotion.

Another possibility, involving a somewhat more competitive relation among the perspectives, is that the situative perspective can provide a kind of synthesis of the behaviorist and cognitive perspectives. According to this possibility, behaviorist analyses study processes of activity, neglecting their contents, while cognitive analyses study contents of activity, including processes that transform those contents, but neglect processes that must be included if activity is to be understood as being affected by and affecting systems other than individual agents. According to this view, the three perspectives may constitute a kind of Hegelian cycle of thesis–antithesis–synthesis (Greeno & Moore, 1993), in which behaviorism provides a thesis that focuses on external aspects of activity, the cognitive view provides an antithesis that focuses on internal informational aspects, and the situative view may develop as a synthesis that unifies the strengths of the two earlier approaches. This view supports an expectation of theoretical developments that will show how principles of individual behavior and of information processing can be understood as special cases of more general principles of interactive functioning.

## Issues of Understanding and Facilitating Practice

In our discussions of issues of educational practice, we have tried to show how the theoretical perspectives that we consid-ered can be used to understand principles that are inherent, as assumptions, in current practices or in practices that people want to have. In our view, the role of theory in practice is not to prescribe a set of practices that should be followed, but rather to assist in clarifying alternative practices, including understanding of ways that aspects of practice relate to alternative functions and purposes of activity. We believe that the educational principles that are expressed in alternative theoretical perspectives can all be valid as bases of practice. Alternative principles can be complementary, but they can also be in conflict. The challenges of practice involve finding patterns of activity that advance multiple values when they are compatible and balance values when they are inconsistent.

The principles articulated in this chapter are first approximations, and further critical discussion may lead to clearer and more coherent expressions of practical assumptions. We also recognize that the issues that we have discussed—learning environments, curriculum, and assessment—are a small subset of the issues that are critical in educational practice. We believe that other issues also can be informed by the kind of discussion we have begun to develop in this chapter, perhaps organized by the same theoretical perspectives that we have used.

As one example of such a prospect, consider issues of teaching practice. The behaviorist perspective suggests a focus on efficiency of conveying information and training skill, and emphasizes teaching practices that involve well-organized routines of classroom activity, with clear plans and goals. The cognitive perspective suggests focusing on teaching as a kind of coaching, emphasizing teachers' understanding of and attention to students' thinking in order to identify potential improvement that they can guide and encourage. The situative perspective suggests a focus on teachers as mentors who represent communities of practice in the society. As such, they engage in the professional activities of creating and using disciplinary knowledge, exemplify valued practices of these communities, and guide students as they become increasingly competent practitioners.

As another example, consider issues of valuing diversity among students. The behaviorist perspective suggests a focus on equity of access and opportunity to acquire valued knowledge and supports development of practices that ensure that all students can achieve a satisfactory level of basic knowledge. The cognitive perspective suggests a focus on differences among students in their interests and engagement in the concepts and methods of subject matter domains, in the understandings that they bring to school activities, and in their learning strategies and epistemological beliefs, and supports development of practices in which these multiple interests, understandings, and approaches are resources that enrich the educational experiences of all students. The situative perspective suggests a focus on school learning as the activities of communities of practice whose members—the teachers and students—are participants in many communities outside of school, and whose main function is to help prepare students for satisfying and effective participation in multiple communities of the society in their later lives. This perspective encourages the development of social arrangements in school that can reinforce and complement students' family and other nonschool social communities and the development of students' and teachers' identities through meaningful participation in social and professional communities that create and use subject matter knowledge.

Needless to say, discussions of these and other crucial educational issues require much careful thought and attention to the diversity of practical and theoretical work that has been and is being carried out regarding them. Our hope and belief is that discussions along these lines may contribute to that work.

## Advancing Practical Theory

We are convinced that there is a significant shift occurring in the relation between theoretical and practical work and progress in educational psychology. We have focused much of our attention in this chapter on a kind of research that includes developmental work in designing learning environments, formulating curricula, and assessing achievements of cognition and learning and, simultaneously, on efforts to contribute to fundamental scientific understanding. In research and development of this kind, questions about a theory are not limited to whether it is coherent and yields accurate predictions; we also ask, as a central question, whether it works—that is, do the concepts and principles of the theory inform practice in productive ways. It becomes a task of research to develop and analyze new possibilities for practice, not just to provide inspiring examples, but also to provide analytical concepts and principles that support understanding of the examples and guidance for people who wish to use the examples as models in transforming their own practices.

This trend is not a simple combination of traditional basic and applied research. It involves a different conceptualization of what research and practical reform are. We believe that, as A. L. Brown and Campione (1994; A. L. Brown, 1994) and J. S. Brown (1991) have argued, reforming practices requires transformations of people's understanding of principles that are assumed—perhaps implicitly—in the practices, and that theoretically oriented research can assist in identifying those principles and suggest ways of accomplishing the transformations. At the same time, we believe that by embedding research in the activities of practical reform, the theoretical principles that are developed will have greater scientific validity than those that have been developed primarily in laboratory work and in disinterested observations of practice, because they will have to address deeper questions of how practices function and develop.

## References

Anderson, J. R. (1983). *The architecture of cognition*. Cambridge, MA: Harvard University Press.

Anderson, J. R., Boyle, C. F., Corbett, A. T., & Lewis, M. W. (1990). Cognitive modeling and intelligent tutoring. *Artificial Intelligence, 42,* 7–50.

Anderson, J. R., Boyle, C. F., & Reiser, B. J. (1985). Intelligent tutoring systems. *Science, 228,* 456–462.

Aronson, E. (1978). *The jigsaw classroom*. Beverly Hills, CA: Sage.

Barwise, J., & Perry, J. (1983). *Situations and attitudes*. Cambridge, MA: MIT Press.

Bassok, M., & Holyoak, K. J. (1989). Interdomain transfer between isomorphic topics in algebra and physics. *Journal of Experimental Psychology: Learning, Memory, and Cognition, 15,* 153–166.

Belenky, M. F., Clinchy, B. M., Goldberger, N. R., & Tarule, J. M. (1986). *Women's ways of knowing*. New York: Basic Books.

Bereiter, C., & Scardamalia, M. (1987). *The psychology of written composition*. Hillsdale, NJ: Lawrence Erlbaum Associates.

Berlyne, D. E. (1960). *Conflict, arousal, and curiosity*. New York: McGraw-Hill.

Bickhard, M. H., & Richie, D. M. (1983). *On the nature of representation: A case study of James Gibson's theory of perception*. New York: Praeger.

Binet, A. (1909). *Les Idées modernes sur les infants*. Paris: Flammarion.

Britten, B. K., & Gülgöz (1991). Using Kintsch's computational model to improve instructional text: Effects of repairing inference calls on recall and cognitive structures. *Journal of Educational Psychology, 83,* 329–345.

Brophy, J. E., & Good, T. L. (1986). Teacher behavior and student achievement. In M. C. Wittrock (Ed.), *Handbook of research on teaching* (3rd ed, pp. 328–375). New York: Macmillan.

Brown, A. L. (1978). Knowing when, where, and how to remember: A problem of metacognition. In R. Glaser (Ed.), *Advances in instructional psychology* (Vol. 1, pp. 77–166). Hillsdale, NJ: Lawrence Erlbaum Associates.

Brown, A. L. (1989). Analogical learning and transfer: What develops? In S. Vosniadou & A. Ortony (Eds.), *Similarity and analogical reasoning* (pp. 369–412). Cambridge, England: Cambridge University Press.

Brown, A. L. (1992). Design experiments: Theoretical and methodological challenges in creating complex interventions in classroom settings. *Journal of the Learning Sciences, 2,* 141–178.

Brown, A. L. (1994). The advancement of learning. *Educational Researcher, 23*(8), 4–12.

Brown, A. L., Ash, D., Rutherford, M., Nakagawa, K., Gordon, A., & Campione, J. (1993). Distributed expertise in the classroom. In G. Salomon (Ed.), *Distributed cognitions: Psychological and educational considerations* (pp. 188–228). Cambridge, England: Cambridge University Press.

Brown, A. L., & Campione, J. C. (1977). Training strategic study time apportionment in educable retarded children. *Intelligence, 1,* 94–107.

Brown, A. L., & Campione, J. C. (1981). Inducing flexible thinking: A problem of access. In M. Friedman, J. P. Das, & N. O'Connor (Eds.), *Intelligence and learning* (pp. 515–529). New York: Plenum Press.

Brown, A. L., & Campione, J. C. (1994). Guided discovery in a community of learners. In K. McGilly (Ed.), *Classroom lessons: Integrating cognitive theory and classroom practice* (pp. 229–270). Cambridge, MA: MIT Press/Bradford.

Brown, A. L., & Kane, M. J. (1988). Preschool children can learn to transfer: Learning to learn and learning from example. *Cognitive Psychology, 20,* 493–523.

Brown, D. E., & Clement, J. (1989). Overcoming misconceptions via analogical reasoning: Abstract transfer versus explanatory model construction. *Instructional Science, 18,* 237–262.

Brown, J. S. (1991, January–February). Research that reinvents the corporation. *Harvard Business Review,* pp. 102–111.

Brown, J. S., Burton, R. R., & deKleer, J. (1982). Pedagogical, natural language and knowledge-engineering techniques in SOPHIE I, II, and III. In D. Sleeman & J. S. Brown (Eds.), *Intelligent tutoring systems* (pp. 227–282). New York: Academic Press.

Brown, J. S., Collins, A., & Duguid, P. (1989). Situated cognition and the culture of learning. *Educational Researcher, 18,* 32–42.

Brownell, W. A. (1935). Psychological considerations in the learning and teaching of arithmetic. In *The teaching of arithmetic: Tenth yearbook of the National Council of Teachers of Mathematics*. New York: Columbia University Press.

Bruner, J. S. (1960). *The process of education*. Cambridge, MA: Harvard University Press.

Burton, R. R., & Brown, J. S. (1982). An investigation of computer coaching for informal learning activities. In D. Sleeman & J. S. Brown (eds.), *Intelligent tutoring systems* (pp. 79–98). New York: Academic Press.

Carey, S. (1985). *Conceptual change in childhood*. Cambridge, MA: MIT Press/Bradford.

Carey, S., & Gelman, R. (Eds.). (1991). *The epigenesis of mind: Essays on biology and cognition*. Hillsdale, NJ: Lawrence Erlbaum Associates.

Carpenter, T. P., Fennema, E., Peterson, P. L., Chiang, C.-P., & Loef, M. (1989). Using knowledge of children's mathematic thinking in classroom teaching: An experimental study. *American Educational Research Journal, 26*, 499–531.

Carver, S. M. (1990, April). Integrating interactive technologies into classrooms. Paper presented at the annual meeting of the American Educational Research Association, Boston, MA.

Case, R. (1985). *Intellectual development: Birth to adulthood*. Orlando, FL: Academic Press.

Case, R. (1991). A developmental approach to remedial instruction. In A. McKeough & J. L. Lupart (Eds.), *Toward the practice of theory-based instruction* (pp. 114–147). Hillsdale, NJ: Lawrence Erlbaum Associates.

Case, R. (1992). Neo-Piagetian theories of cognitive development. In R. J. Sternberg & C. A. Berg (Eds.), *Intellectual development* (pp. 161–196). New York: Cambridge University Press.

Cazden, C. B. (1986). Classroom discourse. In M. C. Wittrock (Ed.), *Handbook of research on teaching* (3rd ed., pp. 432–463). New York: Macmillan.

Chambliss, M. J., & Calfee, R. C. (1996). *Textbooks for learning: Nurturing children's minds*. New York and London: Blackwell.

Chi, M. T. H., Bassok, M., Lewis, M. W., Reimann, P., & Glaser, R. (1989). Self-explanations: How students study and use examples in learning to solve problems. *Cognitive Science, 13*, 145–182.

Chi, M. T. H., Slotta, J. D., & de Leeuw, N. (1994). From things to processes: A theory of conceptual change for learning science concepts. *Learning and Instruction, 4*, pp. 27–43.

Clark, H. H. (1992). *Arenas of language use*. Chicago: University of Chicago Press, and Stanford, CA: Center for the Study of Language and Information.

Cobb, P., Wood, T., & Yackel, E. (1990). Classroom as learning environments for teachers and researchers. In R. B. Davis, C. A. Maher, & N. Noddings (Eds.), *Constructivist views on teaching and learning mathematics* (*Journal for Research in Mathematics Education* Monograph No. 4, pp. 125–146). Reston, VA: National Council of Teachers of Mathematics.

Cobb, P., Wood, T., Yackel, E., Nicholls, J., Wheatley, G., Trigatti, B., & Perlwitz, M. (1991). Assessment of a problem-centered second-grade mathematics project. *Journal for Research in Mathematics Education, 22*, 3–29.

Cognition and Technology Group at Vanderbilt. (1990). Anchored instruction and its relationship to situated cognition. *Educational Researchers, 19*(5), pp. 2–10.

Cognition and Technology Group at Vanderbilt. (1994). From visual word problems to learning communities: Changing conceptions of cognitive research. In K. McGilly (Ed.), *Classroom lessons: Integrating cognitive theory and classroom practice* (pp. 157–200). Cambridge, MA: MIT Press/Bradford.

Cohen, E. G. (1986). *Designing groupwork*. New York: Teachers College Press.

Cole, M., Gay, J., Glick, J. A., & Sharp, D. W. (1971). *The cultural context of learning and thinking*. New York: Basic Books.

Collins, A. (1992). Toward a design science of education. In E. Scanlon & T. O'Shea (Eds.), *New directions in educational technology* (pp. 15–22). Berlin: Springer.

Collins, A., Brown, J. S., & Newman, S. E. (1989). Cognitive apprentice-ship: Teaching the craft of reading, writing, and mathematics. In L. B. Resnick (Ed.), *Knowing, learning, and instruction: Essays in honor of Robert Glaser*. Hillsdale, NJ: Lawrence Erlbaum Associates.

Collins, A., Hawkins, J., & Carver, S. M. (1991). A cognitive apprenticeship for disadvantaged students. In B. Means, C. Chelemer, & M. S. Knapp (Eds.), *Teaching advanced skills to at-risk students* (pp. 216–243). San Francisco: Jossey-Bass.

Collins, A., Hawkins, J., & Frederiksen, J. (1993). Three different views of students: The role of technology in assessing student performance. *Journal of the Learning Sciences, 3*, 205–217.

Confrey, J. (1990). A review of the research on student conceptions in mathematics, science, and programming. In C. B. Cazden (Ed.), *Review of Research in Education* (Vol. 1, pp. 3–56). Washington, DC: American Educational Research Association.

Cuban, L. (1984). *How teachers taught: Constancy and change in American classrooms, 1890–1980*. New York: Longman.

Devlin, K. (1991). *Logic and information*. Cambridge, England: Cambridge University Press.

Dewey, J. (1896). The reflex arc concept in psychology. *Psychological Review, 3*, 357–370.

Dienes, Z. P. (1966). *Mathematics in the primary school*. London: Macmillan.

diSessa, A. (1982). Unlearning Aristotelian physics: A study of knowledge-based learning. *Cognitive Science, 6*, 37–75.

diSessa, A. (1985). Learning about knowing. In E. L. Klein (Ed.), *Children and computers. New directions for child development* (No. 28, pp. 97–124). San Francisco: Jossey-Bass.

diSessa, A., Hammer, D., & Sherin, B. (1991). Inventing graphing: Meta-representational expertise in children. *Journal of Mathematical Behavior, 10*, 117–160.

Dweck, C. S., & Bempechat, J. (1983). Children's theories of intelligence. In S. G. Paris, G. M. Olson, & H. W. Stevenson (Eds.), *Learning and motivation in the classroom* (pp. 239–256). Hillsdale, NJ: Lawrence Erlbaum Associates.

Dweck, C. S., & Legett, E. L. (1988). A social-cognitive approach to motivation and personality. *Psychological Review, 95*, 256–273.

Eckert, P. (1989). *Jocks and burnouts*. New York: Teachers College Press.

Eckert, P. (1990). Adolescent social categories: Information and science learning. In M. Gardner, G. J. Greeno, F. Reif, A. H. Schoenfeld, A. diSessa, & E. Stage (Eds.), *Toward a scientific practice of science education* (pp. 203–218). Hillsdale, NJ: Lawrence Erlbaum Associates.

Ernst, G. W., & Newell, A. (1969). *GPS: A case study in generality and problem solving*. New York: Academic Press.

Estes, W. K. (1959). The statistical approach to learning theory. In S. Koch (Ed.), *Psychology: A study of a science* (Vol. 2, pp. 380–491). New York: McGraw-Hill.

Fawcett, H. (1938). *The nature of proof*. New York: Teachers College, Columbia University.

Feigenbaum, E. A. (1989). What hath Simon wrought? In D. Klahr & K. Kotovsky (Eds.), *Complex information processing: The impact of Herbert A. Simon* (pp. 165–182). Hillsdale, NJ: Lawrence Erlbaum Associates.

Fernandez, C., Yoshida, M., & Stigler, J. W. (1992). Learning mathematics from classroom instruction: On relating lessons to pupils' interpretations. *Journal of the Learning Sciences, 3*, 333–365.

Flavell, J., Green, F. L., & Flavell, E. R. (1986). Development of knowledge about the appearance-reality distinction. *Monographs of the Society for Research in Child Development, 51*(1, Serial No. 212).

Flavell, J., & Wellman, H. M. (1977). Metamemory. In R. V. Kail, Jr., & J. W. Hagen (Eds.), *Perspectives on the development of memory and cognition*. Hillsdale, NJ: Lawrence Erlbaum Associates.

Frederiksen, J. R., & Collins, A. (1989). A systems approach to educational testing. *Educational Researcher, 18*, 27–32.

Gagné, R. M. (1965). *The conditions of learning*. New York: Holt, Rinehart & Winston.

Gagné, R. M. (1968). Learning hierarchies. *Educational Psychologist, 6,* 1–9.

Galanter, E. (Ed.). (1968). *Automatic teaching: The state of the art.* New York: Wiley.

Gardner, H. (1983). *Frames of mind: The theory of multiple intelligences.* New York: Basic Books.

Gardner, M., Greeno, J. G., Reif, F., Schoenfeld, A. H., diSessa, A., & Stage, E. (Eds.). (1990). *Toward a scientific practice of science education.* Hillsdale, NJ: Lawrence Erlbaum Associates.

Gattegno, C. (1963). *For the teaching of elementary mathematics.* Mount Vernon, NY: Cuisenaire Company of America.

Gelman, R., & Gallistel, C. R. (1978). *The child's understanding of number.* Cambridge, MA: Harvard University Press.

Gentner, D., & Stevens, A. L. (Eds.). (1983). *Mental models.* Hillsdale, NJ: Lawrence Erlbaum Associates.

Gibson, J. J. (1966). *The senses considered as perceptual systems.* Boston: Houghton Mifflin.

Gibson, J. J. (1986). *An ecological approach to visual perception.* Hillsdale, NJ: Lawrence Erlbaum Associates. (Original work published 1979)

Gick, M., & Holyoak, K. (1983). Schema induction and analogical transfer. *Cognitive Psychology, 15,* 1–38.

Gilligan, C., Ward, J. V., Taylor, J. M., & Bardige, B. (Eds.) (1988). *Mapping the moral domain: A contribution of women's thinking to psychological theory and education.* Cambridge, MA: Center for the Study of Gender, Education, and Human Development, Harvard University Graduate School of Education.

Ginsburg, H., & Opper, S. (1969). *Piaget's theory of intellectual development: An introduction.* Englewood Cliffs, NJ: Prentice Hall.

Glaser, R. (1984). Education and thinking: The role of knowledge. *American Psychologist, 39,* 93–104.

Glaser, R. (1994). Criterion-referenced tests: Part I. Origins. Part II. Unfinished business. *Educational measurement: Issues and practice. 13,* 9–11; 27–30.

Goldman, S. (in press). Mediating micro-worlds: Collaboration on high school science activities. In T. Koschman (Ed.), *Computer support for collaborative work.* Hillsdale, NJ: Lawrence Erlbaum Associates.

Greeno, J. G. (1995). Understanding concepts in activity. In C. A. Weaver III, S. Mannes, & C. R. Fletcher (Eds.). *Discourse comprehension: Essays in honor of Walter Kintsch* (pp. 65–96). Hillsdale, NJ: Lawrence Erlbaum Associates.

Greeno, J. G., & Moore, J. L. (1993). Situativity and symbols: Response to Vera and Simon. *Cognitive Science, 17,* 49–60.

Greeno, J. G., & Simon, H. A. (1989). Problem solving and reasoning. In R. C. Atkinson, R. J. Herrnstein, G. Lindzey, & R. D. Luce (Eds.), *Stevens' handbook of experimental psychology* (2nd ed.). *Vol. 2. Learning and cognition* (pp. 589–672). New York: Wiley.

Greeno, J. G., Smith, D. R., & Moore, J. L. (1993). Transfer of situated learning. In D. K. Detterman & R. J. Sternberg (Eds.), *Transfer on trial: Intelligence, cognition, and instruction* (pp. 99–167). Norwood, NJ: Ablex.

Guilford, J. P. (1967). *The nature of human intelligence.* New York: McGraw-Hill.

Gumperz, J. J. (1982). *Discourse strategies.* Cambridge, England: Cambridge University Press.

Guthrie, E. R. (1935). *The psychology of learning.* New York: Harper.

Halford, G. S. (1993). *Children's understanding: The development of mental models.* Hillsdale, NJ: Lawrence Erlbaum Associates.

Hall, R. P., Knudsen, J., & Greeno, J. G. (in press). A case study of systemic attributes of assessment technologies. *Educational Assessment.*

Harel, I. (1991). *Children designers: Interdisciplinary constructions for learning and knowing mathematics in a computer-rich school.* Norwood, NJ: Ablex.

Harlow, H. F., & Zimmerman, R. R. (1958). The development of affectional responses in infant monkeys. *Proceedings of the American Philosophical Society, 102,* 501–509.

Hatano, G., & Inagaki, K. (1987). Everyday and school biology: How do they interact? *Quarterly Newsletter of the Laboratory of Comparative Human Cognition, 9,* 120–128.

Hatano, G., & Inagaki, K. (1991). Sharing cognition through collective comprehension activity. In L. B. Resnick, J. M. Levine, & S. D. Teasley (Eds.), *Perspectives on socially shared cognition* (pp. 331–348). Washington, DC: American Psychological Association.

Hayes, J. R. (1981). *The complete problem solver.* Philadelphia: Franklin Institute Press.

Hendrickson, G., & Schroeder, W. H. (1941). Transfer of training in learning to hit a submerged target. *Journal of Educational Psychology, 32,* 205–213.

Holland, J. H., Holyoak, K. J., Nisbett, R. E., & Thagard, P. R. (1986). *Induction: Processes of inference, learning, and discovery.* Cambridge, MA: MIT Press.

Hull, C. L. (1943). *Principles of behavior: An introduction to behavior theory.* New York: Appleton-Century.

Huot, B. (1990). The literature of direct writing assessment: Major concerns and prevailing trends. *Review of Educational Research, 60,* 237–263.

Hutchins, E. (1993). Learning to navigate. In S. Chaiklin & J. Lave (Eds.), *Understanding practice: Perspectives on activity and context* (pp. 35–63). Cambridge, England: Cambridge University Press.

Hutchins, E. (1995). *Cognition in the wild.* Cambridge, MA: MIT Press.

Johnson-Laird, P. N. (1983). *Mental models: Towards a cognitive science of language, inference, and consciousness.* Cambridge, MA: Harvard University Press.

Judd, C. H. (1908). The relation of special training to general intelligence. *Educational Review, 36,* 28–42.

Just, M. A., & Carpenter, P. A. (1980). A theory of reading: From eye fixations to comprehension. *Psychological Review, 87,* 329–354.

Kaput, J. J. (1989). Linking representations in the symbol systems of algebra. In S. Wagner & C. Kieran (Eds.), *Research issues in the learning and teaching of algebra* (pp. 167–194). Reston, VA: Lawrence Erlbaum Associates and National Council of Teachers of Mathematics.

Katona, G. (1940). *Organizing and memorizing: Studies in the psychology of learning and teaching.* New York: Columbia University Press.

Keil, F. C. (1989). *Concepts, minds, and cognitive development.* Cambridge, MA: MIT Press/Bradford.

Kintsch, W. (1994). Text comprehension, memory, and learning. *American Psychologist, 49,* 294–303.

Kintsch, W., & van Dijk, T. A. (1978). Toward a model of text comprehension and production. *Psychological Review, 85,* 363–394.

Laboratory of Comparative Human Cognition. (1982). A model system for the study of learning difficulties. *Quarterly Newsletter of the Laboratory of Comparative Human Cognition, 4,* 39–66.

Lampert, M. (1990). When the problem is not the question and the solution is not the answer: Mathematical knowing and teaching. *American Educational Research Journal, 17,* 29–64.

Lashley, K. S. (1951). The problem of serial order in psychology. In L. A. Jeffress (Ed.), *Cerebral mechanisms in behavior.* New York: Harcourt Brace.

Latour, B., & Woolgar, S. (1986). *Laboratory life: The construction of scientific facts.* Princeton, NJ: Princeton University Press. (Originally published 1979)

Lave, J. (1988). *Cognition, in practice.* Cambridge, England: Cambridge University Press.

Lave, J., & Wenger, E. (1991). *Situated learning: Legitimate peripheral participation.* Cambridge, England: Cambridge University Press.

Lepper, M. R., & Greene, D. (1979). *The hidden costs of reward.* Hillsdale, NJ: Lawrence Erlbaum Associates.

Lesgold, A., Lajoie, S., Bunzo, M., & Eggan, G. (1988). Sherlock: A coached practice environment for an electronics troubleshooting job. Pittsburgh, PA: Learning Research and Development Center, University of Pittsburgh.

Lesgold, A. M., & Perfetti, C. A. (1978). Interactive processes in reading comprehension. *Discourse Processes, 1,* 323–336.

Levine, J. M., Resnick, L. B., & Higgins, E. T. (1993). Social foundations of cognition. *Annual Review of Psychology, 44,* 585–612.

Levine, M. (1988). *Effective problem solving.* Englewood Cliffs, NJ: Prentice Hall.

Lewis, C. (1988). Why and how to learn why: Analysis-based generalization of procedures. *Cognitive Science, 12,* 211–256.

Lewis, M. W., & Anderson, J. R. (1985). Discrimination of operator schemata in problem solving: Learning from examples. *Cognitive Psychology, 17,* 26–65.

Linn, M. C. (1992). The computer as learning partner: Can computer tools teach science? In K. Sheingold, L. G. Roberts, & S. M. Malcolm (Eds.), *This year in school science 1991: Technology for teaching and learning.* Washington, DC: American Association for the Advancement of Science.

Linn, M. C., Songer, N. B., Lewis, E. L., & Stern, J. (1993). Using technology to teach thermodynamics: Achieving integrated understanding. In D. L. Ferguson (Ed.), *Advanced educational technologies for mathematics and science* (Vol. 107, pp. 5–60). Berlin: Springer.

Lipman, M. (1985). Thinking skills fostered by philosophy for children. In J. W. Segal, S. F. Chipman, & R. Glaser (Eds.), *Thinking and learning skills: Vol. 1. Relating instruction to research* (pp. 83–108). Hillsdale, NJ: Lawrence Erlbaum Associates.

Lipman, M. (1991). *Thinking in education.* Cambridge, England: Cambridge University Press.

Lynch, M. (1993). *Scientific practice and ordinary action: Ethnomethodology and social studies of science.* New York: Cambridge University Press.

Malone, T. W. (1981). Toward a theory of intrinsically motivating instruction. *Cognitive Science, 4,* 333–369.

Marton, F., Hounsell, D. J., & Entwhistle, N. (1984). *The experience of learning.* Edinburgh: Scottish Academic Press.

McCloskey, M. (1983). Naive theories of motion. In D. Gentner & A. L. Stevens (Eds.), *Mental models* (pp. 299–323). Hillsdale, NJ: Lawrence Erlbaum Associates.

McDermott, R. P. (1993). The acquisition of a child by a learning disability. In S. Chaiklin & J. Lave (Eds.), *Understanding practice: Perspectives on activity and context* (pp. 269–305). Cambridge, England: Cambridge University Press.

Mehan, H. (1979). *Learning lessons.* Cambridge, MA: Harvard University Press.

Miller, J. R., & Kintsch, W. (1980). Readability and recall of short prose passages: A theoretical analysis. *Journal of Experimental Psychology: Human Learning and Memory, 6,* 335–354.

Minstrell, J. (1989). Teaching science for understanding. In L. B. Resnick & L. E. Klopfer (Eds.), *Toward the thinking curriculum: Current cognitive research* (pp. 129–149). Alexandria, VA: Association for Supervision and Curriculum Development.

Mislevy, R. J. (1993). *Linking educational assessments: Issues, concepts, methods, and prospects.* Princeton, NJ: Policy Information Center, Educational Testing Service.

Moll, L. C., Tapia, J., & Whitmore, K. F. (1993). Living knowledge: The social distribution of cultural resources for thinking. In G. Salomon (Ed.), *Distributed cognitions: Psychological and educational considerations* (pp. 139–163). Cambridge, England: Cambridge University Press.

Moll, L. C., & Whitmore, K. F. (1993). Vygotsky in classroom practice: Moving from individual transmission to social transaction. In E. A. Forman, N. Minick, & C. A. Stone (Eds.), *Contexts for learning: Sociocultural dynamics in children's development* (pp. 19–42). New York: Oxford University Press.

Montessori, M. (1964). *Advanced Montessori method.* Cambridge, MA: Robert Bently. (Original work published 1917)

Moore, J. L. (1993). Comparisons of a physical model and computer representations in reasoning and learning about linear functions. Unpublished doctoral dissertation, Stanford University, Palo Alto, CA.

Moschkovich, J. (Chair). (1994, April). *Learning mathematics in the context of design projects.* Symposium conducted at the annual meeting of the American Educational Research Association, New Orleans, LA.

Moses, R. P., Kamii, M., Swap, S. M., & Howard, J. (1989). The Algebra Project: Organizing in the spirit of Ella. *Harvard Educational Review, 59,* 423–443.

Mullis, I. V. S. (1980). Using the primary trait system for evaluating writing. *National Assessment of Educational Progress Report.* Denver, CO: Education Commission of the States.

Nesher, P. (1989). Microworlds in education: A pedagogical realism. In L. Resnick (Ed.), *Knowing, learning, and instruction: Essays in honor of Robert Glaser* (pp. 187–216). Hillsdale, NJ: Lawrence Erlbaum Associates.

Newell, A. (1980). One final word. In D. T. Tuma & F. Reif (Eds.), *Problem solving and education: Issues in teaching and research* (pp. 175–189). Hillsdale, NJ: Lawrence Erlbaum Associates.

Newell, A. (1990). *Unified theories of cognition.* Cambridge, MA: Harvard University Press.

Newell, A., & Simon, H. A. (1972). *Human problem solving.* Englewood Cliffs, NJ: Prentice Hall.

Nisbett, R. E., Fong, G. T., Lehman, D. R., & Cheng, P. W. (1987). Teaching reasoning. *Science, 238,* 625–631.

Norman, D. A. (1988). *The design of everyday things.* New York: Basic Books.

Nunes, T., Schliemann, A. D., & Carraher, D. W. (1993). *Street mathematics and school mathematics.* Cambridge, England: Cambridge University Press.

Ochs, E., Jacoby, S., & Gonzalez, P. (1994). Interpretive journeys: How physicists talk and travel through graphic space. *Configurations, 2,* 151–172.

Ohlsson, S., & Rees, E. (1991). The function of conceptual understanding in the learning of arithmetic procedures. *Cognition and Instruction, 8,* 103–179.

Osgood, C. E. (1949). The similarity paradox in human learning. *Psychological Review, 56,* 132–143.

Palincsar, A. S., & Brown, A. L. (1984). Reciprocal teaching of comprehension-fostering and monitoring activities. *Cognition and Instruction, 1,* 117–175.

Packer, M. J. (1985). Hermeneutic inquiry in the study of human conduct. *American Psychologist, 40,* 1081–1093.

Papert, S. (1980). *Mindstorms: Children, computers, and powerful ideas.* New York: Basic Books.

Pea, R. (1993). Practices of distributed intelligence and designs for education. In G. Salomon (Ed.), *Distributed cognitions* (pp. 47–87). New York: Cambridge University Press.

Pea, R., Sipusic, M., & Allen, S. (in press). Seeing the light on optics: Classroom-based research and development of a learning environment for conceptual change. In Strauss, S. (Ed.), *Development and learning environments.* Norwood, NJ: Ablex.

Piaget, J. (1929). *The child's conception of the world* (J. & A. Tomlinson, Trans.). New York: Harcourt, Brace & World.

Piaget, J. (1932). *The moral judgment of the child* (M. Worden, Trans.). New York: Harcourt, Brace & World.

Piaget, J. (1970). *Science of education and the psychology of the child* (D. Coleman, Trans.). New York: Orion Press. (Original work published 1935 and 1969)

Piaget, J. (1972). *The child's conception of physical causality* (M. Gabain, Trans.). Totowa, NJ: Littlefield, Adams. (Original work published 1927)

Polya, G. (1945). *How to solve it.* Princeton, NJ: Princeton University Press.

Reigeluth, C. M. (Ed.). (1983). *Instructional design theories and models: An overview.* Hillsdale, NJ: Lawrence Erlbaum Associates.

Reil, M. M., & Levin, J. A. (1990). Building electronic communities: Success and failure in computer networking. *Instructional Science, 19,* 145–169.

Rescorla, R. A., & Wagner, A. R. (1972). A theory of Pavlovian conditioning: Variations in the effectiveness of reinforcement and nonreinforcement. In A. Black & W. F. Prokasy (Eds.), *Classical conditioning: II. Current research and theory* (pp. 64–99). New York: Appleton-Century-Crofts.

Resnick, L. B. (1987a). *Education and learning to think.* Washington, DC: National Academy Press.

Resnick, L. B. (1987b). Learning in school and out. *Educational Researcher, 16,* 13–20.

Resnick, L. B. (1989). Developing mathematical knowledge. *American Psychologist, 44,* 162–169.

Resnick, L. B. (1994). Performance puzzles. *American Journal of Education, 102,* 511–526.

Resnick, L. B., Bill, V. L., Lesgold, S. B., & Leer, M. N. (1991). Thinking in arithmetic class. In B. Means, C. Chelemer, & M. S. Knapp (Eds.), *Teaching advanced skills to at-risk students* (pp. 27–53). San Francisco: Jossey-Bass.

Resnick, L. B., Levine, J. M., & Teasley, S. D. (Eds.). (1991). *Perspectives on socially shared cognition.* Washington, DC: American Psychological Association.

Resnick, L. B., & Omanson, S. F. (1987). Learning to understand arithmetic. In R. Glaser (Ed.), *Advances in instructional psychology* (Vol. 3, pp. 41–96). Hillsdale, NJ: Lawrence Erlbaum Associates.

Resnick, L. B., & Resnick, D. P. (1991). Assessing the thinking curriculum: New tools for education reform. In B. R. Gifford & M. C. O'Connor (Eds.), *Changing assessment: Alternative views of aptitude, achievement, and instruction* (pp. 37–75). Boston: Kluwer.

Roschelle, J. (1992). Learning by collaboration: convergent conceptual change. *Journal of the Learning Sciences, 2,* 235–276.

Roth, K. J. (1986). *Conceptual-change learning and student processing of science texts* (Research Series No. 167). East Lansing, MI: Institute for Research on Teaching, Michigan State University.

Rumelhart, D. E., Hinton, G. F., & Williams, R. J. (1986). Learning internal representations by error propagation. In D. E. Rumelhart, J. L. McClelland, & the PDP Research Group (Eds.), *Parallel distributed processing: Explorations in the microstructure of cognition: Vol. 1. Foundations* (pp. 318–362). Cambridge, MA: MIT Press/radford.

Rumelhart, D. E., McClelland, J. L., & the PDP Research Group (Eds.), (1986). *Parallel distributed processing: Explorations in the microstructure of cognition: Vol. 1. Foundations.* Cambridge, MA: MIT Press/Bradford.

Saxe, G. (1990). *Culture and cognitive development: Studies in mathematical understanding.* Hillsdale, NJ: Lawrence Erlbaum Associates.

Sayeki, Y., Ueno, N., & Nagasaka, T. (1991). Mediation as a generative model for obtaining an area. *Learning and Instruction, 1,* 229–242.

Scardamalia, M., & Bereiter, C. (1991). Higher levels of agency for children in knowledge building: A challenge for the design of new knowledge media. *Journal of the Learning Sciences, 1,* 37–68.

Scardamalia, M., Bereiter, C., & Lamon, M. (1994). The CSILE project: Trying to bring the classroom into World 3. In K. McGilly (Ed.), *Classroom lessons: Integrating cognitive theory and classroom practice* (pp. 201–228). Cambridge, MA: MIT Press/Bradford.

Schegloff, M. A. (1991). Conversation analysis and socially shared cognition. In L. B. Resnick, J. M. Levine, & S. D. Teasley (Eds.), *Perspectives on socially shared cognition* (pp. 150–171). Washington, DC: American Psychological Association.

Schoenfeld, A. H. (1985). *Mathematical problem solving.* Orlando, FL: Academic Press.

Schoenfeld, A. H. (1987). What's all the fuss about metacognition? In

A. H. Schoenfeld (Ed.), *Cognitive science and mathematics education* (pp. 189–216). Hillsdale, NJ: Lawrence Erlbaum Associates.

Schoenfeld, A. H. (1988). When good teaching leads to bad results: The disasters of "well-taught" mathematics courses. *Educational Psychologist, 23,* 145–166.

Schwab, J. J. (1978). *Science, curriculum, and liberal education: Selected essays* (I. Westbury & N. J. Wilkof, Eds.). Chicago: University of Chicago Press.

Schwartz, J. L., Yarushalmy, M., & Wilson, B. (Eds.). (1993). *The geometric supposer: What is it a case of?* Hillsdale, NJ: Lawrence Erlbaum Associates.

Schwarz, B. B., Kohn, A. S., & Resnick, L. B. (1993/1994). Positives about negatives: A case study of an intermediate model for signed numbers. *Journal of the Learning Sciences, 3,* 37–92.

Singley, M. K., & Anderson, J. R. (1989). *The transfer of cognitive skill.* Cambridge, MA: Harvard University Press.

Sizer, T. (1992). *Horace's school: Redesigning the American high school.* Boston: Houghton Mifflin.

Skinner, B. F. (1938). *The behavior of organisms: An experimental analysis.* New York: Appleton-Century-Crofts.

Skinner, B. F. (1953). *Science and human behavior.* New York: Macmillan.

Skinner, B. F. (1958). Teaching machines. *Science, 128,* 969–977.

Slavin, R. E. (1983). *Cooperative learning.* New York: Longman.

Smith, F. (1988). *Joining the literacy club.* Portsmouth, NH: Heinemann.

Smith, J. P., III, diSessa, A. A., & Roschelle, J. (1993/1994). Misconceptions reconceived: A constructivist analysis of knowledge in transition. *Journal of the Learning Sciences, 3,* 115–164.

Spearman, C. (1904). "General intelligence" objectively determined and measured. *American Journal of Psychology, 15,* 201–293.

Steffe, L. P., Cobb, P., & von Glasersfeld, E. (1988). *Construction of arithmetical meanings and strategies.* New York: Springer.

Stein, M. K., Silver, E., & Smith, M. S. (in press). Mathematics reform and teacher development: A community of practice perspective. In J. G. Greeno & S. V. Goldman (Eds.), *Thinking practices: A symposium on mathematics and science learning.* Hillsdale, NJ: Lawrence Erlbaum Associates.

Stevens, A., & Roberts, B. (1983). Quantitative and qualitative simulation in computer-based training. *Journal of Computer-Based Instruction, 10,* 16–19.

Stigler, J. W., & Perry, M. (1988). Mathematics learning in Japanese, Chinese, and American classrooms. In G. Saxe & M. Gearhart (Eds.), *Children's mathematics.* San Francisco: Jossey-Bass.

Stodolsky, S. S. (1988). *The subject matters: Classroom activity in math and social studies.* Chicago: University of Chicago Press.

Suppes, P., & Morningstar, M. (1972). *Computer-assisted instruction at Stanford, 1966–68.* New York: Academic Press.

Terrace, H. S. (1966). Stimulus control. In W. K. Honig (Ed.), *Operant behavior: Areas of research and application* (pp. 271–344). New York: Appleton-Century-Crofts.

Tharp, R. G. (1989). Psychocultural variables and constants: Effects on teaching and learning in schools. *American Psychologist, 44,* 349–366.

Thorndike, E. L. (1903). *Educational psychology.* New York: Lemke & Buechner.

Thorndike, E. L. (1917–1924). *The Thorndike arithmetics.* Chicago: Rand McNally.

Thorndike, E. L. (1922). *The psychology of arithmetic.* New York: Macmillan.

Thorndike, E. L. (1931). *Human learning.* New York: Century.

Thurstone, L. L. (1938). Primary mental abilities. *Psychometric Monographs, 1* (Whole No.).

Tolman, E. C. (1932). *Purposive behavior in animals and men.* New York: Century.

Triesman, P. U. (1990). Teaching mathematics to a changing population: The Professional Development Program at the University of California,

Berkeley. Part I. A study of the mathematics performance of black students at the University of California, Berkeley. In N. Fisher, H. Keynes, & P. Wagreich (Eds.), *Mathematicians and education reform* (pp. 33–46). Washington, DC: American Mathematical Society.

Turvey, M. (1990). Coordination. *American Psychologist, 45,* 938–953.

Turvey, M. (1992). Ecological foundations of cognition: Invariants of perception and action. In H. L. Pick, Jr., P. van den Broek, & D. C. Knill (Eds.), *Cognition: Conceptual and methodological issues* (pp. 85–117). Washington, DC: American Psychological Association.

Underwood, B. J., & Schulz, R. W. (1960). *Meaningfulness and verbal learning.* Philadelphia: Lippincott.

VanLehn, K. (1989). Problem solving and cognitive skill acquisition. In M. Posner (Ed.), *Foundations of cognitive science* (pp. 527–580). Cambridge, MA: MIT Press/Bradford.

VanLehn, K. (1990). *Mind bugs: The origins of procedural misconceptions.* Cambridge, MA: MIT Press/Bradford.

VanLehn, K., Jones, R. M., & Chi, M. T. H. (1992). A model of the self-explanation effect. *Journal of the Learning Sciences, 2,* 1–60.

Wellman, H. M. (1990). *The child's theory of mind.* Cambridge, MA: MIT Press/Bradford.

Wenger, E. (1987). *Artificial intelligence and tutoring systems: Computational and cognitive approaches to the communication of knowledge.* Los Altos, CA: Morgan Kaufmann.

Wertheimer, M. (1959). *Productive thinking* (enlarged ed.). New York: Harper & Row. (Original work published 1945)

White, B., & Frederiksen, J. (1990). Causal model progressions as a foundation for intelligent learning environments. *Artificial Intelligence, 24,* 99–157.

White, B. Y. (1983). Sources of difficulty in understanding Newtonian dynamics. *Cognitive Science, 7,* 41–65.

White, B. Y. (1993). ThinkerTools: Causal models, conceptual change, and science education. *Cognition and Instruction, 10,* 1–100.

White, R. W. (1959). Motivation reconsidered: The concept of competence. *Psychological Review, 66,* 297–333.

Whitehead, A. N. (1916). *The aims of education.* Address to the British Mathematical Society, Manchester, England.

Wiggins, G. (1989, May). A true test: Toward more authentic and equitable assessment. *Phi Delta Kappan,* pp. 703–713.

Winograd, T., & Flores, F. (1986). *Understanding computers and cognition: A new foundation for design.* Norwood, NJ: Ablex.

Wiser, M., & Kipman, D. (1988). The differentiation of heat and temperature: An evaluation of the effect of microcomputer models on students' misconceptions (Report TR88-20). Cambridge, MA: Educational Technology Center, Harvard University.

Workplace Project. (1991). *Workplace project* (videotape). Palo Alto, CA: Systems Science Laboratory, Xerox Palo Alto Research Center.

Yackel, E., Cobb, P., & Wood, T. (1991). Small-group interactions as a source of learning opportunities in second-grade mathematics. *Journal for Research in Mathematics Education, 22,* 390–408.

# PROBLEM-SOLVING TRANSFER

## Richard E. Mayer

UNIVERSITY OF CALIFORNIA, SANTA BARBARA

## Merlin C. Wittrock

UNIVERSITY OF CALIFORNIA, LOS ANGELES

*Problem-solving transfer* occurs when a person uses previous problem-solving experience to devise a solution for a new problem. A primary goal of education is to promote effective problem-solving transfer, that is, to prepare students to solve problems that they have not previously encountered. Accordingly, for nearly a century, educational psychologists have sought to understand the conditions under which students use prior school learning to improve problem-solving performance in new situations, and to help students use what they have learned from previous problems to solve new problems.

More than 50 years ago, the Gestalt psychologist Max Wertheimer eloquently summarized questions concerning problem-solving transfer that are still the focus of modern educational theory and research:

Why is it that some people, when they are faced with problems, get clever ideas, make inventions and discoveries? What happens, what are the processes that lead to such solutions? What can be done to help people to be creative when they are faced with problems? (Luchins & Luchins, 1970, p. 1)

Equipped with research methods and theories not available until recently, educational psychologists have begun to make progress toward answering Wertheimer's questions. This chapter is the latest installment in an ongoing exploration of how educational experiences can help students get clever ideas when they are faced with problems. This chapter defines key terms, summarizes the history of research on problem-solving transfer, reviews recent research on teachable aspects of problem solving, and offers a view of future research on problem-solving transfer.

## INTRODUCTION TO PROBLEM-SOLVING TRANSFER

To understand *problem-solving transfer*, it is first necessary to define key terms.

## Problem Solving

Problem solving is cognitive processing directed at achieving a goal when no solution method is obvious to the problem solver (Mayer, 1992b). According to this definition, problem solving has four main characteristics. First, problem solving is *cognitive*—it occurs within the problem solver's cognitive system and can be inferred indirectly from changes in the problem solver's behavior. Second, problem solving is a *process*—it involves representing and manipulating knowledge in the problem solver's cognitive system. Third, problem solving is *directed*—the problem solver's thoughts are motivated by goals. Fourth, problem solving is *personal*—the individual knowledge and skills of the problem solver help determine the difficulty or ease with which obstacles to solutions can be overcome.

A *problem* occurs when a problem solver wants to transform a problem situation from the given state into the goal state but lacks an obvious method for accomplishing the transformation. In his classic monograph, *On Problem-Solving*, Duncker (1945, p. 1) defined a problem as follows:

A problem arises when a living creature has a goal but does not know how this goal is to be reached. Whenever one cannot go from a given situation to the desired situation simply by action, then there has to be recourse to thinking. Such thinking has the task of devising some action which may mediate between the existing and desired situations.

In short, a problem occurs when a problem solver has a goal but lacks an obvious way of achieving the goal. This definition is broad enough to capture a wide range of problems ranging from producing an essay on whether or not students should be allowed to choose the subjects they will study in school (Scardamalia, Bereiter, & Goelman, 1982) to determining how to get 3/4 of 2/3 of a cup of cottage cheese (Lave, 1988). Today, problem solving cannot be limited to "living creatures." Within a few years of the publication of Duncker's monograph, the

We gratefully acknowledge the many useful comments of David Berliner, Susan Chipman, Martin Covington, Marshall Farr, and Gavriel Salomon, who reviewed an earlier version of this chapter.

electronic computer was born. Indeed, the field of artificial intelligence is devoted to problem solving by machines.

Problems may be classified as well defined or ill defined. In well-defined problems, the given state, goal state, and the allowable operators are specifically clear to the problem solver. For example, a computation problem such as $1.27 \times 0.28$ = _____ is well defined because the given state is $1.27 \times 0.28$ = _____, the goal state is a numerical answer, and the allowable operators are the procedures of decimal multiplication. Similarly, a grammar problem such as "the plural of half is _____" is well defined because the given state is "half," the goal state is to create a specific word, and the operators are to change $f$ to $v$ and add the suffix -es. In ill-defined problems, the given state, goal state, and allowable operators are not specifically clear to the problem solver. For example, the instruction "write an essay on how to end the economic recession" or "write a computer program that will serve as a teacher's gradebook" is an ill-defined problem because allowable operators are not clear and, to some extent, the goal is not well specified. Educational materials often emphasize well-defined problems although most real problems are ill defined.

Problems may also be classified as routine and nonroutine. A routine problem is one for which the problem solver already possesses a ready-made solution procedure. For example, if a student has learned the procedure for long division of whole numbers through a long series of practice problems, then a new long-division problem represents a routine problem. In contrast, a nonroutine problem is one for which the problem solver does not have a previously learned solution procedure. For example, a young student who does not yet know all the addition facts may solve the problem $3 + 5 =$ _____ as follows: "I can take 1 from the 5 and give it to the 3, 5 minus 1 is 4, 3 plus 1 is 4, and 4 plus 4 is 8, so the answer is 8." This student has invented a new solution procedure. Although routine problems form the core of many educational lessons, difficult real-world problems are generally nonroutine.

Problem solving can be analyzed in subprocesses, including representing, planning, and executing. Representing occurs when a problem solver converts an externally presented problem, such as a word problem in a mathematics book, into an internal mental representation, such as a "situation model" of the word problem. Planning involves devising and monitoring a method for solving a problem, such as breaking a problem into parts. Executing occurs when a problem solver actually carries out planned operations, such as making arithmetic calculations to solve a word problem. Although executing is emphasized in classroom instruction, the major difficulty for most problem solvers involves representing and planning.

## Transfer

*Transfer* occurs when a person's prior experience and knowledge affect learning or problem solving in a new situation. Thus, transfer refers to the effect of knowledge that was learned in a previous situation (task A) on learning or performance in a new situation (task B). Cormier and Hagman (1987, p. 1) note that "transfer of learning occurs whenever prior-learned knowledge and skills affect the way in which new knowledge and skills are learned and performed." Furthermore, the definition of transfer includes the stipulation that the previous and new situations differ from one another. For example, Salomon and Perkins (1989, p. 115) distinguish between "mere learning" and transfer: Mere learning occurs when previous learning affects subsequent performance on the same task (e.g., a child who has learned to solve one-column addition problems takes a test on one-column addition problems), whereas transfer occurs when previous learning affects subsequent performance on a different task (e.g., a child who has learned to solve one-column addition problems subsequently learns to solve one-column subtraction or two-column addition problems). According to cognitive theories of transfer reviewed in this chapter, transfer is mediated by the problem solver's cognitive and metacognitive strategies. (See also chapter 2.)

It is useful to distinguish between *positive transfer* and *negative transfer*. Positive transfer occurs when previous problem-solving experience (or learning) facilitates performance on solving new problems (or new learning); negative transfer occurs when previous problem-solving experience (or learning) hinders performance on solving new problems (or new learning). A typical problem-solving transfer paradigm consists of an experimental group that learns how to solve problem A and then tries to solve problem B, and a control group that does not learn how to solve problem A and then tries to solve problem B. If the experimental group solves problem B more rapidly or efficiently than the control group, positive transfer is exhibited; if the experimental group solves problem B less quickly or efficiently than the control group, negative transfer is exhibited. By convention, educational psychologists may use the term "transfer" to denote positive transfer.

It is also useful to distinguish between *knowledge transfer* and *problem-solving transfer*. Knowledge transfer (or transfer of knowledge) occurs when prior learning (task A) affects new learning (task B). Typically, prior learning is measured by an achievement test (e.g., percent correct on task A) and new learning is measured by ease of learning (e.g., time to master task B). For example, knowledge transfer occurs when a child who has mastered addition facts for all single-digit problems (task A) requires less time to learn two-column addition (task B) than a child who has not.

Problem-solving transfer occurs when prior problem-solving experience (task A) affects solving a new problem (task B), that is, when a problem solver uses previous experience with one kind of problem to help solve a different kind of problem. Typically, prior experience is measured by performance on task A (e.g., percent correct or type of method used on solving old problems) and new problem solving is measured by performance on task B (e.g., percent correct or type of method used on solving new problems). For example, problem-solving transfer occurs when a student who has been taught how to solve two-step word problems to 100 percent accuracy is subsequently able to solve three-step word problems better than a student who was not taught about two-step problems. In a transfer study, Wittrock (1978) taught children to solve problems by attending to one dimension (brightness) and then measured transfer to solving problems that involved attending to two dimensions (size and brightness). The trained group solved 100 percent of the training problems and 29 percent of the transfer problems, whereas the control group solved only 7 percent of the transfer problems.

Many strong claims have been made for the importance

of transfer in education. Transfer makes survival possible by allowing humans to adapt to new situations. Schools are not able to teach students everything they will need to know, but rather must equip students with the ability to transfer—to use what they have learned to solve new problems successfully or to learn quickly in new situations. Transfer is a pervasive characteristic of human cognition: New learning always depends on previous learning, new problem solving is always influenced by prior problem solutions.

*Issues in Transfer.* The study of transfer raises several crucial issues. The first issue concerns the role of conscious effort in transfer. Salomon and Perkins (1989) have distinguished between *high-road transfer* and *low-road transfer*. High-road transfer is effortful and conscious; it occurs when a problem solver actively thinks about the connections between the current problem and previous experience. For example, high-road transfer occurs when a person figures out how to find the volume of a frustum of a pyramid by using prior knowledge about how to find the volume of a pyramid (Polya, 1965). Low-road transfer is automatic and does not require conscious attention; it occurs when a problem solver automatically uses prior knowledge in solving a new problem. For example, for most English-literate adults, applying appropriate decoding procedures in reading this sentence involves low-road transfer.

A second issue concerns problem-solving methods—*weak* versus *strong methods*. Weak methods are general problem heuristics that can be applied to a wide variety of domains; for example, the strategy of means-ends analysis is used in computer simulations aimed at general problem solving ranging from logic problems to game playing (Newell & Simon, 1972). Strong methods are problem-solving procedures that are specific to a domain, such as a method that applies only to solving physics word problems (Larkin, McDermott, Simon, & Simon, 1980). Research on expertise often suggests that experts in a given domain rely mainly on strong methods whereas novices rely on weak methods (Chi, Glaser, & Farr, 1988; Ericsson & Smith, 1991; Mayer, 1992b; Smith, 1991; Sternberg & Frensch, 1991). However, some researchers have argued that problem solvers can learn to use strong methods that have been contextualized into specific domains (Perkins, Schwartz, & Simmons, 1988; Singley & Anderson, 1989).

A third issue concerns what is transferred—*specific responses* or *general principles*. For example, Thorndike (1903) emphasized the specificity of transfer by arguing that transfer can occur only when specific behaviors learned in the course of solving one problem can be used to solve at least part of a new problem. For example, single-column addition is a skill that transfers to multicolumn addition because multicolumn addition requires the ability to add single columns. In contrast, Wertheimer (1945/1959) emphasized the generality of transfer by arguing that general principles learned in solving one problem can be used to solve new problems. For example, a student given two short blocks and a long block learns to make a bridge with the two short blocks as the vertical bases and the long block as the horizontal crosspiece. Then, when given two long blocks and a short one, the student eventually builds a bridge with two long blocks as the vertical bases and the short one as the crosspiece. In this case, the student transfers the general principle of bridge building without transferring the specific

responses of using the short blocks as vertical bases and a long block as a horizontal crosspiece. In some cases, what is transferred may be cognitive or metacognitive strategies. The historical development of these issues is explored in the next section.

## HISTORICAL REVIEW: FOUR VIEWS OF TRANSFER

Research and theoretical investigations in learning and cognition have produced four views of transfer: general transfer of general skills, specific transfer of specific behaviors, specific transfer of general skills, and metacognitive control of general and specific strategies.

### Formal Discipline: General Transfer of General Skill

As the curtain opened on the scientific study of education at the start of the 20th century, a prevailing view of problem-solving transfer was derived from faculty psychology—namely, the idea that intellectual performance depended on certain mental faculties such as memory, attention, and judgment. According to this view, training of basic mental functions was thought to have general effects that would transfer to new situations. For example, Binet (cited in Wolf, 1973, p. 207) proposed that students could improve their minds through mental exercises aimed at helping them "to observe better, to listen better, to retain and to judge better." Binet (cited in Wolf, 1973, p. 207) called these techniques "mental orthopedics" and argued that "with practice and training ... we can augment a child's attention, his memory, his judgment—making him literally to become more intelligent than he was before."

An important educational application of this general transfer view was the doctrine of formal discipline—the idea that certain school subjects such as Latin and geometry improved students' minds by making their thinking more logical and disciplined. For example, the establishment of Latin schools was based on the idea that learning classical subjects would help students acquire good mental habits. Rippa (1980) has pointed out that the first public Latin school in the United States was established in Boston in 1635 for sons of the colonial elite, and that its curriculum eventually included reading, writing, and speaking of Latin as well as some knowledge of Greek and mathematics. Although the Latin school movement was strong into the 19th century, its demise came about through the need to prepare the general population for work in an industrialized society and through the accumulation of educational research, which is reviewed in the next section.

### Associationism: Specific Transfer of Specific Behaviors

The birth of the new science of educational psychology in the early 1900s brought with it a view of transfer based on associationist theory, namely, the idea that transfer involves the application of identical behaviors from an initially learned task to the new task. According to the specific transfer view, learning of A will help a person learn B only if B contains elements that are identical to A. For example, learning to solve single-column addition problems helps a student learn to solve two-column addition problems because single-column addition is a component skill required for two-column addition. The most popular version of the specific transfer view was named the "theory of identical elements" by Thorndike and his colleagues, who were the first to study transfer systematically in educational settings (Singley & Anderson, 1989; Thorndike, 1924; Thorndike & Woodworth, 1901).

Thorndike and colleagues proposed the specific transfer view as an alternative to the doctrine of formal discipline. In a series of classic studies, Thorndike (1923, 1924) disproved the doctrine of formal discipline by showing that, on tests of intellectual development or reasoning, students who studied Latin and geometry performed no better than students who studied other subjects. The failure to find general transfer led Thorndike to doubt the alleged effects of the study of Latin and other classical subjects on mental discipline. Instead, he argued that transfer would occur when the specific content of one subject was needed to learn another subject. Accordingly, an educational implication was that the curriculum should be analyzed into specific behaviors and taught in sequence so that lower level basic skills were taught before the higher level skills that included them. Drill and practice on specific skills became the hallmark of the specific transfer view of transfer. This view was questioned by Judd (1939), who proposed that transfer depended not on identical elements but on emphasizing the general principles or generalizations during teaching (Charles, 1987), a view that is reviewed in the next section.

## Gestalt Psychology: Specific Transfer of General Skills

A third view of transfer, emerging from Gestalt psychology, is that high-road transfer occurs when the same general strategy that was previously learned in task A is also required in current learning or performing in task B. Consistent with the specific transfer view, the specific transfer of general skills view holds that transfer occurs only when task A and task B require application of the same component process. However, in contrast to the specific transfer view, the component process that transfers from task A to task B can be a general strategy or a principle rather than a specific behavior. In accord with the general transfer view, this view retains the idea that certain skills can have a broad domain of application extending beyond specific behaviors in the initial learning situations. In contrast to the general transfer view, the skills learned in task A must be related specifically to the requirements of task B.

Gestalt psychologists, while accepting transfer of specific responses as one form of transfer, emphasized transfer of general skills as a second form of transfer. According to the specific transfer of general skills view, learning to solve one type of problem can help students solve new problems even when there are no identical components in the two tasks. In such a case, students may learn a general principle or a strategy in one situation that they subsequently apply to solving problems in a different situation. Bower and Hilgard (1981, p. 323) summarized the Gestalt view as follows:

A pattern of dynamic relationship discovered or understood in one situation may be applicable to another. There is something in common

between the earlier learning and the situation in which transfer is found, but what exists is not identical piecemeal elements but common patterns, configurations, or relationships. One of the advantages of learning by understanding rather than by rote is that understanding is transposable to wider ranges of situations, and less often leads to erroneous applications of old learning.

Building on earlier research demonstrating transfer of general principles (Judd, 1908; Ruger, 1910), the Gestalt psychologists were among the first to provide substantial empirical evidence for transfer of a general principle from one situation to another (Katona, 1940; Wertheimer, 1945/1959). For example, Katona taught students to solve card trick problems and matchstick problems by a rote method, in which they memorized the required series of actions, or by a meaningful method, in which students learned an underlying principle. Students who learned by memorizing tended to perform slightly better on solving the original problem than did students who learned by understanding, but understanders performed much better than memorizers on transfer problems. Katona (1940, p. 53) asserted that "learning by memorizing is a different process from learning by understanding." In learning by understanding a student discovers a principle or a relationship that can be applied to a different problem, but in learning by memorizing a student learns specific responses that can be applied only to problems requiring those behaviors.

An instructional implication is the following: When problem-solving transfer is a goal, then meaningful methods of instruction are more useful than rote methods such as Thorndike's drill and practice. Instead of rote methods of instruction, Katona suggested a method of guided discovery and learning from examples as ways of helping students to learn how to solve problems. Although the Gestaltist emphasis on transferable problem-solving strategies provided a fundamental alternative to the transfer of specific behavior view, the Gestaltists failed to explain how people learn to manage and control their strategies—a topic explored in the next section.

## Cognitive Science: Metacognitive Control of General and Specific Skills

The fourth view of transfer emerging from the cognitive science revolution emphasizes the role of metacognition. Metacognition refers to "knowledge concerning one's own cognitive processes" that is used in "monitoring and consequent regulation and orchestration of those processes" (Flavell, 1976, p. 232). This definition is consistent with the idea that metacognition involves awareness of one's cognitive processes, monitoring of one's cognitive processes, and regulation of one's cognitive processes (Brown, Bransford, Ferrara, & Campione, 1983; Haller, Child, & Walberg, 1988; Morris, 1990). Metacognitive processes include assessing the requirements of the problem, constructing a solution plan, selecting an appropriate solution strategy, monitoring progress toward the goal, and modifying the solution plan when necessary. In the metacognitive transfer view, successful transfer occurs when the problem solver is able to recognize the requirements of the new problem, select previously learned specific and general skills that apply to the new problem, and monitor their application in solving the new problem. The problem solver is seen as an active participant in the problem-solving process, one who must manage the way that prior knowledge is used to solve a new problem.

The metacognitive view of transfer combines features of the previous three views: transfer to a new problem is enhanced when students have learned relevant general and specific processes as well as techniques for selecting and monitoring them. Consistent with the general transfer view, metacognition depends on extremely general intellectual skills—skills that presumably develop through mental exercise in solving or observing the solution of a wide variety of problems. However, in contrast to the general transfer of skills view, metacognition is viewed as a collection of high-level skills rather than as a single monolithic ability. Consistent with the specific transfer of general skills view, problem solvers need to possess knowledge of general principles or relationships, and consistent with the specific transfer of specific behaviors view, problem solvers also need domain-specific skills. However, in contrast to these views, the description of general and specific prerequisites for transfer involve more precise descriptions of information-processing processes and strategies. In the metacognitive view of transfer, problem solvers are managers of their general and specific knowledge; they need to possess relevant specific and general knowledge, but they need to know also how to use that knowledge in the context of problem solving.

For example, in developing a theory of intelligence, Sternberg (1985, 1990) found it necessary to include *metacomponents*—general cognitive processes used in planning, monitoring, and evaluating. Accordingly, some important metacognitive processes include

recognizing the existence of a problem, deciding upon the nature of the problem confronting them, selecting a set of lower order processes to solve the problem, selecting a strategy into which to combine these components, selecting a mental representation upon which the components and strategy can act, allocating one's mental resources, monitoring one's problem solving as it is happening, and evaluating one's problem solving after it is done. (Sternberg, 1990, p. 269)

Siegler and Jenkins (1989) have demonstrated the role of strategy selection in problem solving—that is, problem solvers have a variety of strategies available and must choose the most appropriate ones for a given situation.

An instructional implication of the metacognitive view is that students need to learn when to use various cognitive processes, including being aware of their processes, monitoring their cognitive processes, and regulating their cognitive processes. These implications neatly complement those of the specific transfer of general skills view.

## CURRENT RESEARCH: TEACHABLE ASPECTS OF PROBLEM SOLVING

We begin with a somewhat disappointing body of research: Problem-solving transfer seems to be rare. Laboratory studies have shown that learning how to solve a problem often does not help students solve a subsequent problem that looks different but can be solved in the same way (Reed, Ernst, & Banerji, 1974; Gick & Holyoak, 1980, 1983; Hayes & Simon, 1977; Simon & Reed, 1976). For example, after learning to solve a

story problem involving mixtures of 6 percent and 12 percent boric acid, most problem solvers were unable to solve a mixture problem involving nuts costing $1.65 and $2.10 a pound, even though the test problem could be solved using the same procedure as the previously learned problem (Reed, 1987). Similarly, in spite of claims for thinking skills programs aimed at general improvement in intellectual ability, classroom studies often fail to test for or to reveal convincing evidence that such programs result in general transfer to new kinds of problems (Chipman, Segal, & Glaser, 1985; Nickerson, Perkins, & Smith, 1985; Segal, Chipman, & Glaser, 1985). For example, the CoRT program (Cognitive Research Trust) is a popular thinking skills program that has been used in over 5,000 classrooms in ten nations (de Bono, 1985), but "after 10 years of widespread use we have no adequate evidence concerning ... the effectiveness of the program" (Polson & Jeffries, 1985, p. 445). Finally, field studies reveal that problem solvers generally fail to apply school-taught mathematics procedures to solve mathematics problems they encounter out of school (Lave, 1988; Rogoff & Lave, 1984; Schliemann & Acoily, 1989). For example, when asked to determine which of two cans of peanuts was a better buy in a supermarket, a 10-ounce can for 90 cents or a 4-ounce can for 45 cents, students rarely used the school-taught strategy of computing the unit price for each can. Instead they invented a ratio strategy, such as noting the 10-ounce can was the better buy because it cost twice as much as the 4-ounce can but contained more than twice many ounces (Lave, 1988). In short, those people looking for an easy way to promote problem-solving transfer—in the laboratory, in the classroom, or outside the classroom—are not likely to be comforted by the existing scientific research base on transfer.

Despite past failures, the search for teachable aspects of problem solving continues. Current research and practice in problem-solving transfer often can be traced to one of the four views of transfer summarized in the previous section. At the heart of current research and practice is the role of specificity and generality in transfer from the learned task A to the new task B: Does transfer to a completely new situation (task B) occur through improving one's mind by learning special mind-broadening material (task A)? An instructional implication of this general transfer of general skills view is that students need practice in solving problems within a separate problem-solving curriculum—a curriculum aimed at improving students' general intellectual ability. Does transfer occur only when at least some of the behaviors in task A are identical to the behaviors in task B, as in the specific transfer of specific behaviors view? If specific transfer is the only available route, instruction should focus on improving performance on specific basic skills that are components of larger tasks. Does meaningful learning of general principles from task A transfer to new problems that can be solved using the same general principles, as in the specific transfer of general skills view? This view has implications for the content and method of instruction: Instead of focusing on specific facts and behaviors, the content of instruction should be an understanding of general principles and patterns. In addition to drill and practice on basic skills, students need to learn by understanding in order to know how to apply newly acquired principles to a wide variety of situations. Or, does transfer depend on learning metacognitive skills, including techniques for selecting, monitoring, and evaluating one's existing problem-solving strategies? This view emphasizes the need for autonomous learners who actively control their problem-solving processes. The following discussion provides examples of current research on *improving the mind,* which follows from the general transfer view; *teaching basic skills* needed for thinking tasks, which follows from the transfer of specific behaviors view; and *teaching for understanding, teaching by analogy,* and *teaching thinking strategies,* which tap aspects of the transfer of general skills view and the metacognitive view.

## Improving the Mind

The general transfer of general skills view suggests that transfer can be improved through mental exercise on special tasks that are known to improve mental functioning. Although the doctrine of formal discipline was discredited by Thorndike's (1924) transfer experiments, the search for mind-broadening subject matter continues even in the current literature. For example, Snow (1982, p. 29) asserted that "education is primarily an aptitude development program," and Detterman (1982, p. vii) asked, "How and how much can intelligence be increased?" The search for ways to improve students' intellectual ability has sometimes led to a search for a "new Latin"—a subject matter that would make students smarter overall.

One of the most massive attempts to improve students' minds is Project Head Start, a U.S. government program established in 1965 to improve the intellectual ability and academic achievement of preschool children from low-income homes. Although no specific preschool curriculum was mandated, a goal was to provide preschool experiences for children that would foster their intellectual and academic development. Unfortunately, studies of Project Head Start generally have not identified specific techniques for promoting transfer that have long-term effects on intellectual and academic performance (Carter, 1984; Caruso, Taylor, & Detterman, 1982).

More recently, some scholars have offered a much more focused prescription for improving students' minds. Although Latin is no longer proposed as a source of general transfer, experts have argued that computer programming languages such as LOGO may be a sort of new Latin that could have widespread effects on general cognitive development (Papert, 1980). According to this view, when children learn through discovery how to give instructions to computers in LOGO, "powerful intellectual skills are developed in the process" (Papert, 1980, p. 60). Throughout the 1980s and 1990s researchers have sought to test the claims for computer programming as a vehicle for teaching general problem-solving skills and for discovery as the ideal instructional method.

What are the cognitive consequences of learning to interact with a computer in an unrestricted and nonguided environment? As computer programming in languages such as LOGO became more common in schools in the 1980s, it became clear that students often failed to learn the basics of the language, much less how to transfer what they had learned to new situations (Dalbey & Linn, 1985; Kurland & Pea, 1985; Linn, 1985; Mayer & Fay, 1987; Pea & Kurland, 1984; Perkins, 1985).

For example, in an early unpublished study by Papert and colleagues, 16 students at a school in Brookline, Massachusetts, received 35 hours of hands-on, nondirective programming experience in LOGO as advocated by Papert. In reviewing the results, Nickerson et al. (1985, p. 277) noted that although some students acquired specific programming skills, "we are less certain that they developed powerful general skills." In another early LOGO study conducted by Pea and Kurland at the Bank Street College of Education in New York, approximately 50 students received 25 hours of hands-on, nondirective instruction in LOGO. The results revealed that students performed poorly on predicting what LOGO command would do and tended to write programs "without really comprehending how programs worked" (Nickerson et al., 1985, p. 277).

Learning the rudiments of LOGO is a difficult and time-consuming activity, and transferring the general skill to other domains occurs rarely. In a careful comparison study, Pea and Kurland (1984) reported no major differences on tests of general planning skill between students who had learned LOGO and those who had not. In reviewing the LOGO transfer research, Dalbey and Linn (1985, p. 267) found that "students who learn LOGO fail to generalize this learning to other tasks," and Perkins (1985, p. 12) concluded that the research literature demonstrated "no transfer of skill and poor learning within LOGO itself." Instead, learning to write computer programs appears to transfer most successfully to nonprogramming tasks that are highly similar to the original programming tasks (Clements, 1986; Clements & Gullo, 1984; De Corte, Verschaffel, & Schrooten, 1992; Mayer, 1988, 1992a).

In summary, modern attempts to find mind-improving subject matter, such as the Head Start program in preschools or the teaching of LOGO in elementary and secondary schools, have been no more successful than were historical attempts to use Latin as a vehicle for improving students' minds. Instead, a consistent theme is that a short course of study in one subject matter area does not have enduring effects on solving radically different problems in other subject matter domains.

## Teaching Basic Skills

In contrast to the general transfer of general skills view, the specific transfer of specific behaviors view suggests that instruction should focus on teaching basic skills that are components of many subsequently encountered tasks, such as basic word-decoding skills that form the basis for higher forms of reading, grammatical construction skills that form the basis for higher forms of writing, and computational skills that form the core of higher level mathematical problem solving. For example, classic work on learning hierarchies by Gagné (1968) and more recent research on the development of problem-solving skills in children by Case (1985) and Seigler (1989) have shown how automation of low-level component skills enables the learner to build higher level cognitive skills. Automated skills require little or no conscious attention when they are applied; since attention is a limited resource, automation of low-level skills allows problem solvers to direct their attention to higher level tasks such as planning and monitoring the solution process. Similarly, Anderson and colleagues (Anderson, 1983, 1990; Singley & Anderson, 1989) have shown how the acquisition of cognitive skills progresses from effortful performance requiring conscious attention to automatic performance that does not require attention.

Effective problem solving often depends on automated component skills—that is, on component skills that can be used without overloading the student's memory capacity. Therefore, a major constraint on effective problem solving may be a lack of automated component skills. Two methods for overcoming this problem are mastery/automaticity methods, in which students master component skills before moving on to higher level problem tasks, and constraint removal methods, in which problem-solving tasks are presented in ways that minimize the need for component skills.

*Mastery/Automaticity Methods.* In mastery or automaticity methods, students receive drill and practice on component skills until the skills have become automatic. For example, in reading, comprehension depends on mastering of lower level skills such as decoding of words. To help students become more automatic in their decoding, Samuels (1979) and LaBerge and Samuels (1974) developed the method of repeated readings, in which a student reads a short passage aloud over and over until the reading rate is fast and the error rate is low. This procedure is then repeated with a new passage, and so on. The procedure allows students to increase their fluency, that is, to become automatic in their decoding of passages. As students automate their decoding skills, they can devote more attentional capacity to comprehending the passage. Similar techniques apply to writing, mathematics, and other problem-solving domains.

*Constraint Removal Methods.* If mastery/automaticity methods were the only ones available, early childhood education would not have to provide many opportunities for students to engage in problem solving. An alternative method that allows novices to gain problem-solving experience, and presumably enjoyment, in a new domain is constraint removal—that is, creating problem-solving tasks that do not require attention-demanding skills. For example, in writing an essay, young writers may lack automated motor skills (such as handwriting) and automated grammatical skills (such as spelling and punctuation). To remove these motoric and grammatical constraints on effective writing, students can be asked to dictate their essays (Scardamalia et al., 1982) or instructed not to worry about handwriting, spelling, and punctuation when they write (Glynn, Britton, Muth, & Dugan, 1982; Read, 1981). Such methods allow students to devote more of their attention to organizing and planning a good essay and generally result in longer and better written essays. Similar techniques can be applied to reading comprehension (e.g., listening rather than reading) and mathematics (e.g., using calculators or simply describing what needs to be done to solve word problems).

In summary, even when the focus of instruction is on high-level effortful problem solving, instructional methods must be sensitive to the need for low-level automated component skills.

## Teaching for Understanding

The specific transfer of general skills view suggests that the way in which students learn a new cognitive skill will influence their ability to apply that skill in new situations. Although two instructional methods may lead to equivalent retention of the material, one instructional method may be more successful than the other in leading to transfer. For example, in accord with the Gestalt psychologists, Ausubel (1968, p. 10) proposed that "rotely and meaningfully learned materials are represented and

organized quite differently in the student's psychological structure of knowledge." Rote learning leads to poor problem-solving transfer whereas meaningful learning promotes good problem-solving transfer. It follows that when transfer of a general principle or pattern is a goal of instruction, the preferred instructional method is one that leads to meaningful learning.

According to this view, meaningful learning is a process in which learners must actively construct their own learning outcomes (Ausubel, 1968; Bruner, 1961; Mayer, 1987, 1992c; Resnick, 1989; Wittrock, 1974b, 1990; Wittrock, Marks, & Doctorow, 1975). In his influential theory of meaningful learning, Ausubel (1968, pp. 38–39) proposed that meaningful learning occurs when a learner "relates new material nonarbitrarily and substantively to his cognitive structure" and that it depends on "potentially meaningfully material" (that is, the material has the potential of making sense) and a "meaningful learning set" (that is, the learner possess and uses relevant cognitive structure during learning). More recently, Wittrock (1990, p. 349) noted that "to learn with understanding a learner must actively construct meaning," and Mayer (1992c) argued that "the learner is an active processor of information who is trying to make sense out of the presented material."

*The Conditions of Meaningful Learning.* To promote transfer, an instructional method must elicit cognitive processes in the learner that are required for meaningful learning. Mayer (1984, 1987) has suggested three cognitive conditions for meaningful learning: *selecting* relevant information, *organizing* information into a coherent structure, and *integrating* current information with relevant existing knowledge. Similarly, Sternberg (1985, 1990) has described three knowledge acquisition components within his theory of intelligence: *selective encoding, selective combination,* and *selective comparison,* and Wittrock (1990, 1991) has shown the importance of learner generation of two types of meaningful relations—between the information and experience, and among the parts of the information.

First, when learners engage in the cognitive process of selecting (or selective encoding), they focus attention on relevant pieces of the presented information. This process is characterized as "selecting information from the text and adding that information to working memory" (Mayer, 1984, p. 32) and as "sifting out of relevant from irrelevant information" (Sternberg, 1985, p. 107). As shown in Figure 3–1, selecting (or selective encoding) is represented by the arrow from SM to STM, that is, by the transfer of selected pieces of information from a rapidly decaying sensory memory to active consciousness in short-term memory.

Second, when learners engage in the cognitive process of organizing (or selective combination), they are building internal connections among the selected pieces of information. This process involves "organizing the selected information in working memory into a coherent whole" (Mayer, 1984, p. 32) and "combining selectively encoded information in such a way as to form an integrated ... internally connected whole" (Sternberg, 1985, p. 107). Organizing (or selective combination) is represented by the arrow from STM to STM in Figure 3–1, that is, as the learner mentally manipulates information already in short-term memory.

Third, when learners engage in the cognitive process of integrating (or selective comparison), they build external con-

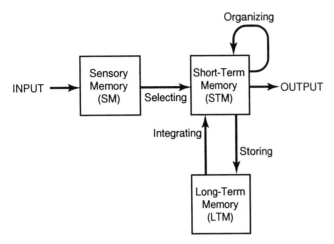

FIGURE 3-1. A Human Information-Processing System

nections between new incoming information and relevant existing knowledge. This process consists of "connecting the organized information to other familiar knowledge structures already in memory" (Mayer, 1984, p. 33) and "relating newly acquired or retrieved information to old knowledge so as to form an externally connected whole" (Sternberg, 1985, p. 107). In Figure 3-1 this process is indicated by the arrow from LTM to STM, that is, by the arrow connecting existing knowledge from LTM to incoming information being built in STM. In a recent series of experiments, Wittrock (1990) found that learner generation of internal and external relations produced large gains in comprehension and transfer.

In addition to possessing these kinds of basic learning processes, self-regulated learners must know how to monitor and control these learning processes in order to achieve a desired goal. It follows that effective instructional methods will ensure that students successfully select relevant information, build internal connections, and build external connections. Three kinds of instructional methods aimed at achieving meaningful learning are structure-based methods, generative methods, and analogy-based methods.

*Structure-Based Methods.* One way to engage active learning processes is to use structure-based methods, in which the learner is given concrete objects that can be manipulated. The purpose of structure-based methods is to help the learner build connections between a familiar, concrete situation and a more abstract concept or rule. For example, in mathematics instruction, "concrete manipulatives" such as bundles of sticks, beads on sticks, or Dienes blocks can be used to help the learner understand simple computational procedures (Brownell & Moser, 1949; Dienes, 1960; Montessori, 1964). In science instruction, hands-on activities are used in which students make predictions and then participate in an actual experiment to test the prediction (Champagne, Gunstone, & Klopfer, 1985). More recently, structure-based methods have been applied to computerized instructional systems, such as White's (1984) computer game for teaching Newton's laws of motion. It was noted over a decade ago by Resnick & Ford (1981) that there is surprisingly little research on the effects of structure-oriented methods on students' classroom learning. That has not changed.

*Generative Methods.* Generative methods require that learners generate relations during learning between their experience and the information to be learned. For example, asking elementary school students to generate summaries of the paragraphs of a text (Doctorow, Wittrock, & Marks, 1978) or to construct verbal and imaginal relations between stories and their experience (Linden & Wittrock, 1981) sizably increases comprehension—from 50 percent to 200 percent—compared with results in control groups that do not engage in these generative activities.

Among high school students, generative strategies that lead students to construct verbal and graphical relations between concepts in economics and their experience increases comprehension and the transfer of economics principles (Kourilsky & Wittrock, 1987). Generative teaching procedures that encourage high school students to relate principles of economics to their experience and to revise their preconceptions about economics sizably increase comprehension and the transfer of concepts in economics as compared with results in controls (Kourilsky & Wittrock, in press).

Asking college students to take notes on a textbook lesson or classroom lecture can encourage learners to select relevant information, organize it coherently, and relate it to their past experience (Kiewra, 1991; Peper & Mayer, 1978). Asking college students to answer simple factual questions during learning can guide their selecting processes, whereas asking them to answer integrative questions can encourage organizing and integrating (Mayer, 1975). Asking college students to generate analogies as they read a text facilitates their construction of relations between the information and their experience, and thus increases their comprehension (Wittrock & Alesandrini, 1990). Generative learning has also been studied in mathematics teaching (Peled & Wittrock, 1990; Wittrock, 1974a), science education (Osborne & Wittrock, 1983, 1985), and geography teaching (Mackenzie & White, 1981). Wittrock (1974b, 1990) has presented a model of generative learning and, in another source (Wittrock, 1991), a model of generative teaching.

*Discovery Methods.* Another technique for encouraging active learning is discovery. In discovery methods, a problem is presented for the student to solve. In pure discovery, no guidance is provided, whereas in guided discovery, the teacher provides enough guidance to ensure that the learner discovers the rule or principle to be learned. Although discovery was advocated for many large-scale curriculum development projects in the 1960s (Bruner, 1961), subsequent research showed that pure discovery was not as effective as guided discovery in promoting problem-solving transfer (Shulman & Kieslar, 1966). Presumably, under pure discovery, many students fail to select the relevant information because they are unable to invent the rule or principle; under guided discovery, students are prompted to find the rule or principle but also are actively involved in building connections between the material and existing knowledge.

Each of these three kinds of instruction—structure-oriented, generative, and discovery—is intended to encourage the learner to actively engage the cognitive processes of selecting, organizing, and integrating during learning. However, meaningful or rote learning can occur under any of these active methods of instruction as well as under less active methods of instruction such as from reading a lesson or listening to a lecture. Whether learning is meaningful or rote depends on the cognitive processing of the learner during learning rather than on how much physical activity the learner engages in during learning. More research is needed to pinpoint how instructional manipulations affect specific cognitive processes during learning. The affects of the social and material context on these processes, as discussed in chapter 2, is still unknown.

## Teaching by Analogy

Another approach to the specific transfer of general skills involves *analogical transfer* which occurs when learners solve a new problem by using what they know about a related problem that they can solve. The known problem is called the *base* (or *source*) and the new problem is called the *target*. More specifically, Vosniadou and Ortony (1989, p. 6) define analogical transfer as "transfer of relational information from a domain that already exists in memory . . . to a domain to be explained."

The target and base problems contain *surface features*, such as specific characters and objects in the problems, and *structural features*, such as the relations among the elements in the problem. A base problem is an analogue (or partial analogue) when it shares the same (or similar) underlying structure as a target problem even if it does not share many surface similarities. For example, in the missionaries and cannibals problem, the problem solver must figure out how to get three cannibals and three missionaries across a river using a boat that can hold one or two persons while ensuring that the cannibals never outnumber the missionaries on either side of the river. In the jealous husbands problem, the problem solver must figure out how to get three jealous husbands and their wives across a river using a boat that can hold one or two persons while ensuring that no woman is left in the company of men without her husband being present. The two problems have certain surface similarities, namely, both involve a boat and a river crossing. However, they also share certain important structural similarities: the missionaries correspond to the husbands, the cannibals correspond to the wives, and the rule that the cannibals cannot outnumber the missionaries corresponds partially to the rule that each wife must accompany her husband.

Once a person learns to solve one of these problems (base), that problem-solving procedure can be used to help generate a solution for the other (target). To make use of the partial analogy between the problems, problem solvers need to focus on the problems' structural similarities while ignoring dissimilarities in their surface features. However, in spite of strong claims made for the pervasiveness of analogical transfer (Polya, 1957), Reed et al. (1974) found that solving one version of the river crossing problem did not facilitate solving the other. Similarly, Hayes and Simon (1977) found that learning to solve one version of the Tower of Hanoi problem often did not facilitate solving an isomorphic version of the problem, and Gick and Holyoak (1980, 1983, 1987) found that solving a version of Duncker's (1945) classic radiation problem worded in a military context often did not ensure that people would be able to solve a structurally identical version of the problem worded in a medical context. These studies represent a disturbing pattern of findings in which people often fail to realize that a solution that they have devised to solve a problem in one domain can be used to solve a structurally equivalent or similar problem in another domain.

This section explores three cognitive conditions for successful analogical transfer—recognition, abstraction, and mapping. *Recognition* occurs when someone who is confronted with a new problem is reminded of a potential analogue (or base problem). *Abstraction* occurs when a problem solver abstracts the general principle or strategy used to solve the base problem. *Mapping* occurs when a problem solver successfully uses that knowledge to solve the target problem. An important educational hypothesis is that each of these processes can be enhanced through instruction.

One source of difficulty in analogical transfer is that problem solvers may fail to recognize a problem in their memory that is analogous to the problem they are currently trying to solve. For example, Gick and Holyoak (1983) asked subjects to read and recall several stories; later, they were asked to solve a problem (target) that was structurally identical to one described in one of the stories (base). In the story for the base problem, a general's problem was to use streams of troops that could vary in size to attack a fortress that was at the hub of many roads, each of which contained mines that would explode if exposed to sufficient weight; the solution was to disperse the troops into small groups traveling along each road and converging on the fortress. On the subsequent problem-solving task, the students' task was to determine how to use rays that could vary in intensity to eliminate an inoperable tumor, without harming the healthy tissue that surrounded it; the solution, analogous to the convergence solution in the fortress problem, was to focus several weak rays so they all converged on the tumor. In this case, the tumor problem and the fortress problem share crucial structural features: The tumor is like the fortress, the surrounding tissue is like the mined roads, the rays that can vary in intensity are like the streams of attacking troops that can vary in size, and the solution principle of focusing weak rays that converge on the tumor is analogous to focusing small groups of troops that converge on the fortress. The results showed that most subjects did not think of the convergence solution to the tumor problem unless the experimenter explicitly stated that one of the stories contained a hint for how to solve the tumor problem. These results suggest that a major impediment to successful analogical transfer is failure to recognize that a previous problem can be used to help solve a current problem.

A second difficulty involves the abstraction process. Once a problem solver recognizes one or more base problems as potential analogues, the problem solver may fail to abstract structural features from these base problems. For example, Gick and Holyoak (1983) asked some subjects to read two stories and then later to solve the tumor problem. Subjects were far more successful in solving the tumor problem if they read two stories that were structurally identical to the tumor problem but dissimilar in their surface content than if they read one story that was structurally identical and one that was irrelevant to the tumor problem. Apparently, exposure to two analogues allowed the subjects to abstract the structural principle of convergence, whereas exposure to only one analogue often did not.

A third difficulty in analogical transfer involves making appropriate connections between the solutions for the base and the target problems. When the base and the target problems have analogous structures but appear to be highly dissimilar based on their surface features, problem solvers may be less likely to use the structure of the base to solve the target problem. For example, Holyoak and Koh (1987) asked subjects to read and summarize a story describing a problem and solution concerning a light bulb; then subjects were asked to solve the tumor problem. When the light bulb and tumor stories shared many surface similarities, problem solvers were likely to show problem-solving transfer; when the stories seemed dissimilar based on surface features, problem solvers were much less likely to transfer unless they were explicitly told to use the light bulb story to solve the tumor problem.

Research on analogical transfer yields important educational implications, such as using analogical models in teaching scientific problem solving and using worked-out examples in teaching mathematical problem solving. For example, in scientific problem solving, students can use a water-flow model or a moving-crowd model to answer questions about current and voltage in electrical circuits (Gentner & Gentner, 1983). In a water-flow model, water is analogous to electrons, pipes are analogous to wires, pumps are analogous to batteries, and an obstruction in a pipe is analogous to a resistor. In a moving-crowd model, mice are analogous to electrons, corridors are analogous to pipes, loudspeakers are analogous to batteries, and a gate in a corridor is analogous to a resistor. Gentner and Gentner (1983) found that students who used the water-flow model to solve electrical circuit problems performed better on questions involving serial batteries, whereas students who used a moving-crowd model performed better on questions involving serial resistors. Apparently, students reason about a new technical domain (electrical circuits) by using a familiar analogue, and the type of analogue they use influences their problem-solving performance. Similarly, Mayer (1989a) has shown that explicit instruction concerning familiar analogical models can help students read a scientific text and use the information to solve problems.

Gentner (1983, 1989) has proposed structure mapping theory to account for analogical reasoning in which knowledge about a familiar system (such as a hydraulic system) can be used to foster reasoning about another system (such as an electrical circuit). Each system consists of specific objects with features and abstract relations among them. For example, in analogical transfer, the two systems have dissimilar specific features (e.g., a pipe is not a wire, water is not electrons) but similar general relations (e.g., "water flow decreases with pipe narrowness" is based on the same general relation as "current decreases with resistance"). People may fail to reason analogically when they are unable to ignore differences in the surface features of the two systems, such as the electrical versus the hydraulic context, or when they are unable to abstract the relevant relations in the systems, such as the relations among water flow, water pressure, and pipe narrowness in the hydraulic system and the relations among current, voltage, and resistance in the circuit system.

In mathematical problem solving, students can use previous experience with a worked-out example problem to guide thinking on a new problem that has the same or similar structure. In order to examine this idea, Reed (1987) provided students with a step-by-step description of how to solve a mixture problem such as, "A nurse mixes a 6 percent boric acid and a 12 percent boric acid solution. How many pints of each are needed to make 4.5 pints of an 8 percent boric acid solution?" Before and after receiving this training, students were asked to solve problems that were identical or similar in structure to the example problem. For example, a problem with the same structure as the example problem is: "A grocer mixes peanuts worth $1.65 and almonds worth $2.10 per pound. How many pounds of each are needed to make 30 pounds of a mixture worth $1.83 a pound?" A problem with a similar structure to the example problem is: "One alloy of copper is 20 percent pure copper and another is 12 percent pure copper. How much of each alloy must be melted together to obtain 60 pounds of alloy containing 10.4 pounds of copper?" Students were unable to solve problems like these before receiving the worked-out example. After training with the worked-out example, students solved about half of the same-structure problems and 10 percent of the similar-structure problems.

This finding shows that students do not always transfer what they have learned about solving one problem to solving other problems that could be solved the same or nearly same way. Following Gentner's (1983, 1989) structure mapping theory, Reed (1987) proposed that the failure to transfer is related to a difficulty in matching the structural features of the presented problems (the target) with the structural features of the worked-out example problem (the base), such as recognizing that 6 percent acid, 12 percent acid, 8 percent acid, and 4.5 pints in the example problem correspond respectively to $1.65, $2.10, $1.83, and 30 pounds in the grocer problem.

An important process in analogical transfer is for students to remember an example problem that is relevant to solving the current problem. For example, Ross (1987, 1989) asked students to read a text on probability theory that included worked-out examples and subsequently to solve some probability problems. Most students produced correct solutions when a test problem reminded them of an appropriate example problem and most students failed when a test problem did not remind them of an appropriate example problem. Similarly, when students are given access to a detailed worked-out example while they work on solving a structurally identical story problem, they are far more successful than when they are not given access to a worked-out example problem (Reed, Dempster, & Ettinger, 1985). Successful and unsuccessful problem solvers differ in the way they use worked-out examples. For example, Novick (1988) found that expert mathematical problem solvers are far more likely to make use of relevant worked-out examples than novices when they are given a related problem to solve. In a more detailed study, Chi, Bassock, Lewis, Riemann, and Glaser (1989) asked physics students to think aloud as they read a physics lesson that included worked-out examples, and then to take a test that included problems that could be solved by the same kinds of methods as the examples. Unsuccessful problem solvers were more likely to reread the example problem than successful problem solvers, who were more likely to focus on specific information in the example problem.

Finally, worked-out examples are most useful when they are structurally similar to the target problems and when students actively work on understanding the example problems. For example, Chi et al. (1989) asked students to think aloud as they studied a physics text containing example problems. Students who generated many comments about the example problems, such as explanations for various steps in the solution, performed much better on solving subsequent physics problems than students who did not produce many explanative comments while studying the example problem. In another study, Zhu and Simon (1987) asked students to think aloud as they learned to factor quadratic equations. The students received worked-out example problems, such as $x^2 = 5x + 6 = (x + 2)(x + 3)$, followed by exercise problems that could be solved using the same methods, such as $x^2 + 11x + 18 =$ _____. In striving to solve the exercise problems, students actively analyzed the solution process in the example problems, a technique that ultimately resulted in most students solving the exercise problems. Cooper and Sweller (1987) found that students were better able to solve equation problems if they had received practice in examining relevant worked-out examples than if they had received practice actually solving the example problems. This line of research helps to clarify the conditions under which students are able to transfer what they learn from the worked-out examples to solving new problems.

In summary, research on thinking by analogy is aimed at determining the conditions for what Vosniadou and Ortony (1989, p.14) call "productive analogy"—a situation in which a problem solver uses a familiar example or model (the base problem) to help derive a method of solving a new problem (the target problem). Productive analogy occurs when a problem solver recognizes that a base problem is analogous to a target problem, abstracts the structural relations from the base, and maps these relations to the target. This growing research area has potential for making contributions to the educational psychology of problem-solving transfer.

## Teaching Thinking Skills

The two previous sections explored techniques for teaching in ways that promote transfer of general principles or relations by using meaningful methods of instruction or by teaching by analogy. This section examines a third way to promote specific transfer of general skills: direct instruction in how to solve problems. This approach is sometimes referred to as teaching of thinking skills (Baron & Sternberg, 1987; Chipman et al., 1985; Halpern, 1992; Nickerson et al., 1985; Segal et al., 1985). *Thinking skills* are behaviors and thoughts that the problem solver engages in during problem solving that are intended to influence the problem solver's representation of a problem and the planning and monitoring of problem-solving solutions.

*Teaching Thinking Skills Courses.* Many thinking skills programs and courses have been developed in order to teach problem-solving skills that will transfer (Chance, 1986; Segal et al., 1985). Mayer (1989b) has identified three issues that must be considered in teaching thinking skills: what to teach, how to teach, and where to teach. Concerning what to teach, should instruction aim to improve thinking as some monolithic ability or to improve a collection of smaller component skills? Concerning how to teach, should instruction focus on the product of problem solving, by rewarding students for getting the right answer, or on the process of problem solving, by helping students describe the methods used to solve problems? Concerning where to teach, should instruction occur in a separate context-free environment or within the context of specific existing courses? A comparison of successful and unsuccessful programs reveals that teaching thinking skills is most effective when the curriculum focuses on a collection of component skills, such as how to represent problems, rather than on improving the mind in general; the methods emphasize problem-solving processes such as modeling the processes of experts rather than solely getting the right answer; and the expectations for transfer are modest, such as students being able to solve similar kinds of problems rather than being able to solve problems in different subject domains.

For example, in one of the first studies on teaching of thinking skills, Bloom & Broder (1950) sought to teach college students how to solve examination problems in various subject domains. As part of the training, students listened to successful problem solvers describe their thought processes as they solved examination problems, students described their own thought processes on the same problems, and students noted differences between how they and the experts solved problems. This training resulted in significantly higher scores on the examinations than for students who did not receive the training. Consistent with the three criteria for successful instruction in thinking skills, the training focused on component skills, such as how to analyze a problem into parts; emphasized process, such as comparing one's own method with that of an expert; and taught within a context that was similar to the final test.

Perhaps the most studied thinking skills program is the Productive Thinking Program, a problem-solving course for elementary school children (Covington, Crutchfield, & Davies, 1966; Covington, Crutchfield, Davies, & Olton, 1974). The program consists of 15 cartoonlike booklets that describe various mystery or detective stories in which two children, Lila and Jim, try to solve the case. Throughout the booklet the reader is asked to generate hypotheses, find relevant information to test the hypotheses, and engage in other problem-solving activities. Students who take the course tend to show larger pretest-to-posttest gains than control students on solving problems like those in the booklet, but "there is only limited and consistent evidence of transfer to dissimilar problems" (Mansfield, Busse, & Krepelka, 1978, p. 531). Again, this program meets the three criteria of teaching component skills such as how to generate and evaluate hypotheses, using models who describe their thought processes, and finding evidence mainly for near but not far transfer.

Another well-documented attempt to teach thinking skills is Feuerstein's Instrumental Enrichment program (1980; Feuerstein, Jensen, Hoffman, & Rand, 1985). Students who were labeled as mentally retarded based on traditional tests of intellectual ability were given problem-solving classes that met several times per week over the course of several years. In a typical lesson, the teacher presented an unfamiliar problem, asked the students to work on it, and then led a class discussion in methods for solving the problem. In this way students could compare their thought processes with those of others. Evaluation studies revealed that students in the Instrumental Enrichment program showed greater pretest-to-posttest gains on tests of nonverbal intelligence than students given conventional instruction. Although the program appears to be effective, Chance (1986, p. 85) has pointed out that it "requires a considerable investment of student time," and Bransford, Arbitman-Smith, Stein, and Vye

(1985, p. 201) have commented that the training emphasizes "training students to solve certain types of problems so they will be able to solve similar problems on their own." Again, the program meets the three criteria of teaching component skills, focusing on the problem-solving process, and achieving near but not far transfer.

***Teaching Domain-Specific Thinking Skills.*** If thinking skills courses foster transfer to similar types of problems but not to structurally different types of problems, a reasonable approach to teaching thinking skills is to incorporate the training of problem-solving skills within specific subject domains such as mathematical, scientific, historic, or literary problem solving. For example, one important kind of thinking skill involves problem representation—converting the problem-as-presented into an internal mental representation of the problem. Polya (1957) called this process "understanding the problem" and emphasized it as a key to mathematical problem solving.

For example, Riley, Greeno, and Heller (1983) found that young students had difficulty understanding problems that contained sentences such as, "Tom has five more marbles than Joe" and would sometimes recall the sentence as "Tom has five marbles." One explanation is that young students lack the appropriate schema for the relational situation described in the problem. Similarly, Lewis and Mayer (1987) found that adults often misunderstood relational statements in word problems, such as "Gas at ARCO costs $1.13 per gallon. This is 5 cents less per gallon than gas at Chevron." In an instructional study, Lewis (1989) taught students how to represent arithmetic word problems by translating sentences from the problem into a diagram based on a number line. Practice in converting sentences into diagrams was effective in subsequently reducing errors on other types of arithmetic word problems.

Once a problem has been represented, the next step is "to devise a plan" (Polya, 1957). Planning often involves breaking a problem into smaller parts, such as determining each of the computational steps that must be carried out to solve a word problem. For example, Schoenfeld (1985) was able to dramatically improve performance on mathematical problem-solving tests by teaching students problem-solving strategies such as breaking a problem down into parts or finding a related problem. In summary, thinking skills such as how to represent problems and how to plan solutions have been successfully taught within a variety of subject domains (Pressley, 1990).

Courses and training programs in various domains differ in their effects on transfer. Lehman, Lempert, and Nisbett (1988) studied the transfer produced by graduate study in psychology, medicine, law, and chemistry. They found that graduate training in psychology and medicine increased transfer of statistical reasoning to everyday problems, probably because study in those two areas involved using quantitative methods to solve practical problems. Training in law increased the ability to reason logically about complex practical problems, probably because the study of law centers on the application of logic and the principles of law to specific complex and practical cases. However, graduate training in chemistry did not increase the transfer of principles of chemistry to the study of complex, everyday problems, probably because graduate training in chemistry focuses on the laboratory study of basic problems, which does not often involve applications to everyday problems.

***Teaching Metacognitive Skills.*** A closely related approach to teaching for transfer involves teaching students how to use metacognitive skills. Knowing how to use a cognitive skill such as representation or planning must be complemented by knowing when and where to use it. For example, Pressley (1990, p. 9) noted that "good strategy users evaluate whether the strategies they are using are producing progress toward goals they have set for themselves" and also consider "the benefits that follow from using the procedures and the amount of effort required to carry out strategies." Flavell (1970) found that older children are more likely to spontaneously employ useful learning strategies than younger children, suggesting that metacognitive strategies may develop with experience.

Methods for teaching metacognitive strategies have been used to increase attention and reading comprehension. Douglas, Parry, Martin, and Garson (1976) developed a metacognitive training program that used self-verbalization, modeling, self-monitoring, and self-reinforcement to teach 7- and 8-year-old hyperactive children to control their attention. Camp (1980) used a "stop, look, and listen" strategy to teach impulsive elementary school boys to control their attention by asking themselves what problem they faced, how they planned to solve their problem, whether they were following their problem-solving plan, and how well they did with their problem. Each of these different programs increased control of attention and reading ability, although reading was not taught in either of them. The effects of the teaching transferred to improve school performance of the learners in the programs.

In reading comprehension, methods for teaching metacognitive strategies have produced large gains in performance. Linden and Wittrock (1981) showed a 50 percent gain in reading comprehension when fourth graders learned strategies for generating images and verbal relations between the text and their experiences as they read stories. Palincsar and Brown (1984) reported large gains in comprehension by using reciprocal teaching methods to teach a metacognitive strategy of comprehension fostering and comprehension monitoring. Wittrock and Kelly (1984) taught functionally illiterate young adults a metacognitive strategy that involved learning in sequence to generate summaries, inferences, and main ideas as they read expository text. Compared with a control group, the metacognitive strategy enhanced reading comprehension and transfer by 20 percent.

Metacognitive skills have also been taught within the context of mathematical problem solving. For example, Cardelle-Elawar (1992) provided classroom instruction to low-performing sixth-grade children on how to use linguistic, strategic, and procedural knowledge to solve mathematical story problems. For example, within each of 30 daily lessons, the teacher helped students learn to recognize when they did not understand the meaning of a word, did not have all the needed information to solve the problem, did not know how to break the problem into steps, or did not know how to carry out a computation. Trained students showed large pretest-to-posttest gains in mathematics achievement and attitudes toward mathematics, whereas control students did not. Apparently, learning to monitor and control one's cognitive processes for solving mathematics problems in the classroom transferred positively to solving other types of mathematics problems on a written test.

Metacognitive skills seem to facilitate transfer and problem solving across different ability levels. For example, Swanson (1990) found that regardless of their aptitudes, fourth and fifth graders with high metacognitive ability outperformed fourth and fifth graders with low metacognitive ability on tests of problem solving. In a review of more than 100 studies on the training of learning strategies, Belmont, Butterfield, and Ferretti (1982) identified seven studies that produced transfer effects on the cognitive functioning of young and mentally retarded children. Six of the seven studies showed that significant transfer occurred only when there was instruction in self-management skills—such as goal setting, strategy planning, and self-monitoring—in addition to training in specific skills involved in the transfer. Training in these self-management skills also shows one way that the teaching of metacognitive skills can increase transfer and problem solving among learners of different ability levels.

Problem-solving transfer seems to depend on domain-specific (or content-specific) knowledge as well as on cognitive and metacognitive strategies. These cognitive and metacognitive strategies can be taught to students of different ability levels, who can learn them and can transfer them to control their attention, to read with comprehension, and to solve problems that occur in everyday school situations. Although not featured in this chapter, learning communities in which these strategies are modelled and valued might be particularly effective in promoting their use (see chapter 2).

## CONCLUSION

A persistent theme within educational psychology has been the need to help students be able to transfer what they have learned to new situations and be able to solve problems that they were not explicitly taught to solve. Recent advances in educational and cognitive psychology have changed the way that educators look at the thorny relationship between teaching and transfer. In particular, advances have come about through changes in the focus of educational psychologists, including a focus on problem-solving process rather than on product, a focus on problem solving within specific situations rather than on problem solving that is abstract or context-free, and a focus on individual problem solvers rather than on group means. Armed with an array of cognitive theories that did not exist a generation ago, educational and cognitive psychologists have begun to understand the conditions for transfer.

This chapter reviewed several different views of transfer and examined the instructional implications that could be derived from each view. The general transfer of general skills view suggests a focus on improving the mind through teaching of mind-broadening material and mental exercises. However, the lack of documented success at promoting problem-solving transfer suggests that other views may be more fruitful. The specific transfer of specific behaviors view has yielded a successful focus on mastery of specific basic skills but has failed to address the broader issue of whether more general principles and processes can be taught. The specific transfer of general skills approach and the metacognitive view suggest meaningful methods of instruction, teaching by analogy, and direct instruction in thinking skills—that is, a focus on teaching for transfer. This review has shown that under appropriate conditions, students can learn to improve their problem-solving transfer.

In spite of recent progress, some scholars continue to raise questions about the very existence of transfer. Others seek to understand more clearly the conditions under which it does and does not occur (Detterman & Sternberg, 1992). Future research is needed to determine the mechanisms by which students learn and transfer general principles and processes from one problem to another. What is the optimal generality of a general skill? How should a general skill be connected to specific problems during instruction? Is transfer always limited to problems that have the same or similar structure as the learned problems? What are the characteristics of people who are able to generate clever solutions when confronted with a new problem? Although progress has been made, the search for teachable aspects of problem solving is not complete.

## References

Anderson, J. R. (1983). *The architecture of cognition.* Cambridge, MA: Harvard University Press.

Anderson, J. R. (1990). *Cognitive psychology and its implications* (3rd ed.). New York: Freeman.

Ausubel, D. P. (1968). *Educational psychology: A cognitive view.* New York: Holt, Rinehart & Winston.

Baron, J. B., & Sternberg, R. J. (1987). *Teaching thinking skills: Theory and practice.* New York: Freeman.

Belmont, J. M., Butterfield, E. C., & Ferretti, R. P. (1982). To secure transfer of training, instruct self-management skills. In D. K. Detterman & R. J. Sternberg (Eds.), *How and how much can intelligence be increased?* (pp. 147–154). Norwood, NJ: ABLEX.

Bloom, B. S., & Broder, L. J. (1950). *Problem-solving processes of college students.* Chicago: University of Chicago Press.

Bower, G. H., & Hilgard, E. R. (1981). *Theories of learning* (5th ed.). Englewood Cliffs, NJ: Prentice-Hall.

Bransford, J. D., Arbitman-Smith, R., Stein, B. S., & Vye, N. J. (1985). Improving thinking and learning skills: An analysis of three approaches. In J. W. Segal, S. F. Chipman, & R. Glaser (Eds.), *Thinking and learning skills* (Vol. 1). Hillsdale, NJ: Erlbaum.

Brown, A. L., Bransford, J., Ferrara, R., & Campione, J. (1983). Learning, remembering, and understanding. In P. H. Mussen (Ed.), *Handbook of child psychology* (Vol. 3). New York: Wiley.

Brownell, W. A., & Moser, H. E. (1949). Meaningful versus mechanical learning: A study on grade 3 subtraction. In *Duke University research studies in education* (No. 8). Durham, NC: Duke University Press.

Bruner, J. (1961). The act of discovery. *Harvard Educational Review, 31,* 21–32.

Camp, B. W. (1980). Two psychoeducational treatment programs for young aggressive boys. In C. K. Whalen & B. Hecker (Eds.), *Hyperactive children: The social ecology of identification and treatment* (pp. 191–219). New York: Academic Press.

Cardelle-Elawar, M. (1992). Effects of teaching metacognitive skills to students with low mathematics ability. *Teaching & Teacher Education, 8,* 109–121.

Carter, L. F. (1984). The sustaining effects study of compensatory and elementary education. *Educational Researcher, 13,* 4–13.

Caruso, D. R., Taylor, J. J., & Detterman, D. K. (1982). Intelligence research and intelligent policy. In D. K. Detterman & R. J. Sternberg (Eds.), *How and how much can intelligence be increased?* (pp. 45–66). Norwood, NJ: ABLEX.

Case, R. (1985). *Intellectual development: Birth to adulthood*. Orlando, FL: Academic Press.

Champagne, A. B., Gunstone, R. F., & Klopfer, L. E. (1985). Effecting changes in cognitive structures among physics students. In H. T. West & A. L. Pines (Eds.), *Cognitive structure and conceptual change*. Orlando, FL: Academic Press.

Chance, P. (1986). *Thinking in the classroom: A survey of programs*. New York: Teachers College Press.

Charles, D. C. (1987). The emergence of educational psychology. In J. A. Glover & R. R. Ronning (Eds.), *Historical foundations of educational psychology* (pp. 17–38). New York: Plenum.

Chi, M. T. H., Bassok, M., Lewis, M. W., Reimann, P., & Glaser, R. (1989). Self explanations: How students study and use examples in learning to solve problems. *Cognitive Science, 13,* 145–182.

Chi, M. T. H., Glaser, R., & Farr, M. J. (1988). *The nature of expertise*. Hillsdale, NJ: Erlbaum.

Chipman, S. F., Segal, J. W., & Glaser, R. (Eds.). (1985). *Thinking and learning skills* (Vol. 2). Hillsdale, NJ: Erlbaum.

Clements, D. H. (1986). Effects of LOGO and CAI environments on cognition and creativity. *Journal of Educational Psychology, 78,* 309–318.

Clements, D. H., & Gullo, D. F. (1984). Effects of computer programming on young children's cognition. *Journal of Educational Psychology, 76,* 1051–1058.

Cooper, G., & Sweller, J. (1987). Effects of schema acquisition and rule automation on mathematical problem-solving transfer. *Journal of Educational Psychology, 79,* 347–362.

Cormier, S. M., & Hagman, J. D. (Eds.). (1987). *Transfer of learning*. San Diego: Academic Press.

Covington, M. V., Crutchfield, R. S., & Davies, L. B. (1966). *The productive thinking program*. Berkeley, CA: Brazelton.

Covington, M. V., Crutchfield, R. S., Davies, L. B., & Olton, R. M. (1974). *The productive thinking program*. Columbus, OH: Merrill.

Dalbey, J., & Linn, M. C. (1985). The demands and requirements of computer programming: A literature review. *Journal of Educational Computing Research, 1,* 253–274.

de Bono, E. (1985). The CoRT thinking program. In J. W. Segal, S. F. Chipman, & R. Glaser (Eds.). *Thinking and learning skills* (Vol. 1, pp. 363–388). Hillsdale, NJ: Erlbaum.

De Corte, E., Verschaffel, L., & Schrooten, H. (1992). Cognitive effects of learning to program in Logo: A one-year study with sixth graders. In E. De Corte, M. C. Linn, & L. Verschaffel (Eds.), *Computer-based learning environments and problem solving* (pp. 207–228). Berlin: Springer-Verlag.

Detterman, D. K. (1982). Foreword. In D. K. Detterman & R. J. Sternberg (Eds.), *How and how much can intelligence be increased?* (pp. vii–viii). Norwood, NJ: ABLEX.

Detterman, D. K., & Sternberg, R. J. (Eds.). (1992). *Transfer on trial: Intelligence, cognition, and construction*. Norwood, NJ: ABLEX.

Dienes, Z. P. (1960). *Building up mathematics*. New York: Hutchinson Educational.

Doctorow, M. J., Wittrock, M. C., & Marks, C. B. (1978). Generative processes in reading comprehension. *Journal of Educational Psychology, 70,* 109–118.

Douglas, V. I., Parry, P., Martin, P., & Garson, C. (1976). Assessment of a cognitive training program for hyperactive children. *Journal of Abnormal Child Psychology, 4,* 389–410.

Duncker, K. (1945). On problem-solving. *Psychological Monographs, 58*(5) (Whole No. 270).

Ericsson, K. A., & Smith, J. (Eds.). (1991). *Toward a general theory of expertise*. Cambridge, England: Cambridge University Press.

Feuerstein, R. (1980). *Instrumental enrichment: An intervention program for cognitive modifiability*. Baltimore: University Park Press.

Feuerstein, R., Jensen, M., Hoffman, M. B., & Rand, Y. (1985). Instrumental enrichment, an intervention program for structural cognitive modifiability: Theory and practice. In J. W. Segal, S. F. Chipman, & R. Glaser (Eds.), *Thinking and learning skills* (Vol. 1). Hillsdale, NJ: Erlbaum.

Flavell, J. (1976). Metacognitive aspects of problem solving. In L. B. Resnick (Ed.), *The nature of intelligence* (pp. 231–236). Hillsdale, NJ: Erlbaum.

Flavell, J. H. (1970). Developmental studies of mediated learning. In H. W. Reese & L. P. Lipsitt (Eds.), *Advances in child development and behavior* (Vol. 5). New York: Academic Press.

Gagné, R. (1968). Learning hierarchies. *Educational Psychologist, 6,* 1–9.

Gentner, D. (1983). Structure mapping: A theoretical framework. *Cognitive Science, 7,* 155–170.

Gentner, D. (1989). The mechanisms of analogical learning. In S. Vosniadou & A. Ortony (Eds.), *Similarity and analogical reasoning* (pp. 199–241). Cambridge, England: Cambridge University Press.

Gentner, D., & Gentner, D. R. (1983). Flowing waters or teeming crowds: Mental models of electricity. In D. Gentner & A. L. Stevens (Eds.), *Mental models* (pp. 99–130). Hillsdale, NJ: Erlbaum.

Gick, M. L., & Holyoak, K. J. (1980). Analogical problem solving. *Cognitive Psychology, 12,* 306–355.

Gick, M. L., & Holyoak, K. J. (1983). Schema induction and analogical transfer. *Cognitive Psychology, 15,* 1–38.

Gick, M. L., & Holyoak, K. L. (1987). The cognitive basis for knowledge transfer. In S. M. Cormier & J. D. Hagman (Eds.), *Transfer of learning* (pp. 9–57). New York: Academic Press.

Glynn, S. M., Britton, B. K., Muth, D., & Dogan, N. (1982). Writing and revising persuasive documents: Cognitive demands. *Journal of Educational Psychology, 74,* 557–567.

Haller, E. P., Child, D. A., & Walberg, H. J. (1988). Can comprehension be taught? *Educational Researcher, 17,* 5–8.

Halpern, D. F. (Ed.). (1992). *Enhancing thinking skills in the sciences and mathematics*. Hillsdale, NJ: Erlbaum.

Hayes, J. R., & Simon, H. A. (1977). Psychological differences among problem isomorphs. In N. J. Castellan, P. B. Pisoni, & G. R. Potts (Eds.), *Cognitive theory* (Vol. 2, pp. 21–41). Hillsdale, NJ: Erlbaum.

Holyoak, K. L., & Koh, K. (1987). Surface and structural similarity in analogical transfer. *Memory & Cognition, 15,* 332–340.

Judd, C. H. (1908). The relation of special training and general intelligence. *Educational Review, 36,* 28–42.

Judd, C. H. (1939). *Educational psychology*. New York: Houghton Mifflin.

Katona, G. (1940). *Organizing and memorizing*. New York: Columbia University Press.

Kiewra, K. H. (1991). Aids to lecture learning. *Educational Psychologist, 26,* 37–54.

Kourilsky, M., & Wittrock, M. C. (1987). Verbal and graphical strategies in the teaching of economics. *Teaching and Teacher Education, 3,* 1–12.

Kourilsky, M., & Wittrock, M. C. (in press). Generative teaching: An enrichment strategy for the learning of economics in cooperative groups. *American Educational Research Journal*.

Kurland, D. M., & Pea, R. D. (1985). Children's mental models of recursive LOGO programs. *Journal of Educational Computing Research, 1,* 235–244.

LaBerge, D., & Samuels, S. J. (1974). Toward a theory of automatic information processing in reading. *Cognitive Psychology, 6,* 293–323.

Larkin, J. H., McDermott, J., Simon, D. P., & Simon, H. A. (1980). Expert and novice performance in solving physics problems. *Science, 208,* 1335–1342.

Lave, J. (1988). *Cognition in practice*. Cambridge, England: Cambridge University Press.

Lehman, D. R., Lempert, R. O., & Nisbett, R. E. (1988). The effects of graduate training on reasoning. *American Psychologist, 43,* 431–442.

Lewis, A. B. (1989). Training students to represent arithmetic word problems. *Journal of Educational Psychology, 81,* 521–531.

Lewis, A. B., & Mayer, R. E. (1987). Students' miscomprehension of relational statements in arithmetic word problems. *Journal of Educational Psychology, 79,* 363–371.

Linden, M., & Wittrock, M. C. (1981). The teaching of reading comprehension according to the model of generative learning. *Reading Research Quarterly, 17,* 44–57.

Linn, M. C. (1985). The cognitive consequences of programming instruction in classrooms. *Educational Researcher, 14,* 14–16, 25–29.

Luchins, A. S., & Luchins, E. H. (1970). *Wertheimer's seminars revisited: Problem solving and thinking* (Vol. 1). Albany, NY: State University of New York.

Mansfield, R. S., Busse, T. V., & Krepelka, E. J. (1978). The effectiveness of creativity training. *Review of Educational Research, 48,* 517–536.

Mayer, R. E. (1975). Forward transfer of different reading strategies evoked by test-like events in mathematics text. *Journal of Educational Psychology, 67,* 165–169.

Mayer, R. E. (1984). Aids to prose comprehension. *Educational Psychologist, 19,* 30–42.

Mayer, R. E. (1987). *Educational psychology: A cognitive approach*. Boston: Little, Brown.

Mayer, R. E. (Ed.). (1988). *Teaching and learning computer programming*. Hillsdale, NJ: Erlbaum.

Mayer, R. E. (1989a). Models for understanding. *Review of Educational Research, 59,* 43–64.

Mayer, R. E. (1989b). Teaching for thinking: Research on the teachability of thinking skills. In I. S. Cohen (Ed.), *The G. Stanley Hall Lecture Series* (Vol. 9). Washington, DC: American Psychological Association.

Mayer, R. E. (1992a). Teaching for transfer of problem-solving skills to computer programming. In E. De Corte, M. C. Linn, & L. Verschaffel (Eds.), *Computer-based learning environments and problem solving* (pp. 193–206). Berlin: Springer-Verlag.

Mayer, R. E. (1992b). *Thinking, problem solving, cognition* (2nd ed.). New York: Freeman.

Mayer, R. E. (1992c). Guiding students' cognitive processing of scientific information. In M. Pressley, K. Harris, & J. Guthrie (Eds.), *Promoting academic competence and literacy: Cognitive research and instructional innovation* (pp. 243–258). Orlando, FL: Academic Press.

Mayer, R. E., & Fay, A. L. (1987). A chain of cognitive changes with learning to program in Logo. *Journal of Educational Psychology, 79,* 269–279.

Mackenzie, A. W., & White, R. T. (1982). Fieldwork in geography and long-term memory structures. *American Educational Research Journal, 19,* 623–632.

Montessori, M. (1964). *Advanced Montessori method*. Cambridge, MA: Bentley.

Morris, P. F. (1990). Metacognition. In M. W. Eysenck (Ed.), *The Blackwell dictionary of cognitive psychology* (pp. 225–229). Oxford, UK: Basil Blackwell.

Newell, A., & Simon, H. A. (1972). *Human problem solving*. Englewood Cliffs, NJ: Prentice-Hall.

Nickerson, R. S., Perkins, D. N., & Smith, E. E. (1985). *The teaching of thinking*. Hillsdale, NJ: Erlbaum.

Novick, L. R. (1988). Analogical transfer, problem similarity, and expertise. *Journal of Experimental Psychology: Learning, Memory, and Cognition, 14,* 510–520.

Osborne, R. J., & Wittrock, M. C. (1983). Learning science: A generative process. *Science Education, 67,* 489–504.

Osborne, R. J., & Wittrock, M. C. (1985). The generative learning model and its implications for science education. *Studies in Science Education, 12,* 59–87.

Palincsar, A. M., & Brown, A. L. (1984). Reciprocal teaching of comprehension fostering and comprehension monitoring activities. *Cognition and Instruction, 1,* 117–175.

Papert, S. (1980). *Mindstorms*. New York: Basic Books.

Pea, R. D., & Kurland, D. M. (1984). On the cognitive effects of learning computer programming. *New Ideas in Psychology, 2,* 137–168.

Peled, Z., & Wittrock, M. C. (1990). Generative meanings in the comprehension of word problems in mathematics. *Instructional Science, 19,* 171–205.

Peper, R. J., & Mayer, R. E. (1978). Note taking as a generative activity. *Journal of Educational Psychology, 70,* 514–522.

Perkins, D. N. (1985). The fingertip effect: How information-processing technology shapes thinking. *Educational Researcher, 14,* 11–17.

Perkins, D. N., Schwartz, S., & Simmons, R. (1988). Instructional strategies for the problems of novice programmers. In R. E. Mayer (Ed.), *Teaching and learning computer programming* (pp. 153–178). Hillsdale, NJ: Erlbaum.

Polson, P. G., & Jeffries, R. (1985). Instruction in general problem-solving skills: An analysis of four approaches. In J. W. Segal, S. F. Chipman, & R. Glaser (Eds.), *Thinking and learning skills* (Vol. 1, pp. 417–455). Hillsdale, NJ: Erlbaum.

Polya, G. (1957). *How to solve it*. Garden City, NY: Doubleday/Anchor.

Polya, G. (1965). *Mathematical discovery*. New York: Wiley.

Pressley, M. (1990). *Cognitive strategy instruction that really improves children's academic performance*. Cambridge, MA: Brookline.

Read, C. (1981). Writing is not the inverse of reading for young children. In C. H. Frederiksen & J. F. Dominic (Eds.), *Writing* (Vol. 2). Hillsdale, NJ: Erlbaum.

Reed, S. K. (1987). A structure-mapping model for word problems. *Journal of Experimental Psychology: Learning, Memory, and Cognition, 13,* 124–139.

Reed, S. K., Dempster, A., & Ettinger, M. (1985). Usefulness of analogous solution for solving algebra word problems. *Journal of Experimental Psychology: Learning, Memory, and Cognition, 11,* 106–125.

Reed, S. K., Ernst, G. W., & Banerji, R. (1974). The role of analogy in transfer between similar problem states. *Cognitive Psychology, 6,* 436–450.

Resnick, L. B. (1989). Introduction. In L. B. Resnick (Ed.), *Knowing, learning, and instruction: Essays in honor of Robert Glaser*. Hillsdale, NJ: Erlbaum.

Resnick, L. B., & Ford, W. (1981). *The psychology of mathematics for instruction*. Hillsdale, NJ: Erlbaum.

Riley, M., Greeno, J. G., & Heller, J. (1983). The development of children's problem solving ability in mathematics. In H. Ginsberg (Ed.), *The development of mathematical thinking*. New York: Academic Press.

Rippa, S. A. (1980). *Education in a free society: An American history*. New York: Longman.

Rogoff, B., & Lave, J. (Eds.). (1984). *Everyday cognition: Its development in social context*. Cambridge, MA: Harvard University Press.

Ross, B. H. (1987). This is like that: The use of earlier problems and the separation of similarity effects. *Journal of Experimental Psychology: Learning, Memory, and Cognition, 13,* 629–639.

Ross, B. H. (1989). Distinguishing types of superficial similarities: Different effects on the access and use of earlier problems. *Journal of Experimental Psychology: Learning, Memory, and Cognition, 15,* 456–468.

Ruger, H. A. (1910). The psychology of efficiency. *Archives of Psychology, 2,* No. 15.

Salomon, G., & Perkins, D. (1989). Rocky roads to transfer: Rethinking mechanisms of a neglected phenomenon. *Educational Psychologist, 24,* 113–142.

Samuels, S. J. (1979). The method of repeated readings. *The Reading Teacher, 32,* 403–408.

Scardamalia, M., Bereiter, C., & Goelman, H. (1982). The role of production factors in writing ability. In M. Nystrand (Ed.), *What writers know* (pp. 173–210). New York: Academic Press.

Schliemann, A. D., & Acoily, N. M. (1989). Mathematical knowledge developed at work: The contribution of practice versus the contribution of schooling. *Cognition and Instruction, 6,* 185–221.

Schoenfeld, A. (1985). *Mathematical problem solving.* Orlando, FL: Academic Press.

Segal, J. W., Chipman, S. F., & Glaser, R. (Eds.). (1985). *Thinking and learning skills* (Vol. 1). Hillsdale, NJ: Erlbaum.

Shulman, L. S., & Kieslar, E. R. (1966). *Learning by discovery.* Chicago: Rand McNally.

Siegler, R. J. (1989). Mechanisms of cognitive growth. *Annual Review of Psychology, 40,* 353–379.

Siegler, R. J., & Jenkins, E. (1989). *How children discover new strategies.* Hillsdale, NJ: Erlbaum.

Simon, H. A., & Reed, S. K. (1976). Modeling strategy shifts in a problem solving task. *Cognitive Psychology, 8,* 86–97.

Singley, M. K., & Anderson, J. R. (1989). *The transfer of cognitive skill.* Cambridge, MA: Harvard University Press.

Smith, M. U. (Ed.). (1991). *Toward a unified theory of problem solving.* Hillsdale, NJ: Erlbaum.

Snow, R. E. (1982). The training of intellectual aptitude. In D. G. Detterman & R. J. Sternberg (Eds.), *How and how much can intelligence be increased?* (pp. 1–37). Norwood, NJ: ABLEX.

Sternberg, R. J. (1985). *Beyond IQ: A triarchic theory of human intelligence.* Cambridge, England: Cambridge University Press.

Sternberg, R. J. (1990). *Metaphors of mind: Conceptions of the nature of intelligence.* Cambridge, England: Cambridge University Press.

Sternberg, R. J., & Frensch, P. A. (Eds.). (1991). *Complex problem solving: Principles and mechanisms.* Hillsdale, NJ: Erlbaum.

Swanson, H. L. (1990). Influence of metacognitive knowledge and aptitude on problem solving. *Journal of Educational Psychology, 82,* 306–314.

Thorndike, E. L. (1903). *Educational psychology.* New York: Lemke & Buechner.

Thorndike, E. L. (1923). The influence of first-year Latin upon the ability to read English. *School and Society, 17,* 165–168.

Thorndike, E. L. (1924). Mental discipline in high school studies. *Journal of Educational Psychology, 15,* 1–22, 83–98.

Thorndike, E. L., & Woodworth, R. S. (1901). The influence of improvement in one mental function upon the efficiency of other functions. *Psychological Review, 8,* 247–261.

Vosniadou, S., & Ortony, A. (Eds.). (1989). *Similarity and analogical reasoning.* Cambridge, England: Cambridge University Press.

Wertheimer, M. (1945/1959). *Productive thinking.* New York: Harper & Row.

White, B. Y. (1984). Designing computer games to help physics students understand Newton's laws of motion. *Cognition and Instruction, 1,* 69–108.

Wittrock, M. C. (1974a). A generative model of mathematics learning. *Journal for Research in Mathematics Education, 5,* 181–197.

Wittrock, M. C. (1974b). Learning as a generative process. *Educational Psychologist, 11,* 87–95.

Wittrock, M. C. (1978). Developmental processes in learning from instruction. *Journal of Genetic Psychology, 132,* 37–54.

Wittrock, M. C. (1990). Generative processes of comprehension. *Educational Psychologist, 24,* 345–376.

Wittrock, M. C. (1991). Generative teaching of comprehension. *Elementary School Journal, 92,* 167–182.

Wittrock, M. C., & Alesandrini, K. (1990). Generation of summaries and analogies and analytic and holistic abilities. *American Educational Research Journal, 27,* 489–502.

Wittrock, M. C., & Kelly, R. (1984). *Teaching reading comprehension to adults in basic skills courses* (Final Report, Vols. 1–3). Los Angeles: University of California, School of Education.

Wittrock, M. C., Marks, C. B., & Doctorow, M. J. (1975). Reading as a generative process. *Journal of Educational Psychology, 67,* 484–489.

Wolf, T. H. (1973). *Alfred Binet.* Chicago: University of Chicago Press.

Zhu, X., & Simon, H. A. (1987). Learning mathematics from examples and by doing. *Cognition and Instruction, 4,* 137–166.

# · 4 ·

# THEORIES AND PRINCIPLES OF MOTIVATION

## Sandra Graham

UNIVERSITY OF CALIFORNIA, LOS ANGELES

## Bernard Weiner

UNIVERSITY OF CALIFORNIA, LOS ANGELES

Early humans no doubt constructed bridges well before engineering courses and knowledge of the laws of physics existed; primitive healers attained cures well before medical courses and knowledge of the laws of biology existed; and achievement strivings in others were fostered well before self-instructional tapes and knowledge of the laws of motivation existed. But it is also true that the laws of physics aided the construction of the Golden Gate Bridge and the laws of biology helped eradicate smallpox. In a similar vein, theories of motivation may assist in the creation of rules to enhance human performance. We acknowledge at the outset that this motivational goal is presently more a dream than a reality and will not reach fruition in the reader's lifetime. Thus, those beginning this chapter with the anticipation that after reading the final paragraph they can go back into the classroom and soon have all the students working with intensity and positive affect will be disappointed.

This does not mean that effective principles of motivation do not exist, as Deborah Stipek illustrates in the following chapter. But a belief about motivation or a specific guide to conduct is far from a theory. For example, it is common knowledge that if a person is engaged in an activity that is interesting, engrossing, and involving, and the person is oblivious to all else, then motivation is high. Intensity, persistence, and other indicators of motivation will thereby be augmented. Psychologists are well aware of this fact, and one approach to enhancing motivation stresses "intrinsic" motivation (Deci, 1975), or motivational "flow" (Csikszentmihalyi, 1975), where conditions are created that increase interest so that learning and mastery are sought for their own sake. This reasonable and in all likelihood correct principle of motivation is shared by prescientific societies and motivational engineers alike. But a guideline for behavior is far from a theory of motivation.

Numerous other principles of motivation have been proposed, and they tend to be in agreement with the thoughts of lay consumers of this knowledge. For example, it has been argued that the search for knowledge will be impeded if other motivations necessary for survival, such as hunger, are more

pressing (Maslow, 1943); that positive benefits accruing from performance will increase the likelihood of subsequent repetitions of this desired behavior (Skinner, 1953); that students will be positively motivated if they are more concerned with mastery of the material than with doing better than others (Nicholls, 1984); and that contexts should be established so that students perceive themselves as personally responsible for performance rather than as passive recipients controlled by outside forces (deCharms, 1972). All of these examples depict reasonable beliefs that can be incorporated into educational programs, with some likelihood of augmenting motivation and performance. They are not, however, theories of motivation.

## WHAT IS A MOTIVATIONAL THEORY?

To address this question, let us begin with a definition of motivation. Motivation is the study of why people think and behave as they do. In the context of academic achievement, motivational concerns would be addressed if we were to ask, for example, why some students complete tasks despite enormous difficulty, while others give up at the slightest provocation, or why some students set such unrealistically high goals for themselves that failure is bound to occur.

Another way to capture the concept of motivation is to think about a typical achievement behavior, such as studying for an examination, and to view it as a temporal sequence that is started, sustained, directed, and finally terminated. Motivational psychologists would want to examine what the individual is doing, or the *choice* of behavior; how long it takes before an individual initiates the activity, or the *latency* of behavior; how hard the person actually works at the activity, or the *intensity* of behavior; how long the individual is willing to remain at the activity, or the *persistence* of behavior; and what the individual is thinking and feeling while engaged in the activity, or the *cognitions* and *emotional reactions* accompanying the behavior. Note that this is quite different from the study of learning,

---

This chapter was written while the authors were supported by grant No. DBS-9211982 from the National Science Foundation.

which has to do with what has already been or is being formed. Educators sometimes confuse the goals of psychologists who study motivation with the goals of those who study learning.

With these definitional issues behind us, let us now turn to what is meant by a theory of motivation. In what ways do theories differ from specific explanations or rules? And why should a theory of motivation provide better (or worse) guidelines for motivational augmentation than would a set of specific explanations or rules?

We construe a theory to be a network of constructs, related to one another by a precise set of rules, with some or all of these constructs linked with an operational language. For example, consider Clark Hull's drive theory of motivation (Hull, 1943, 1951). Although this conception no longer has great impact in psychology, it was the most influential approach in the decades from 1940 to 1960. In its simplest form, the theory states that behavior is a function of drive multiplied by habit: $B = f(D \times H)$. Thus, two constructs, drive and habit, are linked in a clearly specified mathematical manner (multiplicative). Furthermore, drive is determined by factors like hours of deprivation of a commodity necessary for survival, and habit by the number of times a response has been rewarded in a particular situation. Described in this very incomplete manner, drive theory meets some of the criteria necessary for a conception to be labeled as a *theory*—multiple concepts, linked in a definitive manner, and identified with observable indicators.

There are other differences between a theory and a specific explanation in addition to the number of constructs involved and the preciseness of their postulated interrelations. A "good" theory should be able to explain diverse phenomena across a range of disparate situations. That is, a scientific theory entails general laws that transcend particular instances. For example, when a layperson explains why one is drinking water, he or she may state that the person is thirsty. A motivational engineer with the goal of inducing subsequent drinking behavior may deprive the person of water, offer this individual some salty peanuts, and the like. These motivational manipulations will surely "work," i.e., increase the behavior that is desired. In a similar manner, when a person accounts for why another is eating, he or she is likely to explain that the person is hungry; motivational engineers with the goal of increasing food consumption at a point in time surely will be able to establish conditions that heighten eating behavior, such as food deprivation, filling the room with a tantalizing odor, and so forth. But a motivational theorist, unlike the layperson or engineer, would attempt to use the same constructs and theory of action to interpret instances of both water intake and food consumption. The theorist might postulate, for example, that behavior is directly related to the amount of deprivation (whether water or food) and the level of arousal (whether induced by the eating of peanuts or by the aroma of food). Thus, the same concepts are applied to disparate motivational domains, and the analysis shifts from concrete instances to abstract issues involving the presence of any need. One of the goals of science is the development of such general explanatory principles. The objective is to develop a language, an explanatory system, a conceptual representation, or what is more commonly termed a theory, that is applicable across many domains of behavior and provides insights into (accurate predictions about) why behavior is initiated, maintained, directed, and so forth.

The more abstract the language and the greater the generality, the "better" is the theory. However, the further one departs from the specific instance under consideration, the less applicable is the theory to a specific context. For example, stating that behavior is a function of amount of deprivation and level of arousal does not provide the teacher with a clear set of engineering tools to alter performance in the classroom. In the long run, it may indeed be the case, as the motivational psychologist Kurt Lewin (1936) stated, that "nothing is as practical as a good theory." But in the short run, and when the science is as nascent as the field of motivation, then this epigram is not correct. In fact, there may be little as impractical as a theory, and nothing as practical as a good, concrete rule with little generality beyond the issue being considered. Surely, for example, making a task interesting will be a better step toward increasing classroom motivation than postulating that behavior is a function of drive × habit.

In spite of the above statement, this chapter, should not be interpreted as opposed to theoretical development, for it is written by two theoretically oriented motivational psychologists. Rather, it is merely conveying reality (as we interpret it) at this point in the maturation of the field of motivation. Furthermore, theories have goals and benefits other than the possibility of application. The aim of theoretical understanding is to be able to incorporate disparate phenomena in as parsimonious a manner as possible. Such conceptual systems are of value with or without practical implications; and they allow for a more complete understanding of human behavior by grasping the core aspects of motivated action.

## HISTORY OF THE SCIENTIFIC STUDY OF THEORIES OF MOTIVATION

The development of theory in the field of motivation has had disparate impact at different points in history. Thus, prior to examining both general theories and specific principles of motivation that have been proposed, we think it is beneficial to provide an overview of the growth and changes in this field of study. This allows us to introduce the theories and principles that we later review by first placing them in their broader historical context.

History is a constructive process. Just as one can subscribe to different psychological theories, so one can advocate different historical interpretations of a field. Our construction of history should be understood as only one among a number of possible viewpoints. Our interpretation was shaped by our training as experimentalists who believe that motivational principles applied to the classroom should meet the tenets of science. This history therefore has a decidedly empirical focus in tracing those theories that have been most subject to experimental testing.

There have been a few major trends in the scientific study of motivation, which had its origin around 1930. First, and particularly germane to this chapter, there has been a general shift from the creation of all-encompassing, broad theories to a focus on narrower, more bounded "mini"-theories and the analysis of specific aspects of motivated behavior. This is true not only for general psychologists but also for educational psychologists, who have withdrawn from the pursuit of general conceptions of behavior to a consideration of theories of

TABLE 4–1. Contents of the Chapters on Motivation in the Encyclopedia of Educational Research, 1941–1990

| P. T. Young (1941 and 1950) | M. Marx (1960) | B. Weiner (1969) | S. Ball (1982) | B. Weiner (1990) |
|---|---|---|---|---|
| Need and activity level | Theories | Theories | Attribution theory | Cognitions |
| Appetite and aversion | Techniques | Associative | Achievement motivation | Causal attributions |
| Equilibrium and homeostasis | Drive and learning | Drive | Anxiety | Self-efficacy |
| Chemical controls | Drive and frustration | Cognitive | Self-esteem | Learned helplessness |
| Neural structures | Activation of drives | Psychoanalytic | Curiosity | Individual differences |
| Incentives | and motives | Topics | Minor areas | Need for achievement |
| Defense mechanisms | Reward | Curiosity (exploratory | Level of aspiration | Anxiety about failure |
| Degree of motivation | Knowledge of re- | behavior) | Affiliation | Locus of control |
| Educational applications | sults | Affiliation | Biochemical correlates | Attributional style |
| Praise and reproof | Fear and anxiety | Imbalance (dissonance) | Reinforcement theory | Environmental determi- |
| Success and failure | Arousal | Frustration | | nants |
| Knowledge of results | | Aggression | | Cooperation versus com- |
| Cooperation and compe- | | Relation to processes | | petition (goal |
| tence | | Learning | | structure) |
| Reward and punishment | | Perception | | Intrinsic versus extrinsic |
| | | Memory | | rewards |
| | | | | Praise |

Note. From "History of motivational research in education," by. B. Weiner. *Journal of Educational Psychology, 82,* 1990, pp. 616–622.

achievement behavior and principles that might augment or inhibit achievement strivings.

A second trend in the field of motivation has been a shift in the types of theories and principles proposed, from those conceiving of the person as machinelike, without conscious awareness or volition and controlled by environmental forces, to perceptions of individuals as rational scientists, decision makers, information processors, self-determining, and having other characteristics associated with an active mind (see Weiner, 1992). This change was part of the better known general shift in psychology away from mechanism and toward cognitive views of the dynamics of behavior.

One way to document these and other trends in the history of the study of motivation is to perform a content analysis of the chapters on motivation in the standard source book, *The Encyclopedia of Educational Research* (see Weiner, 1990). This volume has been published each decade, starting in 1941, and six chapters examine the motivation research conducted between 1930 and 1990 (Table 4–1).

## The Mechanistic Period: 1930–1960

The first two motivation chapters in the *Encyclopedia of Educational Research* were written by Paul Young (1941, 1950). Table 4–1 reveals that the major research concerns of the day were activity level, appetites and aversions, homeostasis, chemical controls and neural structures, incentives, defense mechanisms, and degrees of motivation (the Yerkes–Dodson law of optimal motivational level). These topics were primarily associated with drive theory, the most dominant of the early theories of motivation. This conception is reviewed in greater detail later in the chapter. Some specific concerns of educational psychologists also were represented in the 1930s to 1950s, including praise and reproof, success and failure, knowledge of results (feedback), cooperation and competition, and reward and punishment. In contrast to the themes associated with drive

theory, the preoccupations of educational psychologists were less clearly tied to any formal conceptions of motivation.

Why were these the main fields of research when the scientific study of motivation was initiated? At first, the experimental analysis of motivation (the Latin root of *motive* means "to move") was linked with the search for the motors of behavior and was associated with mechanical concepts such as instinct, drive, arousal, need, and energization. Motivational psychologists in the 1930s to 1950s were especially concerned with what moved a resting organism to a state of activity. Accordingly, hungry rats were deprived of food and curious monkeys were placed in rooms without visual stimulation. It was believed that a discrepancy between an ideal "off" state and a less than ideal "on" state (i.e., the presence of a need) would be detected by the organism and activity would be initiated until the disequilibrium was reduced to zero (i.e., homeostasis was attained). It was presumed to be hedonic (pleasurable) to be in a state of balance, free of needs, and homeostatic mechanisms were believed to be automatically activated to maintain this equilibrium, such as shivering when the organism was too cold and sweating when the organism was too warm. Hence, researchers examined the effects of a variety of need states on a variety of indexes of motivation, including speed of learning.

The concept of a deprived organism living in an environment of limited resources gave a functionalistic, Darwinian flavor to the field of motivation, which between 1930 and 1960 was dominated by Clark Hull and Kenneth Spence, the moving forces behind drive theory. This foundation was far removed from issues in the classroom. Indeed, motivational theorists thought that human behavior was too complex to study directly and therefore not readily amenable to experimental manipulation, which at that point in history connoted deprivation of something necessary for survival. Hence, another characteristic in the study of motivation during this early period was a reliance on nonhuman subjects, who could indeed be deprived.

Melvin Marx (1960), in the next *Encyclopedia* chapter, also linked motivation with energy and drive level. He examined the topics of drive and learning, drive and frustration, activation of drives, rewards, knowledge of results, fear and anxiety (which were learned drives), and arousal, all within the Hull–Spence tradition, and all with little or no relevance to the concerns of educational psychologists.

## The Arrival of Cognition: 1960–1970

In 1969, four theoretical approaches dominated motivation: associationistic theory (John Watson), drive theory (Hull and Spence), cognitive theory (Kurt Lewin and John Atkinson), and psychoanalytic theory (Sigmund Freud) (see Table 4–1). The theories of Lewin and Atkinson, which followed Hull's in their impact on motivational psychology, will be examined in detail later in this chapter. The specific research areas analyzed in the decade of the 1960s included exploratory behavior, affiliation, balance (dissonance), frustration, and aggression. Furthermore, motivation was related to the other process areas of learning, perception, and memory. Although Hull and Spence and the drive concept remained influential, studies on drive, energy, arousal, homeostasis, and the other mainstays of drive theory received less attention.

Major changes therefore had taken place, some starting before Marx (1960) wrote his chapter and others flowering in the 1960s. The most important change was the general shift in psychology away from mechanism and toward cognition. For example, proponents of the psychology of Edward Thorndike (1911), which was incorporated by Hull, believed that a reward would automatically increase the probability of the immediately prior response, thus augmenting the likelihood of that behavior when the organism was in that same environment. It gradually became evident, however, that reward is associated with a variety of cognitions: A reward might convey to the recipient that he or she is being coerced or that the expectations of others are low. Each of these connotations could have a different motivational implication.

When the cognitive approach to motivation carried the day, the result was not just a different theoretical orientation, but also a new empirical outlook. For example, researchers began to concentrate on human rather than on nonhuman behavior. It became as respectable to generalize from human to nonhuman behavior as vice versa. So, just as Hull speculated about human motivation based on the observation of rats, so Lewin mused about the behavior of rats based on the study of humans! Furthermore, issues associated with success and failure and achievement strivings formed the heart of the theoretical and empirical study of motivation. This interest arose in part because of the manifest importance of achievement strivings in human behavior. In addition, success and failure could be readily manipulated in the laboratory, and their effects on subsequent performance determined, with no more difficulty than depriving lower organisms of food and testing the effects of deprivation on performance. Finally, many naturally occurring instances of achievement outcomes could be subject to field research, including success and failure in the classroom, thus opening a door for educational researchers.

By 1970, motivational research had become almost synonymous with achievement motivation research. Educational psychology thus moved into the spotlight and out of the shadows portrayed in the reviews by Young (1941, 1950) and Marx (1960). Of course, other aspects of human motivation were studied in the 1960s, including affiliative behavior and cognitive balance. But these paled in comparison to the attention given to achievement strivings.

The cognitive motivational theorists remained wedded to the "grand formal theory" approach of Hull and Spence. They set as their task the isolation of the determinants of behavior and the specification of the mathematical relations among these factors. This is illustrated in the dominant Motive × Probability × Incentive formula of Atkinson (1957, 1964) and the closely related theories of Lewin (1935) and Julian Rotter (1954). All of these conceptions were known as expectancy-value theories, according to which motivation is determined by what one expects to get and the likelihood that one will get it. Thus, cognitions were presumed to play a key role in motivated behavior. Further, it became accepted that organisms are always active and, as a result, the key dependent variables in motivation became choice and persistence, indicators of the direction of behavior. Finally, although the scientific goal remained the development of general motivational theories, virtually the only testing ground for these theories was the context of achievement strivings. Thus, a disparity was created between the broad objectives of the theories and their narrow empirical focus.

With, on the one hand, the waning of mechanism, drive, and homeostasis as the loci of investigation and the gradual decline in research using lower organisms as subjects, and on the other hand the advent of cognitivism, rational-person metaphors, achievement strivings, and the study of human motivation, there came another important research direction. Attention shifted to the study of individual differences, with persons characterized as high or low in achievement needs, high or low in anxiety, high or low in internal control, and high or low in other characteristics presumed to bear on motivated activity. For the educational psychologist interested in individuals who performed poorly in the classroom, this was an important and a compatible shift.

## Contemporary Motivation Research: 1970–1990

The next motivation chapter in the *Encyclopedia of Educational Research* was written by Samuel Ball (1982). The topics he covered included attribution theory, achievement motivation, anxiety, and, to a much lesser extent, level of aspiration, affiliation, biochemical correlates of motivation, and reinforcement (see Table 4–1). Ball's chapter documented a continuation of the trends observed in the 1960s, among them the continued decline of the broad theories proposed by Hull, Lewin, Atkinson, and Rotter, although attribution theory as a growing field was added to these general theories; an even greater focus on human behavior, particularly achievement strivings; an increasing range of cognitions documented as having motivational significance, including causal ascriptions; and an enduring interest in individual differences in achievement needs, anxiety about failure, and perceptions of control. During the 1970s, the study of nonhuman motivation (excluding the physiological mechanisms of hunger, thirst, and so forth) and the associated drive concept virtually vanished, not that many years after the heyday of Hull and Spence.

In the 1990s the motivation topics include cognitions (e.g., causal attributions), individual differences in motivation (e.g., need for achievement), and environmental influences on motivation (e.g., competitive versus cooperative contexts). Because most of these topics are reviewed in the remainder of this chapter, we conclude this section on history with the following general impressions:

1. The sweeping theories have for the most part faded away. What remain are varieties of cognitive approaches to motivation. The main theoretical conceptions today are based on the interrelated cognitions of causal attributions, efficacy and control beliefs, and thoughts about the goals toward which the subject is striving.

2. Achievement desires remain at the center of the study of motivation. There are pockets of research on power motivation, affiliation, exploratory behavior, altruism, aggression, and other social motivations, but these are of secondary concern. As already indicated, this orientation greatly limits the generality of the theories that have been proposed. On the other hand, for those solely interested in classroom achievement striving and engineering goals, the lack of theoretical generality need not be of great concern.

3. Within the achievement field, new approaches are vying to share the dominance heretofore held by need for achievement and causal ascriptions. These approaches embrace the linked concepts of task versus ego involvement, competitive versus cooperative goal structures, and intrinsic versus extrinsic rewards.

### Overview of the Remainder of the Chapter

Bearing in mind these thoughts about theory definition (a network of interrelated concepts linked with a data language) and the history of motivational research (from broad mechanistic theories to a more specific focus on cognitive principles germane to achievement strivings), we now turn to a review of motivational theories and achievement-related principles. The review first covers five general theories that have dominated the scientific study of motivation: Hull's drive theory, Lewin's field theory, Atkinson's theory of achievement strivings, Rotter's social learning theory, and attribution theory as espoused by Heider, Kelley, and Weiner. Although some of these broad theories no longer have great impact, they nonetheless spawned a number of contemporary constructs with less breadth but more relevance to classroom motivation. We then turn to six contemporary motivation constructs concerned with achievement strivings. Three constructs generally address concerns about ability or its absence: self-worth, self-efficacy, and helplessness beliefs. As will be seen, these three constructs are, in part, the legacy of expectancy-value theories. The remaining three constructs we examine relate to the cognitive and affective consequences of different achievement goals. Under this broad rubric we review research on task versus ego involvement, intrinsic versus extrinsic incentives, and cooperative versus competitive goal structures. We conclude the chapter with a discussion of general issues in the study of motivation that we consider important for future research.

## GENERAL THEORIES OF MOTIVATION

The five general theories reviewed in this section are described in Table 4–2. We will return to a discussion of the contrasting features of these theories in the section summary. For now, we suggest that the reader refer to Table 4–2 as each theory is presented.

### Hull's Drive Theory

In the early 1990s, there was ferment about the general laws of mechanics, the notion that energy could be transformed in a myriad of ways. It was in this atmosphere that Clark Hull, an early robotic engineer, formulated his general theory of motivation and linked it with experimental psychology. It is uncertain whether Hull should be credited with the formulation of the first experimentally guided motivational theory, for both Kurt Lewin (discussed next in this chapter) and Edward Tolman (whose theory is not examined) were developing their conceptions at about the same time as Hull. But there is no doubt that Hull was the first dominant motivational theorist in America.

Hullian theory was partly derived from the laws of learning. To explain learning, Hull accepted the well-known Law of Effect proposed by Thorndike (1911). That law states that when a stimulus-response bond is followed by a satisfying state of affairs, the strength of the bond increases. Conversely, when a stimulus-response bond is followed by an annoying state of affairs, the strength of the bond is weakened. Hull accepted that reinforcement provided the necessary grounding for the establishment of stimulus-response connections, which he labeled *habits*.

***The Drive Concept.*** Prior to Hull's work, motivational concepts were used to explain a different set of phenomena than those focused on by learning theorists. The behaviors set aside for motivation were grouped under the term "instinctive," the so-called inner urges that were striving for expression. However, in the face of severe criticism, such as lack of agreement on how many instincts there were and how they could be identified, the use of instinct as an explanatory principle began to wane. It often happens in science, however, that a theory or construct does not die—it is replaced. The concept of instinct was replaced by that of drive.

Hull (1943) suggested that it was a physiological deficit, or a need, and not an instinct, that instigated the organism to undertake behaviors that then resulted in the offset of the need. Stimulus-response linkages (habits) could provide the direction but not the energy required for action. According to Hull, for prior associations to be displayed, there had to be some unsatisfied need that in turn produced a drive to action. Drive, then, resulted from physiological disequilibrium and instigated behaviors that returned the organism to a state of equilibrium. Furthermore, drive was considered to be a nondirective energizer of behavior—any extant need would evoke whatever associative linkage was highest in the organism's habit structure.

In addition, Hull specified a mathematical relation between the drive (energy) and habit (direction) determinants of behavior such that

$$Behavior = Drive \times Habit$$

Because the relationship is multiplicative, if there was no deprivation (e.g., drive = 0), the organism would not act at all, no matter how strong the habit. Thus, passivity indicated a satisfied

TABLE 4–2. Characteristics of the Theories of Motivation

| | Motivation Theory | | | | |
|---|---|---|---|---|---|
| | Drive: Hull | Field: Lewin | Achievement: Atkinson | Social Learning: Rotter | Attribution: Heider, Kelley, Weiner |
| 20-year time span | 1940–60 | 1940–60 | 1960–80 | 1960–90 | 1970–90 |
| Homeostasis | Yes | Yes | No | No | No |
| Mathematical model | Yes | Yes | Yes | Yes | No |
| Individual Difference | Anxiety | None | Need achievement | Locus of control | None |
| Focus and range | Food and water deprivation; learning | Task recall; conflict; aspiration level | Task choice | Expectancy in skill vs. chance situations | Achievement, affect, helping |

organism. If the relation between drive and habit were additive, then, if there were many reinforcements for behavior (strong habit), that behavior would be undertaken even in the absence of need. The behavior then would not be functional, which was a basic tenet of motivational approaches in Hull's era.

Hull's formulation generated a vast amount of research in such areas as conflict, frustration, fear, social facilitation, and cognitive dissonance (see reviews in Atkinson, 1964; Bolles, 1967; Cofer & Appley, 1964; Weiner, 1992). Many of the empirical investigations were undertaken to support one or more of the following assertions:

1. Drive energizes behavior. This was documented by demonstrating that without the presence of needs, behavior would not be instigated.
2. Drive and habit relate multiplicatively. This was documented by manipulating both variables and showing their interactive effect on performance.
3. Drive is a pooled energy source. This was examined by varying two needs simultaneously and showing that they both activated the same response.

*Anxiety and Learning.* Among the most novel and influential aspects of research guided by drive theory were studies that related anxiety level to learning, a topic of particular relevance to educational psychologists. Spence (1958) and his colleagues contended that scores on an anxiety scale could be used to infer drive level, for anxiety, like need, was considered an aversive stimulus. These researchers then applied the drive × habit conception to the learning of simple and complex verbal tasks. A simple task is one in which the correct response is dominant in the person's response hierarchy. An example would be a paired associates task where *day* is the correct response to the stimulus word *night.* Although individuals have been exposed to many associations involving the word *day,* the association with *night* has probably occurred more often and thus has the greatest habit strength. According to Spence, anxiety energizes the correct response to a greater extent than it evokes the incorrect response, and therefore increases the speed of learning. Thus, an increase in the level of drive (anxiety) should result in faster learning and fewer errors.

With complex tasks, on the other hand, drive theorists hypothesized that the heightening of drive would interfere with performance. A complex task is one in which there are many

competing response tendencies, all of which are relatively weak in habit strength. The effect of high anxiety as an energizer is to increase the strength of many incorrect tendencies, thereby interfering with the correct response tendency. An interaction is therefore predicted between drive level and performance on easy and complex tasks. Given an easy task, individuals high in anxiety (drive) would be expected to perform better than those low in anxiety. Given a difficult task, in contrast, those high in anxiety would be expected to perform worse.

Empirical studies conducted by Spence and his colleagues generally supported the interaction predicted by drive theory (see Spence, 1958). Thus, general laws of motivation based initially on animal research were successfully applied to predict the speed of human learning. This was indeed an impressive accomplishment.

The main contribution of drive theory was the systematic and precise exploration of motivated behavior from a mechanistic perspective. Drive theorists provided an exemplar for the scientific and experimental study of motivation. They carefully identified the determinants of behavior, specified their relations, created a mathematical model, and deduced predictions from that model that were tested in carefully controlled laboratory settings. This theory did not generate suggestions to increase classroom performance, but instead addressed the fundamental laws of motivation.

## Lewin's Field Theory

Like Hull's drive conception, Kurt Lewin's field theory flourished during the 25-year period between 1935 and 1960. Lewin was guided by basic principles of Gestalt psychology. The Gestaltists argued that a behavioral "field," like physical and perceptual fields, would "seek" an arrangement of simplicity and "goodness," as illustrated in the symmetrical shape assumed by a drop of oil in water, the perception of a circle when such a shape is not fully closed, and the perception of faces as symmetrical when, in fact, they are not. The Gestaltists observed that if a point of light was presented in a dark context, the eye would be drawn to it. A tension would arise in the visual field, and some action would be taken to reduce this tension. Kurt Koffka (1935), a leading Gestalt psychologist, stated: "Theoretically, there is no difference between eye movements and such movements of the whole body as are executed in order, say, to quench one's thirst" (p. 626). A person attaining a goal corresponds to a simple figure, the Gestaltists suggested.

The language of Gestalt psychology, developed primarily to account for perceptual phenomena, was adopted by Lewin for the interpretation of motivated behavior. Known as field theory, Lewin's basic theoretical statement held that behavior is determined by both the person (P) and the environment (E):

$$\text{Behavior} = f(\text{P, E})$$

According to Lewin, the motivational force on the person to reach an environmental goal is determined by three factors: tension ($t$), or the magnitude of a need; valence ($G$), or the properties of the goal object; and the psychological distance of the person from the goal (represented by the letter $e$). Specifically,

$$\text{Force} = f(t, G)/e$$

Each of these factors and their interrelations have specific meanings in Lewinian terms. When a person experiences a need, desire, or intent, he or she is in a state of tension ($t$). For example, hunger produces a state of tension in the individual, who is then directed toward the goal of eating. Once the goal is attained, tension is eliminated. But for Lewin, needs are not related only to bodily functions and survival. The intent to complete a task or to solve a problem produces similar states of tension. Goals ($G$) become attractive, that is, acquire positive valence, to the extent that they can satisfy needs. For example, if one is hungry, the sight of a sumptuous meal acquires positive valence, as does locating a misplaced book if one's need is to find this lost object. Note also that in Lewin's formula, the psychological distance of the person from the goal ($e$) is inversely related to the magnitude of motivation. Thus, the closer one is to the goal (i.e., $e$ approaches 0), the greater is the motivational force. This Lewinian principle is illustrated, for example, by the tired distance runner who sprints when the finish line is in sight, or by the reader who is totally engrossed in the final chapter of an engaging novel.

Few theoretical approaches have been as fruitful as Lewinian theory. Among the diverse motivational phenomena examined are frustration (which was shown to result in regressive behavior); substitution (the replacing of one goal with another when the initially desired goal could not be attained); and level of aspiration (which tends to increase after success and decrease after failure). Here we focus on two motivational phenomena that illustrate the application of Lewinian principles: conflict and task recall.

*Conflict.* Imagine a situation in which a student receives an academic prize in the form of a monetary award. The rules stipulate that the prize can be either a $10,000 cash stipend or applied toward payment of tuition and fees for the next academic year. The student must decide how she wants the award allocated. In Lewinian terms, this represents an approach-approach conflict: The person must choose between two attractive (positively valenced) goals. Lewin regards such conflicts as relatively unstable and easily resolvable. For example, a simple change in cognition (e.g., "I don't want to have to worry about tuition next year") can alter the relative attractiveness of the two goals, thus motivating the individual to move toward the more attractive alternative.

In contrast, consider a situation in which a child is told by his teacher that he must remain in the classroom either during recess or immediately after lunch as punishment for classroom misbehavior. This depicts an avoidance-avoidance conflict inasmuch as the choices are between two negatively valenced alternatives. Lewin argued that avoidance-avoidance conflicts are less easily resolvable than approach-approach conflicts. As one approaches one of the aversive alternatives, the tendency to avoid that goal becomes even stronger. Thus the individual will vacillate between the two undesirable alternatives. Lewin's hypotheses have been supported in experimental studies documenting longer response latencies (implying more conflict) for avoidance-avoidance than for approach-approach hypothetical conflicts.

*Task Recall.* Lewin's student, Bluma Zeigarnik (1927), documented that people are more likely to remember tasks that they are not allowed to complete than those that are completed. Labeled the Zeigarnik effect, the greater recall of unfinished tasks derives from Lewin's conception of tension. The person's desire to reach a goal such as solving a set of anagrams corresponds to a state of tension. This tension leads not only to actual movement toward the goal, but also to thoughts about that goal. If the goal is not reached—for example, if the task is interrupted—the tension persists, as do thoughts about the goal. Hence, there is greater recall of unfinished than finished tasks. Although subsequent experimental studies called into question the robustness of the Zeigarnik effect (see Weiner, 1972), the predictions are unique to Lewin's formulation and are not readily explainable within other motivational frameworks.

*Summary.* Lewinians conceptualized motivation in terms of tensions that move the individual toward goals of varying psychological distance. Hullians conceptualized the same phenomena in terms of drive level and habit strength. Even though their motivational formulas are different, both Lewin and Hull reached similar conclusions about what determines motivated behavior: needs of the person (drive or tension), properties of the goal object (incentives), and a directional variable (habit or psychological distance). Further, both advocated that the goal of motivational theory is to identify the determinants of behavior and specify their mathematical relationships. Unlike drive theorists, however, Lewinians were concerned almost exclusively with complex human behavior as opposed to the behavior of nonhuman organisms. In addition, whereas drive theorists excelled in demonstrating how motivational theorists ought to function as experimenters, conducting well-controlled laboratory investigations, the main contribution of the field theorists was in pointing out the broader goals of a theory of motivation, using whatever experimental methods were available. Few conceptions have been able to incorporate the breadth of motivational phenomena addressed by field theory.

## Expectancy-Value Theories

Studies conducted by Tolman and his colleagues during the 1930s (see Tolman, 1932) suggested that animals learn expectancies—what will follow if and when a particular response is made—rather than specific habits. In motivational theories, the concept of expectancy slowly began to replace the concept of habit in descriptions of the learning process, a change consistent with the more general cognitive emphasis being exhibited by learning theorists. The concept of drive also came under increasing scrutiny. As the belief that organisms are always active gained acceptance, the field of motivation shifted from the study of what turns organisms "on" or "off" to an interest in the direction of behavior, or what choices are made. This shift led to increased attention being paid to incentives, as well as to expectancies, which Tolman had documented as necessary for performance.

The growing recognition of expectancies and incentives as determinants of motivation resulted in what is known as expectancy-value theory. The basic assumptions of expectancy-value theory are in accord with commonsense thinking about motivated behavior: What behavior is undertaken depends on the perceived likelihood that the behavior will lead to the goal, and on the subjective value of that goal. Furthermore, it is assumed that at any given moment individuals are faced with an array of alternative goals, each of which has its own subjective likelihood of attainment and assigned value. The expectancies and values are combined to yield a motivational tendency; the strongest motivational value "wins," that is, is expressed in action.

Expectancy-value theory was adopted by John Atkinson and Julian Rotter, the next two theorists to be examined. Their theories dominated the study of motivation for nearly 20 years, from the early 1960s up to about 1980.

***Atkinson's Theory of Achievement Motivation.*** Like Hull and Lewin, Atkinson (1957, 1964) attempted to isolate the determinants of behavior and then to specify the mathematical relations between the components of his theory. However, Atkinson diverged from Hull and Lewin in concentrating on individual differences in achievement motivation.

In its simplest form, Atkinson's theory states that the tendency to approach an achievement-related goal ($T_s$) is a product of three factors: the need for achievement or the motive for success ($M_s$), the probability that one will be successful at the task ($P_s$), and the incentive value of success ($I_s$). These components were presumed to be multiplicatively related:

$$T_s = M_s \times P_s \times I_s$$

In this equation, $M_s$ represents the achievement motive, a relatively stable or enduring disposition to strive for success. $M_s$ was presumed to be learned early in life and to be shaped by particular childrearing practices. The strength of the achievement motive typically has been measured using projective techniques such as the Thematic Apperception Test (TAT). Subjects write imaginative stories to pictorial stimuli, and these verbal protocols are then scored for their amount of achievement imagery.

$P_s$, or the probability of success, refers to a cognitive expectancy or the anticipation that an instrumental action will lead to the goal. Operationally, this expectancy variable has usually been defined in terms of the normative difficulty of a task. For example, research participants might be told: "Our norms indicate that _____ percent of the students your age and ability level are able to solve these puzzles" (Feather, 1961). The value of $P_s$ thus ranges from 0 to 1, where lower percentages of successful problem solvers depict normatively more difficult

tasks. Finally, the third determinant of motivated behavior, $I_s$, is the incentive value of success. Atkinson postulated that $I_s$ is inversely related to $P_s$: $I_s = 1 - P_s$. This was because the incentive value of success was presumed to be an affect labeled "pride in accomplishment." It was reasoned that greater pride is experienced following success at a difficult task (low $P_s$) than following success at an easy task (high $P_s$); hence, probability and incentive were specified to be negatively related.

This presumption, and the multiplicative relations specified in the model, had surprising and far-reaching motivational consequences. First, motivation was presumed to vary systematically as a function of $P_s$ at the task, with motivation maximum at tasks of intermediate difficulty (i.e., $P_s = 0.50$). Furthermore, the strength of motivation decreased symmetrically as $P_s$ increased or decreased from the level of intermediate difficulty. In addition, Atkinson (1957) further predicted that the greater one's desire to succeed (i.e., the higher the value of $M_s$), the more attracted that individual would be to tasks of intermediate difficulty. Conversely, the less a person cared about achievement success (i.e., the lower the value of $M_s$), the more likely that person would be to select a very easy or very difficult task. These derivations resulted in Atkinson's theory being considered a theory of achievement-related risk-taking.

This conception had many implications for classroom motivation. In one nonobvious conclusion, Atkinson (1964) reasoned that ability grouping (where all performers were of equal ability and thus $P_s$ approached 0.50), would be most beneficial to students high in achievement needs. He suggested creating environments of intermediate difficulty for those motivated by achievement desires. These types of prediction, and a desire to examine the dynamics of behavior among those considered to be high or low in achievement needs, were among the reasons why this conception was so dominant in the field of motivation. As indicated earlier, Atkinson remained committed to the development of a general theory of motivation; however, he confined his empirical interests to the study of achievement motivation, and thus the theory was particularly influential among educational psychologists.

***Rotter's Social Learning Theory.*** Julian Rotter's social learning theory also was concerned with the choices that individuals make when confronted with a number of possible alternative ways of behaving. To explain choice, or the direction of behavior, Rotter (1954) attempted to integrate two major approaches in American psychology: the stimulus-response or reinforcement position, as exemplified primarily by Skinner and, to a lesser extent, by Hull, and the cognitive or field position advocated by Tolman, Lewin, and subsequently by Atkinson.

The motivational model formulated by Rotter is entirely consistent with the general expectancy-value perspective. According to Rotter, motivation is a function of expectancy (E) and reinforcement value (RV):

$$\text{Behavior} = f(\text{E, RV})$$

That is, we engage in actions with the highest expectancy of bringing the most rewarding goal. But how these factors were mathematically related (e.g., multiplicatively, additively) remained unspecified.

In Rotter's terms, reinforcement value (RV) referred to "the degree of preference for any reinforcement . . . if the possibility of their occurring were all equal" (Rotter, 1954, p. 107). Thus, reinforcement value was a relative or comparative term. This value component in the model was never greatly elaborated, inasmuch as Rotter devoted most of his attention to the expectancy variable and its determinants.

According to Rotter, expectancies for success were primarily determined by one's past history in the specific situation under consideration as well as by experiences in similar circumstances. Thus, for example, a person's beliefs about succeeding on a chemistry quiz would be influenced not only by prior experiences on chemistry examinations, but also by general success and failure on school tests (or what are termed generalized expectancies). The more novel a situation, the greater the importance of generalized expectancies in determining immediate beliefs. Hence, if a person had never taken a chemistry quiz before, that person's expectancy of success would be determined primarily by other school-related experiences.

In addition to these two factors, expectancy was determined by the perception of the characteristics of the task. Expectancies of success in skill-related situations were more differentially influenced by prior success and failure than were expectancies of success in chance-related contexts. In skill-determined tasks, where outcomes are determined by one's own abilities and effort, expectancies increase after success and decrease after failure. But in chance-determined tasks, such as the flip of a coin or the throw of a die, probabilities remain relatively unchanged following success or failure.

This analysis led Rotter (1966) to examine individual differences in more generalized perceptions of situations as skill versus chance-determined and to his well-known distinction between internal versus external control of reinforcement. Beliefs concerning personal responsibility for a reward have been postulated to constitute a personality dimension. At one end of this dimension is the person with an internal locus of control—the individual who thinks of herself as completely responsible for her behavior and reinforcements. At the other extreme is the person with an external locus of control—the individual who sees powerful others, luck, or circumstances beyond his or her control as responsible for behavior and reinforcements. Interpretations of Rotter's conception have tended to assume implicitly that to have an internal locus of control (i.e., to perceive outcomes as skill-determined) is the more adaptive motivational state. Internality on locus of control should therefore be positively related to any number of desirable outcomes, including high achievement strivings. Although empirical studies document positive associations between internal locus of control and academic achievement, the strength of this linkage is relatively weak (Findley & Cooper, 1983).

Individual differences in locus of control have been the subject of hundreds of research investigations. In the 1960s and 1970s the construct basically took on a life of its own that was far removed from its expectancy-value roots. Nonetheless, Rotter made many contributions to motivation theory. Among the significant accomplishments of this approach was that social learning theorists, by initiating the study of personal control, returned to a major motivational issue derived from philosophy—free will and its psychological consequences. Further, inasmuch as expectancy of success is a key determinant of classroom motivation and performance, the social learning theorists focused on a variable of central interest to educational

psychologists. Finally, with its emphasis on locus of control, social learning theory provided a foundation for an attributional analysis of perceived causality.

## Attribution Theory

Attribution theory has its roots in the writings of Fritz Heider (1958) and the subsequent contributions of Harold Kelley (1967, 1971) and Bernard Weiner (1985, 1986). Attribution theorists construe humans as scientists seeking to understand the world around them and using naive statistical techniques, including principles of covariation, to reach causal conclusions. As applied to motivation, attribution theory falls under the broad rubric of expectancy-value approaches. However, rather than specifying mathematical relations between components, this theory presumes that motivation is best represented as a temporal process initiated with an event and ending with some behavior or behavioral intention.

In the achievement domain, where attribution theory has been most thoroughly examined, it has been documented that causal search is undertaken to determine the causes of success and failure. This search is most likely to be initiated when unexpected and important events end in failure, such as a low grade given to a good student. Among the most prevalent inferred causes of success and failure are ability, effort, task ease or difficulty, luck, mood, and help or hindrance from others. These inferences are in part based on informational variables, including past performance and social norms. Hence, for example, if one fails an examination and has failed frequently in the past, while others are successful on this examination, then the current failure is likely to be ascribed to lack of ability (see Kelley, 1967).

The motivational consequences of causal ascriptions have been related to the underlying properties of phenomenal causality, or the characteristics that all causes share in varying degrees. Three dimensions of causality have been identified: locus, stability, and controllability (see Weiner, 1986). Locus refers to the location of a cause as internal or external to the actor; stability connotes the invariance of a cause over time; and controllability concerns the extent to which the cause is subject to volitional alteration. Hence, for example, aptitude is considered internal to the actor, stable over time, and uncontrollable, whereas chance or luck typically is conceived as external to the actor, variable, and also uncontrollable.

The locus dimension of causality determines whether pride and self-esteem are altered following success or failure. Internal attributions result in enhanced self-esteem after success and decreased self-esteem after failure, whereas this is not true given external causes of success and failure. Pride and self-esteem have been documented to promote achievement strivings; internal ascriptions therefore are positive motivators following goal attainment.

The stability dimension of causality influences subjective expectancy of success. If a positive outcome is ascribed to a stable cause, such as aptitude, then future success will be anticipated. In a similar manner, negative outcomes attributed to stable causes lead to inferences that future success is unlikely. Hence, persistence in the face of failure is augmented when attributions are made to unstable causes such as insufficient effort and bad luck (see review in Weiner, 1986). Guided by this linkage, achievement change programs have been developed that attempt to induce individuals to ascribe failure to lack of effort (an unstable cause) rather than to low ability (a stable cause). Many successful programs have been described in which retrained subjects have reported greater attributions to lack of effort following failure as well as increments in achievement strivings (see Forsterling, 1985).

Finally, the controllability dimension of causality is related to a number of affects with motivational implications, including anger, guilt, pity, and shame. Specifically, if one is prevented from success by factors that others could have controlled (e.g., noise, bias), then anger is experienced; guilt is felt when one fails or breaks a social contract because of internally controllable causes, such as lack of effort or negligence; pity and sympathy are expressed toward others who do not attain their goals because of uncontrollable causes, including lack of ability or a physical handicap; and shame (humiliation, embarrassment) is a dominant reaction when one fails because of internally uncontrollable causes such as low ability (see reviews in Graham, 1991; Weiner, 1986).

These emotional reactions also can serve as attributional cues. For example, if a teacher expresses pity and sympathy following a pupil's failure, that student tends to make low ability attributions for his or her failure (Graham, 1984). Hence, pity undermines beliefs about ability. Conversely, anger tends to promote the belief by the recipient of this emotional message that he or she has not tried hard enough (see Graham, 1990).

The various affective experiences also serve as goads, that is, they provide "instructions" to undertake particular activities. Pity toward others gives rise to helping and reward, whereas anger generates neglect and perhaps punishment when the other is in need. Thus, shy pupils in the classroom tend to elicit more help from the teacher than aggressive or hyperactive children, in part because shyness is perceived as less subject to volitional change than is aggressiveness (Brophy & Rohrkemper, 1981). In addition, students who do not try in the classroom are reacted to with anger by their teachers and are evaluated negatively, with maximum punishment dispensed to students who have ability but do not exert effort and fail. Conversely, pupils low in ability who succeed because of extra exertion receive the most positive evaluations from others. Guilt and shame, like pity and anger, also have motivational effects. Guilt tends to promote goal-directed activity, whereas shame gives rise to task withdrawal and is a motivational inhibitor.

To illustrate how principles from attribution theory relate to achievement strivings, consider the following two achievement scenarios with quite different consequences, followed by their attributional interpretations:

1. Jane fails her math examination and then seeks tutoring and increases her study time.
2. Susan fails her math examination and decides to drop out of school.

In the first scenario, where following failure the student studies harder, a negative outcome is experienced. Negative outcomes give rise to a search to understand why the goal was not attained. Let us assume that Jane has performed well in the past but on this particular test she performs poorly while others do well. Because the outcome is at variance with social norms,

Jane attributes the failure to herself. And because the outcome is also at variance with her past behavior, the attribution is to an unstable factor—lack of adequate preparation and study time. As previously stated, these causes are perceived as internal and unstable, and also as controllable. Because the causes are unstable, Jane maintains a reasonable expectation of success in the future and is hopeful. Because the causes are controllable by Jane, she experiences guilt, while her teacher and parents are angry and criticize her. High expectations of future success, along with hopefulness and guilt, enable her to overcome her feelings of sadness and weakened self-esteem. These thoughts and affects result in renewed goal strivings and an increase in motivation to perform better on the next examination.

In the second scenario, Susan also is described as failing her examination, but instead of resolving to study harder she drops out. This failure also elicits causal search. Let us assume that Susan has in the past failed examinations on which others did well. Hence, Susan ascribes failure to herself. She attributes her poor performance to low ability, which is internal, stable, and uncontrollable. Because the cause is internal, Susan's self-esteem is lowered; because the cause is stable, Susan anticipates future failure and feels helpless; and because the cause is uncontrollable, Susan feels ashamed and humiliated. In addition, her parents and teacher feel sorry for her and communicate this without criticism, furthering her disbelief in her own competence. Thus, in this achievement situation, Susan has a low expectation of future success and is feeling sad. She also feels low in self-worth, hopeless, and ashamed. Such maladaptive thoughts and feelings decrease achievement strivings and result in withdrawal from the setting.

In sum, attribution theorists contend that persons are naive scientists, trying (sometimes biasedly) to understand the causal structure of the world. The causal decisions reached, through the mediational role of their underlying properties, influence expectancy and affect. These, in turn, influence a variety of motivational variables. Among the main contributions of this approach has been recognition of an increasing number of cognitive determinants of action, as well as specifying the important role of emotion in motivation. The theory therefore has greatly expanded the postulated processes that mediate between the onset of a stimulus and the behavioral response to that stimulus.

## Summary

In this section we have attempted to provide an overview of five major theories of motivation and place them within their historical context. To conclude this review, Table 4–2 compares and contrasts the theories along a number of dimensions.

Table 4–2 first lists the individuals most closely associated with each theory and the 20-year time span during which the major contributions of a theory were made. As indicated both in the table and in the earlier discussion of historical trends, the era of the "grand" theories of Hull, Lewin, and Atkinson has long since passed, and interest in Rotter's social learning theory has clearly waned. Research on attribution theory and its application to achievement concerns has continued to flourish, and this appears to be the dominant contemporary theory of motivation.

The earlier theories of Hull and Lewin postulated that the basic mechanism of motivation is homeostasis—the tendency to seek a balanced state where forces are in equilibrium and there are no extant needs. This principle has lost favor and is not represented in either the expectancy-value theories of Atkinson and Rotter or contemporary attribution theory. Complex human motivations, such as the desire to attain success, win friends, gain power, or help others, fall beyond the range of convenience of homeostatic explanations.

Four of the five theories agree that the basic principle or "spring" of action is hedonism; that is, individuals are motivated to maximize pleasures and minimize pains. Only attribution theory adheres to the principle of mastery, which assumes that knowing and understanding are important in promoting action. At times, truth is sought (e.g., "Why did I fail the exam?"), even though that knowledge might cause great displeasure.

One of the hallmarks of a good theory of motivation is that it consists of a set of principles that are related to one another in a clearly specified manner. Four of the five theories attempted to specify these relations in mathematical or quasi-mathematical models. The theories and their constructs—$D \times H$ (Hull), $t$, $G/e$ (Lewin), $M_s \times P_s \times I_s$ (Atkinson), E & RV (Rotter)—are alike in that each specifies a person variable (a temporary need state or trait), an environmental variable (incentive or value), and a learning component (habit, psychological distance, or expectancy) as the determinants of behavior. Attribution theory has not undertaken this kind of mathematical specification, although clearly it, too, comprises sets of interrelated constructs.

Table 4–2 further shows that three of the conceptions (Hull's drive theory, Atkinson's achievement theory, Rotter's social learning theory) incorporate individual differences as determinants of motivation. Atkinson and Rotter in particular greatly relied on the respective measurement of the achievement motive and locus of control. Problems associated with the measurement of motivational traits as well as their cross-situational generality no doubt contributed to the relative demise of these two theories, a point we return to later.

Finally, Table 4–2 distinguishes the five theories according to their focus, or what the theory has strived to predict; and their range, or what broader facets of motivated behavior are amenable to explanation. Each theory can explain some phenomena with some degree of insight and accuracy, while other phenomena are beyond its range of convenience. For example, Hullian drive theory cannot explain expectancy shifts at skill and chance tasks any more than social learning theory can account for the energizing effects of hunger or anxiety. Similarly, Atkinson's theory is most relevant to choice among tasks that differ in perceived difficulty, but it cannot be enlisted to explain recall of interrupted tasks (the purview of Lewinian field theory), and attribution theory is most capable of accounting for the relations between emotions and subsequent achievement strivings. In sum, there may not be a single encompassing principle that transcends all of the theories of motivation presented here. Rather, each has its own legacy that influenced subsequent developments in the field, and each has contributed to our understanding of the determinants of motivation in its own unique way.

## CONTEMPORARY MOTIVATION CONSTRUCTS RELATED TO ACHIEVEMENT STRIVINGS

In this section we turn from general theories and broad applications to the more specific motivation constructs pertinent to achievement strivings. Here the reader may find more overlap with the issues raised in Stipek's chapter, because the six constructs described here have been popular in educational psychology research. All have been studied with school-aged children, and all have clear implications for classroom motivation. Table 4–3 provides an overview of the defining features of each construct. For clarity of presentation, we offer this summary information, and suggest that the reader refer to the table as each topic is considered.

### Constructs Concerned With Ability Self-Perception

If there is one principle consistently agreed upon in contemporary motivation research, that principle is that self-perception of low ability and self-statements such as "I cannot" have severely debilitating consequences. Each of the following three contemporary constructs offers a particular perspective on the topic of self-perceived ability. To be consistent with the current motivation literature, we refer to them as theories, although they do not fit our working definition of a theory as a set of interrelated principles applicable across broad motivational domains. Furthermore, because all these approaches to some degree employ concepts derived from the various theories of motivation reviewed earlier, we contrast them where appropriate with the principles and guiding assumptions of those theories.

*Self-Worth Theory.* Ability self-perception is the central construct in self-worth theory as articulated by Covington, inasmuch as people are believed to be primarily motivated by the need to perceive themselves as competent (Covington, 1992; Covington & Beery, 1976). Simply put, Covington proposed that to be worthy is to be able. Because society places such high value on one's ability to achieve, self-worth theorists argue that students of all ages go to great lengths to protect a sense of their own ability.

Covington and his colleagues have documented a number of self-protective strategies that students use to maintain positive academic self-regard. Most of these tactics are attributional in nature. Covington (1984) stated that "as a group these strategies seek to shift the personal causes of failure away from the internal attribution of ability and toward external factors beyond the individual's control or responsibility" (p. 83). The strategies include (a) setting unrealistically high goals, so that failure can be attributed to task difficulty rather than to lack of ability; (b) using self-handicapping techniques, such as procrastinating or not studying at all; and (c) excuse-giving, that is, attributing failure to uncontrollable factors such as poor teaching or illness. For example, Covington and Omelich (1979) documented that college students reported they would feel the least shame for test failure that they could attribute to lack of effort (which does not then implicate ability) along with the availability of an excuse for not trying. The greatest reported shame, in contrast, occurred under conditions of high effort accompanied by test failure (which implicates low ability).

Although many of the analyses and empirical findings of self-worth theory derive from attribution principles, there are also fundamental differences between the two conceptions. Whereas self-worth theory conceives ability attributions as the prime determinant of self-esteem, attribution theory employs

TABLE 4–3. Characteristics of Six Contemporary Motivation Constructs

| | | | Characteristic | | |
|---|---|---|---|---|---|
| Construct | Theorist(s) | Basic Assumptions | Core Experimental Manipulations or Independent Variables | Key Empirical Findings | Theoretical Overlap[a] |
| Self-worth | Covington (1984, 1992) | Self-acceptance (worth) is achieved in school with high ability | Causes of success and failure | Students use excuses, self-handicapping, and false effort to protect the perception of high ability | |
| Self-efficacy | Bandura (1991) Schunk (1989, 1991) | Perceptions that one "can" are among the main determinants of motivation and performance | Self-perception of "can" by means of specific learning experiences and modeling | Inductions of the belief that "I can" through modeling, persuasion, etc., enhances performance | |
| Learned helplessness | Seligman (1975) Dweck & Leggett (1988) | Perceptions that one "cannot" lead to motivational, cognitive, and affective deficits | Noncontingent failure; individual differences, assessment of causal beliefs | The belief that "I cannot" is associated with giving up in the face of failure and depression | Task involvement = Mastery = Intrinsic motivation |
| | | | | Children can be distinguished as "mastery-oriented" or "helpless" | |
| Task vs. ego involvement | Nicholls (1978, 1984) | Disparate learning environments elicit a focus on either the task or on comparing oneself to others | Task instructions | Task involvement leads to greater persistence and more positive affect than ego involvement | Ego involvement = Performance goals = Competitive structure |
| Intrinsic vs. extrinsic motivation | Lepper et al (1973) Deci & Ryan (1985) | People have innate tendency to strive for self-determination and competence | Reward contingencies; task instructions | Rewards perceived as controlling (rather than informational) decrease intrinsic motivation | |
| Cooperative vs. competitive goals | Deutsch, (1949a,b) Ames (1984) | Different incentive or goals structures elicit distinct motivational orientations | Interpersonal structure of task performance and evaluation | Cooperative goals result in higher performance and more accurate self-perception | |

[a]Equals sign connotes similarity between constructs.

a higher order theoretical construct—the causal dimension of locus—to account for increments and decrements in self-esteem. As the dominant internal attributions for success and failure, both ability and effort are important antecedents of esteem-related affect. At times, therefore, high effort even with low ability may result in enhanced self-worth, as when individuals feel that they have fulfilled their potential through hard work (Brown & Weiner, 1984). Self-worth theorists take a more extreme position than do attribution theorists in their belief that the influence of perceived effort expenditure on positive self-regard is entirely mediated by its effect on ability self-perception.

At a more general level, self-worth and attributional formulations also take disparate theoretical positions on what constitutes the basic motivator or "spring of action." With its emphasis on maintenance and protection of high personal esteem, self-worth theory is compatible with the belief that the hedonic principle of maximizing rewards and minimizing punishments is the main determinant of behavior. It is also consistent with a line of thinking and research in motivational psychology that holds that people are primarily guided by self-enhancement motives. In other words, individuals seek information that has positive implications for self-esteem and avoid information that

has negative implications (see, for example, Strube & Roemmele, 1985). Attribution theory, on the other hand, is guided by the belief that people are motivated by the need for mastery, or accurate self-assessment, even when such knowledge may have negative implications for self-esteem. Underlying this position is the assumption that a realistic appraisal of one's abilities (both high and low) leads to adaptive functioning. This remains a complex theoretical issue, and there is ongoing debate in the psychological literature as to whether individuals are best served by accurate and realistic beliefs about themselves or by illusory and self-protective beliefs (see Taylor & Brown, 1988).

*Self-Efficacy.* Self-efficacy is an ability construct, popularized by Bandura (1977, 1986, 1989), that refers to individuals' beliefs about their capabilities to perform well. When confronted with a challenging task, a person would be enlisting an efficacy belief if she asked herself, "Am I able to do it?" or "Do I have the requisite skills to master this task?" Bandura (1989) underscored the motivational role of self-efficacy when he stated that "people's self-efficacy beliefs determine their level of motivation, as reflected in how much effort they will exert in an endeavor and how long they will persevere in the face of obstacles. The stronger the belief in their capabilities, the greater and more persistent are their efforts" (p. 1176). Band-ura's claims are supported by a large empirical literature documenting the influence of efficacy beliefs not only on achievement behavior, but also on such health-related concerns as coping and stress, anxiety, pain tolerance, and the management of phobias (Bandura, 1986). This broad application across many domains of behavior is one of the strengths of the self-efficacy construct and probably the best explanation for its enormous popularity in contemporary motivation research.

Schunk (1991) has provided the most up-to-date empirical review of the relations between efficacy self-percepts and achievement strivings. In a typical experiment with children (e.g., Bandura & Schunk, 1981), a subject might be shown a series of arithmetic problems and asked to estimate on a 100-point scale the likelihood that he or she would be able to solve each problem. Subjects might also be required to indicate how certain they are about their estimates. Both of the judgments constitute measures of self-perceived efficacy. In correlational designs, a self-efficacy variable often is created by combining items from more general scales that elicit extent of agreement with such statements as "I know that I will be able to learn the material from this class" and "I expect to do well in this class" (e.g., Pintrich & DeGroot, 1990). In research using either of these rating procedures, it has been found that high self-efficacy and improved performance result when children (a) adopt short-term over long-term goals, inasmuch as progress is easier to judge in the former case; (b) are taught to use specific learning strategies, such as outlining and summarizing, both of which increase attention to the task; and (c) receive performance-contingent rewards versus reward for merely engaging in a task, because only in the former case does reinforcement signal task mastery. All of these instructional manipulations are assumed to increase the belief that "I can do it," which then increases both effort and achievement.

Unlike ability self-ascriptions in attribution theory, which are explanations for past events, efficacy beliefs are future-oriented. They are conceptualized as expectations for personal mastery of subsequent achievement tasks. As such, self-perceived efficacy more closely resembles the expectancy construct in attribution research. Indeed, efficacy theorists believe that causal attributions are one of the determinants of efficacy beliefs (Bandura, 1986; Schunk, 1989). However, unlike attribution theorists, who focus on perceived stability of causes as a (the) major antecedent of expectancy, efficacy theorists have articulated a much more extensive set of antecedents, including prior accomplishments, modeling, persuasion from others, and emotional arousal. For example, physiological symptoms signaling anxiety, such as rapid heart rate or sweaty palms, might function as cues to the individual that she or he is not likely to be successful at a particular task.

Less clear, however, are the theoretical distinctions between efficacy beliefs and Rotter's (1966) historically prior construct of expectancy over control of reinforcements. Recall that Rotter labeled the belief that outcomes are contingent on one's own behavior or characteristics as internal locus of control. In his more recent theorizing, Bandura (1989) described self-efficacy as "people's beliefs about their capabilities to exercise control over events that affect their lives" (p. 1175). Some social learning theorists (e.g., Corcoran, 1991) have pointed out the theoretical overlap of this conception of self-efficacy with Rotter's con-struct. Because the same behavioral predictions can be made about the person with internal locus of control or high perceived self-efficacy, it has even been suggested that the differences between the two theories are more semantic than conceptual (Kirsch, 1985).

Bandura (1991) maintained that the conceptual and empirical nonequivalence of locus of control and self-efficacy is well supported, and the debate between the two camps remains lively. What cannot be disputed is Bandura's argument that self-efficacy has been a much more consistent predictor of behavior and behavior change than has locus of control or any of the other closely related expectancy variables. Efficacy beliefs have been related to the acquisition of new skills and to the performance of previously learned skills at a level of specificity not found in any of the other motivation conceptions that include an expectancy construct.

*Helplessness Beliefs.* Whereas efficacy self-percepts capture the lay understanding of "I can," helplessness beliefs symbolize shared agreement about the meaning of "I cannot." How people deal with the perception that there is no relation between their own behavior and their outcomes has been the cornerstone of learned helplessness theory (e.g., Seligman, 1975). According to this formulation, a state of helplessness exists when failures are perceived as insurmountable, or more technically, when noncontingent reinforcement results in a perception that events are uncontrollable. This belief often is accompanied by passivity, loss of motivation, depressed affect, and performance deterioration. Helplessness becomes a *learned* phenomenon when individuals inappropriately generalize from an experience with noncontingency in one situation to subsequent situations where control is in fact possible. A prototypical example is the successful student who unexpectedly fails despite high effort and then becomes virtually incapable of completing work that was easily mastered prior to failure.

Causal interpretations of failed events proved to be particularly important (Abramson, Seligman, & Teasdale, 1978) and learned helplessness theory now has a decidedly attributional focus. Helplessness theorists maintain that when individuals encounter failures, they ask, "Why?" Explanations for failure are then classified according to underlying causal dimensions, much as they are in contemporary attribution theory. Three dimensions are identified in the helplessness model, and each is linked to a particular psychological consequence. First, if a person explains negative outcomes with internal causes, he or she suffers greater loss in self-esteem than when the same outcome is explained by enlisting external causes. (This is similar to the locus-esteem relation in attribution theory.) Second, if people explain aversive events with stable causes, the negative consequences accruing from a state of helplessness last longer than when explanations endorse unstable causes. (This closely corresponds to the stability-expectancy linkage in attribution theory.) Third, causes perceived as global, that is, generalizable across situations and contexts, lead to more pervasive deficits than causes perceived as specific. (The inclusion of a globality dimension of causality is unique to helplessness theory.) Thus, the people most vulnerable to helplessness beliefs and their consequences are those who attribute failure to internal, stable, and global factors.

Helplessness theory has had its major impact in the clinical literature, where it is recognized as an important cognitive model of depression (Abramson, Metalsky, & Alloy, 1989). However, two lines of research that are particularly pertinent to helplessness beliefs in the achievement domain have also evolved from the theory. One research direction has been concerned with individual differences in the perceived causes of helplessness, or what has been called explanatory style. The second body of pertinent work has examined the cognitive and motivational differences between children characterized as helpless versus mastery-oriented.

*Explanatory Style.* Historically, learned helplessness theorists were experimental psychologists concerned with helplessness as a phenomenological *state* that could be manipulated and studied in the laboratory. In recent years, however, increasing attention has been given to the possibility of individual differences between people in their habitual tendency to explain outcomes in one way or another. Peterson and Seligman (1984) labeled this tendency explanatory style, but the same construct is often referred to in the literature as attributional style. Some people typically explain bad events by pointing to characteristics that are internal, stable, and global (e.g., "I'm always a failure no matter what I do"). These individuals are believed to have a *pessimistic* explanatory style. The other end of the continuum is anchored by individuals whose interpretations of bad events usually evoke momentary and specific causes (e.g., "I just happened to be in the wrong place at the wrong time"). Such individuals are characterized as having an *optimistic* explanatory style.

To measure explanatory style, individuals are presented with hypothetical negative events, such as school failure or social rejection. They report the major cause for the outcome and then rate that cause on the three dimensions of locus, stability, and globality. These dimension ratings are then summed to determine a person's attributional score. Other measurement techniques have also been developed, including content analysis of archival material such as presidential speeches, personal diaries, and the sports pages.

Proponents of explanatory style as a trait have made bold claims about its relationship to a number of life events, including academic achievement. In a review of the achievement literature, Peterson (1990) reported a number of studies indicating that a pessimistic explanatory style is positively related to poor school grades, diminished help-seeking behavior, lower aspiration levels, ill-defined achievement goals, and ineffective use of learning strategies. There is even some evidence for the long-term predictability of explanatory style. For example, Peterson, Seligman, and Vaillant (1988) documented that a pessimistic explanatory style in young adulthood is a risk factor for poor mental health in middle and later adulthood.

Does explanatory style qualify as a genuine personality trait that measures individual differences in a motivation construct? That is, should we view it as central to understanding the role of helplessness beliefs on subsequent achievement strivings, in the same way that we view individual differences in the achievement motive ($M_s$) and variations in locus of control in the respective theories of Atkinson and Rotter? Critics of explanatory style, like critics of personality approaches in general, continue to raise questions about the cross-situational generality of the trait as well as problems in its measurement.

Regarding measurement, for example, Carver (1989) takes issue with the use of a composite score summing across dimensions (locus, stability, globality) when each dimension theoretically predicts a different consequence (self-esteem, chronicity, generality). It is also clear that explanatory style as a predictor of achievement strivings can be completely overriden by strong situational factors (Anderson, 1983). It is not likely, for example, that a failing student's perceived personal competence will be greatly influenced by a causal disposition if her teacher is giving her heavy doses of feedback that implicate low ability. Anderson and his colleagues reviewed the status of explanatory style in what is perhaps the most balanced statement to date (Anderson, Jennings, & Arnoult, 1988). These authors concluded that explanatory style "does not appear to be as general or cross-situationally consistent as originally thought. Neither is it so situationally specific as to cease being a meaningful individual difference construct" (p. 989).

*Helpless Versus Mastery-Oriented Children.* Many of the affective, cognitive, and behavioral consequences of helplessness beliefs have been examined in school-aged children by Dweck and her colleagues (see review in Dweck & Leggett, 1988). These researchers have shown that children who initially are of equal ability display one of two distinct motivational patterns in response to challenging tasks where failure is possible. Some children reveal what Dweck describes as a helpless response pattern to academic challenge: They focus on personal inadequacies, often make spontaneous attributions to lack of ability, express negative affect, including boredom and anxiety, and show marked deterioration in actual performance. In other words, they display the classic symptoms associated with learned helplessness. In contrast, other children maintain what has been characterized as a mastery-oriented approach to imminent failure: These children focus on the task rather than on their abilities, often avoiding attributions altogether; they display positive affect, indicating enjoyment of challenge; and they generate solution-oriented strategies that lead to performance enhancement.

Inasmuch as helpless-response and mastery-oriented children appear not to differ in general ability, other factors must account for their disparate reactions in the face of failure. One such factor, proposed by Dweck and Leggett (1988), addresses the children's implicit theories about the meaning of ability. Helpless children are what Dweck and Leggett label *entity* theorists: They believe that ability is basically fixed and uncontrollable, as when they endorse such statements as "You can learn new things, but how smart you are stays pretty much the same" (Dweck & Leggett, 1988, p. 263). But mastery children think more like *incremental* theorists because they believe that ability is both modifiable and enhanceable. They are therefore more likely to endorse a statement such as "Smartness is something you can increase as much as you want to." It is not difficult to see how these different implicit theories can be related to the achievement-related cognitions and behaviors characteristic of mastery-oriented versus helpless-response children. Children who subscribe to the incremental conception of ability prefer challenging tasks so that they can increase their ability and also achieve greater mastery. On the other hand, students who support the entity conception of ability avoid challenge because their primary concern is with the adequacy of their presumably fixed ability.

The reader might have detected some theoretical overlap between Dweck's entity-incremental distinction and attribution theory's classification of ability along the stability dimension. In essence, individuals who subscribe to an entity view perceive ability as stable, whereas those who endorse an incremental view perceive ability as unstable. It is fully consistent with attribution theory that for some individuals ability might be perceived as unstable. However, attribution researchers have displayed inadequate attention to unstable ability, given the theory's empirical emphasis on the negative consequences of low-ability perceptions and the unquestioned acceptance of a priori classification of causes along the locus, stability, and controllability causal dimensions (see Weiner [1983] for a discussion of this issue). The entity–incremental distinction proposed by Dweck and Leggett serves as a useful reminder for motivation researchers about the importance of subjective perceptions of the meaning of ability.

*Concluding Comments About Ability Perceptions.* The belief that "I can" (self-efficacy), "I cannot" (helplessness), and preoccupation with avoiding public recognition of the latter (self-worth) all characterize contemporary motivation research on self-perceived ability. These topics reflect what is probably the main new direction in the field of motivation—the study of the self. If we add to this list the constructs of self-concept (e.g., Markus & Nurius, 1986), self-focus (e.g., Duval & Wicklund, 1972), self-handicapping (e.g., Jones & Berglas, 1978), self-monitoring (e.g., Snyder & Gangestad, 1986), and the remainder of the "self" vocabulary then it is evident that the self is on the verge of dominating the field of motivation.

## Constructs Concerned with Achievement Goals

Motivation is often defined as goal-directed activity. Many contemporary researchers have picked up on this theme as achievement strivings are increasingly described in terms of the student's goals or purposes for task engagement. For example, Dweck distinguishes mastery-oriented and helpless children not only in terms of their implicit theories about ability, but also according to the achievement goals that they adopt (Elliott & Dweck, 1988). Mastery-oriented children are more likely to be pursuing *learning* goals, where their intent is to master the task and acquire new skills. Helpless children, on the other hand, appear to adopt *performance* goals, in which their purpose is to demonstrate that they have adequate ability and avoid giving evidence that they have low ability. Because students who pursue performance goals often see their ability as threatened in situations of challenge, they are particularly vulnerable to informational cues that might convey low ability. Two themes have emerged from this literature, of which the Dweck approach is illustrative. First, in any achievement context, goals provide the mechanism or filter through which incoming information is processed and interpreted (Ames & Ames, 1989). Second, certain types of goals are more conducive to achievement strivings than others. In the following sections we discuss task versus ego involvement, intrinsic versus extrinsic motivation, and cooperation versus competition as examples of disparate goals that have differential effects on self-perception and achievement strivings (see Table 4–3).

*Task Involvement versus Ego Involvement.* In recent years, much has been written about learning environments that are structured to be task-involving rather than ego-involving, a distinction most closely associated with the work of Nicholls (1984, 1989, 1992). According to Nicholls, task-involving states are those where one's goal is to master the task. Greater understanding or acquisition of new tasks is considered an end in itself. In ego-involving states, by contrast, the primary goal is to demonstrate high ability relative to others or to conceal low ability. Unlike a task-focused context, which emphasizes personal accomplishment and preference for moderately challenging tasks, an ego-focused context connotes highly evaluative situations in which the emphasis is on comparison with others.

Task- versus ego-involving goals have been created by a variety of experimental manipulations, such as telling subjects that the task is a game versus a test (e.g., Graham & Golan, 1991), focusing their attention on the intrinsic value of the task versus doing better than others (Jagacinski & Nicholls, 1984, 1987), or having teachers provide written comments on student assignments rather than letter grades (Butler, 1987). The distinct motivational states elicited by these manipulations have been shown to have disparate consequences for students' self-perception and performance. For example, compared to ego-involved individuals, task-involved learners make fewer low-ability attributions for failure (Nicholls, 1984; Jagacinski & Nicholls, 1987), feel more pride in success resulting from effort (Jagacinski & Nicholls, 1984), and are more likely to be interested in the task and to actually perform better (Butler, 1987; Stipek & Kowalaski, 1989). The general premise underlying all of these findings is that because task-involved subjects believe more in the efficacy of effort, they work harder and therefore experience more positive outcomes.

In his theoretical argument for the task versus ego distinction, Nicholls (1984) also viewed different conceptions of ability as integrally related to particular achievement goals. Some individuals employ a *differentiated* concept of ability. They view ability as capacity, where assessing one's own competence involves comparison with the efforts and outcomes of others. For example, if I try hard while others succeed with less effort, this implies that I am less able. Other individuals entertain a *less differentiated* conception of ability. Greater effort followed by success implies mastery and increased ability, irrespective of the performance of others. If I try hard and master even a difficult task, that leads me to the inference that I have high ability. Although mature learners understand, or can think about, ability in either its differentiated or less differentiated sense, which conception they employ depends on whether their goals are task- or ego-related. Nicholls maintained that task-involving contexts are those in which the less differentiated conception of ability is employed (i.e., effort and mastery connote ability), whereas ego-involving contexts are those in which the more differentiated conception is salient (i.e., ability is judged in relation to the performance of others).

The task–ego distinction has much in common with Dweck's conception of learning versus performance goals. Indeed, the experimental manipulation of goals in Elliott and Dweck's

(1988) study is remarkably like that described in many of the studies manipulating task versus ego orientation. Nicholls and Dweck are also alike in that two different conceptions of ability define one's achievement-related goals. Viewing ability as a fixed entity is not unlike thinking of ability as capacity in the differentiated sense, just as conceiving of ability as incremental resembles the undifferentiated conception of ability as synonymous with effort and mastery. Thus, greater theoretical distinctions need to be made between these two conceptions, an issue we return to in the final section of this chapter.

*Intrinsic versus Extrinsic Incentives.* One of the truisms of education is that it is more adaptive to be intrinsically rather than extrinsically motivated, and that schooling as we know it often undermines children's natural (intrinsic) desire to learn. Motivation research in the achievement domain has elaborated on this pervasive belief by documenting that children and adults with initial interest in a task (intrinsic motivation) lose some of that interest when an external reward (extrinsic motivation) is offered for performing that task (see reviews in Morgan, 1984; Deci & Ryan, 1985). This basic phenomenon, known as the undermining effect of extrinsic reward, has been shown with experimental tasks as simple as playing with colorful markers or as complex as mastering difficult verbal passages, and with both symbolic and tangible rewards including grades, medals, gold stars, food, and even money. Motivational indices examined include choice and persistence at a task in the absence of reward, as well as self-reported interest and enjoyment. For example, in one often cited study (Lepper, Greene, & Nisbett, 1973), young children who received an expected "good player certificate" for engaging in a drawing activity showed less subsequent interest in that activity than did children who did not receive such an award. The 100 or more published studies on this topic following the investigation by Lepper et al. (1973) used variants of this basic paradigm and reported similar findings.

Among the more prevalent theoretical explanations for the undermining effect of rewards on motivation, and the one most compatible with a goal framework, is cognitive evaluation theory, as articulated by Deci and Ryan (1985). According to this conception, intrinsic motivation is displayed when one's goal to feel both self-determining and competent is achieved. Self-determination implies the experience of choice, autonomy, or an internal locus of causality. Competence, in turn, connotes the satisfaction derived from exercising or extending one's capabilities. If a person's feelings of self-determination and competence are enhanced by a reward, then the reward context is intrinsically motivating. Conversely, if rewards lessen one's sense of self-determination and competence, then they undermine intrinsic motivation.

This analysis implies that extrinsic incentives are not always detrimental to intrinsic motivation, a finding that Deci and Ryan explain by contrasting two possible functions of rewards. Rewards can be *controlling* in the sense that they are experienced as pressure to think, feel, and act in a particular way; that is, they exert control over the behavior on which they are contingent. But rewards can also be *informational* to the degree that they provide feedback about how well one is doing; in other words, they signal competence and mastery. When the controlling function of rewards is dominant, intrinsic motivation is undermined, but when the informational aspect is more salient, motivation is enhanced.

Manipulations of reward as controlling or informational have been relatively simple and straightforward in experimental studies. For example, Ryan, Mims, and Koestner (1983) induced controlling rewards for college students working on a puzzle by telling them that they would receive three dollars for their performance but that they "should try as hard as possible because I expect you to perform up to standards on these puzzles" (p. 745). Subjects in the informational condition were promised the same reward but told only to "do as well as you can." The results of this study revealed that controlling rewards diminished intrinsic motivation (i.e., amount of time later spent on the task), even when the reward had been made contingent on high performance. Thus, sources of positive evaluation such as good grades cannot be motivational enhancers, if at the same time they instigate constraints or pressure to perform in a particular way. In a more recent study of cognitive learning in fifth grade children that used a similar manipulation, Grolnick and Ryan (1987) documented less interest in the task that used controlling rather than informational feedback, and also less conceptual learning.

The basic propositions of cognitive evaluation theory as an interpretation of the undermining effects of extrinsic rewards are compatible with ideas concerning personal control and freedom introduced in Rotter's social learning theory. In Rotter's view, a core aspect of personality is the extent to which people see themselves as having control over outcomes. Deci and Ryan, on the other hand, view the quest for control as a fundamental human motive that can be either facilitated or inhibited by environmental factors like reward contingencies.

The approach followed by Deci and Ryan is also consistent with humanistic beliefs that there is an internal, biological tendency to develop fully the capacities and talents that have been inherited, and that there is a central motivation to grow and enhance the self (see Maslow, 1971; Rogers, 1963). Thus, it is presumed that there is an "inner push" that propels people to master their environments (deCharms, 1972). These conceptions therefore embrace such concepts as self-regulation and autonomy, which are seen by some educational psychologists as fundamental to classroom learning. Indeed, because the use of reward, evaluation, and other forms of "constraint" discussed by cognitive evaluation theory are so pervasive in American education, the body of empirical work on intrinsic versus extrinsic incentives has probably received more attention in education as an application of motivation research than have any of the other constructs or theories included in this review.

*Cooperative, Competitive, and Individualistic Goal Structures.* As a method of teaching (and rewarding) students, cooperative learning has become extremely popular during the past two decades (see Slavin, 1985). In this method, students work together in small mixed-ability groups where they are expected to help one another learn or complete a task. From a motivational perspective, cooperative learning is of interest because it is based on a theory of incentive structures and their relation to particular goals. As elaborated by Deutsch (1949b), this theory also uses the language of Lewin's field theory of motivation.

To conceptualize how the need states, or tensions, of different individuals can be related, Deutsch described three different types of goal or incentive structures. A cooperative incentive structure exists when two or more individuals are rewarded based on their performance as a group. Any one member can attain his or her own goal (e.g., academic recognition) only if the other members also attain theirs. A competitive incentive structure is one in which two or more individuals are compared with one another and only the best performing individuals are rewarded. In the strictest sense, a competitive structure exists when any one individual can attain his or her goal only if other participants do not obtain theirs. Finally, an individualistic incentive structure is one where persons are rewarded for their own performance, irrespective of the outcomes of others.

Since Deutsch first offered these distinctions, there has been considerable research on the effects of incentive structure on performance. In his own experimental research, Deutsch (1949a) predicted and found higher productivity when individuals worked in cooperative as opposed to competitive groups. More recent reviews focusing on school achievement outcomes reveal some disagreement about the effectiveness of cooperative systems. Johnson, Maruyams, Johnson, Nelson, and Skon (1981) conducted a meta-analysis of well over 100 studies on this topic and concluded that cooperative structures across the board resulted in higher achievement and productivity than either competitive or individualistic incentives. In a later review, however, Cotton and Cook (1982) questioned this interpretation, arguing instead that the superiority of cooperative reward systems over the other two depended on many situational factors, including degree of interdependence, type of task, and size of the group. Cooperative structures appeared to work best with large groups working very interdependently on complex tasks.

In a later review involving only children in elementary and secondary school, Slavin (1983) also took an interactional approach. He suggested that cooperative incentives lead to better academic achievement only in situations where group members receive a group reward that is based on the assessment of individual learning. Thus, for example, an effective cooperative incentive structure for math learning would be one where the group reward is based on the average or sum of each member's performance on tests of individual achievement. Successful cooperative methods, according to Slavin, are those where individuals are held accountable to the group and there is substantial peer pressure for all students to perform to the best of their abilities. Simply working together on a task and then being evaluated solely on the basis of individual performance led to no better outcome than the more traditional competitive or individualistic goal structures.

In the research reviewed by Slavin (1983) and Johnson et al. (1981), the focus was on performance outcomes, with motivation only inferred to be higher under reward structures with more positive outcomes. Ames (1984) specifically applied a motivational analysis to the three types of goal structures, suggesting that each is related to a distinct motivational system. Competition elicits what Ames referred to as an egoistic motivational system. The emphasis is on ability and outperforming others. Not unlike Covington's (1992) self-worth conception and Nicholls's (1984) ego-involving context, competitive goal structures elicit the desire to demonstrate high ability and maximize the associated feelings of pride, and to avoid demonstrating low ability with its linked emotion of shame.

Individualistic goal structures, in contrast, elicit a mastery motivational orientation where the focus is on effort and competing against one's own standard of excellence. Finally, cooperative goal structures elicit what Ames referred to as a moral motivational orientation where the focus is on how willing one is to exert effort to aid group members. Individuals try hard in order to serve the group's needs and therefore demonstrate social responsibility. At their best, then, cooperative reward systems instigate group members to pay attention to one another's efforts, to reinforce individual members' efforts that improve group performance, and to blame or otherwise apply social disapproval to members perceived as not contributing to group goals. Ames's research has been quite consistent in documenting the positive consequences of cooperative systems on children's self-perception, perception of others, and actual achievement (Ames, 1992).

***Concluding Comments About Achievement Goals.*** In this section we considered three contemporary motivation constructs that fall under the broad rubric of achievement goals. Each described either a context for learning (task involvement versus ego involvement) or a set of incentive structures (informational versus controlling rewards and cooperative versus competitive learning) that was linked to particular achievement goals. None of these topics achieves the status of a theory of motivation in the sense that there are sets of interrelated constructs, linked with an operational language, and broadly applicable to domains other than achievement. However, each suggests one or more principles or guides to achievement-related behavior that can be incorporated into classroom instructional processes. For example, it is evident from this research that motivation is likely to be enhanced if the learner is allowed to focus on the task rather than on outperforming others, if rewards signal competence rather than external constraints, and if students are encouraged to work in collaboration with others rather than alone or in competition.

## GENERAL ISSUES IN THE STUDY OF MOTIVATION

To facilitate presentation of both the theories and principles of motivation in the preceding sections, we have bypassed a number of important and complex issues. For example, little has been said about the role of individual differences in the study of motivation; we have only alluded to the problem of theoretical overlap among constructs; and we have not at all addressed issues such as the development of motivation and the possibility of motivational change. All of these issues are of particular concern to educational psychologists who study motivation. We turn to these complex issues now, not to offer solutions, but to assure readers that we are aware of some of the problems and to invite them to aid in their resolution.

### Individual Differences in Motivation

In the historical review of motivation research, we commented on the rise and fall of the study of individual differences in motivation. Among the earlier theorists, Atkinson (1964) and Rotter (1966) were especially persuasive in arguing that individual differences play a central role in the study of motivational processes. In Atkinson's theory of achievement strivings, persons labeled high in the achievement motive are predicted to display different risk-taking behavior than persons low in that motive. And in Rotter's social learning theory, persons classified as internal on locus of control are predicted to have different generalized expectancies for success than those labeled external. Differences among individuals are therefore central to testing both of these conceptions.

But both theories have fallen prey to all of the complex issues and obstacles faced by trait approaches, particularly their lack of cross-situational generality (e.g., Mischel, 1973). For example, people do not demonstrate high achievement needs in all situations, nor are they equally motivated to exert internal control across diverse settings. Neither Atkinson's nor Rotter's formulation fully acknowledges this possibility. Thus, hypotheses using achievement needs or perceptions of control as predictor variables have often been disconfirmed, and the influence of both theories has waned.

On the other hand, the growing visibility of research on explanatory style suggests a renewed interest in individual differences, as does the shift in learned helplessness research toward viewing helplessness and mastery orientation in a dispositional framework (Dweck & Leggett, 1988). Moreover, research on trait anxiety in achievement contexts continues to thrive. But given the difficulties of personality measurement and the situational specificity of behavior, we believe that a more fruitful approach at this time might be to search first for general laws of motivation rather than explore the possibility of complex person × situation interactions. Once accomplished, this search can be followed by the inclusion of individual differences to refine the generalizations that have been made or to uncover more complex associations that might have been overlooked. Others, of course, may have different views on this complex issue.

## Developmental Factors

Most of the theories and all of the achievement-related contemporary constructs that we reviewed incorporate cognitions of varying complexity. Based on these conceptions, we described a constellation of maladaptive motivational patterns that included attributing failure to low aptitude, having low expectations for success, perceiving outcomes as uncontrollable, and being overly concerned with demonstrating high ability and concealing low ability. All of these beliefs make students more vulnerable to the negative consequences of achievement failure.

There is a vast amount of empirical support for these linkages between cognitions and achievement-related behavior from middle childhood on. The findings are less clear, however, in the case of young children. Developmental research suggests that children younger than about third grade are much less vulnerable to the cognitive-motivational deficits described above. For example, studies show that early elementary school-aged children have very high self-ratings of ability, high expectations, and tend not to display learned helplessness after unexpected failure (see Stipek, 1984, for a review). Young children also are not as susceptible to the low ability inferences that can be communicated through teacher feedback, such as praise for success at an easy task (Barker & Graham, 1987).

Many of these observed differences between younger and older research participants can be traced to cognitive-developmental changes in children's understanding of achievement-related cognitions. For example, Covington's self-worth argument, Dweck's helplessness model, Nicholls' task–ego distinction, and some predictions of attribution theory are based on an understanding and use of what is called a compensatory schema concerning effort and ability. Understanding a compensatory schema means that effort and ability are perceived as inversely related such that the higher one's perceived effort given success at a task, the lower is one's perceived ability, and vice versa. Yet developmental research indicates that children do not understand the compensatory schema before about age 9. Rather, they tend to expect ability and effort to covary positively. The student who tries harder is believed to be smarter, a phenomenon that Kun (1977) labeled the "halo schema" (also see Nicholls, 1978). From a motivational perspective, therefore, young children's thinking naturally resembles the more adaptive belief patterns of mastery-oriented children who endorse an incremental theory of ability (Dweck & Leggett, 1988) or task-involved individuals who employ the less differentiated conception of ability (Nicholls, 1984).

For the educational psychologist concerned with motivation research, these developmental findings suggest that the cognitive models elaborated in the "adult" motivation literature may require some modification when applied to the study of achievement strivings among very young children. These modifications require sensitivity to the cognitive maturity of research subjects. It does not make much sense, for example, to predict helplessness beliefs in a 6-year-old if children of that age do not perceive low ability as something stable and uncontrollable.

But paralleling *age*-related cognitive growth are systematic *grade*-related changes in classroom environments that must also play a role in developmental differences in achievement strivings. For example, as children progress through elementary school, there is increasing focus on ability assessment and comparison with others through such common classroom practices as letter grades, report cards, ability grouping, and movement from a mastery to a competitive feedback orientation (e.g., Eccles, Midgley, & Adler, 1984; Stipek & Daniels, 1988). All of these practices operate to enhance the conception of ability where being smart means being smarter than others but having to try less hard, and doing well means succeeding on hard tasks at which others encounter difficulty. Therefore, the degree to which motivationally maladaptive cognitions become salient will be influenced by both cognitive growth across age and by changes in classroom environments across grade. The motivation researcher with a developmental focus needs to take into account both of these important determinants of perceived personal competence and other achievement-related beliefs.

## Pulling Apart the Theoretical Overlap Between Constructs

A myriad of constructs, including most that we reviewed here, compose the contemporary motivation literature. While each of these constructs has its own set of defining characteristics and empirical findings, the theoretical distinctions between some of the constructs often remain unclear. We noted earlier, for example, that the task–ego distinction has some conceptual overlap with Dweck's conception of learning versus performance goals. It also is not clear how self-efficacy differs from expectancy for future success, whether being mastery-oriented is any different from being task-involved, and whether incremental versus entity theories of ability can be distinguished from an attributional analysis of ability as varying along the stability dimension. In short, motivation researchers need to find ways to distinguish their constructs better, both theoretically and empirically.

It has been suggested that motivational factors influence particular cognitive processes, such as encoding of information or attention deployment, and that these information processing components then more directly influence performance. Perhaps one way to distinguish particular motivational states might be to relate them to particular cognitive processes. In efforts along these lines, Graham and Golan (1991) reported that the motivationally maladaptive effects of ego involvement (compared with involvement) occur more at the retrieval stage of information processing than at the encoding stage. For individuals induced to focus on their ability rather than on mastery, the difficulty may lie not so much in placing information in memory as in accessing that information. Other motivational states, in contrast, appear to be linked to different stages of information processing. For example, Pittman and D'Agostino (1989) have shown that perceived noncontingency (as in the learned helplessness theory) can have positive effects on encoding but not on retrieval of verbal information. Pittman and D'Agostino argued that control-deprived subjects encode new information more carefully as part of their attempt to regain control of their environment.

These sets of findings intimate that motivational constructs might be distinguished by whether they influence new learning (encoding) or whether they facilitate or interfere with an individual's ability to demonstrate what has been learned already (retrieval). We think that a systematic mapping of distinct motivational states onto particular sets of cognitive processes might be a useful step toward the goal of greater conceptual clarity in motivation research.

## Motivation Change

By identifying the determinants of motivation, the theories and principles presented in this chapter also provide suggestions for motivational change. Thus, increasing success expectancies, altering attributions for failure from stable to unstable, changing reward practices in the classroom to emphasize their informational rather than controlling aspect, and altering the perception of ability so that ability is seen as unstable rather than stable are some of the techniques that could be used to enhance motivation. Indeed, many motivational programs have already been tested in both laboratory and clinical settings, and are proving successful (e.g., Forsterling, 1985, 1988; Perry, Hechter, Menec, & Weinberg).

From the literature, it appears that two types of motivational change programs could be pursued. One approach focuses on particular individuals, with the goal of changing their cognitions to be more adaptive. This approach would require the selection and treatment of individuals who, for example, ascribe their failures to stable causes. The other type of change program could be introduced into the general classroom, for it is assumed that all individuals would benefit, for example, from comparing their performance with their own prior performance rather than with others' performance, thereby promoting task rather than ego involvement.

But both of these approaches assume that students value success and are underperforming because of some motivational deficit located either within the person or within the learning context. Unfortunately, the most chronic and pervasive motivational problems are evident in children neither wanting to learn, nor to try. Principles such as task involvement, mastery focus, and unstable attributions for failure then become somewhat irrelevant.

The question thus shifts to a larger and more difficult one: How can we get "unmotivated" children to accept the basic premise that learning, schooling, and mastery of the material that adults prescribe are important? That is, how can there be internalization of attitudes that reflect, "Trust us. We know what is best for you, and if you do it, you will not only like it, but it will help you better yourself in our world"?

We cannot supply an answer to this question, for it lies at the root of problems in contemporary American culture. It involves lack of motivation not only in school, but also on the job. It touches upon not only the lack of equality in our system of distributive justice, but also on a perception of the impossibility of meaningful goal attainment. A change program to treat this larger population of motivationally impaired individuals would have to involve not only the school setting, but also the parents, the principal, the pastor, the policy makers, and the president. This is a task for all of society.

When one talks about the laws of learning, it is assumed that the person is exposed to the material and is attending. When one examines the laws of perception, it is assumed that the perceiver has his or her eyes open. And when one examines the laws of motivation, it is presumed that the student prefers to do better. Without this, motivational enhancement is not possible.

## CONCLUSION

In this chapter, we reviewed some of the history of the study of motivation, the most important and general theoretical conceptions, and more specific principles that pertain to achievement strivings. Motivation is a rich and changing field that has witnessed much progress in its relatively short history. In the 60 years since the insights of Hull and Spence, there have been major upheavals in the field (the shift from mechanism to cognition); new theories and concepts have been introduced (such as causal attributions, learned helplessness, and self-efficacy); and novel research directions have been followed (such as the finding that reward at times can decrease motivation).

We stated at the beginning of this undertaking that readers should not finish this chapter with the hope that they can go into classrooms and institute immediate changes. Perhaps we have been too guarded. Principles have been suggested that readers can follow. Many have good theoretical and empirical grounding. For example, we now know the positive motivational consequences of attributing failure to lack of effort, of selecting tasks of intermediate difficulty, and of having students focus on the task rather than on the self. Thus, there has been a marriage between theory and empirical research, which we indicated at the outset guided our selection of topics for review. The full testing of these principles in classroom settings is a major task we see for future motivation research.

# References

Abramson, L., Seligman, M., & Teasdale, J. (1978). Learned helplessness in humans: Critique and reformulation. *Journal of Abnormal Psychology, 87,* 49–74.

Abramson, L., Metalsky, G., & Alloy, L. (1989). Hopelessness depression: A theory-based subtype of depression. *Psychological Review, 96,* 358–372.

Ames, C. (1984). Competitive, cooperative, and individualistic goal structures: A motivational analysis. In R. Ames & C. Ames (Eds.), *Research on motivation in education* (Vol. 1, pp. 177–207). New York: Academic Press.

Ames, C. (1992). Achievement goals and the classroom motivational climate. In D. Schunk & J. Meece (Eds.), *Student perceptions in the classroom* (pp. 327–348). Hillsdale, NJ: Erlbaum.

Ames, C., & Ames, R. (1989). Introduction. In C. Ames & R. Ames (Eds.), *Research on motivation in education* (Vol. 3, pp. 1–10). New York: Academic Press.

Anderson, C. (1983). Motivational and performance deficits in interpersonal settings: The effects of attributional style. *Journal of Personality and Social Psychology, 45,* 1136–1147.

Anderson, C., Jennings, D., & Arnoult, L. (1988). Validity and utility of the attributional style construct at a moderate level of specificity. *Journal of Personality and Social Psychology, 55,* 979–990.

Atkinson, J. (1957). Motivational determinants of risk-taking behavior. *Psychological Review, 64,* 359–372.

Atkinson, J. (1964). *An introduction to motivation.* Princeton, NJ: Van Nostrand.

Ball, S. (1982). Motivation. In H. E. Mitzel (Ed.), *Encyclopedia of educational research* (5th ed., pp. 1256–1263). New York: Macmillan.

Bandura, A. (1977). Self-efficacy: Toward a unifying theory of behavioral change. *Psychological Review, 84,* 191–215.

Bandura, A. (1986). *Social foundations of thought and action: A social-cognitive theory.* Englewood Cliffs, NJ: Prentice-Hall.

Bandura, A. (1989). Human agency in social cognitive theory. *American Psychologist, 44,* 1175–1184.

Bandura, A. (1991). Human agency: The rhetoric and the reality. *American Psychologist, 46,* 157–162.

Bandura, A., & Schunk, D. (1981). Cultivating competence, self-efficacy, and intrinsic interest through proximal self-motivation. *Journal of Personality and Social Psychology, 41,* 586–598.

Barker, G., & Graham, S. (1987). Developmental study of praise and blame as attributional cues. *Journal of Educational Psychology, 79,* 62–66.

Bolles, R. C. (1967). *Theory of motivation.* New York: Harper & Row.

Brophy, J., & Rohrkemper, M. (1981). The influence of problem ownership on teachers' perceptions of strategies for coping with problem students. *Journal of Educational Psychology, 73,* 295–311.

Brown, J., & Weiner, B. (1984). Affective consequences of ability versus effort ascriptions: Controversies, resolutions, and quandaries. *Journal of Educational Psychology, 76,* 146–158.

Butler, R. (1987). Task-involving and ego-involving properties of evaluation: Effects of different feedback conditions on motivational perceptions, interest, and performance. *Journal of Educational Psychology, 79,* 474–482.

Carver, C. (1989). How should multifaceted personality constructs be tested? Issues illustrated by self-monitoring, attributional style, and hardiness. *Journal of Personality and Social Psychology, 56,* 577–585.

Cofer, C. N., & Appley, M. H. (1964). *Motivation: Theory and Research.* New York: Wiley.

Corcoran, K. (1991). Efficacy, "skills," reinforcement, and choice behavior. *American Psychologist, 46,* 155–157.

Cotton, J., & Cook, M. (1982). Meta-analyses and the effects of various reward systems: Some different conclusions from Johnson et al. *Psychological Bulletin, 92,* 176–183.

Covington, M. (1984). The motive for self-worth. In R. Ames & C. Ames (Eds.), *Research on motivation in education* (Vol. 1, pp. 77–113). New York: Academic Press.

Covington, M. (1992). *Making the grade: A self-worth perspective on motivation and school reform.* New York: Cambridge University Press.

Covington, M., & Beery, R. (1976). *Self-worth and school learning.* New York: Holt, Rinehart, & Winston.

Covington, M., & Omelich, C. (1979). Are causal attributions causal? A path analysis of the cognitive model of achievement motivation. *Journal of Personality and Social Psychology, 37,* 1487–1504.

Csikszentmihalyi, M. (1975). *Beyond boredom and anxiety.* San Francisco: Jossey-Bass.

deCharms, R. (1972). Personal causation training in the schools. *Journal of Applied Social Psychology, 3,* 95–113.

Deci, E. (1975). *Intrinsic motivation.* New York: Plenum Press.

Deci, E., & Ryan, R. (1985). *Intrinsic motivation and self-determination in human behavior.* New York: Plenum Press.

Deutsch, M. (1949a). A theory of cooperation and competition. *Human Relations, 2,* 129–152.

Deutsch, M. (1949b). An experimental study of the effects of cooperation and competition upon group process. *Human Relations, 2,* 199–231.

Duval, S., & Wicklund, R. (1972). *A theory of objective self-awareness.* New York: Academic Press.

Dweck, C., & Leggett, E. (1988). A social cognitive approach to motivation and personality. *Psychological Review, 95,* 256–273.

Eccles, J., Midgley, C., & Adler, T. (1984). Grade-related changes in the school environment: Effects on achievement motivation. In J. Nicholls (Ed.), *Advances in motivation and achievement* (Vol. 3, pp. 283–331). Greenwich, CT: JAI Press.

Elliott, E., & Dweck, C. (1988). Goals: An approach to motivation and achievement. *Journal of Personality and Social Psychology, 54,* 5–12.

Feather, N. T. (1961). The relationship of persistence at a task to expectation of success and achievement-related motives. *Journal of Abnormal and Social Psychology, 63,* 552–561.

Findley, M., & Cooper, H. (1983). Locus of control and academic achievement: A literature review. *Journal of Personality and Social Psychology, 44,* 419–427.

Forsterling, F. (1985). Attributional retraining: A review. *Psychological Bulletin, 98,* 495–512.

Forsterling, F. (1988). *Attribution theory in clinical psychology.* New York: Wiley.

Graham, S. (1984). Communicating sympathy and anger to black and white students: The cognitive (attributional) consequences of affective cues. *Journal of Personality and Social Psychology, 47,* 40–54.

Graham, S. (1990). On communicating low ability in the classroom: Bad things good teachers sometimes do. In S. Graham & V. Folkes (Eds.), *Attribution theory: Applications to achievement, mental health, and interpersonal conflict* (pp. 17–36). Hillsdale, NJ: Erlbaum.

Graham, S. (1991). A review of attribution theory in achievement contexts. *Educational Psychology Review, 3,* 5–38.

Graham, S., & Golan, S. (1991). Motivational influences on cognition: Task involvement, ego involvement, and depth of information processing. *Journal of Educational Psychology, 83,* 198–194.

Grolnick, W., & Ryan, R. (1987). Autonomy in children's learning: An experimental and individual difference investigation. *Journal of Personality and Social Psychology, 52,* 890–898.

Heider, F. (1958). *The psychology of interpersonal relations.* New York: Wiley.

Hull, C. (1943). *Principles of behavior.* New York: Appleton-Century-Crofts.

Hull, C. (1951). *Essentials of behavior.* New Haven: Yale University Press.

Jagacinski, C., & Nicholls, J. (1984). Conceptions of ability and related affects in task involvement and ego involvement. *Journal of Educational Psychology, 76,* 909–919.

Jagacinski, C., & Nicholls, J. (1987). Competence and affect in task involvement and ego involvement: The impact of social comparison information. *Journal of Educational Psychology, 79,* 107–114.

Johnson, D., Maruyams, G., Johnson, R., Nelson, D., & Skon, L. (1981). Effects of cooperative, competitive, and individualistic goal structures on achievement: A meta-analysis. *Psychological Bulletin, 89,* 47–62.

Jones, E., & Berglas, S. (1978). Control of attributions about the self through self-handicapping strategies: The appeal of alcohol and the role of underachievement. *Personality and Social Psychology Bulletin, 4,* 200–206.

Kelley, H. (1967). Attribution theory in social psychology. In D. Levine (Ed.), *Nebraska symposium on motivation* (Vol. 15, pp. 192–238). Lincoln: University of Nebraska Press.

Kelley, H. (1971). *Attribution in social interaction.* New York: General Learning Press.

Kirsch, I. (1985). Self-efficacy and expectancy: Old wine with new labels. *Journal of Personality and Social Psychology, 49,* 823–830.

Koffka, K. (1935). *Principles of Gestalt psychology.* New York: Harcourt.

Kun, A. (1977). Development of the magnitude-covariation and compensation schemata in ability and effort attributions of performance. *Child Development, 48,* 862–873.

Lepper, M., Greene, D., & Nisbett, R. (1973). Undermining children's intrinsic interest with extrinsic rewards: A test of the "overjustification" hypothesis. *Journal of Personality and Social Psychology, 28,* 129–137.

Lewin, K. (1935). *A dynamic theory of personality.* New York: McGraw-Hill.

Lewin, K. (1936). *Principles of topological psychology.* New York: McGraw-Hill.

Markus, H., & Nurius, P. (1986). Possible selves. *American Psychologist, 41,* 954–969.

Maslow, A. (1943). A theory of human motivation. *Psychological Review, 50,* 370–396.

Maslow, A. (1971). *The farther reaches of human nature.* New York: Viking.

Marx, M. (1960). Motivation. In C. W. Harris (Ed.), *Encyclopedia of educational research* (3rd ed., pp. 888–901). New York: Macmillan.

Mischel, W. (1973). Toward a cognitive-social learning reconceptualization of personality. *Psychological Review, 80,* 252–283.

Morgan, M. (1984). Reward-induced decrements and increments in intrinsic motivation. *Review of Educational Research, 54,* 5–30.

Nicholls, J. (1978). The development of the concepts of effort and ability, perception of own attainment, and the understanding that difficult tasks require more ability. *Child Development, 49,* 800–814.

Nicholls, J. (1984). Achievement motivation: Conceptions of ability, subjective experience, task choice, and performance. *Psychological Review, 91,* 328–346.

Nicholls, J. (1989). *The competitive ethos and democratic society.* Cambridge, MA: Harvard University Press.

Nicholls, J. (1992). Students as educational theorists. In D. Schunk & J. Meece (Eds.), *Student perceptions in the classroom* (pp. 267–286). Hillsdale, NJ: Erlbaum.

Perry, R., Hechter, F., Menec, V., & Weinberg, L. (1993). Review of achievement motivation and performance in college students from an attributional retraining perspective. *Research in Higher Education, 34,* 687–723.

Peterson, C. (1990). Explanatory style in the classroom and on the playing field. In S. Graham & V. Folkes (Eds.), *Attribution theory: Applications to achievement, mental health, and interpersonal conflict* (pp. 53–75). Hillsdale, NJ: Erlbaum.

Peterson, C., & Seligman M. (1984). Causal explanations as a risk factor for depression: Theory and evidence. *Psychological Review, 91,* 347–374.

Peterson, C., Seligman, M., & Vaillant, G. (1988). Pessimistic explanatory style is a risk factor for physical illness: A thirty-five year longitudinal study. *Journal of Personality and Social Psychology, 55,* 23–27.

Pintrich, P., & DeGroot, E. (1990). Motivational and self-regulated learning components of classroom academic performance. *Journal of Educational Psychology, 82,* 33–40.

Pittman, T., & D'Agostino, P. (1989). Motivation and cognition: Control deprivation and the nature of subsequent information processing. *Journal of Experimental Social Psychology, 25,* 465–480.

Rogers, C. (1963). Actualizing tendency in relation to "motives" and to consciousness. In M. Jones (Ed.), *Nebraska symposium on motivation* (pp. 1–24). Lincoln: University of Nebraska Press.

Rotter, J. (1954). *Social learning and clinical psychology.* Englewood Cliffs, NJ: Prentice Hall.

Rotter, J. (1966). Generalized expectancies for internal versus external control of reinforcement. *Psychological Monographs, 80,* 1–28.

Ryan, R., Mims, V., & Koestner, R. (1983). Relation of reward contingency and interpersonal context to intrinsic motivation: A review and test of cognitive evaluation theory. *Journal of Personality and Social Psychology, 45,* 736–750.

Schunk, D. (1989). Self-efficacy and achievement behaviors. *Educational Psychology Review, 1,* 173–208.

Schunk, D. (1991). Self-efficacy and academic motivation. *Educational Psychologist, 26,* 207–232.

Seligman, M. (1975). *Helplessness: On depression, development, and death.* San Francisco: Freeman.

Skinner, B. G. (1953). *Science and human behavior.* New York: Macmillan.

Slavin, R. (1983). When does cooperative learning increase student achievement? *Psychological Bulletin, 94,* 429–445.

Slavin, R. (1985). An introduction to cooperative learning research. In R. Slavin, S. Sharan, S. Kagan, R. Hertz-Lazarowitz, C. Webb, & R. Schmuck (Eds.), *Learning to cooperate, cooperating to learn* (pp. 5–16). New York: Plenum Press.

Snyder, M., & Gangestad, S. (1986). On the nature of self-monitoring: Matters of assessment, matters of validity. *Journal of Personality and Social Psychology, 43,* 123–135.

Spence, K. (1958). A theory of emotionally based drive (D) and its relation to performance in simple learning situations. *American Psychologist, 13,* 131–141.

Stipek, D. (1984). The development of achievement motivation. In R. Ames & C. Ames (Eds.), *Research on motivation in education* (Vol. 1, pp. 145–174). New York: Academic Press.

Stipek, D., & Daniels, D. (1988). Declining perceptions of competence: A consequence of changes in the child or the educational environment. *Journal of Educational Psychology, 80,* 352–356.

Stipek, D., & Kowalski, P. (1989). Learned helplessness in task-orienting versus performance-orienting testing conditions. *Journal of Educational Psychology, 81,* 384–391.

Strube, M., & Roemmele, L. (1985). Self-enhancement, self-assessment, and self-evaluative task choice. *Journal of Personality and Social Psychology, 49,* 981–993.

Taylor, S., & Brown, J. (1988). Illusion and well-being: A social psychological perspective on mental health. *Psychological Bulletin, 103,* 193–210.

Thorndike, E. (1911). *Animal intelligence.* New York: Macmillan.

Tolman, E. C. (1932). *Purposive behavior in animals and men.* New York: Appleton-Century-Crofts.

Weiner, B. (1969). Motivation. In R. Ebel (Ed.), *Encyclopedia of Educational Research, Fourth Edition* (pp. 877–887). New York: Macmillan, 1969.

Weiner, B. (1972). *Theories of motivation: From mechanism to cognition.* Chicago: Rand McNally.

Weiner, B. (1983). Some methodological pitfalls in attribution research. *Journal of Educational Psychology, 75,* 530–543.

Weiner, B. (1985). An attributional theory of achievement motivation and emotion. *Psychological Review, 92,* 548–573.

Weiner, B. (1986). *An attributional theory of motivation and emotion.* New York: Springer-Verlag.

Weiner, B. (1990). History of motivational research in education. *Journal of Educational Psychology, 82,* 616–622.

Weiner, B. (1992). *Human motivation: Metaphors, theories, and research.* Newbury Park, CA: Sage.

Weiner, B. (1992). Motivation. In M. Alkin (Ed.), *Encyclopedia of educational research* (6th ed, pp. 860–965). New York: Macmillan.

Young, P. (1941). Motivation. In W. Monroe (Ed.), *Encyclopedia of educational research* (pp. 735–742). New York: Macmillan.

Young, P. (1950). Motivation. In W. Monroe (Ed.), *Encyclopedia of educational research* (rev. ed., pp. 755–761). New York: Macmillan.

Zeigarnik, B. (1927). Über das Behalten von erledigten und unerledigten Handlungen. *Psychologische Forschung, 9,* 1–85.

# ◆ *5* ◆

# MOTIVATION AND INSTRUCTION

## *Deborah J. Stipek*

UNIVERSITY OF CALIFORNIA, LOS ANGELES

Research exploring the critical question of what motivates human behavior has a long and distinguished history, but only relatively recently has behavior in educational settings been a central concern. The field of achievement motivation has matured rapidly, however, generating a great deal of practical knowledge about how instructional practices affect students' motivation.

This chapter examines the implications of motivation theory and research for designing instructional programs to maximize students' motivation. A motivated student is conceptualized as someone who is actively engaged in the learning process. Students who are engaged approach challenging tasks eagerly, exert intense effort using active problem-solving strategies, and persist in the face of difficulty. Motivated students focus on developing understanding and mastering skills; they are enthusiastic and optimistic; and they take pleasure in academic tasks and pride in their achievements. Students who are not motivated are passive; they exert little effort and give up easily. When they do exert effort it is for extrinsic reasons, such as to avoid punishment or obtain some reward unrelated to the task itself. They do not enjoy school tasks and avoid them whenever they can.

The studies described here—both experimental and classroom-based—provide compelling evidence for the importance of teachers' instructional decisions. Study after study demonstrates that although students bring some motivational baggage—beliefs, expectations, and habits—to a class, the immediate instructional context strongly affects their motivation. Decisions about the nature of tasks, how performance is evaluated, how rewards are used, how much autonomy students have, and myriad other variables under a teacher's control largely determine students' motivation. Fortunately, research also suggests particular strategies that teachers can use to have a positive influence on students' motivation.

Over the past several decades, theorists' conceptions of motivation and assumptions about the factors that affect behavior in achievement situations have changed. (See chapter 4 for a detailed discussion of these theoretical shifts.) *Reinforcement theory* dominated the educational literature until the early 1960s. According to traditional reinforcement theory, individuals exhibit a particular behavior in achievement or other settings as a function of their reinforcement history relevant to that behavior—i.e., whether the behavior has been rewarded or punished in the past.

By the early 1960s, most motivation theorists found such mechanistic assumptions about behavior unsatisfactory, and focused instead on cognitive mediators of human behavior in achievement and other situations. *Cognitive motivation* researchers do not rule out extrinsic reinforcement as a factor in achievement behavior. They claim, however, that cognitions, such as expectations, mediate the effect of rewards: What is important is not whether one has been rewarded in the past for the behavior but whether one *expects* to be rewarded in the future.

Atkinson (1964), who played a major role in introducing cognitions into the study of achievement motivation, proposed that achievement behavior is determined also by the desirability or "incentive value" of the achievement goal; individuals are not likely to persist in a task if there is no perceived value in completing it, even if they expect to succeed. Beginning in the early 1960s, motivation researchers primarily studied the effect of expectations and values on achievement behavior.

Cognitive theorists have recently examined the mediating effects of a number of different beliefs associated with expectations—perceptions of one's ability, perceptions of one's control over achievement outcomes, and perceptions of the causes of those outcomes. The conceptualization of achievement values has also broadened. Atkinson conceptualized values narrowly in terms of two expected emotional reactions, pride and shame. Since Atkinson's theory was first developed, achievement motivation theorists have included in their concept of achievement values the characteristics of tasks and the needs, goals, and values of the person.

*Intrinsic motivation* theorists further expanded the notion of values. Intrinsic motivation theory is based on the assumption that humans are naturally motivated to develop their intellectual and other competencies and to take pleasure in their accomplishments (White, 1959). Part of the value of striving to achieve something is the intrinsic pleasure one feels from developing understanding and mastery. Intrinsic motivation researchers have examined factors that foster or inhibit human beings' intrinsic desire to engage in intellectual tasks.

The most recent development in the achievement motivation literature is a focus on *goals*. Early research on achievement motivation examined primarily *whether* individuals approached and persisted at achievement tasks. Many motivation theorists now believe that the *reason* for engaging in a task is just as important as the level of effort expended, the degree of persistence, or any other observable behavior. Researchers have therefore begun to examine the causes and consequences of different goal orientations. Evidence is beginning to suggest, for example, that a goal of developing understanding results in more conceptual learning and more enjoyment than the goal of demonstrating ability or outperforming peers.

This chapter is organized into four sections, that address the factors believed to explain behavior in achievement situations: extrinsic reinforcement, cognitions, values (especially intrinsic values), and goals. Although different factors have been emphasized at different times in the history of research on achievement motivation, all are assumed to play a role. Thus, teachers who want to provide an educational program that maximizes student motivation must attend to all of these sets of factors.

The order in which these factors are addressed here roughly follows the order in which they emerged in the history of motivation theory and research. Discussed first, but only briefly, are some practical implications of research on extrinsic factors affecting achievement behavior. The second section summarizes research on cognitions that are known to influence behavior in achievement settings. This section also discusses instructional strategies that maintain positive perceptions of ability and self-efficacy, high expectations for success, and perceptions of control over achievement outcomes. The third section focuses on the intrinsic value of achievement tasks with a brief discussion of utility value and attainment value. The fourth and final section is on students' goals in achievement contexts and the effects that different goals have on effort and performance.

## EXTRINSIC REINFORCEMENT

For many years a reinforcement model of motivation dominated the educational psychology literature. Achievement behavior, like all other behavior, was assumed to be explained entirely by reinforcement contingencies. Reinforcement theory is derived from Thorndike's (1911) so-called law of effect. (See chapter 4 for a more extended theoretical discussion.) According to this law, also embraced by Hull (1943), a stimulus-response bond is strengthened when it is followed by a positive (or satisfactory) outcome and weakened when it is followed by an unsatisfactory outcome.

Skinner (1974) elaborated on the law of effect by systematically manipulating consequences and then studying their effects on behavior. He defined positive reinforcers as consequences that increased the probability of behaviors they were made contingent on, and negative reinforcers as consequences that increased the probability of a behavior by taking something away or reducing its intensity. Punishment Skinner defined as a negative or unpleasant consequence to behavior that reduced the probability of the behavior.

The educational implications of reinforcement are straightforward: The teacher makes positive reinforcers contingent on desired behavior and punishment contingent on undesired behavior. Thus, good grades, praise, and privileges may be used to reinforce effort on assignments, and bad grades or loss of privileges may serve as punishment for low effort. The teacher constantly criticizing a student for not working can serve as a negative reinforcement; effort should increase if it results in reduced criticism. The simplicity of the theory is no doubt a major reason for its long-standing central role in educational psychology and its widespread classroom application.

In addition to promoting these widely accepted practices, reinforcement theorists have inspired the development of many elaborate behavior modification programs and "token economies" in educational settings (Alschuler, 1968; H. Cohen, 1973; Kazdin, 1975; McLaughlin & Williams, 1988; O'Leary, 1987; Sulzer-Azaroff & Mayer, 1986). A program developed by H. Cohen (1973) for a difficult group of adolescent boys in a residential home illustrates the comprehensive use of reinforcement principles to shape students' behavior. Most of the students in Cohen's study had dropped out of school, and many had been found guilty of crimes. These boys were given points that could be exchanged for goods, services, and special privileges, such as recreational time in a lounge, books, magazines, extra clothing, mail-order supplies, a private shower, or a private room for sleeping and entertaining. Reinforcement was made contingent on academic achievement and behaviors that enhanced achievement. Despite a long history of failed attempts to increase the motivation of these boys, their academic achievement improved dramatically under this token economy system.

Motivation theorists have pointed out a number of problems with reliance on extrinsic reinforcement to motivate desired achievement-related behaviors. (See Stipek, 1993, chapter 3, for a review.) First, traditional rewards used in most American classrooms are not universally effective. Grades, for example, are ineffective as rewards or punishment for students who do not value high grades. Some students (particularly very poor achievers) do not have a realistic chance of obtaining classroom rewards, since such rewards are typically based to some degree on relative performance. Second, it is difficult to reinforce some of the most important learning-related behaviors, such as attentiveness or active problem solving. Students often look attentive when they are not. As a result, teachers usually reward good performance, which for some students is achieved without much effort and for others may be unachievable even with considerable effort. Thus, a child who completes a task without really trying is rewarded, while a child who works very hard but is not able to complete a task is not rewarded. Third, the effect of extrinsic rewards is short-lived. Students cannot be expected to continue to display the desired behaviors when no rewards are available. Fourth, there is considerable evidence, reviewed in a later section, that under some circumstances, rewards can undermine students' intrinsic interest in tasks. These practical problems, as well as theoretical developments in the field, have contributed to a shift of focus away from extrinsic rewards as a strategy for motivating children.

## Cognitive Mediation

Traditional behavior modification programs, including token economies, such as the one developed by H. Cohen, assume that reinforcements have a direct effect on behavior. In recent years, however, most theorists who continue to stress the importance of extrinsic contingencies on behavior have assumed that the effects of those contingencies are mediated by cognitions. Much of the current work that has evolved from reinforcement theory has been influenced by the Russian psychologists Vygotsky (1962, 1978) and Luria (1961), who believed that humans' symbolic representational ability, and especially their ability to use language, allows them to control their own behavior in ways that animals cannot. Humans are able to anticipate, plan, and direct their actions *before* implementing them. Accordingly, in many current classroom applications of reinforcement principles, students play a more active role in manipulating the stimulus conditions that influence their behavior than they did under traditional behavior modification programs. Researchers have developed strategies, referred to as *cognitive behavior modification,* that require students to take more responsibility for managing their behavior.

***Cognitive Behavior Modification.*** Hallahan and Sapona (1983) define cognitive behavior modification (CBM) as "the modification of overt behavior through the manipulation of covert thought processes" (p. 616). It is similar to approaches based on traditional reinforcement theory both because it is designed to change observable behavior and because reinforcement principles are assumed to be operating. But it is different in the sense that the treatment involves modifying a person's cognitive operations in order to achieve a change in his or her behavior. When CBM approaches are used, the teacher is not the sole determiner of reinforcement contingencies and dispenser of rewards, as is the case in behavior modification programs, like token economies, that are based on strict reinforcement theory. Rather, cognitive behavior modification requires children to take more responsibility—by monitoring their own behavior, setting their own goals and standards, or administering their own rewards (Meichenbaum, 1977). The use of CBM reflects a general trend toward giving more attention to students' own role in the learning process—referred to as "self-regulated learning" (see Zimmerman & Schunk, 1989). Learning theorists interested in promoting more self-regulated learning focus on behavioral strategies such as self-recording and self-reinforcement, while more cognitive theorists, discussed below, focus on metacognitive strategies, such as setting goals, planning procedures, and monitoring understanding (Ainley, 1993; Pintrich & De Groot, 1990; Pintrich & Schrauben, 1992).

Proponents of CBM approaches assume several important advantages. When students become more involved in regulating their own behavior, desirable behaviors are expected to be maintained longer after the rewards are withdrawn. Personal involvement should also lead to greater generalization of the desired behavior outside of the setting in which the rewards were originally given. In general, CBM is believed to result in less reliance on external agents to control behavior (Mace & Kratochwill, 1988).

One of the simplest CBM methods used to involve students in regulating their own behavior is to have them record their behavior. *Self-recording* has been found to influence behavior, even without tangible reinforcements—an outcome referred to as "reactivity" (Mace, Belfiore, & Shea, 1989). Children may be asked to record, for example, the duration of an activity (like reading after school each day), the frequency of a particular behavior (completing assignments, forgetting homework), or the level of performance (number of spelling words spelled correctly on weekly quizzes). A few researchers have found that self-monitoring is more effective in increasing desired behaviors than in decreasing undesirable behaviors (e.g., Litrownik & Freitas, 1980). It has been shown to be enhanced by training (Mace & Kratochwill, 1988) and by having a predetermined performance standard to work toward (Kazdin, 1974).

*Self-reinforcement* has also been used in achievement contexts (Bornstein & Quevillon, 1976; Masters & Santrock, 1976). For example, children are allowed to reward themselves with desired activities (playing with the pet gerbil) or with tangible rewards, for completing their work or achieving a certain standard.

A number of researchers have observed that children with learning problems often lack metacognitive skills that provide an awareness of what knowledge, strategies, and resources are needed to perform a task effectively. They may also lack self-regulation skills, such as the ability to plan and evaluate the effectiveness of ongoing activities (Hallahan & Sapona, 1983). These skills can be enhanced by teaching children to verbalize instructions (see, for example, Swanson & Scarpati, 1985). In some cases children are given reminders (such as a card taped to their desk) of the sequence of steps they need to follow to complete a task.

Reinforcement theorists view CBM strategies as a complement to rather than as a substitute for external reinforcement (Mace et al., 1989). According to the theory, individuals control their own behavior only in the sense that they alter the consequences of their actions. The extrinsic consequences ultimately determine future behavior.

Cognitive behavior modification is not without practical problems. Studies have shown, for example, that children tend to select lenient performance standards when given an option (Rosenbaum & Drabman, 1979; Wall, 1983), and they also cheat when allowed to reinforce themselves (Speidel & Tharp, 1980). These are not insurmountable problems. Incentives can be given to encourage students to set challenging standards, and cheating can be monitored. But they suggest that CBM strategies are not always easy to implement.

In addition to these practical problems, most current motivation theorists find reinforcement theory itself inadequate as an explanation of behavior. Although in recent formulations individuals are believed to be able to direct their own behavior by affecting their own reinforcement contingencies, behavior is assumed to be ultimately controlled by its consequences. According to cognitive theories of achievement motivation, to which we now turn, behavior is affected by cognitions themselves, with real consequences playing a less critical role.

## ACHIEVEMENT-RELATED COGNITIONS

Fundamental to most theories of cognition is the idea that whether individuals have been rewarded for achievement behaviors in the past is less important than whether they *expect* to be rewarded in the future. Bandura (1977b, 1986) has further pointed out that expectations for reinforcement are influenced by factors (such as verbal persuasion and observation) other than an individuals' own reinforcement history.

An *expectation of rewards,* both tangible and intangible, is the cognitive mediator that theorists have given the most attention to, but a number of related cognitive constructs may also explain behavior in achievement contexts. Rotter (1966) proposed that whether individuals expect their behavior to be rewarded depends to some degree on their *perceptions of control over outcomes*. He claims that individuals believe they are in control of rewards (to have an "internal locus of control") only when they believe that rewards are contingent on their personal characteristics or behavior. Weisz (1986, 1990) added that in addition to a belief in contingency, a perception of control over outcomes requires individuals to believe they are competent to produce the behavior on which the desired outcome is contingent. Cognitive motivation researchers have therefore studied *perceptions of ability*. Bandura's (1977a, 1982a, 1982b, 1986) construct, *self-efficacy,* contains elements of both expectancies and perceived ability; self-efficacy refers to individuals' judgments of their performance capabilities—that is, whether they are capable of succeeding—on a particular type of task.

Weiner (1986, 1992) emphasizes the importance of individuals' *attributions*—their perceptions of the cause of achievement outcomes. He pointed out that whether rewards are perceived to be contingent on one's own characteristics or behavior is only one dimension of causality that has implications for behavior. The stability of the cause and whether the individual actually controls it are equally important. For example, past outcomes attributed to stable causes (such as ability) are predictive of future outcomes, but outcomes attributed to unstable causes (like luck) are not. Past outcomes attributed to controllable causes (such as effort) similarly have different implications for possible future outcomes than past outcomes attributed to uncontrollable causes (like stable ability).

The following discussion reviews research supporting the claim that cognitions do affect behavior in achievement contexts. There follows a description of particular teacher behaviors and instructional practices that have been shown to affect students' cognitions. The discussion is not organized by cognitive constructs because the cognitions believed to mediate behavior in achievement situations are highly interrelated. For example, students who perceive themselves to be academically competent are more likely than students who believe themselves to be academically *in*competent to attribute success to a stable cause (their own competence), to believe they have control over achievement outcomes, to rate their self-efficacy high on a particular academic task, and to expect future success on school tasks. Because educational practices that affect one belief are likely to affect most of the other beliefs, these achievement-related cognitions are treated as a package in most of the following discussion.

## Effects of Achievement-Related Cognitions on Behavior and Emotions

It is important to understand how instructional practices affect cognitions because these cognitions influence students'

behavior and emotions in achievement contexts. A compelling illustration of the effect of cognitions on behavior is seen in work on learned helplessness.

Dweck and her colleagues have found that children who attribute achievement failure primarily to controllable causes, such as effort or strategy, typically persist and use effective problem-solving strategies when they encounter difficulty. In contrast, children who attribute failure to causes they do not control tend to react to initial failure with maladaptive or helpless behavior, employing strategies that have already failed or simply giving up (see Diener & Dweck, 1978; Dweck, 1975; Dweck & Elliott, 1983; Dweck & Reppucci, 1973). Thus, students who believe rewards are not contingent on their behavior will not exert effort to succeed.

According to Weisz's (1986) analysis, helplessness also occurs in situations in which the outcome is contingent on an individual's behavior but the individual believes he or she lacks the competence to manifest the behavior on which a positive outcome depends. For example, a student may believe that a good grade is contingent on giving correct responses but may become helpless because he does not believe he has the ability to find the correct responses.

Support for relationships between students' control-related beliefs—including both contingency and competency beliefs—and their behavior in achievement settings is seen in research conducted by Skinner, Wellborn, and Connell (1990; see also Connell and Wellborn, 1991). In a correlational study of upper elementary school students, they found that students' beliefs about how much control they had over achievement outcomes, as well as their beliefs about contingency and their competencies, were strongly associated with teachers' ratings of students' level of engagement in classroom activities.

The negative consequences of low perceived competence on achievement behavior may be exacerbated in contexts that engender concerns about performance. Support for this proposal is seen in research reviewed by R. Ames (1983) that suggested that students who have low perceptions of their ability are especially reluctant to seek help when they are concerned about how competent they look.

Self-efficacy beliefs have also been shown to affect achievement-related behavior and learning. Collins (1982), for example, identified students who were low, average, and high in mathematical ability on the basis of scores on standardized tests. Within each ability group students with relatively high perceptions of self-efficacy solved more problems correctly and chose to rework more problems that they had missed than students low in perceived self-efficacy. Self-efficacy perceptions, therefore, predicted achievement behavior over and above actual ability level. Pintrich and De Groot (1990) report a study in which self-efficacy was strongly associated with the use of constructive cognitive strategies and self-regulated learning (e.g., trying to make connections between textbook and classroom instruction, rereading material, making outlines), independent of prior achievement (see also Locke, Frederick, Lee, & Bobko, 1984). Finally, Schunk has shown repeatedly that raising children's perceptions of self-efficacy enhances their performance on academic tasks (see Schunk, 1983a, 1984b, 1989, 1991).

In addition to directly affecting behavior, cognitions have an impact on emotional reactions in educational settings, which are assumed, in turn, to affect achievement-related behavior. Thus, for example, in Atkinson's (1964) theory, expectations for success on a task affect anticipated pride (which engenders task-approach behavior) and shame (which engenders task-avoidance behavior); the higher the perceived probability of success, the less pride anticipated for success and the more shame anticipated for failure.

Weiner (1986) and his colleagues have demonstrated that some emotional reactions to success and failure (assessed by ratings) are affected by perceptions of what caused an outcome. Subjects claim that they experience pride and shame, for example, only when outcomes are attributed to personal characteristics (e.g., ability) or behavior (e.g., effort). Guilt is rated high only when negative outcomes are attributed to controllable causes. Weiner assumes that these emotions, in turn, stimulate approach behaviors (in the cases of pride and guilt) and avoidance behaviors (in the case of shame) in future achievement situations. Support for the proposed effects of emotions on achievement behavior comes from a study by Covington and Omelich (1984a) in which college students' guilt about their performance on one midterm was associated with enhanced effort and performance on the next midterm, whereas humiliation over past performance was associated with subsequent decreased effort and performance.

Because of the importance of achievement-related beliefs and resultant emotions, it is useful to know how beliefs are affected by different instructional approaches and other aspects of educational settings. The following discussion describes research on the effects of achievement contexts on students' expectations for success, perceptions of control over achievement outcomes, perceptions of academic competence, and perceptions of the cause of achievement outcomes.

## Effects of Instructional Practices and the Classroom Context on Achievement-Related Cognitions

Clear and consistent implications for classroom practice can be derived from research on factors affecting achievement-related cognitions. This discussion reviews research on the nature of tasks, as well as many aspects of the instructional context, including the criteria for, and administration of, evaluation and rewards; the social organization of the classroom; and teacher behavior toward children and emotional displays. Both experimental and classroom-based studies are reviewed because both have implications for educational practice.

*Difficulty Level of Tasks.* Students' judgments about the difficulty level of school tasks clearly affect their achievement-related cognitions. Tasks perceived by the student as difficult (in relation to his or her skill level) engender lower expectations for success, perceptions of control, and perceptions of self-efficacy than easy tasks. Giving students easy assignments, however, is not an effective strategy for maintaining positive achievement-related cognitions. Although easy tasks produce high expectations for success, people usually assume that success on easy tasks does not require high ability (Nicholls & Miller, 1984). As a result, easily achieved success does not contribute to positive judgments of competence, nor does it produce feelings of pride and satisfaction (Atkinson, 1964).

Furthermore, tasks that are completed without much effort are not intrinsically interesting.

Motivation researchers, therefore, recommend tasks of intermediate difficulty—tasks that students can complete but only with some effort, so as to engender feelings of increasing competence and pride. Bandura, Schunk, and others have proposed breaking down long-term, *distal goals* into smaller units, or *proximal goals,* as a strategy for calibrating the difficulty of tasks (Bandura, 1981; Locke, Shaw, Saari, & Latham, 1981; Manderlink & Harackiewicz, 1984; Schunk, 1984a, 1990, 1991). Proximal goals allow students to receive continual feedback that conveys a sense of developing mastery while they work toward a long-term goal that might otherwise appear too difficult.

In a demonstration of the motivational value of proximal goals, Bandura and Schunk (1981) gave elementary-school-aged children seven sets of subtraction problems to work on over seven sessions. Children were told either to complete one set each session (proximal goal), to complete all seven sets by the end of the seventh session (distal goal), or simply to work on the problems. The proximal goal situation produced higher self-efficacy and subtraction skill than the other two instructions. Students in the distal goal condition performed no better than students who were given no specific goal (see also Schunk, 1983b, 1986; Schunk & Rice, 1989).

In a study of first and second graders, Gaa (1973) demonstrated that giving children experience in setting proximal goals helped them develop skills in setting appropriate goals for themselves—ones that are challenging but likely to be achieved. Children who met weekly with an experimenter to set goals for the next week and to discuss achievements relative to the previous week's goals attained a higher level of reading achievement and also set more appropriate goals at the end of the intervention than children who were not given experience in setting and reviewing personal goals (see also Gaa, 1979; Tollefson, Tracy, Johnsen, Farmer, & Buenning, 1984; Schunk, 1985, 1991.) In general, researchers have found that involving children in the goal-setting process raises self-efficacy (Schunk, 1985) and enhances performance (Hom & Murphy, 1985).

In summary, challenging tasks that can be accomplished with some effort result in the most positive achievement-related beliefs in students. Clear and frequent feedback indicating developing competencies is important and can be achieved in some achievement contexts by breaking down long-term goals into proximal goals that can be reached in a relatively brief amount of time.

*Task Differentiation.* Rosenholtz and Simpson (1984a, 1984b) have demonstrated that the degree to which tasks are differentiated across students and over time affect students' judgments about their own ability relative to classmates' ability as well as the way they conceptualize ability (see also Rosenholtz & Rosenholtz, 1981; Rosenholtz & Wilson, 1980; Simpson, 1981; Simpson & Rosenholtz, 1986). They claim that an undifferentiated ("unidimensional") academic task structure—in which all students work on the same task, using the same materials, and are expected to produce the same responses—promotes social comparison. Also, the more that tasks are similar from day to day, the more likely it is that individual students will consistently perform at the same level relative to others. Thus, undifferentiated tasks can be expected to promote a conception of ability as a stable trait similar to the concept of IQ. Rigid ability grouping and public evaluation are often associated with a unidimensional task structure, and these factors most likely reinforce perceptions of ability as stable, stratified (i.e., highly unequal), measurable, and consensual—that is, as something that has an objective reality that can be perceived by others and the self. This concept of ability is similar to what Dweck (1986; Dweck & Elliott, 1983) refers to as an "entity" theory.

In differentiated ("multidimensional") task structures, on any day different students may work on several different kinds of tasks, and from day to day the types of tasks students are given vary. This task structure results in less consistency in students' relative performance from task to task and from day to day and makes social comparison more difficult. When students' performance varies from task to task, they are more likely to view skill development as incremental and domain-specific.

Rosenholtz and Simpson (1984a) explain that task structure and the publicness of performance outcomes influence classroom processes in several mutually reinforcing ways. They influence (a) the distribution of actual performances, (b) the amount of information available to students concerning their own and their classmates' performances, (c) the degree to which information about the self and others is comparable, and (d) the level of consistency in performance for any one student. These consequences, in turn, affect the way students form perceptions about their own ability.

Research findings are generally supportive of this analysis. Pepitone (1972) demonstrated experimentally that uniformity in curricular tasks resulted in greater social comparison behavior ("I got fewer wrong than you") than differentiation in tasks. Studies also show that both teachers' evaluations of students and students' evaluations of themselves and their peers are more stratified (that is, there is greater dispersion in judgments) in unidimensional than in multidimensional classrooms (Rosenholtz & Rosenholtz, 1981; Rosenholtz & Simpson, 1984b). Similarly, children's self-perceptions in unidimensional classrooms correspond more strongly to teacher evaluations (Rosenholtz & Rosenholtz, 1981; Simpson, 1981). Students also tend to agree with each other on their own and their classmates' relative ability in unidimensional classrooms (Rosenholtz & Simpson, 1984a). In short, compared to multidimensional classrooms, all actors in unidimensional classrooms agree more closely in their ratings of particular students.

There is also evidence that students define schoolwork more narrowly in unidimensional classrooms. In a study of third graders, Simpson (1981) asked students to rate their ability in "schoolwork" in general and in five specific curriculum areas—arithmetic, reading, social studies, art, and athletics. In unidimensional classrooms, students' ratings of their ability in schoolwork were determined to a significant degree by their ratings in only three areas—arithmetic, reading, and social studies. In multidimensional classrooms, ratings in these three areas were not as strongly associated with students' ratings of their overall ability in schoolwork. Thus, in multidimensional classrooms students could build their self-confidence by performing well in a variety of domains.

Mac Iver (1987), however, has demonstrated that task structure needs to be considered in the context of other variables in classroom instruction. He found, for example, that in multidi-

mensional classrooms in which grades were heavily emphasized, students were highly reliant on adult evaluations in judging their own math ability. Apparently the grades provided a standardized, easily comparable criterion and, when given frequently, they overrode the multiple performance dimensions created by a differentiated task structure. In a second study, Mac Iver (1988) found that an undifferentiated task structure did not result in considerable dispersion in students' perceptions of their ability when the ability level of students was homogeneous. He proposed that an undifferentiated task structure resulted in low stratification in this situation because students focused their attention on the homogeneous group they were assigned to rather than on the variation of ability levels within their group.

Taken together, this body of research provides strong evidence for the effects of task differentiation on students' judgments of ability. Mac Iver's research, however, suggests the importance of examining task structure in concert with other classroom practices, including variables such as evaluation and between-class ability grouping.

*Ability Grouping and Tracking.* Ability grouping and tracking are among the most widely used and also the most controversial strategies for organizing classroom instruction. As Rosenholtz and her colleagues point out, grouping students by ability facilitates comparisons, especially if the composition of the groups is stable and the relative level of the groups is salient.

The effect of ability grouping and tracking on students' judgments of their competence depends on the frame of reference they use to judge their ability. To the degree that students base their judgments of their own ability on their *performance compared with the immediate group or track,* relatively low performers should have higher perceptions of their competence when grouped or tracked with other low performers than when they are heterogeneously grouped (and thus have very high-performing classmates to compare themselves with). High performers would have higher perceptions of their competence when heterogeneously grouped than when grouped with equally high-performing peers because in a heterogeneous group they would have low-performing classmates to compare themselves with. If, on the other hand, students base their self-ratings of ability on their *group membership,* high-performing students should rate their ability higher and low-performing students should rate their ability lower when grouped or tracked.

Eder (1983) provided ethnographic evidence indicating that as early as in the first grade, children use both frames of reference—their own performance compared with that of members of their immediate group, and the standing of their group relative to other groups. The effect of grouping or tracking, therefore, should vary according to the relative salience of performance differences between versus within groups.

To the degree that differences among students *within* the group or track are salient, students' performance relative to other students within their group should affect their perceptions of their own ability. This would be true, for example, in a reading group in which children listened to each other read, or in a tracked class in which the teacher made students' performances on tests public. To the degree that differences *between* groups in a classroom or in a school are salient, students' group placement should affect their perceptions of competence. Group differences would be salient if the teacher regularly announced to the whole class each ability group's assignment, emphasizing differences between groups in the level of difficulty, or if the teacher continually reminded a class which track it was in. Variations related to these variables across studies may explain the inconsistent findings in research on how ability group placement affects students' perceptions of their competence (see Goldberg, Passow, & Justman, 1966; Weinstein, 1976).

There is some evidence suggesting that group membership is more salient for within-class ability grouping than for between-class grouping or tracking. In one study low-achieving students rated their ability lower when they were placed in the low-ability group within a class than when they were in homogeneous low-ability classes. Likewise, high-ability students rated their ability higher when they were grouped within the class than when they were placed in a high-ability class (Reuman, 1989). The results indicated that high-ability grouped students benefited from within-class grouping because they compared themselves to students in lower groups. Low-ability students benefited from between-class groupings because they based their perceptions of their ability primarily on comparisons with the low-ability students in their class.

Children do not necessarily choose a frame of reference that will result in the most positive judgment. Renick and Harter (1989) found that most of the mainstreamed learning-disabled students they studied spontaneously compared their academic performance to that of nondisabled children in their regular classroom. This was found even though they rated themselves higher when they were specifically asked to rate their competence relative to students in the learning-disabled class they attended for part of the day. Their global self-worth ratings were also better predicted by their perceptions of their competence relative to their nondisabled classmates than by their perceptions of their competence relative to that of other learning-disabled children.

In summary, the effect of ability grouping and tracking on students' judgments of their competence is not straightforward. The above analysis suggests that low-achieving children benefit, in terms of their perceived competence, from between-class grouping and are disadvantaged by within-class grouping. The opposite appears to be true for high-achieving students.

*Criteria for Success.* Criteria for evaluation have important implications for students' achievement-related cognitions. C. Ames and her colleagues have studied the effects of the criteria used for determining success (which they refer to as the "goal structure") on students' achievement-related cognitions (see C. Ames, 1984, 1986; C. Ames & R. Ames, 1984, for reviews). They have compared, for example, competitive criteria, in which success is defined as performing better than classmates, with individual or mastery criteria, in which success is defined as personal improvement or meeting a predetermined standard.

Research has shown, first, that the criteria for success influence students' perceptions of the cause of success and failure (their attributions). Children emphasize ability (and sometimes luck) more when interpreting their performance in competitive contexts, and they emphasize effort more in situations in which success is determined by group performance, personal improvement, or meeting a preestablished standard (C. Ames, 1978, 1981; C. Ames & R. Ames, 1978, 1981; C. Ames, R. Ames, & Felker, 1977; Rheinberg, 1983).

A study by C. Ames and R. Ames (1981) demonstrated that criteria for success also affect how children evaluate themselves. Children were given an opportunity to establish a personal performance history on a task (success or failure). They were then introduced to one of two types of criteria for success: competitive (involving comparison with another child) or individualistic (based on self-improvement). When the children were subsequently asked a series of questions, their self-reward and feelings of satisfaction in the competitive situation were based on whether they won or lost, not on the quality of their own performance. Children in the individualistic condition focused on their personal history with the task (i.e., whether they improved).

Covington and Omelich (1984b) showed additional benefits to a mastery standard for success rather than one based on competition. They found that undergraduate psychology students who were graded using a mastery standard (in which grades were determined by what score the student attained) perceived the grading system to be fairer and more responsive to effort than students who were graded using a competitive, norm-referenced standard. The students in the mastery condition also aspired to a higher grade and had more self-confidence about being able to achieve a high grade.

There is evidence that very young children (below the second grade) have a strong disposition to use a mastery standard and to emphasize effort as the cause of achievement (Blumenfeld, Pintrich, & Hamilton, 1986; Harter & Pike, 1984; Stipek, 1981). This suggests that a competitive goal structure may not affect them as much as it would older children. The mastery orientation may be explained in part by limitations in young children's cognitive abilities. For example, they may not be able to make as much sense of comparative information as older children. It is also possible that young children tend to have a mastery orientation partly because competition is stressed less by teachers in the first few grades of school.

Mastery Learning Programs.    Defining success as mastering a predetermined standard is a central feature of the various mastery-based educational programs that have been developed by Bloom (1971, 1974, 1976, 1981) and others. The fundamental assumption underlying mastery learning models is that nearly all students can learn the basic school curriculum, but that some take longer than others. Providing students who learn more slowly with more time to gain skills therefore allows all students to master the curriculum. Making success available to all students should, moreover, engender a perception of control over achievement outcomes, perceptions of self-efficacy, and high expectations for success.

Mastery learning programs such as Bloom's Learning for Mastery (LFM) program (Bloom, Hastings, & Madaus, 1971) and Keller's (1968) Personalized System of Instruction (PSI) have been implemented in schools throughout the world, and their effects on motivation and learning have been extensively evaluated. Evaluations suggest that mastery learning programs have positive effects on attitudes and achievement, particularly for weaker students (Guskey & Pigott, 1988; C-L. Kulik, J. Kulik, & Bangert-Drowns, 1990; J. Kulik, C-L. Kulik, & Cohen, 1979).

They are not, however, entirely effective in achieving motivation-related goals, such as focusing students' attention on improving their own skills as opposed to competing against classmates. Informal observations of mastery-based programs suggest that it is difficult to eliminate students' interest in comparing their performance with that of classmates (Buckholdt & Wodarski, 1974; Crockenberg & Bryant, 1978; Levine, 1983). Researchers have therefore sought ways to use competition to motivate students without negative effects.

Cooperative Incentive Structures.   An instructional strategy that has been proposed to use competition to good advantage pits groups of students of equal skill levels against each other (E. Cohen, 1986; D. Johnson & R. Johnson, 1985b, 1989; Slavin, 1984; Slavin, Sharan, Kagan, Hertz-Lazarowitz, Webb, & Schmuck, 1985). Slavin (1983a, 1983b, 1984) claims, on the basis of reviews of research on cooperative learning programs, that the highest level of motivation and learning occurs when each student's reward is contingent on the performance of all group members—what he refers to as a "cooperative incentive structure." By combining high- and low-performing students in groups, so that all groups have a roughly equal chance of winning, and by making rewards contingent on the group's performance, cooperative incentive structures equalize opportunities for rewards. In this way a group reward structure can relieve motivation problems that many low-ability students have in individual competitive situations in which they have no hope of "winning."

Evidence suggests further that when rewards are based on the sum of all the members' performances, simply being a member of a successful group allows all students some of the advantages of success, such as high self-perceptions of ability, satisfaction, and peer esteem (C. Ames, 1981; C. Ames & Felker, 1979). Because cooperative incentive structures give all students an equal chance at being a member of the winning team, they also focus students' attention on effort as a cause of outcomes, rather than on ability (see C. Ames & R. Ames, 1984).

Cooperative learning approaches have other potential motivational benefits. By rewarding groups as well as individuals for their academic achievement, peer norms favor rather than oppose high achievement (see D. Johnson & R. Johnson, 1985b; Sharan, 1980, for reviews). Studies have found that students in cooperative incentive structures are more likely than students in individual competitive situations to agree with such statements as "Other children in my class want me to work hard" (see Hulton & DeVries, 1976). Research has also shown that students in cooperative incentive structures are more likely to tutor, help, and encourage classmates than students in individualistic competitive structures (see D. Johnson & R. Johnson, 1985a, 1985b).

To summarize, the weight of the evidence on goal structures supports the use of improvement or mastery-based criteria over competitive criteria for success. Competition is only effective in maximizing students' motivation when the game is fair—that is, when all students have a roughly equal chance of winning and when effort determines the outcome. A cooperative incentive structure is one competitive strategy that teachers can use to minimize the negative effects that competition has on children's achievement-related cognitions, especially in classrooms where students vary in their academic skill levels.

*Contingency of Rewards.* Few studies have directly assessed the effect of the contingency of rewards on children's perceptions of control over achievement outcomes. Control theory (Rotter, 1966; Weisz, 1986, 1990), however, has clear implications for classroom practice: Teachers who dispense rewards indiscriminately or unpredictably, or teachers who are biased, should engender perceptions of low control. Support for this assumption comes from one study by Schunk (1983c). Children who were given rewards contingent on their actual performance in a division task had a higher sense of self-efficacy than children who were rewarded for their participation, regardless of their performance.

Brophy (1981) and colleagues' observations of classrooms have revealed that teachers do not always reinforce good performance or even high effort. Anderson, Evertson, and Brophy (1979) found, for example, that teachers were slightly more likely to give praise following reading turns containing mistakes than following errorless reading turns. These teachers may have been using praise to encourage poor-performing children to try harder. Despite these good intentions, however, praise and other rewards that are not consistently contingent on effort and good performance most likely undermine perceptions of control over achievement outcomes. Teachers' lack of consistency and clarity in reward contingencies may explain why some children in Connell's (1985) study claimed not to know what caused success and failure in their classroom.

A study by Dweck, Davidson, Nelson, and Enna (1978) suggests possible gender differences in classroom contingencies. They observed in fourth- and fifth-grade classrooms that although boys were criticized more often than girls, most of the criticism boys received concerned conduct or failure to follow directions. In contrast to the boys, most of the small amount of criticism the girls received concerned the quality of their academic performance. The authors suggest that boys may therefore view negative feedback as less relevant to their intellectual abilities than do girls.

## Communication of Teacher Expectations

The *Pygmalion* study by Rosenthal and Jacobson (1968) was the first to suggest that teachers' expectations, even when based on false information, can influence young students' learning. Since that classic study, many researchers have examined ways in which teachers might influence students' achievement-related beliefs by sometimes unintentionally communicating their own convictions about students' ability to achieve. Traditionally, research on teachers' expectations focused on variations in teachers' behavior toward students for whom they had high or low expectations. Most of these studies, however, assessed the effect of differential teacher behavior on achievement rather than on achievement-related beliefs.

An exception to the focus on teacher behavior and student achievement is work by Weinstein and her colleagues, which examined students' *perceptions* of teachers' behavior and the effects of these perceptions on their own performance expectations. Their research indicates that there is great variability in the degree to which teachers are perceived as behaving differently toward high and low achievers (see Weinstein, 1985, 1989), and that the degree of differentiation has implications for students' own performance expectations.

Brattesani, Weinstein, and Marshall (1984), for example, asked students whether their teacher treated high- and low-achieving students differently, as well as how the teacher treated them. In classrooms in which students claimed that teachers behaved differently toward high and low achievers ("high differential treatment" classrooms), students' expectations for their performance were more strongly associated with teachers' expectations than they were in "low differential treatment" classrooms. Age is also a factor. As early as first grade, children demonstrated their awareness of teachers' differential behavior toward high and low achievers. Yet one study found that children in early elementary school were less likely to report negative treatment toward *themselves* than were upper-elementary-school-aged children (Weinstein, Marshall, Sharp, & Botkin, 1987). Their expectations for themselves also conformed less to their teachers' expectations.

Teacher Attributional Statements.    Attribution researchers have examined *how* differential teacher behavior might affect students' achievement-related beliefs. These studies have focused on attributional statements—statements about the cause of performance outcomes—made directly to individuals, as well as more subtle ways in which teachers communicate their own expectations and perceptions of a student's competence. Their purpose is to understand primarily how teachers convey their beliefs about their students' ability to succeed, thus influencing students' own expectations and beliefs.

Both attribution and self-efficacy theorists have assessed the effect of attribution statements (statements directly referring to the cause of an individual's performance) on the individual's perceptions of the cause of achievement outcomes and on their behavior and learning. The effect of attribution statements has been demonstrated primarily in interventions—referred to as "attribution retraining"—designed to change the attributions children make for their performance outcomes.

Dweck's (1975) pioneering study is illustrative. She identified children who showed the attributional pattern associated with learned helplessness; that is, they tended not to take personal responsibility for outcomes and underemphasized the role of effort. Their performance following the occurrence of failure was impaired, as would be predicted from attribution theory. During 25 daily training sessions, half of these children were given a heavy dose of success and half received attribution retraining. The attribution retraining group had many successes, but several failures were also programmed each day. When failure occurred the experimenter explicitly commented to the child that the failure was due to a lack of effort. At the end of the training the children in the attribution retraining condition, but not the children in the success-only condition, attributed outcomes more to effort than they had before the training. Attribution-retraining children also showed improvement in their response to failure; they persisted, using appropriate problem-solving strategies, rather than giving up. Children who had been in the success-only group showed no improvement in their response to failure. Some of these children even showed a tendency to react somewhat more adversely to failure than they had before the start of the treatment. This and many subsequent studies have demonstrated that improvement in effort and performance can be achieved by explicitly focusing individuals'

attention on effort as causes of their performance (see Forsterling, 1985, for a review).

Although there appear to be benefits to attributing failure to low effort, focusing on effort as a cause of success may be less desirable. Schunk (1982, 1984a, 1984b) claims, on the basis of self-efficacy theory, that effort attribution training is effective because it implicitly gives students who have failed the message that they have the competency to succeed on the task. He suggests that teachers can accomplish this more directly by attributing success to ability, and he has demonstrated in several studies that explicit ability attributions for success raise children's perceptions of their self-efficacy and their performance in math (Schunk, 1983a, 1984b).

Schunk cautions against attributing students' success to effort because this can actually undermine feelings of competence. This was demonstrated in a study in which third graders were told, while they were working on subtraction problems, either "You're good at this" or "You've been working hard," or both (Schunk, 1983a). The children who received only the ability attribution judged themselves the most efficacious and solved the highest number of posttest problems (see also Schunk, 1984b). Schunk suggests that attributing success to effort reduces children's perceptions of their ability because they believe that success requiring high effort indicates lower ability than success achieved without much effort.

The effectiveness of attributional feedback should vary, to some degree, as a function of how far along a student is in developing a skill. Effort feedback should be most effective in the early stages of learning, when effort is necessary to succeed. As skills develop, less effort should be required to succeed at the same task. Consequently, students should find ability attributions more credible.

Several researchers have suggested that when failure occurs, *strategy* attributions might have advantages over effort attributions (Clifford, 1984; Reid & Borkowski, 1987). It is reasonable to expect children who do poorly despite considerable effort to be confused and discouraged when a teacher suggests that their poor performance is caused by poor effort. In contrast to an effort attribution, a strategy attribution provides recognition of students' efforts and conveys a positive, and potentially constructive, suggestion that the child needs to try an alternate approach to the problem.

There is, however, little evidence for the value of strategy versus effort attributions. C. Anderson and Jennings (1980) found in their study of college students that experimentally induced strategy attributions, compared to ability attributions, resulted in higher expectations after failure. The benefits of focusing children's attention on strategy as well as effort were demonstrated in a study by Borkowski, Weyhing, and Carr (1988). This study did not, however, demonstrate any advantages of focusing on strategy rather than on effort.

Attribution retraining studies have provided useful information about the effects of encouraging particular student attributions on effort and performance. Although most studies of the effect of attribution statements have been done in controlled, experimental contexts, the results of the experimental studies strongly suggest that what teachers say in classrooms should affect students' achievement-related benefits.

Emotional Displays.    Teachers' emotional reactions to success and failure also have been shown to affect children's causal attributions and expectations for success. This work is based on the empirically supported assumption that individuals believe that emotional reactions reflect a person's perception of the cause of behavior (see Weiner, 1986). Thus, for example, children as young as 6 years understand that anger is aroused when another's failure is attributed to controllable factors, such as lack of effort, and by about the age of 9 years they understand that pity is aroused when another's failure is perceived to be caused by uncontrollable causes (Weiner, Graham, Stern, & Lawson, 1982; see also Graham, 1990, 1991). Students gain information about their teachers' beliefs concerning the cause of their performance outcomes by attending to the teachers' emotional reactions.

Graham (1984) demonstrated that teachers' emotional responses can also affect students' *self*-perceptions. An experimenter expressed either mild anger or pity to children who had experienced failure. Children who had the sympathetic experimenter were more likely to attribute their failure to a lack of ability than children who had an angry experimenter. The latter were more likely to attribute their failure to a lack of effort. Children who received pity also had lower expectations for success in the future than children who received an angry response from the experimenter. Thus, by simply expressing an emotion the experimenter influenced children's perceptions of the cause of their failure and their expectations regarding future outcomes. These findings demonstrate ways in which well-intentioned teacher behavior may be detrimental to students' achievement-related beliefs.

Praise.   Another counterintuitive finding concerns the effect of praise on students' achievement-related beliefs. Praise given to one student but not to another for the same level of performance, or praise for success on an easy task, appears to have negative effects, at least for older children and adults (Meyer, 1982). Praise lowers rather than enhances self-confidence under these circumstances because it can be interpreted by a student as evidence that the teacher has a low perception of his or her ability. Criticism following poor performance can, under some circumstances, be interpreted as an indication of the teacher's high perception of the student's ability.

Praise can have negative effects and criticism positive effects on children's self-confidence. Parsons, Kaczala, and Meece (1982) found in the 20 fifth- to ninth-grade math classrooms they observed that frequent criticism for the quality of students' work was *positively* related to the students' self-concept of their math ability and to their future expectations. Praise was unrelated to math self-concept, although boys who were not praised tended to believe that their teachers had high expectations for them. The researchers concluded that teachers who avoid criticism and give praise freely overlook the power of the context in determining the meaning of the message. They suggest that well-chosen criticism can convey as much positive information as praise.

Praise and criticism can have these paradoxical effects because they are assumed to be associated with the level of perceived effort (i.e., high effort deserves praise and low effort deserves criticism) and because individuals perceive effort and ability to be inversely related, in the sense that given equal outcomes, the person who tried harder is judged as lower in

ability (Nicholls & Miller, 1984). Accordingly, if two children succeed and the teacher praises only one of them, the observer assumes that the praised child must have worked harder to achieve the same success as the other child, and therefore must be less able. If two children fail and only one is criticized, the observer assumes that the criticized child must not have worked as hard as the other child, and must therefore be higher in ability.

This analysis assumes a complex reasoning process that young children do not understand. Although children appreciate the relationship between praise and effort and make inferences about effort as young as age 5 (Harari & Covington, 1981; Weiner & Peter, 1973), they do not understand the inverse relationship between effort and ability until about age 11 (Nicholls & Miller, 1984). Research has shown that children below about age 11 do not rate a child they observe being praised by the teacher as lower in ability, or a child they observe being criticized as higher in ability, than a child the teacher did not praise or criticize (Barker & Graham, 1987).

Helping.   Helping behavior can also give students a message that they are perceived as low in ability. Meyer (1982) described a study by Conty in which the experimenter offered unrequested help either to the subject or to another individual in the room working on the same task. Compared to those who simply observed another student being helped, the subjects who were offered help claimed to feel more negative emotions (incompetence, anger, worry, disappointment, distress, anxiety) and fewer positive emotions (confidence, joy, pride, superiority, satisfaction). Graham and Barker (1990) reported that children as young as 6 years rated a student whom they observed being offered help by the teacher as lower in ability than the student who was not offered help.

The effect of help on ability judgments and emotional reactions can again be explained by an attributional analysis. Research has shown that in a variety of contexts, individuals are more likely to help others when their need is perceived to be caused by uncontrollable factors, such as low ability, than when their need is attributed to controllable factors, such as insufficient effort (see Weiner, 1986, 1992). This was shown in a classroom study by Brophy and Rohrkemper (1981) in which teachers expressed a greater commitment to help problem students when the causes of need were uncontrollable factors, such as low ability or shyness, than when the problems were attributed to controllable factors, such as lack of effort. Graham and Barker's (1990) results, mentioned above, suggest that a negative judgment of competence for a helped child also requires less complex reasoning. The 6-year-olds in their study may simply have learned that teachers help classmates who do poorly on schoolwork (and who are therefore lacking in competence) more than they help classmates who do well.

This research does not indicate that teachers should never be sympathetic or that they should refuse to praise or help children. It does, however, demonstrate that sympathizing, praising, and offering help to students can have implications for their perceptions of competence, and it suggests the importance of the context in which sympathy, praise, and help are given. Teachers should carefully evaluate whether one child is being offered help when others are not.

## Summary

Students enter each new classroom with a set of achievement-related beliefs, including expectations for success, perceptions of academic competence and self-efficacy, perceptions of control over achievement outcomes, and perceptions of the cause of those outcomes. Negative expectations, negative perceptions of competence, and maladaptive attributions are not easy to change because children interpret events in ways that are consistent with their beliefs. The immediate achievement context can, however, influence achievement-related cognitions in important ways that affect effort and learning. Beliefs that have been shown to be associated with high levels of engagement in intellectual activities are listed in Figure 5–1. Factors shown to foster positive achievement-related beliefs also are summarized in Figure 5–1.

Although much of the evidence for these general principles is based on experimental research, these guidelines are relevant to regular classrooms. Teachers who apply these motivation principles in their classrooms should be able to foster positive achievement-related cognitions, even in students who enter their classroom with negative beliefs about their ability to succeed.

## INTRINSIC VALUE

Individuals forgo opportunities to engage in achievement tasks not only when they expect to fail, but also when they do not expect to enjoy the work or when they do not value the success it might bring. Values are, accordingly, assumed to affect achievement behavior in most prominent theories of achievement motivation (see chapter 4).

As mentioned above, in Atkinson's (1964) Expectancy × Value theory, values are defined narrowly in terms of task-related incentives—expected pride in success and expected shame over failure. Success at a task with a high probability of success is expected to engender less pride, and therefore to have less value, than success at a task with a low probability of success.

Recent theorists have conceptualized values more broadly. Eccles (1983) proposed three kinds of values that influence choices and effort on academic tasks. (a) *Intrinsic value* is the immediate enjoyment one gets from doing a task. (b) *Attainment value* is the subjective importance of doing well on a task or in a particular achievement domain. Importance is determined by how a task or the domain fulfills the individual's needs. Attainment value concerns the relevance of an activity to an individual's self-concept. (c) *Utility value* is the perceived usefulness of a task as a means to achieve goals that might not be related to the task itself. For example, developing competencies in chemistry would have considerable utility value for a college student hoping to be admitted to medical school.

This discussion focuses on intrinsic value because it has been studied far more than attainment or utility value. Furthermore, most of the research on attainment and utility value has been done to explore gender differences, especially in participation in math courses and professions. (This research is discussed in chapter 12 of this volume.)

---

### CLASSROOM PRACTICES

**Tasks**

Design challenging tasks (that can be completed with a reasonable amount of effort).

Divide difficult tasks into subgoals that are achievable without requiring excessive effort.

Differentiate tasks across students and over time.

**Criteria for Success, Evaluation, and Rewards**

Define success in terms of mastery and personal improvement rather than in terms of performance relative to others.

If competition is used, make sure all students have an equal chance of "winning."

Provide clear and frequent feedback conveying developing competence.

Make rewards contingent on effort, improvement, and good performance.

**Teacher Behavior Toward Students**

Avoid unnecessary differential treatment of high and low achievers.

Focus on effort and strategy as the primary causes of failure, effort and ability as the causes of success.

Avoid subtle expressions conveying a perception of low ability (e.g., overly sympathetic responses for failure, praise for success on easy tasks, unnecessary help).

↓

### STUDENT BELIEFS

High expectations for success in general and in particular task situations (self-efficacy)

Perception of self as academically competent

Perception of control over achievement outcomes, including: (1) belief that rewards are contingent on behavior, and (2) belief that one has ability to produce behavior upon which rewards are contingent

Belief that poor outcomes are attributable to low effort or poor strategy, good outcomes are attributable to effort and ability

↓

### STUDENT OUTCOMES

Approach tasks willingly; seek help

Exert high effort, using constructive cognitive strategies

Persist in the face of difficulty

Take pride in success

FIGURE 5–1 Enhancing motivation by fostering positive achievement-related beliefs.

### Concept of Intrinsic Motivation

Several decades ago, motivation theorists recognized that individuals engage in tasks for reasons other than external reinforcement. They argued that humans are *naturally disposed* to seek opportunities to develop competencies—that mastering tasks and developing competencies are intrinsically pleasurable. In 1959, White published a now classic paper presenting evidence that an intrinsic "need" to feel competent is an innate characteristic of all humans and that such behaviors as exploration and attempts at mastery are best explained by this innate motivational force. Piaget (1952) similarly claimed that humans are naturally inclined, from the first day of life, to practice and develop new skills. This presumed innate need is usually referred to in the psychological literature as intrinsic motivation.

DeCharms, Deci, Ryan, and other achievement motivation theorists claim that humans have a natural need to feel *self-determining,* in addition to a need to feel competent. People want to believe they are engaging in activities of their own volition rather than to achieve some external reward or to avoid punishment (deCharms, 1976, 1984; Deci, 1975; Deci & Ryan, 1985). They argue that activities have more intrinsic value when individuals perceive themselves as the cause of their own behavior—when they perceive themselves as the *locus of causality*—than when they believe they are engaging in the activity because of rewards, constraints, or a desire to please another person, when the locus of causality is external.

Ryan and colleagues claim that a perception of personal causality has a positive effect on motivation, even if it does not enhance enjoyment (Deci, Eghrari, Patrick, & Leone, 1994; Ryan & Connell, 1989; Ryan, Connell, & Deci, 1985; Ryan, Connell, & Grolnick, 1992; Ryan & Stiller, 1991). They point out that children often work hard on assigned tasks that are not intrinsically interesting and for which no reinforcement is expected because they have *internalized* achievement values. They have learned from parents, teachers, and others that achievement behaviors are valued in our society, and they have taken on these values as their own. Thus, they experience their efforts on achievement tasks, even uninteresting ones, as being self-determined. The feelings of self-determination that come from the internalization of achievement values provide many of the same advantages as intrinsic interest.

## Advantages of Intrinsic Motivation

Many achievement motivation theorists consider intrinsically motivated behavior more desirable than extrinsically motivated behavior. First, intrinsically motivated individuals are not dependent on consequences external to their behavior, whereas extrinsically motivated individuals cease working when extrinsic rewards are not available (Stipek, 1993, chapter 3). Second, the same conditions that produce greater intrinsic motivation foster better conceptual learning (although not better rote recall) than conditions that engender an external locus of causality (Grolnick & Ryan, 1987). Comprehension also has been shown to be associated with intrinsic interest (Ryan, Connell, & Plant, 1990) and personal interest (see Hidi, 1990, for a review).

The benefits of practices that foster intrinsic motivation should be seen in children's achievement-related behavior outside of as well as in the classroom—an effect Maehr (1976) referred to as "continuing motivation." Extrinsic rewards that control students' learning behaviors convey to students the message that learning is not satisfying or enjoyable and should be engaged in only to obtain rewards or avoid punishment. Classroom instructional practices that sustain children's natural curiosity and intrinsic interest in learning no doubt contribute to their perception of learning as something that is enjoyable and nurture their desire to engage in learning tasks in other settings.

Studies have found, moreover, that an emphasis on extrinsic reasons for engaging in tasks can undermine creativity and cognitive flexibility. For example, in a study reported by Amabile (1983), judges rated art work by female college students who expected to be graded as less creative than the work of those who did not expect to be graded. In a study by McGraw and McCullers (1979), college students who were promised monetary rewards for solving a series of problems had more difficulty "breaking set" (solving a problem that had a different solution from the previous problems) than students who did not expect a monetary reward. The reason for the negative effect of extrinsic motivation on conceptual and creative thinking is not clear, although Amabile (1983) has suggested that extrinsic contingencies can create an instrumental focus that narrows attention and orients individuals to take the quickest and easiest solution.

Given the advantages of intrinsic motivation, research suggesting age-related declines in children's desire to engage in intellectual activities for their own pleasure is troubling. Harter (1981b), for example, found steady declines from the third through the ninth grade on her intrinsic motivation subscales measuring *preference for challenge, curiosity and interest,* and *independent mastery.* Other investigators have reported age-related declines in the perceived value and enjoyment of academic activities in specific domains, such as math (Eccles, 1983; Wigfield, Eccles, Mac Iver, Reuman, & Midgley, 1991. See also chapter 7.).

Eliminating extrinsic motivation from the classroom is neither realistic nor desirable. Little is known about its productive place in educational settings or ways in which it might effectively interact with or complement intrinsic motivation. Research typically pits intrinsic and extrinsic motivation against each other, with the implicit assumption that they are mutually exclusive or that one operates at the expense of the other. The most frequently used scale, for example, forces a choice between intrinsic and extrinsic responses (Harter, 1981b). A recent study suggests that these two orientations have different developmental trajectories and might operate independently (Lepper, Sethi, Dialdin, & Drake, in press). Future research is needed to explore potential compatibilities between these two motivational orientations and the implications for educational practice.

While not all motivation researchers are willing to disavow the use of extrinsic motivation in educational settings, none dispute the value of intrinsic motivation. Fortunately, there is research on instructional strategies that affect students' perceptions of causality and their intrinsic motivation. This research, discussed below, suggests ways to maximize student intrinsic interest in the learning process.

## Effect of Rewards

The most thoroughly researched variable believed to influence intrinsic motivation is the availability of extrinsic rewards. Research has shown that under certain conditions offering extrinsic rewards for engaging in tasks actually *undermines* intrinsic motivation. This effect is illustrated in a study by Lepper, Greene, and Nisbett (1973). One group of children was offered a reward—a "Good Player" certificate—for playing with Magic Markers, and another group was not. Subsequently, the children who had previously received the reward for playing with the Magic Markers did not spend as much free time on the activity as children who had not previously received a reward, nor as much time as a third group that was unexpectedly offered the reward. The quality of the rewarded children's pictures also declined markedly once the reward was withdrawn.

According to Morgan's (1984) review, 70 or 80 published studies have used a paradigm similar to these two studies to examine the effects of reward on subsequent engagement in various activities (see also reviews by Bates, 1979; Deci & Ryan, 1985; Lepper, 1983; Notz, 1975; Pittman, Boggiano, & Ruble, 1983; Ryan, Connell, & Deci, 1985). These studies suggest that external rewards can undermine intrinsic interest in a task.

It is noteworthy that this observed effect of extrinsic rewards is inconsistent with reinforcement theory. According to reinforcement theory, a reward made contingent on a behavior will increase the frequency of the behavior. When it is withdrawn the behavior should return to baseline, but it should not dip below baseline, as has been found in many studies.

Intrinsic motivation theorists assume that the negative effect a reward has on behavior after it is withdrawn can be explained only by cognitive processes. Self-attribution theorists propose that when a reward is offered, an individual perceives the reward as the reason for engaging in the activity, even though he or she would have been intrinsically motivated to do the task without the reward. The person therefore ceases the activity when the reward is withdrawn.

Cognitive evaluation theorists conceptualize motivation on a continuum rather than in terms of an internal–external dichotomy; intrinsic motivation is believed to be proportional to the *degree* to which individuals perceive their behavior to be self-determined or volitional rather than controlled by others, by rewards, or by intrapsychic forces like guilt or a sense of obligation (Deci, Vallerand, Pelletier, & Ryan, 1991; Rigby, Deci, Patrick, & Ryan, 1992; Ryan & Connell, 1989; Ryan & Stiller, 1991). Deci and Ryan (1985) claim that rewards cause individuals to shift away from an internal and toward an external locus of causality on this continuum by creating a feeling of being controlled and by interfering with a feeling of self-determination. Their argument is supported by evidence that other practices that make external reasons for doing a task salient also undermine intrinsic motivation. Those practices include close monitoring (Lepper & Greene, 1975; Plant & Ryan, 1985), imposing deadlines (Amabile, DeJong, & Lepper, 1976), imposing goals (Manderlink & Harackiewicz, 1984), and threats of punishment (see Deci & Ryan, 1987).

Rewards, however, can be used in different ways and for different purposes, and the research reviewed next suggests that their effects on locus of causality, and thus on intrinsic motivation, are determined by how they are used as much as by whether they are used.

### Controlling versus Information Function of Rewards

Lepper (1981), Deci (1975), and Bandura (1982b) all distinguish between two uses of rewards in classrooms: as an *incentive* to engage in tasks (that is, to control behavior) and as

*information* about mastery (see also Deci & Ryan, 1985; Ryan et al., 1985).

Rewards used to control behavior (as well as other instructional practices, such as close monitoring of performance) can shift students away from a perception of autonomy and personal causation and toward a perception of external causation. Such rewards undermine intrinsic motivation. Task-contingent rewards (those based on engaging in the task) are nearly always experienced as controlling.

Performance-contingent rewards (those based on achieving a specified level of performance) vary in their effects on intrinsic motivation, depending on several factors. Deci and Ryan (1985) point out that the interpersonal context in which performance-contingent rewards are given can affect whether they are perceived as controlling or informational. Praise (Ryan, 1982) and monetary rewards (Ryan, Mims, & Koestner, 1983), for example, have been found in experimental studies to undermine intrinsic motivation when a comment that conveys a desire to control, such as "you're doing as you should," was made when the reward was given. When the reward was not accompanied by the controlling comment, it did not undermine intrinsic motivation (see also Enzle & Ross, 1978; Harackiewicz, 1979; Pittman, Davey, Alafat, Wetherill, & Kramer, 1980; Rosenfield, Folger, & Adelman, 1980). Other rewards, such as good grades, can be interpreted as informative or controlling, depending on what the teacher emphasizes. Presumably, the teacher who constantly reminds students that if they don't pay attention they won't get a good grade focuses attention on the controlling function of grades; the teacher who emphasizes the positive information about mastery contained in a good grade focuses attention on the information value.

Students' histories of rewards may also influence the degree to which they perceive rewards as informational or controlling. This is suggested by a study by Pallak, Costomiris, Sroka, and Pittman (1982). They found that good-play awards were interpreted as providing competence information (and thus increased intrinsic motivation) by children in schools where symbolic rewards were used regularly to signify competence, and as an effort to control their behavior (thus decreasing intrinsic motivation) by children in schools where they had not been typically used.

Rewards containing information about competence can sustain or even enhance intrinsic motivation by increasing perceptions of competence or self-efficacy (Boggiano & Ruble, 1979; Karniol & Ross, 1977; Rosenfield, Folger, & Adelman, 1980). The competence feedback implicit in praise is presumably why, in most studies, praise, although external, does not reduce intrinsic motivation (Anderson, Manoogian, & Reznick, 1976; Blanck, Reis, & Jackson, 1984; Deci, 1971, 1972; Dollinger & Thelen, 1978; Pittman et al., 1980; Swann & Pittman, 1977; see Arkes, 1978, for a review). The social reinforcement presumably functions primarily as an indication of competence, which enhances intrinsic motivation, rather than as external control.

One problem with performance-contingent rewards, however, is that they maintain or enhance intrinsic motivation only if the feedback is positive (Boggiano & Ruble, 1979; Rosenfield et al., 1980; Ryan et al., 1983). Negative feedback (e.g., criticism) suggesting *in*competence undermines intrinsic motivation, especially if the individual doubts his or her ability ultimately to demonstrate competence.

*Summary.* The research discussed here suggests that the effect of rewards is not straightforward. Rewards undermine intrinsic interest to the degree that they are perceived to be controlling, and the controlling function can be conveyed in variable and subtle ways. Studies indicate, furthermore, that other practices (close monitoring, emphasizing deadlines, threats of punishment) also interfere with intrinsic motivation by fostering the perception of an external locus of causality. When the information value of rewards is salient—that is, when rewards are interpreted as conveying positive information about competence—they can actually increase intrinsic motivation.

Deci and his colleagues assume that a need to be self-determining is a universal human characteristic. It is, nevertheless, conceivable that people in cultures that stress individualism and autonomy are most negatively affected by attempts to control their behavior. Perhaps rewards used to control behavior would not affect intrinsic interest as much in cultures in which obedience and group cohesiveness were stressed.

## Effect of Evaluation

When teachers stress evaluation, they orient students' attention toward external reasons for engaging in school tasks and thus undermine students' perceptions of internal causality and intrinsic interest. Kage and Namiki (1990), for example, found that junior high school students who were given a series of quizzes that counted toward their grade expressed less interest in the material than students who had been given the quizzes as a means of monitoring their own learning.

An emphasis on external evaluation undermines intrinsic motivation in part because it engenders concerns about performance. Other practices that focus attention on performance, or on how intelligent one appears (referred to as an ego or performance orientation), have also been shown to undermine feelings of self-determination and consequently intrinsic motivation. Ryan (1982), for example, reported that subjects who were told that their performance on a task reflected creative intelligence (and thus who were ego involved) displayed less subsequent intrinsic motivation than subjects to whom the statement about intelligence was not made. Ryan (1982) explains that ego involvement represents a kind of internal control or pressure that people apply to themselves; being pressured by these internal constraints (i.e., a feeling that it is necessary to do well to prove one's self-worth) undermines intrinsic motivation in the same way that external pressures undermine it.

The undermining effect of evaluation appears to be strongest for difficult tasks. Hughes, Sullivan, and Mosley (1985) reported that children who were told that their performance on a difficult task was confidential were more likely to return to the task voluntarily than children who were told that their performance would be evaluated by their teacher. Teacher evaluation did not undermine interest in an easy task. Thus, the combination of being given a difficult task and being told that the teacher would evaluate performance had the most negative effects on intrinsic interest.

Task difficulty was also a relevant factor in a study by Maehr and Sallings (1972). They told eighth-grade boys either that the results of an easy or a difficult task would be reported to the teacher or that the task was "just for fun." Students who believed that their score would be reported were more likely to be

interested in doing another task if the first task had been easy than if the first task had been challenging. Students who were told that the task was for fun were more likely to want to do another task if the first task had been challenging. Similar findings were reported in a study of Iranian fifth graders (Salili, Maehr, Sorensen, & Fyans, 1976).

The *nature* of evaluation also influences its effect on intrinsic motivation. Like rewards, evaluations are better for student motivation if they provide substantive information about competencies. The more information contained in evaluation, the less likely that it will undermine intrinsic interest.

At least two studies have compared the effects on intrinsic motivation of substantive evaluation (written comments about strengths and weaknesses) versus letter grades. The former conveys information to the student about the nature of his or her competencies or steps needed for improvement; the latter do not. Butler and Nisan (1986) either made substantive positive and negative comments on sixth-grade students' papers, with no grade, or they gave numerical (normatively distributed) grades with no comments. Students who received comments claimed to find the tasks more interesting, were more likely to attribute their effort on the task to their interest, and were more likely to attribute success to their interest and effort than those children who received grades. The students who had received comments also performed better on a task requiring creativity. In a later study by Butler (1988), students who received written comments with substantive suggestions for improvement maintained high interest in a task, whereas grades, with and without comments, undermined both interest and performance.

In an experimental study, both global praise (e.g., "very good") and normatively distributed grades resulted in lower interest and desire to engage further in an activity than feedback containing both reinforcement and goal-setting comments (e.g., "You thought of quite a few ideas"; "Maybe it is possible to think of more unusual, original ideas"; Butler, 1987).

Thus, even substantive comments implying a lack of complete mastery can have a positive effect on intrinsic motivation. Presumably, negative comments would be effective only if they were very mild, as in this study, and given in a classroom context in which errors or initial failures were accepted as a natural part of learning and in which students were confident that they would ultimately succeed.

A study by Harackiewicz, Abrahams, and Wageman (1987) suggests that whether external evaluation has a positive or negative effect on intrinsic motivation also depends on the criteria used. Although evaluation based on social norms reduced intrinsic interest in a task, evaluation based on achieving a predetermined score actually *increased* interest. These results suggest that mastery-based evaluation is preferable to competitive or normative evaluation for maintaining intrinsic interest in tasks as well as for maintaining positive achievement-related cognitions, as discussed above.

Evaluation can have an indirect effect on intrinsic interest by influencing the difficulty level of students' choice of tasks, which in turn affects the intrinsic value of tasks. This mediating effect of evaluation was demonstrated in a study by Harter (1978) in which elementary schoolchildren were asked to solve anagrams at four difficulty levels. Half of the subjects were told that the task was a game and half were told that it was a school-type task for which they would receive letter grades. Under the game condition, children chose and verbalized their preference for optimally challenging problems. Those children working for grades chose significantly easier anagrams to perform, expressed less pleasure (smiling) when they solved a problem, and verbalized more anxiety. In a follow-up study (described in Harter, 1992) children who were told they would be graded on their performance chose to do anagrams with one fewer letter than the anagrams they were previously able to solve in a nongraded practice session. Thus, under graded conditions children chose to do tasks they were certain they could do, even though these tasks were not challenging and thus presumably not intrinsically motivating.

Other studies provide further evidence that individuals select easier tasks under externally rewarded in contrast with unrewarded conditions (Boggiano, Pittman, & Ruble, 1982; Pearlman, 1984; Pittman, Emery, & Boggiano, 1982; Shapira, 1976). In the Pittman et al. (1982) study, the preference for a simple version of a task even carried over to a situation in which the original reward contingencies were no longer in effect.

In summary, evaluation, especially for difficult tasks, tends to undermine intrinsic interest either directly, by undermining perceptions of internal causality, or indirectly, by encouraging the selection of easy tasks. Substantive evaluation that provides information about competencies and guidance for future efforts, and evaluation that is based on mastery rather than social norms, however, appear not to have these negative effects and can even enhance intrinsic interest in academic tasks.

## Effect of Competition

A few researchers have suggested that individual competition can heighten an individual's perception of external control, even though it can also provide positive information about competence. To demonstrate this effect experimentally, Deci, Betley, Kahle, Abrams, and Porac (1981) gave college students puzzles to complete with two different instructions. One group was told to try to win (solve the puzzles faster than the other person) and the other group was told to work quickly. Subjects in the competition condition spent less time working on similar puzzles they were subsequently given during a free-choice period than subjects who had not competed. Further evidence for the undermining effect of competition comes from the negative association Fry and Coe (1980) found between the level of competitiveness in junior and senior high schools and students' ratings of their enjoyment in learning (see also Vallerand, Gauvin, & Halliwell, 1986).

These studies suggest that in the long term, competition might focus students' attention on external reasons for engaging in a task and away from its intrinsic interest. Thus, they may be less likely to return to the activity voluntarily after engaging in competition. This effect, however, has to be balanced against the short-term benefits of competition, such as the group competition included in many cooperative learning programs. In addition to allowing all students an equal chance of winning, teachers should limit competition to tasks that are difficult to make fun. For example, competition might be used to get students to memorize the multiplication tables but might not be advisable for assignments involving math word problems, which can be very engaging.

## Effect of Personal Choice

Students' perceptions of personal causality—their sense that they chose to engage in an activity—and thus their intrinsic motivation are affected by how much control they have over their learning activities. This was demonstrated in a study by Deci, Nezlek, and Sheinman (1981). In classrooms in which teachers tended to select controlling behavior as appropriate responses to vignettes of typical problems that arise in school (for example, students not completing their assignments) fourth- through sixth-grade students scored relatively low on Harter's (1981b) measure of intrinsic motivation by the end of the first six weeks of school (see also Deci, Schwartz, Sheinman, & Ryan, 1981; Patrick, Skinner, & Connell, 1993).

Matheny and Edwards (1974) assessed the effects of increasing student choice and responsibility for learning in 25 elementary classrooms, grades one through seven. Teachers were trained to (a) give students some flexibility and responsibility for determining when they completed assignments; (b) allow students to score most of their own written work and to evaluate their progress in individual conferences with the teacher; (c) contract with students for long-range assignments; and (d) set up independent learning centers. Children's perceptions of their control over academic outcomes increased most in classes in which the above strategies were implemented, and teachers who were most successful in implementing these strategies had the highest number of students who gained at least a month in reading achievement for every month in school.

Apparently, intrinsic motivation can be enhanced by providing only a modest amount of choice. Zuckerman, Porac, Lathin, Smith, and Deci (1978) simply gave some of the subjects in their study an opportunity to select which three of six puzzles they would work on during an experiment. Subjects who were given choices were more intrinsically motivated to engage in puzzle solving subsequent to the 30-minute experimental period than subjects who had worked on the same sets of puzzles but without any choices. In a similar experimental study, Swann and Pittman (1977) told some children they could choose one of three puzzles. The experimenters actually controlled which puzzle children worked on by saying, before children had a chance to make a selection, that as long as they were sitting in front of activity B, why didn't they begin with it. Even this illusion of choice resulted in greater intrinsic motivation than was shown by subjects who were not told they could choose.

The benefits of greater student autonomy have been demonstrated also at the high school level. In one study, high school science students who were encouraged to organize their own experiments showed more care and involvement in laboratory work than those who were given detailed instructions and directions (Rainey, 1965). Pascarella, Walberg, Junker, and Haertel (1981) report that in classrooms where students had relatively greater control over learning the students were more interested in science.

DeCharms (1976) conducted one of the most comprehensive and compelling studies of the effect of increased student autonomy. His program was designed to change students from "pawns" (reactive, with little sense of personal causation) to "origins" (responsible, instrumental, and having an internal locus of causality). Teachers were encouraged to give children more responsibility over their school program, including opportunities to set their own goals and make decisions about how to reach those goals. Children were given some choice in the tasks they did and when to do them, and they were encouraged to take personal responsibility, both for accomplishing goals and for failing to meet them.

DeCharms (1976, 1984) found that in schools serving mostly low-income African-American students, the sixth- and seventh-graders who had been in the nine experimental "origins" classrooms made greater achievement gains than students in the control group classrooms. The advantage of the origin group persisted through the eighth grade, even though neither group continued training that year. The origin group also had a better high school completion rate than the control group.

Ryan and Grolnick (1986) point out that students' perceptions of autonomy can vary even within a classroom. They found, furthermore, that the variation in children's perceptions of control within a classroom was significantly associated with their perceptions of competence and global self-worth.

These variations in perceptions of control may be explained by the fact that teachers give more autonomy to some children than to others in the same class. Whatever the explanation, the evidence strongly suggests that giving some choice and providing opportunities for personal responsibility enhance students' perceptions of personal causality and intrinsic interest in school tasks.

## Effect of Task Characteristics

The factors discussed so far affect students' intrinsic interest in tasks indirectly, primarily by influencing their perceptions of personal causality. Even when students have a perception of personal control, however, they will not choose or be intrinsically motivated to complete tasks that are very easy, very hard, boring, repetitive, or meaningless. Theory and research provide clear guidelines regarding the qualities of tasks that are likely to engage students' interest. Four qualities are discussed below.

### 1. Moderate Level of Difficulty

The importance of moderately difficult tasks is strongly suggested by intrinsic motivation theory. Information-processing theorists (e.g., Berlyne, 1966; Hunt, 1965; Kagan, 1972), for example, claim that optimal arousal and interest are generated by a *moderate* discrepancy between an external stimulus (or task) and an individual's representations (or skill level). Accordingly, tasks that are very easy and are completed with little effort and tasks that are difficult and can be completed only with extraordinary effort or not at all are not intrinsically interesting. According to other theorists (Deci, 1975; Piaget, 1952; White, 1959), intrinsic interest derives primarily from the feelings of competence that are associated with working on and completing tasks, and only moderately difficult tasks engender feelings of competence when they are completed.

Moderately difficult tasks have direct benefits for learning as well as for motivation. Piaget (1952) claims that children learn best when they engage in tasks that challenge their current intellectual structures (i.e., create intellectual "disequilibrium") but are not too difficult for them to master eventually. Vygotsky (1962, 1978) similarly recommends instruction that is within children's "zone of proximal development"—too difficult for

them to master immediately on their own, but not too difficult for them to master with some assistance.

The importance of moderate difficulty is supported by Brophy and Good's (1986) review of research on teaching and learning (see also Brophy & Alleman, 1991). They concluded that engagement rates, as well as achievement gains, were enhanced when teachers gave students assignments that they could complete successfully if they invested reasonable effort. Assignments that were confusing or frustrating resulted in low engagement.

Children's preference for moderately difficult tasks was demonstrated in a study by Danner and Lonky (1981) in which children were given experience with three classification tasks of varying levels of difficulty and then told they could spend time working on any of the three tasks. Children spent the most time with and rated as most interesting the tasks that were one step ahead of their previously tested level of classification skill. Additional evidence for the value of moderately difficult tasks comes from Boggiano et al. (1982), who found that children preferred to work on tasks of intermediate difficulty as long as a reward was not made contingent on their performance (see also Shapira, 1976, for a study using college students). Similarly, McMullin and Steffen (1982) found that when subjects worked on puzzles that got slightly more difficult on each trial, they displayed more subsequent intrinsic motivation than when the difficulty level remained constant.

The positive effect that feelings of competence have on intrinsic interest is apparent in studies showing that children who believe they are academically competent are more intrinsically interested in school tasks than students who have a low perception of their academic competence (Boggiano, Main, & Katz, 1988; Gottfried, 1990; Harter, 1981a; Harter & Connell, 1984; Harter & Jackson, 1992). A causal relationship is suggested by the results of a study conducted by Mac Iver, Stipek, and Daniels (1991). These investigators assessed, at the beginning and end of the semester, junior and senior high school students' perceptions of their competence and intrinsic interest in a course they were taking at school. Analyses revealed that interest changed in the direction that perceived competence changed. That is, students whose perception of competence increased over the course of the semester rated the subject as more interesting at the end of the semester than at the beginning, and students whose perception of competence decreased rated the subject as less interesting at the end of the semester (see also Harter, Whitesell, & Kowalski, 1992).

Although one would expect high interest to lead to greater investment and thus greater competence, the results of the Mac Iver et al. study strongly suggest that causality also goes in the other direction—that feelings of competence actually contribute to students' interests. In this study, causal models with change in interest predicting change in perceptions of competence did not explain the data nearly as well as the model with change in perceptions of competence included as a predictor of change in interest. These data have important implications for instruction. They suggest that strategies to induce students to engage in activities they are not initially interested in doing should enhance their interest if they experience success.

The importance of feelings of competence and therefore of adjusting the difficulty level of tasks to students' competency levels is one of the most self-evident and commonly violated principles of motivation. It is not fun to engage in an activity that makes one feel *in*competent or stupid. It is not surprising, therefore that students who have relatively poor skills do not enthusiastically approach tasks that are appropriate for their more skilled classmates. This is especially true when success is defined normatively. In this case, some students will feel incompetent, regardless of their level of effort or improvement. Knowing this, of course, does not make it easy to provide appropriately difficult tasks for 25 to 35 students with varying skill levels.

### 2. Novelty and Complexity

Brophy (1986) stresses the importance of variety in tasks, a claim that is consistent with the proposals of information-processing theorists that individuals are naturally motivated to seek novelty, complexity, and surprise (Berlyne, 1966; Hunt, 1965; Kagan, 1972). A few studies have been conducted to assess the effects of fantasy and other embellishments. They typically involve computer-assisted instruction (CAI), partly because CAI makes it easy to vary such task variables systematically. Embellishments (e.g., balloons popping, music, graphics) that increase the complexity and surprise qualities in CAI have been shown to have positive effects on motivation (see Lepper, 1985; Lepper & Cordova, 1992; Lepper & Malone, 1987; Malone, 1981a, 1981b; Malone & Lepper, 1987; Parker & Lepper, 1992). There is evidence, however, suggesting that girls and boys may respond differently to some embellishments. Malone (1981a) found in one study that music increased the intrinsic appeal of a fraction-learning game for girls but decreased the appeal for boys, whereas fantasy enhanced the appeal of the game for boys but not for girls.

Lepper and Cordova (1992) concluded in their review of CAI research that relatively minor motivational embellishments providing a fantasy context produced heightened interest in the learning activity and often better learning. Research is not available on the effects of embellishments or the inclusion of fantasy on instruction delivered through other media. It is perhaps self-evident that interest is difficult to maintain in situations in which there is little variety in tasks from day to day. Blumenfeld (1992) cautions, however, that variety for the sake of variety may not enhance meaningful engagement. She points out that dramatic and extraneous aspects of tasks, such as fantasy or exotic materials, can distract students' attention from the content or the problem to be solved. Teachers should take care, therefore, to avoid the kind of novelty that might interfere with students' attention to the learning goals of the task. The same caution is in order with regard to other strategies employed to make tasks fun. Although students may be especially likely to engage in fun activities, producing fun is not sufficient. Students' enthusiasm and excitement should not be mistaken for pleasure engendered by the development of new understanding and competency.

### 3. Personal Meaningfulness

Most motivation theorists encourage the development of tasks that have some personal meaning for students (e.g., Brophy, 1987; Stipek, 1993). The value of personal meaningfulness was demonstrated in a study by Anderson, Shirey, Wilson, and

Fielding (1987) in which students' interest in reading materials was as important a determinant of their learning and recall of sentences as were reading comprehension scores and 30 times more important than the readability index. Similarly, Asher and his colleagues (Asher, 1981; Asher, Hymel, & Wigfield, 1978) reported that the interest value of materials was an important predictor of students' memory for the subject matter contained in the materials (see also Garner, Alexander, Gillingham, Kulikowich, & Brown, 1991; Garner, Gillingham, & White, 1989; Schiefele, 1991; Shirey & Reynolds, 1988).

Personal meaningfulness was manipulated experimentally in a study by Anand and Ross (1987). Fifth- and sixth-grade students liked and learned more from a version of a CAI program that included personalized information (the child's favorite teacher, friend, or food) than from a version that used general referents.

Further evidence for the value of personally meaningful tasks comes from Meece's (1991) observations of classrooms in which students had either a very high or a very low level of motivation to increase their knowledge of science. Adapting instruction to the personal interests of students was a distinguishing feature of the high-motivation classrooms.

### 4. Introduction of Tasks

What teachers say when they introduce a new task can also affect students' enthusiasm. This was demonstrated in a study by Malone and Lepper (1987) in which children who had a CAI task involving fractions presented to them as a game spent about 50 percent more time working on it than children who had the same task introduced as a drill.

Brophy, Rohrkemper, Rashid, and Goldberger (1983) assessed the relationship between how teachers introduced tasks and the level of student engagement in intermediate-grade mathematics classrooms. Students were found to be less engaged on tasks that teachers introduced with negative comments such as, "You'll have to work real quietly, otherwise you'll have to do more assignments"; "This test is to see who the really smart ones are" (described in Brophy, 1987, p. 204).

## Relationships

Recently motivation researchers have begun to investigate the effect of children's relationships with teachers and their peers on academic motivation. Connell and Wellborn (1991) claim that "relatedness" is one of three basic human needs, along with feelings of competence and autonomy. (See also Ryan & Powelson, 1991.) Relatedness, in their framework, encompasses the need to feel securely connected to individuals in the social context and the "need to experience oneself as worthy and capable of love and respect" (p. 51). Their research has shown that students' feelings of relatedness to their teacher and classmates are strong predictors of their cognitive, behavioral, and emotional engagement in classroom activities.

Skinner and Belmont (1993) assessed teachers' perceptions of their involvement with their students with a measure that included items about their affection (how much they liked, appreciated, and enjoyed the student), their attunement (understanding, sympathy, and knowledge about the student), and dependability (availability in case of need). Using similar items, students rated their own involvement with their teachers. Teachers' rating of their involvement with students in the fall strongly predicted students' self-perceptions (relatedness to the teacher, feelings of autonomy) assessed in the spring, which in turn predicted students' engagement in classroom activities.

Goodenow (1993) measured middle-school students' perceptions of the social-emotional quality of a class for them, focusing on their own sense of belonging and personal support from their teachers. These perceptions explained over one third of the variance in students' assessment of the interest, importance, and value of the academic work of the class.

This is a new area of research, but findings so far suggest the value of a social context that is accepting and supportive—where each student is valued regardless of his or her academic skills or performance relative to others. Relationships with their teachers may be particularly important factors in the motivation of young children, who have not yet fully differentiated the roles of teachers and parents (Pianta & Steinberg, 1992).

## Summary

Theory and research on intrinsic motivation suggest the importance of two variables—perceptions of self-determination (that one is working on a task for personal rather than external reasons), and perceptions of mastery and competence. Students' intrinsic motivation is maximized by instructional approaches that foster these beliefs, which in turn engender conceptual understanding and creativity. The relationships among the variables discussed in this section are summarized in Figure 5–2.

When school tasks are not intrinsically interesting, students turn their attention to other reasons for doing them (or they do not do them at all). The following discussion examines students' goals as students are engaged in intellectual activities.

---

## GOALS

---

Early achievement motivation researchers (e.g., Atkinson, 1964) measured *whether* subjects approached a task; researchers now are just as likely to ask subjects *why* they approach a task, or to assess the nature of their involvement. Reflecting on this shift, C. Ames (1992) points out that in the past, motivation was typically equated with quantitative changes in behavior, with little attention to the qualitative changes that have important implications for learning, such as how students view themselves in relation to tasks, and particularly how much they value effort and effort-based strategies.

The quality of students' engagement has been examined primarily in the context of a recent distinction made between *learning* goals (referred to by some researchers as "mastery" or "task" goals) and *performance* goals (also referred to as "ego" goals) (see C. Ames, 1992; Blumenfeld, 1992; Maehr, 1984; Meece, 1991; Nicholls, 1983). Learning goals concern developing skills and understanding or achieving a sense of mastery. Students who are more concerned about developing skills and completing a task than about getting a good grade or public recognition have learning goals. Students with performance goals are more concerned about appearances—about *looking* smart or avoiding looking incompetent (rather than

**CLASSROOM PRACTICES**

**Use of Rewards**

Use rewards only when necessary.

Emphasize the informational rather than the controlling purpose of rewards.

Make rewards contingent on mastery or a performance level that each student can achieve with effort (so that positive information about competency is likely.)

Minimize use of other practices that focus students' attention on extrinsic reasons for engaging in tasks (e.g., close monitoring, salient deadlines, threats of punishment, competition).

**Evaluation**

De-emphasize external evaluation, especially for challenging tasks.

Provide substantive, informative evaluation that is based on mastery rather than on social norms.

**Tasks**

Give moderately difficult tasks.

Vary format and nature of tasks.

Give tasks that are personally meaningful.

Allow choice in tasks.

**MEDIATING BELIEFS/FEELINGS**

Perception of self-determination

Feelings of mastery and competence

**STUDENT OUTCOMES**

Intense engagement

Conceptual understanding

Cognitive flexibility

Creativity

Enjoyment

FIGURE 5–2 Enhancing intrinsic motivation.

*being* competent). Looking smart is usually defined as performing better than others and sometimes can be achieved without any learning. A central feature of performance goals is a need for public recognition for superior performance. Thus, a student who works primarily for good grades or teacher praise has performance goals. This distinction in types of goal is related to the intrinsic–extrinsic distinction discussed earlier: Learning goals are intrinsic and performance goals are extrinsic because the goal is not related to the task itself.

As with most motivation constructs, some researchers focus on stable individual differences (that is, they conceptualize beliefs or behavior in terms of traits) and others focus on the effects of the immediate context (although most researchers recognize that both individual dispositions and the immediate environment are important). With regard to goals, Dweck (1986;

Smiley & Dweck, 1994) stresses stable individual differences more than most theorists. She claims that goals are to some degree a consequence of an individual's concept of ability, either as a trait (leading to performance goals) or as something that changes with effort and practice (leading to mastery goals). C. Ames (1992; C. Ames & Archer, 1988), Blumenfeld (1992), and Meece (1991) conceptualize goals less in terms of stable individual differences and more as a consequence of the immediate instructional context.

Dweck (1986) has proposed that learning goals and performance goals have very different implications for the quality of students' motivation, including how they behave in achievement settings and how they interpret performance outcomes (see also Dweck & Elliott, 1983; Dweck & Leggett, 1988; Elliott & Dweck, 1988; Heyman, 1992; Lepper, 1988; Nicholls, Cobb, Wood, Yackel, & Patashnick, 1990). According to Dweck's theoretical analysis, students with learning goals seek challenging tasks that provide opportunities to develop new competencies, regardless of whether they perceive themselves as high or low in ability relative to others. When they encounter difficulty, they assume that their current strategy is inappropriate and needs to be changed, or that they are not trying hard enough. Accordingly, they analyze their strategy and redouble their efforts. For students with learning goals, judgments of competence are based on the amount of effort expanded and on whether real learning or mastery was achieved.

Dweck suggests that because students with performance goals are not focused on their own developing competencies, they judge their competence in terms of their performance relative to others or by external feedback rather then in terms of their own gains in understanding or mastery. Those who are confident in their ability choose moderately difficult tasks to allow them to display their competence. Because they are confident that they will succeed, they engage in effective strategies when they encounter difficulty, as do students with learning goals. But because their goal is to *look* competent (as opposed to *being* competent), they may use shortcuts that achieve their immediate goal but do not actually foster learning (see also Covington, 1992; Nicholls, 1983).

Dweck proposes further that students who have performance goals and lack self-confidence choose easy tasks to avoid displaying incompetence. When they encounter difficulty, they engage in self-defeating strategies to avoid the perception of being low in ability, or they give up because they lack confidence in their ability to demonstrate competence.

Studies have supported Dweck's claim that learning goals (a task or mastery orientation) are associated with moderate risk taking and willingness to engage in challenging tasks. In one study, children who were task oriented were more likely than performance oriented children to select a task described to them as difficult but helpful in promoting skill development (Elliott & Dweck, 1988). Most performance-oriented children selected a task they were told would not teach them anything new but on which they could demonstrate their competence. In another study students who perceived their classroom as relatively more mastery oriented claimed thcy would prefer a science project that would be difficult but would result in new learning over an easy project (C. Ames & Archer, 1988; see also Nicholls, 1984).

Task orientation is also associated with more adaptive perceptions of what causes success and failure. In the C. Ames and Archer (1988) study, students who perceived their classroom to be more performance oriented tended to attribute failure to low ability—an undesirable attribution, because students who believe they cannot change their own ability have no reason to exert effort in the future. In contrast, students who perceived their classroom to be mastery oriented tended to attribute success to high effort and effective learning strategies. Similarly, in a study of second graders, Nicholls et al. (1990) found that a task orientation was associated with the belief that success was caused by interest and effort to understand; students who were more ego oriented believed that success was caused by efforts to compete with classmates. (See Duda & Nicholls, 1992, for similar findings for both academics and athletics.)

Students' perceptions of the implications of their efforts also vary as a function of their goals. For students with mastery goals, more effort is associated with greater feelings of competence. For a performance-oriented individual, high effort can suggest low ability. This was illustrated in studies conducted by Jagacinski and Nicholls (1984) in which students were asked to imagine or recall times they had succeeded with high or low effort under task-involving or ego-involving conditions. When students imagined ego-involving conditions, they judged their ability higher and claimed they would feel better if they had applied low effort and others had needed high effort than if they had applied high effort and others had used low effort (see also Jagacinski & Nicholls, 1987). The opposite was found under task-involving conditions, where high effort was associated with judgments of high ability. This paradoxical effect was observed presumably because individuals with performance goals typically measure success in normative terms—that is, by their performance relative to classmates'—and because, as mentioned above, these individuals perceive effort and ability to be inversely related (Nicholls & Miller, 1984).

The negative consequences of the belief that high effort implies low ability are vividly described by Covington and Beery (1976; see also Covington, 1992, chapter 4). They discuss the dilemma faced by performance-oriented students who are not confident of success. If they try and fail, their failure will provide unambiguous evidence of their low ability. If they do not try they will have an explanation, aside from low ability, for their failure, but they may be punished. This is why Covington and Omelich (1979) refer to effort as a "double-edged sword."

The dilemma leads some students to engage in behavior that may, in the short term, protect them from an image of incompetence but in the long term will interfere with learning and achievement (Covington, 1992; Covington & Beery, 1976). To avoid demonstrating low ability, some students simply do not try, or they cheat. Others resort to more subtle but no more constructive strategies. For example, they may procrastinate, make excuses, work half-heartedly, or set unrealistic goals.

Mastery versus performance goals also have implications for students' attention while they work on tasks. Nicholls (1979, 1983) claims that students focus on the process of completing a task when they are motivated to learn or master. Performance goals are associated with attention on the self, and especially on external evaluations of the self.

A study by Peterson and Swing (1982) illustrates this distinction. One of the students they observed doing a math assignment looked as if she were paying good attention throughout the lesson. However, when subsequently asked what she thought about during the lesson, she commented that her first thought was, "Since I was just beginning, I was nervous, and I thought maybe I wouldn't know how to do things . . . ," (p. 486). After a later lesson segment, she responded, "Well, I was mostly thinking . . . I was making a fool of myself" (p. 486). In contrast, a task-oriented child responded to the same question by describing in some detail the strategies she used to solve the problems.

Csikszentmihalyi (1975) refers to the intense involvement associated with a task orientation as *flow*. Individuals experiencing flow are so intensely attentive to the task they may lose awareness of time and space. Great artists and scholars have reported that they experience flow when working in their field. People who are known for their creativity have claimed to be in a flow state when they did their best work (Nicholls, 1983).

A task orientation is also associated with the use of effective problem-solving strategies. In one study students scoring high on a measure of task orientation in science reported relatively greater use of active metacognitive strategies (e.g., reviewing material not understood, asking questions as they worked, making connections between current problems and past problems), and less use of "superficial engagement" (copying, guessing, skipping questions) than children who claimed to be relatively more ego-oriented (Meece, Blumenfeld, & Hoyle, 1988; reanalyzed in Meece & Holt, 1993). C. Ames and Archer (1988) found, similarly, that the more students perceived their junior high school classroom to support mastery rather than performance goals, the more they reported engaging in active learning strategies (planning, organizing material, setting goals) that are known to facilitate learning. And Nolen (1988) found that the higher the task orientation of junior high students who were asked to read a passage from a science magazine, the more they used deep processing strategies (e.g., discriminating important information from unimportant information, trying to figure out how new information fits with what one already knows, and monitoring comprehension). (See also Ainley, 1993; Pintrich & Schrauben, 1992.)

Researchers have also demonstrated the disadvantages of an ego orientation with regard to problem-solving strategies by manipulating subjects' attention on laboratory tasks. They have, for example, shown that interventions creating a self-focus, such as placing a mirror or video camera near subjects, impair performance on cognitive tasks (e.g., Brockner, 1979; Elliott & Dweck, 1988).

The findings of laboratory studies have been consistent with Dweck's (1986) proposal that an ego or performance orientation undermines effective problem solving for children who have doubts about their competence more than for self-confident children. Elliott and Dweck (1988) experimentally induced performance or learning goals of performance. They also manipulated children's perceptions of skill on a task. When performance-oriented children who had low self-confidence encountered difficulty, their problem-solving strategies deteriorated. This did not occur for performance-oriented children with high self-confidence. Learning- or mastery-oriented children's strategies were not affected by whether they had high or low confidence in their ability. Brockner (1979) also found that the video camera and mirror resulted in impaired performance only for subjects who had low self-esteem.

In addition to promoting active problem solving, a task orientation permits individuals to experience greater pleasure and greater emotional involvement in the work at hand. In the C. Ames and Archer (1988) study mentioned above, the more that students perceived their classroom as supporting mastery goals, the more they liked the class. In a study by Duda and Nicholls (1992), a task orientation was associated with satisfaction and enjoyment in both academics and athletics, and an ego orientation was associated with boredom in academics. Elliott and Dweck (1988) reported that many of the children in a performance-oriented condition who had low perceptions of their ability spontaneously expressed negative feelings about the task with comments like, "After this (problem), then I get to go?" "This is boring," or "My stomach hurts" (p. 10). Children who were task oriented rarely made such comments, whether or not they believed they were competent at the task.

Finally, goals affect what students learn. This was demonstrated by Benware and Deci (1984), who asked two groups of college students to learn material from an unfamiliar passage on neurophysiology. To create different goals, they told one group that they would be tested on the material and another group that they would be teaching the material to other students. Both groups spent the same amount of time learning the material. The two groups did not differ in their rote learning, but the group that was told they would teach the material to others demonstrated greater conceptual understanding than the group that expected to be tested. Thus, the manipulated goal influenced how subjects learned the material. In another study, certain fifth- and sixth-grade students were experimentally manipulated to be ego involved. Compared with students in whom a task orientation had been experimentally manipulated, these students showed poorer word recall at deep processing levels (having to do with meaning) but not at shallow levels (having to do with the sound of the word; Graham & Golan, 1991).

The research described above strongly suggests the value of learning goals. Learning goals are presumably engendered by most of the instructional practices listed in Figure 5–2 that foster intrinsic interest in tasks. Two recent studies, described below, that specifically examined relationships between classroom practices and students' goal orientations can be added to this list. (See Figure 5–3 for a summary of these other instructional practices that engender learning goals.)

In one of the few qualitative studies of students' goal orientations, Meece (1991) describes elementary and middle school science classrooms that engendered different student goals. Observers collected detailed data on science lessons taught by two teachers whose students scored particularly high on questionnaire measures of mastery orientation, two teachers whose students were particularly low on mastery orientation (and high on performance orientation), and one teacher whose students were intermediate on the goal-orientation scales.

A number of instructional practices differentiated classrooms in which students were more or less mastery oriented. First, students in mastery-oriented classrooms were given more diverse opportunities to demonstrate mastery, including making graphs, charts, or diagrams. In classrooms in which students were more performance oriented, competence was demonstrated almost exclusively by answering oral or written questions.

Second, the material and instruction in high mastery-ori-

---

**CLASSROOM PRACTICES** [a]

Provide diverse opportunities to demonstrate mastery.

Adapt instruction to students' knowledge, understanding, and personal experience.

Provide opportunities for exploration and experimentation.

Define success in terms of improvement.

Emphasize effort, learning, and working hard rather than performing or getting the right answer.

Treat errors and mistakes as a normal part of learning.

[a] In addition to practices listed in Figure 5–2.

↓

**STUDENT GOALS**

To master tasks

To understand

To develop skills

To learn

↓

**STUDENT OUTCOMES**

*Students will:*

Be intensely attentive to tasks/learning

Select challenging tasks, take risks

Persist in the face of difficulty

Use effective problem-solving strategies (e.g., planning, organizing, monitoring)

Attribute outcome to effort and strategy rather than to stable ability

Learn at a conceptual level

Feel pleasure and satisfaction

FIGURE 5–3 Fostering learning goals.

ented student classrooms were more likely to be adapted to students' knowledge, understanding, and personal experience. Teachers in the two performance-oriented classrooms used unfamiliar terms and failed to relate new concepts to students' personal knowledge. Teachers in mastery-oriented classrooms were also more likely to point out the value of science learning to students' lives outside of school.

All of the classrooms provided some opportunities for students to select materials and procedures, but the mastery-oriented classrooms provided more opportunities, and other factors (time pressure, emphasis on completing tasks) present in the performance-oriented classrooms detracted from students' ability to explore and experiment on their own. Performance-oriented classrooms also required more teacher assistance (and therefore allowed less student autonomy) because the tasks were too difficult or required skills and knowledge that students lacked.

Teachers in performance-oriented classrooms emphasized

tests and evaluation more than teachers in mastery-oriented classrooms; students were routinely reminded of tests, and evaluation was fairly public. Grades and evaluation were not salient in mastery-oriented classrooms.

Although small-group activities were used in all of the classrooms observed, students in mastery-oriented classrooms were more likely to be given tasks that required a group product. The importance of teamwork was stressed more than in performance-oriented classrooms, where group activities often involved only sharing materials.

Other characteristics of classrooms that foster mastery goals were revealed in a study by C. Ames and Archer (1988) in which students were asked to rate the degree to which they felt teacher behaviors and classroom practices believed to foster a mastery orientation were present in their classroom. The researchers found that certain classroom characteristics formed a coherent scale and predicted student variables associated with mastery goals. Students who attributed success to effort and strategy and who engaged in active learning strategies came from classrooms in which (a) success was defined in terms of improvement and progress, (b) effort, learning, and working hard on challenging tasks were emphasized, (c) teachers focused on how students were learning rather than on how they performed, and (d) errors and mistakes were treated as a natural part of learning. These students had a relatively positive attitude toward the class while students in classrooms that stressed relative performance, and did not have the qualities described above, had more negative attitudes toward their class and tended to attribute failure to low ability.

The shift toward a more qualitative analysis of motivation, reflected in research on student goals, has added an important new dimension to the field of achievement motivation. Although work in this area is relatively new, it has already revealed important connections among instructional practices, qualitative aspects of students' engagement on tasks, and learning. Research on student goals will no doubt continue and is likely to generate a number of practically useful findings.

## CONCLUSION

This chapter has treated various instructional practices independently—the use of rewards, the nature of tasks, criteria for evaluation. Although studies have not examined different combinations of practices specifically, it is safe to assume that the instructional practices discussed depend on each other for their effectiveness. A comprehensive approach to classroom intervention is therefore essential for improving student learning. (See Maehr & Midgley, 1991, for a specific proposal of a schoolwide approach to enhancing students' motivation.) Indeed, implementing a single recommendation can actually undermine positive student motivation.

Consider, for example, providing students more choice in tasks. If choice is given in a classroom in which performance outcomes and external evaluation are stressed, students are likely to select easy tasks that will not help them develop new skills. These traditional practices most likely explain why Clifford and her colleagues found that when given a choice, children tended to select tasks that offered very little risk of failure; the older the children in their studies, the less willing they were to take academic risks (see Clifford, 1991, for a review). Only in a context in which errors and initial failures are considered a natural part of learning and in which evaluation is based primarily on effort and personal improvement will students select tasks that challenge their current skill levels.

Changing the emphasis and nature of evaluation likewise requires attention to other practices as well. The teacher who does not emphasize external evaluation but gives boring, too easy, or too difficult tasks, for example, is more likely to encourage off-task behavior than high effort on assignments or the use of effective problem-solving strategies. Indeed, if tasks are repetitive, irrelevant, and boring, none of the principles discussed in this chapter will improve children's motivation.

In addition to the interactive effects of classroom practices, students' developmental levels, histories, and expectations must be considered in making instructional decisions. For example, suddenly eliminating external rewards for a class of students accustomed to working for rewards will result in less, not more, effort. Students need to be weaned slowly from their dependence on external rewards. Providing more challenging tasks that take effort and persistence to complete will discourage rather than motivate children who have a long history of failure or who lack self-confidence. Such children may initially need a heavy dose of encouragement and praise for their efforts, and will need to be introduced slowly to tasks that they cannot complete easily. Giving more responsibility for selecting and completing tasks to students who have had no experience assessing their own competencies or working independently can also be counterproductive. Some children initially need help in developing the skill of diagnosing their own understanding and mastery level, and they need guidance in how to select and plan what needs to be done to complete tasks.

In summary, the principles discussed in this chapter are well supported by research, but they must be applied thoughtfully and with careful consideration of how classroom practices support or undermine each other and with an awareness of students' histories and expectations.

In future research it would be useful to examine directly how various practices interact with each other in their effects on student motivation. Intervention programs in real educational settings, which systematically vary different combinations of practices, would be especially useful.

The principles of instruction discussed in this chapter are intuitively appealing and make sense to most practitioners. They run counter to prevailing practice (Goodlad, 1984), however, in part because they are not easy to implement in real classrooms. It takes a great deal of skill for teachers to deliver the differentiated instructional program that is suggested by these principles. And teachers are rarely given time to prepare the kind of personally meaningful and intrinsically interesting tasks suggested. Finally, it takes more self-confidence than most teachers have to give students the level of control over their educational program that is recommended by motivation researchers.

Qualitative research would help flesh out these general principles and clarify their classroom implications. Teachers would benefit greatly from ethnographic studies, like the one on science instruction described by Meece (1991), which provides a vivid picture of effective and ineffective classroom practices.

Fortunately, however, there is no need to wait for further research to improve students' motivation and achievement. Much is already known about those instructional strategies that have positive effects on children's motivation. Implementing these strategies is not easy. And teachers will always be faced with their students' motivational baggage—negative beliefs, values, and habits that interfere with learning—as well as other problems over which teachers have little control, such as hunger, emotional disturbances, or limited English ability. But teachers' hands are far from tied. The research described in this chapter provides compelling evidence for the importance, and thus the potential, of the immediate learning environment. The goal mentioned at the beginning of the chapter—for students to be actively and enthusiastically engaged in developing their intellectual skills—is challenging but achievable.

## References

Ainley, M. (1993). Styles of engagement with learning: Multidimensional assessment of their relationship with strategy use and school achievement. *Journal of Educational Psychology, 85,* 395–405.

Alschuler, A. (1968). *How to increase motivation through climate and structure* (Working Paper No. 8-313). Cambridge, MA: Harvard University, Graduate School of Education, Achievement Motivation Development Project.

Amabile, T. (1983). *The social psychology of creativity.* New York: Springer.

Amabile, T., DeJong, W., & Lepper, M. (1976). Effects of externally imposed deadlines on subsequent intrinsic motivation. *Journal of Personality and Social Psychology, 34,* 92–98.

Ames, C. (1978). Children's achievement attributions and self-reinforcement: Effects of self-concept and competitive reward structure. *Journal of Educational Psychology, 70,* 345–355.

Ames, C. (1981). Competitive versus cooperative reward structure: The influence of individual and group performance factors on achievement attributions and affect. *American Educational Research Journal, 18,* 273–288.

Ames, C. (1984). Competitive, cooperative and individualistic goal struc-

tures: A cognitive-motivational analysis. In R. Ames & C. Ames (Eds.), *Research on motivation in education: Vol. 1. Student motivation* (pp. 177–207). New York: Academic Press.

Ames, C. (1986). Conceptions of motivation within competitive and noncompetitive goal structures. In R. Schwarzer (Ed.), *Self-related cognitions in anxiety and motivation* (pp. 229–245). Hillsdale, NJ: Lawrence Erlbaum Associates.

Ames, C. (1992). Classrooms: Goals, structures, and student motivation. *Journal of Educational Psychology, 84,* 261–271.

Ames, C., & Ames, R. (1978). Thrill of victory and agony of defeat: Children's self and interpersonal evaluations in competitive and non-competitive learning environments. *Journal of Research and Development in Education, 12,* 79–81.

Ames, C., & Ames, R. (1981). Competitive versus individualistic goal structures: The salience of past performance information for causal attributions and affect. *Journal of Educational Psychology, 73,* 411–418.

Ames, C., & Ames, R. (1984). Goal structures and motivation. *Elementary School Journal, 85,* 39–52.

Ames, C., Ames, R., & Felker, D. (1977). Effects of competitive reward structure and valence outcome on children's achievement attributions. *Journal of Educational Psychology, 69,* 1–8.

Ames, C., & Archer, J. (1988). Achievement goals in the classroom: Students' learning strategies and motivation processes. *Journal of Educational Psychology, 80,* 260–267.

Ames, C., & Felker, D. (1979). An examination of children's attribution and achievement-related evaluations in competitive, cooperative, and individualistic reward structures. *Journal of Educational Psychology, 71,* 413–420.

Ames, R. (1983). Help-seeking and achievement orientation: Perspectives from attribution theory. In B. DePaulo, A. Nadler, & J. Fisher (Eds.), *New directions in helping* (pp. 165–188). New York: Academic Press.

Anand, P., & Ross, S. (1987). A computer-based strategy for personalizing verbal problems in teaching mathematics. *Educational Communication and Technology Journal, 35,* 151–162.

Anderson, C., & Jennings, D. (1980). When experiences of failure promote expectations of success: The impact of attributing failure to ineffective strategies. *Journal of Personality, 48,* 393–407.

Anderson, L., Evertson, C., & Brophy, J. (1979). An experimental study of effective teaching in first-grade reading groups. *Elementary School Journal, 79,* 193–223.

Anderson, R., Manoogian, S., & Reznick, J. (1976). The undermining and enhancing of intrinsic motivation in preschool children. *Journal of Personality and Social Psychology, 34,* 915–922.

Anderson, R., Shirey, L., Wilson, P., & Fielding, L. (1987). Interestingness of children's reading materials. In R. Snow & M. Farr (Eds.), *Aptitude, learning, and instruction: III. Conative and affective process analyses* (pp. 287–299). Hillsdale, NJ: Lawrence Erlbaum Associates.

Arkes, H. (1978). Competence and the maintenance of behavior. *Motivation and Emotion, 2,* 201 211.

Asher, S. (1981). Topic interest and children's reading comprehension. In R. Spiro, B. Bruce, & W. Brewer (Eds.), *Theoretical issues in reading comprehension* (pp. 525–534). Hillsdale, NJ: Lawrence Erlbaum Associates.

Asher, S., Hymel, S., & Wigfield, A. (1978). Influence of topic interest on children's reading comprehension. *Journal of Reading Behavior, 10,* 35–47.

Atkinson, J. (1964). *An introduction to motivation.* Princeton, NJ: Van Nostrand.

Bandura, A. (1977a). Self-efficacy: Toward a unifying theory of behavioral change. *Psychological Review, 84,* 191–215.

Bandura, A. (1977b). *Social learning theory.* Englewood Cliffs, NJ: Prentice Hall.

Bandura, A. (1981). Self-referent thought: A developmental analysis of self-efficacy. In J. Flavell & L. Ross (Eds.), *Social cognitive development: Frontiers and possible futures* (pp. 200–239). Cambridge, England: Cambridge University Press.

Bandura, A. (1982a). The self and mechanisms of agency. In J. Suls (Ed.), *Psychological perspectives on the self: Vol. 1* (pp. 3–39). Hillsdale, NJ: Lawrence Erlbaum Associates.

Bandura, A. (1982b). Self-efficacy mechanism in human agency. *American Psychologist, 37,* 122–147.

Bandura, A. (1986). *Social foundations of thought and action: social cognitive theory.* Englewood Cliffs, NJ: Prentice Hall.

Bandura, A., & Schunk, D. (1981). Cultivating competence, self-efficacy, and intrinsic interest through proximal self-motivation. *Journal of Personality and Social Psychology, 41,* 586–598.

Barker, G., & Graham, S. (1987). Developmental study of praise and blame as attributional cues. *Journal of Educational Psychology, 79,* 62–66.

Bates, J. (1979). Extrinsic reward and intrinsic motivation: A review with implications for the classroom. *Review of Educational Research, 49,* 557–576.

Benware, C., & Deci, E. (1984). Quality of learning with an active versus passive motivational set. *American Educational Research Journal, 21,* 755–765.

Berlyne, D. (1966). Curiosity and exploration. *Science, 153,* 25–33.

Blanck, P., Reis, H., & Jackson, L. (1984). The effects of verbal reinforcements on intrinsic motivation for sex-linked tasks. *Sex Roles, 10,* 369–387.

Bloom, B. (1971). Mastery learning and its implications for curriculum development. In E. W. Eisner (Ed.), *Confronting curriculum reform* (pp. 17–55). Boston: Little, Brown.

Bloom, B. (1974). An introduction to mastery learning theory. In J. H. Block (Ed.), *Schools, society, and mastery learning* (pp. 3–14). New York: Holt, Rinehart & Winston.

Bloom, B. (1976). *Human characteristics and school learning.* New York: McGraw-Hill.

Bloom, B. (1981). *All our children learning.* New York: McGraw-Hill.

Bloom, B., Hastings, J., & Madaus, G. (1971). *Handbook on formative and summative evaluation of student learning.* New York: McGraw-Hill.

Blumenfeld, P. (1992). Classroom learning and motivation: Clarifying and expanding goal theory. *Journal of Educational Psychology, 84,* 272–281.

Blumenfeld, P., Pintrich, P., & Hamilton, V. (1986). Children's concepts of ability, effort, and conduct. *America Educational Research Journal, 23,* 95–104.

Boggiano, A., Main, D., & Katz, P. (1988). Children's preference for challenge: The role of perceived competence and control. *Journal of Personality and Social Psychology, 54,* 134–141.

Boggiano, A., Pittman, T., & Ruble, D. (1982). The mastery hypothesis and the overjustification effect. *Social Cognition, 1,* 38–49.

Boggiano, A., & Ruble, D. (1979). Competence and the overjustification effect: A developmental study. *Journal of Personality and Social Psychology, 37,* 1462–1468.

Borkowski, J., Weyhing, R., & Carr, M. (1988). Effects of attributional retraining on strategy-based reading comprehension in learning-disabled students. *Journal of Educational Psychology, 80,* 46–53.

Bornstein, P., & Quevillon, R. (1976). The effects of a self-instructional package on overactive preschool boys. *Journal of Applied Behavior Analysis, 9,* 179–188.

Brattesani, K., Weinstein, R., & Marshall, H. (1984). Student perceptions of differential teacher treatment as moderators of teacher expectation effects. *Journal of Educational Psychology, 76,* 236–247.

Brockner, J. (1979). Self-esteem, self-consciousness, and task performance: Replications, extensions, and possible explanations. *Journal of Personality and Social Psychology, 37,* 447–461.

Brophy, J. (1981). Teacher praise: A functional analysis. *Review of Educational Research, 51,* 5–32.

Brophy, J. (1986). *Socializing student motivation to learn* (Institute for Research Teaching Research Series No. 169). East Lansing, MI: Michigan State University.

Brophy, J. (1987). On motivating students. In D. Berliner & B. Rosenshine (Eds.), *Talks to teachers* (pp. 201–245). New York: Random House.

Brophy, J., & Good, T. (1986). Teacher effects. In M. Wittrock (Ed.), *Handbook of research on teaching* (3rd ed., pp. 328–375). New York: Macmillan.

Brophy, J., & Rohrkemper, M. (1981). The influence of problem ownership on teachers' perceptions of and strategies for coping with problem students. *Journal of Educational Psychology, 73,* 295–311.

Brophy, J., Rohrkemper, M., Rashid, H., & Goldberger, M. (1983). Relationships between teachers' presentations of classroom tasks and students' engagements in those tasks. *Journal of Educational Psychology, 75,* 544–552.

Buckholdt, D., & Wodarski, J. (1974, August). *The effects of different reinforcmeent systems on cooperative behaviors exhibited by children in classroom contexts.* Paper presented at the annual meeting of the American Psychological Association, New Orleans, LA.

Butler, R. (1987). Task-involving and ego-involving properties of evaluation: Effects of different feedback conditions on motivational perceptions, interest, and performance. *Journal of Educational Psychology, 79,* 474–482.

Butler, R. (1988). Enhancing and undermining intrinsic motivation: The effects of task-involving and ego-involving evaluation on interest and performance. *British Journal of Educational Psychology, 58,* 1–14.

Butler, R., & Nisan, M. (1986). Effects of no feedback, task-related comments, and grades on intrinsic motivation and performance. *Journal of Educational Psychology, 78,* 210–216.

Clifford, M. (1984). Thoughts on a theory of constructive failure. *Educational Psychologist, 19,* 108–120.

Clifford, M. (1991). Risk taking; Theoretical, empirical, and educational considerations. *Educational Psychologist, 26,* 263–297.

Cohen, E. (1986). *Designing groupwork.* New York: Teachers College Press.

Cohen, H. (1973). Behavior modification in socially deviant youth. In C. Thoresen (Ed.), *Behavior modification in education: Seventy-second yearbook of the National Society for the Study of Education, 72* (Pt. I, pp. 291–314). Chicago: University of Chicago Press.

Collins, J. (1982, March). *Self-efficacy and ability in achievement behavior.* Paper presented at the annual meeting of the American Educational Research Association, New York.

Connell, J. (1985). A new multidimensional measure of children's perceptions of control. *Child Development, 56,* 1018–1041.

Connell, J., & Wellborn, J. (1991). Competence, autonomy, and relatedness: A motivational analysis of self-system processes. In M. Gunnar & L. Sroufe (Eds.), *Self processes in development. Minnesota Symposia on Child Psychology: Vol. 23* (pp. 43–77). Chicago: University of Chicago Press.

Covington, M. (1992). *Making the grade: A self-worth perspective on motivation and school reform.* Cambridge, England: Cambridge University Press.

Covington, M., & Beery, R. (1976). *Self-worth and school learning.* New York: Holt, Rinehart & Winston.

Covington, M., & Omelich, C. (1979). Effort: The double-edged sword in school achievement. *Journal of Educational Psychology, 71,* 169–182.

Covington, M., & Omelich, C. (1984a). An empirical examination of Weiner's critique of attribution research. *Journal of Educational Psychology, 76,* 1214–1225.

Covington, M., & Omelich, C. (1984b). Task-oriented versus competitive learning structures: Motivational and performance consequences. *Journal of Educational Psychology, 7,* 1038–1050.

Crockenberg, S., & Bryant, B. (1978). Socialization: The "implicit curriculum" of learning environments. *Journal of Research Development in Education, 12,* 69–78.

Csikszentmihalyi, M. (1975). *Beyond boredom and anxiety.* San Francisco: Jossey Bass.

Danner, F., & Lonky, E. (1981). A cognitive-developmental approach to the effects of rewards on intrinsic motivation. *Child Development, 52,* 1043–1052.

deCharms, R. (1976). *Enhancing motivation.* New York: Irvington.

deCharms, R. (1984). Motivating enhancement in educational settings. In R. Ames & C. Ames (Eds.), *Research on motivation in education: Vol 1. Student motivation* (pp. 275–310). New York: Academic Press.

Deci, E. (1971). The effects of externally mediated rewards on intrinsic motivation. *Journal of Personality and Social Psychology, 18,* 105–115.

Deci, E. (1972). Intrinsic motivation, extrinsic reinforcement, and inequity. *Journal of Personality and Social Psychology, 22,* 113–120.

Deci, E. (1975). *Intrinsic Motivation.* New York: Plenum Press.

Deci, E., Betley, G., Kahle, J., Abrams, L., & Porac, J. (1981). When trying to win: Competition and intrinsic motivation. *Personality and Social Psychology, 7,* 79–83.

Deci, E., Eghrari, H., Patrick, B., & Leone, D. (1994). Facilitating internalization: The self-determination theory perspective. *Journal of Personality, 62,* 121–142.

Deci, E., Nezlek, J., & Sheinman, L. (1981). Characteristics of the rewarder and intrinsic motivation of the rewardee. *Journal of Personality and Social Psychology, 40,* 1–10.

Deci, E., & Ryan, R. (1985). *Intrinsic motivation and self-determination in human behavior.* New York: Plenum Press.

Deci, E., & Ryan, R. (1987). The support of autonomy and the control of behavior. *Journal of Personality and Social Psychology, 53,* 1024–1037.

Deci, E., Schwartz, A., Sheinman, L., & Ryan, R. (1981). An instrument to assess adults' orientations toward control versus autonomy with children: Reflections on intrinsic motivation and perceived competence. *Journal of Educational Psychology, 73,* 643–650.

Deci, E., Vallerand, R., Pelletier, L., & Ryan, R. (1991). Motivation and education: The self-determination perspective. *Educational Psychologist, 26,* 325–346.

Diener, C., & Dweck, C. (1978). An analysis of learned helplessness: Continuous changes in performance, strategy, and achievement cognitions following failure. *Journal of Personality and Social Psychology, 36,* 451–462.

Dollinger, S., & Thelen, M. (1978). Overjustification and children's intrinsic motivation: Comparative effects of four rewards. *Journal of Personality and Social Psychology, 36,* 1259–1269.

Duda, J., & Nicholls, J. (1992). Dimensions of achievement motivation in schoolwork and sport. *Journal of Educational Psychology, 84,* 290–299.

Dweck, C. (1975). The role of expectations and attributions in the alleviation of learned helplessness. *Journal of Personality and Social Psychology, 31,* 674–685.

Dweck, C. (1986). Motivational processes affecting learning. *American Psychologist, 41,* 1040–1048.

Dweck, C., Davidson, W., Nelson, S., & Enna, B. (1978). Sex differences in learned helplessness: II. The contingencies of evaluative feedback in the classroom. III. An experimental analysis. *Developmental Psychology, 14,* 268–276.

Dweck, C., & Elliott, E. (1983). Achievement motivation. In P. Mussen (Ed.), *Handbook of child psychology: Vol. IV. Socialization, personality, and social development* (pp. 643–691). New York: Wiley.

Dweck, C., & Leggett, E. (1988). A social-cognitive approach to motivation and personality. *Psychological Review, 95,* 256–273.

Dweck, C., & Reppucci, N. (1973). Learned helplessness and reinforcement responsibility in children. *Journal of Personality and Social Psychology, 25,* 109–116.

Eccles, J. S. (1983). Expectancies, values, and academic behavior. In J. T. Spence (Ed.), *Achievement and achievement motives: Psychological and sociological approachess* (pp. 77–146). San Francisco: Freeman.

Eder, D. (1983). Ability grouping and students' academic self-concepts: A case study. *Elementary School Journal, 84,* 149–161.

Elliott, E., & Dweck, C. (1988). Goals: An approach to motivation and achievement. *Journal of Personality and Social Psychology, 54,* 5–12.

Enzle, M., & Ross, J. (1978). Increasing and decreasing intrinsic interest with contingent rewards: A test of cognitive evaluation theory. *Journal of Experimental Social Psychology, 14,* 588–597.

Forsterling, F. (1985). Attributional retraining: A review. *Psychological Bulletin, 98,* 495–512.

Fry, P., & Coe, K. (1980). Interaction among dimensions of academic motivation and classroom social climate: A study of the perceptions of junior high and high school pupils. *British Journal of Educational Psychology, 50,* 33–42.

Gaa, J. (1973). Effects of individual goal-setting conferences on achievement, attitudes, and goal-setting behavior. *Journal of Experimental Education, 42*, 22–28.

Gaa, J. (1979). The effects of individual goal-setting conferences on academic achievement and modification of locus of control orientation. *Psychology in the Schools, 16*, 591–597.

Garner, R., Alexander, P., Gillingham, M., Kulikowich, J., & Brown, R. (1991). Interest and learning from text. *American Educational Research Journal, 28*, 643–659.

Garner, R., Gillingham, M., & White, C. (1989). Effects of "seductive details" on macroprocessing and microprocessing in adults and children. *Cognition and Instruction, 6*, 41–57.

Goldberg, M., Passow, A., & Justman, J. (1966). *The effects of ability grouping*. New York: Teachers College Press.

Goodenow, C. (1993). Classroom belonging among early adolescent students: Relationships to motivation and achievement. *Journal of Early Adolescence, 13*, 21–43.

Goodlad, J. (1984). *A place called school*. New York: McGraw-Hill.

Gottfried, A. (1990). Academic intrinsic motivation in young elementary school children. *Journal of Educational Psychology, 82*, 525–538.

Graham, S. (1984). Communicating sympathy and anger to black and white children: The cognitive (attributional) consequences of affective cues. *Journal of Personality and Social Psychology, 47*, 14–28.

Graham, S. (1990). Communicating low ability in the classroom: Bad things good teachers sometimes do. In S. Graham & V. Folkes (Eds.), *Attribution theory: Applications to achievement, mental health, and interpersonal conflict* (pp. 17–36). Hillsdale, NJ: Lawrence Erlbaum Associates.

Graham, S. (1991). A review of attribution theory in achievement contexts. *Educational Psychology Review, 3*, 5–39.

Graham, S., & Barker, G. (1990). The downside of help: An attributional-developmental analysis of helping behavior as a low ability cue. *Journal of Educational Psychology, 82*, 7–14.

Graham, S., & Golan, S. (1991). Motivational influences on cognition: Task involvement, ego involvement, and depth of information processing. *Journal of Educational Psychology, 83*, 187–194.

Grolnick, W., & Ryan, R. (1987). Autonomy in children's learning: An experimental and individual difference investigation. *Journal of Personality and Social Psychology, 52*, 890–898.

Gusky, T., & Pigott, T. (1988). Research on group-based mastery learning programs: A meta-analysis. *Journal of Educational Research, 8*, 197–216.

Hallahan, D., & Sapona, R. (1983). Self-monitoring of attention with learning-disabled children: Past research and current issues. *Journal of Learning Disabilities, 16*, 616–620.

Harackiewicz, J. (1979). The effects of reward contingency and performance feedback on intrinsic motivation. *Journal of Personality and Social Psychology, 37*, 1352–1363.

Harackiewicz, J., Abrahams, S., & Wageman, R. (1987). Performance evaluation and intrinsic motivation: The effects of evaluative focus, rewards, and achievement orientation. *Journal of Personality and Social Psychology, 53*, 1015–1023.

Harari, O., & Covington, M. (1981). Reactions to achievement from a teacher and a student perspective: A developmental analysis. *American Educational Research Journal, 18*, 15–28.

Harter, S. (1978). Pleasure derived from challenge and the effects of receiving grades on children's difficulty level choices. *Child Development, 49*, 788–799.

Harter, S. (1981a). A model of mastery motivation in children: Individual differences and developmental change. In W. Collins (Ed.), *Minnesota Symposia on Child Psychology: Vol. 14* (pp. 215–255). Hillsdale, NJ: Lawrence Erlbaum Associates.

Harter, S. (1981b). A new self-report scale of intrinsic versus extrinsic orientation in the classroom: Motivational and informational components. *Developmental Psychology, 17*, 300–312.

Harter, S. (1992). The relationship between perceived competence, affect, and motivational orientation within the classroom: Process and patterns of change. In A. Boggiano & T. Pittman (Eds.), *Achievement and motivation: A social-developmental perspective* (pp. 77–114). Cambridge: Cambridge University Press.

Harter, S., & Connell, J. (1984). A comparison of alternative models of the relationships between academic achievement and children's perceptions of competence, control, and motivational orientation. In J. Nicholls (Ed.), *The development of achievement-related conditions and behavior* (pp. 219–250). Greenwich, CT: JAI Press.

Harter, S., & Jackson, B. (1992). Trait vs. nontrait conceptualizations of intrinsic/extrinsic motivational orientation. *Motivation and Emotion, 16*, 209–230.

Harter, S., & Pike, R. (1984). The pictorial scale of perceived competence and social acceptance for young children. *Child Development, 55*, 1969–1982.

Harter, S., Whitesell, N., & Kowalski, P. (1992). Individual differences in the effects of educational transitions on young adolescents' perceptions of competence and motivational orientation. *American Educational Research Journal, 29*, 777–807.

Heyman, G. (1992). Achievement goals and intrinsic motivation: Their relation and their role in adaptive motivation. *Motivation and Emotion, 16*, 231–247.

Hidi, S. (1990). Interest and its contribution as a mental resource for learning. *Review of Educational Research, 60*, 549–571.

Hom, H., & Murphy, M. (1985). Low need achievers' performance: The positive impact of a self-determined goal. *Personality and Social Psychology Bulletin, 11*, 275–285.

Hughes, B., Sullivan, H., & Mosley, M. (1985). External evaluation, task difficulty, and continuing motivation. *Journal of Educational Research, 78*, 210–215.

Hull, C. (1943). *Principles of behavior*. New York: Appleton-Century-Crofts.

Hulton, R., & DeVries, D. (1976). *Team competition and group practice: Effects on student achievement and attitudes* (Report No. 212). Baltimore: Johns Hopkins University, Center for Social Organization of Schools.

Hunt, J. McV. (1965). Intrinsic motivation and its role in psychological development. in D. Levine (Ed.), *Nebraska Symposium on Motivation: Vol. 13* (pp. 189–282). Lincoln: University of Nebraska Press.

Jagacinski, C., & Nicholls, J. (1984). Conceptions of ability and related affects in task involvement and ego involvement. *Journal of Educational Psychology, 76*, 909–919.

Jagacinski, C., & Nicholls, J. (1987). Competence and affect in task involvement and ego involvement: The impact of social comparison information. *Journal of Educational Psychology, 79*, 107–114.

Johnson, D., & Johnson, R. (1985a). The internal dynamics of cooperative learning groups. In R. Slavin, S. Sharan, S. Kagan, R. Hertz-Lazarowitz, N. Webb, & R. Schmuck (Eds.), *Learning to cooperate, cooperating to learn* (pp. 103–124). New York: Plenum Press.

Johnson, D., & Johnson, R. (1985b). Motivational processes in cooperative, competitive, and individualistic learning situations. In C. Ames & R. Ames (Eds.), *Research on motivation in education: Vol. 2. The classroom milieu* (pp. 249–286). Orlando, FL: Academic Press.

Johnson, D., & Johnson, R. (1989). Toward a cooperative effort. *Educational Leadership, 46*, 80–81.

Kagan, J. (1972). Motives and development. *Journal of Personality and Social Psychology, 22*, 51–66.

Kage, M., & Namiki, H. (1990). The effects of evaluation structure on children's intrinsic motivation and learning. *Japanese Journal of Educational Psychology, 38*, 36–45.

Karniol, R., & Ross, M. (1977). The effect of performance-relevant and performance-irrelevant rewards on children's intrinsic motivation. *Child Development, 48*, 482–487.

Kazdin, A. (1974). Self-monitoring and behavior change. In M. Mahoney & C. Thoresen (Eds.), *Self-control: Power to the person* (pp. 218–246). Monterey, CA: Brooks-Cole.

Kazdin, A. (1975). Recent advances in token economy research. In M. Hersen, R. Eisler, & P. Miller (Eds.), *Progress in behavior modifications: Vol 1* (pp. 233–274). New York: Academic Press.

Keller, F. (1968). Goodbye, teacher. . . . *Journal of Applied Behavior Analysis, 1,* 79–89.

Kulik, C-L., Kulik, J., & Bangert-Drowns, R. (1990). Effectiveness of mastery learning programs: A meta-analysis. *Review of Educational Research, 60,* 265–299.

Kulik, J., Kulik, C-L., & Cohen, P. (1979). A meta-analysis of outcome studies of Keller's Personalized System of Instruction. *American Psychologist, 34,* 307–318.

Lepper, M. (1981). Intrinsic and extrinsic motivation in children: Detrimental effects of superfluous social controls. In A. Collins (Ed.), *Aspects of the development of competence. Minnesota Symposia on Child Psychology: Vol. 14* (pp. 155–214). Hillsdale, NJ: Lawrence Erlbaum Associates.

Lepper, M. (1983). Extrinsic reward and intrinsic motivation: Implications for the classroom. In J. Levine & M. Wang (Eds.), *Teacher and student perceptions: Implications for learning* (pp. 281–317). Hillsdale, NJ: Lawrence Erlbaum Associates.

Lepper, M. (1985). Microcomputers in education. *American Psychologist, 40,* 1–18.

Lepper, M. (1988). Motivational considerations in the study of instruction. *Cognition and Instruction, 5,* 289–309.

Lepper, M., & Cordova, D. (1992). A desire to be taught: Instructional consequences of intrinsic motivation. *Motivation and Emotion, 3,* 187–208.

Lepper, M., & Greene, D. (1975). Turning play into work: Effects of adult surveillance and extrinsic rewards on children's intrinsic motivation. *Journal of Personality and Social Psychology, 31,* 479–486.

Lepper, M., Greene, D., & Nisbett, R. (1973). Undermining children's intrinsic interest with intrinsic rewards: A test of the overjustification hypothesis. *Journal of Personality and Social Psychology, 28,* 129–137.

Lepper, M., & Malone, T. (1987). Intrinsic motivation and instructional effectiveness in computer-based education. In R. Snow & M. Farr (Eds.), *Aptitude, learning, and instruction: III. Conative and affective process analysis* (pp. 255–286). Hillsdale, NJ: Lawrence Erlbaum Associates.

Lepper, M., Sethi, S., Dialdin, D., & Drake, M. (in press). In S. Luther, J. Burack, D. Cicchetti, & J. Weisz (Eds.), *Developmental perspectives on risk and psychopathology.* New York: Cambridge University Press.

Levine, J. (1983). Social comparison and education. In J. Levine & M. Wang (Eds.), *Teacher and student perceptions: Implications for learning* (pp. 29–55). Hillsdale, NJ: Lawrence Erlbaum Associates.

Litrownik, A., & Freitas, J. (1980). Self-monitoring in moderately retarded adolescents: Reactivity and accuracy as a function of valence. *Behavior Therapy, 11,* 245–255.

Locke, E., Frederick, E., Lee, C., & Bobko, P. (1984). Effect of self-efficacy, goals and task strategies on task performance. *Journal of Applied Psychology, 69,* 241–251.

Locke, E., Shaw, K., Saari, L., & Latham, G. (1981). Goal setting and task performance: 1969–1980. *Psychological Bulletin, 90,* 125–152.

Luria, A. (1961). *The role of speech in the regulation of normal and abnormal behaviors.* New York: Liveright.

Mace, F., Belfiore, P., & Shea, M. (1989). Operant theory and research on self-regulation. In B. Zimmerman & D. Schunk (Eds.), *Self-regulated learning and academic achievement: Theory, research, and practice* (pp. 27–50). New York: Springer.

Mace, F., & Kratochwill, T. (1988). Self-monitoring. In J. Will, S. Elliott, & F. Gresham (Eds.), *Handbook of behavior therapy in education* (p. 489–522). New York: Plenum Press.

Mac Iver, D. (1987). Classroom factors and student characteristics predicting students' use of achievement standards during ability self-assessment. *Child Development, 58,* 1258–1271.

Mac Iver, D. (1988). Classroom environments and the stratification of pupils' ability perceptions. *Journal of Educational Psychology, 80,* 495–505.

Mac Iver, D., Stipek, D., & Daniels, D. (1991). Explaining within-semester changes in student effort in junior high school and senior high school courses. *Journal of Educational Psychology, 83,* 201–211.

Maehr, M. (1976). Continuing motivation: An analysis of a seldom considered educational outcome. *Review of Educational Research, 46,* 443–462.

Maehr, M. (1984). Meaning and motivation: Toward a theory of personal investment. In R. Ames & C. Ames (Eds.), *Research on motivation in education: Vol. 1. Student motivation* (pp. 115–144). Orlando, FL: Academic Press.

Maehr, M., & Midgley, C. (1991). Enhancing student motivation: A schoolwide approach. *Educational Psychologist, 26,* 399–427.

Maehr, M., & Stallings, W. (1972). Freedom from external evaluation. *Child Development, 43,* 117–185.

Malone, T. (1981a). Toward a theory of intrinsically motivating instruction. *Cognitive Science, 4,* 333–369.

Malone, T. (1981b). What makes computer games fun? *Byte, 6,* 258–277.

Malone, T., & Lepper, M. (1987). Making learning fun: A taxonomy of intrinsic motivation for learning. In R. Snow & M. Farr (Eds.), *Aptitude, learning, and instruction: Vol. III. Conative and affective process analysis* (pp. 223–253). Hillsdale, NJ: Lawrence Erlbaum Associates.

Manderlink, G., & Harackiewicz, J. (1984). Proximal vs. distal goal setting and intrinsic motivation. *Journal of Personality and Social Psychology, 47,* 918–928.

Masters, J., & Santrock, J. (1976). Studies in the self-regulation of behavior: Effects of contingent cognitive and affective events. *Developmental Psychology, 12,* 334–348.

Matheny, K., & Edwards, C. (1974). Academic improvement through an experimental classroom management system. *Journal of School Psychology, 12,* 222–232.

McGraw, K., & McCullers, J. (1979). Evidence of a detrimental effect of extrinsic incentives on breaking a mental set. *Journal of Experimental Social Psychology, 15,* 285–294.

McLaughlin, T., & Williams, R. (1988). Token economy. In J. Witt, S. Elliott, & F. Gresham (Eds.), *Handbook of behavior therapy in education* (pp. 469–487). New York: Plenum Press.

McMullin, D., & Steffen, J. (1982). Intrinsic motivation and performance standards. *Social Behavior and Personality, 10,* 47–56.

Meece, J. (1991). The classroom context and students' motivational goals. In M. Maehr & P. Pintrich (Eds.), *Advances in motivation and achievement: Vol. 7* (pp. 261–285). Greenwich, CT: JAI Press.

Meece, J., Blumenfeld, P., & Hoyle, R. (1988). Students' goal orientations and cognitive engagement in classroom activities. *Journal of Educational Psychology, 80,* 514–523.

Meece, J., & Holt, K. (1993). A pattern analysis of students' achievement goals. *Journal of Educational Psychology, 85,* 582–590.

Meichenbaum, D. (1977). *Cognitive behavior modification.* New York: Plenum Press.

Meyer, W. (1982). Indirect communications about perceived ability estimates. *Journal of Educational Psychology, 74,* 888–897.

Morgan, M. (1984). Reward-induced decrements and increments in intrinsic motivation. *Review of Educational Research, 54,* 5–30.

Nicholls, J. (1979). Quality and equality in intellectual development: The role of motivation in education. *American Psychologist, 34,* 1071–1083.

Nicholls, J. (1983). Conception of ability and achievement motivation: A theory and its implications for education. In S. Paris, G. Olson, & H. Stevenson (Eds.), *Learning and motivation in the classroom* (pp. 211–237). Hillsdale, NJ: Lawrence Erlbaum Associates.

Nicholls, J. (1984). Achievement motivation: Conceptions of ability, subjective experience, task choice, and performance. *Psychological Review, 91,* 328–346.

Nicholls, J., Cobb, P., Wood, T., Yackel, E., & Patashnick, M. (1990). Assessing students' theories of success in mathematics: Individual and classroom differences. *Journal for Research in Mathematics Education, 21,* 109–122.

Nicholls, J., & Miller, A. (1984). Conceptions of ability and achievement motivation. In R. Ames & C. Ames (Eds.), *Research on motivation in education: Vol. 1. Student motivation* (pp. 39–73). New York: Academic Press.

Nolen, S. (1988). Reasons for studying: Motivational orientations and study strategies. *Cognition and Instruction, 5,* 269–287.

Notz, W. (1975). Work motivation and the negative effects of extrinsic rewards: A review with implications for theory and practice. *American Psychologist, 30,* 804–891.

O'Leary, K. (1978). The operant and social psychology of token systems. In A. Catania & T. Brigham (Eds.), *Handbook of applied behavior analysis: Social and instructional processes* (pp. 179–207). New York: Irvington.

Pallak, S., Costomiris, S., Sroka, S., & Pittman, T. (1982). School experience, reward characteristics, and intrinsic motivation. *Child Development, 53,* 1382–1391.

Parker, L., & Lepper, M. (1992). The effects of fantasy contexts on children's learning and motivation: Making learning more fun. *Journal of Personality and Social Psychology, 62,* 625–633.

Parsons, J., Kaczala, C., & Meece, J. (1982). Socialization of achievement attitudes and beliefs: Classroom influences. *Child Development, 53,* 322–339.

Pascarella, E., Walberg, H., Junker, L., & Haertel, G. (1981). Continuing motivation in science for early and late adolescents. *American Educational Research Journal, 18,* 439–452.

Patrick, B., Skinner, E., & Connell, J. (1993). What motivates children's behavior and emotions? Joint effects of perceived control and autonomy in the academic domain. *Journal of Personality and Social Psychology, 65,* 781–791.

Pearlman, C. (1984). The effects of level of effectance motivation, IQ, and a penalty/reward contingency on the choice of problem difficulty. *Child Development, 55,* 537–542.

Pepitone, E. (1972). Comparison behavior in elementary school children. *American Educational Research Journal, 9,* 43–63.

Peterson, P., & Swing, S. (1982). Beyond time on task: Students' reports of their thought processes during classroom instruction. *Elementary School Journal, 21,* 481–491.

Piaget, J. (1952). *The origins of intelligence in children.* New York: Norton.

Pianta, R., & Steinberg, M. (1992). Teacher-child relationships and the process of adjusting to school. *New Directions for Child Development, 57,* 61–80.

Pintrich, P., & De Groot, E. (1990). Motivational and self-regulated learning components of classroom academic performance. *Journal of Educational Psychology, 82,* 33–40.

Pintrich, P., & Schrauben, B. (1992). Students' motivational beliefs and their cognitive engagement in classroom academic tasks. In D. Schunk & J. Meece (Eds.), *Student perception in the classroom* (pp. 149–183). Hillsdale, NJ: Lawrence Erlbaum Associates.

Pittman, T., Boggiano, A., & Ruble, D. (1983). Intrinsic and extrinsic motivational orientations: Limiting conditions on the undermining and enhancing effects of reward on intrinsic motivation. In J. Levine & M. Wang (Eds.), *Teacher and student perceptions: Implications for learning* (pp. 317–340). Hillsdale, NJ: Lawrence Erlbaum Associates.

Pittman, T., Davey, M., Alafat, K., Wetherill, K., & Kramer, N. (1980). Informational versus controlling verbal rewards. *Personality and Social Psychology Bulletin, 6,* 228–233.

Pittman, T., Emery, J., & Boggiano, A. (1982). Intrinsic and extrinsic motivational orientations: Reward-induced changes in preference for complexity. *Journal of Personality and Social Psychology, 42,* 789–797.

Plant, R., & Ryan, R. (1985). Intrinsic motivation and the effects of self-consciousness, self-awareness, and ego-involvement: An investigation of internally-controlling styles. *Journal of Personality, 53,* 435–449.

Rainey, R. (1965). The effects of directed vs. non-directed laboratory work on high school chemistry achievement. *Journal of Research in Science Teaching, 3,* 286–292.

Reid, M., & Borkowski, J. (1987). Causal attributions of hyperactive children: Implications for teaching strategies and self-control. *Journal of Educational Psychology, 79,* 296–307.

Renick, J., & Harter, S. (1989). Impact of social comparisons on the developing self-perceptions of learning disabled students. *Journal of Educational Psychology, 81,* 631–638.

Reuman, D. (1989). How social comparison mediates the relation between ability-grouping practices and students' achievement expectancies in mathematics. *Journal of Educational Psychology, 81,* 178–189.

Rheinberg, F. (1983). Achievement evaluation: A fundamental difference and its motivational consequences. *Studies in Educational Evaluation, 9,* 185–194.

Rigby, C., Deci, E., Patrick, B., & Ryan, R. (1991). Beyond the intrinsic-extrinsic dichotomy: Self-determination in motivation and learning. *Motivation and Emotion, 16,* 165–184.

Rosenbaum, M., & Drabman, R. (1979). Self-control training in the classroom: A review and critique. *Journal of Applied Behavior Analysis, 12,* 467–485.

Rosenfield, D., Folger, R., & Adelman, H. (1980). When rewards reflect competence: A qualification of the overjustification effect. *Journal of Personality and Social Psychology, 39,* 368–376.

Rosenholtz, S., & Rosenholtz, S. (1981). Classroom organization and the perception of ability. *Sociology of Education, 54,* 132–140.

Rosenholtz, S., & Simpson, C. (1984a). Classroom organization and student stratification. *Elementary School Journal, 85,* 21–38.

Rosenholtz, S., & Simpson, C. (1984b). The formation of ability conceptions: Developmental trend or social construction? *Review of Educational Research, 54,* 31–63.

Rosenholtz, S., & Wilson, B. (1980). The effect of classroom structure on shared perceptions of ability. *American Educational Research Journal, 17,* 75–82.

Rosenthal, R., & Jacobson, L. (1968). *Pygmalion in the classroom: Teacher expectation and pupils' intellectual development.* New York: Holt, Rinehart & Winston.

Rotter, J. (1966). Generalized expectancies for internal versus external control of reinforcement. *Psychological Monographs, 1* (Whole No. 609).

Ryan, R. (1982). Control and information in the intrapersonal sphere: An extension of cognitive evaluation theory. *Journal of Personality and Social Psychology, 43,* 450–461.

Ryan, R., & Connell, J. (1989). Perceived locus of causality and internalization: Examining reasons for acting in two domains. *Journal of Personality and Social Psychology, 57,* 749–761.

Ryan, R., Connell, J., & Deci, E. (1985). A motivational analysis of self-determination and self-regulation. In C. Ames & R. Ames (Eds.), *Research on motivation in education: Vol. 2. The classroom* (pp. 13–51). New York: Academic Press.

Ryan, R., Connell, J., & Grolnick, W. (1992). When achievement is not intrinsically motivated: A theory of internalization and self-regulation in school. In K. Boggiano & T. Pittman (Eds.) (1992). *Achievement and motivation: A social developmental perspective* (pp. 167–188). Cambridge UK: Cambridge University Press.

Ryan, R., Connell, J., & Plant, R. (1990). Emotions in nondirected text learning. *Learning and Individual Differences, 2,* 1–17.

Ryan, R., & Grolnick, W. (1986). Origins and pawns in the classroom: Self-report and projective assessments of individual differences in children's perceptions. *Journal of Personality and Social Psychology, 50,* 350–358.

Ryan, R., Mims, V., & Koestner, R. (1983). The relationship of reward contingency and interpersonal context to intrinsic motivation: A review and test using cognitive evaluation theory. *Journal of Personality and Social Psychology, 45*, 736–750.

Ryan, R., & Powelson, C. (1991). Autonomy and relatedness as fundamental to motivation and education. *Journal of Experimental Education, 60*, 49–66.

Ryan, R., & Stiller, J. (1991). The social contexts of internalization: Parent and teacher influences on autonomy, motivation, and learning. In P. Pintrich & M. Maehr (Eds.), *Advances in motivation and achievement* (Vol. 7, pp. 115–149). Greenwich, CT: JAI Press.

Salili, F., Maehr, M., Sorensen, R., & Fyans, L. (1976). A further consideration of the effects of evaluation on motivation. *American Educational Research Journal, 13*, 85–102.

Schiefele, U. (1991). Interest, learning, and motivation. *Educational Psychologist, 26*, 299–323.

Schunk, D. (1982). Effects of effort and attributional feedback on children's perceived self-efficacy and achievement. *Journal of Educational Psychology, 74*, 548–556.

Schunk, D. (1983a). Ability versus effort attributional feedback: Differential effects on self-efficacy and achievement. *Journal of Educational Psychology, 75*, 848–856.

Schunk, D. (1983b). Developing children's self-efficacy and skills: The roles of social comparative information and goal setting. *Contemporary Educational Psychology, 8*, 76–86.

Schunk, D. (1983c). Reward contingencies and the development of children's skills and self-efficacy. *Journal of Educational Psychology, 75*, 511–518.

Schunk, D. (1984a). Self-efficacy perspective on achievement behavior. *Educational Psychologist, 19*, 48–58.

Schunk, D. (1984b). Sequential attributional feedback and children's achievement behaviors. *Journal of Educational Psychology, 76*, 1159–1169.

Schunk, D. (1985). Participation in goal setting: Effects on self-efficacy and skills of learning disabled children. *Journal of Special Education, 19*, 307–317.

Schunk, D. (1986). Children's social comparison and goal setting in achievement contexts. In L. Katz (Ed.), *Current topics in early childhood education* (pp. 62–84). Norwood, NJ: Ablex.

Schunk, D. (1989). Social cognitive theory and self-regulated learning. In B. Zimmerman & D. Schunk (Eds.), *Self-regulated learning and academic achievement: Theory, research and practice* (pp. 83–110). New York: Springer.

Schunk, D. (1990). Goal setting and self-efficacy during self-regulated learning. *Educational Psychologist, 25*, 71–86.

Schunk, D. (1991). Goal setting and self-evaluation: A social cognitive perspective on self-regulation. In M. Maehr & P. Pintrich (Eds.), *Advances in motivation and achievement: Vol. 7* (pp. 85–113). Greenwich, CT: JAI Press.

Schunk, D., & Rice, J. (1989). Learning goals and children's reading comprehension. *Journal of Reading Behavior, 21*, 279–293.

Shapira, Z. (1976). Expectancy determinants of intrinsically motivated behavior. *Journal of Personality and Social Psychology, 34*, 1235–1244.

Sharan, S. (1980). Cooperative learning in small groups: Recent methods and effects on achievement, attitudes, and ethnic relations. *Review of Educational Research, 50*, 241–271.

Shirey, L., & Reynolds, R. (1988). Effect of interest on attention and learning. *Journal of Educational Psychology, 80*, 159–166.

Simpson, C. (1981). Classroom structure and the organization of ability. *Sociology of Education, 54*, 120–132.

Simpson, C., & Rosenholtz, S. (1986). Classroom structure and the social construction of ability. In J. Richardson (Ed.), *Handbook of theory and research for the sociology of education* (pp. 113–138). New York: Greenwood Press.

Skinner, B. (1974). *About behaviorism*. New York: Knopf.

Skinner, E., & Belmont, M. (1993). Motivation in the classroom: Reciprocal effects of teacher behavior and student engagement across the school year. *Journal of Educational Psychology, 85*, 571–581.

Skinner, E., Wellborn, J., & Connell, J. (1990). What it takes to do well in school and whether I've got it: A process model of perceived control and children's engagement and achievement in school. *Journal of Educational Psychology, 82*, 22–32.

Slavin, R. (1983a). *Cooperative learning*. New York: Longman.

Slavin, R. (1983b). When does cooperative learning increase student achievement? *Psychological Bulletin, 94*, 429–445.

Slavin, R. (1984). Students motivating students to excel: Cooperative incentives, cooperative tasks, and student achievement. *Elementary School Journal, 84*, 53–63.

Slavin, R., Sharon, S., Kagan, S., Hertz-Lazarowitz, N., Webb, N., Schmuck, R. (Eds.) (1985). *Learning to cooperate, cooperating to learn*. New York: Plenum Press.

Smiley, P., & Dweck, C. (1994). Individual differences in achievement goals among young children. *Child Development, 65*, 1723–1743.

Speidel, G., & Tharp, R. (1980). What does self-reinforcement reinforce? An empirical analysis of the contingencies in self-determined reinforcement. *Child Behavior Therapy, 2*, 1–22.

Stipek, D. (1981). Children's perceptions of their own and their classmates' ability. *Journal of Educational Psychology, 73*, 404–410.

Stipek, D. (1993). *Motivation to learn: From theory to practice*. Needham Heights, MA: Allyn & Bacon.

Sulzer-Azaroff, B., & Mayer, G. (1986). *Achieving educational excellence*. New York: Holt, Rinehart & Winston.

Swann, W., & Pittman, T. (1977). Initiating play activity of children: The moderating influence of verbal cues on intrinsic motivation. *Child Development, 48*, 1128–1132.

Swanson, H., & Scarpati, S. (1985). Self-instruction training to increase academic performance of educationally handicapped children. *Child and Family Behavior Therapy, 6*, 23–39.

Thorndike, E. (1911). *Animal intelligence*. New York: Macmillan.

Tollefson, N., Tracy, D., Johnsen, E., Farmer, A., & Buenning, M. (1984). Goal setting and personal responsibility training for LD adolescents. *Psychology in the Schools, 21*, 224–233.

Vallerand, R., Gauvin, L., & Halliwell, W. (1986). Negative effects of competition on children's intrinsic motivation. *Journal of Social Psychology, 126*, 649–657.

Vygotsky, L. (1962). *Thought and language*. Cambridge, MA: MIT Press.

Vygotsky, L. (1978). *Mind in society: The development of higher psychological processes*. Cambridge, MA: Harvard University Press.

Wall, S. (1983). Children's self-determination of standards in reinforcement contingencies: A re-examination. *Journal of School Psychology, 21*, 123–131.

Weiner, B. (1986). *An attributional theory of motivation and emotion*. New York: Springer.

Weiner, B. (1992). *Human motivation: Metaphors, theories and research*. London: Sage Publications.

Weiner, B., Graham, S., Stern, P., & Lawson, M. (1982). Using affective cues to infer causal thoughts. *Developmental Psychology, 18*, 278–286.

Weiner, B., & Peter, N. (1973). A cognitive-developmental analysis of achievement and moral judgments. *Developmental Psychology, 9*, 290–309.

Weinstein, R. (1976). Reading group membership in first grade: Teacher behaviors and pupil experience over time. *Journal of Educational Psychology, 68*, 103–116.

Weinstein, R. (1985). Student mediation of classroom expectancy effects. In J. Dusek (Ed.), *Teacher Expectancies* (pp. 329–350). Hillsdale, NJ: Lawrence Erlbaum Associates.

Weinstein, R. (1989). Perceptions of classroom processes and student motivation: Children's views of self-fulfilling prophecies. In C. Ames & R. Ames (Eds.), *Research on motivation in education: Vol. 3. Goals and cognitions* (pp. 187–221). New York: Academic Press.

Weinstein, R., Marshall, H., Sharp, L., & Botkin, M. (1987). Pygmalion and the student: Age and classroom differences in childen's awareness of teacher expectations. *Child Development, 58,* 1079–1093.

Weisz, J. (1986). Understanding the developing understanding of control. In M. Perlmutter (Ed.), *Cognitive perspectives on children's social and behavioral development. Minnesota Symposia on Child Psychology: Vol. 18* (pp. 219–278). Hillsdale, NJ: Lawrence Erlbaum Associates.

Weisz, J. (1990). Development of control-related beliefs, goals, and styles in childhood and adolescence: A clinical perspective. In K. Schaie, J. Rodin, & C. Schooler (Eds.), *Self-directedness: Cause and effects throughout the life course* (pp. 103–145). Hillsdale, NJ: Lawrence Erlbaum Associates.

White, R. (1959). Motivation reconsidered: The concept of competence. *Psychological Review, 66,* 297–333.

Wigfield, A., Eccles, J., MacIver, D., Reuman, D., & Midgley, C. (1991). Transitions during early adolescence: Changes in children's domain-specific self-perceptions and general self-esteem across the transition to junior high school. *Developmental Psychology, 27,* 552–565.

Zimmerman, B., & Schunk, D. (Eds.). (1989). *Self-regulated learning and academic achievement: Theory, research, and practice.* New York: Springer.

Zuckerman, M., Porac, J., Lathin, D., Smith, R., & Deci, E. (1978). On the importance of self-determination for intrinsically motivated behavior. *Personality and Social Psychology Bulletin, 4,* 443–466.

# DEVELOPMENT AND INDIVIDUAL DIFFERENCES

# ·6·

# CHILDREN BECOMING STUDENTS

## Scott G. Paris

UNIVERSITY OF MICHIGAN, ANN ARBOR

## Anne E. Cunningham

UNIVERSITY OF WASHINGTON, SEATTLE

A central theme throughout childhood is "becoming"—becoming less childlike, less dependent, and less naive while simultaneously becoming more skilled, more knowledgeable, and more cooperative. The foundations for lifelong learning are established as children develop abilities to select and direct their own behavior. Schooling fosters these accomplishments because it enculturates children into progressively larger spheres of society, with each new level providing more challenges and more responsibilities. Schooling encompasses socialization processes as well as the cognitive acquisition of knowledge; it includes the "hidden curriculum" attained by students as well as the explicit curriculum taught by teachers and educational materials. The focus in this chapter is student centered because we want to examine children developing within the context of schools. In particular, we examine how they acquire learning strategies and motivational orientations that help them become successful students. It is the intersection of maturation and learning, of development and education, that defines critical themes of becoming and that undergirds many issues in educational psychology, practice, and policy.

The connection between human development and schooling is so natural that one might expect a plethora of theories on the topic and a flood of research during the past 100 years. But surprisingly, for most of the 20th century there has been relatively little developmental research and theory building within educational contexts, compared to the large number of analytical studies of individual differences, pedagogical teaching methods, and general axioms of human learning. The contributions of Binet, Hall, Dewey, Piaget, Montessori, Bruner, and Vygotsky to theories of child development and education have been more influential in the past 20 years than at any other time in the past century. Developmental psychology historically has contributed *indirectly* to educational practices through the implications of research for appropriate learning and teaching techniques, rather than by direct study of children in schools or analyses of the longitudinal consequences of schooling (e.g.,

Bruner, 1961; Vygotsky, 1978). Only recently has the relation between educational and developmental psychology become more symbiotic, in part because of the increase in cognitive research since 1970, in part because pluralistic research has replaced the theoretical and methodological hegemony of behaviorism and experimental psychology that dominated most research in the 20th century. The relation between educational and developmental psychology has also become more reciprocal and balanced, with educational research on children in schools throughout the world informing theories of human development as much as the converse.

This chapter begins with a brief overview of the historical connections between developmental and educational psychology, with special reference to some key theorists. Then volumes of the *Journal of Educational Psychology* published since 1910 are sampled for clues about historical trends in developmental research in education. Next, contemporary issues in learning, curriculum, instruction, and assessment are examined from a developmental perspective to serve as guideposts for interpreting studies reviewed in the rest of the chapter. After this retrospective survey of educational psychology, children's academic development is examined chronologically according to three levels of schooling—preschool, primary grades, and upper elementary grades—with particular attention paid to the transitions into each one. Several key issues are examined at each age period as representative of developmental issues and research in educational psychology. The last section of the chapter discusses two developmental themes in schooling that help to integrate developmental research in educational psychology. Those themes are (a) children's emerging theories about education and (b) the integration of cognitive and motivational strategies for self-regulated learning during childhood. Those themes were selected for discussion because they are enduring issues for both developmental and educational psychology, they influence many aspects of children's learning and motivation in school, and they have been salient issues in recent research and are likely to remain popular in the future.

The authors appreciate the helpful suggestions provided by Keith Stanovich and Fred Morrison.

## HISTORICAL CONNECTIONS BETWEEN DEVELOPMENTAL AND EDUCATIONAL PSYCHOLOGY

Throughout the 19th century, a variety of scientists, philosophers, educators, and other professionals contributed to studies of developmental issues in education. The biographies and contributions of many of these influential people, including Darwin, Hall, Binet, Baldwin, Dewey, Freud, Piaget, Watson, Gesell, Vygotsky, Stern, Werner, and others, are included in the 1992 centennial issues of the journal *Developmental Psychology*. Few of these pioneers were trained as teachers or psychologists, so they often influenced education through the force of their personalities as well as the popularity of their ideas. Their influence devolved from a mixture of practical advice, broad developmental theories and frameworks, and the appeal of scientific methods of inquiry.

### Early Influences on Developmental Approaches to Education

In the early 19th century, several European theorists had profound effects on education. Rousseau proposed in his book *Emile* that children should discover concepts and reason by active inquiry and manipulation. His focus on maturation and discovery rather than didactic drill was a pronounced shift to a child-centered curriculum that influenced others. For example, Johann Pestalozzi, a Swiss lawyer, developed a model school that emphasized growth, kindness, and understanding instead of the acquisition of information by recitation of correct answers and punishment for errors. Friedrich Froebel applied similar ideas to kindergartens in which cooperative and creative activities were viewed as the foundation for learning. By the end of the 19th century, these practices had been translated into pedagogical principles by Johann Herbart, William James, and others.

The European ideas were imported into America by Horace Mann and others who popularized moral education and compulsory schooling because they viewed education as a social vehicle for enhancing personal development. For example, Hilgard (1987, and chapter 31) traced the European influences to several key American educators. William Harris was a school administrator in St. Louis who incorporated kindergartens into public schools and introduced the graded curriculum and promotion by ability to the next grade. Harris also emphasized teaching reading with phonetic methods and introduced a transitional alphabet as a method of instruction. At the same time, Colonel Francis Parker reformed schools in Massachusetts by emphasizing teacher-designed materials rather than a set curriculum to be mastered by everyone. In 1890 he was given 2 million dollars to establish a private school based on his philosophy and a teacher training institute in Chicago that would later become part of the University of Chicago. Subsequently, scholars such as John Dewey and G. Stanley Hall capitalized on the child study movement and teacher training institutes to test and spread their ideas about education and development.

The philosophical underpinnings of educational reform movements based on moral, social, and cognitive development during the 19th century came from several sources, according to Hilgard (1987) and Walberg and Haertel (1992). One contributing view was derived from British empiricism, which presumed that sensory impressions were written onto the mind as if it were a blank slate and complex ideas were compounded from simpler ones. A second view, derived from British associationism, was that ideas became associated through contiguity and practice and could be reconstituted through mental chemistry. A third philosophical contribution was based on the rationalism of Kant, which posited that categories in the mind help to transform and interpret knowledge rather than copy it directly from sensory experiences. A fourth viewpoint arose from Darwin's ideas about evolution and proposed that individual development mirrors the development of species (that is, ontogeny recapitulates phylogeny).

These philosophical positions were linked with contemporary methods of scientific inquiry, but some methods were obstacles to developmental research. For example, one popular scientific method was Wundt's introspectionism, which was particularly unsuited for children. He said,

During the earlier periods of the child's life, experimental methods are hardly applicable at all. The results of experiments which have been tried on very young children must be regarded as purely chance results, wholly untrustworthy on account of the great number of sources of error. For these reasons, it is an error to hold, as is sometimes held, that the mental life of adults can never be fully understood except through the analysis of the child's mind. The exact opposite is the true position to take. (Wundt, 1907, p. 336)

Cairns and Ornstein (1979), who cite this quotation, note that developmental psychology had a shaky foundation because most of the methods used by psychologists in the 19th century were not appropriate for children. Although introspection, along with reaction times and psychophysical measurements, provided useful data from adults, the methods did not work well with children. Consequently, early approaches to educational psychology were often based more on prescriptions for teachers based on inference from findings with adults or animals rather than on direct information about the way students learn and become motivated. It is also apparent that many psychologists assumed that general laws of learning could be derived from research on adults or animals and applied to children with equal validity. Other early methods were equally constraining. For example, Galton established psychological laboratories in England at the end of the 19th century to measure individual differences among people in sensory experiences that were based loosely on tenets of evolutionary theory and faculty psychology. Galton viewed intelligence as innate and measurable by individual mental abilities, a view that would have an enduring impact on educational psychology. Only a few scientists, such as Binet, in France, began to test and interview children about their knowledge, memory, and problem-solving techniques with methods that were designed specifically for children.

### Progress During the Early 20th Century

From the beginning, the field of educational psychology has been concerned with issues related to children and development. However, there has been little consensus on a coherent theory or framework, according to Walberg and Haertel (1992). They identified the diversity within educational psychology by quoting an editorial in the first issue of the *Journal of Educational Psychology*, published in 1910:

Educational psychology will then be regarded as including not only the well-known field covered by the average text-book—the psychology of sensation, instinct, attention, habit, memory, the technique and economy of learning, the conceptual processes, etc.—but also problems of mental development—heredity, adolescence, and the inexhaustible field of child-study—the study of individual differences, of retarded and precocious development, the psychology of the "special class," the nature of mental endowments, the measurement of mental capacity, the psychology of mental tests, the correlation of mental abilities, the psychology of special methods in the several school branches, the important problems of mental hygiene; all these, whether treated from the experimental, the statistical or the literary point of view, are topics and problems which we deem pertinent for consideration in a *Journal of Educational Psychology*. (pp. 1–2)

Perhaps the diversity of topics and the lack of a guiding theory made the field susceptible to the influence of a few key people. Hilgard (1987, and chapter 31) identified Dewey's pragmatism and Thorndike's positivistic research as two of the significant influences on American education in the first half of the 20th century. Dewey was both a philosopher and a psychologist who was aware of the ideas of European philosophers. Encouraged to go to graduate school by W. Harris, Dewey studied with G. S. Hall at Johns Hopkins University and later shaped progressive education at the universities of Michigan and Chicago, where he taught. (In fact, Dewey's children attended Colonel Parker's innovative school in Chicago and influenced Dewey's thinking on the role of effort and interest in children's motivation.) Dewey proposed a social and ecological model of psychology that should, he thought, be studied and applied to important social and educational problems. He created a child-centered approach to curriculum and instruction that emphasized what are referred to today as self-regulated learning strategies. According to Hilgard (1987), "[h]is emphasis was upon intelligent problem solving, in which each child solves the problems that are confronted by selecting appropriate materials and methods and by learning to adapt these materials and methods to his or her ends" (p. 674).

Dewey criticized conventional psychology for its overemphasis on maturation and adherence to laboratory methods (Cahan, 1992). Dewey disapproved of Rousseau's metaphor of children growing and learning naturally, as seeds sprout into plants. Instead, he emphasized the plasticity of development and the power of classroom practices to change the course of children's development. This fit his views of education as a means of directing children's thinking toward desirable social goals. Dewey's conceptual approach emphasized similar processes of knowledge acquisition across ages rather than in distinct stages in development. For Dewey, the difference between children and adults was in terms of the means and goals they used. "There are different objects to think about, and different purposes for which to think, because children and grownups have different kinds of acts to perform—different lines of occupation" (Dewey, 1913, p. 370).

Dewey's perspective on education and development may be more relevant and influential today than it was during his lifetime (Cahan, 1992). Dewey's emphasis on functionalism and the developmental changes in means-ends relations is consistent with current interpretations of strategies and instrumental actions (Skinner, 1985). Dewey's views on learning and instruction emphasize discovery and scientific reasoning with genuine problems, a view consistent with contemporary views of situated learning (J. S. Brown, Collins, & Duguid, 1989; Lave & Wenger, 1991; and chapter 2) and anchored instruction (Cognition and Technology Group at Vanderbilt, 1990; and chapter 25). His focus on relevance, social goals, and multiple layers of context is consistent with the views of Vygotsky, Bruner, Bronfenbrenner, Cole, and Rogoff. Cahan (1992) surmises that Dewey had less influence in his time than now because his ideas reached beyond the empirical methods of psychology and education. Dewey's pedagogy emphasized social and political values in an emerging field that wanted to avoid those issues by appealing to the apparent rigor and neutrality of the scientific method.

Thorndike, although a colleague of Dewey's at Teachers College for many years, established an approach to educational psychology that was considered different from Dewey's. Thorndike wanted to improve classroom instruction and assessment of student achievement, and he wanted to base his work on empirical data. His emphasis on reductionistic approaches to cognition and his reliance on quantitative analyses capitalized on the popularity of the scientific method; consequently, his influence on the field was greater than Dewey's emphasis on "progressive education." Thorndike analyzed the essential words, calculations, and component skills involved in reading and arithmetic. His preferred instructional method was to drill children on the skills, with appropriate reinforcement to strengthen their habits of mind. His methods were based on associations and the "law of effect," constructs that were in the mainstream of behavioristic psychology from 1910 to 1950. The essential skills, concepts, and vocabulary items, once identified for instruction, were relatively easy to measure through objective tests, so he designed many types of achievement tests. Thorndike contributed greatly to making standardized testing respectable and popular.

Dewey and Thorndike were pioneers who influenced educational psychology through the students they taught, the faculty whom they hired, the textbooks they wrote, and the power of the ideas they espoused for changing teaching practices. Their impact was direct through each of these avenues. In contrast, developmental psychology had less direct influence on education. The child study movement, begun by Hall, embedded in changes in social science research, and fostered by philanthropic patronage, led to the establishment of a handful of funded research centers in the United States and Canada during the 1920s and 1930s. (See Smuts and Hagen, 1985, for an excellent review of the history of the child study movement.) The child study centers helped to establish the foundation for longitudinal and experimental research on children, but they had only a small impact on contemporary education. Their influence, like that of the progressive education movement, would reappear in the 1960s amid renewed interest in programs for children and increased federal spending on education.

The most enduring influence of developmental psychology in the early part of the 20th century may have been the focus on intelligence testing. The work of Binet and Simon in France was imported into the United States by Louis Terman and used to create the Stanford-Binet Intelligence Test. The method appealed to psychologists interested in individual differences in mental abilities, the philosophy was consistent with views on the hereditary basis of intelligence, the test was consistent with the new (at that time) quantitative approaches for measuring psychological characteristics with the scientific method, and the test had educational utility for identifying differences among children in academic achievement. Thorndike's research and test development were entirely consistent with this parallel movement. Indeed, the field of educational psychology was uniform in its acceptance of reductionistic and laboratory methods of research with concomitant behavioral approaches to instruction, curriculum, and assessment. The only exception may have been the cognitive research initiated by Piaget and Vygotsky, which would become popular much later.

## Changes During the Second Half of the 20th Century

Behaviorism dominated American psychology until the 1960s and 1970s, with consequences for both the nature and quantity of developmental studies in education. For example, Stevenson (1983) traced research on children's learning during the 20th century and found that most of the studies were investigations of general laws of learning based on conditioning, verbal learning, discrimination learning, and concept formation—the same kinds of studies conducted with human adults as well as in rats, monkeys, and pigeons. Researchers paid little attention to children's developmental stages and learning processes and were not concerned with the relevance of research to academic situations. Although experimental studies of children's learning peaked in popularity in the 1960s, with over a thousand articles published, they all but disappeared in the 1970s.

The synergy between developmental and educational psychology was reestablished with the advent of the cognitive revolution in American psychology. During the 1970s interest was revitalized in Piaget's stages and claims, although the most enduring part of his theory for education may be the constructivist philosophy that undergirds it. For example, a recent book published by the Association for Supervision and Curriculum Development is titled, *The Case for Constructivist Classrooms* (Brooks & Brooks, 1993). Constructivist claims have a long history that includes the pioneering work of Alfred Binet and James Mark Baldwin at the turn of the century, Pierre Janet, and Piaget's colleagues who postulated cognitive operations that were related to educational objectives and instructional methods. Since the 1960s, information-processing theories have guided much of the research on children's thinking. Many of the seminal developmental studies of children have been conducted on children learning literacy, mathematics, and science (e.g., A. Brown, Bransford, Ferrara, & Campione, 1983; Perkins & Simmons, 1988). During the 1980s and 1990s, American educational psychologists rediscovered the work of Soviet researchers such as Vygotsky, Bahktin, and Luria, who created sociohistorical-cultural accounts of learning and development (e.g., Rogoff, 1990; Wertsch, 1991). Research in the 1990s reflects an eclectic mix of these constructivist, cognitive, and cultural theories.

Historical analyses become more difficult as they become more contemporary, but three trends became apparent in the past 10 years. First, constructivistic approaches to development have been combined with information-processing approaches in creative ways. For example, Case (1992) has created a neo-Piagetian theory of development that emphasizes increasing mental capacity with age through changes in central conceptual structures. Each advance in conceptual reorganization allows more complex reasoning. Case (1993) and his colleagues have applied the theory to educational issues in assessment, early education, curriculum, and remedial instruction. Siegler and Jenkins (1989) have shown how children construct their own quantitative reasoning strategies as they learn arithmetic. Other theorists have devised similar cognitive developmental theories of qualitative changes in thinking through increasingly sophisticated information processing that can be applied to educational issues (e.g., Fischer, 1980; Halford, 1982; Sternberg, 1988).

Second, increasing attention has been given to cultural contexts of education and development. For example, Stevenson and Stigler (1992) interpret achievement differences between American and Asian children in terms of different motivational orientations in the two cultures and different educational practices of parents and teachers. Within the United States there has been more and more research on ethnic identity, social class, and subcultural influences on education and development in order to understand the diversity within American educational contexts (e.g., Tharp & Gallimore, 1988, and chapter 11). For example, Heath (1983) showed how family practices and values in different communities promote particular kinds of literacy use. She found that some white families asked their children questions and encouraged school-like discussions, but other white families reinforced more passive roles, and many black families emphasized affective and creative expressions. The congruence between participation in literacy at home and school may contribute to the differential academic success of children from the different communities. Culturally sensitive research has stimulated new conceptualizations of the interplay among cultural factors, development, and education.

Third, there have also been increases in research on children's social development and motivation in academic settings since the 1960s. Much of the attention has focused on how children develop intrinsic motivation, cooperation, and feelings of self-competence and self-worth (Covington, 1992; Harter, 1983; Stipek, 1993, and chapter 5). For example, A. E. Gottfried, Fleming, and A. W. Gottfried (1994) conducted a longitudinal analysis of 9- to 10-year-old children's intrinsic motivation and the role of parents' motivational practices. They found that children's academic intrinsic motivation was highest when mothers (a) emphasized task involvement and pleasure in learning and (b) avoided extrinsic rewards and punishments for academic behavior. Other studies have examined how children cooperate with others and develop positive peer relationships. There has also been increasing popularity of self-referenced systems of motivation (e.g., self-control, self-efficacy, self-regulation) with an emphasis on children's understanding of "possible selves" as instrumental in shaping their expectations and aspirations in school (Markus & Nurius, 1986).

Although the cross-fertilization of developmental psychology and education has increased substantially in recent years, there has been more borrowing of ideas from developmental psychology for applications to education than the reverse. This

TABLE 6–1. Historical Analysis of Numbers of Articles on Various Topics in *Journal of Educational Psychology*

| Topic | 1910 | 1930 | 1950 | 1970 | 1990 |
|---|---|---|---|---|---|
| Nonempirical papers/essays | 40 | 8 | 3 | 0 | 0 |
| Subject area knowledge/performance | 3 | 4 | 4 | 8 | 14 |
| Learning and cognition | 1 | 2 | 1 | 13 | 15 |
| Motivation/achievement | 3 | 2 | 2 | 9 | 7 |
| Attitudes/self-perceptions | 0 | 2 | 1 | 6 | 8 |
| Cooperation/tutoring/helping | 0 | 0 | 0 | 0 | 4 |
| Individual differences | 0 | 2 | 4 | 1 | 8 |
| Teaching/teacher evaluations | 1 | 0 | 0 | 0 | 9 |

TABLE 6–2. Historical Analysis of Numbers of Articles in *Journal of Educational Psychology* According to Ages Studied and Methods Used

| | 1910 | 1930 | 1950 | 1970 | 1990 |
|---|---|---|---|---|---|
| **Age Groups Studied** | | | | | |
| Preschool (0–5 yr) | 0 | 0 | 0 | 2 | 1 |
| Elementary school (6–13 yr) | 2 | 6 | 3 | 16 | 30 |
| High School (14–18 yr) | 1 | 0 | 1 | 2 | 8 |
| College and Adults (>19 yr) | 5 | 6 | 8 | 17 | 24 |
| **Methods Used** | | | | | |
| Cross-sectional | 8 | 12 | 12 | 37 | 53 |
| Longitudinal | 0 | 0 | 0 | 0 | 12 |

conclusion is derived from Walberg and Haertel's (1992) analysis of citations, which shows that three top developmental journals (*Child Development, Journal of Experimental Child Psychology,* and *Developmental Psychology*) were among the top 22 journals cited in 1988 by articles in core educational psychology journals. However, none of these developmental journals was among the top 30 journals that cited more frequently the core educational psychology journals. This trend appears to be changing as more traditional developmental journals publish articles about children in school settings. The cross-fertilization is also evident in the greater number of journals that publish articles that combine both developmental and educational analyses. The next section summarizes historical trends in the developmental issues studied and the methods used as a means of introducing current issues in contemporary research in educational psychology.

## ANALYSIS OF ISSUES IN THE JOURNAL OF EDUCATIONAL PSYCHOLOGY

To identify the major issues and methods studied during the 20th century in educational psychology, we analyzed all of the articles published in the *Journal of Educational Psychology* in the years 1910, 1930, 1950, 1970, and 1990. We categorized each article in the lead issue of the chosen decades according to the topic investigated, age range studied, and method used. Some articles covered more than one topic or age range, so the central features of each article were used to avoid counting articles in more than one category. The scheme was not intended to be precise but rather to provide a historical frame of reference to identify the importance of contemporary issues and methods.

Table 6–1 shows the numbers of articles devoted to various topics. Several trends are clear. First, until the 1950s, a large number of articles in the *Journal of Educational Psychology* were devoted to nonempirical studies. Second, the majority of empirical research has been devoted to analyses of students' performance in particular subject areas, such as mathematics, science, social studies, and language arts. Third, from 1970 on, there was a sharp increase in the number of articles published on learning and cognition. Fourth, there has always been a strong emphasis in the journal on motivation and achievement in educational psychology, but in the past two decades, research has become more differentiated into topics included under self-perceptions and attitudes.

Table 6–2 includes an analysis of the age groups studied in the analyzed articles. Surprisingly, most studies have focused on college students and adults. During the past 20 years there was a sharp increase in the study of elementary school students, but there have been relatively few studies of preschoolers and high school students across the decades. This classification is slightly misleading, however, because many of the studies were cross-sectional and included multiple age groupings, often comparing children with adults. In fact, *all* of the empirical studies reported in the journal articles reviewed through 1970 used cross-sectional methods. In 1990, 12 of the 65 articles used longitudinal research methods. It appears that longitudinal analyses and studies of preschool children and adolescents have not been the central concerns of the *Journal of Educational Psychology* historically, but the variety of developmental ages studied and methods used has increased greatly in the past 20 years.

Developmental studies have historically compared children of different ages and abilities with one another, so the types of comparisons made within these various studies were also examined. The results are shown in Table 6–3. Comparisons between genders have been the most frequent characteristic examined, followed by IQ scores and then race. None of the examined articles compared handicapping conditions among subjects, and only a few compared schools.

This cursory historical analysis reveals that both the total number of articles published in the *Journal of Educational Psychology* and the percentage of articles devoted to empirical research have increased substantially. Moreover, the research base has been dominated historically by studies of adults or comparisons of performance between adults and children. Research studies on preschoolers and adolescents have been less frequent, and longitudinal studies of children's educational accomplishments were rare until recently. The increasing popularity of developmental issues within the field of educational psy-

TABLE 6–3. Historical Analysis of Numbers of Articles in *Journal of Educational Psychology* Devoted to Various Comparisons

| Comparison Groups | 1910 | 1930 | 1950 | 1970 | 1990 |
|---|---|---|---|---|---|
| Sexes | 2 | 4 | 3 | 10 | 20 |
| Intelligence/IQs | 0 | 2 | 1 | 6 | 8 |
| Races | 0 | 0 | 1 | 1 | 2 |
| Schools | 0 | 1 | 0 | 2 | 1 |

chology since 1970 may be traced to the "cognitive revolution" throughout psychology. This is certainly reflected in the increasing number of research articles devoted to learning and cognition since that time. It may also be apparent in the cognitive focus of research on students' academic performance as well as their motivation. Since the 1970s there has been an upsurge in the number of articles devoted to students' motivation in school, but most motivational theories have emphasized cognitive aspects of students' attributions, goals, self-perceptions, self-concepts, and attitudes. The convergence of cognitive, motivational, and developmental analyses in published articles reflects the contemporary concern for "student-centered" education. Research on curriculum, instruction, and assessment has increasingly drawn on developmental research in order to gauge the impact and effectiveness of educational practices on different students. These trends are also evident in the large number of journals established in the past 20 years that examine issues spanning developmental, cognitive, social, cultural, and educational psychology.

## OVERVIEW OF CONTEMPORARY ISSUES

The traditional mission of education has been to inculcate knowledge in children, and the preferred pedagogy has emphasized didactic instruction. In the classroom, these concepts have been translated into "skill and drill" activities that have historical roots in tasks such as the memorization of religious material and Latin conjugations. Today in most primary school classrooms, American children spend a majority of their time filling in worksheets, taking spelling tests, answering questions, practicing handwriting, memorizing facts, and making arithmetic calculations. These pedagogical techniques have become increasingly criticized because they fail to engage students in thoughtful strategies for learning and because the skills fail to transfer to other domains. Repetitive drills also create boredom for able students and frustration for less able students so that the motivational consequences as well as the cognitive consequences of these activities are constraining (Rohrkemper & Corno, 1988). Thus, contemporary educational issues are embedded in developmental questions such as: How do children acquire conceptual understanding of literacy, mathematics, and science? How do children learn to apply and transfer their problem-solving skills? How can curricula and instruction be designed to promote students' motivation and self-regulated learning? How can assessment practices document children's talents, weaknesses, and accomplishments?

Developmental studies of students' learning have shifted from behavioral to cognitive and from factual to conceptual. Whether children are learning about science or social studies, contemporary educators want children to understand the scientific concepts and historical issues at stake in their understanding and not simply to memorize a list of facts. A contemporary issue in children's learning is a shift from teacher-directed to student-centered learning. Although this has been a building block of many theories since Dewey, overly didactic approaches have not enabled children to construct their own understanding or their own strategies for learning. The acquisition of information through acquiescence to the authority of a teacher may lead to "inert knowledge" or lack of transfer rather

than self-directed learning (Corno, 1986). Reflection, metacognition, and motivation are intertwined in the three contemporary issues of self-regulated learning, conceptual understanding, and students' construction of knowledge.

The current issues in curriculum reform are tightly wedded to new directions in children's learning. The main criticism of traditional curricula has been the emphasis on the decontextualized knowledge that students were forced to learn for no apparent purpose other than to recall it at the time of testing. Curricula that are defined by textbooks and workbooks and given to students regardless of their background knowledge and interests often result in presentations of fragmented information to students. Teachers have been increasingly required to administer a curriculum by marching children through a sequence of materials and tests, and they have less often been allowed or encouraged to make the curriculum coherent, meaningful, or interesting for children. One contemporary issue in curriculum considerations is a focus on integrated knowledge across domains. Pedagogical techniques that integrate literacy and social studies or science and mathematics, for example, are seen as fertile areas for children to construct knowledge and understand concepts rather than facts (Steipen & Gallagher, 1993). A second issue concerns the purposes for learning. Although traditional activities were performed primarily for obedience and completion, today's teachers are concerned with authentic purposes for learning, such as writing to other people, reading in order to follow directions or conduct research, or searching for information in order to construct projects and conduct experiments (Blumenfeld, Soloway, Marx, Krajcik, Guzdial, & Palincsar, 1991).

Contemporary issues in instruction include a focus on thoughtfulness and collaboration. One trend is a greater concern for teaching thinking strategies. Sometimes this may be done through direct instruction or explanation, but it is often promoted through Socratic discussions, problem-based learning, inquiry, and other techniques that promote metacognition and discovery (Gaskins, Anderson, Pressley, Cunicelli, & Satlow, 1993). These sociocognitive transactions among students and teachers "make thinking public," which allows students to share, evaluate, and model thinking strategies in any domain. A second trend is for teachers to act less as information givers and more as coaches, mentors, or resources (Paris, Wixson, & Palincsar, 1986). Instruction is "scaffolded" because it provides information in a developmentally appropriate way in levels, sequence, and rate of presentation. A third important issue is the role of social collaboration in facilitating learning (Slavin, 1983; Webb, 1985). Individual seat work and solitary learning are giving way to collaborative learning in which children seek other people, peers as well as adults, as resources for feedback and motivation. Instruction is designed to promote help seeking and help giving with appropriate tutoring so that children can appreciate and model effective strategies in their own teaching and learning.

Assessment has undergone radical changes because of these shifts in learning, curriculum, and instruction (Resnick & Resnick, 1990). Traditional approaches to assessment were tightly connected to a compartmentalized curriculum by a scope and sequence chart of skills. Testing was often conducted to ensure skill mastery and to indicate areas in need of reteaching. Repeated testing and mastery learning promoted a piecemeal curriculum of decontextualized facts. The shift today is away from skill-based standardized and commercially prepared tests and toward the teacher's creation of authentic assessments of students' actual performance (Calfee & Hiebert, 1990; Madaus & Tan, 1993; Valencia, Hiebert, & Afflerbach, 1994). These performance measures may include oral presentations, physical projects, or demonstrations of knowledge and skill in students' portfolios.

A second trend in assessment is a shift from normative to criterion-referenced standards of performance. Norm-referenced tests of achievement focus on relative success based on competition and social comparison, whereas criterion-referenced assessments focus on the individual's development of knowledge and skills. A third trend in assessment is away from passive and summative evaluation and toward dynamic and formative kinds of assessment. This means that teachers assess children's knowledge and motivation in a variety of ways and situations in order to increase the specificity of their diagnosis and to aid them in prescribing effective instructional alternatives for each child. Assessment that is based on performance of students striving for authentic goals and administered in a dynamic, diagnostic manner can support the contemporary trends in learning, curriculum, and instruction in a coherent manner (Wolf, Bixby, Glenn, & Gardner, 1991). Authentic assessment is beneficial for children because (a) it is predicated on sensitivity to individual differences among students, (b) it focuses on individual gains and growth, and (c) it promotes reflection and self-regulated learning (Paris & Ayres, 1994).

In the following sections, we trace children's development in schools by noting the critical developmental issues and milestones that they encounter. Most youngsters are eager to be engaged in schooling and to wear the mantle of "student," even though many of the duties and responsibilities remain vague and mysterious. Whether they begin attending schools as 2- or 6-year-olds, children display great enthusiasm for, but little conceptual understanding of, their roles (L. Weinstein, 1984). For example, preschoolers often equate academic ability with social behavior. When Stipek and Tannatt (1984) asked preschoolers to explain which of their classmates were smart, children usually described good students as the ones who stayed in their seats, obeyed the teacher, and did not tease other children. However, children's concepts about school, especially concepts about themselves as students, crystallize rapidly, so that by 11 or 12 years of age, most children have formed stable concepts of their own distinct academic abilities (Marsh, 1986; Stipek & Mac Iver, 1989). Children's rapid conceptual growth is matched by ever-increasing challenges during elementary and middle school. These transitional points may be marked by greater academic demands, special teachers for different subjects, and adjustments to new schools. Each transition allows children to establish new roles and expectations in different contexts. These changes continue throughout adolescence, which serves as a bridge to college and work for students becoming young adults. Each new challenge met and conquered is emancipating for children, a developmental milestone on a long road to independence.

## PRESCHOOL: READINESS AND PREPARATION

This chapter's emphasis on children *becoming* students blurs the onset of any distinct age, stage, or transition to school because today's children encounter educational agenda and agents in many ways before they become fully enrolled students. Relatively few children around the world enter kindergarten without some type of preschool experience that prepares them for the increasingly formal world of schooling. For example, parents in every culture recognize the value of education and often begin to introduce language games, books, and number concepts to 2- and 3-year-olds (Hess & Holloway, 1984). Adults who continue their education and siblings who share their educational experiences bring the jargon, tools, and work of school into the home. Television has introduced *Sesame Street* and similar educational programs to children in the most remote locations. As 3-, 4-, and 5-year-olds encounter school or school-like experiences, adults introduce them to learning environments with culturally specified procedures, resources, and expectations that allow children to participate in school-like activities as apprentices (Rogoff, 1990). Schooling is not an abrupt transition from home life to school life for most children in industrialized countries around the world, although the kind of preparation that children receive varies widely by social, cultural, and economic status of families.

The age at which children enter school, across America and the world, ranges from 3 to 7 years generally, although the length of the school day, the rigor of the academic activities, and the expectations of teachers vary widely. Similarly, educational policies for determining children's readiness for school, their grouping by age or ability, the curriculum provided to young children, and compensatory programs for those who are unprepared vary across history and culture. These are issues of human development because the underlying dimension for evaluating young children's transition to school is their readiness to learn. *Readiness* has been defined in terms of normative developmental expectations as well as specific content knowledge and skills deemed prerequisite for schooling. This section considers four developmental issues of young children's education: the philosophy of early childhood education programs, compensatory preschool education, age and readiness for school entry, and retention policies in kindergarten.

### Theoretical Foundations for Early Childhood Education

Developmental psychologists have had a large impact on the philosophy of early childhood educational programs. The work of Froebel, Freud, G. Stanley Hall, Gesell, Piaget, Montessori, Bruner, and Vygotsky have all influenced young children's education because the content, sequence, and methods of most early childhood education programs have been based on developmental theories and research (Franklin & Biber, 1977). The theoretical positions of early childhood education programs can be characterized according to three dominant positions: the maturational-socialization view, the cultural transmission (sometimes equivalent to a behavioristic) approach, and the cognitive developmental position. The maturational-socialization view has its philosophical roots in the work of Rousseau and its psychological roots in the theories of Gesell. In this view, development is seen as a natural unfolding of biological structures that are encouraged and supported by environmental stimulation or intervention. The function of education is therefore to provide positive social and emotional experiences that allow young children to reach their potential, which is determined by each child's "internal clock." This view was more popular before 1960 in the United States, yet vestiges of this approach are still evident in early childhood programs that emphasize socialization, physical coordination, and the development of cooperative play.

The cultural transmission model of early childhood education has philosophical roots in the work of John Locke and the behavioral theories of Thorndike and Skinner. It has undergone considerable change as the field of educational psychology has shifted from behavioristic to cognitive approaches. In the traditional transmission model, the role of preschool education is to prepare children for formal educational experiences and to socialize children into their future roles as responsible citizens. Therefore, education should provide a structured and carefully sequenced series of activities that will provide children with the knowledge, skills, and values required by society. This model emphasizes the shaping, conditioning, and guidance provided by adults and is equivalent to the traditional model of education that Dewey criticized as more adult than child centered. This model gives rise to didactic methods of instruction for young children. (More recently, the cultural transmission model has been transformed by sociogenic approaches inspired by Vygotsky and Dewey to allow greater flexibility in enculturation, with more credit given to the child's interests and the importance of adult support.)

The cognitive developmental approach to early childhood education is more recent than the first two models and is derived primarily from the psychological theories of Piaget, Bruner, and Vygotsky. The model treats development as the result of interactions between the individual's maturational level and the quality of experience in the environment. Children's adaptation depends on both the individual and the opportunities afforded in the physical and social environment. In this view, the role of preschool education is to foster the child's adaptation and construction of more complex cognitive organization by creating opportunities for meaningful and challenging experiences. This view has given rise to many educational programs that structure the environment for young children and seek to explain differences in the "readiness" of young children for schooling in terms of differences in their environmental opportunities. Most early childhood educational programs are modeled on one of these three broad ideologies (Fein & Schwartz, 1982), but there is wide variability in what children experience in schools within as well as across these general approaches.

Another dimension on which to contrast approaches to early childhood education is the locus of change. Some approaches tend to be more child centered, whereas others are more teacher centered (Beller, 1973), although the distinction between these programs has become a point of contention. Child-centered programs are based on the assumption that children learn at their own rates through exploration of their environment, manipulation of objects, and social interaction. The integrity of the "whole child" is emphasized and educational activities are directed toward the child's general growth and development in social, emotional, physical, and intellectual spheres (Weikart, 1989). Teacher-centered approaches place less emphasis on free play, learning centers, and children's unsupervised activities. Instead, teaching is based on guidance, practice, and direct instruction. The curriculum is usually constructed with sequential lessons that emphasize specific skills. Teachers control the majority of activities, and they impart specific skills and knowledge, often related to early mathematical concepts and literacy behaviors.

Many studies have been conducted to examine the relative benefits of child-centered versus teacher-centered approaches. It appears that academic programs that are teacher centered impart more knowledge to children initially because children in these programs show significantly greater gains on measures of reading and math achievement as well as higher gains in IQ scores (Karnes, Schwedel, & Williams, 1983). It is not surprising that young children can learn beginning concepts in mathematics and literacy from 3 to 5 years of age and thus accelerate their knowledge base, but these studies were criticized on several grounds. First, many of the studies have been conducted with children of lower socioeconomic status who may show the most substantial gains when provided with activities not usually available in their home. Little research has assessed the effects of early childhood education programs on middle- and upper-class children (Brand & Welch, 1989). Second, despite the initial gains in aptitude and achievement, many studies have shown that the initial advantages of teacher-centered programs disappear by third grade (Miller & Bizzell, 1983). Third, critics of teacher-centered approaches have argued that didactic instruction may actually lead to lower levels of self-esteem (Katz, 1987), feelings of learned helplessness, undue stress (Burts, Hart, Charlesworth, & Kirk, 1990; Elkind, 1987; Kamii, 1985) and overall lack of interest in school activities. Fourth, advocates of child-centered programs argue that social and emotional development is fostered better in child-centered approaches. Many researchers have found no differences in either psychosocial or academic achievement (Schweinhart, Weikart & Larner, 1986).

What are the benefits of early childhood education? There are clear and enduring benefits of educational programs for 3- to 5-year-olds, regardless of the philosophy, curriculum, or instruction. The particular advantages depend on the individual children being served, which may explain the lack of consistent differences between child-centered and teacher-centered programs. We believe that one approach or one type of program is not universally better than another; rather, some programs match some children better than others. When preschool children have supportive home environments in which social rules and cognitive challenges are provided by adults, teacher-centered instruction may be less important than opportunities to play with others and explore new activities. Yet for many children who enter early childhood education programs without home support for cognitive and social tasks, more didactic methods may be appropriate. Comparative research that pits one approach against another has traditionally been unsuccessful because the studies often confound variables such as content and materials, teaching processes, classroom structure, and the backgrounds of children in the programs. Thus, future research may be more useful if it examines the fit between children's abilities and needs and the specific content and opportunities provided by the curriculum (Cunningham, 1993). This "goodness of fit" approach might serve children better and give credibility to the wide variety of approaches that are used with young children.

## Compensatory Preschool Education

Programs for compensatory education in preschool represent a special category of early childhood education. These programs were developed in the United States in the 1960s with the explicit goal of meeting the needs of disadvantaged children—those children who were unlikely to attend preschool before beginning kindergarten or first grade. Compensatory education is set in a historical context of social intervention designed to provide equity and opportunity to young children who were disadvantaged by economics, immigration, race, or handicap. The prime example of compensatory education is the federal program Project Head Start, although it should be noted that many states have their own preschool programs.

The need for compensatory education programs has *increased* since its inception in the 1960s because of the increasing number of young children living in disadvantaged circumstances. For example, 22 percent of children below the age of 5 live in poverty, according to the U.S. Census Bureau (Reed & Sautter, 1990). Many of these children will continue to grow up in destitute environments that constrain their growth, development, and education. According to the National Center for Clinical Infant Programs (1986), 25 percent, or nearly 1 million infants born in the United States each year in the 1980s, were born into families living in poverty, and 20 percent were born to single mothers. Approximately 10 percent of infants, or 370,000 babies per year, were exposed to illegal drugs prenatally, and one study at an inner city Detroit hospital showed that 43 percent of women who delivered babies had taken illegal drugs during pregnancy (Angell, 1989). Children born to minority families face great risk of low birth weight, poverty, and exposure to drugs. They also may be raised in families headed by adolescent or single mothers and may live in environments that pose additional risks to their academic success. Thus, the children served by compensatory education programs encounter many potential difficulties for a broad spectrum of reasons.

Project Head Start represents the largest and primary source of federal funds for early childhood education, although Head Start currently serves only 24 percent of the 3- to 5-year-olds living in poverty (Schweinhart, Barnes, & Weikart, 1993). Head Start was designed to address young children's health, social, and educational needs (Zigler & Valentine, 1979). It is a multidisciplinary program that emphasizes children's social and emotional development by encouraging curiosity, self-discipline, and self-confidence. The importance of self-worth and dignity for the child and family is stressed, as is the development of a responsible attitude toward society. The development of children's intellectual capabilities and, more specifically, their preparation for schooling were never the central components of Head Start. Yet early evaluations of the effectiveness of Head Start focused almost exclusively on intellectual gains made by children.

It is important to recognize that Project Head Start was based on the developmental theories of such psychologists as J. McVickers Hunt, Benjamin Bloom, Jean Piaget, Jerome Bruner, and others who stressed environmental rather than maturational factors as the primary influence on child development. Edward Zigler, the founding father and leading advocate of Head Start, emphasized the social and emotional aspects of development for disadvantaged children as a more critical component of

readiness than specific academic skills and knowledge. Thus, it is ironic that the initial evaluations of the success of Head Start were often based on cognitive measures and academic achievements. Many of these early evaluations, such as the Westinghouse Report (Cicerelli, 1969), found short-term gains in IQ scores and academic achievement among Head Start children, but the initial success faded out by third grade. The failure of research to substantiate long-term benefits of compensatory education programs such as Head Start led to a reappraisal of the curricula as well as the assumptions of the programs during the 1970s. In 1985, a comprehensive review of more than 200 separate Head Start evaluation studies was published (McKey, Condelli, Ganson, Barrett, McConkey, & Plantz, 1985). This review found that Head Start had significant short-term positive effects on cognitive and socioemotional development. There were also positive long-term effects such as improved physical health, motor skills, and nutrition of the participants. However, these studies also found a gradual fadeout of cognitive gains.

In an effort to find evidence of long-term effects that could be used to preserve federal support for Head Start, a consortium of independent investigators who agreed to pool their evaluation of early education programs was established in 1975. The analysis of these projects was reported by the Consortium for Longitudinal Studies (1983), which found significant short-term and long-term benefits. Children in Head Start programs showed significantly higher IQ scores 1 or 2 years after participation in the program, but the advantage gradually faded. The early advantages in mathematics and reading also began to fade by third or fourth grade. However, children who participated in Head Start were significantly less likely to be placed in special education or retained in grade throughout elementary school. They were also more likely to complete high school.

Takanishi and DeLeon (1994) argue that Head Start has been evaluated inadequately and with unfair expectations. They say that Head Start cannot inoculate preschoolers from all future influences when children continue to live in dangerous or unsupportive environments:

> Much of the research focused on Head Start has been obsessed with long-term effects and a corollary issue, fadeout effects. . . . More attention should be focused on the transitions from Head Start to successive educational environments and their relationship with family and neighborhood factors in shaping outcomes at different developmental stages. That fadeout effects have been attributed to weak or ineffective Head Start programs without an examination of the children's experiences after Head Start seems amazing in retrospect. (p. 121)

Zigler and Styfco (1994) say that the need for Head Start is greater than ever in the United States and that current research needs to be expanded to reveal the benefits and new directions for Head Start. They advocate changes in Head Start so that services are provided earlier to families with children at risk, the training of staff improves, and there is more continuity from Head Start to the educational curriculum experienced in elementary school. They also advocate more realistic expectations and increased funding for services and research:

> The empirical literature thus delivers good news and bad news. The bad news is that neither Head Start nor any preschool program can inoculate children against the ravages of poverty. Early intervention

simply cannot overpower the effects of poor living conditions, inadequate nutrition and health care, negative role models, and substandard schools. But good programs can prepare children for school and possibly help them develop better coping and adaptation skills that will enable better life outcomes, albeit not perfect ones. (p. 129)

The positive benefits of compensatory programs for early childhood education have been confirmed in other reviews. For example, Ramey, Bryant, and Suarez (1984) found that 11 of 14 programs for infants through preschoolers had positive effects on children's intellectual development in Project Giant Step (J. I. Layzer, Goodson, & Layzer, 1990). This is a New York City project that provides half-day preschool programs to 18,000 low-income 4-year-olds as well as supplementary services for their families. The long-term follow-up of students in the Perry Preschool Project (Berrueta-Clement, Schweinhart, Barnett, Epstein, & Weikart, 1984) found better social adjustment, more employment, and less welfare dependence at age 19 for children who had participated in compensatory educational programs as preschoolers. Both the Perry study and the Syracuse study (Lally, Mangione, & Honig, 1988) reported that preschool program participants have lower delinquency and arrest rates as adolescents. Thus, compensatory education programs have had a positive impact upon intellectual, academic, and social development of a low-socioeconomic status, primarily black, high-risk population that have been the typical participants in Head Start programs.

## Entry into Formal Schooling

The transition into formal schooling has become a prolonged process for many students. They often enroll in preschool or daycare programs from age 2 to 4, and in early childhood programs or formal kindergartens before beginning first grade. The policies for kindergarten are variable. Some states require it and some do not; some provide half days and some full days. This policy contrasts sharply with other countries, such as the United Kingdom, Australia, New Zealand, and Japan, where full-day school attendance is common for 5-year-olds. The variability in kindergarten policies throughout U.S. schools is puzzling because most educators recognize the value of kindergarten experiences. For example, Entwisle, Alexander, Cadigan, and Pallas (1987) found that children who attended kindergarten most frequently made greater gains in reading and math in first grade than children who had less kindergarten. Extra kindergarten did not just socialize children into school roles, it boosted academic skills. Furthermore, this advantage was more marked for African-American than Caucasian children.

Not only are the length and abruptness of the transition to formal schooling variable, the basis for school entry is also controversial. One method used to determine school enrollment is age, but historically, the entrance age has been steadily increasing in U.S. kindergartens. The second method for certifying school entry is grouping children by ability. However, the small number of research studies that have investigated grouping by age or ability has produced mixed results. For example, grouping children by ability proves occasionally to be effective for children who are older and more skilled (Dahlof, 1971; Eschel & Klein, 1978; Hart, 1967; Jackson, 1975) but is generally detrimental for less skilled students (Oakes, 1981). A substantial body

of research has focused on the educational and social cost of homogeneous ability grouping (Hadermann, 1976; Holmes & Matthews, 1984; Kirp, 1974; Lefkowitz, 1972; Oakes, 1985). Nevertheless, there is a trend toward more homogeneous grouping of children in primary grades (Smith & Shepard, 1987). Each of these approaches to school entry is briefly examined below.

*Eligibility According to Age.* Three trends in American education have helped cause an increase in grouping children by age in primary grades. First, there has been a greater emphasis on academic training of skills and knowledge for children in kindergarten and first grade. Second, there has been more emphasis on the standardization of an educational curriculum in primary grades and higher expectations for students. Third, many parents want their children to be above average in physical and social skills for their cohort, so they delay entry into school. These forces have inadvertently raised the age at which children begin formal schooling in the United States.

Over the past 30 years, there has been a trend also to raise the age at which children are legally eligible to enter kindergarten. In 1958, for example, 4-year-old children whose birth dates were after December 1 were not allowed to enter kindergarten. During the 1970s, that cutoff date was moved back to October 1 in many districts. In the 1980s the trend was toward an earlier cutoff date of June 1 in some areas of the country (Siegal & Hanson, 1991). As a consequence, most American children are now 5 years old when they begin kindergarten and 14 when they begin high school.

Increasing the school entrance age was partly a consequence of research that showed that younger children do not perform as well as older children in their class (Langer, Kalk, & Searls, 1984), are more likely to be considered at risk for maladjustment (Weinstein, 1968–1969), and also are more likely to be labeled as learning disabled (Diamond, 1983). Differences among children are already evident in first grade (Shepard & Smith, 1986). These facts may not be surprising, since young children in first grade may be 11 months behind their older classmates. Is this good evidence for using chronological age as the criterion for school readiness? Is the solution simply to raise the age of school entrance? No, because excluding the youngest children from a group becomes a never-ending process. Age is relative within a classroom. The mean age of the group may change, but there is still a distribution of oldest to youngest students that begs the question of whether they should be grouped by age or by ability. When homogeneous groups are created by eliminating younger students, the mean age is merely shifted upward, and the apparent increase in test scores may arise simply because the new scores belong to a different and older group of students. The younger students have not become smarter, they have just been excluded. The other benefit realized from raising the entrance age, namely, the smaller class size, is also only temporary.

Readiness for school depends on the situations in which children grow up and on the norms and values of the culture. Different policies and expectations lead to widely different patterns of school entry. In England, children begin public school when they are 4 years old, whereas children in Sweden and the Soviet Union begin formal schooling at 7 years (Austin, De Vries, Thirion, & Stukat, 1975; Baranova & Rozyeva, 1985).

In many English-speaking countries, it is not uncommon to find 4½-year-olds in full-day school. The paradox is that older children, no matter what age, are praised and younger children, no matter what age, are criticized because the comparisons between them are made inappropriately. One researcher concluded that it "seems school personnel complain in every society about how poorly young children perform. The only problem with the examples used is that the children are all of different ages, seven, six, and five" (Gredler, 1980, p. 240).

These age differences are not very significant, though, because there is such wide variability in basic skills within the classroom. Moreover, Shepard and Smith (1986) have pointed out that the disadvantage that younger children experience relative to their older peers is a combination of age and ability. For example, when Shepard and Smith (1986) examined their data by children's ability, there was no difference in achievement between the youngest and oldest age groups for children who were above the 75th or 50th percentile points of their respective age intervals. The largest differences between young and older students in first grade were found for children who scored below the 25th percentile. Thus, the age differences in performance between younger and older students tend to be attributed to a combination of age, ability, and teacher bias.

*Grouping by Ability.* Many educators are dissatisfied with school entry based on age alone and have argued instead that children's school entry should be determined by ability or achievement. Traditionally these ability groupings have been determined by specific academic achievements or needs such as physical handicaps, mental handicaps, or learning disabilities. It should also be noted that some parents delay the school entry of boys so that their physical and social development might be advanced compared with that of their classmates, a presumed advantage when the boys begin dating and participating in organized sports. Some parents are motivated by ambitions for their children's athletic or academic competitiveness. Some teachers are motivated to group children by ability in order to facilitate instruction with a more homogeneous range of abilities in their classrooms. Grouping children in kindergarten according to special physical or mental needs may often benefit both teachers and students, yet even this ability grouping procedure, like others, has been controversial (Madden & Slavin, 1983).

The underlying issue in grouping by ability is children's readiness for learning. Two different methods have been used to identify children's early abilities and their placement into first grade. The first is to assess developmental age as measured by maturation of physical, intellectual, social, and emotional behavior. The tasks and instruments used to measure readiness and the philosophy underlying their use are clearly associated with a maturational point of view. The second method is more closely associated with the transmission model of teaching and uses academic achievement tests to determine children's specific abilities, usually in math, reading, and writing. The derived scores are based on developmental ages rather than chronological ages. The concept of developmental age is controversial, partly because it is not clear how the construct is measured, and partly because it is unclear how developmental age is related to success in the primary grades. It is also important to recognize that a test of developmental age might be based on

information and experiences that have not been available to some children, and therefore the tests may be unfair.

The issue of ability grouping for school entry is hotly debated by school researchers and practitioners who favor placement by developmental age (DiPasquale, Moule, & Flewelling, 1980; Donofrio, 1977; Wood, Powell, & Knight, 1984) and by those who question the validity of the construct (Bear & Modlin, 1987; Meisels, 1988; Shepard & Smith, 1988). Some states, such as Georgia and Minnesota, sort children by achievement for entrance into first grade, yet there is wide variability even within school districts. Smith and Shepard (1987), for example, found that some schools retained virtually no kindergarteners, whereas other schools retained as many as a third of the students in kindergarten before entering first grade. The tests and the cutoff scores can be used as political instruments to shape policies and opportunities.

## Retention in Kindergarten

The concept of readiness translates directly into educational policies affecting children's age of school entry, the kinds of instruments used to assess developmental readiness, and the practices for retaining children in kindergarten. Retention in early childhood programs is essentially the practice of having a child stay back a year, either at home, in preschool, in kindergarten, or in a readiness class (see Plummer, Lineberger, & Graziano, 1986, for a review). Social promotion is the practice of allowing children to enter the next grade (usually first grade, in this case) despite doubts concerning the child's present capabilities. The popularity of retention and social promotion has fluctuated widely during the past century.

The arguments in favor of retention are based on predictions about the child's developmental trajectory. First, "immature" children may perform below the level of most of their classmates and therefore be unable to participate in routine academic activities. Second, if children cannot participate or compete at the same level as their classmates, they will experience frustration, apathy, and low self-esteem and have discipline problems. Third, retention allows underachievers to master skills; it provides time to mature and it fosters success on school-related tasks. Fourth, retention allows teachers to provide better instruction because they are teaching a more homogeneous group of students who exhibit fewer disciplinary problems (Carstens, 1985).

In contrast, the arguments in favor of promoting children to kindergarten and first grade despite their lack of preparation and readiness are based more on social and economic factors. First, retention is financially costly and adds another year to the 13-year educational system. Second, children identified for retention often come from families that are poor, minority, or recent immigrants to the United States. They may be stigmatized or segregated by this educational policy (Carstens, 1985). Third, there have been criticisms of the instruments used to screen children. Some researchers argue that the children are too young and the tests are too unreliable to predict whether an individual child will succeed or fail later in school. Fourth, children who are placed in a homogeneous group of other children "not ready" for formal school will be in an unstimulating and socially pejorative environment that may be boring. Fifth, children who are held back will be larger, older, and more socially mature than their classmates and may have difficulties with social relationships.

Jackson (1975) surveyed more than 100 studies of retention and promotion policies and analyzed 44 original research studies. The majority of the studies suffered from one or more of the following weaknesses: (a) the studies failed to sample children from varied populations of students; (b) the studies failed to define the treatments children received as a result of being retained or promoted; (c) the studies were short term and not longitudinal, thereby limiting analysis of the long-term affects of retention practices; or (d) they failed to examine the interactions between treatment conditions and student characteristics. Jackson concluded, "Educators who retain pupils in a grade do so without valid research evidence to indicate that such treatment will provide greater benefits to students with academic or adjustment difficulties than will promotion to the next grade" (p. 627). This pessimistic conclusion has not changed much in the past 20 years. Whether retention is based on chronological age or general achievement, there seems little merit in retention based on a loosely defined concept of developmental readiness.

The concept of maturational readiness as determined by test instruments has come under attack for several reasons, including the test items, testing procedures, and discriminatory consequences of the results. For example, the Gesell Preschool Readiness Test (Haines, Ames, & Gillespie, 1980) is administered to half a million children each year and is used to screen them for kindergarten and first-grade entry. The Gesell test contains items designed to measure motor, cognitive, language, and personal-social development, but it has poor reliability and validity and contains many items that are virtually identical to those on IQ tests (Bear & Modlin, 1987; Kaufman, 1985; Naglieri, 1985). Thus, some of the tests used to measure school readiness are suspect, and there is little empirical support for the practice of retaining children on the basis of developmental age.

When children are retained on the basis of specific academic achievement, it is hoped that the extra year provides compensatory experiences that will foster future development. Unfortunately, the research does not support this prediction. Bell (1972) studied children with low achievement test scores who were recommended by their teachers for retention. Some of these children were retained and some went directly into first grade. It was found that the children who were retained had lower achievement and lower self-esteem scores at the end of the next year. Several other studies have confirmed that retention has a negative impact on both achievement test scores and indicators of socioemotional health (Gredler, 1984; Holmes & Matthews, 1984; Rose, Medway, Cantrell, & Marcus, 1983). Even when retention leads to slight improvement among children, those advantages disappear by the third grade.

It is also worthwhile to distinguish children who are held *back* after kindergarten from those children who are held *out* of kindergarten. Teachers may elect to hold children back after poor performance in kindergarten, but parents are usually the ones who choose to delay their children's initial entry into school. This is often done to ensure that the child performs near the top of the class in academics and sports. The irony is that these two different motives for helping children achieve often produce a kindergarten class with large differences in performance. Thus, heterogeneous classes, which pose more problems for teachers, may be the consequence of poor retention policies by teachers and parents.

There are few, if any, benefits of retaining children in kindergarten or first grade based on their lack of school readiness or lack of academic skills. The notion of developmental readiness for school is largely an artifact of a maturational position that is common folklore but not a central premise of current educational theories of learning, motivation, or self-concept development. This example points out how educational policies are often founded on naive or outdated conceptions of human development. It also illustrates the wide variability in young children's preparation for school, the poor predictability of tests given to young children, and the difficulty of conducting research when the variability of children and educational programs is so great. Despite the appeal of uniform educational policies based on age, ability, or curriculum, there is little consensus across countries in the world or across states in the United States regarding the appropriate age to begin school, the appropriate way to identify children for school entry, or which curriculum is generally better than another. These conclusions should lead developmental and educational researchers to focus more on the fit between individual children and their educational environments rather than on the effectiveness of treatments or homogeneous groups of children as main effects in traditional comparative designs. More detailed analyses of individual differences and the goodness of fit between the needs of individual children and the resources of specific educational environments needs to be conducted.

## FOUNDATIONS FOR LEARNING: GRADES 1 THROUGH 3

There are dramatic changes during the primary grades as children progress from 6-year-old new first graders to 9-year-old school veterans. Whether viewed as the transition to concrete operational thinking in Piagetian terms, as the acquisition of well-practiced knowledge organization and cognitive strategies, or as enculturation into the environment of schooling, these 3 years provide a foundation for children's academic careers. In a study of 1,500 school dropouts, Lloyd (1978) found that the best predictor of school leaving was IQ scores, the next best predictor was achievement test scores, then retention in a previous grade, and then grade point average by the time students were in third grade. Other studies confirmed that high school dropouts encounter early difficulties in the primary grades and are often retained. Retention in primary grades leads to nearly an 80 percent chance of becoming a school dropout (Fitzsimmons, Cheever, Leonard, & Maconovich, 1969; Howard & Anderson, 1978). Along with academic measures of achievement, other strong predictors of future delinquency and criminal behavior in adulthood include acting-out behavior, antisocial behavior, and emotional difficulties in primary grades (Loeber, 1985; Steinberg, 1987). Thus, children's social and cognitive development during the primary grades may set the stage for future successes or failures in their broader achievements and adjustments.

Research in educational psychology during the past 20 years has given greater attention to academic and social foundations of children's learning. The following discussion highlights two aspects of children's development during primary grades that embrace central issues such as the relationship between home and school, cognitive skills and precursors to academic achievement, and educational programs that respond to distinctive needs of students. The discussion considers first the achievements of a subgroup of students, minority children, because assimilation into school and early achievements are particularly difficult for some of them. Second, the discussion considers the early development of literacy, because it is a crucial academic domain that enables future learning and embodies many significant developmental issues.

## Achievement of Minority Children in Primary Grades

American society has become increasingly diverse throughout the 20th century. African Americans, Asian Americans, Hispanic Americans, and Native Americans now account for about one third of the U.S. population (Spencer, 1990). Indeed, many argue that by the year 2000 these groups will together constitute a new majority (McLoyd, 1990). It is important to consider the many differences in beliefs and practices among cultural groups and between social classes. Teachers are often unaware of the different cultural meanings that minority children have learned in their communities and attach to schooling. Native American children, for example, often find it difficult to adapt to the socially competitive and comparative nature of traditional classrooms. In their culture, children are taught to share not only things but knowledge and information as well. The individual nature of the traditional classroom often conflicts with the values and beliefs of minority children. As a result, Native American children are often regarded as lazy and unmotivated. Other minority children, for example, African Americans and Hispanics, especially from lower socioeconomic backgrounds, face similar discrimination (Garcia-Coll, 1990). The growing diversity of children and their subsequent differences in behavior, attitude, values, language, and achievement are one of the challenges schools must meet in the future.

Because of their differences, the transition to the academic life of school is particularly important for children from lower socioeconomic backgrounds. Instead of decreasing in numbers since the politically inspired War on Poverty, the number of children living in poverty has increased dramatically since 1980. A recent study by the General Accounting Office found that during the 1980s, the number of infants and toddlers living in poverty rose 26 percent, from 1.8 million to 2.3 million. Another study prepared for the Carnegie Corporation (1993) showed that 3 million children, or nearly 25 percent of U.S. infants and toddlers, were living in poverty in 1990. Children now represent the largest group of America's poor. By 1989, children accounted for 40 percent of all individuals living below the poverty line (National Center for Children in Poverty, 1990). Are these just infants and young children? No—many are school-aged children between 6 and 11 years old. Of this age group, 20 percent live below the poverty line (Reed & Sautter, 1990). The demographics of poverty have shifted substantially in the past 20 years. Although 90 percent of the elderly poor receive significant benefits and their lot has markedly improved over the past 20 years, the same cannot be said for children. The incidence of poverty among children has increased greatly and the consequences of this shift extend beyond children's health

and education to affect the general economic and social well-being of communities. Many social policy analysts argue that the same safeguards provided for the elderly should be provided for children (Committee for Economic Development, 1988).

The causes of increasing poverty are numerous, but some of the contributing factors are salient. The number of children living in single-parent households has been increasing steadily for years. One in every four children now lives in a single-parent family, with women heading about 90 percent of them (Hetherington, Stanley-Hagen, & Anderson, 1989). The proportion is even higher among African-American families, where one out of every two families is headed by a single parent (National Center for Children in Poverty, 1990). Clearly, children from these families face additional challenges in their transition from home to school environment simply as a result of their differences in resources. Of course, single-parent families are not the only cause of poverty, because half of the nation's poor children live with both parents (U.S. Bureau of the Census, 1987). Many argue that the shift from a manufacturing economy to a service economy has been a significant factor in the growth of poverty. Many families are working harder but getting poorer in the United States (Reed & Sautter, 1990). Others emphasize the changes in federal assistance policies that have made it increasingly difficult to receive financial assistance from the government (Garwood, Hartman, Philips, & Zigler, 1989). Although two thirds of poor Americans are white, the *rate* of poverty is higher for children of color. Four out of nine African-American children are poor and three out of eight Hispanic children are poor, compared to one out of seven white children who are poor (Children's Defense Fund, 1990). It is projected that these ratios for minority families will continue to increase in the next decade unless significant policy changes are made.

One solution put forth to ease minority children's transition to academic life is to coordinate all social services within the school setting. Schools would broaden their scope to function as community centers offering family support services to alleviate the social, psychological, and health problems faced by minority children. Because the traditional sources of support (e.g., health, nutrition, neighborhood programs) are often fragmented or unavailable for all children, some argue that linking social services with academic programs can provide greater access and continuity of service to minority children and their families. Critics argue that schools are not adequately meeting the needs of lower socioeconomic groups to overcome the barriers that exist (Alexander & Entwisle, 1988; McAdoo, 1988). Inevitably, changes are needed within the system to assist children, parents, and teachers to surmount the increasing diversity of cultures and the economic disadvantages experienced by these groups.

The transition to the academic life of school is particularly important for minority and low-socioeconomic-status children, who traditionally have less preparation for school environments that embody middle-class values in behavior, language, and achievement patterns. Comer (1989) describes the first 3 or 4 years of school as a critical period that must provide positive interactions and "bonding" between the child and the school staff in order to give the child the discipline and skills needed to succeed. It is children's commitment to school goals, attitudes, cooperation, attention, persistence, and effort (Comer, 1989), coupled with advances in literacy, math, and problem-solving skills, that are so critical for future success. Teachers' perceptions of children are important in these primary years because they affect the placement of children in groups as well as expectations, attitudes, and behaviors during instruction. Early developmental accomplishments also affect teachers' decisions about retention and placement in special education classes during primary grades.

All of these factors can influence children's self-concept and expectations. Alexander and Entwisle (1988), in their Beginning School Study in Baltimore, found that achievement patterns in the primary grades persisted at higher levels, especially for minority children. They said,

There is good reason to think that how the children make the transition to full-time schooling will have implications both profound and long-lasting—whether the children are black or white. Additionally, though, . . . we think it likely that the academic difficulties experienced by many minority youngsters are peculiarly traceable to adjustment problems and patterns of underachievement that began in the first years of formal schooling. (p. 3)

Clark (1983) asserted that the school difficulties of low-socioeconomic-status black high school students began in the primary grades. None of the low achievers recalled positive interactions with teachers or encouragement in their early school experiences, whereas students who were successful often reported early and positive support from teachers. Holliday (1985), in her study of 9- and 10-year-old black children, also found that the lack of success in young black children's achievement efforts often transformed their behavior into learned helplessness. Alexander and Entwisle (1988) found that minority and majority children began first grade with similar achievement scores but that the scores of minority children dropped below the scores of majority children by the end of first grade. The gap continued to widen on both report card marks and achievement test scores throughout the primary years.

Reynolds (1989) studied 1,500 minority children in Chicago in publicly funded kindergarten programs and found that achievement in reading and math at second grade was significantly predicted by achievement in kindergarten and first grade. Children's motivation, school attendance, and parent involvement also had significant effects. Speece and Cooper (1990) identified multivariate profiles of first-grade children identified at risk for school failure based on patterns resembling mild mental retardation, specific learning disabilities, and language disabilities. Both of these studies show that there is developmental continuity in school success or school failure based on the achievements of children in primary grades. Minority children, and those with specific handicapping conditions, are at risk for future academic failure unless those problems are prevented or remediated in the primary grades.

## Literacy Development in the Primary Grades

The development of literacy again raises the issue of readiness to learn. In a classic study, Morphett and Washburne (1931) reviewed the existing literature and concluded that children's reading usually began at age 6½ years, so that was the appropriate time to begin formal reading instruction. For most of the 20th century, in most countries around the world, reading

instruction has begun at approximately 6 to 7 years of age. Recent research has questioned the wisdom of that delayed exposure to reading, partly because it presumes a maturational readiness view of literacy and partly because preschoolers today are exposed to enormous amounts of literacy and environmental print before they are taught formally how to read and write. Clearly, literacy development before school reflects the practices of the child's society, culture, and family (Heath, 1983; Scribner & Cole, 1981; Teale & Sulzby, 1986) as well as maturational factors. The field of emergent literacy has focused on the percursors to formal reading and writing and has shown that substantial literacy development occurs before age 6 (e.g., Ferreiro & Teberosky, 1982; Sulzby & Teale, 1991). For example, Teale and Sulzby (1986) have shown that shared book reading, adult guidance in early comprehension of stories, and early attempts to write in unconventional forms are important precursors to literacy.

Children also differ in their command of the language upon entry to school (Heath, 1983). Differences in vocabulary development as well a familiarity with formal language vary widely among prereaders. In their longitudinal study of children from preschool through elementary school, Snow (1991) and her colleagues demonstrated a strong link between young children's oral language competencies and later reading development. Snow and Dickinson (1991) assert that there are certain types of language skills associated with written language that are critical for later reading. In contrast to previous work suggesting that these language skills arise from direct contact with print, Snow and her colleagues argue that the language skills that support reading arise as a result of a variety of interactive experiences during which children learn to use and understand decontextualized language (i.e., talk that extends beyond the immediate, factual story into the realm of possibilities and ideas). This is consistent with a continuous view of literacy development from early, socially contextualized utterances of oral language to the decontextualized meaning of texts.

Thus, oral language provides a foundation for literacy, a base that may be inadequate for many children. Indeed, in a survey conducted by the Carnegie Foundation for the Advancement of Learning, over 50 percent of the kindergarten teachers surveyed reported "language deficiencies" as the biggest obstacle to their students' readiness for school (Boyer, 1991). Others have taken an even stronger position. Halliday (1975) asserted that "educational failure is language failure." The important bridge between oral language and early reading and writing is at the heart of the whole-language philosophy for teaching literacy to young children (Goodman, 1986).

*Early Reading Development.* Three developmental accomplishments are particularly crucial for early reading success. First, there must be an awareness of the relationship between sounds and symbols in print, phonological decoding and recoding. Second, there must be an awareness of the purposes of reading and initial concepts about print, such as the direction one reads and the meaning of punctuation marks. Third, beginning readers must develop strategies for decoding and comprehending the meaning of print. Each of these is considered briefly.

The importance of phonological processing skills in early reading acquisition has been firmly established (e.g., Adams,

1990; Brady & Shankweiler, 1991; Bruck & Treiman, 1990; Catts, 1991; Cunningham, 1990; Stanovich, 1986; Stanovich, Cunningham, & Feeman, 1984; Vellutino & Scanlon, 1987; Wagner & Torgesen, 1987; Yopp, 1988). Certainly by age 5, children need to be able to identify distinctive sounds with individual letters, to identify rhymes, and to identify similarities and differences between sounds. Early reading depends on the ability to segment phonemes as well as to blend phonemes, and to associate these distinctive sounds with letter patterns. Is phonemic awareness a cause or a consequence of early reading development? The outcomes of various training studies indicate that phonemic awareness can be taught directly and has subsequent positive benefits for the reading abilities of early elementary schoolchildren (Bradley & Bryant, 1983; Cunningham, 1990; Lundberg, Frost, & Petersen, 1988; Treiman & Baron, 1983). Indeed, Cunningham (1990) found that three combined measures of phonemic awareness accounted for more than half of the variance in kindergarten and first-grade children's reading achievement at the end of the year. It appears that phonemic awareness is both a cause and a consequence of early reading development because it is interwoven in daily instruction and literacy achievement in school.

Much less attention in beginning reading has focused on variance in orthographic processing efficiency, that is, individual differences in the ability to form, store, and access orthographic representations. Some research suggests that orthographic processing skills may be separable from phonological skills as a determinant of individual differences in reading ability (e.g., Bryant & Impey, 1986; Freebody & Byrne, 1988; Treiman, 1983), especially in older children and adults (Cunningham & Stanovich, 1990, 1992; Stanovich & Cunningham, 1992). In a study of first-grade readers, Cunningham and Stanovich (1993) found that orthographic processing ability accounted for variance in word recognition ability even after the variance in multiple phonological processing measures had been partialed out, thus demonstrating that the development of print-specific knowledge is not entirely dependent on phonological processing skill.

Another important aspect of early literacy is awareness of concepts about print. Children's understanding of the relations among the forms and functions of speech and print is crucial for learning to read and write. For example, Clay (1979) found that beginning readers often did not understand that print rather than pictures tell the story, and they were confused about the direction that one reads print on the page. In an interview of first graders, Weintraub and Denney (1965) found that only 20 percent of the children understood that reading is a cognitive activity that helps learning. Many first graders believe that reading is a "stand-up, sit-down" social participation (Johns, 1984) or simply saying the words on the page (Bondy, 1990). Children need to become aware of the nature and purposes for reading as well as the technical features. Acquiring new vocabulary permits the young child to talk and think about the activity of reading itself. Becoming facile with the technical features—letter, word, sentence, sound—requires a level of linguistic awareness (Liberman, 1973) that helps children conceptualize literacy and reflect on their own reading and writing.

Children develop early awareness of the dimensions of reading from their early exposure to print, usually in joint bookreading activities with adults (Snow & Ninio, 1986). These scaf-folded interactions provide crucial opportunities for learning initial concepts about print. Between the ages of 3 and 5 years, children improve dramatically in their ability to identify and name letters and to discriminate the visual and auditory aspects of print (Hiebert, 1981). Lomax and McGee (1987) studied children's awareness of different aspects of reading from 3 to 7 years and found a dramatic increase in metacognition between 3- and 4-year-olds. Lomax and McGee proposed that the early concepts about print form a foundation for subsequent reading development.

The third aspect of children's early reading development is the appreciation of strategies for deciphering words and meaning. Many young readers show a casual disregard for monitoring comprehension while reading and apparently have little sense of the need to use strategies to correct their poor understanding (Garner, 1987; Markman & Gorin, 1981). The most common strategies that beginning readers use are to skip unknown words or to guess. They rarely use context and prior knowledge to guide their comprehension of unfamiliar words. Likewise, children in the primary grades have only a modest understanding of the variety of reading strategies that they might use before, during, and after reading (Paris, Wasik, & Turner, 1990). Baker (1984) observed that children focused on different standards when they tried to evaluate their comprehension. Young children focused primarily on individual words whereas older children evaluated the meaning according to multiple standards. Comprehension strategies and standards are used much less frequently than word attack strategies for decoding the sounds of print.

***The Development of Writing.*** The development of reading and writing go hand in hand. Long before children are able to read print or use writing in a conventional manner, they use scribbling and letterlike forms to convey the meaning of a text (Mason & Allen, 1986). These nonconventional literacy behaviors are developmental approximations to conventional reading and writing (Sulzby, 1985). They are motivated by children's desire to express and communicate their ideas through print and to imitate the textual forms of communication that they experience in the environment.

Learning to write requires the mastery of an abstract symbol system and the mechanical production of print with a writing tool; thus, it makes several demands on the cognitive and physical abilities of children. Writing also involves a number of rule-governed conventions—spelling, punctuation, formatting—that are uniquely associated with a printed text. Furthermore, writing usually occurs as an isolated activity and requires the writer to imagine the audience. Scardamalia and Bereiter (1986) assert that written language does not consist only of knowledge and skills added to oral language abilities, but it involves "a radical conversion from a language production system dependent upon inputs of every level from a conversational partner to a system capable of functioning autonomously" (p. 783). Thus, the development of writing involves complex cognitive and social processes that extend young children's basic oral competence.

When 3- to 4-year-olds begin to write, their early notions seem more closely related to drawing than to conventional print (Dyson, 1983). At this age, children create meaningful graphics, such as letters and letterlike forms, and talk about them. Only gradually does writing begin to be recognized as "talk written down." Clay (1979) observed that 4- to 7-year-old children discover various principles associated with print as they move from drawing to the production of letterlike graphics. They discover the *flexibility principle* (by varying letter forms, new letters can be produced), the *recurring principle* (the same shapes can be used repeatedly), and the *generative principle* (a limited number of signs can be used in different combinations). It is clear that young children's early attempts to write reflect both an active construction of meaning and an abstraction of cognitive principles for producing print.

Ferreiro (1985) asserts that research has focused too heavily on the figurative aspects of children's writing. She emphasizes the conceptual aspects of children's early compositions: When children "put physical marks on paper, they put into play their hypotheses about the meaning of graphic representation" (p. 225). Ferreiro interviewed children about their concepts of written language and identified five sequential levels of writing ranging from undifferentiated letter strings to writing forms that are read globally to conventional and alphabetic writing. Sulzby (1986) has examined children's written language as they create stories. She has documented and described a variety of emergent forms of writing ranging from scribbling to drawing to random letter strings to invented spellings to conventional spellings in a regular sequence. The legitimization of invented spelling in kindergarten and first grade has been promoted by educators who advocate whole-language curricula, because whole language is predicated on the integration of reading, writing, speaking, and listening in a developmental framework that emphasizes the child's discovery and use of increasingly sophisticated forms of communication. Both Sulzby and Dyson emphasize that children use different emergent forms of writing to accomplish various tasks. Thus, by 5 to 6 years of age, children show an awareness of the audience, and the purpose of the task, and construct appropriate approximations to print when they communicate. Such variations may reveal advancing cognitive notions of writing, but they also make it difficult to identify developmental stages in children's literacy.

A cognitive processing model that provides a framework for understanding variation in writing across tasks has been proposed by Flower and Hayes (1981). The model proposes that children have limited cognitive resources to devote to the complex task of writing. The cognitive overload generated by the multiple demands for writing may cause children to lose sight of high-level compositional goals and focus instead on the task of producing print. Such a focus on the mechanics of text production might explain the relative lack of attention to comprehension monitoring in reading and writing until these lower level aspects of text production and decoding become automated. Thus, there are parallels among (a) children's developing reading and writing competence, (b) their automatic use of component skills, and (c) their growing awareness of strategies for monitoring and repairing the comprehensibility of text.

## Family Environment and Literacy Development

Literacy activities of children vary tremendously among families of different cultural and economic backgrounds (Hess & Holloway, 1984). For example, Teale (1986) found that some children have as many as 1,000 hours of "lap time" with parents

sharing literacy, whereas others may begin kindergarten without much experience of, or adult guidance in, reading and writing. Some environments have prepared some children more for school-based literacy learning than others. Edwards (1989) found that low-income, undereducated mothers did not provide the same level of lap-time reading. She attempted to train the mothers to read to their children but observed that despite extensive training, the mothers did not learn to talk with their children, elaborate, ask questions, or discuss illustrations. Edwards argues that in many homes the mothers themselves are limited by their own low level of literacy skills. Research has shown important links among the time that young children spend with parents, the literate environment in the home, and children's later reading fluency. Hewison and Tizard (1980), in their study of British infant and middle schools, found that parental attitudes were important, but the most predictive factor was whether the parent "coached" the child. In middle school, the factor that was the best predictor of later reading success was whether the mother heard the child read as opposed to reading to the child. The quality of parental behavior and other measures of family environment appear to describe the family's influence on school achievement more accurately and specifically than do socioeconomic factors (e.g., Barth & Parke, 1993; Hess, Holloway, Dickson, & Price, 1984).

The home literacy environments of children from low-socio-economic-status backgrounds can be quite different from school literacy practices (Heath, 1983). Children judge the value of literacy by observing the behavior of adults in their homes, and these value judgments may affect achievement in school. Clear links, for example, are seen between children's leisure reading habits and parents' level of literacy support (Neuman, 1986). If parents do not value or participate in literacy activities, young children do not observe the personal, economic, and social benefits of reading (Fitzgerald, Spiegel, & Cunningham, 1991). This is why many literacy programs aim to promote literacy of all family members through intergenerational reading and writing activities.

Literacy-rich environments offer many opportunities for joint activities, but they are also rich in print. The mere availability and exposure to text may have benefits for young children's literacy. Recent studies examining components of reading ability corroborate the research indicating that book-reading practices of families promote the development of skilled reading at a processing level. For example, Cunningham and Stanovich (1993) found that orthographic processing knowledge was linked to individual differences in children's experiential history of literacy activities. Thus, early differences in knowledge about orthography may create environmentally linked orthographic variance that is independent of phonological processing differences among children. The seminal work of Maclean, Bryant, and Bradley (1988) on preschool children's knowledge of nursery rhymes also demonstrate the link between the literacy environment and early phonological and orthographic processing skills. It is likely that the richness and coaching provided in children's early literacy environments may promote the development of specific skills and knowledge that then serve to enable more efficient subsequent reading (Cunningham, Stanovich, & West, 1994).

How can schools provide appropriate educational experiences for children when they enter with such diverse backgrounds and literacy skills? Tracking and sorting children at school entry does not foster equal opportunities and runs the risk of social discrimination. For many educators, it is becoming clear that teachers and schools must find new ways to accommodate the diversity of students and families they serve. Feitelson (1987) studied literacy development in Israeli families and pointed out that the educational establishment needs to be responsible for tasks that teachers in highly industrialized or stable communities often expect parents to perform. She argues that "schools cannot be allowed to depend only upon parents' ability to prepare their children for these tasks and experiences" (p. 176). This view is shared by many educators in the United States. The increasing cultural, ethnic, familial, and economic diversity of children may force schools to provide surrogate family environments.

## Programs for Home-to-School Literacy

Numerous programs have been developed over the past decade that focus on children's literacy development and home-to-school links. One of the earliest programs was begun in 1963 by the Verbal Interaction Project (Levenstein, 1988). This program is based on the principle that mother–child talk builds a foundation for later literacy development. It is geared toward families with children between the ages of 2 and 4 from lower socioeconomic backgrounds. This outreach program provides services to mothers and children in their own homes. Participating families are given books, toys, and other literacy instruments. Although the mother is considered the primary teacher, a home visitor teaches the mother literacy skills and models appropriate verbal interactions between mother and child. Results of these interventions showed a common pattern of home intervention studies. In general, the children displayed better attitudes toward reading and schooling, experienced lower rates of grade retention and placement in special education classes, and had higher reading achievement through the seventh grade (Levenstein, 1988).

Another preventive program designed specifically for parents is PACE (Parent and Child Education), founded in 1986 by the state of Kentucky. PACE was founded in the belief that parents' inadequate education perpetuated a cycle of academic failure in their children. Several factors are examined in this program, including parental attitudes toward literacy and their effect on children's literacy development, the relation between parental educational level and children's achievement, and finally parenting style. The program focuses on developing oral and preliteracy skills in young children, vocational training for parents, and parent–child workshops in early childhood education. Results show that children in PACE display higher test scores on entering school than their nonprogram peers. Also, 90 percent of the participating children ranked average or above average in their attitudes toward school and motivation to learn. Parents reported higher self-esteem and increased time reading to their children (Hibpshman, 1989).

During the late 1980s, a series of programs was launched under the rubric of Even Start. These programs are all designed to promote family literacy skills, especially the development of children from birth to 8 years old. More than 20 states now offer Even Start programs. One well-known program is Arkansas's HIPPY (Home Instruction Program for Preschool Youngsters),

which serves 4,500 children and their parents. In this program, parents work for 2 years, 30 weeks a year, and 15 minutes a day, 5 days a week, in the school setting. In addition, parents receive education and vocational training while their children are in preschool classes. The program disseminates information on parenting skills as well as community resources. A major focus of the program is to involve parents in activities with their children and model appropriate skills and behaviors (Boyer, 1991).

Intervention programs designed to provide links between the home and school environment appear to be effective in helping children in their transition to becoming a student (e.g., Gotts, 1980; Pfannensteil & Seltzer, 1989; Scott, 1976; Zigler & Muenchow, 1992), especially when the home environment is markedly different from the school setting. The critical variables, however, that influence the children's achievement are not completely understood. For example, White, Taylor, and Moss (1992) argue that there is not sufficient evidence to support the notion that parental intervention is effective in enhancing children's academic achievement. A key factor, however, is creating a bridge between beliefs, values, and practices in the home and school so that they mutually support children's education (Hess & Holloway, 1984).

## Individual Differences in Readiness for Literacy

Many researchers question whether the construct of readiness is useful for understanding the nature of the child's transition from home to school. They focus instead on individual differences in cognitive, linguistic, and academic skills. In a longitudinal study of kindergarten and first-grade students, Morrison, Griffith, and Williamson (1993) investigated the individual differences in literacy skills among children on entrance into kindergarten and tracked them through early elementary school. At the beginning of their kindergarten year, large differences among the children were found. Their findings revealed substantial differences in vocabulary (age-level equivalents as wide as 7 years). Equally large differences were found on their measure of reading skills.

Schooling provides the opportunity to diminish initially large differences in literacy among children. Morrison et al. (1993) hypothesized that the large individual differences found at school entry would begin to decrease systematically. Instead, their data showed that none of their measures ever reliably decreased over the first 2 years of school. On two of their four outcome measures, reading and receptive vocabulary, the initial differences were maintained, and on the others, mathematics and cultural knowledge, the initial differences were amplified. Their findings revealed that a child's relative standing across cognitive and academic skills remains reasonably stable over the beginning years of school. The stability of these initial relationships was found in a longitudinal study of first- to fourth-grade students by Juel (1988) as well. The probability that a child would remain a poor reader at the end of fourth grade if the child was a poor reader at the end of first grade turned out to be .88. The probability that a child would become an average reader in fourth grade if he or she was a poor reader in first grade was only .13. Juel points out that due to their poor skill level, poor readers simply cannot read as much as better readers and therefore are exposed to less print. By the end of first grade, the good readers had seen, on average, 18,681 words in running text, whereas the poor readers had seen 9,975 words, about half as many. This inequality in print exposure was magnified as the years progressed (see also Anderson, Wilson, & Fielding, 1987).

The magnification over time of initial differences in cognitive abilities such as literacy demonstrates the cumulative advantage phenomenon described by Stanovich (1986). These "Matthew effects," whereby the rich get richer and the poor get poorer, appear to be "inextricably embedded within the developmental course of reading progress" (p. 381). Given the present U.S. system of education, in which social comparison is reinforced through instructional and assessment practices, it appears that the gulf between good and poor readers will become wider with each passing year in school. Thus, the primary years of schooling and children's early literacy are fundamental to children's developmental accomplishments in school.

## LEARNING TO LEARN IN GRADES 4 THROUGH 8

During the upper elementary grades and middle school, students experience profound changes in school environments and agenda. No longer do students spend the entire day with the same teacher or same students. Their classes focus on increasingly specialized domains and their academic progress is evaluated publicly at more frequent intervals. Upper elementary grades and middle school demand greater detailed and organized knowledge from students through changes in the curriculum, homework, and assessment practices. Students also undergo more frequent and more explicit social comparisons that have pronounced effects on children's orientation to school. This section reviews developmental changes in students' learning strategies, motivation, and help seeking as they approach adolescence. The discussion summarizes the major changes in Grades 4 through 8 in terms of students' emerging theories about schooling and their emerging habits of self-regulated learning.

### Acquiring and Honing Personal Learning Strategies

With each advancing year in school, children encounter more challenging tasks that require a greater variety of learning strategies. Some of these strategies are domain-specific, for example, algorithms for multiplying and dividing or sequential strategies for conducting a science experiment. There are other strategies, however, that can be used across a variety of disciplines and are more characteristic of general thinking strategies. These include strategies for planning, monitoring, and revising one's understanding or actions. Weinstein and Mayer (1986) identified several major categories of these general learning strategies. (a) Rehearsal strategies (for basic and complex tasks) promote memorization through repetition and practice. (b) Elaboration strategies (for basic and complex tasks) extend information so that it is connected to additional schemes, events, and frameworks. (c) Organizational strategies (for basic and complex tasks) transform the information into new categories and relations that are recalled through familiar and multiple retrieval cues. (d) Comprehension-monitoring strategies are tac-

tics that are used to evaluate and improve the sensibility of information that is read, heard, spoken, or written. (e) Affective strategies help to manage emotions such as reducing anxiety so that interpretation of events does not lead to feelings of helplessness or hopelessness. Motivation and metacognition are interwoven in the use of these kinds of learning strategies that promote self-appraisal and self-management of cognitive resources (Paris & Winograd, 1990).

Although there is no consensus on a single taxonomy of learning strategies, there is general agreement about the kinds of knowledge that students need to acquire about strategies in order to use them independently (Garner, 1990). One type of information that children acquire about academic strategies is *declarative knowledge,* or knowing what particular strategies are available or required. For example, beginning readers usually understand that they can use context to figure out the meaning of new vocabulary words, even though they may need considerable instruction on how and when to use contextual cues. A second aspect of metacognition about strategies is *procedural knowledge*. When children understand the procedures for learning a strategy, they know how it is applied and can follow the steps to use it. For example, children are often taught how to use rules for place-value borrowing in arithmetic, how to write five-paragraph essays in report writing, and how to use graphic organizers like webs, diagrams, and charts.

However, knowing what to do, and knowing how to do it, are often insufficient. A great deal of research has shown that children need the metacognitive knowledge about when strategies should be applied and why they are effective. This has been called *conditional knowledge* (Paris, Lipson, & Wixson, 1983) because it specifies the conditions under which strategies are appropriate. Conditional knowledge helps to establish the causal connection between the use of a strategy and successful performance. A thorough understanding of learning strategies usually includes all three types of knowledge, although students may not be aware of them without reflection or prompting. This is why research on learning strategies has so often used interventions designed to promote greater awareness and use of strategies. During the past 15 years, there have been many instructional intervention studies designed to promote metacognition about literacy (e.g., Duffy, Roehler, Sivan, Rackliffe, Book, Meloth, Vavrus, Wesselman, Putnam, & Bassiri, 1987; Palincsar & Brown, 1984; Paris, Cross, & Lipson, 1984; Pressley, Goodchild, Fleet, Zajchowski, & Evans, 1989). A special issue of *The Elementary School Journal* (see, for example, Duffy, 1993) on strategy instruction describes various programs that all show how dialogues among students, instructional transactions, and explanations about strategies are essential in classroom conversations. These instructional interactions promote metacognition because they encourage children to construct and apply appropriate strategies for reading and writing while also discussing, defending, teaching, and sharing the tactics.

The orchestration of metacognition, strategy knowledge, and motivation has been described by Borkowski, Carr, Rellinger, and Pressley (1990) as part of the "good strategy-user" model. There are three components to this model. The first is specific strategy knowledge, in which children acquire procedural, declarative, and conditional knowledge about particular strategies. The second component includes general strategy knowledge and attributional beliefs that help children understand the effort required to apply a strategy and the causal attribution between the strategy and successful performance. The third component is metacognitive acquisition procedures, which are strategies that regulate other strategies. These boil down to self-experimentation and self-evaluation, and may reflect general characteristics of thinking and motivation. Successful strategy users, therefore, have a great deal of knowledge about specific strategies, the settings in which they are appropriate, and the motivational requirements to use them.

Literacy affords a good arena in which to study strategies, and a convenient way to examine the strategies that children acquire about literacy is to divide them according to strategies used before reading and writing, during reading and writing, and after reading and writing.

Before children begin to read, it is useful to preview texts and to establish a purpose for reading. It may also be useful to make inferences from the text source, titles, pictures, and skimming of information before one begins to read. However, these strategies are difficult for many children throughout elementary school (Paris, Wasik, & Turner, 1990). Similar kinds of strategies facilitate writing, but 8- to 12-year-olds are often reluctant to use brainstorming, semantic webs, and peer discussions to guide their initial drafts. Instruction in prewriting and prereading strategies has consistently shown positive beliefs for elementary school students, particularly those students who have learning disabilities related to literacy (Wong, 1987).

One of the key strategies that children learn to use as they read is to make inferences and elaborate the meaning from text. However, without explicit instructions, 10- to 12-year-old children often focus on the literal meaning of the text rather than transforming it into their own words and ideas (Johnston & Afflerbach, 1985). In addition, children in upper elementary grades have difficulty identifying main ideas and difficulty distinguishing important from unimportant information. The focus on literal meaning and the inability to distinguish main ideas may arise from inappropriate comprehension goals or the lack of appropriate strategies employed while reading. In the same vein, children often fail to monitor and repair their writing when they are engaged in the task. They often do not re-read for comprehensibility or use topic sentences and main ideas to organize their writing.

When children finish reading a passage, they often do not look back in texts to check their understanding or make good summaries. For example, Brown and Day (1983) found that fifth and seventh graders, when trying to summarize a passage, tended to recall bits of information in the same sequence as the text and did not plan their summaries effectively. They often ran out of space on the page before they had completed their summaries. Taylor (1986) studied fourth and fifth graders' summarization skills and found that the good summarizers planned effectively, used text structure as an aid in selecting important ideas, and recorded information in their own words. Winograd (1984) found a similar pattern among eighth graders who were asked to summarize. Again, there is a parallel with writing strategies. Students who are asked to revise frequently make superficial changes and fail to appreciate the audience's perspective or monitor the comprehensibility of their text. Children who use effective strategies for revising may follow the advice of a peer, may re-read their own writing from a different perspective, and are more likely to embellish ideas as they revise.

Considerable research has shown that many children do not acquire effective academic strategies by the time they enter high school (Pintrich & De Groot, 1990). Whether it is due to lack of awareness, lack of practice, or lack of motivation, the failure to employ effective strategies before, during, and after a task usually hinders reading comprehension and written communication. During the past 15 years, the number of demonstrations of effective instructional interventions that promote children's strategy use has grown. For example, Ashman and Conway (1993) describe how process-based instruction (PBI) can provide children with general and specific strategies. PBI involves a time line of activities that emphasize cuing, acting, monitoring, and verifying strategy use. Teachers help students apply plans for strategic problem solving across the curriculum. Harris and Graham (1992) taught children a variety of practical strategies for organizing, planning, and revising their compositions. They taught six different self-instructional tactics to promote self-regulation: (a) identify the problem, (b) focus on the task, (c) apply the strategies, (d) evaluate performance, (e) cope with anxiety and maintain self-control, and (f) apply self-reinforcement. They also encourage teachers to instruct children in general schemes for goal setting and self-assessment.

These programs of strategy instruction incorporate several key features of successful interventions. One key feature is to provide a rich variety of strategies that children can use on academic tasks. Second, teachers share specific strategy information among children—the procedural, declarative, conditional knowledge that is required for students to become aware of how, when, and why to apply strategies (Paris, 1991). A third important principle is the causal attribution of improved performance to the effective application of the strategy. A fourth principle is that effective strategies can be learned effectively from peers during discussion and tutoring (Palincsar & Brown, 1984). Fifth, academic strategies are part of larger plans for managing one's effort, resources, and emotions. Finally, it is important for effective strategies to be embedded in daily activities so that teachers and students have the opportunity to employ the strategies in authentic activities throughout the curriculum.

## Motivational Orientations

Until the 1970s, educational psychologists usually explained students' motivation in behavioral terms of habits, rewards, punishments, contingencies, and schedules of reinforcement. Motivation was largely considered a property provided by other people or the environment in response to needs or drives of the individual. These views are hardly evident today. They were swept away by cognitive theories of students' motivation that have dominated research during the past 25 years (see chapters 3 and 4). Contemporary approaches to children's academic motivation examine cognitive and situational factors that underlie academic choices, effort, persistence, and strategies (Paris & Turner, 1994). The underlying question today in children's academic achievement motivation is, Why does a child choose to act in a particular manner? The search for motivational explanations instead of behavioral patterns of responses has led to the examination of a wide variety of constructs, including personal attributions, goals, self-perceptions of competence, risk taking, and intrinsic motivation. These various theories are reviewed in chapters 4 and 5. Here it is important to describe how these various motivational processes develop in school-aged children and how they influence children's learning over time.

***Attributions for Success and Failure.*** Bernard Weiner (1985) has articulated an attributional theory of achievement motivation based on the internal and external perceived causes for success and failure. These causes can be further subdivided according to whether they are stable or unstable and controllable or uncontrollable. According to Weiner and others, it is the students' perceived causal explanations that can lead to particular emotional reactions and motivational orientations. For example, Stevenson and Stigler (1992) have suggested that children in China and Japan are primarily motivated to achieve in school because they attribute success to effort and hard work, whereas American children may expend less effort because they believe that success is more likely to be due to innate ability. The different attributions for success lead to different expectations and investments of effort and may underlie part of the difference in achievement between students in Asian and American schools, according to Stevenson and Stigler (1992).

There have been many applications of attribution theory to children's educational success or failure. Two general findings will illustrate the power of this motivational construct. First, students' passivity and learned helplessness may be a result of inappropriate attributions (Kistener, Osborne, & LeVerrier, 1988). If students attribute their academic failures to low ability, they believe that further effort cannot overcome failure. When teachers exhort children to try harder and the students find that greater effort leads to no difference in learning or understanding, children's interpretation of their own low ability is reinforced and they quit trying (Johnston & Winograd, 1985). It is the cumulative impact of children's counterproductive attributions that begins to diminish their optimism about their own competence and self-efficacy. Lower expectations about one's own efforts and abilities then decrease risk taking and the search for academic challenges, which then leads to passivity or success on easy tasks.

Second, gender differences in math achievement may be influenced by different attributional patterns (see chapters 7 and 12). For example, girls may attribute their failure in mathematics to low ability, whereas boys may attribute failure in mathematics to insufficient effort. Conversely, girls may attribute success in mathematics to high effort, whereas boys may attribute success to high ability. Such causal attributions lead girls to quit trying and boys to try harder on future math problems. Of course, children's attributions reflect the influence of other people and classroom settings. Through their emotions, expectations, and encouragement, teachers may convey different expectations about boys and girls, minority and majority students, and high and low achievers. When children feel that teachers hold low expectations for them, feel pity for them, and provide them with modest goals, students may perceive that teachers attribute limited ability to the students. Motivational orientation such as learned helplessness, low expectations, and stereotypical bias are the result of subtle and cumulative factors for many years. It is unusual to find these motivational orientations in children below 8 years of age but these attributional patterns become more pronounced by middle school.

***Motivational Goals.*** Although children attribute success and failure in school to distinct sources, those attributions can be influenced by the motivational goals that are adopted. For example, Ames and Ames (1984) assert that a competitive classroom environment provides an attributional focus on personal ability, whereas a cooperative or mastery orientation in a classroom places an attributional focus on effort. Many theorists have argued that American schools provide highly competitive environments in which students' performances are compared (Nicholls, 1989). If all students try hard, then explanations of differences usually focus on differences in ability. Thus, classroom value orientations influence students' motivational orientations. When teachers emphasize "doing your best," "helping others," or "task engagement," then children will give more attention to effort and mastery. These patterns of attributions and goals lead to different self-perceptions. Competitive orientations often lead to negative self-perceptions and anxiety, whereas orientations to effort do not affect children's self-esteem to the same extent. Thus, schools socialize children into different motivational orientations, which in turn leads to different attributional causes for success and failure, which in turn leads to different emotional reactions and self-esteem (Anderman & Maehr, 1994).

Goal orientation of students is linked to age, partly because the classroom climate and organization change as children proceed through school (C. Ames & Archer, 1988). As children confront more instances of social comparison in higher grades, they are more likely to adopt competitive goals and focus on ability attributions. Paradoxically, this orientation can inhibit effort from children who are unsuccessful because if they try hard and fail, they only confirm their suspicion of low ability. This is why Covington (1992) calls effort a "double-edged sword." When effort does not lead to success, students usually attribute failure to low ability, make excuses, decrease future effort, and internalize shame and humiliation about their low ability. Remediation of these cycles of failure requires instruction about better strategies for learning, not simply exhortations to try harder (Corno, 1992).

***Perceptions of Competence.*** Children's motivation in school is determined in part by the perceptions they have of their own academic abilities. The fundamental tenet of this approach is that students' perception of their own ability, control, efficacy, and effort will guide their actions. It is derived from social psychologists such as Harold Kelly and Fritz Heider and is evident in current work on the role of self schemas. It is also consistent with the constructivist position in developmental psychology, in which children's idiosyncratic constructions of the world move from egocentric to normative concepts (Harter, 1983). The general picture of children's motivational development is that they are optimistic about themselves during the early years of schooling and gradually become realistic (i.e., more pessimistic) about their academic abilities as they progress through school. In fact, Stipek (1981) found that more than 80 percent of children in a first-grade class thought they were the best student in the class. Older students have more accurate pictures of their own competence, but they often believe that ability and intelligence have fixed capacities. Older students begin to regard intelligence as a trait that varies among people and may over- or underestimate their own competence. The developmental changes in these concepts and the consequences for academic learning and motivation have been popular areas of research.

Nicholls (1990) summarized his program of research in which he investigated the development of children's understanding of ability and the meanings they attach to related terms. For example, he found that 5-year-olds had difficulty differentiating the concepts of luck and skill. By 12 years of age, however, skill and luck outcomes were clearly distinguished, and effort was seen to affect outcomes only on skill tasks. Nicholls and his colleagues also examined how children distinguished the concepts of difficulty and ability. Preschoolers often equate difficulty and ability because they reason that tasks that are hard for them indicate to them that they do not have sufficient ability to complete the tasks. Gradually, children acquire an objective concept of difficulty and then a normative concept of difficulty. Those tasks that can be completed by fewer of a child's peers are regarded as requiring higher ability. Thus, by middle childhood, children distinguish self-referenced views of difficulty from norm-referenced views of difficulty. However, a negative consequence of this conceptual advance is a heightened sensitivity to one's relative standing among peers and to social comparisons.

Perhaps the most fundamental distinction that children make about their own competence is the distinction between ability and effort, a distinction that is critical for the attributions they make about the perceived causes of success and failure. Nicholls (1990) identified four levels of differentiation. Until age 5 or 6, children often equate effort or outcome with ability. For example, they see that people who try harder are smarter or people who are more successful have more ability. This gives way to an interpretation of effort as the cause of outcomes in which the proportion of effort is equal to the proportion of success. By fourth or fifth grade, however, effort and ability become differentiated and are regarded as sometimes independent. The final stage is achieved by early adolescence, in which ability is regarded as capacity that varies among people. Children reason that low ability may diminish the effects of effort and high ability may increase the positive consequences of effort on academic performance. They also reason that high effort is required to compensate for lower ability. One negative outcome of this differentiated view of ability and effort is that young adolescents view high effort as an indicator of lower ability, and so they may not expend effort or they may disguise it to their peers.

Children also show a progressive differentiation of general ability from intelligence. Until 7 or 8 years of age, children regard intelligence as a general measure of success in all activities. After 8 years of age, though, they see intelligence as more restricted to academic and cognitive activities. Nicholls (1990) suggests that children's differentiated notions of intelligence parallel children's distinct concepts of ability and effort that occur somewhat later. By middle adolescence, intelligence is regarded as having two components. One component is based on verbal intelligence, which is similar to the construct of crystallized intelligence, whereas the second component reflects abstract reasoning, which is more like the construct of fluid intelligence. Young adolescents consider abstract intelligence and fluid reasoning abilities to be part of an individual's intellectual capacity and thus relatively unaffected by practice and instruction.

The developmental differentiation of the concept of ability from skill, difficulty, and effort is fostered by cognitive development as well as feedback in academic settings. Parents, teachers, and peers all provide information about the relative performance standing of individuals that promotes conceptualizations of ability as capacity and intelligence as unalterable. Nicholls (1990) points out that these concepts are embedded in a social meritocracy in American schools. Whether or not children use these concepts to guide their behavior may depend greatly on the goal orientations they adopt in specific settings. Nicholls argues that classrooms that promote ability comparisons and ego involvement reinforce a notion of ability as fixed capacity and promote normative comparisons in which a sizable number of children must perceive themselves as below average. In contrast, classrooms that emphasize task involvement or mastery goals place a premium on effort and comparisons of longitudinal growth. Thus, classrooms with a task focus might promote motivation and learning to a greater extent than classrooms with a focus on individual ability.

Many researchers have examined the accuracy of children's perceptions of their own abilities. In general, it appears to be harmful to greatly overestimate or underestimate one's competence. The most motivating perspective may be a slightly optimistic view of one's own competence relative to one's actual achievements. Phillips and Zimmerman (1990) found that many children had "illusions of incompetence" because they seriously underestimated their own ability. They interviewed high-achieving third, fifth, and ninth graders and found generally that they had unrealistically low expectations for success, believed that adults and teachers had unfavorable impressions about their own abilities, showed reluctance to sustain their efforts on difficult tasks, and showed more anxiety about evaluation and social comparison to other children.

Does the illusion of incompetence change with age? Phillips and Zimmerman (1990) found that children's actual achievement scores as well as their perceptions of competence were relatively stable over time. But interestingly, the correlations between students' perceptions and their actual test scores were modest, $rs = .27–.36$, which indicates that students' perceptions of their own abilities are not calibrated accurately. There is a striking developmental difference in the way boys and girls perceive their own academic competence. In third and fifth grades, boys and girls were equally distributed in the low, average, and high perceived-competence groups. By ninth grade, though, girls were substantially overrepresented in the low perceived-competence groups and underrepresented in the group with high self-perceptions. This is consistent with research on math achievement in which girls exhibit equal performance and equal perceptions of competence to boys in elementary school, but gradually lower their perceptions of their own abilities as they proceed to high school.

Why do girls show a developmental trend of greater pessimism about their own perceived abilities? Phillips and Zimmerman (1990) suggest that parents convey sex-linked beliefs about their children's abilities and likely achievements. Parents regarded school as more difficult for daughters than for sons. Likewise, girls thought that their mothers had significantly lower expectations for their academic performance than for boys' performance. This pattern of gender-linked beliefs, lower standards for girls, and girls' perceptions of lower parental expectations is consistent with gender-linked changes in self-perceptions of mathematics ability and motivation (see chapter 7, this volume). It appears that children are socialized into student roles by parents, who may hold widely differing expectations and beliefs for boys and girls, and that these socializing factors, rather than intellectual ability alone, shape children's academic motivation.

Children who underestimate their own academic abilities undermine their own learning and academic achievement. One consequence of low perceptions of ability is decreased effort in schoolwork. Children reason that high effort will reveal to their classmates only that they have low ability, or that success with high effort will confirm in their own mind that they have low ability, so they expend less effort to avoid the negative attributions by themselves or other people. A second consequence of exaggerated pessimism is that students invest their energies in other areas. For example, they may avoid schoolwork and expend extra effort in social, athletic, or musical activities. If they choose this tactic, they often maintain a positive sense of self-worth and a highly restricted view of low academic competence. However, some students generalize their lower perceptions of competence to other areas of achievement and may drop out of school or engage in antisocial behavior. It is an ironic self-fulfilling prophecy that the inaccurate perceptions may lead to a host of counterproductive behaviors that inhibit academic achievement and learning. Parents and teachers may unwittingly contribute to the illusion of incompetence when they emphasize grades, achievement, and social comparisons as the basis of evaluating individual self-worth (Covington, 1992).

It is worth mentioning that some students have a different kind of miscalibrated assessment of their own ability. Some students with low or average academic achievements have exaggeratedly positive views of their own competence. Stevenson, Chen, and Uttal (1990) found that minority students in inner cities often had highly positive views of their competence and achievement, despite having low test scores. These "illusions of competence" may result from an unchallenging curriculum, inflated praise from teachers and parents, or compensatory reactions from the students. Unfortunately, miscalibrated optimism can also lead to reduced effort, reduced persistence, and inhibited future achievement. It appears, therefore, that students who have excessively pessimistic or optimistic views of their own competence may not invest appropriate effort in academic work and may encounter difficulty dealing with feedback that is discordant with their own self-evaluations.

## The Development of Help Seeking

Students who are competent and confident know how to seek help in classrooms. They know who can provide useful help and under what conditions help can be sought. Academic help seeking is a topic at the intersection of children's motivation and strategic learning because it depends on both children's motivational goals and the instrumental strategies they use to seek help. Historically, help seeking has been regarded negatively as a manifestation of children's overdependency on other people. In this view, help seeking should be avoided because it prevents the development of self-sufficiency and may be an indicator of low ability. Nelson-Le Gall (1985) has contrasted this dependency-oriented help seeking with an instrumental

or mastery-oriented help seeking in which students use other people as resources in positive ways. This is an important distinction, because students who seek help for instrumental reasons can use other people to answer questions and provide scaffolding for their own learning, whereas students who seek help from others in order to complete their work often undermine their own learning. Instrumental help seeking is therefore a consequence of mastery-orientated learning goals, whereas dependency-oriented help seeking is undertaken to preserve or enhance self-esteem while avoiding genuine effort and learning.

Help seeking varies as a function of the age of the student, the characteristics of the help provider, and the characteristics of the instructional setting. Consider first some general developmental changes in help seeking. Wood, Bruner, and Ross (1976) observed that 3-year-olds usually ignored a tutor, but 4- and 5-year-olds asked questions when they experienced difficulty with a problem. Myers and Paris (1978) interviewed second and sixth graders about strategies they used to enhance reading comprehension and found that sixth graders were more likely than second graders to seek help from others. As they progress through elementary school, children become more aware of the characteristics of effective helpers. Young children focus more on helpers who are polite, kind, and nice, whereas students in middle and upper grades are more concerned with academic tasks, so they choose helpers who are competent and skilled (Nelson-Le Gall & Gumerman, 1984). With age and practice, children understand who can provide help, how to signal for help, and how to use the help provided in order to solve specific academic problems (Newman & Goldin, 1990).

In addition to greater awareness of strategic and adaptive help seeking, there are also age-related changes in children's attitudes and beliefs about seeking help with schoolwork. Newman and Schwager (1993) studied students' perceptions of teachers and classmates in relation to seeking help in mathematics. In general, students in Grades 3, 5, and 7 preferred teachers to classmates as helpers because the teacher was viewed as a better facilitator and less likely to think students were "dumb" for asking questions. At all three grade levels, a warm, positive relationship with the teacher was important, but among older students, who were more task oriented, the classroom climate and a sense of encouragement for asking questions influenced whether or not students sought help. Seventh graders also showed more concern about the potential embarrassment of publicly seeking help and asking questions. It is likely that the greater social comparison and anxiety about peer perceptions inhibit help seeking among older students. However, at all grade levels, students were more likely to ask questions if they did not think they were the only ones in the class seeking help. A final age-related difference observed by Newman and Schwager (1993) was in the perceived usefulness of help seeking. Children in Grades 5 and 7 believed more strongly that asking questions is a positive strategy that smart students use. In fact, high achievers in high school and college do seek information and social assistance more often than low achievers (Karabenick & Knapp, 1991; Zimmerman & Martinez-Pons, 1986).

These age-related differences are difficult to disentangle from age-related differences in educational practices. As children progress from elementary to middle school, more emphasis is placed on ability grouping, tracking, social comparative assessment, and explicit discussion among peers about relative abilities. When comparison and competition among students are emphasized in classrooms, help seeking seems to be diminished. However, when cooperative learning, reciprocal teaching, and peer tutoring are evident in the classroom, help seeking is more likely to be observed (Newman, 1994; Webb, 1985).

Several other student characteristics are associated with help seeking. Children who have positive self-perceptions of their own ability in school generally show greater levels of task engagement and help seeking. Although they may not need to seek help as often, when the need arises, they seek assistance readily. A second important factor is students' perceptions of control in the classroom. Newman and Schwager (1992) suggest that

the following children are relatively unlikely to seek help adaptively; (a) those who do not expect to do well, (b) those who are in the dark about what it takes to do well, and (c) those who believe that ability, powerful others, and luck are what it takes, but believe that they themselves are *not* smart, *not* liked by the teacher, and *not* lucky. In other words, those who feel they do not have control over their own academic success—perhaps because they do not know what is important or because they perceive they do not have access to what is important—are expected to be disengaged in the classroom. (p. 129)

A third factor that influences help seeking is students' motivational orientation. Nelson-Le Gall and Jones (1990) found that third and fifth graders who were intrinsically motivated and strived for independent mastery were more likely to seek academic help through hints, rather than seeking the answers directly. In contrast, children who were characterized as extrinsically motivated were just as likely to prefer receiving the answers as hints. Newman (1990) also found that students in Grades 3, 5, and 7 who showed a strong preference for challenge also were likely to seek help. Thus, students who believe that personal control and challenge are important for learning in school are likely to seek help from others when they encounter difficulties.

Students seek help for many different reasons, some for dependence and some for independence. Some help is sought for learning and mastery goals, whereas other help is sought for completing the task at hand. It is important to understand both the motivational orientation as well as the strategic utility of help seeking to understand how and why students seek or avoid seeking help. It is clear that with increasing age and experience, students become aware of when and how to seek help while also avoiding potential embarrassment or threats to their self-esteem. It is likely that particular classroom climates and instructional practices create situations in which students feel comfortable or uneasy seeking help, and therefore developmental changes in help seeking must be interpreted relative to situational features.

## DEVELOPMENTAL CONTINUITIES IN BECOMING A STUDENT

Children are socialized into the roles of students with expectations, beliefs, and strategies that are provided by parents and teachers. Within this fabric of cultural habits and standards,

children weave their individual talents, abilities, and motivation as they become students. Although children develop dramatically between 3 and 13 years of age on many dimensions, consistency in the environment and predictable developmental accomplishments bring stability to the patterns of change. We chart two general features of children's enculturation into the world of schooling as a conclusion to this chapter. The first theme emphasizes children's emerging theories about education—their notions about school activities, teachers, and their academic selves. The second theme is action-based and considers how children become academically self-regulated with cognitive, behavioral, and motivational strategies.

### Theories of Schooling Constructed by Children

Before children start school, they are exposed to practices and expectations about school from their siblings and parents. Preschool experiences teach children about routines in school settings, the social requirements for working in groups, and the respective roles of students and teachers. Thus, by age 4 to 5 years, most children have a rudimentary scheme for school based on their particular experiences and activities. These concepts are often highly idiosyncratic and erroneous but they reveal how children make sense of their experience and how they anticipate future schooling. Entwisle, Alexander, Pallas, and Cadigan (1987) suggest that children's academic self-image emerges in the period of home-to-school transition: "[W]e see the academic self-image as one part of a theory that children unwittingly construct for themselves about themselves. Children make and test hypotheses about their 'self' and revise their concepts accordingly" (p. 1192). Children's early concepts about school will later become coherent beliefs that motivate particular actions, and thus they may be regarded as preliminary theories about education (Paris & Byrnes, 1989). Every year of schooling adds rich knowledge to these theories and reveals the interplay of idiosyncratic experience, developmental abilities of children, and the constructive nature of children's theory building.

Children's understanding of who is successful in school depends on their understanding of the concepts of ability, intelligence, and achievement. As we have seen in Nicholls's research, there is a growing differentiation of these terms throughout childhood. Children in the first and second grades generally judge ability across cognitive, social, and physical domains and consider children who are praised for their performance to be "good" and "smart." They believe that trying hard, completing tasks, and receiving teacher praise are all signs of high academic competence (Blumenfeld, Pintrich, Meece, & Wessels, 1982). By the time children reach middle school, they base their evaluations of academic competence on grades, ability grouping, and other readily observable social comparisons of success (Stipek & Mac Iver, 1989). Academic self-perceptions become differentiated from social and athletic competence and become highly distinct by subject matter by early adolescence.

As children gain greater understanding of the concepts of effort and ability, they change the way they view academic competence. For example, Dweck and Bempechat (1983) suggest that young children are "incremental theorists" because they believe that increments in effort yield increments in ability. Thus, trying hard makes people smarter, and smart people try harder. But this theory of effort slowly gives way to an "entity theory" according to which academic ability is a fixed capacity and cannot be easily changed by one's effort. Self-referenced theories often provide illusions of competence or incompetence and can subvert students' appropriate effort and motivation in school. Thus, it is not just the accuracy of children's emerging theories that is important, but also how they act on the information that they construct.

With each year of schooling, children acquire a better understanding of instructional and assessment activities in the classroom. Although they may have only a vague idea in first grade about the difference between worksheets and authentic problem-solving skills, repeated experiences lead them to form concepts about reading, math, and science based on the nature of these activities. That is why some children in first and second grades regard literacy as simply reading aloud or completing worksheets, whereas other children regard reading and writing as forms of communication for more functional purposes. By middle school, some children regard the exchange of effort for grades as a "piece work" labor system (Doyle, 1983). By adolescence, these students may have detached themselves from the academic goals of school because they find classrooms too frustrating or boring. In contrast, other students who have mastery goals, positive self-concepts of their own ability, and good understanding of how strategies promote learning and motivation exhibit high levels of persistence and achievement.

With experience, children become increasingly able to perceive the classroom climate and environment. For example, Meece, Blumenfeld, and Puro (1989) examined the engagement and motivation of fifth- and sixth-grade students in different science lessons. They found that students were more actively engaged and had higher levels of mastery motivation when the teachers provided challenging activities, were responsive to students' needs and interests, supported peer relations, and emphasized the intrinsic value of learning. The progressive "fit" between students' motivation and teachers' instruction reflects the mutual readings of the classroom by teacher and students. Students are also progressively better able to understand teachers' intentions and assignments although there are occasionally mismatches that undermine learning (Winne & Marx, 1982).

Finally, it is clear that students learn a great deal about assessment practices in school. Until Grade 3 or 4, students remain optimistic and enthusiastic about all kinds of classroom assessments of learning. By eighth grade, however, many students discriminate the value of teacher-made tests from standardized testing. They often become suspicious about the validity and usefulness of standardized achievement testing (Paris, Lawton, Turner, & Roth, 1991). The developing disillusionment about assessment practices can reinforce students' negative views of their academic performance and of school. When high-stakes testing is perceived as a threat to students' self-perceptions of ability, they may undermine the results by cheating or trying half-heartedly. Such practices sabotage the validity of the test and prohibit attributions of low ability based on the test scores.

Children's theories about school include many specific concepts about what they are required to do and why the tasks are important. Their reasons for working hard in school are often tied to their social cognitions about other people. There-

fore, young children try hard because effort is regarded as virtuous, praised by teachers, and respected by peers. Older children have more complex ideas about effort that may lead them to regard high effort as risky. In a similar vein, children may avoid using strategies that appear too effortful or too elementary because of the reflections they cast on students' attributions of ability. Thus, theories about education are guided by defensiveness to avoid failure and threats to self-worth as much as they are guided by achievement goals and demonstrations of competence (Covington, 1992).

## Integration of Skill and Will in Self-Regulated Learning

As children build theories about schooling, they act according to their beliefs. It is the integration of beliefs, strategies, control, and self-perceptions that result in coherent self-regulated learning (Zimmerman, 1989). For example, Anderson, Stevens, Prawat, and Nickerson (1988) observed children in third- and fourth-grade classrooms to examine how teaching practices led to different patterns of self-regulation. They found:

When teachers explicitly structure information about the task environment that focuses students' attention on predictable and sensible relationships, they are contributing to students' knowledge about contingencies and, thus, their sense of what controls outcomes. Once knowledge of control is established, then it is necessary for teachers to provide the expectations and opportunities for students to practice self-regulation of task performance. Thus, once students know that task-performance outcomes have reasonable explanations, they can learn that they themselves are important causal influences (i.e., they begin to develop an internal locus of control). When practice in self-regulation is successful (which requires skillful selection and presentation of tasks by the teacher), students see that they are indeed the cause of successful performance and then self-esteem may increase. (p. 294)

It is the link between students' theories and teachers' practices that leads to particular actions. Consider what it takes for students to become strategic problem solvers and independent learners. They must acquire the cognitive resources and the motivational dispositions to plan, evaluate, monitor, and revise their actions systematically as they learn. This orientation is not taught by didactic methods, according to Duffy (1993). He has examined how teachers and students react to instruction that focuses on cognitive strategies for reading and surmises that strategy instruction requires teachers to help students build conceptual models of strategic problem solving using metacognitive dialogues and flexible instruction. It is the conceptual model, or theory of the tasks and strategies, that allows students to transfer tactics across problems and situations.

Nicholls (1992) argues that children create many idiosyncratic theories about school but that two general theories reflect their task or ego orientations in school. Students who develop a theory that is task oriented focus on mastery and personal effort, whereas those who hold ego-oriented theories focus on social comparison of abilities. According to Nicholls,

From grade two and up (and probably before then), it is possible to identify ego-oriented students who, more than those low in ego-orientation, see high ability (as they construe it) as necessary for academic success. At any developmental level, the important individual differences in theories about school work are differences in *use* of concepts such as ability, not in the *nature* of the concepts students have available. At all ages, ego-oriented students give their concepts of ability a major role in their interpretations of academic outcomes, whereas task-oriented students rely more on concepts of collaboration and understanding. (p. 274)

Thus, self-regulation is the consequence of clear understanding of teachers' practices and a motivational orientation in school. These dispositions and concepts of students lead them to invest effort and make choices differentially, and thus they are self-regulated to maximize their feelings of confidence and satisfaction. Self-regulation requires personal will power, or volition, which is manifested in strategies that protect a commitment to selected goals (Corno, 1989). This view of academic motivation emphasizes the intrinsic motivation and self-determinism of students (Deci, Vallerand, Pelletier, & Ryan, 1991). Intrinsic motivation includes students' persistence and effort for the enjoyment of the task itself. Intrinsic motivation is enhanced when students have choices, challenges, and collaborative learning, and when the consequences of their performance increase students' feelings of self-efficacy (Paris & Turner, 1994). In one sense, intrinsic motivation is a complex, positive theory of action in the classroom that students hold about themselves and their task engagement in school.

As they progress through elementary school, students acquire more effective learning strategies for taking tests, completing homework, filling out worksheets, writing reports, conducting research, and collaborating with others. They become "good strategy users" while simultaneously developing tactics for negotiating daily activities in the classroom. These strategies integrate cognitive and motivational tactics. It is the fusing of "skill and will" that is at the heart of self-regulated learning (McCombs & Marzano, 1990; Paris & Cross, 1983). This means that children's performance in school cannot be analyzed simply as a set of strategies, plans, goals, or attributions, because such analyses are incomplete. A more thorough understanding about why students act in particular ways is gained if we examine the concepts, beliefs, and theories that they hold and chart the ways that their theories change with educational experiences.

## CONCLUSIONS

Schools provide the first and most important transition for children from the shelter of their families to the larger social world of work and cooperation. Around the world, children develop many of their lifelong skills and motivational orientations in school. Therefore, educational psychology has a fundamental role to play in conducting research on young children's development and schooling and in establishing policies that enhance educational practices. We have discussed the large variability in preschool experiences and entry into formal schooling around the world. The policies regarding school entry and early retention need to be reexamined in light of educational research. Many children, especially those who are economically and socially disadvantaged, start their educational careers behind other children and many never catch up. Compensatory programs and educational innovations are needed to provide full opportunities for all children to succeed in school.

In addition to a good start, children need the sustained resources of teachers and parents throughout elementary and middle school to acquire effective cognitive strategies and motivational orientations to school. Although we described many examples of children's literacy, similar examples could be drawn from children's mathematical and scientific reasoning. In all subject areas, it is important to provide authentic and challenging activities for teaching and assessing students' knowledge so that they construct appropriate theories about education and positive theories about their own self-efficacy. The foundation provided by elementary education is crucial for the continued development of children. Children's academic self-perceptions and their theories about education are formed during childhood and have long-lasting consequences. Self-regulated students become productive citizens who value education and foster learning among others because the lessons they learn on their developmental journeys of becoming students are passed on from one generation to the next.

## *References*

Adams, M. J. (1990). *Beginning to read: Thinking and learning about print*. Cambridge, MA: MIT Press.

Alexander, K. L., & Entwisle, D. R. (1988). Achievement in the first 2 years of school: Patterns and processes. *Monographs of the Society for Research in Child Development, 53*(2, Serial No. 218).

Ames, C., & Ames, R. (1984). Goal structures and motivation. *Elementary School Journal, 85*, 39–52.

Ames, C., & Archer, J. (1988). Achievement goals in the classroom: Students' learning strategies and motivation processes. *Journal of Educational Psychology, 80*, 260–267.

Anderman, E. M., & Maehr, M. L. (1994). Motivation and schooling in the middle grades. *Review of Educational Research, 64*, 287–309.

Anderson, L. M., Stevens, D. D., Prawat, R. S., & Nickerson, J. (1988). Classroom task environments and students' task-related beliefs. *Elementary School Journal, 88*, 281–295.

Anderson, R. C., Wilson, P. T., & Fielding, L. G. (1987). Growth in reading and how children spend their time outside of school. *Reading Research Quarterly, 23*, 285–303.

Angell, D. E. M. (1989, September 13). 42.7% of mothers at Hutzel used drugs, study shows. *Detroit News*, p. 1.

Ashman, A., & Conway, R. (1993). *Using cognitive methods in the classroom*. London: Routledge.

Austin, G., DeVries, A., Thirion, A., & Stukat, K. (1975). Early childhood education in three countries. *International Journal of Early Childhood, 7*, 157–165.

Baker, L. (1984). Spontaneous versus instructed use of multiple standards for evaluating comprehension: Effects of age, reading proficiency, and type of standard. *Journal of Experimental Child Psychology, 38*, 289–311.

Baranova, T. I., & Rozyeva, N. S. (1985). From the history of the experimental teaching of six-year-old children in the USSR. *Soviet Education, 22*, 38.

Barth, J. M., & Parke, R. D. (1993). Parent-child relationship influences on children's transition to school. *Merrill-Palmer Quarterly, 39,* 173–195.

Bear, G. G., & Modlin, P. D. (1987). Gesell's developmental testing: What purpose does it serve? *Psychology in the Schools, 24,* 40–44.

Bell, M. (1972). *A study of the readiness room in a small school district in suburban Detroit, Michigan.* Unpublished doctoral dissertation, Wayne State University.

Beller, E. K. (1973). Research on organized programs of early education. In R. Travers (Ed.), *Second handbook of research on teaching* (pp. 530–600). Chicago: Rand McNally.

Berrueta-Clement, J. R., Schweinhart, L., Barnett, W., Epstein, A., & Weikart, D. (1984). *Changed lives: The effects of the Perry preschool program on youths through age 19.* Ypsilanti, MI: High/Scope Educational Research Foundation.

Blumenfeld, P. C., Pintrich, P., Meece, J., & Wessels, K. (1982). The formation and role of self-perceptions of ability in elementary classrooms. *Elementary School Journal, 82,* 401–420.

Blumenfeld, P. C., Soloway, E., Marx, R. W., Krajcik, J. S., Guzdial, M., & Palincsar, A. S. (1991). Motivating project-based learning. *Educational Psychologist, 26,* 369–398.

Bondy, E. (1990). Seeing it their way: What children's definitions of reading tell us about improving teacher education. *Journal of Teacher Education, 41,* 33–45.

Borkowski, J., Carr, M., Rellinger, E., & Pressley, M. (1990). Self-regulated cognition: Interdependence of metacognition, attributions, and self-esteem. In B. F. Jones & L. Idol (Eds.), *Dimensions of thinking and cognitive instruction* (pp. 53–92). Hillsdale, NJ: Lawrence Erlbaum Associates.

Boyer, E. (1991). *Ready to learn: A mandate for the nation.* Princeton: Carnegie Foundation for the Advancement of Learning.

Bradley, L., & Bryant, P. (1983). Categorizing sounds and learning to read: A causal connection. *Nature, 301,* 419–424.

Brady, S., & Shankweiler, D. (Eds.). (1991). *Phonological processes in literacy.* Hillsdale, NJ: Lawrence Erlbaum Associates.

Brand, H. J., & Welch, K. (1989). Cognitive and social-emotional development of children in different preschool environments. *Psychological Reports, 65,* 480–482.

Brooks, J. G., & Brooks, M. G. (1993). *The case for constructivist classrooms.* Alexandria, VA: Association for Supervision and Curriculum Development.

Brown, A., Bransford, J., Ferrara, R., & Campione, J. (1983). Learning, remembering, and understanding. In J. H. Flavell & E. M. Markman (Eds.), *Carmichael's manual of child psychology* (Vol. 1, pp. 77–166). New York: Wiley.

Brown, A., & Day, J. (1983). Macrorules for summarizing text: The development of expertise. *Journal of Verbal Learning and Verbal Behavior, 22,* 1–14.

Brown, J. S., Collins, A., & Duguid, P. (1989). Situated cognition and the culture of learning. *Educational Researcher, 18,* 32–42.

Bruck, M., & Treiman, R. (1990). Phonological awareness and spelling in normal children and dyslexics: The case of initial consonant clusters. *Journal of Experimental Child Psychology, 50,* 156–178.

Bruner, J. (1961). *The process of education.* Cambridge, MA: Harvard University Press.

Bryant, P., & Impey, L. (1986). The similarities between normal readers and developmental and acquired dyslexics. *Cognition, 24,* 121–137.

Burts, D. C., Hart, C. H., Charlesworth, R., & Kirk, L. (1990). A comparison of frequencies of stress behaviors observed in kindergarten children in classrooms with developmentally appropriate versus developmentally inappropriate instructional practices. *Early Childhood Research Quarterly, 5,* 407–423.

Cahan, E. D. (1992). John Dewey and human development. *Developmental Psychology, 28,* 205–214.

Cairns, R. B., & Ornstein, P. A. (1979). Developmental psychology. In E. Hearst (Ed.), *The first century of experimental psychology* (pp. 459–512). Hillsdale, NJ: Lawrence Erlbaum Associates.

Calfee, R., & Hiebert, E. (1990). Classroom assessment of reading. In R. Barr, M. Kamil, P. Mosenthal, & P. D. Pearson (Eds.), *Handbook of reading research* (2nd ed., pp. 281–309). New York: Longman.

*Carnegie Foundation Report* (1993). New York: Carnegie Corporation of New York.

Carstens, A. (1985). Retention and social promotion for the exceptional child. *School Psychology Review, 14,* 48–63.

Case, R. (1992). *The mind's staircase: Exploring the conceptual underpinnings of children's thought and knowledge.* Hillsdale, NJ: Lawrence Erlbaum Associates.

Case, R. (1993). Theories of learning and theories of development. *Educational Psychologist, 28,* 219–233.

Catts, H. W. (1991). Early identification of reading disabilities. *Topics in Language Disorders, 12,* 1–16.

Children's Defense Fund (1990). *Children 1990: A report card, briefing book, and action primer.* Washington, DC: Children's Defense Fund.

Cicerelli, V. G. (1969). *The impact of Head Start: An evaluation of the effects of Head Start on children's cognitive and affective development.* Report presented to the Office of Economic Opportunity, No. PB-184-328. Washington, DC: Westinghouse Learning Corporation.

Clark, R. M. (1983). *Family life and school achievement: Why poor black children succeed or fail.* Chicago: University of Chicago Press.

Clay, M. M. (1979). *The early detection of reading difficulties.* Auckland, NZ: Heinemann.

Cognition and Technology Group at Vanderbilt, The. (1990). Anchored instruction and its relationship to situated cognition. *Educational Researcher, 19,* 2–10.

Comer, J. P. (1989). Poverty, family, and the black experience. In G. Miller (Ed.), *Giving children a chance: The case for more effective national policies* (pp. 109–130). Washington, DC: Center for National Policy Press.

Committee for Economic Development (1988). *Children in need: Investment strategies for the educationally disadvantaged.* New York: Committee for Economic Development.

Consortium for Longitudinal Studies (Ed.). (1983). *As the twig is bent: Lasting effects of preschool programs.* Hillsdale, NJ: Lawrence Erlbaum Associates.

Corno, L. (1986). The metacognitive control components of self-regulated learning. *Contemporary Educational Psychology, 11,* 333–346.

Corno, L. (1989). Self-regulated learning: A volitional analysis. In B. J. Zimmerman & D. H. Schunk (Eds.), *Self-regulated learning and academic achievement* (pp. 111–141). New York: Springer.

Corno, L. (1992). Encouraging students to take responsibility for learning and performance. *Elementary School Journal, 93,* 69–83.

Covington, M. C. (1992). *Making the grade.* Cambridge, England: Cambridge University Press.

Cunningham, A. E. (1990). Explicit versus implicit instruction in phonemic awareness. *Journal of Experimental Child Psychology, 50,* 429–444.

Cunningham, A. E. (1993). Eeny, meeny, miny, moe: Testing policy and practice in early childhood education. In B. R. Gifford (Ed.), *Policy perspectives on educational testing* (pp. 229–294). Boston: Kluwer.

Cunningham, A. E., & Stanovich, K. E. (1990). Assessing print exposure and orthographic processing skill in children: A quick measure of reading experience. *Journal of Educational Psychology, 82,* 733–740.

Cunningham, A. E., & Stanovich, K. E. (1992). Tracking the unique effects of print exposure: Associations with vocabulary, general knowledge, and spelling. *Journal of Educational Psychology, 83,* 264–274.

Cunningham, A. E., & Stanovich, K. E. (1993). Children's literacy environments and early word recognition subskills. *Reading and Writing: An Interdisciplinary Journal, 5,* 193–204.

Cunningham, A. E., Stanovich, K. E., & West, R. F. (1994). Literacy environment and the development of children's cognitive skills. In E. M. H. Assink (Ed.), *Literacy Acquisition and Social Context* (pp. 70–90). London: Harvester Wheatsheaf.

Dahlof, U. S. (1971). *Ability grouping, content validity, and curriculum process analysis.* New York: Teachers College Press.

Deci, E. L., Vallerand, R. J., Pelletier, L. G., & Ryan, R. M. (1991). Motivation and education: The self-determination perspective. *Educational Psychologist, 26,* 325–346.

Dewey, J. (1913). Reasoning in early childhood. In J. A. Boydston (Ed.), *The middle works of John Dewey, 1899–1924* (Vol. 7, pp. 369–376). Carbondale, IL: Southern Illinois University Press.

Diamond, G. H. (1983). The birthdate effect: A maturational effect. *Journal of Learning Disabilities, 16,* 161–164.

DiPasquale, G., Moule, A., & Flewelling, R. (1980). The birthdate effect. *Journal of Learning Disabilities, 13,* 4–8.

Donofrio, A. F. (1977). Grade repetition: Therapy of choice. *Journal of Learning Disabilities, 10,* 28–30.

Doyle, W. (1983). Academic work. *Review of Educational Research, 53,* 159–200.

Duffy, G. G. (1993). Rethinking strategy instruction: Four teachers' development and their low achievers' understanding. *Elementary School Journal, 93,* 231–247.

Duffy, G., Roehler, L., Sivan, E., Rackliffe, G., Book, C., Meloth, M., Vavrus, L., Wesselman, R., Putnam, J., & Bassiri, D. (1987). Effects of explaining the reasoning associated with using strategies. *Reading Research Quarterly, 22,* 347–368.

Dweck, C., & Bempechat, J. (1983). Children's theories of intelligence: Consequences for learning. In S. Paris, G. Olson, & H. Stevenson (Eds.), *Learning and motivation in the classroom* (pp. 239–256). Hillsdale, NJ: Lawrence Erlbaum Associates.

Dyson, A. (1983). The role of oral language in early writing. *Research in the Teaching of English, 17,* 1–30.

Edwards, P. A. (1989). Supporting low SES mothers' attempts to provide scaffolding for book reading. In J. B. Allen & J. M. Mason (Eds.), *Risk makers, risk takers, risk breakers: Reducing the risks for young literacy learners* (pp. 220–250). Portsmouth, NH: Heinemann Educational Books.

Elkind, D. (1987). *Miseducation: Preschoolers at risk.* New York: Knopf.

Entwisle, D. R., Alexander, K. L., Cadigan, D., & Pallas, A. M. (1987). Kindergarten experience: Cognitive effects or socialization? *American Educational Research Journal, 24,* 337–364.

Entwisle, D. R., Alexander, K. L., Pallas, A. M., & Cadigan, D. (1987). The emergent academic self-image of first-graders: Its response to social structure. *Child Development, 58,* 1190–1206.

Eschel, Y., & Klein, A. (1978). The effects of integration and open education on mathematics achievement in the early grades in Israel. *American Educational Research Journal, 15,* 319–323.

Fein, G., & Schwartz, P. (1982). Developmental theories in early education. In B. Spodek (Ed.), *Handbook of research in early childhood education* (pp. 86–103). New York: Free Press.

Feitelson, D. (1987). Reconsidering the effects of school and home for literacy in a multicultural cross language context: The case of Israel. In D. A. Wagner (Ed.), *The future of literacy in a changing world* (pp. 174–185). Oxford: Pergamon Press.

Ferreiro, E. (1985). Literacy development: A psychogenetic perspective. In D. Olson, N. Torrance, & A. Hildyard (Eds.), *Literacy, language, and learning* (pp. 217–228). Cambridge, England: Cambridge University Press.

Ferreiro, E., & Teberosky, A. (1982). *Literacy before schooling.* Exeter, NH: Heinemann.

Fischer, K. W. (1980). A theory of cognitive development: The control and construction of hierarchies of skills. *Psychological Review, 87,* 477–531.

Fitzgerald, J., Spiegel, D. L., & Cunningham, J. W. (1991). The relationship between parental literacy level and perceptions of emergent literacy. *Journal of Reading Behavior, 23,* 191–213.

Fitzsimmons, S. J., Cheever, J., Leonard, E., & Macunovich, D. (1969). School failures: Now and tomorrow. *Developmental Psychology, 1,* 134–146.

Flower, L., & Hayes, R. (1981). A cognitive process theory of writing. *College Composition and Communication, 32,* 365–388.

Franklin, M. B., & Biber, B. (1977). Psychological perspectives and early childhood education: Some relations between theory and practice. In L. Katz (Ed.), *Current topics in early childhood education* (Vol. 1, pp. 1–32). Norwood, NJ: Ablex.

Freebody, P., & Byrne, B. (1988). Word-reading strategies in elementary school children: Relations to comprehension, reading time, and phonemic awareness. *Reading Research Quarterly, 23,* 441–453.

Garcia-Coll, C. (1990). Developmental outcome of minority infants: A process-oriented look at our beginnings. *Child Development, 61,* 270–289.

Garner, R. (1987). *Metacognition and reading comprehension.* Norwood, NJ: Ablex.

Garner, R. (1990). When children and adults do not use learning strategies: Toward a theory of settings. *Review of Educational Research, 60,* 517–529.

Garwood, S., Hartman, A., Philips, D., & Zigler, E. (1989). As the pendulum swings: Federal agency programs for children. *American Psychologist, 44,* 434–440.

Gaskins, I. W., Anderson, R. C., Pressley, M., Cunicelli, E. A., & Satlow, E. (1993). Six teachers' dialogues during cognitive process instruction. *Elementary School Journal, 93,* 277–304.

Goodman, K. (1986). *What's whole in whole language?* Portsmouth, NH: Heinemann.

Gottfried, A. E., Fleming, J. S., & Gottfried, A. W. (1994). Role of parental motivational practices in children's academic intrinsic motivation and achievement. *Journal of Educational Psychology, 86,* 104–113.

Gotts, E. E. (1980). Long-term effects of a home oriented preschool program. *Childhood Education, 56,* 228–234.

Gredler, G. R. (1980). The birthdate effect: Fact or artifact? *Journal of Learning Disabilities, 13,* 239–242.

Gredler, G. R. (1984). Transition classes: A viable alternative for the at-risk child? *Psychology in the Schools, 21,* 463–470.

Hadermann, K. F. (1976). Ability grouping: Its effect on learners. *National Association of Secondary School Principals Bulletin, 60,* 85–89.

Haines, J., Ames, L. B., & Gillespie, C. (1980). *The Gesell preschool test manual.* Lumberville, PA: Modern Learning Press.

Halford, G. S. (1982). *The development of thought.* Hillsdale, NJ: Lawrence Erlbaum Associates.

Halliday, M. A. K. (1975). *Learning how to mean.* New York: Elsevier North-Holland.

Harris, K. R., & Graham, S. (1992). *Helping young writers master the craft: Strategy instruction and self-regulation in the writing process.* Cambridge, MA: Brookline Books.

Hart, R. H. (1967). The effectiveness of an approach to the problem of varying abilities in teaching reading. In M. P. Franklin (Ed.), *School organization: Theory and practice* (pp. 443–448). Chicago: Rand McNally.

Harter, S. (1983). Developmental perspectives on the self-system. In P. Mussen (Ed.), *Handbook of child psychology: Vol. 4. Socialization, personality, and social development* (pp. 275–385). New York: Wiley.

Heath, S. B. (1983). *Ways with words: Language, life, and work in communities and classrooms.* Cambridge, England: Cambridge University Press.

Hess, R. D., & Holloway, S. D. (1984). Family and school as educational institutions. In R. D. Parke (Ed.), *Review of child development research* (Vol. 7, pp. 179–222). Chicago: University of Chicago Press.

Hess, R. D., Holloway, S. D., Dickson, W., & Price, G. (1984). Maternal variables as predictors of children's school readiness and later achievement in vocabulary and mathematics in sixth grade. *Child Development, 55,* 1902–1912.

Hetherington, E. M., Stanley-Hagen, M. S., & Anderson, E. R. (1989). Marital transition: A child's perspective. *American Psychologist, 44,* 2, 303–312.

Hewison, J., & Tizard, J. (1980). Parental involvement and reading attainment. *British Journal of Educational Psychology, 50,* 209–215.

Hibpshman, T. (1989). *An explanatory model for family literacy programs.* Frankfort, KY: Kentucky Department of Education.

Hiebert, E. H. (1981). Developmental patterns and interrelationships of preschool children's print awareness. *Reading Research Quarterly, 16,* 236–260.

Hilgard, E. R. (1987). *Psychology in America: A historical survey.* San Diego: Harcourt Brace Jovanovich.

Holliday, B. G. (1985). Towards a model of teacher-child transactional processes affecting black children's academic achievement. In M. B. Spencer, G. K. Brookins, & W. R. Allen (Eds.), *Beginnings: The social and affective development of black children* (pp. 117–131). Hillsdale, NJ: Lawrence Erlbaum Associates.

Holmes, C., & Matthews, K. (1984). The effects of nonpromotion of elementary and junior high school pupils: A meta-analysis. *Review of Educational Research, 54,* 225–236.

Howard, M. A. P., & Anderson, R. J. (1978). Early identification of potential school dropouts: A literature review. *Child Welfare, 4,* 221–231.

Jackson, G. B. (1975). The research evidence on the effects of grade retention. *Review of Educational Research, 45,* 613–635.

Johns, J. (1984). Students' perceptions of reading: Insights from research and pedagogical implications. In J. Downing & R. Valtin (Eds.), *Language awareness and learning to read* (pp. 57–77). New York: Springer.

Johnston, P., & Afflerbach, P. (1985). The process of constructing main ideas from text. *Cognition & Instruction, 2,* 207–232.

Johnston, P., & Winograd, P. (1985). Passive failure in reading. *Journal of Reading Behavior, 17,* 279–301.

Juel, C. (1988). Learning to read and write: A longitudinal study of 54 children from first through fourth grades. *Journal of Educational Psychology, 4,* 437–447.

Kamii, C. (1985). Leading primary education toward excellence: Beyond worksheets and drill. *Young Children, 40,* 3–9.

Karabenick, S. A., & Knapp, J. R. (1991). Relationship of academic help-seeking to the use of learning strategies and other instrumental achievement behavior in college students. *Journal of Educational Psychology, 83,* 221–230.

Karnes, M. B., Schwedel, A. M., & Williams, M. B. (1983). A comparison of five approaches for educating young children from low-income homes. In the Consortium for Longitudinal Studies (Eds.), *As the twig is bent . . . Lasting effects of preschool programs* (pp. 133–170). Hillsdale, NJ: Lawrence Erlbaum Associates.

Katz, L. G. (1987). Early education: What should young children be doing? In S. L. Kagan & E. F. Zigler (Eds.), *Early schooling: The national debate* (pp. 151–167). New Haven: Yale University Press.

Kaufman, N. L. (1985). Review of the McCarthy Screening Test. In O. K. Buros (Ed.), *The eighth mental measurement yearbook.* Highland Park, NJ: Gryphon Press.

Kirp, D. L. (1974). Student classification, public policy, and the courts. *Harvard Educational Review, 44,* 7–52.

Kistener, J., Osborne, M., & LeVerrier, J. (1988). Causal attributions of learning-disabled children: Developmental patterns and relation to academic progress. *Journal of Educational Psychology, 80,* 82–89.

Lally, J. R., Mangione, P. L., & Honig, A. S. (1988). The Syracuse University Family Development Research Program: Long-range impact of an early intervention with low-income children and their families. In D. R. Powell (Ed.), *Parent education as early childhood intervention: Emerging directions in theory, research, and practice* (pp. 79–104). Norwood, NJ: Ablex.

Langer, P., Kalk, J. M., & Searls, D. T. (1984). Age of admission and trends in achievement: A comparison of blacks and caucasians. *American Educational Research Journal, 21,* 61–78.

Layzer, J. I., Goodson, B. D., & Layzer, J. A. (1990). *Evaluation of Project Giant Step. Year two report: The study of program effects.* Executive summary. Cambridge, MA: Abt Associates.

Lave, J., & Wenger, E. (1991). *Situated learning: Legitimate peripheral participation.* Cambridge, England: Cambridge University Press.

Lefkowitz, L. J. (1972). Ability grouping: Defacto segregation in the classroom. *Clearing House, 46,* 293–297.

Levenstein, P. (1988). *Messages from home: The mother-child home program and the prevention of school disadvantage.* Columbus: Ohio State University Press.

Liberman, I. Y. (1973). Segmentation of the spoken word and reading acquisition. *Bulletin of the Orton Society, 23,* 65–77.

Lloyd, D. N. (1978). Prediction of school failure from third-grade data. *Educational and Psychological Measurement, 38,* 1193–1200.

Loeber, R. (1985). Patterns and development of antisocial child behavior. *Annals of Child Development, 2,* 77–116.

Lomax, R. G., & McGee, L. M. (1987). Young children's concepts about print and reading: Toward a model of word reading acquisition. *Reading Research Quarterly, 22,* 237–256.

Lundberg, I., Frost, J., & Petersen, O. P. (1988). Effects of an extensive program for stimulating phonological awareness in preschool children. *Reading Research Quarterly, 23,* 263–284.

Maclean, M., Bryant, P., & Bradley, L. (1988). Rhymes, nursery rhymes, and reading in early childhood. In K. E. Stanovich (Ed.), *Children's reading and the development of phonological awareness* (pp. 11–38). Detroit: Wayne State University Press.

Madaus, G. F., & Tan, A. G. A. (1993). The growth of assessment. In G. Cawelti (Ed.), *Challenges and achievements of American education* (pp. 53–79). Alexandria, VA: Association for Supervision and Curriculum Development.

Madden, N. A., & Slavin, R. E. (1983). Mainstreaming students with mild handicaps: Academic and social outcomes. *Review of Educational Research, 53,* 519–569.

Markman, E. M., & Gorin, L. (1981). Children's ability to adjust their standards for evaluating comprehension. *Journal of Educational Psychology, 73,* 320–325.

Markus, H. R., & Nurius, P. (1986). Possible selves. *American Psychologist, 41,* 954–969.

Marsh, H. (1986). Verbal and math self-concepts: An internal/external frame of reference model. *American Educational Research Journal, 23,* 129–149.

Mason, J., & Allen, J. (1986). A review of emergent literacy with implications for research and practice in reading. In E. Rothkopf (Ed.), *Review of research in education* (Vol. 13, pp. 3–47). Washington, DC: American Educational Research Association.

McAdoo, H. P. (Ed.). (1988). *Black families.* Newbury Park, CA: Sage.

McCombs, B. L., & Marzano, R. J. (1990). Putting the self in self-regulated learning: The self as agent in integrating skill and will. *Educational Psychologist, 25,* 51–69.

McKey, R. H., Condelli, L., Ganson, H., Barrett, B., McConkey, C., & Plantz, M. (1985). *The impact of Head Start on children, family, and communities: Final Report of the Head Start Evaluation, Synthesis, and Utilization Project* (DHHS Publication No. OHDS 85-31193). Washington, DC: U.S. Government Printing Office.

McLoyd, V. C. (1990). Minority children: Introduction to special issue. *Child Development, 61,* 2, 263–266.

Meece, J. L., Blumenfeld, P. C., & Puro, P. (1989). A motivational analysis of elementary science learning environments. In M. Matyas, K. Tobin, & B. Fraser (Eds.), *Looking into windows: Qualitative research in science education* (pp. 13–23). Washington, DC: American Association for the Advancement of Science.

Meisels, S. (1988). Developmental screening in early childhood: The interaction of research and social policy. *Annual Review of Public Health, 21,* 527–550.

Miller, L. B., & Bizzell, R. P. (1983). Long-term effects of four preschool programs: Sixth, seventh, and eighth grades. *Child Development, 54,* 727–741.

Morphett, M. V., & Washburne, C. (1931). When should children begin to read? *Elementary School Journal, 31,* 496–503.

Morrison, F. J., Griffith, E. M., & Williamson, G. L. (1993). Two strikes from the start: Individual differences in early literacy. Paper presented at the biennial meeting of the Society for Research in Child Development, New Orleans.

Myers, M., & Paris, S. G. (1978). Children's metacognitive knowledge about reading. *Journal of Educational Psychology, 70,* 680–690.

Nagalieri, J. A. (1985). Normal children's performance on the McCarthy Scales, Kaufman Assessment Battery, and Peabody Individual Achievement Test. *Journal of Psychoeducational Assessment, 3,* 123–129.

National Center for Children in Poverty. (1990). *Five million children: A statistical profile of our poorest young children.* New York: Columbia University School of Public Health.

National Center for Clinical Infant Programs. (1986). *Infants can't wait: The numbers.* Washington, DC: National Center for Clinical Infant Programs.

Nelson-Le Gall, S. (1985). Help-seeking behavior in learning. In E. W. Gordon (Ed.), *Review of research in education* (Vol. 12, pp. 55–90). Washington, DC: American Educational Research Association.

Nelson-Le Gall, S., & Gumerman, R. A. (1984). Children's perceptions of helpers and helper motivation. *Journal of Applied Developmental Psychology, 5,* 1–12.

Nelson-Le Gall, S., & Jones, E. (1990). Cognitive-motivational influences on the task-related help-seeking behavior of black children. *Child Development, 61,* 581–589.

Neuman, S. B. (1986). The home environment and fifth grade students' leisure reading. *Elementary School Journal, 86,* 334–343.

Newman, R. S. (1990). Children's help-seeking in the classroom: The role of motivational factors and attitudes. *Journal of Educational Psychology, 82,* 71–80.

Newman, R. S. (1994). Adaptive help seeking: A strategy of self-regulated learning. In D. Schunk & B. Zimmerman (Eds.), *Self-regulation of learning and performance: Issues and educational applications* (pp. 283–301). Hillsdale, NJ: Lawrence Erlbaum Associates.

Newman, R. S., & Goldin, L. (1990). Children's reluctance to seek help with schoolwork. *Journal of Educational Psychology, 82,* 92–100.

Newman, R. S., & Schwager, M. T. (1992). Student perceptions and academic help-seeking. In D. H. Schunk & J. L. Meece (Eds.), *Student perceptions in the classroom* (pp. 123–146). Hillsdale, NJ: Lawrence Erlbaum Associates.

Newman, R. S., & Schwager, M. T. (1993). Students' perceptions of the teacher and classmates in relation to reported help seeking in math class. *Elementary School Journal, 94,* 3–17.

Nicholls, J. G. (1989). *The competitive ethos and democratic education.* Cambridge, MA: Harvard University Press.

Nicholls, J. G. (1990). What is ability and why are we mindful of it? A developmental perspective. In R. J. Sternberg & J. Kolligan (Eds.), *Competence considered* (pp. 11–40). New Haven: Yale University Press.

Nicholls, J. G. (1992). Students as educational theorists. In D. Schunk & J. Meece (Eds.), *Student perceptions in the classroom* (pp. 267–286). Hillsdale, NJ: Lawrence Erlbaum Associates.

Oakes, J. (1981). A question of access: Tracking and curriculum differentiation in a national sample of English and mathematics classes. *A study of schooling.* Technical Report No. 24. Los Angeles: University of California.

Oakes, J. (1985). *Keeping track.* New Haven: Yale University Press.

Palincsar, A. S., & Brown, A. (1984). Reciprocal teaching of comprehension-fostering and comprehension-monitoring activities. *Cognition and Instruction, 1,* 117–175.

Paris, S. G. (1991). Assessment and remediation of metacognitive aspects of reading comprehension. *Topics in Language Disorders, 12,* 32–50.

Paris, S. G., & Ayres, L. R. (1994). *Becoming reflective students and teachers with portfolios and authentic assessment.* Washington, DC: American Psychological Association.

Paris, S. G., & Byrnes, J. P. (1989). The constructivist approach to self-regulation and learning in the classroom. In B. Zimmerman & D. Schunk (Eds.), *Self-regulated learning and academic achievement: Theory, research, and practice* (pp. 169–200). New York: Springer.

Paris, S. G., & Cross, D. R. (1983). Ordinary learning: Pragmatic connections among children's beliefs, motives, and actions. In J. Bisanz, G. Bisanz, & R. Kail (Eds.), *Learning in children* (pp. 137–169). New York: Springer.

Paris, S. G., Cross, D. R., & Lipson, M. Y. (1984). Informed strategies for learning: A program to improve children's reading awareness and comprehension. *Journal of Educational Psychology, 76,* 1239–1252.

Paris, S. G., Lawton, T. A., Turner, J. C., & Roth, J. L. (1991). A developmental perspective on standardized achievement testing. *Educational Researcher, 20,* 12–20.

Paris, S. G., Lipson, M. Y., & Wixson, K. (1983). Becoming a strategic reader. *Contemporary Educational Psychology, 8,* 293–316.

Paris, S. G., & Turner, J. T. (1994). Situated motivation. In P. Pintrich, C. Weinstein, & D. Brown (Eds.), *Student motivation, cognition, and learning: Essays in honor of Wilbert J. McKeachie.* Hillsdale, NJ: Lawrence Erlbaum Associates.

Paris, S. G., Wasik, B. A., & Turner, J. C. (1990). The development of strategic readers. In R. Barr, M. Kamil, P. Mosenthal, & P. D. Pearson (Eds.), *Handbook of reading research* (2nd ed., pp. 609–640). New York: Longman.

Paris, S. G., & Winograd, P. W. (1990). How metacognition can promote academic learning and instruction. In B. J. Jones & L. Idol (Eds.), *Dimensions of thinking and cognitive instruction* (pp. 15–51). Hillsdale, NJ: Lawrence Erlbaum Associates.

Paris, S. G., Wixson, K. K., & Palincsar, A. M. (1986). Instructional approaches to reading comprehension. In E. Rothkopf (Ed.), *Review of research in education* (pp. 91–128). Washington, DC: American Educational Research Association.

Perkins, D. N., & Simmons, R. (1988). Patterns of misunderstanding: An integrative model for science, math, and programming. *Review of Educational Research, 58,* 303–326.

Pfannensteil, J. C., & Seltzer, D. A. (1989). New parents as teachers: Evaluation of an early parent education program. *Early Childhood Research Quarterly, 4,* 1–18.

Phillips, D. A., & Zimmerman, M. (1990). The developmental course of perceived competence and incompetence among competent children. In R. J. Sternberg & J. Kolligian (Eds.), *Competence considered* (pp. 41–66). New Haven: Yale University Press.

Pintrich, P. R., & De Groot, E. V. (1990). Motivational and self-regulated learning components of classroom academic performance. *Journal of Educational Psychology, 82,* 33–40.

Plummer, D. L., Lineberger, M. H., & Graziano, W. G. (1986). The academic and social consequences of grade retention: A convergent analysis. In L. G. Katz (Ed.), *Current topics in early childhood education* (Vol. 6, pp. 224–252). Norwood, NJ: Ablex.

Pressley, M., Goodchild, R., Fleet, J., Zajchowski, R., & Evans, E. D. (1989). The challenges of classroom strategy instruction. *Elementary School Journal, 89,* 301–342.

Ramey, C. T., Bryant, D. M., & Suarez, T. M. (1984). Preschool compensatory education and modifiability of intelligence: A critical review. In D. Detterman (Ed.), *Current topics in human intelligence* (pp. 247–296). Norwood, NJ: Ablex.

Reed, S., & Sautter, R. C. (1990). Children of poverty: The status of 12 million young Americans. *Phi Delta Kappan, 71,* 10, 785–790.

Resnick, L., & Resnick, D. (1990). Tests as standards of achievement in school. In *The uses of standardized tests in American education* (pp. 63–80). Princeton: Educational Testing Service.

Reynolds, A. (1989). Early schooling of children at risk. Unpublished dissertation, University of Illinois at Chicago.

Rogoff, B. (1990). *Apprenticeship in thinking: Cognitive development in social context.* Oxford: Oxford University Press.

Rohrkemper, M., & Corno, L. (1988). Success and failure on classroom tasks: Adaptive learning and classroom teaching. *Elementary School Journal, 88,* 297–312.

Rose, J. S., Medway, F. J., Cantrell, V. L., & Marcus, S. H. (1983). A fresh look at the retention-promotion controversy. *Journal of School Psychology, 21,* 201–211.

Scardamalia, M., & Bereiter, C. (1986). Written composition. In M. Wittrock (Ed.), *Handbook of research on teaching* (3rd ed., pp. 778–803). New York: Macmillan.

Scribner, S., & Cole, M. (1981). *The psychology of literacy.* Cambridge, MA: Harvard University Press.

Schweinhart, L. J., Barnes, H. V., & Weikart, D. P. (1993). *Significant benefits: The High/Scope Perry Preschool Study through age 27.* Monographs of the High/Scope Educational Research Foundation, No. 10. Ypsilanti, MI: High/Scope Press.

Schweinhart, L. J., Weikart, D. P., & Larner, M. B. (1986). Consequences of three preschool curriculum models through age 15. *Early Childhood Research Quarterly, 1,* 15–45.

Scott, R. (1976). Home Start: Third-grade follow-up assessment of a family centered preschool enrichment program. *Psychology in the Schools, 13,* 435–438.

Shepard, L. A., & Smith, M. L. (1986). Synthesis of research on school readiness and kindergarten retention. *Educational Leadership, 44,* 78–86.

Shepard, L. A., & Smith, M. L. (1988). Escalating academic demand in kindergarten: Counterproductive policies. *Elementary School Journal, 89,* 135–146.

Siegal, D. F., & Hanson, R. A. (1991). Kindergarten educational policies: Separating myth from reality. *Early Education and Development, 2,* 5–30.

Siegler, R. S., & Jenkins, E. (1989). *How children discover new strategies.* Hillsdale, NJ: Lawrence Erlbaum Associates.

Skinner, E. A. (1985). Action, control judgments, and the structure of control experience. *Psychological Review, 92,* 39–58.

Slavin, R. (1983). *Cooperative learning.* New York: Longman.

Smith, M. L., & Shepard, L. A. (1987). What doesn't work: Explaining policies of retention in the early grades. *Phi Delta Kappan, 69,* 129–134.

Smuts, A. B., & Hagen, J. W. (1985). History and research in child development. *Monographs of the Society for Research in Child Development, 50*(4–5, Serial No. 211).

Snow, C. E. (1991). Theoretical basis for relationships between language and literacy in development. *Journal of Research in Childhood Education, 6,* 5–20.

Snow, C. E., & Dickinson, D. K. (1991). Some skills that aren't basic in a new conception of literacy. In A. Purves & T. Jennings (Eds.), *New conceptions of literacy* (pp. 179–191). Albany, NY: SUNY Press.

Snow, C. E., & Ninio, A. (1986). The contracts of literacy: What children learn from learning to read books. In W. H. Teale & E. Sulzby (Eds.), *Emergent literacy: Writing and reading* (pp. 116–138). Norwood, NJ: Ablex.

Speece, D. L., & Cooper, D. H. (1990). Ontogeny of school failure: Classification of first-grade children. *American Educational Research Journal, 27,* 119–140.

Spencer, M. B. (1990). Development of minority children. *Child Development, 61,* 270–289.

Stanovich, K. E. (1986). Matthew effects in reading: Some consequences of individual differences in the acquisition of literacy. *Reading Research Quarterly, 21,* 360–407.

Stanovich, K. E., & Cunningham, A. E. (1992). Studying the consequences of literacy within a literate society: The cognitive correlates of print exposure. *Memory and Cognition, 20,* 51–68.

Stanovich, K. E., Cunningham, A. E., & Feeman, D. J. (1984). Intelligence, cognitive skills, and early reading progress. *Reading Research Quarterly, 19,* 278–303.

Steinberg, L. (1987). Familial factors in delinquency: A developmental perspective. *Journal of Adolescent Research, 2,* 255–268.

Steipen, W., & Gallagher, S. (1993). Problem-based learning: As authentic as it gets. *Educational Leadership, 50,* 25–28.

Sternberg, R. S. (1988). *The triarchic mind: A new theory of human intelligence.* New York: Viking.

Stevenson, H. W. (1983). How children learn: The quest for a theory. In P. Mussen (Ed.), *Handbook of child psychology* (Vol. 1, pp. 213–236). New York: Wiley.

Stevenson, H. W., Chen, C., & Uttal, D. (1990). Beliefs and achievement: A study of black, white, and Hispanic children. *Child Development, 61,* 508–523.

Stevenson, H. W., & Stigler, J. (1992). *The learning gap.* New York: Summit Books.

Stipek, D. J. (1981). Children's perceptions of their own and their classmates' ability. *Journal of Educational Psychology, 73,* 404–410.

Stipek, D. J. (1993). *Motivation to learn: From theory to practice.* Boston: Allyn & Bacon.

Stipek, D. J., & Mac Iver, D. (1989). Developmental change in children's assessment of intellectual competence. *Child Development, 60,* 521–538.

Stipek, D. J., & Tannatt, L. M. (1984). Children's judgments of their own and their peers' academic competence. *Journal of Educational Psychology, 76,* 75–84.

Sulzby, E. (1986). Writing and reading: Signs of oral and written language organization in the young child. In W. H. Teale & E. Sulzby (Eds.), *Emergent literacy: Writing and reading* (pp. 50–89). Norwood, NJ: Ablex.

Sulzby, E. (1985). Children's emergent reading of favorite storybooks: A developmental analysis. *Reading Research Quarterly, 20,* 458–481.

Sulzby, E., & Teale, W. H. (1991). Emergent literacy. In R. Barr, M. L. Kamil, P. Mosenthal, & P. D. Pearson (Eds.), *Handbook of reading research* (Vol. 2, pp. 727–757). New York: Longman.

Takanishi, R., & DeLeon, P. H. (1994). A Head Start for the 21st century. *American Psychologist, 49,* 120–122.

Taylor, R. J. (1986). Receipt of support from family among black Americans: Demographic and familial differences. *Journal of Marriage and the Family, 48,* 67–77.

Teale, W. H. (1986). Home background and young children's literacy development. In W. H. Teale & E. Sulzby (Eds.), *Emergent literacy: Writing and reading* (pp. 173–206). Norwood, NJ: Ablex.

Teale, W. H., & Sulzby, E. (1986). *Emergent literacy: Writing and reading.* Norwood, NJ: Ablex.

Tharp, R. G., & Gallimore, R. (1988). *Rousing minds to life: Teaching, learning, and schooling in social context.* Cambridge, England: Cambridge University Press.

Treiman, R. (1983). The structure of spoken syllables: Evidence from novel word games. *Cognition, 15,* 49–74.

Treiman, R., & Baron, J. (1983). Phonemic-analysis training helps children benefit from spelling-sound rules. *Memory and Cognition, 11,* 382–389.

U.S. Bureau of the Census (1987). *Who's minding the kids?* Current Population Reports, Series P-70, No. 9. Washington, DC: Government Printing Office.

Valencia, S. W., Hiebert, E. H., & Afflerbach, P. P. (1994). *Authentic reading assessment: Practices and possibilities.* Newark, DE: International Reading Association.

Vellutino, F. R., & Scanlon, D. M. (1987). Phonological coding, phonological awareness, and reading ability: Evidence from longitudinal and experimental study. *Merrill Palmer Quarterly, 33,* 321–363.

Vygotsky, L. S. (1978). *Mind in society.* Cambridge, MA: Harvard University Press.

Wagner, R. K., & Torgesen, J. K. (1987). The nature of phonological processing and its causal role in the acquisition of reading skills. *Psychological Bulletin, 101,* 192–212.

Walberg, H. J., & Haertel, G. D. (1992). Educational psychology's first century. *Journal of Educational Psychology, 84,* 6–19.

Webb, N. M. (1985). Student interaction and learning in small groups: A research summary. In R. Slavin, S. Sharan, S. Kagan, R. Hertz-Lazarowitz, N. Webb, & R. Schmuck (Eds.), *Learning to cooperate, cooperating to learn* (pp. 147–172). New York: Plenum Press.

Weikart, D. P. (1989). Hard choices in early childhood care and education: A view to the future. *Young Children, 44,* 25–30.

Weiner, B. (1985). An attribution theory of achievement motivation and emotion. *Psychological Review, 92,* 548–573.

Weinstein, C., & Mayer, R. (1986). The teaching of learning strategies. In M. Wittrock (Ed.), *Handbook of research on teaching* (pp. 315–327). New York: Macmillan.

Weinstein, L. (1968–1969). School entrance age and adjustment. *Journal of School Psychology, 7,* 209–228.

Weinstein, R. (1984). Student perceptions of schooling. *Elementary School Journal, 83,* 287–312.

Weintraub, S., & Denney, P. T. (1965). What do beginning first graders say about reading? *Childhood Education, 41,* 326–327.

Wertsch, J. V. (1991). *Voice of the mind.* Cambridge, MA: Harvard University Press.

White, K. R., Taylor, M. J., & Moss, V. D. (1992). Does research support claims about benefits of involving parents in early intervention programs? *Review of Educational Research, 62,* 91–125.

Winne, P. H., & Marx, R. W. (1982). Students' and teachers' views of thinking processes involved in classroom learning. *Elementary School Journal, 82,* 493–518.

Winograd, P. N. (1984). Strategic difficulties in summarizing texts. *Reading Research Quarterly, 19,* 404–425.

Wolf, D., Bixby, J., Glenn, J., & Gardner, H. (1991). To use their minds well: Investigating new forms of student assessment. In G. Grant (Ed.), *Review of Research in Education, 17* (pp. 31–74). New York: American Educational Research Association.

Wong, B. Y. L. (1987). Metacognition and learning disabilities. *Learning Disability Quarterly, 10,* 189–195.

Wood, D., Bruner, J., & Ross, G. (1976). The role of tutoring in problem solving. *Journal of Child Psychology and Psychiatry, 17,* 89– 100.

Wood, C., Powell, S., & Knight, R. C. (1984). Predicting school readiness: The validity of developmental age. *Journal of Learning Disabilities, 17,* 8–11.

Wundt, W. (1907). *Outlines of psychology* (C. H. Judd, trans.). New York: Stechert.

Yopp, H. K. (1988). The validity and reliability of phonemic awareness tests. *Reading Research Quarterly, 23,* 169–177.

Zigler, E., & Muenchow, S. (1992). *Head Start: The inside story of America's most successful educational experiment.* New York: Basic Books.

Zigler, E., & Styfco, S. J. (1994). Head Start: Criticisms in a constructive context. *American Psychologist, 49,* 127–132.

Zigler, E., & Valentine, J. (Eds.). (1979). *Project Head Start: A legacy of the War on Poverty,* New York: Free Press.

Zimmerman, B. J. (1989). Models of self-regulated learning and academic achievement. In B. Zimmerman & D. Schunk (Eds.), *Self-regulated learning and academic achievement: Theory, research, and practice* (pp. 1–25). New York: Springer.

Zimmerman, B. J., & Martinez-Pons, M. (1986). Development of a structured interview for assessing student use of self-regulated learning strategies. *American Educational Research Journal, 23,* 614–628.

# DEVELOPMENT BETWEEN THE AGES

# OF 11 AND 25

## Allan Wigfield

UNIVERSITY OF MARYLAND, COLLEGE PARK

## Jacquelynne S. Eccles

UNIVERSITY OF MICHIGAN, ANN ARBOR

## Paul R. Pintrich

UNIVERSITY OF MICHIGAN, ANN ARBOR

This chapter discusses development across a fascinating part of the life span—early adolescence, adolescence, and young adulthood. The time span covered is one in which individuals experience many changes, including the biological changes associated with puberty and the social and educational changes resulting from transitions from junior high to high school, from high school to college or the work force, and from college to the work force. During this period individuals make many choices and have many experiences that can direct the course of the rest of their adult lives. These choices include, among others, whether or not to stay in school, what career or occupation to undertake, and whether or not to get married. Despite their obvious importance, until recently the adolescent and young adult periods did not receive as much attention as childhood in the developmental literature. This has changed during the last decade, however; evidence of that change includes the new Society for Research on Adolescence, new journals on adolescence, and increased interest in postsecondary education, as shown by the Office of Educational Research and Improvement's funding of a center on postsecondary education focused on learning and thinking.

In this chapter we attempt to convey the most important changes occurring during this part of life, focusing in particular on changes in characteristics related to adolescents' and young adults' school performance. We discuss changes in characteristics such as self-concept, motivation, cognition, and achievement, and some factors that influence changes in these characteristics. To convey these changes best, the chapter is organized chronologically and with a developmental focus, beginning with early adolescence and moving through the adolescent period to young adulthood.

In conceptualizing how development occurs, theorists have proposed different theoretical models that can be classified into two metatheoretical types, organismic and contextual. Each type relies on different assumptions and metaphors for the description of change and development (Lerner, 1986; Pepper, 1942; Pintrich, 1990). Organismic models use a metaphor that highlights the individual organism as it develops through its active construction and organization of the environment. Organismic models also tend to assume that development is characterized by an epigenetic pattern of change involving qualitative and discontinuous growth. According to such models, an individual's cognitive, social, or personal development at higher levels of development is distinctly different from that at lower levels, involving not just quantitatively more of some function or structure but qualitatively new functions, structures, or organizations. In addition, many, although not all, organismic models assume that there is a teleological end point or final stage

The research of Eccles, Wigfield, and their colleagues described in this chapter was supported by grants from the National Institute of Child Health and Human Development (HD17553 and HD31724) to Jacquelynne Eccles and a grant from the National Science Foundation (BNS-8510504) to Jacquelynne Eccles and Allan Wigfield. We thank all of our colleagues for their assistance in the studies reported herein. Special thanks go to David Reuman, Harriet Feldlaufer, Douglas Mac Iver, Dave Klingel, and Jan Jacobs as well as all of the teachers, school personnel, and students who agreed to participate in these studies. Paul R. Pintrich thanks his colleagues Teresa Garcia, Malcolm Lowther, Bill McKeachie, and Joan Stark for their helpful comments on an earlier draft of the section on late adolescence and young adulthood. All three authors also thank John Mergendoller for his review and constructive comments on the entire chapter.

of development (e.g., formal operations in Piagetian theory) that some individuals will reach over the course of their life (Lerner, 1986; Pintrich, 1990).

In contrast, contextual models use a basic metaphor of the "historical event" as the key organizer of development, thereby shifting the focus away from the individual to the context. Contextual models emphasize the nature of the individual's interactions with others in different situations and different environments over the life course as the main influence on development (Higgins & Parsons, 1983; Lerner, 1986; Pintrich, 1990). Although contextual models such as Vygotskian theory and different life-span theories focus on the importance of the contextual and situational demands on the individual, theorists working in those frameworks also argue that change is an active, constructive, and dialectical process among the multiple contextual determinants of change and the individual's personal construal of these determinants (Pintrich, 1990). Contextual models have been gaining greater prominence in both psychology and education.

We include these contextual models in this chapter in two ways. First, we highlight recent contextual theoretical models of the development of adolescents' and young adults' cognition and self-concepts; these models are a special focus in the section on later adolescent and young adult development. Second, we highlight different contexts of development that adolescents and young adults experience—the school, family, and peer group—and examine how each influences adolescent and young adult development. We focus on the important changes that occur in these contexts during this time period—the school transitions, the "distancing" in parent–child relations, and the emerging influence of the peer group during early and middle adolescence. Because this book is on educational psychology, the larger part of the discussion is devoted to the influence of school contexts on development. Peer group and family relations are discussed most extensively in the section on early and middle adolescence. We also consider how different developmental trajectories, both positive and negative, across this period can be understood. For instance, we discuss adolescents who drop out of school versus those who enroll and succeed in college. In each section we group differences in the characteristics we discuss, with a particular focus on gender and race differences.

Most of our own theoretical and empirical work has concerned adolescents' and young adults' achievement motivation, achievement beliefs and attitudes, the relation of these beliefs to student cognition and strategy use, and their influence on students' performance in school (e.g., Eccles, 1984a, 1984b; Eccles, Adler, & Meece, 1984; Eccles & Wigfield, 1985; Eccles et al., 1983; Meece, Wigfield, & Eccles, 1990; Pintrich, 1988, 1989; Pintrich & De Groot, 1990; Pintrich & Garcia, 1991; Wigfield & Eccles, 1992; Wigfield, Eccles, Mac Iver, Reuman, & Midgley, 1991). For this reason, our emphasis will be on research that has examined students' motivation and cognition and the relation of these factors to students' achievement, an emphasis that seems appropriate to a handbook on educational psychology. Because the research in these areas across the age span under consideration is voluminous, we have had to be selective in our review. Wherever possible we make suggestions about where readers can find more information on topics that they find to be of particular interest.

# DEVELOPMENT DURING EARLY AND MIDDLE ADOLESCENCE

During the early adolescent years children experience the biological and social changes associated with puberty. Most adolescents also make two important school transitions during early and middle adolescence: moving from elementary to middle school or junior high school, and then from middle school to high school. Different theorists (e.g., Blyth, Simmons, & Carlton-Ford, 1983; Eccles & Midgley, 1989; Hill & Lynch, 1983; M. Rosenberg, 1986; Simmons, Blyth, Van Cleaves, & Bush, 1979) have proposed that these changes have significant impact on a variety of developmental outcomes. Many children make these changes relatively easily. Others, however, have difficulty with one or another of these changes and as a result are at risk for a number of unfortunate developmental outcomes, such as dropping out of school, drug abuse, and delinquency. We begin our discussion of these changes with a consideration of the biological changes that occur during early adolescence.

## Biological Changes Associated With Puberty

The biological changes associated with puberty are the most dramatic ones that individuals experience during their lifetimes (outside of prenatal development), and these changes have often been used to characterize the early adolescent period as a period of "storm and stress" (Hall, 1904), during which there is a great deal of conflict between children, parents, and teachers (e.g., Blos, 1979; Freud, 1958). We have heard teachers (and parents) say, "If we could just lock kids up for those years, things would be fine!" While it is undeniable that major physical changes occur during early adolescence, many researchers now believe that the characterization of this time period as one of storm and stress is an overstatement (see, e.g., Brooks-Gunn & Reiter, 1990; Dornbusch, Petersen, & Hetherington, 1991). Yet recently Lerner, Entwisle, and Hauser (1994) again used the term "crisis" in their description of the state of contemporary American adolescents. Whether or not adolescents are in crisis, the biological changes they go through do have many influences on their behaviors and thoughts.

A complete review of those biological changes is beyond the scope of this chapter (see Adams, Montemayor, & Gullotta, 1989; Brooks-Gunn & Reiter, 1990; Buchanan, Eccles, & Becker, 1992; Malina, 1990; and Paikoff & Brooks-Gunn, 1990, for a thorough discussion of these changes). Briefly, during early adolescence children undergo a growth spurt and develop secondary sex characteristics as a result of activation of the hormones controlling these physical developments. The processes by which the hormones become activated are not well understood, but their effects are clear. One important point to note is that the timing of puberty is quite different for girls and boys. Girls enter puberty approximately 18 months before boys do, which means that during early adolescence girls and boys of the same chronological age are at quite different points in their physical development, a fact that is readily apparent to anyone observing in middle grades classrooms. There now is a large literature on the effects of early versus late maturity for boys and girls. There is some consensus that for boys, early maturity is advantageous, particularly with respect to their participation in sports activities (see Malina, 1990) and social standing in school (Petersen, 1985). For girls, early maturity can be problematic, since they will be the first to experience pubertal changes and thus can feel "out of sync" with their agemates (see Petersen, 1988; Simmons & Blyth, 1987). In fact, Simmons and her colleagues (1979) report that early-maturing girls have the lowest self-esteem and the most difficulty adjusting to school transitions, particularly the transition from elementary to junior high school. Like early-maturing girls, later maturing boys also may have some difficulties as a result of their physical development being out of synchrony with their agemates' development.

Magnusson and Stattin have traced the long-term consequences of early maturation in females (Magnusson, 1988; Stattin & Magnusson, 1990). Early-maturing girls in Sweden obtain less education and marry earlier than their later maturing peers despite no initial differences in achievement levels. The authors present evidence that this effect is mediated through the association of early maturation with involvement with older adolescents: Early-maturing females are more likely to join older peer groups and to begin dating older males; in turn, the early-maturing girls in these peer groups are more likely to drop out of school and get married, perhaps because school achievement is not valued by their peer social network, while early entry into the job market and early marriage are. These results are consistent with the oft-cited finding that underachievement in males tends to begin in early elementary school, while underachievement in females is more likely to begin in early adolescence. Clearly, there is a need to understand the link between pubertal development and school achievement better, particularly for females.

Recently a number of researchers have been assessing how the hormonal changes that occur in early adolescence relate to children's behavior at this time. Both Paikoff and Brooks-Gunn (1990) and Buchanan et al. (1992) have proposed several different possible models to account for these relations, ranging from models that propose a direct link between hormonal change and behavior to models that propose mediated and cumulative effects—that is, the hormones' effects on behavior are said to be mediated through the physical changes in children's bodies and the social experiences early adolescents have. There is some interesting evidence for the relatively direct effects of hormones on behaviors such as aggression (Olweus, Mattsoon, Schalling, & Low, 1980, 1988; Susman, Inof-Germain, Nottelmann, Loriaux, Cutler, & Chrousos, 1987), sexuality (Udry, 1988), and mood swings (Buchanan, 1989; Buchanan et al., 1992). However, many researchers (e.g., Buchanan et al., 1992; Petersen & Taylor, 1980) have adopted the mediated effects model, arguing that hormones affect behavior indirectly through their impact on secondary sex characteristics, or in combination with social and personality factors. As an example of the latter kind of effect, Brooks-Gunn and Warren (1988) reported that pubertal changes influenced girls' body image and descriptions of themselves; for instance, breast development was associated with a positive body image, superior adjustment, and positive peer relations. These psychological differences likely influence other psychological and behavior outcomes, such as school achievement. To give an example of how pubertal changes can influence children's relations with others, Steinberg (1987, 1988) argued that parent–child rela-

tions change most at the peak of pubertal development, a point we return to later.

These physical changes are not the only changes early adolescents face; they also undergo school transitions and important social changes as well. Those researchers adopting a cumulative effects model (e.g., Simmons & Blyth, 1987; Simmons, Burgeson, Carlton-Ford, & Blyth, 1987) argue that it is the combination of changes occurring in early adolescence that can be problematic for some early adolescents. Pubertal change, school transitions, social changes such as dating, and potential family changes all can occur at this time. If several of those changes are negative, children can be at risk for developmental problems such as lowered self-esteem and early sexual activity (Simmons et al., 1987). Again, because girls enter puberty earlier than boys do, they are more likely to be coping with pubertal changes at the same time they make the middle grades school transition, and thus are more likely to face multiple transitions simultaneously.

One important educational implication of this work concerns the issue of timing for the transition from elementary to secondary school. Because of the difficulties of coping with several transitions at once, some researchers have argued that middle grades school should begin earlier, so that students make the school transition before they enter puberty. The recent movement in many parts of the country to make middle grades schools more like elementary schools and less like traditional junior high schools also reflects concern over the variety of changes early adolescents have to face. Others have argued that a kindergarten through eighth grade organizational structure may be most beneficial to early adolescents. There is increasing awareness among educators that this is a unique developmental phase that requires careful structuring of educational environments (see further discussion later in this chapter).

In sum, the physical changes that occur at adolescence are dramatic, and they have been shown to relate to emotional and behavioral changes occurring at that time. Although many adolescents have little difficulty going through these changes, they can be a source of problems for some, particularly when other social and psychological changes occur at the same time. Developmental researchers recently have done much important work on the impact of these changes on different behaviors; now educational researchers need to pay more attention to how these physical changes influence early adolescents' school performance, interactions with peers, and interactions with teachers. We will refer to the effects of these changes in later sections of this chapter.

## Changes in Cognition and Achievement During Early and Middle Adolescence

A great deal has been written about how children's thinking changes during the adolescent years (e.g., see Byrnes, 1988; Keating, 1990), and many chapters in this *Handbook* are devoted to students' cognition and information processing (see in particular chapters 2, 3, and 8, as well as the chapters on learning in different subject areas). Because of this coverage we discuss this issue rather briefly in this section. We provide more detailed discussion of how cognition changes during this part of the life span in the section on development during the college years, because many of those changes reach fruition during that developmental period.

In summarizing how children's thinking changes as they go through adolescence, the most important changes to note are the increasing ability of children to think abstractly, to consider the hypothetical as well as the real, to engage in more sophisticated and elaborate information-processing strategies, to consider multiple dimensions of a problem at once, and to reflect on oneself and on complicated problems (see Keating, 1990, for more complete discussion). Abstract thought and hypothetical thinking are of course hallmarks of Piaget's formal operations stage, the stage that he and his colleagues stated should emerge during adolescence (e.g., Piaget, 1952; Piaget & Inhelder, 1973). Although currently there is much debate over exactly when these kinds of cognitive processes emerge and although many researchers question whether the emergence of these processes reflects global stage-like changes in cognitive skills as described by Piaget, most theorists do agree that these kinds of thought processes are more characteristic of adolescents' cognition than of younger children's cognition (e.g., see Fischer, 1980).

Many cognitive theorists have assessed more specific information-processing skills, cognitive learning strategies, and metacognitive skills (see Bjorklund, 1989; A. L. Brown, Bransford, Ferrara, & Campione, 1983; Pressley, Borkowski, & Schneider, 1987; Weinstein & Mayer, 1986; and chapters 2, 3, 5, 6, and 8), and how those skills and strategies change over the course of development. This work demonstrates a steady increase in children's information-processing skills and use of more sophisticated learning strategies, in their knowledge of a variety of different topics and subject areas, in their ability to apply their knowledge to new learning situations, and in their awareness of their strengths and weaknesses as learners. One major implication of this work on children's cognitions and strategy use is that adolescents should be more efficient, sophisticated learners, ready to cope with relatively advanced topics in many different subject areas. However, Keating (1990) argued that these changes do not necessarily make adolescents better thinkers, particularly during the early adolescent years. They need more experience with these skills before the skills become very useful (see further discussion of these issues under "Cognitive Development in Late Adolescence and Young Adulthood," below).

Along with their implications for children's learning, these changes in children's thinking have important implications for individuals' self-concepts, thoughts about their future, and understanding of others. As we discuss in more detail below, theorists such as Erikson (1963) and Harter (1990b) view the adolescent years as a time of change in children's self-concepts, as they consider what possibilities are available to them and try to come to a deeper understanding of themselves. These sorts of self-reflections require the kinds of higher order cognitive processes just discussed. During early adolescence and adolescence individuals also become much more interested in understanding others' internal psychological characteristics, and friendships become based more on perceived similarity in these characteristics. Again, these sorts of changes in person perception reflect the broader changes in cognition that occur at this time.

During the 1980s many researchers examined the ways in which children and adolescents regulate their cognition and learning in educational settings. Zimmerman (1989b) stated that students are self-regulated when "they are metacognitively, motivationally, and behaviorally active participants in their own learning processes" (p. 4). As Zimmerman (1989a, 1989b), Schunk (1991a), Pintrich and De Groot (1990), and others have discussed, students who are self-regulated are more likely to use effective learning strategies, be meaningfully engaged in their own learning, and attain their academic goals. From a developmental perspective, as children's cognitive skills increase and they have more experience in educational settings, they should be able to regulate their learning better, and so be able to do more complicated and elaborate achievement tasks. Zimmerman and others have argued that helping students become self-regulated learners should be an important educational goal.

These changes in cognitive skills and the ability to regulate behavior are used as a rationale for special middle grades schools, in which students purportedly learn more challenging material. However, observational studies of seventh-grade classrooms in traditional middle schools show that the intellectual level of content taught in these classrooms often is *lower* than the intellectual level of content in elementary school classrooms, which could contribute to the decrease in academic engagement of some students (see Eccles, Wigfield, Midgley, et al. 1993, and further discussion later). In addition, these advances in information-processing skills do not necessarily translate into better school performance. Several investigators have found that grades for many early adolescents decline following the transition to junior high (see Simmons & Blyth, 1987), and that this lower performance is predictive of later dropping out (Finn, 1989; Roderick, 1992; Rumberger, 1987). These declines reflect in part the stricter grading standards in junior high and high school (see Blyth, Simmons, & Bush, 1978; Kavrell & Petersen, 1984; Schulenberg, Asp, & Petersen, 1984; and further discussion later), but they also reflect some students' difficulties in dealing with the transition to middle grades schools, and subsequent disengagement from academic pursuits.

There has been continuing debate over how much schooling can influence cognitive development and achievement outcomes. In discussing secondary schools' effects on educational attainment, Entwisle (1990) concluded from her review of relevant research that the effects of school quality on educational attainment are relatively small, and that achievement test gains in high school are relatively small. She pointed to adolescents' abilities and social class standing as more crucial variables explaining educational attainment. Keating (1990) also discussed how increases in achievement slow during adolescence. However, he also argued that a number of factors in the school setting can influence cognitive development and success in school: the amount of meaningful material introduced, how the training of thinking skills is (or is not) embedded in detailed content knowledge, and the ways in which teachers foster (or don't foster) critical thinking skills. In a recent review Ceci (1991) marshaled evidence to show, first, that schooling has a strong influence on IQ, so that children who stay in school longer have higher IQ scores; and second, that aspects of school quality such as the pacing of lessons, curricular demands and attainments, and class organization, along with the sheer quantity of schooling, also influence children's cognitive development. However, the specific ways in which the indicators of school quality influence IQ and cognitive processes was not completely clear from his review. From this work it appears that school's influence on IQ and achievement does diminish during adolescence, but still has significant effects.

*Group Differences in Cognition and Performance.* Group differences in academic performance between minority and majority adolescents are well documented and often increase during secondary school (see Parham & Parham, 1989). Although some ethnic groups (particularly Asian Americans) continue to excel in school and on standardized tests, other minority students (particularly African Americans and Hispanics) fare less well in the secondary school years. Compared to whites and Asians, adolescents from these groups continue to perform worse on standardized achievement tests and enroll in more remedial and less advanced courses (Council of the Great City Schools, 1992; Rumberger, 1987; Slaughter-Defoe, Nakagawa, Takanishi, & Johnson, 1990). The latter difference is especially marked for math and science. African-American and Hispanic adolescents also drop out of high school at substantially higher rates than do white or Asian students (Rumberger, 1987), although the drop out rate among African-American students has leveled lately.

In contrast to these widening differences between ethnic groups, the pattern for gender differences is less consistent. Boys' and girls' grades do not differ substantially during secondary school and college; and in fact girls often outperform boys even in math and science (see Linn & Hyde, 1989; Vetter, 1992). Comparisons on standardized test performances and course enrollments show a different pattern: There are gender differences favoring males on both of these indicators for math and physical science achievement, even among the highly gifted and talented (Eccles & Harold, 1992; Vetter, 1992; White, 1992). In contrast, females are more likely than males to enroll in advanced courses in language and literature.

Many researchers have tried to explain these ethnic group and gender differences in achievement performance and choice. Explanations have focused on differences in quality of instruction, differences in cognitive and learning styles, differences in aptitude, and differences in self, social, and motivational factors. Much of the work on the first three of these explanations is reviewed elsewhere in this volume (see chapters 9, 11, 12, and 15). We turn next to a discussion of self, social, and motivational factors that are a crucial aspect of adolescent development and that also help explain individual and group differences in school achievement.

## Adolescents' Self-Concepts, Achievement Beliefs, and Achievement Values

In this section we consider work on different aspects of children's self-beliefs, including their general self-concepts and beliefs focused more on their achievement activities (readers interested in these topics also should see chapters 4, 5, and 9, this volume). The specific achievement beliefs we focus on come from recent theoretical and empirical work on the nature of adolescents' achievement motivation and include adolescents' sense of competence and efficacy for different activities, their valuing of those activities, and the goals they have for

different activities. Adolescence is a time during which these beliefs change in important ways. It is also a time in which many more choices and options become available to adolescents, which means that the beliefs they have about different activities can have more substantial effects on their behavior. For instance, earlier in school students have little choice about which subjects to take, and so even if they believe they lack competence for a particular subject and don't like it much, they still have to take it. In high school students can make choices about whether to continue taking classes in areas like math and science. As we will see, their beliefs about those subjects, as well as their performance in them, have a strong impact on these choices. Thus, to understand adolescents' specific choices of which activities to pursue and more general choices about whether or not to stay in school, we must understand how their self-beliefs change during adolescence.

*Self-Concept and Identity Development During Early and Middle Adolescence.* Research on adolescents' general self-concept has burgeoned in the past decade. Adolescence has long been thought to be a time of great change in children's self-concepts; in Erikson's (1963) groundbreaking work, he characterized adolescence as the time in which individuals searched for their identity, either finding it or sinking into role confusion. More recently, Harter (1990b) has discussed how during middle adolescence the self-concept is both less integrated and more unstable than at earlier or later time periods, and that perceived inconsistencies or conflicts in one's characteristics were a source of great concern during this period (see also M. Rosenberg, 1986; Simmons & Blyth, 1987; Simmons, Rosenberg, & Rosenberg, 1973). Thus, like Erikson, Harter proposed that a major task of adolescence is to integrate the disparate aspects of self.

One hallmark of recent research on adolescents' general self-concepts is that much of it is more theoretically based than earlier work (see Byrne, 1984; Harter, 1990a, 1990b; Wigfield & Karpathian, 1991). Also, researchers have focused on more particular aspects of self-concept rather than just measuring individuals' general sense of themselves, and have developed measures of self-concept that have better psychometric properties and convergent and divergent validity (see Byrne, 1984; Wigfield & Karpathian, 1991; and Wylie, 1989, for further discussion). Byrne (1984) discussed different theoretical models of the self-concept. Three of these models have received the most research attention. First is the nomothetic position that the self-concept is unidimensional. Second is a taxonomic model that proposes a multifaceted self-concept with the facets relatively distinct, and also a more general self-concept factor (e.g., see Harter, 1985, 1986). Third is a hierarchical model that posits multiple facets of the self-concept arranged in a hierarchy, with more specific aspects of the self-concept at the base and the general self-concept at the apex (e.g., see Marsh, 1990b; Marsh & Shavelson, 1985; Shavelson, Hubner, & Stanton, 1976). Most researchers now reject the nomothetic model, but there continues to be debate between proponents of taxonomic models and hierarchical models.

Marsh and his colleagues have done a great deal of empirical work to examine the structure of self-concept, utilizing Shavelson et al.'s (1976) hierarchical model of the self-concept as the theoretical basis for their work. They developed three different scales to measure children's self-concept, called the

Self-Description Questionnaire (SDQ) I, II, and III, for use with different-aged children and adolescents. These scales contain subscales that assess children's self-concepts in many different activity domains, including both academic and nonacademic activities. The primary constructs assessed on these questionnaires are children's and adolescents' beliefs about their ability and liking for each of the activity domains assessed.

Extensive factor-analytic work with these scales has shown, first, that the items in each domain form separate factors, with these factors emerging in children as young as kindergarten and first-grade children (see Marsh, Craven, & Debus, 1991; Marsh & Hocevar, 1985; see also Eccles, Wigfield, Harold, & Blumenfeld, 1993, for further evidence of young children's differentiated beliefs about their abilities). That is, there are clearly separate dimensions of self-concept even in very young children. Second, during middle childhood and early adolescence children's self-concepts appear to be organized hierarchically (e.g., Marsh, 1990b; Marsh & Hocevar, 1985; Marsh & Shavelson, 1985); however, the model is more complex than the one originally proposed by Shavelson et al. (1976). Interestingly, during later adolescence there is less evidence for a hierarchical self-concept. Marsh and O'Neill (1984) and Marsh and Shavelson (1985), using SDQIII, found that the 13 SDQIII scales were very clearly defined. However, correlations among these factors were very low (averaging .09), leading Marsh and Shavelson to conclude that late adolescents' self-concepts, though multifaceted, are not hierarchically organized. As noted earlier, Harter (1990b) also proposed that the self-concept is less integrated and more unstable during middle adolescence. Marsh and O'Neill's results may reflect this "disintegrated" self. These findings suggest an intriguing pattern in self-concept development across childhood and adolescence: from differentiated and hierarchical to differentiated into quite distinct components. We know less about how these components of self-concept are organized during the college years and after, because researchers have not assessed this issue as frequently in those populations. The research on self and identity processes during the college years and later has taken more of a process approach (see discussion below).

Researchers also have examined how children's and adolescents' general self-esteem changes (see M. Rosenberg, 1986, for a review). Simmons et al. (1973) showed that following the transition to junior high school, early adolescents' general self-esteem is lower and less stable and their self-consciousness is higher, though there has been some debate about how prevalent these negative changes in general self-esteem are. In our work (Eccles, Wigfield, Flanagan, Miller, Reuvman, & Yee, 1989; Wigfield et al., 1991), we found children's self-esteem to be lowest immediately after the transition into junior high school in seventh grade but increased during the seventh-grade year. In their longitudinal work Blyth et al. (1983) and Simmons et al. (1979) found that for most children, self-esteem scores increased across adolescence (see also Dusek & Flaherty, 1981; Nottelmann 1987; O'Malley & Bachman, 1983). In Simmons's work and Blyth's work, white girls making the transition to junior high school were the only group to show consistent evidence of declines in self-esteem. Eccles and her colleagues (Eccles & Midgley, 1989; Eccles, Wigfield, Midgley, et al., 1993) and Simmons and her colleagues (Blyth et al., 1983; Simmons & Blyth, 1987; Simmons et al., 1973, 1979) have postulated that

these changes in early adolescents' self-beliefs are due in part to changes in the school environment that occur following the transition to junior high; these changes are discussed in more detail later.

Which specific components of children's self-concepts relate most strongly to their overall self-esteem or self-worth at different ages has been an important research topic in this area. Harter (1985, 1986) reported that during childhood and adolescence children's perceptions of competence correlated positively with one another and with their general self-worth, with the correlations between these constructs ranging between .40 and .67 (these correlations are somewhat lower in Marsh's work, though still significant). Harter also found that during the elementary school years and adolescence perceptions of physical appearance and social acceptance relate most strongly to children's feelings of self-worth (see Harter, 1990a, 1990b). These findings probably will come as no surprise to teachers and others working with early adolescents. Social status and physical appearance often seem to be much more important to adolescents than more mundane things like school success. The great changes in physical appearance occurring at this time likely are a major reason why adolescents are so concerned about their appearance.

A more difficult issue is determining exactly *how* the specific aspects of self-concept may influence general self-worth. Taking a broad perspective on this issue that she derived from William James, Harter (1985, 1990a) posited that individuals' general self-worth is determined in part by the synchrony between their sense of competence at different activities and the importance of those activities to them. Doing well on activities that are important should foster positive general self-worth. Harter has found support for this notion in her empirical work: Children who believe they are good at activities they think are important have more positive general self-worth than do children who believe certain activities are important but do not think they are competent at those activities.

In their discussion of how specific aspects of self-concept relate to one's overall sense of self, Marsh and Shavelson (1985) argued against merely summing scores from different subscales to form a total score. Instead, they proposed that a weighted combination of self-concept facets would be a more appropriate method. However, Marsh and Shavelson stated that it is not known exactly how individuals would engage in the process of weighting different aspects of the self-concept in determining general self-concept, a problem also noted by Harter (1986). This equation likely differs from individual to individual, although as we have seen, beliefs about physical appearance and social acceptance appear to have relatively large weights for most adolescents. Further assessment of this issue should be a priority for self-concept research in the 1990s.

This issue also has very important implications for students' school engagement. To the extent that adolescents do well in school and believe it is important, they should remain engaged in academic activities. If either their performance decreases or they begin to decide that school is not important, then their engagement will decrease. As we just noted, the importance of school often decreases during adolescence because many adolescents begin to see social activities as more important to them at this time, and they like those activities much more than they like academic tasks (see Eccles et al., 1989; Wigfield et al., 1991).

*Links of General Self-Concept to School Achievement.* There has been a running debate among educational researchers concerning the direction of causality in this relationship. Some have argued that achievement determines self-concept. Others take a "self-concept enhancement" approach, arguing that increases in self-concept can improve achievement (see Byrne, 1984; Calsyn & Kenny, 1977, for more complete discussion of these different views). In earlier reviews, Hansford & Hattie (1982) concluded that general self-concept and achievement were only moderately related. Scheier and Kraut (1979) argued that programs attempting to boost children's general self-concept had little effect on their achievement; thus they strongly rejected the self-concept enhancement view. These reviewers focused primarily on general self-concept; the more recent work just discussed suggests that specific aspects of self-concept relate more closely to achievement in a given area than does general self-concept (see Byrne, 1984; Eccles & Wigfield, 1985; Wigfield & Karpathian, 1991, for more detailed discussion). However, based on her review of studies of more specific aspects of self-concept and achievement Byrne (1984) concluded that causal predominance in this relationship still had not been established.

Two recent studies have addressed the issue of causality in the self-concept/achievement relation, using more sophisticated designs than in many previous studies. Skaalvik and Hagtvet (1990) look at longitudinal relations between academic self-concept of ability, general self-esteem, and school achievement in third- and fourth-grade and sixth- and seventh-grade cohorts of Norwegian students. They hypothesized that academic achievement would predict academic self-concept of ability more strongly than vice versa, and that self-concept of ability would predict general self-esteem more strongly than would academic achievement. Their structural equation modeling analyses provided some support for these hypotheses in both cohorts; however, important cohort effects emerged. For the younger cohort, academic achievement more strongly predicted self-concept of ability than vice versa, but in the older cohort there was some evidence that the relationship between the two variables was reciprocal. Results of this study thus show that there are age differences in the nature of the relation between self-concept and achievement.

In a longitudinal panel study, Marsh (1990a) examined relations at four time points between ability perceptions and grades in a sample of high school males. Prior ability perceptions and grades influenced subsequent grades, but subsequent ability perceptions were most strongly influenced by prior ability perceptions. In fact, previous grades did not relate to subsequent ability perceptions at any of the time points. Based on these findings, Marsh concluded that "the effects of academic self-concept were 'causally predominant' over those of reported grades, and these results provide strong support for the self-concept enhancement model of the relation between self-concept and achievement" (p. 651). These findings contradict Scheier and Kraut's (1979) point that self-concept is not causal, but need replication before this conclusion is fully supported. The relations between these constructs are complex, and it will be difficult to prove conclusively a causal direction in these relations. It is more likely that the relations between self-concept and achievement are reciprocal, at least by the middle school years. That is,

students' achievement outcomes should continue to influence their self-concepts, and these beliefs could then influence subsequent achievement (see Eccles & Wigfield, 1985; Marsh, 1990a; Wigfield & Karpathian, 1991, for further discussion). Adolescents' more specific achievement beliefs also can influence their achievement behaviors; we consider that topic next.

*Adolescents' Specific Achievement Beliefs and Achievement Motivation.* Work on motivation and achievement-related beliefs also flourished in the 1980s and 1990s. As discussed in more detail in chapters 4 and 5 in this volume, much of this work has taken the broad perspective that children's *interpretations* of their achievement outcomes are the critical mediators of subsequent achievement behavior. For that reason, children's beliefs about their accomplishments have been studied extensively. The beliefs receiving the most attention include attributions for success and failure (Weiner, 1979, 1985, 1986), competence beliefs (Blumenfeld, Pintrich, Meece, & Wessels, 1982; Covington, 1984; Dweck & Elliott, 1983; Eccles et al., 1983; Harter, 1982; Nicholls, 1984, 1990; Stipek & Mac Iver, 1989), perceptions of efficacy at different tasks (Bandura, 1986; Schunk, 1991a, 1991b), perceptions of control over outcomes (Connell, 1985; Skinner, 1990), achievement goals (C. Ames, 1992; Dweck & Leggett, 1988; Nicholls, 1984; Wentzel, 1989), and achievement values (Eccles et al., 1983; Wigfield & Eccles, 1992). Still other work has focused on children's intrinsic versus extrinsic motivation (Deci & Ryan, 1985; Harter, 1981a, 1981b), and children's anxiety (Wigfield & Eccles, 1989). An important feature of much of this work has been the focus on relatively specific beliefs rather than on more global beliefs such as self-concept.

Researchers looking at how these beliefs change during early adolescence and adolescence often have found that adolescents' beliefs and values become more negative (see Eccles, Midgley, & Adler, 1984; Eccles & Midgley, 1989; Harter, 1990b; Stipek & Mac Iver, 1989, for reviews). Many early adolescents become more anxious about school (Fyans, 1979; Harter, Whitesell, & Kowalski, 1992) and have lower academic intrinsic motivation (Harter, 1981b; Harter et al., 1992). Early adolescents have lower ability self-concepts than do their younger peers (Eccles, Adler, & Meece, 1984; Eccles et al., 1983, 1989; Marsh, 1989; Wigfield et al., 1991). In a summary of his cross-sectional studies of age differences in aspects of self-concept, Marsh (1989) reported that children's beliefs about their ability in a variety of different activity domains show quadratic effects that are U shaped: lower in eighth and ninth grade than in seventh grade, and higher in tenth and eleventh grade. Some studies suggest that early adolescents' beliefs about mathematics become particularly negative (Brush, 1980; Eccles, Adler, & Meece, 1984). Because most of these studies were done in schools, they included only adolescents who were at least engaged enough in school to still be there; the achievement beliefs of adolescents' dropping out may become even more negative at earlier ages.

The work on achievement goals also suggests change across age. Nicholls (1979, 1984) defined two major kinds of goal orientations that children have, ego involvement and task involvement (see Dweck & Elliott, 1983, for a complementary analysis). Individuals adopting an ego-involving orientation seek to maximize favorable evaluations of their competence and minimize negative evaluations of competence. Questions like "Will I look smart?" and "Can I outperform others?" reflect ego-involved goals. With task involvement, individuals focus on mastering tasks and increasing competence at different tasks. Questions such as "How can I do this task?" and "What will I learn?" reflect task involvement. Nicholls has discussed that when children focus on ego-involved goals, they try to outperform others, and are more likely to do tasks they know they can do. Task-involved children choose challenging tasks and are more concerned with their own progress than with outperforming others. Researchers (e.g., Nicholls, 1979) have suggested that ego-involved goals become more dominant during secondary school.

Wentzel (1989) assessed a broader set of goals obtained from interviews with adolescents. Some of these are similar to Nicholls's (1979) task goals, including "being a successful student," "learning new things," "understanding new things," and "doing one's best." Other academic goals, like "being better than others," are more like Nicholls's ego goals. Some of the goals concern social aspects of school (making friends, winning approval, being helpful, getting others to help, being dependable and responsible), and others concern enjoyment of school (having fun). Wentzel found that high-, middle-, and low-achieving adolescents had quite different sets of goals; the high achievers focused more on several of the achievement-related goals and social responsibility. The middle achievers and low achievers focused more on social interaction goals, and low achievers in particular stated they did not try to win others' approval or be successful. Wentzel (1989) has not looked at how these goals might differ in older and younger children. One possible change would be that for many children, social goals may become more critical than academic goals, especially during early adolescence. Further, the differences between high, middle, and low achievers may become more pronounced during adolescence, as some children continue to do well in school and others struggle. Those doing poorly may especially seek goals other than academic ones in school, or reject school altogether (see Finn, 1989; Rumberger, 1987). How individuals choose among these different goals should have an effect on their engagement in school.

*Relations of Specific Achievement Beliefs and Values to Academic Performance and Choice.* Some researchers have examined how adolescents' specific achievement beliefs relate to their academic achievement and choice of activities. For instance, researchers interested in children's and adolescents' self-efficacy for different tasks have posited that efficacy beliefs relate to individuals performance, persistence, and choice of different activities (e.g., Bandura, 1986; Schunk, 1991b; Zimmerman, Bandura, & Martinez-Pons, 1992). In their expectancy-value approach to this issue, Eccles, Wigfield, and their colleagues have extensively examined these relations in studies done with late-elementary-school- through high-school-aged students (e.g., Eccles, 1984a, 1984b; Eccles, Adler, & Meece, 1984; Eccles et al., 1983; Meece et al., 1990). Two fundamental findings emerge from this work. First, children's perceptions of ability and expectancies for success are the strongest predictors of subsequent grades in math and English, predicting those outcomes more strongly than either previous grades or achievement values. Second, children's achievement values such as liking of tasks, importance attached to them, and their

usefulness are the strongest predictors of children's intentions to continue math and actual decisions to do so (see Wigfield, 1994; Wigfield & Eccles, 1992, for more complete reviews; see also Feather, 1982, 1988, for work on how students' values relate to their choice of college major). As we discussed earlier, given the increasing opportunities for choice among different academic courses during middle adolescence, the finding that adolescents' achievement values relate most strongly to their choices is particularly important. We know less about the processes by which adolescents come to value and devalue different activities; understanding these processes should be a research priority for the later 1990s.

Pintrich and his colleagues have examined how adolescents' expectancies and values for different school subjects relate to their use of cognitive strategies as well as to their achievement performance (Pintrich & De Groot, 1990; Pintrich & Garcia, 1991; Pintrich & Schrauben, 1992). This work is important because these researchers have specifically examined links between cognition and motivation. Pintrich and his colleagues have found that students' perceived self-efficacy and values relate positively to their use of cognitive strategies and self-regulation. The relations between achievement values, strategy use, and self-regulation are stronger than those between self-efficacy, strategy use, and self-regulation. They also found that expectancies relate more strongly to performance than do achievement values. However, in predicting performance from the motivational variables, strategy use, and perceived self-regulation, they found that it is the cognitive strategy and self-regulation scales that directly predict performance. The effects of self-efficacy and values on performance appear to be mediated through the cognitive variables. Pintrich and De Groot argued that students' self-efficacy may facilitate their cognitive engagement, and their achievement values relate to their choice of whether to become engaged, but their use of cognitive strategies and self-regulation relate more directly to performance.

Most of the research just discussed concerns how children's motivation relates to their performance and choice. In contrast, Kuhl (1985, 1987) has argued that motivation does not directly determine these outcomes, but instead only leads the individual to action beyond motivation. Once the individual undertakes an action, Kuhl posited that volitional processes take over and determine whether or not the intention is fulfilled (see also Corno, 1989, 1993). Thus, along with understanding motivational processes, Kuhl proposed that we need to understand how individuals control (or do not control) the motivated actions they undertake. He proposed several different volitional strategies individuals can use to help them carry through their plans: selective attention, encoding control, emotional control, motivational control, environmental control, and parsimony of information processing. Corno (1993) has discussed possible relations between motivational and volitional processes, and how students implement the motivated decisions they make through volitional strategies like those discussed by Kuhl.

In the work both on motivation and volition, we now need more studies of the processes involved in these evolving relations, and studies of different developmental trajectories in both these achievement-related characteristics and their relation to school performance and choice. We also need to look more closely at exactly how achievement beliefs, motivation, and volition relate to students' cognition and regulation of their learning and actual conceptual change (see Pintrich, Marx, & Boyle, 1993; Wigfield, 1993; and chapter 9 for further discussion). We are encouraged that many researchers now are proposing more specifically how motivation, volition, and cognition relate, but much work remains to be done before we have a clear understanding of those relations.

### Group Differences in Self-Concept, Motivation, and School Performance During Adolescence

Gender Differences.   Though sex typing itself occurs in the preschool years (see Huston, 1983), several researchers have suggested that engaging in gender-role appropriate activities may become quite important to early adolescents, as they try to conform more to gender-role stereotypes once they enter puberty (Eccles, 1987; Hill & Lynch, 1983). Hill & Lynch labeled this phenomenon gender-role intensification. This phenomenon may lead early adolescents to have less positive beliefs and be less involved in activities that they see as less appropriate to their own gender. For instance, girls who believe that math is not appropriate for females and who wish to conform to perceived feminine roles may decide to discontinue taking math when that possibility becomes available, even if they are doing very well in that subject.

Rosenberg (1986) suggested that girls are more affected by the physical changes occurring at puberty and thus their self-concepts are more volatile than those of boys during this time period. Simmons and Blyth (1987) found that the junior high transition had a negative effect only on girls' self-esteem; our own work did not replicate this finding (Eccles et al., 1989; Wigfield et al., 1991). However, in our studies and those of others, boys reported higher self-esteem than did girls during early adolescence (e.g., Blyth et al., 1983; Marsh, 1989; Nottelmann, 1987; Rosenberg & Simmons, 1972; Simmons et al., 1979). We are unsure whether this finding reflects "true" gender differences in self-esteem or response bias, since boys tend to be more self-congratulatory than girls in their responses to self-report measures, while girls may be more modest in their self-reports (Eccles, Adler, & Meece, 1984).

There are many gender differences in children's competence beliefs for activities in different domains. We find these differences to be particularly intriguing in light of recent evidence that actual achievement and test score differences between boys and girls are decreasing. In an important article Linn and Hyde (1989) presented a meta-analysis of recent work on sex differences in verbal, mathematics, and science aptitude test performance. They concluded that sex differences in verbal ability now are negligible; differences in quantitative skills show that girls' computation skills are better at all ages and boys do better on mathematics conceptual "word" problems in high school, though again these differences have decreased in the past 15 years; and differences in science knowledge and process still favor boys, though they also are decreasing and appear to reflect experiential differences between boys and girls in science.

Despite these achievement findings, gender differences in self-perceptions remain. In our work adolescent boys had higher competence beliefs for sports and math than did adolescent girls, and the girls had higher competence beliefs for English (see Eccles et al., 1983, 1989; Wigfield et al., 1991). Marsh (1989) also reported many gender differences in response to his self-concept scales, though he noted that the gender differences explained only about 1 percent of the variance in responses. Across all three SDQ measures boys' physical appearance, physical ability, and math self-concept scores were higher than those of girls, whereas girls' scores were higher for verbal/reading and general school subscales. Interestingly, there were few age-by-sex interactions in children's and adolescents' responses to our measures or those of Marsh, suggesting that the gender differences neither increase nor decrease in magnitude across age. Recently, Eccles et al. (1993) found that many of these differences in competence beliefs occur in children as young as first graders.

Eccles, Wigfield, and their colleagues have found differences also in boys' and girls' valuing of different tasks. Boys like sports and rate sports activities as more important than do girls, whereas the opposite pattern occurs for social activities and English. There were no differences in math (Eccles et al., 1989; Wigfield et al., 1991). Although it is encouraging that boys and girls like math similarly and think it equally important, the fact that girls have less positive views of their ability in math could be problematic. If these trends continue into high school, which they seem to do (e.g., Eccles et al., 1983; Wigfield, 1984), girls should be less likely than boys to take optional advanced-level math courses. This potential problem could be further exacerbated by the fact that girls report liking social activities so much more than math; social activities also could interfere with continued participation in mathematics.

Differences for Minority Adolescents.   Less is known about motivational differences across adolescents from different racial and ethnic groups, although work in this area is growing (see Berry & Asamen, 1989; Graham, 1989, 1994; and Slaughter-Defoe et al., 1990, for a review of some of this work). Of the work that has been done, most has concerned African-American adolescents and has attempted to explain the achievement difficulties many African-American adolescents experience. In her discussion of this problem, Graham (1989) stated, "Far too many minority children perform poorly in school not because they lack basic intellectual capacities or specific learning skills but because they have low expectations, feel hopeless, lack interest, or give up in the face of potential failure" (p. 40). In reviewing the research on differences between black and white students on motivational constructs such as locus of control and achievement attributions, Graham (1994) concluded that the (relatively small) literature in each area showed that differences between those groups are not very large, and often were not found. Further, she argued that many existing studies have not adequately distinguished between race and socioeconomic status, thus confounding the effects of those two variables. Graham (1989, 1994) stated that we do not yet have adequate theories explaining achievement motivation in African-American children and adolescents, and she called for theoretical work focusing on cognitive motivational variables such as attributions, achievement goals and values, and beliefs about ability and efficacy. We strongly concur with this suggestion but believe current theoretical models such as expectancy-value theory, self-efficacy theory, and attribution theory could be utilized. To give two examples of the importance of these kinds of variables in minority adolescents' achievement, Gurin and Epps (1974) found that perceived efficacy was an important predictor of academic achievement among black adolescents. Hale-Benson (1989) also pointed to the importance of beliefs about *academic* efficacy, as contrasted to *personal* efficacy, to the achievement of African-American children, particularly boys. Interestingly, in discussing the high achievement of many Asian children, researchers have noted that those children often seem to focus on *effort* rather than ability or efficacy as a cause of their achievement (see Holloway, 1988).

Other researchers have looked at differences in components of self-concept between white and black children. Often there are no differences between groups in general self-concept or self-esteem (see Powell, 1989). However, Hare (1985) found that black adolescents' academic self-concepts were lower than those of black *children,* and he postulated that this was due to the adolescents' increasingly clear understanding of their relatively poor academic perfomance. Other studies have indicated that academic self-concept is not predictive of general self-esteem for African-American children (Bledsoe, 1967; Hare, 1977), suggesting that academic self-concept is not of critical importance to African-American children's sense of worth. Indeed, some studies have shown that possessing academic skills actually works against African-American students' social acceptance by their peers (McDermott, 1987; see also Fordham & Ogbu, 1986). Similarly, in looking at African-American students' performance in college, Steele (1992) has suggested that they develop an ambivalent orientation to academic achievement. Confronted throughout their school career with mixed messages about their competence and their potential, they lower the value they attach to academic achievement. Fordham and Ogbu have made a similar argument linking African-American students' perception of limited future job opportunities to lowered motivation to work hard on academic achievement. They argue that society and schools give African-American youth the dual message that academic achievement is unlikely to lead to positive adult outcomes for them and that they are not valued by the system. In response to these messages, African-American youth create an oppositional culture that rejects the value of academic achievement. Ogbu (1992) has discussed cogently how this dynamic is different for forced minorities (African Americans) than for voluntary minority immigrant groups (recent immigrants from Asia).

Thus, in considering performance and motivational differences across different ethnic and minority groups, it is essential to point out that such differences must be considered in light of larger contextual issues that influence development. Indeed, several researchers have pointed out the importance of taking a contextual view of minority achievement. For example, Spencer and Markstrom-Adams (1990) discussed identity formation (or self-concept development) during childhood and adolescence in different groups of minority children. They argued that in forming their identities, minority children have to deal with several difficult issues that majority adolescents do not face, such as the often negative view of their group held by many members of the majority society, conflict between the values of their group and those of the larger society, and lack of "identity-achieved" adults in their group who could serve as models for them. These difficulties sometimes impede identity formation in minority adolescents, leading to identity diffusion or possibly an inadequate exploration of different identities that the adolescent could take on. In discussing some of these same issues, W. E. Cross (1987) posited that to understand identity development in African-American children and adolescents, their personal identities and orientation to their racial group both must be understood. For instance, some African-American adolescents may have positive personal identities but be less positive about their racial group as a whole, whereas others may have negative personal identities but positive orientations toward their group. Cross argued that many researchers have confounded these two constructs in their studies, leading to confusion in our understanding of identity development in African-American adolescents.

Research on these issues, while growing, still is lacking, and like Graham's (1989, 1994) suggestion that more research be done on minority children's motivation in achievement settings, Spencer and Markstrom-Adams (1990) called for more research on the processes involved in the self-concept development of children from different ethnic and racial groups. We concur strongly with these recommendations and believe such work would make a very important contribution to both theory and application in these areas. At present we do not know enough to say whether or not current theoretical models are adequate for describing the development of self-concept and motivation in different groups of adolescents, or whether new models will need to be developed. As a result, it often is difficult to formulate appropriate intervention strategies to help minority children struggling with school. Certainly these topics should be a research priority for the later 1990s.

Finally, in thinking about the achievement and motivation of minority youth, it is important to consider the context of schooling and bear in mind the quality of the educational institutions that serve these youth. Thirty-seven percent of black youth and 32 percent of Hispanic youth, compared to 5 percent of white and 22 percent of Asian youth, are enrolled in the 47 largest city school districts in this country. Twenty-eight percent of these youths live in poverty and 55 percent are eligible for free or reduced-cost lunches, suggesting that class may be as important as (or more important than) race in the differences that emerge. Teachers in these schools report feeling less safe than teachers in other school districts, dropout rates are highest in these schools, and achievement levels at all grades are the lowest (Council of the Great City Schools, 1992). Finally, schools that serve this population are less likely than schools serving advantaged populations to offer either high-quality remedial services or advanced courses and courses that facilitate the acquisition of higher order thinking skills and active learning strategies (Mac Iver & Epstein, 1991). Even children who are extremely motivated may find it difficult to perform well under these educational circumstances.

## Friendships and the Peer Group in Early and Middle Adolescence

Another major difference between children and adolescents concerns adolescents' more extensive involvement in social activities, sports activities, and a variety of other extracurricular activities. We have found that early adolescents rate social activities as very important to them and like them more than other activities, especially more than academic activities (Eccles et al., 1989; Wigfield et al., 1991). Indeed, activities with peers, peer acceptance, and appearance can take precedence over school activities during this time period, often to the chagrin of parents and teachers. In fact, as mentioned earlier, Harter (1990a) found that early adolescents' physical appearance and social acceptance are the most important predictors of their general self-esteem, more important than their perceptions of their own cognitive competence (see also Harter, 1992, for discussion of some dangers in this pattern).

Children's friendships undergo some important changes during adolescence (see Berndt & Perry, 1990; Damon & Hart, 1987; Savin-Williams & Berndt, 1990; Selman, 1980). Sullivan (1953) suggested that adolescent friendships are characterized more by fulfilling intimacy needs than are earlier friendships, and indeed most research shows that children state that friends are those with whom one can share intimate thoughts (this depiction may be somewhat more true for girls; see Douvan & Adelson, 1966). In addition, adolescents state that their friends share similar psychological characteristics, interests, and values, and that friends should be loyal to one another (see Berndt & Perry, 1990; Savin-Williams & Berndt, 1990). Many of these changes in adolescents' conceptions of friendships can be linked to changes in their growing cognitive skills, increased perspective-taking ability, and more varied social experiences (see Eisenberg, 1990; Selman, 1980). Yet Elkind (1967, 1985) proposed that many adolescents become more egocentric and self-focused at adolescence, thinking the world revolves around them (see Lapsley & Murphy, 1985, for an alternative view). Such egocentrism might reflect adolescents' struggles with their newly developed thinking skills (Keating, 1990).

Perhaps because of the importance of social acceptance during adolescence, friendships during this time period often are characterized by their organization into cliques and groups (see B. B. Brown, 1990; Eder, 1985). Adolescents often form relatively rigid groups that sometimes differ in overall status in the school. For instance, T. B. Perry (1987) found that more popular children tended to have friends who also were more popular, whereas less popular children's friends also were less popular. One reason for the existence of these cliques is to help adolescents establish a sense of identity; belonging to a group is one way to solve the problem of "who am I." A second (and related) phenomenon is that children's conformity to their peers peaks during early adolescence; children are most likely to go along with others' wishes at this time (see Hartup, 1983). This also has been related to the overwhelming importance of social acceptance to adolescents, as well as to children's developing identity. Individuals less certain of their own identities may be more likely to conform to others'.

In the popular literature, much has been written about how conformity to peers can create many problems for adolescents, and that "good" children often are corrupted by the negative influences of peers. The problem of adolescent gangs engaging in various deviant behaviors also has received a great deal of media attention, and indeed gangs do pose serious social problems in many cities. However, although pressure from peers to engage in misconduct does increase during adolescence (see B. B. Brown, 1990), many researchers disagree with the simplistic view that peer groups often have a bad influence on adolescents. Hartup (1983) discussed how most adolescents tend to agree more with their parents' views on major issues such as morality, the importance of education, politics, and religion. Peers had more of an influence on things such as dress and clothing styles, music, and activity choice. B. B. Brown

(1990) reviewed studies showing that it is poor parenting that sometimes leads children to get in with a "bad" peer group, rather than the peer group pulling the child into difficulties. He also argued that adolescents usually seek out similar peers; those involved in sports will have other athletes as friends, those serious about school will seek academic friends, and those less involved in school may belong to groups with similar attitudes. In one example of this kind of influence, Bain and Anderson (1974) discussed work showing that adolescents whose friends planned to go to college themselves were more likely to attend college. Thus the peer group acts more to reinforce predispositions than to change adolescents' characteristics in a major way.

Social acceptance also has been shown to relate to a variety of positive mental health outcomes, both before and during adolescence (see Parker & Asher, 1987). For instance, T. B. Perry (1987) found that adolescents who were satisfied with their friendships reported higher self-esteem. Miller and Berndt (1987) reported that children whose friendships had more positive characteristics were themselves more involved in school and received better grades. And Berndt and Hawkins (1987) found that children with good friendships during sixth grade were more popular in seventh grade, following the transition to junior high school. Unfortunately, school transitions often disrupt children's friendships, perhaps causing some difficulties in these important psychological outcomes. In our study of how the transition to junior high school influenced children's perceptions of social ability, we found a dramatic decrease in those beliefs immediately after the transition. Fortunately, this effect moderated during the seventh-grade year, though children's perceptions of their social ability at the end of seventh grade still were lower than they were at the end of sixth grade, before the transition (Wigfield et al., 1991).

How do children's friendships relate to their school achievement? From B. B. Brown's (1990) review (see also chapter 26, this volume), it appears that friends potentially can have both positive and negative effects on school achievement. High-achieving children who seek out other high achievers as friends could end up performing better as a result of their interactions with these other children. In contrast, low achievers whose friends are primarily other low achievers may begin to do even worse in school. There is evidence to indicate that low achievers do tend to gravitate together in class (see McMichael, 1980). Given the importance of social acceptance to adolescents, children lacking friends may not get involved in extracurricular activities, and their school performance may suffer as well. Rejected children are at risk for numerous negative social and psychological outcomes (see Asher & Coie, 1990). One way that positive social interaction has been facilitated in classrooms is through cooperative learning (see Johnson & Johnson, 1987; Mergendoller & Marchman, 1987; Slavin, 1990). Generally, research on the effects of cooperative learning show that when it is used in classrooms, children are more accepting of one another, and fewer children are socially isolated. Thus the greater use of such techniques could mitigate the effects of peer rejection on students' achievement.

## Group Differences in Children's Friendships

Relations between boys and girls undergo obvious and important changes during adolescence. Most researchers doing sociometric studies of children's friendships during elementary school ask children for same-sex ratings of their friendships, because same-sex friendships are most prevalent at that time. During early adolescence cross-sex interactions become more prevalent, although interactions between the sexes are often awkward initially. In her observational study of friendships in a middle school, Schofield (1980) found that boys and girls often did not interact much, although some cross-sex friendships were developing. More important, in talking with boys and girls she found that they were very aware that they soon would be dating, and many of the awkward interactions between boys and girls featured teasing, pushing and shoving, and halting conversation seemed to reflect that awareness. Because of this awareness of the imminence of dating, Schofield described boys and girls as having "complementary" social identities.

The work by Magnusson and Stattin (Magnusson, 1988; Stattin & Magnusson, 1990) extends this idea into the high school years and beyond. They report that some young women (early maturers especially) are particularly likely to be channeled into complementary relations with their male peers. Because these females look sexually mature, they are more likely to become involved with older peers, particularly with older male peers who interact with them in terms of reciprocal gender roles. As the young women get caught up in this peer social system, they shift their attention from academic activities into heterosocial activities and roles. As a result, they lower their educational aspirations and, in fact, end up obtaining less education than other females, often marrying and becoming parents earlier instead. Thus, what appears initially as a charming set of complementary social identities can have quite negative consequences for some females (especially those who mature early) as their social identity detracts from educational focus and attainment.

Relations across different ethnic and racial groups do not seem as complementary. In Schofield's (1980) study, despite strong efforts by school staff to create mixed groups of children in different school activities, children would resegregate at the first opportunity they had. In addition, different groups in the school did not have extremely positive views of one another; in many instances white students thought black students were aggressive, disruptive, and poor achievers, whereas black students thought white students were conceited and racist. As a result of these patterns Schofield suggested that black and white children have conflicting rather than complementary social identities. These patterns may be exacerbated by the separate neighborhoods in which children of different races often live. DuBois and Hirsch (1990) found that 80 percent of both black and white early adolescents said they had friends from other races at school. However, only 25 percent of the adolescents said that they had friends from other races in their neighborhoods. One way to increase cross-race friendships is the use of cooperative learning in the classroom; Slavin (1990) and Johnson and Johnson (1987) reported that both cross-race acceptance and interaction increase when more cooperative learning is used. The promotion of positive social relations among different groups will become even more important as our schools continue to become more diverse.

It is also important to consider the possible impact of peer groups on achievement behavior. As noted above, the recipro-cal gender-role peer interactions of early-maturing females appear to have a negative effect on their academic achievement. Similar processes have been suggested for various ethnic groups. As noted earlier, several investigators have suggested, and provided evidence, that black youth are likely to receive less peer support for academic achievement than white youth (e.g., Fordham & Ogbu, 1986). Steinberg, Dornbusch, and Brown (1992) concluded, based on their recent study of ethnic differences in achievement in California and Wisconsin, that both the lower performance of African Americans and Hispanics and the higher performance of whites and Asians are more a result of ethnic differences in peer support for academic achievement than a result of ethnic differences in either the value parents attach to education or the youths' beliefs regarding the likely occupational payoff for academic success. Yet family relations continue to have an important impact on adolescents' school achievement and many other aspects of their development. We consider family relations during adolescence next.

## Changes in Family Relations During Early and Middle Adolescence

A prevalent view holds that relations between parents and adolescents are much stormier than parent–child relations or relations between parents and their adult children. This view is more common in the clinical literature (e.g., Blos, 1979; Freud, 1958) and in anecdotal reports from some parents than it is in the research literature (e.g., Buchanan et al., 1992; Collins, 1990; Dornbusch et al., 1991; Petersen, 1988). Although the extent of actual disruption in parent–adolescent relations is debated, there is little question that parent–child relations do change during adolescence. As adolescents become physically mature they often seek more independence and autonomy and may begin to question family rules and roles. One clear finding is that parents and adolescents do have more conflicts than are reported in earlier parent–child relations, with those conflicts often centering on things like dress and appearance, chores, and dating (see Collins, 1990; Paikoff & Brooks-Gunn, 1990, for reviews). These conflicts appear to be especially likely when families experience different kinds of stress, particularly the stresses associated with economic hardships (McLoyd, 1990), and discord among family members (see Barber & Eccles, 1992; Hauser & Bowlds, 1990). Unfortunately, in U.S. society today more families are experiencing these kinds of economic and social difficulties, and so more conflicts will be likely. Yet, as mentioned earlier, many researchers find that parents and adolescents agree more than they disagree on core values such as beliefs about the importance of education, political beliefs, and spirituality (see Hartup, 1983).

Other ways in which relations between parents and adolescents differ from earlier parent–child relations is that they have fewer interactions and do fewer things together outside the home. This is perhaps best illustrated by the horror many adolescents express at being with their parents at places like shopping malls, where their friends might be. Also, especially during puberty, affective relations can be more negative, and girls in particular report feeling less accepted by parents (see Collins, 1990, for a more thorough review). In fact, Steinberg (1989) has argued that puberty has a special role in this distancing in relations between adolescents and parents. He argued for an evolutionary basis for this distancing, citing evidence from non-human primates that puberty is the time when parents and offspring often go their separate ways. Because human parents and adolescents usually continue to live together for a long time after adolescents go through puberty, distancing rather than complete separation may be the evolutionary vestige in humans. Although he did not take an evolutionary perspective, Collins (1990) wrote that the distancing in parent–adolescent relations has great functional value for adolescents, in that it fosters their individuation from their parents, allows them to try more things on their own, and develops their own competencies and efficacy.

One arena in which this distancing may not be as advantageous is in parents' involvement in their adolescents' education. Most studies of parental involvement in schooling show that it is highest in elementary school and drops off after that (see Eccles & Harold, 1993, in press; Epstein, 1991). There are many reasons why this occurs. One reason is the structure of the schools themselves. Elementary schools are smaller and often located in the neighborhood, and children usually have just one teacher most responsible for their education. Secondary schools are much larger, more diffuse, and adolescents have a different teacher for each subject area. Parents often find this larger and more bureaucratic institution harder to deal with. At the same time, during adolescence children also may make it clear they do not want their parents to be as directly involved in their school activities, either at home or at school. Yet numerous studies indicate that continued parental involvement in their children's education is a critical factor in their school performance (see Eccles & Harold, 1993, in press; Epstein, 1991, for reviews). This has been demonstrated also in studies of African-American adolescents (see Hale-Benson, 1989; Jenkins, 1989); indeed, one hallmark of Comer's (1988) school reform programs is to enhance parental involvement in many different aspects of schooling.

Although the contextual factors associated with different school environments have a strong influence on parents' involvement or lack of involvement in their children's schooling, and thus may influence adolescents' school achievement, organismic factors also are important. Parenting style is one such factor, and developmental psychologists have explored how parents' styles of interaction and discipline with their children influence a host of children's developmental outcomes. Baumrind (1971) identified several different broad parental styles, the three most prominent being authoritarian, permissive, and authoritative. Authoritarian parents are those who have strict rules in place, allow little give-and-take about those rules, and use assertive discipline strategies. Permissive parents essentially leave children to their own devices and discipline them infrequently. Authoritative parents provide rules and structure, but discuss those rules with their children and show some flexibility in how the rules are applied. In addition, they are warm and accepting of their children. Baumrind found that the authoritative parenting style was associated with many positive developmental outcomes, more so than either the authoritarian or permissive styles. In a study with adolescents, Dornbusch, Ritter, Leiderman, Roberts, and Fraleigh (1987) assessed how these different parenting styles related to high school students' grades. In support of Baumrind's work, the

authoritative parents tended to have adolescents who did better in school, whereas both authoritarian and permissive parents did not.

This brief review highlights the importance of both contextual factors (characteristics of the school environment) and organismic factors (parenting styles) in influencing both parental involvement in school and parental impact on adolescents' achievement. Finding ways to maintain parental involvement in their children's education during the middle and high school years remains an important priority.

## SCHOOL TRANSITIONS AND ADOLESCENT DEVELOPMENT

Very few developmental periods are characterized by so many changes at so many different levels as is adolescence. The changes during adolescence relate to pubertal development, social role redefinitions, cognitive development, school transitions, and the emergence of sexuality. With rapid change comes a heightened potential for both positive and negative outcomes. And, although most individuals pass through this developmental period without excessively high levels of "storm and stress," many individuals do experience difficulty during this period (see Dryfoss, 1990). As a result, a substantial portion of America's adolescents are not succeeding as well as might be hoped: Between 15 percent and 30 percent (depending on ethnic group) drop out of school before completing high school; adolescents as a group have the highest arrest rate of any age group; and increasing numbers of adolescents consume alcohol and other drugs on a regular basis (McCord, 1990; Office of Educational Research and Improvement, 1988). Many of these problems appear to begin during the early adolescent years (Carnegie Council on Adolescent Development, 1989). Is there something unique about this developmental period that puts individuals at greater risk for difficulty as they pass through it? In this section, we look more closely at this question, reviewing evidence for the hypothesis that some of the negative psychological changes associated with adolescent development result from a mismatch between the needs of the developing adolescent and the opportunities afforded them in their school environment. Thus we will be discussing an important context, the school environment, in which adolescent development takes place. We focus especially on the transition from elementary to middle or junior high school, but also discuss the transition into high school.

### The Middle Grades School Transition

Evidence suggests that the early adolescent years mark the beginning for some individuals of a downward spiral that can lead to academic failure and school dropout. For example, both Roderick (1992) and Simmons and Blyth (1987) found a marked decline in some early adolescents' school grades as they moved into junior high school. The magnitude of this decline was predictive of subsequent school failure and dropout. Similar declines have been documented for such motivational constructs as interest in school (Epstein & McPartland, 1976), intrinsic motivation (Harter, 1982), self-concepts/self-perceptions (Eccles, Midgley, & Adler, 1984; Simmons et al., 1979), and confidence in one's intellectual abilities, especially following failure (Parsons & Ruble, 1977). There are also reports of increases during early adolescence in such negative motivational and behavioral characteristics as test anxiety (Wigfield & Eccles, 1989), learned helplessness responses to failure (Rholes, Blackwell, Jordan, & Walters, 1980), a focus on self-evaluation rather than task mastery (Nicholls, 1990), and both truancy and school dropout (Rosenbaum, 1976; see Eccles & Midgley, 1989; Eccles, Midgley, & Adler, 1984, for full reviews). Although these changes are not extreme for most adolescents, there is sufficient evidence of a gradual decline in various indicators of academic motivation, behavior, and self-perception over the early adolescent years to make one wonder what is happening (see Eccles & Midgley, 1989). Although few studies have gathered information on ethnic or social class differences in these declines, we do know that academic failure and dropout is especially problematic among some ethnic groups and among youth from low-socioeconomic-status communities and families (e.g., Hauser, 1991). It is probable, then, that these groups will show declines in academic motivation and self-perception as they move into and through the secondary school years.

A variety of explanations have been offered to explain these negative changes. Some have suggested that such declines result from the intrapsychic upheaval assumed to be associated with early adolescent development (e.g., Blos, 1965). Others have suggested that it is the coincidence of the timing of multiple life changes. For example, Simmons and her colleagues have suggested that the coincidence of the junior high school transition with pubertal development accounts for the declines in the school-related measures and self-esteem, particularly for females (e.g., Blyth et al., 1983; Simmons & Blyth, 1987). Still others suggest that it is the nature of the junior high school environment rather than the transition per se that is important (e.g., Eccles & Midgley, 1989; Eccles, Midgley, & Adler, 1984). Drawing on person–environment fit theory (see Hunt, 1975), Eccles and Midgley (1989) proposed that the negative motivational and behavioral changes associated with early adolescence could result from the fact that traditional junior high schools are not providing appropriate educational environments for early adolescents. According to person–environment theory, behavior, motivation, and mental health are influenced by the fit between the characteristics individuals bring to their social environments and the characteristics of these social environments. Individuals are not likely to do well or to be motivated if they are in social environments that do not fit their psychological needs. If the social environments in the typical middle grades schools do not fit well with the psychological needs of adolescents, then person–environment fit theory predicts a decline in adolescents' motivation, interest, performance, and behavior as they move into this environment.

Evidence for this perspective is reviewed in this section. But in order to understand the role school environments might play in beginning negative motivational changes at early adolescence, two types of evidence need to be considered: evidence drawn from studies that follow the standard environmental influences approach, and evidence from studies that adopt a developmental variant on the person–environment fit paradigm, or, as Eccles and Midgley term it, the stage–environment fit approach (see Eccles & Midgley, 1989).

*General Environmental Influences Model.* Work in a variety of areas has documented the impact of various classroom and school environmental characteristics on motivation. For example, literature on big schools versus small schools has demonstrated the motivational advantages of small secondary schools, especially for marginal students (Barker & Gump, 1964). Similarly, the literature on teacher efficacy has documented the positive student motivational consequences of high teacher efficacy (Ashton, 1985; Brookover, Beady, Flood, Schweitzer, & Wisenbaker, 1979). Finally, organizational psychology has demonstrated the importance of participatory work structures on worker motivation (Lawler, 1976). The point is, there may be systematic differences between the academic environments of typical elementary schools and those of typical junior high schools and middle schools; if so, those differences could account for some of the motivational changes seen among early adolescents as they make the transition into junior high school or middle school. In other words, the motivational problems seen in early adolescence may be a consequence of the type of school environment these students are forced to adapt to rather than characteristic of the developmental period per se (see Higgins & Parsons, 1983, for a full elaboration of this argument). The same argument could be made for the problems associated with the transition to high school and college; these transitions are discussed later in this chapter.

*Developmental Stage-Environment Fit Model.* A slightly different analysis of the possible environmental causes of the motivational changes associated with the junior high school transition draws on the idea of person–environment fit. Such a perspective leads one to expect negative motivational consequences for individuals when they are in environments that do not fit well with their needs (Hunt, 1975; Lewin, 1935). At the most basic level, this perspective suggests the importance of looking at the fit between the needs of early adolescents and the opportunities afforded them in the traditional junior high school environment. A poor fit would help explain the declines in motivation associated with the transition to either junior or senior high school.

An even more interesting way to use the person–environment fit perspective is to put it into a developmental framework. Hunt (1975) argued for the importance of adopting a developmental perspective on person–environment fit in the classroom. He suggested that teachers need to provide the optimal level of structure for children's current levels of maturity while at the same time providing a sufficiently challenging environment to pull the children along a developmental path toward higher levels of cognitive and social maturity. Eccles and Midgley (1989) extended this perspective to an analysis of the motivational declines associated with the junior high school transition. They suggested that different types of educational environments may be needed for different age groups in order to meet the individual's developmental needs and to foster continued developmental growth. Exposure to the developmentally appropriate environment would facilitate both motivation and continued growth. In contrast, exposure to a developmentally inappropriate environment, especially a developmentally regressive environment, was predicted to create a particularly poor person–environment fit, which in turn would lead to declines in motivation and in attachment to the goals of the institution. Imagine two trajectories, one a developmental trajectory of individual growth, the other a trajectory of environmental change across the school years. Positive motivational consequences are predicted when these two trajectories are in synchrony with each other, that is, when the environment is both responsive to the changing needs of the individual and offers the kinds of stimulation that will propel continued positive growth. In other words, transition to a facilitative and developmentally appropriate environment, even at this vulnerable age, should have a positive impact on children's perceptions of themselves and their educational environment. In contrast, negative motivational consequences are predicted when these two trajectories are out of synchrony. If this is true, then a transition into a developmentally inappropriate educational environment should result in the types of motivational declines that have been identified as occurring with the transition into junior high school.

This analysis suggests a set of researchable theoretical and descriptive questions. First, what are the developmental needs of the early adolescent? Second, what kind of educational environment would be developmentally appropriate in terms of both meeting these needs and stimulating further development? Third, what are the most common changes in the academic environment before and after the transition to middle or junior high school? Fourth, and most important, are these changes compatible with the physiological, cognitive, and psychological changes early adolescents experience? Or is there a developmental mismatch between maturing early adolescents and the classroom environments they experience before and after the transition to the junior high school—a mismatch that results in a deterioration in academic motivation and performance for some children? Finally, can a similar analysis be used to understand motivational changes associated with the transition to high school and college, or from school to work?

***Stage-Environment Fit and the Transition to Junior High School.*** Eccles and Midgley (1989) argued that there are developmentally inappropriate changes at the junior high school in a cluster of classroom organizational, instructional, and climate variables, including task structure, task complexity, grouping practices, evaluation techniques, motivational strategies, locus of responsibility for learning, and quality of teacher–student and student–student relationships. They argued that these changes contribute to the negative change in students' motivation and achievement-related beliefs assumed to coincide with the transition into junior high school. The research of Eccles, Midgley, Wigfield, and their colleagues, as well as the little other available research, provides support for these suggestions. This research is summarized below (see also Arderman & Maehr, 1994).

Remarkably few empirical studies have focused on differences in the classroom or school environment across grades or school levels. Most descriptions have focused on school-level characteristics such as school size, degree of departmentalization, extent of bureaucratization, and so on. For example, Simmons and Blyth (1987) pointed out that most junior high schools are substantially larger (by several orders of magnitude) than elementary schools, and instruction is also more likely to be organized and taught departmentally. As a result of both of these differences, junior high school teachers typically teach several different groups of students each day and are unlikely to teach any particular students for more than 1 year. In addition, students typically have several teachers each day with little opportunity to interact with any one teacher on any dimension except the academic content of what is being taught and disciplinary issues. Thus, the opportunity for forming close relationships between students and teachers is effectively eliminated at precisely the point in the students' development when they have a great need for guidance and support from nonfamilial adults (see Carnegie Council on Adolescent Development, 1989). Such changes in student–teacher relationships, in turn, are likely to undermine the sense of community and trust between students and teachers, leading to a lowered sense of efficacy among the teachers, an increased reliance on authoritarian control practices by the teachers, and an increased sense of alienation among the students. Such changes are also likely to decrease the probability that any particular student's difficulties will be noticed early enough to get the student necessary help, thus increasing the likelihood that students on the edge will be allowed to slip onto negative trajectories leading to increased school failure and dropout.

Although differences on these characteristics can have important effects on teacher beliefs and practices and on student alienation and motivation, until quite recently those links were rarely assessed. Most attempts to assess the classroom environment have included only one grade level and have related differences in the environment to student outcomes, particularly scores on achievement tests. Little research has focused on systematic differences between the classroom environment of elementary and junior high or middle schools. But looking across the various relevant studies, six patterns emerge with a fair degree of consistency.

*Authority Relationships.* First, despite the increasing maturity of students, junior high school classrooms, as compared with elementary school classrooms, are characterized by a greater emphasis on teacher control and discipline and fewer opportunities for student decision-making, choice, and self-management (e.g., Brophy & Everston, 1976; Lounsbury, Marani, & Compton, 1980; Midgley & Feldlaufer, 1987; Midgley, Feldlaufer, & Eccles, 1988a,b; Moos, 1979). For example, Brophy, Everston, and their colleagues found consistent evidence that junior high school teachers spend more time maintaining order and less time actually teaching than elementary school teachers (Brophy & Everston, 1976). Similarly, Midgley et al. (1988b) found that sixth-grade elementary school math teachers reported less concern with controlling and disciplining their students than these same students' seventh-grade junior high school math teachers reported one year later.

Similar differences emerge on indicators of students' opportunity to participate in decision-making regarding their own learning. For example, Ward and her colleagues found that upper elementary school students are given more opportunities to take responsibility for various aspects of their schoolwork than seventh-grade students in a traditional junior high school (Ward, Mergendoller, Tikunoff, Rounds, Dadey, & Mitman, 1982). Similarly, Midgley and Feldlaufer (1987) reported that both seventh graders and their teachers in the first year of junior high school indicated less opportunity for students to participate in classroom decision-making than did these same students and their sixth-grade elementary school teachers one year earlier. In addition, using a measure developed by P. Lee, Statuto, and Kedar-Voivodas (1983) to assess the congruence between the adolescents' desire for participation in decision-making and their perception of the opportunities for such participation, Midgley and Feldlaufer (1987) found a greater discrepancy when the adolescents were in their first year in junior high school than when these same adolescents were in their last year in elementary school. Clearly, the fit between the adolescents' desire for autonomy and their perception of the extent to which their school affords them opportunities to exchange in autonomous behavior had decreased during the junior high school transition.

As outlined earlier, person–environment fit theory suggests that such mismatch between young adolescents' desires for autonomy and control and their perception of the opportunities in their environments should result in a decline in the adolescents' intrinsic motivation and interest in school. More specifically, given the general developmental progression toward increased desire for independence and autonomy during early adolescence, Eccles and Midgley (1989) predicted that adolescents who experience decreased opportunities for participation in classroom decision-making along with increased desires for greater participation in such decisions should be at particularly high risk for negative motivational outcomes. In a longitudinal analysis of the P. Lee et al. (1983) measure, Mac Iver and Rueman (1988) provided some support for this prediction. They compared the changes in intrinsic interest in math for adolescents reporting different patterns of changes in the match between their desire for participation in classroom decision-making and their perception of the opportunity for such decision-making across the junior high school transition. Consistent with the prediction, it was the adolescents who thought that their seventh-grade math classrooms were putting greater constraints on their preferred level of participation in classroom decision-making than did their sixth-grade math classrooms who showed the most marked declines in their intrinsic interest in math as they moved from sixth grade into seventh grade.

Another way to look at stage–environment mismatch is to look for differences between children of the same age who are at different maturational levels. C. L. Miller (1986) and her colleagues adopted just such a strategy with the Michigan Study of Adolescent Life Transitions (MSALT). They focused on individual differences between sixth-grade girls at different stages of pubertal development in the match between the girls' desire for decision-making opportunities and their perceptions of the opportunity for such decision-making in their classrooms. Consistent with the intraindividual longitudinal pattern of age-related change reported above, the more physically mature female adolescents expressed a greater desire for input into classroom decision-making than did their less developmentally mature female classmates (C. L. Miller, 1986). Unfortunately, as was true for the longitudinal results, the more physically mature females did not perceive greater opportunities for participation in classroom decision-making. Although girls of varying degrees of pubertal development were in the same classrooms, the more physically mature ones (i.e., the early developers) reported fewer opportunities for participation in classroom decision-making than did their less mature female peers (i.e., the on-time and late developers).

These maturational differences are even more striking when one looks at the within-year changes in these female adolescents' perceptions of the opportunities they have to participate in classroom decision-making. Miller calculated the mean change in these females' perceptions of opportunities from fall to the spring testing and then looked at this change as a function of their pubertal status. The early-maturing females showed a negative change (a decline) over the course of the school year in the extent to which they felt they could participate in classroom decision-making. In contrast, the late-maturing females in these same classrooms showed a positive change (an increase) over the course of the school year (C. L. Miller, 1986). How could this be, given that these adolescents were in the same classrooms? Did the teachers actually treat these adolescent females differently—i.e., did the teachers respond to earlier physical maturity with more controlling behavior? Or did the adolescents perceive a similar environment differently—i.e., did the early-maturing adolescents perceive the same level of adult control as providing less opportunity for self-control than did the later maturing adolescents? Evidence from educational psychology, developmental psychology, and general psychology suggests that either or both of these explanations could be accurate: Teachers do respond differently to various children in the same classroom, depending on a variety of characteristics (Brophy & Evertson, 1976), and people do perceive similar environments differently depending on their cognitive and/or motivational orientation (see Baron & Graziano, 1991). More detailed classroom observations are needed to determine the exact nature of the relation between teachers' behavior and adolescents' perceptions. But, more important for the issues central to this discussion, the degree of mismatch between the female adolescents' desire for input and their perception of these opportunities in their classroom environment was related to their pubertal maturity, with the mismatch greater among the more physically mature female adolescents than among the less mature.

These last results are especially interesting in light of the finding by Simmons and her colleagues (e.g., Simmons & Blyth, 1987; Simmons et al., 1979) that it is the more physically mature girls who are also involved in dating who respond to the transition to junior high school with increased levels of truancy and school misconduct and decreased self-esteem. Simmons et al. (1979) and Simmons and Blyth (1987) have explained this result in terms of multiple risks—these girls are the early adolescents who are experiencing school and pubertal transitions simultaneously. Alternatively, it is possible that it is the mismatch between their desire for a less controlling adult environment and their perceptions of a decline in the actual opportunity for participation that puts these females at risk for the most negative motivational outcomes.

Affective Relationships.  Second, junior high school classrooms, as compared with elementary school classrooms, are characterized by a less personal and less positive teacher–student relationship (see Eccles & Midgley, 1989). For example, in a study by Trebilco, Atkinson, and Atkinson (1977), students reported less favorable interpersonal relations with their teachers after the transition to secondary school than before. Similarly, Feldlaufer, Midgley, and Eccles (1988) found that both students and observers rated junior high school math teachers as less friendly, less supportive, and less caring than the teachers these same students had 1 year earlier in the last year of elementary school. The seventh-grade teachers in this study also reported that they trusted the students less than did these students' sixth-grade teachers (Midgley et al., 1988b).

Research on the effects of classroom climate indicates that the quality of student–teacher relationships is associated with students' academic motivation and attitudes toward school (e.g., Fraser & Fisher, 1982; Moos, 1979; Trickett & Moos, 1974). Consequently, there is reason to believe that transition into a less supportive classroom will impact negatively on early adolescents' interest in the subject matter being taught in that classroom. Midgley et al. (1988a) tested this hypothesis. As predicted, it was the early adolescents who moved from elementary teachers they perceived to be high in support to junior high school teachers they perceived to be low in support who showed the commonly reported decline in the value they attached to math; in contrast, the early adolescents who moved from teachers they perceived to be low in support to teachers they perceived to be high in support showed an increase in the value they attached to math. These differences were especially marked among the low-achieving students, suggesting that low-achieving students are particularly at risk when they move to less facilitative classroom environments following a school transition.

Organization of Instruction.    Third, the shift to junior high school is associated with an increase in practices such as whole-class task organization and between-classroom ability grouping (see Eccles & Midgley, 1989). For example, in the MSALT study, whole-group instruction was the norm in the seventh grade, small-group instruction was rare, and individualized instruction was not observed at all. In contrast, the sixth-grade teachers mixed whole- and small-group instruction within and across subjects areas (Rounds & Osaki, 1982). Similar shifts toward increased whole-class instruction, with most students working on the same assignments at the same time, using the same textbooks, and doing the same homework assignments, were evident in the MSALT study (Feldlaufer et al., 1988). In addition, several reports have documented the increased use of between-class ability grouping beginning in junior high school (e.g., Oakes, 1981).

Changes such as these increase social comparison, concerns about evaluation, and competitiveness (see Eccles, Midgley, & Adler, 1984; Rosenholtz & Simpson, 1984). They may also increase the likelihood that teachers will use normative grading criteria and more public forms of evaluation, both of which negatively affect many early adolescents' self-perceptions and motivation. These changes may also make aptitude differences more salient to both teachers and students, leading to increased teacher expectancy effects and decreased feelings of efficacy among teachers (see Eccles & Wigfield, 1985).

Teacher Efficacy.    Fourth, junior high school teachers feel less effective as teachers, especially for low-ability students. This was one of largest differences found between sixth- and seventh-grade teachers in the MSALT study. Seventh-grade teachers in these junior high schools reported much lower confidence in their teaching efficacy than did the sixth-grade elementary school teachers in the same school districts (Midgley et al., 1988b). Others have reported similar results. W. Alexander and George (1981) found that teachers in traditional junior high

schools had a lower sense of their teaching efficacy than did teachers in a more innovative middle grades school.

Several studies have documented the impact of teacher efficacy on student beliefs, attitudes, motivation, and achievement. For example, Brookover et al. (1979), using schools as the unit of analysis, found negative correlations between teachers' sense of academic futility and students' self-concept of ability and self-reliance. W. Alexander and George (1981), in the study just mentioned, found that teachers in the more innovative middle grades school had higher expectancies for student success and also were more likely to take personal responsibility for student failure than were the junior high school teachers. Ashton (1985) found that teachers' sense of efficacy related positively to high school students' performance on math and language arts achievement test scores. The more efficacious teachers also were more encouraging and supportive of students.

Given these associations, differences in teachers' sense of efficacy before and after the transition to junior high school could contribute to the decline in early adolescents' beliefs about their academic competency and potential. Midgley, Feldlaufer, and Eccles (1989) tested this hypothesis. They divided their adolescent sample into four groups based on median splits of their math teachers' ratings of their personal teaching efficacy. The largest group of students (559 out of the 1,329 included in these analyses) moved from a high-efficacy sixth-grade math teacher to a low-efficacy seventh-grade math teacher. Another 474 adolescents had low-efficacy teachers both years, 117 moved from low- to high-efficacy teachers, and 179 had high-efficacy teachers both years. As predicted, the adolescents who moved from high-efficacy to low-efficacy teachers during the transition (the most common pattern) ended their first year in junior high school with lower expectancies for themselves in math, lower perceptions of their performance in math, and higher perceptions of the difficulty of math than the adolescents who had experienced no change in teacher efficacy or who had moved from low- to high-efficacy teachers. These effects were especially marked among the low-achieving adolescents. By the end of the junior high school year, the confidence that those low-achieving adolescents who had moved from high- to low-efficacy teachers had in their ability to master mathematics had declined dramatically—a drop that could well mark the beginning of the downward spiral in school motivation that eventually leads to school dropout for so many low-achieving adolescents. It is important to note, however, that this same decline was *not* characteristic of the low-achieving adolescents who moved to high-efficacy seventh-grade math teachers.

Cognitive Level of Academic Content.    Fifth, despite what one might expect, given what we know about cognitive development at this age, there is evidence that classwork during the first year of junior high school requires lower levels of cognitive skill than classwork at the elementary level. One rationale often given for the large, departmentalized junior high school system is its efficiency in providing early adolescents with higher level academic work and more varied academic courses taught by specialists in their fields. It is argued that the early adolescents are ready for more formal instruction in the various subject areas. Two assumptions are implicit in this argument. First, it is assumed that more formal, departmentalized teaching is conducive to the learning of higher order cognitive processes.

Second, it is assumed that children in junior high school are undertaking higher order learning tasks in their departmentalized courses. Both of these assumptions can be questioned. For example, in an observational study of 11 junior high school science classes, only a very small proportion of tasks required higher level creative or expressive skills; the most frequent activity involved copying answers from the board or textbook onto worksheets (Fleming & Chambers, 1983; Mergendoller, Marchman, Mitman, & Packer, 1988). Similarly, Walberg, House, and Steele (1973) rated the level of complexity of student assignments across Grades 6 to 12 according to Bloom's taxonomy of educational objectives. The proportion of low-level activities peaked in Grade 9, the first year after the students in this district made the transition into secondary school. Both of these studies, as well as other studies, suggest that the actual cognitive demands made on adolescents decrease rather than increase as they make the transition from primary school into secondary school. No one has researched the impact of this decline in the cognitive demands placed on students, but one could speculate that its impact is likely to be negative, especially in light of the more rigorous grading practices often associated with this school transition (see review below). Although the students have been led to believe that they are moving to a more challenging school environment, they may well find themselves in classes that are reviewing the material they learned in elementary school, and they are likely to be given lower grades for their work. As we shall see below, this experience is not likely to facilitate their motivation.

Grading Practices.   Finally, junior high school teachers appear to use a higher standard in judging students' competence and in grading their performance than do elementary school teachers (see Eccles & Midgley, 1989). There is no stronger predictor of students' self-confidence and efficacy than the grades they receive. If grades change, then we would expect to see a concomitant shift in the adolescents' self-perceptions and academic motivation. There is evidence that junior high school teachers use stricter and more social comparison–based standards than elementary schoolteachers to assess student competency and to evaluate student performance, leading to a drop in grades for many early adolescents as they make the transition into junior high school. For example, Finger and Silverman (1966) found that 54 percent of the students in New York State schools experienced a decline in their grades when they moved into junior high school. Similarly, Simmons and Blyth (1987) found a greater drop in grades between sixth and seventh grade for adolescents making the transition to junior high school at this point than for adolescents enrolled in kindergarten through eighth grade schools. Roderick (1992) found a similar difference in the likelihood of a grade drop between fifth and sixth grade, depending on whether the students moved into a middle school or remained in a kindergarten through sixth grade elementary school between these two grades. Finally, the decline in grades is not matched by a decline in the adolescents' scores on standardized achievement tests, suggesting that the decline reflects a change in grading practices rather than a change in the rate of students' learning (Kavrell & Petersen, 1984). Imagine what this decline in grades might do to early adolescents' self-confidence, especially in light of the fact that the material is not likely to be more intellectually challenging.

Although neither Simmons and Blyth nor Roderick looked at this specific question, both documented the impact of this grade drop on subsequent school performance and dropout. Even controlling for a youth's performance prior to the school transition, the magnitude of the grade drop following the transition into either junior high school or middle school is a major predictor of early school leaving in both studies.

*Summary.*  Changes such as those reviewed in the last several pages are likely to have a negative effect on many children's motivational orientation toward school at any grade level. But Eccles and Midgley (1989) have argued that these types of school environmental changes are particularly harmful in early adolescence, in light of what is known about psychological development during this stage of life. Evidence from a variety of sources suggests that early adolescent development is characterized by increases in desire for autonomy, peer orientation, self-focus and self-consciousness, salience of identity issues, concern over heterosexual relationships, and capacity for abstract cognitive activity (see B. B. Brown, 1990; Eccles & Midgley, 1989; Harter, 1990b; Katchadourian, 1990; Keating, 1990; Simmons & Blyth, 1987). Simmons and Blyth have argued that adolescents need a reasonably safe and an intellectually challenging environment to adapt to these shifts, an environment that provides a "zone of comfort" as well as new opportunities for growth. In light of these needs, the environmental changes often associated with the transition to junior high school seem especially harmful in that they emphasize competition, social comparison, and ability self-assessment at a time of heightened self-focus; they decrease decision-making and choice at a time when the desire for control is growing; they emphasize lower level cognitive strategies at a time when the ability to use higher level strategies is increasing; and they disrupt social networks at a time when adolescents are especially concerned with peer relationships and may be in special need of close adult relationships outside of the home. The nature of these environmental changes, coupled with the normal course of individual development, is likely to result in a developmental mismatch so that the fit between the early adolescent and the classroom environment is particularly poor, increasing the risk of negative motivational outcomes, especially for adolescents who are having difficulty succeeding in school academically. One important task for researchers in the 1990s is to assess whether the kinds of mismatch between school environments and early adolescent development we have discussed can be generalized to early adolescents in different kinds of educational settings (e.g., rural vs. urban schools; rich vs. poorer schools) or to different groups of early adolescents (see Berliner, 1989).

## The Transition to High School

Although there has been less work on the transition to high school than on the transition to junior high school, the work on high school environments suggests that many of the same problems noted earlier for the junior high school transition characterize the transition into high school as well. Several of the changes are continued and exaggerated. For example, high schools are typically even larger and more bureaucratic than junior high and middle schools. Based on arguments related to the economies of scale, most public school districts have moved toward consolidation at the secondary school level. It was hoped that consolidation would increase efficiency and provide more equal educational opportunities for all students in the district. In a major review of the impact of high school organization on teachers and students. Bryk, Lee, and Smith (1990) concluded that

these aims . . . have not been achieved. The incidence of dropping out . . . increased through the 1970's and remains depressingly high, with rates in excess of 50 percent not uncommon in urban schools; . . . [T]he expansion of school bureaucracy . . . has contributed to student passivity and teacher alienation, both of which are now pervasive. A system of mass education relying on processes of specialization and centralization has promoted a breakdown in human commitment. . . . . These forces appear especially disruptive in large urban districts. (p. 201)

They go on to give numerous examples of how the sense of community among teachers and students is undermined by school size and bureaucratic structure (e.g., Bryk & Driscoll, 1988; Newmann, 1981). Teachers do not know each other and do not know the students. Little effort is made to make the instruction relevant to the students. There is little opportunity for students and teachers to get to know each other and, as a consequence, there is distrust between them and little attachment to a common set of goals and values. As was true of the transition into junior high school, there is little opportunity for the students to form a mentorlike relationship with a nonfamilial adult. It is predictable that such an environment will undermine the motivation and involvement of many students, especially those who are not doing particularly well academically, those not enrolled in the favored classes, and those who become alienated from the values of the adults in the high school. But few studies have actually followed students through this transition in order to test this hypothesis; and even fewer studies have investigated ways in which existing high schools could be modified to overcome some of these problems. Designing and evaluating such interventions is an important challenge for the 1990s.

Also for reasons of efficiency, most large public high schools have organized instruction around curricular tracks that sort students into different groups. As a result, there is even greater diversity in the educational experiences of high school students than of middle grades students. Unfortunately, this diversity is often associated more with the students' social class and ethnic group than with differences in the students' talents and interest (Lee & Bryk, 1989). As a result, curricular tracking has served to reinforce social stratification rather than foster optimal education for all students, particularly in large schools (Lee & Bryk, 1989). Lee and Bryk have shown that average school achievement levels do not benefit from this curricular tracking—quite the contrary. Evidence comparing Catholic high schools with public high schools suggests that average school achievement levels are increased when all students are required to take the same challenging curriculum. This conclusion is true even after one has controlled for student selectivity factors. A more thorough examination of how the organization and structure of our high schools influence cognitive, motivational, and achievement outcomes should be an important task for research in the 1990s. During the 1980s we learned much about the transition

from elementary to junior high school; now it is time to look more closely at transitions into and out of high school.

*Leaving High School Early: The Problem of Dropping Out.* One major difference between middle school and high school is that there are many more social and educational choices available to high school students, choices that can have both positive and negative consequences. The educational choices students face include the kinds of classes they will continue to take in high school; for example, whether to focus on academically oriented or vocationally oriented courses. A more fundamental educational decision is whether or not to stay in school at all. Along with these choices about schooling and academics, high school students (and, increasingly, middle school students) face a variety of social choices as well: how sexually active to become, whether or not to use drugs and alcohol, and whether or not to engage in different kinds of deviant or criminal behaviors. Some adolescents struggle with eating disorders. Others, for a variety of reasons, decide that they cannot cope with their circumstances, and commit suicide. These distressing choices, and the troubling statistics showing higher levels of teen pregnancy, adolescent drug use, and adolescent crime and violence, indicate that more and more adolescents are engaging in what McCord (1990) calls problem behaviors (see also Dryfoss, 1990; Lerner et al., 1994). A complete review of the work on these problem behaviors is outside the scope of this chapter; interested readers should consult Hauser and Bowlds (1990) and McCord (1990) for excellent discussions of stress, coping, and problem behaviors that occur during adolescence. Because we are focusing primarily on academic outcomes in this chapter, in this section we focus on the issue of dropping out of school.

In middle or junior high school students can disengage from school by not trying, acting out, or being truant; however, they still are required to be in school. At age 16 students can make the decision to leave school, and unfortunately, many choose to do so. Although there is debate about the exact numbers of students dropping out (see Rumberger, 1987), the numbers are large enough to be a major social problem. Further, a disproportionate number of African-American and Hispanic students leave high school before graduating; in some school districts as many as 50 percent or more of these students leave school before completing their degree work (Bryk et al., 1990). Entwisle (1990) reviewed the work that has examined the characteristics of students more likely to drop out of high school (see also Rumberger, 1987). These characteristics include low ability, low achievement, coming from a poverty background, working too many hours while trying to go to school, and early pregnancy. Entwisle pointed out that adequate prospective studies that could be used to identify which children would be most likely to drop out are lacking. Work that is available, however, suggests that students who do poorly in elementary school, who exhibit serious behavior problems in school, and who are truant on a frequent basis will be more likely to drop out of high school. Finn (1989) discussed how these problems often are interrelated. Understanding the factors related to dropping out certainly is important; however, Rumberger argued for the need to understand better *processes* related to dropping out, rather than just listing factors associated with the problem. In beginning to address that issue, Finn argued for a participation-identification model of the dropout process, stating that students who participate less in academic and nonacademic activities in school, beginning in elementary school, will identify less with the educational process and ultimately will be more likely to drop out of school.

As part of participation-identification processes, Finn pointed to the importance of valuing of school, a construct we have discussed in this chapter and elsewhere (e.g., Eccles et al., 1983; Wigfield, 1994; Wigfield & Eccles, 1992). Students who do not value math will be more likely to opt out of math when they no longer have to take it. Do adolescents' specific achievement values relate to their bigger decision about dropping out or staying in school? Assessing students' particular subjective values over the school years may help predict which students will become disengaged from school and could provide a better model for how students' achievement-related beliefs influence their decisions to stay in or leave school. Most researchers examining how students' beliefs relate to dropping out of school have focused on students' general self-esteem, a construct that may be too broad to have much predictive utility in explaining specific decisions like dropping out of school (see Finn, 1989, for a critique of the self-esteem explanation of dropping out of school).

We have been discussing dropping out of school as a choice; however, many students drift into dropping out of school rather than consciously deciding to do so. That is, the circumstances of their lives are such that continuing to go to school would be very difficult. These circumstances include the economic pressure many poor students face, discrimination, and poor schools, to name just a few. These circumstances play a major role in influencing some students to drop out (see Finn, 1989; Rumberger, 1987). For the students who do make a more conscious decision that school is not for them, the relative contribution of both specific achievement values and more general valuing of education also plays a significant role, one that has not been addressed sufficiently.

One of the major outcomes of dropping out of school is that it seriously reduces the adolescent's chances of obtaining a well-paying job (see Rumberger, 1987). Rumberger estimated that the economic and social costs of dropping out both to the individual and to our society at large run into the billions of dollars. Not only do individuals who drop out lose potential earnings, but society often has to provide more extensive social services for dropouts, because they are more likely to engage in some or all of the problem behaviors that McCord (1990) discussed. Although receiving a high school diploma may alleviate some of these problems, in today's society a high school degree no longer ensures reasonable job prospects. When U.S. society was an industrial society, a high school diploma often was enough to guarantee access to reasonably well-paying and secure jobs. As we move into a postindustrial society, that no longer is the case; indeed, some students now may be dropping out of high school because they realize a high school diploma will not mean much to them in terms of job prospects. Rumberger (1987) and Finn (1989) both discussed the need for intervention programs to keep more students in school, programs that focus on giving those students skills they will need in the workplace. Encouraging more students to stay in school, and finding meaningful and rewarding things for them to do after they finish high school, is an important challenge for the later 1990s. This challenge is important enough that the Clinton

administration already is talking about ways to restructure high schools so that students not going to college receive adequate technical skill training so that they can obtain good jobs in the increasingly technological workplace.

Other students finish high school and move on to the world of work, or to college. What happens to them? That is the broad focus of the next section.

## DEVELOPMENTAL CHANGES DURING LATE ADOLESCENCE AND YOUNG ADULTHOOD

This section describes the important changes that occur after the high school years. As in the previous section, we focus first on changes in later adolescents' and young adults' cognition, self-concepts, and motivation. We briefly consider group differences in these important constructs. We then discuss how individuals cope with the transitions from high school to college, and from college to the work force, although space limitations curtail the discussion on transitions. We realize that there are many individuals who do not go on to college and that the trajectories of development may be somewhat different for them (see McCall, Evahn, & Kratzer, 1992). Nevertheless, we focus on college students because this is a handbook on educational psychology, and the college classroom is an important site for development, learning, and instruction.

As we discussed earlier, both psychological and educational theory and research are moving away from organismic models that highlight the individual without giving equal or more weight to the context, and toward more contextual models (Bruner, 1990; Pintrich, 1994). However, organismic models that focus on the individual have to date been the most frequently used models in research on college students and are representative of much of the research reviewed in this section. In contrast, research on adults has tended to rely on a life-span approach to development and seems to represent an adequate integration of the tensions between organismic and contextual perspectives (Lerner, 1986). These life-span approaches (see Abeles, 1987; Baltes, 1987; Baltes & Schaie, 1973; Featherman, 1983) assume that development can be both quantitative and qualitative and is ongoing across all ages, not just limited to certain ages like childhood and adolescence, as suggested in many organismic models. In addition, life-span approaches generally describe development as being multidimensional (changes occur across biological, social, cognitive, and affective dimensions); multidetermined (changes can be a function of biological, social, physical, psychological, and historical events); and multidirectional (changes can occur in different patterns and trajectories, depending on both individual and situational factors; change is not necessarily directed along a single path to a particular end point such as formal operations). Finally, a recent assumption of the life-span approach is that the process of development is a dynamic relation between growth (gain) and decline (loss), with a larger ratio of gains to losses early in life but the ratio declining with age (Baltes, 1987). Of course, along with life-span approaches there are other contextual models, including Vygotskian, constructivist, and postmodern deconstructionist views, available to guide future research and thinking. One of the key issues for future research on adolescents and young adults is the specification and refinement of these different contextual models and their application to classic problems in educational psychology such as classroom learning and motivation.

## Cognitive Development in Late Adolescence and Young Adulthood

We discussed earlier how cognition changes during adolescence; we build on that discussion in this section. To recapitulate briefly, in terms of research on adolescent thinking and cognitive development, Piagetian theory (Inhelder & Piaget, 1958) is the standard model, with the fourth stage, formal operations, representing the sine qua non of mature thinking. The hallmarks of formal operational thinking (cf. Flavell, Miller, & Miller, 1993; Keating, 1980, 1990) include (a) abstract thinking, or the ability to think about possibilities beyond concrete reality; (b) propositional thinking, or the ability to think about logical relations among ideas, concepts, propositions, and cognitive operations; (c) combinatorial thinking, or the ability to generate different possible combinations of ideas and cognitive operations; (d) hypothetical-deductive thinking, or the ability to think scientifically, including the ability to define and control variables and to generate, test, and revise hypotheses; (e) the ability to regulate cognition, including the ability to define a problem, select a strategy, and revise options in the course of solving a problem, (f) metacognition, or the ability to think about cognitive processes, memory, learning, language, and thinking; and (g) the ability to be self-reflective about not just cognitive processes but also issues such as identity, existence, morality, and personal relationships.

The second decade of life is when much of this thinking should develop, especially the latter third (18–20 years), when many students are in college. In fact, in classic Piagetian theory, most college students should have attained formal operations. However, the research on college students suggests that almost half have not acquired formal operations by their freshmen year (Pascarella & Terenzini, 1991). In addition, the few longitudinal studies of college students (e.g., Eisert & Tomlinson-Keasey, 1978; Mentkowski & Strait, 1983) have shown very small gains in formal operational thinking from freshman to senior years. Moreover, depending on the sample (including both secondary- and post-secondary-school students) and the nature of the assessment tasks, the results can range from zero to 100% of the sample demonstrating formal operations, with most estimates in the 40 percent to 70 percent range (King, 1986; Neimark, 1983; Pascarella & Terenzini, 1991).

Obviously, there are difficulties in the operational definition and assessment of formal operations (Keating, 1980, 1990). These formal operations are typically assessed by interviewing students regarding their strategies for solving a variety of Piagetian-type tasks such as conservation, the balance beam problem, the pendulum problem, and their reasoning on syllogisms or the creation of combinations. These tasks are decontextualized and often do not accurately reflect students' knowledge on academic or school tasks (Keating, 1980; King, 1986; Laboratory of Comparative Human Cognition, 1983). In addition, the problem of intraindividual differences in the level of reasoning depending on the domain assessed remains a major problem for

any strong stage model (in Piagetian terms, the problem of horizontal decalage). For example, DeLisi and Staudt (1980) found that college students majoring in physics, political science, and English were more likely to display formal operational reasoning on problems relevant to their discipline when presented with the traditional pendulum problem (physics), a political socialization problem, or a literary analysis problem. This type of domain specificity of reasoning suggests that students' thinking may depend more on their knowledge in a particular subject area and on the type of task presented to them than on any broad general logical structure such as a stage of formal operations (cf., A. L. Brown et al., 1983; Gelman & Baillarageon, 1983; Glaser, 1984). Accordingly, there has been a move away from strong stage formalizations such as Piagetian formal operations in the study of adolescent cognitive development (Keating, 1990; Pintrich, 1990).

There are, however, more recent post-Piagetian or neo-Piagetian models that describe cognitive development beyond formal operations (e.g., Case, 1985, 1992; Demetriou, Efklides, & Platsidou, 1993; Fischer, 1980). These models are organismic and assume that cognitive development is hierarchical, with later stages dependent on the attainment of earlier stages such as formal operations. These models do propose stage-related descriptions of thinking, but they tend to use a "soft" stage model where stages can be more domain specific and related to actual experience rather than "hard" stage models where development is universal and not context dependent (Kohlberg & Armon, 1984). As Campbell (1993) points out, there are different variations on this domain-specific stage development notion, with the weakest version suggesting that development is the same in different domains but that the pace of development varies (e.g., Fischer, 1980). Stronger versions include the idea that there can be different steps in different domains (e.g., Turiel & Davidson, 1986) and the strongest version is that development follows different processes in different domains (e.g., Keil, 1990). The nature and definition of a stage is one of the key issues in current cognitive developmental theory and research in adolescence and adulthood. In addition, the neo-Piagetian proposal that development is stagelike but can vary by domain still leaves unresolved questions regarding the nature of domains. These questions include (a) How are domains to be identified? (b) What are the boundaries between domains? (c) Do these boundaries remain fixed or do they change with development? and (d) Within a "domain," are there subdomains and subsubdomains (see Campbell, 1993)?

Fischer and his colleagues (Fischer, 1980; Fischer, Hand, & Russell, 1984; Fischer & Kenny, 1986; Fischer, Kenny, & Pipp, 1990) have proposed a skill theory of development that builds on Piagetian theory but does not assume universal change in cognition across domains. For instance, this model accepts horizontal decalage as both theoretically and empirically important rather than as something to be explained away. Fischer argues that skill development is domain specific as a function of individual differences in aptitude and motivation as well as variations in environmental conditions that might support or discourage skilled performance. He uses the same construct as Vygotsky's zone of proximal development, albeit labeled range of development, to describe the difference between displaying a skill under conditions of optimal support and not being able to use a skill in many ordinary environmental conditions

(Fischer et al., 1990). There are ten levels in skill theory, with levels 7 through 10 emerging between 10 and 25 years of age. Levels 7 and 8 (approximately ages 10–15) parallel many of the operations subsumed under formal operations concerning the use of abstractions and the coordination of two abstractions. Level 9 (ages 19–21) involves building abstract systems in which a number of different abstractions (intention, responsibility, morality) can be related to one another in complex ways. Finally, level 10 (ages 24–26) involves the integration of two or more abstract systems from level 9 to form a general theory or generate general principles such as an overall epistemological framework (Fischer et al., 1990). This model represents an integration of organismic and life-span views and provides a useful theoretical model that can be applied to development in many domains, not just cognition. For example, Harter (1990c) has suggested that the development of a general ability to coordinate and integrate abstractions serves an adaptive function for adolescents as they become better able to cope with their multiple, and potentially conflicting, self-concepts. Recently, Kitchener, Lynch, Fischer, & Wood (1993) mapped the development of epistemological thinking onto Fischer's skill levels.

In another model that describes thinking beyond formal operations, Commons and his colleagues (Commons & Richards, 1984a, 1984b; Commons, Richards, & Kuhn, 1982) have described postformal stages of development that go beyond the reasoning about variables indicative of formal operations to reasoning about systems of variables (fifth stage) to reasoning about paradigms (sixth stage). These abilities to think systematically and paradigmatically would be especially relevant to college courses requiring students to compare and contrast different theories and paradigms, such as courses in the social sciences or education. A related model includes the empirical research on college students' ability to think dialectically (Basseches, 1980, 1984, 1986) based on Riegel's (1973, 1975, 1976) suggestion that a fifth stage of development beyond formal operations would involve dialectical thinking. Basseches has described 24 schemas or dialectical operations, among which are the ability to look for and recognize examples of the dialectic inherent in competing principles, models, or theories (cf. the systematic and paradigmatic thinking of Commons) and the ability to use dialectical logic to analyze different systems of knowledge and theories in terms of their context and relationships to each other (Basseches, 1986). The ability to use these operations would be related to students' and teachers' understanding of many of the neo-Vygotskian and situated cognition models that emphasize the situational, contextual, and dialectical nature of behavior. To the extent that students in educational psychology courses at the undergraduate or graduate level are not able to use these dialectical schemas, this model would predict that they would have difficulty in those courses.

Another developmental model that addresses some of the same issues and has enjoyed popularity in the research literature on higher education as well as in the literature on college student counseling and faculty improvement is W. G. Perry's (1970, 1981) model of college student development. In contrast to the emphasis on the formal logic of students' reasoning, as described above, Perry has been more concerned with the content of college students' epistemological reasoning about the intellectual and moral relativism often encountered in the course of a college education. The nine stages and transitions are quite detailed (see W. G. Perry, 1970, 1981), but the initial positions describe students who are moral and intellectual absolutists and believe that there are correct solutions for every moral and intellectual problem and rely on authorities to teach them the proper answers. The middle positions in Perry's scheme are characterized by the discovery of relativistic answers to problems and contextual reasoning about issues. In these stages authorities are perceived as other individuals who have beliefs and opinions that may be helpful to the student in understanding the moral and intellectual issues, but authorities' beliefs may be challenged on contextual and relativistic grounds. The final stages in Perry's model describe students as developing a set of personal values to which they become committed as an expression of their own identity. This personal commitment helps the student cope with the relativity inherent in many intellectual and moral issues and allows the student to move away from absolutism and idealism to the pragmatic considerations and commitments of adulthood (Labouvie-Vief, 1982).

Besides the methodological issues concerning operationalization and measurement (use of interviews and reliable coding of responses) and sampling (original developmental scheme based on a longitudinal study of 84 undergraduate men from Harvard), one of the theoretical difficulties with Perry's description of the stages of college student development is that it seems to blur some important distinctions between intellectual, moral, and identity development. In particular, the model seems to shift away from the epistemological concerns of stages 1 through 5 to identity issues in stages 6 through 9 (Pascarella & Terenzini, 1991). Following this criticism, Kitchener and her colleagues developed the reflective judgment model, which focuses solely on the development of individuals' beliefs and assumptions about the nature of knowledge or forms of epistemic cognition (King & Kitchener, 1994; King, Kitchener, Davison, Parker, & Wood, 1983; Kitchener, 1983, 1986; Kitchener & King, 1981; Kitchener et al., 1993). This includes individuals' understandings about what can and cannot be known (e.g., how a child learns), how they can come to know something (e.g., through experience, research, intuition, etc.), and how certain they can be in their knowledge (e.g., absolutely, probabilistically). These assumptions about the nature of knowledge influence how individuals will justify their beliefs, identify and define problems, seek solutions, and revise their problem-solving behavior (Kitchener, 1986; cf. Arlin, 1986; Pintrich et al., 1993; Posner, Strike, Hewson, & Gertzog, 1982). The model proposes that there are seven stages that characterize the different levels of epistemic cognition. Individuals in the first stage believe that reality can be understood through direct observation, that there is no uncertainty in this knowledge, and that there is therefore no need to justify one's beliefs. The second and third stages reflect a move away from these absolutist beliefs, although there is still an assumption of a true reality and an assumption that differences in perceptions of reality are due to false claims or uncertainty. Direct observation and knowledgeable authorities provide a means of deciding among competing claims in these stages. In the fourth and fifth stages reality is seen as subjective and dependent on individuals' perceptions and experience. Accordingly, in this world view, beliefs are not certain and can be developed only through a reliance on data, logic, and rules of inquiry that are applicable to a specific context.

In the final two stages, there is a move away from the purely relativistic thinking of the fourth and fifth stages to beliefs that reality is constructed through personal interpretations and that appropriate methods (e.g., personal evaluation of the opinions of experts, critical inquiry, or synthesis) are available for evaluating the evidence for different world views. This leads to the development of a personal world view that acknowledges that some claims about reality are better or more complete than others (Kitchener, 1986).

Baxter Magolda (1992) and Kuhn (1991) also have examined the development of epistemological reasoning. Baxter Magolda interviewed 70 male and female college students over the course of 5 years, from their first year in college to 1 year after graduation. She found that students' responses to her open-ended interviews about the nature of learning and knowledge evolved over time through four levels, from a focus on absolute knowing (knowledge is certain) through transitional knowing (knowledge is partially certain, partially uncertain), to independent knowing (all knowledge is uncertain), to the final level of contextual knowing (knowledge is contextual and judged on the basis of evidence within a certain domain or context). Kuhn's cross-sectional study of individuals ranging in age from middle adolescence (14–15 years old) to adulthood (through the 20s, 40s, and 60s) found a similar shift across age groups from an absolutist to a multiplist to an evaluative perspective on the nature of knowledge and epistemology.

The development of epistemological thinking is an important aspect of a college education. It appears that there is a developmental shift over time (in both cross-sectional and longitudinal studies), with upperclass students demonstrating higher levels of thinking about the nature of knowledge, evidence, and rules of inquiry, with the biggest shift often coming between the first and second years of college (Pascarella & Terenzini, 1991). In addition, even when age, socioeconomic status, and general ability differences between those who attend and those who do not attend college are controlled for, there appears to be a strong effect of a college education on students' ability to reason about epistemological issues (Kuhn, 1991; Pascarella & Terenzini, 1991).

Although an important outcome of college, these models of epistemological reasoning still focus on general reasoning schemas that cut across domains, reflecting the authors' general organismic metatheory. There is a need for more research on the domain specificity of students' reasoning in line with the assumptions of a life-span approach. For example, Donald (1990) has shown that experts in certain disciplines (professors in both basic and applied fields of study in physics, psychology, and English) use different methods for determining truth and verifying knowledge claims and make differential use of conceptual models and empirical evidence. It would seem likely that students majoring in the different disciplines might reason differently, depending on the principles used by their professors. Moreover, Kuhn (1991) found domain and intraindividual differences in students' reasoning and epistemological theories about school failure, unemployment, and recidivism in criminals (three social science topics), suggesting a role for content knowledge within a discipline. Accordingly, there is a need for more research on how these general reasoning schemas interact with students' content and disciplinary knowledge in specific domains. For example, Schommer and her colleagues (Schom-

mer, 1990; Schommer, Crouse, & Rhodes, 1992) showed that college students' beliefs about the nature of knowledge and learning influenced their comprehension and metacognition. Students who believed that knowledge is simple (knowledge consists of isolated facts), that learning occurs quickly, and that knowledge is unchanging were lower in metacognitive comprehension monitoring and actual comprehension, even when prior knowledge was taken into account. These two studies focused on specific domains (statistics, psychology, health/nutrition) and parallel some of the findings for students' beliefs about mathematics (Schoenfeld, 1983, 1985).

Research on these epistemological beliefs and the role they play in student learning, cognition, and motivation is just beginning but promises to be an important area of future endeavor as traditional scientific and rational models of thinking and reasoning are called into question by constructivist, deconstructionist, and feminist scholars. Research is needed on how and why certain types of epistemological beliefs may influence students' thinking and learning. In addition, research on epistemological beliefs is important for understanding not just student learning, but also teacher development, learning, and education (Pintrich, 1990). It may be that an important goal of teacher education involves changing novice teachers' absolutist beliefs about education toward a more evaluative and reflective belief system about education. Finally, the vast majority of this research has focused on college students, but it is likely that the genesis of these epistemological beliefs occurs earlier, in junior high and high school. In one of the few studies that has examined high school students, Schommer (1993) found the same pattern of epistemological beliefs as she found in college students. Clearly, these beliefs begin to develop earlier than the freshman year in college, but there is little research on the early development of these beliefs and the roles that different school contexts may play in that development.

At the same time, a great deal of conceptual and definitional work remains to be done. The general epistemological beliefs about knowledge and reasoning that are a concern of W. Perry and Kitchener are not the same as beliefs about how to learn in mathematics (Schoenfeld, 1983), or how to learn in general (Baxter Magolda, 1992). Nor are they a general orientation to the source of knowledge (Belenky, Clinchy, Goldberger, & Tarule, 1986). There has been a tendency to label a variety of beliefs as epistemological beliefs (e.g., learning is innate, success is unrelated to hard work; see Schommer et al., 1992) when some of these beliefs may be better classified as motivational beliefs. These different beliefs may be related and general epistemological beliefs may have some motivational "force" to inspire more cognitive engagement, but there needs to be more theoretical and empirical work on the nature of these beliefs and the different functions they may play in learning.

In addition, there has been very little research on how gender, ethnicity, and socioeconomic differences may influence students' reasoning and their beliefs. Belenky et al. (1986) interviewed college women about their epistemological beliefs and found that some women emphasized a more connected and empathic reasoning style beyond their earlier absolutist and multiplist stages. They suggested that this trajectory may be an equally valid path for the development of reasoning, in contrast to the final stages of Perry's or Kitchener's models, which rely on a more traditional scientific paradigm as the epitome of sophisticated thinking. At the same time, Baxter Magolda (1992) and Kuhn (1991), who included both men and women in their samples, did not find very important gender differences in epistemological reasoning; this result contrasts with the work of researchers such as Belenky et al. (1986) or Gilligan (1982). In this sense the argument of Belenky et al. parallels other feminist critiques (e.g., Gilligan, 1982; Noddings, 1984) of Kohlberg's and Piaget's models of development. The nature of these gender differences and of potential ethnic or class differences needs to be explored in more detail in future research. At the same time, the basic construction and search for differences along gender, ethnicity, or class lines can paradoxically reify some of the bias and inequality inherent in the social structures that create the need to examine questions of differences (Hare-Mustin & Marecek, 1988). Accordingly, future research needs to be sensitive to this issue and to the possibility that, given a life-span perspective that emphasizes contextual influences and experiences, there probably are important individual differences within the broad categories of gender, class, or ethnicity.

In summary, current research on cognitive development in the college years has addressed issues of both the content and form of thinking. As domain-specific and contextual models become more important and researchers move away from very general Piagetian and information-processing models, issues regarding the content of students' thinking will become even more important. There is a great need for research on students' understanding of disciplinary and epistemological knowledge, not just the domain-specific declarative knowledge represented in college courses. It appears that acquisition of domain-specific and discipline-specific knowledge is one of the key cognitive abilities that college students acquire as they major in different areas (Snow & Swanson, 1992), paralleling the cognitive development of very young children (Wellman & Gelman, 1992). Accordingly, research on late adolescent thinking in the next decade needs to develop in-depth descriptions of students' theories and frameworks for thinking in these different domains.

## Self-Concept and Motivation in Late Adolescence and Young Adulthood

*Identity Development: General Models.* Paralleling the Piagetian view of cognitive development, many of the traditional organismic models of social and personal development conceptualize development as evolving over time in terms of both the objective events (i.e., physical, social, biological) that occur at certain chronological ages or stages in the development of the individual as well as the more subjective, psychological issues that these events seem to evoke in individuals (e.g., Erikson, 1963; Levinson, 1978; Neugarten, 1968; Veroff & Veroff, 1980). As Brim and Ryff (1980) point out, biological maturational events, social role changes in marital, career, and family status, and changes in the physical environment as a result of relocation, physical injuries or illness, or changes in physical appearance are all objective events that individuals must cope with as they develop. These events provide one aspect of the context that help shape individuals' social and personal development.

Traditional stage models propose that these contextual events are usually age dependent and in the course of normal development most individuals will cope with the psychological

issues elicited by these events at approximately the same time. For instance, regarding self-concept development, during the college years, the issue of identity remains the most salient (Chickering, 1969; Erikson, 1963; Marcia, 1980). Research has focused on the dimensions of identity as well as the structure and form of the developmental patterns. For example, one of the most popular models in the literature on higher education is Chickering's (1969) model of the seven vectors or domains of college student identity development (achieving competence, managing emotions, developing autonomy, establishing a stable identity, developing interpersonal relations, developing purpose [including career goals], and developing integrity). Development within and across these domains is assumed to show directional change following the general orthogenetic principle of increased differentiation and integration. It appears that there is development in these areas in the course of a student's four years in college, but there is very little evidence that attending college per se influences the course of development (Pascarella & Terenzini, 1991). This would be expected, in that the seven domains reflect normative life tasks most individuals confront in U.S. society regardless of college attendance.

A model that has focused more on the form of identity development is Marcia's (1980) extension of Erikson's identity versus diffusion stage. Marcia proposes that there are two dimensions of identity, presence or absence of a crisis and extent of personal commitment to an occupation and an ideology. By crossing these two dimensions, a 2 by 2 matrix is formed, generating four different individual modes or personal styles for coping with the identity issue. The most adaptive mode is labeled *identity achievement* and represents students who have experienced a crisis, wrestled with the issues, and made a commitment to a particular identity. In contrast, students who have made a commitment to an identity but who have not experienced a crisis are said to be in *foreclosure status*, suggesting a too early resolution of identity (e.g., going along with a parentally chosen occupation). The *identity diffusion mode* is represented by students who have not made any commitments and may or may not have experienced a crisis. Finally, the *moratorium mode* reflects students who are actively in crisis but have only a vague commitment (Marcia, 1980). Although these four distinct modes were originally seen as mutually exclusive categories of stable individual differences, current theorizing suggests that they may represent a normative developmental sequence (Harter, 1990c; Waterman, 1982, 1985). In addition, Waterman (1982), in line with a life-span perspective, has suggested that there may be alternative trajectories of identity development, with the potential for diffusion and moratorium to reappear after the attainment of identity achievement. Finally, Marcia's empirical work on this model remains limited, and we do not know the extent to which it can be generalized.

*Identity Development: Domain-Specific and Social Cognitive Models.* As in the area of cognitive development, general stage models provide an important description of self-concept development. However, recent research has taken a more social cognitive and life-span perspective and focused on the domain-specific features of development, intraindividual and individual differences in development, and contextual influences on development. This general constructivist approach has suggested that a variety of idiosyncratic, personal, and contextual construals of the general life events and psychological issues are experienced by individuals over the life course. The resolution of identity issues is an important psychological event in most people's lives, but there is a great deal of variability in how these issues are defined, represented, and resolved.

There are a number of models of this process, including life tasks (Cantor & Kihlstrom, 1987), current concerns (Klinger, 1977), personal projects (Little, 1983), and life themes (Csikszentmihalyi, 1985). In these constructivist models, an individual's life tasks may not follow a proscribed, universal pattern of development (e.g., identity and generativity issues may be resolved before intimacy issues). For example, in a series of studies of college students, Cantor and her colleagues (see Cantor & Kihlstrom, 1987) found that students could identify a number of concerns that were personally demanding and guided their activities. These included academic goals (doing well, getting organized) as well as social goals (making friends, being on their own, and establishing an identity). Eisenhart and Holland (e.g., Eisenhart, 1990; Holland & Eisenhart, 1988) in an ethnographic study of 23 college women found that negotiating male–female intimate relationships was a major life task of the transition to college. In addition, they noted that there were a number of different strategies the women used to resolve the difficulties surrounding these relationships but that the range of strategies was limited by certain peer group beliefs. As Cantor and Kihlstrom (1987) pointed out, these concerns reflect normative life tasks (i.e., achievement, intimacy, independence) that would be predicted by most developmental models (e.g., Erikson, 1963; Veroff & Veroff, 1980). However, the life-task approach, in line with the assumptions of a life-span contextual approach, differs in assuming that individuals will define these issues somewhat differently and will seek different strategies for solution. For example, some students defined independence in terms of coping without parental support, while others concentrated on more practical matters such as money management. In addition, students had very different problem-solving strategies as a function of their personal construal of college life tasks (Cantor & Kihlstrom, 1987). Accordingly, this model suggests that all college students will have to cope with issues related to achievement, identity, and intimacy and that a more microgenetic, intraindividual, and contextual analysis will be revealed, not a linear developmental sequence as in classic organismic models. In this developmental model, a variety of personal construals, strategies, and developmental trajectories describe social development in different contexts.

Although there are a number of social cognitive models, one commonality is that the notion of a life task (or current concern or personal project) includes an individual's representation of both a goal for the task and a strategy for solving the task. Thus, this approach describes personal development in terms of both motivational components (goals, self-beliefs) and cognitive components (strategies for problem solving and self-regulation). This conceptualization of personal and social development makes explicit the links with more general cognitive models of learning and thinking. In fact, the life-task approach of Cantor and Kihlstrom (1987) is isomorphic with models of cognition based on declarative and procedural knowledge. This basic distinction about knowing what and knowing how can be applied to traditional motivational and cognitive constructs to generate a framework for the analysis of motivational self-

knowledge and motivational strategies and cognitive knowledge and cognitive strategies. Garcia and Pintrich (1994) have proposed just such a framework to examine the role of content and self-knowledge and motivational and cognitive strategies in the academic domain. Accordingly, in terms of motivational and social development, there should be changes in both self-knowledge and strategies for regulating the self over the life span.

### Self-Schemas and Motivation

A number of models propose that motivational self-knowledge is an important construct, and *self-schemas* (Markus & Nurius, 1986) provide a way to link a variety of motivational constructs such as goals, beliefs, aspirations, motives, and affect into an organized cognitive framework (Markus & Nurius, 1986). Self-schemas are the individually constructed, dynamic, contextual, and flexible organizations of knowledge about oneself. A self-schema is similar to the traditional self-concept (Wigfield & Karparthian, 1991) in its content but functions as a much more situated, dynamic, and cognitive representation of the self than the somewhat static view implicit in traditional self-concept research. Self-schemas function as personal construals of goals and provide a self-regulatory function for individual cognition, emotion, and motivation (Markus & Kitayama, 1991). In particular, the self-schema construct includes the notion of a "possible self," which refers to a positive self-image that a person would like to become (e.g., a good learner, tennis player, spouse, parent), which can function as a goal to approach, as well as negative future self-schemas that we strive to avoid (e.g., poor, unemployed, homeless).

The developmental trajectories of self-schemas in the college years have not been investigated in many studies. In a cross-sectional study of possible selves across the life span, Cross and Markus (1991) queried 183 individuals ranging in age from 18 to 86 about their hoped-for and feared selves. They found that the younger college students (ages 18–24 years) had higher ratings of instrumentality in terms of believing that they could bring about hoped-for selves and avoid feared selves. In addition, younger individuals generated more possible selves but reported fewer strategies or actions undertaken to accomplish these selves. In contrast, the older individuals reported doing more to bring about a more limited number of possible selves. This result is in line with general theories of identity and personal development that suggest that over the course of the life span, individuals develop more focused and enacted personal identities, in contrast to the myriad of possibilities that younger adolescents think about abstractly but do not necessarily attempt to actualize. Accordingly, these results highlight the need to examine both self-schemas and the strategies to accomplish them in the course of development.

There has not been much empirical research on self-schemas in academic settings, but Garcia and Pintrich (1994) have outlined how academic self-schemas might be related to the use of various cognitive and motivational self-regulatory strategies in an academic setting. They propose that self-schemas function as "declarative knowledge of the self" that can influence the activation and use of various motivational strategies (self-handicapping, defensive pessimism) as well as cognitive learning strategies (elaboration, comprehension monitoring). The utility of the self-schema construct for research in educational psychology awaits further empirical research, but preliminary correlational studies with junior high and college students (see Garcia & Pintrich, 1993; Pintrich & Garcia, 1993; Pintrich, Garcia, & De Groot, 1994) suggest that students with positive academic self-schemas are more likely to report using more cognitive learning strategies (e.g., elaboration) and self-regulatory strategies (e.g., comprehension monitoring).

### Links Between Motivation and Achievement Behavior

Although few studies are developmental in design, a number of studies have examined the motivational strategies used by college students to accomplish life tasks or achieve possible selves. These strategies, such as self-handicapping, defensive pessimism, and reevaluation of task value and interest (Garcia & Pintrich, 1994) are used by students to control their effort and motivation and parallel Kuhl's self-regulatory strategies of motivation and emotion control (Kuhl, 1992). These motivational strategies may be automatic, habitual, and used without awareness and intentionality, but they can be brought under the intentional control of the learner (cf. Paris, Lipson, & Wixson, 1983; Schneider & Pressley, 1989). They influence students' motivated behavior in terms of choice, level of activity, and persistence at a task (see Garcia & Pintrich, 1994).

Self-handicapping refers to the creation of obstacles or withdrawal of effort to make potential failure less indicative of ability (Baumeister & Scher, 1988; Tice & Baumeister, 1990). For example, procrastination before an exam can have beneficial effects on ability attributions because failure can be attributed to lack of effort, while success can be attributed to ability (Covington, 1992; Covington & Omelich, 1979). For the self-handicapper, protection of self-worth is the most important goal, so not putting forth effort, although jeopardizing actual performance, maximizes the potential for positive self-ascriptions. College students use a variety of self-handicapping strategies that can have detrimental influences on their cognitive engagement as well as their actual learning (Covington, 1992).

Another type of motivational strategy is defensive pessimism, which refers to the setting of low expectations for performance but coupling those low expectations with an increase in effort in order to gain control over anxiety (Cantor & Norem, 1989; Norem & Cantor, 1986, 1990). Defensive pessimists seem to activate a negative self-schema (e.g., "I'm not prepared for this test," "This course is so hard, and I really don't understand it."), which generates anxiety about doing well, which then leads to increased effort to overcome the anxiety. In this sense, the negative self-schema serves as a negative goal for students to avoid, and they harness the fear of becoming that possible self to increase their effort. Accordingly, high levels of self-regulation (increased effort, as in defensive pessimism) need not always be driven by perceptions of high efficacy and competence (cf. Kuhl, 1987; Paris & Newman, 1990; Pintrich & Schrauben, 1992; Schunk, 1994); they can also arise from concerns about lack of efficacy and competence. At the same time, Norem and Cantor (1990) reported longitudinal data suggesting that over the course of several years of college life there was eventually a cost for defensive pessimists in terms of lower levels of academic achievement. Norem and Cantor suggested that this decline may be a function of accumulated stress from

higher levels of anxiety over several years, increased self-expectations, and less social support from friends. Future research needs to examine under what conditions and for which individuals self-efficacy and higher levels of self-regulation are linked in a positive fashion, in contrast to the negative relations between efficacy, anxiety, and self-regulation for individuals using a defensive pessimism strategy. In addition, there is a need for research regarding the intraindividual stability in contrast to the situational or domain specificity of these motivational strategies (e.g., differences in use of these strategies in academic, work, or social domains). Finally, there is a clear need for developmental research on the ontogenesis of these motivational strategies, since Norem and Cantor's work suggests that they are available to students when they enter college. In addition, there is a need for research that extends these constructs to how individuals cope with transitions and life tasks after college (e.g., adjustments to work, marriage, and family).

Although the links between these specific motivational strategies and students' actual cognitive engagement have not been tested yet, there is a fairly large literature on how various motivational beliefs are linked to college students' use of different cognitive and self-regulatory strategies (Pintrich & Schrauben, 1992). For example, as discussed briefly earlier, Pintrich and his colleagues have shown in both early adolescents and college students that positive motivational beliefs such as high self-efficacy, a focus on mastery goals, and a belief in control over learning and lower levels of anxiety are positively related to deeper levels of cognitive processing, including the use of elaborative and metacognitive strategies (e.g., Pintrich, 1989; Pintrich & De Groot, 1990; Pintrich & Garcia, 1991). R. P. Perry and his colleagues (e.g., R. P. Perry & Magnusson, 1989) have shown that an attributional style that focuses on positive beliefs about control also have a positive effect on learning and performance. In addition, there has been work on how different classroom characteristics influence these motivational beliefs (R. P. Perry, 1991).

### Group Differences in Cognition, Motivation, and Achievement

Research on gender and ethnic differences in college students' cognition, motivation, and achievement has yielded somewhat mixed results. On the one hand, there are a large number of studies that report gender and ethnic differences in many different kinds of outcomes, including cognitive abilities, self-concept, motivation, attitudes, and achievement (see Pascarella & Terenzini, 1991). Pascarella & Terenzini reported few group differences in cognitive outcomes such as postformal reasoning or critical thinking, although they did note that some gender differences seemed to emerge on the social outcomes such as motivation and self-concept. In most cases, these gender differences paralleled the findings discussed earlier in this chapter in respect to younger children. Females are more likely to have lower perceptions of their efficacy and self-concept than males, although their actual achievement does not differ greatly from that of males.

On the other hand, much of this research on group differences in college students has not been explicitly designed to focus on these differences, so there is a lack of theoretical sophistication about why differences might emerge in the college context. Moreover, many of the studies are fraught with methodological problems, including sampling problems that confound ethnicity with socioeconomic class (see Graham, 1992, 1994) or the use of very small samples and case studies that are difficult to generalize to a diverse college population, measurement problems due to the use of measures with poor psychometric properties, and design issues where age, differential experience, and contexts (community college vs. four-year college/university) are confounded with gender, class, and ethnicity. Needless to say, there is a great need for research on these topics that would overcome these methodological problems. More important, however, there is a need for thoughtful research on theoretically based models that would explain the ontogenesis of gender and ethnic differences. In particular, well-designed research is needed to test whether there is a need for alternative theoretical models that propose the existence of other psychological, sociological, or anthropological constructs and mechanisms for gender and ethnic differences (e.g.Ogbu's (1992) involuntary minority argument). In contrast, it may be that the current array of models and constructs is sufficient in terms of functional psychological mechanisms for explaining differences, although there may be important group differences in the *content* of such constructs and mechanisms. For example, attributional theory (see Graham 1992, 1994) and expectancy-value models in the motivational domain may be able to describe group differences by gender and ethnicity without recourse to other psychological constructs. Different groups may simply have different types of attributional patterns and motivational beliefs about their expectancies and values for academic work that lead to group differences in behavior and achievement. In the same way, there may be large differences in the content of cognitive schemas, knowledge, and the types of cognitive and motivational strategies used by different groups that lead to differences. On the other hand, these models may have to be adapted to include other constructs to help understand observed differences, as Spencer and Markstrom-Adams (1990) proposed in their discussion of identity development in minority youth. Future research will have to grapple with these theoretical and methodological issues, as research on group differences will continue to be an important topic of research into the 21st century.

## TRANSITIONS AND CONTEXTUAL INFLUENCES ON DEVELOPMENT IN LATE ADOLESCENCE AND YOUNG ADULTHOOD

The literature on the influence of college on student development is vast and beyond review in the present chapter. However, there is an extremely important book on the effects of college on students by Pascarella and Terenzini (1991) that represents a monumental effort to review all the research published in this area since 1967 (over 3,000 studies). Anyone interested in how college influences any aspect of student development, from cognition to motivation to values to personality to moral development, should start with this book. More recently, Astin (1993) updated his classic book, *Four Critical Years* (Astin, 1977) and presented the results of a new longitudinal study of how various college characteristics influence stu-

dent development over the 4 years of college. At the same time, much of this research in higher education that has examined contextual effects has not focused on psychological constructs that parallel the characteristics of middle schools discussed earlier, nor has it focused much on classroom-level analyses. Instead, many higher education researchers, given their sociological background and interest in higher education policy, have concentrated on macrolevel, sociological questions such as the general net effect of attending college (the value-added question), between-college differences (e.g., differences due to institutional type, size, or selectivity), and within-college differences in experience (differences due to academic major, residence arrangement, involvement in extracurricular activities, peer group characteristics; see Astin, 1993, and Pascarella & Terenzini, 1991). This information has important implications for college administrators but is less relevant to building psychological models of development, learning, and classroom teaching.

The research that has been done on the psychological dimensions of the college classroom has been conducted mainly following a general process–product paradigm of research on college teaching (see reviews by Murray, 1991; and R. P. Perry, 1991). In the previous section on transitions to junior high, six dimensions of classrooms (authority relations, affective relations, organization of instruction, teacher efficacy, cognitive level of academic content, and grading practices) were identified as having an important influence on cognitive and social development. Most of the research on processes in college classrooms that have a positive influence on cognition and motivation would fit into two of those dimensions, affective relations and organization of instruction. Both Murray (1991) and R. P. Perry (1991) found that the dimensions of instructor clarity, organization, and expressiveness and interestingness in lecturing (all aspects of organization of instruction) are correlated positively wth cognitive engagement and motivation. Given the overwhelming predominance of lectures in college classrooms, most of the classroom process research has focused on how to improve lectures, and so has not addressed issues of alternative activity structures. The other important aspects of this process research found that appropriate and timely feedback and opportunities for interaction with the instructor (aspects of affective relations) are also positively related to college students' cognition and motivation (Murray, 1991; R. P. Perry, 1991).

The other dimensions have been less researched, although there is some evidence that the cognitive level of academic content, defined in terms of the types of assessment tasks and evaluation procedures used, is at a fairly low level in most college classrooms, with the expected results of lowering cognition and motivation (Crook, 1988). In addition, there is little research on the authority structures and grading practices in college classrooms. Most college classrooms do not allow for much control and autonomy of tasks or grading practices, although they may allow for some choice of topics (McKeachie, Pintrich, Lin, Smith, & Sharma, 1990). Covington (1992) has shown that grading on a curve and the competition it engenders can have detrimental effects on cognition and motivation at all grade levels, including college classrooms. Most of this research on these dimensions of authority relations, cognitive level of tasks, and grading practices suggests that these aspects of the college classroom are very similar to the negative aspects of junior high classrooms reviewed above. Indeed, in the college classroom these aspects may be even more negative. Interestingly, there has been little discussion and even less research on the developmental person–environment mismatch resulting from the negative aspects of college classrooms imposed on students who are likely to be cognitively ready for higher level tasks and more independence. Of course, there is a large self-selection process operating, whereby only some students go on to college, in comparison to all children under age 16 attending junior high. These students may have the self-schemas and coping strategies that allow them to adapt to this type of instruction in college. These students also have the freedom to choose their major, and can take a variety of electives; thus, they have more choices than students in secondary schools. In addition, the freedom college students have outside the classroom may allow them to meet their developmental "needs" for autonomy and independence elsewhere, if those needs are not met in the classroom. Nevertheless, there is a need for much more developmental research on the cognitive and motivational aspects of college classroom tasks, authority structures, and grading practices, following the analysis of Doyle (1983) in kindergarten through Grade 12 classrooms. In addition, this research must move beyond process–product and descriptive research paradigms to more constructivist approaches that address how students interpret and construct meaning for themselves, set goals, and develop various motivational and cognitive strategies for coping with the various classroom contexts they encounter over the course of their college career.

*The Transition from High School to College.* In terms of student development, the transition to college is often a difficult one for many students. Attrition is highest in the first 2 years of college, especially the first year (Pascarella & Terenzini, 1991). A great deal of research has examined this issue, with most of it guided by a general person–environment fit model (see Tinto, 1987) which proposes that students' entry level cognitive skills and their goals and motivation for college interact with the institutional characteristics of the college, defined in terms of academic integration (e.g., involvement in and support for learning) and social integration (e.g., involvement in and support for social and extracurricular activities), which then produce a "decision" to either stay in or leave college. This research has been very important because it suggests that the nature of the actual experiences and interactions that students have with faculty and other students and students' interpretations of these experiences are the most important mediators of college dropout, rather than macrolevel institutional characteristics per se. This work also has generated a literature on programs to improve student retention through integrative first-year experiences and various academic and social programs (e.g., Noel, Levitz, & Saluri, 1985; Upcraft & Gardner, 1989). In particular, these programs often have focused on the retention of minority students, given their much higher attrition rate in general (e.g., Nettles, 1988).

The general model that underlies much of this research on student attrition has been a functional one that has examined the interaction of an individual's cognitive and motivational characteristics with the various characteristics of the institutional setting. In contrast, more recent sociological and anthropologi-

cal models have stressed social and cultural reproduction models whereby race, class, and gender are important considerations in the construction and reproduction of inequities in schools at all levels (e.g., Trueba, 1988). At the same time, cognitive anthropology and cultural psychology perspectives (e.g., Tharp & Gallimore, 1988; Trueba, 1988) on these issues have suggested the need for more microanalytic research on how individuals within different ethnic groups (e.g., African Americans, Latinos, Native Americans) vary in their coping strategies and their success. For example, a number of researchers have pointed out that within those different ethnic groups there are individuals who are successful in school and achieve academic success, thereby bringing into question global explanations regarding differences in minority achievement based on a typology of ethnic groups in terms of their immigrant status (e.g., Pottinger, 1989; Betoncourt & Lopez, 1993; Trueba, 1988). Similar arguments have been made in terms of gender differences in achievement in math and science (McDade, 1988). From our more psychological perspective, this is a much-needed addition to the more macrolevel sociological and cultural explanations for race, class, and gender differences and a trend that we hope continues into the 21st century.

*The Transition to the World of Work.* The transition to the world of full-time work is not an easy one, whether it occurs after high school or after college. Although a great deal of research has examined the influence of working while in high school on adolescent development (e.g., Fine, Mortimer, & Roberts, 1990; Greenberger & Steinberg, 1986), there is less developmental and psychological research on the effects of full-time work on adolescent and early adult development after formal schooling is completed. Most of the research that has examined this issue has taken sociological and economic perspectives and considered questions of access, opportunity, and equity in terms of race, class, and gender differences (e.g., Borman, 1991; Valli, 1986; Weis, 1990; Willis, 1977). In fact, there have been recent calls for more developmental and longitudinal research on the transition to work for individuals who do not go on to college. At the same time, it is clear that future psychological research on the transition to work needs to examine the person–environment fit as discussed in the research presented earlier on the transition to middle school, not just examine the psychology of the adolescent or the sociology of the work context in isolation from one another.

The transition from school to work is usually seen as a difficult one, because of the discontinuities between the nature of schools and the nature of work settings (Candy & Crebert, 1991; Marshall, 1988; Resnick, 1987). There are a number of dimensions along which the two may differ, paralleling the organizational and structural dimensions that can be used to distinguish secondary schools from elementary schools, although there may be greater discontinuities between schools and work settings than between elementary and secondary schools. Alternatively, there may be greater discontinuities between discrete work settings, depending on the nature of those settings (e.g., traditional manufacturing settings vs. traditional service organizations vs. knowledge-generating companies). Two major differences are the nature of the activities or work to be done and the procedures and cognitive operations necessary to accomplish the work. As Resnick (1987) has pointed out, U.S. public schools often focus on individual production or performance, whereas work settings emphasize socially shared performances. In addition, Resnick noted that work settings often provide a variety of tools and contextual supports for accomplishing the task, in contrast to the emphasis on "unaided" thought in schools. Finally, Resnick proposed that schools tend to focus on the teaching of generalizable cognitive skills and on working with symbols and abstract ideas rather than on situated competencies and contextualized reasoning, as in work settings. Candy and Crebert (1991) suggested that these same differences characterize not just differences between kindergarten through Grade 12 education and work settings, but that postsecondary classrooms actually exacerbate these differences, making it even more difficult for college graduates to make the transition to the world of work. Accordingly, it would be expected that there may be a discontinuity between the students' knowledge and cognitive capabilities and the work setting, depending on the nature of the work in the specific setting. There is a need for more research on this issue, particularly longitudinal research that examines intra- and interindividual differences over time and across different work contexts, rather than just simple descriptive contextual studies of what individuals do in their work settings.

Besides the nature of the work, the reward, evaluation, authority, and participation structures may be different in school and work settings (Borman, 1991; Marshall, 1988). While schools may operate under a performance/grade exchange system focused on individual performance, the distribution of rewards in work settings is often based on group or unit performance. In addition, the importance of the extrinsic rewards (financial, status, power) or sanctions (loss of job) may be greater in work settings. Evaluation and authority structures may also vary. In a classroom setting, the teacher is most often the evaluator and authority figure. In work settings, there may be numerous evaluators (co-workers, supervisors, clients) who may use different evaluation criteria. In addition, in some work settings there may be clear authority structures with very little worker autonomy (e.g., traditional manufacturing positions) or more ambiguous authority structures where the individual is allowed more autonomy and choice. Finally, there may be differences in the participation structures. Traditionally, classrooms have forced students to work individually, although this may be changing with the rise in the use of cooperative learning in kindergarten through Grade 12 education. Most college courses still require students to work individually (to allow students to do otherwise is "cheating" to many professors). In contrast, most work settings require some type of interaction between co-workers. In fact, lack of interpersonal skills and inability to work collaboratively are often seen as more of a problem by employers than lack of knowledge or lack of cognitive skills. At the same time, there may be work settings that do not allow much interaction between co-workers (see Borman, 1991). Accordingly, given the obvious within-work setting differences, research on the school-to-work transition needs to examine not only the transition to work, but the nature and quality of that work experience, in the same way that research on the transition to middle school has examined not just the transition itself but the nature and structures of middle schools and their fit to the individual students that move into them. In light of the findings in the educational literature on the effects of different reward, authority, evaluation, and participation structures on student motivational beliefs (e.g., C. Ames, 1992; Maehr & Midgley, 1991), it would be expected that there would be similar findings for the work settings, although Fine et al. (1990) note that there has been little research on work setting and motivational beliefs. At the same time, it is important to examine not just the effects of the work setting, but how individuals construct their own meaning of the work setting in light of their own motivational goals, beliefs, and values (cf. Borman, 1991; Maehr & Braskamp, 1986).

In summary, in both the transition to college and the transition to work literatures, there are a number of different models of the effects, from macrolevel sociological and economic to more microlevel sociolinguistic, cognitive anthropological, and psychological models. In terms of future psychological research, we need to incorporate the insights from cultural anthropology and sociology about the importance of context and culture. At the same time, psychological models have much to offer in terms of conceptualizing how individuals construct meaning in the context and how they develop different cognitive and motivational schemas and strategies for negotiating the demands of the transition. In addition, researchers need to begin to examine not just the positive or negative effects of transitions in terms of producing discontinuous change, but also how transitions might accentuate preexisting individual differences, thereby producing continuous change (e.g., Caspi & Bem, 1990; Caspi & Moffitt, 1991). In this way, our models will begin to describe and understand both the role of different contexts and the role of the individual in constructing and creating individual trajectories of development over the life course from 11 to 25 years. In turn, this will allow for the development of better educational contexts to change and improve the developmental trajectories of all children in junior high, high school, and college classrooms.

## CONCLUSION

We have come to the end of our description of development between the ages of 11 and 25. As we reflect on the information presented in this chapter, we are encouraged by the amount we have learned in the past 10 to 15 years about the nature of development during this part of the life span, as well as how different school and classroom environments affect students' development. We are excited about the growing emphasis on contextual models of development in psychological and educational theory. We also are encouraged by the application of this knowledge about adolescent and young adult development to educational practice, as best shown by reform efforts in middle school education occurring across the country. Yet, as we have pointed out throughout the chapter, much remains to be done, both in developmental research and in applying that research to education. We close by highlighting several areas in which more work is necessary. Despite the growing awareness and concern about the need to know more about the different groups that make up our increasingly diverse society, the amount of research on those groups still lags behind the research on white, middle-class adolescents and young adults, as Graham (1992, 1994) has discussed cogently. As research on these groups accumulates we will better know how current theoretical models of development will need to be modified to explain development in the various groups in our society. This knowledge also will be very useful in developing educational programs to serve these adolescents and young adults. We have noted that middle school reform efforts are ongoing in many parts of the country; researchers need to assess these efforts to see if they are resulting in more positive developmental outcomes for early adolescents. We also now need to focus more on the transitions to high school and college, and to develop programs and practices to ease those transitions. We hope that by the time the chapter on development during adolescence and young adulthood is written for the next edition of this *Handbook,* much of this information will be available.

# References

Abeles, R. P. (1987). *Life-span perspectives and social psychology.* Hillsdale, NJ: Lawrence Erlbaum Associates.

Adams, G. R., Montemayor, R., & Gullotta, T. P. (Eds.). (1989). *Biology of adolescent behavior and development.* Newbury Park, CA: Sage.

Alexander, W., & George, P. (1981). *The exemplary middle school.* New York: Holt, Rinehart, & Winston.

Ames, C. (1992). Classrooms: Goals, structures, and student motivation. *Journal of Educational Psychology, 84,* 261–271.

Arderman, E. M., & Maehr, M. L. (1994). Motivation and schooling in the middle grades. *Review of Educational Research, 64,* 287–309.

Arlin, P. K. (1986). Problem finding and young adult cognition. In R. A. Mines & K. S. Kitchener (Eds.), *Adult cognitive development: Methods and models* (pp. 22–32). New York: Praeger.

Asher, S. R., & Coie, J. (Eds.). (1990). *Peer rejection in childhood.* Cambridge, England: Cambridge University Press.

Ashton, P. (1985). Motivation and the teacher's sense of efficacy. In C. Ames & R. Ames (Eds.), *Research on motivation in education* (Vol. 2, pp. 141–171). Orlando, FL: Academic Press.

Astin, A. W. (1977). *Four critical years.* San Francisco: Jossey-Bass.

Astin, A. W. (1993). *What matters in college: Four critical years revisited.* San Francisco: Jossey-Bass.

Bain, R. K., & Anderson, J. G. (1974). School context and peer influences on educational plans of adolescents. *Review of Educational Research, 44,* 429–445.

Baltes, P. B. (1987). Theoretical propositions of life-span developmental psychology: On the dynamics of growth and decline. *Developmental Psychology, 23,* 611–626.

Baltes, P. B., & Schaie, K. W. (1973). *Life-span developmental psychology.* New York: Academic Press.

Bandura, A. (1986). *Social foundations of thought and action: A social cognitive theory.* Englewood Cliffs, NJ: Prentice-Hall.

Barber, B. L., & Eccles, J. S. (1992). Long-term influence of divorce and single parenting on adolescent family- and work-related values, behaviors, and aspirations. *Psychological Bulletin, 111,* 108–126.

Barker, R., & Gump, P. (1964). *Big school, small school: High school size and student behavior.* Stanford, CA: Stanford University Press.

Baron, R. M., & Graziano, W. G. (1991). *Social psychology.* New York: Holt, Rinehart, & Winston.

Basseches, M. (1980). Dialectical schemata: A framework for the empirical study of the development of dialectical thinking. *Human Development, 23,* 400–421.

Basseches, M. (1984). *Dialectical thinking and adult development.* Norwood, NJ: Ablex.

Basseches, M. (1986). Dialectical thinking and young adult cognitive development. In R. A. Mines & K. S. Kitchener (Eds.), *Adult cognitive development: Methods and models* (pp. 33–56). New York: Praeger.

Baumeister, R., & Scher, S. (1988). Self-defeating behavior patterns among normal individuals: Review and analysis of some common self-destructive tendencies. *Psychological Bulletin, 104,* 3–22.

Baumrind, D. (1971). Current patterns of parent authority. *Developmental Psychology Monographs, 4*(1, Pt. 2).

Baxter Magolda, M. (1992). *Knowing and reasoning in college.* San Francisco: Jossey-Bass.

Belenky, M., Clinchy, B., Goldberger, N., & Tarule, J. (1986). *Women's ways of knowing.* New York: Basic Books.

Berliner, D. C. (1989). Furthering our understanding of motivation and environments. In C. Ames & R. Ames (Eds.), *Research on motivation in education* (Vol. 3, pp. 317–342). San Diego: Academic Press.

Berndt, T. J., & Hawkins, J. A. (1987). *The contribution of supportive friendships to adjustment after the transition to junior high school.* Unpublished manuscript, Purdue University, Lafayette, IN.

Berndt, T. J., & Perry, T. B. (1990). Distinctive features of early adolescent friendships. In R. Montemayor, G. R. Adams, & T. P. Gullotta (Eds.), *From childhood to adolescence: A transitional period?* (pp. 269–287). Newbury Park, CA: Sage.

Betoncourt, H., & Lopez, J. (1993). The story of culture, ethnicity, and race in American psychology. *American Psychologist, 48,* 629–637.

Bjorklund, D. (1989). *Children's thinking: Developmental function and individual differences.* Pacific Grove, CA: Brooks-Cole.

Bledsoe, J. (1967). Self-concept of children and their intelligence, achievement, interests, and anxiety. *Childhood Education, 43,* 436–438.

Blos, P. (1965). The initial stage of male adolescence. *Psychoanalytic Study of the Child, 20,* 145–164.

Blos, P. (1979). *The adolescent passage.* New York: International Universities Press.

Blumenfeld, P., Pintrich, P. R., Meece, J., & Wessels, K. (1982). The formation and role of self-perceptions of ability in elementary school classrooms. *Elementary School Journal, 82,* 401–420.

Blyth, D. A., Simmons, R. G., & Bush, D. (1978). The transition into early adolescence: A longitudinal comparison of youth in two educational contexts. *Sociology of Education, 51,* 149–162.

Blyth, D. A., Simmons, R. G., & Carlton-Ford, S. (1983). The adjustment of early adolescents to school transitions. *Journal of Early Adolescence, 3,* 105–120.

Borman, K. (1991). *The first "real" job: A study of young workers.* Albany: SUNY Press.

Brim, O. G., & Ryff, C. D. (1980). On the properties of life events. In P. B. Baltes & O. G. Brim (Eds.), *Life-span development and behavior* (pp. 368–388). New York: Academic Press.

Brookover, W., Beady, C., Flood, P., Schweitzer, J., & Wisenbaker, J. (1979). *School social systems and student achievement: Schools can make a difference.* New York: Praeger.

Brooks-Gunn, J., & Reiter, E. O. (1990). The role of pubertal processes. In S. S. Feldman & G. R. Elliott (Eds.), *At the threshold: The developing adolescent* (pp. 16–53). Cambridge, MA: Harvard University Press.

Brooks-Gunn, J., & Warren, M. P. (1988). The psychological significance of secondary sexual characteristics in 9- to 11-year old girls. *Child Development, 59,* 161–169.

Brophy, J. E., & Evertson, C. M. (1976). *Learning from teaching: A developmental perspective.* Boston: Allyn & Bacon.

Brown, A. L., Bransford, J. D., Ferrara, R. A., & Campione, J. C. (1983). Learning, remembering, and understanding. In J. H. Flavell & E. M. Markman (Eds.), *Handbook of child psychology: Vol. 3. Cognitive development,* 4th ed. (pp. 77–166). New York: Wiley.

Brown, B. B. (1990). Peer groups and peer cultures. In S. S. Feldman &

G. R. Elliott (Eds.), *At the threshold: The developing adolescent* (pp. 171–196). Cambridge, MA: Harvard University Press.

Bruner, J. S. (1990). *Acts of meaning*. Cambridge, MA: Harvard University Press.

Brush, L. (1980). *Encouraging girls in math*. Cambridge, MA: Abt.

Bryk, A. S., & Driscoll, M. E. (1988). *The school as community: Theoretical foundations, contextual influences, and consequences for students and teachers*. Madison, WI: University of Wisconsin, National Center on Effective Secondary Schools.

Bryk, A. S., Lee, V. E., Smith, J. B. (1990). High school organization and its effects on teachers and students: An interpretative summary of the research. In J. Witte & W. Clure (Eds.), *Choice and control in American education* (pp. 135–226). London: Falmer Press.

Buchanan, C. M. (1989, April). *Hormone concentrations and variability: Associations with self-reported moods and energy in early adolescent girls*. Paper presented at the meeting of the Society for Research on Child Development, Kansas City, MO.

Buchanan, C. M., Eccles, J. S., & Becker, J. B. (1992). Are adolescents the victims of raging hormones? Evidence for activational effects of hormones on moods and behaviors at adolescence. *Psychological Bulletin, 111*, 62–107.

Byrne, B. M. (1984). The general/academic self-concept nomological network: A review of construct validation research. *Review of Educational Research, 54*, 427–456.

Byrnes, J. B. (1988). Formal operations: A systematic reformulation. *Developmental Review, 8*, 1–22.

Calsyn, R., & Kenny, D. (1977). Self-concept of ability and perceived evaluations by others: Cause or effect of academic achievement? *Journal of Educational Psychology, 69*, 136–145.

Campbell, R. (1993). Commentary: Epistemological problems for neo-Piagetians. *Monographs of the Society for Research in Child Development, 58* (Serial No. 234).

Candy, P., & Crebert, R. (1991). Ivory tower to concrete jungle: The difficult transition from the academy to the workplace as learning environments. *Journal of Higher Education, 62*, 570–592.

Cantor, N., & Kihlstrom, J. (1987). *Personality and social intelligence*. Englewood Cliffs, NJ: Prentice Hall.

Cantor, N., & Norem, J. (1989). Defensive pessimism and stress and coping. *Social Cognition, 7*, 92–112.

Carnegie Council on Adolescent Development. (1989). *Turning points: Preparing American youth for the 21st century*. New York: Carnegie Corporation.

Case, R. (1985). *Intellectual development: Birth to adulthood*. Orlando, FL: Academic Press.

Case, R. (1992). *The mind's staircase*. Hillsdale, NJ: Lawrence Erlbaum Associates.

Caspi, A., & Bem, D. (1990). Personality continuity and change across the life course. In L. Pervin (Ed.), *Handbook of personality: Theory and research* (pp. 549–575). New York: Guilford Press.

Caspi, A., & Moffitt, T. (1991). Individual differences are accentuated during periods of social change: The sample case of girls at puberty. *Journal of Personality and Social Psychology, 61*, 157–168.

Ceci, S. J. (1991). How much does schooling influence general intelligence and its cognitive components? *Developmental Psychology, 27*, 703–722.

Chickering, A. W. (1969). *Education and identity*. San Francisco: Jossey-Bass.

Collins, W. A. (1990). Parent-child relationships in the transition to adolescence: Continuity and change in interaction, affect, and cognition. In R. Montemayer, G. R. Adams, & T. P. Gullotta (Eds.), *From childhood to adolescence: A transitional period?* (pp. 85–106). Beverly Hills, CA: Sage.

Comer, J. P. (1988). Educating poor minority children. *Scientific American, 259*(5), 42–48.

Commons, M. L., & Richards, F. A. (1984a). A general model of stage theory. In M. Commons, F. A. Richards, & C. Armon (Eds.), *Beyond formal operations: Late adolescent and adult cognitive development* (pp. 120–140). New York: Praeger.

Commons, M. L., & Richards, F. A. (1984b). Applying the general stage model. In M. L. Commons, F. A. Richards, & C. Armon (Eds.), *Beyond formal operations: Late adolescent and adult cognitive development* (pp. 141–157). New York: Praeger.

Commons, M. L., Richards F. A., & Kuhn, D. (1982). Systematic and metasystematic reasoning: A case for levels of reasoning beyond Piaget's stage of formal operations. *Child Development, 53*, 1058–1069.

Connell, J. P. (1985). A new multidimensional measure of children's perceptions of control *Child Development, 56*, 1018–1041.

Corno, L. (1989). Self-regulated learning: A volitional analysis. In B. J. Zimmerman & D. H. Schunk (Eds.), *Self-regulated learning and academic achievement: Theory, research and practice* (pp. 111–141). New York: Springer.

Corno, L. (1993). The best-laid plans: Modern conceptions of volition and educational research. *Educational Researcher, 22*, 14–22.

Council of the Great City Schools. (1992). *National urban education goals: Baseline indicators, 1990–91*. Washington, DC: Council of the Great City Schools.

Covington, M. V. (1984). The motive for self-worth. In R. Ames & C. Ames (Eds.), *Research on motivation in education* (Vol. 1, pp. 77–113). New York: Academic Press.

Covington, M. V. (1992). *Making the grade: A self-worth perspective on motivation and school reform*. Cambridge, England: Cambridge University Press.

Covington, M. V., & Omelich, C. (1979). Effort: The double-edged sword in school achievement. *Journal of Educational Psychology, 71*, 169–182.

Crook, T. (1988). The impact of classroom evaluation practices on students. *Review of Educational Research, 58*, 438–481.

Cross, S., & Markus, H. (1991). Possible selves across the life span. *Human Development, 34*, 230–255.

Cross, W. E. (1987). A two-factor theory of black identity: Implications for the study of identity development in minority children. In J. S. Phinney & M. J. Rotherman (Eds.), *Children's ethnic socialization: Pluralism and development* (pp. 117–134). Newbury Park, CA: Sage.

Csikszentmihalyi, M. (1985). Emergent motivation and the evolution of the self. In D. Kleiber & M. Maehr (Eds.), *Advances in motivation and achievement: Motivation and adulthood* (pp. 93–119). Greenwich, CT: JAI Press.

Deci, E. L., & Ryan, R. M. (1985). *Intrinsic motivation and self-determination in human behavior*. New York: Plenum Press.

DeLisi, R., & Staudt, J. (1980). Individual differences in college students' performance on formal operations tasks. *Journal of Applied Developmental Psychology, 1*, 108–208.

Demetriou, A., Efklides, A., & Platsidou, M. (1993). The architecture and dynamics of developing mind. *Monographs of the Society for Research in Child Development, 58* (Serial No. 234).

Donald, J. (1990). University professors' views of knowledge and validation processes. *Journal of Educational Psychology, 82*, 242–249.

Dornbusch, S. M., Petersen, A. C., & Hetherington, E. M. (1991). Projecting the future of research on adolescence. *Journal of Research on Adolescence, 1*, 7–18.

Dornbusch, S. M., Ritter, P. L., Leiderman, P. H., Roberts, D. F., & Fraleigh, M. J. (1987). The relation of parenting style to adolescent school performance. *Child Development, 58*, 1244–1257.

Douvan, E., & Adelson, J. (1966). *The adolescent experience*. New York: Wiley.

Doyle, W. (1983). Academic work. *Review of Educational Research, 53*, 159–199.

Dryfoss, J. G. (1990). *Adolescents at risk: Prevalence and prevention*. New York: Oxford University Press.

Dubois, D. L., & Hirsch, B. J. (1990). School and neighborhood friendship patterns of blacks and whites in early adolescence. *Child Development, 61,* 524–536.

Dusek, J. B., & Flaherty, J. F. (1981). The development of the self-concept during the adolescent years. *Monographs of the Society for Research in Child Development, 46*(4, Serial No. 191).

Dweck, C. S., & Elliott, E. S. (1983). Achievement motivation. In E. M. Hetherington (Ed.), *Handbook of child psychology: Vol. IV. Socialization, personality, and social development,* 4th ed. (pp. 643–691). New York: Wiley.

Dweck, C. S., & Leggett, E. L. (1988). A social-cognitive approach to movitation and personality. *Psychological Review, 95,* 256–273.

Eccles, J. S. (1984a). Sex differences in achievement patterns. In T. Sonderegger (Ed.), *Nebraska Symposium on Motivation, 32,* 97–132. Lincoln, NE: University of Nebraska Press.

Eccles (Parsons), J. S. (1984b). Sex differences in mathematics participation. In M. Steinkamp and M. L. Maehr (Eds.), *Advances in motivation and achievement* (Vol. 2, pp. 93–137). Greenwich, CT: JAI Press.

Eccles, J. S. (1987). Gender roles and women's achievement-related decisions. *Psychology of Women Quarterly, 11,* 135–172.

Eccles, J. S., Adler, T. F., Futterman, R., Goff, S. B., Kaczala, C. M., Meece, J., & Midgley, C. (1983). Expectancies, values and academic behaviors. In J. T. Spence (Ed.), *Achievement and achievement motives* (pp. 75–146). San Francisco: Freeman.

Eccles, J. S., Adler, T., & Meece, J. L. (1984). Sex differences in achievement: A test of alternate theories. *Journal of Personality and Social Psychology, 46,* 26–43.

Eccles, J. S., & Harold, R. D. (1992). Gender differences in educational and occupational patterns among the gifted. In N. Colango, S. G. Assouline, & D. L. Amronson (Eds.), *Talent development: Proceedings from the 1991 Henry B. and Jocelyn Wallace National Research Symposium on Talent Development* (pp. 3–29). Unionville, NY: Trillium Press.

Eccles, J. S., & Harold, R. D. (1993). Parent-school involvement during the early adolescent years. *Teachers College Record, 94,* 568–587.

Eccles, J. S., & Harold, R. D. (in press). Family involvement in children; and adolescents' schooling. In A. Booth & J. Dunn (Eds.), *Family-school links: How do they affect educational outcomes?* Hillsdale, NJ: Lawrence Erlbaum Associates.

Eccles, J. S., & Midgley, C. (1989). Stage-environment fit: Developmentally appropriate classrooms for young adolescents. In C. Ames & R. Ames (Eds.), *Research on motivation in education* (Vol. 3, pp. 139–186). San Diego: Academic Press.

Eccles, J. S., Midgley, C., & Adler, T. (1984). Grade-related changes in the school environment: Effects on achievement motivation. In J. G. Nicholls (Ed.), *The development of achievement motivation* (pp. 283–331). Greenwich, CT: JAI Press.

Eccles, J. S., & Wigfield, A. (1985). Teacher expectancies and student motivation. In J. B. Dusek (Ed.), *Teacher expectancies* (pp. 185–226). Hillsdale, NJ: Lawrence Erlbaum Associates.

Eccles, J. S., Wigfield, A., Flanagan, C., Miller, C., Reuman, D., & Yee, D. (1989). Self-concepts, domain values, and self-esteem: Relations and changes at early adolescence. *Journal of Personality, 57,* 283–310.

Eccles, J. S., Wigfield, A., Harold, R. D., & Blumenfeld, P. B. (1993). Age and gender differences in children's achievement self-perceptions during the elementary school years. *Child Development, 64,* 830–847.

Eccles, J. S., Wigfield, A., Midgley, C., Reuman, D., Mac Iver, D., & Feldlaufer, H. (1993). Negative effects of traditional middle schools on students' motivation. *Elementary School Journal, 93,* 553–574.

Eder, D. (1985). The cycle of popularity: Interpersonal relations among female adolescents. *Sociology of Education, 58,* 154–165.

Eisenberg, N. (1990). Prosocial development in early and mid-adolescence. In R. Montemayor, G. R. Adams, & T. P. Gullotta (Eds.), *From childhood to adolescence: A transitional period?* (pp. 240–268). Newbury Park, CA: Sage.

Eisenhart, M. (1990). Learning to romance: Cultural acquisition in college. *Anthropology and Education Quarterly, 21,* 19–40.

Eisert, D., & Tomlinson-Keasey, C. (1978). Cognitive and interpersonal growth during the college freshman year: A structural analysis. *Perceptual and Motor Skills, 46,* 995–1006.

Elkind, D. (1967). Egocentrism in adolescence. *Child Development, 38,* 1025–1034.

Elkind, D. (1985). Egocentrism redux. *Developmental Review, 5,* 218–226.

Entwisle, D. R. (1990). Schooling and the adolescent. In S. S. Feldman & G. R. Elliott (Eds.), *At the threshold: The developing adolescent* (pp. 197–224). Cambridge, MA: Harvard University Press.

Epstein, J. L., & McPartland, J. M. (1976). The concept and measurement of the quality of school life. *American Educational Research Journal, 13,* 15–30.

Epstein, J. S. (1991). School and family connections: Theory, research, and implications for integrating sociologies of education and families. In D. G. Unger & M. B. Sussman (Eds.), *Families in community settings: Interdisciplinary perspectives* (pp. 99–126). New York: Haworth Press.

Erikson, E. H. (1963). *Childhood and society.* New York: Norton.

Feather, N. T. (1982). Human values and the prediction of action: An expectancy-value analysis. In N. T. Feather (Ed.), *Expectations and actions: Expectancy-value models in psychology* (pp. 263–289). Hillsdale, NJ: Lawrence Erlbaum Associates.

Feather, N. T. (1988). Values, valences, and course enrollment: Testing the role of personal values within an expectancy-value framework. *Journal of Educational Psychology, 80,* 381–391.

Featherman, D. L. (1983). Life-span perspectives in social science research. In P. B. Baltes & O. G. Brim (Eds.), *Life-span development and behavior* (pp. 1–57). New York: Academic Press.

Feldlaufer, H., Midgley, C., & Eccles, J. S. (1988). Student, teacher, and observer perceptions of the classroom environment before and after the transition to junior high school. *Journal of Early Adolescence, 8,* 133–156.

Fine, G., Mortimer, J., & Roberts, D. (1990). Leisure, work, and the mass media. In S. Feldman & G. Elliott (Eds.), *At the threshold: The developing adolescent* (pp. 225–252). Cambridge, MA: Harvard University Press.

Finger, J. A., & Silverman, M. (1966). Changes in academic performance in the junior high school. *Personnel and Guidance Journal, 45,* 157–164.

Finn, J. D. (1989). Withdrawing from school. *Review of Educational Research, 59,* 117–142.

Fischer, K. (1980). A theory of cognitive development: The control and construction of hierarchies of skills. *Psychological Review, 87,* 477–531.

Fischer, K., Hand, H., & Russell, S. (1984). The development of abstractions in adolescence and adulthood. In M. S. Commons, F. A. Richards, & C. Armon (Eds.), *Beyond formal operations: Late adolescent and adult cognitive development* (pp. 43–73). New York: Praeger.

Fischer, K., & Kenny, S. (1986). Environmental conditions for discontinuities in the development of abstractions. In R. A. Mines & K. S. Kitchener (Eds.), *Adult cognitive development: Methods and models* (pp. 57–75). New York: Praeger.

Fischer, K., Kenny, S., & Pipp, S. (1990). How cognitive processes and environmental conditions organize discontinuities in the development of abstractions. In C. Alexander, E. Langer, & R. Oetzel (Eds.), *Higher stages of development* (pp. 162–187). New York: Oxford University Press.

Flavell, J. H., Miller, P., & Miller, S. (1993). *Cognitive development.* Englewood Cliffs, NJ: Prentice Hall.

Fleming, M., & Chambers, B. (1983). Teacher-made tests: Windows on the classroom: In W. R. Hathaway (Ed.), *Testing in the schools*. San Francisco: Jossey-Bass.

Fordham, S., & Ogbu, J. (1986). Black students' school success: Coping with the burden of "acting white." *Urban Review, 18*, 176–205.

Fraser, B. J., & Fisher, D. L. (1982). Predicting students' outcomes from their perceptions of classroom psychosocial environment. *American Educational Research Journal, 19*, 498–518.

Freud, A. (1958). *Adolescence: Psychoanalytic study of the child* (Vol. 13). New York: Academic Press.

Fyans, J. (1979). *Test anxiety, test comfort, and student achievement test performance*. Paper presented at the Educational Testing Service, Princeton, NJ.

Garcia, T., & Pintrich, P. R. (1993, April). *Self-schemas, motivational strategies, and self-regulated learning*. Paper presented at the annual meeting of the American Educational Research Association, Atlanta, GA.

Garcia, T., & Pintrich, P. R. (1994). Regulating motivation and cognition in the classroom: The role of self-schemas and self-regulatory strategies. In B. J. Zimmerman & D. H. Schunk (Eds.), *Self-regulation of learning and performance: Issues and educational applications* (pp. 127–153). Hillsdale, NJ: Lawrence Erlbaum Associates.

Gelman, R., & Baillarageon, R. (1983). A review of some Piagetian concepts. In J. H. Flavell & E. M. Markman (Eds.), *Handbook of child psychology: Vol. 3. Cognitive development* (pp. 167–230). New York: Wiley.

Gilligan, C. (1982). *In a different voice: Psychological theory and women's development*. Cambridge, MA: Harvard University Press.

Glaser, R. (1984). Education and thinking: The role of knowledge. *American Psychologist, 39*, 93–105.

Graham, S. (1989). Motivation in Afro-Americans. In G. L. Berry & J. K. Asamen (Eds.), *Black students: Psychosocial issues and academic achievement* (pp. 40–68). Newbury Park, CA: Sage.

Graham, S. (1992). "Most of the subjects were white and middle class": Trends in published research on African Americans in selected APA journals 1970–1989. *American Psychologist, 47*, 629–639.

Graham, S. (1994). Motivation in African Americans. *Review of Educational Research, 64*, 55–117.

Greenberger, E., & Steinberg, D. (1986). *When teenagers work: The psychological and social costs of adolescent employment*. New York: Basic Books.

Gurin, P., & Epps, E. (1974). *Black consciousness, identity, and achievement*. New York: Wiley.

Hale-Benson, J. (1989). The school learning environment and academic success. In G. L. Berry & J. K. Asamen (Eds.), *Black students: Psychosocial issues and academic achievement* (pp. 83–97). Newbury Park, CA: Sage.

Hall, G. S. (1904). *Adolescence: Its psychology and its relations to anthropology, sex, crime, religion, and education*. New York: Appleton.

Hansford, B. C., & Hattie, J. A. (1982). The relationship between self and achievement/performance measures. *Review of Educational Research, 52*, 123–142.

Hare, B. R. (1977). Racial and socioeconomic variations in preadolescent area-specific and general self-esteem. *International Journal of Intercultural Relations, 1*, 31–51.

Hare, B. R. (1985). Stability and change in self-perceptions and achievement among black adolescents: A longitudinal study. *Journal of Black Psychology, 11*, 29–42.

Hare-Mustin, R., & Marecek, J. (1988). The meaning of difference: Gender theory, postmodernism, and psychology. *American Psychologist, 43*, 455–464.

Harter, S. (1981a). A model of intrinsic mastery motivation in children: Individual differences and developmental change. In W. A. Collins (Ed.), *Minnesota Symposia on Child Psychology, 14*, 215–255. Hillsdale, NJ: Lawrence Erlbaum Associates.

Harter, S. (1981b). A new self-report scale of intrinsic versus extrinsic orientation in the classroom: Motivational and informational components. *Developmental Psychology, 17*, 300–312.

Harter, S. (1982). The perceived competence scale for children. *Child Development, 53*, 87–97.

Harter, S. (1985). Competence as a dimension of self-evaluation: Toward a comprehensive model of self-worth. In R. Leahy (Ed.), *The development of the self* (pp. 55–121). New York: Academic Press.

Harter, S. (1986). Processes underlying the construction, maintenance and enhancement of the self-concept in children. In J. Suls & A. C. Greenwald (Eds.), *Psychological perspectives on the self* (Vol. 3, pp. 137–181). Hillsdale, NJ: Lawrence Erlbaum Associates.

Harter, S. (1990a). Causes, correlates and the functional role of self-worth: A life-span perspective. In R. J. Sternberg & J. Kolligian (Eds.), *Competence considered* (pp. 67–97). New Haven: Yale University Press.

Harter, S. (1990b). Processes underlying adolescent self-concept formation. In R. Montemayer, G. R. Adams, & T. P. Gullotta (Eds.), *From childhood to adolescence: A transitional period?* (pp. 205–239). Newbury Park, CA: Sage.

Harter, S. (1990c). Self and identity development. In S. Feldman & G. Elliott (Eds.), *At the threshold: The developing adolescent* (pp. 352–387). Cambridge, MA: Harvard University Press.

Harter, S. (1992). Visions of self: Beyond the me in the mirror. In J. Jacobs (Ed.), *Nebraska symposium on motivation* (Vol. 40, pp. 99–144). Lincoln, NE: University of Nebraska Press.

Harter, S., Whitesell, N., & Kowalski, P. (1992). Individual differences in the effects of educational transitions on children's perceptions of competence and motivational orientation. *American Educational Research Journal, 29*, 777–808.

Hartup, W. W. (1983). Peer relations. In P. H. Mussen (Ed.), *Handbook of child psychology: Vol. IV. Socialization*, 4th ed. (pp. 103–196). New York: Wiley.

Hauser, R. M. (1991). What happens to youth after high school? *Focus, 13*, 1–13.

Hauser, S. T., & Bowlds, M. K. (1990). Stress, coping, and adaptation. In S. S. Feldman & G. R. Elliott (Eds.), *At the threshold: The developing adolescent* (pp. 388–413). Cambridge, MA: Harvard University Press.

Higgins, E. T., & Parsons, J. E. (1983). Social cognition and the social life of the child: Stages as subcultures. In E. T. Higgins, D. W. Ruble, & W. W. Hartup (Eds.), *Social cognition and social behavior: Developmental issues*. New York: Cambridge University Press.

Hill, J. P., & Lynch, M. E. (1983). The intensification of gender-related role expectations during early adolescence. In J. Brooks-Gunn & A. C. Petersen (Eds.), *Girls at puberty* (pp. 201–228). New York: Plenum Press.

Holland, D., & Eisenhart, M. (1988). Moments of discontent: University women and the gender status quo. *Anthropology and Education Quarterly, 19*, 115–138.

Holloway, S. (1988). Concepts of ability and effort in Japan and the U.S. *Review of Educational Research, 58*, 327–346.

Hunt, D. E. (1975). Person-environment interaction: A challenge found wanting before it was tried. *Review of Educational Research, 45*, 209–230.

Huston, A. (1983). Sex-typing. In P. H. Mussen (Ed.), *Handbook of child psychology* (Vol. IV, 4th ed., pp. 387–467). New York: Wiley.

Inhelder, B., & Piaget, J. (1958). *The growth of logical thinking from childhood to adolescence*. New York: Basic Books.

Jenkins, L. E. (1989). The black family and academic achievement. In G. L. Berry & J. K. Asamen (Eds.), *Black students: Psychosocial issues and academic achievement* (pp. 138–152). Newbury Park, CA: Sage.

Johnson, D. W., & Johnson, R. T. (1987). *Learning together and alone*. Englewood Cliffs, NJ: Prentice Hall.

Katchadourian, H. (1990). Sexuality. In S. G. Feldman & G. R. Elliott

(Eds.), *At the threshold: The developing adolescent* (pp. 330–351). Cambridge, MA: Harvard University Press.

Kavrell, S. M., & Petersen, A. C. (1984). Patterns of achievement in early adolescence. In M. L. Maehr (Ed.), *Advances in motivation and achievement* (Vol. 4, pp. 1–35). Greenwich, CT: JAI Press.

Keating, D. P. (1980). Thinking processes in adolescence. In J. Adelson (Ed.), *Handbook of adolescence psychology* (pp. 211–246). New York: Wiley.

Keating, D. P. (1990). Adolescent thinking. In S. S. Feldman & G. R. Elliott (Eds.), *At the threshold: The developing adolescent* (pp. 54–89). Cambridge, MA: Harvard University Press.

Keil, F. (1990). Constraints on constraints: Surveying the epigenetic landscape. *Cognitive Science, 14,* 135–168.

King, P. M. (1986). Formal reasoning in adults: A review and critique. In R. A. Mines & K. S. Kitchener (Eds.), *Adult cognitive development: Methods and models* (pp. 1–21). New York: Praeger.

King, P., & Kitchener, K. S. (1994). *Developing reflective judgment: Understanding and promoting intellectual growth and critical thinking in adolescents and adults.* San Francisco: Jossey-Bass.

King, P. M., Kitchener, K. S., Davison, M. L., Parker, C. A., & Wood, P. K. (1983). The justification of beliefs in young adults: A longitudinal study. *Human Development, 26,* 106–116.

Kitchener, K. S. (1983). Cognition, metacognition, and epistemic cognition. A three-level model of cognitive processing. *Human Development, 26,* 222–232.

Kitchener, K. S. (1986). The reflective judgment model: Characteristics, evidence, and measurement. In R. A. Mines & K. S. Kitchener (Eds.), *Adult cognitive development: Methods and models* (pp. 76–91). New York: Praeger.

Kitchener, K. S., & King, P. M. (1981). Reflective judgment: Concepts of justification and their relationship to age and education. *Journal of Applied Developmental Psychology, 2,* 89–116.

Kitchener, K. S., Lynch, C., Fischer, K., & Wood, P. (1993). Developmental range of reflective judgment: The effect of contextual support and practice on developmental stage. *Developmental Psychology, 29,* 893–906.

Klinger, E. (1977). *Meaning and void: Inner experience and the incentives in people's lives.* Minneapolis: University of Minnesota Press.

Kohlberg, L., & Armon, C. (1984). Three types of stage models used in the study of adult development. In M. L. Commons, F. A. Richards, & C. Armon (Eds.), *Beyond formal operations: Late adolescent and adult cognitive development* (pp. 383–394). New York: Praeger.

Kuhl, J. (1985). Volitional mediators of cognition-behavior consistency: Self-regulatory processes and action versus state orientation. In J. Kuhl & J. Beckman (Eds.), *Action control: From cognition to behavior* (pp. 101–128). Berlin: Springer.

Kuhl, J. (1987). Action control: The maintenance of motivational states. In F. Halisch & J. Kuhl (Eds.), *Motivation, intention, and volition* (pp. 279–307). Berlin: Springer.

Kuhl, J. (1992). A theory of self-regulation: Action versus state orientation, self-discrimination, and some applications. *Applied Psychology: An International Review, 41,* 97–129.

Kuhn, D. (1991). *The skills of argument.* Cambridge, England: Cambridge University Press.

Laboratory of Comparative Human Cognition. (1983). Culture and cognitive development. In W. Kessen (Ed.), *Handbook of child psychology: History, theory, and methods,* 4th ed. (Vol. 1, pp. 295–356). New York: Wiley.

Labouvie-Vief, G. (1982). Dynamic development and mature autonomy: A theoretical prologue. *Human Development, 25,* 161–191.

Lapsley, D., & Murphy, M. (1985). Another look at the theoretical assumptions of adolescent egocentrism. *Developmental Review, 5,* 201–217.

Lawler, E. E. (1976). Control systems in organizations. In M. D. Dunnette

(Ed.), *Handbook of industrial and organizational psychology.* Chicago: Rand McNally.

Lee, P., Statuto, C., & Kedar-Voivodas, G. (1983). Elementary school children's perceptions of their actual and ideal school experience: A developmental study. *Journal of Educational Psychology, 75,* 838–847.

Lee, V. E., & Bryk, A. S. (1988). Curriculum tracking as mediating the social distribution of high school achievement. *Sociology of Education, 24,* 78–94.

Lee, V. E., & Bryk, A. S. (1989). A multilevel model of the social distribution of high school achievement. *Sociology of Education, 62,* 172–192.

Lerner, R. (1986). *Concepts and theories of human development.* New York: Random House.

Lerner, R. M., Entwisle, D. R., & Hauser, S. T. (1994). The crisis among contemporary American adolescents: A call for the integration of research, policies, and programs. *Journal of Research on Adolescence, 4,* 1–4.

Levinson, D. (1978). *The seasons of a man's life.* New York: Ballantine Books.

Lewin, K. (1935). *A dynamic theory of personality.* New York: McGraw-Hill.

Linn, M. C., and Hyde, J. S. (1989). Gender, math, and science. *Educational Researcher, 18,* 17–27.

Little, B. (1983). Personal projects: A rationale and methods for investigation. *Environmental Behavior, 15,* 273–309.

Lounsbury, J. H., Marani, J. V., & Compton, M. F. (1980). *The middle school in profile: A day in the seventh grade.* Fairborn, OH: National Middle School Association.

Maehr, M. L., & Midgley, C. (1991). Enhancing student motivation: A schoolwide approach. *Educational Psychologist, 26,* 399–427.

Mac Iver, D. J., & Reuman, D. A. (1988, April). *Decision-making in the classroom and early adolescents' valuing of mathematics.* Paper presented at the annual meeting of the American Educational Research Association, New Orleans.

Mac Iver, D. J., & Epstein, J. L. (1991). *How equal are opportunities for learning in disadvantaged and advantaged middle grades schools?* Unpublished manuscript. Johns Hopkins University, Center for Research on Effective Schooling for Disadvantaged Students, Baltimore.

Maehr, M. L., & Braskamp, L. (1986). *The motivation factor: A theory of personal investment.* Lexington, MA: Lexington Books, D. C. Heath.

Magnusson, D. (1988). *Individual development from an interactional perspective.* Hillsdale, NJ: Lawrence Erlbaum Associates.

Malina, R. M. (1990). Physical growth and performance during the transitional years (9–16). In R. Montemayor, G. R. Adams, & T. P. Gullotta (Eds.), *From childhood to adolescence: A transitional period?* (pp. 41–62). Newbury Park, CA: Sage.

Marcia, J. (1980). Identity in adolescence. In J. Adelson (Ed.), *Handbook of adolescent psychology* (pp. 159–187). New York: Wiley.

Markus, H., & Kitayama, S. (1991). Culture and the self: Implications for cognition, emotion, and motivation. *Psychological Review, 98,* 224–253.

Markus, H., & Nurius, P. (1986). Possible selves. *American Psychologist, 41,* 954–969.

Marsh, H. W. (1989). Age and sex effects in multiple dimensions of self-concept: Preadolescence to early adulthood. *Journal of Educational Psychology, 81,* 417–430.

Marsh, H. W. (1990a). Causal ordering of academic self-concept and academic achievement: A multivariate, longitudinal panel analysis. *Journal of Educational Psychology, 82,* 646–656.

Marsh, H. W. (1990b). The structure of academic self-concept: The Marsh/Shavelson model. *Journal of Educational Psychology, 82,* 623–636.

Marsh, H. W., Craven, R. G., & Debus, R. (1991). Self-concepts of young children 5 to 8 years of age: Measurement and multidimensional structure. *Journal of Educational Psychology, 83,* 377–392.

Marsh, H. W., & Hocevar, D. (1985). The application of confirmatory factor analyses to the study of self-concept: First and higher-order factor structures and their invariance across age groups. *Psychological Bulletin, 97,* 562–582.

Marsh, H. W., & O'Neill, R. (1984). Self-description questionnaire III: The construct validity of multidimensional self-concept ratings by late adolescents. *Journal of Educational Measurement, 21,* 153–174.

Marsh, H. W., & Shavelson, R. (1985). Self-concept: Its multifaceted hierarchical structure. *Educational Psychologist, 20,* 107–123.

Marshall, H. (1988). Work or learning: Implications of classroom metaphors. *Educational Researcher, 17,* 9–16.

McCall, R., Evahn, C., & Kratzer, L. (1992). *High school underachievers: What do they achieve as adults?* Newbury Park, CA: Sage.

McCord, J. (1990). Problem behaviors. In S. S. Feldman & G. R. Elliott (Eds.), *At the threshold: The developing adolescent* (pp. 414–430). Cambridge, MA: Harvard University Press.

McDade, L. (1988). Knowing the "right stuff": Attrition, gender, and scientific literacy. *Anthropology and Education Quarterly, 19,* 93–114.

McDermott, R. (1987). Achieving school failure: An anthropological approach to literacy and social stratification. In G. Spindler (Ed.), *Education and cultural process: Anthropological approaches* (2nd ed.). Prospect Heights, IL: Waveland Press.

McKeachie, W. J., Pintrich, P. R., Lin, Y-G., Smith, D., & Sharma, R. (1990). *Teaching and learning in the college classroom: A review of the research literature.* Ann Arbor, MI: NCRIPTAL—University of Michigan.

McLoyd, V. C. (1990). The impact of economic hardship on black families and children: Psychological distress, parenting, and socioemotional development. *Child Development, 61,* 311–346.

McMichael, P. (1980). Reading difficulties, behavior, and social status. *Journal of Educational Psychology, 72,* 76–86.

Meece, J. L., Wigfield, A., & Eccles, J. S. (1990). Predictors of math anxiety and its consequences for young adolescents' course enrollment intentions and performances in mathematics. *Journal of Educational Psychology, 82,* 60–70.

Mentkowski, M., & Strait, M. (1983). *A longitudinal study of student change in cognitive development, learning styles, and generic abilities in an outcome-centered liberal arts curriculum.* (Final report to the National Institute of Education, Research Report No. 6.) Milwaukee, WI: Alverno College, Office of Research and Evaluation.

Mergendoller, J. R., & Marchman, V. L. (1987). Friends and associates. In V. Richardson-Koehler (Ed.), *Educator's handbook: A research perspective* (pp. 297–328). New York: Longman.

Mergendoller, J. R., Marchman, V. L., Mitman, A. L., & Packer, M. J. (1988). Task demands and accountability in middle-grade science classes. *Elementary School Journal, 88,* 251–265.

Midgley, C., & Feldlaufer, H. (1987). Students' and teachers' decision-making fit before and after the transition to junior high school. *Journal of Early Adolescence, 7,* 225–241.

Midgley, C., Feldlaufer, H., & Eccles, J. S. (1988a). Student/teacher relations and attitudes toward mathematics before and after the transition to junior high school. *Child Development, 60,* 375–395.

Midgley, C., Feldlaufer, H., & Eccles, J. S. (1988b). The transition to junior high school: Beliefs of pre- and post-transition teachers. *Journal of Youth and Adolescence, 17,* 543–562.

Midgley, C., Feldlaufer, H., & Eccles, J. S. (1989). Change in teacher efficacy and student self- and task-related beliefs during the transition to junior high school. *Journal of Educational Psychology, 81,* 247–258.

Miller, C. L. (1986, April). *Puberty and person-environment fit in the classroom.* Paper presented at a meeting of the American Educational Research Association, San Francisco.

Miller, K. E., & Berndt, T. J. (1987, April). *Adolescent friendship and school orientation.* Paper presented at a meeting of the Society for Research in Child Development, Baltimore.

Moos, R. H. (1979). *Evaluating educational environments.* San Francisco, CA: Jossey-Bass.

Murray, H. (1991). Effective teaching behaviors in the college classroom. In J. Smart (Ed.), *Higher education: Handbook of theory and research* (Vol. 7, pp. 135–172). New York: Agathon Press.

Neimark, E. D. (1983). Adolescent thought: Transition to formal operations. In B. Wolman (Ed.), *Handbook of developmental psychology* (pp. 486–502). Englewood Cliffs, NJ: Prentice Hall.

Nettles, M. (1988). *Toward black undergraduate student equality in American higher education.* New York: Greenwood Press.

Neugarten, B. (1968). *Middle age and aging.* Chicago: University of Chicago Press.

Nicholls, J. G. (1979). Quality and equality in intellectual development: The role of motivation in education. *American Psychologist, 34,* 1071–1084.

Nicholls, J. G. (1984). Achievement motivation: Conceptions of ability, subjective experience, task choice, and performance. *Psychological Review, 91,* 328–346.

Nicholls, J. G. (1990). What is ability and why are we mindful of it? A developmental perspective. In R. J. Sternberg & J. Kolligian (Eds.), *Competence considered* (pp. 11–40). New Haven: Yale University Press.

Noddings, N. (1984). *Caring.* Berkeley: University of California Press.

Noel, L., Levitz, R., & Saluri, D. (Eds.). (1986). *Increasing student retention: Effective programs and practices for reducing the dropout rate.* San Francisco: Jossey-Bass.

Norem, J., & Cantor, N. (1986). Defensive pessimism: Harnessing anxiety as motivation. *Journal of Personality and Social Psychology, 51,* 1208–1217.

Norem, J., & Cantor, N. (1990). Cognitive strategies, coping, and perceptions of competence. In R. Sternberg & J. Kolligian (Eds.), *Competence considered* (pp. 190–204). New Haven: Yale University Press.

Nottelmann, E. D. (1987). Competence and self-esteem during the transition from childhood to adolescence. *Developmental Psychology, 23,* 441–450.

Oakes, J. (1981). *Tracking policies and practices: School by school summaries. A study of schooling* (Tech. Rep. No. 25). Los Angeles: University of California, Graduate School of Education.

Office of Educational Research and Improvement. (1988). *Youth Indicators 1988.* Washington, DC: U.S. Government Printing Office.

Ogbu (1992). Understanding cultural diversity and learning. *Educational Researcher, 21,* 5–14.

Olweus, D., Mattsoon, A. Schalling, D., & Low, H. (1980). Testosterone, aggression, physical, and personality dimensions in normal adolescent males. *Psychosomatic Medicine, 42,* 153–169.

Olweus, D., Mattsoon, A., Schalling, D., & Low, H. (1988). Circulating testosterone levels and aggression in adolescent males: A causal analysis. *Psychosomatic Medicine, 50,* 261–272.

O'Malley, P. M., & Bachman, J. G. (1983). Self-esteem changes and stability between ages 13 and 23. *Developmental Psychology, 19,* 257–268.

Paikoff, R. L., & Brooks-Gunn, J. (1990). Physiological processes: What role do they play during the transition to adolescence? In R. Montemayor, R. G. Adams, & T. P. Gullotta (Eds.), *From childhood to adolescence: A transitional period?* (pp. 63–81). Newbury Park, CA: Sage.

Parham, W. D., & Parham, T. A. (1989). The community and academic achievement. In G. L. Berry & J. K. Asamen (Eds.), *Black students: Psychosocial issues and academic achievement* (pp. 120–137). Newbury Park, CA: Sage.

Paris, S., Lipson, M., & Wixson, K. (1983). Becoming a strategic reader. *Contemporary Educational Psychology, 8,* 293–316.

Paris, S., & Newman, R. (1990). Developmental aspects of self-regulated learning. *Educational Psychologist, 25,* 87–102.

Parker, J. G., & Asher, S. R. (1987). Peer relations and later personal adjustment: Are low accepted children "at risk"? *Psychological Bulletin, 102,* 357–389.

Parsons, J. E., & Ruble, D. N. (1977). The development of achievement-related expectancies. *Child Development, 48,* 1975–1979.

Pascarella, E. T., & Terenzini, P. T. (1991). *How college affects students.* San Francisco: Jossey-Bass.

Pepper, S. C. (1942). *World hypotheses.* Berkeley, CA: University of California Press.

Perry, R. P. (1991). Perceived control in college students: Implications for instruction in higher education. In J. Smart (Ed.), *Higher education: Handbook of theory and research* (Vol. 7, pp. 1–56). New York: Agathon Press.

Perry, R. P., & Magnusson, J. L. (1989). Causal attributions and perceived performance: Consequences for college students' achievement and perceived control in different instructional conditions. *Journal of Educational Psychology, 81,* 164–172.

Perry, T. B. (1987). *The relation of adolescents' self-perceptions to their social relationships.* Unpublished doctoral dissertation, University of Oklahoma, Norman, OK.

Perry, W. G. (1970). *Forms of intellectual and ethical development in the college years: A scheme.* New York: Holt, Rinehart, & Winston.

Perry, W. G. (1981). Cognitive and ethical growth: The making of meaning. In A. W. Chickering (Ed.), *The modern American college* (pp. 76–116). San Francisco: Jossey-Bass.

Petersen, A. (1985). Pubertal development as a cause of disturbance: Myths, realities, and unanswered questions. *Genetic, Social and General Psychology Monographs, 111,* 205–232.

Petersen, A. (1988). Adolescent development. *Annual Review of Psychology, 39,* 583–607.

Petersen, A., & Taylor, B. (1980). The biological approach to adolescence: Biological change and psychosocial adaptation. In J. Adelson (Ed.), *Handbook of the psychology of adolescence* (pp. 117–155). New York: Wiley.

Piaget, J. (1952). *The origin of intelligence in children.* New York: International Universities Press.

Piaget, J., & Inhelder, B. (1973). *Memory and intelligence.* London: Routledge & Kegan Paul.

Pintrich, P. R. (1988). A process oriented view of student motivation and cognition. In J. S. Stark & L. Metz (Eds.), *Improving teaching and learning through research: New directions for institutional research, 57* (pp. 55–70). San Francisco: Jossey-Bass.

Pintrich, P. R. (1989). The dynamic interplay of student motivation and cognition in the college classroom. In C. Ames & M. Maehr (Eds.), *Advances in motivation and achievement: Vol. 6. Motivation enhancing environments* (pp. 117–160). Greenwich, CT: JAI Press.

Pintrich, P. R. (1990). Implications of psychological research on student learning and college teaching for teacher education. In W. R. Houston (Ed.), *Handbook of research on teacher education* (pp. 826–857). New York: Macmillan.

Pintrich, P. R. (1994). Continuities and discontinuities: Future directions for research in educational psychology. *Educational Psychologist, 29,* 137–148.

Pintrich, P. R., & De Groot, E. (1990). Motivational and self-regulated learning components of classroom academic performance. *Journal of Educational Psychology, 82,* 33–40.

Pintrich, P. R., & Garcia, T. (1991). Student goal orientation and self-regulation in the college classroom. In M. L. Maehr & P. R. Pintrich (Eds.), *Advances in motivation and achievement* (Vol. 7, pp. 371–402). Greenwich, CT: JAI Press.

Pintrich, P. R., & Garcia, T. (1993, August). *Possible selves as goals and their role in self-regulated learning.* Paper presented at the annual meeting of the American Psychological Society, Chicago.

Pintrich, P. R., Garcia, T., & De Groot, E. (1994, April). *Positive and negative self-schemas and self-regulated learning.* Paper presented at the annual meeting of the American Educational Research Association, New Orleans.

Pintrich, P. R., Marx, R. W., & Boyle, R. A. (1993). Beyond cold conceptual change: The role of motivational beliefs and classroom contextual factors in the process of conceptual change. *Review of Educational Research, 63,* 167–199.

Pintrich, P. R., & Schrauben, B. (1992). Students' motivational beliefs and their cognitive engagement in classroom academic tasks. In D. H. Schunk & J. L. Meece (Eds.), *Student perceptions in the classroom* (pp. 149–183). Hillsdale, NJ: Lawrence Erlbaum Associates.

Posner, G., Strike, K., Hewson, P., & Gertzog, W. (1982). Accommodation of a scientific conception: Toward a theory of conceptual change. *Science Education, 66,* 211–227.

Pottinger, R. (1989). Disjunction to higher education: American Indian students in the southwest. *Anthropology and Education Quarterly, 20,* 327–344.

Powell, G. J. (1989). Defining self-concept as a dimension of academic achievement for inner city youth. In G. L. Berry & J. K. Asamen (Eds.), *Black students: Psychosocial issue and academic achievement* (pp. 69–82). Newbury Park, CA: Sage.

Pressley, G. M., Borkowski, J. G., & Schneider, W. (1987). Cognitive strategies: Good strategy users coordinate metacognition and knowledge. In R. Vasta & G. Whitehurst (Eds.), *Annals of child development, 5,* 89–129. Greenwich, CT: JAI Press.

Resnick, L. (1987). Learning in school and out. *Educational Researcher, 16,* 13–20.

Rholes, W. S., Blackwell, J., Jordan, C., & Walters, C. (1980). A developmental study of learned helplessness. *Developmental Psychology, 16,* 616–624.

Riegel, K. (1973). Dialectical operations: The final period of cognitive development. *Human Development, 16,* 346–370.

Riegel, K. (1975). Toward a dialectical theory of development. *Human Development, 18,* 50–64.

Riegel, K. (1976). The dialectics of human development. *American Psychologist, 31,* 689–700.

Roderick, M. (1992). *School transition and school dropout: Middle school and early high school antecedents to school leaving.* Unpublished manuscript, School of Social Service Administration, University of Chicago.

Rosenbaum, J. E. (1976). *Making inequality: The hidden curriculum of high school tracking.* New York: Wiley.

Rosenberg, M. (1986). Self-concept from middle childhood through adolescence. In J. Suls & A. G. Greenwald (Eds.), *Psychological perspectives on the self* (Vol. 3, pp. 107–136). Hillsdale, NJ: Lawrence Erlbaum Associates.

Rosenberg, M., & Simmons, R. G. (1972). *Black and white self-esteem: The urban school child* (Arnold M. and Caroline Rose Monograph Series). Washington, DC: American Sociological Association.

Rosenholtz, S. J., & Simpson, C. (1984). The formation of ability conception: Developmental trend or social construction? *Review of Educational Research, 54,* 301–325.

Rounds, T. S., & Osaki, S. Y. (1982). *The social organization of classrooms: An analysis of sixth- and seventh-grade activity structures* (Report EPSSP-82-5). San Francisco: Far West Laboratory.

Rumberger, R. W. (1987). High school dropouts: A review of issues and evidence. *Review of Educational Research, 57,* 101–122.

Savin-Williams, R. C., & Berndt, T. J. (1990). Friendship and peer relations. In S. S. Feldman & G. R. Elliott (Eds.), *At the threshold: The developing adolescent* (pp. 277–307). Cambridge, MA: Harvard University Press.

Scheier, M. A., & Kraut, R. E. (1979). Increasing educational achievement via self-concept change. *Review of Educational Research, 49,* 131–150.

Schneider, W., & Pressley, M. (1989). *Memory development between 2 and 20.* New York: Springer.

Schoenfeld, A. (1983). Beyond the purely cognitive: Belief systems, social cognitions, and metacognitions as driving forces in intellectual performance. *Cognitive Science, 7*, 329–363.

Schoenfeld, A. (1985). *Mathematical problem solving*. New York: Academic Press.

Schofield, J. W. (1980). Complementary and conflicting identities: Images and interactions in an interracial school. In S. R. Asher & J. Gottman (Eds.), *The development of children's friendships* (pp. 55–90). New York: Cambridge University Press.

Schommer, M. (1990). Effects of beliefs about the nature of knowledge on comprehension. *Journal of Educational Psychology, 82*, 498–504.

Schommer, M. (1993). Epistemological development and academic performance among secondary school students. *Journal of Educational Psychology, 85*, 406–411.

Schommer, M., Crouse, A., & Rhodes, N. (1992). Epistemological beliefs and mathematical text comprehension: Believing it is simple does not make it so. *Journal of Educational Psychology, 84*, 435–443.

Schulenberg, J. E., Asp, C. E., & Petersen, A. C. (1984). School from the young adolescent's perspective: A descriptive report. *Journal of Early Adolescence, 4*, 107–130.

Schunk, D. H. (1991a). Goal setting and self-evaluation: A social cognitive perspective on self-regulation. In M. L. Maehr & P. R. Pintrich (Eds.), *Advances in achievement and motivation, 7*, 85–113. Greenwich, CT: JAI Press.

Schunk, D. H. (1991b). Self-efficacy and academic motivation. *Educational Psychologist, 26*, 233–262.

Schunk, D. H. (1994). Self-regulation of efficacy and attributions in academic settings. In D. H. Schunk & B. C. Zimmerman (Eds.) *Self-regulation of learning and performance: Issues and educational applications* (pp. 75–99). Hillsdale, NJ: Lawrence Erlbaum Associates.

Selman, R. L. (1980). *The growth of interpersonal understanding*. New York: Academic Press.

Shavelson, R. J., Hubner, J. J., & Stanton, G. C. (1976). Self-concept: Validation of construct interpretations. *Review of Educational Research, 46*, 407–441.

Simmons, R. G., & Blyth, D. A. (1987). *Moving into adolescence: The impact of pubertal change and school context*. Hawthorn, NY: Aldine de Gruyter.

Simmons, R. G., Blyth, D. A., Van Cleaves, E. F., & Bush, D. (1979). Entry into early adolescence: The impact of school structure, puberty, and early dating on self-esteem. *American Sociological Review, 44*, 948–967.

Simmons, R. G., Burgeson, R., Carlton-Ford, S., & Blyth, D. (1987). The impact of cumulative change in adolescence. *Child Development, 58*, 1220–1234.

Simmons, R. G., Rosenberg, M. F., & Rosenberg, M. C. (1973). Disturbance in the self-image at adolescence. *American Sociological Review, 38*, 553–568.

Skaalvik, E. M., & Hagtvet, K. A. (1990). Academic achievement and self-concept: An analysis of causal predominance in a developmental perspective. *Journal of Personality and Social Psychology, 58*, 292–307.

Skinner, E. A. (1990). Age differences in the dimensions of perceived control during middle childhood: Implications for developmental conceptualizations and research. *Child Development, 61*, 1882–1890.

Slaughter-Defoe, D. T., Nakagawa, K., Takanishi, R., & Johnson, D. J. (1990). Toward cultural/ecological perspectives on schooling and achievement in African- and Asian-American children. *Child Development, 61*, 363–383.

Slavin, R. E. (1990). *Cooperative learning: Theory, research, and practice*. Englewood Cliffs, NJ: Prentice Hall.

Snow, R., & Swanson, J. (1992). Instructional psychology: Aptitude, adaptation, and assessment. *Annual Review of Psychology, 43*, 583–626.

Spencer, M. B., & Markstrom-Adams, C. (1990). Identity processes among racial and ethnic minority children in America. *Child Development, 61*, 290–310.

Stattin, H., & Magnusson, D. (1990). *Pubertal maturation in female development*. Hillsdale, NJ: Lawrence Erlbaum Associates.

Steele, C. (1992, April). *Assessing the challenges of increasing and varied minority populations*. Paper presented at the annual meeting of the American Educational Research Association, San Francisco.

Steinberg, L. (1987). Impact of puberty on family relations: Effects of pubertal status and pubertal timing. *Developmental Psychology, 23*, 451–460.

Steinberg, L. (1988). Reciprocal relations between parent-child distance and pubertal maturation. *Developmental Psychology, 24*, 122–128.

Steinberg, L. (1989). Pubertal maturation and parent-adolescent distance: An evolutionary perspective. In G. Adams, R. Montemayor, & T. Gullotta (Eds.), *Advances in adolescent development* (Vol. 1). Beverly Hills, CA: Sage.

Steinberg, L., Dornbusch, S. M., & Brown, B. B. (1992). Ethnic differences in adolescent achievement: An ecological perspective. *American Psychologist, 47*, 723–729.

Stipek, D., & Mac Iver, D. (1989). Developmental change in children's assessment of intellectual competence. *Child Development, 60*, 521–538.

Sullivan, H. S. (1953). *The interpersonal theory of psychiatry*. New York: Norton.

Susman, E. J., Inoff-Germain, G., Nottelmann, E. D., Loriaux, D. L., Cutler, C. B., & Chrousos, G. P. (1987). Hormones, emotional dispositions, and aggressive attributes in young adolescents. *Child Development, 58*, 1114–1134.

Tharp, R., & Gallimore, R. (1988). *Rousing minds to life: Teaching, learning, and schooling in social context*. Cambridge, England: Cambridge University Press.

Tice, D., & Baumeister, R. (1990). Self-esteem, self-handicapping, and self-presentation: The strategy of inadequate practice. *Journal of Personality, 58*, 443–464.

Tinto, V. (1987). *Leaving college: Rethinking the causes and cures of student attrition*. Chicago: University of Chicago Press.

Trebilco, G. R., Atkinson, E. P., & Atkinson, J. M. (1977, November). *The transition of students from primary to secondary school*. Paper presented at the annual conference of the Australian Association for Research in Education, Canberra.

Trickett, E. J., & Moos, R. H. (1974). Personal correlates of contrasting environments: Student satisfactions in high school classrooms. *American Journal of Community Psychology, 2*, 1–12.

Trueba, H. (1988). Culturally-based explanations of minority students' academic achievement. *Anthropology and Education Quarterly, 19*, 270–287.

Turiel, E., & Davidson, P. (1986). Heterogeneity, inconsistency, and asynchrony in the development of cognitive structures. In I. Levin (Ed.), *Stage and structure*. Norwood, NJ: Ablex.

Udry, J. R. (1988). *Biosocial models of adolescent problem behaviors*. Unpublished manuscript.

Upcraft, L., & Gardner, J. (1989). *The freshman year experience: Helping students survive and succeed in college*. San Francisco: Jossey-Bass.

Valli, L. (1986). *Becoming clerical workers*. Boston: Routledge & Kegan Paul.

Veroff, J., & Veroff, J. B. (1980). *Social incentives: A life-span developmental approach*. New York: Academic Press.

Vetter, B. (1992). Ferment: yes, progress: maybe, change: slow. *Mosaic, 23*, 34–41.

Walberg, H. J., House, E. R., & Steele, J. M. (1973). Grade level, cognition, and affect: A cross-section of classroom perceptions. *Journal of Educational Psychology, 64*, 142–146.

Ward, B. A., Mergendoller, J. R., Tikunoff, W. J., Rounds, T. S., Dadey, G. J., & Mitman, A. L. (1982). *Junior high school transition study: Executive summary*. San Francisco: Far West Laboratory.

Waterman, A. (1982). Identity development from adolescence to adulthood: An extension of theory and review of research. *Developmental Psychology, 18*, 341–358.

Waterman, A. (1985). Identity in the context of adolescent psychology. In A. Waterman (Ed.), *Identity in adolescence: Processes and contents* (pp. 5–24). San Francisco: Jossey-Bass.

Weiner, B. (1979). A theory of motivation for some classroom experiences. *Journal of Educational Psychology, 71*, 3–25.

Weiner, B. (1985). An attributional theory of achievement motivation and emotion. *Psychological Review, 92*, 548–573.

Weiner, B. (1986). *An attributional theory of motivation and emotion*. New York: Springer.

Weinstein, C. E., & Mayer, R. E. (1986). The teaching of learning strategies. In M. Wittrock (Ed.), *Handbook of research on teaching* (pp. 315–327). New York: Macmillan.

Weis, L. (1990). *Working class without work: High school students in a de-industrializing economy*. New York: Routledge.

Wellman, H., & Gelman, S. (1992). Cognitive development: Foundational theories of core domains. *Annual Review of Psychology, 43*, 337–375.

Wentzel, K. R. (1989). Adolescent classroom grades, standards for performance, and academic achievement. An interactionist perspective. *Journal of Educational Psychology, 81*, 131–142.

White, P. E. (1992). *Women and minorities in science and engineering: An update*. Washington, DC: National Science Foundation.

Wigfield, A. (1984, April). *Relationship between ability perceptions, other achievement-related beliefs, and school performance*. Paper presented at the meeting of the American Educational Research Association, New Orleans, LA.

Wigfield, A. (1993). Why do I have to learn this? Adolescents' valuing of school. In P. R. Pintrich & M. L. Maehr (Eds.), *Advances in motivation and achievement, 8*, pp. 99–138. Greenwich, CT: JAI Press.

Wigfield, A. (1994). The role of children's achievement values in the regulation of their learning outcomes. In D. H. Schunk & B. J. Zimmerman (Eds.), *Self-regulation of learning and performance: Issues and educational applications* (pp. 101–124). Hillsdale, NJ: Lawrence Erlbaum Associates.

Wigfield, A., & Eccles, J. S. (1989). Test anxiety in elementary and secondary school students. *Educational Psychologist, 24*, 159–183.

Wigfield, A., & Eccles, J. S. (1992). The development of achievement task values: A theoretical analysis. *Developmental Review, 12*, 265–310.

Wigfield, A., Eccles, J., Mac Iver, D., Reuman, D., & Midgley, C. (1991). Transitions at early adolescence: Changes in children's domain-specific self-perceptions and general self-esteem across the transition to junior high school. *Developmental Psychology, 27*, 552–565.

Wigfield, A., & Karpathian, M. (1991). Who am I and what can I do? Children's self-concepts and motivation in achievement situations. *Educational Psychologist, 26*, 233–262.

Willis, P. (1977). *Learning to labor: How working class kids get working class jobs*. New York: Columbia University Press.

Wylie, R. C. (1989). *Measures of the self-concept*. Lincoln, NE: University of Nebraska Press.

Zimmerman, B. J. (1989a). A social cognitive view of self-regulated learning. *Journal of Educational Psychology, 81*, 329–339.

Zimmerman, B. J. (1989b). Models of self-regulated and academic achievement. In B. J. Zimmerman & D. H. Schunk (Eds.), *Self-regulated learning and academic achievement: Theory, research, and practice* (pp. 1–25). New York: Springer.

Zimmerman, B. J., Bandura, A., & Martinez-Pons, M. (1992). Self-motivation for academic attainment: The role of self-efficacy beliefs and personal goal setting. *American Educational Research Journal, 29*, 663–676.

# ·8·

# INDIVIDUAL DIFFERENCES IN
# COGNITIVE FUNCTIONS

## Jan-Eric Gustafsson
UNIVERSITY OF GÖTEBORG, SWEDEN

## Johan Olav Undheim
UNIVERSITY OF TRONDHEIM, NORWAY

Individual differences are easily recognized in any area of performance. The learning performances expected to take place in classrooms are no exception, and individual differences are indeed conspicuously present in school. This is partly due to the fact that the social context of the classroom invites comparisons: Students of approximately the same age work on the same set of tasks, with results that are easily comparable and that often have consequences for the future lives of the students. Thus, in the school context, individual differences in performance are of great importance to students, teachers, parents, counselors, and everyone else involved.

This chapter focuses on individual differences in cognitive functions, while chapter 9 focuses on individual differences in affective and conative functions. Both chapters discuss research on how individual differences should be conceptualized and identified. Other issues discussed concern how instruction and the educational system may take individual differences into account, and what factors, including educational ones, affect the development of individual differences.

The oldest, the most influential, and the most criticized approach to the study of individual differences is the psychometric one. This approach, which dates back to the late 19th century, relies on psychological tests that yield scores on quantitative scales. These scores may be analyzed by statistical methods to identify the dimensions of ability that form the structure of individual differences.

The psychometric approach has resulted in the technology of mental testing, which has had a profound impact on society. However, the approach has been criticized for failing to provide deeper theoretical insights into the nature of intelligence (see, e.g., L. B. Resnick, 1976). As has been pointed out, the approach is product oriented and fails to specify the processes by which problems are solved. Since the late 1960s a second, process-oriented approach to the understanding of individual differences has evolved. Starting from the cognitive research that models the human mind as an information-processing system, process-oriented researchers have designed experimental procedures to locate the processes underlying performance. Other researchers have tried to find sources of individual differences in biological and neuropsychological factors; yet others have sought explanations in cultural and sociological factors (see, e.g., R. J. Sternberg, 1990).

This chapter discusses the psychometric and the process-oriented approaches, in that order of priority. The emphasis on the psychometric approach stems in part from its historical importance, which makes it necessary to understand the fundamental concepts of this approach, but there are other reasons as well. Although the psychometric approach appeared to have reached a dead end in the 1960s, important progress with this approach has been made in recent decades. It now seems possible to reconcile conflicting views concerning the structure of cognitive abilities and to approach both old and new problems with more powerful conceptual and methodological tools. The fact that both authors of this chapter are more familiar with the psychometric approach undoubtedly also has influenced our priorities.

We also want to emphasize that most other chapters of this *Handbook* present theories, methods, and empirical results that are highly relevant to any student of individual differences in cognitive functions, but this is particularly true for chapters 1 through 7. We have already referred to chapter 9, which discusses individual differences in affective and conative functions. Chapter 10 also deals with individual differences, with a focus on exceptionality.

We would like to express our gratitude to John B. Carroll, Richard E. Snow, and Robert J. Sternberg for their invaluable comments on previous versions of this chapter.

## BASIC OBSERVATIONS OF INDIVIDUAL DIFFERENCES

### Conceptions and Measures of Individual Differences in Cognitive Functions

All research starts from a conception of the phenomenon under study. Researchers and lay persons have conceptions about the nature of individual differences, and it may be suitable to start with a discussion of some of these conceptions.

*Conceptions of Individual Differences Among Children and Adults.* Research on people's conceptions of individual differences has investigated, among other things, the concept of intelligence (e.g., Berg & Sternberg, 1985; R. J. Sternberg, Conway, Ketron, & Bernstein, 1981), and how differences in children's intelligence might account for differences in achievement. Berg and Sternberg (1985) found that adults distinguished between three different aspects of intelligence: practical problem-solving ability ("reasons logically and well," "identifies connections among ideas," "sees all aspects of a problem"), verbal ability ("speaks clearly and articulately," "is verbally fluent," "converses well"), and social competence ("accepts others for what they are," "displays interest in the world at large"). As was pointed out by R. J. Sternberg (1990, p. 60), the problem-solving dimension and the verbal dimension clearly resemble the major dimensions in Cattell and Horn's hierarchical model of ability (discussed below).

Children, too, seem to make similar distinctions. Cain and Dweck (1990) found that children account for differences in achievement outcomes through an implicit theory of intelligence, according to which intelligence is a combination of knowledge, capacity, and effort. It thus seems that both adults and children have a multifaceted conception of individual differences in intelligence and school achievement, with a distinction between acquired knowledge, on the one hand, and a capacity for problem solving and reasoning on the other.

*Expert Definitions of Intelligence.* The concept of intelligence has a central place in research on individual differences. During the first decades of the 20th century, measures of general intellectual ability were constructed, but it proved difficult to agree on a definition of intelligence. In 1921 the editors of the *Journal of Educational Psychology* invited 14 experts to give their views on the nature of intelligence and its measurement. A wide variety of definitions were suggested, such as the ability to carry on abstract thinking, the ability to learn, and the ability to adapt to new situations (see R. J. Sternberg, 1990, p. 35, for a summary). Even though many definitions focused on similar aspects, there was a considerable lack of agreement. Decades later R. J. Sternberg and Detterman (1986) repeated the 1921 symposium and asked two dozen contemporary experts to define intelligence. Again, a diverse set of responses was obtained. A multifaceted framework of the responses was proposed that distinguished (among other things) among those who see the locus of intelligence as within the individual, as within the environment, or as within the interaction between the individual and the environment. However, even though diverse viewpoints were obtained, 50 percent of all respondents

mentioned attributes of higher level processing, such as abstract reasoning, problem solving, and decision making, as important aspects of intelligence (see also Snyderman & Rothman, 1987). These aspects are emphasized in the nonexpert conceptions as well, so despite the diversity there does seem to be agreement among both experts and nonexperts.

### Measures of Individual Differences

The scientific study of individual differences in cognitive functions is closely related to the use of tests. A test may be broadly defined as "a systematic procedure for observing behavior and describing it with the aid of numerical scales or fixed categories" (Cronbach, 1990, p. 32). Usually attempts are made to standardize the situation and presentation of tasks so that tests yield scores that are comparable across individuals, times, and places. Tests may be "objective" in the sense that no human judges observe or rate performance; multiple-choice or true–false items are typical examples. Other tests allow room for disagreement between observers, and sometimes great effort must be spent to train evaluators in observation and rating procedures.

Tests are usually composed of items. The items may be arranged into subtests, whose scores may be combined to yield an overall score. Sometimes the subtest scores are referred to as test scores and the whole set of tests is called a test battery.

Here we are interested in a certain subclass of tests, namely mental, cognitive, or intelligence tests. There seems to be no agreed-upon definition that clearly distinguishes mental tests from other tests. Jensen (1987a, p. 88) refers to the negative criterion that the variance in task performance should not be associated with individual differences in physical capacity. Guttman and Levy (1991, p. 82; see also Guttman, 1965a) suggest that an intelligence test item should ask about an objective rule for which responses can be ordered from "very right to very wrong." Both Jensen's and Guttman's definitions are quite broad, however, and a great variety of tests are covered. The tests may involve different sensory modalities for presentation and response (e.g., visual, oral, kinesthetic), different kinds of stimulus material (e.g., words, figures, numbers, letters, physical objects, pictures), and different types of task requirements (e.g., discrimination, generalization, recall, recognition, naming, comparison, decision, inference).

To make our presentation more concrete, we next describe a few of the major tests of intelligence. For detailed information on these and other tests, see Anastasi (1988), Cronbach (1990), Murphy and Davidshofer (1988), and the descriptions and reviews of tests compiled in the *Mental Measurements* yearbooks (e.g., Buros, 1978; Kramer & Conoley, 1992).

*The Stanford-Binet Intelligence Scale.* The fourth edition of the Stanford-Binet Intelligence Scale (R. L. Thorndike, Hagen, & Sattler, 1986) is a descendant of the first intelligence scale, developed by Binet and Simon in France in the early 1900s. Carroll (1982) observed that "despite a number of revisions (Goddard, 1908; Terman, 1916; Terman & Merrill, 1937, 1960), the content of the present 'Stanford-Binet' scale can in most cases be traced back to that of the original scale" (p. 33). However, after the last revision, the structure of the test is quite different. The fourth edition is organized into four different

TABLE 8–1. Subtests of WISC-III

| Subtest | Example[a] or Type of Task |
|---|---|
| Information | "Who was Thomas Jefferson?" |
| Comprehension | "Why is it important to use zip codes when you mail letters?" |
| Similarities | "In what way are corn and macaroni alike? How are they the same?" |
| Vocabulary | "What do we mean by 'protect'?" |
| Arithmetic | "Dick had 13 pieces of candy and gave away 8. How many did he have left?" |
| Digit Span | Repeat sequences of numbers forward and backward. |
| Block Design | Construct a pattern shown on a card out of colored blocks. |
| Picture Completion | Fill in a missing detail in presented picture. |
| Picture Arrangement | Place a series of cartoon panels in a meaningful sequence. |
| Object Assembly | Put together parts to make an object. |
| Coding | Put symbols as fast as possible beneath numbers according to a code which remains available. |
| Symbol Search | Scan two groups of shapes and indicate whether any shapes are common to the groups. |
| Mazes | Draw a line from the center to the exit of a maze without entering any blocked passages or crossing through walls. |

[a]Examples taken from Cronbach (1990, p. 246).

sections: a Verbal section, with subtests such as Vocabulary, Comprehension, and Absurdities; a Quantitative section, involving, for example, Number Series; an Abstract/Visual section with subtests such as Pattern Analysis, Copying, and Matrices; and a Memory section comprising subtests such as Memory for Digits and Memory for Objects. The test is designed to measure overall ability from ages 2 to 23, but only subtests and items appropriate to the age and ability of the examinee are administered. The test yields an overall score called the Composite Standard Age Score, or CSAS, as well as a Standard Age Score for each of the sections.

*The Wechsler Intelligence Scale for Children.* Wechsler developed measures of general ability in the 1930s, primarily to obtain a clinically useful scale of the intellectual functioning of adults. The original Wechsler-Bellevue Scale (Wechsler, 1939) has been followed by several revisions (Wechsler, 1974, 1991) and extensions to younger age groups. The Wechsler test system (Matarazzo, 1972) has long been the dominant individual test (Cronbach, 1990, p. 243), particularly for children.

The Wechsler Intelligence Scale for Children—Third Edition (WISC-III; Wechsler, 1991, 1992) covers the age range from 6 to 16 and consists of 13 subtests, which are listed in Table 8–1, along with an example or brief description of each. The subtests are divided to provide Verbal and Performance IQ scores, and a Full Scale IQ score is determined from all the subtests.

*The Kaufman Assessment Battery for Children.* This more recent test (Kaufman & Kaufman, 1983) is designed for ages 2½ to 12½. It is divided into two major sections, Mental Pro-

cessing and Achievement. The Achievement scales measure vocabulary, reading comprehension, general knowledge, and knowledge of arithmetic. The Mental Processing scales are divided into Sequential Processing and Simultaneous Processing tests. Sequential processing is employed when problems are solved step by step, as in a digit span test. Simultaneous processing is involved when multiple pieces of information must be integrated to solve a problem, such as in a matrices task. In addition to scores on individual subtests, five global scale scores are reported, an Achievement score and scores for Sequential Processing, Simultaneous Processing, Mental Processing, and a nonverbal score.

*Discussion.* Intelligence tests have been in use for over a century and continue to appear in new revisions. Such tests evoked much criticism and controversy (see, e.g., Cronbach, 1975a). For example, Neisser (1976) argued that the problems found on such tests are well defined but trivial, with only one correct answer, where all the information needed is supplied with the task. Such problems were labeled "academic" by Neisser, who saw them as quite different from the problems of everyday life.

Recently there has been increasing interest in what has been termed practical intelligence (R. J. Sternberg & Wagner, 1986, 1989), or performance on tasks of the kind encountered in everyday life. For example, Fredriksen (1986) described tests that are close to real-life problems, such as the in-basket test, which simulates the problem solving required of, for example, government administrators and school principals. Wagner and Sternberg (1986) argued that to achieve success in an occupation it is necessary to learn and apply information that is never explicitly taught. Such tacit knowledge is not captured by traditional tests but requires tests that resemble the tasks found in the everyday world.

In a parallel trend, there has been in the field of educational measurement a rapid development of modes of assessment that require students to create answers or products of their own. Such performance assessment is seen as an alternative to standardized objective paper-and-pencil tests (e.g., Gardner, 1992; Resnick & Resnick, 1992). These more realistic tasks represent exciting new sources of information about individual differences in abilities, knowledge, and skill. In the final section of this chapter we explore how the more traditional modes of measurement relate to the newer modes of assessment.

## THE STRUCTURE OF INDIVIDUAL DIFFERENCES IN COGNITIVE FUNCTIONS

All sciences need systems of description and classification. In the field of research on individual differences, these issues have received much attention, and in the psychometric approach techniques have been developed for measuring and sorting abilities. In this section we describe the fundamental concepts and techniques of this research.

### Fundamental Psychometric Concepts

Performances on different mental tests tend to be positively intercorrelated (e.g., Guttman & Levy, 1991; Spearman, 1927;

TABLE 8–2. Correlations Among the Subtests in the WISC-III Battery (U.S. Norming Sample, 11-Year-Olds, N = 200)

|  | Inf. | Sim. | Ari. | Voc. | Com. | DS | PCom. | CD. | PA | BD | OA | SS | Mz. |
|---|---|---|---|---|---|---|---|---|---|---|---|---|---|
| Information | 1.00 | | | | | | | | | | | | |
| Similarities | 0.66 | 1.00 | | | | | | | | | | | |
| Arithmetic | 0.55 | 0.61 | 1.00 | | | | | | | | | | |
| Vocabulary | 0.67 | 0.67 | 0.55 | 1.00 | | | | | | | | | |
| Comprehension | 0.47 | 0.61 | 0.48 | 0.63 | 1.00 | | | | | | | | |
| Digit Span | 0.33 | 0.36 | 0.53 | 0.33 | 0.26 | 1.00 | | | | | | | |
| Picture Completion | 0.48 | 0.49 | 0.38 | 0.44 | 0.39 | 0.27 | 1.00 | | | | | | |
| Coding | 0.18 | 0.22 | 0.27 | 0.23 | 0.26 | 0.28 | 0.19 | 1.00 | | | | | |
| Picture Arrangement | 0.33 | 0.29 | 0.15 | 0.35 | 0.25 | 0.15 | 0.37 | 0.17 | 1.00 | | | | |
| Block Design | 0.38 | 0.46 | 0.51 | 0.38 | 0.35 | 0.27 | 0.54 | 0.27 | 0.30 | 1.00 | | | |
| Object Assembly | 0.36 | 0.43 | 0.39 | 0.40 | 0.32 | 0.20 | 0.47 | 0.23 | 0.35 | 0.54 | 1.00 | | |
| Symbol Search | 0.31 | 0.29 | 0.34 | 0.34 | 0.30 | 0.21 | 0.32 | 0.51 | 0.29 | 0.47 | 0.33 | 1.00 | |
| Mazes | 0.09 | 0.11 | 0.14 | 0.09 | 0.06 | 0.11 | 0.07 | 0.14 | 0.15 | 0.17 | 0.19 | 0.17 | 1.00 |
| Mean correlation: | 0.37 | 0.43 | 0.41 | 0.42 | 0.37 | 0.28 | 0.37 | 0.25 | 0.26 | 0.39 | 0.35 | 0.32 | 0.13 |

L. L. Thurstone, 1947). This principle of a "positive manifold" (L. L. Thurstone, 1947) may be illustrated by the intercorrelations among the subscales of the WISC-III battery. Table 8–2 presents results from the U.S. norming sample (Wechsler, 1991) for the age group of 11-year-olds. All correlations are positive and range between a low of .06 (Comprehension and Mazes) to a high of .67 (Information and Vocabulary). The means of correlations between one subtest and the other subtests vary less (between a low of .13 for Mazes and a high of .43 for Similarities). These values also support the conclusion that the subscales are positively related. However, closer scrutiny of the correlations indicates patterns of similarities and differences among the subtests. For example, Information, Similarities, Vocabulary, and Comprehension are more highly correlated among themselves than they are with the other tests; and Block Design and Object Assembly are highly correlated. This suggests that different subgroups of tests reflect different abilities.

Observations such as these form the basis for the factor-analytic approach. There is an obvious need for a simplified description in terms of a more limited set of concepts than those used to describe the tasks themselves. Research on the structure of individual differences aims to identify such concepts. More specifically, this research has sought to determine the answers to two basic questions, namely (a) how many dimensions are needed to describe individual differences in cognitive performance? and (b) what are the interrelationships among the dimensions of ability? The purpose thus has been to develop a system of classification, or a taxonomy of abilities.

A century of research has sought to uncover the structure of individual differences. Different schools of thought have proposed different systems of classification. Despite considerable controversy over this history, it is now possible to see the contours of a unified structural model. Before discussing these advances, we present some of the methodological tools employed in the research.

*Measurement Concepts.* Progress in research on individual differences has been closely linked to the development of new mathematical, statistical, and computational techniques, and attempts to solve substantive research problems have led to

the development of new techniques and methods. Particularly in the early phases of development of differential psychology there was a close interplay between theoretical and methodological advances.

Building on the work of Francis Galton and Karl Pearson, among others, Spearman (1904a, 1904b) laid the foundation for two of the most important methodological subfields of relevance to research on individual differences: factor analysis and measurement theory (or "mental test theory"). The aim of factor analysis is to identify a limited set of dimensions of ability that may account for individual differences in performance. Test theory is concerned with characteristics of the measurements of performance. As may be understood from their common origin, factor analysis and test theory are intimately related. However, as has been noted by Carroll (1982), "the specialties tend to be quite separate: they are usually treated in different university courses and taught by different specialists, who tend to publish in different sets of journals" (p. 45).

These disciplines are complex and cannot be presented here. However, because factor analysis plays such an important role in the psychometric approach to individual differences, it is essential that the fundamental characteristics of this technique be understood. Some basic concepts and principles of factor analysis are therefore presented later with concrete examples.

Performance on an item in a test usually is judged to be right or wrong. From the performance of the examinees on the items, the test-theoretic models aim to estimate the examinees' level on an underlying, unobservable, or latent variable (ability). Different test-theoretic models make different assumptions about the form of the relationship between observable performance and the latent variable. Classic test theory and its modern developments (e.g., Cronbach, Gleser, Nanda, & Rajaratnam, 1972; Jöreskog, 1971; Lord & Novick, 1968) assume a simple linear regression of the observed sum of correct answers on ability. Modern test theory (e.g., Hambleton, 1989; Lord, 1980), in contrast, assumes a nonlinear relationship between the latent variable and the probability of a correct answer on an item. Within this approach, different models make different assumptions: The one-parameter model (Rasch, 1960), for example, assumes that the same relation holds for each and every item, while the so-called two- and three-parameter models allow different relations for different items.

The idea of an unobservable ability variable accounting for observable performance thus is central to both factor analysis and test theory. However, this idea can be confusing and misleading. Snow and Lohman (1989) argued that

sign-trait interpretations of test scores and their intercorrelations are superficial summaries at best. At worst, they have misled scientists, and the public, into thinking of fundamental, fixed entities, measured as amounts. (p. 317)

Such a reified view has, indeed, been frequent in research on individual differences (e.g., Gould, 1981; Humphreys, 1985), and for some researchers it has been a reason to reject the psychometric approach as fundamentally flawed and biased (e.g., Keating, 1984). However, the latent variable need not be conceived of as a singular entity, except as a convenient summary. In recent cognitive research on psychometric tasks, for example, rich descriptions of the processes involved in solving test items have been obtained. Sometimes, however, it is neither possible nor desirable to obtain detailed information about the psychological processes underlying a score. The concept of ability (or latent variable) is useful because it allows description and analysis of intellectual performance across tasks. In the psychometric approach, variance is partialed out of specific tasks to determine dimensions that span several tasks. Summation of scores over items and tests is a simple way to partial out task-specific variance. However, the modern test-theoretic models offer much more refined techniques for aggregation of scores, and for investigating whether the conditions for aggregation are fulfilled.

Thus, the notion of a latent variable is just a mathematical and conceptual tool, or, as Carroll (1993) put it, "a calculational convenience, as it were, in linking together a particular series of observations" (p. 23). This tool makes it possible to study individual differences in performance over several tasks. We may consider a situation in which a large number of interchangeable measures represent the same domain or construct. Suppose, for example, that we aim to measure the level of vocabulary knowledge among a group of persons. Not only is there a very large number of possible words to choose from (around 500,000 in English), but we may also present the target word in a large number of ways (e.g., with or without context, in different typographical layouts, in groups of different sizes, etc.). The examinee may also be requested to give the response in many different ways. We may thus construct an infinite number of vocabulary items that may be combined into an infinite number of tests.

If two or more of these tests are given to a group of examinees we would expect them to yield roughly the same results, so that the rank ordering according to level of performance on one test would agree with the rank ordering according to level of performance on another test. However, we cannot expect perfect agreement, because there are many circumstances that may cause an examinee to achieve a higher score on one test than on another. The examinee may be lucky or unlucky with the particular selection of words in a test; the modes of presentation and response for a test may give the examinee an advantage or a disadvantage; the external circumstances under which the tests were taken may have varied; different raters of performance, who are more or less lenient, may be involved; and so on. A large number of factors thus may cause measurements intended to measure the same ability to give different results. Conceptually, however, we can imagine that all items could be presented to a person in an unbiased manner. The result thus obtained would be a value on a latent variable. We thus invoke the latent variable without making any assumptions about the processes involved in acquiring vocabulary or in responding to the test. Nor do we assume that the latent variable represents a fixed, unchangeable amount of ability.

The test-theoretic models are statistical models, and they have no strong foundation in psychological theory. Because the models have no prior justification, they must be justified on the basis of their results. The models also make assumptions that may be too simplistic for real situations, such as assuming statistical independence to hold between performance on different items (see Snow & Lohman, 1989, p. 267, for descriptions of situations in which this is not true).

Humphreys (1962, 1985) also has criticized test theory for relying on assumptions of unidimensionality and homogeneity. These assumptions often imply that tests should be splintered into more homogeneous subsets of items, with the consequence that researchers would have to deal with thousands of tests and almost as many factors. However, even though tests are made statistically homogeneous, they may be psychologically complex. This is because any particular "test is an inextricable combination of content, operation, product, and so on. Factor purity is not equivalent to psychological purity" (Humphreys, 1985, p. 206).

The studies relying on psychometric techniques may be described as technically sophisticated but psychologically naive. The studies mainly have aimed to investigate the broad structural issues, however, and for these purposes it may be argued that the psychometric techniques are quite appropriate. We will return to a discussion of the advantages and disadvantages of different methodological approaches.

## Taxonomies of Cognitive Abilities

Psychometric techniques have been employed in many studies aimed at resolving the problem of the structure of abilities. This research has resulted in a proliferation of models that include different numbers of dimensions of individual differences and assume different types of relations among the dimensions. However, structural models of abilities have been erected not only on the basis of results from multivariate statistical analyses. Thus, Gardner (1983), R. J. Sternberg (1985), and others have proposed structural models that rely on other types of evidence, such as experimental, developmental, neuropsychological, and cross-cultural research. These models are also described below.

*General Cognitive Ability.* Whether a test of intelligence yields subscores for different domains of performance or not, it typically yields an overall score as an index of general intellectual ability. In the world of practical applications, these scores are heavily relied on, and the notion of general cognitive ability is firmly entrenched. Indeed, as Scarr (1989) observed, "no concept in the history of psychology has had or continues to have as great an impact on everyday life in the Western world" (p. 75).

Several comprehensive historical accounts of the development of the theory and practice of intelligence measurement have been published (Carroll, 1982, 1993; DuBois, 1970; R. M. Thorndike & Lohman, 1990), so the history will not be described here. However, to understand the major positions on theoretical and empirical issues, it is instructive to look at the developments during the first few years of the 20th century.

During these years the first practically useful intelligence scale was developed by Binet and Simon (1905, 1908). Both Binet and other researchers (e.g., J. M. Cattell, 1890; Galton, 1883) had previously tried to construct mental tests with simple tasks such as speed of reaction, sensory discrimination, and word association. The new scale, however, was composed of more complex tasks. The tasks varied, but most required understanding of language and the ability to solve problems of both verbal and nonverbal kinds. This scale met with great success.

Spearman (1904b) presented the first formalized model of the structure of cognitive abilities. He assumed that performance on any intellectual task is affected by two factors: one general, which is common to all tasks ($g$), and one that is specific to the task ($s$). Testing the model on several different sets of variables, comprising among other things psychophysical assessments, ratings of intelligence, school marks, and psychological tests, Spearman concluded that in most cases one common factor was sufficient to account for the correlations among the variables.

One might expect the work of Binet and of Spearman to have been mutually supportive. That was not the case, however. Binet was aware of Spearman's work but criticized it as empirically inadequate (Binet, 1905). Spearman (1927) argued that the procedures used in developing Binet's tests, as well as the theoretical framework, were quite incompatible with his own position. Binet saw the score as representing an average of several abilities, but Spearman argued that the conception of general mental ability as an average led to insurmountable theoretical problems. The domains to be sampled must be determined, the sampling must be representative, the scale units must be compatible, and so on. Spearman (1927) thus claimed that:

*No genuine averaging, or sampling, of anybody's abilities is made, can be made, or even has really been attempted.* When Binet borrowed the idea of such promiscuous pooling, he carried it into execution with a brilliancy that perhaps no other living man could have matched. But on the theoretical side, he tried to get away too cheaply. (p. 71; emphasis in original)

Thus, from the beginning the work on general intelligence has developed along two different lines that have had little contact. One tradition has been oriented toward the development of practically useful tests. Within this tradition the IQ tests have been developed, with a close look at the predictive validities of the tests, particularly against scholastic criteria. The other tradition has attempted to identify the nature of the general factor through factor analytic means.

To be more concrete we will consider some simple factor models for the WISC scales presented in Table 8–1. The simplest explanation for the positive correlations among the scales (Table 8–2) is that performance on all the scales to a certain extent has a common cause. A simple model that captures this situation is

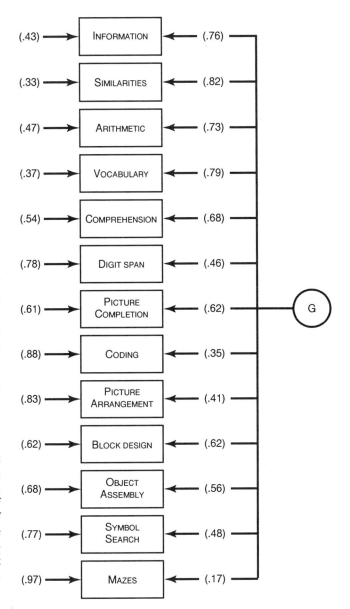

FIGURE 8–1. A One-Factor Model for the WICS-III Battery

shown in Figure 8–1. This model specifies performance on each of the WISC scales to be influenced by two unobservable (latent) variables. One of these (G) is assumed to affect performance on all the tests. The other variables are different for each of the scales, and represent the examinees' competence to deal with the items in a particular scale (over and above the level determined by G), the amount of luck in guessing, and all other factors that affect performance on a specific scale.

Algebraically, the model shown in Figure 8–1 may be expressed as a linear additive regression model, with the WISC scales as dependent variables and the latent variables as independent variables. This is a factor-analytic model and it is virtually identical to the original Spearman (1904b) model. The model assumes that an observed score for an examinee may be accounted for in terms of a weighted sum of scores on a limited set of underlying unobservable variables. The basic principles of factor analysis are simple, but the mathematical solutions tend to be complicated, and there are several different factor-analytic approaches (see, e.g., Gorsuch, 1983; Harman, 1967; Loehlin, 1992; McDonald, 1985; Mulaik, 1972).

In the most recently developed methods of factor analysis, the researcher proposes a particular model with a specified number of factors and a hypothesized pattern of relations between observed and latent variables. Parameters in this model may then be estimated from data. The model-fitting process also yields a statistical test of whether the model fits the data or not, as well as tests of the significance of individual parameters. This hypothesis-testing technique, which is frequently called "confirmatory" factor analysis (which, incidentally, is quite inappropriate a label, because models can be only rejected, never confirmed) is available in several easy-to-use computer programs (e.g., the EQS program by Bentler, 1992; the CALIS program within the SAS, 1990, system; the LISCOMP program by Muthén, 1988; or the LISREL program by Jöreskog & Sörbom, 1989, 1993). Estimates can thus be obtained of the amount of influence of the G variable on the WISC scales and of the amount of variance in the e variables. It would, however, carry too far to describe the technicalities of specification and estimation, so the interested reader is referred to the texts by Loehlin (1992) and Bollen (1989).

The results obtained with the LISREL program have been entered into Figure 8–1. The coefficients for the relations between the G factor and the WISC scales are called *factor loadings*. These are regression coefficients for the regression of the observed variables on the latent variable, but here they are standardized and may be interpreted as coefficients of correlation. The factor loadings range between .17 (for Mazes) and .82 (for Similarities). The square of the factor loading represents the amount of variance accounted for by the latent variable in the observed variable. Thus, the G factor accounts for 3 percent of the variance on the Mazes subtest and for 67 percent of the variance on the Similarities subtest.

Factor analysis thus divides the variance in an observed variable into two parts, one part that is due to the common factors (here the single G factor) and one that is unique to the variable. The unique variance in turn is often divided into two parts, one called *specificity*, which is the reliable part of the unique variance, and the other part called *error variance,* which represents random sources of influence. The specific factors cause performance to be higher or lower than could be expected from the common factors, such as knowledge and skills that are important in a particular domain. However, the specificity cannot be separated from the error variance unless there are at least two measures from each domain.

From this one-common-factor model it follows mathematically that the correlation between any two scales should be equal to the product of the factor loadings for the scales. If we compute all the correlations predicted from the model and compare them with the actually observed correlations, we would expect only random deviations. However, if the model is not appropriate for the data, we will get large deviations between the predicted and the observed correlations. The technique of confirmatory factor analysis summarizes the many comparisons into a global $\chi^2$ measure of goodness-of-fit. If this measure is large in relation to the degrees of freedom, the model must be rejected. For the present model the $\chi^2$ value is 218.4, with 65 degrees of freedom (*df*). This is highly significant, so we must conclude that the one-factor model does not fit the WISC scales.

The factor-analytic procedure devised by Spearman (1904b) also offered a crude and cumbersome method for investigating model fit. Even though the first study indicated good fit (Spearman, 1904b), later studies by Spearman and others showed that the simple one-factor model was unable to reproduce the observed correlations. An acceptable model must thus be more complex in the sense that it includes more dimensions.

Before looking at alternative models there is reason, however, to consider another way of defining the general factor, based on so-called principal components. In principal component analysis (Hotelling, 1933), the observed variables are transformed into new uncorrelated (orthogonal) variables in such a way that the first component accounts for the largest proportion of the total variance, the second largest principal component for the second largest proportion, and so on. Some researchers identify the general factor as the first principal component (or the first principal factor, which is similarly defined) in a matrix of intercorrelations between test performances (see, e.g., Ceci, 1990a; Jensen, 1980, 1982, 1987a). However, with this approach the nature of the general factor varies as a function of which particular tests are included in the matrix (e.g., Horn, 1989; L. L. Thurstone, 1947). If there are many verbal tests in one battery and many spatial tests, for example, in another battery, the first principal components of these two test batteries will define different "general" factors.

The problems of identifying a general intellectual factor through factor analysis have not prevented the development and use of tests that combine a variety of different tasks. Such tests have, however, been presented under a plethora of labels (e.g., IQ, intelligence, mental ability, scholastic ability, academic ability), and from analytic and taxonomic points of view it is extremely difficult to find any order among these notions and measures.

***Multiple Abilities.*** Spearman (1927) was aware that his model was refuted by the empirical results, but he continued to emphasize the *g* factor and argued that the deviations from the hypothesized model were due to correlations among *s* factors, caused by a more or less superficial overlap among certain tasks. The Spearman model, however, was abandoned by most researchers when L. L. Thurstone (1938) proposed an alternative model, formulated in terms of a limited set of specialized intellectual abilities, each of which is important for performance in limited domains of tasks.

Thurstone (1931, 1938, 1947) developed factor analysis to encompass multiple common factors, and modern versions of these techniques still represent the dominant form of factor analysis. Multiple-factor analysis permits identification of the number of independent dimensions required to account for the correlations among a set of tests. In this model, too, it is assumed that a person's score on a particular test is accounted for by one or more latent variables.

In the techniques invented by Thurstone, which are now called exploratory factor analysis, no assumptions are made about the number of latent variables or about a particular pattern of relationships between latent and observed variables. The solutions are not mathematically unique, however, so any solution may be transformed (rotated) into an infinite number of alternative solutions. The transformation may be done in such a manner that the factors are uncorrelated (orthogonal rotation) or correlated (oblique rotation). Thurstone (1947) proposed that a solution should have a "simple structure" in the sense that each factor should be associated with a subset of the observed variables, and each observed variable should be influenced by only one or a few factors. The simple structure criteria have been implemented in computer programs for exploratory factor analysis, so that the solution is numerically optimized according to these criteria. One of the best-known algorithms for orthogonal rotation is called the Varimax solution (Kaiser, 1958), and a frequently used algorithm for oblique rotation is Promax (A. E. Hendrickson & White, 1964).

Thurstone also was an inventive creator of test items. In a large-scale study he administered a battery of 56 tests to a sample of 240 university students and, with the newly developed factor-analytic technique, he identified about a dozen "primary" factors, nine of which were found interpretable (Spatial, Perceptual, Numerical, Verbal, Memory, Word Fluency, Inductive, Arithmetical Reasoning, and Deduction) (L. L. Thurstone, 1938). Thurstone reported that there was no sign of the general factor, and he thus replaced this factor with his set of specialized abilities.

After Thurstone's pioneering work, which was replicated and extended in several studies (e.g., L. L. Thurstone, 1944; Thurstone & Thurstone, 1941), the "primary mental abilities" were subjected to much research. French (1951) presented the first survey of findings from multiple-factor analysis and listed some 60 factors of ability and achievement. Later reviews (e.g., Carroll, 1989, 1993; R. B. Cattell, 1987; Ekstrom, French, & Harman, 1976; French, Ekstrom, & Price, 1963; Guilford, 1967; Guilford & Hoepfner, 1971; Horn, 1976; Pawlik, 1966) have subtracted some of the factors on this list, but have also added quite a few.

The Guilford (1967) structure-of-intellect (SOI) model may be seen as an attempt to create a taxonomy of the primary type of abilities. According to this facet model (see discussion of the radex model below), each test and factor may be classified into a three-dimensional system, with "content," "operation," and "product" as facets. There are four different contents (figural, symbolic, semantic, and behavioral), five different operations (cognition, memory, divergent production, convergent production, and evaluation), and six different products (units, classes, relations, systems, transformations, and implications). Combining the elements of the three facets in all possible ways yields 120 expected factors. Guilford (1972; see also Guilford & Hoepfner, 1971) showed that almost all the primary factors previously found might be classified into the SOI model and that new instruments could be developed to measure factors predicted by the model.

The SOI model assumes all the factors to be orthogonal, and although Guilford's intention was to organize and understand the growing number of ability factors, he actually contributed more than anyone else to the proliferation of dimensions. Subsequent studies also have found the empirical basis for many of Guilford's proposed factors wanting (Carroll, 1993; Horn, 1967; Horn & Knapp, 1973, 1974; Undheim, 1979; Undheim & Horn, 1977), and the logical validity of the whole model has been challenged (e.g., Carroll, 1968, 1972, 1993).

The most recent and most ambitious attempt to create order among the primary abilities is represented by Carroll's (1993) work. Carroll has assembled and reanalyzed a large number of matrices of correlations among tests of cognitive abilities. A modern form of exploratory factor analysis has been applied in a consistent way across no fewer than 468 matrices. The analysis has been conducted in several steps and has resulted in a hierarchical model, which is described more fully later in the chapter. Here we concentrate on the results from the first step, which has yielded a large set of narrow abilities.

At the first-order level the reanalysis has identified at least some 60 named factors. Some of these factors appear in a large number of reanalyses; others have been located in only a few of the correlation matrices. Table 8–3 lists and describes some 35 factors identified in at least 10 studies. Several of these first-order factors had been identified in the 1930s and 1940s by Thurstone and his collaborators and have since been identified in a large number of studies (e.g., I, RG, V, MS, VZ, S, CF, P, N, FW, FI). Other factors have been detected through a more detailed analysis of particular domains, and these factors often are subfactors below another ability. For example, V is rather broadly defined as reflecting vocabulary knowledge and reading comprehension, but there are also several factors that represent more specific abilities in this domain (e.g., VL, RC, RD, RS).

Carroll's reanalysis also uncovered abilities in domains that have not been so frequently studied. These abilities are not included in Table 8–3 because they have been found in relatively few studies, but it is worthwhile to consider them briefly. One of these concerns auditory perception, where Carroll is able to differentiate among about a dozen factors. Some of these factors reflect hearing acuity for different kinds of material; others express individual differences in ability to discriminate between tones with respect to attributes such as pitch, timbre, intensity, duration, and rhythm; and still other factors reflect musicality and judgments of complex relations among tonal patterns.

Speed of performing simple tasks, such as reaction time measured in simple detection or choice tasks, also defines first-order factors. Among these are factors for simple reaction time, choice reaction time, and semantic processing speed.

According to the criteria adopted by Carroll, correlation matrices that included only measures of school achievement were not to be selected. However, such measures were included in some of the selected studies, and they readily define both broad factors such as "General School Achievement" and narrower factors such as "Achievement and Knowledge in Mathematics and Science" and "Mechanical and Technical Knowledge."

We will return to an evaluation of the research on narrow ability factors using multiple-factor analysis, but first we consider a more concrete example. Insofar as a one-factor model does not fit the WISC data, it is reasonable to investigate models with two or more factors. Several exploratory factor analyses of the WISC have been presented (see, e.g., A. S. Kaufman, 1975), and they typically produce two factors: a Verbal Comprehension (VC) factor related to Information, Vocabulary, Comprehension, and Similarities; and a Perceptual Organization (PO) factor loaded by Picture Completion, Picture Arrangement, Block Design, Object Assembly, and Mazes. Sometimes a third factor, called Freedom from Distractability (FD), is identified. The scales Digit Span, Arithmetic, and Coding tend to load on

TABLE 8–3. Summary of Primary Factors Identified by Carroll (1993)

| Factor Name | Label | Factor Description |
|---|---|---|
| General Sequential Reasoning | RG | ". . . tasks or tests that require subjects to start from stated premises, rules, or conditions and engage in one or more steps of reasoning to reach a conclusion." (p. 245) |
| Induction | I | ". . . tasks or tests that present subjects with materials that are governed by one or more implicit rules, or that exhibit or illustrate certain similarities or contrasts. The subject's task is to discover the rules that govern the materials or the similarities and contrasts on which rules can be based, and then to exhibit that discovery in some way." (p. 245) |
| Quantitative Reasoning | RQ | ". . . tasks or tests that require subjects to reason with concepts involving quantitative or mathematical relations in order to arrive at correct conclusions. The reasoning processes can be either inductive or deductive, or both." (p. 246) |
| Piagetian Reasoning | RP | ". . . reside in Piagetian reasoning tasks. The relation . . . to factors RG, I, and RQ is unclear because research has not been adequate to reveal or clarify such relations." (p. 246) |
| Language Development | LD | ". . . general development in spoken native language skills. Best measured by oral or listening vocabulary tests, but can also be measured by tests in which listening comprehension of langugage materials of increasing difficulty is involved." (p. 153) |
| Verbal (Printed) Language Comprehension | V | Vocabulary knowledge and reading comprehension |
| Lexical Knowledge | VL | Vocabulary knowledge |
| Reading Comprehension | RC | Reading comprehension |
| Reading Decoding | RD | Word recognition and decoding |
| Reading Speed | RS | Reading speed |
| Cloze Ability | CZ | Items requiring subjects to supply words that have been deleted in a prose passage |
| Spelling Ability | SG | Correct spelling of words |
| Phonetic Coding | PC | Encoding and remembering phonetic and graphemic material |
| Grammatical Sensitivity | MY | ". . . awareness and knowledge of the grammatical features of the native language, quite apart from the skill with which the individual employs those features in using the native language in listening, speaking, reading, and writing." (p. 174) |
| Foreign Language Aptitude | LA | Aptitude to acquire foreign language |
| Communication Ability | CM | ". . . general skills in communication, often involving listening and speech production, with or without involvement of reading and writing." (p. 177) |
| Listening Ability | LS | ". . . listen to spoken prose." (p. 178) |
| Oral Production | OP | Oral production |
| Writing Ability | WA | Writing ability |
| Foreign Language Proficiency | KL | Proficiency in foreign language |
| Memory Span | MS | "An ability indicated by the amount of material (verbal, numerical, or figural) that the individual can immediately recall, in its correct order, after one exposure to that material." (p. 302) |
| Associative Memory | MA | "The ability to form arbitrary associations in stimulus material such that on testing, the individual can recall what stimulus is paired with another, or recognize, in a series of test stimuli, what stimuli were experienced in a study phase." (p. 302) |
| Free Recall Memory | M6 | "Indicated by the fact that some individuals, after a study phase, are able in a test phase to recall more (arbitrarily unrelated) material from the study phase than others, when the amount of material to be remembered exceeds the individual's memory span." (p. 302) |
| Meaningful Memory | MM | "Indicated by the fact that some individuals, after a study phase, are able to recall (reproduce) or recognize more material from a study phase than others, when the material in the study phase has meaningful interrelations." (p. 302) |
| Visual Memory | MV | "The ability to form, in a study phase, a mental representation (or possibly an image) of visual material that is presented, when the visual material is not readily codable in some modality other than visual, and to use that representation in responding in a test phase by recognition or recall." (p. 302) |
| Visualization | VZ | "Ability in manipulating visual patterns, as indicated by level of difficulty and complexity in visual stimulus material that can be handled successfully, without regard to the speed of task solution." (p. 362) |
| Spatial Relations | SR | "Speed in manipulating relatively simple visual patterns by whatever means (mental rotation, transformation, or otherwise)." (p. 363) |
| Closure Speed | CS | "Speed in apprehending and identifying a visual pattern, without knowing in advance what the pattern is, when the pattern is disguised or obscured in some way." (p. 363) |
| Flexibility of Closure | CF | "Speed in finding, apprehending and identifying a visual pattern, knowing in advance what is to be apprehended, when the pattern is disguised or obscured in some way." (p. 363) |
| Perceptual Speed | P | "Speed in finding a known visual pattern, or in accurately comparing one or more patterns, in a visual field such that the patterns are not disguised or obscured." (p. 363) |
| Hearing and Speech Threshold | UA, UT, and UU | Hearing acuity for different kinds of materials |

TABLE 8–3. *(Continued)*

| Factor Name | Label | Factor Description |
|---|---|---|
| Speech Sound Discrimination | US | Speech sound discrimination (p. 392) |
| General Sound Discrimination | U3 | "Discrimination of tones and sequences of tones with respect to basic attributes such as pitch, intensity, duration, and rhythm." (p. 392) |
| Sound–Frequency Discrimination | U5 | "Discrimination of tones with respect to pitch and timbre." (p. 392) |
| Sound—Intensity/Duration Discrimination | U6 | "Discrimination of tones with respect to intensity, or (possibly) discrimination of tonal patterns with respect to temporal, rhythmical aspects." (p. 392) |
| Auditory Cognitive Relations | UI | ". . . judgments of complex relations among tonal patterns." (p. 392) |
| Resistance to Auditory Stimulus Distortion | UR | ". . . ability to resist or overcome the effects of distortions of speech stimuli that occur through masking or other types of interposition of extraneous auditory stimuli." (p. 383) |
| Ideational Fluency | FI | "Speed in thinking of, and reporting (usually in writing) a series of different verbal responses falling in a specific class." (p. 438) |
| Naming Facility | NA | "Speed in evoking and reporting (orally or in writing) an accepted name for a given thing, as cued by the thing itself or a picture of it, or in some other appropriate way." (p. 438) |
| Associational Fluency | FA | "Speed in thinking of, and reporting (usually in writing) a series of different verbal responses that are semantically associated with a given stimulus." (p. 439) |
| Expressional Fluency | FE | "Speed in thinking of, and reporting (usually in writing) a series of syntactically coherent verbal responses under highly general or more specific cueing conditions." (p. 439) |
| Word Fluency | FW | "Speed in thinking of, and reporting (usually in writing) one or more language units (usually, words) that have specified phonemic or (more usually) graphemic properties." (p. 439) |
| Sensitivity to Problems | SP | "Speed and success in thinking of, and reporting (usually in writing) solutions to 'practical' problems, or new ways of using objects." (p. 439) |
| Originality/Creativity | FO | "Speed and success in thinking of, and reporting (usually in writing) unusual or original verbal/ideational responses to specified tasks." (p. 439) |
| Figural Fluency | FF | "Speed and success in producing (usually by drawing) a variety of 'figural' responses to specified tasks." (p. 439) |
| Figural Flexibility | FX | "Speed and success in dealing with figural tasks that require a variety of approaches to a solution." (p. 439) |

Note: References in Factor Description column are to page numbers in Carroll (1993).

this factor. Factor analyses of the newly revised WISC-III battery, which includes an additional subscale, indicate that a Speed factor may be identified as well (Wechsler, 1991).

If we specify the number of factors and their relations to the WISC scales, the model may be estimated with a program for confirmatory factor analysis, just as was done with the one-factor model. In the first step a model with two correlated factors (VC and PO) was tested. As shown in Figure 8–2, this model hypothesizes a pattern of relations between factors and subtests based on the results obtained in the exploratory analyses. The fit of this model is not perfect ($\chi^2 = 140.7$, $df = 64$), but the model fits considerably better than the one-factor model. A three-factor model that includes the FD factor as well also has been fitted. The overall fit of this model is somewhat better than the two-factor model ($\chi^2 = 112.4$, $df = 62$). However, an even better fit is obtained when a Speed factor is included as a fourth factor in the model ($\chi^2 = 79.1$, $df = 59$, $p < .04$).

As may be seen in Figure 8–3, the factor loadings describe a pattern of relations between the four factors VC, PO, FD, and Speed and the 13 subscales that conforms excellently to the results obtained in previous research. However, the four factors are highly correlated. The correlation between VC and PO is .72; between VC and FD it is .74; and between PO and FD the correlation is .62. Thus, there is considerable overlap between the factors, and this overlap is left unanalyzed and unexplained in this type of model.

The models that postulate multiple correlated abilities have

been and remain widely accepted. Nevertheless, there is growing disenchantment with the multiple-factor models. Several critics have pointed to the limited utility of multiple-factor analysis for describing the structure of ability. Humphreys (1962, 1985), for example, noted that this form of analysis tends to yield very narrow factors. In the limit, each factor is identified by a set of parallel tests, which implies that factor analysis identifies as many dimensions as there are types of test items.

In practical applications, too, the value of the primary abilities has been questioned (e.g., Ree & Earles, 1991a; R. L. Thorndike, 1985). Differential aptitude batteries seem not to have differential predictive power for achievement in different subject matter areas (see, e.g., Carroll, 1982; McNemar, 1964). In the research on aptitude–treatment interactions (ATIs; see below) narrow ability concepts also have failed to live up to expectations. On the basis of a large review of ATI research, Cronbach and Snow concluded:

whereas we had expected specialized abilities rather than general abilities to account for interactions, the abilities that most frequently enter into interactions are general. Even in those programs of research that started with specialized ability measures and found interactions with treatment, the data seem to warrant attributing most effects to a general ability. (1977, pp. 496–497)

Thus, even though models with correlated narrow abilities fit data well, broader abilities may be needed for both theoretical and practical reasons.

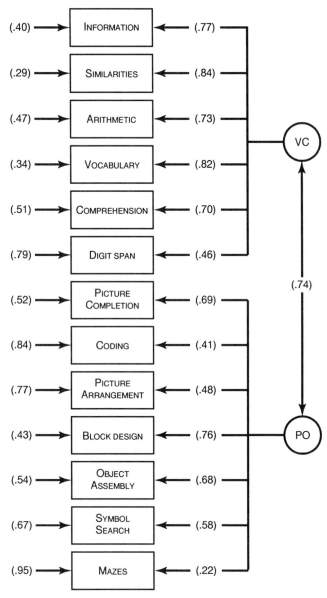

FIGURE 8–2. An Oblique Two-Factor Model for the WISC-III Battery

*Hierarchical Approaches.* Since about the mid-70s there has been a resurgence of interest in broad factors of ability, primarily as a result of disenchantment with the results obtainable with the narrow abilities. As an alternative, interest has focused on hierarchical models of abilities (see Lohman, 1989, p. 334).

A hierarchical model may be constructed through factoring of correlations among the factors, using the same factor-analytic principles as when observed variables are analyzed. For example, it may be hypothesized that a single "second-order" factor is sufficient to account for the intercorrelations among the factors. If a single factor cannot account for the correlations among the factors, we may introduce one or more additional second-order factors. Should we end up with several second-order factors, these may be correlated. To account for these correlations a third-order factor may be introduced, and so on. Thus,

with this approach a hierarchy of factors is built, starting from below with a large number of narrow first-order factors and ending at the top of the hierarchy with one, or a few, broad higher order factors. Such a model may be transformed into a model with orthogonal factors, all of which are directly related to the observed variables (Schmid & Leiman, 1957).

It is not necessary, however, to stack the factors on top of one another. In an alternative approach, orthogonal factors are allowed to span a broader or narrower range of observed variables. A general factor is typically fitted first, after which successively narrower factors are fitted to the residual correlations (see, e.g., Gustafsson & Balke, 1993). Such an approach has been favored in the British research on the structure of abilities (e.g., P. E. Vernon, 1961).

The most popular hierarchical model is the theory of fluid and crystallized ability developed by Raymond B. Cattell and John L. Horn. However, other researchers also have contributed importantly to the development and dissemination of the theory (e.g., Cronbach, 1984, 1990; Snow, 1980, 1981). The theory was first formulated by Cattell (1943), who argued that there is not one general factor of intelligence but two, which he called fluid and crystallized intelligence. However, clear empirical support was not demonstrated until considerably later (e.g., R. B. Cattell, 1963; Horn, 1968; Horn & Cattell, 1966). Through factorization of tests or factors representing primary abilities, Cattell and Horn identified several second-order factors, or broad abilities. The two dimensions of central importance in the Cattell and Horn formulation are fluid intelligence (Gf) and crystallized intelligence (Gc), and the whole theory is often referred to as Gf-Gc theory. Both these dimensions reflect the capacity for abstraction, concept formation, and perception and eduction of relations. The Gc dimension, however, is thought to reflect individual differences associated with systematic influences of acculturation and is central in tasks of a verbal-conceptual nature. The V factor and school achievement factors load highly on Gc. The Gf dimension is thought to reflect effects of biological and neurological factors and factors such as incidental learning. However, while Gf was originally hypothesized to reflect genetic potential to a larger extent than Gc, the evidence indicates that the heritability of Gf and Gc is about equal (see Horn & Hofer, 1992, p. 61). Gf is most strongly shown in new and complex tasks. I and RG (see Table 8–3) are examples of factors that load on Gf.

In the early formulation of Gf-Gc theory, Horn (1966) and Horn and Cattell (1966) identified some additional second-order factors: General Visualization (Gv), General Speediness (Gs), and General Fluency (Gr). In later research (see, e.g., Horn, 1978, 1980, 1986, 1989; Horn & Stankov, 1982; Stankov & Horn, 1980) the list of second-order factors has been considerably expanded and a hierarchical model based on levels of functions has been proposed.

The Horn (1986, 1989) model organizes the abilities within an information-processing hierarchy with levels of sensory reception, associational processing, perceptual organization, and relation eduction. This model strongly resembles a hierarchical model proposed by Burt (1949; see Horn, 1978). The perceptual organization level, which provides input to the Gf-Gc processes, includes Gv and a factor of General Auditory (Ga) competence, reflecting capacities for dealing with the complexities of sound. This level also includes a General Speed dimension (Gs). The

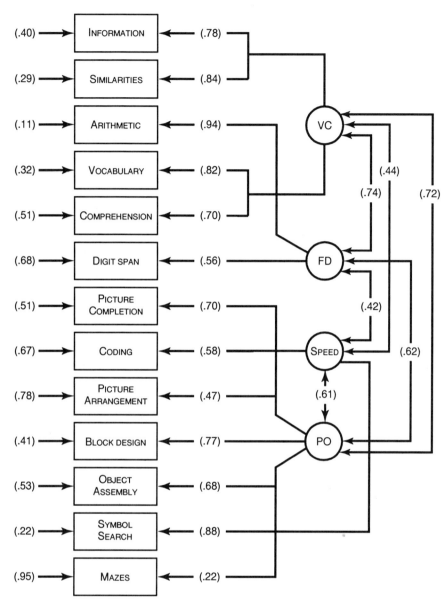

FIGURE 8-3. An Oblique Four-Factor Model for the WISC-III Battery

level of associational processing includes two dimensions representing memory capacities. One of these, short-term acquisition and retrieval (SAR), reflects the capacity to store and retrieve information over such short periods of time as a minute or two, while the other, tertiary storage and retrieval (TSR), identifies an ability to retrieve information stored a considerable time before the measurement. At the lowest level—the one of sensory reception—one factor represents the acuity of visual sensory detectors (vSD) and another represents the acuity of auditory sensory detectors (aSD).

R. B. Cattell (1971, 1987) also has developed the Gf-Gc theory into a hierarchical model that uses concepts quite different from those used by Horn. The so-called triadic theory includes abilities of three different kinds. "General capacities" (e.g., Gf, Gs, Gr) represent limits to brain action as a whole. Another class of abilities is referred to as "provincial powers."

These correspond to sensory area factors, such as visualization, auditory structuring ability, and motor and kinesthetic abilities. The third class of abilities is referred to as "agencies," which are abilities to perform in different areas of cultural content. The agencies largely correspond to primary abilities. According to the triadic theory the three kinds of abilities combine in joint action in observed behavior (R. B. Cattell, 1987, p. 366).

Cattell has reported a few studies in which a third-order general factor was introduced. This factor has been found to be highly related to Gf and has been interpreted by Cattell as a "historical" Gf—"the fluid ability of yesteryear, which fathered the present fluid ability directly and begot the present crystallized ability out of past experiences" (R. B. Cattell, 1987, p. 141).

As has already been mentioned, Carroll (1993) has formulated a hierarchical model with factors of three degrees of generality. Carroll calls his model the three-stratum model, using the term "stratum" rather than the technical term "order" to indicate a more absolute reference than is allowed by factor analysis. The problem, of course, is that a factor that may appear at the second-order level in one analysis, may appear at the first- or third-order level in another analysis, depending on whether there is a smaller or larger number of variables.

The three-stratum division corresponds to a classification of abilities in the categories narrow, broad, and general. The abilities presented in Table 8–3 belong to the category of narrow abilities. Carroll also has identified some 10 broad and general abilities, which are briefly characterized below.

*General Intelligence* (G). A large number of the reanalyses yielded a factor (first-, second-, or third-order) that could be classified as general intelligence because it had loadings for variables in several different domains. In Carroll's three-stratum model the factor is classified as belonging to the third stratum. The loadings usually are high for Induction (I) and other factors involving complex reasoning tasks (e.g., RQ, VZ, CF, V) and low for psychomotor and speed factors (e.g., MS, SP). According to Carroll this suggests that the g factor involves complex higher order cognitive processes.

*Fluid Intelligence* (Gf or 2F; in Carroll's notation the stratum to which a broad ability belongs is indicated by a number in the factor label). In most studies this factor dominates reasoning factors such as I, VZ, RG, and RQ, but other factors have also been found to have substantial relations with Gf (e.g., FI, SR, P, MS, CF). The factor thus involves difficult tasks of induction, reasoning, problem solving, and visual perception.

*Crystallized Intelligence* (Gc or 2C). This factor also is classified as belonging to the second stratum. First-order factors with high loadings on Gc tend to involve language and reading skills (e.g., V, LD, RC, SS) and declarative knowledge in wide areas (e.g., General Information). Factors involving numerical content (e.g., RG, N) have also been found to have substantial loadings on Gc. It should be observed, however, that the tests measuring these abilities most often are verbal and that the numerical skills are acquired through schooling, which tend to emphasize verbal communication. The Gc factor may thus be interpreted as a broad verbal factor.

*General Memory and Learning* (Gy or 2Y). Carroll identified a second-stratum memory factor that spans narrow factors reflecting short-term acquisition of material, such as MA, MS, and MM. However, he also reported strong indications of several second-order memory factors, even though the currently available evidence does not make it possible to identify these factors with precision.

*Broad Visual Perception* (Gv or 2V). This factor dominates narrow factors that involve manipulation of figural information (e.g., VZ, SR, CF, P). Carroll interpreted 2V as a general ability to deal with visual form, particularly when perception or mental manipulation is complex and difficult.

*Broad Auditory Perception* (Ga or 2U). Few studies have investigated the structure of individual differences in the auditory domain, but according to Carroll there is sufficient evidence for at least one broad auditory perception factor. This factor spans a broad range of narrow factors reflecting hearing acuity, discrimination of sound features, and musicality. Carroll hypothesized that an important component of 2U is the degree to which the individual can cognitively control the perception of auditory stimulus inputs.

*Broad Retrieval Ability* (Gr or 2R). This factor dominates a large set of narrow factors involving tasks designed to reflect originality and quickness of retrieving symbols (e.g., FI, FO, FE, FA, FF, SP, FA). A central element in this factor seems to be the capacity readily to call up concepts, ideas, and names from long-term memory. According to Carroll, this domain is in need of further research to clarify the structure and obtain more precise interpretations.

*Broad Cognitive Speediness.* The higher order analyses conducted by Carroll yielded more than one factor involving speed. One factor (Gs or 2S) is involved in narrow factors assessing relatively simple tasks administered under time constraints (e.g., P, N). Another factor (Gt or 2T) dominates various kinds of reaction time tasks, such as the Hick paradigm (see below). A third factor (General Psychomotor Speed; Gp or 2P) is primarily concerned with the speed of finger, hand, and arm movements.

From these descriptions it is obvious that Carroll's mapping of the higher order ability structure largely coincides with previous results, except that it is more comprehensive than any previous account.

The hierarchical approach thus rediscovers the broad abilities as structures imposed on the primary abilities. However, the broad abilities did not vanish as completely from the British research scene as they did from the American scene. In British research the g factor in the Spearman tradition was preserved, but group factors of great importance were also detected.

The British researchers have relied on the so-called hierarchical group-factor technique (e.g., Burt, 1941; Harman, 1967). This technique starts by first extracting the general factor and then extracting group factors that get successively narrower. The most influential summarization of the results achieved with this technique is that of P. E. Vernon (1950, 1961, 1965). At the top of his hierarchical model is the g factor. The model also includes two major group factors: the verbal-numerical-educational (*v: ed*) factor, and the practical-mechanical-spatial-physical (*k: m*) factor. Given a sufficient number of tests, these major group factors may be subdivided into several minor group factors. Thus, the *v: ed* factor subdivides into different scholastic factors such as *v* (verbal) and *n* (numerical) group factors. The *k: m* factor may be subdivided into minor group factors such as perceptual, spatial, and mechanical abilities. In contrast to the American tradition, however, British research has placed relatively little emphasis on the minor group factors.

There are both similarities and differences between the Gf-Gc model and the Vernon model (for discussions about the respective advantages of these models, see R. B. Cattell, 1963; Humphreys, 1967; Vernon, 1969). The Gc and the *v: ed* factors are virtually identically described, and the characterizations of Gv and *k: m* largely overlap. But there is no general factor in the Gf-Gc model and the Vernon model does not recognize any major group factor that clearly corresponds to Gf, even though this factor has tentatively been equated with the *k: m* factor (see, e.g., Humphreys, 1967; R. J. Sternberg, 1990, p. 95).

However, comparisons between the hierarchical models using modern confirmatory factor analysis (e.g., Gustafsson, 1984, 1988; Undheim, 1981; Undheim & Gustafsson, 1987) show that the difference between the American and the British hierarchies is more apparent than real. In these comparisons higher order factor models have been extended to include a third-level factor as well. This has led to the discovery that the correlation between the second-order Gf factor and the third-order G factor is so close to unity that these factors must be considered identical. This explains why there is no Gf factor among the major group factors in the Vernon model. The reason is that the G factor accounts for all the systematic variance in the tests, leaving no variance for a subordinate Gf factor to account for.

The differences in the patterns of result of the American and the British hierarchical factorists thus are due to the way in which the analyses have been performed. The Gf-Gc model is, as it were, constructed with the first-order factors as building blocks for the second-order factors. With the technique of higher order factor analysis, the analysis is conducted from the bottom up. In the factor-analytic techniques, used in the British tradition, the analysis starts at the top and goes down, fitting the g factor first and then adding successively narrower factors.

If these two ways of approaching the correlation matrix are both correct, they should uncover the same hierarchical structure. The reason they have not is that the analysis in both cases has stopped too early. If the bottom-up approach adopted in the Gf-Gc model is extended to include a level above the second-order factors, this approach yields a general factor as well; and if the top-down approach employed in the Vernon model is extended down below the level of major group factors it yields a large number of narrow factors that correspond to the primary abilities. In both cases the result is a hierarchy with factors at three levels, and these factors have similar interpretations.

Before leaving the hierarchical models, it is interesting to consider the possibility of fitting such a model to the WISC-III battery, so a few simple models have been fitted to the standardization data in Table 8–2 (see also Gustafsson, 1992). The first hierarchical model considered introduces a second-order general factor (Gen) with relations to VC, PO, FD, and Speed. In this model the Gen factor attempts to account for the intercorrelations among the first-order factors in the same way that the first-order factors attempt to account for the intercorrelations among the observed variables. This model does not fit quite as well as does the model with four correlated factors ($\chi^2 = 90.5$, $df = 61$, $p < .01$). It does fit better than the three-factor model, however, and for our purposes the model may be considered acceptable. The model yields very high estimates of the relations between the Gen factor and the lower order factors: .89 for VC, .82 for PO, .80 for FD, and .58 for Speed. This analysis thus supports the presence of a general factor in the WISC-III battery.

Another hierarchical model includes a general factor with relations to all tests (G; the symbol g refers in this text only to Spearman's general factor). The model also includes a hypothesized broad verbal factor (Gc'; the prime symbol is used to indicate a residual factor, which does not include variance from the general factor) with assumed relations to Information, Similarities, Vocabulary, and Comprehension, and a broad spatial-figural factor (Gv'), hypothesized to be loaded by Picture Completion, Picture Arrangement, Block Design, Object Assembly, and Symbol Search. A narrow Speed factor with relations to Coding and Symbol Search is also hypothesized. All factors are assumed to be orthogonal.

According to this model most of the observed variables are influenced by two latent variables, so the model does not adhere to Thurstone's ideal of simple structure. It follows from the hierarchical approach, however, that the observed variables simultaneously reflect variance from several factors of different degrees of generality, so the simple structure ideal does not seem reasonable from this perspective. In this model the less general factors do not contain any variance from the more general factors, and the type of model is referred to as a nested-factor model (see Gustafsson & Balke, 1993).

This model fits the data about as well as does the model with four oblique factors. However, the fit is somewhat improved if relations are allowed between Gc' and Picture Completion and Gc' and Picture Arrangement as well (see Gustafsson, 1992). Also, the estimate of the relation between Gc' and Arithmetic was so close to zero that it could be assigned a fixed value of zero, as were a few other relations. With these changes an improved fit was obtained ($\chi^2 = 64.7$, $df = 53$, $p < .13$). As may be seen in Figure 8–4, the loadings do in most cases conform to expectations. Several tests have high loadings on G, the loadings being lower than .5 for six tests only (Picture Completion, Coding, Picture Arrangement, Object Assembly, Symbol Search, and Mazes). As may be expected, Vocabulary and Information have the highest of Gc' loadings, and Block Design and Object Assembly load interest on Gv'. The loadings of the two performance tests, Picture Completion and Picture Arrangement, on Gc' may seem surprising against the background of previous research on the structure of WISC. The relations are not unreasonable, however. The Picture Completion subtest requires identification of missing parts of familiar objects, and a verbal response is required. In Picture Arrangement the task is to arrange a set of pictures in the right order so that they tell a story that makes sense. Examinees who have rich experience of stories from books and other media are likely to perform better on this task. We return to a discussion of the hierarchical model for WISC-III later in the chapter.

*The Radex Model.* The models described so far have a strong association with factor analysis. Multidimensional scaling (Guttman, 1968; Shepard, Romney, & Nerlove, 1972) is another method used in studies of the organization of abilities. This technique takes the correlations to represent degree of similarity between the tests and constructs an *n*-dimensional space within which the tests are represented as a geometric configuration of points. Nonmetric multidimensional scaling methods, which use only rank order information, are applicable under mild assumptions about the nature of the data, and they do tend to yield relatively simple solutions in which only two or three dimensions need to be used. These dimensions are interpretable in terms of facets that represent structural characteristics of the tests (e.g., content, process requirements, response modes).

Guttman (1954, 1965b; Guttman & Levy, 1991) formulated the so-called radex (*rad*ial *ex*pansion of complexity) model partly through nonmetric scaling analyses of some of the L. L. Thurstone (1938) and Thurstone and Thurstone (1941) data. The radex model involves two simultaneous orderings of tasks: one ordering according to complexity, which results in the correlational pattern known as the *simplex* pattern; and one ordering according to content, which results in the *circumplex* pattern of correlations. Guttman (1954) predicted that these patterns would combine in such a way that the less complex

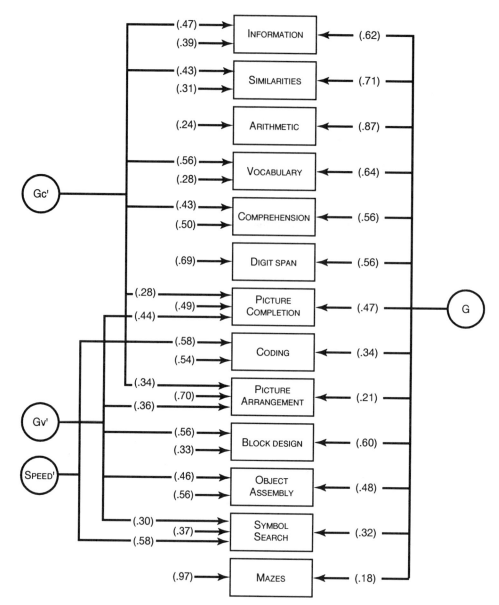

FIGURE 8–4. A Nested-Factor Model with Four Orthogonal Factors for the WISC-III Battery

tests would fall closer to the center of a two-dimensional space and the more complex tests would appear at the periphery. The content dimensions would appear as triangular areas containing verbal, figural, and numerical tests, for example. Guttman (1965a) found, however, that the less complex tests used in the Thurstone studies tended to appear toward the periphery. Thus, "the radex seemed to represent a radial expansion of simplicity" (Snow, Kyllonen, & Marshalek, 1984, p. 58). This led Guttman to leave the notion of complexity in favor of a distinction between analytic and achievement tests, or between rule inferring and rule applying.

The latest version of the Guttman structural model relies on the facet model (e.g., Guttman, 1965a, 1965b; Guttman & Levy, 1991). Each facet consists of a set of elements that permits classification of the test items according to content or other characteristics. Typically several facets are employed to obtain

a multiway simultaneous classification of test items, as is the case for Guilford's SOI model.

Guttman and Levy (1991) presented a three-dimensional scaling model for the WISC-R battery based on a three-facet model. The Format of Communication facet represents the medium of the test items and has three elements: verbal, numerical, and geometric-pictorial. The Rule Task facet refers to the kind of task to be performed and has two major elements: inference, requiring the examinee to infer a rule from examples or hints and application, requiring application of a previously learned or explicitly presented rule. Rule-application items based on short-term memory have been classified into a separate, third element called learning. The Mode of Expression facet represents the way in which the examinee gives the response, and it too has three elements: oral response, response by manual manipulation, and response through paper and pencil. In an

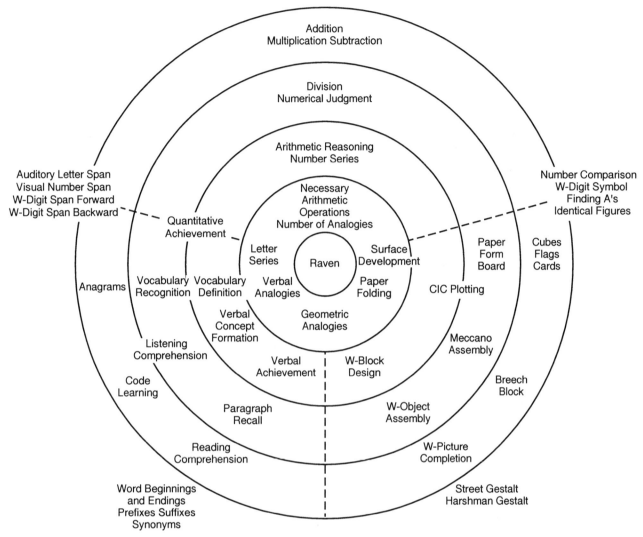

FIGURE 8–5. A Schematic Representation of the Radex Model From Snow and Lohman (1989). Reproduced with permission.

empirical application of the scaling methods to norming data for the WISC-R (Guttman & Levy, 1991) a three-dimensional solution was obtained that provides support for the model. However, the empirical basis is still too limited to allow any definite conclusion to be drawn about the three-facet model, but it does seem worthwhile to investigate it on larger batteries.

Another structural model has been formulated on the basis of multidimensional scaling analyses by Snow et al. (1984; see also Marshalek, Lohman, & Snow, 1983). This model extends Guttman's ideas about complexity as a fundamental characteristic of tests, and it is also interesting because it provides a direct link to the hierarchical model of intelligence derived from factor analysis. A schematic version of the model is presented in Figure 8–5. This model summarizes results obtained in reanalyses of several very large correlation matrices, including, among others, the Thurstone matrices. In the center of the radex map there are complex tests (e.g., Raven, Letter Series, Geometric Analogies), which typically load on I and Gf. These tests are based on different kinds of content, but content differences seem unimportant in the complex problem-solving tasks included in these

tests. However, the rest of the radex is divided into content areas (verbal, numerical, and figural), and within each content area the tests are ordered according to complexity. In the numerical domain, for example, tasks requiring application of arithmetic skills (Addition, Subtraction, and Multiplication) are closest to the periphery; tasks requiring more problem solving (Division, Numerical Judgment) are closer to the center; and closest to the center are the highly complex tests Arithmetic Reasoning and Number Series. In the other content areas as well we find such progressions from less complex to more complex tasks.

Snow et al. (1984) also compared the representation of the tests in a two-dimensional space defined by multidimensional scaling and the representation according to a hierarchical factor model. They estimated the loadings of each test on the general factor, defined as the first principal factor, and showed that the factor loadings were almost perfectly related to the level of complexity of the tests, as determined by the multidimensional scaling. The content areas identified in the radex model are also quite easy to identify with the broad abilities identified in the hierarchical factor model (i.e., verbal = Gc, figural = Gv). Thus, even though the representations are quite different mathematically and conceptually, a closer analysis shows the different models to be not only compatible at a general level but also interconvertible.

*Alternative Theoretical Models.* Taxonomies of abilities have also been proposed within several theoretical frameworks that address structural questions. We briefly describe three of these—R. J. Sternberg's (e.g., 1985) triarchic theory, the theory of experimental structuralism of Demetriou and Efklides (e.g., 1985), and Gardner's (1983) theory of multiple intelligence.

R. J. Sternberg (1985) has proposed an encompassing theory of intelligence that includes three subtheories: a computational subtheory, which accounts for the mental mechanisms that underlie intelligent behavior; a contextual subtheory, which deals with intelligence in its sociocultural context; and an experiential subtheory, which specifies the situations and tasks in which intelligence is demonstrated. The theory has been investigated in a massive series of studies, some of which will be touched on in later sections.

According to Sternberg's theory, the mental mechanisms that underlie intelligent performance can be described in terms of three basic kinds of processing components: metacomponents, performance components, and knowledge acquisition components. Metacomponents are higher order executive processes that plan, monitor, and evaluate the lower order processes represented by the performance components. The number of performance components is quite large, and many, but not all, of these components are specific to narrow classes of tasks. The role of the knowledge acquisition components, finally, is to acquire the information that is operated on by the metacomponents and performance components.

The contextual subtheory argues that to understand intelligence, one must also understand how thought is intelligently translated into action in different contextual settings. Sternberg proposes that intelligence should be understood in part in terms of the individual's attempts to adapt to, select, and shape real-world environments. The term "practical intelligence" emphasizes the need for seeing action options as part of intelligence.

The experiential subtheory recognizes the importance of a person's previous experience of a task to the possibility of using that task in assessment of intelligence. The theory states that intelligence is best measured when the tasks or situations are either relatively novel or in the process of becoming automatized.

Sternberg's componential subtheory is discussed at some length in later sections of this chapter. The categories of abilities employed in the Sternberg theory and proposed test (see R. J. Sternberg, 1992) overlap to a large extent with those employed in the other taxonomic systems. The content categories are the same as those employed by Guttman, and these can easily be translated into dimensions in the factorial systems. Among the process categories the componential aspect of intelligence clearly coincides with Gf (or *g*). The other process categories, however, are not so easily translated into categories of the other taxonomic systems. This is because at least some of the tasks are quite new and empirical data are still lacking. It may be asked, however, to what extent the measures of ability to cope with novelty and the measures of the practical aspects of intelli-

gence are really distinguishable from Gf. A penetrating discussion of Sternberg's theory is provided by Messick (1992).

Demetriou and Efklides (e.g., 1985, 1987, 1988, 1994; Demetriou, Efklides, & Platsidou, 1993) have formulated a theory, called *experiential structuralism*, that integrates a developmental approach with a concern for individual differences. The theory argues that the mind develops at three levels. The first refers to a general processing system, which determines the potential to develop cognitive strategies and skills. Important aspects of this system are its speed of processing, control of processing, and efficiency of storage. The second level refers to a metacognitive system that governs self-understanding and self-regulation. The third involves several "specialized structural systems" (SSSs), which are responsible for the representation and processing of different reality domains.

The SSSs may be seen as complexes of abilities that have been empirically identified in longitudinal and experimental as well as psychometric studies. The SSSs are also differentiated on the basis of a set of more fundamental theoretical principles, referring, among other things, to applicability to different reality domains and the employment of different processing mechanisms and modes of representation. The following five SSSs have been described:

- The *Qualitative-Analytic* SSS is a complex of analytic abilities that enables the person to operate on categorical, matrix, and serial structures.
- The *Quantitative-Relational* SSS is concerned with the quantitative aspects of reality and thus is involved both in simple arithmetic and in more advanced mathematical thinking.
- The *Causal-Experimental* SSS enables the person to extract causal relations from reality. This complex involves combinatorial, hypothesis formation, experimental, and model construction abilities.
- The *Imaginal-Spatial* SSS enables the person mentally to visualize elements or parts in relation to each other.
- The *Verbal-Propositional* SSS enables treatment of information coded in verbal form and processed through propositional reasoning.

The theory of experiential structuralism has its roots in developmental psychology rather than in differential psychology, and it has brought new concepts, tasks, and methods to the research on individual differences. In particular the theory contributes a much more detailed understanding of the structure and nature of reasoning abilities than has been achieved in previous differential research. At a general level the model is quite compatible with a hierarchical model of abilities because it specifies both general sources of individual differences and domain-specific ones, even though the actual overlap between the dimensions specified within the theory of experiential structuralism and the psychometric models remains to be investigated in detail (see, however, Carroll, Kohlberg & DeVries, 1984, for an earlier study of relations between psychometric and developmental measures of intelligence).

Gardner (1983) has suggested an alternative classification of abilities that was developed primarily from sources of information other than psychometric techniques. A set of criteria or "signs" has been established, as many as possible of which should be met for distinguishing an independent "intelligence." One important sign is potential isolation by brain damage, where neuropsychological evidence of the consequences of lesions of a specified area in the brain is considered. The existence of idiots savants, prodigies, and other exceptional individuals with a highly uneven profile of abilities may provide evidence for a particular intelligence. Other important criteria are an identifiable core operation or set of operations and a distinctive developmental history, along with a definable set of expert end-state performances. On the basis of an extensive review of literature from several different areas, such as developmental psychology, neuropsychology, and cross-cultural research, Gardner has proposed a list of seven intelligences:

- *Linguistic intelligence* includes the skills involved in reading, writing, listening, and talking. Poetry is the prime example of application of linguistic intelligence because it involves sensitivity not only to the meaning of words but also to the order of words, to the sounds, rhythms, and inflections of words, and to different functions of language.

- *Logical-mathematical intelligence* enters, for example, mathematical and scientific thinking, the solving of logical puzzles, and a wide range of situations met in everyday life that require analysis and judgment.

- *Spatial intelligence* affects the accurate perception of the visual world, transformations and modifications of the initial perceptions, and recreation of visual experiences when the physical stimuli are no longer present. This intelligence is important in activities such as navigation, piloting a plane, drawing, and playing chess.

- *Musical intelligence* is involved in the production of music, such as singing, playing an instrument, and composing, and to some extent in appreciating music.

- *Bodily kinesthetic intelligence* enters into activities where the body or different portions of it are used, such as dancing, athletics, acting, and surgery.

- *Interpersonal intelligence* is important in relations with other persons and represents abilities to discern other persons' moods, temperaments, motivations, and intentions.

- *Intrapersonal intelligence* involves the ability to understand oneself, for example, to understand one's emotions and to behave in ways that are appropriate to one's needs, goals, and abilities.

The theory of multiple intelligences is strongly biologically influenced and assumes, like other modular theories (e.g., Fodor, 1983), the existence of independently working brain organizations. The intelligences are assumed to work in concert in the solution of a particular problem; a mathematical word problem thus involves both linguistic intelligence and logical-mathematical intelligence, and it may well involve the personal intelligences as well. Gardner assumes, however, the intelligences to be independent in the sense that the level of performance achieved by one intelligence is not related to the level achieved by the other intelligences.

All intelligences proposed by Gardner represent domains of performance studied in previous work on individual differences, even though some of them have received more attention than others. In fact, several of the intelligences seem to overlap

almost perfectly with ability constructs in psychometric models (see Carroll, 1993, p. 641; Messick, 1992). This is true for linguistic intelligence, for example, which is very close to Gc (or $v : ed$) and for spatial intelligence, which is close to Gv (or $k : m$). Logical-mathematical intelligence overlaps to a large extent with Gf. However, even though the Gardner intelligences seem largely compatible with the psychometrically identified abilities, they are assumed to be uncorrelated. Gardner has suggested that the observed correlation among the psychometric abilities is due to the fact that "most tests of intelligence are paper-and-pencil exercises which rely heavily on linguistic and logical-mathematical abilities" (1983, p. 321). However, strong correlations are observed also for tests that are oral and manipulative (e.g., WISC and Stanford-Binet). It seems, furthermore, that Gardner is open to the possibility that logical-mathematical intelligence is important in the construction and perception of analogies and metaphors that cut across different intellectual domains. Gardner (1983) has argued that "it may be the particular hallmark of logical-mathematical intelligence to perceive patterns wherever they may be" (p. 290). However, if logical-mathematical intelligence is ascribed general capacities of pattern perception, that implies that it must be as general an ability as is Gf and cause correlations between performances in different domains. It is also interesting to note that Gardner reports the logical-mathematical abilities to be less clearly naturally localized than the other abilities, which supports the interpretation of logical-mathematical ability as a more general ability.

***Conclusions About the Structure of Abilities.*** The conflict between alternative models of the structure of intelligence has in previous research been a major problem. The fact that factor analysis seems to support mutually conflicting models even led Sternberg to the conclusion that factor analysis has "failed because it has been too successful in supporting, or at least in failing to disconfirm, too many alternative models of intelligence" (R. J. Sternberg, 1981b, p. 143).

However, even though on the surface the models seem quite different, much as maps employing different cartographic notations look different (cf. R. J. Sternberg, 1990, pp. 6–7), it should not be concluded that all models are contradictory or arbitrary. Nor should it be concluded that all models are acceptable; some models should in fact be rejected as false.

One of the issues of longest standing has been the question of whether there exists a general cognitive factor or not. Ever since Thurstone, researchers working within the tradition of multiple-factor analysis have tended to argue against the existence of such a dimension. However, as we have seen, when the correlation among the factors are analyzed, broad abilities emerge.

Only if the multiple-factor model specifies the factors to be uncorrelated is it fundamentally incompatible with a solution that allows for broad abilities as well. Guilford (1967) based the SOI model on results from factor-analytic studies, relying on an orthogonal model. However, it is possible to represent a rather substantial correlation between factors in an orthogonal factor model in the form of small loadings scattered on several factors. Such loadings typically would be small enough to remain unreported, and in any case they would be difficult to interpret. Thus, the fact that orthogonal multiple-factor models have been fitted to ability data cannot be taken as evidence against the notion of broad abilities (see also Horn and Knapp's [1973, 1974] criticism of the Guilford procedures). Further, Guilford (1981, 1985) changed his position to allow correlations among the abilities in the SOI model and hypothesized a large number of second- and third-order factors along the dimensions of the model (see Brody, 1992, pp. 32–34, for a presentation and evaluation of this hierarchical model; see also Messick, 1992). Guilford's orthogonal SOI model must therefore be rejected.

Gardner's model of multiple intelligences also involves claims about orthogonality. However, these claims seem empirically unfounded and difficult to defend theoretically, so at least in this respect Gardner's model must be rejected as well (cf. Messick, 1992).

In contrast, the empirical evidence in favor of a hierarchical arrangement of abilities is overwhelming, even though different theoreticians specify a somewhat different number of levels. Horn (e.g., 1989), among others, has strongly argued against a hierarchy with a general factor at the apex. Cattell, who accepts a model with a single general factor ("historical Gf") at the top, has made the point that it is impossible to prove an ability to be truly general because it is always possible to find one or more performances unrelated to it (R. B. Cattell, 1987, pp. 101–102).

Nevertheless, there appears to be considerable support for Carroll's (1993) classification of abilities into three categories: general, broad, and narrow abilities. The narrow or first-stratum abilities correspond to primaries in the Thurstone tradition, and the best present estimate of their number is around 60. Several of these factors are briefly described in Table 8–3. However, not even Carroll's list of first-stratum factors is likely to be the final and complete one. As new tasks are invented and nontraditional domains are investigated more thoroughly, the number of narrow factors is likely to increase.

The broad or second-stratum abilities correspond closely to the abilities identified by Cattell and Horn, and several of them are close to the major group factors identified in the British research. Among the eight broad abilities interpreted by Carroll, some are well identified (i.e., Gf, Gc, Gv, and Gr), while the other broad abilities are based on a less solid empirical foundation. Thus, as further research is conducted on the nature of the higher stratum abilities, some additional broad abilities may come to be identified.

The general or third-stratum factor that emerges from Carroll's analyses has the highest relations with Gf, Gc, Gr, and Gv. However, even though the Gf factor tends to have the highest loading on G, the loadings are not quite so close to unity as has been found in the analyses employing confirmatory techniques. One reason for this finding is that many of the matrices reanalyzed by Carroll include a limited set of variables, often overrepresenting a particular domain (see, e.g., Undheim, 1981). Another reason may be that the exploratory technique employed by Carroll is not powerful enough to establish the close connection between Gf and g (Undheim & Gustafsson, 1987). Further analyses of existing data should be conducted to determine the reason for this discrepancy between Carroll's analyses and the third-order analyses based on confirmatory factor analysis. It may be concluded, however, that a three-stratum hierarchical model does manage to organize and classify most cognitive abilities, even though the measures were originally conceptualized and developed within conflicting theoretical frameworks. In this sense the three-stratum model may be regarded as a unified structural model.

However, there are at least two different ways of conceptualizing the relations between factors at different levels of a hierarchy. Researchers who rely on the bottom-up, higher order modeling approach tend to regard the first-order, primary factors as indivisible. However, in the top-down, nested-factor approach, factors at lower levels in the hierarchy are automatically freed from the variance due to the broader factors. Thus, the lower order factors are split up into two or more parts: one due to the lower order factor, and one due to the higher order factors. We may thus distinguish between two types of hierarchical models: one that assumes no relations between factors at different levels and one that includes relations from higher levels to lower levels. The former types of models will be referred to as weak hierarchical models, and the latter types will be referred to as strong hierarchical models. The Cattell and Horn models belong to the category of weak models, while the Carroll (1993) model, the Vernon model, the Undheim (1981) model, and the nested-factor model presented here for the WISC-III battery all are examples of strong hierarchical models.

There is reason to look somewhat more closely at the implications of these two ways of interpreting hierarchical models. For example, in the weak hierarchical model, individual differences in acquired knowledge over broad content areas are represented by the Gc dimension, but in the strong hierarchical model they are represented by two dimensions, namely G and Gc' (remember that the prime symbol is used to indicate a residual factor). To capture individual differences in a narrower class of tasks, such as vocabulary, the weak hierarchical model defines a separate dimension (e.g., V). The strong hierarchical model, in contrast, decomposes individual differences in word knowledge into three sources of variance: Gf, Gc', and V'. In an even narrower class of vocabulary items, such as word knowledge in a specific content area, the strong hierarchical model would involve Gf, Gc', and V', plus one or more content-related factors, while the weak hierarchical model would specify yet another ability.

Previous research has rarely made any connections between the levels of hierarchical models. Such empirically based connections require a large number of tests for each person, since otherwise neither the higher order nor the lower order factors can be estimated. Also, the statistical and computational techniques for efficient estimation of strong hierarchical models were not available until the confirmatory techniques appeared. Thus, even though there are some early exceptions (e.g., Hultsch, Hertzog, & Dixon, 1984; Jackson, Donaldson, & Cleland, 1988), only scattered studies have actually employed strong hierarchical models (e.g., Carroll, 1993, pp. 647–653; Gustafsson, 1989, 1994; Gustafsson & Balke, 1993). Much empirical research must therefore be conducted before the value of the strong hierarchical approach can be judged.

The close correspondence between the hierarchical approach and the structural description contributed by the radex model has already been demonstrated. Thus, the conclusion that the hierarchical model provides a useful approach implies acceptance of the radex model as well. However, the two approaches do not yield identical results, and both models seem to have advantages and disadvantages.

Although the verbal element of the content facet roughly

corresponds to Gc, in the hierarchical model this factor is more broadly defined to represent degree of acquisition of culturally valued knowledge and skills. In Western society such knowledge and skills tend to be heavily verbally dominated, which makes it reasonable to equate the Gc (or rather Gc′) dimension with the verbal element of the content facet. It is, however, an urgent theoretical and empirical task to determine whether Gc′ includes components that go beyond verbal content.

The content facet also includes a numerical element, but there is no broad ability dimension representing numerical or quantitative ability in the hierarchical model. This is because the variance associated with complex numerical tests (e.g., number series) is captured by Gf, and because quantitative achievement tests are related to Gc as well. The radex plots indicate that the empirical evidence in favor of the numerical element of the content facet is not particularly strong, so one possible resolution of the conflict between the radex model and the hierarchical model might be to drop the numerical element of the content facet. This issue needs to be clarified in further research.

One of the obvious advantages of the nonmetric scaling technique on which the radex model is based is that it is applicable under very mild assumptions about the nature of the data. Also, as noted by Snow and Lohman (1989), the radex model does not easily allow for a reified mode of thinking in terms of fixed entities that exist within persons.

The advantages of the dimensional approach reside in its analytical power. Thus, in the nonmetric analysis each point in the space is an undecomposable product of several dimensions, which makes it impossible, for example, to make comparisons between the means of different groups of persons in terms of the facet elements (cf. Gustafsson, 1992). At least if one can accept the statistical assumptions, it is possible to use the dimensional approach for studies of mean differences and correlates of the dimensions. The approaches thus seem to have complementary advantages and disadvantages, and frequently both should be used in parallel.

***Characteristics of the General Factor.*** For a long time the general factor was more or less banned from the scientific scene, but with its prominent position in the hierarchical model this dimension is brought back as a central dimension of individual differences. In future research and application it is essential, however, that the G factor be ascribed a proper amount of influence and that the degree of importance of this factor be neither overrated nor underrated.

Proponents of the G factor tend to argue that this factor is of the greatest importance for predicting every kind of intellectual performance (see, e.g., Jensen, 1987a). However, from the hierarchical model it follows that the degree of importance of the G factor above all is a function of how broad or narrow a domain of performance is being predicted. Thus, performance on a specific intellectual task may be related only trivially to the G factor, but a measure of performance over a wider area, such as school achievement over the course of a year, may be highly related to the G factor. To clarify this issue, we will consider a concrete example.

In Figure 8–4 a strong hierarchical model for the WISC-III is presented. The model includes a general factor (G); the Gc′ factor, with an emphasis on the verbal subtests; the Gv′ factor, with an emphasis on the performance subtests; and a narrow Speed′ factor. In the orthogonal nested-factor model the squared factor loading represents the amount of variance accounted for by the latent variable in a particular subtest, and these estimates are presented in Table 8–4. The G factor accounts for between 4% and 76% of the variance in the subtests. The Gc′ factor tends to contribute somewhat less to variance than the G factor. However, Information, Similarities, Vocabulary, and Comprehension have a rather substantial proportion of their variance from Gc′. The Gv′ factor accounts for at least as much variance as does the G factor in several performance tests. In all subtests the error component is substantial, and in several of the subtests it is the overwhelmingly largest source of variance.

The G factor in the present model is not very well defined, and there is little basis for claiming equivalence with Gf. The analysis nevertheless indicates that the variance of each WISC-III subtest is decomposable into several sizable components, among which the one due to G typically is not the most important one. The subtests have, however, been constructed to yield a total score (i.e., Full Scale IQ), and it may be asked which sources of variance are present in this score. Assuming that standard scores on subtests are summed to form the total score, which is approximately true for WISC-III, the factor loadings may be used to determine the relative contributions of the factors to the total score variance. Because the model is orthogonal it is easy to show that the total score variance is a function of the sum of the square of the summed (over variables) factor loadings (cf. Reuterberg & Gustafsson, 1992). The procedure is demonstrated in Table 8–4, and it may be seen that out of a total (predicted) variance of 62.87 about 10 percent is due to error. No less than 71 percent of the total variance is due to the G factor, 10 percent to Gc′, 7 percent to Gv′, and 2 percent to Speed′.

Thus, even though all the subtests are quite heterogeneous and get a relatively small part of their variance from G, the variance of the summed score (i.e., the Full Scale IQ score) is almost totally dominated by G (cf. Cronbach, 1951). The sum has a loading as high as .84 (i.e., the square root of .71) on the G factor. This is because the variance of a total score that is formed by summing over subscores is influenced by a particular factor in proportion to the square of the number of subscores that the factor is involved in. Thus, the size of loadings is relatively unimportant compared to the number of tests influenced by a factor.

The same line of reasoning extends down to the item level. If we were to construct a factor model for item-level data we would find that the broad factors account for only small fractions of the variance (5 percent to 10 percent, say) of each item, with item-specific components typically accounting for the major part of the variance.

Thus, broad abilities account for a relatively small proportion of variance in specific tasks but for a substantial proportion of the variance in scores that are aggregated over several tasks. This principle reinforces the view that at present, the most useful structural description may be obtained with a rather limited set of broad ability concepts, but we must be careful not to overemphasize the power of the broad dimensions as predictors of performance in a particular task.

Models of ability that include a general factor have been criticized for defining a noninvariant G factor (see, e.g., L. L.

TABLE 8–4. Sources of Variance in WISC-III According to a Hierarchical Model

| Subtest | G | | Gc′ | | Gv′ | | Speed′ | | Error |
|---|---|---|---|---|---|---|---|---|---|
| | b | var. | b | var. | b | var. | b | var. | var. |
| Information | .62 | .38 | .47 | .22 | | | | | .39 |
| Similarities | .71 | .50 | .43 | .18 | | | | | .31 |
| Arithmetic | .87 | .76 | | | | | | | .24 |
| Vocabulary | .64 | .41 | .56 | .31 | | | | | .28 |
| Comprehension | .56 | .31 | .43 | .18 | | | | | .50 |
| Digit Span | .56 | .31 | | | | | | | .69 |
| Picture Completion | .47 | .22 | .28 | .08 | .44 | .19 | | | .49 |
| Picture Arrangement | .21 | .04 | .34 | .12 | .36 | .13 | | | .70 |
| Block Design | .60 | .36 | | | .56 | .31 | | | .33 |
| Object Assembly | .48 | .23 | | | .46 | .21 | | | .56 |
| Coding | .34 | .12 | | | | | .58 | .34 | .54 |
| Symbol Search | .42 | .18 | | | .30 | .09 | .58 | .34 | .37 |
| Mazes | .18 | .03 | | | | | | | .97 |
| Sum | 6.66 | | 2.51 | | 2.12 | | 1.16 | | 6.37 |
| Contribution to total score variance (= square of summed loadings) | 44.36 | | 6.30 | | 4.49 | | 1.35 | | 6.37 | Total 62.87 |
| Variance contribution (%) | 71 | | 10 | | 7 | | 2 | | 10 | 100 |

Note: b = loading of subtest on factor; var. = variance explained in the subtest.

Thurstone, 1947), and the hierarchical group-factor techniques developed and used in the British research on abilities (e.g., Burt, 1944; P. E. Vernon, 1961) have not been much used elsewhere. The hierarchical group-factor analysis is carried out by assessing loadings on a general factor first, and then analyzing residual correlations in groups of tests. However, the nature of the general factor may change with the composition of the test battery, and if the general factor changes, the residual factors change as well. Thus, these approaches may be criticized for being arbitrary (e.g., Horn, 1989), even though several recent studies indicate a high level of correlation between estimates of loadings on the G factor from different collections of tests (see, e.g., R. L. Thorndike, 1987) and very high correlations of estimates of the G factor across different methods of estimation (e.g., Ree & Earles, 1991b).

However, the identity between Gf and g, which has been at least tentatively established, should make it possible to identify a general factor that is as invariantly defined as is Gf. Gustafsson (1994) fitted three nested-factor models to partially overlapping sets of variables, the largest of which contained 20 variables and the smallest of which included only 7 variables. Judging from the estimates of loadings of the variables common to all models, the general factor was almost perfectly invariant over the three models. The reason for this invariance was that the models were specified without any residual Gf factor. This causes the G factor to coincide with the Gf factor, and to be as invariantly defined as any latent variable within a regular analysis based on simple structure criteria. It must be noted, however, that if a nested-factor model is fitted to a set of variables and such a constraint is not imposed, the general factor will be as poorly defined as in any principal factor analysis.

*Conclusions.* Our review of research on the number of dimensions needed to describe individual differences in performance

suggests a model with a relatively limited set of broad abilities and a rather large set of narrow abilities. To understand the relative importance of broad and narrow abilities it also seems that they must be considered simultaneously.

In the remaining parts of this chapter we will consider research that has related measures of cognitive abilities to other variables. In this research different measures of general cognitive ability have dominated, but measures of narrow abilities have been employed as well. Both kinds of measures have generally been interpreted within nonhierarchical frameworks, but they are nevertheless correlated with the dimensions identified in the hierarchical model. The amount of correlation is generally not known, but it seems that many tests of general cognitive ability have such a verbal bias that they represent a mixture of G (or Gf) and Gc. Thus, tests that aim to measure general intelligence cannot be claimed to be pure measures of G at the apex of the hierarchical model, even though at least some tests should have a large amount of overlap with this factor. This creates problems of interpretation and comparability of results from studies where different tests carrying the same label have been used. To a certain extent this problem can be solved through reanalysis of existing data, but above all it must be addressed in the design and analysis of future studies.

## PROCESS ASPECTS OF INDIVIDUAL DIFFERENCES IN COGNITIVE FUNCTIONS

The psychometric taxonomic approach provides little information about which processes lead to successful performance, or what distinguishes the mode of operation of persons low or high on an ability dimension. Around the mid-1970s such questions were asked by several researchers (e.g., Estes, 1974; Glaser, 1972; E. Hunt, Frost, & Lunneborg, 1973; L. B. Resnick,

1976; Snow, 1980; R. J. Sternberg, 1977), and since then vigorous efforts have been made to increase our understanding of the processes behind individual differences in cognitive performance.

This research has relied on the progress made in cognitive experimental psychology. In the early and mid-1970s cognitive psychology was heavily influenced by information-processing models derived from analogies to computer functioning. Thus, to the modern cognitive psychology of individual differences the computer has become a metaphor for theory as well as a medium for the realization and evaluation of it (Snow & Lohman, 1989; R. J. Sternberg, 1990).

In this part of the chapter we provide an overview of some of the methods and results of the research aimed at a process-based understanding of individual differences. A more extensive review has been provided by Snow and Lohman (1989) in a publication that is also a rich source of interesting hypotheses to guide further research.

We have organized the review of results from individual differences studies of cognitive processes around the main ability constructs of psychometric research. The discussion is thus concentrated on some of the major ability factors at the second and third strata, that is, on G/Gf, Gc, and Gv. Most of the research has involved tasks belonging to these domains. Along with the presentation and discussion of substantive results, basic methodological concepts and procedures are also described.

## Process Interpretations of General Intelligence

In a crude classification, two general approaches to the study of processes underlying individual differences in intelligence may be distinguished. These were labeled the cognitive-correlates approach and the cognitive-components approach by Pellegrino and Glaser (1979). In the first approach, performance on tasks believed to involve certain basic processing skills is related to psychometric ability tests. In the cognitive-components approach the aim is to develop processing models of existing psychometric measures, finding ways to decompose complex tasks into simpler components.

When individual difference dimensions are analyzed in terms of relatively simple tasks, it is assumed that intelligence and other complex characteristics can be understood through a bottom-up analysis of simple processes. Ideally, then, the simple information-processing tasks reflect individual differences in efficiency of neural functioning and are free from influences of schooling and other cultural factors. We will start by reviewing studies of relations between measures of general intelligence and certain quite simple measures.

*Psychophysical Measures.* Research on reaction time (RT) has come to epitomize a revitalization of old paradigms for studying intelligence. Relationships between intelligence and RT were studied more than a century ago by Galton (1883) and J. M. Cattell (1890). The relations turned out to be low or nonexistent, however (e.g., Wissler, 1901), so the research more or less came to a halt.

Jensen (e.g., 1982, 1985, 1987a; see also P. A. Vernon, 1987) developed an apparatus for securing different parameters of choice RT and formulated a theoretical rationale for why rela-

tions between RT and intelligence should be expected. Jensen's analyses of choice RT are based on Hick's (1952) research, which proposed that RT increases as a linear function of the increase in the amount of information. Better reasoners are expected to be faster overall (low RT). Also, the increase in RT as the number of choices grows is expected to be less for good reasoners. In other words, intelligence is expected to be related to speed of processing information of increasing complexity.

Jensen (1987b) reviewed a number of studies using the Hick paradigm. Averaging data from 32 studies, Jensen found a mean correlation of −.25 between intelligence measures and intercept, −.28 with slope, and −.32 with mean RT. These correlations have been corrected for attenuation due to restriction of range and imperfect reliability. The results were interpreted by Jensen (1987b) in terms of individual differences in elementary cognitive processes. Slow processing is assumed to lead to an incapacity to handle complex problems in which a large amount of information must be dealt with.

Another reliable finding is that variation in RT, as measured by the standard deviation of RT, is the parameter showing the highest negative correlation with traditional intelligence measures (Jensen, 1982, 1987b). G. E. Larson and Alderton (1990) conducted a more refined analysis by decomposing the global variability index into its constituent RTs. They found that the slowest trials were of greatest importance to variability and to the relationship between variability and general intelligence. This finding indicates that subjects of high intelligence more consistently maintain an optimal level of performance than subjects of low intelligence. Several different interpretations of these results are possible (see, e.g., Brody, 1992, pp. 60–62). It may be that persons of higher intelligence are more skilled at controlling their attention, which skill may have developed in response to the requirements of schooling. Another possibility is that there are differences in the efficiency of basic neurological processes (Eysenck, 1993; Jensen, 1985) that also cause individual differences in skills measured by tests of intelligence.

Critics of RT research have argued that correlations on the order of .3 are too low to demonstrate a more fundamental characteristic of intelligence (Kline, 1990; R. J. Sternberg, 1985). Questions have been raised also as to the applicability of Hick's law to all subjects (Barrett, Eysenck, & Lucking, 1986). Further, Brody (1992, p. 53) has pointed out that the data indicate that slope measures are not as highly related to intelligence as would be expected from the theory, which states that such measures provide an index of the rate of processing information. Carroll (1981) suggested that the cognitive tasks and psychometric tests may be related because they share a common speed factor. Similarly, Sternberg (1990, p. 116) suggested that the relatively low correlations attained might be because psychometric tests draw on lower level perceptual and memory abilities that do not provide a theoretical grounding for the complex kinds of information processing called intelligence.

Another psychophysical measure of simple information processing that has been related to general intelligence is inspection time (IT), or the minimal duration of a single inspection a person requires to apprehend a stimulus. The original IT task involved tachistoscopic presentations of different durations of two lines of unequal length, a procedure used to estimate the minimal exposure time needed to judge which of the two lines was longer (Vickers, Nettlebeck, & Willson, 1972). IT measures have also been developed for tasks in other modalities, such as auditory pitch discrimination and tactile discrimination.

Kranzler and Jensen (1989) used meta-analysis to summarize the results of 31 studies that used IT measures. A mean correlation of −.29 (−.49, after correction for attenuation and restriction of range) was found with intelligence. Excluding studies criticized on methodological grounds by Nettlebeck (1987), an even higher estimate was obtained (−.54, corrected). The correlation between intelligence and measures of IT thus seems higher than for measures of RT. We will return to a discussion of possible interpretations of the relations.

Some recent studies have investigated relations between performance on measures of simple information processing administered during the first year of life and performance on measures of intelligence administered in early childhood. Measures of habituation (or novelty preference) estimate the decrement in attention following repeated presentation of a stimulus and are obtained, for example, by observing the direction of a child's gaze.

Bornstein (1989; see also Brody, 1992, pp. 71–77, and Fagan, 1984) summarized results from 14 studies investigating relations between early measures of habituation and measures of intelligence administered between ages 2 and 8. The correlations ranged between .28 and .77. Brody (1992, p. 73) computed the weighted average of the correlations to be .44 and estimated the disattenuated correlation to be at least .70.

As was observed by Brody, both IT measures and infant habituation indices may at least in a superficial and metaphorical sense be construed as measures of the speed and accuracy of processing stimulus information. So far there is no research investigating relations among these measures. The internal consistency of these preference measures is, however, sometimes disturbingly low (Benasich & Bejar, 1992). Also, there is little evidence that studies that employ measures with higher reliability show better prediction, which indicates that corrections for attenuation should be cautiously applied. Interobserver reliability is reported to be high, but this measure is not sensitive to common subjective elements in the judgment of preferred attention, such as those related to the fact that a parent always accompanies the child. More well-controlled studies should thus be conducted before strong conclusions are made about the predictive power of early measures of novelty preference.

Recently, various biological measures have been related to scores on psychometric instruments. The base of findings is as yet too weak to allow any strong conclusions to be drawn about relations between intelligence and parameters derived from biological measures, but a brief description of the measures employed in current research certainly is worthwhile.

Average evoked potentials (AEPs) are measures of the electrical activity of the brain evoked by an external stimulus, such as a light flash or a beep. D. E. Hendrickson and Hendrickson (1980) derived a measure (the "string" measure) that yields high values for complex waveforms and low values for simple waveforms. A simple waveform is hypothesized to be due to many errors of transmission and to be indicative of a low level of intelligence. Several studies using the string measure (see Deary & Caryl, 1993, for a review; see also P. A. Vernon, 1991) have obtained considerable correlations. Schafer (1982) con-

structed a measure of neural adaptability based on the difference in evoked-potential amplitude between unexpected and expected stimuli, which in several studies has been shown to yield high correlations. However, several failures to replicate relations with AEP measures have also been reported, and the causes of these failures remain to be identified (Deary & Caryl, 1993).

Cerebral glucose metabolism rates (GMRs) provide an index of brain activity (e.g., Haier et al., 1988), determined through the use of positron emission tomography (PET). This technology may be used to determine overall brain activity, as well as which parts of the brain were most active during performance on a task. So far only a few studies, each with a small number of subjects, have been conducted. The results indicate that persons with higher test scores have lower GMRs, which indicates that they expend less energy than lower scoring persons (P. A. Vernon, 1991). Further work will show if these results replicate or not.

Nerve conduction velocity (NCV) is a measure of the speed with which electrical impulses are transmitted by the nervous system. It is measured peripherally (e.g., in the arm) and noninvasively. A couple of studies have shown positive relations (.40–.50) between intelligence and NCV (see P. A. Vernon, 1991), but failures to replicate have also been reported (Reed & Jensen, 1991). Again, further work is necessary.

P. A. Vernon (1991; see also Eysenck, 1988, 1993) argued that the biological and RT correlates of intelligence support a neural efficiency model of intelligence that accounts for individual differences in broad intellectual ability in terms of the speed and efficiency of execution of basic neurophysiological processes. Other interpretations are also possible, however, including ones that see the biological measures as being affected by differences in intelligence (see, e.g., R. J. Sternberg, 1990, p. 177). Thus, it should not be assumed automatically that physiological measures explain the cognitive measures, let alone the construct of intelligence.

***Correlates with Experimental Task Parameters.*** In the study of cognitive correlates of intelligence, several tasks based on well-defined paradigms in cognitive psychology have been employed.

One example is a set of stimulus-comparison tasks developed by Posner and Mitchell (1967), based on the subtractive-factors method. This method, which originated with Donders (1868/1969), aims at determining the duration of processing stages in a task. In the Posner task, subjects are required to compare letters of the alphabet and to respond yes if and only if the two letters are physically identical (aa or AA). A second task of letter comparisons uses the same stimulus material but requires a yes answer if the two letters have the same name (Aa and aA in addition to aa and AA). An information-processing model of Task 1 would posit the processing stages of registering the physical stimuli as well as encoding, comparing, and responding to these. Presumably, Task 2 includes all these processes plus the process to retrieve the name codes associated with the two stimulus representations. Thus, the difference between time to respond on Task 2 and time to respond on Task 1 is an estimate of the duration of this retrieval stage. The resulting score has been called the NIPI difference (for Name Identity minus Physical Identity) and has been used as a measure of speed of lexical access in several studies. E. B. Hunt (1978), who was one of the first researchers to study relations between intelligence and experimentally derived processing parameters, found that the NIPI measure was inversely related to measures of verbal ability, implying faster access to long-term memory codes for verbal material for subjects high in verbal ability.

Shepard and Metzler (1971) have developed a much used technique for analyzing processing in spatial tasks. They showed that the time taken to mentally rotate a figure is a monotonically increasing function of the angle of rotation of the figure. The slope of this function is a measure of the speed of mental rotation, and this measure has been related to psychometric instruments assessing spatial and other ability factors.

In another method called the additive-factors method (S. Sternberg, 1969, 1975), variable amounts of processing in different stages are modeled in a way similar to the mental rotation tasks. A memory search task developed by S. Sternberg may give some idea of the additive-factors method (see Chiang & Atkinson, 1976). This task first requires memorization of a 2-, 3-, 4-, or 5-letter or -digit string, and then a decision is to be made whether a particular letter or digit is or is not in the set. A visual search task may reverse the procedure: A single letter or digit is stored, and the variable string is then presented, requiring the subject to indicate whether or not the stored symbol is in the presented string. Each task yields a slope for RT as a function of string size and an intercept parameter. Although the two tasks are assumed to involve the same sequence of four processing stages or components (encoding, comparison, decision, and response), the parameter estimates reflect variance from different combinations of stages. Analysis of common variance among the different parameters may thus give indications of which stages produce important individual differences and may be retained as individual difference constructs for subsequent analyses (see Snow, 1978, and Snow & Lohman, 1989, for a detailed analysis of this empirical example).

Several studies have been conducted in which a battery of laboratory tasks has been administered along with a battery of psychometric tasks measuring general and specific abilities (e.g., Keating & Bobbitt, 1978; Keating, List, & Merriman, 1985; McGue & Bouchard, 1989). One purpose of these studies has been to investigate discriminant and convergent validity of specialized abilities (e.g., verbal and spatial abilities), and results relevant to these questions are considered in later sections. It is also of great interest, however, to see to what extent relations exist between general intelligence and the processing parameters. We focus on one study that allows some tentative conclusions to be drawn about such relations.

McGue and Bouchard (1989) used three experimental tasks, one from each of the three experimental paradigms described above; the Posner measure of RT for name and physical identity judgments of letters; the Shepard–Metzler measure of time to judge visually rotated figures as being the same as or different from a comparison figure; and the Sternberg measure of the time taken to identify a probe digit as belonging to a previously presented set of digits. For each of these tasks they derived slope and intercept measures. They also administered a battery of cognitive tests to measure verbal (V), spatial (S), perceptual (P), and visual memory (VM) abilities.

The results gave some evidence for convergent and discrimi-

nant validity. Thus, the V score had the highest relation with the NIPI parameter, and the S score the highest relation with parameters derived from the Shepard–Metzler task. But there also were significant relations between the V score and parameters from all the other tasks, and the S score was significantly correlated with the intercept parameter in every task. The other ability measures showed similar generality of relations. Thus, even though the ability measures were not combined into a measure of general intelligence, these results clearly indicate the pervasive importance of the general factor. It is, of course, of great theoretical and methodological significance that theoretically based measures of content-specific processing parameters predict abilities in other content areas, but it seems that the consequences of this have not been adequately taken into account in the design and interpretation of studies in this area (see, e.g., the discussion by Brody, 1992, pp. 92–94, about the conclusions drawn by Keating et al., 1985).

Along with Brody (1992, p. 95) it is also worth noting that in the McGue and Bouchard study, as in most other studies, the intercept measures, which capture the individual's overall level of performance, are more highly related to the psychometric tasks than are the slope parameters. The correlations also are rather low in absolute value, and only rarely do they exceed .30.

***Correlates with Task Complexity and Novelty.*** There are many indications in the psychometric literature that a higher degree of task complexity is associated with higher correlations with intelligence (e.g., Jensen & Figueroa, 1975; Snow et al., 1984). Task parameters have also been systematically varied to explore this relationship.

The results show that choice RT is more highly correlated with intelligence than is simple RT, and that tasks that involve more choices have higher correlations than tasks with fewer choices. Complications of the response rules in choice RT tasks, as in the Odd-Man-Out paradigm (Frearson & Eysenck, 1986), cause an increase in the amount of correlation with intelligence. G. Larson, Merritt, and Williams (1988) constructed an even more complex task, called Mental Counters, which requires subjects to hold, revise, and store three counter values under severe time pressure. Correlations with a G estimate were considerably higher with the Mental Counters task than with ordinary choice RT tasks.

G. Larson et al. (1988) suggested interpretations along two different lines of the effect of task complexity. A structural interpretation assumes that G may be defined as the universe of cognitive operations, and that the correlation with G is a function of the extent to which the universe is sampled. Complex tasks include many cognitive operations and yield, therefore, high correlations with G. Another interpretation, formulated in terms of limited energy resources, hypothesizes that individuals vary in their ability to keep and transform short-term memory representations (or working memory; see Baddeley, 1986).

Another technique to increase complexity is to ask subjects to work on two different tasks at the same time. Stankov (e.g., 1987, 1988; Roberts, Beh, & Stankov, 1988) has reported results from such dual-task studies that support the prediction that higher G loadings are obtained when another task competes for attentional resources than when the task is performed in isolation.

R. J. Sternberg (1981a, 1985) has suggested that intelligence is best reflected in tasks that cannot be solved in a habitual manner, and that, therefore, higher correlations with intelligence are to be expected with tasks that are relatively novel, or nonentrenched, than tasks that can be solved with practiced algorithms (entrenched tasks). R. J. Sternberg and Gastel (1989) varied the degree of nonentrenchment by using either familiar or counterfactual presuppositions in a statement verification task. There was a tendency for decision time on tasks involving counterfactual presuppositions to be more highly related to Gf than on the tasks involving familiar presuppositions. Sternberg and Gastel interpreted these results as providing support for the theory about the importance of novelty. G. E. Larson (1990), however, challenged this interpretation, arguing that in the nonentrenched condition the task is more complex, because subjects must actively maintain a new presupposition in memory and simultaneously process a series of statements. Thus, according to Larson, complexity theory provides a more appropriate and parsimonious interpretational framework.

The evidence regarding the importance of novelty thus allows alternative interpretations. However, from the hierarchical model it seems reasonable to make the deduction that entrenched tasks are not the best measures of the general factor, because such tasks would tend to involve a substantial amount of Gc variance. This line of reasoning thus supports the novelty theory in a somewhat indirect manner. However, it should also be observed that Raaheim (1988) has proposed a theory, along with some supporting evidence, that tasks that are too novel do not reflect intelligence well. This would indicate that the degree of novelty is nonlinearly related to the degree to which a task is correlated with intelligence.

*Cognitive Correlates of Intelligence—Discussion.* The research on correlates of intelligence with parameters of laboratory tasks has established correlations with several tasks (e.g., RT, IT, infant habituation, AEP, NCV) that tend to be in the range of .30 to .50. It may be argued that some of these correlations are too low to tell anything of interest, but it also seems that some of the correlations are sufficiently high to warrant speculation about possible mechanisms. It must, of course, be stressed that even though correlations are obtained with laboratory tasks or biological measures, the direction of causality is ambiguous. In the presentation several examples have been given of a possible influence of intelligence on the experimental measures, and other plausible explanations of this kind certainly are possible (see, e.g., R. J. Sternberg, 1990, p. 177, for alternative interpretations of the correlation between AEPs and intelligence).

Ceci (1990a, 1990b) in particular has argued against the physiological view, in which it is assumed that causal inferences may be made from microlevel laboratory measures of processing efficiency to macrolevel measures of intelligence. According to Ceci, performance on the microlevel tasks is also affected by factors other than individual differences in central nervous system efficiency, such as knowledge base differences, which are at least partly environmentally and motivationally determined. Any simple, unidirectional path of influence from laboratory or physiological measures thus cannot be taken for granted. This problem, along with the fact that correlations tend to be modest in size, indicates that simple parameters derived from laboratory tasks or physiological measures will not automatically provide insight into the mechanisms of individual differences in intelligence.

Brody (1992) argued, however, that Ceci's criticism does not seem to apply to the results obtained with stimuli such as flashing lights, line length, and tones differing in pitch (p. 77). According to Brody, the nontrivial correlations with intelligence that have been obtained with such tasks indicate that the ability to process information accurately and rapidly is of importance, and particularly important is the ability to notice differences between stimuli under difficult conditions (Brody, 1992, p. 77).

This idea may be related to one of the three fundamental qualitative principles of cognition postulated by Spearman (1923), namely, the principle of "apprehension of experience," or what today might be called encoding of stimuli. Following Spearman, the other two principles ("eduction of relations," or inductive inference; and "eduction of correlates," or application of relations) have received most attention as ingredients of intelligence. However, Brody's review of the literature clearly demonstrates that more attention should be devoted to individual differences in discrimination and encoding of incoming stimuli.

Much evidence indicates, nevertheless, that manipulation of complex and abstract information, particularly under difficult conditions, to a particularly high degree requires G. Research also has been directed at such tasks, with the aim of achieving a better understanding of the processes involved in solving complex tasks. We consider such research next.

*Components, Metacomponents, and Strategies.* In the process-analytic approaches considered so far, performance on more or less well-understood laboratory tasks was related to performance on psychometric tasks. We now consider approaches that attempt to understand performance on the complex tasks themselves, through modeling of performance. A breakthrough in this line of research occurred when R. J. Sternberg (1977, 1980) developed a methodology, called componential analysis, for modeling performance on relatively complex reasoning tasks. Componential analysis may be said to combine the subtractive and additive methods of process analysis. Also, Sternberg recognized that the type of regression model proposed by Clark and Chase (1972) for sentence verification tasks could be performed on individual data.

Componential analysis typically involves formulation and testing of a complete and complex theory of performance on a task. It is assumed that task performance may be analyzed in terms of a limited set of elementary components that combine according to different rules. If estimates of the efficiency of components can be obtained for each person, and if the components can be shown to have generality over tasks, a strong basis for a process-oriented theory of individual differences is obtained.

R. J. Sternberg (1977) proposed that analogy items require at least five component processes. These processes are confounded in the full task of solving an analogy, but Sternberg showed that these components may be unconfounded. Through administration of tasks involving different numbers and sequences of hypothesized component processes, estimates of the time required to perform each process may be obtained. Detailed descriptions of the procedures of componential analysis are provided by Sternberg (1977, 1985) and Snow and Lohman (1989).

In the process-analytic research, time measures rather than number of correct answers have been studied. The power/speed distinction has been a recurring issue in psychometric research. In a review of studies, Horn and Hofer (1992) argued for a separate factor of "correct decision speed" in complex reasoning. Nonetheless, when time measures have acceptable reliability and subject samples are reasonably heterogeneous, time measures of tasks involving fluid-analytic reasoning correlate quite substantially with the number of rights on traditional fluid-analytic tasks (R. J. Sternberg & Gardner, 1983). Thus, cognitive-process analyses using time measures are clearly relevant to the unpacking of this broad ability factor.

A wide range of inductive and deductive reasoning tasks have now been subjected to componential analysis through the work of S. E. Embretson (1985, 1986), Pellegrino and Glaser (1980, 1982), R. J. Sternberg (1982, 1985), and many others. Reviews of this work are available from Goldman and Pellegrino (1984), R. J. Sternberg (1985), and Snow and Lohman (1989). A study by Sternberg and Gardner (1983) exemplifies an attempt to demonstrate commonalities in information processing on fluid ability tasks.

Three traditional formats of fluid ability reasoning were studied: analogies, series, and classifications. The analogy items were of the form A : B : : C : (D$_1$, D$_2$); that is, A is to B as C is to one of two given D alternatives; and the other tasks also had a traditional structure. The model assumed that solving such items required seven different component processes: encoding (activating information in long-term memory), inferencing (discovering relationships between two concepts already encoded), mapping (inferring the relationship between the A and C terms above), application (generating a term that is related to C in the same way that A is related to B, or "educing correlates"), comparison (comparing the generated answer to the options provided), justification (recycling through some or all of the previous model steps in order to evaluate the chosen solution), and responding (response time combined with preparatory time and other unspecified sources of variance).

In the analysis, Sternberg and Gardner combined the three components, inference, mapping, and application, into one "reasoning" component in order to increase the reliability of individual parameter estimates and to make component scores across tasks and contents more comparable. Since each task was represented by three kinds of contents (verbal, schematic pictorial, and geometric), correlations of component scores for contents were collapsed over tasks and correlations for tasks were collapsed over contents. Correlations of corresponding components (i.e., components with the same name) ranged from −.08 to .80, with a median of .43. Correlations among noncorresponding components were on the average somewhat lower (.24). Sternberg and Gardner interpreted this correlation boundary as providing some convergent and discriminant validity for the hypothesis of unities in inductive reasoning components. It may be noted, however, that the Sternberg and Gardner study found little evidence for the unity of encoding and justification components across tasks or contents. It is also interesting to note that all components tend to show relatively high correlations, which indicates that it is necessary to reintroduce G to account for these correlations. This in turn presents a problem for the componential approach as an attempt to understand complex intellectual behavior. It thus seems that the components are afflicted by similar interpretational problems as are the latent variables of the psychometric approach.

Lohman (1994) made explicit another fundamental problem in research that aims to account for individual differences in terms of estimated components. He observed that the most consistent correlations with test performance are typically obtained with the intercept parameter. From a componential perspective this result is unexpected, but not from an individual difference perspective, because "[t]he intercept, which is the residual or wastebasket term in componential models, is actually the locus of individual difference variance that is consistent across trials, whereas component scores, which capture consistent variation in item difficulty, commonly explain residual individual variance" (Lohman, 1994, p. 7). Lohman thus concluded that attempts to isolate individual differences in performance on homogeneous tasks from component scores cannot succeed. Instead, he emphasized studies of individual differences in approaches to tasks.

Multiple-strategy models, which capture such individual differences, have also been formulated and tested. These models indicate that strategy shifts do occur, with subjects high on fluid-analytic reasoning showing the greatest flexibility (Kyllonen, Lohman, & Woltz, 1984). Snow and Lohman (1989) argued that such findings suggest that a theory of fluid-analytic reasoning ability must include alternative component processes, organized into multiple strategies, among which persons shift during performance.

There also is evidence for developmental changes in strategies on reasoning tasks. Younger children and less able students are less likely to understand that the C and D relationship must mirror the A : B relation of an analogy problem, and they thus rely more on associative relatedness to the C term than on analogical reasoning (Goldman, Pellegrino, Parseghian, & Sallis, 1982; Pellegrino, 1985; R. J. Sternberg & Rifkin, 1979). Even more advanced subjects may revert from the rule-oriented procedure implied by Sternberg's components to various other approaches, including associations, partial rules, and response elimination, and sometimes working backward from the alternative solutions given (Bethell-Fox, Lohman, & Snow, 1984; Embretson, Schneider, & Roth, 1986; Snow, 1980; Whiteley & Barnes, 1979).

Snow (e.g., 1981; see also Snow & Yalow, 1982) has proposed that crystallized and fluid intelligence correspond to two somewhat different transfer functions. Crystallized intelligence represents the organization of more formal educational experiences into functional cognitive systems that can aid further learning in educational situations. The transfer is thought to encompass both specific knowledge and such organized processing strategies as academic learning skills. Crystallized intelligence, then, is thought of as representing previously constructed assemblies of performance processes that are retrieved as a system and applied anew in instructional or other performance situations not unlike those experienced in the past. Fluid ability, on the other hand, is thought to represent the transfer resulting from many incidental learning experiences, or at least more indirectly taught skills and strategies. Thus, fluid intelligence represents new assemblies, or the flexible reassembly, of performance processes needed for more extreme adaptations to novel situations (Snow & Yalow, 1982, pp. 519–520).

Several researchers have suggested that overall efficiency of the cognitive system may be due to metacognitive functioning. Metacomponents, metacognitive processes, or "executive" components (as opposed to performance components) are higher order control processes used for executive planning, monitoring, and evaluation of one's performance on a task (Brown, 1978; Campione & Brown, 1978). Examples of such components may be the recognition that a problem exists, the definition of just what the problem is, the selection and combination of performance components to use, the decision on how to allocate attentional resources, the choice of representation, and so forth (see R. J. Sternberg, 1990, p. 121). Metacomponents are assumed to have a high degree of intertask generality and are hypothesized to be highly related to intelligence.

So far, however, there is little empirical support for this hypothesis. Brody (1992, p. 117–120) reviewed several studies reported by Sternberg and his co-workers in which attempts were made to isolate metacomponents experimentally. He concluded that there is little evidence of generality of the metacomponents and that the relationships between metacomponents and general intelligence are weak. Further work is thus needed on the identification of metacomponents.

*Computer Simulations.* The computer simulation methodology developed in modern cognitive psychology has been applied in individual differences research as well. For example, computer simulations of Thurstone Letter Series have been carried out to address the problem of representativeness of item or domain sampling (see Butterfield, Nielsen, Tangen, & Richardson, 1985; Kotovsky & Simon, 1973). Carpenter, Just, and Schell (1990) constructed two versions of a computer program designed to solve the Raven test. One version was intended to simulate the performance of the best-performing students in a sample of college students, which was studied with verbal protocol analysis and eye movement recordings, and the other version was designed to simulate the performance of the median-performing student. The performance of the programs was quite close to the performance of the human subjects, so it seems that they capture at least some aspects of performance on the Raven test. The computer simulation involved an incremental development of hypotheses and repeated reiterative testing of these hypotheses. The simulation also indicated the importance of the ability to decompose problems into smaller parts and to manage a hierarchy of goals and subgoals generated by this problem decomposition, with heavy demands on working memory.

This characterization may be taken as a specification of processes involved in intelligence, even though it is obviously not a complete theory of intelligence. The programs lack generality, because they are able to solve only Raven problems. Another limitation of the simulation is that the model omits perceptual encoding as a source of individual differences in performance (cf. Brody, 1992, p. 124). There also is strong evidence that the perceptual characteristics of the items are powerful determinants of task difficulty (K. Richardson, 1991).

In studies of problem solving, the process of finding a solution to a problem is often visualized as a search through paths in the problem space. The research has tended to concentrate on the strategies that effective problem solvers use relative to ineffective subjects. Thus, much of the literature on problem solving is concerned with metacognitive components, although most often the influence of specific strategies has been investigated. Even so, some strategies are general to many situations, such as heuristics, examples of which are means/ends analysis and subgoaling. However, very little research has been done on the cross-task consistency of the heuristics.

*Conclusions.* The research reviewed here is all quite recent and it has been conducted along a multitude of lines, so strong conclusions are not to be expected. It is obvious, however, that a great amount of progress has been made and that several promising lines of research may be pursued to clarify which processes contribute to individual differences in general intelligence.

Before discussing different attempts at characterizing general intelligence in process terms, we will briefly consider a distinction between two different ways of regarding G, namely, as unitary or as multiply determined. Spearman (e.g., 1927) tended to interpret *g* as a singular entity related to the overall energy of the mind. An alternative interpretation was proposed by Thomson (1916), who showed that the G factor may be accounted for if it is assumed that there is a large number of bonds or units in the mind, a subset of which is sampled by any ability test. The correlation between two tests would be determined by the number of bonds they share in common, which is high for some pairs of tests and low for other pairs. Thus, according to Thomson, the G factor could be better explained with reference to the operation of the laws of chance than by assuming that G is a single theoretical entity.

The heated debate between Thomson and Spearman did not end in victory for one of the two interpretations (see Brody, 1992, pp. 10–13, for a summary and for references). Both interpretations explain the existence of a general factor, but they are not precise enough to make differential predictions that can be tested empirically (cf. Loevinger, 1951). Rather, the interpretations may be regarded as different metaphors that "may have different theoretical consequences and may lead investigators to suggest different research problems" (Brody, 1992, p. 12).

Among contemporary theoreticians it is possible to identify some with a strong affinity for Thomson's "anarchic" metaphor and some who lean more toward Spearman's "monarchic" view. Humphreys (1985, 1989), for example, has formulated an interpretation along Thomson's lines of the general factor in terms of a large number of determinants. Snow and Lohman (1989) also took this position, arguing against interpretations of test scores in terms of fixed entities measured as amounts. They pointed out that latent variables need not be conceived of as singular entities and observed that in recent cognitive research on psychometric tasks the latent ability variable is not considered univocal, except that it is a convenient summary of amount correct regardless of which processes were involved in solving the items. This position is much more in line with Thomson's thinking than with Spearman's. Others, such as Eysenck (1988), argue, however, that Spearman's principles of eduction of correlates and relations provide the best understanding of G.

Kranzler and Jensen (1991) conducted an empirical study to answer the question of whether G is unitary or a collection of independent processes. They estimated G from a battery of paper-and-pencil tests, and they also administered a large battery of elementary cognitive tasks (ECTs). The ECTs included the Hick and Odd-Man-Out paradigms, inspection time, visual search, memory search, and the Posner paradigm. Ten principal component dimensions were derived from the intercorrelations among the ECTs, from which the G factor was predicted. Four of the components were found to contribute significantly to the prediction of G. On the basis of this result, Kranzler and Jensen concluded that individual differences in G reflect at least four independent components of variance, and that G therefore is not unitary.

In a criticism of the Kranzler and Jensen study, Carroll (1991) argued, however, that the procedures used do not allow this conclusion to be drawn from the empirical results unless the unrealistic assumption is made that a perfectly pure measure of G has been obtained. Carroll also made the point that if the G factor contains different and less than perfectly correlated processes, this would be detectable by factor analysis and would cause the appearance of lower order factors.

Thus, from the psychometric point of view, it is an assumption that G may be conceived of as a unitary dimension, and there is no point in investigating this empirically with correlational methodology. However, at an individual level it is obvious that performance is constituted by a complex set of processes, strategies, skills, and pieces of knowledge, insight into which should also help explain different levels of performance. If anything, there is thus a complementary relationship between the unitary and the complex views on the nature of G.

The results of both the cognitive-correlates and cognitive-components approaches show that there are correlations between intelligence and different process measures. The process measures also tend to be correlated among themselves. This tends to weaken their power as explanatory constructs, because in the limit it would be necessary to introduce a G factor to account for these correlations. However, even though it does not seem possible to identify a narrow set of clearly delimited processes that would explain individual differences in intelligence, there do seem to be clear patterns and tendencies among the results, and many interesting directions to follow in future research.

A major finding that emerges from almost all approaches employed in the process-analytic research is that task complexity exerts a strong influence on the amount of G involvement in performance differences. Thus, the amount of information that must be kept active at one and the same time seems to be a strongly determining factor. Further research to elucidate the mechanisms involved can and should entail different methodological approaches within different theoretical frameworks.

As an example, let us consider one concept that has been shown to yield interesting theoretical results and promises to be particularly useful in future research—the concept of working memory. The capacity of this hypothesized central processor for temporary storage and manipulation of information (see, e.g., Baddeley, 1986) may be hypothesized to be highly related to reasoning ability. It will be recalled, for example, that Carpenter et al. (1990) in their analysis of what is measured by the Raven Progressive Matrices test concluded that it reflects "the ability to induce relations and the ability to dynamically manage a large set of problem solving goals in working memory" (p. 404).

Kyllonen and Christal (1989) have formulated a relatively simple model of the cognitive architecture. In their terms, the model assumes an input system, a procedural memory, a declarative memory, and a response system. A working memory is also postulated as a short-term storage and information-exchange system and is involved whenever tasks require simultaneous processing and storage of information. Thus, working memory capacity is hypothesized to influence performance on almost every task. In particular, however, working memory limitations are hypothesized to affect performance on complex tasks that require simultaneous storage and processing of several pieces of information. From this model it follows that individual differences in working memory capacity should closely parallel individual differences in general intelligence. Kyllonen and Christal (1990) reported a study that provides empirical support for the hypothesis that the general factor and working memory capacity are highly correlated dimensions of individual differences. There is thus both theoretical and empirical support for the concept of working memory capacity in explaining individual differences in general intelligence.

## Process Interpretations of Crystallized Intelligence

The correlational evidence indicates that Gc is strongly biased toward verbal educational knowledge and that it represents declarative knowledge structures in many areas. A process interpretation of Gc is made difficult by the fact that many of the processes that account for individual differences in Gc do not occur when the test is taken, but have occurred over the whole course of development of knowledge and skills. Another problem is that verbal abilities to a large extent overlap with general intellectual ability. This is in particular true for vocabulary tests, which tend to have the highest loadings on the general factor (see, e.g., Jensen, 1980). Thus, many of the processes that have been associated with performance on verbal tests may be interpreted more parsimoniously in terms of general intellectual ability, even though the design limitations of the studies rarely make it possible to disentangle effects associated with G and Gc.

***Cognitive Correlates of Crystallized Intelligence.*** The approach to process analysis that has been labeled the cognitive-correlates approach started by investigating language and verbal abilities (see E. B. Hunt, 1985; Perfetti, 1985). Initially, interest was concentrated on lexical processes. Hunt's studies using the Posner paradigm suggested that verbal ability was related to lexical access time for letter names (E. B. Hunt, Lunneborg, & Lewis, 1975). Verbal ability also was found to be related to access time for words, with a higher relationship when the lexical decision became more complex (Goldberg, Schwartz, & Stewart, 1977). Ease of word identification for high-ability readers also includes less negative effects of letter degrading (Perfetti & Roth, 1981).

Snow and Lohman (1989, p. 295) suggested that certain basic verbal processing skills involve the ability to create, retain, and transform information coded in such a way that information about order of elements is preserved. Even though individual differences in such skills account for only a small proportion of the total variance in Gc, the proportion accounted for is larger if only the Gc residual is taken into account.

The above are examples of a bottom-up approach. Experimental research also suggests that top-down approaches are used and that there is an interaction of the two approaches (see Rumelhart, 1977). According to a bottom-up model, information is passed from low-level processes, such as detection of lines and angles, through intermediate levels, such as letter identification, on to recognition of a word. A top-down model indicates that information may also flow in the other direction. Thus, a word, once activated, activates letters, and these can activate letter features. The top-down account also introduces context effects on letter perception, word perception, and even sentence perception. The suggestion that "high verbal" people are facile at recognizing letters and words thus opens up many more possibilities than would be implied by "elementary information processes."

Top-down models have been particularly concerned with the effect of previous or surrounding words on word recognition. Research has also been concerned with the comprehension of sentences as such, suggesting "propositions" to be abstract units of elementary meaning that combine to make up the meaning of a sentence (see Kintsch, 1974). Comprehension at this level is seen as a matter of encoding word meanings and propositions in working memory, assembling and integrating them, and transferring them to long-term memory. Individual differences research has tried to find evidence for the impact of such differences in top-down processing. For instance, high-ability readers have been shown to have better memory capacity than low-ability readers in general; also the high-ability children remember verbatim words from the sentence read and from the preceding sentence better than low-ability children (Goldman, Hogaboam, Bell, & Perfetti, 1980). The memory differences between high- and low-ability children are found when texts are heard as well as read, and high-ability adult readers remember more spoken words than do low-ability readers.

Top-down models imply that some processes involved in language understanding are "inference driven," which suggests the influence of reasoning. Although individual differences in the inference-driven processing part of such top-down approaches have not been studied extensively, findings do suggest that reasoning ability is important for acquiring word meanings. Several studies indicate that word meanings can and must be acquired through contextual inference, where processes of reasoning and problem solving are applied to the information given to infer the meaning of a word (R. J. Sternberg & Powell, 1983; van Daalen-Kapteijns & Elshout-Moor, 1981; Werner & Kaplan, 1950). Such learning from context probably explains the strong relationship between vocabulary and general intelligence. This does not preclude, of course, that a higher vocabulary level facilitates learning from context (see R. J. Sternberg, 1990, p. 150), or that variation in amount of language exposure is another important factor in acquisition of vocabulary (Huttenlocher, Haight, Bryk, Seltzer, & Lyons, 1991).

Research also suggests that high-ability readers use context information to their advantage, including the exclusion of context when context-free word recognition is faster (Perfetti & Roth, 1981). Thus, lower-ability students seem more dependent on context, a dependence that may be a way of compensating for less proficient lower level word-recognition skills (see Stanovich, 1981).

*Knowledge-Based Approaches.* A knowledge-based approach may be seen as a somewhat separate approach that focuses on the role of prior information in the acquisition of new information. In most such studies, the term *knowledge* refers to domain-specific knowledge. Often researchers in this vein actually de-emphasize process differences between high- and low-ability individuals, or between experts and novices, stressing differential knowledge structures. The term *schemata* has been used for such structures (see, e.g., Spiro, 1980), and the term *script* has been used to designate some well-learned schemata that decribe standard situations (Schank & Abelson, 1977).

The study of expertise in various fields has evolved into an approach of its own, allowing insights into the nature of skilled performance in different fields. In a classic study, Chase and Simon (1973) showed that chess players with high levels of expertise had very good memory for the location of pieces in representative chess positions, but not for chessboards with randomly placed pieces. On the basis of this study and other results, Chase and Simon (1973) suggested that the superior performance of the expert is due to the availability of a base of stored knowledge of relevant positions and methods (see also de Groot, 1965). They also noted that it takes thousands of hours to build up such an elaborate repertoire of information, which implies that practice must be a major factor in the acquisition of skill. Following the lead of this work, a considerable number of studies have been performed on the nature of expertise, in chess (Charness, 1991) and in other fields (see, e.g., Chi, Glaser, & Farr, 1988).

Ericsson and J. Smith (1991) identified three steps in the expertise approach. The first step involves finding or designing tasks that, under standardized laboratory conditions, capture the essence of superior performance in the appropriate domain. So far there are relatively few examples of such tasks, but memory tasks have proved convenient to use and have yielded interesting results (e.g., Egan & Schwartz, 1979; Morris, Tweedy, & Gruneberg, 1985; Spilich, Vesonder, Chiesi, & Voss, 1979). Ericsson and Smith (1991, p. 18) argue, however, that the processes underlying memory performance may only partially account for the superior performance of experts.

After appropriate tasks have been identified, the second step involves application of the methods of analysis of cognitive psychology to analyze the nature of expert performance. One approach relies on extensive case studies of single subjects who are expert performers in a particular domain of tasks, such as mental calculations (e.g., Howe & Smith, 1988) or memory (e.g., Ericsson, 1985). A more frequently used method consists of comparisons of think-aloud verbalizations of groups of experts and novices, through which a wide range of differences has been identified. For example, in problem solving, novices generate step-by-step solutions, while experts tend to retrieve a solution method as part of the immediate comprehension of the task (e.g., Anzai, 1991; Chi, Glaser, & Rees, 1982). Other studies have focused on comparisons between experts and novices with respect to tasks designed to investigate particular aspects of performance. For example, when physicists and novices are given the task to categorize problems from elementary physics, the experts sort them by the physical principles involved, whereas novices sort on the basis of surface characteristics (Chi et al., 1981).

The third step involves specification of the mechanisms accounting for superior performance, and several more or less elaborated theories and models have been proposed. One approach emphasizes the direct relation between improvement in performance and amount of practice that has been established in some task domains (e.g., Newell & Rosenbloom, 1981). Other theoretical accounts focus on the development of skilled memory to rapidly store and retrieve information in long-term memory (e.g., Chase & Ericsson, 1981). Still another theoretical approach focuses on the ability to plan and reason, and emphasizes the necessity in many domains to represent and integrate large amounts of information through processes of reasoning and interpretation. It seems unlikely, however, that one single theoretical account will prove to be sufficient (cf. Ericsson & Smith, 1991, p. 32).

Several studies have shown level of expertise in a particular domain to be a more powerful determinant of further learning than general mental ability. Schneider, Körkel, and Weinert (1990) summarized two studies with fourth- to eighth-grade children as subjects which indicated that domain-specific knowledge was more important than general cognitive abilities in determining performance on a learning task. Ceci and Liker (1986) showed that adults with low scores on intelligence tests were capable of complex reasoning processes in selecting race-track winners. These studies thus indicate that domain-specific knowledge can sometimes compensate for lack of general cognitive abilities. However, an absence of relations is not easily established, so such results should be carefully interpreted.

*Conclusion.* The cognitive science research has clearly shown the important role of knowledge structures for acquisition of new knowledge, and for cognition in general. Crystallized ability is probably best interpreted as representing individual differences in available knowledge. Several of the other chapters in this *Handbook* describe how such knowledge structures are developed in different domains. Obviously, however, process differences determine individual differences in the development of knowledge structures as well. But what started with research on rather elementary processes has evolved into research on a range of processes, including quite complex strategies. In a summary account, E. B. Hunt (1985) pointed to the range of "processes" needed to account for individual differences in verbal ability—from "automatic, involuntary acts of lexical identification to the planned strategies people use to extract meaning from lengthy texts" (E. B. Hunt, 1985, p. 55). Thus, the cognitive-correlates approach started out to explain verbal ability, but some of the explaining variables now are as complex as verbal ability itself.

However, many of the reported studies have examined the relation of process variables to verbal tasks, not to verbal ability as a class or domain of cognitive behavior. The hierarchical model described in the previous section implies, when interpreted in the strong form, that a positive relation between a process variable and some verbal tests may indicate a relation to general intelligence, to fluid intelligence, to any of the other broad second-stratum ability factors, or to any of the many factors at the first stratum. There is similar confusion with respect to the process variables; we do not know if an observed relation is specific to the process variable that happened to be measured or is general to a class of variables. To obtain better empirical precision and greater theoretical clarity, it may thus be worth-

while to adopt multivariate, hierarchical approaches for both the process and the psychometric variables.

## Process Interpretations of Broad Visual Perception Ability

The factor-analytic evidence indicates that Gv presents a broad ability to deal with visual forms, particularly those that would be characterized as figural or geometric. Spatial tests have always shown quite large correlations with general reasoning tests. In fact, sometimes it has been difficult to differentiate Gv from Gf, especially when Gv is dominated by Vz (Marshalek et al., 1983).

A theoretical issue that is of some importance for the interpretation of Gv concerns the representation of visual information. Pylyshyn (1981) claimed that spatial knowledge is represented internally as abstract propositions, while Kosslyn (1981) defended a functional role for quasi-pictorial images. Anderson (1978) argued that it is difficult to resolve this debate empirically, but has since argued for multiple memory codes (1983, 1985). Thus, experimental studies of spatial cognition have suggested that there is one type of knowledge code that preserves configurational information, while there is also another one that is more conceptual and abstract. Kosslyn (1981) talks about literal versus propositional codes, and Anderson (1983) refers to a perceptual-based code and a meaning-based code. Studies indicate that the knowledge codes are each operated on by different types of processes. The literal type tends to be transformed by analogue processes, such as rotation and transposition. The propositional or meaning-based code may use processes of the same kind as suggested for general procedural knowledge used in conceptual information handling.

In contrast to the knowledge-intensive Gc tasks, spatial tasks are process intensive, and a considerable amount of cognitive experimental research has been conducted. The research has employed the same techniques and approaches as have been used in process analyses of Gf tasks. In particular, the research has aimed at formulating process models for existing tests, or types of items, such as paper folding (e.g., Kyllonen, Lohman, & Snow, 1984), surface development, and form board items (e.g., Lohman, 1988).

Lohman (1988; see also Lohman & Kyllonen, 1983; Snow & Lohman, 1989) constructed form board items in which several sources of difficulty, such as amount of rotation and number of elements to be synthesized, were systematically varied. Correlations between subscores derived from this faceted design and spatial ability factors varied systematically according to the information-processing requirements of the items. Thus, the correlation with the Vz factor increased systematically with the number of synthesis operations required. However, when complexity was increased further by requiring addition of more stimuli and rotation, the correlation with Vz decreased and correlations with a Memory Span factor increased. Snow and Lohman pointed out that this analysis "helped demonstrate the fact that various spatial factors are arbitrary points in a continuous, but multidimensional, space" (p. 291). One problem with this analysis, however, is that it does not show which components of the Vz factor (i.e., G, Gv', or Vz') are involved in this changing pattern of correlations. If a strong hierarchical model is fitted to an appropriate battery of cognitive tests, this could be investigated in further research. Such studies would provide further information not only about spatial abilities, but also about the nature of the general factor.

The same data were also used for information-processing analyses of how subjects perform different task steps. Different hypotheses were formulated and tested by regressing latencies for the particular task step on relevant task characteristics (see Kyllonen, Lohman, & Woltz, 1984; Lohman, 1988). The results showed that on each of the task steps most subjects shifted between different strategies. Snow and Lohman (1989) suggested that the high correlation between Vz tasks and Gf may be caused by the circumstances that "both types of tasks require flexible adaptation of solution strategies to changing item demands. Thus, most complex spatial tests are probably better characterized as figural reasoning tests with a spatial component than as measures of one or more uniquely spatial processes" (Snow & Lohman, 1989, p. 291).

Analyses of less complex spatial tasks have revealed more clear-cut differences between strategies. Cooper (1982) analyzed a visual comparison task and identified two markedly different strategies, one serial and analytic and the other parallel and holistic. However, even though there seemed to be marked individual differences in the adoption of one strategy or the other, it is not clear how these strategies relate to performance on tests of spatial abilities.

The Shepard–Metzler (1971) paradigm (see earlier discussion) has also been a starting point for research on mental rotation, for example, on items of the kind that reflect the Spatial Relations (SR) factor. Pellegrino and Kail (1982) investigated a task that required subjects to determine whether two figures could be rotated into congruence. Slope and intercept parameters for decision time were determined from a series of items that varied the angular separation between the figures. Only the intercept parameter correlated with spatial test performance in a sample of children, whereas both slope and intercept parameters predicted test performance in samples of adolescents and adults. However, model fits were poor for a large proportion of subjects in the sample of children, and it may be that slopes provide meaningful and dependable information only for subjects well fitted by the model. This indicates, in turn, that one interesting individual differences variable is whether a person fits a particular model or not (cf. Snow, 1980).

Salthouse, Babcock, Mitchell, Palmon, and Skovronek (1990) investigated three alternative hypotheses about which processing factors account for individual differences in spatial visualization ability. According to one, the "representational quality" hypothesis, individual differences in the effectiveness with which accurate and complete internal representations of spatial information are generated (e.g., Cooper & Mumaw, 1985; Poltrock & P. Brown, 1984) account for differences in spatial visualization ability. The "transformation-efficiency" hypothesis emphasizes individual differences in the efficiency of executing spatial transformations. This hypothesis is supported by evidence showing a relationship between visualization ability and speed of mental rotation (e.g., Just & Carpenter, 1985; Lansman, 1981). According to the third, the "preservation-under-transformation" hypothesis, differences in the ability to preserve an internal spatial representation during the transformation process account for individual differences in spatial visualization ability.

Salthouse et al. (1990) studied these hypotheses in two experiments in which students at a technical university were classified into a low group and a high group according to level of spatial visualization ability. These groups were given tasks that required a different number of transformations or made different memory demands. The pattern of results did not, however, provide convincing support for any of the three hypotheses in their original form. The preservation-under-transformation hypotheses seemed best supported, but it was also observed that any kind of concurrent processing, not just spatial transformations, seemed to be the essential aspect. Salthouse et al. suggested that low-spatial subjects may lose more information during processing because they require more "work space" than high-spatial subjects. Thus, "high- and low-spatial subjects may be equally proficient in storage or processing when either is carried out separately, but when performed in combination one or both aspects may be impaired in low-spatial subjects because the joint demands exceed the available capacity" (p. 228). This explanation suggests that limitations on working memory may be important for understanding individual differences in spatial visualization ability as well, which also indicates the importance of studying individual differences in Gf along with individual differences in broad visualization ability.

## Discussion and Conclusions

It has been possible to present only small samples of all the research relevant for understanding process aspects of cognitive abilities, and it should also be emphasized that much research covered in later sections of this chapter is highly relevant for the interpretation of cognitive abilities. Therefore, no attempt is made here to formulate more integrated theoretical accounts of the dimensions of ability. This is, however, one of the great challenges of future research.

There is reason, however, to discuss relations between the different approaches to the study of intelligence at somewhat greater length. The process-oriented research, some of which is guided by the computer metaphor, has contributed interesting results and helped revitalize the field of intelligence. However, the computational, cognitive science research is sometimes presented and conceived as a newer and better alternative to the psychometric, differential approach. In our opinion, the two approaches should be seen as complementary and oriented toward different phenomena. The possibilities for mutual exchange seem largely unexploited, however, so another challenge for future research is to develop new models for integration of the psychometric and the cognitive science approaches.

The structural analysis shows that individual differences in cognitive performance may be described in terms of several sources of variance, some of which are broad and some of which are narrow. This formulation is based on a particular set of assumptions, however. The fact that the approach is a differential one implies that only domains in which there are individual differences in performance may be fruitfully approached, and that the concept of ability plays a central role.

The ability concept makes it possible to capture performance consistencies that span several domains. This is achieved through partialing out a specific task variance, which is typically done through summation of scores over items and over tests. In this way more generalized dimensions are identified, which capture a part of the variance in specific tasks but always leave a part—and typically a large part—of the variance unaccounted for. The major advantages thus are generality and availability of abstract concepts that refer to across-task consistencies associated with persons.

The psychometric approach is group centered, and the central concepts tend to lose their meaning when brought down to the individual level. Thus, the statement that the observed variance on a vocabulary test, say, may be attributed to a certain set of factors (e.g., Gf, 30 percent; Gc', 20 percent; V', 20 percent) only has meaning as a statement that refers to a distribution of scores. When interpreted at this level, the statement gives valuable information about the test, and it also provides some further information of value for the interpretation of the ability factors. However, the statement should not be interpreted to mean that any single person uses a certain proportion of Gf, Gc', and V' to solve vocabulary tasks.

It is true that the factor-analytic model, when formulated as a regression equation, does specify an individual's performance to be a weighted sum of the individual's abilities, according to a linear, additive, compensatory model (see, e.g., H. Harman, 1967). As a model for task performance at the individual level, however, this formulation does not make much psychological sense, particularly since we may not even want to make the assumption that abilities exist within persons as entities. However, as shown by Carroll (1993), violations of the assumptions of the factor-analytic model are not necessarily serious, as long as we do not interpret the results as indicating that the linear, additive model is true for each individual in the sample.

Most of the research conducted with the aim of understanding individual differences in process terms involves a detailed study of one or a limited number of tasks. This is particularly true for the cognitive-components approach, but the cognitive-correlates approach is also strongly associated with a limited number of task paradigms. Close study of particular tasks brings the advantage of a good understanding of performance on these tasks. However, as long as a task is a less than perfect measure of intelligence, understanding of task performance will not automatically lead to an understanding of individual differences in ability. The reason for this, of course, is that task performance involves both general sources of variance, which are the ones we want to understand, and task-specific and other narrow sources of variance, which may be of interest in themselves but are of no interest for understanding broad dimensions of individual differences. A process model that accounts for performance on a single type of task cannot differentiate these sources of variance. Even on tasks that are regarded as the best measures of intelligence, the general sources of variance account for only a small fraction of the variability. This may be one reason why attempts to understand intelligence in terms of a componential decomposition of performance on complex tasks has tended to show diminishing returns (cf. Kyllonen & Christal, 1990, p. 427; Undheim, 1994). Although such modeling of task performance yields much information about sources of difficulty on that particular task, we are not much informed about the general sources of variance. The cognitive-correlates approach has a similar limitation in that particular tasks are related to other tasks, although often more complex ones. On the other hand, descriptions of individual differences in terms of general intelligence and other broad constructs provide little information about actual functioning on particular tasks. Thus, one of the major challenges for future research is to develop approaches that allow meaningful statements about relations between generalized dimensions of individual differences and specific task performance.

## SOURCES OF VARIANCE IN COGNITIVE ABILITIES

Some of the most intensely studied and debated questions in the field of differential psychology concern those factors which cause differences in performance. Research aimed at determining the relative influence of genetic and environmental factors is one important example, as is research focused on effects of performance of group belongingness (e.g., sex, race, culture). Time is another important source of variance that has been investigated in research on the degree of stability of individual differences and in life-span developmental research.

The research on sources of variance in cognitive abilities is of immense theoretical and practical importance, and it has great social and political relevance as well (Cronbach, 1975a). But the work is much too vast to be comprehensively described here. Therefore, we indicate only main results and research approaches, and provide references for further reading.

It seems that concepts of abilities are often associated with beliefs about hereditary causation and fixedness over time, with little room for influence from environment and context. We want to stress, however, that the concept of ability itself implies no such assumption. The ability concept is based on the assumption that performance consistencies may be analyzed in terms of dimensions that span several tasks, while questions about degree of heredity and amount of stability over time are to be answered through empirical research (see also Undheim, 1994).

### Genes and Environments

Nature (or genes) and nurture (or environment) are two main classes of factors that may be invoked to account for individual differences in cognitive ability. Much research has sought to determine the relative influence of these categories of factors, amid considerable discussion and controversy.

Two main approaches to the study of genetic influences on behavior can be distinguished. One, which may be called the gene-centered approach, focuses on the consequences of a known genetic or chromosomal disorder for intellectual functioning. The other approach, which may be called the trait-centered or the biometrical approach (or the behavior genetics approach), is much broader and provides information about the relative importance of environmental and genetic factors as sources of variance in a group of persons.

*The Gene-Centered Approach.* Some known disorders, such as Klinefelter's syndrome, Turner's syndrome, and Down's syndrome (Willerman, 1979), imply disorders in intellectual functioning. Down's syndrome, of which there are several kinds, is due to an extra quantity of the genetic material from chromosome 21. The syndrome is associated with very low measured intelligence and accounts for about 10 percent of all cases of mental retardation. Similar chromosomal disorders have been identified, such as trisomy 13 and 18. Others involve partial deletions of a particular chromosome, such as one called *cri du chat* ("cry of the cat"), so called because the infant makes a catlike sound. This disorder is due to deletion of the short arm of chromosome 5 and is associated with severe mental retardation.

Turner's syndrome is characterized by only one sex chromosome (XO) instead of the normal two (XX). This syndrome has less severe consequences for intellectual development than *cri du chat* syndrome but is associated with consistent deviations in the profile of intellectual abilities, with a lower level of performance on tests requiring spatial organization relative to verbal abilities, among affected females. Klinefelter's syndrome is characterized by an XXY sex chromosome complement. The latter is not associated with any deficiency in spatial ability but is associated with an increased incidence of mental retardation.

Many disorders leading to mental retardation are associated with recessive genes. Phenylketonuria (PKU) is an interesting example of recessive gene functioning with severe consequences when left untreated, but a complete reversal of the prognosis if treatment is provided at birth (Paine, 1957). This autosomal recessive disorder is related to inability to metabolize phenylalanine. About 0.5 to 1 percent of the population are carriers of the gene, and in keeping with classic Mendelian laws the disorder occurs in one of four children of parents who are both carriers of the gene. A rather effective preventive therapy involves diets low in phenylalanine. If the newborn screening test for PKU is administered and therapy is carried out, the biochemical abnormalities are to a large extent reversed.

The gene-centered approach indicates that specific genetic effects account for a certain proportion of cases in the extreme lower tail of the distribution for intellectual abilities. Although data on environmental effects on behavior characteristics are not always so clear-cut, PKU is an interesting case exemplifying dramatic effects environmental change can have on a wholly genetic disease.

***The Behavior Genetic Approach.*** In behavior genetics research, genetic and environmental sources of variance within populations are studied, and attempts are made to determine their relative importance. Heritability as a technical term (denoted $h^2$) is defined as the proportion of total variation in a trait that is caused by genetic variance. It is important to emphasize that high heritability is not equivalent to demonstrating that the expression of a trait is the direct result of genetic action, as is the case with the gene-centered approach. Rather, it is an estimate of the amount of genetically caused variance in the trait within a population. In other words, heritability research tries to disentangle the extent to which differences in a trait are the result of differences in genetic makeup. A heritability index of 0.7, for example, means that 70 percent of the variance in ability scores is due to genes, not that 70 percent of a particular score achieved on the ability test is due to gene action. The heritability index is relative also in the sense that it is a function of the amount of environmental variation. Thus, the heritability index for height is probably larger in, say, the Scandinavian countries than in most countries of Africa. This is so because

the environmental variation of relevance to height, particularly nutritional variation, is much larger in most regions in Africa.

This does not imply that heritability estimates are artifactual and of no importance. If the estimate falls short of 1.0, this is evidence for environmental influences, and if it is greater than zero, it indicates the presence of genetic action. However, it is difficult to interpret an estimate of a given size, because the actual amount of environmental variation is rarely known. If the environmental conditions for intellectual development vary enormously, heritability estimates will be low, even though genetic mechanisms might be important for intellectual potential. It may be added that environmental homogeneity is the goal of many educational and social reforms and is generally regarded as a desirable condition. However, to the extent that we approach this goal of equal opportunity, heritability estimates will go up, which seems paradoxical.

Heritability for a behavioral index can be estimated from the correlations among relatives. This can be done in several ways, such as by comparing the amount of similarity between identical or monozygotic twins and fraternal or dizygotic twins or by performing a consanguinity analysis of the degree of similarity as a function of genetic similarity (e.g., Vandenberg & Vogler, 1985). Other powerful approaches involve the study of children adopted early in life whose biological and adoptive parents have been tested with intelligence measures, or studies of monozygotic twins who have been separated early in life.

The behavior genetic approach may be understood as an attempt to partition variance (e.g., Bouchard, 1993). A first division separates genetic and environmental sources of variance, but these components may be further subdivided. Environmental variance has two components, within-family variance and between-family variance. Between-family variance refers to variations associated with being reared in different families. It is this source of variance that is generally considered when we think of environmental influences on intelligence. Within-family environmental influences are environmental influences attributable to different experiences of individuals reared in the same family. This category includes events that occur within the context of the family, such as differential treatment of siblings being reared together, as well as events that occur outside the family context, such as friendships that are not shared with other members of the family.

If we assume that more than one gene is at work, genetic variance may be partitioned into additive genetic variance and nonadditive genetic variance. Additive genetic variance reflects the combined effect of independent genes influencing a phenotype. Nonadditive genetic influences may be due to dominance of one gene or one set of genes over another, or to interactive effects of genes.

In the simplest models, genetic and environmental variance components simply add up to the total variance, but much evidence indicates complications. First of all, assortative mating must be taken into account. This term refers to the phenomenon that the parents are more similar with respect to some characteristic than would be expected from random mating alone. One effect of assortative mating is that siblings are more alike than would be the case if mating was random. There also may be sources of variance that involve combinations of genetic and environmental components. Genetic–

environmental covariance is one such source of variance, created by correlations between genes and environments, while genetic–environmental interaction involves the possibility that different genotypes respond differently to the same environment.

More specifically, covariance between genes and environment means that different genotypes are selectively subjected to different environmental treatments. Plomin, DeFries, and Loehlin (1977) discussed three conceptually distinct types of such covariance. The passive type is present when the parents provide their children with both good genes and a good environment. The reactive type of covariance occurs when teachers and others systematically furnish different environments to children of different perceived potentials. The active type of covariance is created when the children actively seek out environments that are suitable to their genetic propensities. Genetic–environmental interaction, finally, would be present if the influence of genes varied in different environments (see Wachs, 1992, for an extended discussion about the interrelationships of environmental and organismic factors).

This sketchy outline of possible sources of variance indicates some of the difficulties of the behavior genetics approach. In applications to actual data, estimates of all these sources of variance are rarely possible. Different assumptions in different studies have led to inconsistent results and disagreements over the interpretations of results. Other difficulties add to this complexity as well. For example, the group of identical twins reared apart is relatively small and may not be representative, so generalization is limited. Similarly, there are difficulties in extrapolating from adoption studies. It is possible that adopted children's relationship with their adoptive parents is different from that of natural children. Thus, it should come as no surprise that conclusions have differed widely, ranging from Kamin's (1974) claim that there is no evidence for genetic factors in intellectual abilities to Jensen's (1969) conclusion that the major share of the population variance is genetically determined.

However, recent reviews of studies that provide quantitative estimates of the relative importance of genetic and environmental influences on intelligence test scores (e.g., N. D. Henderson, 1982; Loehlin, Willerman, & Horn, 1988) agree that there is considerable influence from both categories of factors, even though the actual quantitative estimates tend to vary. One reason for the different estimates is that models varying in level of complexity and sophistication tend to yield different estimates. However, the estimates vary over time and populations, as is shown by several studies reviewed by Brody (1992, pp. 151–153). This finding clearly demonstrates that heritability is not a characteristic of a particular variable but is a population-dependent measure.

Developments in statistical methods for estimating and testing path-analytic models now provide the behavior genetics approach with more powerful tools than were previously available (see Plomin, DeFries, & Fulker, 1988, chapter 8, for an introduction). Recently, general purpose software systems such as LISREL (Jöreskog & Sörbom, 1989) have been used to estimate and test different models (see Chipuer, Rovine, & Plomin, 1990, for a detailed description of how this can be done). Chipuer et al. (1990; see also Loehlin, 1989) used an updated summary of correlations between persons having different family relations, compiled by Bouchard and McGue (1981), to compare models that made different assumptions about which sources of variance should be taken into account, such as additive and nonadditive genetic factors and shared and nonshared environmental factors. The model tests showed that a satisfactory fit between model and data was not achieved unless the model included both an additive and a nonadditive genetic component, as well as different estimates of the amount of influence of shared and nonshared environment for different categories of relatives.

Estimates derived from the final model indicate that 51 percent of the variance is due to genetic factors (32 percent from the additive genetic component and 19 percent from the nonadditive genetic component) and 49 percent is due to environmental factors. The environmental variance was divided into an estimate of the effect of the environment that is shared by all the members of a family and an estimate of the effect of nonshared environment. For siblings, these two factors were estimated to be of about the same amount of importance, while for twins the shared environment was estimated to be of considerably greater importance than the nonshared environment.

Research on the differential heritability of Gf and Gc has been conducted as well, but no clear conclusion has been reached. According to Horn (1989), there is no evidence that Gf is under stronger genetic influence than Gc. However, R. B. Cattell (1982) interpreted the available data as supporting the hypothesis that Gf is more highly heritable than is Gc. One reason for the different conclusions may be that Cattell recommends that studies of the inheritance of lower order factors should rely on what he calls stub factors, or the variance that is left when the influence from higher order factors has been partialed out. So far, however, few studies employing a strong hierarchical approach have been conducted.

Studies of genetic influences on narrow abilities are less common than studies of genetic influences on general ability. However, Vandenberg (1968) found that among the subtests in Thurstone's Primary Mental Abilities Battery the Verbal, Space, and Word Fluency subtests were more heritable than were the Number, Reasoning, and Memory subtests. Other studies, too, indicate a relatively weak genetic involvement in memory abilities (see McGue & Bouchard, 1989; Plomin, 1988, pp. 9–16). Again, however, it seems essential that future research achieve a clear separation of the more general and the more specific sources of variance in measures of narrow abilities.

***Within- and Between-Family Environmental Effects.*** The separation of effects of shared and nonshared environment is a relatively recent development in behavioral genetics research and one that has yielded interesting results, particularly so when applied in a developmental perspective (see Plomin, 1988). For example, Scarr and Weinberg (1976) conducted an adoption study of adolescent subjects and found that the effects of shared environment decreased in importance after childhood as extrafamilial factors became more influential. Such results, which indicate an increased importance of nonshared environment, has caused a greater focus on those environmental influences within families that cause siblings to be different (Plomin & Daniels, 1987), rather than on between-family differences that are captured by global background factors related to socioeconomic status, for example (see Plomin, 1988). It would, however, be of great interest to know which particular environmental factors within these different categories are important. Several research findings have been reported.

One approach to investigating between-family differences is to study variations in parental socialization practices and other aspects of the home environment and then to relate these to variations in children's performance. The Caldwell Home Inventory (e.g., Caldwell & Bradley, 1978) is one such instrument that has been used in several large-scale longitudinal studies. Brody (1992, pp. 168–172) reviewed this research and concluded that there is a positive relationship between qualities of the home environment and intellectual development. He also noted, however, that it is not possible to infer with certainty that the measured environmental factors are causally involved, because (a) characteristics of the child may affect the treatment that he or she receives in the family, (b) genetic factors of the parents may influence the environmental factors, and (c) there may be a genetic covariance between children and parents.

The difficulties encountered in attempts to draw causal conclusions from quasi-experimental studies are not easily solved, and the possibilities for conducting well-controlled experimental studies in this area are very limited indeed. However, results from studies of educational interventions, which are reviewed in the next section, are relevant here as well. These studies do indicate that substantial short-term effects may be achieved, but that the lasting effects may be more limited. In line with this observation, Brody (1992) concluded a review of between-family environmental effects with the statement: "It may very well be the case that variations in parenting styles and the adequacy of the home environment have important influences on the early intellectual development of children. These influences may fade and be of diminishing importance for mature intellectual development" (p. 173).

Environmental variables studied as between-family variables may also be examined for their contributions to differences between children within the same family. Differential parental treatment and differential exposure to peers, teachers, and media are a few examples of systematic nonshared environmental factors. Family composition differences caused by birth order effects is another source of nonshared environmental variance. As well, there are nonsystematic sources of variance, such as errors of measurement, and illnesses and accidents. The combined effect of all the nonshared environmental influences is substantial, but little is known about the relative importance of different factors.

Family composition is so far the only factor that has received substantial attention, and in large sets of data a systematic if complex pattern of relations among birth order, family size, and intelligence has been found (Belmont & Marolla, 1973). Zajonc and Markus (1975) formulated a theoretical model, called the confluence model, to account for these relations. According to this model the family furnishes its growing members with an intellectual environment that is a function of the average intellectual level of all its members. The model specifies the average level of intelligence in a family of two adults and no children to be 100. When a child is born into the family, the average intelligence level decreases to 66.7 (i.e., (100 + 100 + 0)/3). If a second child is born into the family before the first child has reached the adult level of intelligence, the average level of family intelligence experienced by the second child will be lower than that of the first child (e.g., (100 + 100 + 20 + 0)/4 = 55, if the first child has reached a level of 20).

The model predicts negative correlations between family size and intelligence and between birth order and intelligence. However, the model is able to account also for the tendency toward increasing levels of intelligence for later-born children in large families, because several of the earlier-born children have reached the adult level of intelligence. The model overpredicts the intelligence of only and last-born children, which, Zajonc and Markus hypothesize, occurs because children in these categories are deprived of the opportunity to teach younger siblings.

The confluence model fits the Belmont and Marolla data quite well, but negative findings have also been reported. For example, Marjoribanks and Walberg (1975) found that the relations among birth order, family size, and intelligence were different in different social classes, an observation that was not expected from the model. Gailbraith (1982) also demonstrated that the confluence model failed empirical tests, and he identified problems with the formal, mathematical aspects of the model as well. Further work remains to be done in this area.

The biological environment in a broad sense, including the prenatal environment, the birth process, and toxic and nutritional factors, is likely to influence intellectual development as well. Brody (1992, pp. 206–214) reviewed several studies of relations among biological factors and found evidence that many such factors (e.g., mother's alcohol intake during pregnancy, birth trauma, environmental lead, nutrition) exert small but consistent effects on intellectual performance.

*Conclusions.* The results from research on the relative effects of nature and nurture on individual differences indicate that these broad categories of factors account for approximately equal amounts of variance. There is growing awareness, however, that estimates of heritability vary over time, culture, and age levels. Paradoxically, behavior genetics research also has pointed to quite substantial environmental effects, particularly from those nonshared environmental factors that cause children in the same family to be different. So far, however, research has not identified the particular environmental factors in the home environment that are most important; this is an urgent task for future work. As discussed next, however, there is ample evidence that the quality and quantity of education relate positively to intellectual development. However, we do not know whether this is mainly an effect on Gc rather than on Gf or general intelligence. In general, there is little hard evidence on differential heritability of the different dimensions of ability, and we know virtually nothing about the relative importance of within- and between-family environments for individual differences in different categories of abilities.

## Time as a Source of Variance: Stability and Change

In the psychometric literature, *change* may refer to absolute changes in the level of performance on specific tasks, to changes in ability structure with age, or to changes in the level of performance on estimated ability constructs. *Stability* usually refers to stability of relative position in the group, as measured by a correlation coefficient. As for absolute change, Stern's index of IQ as mental age divided by chronological age was based on rapid age-related changes in level of performance. This index later proved inadequate, partly because absolute changes in level of performance after age 15 are small relative to age changes. Measurement of absolute change is methodologically difficult, and even when only relative change is measured, for example, in terms of standard deviation (SD) units, artifacts of measurement are likely to be present.

One problem is that the sources of variance accounting for task performance may change over time. Thus, with the advent of multiple-factor analysis, changes of ability structure over time came into focus. The most popular idea has been the factor differentiation hypothesis (Garrett, 1946), according to which abilities are more clearly separated with advancing age. Although most reviewers conclude that there is evidence for this hypothesis (see, e.g., R. J. Sternberg, 1990, p. 101), the question is far from settled, primarily because of the difficult measurement problems encountered.

Research on changes in adulthood has been tied largely to Gf-Gc theory. The characteristics of fluid and crystallized ability were partly based on the notion of differential development of these two dimensions of ability over the life span. Horn and Cattell (1966) interpreted their findings to support the idea that Gc increases over the life span, whereas Gf increases up until the 20s and decreases slowly thereafter. However, one methodological problem in cross-sectional analyses of the effects of age on intelligence is that age and cohort effects are confounded (see, e.g., Brody, 1992, p. 235). Longitudinal studies also have methodological problems. Thus, samples generally cannot be maintained intact, which implies that samples of elderly who persist in longitudinal studies are increasingly nonrepresentative subsamples of the population. The best solution therefore is to combine cross-sectional and longitudinal studies in a systematic way.

Some researchers take the position that there is little or no decline in abilities as a function of age (e.g., Baltes & Schaie, 1976). In contrast, Horn and Hofer (1992) interpret the available evidence as indicating that Gf, Gs, and short-term memory (Gsm) steadily decrease from the early 20s, that Gv increases into the 30s and early 40s and then decreases, while Gc increases into the 60s before any decline is indicated. Further research in this area would need to address questions about the mechanisms behind the age-related changes in abilities.

Research on the stability of general intelligence from correlational studies indicates that after about age 10 this characteristic is quite stable, with very high correlations between measurements separated by shorter time intervals (Bloom, 1964). Estimates of the actual degree of correlation vary somewhat between studies, however. Bloom (1964) concluded that intelligence at the age of 13 predicts at least 90 percent of the true variance in intelligence at the age of 18. Härnqvist (1968a, 1968b, 1973) obtained somewhat lower estimates in two studies, one studying changes between ages 13 and 18, and the other with an interval of 1 year between measurements. Humphreys (1989) concluded that the true correlation between ability at two ages is about .96 raised to the power of the number of years between the first test and the retest. For a 10-year period the expected true correlation would be about .63 to .70. However, the principle of "stability through aggregation" applies here too. Thus, if mean scores computed for two or three successive years are related over time, higher relations are

found. For example, using data from the Berkeley growth study (Jones & Bayley, 1941), Brody showed that a mean score for ages 5, 6, and 7 correlated .86 with a mean score for ages 17 and 18.

Results from studies of the stability of specific abilities are less consistent than those obtained in the study of general intelligence. In some studies coefficients of stability are almost as high for specific abilities as for general ability (e.g., Meyer & Bendig, 1961), while in others lower degrees of stability have been found. Härnqvist (1968a, 1968b, 1973) and Balke-Aurell (1982) found a rather low degree of stability between ages 13 and 18 for a contrast between verbal and spatial abilities. One reason for these different results is that some researchers define the narrow abilities as including variance from a general factor, while others first extract the variance due to general intelligence (cf. Härnqvist, 1973; Tyler, 1958). Gustafsson and Undheim (1992) separated broad and narrow dimensions of intelligence in a strong hierarchical model and studied the stability of these dimensions between ages 12 and 15. The true correlation for Gf over time was estimated to be around .92, which is a value close to what was expected from Humphreys's (1989) rule. For the Gv' dimension, virtually perfect stability was found. This result needs replication before it may be concluded that individual differences in Gv' are particularly stable, but the study demonstrates that a different pattern of results may emerge when a strong hierarchical model is applied.

## Group Differences as a Source of Variance in Cognitive Functioning

Empirical findings concerning differences in level of performance between males and females, blacks and whites, and other groups identified by physical or social characteristics have generated considerable controversy during the 20th century (e.g., Cronbach, 1975a). Group differences, although often found, tend to be small relative to individual differences within groups. There is, for example, a difference of about 1 SD unit between the performance of U.S. blacks and whites on commonly used tests of general intelligence (Loehlin, Lindzey, & Spuhler, 1975), whereas individual differences within these groups span about 6 SD units. Gender differences tend to be much smaller than race differences, so for both gender and race the ratio of within-group to between-group variability in intelligence scores is large.

Even so, group differences are not unimportant. With a group difference of 1 SD unit, about 16 percent of the group with the lower mean score is above the mean of the higher group. However, even small group differences have considerable impact on the relative number of persons at the extremes of the distribution. For example, when the 10 percent highest scoring individuals are selected from two groups with a 1 SD unit difference, eight times as many individuals come from the group with the higher mean as from the group with the lower mean. Thus, in highly selective situations, even small group differences may have considerable practical impact.

*Gender Differences.* In a comprehensive review of gender differences in cognitive abilities, Maccoby and Jacklin (1974) discussed several methodological problems in such research. Thus, editorial fashion in publication makes it less likely that studies showing no difference will be reported than studies showing differences. Sample selection is another source of bias. For example, boys are more likely than girls to drop out of high school, which may cause high school girls to be compared with a somewhat more select group of boys. Bias may also be due to differential course taking among boys and girls (see, e.g., Fennema & Sherman, 1977). Unfortunately, few studies have been able to control for effects of attrition.

To interpret gender differences in particular psychological constructs, the factor structures should be identical for males and females. According to Carroll's (1993) review of the factor-analytic literature, studies of factor structure invariance across groups of males and females are limited. However, most data sets yielded about the same number of factors, and cross-identification of factors generally was good, with a somewhat higher degree of invariance for higher order factors than for lower order factors. Some differences were observed, however, chiefly with respect to reading, mathematical reasoning, and spatial skills. Nevertheless, the overall impression is that the assumption of invariance of factor structure is generally supported.

Much work in differential psychology conducted during the early decades of the 20th century was motivated by a desire to demonstrate that females were not inherently inferior to males (Tyler, 1965, p. 239), and the main finding was that girls did about as well as boys on tests of intellectual functioning. Eventually the construction of some tests of general ability came to be based on the assumption of equivalence, and items and subtests were balanced so that the total score would not give an advantage to either sex (Matarazzo, 1972; McNemar, 1942). This implies, unfortunately, that these tests cannot be used to study gender differences in level of general intellectual ability. Indirect evidence indicates, nevertheless, that there are no substantial gender differences with respect to general ability. There is no evidence that the balancing procedure has detracted from the validity of the scales for predicting performance in school or in work.

Meta-analysis has become the preferred way of summarizing empirical results on gender differences in level of performance. Hyde and Linn (1988) analyzed 165 studies (involving over a million subjects) of gender differences on verbal tests. They found a declining female superiority, from an effect size of .23 for studies published before 1973 to an effect size of .10 for later studies. There is also evidence that verbal fluency tasks, which typically require written responses, are the domain of verbal abilities for which the largest gender difference has been observed (see Tyler, 1965, p. 244).

In the area of mathematics, male superiority has been found, but not with respect to speediness and accuracy of numerical operations (Feingold, 1988). Hyde, Fennema, and Lamon (1990) found evidence of a changing trend in gender differences in mathematical performance as well, with older studies showing a larger effect size favoring males than more recent studies. The results also indicated that unselected samples and samples selected for above-average math performance gave a different pattern of results. Males are more likely to outperform females in more select samples (see Brody, 1992, pp. 319–320). The Johns Hopkins talent search studies also show that the ratio of males to females increases from 2 : 1 when a cutting score of 500 on the SAT math section is used to 13 : 1 when a cutting score of 700 is used (Benbow, 1988; Benbow & Stanley, 1981).

Similar results have been found in studies using more representative samples (Lubinski & Humphreys, 1990; Undheim & Nordvik, 1992). These findings indicate that variability among males in mathematical performance is larger than variability among females.

Interpretations of results in this area are made difficult, however, by the fact that mathematical reasoning is not particularly well defined as an ability construct. Carroll (1993) reported less than satisfactory congruence of mathematical reasoning factors across groups of males and females. As has already been discussed, there is also the question of whether mathematical/numerical reasoning is part of Gc or should be regarded as a broad domain of its own. When this issue is addressed in future research, gender differences with respect to structure should also be investigated.

Linn and Petersen (1985) used meta-analysis to synthesize the empirical research on gender differences in visual-spatial abilities published after the Maccoby and Jacklin (1974) review and prior to 1982. They obtained a mean effect of .44 for spatial perception, .73 for measures of rotation, and .13 for measures of visualization. There was little evidence for age differences in these effect sizes. There was evidence, however, for diminishing gender differences on many kinds of visual-spatial tasks.

In this area, too, the interpretation of results is complicated by the fact that the congruence of ability factors across groups of males and females is not always good. Carroll (1993) reported results that indicate that females have a less differentiated structure of narrow abilities in this domain than do males, and it has been suggested that girls to a greater extent than boys tend to solve visual-spatial tasks through verbal and reasoning processes.

In conclusion, in almost all domains there is strong evidence that gender differences in performance are diminishing. The changes in the educational and professional aspirations of females in Western industrialized nations toward traditional male professions are consistent with the cognitive data. For example, the number of female students enrolled in and graduating from schools of engineering and architecture has increased dramatically (for a discussion, see Halpern, 1992). The differences that remain are likely to be related to factors such as parental beliefs and pressures, gender roles, activity stereotypes, and goals and expectations of success (see Eccles [Parsons] et al., 1983; Eccles & Harold, 1992).

Biological factors may account for some differences as well. The findings that are most difficult to explain by psychosocial hypotheses relate to performances that are not socially valued, in school or out of school, and thus not subject to obvious bias in terms of differential values and investments of time and effort. The largest and most reliable differences of this kind belong to the domain of visual-spatial performances, and Halpern (1992) argued that at least some of these are difficult to explain through environmental hypotheses. It has been suggested that a difference in cerebral lateralization among males and females may account for the male superiority in performance on certain spatial tests. Another biologically oriented hypothesis attempts to relate gender differences in abilities to hormonal differences. Thus, Kimura and Hampson (1993) concluded that if androgens are present early in life, this may affect the development of certain motor skills and spatial and mathematical abilities. If they are not present, the development of small-amplitude intrapersonal motor skill, verbal fluency, and perceptual speed is favored. They also reported evidence that the pattern of performance varies as a function of fluctuation in hormone status. However, studies in this area rarely provide unambiguous findings in support of clearly articulated theoretical assertions (see Brody, 1992, pp. 324–328). Thus, further research is needed before the precise nature of the biological differences that may contribute to gender differences in performance on ability tests is known.

*Racial and Ethnic Differences.* As already mentioned, a 1 SD difference in level of performance on tests of general intelligence exists between the U.S. black and white populations. Part of this difference is associated with differences in socioeconomic background between the racial groups, however. The black–white difference in performance has been approximately constant for several decades (Loehlin et al., 1975), and it also seems to be fairly constant over the life span, at least after age 3 (see Brody, 1992, p. 282–283).

The pattern of differences is not constant over different types of cognitive measures, however. Jensen and Reynolds (1982; see also Gustafsson, 1992) found that black children outperformed white children on associative memory tasks. There also is evidence that black samples tend to do better on tests of verbal ability than on tests of spatial and numerical reasoning (see Stodolsky & Lesser, 1967). Jensen (1985) has presented some evidence in support of the so-called Spearman hypothesis, according to which the size of the black–white difference is a function of the G loading of the test. The relations are rather weak, however, and Jensen's conclusions have been criticized on both empirical and conceptual grounds (see Brody, 1992, pp. 284–287, for a summary of this discussion).

It is a simple matter to conclude that there is a difference in level of performance on tests of intelligence between blacks and whites, but the interpretation of this difference has caused considerable controversy. One issue is whether the test scores have the same meaning in samples of blacks and whites, or if there is such a bias that it is necessary to know the race of the person tested to interpret the scores. The issue of bias in mental testing (e.g., Jensen, 1980) has been investigated, for example, with factor analysis to study factorial invariance, with regression analysis to see if the predictive validity of tests is the same in both groups, and with item analysis techniques to investigate possible biasing effects of item characteristics. Brody (1992, pp. 287–296) reviewed this literature and concluded that the black–white difference is not due to bias in the tests employed.

Another controversial issue is whether the black–white difference is due to genetic or environmental sources of variance. Jensen (1973) suggested that at least one-half of the IQ difference is attributable to genetic factors, but many argue that the environmental differences are primary. It must be emphasized that even though heritability may be high within both black and white populations, the racial difference may be entirely environmental. This is because the sources of between-group differences may be different from the sources of within-group differences (see MacKenzie, 1980, 1984). As was observed by Bock and Moore (1986), the average stature in European, American, and Asian populations has increased nearly 1 SD unit in two generations, mainly as a function of better nutrition. Within these populations measures of stature have at least as high heritability as has IQ, which demonstrates that between-group differences may be caused by environmental factors, and within-group differences by a combination of genetic and environmental factors.

Another example of a between-group difference in test performance of the same order of magnitude as the racial difference is provided by the increase in test scores of about 1 SD since the 1930s (see below). This increase in level of performance between successive generations is due to environmental factors, such as improved quality and quantity of education. As has been argued by Flynn (1980, 1984, 1987a, 1987b), this change indicates that there do exist environmental factors that may account for a 1 SD difference in IQ.

Brody (1992, pp. 296–310) reviewed the literature on reasons for black–white differences in test scores and argued that the best source of evidence is provided by transracial adoption studies. The relatively few studies available (e.g., Scarr & Weinberg, 1976) do seem to indicate that environmental factors are more important than genetic factors. Brody concluded, "While it may be difficult to definitively rule out a genetic hypothesis on the basis of the available evidence, I think that it is also fair to say that there is no convincing direct or indirect evidence in favor of a genetic hypothesis of racial differences in IQ" (p. 309).

Bock and Moore (1986) conducted a large survey study of sociocultural factors in performance on the Armed Services Vocational Aptitude Battery (ASVAB). They interpreted the typical pattern of observed differences between the black and white populations in terms of cultural differences that are "reflected in the way children are oriented to the social and object environment, modes of communication, and tolerance for varying levels of sensory stimulation" (p. 83). In a similar approach Humphreys (1988) identified what he labeled the "inadequate learning syndrome" (ILS), which is characterized by substantial deficits in basic academic skills and information. To eliminate the ILS, which is more prevalent among blacks, substantial efforts are needed throughout the education system as well as during the preschool years. Humphreys also emphasized that "ILS in an individual student is affected by the prevalence of ILS among parents and other relatives, neighborhood adults, and peers. It is embedded in a complex of problems that include teen pregnancy, illegitimacy, female-headed families, welfare, drugs, prostitution, and violent crime" (Humphreys, 1988, p. 259). Environmental sources of differences in performance, even if it is known which they are, may indeed be as difficult to remedy as any genetic source.

*Socioeconomic Differences.* The relationship between measured abilities and socioeconomic level (own or parental) is one of the best-documented findings in the history of mental tests (Tyler, 1965, p. 336). The correlation between the socioeconomic level of parents and the school performance of their children is close to .5 (Lavin, 1965). The association tends to be somewhat higher in elementary school and somewhat lower in high school or secondary school, which is probably due to restrictions on variability in the latter case. K. R. White (1982) conducted a meta-analysis of studies of the relation between socioeconomic background and scores on tests of general mental ability, and found a correlation of .33.

The relative importance of socioeconomic background and

measured intelligence for school achievement has been studied with path-analytic techniques (e.g., O. D. Duncan, Featherman, & Duncan, 1972). The results support the general conclusion that a person's social background is important for educational attainment, but that individual differences in intelligence estimated by scores obtained early in the person's educational career account for a larger part of the variance in educational attainment. However, a recent study by C. R. Henderson and Ceci (1992) questioned this conclusion. Using Project Talent data, they related SES and intelligence to educational attainment to show that while both parents' SES and IQ related significantly to educational attainment, the SES background seemed to be the most potent. In this model, parents' SES was placed at the very start of the paths explored, which reduced IQ to a residual variable. Although Henderson and Ceci (1992) concluded that it is better to be born rich than smart, a recent Scandinavian study using similar methodology concluded otherwise (Nordvik & Undheim, 1993). It would not be unreasonable to expect cross-cultural differences regarding the interplay of SES and ability, but the question is still open. In any case, the message is that socioeconomic background accounts for variance in measures of intelligence, as well as in educational and occupational variables.

## Discussion and Conclusions

The research reviewed here clearly shows that a multitude of factors influence level of performance on intelligence tests. Genetic and environmental categories of factors seem to exert roughly equal amounts of influence. Thus, even the relatively limited range of environmental variation represented in the behavior genetics studies is a powerful source of individual differences. It also must be emphasized that the partitioning of variance in behavior genetics research strictly refers to differences between individuals; the results do not account for group differences in performance, nor do they imply limits to the effects that can be achieved through environmental manipulations.

Many more specific environmental factors have been identified as important, even though the effect of each variable typically is small. The concerted action of many factors may thus be necessary to achieve substantial change. In the next section we consider the influence of education on intelligence, which does seem to indicate that considerable effects may be achieved.

## ABILITY DIFFERENCES IN RELATION TO LEARNING AND INSTRUCTION

Much research has investigated individual differences in relation to learning and instruction. We have chosen to organize our exposition in three major sections, according to a simple input–process–output model of instruction.

In the first section individual differences are seen as input variables to processes of instruction, the duration of which may range from a few minutes to several years. This research thus investigates aptitudes for learning from an instructional process that is more or less fixed. In the next section individual differences during the course of learning and instruction are investigated. Several different approaches have been employed to adapt the processes of instruction to accommodate individual

differences, such as ability grouping and different methods of individualization. In the last section, individual differences are treated as outcomes of instructional and educational processes that either explicitly aim to affect individual differences variables or have other aims but nevertheless affect more generalized characteristics of individuals.

This simple organization of the material allows treatment of the major issues of the field. Many issues cannot be addressed, however, so the reader is advised to consult the more comprehensive review by Snow and Yalow (1982).

## Cognitive Abilities as Aptitudes for Learning and Instruction

According to Snow (1991), the term *aptitude* originally had a meaning close to readiness, suitability, susceptibility, or potential for development, given specified situations. However, he also observed that the meaning of the term has become more and more narrow:

Specifically in English, aptitude was gradually equated with intelligence, and capacity in the 16th, 17th, and 18th centuries, then misinterpreted and generalized as a single-rank-order of "general intellectual fitness for any situation" in the 19th century, and then captured in this condition by the mental testing movement in the 20th century. (Snow, 1991, p. 250)

Thus, in English the term aptitude has come to be associated with capacity as a generalized trait and fixed entity. Snow (1991; see also Cronbach & Snow, 1977) and others have shown that a broader conception of aptitude is necessary that would allow for multidimensionality and situational specificity. There is reason, however, to consider the approaches and results of research that has been conducted from the narrower, psychometric point of view.

*General Cognitive Ability and Learning.* The relationship between intelligence and learning ability has proved difficult to determine empirically. Woodrow (1946) conducted a series of widely cited studies that seemed to demonstrate that brighter students did not improve more rapidly with practice on tasks such as analogies and addition than did the less bright students. Allison (1960) and Stake (1961) related performance on reference batteries of ability tests to a variety of rote memory and conceptual learning tasks within the framework of a factor-analytic, multiple-factor model. Some relations were found, but a clear structure of relations could not be established. However, these negative conclusions were due to problems of measurement and conceptualization of both learning and ability (see Snow et al., 1984; Humphreys, 1979). Cronbach and Snow (1977) reanalyzed the early studies and demonstrated that ability tests do correlate with learning. They also concluded that "[a] concept of general mental ability is adequate to account for nearly all the correlations observed, except where a separate rote-memory factor is pertinent" (p. 142).

Snow et al. (1984) reanalyzed the Allison and Stake matrices again, this time using nonmetric multidimensional scaling. They showed that the ability and learning correlations fit the radex model and that it is possible to identify both a content facet and a complexity continuum among the learning tasks, even though the tasks studied tended to be of only low or intermediate complexity. Thus, the same taxonomic structure as was identified on the basis of the correlational research on abilities applies, to a certain extent, to learning tasks.

Measures of intelligence administered during childhood and adolescence predict amount of schooling quite well. For example, in a Swedish study Härnqvist (1990) was able to account for some 60% of the variance in level of education achieved at age 32 using an optimally weighted set of measures, with general cognitive level as the strongest partial predictor. On the basis of analyses of several sets of data, O. D. Duncan, Featherman, and Duncan (1972) estimated that intelligence accounted for 29% of the variance in amount of education, when socioeconomic background was controlled for.

Correlations between measures of general intelligence and later measures of educational achievement have been found to be around .50, with some systematic variation as a function of the age level of the students (for reviews, see R. B. Cattell & Butcher, 1968; Jensen, 1980, pp. 316–337; Lavin, 1965). Thus, correlations tend to be higher (.60 to .70) at elementary school levels and lower in college and graduate school (Jensen, 1980). The restriction of ability range at higher levels of the educational system as a function of student selection and self-selection may be one reason for this pattern. Other possible explanations are that abilities and achievement differentiate as a function of maturation (Garrett, 1946) and education (Anastasi, 1970).

Correlations between ability and achievement tend to vary considerably from one study to another, however. Such a pattern is typical of studies of the validity of ability tests as predictors of outcomes in many fields, such as work performance. The variability of validity coefficients has been interpreted in terms of situational specificity, which would limit the possibility of generalizing from one situation to another. However, during the 1980s techniques of validity generalization (Schmidt & Hunter, 1981; Schmidt, Pearlman, Hunter, & Hirsh, 1985; see also Sackett, Tenopyr, Schmidt, & Kahn, 1985), based on meta-analytic approaches, demonstrated that the major part of the variance in observed validity coefficients can be explained by sampling error (Schmidt & Hunter, 1981). However, when jobs are grouped into job families on the basis of their level of complexity, the magnitude of the relation between performance and general mental ability increases as a function of job complexity (see Lubinski & Dawis, 1992, for a short presentation). This finding parallels the laboratory findings of the effects of variations in level of complexity in laboratory tasks. To our knowledge, such meta-analyses have not yet been conducted with educational achievement as the criterion. However, for the categories of jobs with the highest levels of complexity, correlations with general cognitive ability similar to those obtained with educational criteria were observed (.45 to .58).

Analyses of the nature of school learning have been a source of hypotheses about reasons for the relationship between general cognitive ability and school achievement. L. B. Resnick (1976) argued that intelligence may be regarded as the ability to learn from incomplete instruction. Studies of learning and instruction in high school geometry (e.g., Greeno, 1980) indicate that conventional texts and classroom lessons often leave important background features implicit, and that the example exercises are often insufficient to allow development of generalizable cognitive skills. Snow and Yalow (1982, p. 518) observed

that such incomplete instruction and exercise put heavy demands on "eduction of relations and correlates," which are two of the processes that Spearman (1923) viewed as central to intelligence. It remains to be specified, however, how instruction should be changed to effect a change in the amount of relation between intelligence and school achievement. This is a major challenge for future research.

*Specific Cognitive Abilities and Scholastic Achievement.* Several studies have investigated whether the amount of explained variance in educational achievement may be increased if several narrow abilities are used as predictors. However, differential aptitude batteries seem not to have differential predictive power for achievement in different subject matter areas (see, e.g., Carroll, 1982; McNemar, 1964; Ree & Earles, 1991a; R. L. Thorndike, 1985). Even though these and other studies demonstrate the pervasive role of general ability in prediction, there is nevertheless scattered evidence that specific abilities could make a contribution (Cronbach, 1990). Carroll (1982, p. 84) noted that the available multifactor batteries do not provide sufficiently clear measures of general and special skills factors to allow determination of the relative importance of these factors in predicting achievement.

Gustafsson and Balke (1993) applied a strong hierarchical model with latent variables to more clearly identify general and specific abilities. For a battery of aptitude tests administered to sixth-grade students, a confirmatory factor model was fitted with a general factor and several orthogonal residual factors. Among these were both broad abilities (Gc and Gv) and narrow factors. A model was also fitted to course grades obtained in the ninth grade, which included a general school achievement factor and domain-specific achievement factors in areas such as science and mathematics, social science, language, and spatial-practical performance. Some 40% of the variance in general school achievement could be accounted for by G and Gc'. However, larger proportions of variance were accounted for in the domain-specific achievement factors, and different aptitude factors were important in different domains. This study thus indicates that differentiation among at least a limited number of broad abilities may be worthwhile.

*Cognitive Abilities and Skill Acquisition.* Fleishman (1967) summarized findings from studies of relations between ability and skill acquisition over time and concluded that broad intellectual abilities are more highly correlated with early task performance, whereas narrow intellectual abilities (e.g., Perceptual speed, P) are more highly correlated with performance late in practice. Using a more refined methodology that combines correlational and information-processing techniques, Ackerman (e.g., 1986, 1987, 1988, 1989) has shown how information-processing requirements of tasks affect ability–performance relations during practice. According to the Ackerman model, skill acquisition is composed of three phases, cognitive, associative, and autonomous, each of which draws on different abilities.

The cognitive phase involves understanding of the task requirements (i.e., rules and goals of the task, appropriate strategies, and so on). Individual differences in performance during this phase are mainly related to general ability, and particularly so for novel and complex tasks. For tasks that are consistent (i.e., where the learner can deal with inputs and outputs in an unvarying manner from situation to situation), the influence of general abilities diminishes with practice. During the cognitive phase, task-appropriate broad-content abilities also are important; an example is verbal ability for tasks that involve processing of semantic material.

During the associative phase, the learner puts together an appropriate sequence of cognitive and motor processes required to perform the task. The cognitive load on the learner is reduced when goals and procedures are moved from working memory to long-term memory, so that the relation with general ability diminishes. During this phase there is an initially increasing association between perceptual speed ability and performance. However, as learners reach a level of performance where their psychophysical abilities impose limitations on performance, the importance of perceptual speed decreases.

During the autonomous phase, finally, the skill is automatized and can be performed with little attention. Individual differences in the final level of performance reached are more dependent on noncognitive motor abilities than on cognitive abilities.

Ackerman's theory is considerably more elaborate than is evident from this brief description. It also attempts to consider motivational differences in learning (see chapter 9, this volume), and it specifies in detail how task characteristics such as consistency, complexity, and transfer may be expected to influence the relationship between ability and performance. Several of these hypotheses have been tested in empirical research, but much work remains to be done in this fascinating field.

*Conclusions.* To summarize, there are relations among measures of cognitive abilities and learning that seem to vary over both different measures of abilities and different learning tasks. In previous sections a considerable amount of work on taxonomic models of cognitive tasks was presented. However, there seems to be a need for a more full-fledged taxonomy of learning skills that would serve as a tool both for basic research and for determining the limits of generalizability from research to practical applications.

Kyllonen and Shute (1989) proposed a taxonomy that is a synthesis of the rational taxonomies proposed by Bloom (1956) and Gagné (1985), the correlational taxonomy, as exemplified by the radex model, and taxonomies based on information-processing models (e.g., J. R. Anderson, 1983). The Kyllonen and Shute taxonomy classifies learning skills according to three major dimensions: knowledge type, instructional environment, and domain.

The knowledge type dimension makes a fundamental distinction between declarative knowledge ("know that") and procedural knowledge ("know how"). Subcategories of declarative knowledge can be arranged by complexity, from propositional knowledge to schemata, or packets of related propositions. Subcategories of procedural knowledge may also be distinguished, such as simple productions, skills, and automatic skills. Procedural knowledge can also be arranged by generality, from a narrow to a broad range of applicability. Another knowledge type identified by Kyllonen and Shute is the mental model, which involves multiple skills applied to elaborate schema.

The instructional environment dimension is characterized according to the amount of student control in the learning process. At one end rote learning involves little student control;

at the other end learning by observation and discovery involves much student control. In between these extremes are didactic learning by textbook or lecture, learning by practice, learning by analogy, and learning from examples.

The domain dimension reflects the importance of subject matter in learning. Kyllonen and Shute suggested that one critical aspect of the domain dimension is whether a subject matter taps quantitative/technical knowledge or verbal knowledge. They also proposed that the relative importance of speed versus quality in decision-making may be a critical domain dimension.

This taxonomy is not yet fully developed or tested but it does seem useful for organizing research results, and for formulating hypotheses about relations between cognitive abilities and learning.

## Adapting Instruction to Individual Differences

The research considered above has demonstrated substantial relations between measures of broad factors of ability and school achievement. It may be asked if it is possible to modify these relations through adapting instruction to individual differences.

*Mastery Learning.* Bloom (1974) suggested that the relationship between general intelligence and school achievement could be reduced if slow learners were allocated a sufficient amount of time to master the material before they were presented with new material. According to Bloom, use of so-called mastery learning procedures (see Block & Anderson, 1975) would prevent pupils from developing cumulative deficits and would cause individual differences in achievement to diminish.

Slavin (1987a) reviewed research on mastery learning and noted that studies reporting dramatic effects of mastery learning tended to be of short duration. For studies of longer duration there was no effect of mastery learning. The studies reviewed did not support Bloom's prediction that the time needed for mastery would decrease for slow learners. Thus, if the students who learn rapidly are given new material as they master old material, and the slow students are allowed the time they need to achieve mastery before new material is introduced, the range of material taught in an ordinary classroom becomes large. It thus seems that mastery learning procedures suffer from limitations as a means for reducing individual differences in performance.

*Aptitude-Treatment Interactions.* Relations between aptitude and achievement might be possible to influence through changes in the curriculum, the instructional method, the organization of teaching, or through another kind of "treatment" change. Figure 8–6 displays three possible patterns of outcome when outcome is regressed upon aptitude within two treatments (A and B). In Figure 8–6A the two regression lines are parallel, and for every score on aptitude, the level of outcome is higher in treatment A by the same amount. According to this figure there are main effects both for aptitude and for treatment; that is, persons with high aptitude scores outperform persons with low aptitude scores by the same amount in both treatments, and those receiving treatment A outperform those receiving treatment B by the same amount for every level of aptitude. In Figure 8–6C the two regression lines cross, implying that per-

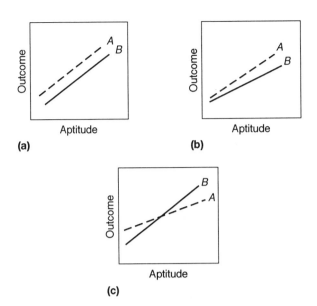

FIGURE 8–6. Possible Relations Between Aptitudes and Outcomes in Two Treatments

sons scoring higher than the aptitude score at the cross-over point achieve a higher result with treatment B, while persons with a lower aptitude score achieve a higher score with treatment A. Here there is an aptitude–treatment interaction (ATI), because the effect of treatment varies as a function of aptitude. A simple analysis of mean differences between treatments would show no difference, so in this case there is no main effect for treatment. However, even though the difference between persons scoring high and persons scoring low on the aptitude variable is larger in treatment B than in treatment A, there is a difference in the same direction for both treatments. There is thus a main effect for aptitude, as well as an interaction effect.

In Figure 8–6B, too, the regression lines are nonparallel, but they do not cross within the range of the aptitude variable. There is a difference in favor of treatment A over the whole range of aptitude, but the difference is larger for higher scores on the aptitude variable than for lower scores. This is a so-called *ordinal* interaction effect, while the interaction with crossing regression lines is called a *disordinal* interaction.

Both types of ATI are highly interesting from a theoretical point of view, but from an applied point of view interest has focused on disordinal interactions. This is because such interactions would imply that choice of different treatments for different subgroups of students would reduce individual differences in outcomes. In fact, Cronbach and Gleser (1965) demonstrated that the differential treatment of persons classified into different groups assumes, implicitly or explicitly, the existence of a disordinal interaction.

ATI research was originated by Cronbach (1957, 1967), who argued that correlational, differential research should be combined with experimental research in a systematic study of interactions between aptitudes and treatments. This kind of study would represent a unification of the two disciplines of scientific psychology (Cronbach, 1957), and it would also be of interest from the point of view of individualization of instruction. In

the late 1960s many researchers started to investigate ATIs. This early research was reviewed by Cronbach and Snow (1977; see also Berliner & Cahen, 1973), who concluded that many single studies showed strong ATI effects. However, inconsistent results also were common, so that no particular conclusion could be generalized to serve as a basis for instructional practice. Cronbach and Snow attributed a part of these inconsistencies to methodological weaknesses among the studies, such as inadequate statistical analysis, low statistical power to detect interactions, poorly understood aptitude variables, unclear differentiation of treatments, and no separation of effects at individual and classroom levels. They also emphasized the inherent complexity of social and behavioral research, where higher order interactions involving several variables are the rule rather than the exception (see Cronbach, 1975b).

In subsequent research many of the methodological problems that afflicted the early studies were amended, and several tentative generalizations have been formulated (e.g., Snow, 1977, 1989; Snow & Lohman, 1984; Snow & Yalow, 1982). These generalizations tend to involve cognitive, conative, and affective variables simultaneously, so several examples are given in chapter 9. Here we consider only some results obtained with cognitive variables.

In the early phases of ATI research, hypotheses were often formulated in terms of narrow abilities. However, contrary to expectations (see Cronbach, 1967), most interactive effects involving cognitive variables have been detected with general ability, even though there is almost always a main effect for general ability as well. The strongest and most consistently replicated interaction with G involves treatments that differ in the structure and completeness of instruction (Snow & Lohman, 1984; Snow & Yalow, 1982).

Treatments with a high degree of structure exercise a high level of external control of the learning activities through control of the sequence of pacing, feedback, and reinforcement. In such treatments the instructional tasks are broken down into small units, and presentations are concrete and explicit. Instructional methods characterized as expository, direct instruction, teacher-controlled, or drill-and-practice are instances of high structure. Such treatments seem to be beneficial for learners with low general ability.

In treatments with a low degree of structure, learners must act more independently, and they must on their own contribute inferences and generalizations that are not explicitly provided. Instructional methods described as indirect, inductive, discovery-oriented or learner-controlled are examples of low-structure treatments. In such treatments learners with a high level of general ability tend to do well, whereas those with a low level of ability tend to do poorly. Thus, in high-structure treatments there is a shallower slope of outcome on general ability, while in low-structure treatments the slope is steeper.

Snow (1989) suggested that these effects may be accounted for in terms of the greater complexity and difficulty of the low-structure treatments, which provides a motivating challenge for learners high in general ability but leaves less able learners helpless, anxious, or unmotivated. High-structure treatments reduce complexity, from which the less able learners benefit. However, such treatments may become boring for able learners, and the mode of presentation may interfere with the able learner's own preferred processing style.

The complexity of the field of ATI research is clearly illustrated by the fact that Whitener (1989), in a review employing meta-analytic techniques of nine studies of interactions between prior achievement and amount of instructional support, reached the conclusion that there is a steeper regression on aptitude in high-instructional-support treatments than in low-instructional-support treatments. In a superficial comparison at least, this conclusion is the opposite of the one drawn by Snow.

There may be several explanations for these discrepant conclusions, but here we can consider only a few. Whitener formulated the ATI hypothesis in terms of prior achievement or Gc, while Snow's interpretation is formulated in terms of Gf. In the empirical studies distinctions have not generally been made between these broad abilities, but it seems likely that the studies reviewed by Snow to a larger extent have employed aptitude variables capturing Gf rather than Gc. However, if the high-instructional-support/high-structure treatment is similar to the kind of teaching experienced by the students before the experiment, it seems likely that those students who have previously been successful (i.e., high-Gc students) will continue to be so in this treatment. In future empirical research and reviews it thus seems worthwhile to try to separate Gf and Gc, and also to take the instructional history of the students into account.

Should it be found that Gf and Gc are involved in opposed interactions, the implications would be interesting. According to the strong hierarchical model, Gc is a mixture of the two components Gf and Gc'. Thus, if a single measure of Gc is used in an ATI study, it could happen that the within-treatment regressions appear parallel when in fact there are interactions with Gf and Gc' in opposite directions. To establish such effects it is necessary to administer a battery of ability tests and use a strong hierarchical model to decompose the test variance into components of different degrees of generality.

Gustafsson (1989) adopted such a technique in a reanalysis of a study investigating interactions between presentation modality (i.e., reading vs. listening) and cognitive abilities. The result indicated that Gv', as predicted, had a steeper slope in the listening treatment, whereas Gf had a less steep slope in this treatment. However, these results could not be detected in the original analysis of the data because that analysis relied on Gv, in which the opposite effects for Gf and Gv' cancelled. The results from this reanalysis are tentative, but they do suggest that further reanalyses based on a strong hierarchical model should be conducted.

ATI research has been accused of having failed to demonstrate that interactions exist (e.g., Bracht, 1970). There is no doubt, however, that the empirical research has demonstrated the existence of ATIs, even though the research has not yet arrived at such a strong foundation of knowledge that applications may be built on it. However, this is a characteristic that ATI research shares with most areas of educational research, and it should be viewed as a challenge rather than as the final result.

*Ability Grouping.* The terms "ability grouping," "streaming," and "tracking" refer to teaching practices according to which students who seem to be similar in ability are brought together. However, such practices vary greatly in flexibility and duration of placement and in the extent to which the teaching is actually adapted to the needs of different groups of students (Oakes,

Gamoran, & Page, 1991). Furthermore, few questions about classroom organization have been so controversial or inspired so much research.

Reviews of studies of the efficacy and usefulness of ability grouping have failed to demonstrate any clear and strong effects (Carroll, 1982, p. 88), but, as was noted by Kulik and Kulik (1982), the emphasis of the reviewers has changed over the years. In the 1950s reviewers often concluded that grouping could be especially beneficial for high-aptitude students, whereas recent reviews focus on negative effects on self-concept and motivation for disadvantaged students.

In this context we can mention only a few examples of conclusions from recent reviews of research. According to Slavin (1987b), there seems to be no overall effect of ability grouping at the elementary school level, even though increases in the inequality of achievement indicate differential effects on different groups of students. A meta-analysis of effects of ability grouping at the secondary school level by Kulik and Kulik (1982) indicated a small effect (.10 SD). However, especially clear effects were found when high-ability students received enriched instruction, while effects for average or below-average students were close to zero. There is also evidence that high-track students in tracked secondary schools benefit more than comparable students in lower track classes (Gamoran & Mare, 1989).

It seems, however, that outcome-centered studies, which treat the instructional process as a "black box," provide only limited insights into the nature of ability grouping. One example of this is the reanalysis by Dahllöf (1971) of a large comparative study by Svensson (1962). In the original study it was concluded that there was no difference in level of achievement between a differentiated and an undifferentiated curriculum. However, by including process data collected within another project, Dahllöf showed that the high-track group in the differentiated curriculum had indeed progressed further. Another example is provided by the work of Oakes (1985), who, by looking at the process of instruction, demonstrated that clear differences existed favoring upper tracks with respect to the content and quality of instruction, the patterns of teacher–student and student–student relationships, the expectancies of teachers, and so on. There was thus an unequal distribution of school resources over tracks, the effects of which were contaminated by any effects that homogeneity of grouping may have had as such. Another major problem with ability grouping is that the individual differences in actual subject matter achievement are still quite large. A mean correlation of about .50 between general ability and academic subjects implies a reduction of variance of 25 percent. With correlations between achievements in different subjects of, say, .60 to .70, there will be large achievement differences in ability-grouped classrooms. It is unlikely that the teaching has accommodated well to this situation.

*Conclusion.* So far little progress has been made in attempts to reduce the relationship between intelligence and education. However, Brody (1992, p. 264) noted that cross-cultural comparisons may be one way to put the importance of intellectual differences in perspective. A study by Stevenson et al. (1990) found fifth-grade children in Beijing to average 1.3 SD higher on a test battery of mathematical knowledge than children in Chicago of comparable age. These differences may be accounted for in terms of differences in curriculum, rather than in terms of intellectual differences between Chinese and U.S. children. Thus, studies of performance differences at an international level may be one way of putting both individual and national differences in perspective.

## Effects of Education on Intelligence

The development and cultivation of general skills of thinking and learning are important goals of education, so intelligence must be treated as an important outcome of education as well (e.g., Snow & Yalow, 1982). The effects on cognitive abilities of both short-term instructional programs and long-term educational experiences have been studied. This research is briefly reviewed below.

*Amount of Education and Intelligence.* Randomized experiments cannot be employed to investigate the effects of variations in quality and quantity of education on intelligence, so quasi-experimental designs have been relied on. In these, initial differences among groups receiving different amounts of education have been controlled for with statistical methods. Several large-scale studies have demonstrated a positive effect on intelligence of amount of education (e.g., Husén & Tuijnman, 1991; Härnqvist, 1968a, 1968b; Lorge, 1945). For example, Härnqvist (1968a, 1968b) found that students who had an academically oriented education gained more than 0.5 SD in intelligence after covariance-analytic control of initial differences, relative to students with less academic secondary school education. It cannot be guaranteed, however, that the statistical control of initial differences in intelligence fully takes into account all the relevant differences. For example, Brody (1992) pointed out that groups with different amounts of education may differ in intellectual interests, and these differences may cause the observed changes in intelligence. Even though studies of effects of interests on changes in cognitive abilities do not indicate any important effects (see, e.g., Gustafsson & Undheim, 1992), it is in principle impossible to infer causation with certainty from quasi-experimental designs. Thus, evidence concerning effects of education on intelligence must also be sought elsewhere.

Ceci (1990a) argued that studies in several different areas, taken collectively, provide strong evidence of effects of education on intelligence. There is, thus, a small but reliable decrement in intelligence test performance during summer vacations (e.g., Jencks et al., 1972). For every year of delayed entry into formal schooling there is a decrement in IQ (e.g., Freeman, 1934; Sherman & Key, 1932), and relative scores decrease between 1 and 2 IQ points on average for each year of high school not finished (e.g., de Groot, 1951; Husén, 1951).

Further evidence of the role of education is provided in a study by Cahan and Cohen (1989), who investigated the influence of schooling by comparing pupils in the same grade who differed in age with pupils in different grades. Using a regression procedure they estimated that the gain in test scores associated with 1 year of schooling was 0.275 SD. It has also been shown that early school entry is associated with improved test performance (P. Baltes & Reinert, 1969). Furthermore, sociological studies show that blacks who migrated from the U.S. South to the North between the two world wars increased their test

scores as a function of the improved schooling received (Lee, 1951).

These sources of evidence, along with others that will be considered below, indicate that there is a direct causal link from schooling to measured intelligence. Ceci (1990a, pp. 71–72) suggested that schooling influences performance on intelligence tests through a combination of direct instruction of factual knowledge and indirect modes or styles of thinking and reasoning, which favor disembedded ways of thinking about the world. So far, however, there is little detailed evidence concerning the nature of the mechanisms through which schooling exerts its influence on cognitive development.

*Changes in the Population's Level of Intelligence over Time.* Cohort studies have revealed striking improvements on tests between successive generations. Flynn (1984) used data from standardization samples in the United States of different versions of the Wechsler and Binet tests, and estimated that IQ increased by almost 1 SD between 1932 and 1978. Flynn (1987a) extended the analysis to 14 industrialized countries and concluded that increases could be found in almost all countries.

Substantial increases in test scores were also observed between World War I and World War II—effects that were explained with reference to the increased amount of formal education (see also Humphreys, 1989). For the post-World War II cohorts the increases in performance are not associated with any substantial improvements in the amount of education received, even though there may have been quality improvements. The fact that a larger increase in performance has been observed for nonverbal tasks than for verbal tasks also has created doubts about what role wider access to education has played in causing the changes.

However, increased quality and quantity of education should not be ruled out as determinants of the increased level of performance (cf. Husén & Tuijnman, 1991). The considerably larger increase for nonverbal tasks of the Gf type than for verbal tasks may reflect a true change in the profile of ability, but it may also be due to an increase in the level of difficulty of the verbal (typically vocabulary) items. So far no attempt has been made to differentiate between the two interpretations, but reanalyses of existing data with modern techniques of item analysis (see chapter 25) might reveal changes in level of difficulty of the verbal items.

A study by Härnqvist and Stahle (1977) demonstrated that quality aspects may be important, too. They found that an increase in girls' test scores, and particularly so on a spatial visualization test, was related to a change from a tracked to a nontracked curriculum. Teasdale and Owen (1989) found that the increase in performance observed in Danish data was much larger at lower levels than at higher levels, a difference which they attributed to improved remedial education in Danish schools. It thus seems that a deeper understanding of the nature and causes of the massive IQ gains would require a much more detailed analysis of changes for different groups of individuals, which in turn should be related to changes in demographic, educational, and other societal factors.

Flynn (1987b) has argued that the massive test score gains show that intelligence tests are not good measures of true underlying ability because there is no evidence that the increases are associated with increases in academic achievement and academic accomplishments. According to Flynn, the tests are unduly influenced by cultural and environmental factors, and "they fail completely when they attempt to bridge the cultural distance that separates generations in modern industrial societies" (Flynn, 1987b, p. 25). Flynn's observation that group differences may be caused by factors other than those hypothesized to be measured by the test is very important, particularly in light of the social and political importance attached to group differences in performance. However, Flynn's argument largely rests on the absence of dramatic increases in the number of very high-scoring persons, which would be expected from an upward shift of 1 SD of the distribution. Thus, until more detailed analyses have been conducted to identify which groups of persons account for the increase in performance and which factors are associated with the change, Flynn's far-reaching conclusions should be viewed with skepticism.

***Interventions to Increase Intelligence.*** Attempts to increase intelligence by changing the environment of the child has a long history (Detterman & Sternberg, 1982; Spitz, 1986), but developments during the 1960s are particularly important. In 1965 Project Head Start was begun with the aim of providing an enriched environment for disadvantaged children that would increase their intelligence and their ability to benefit from education. The Head Start program consists mainly of preschool centers that offer programs up to 9 months long. Reviews of evaluations of effects indicate a clear increase in test performance as a result of participation in Head Start (e.g., Haskins, 1989; Royce, Darlington, & Murray, 1983). But the gains diminish over time, and after a few years children with Head Start do not maintain an advantage in cognitive performance over non-Head Start children (McKey et al., 1985). However, it should be emphasized that there are important short-term and long-term effects of Head Start other than performance on intelligence tests (see, e.g., Scott-Jones, 1992), such as effects on health (Haskins, 1989) and on the local communities (McKey et al., 1985).

Project Follow Through was designed to extend the Head Start interventions as a response to preliminary evidence that Head Start achieved only short-term gains. In Follow Through a large variety of different educational models were tried for kindergarten and elementary schoolchildren. However, in a summary of an evaluation carried out over a 4-year period, Spitz (1986) concluded that "experience in Follow Through programs had no effect on intelligence, as measured by the Colored Progressive Matrices Test" (p. 93).

The Milwaukee Project provided an intensive preschool educational intervention to a small group of children of mothers with a low IQ. Early reports of dramatic effects on measured intelligence seem not, however, to be accompanied by any effects on academic performance in fourth grade (see Garber, 1988). Brody (1992) reviewed this program, along with other preschool interventions intended to increase intelligence, and concluded that "[t]here is no credible evidence that experimental interventions during the preschool years will create enduring changes in performance on tests of intelligence" (p. 178).

It is important, however, that the somewhat disappointing pattern of immediate gains that then fade away is put into proper perspective. Zigler, Styfco, and Gilman (1993) posed the question, "Do we really want to believe that a year in preschool can ultimately shape the course of a human life?" (p. 21). They went on to argue that:

It is shocking that so many have chosen to focus on a year or two when the child was a pre-schooler, and have disregarded the many subsequent years of development, exalted a single experience over myriad others, and are now putting their hopes and money on early childhood programs as the solution—not part of a solution—to pervasive social problems. (p. 21)

In future policy initiatives it thus seems essential that more reasonable expectations be formulated and more detailed investigations be conducted into how the immediate gains may be sustained and developed.

In addition to compensatory programs, a wide range of methods and procedures for teaching thinking have been devised. Nisbet (1991) made a distinction between the "skills" approach and the "infusion" approach. According to the latter, thinking skills are best developed if throughout the curriculum methods of teaching are adopted that stimulate development of intellectual skills, such as problem-based teaching and learning, and the use of information technology and computers. The skills approach instead focuses on identifiable thinking skills abstracted from their contexts. There are now numerous cognitive skills programs (e.g., de Bono, 1976; Feuerstein, Rand, Hoffman, & Miller, 1980; Lipman, Sharp, & Oscanyan, 1980; see also Maclure & Davies, 1991). Several such programs are comprehensively reviewed and discussed by Chipman, Segal, and Glaser (1985), L. B. Resnick (1987), Segal, Chipman, and Glaser (1985), and R. J. Sternberg and Bhana (1986). However, as was observed by Sternberg and Bhana (1986), much of the empirical information has resulted from studies that leave a lot to be desired from a scientific point of view.

Blagg (1991) reported results from a large and relatively well-controlled empirical study conducted in England of the Feuerstein et al. (1980) Instrumental Enrichment (FIE) program. This program is intended to correct a long list of cognitive deficits (e.g., unplanned and unsystematic behavior, inability to consider two sources of information at once, lack of comparative behavior) through a series of instruments, each of which emphasizes a particular cognitive function. Examples of materials in the program include tasks that require students to identify geometric figures within amorphous arrays of dots (cf. tasks for measuring flexibility of closure), comparison tasks that require students to identify differences among similar-looking objects, categorization tasks, and series tasks. The evaluation was done in four secondary schools, in which low-achieving 14-year-old students were taught the Feuerstein program for an average of 112 hours. However, the study failed to demonstrate any increase in performance on intelligence tests, nor was there any evidence that the program had any effects on school achievement or study skills. Spitz (1986, pp. 173–182) also reviewed studies of the Feuerstein program without finding much evidence that the positive results obtained by Feuerstein with Israeli immigrants could be generalized to other cultural settings.

Stankov (1991) summarized results from a series of studies investigating effects of training on Gf and Gc. The theoretical starting point of the research has been that Gf and Gc should both be affected by training, but that different exercises may produce differential effects on these abilities. Among the studies considered was an extended intervention study conducted by Kvashchev in Yugoslavia. An experimental group of classes was provided with 3 to 4 hours per week of training in creative problem solving for 3 years. Effects were evaluated with a battery of 28 tests, and the results indicated an increase in both Gf and Gc performance. Stankov thus concluded that the creative problem-solving exercises "have qualities that are affecting, through transfer, both the formal learning reflected in Gc and also the casual learning processes of Gf that are typically not specifically taught in school" (Stankov, 1991, p. 103).

Stankov also reported a series of practice studies in which practice curves for single and competing tasks have been compared. The studies indicate that tasks may be differentiated into those that depend on automatic processing (perceptual abilities, crystallized abilities) and those that depend on controlled, resource-limited processing (short-term memory, fluid intelligence).

Klauer (1990) has formulated a "neo-Spearman" process theory of inductive reasoning which specifies that inductive reasoning is a process of discovering regularities by finding identity and difference with respect to attributes of and relations between objects. The theory has been tested in an extended series of experiments in which subjects have been trained to adopt a strategy that should lead to improvements with respect to certain tasks, but to no improvements on other tasks. The experimental results generally support predictions and indicate that considerable transfer effects may be achieved.

*Practice and Coaching.* Much attention has been devoted to investigations of the effectiveness of training intended to increase scores on specific tests, such as college entrance tests (for a review, see Bond, 1989). Coaching on a test may take many different forms, such as instruction in test wiseness, specific instruction about how to solve a particular type of item, or instruction in a broad content domain. Studies of the effect of coaching on the SAT indicate that it is possible to increase performance (e.g., Anastasi, 1981), even though effects are rather small. Messick and Jungeblut (1981) demonstrated that the effect is nonlinearly related to the duration of the intervention, such that gains are larger at the beginning of an intervention program and the expected increments from coaching decline. However, coaching not accompanied by practice appears to be ineffective (Jensen, 1980). Simple unassisted practice also has effects—particularly for students without previous test-taking experience—on group paper-and-pencil tests and on speeded tests (see Bond, 1989). It seems, however, that transfer of training is relatively small, which demonstrates that the changes are restricted to observable test performance and should not be interpreted as effects on intelligence.

## Discussion and Conclusions

The research results indicate strong effects of schooling on test performance and suggests that experimental interventions also may produce substantial changes in performance. How-

ever, long-term effects appear more difficult to achieve than short-term effects.

One possible interpretation of the difficulty in achieving enduring changes is that the relatively brief interventions of the programs are insufficient to compensate for the effects of an environment that is not conducive to intellectual development, as this is measured in the studies. According to this view, additional interventions at higher age levels are needed (cf. Scott-Jones, 1992). According to another interpretation, the strong effects achieved in the younger age groups are due to similarities in the teaching and in the instruments used to measure intelligence. Thus, according to this view, "the training did not change the basic intelligence, it merely provided them with skills that will not generalize to novel tasks" (Spitz, 1986, p. 112). Along a similar line of reasoning it may be argued that the results from the developmental behavior genetic research (see above), which indicate that the effects of shared environment decrease with age, provide an explanation for the results from the intervention studies as well (cf. Spitz, 1992). According to the latter view there is little hope that any substantial, enduring effects may be achieved.

Even though the research on attempts to improve intelligence provides little ground for optimism, it certainly cannot be claimed that interventions to improve the intellectual environment have proved ineffective. In fact, the quite dramatic increases in intelligence during the past 50 years, and the strong effects of education on intelligence, do show that environmental variations may be effective enough. The problem seems to be that at present, little is known about which particular factors are important. The large effects may be due to the combined effect of a large number of factors, all of which exert a small positive effect on intelligence. Whether this is true or not, it is an urgent task for further research to identify which factors or sets of factors are involved in the increased level of intelligence.

## FINAL REMARKS

Research on individual differences in cognitive functions is one of the oldest fields of educational psychology. A striking characteristic of this field of research is that great applied advances were made early, with profound practical implications, through the creation of the technology of mental testing. This was done during the first decades of the 20th century, "leaving only matters of refinement for the period 1935 to the present" (Carroll, 1982, p. 31). However, the level of theoretical sophistication has never matched the success in the applied field, and many of the research activities throughout the century may be described as a search for the missing theory. In this search, periods of stagnation have been followed by periods of progress. For example, R. B. Cattell (1971) argued that after the pioneer work of Binet, Burt, Piaget, Spearman, and Thurstone, little progress was made. Cattell even described the field of intelligence between 1940 and 1970 as an "ant-like industry regarding psychometric details, a retrogressive drift in stagnant waters into pre-Spearman chaos" (R. B. Cattell, 1971, p. x).

We do believe that true advances have been made in the decades that have passed since Cattell made his statement. The present chapter has tried to convey these strides within the psychometric field; among these are Cattell's own contributions, and many others, including Carroll's (1993) monumental reanalysis of hundreds of factor matrices. We also have recorded new approaches to individual differences research, most important the research based on the information-processing approach in the 1970s and 1980s. We have noted as well a fading of the expectations of this approach, even though important gains have been made, and will continue to be made, within the process-oriented research.

Questions about the structure and nature of basic traits, along with questions about stability, change, heritability, and environmental maleability, continue to be central to the field of research on cognitive abilities. This is true for the field of personality as well. It is interesting to note three separate parallels between the latest development in personality research and that in research on cognitive abilities. First, in the former field there is a growing consensus as to the set of major personality variables referred to as "the big five" (see McCrae & Costa, 1990). In psychometric research on cognitive abilities, too, there is growing consensus as to five or six major dimensions of ability: fluid-analytic or general ability (Gf or $g$), crystallized or verbal-educational ability (Gc), broad visualization (Gv), broad speediness (Gs), and broad fluency (Gr). Second, in personality research as well as in cognitive research, there is evidence for a considerable degree of stability of these major dimensions. And third, there are parallels between the heated debate over person variance versus situational variance in personality research, spurred by Mischel's (1968) writings, and the question of task- or domain-specific knowledge versus broad abilities. In both cases the solution to the problem is the same: The observed variance is dominated by situational and task-specific variance when single behavioral incidents are examined, but broad personality traits and abilities are strongly predictive of observed variance in the long run, when behavior is aggregated over several situations and tasks.

Throughout this chapter we have discussed possible directions for future research, and we will not repeat those discussions here. There is reason, however, to discuss a few issues of general importance, such as the concepts of ability and intelligence and the future of standardized tests in research and practice.

We will first reconsider the relations between the psychometric approach, on the one hand, and psychophysical, biological, and cognitive science approaches on the other. These newer approaches are often presented as alternatives to psychometry. In particular, cognitive science research is sometimes seen as providing so much information that once performance on every task is modeled for every individual, there is no need for measures that reflect individual differences in level of performance across several tasks (e.g., O'Connor, 1992, p. 19). However, quite apart from the practical and theoretical problems involved in accomplishing such a process modeling (cf. Lohman, 1994), there are other reasons why the generalized concepts that refer to broad abilities are not going to disappear. One reason is that the phenomena of consistency and stability of individual differences are much too important theoretically and practically not to be captured by appropriate constructs. Such constructs cannot refer to specific tasks, but must necessarily be more abstract.

Another reason is that the broad ability constructs may be needed in the task-specific modeling as well. Much current cog-

nitive science research emphasizes the "situatedness" (see Lave, 1988; and chapter 2) of human cognition and the importance of particular contexts and tasks. Somewhat paradoxically, the decomposition of variance into broad and narrow components, which indicates that task-specific sources of variance are the most important ones, may be interpreted as providing some support for such views. However, the psychometric research also indicates that a certain proportion of variance in performance on any specific task (around 10%, say), may be accounted for in terms of broad ability factors. Some progress has been made in understanding how task characteristics (e.g., complexity, novelty, content) affect the relation between performance and broad ability factors, but so far there are only few examples of successful integration of broad abilities into process models. This is a challenging task for future research.

The concept of intelligence is one of the most intensely discussed and researched concepts in educational psychology. There is little hope that it will ever be possible to achieve a generally agreed-upon definition of this concept. However, from an empirical point of view, considerable progress has been made in clarifying the nature of intelligence. Thus, Carroll (1993) argued that the concept of intelligence

is . . . an inexact, unanalyzed popular concept that has no scientific status unless it is restated to refer to the abilities that compose it. . . . The long-discussed problem of defining intelligence is transformed into one of defining the various factorial constructs that underlie it and specifying their structure. (p. 627)

We agree with Carroll, but there may be reason not to overemphasize the distinction between the empirically based definition and other notions. Thus, the major dimensions of the hierarchical model of the structure of cognitive abilities are also those that seem to be the most salient ones in both lay and expert implicit theories of intelligence.

The standardized test is a frequently used tool, both in applied settings and for purposes of research, and there is reason to assume that tests will play important roles in the future as well. However, as a function of recent developments in methods and techniques of measurement, there is also reason to expect that the technology of testing may change in the future.

During the past decade there was a strong trend toward the development of new methods of assessment and measurement, with an emphasis on measurement of practical intelligence and the use of more realistic, complex and natural tasks. This is an important and interesting development, and we may expect further progress in the development of new forms of measurement.

Standardized tests serve well when the purpose is to obtain information that may be analyzed in terms of multiple underlying dimensions of individual differences. However, in the psychometric approach the tasks themselves often are not considered to be of much interest in themselves. The orientation toward practical intelligence and realistic tasks involves a focus on tasks of intrinsic interest, and often the purpose is to assess qualities of performance in a given domain, without any attempt to account for individual differences in performance in terms of underlying dimensions. However, particularly when used as a basis for statements about individual differences in performance, realistic tasks provide challenges of both methodological and theoretical kinds. The tasks typically are time-consuming to perform and to score, so generally fewer tasks are presented than in a traditional standardized test. The possibilities for reducing the influence of unwanted sources of variance through aggregation over several tasks thus are more limited, which implies that in comparison with a typical standardized test, factors associated with the tasks and the situation will be more important sources of variance than will the broad dimensions of individual differences. We want to emphasize, however, that these are differences of degree rather than differences of kind. Thus, multidimensionality and complexity seem to be common characteristics of all instruments for measurement of individual differences in cognitive functions.

Above all, however, realistic tasks provide theoretical challenges for future research on individual differences in cognitive functions. Messick (1992, p. 380) observed that current theories of intelligence do not deal very well with the role of knowledge in intellectual functioning or with the role of ability in the acquisition of knowledge. Realistic tasks typically involve active use of knowledge, so that to understand individual differences in processes and performance on such tasks, the interplay between cognitive abilities and knowledge must be understood.

It is also necessary to understand the affective and conative aspects of performance, the focus of chapter 9. Messick (1992) stated our needs as well:

What is needed is a theoretical perspective that comprehends the interplay of abilities, knowledge, and personality in intellectual functioning—or else we need some basis for clearly distinguishing intelligence from knowledge in cognitive processing as well as for distinguishing both of them from the motivational, affective and volitional aspects of cognitive processing. (p. 381)

These are some of the major challenges for future research on individual differences. Some starting points for an integrated treatment of cognitive, affective, and conative aspects of individual differences in performance are provided in the next chapter.

## References

Ackerman, P. L. (1986). Individual differences in information processing: An investigation of intellectual abilities and task performance during practice. *Intelligence, 10,* 109–139.

Ackerman, P. L. (1987). Individual differences in skill learning: An integration of psychometric and information processing perspectives. *Psychological Bulletin, 102,* 3–27.

Ackerman, P. L. (1988). Determinants of individual differences during skill acquisition: A theory of cognitive abilities and information processing. *Journal of Experimental Psychology: General, 117,* 299–329.

Ackerman, P. L. (1989). Individual differences and skill acquisition. In P. L. Ackerman, R. J. Sternberg, & R. Glaser (Eds.), *Learning and individual differences: Advances in theory and research* (pp. 165–217). New York: Freeman.

Allison, R. B. J. (1960). Learning parameters and human abilities. Unpublished doctoral dissertation, Educational Testing Service and Princeton University, Princeton, NJ.

Anastasi, A. (1970). On the formation of psychological traits. *American Psychologist, 25,* 899–910.

Anastasi, A. (1981). Coaching, test sophistication, and developed abilities. *American Psychologist, 36,* 1086–1093.

Anastasi, A. (1988). *Psychological testing* (6th ed.). New York: Macmillan.

Anderson, J. R. (1978). Arguments concerning representations for mental imagery. *Psychological Review, 85,* 249–277.

Anderson, J. R. (1983). *The architecture of cognition.* Cambridge, MA: Harvard University Press.

Anderson, J. R. (1985). *Cognitive psychology and its implications.* New York: Freeman.

Anzai, Y. (1991). Learning and use of representations for physics expertise. In K. A. Ericsson & J. Smith (Eds.), *Toward a general theory of expertise: Prospects and limits* (pp. 64–92). Cambridge, England: Cambridge University Press.

Baddeley, A. D. (1986). *Working memory.* Oxford: Clarendon Press.

Balke-Aurell, G. (1982). *Changes in ability as related to educational and occupational experience.* Göteborg, Sweden: Acta Universitatis Gothoburgensis.

Baltes, P., & Reinert, G. (1969). Cohort effects in cognitive development in children as revealed by cross-sectional sequences. *Developmental Psychology, 1,* 169–177.

Baltes, P. B., & Schaie, K. W. (1976). On the plasticity of intelligence in adulthood and old age: Where Horn and Donaldson fail. *American Psychologist, 31,* 720–725.

Barrett, F. C., Eysenck, H. J., & Lucking, S. (1986). Reaction time and intelligence: A replicated study. *Intelligence, 10,* 9–40.

Belmont, L., & Marolla, F. A. (1973). Birth order, family size, and intelligence. *Science, 182,* 1096–1101.

Benasich, A. A., & Bejar, I. I. (1992). The Fagan test of intelligence: A critical review. *Journal of Applied Psychology, 13,* 153–171.

Benbow, C. P. (1988). Sex differences in mathematical reasoning ability in intellectually talented preadolescents: Their nature, effects, and possible causes. *Behavioral and Brain Sciences, 11,* 169–232.

Benbow, C. P., & Stanley, J. C. (1981). Mathematical ability: Is sex a factor? *Science, 212,* 118–119.

Bentler, P. M. (1992). *EQS: Structural equations program manual.* Los Angeles: BMDP Statistical Software.

Berg, C. A., & Sternberg, R. J. (1985). A triarchic theory of intellectual development during adulthood. *Developmental Review, 5,* 334–370.

Berliner, D. C., & Cahen, L. S. (1973). Trait-treatment interactions and learning. In F. N. Kerlinger (Ed.), *Review of research in education* (Vol. 1, pp. 58–94). Itasca, IL: Peacock.

Bethell-Fox, C. E., Lohman, D. F., & Snow, R. E. (1984). Adaptive reasoning: Componential and eye movement analysis of geometric analogy performance. *Intelligence, 8,* 205–238.

Binet, A. (1905). Analyse de C. E. Spearman, "The proof and measurement of association between two things" et "General intelligence objectively determined and measured." *Année Psychologique, 11,* 623–624.

Binet, A., & Simon, T. (1905). Méthodes nouvelles pour le diagnostic du niveau intellectuel des anormaux [New methods for diagnosing the intellectual level of abnormals]. *Année Psychologique, 11,* 191–336.

Binet, A., & Simon, T. (1908). Le développment de l'intelligence chez les enfants [The development of intelligence in children]. *Année Psychologique, 14,* 1–94.

Blagg, N. (1991). *Can we teach intelligence? A comprehensive evalua-

*tion of Feuerstein's Instrumental Enrichment Program*. Hillsdale, NJ: Lawrence Erlbaum Associates.

Block, J. H., & Anderson, L. W. (1975). *Mastery learning in classroom instruction*. New York: Macmillan.

Bloom, B. S. (1956). *Taxonomy of educational objectives: Cognitive domain. Handbook I*. New York: McKay.

Bloom, B. S. (1964). *Stability and change in human characteristics*. New York: Wiley.

Bloom, B. S. (1974). Time and learning. *American Psychologist, 29*, 682–688.

Bock, R. D., & Moore, E. G. J. (1986). *Advantage and disadvantage: A profile of American youth*. Hillsdale, NJ: Lawrence Erlbaum Associates.

Bollen, K. A. (1989). *Structural equations with latent variables*. New York: Wiley.

Bond, L. (1989). The effects of special preparation on measures of scholastic ability. In R. Linn (Ed.), *Educational measurement* (3rd ed., pp. 429–444). New York: Macmillan.

Bornstein, M. H. (1989). Stability in early mental development: From attention and information processing in infancy to language and cognition in childhood. In M. H. Bornstein & N. A. Krasnegor (Eds.), *Stability and continuity in mental development*. Hillsdale, NJ: Lawrence Erlbaum Associates.

Bouchard, T. J., Jr. (1993). The genetic architecture of human intelligence. In P. A. Vernon (Ed.), *Biological approaches to the study of human intelligence* (pp. 33–138). Norwood, NJ: Ablex.

Bouchard, T. J., Jr., & McGue, M. (1981). Familial studies of intelligence: A review. *Science, 212*, 1055–1059.

Bracht, G. H. (1970). Experimental factors related to aptitude-treatment interactions. *Review of Educational Research, 40*, 627–645.

Brody, N. (1992). *Intelligence* (2nd ed.). San Diego, CA: Academic Press.

Brown, A. L. (1978). Knowing when, where, and how to remember: A problem of metacognition. In R. Glaser (Ed.), *Advances in instructional psychology* (Vol. 1, pp. 77–165). Hillsdale, NJ: Lawrence Erlbaum Associates.

Buros, O. K. (Ed.). (1978). *The eighth mental measurements yearbook*. Highland Park, NJ: Gryphon Press.

Burt, C. (1941). *The factors of the mind: An introduction to factor analysis in psychology*. New York: Macmillan.

Burt, C. (1944). Mental abilities and mental factors. *British Journal of Educational Psychology, 14*, 85–94.

Burt, C. (1949). The structure of the mind: A review of the results of factor analysis. *British Journal of Educational Psychology, 19*, 100–111, 176–199.

Butterfield, E. C., Nielsen, D., Tangen, K. L., & Richardson, M. B. (1985). Theoretically based psychometric measures of inductive reasoning. In S. E. Embretson (Ed.), *Test design: Developments in psychology and psychometrics* (pp. 77–148). New York: Academic Press.

Cahan, S., & Cohen, N. (1989). Age versus schooling effects on intelligence development. *Child Development, 60*, 1239–1249.

Cain, K. M., & Dweck, C. S. (1990). The development of children's conception of intelligence: A theoretical framework. In R. J. Sternberg (Ed.), *Advances in the psychology of human intelligence* (Vol. 5, pp. 47–82). Hillsdale, NJ: Lawrence Erlbaum Associates.

Caldwell, R., & Bradley, R. (1978). *Home observation for measurement of the environment*. Little Rock: University of Arkansas.

Campione, J. C., & Brown, A. L. (1978). Toward a theory of intelligence: Contributions from research with retarded children. *Intelligence, 2*, 279–304.

Carpenter, P. A., Just, M. A., & Shell, P. (1990). What one intelligence test measures: A theoretical account of the processing in the Raven Progressive Matrices test. *Psychological Review, 97*, 404–431.

Carroll, J. B. (1968). Review of J. P. Guilford's *The nature of human intelligence* (New York: McGraw-Hill, 1967). *American Educational Research Journal, 5*, 249–256.

Carroll, J. B. (1972). Stalking the wayward factors: Review of J. P. Guilford & R. Hoepfner's *The analysis of intelligence* (New York: McGraw-Hill, 1971). *Contemporary Psychology, 17*, 321–324.

Carroll, J. B. (1981). Ability and task difficulty in cognitive psychology. *Educational Researcher, 10*, 11–21.

Carroll, J. B. (1982). The measurement of intelligence. In R. J. Sternberg (Ed.), *Handbook of human intelligence* (pp. 29–120). New York: Cambridge University Press.

Carroll, J. B. (1989). Factor analysis since Spearman: Where do we stand? What do we know? In R. Kanfer, P. L. Ackerman, & R. Cudeck (Eds.), *Abilities, motivation, and methodology: The Minnesota Symposium on Learning and Individual Differences* (pp. 43–67). Hillsdale, NJ: Lawrence Erlbaum Associates.

Carroll, J. B. (1991). No demonstration that *g* is not unitary, but there's more to the story: Comment on Kranzler and Jensen. *Intelligence 15*(4), 423–436.

Carroll, J. B. (1993). *Human cognitive abilities. A survey of factor-analytic studies*. Cambridge, England: Cambridge University Press.

Carroll, J. B., Kohlberg, L., & DeVries, R. (1984). Psychometric and Piagetian intelligences: Toward resolution of controversy. *Intelligence, 8*, 67–91.

Cattell, J. M. (1890). Mental tests and measurements. *Mind, 15*, 373–381.

Cattell, R. B. (1943). The measurement of adult intelligence. *Psychological Bulletin, 40*, 153–193.

Cattell, R. B. (1963). Theory of fluid and crystallized intelligence: A critical experiment. *Journal of Educational Psychology, 54*, 1–22.

Cattell, R. B. (1971). *Abilities: Their structure, growth, and action*. Boston: Houghton Mifflin.

Cattell, R. B. (1982). *The inheritance of personality and ability: Research methods and findings*. New York: Academic Press.

Cattell, R. B. (1987). *Intelligence: Its structure, growth and action*. North-Holland: Elsevier.

Cattell, R. B., & Butcher, J. (1968). *The prediction of achievement and creativity*. Indianapolis: Bobbs-Merrill.

Cattell, R. B., & Horn, J. L. (1978). A check on the theory of fluid and crystallized intelligence with description of new subtest designs. *Journal of Educational Measurement, 15*(3), 139–164.

Ceci, S. J. (1990a). *On intelligence . . . more or less: A bio-ecological treatise on intellectual development*. Englewood Cliffs, NJ: Prentice Hall.

Ceci, S. J. (1990b). On the relation between microlevel processing efficiency and macrolevel measures of intelligence: Some arguments against current reductionism. *Intelligence, 14*(1), 141–150.

Ceci, S. J., & Liker, J. (1986). A day at the races: A study of IQ, expertise, and cognitive complexity. *Journal of Experimental Psychology: General, 115*, 255–266.

Chang, A., & Atkinson, R. C. (1976). Individual differences and interrelationships among a select set of cognitive skills. *Memory & Cognition, 4*, 661–672.

Charness, N. (1991). Expertise in chess: The balance between knowledge and search. In K. A. Ericsson & J. Smith (Eds.), *Toward a general theory of expertise: Prospects and limits* (pp. 39–63). Cambridge, England: Cambridge University Press.

Chase, W. G., & Ericsson, K. A. (1981). Skilled memory. In R. J. Anderson (Ed.), *Cognitive skills and their acquisition* (pp. 141–189). Hillsdale, NJ: Lawrence Erlbaum Associates.

Chase, W. G., & Simon, H. A. (1973). The mind's eye in chess. In W. G. Chase (Ed.), *Visual information processing*. New York: Academic Press.

Chi, M. T. H., Feltovich, P. J., & Glaser, R. (1981). Categorization and representation of physics problems by experts and novices. *Cognitive Science 5*, 121–152.

Chi, M. T. H., Glaser, R., & Farr, M. J. (Eds.). (1988). *The nature of expertise*. Hillsdale, NJ: Lawrence Erlbaum Associates.

Chi, M. T. H., Glaser, R., & Rees, E. (1982). Expertise in problem solving.

In R. J. Sternberg (Ed.), *Advances in the psychology of human intelligence* (Vol. 1, pp. 1–75). Hillsdale, NJ: Lawrence Erlbaum Associates.

Chipman, S. F., Segal, J. W., & Glaser, R. (Eds.). (1985). *Thinking and learning skills: Current research and open questions* (Vol. 2). Hillsdale, NJ: Lawrence Erlbaum Associates.

Chipuer, H. M., Rovine, M. J., & Plomin, R. (1990). LISREL modeling: Genetic and environmental influences on IQ revisited. *Intelligence, 14,* 11–29.

Clark, H. H., & Chase, W. G. (1972). On the process of comparing sentences against pictures. *Cognitive Psychology, 3,* 472–517.

Cooper, L. A. (1982). Strategies for visual comparison and representation: Individual differences. In R. J. Sternberg (Ed.), *Advances in the psychology of human intelligence* (Vol. 1, pp. 77–124). Hillsdale, NJ: Lawrence Erlbaum Associates.

Cooper, L. A., & Mumaw, R. J. (1985). Spatial aptitude. In R. F. Dillon (Ed.), *Individual differences in cognition* (Vol. 2, pp. 221–253). Orlando, FL: Academic Press.

Cronbach, L. J. (1951). Coefficient alpha and the internal structure of tests. *Psychometrika, 16,* 297–334.

Cronbach, L. J. (1957). The two disciplines of scientific psychology. *American Psychologist, 12,* 671–684.

Cronbach, L. J. (1967). How can instruction be adapted to individual differences? In R. M. Gagné (Ed.), *Learning and individual differences* (pp. 23–39). Columbus, OH: Merrill.

Cronbach, L. J. (1975a). Five decades of public controversy over mental testing. *American Psychologist, 30,* 1–14.

Cronbach, L. J. (1975b). Beyond the two disciplines of scientific psychology. *American Psychologist, 30,* 116–127.

Cronbach, L. J. (1984). *Essentials of psychological testing* (4th ed.). New York: Harper & Row.

Cronbach, L. J. (1990). *Essentials of psychological testing* (5th ed.). New York: Harper & Row.

Cronbach, L. J., & Gleser, G. C. (1965). *Psychological tests and personnel decisions* (2nd ed.). Urbana: University of Illinois Press.

Cronbach, L. J., Gleser, G. C., Nanda, H., & Rajaratnam, N. (1972). *The dependability of behavioral measurements: Theory of generalizability for scores and profiles.* New York: Wiley.

Cronbach, L. J., & Snow, R. E. (1977). *Aptitudes and instructional methods.* New York: Irvington.

Dahllöf, U. (1971). *Ability grouping, content validity and curriculum process analysis.* New York: Columbia University, Teachers College Press.

Deary, I. J., & Caryl, P. G. (1993). Intelligence, EEG and evoked potentials. In P. A. Vernon (Ed.), *Biological approaches to the study of human intelligence* (pp. 259–315). Norwood, NJ: Ablex.

de Bono, E. (1976). *Teaching thinking.* London: Temple Smith.

de Groot, A. D. (1951). War and the intelligence of youth. *Journal of Abnormal and Social Psychology, 46,* 577–597.

de Groot, A. D. (1965). *Thought and choice in chess.* The Hague: Mouton.

Demetriou, A., & Efklides, A. (1985). Structure and sequence of formal and postformal thought: General patterns and individual differences. *Child Development, 56,* 1062–1091.

Demetriou, A., & Efklides, A. (1987). Towards a determination of the dimensions and domains of individual differences in cognitive development. In E. De Corte, H. Lodewijks, R. Parmentier, & P. Span (Eds.), *Learning and instruction: European research in an international context* (Vol. 1, pp. 41–52). Oxford/Leuven: Pergamon/University of Leuven Press.

Demetriou, A., & Efklides, A. (1988). Experiential structuralism and neo-Piagetian theories: Toward an integrated model. In A. Demetriou (Ed.), *The neo-Piagetian theories of cognitive development: Toward an integration* (pp. 173–222). Amsterdam: North-Holland, Elsevier.

Demetriou, A., & Elfklides, A. (1994). Structure, development, and dynamics of mind: A meta-Piagetian theory. In A. Demetriou & A. Efklides (Eds.), *Intelligence, mind, and reasoning: Structure and development* (pp. 75–109). Amsterdam: North-Holland.

Demetriou, A., Efklides, A., & Platsidou, M. (1993). Experiential structuralism: A frame for unifying cognitive developmental theories. *Monographs of the Society for Research in Child Development, 58* (Serial No. 234).

Detterman, D. K., & Sternberg, R. J. (Eds.). (1982). *How and how much can intelligence be increased?* Norwood, NJ: Ablex.

Donders, F. C. (1969). On the speed of mental processes (W. G. Koster, Trans.). *Acta Psychologica, 30,* 412–431. (Original work published 1868)

DuBois, P. H. (1970). *A history of psychological testing.* Boston: Allyn & Bacon.

Duncan, O. D., Featherman, D. L., & Duncan, B. (1972). *Socioeconomic background and achievement.* New York: Seminar Press.

Eccles, J. S., & Harold, R. D. (1992). Gender differences in educational and occupational patterns among the gifted. In N. Colangelo, S. G. Assouline, & D. L. Ambroson (Eds.), *Talent development: Proceedings from the 1991 Henry B. Wallace National Research Symposium on Talent Development.* Unionville, NY: Trillium Press.

Eccles (Parsons), J. S., Adler, T. F., Futterman, R., Goff, S. B., Kacwala, C. M., Meece, J. L., & Midgley, C. (1983). Expectations, values, and academic behaviors. In J. T. Spence (Ed.), *Perspectives on achievement and achievement motivation.* San Francisco: Freeman.

Egan, D. E., & Schwartz, B. J. (1979). Chunking in recall of symbolic drawings. *Memory and Cognition, 7,* 149–158.

Ekstrom, R. B., French, J. W., & Harman, H. H. (1976). *Manual for kit of factor-referenced cognitive tests, 1976.* Princeton, NJ: Educational Testing Service.

Embretson, S. E. (1985). Multicomponent latent trait models for test design. In S. E. Embretson (Ed.), *Test design: Developments in psychology and psychometrics* (pp. 195–218). New York: Academic Press.

Embretson, S. E. (1986). Intelligence and its measurement: Extending contemporary theory to existing tests. In R. J. Sternberg (Ed.), *Advances in the psychology of human intelligence* (Vol. 3, pp. 335–368). Hillsdale, NJ: Lawrence Erlbaum Associates.

Embretson, S. E., Schneider, L. M., & Roth, D. L. (1986). Multiple processing strategies and the construct validity of verbal reasoning tests. *Journal of Educational Measurement, 23*(1), 13–32.

Ericsson, K. A. (1985). Memory skills. *Canadian Journal of Psychology, 39,* 188–231.

Ericsson, K. A., & Smith, J. (1991). Prospects and limits of the empirical study of expertise: An introduction. In K. A. Ericsson & J. Smith (Eds.), *Toward a general theory of expertise: Prospects and limits* (pp. 1–38). Cambridge, England: Cambridge University Press.

Estes, W. K. (1974). Learning theory and intelligence. *American Psychologist, 29,* 740–749.

Eysenck, H. J. (1988). The concept of "intelligence": Useful or useless? *Intelligence, 12*(1), 1–16.

Eysenck, H. J. (1993). The biological basis of intelligence. In P. A. Vernon (Ed.), *Biological approaches to the study of human intelligence* (pp. 1–32). Norwood, NJ: Ablex.

Fagan, J. F. (1984). The relationship of novelty preferences during infancy to later intelligence and later recognition memory. *Intelligence, 8,* 339–346.

Feingold, A. (1988). Cognitive gender differences are disappearing. *American Psychologist, 43,* 95–103.

Fennema, E., & Sherman, J. (1977). Sex-related differences in mathematics achievement, spatial visualization and affective factors. *American Educational Research Journal, 14,* 51–71.

Feuerstein, R., Rand, Y., Hoffman, M., & Miller, R. (1980). *Instrumental enrichment.* Baltimore, MD: University Park Press.

Fleishman, E. A. (1967). Individual differences in motor learning. In

R. M. Gagné (Ed.), *Learning and individual differences*. Columbus, OH: Merrill.

Flynn, J. R. (1980). *Race, IQ and Jensen*. London: Routledge & Kegan Paul.

Flynn, J. R. (1984). The mean IQ of Americans: Massive gains 1932–78. *Psychological Bulletin, 95*, 29–51.

Flynn, J. R. (1987a). Massive IQ gains in 14 nations: What IQ tests really measure. *Psychological Bulletin, 101*, 171–191.

Flynn, J. R. (1987b). The ontology of intelligence. In J. Forge (Ed.), *Measurement, realism and objectivity* (pp. 1–40). Dordrecht, The Netherlands: Reidel.

Fodor, J. A. (1983). *The modularity of mind: An essay on faculty psychology*. Cambridge, MA: MIT Press.

Frearson, W. M., & Eysenck, H. J. (1986). Intelligence, reaction time (RT) and a new "odd-man-out" RT paradigm. *Personality and Individual Differences, 7*, 807–817.

Freeman, F. S. (1934). *Individual differences*. New York: Henry Holt.

Fredriksen, N. (1986). Toward a broader conception of human intelligence. In R. J. Sternberg & R. K. Wagner (Eds.), *Practical intelligence: Origins of competence in the everyday world* (pp. 84–116). Cambridge, England: Cambridge University Press.

French, J. W. (1951). The description of aptitude and achievement tests in terms of rotated factors. *Psychometric Monographs, 5*.

French, J. W., Ekstrom, R. B., & Price, L. A. (1963). *Manual and kit of reference test for cognitive factors*. Princeton, NJ: Educational Testing Service.

Gagné, R. M. (1985). *The conditions of learning and theory of instruction*. New York: Holt, Rinehart & Winston.

Gailbraith, R. C. (1982). The confluence model and six divergent data sets: Comments on Zajonc and Bargh. *Intelligence, 6*, 305–310.

Galton, F. (1883). *Inquiries into human faculty and its development*. London: Macmillan.

Gamoran, A., & Mare, R. (1989). Secondary school tracking and educational inequality: Compensation, reinforcement, or neutrality? *American Journal of Sociology, 94*, 1146–1183.

Garber, H. L. (1988). *The Milwaukee Project: Preventing mental retardation in children at risk*. Washington, DC: American Association on Mental Retardation.

Gardner, H. (1983). *Frames of mind: The theory of multiple intelligences*. New York: Basic Books.

Gardner, H. (1992). Assessment in context: The alternative to standardized testing. In B. R. Gifford & M. C. O'Connor (Eds.), *Changing assessments: Alternative views of aptitude, achievement and instruction* (pp. 77–119). Boston: Kluwer.

Garrett, H. E. (1946). A developmental theory of intelligence. *American Psychologist, 1*, 372–378.

Glaser, R. (1972). Individuals and learning: The new aptitudes. *Educational Researcher, 1*, 5–13.

Goddard, H. H. (1908). The Binet and Simon tests of intellectual capacity. *The Training School, 5*, 3–9.

Goldberg, R. A., Schwartz, S., & Stewart, M. (1977). Individual differences in cognitive processes. *Journal of Educational Psychology, 69*, 9–14.

Goldman, S. R., Hogaboam, T. W., Bell, L. C., & Perfetti, C. A. (1980). Short-term retention of discourse during reading. *Journal of Educational Psychology, 72*, 647–655.

Goldman, S. R., & Pellegrino, J. W. (1984). Deductions about deduction: Analyses of developmental and individual differences. In R. J. Sternberg (Ed.), *Advances in the psychology of human intelligence* (Vol. 2, pp. 147–197). Hillsdale, NJ: Lawrence Erlbaum Associates.

Goldman, S. R., Pellegrino, J. W., Parseghian, P. E., & Sallis, R. (1982). Developmental and individual differences in verbal analogical reasoning by children. *Child Development, 53*, 550–559.

Gorsuch, R. L. (1983). *Factor analysis* (2nd ed.). Hillsdale, NJ: Lawrence Erlbaum Associates.

Gould, S. J. (1981). *The mismeasure of man*. New York: Norton.

Greeno, J. G. (1980). Some examples of cognitive task analysis with instructional implications. In R. E. Snow, P. A. Federico, & W. E. Montague (Eds.), *Aptitude, learning, and instruction: Vol. 2. Cognitive process analysis of learning and problem-solving*. Hillsdale, NJ: Lawrence Erlbaum Associates.

Guilford, J. P. (1967). *The nature of human intelligence*. New York: McGraw-Hill.

Guilford, J. P. (1972). Thurstone's primary mental abilities and structure-of-intellect abilities. *Psychological Bulletin, 77*, 129–143.

Guilford, J. P. (1981). Higher-order structure-of-intellect abilities. *Multivariate Behavioral Research, 16*, 411–435.

Guilford, J. P. (1985). The structure-of-intellect model. In B. B. Wolman (Ed.), *Handbook of intelligence: Theories, measurements, and applications* (pp. 225–266). New York: Wiley.

Guilford, J. P., & Hoepfner, R. (1971). *The analysis of intelligence*. New York: McGraw-Hill.

Gustafsson, J-E. (1984). A unifying model for the structure of intellectual abilities. *Intelligence, 8*, 179–203.

Gustafsson, J-E. (1988). Hierarchical models of individual differences in cognitive abilities. In R. J. Sternberg, *Advances in the psychology of human intelligence* (Vol. 4, pp. 35–71). Hillsdale, NJ: Lawrence Erlbaum Associates.

Gustafsson, J-E. (1989). Broad and narrow abilities in research on learning and instruction. In R. Kanfer, P. L. Ackerman, & R. Cudeck (Eds.), *Abilities, motivation, and methodology: The Minnesota Symposium on Learning and Individual Differences* (pp. 203–237). Hillsdale, NJ: Lawrence Erlbaum Associates.

Gustafsson, J-E. (1992). The relevance of factor analysis for the study of group differences. *Multivariate Behavioral Research, 27*(2), 239–247.

Gustafsson, J-E. (1994). Hierarchical models of intelligence and educational achievement. In A. Demetriou & A. Efklides (Eds.), *Intelligence, mind, and reasoning: Structure and development* (pp. 45–73). Amsterdam: North-Holland.

Gustafsson, J-E., & Balke, G. (1993). General and specific abilities as predictors of school achievement. *Multivariate Behavioral Research, 28*(4), 407–434.

Gustafsson, J-E., & Undheim, J. O. (1992). Stability and change in broad and narrow factors of intelligence from ages 12 to 15 years. *Journal of Educational Psychology, 84*(2), 141–149.

Guttman, L. (1954). A new approach to factor analysis: The radex. In P. F. Lazarsfeld (Ed.), *Mathematical thinking in the social sciences* (pp. 216–257). Glencoe, IL: Free Press.

Guttman, L. (1965a). A faceted definition of intelligence. *Studies in Psychology, Scripta Hierosolymitana, 14*, 166–181.

Guttman, L. (1965b). The structure of interrelations among intelligence tests. In *Proceedings of the 1964 Invitational Conference on Testing Problems*. Princeton, NJ: Educational Testing Service.

Guttman, L. (1968). A general nonmetric technique for finding the smallest coordinate space for a configuration of points. *Psychometrika, 33*, 469–506.

Guttman, L., & Levy, L. (1991). Two structural laws for intelligence tests. *Intelligence, 15*(1), 79–104.

Haier, R. J., Siegel, B. J., Neuchterlein, K. H., Hazlett, M. E., Wu, T. C., Paek, J., Browning, H. L., & Buchsbaum, M. S. (1988). Cortical glucose metabolic rate correlates of reasoning and attention studied with positron emission tomography. *Intelligence, 12*, 199–217.

Halpern, D. (1992). *Sex differences in cognitive abilities* (2nd ed.). Hillsdale, NJ: Lawrence Erlbaum Associates.

Hambleton, R. K. (1989). Principles and selected applications of item response theory. In R. L. Linn (Ed.), *Educational Measurement* (3rd ed., pp. 147–200). New York: American Council on Education/Macmillan.

Harman, H. (1967). *Modern factor analysis*. Chicago: University of Chicago Press.

Haskins, R. (1989). Beyond metaphor: The efficacy of early childhood education. *American Psychologist, 44*, 274–282.

Henderson, C. R., & Ceci, S. J. (1992). Is it better to be born rich or smart? A bioecological analysis of the contributions of IQ and socioeconomic status to adult income. In K. R. Billingsly, H. Brown, & E. Devohaves (Eds.), *Scientific excellence in supercomputing*. Athens, GA: Baldwin Press.

Henderson, N. D. (1982). Human behavior genetics. *Annual Review of Psychology, 33*, 403–440.

Hendrickson, A. E., & White, P. O. (1964). A quick method for rotation to oblique simple structure. *British Journal of Statistical Psychology, 17*, 65–70.

Hendrickson, D. E., & Hendrickson, A. E. (1980). The biological basis of individual differences in intelligence. *Personality and Individual Differences, 1*(1), 3–33.

Hick, W. E. (1952). On the rate of gain of information. *Quarterly Journal of Experimental Psychology, 4*, 11–26.

Horn, J. L. (1966). Integration of structural and developmental concepts in the theory of fluid and crystallized intelligence. In R. B. Cattell (Ed.), *Handbook of multivariate experimental psychology*. Chicago: Rand McNally.

Horn, J. L. (1967). On subjectivity in factor analysis. *Educational and Psychological Measurement, 27*, 811–820.

Horn, J. L. (1968). Organization of abilities and the development of intelligence. *Psychological Review, 72*, 242–259.

Horn, J. L. (1976). Human abilities: A review of research and theory in the early 1970s. *Annual Review of Psychology, 27*, 437–485.

Horn, J. L. (1978). Human ability systems. In P. B. Baltes (Ed.), *Life-span development and behavior* (pp. 211–256). New York: Academic Press.

Horn, J. L. (1980). Concepts of intellect in relation to learning and adult development. *Intelligence, 4*, 285–317.

Horn, J. L. (1986). Intellectual ability concepts. In R. J. Sternberg (Ed.), *Advances in the psychology of human intelligence* (Vol. 3, pp. 35–77). Hillsdale, NJ: Lawrence Erlbaum Associates.

Horn, J. L. (1989). Models of intelligence. In R. L. Linn (Ed.), *Intelligence: Measurement, theory and public policy* (pp. 29–73). Urbana: University of Illinois Press.

Horn, J. L., & Cattell, R. B. (1966). Refinement and test of the theory of fluid and crystallized intelligence. *Journal of Educational Psychology, 57*, 253–270.

Horn, J. L., & Hofer, S. M. (1992). Major abilities and development in the adult period. In R. J. Sternberg & C. Berg (Eds.), *Intellectual development* (pp. 44–99). Cambridge, England: Cambridge University Press.

Horn, J. L., & Knapp, J. R. (1973). On the subjective character of the empirical base of Guilford's structure-of-intellect model. *Psychological Bulletin, 80*, 33–43.

Horn, J. L., & Knapp, J. R. (1974). Thirty wrongs do not make a right: Reply to Guilford. *Psychological Bulletin, 81*, 502–504.

Horn, J. L., & Stankov, L. (1982). Auditory and visual factors of intelligence. *Intelligence, 6*, 165–185.

Hotelling, H. (1933). Analysis of a complex of statistical variables into principal components. *Journal of Educational Psychology, 24*, 417–441, 498–520.

Howe, M. J. A., & Smith, J. (1988). Calendar calculating in "idiot savants": How do they do it? *British Journal of Psychology, 79*, 371–386.

Hultsch, D. F., Hertzog, C., & Dixon, R. A. (1984). Text recall in adulthood: The role of intellectual abilities. *Developmental Psychology, 20*(6), 1193–1209.

Humphreys, L. G. (1962). The organization of human abilities. *American Psychologist, 17*, 475–483.

Humphreys, L. G. (1967). Critique of "Theory of fluid and crystallized intelligence: A critical experiment." *Journal of Educational Psychology, 58*, 129–136.

Humphreys, L. G. (1979). The construct of general intelligence. *Intelligence, 3*, 105–120.

Humphreys, L. G. (1985). General intelligence: An integration of factor, test and simplex theory. In B. B. Wolman (Ed.), *Handbook of intelligence: Theories, measurements, and applications* (pp. 201–224). New York: Wiley.

Humphreys, L. G. (1988). Trends in levels of academic achievement of blacks and other minorities. *Intelligence, 12*(3), 231–260.

Humphreys, L. G. (1989). Intelligence: Three kinds of instability and their consequences for policy. In R. L. Linn (Ed.), *Intelligence: Measurement, theory and public policy* (pp. 193–216). Urbana: University of Illinois Press.

Hunt, E. B., Frost, N., & Lunneborg, C. (1973). Individual differences in cognition: A new approach to intelligence. In G. H. Bower (Ed.), *Psychology of learning and motivation* (Vol. 3). New York: Academic Press.

Hunt, E. B. (1978). Mechanisms of verbal ability. *Psychological Review, 85*, 109–130.

Hunt, E. B. (1985). Verbal ability. In R. J. Sternberg (Ed.), *Human abilities: An information-processing approach* (pp. 31–58). New York: Freeman.

Hunt, E. B., Lunneborg, C., & Lewis, J. (1975). What does it mean to be high verbal? *Cognitive Psychology, 7*, 194–227.

Husén, T. (1951). The influence of schooling upon IQ. *Theoria, 17*, 61–88.

Husén, T., & Tuijnman, A. (1991). The contribution of formal schooling to the increase in intellectual capital. *Educational Researcher, 20*, 17–25.

Huttenlocher, J., Haight, W., Bryk, A., Seltzer, M., & Lyons, T. (1991). Early vocabulary growth: Relation to language input and gender. *Developmental Psychology, 27*(2), 236–248.

Hyde, J. S., Fennema, E., & Lamon, S. J. (1990). Gender differences in mathematics performance: A meta-analysis. *Psychological Bulletin, 107*, 139–155.

Hyde, J. S., & Linn, M. C. (1988). Gender differences in verbal ability: A meta-analysis. *Psychological Bulletin, 104*, 153–169.

Härnqvist, K. (1968a). Relative changes in intelligence from 13 to 18: I. Background and methodology. *Scandinavian Journal of Educational Research, 9*, 50–64.

Härnqvist, K. (1968b). Relative changes in intelligence from 13 to 18: II. Results. *Scandinavian Journal of Psychology, 9*, 65–82.

Härnqvist, K. (1973). Canonical analyses of mental test profiles. *Scandinavian Journal of Psychology, 14*, 282–290.

Härnqvist, K. (1990). Long-term effects of education. In K. Härnqvist & N. E. Svensson (Eds.), *Swedish research in a changing society* (pp. 323–338). Hedemora, Sweden: Gidlunds.

Härnqvist, K., & Stahle, G. (1977). *An ecological analysis of test score changes over time* (Reports from the Institute of Education, University of Göteborg, No. 64). Göteborg, Sweden: University of Göteborg.

Jackson, N. E., Donaldson, G. W., & Cleland, L. N. (1988). The structure of precocious reading ability. *Journal of Educational Psychology, 80*(2), 234–243.

Jencks, C., Smith, M., Acland, H., Bane, M. J., Cohen, D., Gintis, H., Heyns, B., & Michelson, S. (1972). *Inequality: A reassessment of the effects of family and schooling in America*. New York: Basic Books.

Jensen, A. R. (1969). How much can we boost IQ and scholastic achievement? *Harvard Educational Review, 39*, 1–123.

Jensen, A. R. (1973). *Educability and group differences*. London: Methuen.

Jensen, A. R. (1980). *Bias in mental testing*. New York: Free Press.

Jensen, A. R. (1982). The chronometry of intelligence. In R. J. Sternberg (Ed.), *Advances in the psychology of human intelligence* (Vol. 1, pp. 255–310). Hillsdale, NJ: Lawrence Erlbaum Associates.

Jensen, A. R. (1985). The nature of the black-white difference on various psychometric tests: Spearman's hypothesis. *Behavioral and Brain Sciences, 8,* 193–263.

Jensen, A. R. (1987a). The *g* beyond factor analysis. In R. R. Ronning, J. A. Glover, J. C. Conley, & J. C. Witt (Eds.), *The influence of cognitive psychology on testing* (Buros-Nebraska Symposium on Measurement and Testing, Vol. 3, pp. 87–142). Hillsdale, NJ: Lawrence Erlbaum Associates.

Jensen, A. R. (1987b). Individual differences in the Hick paradigm. In P. A. Vernon (Ed.), *Speed of information-processing and intelligence* (pp. 101–175). Norwood, NJ: Ablex.

Jensen, A. R., & Figueroa, R. A. (1975). Forward and backward digit-span interaction with race and IQ: Predictions from Jensen's theory. *Journal of Educational Psychology, 67,* 882–893.

Jensen, A. R., & Reynolds, C. R. (1982). Race, social class and ability patterns on the WISC-R. *Personality and Individual Differences, 3,* 423–438.

Jones, H. E., & Bayley, N. (1941). The Berkeley Growth Study. *Child Development, 12,* 167–173.

Just, M. A., & Carpenter, P. A. (1985). Cognitive coordinate systems: Accounts of mental rotation and individual differences in spatial ability. *Psychological Review, 92,* 137–171.

Jöreskog, K. G. (1971). Statistical analysis of sets of congeneric tests. *Psychometrika, 36,* 109–133.

Jöreskog, K. G., & Sörbom, D. (1989). *LISREL 7: A guide to the program and applications.* Chicago: SPSS.

Jöreskog, K. G., & Sörbom, D. (1993). *LISREL 8: Structural equation modelling with the SIMPLIS command language.* Chicago: Scientific Software International.

Kaiser, H. F. (1958). The varimax criterion for analytic rotation in factor analysis. *Psychometrika, 23,* 187–200.

Kamin, L. J. (1974). *The science and politics of IQ.* New York: Wiley.

Kaufman, A. S. (1975). Factor analysis of the WISC-R at eleven age levels between 6½ and 16½ years. *Journal of Consulting and Clinical Psychology, 43,* 135–147.

Kaufman, A. S., & Kaufman, N. L. (1983). *Kaufman Assessment Battery for Children: Interpretive manual.* Circle Pines, MN: American Guidance Service.

Keating, D. P. (1984). The emperor's new clothes: The "new look" in intelligence research. In R. J. Sternberg (Ed.), *Advances in the psychology of human intelligence* (Vol. 2, pp. 1–46). Hillsdale, NJ: Lawrence Erlbaum Associates.

Keating, D. P., & Bobbitt, B. L. (1978). Individual and developmental differences in cognitive-processing components of mental ability. *Child Development, 49,* 155–167.

Keating, D. P., List, J. A., & Merriman, W. E. (1985). Cognitive processing and cognitive ability: A multivariate validity investigation. *Intelligence, 9,* 149–170.

Kimura, D., & Hampson, E. (1993). Neural and hormonal mechanisms mediating sex differences in cognition. In P. A. Vernon (Ed.), *Biological approaches to the study of human intelligence* (pp. 375–397). Norwood, NJ: Ablex.

Kintsch, W. (1974). *The representation of meaning in memory.* Hillsdale, NJ: Lawrence Erlbaum Associates.

Klauer, K. J. (1990). A process theory of inductive reasoning tested by the teaching of domain-specific thinking strategies. *European Journal of Psychology of Education, 5*(2), 191–206.

Kline, P. (1990). *Intelligence: The psychometric view.* London: Routledge.

Kline, P. (1991). Sternberg's components: Non-contingent concepts. *Personality and Individual Differences, 12*(9), 873–876.

Kosslyn, S. M. (1981). The medium and the message in mental imagery: A theory. *Psychological Review, 88,* 46–66.

Kotovsky, K., & Simon, H. A. (1973). Empirical tests of a theory of human acquisition of concepts for sequential events. *Cognitive Psychology, 4,* 399–424.

Kramer, J. J., & Connley, J. C. (1992). *The eleventh mental measurements yearbook.* Lincoln: University of Nebraska Press.

Kranzler, J. H., & Jensen, A. R. (1989). Inspection time and intelligence: A meta-analysis. *Intelligence, 13,* 329–347.

Kranzler, J. H., & Jensen, A. R. (1991). The nature of psychometric *g*: Unitary process or a number of independent processes? *Intelligence, 15*(4), 397–422.

Kulik, C-C., & Kulik, J. A. (1982). Effects of ability grouping on secondary school students: A meta-analysis of evaluation findings. *American Educational Research Journal, 19,* 415–428.

Kyllonen, P. C., & Christal, R. E. (1989). Cognitive modeling of learning abilities: A status report of LAMP. In R. Dillon & J. W. Pellegrino (Eds.), *Testing: Theoretical and applied issues* (pp. 146–173). New York: Freeman.

Kyllonen, P. C., & Christal, R. E. (1990). Reasoning ability is (little more than) working-memory capacity. *Intelligence, 14*(4), 389–433.

Kyllonen, P. C., Lohman, D. F., & Snow, R. E. (1984). Effects of aptitudes, strategy training, and task facets on spatial task performance. *Journal of Educational Psychology, 76,* 130–145.

Kyllonen, P. C., Lohman, D. F., & Woltz, D. J. (1984). Componential modeling of alternative strategies for performing spatial tasks. *Journal of Educational Psychology, 76*(6), 1325–1345.

Kyllonen, P. C., & Shute, V. J. (1989). A taxonomy of learning skills. In P. L. Ackerman, R. J. Sternberg, & R. Glaser (Eds.), *Learning and individual differences: Advances in theory and research* (pp. 117–163). New York: Freeman.

Lansman, M. (1981). Ability factors and the speed of information processing. In M. Friedman, J. P. Das, & N. O'Connor (Eds.), *Intelligence and learning* (pp. 441–457). New York: Plenum Press.

Larson, G., Merritt, C. R., & Williams, S. E. (1988). Information processing and intelligence: Some implications of task complexity. *Intelligence, 12*(2), 131–147.

Larson, G. E. (1990). Novelty as "representational complexity": A cognitive interpretation of Sternberg and Gastel (1989). *Intelligence, 14*(2), 235–238.

Larson, G. E., & Alderton, D. L. (1990). Reaction time variability and intelligence: A "worst performance" analysis of individual differences. *Intelligence, 14*(3), 309–325.

Lave, J. (1988). *Cognition in practice.* New York: Cambridge University Press.

Lavin, D. E. (1965). *The prediction of academic performance.* New York: Wiley.

Lee, E. S. (1951). Migration: A Philadelphia test of the Klineberg hypothesis. *American Sociological Review, 16,* 227–232.

Linn, M. C., & Petersen, A. C. (1985). Emergence and characterization of sex differences in spatial ability: A meta-analysis. *Child Development, 56,* 1479–1498.

Lipman, M., Sharp, A. N., & Oscanyan, F. S. (1980). *Philosophy in the classroom.* Philadelphia: Temple University Press.

Loehlin, J. C. (1989). Partitioning environmental and genetic contributions to behavioral development. *American Psychologist, 44,* 1285–1292.

Loehlin, J. C. (1992). *Latent variable models. An introduction to factor, path, and structural analysis* (2nd ed.). Hillsdale, NJ: Lawrence Erlbaum Associates.

Loehlin, J. C., Lindzey, G., & Spuhler, J. M. (1975). *Race differences in intelligence.* San Francisco: Freeman.

Loehlin, J. C., Willerman, L., & Horn, J. M. (1988). Human behavior genetics. *Annual Review of Psychology, 33,* 101–133.

Loevinger, J. (1951). Intelligence. In H. Nelson (Ed.), *Theoretical foundations of psychology.* New York: Van Nostrand.

Lohman, D. F. (1988). Spatial abilities as traits, processes, and knowledge. In R. J. Sternberg (Ed.), *Advances in the psychology of human intelligence* (Vol. 4, pp. 181–248). Hillsdale, NJ: Lawrence Erlbaum Associates.

Lohman, D. F. (1989). Theory and research in intelligence. *Review of Educational Research, 59*(4), 333–373.

Lohman, D. F. (1994). Component scores as residual variation (or why the intercept correlates best). *Intelligence, 19*(1), 1–11.

Lohman, D. F., & Kyllonen, P. C. (1983). Individual differences in solution strategy on spatial tasks. In R. F. Dillon & R. R. Schmeck (Eds.), *Individual differences in cognition* (Vol. 1, pp. 105–135). New York: Academic Press.

Lord, F. M. (1980). *Applications of item response theory to practical testing problems.* Hillsdale, NJ: Lawrence Erlbaum Associates.

Lord, F. M., & Novick, M. R. (1968). *Statistical theories of mental test scores.* Reading, MA: Addison-Wesley.

Lorge, I. (1945). Schooling makes a difference. *Teachers College Record, 46,* 483–492.

Lubinski, D., & Dawis, R. V. (1992). Aptitudes, skills, and proficiencies. In M. D. Dunnette (Ed.), *Handbook of industrial and organizational ability* (2nd ed., Vol. 3, pp. 1–59). Palo Alto, CA: Consulting Psychologists Press.

Lubinski, D., & Humphreys, L. G. (1990). A broadly based analysis of mathematical giftedness. *Intelligence, 14,* 327–355.

Maccoby, E. E., & Jacklin, C. N. (1974). *The psychology of sex differences.* Stanford, CA: Stanford University Press.

MacKenzie, B. (1980). Hypothesized genetic racial differences in IQ: A criticism of three proposed lines of evidence. *Behavior Genetics, 10,* 225–234.

MacKenzie, B. (1984). Explaining race differences in IQ: The logic, the methodology, and the evidence. *American Psychologist, 39,* 1214–1233.

Maclure, S., & Davies, P. (Eds.). (1991). *Learning to think: Thinking to learn.* Oxford: Pergamon Press.

Marjoribanks, K., & Walberg, H. J. (1975). Family environment: Sibling constellation and social class correlates. *Journal of Biosocial Science, 7,* 15–25.

Marshalek, B., Lohman, D. F., & Snow, R. E. (1983). The complexity continuum in the radex and hierarchical models of intelligence. *Intelligence, 7,* 107–128.

Matarazzo, J. D. (1972). *Wechsler's measurement and appraisal of adult intelligence* (5th ed.). Baltimore, MD: Williams & Wilkins.

McCrae, R. R., & Costa, P. T., Jr. (1990). *Personality in adulthood.* New York: Guilford.

McDonald, R. P. (1985). *Factor analysis and related methods.* Hillsdale, NJ: Lawrence Erlbaum Associates.

McGue, M., & Bouchard, T. J., Jr. (1989). Genetic and environmental determinants of information processing and special mental abilities: A twin analysis. In R. J. Sternberg (Ed.), *Advances in the psychology of human intelligence* (Vol. 5, pp. 7–46). Hillsdale, NJ: Lawrence Erlbaum Associates.

McKey, R., Condelli, L., Ganson, H., Barrett, B., McDonkey, C., & Plantz, M. (1985). *The impact of Head Start on children, families, and communities: Head Start Synthesis Project.* Washington, DC: U.S. Government Printing Office.

McNemar, Q. (1942). *The revision of the Stanford-Binet scale.* Boston: Houghton-Mifflin.

McNemar, Q. (1964). Lost: Our intelligence? Why? *American Psychologist, 19,* 871–882.

Messick, S. (1992). Multiple intelligences or multilevel intelligences? Selective emphasis on distinctive properties of hierarchy: On Gardner's *Frames of Mind* and Sternberg's *Beyond IQ* in the context of theory and research on the structure of human abilities. *Psychological Inquiry, 3*(4), 365–384.

Messick, S., & Jungeblut, A. (1987). Time and method in coaching for the SAT. *Psychological Bulletin, 89,* 191–216.

Meyer, W. J., & Bendig, A. W. (1961). A longitudinal study of mental abilities. *Journal of Educational Psychology, 52,* 50–60.

Mischel, W. (1968). *Personality and assessment.* New York: Wiley.

Morris, P. E., Tweedy, M., & Gruneberg, M. M. (1985). Interest, knowl-edge and the memorization of soccer scores. *British Journal of Psychology, 76,* 415–425.

Mulaik, S. A. (1972). *The foundations of factor analysis.* New York: McGraw-Hill.

Murphy, K. R., & Davidshofer, C. O. (1988). *Psychological testing: Principles and applications.* Englewood Cliffs, NJ: Prentice Hall.

Muthén, B. (1988). *LISCOMP User's Guide.* Mooresville, IL: Scientific Software.

Neisser, U. (1976). General, academic, and artificial intelligence. In L. Resnick (Ed.), *The nature of intelligence* (pp. 134–144). Hillsdale, NJ: Lawrence Erlbaum Associates.

Nettlebeck, T. (1987). Inspection time and intelligence. In P. A. Vernon (Ed.), *Speed of information-processing and intelligence.* Norwood, NJ: Ablex.

Newell, A., & Rosenbloom, P. S. (1981). Mechanisms of skill acquisition and the law of practice. In J. R. Anderson (Ed.), *Cognitive skills and their acquisition* (pp. 1–55). Hillsdale, NJ: Lawrence Erlbaum Associates.

Nisbet, J. (1991). Methods and approaches. In S. Maclure & P. Davies (Eds.), *Learning to think: Thinking to learn* (pp. 177–185). Oxford: Pergamon Press.

Nordvik, H., & Undheim, J. O. (1993). *Cognitive abilities in the prediction and understanding of achievement.* Paper presented at the 5th European Conference of EARLI, Aix-en-Provence, France, August 31–September 5.

Oakes, J. (1985). *Keeping track: How schools structure inequality.* New Haven, CT: Yale University Press.

Oakes, J., Gamoran, A., & Page, R. (1991). Curriculum differentiation: Opportunities, consequences, and meanings. In P. Jackson (Ed.), *Handbook of Research on Curriculum.* New York: Macmillan.

O'Connor, M. C. (1992). Rethinking aptitude, achievement, and instruction: Cognitive science research and the framing of assessment policy. In B. R. Gifford & M. C. O'Connor (Eds.), *Changing assessments: Alternative views of aptitude, achievement and instruction* (pp. 9–35). Boston: Kluwer.

Paine, R. S. (1957). The variability in manifestations on untreated patients with phenylketonuria (phenylpyruvia aciduria). *Pediatrics, 20,* 290–301.

Pawlik, K. (1966). Concepts and calculations in human cognitive abilities. In R. B. Cattell (Ed.), *Handbook of multivariate experimental psychology.* Chicago: Rand McNally.

Pellegrino, J. W. (1985). Inductive reasoning ability. In R. J. Sternberg (Ed.), *Human abilities: An information-processing approach* (pp. 195–225). San Francisco: Freeman.

Pellegrino, J. W., & Glaser, R. (1979). Cognitive correlates and components in the analysis of individual differences. In R. J. Sternberg & D. K. Detterman (Eds.), *Human intelligence: Perspectives on its theory and measurement* (pp. 61–88). Norwood, NJ: Ablex.

Pellegrino, J. W., & Glaser, R. (1980). Components of inductive reasoning. In R. E. Snow, P. A. Federico, & W. E. Montague (Eds.), *Aptitude, learning, and instruction: Vol. 1. Cognitive process analyses of aptitude* (pp. 177–218). Hillsdale, NJ: Lawrence Erlbaum Associates.

Pellegrino, J. W., & Glaser, R. (1982). Analyzing aptitudes for learning: Inductive reasoning. In R. Glaser (Ed.), *Advances in instructional psychology* (Vol. 2, pp. 269–345). Hillsdale, NJ: Lawrence Erlbaum Associates.

Pellegrino, J. W., & Kail, R. (1982). Process analyses of spatial aptitude. In R. J. Sternberg (Ed.), *Advances in the psychology of human intelligence* (Vol. 1, pp. 311–366). Hillsdale, NJ: Lawrence Erlbaum Associates.

Perfetti, C. A. (1985). Reading ability. In R. J. Sternberg (Ed.), *Human abilities: An information-processing approach.* New York: Freeman.

Perfetti, C. A., & Roth, S. (1981). Some of the interactive processes in reading and their role in reading skill. In A. M. Lesgold & C. A. Perfetti (Eds.), *Interactive processes in reading.* Hillsdale, NJ: Lawrence Erlbaum Associates.

Plomin, R. (1988). The nature and nurture of cognitive abilities. In R. J. Sternberg (Ed.), *Advances in the psychology of human intelligence* (Vol. 4, pp. 1–33). Hillsdale, NJ: Lawrence Erlbaum Associates.

Plomin, R., & Daniels, D. (1987). Why are two children in the same family so different from each other? *Behavioral and Brain Sciences, 10,* 44–54.

Plomin, R., DeFries, J. C., & Fulker, D. W. (1988). *Nature and nurture during infancy and early childhood.* Cambridge, England: Cambridge University Press.

Plomin, R., DeFries, J. C., & Loehlin, J. C. (1977). Genotype-environment interaction and correlation in the analysis of human behavior. *Psychological Bulletin, 84,* 309–322.

Poltrock, S. E., & Brown, P. (1984). Individual differences in visual imagery and spatial ability. *Intelligence, 8,* 93–138.

Posner, M. I., & Mitchell, R. F. (1967). Chronometric analysis of classification. *Psychological Review, 74,* 392–409.

Pylyshyn, Z. W. (1981). The imagery debate: Analogue media versus tacit knowledge. *Psychological Review, 87,* 16–45.

Raaheim, K. (1988). Intelligence and task novelty. In R. J. Sternberg, *Advances in the psychology of human intelligence* (Vol. 4, pp. 73–97). Hillsdale, NJ: Lawrence Erlbaum Associates.

Rasch, G. (1960). *Probabilistic models for some intelligence and attainment tests.* Copenhagen: Danish Institute for Educational Research.

Raven, J. K. C. (1938). *Progressive Matrices: Sets A, B, C, D & E.* London: H. K. Lewis.

Ree, M. J., & Earles, J. A. (1991a). Predicting training success: Not much more than g. *Personnel Psychology, 44*(2), 321–332.

Ree, M. J., & Earles, J. A. (1991b). The stability of g across different methods of estimation. *Intelligence, 15,* 271–278.

Reed, T. E., & Jensen, A. R. (1991). Arm nerve conduction velocity (NCV), brain NCV, reaction time, and intelligence. *Intelligence, 15,* 33–47.

Resnick, L. B. (Ed.). (1976). *The nature of intelligence.* Hillsdale, NJ: Lawrence Erlbaum Associates.

Resnick, L. B. (1987). *Education and learning to think.* Washington, DC: National Academy Press.

Resnick, L. B., & Resnick, D. P. (1992). Assessing the thinking curriculum: New tools for educational reform. In B. R. Gifford & M. C. O'Connor (Eds.), *Changing assessments: Alternative views of aptitude, achievement and instruction* (pp. 37–75). Boston: Kluwer.

Reuterberg, S-E., & Gustafsson, J-E. (1992). Confirmatory factor analysis and reliability: Testing measurement model assumptions. *Educational and Psychological Measurement, 52,* 795–811.

Richardson, K. (1991). Reasoning with Raven—in and out of context. *British Journal of Educational Psychology, 61*(2), 129–138.

Roberts, R. D., Beh, H. C., & Stankov, L. (1988). Hick's law, competing-task performance, and intelligence. *Intelligence, 12,* 111–130.

Royce, J. M., Darlington, R. B., & Murray, H. (1983). Pooled analyses: Findings across studies. In Consortium for Longitudinal Studies (Ed.), *As the twig is bent . . . Lasting effects of preschool programs.* Hillsdale, NJ: Lawrence Erlbaum Associates.

Rumelhart, D. E. (1977). *An introduction to human information processing.* New York: Wiley.

Sackett, P. R., Tenopyr, M. L., Schmidt, N., & Kahn, J. (1985). Commentary on forty questions about validity generalization and meta-analysis. *Personnel Psychology, 38,* 697–798.

Salthouse, T. A., Babcock, R. L., Mitchell, D. R. D., Palmon, R., & Skovronek, E. (1990). Sources of individual differences in spatial visualization ability. *Intelligence, 14,* 187–230.

SAS Institute (1990). *SAS/STAT user's guide (version 6)* (4th ed.). Cary, NC: SAS Institute.

Scarr, S. (1989). Protecting general intelligence: Constructs and consequences for interventions. In R. L. Linn (Ed.), *Intelligence: Measurement, theory and public policy* (pp. 74–118). Urbana: University of Illinois Press.

Scarr, S., & Weinberg, R. A. (1976). I.Q. test performance of black children adopted by white families. *American Psychologist, 31,* 726–739.

Schafer, E. P. W. (1982). Neural adaptability: A biological determinant of behavioral intelligence. *International Journal of Neuroscience, 17,* 183–191.

Schank, R., & Abelson, R. P. (1977). *Scripts, plans, goals, and understanding.* Hillsdale, NJ: Lawrence Erlbaum Associates.

Schmid, J., & Leiman, J. M. (1957). The development of hierarchical factor solutions. *Psychometrika, 22,* 53–61.

Schmidt, F. L., & Hunter, J. E. (1981). Employment testing: Old theories and new research findings. *American Psychologist, 26,* 1128–1137.

Schmidt, F. L., Pearlman, K., Hunter, J. E., & Hirsh, H. R. (1985). Forty questions about validity generalization and meta-analysis. *Personnel Psychology, 38,* 697–789.

Schneider, W., Körkel, J., & Weinert, F. E. (1990). Expert knowledge, general abilities, and text processing. In W. Schneider & F. E. Weinert (Eds.), *Interactions among aptitudes, strategies, and knowledge in cognitive performance* (pp. 235–251). New York: Springer.

Scott-Jones, D. (1992). Family and community interventions affecting the development of cognitive skills in children. In T. G. Sticht, M. J. Beeler, & B. A. McDonald (Eds.), *The intergenerational transfer of cognitive skills: Vol. I. Programs, policy, and research issues* (pp. 84–108). Norwood, NJ: Ablex.

Segal, J. W., Chipman, S. F., & Glaser, R. (Eds.). (1985). *Thinking and learning skills: Vol. 1. Relating instruction to research.* Hillsdale, NJ: Lawrence Erlbaum Associates.

Shepard, R. N., & Metzler, J. (1971). Mental rotation of three dimensional objects. *Science, 171,* 701–703.

Shepard, R. N., Romney, A. K., & Nerlove, S. B. (Eds.). (1972). *Multidimensional scaling: Theory and applications in the behavioral sciences* (Vol. 1). New York: Seminar Press.

Sherman, M., & Key, C. B. (1932). The intelligence of isolated mountain children. *Child Development, 3,* 279–290.

Slavin, R. E. (1987a). Mastery learning reconsidered. *Review of Educational Research, 57,* 175–213.

Slavin, R. E. (1987b). Ability grouping and student achievement in elementary schools: A best-evidence synthesis. *Review of Educational Research, 57,* 293–336.

Snow, R. E. (1977). Research on aptitudes: A progress report. In L. S. Shulman (Ed.), *Review of Research in Education.* Itasca, IL: Peacock.

Snow, R. E. (1978). Theory and method for research on aptitude processes. *Intelligence, 2,* 225–278.

Snow, R. E. (1980). Aptitude processes. In R. E. Snow, P. A. Federico, & W. E. Montague (Eds.), *Aptitude, learning, and instruction: Vol. 1. Cognitive process analysis of aptitude* (pp. 27–64). Hillsdale, NJ: Lawrence Erlbaum Associates.

Snow, R. E. (1981). Toward a theory of aptitude for learning: I. Fluid and crystallized abilities and their correlates. In M. P. Friedman, J. P. Das, & N. O'Connor (Eds.), *Intelligence and learning* (pp. 345–362). New York: Plenum Press.

Snow, R. E. (1989). Aptitude-treatment interaction as a framework for research on individual differences in learning. In P. L. Ackerman, R. J. Sternberg, & R. Glaser (Eds.), *Learning and individual differences: Advances in theory and research* (pp. 13–59). New York: Freeman.

Snow, R. E. (1991). The concept of aptitude. In R. E. Snow & D. E. Wiley (Eds.), *Improving inquiry in social science* (pp. 249–284). Hillsdale, NJ: Lawrence Erlbaum Associates.

Snow, R. E., Kyllonen, P. C., & Marshalek, B. (1984). The topography of ability and learning correlations. In R. J. Sternberg (Ed.), *Advances in the psychology of human intelligence* (Vol. 2, pp. 47–104). Hillsdale, NJ: Lawrence Erlbaum Associates.

Snow, R. E., & Lohman, D. F. (1984). Toward a theory of cognitive aptitude for learning from instruction. *Journal of Educational Psychology, 76,* 347–376.

Snow, R. E., & Lohman, D. F. (1989). Implications of cognitive psychology for educational measurement. In R. Linn (Ed.), *Educational measurement* (3rd ed., pp. 263–331). New York: Macmillan.

Snow, R. E., & Yalow, E. (1982). Education and intelligence. In R. J. Sternberg (Ed.), *Handbook of human intelligence* (pp. 493–585). Cambridge, England: Cambridge University Press.

Snyderman, M., & Rothman, S. (1987). Survey of expert opinions on intelligence and aptitude-testing. *American Psychologist, 42,* 137–144.

Spearman, C. (1904a). The proof and measurement of association between two things. *American Journal of Psychology, 15,* 72–101.

Spearman, C. (1904b). "General intelligence," objectively determined and measured. *American Journal of Psychology, 15,* 201–293.

Spearman, C. (1923). *The nature of 'intelligence' and the principles of cognition.* London: Macmillan.

Spearman, C. (1927). *The abilities of man.* London: Macmillan.

Spilich, G. J., Vesonder, G. T., Chiesi, H. L., & Voss, J. F. (1979). Text processing of domain-related information for individuals with high and low domain knowledge. *Journal of Verbal Learning and Verbal Behavior, 18,* 275–290.

Spiro, R. J. (1980). Constructive processes in prose comprehension and recall. In R. J. Spiro, B. C. Bruce, & W. F. Brewer (Eds.), *Theoretical issues in reading comprehension.* Hillsdale, NJ: Lawrence Erlbaum Associates.

Spitz, H. H. (1986). *The raising of intelligence: A selected history of attempts to raise retarded intelligence.* Hillsdale, NJ: Lawrence Erlbaum Associates.

Spitz, H. H. (1992). Early childhood intervention. In T. G. Sticht, M. J. Beeler, & B. A. McDonald (Eds.), *The intergenerational transfer of cognitive skills: Vol. 1. Programs, policy, and research issues* (pp. 17–31). Norwood, NJ: Ablex.

Stake, R. E. (1961). Learning parameters, aptitudes, and achievement. *Psychometric Monographs, 9.*

Stankov, L. (1987). Competing tasks and attentional resources: Exploring the limits of the primary-secondary paradigm. *Australian Journal of Psychology, 39,* 123–137.

Stankov, L. (1988). Single tests, competing tasks and their relationship to broad factors of intelligence. *Personality and Individual Differences, 9,* 25–33.

Stankov, L. (1991). The effects of training and practice on human abilities. In H. A. H. Rowe (Ed.), *Intelligence: Reconceptualization and measurement* (pp. 97–117). Hillsdale, NJ: Lawrence Erlbaum Associates.

Stankov, L., & Horn, J. L. (1980). Human abilities revealed through auditory tests. *Journal of Educational Psychology, 72,* 21–44.

Stanovich, K. E. (1981). Attentional and automatic context effects in reading. In A. M. Lesgold & C. A. Perfetti (Eds.), *Interactive processes in reading.* Hillsdale, NJ: Lawrence Erlbaum Associates.

Sternberg, R. J. (1977). *Intelligence, information processing, and analogical reasoning: The componential analysis of human abilities.* Hillsdale, NJ: Lawrence Erlbaum Associates.

Sternberg, R. J. (1980). Sketch on a componential subtheory of human intelligence. *Behavioral and Brain Sciences, 3,* 573–614.

Sternberg, R. J. (1981a). Intelligence and nonentrenchment. *Journal of Educational Psychology, 73,* 1–16.

Sternberg, R. J. (1981b). Nothing fails like success: The search for an intelligent paradigm for studying intelligence. *Journal of Educational Psychology, 73,* 142–155.

Sternberg, R. J. (1982). Reasoning, problem solving, and intelligence. In R. J. Sternberg (Ed.), *Handbook of human intelligence* (pp. 225–307). Cambridge, England: Cambridge University Press.

Sternberg, R. J. (1985). *Beyond IQ: A triarchic theory of human intelligence.* Cambridge, England: Cambridge University Press.

Sternberg, R. J. (1990). *Metaphors of mind. Conceptions of the nature of intelligence.* Cambridge, England: Cambridge University Press.

Sternberg, R. J. (1992). CAT: A program of comprehensive abilities testing. In B. R. Gifford & M. C. O'Connor (Eds.), *Changing assessments: Alternative views of aptitude, achievement and instruction* (pp. 213–274). Boston: Kluwer.

Sternberg, R. J., & Bhana, K. (1986). Synthesis of research on the effectiveness of intellectual skills programs: Snake-oil remedies or miracle cures? *Educational Leadership, 44*(2), 60–67.

Sternberg, R. J., Conway, B. E., Ketron, J. L., & Bernstein, M. (1981). People's conception of intelligence. *Journal of Personality and Social Psychology, 41,* 37–55.

Sternberg, R. J., & Detterman, D. K. (Eds.). (1986). *What is intelligence? Contemporary viewpoints on its nature and definition.* Norwood, NJ: Ablex.

Sternberg, R. J., & Gardner, M. K. (1983). Unities in inductive reasoning. *Journal of Experimental Psychology, 112*(1), 80–116.

Sternberg, R. J., & Gastel, J. (1989). Coping with novelty in human intelligence: An empirical investigation. *Intelligence, 13*(2), 187–197.

Sternberg, R. J., & Powell, J. S. (1983). Comprehending verbal comprehension. *American Psychologist, 38,* 878–893.

Sternberg, R. J., & Rifkin, B. (1979). The development of analogical reasoning processes. *Journal of Experimental Child Psychology, 27,* 195–232.

Sternberg, R. J., & Wagner, R. K. (Eds.). (1986). *Practical intelligence: Nature and origins of competence in the everyday world.* New York: Cambridge University Press.

Sternberg, R. J., & Wagner, R. K. (1989). Individual differences in practical knowledge and its application. In P. L. Ackerman, R. J. Sternberg, & R. Glaser (Eds.), *Learning and individual differences: Advances in theory and research* (pp. 255–278). New York: Freeman.

Sternberg, S. (1969). Memory-scanning: Mental processes revealed by reaction time experiments. *American Scientist, 57,* 421–457.

Sternberg, S. (1975). Memory-scanning: New findings and current controversies. *Quarterly Journal of Experimental Psychology, 27,* 1–32.

Stevenson, H. W., Lee, S., Chen, C., Lummis, M., Stigler, J., Fan, L., & Ge, F. (1990). Mathematics achievement of children in China and the United States. *Child Development, 61,* 1053–1066.

Stodolsky, S. S., & Lesser, G. (1967). Learning patterns in the disadvantaged. *Harvard Educational Review, 37,* 546–593.

Svensson, N. E. (1962). *Ability grouping and scholastic achievement: Report on a five-year follow-up study in Stockholm.* Stockholm: Almqvist & Wiksell.

Teasdale, T. W., & Owen, D. R. (1989). Continuing secular increases in intelligence and a stable prevalence of high intelligence levels. *Intelligence 13*(3), 255–262.

Terman, L. M. (1916). *The measurement of intelligence.* Boston: Houghton Mifflin.

Terman, L. M., & Merrill, M. A. (1937). *Measuring intelligence: A guide to the administration of the new revised Stanford-Binet tests of intelligence.* Boston: Houghton Mifflin.

Terman, L. M., & Merrill, M. A. (1960). *Stanford-Binet Intelligence Scale: Manual for the third revision. Form L-M.* Boston: Houghton Mifflin.

Thomson, G. H. (1916). A hierarchy without a general factor. *British Journal of Psychology, 8,* 271–281.

Thorndike, R. L. (1985). The central role of general ability in prediction. *Multivariate Behavioral Research, 20,* 241–254.

Thorndike, R. L. (1987). Stability of factor loadings. *Personality and Individual Differences, 8,* 585–586.

Thorndike, R. L., Hagen, E. P., & Sattler, J. M. (1986). *The Stanford-Binet Intelligence Scale, Fourth Edition: Technical Manual.* Chicago: Riverside.

Thorndike, R. M., & Lohman, D. F. (1990). *A century of ability testing.* Chicago: Riverside.

Thurstone, L. L. (1931). Multiple factor analysis. *Psychological Review, 38,* 406–427.

Thurstone, L. L. (1938). Primary mental abilities. *Psychometric Monographs, 1.*

Thurstone, L. L. (1944). *A factorial study of perception*. Chicago: University of Chicago Press.

Thurstone, L. L. (1947). *Multiple factor analysis*. Chicago: University of Chicago Press.

Thurstone, L. L., & Thurstone, T. G. (1941). Factorial studies of intelligence. *Psychometric Monographs, 2*.

Tyler, L. E. (1958). The stability of patterns of primary mental abilities among grade school children. *Educational and Psychological Measurement, 18*(4), 769–774.

Tyler, L. E. (1965). *The psychology of human differences*. New York: Appleton-Century-Crofts.

Undheim, J. O. (1979). Capitalization on chance: The case of Guilford's memory abilities. *Scandinavian Journal of Psychology, 20*, 71–76.

Undheim, J. O. (1981). On intelligence: II. A neo-Spearman model to replace Cattell's theory of fluid and crystallized intelligence. *Scandinavian Journal of Psychology, 22*, 181–187.

Undheim, J. O. (1994). Taking stock of what there is: The case of cognitive abilities. In A. Demetriou & A. Efklides (Eds.), *Intelligence, mind, and reasoning: Structure and development* (pp. 29–44). Amsterdam: North-Holland.

Undheim, J. O., & Gustafsson, J-E. (1987). The hierarchical organization of cognitive abilities: Restoring general intelligence through the use of linear structural relations (LISREL). *Multivariate Behavioral Research, 22*, 149–171.

Undheim, J. O., & Horn, J. L. (1977). Critical evaluation of Guilford's structure-of-intellect theory. *Intelligence, 1*, 65–81.

Undheim, J. O., & Nordvik, H. (1992). Socio-economic factors and sex differences in an egalitarian educational system: Academic achievement in 16-year-old Norwegian students. *Scandinavian Journal of Educational Research, 36*, 87–98.

van Daalen-Kapteijns, M. M., & Elshout-Moor, M. (1981). The acquisition of word meanings as a cognitive learning process. *Journal of Verbal Learning and Verbal Behavior, 20*, 386–399.

Vandenberg, S. G. (1968). The nature and nurture of intelligence. In D. C. Glass (Ed.), *Genetics* (pp. 3–58). New York: Rockefeller University Press.

Vandenberg, S. G., & Vogler, G. P. (1985). Genetic determinants of intelligence. In B. B. Wolman (Ed.), *Handbook of intelligence: Theories, measurements, and applications* (pp. 3–57). New York: Wiley.

Vernon, P. A. (Ed.). (1987). *Speed of information-processing and intelligence*, Norwood, NJ: Ablex.

Vernon, P. A. (1991). Studying intelligence the hard way. *Intelligence, 15*(4), 389–395.

Vernon, P. A. (Ed.). (1993). *Biological approaches to the study of human intelligence*. Norwood, NJ: Ablex.

Vernon, P. E. (1950). *The structure of human abilities*. London: Methuen.

Vernon, P. E. (1961). *The structure of human abilities* (2nd ed.). London: Methuen.

Vernon, P. E. (1965). Ability factors and environmental influences. *American Psychologist, 20*, 723–733.

Vernon, P. E. (1969). *Intelligence and cultural environment*. London: Methuen.

Vickers, D., Nettlebeck, T., & Willson, R. J. (1972). Perceptual indices of performance: The measurement of "inspection time" and "noise" in the visual system. *Perception, 1*, 263–295.

Wachs, T. D. (1992). *The nature of nurture*. Newbury Park, CA: Sage.

Wagner, R. K., & Sternberg, R. J. (1986). Tacit knowledge and intelligence in the everyday world. In R. J. Sternberg & R. K. Wagner (Eds.), *Practical intelligence: Nature and origins of competence in the everyday world* (pp. 51–83). New York: Cambridge University Press.

Wechsler, D. (1939). *The measurement of adult intelligence*. Baltimore, MD: Williams & Wilkins.

Wechsler, D. (1974). *Manual for the Wechsler Intelligence Scale for Children—Revised*. New York: Psychological Corporation.

Wechsler, D. (1991). *Manual for the Wechsler Intelligence Scale for Children—Third edition*. San Antonio, TX: Psychological Corporation.

Wechsler, D. (1992). *Manual for the Wechsler Intelligence Scale for Children—Third edition UK*. Sidcup, Kent, England: Psychological Corporation.

Werner, H., & Kaplan, E. (1950). The acquisition of word meanings: A developmental study. *Monographs of the Society for Research in Child Development, 15*(1, Serial No. 51).

White, K. R. (1982). The relation between socioeconomic status and academic achievement. *Psychological Bulletin, 81*, 461–481.

Whitely, S. E., & Barnes, G. M. (1979). The implications of processing event sequences for theories of analogical reasoning. *Memory & Cognition, 7*(4), 323–331.

Whitener, E. M. (1989). A meta-analytic review of the effect on learning of the interaction between prior achievement and instructional support. *Review of Educational Research, 59*(1), 65–86.

Willerman, L. (1979). *The psychology of individual and group differences*. San Francisco: Freeman.

Wissler, C. (1901). The correlation of mental and physical traits. *Psychological Monographs, 3*, 1–62.

Witkin, H. A., Oltman, P. K., Raskin, E., & Karp, S. A. (1971). *A manual for the Embedded Figures tests*. Palo Alto: Consulting Psychologists Press.

Woodrow, H. (1946). The ability to learn. *Psychological Review, 53*, 147–158.

Zajonc, R. B., & Markus, G. B. (1975). Birth order and intellectual development. *Psychological Review, 87*, 74–88.

Zigler, E., Styfco, S. J., & Gilman, E. (1993). The national Head Start program for disadvantaged preschoolers. In E. Zigler & S. J. Styfco (Eds.), *Head Start and beyond* (pp. 1–41). New Haven, CT: Yale University Press.

# · 9 ·

# INDIVIDUAL DIFFERENCES IN AFFECTIVE AND CONATIVE FUNCTIONS

## Richard E. Snow
STANFORD UNIVERSITY

## Lyn Corno
TEACHERS COLLEGE, COLUMBIA UNIVERSITY

## Douglas Jackson III
STANFORD UNIVERSITY

The human mind has long thought to have three aspects; cognition, conation, and affection (Hilgard, 1980). Although these aspects must ultimately be understood in combination, psychology has routinely divided attention among them. The division has limited progress in educational psychology, especially in work on individual differences in relation to learning and development, because it has encouraged research to focus exclusively on one or another aspect alone. Usually the focus has been on cognition. However, many important student aptitude and achievement differences are not strictly cognitive; many are affective or conative, and many may better be treated as blends. Important aspects of teacher and administrator functioning also go well beyond the cognitive.

Given the triadic distinction, this chapter emphasizes research on affective and conative functions in education. But it attempts to relate to the work on cognitive differences reviewed by Gustafsson and Undheim in chapter 8, and it looks forward to new forms of research that examine cognition, conation, and affect together. It reviews evidence on affective and conative differences in relation to research on learning, teaching, instruction, and educational development. It also suggests how researchers can use the evidence and methods of differential psychology to reach new understandings of human functioning in education. In addition to chapter 8, our work bears reading in relation to chapters 4, 5, 6, and 7, because it treats individual differences in some of the same psychological functions addressed there.

## HISTORY, SYSTEMS, AND JUSTIFICATION

We begin by placing the discussion in historical context, delimiting its scope and organization, reviewing terminology and methods, and identifying historically important problems that still exist today. We do not recount history in detail.

### Definitions

The traditional definitions, excerpted here from those given by English and English (1958), are as follows:

Historically three modes of mental functioning were usually distinguished: *Cognition, conation* (or volition), and *affect* (more often called *affection*). (p. 15). In most systems *cognition, affection* and *conation* are the three categories under which all mental processes are classified. (pp. 92–93) Some writers, however, combined conation and affection. (p. 15)

- *Cognition*—A generic term for any process whereby an organism becomes aware or obtains knowledge of an object . . . It includes *perceiving, recognizing, conceiving, judging, reasoning* . . . [I]n modern usage sensing is usually included under cognition. (p. 92)
- *Affection*—A class name for *feeling, emotion, mood, temperament* . . . a single feeling-response to a particular object or idea . . . the general reaction toward something liked or disliked . . . the

The work reported in this chapter was supported in part by a subcontract to Stanford University from the Center for Research on Evaluation, Standards and Student Testing, University of California, Los Angeles, under grant No. R117G10027, U.S. Department of Education/OERI. The authors thank Noel Entwistle, Jan-Eric Gustafsson, Samuel Messick, Henry Braun, Lee Cronbach, and Wilbert McKeachie for their many constructive criticisms and suggestions.

dynamic or essential quality of an emotion; the energy of an emotion. (p. 15)

*Conation*—That aspect of mental process or behavior by which it tends to develop into something else; an intrinsic "unrest" of the organism . . . almost the opposite of *homeostasis*. A *conscious* tendency to act; a conscious striving. . . . It is now seldom used as a specific form of behavior, rather for an aspect found in all. Impulse, desire, volition, purposive striving all emphasize the conative aspect. (p. 104)

As Hilgard (1980) traced it, this triadic conception of mind was central to psychological theory for 200 years. But its use died out in the early 1900s as North American psychology developed as a laboratory experimental science, increasingly committed to behaviorism. Faculty and instinct psychologies were rejected, as was the need for any comprehensive classification of mental processes or functions. McDougall (1923) was apparently the last to use the three terms in any general way.

But theorists interested in individual differences in cognitive abilities continued to acknowledge affective and conative aspects of performance as important forces, and McDougall (1933) retained the distinction even as he described these forces as propensities rather than instincts. Spearman (1927) devoted several chapters to the relation of intelligence to perseveration, self-control, fatigue, and effort, attributing oscillations and inconsistencies in cognitive efficiency to such conative influences. Thurstone (1924, 1948) discussed performance as purposive and willful, as an interaction of intelligence, motivation, inhibition, and temperament; he argued that reaction time measures for different kinds of responses should reflect both abilities and temperaments, thereby erasing distinctions between them. Wechsler (1950) argued against the definition of intelligence as a strictly cognitive construct, noting that adaptation and achievement in intellectual performance also involved the need for achievement, interest, purposeful consistency, and perseveration as important conative aspects. Guilford (1959) found that different persons exhibited differential preferences for or interests in different types of thought processes such as wishful thinking, convergent versus divergent thinking, and dichotomous thinking. He showed that various temperament factors influenced the maintenance of cognitive activity. Cattell (1971) also represented ability, temperament, and dynamic traits as three basic modalities in his theory. He devoted much research to the study of their interaction (see Messick, 1987, for a deeper discussion of all this work).

Thus, there is a significant history of research in differential psychology that acknowledged the triadic interaction even as mainstream theoretical psychology ignored it. In recent decades, cognitive psychology has become ascendant and is even now being extended to yield cognitive theories of emotion and motivation. That is all to the good. However, as Hilgard (1980) suggested, there will always be divisions of labor, and emphases will wax and wane. Maintaining the triad calls attention to aspects of psychological reality that are being neglected at each juncture.

## Why Study Affective and Conative Differences in Education?

For both practical and theoretical reasons, educational psychology has always included an emphasis on affective and conative as well as cognitive individual differences. Human diversity is ubiquitous in education, and this poses both problems and possibilities. Teachers and educational designers need to understand student variations in attitude, motivation, and style as well as ability. They need to adapt instruction to the strengths, weaknesses, preferences, and predilections of different students. They also seek to identify and capitalize on individuality and promote its further development. Students in turn, need to adapt to personality differences among teachers and other students. Diversity in the school community has to be considered in governance and in the provision of services. Evaluation studies need to examine treatment effects with respect to a variety of individual differences among those treated, because a program or policy cannot be judged generally good or worthy of adoption or continuance if it serves some fraction of its constituents badly. Finally, the assessment of educational outcomes has to be both differential and multivariate, especially including affective and conative measures, as soon as one admits that the school community values goals beyond cognitive achievement.

It is commonly said that education needs ways to capitalize on individual strengths where possible and to compensate for individual weaknesses where necessary, intervening to remediate where weaknesses can be removed directly or to circumvent them when they cannot (Corno & Snow, 1986). The need for these adaptive functions is fully as important in the affective and conative domains as it is in the cognitive domain, although the forms taken by these adaptations may differ. We return to the adaptation problem at several later points.

On the theoretical side, we argue that the phenomena of individual differences are of substantial scientific interest in their own right; thus, differential research should at least proceed in parallel with research aimed at general principles. More important, we think, is the likelihood that generalizations about teaching and learning cannot be validated without studying person differences and situation differences jointly. Especially in research on affective and conative functions, it has long been known that individual variations appear to play a central mediating role (see, e.g., Lazarus, 1993). In other words, advances in theory require that differential research proceed in interaction with the search for general laws. Alas, five old arguments are still used today to justify the rejection of individual difference considerations in psychology generally and in educational psychology in particular. These arguments are most often leveled against the study of affective and conative differences. They are:

1. Individual differences in personality, including affect, conation, and the like, do not really exist. They are epiphenomena that arise from more basic behavioral and physiological functions and will be dropped from consideration as soon as these basic functions are understood.
2. Such differences exist, but only as within-person variations arising from the characteristics of specific situations and changes therein; between-person differences are unstable and ungeneralizable.
3. Such differences exist both within persons and between persons but cannot be understood or measured properly without first having general theories. Individual differences can then be included to reach subsidiary principles and boundary conditions on the general theories.

4. Such differences exist but cannot be measured reliably at present. Educational psychologists should wait to consider them until others do the measurement development work.
5. Such differences can be measured reliably, but the resulting plethora of constructs and measures defies organization into useful taxonomies or theories. Educational psychologists should wait until others provide such organizations.

The first position was espoused by early behaviorists (e.g., Watson, 1930). It counts on reduction to simple learning principles, or even to neurophysiology. But reductionism as explanation has been rejected on both philosophical and psychological grounds. Research has to proceed at molar and molecular levels in parallel because each level has its own properties; also, advances at each level help guide work at other levels. Even if one could hope for eventual explanation by reduction, one cannot expect educators to shelve their problems for decades while waiting for psychology to catch up. There are obvious affective and conative problems in schools today; useful assessments and treatments are needed even if explanations for them must come later.

The second position also originated in behaviorism but is now embraced by other theorists. It is the situationist (versus personologist) argument that arose from the oft-noted low correlations of traditional personality measures with important behavioral criteria (Mischel, 1968). In this view, the situation is all-powerful; with the possible exception of intelligence, there are no enduring, stable personality traits. But the debate over whether person or situation variation was more important has since been displaced by one or another form of Person × Situation interactionism; it is recognized that either person or situation main effects, or both, can be powerful in different levels and contexts, but also that the interaction between them may often be the most important focus. Cronbach (1957) defined one basic approach to interaction. Related approaches have been taken up in personality research (Endler & Magnusson, 1976; Magnusson & Endler, 1977; Mischel, 1983, 1984), clinical and counseling psychology (Dance & Neufeld, 1988; Shoham-Salomon & Hanna, 1991), and developmental psychology (Magnusson & Allen, 1983; Wachs & Plomin, 1991), as well as educational research (Cronbach & Snow, 1977; Snow, 1989a). Other interactionist views are evident in behavior genetics (Wachs & Plomin, 1991) and social psychology (Ross & Nisbett, 1991), even though these two fields have usually seemed to champion person characteristics or situation characteristics, respectively. There are also some new forms of transactionism (with historical roots in perception psychology) now being used to interpret such interactions (Snow, 1994).

The third argument is perhaps the most prevalent today. It derives partly from the second view and also spawns the more specialized admonitions to educational psychologists found in the fourth and fifth arguments. Its early advocate was Hull (1945), who believed that individual differences could be accounted for as parameter variations within a uniform general process model of all human learning. A similar, neobehaviorist position was argued by Berlyne (1968). Weiner (1986; see also chapter 4, this volume) restated it for personality research as follows:

given the difficulties of personality measurement and the situational specificity of behavior, it will be more fruitful to search first for general

laws rather than explore Person × Situation interactions. This can then be followed, if necessary, by the inclusion of individual differences to refine the generalizations that have been made or to uncover more complex associations that might have been overlooked. (p. 11)

In other words, if arguments 2, 4, and 5 are correct, we should emphasize Hullian generalities and leave the secondary perturbations of individual differences to those who come in later to sweep up. The trouble is that arguments 2, 4, and 5 are not correct; they are rejected not only by the evidence on interactions but also by many other advances in personality research (see, e.g., Pervin, 1990; Saklofske & Zeidner, 1995). It is clear that stable personality differences exist and can be measured, and they cohere in ways that allow taxonomy and theory (McCrae & Costa, 1994). Further, it is increasingly evident that the general laws preferred in argument 3 cannot be found *without* exploring Person × Situation interactions. One always needs to test boundary conditions to decide what principles are candidates for generalization. Both persons and situations are formidable sources of variations that pose boundaries. Replications often fail, indicating that interactions are present. When interactions are examined, it is often found that generalizations hold only within narrowly specified boundary conditions, if at all; of course, the same concern applies to interaction findings themselves, because there are always higher order interactions to be checked (Cronbach, 1975). One may hope to find important educational situations where limited generalizations hold—where local theories may be stated, used, and then monitored as times, conditions, and populations change (Snow, 1977a). But one cannot identify these without carrying along at least the most apparently relevant individual difference constructs and measures in some form from the start. Similarly, one may hope to define "aptitude complexes" (Snow, 1987) or "acquired contextual modules" (Bereiter, 1990) as compound person characteristics accumulated over learning experience in particular types of situations. But again, one must study person differences and situation differences jointly to do this. The Person × Situation interaction problem is also revisited at several later points in this chapter.

The fourth and fifth arguments can also be dismissed on other grounds. Educational psychology cannot wait for others to develop theories or measures. Beyond the everyday needs of applied research, development, and practice noted earlier, educational psychology has its own basic science agenda. Indeed, the distinction between "basic" and "applied" research no longer works in many instances (see Greeno, 1980; chapter 2, this volume). Theories and measures are not just developed in laboratories and applied in the field. Rather, the basic phenomena of concern to educational psychology are situated in the field; they exist in certain unions of persons, performance conditions, and educational environments and must be understood in the terms of those contexts. One can import theory and method from other contexts as they help. But to explain affective, conative, and cognitive functions, and individual differences in them, in learning mathematics or appreciating history or teaching art, is to understand them fundamentally *in situ*.

## What Should Be Studied, and How?

Given that we need to study individual differences within educational settings for both theoretical and practical reasons, the important questions of which ones to study and how to study them remain. Affective and conative differences appear more numerous than cognitive abilities. We need a priority list. We also need good research methods.

*The Need for Taxonomy.* Cronbach (1957) once likened the field of correlational psychology to the Holy Roman Empire, as contrasted with the Tight Little Island of experimental psychology. He clearly had in mind the far-flung reaches of research on affective and conative differences, as well as the various categories of cognitive ability. In the ensuing decades, cognitive differential psychology converged on a fairly unified model of ability factor structure and made significant advances in the analysis of process differences associated with different abilities in this structure (see Carroll, 1993; Lohman, 1989b; Sternberg, 1985; chapter 8, this volume). However, over the same decades, most of the many provinces of affective and conative differences remained isolated, studied only in local explorations. Despite some heroic speculations (e.g., Royce & Powell, 1983) the domain has remained largely fragmented—unorganized, undefined as a field, and thus underappreciated.

The first major problem in this diverse field, then, is to define and structure it in a way that promotes new lines of programmatic research and useful theorizing. We can then face the above arguments about the field and many other issues more squarely. But it is important not to adopt one particular theoretical view to the exclusion of others, lest important phenomena or methods of studying them be left out. It is also important not to belabor definitions unduly, even while seeking common agreement on some convenient and useful terminology. As Izard, Kagan, and Zajonc (1984) noted in their overview of the emotion–cognition–behavior complex:

> Although definition is a current issue, we recognize that at some stages of development a given discipline may well refrain from setting up strict formal demands upon its definitions. The more specific the definition, the sharper the boundary it draws among phenomena. And at some stages of knowledge it isn't always clear where the boundaries should be. . . . for example, if one defines emotion so as to exclude interest, we might have difficulty in dealing with surprise and boredom. (p. 4)

In seeking to establish some structure in the present chapter, therefore, it is important that we, and all readers, keep in mind that boundaries and relations between different domains are fuzzy.

*Relations to Student Learning and Development.* An important goal for educational psychology is to discover the ways in which affective and conative differences among students influence learning and cognitive performance, both on immediate school tasks and in long-range educational development, and vice versa. But one should not routinely expect simple, straightforward monotone relations between dimensional measures of student personality and indicators of educational value. In contrast to the prevailing linear relations among cognitive measures, relations for affective and conative measures may be curvilinear; some theories even predict this. Further complicating the picture, other student characteristics may also moderate the relationships. And personality–achievement relations will likely also depend on subject matter, grade level, instructional conditions and contexts, teachers, and many other factors.

Nonetheless, much early work on affective and conative factors in relation to educational achievement was limited to a search for simple monotone predictions. In this chapter we note that work briefly, for what leads it may supply to further research, along with examples of more recent work that takes a more complex view.

*Outcomes of Instruction.* Most affective and conative constructs that have been studied in relation to instruction have been treated as predispositions, even though many can also be viewed as outcomes of instruction. For example, various educational influences might serve to increase conscientiousness, sociability, interest, or openness to new ideas, or to reduce impulsivity or anxiety. Personal counseling and psychotherapy often have these goals. Such variables may be useful criteria in broad educational evaluations. Of course, instruction designed specifically to affect personality faces ethical questions that cognitive instructional psychology usually can ignore. Beyond these lie constructs that range from traitlike to fairly specific responses and that clearly represent both pre- and postdispositions simultaneously. For example, positive student interest in history or physics or some particular kind of art is just as likely to be seen as an important goal of instruction as it is an important aspect of readiness to learn; indeed, such an attitude is a goal precisely because it is an aspect of readiness for future learning as well as of appreciation of a subject matter domain for its own sake. Certainly, positive values for democracy and good citizenship are important goals of education, as are healthy beliefs about education, society, and self. They can be assessed as either readiness or goal attainment.

The founding fathers of educational psychology had much to say about affective and conative goals (see, e.g., Dewey, 1913; James, 1890/1983; Judd, 1927; Thorndike, 1935). Much early effort went into assessing these goals (Stern, 1963), defining them as explicit objectives (Krathwohl, Bloom, & Masia, 1964), and studying teacher effects on them (Khan & Weiss, 1973). Unfortunately, relatively little modern research specifically addresses affective and conative outcomes of instruction and how best to conceptualize or assess them. We include examples where possible.

*Teachers and Administrators.* There was also much early research on teacher personality (see Getzels & Jackson, 1963), its role in classroom life (P. W. Jackson, 1968), and teacher training for affective roles (G. I. Brown, 1975). More recently, individual differences among teachers have been studied in relation to particular adaptations of teaching methods (Corno & Snow, 1986) and to teacher expectancies about particular students (Brophy, 1985). But most research today builds the cognitive psychology of teaching.

*Choice of Focus for This Chapter.* Given the present state of research on affective and conative differences in education, we have chosen to focus the discussion on individual constructs we consider most important for future research and on building a taxonomy within which these constructs can be located, studied, and interrelated. We include selected examples of empirical relations between measures of these constructs and measures

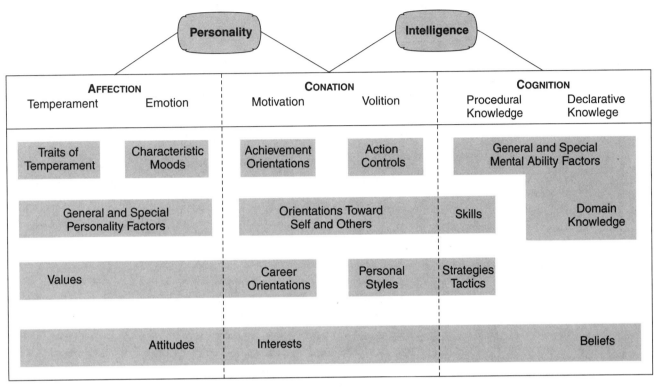

FIGURE 9–1. A Provisional Taxonomy of Individual
Difference Constructs

of student learning and development. We also select example studies to suggest the range of measurement and methodological approaches that might be used in further work. We do not review in detail the present state of validation of each construct.

## Taxonomy and Terminology

We start with the provisional taxonomy of person differences shown in Figure 9–1 and discuss its major distinctions here. Each of its categories is then subdivided and elaborated in later sections of this chapter. Each category holds a number of individual difference constructs. But we expect that continuing research will revise some constructs, reclassify others, create new ones, and substantially change the taxonomic array. We begin with person constructs because these are the poles around which research evidence has accumulated to date. No comparable taxonomy of situations has emerged, although advances have been made in this direction. Person–situation interaction research has also begun developing new kinds of reciprocal and transactive constructs, but their value is as yet unproven empirically. And more "whole person" views of person–situation transaction are yet to be well articulated. These recent developments are reviewed later.

At the top of Figure 9–1, the everyday constructs of *intelligence* and *personality* are shown as superordinate but cloudy. Both terms are vague and value-laden in popular discourse, and likely to promote simplistic thinking and misunderstanding in educational discussions. Also, intelligence in many definitions comprises aspects of both cognition and conation (Snow,

1989b; Sternberg & Detterman, 1986), as suggested in the figure by the connections to each; similarly, personality comprises aspects of both conation and affect. Indeed, the term "personality" is often taken to subsume all aspects of individual human psychology, including intelligence. We thus try to avoid these terms except in generic usage. We recommend instead the triad of cognition, conation, and affect. It rests on two more clearly defined functions—cognition and affect—and brings conation explicitly back to equal status after a long hiatus.

Each of these three domains has two subdivisions in Figure 9–1, chosen to make further theoretical distinctions we think deserve attention, even though all kinds of individual difference constructs may not map clearly onto them. For example, some cognitive theories distinguish between declarative and procedural knowledge, or more simply knowledge and skill, even though ability constructs such as verbal or spatial or mathematical ability combine aspects of both. Similarly, affection can be subdivided into temperament and emotion even though personality factor interpretations rely on aspects of both. Temperament is usually taken to refer to more constitutional, biologically based characteristics that are relatively less situation dependent, whereas emotion usually refers to feeling states that are more directly situation dependent. As with the ability category, the personality factor category is centered in the affect column for this reason. Under the ability and personality factor categories, we place other cognitive and affective categories to reflect their primary emphases. Thus, knowledge structures and beliefs relate more to declarative knowledge differences, whereas cognitive skills, strategies, and tactics relate more to procedural knowledge differences. Traits interpreted as largely biological are considered temperament differences, whereas characteristic mood states are listed as emotional differences. But this does not imply a pairwise trait-versus-process contrast across columns. Each column can contain stable, traitlike response tendencies. The term "characteristic mood" was chosen rather than "affects" or "feelings" to imply a relatively stable state of readiness for particular kinds of emotional response. Values and attitudes are also connected to temperament and emotion columns, respectively. Values appear more permanent and temperament-like, but attitudes can be quite stable tendencies to respond characteristically to particular situations.

In contrast to the cognitive and affective domains, conation and its subdivision into motivation and volition needs more justification and definition here. Historically, European psychology was much concerned with volition, or will, whereas North American psychology emphasized motivation to the exclusion of volition. The difference arose because mainstream American behaviorism was receptive to the concept of motivation (as drive) but rejected anything smacking of mentalism and especially of will (as in "free will"). Also, Lewin (1926) rejected Ach's (1910) theory of volition, in which intention-action control processes were central, replacing them with needs and their related valences in an all-encompassing motivation theory. Lewin emigrated to the United States and influenced American personality and social psychology; Ach did not (see Kuhl, 1984; Kuhl & Beckmann, 1985).

Understanding the choices individuals make has been the primary concern of most theories of human motivation. The problem of choice has been important because it is assumed that once we know what goal a person has chosen and what action he or she will take to attain that goal, then we should be able to predict that person's behavior (Kuhl, 1986). For example, the classic expectancy-value model of motivation (e.g., Atkinson & Feather, 1966; Atkinson & Raynor, 1974) uses two parameters to predict an individual's behavior: the expectation that an action can be performed to yield the desired results, and the personal value of all the outcomes based on that action. According to this expectancy-value theory, all individuals' behavior is a function of a consistent algebraic relationship between these two parameters. But Kuhl (1977, 1982) found that people use idiosyncratic and highly context-specific rules to combine expectancies and values, sometimes basing decisions only on value information, at other times using only expectancy information, and at still other times combining them distinctively. These and other data suggested that, beyond expectancy-value theory, "additional processes had to be postulated to mediate the implementation and maintenance of intentions" (Kuhl, 1990, p. 2). Heckhausen and Kuhl (1985) thus developed action-control theory, to consider intentional states as distinct from motivational states. The predecisional state is labeled "motivation" and the postdecisional state is labeled "volition." When an individual makes a decision to pursue a particular goal, the motivational state is terminated and the volitional state is begun. Following Corno (1989), "motivational processes mediate the formation of decisions and *promote* decisions whereas volitional processes mediate the enactment of those decisions and *protect* them" (p,. 114, emphasis in the original). The distinction between motivation and volition is necessary because even well-motivated students choosing clear goals may have diffi-

culty enacting their intentions; they may be distracted by internal events, such as task-irrelevant thoughts, or by external exigencies, including the actions of other persons. These motivational and volitional functions seem to be governed by different principles.

The distinction also helps classify and contrast important further subdivisions of individual difference constructs. Motivation concerns wishes, wants, needs, and goals; we place achievement orientations, interests, and various aspects of self-directed orientations here. Volition concerns intentions, efforts, actions, and self-regulation; here we place action controls, personal styles, and some other-directed orientations.

A taxonomic structure like that offered in Figure 9–1 is only a provisional lattice on which to hang theories, hypotheses, and findings as research continues. It serves to ensure that some construct categories are not forgotten, and it provides a list of potentially relevant variables when one sets out to validate a proposed new construct. Further, some theories may bridge categories or columns in the taxonomy. As noted above, the Heckhausen–Kuhl (1985) theory bridges motivation and volition. Weiner's (1986) attribution theory connects motivation and emotion. Kanfer and Ackerman (1989a, 1989b) combine ability and motivation. Also, particular individual difference constructs may be placed in one location in this lattice but may relate in important ways to constructs in other locations. This helps demonstrate that underlying cognitive, conative, and affective functions can mix as constituents of a construct that on its surface appears to be subordinate within one domain. Any such construct to be investigated ought to be placed in a provisional correlational network that helps identify its likely constituents and connections to other parts of the taxonomy.

***Individual Difference Constructs.*** But what are individual difference constructs? And how does one place them in correlational networks?

A construct is a particular kind of scientific concept formed to represent a hypothesized psychological function—that is, some inferred system, structure, process, force, or activity—that can account for regular patterns of observed relations among behavioral measures. When superficially different measures show strong, enduring interrelations, we say they reflect the same hypothetical construct. We infer an underlying commonality among the measures. Even when measures show weak relations, as individual test items often do, we can aggregate to find commonality at the level of latent variable structures (see chapter 8, this volume, for a discussion of measurement and latent variables). To label such a commonality as a construct is also to generalize across a class of situations all of which presumably evoke the psychological function inferred.

Individual difference constructs in particular are designed to account for measured inter- and intraindividual differences in these inferred functions. The measures may be categorical. More typically, they are designed to provide gradations along which different persons can be ordered according to the degree to which they manifest the psychological function of interest. Some constructs and measures are bipolar. The observed differences can also be interpreted as either relatively enduring or transitory, and as either relatively broad or narrow with respect to the range of situations in which they are evoked.

Most constructs listed in Figure 9–1 and discussed in this

chapter are nomothetic, normative descriptions of interindividual differences; that is, each identifies a dimension that is assumed to apply to all persons (at least all within some broad cultural category) on which they differ by degree. However, there are normative constructs that are not truly nomothetic; rather than applying to all persons, they describe normative differences within particular groups of persons in particular contexts that may be irrelevant in other groups or contexts. We discuss these as contextual constructs in a later section. There are also three types of intraindividual constructs. First, there are ipsative constructs that contrast relative levels of different normative dimensions. A difference score showing relative strength in verbal versus spatial ability would be a cognitive example. Some personality and interest inventories require forced choices that contrast different dimensions within persons. Thorndike (1912) had students rank-order their interest and their achievement across different school subjects and produced a correlation as an ipsative measure for each person. A second type of intraindividual construct describes individual change over short or long time periods. Individual inconsistency, gain, or growth measures are examples. Third are so-called idiographic or idiomorphic descriptions of the uniqueness or individuality of a particular person, or the degree to which particular traits are central or salient for that person. Some concepts and methods of potential use in educational psychology have arisen from these approaches (see, e.g., Allport, 1937; Kelly, 1963; Neimeyer, 1985). However, there are special problems of measurement and interpretation involved in working with ipsative, idiographic, and individual change constructs. There are also both controversies and complementarities in relation to nomothetic constructs. To pursue these issues, readers should consult specialized chapters (Caspi & Bem, 1990; Messick, 1983; Rorer, 1990) and leading texts (Cronbach, 1990).

Constructs should be represented by more than one measure; otherwise it is impossible to separate variance attributable to the construct from variance due to particularities of any one measure. These measures in turn should be evaluated in relation to measures of other established constructs. Studying several proposed measures of a construct in relation to sets of other established measures helps locate the proposed measures in an empirical correlational network that displays their convergence on the target construct and their divergence from measures purporting to represent different constructs. Both convergent and discriminant validation are needed (Campbell & Fiske, 1959). Such a correlational network may suggest superstructures wherein several constructs may be meaningfully interconnected in parallel or superordinate–subordinate relations. It may also show the predictive importance of constructs in relation to other variables that theoretically should be expected to reflect related individual differences. Gustafsson and Undheim (in chapter 8) give excellent examples using cognitive abilities. Correlational network research of this sort, moreover, provides tests of taxonomic implications.

*Construct Validation.* Research showing the kind of correlational network in which a construct and its measures can be located provides evidence for construct validity. Embretson (1983) called this evidence of a construct's "nomothetic span," but "nomological validity" is the preferred concept; it implies

both empirical correlational span and theoretical rationale, and avoids confusion with nomothetic versus idiographic (Messick, 1989b). Research that identifies constituent structures and processes thought to underlie the responses depicted by the construct's measures contributes to what Embretson (1983) called "construct representation." In addition to correlational and analytic studies, another important source of evidence on construct validity comes from studies that show interactions between an individual difference construct and an experimental treatment variable; understanding of the construct is demonstrated by manipulating its relation to other constructs and measures experimentally. In educational research, this form of evidence has been called aptitude–treatment interaction, or ATI for short (Cronbach & Snow, 1977; Snow, 1991, 1992). Gustafsson and Undheim (in chapter 8) give some examples of cognitive ATI. We give affective and conative examples in the body of this chapter. Usually, ATI is discussed as a way of validating adaptive or individualized instruction, but it is as much a validation of the aptitude construct itself. Beyond these approaches, many other kinds of considerations, evidence, and methods are also relevant to construct validation (see Messick, 1989b; Wainer & Braun, 1988).

In the abstract, the process is not different from the process of validating any scientific theory. Constructs evolve and are validated progressively through long-term programmatic research. In psychology and education, however, and especially in research on affective and conative differences, researchers often must make do with less. We attempt to build a plausible, provisional interpretation of observed individual differences on measures designed or chosen to reflect a construct of interest. There may be evidence from correlational studies, predictions of educational criteria, and even from some ATI studies. Substantial progress has been made, even though there are as yet relatively few nomological networks in affective and conative research that can be counted on as theoretically clear and stable. And most individual difference constructs in this domain have so far been represented only as psychometric scales or statistical combinations derived from questionnaire items; projective methods and clinical inference, used frequently elsewhere, have not been used much in educational research. Process analyses and ATI studies are still rare. A major issue, too, is the degree to which the meaning of any given construct can be expected to remain stable across persons, situations, and social history. This is the nomothetic versus contextual issue again.

*Traits versus Response Tendencies.* An individual difference construct that is interpreted to be relatively enduring and stable over time, and to apply to a relatively broad range of situations, is likely to be labeled a *trait* for short. This practice is not troublesome if traits are simply conceived of as useful abstractions that provide statistical summaries of response tendencies in defined types of situations (see, e.g., Cronbach, 1990, p. 498 *ff*). The trait label sums up to the point of measurement some aspects of the person's learning history in particular situations and offers a prediction about the person's behavior in similar situations in the future. Unfortunately, the term trait leads many interpreters to impute to the person a predisposition that is general, constant, and inherited; often the disposition is also reified by this label as "a thing in the head." Abilities are most often treated this way in common parlance (see chapter

8, this volume). Thus, the situational aspect of the construct definition is lost, as is the implication that the individual differences may in many cases derive from variations in personal learning history in particular situation types.

Clearly there are differential human features that are wholly or partly genetic and that are in fact or belief linked to personality differences. Eye and hair color, and color blindness, may be traits in the Mendelian sense, as are some specific biological malfunctions that give rise to psychological differences. Other bodily features, such as height and weight, handedness, and the physical configurations that may be regarded as more or less attractive in particular cultures, are both polygenetic and subject to substantial influence from environmental sources; they may also produce psychological differences in interaction with the physical and social environment. Some temperament differences are here called traits because they appear to be largely genetic in origin. Beyond these instances, however, we recommend that the term be used only generically and interpreted only as a response tendency. Alternative generic terms such as *attribute* or *characteristic* will often serve as well. The genetic basis of any given individual difference construct, of course, remains an open question for further research (Plomin, 1994; Plomin, Chipuer, & Loehlin, 1990).

*Types, Traits, Styles, and States.* A further terminological problem concerns the distinction between *types* and *traits*, on the one hand, and *traits*, *styles*, and *states* on the other. *Strategies* and *tactics* are also sometimes distinguished from all these, as are *approaches* and *orientations*. Some of these contrasts may be important, but we should avoid proliferating terms wherever possible.

Type distinctions have been used to characterize individual differences from Hippocrates and Galen in ancient Greece, through Jaensch (1938), Jung (1923), Kretschmer (1925), and Sheldon (1942) in the 20th century. Though most of these old typologies have been rejected as oversimplified or invalid, some survive. One example is the Myers–Briggs Type Indicator (Myers & McCaulley, 1993), which is widely used to assess Jung's theoretical distinctions (see Pittenger, 1993). However, its scores can be treated as continuous trait measures; categorical type interpretations are not required. Indeed, hierarchical factor models of personality can treat types as higher order factors composed of combinations of trait factors from the next lower level, and this is consistent with Jung's theory (H. J. Eysenck & M. W. Eysenck, 1985). Beneath the trait factors would be still lower order factors representing habits, with specific responses to particular items or measures at the base. This sort of hierarchy is shown schematically in Figure 9–2. As an example, introversion is both a Jungian type construct and a higher order factor combining persistence, shyness, accuracy, and other trait factors. In turn, these trait factors may be characterized as constellations of habits. Categorical distinctions can also be useful as provisional type constructs while more detailed, multivariate trait descriptions are being sought in continuing research. They may even be more meaningful in communication with parents and teachers; category labels such as "bullies" and "victims" provide an example to be described below.

Also shown schematically in Figure 9–2 is another kind of hierarchical continuum, ranging from traits through styles, strategies, and tactics to states at the bottom; in the middle, orientations and approaches connect to styles and strategies, respectively. Constructs at any of these levels may relate instrumentally to learning outcomes; indeed, any of these constructs may be treated as a particular learning outcome itself. And learning experiences in situations accumulate; tactics, strategies, and styles appropriate to particular types of situations develop, and the developing persons seek out the types of situations that fit them in some personal sense. The result is continuing pursuit of achievement in a particular field. Field achievements as constructs return us to the level of traits and types (and also perhaps to the level of stereotypes) because development in a career field means taking on the styles, values, and beliefs of a field as well as building the requisite abilities and knowledge. Also, in a figurative sense, career fields select personalities. It is not surprising, then, that we come to think of accountants, artists, engineers, lawyers, poets, and truck drivers as having distinct and different personalities. Different kinds of students choose different subjects in school, but different subjects also draw in, develop, and retain different kinds of students. Teaching as a professional field may also attract and fit certain kinds of personalities and not others; even success in teaching in particular disciplines, such as science versus social studies, might reflect particular patterns of personality (see Getzels & Jackson, 1963).

Style constructs can also be thought of as intersections or combinations of cognitive ability and personality characteristics described as characteristic modes of attending, perceiving, and thinking, or of information processing in general. Style definitions emphasize task types and performance processes rather than the content or level of performance (Messick, 1987, 1994). In much common usage, style constructs are traitlike, at the same level of generality as ability and personality factors, but with the added implication of conscious preference. Some theorists emphasize this implication of choice, but others think of choice as strategic and situated with style as automatic and basic. However, there are both conceptual and methodological problems here. Some style constructs are not easily distinguished from ability constructs because they are measured using maximum performance tasks; on such tasks, one cannot choose to perform better than one is able to perform. Field independence–dependence (Witkin & Goodenough, 1981) is an example of such a construct. Other style constructs mix maximum and typical performance measures. An example here is reflection–impulsivity, which is defined by a mixture of error and time scores. Still others rest on typical self-reports and are difficult to distinguish from personality traits.

Some theorists also build up from correlations among specific responses to style constructs at the trait level. Schmeck (1988a, 1988b) has used questionnaire items about learning or study tactics; examples of such tactics might be contrasting the elements of key concepts or using imagery to connect them. Factor analyses of these item intercorrelations yield strategies, defined as consistent combinations of tactical procedures that implement a plan. Questions that ask about general tactics and strategies rather than behavior in particular courses can then be interpreted as styles. Presumably, factors that combine strategies identify styles, just as factors that combine habits define traits in the Eysenckian view. Both Schmeck and Entwistle (see Schmeck, 1988b) recommend that we reserve the term *style* for cognitive style constructs such as field independence or

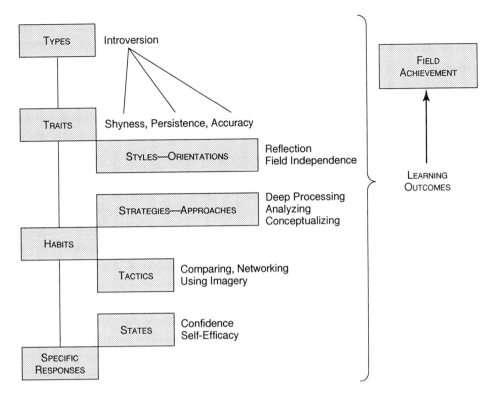

FIGURE 9–2. Schematic Representation of Different Levels of Referent Generality for affective and conative aptitude constructs related to learning outcomes and field achievements.

reflection–impulsivity. Learning style constructs relating to performance in educational settings would then better be called *orientations*, according to Beaty (1995). These orientations would represent consistent preferences for different courses, but also for particular approaches to learning—that is, learning strategies—resulting from the person's personality traits, cognitive styles, motives and intentions, and perceptions of the course and context. Beaty (1995) also distinguishes a higher level of student orientations to education in general, contrasting vocational, academic, personal, and social orientations, for example. These orientations suggest value constructs and also might be expected to correlate with Holland's (1973) personality types based on career interests.

Thus, as exemplified in Figure 9–2, a person might be highly introverted, showing particularly the traits of shyness, persistence, and accuracy, but might also show a reflective and field-independent style. One might observe a combination of deep study orientation, involving the strategies of conceptualization and analysis, and the particular tactics of comparing, networking, and use of visual imagery in learning. Coupled with an academic orientation toward higher education and the motivation to gain secure, supportive, and satisfying employment, the resulting domain of field achievement might be pursuit of a scholarly career.

Finally, states are momentary reports about "How I feel now, in this situation," whereas reports about traits are attempts to define an average or typical response for a class of situations.

Examples of state constructs are feelings of confidence and self-efficacy at a point in learning. States are usually measured with a few simple and direct, on-the-spot questions, and they will fluctuate within persons from day to day, even from minute to minute, as well as from situation to situation. Those who favor the situationist view of personality emphasize this within-person variation in states. But it is difficult to show that state and trait measures are independent; they will usually be related. State intensity may often be some multiplicative function of situational stimulus strength and typical trait level.

*Contextual Constructs.* The levels of Figure 9–2 suggest different levels of referent generality (Coan, 1964) for affective and conative constructs. That is, each level represents a different degree of broad versus narrow generalization of stability of individual differences across time and situation. Traits and styles stand at a higher level of referent generality than do habits and strategies. It is important in research to keep track of the level on which constructs appear to stand. Each level also reflects a different degree of constraint on the observation situation. A student's specific response in a particular time and place will be interpreted as a state. As consistency of aggregated response across times and situations is observed, tactics, habits, strategies, and then styles and traits may be inferred. The levels of referent generality suggest the breadth of contexts over which one generalizes, even though these contexts remain largely unspecified.

But there are constructs that are defined to apply only to

particular types of contexts or situations (or groups of persons); we call these *contextual* constructs. Indeed, their definitions often arise explicitly from the union of persons and situations of particular sorts. Most trait constructs only vaguely imply situational characteristics. For example, shyness implies behavior in relation to social situations; persistence typically implies effortful work situations. Note, however, that shyness can be manifested in the avoidance or control of social situations, and can be felt when the person is alone, in fantasies or dreams. Persistence too can persist mentally, away from the actual work situation. For some other contextual constructs, the relevant situations are explicitly but broadly identified. Mathematics anxiety concerns anxiousness in the presence of mathematical symbols and problems. Test anxiety concerns situations involving the expectation of evaluation. Again, such anxieties can be manifested in anticipation of situations not yet faced, and in general self-concepts. As further examples, Bereiter's (1990) acquired contextual modules of public speaking ability and intentional learning style are dispositions specialized in and for particular sorts of situations. They too can be manifested overtly or covertly outside of the situations that help define them.

Formal educational contexts provide a particularly important collection of situations with which persons interact as they develop. And constructs linked to these contexts and development in them should be uniquely important for educational psychology. Persistence, math and test anxiety, public speaking, and intentional learning style are obvious examples of educational psychological constructs. So too are constructs representing approaches to learning and studying (Entwistle, 1987a, 1988). One can entertain even more specialized and localized style constructs that pertain to learning math or science in a particular curriculum reform, or learning through exploration in computerized microworlds, or satisficing in a particular high school's physical education classes.

But a major issue arises. Are nomothetic, normative constructs derived from general psychology the place to start in seeking understanding of individual differences in education? Shyness and persistence are such general characteristics. Or does adaptation to particular educational contexts produce differential constructs closer and thus more useful in understanding local educational phenomena? The question is partly which came first, and partly it is one of research strategy: Should we stay close to constructs from general psychology, using its nomological network but limiting ecological validity and potential teacher comprehension and use, or should we stay close to classroom experience, building ecologically valid constructs that teachers can use but that become an island universe without support from general psychological theory?

Perhaps, some kind of theoretical two-way street is possible. There have been attempts to forge person–situation units useful for differential theory in the past; Lewin (1951) sought to characterize persons in their own physical, perceptual, and social fields, and Murray (1938) similarly emphasized need–press units, for example. Some current theorists argue that the most useful individual difference constructs will be those derived from analyses of person–situation interactions and transactions, using both general constructs and rich local descriptions. These will be descriptions of person–situation unions in which definition depends on characteristics of both and cannot be located in persons' heads or in situational stimulus structures alone.

They will also thus be conditional, specifying the local contextual conditions in which the individual difference is exhibited. One example is Mischel's (1990) program of research on children's self-regulatory behavior in situations that require waiting for desired goals. He was able to identify experimentally the delay conditions that identified stable individual differences as well as the strategies involved in successful delaying of gratification. Although context dependent, his constructs and measures nonetheless predicted cognitive and social coping and school achievement in later years. Snow has argued (1991, 1992) that all aptitudes—cognitive, conative, and affective—are contextual constructs in this sense, and that an important goal for educational psychology is to discover the instructional conditions in which each apparently general or local, or even idiographic, individual difference construct does and does not serve as aptitude. Development of this kind of situativity theory is now advancing (Greeno, 1989; see also chapter 2, this volume), although the work has not yet addressed individual differences in affective and conative functions.

## A Classic Example

Although there are many old classics in research on affective and conative differences, one study stands out both for its size and status and for the sweeping generalization often attributed to its results. We revisit it here as an example of general trait versus contextual construct interpretation in a large, well-conducted research program. There are also some methodological lessons.

In 1926, a 5-year project called the Character Education Inquiry began at Teachers College, Columbia University, under the supervision of E. L. Thorndike. It was motivated by concern over how to evaluate moral education, and so sought to build and study a large array of behavioral measures of hypothesized aspects of character, such as honesty, helpfulness, cooperation, inhibition, persistence, moral knowledge and attitude. These measures were then used to survey individual differences among thousands of schoolchildren in Grades 5 through 8 in a variety of locations. Results were reported in three volumes, covering deceit (Hartshorne & May, 1928), service and self-control (Hartshorne, May, & Maller, 1929), and the organization of character (Hartshorne, May, & Shuttleworth, 1930). We focus on the first report here, but briefly mention the others.

The battery of deception tests included measures of cheating on classroom work, athletic contests, party games, and homework, but also measures of lying and stealing. The principal conclusion was based mainly on the intercorrelations among these measures. Hartshorne and May (1928) considered these correlations low in general and noted that they declined in size as test situations became more dissimilar. Other evidence also showed that situational factors such as the ease of cheating, the payoff, or the risk involved influenced the likelihood of deceit. Hartshorne and May concluded that

an individual's honesty or dishonesty consists of a series of acts and attitudes to which these descriptive terms apply. The consistency with which [s]he is honest or dishonest is a function of the situations in which [s]he is placed in so far as (1) these situations have common elements, (2) [s]he has learned to be honest or dishonest in them, and (3) [s]he has become aware of their honest or dishonest implications or consequences. (Book I, p. 380)

TABLE 9–1. Intercorrelations Among Dishonesty Scores in Nine Kinds of Deceit Situations

| | A | B | C | D | E | F | G | H | I |
|---|---|---|---|---|---|---|---|---|---|
| A. Copying from scoring keys (3) | **87** **70** | 45 | 40 | 40 | 17 | 29 | 12 | 14 | 35 |
| B. Adding scores after time limit (6) | 29 | **82** **44** | 37 | 42 | 19 | 34 | 17 | 17 | 25 |
| C. Peeping in closed eyes conditions (3) | 28 | 22 | **72** **46** | 30 | 23 | 10 | 25 | 20 | 11 |
| D. Faking solutions to puzzles (3) | 29 | 26 | 20 | **75** **50** | — | 30 | 12 | 35 | 26 |
| E. Getting forbidden help on homework (1) | 15 | 14 | 19 | — | **24** **24** | 14 | −02 | −01 | 40 |
| F. Faking athletic records (4) | 20 | 19 | 06 | 18 | 09 | **77** **46** | 12 | 28 | 23 |
| G. Faking, peeping, and stealing in party games (3) | — | — | — | — | — | — | **—** | 21 | 00 |
| H. Stealing money from a box (1) | 13 | 13 | 16 | 28 | −01 | 16 | — | **—** | 13 |
| I. Lying about conduct in general (1) | 31 | 25 | 16 | 21 | 40 | 00 | — | 13 | **84** **84** |

*Note:* Table based on *Studies of the Nature of Character: I. Studies in Deceit* by H. Hartshorne and M. A. May, 1928, New York: Macmillan. Adapted with permission.

*Note:* Decimals omitted. Numbers of measures for each situation are shown in parentheses. Dashes indicate unreported values.

No one is honest or dishonest by "nature." (Book I, p. 412)

[H]onesty or dishonesty is not a unified trait in children of the ages studied, but a series of specific responses to specific situations. (Book II, p. 243).

Although Hartshorne and May considered their measures and data carefully and discussed various complexities, they seemed to adopt their "doctrine of specificity" (Book II, p. 242) too sharply. Their distinction between general trait and situated response was all or none; apparently to qualify, a "trait" had to be about as ever present as eye color. For example, they expected that a useful predictive validity from present to future measures of honesty required an intercorrelation of .90 or better (Book II, p. 125). Unfortunately, their capsule conclusions have been widely cited as counting heavily against the contrasting "doctrine of traits" (see, e.g., Mischel, 1968).

This chapter need not spend pages pitting the doctrine of specificity and the doctrine of traits against one another; it has already been argued that Person × Situation interaction and the idea of bounded or contextualized individual difference constructs is often the more useful model. It is so in this case. Given all the Hartshorne–May evidence, it seems clear that neither general trait nor specific response models fit the data. Table 9–1 shows the correlations among their measures of dishonesty. Above the main diagonal are correlations between the summed measures for each kind of deceit situation. Below the main diagonal are averages of individual measure correlations across the different kinds of situations. Reliability estimates for the two sets of scores appear in the shaded boxes along the diagonal. The lower value is the average correlation among the measures in each situation. The upper value is the estimate for the sum of these measures, stepped up from the average intercorrelation using the Spearman–Brown formula. Dashes indicate unreported values.

Hartshorne and May (1928, Book I, p. 383) emphasized the correlations below the diagonal, within and between kinds of situations. Thus, the average intercorrelation among classroom test copying scores is .70, but the average intercorrelation between these measures and cheating on classroom speed tests is only .29. For cheating in athletic contests, this average is only .20. These latter values are indeed low. However, the within-situation averages seen as reliability estimates are also quite low; the tests are short and the copying, speed, and athletic scores are difference scores, a notoriously troublesome form of measure. Summing the measures within situations increases reliability and allows stronger correlations to stand out above the main diagonal. The classroom measures are now especially noteworthy; indeed, if these values, ranging from .30 to .45, are corrected for unreliability in each, they then range from .41 to .54. It would appear that we have a contextual construct: The tendency to cheat in classroom test situations shows sufficient convergent validity to be measured and studied as a unified construct, at least provisionally. It also shows enough relation to cheating in athletics, and to the admittedly weak measures of lying and stealing, that some further studies along these lines would seem justified; what boundary to place on the contextual construct is an empirical question. Furthermore, Burton (1963) reached a conclusion similar to ours. He factor analyzed the matrices in Table 9–1 and also the matrix of correlations corrected for unreliability. All three analyses yielded essentially the same pattern: a strong central factor representing classroom honesty and small separate factors for athletic cheating and perhaps lying. Burton also showed that a Guttman Simplex model fit the correlation pattern reasonably well, especially for the classroom measures. Both these procedures work well in helping to define provisional boundaries for the contextual construct (see Burton, 1963, for reviews of other early research on character).

Other evidence supporting a consistent construct interpretation is given by Hartshorne and May (1928) themselves. For example, cognitive ability correlated with classroom academic cheating in the range of −.30 to −.50, whereas for cheating on puzzles, in athletics, and at parties, the correlations ranged from −.10 to −.24. Ability relations with stealing and lying were also notably negative, −.13 to −.35 respectively. All these relations are complicated by distribution problems and the use of various estimation, correction, and partialing formulas in different samples; for example, the incidence of deceit increased slightly with age, which was then partialed out of some correlation estimates. Nevertheless, the correlations of honesty with ability are consistent. Furthermore, the correlation between teacher ratings of student honesty and student classroom measures of honesty was about .40; comparable correlations between teacher ratings and student tests of general ability were about .50. Also reported were significant relations of honesty with socioeconomic level, emotional stability, teacher ratings on deportment, and resistance to suggestion. Instructions indicating that scores would count on monthly reports increased the incidence of cheating, but other experimental manipulations of test instructions (e.g., concerning student competition) had no effect. Thus, the desire to do well on classroom exercises seemed to be the primary motive for cheating and this was not otherwise manipulable; this suggests "need for achievement" as another corollary individual difference.

Finally, as Hartshorne and May (1928) noted, many children did not cheat at all. In the later work (Hartshorne, May, & Shuttleworth, 1930), it was reported that a total honesty score correlated .38 to .42 with moral knowledge tests and .48 with teacher and other student ratings of reputation in several samples, and that an honesty integration score reflecting each child's consistency across the honesty tests (without the party tests) showed marked individual differences. The authors concluded,

The doctrine of specificity holds for children in general but holds with very different force for different children. [Referring to points (1) and (2) in the previous passage quoted above, they go on] Our present data show that children differ among themselves. . . . Some children have learned to be honest or dishonest in more situations or have become acutely aware of the honest or dishonest implications of these situations than have children in general. Their behavior, as a result, is relatively consistent. . . . Another proportion of children have either not as yet learned to be either honest or dishonest in different situations or are not as yet aware of the implication of these situations for honesty or dishonesty. Their behavior is relatively inconsistent. They are at the mercy of the varying temptations of every changing moment. (pp. 308–309)

*Conclusion.* In short, classroom honesty is a significant individual difference—a phenomenon of importance to teachers and educational administrators, as well as students and parents, whether or not it is general across all domains of human conduct. That it may be connected primarily to conventional school situations, and even bounded therein, does not lessen its status or use as a relatively stable construct to be studied further in relation to persons and situations within that context. The finding that children differ in their consistency with respect to honesty is an important added feature of the construct and perhaps also of the age group studied; it was echoed decades later by Bem (see Bem & Allen, 1974; Bem & Funder, 1978) as a general observation about individual differences in consistency. What Hartshorne and May observed increasing in their age range might have been the *formation* of a traitlike dimension of schoolwork honesty that combines affective, conative, and cognitive aspects of educational behavior.

In the later studies, small batteries of behavioral tests of service (e.g., class loyalty, generosity, cooperation) and of self-control (e.g., persistence, inhibition) showed variable but useful reliability and were not highly interrelated. Tests of moral knowledge and attitude showed both high reliability and intercorrelation. In turn, these measures showed variable relation to classroom and student background characteristics. In their final conclusions, Hartshorne and May maintained that "In proportion as situations are alike, conduct is correlated. In proportion as situations are unlike, conduct is uncorrelated . . . [but also that] amount and consistency of character tend to go together. (pp. 373 *ff*).

*A Caution.* As this chapter proceeds, we try to show where some other old but potentially important constructs are buried, but we cannot stop to exhume each one for an autopsy. Similarly, we try to identify new constructs of importance to education, but we cannot evaluate carefully every study in the current explosion of new work. Readers must do this for each construct of interest in relation to their own ongoing theory, research, or practice. It is treacherous to rely only on what authors and reviewers say about a study. This is shown in our review of the character project, but it applies as well to other work, including our review of it.

## AFFECTIVE CONSTRUCTS OF TEMPERAMENT AND EMOTION

Returning now to Figure 9–1, our discussion of particular constructs proceeds from upper left to lower right, but the flow sometimes moves across rows, sometimes down columns. This is because relations between construct categories sometimes seem closer in one direction than another; we also sometimes combine adjacent categories for discussion in a common section. Our treatment of each construct within categories is necessarily brief. Because we think it important to emphasize the large range of possibilities for further reseach, we have opted for breadth rather than depth of coverage. Even with this, we hardly cover all constructs that could be listed in the taxonomy; we add representative references for broader and deeper reading where possible.

According to Allport (1961, p. 34), "temperament refers to the characteristic phenomena of an individual's emotional nature, including . . . susceptibility to emotional stimulation . . .

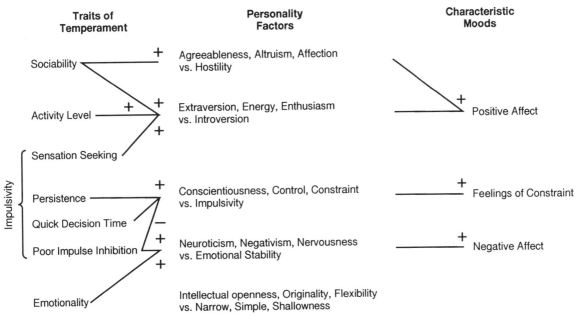

FIGURE 9–3. Schematic Network of Relations Among Temperament Traits, the Big Five Personality Factors, and Characteristic Moods

customary strength and speed of response . . . prevailing mood, and all the peculiarities of fluctuation and intensity in mood. . . ." Buss and Plomin (1984, p. 84) narrowed the definition; for them, temperaments are "inherited personality traits present in early childhood" that influence the development of adult personality. Eastern European research, developing from Pavlov's typology (see Gray, 1964), also distinguishes sharply between temperament and personality; the former concerns innate types reflecting individual differences in strength and speed, mobility, and balance of the nervous system as a function of biological evolution, whereas the latter concerns traits reflecting social learning and historical influences on the person (Strelau, 1983). Whether temperament and emotion categories are considered distinct or not, or singular and global, or highly multivariate and differentiated, most theorists agree that some subset of affective individual differences are heavily rooted in the biological substrate of behavior and are highly heritable, even though influenced by developmental experiences and displayed as a function of person–situation interaction. We call the constructs in this subset *traits of temperament* and separate them both from *characteristic emotional moods* and from *personality factors* presumed to derive as much or more from personal learning history. The three sets of constructs and some interrelations are shown in Figure 9–3. We take up temperaments, then moods, then personality factors in between.

## Traits of Temperament

Buss and Plomin (1984) define and measure three traits of normal temperament: activity level, sociability, and emotionality. The first concerns behavioral energy, including both vigor and tempo; vigor may be like Allport's customary strength or

intensity, whereas tempo may be like Allport's customary speed. Sociability represents need for social interaction and shared rather than solitary activities. Emotionality refers to physiological arousal associated with the emotions of distress, anger, or fear. It is of course possible to imagine subdivisions of sociability and emotionality analogous to the vigor/tempo distinction under activity level. Sociability might be expressed in either intensity or frequency of need for social contact. Similarly, emotionality could be expressed as either intensity or frequency of emotional response, or both. Some research suggests that this latter distinction may be particularly important. Individuals differ in how frequently they experience positive or negative moods but differ independently in how strongly they feel these moods when they do feel them; those persons who experience strong positive emotions may also be the persons who experience strong negative emotions (Larsen & Diener, 1987).

In earlier work, Buss and Plomin (1975) investigated impulsivity as a fourth temperament trait, consisting of four aspects: sensation seeking, persistence, quick decision time, and poor impulse inhibition. In later work this construction was dropped, presumably because the measures proved complex, with multiple relations to other constructs. We retain it here, however, and list its parts along with the other three temperament constructs in Figure 9–3, because we see the parts as important in education regardless of whether or not they cohere as a unified temperament construct. Impulsivity is later discussed as a personal style, persistence as a volitional construct, and sensation seeking as a personality construct. This provides a good example of potential interconnectedness across rows and columns in Figure 9–1.

Eastern European researchers have studied some of the same or similar temperament traits for decades (Strelau, 1983). Early studies in the Pavlovian tradition measured strength of excitation of the nervous system as efficiency and sensitivity with respect to stimulus thresholds, and contrasted individuals with "strong" versus "weak" nervous systems in relation to memory efficiency and styles of action in academic performance. Strong individuals are said to do well when memory tasks involve large amounts of difficult but relatively meaningless material; weak individuals are more efficient in recall of meaningful text. However in academic work, evidence suggests that weak children are more prone to fatigue, needing more relaxation, silence, and solitude during homework than strong children, who, in contrast, show more need for warmup but then do homework at a stretch; they function more efficiently without the need for preparatory plans and are liable to increased intellectual activity but shorter performance duration during tension or stress, relative to weak children. A further observation is that concentration and attention to high school learning tasks is lower under stressful conditions for weak students than for strong students.

Continuing research by Strelau (1983) and others has advanced these and several related lines of work. Based on the Pavlovian tradition, self-report inventories have been developed for use as substitutes for observational diagnoses and laboratory methods of measurement. Scales for strength of excitation, strength of inhibition, and mobility of nervous processes are included in one. Another inventory on the temporal aspects of temperament yields two dimensions, representing the persistence or perseverance and the tempo or liveliness of behavior. For Strelau the major dimensions of temperament are reactivity (intensity of reaction to stimulus situations) and activity (amount and range of stimulative activities undertaken). Individuals seek to maintain optimal activation. The higher the reactivity, the less need there is for stimulating activity, and vice versa. High- and low reactive persons thus differ in their preference for low- and high-stimulation activities, respectively. The contrast relates to arousability (see Farley, 1981, 1985) and to the activity level and sensation-seeking constructs of Buss and Plomin (1975, 1984) and others (see subsequent discusson, this chapter). As summarized by Strelau (1983), the evidence suggests that high-reactive persons avoid stress and tension that might reduce productivity, taking breaks to avoid overstimulation and alternating activities to give particular mental functions rest; low-reactive persons don't need rest breaks—they seek the stimulating novelty and complexity that high reactives minimize. In contrast to low reactives, high-reactive learners prefer concrete over abstract tasks and algorithmic over heuristic instruction. They also engage in more auxiliary actions while attempting text comprehension, such as underlining, making notes and summaries, segmenting the text, and reviewing. Both preference for type of instruction and tendency toward auxiliary learning strategies show clear ATI patterns. Strelau's (1983) conclusion was that

all experiments aimed at manipulating the functional structure of action by using different kinds of instruction, show that high-reactive persons prefer situations which ensure task performance through the use of a large number of auxiliary actions. When forced to perform tasks which contradict their preferences, the high-reactive persons invest more effort or display a lowering of performance level. (p 220).

Strelau also recommended that reactivity and ability be investigated jointly in further work. For further review of contemporary research on temperament, see Strelau, Farley, and Gale (1985, 1986) and Bates and Wachs (1994).

## Characteristic Emotional Moods

Although emotions are usually thought of as states, not traits, it is clear that individuals differ consistently in the mood states they seem to adopt, display, or submit to in given types of situations. A student may exhibit happiness or boredom in particular classes every day or in school all day every day. These are emotional states that seem to have become more general and frequent response tendencies—that is, traits. We call them here characteristic emotional moods, but they have also often been referred to as affects (Tomkins, 1962, 1963) and even as emotion traits (Izard, 1991).

Tellegen (1982, 1985; Watson, Clark, & Tellegen, 1988) has conducted factor-analytic studies of moods using statelike adjectives such as alert, attentive, interested, and proud for positive mood; afraid, guilty, hostile, and nervous for negative mood; and cautious, plodding, reflective, and sensible for constrained mood. These three mood constructs seem to show clear connections to temperament and personality constructs, as shown in Figure 9–3 (see John, 1990). Of course, the positive and negative moods should correlate with each personality factor positively or negatively, depending on which pole is focused on for each dimension.

It was noted that research on the temperament construct of emotionality suggests individual differences in either the frequency or the intensity of both positive and negative emotions. Tellegen's mood state factors do not seem to capture this frequency-intensity distinction but could be used to study it further. There is other evidence that an intensity or activation level aspect of moods is distinguishable (Sjöberg, Svensson, & Persson, 1979). Particularly in school settings, one might expect to find not only pervasive positive or negative emotional moods among different students but also within-person shifts between strong positive and negative emotions connected with different courses or teachers or learning tasks. At present, little is known about how moods become long lasting or pervasive, or how they change as situations change.

Research on these characteristic moods could provide a beginning for a more detailed analysis of individual differences in emotions related to learning in educational situations. Such an analysis could be linked to the explosion of interest in the general psychology of emotions over the past decade. There are now numerous collections and broad reviews, several of which are particularly useful for educational psychology (see, e.g., Frijda, 1986; Izard, 1991; Izard et al., 1984; Lazarus, 1991). This work has shown relations between various emotions and temperament constructs, motivational and volitional processes (including interest and self-regulation), and cognitive functions (e.g., Pekrun, 1992). There are also increasingly interesting cognitive analyses of emotions (e.g., Ortony, Clore, & Collins, 1988) and of children's knowledge about emotions (e.g., Stein & Levine, 1987).

Here are just a few of the possibilities for linkage. It is known that recall of previous experience, including material explicitly learned, can be mood dependent. Learners recall better if their emotional state during recall matches their mood in learning

(Bower, 1981). Thus, students who differ in characteristic mood should differ qualitatively in what they learn, and also quantitatively to the degree that mood during learning and mood during recall differ. It is further known that positive affect induced during learning enhances meaningful cognitive organization and processing; happy students may be more likely to encode new information in ways that connect it more fully and flexibly to existing knowledge, in both obvious and creative ways, and to modify existing knowledge organization in the process (see Isen, Daubman, & Gorgoglione, 1987). This encoding enriches and thus facilitates learning on some tasks (e.g., meaningful accretion, categorization, problem solving, recall) but may impair performance on others (e.g., rote memorization), where an enriched cognitive context may interfere with or distract attention from surface essentials. In other words, a characteristic positive affect may be an aptitude for meaningful learning and problem-solving situations, but not for rote learning. Further, for students desiring personally meaningful learning, encountering learning situations that match or satisfy these desires will elicit positive emotion and subsequently enhanced learning, whereas situations that do not match or that frustrate these concerns elicit indifference or negative emotion (Frijda, 1986). Clearly also, students' emotional response to learning situations depends on their present appraisal of such situations, beyond their match–mismatch, reward–punishment history in similar situations. According to Lazarus (1982):

[T]he concept of appraisal appears to emphasize individual differences and thereby requires complex, even individualized, rules about the determinants of appraisal. (p. 1024)

Concern for individual differences leads inevitably to concern with personal meanings and to the factors that shape such meanings (p. 1022)

[Thus] . . . above all, emotions are individual phenomena and display great variations among individuals; although to some extent people share emotional experiences, and general laws can be formulated about the emotion process, an emotion happens to an individual with a distinctive history who wants, thinks, and confronts specific environments, evaluates their significance, and acts as adaptively as possible.

One major task now is to translate the suggestions and implications of views and findings such as the above into research in educational psychology. But an equally important task is to start in real educational settings to trace the role of affect. We thus cite here three example studies concerned directly with emotion differences and learning in schools.

McCaslin, Tuck, Wiard, B. Brown, LaPage, and Pyle (1994) used both experience sampling and student journals to obtain affective data from fourth graders in a study of cooperative math learning. Their measures included personal affect ratings of positive and the absence of negative emotions ("How I felt in my group today") as well as complementary ("How it was in group today") scales. The latter asked students to recognize elements of their own group-related behavior that may have either enhanced or obstructed the group process and related student affect. Results showed reasonable reliability for each subscale and a moderate positive correlation between students' reports of absent negative experiences in small groups and student achievement. Enhancing and interfering behavior were

related to the absence and presence of negative affect measures, as expected. Perceived interfering behavior showed negative correlations with student achievement as well. Correlations between positive affect, perceived behavior, and achievement were weak, suggesting that the negative emotion–cognition linkages may be most salient for students at this grade level in small-group math tasks.

Boekaerts (1987) investigated "on-line" aspects of affect and motivation in adolescents as they completed math tasks reflective of their regular curriculum. She also developed a Stress and Coping Inventory based on interviews with early adolescents concerning their regularly occurring academic stressors (e.g., tests, homework, failures, and other classroom challenges, including conflicts with teachers and peers) and how they coped. Following work by Lazarus and Folkman (1984), Boekaerts distinguished two modes of coping strategies: problem focused and emotion focused. Students are assumed to prefer one mode of coping, but most coping models allow that individuals may use both forms of coping, even in the same stressful situation. The former includes attempts to alter perceived stressors, often through planful problem solving. The latter refers to attempts to regulate negative emotions related to the stressor or to regain self-control (see also Suls & Fletcher, 1986, for related distinctions identified by other coping research).

Boekaerts's on-line measure asked students to answer questions about their confidence for doing math tasks, their state anxiety, the perceived relevance of the task, and effort expenditure. Path analyses related all of these variables to task performance, a questionnaire measure of fear of failure, and "disengagement." Disengagement was assessed using Kuhl's (1984) Action Control Scale and registered students' reported use of procedures to regulate action in the presence of intrusive thoughts or feelings of anxiety. Students high on disengagement are not preoccupied with failure, but rather mentally disengage from the perturbing situation.

Boekaerts's research demonstrated that students who can control their actions through disengagement tend to have more positive feelings about their performance, lower anxiety, and higher performance on these tasks. Following Kuhl's theory, the control of action through careful monitoring and pointed effort is a regulatory mechanism for state anxiety and ruminating thoughts. In these studies, disengagement is viewed as an adaptive process that helps the student to "restore well-being," and not as a defense mechanism (Boekaerts, 1993, 1994).

Other research by Boekaerts, Hendricksen, and Maes (1987) finds that students who frequently experience academic stressors report more problem-focused than emotion-focused coping and that gender differences occur in these processes. Females more frequently than males reported experiencing interpersonal stressors and tended to report more problem-focused coping. Coping strategies differ by age and ability as well in Boekaerts's studies, suggesting a need to conduct subgroup analyses in continuing research on relationships between emotion and learning, and more generally between personality and intelligence (Boekaerts, 1995).

Pekrun (1994) studied academic emotion as "habitual experiences typical of individual students" (p. 13). Self-ratings of positive and negative academic emotions (in learning and test-taking situations) were correlated with self-regulated learning and achievement in German university courses. The four learning-related emotions identified were joy, anger, anxiety, and boredom. The emotions identified in test situations were joy, hope, relief, anger, anxiety, and hopelessness. The two learning and test subscales of the Academic Emotion questionnaire reliably measure four components for each of the above-mentioned emotions—affective, physiological, cognitive, and motivational. Self-regulated learning strategies were measured by questionnaire (Pintrich, Smith, Garcia, & McKeachie, 1991), and course grades represented academic achievement. Pekrun's results support the distinctiveness of the different categories of emotion identified. In his study, learning- and test-related enjoyment correlated positively with interest, motivation to learn, and self-regulation strategies of time management and effort expenditure. Anger and hopelessness correlated negatively with these variables. Patterns were similar for correlations between positive and negative emotions and achievement. Thus, different academic emotions can be distinguished empirically; these emotions seem to serve different functions in student learning and performance (see also Pekrun, 1992; Pekrun & Frese, 1992).

## Personality Factors

Personality differences go beyond temperaments biologically defined and beyond prevailing moods that reflect long-term positive or negative experience, although they may derive in part from combinations of these sources. Differences also arise from each individual's personal and social learning history within particular familial and cultural contexts. There is a long tradition of research on personality differences shown in self-report questionnaires, in ratings by others, and in the person-descriptive features of language.

***The Big Five Model.*** After decades of factor-analytic research on personality differences, a clear convergence of evidence seems now at hand that organizes the many dozens of subordinate constructs and measures under five superdimensions (see John, 1990, for the history). As shown in Figure 9–3, the five are *agreeableness versus hostility* (including such other factor labels as friendliness, compliance, likability, and sociability); *extraversion versus introversion* (including surgency, assertiveness, ambition, and power); *conscientiousness* (including responsibility, dependability, self-control, and will to achieve); *neuroticism versus emotional stability* (including anxiety, emotionality, emotional control, and adjustment); and *intellectual openness* (including intelligence, culture, independence, and flexibility). These five major personality factors are connected in Figure 9–3 with the temperament traits described previously, as well as with the emotional moods. Average mood (and also mood variability) is associated with extraversion; negative mood is related to neuroticism (Hepburn & Eysenck, 1989). It is noteworthy that the temperaments also map reasonably well onto three of these more molar personality dimensions. The other two major dimensions connect to other parts of the taxonomy in Figure 9–1. *Intellectual openness* is intelligence, but defined more broadly to include cognitive abilities in concert with an affective-conative style of open, independent, flexible inquiry. Presumably this dimension is close to G and Gf as defined by Gustafsson and Undheim (chapter 8, this volume). Although *conscientiousness* seems to be the popular label, Dig-

man (1990) has suggested that "will to achieve" or simply "will" is the better term; this connects the interpretation of this factor back to Webb's (1915) early factor-analytic study of character and intelligence and also to the early German psychology of will, which in turn connects to our category of volition, as noted earlier. There are also dimensions of social behavior identified by Bales (1970) and Wiggins (1979) that connect closely with the agreeableness and extraversion dimensions of the Big Five.

For a detailed summary of the factor-analytic research supporting the five-factor model, see Digman (1990) and John (1990). Also, Hofstee, De Raad, and Goldberg (1992) offer an integration of the five-factor and circumplex models of trait structure that may be an important alternative to hierarchical factor models of the sort appropriate for the ability domain (see chapter 8, this volume). Here discussion is limited to each superdimension taken individually.

***Extraversion, Introversion, and Learning.*** Among children, extraversion seems associated with higher school achievement, whereas among adolescents and adults introverts show higher achievement than extraverts. Introverts also appear to perform better under structured learning conditions; extraverts seem better off with less external structure. It would appear, then, that the organizational structure of conventional secondary level instruction favors introverts. On the other hand, extraverts seem less able than introverts to maintain concentration under independent learning conditions, such as library study or homework. In summarizing this research, Eysenck and Eysenck (1985) noted that relations may be reciprocal. Able learners may become more introverted over time, especially as more advanced or difficult academic work requires more effort and concentration, and the greater social engagement of extraverts may distract them from or diminish their academic work. Noteworthy here, however, is the finding by Entwistle and Wilson (1970) that extraverts with academic motivation and good study habits were as effective as introverts. So a further question for research concerns how and why personality differences are manifested in different learning activities and styles.

M. W. Eysenck (1981) also summed up much of the literature on the relation of extraversion/introversion to cognitive processes involved in learning and memory. Most studies were laboratory experiments using verbal tasks. The more robust and important research findings were listed by him as follows

Reward enhances the performance of extraverts more than introverts, whereas punishment impairs the performance of introverts more than extraverts.

Introverts are more susceptible than extraverts to distraction.

Introverts are more affected than extraverts by response competition.

Introverts take longer than extraverts to retrieve information from long-term or permanent storage, especially non-dominant information.

Introverts have higher response criteria than extraverts.

Extraverts show better retention-test performance than introverts at short retention intervals, but the opposite happens at long retention intervals.

In general, introverts seem to display higher motivational baselines and higher aspirations for their performance than do extraverts, and so invest their cognitive resources more fully. They may thus be less affected by rewards, more affected by distractions, competition, and punishments, and more focused

FIGURE 9–4. Relationship of Achievement to extraversion and neuroticism for boys, girls, and Total Sample of 13-year-old Scottish Students

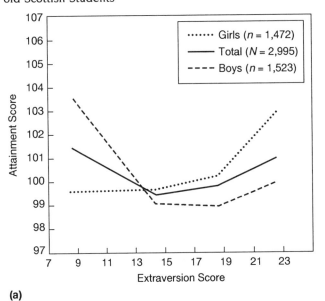

(a)

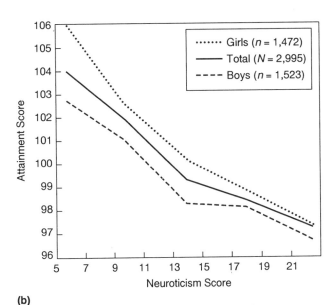

(b)

*Source*: "Neuroticism and School Attainment: A Linear Relationship?" by N. Entwistle and S. Cunningham, *British Journal of Educational Psychology, 38,* pp. 123–132. Adapted by permission.

on the costs and worries of less than optimal performance than are extraverts.

A large study of middle school children by N. Entwistle and Cunningham (1968) introduced an interesting complication to this summary. Extraversion scores showed a curvilinear relation to teacher rankings on academic attainment, and different patterns for males and females. As shown in Figure 9–4A, males were ranked higher by their teachers if introverted, whereas females were ranked higher if extraverted. The attainment scores may reflect gender-linked personality differences in learning. It

may also be that females act out their classroom extraversion in more socially acceptable ways than do males, on average.

Entwistle and Cunningham also studied neuroticism, with the result shown in Figure 9–4B. The negative linear trend for both gender groups is consistent with much other evidence on schoolchildren: Emotionally stable students show higher achievement than neurotic students. When extroversion and neuroticism were crossed, it was the stable extravert females and stable introvert males who showed highest attainment scores.

*Neuroticism, Anxiety, Impulsivity and Learning.* As noted above, Figure 9–4 displays a frequent finding of a negative relation between neuroticism or anxiety measures and learning outcome measures. But this relation is moderated by other factors. It can be strongly negative among unselected schoolchildren, only mildly negative among high school students, and even mildly positive among college students. This suggests higher order interaction with cognitive ability. There is strong evidence of ability × anxiety × treatment interaction with high-structure versus low-structure instructional methods. But there is also a moderating effect of learning task difficulty and type and strength of reward and punishment (for details, see Eysenck & Eysenck, 1985; Snow, 1977b, 1989a).

Neuroticism and anxiety are considered synonymous by some researchers, but not by others (e.g., Gray, 1973, 1982). The reward and punishment point also relates to Gray's theory, which brings in the construct of impulsivity—an apparent opposite of conscientiousness and closely related to the impulsivity temperament hypothesized by Buss and Plomin (1975). Figure 9–5 shows Gray's proposal. Anxiety increases from stable extravert to neurotic introvert. Impulsivity increases from stable introvert to neurotic extravert. Also, anxiety reflects sensitivity to cues for punishment, whereas impulsivity reflects sensitivity to cues for reward. Therefore, the anxious person should perform better under threat of punishment, whereas the impulsive person should do better with rewards and praise. Note that the regions of anxiousness and impulsivity overlap in response to reward and punishment. In other words, neuroticism equals anxiety plus impulsivity and reflects sensitivity to both reward and punishment.

Extraversion/introversion represents a balance; extraverts are more sensitive to reward, introverts are more sensitive to punishment. Various sources of evidence support these ideas in relation to learning (see Gray, 1982). However, there are major complications. A program of work by Revelle (1989) on these and related personality–performance relationships suggests that different task demands (e.g., demand for transfer or memory), arousal conditions (e.g., time of day, caffeine intake), and outcome measures (e.g., accuracy, persistence) can have significant interacting effects. Also, it is not clear for educational settings how and why threat of punishment should help anxious learners, especially over some duration. Contrasting evidence suggests that anxious learners are helped by reducing threat, formality, and competition (Birney, Burdick, & Teevan, 1969). Further work in educational settings is needed on these points. Also, much further work on anxiety and instruction, referred to later under evaluation anxiety, needs to be considered.

*Subordinate Personality Factors.* Many factor theorists agree that personality differences can be represented hierarchically,

FIGURE 9–5. Schematic Representation of Gray's Hypothesis for Interrelationships Among Anxiety, Impulsivity, Neuroticism, and Extraversion

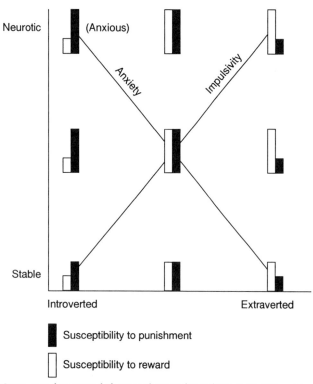

Neurotic     (Anxious)

Stable

Introverted              Extraverted

■ Susceptibility to punishment

□ Susceptibility to reward

*Source:* Based on "Causal Theories of Personality and How to Test Them," by J. A. Gray, 1973, in *Multivariate Analysis and Psychological Theory*, edited by T. R. Royce, London: Academic Press, pp. 409–463. Adapted by permission.

much as are cognitive abilities. The broad, Big Five constructs would be at the top, with successively narrower constructs at middle levels, and specific dispositions and responses at the bottom level, as suggested by the levels of Figure 9–2. This hierarchical conceptualization of personality reflects the observation that significant correlations often occur among personality measures, and also among factors. However, in contrast to the ability domain, personality dimensions are more loosely interrelated; some correlations are negative, some are unstable, and some may well be nonlinear. There is also continuing disagreement concerning how best to name and define many of the factors in the middle range below the Big Five level, which factors belong to which subordinate level, and which levels of the hierarchy are most important. New studies and reanalyses of old data continue (see, e.g., Costa & McCrae, 1988; H. J. Eysenck, 1977; Guilford, 1975), but none has yet attempted a comprehensive reanalysis using consistent methodology, as Carroll (1993) has done for the cognitive ability domain. It is therefore premature to attempt for personality factors anything like the cognitive hierarchical structure offered by Gustafsson and Undheim (chapter 8, this volume) for abilities (see also Hofstee et al., 1992).

It is worthwhile, however, to show a sampling of the variety of subordinate constructs available from some of the long-standing and widely used assessment instruments. Table 9–2 includes four columns for four theorists whose work can be considered central. Guilford (1959; Guilford & Zimmerman,

1949) and Cattell (1965; Cattell, Eber, & Tatsuoka, 1970) were among the first to develop multidimensional personality assessments in the factor-analytic tradition. D. N. Jackson (1984) developed his instrument to reflect Murray's (1938) theory of manifest needs. Gough (1987) used empirical group comparisons based on peer ratings of high school and college students as well as factor analysis.

It is clear that the four lists are similar, but also that each includes unique factors. Potential problems as well as potential progress may be represented here. Factor measures with the same or similar names may in fact reflect different qualities, and factor measures with different names may nonetheless reflect the same qualities. In other words, there may be examples of both the jingle and the jangle fallacies here.

Factor analysis of correlations across the four lists would probably reproduce the Big Five dimensions and might identify other factors as well. However, although the Big Five solution seems robust across diverse samples, cultures, and measuring instruments, some theorists believe it leaves out important aspects of personality that are included when a more differentiated and complex view is taken. Mershon and Gorsuch (1988), for example, examined the relationship between differing numbers of factors and criterion data from 16 studies. They concluded that when factor extraction was increased from 6 to 16, most studies showed a substantial increase in percentage of criterion variance accounted for. Unless a factor analysis is designed to be hierarchical, it will ignore variance specific to any one personality dimension or scale. Only the covariation among the primary scales listed in Table 9–2 would be included in the five resulting second-order factors; the specific and content-related aspects of the primary scales would usually be dropped. Yet it may be the specific or content-related components of a personality dimension that best represent the construct of interest in some educational situation under study. For example, neuroticism includes aggression and anxiety, among other dimensions, but aggression and anxiety differ in important ways. Extraversion includes both exhibition and dominance, and introversion includes both reflectiveness and restraint, but each of these constructs has unique meaning in its own right. Perhaps some of the controversy in naming the Big Five dimensions stems from problems such as these, where the superconstruct coordinates but does not capture the several constituent dimensions. Perhaps research on personality differences needs to include and study broad, narrow, and specific factors simultaneously; this is the recommendation from ability factor research (see chapter 8, this volume).

There have been many attempts over the years to correlate these multiple dimensions of personality with multiple dimensions of student school achievement, and also achievement in industrial training and job-related performance. As noted earlier, however, large surveys of linear correlations may provide markers to show where more analytic research might dig deeper, and certainly large and stable linear correlations can be used to support decision rules for selection or classification. But often such correlations are unsatisfying because they do not afford analytic interpretations.

Table 9–3 provides one example from a study relating scores on Cattell's High School Personality Questionnaire to teacher ratings and Stanford Achievement Test scores for a sample of U.S. seventh graders from a small midwestern city (Cattell &

TABLE 9-2. Primary Personality Factors Available from Four Assessment Instruments

| Guilford–Zimmerman (1949): Temperament Survey | Cattell, Eber & Tatsuoka (1970): 16 Personality Factors | Jackson (1984): Personality Research Form | Gough (1987): California Psychological Inventory |
|---|---|---|---|
| General Activity | Reserved vs. Outgoing | Abasement | Femininity |
| Ascendance | Less Intelligent vs. More Intelligent | Achievement | Achievement via Conformance |
| Sociability | Emotional vs. Stable | Affiliation | Sociability |
| Self-Restraint | Humble vs. Assertive | Aggression | Tolerance |
| Reflectiveness | Sober vs. Happy-go-lucky | Autonomy | Good Impression |
| Emotionality | Expedient vs. Conscientious | Change | Flexibility |
| Depression | Shy vs. Venturesome | Cognitive Structure | Social Presence |
| Calmness vs. Nervousness | Tough-minded vs. Tender-minded | Defendence | Socialization |
| Confidence vs. Inferiority | Trusting vs. Suspicious | Dominance | Dominance |
| Objectivity | Practical vs. Imaginative | Endurance | Capacity for Status |
| Friendliness | Forthright vs. Shrewd | Exhibition | Self-Acceptance |
| Good Personal Relations | Placid vs. Apprehensive | Harm Avoidance | Communality |
| Masculinity vs. Femininity | Conservative vs. Experimenting | Impulsivity | Responsibility |
| | Group-tied vs. Self-Sufficient | Nurturance | Flexibility |
| | Casual vs. Controlled | Order | Sense of Well-being |
| | Relaxed vs. Tense | Play | Self-Control |
| | | Sentience | Intellectual Efficiency |
| | | Social Recognition | Psychological Mindedness |
| | | Succorance | Achievement via Independence |
| | | Understanding | |
| | | Infrequency | |
| | | Desirability | |

TABLE 9-3. Correlations of School Achievement Measures with Personality Factors

| | Intellectual Openness | | Agreeableness | Extraversion | | Conscientiousness | | Neuroticism |
|---|---|---|---|---|---|---|---|---|
| | Intelligence | Resourcefulness | Reserved | Dominance | Surgency | Conscientiousness | Will power | Neuroticism |
| | B | $Q_2$ | A | E | F | G | $Q_3$ | C |
| **Teacher ratings** | | | | | | | | |
| Sports Interest | 35* | 07 | 15 | 18* | 16* | 14 | 01 | 08 |
| Sports Achievement | 39* | 11 | 30* | 23* | 05 | 24* | 12 | 09 |
| Social Adjustment | 35* | 12 | 21* | 27* | 11 | 24* | 13 | 09 |
| Leadership | 45* | 14 | 21* | 23* | 15 | 28* | 14 | 10 |
| Good Behavior | 18* | 15 | 13 | 28* | −09 | 18* | 26* | −10 |
| Academic Interest | 53* | 30* | 26* | 26* | 07 | 37* | 19* | 07 |
| Personal Adjustment | 41* | 29* | 20* | 21* | 01 | 31* | 18* | 11 |
| **Test scores** | | | | | | | | |
| Total Score | 62* | 35* | 17* | 22* | 02 | 34* | 18* | 02 |
| Paragraph Meaning | 57* | 35* | 15 | 14 | 05 | 32* | 14 | 03 |
| Word Meaning | 58* | 32* | 04 | 08 | −01 | 29* | 13 | −02 |
| Spelling | 53* | 18* | 25* | 30* | 16* | 33* | 05 | 03 |
| Language | 53* | 22* | 21* | 24* | 02 | 34* | 13 | 00 |
| Arithmetic Reasoning | 54* | 35* | 19* | 10 | −02 | 31* | 12 | 04 |
| Personal Adjustment | 46* | 26* | 19* | 22* | 01 | 36* | 03 | −08 |

Note: Based on *The Prediction of Achievement and Creativity* (p. 187) by R. B. Cattell and H. J. Butcher, 1968, New York: Bobbs-Merrill. Adapted by permission.

Note: N = 153; $r_{05}$ = .16. Decimals are omitted. An asterisk (*) indicates correlations significant at $p < .05$.

Butcher, 1968). The table gives simple correlations for eight factors; we group these into clusters to correspond roughly to the five-factor model discussed previously. We have omitted from the table results for six other personality factors because they showed no interesting correlations. As usual, a general intelligence measure produced substantial correlation with almost all teacher and achievement test criteria. However, the number of significant correlations for personality measures here is noteworthy; none is large, but many are appreciable and deserving of further consideration in research on cognitive outcomes. When considering educational outcomes beyond the strictly cognitive, many other relations are especially interesting. Multiple correlational analysis showed that the personality measures added substantially to the criterion variance accounted for, beyond that due to ability alone; for about half the teacher ratings and half the test criteria, an increase in $R$ due to the personality addition was statistically significant.

## Selected Affective Complexes

Just as uncertainty remains as to how best to organize the middle range of personality factors in the Big Five model, there may also be important superordinate constructs not well characterized by combinations of factors at either level (Wiggins & Pincus, 1992). These constructs might take the form of broad dimensions, profiles, or types; or they might best be treated as blends, syndromes, compounds, or complexes. We discuss briefly several examples of such complex constructs that may be particularly relevant for new research in educational psychology.

*Authoritarianism.* A classic study of personality differences emerged from recognition during World War II that some human beings, although apparently intelligent, educated, and independent citizens in many respects, could harbor irrational superstitions, prejudices, and religious and racial hatreds, and could be both ruthlessly aggressive and blindly submissive to authority in pursuing them. To understand the emergence of this apparently new personality type, Adorno, Frenkel-Brunswik, Levinson, and Sanford (1950/1982) conducted interview and questionnaire studies to assess tendencies toward anti-Semitism, fascism, and ethnocentrism more generally. Their analysis produced the concept of the "authoritarian personality" and its ideal opposite, the "genuine liberal." Their discussion defines the two types while also exemplifying careful, qualified use of typological constructs:

[A] basically hierarchical, authoritarian, exploitive parent–child relationship is apt to carry over into a power-oriented, exploitively dependent attitude toward one's sex partner and one's God and may well culminate in a political philosophy and social outlook which has no room for anything but a desperate clinging to what appears to be strong and a disdainful rejection of whatever is relegated to the bottom. The inherent dramatization likewise extends from the parent–child dichotomy to the dichotomous handling of social relations as manifested especially in the formation of stereotypes and of ingroup–outgroup cleavages. Conventionality, rigidity, repressive denial, and the ensuing break-through of one's weakness, fear and dependency are but other aspects of the same fundamental personality pattern, and they can be observed in personal life as well as in attitudes toward religion and social issues.

On the other hand, there is a pattern characterized chiefly by affec-

tionate, basically equalitarian, and permissive interpersonal relationships. This pattern encompasses attitudes within the family and toward the opposite sex, as well as an internalization of religious and social values. Greater flexibility and the potentiality for more genuine satisfactions appear as results of this basic attitude.

However, the two opposite types of outlook must by no means be regarded as absolutes. They emerge as a result of statistical analysis and thus have to be considered as syndromes of correlating and dynamically related factors. They consist in accumulations of symptoms frequently found together but they leave plenty of room for variations of specific features. Furthermore, various distinct subtypes are found within each of the two major patterns. Above all, two subvarieties of the ethnically prejudiced must be distinguished: the conventional and the psychopathic. Many more subvarieties can be distinguished on the basis of differential preoccupation with this or that particular trait that is alleged to exist in an ethnic minority. Our prejudiced subjects, however, are on the whole more alike as a group than are the unprejudiced. The latter include a great variety of personalities; many, on the surface at least, have no more extreme variants in common than the absence of a particular brand of hostility.

Indications are that there may be more similarity, within the major types, at the core than at the surface. This holds especially for the highly prejudiced subject, with his great variety of rationalizations and behavioral manifestations of prejudice. (pp. 475–476)

Research on the authoritarian complex and on various measurement and methodological problems connected with it declined over the years, but recent work has reaffirmed its validity and improved its measurement (see Christie, 1991; Stone & Lederer, 1991). Factor-analytic work by Kline and Cooper (1984; see also Kline, 1993) in particular shows a clear dimension associated with obsessiveness, conscientiousness, rigidity, and control that seems distinct from other major personality dimensions. Their study also suggested that a dogmatism scale developed by Rokeach (1960) to generalize the authoritarian concept to cover rigidity of both right- and left-wing beliefs probably reflects a distinct aspect deserving separate study (see also Christie, 1991).

Authoritarianism is not merely a remnant of World War II. It is not limited to anti-Semitic or fascist ideology. It is a multifaceted complex that includes aspects related to aggression and submission to authority as well as rigidity and stereotypy in ethnocentric, political, and socioeconomic beliefs. Perhaps most important, ethnocentrism in some degree may be a fundamental characteristic of all human beings, in all times, and thus an enduring problem for education. Change in ethnocentric thinking and attitudes may be a critical educational goal. In the extreme, rigid, prejudicial ingroup–outgroup thinking can have deep, even explosive negative consequences for the school community and thus for the whole educational enterprise. Work on modern problems of ethnic diversity, ethnocentrism, and aggression in education would do well to start with a review of the research on authoritarianism.

*Bullies and Victims.* The work of Olweus (1979, 1984, in press) is a good example of research on another problem-oriented personality complex related to aggression and which therefore may also relate to authoritarianism. The problem in this instance is bullying at school. Bullying or victimization is indicated when a person is the target, repeatedly over time, of intentionally aggressive acts by one or more other persons that are designed to inflict injury or discomfort; the acts can be physical or mental, direct or indirect (e.g., in the form of social ostracism or isolation), but they always involve a real or implied power difference favoring the bully.

Olweus conducted extensive questionnaire surveys in Scandinavia on the frequency and kinds of bullying. He was able to construct descriptions of children and adolescents who were typically bullies or victims, the patterns of behavior associated with several subgroups, and the family backgrounds and school characteristics related to these patterns. He also gathered evidence from other European countries and the United States.

Bullying is now recognized as a serious and increasing problem for the educational systems of many countries. Some estimates suggest that upward of 30% of the student population may be either bully or victim at some stage of school life. Bullying occurs in all grades, although its incidence declines with grade; as age increases, its form may change from direct physical acts to indirect verbal or social acts. Bullies are often older than their victims. Males tend to be bullied more than females, but males also tend to carry out much of the bullying to which females are subjected. Males show more bullying and use more direct physical aggression; females are more likely to use indirect harassment. Both bullies and victims tend to be stable groups; that is, individual bullies and victims show consistency in this pattern of behavior over time. Survey estimates also suggest that most bullying occurs at school, rather than en route to or from school; that teachers usually do little to stop it; and that most parents are unaware of it. There are large individual differences among schools in the frequency of occurrence of bullying, but these differences are not correlated with school location (urban vs. rural) or school size.

There are typical personality profiles associated with each group, although there are several subgroups. Passive or submissive victims are typically anxious, insecure, cautious, relatively low in self-esteem and in physical strength, and more often socially isolated. Their behavior may signal to bullies that they will not assert themselves or retaliate if attacked. Olweus noted that an important though smaller subgroup consists of provocative victims who display both anxious and aggressive reactions and may be hyperactive and irritating or disruptive for their classmates, thus provoking negative reactions. Victimization has been found to predict poor self-esteem and depression in the years after school.

Bullies are typically aggressive toward teachers and parents as well as other students. On average, they show impulsivity, a need for dominance, a positive self-concept, and little anxiety, insecurity, or empathy for their victims. An important subgroup consists of passive bullies or henchmen—followers who may otherwise show a variety of profiles. Olweus (in press) reported follow-up studies in which about 60% of male bullies in Grades 6 through 9 had one criminal conviction by age 24, and about 40% had three or more convictions. Olweus's work has also produced descriptions of parent–child relations that may lead to later bullying, school and classroom conditions that may support it, and suggestions for teacher and parent programs to combat it.

*Sensation Seekers.* Another personality complex that may be important for education has been labeled "sensation seeking." Although thought of as an aspect of temperament (and impulsivity) by some theorists (see Figure 9–2), it deserves attention as

a broad dimension in its own right (see D. W. Fiske & Maddi, 1961). The construct has been defined as "the need for varied, novel, and complex sensations and experiences and the willingness to take physical and social risks for the sake of such experience" (Zuckerman, 1979, p. 10). Recent research by Björck-Åkesson (1990) has shown that the major dimension should be interpreted more broadly as need or preference versus nonpreference for arousing experiences in everyday activities in general, not necessarily only in novel, complex, or risky situations. In adapting her model for research with school-age students, she also established four subordinate, narrow dimensions—thrill and adventure seeking, new experience seeking, activity, and outgoingness—that capture some aspects of Zuckerman's measures for adults.

Björck-Åkesson (1990) has related her measures to several dimensions of attitudes toward school and also to cognitive ability differences among students in Sweden who were tested in Grade 6 and again in Grade 8. The results suggested that sensation seeking as a broad preference for arousal was related to positive attitudes toward challenges and complexities in school learning and toward working in small groups, and negative attitudes about teachers imposing structure. Also, students high in general ability and in spatial visualization showed increased sensation-seeking tendencies between Grades 6 and 8.

Some of this evidence is consistent with prior studies by Farley (1981, 1985), who theorizes that school environments, instructional procedures, and teacher personalities vary significantly in arousal potential. Traditional, relatively structured classrooms are less arousing, whereas relatively unstructured situations involving inductive teaching, open discussion, and student decision-making are potentially more arousing. The ATI hypothesis is that high-sensation seekers should prefer and excel in high-arousal learning environments, whereas low-sensation seekers should be better fit by low-arousal environments. However, intrinsic arousal levels of students, as distinct from the need for arousal, must also be considered. Farley notes that severe overarousal or underarousal can produce withdrawal or hyperactivity, respectively; adaptive instructional designs are needed to reach and modulate optimal levels of arousal for different learners.

*Some Other Student Personalities.* Thomas and Chess (1977) sought to define profiles of temperament, mood, and personality that would be particularly useful for research in elementary education. They distinguished three profiles, categorizing children as having easy, difficult, or slow-to-warm temperaments; we think of them as complexes or types. The easy child shows regularity, a positive approach to novelty, adaptability, and a moderately positive mood. The difficult child shows irregular biological functions, negative withdrawal from novelty, slow or no adaptation to change, and an intensely negative mood. The slow-to-warm child is characterized by a mildly negative response to new stimuli, a slow but eventually positive adaptation, and a mildly positive or negative mood.

The Thomas–Chess work and other research (see Wang & Lindvall, 1984) suggests that this is an important contrast. Evidence shows that teachers tend to overestimate the abilities of easy students while underestimating the abilities of those in the other two categories, but also that easy students average more task completion and higher achievement. Both easy and difficult students gain more interactions with teachers than slow-to-warm students. The latter rely on teachers to assign work; do not initiate, self-select, or explore learning activities; and display less knowledge of classroom procedures. Difficult students show an external locus of control and low responsibility, and receive low teacher ratings on effort and popularity, relative to other students. Here again further research could aim at helping teachers identify and adapt to these differences constructively, as well as elaborating our understanding of the underlying psychology of the contrast.

Block and Haan (1971) described a different typology of students based on longitudinal studies begun in the 1930s. Their work formed part of the Berkeley Growth Studies (see Clausen, 1993). Although the data came from a different era, the study is unparalleled in its size and duration, and in its range and detail. Of particular interest are student types identified using the Q-sort technique. This procedure uses rules to order personality descriptive variables to describe student personalities in a form suitable for quantitative analysis. The study included data on interests, personality, attitudes, ability, muscular coordination, as well as ratings of the parents and home environment, medical records, and extensive interviews with subjects, parents, teachers, and spouses.

The analysis grouped males and females separately into types based on personality profiles and then used longitudinal data to describe average trajectories for each type. Ego resilients, for example, are one type of males who have had a favorable upbringing, with good ability, health, and physical endowment. By junior high school, ego-resilient males display inner direction, acceptance of responsibility, and respect for parents and peers, but tend to be oversocialized, idealizing parents and too readily feeling guilt. By senior high school, ego resilients have become more interested in the opposite sex, more aware of the importance of power, and more self-confident, but generally maintain continuity in their lives. Other types have much different constellations of personal qualities and concerns. Among females, for example, cognitive copers have moved from relative maladjustment in high school to achieve more education than any of the other types by adulthood. Cognitive copers tend to be physically undistinguished in junior high school, easily fearful, guilt-ridden, and latently angry, but also more concerned with intellectual matters associated with the adult world. By senior high school, the cognitive coper has become more ambitious, intellectual, and effective, though still introspective and constantly in search of identity. By adulthood, cognitive copers demonstrate personal maturity and a sense of competence, and use the validation of external accomplishment to develop substantial confidence.

Although the particular types identified by Block and Haan (1971) may or may not be useful today, types identified using their approach may offer a more holistic picture of students' lives by emphasizing the broader context of upbringing and individual development over the school years. Also, ego resilience seems to be a complex construct of continuing usefulness. Haan (1977) went on to develop assessments for a variety of coping and ego defense mechanisms that appear useful in studying individual differences in personality development.

# CONATIVE CONSTRUCTS OF MOTIVATION AND VOLITION

Motivation and volition are historically intertwined, both in everyday usage and in psychological theory. Together they reflect the conative aspect of human psychological functioning. As defined at the start of this chapter, conation is the tendency to take and maintain purposive action or direction toward goals. Although much work in recent years has concerned issues of motivation, research on volition is increasing, and the distinction between the two domains appears clearer.

Corno (1993, 1994; Corno & Kanfer, 1993) has surveyed the wide variety of conative constructs and processes being studied in contemporary research. Figure 9–6 is adapted from her more detailed schematic flowchart to identify just the categories of individual difference constructs we examine here. As noted earlier, following other theory (Heckhausen & Kuhl, 1985), motivation and volition are seen to form a continuum—a kind of commitment pathway—from contemplating or deliberating over options to enactment or implementation. Consistent with the bulk of theory and research (see chapters 4 and 5, this volume), the domain of motivation is involved with decision-making and choice with respect to individual goals. Within this domain, researchers have identified various personal determinants of decision-making or willingness to engage in learning or performance tasks. These determinants include personal need for achievement and fear of failure, various other intrinsic and extrinsic goals, and future time perspectives with respect to goals; we classify these factors as *achievement orientations*. But two other categories of important determinants of goal choice and motivation are also identified. One encompasses *self-directed orientations* such as self-concept, self-worth, and self-efficacy. The other comprises *values*, *attitudes*, and *interests* in preferred subject matter, tasks, or procedures. Goals related to education are formed as a product of planning and decision-making governed by these influences; through this process, some goals reach the status of explicit intentions (or, in Kuhl's [1984] language, "action schema"; they cross "the Rubicon" to become commitments). Explicit intentions are more likely than other goals to be enacted over the long run, but even these are not accomplished automatically, and controls are necessary to protect intentions whenever there are questions about follow-through, as there are in most academic situations (Corno, 1986; Kuhl, 1984).

Accordingly, the domain of volition includes constructs involved in implementing goals, assisting individuals to carry out their best-laid plans and intentions. One category of individual difference constructs that we call *action controls* is used to handle competing intentions and other distractions affecting attention processes, and other goal-related actions engaged in by individuals to manage available resources in timely and efficient ways. Although these control processes are a relatively new focus of investigation, individual differences among students in predispositions to act deliberately and persist despite distractions were documented long ago (Webb, 1915; see also Sockett, 1988). This category includes recent research on self-regulated learning in relation to schooling (see, e.g., Schunk & Zimmerman, 1994). It also incorporates work on mindfulness, effort, and persistence. Modern research on conation thus in-

FIGURE 9–6. Schematic Representation of Conative Individual Difference Constructs in the Motivation–Volition Cycle

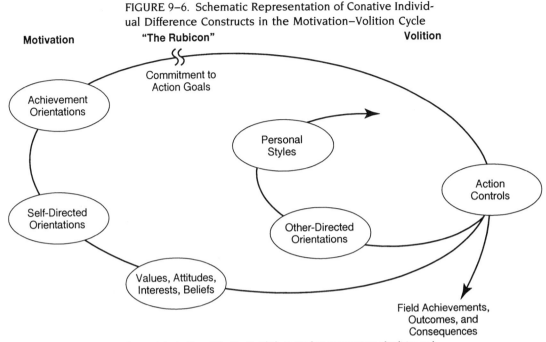

Source: Adapted from "The Best Laid Plans: Modern Conceptions of Volition and Educational Research," by Corno, L. *Educational Researcher*, (1993), *22*(2), 14–22.

cludes efforts to characterize both the factors that initiate and predispose goal setting in individuals and the factors that underlie self-regulation, effort investment, and protective goal striving. These combinations of conative factors are then hypothesized to influence educational outcomes in conjunction with the influence of cognitive abilities, affect, and other personal and situational factors. Cognitive–conative blends that seem to offer molar constructs of use in longitudinal views of education have been called "planful competence" in adolescence (Clausen, 1993) and "productive follow-through" in college (Willingham, 1985).

A second, loosely formed category of *other-directed orientations* is also located under volition because individuals open to external influence from others must at some level permit it, even pursue it, and because individuals must behave intentionally in attempts to influence others. Here we consider characteristics such as persuasability, empathy, and social intelligence. Individuals differ in their relationships to persons and situations outside themselves, and in the extent to which they take these relationships into account in their own decisions. They also differ in their attempts to influence others and in their willingness to be influenced by them. In children, for example, noncompliance is often attributed to "willfulness." These individual differences affect response to education, but to date little is known about the interrelationships of the many and varied other-directed constructs, or even about how best to conceptualize this category.

A third volitional category contains *personal styles*, because many stylistic constructs concerned with learning or studying seem to reflect characteristic differences in volition. We consider major issues for research on styles in general here. The volitional aspect of learning styles we think provides a more promising research target for education than do the many other types of

style constructs. Also considered in this section is the possibility of local development of learning style constructs by or with teachers themselves.

Our discussion proceeds from achievement orientations to action controls, then to orientations toward self and others taken together. Personal styles are then addressed. As initially suggested in Figure 9–1, both other-directed constructs and personal styles overlap with what are usually considered cognitive skills, strategies, and tactics. As was done for the affective column, we conclude this section with some examples of conative complexes. A final section covers values, interests, attitudes and beliefs, a loose collection that crosses all columns of Figure 9–1.

It is important to note at the start that three broad factor-analytic studies of school motivation have provided corresponding outline sketches of much of the conative domain as we have defined it here. The results, summarized in Table 9–4, come from high school students in the United States (Chiu, 1967), the United Kingdom, and Hungary (see Entwistle, Kozeki, & Balarabe, 1988; Snow, 1989b). The columns of Table 9–4 identify the factors obtained in the three studies. The rows associate factors with one another and with the relevant categories from our taxonomy. The achievement orientations, interests, and orientations toward self and others categories appear well represented; the action control category reflects personality factors discussed at the end of this section as parts of some conative complexes.

## Achievement Orientations

The history of research on individual differences in achievement motivation provides a useful example of how educational psychological research in one area of investigation has evolved

TABLE 9–4. Conative Constructs Derived from Three Factor Analyses of
School Motivation

| Our Construct Category | Chiu's Factors | Kozeki's Factors | Entwistle's Factors |
|---|---|---|---|
| Need for achievement | Positive orientation to school learning | Competence through seeking knowledge | Hope for success |
| Evaluation anxiety | | | Fear of failure Instrumental motivation |
| Individual interest | Curiosity | Interest in schoolwork | Intrinsic motivation |
| Independence vs. compliance | Conformity | Responsibility for own actions Independence and self-confidence Compliance with authority | Conscientiousness |
| Social vs. task orientation | Need for social recognition | Identification with teachers Cooperation with peers Warm relations with parents | |

Note: Based on Cognitive-Conative Aptitude Interactions (p. 446) by R. E. Snow. In R. Kanfer, P. L. Ackerman, & R. Cudeck (Eds.) (1989b) *Abilities, Motivation, and Methodology* Hillsdale, NJ: Lawrence Erlbaum Associates. Adapted by permission.

over time. We discuss it under the general heading of achievement orientations to emphasize the different needs, goals, and choices toward which individuals are oriented; achievement motivation is not a singular construct.

*Need for Achievement.* Soon after World War II, Atkinson and McClelland (1948) and their colleagues (e.g., McClelland, Atkinson, Clark, & Lowell, 1953) began a long line of research on one of several need factors in Murray's (1938) need theory of personality. They defined *need for achievement* (or nAch) as a specialized "desire to do something better, faster, more efficiently, with less effort" when judged against a standard of excellence (McClelland, 1961, p. A). In early research, need for achievement was related explicitly to competitiveness, the tendency to measure success against standards, and specific goals or tasks; it was not construed as a general desire to succeed. The term *need for achievement* was used interchangeably with *motive to achieve* or *achievement motivation*; and ultimately the link to need theory blurred.

McClelland et al. (1953) also distinguished two components of achievement motivation that might take primacy or reflect a dominant motivation pattern in individuals, thus differentially influencing risk behavior or choice in achievement situations. *Fear of failure* was defined synonymously with evaluation anxiety (or, in more narrow terms, *test anxiety*) and was considered a potentially dysfunctional aspect of achievement motivation when dominant. This contrasted with the tendency of some individuals toward a dominant pattern of *hope for success* in performance situations, which was considered adaptive.

Research suggests that fear of failure results in a tendency to avoid situations that might lead to failure or to choose tasks in which failure is unlikely. Individuals with this motivational profile also choose situations in which failure is probable but the payoff is high, thus confirming expectations. However, other research shows that some students with high fear of failure choose noncompetitive, nontimed situations and do well in them (Birney et al., 1969), and they can often do passably well in normal academic learning also (Entwistle & Wilson, 1977). In contrast, individuals with a motivational profile dominated by hope for success have been shown to pursue situations in

which there is reasonable opportunity to succeed (i.e., moderately difficult tasks with a moderate payoff), and they often do so. A mathematical model established by Atkinson (1957, 1964) has guided many investigations of these factors on various achievement tasks.

In early studies, McClelland et al. (1953) used scales to assess fear of failure and hope for success adapted from Murray's (1938) Thematic Apperception Test (TAT), a projective procedure. The TAT requires interpretations of ambiguous pictures; the assumption is that respondents' particular motivational profiles or tendencies will be reflected therein. Respondents' stories are scored for relevant themes. McClelland, Atkinson, and others used the scale to investigate experimentally induced need for achievement, as well as individual differences in need for achievement seen as a trait (see, e.g., Atkinson & Birch, 1970).

A second wave of research devised self-report questionnaires to substitute for the TAT. These efforts raised doubts about TAT psychometric properties and, more generally, questioned projective measures (see M. S. Weinstein, 1969; Cronbach, 1990). Concerns included lack of standardization in administration and scoring, as well as the validity of the assumption that responses reflect deep needs rather than intelligence and other factors (Anastasi, 1976).

In a meta-analysis of 105 studies, Spangler (1992) compared TAT and questionnaire measures and concluded that

the correlations between TAT measures of need for achievement with outcomes were on average positive; that these correlations were particularly large for outcomes such as career success measured in the presence of intrinsic, or task-related, achievement incentives; that questionnaire measures of need for achievement were also positively correlated with outcomes, particularly in the presence of external or social achievement incentives; and that on average TAT-based correlations were larger than questionnaire-based correlations. (p. 140)

In other words, Spangler found an interaction between type of measure (TAT vs. questionnaire) and type of performance environment (intrinsic, task-related vs. extrinsic social incentives). Spangler also reported low correlation between TAT and questionnaire measures, suggesting that the two are validly measuring different aspects of achievement motivation.

Current research rests on many different questionnaire measures of need for achievement, each reflecting different links to existing theory as well as different psychometric properties. Ray (1982) reviewed over 70 such measures. D. N. Jackson, Ahmed, and Heapy (1976) further identified several different aspects of achievement motivation reflected in the various available measures. They suggested that, in addition to fear of failure and hope for success, the construct should include acquisitiveness, independence versus conformity, status with others, competitiveness, and concern for excellence (see also Messick, 1989b). Cassidy and Lynn (1989) have offered a questionnaire measure of multidimensional achievement motivation that combines the D. N. Jackson et al. (1976) questionnaire with others' questionnaires (e.g., Lynn, Hampson, & Magee, 1983; Spence & Helmreich, 1983; Warr, Cook, & Wall, 1979).

Most of the widely used self-report questionnaires, regardless of their differing theoretical bases, do seem to predict cognitive performance on high school–and college-level tasks; they also distinguish students in more versus less demanding high school programs and relate positively to teacher ratings of school motivation (Rand, Lens, & Decock, 1989; Lens & DeCruyenaere, 1991). There have also been recent advances in content analysis techniques for the TAT (C. P. Smith, 1992). Both TAT and questionnaire measures have been used with success in ATI research, most notably by McKeachie and his colleagues (see summary in Cronbach & Snow, 1977).

*Evaluation Anxiety.* As noted, the fear of failure dimension of achievement motivation is also the construct widely referred to and studied separately as test anxiety or, more generally, evaluation anxiety. Typical measures are self-report questionnaires designed to reflect individual differences in proneness to fear of failure in evaluative situations generally, not just tests.

In their early work, Mandler and Sarason (1952) interpreted differences in performance of high- and low-test-anxious students as resulting from two learned psychological drives evoked by test situations: task-directed drives and learned anxiety drives. These stimulate opposite and incompatible kinds of behavior: task-directed, relevant efforts to finish the task and thereby reduce the anxiety, versus self-directed, task-irrelevant responses, manifested by insecurity, anticipation of negative outcomes or diminished self-worth and status, and implicit attempts to escape the evaluative situation. Alpert and Haber (1960) labeled these task-directed and task-irrelevant components as facilitating and debilitating anxieties, respectively, and devised a questionnaire to distinguish them. Factor-analytic studies (Liebert & Morris, 1967; Hagtvet, 1984) then suggested that debilitating anxiety divides further into separate components for worry and emotionality. Worry involves cognitive concerns about the consequences of failure, whereas emotionality involves reactions of the autonomic nervous system evoked by evaluative stress. This evaluative stress can be associated with particular content domains or performance situations, such as learning mathematics or using computers, and this in turn may give rise to other specialized reactions such as math anxiety and computer anxiety. Spielberger (1980) applied the concepts of worry and emotionality in the construction and development of another questionnaire system that also provides the distinction between trait and state anxiety.

Based on the above, we can sketch in Figure 9–7 a schematic correlational network for the evaluation anxiety construct. One can think of stable, undifferentiated, or chronic anxiety as a trait difference of which evaluation anxiety is a broadly situated specialization. It is thus a contextual construct. Other, more specifically situated specializations, such as math or computer anxiety, can also be identified. At the other end of the continuum is state anxiety, highly situated and unstable. In some personality theories, as already noted, anxiety is closely connected to neuroticism, introversion, and characteristic negative mood. Evaluation anxiety has an emotionality or physiological arousal component rooted in temperament differences and a worry component that can be interpreted using both volitional and cognitive terms. Worry involves effort diversion as well as worrisome thoughts. Worry intrudes on intended actions, disrupting action control and persistent effort investment. These factors are consistent with Kuhl's (1984) analysis, which posits further that individuals can cope with failure through emotion control. Also, Nicholls (1984) noted that worry may reflect perceived ability deficits as well as fear of failure, and his achievement motivation construct and measure includes work avoidance as well as task orientation and ego orientation (see Nicholls, Patashnick, & Nolen, 1985).

Information-processing interpretations have been offered by Hunsley (1987), Naveh-Benjamin, McKeachie, and Lin (1987), Tobias (1985), and Sieber, O'Neill, and Tobias (1977), among others. Tobias (1985), for example, discussed competing hypotheses as to how anxiety might hinder information processing in learning and performance at different stages of processing. The interference hypothesis suggests that the evaluative threat posed in testing situations impedes the retrieval of already learned information for high-anxious students by reducing their cognitive processing resources. The deficit-skills hypothesis argues that inadequate initial preparation and poor test-taking skills account for the reduced performance of high-anxious students. Tobias cited evidence suggesting that both effects can occur and thus both deserve research. As one suggestion, Naveh-Benjamin and colleagues (1987) have used nonevaluative situations to distinguish students with retrieval problems from students with organizational and other problems. Other summaries of experimental evidence (e.g., Eysenck & Eysenck, 1985; M. W. Eysenck, 1982) suggest that understanding the negative effects of anxiety on performance requires considering task difficulty, which increases negative effects, and the distinction between performance effectiveness and efficiency (which brings effort into the equation): Anxiety degrades efficiency more than it degrades effectiveness because of its effects on effort. Results so far also suggest that anxiety robs working memory resources and limits encoding, organization, and depth of processing in general. The effects appear largely due to the worry component (Morris, Davis, & Hutchings, 1981). Identifying the nature of the relationship between anxiety and cognitive processing could serve as a foundation for designing differential treatment programs for high-anxious students that might be more effective in improving learning and performance than global anxiety reduction programs or study skill improvement programs. It might also lead to measurement techniques based on performance indicators as well as questionnaires.

Attribution theorists have also provided cognitive reinterpre-

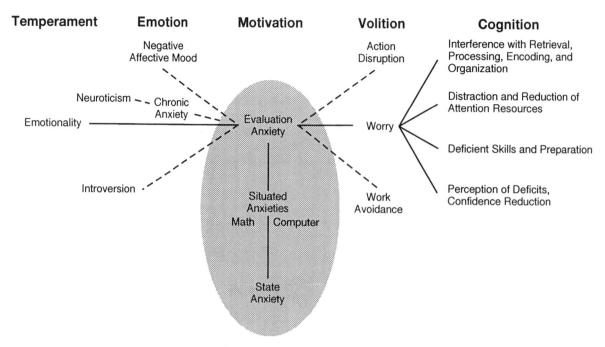

FIGURE 9–7. Schematic Representation of the Correlational Network Relating Evaluation Anxiety to Other Variables Across the Provisional Taxonomy of Figure 9–1

tations of the components of achievement motivation (see, e.g., R. E. Ames & C. Ames, 1984; Weiner, 1986). Rest, Neirenberg, Weiner, & Heckhausen (1973), for example, defined fear of failure to include attributions for failure to internal, stable, uncontrollable factors such as a lack of ability. Work by Dweck (1975) has related students' failure attributions to lack of persistence and coping under failure conditions, and a disbelief in the relationship between effort and outcome; this construct has been labeled "learned helplessness" (Elliott & Dweck, 1988). Other work has connected students' performance attributions to various instructional conditions such as different forms of feedback and reward (e.g., Ames, 1992), as well as to cognitive ability (Butler, 1987). Some researchers view attributional tendencies as habitual, referring to them as attributional or explanatory styles; we consider this construct in our section on personal styles.

Dweck & Leggett (1988) have also argued that fear of failure has a positive, coping aspect that is socially protective for some students, even though it may be maladaptive in school. Hope for success is now seen as related to personal judgments against (often normative) standards of excellence, which can be maladaptive, and these have been linked to self-evaluative emotions such as pride and shame (Kuhl, 1978; Weiner, 1986).

A related construct is Horner's (1968, 1972) fear of success, defined as a "latent, stable personality disposition to become anxious about achieving success" (Horner, 1972, p. 159). It was considered an important variable for women especially. Although fear of success was the focus of a flurry of research, its construct validity has been questioned. Shaver (1976), for example, argued that most of the evidence for fear of success could be accounted for by fear of failure. Heckhausen, Schmalt,

and Schneider (1985) also reviewed this literature and noted that, although the fear of success construct does not explain gender differences in achievement motivation, it has fostered deeper analyses of gender differences in this area; a spectrum of other studies has resulted.

The research literature relating evaluation anxiety to learning and performance relevant to instruction is vast (e.g., Gaudry & Spielberger, 1971; Hagtvet, 1986, 1991; Hagtvet & Min, 1993; Hembree, 1988; Schwarzer, Van der Ploeg & Spielberger, 1982; Van der Ploeg, Schwarzer, & Spielberger, 1983, 1984). As noted before, correlational evidence usually shows a moderate negative relation between anxiety and cognitive performance; this relation is influenced by variations in task difficulty and effort investment, and also by instructional treatment variations. Two recent examples come from studies by Helmke (1988, 1989, 1994) in which an evaluation anxiety measure was correlated with math achievement outcome separately in each of an array of classrooms. Figure 9–8 shows the varying size of these correlations across (a) 39 middle school classrooms and (b) 54 elementary classrooms. Multilevel regression analyses showed that in middle school classrooms, negative effects of anxiety occurred as teachers displayed high time intensity, density of content coverage, and low use of structuring previews and reviews. Particularly important was the student's anxiety score relative to the class average anxiety score. However, in elementary school classrooms, these instructional treatment variables were not important moderators. Rather, an unfavorable social climate and low teacher warmth were associated with negative anxiety effects. The difference in important treatment variation is understandable given the relative emphasis on social-emotional versus cognitive goals at the two grade levels.

FIGURE 9–8. Correlations of Evaluation Anxiety and Academic Achievement in (A) 54 elementary classrooms (German Grade 4) and (B) 39 middle school classrooms (German Grades 5 and 6).

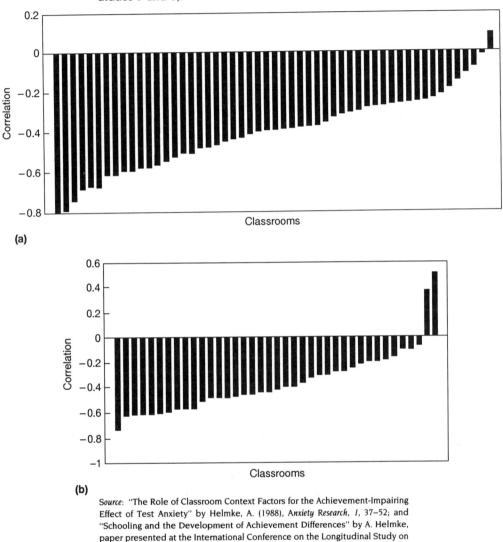

(a)

(b)

*Source*: "The Role of Classroom Context Factors for the Achievement-Impairing Effect of Test Anxiety" by Helmke, A. (1988), *Anxiety Research, 1*, 37–52; and "Schooling and the Development of Achievement Differences" by A. Helmke, paper presented at the International Conference on the Longitudinal Study on the Genesis of Individual Competencies, Max-Planck-Institut for Psychological Research, Munich, Germany, July 22, 1994. Adapted by permission.

Other strong demonstrations of evaluation anxiety operating in interaction with instructional treatment variations to influence educational learning have been summarized by Cronbach and Snow (1977; Snow, 1987, 1989a, 1989b). Typically, highly anxious learners do better with teacher structure and support, whereas they do less well than nonanxious learners when given low-structure or high-pressure-inductive, student-centered instruction, as some of Helmke's data suggest. There have also been interactions involving ability, anxiety, and this treatment contrast; an example is given later. Clearly, grade level moderates these effects also. There are indications, moreover, that evaluation anxiety interacts with test format and test-taking strategy to influence student performance (Schmitt & Crocker, 1981). Unfortunately, it is also the case that most of this research fails to distinguish among the components of evaluation anxiety

or to recognize it as only the negative side of achievement motivation, that is, only half the story of performance in evaluative situations. The positive side—that is, need for achievement—is also aroused and makes a contribution that needs to be studied jointly when explaining differences in learning and test performance (Naveh-Benjamin, McKeachie, Lin, & Tucker, 1986; Rand et al., 1989).

Of particular note in this regard is Len's (1983) demonstration of curvilinear relations of educational achievement with both need for achievement and fear of failure, as shown in Table 9–5. Achievement here is assessed by final oral examinations on the year's course work among Belgian college students. Maximum achievement was shown by students in the middle range on both questionnaires, on average. Achievement was lower among students scoring more toward either end of either

TABLE 9–5. Mean College Examination Scores for Three Levels of Need for Achievement Crossed with Three Levels of Fear of Failure

| Fear of Failure | Need for Achievement | | | |
|---|---|---|---|---|
| | Low | Medium | High | Total |
| High | 49.7 (12) | 52.6 (14) | 50.1 (8) | 50.1 |
| Medium | 53.4 (11) | 60.3 (9) | 58.1 (11) | 57.1 |
| Low | 50.1 (9) | 55.2 (10) | 53.5 (14) | 53.1 |
| Total | 51.1 | 55.5 | 54.1 | |

Note: Based on *Achievement Motivation, Text Anxiety, and Academic Achievement* by W. Lens, 1983, Leuven, Belgium: University of Leuven, Psychological Reports.
Note: Cell sizes in parentheses.

dimension. The result suggests an inverted U relation between arousal and performance, and should also serve as a warning against thoughtless use of linear models in conative measurement.

***Intrinsic versus Extrinsic Achievement Goals.*** Recent reviews of achievement motivation research have suggested that need for achievement is a form of intrinsic motivation (Entwistle, 1987b) but also that the distinction between intrinsic and extrinsically motivated goals, choice behavior, and action is a critical theoretical issue (Lepper, 1988). Consistent with early theories of effectance or competence motivation (e.g., White, 1959), Deci and Ryan (1985) argue that individuals undertake challenge in achievement settings as a function of needs for competence or mastery; these are intrinsic motives. They proposed that individuals differ in these intrinsic motives, and they designed an Academic Self-Regulation Questionnaire (Ryan & Connell, 1989) to distinguish students along this dimension. Various studies by Deci and his colleagues (e.g., Ryan, Connell, & Deci, 1985) suggest that students' level of intrinsic motivation is related to several features of school and classroom environments, including choice, feedback/reward structures, and the amount of teacher surveillance.

People engage in tasks and activities that are intrinsically motivating for their own sake, not to receive some external reward or avoid some negative consequence. "Intrinsically motivated learning is learning that occurs in a situation in which the most narrowly defined activity from which the learning occurs would be done without any external reward or punishment" (Malone & Lepper, 1987, p. 229). Interest in the concept of intrinsic motivation was stimulated in part by White (1959), who argued that curiosity, exploration, and attempts at mastery can be considered expressions of an intrinsic need to deal competently with one's environment (Harter & Connell, 1984). Recent cognitive evaluation theory (Deci & Ryan, 1985) strikes a similar tone. Intrinsically motivated behavior is based in an individual's need to be competent and self-determining and arises from an internal locus of causality in which individuals undertake behavior for its internal rewards, including interest and mastery. Thus, interest may be an emotional outcome or

reward of intrinsic motivation. It may also be an energizing agent for subsequent intrinsic motivation; there is a chicken-and-egg problem here, as at various other points in this chapter.

A few self-report instruments measure aspects of intrinsic motivation. One by Ryan and Connell (1989) for late elementary and middle school students contains subscales for intrinsic motivation and three forms of extrinsic motivation. The same scales are provided by Vallerand, Blais, Briere, and Pelletier (1989) for use with college students; they add a scale for lack of interest or poor motivation for academic material. Harter's (1981) instrument is a forced choice measure of intrinsic versus extrinsic motivation, including subscales for preference for challenge versus easy work; incentive to work to satisfy one's own interest and curiosity versus to please the teacher and obtain good grades; attempts at independent mastery versus dependence on the teacher; independent judgment versus reliance on the teacher's judgment; and internal versus external criteria for success and failure. These subscales are clustered and can be scored for constructs labeled autonomous judgment and intrinsic mastery motivation.

Measures used to assess the presence or degree of intrinsic motivation for a particular person in a particular situation at a particular time need to be designed to represent the person–situation interactional character of the construct, as well as its state-versus-trait aspect. More than most other achievement motivation constructs, intrinsic motivation seems to require more contextual definition involving person, situation, and time; it seems less accessible by conventional questionnaire. In light of the theoretical as well as practical importance of the construct, much more extensive assessment research is needed.

In a rare convergence of findings, several groups of researchers have recently defined two forms of "achievement goal orientations" more or less consistently with definitions of intrinsic and extrinsic motivation (Ames, 1992). These studies demonstrate relationships between different achievement goal orientations and levels of information processing, affect, and behavioral persistence during learning. Table 9–6 shows considerable conceptual and empirical convergence on the nature and role of achievement goal orientations, even though the terminology varies.

So-called task-involved (Nicholls, 1979), learning-oriented (Dweck, 1975), and mastery-focused (Ames, 1984) achievement goal orientations are characteristic of learners who intend to master new skills and develop their knowledge, who value learning, and who believe that with sufficient effort they can expand their intellectual competencies (intrinsic factors). In contrast, individuals who adopt goals that are ego related, performance oriented, and ability focused are concerned about displaying their own competence and succeeding by outperforming others or accomplishing goals with less effort (extrinsic factors) (Ames & Archer, 1988, p. 260). It is noteworthy that these definitions of performance orientations, in contrast to the definitions of learning or mastery orientations, are quite consistent with the original definition of need for achievement offered by McClelland et al. (1953).

Goal orientations are hypothesized to emerge as a function of the salience of mastery versus performance goals in the task situations that students typically encounter in school and at home. Goal orientations are not assumed to generalize over

TABLE 9–6. A Comparison of Three Current Models of Contrasting Student Motivational Orientations

| Basic Theoretical Concepts | | |
| --- | --- | --- |
| Intrinsic Motivation versus Extrinsic Motivation | Task Orientation versus Ego Orientation | Learning Goals versus Performance Goals |
| Intrinsic motivation: activity undertaken for its own sake | Task orientation: educational activity undertaken for the sake of learning itself | Learning goals: educational activity undertaken for the sake of increasing one's own competence |
| Extrinsic motivation (comparative): activity undertaken in order to achieve performance superior to that of others | Ego orientation: educational activity undertaken in order to demonstrate one's high level of ability relative to that of others | Performance goals: educational activity undertaken in order to gain favorable judgments of one's competence compared to that of others. |
| Extrinsic motivation (noncomparative): activity undertaken in order to obtain extrinsic reward or avoid extrinsic punishment | | |

| *Illustrative Situational Factors Demonstrated to Produce an Extrinsic Motivational Orientation, Ego Orientation, or Orientation Toward Performance Goals* | | |
| --- | --- | --- |
| Extrinsic rewards or punishments, expected evaluation of performance, unnecessarily close surveillance, superfluous temporal deadlines, and so forth | Expected evaluation of performance, presentation of activity as test, desire to please teacher, and so forth | Expected evaluation of performance, presentation of activity as test, expectation of potential failure, and so forth |

Note: Based on "Motivational Considerations in the Study of Instruction," by M. R. Lepper, 1988, *Cognition and Instruction*, 5, pp. 289–309. Adapted by permission.

tasks or subject matter domains that lack these salient features (Ames & Archer, 1987, 1988). Indeed, the assessment of goal orientation used by Ames and her colleagues, for example, asks elementary through high school students to rate their classes and teachers on factors that promote mastery versus performance orientations, such as how success is defined and how errors are interpreted, as well as defined goals, teacher orientations toward learning, and grading and grouping practices. Maehr (1991) has shown that the emphasis schools place on different goals affects the motivation of students, with student motivation in later grades tied more directly to the psychological climate of the school. For example, schools that emphasize accomplishment by publicly displaying grades promote performance-related goals (Maehr & Midgley, 1991). C. Ames (1990) and C. Ames and Maehr (1989) have identified strategies for teachers and parents to use to emphasize mastery goals in the classroom and at home. This yearlong intervention resulted in better student attitudes toward school as well as improved learning-related behavior and performance. This work offers important steps toward identifying factors in the instructional situation that promote the appearance of different achievement motivational orientations in students, with student perception providing the medium of communication between person and environment.

Differing achievement goal orientations are thus in part student perceptions of classroom variables, which appear to influence students' attitudes toward school as well as their learning-related behavior and performance (Ames, 1992; Steinkamp & Maehr, 1983, 1984). Elliott and Dweck (1988) have equated such achievement goal orientations with a "program" of cognitive processes. Bereiter (1990) uses a similar metaphor in suggesting that students develop "schoolwork modules" as a function of particular perceptions and experiences in achievement-related situations. These programs or modules—the software of achievement motivation—develop over experience in different environments, differ among students as a result, and thus have differential consequences of substantial importance for long-term learning and educational development.

Dweck and Leggett (1988) suggest that these differences arise from implicit theories of intelligence. An individual with an entity theory of intelligence believes that social and personality attributes are fixed. Such a theory leads to performance goals, and a performance-oriented response to failure. In contrast, an individual with an incremental theory of intelligence believes that social and personality attributes are malleable (Goodnow, 1980). An incremental theory is said to lead to learning goals and a mastery orientation. Implicit theories of intelligence help formulate goals. According to Elliott and Dweck (1988), goal orientation interacts with confidence to influence task choice, performance, and persistence.

Measurement of mastery versus performance orientation depends on student age. Dweck uses effort-related items from Crandall, Katkovsky, and Crandall's (1965) attributional scale to classify primary schoolchildren as mastery or performance oriented. This scale was chosen because past research (Dweck, 1975) showed that the major difference between mastery and performance orientations was in the respective tendency to neglect or emphasize the role of effort in determining failure. Mastery-oriented responses focus on effort as the major cause of failure, resulting in renewed attention to the task. Performance-oriented responses, on the other hand, focus on failure as a result of ability, with additional effort not regarded as helpful. For older children and adolescents, Dweck administers questions that assess students' theories about the nature of intelligence, and infers learning orientation from their responses. For a related approach that investigates the mastery, evaluation, prosocial, and compliance goals that students pursue in relation to achievement, see Wentzel (1989, 1993b).

Students who adopt mastery goal orientations as a result of experiences that reinforce these views appear better able to engage in academic work and to sustain this engagement in the face of difficulty (Ames, 1992; Pintrich, 1990). This relationship is complicated, however, by evidence that extrinsic motivation can facilitate learner engagement when intrinsic motivation is low (Pintrich & Garcia, 1991), as well as indications that both mastery and performance orientations may coexist in individuals; positive effects can result in teaching situations in which performance goals are allowed to exist but are not made salient (Blumenfeld, 1992; Corno, 1992). Such complications in research results serve to deepen our appreciation of the psychology of classroom motivation and the subtleties of individual differences therein. Careful work in this area also has implications for reform in teaching, classroom reward structures, and tasks (see, e.g., Ames, 1992; Blumenfeld, 1992; Marshall & Weinstein, 1986).

In a similar vein, Nicholls et al. (1985) examined high school student's perceptions of the causal attributions related to school success. For example, students who believed that school should enable them to enhance their wealth and status were less likely to be committed to learning for its own sake than students who believed that schools should teach commitment to society, understanding of the world, and high standards. This work is important because it links students' personal goals with their educational ideologies, values, and causal attributions for success. A related approach assesses a broad array of personal goals and personal agency beliefs to capture the multifaceted character of school and life motivation (Ford, 1994).

Goal theory has contributed a framework for guiding recent motivational research, and has served as a source of interventions that focus on changing students' perceptions of classroom- and school-level goal orientations (Anderman & Maehr, 1994). Goal orientations are usually regarded as subordinate to self-efficacy. Students adopting mastery goals have higher self-efficacy for learning than students adopting performance-related goals (Midgley, Anderman, & Hicks, in press).

*Future Time Perspective.* Finally, we consider research by Nuttin and Lens (1985) addressing the hypothesis that the goal objects of individuals' "future time perspectives" are among the factors used to motivate and regulate purposive behavior. This theory bridges between motivation and volition by explicitly connecting individual thinking about goals to the initiation of processes for accomplishing goals.

These authors distinguish future time perspective from positive or negative attitudes or preferential orientations to the past, present, or future. Future time perspective refers to "temporally localized [goal] objects. . . . that occupy [an individual's] mind in a certain situation" (Nuttin & Lens, 1985, p. 21). Time perspective thus has both temporal and spatial aspects. One assertion is that individuals typically extend their viewpoints to consider desired goals in their future; some persons construct longer, more realistic and more accessible perspectives than others, as well as perspectives that are more optimistic and balanced with respect to both proximal and distal goals. A long, realistic, and accessible time perspective facilitates the effectiveness with which individuals can formulate and realize long-term projects. To bring important long-term projects to completion, individuals must regulate and coordinate the many instrumental steps necessary along the way. They must move from plans to the implementation of plans, that is, from motivation to volition.

One hypothesis is that some students are unable to perceive the usefulness of their present studies to a far-distant career, so they put forth insufficient effort in school.

There are five aspects or dimensions of future time perspective: its extension in length or depth, the perceived instrumentality of goal objects within its extension, the density of goal objects within different perceived time periods, the degree of structure relating these objects, and the degree of vividness and realism associated with each perceived goal object (for background and details, see Nuttin, 1984; Nuttin & Lens, 1985; Van Calster, Lens, & Nuttin, 1987).

Individual perspectives on realistic goals have been measured using a sequence of projective-like questionnaires that require respondents to identify their positive and negative goals (e.g., "I hope to complete school"; "I am resolved not to fail to complete school"). These are coded into age-related periods (e.g., ages 6–12, 12–18, 18–25) during which the goal objects are normally reached. Localization of the objects is based on norms established in various social groups, thus avoiding potential measurement issues raised by subjects' personal estimations of normality. Codes are also defined for object categories, including the self, others, material objects, and conceptual entities, as well as behavioral relations.

A forward-looking perspective on realistic goal objects, as measured this way, has been shown to facilitate the effectiveness with which individuals actually realize their long-term goals. These differences relate also to age and contextual variables, and the age–time perspective relationship appears curvilinear (Lens & Gailly, 1980). Although psychometric studies support the construct validity of these measures, such protocol scoring is certainly linked to length of response, and little is known about the cognitive processes that underlie the generation of responses to question stems of this sort. Assessment procedures would benefit from case studies of individuals over time.

This work relates back to Lewin (1931, 1951), who observed that time perspective extends developmentally in childhood through personal, constructive activity. We see in the research of Nuttin and Lens (1985) a new examination of time perspective that links the tendency to form and strive for goal objects to the domain of volition as modern theorists define it (see also Murgatroyd, Rushton, Apter, & Ray, 1978). As William James wrote (1890/1983, p. 1166), "we reach the heart of our inquiry into volition when we ask by what process is it that the thought of any given action comes to prevail stably in the mind."

## Action Controls

The category of action controls includes a variety of self-regulatory mechanisms used to accomplish goals. As indicated earlier, goals are chosen or formed as a motivational function, through decisions about valued outcomes, expectancies for success and related beliefs, as well as through means–end planning. Some goals become explicit intentions (or action schemata) represented symbolically as visions of oneself carrying out certain actions to accomplish goals (Kuhl & Kazen-Saad, 1989; Norman & Shallice, 1986). Symbolic representations of actions are important if goals are to be pursued and accomplished over the long term, but they are insufficient in the face of competing goals that may become dominant along the way.

Educational situations often involve competing goals and the handling of multiple goals over long time periods. Schoolwork presents students with goals that are not always of their own choosing, and these goals may be ambiguous, undervalued, repetitive, or demanding. It also requires the protection of explicit goals from various forms of distraction. Under such conditions, specific action controls can be used to help promote persistence (Corno & Kanfer, 1993; Kuhl & Kazen-Saad, 1989). These same controls can be used to maintain focus on goals that are not perceived as difficult to enact but that require intelligent investment of energy resources, given the number of other commitments.

Included under action controls are (a) the control strategies identified by Kuhl and his colleagues (e.g., Kuhl & Beckmann, 1985; see also Corno, 1989), (b) certain self-regulational processes involved in the management of resources during learning (e.g., Zimmerman & Schunk, 1989), and (c) tendencies toward mindful effort investment and related forms of goal-directed cognition (Salomon, 1991; Rollett, 1987). Our discussion highlights commonalities as well as differences across these subcategories.

*Action versus State Orientation.* Action control theory led to empirical research on an individual difference construct labeled action orientation versus state orientation. Action-oriented individuals tend to take immediate action to achieve their goals. They "are characterized by an intentional focus on a situationally appropriate action plan" (Kuhl & Kraska, 1989, p. 366). They are able to attend successively or even simultaneously to the present state, some future state, discrepancies between present and future states, and appropriate actions that will transform the present state into the desired future state (Kuhl, 1987). In contrast, state-oriented individuals are unable to deal effectively with these elements. They tend to focus on past difficulties and situationally inappropriate intentions. Their behavior is marked by overmaintenance of intentions that are either unrealistic or should be postponed. This results in "fixation on past, present, or future states, for example, on a past failure to attain a goal, on the present emotional consequences of that failure, or on the desired goal state itself" (Kuhl & Kraska, 1989, p. 366).

Kuhl (1981, 1984, 1993) developed self-report measures of action versus state orientation, yielding separate scores for performance-related, failure-related, and decision-related orientations. Moderate correlations between these subscales and measures of test anxiety, extraversion, self-consciousness, achievement motivation, future orientation, and cognitive complexity reflect the theoretically expected overlap with personality and motivation, and at the same time indicate that a sizable proportion of variance in action-orientation scores cannot be accounted for by these variables.

*Action Control Strategies.* In Kuhl's terms, volitional control strategies are mechanisms used by individuals to "manage the maintenance of intentions" (Kuhl & Kazen-Saad, 1989, p. 387). Unlike some other, automatic controls, volitional control is considered higher order and conscious. When information-processing demands are high and competing goals are present, control strategies help maintain focus on intended rather than competing actions. Because this function assumes the capacity for cognitive representation of intentions (i.e., the formation of

action schemata or visualizations of oneself carrying out goals), it develops in part as a function of other cognitive capabilities. According to Kuhl & Kraska (1989), rudimentary forms of volitional control may be observed in young children, but adolescents and adults refine this capability significantly over time.

Kuhl's theory includes a taxonomy of six control strategies that allow students to protect selected intentions from competing action tendencies (see Kuhl, 1984, and Corno, 1986, 1989, for presentations of the complete taxonomy). To illustrate these strategies, suppose that a student needs to support the intention to do homework and inhibit the preference to watch television. The student could use *selective attention,* focusing on sequential aspects of tasks to channel attentional resources toward the academic work while avoiding visual contact with the television set. *Motivation control* would involve self-reinforcement and punishment to emphasize the sense of satisfaction that comes from completing the homework. *Emotion control,* such as reassuring self-speech, could also be used to limit anxiety about the difficulty in starting the homework. *Environmental control,* such as choosing a work environment away from the distraction of the television, could also be used. Finally, the deliberate development of a habitual, preferred way of working (i.e., a *work style*) controls one's actions further by establishing a work environment conducive to perseverance. Institutions fulfill the same purpose by defining a "work ethic" to which employees conform.

Kuhl and Kraska (1989) have developed a measure of strategy uses called the Metamotivational Knowledge Test for Children. This measure consists of pictures depicting situations in which it is difficult to maintain an intention. For example, one picture shows a student working on homework while friends play outside the window. Respondents are asked questions about alternative strategies for maintaining desired intentions and avoiding distractions. Evidence suggests that scores increase almost linearly from Grade 1 to Grade 4 for motivation control, attention control, and coping with failure, but scores for emotion control remain flat, suggesting that emotion control might develop later in childhood. Scores have also correlated positively with teacher ratings of compliance with classroom rules and overall adjustment to school.

In further work, Kuhl and Kraska (1989) developed a computerized performance assessment of action control efficiency. In a children's version, respondents complete a choice reaction time task in part of the screen. Successful performance earns money for toys. Occasionally, while they work, an interesting and uncontrollable distraction appears in another part of the screen, which affects the amount of money they will earn. Children readily understand that interrupting their performance on the speeded task to watch the distraction will reduce their earnings, so they form an intention to avoid this. Children with low strategy knowledge, as measured by Kuhl's metamotivational knowledge measure, tend to show much higher variances, though not longer averages, in response times. According to Kuhl, when children become distracted, they notice that their performance has decreased, so they try to make up for it by increasing their speed on later trials. This measure of volitional efficiency correlates positively with the strategy knowledge measure. Because performance-based measures of volition are rare (see Heckhausen & Gollwitzer, 1987), convergence between scores on this indicator and the self-report measure are particularly noteworthy. Strategy use scores on both measures correlated negatively in these studies with test anxiety assessed by self-report questionnaire.

Another line of research by Kanfer and Ackerman (1989a, 1989b) has examined volitional strategies among military recruits learning to perform an air traffic control simulation task. The demands of this task were especially troublesome for low-ability trainees, in the early learning phases particularly. These trainees reported anxiety and ruminating thoughts when asked to accomplish specific goals during early encounters with the task, and were less likely than high-ability trainees to evidence use of volitional control. This result held even with low-ability trainees who reported high self-efficacy and displayed other constructive patterns of motivation, suggesting that motivation alone was insufficient for successful learning. Kanfer and Ackerman were able to improve the performance of these less able learners and to reduce their self-reported anxiety through pointed instructions in strategies for handling excess worry and anxiety.

*Self-Regulated Learning.* Some recent work has addressed similarities between Kuhl's theory of action control and hypothesized processes that define "self-regulated learning" (Corno & Mandinach, 1983; Corno & Rohrkemper, 1985). As indicated earlier, conceptions of self-regulated learning generally embrace aspects of volitional control along with motivational factors such as self-efficacy and cognitive involvement in learning (Corno, 1986, 1993, 1994; Zimmerman, 1990). Most relevant to our conception of action control are the self- and task-management aspects of self-regulated learning, such as rearranging task environments to make learning easier or more fun, seeking information and assistance from teachers or peers, and selecting the most important information on which to concentrate for longer periods of time.

Research on self-regulated learning has been pursued largely by Schunk (1989) and Zimmerman (1989, 1990) using a social-cognitive perspective derived from Bandura (1977, 1986). Accordingly, the details of these investigations differ from the above in theoretical perspectives and the relative emphases on motivational versus volitional processes (see, e.g., Zimmerman & Schunk, 1989). However, Zimmerman and Martinez-Pons (1986, 1988; Zimmerman, Bandura, & Martinez-Pons, 1992) and Pintrich (1989; Pintrich & DeGroot, 1990; Pintrich, Smith, Garcia, & McKeachie, 1993), in particular, have examined both motivational and volitional aspects of self-regulated learning in correlational studies that demonstrate significant relationships between these factors and learning outcomes in student samples. Even these efforts only begin to put volition into relation with motivation in research on self-regulated learning (Corno & Kanfer, 1993).

Perhaps the greatest similarity between most research on self-regulated learning and the approach adopted by Kuhl is the attempt to characterize students on the basis of expressed strategy use in performance-related situations. Zimmerman and Martinez-Pons (1988) and Pintrich and Garcia (1991) focus directly on relationships between expressed strategy use and adolescent or adult academic achievement. They also include indices of ability and other motivational factors that display relationships with self-reported strategies. In one factor-analytic study with college students, Pintrich and Garcia (1991) found

distinct factors for self-regulated learning, measures of motivation assessed by self-report (e.g., goal orientation, text anxiety, self-efficacy), and academic ability and achievement. The various items reflecting volitional strategies included on both the questionnaire developed by Pintrich and the interview protocol of Zimmerman and Martinez-Pons include resource management (use of time, effort, and other available environmental support) as well as strategies for self-monitoring and self-reinforcement. Reported use of these strategies appears particularly strong when compared with other cognitive strategy use in correlations with achievement and other school accomplishments (see Corno, 1989; Kanfer & Ackerman, 1989a, 1989b). In one study (Zimmerman & Martinez-Pons, 1986), five of the nine reported strategies correlating most strongly with scores on standardized tests of achievement were consistent with Kuhl's taxonomy. Another study (Britton & Tesser, 1991) found that a measure of time management practices used by college students predicted student grades through subsequent years.

Another subcategory of action control strategy might be designated metacognitive or goal-related control, to distinguish it conceptually from Kuhl's work and research on self-regulated learning more generally. Again, however, these categories overlap substantially, so much is to be gained by consolidation through further research. We consider metacognitive control to form the basis for adaptive use of learning strategies, such as deep or elaborative processing (Corno, 1992, 1993, 1994; Entwistle, 1988; Weinstein & Mayer 1986). Metacognitive control is not considered equivalent to deep processing or other learning strategies; rather it supports their use with appropriate timing and flexibility of deployment. Included here also would be monitoring and appraisal processes that help determine the extent to which effort investments are sustained. This relates in turn to notions of supervisory or "executive" control (Ach, 1910; Norman & Shallice, 1986; Wagner & Sternberg, 1987). For other related constructs combining conation and cognition, see Cacioppo & Petty (1982) on "need for cognition" and Pittman & D'Agostino (1989) on "control deprivation."

A significant body of research exists on cognitive learning strategies in educational psychology. This work has been distinct in most respects from strategy research based on theories of volition or social cognition (Pressley & Levin, 1983). Among the more frequently discussed findings in studies of learning strategy induction is the difficulty of obtaining transfer; students who learn strategies during training do not automatically apply them in schoolwork thereafter (Pressley, Goodchild, Fleet, Zajchowski, & Evans, 1989). When transfer does occur, it seems to be fostered by attention during training to issues of self-regulation and control—to well-timed application and follow-through (Dole, Duffy, Roehler, & Pearson, 1991; Paris & Winograd, 1990). Thus, new iterations of work on cognitive strategies might give more attention to conative strategies in attempts to assist students in acquiring and transferring trained strategic capabilities to new learning.

*Mindful Effort Investment versus Effort Avoidance.* Mindfulness involves intentional, purposeful, metacognitively guided employment of nonautomatic, hence effort-demanding, mental processes (Salomon, 1987). A learner rarely applies knowledge and skill automatically as needed. There must be an intention to mobilize and apply knowledge and skill to a new situation. This intention mobilization is mentally taxing; it demands effort investment in mindful application of knowledge and skill. The difference between what a person can do and what a person actually does in a situation indicates the effect of mindful effort investment. Except for the conative, effort aspect, the distinction between mindfulness and mindlessness seems parallel to that between controlled and automatic processing in cognitive psychology.

Mindfulness is a function of stable individual differences but also of situational factors. Different instructional conditions will promote different degrees of mindful effort investment directly. But the learner's perception of the demand characteristics of different situations is also a powerful control on mindfulness (Salomon, 1983, 1984). Persons also differ reliably in their tendency to engage in and enjoy effortful cognitive activity versus their tendency to minimize mental effort in processing incoming information, and there is interaction of this person difference with instructional conditions. Learners high in mindfulness perform better when given loose guidance and enough freedom to work independently, but react negatively when given unduly specific and continuous guidance. The opposite is seen for learners low in mindfulness. High-mindful learners perform better when working alone than in teams. However, in teams that also allow independent activity, highs are unaffected, while low-mindful learners tend to loaf. Mindful learners intentionally seek out opportunities to invest mental effort. They are selective—mindful about some aspects of a situation while ignoring other aspects. Mindlessness occurs when a situation is perceived as familiar, undeserving of effort, or too demanding; and the sequence of events is passively allowed to unfold without the person actively engaging in it (see Langer, 1989; Salomon, 1981, 1983, 1984; Salomon & Leigh, 1984).

On the other hand, there also appears to be a mindful, volitional system aimed at actively avoiding the investment of effort in learning in achievement situations. The person's behavior seems motivated to escape from such situations, mentally or physically or both (Rollett, 1987). Effort avoidance can be distinguished from low need for achievement characterized by laziness or high fear of failure characterized by striving to achieve; a person motivated by effort avoidance shows active mental or physical escape, that is, mindful avoidance, with no intention to succeed. Effort avoidance tendencies seem to derive from frustrating early experiences in a task domain, so the construct is usually domain-specific. But experiencing frustration in many school activities presumably leads to generalized effort avoidance.

Unsupportive, restrictive intervention styles used by parents and teachers appear associated with the emergence of effort avoidance. The more teachers or parents use pressure to motivate such persons, the quicker effort avoidance appears. Effort avoiders try to convince teachers that they are not smart enough to cope with tasks given them. They tend to score lower on group tests than on individual intelligence tests. Their strategies for effort avoidance include working very slowly, working rapidly in slipshod fashion, stopping work when praised, producing feelings of resignation to induce teachers not to push them, and generating various excuses for not working.

Further research needs to distinguish "debilitating" or "defensive" effort avoidance from "intelligent" effort avoidance, that is, the intelligent budgeting of minimal effort to reach desired goals. Effort avoidance may at times be a healthy reaction to exhausting or extremely difficult tasks. Thus, discontinuing work or setting lower standards for performance in such situations needs more study as an adaptive device. Flexible adaptation of mental effort in learning can be construed as serving volitional functions. That is, intelligent investment of limited mental effort, or "satisficing" (Simon, 1982), is a way of increasing the probability of eventual success in accomplishing intended goals. Also, the nature of prior frustrations and the appraisal of situations that lead to effort avoidance are not yet well understood.

Assessment of both effort investment and effort avoidance has relied on questionnaires. Effort investment is reflected in self-reports about the number and kind of nonautomatic mental elaborations a person uses in various situations (Salomon, 1981). The scale has been used successfully in instructional research comparing perceptions of difficulty of television versus reading as learning media; students differentially invest mental effort as a function of these perceptions. The effort avoidance scale includes items such as "I really can't understand why I should know the multiplication tables by heart"; "I can't work when the sun is shining"; "When I'm supposed to write for a long time I get quite tired." The scale has been shown to be unidimensional and to contribute to prediction of learning criteria even with fear of failure partialed out (Rollett, 1987). No research as yet seems to have included both investment and avoidance measures in the same study.

Pintrich and Schrauben (1992) have reviewed other research relating student motivational factors to efforts to learn, including studies by Dweck (1986), Nolen (1988), and Entwistle (1981). Collectively, this work shows a strong association between certain perceptions of self and task and well-timed effort investment in learning. Adopting a learning mastery goal orientation in particular promotes higher engagement. In contrast, self-perceptions of high ability, or efficacy for academic achievement, show less substantial relationships with cognitive engagement outcomes (Ames, 1992; Kanfer & Ackerman, 1989). Particularly strong volition, then, may be a sense of inadequacy in hiding (Corno, 1994).

## Orientations Toward Self and Others

Beneath achievement orientations and action controls in Figure 9–1, we distinguish two further categories of conative constructs to represent orientations toward self and orientations toward other persons and social tasks. Perhaps the two could as well be considered just another group of affective or personality factors; in a sense, all responses to personality questionnaires are reports of perceptions of self. Perhaps the cognitive aspect could be emphasized also; these two categories could include the abilities Gardner (1983) labels intrapersonal and interpersonal intelligence, respectively. But there is value for research purposes in maintaining the separation from affective and cognitive functions, at least provisionally. Self-directed constructs such as self-concept or self-image as a learner seem fundamentally motivational in function, more closely tied than personality constructs to self-perceptions with respect to particular performance contexts or goals. Similarly, other-directed constructs such as empathy, persuasibility, or Machiavellianism seem fundamentally volitional. They include sensitivity or receptiveness to social information and the ability to judge environmental influences, including the motives, goals, and personalities of other persons. But they also define and are defined by distinct and purposeful patterns of action with respect to other persons and social situations. Finally, orientations toward self and toward others must be fundamentally intermingled; each helps define the other. Thus we discuss them together here.

*Self-Concept.* Self-concept is a broad, multidimensional construct comprised of complex and dynamic systems of self-perceptions, each perception having a corresponding value (Purkey, 1983). Self-concept includes both self-knowledge and an evaluation of the value or worth of one's own abilities, actions, or products. Individuals have different self-concepts in different ability domains, such as academic, social, and physical. These broad domains can be further subdivided to differentiate self-concept in mathematics from self-concept in English, and still further subdivided to yield self-concepts for particular tasks. Self-concept can be equated with Bandura's (1977) perceived self-efficacy when it is applied to individuals' "judgments of their capabilities to organize and execute courses of action required to attain designated types of performances" (Bandura, 1986, p. 391).

Self-concept researchers have frequently distinguished the descriptive, cognitive aspect (e.g., "I can read well") from the evaluative, affective aspect ("I feel good about how I read") (Rosenberg, 1979; Skaalvik, 1990). The affective dimension is often referred to as self-esteem and emphasizes self-worth and self-respect (Schunk, 1991). The relation between overall self-esteem and particular aspects of self-concept has been a topic of debate since James (1890/1983) argued that one must understand people's narrow and idiosyncratic self-perspectives before one can fully understand their global self-appraisals.

Some researchers regard self-concepts as domain-specific constructs that include academic self-concept, verbal self-concept, mathematical self-concept, or physical ability self-concept, to name a few; some assume a hierarchical organization of these constructs (Harter, 1982, 1985a, 1985b, 1986; Marsh, 1984; Shavelson, Hubner, & Stanton, 1976). Most frequently, especially in earlier work, self-concept is defined either by summing over different dimensions of self-concept, such as mathematics, English, and physical ability (e.g., Coopersmith, 1967; Sears, 1963), or by computing a higher order factor score from intercorrelations among measures for different self-concept domains. The difficulty here is that the meaning of general self-concept changes depending on the particular self-concept measures researchers include in their analyses. Other problems with early self-concept research are identified in Wylie's (1979, 1989) exhaustive review; they include infirmities in instruments designed to measure self-concept, poor theoretical rationales for many of the studies, weaknesses in research methodology, and inconsistent findings.

Multiple-construct measures of self-concept often include a scale to measure a specific, unidimensional and superordinate facet of self that refers to self-confidence, self-competence, or self-esteem. Items from these scales do not contain items from the various facets of self-concept but measure a general sense of self-competence that is applicable across the areas of an individual's life. This is the approach of Rosenberg (1965, 1979),

Harter (1982, 1983), and Marsh (1988). Surprisingly, this "self-esteem" dimension of self-concept is often poorly correlated with measures of more specific dimensions of self-concept, despite factor-analytic studies showing that it is internally consistent, highly reliable, and clearly separable from other factors.

Interest in the self-concept is fueled in part by the belief that improving students' academic self-concepts will yield concomitant improvements in student motivation for learning and thus academic performance (Byrne, 1984). Calsyn and Kenny (1977) refer to this as the self-enhancement model. Alternatively, a skill development model suggests that an enhanced academic self-concept results from academic achievement. Several longitudinal studies (Shavelson & Bolus, 1982; Byrne, 1986; Marsh, 1989) have sought to establish causal relations between self-concept and academic achievement but have yielded mixed results, depending on how academic achievement was measured (Marsh, 1991). When achievement is inferred from school grades, academic self-concept seems to drive achievement (Shavelson & Bolus, 1982). When achievement is inferred from standardized test scores, it appears to influence self-concept (Newman, 1984; see also Marsh, 1986). When the achievement measure reflects both grades and test scores, neither predominates (Byrne, 1986). Marsh (1990) suggested that prior academic self-concept exerts more influence over school grades because grades are more susceptible to motivational and volitional influences. Helmke (1989) has shown that self-concept of ability predicts achievement differently in different classrooms, as another example of ATI. In classrooms where teacher supportive contact with individual students was high, self-concept–achievement relations were low; in classrooms with low teacher support, achievement was highly related to individual student self-concept.

Self-concept is also important because it is viewed as a desirable outcome of education. Yet most educational programs and evaluations of interventions have failed to demonstrate improved self-concept, particularly when global self-concept measures have been used as criteria (Marsh, 1990; Scheirer & Kraut, 1979; Wylie, 1979). Some results even suggest that interventions that improve performance in a particular domain may reduce self-concept in that domain because competition among learners can produce frame-of-reference effects harmful to individuals' self-concepts (Marsh & Peart, 1988). It is also possible that such influences produce less positive but more realistic self-images. Marsh (1990) reported positive results when repeated measures designs were used with large samples of students, and when the self-concept measures used as outcome variables were defined narrowly, targeted to the intervention domains.

Another perspective on the motivational influence of self-concept on behavior regards the self-concept as a set of cognitive schemas (Markus, 1977; Markus & Nurius, 1986). According to Markus and Nurius, people create representations of what they think they might become, what they would like to become, and what they are afraid of becoming in the future. Here, self-concepts or "possible selves" serve to represent motives "by giving specific cognitive form to the end states (goals and threats), to the associated plans or pathways for achieving them, and to the values and affect associated with them" (Markus & Nurius, 1986, p. 961). These self-schemas affect which goals one chooses to pursue (Schlenker, 1985; Wicklund & Gollwitzer, 1982) and how much effort and persistence one will devote to achieving them (Ruvolo & Markus, 1986).

*Self-Worth.* Another related construct is self-worth, which has at its core the assumption that "the search for self-acceptance is the highest human priority" (Covington, 1992, p. 74). According to self-worth theory, students have a compelling need to protect their sense of worth or personal value. A sense of worth depends on a student's level of performance, self-estimate of ability, and degree of effort expended. Of these influences, self-perception of ability exerts the most influence on self-worth, especially for older students, because it is strongly associated with success (Covington, 1992) and because students prefer to achieve through ability rather than effort (J. Brown & Weiner, 1984). For many students, the mere perception of high ability guarantees a positive self-identity in school, and its absence triggers feelings of shame or humiliation.

Effort is also an important source of self-worth and is reinforced in learning contexts by teachers who value a work ethic. Students learn that effort is important to learning but that ability is a predictor of future occupational success. They also learn that high effort paired with failure implies low ability. This is the crux of self-worth theory: that expanding effort is a double-edged sword; despite the enhanced self-worth that results from making an effort, there is also a risk that failure will occur, suggesting low ability and leading to feelings of shame or humiliation.

Self-worth theory has roots in both attribution theory and achievement motivation theory. It emphasizes the role of self-perceptions of the causes of successes and failures as major determinants of future achievement behavior, and it shares with attribution theory the implication that failure can act as either a positive or negative reinforcer, depending on whether it is perceived as due to lack of effort or to lack of ability. But it provides a richer account of school achievement dynamics by taking into consideration students' motives. For example, attribution theory has difficulty explaining why some students who attribute failure to lack of effort will try harder in the future, whereas others will simply give up. Self-worth theory explains this result by suggesting that some students try to avoid the ability-linked emotion of humiliation associated with high effort and failure by not trying. Other students try to avoid the effort-linked emotion of guilt by trying harder, avoiding failure by being successful.

Several failure-avoiding tactics can be understood in the context of the self-worth construct. These tactics aim to shift the perceived causes of failure from stable, internal factors like ability to external or unstable factors beyond the individual's control. By setting unrealistically high goals, a student's failure will not be perceived as due to lack of ability or effort. Similarly, procrastination also creates an excuse should a student fail— time was insufficient for effort to succeed. Moreover, success that occurs despite procrastination implies very high ability.

Self-worth theory has educational implications for teachers. The preoccupation with ability as a determinant of self-worth may be unavoidable, but teachers can encourage students to find other sources of worth beyond ability, such as pride in work that is completed well, or the feelings of success that arise from self-improvement. Instructional treatments based on mastery learning and cooperative learning can be arranged to emphasize within-self comparisons and directed effort, or the rewards of teamwork rather than competition with peers (Covington, 1984).

Support for self-worth theory comes from achievement motivation and attribution research as well as from several studies by Covington and his colleagues (see Covington, 1992). One study explored affective reactions to test failure experiences in college students. Participants were asked to rate their ability, degree of humiliation (an ability-linked affect), and guilt (an effort-linked affect), depending on how much they studied (high vs. low effort). Degree of effort accounted for all the variation in guilt reactions, but perceptions of inability accounted for most of the variation in humiliation. Further, trying hard increased perceptions of inability, causing a further increase in humiliation. Apparently, although high effort reduces feelings of guilt, it can cause humiliation by decreasing perceptions of ability. The implication is that students must exert sufficient effort to avoid teacher punishment and feelings of guilt, but not so much as to risk the humiliation of failing after trying hard. Thus, paired with the predominance of ability perceptions over effort perceptions, students are likely to "endure the pangs of guilt rather than the humiliation of incompetency" (Covington, 1984, p. 10).

*Self-Efficacy.* Another important construct in achievement behavior is self-efficacy, initially concerned with individuals' perceived ability to control performance in emotionally difficult situations, but broadened later to include virtually all performance activities. Self-efficacy can be defined as individuals' "judgment of their capabilities to organize and execute courses of action required to attain designated types of performances" (Bandura, 1986, p. 391). In an educational context, self-efficacy refers to students' expectations about their ability to complete specific academic tasks successfully or achieve specific goals (Schunk, 1985). Although self-efficacy beliefs are often considered statelike and task-specific, more general measures now exist to represent more pervasive perceptions across arrays of tasks (Schwarzer, 1992).

The sense of self-efficacy is hypothesized to affect individuals' activity choices, effort, and persistence. Learners who are unsure of their ability to complete a task will often avoid it or give up more easily when they encounter difficulties. An initial sense of self-efficacy varies as a function of prior experience and perceived ability in particular tasks. It is refined through success and failure on similar tasks, observations of others, and social influence from others. Once a sense of efficacy develops for particular situations, it is resistant to change (Bandura, 1986).

Self-efficacy can thus develop as a stable contextual construct and person characteristic as a predictor. There is evidence that self-efficacy predicts a broad range of outcomes, including academic achievements, athletic performance, social skills, career choices, pain tolerance, coping with feared events, and recovery from heart attacks (Bandura, 1986). For example, Pintrich and DeGroot (1990) intercorrelated student performance, self-regulation, self-efficacy, and intrinsic motivation measures among seventh graders. Regression analyses showed that self-efficacy, self-regulation, and test anxiety predicted performance better than intrinsic motivation measures. Intrinsic motivation influenced performance only indirectly through its relation to self-regulation and cognitive strategy use, regardless of prior achievement.

Self-efficacy appears related to a diversity of other constructs, including coping ability, depression, phobic disability, health behavior, smoking cessation, and disease recovery (Schwarzer, 1992). Among educational constructs, self-efficacy is related to self-concept, outcome expectations, and the perceived value of outcomes. It also relates to locus of control, since positive outcome expectations are presumably beliefs about the strength of the link between successful performance and desired outcomes.

*Locus of Control.* The locus of control construct distinguishes people's beliefs about their own internal versus external sources of control over personal outcomes (Rotter, 1966). Some individuals believe outcomes are strongly associated with their actions, whereas others believe that outcomes are due to luck, fate, or other persons' influences. DeCharms (1968) made it a type construct, referring to "origins" and "pawns." It thus bridges the categories of self-directed and other-directed orientations. It has also prompted volumes of research interest over the past several decades (see Lefcourt, 1982, 1991). Internals, in contrast to externals, are more willing to defer gratification (Zythoskee, Strickland, & Watson, 1971), more persistent when facing difficult tasks (Karabenick & Srull, 1978; Srull & Karabenick, 1975), more accurate in judging the lapse of a minute (Walls & Smith, 1970), and have longer future time perspectives (Platt & Eisenmann, 1968; Shybut, 1968). Recently, the simple internal versus external distinction has been eclipsed by attribution theory with its elaborated $2 \times 2 \times 2$ classification of causal attributions; in addition to internal or external, causes could result from stable or unstable factors, and be controllable or uncontrollable (Weiner, 1986). Further, the global measure originating from Rotter's (1966) work has proved not to represent a dimension with broad, coherent definition (Kline, 1993). Recent work has thus specialized a variety of measures tailored to particular populations, goals, and contexts (Lefcourt, 1991). For example, one specialized measure of use in educational research assesses children's beliefs about their control over and responsibility for successful achievement in school (Crandall, Katkovsky, & Crandall, 1965). There is evidence that high versus low internality predicts teacher-graded and test-measured achievement, and that high internality is positively associated with time and effort investment in free-time intellectual activities, at least for boys. In turn, some items from this instrument have been used by Dweck (1986) to distinguish children's incremental versus fixed-entity beliefs about intelligence and the resulting mastery versus performance orientations in school work.

*Social Ability.* The other-directed construct with the longest history in empirical research is so-called social intelligence, defined by Thorndike (1920) as sensitivity to others and the ability to act wisely in human relations. Thorndike argued that social competence was a critical element of human ability. Some new theorists place social intelligence at the center of personality (Cantor & Kihlstrom, 1987), although their definition emphasizes declarative and procedural knowledge used to guide personal-social life rather than affective and conative factors. Others (A. P. Fiske, 1992) have sought to identify the elementary forms of social relations with which children and

adults become competent without addressing individual differences directly. We call the construct "social ability" to deemphasize the overblown claim inherent in the term "intelligence," but also to place it at a level appropriate for contrast with academic abilities. Educators have lamented all along that disproportionate emphasis is placed on the limited domain of academic abilities, even as social and interpersonal competence and other qualities important not only to student success but to success, health, and happiness in everyday life are ignored (O'Sullivan & Guilford, 1975; Wentzel, 1989). But attempts to identify the abilities associated with social functioning have been frustrated because most attempted measures have proved empirically indistinguishable from measures of verbal ability (Ford & Tisak, 1983; Moss, Hung, & Omwake, 1949; Stricker & Rock, 1990). Modern differential research has thus sought to refine existing definitions and develop new measures.

From their literature review, Walker and Foley (1973) concluded that definitions of social ability identify two dimensions: the ability to decode social information, including the ability to understand nonverbal cues and make accurate social inferences, and the ability to behave adaptively and effectively in social situations. They also noted that some research seemed circular, defining social skill as performance on any test that includes a social skill measure.

Work on the first component—decoding of social information—has been pursued by anthropologists and social psychologists interested in nonverbal communication. Several measures of this facility have been studied extensively in relation to other social and personality variables. Such measures include the Profile of Nonverbal Sensitivity (Rosenthal, Hall, DiMatteo, Rogers, & Archer, 1979) and the Social Interpretations Test (Archer & Akert, 1977a, 1977b, 1980). For example, high scorers on the profile tend to be even-handed with others, better adjusted, less rigid, and more extraverted; scores have been found to be positively correlated with age but largely uncorrelated with academic ability and achievement, socioeconomic status, or race.

Sternberg's (1990) theory of intelligence (see chapter 8, this volume) includes a contextual subtheory that is concerned with mental activity directed toward adapting to real life events and contexts; one aspect of this activity is the ability to decode nonverbal social cues. In one study (Barnes & Sternberg, 1989), students viewed photographs of romantically involved couples and persons in supervisor—subordinate relationships, of which some were real-life pairs and others were paired actors, and had to identify which photographs were of real-life pairs. Accuracy on the two tasks was uncorrelated, suggesting that skill here may be quite context specific. But accuracy on identifying real-life and cosmetic romantic couples did correlate, as expected, with scores on other existing measures of social intelligence.

Many other studies have focused on intercorrelations among testlike measures of social abilities. Guilford (1967) reviewed older research as well as a series of factor analyses on the behavioral content region of his Structure of Intellect model (see also Guilford & Hoepfner, 1971; O'Sullivan & Guilford, 1975). In this work, social intelligence-like ability tests were constructed by crossing behavioral content mainly with the cognition and divergent thinking operations. For example, some tests might ask examinees to interpret facial expressions.

Others might require generating numerous solutions to social problems. Although some social behavioral ability factors were identified in this work, it has generally been difficult to show that these factors are distinct from general or verbal abilities. Keating's (1978) study is an indication of the difficulty. He correlated traditional measures of cognitive ability and social intelligence and found no evidence of a distinct social domain.

Another approach emphasizes the second aspect identified by Walker and Foley (1973)—that social competence is demonstrated by social behavior that results in successful outcomes. Research by Ford and Tisak (1983) included several measures of behavioral effectiveness. One measure, the Social Competence Nomination Form, presented hypothetical situation descriptions containing detailed behavioral and contextual referents involving peers, parents, or teachers and asked respondents to nominate three boys and three girls in their grade who they believed would be most effective in the situation described. There were also self-assessments of social competence, a behavioral observation measure of social intelligence based on an interview, and a self-report measure of empathy. Correlations showed that the social competence measures demonstrated convergent validity and some degree of discriminant validity from academic achievement measures. Factor analysis revealed a distinct social intelligence factor, and regression analysis confirmed the greater power of the social measures to predict a behavioral criterion of social effectiveness. Ford and Tisak (1983) thus showed that the social domain is empirically distinguishable from the academic domain when behavioral measures are used. L. T. Brown and Anthony (1990) replicated these findings with college students, but also found that self-assessments of social intelligence were largely unrelated to peer assessments.

Sternberg (1992) has noted that measuring social intelligence in terms of actual behavioral success confounds successful performance due to social skills with other potential causes of social success, such as physical attractiveness, clothing tastes, willingness to use humor, and egocentrism. Although Ford and Tisak (1983) downplayed their findings of significant correlations between academic and social intelligence measures, it is reasonable to expect general ability to relate to social functioning and to the development of knowledge, skills, and effective strategies important to demonstrating successful behavioral outcomes. Nonetheless, Ford and Tisak's (1983) procedure provided a clear criterion for judging social competence beyond simple understanding or knowledge of social cues, which may not coincide with the intelligent *use* of that knowledge in attaining social goals (L. T. Brown & Anthony, 1990). Because volition is defined more generally to involve use of knowledge to accomplish goals, this aspect of social intelligence appears particularly associated with parts of the volitional domain (see also Wentzel, 1991, 1993a, for a discussion of social ability in relation to goal accomplishment in students). In addition, the distinction between social intelligence factors defined by self- versus other ratings parallels our distinction between self- and other-directed constructs, as well as Gardner's (1983) distinction between intrapersonal and interpersonal intelligences.

According to Gardner and Hatch (1989, p. 6), intrapersonal intelligence, the self-directed construct, is "access to one's own feelings and strengths and the ability to discriminate among them and draw upon them to guide behavior." Interpersonal intelligence, the other-directed construct, is the capacity "to discern and respond appropriately to the moods, temperaments, motivations, and desires of other people." There is as yet no evidence to show whether assessments of these functions correlate with the other measures discussed above. But Gardner and Sternberg have sought to teach these skills to schoolchildren. Sternberg (1992) reported significant differences favoring treated students over control students on standardized tests in several schools using the program, but treatment effects varied between schools. The work now seeks to identify the particular school elements that predispose to a positive response to treatment.

This work echoes an earlier experiment by Corno (1980; Corno, Mitman, & Hedges, 1981) in which parents and third-grade students worked together on reading activities that taught them the meaning of social cues in classroom teaching behavior, their functions in helping students learn, and what students can do to help themselves decode the structure of lessons. That study found significant effects favoring treated students on standardized tests of verbal ability as well as attitude toward school and self-esteem in both class- and individual-level analyses. School variance was less significant, however, than variance in student completion rates. But students completed this program individually within classrooms, and not in groups, as in the Gardner–Sternberg project. Completion rates correlated significantly with measures of general ability (suggesting that the activities posed challenges for many students of this age), and greater completion generally resulted in higher adjusted achievement and attitude. Thus, another key to academic learning may be found in individual differences in the ability to "read" classroom social environments and the patterns of teacher behavior that provide cues to the structures of lessons and student participation demands.

A construct of social intelligence should also include the ability to make correct social inferences or predictions about other people's behavior, as Walker and Foley (1973) noted. A small study by Fancher (1966) on this aspect shows how subtle may be the relations between social and cognitive abilities. Students were asked to predict the social behavior of others in particular situations based purely on personality descriptions of those persons. For student judges high in mathematical reasoning ability, accuracy in prediction of others came with the use of a few broad traits to characterize those others. For judges high in verbal abilities, highly differentiated characterizations were best for prediction. This suggests that accuracy in social inference depends on matching one's style of perceiving and describing other persons with one's own profile of cognitive strengths and weaknesses.

This observation returns us to the cognitive knowledge base of personal-social functioning and the recognition that this knowledge base is highly idiosyncratic. New attempts to develop assessments of personal knowledge patterned on Kelly's (1955) idiographic methods appear promising (see Cantor & Kihlstrom, 1987, for a review), although they are so far more relevant to psychotherapeutic use than to education.

*Empathy.* Another disposition that seems to stand alone and yet may be an aspect of social intelligence as well involves the vicarious sharing of perceived affective or conative states of others—in short, empathy. The construct has a long history and many definitions involving attention to emotional cues, social perspective taking, cognitive understanding and inferring of others' affective or conative functioning, and imaginative and imitative action; it is also necessary to avoid confusions with sympathy (i.e., feeling *for* without feeling *with* someone), personal distress (in reaction to another's distress), and projection (ascribing one's own state to another) (see Eisenberg & Strayer, 1987).

Zahn-Waxler, Robinson, and Emde (1992) define empathy simply as the "experience of others' emotional, physical, or psychological states" (p. 1038). Because empathy reflects the capacity to "'read' others' emotions, to understand their motives and intentions, and to be positively invested in interpersonal relationships" (p. 1038), it is presumed to have important adaptive value, even survival value in evolutionary terms. In other words, it is believed that empathy mediates prosocial behavior. Certainly, substantial evidence argues that empathy (and sympathy) relates positively to voluntary efforts to help others, although such intentions are not necessary consequences of empathy (Eisenberg & Strayer, 1987).

Studies measuring empathy have been based on picture story verbalizations, social behavioral observations, facial and gestural measures, self-report questionnaires, and physiological measures. Children's prosocial behavior, facial expressions, and attempts to understand the nature of others' distress have been found to reflect stable individual differences as early as 2 years of age (see Zahn-Waxler, Cummings, Iannotti, 1986). These differences also appear age related, with reparative behavior toward others increasing consistent with cognitive development (Hoffman, 1975; Zahn-Waxler, Radke-Yarrow, Wagner, & Chapman, 1992). Individual differences show continuity and stability at least to adolescence, although cognitive and affective aspects of empathy may weigh differently for different children; some appear more emotional and some more analytic in response to another's distress. Parental and social factors that seem to promote the development of empathy include secure early attachment, parental affection, the availability of empathic models, parental use of inductive discipline encouraging imaginal empathy, encouragement of self-concept as well as perceived similarity to others, and discouragement of excessive interpersonal competition (Barnett, 1987). Intervention research on empathy has also found positive influences for environmental socialization factors such as affective qualities in parental relationships and friends (Costin & Jones, 1992; Hoffman, 1994). Given its survival value, empathy may have a biological basis as well, and there appear to be gender differences even in newborns (Eisenberg & Lennon, 1983; see also the evidence on heritability reviewed by Zahn-Waxler, Robinson et al., 1992).

Empathy is presumably promoted in moral education and development programs. It clearly plays a role in classroom instruction through the necessary skills of prosocial behavior, cooperation and turn taking, and affective bonding with teachers and peers. Children who display these capabilities in elementary school tend to be better liked by other children and teachers, which helps to create more favorable conditions for academic success during adolescence (Wentzel, 1993a, 1993b). In one study Wentzel (1991) found that adolescents who displayed socially responsible behavior in school had significantly higher grade point averages than students who did not when cognitive factors and other behavior were controlled for statistically. Social responsibility was assessed in this study by peer nomination.

*Machiavellianism.* Machiavellian personalities aim subtly but deliberately to manipulate other persons and situations to their own best interests (Christie & Geis, 1970). The strongly Machiavellian or "cool syndrome" person tries to initiate and control situations without respect for other persons' goals, resists external social influence, and can function in these ways even in emotionally tense situations. The strongly Machiavellian person is a low-reactive temperament in Strelau's (1983) terms, showing detachment and low emotionality in relations with others, but not hostility or vindictiveness (Wrightsman, 1991). Persons weak in Machiavellian tendencies—those with the "soft touch" syndrome—are submissive, susceptible to social influence and persuasion, and generally attentive to other persons and social conventions. There is some evidence that Machiavellianism is a multifaceted construct, with separate belief constructs for deceit, flattery, immorality, and cynicism (O'Hair & Cody, 1987).

The Machiavellian person has come to be seen as someone who uses guile, deceit, and opportunism to manipulate others to his or her own purposes (Christie & Geis, 1970). It is important to note, however, that scholars disagree on this negative attribution as an appropriate characterization of Machiavelli, the historical figure. According to Berlin (1980), Machiavelli regarded traditional morality as utopian and thus impractical, so he emphasized the practical, realistic side of politics, urging that people avoid self-delusion. With this interpretation, we might see Machiavelli as an early contributor to the theory of practical intelligence (Sternberg & Wagner, 1986). Whether Machiavellianism is interpreted positively or negatively, research on this personality type has turned up some findings relevant to educational psychology.

Children high in Machiavellianism are less empathetic, rated as less helpful by teachers, and more likely to choose self-oriented reasons for engaging in helpful behavior (Barnett & Thompson, 1984). Among college students, Machiavellian attitudes are related to success in speech communication courses (Jandt, 1975; Burgoon, 1971). Among school principals, Machiavellian attitudes are positively related to perceived level of stress (Fortin, 1989), external locus of control, low job satisfaction (Richford & Fortune, 1984; Volp & Willower, 1977) and high job mobility, but are unrelated to teacher ratings of principal effectiveness, loyalty to the principal and school, or openness of the school climate (Hoy, Rees, & Williams, 1973).

*Persuasibility.* The person with weak Machiavellian tendencies is thought to be especially susceptible to influence and persuasion by others. In research on attitude formation and change, the related construct of persuasibility has been studied. Hovland and Janis (1962) defined persuasibility as variability in sensitivity to one or more classes of influential communications or propaganda, including media such as film, speech, or text. Communications research suggests that persons who are persuasible are readily influenced in opinion, attitude, and belief by external messages, and that yielding to persuasive argument, through comprehension and acceptance of new information, is a major route to attitude change. Unfortunately, although much of education aims to persuade, this construct has been

FIGURE 9–9. Probability of Reception, Yielding, and Attitude Change as a Function of Message Recipients' Level of Intelligence

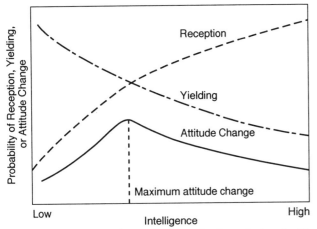

Source: Based on "Attitude Change: The Information-Processing Paradigm" by W. J. McGuire, pp. 108–141 in *Experimental Social Psychology*, edited by G. G. McClintock, 1972, New York: Holt, Rinehart & Winston. Adapted by permission.

almost totally neglected in educational psychology. In a later section, we touch on a variety of other issues in attitude research (see also Eagly & Chaiken, 1993). Here we address one central model that also connects persuasibility to other student differences.

Following from the early work of Hovland and Janis (1962), the program of research by McGuire (1968, 1972, 1985, 1990) may provide the most interesting and useful base for education-related research. McGuire proposed an information-processing model of persuasion with several stages such as presentation of the message, followed by attention, comprehension, yielding, retention, and action (different terms and numbers of stages have been used in different presentations). Most important for our purposes is his retention–yielding model, which posits a curvilinear relation between the probability of reception, yielding, and attitude change, on the one hand, and individual differences in intelligence, self-esteem, and anxiety on the other (see Figure 9–9). The interpretation for intelligence, as an example, is that message recipients' attention and comprehension of a message likely increase with intelligence, but yielding and attitude change as a result likely decrease. The model also includes a contextual moderation principle. With complex, well-argued messages, reception is more important than yielding, and intelligence should relate positively to attitude change. With simple and poorly argued messages, where yielding is more important than reception, intelligence should relate negatively to attitude change. Although the evidence relating to this model is understandably complex, meta-analysis of the literature has supported the curvilinear hypothesis for self-esteem; the intelligence–persuasion relationship has also found weak support so far (Rhodes & Wood, 1992).

The psychological construct of persuasibility is not satisfactorily measured in most research that equates it with attitude change (Ercikan, 1991; Hovland & Janis, 1962). As noted, persuasibility has elements in common with deep personality characteristics prominently associated not only with cognitive and

motivational functions but also with volitional functions; conformity and reactance are examples, in addition to intelligence, self-esteem, and anxiety. We discuss conformity as part of a conative complex in a later section. Reactance derives from Brehm (1966), who posited that persons react against and attempt to remove imposed behavioral constraints they perceive as reducing freedom or personal control (see Deci & Ryan, 1985; McCaslin & Good, 1992). It also relates to work by Pittman and D'Agostino (1989), which shows control-deprived subjects to work more carefully as they learn and try to regain control.

## Personal Styles

No category we have covered contains a more voluminous, complex, and controversy-laced literature than that of personal styles. There is a long, diverse history, many continuing research programs, and a current explosion of interest (see Messick, 1994). Particularly in education, however, there are also many new, as yet unvalidated constructs and claims about practical use. Even much studied constructs are often poorly represented by the measures chosen. However, most of the complexities are beyond our current purview. We limit our review to some conceptual issues and an overview of learning style and strategy assessments, followed by two selected examples of overarching constructs with substantial foundation in educational research and practice settings.

*Kinds and Characteristics of Style Constructs.* A style can be defined simply as a strategy used consistently across a class of tasks. A strategy is an action plan composed of organized tactics, and a tactic is a possible move, overt or covert, within that plan. In reverse, the moves actually used in performing a specific task are indicants of tactics, the organization of which signifies a strategy; its generalization across tasks is then a style (see Schmeck, 1983, 1988b; Snowman, 1986). Some learning styles often have this construction. More typically, however, style constructs are defined not simply as consistent strategies but more deeply as characteristic habitual or preferred ways in which individuals adapt to the demands and affordances of situations involving cognitive or social performance. Messick (1994) emphasizes that

styles are self-consistent regularities in the manner or form of human activity. . . . [S]tyles are both integrative and pervasive. Because these personal styles refer to consistencies in the *way* psychological substance is processed rather than to consistencies in the substance itself, they may entail mechanisms for the organization and control of processes that cut across substantive areas. (p. 121, emphasis in original)

Six kinds of style constructs have been studied: *cognitive styles*, involved in perception and thinking (e.g., field independence vs. dependence, reflection–impulsivity), *learning styles*, involved in approaches to learning and studying (e.g., deep vs. surface processing, comprehension-learning versus operation-learning), *expressive styles*, involved in verbal or nonverbal communication (e.g., tempo, constricted vs. expansive), *response styles*, involved in self-perception and self-report (e.g., acquiescence, deception), *defensive styles*, involved in accommodating anxiety and conflict (e.g., obsessive–compulsive, hysterical), and *cognitive controls*, a subset of stylelike but function-specific and unipolar controls on attention and behavior (e.g., strong vs. weak automatization, constricted vs. flexible control). For more complete listings of constructs in each category, see Messick (1976, 1987).

We emphasize learning styles and strategies here, but we make no sharp distinction between learning styles and cognitive styles, or between styles and approaches. A learning style construct would presumably encompass both one's approach to learning, studying, and problem-solving tasks and one's approach to the characteristic cognitive activities and information-processing operations typically used during task performance.

Some theorists deemphasize consistency across situations to interpret multiple styles as choices to fit different situations; flexible shifts in style are thus the focus, but flexible adaptation of information processing is taken as a mark of learning ability as well as of style or strategy (Battig, 1979; Kyllonen, Lohman, & Woltz 1984; Snow, 1981). Choice is not necessarily characteristic of style. We said "habitual or preferred" above because some stylistic aspects of performance may be habitual but distinctly not preferred; procrastination or overarousal are obvious examples. However, many individual differences in style include variations in preferred modes of task performance, and may also refer to preferred environmental and social conditions in which such performance is undertaken. Some style constructs also seem to include cognitive skill components. Thus, there is concern that some of the more widely known style constructs, notably field independence, either cannot be reliably distinguished from fluid-analytic ability or need substantial redefinition with respect to it (Cronbach, 1990; Linn & Kyllonen, 1981; McKenna, 1984, 1990). Other substantive and methodological criticisms have been raised concerning various style constructs and measures (e.g., Curry, 1990; Tiedeman, 1989). However, new research is beginning to evaluate these criticisms, comparing multiple constructs and measures in the same studies (Curry, 1991). And the complexities of measurement and construct validation in this field are becoming more widely recognized. As Messick (1994) pointed out, criticisms of style research often fail to reflect subtle distinctions in the developing theories, to distinguish measures from constructs, or to appreciate sources of inconsistency that afflict many other fields of research, not just work in styles.

Furthermore, theorists such as Messick (1987, 1989a, 1993, 1994) see style constructs as linkages or bridges between traditional ability and personality constructs, and as more directly representing processes than either; styles are both expressions of personality in action and expressions of preferred or habitual utilization of abilities. Baron (1982) would interpret impulsivity this way—as a speed versus accuracy trade-off that can be reliably measured and manipulated in particular situations (see Lohman, 1989a). In turn, learning styles link cognitive styles with learning strategies and outcomes. Schmeck (1988b) also would place learning styles between personality traits and learning strategies in a causal chain to learning outcomes. He interprets style as an expression of personality in a situation, a preferred learning strategy, but also including aspects of motivation, affect, and cognitive style. Biggs (1988; Biggs & Collis, 1982), Entwistle (1987a, 1988), and Hunt (1971; Hunt & Sullivan, 1974) also emphasize motivational as well as cognitive analysis of stylistic differences and consider the relations between learning and teaching styles. Despite the complexities, there is persis-

tent research advocating some old-style distinctions, such as field independence versus dependence (Globerson & Zelniker, 1989; Wapner & Demick, 1991; Witkin & Goodenough, 1981) and verbalization versus visualization (Richardson, 1977; Cohen & Saslona, 1990). In addition, many studies propose other distinctions, such as holistic versus serialist learning and memory organization (Pask, 1976, 1988); mental self-government styles (Sternberg, 1990); attributional styles (Anderson, 1983; Anderson, Jenning, & Arnoult, 1988); certainty versus uncertainty orientations (Sorrentino & Short, 1985; Huber, 1990); thinking dispositions (Perkins, Jay, & Tishman, 1993); convergent versus divergent thinking (Hudson, 1966); learning by divergence, assimilation, convergence, or accommodation (Kolb, 1978, 1981; Marshall & Merritt, 1986); and preferences for extraversion versus introversion, sensing versus intuition, thinking versus feeling, and judgment versus perception (Myers & McCaulley, 1993). There are also new conceptualizations of styles to characterize ethnic group differences (see Cole, 1985; Gordon, 1988; Tharp, 1989) and differential modes of human–computer interaction (Kyllonen & Shute, 1989; Snow, 1980).

There is thus a long list of style assessment instruments and an even longer list of learning style constructs and constituents. Table 9–7 lists the style and strategy constructs represented in four major current programs, together with key references, to provide a reasonably broad sample of each kind of construct. The table makes clear some of the conceptual and definitional problems referred to earlier. Keefe's (1987, 1988; Keefe & Monk, 1988) assessment inventory, for example, includes cognitive ability tests. Direct performance scores on these tests should not be called style. Several of the inventories overlap, showing apparently similar affective and conative scales that may not be empirically similar. Each inventory also includes apparently unique constructs, although different labels do not guarantee empirical distinction.

That is a problem for research on styles and strategies, just as it is for research on any other individual difference constructs. Investigators should be free, even encouraged, to build instruments to fit their own theoretical and practical needs. But both the jingle and the jangle fallacies apply. Because scale labels such as those in Table 9–7 are taken as theoretical claims, and because they are used as aptitude constructs to differentiate instructional treatment among different learners, a heavy burden of validation weighs on the investigator (Snow, 1992).

Style constructs seem to need a different theoretical and measurement framework, and perhaps also a different approach to validation, than ability constructs and most other affective and conative constructs. Perhaps there need to be multiple approaches, insofar as style (and strategy) constructs exist at different levels of referent generality and in different networks of associated constructs and evidence. One suggestion is to recognize explicitly the bipolar contrastive character of many style constructs by constructing ipsative contrast scores; in this way, relative strengths, preferences, predilections, and alternative action tendencies could be represented as intraindividual as well as interindividual differences. Messick (1994) demonstrated how this construction clarifies the meaning and measurement of field independence versus field dependence and eliminates some of the criticisms. Careful definition of other such constructs as bipolar, with careful examination of the value-differentiated character of each pole, could prove a major

TABLE 9–7. Scales Included in Four Learning Styles and Strategies Questionnaires

| Keefe (1988) | | Pintrich Smith et al. (1991) | |
|---|---|---|---|
| Cognitive Skills | | Value Components | |
| Analytic Skill | Embedded figures identification | Intrinsic Goal Orientation | Prefer challenging, arousing learning |
| Spatial Skill | Pattern recognition, visualization | | |
| Discrimination Skill | Size comparison, attention control | Extrinsic Goal Orientation | Prefer good grades |
| Categorization Skill | Consistency in narrow vs. broad inclusion | Task value | This course is interesting, important, useful |
| Sequential Processing Skill | Recognition of seriation of shapes | Expectancy Components | |
| | | Control Beliefs | If I study I will get good grades |
| Simultaneous Processing Skill | Gestalt closure recognition | Perceived Competence | I am a good student |
| | | Self-Efficacy | Beliefs about successful performance in a particular domain |
| Memory Skill | Leveling vs. sharpening in figure sequence | | |
| | | Expectancy of Success | I expect to do well in this course |
| Verbal-Spatial Preference | Choice of meaning pairs | | |
| Perceptual response | Visual, auditory, or motor-kinesthetic modality preference | Affective Components | |
| | | Test Anxiety | Concern for being evaluated |
| Study and Instructional Preferences | | Cognitive Strategies | |
| Persistence Orientation | Willingness to complete difficult tasks | Rehearsal | Repeat material over and over until it is learned |
| Verbal Risk Orientation | Willingness to state opinions | Selection | Deciding what to study |
| Manipulative Preference | Preference for hands-on learning | Organization | Deciding how to arrange study topics |
| Study Time Preference | Early morning, late morning, afternoon, or evening preference | Elaboration | Exploring details of the study material |
| Grouping Preference | Preference for whole class, small-group, or dyadic learning | Metacognition | Understanding of how to learn and study |
| Posture Preference | Formal vs. informal body positions for learning | Surface Processing | Tries to do minimum work to satisfy the teacher |
| Mobility Preference | Stationary vs. mobile studying | Critical Thinking | Wants to know why things work the way they do |
| Sound Preference | Silence vs. background sound for studying | Original Thinking | Innovative and creative approach to learning |
| Lighting Preference | Higher vs. lower illumination | | |
| Temperature Preference | Warmer vs. cooler settings | Resource Management | |
| | | Time and Study | Sets aside time for studying |
| | | Study Environment | Studies in an environment free from distractions |
| Schmeck et al. (1977) | | Effort | Puts forth effort when studying |
| Academic Self-Concept | | Help-Seeking Behavior | Willing to ask for help when confronted with problems |
| Intrinsic Motivation | Learn what I am told to | | |
| Self-Efficacy | Trouble planning, studying, remembering | | |
| | | Weinstein et al. (1988): Learning and Study Strategies Inventory | |
| Non-Reiterative Processing | Rote memorizing | Anxiety | Worry about school, grades, tests |
| Self-Esteem | Worry about being wrong | Attitude | Success in school is clear goal |
| | | Concentration | Task attention vs. distraction, day dreaming |
| Reflective Processing | | | |
| Deep Processing | Try to understand, interpret, reflect | Information Processing | Active organization and elaboration |
| Elaborative Processing | Relate to other situations | Motivation | Willing to work hard, self discipline |
| Self-Expression | Personalize, paraphrase, play with ideas | Scheduling | Manages time, planning |
| | | Selecting Main Ideas | Identifies key points to learn |
| Agentic Processing | | Self-Testing | Reviews regularly, prepares for class |
| Conventional | Rational, reflective, careful, complete | | |
| Serial Processing | Persistent, step-by-step, finish tasks in order | Study Aids | Uses practice, examples, headings, diagrams |
| Fact Retention | Careful effort on all details | Test strategies | Prepares for tests, test-taking |
| Methodical Study | Schedule studying, no cramming | | |

advance. A similar approach might also sharpen definitions and assessments in other areas of research on affective and conative differences.

Another advance might come from more explicit interpretation of styles within a model of person–situation interaction and adaptation. Perhaps learning styles are not best treated as distinguishable traitlike constructs on par with other dimensions in Figure 9–1. Rather, each may be a complex result of multiple differences from Figure 9–1 acting jointly in interaction with the demands and affordances of particular performance situations. The learning activities observable during present performance and the preferences and habits arising from previous learning performance should not, from this perspective, be reified as distinct, stable traits. They may be better treated as indicators of mediating functions in the personality–performance interface. There would thus be relatively few but more molar constructs reflecting broad contrasts in the dynamics of the personality–task interface during learning in particular instructional environments. It is not clear that these constructs should be considered styles equivalent to all the other style constructs. As noted previously, Entwistle (1988) would prefer to distinguish style from approach, which might better describe these more molar, dynamic, and contextual learner differences. Again, Bereiter's (1990) "acquired conceptual modules" might serve as well (see also Entwistle, 1995a, 1995b). In the next sections, we consider two constructs that might be interpreted in this way.

*Deep versus Surface Approaches to Learning.* One of these more pervasive constructs distinguishes between deep and surface approaches to the processing of information in learning situations (Entwistle, 1987a; Marton, Hounsell, & Entwistle, 1984; Marton & Säljö, 1976). We think this distinction summarizes the effective result in learning activities of a large number of other style and strategy differences. That is, many other kinds of differences can have the effect of producing deep or surface processing; if so, these other differences are functionally equivalent. Also, while this result may be interpreted in cognitive information-processing terms, it clearly reflects differences in intention or commitment to learn, which is a broader conative construct. Thus, this construct links back to the previous discussions of task-, learning-, and mastery-oriented goals, and to action control, self-regulation, and mindfulness as well.

In the deep processing approach to learning, learners regard the learning material (text, problem, etc.) as the means by which to gain an understanding of the underlying meaning of the material. In the surface approach, learners regard the particular learning material as what needs to be learned, without attempting to link it to a larger conceptual framework. Students who are intrinsically motivated and who learn for the sake of learning, with less concern about their performance or others' evaluations of their performance, are more likely to use a deep approach. Learning is viewed primarily as constructing meaning as an interpretive process of understanding reality. A surface approach is likely to occur when students are motivated to fulfill the demands placed on them by others, so it relates more to extrinsic motivation and evaluation anxiety and is particularly sensitive to assessment procedures. Learning is regarded as a passive transmission of what is found in learning materials to the brain of the learner, with particular emphasis on memoriza-

tion in knowledge acquisition. The deep versus surface dichotomy has elements that are both state- and traitlike. Marton et al. (1984) described it as not "a stable characteristic of the student, but rather . . . a relation between the student's perception of a task and his approach to it" (p. 135). Yet research has implied that it is "to some extent a stable characteristic of the student—or at least that some students [adopt] consistent approaches across a range of different study tasks" (p. 213). The relationship between deep versus surface approaches and performance is of course indirect. Successful performance can be achieved through either approach with effort, depending on what kinds of outcome are scored. The deep approach will lead to far greater understanding than the surface approach, and will correlate with learning outcomes especially when understanding is emphasized.

Both questionnaire and interview assessment methods have been developed, and there is now solid evidence on the deep versus surface distinction as important in learning. There is also evidence for another distinct approach, called "strategic," to represent learners whose activities aim mainly at impressing instructors and obtaining the highest possible grade by whatever means or process is necessary (Entwistle & Ramsden, 1983). These distinctions have now been related to student abilities, other learning skills and strategies, and confidence and motivation (see Tait & Entwistle, in press). Also, Pintrich and Schrauben (1992) have connected deep versus surface processing to other measures of conation. Their review of research in this area related deep processing to mastery goal orientation, subject matter interest, intrinsic motivation, and aspects of self-regulated learning. Probably, mindfulness and deep processing are also closely related. Surface processing is related to performance goals and extrinsic motivation. Although not discussed by Pintrich and Schrauben (1992), the strategic approach probably reflects some aspects of self-regulated learning and an ego orientation; it may also result when learners adopt both mastery and performance goals, as some theorists have suggested (e.g., Blumenfeld, 1992; Corno, 1992).

The questionnaire measure for deep processing includes scales for intention to understand, active interest, relating ideas, and use of evidence. Representing the surface approach are scales for intention to reproduce, passive learning, unrelated memorizing, and fear of failure. The questionnaire measure for the strategic approach includes intention to excel, alertness to assessment demands, study organization, and time management. Some scales for lack of direction and interest and for academic self-confidence are also added (see Tait & Entwistle, in press).

Entwistle (1988) has taken steps to relate his inventory to Schmeck's instruments, represented in Table 9–7. Building abbreviated versions of both, he was able to report substantial correlations between some similar scales and a combined factor analysis; this yielded distinct dimensions combining (1) deep approach, elaborative processing, and intrinsic motivation; (2) surface approach, fear of failure, and orientation to task details; (3) disorganized study methods and social motivation; and (4) achieving orientation and strategic approach (though this last factor was not consistent across the college student samples). It does seem that high first-dimension scores might reflect independent, intentional learning, and perhaps also a task orientation that contrasts with social orientation, as in the third dimension here. A correlational network of this sort remains to be developed. But Entwistle (1988) has summarized many aspects of intention, performance, and learning outcome differences associated with the contrasting deep, surface, and strategic approaches.

A closely related set of approaches to learning constructs is measured by Biggs's (1987, 1991) self-report Learning Process Questionnaire, which yields scores for deep, achieving, and surface approaches. A study by Ainley (1993) used this questionnaire to investigate how student beliefs and goals are associated with different styles of engagement in learning and both school achievement and the strategies students use when preparing for examinations. Ainley used cluster analysis techniques to identify six clusters of high school students across general ability and the three approaches to learning constructs. She labeled these clusters detached, committed, hopeful, engaged, disengaged, and keen-to-do-well. For example, detached students were highly able students who scored well below average on achieving and surface approaches but had average scores on the deep approach, suggesting a low level of involvement. Students from these six clusters reported using different examination preparation strategies, with committed and engaged students using active, transformational strategies but keen-to-do-well and hopeful but less able students using passive, reproductive strategies. These six clusters were also related to students' achievement as measured by school grades and a statewide examination, with committed students scoring most highly.

Ainley's (1993) study is unusual because it took into account the multidimensional character of student styles of engagement with learning through cluster analysis techniques (but see also Pintrich, 1989). This approach is much needed in educational research and complements studies that emphasize the independent effects of similar constructs.

*Conceptual Level.* One theory of personality development defines a dimension of conceptual complexity and interpersonal maturity along which children move as they grow and learn (Harvey, Hunt, & Schroder, 1961). This dimension also characterizes individual differences at a given age, contrasting concrete experience, conceptual simplicity, and external, dependent orientations in relation to others versus abstract conceptualization and internal, interdependent orientations with respect to others; the dimension is called conceptual level for short. The measure uses paragraph-completion tests that are essentially projective. The high-scoring person perceives the environment as both differentiated and integrated, thinks abstractly, and shows maturity in social relations. The low-scoring person perceives stereotypically and thinks in terms of concrete experience. Some evidence suggests that the difference correlates also with moral maturity, ego development, and future time perspective.

Hunt (1971, 1975, 1977; Hunt & Sullivan, 1974) in particular developed the assessment of conceptual level for use in educational research. He saw it as a style construct, enabling matches between student and teacher (or teaching method) for optimum social and cognitive benefit. The original theory specified varied situation types with which conceptual level would interact. One line of Hunt's research singled out high versus low structure of the teaching–learning situation, such as didactic versus dis-

covery or teacher-centered versus learner-centered instruction, as the matching treatment variable. Cronbach and Snow (1977) reviewed several studies of this hypothesis, concluding that low-conceptual-level students are apparently helped by more directive teaching, whereas high-level students benefit when given more independent control of the learning situation. Hunt's positive results also line up with other findings we have cited showing that ability and anxiety often yield similar ATI patterns. But the relations between ability, anxiety, and conceptual level remain unclear and may be quite complicated. In some work, with ability partialed out, conceptual level differences related positively with achievement in college social science and humanities courses but negatively with achievement in engineering courses (Hunt & Sullivan, 1974). The difference could be attributed to a memorization emphasis in engineering compatible with low conceptual level and an abstract conceptual emphasis in social science and humanities compatible with high conceptual level (given control of ability differences). Given such results, one might also expect relations between conceptual level and the deep versus surface approaches to learning just discussed.

A broader review by Miller (1981) covered various issues concerned with the original theory as well as later studies of the conceptual-levels-matching hypothesis. He concluded that the theory was reasonably well supported despite various aspects that needed further work. Meanwhile Hunt (1987) implemented conceptual levels matching in several public schools. Although grouping students by conceptual level seemed to work as intended, by Hunt's observation, the most important effect of style grouping seemed to be the freedom it provided teachers to adapt in other ways to students with other stylistic differences and needs. From several years of experience in dealing with learning and teaching style variations in these schools, Hunt recommended that no learning style construct be imposed from outside, but rather that teachers be helped to define appropriate and useful styles for themselves and their students. Hunt's theoretical ideas were derived significantly from those of Lewin (1951) and Kelly (1955). In proposing that nomothetic style constructs be set aside in favor of idiosyncratically defined styles, he has reasserted Kelly's emphasis on personal idiographic constructs. When teachers can define or choose style distinctions for themselves that best fit their own local context, they are also more likely to understand and use them effectively. Such local contextual constructs could be much more useful in guiding adaptation to moment-to-moment student needs. Whether they would serve as well for the week-to-week or month-to-month adaptations envisioned in earlier matching or ATI research is an empirical question.

Hunt's (1987) notion of helping teachers build their own contextually tuned style constructs runs some risk of overdifferentiating among learners by bringing too many style distinctions into attention or by misguiding attempts at adaptive teaching by centering on invalid distinctions; either move would be counterproductive. But that is already a threat, given the many style systems being proposed for teacher use today. At least Hunt's approach would bring teacher judgments about what style adaptations are most important to their own contexts back to center-stage focus. It might also allow teacher priorities in practice to work against the overdifferentiation evident in some externally imposed style systems.

## Selected Conative Complexes

*Flow.* One important compound of affective, conative and cognitive experience during learning is called *flow* by M. Csikszentmihalyi (1990). Flow is a state of optimal experience characterized by total concentration and absorption in a challenging activity that engenders a sense of control, interest, enjoyment, even exhilaration. Flow is said to be autotelic because it contains its own goal. During flow states, individuals are engaged in the intrinsically motivated development of skills and understandings without conscious deliberation or problem solving but with a keen interest in pursuing the task, not for extrinsic rewards or feedback but for the intrinsic affect or feeling of performance. Energy is so intensely directed to the task that other subjects or problems are ignored completely. Dewey (1913, 1964/1934) described this kind of deep experiential learning as a distinct and special life episode in which one feels a sense of unity among diverse aspects of experience. Lewin (1951) also discussed this kind of "in-the-moment" detachment. A deep processing style may also tie in. Although flow is usually described as a state, there are substantial individual differences; some students experience it often, others rarely or never.

To assess flow, M. Csikszentmihalyi and his colleagues have employed a procedure called the experience sampling method (see Csikszentmihalyi & Csikszentmihalyi, 1988). Students agree to carry an electronic pager with them for a fixed period of time. Signals are sent to the pagers at random intervals to cue students to complete self-report measures describing their current situations and emotional and cognitive states at that moment. Items concern mood with respect to both potency and affect, feelings of challenge, concentration, intrinsic motivation, self-esteem, goal importance, and self-estimated skill in the activity at hand. Flow states seem to occur especially in situations where the person perceives both challenge and skill to be equally high. Current studies represent flow both as an intraindividual experience varying within persons and as an individual difference factor.

So far, the research has shown that individuals differ drastically in how much time they spend in situations that promote flow. But M. Csikszentmihalyi and Nakamura (1989) also emphasize other person characteristics they call metaskills:

The flow model suggests that to derive enjoyment from life reliably requires the ability to get into flow, stay in it, and make the process evolve. We hypothesize that this depends on a capacity to structure interactions with the environment in ways that facilitate flow. . . . [T]his would seem to depend on having assigned to other experiences the functions performed by games and other autotelic activities that are deliberately structured to provide experiential rewards. Specifically, the characteristics of the autotelic activity correspond to capacities (1) to focus attention on the present moment and the activity at hand; (2) to define one's goals in an activity and identify the means for reaching them; and (3) to seek feedback and focus on its information aspects. In addition to these abilities, the dependence of enjoyment on a balancing of challenges and skill suggests the importance of a capacity to continuously adjust this balance, by using anxiety and boredom as information, and identifying new challenges as skills grow. In relation to this, a capacity to tolerate the anxiety-provoking interactions that test one's skills also appears to be important. Finally, we suspect other metaskills have their effect outside of the particular interaction; these would include the ability to delay gratification, which seems necessary for the eventual enjoyment of activities that require a significant investment of energy before they start providing intrinsic rewards. (pp. 66–67)

Individual differences in such metaskills are presumed to derive from autotelic family contexts; some parents create conditions that promote intrinsic motivation in family activities and model its characteristics therein. In further studies of talented students who did or did not take advantage of their opportunities, the so-called complex families that offered continuity of support and involvement, mixed with challenging opportunities and freedom to pursue them individually, were the most successful. It was also noted that teachers differ in promoting flow much as do parents. Flow teachers visibly nurture their own interests, arrange classroom conditions to emphasize intrinsic rewards, and minimize extrinsic pressures for competition, grades, and rules. They also "read" the shifting needs of different students, adapt to individual interests and styles of learning, and balance intervention, withdrawal, critique, and encouragement in interactions with students (M. Csikszentmihalyi, Rathunde, & Whalen, 1993).

An example of flow measures used in combination with measures of interest, achievement motivation, ability, and achievement in high school mathematics comes from Schiefele and M. Csikszentmihalyi (in press). In this case experience sampling focused on math class time. The experience dimensions studied were potency (active–passive, strong–weak moods), affect (happy–sad, cheerful–irritable moods), concentration, intrinsic motivation, self-esteem, importance of present activity, and perceived skill in it. The flow measures were used first as indicators of quality of experience in math class, to be predicted by other measures, and then as predictors of achievement along with the other measures. Results showed prior math interest to be the strongest predictor of potency, intrinsic motivation, self-esteem, and perceived skill. Ability and achievement motivation showed only weak relations with reported experience. Math achievement was predicted by ability and interest but not by the quality experience indicators. The authors suggest that experience sampling provides an important outcome measure for further work. Quality of classroom experience, including affective mood, interest, and intrinsic motivation, has not been a major focus of research on mathematics teaching, relative to cognitive objectives, but it may be equally crucial.

### *The Independent-Intentional Learner.*

Another example of an aptitude complex combines affective and conative dimensions with ability. We place it here also because it cries out for further analysis of the learning styles and strategies associated with each profile.

Two of the subordinate personality factors in Table 9–2 are *achievement via independence* (Ai) and *achievement via conformance* (Ac). Both reflect positive self-reports. Ac refers to achievement when tasks and performance situations are well defined and externally structured. High-Ac persons are described as capable, cooperative, organized, responsible, persistent, industrious, and sincere. In contrast, Ai refers to achievement in performance tasks and situations where individual initiative is required and rewarded. High-Ai persons are described as mature, forceful, demanding, independent, and self-reliant. Factor-analytic studies tend to group the two scales with other scales to create more general personality constructs; the Ai scale is grouped with intellectual efficiency and flexibility as part of intellectual openness, the fifth of the Big Five dimensions in Figure 9–3, whereas the Ac scale is grouped with conformity, responsibility, compliance, and conscientiousness, the third dimension in Figure 9–3.

Most important for present purposes, however, is the tendency for students with opposite profiles on these two dimensions to achieve in alternative instructional environments matched to their strengths. In several ATI studies, students high in Ac relative to Ai were more successful when presented with instruction that was formally structured and demanding of conformity, whereas students high in Ai relative to Ac did better with instruction that emphasized student initiative and independence (Domino, 1968, 1971; Peterson, 1976; Porteus, 1976; Snow, 1977b). The consistent results suggest that better learning outcome occurs when the instructor's teaching style is matched to this student personality profile.

Two of the high school studies showing this ATI pattern also included crystallized verbal ability (Gc) and test anxiety (Ax) as additional aptitude measures. These measures produced a similar ATI pattern with instructional treatments. Students with moderate to high Gc and moderate to low Ax did best with less teacher structuring and more student initiative; students quite high or quite low in both Gc and Ax did best with more teacher structuring and less student independence. There were, moreover, correlations among the four aptitude measures; Gc showed moderate positive correlations with Ai, slightly less so with Ac, and Ax correlated negatively with all three, especially Ac. There is some further evidence that these aptitude differences correlate with different patterns of study habits and attitudes among college students (Rutkowski & Domino, 1975), and show strong correlation also with some achievement motivation measures (J. H. Morris & Snyder, 1978).

In other words, there is a four-way aptitude space that can be divided into two regions, one in which teacher-controlled instruction is expected to be best and one in which optimum structure is obtained more by student initiative and independent action. An aptitude profile of moderate to high Gc, moderate to low Ax, and Ai higher than Ac fits the more independent, student-controlled instructional treatment. This aptitude complex for student initiative in learning seems similar to what Bereiter (1990) has described as the profile of the "intentional" learner, but "independent" learner would also be a good descriptor. A profile showing distinctly high Ax with high Gc, or low Ax with low Gc, and Ac higher than Ai, better fits the teacher-controlled instructional treatment. Perhaps this latter aptitude complex might be termed the "compliant" learner. Although one might hope to design educational treatments in which all students would eventually acquire an independent-intentional aptitude profile, it is important to recognize the interim needs of students showing the compliant profile. Perhaps for them, more teacher control is needed in early stages to promote gradual change to more effective independent learning in later stages of instruction. At least, identifying this complex aptitude contrast allows research to pursue deeper understanding of the compound and its developmental and educational implications (see Snow, 1987).

A particularly important next step for research would be to connect individual differences in learning strategies and tactics

to these profiles. The correlations with study habits, attitude, and strategy questionnaires provide some clues to pursue. Beyond this, more direct assessment of learning activities and perceptions of learners with different profiles in the contrasting instructional environments could provide a rich description of this potentially important complex.

***Task versus Social Orientation.*** Several pairs of constructs in our review seem explicitly or implicitly to contrast task orientation versus social orientation. Sociability, extraversion, most of the other-directed constructs, even achievement via conformity suggest the person's emphasis on or attention to social relations. On the other hand, achievement via independence, action controls, need for achievement, and some aspects of self-directed constructs concern person–task relations pursued individually, perhaps even antisocially. Also, as Spangler (1992) noted, some measures of motivation have functioned better with task-related incentive situations, others with social incentive situations. It thus may be useful to develop a more molar, complex contrast between task and social orientation; in educational situations there are often frequent shifts between individual and group work, and in recent years there has been increasing emphasis on cooperative learning in small groups (Slavin, 1983).

One brief example can suggest how such a contrast might work in small-group instruction while also showing how data analysis with affective and conative individual difference variables can help do detective work in educational program evaluations. It comes from an evaluation of a new curriculum for Dutch first-year (18-year-old) medical students (Wijnen & Snow, 1975; see also Snow, 1977b). As part of the study, aptitude–outcome relations were plotted for each 4-week instructional block over the year. Instruction in each block proceeded by problem- or case-based small-group discussion among students, without teachers—a radical departure from the teacher-directed lecture and recitation often found in Dutch and U.S. high schools and colleges.

Figure 9–10A shows plotted scores for 49 students on a verbal ability pretest and an achievement post test covering the first 4-week block of instruction. The solid regression line shown (corresponding to $r = .48$) is fitted to all points taken together, but the distribution appears curvilinear; particularly among high-ability students, it appears as if two bivariate distributions, running in contrary direction, have overlapped to reduce the overall relation of ability to learning outcome. An informal analysis used rules for fitting ellipses and partitioning the scatterplots into area groups, labeled by letter, as shown in Figure 10A. The continuum represented by persons labeled A, B, or C yields the strongest ability–outcome relation. Then, personality scales administered at pretest were used to identify variables associated with the continuum distinguishing persons labeled B, D, E, or F. It was found that students labeled E or F described themselves as more independent and more motivated to achieve than did B and D students. Together with A students, they also appeared less altruistic, less interpersonally oriented, and more task oriented than did students of other groups. F students also showed the highest facilitating anxiety and the lowest debilitating anxiety scores. B students were the most interpersonally oriented and the least task oriented, on average, of all the groups. The resulting hypothesis is that high-ability students who are also highly motivated and oriented

FIGURE 9-10. Scatterplots for Three Instructional Blocks Using Verbal Analogies Test Scores as Aptitude and Achievement Test Scores for Block I (A), Block III (B), and Block V (C) as Outcomes

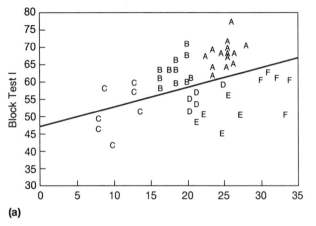

(a)

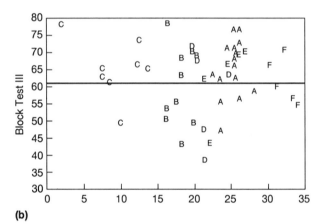

(b)

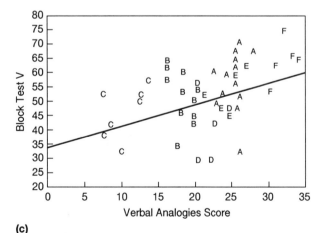

(c)

Source: Based on *Implementing an Evaluation System for Medical Education* by W. H. F. W. Wijnen and R. E. Snow, 1975, Technical Report No. 1, Maastricht, The Netherlands: Medische Faculteit Maastricht.

toward independent task activity do poorly in this instructional method, because it demands a large amount of cooperative interpersonal activity in learning. Middle-ability students who value the interpersonal interaction perhaps more than the task activity do as well as or better than many high-ability students.

These students were then followed through successive 4-week blocks of instruction. Figures 10B and 10C show example scatterplots for two later blocks, in which students are identified by their area groups from the first block. The F students appear gradually to adapt to the instructional situation, emerging at the top of the class by the fifth block (i.e., the 20th week, when content also became more difficult and more biomedical in character). Some B, D, and A students seem to be falling out of the distribution across this same sequence. Perhaps the novelty of the interpersonal instructional situation and their initial success in it are not sustaining. Thus, the aptitude complex that accounts for performance at an early stage shifts in later stages of instruction; what at first appeared to be an aptitude for this kind of instruction may appear later to be an inaptitude, and vice versa.

Although different measures were used in this situation than in those described in the independence-conformance complex, it is not hard to see the F students as comparable to the high-G, high-At, low-Ax students discussed there. Instruction was student centered in the extreme, but it was socially centered, which apparently conflicted at first with these students' independent, task-oriented styles of work until they adapted to it or overcame it. This emphasizes the importance of detailed analysis of aptitudes and treatments over time. It also provides an indirect argument in support of multivariate aptitude description even in educational experiments and evaluations not specifically concerned with individual differences.

***Other Complexes.*** Many other complexes might be proposed, especially as one studies particular educational contexts in which people perform, and differ significantly from one another in the process. Leadership is an example of a complex previously studied in business and military settings (see Fiedler & Garcia, 1987; Hogan, Curry, & Hogan, 1994). The combinations of qualities that make a good leader vary from situation to situation. To our knowledge, leadership as a person–situation interaction complex has not been studied as it varies among teachers and educational administrators in different schools or school systems. In government organizations, innovative performance has been shown to be related to one kind of complex of personal characteristics in group-centered organizational climates and to a different complex in rule-centered climates (Forehand, 1968). Some research on administrator personality and interactional hypotheses involving organizational climate has included school administrators (Frederiksen, Jensen, & Beaton, 1972; Hemphill, Griffiths, & Frederiksen, 1962). New research on school and department collegiality and morale may also suggest such hypotheses (see, e.g., Talbert, McLaughlin, & Rowan, 1993).

## VALUES, INTERESTS, ATTITUDES, AND BELIEFS

We conclude our taxonomy with a broad, diverse, loose category that cuts across all three columns of Figure 9–1 and contains potentially thousands of idiosyncrasies. We think of values and attitudes as affective, interests as both affective and motivational, and beliefs as having volitional as well as cognitive significance. However, because of their strong interrelation, even occasional interchangeability, values and attitudes, interests, and beliefs are best discussed together. Values and career orientations are also discussed together here. They could have been treated earlier in proximity to personality factors, because they are often interpreted as manifestations of personality and studied as such empirically. But molar values and career orientations must also be connected to the more molecular level of attitudes, topical interests, and beliefs. There may thus be theoretical value in fitting them here.

Attitudes are usually thought of as internal states that express, overtly or covertly, positive or negative evaluative responses to an object, person, or condition (Eagly & Chaiken, 1993). But cognitive representation and behavioral response are also emphasized, and values are added as higher-order evaluative standards (see Olson & Zanna, 1993, for elaborated definitions). Rokeach (1968) interrelated values, attitudes, and beliefs as follows:

An attitude is a relatively enduring organization of beliefs around an object or situation predisposing one to respond in some preferential manner. (p. 112)

A belief is any simple proposition, conscious or unconscious, inferred from what a person says or does, capable of being preceded by the phrase "I believe that...." (p. 113)

[A] value is seen to be a disposition of a person just like an attitude, but more basic than an attitude, often underlying it.... a value [is] a type of belief, centrally located within one's total belief system, about how one ought or ought not to behave, or about some end-state of existence worth or not worth attaining. Values are thus abstract ideals, positive or negative, not tied to any specific attitude object or situation, representing a person's beliefs about ideal modes of conduct and ideal terminal goals.... (p. 124)

An adult probably has tens or hundreds of thousands of beliefs, thousands of attitudes, but only dozens of values. A *value system* is a hierarchical organization—a rank ordering—of ideals or values in terms of importance. To one person truth, beauty, and freedom may be at the top of the list, and thrift, order, and cleanliness at the bottom; to another person, the order may be reversed. (p. 124)

An interest, then, seems to be a blend of positive affect and attitude, involving selective attention, a feeling of intrinsic preference, and an energizing motivational effect (Tomkins, 1962). Interests can be fairly specific, as in interest in a specific course or topic, or as broad as values; interest in all things aesthetic or social, for example. Some career interests display this breadth, so we refer to them as orientations.

## Values and Career Orientations

Beaty (1995) contrasts vocational, academic, personal, and social orientations toward education. These would appear to be educational values by our definition. The Allport–Vernon–Lindzey Study of Values (1960) provides assessment of six classes of values and their relative importance to the individual: theoretical, social, political, religious, aesthetic, and economic.

Holland (1973, 1985) has developed a personality theory, based on career orientations, that depicts six themes and their relative importance for the person: investigative, social, realistic, conventional, artistic, and enterprising. Although this construction derives from Holland's (1985) own instruments for assessing occupational interests, the same list can also be obtained from the homogeneous dimensions of the Strong–Campbell Interest Inventory (see Campbell & Hansen, 1981), which are essentially attitude statements about different school or college subject matter domains. One can also add in some other value dimensions that have been studied in isolation, such as traditionalism, to provide a list of some 20 or so constructs. As seen above, however, there are substantial overlaps; factor analysis would probably reduce the list to a dozen or less.

Although career orientations have long been considered distinct from the personality domain, research in the past decade has demonstrated some strong linkages. The sum of Holland's six themes correlates positively with the healthy dimensions of the Big Five personality model (especially extraversion and openness) and negatively with the neuroticism dimension. Related Holland measures of vocational identity and career attitudes and strategies show similar positive and negative correlational patterns with Big Five dimensions (see Gottfredson, Jones, & Holland, 1993; Holland, 1994; Holland, Johnston, & Asama, in press).

Unfortunately, there is not good evidence that values or career orientations predict success in school or in occupations (Cronbach, 1990). Career interests can predict persistence in a particular educational program, however. Measures of values can distinguish students in different fields of study and different occupational interest groups. They have also shown correlations with behavioral measures of cheating, volunteering, and social activism (Braithwaite & Scott, 1991). Certainly constructs of value and career orientation are useful for counselors and students in promoting self-understanding and thoughtful career planning. At present, we know rather little about the course of interest or value development through schooling. Some value changes across college and social experience have been documented (Hoge & Bender, 1974).

Value differences should be important to study in another connection, namely parental and community views of educational alternatives. Ideological disputes over particular educational reforms in curriculum and teacher selection, or instruction and assessment development, trace back to individual value positions. Seen in this light, such clashes might be understood, reduced, or averted. So far, educational psychological research has rarely entered this arena.

## Individual Interests

Individual content or procedural interest, as opposed to career orientation, is a relatively enduring and stable preference for certain topics, subject areas, or activities (Schiefele, 1991). In an attempt to provide a theoretical definition of individual differences in interest, Schiefele and Krapp (1988) proposed that interest be regarded as a specific form of concrete interaction between person and object, resulting in an enduring, stable disposition or orientation toward the object. They suggest that this interest relationship is expressed in cognitive, emotional, and value terms in which there is strong subjective meaning

TABLE 9–8. Stem and Leaf Diagram Showing
121 Independent Correlations Between Interest
and Achievement

| | |
|---|---|
| .6 | 7 |
| .6 | 04 |
| .5 | 8 |
| .5 | 011223 |
| .4 | 67788999 |
| .4 | 0012223334 |
| .3 | 5555667777888889999 |
| .3 | 000012222333334 |
| .2 | 66666667777777888899999 |
| .2 | 00112222233444 |
| .1 | 55666777778888 |
| .1 | 022334 |
| .0 | 9 |

Note: Diagram is based on all studies reviewed by V. Schiefele, A. Krapp, and A. Winteler in "Interest as a Predictor of Research," pp. 183–211 in The Role of Interest in Learning and Development, edited by K. A. Renninger, S. Hidi, and A. Krapp, 1992, Hillsdale, NJ: Lawrence Erlbaum Associates.

and self-intentionality toward the object. Prenzel (1988) added to the definition qualities of persistence (the maintenance of the relationship by repeated engagements with the object) and selectivity (the stability of content in consecutive engagements over time). In short, maintaining this special person–object relationship leads to interest, which then serves to promote intrinsic motivation. A questionnaire based on these definitions yields scores for the interest constructs and also cognitive competence with respect to the same objects. Further developments focus on assessing the combined "tendency or the willingness to acquire knowledge about the object of interest" (Schiefele, Krapp, & Winteler, 1988, p. 7).

The research based on this and a variety of similar self-report instruments suggests moderate but regular relation to cognitive achievement. Table 9–8 shows a stem and leaf summary of correlations from 121 studies of interest-achievement correlations (see Schiefele, Krapp, & Winteler, 1992). The average is about 10% of achievement variance accounted for by interest differences, but the contrast of correlations of .50 or above for 10 studies and .15 or below for 7 studies cries out for ATI analysis. The display parallels that shown earlier for Helmke's studies of anxiety.

As mentioned previously, there is also evidence that high-interest learners achieve deeper understanding in learning than low-interest learners; they show more elaborated associative structures, more transfer and comprehension, and less restriction to task-specific strategies (Pintrich & Schrauben, 1992). In addition to deeper comprehension, interest leads to more imagery and perhaps a more personal-emotional quality to the knowledge network (Tobias, 1994). But it is not clear how the learning of high-interest learners differs from that of extrinsically motivated learners, or how more specifically interest differences and prior knowledge differences jointly influence the quality of learning outcomes (Schiefele, 1991).

A related line of work refers to content motives reflecting specific subject matter interest. Nenniger (1987) described a content motive in learning as "an enduring, highly general and very stable personality trait that determines the person's sensitivity to situational determinants" (p. 159). In contrast to

achievement motives, content motives may need to be considered as individual difference variables that are modified, even as they affect learning. In several studies, Nenniger has used a questionnaire to assess content-oriented motive toward mathematics. There are separate scales for interest in mathematics and readiness for work in mathematics.

Sjöberg (1983) measured interests in math and science with attitude items that also covered characteristics of fields of study hypothesized to be factors underlying interest in a field. Students who valued logical structure, correct answers, knowledge accumulation through reasoning, opportunity for independent activity, surprising insights, and openness to further development were also those expressing strong interest in math and science. These measures and a general interest factor also correlated with grades. In other work, Hedelin and Sjöberg (1985) found interest in mathematics to decline sharply across Grades 1 to 9 in Sweden. Decline was steeper for females and low achievers but was pronounced also for males and high achievers. Some more spotty declines were also noted for interests in reading and writing.

Further research is addressing the relationship between learning processes and strategies and interest, the emotional aspect of interest, and also the qualitative differences in recall associated with interest (see Renninger, Hidi, & Krapp, 1992). Of concern also are the potential negative influences of interest on learning. Mismatch between individual interest and classroom environment can produce aversive reactions and discouragement. Strong interest may also promote students' concluding that topics are understood after only superficial perusal, misunderstanding of task requirements, or misjudgment of goals and a subsequent overblown sense of competence.

Finally, since working on interesting tasks improves the quality of learning, interest should be considered a desired outcome of education as well as a motivator. Research ought also to look beyond school for evidence that enduring interest is an outcome of education.

## Attitudes

We cannot review here the volumes of work on the structure of attitudes and beliefs (see Eagly & Chaiken, 1993) or the vast catalogue of individual attitude constructs and measures (see Robinson, Shaver, & Wrightsman, 1991). It is the case, however, that some constructs discussed in other sections can be usefully studied as attitude or belief structures (e.g., self-esteem, persuasibility, aspects of anxiety, even authoritarianism). And, although attitudes are usually studied as states that are based on aggregates of beliefs, persons can develop characteristic attitude patterns that become stable individual differences, though not interpreted at the level of values or necessarily connected to specific beliefs. Individual interests, just discussed, may be thought of as positive attitudes that have developed into enduring preferences for particular topics and tasks.

In education, then, persistent positive attitudes toward particular subject matter and activity domains can be treated as equivalent to interests. So might more pervasive attitudes toward schooling in general. Yet the negative side of these attitudes is not well treated as interest. The zero point of interest is presumably disinterest, indifference, even boredom. But negative interest implies antagonism and impetus to action away from the attitude object, not just boredom with it. Thus, although positive attitude toward, and positive interest in, school may be equivalent, the negative attitudes toward school that lead to absenteeism, vandalism, and dropout seem to reflect different dimensions, perhaps qualitatively different interests. There apparently are other attitudes about education-related objects or persons that also require differentiation from interests. Student attitudes toward particular teachers, or types of teachers or students, or styles of behavior, or discussion topics may be examples. In other words, some attitude constructs may best be considered unidimensional and bipolar, whereas others are better treated as bidimensional and unipolar (see Kerlinger, 1984). A similar possibility was noted in connection with style constructs. There are also nondimensional models, such as associative networks, that may better represent attitude and belief structures in some instances.

Educational psychological research has not delved deeply into these aspects of student or teacher attitude structure. Attitude measures have often been used to study teacher personality (see Getzels & Jackson, 1963) and to index extra student outcomes beyond cognitive achievement. Too often, however, student attitude outcomes are reported as isolated treatment effects without further psychological analysis of their meaning or relation to cognitive outcomes. Attitudes toward subject matter, particularly science and math, have become targets for research in their own right as they relate to national priorities for education and careers. But there seems not to have been programmatic research on other education-related attitude systems, beyond the research on interests, for a long time. Such attitude systems might relate to self-concept in specific subject areas, as previously discussed.

## Beliefs

People state opinions, from which their beliefs as well as their attitudes may be inferred. But most research on beliefs related to education has sought to build cognitive theories of "naive" or "folk" physics, biology, psychology, or the like. The goal has been to describe how children or adolescents understand the phenomena in one or another subject matter domain. Though important in their own right for educational research, these cognitive analyses leave out of consideration the affective and conative aspects of these beliefs and so ignore their emotional or motivational role in further learning or performance with respect to them. Beliefs are not strictly cognitive. All concepts carry connotative, evaluative meaning (Osgood, Suci, & Tannenbaum, 1957) as well as denotative meaning, and the frequent finding that some "cognitive" misconceptions are deep-seated and resistant to instruction suggests that they may also have affective roots. Furthermore, analyses aimed at identifying the affective as well as cognitive structure of concepts to be learned might turn up useful suggestions for instructional design. As Lepper and Malone (1987) suggested, curiosity, fantasy, challenge, and various other motivational devices can be used to improve instruction. Interestingness is also a factor to be manipulated in instruction to good effect, and also good affect (Renninger, Hidi, & Krapp, 1992). But the use of these devices, particularly in adapting instruction to individual differences, would be significantly enhanced by better understanding of the affective and conative character of prior knowledge and belief about the concepts to be learned.

*Belief Formation and Volitional Function.* When people read environments, they form situation models or belief systems about essential features, the people who coexist in the environment, and the functions that both features and people serve there. These systems have the appearance of rationality, but in fact they are overly simplified views of reality (Newell & Simon, 1972) that are often sufficiently powerful to exert influence on many aspects of information processing and behavior, both in and outside the familiar environment. They have staying qualities as well (Bem, 1970; Nisbett & Ross, 1980). Perseverance, or the fact that beliefs die hard, implies a strong link to emotion, as noted earlier. Indeed, affective evaluative loadings are acknowledged in many of the numerous denotative and operational definitions of beliefs currently in use (Pajares, 1992).

In contrast, research has rarely considered what might be called the volitional (or intentional and protective maintenance) aspects of beliefs, despite evidence that overcoming powerful beliefs formed on the basis of personal experience is an exceedingly difficult undertaking (Munby, 1982; Nespor, 1987). Preservice teachers' beliefs about learning have been shown to affect their willingness to entertain contradictory ideas (Holt-Reynolds, 1992). And as Nisbett and Ross (1980) noted, individuals will even interpret evidence in direct conflict with their beliefs in ways that appear supportive. Of unyielding and distorted beliefs, Pajares (1992) writes:

It is not simply the emotional qualities of beliefs that are responsible for this. Cognitive and information processing principles are involved . . . and the effect of prior beliefs on memory and interpretation is the result of these principles at work. Individuals use encoding and decoding biases to confirm prior theories when they selectively retrieve material from memory. . . . [B]eliefs color not only what individuals recall but how they recall it, if necessary completely distorting the event recalled in order to *sustain the belief.* (p. 317, emphasis added)

Thus, beliefs (and expectations) that teachers and students form about one another and about school learning, as well as beliefs about subjects to be learned, and relationships between ability, effort, and outcomes as previously described, display intentional and maintenance functions. Such beliefs may exhibit ties to temperament and motivational goal differences, and may be sustained through ties to emotions experienced as these beliefs are formed, *as well as* forms of information processing called protectively into play. Beliefs organized around objects or situations are also characterized by most researchers as predisposing toward action, and measurements of these beliefs include both intention and action components (e.g., Goodman, 1988; Tabachnick & Zeichner, 1984).

*Teacher Expectations and Related Beliefs.* One example of particular interest for education involves research on teacher expectations about individual students—their individual capabilities and limitations, as well as those of classes teachers face from year to year. Much work shows that teacher expectations can influence their classroom behavior, their interactions with students, and sometimes their students' immediate achievement, though not their intellectual growth (see, e.g., Dusek,

1985; Elashoff & Snow, 1971; M. L. Smith & Shepard, 1988). Most important for our purposes is the work of Brophy (1983, 1985) and his colleagues (Brophy & Evertson, 1981; Brophy & Good, 1974). Their studies show individual differences among teachers and also among students that moderate expectancy effects. Susceptibility to such effects thus seems to be an important teacher difference variable. Some teachers in interaction with some students produce positive expectation effects. More typically, however, certain combinations of teachers and students produce negative expectation effects, sometimes of major consequence.

Teachers guided by realistic beliefs and goals who want to help low achievers and will invest effort in extra encouragement and instruction for them are most likely to show positive expectation effects for low achievers. Teachers who hold rigid stereotypic expectations and social class biases and who tend to differentiate their treatment of high and low achievers accordingly are more likely to produce negative expectation effects for low achievers. The majority of teachers fall between these extremes, and the contrast also interacts with other beliefs about teaching and other student characteristics. High school teachers who emphasize content presentation and reward student comprehension and positive attitude may especially help high achievers and hinder low achievers unless they invest directly in helping low achievers. Elementary schoolteachers who emphasize socialization and personal interaction may cover less content but better help low achievers to master it, if they see them as capable of learning. If they see low achievers as limited, their personal-social emphasis may especially hinder these students. The evidence on student characteristics suggests that teacher expectancy effects can be mediated by gender and physical characteristics as well as by differences in prior achievement or ability; especially noteworthy are findings suggesting that dependent, compliant, adult-oriented or other-directed students are more susceptible to teacher expectations than are independent, active, assertive students. Thus, students differ in their tendency to behave in ways consistent with expectations, positive or negative (see Brophy, 1985, for a detailed review; see also chapters 19 and 21, this volume). Of course, interpersonal expectancies exist between students and from students to teachers as well. But these kinds of beliefs have not been much studied.

Other teacher beliefs include efficacy for teaching and personal efficacy and feelings of control over structural aspects of teachers' work (Pajares, 1992). These need more investigation, especially also in relation to beliefs of school administrators and parents.

***Student Beliefs About Self and Situation.*** A growing line of work in recent years concerns student beliefs about school subject matter fields and concepts therein. The aim has been to understand the nature of student prior conceptions and misconceptions and their role in later learning and conceptual change. The approach has been primarily cognitive.

But there are important affective and conative aspects to personal belief systems. Some children believe in the equivalence of ability and effort in influencing performance, and some form naive beliefs about learning from parent–child interactions about the nature of school, teachers, and homework that have major affective and conative effects (Corno & Kanfer, 1993).

Human beings in general show tendencies to form and hold beliefs that serve their own needs, desires, and goals; these beliefs serve ego-enhancement, self-protective, and personal and social control purposes and cause biases in perception and judgment in social situations as a result (Kruglanski, 1989; Kruglanski & Ajzen, 1983). Marked individual differences can be seen in these belief systems, and their effects deserve study in education.

In a sense, most if not all of the constructs discussed in this chapter reflect in some degree individual differences in personal beliefs about self or others, and can be studied as such. Approaching these affective and conative constructs as personal belief systems operating in classroom contexts may offer a new and broader view of teacher–student interaction and of student learning and conceptual development in schools. A start in this direction has been made by Pintrich, Marx, and Boyce (1993), who review four classes of such beliefs: goal beliefs (e.g., intrinsic vs. extrinsic orientations), value beliefs (e.g., intrinsic interests, instrumental value), self-efficacy beliefs (e.g., perceived abilities, confidence), and control beliefs (e.g., perceived internal vs. external control, outcome expectancies). This perspective seems to hold promise for enriching our understanding of the associated constructs discussed previously and also for consolidation with cognitive models of beliefs and conceptual change.

Beliefs about self in relation to different educational learning, teaching, and assessment situations, and also the perception of such situations through this lens, may even mediate the relations between personality and performance. Students differ in their conceptions of learning under different instructional conditions (Säljö, 1975, 1982), they are influenced by their expectations about the form of assessment to be faced (d'Ydewalle, 1984; d'Ydewalle, Swerts, & De Corte, 1983), and their perceptions of the learning environment affect their approaches to learning (see several chapters in Marton et al., 1984, and in Schmeck, 1988a). An early demonstration that perception of the instructional situation can influence personality–achievement relations comes from work in which a blend of teacher control and student control was seen by students as one or the other. Anxious students who perceived the situation as teacher controlled did relatively well, whereas anxious students perceiving student control did poorly (Dowaliby & Schumer, 1973; see also Cronbach & Snow, 1977). Current work in higher education is pursuing the relation of perceptions of teaching and instructional environment to individual differences in approach to learning and studying (Entwistle & Tait, 1990; Meyer, 1991; Tait & Entwistle, in press). The power of beliefs and perceptions to moderate person–situation interactions of this sort deserves much further investigation.

## PROSPECTS FOR THEORY, RESEARCH AND PRACTICE

This chapter has presented a selection of old and new affective and conative constructs deemed important for educational psychology, along with a provisional taxonomy to house them. These constructs and their interrelationships warrant continued research, not only because they represent important influences on learning and development, but also because they themselves often represent intended or unintended educational outcomes. Continuing research aimed at either point needs to elaborate and deepen the definition and validation of each construct in relation to proximal others in a correlational network. This is the line of future research most directly concerned with testing and elaborating the present taxonomy of constructs. We need not belabor this goal further.

But there are at least eight other, interrelated goals for further work on individual differences in affective and conative functions. We discuss each briefly here. The goals are:

1. Understanding the importance of these individual differences in and for education.
2. Understanding how these functions operate in adaptive transaction with educational situations.
3. Deriving a taxonomy of educational situation characteristics that complements that for person characteristics and enriches our understanding of person–situation interaction.
4. Understanding the development and specialization of affective and conative functions in educational settings.
5. Building a functional integration across affective, conative, and cognitive constructs to a whole-person view of human learners as individuals.
6. Building improved assessment, research, and evaluation methodologies in support of the above goals.
7. Investigating the role of differential affective and conative functions among educational personnel other than students.
8. Developing a richer and more productive relationship between the constructs and methods discussed here and the realms of educational practice.

## Importance in Education

We chose constructs for this review based on our sense of theoretical and empirical justification in psychology generally and in relation to important issues in education. The reader may notice, however, that the evidence for educational importance is stronger in some construct categories than in others. Also, the research on different constructs varies in its ecological validity with respect to education. And some constructs seem to be general traits, defined without reference to education, whereas others seem to derive fundamentally from educational experience. Contrast the temperament or personality factors with some of the interests or learning styles and strategies, for examples.

The contrast suggests two research strategies for the future. One would start from general psychological constructs and look for evidence of relation to and specialization in particular educational settings. The other would begin with educational settings, deriving specialized constructs that work within them, and then looking for correlations with general psychology. It is arguable which is ultimately best for understanding and improving education. Staying too close to general constructs defined outside of education risks irrelevance. Staying within the bounds of specialized educational constructs builds an island universe out of communication with the rest of social science. We emphasized contextual constructs as a theoretical goal midway between these extremes, but one can arrive at that midway point from either direction. The best strategy for the short run will likely be to leave room for all these alternatives and let individual differences among investigators operate. Much more evidence is needed before ultimate value to education can be judged.

## Adaptive Transactions in Teaching and Learning

One critically important source of evidence for either research direction is the study of interactions between person characteristics and situation characteristics. Affective and conative aptitudes interact with teaching and instructional treatment alternatives to influence learning. Both general and special constructs are validated in particular educational settings that way. Examples of such interactions were included in this chapter where appropriate. There are many other examples (Cronbach & Snow, 1977; Snow, 1989a, 1994). However, teaching-learning interactions, and person–situation interactions in general need ultimately to be understood as dynamic adaptive unions. One can study person variables and situation variables as though they were independent while acting jointly, or as being interdependent in action. But there are reciprocal and transactive processes also to be accounted for in the person–situation interface (Snow, 1994). Again, the contextual constructs discussed in this chapter offer some important places to start—they represent placeholders where more analytic research might pursue deeper, richer accounts of person-in-situation processes. Furthermore, careful study of individual variation within contexts may give rise to the new kinds of contextual constructs noted above as specifically important in education. Some learning style constructs, such as deep versus surface approaches to learning, seem to have this character.

This view of person-in-situation as adaptive transactive process emphasizes the relational character of affective and conative, as well as cognitive, constructs. Individual differences then are interpreted as existing not in the head of the person alone nor in the structure of the situation alone but in the interface between them. Thus, defining the situation in which some affective or conative construct functions is part of defining the construct. Furthermore, just as situations selectively provide demands and opportunities (Gibson, 1979, called them "affordances") that connect with characteristics of persons, persons also select and sample from their situations. There is an adaptive process through which persons and situations become tuned to one another, for good or ill. An important exercise in further research will be to examine the nature of the particular teaching situations that seem to match or mismatch the affective and conative characteristics of particular students, and then to study the transactive properties of such unions. Individual differences seem to come into play as a function of situational affordances. Situation differences take on particular salience as a function of the person differences they call into play.

In the lengthening history of person–situation interaction research, occasional attention has been paid to this adaptive transactive aspect. Recently, some new beginnings have been made on the cognitive side of this analysis (see chapter 2, this volume), and these include an individual difference perspective (Snow, 1991, 1992, 1994). On the affective–conative side, complex constructs such as sensation seeking and flow begin to reflect this same sense of person–situation union. But the best setting in which to observe and study affective–conative–cognitive functions in adaptive transactions may be tutoring. Research by Lepper and Chabay (1988) and by Swanson (1990; see also Snow, 1994) begins to suggest that cognitive–affective adaptation between tutor and student can be studied from a differential psychological perspective, with potential benefit far beyond the improvement of tutoring alone. Both macro- and microlevel interactions can be studied. There are other real educational settings that support this kind of study, but none are so well designed to permit process analysis.

## Toward a Taxonomy of Learning Situations

To meet the challenge of person-in-situation research, the construction of a taxonomy of situations or, better, of educational affordances in them is needed to match somehow the taxonomy of person characteristics we have here proposed. There have been previous attempts. Some tried to be truly comprehensive (e.g., Sells, 1963). Some reviewed important purposes and methodology (Frederiksen, 1972). Some classified learning tasks according to particular theories of learning or instruction (Kyllonen & Shute, 1989; Melton, 1964; T. A. Ryan, 1981). Some sought empirical dimensions of educational environments based on participant perceptions (Moos, 1979; Pace & Stern, 1958). Some developed taxonomies of performance task requirements (Fleishman & Quaintance, 1984). And, perhaps most important, some concentrated on situation dimensions to which particular person characteristics are adapted, and vice versa (Hettema, 1979, 1989). These advances, in turn, can be situated in even more general approaches to environments and the study of behavior in them (Barker, 1968).

All of these efforts bear review for the suggestions they provide. Yet none fills the educational need fully. Educational psychological research on school learning needs a taxonomy that distinguishes among learning tasks, grouping and classroom learning situations, and school situations in terms that connect the demands and opportunities—the affordances—of different learning situations to the characteristics of learner readiness. Such a provisional taxonomy provides only a start, comparable to our person categories. But it is essential that the theoretically and practically most important person and situation distinctions be brought into interactional research as a priority list. One cannot study all possible combinations. Again, studying learner differences and educational treatment differences jointly may suggest new contextual constructs particularly useful in such settings.

Also needed is a classification of opportunities to learn outside of school. The field of research on educational practice extends beyond classroom tasks and school environments to studies of museums and educational clubs and camps, and to industry, government, and the military. Affective and conative outcomes are often included in statements of objectives for teaching and curriculum in these fields. Factors such as motivation, interest, persistence, self-control, responsibility, compliance, endurance, commitment, and lifelong learning have long been regarded as benchmarks for evaluation. Yet formal evaluations rarely go beyond the cognitive objectives, except by impression and anecdote.

## Development

*The Course of Development.* A further need is a sense of the course of development, differentiation, and specialization, particularly across the school years, of affective and conative differences. The possibility that Hartshorne and May (1928) witnessed the formation of a stable honesty dimension within the educational context of their times while inferring only specificity of response should be a signal that understanding developmental trends is crucial in this field. Developmental research concerning affective and conative functions is addressed in chapters 6 and 7 of this volume. Perhaps this work will follow the cognitive side of psychological research in education, which is now pursuing integrations of differential and developmental approaches to abilities (Case & Edelstein, 1993; Demetriov & Efklides, 1991).

It is also important to note that classroom honesty in the 1920s or authoritarianism in the 1940s may differ from similarly named constructs in the new millennium. Social, cultural, and historical changes may cause changes in personal constructs. This is a different kind of problem for developmental research.

*Heritability.* For most temperament constructs, evidence is substantial that individual difference variance is influenced by hereditary factors. This influence is significant also for the personality factors to which the temperament measures are linked in Figure 9–3 (see Bouchard, 1994; Plomin, 1989, 1994), although heritability estimates are lower for personality than for ability (Loehlin, 1992). There are also implications that genetic factors may underlie individual differences in some broad value dimensions, including some that may relate to authoritarianism. One of these is traditionalism—a belief in the value of rules, authority, discipline, and moral standards.

On the other hand, those differences so far investigated in the conative domain have shown still lower heritability. Loehlin (1992), for example, reported lower heritability estimates for ideals, goals, interests, and activities than for ability and personality measures, and in particular noted how self-concept differences among twins showed striking environmental influences. Perhaps motivational and volitional differences, in contrast to affective dimensions, are more a function of individual home and school experience. However, the development of either affective or conative differences, as they intertwine with one another, has not yet been addressed by programmatic research.

Behavior genetics research will continue to expand, and findings on all these points will likely be elaborated. Other constructs may also be found to show significant heritability. But it is important to keep in mind three points about such findings. First, heritability indices are only population statistics; as with all other empirical statistical estimates, they vary with the ranges of populations and environments studied (as well as with the variance component models on which they are based). Second, just as they attribute individual difference variations to genetic factors in some degree, they underscore the importance of environmental variations. Indeed, research in behavior genetics has done much to sharpen our conceptions of environments (Wachs, 1992) and our focus on the importance of within-family variations in microenvironments (Scarr, 1992). This in turn helps focus more attention on microenvironmental variations in classrooms, schools, and families as they interact with affective and conative characteristics of learners and teachers. Third, it should be remembered that educational research always deals with the phenotype, not with its parts.

## Integration of Affective, Conative, and Cognitive Functions

We also need an integrated model of affective and conative with cognitive functioning and development. There are long-standing debates over the sequence and interdependence of these basic functions in action (see Lazarus, 1982; Zajonc, 1980). There is also a growing tendency in some theoretical work to "cognize" the affective and conative functions rather than consider them jointly with cognition; this loses their dynamic energizing aspect, and also ignores much empirical evidence showing differential relationships. Education appears to provide a good setting in which to study all three functions, both in interaction and in development.

We noted earlier that classic works in differential psychology sought to place cognitive abilities with affective and conative differences in a factor-analytic system (e.g., Cattell, 1971; Guilford, 1959; Thurstone, 1924). There is certainly room for more work along these lines. It is also important, however, to bring modern process-oriented research into the same picture. A program of work by Kanfer and Ackerman (1989a, 1989b; Ackerman, 1989) and their colleagues provides a good example of the possibilities; only brief mention is possible here. Their work began examining ability–conation interactions in complex skill acquisition tasks, manipulating task demand and goal-setting conditions within an ATI paradigm to reach integrative information-processing accounts of individual differences in learning. They then broadened their scope to address developmental issues (Kanfer, 1990) and learning strategy issues (Ackerman & Woltz, 1994) in other kinds of simple learning. Also developed was the construct of typical intellectual engagement, investigated in relation to both ability and personality domains (Goff & Ackerman, 1992). Ensuing argument about the validity of this construct also offers an example of the kind of continuing analysis that is sorely needed in the field represented by this chapter (see Ackerman & Goff, 1994; Rocklin, 1994). Although it is too early to tell just what shape the theory will take as work continues, the program has brought together the right ingredients for one kind of integration, at least within a subset of the learning tasks relevant to educational psychology.

However, another kind of integration is needed, one that views individual human functioning in educational settings as a whole, open, adaptive system, and assesses it as such (see, e.g., Hettema, 1989; Magnusson & Törestad, 1993). Fragmentation of human personality into particular variables and pursuit of multivariate empirical relationships is a fruitful research strategy up to a point. But individuals are more than lists of variables. Somehow we need to find ways to put the fragments and relationships back into a pattern that describes integrated activity. All measurement models—indeed all theoretical abstractions—throw information away. The trick may be to find multiple models that criss-cross in ways that help fill in the information that any one model leaves out.

## Improving Methodology

*Assessment.* It follows that research in this field badly needs improved assessment techniques, both for measuring constructs such as those reviewed and for detecting affective and conative aspects of educational performance more directly. One step in this direction would be to produce a comprehensive listing of techniques and measurement strategies that have already been tried. Another step would be to collect what is known about questionnaire design, the strengths and weaknesses of different formats, and the need for controls on different response styles. Especially important would be the modifications needed for different age levels. So many of today's measures rely on questionnaires developed and used without adequate evaluation that a comprehensive review of this technology seems a logical place to start (see, e.g., D. N. Jackson, 1971; D. N. Jackson & Helmes, 1979).

A related need is review of the accumulated literature on particular assessment techniques and the contrasts between them. Ozer and Reise (1994) and Rorer (1990) offer important general comparisons. Spangler's (1992) review of TAT versus questionnaire measures of achievement motivation provides an invaluable addition to the construct validity discussion in this domain. Other accumulations of research on particular techniques, such as C. P. Smith's (1992) handbook on the TAT, are also extremely valuable. Expanding the catalogue of constructs, measures, and directly related studies beyond that now available (e.g., as in Robinson et al., 1991; Snow, 1989c, 1990; Snow & Jackson, 1994) is a useful further step.

But these reviews should suggest new lines of research that might advance and perhaps radically alter current approaches to assessment. One example is the work of Hettema (1989), who has developed multilevel assessments combining self-report with physiological measures and direct behavioral observation. Barclay (1977) developed a multilevel assessment for classroom use that combines self-reports, peer reports, and teacher ratings in several domains of affective and conative as well as cognitive competencies and social behavior. On another tack, Kline (1973) aimed at producing an information-processing account of responses to projective assessments. Still another line has sought to build process models of response to conventional personality inventory items and to analyze the subjective meaning of such items for different persons (see, e.g., Cliff, 1977; De Boeck, 1978, 1981; Rogers, 1974).

The computer performance task developed by Kuhl, as already noted, is an innovative prototype for many possible performance-based assessments of conative constructs. There have been occasional attempts to develop performance tests and other objective measures in the history of personality research (Cattell & Warburton, 1967; Eysenck & Eysenck, 1985; Kline & Cooper, 1984; Strelau, 1983). We believe much basic research is needed in this direction.

A particularly important advance may come from computer-based free-response techniques. An example comes from Claeys, De Boeck, Van Den Bosch, Biesmans, and Böhrer (1985). Their procedure gives the respondent only this instruction: "Describe your personality as completely as possible, using any personal adjectives you choose. Do not say how you want to be, but say how you really are. Try to use words of common usage." The adjectives are then scored for various personality dimensions, using a computerized dictionary of adjectives and system of weights for each of the personality dimensions, based on expert judgments previously obtained. A series of studies compared this free-response instrument with conventional, fixed-format personality measures representing dimensions such as extraversion, agreeableness, conscientiousness, and neuroticism. Results suggested that the validity of personality assessments might be substantially increased when a free-response self-description instrument is administered first in a battery that includes other, conventional instruments. It appears that free response activates the respondent's personal knowledge structure so as to improve the validity of responses both to free-format instruments and to following fixed-format inventories.

The possibility that the personal knowledge structure individuals bring to bear in self-reports of personality can be activated by free recall to increase the validity of ensuing reports deserves much further research. The rationale of conventional assessments is that individuals reveal their personalities by recognizing themselves as fitting in some degree statements or structures composed by researchers. This approach essentially ignores the individuality of personal self-concepts, as well as the possibility that such self-knowledge may not routinely be consciously available. Free response, on the other hand, allows individuality of response and may also provide a more intensive conscious search of personal knowledge. The free-recall form of reporting personal conceptions is also akin to the open-ended self-report methods used in cognitive research on learner's conceptions of their own learning in particular instructional situations. And computerization of the technique makes it easily used as well as applicable to more focused domains than general personality dimensions. One can imagine descriptor systems designed along the lines of the Belgian free self-report but focused on learning-related motivations, interests, perceptions, and action tendencies, as well as on learning activities in particular situations. It might even be possible to collect such scaled descriptions periodically during learning from instruction. The coordination of these lines of research might produce a richer and more integrated view of the cognitive, affective, and conative psychology of personal knowledge, as well as practical improvements in assessment technology.

*Research Methods.* Beyond the improvement of assessment technology, there is need also to improve research and evaluation methodology. This involves rediscovering and applying old, useful methods as well as inventing new ones. The multitrait-multimethod matrix (Campbell & Fiske, 1959) is an example of a powerful old method not much used currently. On the other hand, advances in the development of factor-analytic and hierarchical modeling techniques, some of which can incorporate multitrait-multimethod comparisons, are now coming rapidly into use. The improvements and clarifications obtainable with latent variable models are clearly demonstrated by Gustafsson and Undheim (chapter 8). There are also now attempts to survey advances in the methodology of differential psychology more broadly to include process analyses and ATI methodology (see, e.g., Reynolds & Willson, 1985). Most examples, however, rely on cognitive abilities. As noted at several points in this chapter, affective and conative differences may not fit some of the assumptions that are conventional in cognitive research.

A thorough review of methodology for this domain specifically is an important next step. Again, holistic as well as analytic viewpoints need to be included (Magnusson & Törestad, 1993).

Beyond, or perhaps beneath, the formal and sophisticated statistical methods, however, there is need for new emphasis on simple exploratory graphical methods such as those advocated by Tukey (1969; see also chapter 30, this volume). The study of affective and conative differences in learning is different enough from cognitive research, and the need for progress in the face of its complexity is great enough, that data analysis should not be prepackaged or blind. We included one example of the value of scatterplotting to make this point. Figure 9–10 demonstrated a variant of the old off-quadrant technique (Marks, 1964), adapted to fit the peculiarities of a sample distribution in hand. The lesson is not to follow this particular procedure. Rather, it is to do this kind of detective work to explore theories, methods, and measures at the level of individual raw data.

Combined with ATI experiments in which manipulations are chosen to explore this individual process level, we may find new avenues to useful theory. The series of studies cited previously by Ackerman and Woltz (1994) provides a good example. Other experimental analyses that attempt to examine cognitive and affective or conative processes at this level are exemplified by Lohman (1989a) with speed–accuracy trade-off and Siegler and Campbell (1989) with confidence differences and strategy choice in arithmetic problems. It is not claimed that results from these endeavors generalize to classrooms. Rather, it is hoped that they will enrich our conceptualizations about affective and conative processes in general, and perhaps provide ideas for new forms of performance-based assessments in education.

## Educational Personnel

Individual differences in affection and conation pervade all fields of educational practice. Schooling outcomes are influenced significantly by parents, teachers, and school administrators, who themselves contend with many of the same affective and conative variations that we have described with respect to students.

*Parents.* Parents face emotional and volitional burdens in attempting to juggle work and family responsibilities with commitments to their children's development both at home and in school. They also face daily the range of responses their children display toward school. Struggles over school-related difficulties in this domain often appear as behavior problems in preschool and continue on in different forms throughout young adulthood (Hartup, 1989). Research on student differences in affective and conative functioning in school will need to trace these functions also to parental and family influences.

*Teachers.* Today's teachers are selected implicitly by the educational system they traverse, as well as by personal home and social factors related to the affective and conative constructs we review. They then undergo an intensive process of teacher education and assessment that leads to further selection. Teacher motivation to teach, sense of self-concept and self-efficacy, attitude toward teaching, goal orientations and style of teaching practice, and tendency toward stress and burnout arise as topics in teacher education, take on real meaning during the inductive years, and continue to influence teachers' long-term performance and commitments to teaching and its various approaches later on (e.g., Ashton & Webb, 1986).

Research on teaching rediscovered teacher cognition in the 1980s and advanced our understanding of teacher thinking, planning, and decision-making in instruction significantly. It appears now to be time to rediscover teacher personality, both as it influences teacher professional development and as it interacts with student affect, conation, and cognition in the classroom. P. W. Jackson's (1968) older work, and Brophy's (1985; Brophy & Evertson, 1981) newer initiatives deserve particular attention in this regard. Important also are the results of inquiries by educational administrators into the roots of teacher incompetence, burnout, and turnover. Bridges (1992), for example, noted that motivation and personality problems are chief factors, after ability deficiencies, underlying judgments of teacher incompetence. And the management of cases of poor performance among teachers requires continuing attention to teacher personality and motivation on the part of the responsible supervisor.

*School Administrators.* Administrative officials, especially department heads, principals, and superintendents, must attend carefully to student, parent, and faculty expectations, motivation, and morale to establish positive emotional climates and leadership at the building and district level. Studies into the dynamics of these intersecting and complex relationships require consideration of affective and conative processes. Although understanding the roles and performance of educational administrators in these respects benefits from research on administration in general, the particular circumstances of educational organizations require special research attention (see Berryman, 1993; Bridges, 1982; Miskel, 1982; and the several relevant chapters in Boyan, 1988).

## Relations to Practice

In the final analysis, the constructs and relations reviewed here are important insofar as they are relevant to educational practice. Thus, it is appropriate to ask in conclusion whether research in this domain has led to any lasting improvements in practice, and if not, why not. A careful review of the relations of theory and research to practice is beyond our scope here. But the impression is strong that a list of changes in practice due clearly to work in this domain would not be long.

Most instructional changes aimed at practical improvements with respect to individual differences have focused on ability and prior knowledge. Even evaluation studies often leave affective and conative characteristics out of consideration. Teachers often talk about affective and conative differences among students, and they also attempt stylistic adaptations to different students along these lines. But the conceptual languages teachers and researchers use in this regard may be only superficially similar; at base they seem to differ significantly. And the generalized research findings may often not seem valid for particular classrooms and schools.

In our section on personal styles, Hunt's (1987) plea for teacher-based constructs of learner style was noted. Entwistle (1987c) also has urged that differential constructs should be ecologically valid for classrooms if we expect teachers to use them and use them well. In addition, we have marked the need for understanding affective and conative differences among teachers and administrators in relation to their performance situations, including their own conceptions of learning and individual differences in others. The point is not to recommend substituting educators' own concepts for the theoretical constructs we have reviewed. Rather, it is to suggest that we try to find a meeting ground where psychological science and the wisdom of practice can learn from and benefit one another. In education, local context, idiosyncrasy, and changing conditions make one kind of construct salient in one particular niche and another in another. What is salient and therefore useful may best be coconstructed by scientist and practitioner working together in particular local contexts. At least, the concepts local educators use to guide and interpret their practice will be enriched thereby, as will the concepts the researcher chooses to study further. At most, theory and practice will merge in producing both understanding of individual differences in education and improved ways of using them.

## *References*

Ach, N. (1910). *Über den Willensakt und das Temperament.* Leipzig: Quelle Meyer.

Ackerman, P. L. (1989). Individual differences in skill acquisition. In P. L. Ackerman, R. J. Sternberg, & R. Glaser (Eds.), *Learning and individual differences: Advances in theory and research* (pp. 164–217). New York: Freeman.

Ackerman, P. L., & Goff, M. (1994). Typical intellectual engagement and personality: Reply to Rocklin (1994). *Journal of Educational Pychology, 86,* 150–153.

Ackerman, P. L., & Woltz, D. J. (1994). Determinants of learning and performance in an associative memory/substitution task: Task constraints, individual differences, volition, and motivation. *Journal of Educational Psychology, 86,* 487–515.

Adorno, T. W., Frenkel-Brunswik, E., Levinson, D. J., & Sanford, R. N. (1982). *The authoritarian personality* (abridged ed.). New York: Norton. (Original work published 1950)

Ainley, M. D. (1993). Styles of engagement with learning: Multidimensional assessment of their relationship with strategy use and school achievement. *Journal of Educational Psychology, 85,* 395–405.

Allport, G. W. (1937). *Personality: A psychological interpretation.* New York: Holt.

Allport, G. W. (1961). *Pattern and growth in personality.* New York: Holt, Rinehart & Winston.

Allport, G. W., Vernon, P. E., & Lindzey, G. (1960). *Study of Values: A scale for measuring the dominant interests in personality* (3rd ed.) Boston: Houghton Mifflin.

Alpert, R., & Haber, R. (1960). Anxiety in academic achievement situations. *Journal of Abnormal and Social Psychology, 61,* 207–215.

Ames, C. (1984). Competitive, cooperative, and individualistic goal structures: A cognitive motivational analysis. In R. E. Ames & C. Ames (Eds.), *Research on motivation in education: Vol. 1. Student motivation* (pp. 177–208). Orlando, FL: Academic Press.

Ames, C. (1990). Motivation: What teachers need to know. *Teachers College Record, 91,* 409–421.

Ames, C. (1992). Classrooms: Goals, structures, and student motivation. *Journal of Educational Psychology, 84,* 261–271.

Ames, C., & Archer, J. (1987). Mothers' belief about the role of ability and effort in school learning. *Journal of Educational Psychology, 18,* 409–414.

Ames, C., & Archer, J. (1988). Achievement goals in the classroom: Students' learning strategies and motivation processes. *Journal of Educational Psychology, 80,* 260–267.

Ames, C., & Maehr, M. L. (1989). *Motivation enhancing environments.* Greenwich, CT: JAI Press.

Anastasi, A. (1976). *Psychological testing.* New York: Macmillan.

Anderman, E. M., & Maehr, M. L. (1994). Motivation and schooling in the middle grades. *Review of Educational Research, 64,* 287–309.

Anderson, C. A. (1983). Motivational and performance deficits in interpersonal settings: The effects of attributional style. *Journal of Personality and Social Psychology, 50,* 1136–1147.

Anderson, C. A., Jenning, D. L., & Arnoult, L. H. (1988). The validity and utility of the attributional style construct at a moderate level of specificity. *Journal of Personality and Social Psychology, 55,* 979–990.

Archer, D., & Akert, R. M. (1977a, October). How well do you read body language? *Psychology Today,* pp. 68–72, 119–120.

Archer, D., & Akert, R. M. (1977b). Words and everything else: Verbal cues in social interpretation. *Journal of Personality and Social Psychology, 35,* 443–449.

Archer, D., & Akert, R. M. (1980). The encoding of meaning: A test of three theories of social interaction. *Sociological Inquiry, 50,* 393–419.

Ashton, P. T., & Webb, R. B. (1986). *Making a difference: Teachers' sense of efficacy and student achievement.* White Plains, NY: Longman.

Atkinson, J. W. (1957). Motivational determinants of risk-taking behavior. *Psychological Review, 64,* 359–372.

Atkinson, J. W. (1964). *An introduction to motivation.* Princeton, NJ: Van Nostrand.

Atkinson, J. W., & Birch, D. (1970). *A dynamic theory of action.* New York: Wiley.

Atkinson, J. W., & Feather, N. T. (Eds.). (1966). *A theory of achievement motivation.* New York: Wiley.

Atkinson, J. W., & McClelland, D. C. (1948). The projective expression of needs: II. The effect of different intensities of the hunger drive on thematic apperception. *Journal of Experimental Psychology, 38,* 643–658.

Atkinson, J. W., & Raynor, J. O. (Eds.). (1974). *Motivation and achievement.* Washington, DC: Winston.

Bales, R. F. (1970). *Personality and interpersonal behavior.* New York: Holt, Rinehart & Winston.

Bandura, A. (1977). Self-efficacy: Toward a unifying theory of behavioral change. *Psychological Review, 84,* 191–215.

Bandura, A. (1986). *Social foundations of thought and action: A social cognitive theory.* Englewood Cliffs, NJ: Prentice Hall.

Barclay, J. R. (1977). *Appraising individual differences in the elementary classroom: Manual of the Barclay Classroom Climate Inventory* (4th ed.). Lexington, KY: Educational Skills Development.

Barker, R. G. (1968). *Ecological psychology: Concepts and methods for studying the environment of human behavior.* Stanford: Stanford University Press.

Barnes, M. L., & Sternberg, R. J. (1989). Social intelligence and decoding of nonverbal cues, *Intelligence, 13,* 263–287.

Barnett, M. A. (1987). Empathy and related responses in children. In N. Eisenberg & J. Strayer (Eds.), *Empathy and its development.* Cambridge, U.K.: Cambridge University Press.

Barnett, M. A., & Thompson, S. (1984, May). *The role of affective perspective-taking ability and empathic disposition in the child's machiavellianism, prosocial behavior, and motive for helping.* Paper pre-

sented at the annual meeting of the Midwestern Psychological Association, Chicago.

Baron, J. (1982). Personality and intelligence. In R. J. Sternberg (Ed.), *Handbook of human intelligence* (pp. 308–351). New York: Cambridge University Press.

Bates, J. E., & Wachs, T. D. (Eds.). (1994). *Temperament: Individual differences at the interface of biology and behavior.* Washington, DC: American Psychological Association.

Battig, W. F. (1979). Are the important "individual differences" between or within individuals? *Journal of Research in Personality, 13,* 546–558.

Beaty, E. (1995). Study contracts and educational orientations. In F. Marton, D. J. Hounsell, & N. J. Entwistle (Eds.), *The experience of learning* (2nd ed.). Edinburgh: Scottish Academic Press.

Bem, D. J. (1970). *Beliefs, attitudes, and human affairs.* Belmont, CA: Brooks/Cole.

Bem, D. J., & Allen, A. (1974). On predicting some of the people some of the time: The search for cross-situational consistencies in behavior. *Psychological Review, 81,* 506–520.

Bem, D. J., & Funder, D. C. (1978). Predicting more of the people more of the time: Assessing the personality of situations. *Psychological Review, 85,* 485–501.

Bereiter, C. (1990). Aspects of an educational learning theory. *Review of Educational Research, 60,* 603–624.

Berlin, I. (1980). *Against the current.* New York: Viking Press.

Berlyne, D. E. (1968). Behavior theory as personality theory. In G. F. Borgatta & W. W. Lambert (Eds.), *Handbook of personality theory and research* (pp. 629–690). Chicago: Rand McNally.

Berryman, S. E. (1993). Learning for the workplace. In L. Darling-Hammond (Ed.), *Review of research in education* (Vol. 19, pp. 343–403). Washington, DC: American Educational Research Association.

Biggs, J. B. (1987). *Student approaches to learning and studying.* Hawthorn, Victoria, Australia: Australian Council for Educational Research.

Biggs, J. B. (1988). Approaches to learning and to essay writing. In R. R. Schmeck (Ed.), *Learning strategies and learning styles* (pp. 185–228). New York: Plenum Press.

Biggs, J. B. (1991). Student learning in the context of school. In J. B. Biggs (Ed.), *Teaching for learning: The view from cognitive psychology* (pp. 7–29). Hawthorn, Victoria, Australia: Australian Council for Educational Research.

Biggs, J. B., & Collis, K. F. (1982). *Evaluating the quality of learning: The SOLO taxonomy.* New York: Academic Press.

Birney, R. C., Burdick, H., & Teevan, R. C. (1969). *Fear of failure.* New York: Van Nostrand-Reinhold.

Björck-Åkesson, E. (1990). *Measuring sensation seeking.* Göteborg, Sweden: Acta Universitatis Gothoburgensis.

Block, J., & Haan, N. (1971). *Lives through time.* Berkeley, CA: Bancroft Books.

Blumenfeld, P. C. (1992). Classroom learning and motivation: Clarifying and expanding goal theory. *Journal of Educational Psychology, 84,* 272–281.

Boekaerts, M. (1987). Situation-specific judgments of a learning task versus overall measures of motivational orientation. In E. De Corte, H. Lodewijks, R. Parmentier, & P. Span (Eds.), *Learning and instruction: European research in an international context* (Vol. 1, pp. 169–179). Leuven, Belgium, and Oxford, U.K.: Leuven University Press and Pergamon Press.

Boekaerts, M. (1993). Being concerned with well-being and with learning. *Educational Psychologist, 28,* 149–167.

Boekaerts, M. (1994, April). *The other side of learning: Allocating resources to restore well-being.* Paper presented at the annual conference of the American Educational Research Association, New Orleans, LA.

Boekaerts, M. (1995). The interface between intelligence and personality as determinants of classroom learning. In D. H. Saklofske & M. Zeidner (Eds.), *International handbook of personality and intelligence,* (pp. 161–183) New York: Plenum Press.

Boekaerts, M., Hendricksen, J., & Maes, S. (1987). *The Stress and Coping Inventory.* Leiden, The Netherlands: Leiden University, Center for the Study of Education and Instruction.

Bouchard, T. J. (1994). Genes, environment, and personality. *Science, 265,* 1700–1701.

Bower, G. H. (1981). Mood and memory. *American Psychologist, 36,* 129–148.

Boyan, N. J. (Ed.). (1988). *Handbook of research on educational administration.* New York: Longman.

Braithwaite, V. A., & Scott, W. A. (1991). Values. In J. P. Robinson, P. R. Shaver, & L. S. Wrightsman (Eds.), *Measures of personality and social psychological attitudes* (pp. 661–753) San Diego: Academic Press.

Brehm, J. W. (1966). *A psychological theory of reactance.* New York: Academic Press.

Bridges, E. M. (1982). Research on the school administrator: The state of the art, 1967–1980. *Educational Administration Quarterly, 18*(3), 12–33.

Bridges, E. M. (1992). *The incompetent teacher* (2nd ed.). London: Falmer Press.

Britton, B. K., & Tesser, A. (1991). Effects of time-management practices on college grades. *Journal of Educational Psychology, 83,* 405–410.

Brophy, J. (1983). Research on the self-fulfilling prophecy and teacher expectations. *Journal of Educational Psychology, 75,* 631–661.

Brophy, J. (1985). Teacher-student interaction. In J. B. Dusek (Ed.), *Teacher expectancies* (pp. 303–322). Hillsdale, NJ: Lawrence Erlbaum Associates.

Brophy, J., & Evertson, C. M. (1981). *Student characteristics and teaching.* New York: Longman.

Brophy, J., & Good, T. (1974). *Teacher-student relationships: Causes and consequences.* New York: Holt, Rinehardt & Winston.

Brown, G. I. (1975). The training of teachers for affective roles. In K. Ryan (Ed.), *Teacher education* (74th Yearbook of the National Society for the Study of Education, Pt. II, pp. 173–203). Chicago: National Society for the Study of Education.

Brown, J., & Weiner, B. (1984). Affective consequences of ability versus effort ascriptions: Controversies, resolutions, and quandaries. *Journal of Educational Psychology, 76,* 146–158.

Brown, L. T., & Anthony, R. G. (1990). Continuing the search for social intelligence. *Personality and Individual Differences, 11,* 463–470.

Burgoon, M. (1971). The relationship between willingness to manipulate others and success in two different types of basic speech communication. *Speech Teacher, 20,* 178–183.

Burton, R. V. (1963). Generality of honesty reconsidered. *Psychological Review, 70,* 481–499.

Buss, A. H., & Plomin, R. (1975). *A temperament theory of personality development.* New York: Wiley.

Buss, A. H., & Plomin, R. (1984). *Temperament: Early developing personality traits.* Hillsdale, NJ: Lawrence Erlbaum Associates.

Butler, G. (1987). Anticipatory anxiety and risk perception. *Cognitive Therapy and Research, 11,* 551–565.

Byrne, B. M. (1984). The general/academic self-concept nomological network: A review of construct validational research. *Review of Educational Research, 54,* 427–456.

Byrne, B. M. (1986). Self-concept/academic achievement relations: An investigation of dimensionality, stability, and causality. *Canadian Journal of Behavior Science, 18,* 173–186.

Cacioppo, J. T., & Petty, R. E. (1982). The need for cognition. *Journal of Personality and Social Psychology, 42,* 116–131.

Calsyn, R. J., & Kenny, D. A. (1977). Self-concept of ability and perceived evaluation of others: Cause or effect of academic achievement? *Journal of Educational Psychology, 69,* 136–145.

Campbell, D. P., & Fiske, D. W. (1959). Convergent and discriminant validation by the multitrait-multimethod matrix, *Psychological Bulletin, 56,* 81–105.

Campbell, D. P., & Hansen, J. C. (1981). *Manual for the SVIB-SCII.* Stanford, CA: Stanford University Press.

Cantor, N., & Kihlstrom, J. F. (1987). *Personality and social intelligence.* Englewood Cliffs, NJ: Prentice-Hall.

Carroll, J. B. (1993). *Human cognitive abilities: A survey of factor-analytic studies.* Cambridge, U.K.: Cambridge University Press.

Caspi, A., & Bem, D. J. (1990). Personality continuity and change across the life course. In L. A. Pervin (Ed.), *Handbook of personality: Theory and research* (pp. 549–569). New York: Guilford Press.

Case, R., & Edelstein, W. (1993). *The new structuralism in cognitive development: Theory and research on individual pathways.* New York: Karger.

Cassidy, T., & Lynn, R. (1989). A multifactorial approach to achievement motivation: The development of a comprehensive measure. *Journal of Occupational Psychology, 62,* 301–312.

Cattell, R. B. (1965). *The scientific analysis of personality.* Baltimore: Penguin Books.

Cattell, R. B. (1971). *Abilities: Their structure, growth, and action.* New York: Houghton Mifflin.

Cattell, R. B., & Butcher, H. J. (1968). *The prediction of achievement and creativity.* New York: Bobbs-Merrill.

Cattell, R. B., Eber, H. W., & Tatsuoka, M. (1970). *The 16 P. F. handbook.* Champaign, IL: Institute for Personality and Ability Testing.

Cattell, R. B., & Warburton, F. W. (1967). *Objective personality and motivational tests.* Urbana: University of Illinois Press.

Chiu, L. H. (1967). *A factorial study of academic motivation.* Unpublished doctoral dissertation, Columbia University, New York.

Christie, R. (1991). Authoritarianism and related constructs. In J. P. Robinson, P. R. Shaver, & L. S. Wrightsman (Eds.), *Measures of personality and social psychological attitudes* (pp. 501–569). San Diego: Academic Press.

Christie, R., & Geis, F. L. (1970). *Studies in Machiavellianism.* New York: Academic Press.

Claeys, W., De Boeck, P., Van Den Bosch, W., Biesmans, R., & Böhrer, A. (1985). A comparison of one free format and two fixed format self-report personality assessment methods. *Journal of Personality and Social Psychology, 49,* 1028–1039.

Clausen, J. A. (1993). *American lives.* New York: Free Press.

Cliff, N. (1977). Further study of cognitive processing models for inventory response. *Applied Psychological Measurement, 1,* 41–49.

Coan, R. W. (1964). Facts, factors and artifacts: The quest for psychological meaning. *Psychological Review, 71,* 123–140.

Cohen, B. H., & Saslona, M. (1990). The advantage of being a habitual visualizer. *Journal of Mental Imagery, 14,* 101–112.

Cole, M. (1985). Mind as a cultural achievement: Implications for IQ testing. In E. Eisner (Ed.), *Learning and teaching the ways of knowing* (pp. 218–249). Chicago: National Society for the Study of Education.

Coopersmith, S. (1967). *The antecedents of self-esteem.* San Francisco: Freeman.

Corno, L. (1980). Individual and class level effects of parent-assisted instruction in classroom memory support strategies. *Journal of Educational Psychology, 72,* 278–292.

Corno, L. (1986). The metacognitive control components of self-regulated learning. *Contemporary Educational Psychology, 11,* 333–346.

Corno, L. (1989). Self-regulated learning: A volitional analysis. In B. Zimmerman & D. Schunk (Eds.), *Self-regulated learning and academic achievement: Theory, research and practice* (pp. 111–142). New York: Springer.

Corno, L. (1992). Encouraging students to take responsibility for learning and performance. *Elementary School Journal, 93,* 69–84.

Corno, L. (1993). The best-laid plans: Modern conceptions of volition and educational research. *Educational Researcher, 22*(2), 14–22.

Corno, L. (1994). Student volition and education: Outcomes, influences, and practices. In D. H. Schunk & B. J. Zimmerman (Eds.), *Self-regulation of learning and performance: Issues and educational applications* (pp. 229–254). Hillsdale, NJ: Lawrence Erlbaum Associates.

Corno, L., & Kanfer, R. (1993). The role of volition in learning and performance. In L. Darling-Hammond (Ed.), *Review of research in education* (Vol. 19, pp. 3–43). Washington, DC: American Educational Research Association.

Corno, L., & Mandinach, E. B. (1983). The role of cognitive engagement in classroom learning and motivation. *Educational Psychologist, 18,* 88–108.

Corno, L., Mitman, A., & Hedges, L. V. (1981). The influence of direct instruction on student self-appraisals: A hierarchical analysis of treatment and aptitude-treatment interaction effects. *American Educational Research Journal, 18,* 39–61.

Corno, L., & Rohrkemper, M. M. (1985). The intrinsic motivation to learn in classrooms. In C. Ames & R. E. Ames (Eds.), *Research on motivation in education* (Vol. 2, pp. 53–90). Orlando, FL: Academic Press.

Corno, L., & Snow, R. E. (1986). Adapting teaching to individual differences among learners. In M. C. Wittrock (Ed.), *Handbook of research on teaching* (3rd ed., pp. 605–629). New York: Macmillan.

Costa, P. T., & McCrae, R. R. (1988). From catalog to classification: Murray's needs and the five-factor model. *Journal of Personality and Social Psychology, 55,* 258–265.

Costin, S. E., & Jones, D. C. (1992). Friendship as a facilitator of emotional responsiveness and prosocial interventions among young children. *Developmental Psychology, 28,* 941–947.

Covington, M. (1984). The self-worth theory of achievement motivation: Findings and implications. *Elementary School Journal, 85,* 5–20.

Covington, M. (1992). *Making the grade.* New York: Cambridge University Press.

Crandall, V. C., Katkovsky, W., & Crandall, V. J. (1965). Childrens' beliefs in their own control of reinforcement in intellectual-academic situations. *Child Development, 36,* 91–109.

Cronbach, L. J. (1957). The two disciplines of scientific psychology. *American Psychologist, 12,* 671–684.

Cronbach, L. J. (1975). Beyond the two disciplines of scientific psychology. *American Psychologist, 30,* 116–127.

Cronbach, L. J. (1990). *Essentials of psychological testing.* New York: Harper & Row.

Cronbach, L. J., & Snow, R. E. (1977). *Aptitudes and instructional methods: A handbook for research on interactions.* New York: Irvington.

Csikszentmihalyi, M. (1990). *Flow: The psychology of optimal experience.* New York: Harper & Row.

Csikszentmihalyi, M., & Csikszentmihalyi, I. S. (Eds.). (1988). *Optimal experience: Psychological studies of flow in consciousness.* New York: Cambridge University Press.

Csikszentmihalyi, M., & Nakamura, J. (1989). The dynamics of intrinsic motivation. In R. E. Ames & C. Ames (Eds.), *Research on motivation in education: Vol. 3. Goals and cognition* (pp. 45–71). New York: Academic Press.

Csikszentmihalyi, M., Rathunde, K., & Whalen, S. (1993). *Talented teenagers: A longitudinal study of their development.* New York: Cambridge University Press.

Curry, L. (1990). *Learning styles in secondary schools: A review of instruments and implications for their use.* Madison: University of Wisconsin, National Center for Effective Secondary Schools.

Curry, L. (1991). Patterns of learning style across selected medical specialities. *Educational Psychology, 11,* 247–277.

Dance, K. A., & Neufeld, R. W. J. (1988). Aptitude-treatment interaction research in the clinical setting: A review of attempts to dispel the "patient uniformity" myth. *Psychological Bulletin, 104,* 192–213.

De Boeck, P. (1978). Validity of a cognitive processing model for responses to adjective and sentence type inventories. *Applied Psychological Measurement, 2,* 369–376.

De Boeck, P. (1981). Individual differences in the validity of a cognitive processing model for responses to personality inventories. *Applied Psychological Measurement, 5,* 481–492.

De Charms, R. (1968). *Personal causation: The internal affective determinants of behavior.* New York: Academic Press.

Deci, E. L., & Ryan, R. M. (1985). *Intrinsic motivation and self-determination in human behavior.* New York: Plenum Press.

Demetriou, A., & Efklides, A. (1991). The development of quantitative-relational abilities from childhood to adolescence: Structure, scaling, and individual differences. *Learning and Instruction, 1,* 19–43.

Dewey, J. (1913). *Interest and effort in education.* New York: Houghton Mifflin.

Dewey, J. (1964). The need for a philosophy of education. In R. D. Archambault (Ed.), *John Dewey on education* (pp. 3–14). Chicago: University of Chicago Press. (Original work published 1934)

Digman, J. M. (1990). Personality structure: Emergence of the five-factor model. *Annual Review of Psychology, 41,* 417–440.

Dole, J., Duffy, G., Roehler, L., & Pearson, P. D. (1991). Moving from the old to the new: Research on reading comprehension instruction. *Review of Educational Research, 61,* 239–264.

Domino, G. (1968). Differential predictions of academic achievement in conforming and independent settings. *Journal of Educational Psychology, 59,* 256–260.

Domino, G. (1971). Interactive effects of achievement orientation and teaching style on academic achievement. *Journal of Educational Psychology, 62,* 427–431.

Dowaliby, F. J., & Schumer, H. (1973). Teacher-centered vs. student-centered mode of college classroom instruction as related to manifest anxiety. *Journal of Educational Psychology, 64,* 125–132.

Dusek, J. B. (Ed.). (1985). *Teacher expectancies.* Hillsdale, NJ: Lawrence Erlbaum Associates.

Dweck, C. S. (1975). The role of expectations and attributions in the alleviation of learned helplessness. *Journal of Personality and Social Psychology, 31,* 674–685.

Dweck, C. S. (1986). Motivational processes affecting learning. *American Psychologist, 41,* 1040–1048.

Dweck, C. S. (1994, August). *Implicit theories on the self.* Paper presented at a meeting of the American Psychological Association, Los Angeles.

Dweck, C. S., & Leggett, E. L. (1988). A social-cognitive approach to motivation and personality. *Psychological Review, 95,* 256–273.

d'Ydewalle, G. (1984). *Motivation and information processing. Psychological Reports.* Leuven, Belgium: University of Leuven.

d'Ydewalle, G., Swerts, A., & De Corte, E. (1983). Study time and test performance as a function of test expectations. *Contemporary Educational Psychology, 8,* 55–67.

Eagly, A. H., & Chaiken, S. (1993). *The psychology of attitudes.* Fort Worth, TX: Harcourt Brace Jovanovich.

Eisenberg, N., & Lennon, J. (1983). Sex differences in empathy and related capacities. *Psychological Bulletin, 94,* 100–131.

Eisenberg, N., & Strayer, J. (1987). *Empathy and its development.* New York: Cambridge University Press.

Elashoff, J. D., & Snow, R. E. (1971). *Pygmalion reconsidered.* Worthington, OH: Charles A. Jones.

Elliott, E. S., & Dweck, C. S. (1988). Goals: An approach to motivation and achievement. *Journal of Personality and Social Psychology, 54,* 5–12.

Embretson, S. (1983). Construct validity: Construct representation versus nomothetic span. *Psychological Bulletin, 93,* 179–197.

Endler, N. S., & Magnusson, D. (Eds.). (1976). *Interactional psychology and personality.* Washington, DC: Hemisphere.

English, H. B., & English, A. C. (1958). *A comprehensive dictionary of psychological and psychoanalytic terms.* New York: Longman's Green.

Entwistle, N. J. (1981). *Styles of learning and teaching.* Chichester, U.K.: Wiley.

Entwistle, N. J. (1987a). Explaining individual differences in school learning. In E. De Corte, H. Lodewijks, R. Parmentier, & P. Span (Eds.), *Learning and instruction: European research in an international context* (Vol. 1, pp. 69–88). Leuven, Belgium, and Oxford, U.K.: Leuven University Press and Pergamon Press.

Entwistle, N. J. (1987b). Motivation to learn: Conceptualizations and practicalities. *British Journal of Educational Studies, 35*, 129–148.

Entwistle, N. J. (1987c). *Understanding Classroom Learning.* London: Hodder & Stoughton.

Entwistle, N. J. (1988). Motivational factors in students' approaches to learning. In R. R. Schmeck (Ed.), *Learning strategies and learning styles* (pp. 21–51). New York: Plenum Press.

Entwistle, N. J. (1995a). Frameworks for understanding as experienced in essay writing and in preparing for examinations. *Educational Psychologist, 39*, 47–54.

Entwistle, N. J. (1995b). Introduction: Influences of instructional settings on learning and cognitive development—Findings from European research programs, *Educational Psychologist, 30*, 1–3.

Entwistle, N. J., & Cunningham, S. (1968). Neuroticism and school attainment: A linear relationship? *British Journal of Educational Psychology, 38*, 123–132.

Entwistle, N. J., Kozeki, B., & Balarabe, J. (1988, April). *Motivation, attributions and approaches to learning in British and Hungarian secondary schools.* Paper presented at the annual meeting of the American Educational Research Association, New Orleans, LA.

Entwistle, N. J., & Ramsden, P. (1983). *Understanding Student Learning.* London: Croom Helm.

Entwistle, N. J., & Tait, H. (1990). Approaches to learning, evaluations of teaching, and preferences for contrasting academic environments. *Higher Education, 19*, 169–194.

Entwistle, N. J., & Wilson, J. D. (1970). Personality, study methods, and academic performance. *Universities Quarterly, 24*, 147–156.

Ercikan, K. (1991). Item response theory models for knowledge, opinion and persuasibility measurement. Unpublished doctoral dissertation, Stanford University, Stanford, CA.

Eysenck, H. J. (1977). Personality and factor analysis: A reply to Guilford. *Psychological Bulletin, 84*, 405–411.

Eysenck, H. J., & Eysenck, M. W. (1985). *Personality and individual differences.* New York: Plenum Press.

Eysenck, M. W. (1981). Learning, memory and personality. In H. J. Eysenck (Ed.), *A model for personality* (pp. 169–203). Berlin: Springer.

Fancher, R. E., Jr. (1966). Explicit personality theories and accuracy of person perception. *Journal of Personality, 34*, 252–261.

Farley, F. H. (1981). Basic process individual differences: A biological based theory of individualization for cognitive, affective and creative outcomes. In F. H. Farley & N. J. Gordon (Eds.), *Psychology and education: The state of the union* (pp. 9–31). Berkeley, CA: McCutchan.

Farley, F. H. (1985). Psychobiology and cognition: An individual-differences model. In J. Strelau, F. H. Farley, & A. Gale (Eds.), *The biological bases of personality and behavior: Vol. 1. Theories, measurement techniques, and development* (pp. 61–73). Washington, DC: Hemisphere.

Fiedler, F., & Garcia, J. E. (1987). *New approaches to leadership: Cognitive resources and organizational performance.* New York: Wiley.

Fiske, A. P. (1992). The four elementary forms of sociality: Framework for a unified theory of social relations. *Psychological Review, 99*, 689–723.

Fiske, D. W., & Maddi, S. R. (1961). *Functions of varied experience.* Homewood, IL: Dorsey Press.

Fleishman, E. A., & Quaintance, M. K. (1984). *Taxonomies of human performance: The description of human tasks.* Orlando, FL: Academic Press.

Ford, M. (1994). *Motivating human behavior.* Oxford, U.K.: Pergamon Press.

Ford, M., & Tisak, M. S. (1983). A further search for social intelligence. *Journal of Educational Psychology, 75*, 197–206.

Forehand, G. A. (1968). On the interaction of persons and organizations. In R. Taguiri & G. H. Litwin (Eds.), *Organizational climate: Explorations of a concept* (pp. 65–82). Boston: Harvard University, Graduate School of Business Administration.

Fortin, J. C. (1989). *Machiavellian behavior and school principals' level of stress* (pp. 1–20). Unpublished manuscript, University of Ottawa, Ottawa, Canada.

Frederiksen, N. (1972). Toward a taxonomy of situations. *American Psychologist, 27*, 114–123.

Frederiksen, N., Jensen, O., & Beaton, A. E. (1972). *Prediction of organizational behavior.* New York: Pergamon Press.

Frijda, N. H. (1986). *The emotions.* New York: Cambridge University Press.

Gardner, H. (1983). *Frames of mind.* New York: Basic Books.

Gardner, H., & Hatch, T. (1989). Multiple intelligences go to school: Educational theory of multiple intelligences. *Educational Researcher, 18*(8), 4–9.

Gaudry, E., & Spielberger, C. D. (1971). *Anxiety and educational achievement.* Sydney: Wiley.

Getzels, J. W., & Jackson, P. W. (1963). The teacher's personality and characteristics. In N. L. Gage (Ed.), *Handbook of research on teaching* (pp. 506–582). Chicago: Rand McNally.

Gibson, J. J. (1979). *The ecological approach to visual perception.* Boston: Houghton Mifflin.

Globerson, T., & Zelniker, T. (1989). *Cognitive style and cognitive development.* Norwood, NJ: Ablex.

Goff, M., & Ackerman, P. L. (1992). Personality-intelligence relations: Assessment of typical intellectual engagement. *Journal of Educational Psychology, 84*, 537–552.

Goodman, J. (1988). Constructing a practical philosophy of teaching: A study of preservice teachers' professional perspectives. *Teaching and Teacher Education, 4*, 121–137.

Goodnow, J. J. (1980). Everyday concepts of intelligence and its development. In N. Warren (Ed.), *Studies in cross-cultural psychology* (Vol. 2, pp. 191–219). Oxford, U.K.: Pergamon Press.

Gordon, E. W. (1988). *Report of the New York State Board of Regents' Panel on Learning Styles.* Albany: New York State Board of Regents.

Gottfredson, G. D., Jones, E. M., & Holland, S. L. (1993). Personality and vocational interests: The relation of Holland's six interest dimensions to five robust dimensions of personality. *Journal of Counseling Psychology, 40*, 518–524.

Gough, H. (1987). *Manual for the California Psychological Inventory.* Palo Alto, CA: Consulting Psychologists Press.

Gray, J. A. (1964). *Pavlov's typology.* Oxford, U.K.: Pergamon Press.

Gray, J. A. (1973). Causal theories of personality and how to test them. In J. R. Royce (Ed.), *Multivariate analysis and psychological theory* (pp. 409–463). London: Academic Press.

Gray, J. A. (1982). A critique of Eysenck's theory of personality. In H. J. Eysenck (Ed.), *A model for personality* (pp. 246–276). Berlin: Springer.

Greeno, J. G. (1980). Psychology of learning, 1960–1980: One participant's observations. *American Psychologist, 35*, 713–728.

Greeno, J. G. (1989). A perspective on thinking. *American Psychologist, 44*, 134–141.

Guilford, J. P. (1959). *Personality.* New York: McGraw-Hill.

Guilford, J. P. (1967). *The nature of human intelligence.* New York: McGraw-Hill.

Guilford, J. P. (1975). Factors and factors of personality. *Psychological Bulletin, 82*, 802–814.

Guilford, J. P., & Zimmerman, W. W. (1949). *The Guilford Zimmerman Temperament Survey: Manual.* Beverly Hills, CA: Sheridan Supply.

Haan, N. (1977). *Coping and defending: Processes of self-environment organization.* New York: Academic Press.

Hagtvet, K. A. (1984). Fear of failure, worry, and emotionality: Their suggestive causal relationships to mathematical performance and state anxiety. In H. M. van der Ploeg, R. Schwarzer, & C. D. Spielberger (Eds.), *Advances in test anxiety research* (Vol. 3, pp. 211–224). Lisse, The Netherlands: Swets & Zeitlinger.

Hagtvet, K. A. (1986, April). *Interaction of anxiety and ability on academic achievement: A simultaneous consideration of parameters.* Paper presented at a meeting of the American Educational Research Association, San Francisco.

Hagtvet, K. A. (1991). Interaction of anxiety and ability on task performance: A simultaneous consideration of parameters. *Zeitschrift für Pädagogische Psychologie, 5,* 111–119.

Hagtvet, K. A., & Min, Y. R. (1993, September). *Differential relations of ability and anxiety to stability and change of a problem solving process.* Paper presented at a meeting of the European Association for Research on Learning and Instruction, Aix-en-Provence, France.

Harter, S. (1981). A new self-report of intrinsic versus extrinsic orientation in the classroom: Motivational and informational components. *Developmental Psychology, 17,* 300–312.

Harter, S. (1982). The perceived competence scale for children. *Child Development, 53,* 87–97.

Harter, S. (1983). Developmental perspectives on the self-system. In P. H. Mussen (Ed.), *Handbook of child psychology* (4th ed., pp. 275–385). New York: Wiley.

Harter, S. (1985a). Competence as a dimension of self-evaluation: Toward a comprehensive model of self-worth. In R. L. Leahy (Ed.), *The development of the self* (pp. 95–121). New York: Academic Press.

Harter, S. (1985b). *Manual for the Self-Perception Profile for Children.* Denver, CO: Psychology Dept., University of Denver.

Harter, S. (1986). *Manual for the Self-Perception Profile for Adults.* Denver, CO: Psychology Dept., University of Denver.

Harter, S., & Connell, J. P. (1984). A model of children's achievement and related self-perceptions of competence, control and motivational orientation. *Advances in Motivation and Achievement, 3,* 219–250.

Hartshorne, H., & May, M. A. (1928). *Studies of the nature of character: I. Studies in deceit.* New York: Macmillan.

Hartshorne, H., May, M. A., & Maller, J. B. (1929). *Studies of the nature of character: II. Studies in service and self-control.* New York: Macmillan.

Hartshorne, H., May, M. A., & Shuttleworth, F. K. (1930). *Studies of the nature of character: III. Studies in the organization of character.* New York: Macmillan.

Hartup, W. W. (1989). Social relationships and their developmental significance. *American Psychologist, 44,* 120–126.

Harvey, O. J., Hunt, D. G., & Schroder, H. M. (1961). *Conceptual systems and personality organization.* New York: Wiley.

Heckhausen, H., & Gollwitzer, P. (1987). Thought contents and cognitive functioning in motivational vs. volitional states of mind. *Motivation and Emotion, 11,* 101–120.

Heckhausen, H., & Kuhl, J. (1985). From wishes to action: The dead ends and short-cuts on the long way to action. In M. Frese & J. Sabini (Eds.), *Goal-directed behavior: Psychological theory and research on action.* Hillsdale, NJ: Lawrence Erlbaum Associates.

Heckhausen, H., Schmalt, H.-D., & Schneider, K. (1985). *Achievement motivation in perspective.* London: Academic Press.

Hedelin, L., & Sjöberg, L. (1985, June). *The attrition of interests in the Swedish compulsory school.* Paper presented at the First European Conference for Research on Learning and Instruction, Leuven, Belgium.

Helmke, A. (1988). The role of classroom context factors for the achievement-impairing effect of test anxiety. *Anxiety Research, 1,* 37–52.

Helmke, A. (1989). Affective student characteristics and cognitive development: Problems, pitfalls, perspectives, *International Journal of Educational Research, 13,* 915–932.

Helmke, A. (1994, July). *Schooling and the development of achievement differences.* Paper presented at the International Conference on the Longitudinal Study on the Genesis of Individual Competencies, Max-Planck-Institut for Psychological Research, Munich, Germany.

Hembree, R. (1988). Correlates, causes, effects, and treatment of test anxiety. *Review of Educational Research, 58,* 47–77.

Hemphill, J. K., Griffiths, D. E., & Frederiksen, N. (1962). *Administrative performance and personality: A study of the principal in a simulated elementary school.* New York: Teachers College, Columbia University.

Hepburn, L., & Eysenck, M. W. (1989). Personality, average mood and mood variability. *Personality and Individual Differences, 10,* 975–983.

Hettema, P. J. (1979). *Personality and adaptation.* Amsterdam: North-Holland.

Hettema, P. J. (1989). *Personality and environment: Assessment of human adaptation.* New York: Wiley.

Hilgard, E. R. (1980). The trilogy of mind: Cognition, affection, and conation. *Journal of the History of Behavioral Sciences, 16,* 107–117.

Hoffman, M. L. (1975). Developmental synthesis of affect and cognition and its implications for altruistic motivation. *Developmental Psychology, 11,* 607–622.

Hoffman, M. L. (1994). Discipline and internalization. *Developmental Psychology, 30,* 26–28.

Hofstee, W. K. B., De Raad, B., & Goldberg, L. R. (1992). Integration of the big five and circumplex approaches to trait structure. *Journal of Personality and Social Psychology, 63,* 146–163.

Hogan, R., Curry, G. J., & Hogan, J. (1994). What we know about leadership: Effectiveness and personality. *American Psychologist, 49,* 493–504.

Hoge, D., & Bender, I. E. (1974). Factors influencing value change among college graduates in adult life. *Journal of Personality and Social Psychology, 29,* 572–585.

Holland, J. L. (1973). *Making vocational choices.* Englewood Cliffs, NJ: Prentice Hall.

Holland, J. L. (1985). *Making vocational choices: A theory of vocational personalities and work environments.* Englewood Cliff, NJ: Prentice Hall.

Holland, J. L. (1994, August). *Some explorations of interest item endorsement rates as signs of personality.* Paper presented at the meeting of the American Psychological Association, Los Angeles, CA.

Holland, J. L., Johnston, J. A., & Asama, N. F. (in press). More evidence for the relationship between Holland's personality types and personality variables. *Journal of Career Assessment.*

Holt-Reynolds, D. (1992). Personal history-based beliefs as relevant prior knowledge in course work. *American Educational Research Journal, 29,* 325–349.

Horner, M. S. (1968). *Sex differences in achievement motivation and performance in competitive and non-competitive situations.* Unpublished doctoral dissertation, University of Michigan.

Horner, M. S. (1972). Toward an understanding of achievement related conflicts in women. *Journal of Social Issues, 28,* 157–175.

Hovland, C. I., & Janis, I. L. (1962). An overview of persuasibility research. In C. I. Hovland & I. L. Janis (Eds.), *Personality and persuasibility.* New Haven, CT: Yale University Press.

Hoy, W. K., Rees, R. T., & Williams, L. B. (1973). *Machiavellianism in the school setting: Teacher–principal relations. Final report.* Washington, DC: National Center for Educational Research and Development.

Huber, G. L. (1990). Motivation by cognitive controversy: A challenge to cooperate for every learner? In H. Mandl, E. De Corte, S. N. Bennett, & H. F. Friedrich (Eds.), *Learning and instruction: European research in an international context* (Vol 2.1., pp. 517–532). Oxford, U.K.: Pergamon Press.

Hudson, L. (1966). *Contrary imaginations.* New York: Schocken.

Hull, C. L. (1945). The place of innate individual and species differences in a natural-science theory of behavior. *Psychological Review, 52,* 55–60.

Hunsley, J. (1987). Cognitive processes in mathematics anxiety and test anxiety: The role of appraisals, internal dialogue, and attributions. *Journal of Educational Psychology, 79*, 388–392.

Hunt, D. E. (1971). *Matching models in education. The coordination of teaching methods with students characteristics*. Toronto: Ontario Institute for Studies in Education.

Hunt, D. E. (1975). *Teachers' adaptation to students: Implicit and explicit matching* (Research and Development Memorandum No. 139). Stanford, CA: Stanford Center for Research and Development in Teaching.

Hunt, D. E. (1977). Conceptual level theory and research as guides to educational practice. *Interchange, 8*, 78–90.

Hunt, D. E. (1987). *Beginning with ourselves in practice, theory, and human affairs*. Cambridge, MA: Brookline Books.

Hunt, D. E., & Sullivan, E. V. (1974). *Between psychology and education*. Hinsdale, IL: Dryden Press.

Isen, A., Daubman, K. A., & Gorgoglione, J. M. (1987). The influence of positive affect on cognitive organization: Implications for education. In R. E. Snow & M. J. Farr (Eds.), *Aptitude, learning and instruction* (Vol. 3, pp. 143–162). Hillsdale, NJ: Lawrence Erlbaum Associates.

Izard, C. E. (1991). *The psychology of emotions*. New York: Plenum Press.

Izard, C. E., Kagan, J., & Zajonc, R. B. (1984). *Emotions, cognition, and behavior*. New York: Cambridge University Press.

Jackson, D. N. (1971). The dynamics of structured personality tests: 1971. *Psychological Review, 78*, 229–248.

Jackson, D. N. (1984). *Manual for the Personality Research Form*. Port Huron, MI: Research Psychologists Press.

Jackson, D. N., Ahmed, S. A., & Heapy, N. A. (1976). Is achievement a unitary construct? *Journal of Research in Personality, 10*, 1–21.

Jackson, D. N., & Helmes, E. (1979). Basic structure content scaling. *Applied Psychological Measurement, 3*, 313–325.

Jackson, P. W. (1968). *Life in classrooms*. New York: Holt, Rinehart & Winston.

Jaensch, E. R. (1938). *Der Gegentypus*. Leipzig: Barth.

James, W. (1983). *The principles of psychology*. Cambridge, MA: Harvard University Press. (Original work published 1890)

Jandt, F. E. (1975). Machiavellianism in the basic course—again (pp. 1–10). Unpublished manuscript. Brockport, NY: State University College.

John, O. P. (1990). The "big five" factor taxonomy: Dimensions of personality in the natural language and in questionnaires. In L. A. Pervin (Ed.), *Handbook of personality: Theory and research* (pp. 66–100). New York: Guilford Press.

Judd, C. H. (1927). *Psychology of secondary education*. New York: Ginn.

Jung, C. G. (1923). *Psychological types*. London: Routledge & Kegan Paul.

Kanfer, R. (1990). Motivation and individual differences in learning: An integration of developmental, differential, and cognitive perspectives. *Learning and Individual Differences, 2*, 221–239.

Kanfer, R., & Ackerman, P. L. (1989a). Dynamics of skill acquisition: Building a bridge between intelligence and motivation. In R. J. Sternberg (Ed.), *Advances in the psychology of human intelligence* (Vol. 5, pp. 83–134). Hillsdale, NJ: Lawrence Erlbaum Associates.

Kanfer, R., & Ackerman, P. L. (1989b). Motivation and cognitive abilities: An integrative/aptitude-treatment interaction approach to skill acquisition. *Journal of Applied Psychology Monograph, 74*, 657–690.

Karabenick, S. A., & Srull, T. K. (1978). Effects of personality and situational variation in locus of control on cheating: Determinants of the "congruence effect." *Journal of Personality, 46*, 72–95.

Keating, D. K. (1978). A search for social intelligence. *Journal of Educational Psychology, 70*, 218–233.

Keefe, J. W. (1987). *Learning style theory and practice*. Reston, VA: National Association of Secondary School Principals.

Keefe, J. W. (Ed.) (1988). *Profiling and utilizing learning style*. Reston, VA: National Association of Secondary School Principals.

Keefe, J. W., & Monk, J. S. (1988). *Learning style profile technical manual*. Reston, VA: National Association of Secondary School Principals.

Kelly, G. A. (1955). *The psychology of personal constructs*. New York: Norton.

Kelly, G. A. (1963). *A theory of personality: The psychology of personal constructs*. New York: Norton.

Kerlinger, F. N. (1984). *Liberalism and conservatism: The nature and structure of social attitudes*. Hillsdale, NJ: Lawrence Erlbaum Associates.

Khan, S. B., & Weiss, J. (1973). The teaching of affective responses. In R. M. W. Travers (Ed.), *Second handbook of research on teaching* (pp. 759–804). Chicago: Rand McNally.

Kline, P. (1973). *New approaches in psychological measurement*. New York: Wiley.

Kline, P. (1993). *Personality: The psychometric view*. London: Routledge.

Kline, P., & Cooper, C. (1984). A construct validation of the Objective Analytic Test Battery (OATB). *Personality and Individual Differences, 5*, 328–337.

Kolb, D. A. (1978). *Learning Style Inventory: Technical manual*. Boston: McBer.

Kolb, D. A. (1981). Learning styles and disciplinary differences. In A. W. Chickering & Associates (Eds.), *The modern American college*. San Francisco: Jossey-Bass.

Krathwohl, D. R., Bloom, B. S., & Masia, B. B. (1964). *Taxonomy of educational objectives: Handbook II. Affective domain*. New York: McKay.

Kretschmer, E. (1925). *Physique and character*. London: Kegan Paul.

Kruglanski, A. W. (1989). *Lay epistemics and human knowledge*. New York: Plenum Press.

Kruglanski, A. W., & Ajzen, I. (1983). Bias and error in human judgment. *European Journal of Social Psychology, 13*, 1–44.

Kuhl, J. (1977). *Mess- und prozesstheoretische Analysen einiger Person- und Situationsparameter der Leistungmotivation* [Personal and situational determinants of achievement motivation: Computer simulation and experimental analysis]. Bonn: Bouvier.

Kuhl, J. (1978). Standard setting and risk preference: An elaboration of the theory of achievement motivation and an empirical test. *Psychological Review, 85*, 239–248.

Kuhl, J. (1981). Motivational and functional helplessness: The moderating effect of state versus action orientation. *Journal of Personality and Social Psychology, 40*, 155–170.

Kuhl, J. (1982). The expectancy-value approach in the theory of social motivation: Elaborations, extensions, critique. In N. T. Feather (Ed.), *Expectations and actions: Expectancy-value models in psychology* (pp. 125–160). Hillsdale, NJ: Lawrence Erlbaum Associates.

Kuhl, J. (1984). Volitional aspects of achievement motivation and learned helplessness: Toward a comprehensive theory of action control. In B. A. Maher (Ed.), *Progess in experimental personality research* (Vol. 12, pp. 99–170). New York: Academic Press.

Kuhl, J. (1986). Motivation and information processing: A new look at decision making, dynamic change, and action control. In R. M. Sorrentino & E. T. Higgins (Eds.), *Handbook of motivation and cognition: Foundations of social behavior* (pp. 404–434). New York: Guilford Press.

Kuhl, J. (1987). Feeling versus being helpless: Metacognitive mediation of failure-induced performance deficits. In F. Weinert & R. Kluwe (Eds.), *Metacognition, motivation, and understanding* (pp. 217–235). Hillsdale, NJ: Lawrence Erlbaum Associates.

Kuhl, J. (1990). *Self-regulation: A new theory for old applications*. Paper presented at the XXII International Congress of Applied Psychology, Kyoto, Japan.

Kuhl, J. (1993). The Self-Regulation Test for Children (SRTC). In F. E. Weinert & W. Schneider (Eds.), *The Munich longitudinal study on the genesis of individual competencies (LOGIC) (Report*

*No. 9, pp. 12–19)*. *Munich: Max-Planck-Institute for Psychological Research.*

Kuhl, J., & Beckmann, J. (1985). Historical perspectives in the study of action control. In J. Kuhl & J. Beckmann (Eds.), *Action control: From cognition to behavior* (pp. 89–100). New York: Springer.

Kuhl, J., & Kazen-Saad, M. (1989). Volition and self-regulation: Memory mechanisms mediating the maintenance of intentions. In W. A. Hersberger (Ed.), *Volitional action* (pp. 387–407). Dordrecht, The Netherlands: Martinus Nijhoff.

Kuhl, J., & Kraska, K. (1989). Self-regulation and metamotivation: Computational mechanisms, development, and assessment. In R. Kanfer, P. L. Ackerman, & R. Cudeck (Eds.), *Abilities, motivation, and methodology* (pp. 343–374). Hillsdale, NJ: Lawrence Erlbaum Associates.

Kyllonen, P. C., Lohman, D. F., & Woltz, D. J. (1984). Componential modeling of alternative strategies for performing spatial tasks. *Journal of Educational Psychology, 76,* 1325–1345.

Kyllonen, P. C., & Shute, V. J. (1989). A taxonomy of learning skills. In P. L. Ackerman, R. J. Sternberg, & R. Glaser (Eds.), *Learning and individual differences* (pp. 117–163) New York: Freeman.

Langer, E. J. (1989). *Mindfulness.* Reading, MA: Addison-Wesley.

Larsen, R., & Diener, E. (1987). Affect intensity as an individual difference characteristic. *Journal of Research in Personality, 21,* 1–39.

Lazarus, R. S. (1982). Thoughts on the relations between emotion and cognition. *American Psychologist, 37,* 1019–1024.

Lazarus, R. S. (1991). *Emotion and adaptation.* New York: Oxford University Press.

Lazarus, R. S. (1993). From psychological stress to the emotions: A history of changing outlooks. *Annual Review of Psychology, 44,* 1–21.

Lazarus, R. S., & Folkman, S. (1984). *Stress, appraisal, and coping.* New York: Springer.

Lefcourt, H. M. (1982). *Locus of control.* Hillsdale, NJ: Lawrence Erlbaum Associates.

Lefcourt, H. M. (1991). In J. P. Robinson, P. R. Shaver, & L. S. Wrightsman (Eds.), *Measures of personality and social psychological attitudes* (pp. 413–493). San Diego, CA: Academic Press.

Lens, W. (1983). *Achievement motivation, test anxiety, and academic achievement.* Psychological Reports. Belgium: University of Leuven.

Lens, W., & DeCruyenaere, M. (1991). Motivation and de-motivation in secondary education: Student characteristics. *Learning and Instruction, 1,* 145–159.

Lens, W., & Gailly, A. (1980). Extension of future time perspective in motivational goals of different age groups. *International Journal of Behavioral Development, 3*(1), 1–17.

Lepper, M. R. (1988). Motivational considerations in the study of instruction. *Cognition and Instruction, 5,* 289–309.

Lepper, M. R., & Malone, T. W. (1987). Intrinsic motivation and instructional effectiveness in computer based education. In R. E. Snow & M. J. Farr (Eds.), *Aptitude, learning and instruction: Vol. 3. Conative and affective process analyses* (pp. 255–296). Hillsdale, NJ: Lawrence Erlbaum Associates.

Lepper, M. R., & Chabay, R. W. (1988). Socializing the intelligent tutor: Bringing empathy to computer tutors. In H. Mandl & A. M. Lesgold (Eds.), *Learning issues for intelligent tutoring systems* (pp. 242–257). New York: Springer.

Lewin, K. (1931). Sachlichkeit und Zwang in der Erziehung zur Realität. *Neue Erziehung, 2,* 99–103.

Lewin, K. (1951). *Field theory in the social sciences.* New York: Harper & Row.

Lewin, K. (1961). Intention, will, and need. In T. Shipley (Ed.), *Classics in psychology* (pp. 1234–1289). New York: Philosophical Library. (Original work published 1926)

Liebert, R., & Morris, L. (1967). Cognitive and emotional components of test anxiety: A distinction and some initial data. *Psychological Reports, 20,* 975, 978.

Linn, M. C., & Kyllonen, P. (1981). The field dependence-independence construct: Some, one, or none. *Journal of Educational Psychology, 73,* 261–273.

Loehlin, J. C. (1992). *Genes and environment in personality development.* Newbury Park, CA: Sage.

Lohman, D. F. (1989a). Estimating individual differences in information processing using speed-accuracy models. In R. Kanfer, P. L. Ackerman, & R. Cudeck (Eds.), *Abilities, motivation, and methodology* (pp. 119–163). Hillsdale, NJ: Lawrence Erlbaum Associates.

Lohman, D. F. (1989b). Human intelligence: An introduction to advances in theory and research. *Review of Educational Research, 59,* 333–373.

Lynn, R., Hampson, S. L., & Magee, M. (1983). Determinants of educational achievement at 16+: Intelligence, personality, home background and school. *Personality and Individual Differences, 4,* 473–481.

Maehr, M. L. (1989). Thoughts about motivation. In C. Ames & R. E. Ames (Eds.), *Research on motivation in education* (Vol. 3, pp. 299–315). New York: Academic Press.

Maehr, M. L. (1991). The "psychological environment" of the school: A focus for school leadership. In P. Thurston & P. Zodhiates (Eds.), *Advances in educational administration* (Vol. 2, pp. 51–81). Greenwich, CT: JAI Press.

Maehr, M. L., & Midgley, C. (1991). Enhancing student motivation: A schoolwide approach. *Educational Psychologist, 26,* 399–427.

Magnusson, D., & Allen, V. L. (1983). *Human development: An interactional perspective.* New York: Academic Press.

Magnusson, D., & Endler, N. S. (Eds.). (1977). *Personality at the crossroads: Current issues in interactional psychology.* Hillsdale, NJ: Lawrence Erlbaum Associates.

Magnusson, D., & Törestad, B. (1993). A holistic view of personality: A model revisited. *Annual Review of Psychology, 44,* 425–451.

Malone, T. W., & Lepper, M. R. (1987). Making learning fun: A taxonomy of intrinsic motivations for learning. In R. E. Snow & M. J. Farr (Eds.), *Aptitude, learning, and instruction: Vol. 3. Conative and affective process analyses* (pp. 223–250). Hillsdale, NJ: Lawrence Erlbaum Associates.

Mandler, G., & Sarason, S. (1952). A study of anxiety and learning. *Journal of Abnormal and Social Psychology, 47,* 166–173.

Marks, M. R. (1964). How to build better theories, tests, and therapies: The off-quadrant approach. *American Psychologist, 19,* 793–798.

Markus, H. (1977). Self-schemas and processing information about the self. *Journal of Personality and Social Psychology, 55,* 858–866.

Markus, H., & Nurius, P. (1986). Possible selves. *American Psychologist, 41,* 954–969.

Marsh, H. W. (1984). Relations among dimensions of self-attributions, dimensions of self-concept, and academic achievements. *Journal of Educational Psychology, 76,* 1291–1308.

Marsh, H. W. (1986). Causal effects of academic self concept on academic achievement: A reanalysis of Newman (1984). Unpublished report, Department of Education, University of Sydney, New South Wales, Australia (Ed 278 684).

Marsh, H. W. (1988). *Self Description Questionnaire: A theoretical and empirical basis for the measurement of multiple dimensions of preadolescent self-concept: A test manual and a research monograph.* San Antonio, TX: Psychological Corp.

Marsh, H. W. (1989). Age and sex effects in multiple dimensions of self-concept: Preadolescence to early childhood. *Journal of Educational Psychology, 81,* 417–430.

Marsh, H. W. (1990). A multidimensional, hierarchical model of self-concept: Theoretical and empirical justification. *Educational Psychology Review, 2,* 77–171.

Marsh, H. W. (1991). Students' evaluations of teaching effectiveness: The stability of mean ratings of the same teachers over a 13-year period. *Teaching and Teacher Education, 7,* 303–314.

Marsh, H. W., & Peart, N. (1988). Competitive and cooperative physical fitness training programs for girls: Effects on physical fitness and on multidimensional self-concepts. *Journal of Sport Exercise Psychology, 10,* 390–407.

Marshall, J. C., & Merritt, S. L. (1986). Reliability and construct validity of the learning style questionnaire. *Educational and Psychological Measurement, 46,* 257–262.

Marshall, J. C., & Weinstein, R. S. (1986). Classroom context of student-perceived differential teacher treatment. *Journal of Educational Psychology, 78,* 441–453.

Marton, F., Hounsell, D. J., & Entwistle, N. J. (Eds.). (1984). *The experience of learning.* Edinburgh: Scottish Academic Press.

Marton, F., & Säljö, R. (1976). On qualitative differences in learning: I. Outcome and process. *British Journal of Educational Psychology, 46,* 4–11.

McCaslin, M., & Good, T. L. (1992). Compliant cognition: The misalliance of management and instruction goals in current school reform. *Educational Researcher, 21*(3), 4–17.

McCaslin, M., Tuck, D., Wiard, A., Brown, B., LaPage, J. & Pyle, J. (1994). Gender composition and small group learning in fourth-grade mathematics. *Elementary School Journal, 94,* 467–482.

McClelland, D. C., Atkinson, J. W., Clark, R. A., & Lowell, E. L. (1953). *The achievement motive.* New York: Appleton-Century-Crofts.

McClelland, D. C. (1961). *The achieving society.* Princeton, NJ: Van Nostrand.

McCrae, R. R., & Costa, P. T., Jr. (1994). The stability of personality: Observations and evaluations. *Current Directions in Psychological Science, 3,* 173–175.

McDougall, W. (1923). *Outline of psychology.* New York: Scribner.

McDougall, W. (1933). *Energies of men.* New York: Scribner.

McGuire, W. J. (1968). Personality and susceptibility fo social influence. In E. F. Borgatta & W. W. Lambert (Eds.), *Handbook of personality theory and research* (pp. 1130–1187). Chicago: Rand McNally.

McGuire, W. J. (1972). Attitude change: The information-processing paradigm. In C. G. McClintock (Eds.), *Experimental social psychology* (pp. 108–141). New York: Holt, Rinehart & Winston.

McGuire, W. J. (1985). Attitudes and attitude change. In G. Lindzey & E. Aronson (Eds.), *Handbook of social psychology* (3rd ed., Vol. 2, pp. 233–346). New York: Random House.

McGuire, W. J. (1990). Dynamic operations of thought systems. *American Psychologist, 45,* 504–512.

McKenna, F. P. (1984). Measures of field dependence: Cognitive style or cognitive ability? *Journal of Personality and Social Psychology, 47,* 593–603.

McKenna, F. P. (1990). Learning implications of field dependence-independence: Cognitive style versus cognitive ability, *Applied Cognitive Psychology, 4,* 425–437.

Melton, A. W. (1964). *Categories of human learning.* New York: Academic Press.

Mershon, B., & Gorsuch, R. L. (1988). Number of factors in the personality sphere: Does increase in factors increase predictability of real-life criteria? *Journal of Personality and Social Psychology, 55,* 675–680.

Messick, S. (Ed.). (1976). *Individuality in learning: Implications of cognitive styles and creativity for human development.* San Francisco: Jossey-Bass.

Messick, S. (1983). Assessment of children. In P. H. Mussen (Ed.), *Handbook of child psychology* (4th ed., pp. 477–526). New York: Wiley.

Messick, S. (1987). Structured relationships across cognition, personality and style. In R. E. Snow & M. C. Farr (Eds.), *Aptitude, learning and instruction: Vol. 3. Conative and affective process analyses* (pp. 35–75). Hillsdale, NJ: Lawrence Erlbaum Associates.

Messick, S. (1989a). *Cognitive style and personality: Scanning and orientation toward affect* (RR-89-16). Princeton, NJ: Educational Testing Service.

Messick, S. (1989b). Validity, In R. L. Linn (Ed.), *Educational measurement* (3rd ed., pp. 13–103). New York: Macmillan.

Messick, S. (1993). *Human abilities and modes of attention: The issue of stylistic consistencies in cognition* (RR-93-43). Princeton, NJ: Educational Testing Service.

Messick, S. (1994). The matter of style: Manifestations of personality in cognition, learning, and teaching. *Educational Psychologist, 29,* 121–136.

Meyer, J. H. F. (1991). Study orchestration: The manifestation, interpretation and consequences of contextualized approaches to studying. *Higher Education, 22,* 297–316.

Midgley, C., Anderman, E. M., & Hicks, L. (in press). Differences between elementary and middle school teachers and students: A goal theory approach. *Journal of Early Adolescence.*

Miller, A. (1981). Conceptual matching models and interaction research. *Review of Educational Research, 51,* 33–84.

Mischel, W. (1968). *Personality and assessment.* New York: Wiley.

Mischel, W. (1983). Alternatives in the pursuit of the predictability and consistency of persons: Stable data that yield unstable interpretations. *Journal of Personality, 51,* 578–604.

Mischel, W. (1984). Convergences and challenges in the search for consistency. *American Psychologist, 39,* 351–364.

Mischel, W. (1990). Personality dispositions revisited and revised: A view after three decades. In L. A. Pervin (Ed.), *Handbook of personality: Theory and research* (pp. 111–132). New York: Guilford Press.

Miskel, C. G. (1982). Motivation in educational organizations. *Educational Administration Quarterly, 18*(3), 65–88.

Moos, R. (1979). *Evaluating educational environments.* San Francisco: Jossey-Bass.

Morris, J. H., & Snyder, R. A. (1978). Convergent validities of the resultant achievement motivation test and the presatie motivatie test with Ac and Ai scales of the CPI. *Educational and Psychological Measurement, 38,* 1151–1155.

Morris, L. W., Davis, M. A., & Hutchings, C. H. (1981). Cognitive and emotional components of anxiety: Literature review and a revised worry-emotionality scale. *Journal of Educational Psychology, 73,* 541–555.

Moss, F. A., Hung, T., & Omwake, K. (1949). *Social Intelligence Test.* Montreal, PQ: Institute of Psychological Research.

Munby, H. (1982). The place of teachers' beliefs in research on teaching thinking and decision making, and an alternative methodology. *Instructional Science, 11,* 201–225.

Murgatroyd, S., Rushton, C., Apter, M., & Ray, C. (1978). The development of the Telic Dominance Scale. *Journal of Personality Assessment, 42,* 519–528.

Murray, H. A. (1938). *Explorations in personality.* Cambridge, MA: Harvard University Press.

Myers, I. B., & McCaulley, M. H. (1993). *Manual: A guide to the development and use of the Myers–Briggs Type Indicator.* Palo Alto, CA: Consulting Psychologists Press.

Naveh-Benjamin, M., McKeachie, W. J., & Lin, Y. G. (1987). Two types of test anxious students: Support for an information processing model. *Journal of Educational Psychology, 79,* 131–136.

Naveh-Benjamin, M., McKeachie, W. J., Lin, Y. G., & Tucker, D. G. (1986). Inferring students' cognitive structures and their development using the "ordered tree technique." *Journal of Educational Psychology, 78,* 130–140.

Neimeyer, R. A. (1985). *The development of personal construct psychology.* Lincoln: University of Nebraska Press.

Nenniger, P. (1987). How stable is motivation by contents? In E. de Corte, H. Lodwijks, R. Parmentier, & P. Span (Eds.), *Learning and instruction: European research in an international context* (Vol. 1, pp. 159–179). London: Pergamon Press.

Nespor, J. (1987). The role of beliefs in the practice of teaching. *Journal of Curriculum Studies, 19,* 317–328.

Newell, A., & Simon, H. A. (1972). *Human problem solving.* Englewood Cliffs, NJ: Prentice Hall.

Newman, R. S. (1984). Children's achievement and self evaluations in mathematics: A longitudinal study. *Journal of Educational Psychology, 76,* 857–873.

Nicholls, J. G. (1979). Development of perception of own attainment and causal attribution for success and failure in reading. *Journal of Educational Psychology, 71,* 94–99.

Nicholls, J. G. (1984). Achievement motivation: Conceptions of ability, subjective experience, task choice, and performance. *Psychological Review, 92,* 328–346.

Nicholls, J. G., Patashnick, M., & Nolen, S. B. (1985). Adolescents' theories of education. *Journal of Educational Psychology, 77,* 683–692.

Nisbett, R. E., & Ross, L. (1980). *Human interference: Strategies and shortcomings of social judgment.* Englewood Cliffs, NJ: Prentice Hall.

Nolen, S. (1988). Reasons for studying: Motivational orientations and study strategies. *Cognition and Instruction, 5,* 269–287.

Norman, D. A. & Shallice, T. (1986). Attention to action: Willed and automatic control of behavior. In R. J. Davidson, G. E. Schwartz, & D. Shapiro (Eds.), *Consciousness and self-regulation: Advances in research* (Vol. 4, pp. 1–18) New York: Plenum Press.

Nuttin, J. (1984). *Motivation, planning, and action.* Leuven, Belgium, and Hillsdale, NJ: Leuven University Press and Lawrence Erlbaum Associates.

Nuttin, J., & Lens, W. (1985). *Future time perspective and motivation.* Leuven, Belgium, and Hillsdale, NJ: Leuven University Press and Lawrence Erlbaum Associates.

O'Hair, D., & Cody, M. J. (1987). Machiavellian beliefs and social influence. *Western Journal of Speech Communication, 51,* 279–303.

Olson, J. M., & Zanna, M. P. (1993). Attitudes and attitude change. *Annual Review of Psychology, 44,* 117–154.

Olweus, D. (1979). Stability of aggressive reaction patterns in males: A review. *Psychological Bulletin, 86,* 852–875.

Olweus, D. (1984). Development of stable aggressive reaction patterns in males. In R. Blanchard & C. Blanchard (Eds.), *Advances in the study of aggression* (Vol. 1.). New York: Academic Press.

Olweus, D. (in press). *Bullying at school: What we know and what we can do.* Oxford, U.K.: Blackwell.

Ortony, A., Clore, G. L., & Collins, A. (1988). *The cognitive structure of emotions.* New York: Cambridge University Press.

Osgood, C. E., Suci, G. J., & Tannenbaum, P. H. (1957). *The measurement of meaning.* Urbana: University of Illinois Press.

O'Sullivan, M., & Guilford, J. P. (1975). Six factors of behavioral cognition: Understanding other people. *Journal of Educational Measurement, 12,* 255–271.

Ozer, D. J., & Reise, S. P. (1994). Personality assessment. *Annual Review of Psychology, 45,* 357–388.

Pace, C. R., & Stern, G. G. (1958). An approach to the measurement of psychological characteristics of college environments. *Journal of Educational Psychology, 49,* 269–277.

Pajares, M. F. (1992). Teachers' beliefs and educational research: Clearing up a messy construct. *Review of Educational Research, 62,* 307–332.

Paris, S. G., & Winograd, P. (1990). Promoting metacognition and motivation of exceptional children. *Remedial and Special Education, 11,* 7–15.

Pask, G. (1976). Styles and strategies of learning. *British Journal of Educational Psychology, 46,* 128–148.

Pask, G. (1988). Learning strategies, teaching strategies, and conceptual or learning style. In R. R. Schmeck (Ed.), *Learning strategies and learning styles* (pp. 83–99). New York: Plenum, Press.

Pekrun, R. (1992). Emotions in learning and achievement. In D. Frey (Ed.) *Proceedings of the 37th Congress of the German Psychological Association at Kiel 1990* (Vol. 2). Gottingen: Hogrefe.

Pekrun, R. (1994, April). Academic emotions in students' self regulated learning. Paper presented at the meeting of the American Education Research Association, New Orleans.

Pekrun, R., & Frese, M. (1992). Emotions in work and achievement. In C. L. Cooper & I. T. Robertson (Eds.), *International Review of Industrial and Organizational Psychology, 7,* 153–200. London: Wiley.

Perkins, D. N., Jay, E., & Tishman, S. (1993). New conceptions of thinking: From ontology to education. In *New conceptions of thinking* [Special issue]. *Educational Psychologist, 28,* 67–85.

Pervin, L. A. (Ed.). (1990). *Handbook of personality: Theory and research.* New York: Guilford Press.

Peterson, P. L. (1976). Interactive effects of student anxiety, achievement orientation, and teacher behavior on student achievement and aptitude. Unpublished doctoral dissertation; Stanford University, Stanford, CA.

Pintrich, P. R. (1989). The dynamic interplay of student motivation and cognition in the college classroom. In C. Ames & M. L. Maehr (Eds.), *Advances in motivation and achievement: Vol. 6. Motivation-enhancing environments* (pp. 117–160). Greenwich, CT: JAI Press.

Pintrich, P. R. (1990). Implications of the psychological research on student learning and college teaching for teacher education. In R. Houston (Ed.), *The handbook of research on teacher education* (pp. 826–857). New York: Macmillian.

Pintrich, P. R., & DeGroot, E. (1990). Motivational and self-regulated learning components of classroom academic performance. *Journal of Educational Psychology, 82,* 33–40.

Pintrich, P. R. & Garcia, T. (1991). Student goal orientation and self-regulation in the college classroom. In M. L. Maehr & P. R. Pintrich (Eds.), *Advances in motivation and achievement: Vol. 7.* (pp. 371–402) Greenwich, CT: JAI Press.

Pintrich, P. R., Marx, R. W., & Boyle, R. A. (1993). Beyond cold conceptual change: The role of motivational beliefs and classroom contextual factors in the process of conceptual change. *Review of Educational Research, 63,* 167–199.

Pintrich, P. R., & Schrauben, B. (1992). Students' motivational beliefs and their cognitive engagement in academic tasks. In D. Schunk & J. Meece (Eds.), *Students' perceptions in the classroom: Causes and consequences* (pp. 149–183) Hillsdale, NJ: Lawrence Erlbaum Associates.

Pintrich, P. R., Smith, D. A. F., Garcia, T., & McKeachie, W. J. (1991). *A manual for the use of the motivated strategies for learning questionaire (MSLQ)* (Tech. Rep. No. 91-B-004). Ann Arbor: University of Michigan, National Center for Research to Improve Postsecondary Teaching and Learning.

Pintrich, R. P., Smith, D. A. F., Garcia, R., & McKeachie, W. J. (1993). Reliability and predictive validity of the Motivated Strategies for Learning Questionnaire (MSLQ). *Educational and Psychological Measurement, 53,* 801–813.

Pittenger, D. J. (1993). The utility of the Myers-Briggs Type Indicator. *Review of Educational Research, 63,* 467–488.

Pittman, T. S., & D'Agostino, P. R. (1989). Motivation and cognition: Control deprivation and the nature of subsequent information processing. *Journal of Experimental Social Psychology, 25,* 465–480.

Platt, J. J., & Eisenmann, R. (1968). Internal-external control of reinforcement, time perspective, adjustment, and anxiety. *Journal of General Psychology, 79,* 121–128.

Plomin, R. (1989). Environment and genes: Determinants of behavior. In *Children and their development: Knowledge base, research agenda, and social policy application* [Special issue]. *American Psychologist, 44,* 105–111.

Plomin, R. (1994). *Genetics and experience: The interplay between nature and nurture.* Thousand Oaks, CA: Sage.

Plomin, R., Chipuer, H. M. & Loehlin, J. C. (1990). Behavioral genetics and personality. In L. A. Pervin (Ed.), *Handbook of personality: Theory and research* (pp. 225–240). New York: Guilford Press.

Porteus, A. W. (1976). *Teacher-centered vs. student-centered instruction. Interaction with cognitive and motivational aptitudes.* Unpublished doctoral dissertation, Stanford University, Stanford, CA.

Prenzel, M. (1988, April). *Conditions for the persistence of interest*. Paper presented at the meeting of the American Educational Research Association, New Orleans.

Pressley, M., Goodchild, F., Fleet, J., Zajchowski, R., & Evans, E. (1989). The challenges of classroom strategy instruction. *Elementary School Journal, 89,* 301–342.

Pressley, M., & Levin, J. (1983). *Cognitive strategy research: Psychological foundations*. New York: Springer.

Purkey, W. W. (1983). Self-concept as learner: An overlooked part of self-concept theory. *Journal of Humanistic Education and Development, 22,* 52–57.

Rand, P., Lens, W., & Decock, D. (1989). *Negative motivation is half the story* (Tech. Rep. No. 41) Psychological Reports. Leuven, Belgium: University of Leuven.

Ray, J. J. (1982). *Self-report measures of achievement motivation: A catalog*. New South Wales, Australia: University of New South Wales. (Eric Document No. ED237523).

Renninger, K. A., Hidi, S., & Krapp, A. (1992). *The role of interest in learning and development*. Hillsdale, NJ: Lawrence Erlbaum Associates.

Rest, S., Neirenberg, R., Weiner, B., & Heckhausen, H. (1973). Further evidence concerning the effects of perceptions of effort and ability on achievement evaluation. *Journal of Personality and Social Psychology, 28,* 187–191.

Revelle, W. (1989). Personality, motivation, and cognitive performance. In R. Kanfer, P. L. Ackerman, & R. Cudeck (Eds.), *Abilities, motivation, and methodology* (pp. 297–341). Hillsdale, NJ: Lawrence Erlbaum Associates.

Reynolds, C. R., & Willson, V. L. (Eds.). (1985). *Methodological and statistical advances in the study of individual differences*. New York: Plenum Press.

Rhodes, N., & Wood, W. (1992). Self esteem and intelligence affect influenceability: The mediating role of message reception. *Psychological Bulletin, 111,* 156–171.

Richardson, A. (1977). Verbalizer-visualizer: A cognitive style dimension. *Journal of Mental Imagery, 1,* 109–126.

Richford, M. L., & Fortune, J. C. (1984). The secondary principal's job satisfaction in relation to two personality constructs. *Education, 105,* 17–20.

Robinson, J. P., Shaver, P. R., & Wrightsman, L. S. (1991). (Eds.). *Measures of Personality and Social Psychological Attitudes*. San Diego, CA: Academic Press.

Rocklin, T. (1994). Relation between typical intellectual engagement and openness: Comment on Goff and Ackerman (1992). *Journal of Educational Psychology, 86,* 145–149.

Rogers, T. B. (1974). An analysis of the stages underlying the process of responding to personality items. *Acta Psychologica, 38,* 205–213.

Rokeach, M. (1960). *The open and closed mind*. New York: Basic Books.

Rokeach, M. (1968). *Beliefs, attitudes, and values*. San Francisco: Jossey-Bass.

Rollett, B. A. (1987). Effort avoidance and learning. In E. De-Corte, H. Lodewijks, R. Parmentier, & P. Span (Eds.), *Learning and instruction: European research in an international context* (Vol. 1, pp. 147–157). Leuven, Belgium, and Oxford, U.K.: Leuven University Press and Pergamon Press.

Rorer, L. G. (1990). Personality assessment: A conceptual survey. In L. A. Pervin (Ed.), *Handbook of personality: Theory and research* (pp. 693–718). New York: Guilford Press.

Rosenberg, M. (1965). *Society and the adolescent self-image*. Princeton, NJ: Princeton University Press.

Rosenberg, M. (1979). *Conceiving the self*. New York: Basic Books.

Rosenthal, R., Hall, J. A., DiMatteo, M.. R., Rogers, P. L., & Archer, D. (1979). *Sensitivity to nonverbal communication: The PONS test*. Baltimore, MD: Johns Hopkins University Press.

Ross, L., & Nisbett, R. E. (1991). *The person and the situation: Perspectives of social psychology*. New York: McGraw-Hill.

Rotter, J. B. (1966). Generalized expectancies for internal vs. external control of reinforcement, *Psychological Monographs, 80* (1, Whole No. 609).

Royce, J. R., & Powell, A. (1983). *Theory of personality and individual differences: Factors, systems, and processes*. Englewood Cliffs, NJ: Prentice Hall.

Rutkowski, K., & Domino, G. (1975). Interrelationship of study skills and personality variables in college students. *Journal of Educational Psychology, 67,* 784–789.

Ruvolo, A. P., & Markus, H. R. (1986). Possible selves and performance: The power of self-relevant imagery. In *Self-knowledge: Content, structure, and function* [Special issue]. *Social Cognition, 10,* 95–124.

Ryan, R. M., & Connell, J. P. (1989). Perceived locus of causality and internalization: Examining reasons for acting in two domains. *Journal of Personality and Social Psychology, 57,* 749–761.

Ryan, R. M., Connell, J. P., & Deci, E. L. (1985). A motivational analysis of self-determination and self-regulation in education. In C. Ames & R. E. Ames (Eds.), *Research on motivation in education: Vol. 2, The classroom milieu* (pp. 13–51). New York: Academic Press.

Ryan, T. A. (1981). Intention and kinds of learning. In G. d'Ydewalle & W. Lens (Eds.), *Cognition in human motivation and learning* (pp. 59–85). Leuven, Belgium, and Hillsdale, NJ: Leuven University Press and Lawrence Erlbaum Associates.

Saklofske, D. H., & Zeidner, M. (1995). *International handbook of personality and intelligence*. New York: Plenum Press.

Säljö, R. (1975). *Qualitative differences in learning as a function of the learner's conception of the task*. Göteborg, Sweden: Acta Universitatis Gothoburgensis.

Säljö, R. (1982). *Learning and understanding: A study of differences in constructing meaning from a text*. Göteborg, Sweden: Acta Universitatis Gothoburgensis.

Salomon, G. (1981). *Communication and education: Social and psychological interactions*. Beverly Hills, CA: Saga.

Salomon, G. (1983). The differential investment of mental effort in learning from different sources. *Educational Psychologist, 18,* 42–50.

Salomon, G. (1984). Television is "easy" and print is "tough": The differential investment of mental effort in learning as a function of perceptions and attributions. *Journal of Educational Psychology, 76,* 647–658.

Salomon, G. (1987, September). *Beyond skill and knowledge: The role of mindfulness in learning and transfer*. Paper presented at the Second European Conference for Research on Learning and Instruction, Tübingen, Germany.

Salomon, G. (1991). Transcending the qualitative-quantitative debate: The analytic and systemic approaches to educational research. *Educational Researcher, 20*(6), 10–18.

Salomon, G., & Leigh, T. (1984). Predispositions about learning from print and television. *Journal of Communication, 20,* 119–135.

Scarr, S. (1992). Developmental theories for the 1990s: Development and individual differences. *Child Development, 63,* 1–19.

Scheirer, M., & Kraut, R. E. (1979). Increasing educational achievement via self-concept change. *Review of Educational Research, 49,* 131–149.

Schiefele, U. (1991). Interest, learning, and motivation. *Educational Psychologist, 26,* 299–323.

Schiefele, U., & Csikszentmihalyi, M. (in press). Motivation and ability as factors in mathematics experience and achievement. *Journal for Research in Mathematics Education*.

Schiefele, U., & Krapp, A. (1988, April). *The impact of interest on qualitative and structural indicators of knowledge*. Paper presented at the meeting of the American Educational Research Association, New Orleans.

Schiefele, U., Krapp, A., & Winteler, A. (1988, April). *Conceptualization and measurement of interest*. Paper presented at the meeting of the American Educational Research Association, New Orleans.

Schiefele, U., Krapp, A., & Winteler, A. (1992). Interest as a predictor of academic achievement: A meta-analysis of research. In K. A. Renninger, S. Hidi, & A. Krapp (Eds.), *The role of interest in learning and development* (pp. 183–211). Hillsdale, NJ: Lawrence Erlbaum Associates.

Schlenker, B. (1985). Identity and self-identification. In B. R. Schlenker (Ed.), *The self and social life* (pp. 65–99). New York: McGraw-Hill.

Schmeck, R. R. (1983). Learning styles of college students. In R. Dillon & R. R. Schmeck (Eds.), *Individual difference in cognition* (Vol. 1, pp. 233–279). New York: Academic Press.

Schmeck, R. R. (1988a). (Ed.). *Learning strategies and learning styles.* New York: Plenum Press.

Schmeck, R. R. (1988b). Strategies and style of learning. In R. R. Schmeck (Ed.), *Learning strategies and learning styles* (pp. 317–345). New York: Plenum Press.

Schmeck, R. R., Rebich, F. D., & Ramanaiah, N. (1977). Development of a self-report inventory for assessing individual differences in learning processes. *Applied Psychological Measurement, 1,* 413–431.

Schmitt, A. P., & Crocker, L. (1981, April). *Improving examinee performance on multiple-choice tests.* Paper presented at the meeting of the American Educational Research Association, Los Angeles.

Schunk, D. H. (1985). Participation in goal setting: Effects on self-efficacy and skills of learning disabled children. *Journal of Special Education, 19,* 307–317.

Schunk, D. H. (1989, March). Attributions and perceptions of efficacy during self-regulated learning by remedial readers. Paper presented at the meeting of the American Educational Research Association, San Francisco.

Schunk, D. H. (1991). Self-efficacy and academic motivation, *Educational Psychologist, 26*(3 & 4), 207–231.

Schunk, D. H. & Zimmerman, B. J. (Eds.). (1994). *Self-regulation of learning and performance: Issues and educational applications.* Hillsdale, NJ: Lawrence Erlbaum Associates.

Schwarzer, R. (1992). *Self-efficacy: Thought control of action.* Washington, DC: Hemisphere.

Schwarzer, R., Van Der Ploeg, H. M., & Spielberger, C. D. (Eds.) (1982). *Advances in Test anxiety research.* Vol. 1, Lisse, The Netherlands: Swets and Zeitlinger.

Sears, P. S. (1963). Self-concept in the service of educational goals. *California Journal for Instructional Improvement, 6,* 3–12.

Sells, S. (Ed.). (1963). *Stimulus determinants of behavior.* New York: Ronald Press.

Shavelson, R. J., & Bolus, R. (1982). Self-concept: The interplay of theory and methods. *Journal of Educational Psychology, 74,* 3–17.

Shavelson, R. J., Hubner, J. J., & Stanton, G. C. (1976). Self-concept: Validation of construct interpretations. *Review of Educational Research, 46,* 407–441.

Shaver, P. (1976). Questions concerning fear of success and its conceptual relatives. *Sex Roles, 2,* 305–320.

Sheldon, W. H. (1942). *The varieties of human temperament.* New York: Harper.

Shoham-Salomon, V., & Hanna, M. T. (1991). Client-treatment interaction in the study of differential change processes. *Journal of Consulting and Clinical Psychology, 59,* 217–225.

Shybut, J. (1968). Time perspective, internal versus external control and severity of psychological disturbance. *Journal of Clinical Psychology, 24,* 312–315.

Sieber, J. E., O'Neil, H. F., & Tobias, S. (1977). *Anxiety, learning, and instruction.* Hillsdale, NJ: Lawrence Erlbaum Associates.

Siegler, R. S., & Campbell, J. (1989). Individual differences in children's strategy choices. In P. L. Ackerman, R. J. Sternberg, & R. Glaser (Eds.), *Learning and individual differences: Advances in theory and research* (pp. 219–254). New York: Freeman.

Simon, H. A. (1982). *Models of bounded rationality.* Cambridge, MA: MIT Press.

Sjöberg, L. (1983). Interest, achievement and vocational choice. *European Journal of Science Education, 5,* 299–307.

Sjöberg, L., Svensson, E., & Persson, L.-O. (1979). The measurement of mood. *Scandinavian Journal of Psychology, 20,* 1–18.

Skaalvik, E. M. (1990). Gender differences in general academic self-esteem and in success expectations on defined academic problems. *Journal of Educational Psychology, 82,* 593–598.

Slavin, R. E. (1983). *Cooperative learning* (Research on Teaching Monograph Series). New York: Longman.

Smith, C. P. (Ed.). (1992). *Motivation and personality: Handbook of thematic content analysis.* New York: Cambridge University Press.

Smith, M. L., & Shepard, L. A. (1988). Kindergarten readiness and retention: A qualitative study of teachers' beliefs and practices. *American Educational Research Journal, 25,* 307–333.

Snow, R. E. (1977a). Individual differences and instructional theory. *Educational Researcher, 6*(10), 11–15.

Snow, R. E. (1977b). Research on aptitudes: A progress report. In L. S. Shulman (Ed.), *Review of research in education* (Vol. 4, pp. 50–105). Itasca, IL: Peacock.

Snow, R. E. (1980). Aptitude processes. In R. E. Snow, P. A. Federico, & W. E. Montague (Eds.), *Aptitude, learning and instruction: Vol 1. Cognitive process analyses of aptitude* (pp. 27–64). Hillsdale, NJ: Lawrence Erlbaum Associates.

Snow, R. E. (1981). Toward a theory of aptitude for learning: Fluid and crystallized abilities and their correlates. In M. P. Friedman, J. P. Das, & N. O'Connor (Eds.), *Intelligence and learning* (pp. 345–362), New York: Plenum Press.

Snow, R. E. (1987). Aptitude complexes. In R. E. Snow & M. J. Farr (Eds.), *Aptitude, learning, and instruction: Vol. 3. Conative and affective process analyses* (pp. 11–34). Hillsdale, NJ: Lawrence Erlbaum Associates.

Snow, R. E. (1989a). Aptitude-treatment interaction as a framework of research in individual differences in learning. In P. L. Ackerman, R. J. Sternberg, & R. Glaser (Eds.), *Learning and individual differences: Advances in theory and research* (pp. 13–59). New York: Freeman.

Snow, R. E. (1989b). Cognitive-conative aptitude interactions in learning. In R. Kanfer, P. L. Ackerman, & R. Cudeck (Eds.), *Abilities, motivation, and methodology* (pp. 435–474). Hillsdale, NJ: Lawrence Erlbaum Associates.

Snow, R. E. (1989c). Toward assessment of cognitive and conative structures in learning. *Educational Researcher, 18*(9), 8–14.

Snow, R. E. (1990). New approaches to cognitive and conative assessment in education. *International Journal of Educational Research, 14,* 455–473.

Snow, R. E. (1991). The concept of aptitude. In R. E. Snow & D. F. Wiley (Eds.), *Improving inquiry in social science* (pp. 249–284). Hillsdale, NJ: Lawrence Erlbaum Associates.

Snow, R. E. (1992). Aptitude theory: Yesterday, today, and tomorrow, *Educational Psychologist, 27,* 5–32.

Snow, R. E. (1994). Abilities in academic tasks. In R. J. Sternberg & R. K. Wagner (Eds.), *Mind in context: Interactionist perspectives on human intelligence* (pp. 3–37). New York: Cambridge University Press.

Snow, R. E., & Jackson, D. N. III. (1994). Individual differences in conation: Selected constructs and measures. In H. F. O'Neill, Jr., & M. Drillings (Eds.), *Motivation: Research and theory* (pp. 71–99). Hillsdale, NJ: Lawrence Erlbaum Associates.

Snowman, J. (1986). Learning tactics and strategies. In G. D. Phye & T. Andre (Eds.), *Cognitive instructional psychology: Components of classroom learning* (pp. 243–275). New York: Academic Press.

Sockett, H. (1988). Education and will: Aspects of personal capability. *American Journal of Education, 96,* 195–214.

Sorrentino, R. M., & Short, J.-A. C. (1985). Uncertainty orientation, motivation, and cognition. In R. M. Sorrentino & E. T. Higgins (Eds.), *The handbook of motivation and cognition: Foundations of social behavior* (pp. 379–403). New York: Guilford Press.

Spangler, W. D. (1992). Validity of questionnaire and TAT measures of need for achievement: Two meta-analyses. *Psychological Bulletin, 112,* 140–154.

Spearman, C. (1927). *The abilities of man.* New York: Macmillan.

Spence, J. T., & Helmreich, R. L. (1983). Achievement related motives and behavior. In J. T. Spence (Ed.), *Achievement and achievement motives: Psychological and sociological approaches* (pp. 7–68). San Francisco: Freeman.

Spielberger, C. D. (1980). *Test Anxiety Inventory ("Test Attitude Inventory"): Preliminary professional manual.* Palo Alto, CA: Consulting Psychologists Press.

Srull, T. K., & Karabenick, S. A. (1975). Effects of personality-situation locus of control congruence. *Journal of Personality and Social Psychology, 32,* 617–628.

Stein, N. L., & Levine, L. J. (1987). Thinking about feelings: The development and organization of emotional knowledge. In R. E. Snow & M. J. Farr (Eds.), *Aptitudes, learning, and instruction: Vol. 3. Conative and affective process analyses* (pp. 165–196). Hillsdale, NJ: Lawrence Erlbaum Associates.

Steinkamp, M. W., & Maehr, M. L. (1983). Affect, ability, and science achievement: A quantitative synthesis of correlational research. *Review of Educational Research, 53,* 369–396.

Steinkamp, M. W., & Maehr, M. L. (1984). Gender differences in motivational orientations toward achievement in school science: A quantitative synthesis. *American Educational Research Journal, 21,* 39–59.

Stern, G. (1963). Measuring noncognitive variables in research on teaching. In N. L. Gage (Ed.), *Handbook of research on teaching* (pp. 399–447). Chicago: Rand McNally.

Sternberg, R. J. (Ed.). (1985). *Human abilities: An information processing approach.* New York: Freeman.

Sternberg, R. J. (Ed.) (1990). *Wisdom: Its nature, origins, and development.* New York: Cambridge University Press.

Sternberg, R. J. (1992, August). Optimizing student potential by teaching practical intelligence for school. Paper presented at the meeting of the American Psychological Association, Washington, D.C.

Sternberg, R. J., & Detterman, D. K. (Eds.). (1986). *What Is intelligence?* Norwood, NJ: Ablex.

Sternberg, R. J., & Wagner, R. K. (1986). *Practical intelligence: Nature and origins of competence in the everyday world.* New York: Cambridge University Press.

Stone, W. F., & Lederer, G. (Eds.). (1991). *Strength and weakness: The authoritarian personality today.* New York: Springer.

Strelau, J. (1983). *Temperament-persaonality-activity.* New York: Academic Press.

Strelau, J., Farley, F. H., & Gale, A. (Eds.). (1985). *The biological bases of personality and behavior: Vol. 1. Theories, measurement techniques, and development.* Washington, DC: Hemisphere.

Strelau, J., Farley, F. H., & Gale, A. (Eds.). (1986). *The biological bases of personality and behavior: Vol. 2. Psychophysiology, performance, and application.* Washington, DC: Hemisphere.

Stricker, L. J., & Rock, D. A. (1990). Interpersonal competence, social intelligence, and general ability. *Personality and individual Differences, 11,* 833–839.

Suls, J., & Fletcher, B. (1986). The relative efficacy of avoidant and nonavoidant coping strategies: A meta-analysis. *Health Psychology, 4,* 249–288.

Swanson, J. H. (1990, April). *The effectiveness of tutorial strategies: An experimental evaluation.* Paper presented at the meeting of the American Educational Research Association, Boston.

Tabachnick, B. R., & Zeichner, K. M. (1984). The impact of the student teaching experience on the development of teacher perspectives. *Journal of Teacher Education, 35*(6), 28–36.

Tait, H., & Entwistle, N. J. (in press). Identifying students at risk through ineffective study strategies. *Higher Education.*

Talbert, J. E., McLaughlin, M. W., & Rowan, B. (1993). Understanding context effects on secondary school teaching. *Teachers College Record, 95,* 45–68.

Tellegen, A. (1982). *Brief manual for the Differential Personality Questionnaire.* Unpublished manuscript, University of Minnesota.

Tellegen, A. (1985). Structures of mood and personality and their relevance to assessing anxiety, with an emphasis on self-report. In A. H. Tuma & J. D. Maser (Eds.), *Anxiety and the anxiety disorders* (pp. 681–716). Hillsdale, NJ: Lawrence Erlbaum Associates.

Tharp, R. G. (1989). Psychocultural variables and constants: Effect on teaching and learning in schools. *American Psychologist, 44,* 349–359.

Thomas, A., & Chess, S. (1977). *Temperament and development.* New York: Brunner/Mazel.

Thorndike, E. L. (1912). The permanence of interests and their relation to abilities. *Popular Science Monthly, 81,* 449–456.

Thorndike, E. L. (1920). Intelligence and its uses. *Harper's Magazine, 140,* 227–235.

Thorndike, E. L. (1935). *Adult interests.* New York: Macmillan.

Thurstone, L. L. (1924). *The nature of intelligence.* Westport, CT: Greenwood Press.

Thurstone, L. L. (1948). Psychological implications of factor analysis. *American Psychologist, 3,* 402–408.

Tiedeman, J. (1989). Measures of cognitive style: A critical review. *Educational Psychologist, 24,* 261–275.

Tobias, S. (1985). Test anxiety: Interference, defective skills, and cognitive capacity. *Educational Psychologist, 20,* 135–142.

Tobias, S. (1994). Interest, prior knowledge, and learning, *Review of Educational Research, 64,* 37–54.

Tomkins, S. S. (1962). *Affect, imagery, consciousness: Vol. I. The positive affects.* New York: Springer.

Tomkins, S. S. (1963). *Affect, imagery, consciousness: Vol. II. The negative affects.* New York: Springer.

Tukey, J. W. (1969). Analyzing data: Sanctification or detective work. *American Psychologist, 24,* 83–91.

Vallerand, R. J., Blais, M. R., Briere, N. M., & Pelletier, L. G. (1989). Construction et validation de l'Echelle de Motivation en Education [Construction and validation of the Academic Motivation Scale]. *Canadian Journal of Behavioral Sciences, 21,* 323–349.

Van Calster, K., Lens, W., & Nuttin, J. R. (1987). *Attitude toward the personal future and its impact on motivation in high school students.* Unpublished report, University of Leuven, Belgium.

Van Der Ploeg, H. M. Schwarzer, R., & Spielberger, C. D. (Eds.) (1983). *Advances in test anxiety research.* Vol. 2., Lisse, The Netherlands: Swets and Zeitlinger.

Van Der Ploeg, H. M. Schwarzer, R., & Spielberger, C. D. (Eds.) (1984). *Advances in test anxiety research.* Vol. 3., Lisse, The Netherlands: Swets and Zeitlinger.

Volp, F. D., & Willower, D. J. (1977). The school superintendent and Machiavellianism. *Education, 97,* 257–262.

Wachs, T. D. (1992). *The nature of nurture.* Newbury Park, CA: Sage.

Wachs, T. D., & Plomin, R. (Eds.). (1991). *Conceptualization and measurement of organism-environment interaction.* Washington, DC: American Psychological Association.

Wagner, R. K., & Sternberg, R. J. (1987). Executive control in reading comprehension. In B. K. Britton & S. M. Glynn (Eds.), *Executive control processes in reading* (pp. 1–20). Hillsdale, NJ: Lawrence Erlbaum Associates.

Wainer, H., & Braun, H. I. (1988). *Test validity.* Hillsdale, NJ: Lawrence Erlbaum Associates.

Walker, R. E., & Foley, J. M. (1973). Social intelligence: Its history and measurement. *Psychological Reports, 33,* 451–459.

Walls, R. T., & Smith, T. S. (1970). Development of preference for delayed reinforcement in disadvantaged children. *Journal of Educational Psychology, 61,* 118–123.

Wang, M. C., & Lindvall, C. M. (1984). Individual differences and school learning environments. *Review of Research in Education, 11,* 161–225.

Wagner, S., & Demick, J. (Eds.). (1991). *Field dependence-independence: Cognitive styles across the life span.* Hillsdale, NJ: Lawrence Erlbaum Associates.

Warr, P., Cook, J., & Wall, T. (1979). Scales for the measurement of some work attitudes and aspects of psychological well-being. *Journal of Occupational Psychology, 52,* 129–148.

Watson, J. B. (1930). *Behaviorism* (rev. ed.). New York: Norton.

Watson, D., Clark, L. A., & Tellegen, A. (1988). Development and validation of brief measures of positive and negative affect: The PANAS scales. *Journal of Personality and Social Psychology, 54,* 1063–1070.

Webb, E. (1915). Character and intelligence. *British Journal of Psychology, Monograph Supplement,* Vol. I. No. III.

Wechsler, D. (1950). Cognitive, conative, and non-intellective intelligence. *American Psychologist, 5,* 78–83.

Weiner, B. (1986). *An attributional theory of motivation and emotion.* New York: Springer.

Weinstein, C. F., & Mayer, R. F. (1986). The teaching of learning styles. In M. C. Wittrock (Ed.), *Handbook of research on teaching* (3rd ed., pp. 315–327). New York: Macmillan.

Weinstein, C. E., Zimmerman, S. A., & Palmer, D. R. (1988). Assessing learning strategies: The design and development of the LASSI. In C. E. Weinstein, E. T. Goetz, & P. A. Alexander (Eds.) *Learning and study strategies* (pp. 25–40). San Diego, CA: Academic Press.

Weinstein, M. S. (1969). Achievement motivation and risk preference. *Journal of Personality and Social Psychology, 13,* 153–172.

Wentzel, K. R. (1989). Adolescent classroom goals, standards for performance, and academic achievement: An interactionist perspective. *Journal of Educational Psychology, 81,* 131–142.

Wentzel, K. R. (1991). Social competence at school: Relation between social responsibility and academic achievement. *Review of Educational Research, 61,* 1–24.

Wentzel, K. R. (1993a). Does being good make the grade? Social behavior and academic competence in middle school. *Journal of Educational Psychology, 85,* 357–364.

Wentzel, K. R. (1993b). Motivation and achievement in early adolescence: The role of multiple classroom goals. *Journal of Early Adolescence, 13,* 14–20.

White, R. W. (1959). Motivation reconsidered: The concept of competence. *Psychological Review, 66,* 297–333.

Wicklund, R. A., & Gollwitzer, P. M. (1982). *Symbolic self-completion.* Hillsdale, NJ: Lawrence Erlbaum Associates.

Wiggins, J. S. (1979). A psychological taxonomy of trait-descriptive terms: The interpersonal domain. *Journal of Personality and Social Psychology, 37,* 395–412.

Wiggins, J. S., & Pincus, A. L. (1992). Personality: Structure and assessment. *Annual Review of Psychology, 43,* 473–504.

Wijnen, W. H. F. W., & Snow R. E. (1975). *Implementing an evaluation system for medical education* (Tech. Rep. No. 1). Maastricht, The Netherlands: Medische Faculteit Maastricht.

Willingham, W. (1985). *Success in college.* New York: College Board.

Witkin, H. A. & Goodenough, D. R. (1981). *Cognitive styles: Essence and origins.* New York: International Universities Press.

Wrightsman, L. S. (1991). Interpersonal trust and attitudes toward human nature. In J. P. Robinson, P. R. Shaver, & L. S. Wrightsman (Eds.), *Measures of personality and social psychological attitudes* (pp. 373–412). San Diego, CA: Academic Press.

Wylie, R. C. (1979). *The self-concept* (Vol. 2). Lincoln: University of Nebraska Press.

Wylie, R. C. (1989). *Measures of self-concept.* Lincoln: University of Nebraska Press.

Zahn-Waxler, C., Cummings, M., & Iannotti, R. J. (1986). (Eds.). *Altruism and aggression: Biological and social origins.* New York: Cambridge University Press.

Zahn-Waxler, C., Radke-Yarrow, M., Wagner, E., & Chapman, M. (1992). Development of concern for others. *Development Psychology, 28,* 126–136.

Zahn-Waxler, C., Robinson, J., & Emde, R. (1992). The development of empathy in twins. *Developmental Psychology, 28,* 1038–1047.

Zajonc, R. B. (1980). Feeling and thinking: Preferences need no inferences. *American Psychologist, 35,* 151–175.

Zimmerman, B. J. (1989). A social cognitive view of self-regulated academic learning. *Journal of Educational Psychology, 81,* 329–339.

Zimmerman, B. J. (1990). Self-regulating academic learning and achievement: The emergence of a social cognitive perspective. *Educational Psychology Review, 2,* 173–201.

Zimmerman, B. J., Bandura, A., & Martinez-Pons, M. (1992). Self-motivation for academic attainment: The role of self-efficacy beliefs and personal goal setting. *American Educational Research Journal, 29,* 663–676.

Zimmerman, B. J., & Martinez-Pons, M. M. (1986). Development of a structured interview for assessing student use of self-regulated learning strategies. *American Educational Research Journal, 23,* 614–629.

Zimmerman, B. J., & Martinez-Pons, M. (1988). Construct validation of a strategy model of student self-regulated learning. *Journal of Educational Psychology, 80,* 284–290.

Zimmerman, B. J., & Schunk, D. H. (Eds.). (1989). *Self-regulated learning and academic acheivement.* New York: Springer.

Zuckerman, M. (1979). *Sensation seeking: Beyond the optimal level of arousal.* Hillsdale, NJ: Lawrence Erlbaum Associates.

Zythoskee, A., Strickland, B. R., & Watson, J. (1971). Delay of gratification and internal versus external control among adolescents of low socioeconomic status. *Developmental Psychology, 4,* 93–98.

# · 10 ·

# EXCEPTIONALITY

## Barbara K. Keogh

UNIVERSITY OF CALIFORNIA, LOS ANGELES

## Donald L. MacMillan

UNIVERSITY OF CALIFORNIA, RIVERSIDE

The study of individual differences has long been a mainstay of educational psychology. In his 1957 address to the American Psychological Association, Cronbach referred to correlational psychology as one of the two disciplines of scientific psychology, arguing for the importance of study of "variation between individuals, social groups, and species" (p. 671). In 1978 Tyler called for the study of "different patterns of mental organization, different repertoires of competencies, and different strategies and styles" (p. 235). Exceptional conditions may be viewed as particular subsets of individual differences, or as representing the extremes of continua of individual variations. The qualitative-quantitative question is fundamental to the conceptualization and definition of exceptionality and influences decisions about assessment, identification, and instruction. It is a recurring issue in subsequent sections of this chapter.

It is important to note that a multitude of individual characteristics (e.g., cognitive, motivational, and personality factors) are important influences on performance. From the perspective of educational psychology, we must consider which individual variants are relevant to educational theory and practice—which are legitimate domains of study. We must also recognize that the knowledge base that composes educational psychology affects or interacts with the content and practice of other disciplines. Indeed, on a service level the strongest links to exceptional conditions are with special education.

Finally, we must acknowledge that our understanding of exceptional conditions and what to do about them is in part a function of political and social influences, not just of scientific knowledge. Because of President John F. Kennedy's personal interest, during his administration federal appropriations for research and training in the field of mental retardation increased dramatically. Some years later Public Law 94-142, the Education of All Handicapped Children Act of 1975, emerged from the background of the civil rights movement of the 1960s and from litigative efforts to guarantee the rights of children with handicaps.

Examination of the transactional influences of educational psychology and the study of exceptional individuals could proceed in a number of directions. We might study how theories, methods of inquiry, and instructional techniques invoked in the field of educational psychology have influenced the selection of theories, methods, and practices used by those studying exceptional individuals. We might also examine the relative influence of educational psychology, vis-à-vis other disciplines and professions, on research and practice with exceptional individuals. It would also be fruitful to examine the particular problems and constraints that confront the researcher concerned with individuals falling at the extremes of distributions, the situation with most groups of exceptional students. The concern for variation is, of course, inconsistent with the emphasis on normative behavior that characterizes much of the research in educational and developmental psychology, and the differences in perspectives have marked consequences for sampling, instrumentation and measurement, design, analysis, and statistical techniques.

In this chapter we focus on three groups of exceptional learners: mildly mentally retarded, learning disabled, and gifted and talented. Although the psychological and educational needs of individuals with more severe handicaps are important, those three groups make up the preponderance of exceptional learners in school. The chapter is organized into five major sections: issues in definition and classification, background and current status, assessment and evaluation of exceptional individuals, program planning for exceptional learners, and implications for conducting research on special populations. A final section

We thank Professors Fred Morrison, H. Lee Swanson, Robert Hodapp, and Edward Zigler for their thoughtful and helpful reviews, and Professor Nancy Robinson for consultation on the gifted sections of this chapter. Preparation of this chapter was supported in part by grants No. HD19124 and HD11944 from The National Institute of Child Health and Human Development to the Sociobehavioral Group of the University of California Los Angeles Mental Retardation Center, and by grants Nos. HC02320002 and H023C80072 from the U.S. Department of Education to the University of California, Riverside.

contains a brief discussion of continuing issues in the education of exceptional individuals.

## ISSUES IN DEFINITION AND CLASSIFICATION

A major substantive question confronting both researchers and practitioners is, what constitutes exceptionality? Some assumed norm, standard, or expectation is implicit in the notion of exceptional, as exceptional conditions are defined in terms of difference from some referent. At issue is different in what way: In health? In age-based developmental expectancies? In socially and legally appropriate behaviors? In grade-level reading achievement? In having an IQ greater than or less than 100? The question is sometimes posed in terms of qualitative or quantitative differences; that is, should exceptional conditions be viewed as separate and discrete syndromes or as extremes of the normal distribution?

The qualitative, syndromal organization of exceptional conditions, characteristic of medical approaches, has historically been applied to extreme and to biologically based conditions, such as genetically based severe or profound mental retardation or psychoses. The quantitative perspective, more consistent with an educational psychology perspective, is widely applied to exceptionality in schooling and usually refers to conditions such as slow learning, mild mental retardation, and learning disabilities—or, at the other end of the continuum, to giftedness. Mental retardation and giftedness represent extremes on the IQ continuum, while learning disabilities are usually defined in terms of placement on a continuum of discrepancy between aptitude and achievement. The quantitative approach has led to reliance on psychometric, statistical models of definition and identification, as educational exceptionality is defined primarily in terms of position on an assumed normal curve, with cutoff points expressed as deviations from the mean.

The psychometric definition, applied at the turn of the century by Binet and Simon (1905) has spawned a multitude of tests and measures aimed primarily at a few major dimensions of individual differences—cognition, achievement, and specific aptitudes. These are obviously educationally important and relevant dimensions, and many of the measurement issues in their assessment have been addressed. It should be noted, however, that the psychometric approach is limited to dimensions of individual difference that are presumed to be normally distributed and are amenable to quantification. Further, placement on a quantitative distribution provides little if any information about other characteristics that affect performance, and provides minimal direction for intervention or treatment.

### Classification Systems

Both qualitative and quantitative approaches have contributed to our understanding of exceptionality but have resulted in somewhat different systems of classification and in reliance on different techniques for identification of individual exemplars of classes or categories. Consider, for example, the diagnostic classification system in the fourth edition of the American Psychiatric Association's *Diagnostic and Statistical Manual of Mental Disorders* (DSM-IV), published in 1994, and the classifi-

cation system used for providing special education services under PL 94-142, the Education of All Handicapped Children Act of 1975, now known as the Individuals with Disabilities Education Act of 1990, or IDEA. Some individuals will be identified in common, but there will be real differences in the characteristics of category members, depending on the approach to definition inherent in the classification system.

As noted by Zigler and Phillips (1961), the nature of categories or classes and definitional criteria varies, in part as a function of purpose. Keogh (1993) has suggested that categories may be useful for advocacy, for provision of services, or for research purposes, but she warned that these nets do not necessarily catch the same individuals. Thus, inferences based on data from one category may not generalize to another. Broadly defined, nonspecific categories may be acceptable, even desirable, for advocacy or for ensuring funding for services; precise and limited categories are necessary for experimental research involving manipulation of single instructional variables or for tests of specific instructional practices.

For the most part, classes of educational exceptionality are neither mutually exclusive nor exhaustive. Traditionally, classification of exceptionality has tended to rely on monothetic typologies in which the presence of particular attributes or characteristics is necessary and sufficient for class membership (Fletcher, Francis, Rourke, S. E. Shaywitz, & B. A. Shaywitz, 1993). An alternative model of classification is the polythetic typology, in which it is not necessary for all attributes to be present; rather, class membership is determined by the presence of some subset of attributes (Blashfield, 1993). The polythetic typology is consistent with the idea of clusters or subgroups within any broad diagnostic class. Within an educational framework the reliance on shared attributes or polythetic models allows, even leads to, conceptual and empirical diversity. To illustrate, classification as gifted is usually determined by IQ *and* by high achievement or evidence of particular talent. Similarly, the American Association on Mental Retardation's definition of mental retardation (Luckasson, 1992) requires that an individual exhibit subaverage general intelligence *and* impairments in two or more of the 10 adaptive skill areas listed; IQ alone or adaptive skill deficiency alone does not define the condition. The main defining criterion of learning disabilities is a discrepancy between ability and achievement, yet a discrepancy alone is not sufficient, as it must be accompanied by one or more of a range of other characteristics (e.g., evidence of a disorder in one or more psychological processes such as perception, language, or attention).

The classification issue is further complicated by problems of identification, that is, the process of assigning individuals to classes. Whereas classification is conceptual, identification is measurement bound (Bailey, 1973) and thus is threatened by inappropriate or technically inadequate measures and by flawed applications and interpretations (Shepard, 1983; Ysseldyke, Algozzine, Regan, & Potter, 1980). As a consequence, assignment of individuals to classes, especially broadly defined classes, does not guarantee homogeneity of characteristics, muddying considerably the efforts of educational psychologists to test methods and to evaluate interventions. Current interest in statistical methods for subtyping (McKinney, 1984; Speece, 1990) is driven in part by the need to reduce the variability found in broad-based categories.

## Challenges to Classification

The classification of children for educational purposes has been a continuing debate for decades (see Heller, Holtzman, & Messick, 1982, or the 2 volumes edited by Hobbs, 1975), and a major focus of the controversy concerns the potentially negative consequences of inaccurate or inappropriate labeling. Once labeled, a child may be segregated, leading to concerns about possible stigmatization, peer rejection, and decrements in self-evaluations. Further questions have to do with the reliability and validity of classification. In this context reliability refers to the degree of diagnostic agreement (i.e., do different diagnosticians or assessors agree that a given child is learning disabled, mentally retarded, or neither?). Descriptive validity refers to the similarity or homogeneity of the individuals identified as members of a given class (e.g., do all gifted children have IQs at least 2 standard deviations [SD] above the mean?) and to the number of meaningful correlates of class membership—how much we know about members of a given classification (Zigler, Balla, & Hodapp, 1984).

Other concerns relate to the effectiveness of special education programs for pupils with exceptional learning needs. Examination of the range of individual differences in achievement in regular education programs indicates that many children with mild learning handicaps do not master the curriculum taught by means of normative instructional methods. However, evidence of the efficacy of special education programs is equivocal. A sizable but methodologically questionable body of research suggests that specialized programs have not led to improved academic performance of problem learners, and a number of professionals have called for a major restructuring of programs (M. C. Reynolds, Wang, & Walberg, 1987; W. Stainback & S. Stainback, 1984; Will, 1986).

The idea that exceptional learners require programs that match their learning needs has been a mainstay of special education. The argument that it is the nature of instruction rather than the rate or intensity of instruction is clearly an aptitude–treatment interaction (ATI) perspective. While that perspective is attractive, evidence demonstrating that instructional methods are differentially effective with problem learners or with categories or classes of learners has been elusive. Problems in documenting ATI effects may be related in part to the nature of the classification systems and the identification procedures used, as the broad-band categories contain individuals who are often characterized more by differences than by commonalities (Speece & Cooper, 1991). A more detailed discussion of ATIs with exceptional learners may be found in the assessment and instructional sections of this chapter.

## Social-Political Influences

The definitions of many exceptional conditions and the operational measures used to identify exemplars vary with time and place. Sociopolitical and economic conditions affect views of exceptionality and of categories or classes, and determine in part the numbers of individuals identified as exemplars of the categories (Keogh, 1994). Changing the IQ cutoff levels from 1 to 2 SD below the mean led to major changes in the numbers of pupils identified as mentally retarded (Zigler & Hodapp, 1986); inclusion of learning disabilities as a special

education category dramatically reduced the numbers of pupils categorized as retarded (MacMillan, 1989a). The availability of other programs such as remedial reading or Title 1 affects the number of pupils referred for special education services (Mehan, Meihls, Herweck, & Crowdes, 1981). Thus, prevalence figures must be interpreted cautiously and should be expected to vary according to geographic location and time.

Despite the limitations of current classification systems, available prevalence figures provide useful information in directing both service and research efforts. The U.S. Office of Special Education Programs (OSEP) reports to Congress annually on the implementation of the IDEA act (previously PL 94-142). Data reported by states are summarized in terms of how many children are served under each of the disability categories as well as the setting (e.g., special day class, resource room) in which they are served. Excluded are OSEP data on gifted students, as they are not a responsibility of that agency.

Figures from the 1990 OSEP report to Congress are shown in Table 10–1. The total number of identified handicapped individuals ages 6 to 21 years approaches 10% of the school population, or nearly 4,000,000 students. Prevalence figures will likely increase substantially in the next years as Public Law 99-457 mandates services for handicapped and "at risk" preschool children ages 3 to 5 years, and offers incentives for identifying and providing services for infants and toddlers to age 3 years. Indeed, figures summarized in OSEP's 15th *Annual Report to Congress* (1993) indicate that 4,994,165 students were served in special education in the 1990–1992 school year; 66,495 were in the birth to age 2 years range, and 422,226 were ages 3 to 5 years. The inclusion of a broader age range of exceptional learners raises interesting and demanding questions for both developmental and educational psychologists, as traditional techniques, methods, and instructional programs will in many cases be inappropriate for the assessment and intervention needs of these young exceptional children.

PL 94-142 was fully implemented during the 1976–1977 school year, and it is instructive to note the changes in prevalence rates within categories, particularly for learning disabled and mildly retarded children. As shown in Table 10–1, there has been a dramatic reduction in the percentage of children served as mentally retarded and a corresponding increase in the number of children served as learning disabled. This shift corresponds to the full implementation of PL 94-142 and its nondiscriminatory testing provision, as well as the sociopolitical attention to the overrepresentation of minority children in programs for the mentally retarded.

## BACKGROUND AND CURRENT STATUS

Early special services for exceptional pupils were limited to individuals with severe handicaps, and the pioneers were primarily physicians, rather than educators or psychologists. Their legacy continues to influence the search for etiology, symptoms, and an exclusionary diagnosis (Forness & Kavale, 1984; MacMillan & Hendrick, 1993). Of direct concern for educational psychologists, services for mildly impaired learners arose in response to practical problems following compulsory attendance laws and a wave of immigration to major urban centers. Early in the 20th century, school officials recognized students

TABLE 10–1. Number and Change in Number of Children Ages 6 to 21 Years Served Under the Education of the Handicapped Act—B

| Handicapping Condition | No. | | Change | |
|---|---|---|---|---|
| | 1976–77 | 1988–89 | No. | (%) |
| Learning disabled | 782,095 | 1,972,135 | 1,190,040 | 152.16 |
| Speech impaired | 1,170,425 | 957,135 | −213,290 | (−18.22) |
| Mentally retarded | 818,718 | 521,782 | −296,936 | (−36.27) |
| Emotionally disturbed | 245,343 | 336,722 | 91,379 | 37.25 |
| Hard of hearing/deaf | 55,116 | 41,010 | −14,106 | (−25.59) |
| Multihandicapped | — | 65,052 | — | — |
| Orthopedically handi-capped | 70,566 | 41,463 | −29,103 | (−41.24) |
| Other health impairment | 115,867 | 46,614 | −69,253 | (−59.77) |
| Visually handicapped | 26,215 | 17,101 | −9,114 | (−34.77) |
| Deaf-blind | — | 789 | — | — |

Note: Data are from Tables AA20 and AA25, *Twelfth Annual Report to Congress on the Implementation of the Education of the Handicapped Act*, compiled and reported by the U.S. Office of Special Education Programs, 1990, Washington, DC: U.S. Department of Education. Figures are reported for 50 states, the District of Columbia, and Puerto Rico.

whose advancement through the grades was slower than expected, or "retarded." Interestingly, in contrast to the medical approach, which focused the problem in the individual (e.g., familial retardation, brain damage), in 1909 Ayres attributed learning failures to curricula that matched the capabilities of only the brightest students. Surveys of school progress during this time confirmed that large numbers of students repeated grades or dropped out, suggesting that the prevailing curricula were inappropriate for a substantial segment of the school population.

Special education services for mildly impaired learners emerged, and pupils were segregated into ungraded classes on the basis of their behavior and achievement. These classes were found in most major cities (see Hendrick & MacMillan, 1989). Terman's publication of *The Measurement of Intelligence* (1916) and *The Intelligence of School Children* (1919) prompted the increased acceptance of ability grouping in the public schools, a grouping system that relied heavily on mental tests, hailed as the new scientific basis for organized instruction. By 1920, intelligence testing influenced how children would be selected for ungraded classes, and IQ became decisive in precluding moderately and severely retarded children from attending schools (Scheerenberger, 1983).

Because segregated versus mainstream placement is a continuing issue, it is important to note that ungraded, separate classes arose in response to a practical problem and that they predated the common use of intelligence tests by nearly 20 years. The contributions of educational psychologists to the special education enterprise would come later, and some of these contributions, especially the use of aptitude tests, would ultimately be the source of major controversy, a point that is discussed later in this chapter.

Historically, the educational response to exceptional individuals developed from practical needs and from social and political concerns. Demands for services for exceptional children have been enhanced by the activities of powerful parent and professional advocacy groups and organizations. These groups have assumed major and continuing roles in assuring and improving services. As an example, the Council for Exceptional Children (CEC) is an umbrella organization concerned with a wide range of exceptional conditions. Organizational subgroups within the CEC include the Association for the Gifted and Talented, the Division for Learning Disabilities, and the Division of Mental Retardation. The American Association on Mental Retardation, the Division on Mental Retardation of the American Psychological Association, and the American Academy on Mental Retardation are professional groups concerned with research issues, while the Association for Retarded Citizens, now known as the Arc, has assumed a strong advocacy role.

Comparable groups in the learning disabilities field, in addition to the Division for Learning Disabilities of the CEC, include the Council for Learning Disorders and the Learning Disabilities Association of America, the last a parent-organized and -governed organization. Major organizations concerned with the gifted and talented include the National Association for Gifted Children, the Gifted Child Society, and the Association for Gifted and Talented Students. There are also a number of organizations that target specific problem conditions, such as the Orton Dyslexia Society, the Association for Children with Down Syndrome, the Autism Society of America, and the United Cerebral Palsy Association.

Many organizations provide information aimed at advancing research and service through journal publication. Some well-known American journals are *Exceptional Children, Remedial and Special Education, Annals of Dyslexia, Teaching Exceptional Children, Exceptionality, American Journal on Mental Retardation, Mental Retardation, Learning Disabilities Research and Practice, Journal of Learning Disabilities, Learning Disabilities Quarterly, Journal for the Education of the Gifted, Gifted Child Quarterly*, and *Gifted-Talented Digest*. In addition, a number of journals in related fields frequently contain content relevant to exceptional individuals, among them the *Journal of Abnormal Psychology, Reading Research Quarterly, Journal of Reading, Journal of Early Intervention, Child Development, Journal of Consulting and Clinical Psychology, Developmental Medicine and Child Neurology, Journal of Child Psychology and Psychiatry*, and the *Journal of Educational Psychology*.

The research and service roles of educational psychologists have increased as the educational needs and rights of exceptional individuals have been recognized. In addition to questions relating to the etiology and expression of exceptional conditions, important issues have to do with appropriateness, quality, and effectiveness of services, implementation strategies, training, and evaluation. These concerns become especially important with the current emphasis on academic excellence in traditional achievement domains. In subsequent sections of this chapter, we discuss these issues in relation to three major categories of exceptionality—mental retardation, learning disabilities, and gifted and talented students.

## Mental Retardation

Following President Kennedy's 1963 message to Congress proposing a national program to combat mental retardation, the study of retardation increased dramatically. This program included comprehensive planning by states, construction of community facilities, university-based research centers, the development of model clinical programs for training professional personnel, and the expansion of maternal, child health, and crippled children's services, emphasizing care of children with mental retardation and developmental disabilities. The creation of the National Institute of Child Health and Human Development and Project Head Start also benefited the field (Tarjan, 1972).

Among those attracted to research and training in mental retardation were psychologists who viewed the study of mental retardation as a way to advance knowledge about normative development, or as a way to test general theories of learning and development. Others were attracted because of the link between poverty and mild mental retardation, seeking to identify environmental factors as possible suppressors of intellectual development (MacMillan, 1989b). The quantitative perspective dominated psychological and educational research, and for purposes of theory testing, individuals who were mentally retarded were seen as differing in degree rather than in kind. Although not differentiated by conventional tests of intelligence and related measures, the mentally retarded population was viewed as containing at least two subgroups of children: genotypically retarded children, and phenotypically retarded children who were genotypically normal (Zigler, 1967). The latter subgroup was of particular interest as it implicated experiential and environmental influences, including the impact of schooling, on retardation.

Researchers of mild mental retardation had for years noted the disproportionately high prevalence of children coming from impoverished families. Indeed, in many studies mild retardation and poverty are so confounded that it is not possible to disentangle the possible independent effects of each. The importance of environment in retardation was fueled by reexamination of the role of experience in intellectual development precipitated by the publication of Hunt's (1961) book, *Intelligence and Experience,* and the work of Benjamin Bloom, described in *Stability and Change in Human Characteristics* (1964). The interests and research of educational psychologists and special educators merged in the 1960s and 1970s as the Johnson administration's War on Poverty included efforts to prevent mild mental retardation and to reduce the risk experienced by children of poverty. Project Head Start and various other early intervention efforts were initiated during this era in an effort to test notions of malleability or plasticity. An excellent review of this history as it applies to efforts to raise the intelligence of mentally retarded individuals is provided by Spitz (1986).

The research literature from the 1960s and 1970s abounds with studies comparing mentally retarded samples with nonretarded samples in efforts to understand how mentally retarded children differed in terms of attention, verbal learning, memorial processes, and the use of mnemonics (see Brooks, Sperber, & McCauley, 1984; Ellis, 1979). The inclusion of mentally retarded subjects in investigations of cognitive theories allowed tests of generalizability and of stage-specific developmental patterns such as those described by Piaget (Weisz & Zigler, 1979). Essentially, the empirical evidence appears to support a similar-sequence hypothesis (see Hodapp, 1990; Mundy & Kasari, 1990, for discussion).

The prevalence of mental retardation has declined dramatically since the 1970s, as definitions and IQ cutoff points have changed. A consequence is that classification as educably retarded is primarily limited to children with IQs of about 65 or lower (Gottlieb, 1981). As a result, the developmental difference controversy (Zigler, 1982) concerning the cognitive functioning of persons with mental retardation of nonorganic origin has become somewhat moot. Few cases of nonorganic mental retardation are clinically identified by the schools. Burack (1990) examined differences in cognitive functioning and development among individuals with mental retardation of different etiologies, such as Down syndrome, fragile X syndrome, and Williams syndrome. Burack found that subjects sharing a common etiology often exhibited strengths and weaknesses that were unique to that group, a finding that suggested that there may be different psychological profiles among children with mental retardation of specific etiologies.

Etiology-specific cross-domain differences have also been identified by Hodapp and Dykens (1994), who argue for considering both specific and general aspects of abilities across and within etiological subgroups of mentally retarded individuals. For example, children with idiopathic infantile hypercalcemia of the Fanconi type (IIHF) exhibit far better verbal than visual-spatial abilities (Udwin, Yule, & Martin, 1987). In contrast, children with Down syndrome exhibit strengths in visual-motor integration and weaknesses in language abilities (Pueschel, Gallagher, Zartler, & Pezzullo, 1987). When children with Down syndrome were compared with children with fragile X syndrome, it was found that boys with fragile X syndrome exhibited their single most delayed development in visual-motor integration, an area of relative strength for children with Down syndrome. Further, no differences were found between simultaneous and sequential processing among subjects with Down syndrome, whereas boys with fragile X syndrome were 2 years behind in sequential processing skills.

Findings suggesting differences in cognitive performance by etiological subgroups suggest possible ATIs and argue for instructional research with subgroups of retarded students. Subgroup differences also have implications for sampling and subject-selection procedures in research. It is likely that no differences by etiology will be found on some measures, but where etiological differences exist, it is essential that samples be constituted in ways that permit testing for differences. The previous use of IQ measurements for stratifying samples of mentally retarded subjects do not reveal such etiological differences in the characteristics under investigation.

## Learning Disabilities

Learning disabilities, with an emphasis on psychological processing functions, emerged in the 1960s as a major category of exceptionality. The term is credited to Samuel Kirk, who referred to problems in "development in language, speech, reading, and associated communication skills needed for social interaction" (S. Kirk, 1963, pp. 2–3). As for other constructed definitions, the specifics of the definition have evolved over time. As an example, the Interagency Committee on Learning Disabilities (1987), a multidisciplinary group representing 13 federal institutes and agencies argued for the inclusion of social skills deficits in the definition (see also Kavanagh & Truss, 1988). This position was explicitly rejected by the U.S. Department of Education and the National Joint Committee on Learning Disorders (1987), and the controversy further muddied the definitional question.

Despite differences in specifics, most definitions incorporate the ideas that learning disabilities (a) represent problem conditions that are different from other achievement-related conditions (mental retardation, slow learning); (b) may be expressed as unexpected difficulties in a range of basic ability domains, such as thinking or spoken or written language; and (c) are presumed to be focused in the individual and due to an underlying neurological condition. A central assumption is that learning-disabled individuals' performance or achievement levels are inconsistent with their intellectual or developmental potential, and that learning-disabled individuals exhibit specific and unexpected failures in some, but not necessarily all, areas of functioning (Keogh, 1990; Stanovich, 1985).

Although the discrepancy definition is defensible on a conceptual level (Keogh, 1988), there have been serious limitations in implementation. Problems have to do with the reliance on inadequate and unsound diagnostic techniques and practices, unreliability of measurement, the choice of discrepancy models and statistical formulas used in computation, and the interpretive significance of discrepancies (see Cone & Wilson, 1981; Reynolds, 1984–1985; Shepard, 1983; Ysseldyke et al., 1980). We underscore the methodological vagaries and problems and emphasize that the heterogeneity evident in any identified group of learning-disabled individuals is a function of both conceptual and operational inconsistencies.

Differences in definitions and in diagnostic practices also reflect disciplinary perspectives. As was true of mental retardation, the origins of the field were in medicine and neurology, as physicians and psychologists attempted to localize neural functions and to link known neurological damage to cognitive and perceptual abilities and learning problems (Goldstein, 1942; Strauss & Lehtinen, 1947). Problems now viewed as learning disabilities have been identified for many years (Doris, 1993; Torgesen, 1991), although under different, sometimes exotic, diagnostic labels: strephosymbolia, congenital word blindness, perceptual and visual-motor disorders, and specific reading or language disabilities. Current approaches reflect interest in neuropsychological, cognitive, and metacognitive processes (see volumes edited by Ceci, 1986; Swanson & Keogh, 1990) and in domain- and content-specific learning disabilities, especially reading and language problems (Pearson, Barr, Kamil, & Mosenthal, 1991).

Whatever the differences in specifics of definition and procedures for identification, the phenomenal changes in prevalence rates must be underscored. Learning disabilities is the fastest growing and single largest category of special education programs, currently providing services to approximately 1.9 million students. As shown in Table 10–1, the number of identified pupils ages 6 to 21 increased by over 152 percent from 1976–1977 to 1988–1989 (OSEP, *Twelfth Annual Report*, 1990), and it is estimated that nationally, learning-disabled pupils represent almost 50 percent of pupils identified for special education services and about 2 percent to 15 percent of all pupils enrolled in public schools (National Association of State Boards of Education, 1992).

The qualitative-quantitative issue raised earlier in this chapter is pertinent in the continuing conceptual questions about learning disabilities. Are learning disabilities unique and qualitatively different conditions, and are they syndromes that are neurologically based? Or does the category identify individuals whose developmental or educational status represents a particular position on an assumed normal distribution curve, as proposed by S. E. Shaywitz, Escobar, B. A. Shaywitz, Fletcher, and Makuch (1992)? In the extreme view, syndromes are presumed to be unitary and relatively discrete, to have specific etiologies, and to require particular interventions or treatments. Targeted processes might be visual-spatial, temporal, attentional, or auditory-processing functions. A problem with the syndrome approach is that specific symptoms or indications are often observed in many presumably discrete conditions, thus raising questions about independence and integrity. The problem is particularly apparent in learning disabilities, where the range of characteristics or attributes within groups of identified individuals is very broad (Keogh, Major-Kingsley, Omori-Gordon, & Reid, 1982). As discussed earlier, the heterogeneity is due in part to the polythetic nature of the classification system as well to limitations of measurement. The limitations of the qualitative or syndrome perspective arise from the overlap of symptoms and the lack of mutual exclusiveness of syndromes, imprecise and unreliable diagnostic techniques and tests, and treatments and interventions of questionable educational appropriateness or effectiveness.

Defining learning disabilities in terms of normal curve assumptions, however, results in confounding learning disabilities and low achievement due to other conditions and restricts identification to quantitatively measurable dimensions of individual differences. The quantitative perspective is operationalized in most regulations governing eligibility for special educational services as a discrepancy between aptitude (IQ) and measured achievement in reading, mathematics, or spelling. This approach obviously places learning disabilities within the framework of schooling, and thus limits identification to school-aged children. Theoretical issues relate to the relationship between intelligence and academic achievement and to a discrepancy definition. Siegel (1990) proposes that IQ be abandoned in the definition of learning disabilities and that two types of academic learning disabilities, reading and arithmetic, be defined on the basis of achievement. Her argument is based in part on the findings that basic cognitive processes are similar across IQ levels and that good readers are found within lower IQ groups. A further issue relates to a possible confound between learning disabilities and low achievement (Ysseldyke, Algozzine, Shinn, & McGue, 1982). Support for learning disabilities as a category distinguishable from low achievement is found in the recent meta-analysis by Kavale, Fuchs, and Scruggs (1994).

## Gifted and Talented

The educational and psychological literature has paid less attention to the gifted and talented than to persons with other exceptional conditions, despite estimates that prevalence rates for giftedness and mental retardation are generally similar, 3 percent to 5 percent of the population (Horowitz & O'Brien, 1985). Reasons for the relative lack of effort directed toward gifted and talented students are not entirely clear but may have to do with the perceived greater personal and educational needs of pupils with handicaps, with an assumption that gifted pupils succeed well without specialized help, and with the general egalitarian tradition in the United States (Zigler & Farber, 1985).

The current push for academic excellence has created a favorable climate for research and program development directed toward gifted and creative students. As for other exceptional conditions, efforts have been limited by continuing definitional inconsistencies and ambiguities at both conceptual and operational levels. Gallagher (1992) questioned whether identification procedures should be directed toward finding potential or aptitude or toward recognizing superior performance. Hoge and Cudmore (1986) and Freeman (1995) emphasized that definitions vary in terms of the breadth of qualities or traits represented and in the nature, composition, and weight of the qualities. Some definitions are focused primarily on a single characteristic (e.g., intellectual potential operationalized as IQ, or specific aptitudes or talents); other, multivariate definitions include a range of abilities or characteristics. Thus, a central question relates to the nature of giftedness: its qualitative and quantitative expression, its breadth or specificity.

The systematic study of giftedness as defined as high intelligence and high achievement emerged primarily from the work of British theorists who adopted a general factor theory of intelligence and who believed that differences in mental abilities were quantifiable through systematic measurement. A tradition operationalized in the early work of Binet and Simon (1905) and still evident today is the reliance on the IQ test for identifying gifted students for eligibility for special programs. In his classic study, Terman (1925) equated giftedness and intellectual superiority and set a minimum quantitative score (IQ = 140) for admission into his sample. His view of intelligence as ability in logical, abstract reasoning was consistent with Spearman's two-factor theory, with the emphasis on $g$, or the "eduction of correlates." In this definition, both historically and currently, it is reasonable to expect that a general ability factor will be expressed in a range of performance domains, that the general factor may be assessed legitimately and accurately, and that high ability or giftedness may be defined in terms of psychometric status. These issues are also discussed in chapter 8.

Challenges to the IQ test as well as recent contributions from developmental and cognitive psychology have yielded an increasing number of different conceptualizations of intelligence and of giftedness (Cattell, 1987; Ceci, 1990; Gardner, 1983; Guilford, 1967; Sternberg & Davidson, 1985, 1986; Thurstone, 1938). These formulations include those based on information-processing, structural, knowledge-based, and con-

textualist theories, as well as those that emphasize multiple intelligences, modular faculties, and specific talents and creativity. Several approaches are briefly described.

For legislative purposes at the federal level, in 1972 Marland defined giftedness in terms of high performance or potential in areas of general intellectual ability, specific academic aptitude, creative or productive thinking, leadership ability, and visual and performing arts. More recently Sternberg (1985) proposed a triarchic theory that is made up of three subtheories. The first, a componential subtheory, specifies internal or metacognitive components (metacomponents, performance components, and knowledge acquisition components); the second has to do with the interaction of the individual and tasks or situations (abilities to deal with novel tasks and to automatize); and the third, or contextual subtheory, addresses aspects of purposive adaptation, selection, and shaping within the cultural context. Sternberg and Davidson (1986) argue that giftedness is "societally defined" (p. 42) and therefore includes components that reflect societal values, such as intellectual skills, artistic skills, niche-fitting skills, and physical skills. From another perspective, Gardner (1983) proposed that there are many intelligences, specifying seven domains: linguistic, logical and mathematical, visual-spatial, bodily-kinetic, musical, interpersonal, and intrapersonal. See also Gruber (1985) and Renzulli (1977) for important conceptual positions. Still unresolved is the issue of general ability or domain specificity.

While the conceptual debate continues, it should be noted that the majority of states in the United States have adopted legal definitions of giftedness that allow for specific academic aptitudes and creativity as well as general intellectual ability as indexed by IQ. In practice, however, the identification of gifted school-aged pupils is based primarily on IQ as determined by standard intelligence tests. As in the assessment of mental retardation and learning disabilities, tests for giftedness often are inaccurately used, reflecting limited understanding of their technical properties as well as a lack of consideration of appropriateness for particular groups or subgroups.

An aspect of conceptualization that runs through many definitions of giftedness relates to the quantitative-qualitative distinction made earlier in this chapter. A widely held intuitive belief suggests that gifted individuals are qualitatively different from nongifted peers, that their information-processing abilities differ in kind, not just in quality or speed. This perspective was challenged by Jackson and Butterfield (1986), who argued that giftedness may be explained by the same cognitive processes that characterize nongifted information processors: "Gifted performance is different from ordinary performance, but it does not appear to be different in any way that would justify the creation of separate cognitive theories of giftedness" (p. 177). This view is consistent with that of Zigler and Farber (1985), who opted for a developmental rather than difference model of both giftedness and retardation. However, Gallagher (1992) suggested that gifted performance is "quantitatively different but, at the extreme, these quantitative differences may result in qualitatively different performance" (p. 544). As with the question of domain specificity or global aptitude, the quantitation-qualification issue is unresolved.

Robinson and Noble (1991), Freeman (1995), and Gallagher (1992) have argued that there are several "special populations" in which gifted students are underidentified and underserved and who deserve attention. These include gifted individuals from minority, low-income, or handicapped groups. They also emphasized that as a group, gifted females, regardless of ethnic or economic status, are particularly likely to be at risk for failing to meet their potential, citing discriminatory identification practices, socialization effects (especially sex-role expectations), limited opportunities, and differential treatment by parents and teachers.

In addition to the groups already discussed, there is some agreement that highly gifted children (IQs more than 4 SD above the mean) may have more social-emotional and adjustment problems than their less gifted peers (Janos & Robinson, 1985; Robinson & Noble, 1991). In a 1942 publication Hollingworth painted a picture of children with IQs above 180 as one of distance from peers in interests and activities, as bored and frustrated in school, and as having serious social and behavior problems, especially in the early school years. These observations were inconsistent with the more positive picture for less highly gifted children, suggesting a nonlinear relation between ability and adjustment (Robinson & Noble, 1991). Although evidence about adjustment is somewhat equivocal, compared with other gifted and "normal" groups, a larger proportion of highly gifted students appear to have adjustment problems. It is reasonable to hypothesize that, just as for other children, it is the nature of the match between child and context rather than high IQ per se that leads to different outcomes.

## Commonalities and Differences Across Conditions

We have framed the discussion of exceptionality around three groups of learners: mildly retarded, learning disabled, and gifted. Differences among the three groups are obvious, yet there are a number of issues in common that deserve consideration. The first has to do with definition and identification. All three exceptional conditions include intellectual level as an important criterion. Because intellectual level is commonly operationalized as IQ, and thus is dependent on test results, issues of ethnic, economic, and gender bias in test content and procedures are relevant. Institutional bias in referral and assessment practices also are likely influences on prevalence rates and thus affect equitable expenditure of resources.

Second, using current definitions, all three categories collect a range of exemplars, bringing into question issues of representativeness and of generalizability of instructional practices and research findings. The heterogeneity within learning-disabled groups and the range of adaptive and behavioral competencies among mentally retarded individuals are well documented. Giftedness as defined by high IQ, and talent as defined by specific aptitudes, also result in differences in exemplars. Thus, programmatic decisions as well as research and evaluation efforts are threatened by reliance on broad-band definitions and by use of system-identified and clinic samples.

Third, programmatic decisions, especially those having to do with segregated or integrated placements, are concerns in all three conditions, although for somewhat different reasons. There have been major challenges to segregated programs for learning-disabled and retarded pupils, based primarily on issues of stigma, lowered and negative self-views, and inadequate instructional programs. Labeling and segregation are also issues for gifted students, as the label may carry negative connotations,

may obscure differences among gifted individuals, may lead to unrealistic self- and other-expectations, and may distance the student from peers; the negative social consequences may be especially detrimental for girls. Specialized programs for gifted students also raise questions of elitism.

Despite these commonalities, differences across groups may affect children's personal/social and educational experiences. One issue relates to attributions about the causes of the condition. The genetic hypothesis is more acceptable for explaining giftedness than for explaining retardation; learning disabilities are regularly attributed to neurological rather than environmental conditions. Differences in economic, ethnic, and gender characteristics within groups are also apparent: Females are underrepresented and males are overrepresented in all three categories; low-economic-status and ethnic minority children are overrepresented in learning disabilities and retarded categories; and males, higher economic status, and ethnic majority children are overrepresented in gifted programs.

The goals and practices of educational interventions also differ, as programs for learning-disabled pupils are usually directed toward specific targets (e.g., reading or math), whereas programs for gifted pupils rely on enrichment or accelerated progress through regular curricula, and programs for retarded pupils currently emphasize lower goals, slower rates, and less academic content. Finally, expectations and aspirations for current performance and long-term outcomes and competencies differ, affecting educational opportunities, curricular and instructional decisions, and expenditure of resources.

## ASSESSMENT AND EVALUATION

Earlier in this chapter we argued that defining categories of exceptionality is a constructive process that is influenced by sociopolitical, economic, and legal conditions. The process of assessment is similarly affected, and thus has changed over time. As already noted, scores on formal IQ tests administered by psychologists became the primary basis for establishing eligibility as gifted or retarded and remain a key ingredient in the discrepancy that defines learning disabilities. Current challenges to the use of traditional assessment approaches have arisen in part from the lack of "curricular validity" and also from the exposition of possible bias in their use with children from ethnic minority backgrounds (see Elliott, 1987; McShane & Cook, 1985). Psychometric tests are often portrayed as unfair and discriminatory. Critics argue that because they are standardized on a white population the content is biased against children from other cultural and linguistic backgrounds, and that a variety of situational factors (e.g., race of examiner, lack of appreciation of nonstandard English, motivational factors) suppress performance, rendering the scores invalid for normative comparisons (see Jensen, 1980; Sattler, 1988, for detailed treatment of these issues).

Alternative approaches to assessment of exceptional learners have relied heavily on assumptions of ATIs. Indeed, the belief that handicapped or problem learners require specialized and individualized instruction has driven assessment practices. Efforts have been directed primarily at specification of in-person aptitudes that are presumed to characterize particular problem conditions and are thought to interact with instruction. Assessment techniques have been developed to address visual and auditory perceptual skills, visual-motor abilities, selective and sustaining attention, cognitive and memorial processes, and, to a lesser extent, motivational and affective characteristics. The Illinois Test of Psycholinguistic Abilities (ITPA) (S. Kirk, McCarthy, & W. Kirk, 1968), for example, targeted processes of auditory and visual reception, visual and auditory sequential memory, visual and auditory association, and so forth—processes presumed to underlie learning and learning problems. The ITPA, along with many of the other "process" measures, has been criticized because of psychometric limitations and because many of the processes presumably tapped were only inferentially linked to learning problems. At issue is whether process deficiencies and learning problems are correlational or causal.

The influence of developmentalists, information-processing theorists, neuropsychologists, and instructional researchers in the educational psychology tradition is also apparent as assessment practices change. Efforts to differentiate the "truly retarded" from the "apparently, but not really, retarded" prompted a number of efforts to develop appropriate and useful assessment procedures. Budoff (1967) used gain/no gain performance on Kohs blocks tasks following instruction as a way of identifying problem learners capable of higher level performance. Jensen (1970) studied the utility of performance on laboratory learning tasks requiring different processes (referred to as Type I and Type II). Mercer and Lewis (1977) devised an elaborate assessment package (System of Multicultural Pluralistic Assessment, or SOMPA) in an effort to provide a more culturally unbiased evaluation. See Swanson's (1991) edited volume on assessment, and the topical issue of *Special Services in the Schools* (1986) for comprehensive reviews of assessment of learning disabilities.

The central importance of language in learning and the well-documented finding of persistent language problems associated with learning disabilities and mental retardation have resulted in a large volume of research directed at linguistic and psycholinguistic functions and techniques of assessment (Johnson, 1988; Tallal, 1988). From a different perspective, neuropsychological techniques have been directed at identifying specific information-processing abilities assumed to underlie or cause learning problems. Examples of several well-known approaches are the Luria-Nebraska and the Halstead-Reitan neuropsychological test batteries (see Hynd & Obrzut, 1986). To date, neuropsychological assessment techniques have had limited direct utility for educational diagnosis or intervention planning, partly because of inadequate psychometric characteristics of many of the measures, problems in construct validity, and the lack of a developmental framework (Obrzut & Boliek, 1991). Also, it is often difficult to make a direct translation from specific neurological test data to school learning tasks. The neuropsychological approaches nonetheless provide interesting and potentially insightful information about the etiology of learning problems.

Because of the criticism of measures of presumed processes and the lack of definitive evidence in support of ATIs, there has been a shift toward direct assessment of problem learners (Lloyd, 1988). In specific, there is increased reliance on practices that are subject matter specific, that are presumed to have curricular validity, that are contextually based, and/or that are derived from accepted models of cognition. A consequence of the move

away from both global psychometric and underlying process orientations is the emerging goal of assessing pupils' responses to instruction—that is, their ability to profit from intervention. Not surprisingly, many of these approaches are characterized by a strong instructional orientation. Specifics of approaches vary considerably but in general reflect either the powerful behaviorist influence or the more recent cognitive perspective. We illustrate with a brief discussion of two widely used approaches to assessment and instruction.

## Criterion-Referenced Measurement

Based on a task analysis of end-point skills, most criterion-referenced assessments are hierarchically ordered, indicating where weaknesses or breakdowns occur in the presumed sequence of skills. Criterion-referenced approaches may be based on expected formal curricula or may be program or curriculum specific (e.g., Howell & Morehead, 1987; Salvia & Hughes, 1990). Deno and L. S. Fuchs's (1987) system of curriculum-based measurement is an example of an approach that is widely used in programs for exceptional learners. Like other curriculum-based assessment approaches, their system is classroom based, includes daily frequency and duration recording, and yields quantitative data. Curriculum-based measurement is used increasingly with exceptional learners because the methods are content and context specific, are focused on individual pupils, provide a detailed record of learning progress and failures, and, within the framework of a specific curriculum, may be used to focus instruction. Limitations include the measurement-driven emphasis, the narrow range of content, and the consequent lack of concern for other relevant processes and influences (see Heshusius, 1991, for critique).

## Cognitive Approaches

Cognitive approaches to assessment with exceptional learners were stimulated by the resurgence of research in cognitive science, by work on children's memory processes, and more recently by interest in Vygotskian theory. Findings in general support the notion that problem learners have less well-developed and less effective metacognitive strategies than do their more successful peers. The generality or specificity of strategies and the relationship of strategy use to particular subject matter areas are still uncertain, but a number of approaches to assessment have in common the goal of identifying memorial and metacognitive skills (see Jacobs & Paris, 1987; Swanson, 1988; Wong, 1988; and chapter 6).

Approaches in the Vygotskian tradition are frequently referred to as dynamic assessment, and emphasize assessment under instructional conditions (Brown & Campione, 1986; Budoff, 1987; Feuerstein, 1979). The notion of assisted or scaffolded performance is central in these techniques, and adherents (see Lidz, 1987) argue that the goal is to tap learners' potential for cognitive change and to identify the processes used in problem solving. Palincsar, Brown, and Campione (1991) suggest that dynamic assessment approaches are based on three major assumptions: the importance of the social context, the need to capture the learner's flexibility, and the goal of prescription rather than prediction.

Dynamic assessment is not a single, standardized approach,

so that specific techniques differ, some approaches relying on well-specified procedures, others allowing almost complete examiner flexibility (see Palincsar et al., 1991, for an overview of models). The test–teach–test models employed by Brown and Campione (1986), Budoff (1967), and Bransford, Delclos, Vye, Burns, and Hasselbring (1987) are relatively formalized, although the content may be subject matter specific or nonspecific, such as puzzles or block design tasks. The Learning Potential Assessment Device (LPAD) (Feuerstein, 1979) is also directed at assessing pupils' responsiveness to instruction, but the techniques are highly individualized and, for the most part, unstandardized. The training materials differ from the content of school curricula and are designed to get at broad cognitive processes presumed to underlie school learning. The lack of formalized pre- and posttest data makes it difficult to assess the effectiveness of the LPAD with exceptional learners.

Dynamic assessment approaches may be particularly useful with pupils evidencing mild retardation or learning disabilities, as their poor performance on psychometric tests may mask their instructional potential. Assisted performance techniques also hold promise of having considerable clinical utility in linking assessment to instruction, thus meeting the criterion of prescription rather than prediction. It should be noted, however, that some cognitive-oriented approaches assume that processes more fundamental than those tapped by intelligence tests can be assessed. However, Tryon (1979) has argued that tests do not measure traits per se, but rather elicit responses to items that permit predictions of behavior or performance in other situations or on other tasks. Thus, he argued that efforts to tap both underlying processes or learning potential presumed to underlie aptitude were illustrative of the "test-trait fallacy."

## Assessing Outcomes

Whereas alternative assessment approaches are focused on instructional variables, a major component of the assessment of exceptional learners has to do with outcomes or achievement. The emphasis on outcomes is particularly important in light of the current emphasis on excellence in American schools and the push toward national testing standards. A consequence of this movement has been the implementation of minimum competency testing in a majority of U.S. states and an increased emphasis on quantitative indices of achievement. The requirement of minimum competency testing of handicapped learners, like issues in achievement testing in general, raises both conceptual and psychometric problems (see Balow, MacMillan, & Hendrick, 1986; MacMillan, Balow, & Widaman, 1988, for detailed discussions). Problem learners often are programmed into nonacademic, vocational tracks, yet the emphasis in testing is on reading, mathematics, and writing, which raises issues of the "curricular validity" of standardized achievement tests. Questions concerning the use of different standards or criteria for performance, the impact of modified administrative procedures, and the relationship of test content to curricular content are essentially unanswered.

## INSTRUCTIONAL PROGRAMS

As noted earlier, the historical response to pupils with learning problems was to limit schooling opportunities, for example

to deny admission or to curtail the number of years in school. Since the turn of the century we have seen regulations "permitting" special education programs modified to mandate services for children with disabilities. The persistent issues confronting educators over the decades concern how and to what extent modifications should be designed to accommodate the special learning needs of the students identified. For some categories of exceptional children (e.g., blind and deaf) the modifications are straightforward and entail bypassing the impaired sensory modality. For mildly retarded, learning-disabled, and gifted students, the answers to instructional questions are not as clear, and the question of what is special about special education is not as readily answered. The modifications afforded mildly handicapped and gifted learners can be grouped into administrative (*where* they are taught), curricular (*what* they are taught), and instructional (*how* they are taught) modifications. We consider first the program accommodations for learning-disabled and mildly retarded learners.

## Administrative Modifications: Where Students Are Taught

The treatment of administrative arrangement as the important modification reflects a belief that where problem learners are placed is more important than what is done with them once they are placed. During the 1930s and 1940s issues focused on special schools versus regular schools; later, the comparison of interest was special classes versus regular classes. Segregated placements have been criticized for isolating children from nonhandicapped peers, thus limiting opportunities for social development. Further, efficacy studies of programs for retarded pupils have failed to show the academic superiority of special classes, despite lower pupil/teacher ratios, the use of specially trained teachers, and higher per-pupil expenditures.

Initially at least, there were few criticisms of special class placements for brain-injured or emotionally disturbed children, likely because the ethnic representation found for mild retardation was not an issue. In addition, assumptions about the etiology of learning disabilities led to treatments designed specifically to address the presumed causes of the behaviors that defined the condition. Based on assumptions of neurological damage, special class environments were created to provide instructional settings believed to minimize the expression of damage. Reduced-stimulation learning environments, for example, as developed by Strauss and Lehtinen (1947) and by Cruickshank, Bentzen, Ratzeberg, and Tannhauser (1961) for educating brain-injured children, were planned specifically to minimize extraneous (presumably disruptive) stimuli by providing instruction in classrooms with severely restricted decors, by placing students in study carrels, by reducing nonessential aspects of materials, and by maintaining well-ordered and nonvarying routines. Early efforts to serve children with visual-perceptual and auditory-perceptual deficits generated specific remedial techniques designed to remediate such problems (Frostig & Horne, 1964; Kephart, 1960).

Because of the strong sentiment against special class placement over the past 20 years, efforts focused on the development of a "continuum of placements," and more recently on mainstreaming, full inclusion, and the Regular Education Initiative (Reynolds et al., 1987; Will, 1986), which calls for "shared responsibility" and a merger of regular and special education. The pressure for mainstreaming mildly handicapped learners has been extended to include those with severe and profound handicaps (Halvorsen & Sailor, 1990), and full inclusion (also referred to as full integration or inclusive education) is a major, if controversial, issue. Strongly supported by The Association for the Severely Handicapped and recently by the National Association of State Boards of Education (1992), full inclusion has been challenged by parent and professional groups concerned about possible loss of needed services for exceptional pupils (see position papers from the Learning Disabilities Association of America, 1993). A major question relates to the ability of the regular system to provide differentiated and individualized programs for exceptional learners, as mandated under PL 94-142 and IDEA.

The basis for full inclusion has been primarily ideological rather than empirical (Lieberman, 1992), and the benefits anticipated by advocates for students with severe disabilities and their regular-class peers await documentation. Support for full inclusion of all exceptional pupils is based mostly on testimonials, endorsements, and beliefs, while critics continue to ask for empirical validation that full inclusion "works." Part of the difficulty lies in the way full inclusion is conceptualized, that is, as the independent or dependent variable. Advocates appear to consider it the dependent variable. Thus, they ask what school, teacher, and structural factors are associated with implementing inclusive programs. On the other hand, those with reservations tend to consider inclusion the independent variable that somehow influences the outcomes of importance, such as improved achievement, greater peer acceptance, more favorable feelings of self, and greater tolerance by nonhandicapped regular-class peers. Evidence supporting the latter concept is absent or extremely limited.

Some of the more extreme positions on inclusion argue for universal placement in regular classes in neighborhood schools as the only placement of choice, thereby challenging the need for a continuum of placements currently available and consistent with IDEA (Taylor, 1988). For example, Laski (1991) launched a frontal attack on the least restrictive environment component of IDEA, calling for its abandonment as hopelessly vague, demeaning, and outmoded. Others, however, point to the need for a continuum of placement options, noting that there is an inherent danger in assuming that any one placement will benefit all children with disabilities without regard for the nature and severity of the conditions.

Available evidence cited in support of full inclusion is limited in that it tends to be based on findings in children with moderate disabilities, not those with profound mental, behavioral, or physical disabilities. Moreover, much of it is focused on preschool or early elementary grade children. As such, the developmental changes that might influence the benefits/costs of inclusion are not currently a matter of record. Finally, the emphasis on where services are delivered is reminiscent of Bronfenbrenner's notion of a "social address" in that it focuses on where interactions occur rather than on the nature and quality of the interactions. As such, placement options might be conceptualized more appropriately as contextual variables in which the interactions of importance occur.

Specific problems in implementing inclusion have been well articulated (see the special issues of *The Journal of Learning* *Disabilities, 21*(1), 1988; *Remedial and Special Education, 11*(3), 1990); and the cogent discussions by D. Fuchs & L. S. Fuchs, 1994, and Kauffman & Hallahan, 1994). Despite the philosophical flavor to much of the debate (Reynolds et al., 1987; W. Stainback & S. Stainback, 1984), efforts are increasing to identify instructional and organizational factors that affect mainstream instruction (Gersten & Woodward, 1990; Kauffman, Gerber, & Semmel, 1988). These factors include the need for workable implementation models, administrative and specialized support, teacher preparation and assistance, and curricular and instructional modifications. Of interest, little attention has been given to the implications of full inclusion for gifted students.

## Curricular Modifications: What Is Taught

Modifications in instructional programs were primarily in terms of *where* exceptional pupils were taught and, to a lesser extent, *how* they were taught (e.g., bypassing the visual modality for blind students). *What* they were taught, that is, goals and curricula, were essentially the same as those for students in regular programs. Remedial programs for learning-disabled students emphasized assistance in coping with the regular curriculum and in achieving normative goals, the special services delivered in resource rooms or pull-out programs. In contrast, for mentally retarded students, the what of the curriculum was different and included lower academic goals and an emphasis on social development and vocational and leisure activity goals. The content of the curriculum reflected the belief that it would prepare the pupils for "real-life" adult functioning that would be productive and satisfying. The effect of nonacademic goals was a common curriculum for students categorized as educable mentally retarded, and services were provided in segregated classes. Examination of early texts and teaching manuals suggests that individualization within programs was limited to rate, not content.

Current legislation mandates placement of all students in the least restrictive environment, and makes the individual education plan central in curricular planning. Goals are to be individually determined, not category based, and wherever possible exceptional students are to be served in regular education classes. The combination of the press for inclusion and the adoption of the resource specialist as the preferred service delivery model has essentially eliminated a specialized curriculum. Mildly retarded students are increasingly exposed to the standard curriculum, reflecting an implicit decision that these children do not require modifications in what they should be taught.

The changes in curriculum and in goals have vast implications for program evaluation efforts as well as for instruction. Specialized curricula and modified goals were possible when students were enrolled in separate classes, and instructional programs were determined by category of disability. It was, thus, possible to compare programs across sites. However, in regular class placement it is not possible to employ between-group designs because the "treatments" for exceptional students are not homogeneous but, in keeping with requirements for individual educational plans, are individualized and thus heterogeneous. The earlier efficacy studies can no longer be conducted. Today, efficacy must be addressed on a case-by-case basis, as each child's program is individually tailored.

## Instructional Modifications: How Students Are Taught

We have already described several instructional modifications designed to accommodate neurological damage presumed to underlie the learning and behavioral problems of some problem learners. In general, two major influences have been particularly influential in educational programming: behaviorism and cognitive psychology. During the 1960s applied behaviorists became actively involved in programs for severely disabled individuals, often working in institutional settings. Their interventions were guided by behavioral principles and theoretical concepts that were adapted to the situational demands of applied settings (MacMillan & Morrison, 1980). This approach provided a guiding philosophy that every child is a candidate to learn and that failure to learn was attributable to tutorial inadequacies, not child factors.

Behaviorists questioned the utility of categories and labels and targeted specific behaviors to be changed, without regard to category of handicap. Early work was predominantly directed toward single subjects, but behavioral principles spread rapidly to the design of entire classrooms (Hewett, 1968) and the use of token economies (O'Leary & Drabman, 1971). The impact of applied behaviorism is apparent not only in special education but also in the practice of school psychology, where standardized instruments and traditional approaches to assessment have been challenged as irrelevant for programming.

The second major influence on programming for exceptional students has its foundation in cognitive theory. Like the approaches to assessment already reviewed in this chapter, current intervention programs from this perspective are focused on training cognitive, especially metacognitive, skills, with these efforts taking a number of forms. The research directed at various aspects of cognitive interventions is impressive in its breadth and its depth. The reader is referred to volumes edited by Ceci (1986), Meyers and Craighead (1984), Scruggs and Wong (1990), and Swanson and Keogh (1990), all of which contain comprehensive reviews and discussion of research and practice from a strategy training perspective. Many of the cognitive programs combine behavioral principles with social learning theory and information-processing models, attempting to improve learning and problem-solving performance through self-regulation techniques, including self-monitoring, self-assessment, self-evaluation, and self-reinforcement (see Lloyd & Landrum, 1990, for review).

From somewhat different perspectives other investigators have developed interventions focused on mnemonic strategies (Mastropieri & Fulk, 1990; Scruggs & Mastropieri, 1992). Borkowski and his colleagues (Borkowski, Johnston, & Reid, 1987) have delineated components of metamemory that are thought to have different developmental histories and are differently influenced by instruction. As noted by many investigators, questions of transfer, generalization, and maintenance are central and not fully answered. Swanson (1988) emphasizes that strategy instruction is a continuum that extends from conscious and highly effortful processing to more automatic, less effort-demanding processing. He proposes a number of principles to guide strategy-training efforts: strategies serve different purposes, strategies are related to learners' knowledge base, comparable performance does not necessarily imply comparable strategies (Swanson, 1993).

A third influence is Vygotskian theory, which is currently a major influence on cognitive approaches, leading to programs that are contextualized and experientially based. The theory of teaching proposed by Tharp and Gallimore (1988) is illustrative of the contextualist-cognitive view. The notion of the zone of proximal development, a central construct in this approach, is especially pertinent and provides a promising direction for assessment and instruction. A further discussion of Vygotskian theory as applied to development and to education may be found in the writings of Brown and Campione (1986), Rogoff (1982), Wertsch (1985), and chapter 2.

## Programs for Gifted and Talented Students

The educational needs of gifted and talented individuals have been acknowledged for many years, yet issues of appropriateness, efficacy, and equity remain. In the 1950s federal legislation provided support for identification and specialized instruction for gifted and talented students. At the same time a number of programs (e.g., advanced placement, the National Merit Scholarship Fund) were developed (Fox & Washington, 1985), and in the 1970s the majority of states developed regulations and guidelines for implementation of special programs for gifted students. The Marland Report (1972) outlined three types of program accommodations for gifted students: different curricula, different instructional strategies, and organizational and administrative accommodations. Gallagher (1992) described curriculum modifications as content acceleration, content enrichment, content sophistication, and content novelty. Administrative accommodations are similar to those found in other special education programs, including special schools or classes, pull-out or resource rooms, and curricular modifications within regular classes, the last operationalized as enrichment or as rapid pacing. Like programs for other exceptional learners, too often the arguments for and against given curricular accommodations appear to reflect philosophical views and advocacy rather than data-based positions.

In general, the evidence suggests that acceleration benefits gifted students academically (J. A. Kulik & C. C. Kulik, 1984). The effects of enrichment programs appear variable, as the content and methods of enrichment programs are themselves varied, some consisting primarily of "busy work" and others providing substantive and relevant content. Whatever the particular administrative structure, a key instructional aspect relates to the faster pacing of instruction and to access to higher level content. An example of the accelerated model is the Study of Mathematically Precocious Youth (Benbow & Stanley, 1983); an example of the enrichment model is the the enrichment triad (Renzulli, 1977).

## Aptitude–Treatment Interactions

The notion of individualized special instructional needs is a fundamental tenet in educational planning for exceptional learners, and an ATI approach is implicit in many programs. L. S. Fuchs and D. Fuchs (1986) challenge the ATI model, arguing that problems include lack of comprehensive knowledge of learners' cognitive abilities, inadequate tests of aptitudes, and incomplete understanding of the scope of possible interactions among learners, teachers, and instructional programs and environments. Speece (1990), however, suggests that ATIs with problem learners have not been adequately tested, and proposes that the complexity of real-life ATIs must be reflected in research models if we are to understand school failure. In Speece's view, major questions to be addressed include the following: How many and which individual difference aptitudes need to be studied? How can we deal with heterogeneity within treatment groups? Can we specify the content and complexity of instruction? What is the appropriate unit of analysis, and what analytic and statistical models are useful for testing interactions?

Speece's suggestions are consistent with those of Corno and Snow (1986), who propose a taxonomy of adaptive teaching that includes aptitudes of intellectual ability and prior achievement, cognitive and learning styles, academic motivation and related personality characteristics, and instructional accommodations (see also chapter 9). Corno and Snow note that some programs for exceptional learners are aimed at developing aptitudes (e.g., cognitive strategy-training programs with learning-disabled or mildly retarded students) and work better with less able than with more able or gifted students. In contrast, some evidence suggests that inductive "discovery learning" is more effective with high-ability students than with low-ability learners (Corno & Snow, 1986). For example, Webb (1982) has demonstrated that grouping patterns (e.g., large versus small groups, high versus low abiilty) have different effects on the math achievements of high- and low-aptitude students. In short, there is increasing evidence to support the idea that ATIs are important in exceptional students' learning, but to date their applied utility has been limited by both substantive and methodological problems.

## Program Evaluation

The extent to which services are effective is central to the special education enterprise. Kauffman, Kameenui, Birman, and Danielson (1990) observed that despite almost 20 years of compliance with PL 94-142 (now IDEA), the evidence suggests that compliance has not resulted in better outcomes. An essential question has to do with the selection of outcomes. How should the effectiveness of specialized services be evaluated? Traditional evaluation of special programs has focused on two major outcomes, achievement and adjustment. As noted previously, such efforts have usually involved between-group designs with *placement* (special day class, resource room, mainstreaming) as the independent variable. The utility of such designs is questionable in light of individualized programming based on individual education plans.

Further, there are questions concerning the curricular validity of standardized achievement tests when used with problem learners, especially those in segregated programs where instruction is focused on elements other than those tapped by tests. Insofar as the students in regular classes are taught reading and math while those in separate classes for retarded students often are not, the utility of achievement tests for reflecting the adequacy of instruction is questionable. Use of grade point average is also troublesome, as it is difficult to equate marks given

students in special programs with those given regular education students. Recent evidence (Wagner et al., 1991) indicates that course marks are inflated for special students mainstreamed into regular secondary school classes.

Efforts to assess "adjustment" outcomes have tended to rely on sociometric data (MacMillan & Morrison, 1984) and on measures of self-attitudes, including self-concept and self-esteem, two goals of special programming. Indeed, one of the goals of special education has been to assist children with learning difficulties so that they could avoid undue failure and resulting self-deprecation. However, measurement of these outcomes has proven elusive when conducted with instruments standardized on nonhandicapped populations. For example, Silon and Harter (1985) found that the four-factor structure of the Perceived Competence Scale with normally developing children was not replicated with students with mild mental retardation, where only two factors were identified. Similarly, issues of differing reliability for scales when subjects have disabilities must also be taken into account. At present the use of scales standardized on nonhandicapped populations renders interpretation of scores risky, at best.

Persistence data have been proposed as an alternative to traditional outcome criteria, and dropout figures are viewed as key indicators of success for educational programs in both regular and special education (MacMillan, Widaman, Balow, Borthwick-Duffy, Hendrick, & Hemsley, 1992). The extant evidence on dropouts of exceptional learners indicates that the magnitude of the problem varies by disability category (Wolman, Bruininks, & Thurlow, 1989). Dropout rates for learning-disabled and behaviorally disordered students have increased and are substantially higher than rates for the general school population and for many other categories of exceptional learners. However, some caution needs to be exercised in interpreting these findings, as dropping out is associated with student characteristics and behaviors (e.g., disciplinary problems) rather than with category affiliation (Wagner et al., 1991). Moreover, inferences about special education effects are limited when exceptional pupils spend 80 percent of their time in regular classes. Clearly, there are continuing problems in the evaluation of special programs. Yet efficacy is central to programmatic decisions as well as to policy decisions and to the allocation of resources.

## METHODOLOGICAL ISSUES IN CONDUCTING RESEARCH

Research on exceptional individuals presents particular problems in addition to those of concern when conducting research on nonhandicapped individuals. Threats to internal and external validity arise in unique ways. The following discussion briefly considers sampling, measurement, and design issues.

### Sampling

Classification of children into categories of educational exceptionality derives primarily from the need for services rather than from researchers' needs for samples with clearly defined population parameters. Moreover, the diagnostic practices used to qualify students as eligible for special education and related services vary as a function of the specific disability, the diagnostician, and the system in which services are delivered. Referral, too, is affected by system variables. Unless a student is nominated or referred by a regular-class teacher, he or she is not evaluated for eligibility. Regular-class teachers differ in terms of tolerance for pupil behaviors, in attributions about good or poor class performance, in expectations related to students' gender and ethnicity, and in their perceptions of administrator's views about the acceptability of high referral rates. It should not be surprising then, that prevalence and the characteristics of identified pupils vary according to classroom, school, and district.

Many subjects in special education research are system identified rather than investigator identified (Keogh & MacMillan, 1983; MacMillan, Meyers, & Morrison, 1980; Morrison, MacMillan, & Kavale, 1985). System identification seriously compromises inferences and generalizations to a larger population of mentally retarded, learning-disabled, or gifted students. Further, because schools select students perceived as needing available services, students who do not meet strict eligibility criteria may be included in study samples (see Keogh et al., 1982). In addition, students who meet criteria for eligibility may not be placed because of parental objection or limited availability of space in special programs. Thus, using "all pupils enrolled in a special day class" or "all pupils enrolled in a resource room program" severely compromises inferences across studies, as a given individual may be placed in a special program in one school but not in another. Indeed, a research subject in one school might serve as a contrast group subject in another. As a consequence, it is virtually impossible to generalize from a given study sample to a known population, because of the idiosyncratic fashion in which system-based identification works.

Additional problems emerge in selecting samples from lists of special education students or from clinic rosters. Such groups represent only a limited, and usually extreme, segment of the problem distribution. Further, in many of the categories of exceptionality, important demographic and subject characteristics (e.g., gender, ethnicity, and socioeconomic status) are not distributed in proportion to their prevalence in the general population. Comparisons of served and nonserved subjects are affected because both system-identified special education groups and clinic rosters contain disproportionately high numbers of males (Richardson, Katz, & Koller, 1986) and of ethnic minority or low-socioeconomic-status children (MacMillan, 1982; Reschly, 1988).

The researcher studying exceptional individuals must make decisions about the desire to generalize findings to those actually identified versus testing for difference among those served on the basis of ethnicity and gender. If the goal of the research requires a sample representative of the larger population of exceptional learners, then the sample will contain different proportions of subjects based on ethnicity and gender. Conversely, if the goal is to test whether male gifted students differ from female gifted students, it is necessary to oversample females in order to reliably estimate the parameter of interest. Clearly, the researcher must be aware of the consequences of sampling decisions relative to the purpose of the research.

The generalization issue is also complicated by geographic effects on identification. We have already noted the consider-

able geographic variation in the percentage of schoolchildren served as educable mentally retarded and as learning disabled (OSEP, *Twelfth Annual Report to Congress,* 1990). As an example, during the 1989 school year, 0.38 percent of the students in New Jersey and 3.26 percent of the students (ages 6 to 17) in Alabama were served as mentally retarded; for learning disabilities, the percentages ranged from 2.06 percent in Georgia to 7.66 percent in Rhode Island. It is unlikely that such variation can be explained in terms of true differences in prevalence. Rather, differences are more likely due to identification criteria and practices, and to the purposes of identification.

The identification of meaningful comparison groups also presents a challenge. To illustrate, consider a comparative study of mentally retarded and nonretarded subjects on a learning task. A common procedure is to match samples on the basis of chronological age (CA) or mental age (MA) estimated from intelligence tests. Some tasks may depend on IQ (i.e., the rate of mental development); thus, the need to isolate whether observed differences are due to CA, MA, or IQ requires multiple comparison groups, one matched on CA and another matched on MA. Even then, there are problems in interpreting main effects and interaction effects when group designs are employed, because of nonlinear relationships between the independent and dependent variables across groups. The issue of CA/MA matches is particularly important in studies of retarded and gifted pupils, where IQ is a major criterion for identification.

## Measurement and Design

As noted earlier in this chapter, classification is measurement free, but identification is measurement specific. Thus, the validity of selection of exceptional pupils is directly tied to assessment techniques and procedures. Yet the technical adequacy of tests commonly used for identification has been widely challenged (see Reynolds, 1984–1985; Shepard, 1983). There is agreement that important points to consider include reliability, the nature of the reference or norming group, and the validity of the tests relative to the constructs or abilities being tested. Reliabilities of .90 or above are commonly accepted as adequate, and a number of the commonly used standardized tests for assessing intelligence and achievement, critical variables in identification of gifted, learning-disabled, and retarded students, have acceptable stability coefficients. However, many tests of specific abilities and presumed processes (including cognitive and neuropsychological functions) are of questionable reliability, lack adequate scaling properties, and provide inappropriate normative data for determining what is normal and what is exceptional performance (Obrzut & Bolick, 1991).

Further, although a number of reliable and well-normed tests are technically defensible, their use with exceptional learners may be questioned. The appropriateness of reference groups, of possible unreliability of scores at extreme ends of distributions, of regression effects, and of the consistency of factor structures across groups and developmental stages, threaten the intepretability of scores. The issues of norms raises a particularly thorny issue. How narrow must the norming group be to permit valid comparison of scores of individuals? In response to these problems, some researchers argue for single-case strategies or for criterion-referenced tests. Whatever the assessment strategy employed, we emphasize that the validity of the findings depends on the adequacy of administration and inference. We emphasize, too, that test selection must be linked to the purpose of testing. Norm-referenced, standardized tests of intelligence and achievement provide information about an individual pupil's standing relative to age-based majority culture expectations; they do not tap cognitive potential, nor do they provide information about individual variations in functional learning skills and knowledge. Thus, they are of limited value in assessing exceptional pupils' instructional needs or readiness.

Important from a program perspective, many of the tests used in assessing exceptional learners, including norm-referenced standardized scales, are of low power for determining change or assessing intervention effects. Slower rates of development, a limited range of competencies tapped, and global summary scores contribute to weak power to demonstrate change. Yet quantitative scores derived from such measures are often required to demonstrate program efficacy and to ensure funding. Closely related, accountability and the need for documentation of program effects have led to the adoption of standard designs and methods developed in psychological research. Single and two-group pre-/posttest designs are common, although there are a number of limitations inherent in these approaches when applied to exceptional children, such as failure to meet requirements ensuring sample homogeneity, restrictions on random assignment, and unknown treatment–subject interactions (Sheehan & Keogh, 1982). Further, statistical approaches that are based on aggregated group data for the most part provide only main effect findings. Single-subject and case history designs are useful but are limited in generalization and in the aggregation of findings and inferences across subjects.

The problem of program evaluation is particularly difficult with exceptional learners, where by law, each child receives schooling under an individual educational plan. Thus the evaluation of treatment is really an evaluation of treatments, and the outcomes are confounded by variability of subjects and of interventions. Even when program characteristics are well defined and structured, the demonstration of effects is threatened by differences in depth and fidelity of implementation so that despite a common program philosophy or orientation, there are variations in programs delivered to individual pupils. Clearly this influences the demonstration of effects presumably due to the content of intervention. The issue can be framed in terms of internal validity: Are the documented changes a function of the program or of some unknown and uncontrolled influences? The threats to internal validity identified by Campbell and Stanley in 1963 are equally relevant today: history, maturation, testing, instrumentation, statistical regression, mortality, and selection–maturation interactions.

## CONTINUING ISSUES AND RESEARCH NEEDS

Although considerable progress has been made in understanding exceptional conditions and in devising appropriate educational programs for them, a number of problems are evident today: equity, identification policies and practices, placement, assessment, and standards and accountability. Each of these is pertinent in the movement for educational reform that is reshaping special education (Kauffman, 1993). It should be noted that most reform movements pay little, if any, attention to exceptional learners or to individual differences among learners. Indeed, many of the reform proposals (e.g., national competency testing, standardized testing of core subjects in Grades 4, 8, and 12, 90 percent high school graduate rate) may be inappropriate and unrealistic for a substantial number of students. It has been argued that the emerging emphasis on academic excellence may be a direct counter to the goal of full inclusion of problem learners (Kauffman, 1989).

If "all means all," as stated in the *America 2000 Sourcebook* (1992) and reaffirmed in Goals 2000: Educate America Act (1992), then reforms must include the particular educational problems and needs of exceptional learners, who constitute 10 percent to 15 percent of the school population.

Based on the material covered in this chapter, we propose several research topics that in our view are especially relevant for educational psychologists. The first has to do with the increasingly broad range of exceptional individuals eligible for services. Recognition of the importance of early intervention, and an emphasis on prevention rather than remediation, means that educational services will be extended to very young children, even to infants. Similarly, the continuing educational needs of exceptional youths and adults require that educational psychologists move beyond the relatively narrow constraints of schooling defined as kindergarten through Grade 12. Further, the addition of autism and traumatic brain injury to the categories of exceptionality recognized by the Office of Special Education Programs of the U.S. Department of Education, combined with the current interest in attention deficit/hyperactivity disorder and prenatal exposure to substance abuse, suggests that the percentage of schoolchildren considered exceptional may be substantially increased. Clearly, the traditional techniques of assessment, measurement, and instruction must change in response to the unique needs of these populations.

A second topic relates to questions of possible etiology-specific patterns of learning and thus to specialized educational needs. A major task is to delineate commonalities and differences in learning strategies between exceptional learners and their nondisabled peers, as well as to identify possible differences in aptitudes within the population of exceptional individuals. The qualitative-quantitative question raised earlier is still unanswered.

A third and closely related challenge has to do with the movement toward fuller inclusion of exceptional students in regular education programs. Inclusion means not just physical placement, but at the very least requires consideration and test of strategies for integration, including implications for personnel and resources. Moreover, the impact of exceptional children on the achievement and attitudes of nonhandicapped classmates warrants evaluation and may require reconsideration of what constitutes effective classrooms and effective schools. The need for empirical evidence of efficacy is particularly important if full inclusion is taken literally and children with severe and profound mental retardation or emotional disturbance are placed in regular classes.

A fourth critical area has to do with the documentation of program outcomes for exceptional learners. Exceptional learners have often been excluded in evaluations of regular education programs; further, many practices found in special education programs are essentially untested. Evaluation of the impact of programs for exceptional learners presents some unique problems and challenges to traditional approaches, yet it is of particular importance in light of the current emphasis on higher standards of performance.

These are not new topics, but have increased urgency given the current needs for educational reform. We caution that good intentions are necessary but not sufficient, and that change is likely to be slow. We argue, too, that changes in educational policies and practices must take into account the broad range of individuals who are viewed as exceptional.

## References

American Psychiatric Association. (1987). *Diagnostic and statistical manual of mental disorders* (3rd ed., rev.). Washington, DC: American Psychiatric Press.

American Psychiatric Association. (1994). *Diagnostic and statistical manual of mental disorders* (4th ed.). Washington, DC: American Psychiatric Press.

*America 2000 Sourcebook*. (1992). Washington, DC: U.S. Department of Education.

Ayres, L. P. (1909). *Laggards in our schools*. New York: Russell Sage Foundation.

Bailey, K. (1973). Monothetic and polythetic typologies and their relation to conceptualization, measurement, and scaling. *American Sociology Review, 38*(1), 18–33.

Balow, I. H., MacMillan, D. L., & Hendrick, I. G. (1986). Local option competency testing: Psychometric issues with mildly handicapped and educationally marginal students. *Learning Disabilities Research, 2*(1), 32–37.

Benbow, C. P., & Stanley, J. C. (1983). An eight-year evaluation of SMPY: What was learned? In C. P. Benbow & J. C. Stanley (Eds.), *Academic precocity: Aspects of its development*. Baltimore: Johns Hopkins University Press.

Binet, A., & Simon, T. (1905). Methods nouvelles pour le diagnostic du nouveau intellectuel des anormaux. *Année Psychologique, 11*, 191–244.

Blashfield, R. K. (1993). Models of classification as related to a taxonomy of learning disabilities. In G. R. Lyon, D. B. Gray, J. F. Kavanagh, & N. A. Krasnegor (Eds.), *Better understanding of learning disabilities* (pp. 17–26). Baltimore: Paul H. Brookes Publishing.

Bloom, B. S. (1964). *Stability and change in human characteristics*. New York: Wiley.

Borkowski, J. G., Johnston, M. B., & Reid, M. K. (1987). Metacognition, motivation, and controlled performance. In S. J. Ceci (Ed.), *Handbook of cognitive, social, and neuropsychological aspects of learning disabilities* (pp. 147–173). Hillsdale, NJ: Lawrence Erlbaum Associates.

Bransford, J. D., Delclos, V. R., Vye, N. J., Burns, M. S., & Hasselbring, T. S. (1987). Approaches to dynamic assessment: Issues, data, and future directions. In C. S. Lidz (Ed.), *Dynamic assessment: Foundation and fundamentals* (pp. 479–496). New York: Guilford Press.

Brooks, P. H., Sperber, R., & McCauley, C. (Eds.). (1984). *Learning and cognition in the mentally retarded*. Hillsdale, NJ: Lawrence Erlbaum Associates.

Brown, A. L., & Campione, J. (1986). Psychological theory and the study of learning disabilities. *American Psychologist, 41*, 1059–1068.

Budoff, M. (1967). Learning potential among institutionalized young adult retardates. *American Journal of Mental Deficiency, 72*, 404–411.

Budoff, M. (1987). The validity of learning potential assessment. In C. S. Lidz (Ed.), *Dynamic assessment: An international approach* (pp. 52–81). New York: Guilford Press.

Burack, J. A. (1990). Differentiating mental retardation: The two-group approach and beyond. In R. M. Hodapp, J. A. Burack, & E. Zigler (Eds.), *Issues in the developmental approach to mental retardation* (pp. 27–48). New York: Cambridge University Press.

Campbell, D. T. & Stanley, J. C. (1963). Experimental and quasi-experimental designs for research on teaching. In N. L. Gage (Ed.), *Handbook of research on teaching* (pp. 171–246). Chicago: Rand-McNally.

Cattell, R. B. (1987). *Intelligence: Its structure, growth, and action*. Amsterdam: Elsevier Science.

Ceci, S. J. (Ed.) (1986). *Handbook of cognitive, social, and neuropsychological aspects of learning disabilities* (Vols. 1 and 2). Hillsdale, NJ: Lawrence Erlbaum Associates.

Ceci, S. J. (1990). *On intelligence—more or less: A bioecological treatise on intellectual development*. Englewood Cliffs, NJ: Prentice Hall.

Cone, T. E., & Wilson, L. R. (1981). Quantifying a severe discrepancy: A critical analysis. *Learning Disability Quarterly, 4*(4), 359–371.

Corno, L., & Snow, R. E. (1986). Adapting teaching to individual differences among learners. In M. C. Wittrock (Ed.), *Handbook of research on teaching* (3rd ed., pp. 605–629). New York: Macmillan.

Cronbach, L. J. (1957). The two disciplines of scientific psychology. *American Psychologist, 12*, 671–684.

Cruickshank, W. M., Bentzen, F. A., Ratzeberg, F. H., & Tannhauser, M. T. (1961). *A teaching method for brain-injured and hyperactive children*. Syracuse: Syracuse University Press.

Deno, S. L., & Fuchs, L. S. (1987). Developing curriculum-based measurement systems for data-based special education problem solving. *Focus on Exceptional Children, 19*(8), 1–16.

Doris, J. (1993). Defining learning disabilities. A history of the search for consensus. In G. R. Lyon, D. B. Gray, J. F. Kavanagh, & N. A. Krasnegor (Eds.), *Better understanding of learning disabilities*. Baltimore: Paul H. Brookes Publishing.

Elliott, R. (1987). *Litigating intelligence*. Dover, MA: Auburn House.

Ellis, N. R. (1979). *Handbook of mental deficiency: Psychological theory and research* (2nd ed.). Hillsdale, NJ: Lawrence Erlbaum Associates.

Feuerstein, R. (1979). *The dynamic assessment of retarded performers: The learning potential assessment device, theory, instructions, and techniques*. Baltimore: University Park Press.

Fletcher, J. M., Francis, D. J., Rourke, B. P., Shaywitz, S. E., & Shaywitz, B. A. (1993). Classification of learning disabilities: Relationships with other childhood disorders. In G. R. Lyon, D. B. Gray, J. F. Kavanagh, & N. A. Krasnegor (Eds.), *Better understanding of learning disabilities* (pp. 27–55) Baltimore: Paul H. Brookes Publishing.

Forness, S. R., & Kavale, K. A. (1984). Education of the mentally retarded: A note on policy. *Education and Training of the Mentally Retarded, 19*, 239–245.

Fox, L. H., & Washington, J. (1985). Programs for the gifted and talented. In F. D. Horowitz & M. O'Brien (Eds.), *The gifted and talented: Developmental perspectives* (pp. 197–221). Washington, DC: American Psychological Association.

Freeman, J. (1995). Annotation: Recent studies of giftedness in children. *Journal of Child Psychology and Psychiatry, 36*(4), 531–547.

Frostig, M., & Horne, D. (1964). *The Frostig program for the development of visual perception*. Chicago: Follett.

Fuchs, D., & Fuchs, L. S. (1994). Inclusive school movement and the radicalization of special education reform. *Exceptional Children, 60*(4), 294–309.

Fuchs, L. S., & Fuchs, D. (1984). Criterion-referenced assessment without measurement: How accurate for special education? *Remedial and Special Education, 5*(4), 25–32.

Fuchs, L. S., & Fuchs, D. (1986). Effects of systematic formative evaluation: A meta-analysis. *Exceptional Children, 53*, 199–208.

Gallagher, J. J. (1992). Gifted persons. In M. C. Alkin (Ed.), *Encyclopedia of educational research* (Vol. 2, pp. 544–549). New York: Macmillan.

Gardner, H. (1983). *Frames of mind: The theory of multiple intelligences.* New York: Basic Books.

Gersten, R., & Woodward, J. (1990). The thinking the regular education initiative: Focus on the classroom teacher. *Remedial and Special Education, 11*(3), 7–16.

Goals 2000. Educate America Act. A Strategy for Reinventing Our Schools. Washington, D.C.: U.S. Department of Education. 1993, pp. 1–5.

Goldstein, K. (1942). *Affects of brain injuries in war.* New York: Grune & Stratton.

Gottlieb, J. (1981). Mainstreaming: Fulfilling the promise? *American Journal of Mental Deficiency, 86,* 115–126.

Gruber, H. E. (1985). Giftedness and moral responsibility: Creative thinking and human survival. In F. D. Horowitz & M. O'Brien (Eds.), *The gifted and talented: Developmental perspectives.* Washington, DC: American Psychological Association.

Guilford, J. P. (1967). *The nature of human intelligence.* New York: McGraw-Hill.

Halvorsen, A. T., & Sailor, W. (1990). Integration of students with severe and profound disabilities: A review of research. In R. Gaylord-Ross (Ed.), *Issues and research in special education* (pp. 110–172). New York: Teachers College Press.

Heller, K. A., Holtzman, W. H., & Messick, S. (1982). *Placing children in special education: A strategy for equity.* Washington, DC: National Science Foundation, National Academy Press.

Hendrick, I. G., & MacMillan, D. L. (1989). Selecting children for special education in New York City: William Maxwell, Elizabeth Farrell, and the development of ungraded classes, 1900–1920. *Journal of Special Education, 22,* 395–417.

Heshusius, L. (1991). Curriculum-based assessment and direct instruction: Critical reflections on fundamental assumptions. *Exceptional Children, 57,* 315–328.

Hewett, F. M. (1968). *The emotionally disturbed child in the classroom.* Boston: Allyn & Bacon.

Hobbs, N. (Ed.) (1975). *Issues in the classification of children* (Vols. I and II). San Francisco: Jossey-Bass.

Hodapp, R. M. (1990). One road or many? Issues in the similar sequence hypothesis. In R. M. Hodapp, J. A. Burack, & E. Zigler (Eds.), *Issues in the developmental approach to mental retardation* (pp. 49–70). New York: Cambridge University Press.

Hodapp, R. M., & Dykens, E. M. (1994). Mental retardation's two cultures of behavioral research. *American Journal on Mental Retardation, 98*(6), 675–687.

Hoge, R. D., & Cudmore, L. (1986). The rise of teacher judgment measures in the identification of gifted pupils. *Teaching and Teacher Education, 2*(2), 181–196.

Hollingworth, L. (1942). *Children above 180 IQ.* New York: World Books.

Horowitz, F. D., & O'Brien, M. (1985). Perspectives on research and development. In F. D. Horowitz & M. O'Brien (Eds.), *The gifted and talented: Developmental perspectives* (pp. 437–454). Washington, DC: American Psychological Association.

Howell, K., & Morehead, M. K. (1987). *Curriculum-based evaluation for special and remedial education.* Columbus, OH: Merrill.

Hunt, J. M. (1961). *Intelligence and experience.* New York: Ronald Press.

Hynd, G. W., & Obrzut, J. E. (1986). Clinical child neurology: Issues and perspectives. In J. E. Obrzut & G. W. Hynd (Eds.), *Child neuropsychology: Clinical practice* (Vol. 2). Orlando, FL: Academic Press.

Interagency Committee on Learning Disabilities (1987). *A report to the Congress.* Washington, DC: U.S. Government Printing Office.

Jackson, N. E., & Butterfield, E. C. (1986). A conception of giftedness designed to promote research. In R. J. Sternberg & J. E. Davidson (Eds.), *Conceptions of giftedness* (pp. 151–181). Cambridge, England: Cambridge University Press.

Jacobs, J. E., & Paris, S. G. (1987). Children's metacognition about reading: Issues in definition, movement, and instruction. *Educational Psychologist, 22*(3, 4), 255–278.

Janos, R. M., & Robinson, N. M. (1985). Psychological development in intellectually gifted children. In F. D. Horowitz & M. O'Brien (Eds.), *The gifted and talented: Developmental perspectives* (pp. 149–195). Washington, DC: American Psychological Association.

Jensen, A. R. (1970). A theory of primary and secondary familial mental retardation. In N. R. Ellis (Ed.), *International review of research in mental retardation* (Vol. 4, pp. 33–105). New York: Academic Press.

Jensen, A. R. (1980). *Bias in mental testing.* New York: Free Press.

Johnson, D. J. (1988). Review of research on specific reading, writing, and mathematical disorders. In J. F. Kavanagh & T. J. Truss, Jr. (Eds.), *Learning disabilities: Proceedings of the national conference* (pp. 79–163). Parkton, MD: York Press.

*Journal of Learning Disabilities* (1988). *21*(1).

Kauffman, J. M. (1989). The Regular Education Initiative as a Reagan-Bush education policy: A trickle-down of the hard-to-teach. *Journal of Special Education, 23,* 256–278.

Kauffman, J. M. (1993). How we might achieve the radical reform of special education. *Exceptional Children, 60*(1), 6–16.

Kauffman, J. M., Gerber, M. M., & Semmel, M. I. (1988). Arguable assumptions underlying the Regular Education Initiative. *Journal of Learning Disabilities, 21,* 6–11.

Kauffman, J. M., & Hallahan, D. P. (Eds.). (1994). *The illusion of full inclusion.* Austin, TX: Pro-Ed.

Kauffman, J. M., Kameenui, E. J., Birman, B., & Danielson, L. (1990). Special education and the process of change: Victim or master of educational reform? *Exceptional Children, 57,* 109–115.

Kavale, K. A., Fuchs, D., & Scruggs, T. E. (1994). Setting the record straight on learning disability and low achievement: Implications for policymaking. *Learning Disabilities Research & Practice, 9*(2), 70–77.

Kavanagh, J. F., & Truss, T. J., Jr. (Eds.). (1988). *Learning disabilities: Proceedings of the national conference.* Parkton, MD: York Press.

Keogh, B. K. (1988). Learning disability: Diversity in search of order. In M. Wang, M. Reynolds, & H. Walberg (Eds.), *Handbook of special education research and practice* (pp. 225–249). London: Pergamon Press.

Keogh, B. K. (1990). Definitional assumptions and research issues. In J. L. Swanson & B. Keogh (Eds.), *Learning disabilities: Theoretical and research issues* (pp. 13–19). Hillsdale, NJ: Lawrence Erlbaum.

Keogh, B. K. (1993). Linking purpose and practice: Social, political and developmental perspectives on classification. In G. R. Lyon, D. B. Gray, J. F. Kavanagh, & N. A. Krasneger (Eds.), *Better understanding of learning disabilities* (pp. 311–323). Baltimore, MD: Paul H. Brookes Publishing.

Keogh, B. K. (1994). What the special education research agenda should look like in the year 2000. *Learning Disabilities Research & Practice, 9*(2), 62–69.

Keogh, B. K., & MacMillan, D. L. (1983). The logic of sample selection: Who represents what? *Exceptional Education Quarterly, 4*(3), 84–96.

Keogh, B. K., Major-Kingsley, S., Omori-Gordon, H., & Reid, H. P. (1982). *A system of marker variables for the field of learning disabilities.* Syracuse: Syracuse University Press.

Kephart, N. C. (1960). *The slow learner in the classroom.* Columbus, OH: Merrill.

Kirk, S. (1963). Behavioral diagnosis and remediation of learning disabilities: *Proceedings of a conference on problems of perceptually handicapped children, 1,* 1–23.

Kirk, S., McCarthy, J., & Kirk, W. (1968). *The Illinois test of psycholinguistic abilities.* Champaign-Urbana; University of Illinois Press.

Kulik, J. A., & Kulik, C. C. (1984). Synthesis of research on effects of accelerated instruction. *Educational Leadership, 42*(2), 84–89.

Laski, F. J. (1991). Achieving integration during the second revolution.

In L. H. Meyer, C. A. Peck, & L. Brown (Eds.), *Critical issues in the lives of people with severe disabilities* (pp. 409–421). Baltimore, MD: Paul H. Brookes Publishing.

Learning Disabilities Association of America. (1993). Position paper on full inclusion of all students with learning disabilities in a regular education classroom. Pittsburgh, PA: Learning Disabilities Association of America.

Lidz, C. S. (Ed.) (1987). *Dynamic assessment: Foundation and fundamentals.* New York: Guilford Press.

Lieberman, L. M. (1992). Preserving special education . . . For those who need it. In W. Stainback & S. Stainback (Eds.), *Controversial issues confronting special education: Divergent perspectives* (pp. 13–25). Boston: Allyn & Bacon.

Lloyd, J. W. (1988). Direct academic intervention in learning disabilities. In M. Wang, M. Reynolds, & H. Walberg (Eds.), *Handbook of Special Education* (pp. 345–366). London: Pergamon Press.

Lloyd, J. W., & Landrum, T. (1990). Self-recording of attending to task: Treatment components and generalization of effects. In T. E. Scruggs & B. Y. L. Wong (Eds.), *Intervention research in learning disabilities* (pp. 235–262). New York: Springer-Verlag.

Luckasson, R. (Ed.). (1992). *Mental retardation: Definition, classification, and systems of support.* Washington, DC: American Association on Mental Retardation.

MacMillan, D. L. (1982). *Mental retardation in school and society* (2nd ed.). Boston: Little, Brown.

MacMillan, D. L. (1989a). Equality, excellence, and the EMR populations: 1970–1989. *Psychology in Mental Retardation and Development Disabilities, 15*(2), 1, 3–10.

MacMillan, D. L. (1989b). Mild mental retardation: Emerging issues. In G. A. Robinson, J. R. Patton, E. A. Polloway, & L. R. Sargent (Eds.), *Best practices in mild mental disabilities* (pp. 1–20). Reston, VA: Council for Exceptional Children, Division on Mental Retardation.

MacMillan, D. L., Balow, I. H., & Widaman, K. F. (1988). Local optional competency testing: Conceptual issues with mildly handicapped and educationally at-risk students. *Learning Disabilities Research, 3*(2), 94–100.

MacMillan, D. L., & Hendrick, J. G. (1993). Evolution and legacies. In J. I. Goodlad & T. C. Lovitt (Eds.), *Integrating general and special education* (pp. 23–48). Columbus, OH: Merrill.

MacMillan, D. L., Meyers, C. E., & Morrison, G. M. (1980). System-identification of learning disabled children: Implications for interpreting and conducting research. *American Journal of Mental Deficiency, 85*, 108–115.

MacMillan, D. L., & Morrison, G. M. (1980). Evolution of behaviorism from the laboratory to special education settings. In B. K. Keogh (Ed.), *Advances in special education* (Vol. 2, pp. 1–28). Greenwich, CT: JAI Press.

MacMillan, D. L., & Morrison, G. M. (1984). Sociometric research in special education. In R. L. Jones (Ed.), *Attitudes and attitude change in special education: Theory and practice* (pp. 93–117). Reston, VA: Council for Exceptional Children.

MacMillan, D. L., Widaman, K. F., Balow, I. H., Borthwick-Duffy, S., & Hendrick, I. G., Hemsley, R. (1992). Special education students exiting the educational system. *Journal of Special Education, 26*(1), 20–36.

Marland, S., Jr. (1972). *Education of the Gifted and Talented.* Report to the U.S. Congress. Washington, DC: U.S. Government Printing Office.

Mastropieri, M. A., & Fulk, B. J. M. (1990). Enhancing academic performance with mnemonic instruction. In T. E. Scruggs & B. Y. L. Wong (Eds.), *Intervention research on learning disabilities* (pp. 102–121). New York: Springer Verlag.

McKinney, J. D. (1984). The search for subtypes of specific learning disability. *Annual Review of Learning Disabilities, 12,* 19–26.

McShane, D., & Cook, V. J. (1985). Transcultural intellectual assessment: Performance by Hispanics on the Wechsler scales. In B. Wolman (Ed.), *Handbook of intelligence* (pp. 737–785). New York: Wiley.

Mehan, H., Meihls, J. L., Herweck, A., & Crowdes, M. S. (1981). Identifying handicapped students. In S. B. Bacharach (Ed.), *Behavior in schools and school districts* (pp. 381–428). New York: Praeger.

Mercer, J. R., & Lewis, J. (1977). *System of multicultural pluralistic assessment: Conceptual and technical manual.* Riverside, CA: University of California, Riverside, Department of Sociology.

Meyers, A. W., & Craighead, W. E. (Eds.). (1984). *Cognitive behavior therapy with children.* New York: Plenum Press.

Morrison, G. M., MacMillan, D. L., & Kavale, K. (1985). System identification of learning disabled children: Implications for research sampling. *Learning Disability Quarterly, 8*(1), 2–10.

Mundy, P., & Kasari, C. (1990). The similar-structure hypothesis and differential rate of development in mental retardation. In R. M. Hodapp, J. A. Burack, & E. Zigler (Eds.), *Issues in the developmental approach to mental retardation* (pp. 71–92). New York: Cambridge University Press.

National Association of State Boards of Education (1992). *Winners all: A call for inclusive education.* The Report of the NASBE Study Group on Special Education. Alexandria, VA: National Association of State Boards of Education. pp. 1–44.

*National Joint Committee on Learning Disabilities.* (1987). Learning disabilities: Issues of definition. *Journal of Learning Disabilities. 20,* 107–108.

Obrzut, J. E., & Boliek, C. A. (1991). Neuropsychological assessment of childhood learning disabilities. In H. L. Swanson (Ed.), *Handbook on the assessment of learning disabilities.* Austin, TX: Pro-Ed.

Office of Special Education Programs. (1990). *Twelfth annual report to Congress on the implementation of the Education of the Handicapped Act.* Washington, DC: U.S. Department of Education.

Office of Special Education Programs. (1993). *Fifteenth annual report to Congress on the implementation of the Individuals with Disabilities Education Act.* Washington, DC: U.S. Department of Education.

O'Leary, K. D., & Drabman, R. (1971). Token reinforcement in the classroom: A review. *Psychological Bulletin, 75,* 379–398.

Palincsar, A. S., Brown, A. L., & Campione, J. C. (1991). Dynamic assessment. In H. L. Swanson (Ed.), *Handbook on the assessment of learning disabilities* (pp. 79–94). Austin, TX: Pro-Ed.

Pearson, D. P., Barr, R., Kamil, M. L., & P. Mosenthal. (1991). *Handbook of reading research.* New York: Longman.

Pueschel, S., Gallagher, P., Zartler, A., & Pezzulo, J. (1987). Cognitive and learning processes in children with Down syndrome. *Research in Developmental Disabilities, 8,* 21–37.

*Remedial and Special Education,* May/June. *11*(3).

Renzuli, J. (1977). *The enrichment triad model: A guide for developing defensible programs for the gifted and talented.* Mansfield Center, CT: Creative Learning Press.

Reschly, D. J. (1988). Minority mild mental retardation over-representation: Legal issues, research findings, and reform trends. In M. C. Wang, M. C. Reynolds, & H. J. Walberg (Eds.), *Handbook of special education: Research and practice* (Vol. 2, pp. 23–41). Oxford, England: Pergamon Press.

Reynolds, C. R. (1984–1985). Critical measurement issues in learning disabilities. *Journal of Special Education, 18*(4), 451–476.

Reynolds, M. C., Wang, M. C., & Walberg, H. J. (1987). The necessary restructuring of special and regular education. *Exceptional Children 53*(5), 391–398.

Richardson, S. A., Katz, M., & Koller, H. (1986). Sex differences in the numbers of children administratively classified as mildly mentally retarded: An epidemiological review. *American Journal of Mental Retardation, 91,* 250–256.

Robinson, N. M., & Noble, K. D. (1991). Social-emotional development and adjustment of gifted children. In M. C. Wang, M. C. Reynolds, &

H. J. Walberg (Eds.), *Handbook of Special Education Research and Practice* (Vol. 4). Oxford, England: Pergamon Press.

Rogoff, B. (1982). Integrating context and cognitive development. In M. E. Lamb, & A. L. Brown (Eds.), *Advances in developmental psychology* (Vol. 2, pp. 125–170). Hillsdale, NJ: Lawrence Erlbaum Associates.

Salvia, J., & Hughes, C. (1990). *Curriculum-based assessment: Testing what is taught.* New York: Macmillan.

Sattler, J. M. (1988). *Assessment of children* (3rd ed.). San Diego: Sattler.

Scheerenberger, R. C. (1983). *A history of mental retardation.* Baltimore, MD: Paul H. Brookes Publishing.

Scruggs, T. E., & Mastropieri, M. A. (1992). Classroom applications of mnemonic instruction: Acquisition, maintenance, and generalization. *Exceptional Children, 58*(3), 219–229.

Scruggs, T. E., & Wong, B. Y. L. (Eds.) (1990). *Intervention research in learning disabilities.* New York: Springer.

Shaywitz, S. E., Escobar, M., Shaywitz, B. A., Fletcher, J. M., & Makuch, R. (1992). Evidence that dyslexia may represent the lower tail of a normal distribution of reading ability. *New England Journal of Medicine, 326*(3), 145–150.

Sheehan, R., & Keogh, B. K. (1982). Design and analysis in the evaluation of early childhood special education programs. *Topics in Early Childhood Special Education, 1*(4), 81–88.

Shepard, L. (1983). The role of measurement in educational policy: Lessons from the identification of learning disabilities. *Educational Measurement Issues and Practice, 2*(3), 4–8.

Siegel, L. S. (1990). IQ and learning disabilities: RIP. In H. L. Swanson & B. K. Keogh (Eds.), *Learning disabilities: Theoretical and research issues.* Hillsdale, NJ: Lawrence Erlbaum Associates.

Silon, E. L., & Harter, S. (1985). Assessment of perceived competence, motivational orientation, and anxiety in segregated and mainstreamed educable mentally retarded children. *Journal of Educational Psychology, 77,* 217–230.

*Special services in the schools.* (1986). Emerging perspectives on assessment of exceptional children, 2(2/3). Binghamton, New York: Haworth Press.

Speece, D. L. (1990). Aptitude-treatment interactions: Bad rap or bad idea? *Journal of Special Education, 24*(2), 139–149.

Speece, D. L., & Cooper, D. H. (1991). Retreat, regroup, or advance? An agenda for empirical classification research in learning disabilities. In L. V. Feagens, E. G. Short, & L. J. Meltzer (Eds.), *Subtypes of learning disabilities* (pp. 33–52). Hillsdale, NJ: Lawrence Erlbaum Associates.

Spitz, H. H. (1986). *The raising of intelligence: A selected history of attempts to raise retarded intelligence.* Hillsdale, NJ: Lawrence Erlbaum Associates.

Stainback, W., & Stainback, S. (1984). A rationale for the merger of special and regular education. *Exceptional Children, 51*(2), 102–111.

Stanovich, K. E. (1985). Explaining the variance in reading ability in terms of psychological processes: What have we learned? *Annals of Dyslexia, 35,* 67–96.

Sternberg, R. J. (1985). *Beyond IQ: A triarchic framework for intelligence.* New York: Cambridge University Press.

Sternberg, R. J., & Davidson, J. E. (1985). Cognitive development in the gifted and talented. In F. D. Horowitz & M. O'Brien (Eds.), *The gifted and talented: A developmental perspective* (pp. 37–74). Washington, DC: American Psychological Association.

Sternberg, R. J., & Davidson, J. E. (Eds.). (1986). *Conceptions of giftedness.* New York: Cambridge University Press.

Strauss, A. A., & Lehtinen, L. E. (1947). *Psychotherapy and education of the brain-injured child* (Vol. 1). New York: Grune & Stratton.

Swanson, H. L. (1988). Learning disabled children's problem solving: Identifying mental processes underlying intelligent performance. *Intelligence, 12,* 261–278.

Swanson, H. L. (Ed.). (1991). *Handbook on the assessment of learning disabilities.* Austin, TX: Pro-Ed.

Swanson, H. L. (1993). Learning disabilities from the perspective of cognitive psychology. In G. R. Lyon, D. B. Gray, J. F. Kavanagh, N. A. Krashegor (Eds.), *Better understanding of learning disabilities.* Baltimore, MD: Paul H. Brookes Publishing.

Swanson, H. L., & Keogh, B. K. (Eds.). (1990). *Learning disabilities: Theoretical and research issues.* Hillsdale, NJ: Lawrence Erlbaum Associates.

Tallal, P. (1988). Developmental language disorders. In J. F. Kavanagh & T. Truss, Jr. (Eds.), *Learning disabilities: Proceedings of the national conference* (pp. 181–272). Parkton, MD: York Press.

Tarjan, G. (1972, October). *Toward accelerated progress in mental retardation.* Paper presented at the first convention of the Federacíon Venezolanga de Padres y Amigos de Ninos Exceptionales (FEVEPANE), Caracas, Venezuela.

Taylor, S. J. (1988). Caught in the continuum: A critical analysis of the principle of the least restrictive environment. *Journal of the Association for Persons with Severe Handicaps, 13,* 41–53.

Terman, L. M. (1916). *The measurement of intelligence.* Boston: Houghton Mifflin.

Terman, L. M. (1919). *The intelligence of school children.* Boston: Houghton Mifflin.

Terman, L. M. (1925). *Mental and physical traits of a thousand gifted children: Their education and development* (Vol. 1). Stanford, CA: Stanford University Press.

Tharp, R. G., & Gallimore, R. (1988). *Rousing minds to life.* Cambridge: Cambridge University Press.

Thurstone, L. L. (1938). Primary mental abilities. *Psychometric Monographs, 1.*

Torgesen, J. K. (1991). Learning disabilities: Historical and conceptual issues. In B. Wong (Ed.), *Learning about learning disabilities.* San Diego: Academic Press.

Tyler, L. E. (1978). *Individuality.* San Francisco: Jossey-Bass.

Tryon, W. W. (1979). The test-trait fallacy. *American Psychologist, 34,* 402–406.

Udwin, O., Yule, W., & Martin, M. (1987). Cognitive abilities and behavioral characteristics of children with idiopathic infantile hypercalcemia. *Journal of Child Psychology and Psychiatry, 28,* 297–309.

Wagner, M., Newman, L., D'Amico, R., Jap, E. D., Butler-Dalin, P., Marder, C., & Cox, R. (1991). *Youth with disabilities: How are they doing?* Menlo Park, CA: SRI International.

Webb, N. M. (1982). Group composition, group interaction, and achievement in cooperative small groups. *Journal of Educational Psychology, 74,* 475–485.

Weisz, J., & Zigler, E. (1979). Cognitive development in retarded and nonretarded persons: Piagetian tests of the similar-sequence hypothesis. *Psychological Bulletin, 86,* 831–851.

Wertsch, J. V. (1985). *Culture, communication, and cognition: Vygotskian perspectives.* Cambridge, England: Cambridge University Press.

Will, M. C. (1986). Educating children with learning problems: A shared responsibility. *Exceptional Children, 52*(5), 411–416.

Wolman, C., Bruininks, R., & Thurlow, M. (1989). Dropouts and dropout programs: Implications for special education. *Remedial and Special Education, 10,* 6–20, 50.

Wong, B. Y. L. (1988). An instructional model for intervention research in learning disabilities. *Learning Disability Research, 4*(1), 5–16.

Ysseldyke, J. E., Algozzine, B., Regan, R., & Potter, M. (1980). Technical adequacy of tests used by professionals in simulated decision-making. *Psychology in the Schools, 17,* 202–209.

Ysseldyke, J. E., Algozzine, B., Shinn, M., & McGue, M. (1982). Similarities and differences between underachievers and students labeled learning disabled. *Journal of Special Education, 16,* 73–85.

Zigler, E. (1967). Familial mental retardation: A continuing dilemma. *Science, 155,* 292–298.

Zigler, E. (1982). Developmental versus difference theories of mental retardation and the problem of motivation. In E. Zigler & D. Balla (Eds.), *Mental retardation: The developmental-difference controversy* (pp. 163–188). Hillsdale, NJ: Lawrence Erlbaum Associates.

Zigler, E., Balla, D., & Hodapp, R. M. (1984). On the definition and classification of mental retardation. *American Journal of Mental Deficiency, 89,* 215–230.

Zigler, E., & Farber, E. A. (1985). Commonalities between the intellectual extremes: Giftedness and mental retardation. In F. D. Horowitz, & M. O'Brien (Eds.), *The gifted and talented: Developmental perspectives* (pp. 387–408). Washington, DC: American Psychological Association.

Zigler, E., & Hodapp, R. M. (1986). *Understanding mental retardation.* New York: Cambridge University Press.

Zigler, E., Phillips, L. (1961). Psychiatric diagnosis: A critique. *Journal of Abnormal and Social Psychology, 63,* 607–618.

# ·11·

# ETHNICITY AND CULTURE IN

# EDUCATIONAL PSYCHOLOGY

## Pedro R. Portes

UNIVERSITY OF LOUISVILLE

## EDUCATION AND CULTURE

Educational psychology confronts at least two major problems today. One problem has to do with the sociocultural factors that make schools ineffectual in educating children from certain cultures. The second problem is even more fundamental, for it concerns the relationship between culture and mind. The school achievement gap among ethnic groups, an index of group-based inequality, has led to many attempts at cure, from multicultural educational programs for students and educators to the incorporation of culture-sensitive books and a variety of instructional methods in the curriculum. Educational psychology has played a minor role in the development of the latter and focused more on testing and basic skills approaches in teaching. Educational psychology seems to favor a methodological approach to "culture-related" educational problems that follow in the tradition of post hoc, aptitude–treatment interaction (ATI) research.

The way educational psychology has dealt with ethnicity and culture mirrors how psychology has addressed those issues in general, chiefly as areas outside its primary research concerns. Ethnicity and culture have been treated mainly as control variables in a literature where a focus on race, a pseudoscientific category, has overshadowed the study of culture and led to dubious assumptions for both theory and research (Zuckerman, 1990). The theories that in the past helped with classroom management, instructional design, or measurement, or that advanced the cause of meaningful learning, have not been able to tackle effectively group-based inequality. Some might argue that educational psychology need not address such limitations, since these lie outside the realm of the individual psyche and of psychology in general. Yet limitations in understanding the

relations among mind, culture, and development are partly responsible for this problem.

Both conceptions of what ethnicity actually is, and ethnocentrism, are rooted in a group's social knowledge base (Stanfield, 1985), just as for any other "groupism" (Sirotnik, 1990). This often leads to the subtle forging of inequality in multicultural contexts, where inequality exists in both access to means and in ends. This bipartite inequality has, in fact, been well documented in the literature (Coleman, 1973, 1990; The Forgotten Half, 1988; Jencks et al., 1972). These inequalities lead to the forging of ethnic or group identities, discourses (A. Portes & Stepick, 1993), and narratives (Martin, 1995). Modern psychology, with its "narrowly focused and compulsively insular camps" (Bevan, 1991), has tended to avoid issues that require attention to the problem of mind and culture. Educational psychology now faces a crisis because of its intimate role in educational practices that leave many children disenfranchised by virtue of poorly understood cultural histories.

Thus, contemporary educational psychology is subject to two critiques. First, it has been largely limited to playing a mediating role among the reigning paradigms in psychology and educational practice. Those paradigms have tended to be acultural, ethnocentric, or both. Second, educational psychology has not capitalized on its strategic field position in advancing the discipline through vigorous theoretical pursuit of those accumulating anomalies in the literature concerning ethnicity and culture. It has not focused on the study of teaching and learning as a joint process from a cultural or a developmental perspective. For example, anomalies are often evident in ATI studies and intervention research. Student characteristics that are culturally based are often treated superficially, and between-group differences tend to be explained nomothetically by "race." Why, for instance, is membership in one (ethnic) group

The author acknowledges the assistance lent by Ronald Gallimore, Luis Moll, Michael Cole, Jaan Valsiner and Elsie Moore in developing this chapter.

related to differences in educational outcomes, independent of socioeconomic status (SES) and other factors? Why are within-group differences ignored? Why are most current research efforts in the discipline so distal to history and culture? Such omissions have left a void that is quickly being filled by scholars from other disciplines. The result of the above limitations has been a fragmented research landscape in educational research that is reflected in disjointed research themes, particularly in basic texts. The study of social and mental development, learning theories, humanistic-wholistic education, cooperative learning, special education, motivation, measurement, and content area research (e.g., science education), and even this *Handbook* itself illustrate the segmentation of the discipline. Each area has different goals and treats cultural factors and differences in a post hoc fashion, often separate from each respective area. From this view, educational pschology has lost an opportunity to steer the mother discipline toward a broader understanding of the human mind.

Educational psychology prospers by addressing culture directly and testing the mettle of extant models and the assumptions inherent in their knowledge base. In developmental and clinical psychology, the acultural bent of research has been recently noted (Sarason, 1981a; Wertsch & Tulviste, 1992). A cultural approach would lead educational psychology to search for ways of unpacking (Whiting, 1980) aggregated group characteristics (e.g., SES, ethnicity, or gender-related beliefs, behaviors, or attitudes) for improving classroom learning and teaching.

Most current educational psychology models tend to approach student characteristics as fixed traits or aptitudes that exist outside the intercultural context that, quite possibly, defines them. Some have argued that at-risk students should change their attributions or that they receive instruction that is too basic, which in turn discourages those already performing below the norm. Others argue for or against whole language learning and inductive methods and in favor of more direct instruction (Delpit, 1986). Today, new educational goals are becoming evident, causing corresponding changes in the goals and methods of measurement and evaluation. However, even culture-sensitive approaches tend to overlook within-group differences that are substantial and resist stereotypy. Matute-Bianchi (1986) identified several categories of students of Mexican background within a single school, and Ogbu (1990) noted five types of successful African-American students. Despite their small numbers, Native and Asian Americans are also more diverse in language and cultural traits than the 12 percent of European Americans who are poor and who constitute the lower end of the distribution of English-speaking whites. An argument can thus be made for educational psychology to align its mediational role and research priorities in a cultural direction. Culture remains a "black box" in the field, one wherein many of the mysteries related to group differences in achievement and to ATI phenomena lie hidden. Ethnicity, a sociobiological construct, still is confounded with class, history, and physical traits, conceptually and in practice (Dominguez, 1986). For the purposes of this chapter, *ethnicity* is treated as a category that involves a contrast among *types* of culture shared by groups differing in history, language, beliefs, physical genotype, or other socially relevant traits. Ethnicity is viewed here essentially as a dialectical construct ("us/them") that reflects distinct

sources of cultural influences on human development in the context of others.

## Pluralism, Demographics, and Equity Concerns

Ethnic and gender differences in access to both means and ends are central to the problem of group-based inequality. Let us examine the current context in which ethnicity and culture have become relevant, even pressing topics for our field. In the 1960s, study of group-based inequality led to the startling finding that educational achievement is minimally related to a host of standard school variables. The latter have been conceptualized as "quality of inputs to schools," with inputs understood as meaning per-pupil expenditures, personnel qualifications, attitudes, salaries, curricula, books, and the like (Coleman, 1966, 1990) that, in turn, account for output indicators such as educational achievement. Student body and teacher characteristics such as beliefs and vocabulary scores, in fact, showed stronger relationships. However, after relevant variables were controlled for, family background characteristics showed the strongest relation to achievement, leading to the conclusion that "the closest portions of the child's social environment—his family and fellow-students—affect achievement most" (Coleman, 1990, p. 74), followed by (the more socially distant) teachers, with little influence from nonsocial aspects of the school environment. Later, Jencks et al. (1972) found that variations in educational opportunity had little influence on occupational status or income, and that the amount of schooling was of greater importance than school performance. The need for rethinking the organization and the very goals of education became evident. These landmark reports and others published since then (U.S. Department of Education, *The Nation's Report Card*, 1995) are often taken as evidence of a decline in educational quality. Yet they also reflect stability and improvement in schooling and in the distribution of student achievement (Berliner & Biddle, 1995; Bruer, 1993). Studies such as Coleman's suggest that the home setting is the fundamental cell in which cultural differences are formed and acquired, and the primary mediator of achievement differences. Unfortunately, this cell is not generally considered with culture in mind when thinking about the design of instruction or the organization of schooling.

Today's pluralism is a relatively recent trend stemming from a change in societal values. Schooling for the masses is a rather recent phenomenon (M. Cole & S. Cole, 1989), as are current beliefs and expectations of equity, particularly with respect to the quality and value of education. As pressure to improve student achievement mounts, group-based inequality becomes more apparent for some. These developments have moved group-based inequality to the forefront of social sciences concerned with education. As will be noted subsequently, educational psychology emerged in the 20th century in a period that was much less concerned about equity, and it evolved in ways not sensitive to group-based inequality or cultural phenomena in general. Instead, from the outset, educational psychology was more concerned with individual differences and the measurement of abilities than with facilitating student learning (Charles, 1988).

## The Bounds of Group-Based Inequality

A clear index of the problem of group-based inequality may be noted in the distribution of wealth. The top 1 percent of the U.S. population increased its wealth from 28 percent in 1973 to 36 percent in 1990 (U.S. Bureau of the Census, 1990). More than a quarter of a century after the Brown decision, over 40 percent of African-American students live in poverty, and income and related indices have dropped significantly during this period (The Forgotten Half, 1988) despite the civil rights movement. The poverty rates for other colonized ethnic minorities are just as alarming because of the increasing number of children entering the cycle of poverty. Over 25 percent of all children grow up in poverty (Hodgkinson, 1991), and the figure is higher for some ethnic groups according to census data. Ethnicity often tends to be associated with differences in SES, speech, and physical traits. This triple marker of ethnic disadvantage is a formidable barrier to learning and development, for both student and schools. The problem of group-based inequality in educational achievement may thus be defined by a social context in which disproportionate numbers of a cultural group are subject to poverty, school failure, and underdevelopment. Unlike the broader issue of social inequality, which is driven by power, oppression, and subordination, group-based inequality in this chapter is focused on issues concerned with learning, teaching, and development in educational psychology, a field that is striving to understand cultural differences.

Most schools are still segregated by ethnicity and social class (Ornstein & Levine, 1989), with minorities constituting the majority in 23 of the 25 largest school districts in the United States, a trend that is increasing (Banks, 1995; Banks & McGee, 1989). A third of all Spanish-speaking students attend schools in which dominant culture children are a small minority, but not insofar as teachers and administrators are concerned. Approximately 90 percent of teachers are white, a fact that misleads many into thinking of the group-based inequality problem as racial, to be solved primarily by increasing the number of nonwhite teachers. Educational inequality today is indexed mainly by four closely correlated measures: years of education completed, dropout rates, grade retention, and subject matter achievement. Over two decades ago, 30 percent of African-American students dropped out of high school, compared to 15 percent for all other students. Soon thereafter, census data became available not only by race but also by ethnicity. As persons from Spanish-speaking background were officially labeled Hispanic by the federal government, a significant decrease in the dropout rates for white, non-Hispanic students occurred (U.S. Bureau of the Census, 1992). By 1991, a significant decrease in dropout rates was evident for white, (8.4 percent) and black (13.3 percent) students, while 37 percent of students of Latin American origin became high school dropouts. Significant variability exists in the latter group, however, with respect to each subgroup's cultural history.

Children from various Native American groups, followed by those of African and certain Latin-American and Asian origins, run the highest risk of being segregated while in school, of dropping out, of receiving the lowest level of curricula, and of experiencing less favorable learning conditions, expectations, and social interactions, relative to majority group children (Goodlad, 1983; Morgan, 1977; Neisser, 1986; Oakes, 1985).

This occurs even when the latter become the numerical minority in school. The end of the baby boom for European Americans and the relatively low middle-class birth rate, along with immigration, has resulted in a seeming "ethnic boom" that, alongside intergenerationally poor European Americans, contributes to a growing underclass. Although immigrant children often do well in school, an increasing number of them must adapt to conditions that engulf colonized minorities. This underclass will be characterized by less, and poorer, education. Even with the projected demographic changes that may cause the numerical majority to become the largest minority by the year 2020, current schooling practices might not measurably change, as is the case in most countries with a minority dominant culture. In the past, the mechanisms of tracking and teacher education ensured inequality. Now there are changes, but other mechanisms such as private education, the end of affirmative action programs, and computer-assisted instruction are likely to emerge as schools "fail" or remain in a state of crisis. However, schools' failure must be considered in light of changes in the cultural-historical context and of new societal goals (Berliner & Biddle, 1995).

Schools seem generally ineffectual in leveling historically determined cultural differences so that only individual differences would remain. The massive inequality of access and achievement that was documented decades ago (Coleman, 1973; Jencks et al., 1972; Murphy, 1988) remains for some ethnic groups. This observation suggests that it is not only pluralism that drives the current prioritization of educational equity for all but also, and perhaps more important, demographic changes in the constitution of increasingly multicultural societies and the changing global economy. Projections based on current levels of inequity are generally viewed as alarming in a society that has generally sought to be associated with democracy and social justice.

Considerable variation exists with students from historically disadvantaged minority groups as well. Although ethnicity has often been associated with low school achievement and SES, it is also associated with high academic achievement for other groups (see, e.g., M. A. Gibson & Ogbu, 1991; Suarez-Orozco, 1987, 1991). It seems, then, that ethnicity mediates development, particularly in areas related to school achievement. The study of ethnicity has attracted only superficial research attention in the field of educational psychology, however. Although it is a category worthy of inquiry in its own right, where the formation of social identities might play a central role, important questions remain with respect to ethnicity and school learning. What exactly about ethnicity mediates development? How does it operate independently of SES? And how may it be studied theoretically in relation to human development?

It is in this context that the question of group-based inequality—selected to bring attention to culture and ethnicity in educational psychology—becomes relevant. Does educational psychology have anything to offer? The traditional answer has been mostly negative, because group-based inequality is regarded mainly as a sociopolitical issue. From a critical pedagogical view, educational psychology may be viewed as part of the group-based inequality problem and may be unable to extricate itself sufficiently to be able to address it. Insofar as the real factors underlying group-based inequality appear to extend beyond individual psychology, educational psychology has little to offer. Research in educational psychology is not concerned with contextual issues, and only a small part of culture-related educational problems can be addressed at the instructional level in schools. In effect, educational psychology may be necessary but is not sufficient, as currently practiced, in eliminating group-based inequality—if that were a societal goal. The argument in this chapter, however, is that educational psychology *does* have something to offer beyond defining "best practice" from a functionalist perspective. The latter has been aimed toward the isolation of "universals" regarding the individual, net of context (Kessen, 1979; Salomon, 1995). Evidence now exists, however, that ethnicity and culture play a central role in critical areas and problems that are at stake in educational psychology. In fact, it seems that if educational psychology is to fully address problems related to learning and teaching and pertinent to human development, a cultural focus and a different unit of analysis will be needed. It should be made clear, then, that addressing the group-based inequality problem is relevant for the discipline rather than for political reasons, and that the discipline should not serve as a tool for promoting certain interests. Rather, the group-based inequality puzzle provides an opportunity for the discipline to investigate how culture is related to development, and to reexamine its underlying goals and assumptions.

## Chapter Plan

This chapter grapples with the issue of how culture and, by extension, ethnicity play a role in key areas that pertain directly to educational psychology. It reviews psychoeducational approaches to group-based inequality that may be operationalized generally by a one standard deviation difference in intellectual performance. Other questions addressed are the following: Why should culture or ethnicity be of concern in educational psychology? How has educational psychology approached ethnicity, and what has the field contributed to understanding culture and educational practice? The goal is to integrate what is generally known about the topic, explore theoretical and methodological issues for integrating culture into the mission of the discipline, and outline problems and future directions for the field. The fields of education and psychology also need to be understood, historically, in their own cultural and historical context, as they have approached issues regarding development, educability, and learning, both at the individual level and at the group level.

## Some Delimitations

Several ways to characterize the relations among culture, ethnicity, and educational outcomes have been described in the literature. The first account of group or population differences in intellectual development was sociobiological in nature (Herrnstein & Murray, 1994; Jensen, 1969) and has thrived well within the psychometric tradition. A second approach to group differences is based on socioeconomic status (Apple, 1982; Bowles & Gintis, 1977, 1988; Coleman, 1966; Jencks et al., 1972; Sewell, Hauser, & Wolf, 1980) as the primary transmitter of inequality. The third approach to group-based differences in educational outcomes is sociocultural and includes history and study of the dynamics that create ethnicity.

The greatest problem in explaining the massive inequality that now exists is that the above factors are substantially con-

founded. For example, some groups' lower academic achievement may be due primarily to their overrepresentation historically at the lower end of the SES distribution and the intergenerational effects of SES conditions, which in turn are associated with physical and cultural characteristics. Low socioeconomic status may be correlated with physical characteristics, with cultural-historical factors, or with both. Language, religion, values, and degree of cultural adaptation into a multicultural context may also account for ethnic group differences, more so than biological traits or social class. Understanding ethnicity's relation to intellectual performance, motivation, and success also requires the analysis of sociocultural contexts in light of significant within-group differences regarding the effects of private schooling, degree of cultural adaptation, and other mediating factors.

For the purposes of the present discussion, explanations based primarily on heredity will be excluded. Writings relevant to this argument are well represented in the literature (Gould, 1981; Lewontin, Rose, & Kamin, 1984; Persell, 1977; Stevenson & Stigler, 1992; Thompson, Detterman, & Plomin, 1991; and chapter 8). This decision still leaves the unwieldy interaction and main effects of the remaining two factors in accounting for variability in human development. While consideration of SES is important in its own right and in its covariance with group differences, the chapter's scope will be limited primarily to culture and ethnicity in ways that allow class to be understood partly as a form of culture. It is worthwhile noting that the relation between SES and academic achievement in the United States might be overestimated. In a review of over 100 studies, K. R. White (1982) found that less than 5 percent of students' academic achievement could be accounted by SES. This chapter primarily offers a cultural and historical view of ethnicity and its links to development and education. Ethnicity is defined here as a sociobiological category that is not simply a subset of culture but implies a dynamic process of adaptation between members of at least one outgroup and those of another (that generally regards its group as nonethnic). In the next section, some historical grounds for the study of culture in relation to mind are summarized.

## ETHNICITY AND CULTURE IN PSYCHOLOGY: A HISTORICAL BRIEF

As the philosophers of the Enlightenment opened the doors to the development of various sciences, psychology was designated to be the most strategic in the study of man. It would, according to Gay (1969), radiate out "to other sciences of man, to the educational, aesthetic, and political" in its course of development. Among the current branches of psychology, educational psychology appears to be most strategically placed to bridge the gap between theory and practice, as well as to serve the "causal and purposive" (Munsterberg, 1915) goals of an emerging psychology. In education, psychology was also considered the master science and resided in colleges of education earlier in the century. A purposive psychology would attend to the meaning-related and sociohistorical aspects of psychology.

In the European philosophical tradition there is a concern for culture/ethnicity as a marker of societal conditions and cultural context. For example, Cahan & S. H. White (1992) noted:

Observations of everyday experiences give truths that are (quoting J. S. Mill) "not absolute, but dependent on some general conditions" . . . (and which are to be) . . . "relied on in so far as there is ground of assurance that those conditions are realized" (p. 864). . . .

But, Mill (1843/1974) said, "When maxims of this sort, collected from Englishmen, come to be applied to Frenchmen, or when those collected from the present day are applied to past or future generations, they are apt to be at fault" (p. 864). Observations of human conduct reveal "not the principles of human nature, but results of those principles under the circumstances in which mankind have happened to be placed" (pp. 861–862).

This passing reference to the issue of cultural differences was suggestive of what would later become a central concern for cultural-educational anthropology, cross-cultural psychology, and, more recently, developmental and educational psychology.

An important antecedent of psychology's consideration of culture and ethnicity is evident in Wundt's less known work on *Völkerpsychologie*. This interest in cultural influences with regard to the development of psychological functions came as a response to ambitious but perhaps premature proposals for the study of the particular traits of different ethnic groups by Moritz Lazarus and Heymann Steinhal during the 1860s (Krewer & Jahoda, 1990) and later by J. Stanley Hall. Wundt considered language, customs, and myths to be the basic components of the *Volksseele* (or mind of the folk), which has also been termed folk psychology (Bruner, 1990). Despite the rich promise prefiguring a cultural psychology, methods that might connect culture and mind were still unknown. Psychology was just beginning to uncover general laws of development and methods at the turn of the century when major intergroup conflicts intervened. These conflicts separated studies of culture from those of mind. The connection between ethnic conflict and warfare seems not only inherent but might explain, to a considerable extent, the reluctance to broach the topic of ethnicity in science.

The decades around the turn of the century were an exciting period as, with relatively unfettered minds, some psychologists struggled to define the direction of the field for the 20th century. Wundt, Hall, Baldwin, Dewey, James, Munsterberg, Stern, Bartlett, Vygotsky, Werner, and Mead all sought to define the boundaries of a psychology that would address truly developmental and cultural processes that appeared intimately related to education. Their early work explored fundamental issues that still remain for psychology (Siguan, 1987).

## The Exclusion of Culture and Ethnicity from Psychology

The departure of the study of culture from the forefront of psychology, particularly in North America, occurred in great part because of two main factors. One was the absence of methodological advances or tools that would lend scientific respect and stability to the field. The beliefs, motives and values, that then prevailed with respect to the scientific approach focused the study of mind in the individual. Paradigms that would satisfy scientific agenda would be the most likely to succeed. The mind–body problem in psychology had resulted in various competing philosophy-based models around the turn of the century. The models that became preeminent were the ones that benefit-

ted most from the discovery of correlation methods and conditioning paradigms, and that operated in the spirit of a "brass instrument" experimental science. These means or methods became instrumental in establishing prevailing microparadigms in psychology, such as individual differences. The development of a particular knowledge base and its direction thus evolved largely on the basis of tools or methods and the questions that could be addressed. Individual differences in mind tended to be studied without cultural properties, or net of them.

The second factor was the interruption of two world wars that not only quieted the voices of seminal thinkers, but also changed the goals of the discipline. North American psychology reigned, and became almost wholly identified with the prevailing causal-objective, behavioral, psychometric paradigms. After the First World War, Western psychology became socially institutionalized and was valued strongly for its potential use in solving practical social and learning problems in the military and in industry, as well as in the community and in schools.

In retrospect, developmental and phenomenological orientations on the Continent seem to have had difficulty entering mainstream Anglo-Saxon psychological thought until recently. Psychology in North America became concerned with problems of selection, measurement, and prediction of behavior, which permitted the reduction of uncertainties, and this concern still prevails (R. J. Gibson, 1994; Sarason, 1981b). Psychological inquiry into matters that might require open-endedness and consideration of contextual factors tended to be discouraged for motives related to rigorous control and the discipline's public respectability. As psychologists began to move away from schools and colleges of education to form psychology departments within divisions of arts and sciences, a primary goal for them was to be regarded as legitimate scientists. Consequently, a focus on experimental, industrial-organizational psychology evolved that defined behavior as the unit of analysis for control and prediction purposes. Why, then, would one expect in that sociopolitical and scientific era a consideration of culture?

Cahan and S. H. White (1992) help to explain how the above occurred. A reductionistic psychology could not serve as a basis for educational practice. Thus, for some scholars, understanding individual development *in relation to* socially organized activities and tools remained a central concern for the field earlier in the 20th century. The role of methods, including Darwin's earlier comparative approach, is important here to illustrate how "means or tools" influence cultural (scientific) knowledge and development. On this issue, Vygotsky wrote:

The methodology of a particular science is formed under the influence of philosophy, but it has its own rules determined by the nature of the subject matter of that science, by the historical development of its conceptual structures. That is why a methodological research on psychological concepts, methods, explanatory principles, is not philosophical "loft" added to science. It appears as a consequence of the requirements of a particular science, it is an integral part of that science. (Vygotsky, 1982, p. 451)

Although a cultural psychology was fathomed in the minds of several pioneers in the field, behaviorism already counted on correlational techniques, classical conditioning and an acceptable unit of analysis for research on simple learning. Behaviorism's consideration of culture was limited mainly to Thorndike's law of set and attitude, which had to be decontextualized with great effort and creativity to be used meaningfully Also, Hall (1911) had expressed some modest interest in linking ethnic psychology to pedagogy in ways that appear not very astute. Of the three main traditions that influenced 20th-century psychology in North America educational psychology remained closest to Thorndike's, and its course has not strayed far from functionalism since (Berliner, 1990). Culture was thus left "packaged" (Whiting, 1980) to include everything outside individual behavior that was not biological. Ethnicity, as a cultural-biological compound, became too messy for scientific study aimed toward isolation and simplification. The influence of Wundt and German psychology ended soon after Munsternberg's influence disappeared from North American psychology, except for some post-World War II emigrés who favored an ecological view.

One final point concerns cross-cultural and, more generally, social psychology. Although it is the one branch of the discipline that would appear most advanced in approaching the mind–culture problem, unfortunately it too has treated culture as an intervening or independent variable. Culture continues to be studied in a post hoc fashion, as an external influence on the mind and on learning and teaching problems in education.

## WHY ETHNICITY IN EDUCATIONAL PSYCHOLOGY?

The ways in which educational psychology has approached ethnicity, as well as the reasons why it should consider the relation between culture and mind, merit attention. How the study of the mind can be employed to facilitate learning and development, particularly for students affected by group-based inequality, is only one reason for including ethnicity in the forefront of the discipline. This is what may be regarded as a social equity motive. It is important particularly when generations of children remain trapped in a cycle of disadvantage in school by virtue of the "nurture" and SES of their natal culture relative to others. This motive drives most approaches that address the needs of most "at-risk," culturally different students (e.g., Brophy, 1988; D. M. Kagan, 1990; Ornstein & Levine, 1989; Perry, 1993). These approaches are generally based on educational psychology, which generally has had a headlock on intervention, at least from the perspective of other disciplines (Trueba, 1988).

The other motive, however, is that in order to fully understand human development, motivation, and related topics, a discipline of mind requires attention to culture as much as to other components related to learning and biological factors. This orientation may be viewed as centered on a scientific advancement motive, one that addresses the isomorphism or linkage between mind and culture. The issue here is one that must ultimately deal with what may be considered a new type of mind–body problem, namely, that of mind and culture. The question of the extent to which cultural history influences social, affective, and intellectual development is not new to psychology, yet it has not been on the agenda of educational psychology as a whole.

With respect to the social equity motive, the problem centers on inequality in academic achievement associated with children

from some ethnic groups and the inability of schools to provide access to equal educational opportunities. Instruction may be delivered in the same way to all children and still not be equal. Equality of opportunity in education seems to convey generally that schools "provide whatever means necessary" to achieve educational outcomes in comparable frequency distributions for students in diverse groups. It is a notion based more on output than on input in schooling. The problem of defining equality centers largely on the meaning given to pluralism in the beliefs of society. This problem becomes alarming when evidence is found that schools are not only ineffective or inept in reducing the educational gap but that they may actually structure inequality (Morgan, 1977; Oakes, 1985, 1991; Ogbu, 1974, 1989; Persell, 1977; Stanfield, 1985). Although schools generally fail to educate some group's children, they also *hinder* their development by the segregation created by labels, such as "at risk." They are instrumental in the creation of the at-risk culture, constructing yet another social identity. Schools may be hazardous for certain groups of students. Labels can be used cleverly and in ways that are not in the interest of their bearers. This has been observed with misuse of the term "special education" for containment rather than for educational purposes, which has a sad history related to placement-testing practices (Mehan, 1992; Mercer, 1974; Oakes, 1985). The power differential is evident not only in the construction of exceptionality but also in the literature on grouping students for instruction. As Oakes (1991) concluded.

The result is that ability-related grouping practices lead to considerable race and class separation, race- and class-linked differences in opportunities to learn, and, ultimately, limited educational and occupational futures for low-income and most minority students. (p. 567)

This concern presses educational psychology, for the literature on effective teaching becomes somewhat irrelevant for children whose "culture brand" or ethnicity is not compatible with that found in school, a situation that also applies to nonminority groups of low SES students as well. Socioeconomic status appears to differentially affect various ethnic groups, possibly because of differences in cultural history that may bind their "freedom of movement" (Valsiner, 1985). The socialization of colonized minority groups' children is different from the socialization of children in the majority group's underclass and middle class, and different again from the socialization of some immigrant groups' children (A. Portes & Rumbaut, 1990; Suarez-Orozco, 1991). The good news is that we need not choose between these two motives, since for the scientific advancement motive to prevail, attention to group differences is indispensable.

### How Educational Psychology Addresses Ethnicity

Research over a quarter of a century ago reported that educational achievement, the main indicator of group-based inequality employed in educational psychology, was unrelated to school differences in a number of inputs, such as per pupil expenditures (Coleman, 1966). The next target of close scrutiny were the organization of personnel, resources, and instructional activities that constitute educational practices. But Coleman claimed that student characteristics showed stronger association with achievement than with school characteristics or family background. Soon after, educational psychology research examined student characteristics in terms of individual differences in response to treatments, locus of control, self-concept, and motivation. This came after a decade of "environmentalism" inspired by Hunt (1961), which led to a series of social experiments in early-age educational interventions (Lazar & Darlington, 1982).

A classic example of research that illustrates how ethnicity was approached then (and now) is the study of Paton, Walberg, and Yeh (1973). Following a criteria-of-effectiveness approach, the study found that relationships between student characteristics and achievement varied significantly, depending on ethnicity. Black students maintained positive self-regard despite lower achievement, which, unlike white students, they tended to attribute to external factors. Family background was related to self-concept, regardless of ethnic membership. Recommendations from these types of studies center on positive reinforcement, particularly for ethnic children (C. A. Clark & Walberg, 1969), on changing their internal attributions (Alschuler, 1972), and on changing various teacher and teaching characteristics and school variables related to achievement (Brophy, 1988; Kounin, 1970). Typically, studies focus on the relation between achievement and some characteristic or treatment, and only cursory attention is given to how culture might affect the development of individual and collective characteristics. Ethnicity is studied superficially and only after a breakdown involving demographic factors is employed in order to account for otherwise "error" variance. The error here, ironically, might lie in not seeking a deeper understanding of a group's differences as instantiations of person–context relationships.

In another example of how ethnicity is typically approached, Mexican- and Anglo-American mother–child dyads were studied in the context of a model replication task by Laosa (1979). The mothers' form of controlling the task differed by ethnicity in ways that suggested greater compatibility between schoolteachers and Anglo mothers' style of interaction. Yet Laosa found that when mothers' educational level was controlled for, ethnic differences in parenting style disappeared (in ways reminiscent of Peal and Lambert's [1962] research on bilingualism and intellectual competence). Across several studies (P.R. Portes, 1982, 1991; Zady, 1994), the correlation between academic achievement and SES or ethnicity became insignificant after parent–child interaction style was controlled for.

Ethnicity and culture remain packaged in most studies. When this basic variable is unpackaged, general inferences made about ethnicity often appear unfounded. In effect, ethnicity is generally investigated in a removed, aseptic manner, much as are other control measures such as age, gender, and SES differences, to produce neat, publishable results. When interactions among these control variables are found, race (which is generally confused with ethnicity) is generally considered troublesome. Yet a myriad of speculations about cultural mediation can be found in many a discussion section of the educational psychology literature. Ethnicity generally remains a proxy for a host of confounded attributes that are packaged along with SES and cultural history.

The study of ethnicity requires greater attention to within-group differences, which may be of greater significance than between-group differences. Yet common practice focuses on the latter. In some cases ethnicity is constituted in ways that mark a historically determined degree of social distance from the mainstream that is narrowed over generations, particularly for some immigrant groups. In others, ethnicity is packaged or shaped differently by ethnocultural history, sometimes in ways that preclude full assimilation for the individual in a given social context. However, most research does not regard ethnicity as a developmental process or as a trait along a continuum, but rather as a fossilized and dichotomous category that one either has or does not have. Ethnicity is presumed to be experienced in the same way by different individuals and to have the same effects on different individuals, with little attention paid to what these effects are or how they are internalized.

Educational psychology has not been directly interested in what ethnicity is—a variable compound constituted by cultural, biological, and historical constants. Nor has it attended to the subjective meaning of ethnicity. Rather, the concern is about what ethnicity is associated *with*, particularly what it "does" to our variables of interest. Research concerned with adapting instruction to student characteristics has centered on ATI studies (Tobias, 1985), which are remotely concerned with ethnicity in general. The outcome of many studies concerning ethnic differences is familiar; most document the need for programs to develop achievement motivation, self-esteem, democratic child-rearing practices, and other traits.

This section of the chapter discussed how educational psychology has generally approached ethnicity in relation to development and learning, and, by extension, the issue of mind in society. In the next section, past and current research models concerning group-based inequality are reviewed.

# APPROACHES TO THE GROUP-BASED INEQUALITY PROBLEM: THREE CULTURAL APPROACHES IN EDUCATION

The literature on ethnicity and inequality reflects various positions relevant to the question of how culture shapes differences in achievement and, more generally, human development. These positions are discussed next as the cultural deficit, the cultural difference, and what will be termed the post-cultural difference approaches. They represent the main avenues for understanding ethnicity as it relates to schooling in our field. Each approach differs conceptually in the analysis of culturally mediated educational inequality and in ways of addressing it.

## The Cultural Deficit Approach

The cultural deficit model is inherent in many of the current programs that respond to and define "at-risk" student populations. These programs aim to acculturate the child by seeking accommodation to the school's academic culture. The motive or the belief here is that the child can thus benefit more fully from education and its rewards. The cultural deficit model draws attention to the adaptiveness in ethnic socialization practices and values relative to a norm, particularly in education.

Basil Bernstein's (1971) insights into social class differences in linguistic codes were later employed to account for ethnic differences in children's intellectual performance. The causal model assumed that parental verbal behavior largely accounted for—or at least indexed—families' cognitive socialization patterns. Studies in the causal mode (Hess & Shipman, 1968; Laosa, 1981; Sigel, 1986) concentrated on the early detection of particular cultural sources of variation in the immediate developmental context of children. In fact, since the middle of the 20th century, parent–child interaction research has been one of the most fertile areas for understanding the unfolding of environmental influences on development.

Bernstein's argument that social class differences are associated with differences in child-rearing or socialization patterns served to explain variability in development. These patterns tend to be self-perpetuating. In the cultural deficit model, the use of language in middle-class homes (the elaborative code) is complex and introduces a broader range of meaning and content that later becomes advantageous to sociocognitive development. Along with different child-bearing techniques, the child's socialization is believed to be more rational, ordered, and self-controlled, and to lead to easier comprehension of complex chains of thought pertinent to forming relations and abstract categories (Ginsberg, 1972).

The lower-class child, in contrast, is exposed to a restricted code of language use and to arbitrary, authoritative discipline that may have negative affective consequences as well. According to Bernstein (1961), this would lead to a "low level of conceptualization, an orientation to a low order of causality, a disinterest in (learning) processes" (pp. 302–303), along with a preference for immediate gratification, which violates a cherished middle-class trait, delay of gratification. Such class-related observations are not much different from ethnic characterizations with regard to low effort (Ogbu, 1992) or other traits.

As Laosa (1981) noted in his review of this literature, most observational studies were interpreted on the basis of Bernstein's initial model (Hess & Shipman, 1968; Kamii & Radin, 1967). This line of research laid the foundation for a host of early-age intervention programs in the 1960s (Dunham, Portes, & Williams, 1984; Lazar & Darlington, 1982) and current ones such as Head Start. The *Zeitgeist* of that time guided community and school programs with learning theory (respondent, operant, social, cognitive), on the one hand, and Piagetian, maturation-based approaches on the other. The notion of a critical period in intellectual development, loosely borrowed from Lorenz's (1952) ethnological work, was employed as a rationale for early educational interventions aimed at the stabilization and maximization of mental development. If intelligence could be boosted during this period of rapid growth, some believed the gap would "disappear," an economic solution that would be maintained later in life. Hunt's (1961) environmental thesis was, in effect, being tested by these grand social experiments that essentially tested early experience effects in compensating for cultural-historical effects.

What is important about these studies for the purposes of this discussion is how the ideas of deficit, of the need for a compensatory "head start," reflected a well-meaning but ethnocentric knowledge base. By ignoring sociocultural and historical lines of development, these social scientists soon found themselves entrenched, defending the meager, sometimes short-lived performance gains achieved against attacks from two fronts. One front argued that educational interventions failed because heredity's weighty determination of measured intelli-

gence (Jensen, 1969), as defined by psychometric theory, had been underestimated. Preschool interventions were also believed to be doomed in achieving group-based equality (i.e., parallel normal distributions in intellectual measures) for "disadvantaged" students since their impact would be neutralized by middle-class families' consequent adjustment in cognitive socialization. The other camp argued that the "delivery capacity" (Dunham, 1973) of these early-age interventions had been insufficient in achieving long-term compensation (Lazar & Darlington, 1983). It presumed that the limited experiences provided to disadvantaged children approximated development in a middle-class culture, and that more of the same was simply needed. During this period, culturally determined language and dialect differences drew much attention in the discussion of deficits as differences. The adaptiveness of culture-specific behavior patterns and "learning styles" also drew attention (Ramirez & Castaneda, 1974) as salient cultural characteristics that might require accommodation or modification.

In sum, the deficit perspective presumed that early "training" of disadvantaged children from low SES groups might overcome the deficit or differences created by some cultures, something that at the time seemed revolutionary and in line with the environmentalism championed by Hunt (1961) with regard to intellectual development. Cultural differences were regarded basically as SES-related problems in socialization that led to mental underdevelopment. Longitudinal evaluations of programs based on this model failed to show lasting scholastic achievement gains on the part of children served (Lazar & Darlington, 1983). Yet these programs proved cost-effective in reducing dropout, absenteeism, and retention rates and suggested that greater investment of resources might have closed the achievement gap.

## The Cultural Difference Approach

Even if social class differences could be eliminated, significant differences in intellectual achievement remain correlated with culture (Steinberg, Dornbusch, & Brown, 1992). A culture's social and economic organization greatly sways communication, learning, and motivational patterns. The cultural difference view (Cole & Bruner, 1971; Kleinfield, 1973; Laosa, 1981) was critical of both the theoretical assumptions and methods inherent in the cultural deficit perspective. The differences in achievement were not viewed in terms of deficits but rather in terms of differences linked to particular cultural conditions. The achievement difference was thought to arise not because one culture is superior to another but because children's cultural experiences with some concepts and skills (particularly those involved in literacy) vary systematically across cultural contexts. Rather than being situated in the child's mind, the deficit was actually a relative difference produced largely by each group's cultural context and history. As Cole and Bruner (1971) noted, the difference model is essentially a deficit model without the assumption that one group is superior to another.

The difference model implies a relation between individual and culture reminiscent of the isomorphism in the mind–body problem in psychology. Rather than correcting or modifying the deficit in "them"—typically children from disempowered outgroups—this model began a line of research that documented cultural differences in daily activity and how these, in turn, resulted in differences in thought, language, and behavior (Cole, Gay, Glick, & Sharp, 1971; Dasen, 1977; Greenfield, 1983; Jahoda, 1980). It has paved the way for multicultural education (Banks, 1995; Gollnick & Chinn, 1986). However, this model has limited value in addressing how cultural differences are to be confronted in education. In more recent ethnographic studies (Heath, 1982; Heath & McLaughlin, 1994; S. Phillips, 1983), the links between language and thought are examined from a cultural difference perspective. The difference model does not explain, however, why some culturally and linguistically different groups of students, many of whom are poor and have language difficulties, are able to rival and sometimes outperform the mainstream group norm, unlike students from colonized minority groups.

## Post-Cultural Difference Models

A large body of literature has emerged in educational psychology and anthropological education that casts grave doubt on the equity of contemporary education. The literature may be described along two fundamental dimensions. One is the extent to which the school *or* the students' culture is to be regarded as most accountable and detrimental to children's adaptation to school. The second is the degree of accommodation required by the schools or the students' culture to make the change. Let's examine what may be regarded as a cultural deficit–related approach, one in which children (and their families) basically must learn to accommodate to the dominant culture in ways that resemble those of successful immigrants in order to end "ethnic school failure" (Foley, 1991). Although the dominant culture is urged to change somewhat, individuals' and their natal group's accommodation is most critical in this first model.

*From Double Stratification to a Folk Theory of Success.* J. U. Ogbu's (1978, 1991, 1992) sociohistorical analysis of the origins of educational inequality in the United States has led to the popularization of a castelike model that describes the status of minorities as voluntary or involuntary. Native, African, and Mexican Americans share a history of oppression and cultural subordination rooted in colonialism that is maintained by the current social system. They are regarded as involuntary minorities. Voluntary minorities or immigrants, on the other hand, perform better in school, although they share impoverishment, suffer discrimination (as do involuntary minorities), and face language problems. Their interpretations of unfavorable conditions and of the host society's organization, along with their motives, differ significantly from those of the involuntary group with respect to having a dual status frame of reference. Voluntary minorities tend to perceive their current status as relatively better than that of their past, and they manage to achieve greater social mobility over time. Their pattern of adaptation resembles that of past European immigrants in spite of differences in ethnic traits that might impose glass ceilings for noncaucasians. A third group, autonomous minorities such as Mormons, Jews, and similar groups, retain their cultural identity while their children tend to be normally distributed in both education and occupational attainments. In accounting for the different achievement

levels in school, Ogbu (1992) distinguishes primary from secondary cultural differences. Primary differences in language or religion, for example, exist before two groups come in contact. Secondary cultural differences arise after initial contact and often are developed by minority groups as adaptation patterns to "cope with their subordination" (Ogbu, 1992, p. 8), which in turn leads to negative psychological adaptation patterns. Pessimism regarding school and occupational success, as well as differences in communication, interaction or learning styles, are part of this definition of cultural difference.

Involuntary minority students are at double risk because both socioeconomic and castelike roles interact to produce a collective state of "learned helplessness" and consequent differences in achievement socialization that are critically significant for any comparative framework involving ethnicity. The learned helplessness assumption posits that learned uncontrollability results in the transmission of cognitive, motivational, and affective patterns that lead to different (cultural) models of success and attribution. Ogbu (1977) argues that this is a critical mechanism for disadvantagement among African Americans that is similar to the Burakumin castelike minority in Japan and probably elsewhere (e.g., Berbers in Morocco, lower-caste groups in India).

The disillusion of African Americans resides in a collective history of disparagement, one in which effort and reward are not generally correlated. This disillusion has a behavioral counterpart, helplessness, which operates at the group level. It is manifested in ambivalence about schooling and in an oppositional group identity that is often driven by low (academic) self-esteem. This single frame of reference leads to distrust of schools and their practices. This frame is linked to the ways education has been designed for involuntary minorities, which has a lamentable history. Ogbu (1992) notes that teachers have mostly conduct expectations rather than academic ones for involuntary minority students, which, along with biased texts, tests, tracking, prejudice by school personnel, and an overall incompetence in dealing with cultural and language differences, leads to a norm of low effort, resistance, opposition, and disillusionment.

Voluntary Minorities and the Ethnicity of Success. Immigrant voluntary minorities typically outperform involuntary minorities in the United States, in part because their frame of reference lies "back home." This allows them to perceive accommodation problems as temporary and relatively less severe. In a recent comparison of successful and less successful minorities (Gibson & Ogbu, 1991; Ogbu, 1992), involuntary minorities such as Chicanos were compared with voluntary minorities also of Mexican origin in the United States, Koreans in Japan with Koreans in the United States, and other similar groups. Key factors relevant to achievement motivation and belief systems were noted that relate to children's academic success. For involuntary minority groups, efforts to raise educational standards in educational reforms may be perceived as another ploy by the dominant culture to maintain and extend an insurmountable advantage. Magnet schools and similar plans still leave most minority students in segregated schools. Self-selection could be one reason why African Americans in private schools have higher test scores than those in public schools but lower scores than white students in private schools. Involuntary minority groups tend to become discouraged academically also because they tend to have less peer support, which has been documented relative to Asian Americans (Steinberg et al., 1992) and other groups. They often live in a context in which their unemployment, infant mortality, and related rates are well above those for the general population.

Problems with Ogbu's Macro Approach. Ogbu points to the low-effort syndrome among African Americans, their failure to develop "effort optimism" (Ogbu, 1992). After generations of institutionalized discrimination and job ceilings, these students develop oppositional tendencies. Although some "castelike" students manifest resistance in classrooms, others do not, suggesting that Ogbu's macromodel has some blind spots. For example, Ogbu's recommendations for change center on bringing about improvements in opportunity structures through vigorous collective action, one area in which the African-American community has been most effective. However, he argues that the African-American community must also work to establish new norms for academic effort and success without losing cultural values and identity. This may be accomplished by channeling children's activities from nonacademic to academic ones, rewarding those efforts equally if not more than those in athletics and entertainment. How this type of collective action is to be organized is not clear. Ogbu suggests that schools need to promote trust through open discussions of differences, mutual responsibility, and collaboration strategies. Programs need to educate involuntary minority groups about the nature of the low-effort syndrome so that they can become more like the successful "alternators" and voluntary immigrants without giving up their cultural identity. He believes that this can be accomplished through "special counseling and related programs" that remain vague. This model tends to be pedagogically impotent and imputes causality on the basis of limited data regarding schools and various minorities' scholastic achievement. It also does not account for the rise of black colleges and universities and the overcoming of barriers by some.

*School-Structured Failure.* In this second post-cultural difference approach, mutual accommodation between the schools and "culturally different" students is also proposed. However, the focus is more on restructuring schools and society than on changing students' culture and communities. The problem here can be defined both as structural (e.g., curricula, school organization, textbooks) and functional (e.g., teaching practices and processes, time on task). From this perspective, student differences in behavioral and attitudinal patterns will be eliminated only after the social conditions that help construct them (at the group level) are addressed. In effect, how can ethnic children (or their development) be expected to be "like others" when they and their cultural niche have shared significantly different experiences? Both interpretative and motivational patterns evolve from experiences and modeling. With this approach, it makes more sense to focus attention on the social context of education before expecting meaningful changes at the individual level. In effect, it is not the involuntary minorities' cultural "deep structure" that accounts for many of the learning problems at schools, but rather the product of intercultural relations that then become reproduced in schools. These relations concern power, stratification, and have a role in reproducing in-

equality. From this perspective, group-based inequality cannot be substantially modified solely through changing a group's beliefs, attitudes, or behavior.

The Means of Schooling. School-based changes in pedagogy, curriculum, and organization strategies have been the bread and butter of educational psychology. However, students' culture is generally presumed constant and considered post hoc in general. These school-based changes have also been on the menu for educational anthropology and related fields that currently address group-based inequality. Under this second model, considerable variability exists both in theory and method. The confluence of the literature here also includes action anthropology, multicultural education, effective schools, and various pedagogical and curricular reforms that attempt accommodation to at-risk students' culturally based differences. Some of these will be discussed, although in-depth analyses are beyond the scope of the chapter. These strategies include current teacher education reforms, state, district-, and school-level educational reforms, revised textbooks, "ability" grouping strategies, bilingual education, ESL, multiethnic education programs (Banks, 1987), and invitational (Purkey & Smith, 1983), humanistic, and holistic educational approaches. All of these strategies may be regarded as collective means through which the relation between inequality and group membership can be mediated.

Changing School Organization of Curriculum and Instruction. School-based accommodation is most representative of educational psychology research, although it extends into bilingual and multicultural education as well. In the multicultural education movement, content is to be infused into the curriculum for various purposes (see Banks, 1987)—for example, to make education more inviting to outgroup members by preserving and respecting their heritage, to reduce the ethnocentrism and prejudice of the majority, to adjust teaching strategies to various learning styles, and to promote new social values consistent with cultural pluralism. There is an underlying assumption that by expanding the cultural awareness of the majority or the cultural breadth of content, equality in educational access might trickle down eventually. Although the proposed changes in attitude and cultural knowledge may be necessary in eliminating inequality, they do not appear sufficient per se. This model's importance lies in moving not only toward cultural pluralism in the curriculum but also toward a new socioeducational goal that aims to forge a multicultural national identity (Banks, 1995; Gay, 1977; Gollnick & Chinn, 1986; Pai, 1990).

Second, many programs of bilingual education are included in the accommodationist approach. Only a few points about this complex and emotional issue will be noted. Although most of the reasons discussed as to why African-American students generally do not achieve in school have been extended to other involuntary minority groups, non-English-speaking students' problems may stem more specifically from school-based practices having to do with curriculum, instructional methods, and the treatment of language differences. Without bilingual education, for example, Spanish-speaking children take 5 to 8 years to reach grade level on tests of academic language (Collier, 1987). With adequate bilingual programs, they typically reach grade level 2 years ahead of those who have had bilingual

TABLE 11–1. School Persistence by Age, Race, and Spanish Origin: Enrolled in School in the United States, 1980

| Group | 18–19 | 20–21 | 22–24 | 25–34 |
|---|---|---|---|---|
| Chinese | 83.9 | 74.0 | 50.7 | 21.9 |
| Japanese | 77.0 | 61.6 | 38.9 | 14.6 |
| Korean | 77.7 | 54.8 | 30.5 | 13.2 |
| Asian Indian | 72.0 | 54.3 | 39.2 | 14.8 |
| Vietnamese | 66.6 | 47.5 | 37.8 | 22.4 |
| Cuban | 65.1 | 44.8 | 28.5 | 12.7 |
| Filipino | 62.7 | 38.3 | 20.2 | 9.6 |
| White, non-Hispanic | 53.1 | 33.6 | 17.4 | 8.5 |
| Black | 51.7 | 28.4 | 15.9 | 9.6 |
| Hawaiian | 42.2 | 21.7 | 13.5 | 7.3 |
| Puerto Rican | 41.8 | 21.7 | 13.1 | 8.0 |
| Mexican | 39.2 | 18.9 | 11.6 | 7.2 |
| American Indian | 38.2 | 19.3 | 12.7 | 8.8 |

(Years Old columns above)

Reproduced by permission. Data originally compiled from U.S. Bureau of the Census, 1983, Tables 123, 160, and 166.

instruction. Another key difference between involuntary and voluntary minority children may lie in pre-first-grade literacy, and literacy support that interacts significantly with the organization of classroom instruction. Involuntary minority children are fairly homogeneous with regard to low SES, literacy, and parental support on school entry. With voluntary minority children, greater variability is found that is related to the SES characteristics and motivation of immigrants. For example, most immigrants are not generally from the lowest class level in their respective countries (A. Portes & Rumbaut, 1990). They often bring cultural capital and helps account for the pattern found in Table 11–1. Children from the latter group are often included in programs related to group-based inequality. Yet their cultural settings appear to differ significantly from those of involuntary minorities with regard to values, beliefs and motives, goals, and ways to achieve those goals. From this view, bilingual education seems most critical, then, for nonimmigrant children of involuntary minority background, although immigrant children may be the most likely to profit from such programs. This issue will likely continue to be debated, particularly as anti-immigration sentiments swell nationally.

Third, the effective schools movement (Brookover, Brady, & Warfield, 1981; Edmonds, 1979; Glasman, 1984; Miller, 1985; Murphy, Weil, Hallinger, & Mitman, 1985) has gained some attention among those concerned about inequality at the structural level. This is essentially a sociological approach that is concerned with different sets of characteristics that range in emphasis from safe, orderly environments and parental involvement to high expectations and instructional leadership. Along with school-based management models and programs that address at-risk populations, such as Levin's (1988) accelerated schools, these strategies for school change tap important variables that may be considered necessary but again insufficient in uprooting inequality, both in terms of access and in terms of long-term outcomes. When applied in conjunction with other strategies, they have been shown to be effective (Comer, Haynes, & Hamilton-Lee, 1989). The latter two approaches are

among the few that have proven successful in attenuating the relation between ethnoculture and school achievement.

Another new definition of the problem of inequality is one centered on student opportunity to learn (Murphy, 1988), which is primarily seen as a function of actions of staff at the district and school levels. This view is based largely on the effective schools model, concerned with the well-documented differences in curricular and pedagogical practices noted earlier. To achieve equity in students' access to favorable conditions in schooling, this model proposes specific changes in three domains: state and federal policies regarding a core curriculum, changes in teacher preparation, and practitioner actions that follow the canons of the effective schools movement (Brookover et al., 1981). However, this literature suffers from methodological weaknesses (see Purkey & Smith, 1983) and seems to be lacking theoretically with respect to the relations between culture and development and those between learning and teaching.

Functional Barriers: Instructional Processes and Quality Control. The process–product model has been linked to rote learning and teaching methods that foster student passivity (Goodlad, 1983) and low-level mental skills (Durkin, 1979), making schools particularly perilous for otherwise competent, healthy children. Disadvantaged students, who often lack basic literacy skills, are more likely to be placed in and kept in low-ability tracks and to receive a different educational fare than the norm. Not only is the educational fare different, but the instruction is of lower quality in the lower tracks (Good & Marshall, 1984), which are often taught by the least prepared teachers (Oakes, 1985). At-risk students are typically found in boring classes that do not require the development of higher level cognitive skills (Davis, 1986; Trimble & Sinclair, 1986). At-risk students also tend to be concentrated in urban areas where teacher turnover and attrition rates are high (Wise, Darling-Hammond, & Berry, 1987) and student–teacher ratios are high. In many instances, low-income children are served by less experienced teachers. Educational research has challenged the notion that teacher expertise—pedagogical expertise or content mastery—does not make a difference (Berliner, 1993; Shulman, 1987). Yet the best teachers are themselves tracked away from serving at-risk populations (Oakes, 1985). "Gifted" education has served to allocate one of the most critical resources away from those most in need. As Darling-Hammond and Green (1990, p. 246) note:

A more refined allocation of teaching resources is occurring now with the proliferation of gifted and talented programs across the country. Teachers who are among the most skilled are offering rich, challenging curricula to select groups of students, on the theory that only a few students can benefit from such curricula and teaching. Yet the distinguishing feature of programs for the gifted and talented frequently turns out to be not the difficulty of the work presented but the quality. Students . . . integrate ideas across fields of study. . . . [They] are asked to think, write, create, develop projects . . . to explore.

The differences between tracks are substantive, particularly in terms of less interactive teaching and the basic academic focus (Good & Marshall, 1984; Oakes, 1985; Zady, 1994). Disadvantaged students receive less academic content in both elementary (Brookover et al., 1981) and secondary schooling (Walberg & Keefe, 1986). Lower curricular expectations, less homework, and lower standards are associated with lower track education (Murphy & Hallinger, 1989). These authors conclude their review of the literature by noting:

At the classroom level, a more limited academic focus, poor use of instructional time, the trading-off of rigorous encounters with material for student compliance, the use of inappropriate pacing, and lower expectations, continue to reduce the opportunity to learn and [the] content coverage for students in lower tracks. (p. 139)

The human capital represented by effective teachers appears to be invested far from "low-ability" groups, who, as noted before, often interfere with their own learning behavior problems (Evertson, 1982; Oakes, 1985), lack of motivation, and resistance (Erickson, 1986). Teacher effects have been scrutinized in educational research (Brophy & Good, 1974, 1986; Persell, 1977; Morgan, 1977; Rosenshine, 1983), along with teacher expectations, an issue that is related to students' self-esteem, motivation, and development. In effect, tracking and curricular differences have produced the most convincing case for the active role of schools in the coconstruction of inequality. As Murphy and Hallinger (1989) note, "equity is not defined by exposure to schooling or patterns of aggregated resources but by access to learning" (p. 135). Significant differences in curricular content and instructional practices occur (Goodlad (1983; Goodlad & Keating , 1990; and Murphy, 1988), and then produce severe problems in what Comer et al. (1989) have deemed "the affective relational" dimension between student and school personnel. Comer noted that by the middle of the elementary school years, adverse school effects on children have produced permanent barriers to success, primarily in terms of the affective domain. A convincing literature exists on the relations between the affective domain in education and school success.

Finally, serious limitations in pedagogical theory underlie many educational practices that appear atheoretical (Good & Weinstein, 1986). The thrust of this literature is to suggest that the solution may lie in providing a more uniform curriculum (or at least in providing the existing one to all students), in developing and distributing competent teachers and improved teaching methods, in raising expectations, and in eliminating tracking. Heterogeneous grouping of students in cooperative learning situations may have positive effects on achievement for all groups (Slavin, 1983). Cooperative learning, along with multicultural education and all the other means already noted, may again be considered necessary, although not sufficient. Whether the effect of these means on student affect and motivation can eliminate group-based inequality remains to be seen.

From the above perspective, two themes emerge with respect to instruction. Effective teaching does correlate with student learning but is not distributed fairly. As a strategic school variable, good teachers represent human capital for which there is great demand, particularly at a time when teacher education programs are severely criticized. There is also considerable variability in factors conducive to effective schooling for disadvantaged students. However, as much variability may be found within ethnic groups in terms of student readiness for school learning or motivation as exists between groups. Each source

of variation is only beginning to be understood contextually. In sum, whereas schools and classroom processes were the black box for Ogbu's model, culture seems to be such for the process–product approach.

*Interpretative Educational Anthropology.* The third and perhaps most promising post-cultural difference approach that has examined cultural factors in understanding school-based inequality is based on ethnographic studies. These have been generally ignored in educational psychology. In spite of criticism about the "sentimental egalitarianism" and "ultrarelativism" leveled at the interpretative tradition (Karabel & Halsey, 1977), educational anthropology has been most useful in revealing the impact of cultural knowledge from the student's perspective and in providing insights into the experiential dimensions of students' cultural context. As with the school-structured approach, what teachers do with students is believed to matter. Educational anthropology has brought a more critical perspective to the issue of group-based inequality by underlining how power relations are manifested in education and showing how disadvantages and at-risk status are constituted by instructional processes, as well as by suggesting ways in which the mismatch problem can be addressed.

The interpretative approach focuses on conditions that lend congruence to children's development in both home and school settings and that lead to success (McDermott, Goldman, & Herve, 1984; Trueba, 1987). Many ethnographic studies build on models based on partnerships that work and lead to school success, which is defined and measured differently in ethnography than in educational psychology. The interpretative approach also focuses on processes in schooling that reproduce socioeconomic and educational inequality; at the same time, it explores the means underlying exceptions of success. Intervening variables that are critical for academic success are examined in context-specific detail and in proximal circumstances (Mehan, 1987). Discontinuities between school and parental teaching styles among low SES minority and majority students have been noted in this literature (Cazden, 1986; Delgado-Gaitan, 1990; Heath, 1982, 1986; Trueba, 1987). Such discontinuities are often addressed by labeling or by the social construction of deficits through institutionalized practices that reproduce failure at various levels—student, students' ethnic group, school, and societal.

Key barriers to school success stemming from language use and socialization are identified and observed across contexts varying in receptivity to cultural differences. For example, Piestrup (1973) found that when the structure of discourse in the classroom was modified to fit the language use patterns in low SES environments of African-American children, performances on standardized reading tests increased significantly relative to the performance of children in regular classrooms. Foster (1989) reports that the success of effective inner-city teachers lies similarly in closing the distance between different interactional styles found at home and school and in paving the way for the affective relational domain associated with school success (Comer, 1991). Native American students' performance increases when classroom participation activities are congruent with the cultural norms of cooperation and sociality rather than with competition and individualism (Phillips, 1983). Moll (1992) found that when Spanish-speaking students' cultural "funds of knowledge" were tapped by schooling practices, improvements in achievement motivation and academic performance could be observed. When students are allowed to deal with cognitively challenging content in bilingual education classes, competencies presumed absent in monolingual classes, which tend to focus only on rote learning, are revealed. Monocultural teachers are then surprised. S. Kagan (1986) noted similar findings with other ethnic minority children. Studies such as those by Heath (1982), Trueba (1987), and Vogt, Jordan, and Tharp (1987) show that the problem of group-based inequality is primarily due to a cultural mismatch in meanings, language use, and other mediational aspects of social interactions that influence learning. Heath (1982) drew attention to speech genres that are essential to school success but that often are not cultivated in some children's natal culture, particularly in cultures unfamiliar with school-based language activities. In many cases, too, these genres are found in language-minority contexts but remain untapped in the prevailing genre of most educational settings.

In sum, low SES socialization practices may fail to prepare children for the demands of the competitive structures organized in most schools. However, it may be that low SES socialization alone is not the culprit for some ethnic groups' school failure, since school practices and structures seem to define and constitute the notion of failure, learning disabilities, and readiness. Both types of practices lead to differences and deficits, depending on one's perspective. These practices interact and tend to compromise some children's adaptation to schooling in ways that seem compounded by ethnicity beyond SES and race. Language and behavior differences and the reactions these typically elicit from monocultural educators appear to forge inequality in access to the means (intellectual or affective) that are necessary for success. Unless low SES families invest in increasing the competencies of children before first grade, schools, like business investors, will shy away from those futures. Working-class parents have less savvy in increasing children's school-relevant worth, and have less time and resources to support children's development even when they have the will to develop competencies. They have a sanguine belief that schools, not they, are in charge of educating children and that they are not to intervene in their schooling (McDermott et al., 1984). The naiveté of this belief is relative, however, since middle-class parents will leave certain areas to schools as well. Some content areas are emphasized more than others, and in the middle-class group, these may coincide with those reinforced in school. Whether it is a question of SES or of cultural savvy relative to demands for school-related compatibilities remains debatable, particularly since school environments are not always constant.

What are some of the critical, alterable variables for restructuring schools from this perspective? What are the prospects of changing the ways cultures of low SES origin place their children "at risk"? How may the cultural capital found in children be invested in and appreciated more fully?

The interpretative school argues for mutual accommodation for both teachers and students in modifying their behavior toward a common goal (Mehan, 1992). The main focus, however, is on the modification of school learning environments through the cooperation of teachers and parents. Teachers are encouraged to approximate the information-processing styles in the child's culture, to provide "psychological safety" (Maslow, 1970) in encouraging student participation and to involve parents.

Interpretative research also places greater attention on the concept of social agency in understanding inequality. According to Mehan (1992), how students make choices under varying social conditions and how their cultural "sphere gains relative autonomy from structural constraints" (p. 8) constitute an important part of interpretative educational anthropology's focus. Studies by Willis (1977) and MacLeod (1987) show that cultural attitudes and action patterns cannot be easily accounted for by structural influences or dominant ideologies. For example, in some contexts, African-American low-income youths attend class, study hard, reject drugs, hold high aspirations, and display high achievement motivation, while their low-income Anglo counterparts do not (MacLeod, 1987). The interpretative approach permits a fuller understanding of mediating factors such as the belief that racial inequality has been checked in the past two decades, that effort can now be rewarded, that effective parent-controlled contingencies exist, and others. In effect, this approach begins to include the notions of culturally mediated action and social agency as alternative explanations to the (SES) determinism inherent in macrosociological models.

Another way this approach addresses school-based inequalities is through the analysis of "constitutive actions and rules" that give meaning and define giftedness, mental retardation, academic and vocational tracks, and so on. Institutionalization of tracking, labeling the mentally retarded, and similar practices, along with their prescribed courses of action, are questioned from this view. Mehan (1992) wrote,

designations like "educationally handicapped," "learning disabled," and "normal" are reflections of students, including their SES, ethnicity, and talent. But my colleagues and I found such designations were influenced by the calendar, educators' work loads, and available funds. These are practical circumstances, not individual characteristics. (p. 15)

As with the other post-cultural deficit/difference models, institutional practices of schools are viewed as causing educational handicaps, rather than the latter being situated in the individual child or her culture. Labeling, as an instrument of the dominant group's cultural knowledge, simply provides a means to constitute a relationship, after which resources can be allocated accordingly. This model calls for the elimination of school-based stratification, as well as for the utilization of the knowledge students bring with them to school in creating new interactional contexts. The model emphasizes the study of context, the dynamic understanding of education, of the ways teachers can and do make a difference, and of power relations. It shows how strategic and economic reorganization of educational practices, at the microlevel of the classroom, account for student success in ways that challenge competing models.

Finally, the interpretative approach reduces the dualism between macro- and microanalyses of inequality. This approach overcomes, in part, limitations inherent in other approaches, including those drawing on macrosociological models (e.g., Apple, 1982; Bourdieu & Passeron, 1977; Bowles & Gintis, 1977; Willis, 1977). Interpretative research has richly described the characteristics of high achievers within each of the most disadvantaged ethnic groups (R. Clark, 1983; Suarez-Orozco, 1991; Wong-Rieger & Quintana, 1987). However, two problems remain that are pertinent to the group-based inequality problem. Will the above descriptions of success in some cases be reproduced in others? Does showing that there are exceptions to the rule in some social contexts take us much further than the other models? What is the explanatory power of any one of these three models and the impact of their recommended interventions? There seems to be general agreement among all three with respect to the schools' role in forging inequality. However, a comprehensive model by which specific school, community, and family variables could be theoretically integrated with respect to student's and teachers' beliefs, daily routines, sense of agency, and competence still requires elaboration.

## Toward a Theoretical Integration

The above perspectives regarding group-based inequality suggest that a cultural approach to education and psychology is needed in integrating various models. Such an approach would likely incorporate the main of learning and instructional literature yet bring about some drastic changes with respect to understanding the social formation of mind. It would have to be based on a sound framework that incorporates culture, history, and social agency with pedagogical means. It would have to break down the various levels inherent in culture and specify ethnicity in order to allow individual-level analyses of development to be considered in recursive terms particularly. Such approach would provide a lingua franca through which an integration of extant models and an interdisciplinary dialogue could take place. It would be an approach to education that would address not only the issue of group-based inequality but also the broader issue of how to better educate everyone in general. A conceptual framework that is not totally new but that has lain dormant psychology will be outlined next. Its history and some of its components are sketched below as they relate to ethnicity in educational psychology and to the larger issue of improving education.

## A CULTURAL-HISTORICAL FRAMEWORK

At a time when the cultural deficit and cultural difference positions were beginning to fuel the polemical fires of the late 1960s and 1970s, a small book by L. S. Vygotsky reappeared in the West. *Thought and Language* (Vygotsky, 1962) and subsequent translations of his work opened the doors to a cultural-historical psychology. The latter integrated key interdisciplinary findings and drew attention to the means through which development is socially influenced. Cultural-historical theory evolved in spite of political censure and the premature death of its main founder in 1934 at the age of 38. It was also slow to enter mainstream Western psychology because of the historical factors noted earlier.

Although it is receiving increased attention in educational psychology, the cultural-historical model remains outside the dominant thrust of the discipline. It might be argued that the model has yet to be validated, or that it lacks grounded methods and empirical data (Belmont, 1995). However, this theory might represent a paradigmatic shift that would allow for the integration of often "uncoordinated compendia of empirical data and techniques" (L. S. Vygotsky, 1993, p. 34) and extension into

new areas. The cultural-historical approach is attractive in part because its diagnosis of the crisis in psychology in the first part of the 20th century still rings true today. The model's influence today owes much to cofounder Alexander Luria's efforts in the West. Its focus on the study of human history (van der Veer & Valsiner, 1991) helps us to understand group differences and lends strong theoretical support to the discipline. This approach is consistent with the cultural context perspective (Cole & Cole, 1989), which may be differentiated from the standard ones based on biological maturation, environment, or their interaction. The same environmental or biological factor "may have quite different consequences for development, depending upon the specific context in which it occurs. The ways people organize the contexts of their activities depend upon the experiences of prior generations. Therefore this perspective includes a third source, the history of the child's social group as brought into the present in the form of culture" (p. 16).

Cultural-historical theory provides a general framework for incorporating culture and ethnicity into psychology, on the one hand, and for understanding group-based inequality on the other. The scientific context and scope of the theory are well described elsewhere (Das, 1995; van der Veer & Valsiner, 1991; L. S. Vygotsky, 1993; Wertsch, 1985a & b, 1991). This section outlines salient aspects of the model to allow for some expansions to be made regarding our understanding of the development of cultural differences in education and their role in psychology.

## The Domains of Cultural-Historical Theory

Van der Veer and Valsiner (1991) and Wertsch (1991) note that Vygotsky's cultural-historical model consists of three major domains of inquiry in explaining the qualitative changes of mind and human development. The first domain is phylogenesis, which is related to comparative psychology. The second domain concerns the cultural-historical line of development (sociogenesis), which relates to how different patterns of collective activity influence, in reciprocal fashion, the development and nature of mediational tools as well as of social identities for individuals and groups. This line is appropriate for studying the emergence, evolution, and consequences of ethnicity. The third domain consists of developmental changes at the individual level, generally in intellectual functioning (microgenesis). This domain is relevant to understanding the individuals' acquisition of higher level functions, social identity formation, and the relative influence of higher level functions on development. This influence may be understood through the mediation of tools and activities and their acquisition.

## Development Mediated by Tools and Materials

The comparative study of human cognition can be discussed in terms of how material and psychological tools influence development. In the cultural-historical framework, higher psychological functions are mediated by material and psychological tools. The latter might include the ideas of other human beings (an example is the influence that some of Vygotsky's contemporaries had in forging this model). The mediation provided by tools helps account for developmental differences and their direction. At the group level, such differences become cultural differences centered on patterns of mediated experience and tool acquisition. As Kozulin and Presseisen (1995) describe Vygotsky's views:

material tools do not exist as individual implements; they presuppose collective use, interpersonal communication and symbolic representation. This symbolic aspect of tool-mediated activity gives rise to a new and important class of mediators. . . . Whereas material tools are directed at the objects of nature, psychological tools mediate humans' own psychological processes. (p. 68)

## Cultural History

The cultural history of groups in a multicultural society often reflects conditions that are related directly to the prevalence of one system of psychological tools relative to others. The psychological and social consequences appear self-evident in explaining and constructing group-based inequality. The first empirical test of this aspect of cultural-historical theory dates back to the 1930s.

Vygotsky and his colleagues employed conceptualization and memory tasks to make inferences about how culture influenced cognitive functions across different ethnocultural contexts in a tradition established partly by Levy-Bruhl (1923). By contrasting the conceptual development of rural Uzbeks in Central Asia with that of schooled Russians, a new psychology began that integrated sociogenetic processes with individual development. Those early studies were seminal in showing how ethnicity, as a marker for sociohistorical development, influenced intellectual development through mediational tools. Other studies have followed in that tradition (Cole & Scribner, 1973; Scribner & Cole, 1981).

Far from concluding that unschooled rural subjects experienced cultural and cognitive deficits when compared with their schooled, urban counterparts, Levy-Bruhl began pondering how culturally organized contexts influence mental and affective development. How individual development is situated or grounded culturally in a variety of socially organized activities was one insight that led Alexei Leontiev, the third founder of cultural-historical theory, to elaborate:

[H]uman psychology is concerned with the activity of concrete individuals, which takes place either in a collective or in a situation in which the subject deals directly with the surrounding world of objects, i.e., at the potter's wheel or the writer's desk, . . . [i]f we removed human activity from the system of social relationships, it would not exist. . . . [T]he human individual's activity is a system in the system of social relations. It does not exist without these relations. (Leontiev, 1981, pp. 46–47)

The question of how external social relations become relevant in the acquisition of higher mental processes is not new (van der Veer & Valsiner, 1991; Wertsch, 1985b). What is seminal here is the idea of mediation by sign systems, an idea that evolved in part from other important thinkers of the time, such as E. Durkeim, L. Levy-Bruhl, R. Thurnwald, J. Baldwin, K. Vossler, E. Cassirer, W. Wundt (van der Veer & Valsiner, 1991).

Mediational tools can alter the patterns of activity (behavior) for an individual or a group. This point is of particular importance in understanding group differences. At the same time,

patterns of activities can serve to maintain stability or promote change in individual and cultural development. This reciprocal relation is important in providing a theoretical rationale for equity-oriented educational and social policies. For example, each advance in individual development is linked to changes in tools or means, and those changes are reflected in the way activities are approached. The acquisition of mediational tools or means accounts for the transition from simple to complex psychological functions, and from one pattern of activity to another. Thus, the study of factors that influence their evolution and acquisition is of primary concern for the field. Mediational means such as language, literature, or calculus not only provide for cultural continuity but also guide cultural and individual development. An important issue that requires still some attention is the specification of characteristics that emerge from the tool–activity connection. Identity formation, motivation, and intellectual competencies are among several domains mediated by symbols, signs, values, or skills found in culture.

## The Law of Cultural Development

Vygotsky's "law of cultural development," which pertains to how humans develop higher psychological functions, was a forerunner of social learning theory:

Any function in the child's cultural development appears twice, or on two planes. First it appears on the social plane, and then on the psychological plane. First it appears between people as an interpsychological category, and then within the child as an interpsychological category. (Vygotsky, 1978, p. 71)

This ontogenetic law lays the groundwork for understanding differences in development associated with ethnicity in terms of tool acquisition and activity. Intercultural contact historically has influenced the acquisition and development of mediational tools that are gradually reflected in different patterns of activity. Differences in socialization activities provided in community and family settings also lend structure to the acquisition of mediational means or tools. From this perspective, a group's beliefs, values, or expectations may be understood partly as acquired mediational tools that filter cultural influences on individual development.

Culture influences normative mental development mainly through how well these mediational tools are reconstructed and amplified from one generation to the next. Cultural influences on cognition, however, seem themselves in turn to be determined by the types of activities prevalent in a group. The cultural history of various groups within a multiethnic society may be associated with differences in activity patterns. The latter have a reciprocal relation to adaptation demands and strategies.

The first law of cultural development might also be extended at the group level. Some functions in a group's cultural development appear at least twice, or on two planes. First they appear in the intercultural plane, and then on the intracultural plane. First they appear between cultural groups, and then they might be assimilated within the group. In cultural adaptation, some ethnic groups modify those functions (Berry, 1980, 1983). Intercultural contact can also change another group's functions, beliefs, and values. Hence, new functions may emerge from intercultural contact as well be reconstructed across loci in an open system.

## A Focus on the Role of Change

In cultural-historical theory, the study of development, which includes learning, is the heart of psychology. As Valsiner (1989) noted, Vygotsky "advanced the general methodological canon for psychology: Only when psychological phenomena are viewed in their process of change can they be adequately explained" (p. 61). Kurt Lewin also emphasized historical analysis as an indispensable methodological tool.

The cultural-historical model emphasizes that individual characteristics related to learning (e.g., personality, identity, motivational, or affective characteristics) require study in their very process of change. An implication here is that a similar principle should hold for the study of ethnicity-related characteristics. The focus on sociogenesis provides an alternative to approaches that essentially accept group stereotypes as fossilized traits that require accommodation. Valsiner (1989) describes clearly the historical approach to the study of mind by noting:

> The "historical" portion of the label cultural-historical refers specifically to the developmental nature of all psychological phenomena. Note that in this context, the term has little in common with the more traditional meaning relating to past events. In cultural-historical thinking, historical implies the connection between past, present and future.
>
> . . . [I]n cultural-historical thinking, individual human beings are considered to play an active role in their (as well as others') psychological development. Previous psychological schools attributed causality to the environment ("nurture") or to inborn and predetermined "essences" in individual persons ("nature"). In either case, the person was believed to play a passive role—as the target of environmental stimulation in the first case or as the "vessel" within which nature's causal essences unfold in the second case. In contrast, cultural-historical thinking emphasizes the instrumental function of the person, who, by acting upon his or her environment with the help of tools or signs, changes his or her development. Note that in this case cultural means "instrumentally created" and is different from the way in which the term is used in contemporary cross-cultural psychology—that is, meaning "specific to a certain group of people who make up a culture." (p. 60).

In extending this model, ethnicity may be regarded as organizing development directly through the cultural tools that prevail and/or are made available. Individuals may be advantaged or constrained by the nature of activities found in their community, which in turn influences the degree and the scope of the tools and signs employed. Yet individuals are relatively free to alter their development by acting on the environment with newly acquired means and schemata. The appropriation of mediational tools is explained in part by the double stimulation method (Vygotsky, 1986) by which individuals or groups convert neutral stimuli and opportunities into means or tools that in turn change development.

## The Role of Activity

A key antecedent to group-based developmental differences may lie in the mediation of valued word meanings, intellectual skills, beliefs, and other means necessary to adapt and thrive in a given cultural setting. Social and historical conditions influence the *activities* that cultural groups typically engage in, particularly those related to meeting the most basic needs. These social conditions are historically intertwined with the issues of access to, and the acquisition of, means for learning and development.

Linking intellectual development to the modes of activity and the tools or means of mediation still remains a methodological challenge. If we begin with the assumption that in order to understand a person's development, it is necessary to consider the organizing principles underlying sociocultural institutions and activities, new units of analysis become necessary. Some of these units have been proposed (Leontiev, 1981). These serve not only to help explain individual development but also psychocultural phenomena such as ethnicity in relation to development and learning.

Three analytic units have been considered (Wertsch, Minick, & Arns, 1984) in activity analysis. The unit of analysis for the study of mind is an actual pattern of activity that exists as a system with its own structure (*deyatel'nost*). This unit allows one to connect the individual with sociocultural/institutional phenomena. The second unit (*deistvie*) is goal-oriented action, a more accepted unit in mainstream psychology that includes expectations associated with a given action. Leontiev's (1981) third unit, operation (*operatsiya*), is concerned with *how* goal-directed action is carried out. Examples relating to the latter, at the collective level, might be desegregation, cooperative learning, tracking, bilingual education, and other collective mediational means. An analysis of the types of activities or operations common to a given group regarded as at risk, underdeveloped, or developing (at both inter- or intranational levels) might again suggest an inherent difference in the means or tools that mediate experience relative to others'. This difference constitutes, in part, the basis for creating disadvantage (or advantage) and the need for "remediation" or interventions that center purposely on introducing specific cultural (instrumental) means into children's development. Introducing these operations at the collective level serves as means for gradually breaking down the barriers associated with group-based inequality.

## The Zone of Proximal Development

The zone of proximal development metaphor is the most visible construct in current educational research related to this framework. This theoretical tool is understood generally as a person's potential for learning maximally with external assistance. Traditionally, psychology has regarded children's development in terms of measured test performance. An important aspect of development has been overlooked that is of equal if not greater importance than that reflected by unassisted behavior. This is the zone of proximal development, defined by those (mental)

> functions that have not yet matured but are in the process of maturation, functions that will mature tomorrow but are currently in an embryonic state. These functions could be termed the "buds" or "flowers" of development rather than the "fruits" of development. The actual developmental level characterizes mental development retrospectively, while the zone of proximal development characterizes mental development retrospectively. (Vygotsky, 1978, pp. 86–87)

To understand the process of internal development more clearly, Vygotsky provided an operationally defined example that is often confused with the definition of the ZPD:

the distance between the actual developmental level as determined by individual problem solving and the level of potential development as determined by problem solving under adult guidance or in collaboration with more capable peers. (p. 86)

For example, two children of the same age and who have the same test scores might appear comparable in terms of maturation and learning ability yet could differ considerably in their learning potential in particular zones or areas of development (e.g., math, history, geography) or in their chances to benefit from external assistance. Their learning potential in a particular content area or zone might differ considerably in terms of achieving success at the next higher level of a task or problem.

Learning activities in the zone of proximal development awaken developmental processes that mature through social interaction with other, generally more advanced individuals. Mastering the use of mediational tools (Wertsch, 1985b) and other theoretical learnings requires these social interactions in creating or expanding various zones of development. In this model, the person's cognitive structure changes as zones of proximal development are created or expanded by oneself or with others' assistance. This subtle contrast lends emphasis to the social foundations of higher level psychological functions. One main implication of the zone of proximal development construct is that it represents where, when, and to a considerable extent how culture meets individual consciousness (M. Cole, 1985). This meeting of culture and mind occurs in settings that provide conditions which facilitate actions at the individual and group level.

*Activity in the Zone of Proximal Development.* The concept of zones of proximal development has drawn great interest in the educational research community partly because it captures the dynamism of a functional, recursive system. As noted by Newman, Griffin, and Cole (1989),

"The interpersonal system" in the ZPD (which can be found also with texts, computers inside and outside "the head") also "constitutes a functional system in the same sense used by Luria." Like our circulatory or digestive systems, activity in sensitive areas produce change in the system. Unlike in those closed systems, however, "activity within a ZPD, an invariant task may occur many times, but how the functional system is constituted may change. (pp. 72–73)

The contrast helps explain much of the semiotic relation between cultural and individual development. One implication of the concept of zones of proximal development concerns educational practices that presume readiness for instruction based on chronological age or past test performance. Age or grade segregation reflects a culture's organization of education, for example, as much as the values associated with speed or power tests, and even the very (Western) concept of time. If it takes children who are less ready in first grade more time to master certain competencies or if others can advance through the existing grades earlier, the present organization of age-graded learning environments becomes instrumental in fossilizing relative gaps in development between individuals or groups. At the group level, the above organization becomes perilous for those whose sociocognitive development and cognitive environments are out of step or less compatible with the mainstream's norms, programs, and expectations. This can occur

affectively, motivationally, and intellectually (e.g., where social promotion is school policy).

In cultural-historical theory, developmental stages simply index age norms in a given sociocultural space and time. Education aimed at "where the student is at" takes on new meaning in societies with increasing ethnic diversity.

*The Zone of Proximal Development and Ethnicity.* Although some cultural-historical ideas are increasingly popular in educational and cognitive-development research at the individual level, they have yet to be employed at the group level or in a broader, social policy context. The zone of proximal development construct has not been applied directly to problems of group-based inequality at the collective level. Cultures do seem to have areas of proximal development, of differential advantages and changing aptitudes that are relative in nature.

Ethnicity may be understood as a psychosocial process that first emerges interculturally before being constructed in the individual. Its meaning and value change as the social relations between groups change (Dominguez, 1986). Yet this process of social construction, which occurs both objectively and subjectively, is central in creating zones of proximal development for individuals within groups. Depending on factors yet to be considered, ethnicity may be conceived of as a primary filter of cultural influences, like gender and class. Many areas or zones of development are created or responded to differentially as a function of this filter. The zone of proximal development heuristic is useful in specifying issues related to how learning and teaching are organized, both in and out of school. This implies that a comprehensive analysis of such organization in a variety of settings is necessary in deploying this heuristic fruitfully. And finally, the major implication here is that teaching and learning are maximized when they target the zone of proximal development, when they help to transform objectively defined competencies into personal capabilities. Many of the current problems in education related to group-based inequality can be understood around this metaphor. The cultural program of the mainstream group generally develops the zone of proximal development of its own members relatively more effectively than that of previously colonized groups.

The emergence of ethnicity at the societal level and individually as well may be understood in terms of means or mediated action (Penuel & Wertsch, 1995). These are involved in the transition from the interpsychological to the intrapsychological plane at the individual level, and in the transition from the intergroup to the intragroup level in multicultural contexts. At the group level, the analysis centered on mediated learning or means helps to account for group-based inequality, particularly its origin, maintenance, and eradication. This model's account of the learning–teaching process and the relation between learning and development also links the topics of schooling and ethnicity. One may study ethnicity as it emerges and moves from the social plane to the individual plane and becomes part of the identity formation process. Students attempt to maintain fidelity as they strive to adopt a social identity, sometimes working harder or hardly, depending on their subjective interpretation of such identity. This model also serves to maximize education by clarifying the jointness of the teaching–learning process and differentiating students' actual and potential development in relation to group membership.

Finally, how may ethnicity, pedagogy, and educational psychology be linked? The ideal study of ethnicity in educational psychology would seem to require attention to the development of mind as it unfolds in different cultural settings, particularly with regard to the ontogeny of particular beliefs, values, and motivation. Such settings involve not only the construction of particular cultural knowledge and intellectual skills but a whole spectrum of human development known as conation (see chapter 9, this volume) that includes motivational and affective domains.

## EXTENDING THE FRAMEWORK

The three main approaches of group-based inequality presented earlier join evidence regarding ethnicity's relation to development. The literature suggests that ethnicity exerts its influence at various levels, from castelike conditions in intergroup relations, the organization of schooling and beliefs, to participant structures (Phillips, 1983), teacher expectations, and practices. Educational failure is selectively constructed for some groups in terms of how instruction is delivered, how school personnel behave, and the beliefs and attitudes of school personnel, students, and communities. The gist of this literature suggests that in the absence of cultural compatibility, many of the goals, operations, and strategies found in mainstream schools are organized in ways that benefit students from some groups more than others.

To understand how ethnicity affects acculturation and development in general, the mind–culture problem needs to be broadened in an overarching theoretical framework that (a) helps integrate findings from various modes of inquiry and (b) advances methods that allow it to be tested. The cultural-historical model serves to integrate the various explanations of group-based inequality in scholastic achievement. However, its relatively new reconstitution in the social sciences requires further extension, methodological advances, and empirical validation. The remainder of this chapter amplifies some of the reaches of the model and its evolving methodologies.

### Culture and the Activity Setting Unit

An analytic unit that incorporates mediated action across social contexts is most pertinent in illustrating how to study development with culture in mind. The activity setting unit evolved from the work of Barker, John and Beatrice Whiting, and Bronfenbrenner (O'Donnell & Tharp, 1990). This unit of analysis serves to specify how culture affects development and to explain group differences in school achievement. The context in which learning–teaching interactions occur is an activity setting. To specify how children's ecocultural niche (Super & Harkness, 1980, 1986) is organized and how it might influence development, the activity setting unit addresses five types of variables:

1. *personnel* present/available for activities
2. *salient cultural values, beliefs, and attitudes that participants bring to various activities*
3. the operations and *task demands* of the activity

4. the *scripts* for conduct that govern the participants' actions
5. the *purposes, motives, or intentions guiding the action.* (Gallimore, Goldenberg, & Weisner, 1993)

These five components require consideration in unpacking culture both objectively and subjectively (Whiting, 1976). It is important to note that the third and fourth variables in this unit relate directly to mediational tools.

The use of the activity setting unit takes some getting used to, both conceptually and methodologically. However, this composite unit helps us avoid some of the dead ends found when individual functioning or learning environments are reduced to something that no longer resembles real-life phenomena (Bronfenbrenner, 1979). Rather than counting the number of books in the home, the hours spent viewing television or doing homework alone, or, as Salomon (1995) notes, dealing with "teacher cognitions without their actions, abilities without motivations," this unit helps connect the individual to the social context. In the study of group factors such as ethnicity, an "intergroup" category, the analysis of two or more settings is also required. For example, in considering a student's achievement motivation or academic self-concept, not only might we consider our objective data from self-reports, or the student's perspective and values, but we might also note those values operating in the student's culture relative to another's. Unpacking ethnicity thus requires attention to an additional cultural variable outside the activity setting unit, that of intergroup relations. That is, the influence of a particular group on the individual often depends on the group's relation to other groups in the larger macroculture. This issue is far more complex than studying classroom or school effects or aggregated variables in a nested design. It requires extending a relatively new concept in the cultural-historical model, agency.

Several researchers have begun to integrate context in their study of human development (Greenfield, 1993; Rogoff, 1982), so only a brief elaboration is presented next. In work with native Hawaiian schoolchildren, cultural incompatibility in certain variables of the activity setting unit were hypothesized to cause school failure (R. Tharp & Gallimore, 1988). In the natal activity setting, children's learning scripts were centered on peer interactions, so that prior to school entry, adults played only a minor teaching role (personnel gap). They believed children should learn mainly on their own, so that literacy skills were not cultivated as in the mainstream. They did not share the middle-class culture's values and scripts that constructed the "achievement motive" and similar characteristics that are compatible with most school settings. In addition, Hawaiian children are not privy to many of the social conventions that facilitate school learning or routines (e.g., carrying a school bag or singing an alphabet song in preschool). R. Tharp and Gallimore (1988) note that part of the activity setting involves not only the content (the what) of activities but also the operations through which activities are carried out (the how), which

arise in the context of culturally generated activities. They are grounded in the ecocultural niche of each family; it is the niche that makes certain activities more salient and important; it is the activities that influence the choice of scripts. (p. 75)

Activity settings help to account for the directional effects of ethnicity on human development, through the task demands, goals, and routine activities embedded in everyday life. These are linked with learning various aptitudes, attitudes, and values. In such settings, formal and informal (hidden) curricula, significant others, and patterns of social interaction relevant to modeling and the acquisition of mediational tools are found. The extent to which mediated learning experiences (that are compatible with those valued in school) occur in these settings determines, to a large extent, the adaptability of students and the agenda for educational interventions. Some settings are helpful in directing development toward some zones more than others. Ethnicity may be understood as a macro-activity setting for cultural mediation that, along with class, needs to be taken into consideration in the design of educational experiences.

## Group and Personal Agency

As noted earlier, group differences in mastering of new cultural knowledge or in school adaptation are not well accounted for by SES. Histories of oppression by one group over another provide a partial, post hoc explanation that remains vague in the specification of change mechanisms. Group differences in the development and reconstruction of mediational tools through schooling provides greater specificity that pertains to the cultural line of development. However, differences in access or exposure to a variety of cultural tools are only part of the problem of group-based inequality in education. A third element is needed in addressing the group-based inequality puzzle. As noted by Wertsch and Tulviste (1992):

one cannot derive an adequate account of mediated action by focusing either on the mediational means or on the individual or individuals initiating and carrying out action in isolation. Instead, both components are inherently involved in such a way that agency is defined as "individual(s)-operating-with-mediational-means. . . ." This account allows for innovation because each concrete use of mediational means by individuals involves some differences from other uses. Indeed, the individual use may vary quite radically from previous uses. On the other hand, however, mediated action is always constrained in certain fundamental ways by the fact that existing cultural tools are used. As a result, any creativity that occurs involves the transformation of an existing pattern of action, a new use for an old tool. (p. 555)

At the group level, one may understand agency in terms of a group's collective action that employs the media, constitutional or natural laws, or other means instrumentally. For example, African Americans generally attempt to overcome inequities by demanding that the rules be changed (Ogbu, 1992). Other groups adopt a "try harder" or a "join them and beat them at it" pattern that then constitutes ethnic stereotypes and that may also form part of the cultural system of a group, at least for some generations. Historically, Jews have employed literacy and other tools as instruments for forging an adaptive cultural identity. Similarly, unwelcomed immigrants variably employ legal and illegal means in their cultural adaptation. Successful new immigrants and established minority groups tend to be those that turn inert social capital and opportunities into stimuli that facilitate adaptation, both economically and educationally. For example, in some ethnic communities, families pool their savings and help establish businesses that then employ mem-

bers of the group. Similarly, the utilization of a community's fund of knowledge (Moll, 1992) can be understood as efforts to employ dormant means collectively. Other groups lobby for bilingual education as a means to ensure that instruction will respond more to their children's potential for learning. Conversely, dominant groups have employed foreign and slave labor as means for their own cultural and economic development, particularly during times when their social knowledge allowed it (Roosens, 1989). Anti-immigrant rhetoric serves as an example of a political means employed in climates where the benefits of cheap labor are outweighed by other factors associated with ethnogenesis.

Individuals as well as groups, then, may alter their own development through various types of agency. The latter may be recognized in terms of a group's work ethic or artistic, business, or athletic talent. Persons and groups may convert neutral and minimally useful stimuli into instrumental means. For example, private school may be employed by individuals and groups to advance their development. However, access to such means is moderated, in turn, by group, intergroup, and individual variables. To extend this model, researchers may focus on modifications and restructuring of variables that may allow greater access to new means, through which students' development and agency may be advanced. Both effective and cognitive domains would be involved.

## Ethnicity and Power Differentials in Learning Environments

Ethnicity, by definition, denotes a cultural difference in socialization and world view that is sometimes weighted by power differentials. In the process of education, for instance, culturally different students become painfully aware not only of the mainstream's world view but also of their own world view—perhaps for the first time in an objective sense (Roosens, 1989). How social identities are constructed in the educational marketplace in turn influences a host of affective and cognitive factors. Terms such as "inner city" or "at risk" serve to locate individuals' development in a social context and to assign common meanings. Subjectively, such terms also serve as means defining the self, the reference group, and their value. The label "at risk" or "disadvantaged" refers not to the child necessarily but rather to the effect of limitations often found in schools that fail in educating children *with* their culture kit (Wertsch & Tulviste, 1992). Disadvantagement involves the notion that "there are large demographically identifiable subpopulations that gain significantly less than others from their interaction with the public schools" (Bereiter, 1970). The structuring of "deficits and disorders" found in school settings is often beyond the control of learners and their communities. When schooling structures disadvantage in the already disadvantaged, it places them and society in an at-risk status. Many children become vulnerable, in a very similar sense as in the clinical literature (e.g., Garmezy, 1991; Rutter, 1979), upon entering school.

From this perspective, the risk for underdevelopment concerns not only the types of mediational tools mastered by students from different groups, but the accumulation and maintenance of limitations during students' formative years. These limitations continue today primarily because of a second type of social knowledge gap that is exposed in a limited understanding of development and culture (the first social knowledge gap was exposed in the cultural deficit belief). Most early-age compensatory programs, for example, may be regarded as re-mediation efforts that aim to establish a new, school-compatible sort of continuity that is rarely maintained. The mediated learning experiences provided are insufficient and organized in ways that are unlikely to alter the achievement gap. It may not be enough to enrich the child's early cognitive development in one temporary setting and simply assume that later, cognitive support will be organized and maintained in school settings. Coordinated, systemic approaches are needed that combine local knowledge, theory-derived means, and mediated activities in bringing about significant change. The latter may not be subject to evaluation by traditional means, including the canon of external validity. This was one of the main learnings from compensatory education programs, which in retrospect appear as experimentations with various activity setting variables. For educational psychology, the implications here are clear. Research aimed at finding not only universals but also local solutions based on the design of learning environments, dynamic assessments of learning potential, and different combinations of person-context variables requires further attention. Providing mediated learning experiences in strategic domains where students' learning potential and agency can be maximized is another important direction.

## INTEGRATING CURRENT RESEARCH

This section examines how well past and current research may be integrated into the cultural-historical framework. Educational interventions generally provide conditions for students to display agency and internal attributions and to acquire new mediational tools and metacognitive strategies. Many of the current research programs in educational psychology can be understood as concerned, at least indirectly, with particular instrumental means with which students may advance their own development. School-based motivational programs such as those devised by Alschuler (1972) or Dweck (1986), or research on student thought processes noted by Wittrock (1986), or ATIs—in fact, most of the topics examined in the present *Handbook*—may be regarded as fitting into the matrix where individual and context meet. Programs aimed at improving children's self-esteem and sense of belonging can be understood as attempts to alter some aspects of the activity setting of the student. The role of certain beliefs, such as those found in a folk incremental theory, as opposed to entity theory (Dweck, 1986), captures one educational setting variable. Teachers and children may learn to regard intelligence and social competence as functions of knowledge and strategy incrementation that are developed primarily through practice and effort. As Marshall and Weinstein (1984) suggest, teachers who share this cognition are likely to favor mastery, cooperation, flexible learning practices, and criterion-referenced performance assessments. In other settings, an entity belief may be found to be as adaptive in its relation to the self-fulfilling prophecy, self-esteem, or other variables.

Surely, most of the extant research in educational psychology is not designed with the cultural context in mind. The argument, however, is that research findings remain useful in providing data points in a matrix that may be reconstructed with culture in mind.

Interventions aimed at changing locus of control or self-esteem, or that change teacher expectations, or that alter strategies used by students are useful from this perspective. However, future research plans in the various subareas of educational psychology require some rethinking and integration.

Educational psychologists tend to believe they have the keys to solve most pedagogical problems, or the means that generally hover beyond the reach of educators who work with less pedagogical knowledge and skills. It would seem that with the clear links between culture and cognition that emerge from the present framework, educational psychology might indeed be in a strategic position to close the group-based achievement gap.

The principal goals of educational research require strategies to increase the range of activities and mediated experiences that students encounter regularly. For some groups, countering the effects of sociohistorically determined disadvantages that multiply on school entry becomes a strategic goal of education. For more advantaged groups of students, the goal is similar in that educational activities are still designed to maximize areas of potential development. The problem of establishing and maintaining the match between zones of proximal development and school learning remains a critically important research problem. This problem requires improvement in dynamic assessments of children's development (Fuerstein, 1990; Brown & Ferrara, 1985; Kozulin & Presseissen, 1995; Minick, 1987; Newman et al., 1989) as well as improvements in designs for responsive educational settings.

In the past, educational psychology research focused extensively on maximizing the external conditions of learning, in particular the types of instructional settings. Today, it seems that a fundamental change for educational psychology research involves more in-depth analyses of developmental and cultural conditions. While attention to learner characteristics, learning environments, and adapting instruction to various ability groups has been prevalent, these areas acquire new meaning within the present framework. Changes associated with increased compatibility and success in one setting may not be effective when implemented for other groups of students. This suggests a need for a developmental approach focused on mediated action (Wertsch, 1991) relative to standard approaches that tend to overlook the cultural situatedness of various operations, goals, and learning potential.

The joining of process–product and information-processing approaches with an evolving cultural-historical model appears to be promising. The future research agenda requires continued improvements with respect to educators' own theoretical understanding and grasp of the "means of assistance" (R. Tharp & Gallimore, 1988), reciprocal teaching, and similar areas that fall squarely on learning and instructional theory. Attention to the assumptions and principles of measurement and evaluation that have driven process–product research and other educational psychology research is also required. Teachers and teacher educators also need to master essential principles relating to their psychocultural mediation of development. Much of the current research on organizing instruction, reforming teacher education, improving parent involvement, and formulating new goals and methods for assessing success can be understood as targeting different aspects of activity settings.

But are the above strategies being carried out consciously in educational psychology? Are these guided by a theory-based systemic plan in mind? For example, new goals such as those associated with educational reforms, the development of thinking skills, or creative problem solving represent one level of the activity setting unit in school. A new set of operations at the macro or micro levels may be driven by new beliefs about education. Improving the education of future teachers reflects an effort to manipulate a school personnel variable, whereas improving parental involvement represents a school-based operation with the goal of affecting children's natal activity setting (i.e., personnel, routines, and other variables).

A main implication here is the need to reinterpret present research findings and practices within a broader framework that allows greater integration of context in the work of educational psychologists. A broader framework helps to situate many current miniresearch paradigms within education and along with their findings. Finally, it helps preclude pseudodebates among different research traditions. Not too long ago, Gagné (1987) reflected on the peaks and valleys of educational psychology, noting "peaks during which worthwhile developments in the parent discipline have been incorporated and used to advantage" (p. 401). It would seem that in the present case, the worthwhile developments do not originate in mainstream (Western) psychology but from a less cultivated "second psychology" (Cahan & White, 1992) that is still to be incorporated into the core of psychology.

## Toward a Broader Perspective

The relation of teaching to cognitive development analyzed earlier by Vygotsky (see van der Veer & Valsiner, 1992, chapter 13) is most pertinent to core issues in educational psychology. For example, instruction as an external means of supporting the processes, learning, or the strategies that students learn to learn (Gagné, 1987, p. 401), forms essential pedagogical knowledge in educational psychology. The model, with its emphases on tool mediation, agency, the zone of proximal development, metacognitive assistance, and related constructs, represents a source of advantage to educational psychology that might allow educational psychology in turn to benefit other branches of psychology and of the social sciences.

More important, perhaps, is the question, "What is it about culture and ethnicity that accounts for significant differences in response to the schooling process and its outcomes?" Note that this question subsumes the different approaches to explaining group-based inequality reviewed earlier. Each approach can be analyzed as lending emphasis to particular context variables or combinations of variables from both objective and subjective perspectives. For example, when researchers discover that students mount resistance in schools or fall prey to the low-effort syndrome, student beliefs are involved that then influence the patterns of behavior observed. Or, when current tracking practices or bilingual education policies are analyzed, a different aspect of the cultural context is in question that influences how personnel act, their beliefs, and the goals they set for students. Ethnicity always implies interrelations among activity settings in which the child's development unfolds. Attention to context variables and the concept of agency can be instrumental in establishing greater student–school compatibilities and in providing optimal teaching and learning conditions for all students. The inclusion of ethnicity and culture allows researchers to consider the influence of settings outside the classroom that influence students' development.

The theoretical and methodological adjustments implied by a cultural model may be viewed as building on many of the advancements in social science research. Advances in areas such as power analysis, causal modeling, or ethnographic methods, along with research programs such as cooperative learning, teacher and student thought processes, learning environments, and others, remain important tools for a unified approach to culture and mind. In addressing the group-based inequality problem as a particular sort of task for the discipline, each of the above areas has a contribution to make in sorting out culture's relation to teaching, learning, and development.

A final set of issues concerns whether a new view of mind, a new world view, may encounter difficulty in asserting itself in the main of the discipline. If a new unit of analysis enters the field, to what extent can the discipline absorb the shift, in both theoretical and methodological terms? The questions that are addressed by the cultural-historical framework are generally different and focus more on developmental change. Finally, the social constructivism inherent in this model often tends to be associated exclusively with a qualitative, phenomenological research tradition by many, although it is not necessarily so. Vygotsky's legacy is clearly that of *social science* (Rizo, 1991), inclusive of the experimental method and based on the belief of the materialist aspects of the psyche. The legacy clearly suggests a salient concern for educational issues regarding teaching, learning, and development that are in the positivist tradition. These and related issues have yet to be addressed in the field as it undergoes its own transformation.

## SUMMARY AND CONCLUSIONS

This chapter considered ethnicity and culture in relation to the development of the human mind and group differences. It documented gross group-based differences in education and interdisciplinary responses to the issue of inequality, and attempted to reframe the problem. The concept of group-based inequality was defined in relation to ethnocultural history and analyzed in terms of mediated experience and activity. The cultural-historical approach was outlined and expanded to address conceptual and methodological issues confronting educational psychology.

Two major questions were raised at the beginning concerning the question of how ethnicity and culture mediate development, teaching, learning, and particularly group-based differences. The first concerned how educational psychology has approached ethnicity. A general theme that emerged was that of the study of ethnicity as a categorical, static variable. The standard factorial approach has accounted for ethnicity as error variance, a preliminary step in the breaking down of demographic, external factors before considering the variable of interest. Some of these factors reflect distal cultural influences. It has been noted that the very motives and beliefs in educational psychology for this approach have been so, mainly in order to examine other, more important questions that lie within the traditional scope of educational psychology. We may understand how each tradition within educational psychology has set forth its beliefs (e.g., objective, scientific psychology), goals, and operations before the field. While some understanding of culture has been found packaged in process–product research, such understanding has not been a priority. It may be that this situation may have been due to the absence of methods or mediational tools with which to incorporate or inject culture into psychology, at least until recently.

Educational psychology has provided fragmentary glimpses of cultural influences and has restricted the culture–mind problem primarily to group-based differences in developmental outcomes. Criteria-of-effectiveness types of research programs (see Berliner, 1990) remain central to educational psychology today, reflecting new extensions of the reigning cognitive paradigm. Educational psychology consists of various research programs such as those addressing cooperative learning, teacher, or student cognitions (Wittrock, 1986), teacher expectations (Cooper & Good, 1983), motivation (Dweck, 1986), instructional design, and other areas that remain important in addressing both equity and excellence concerns. These areas of research examine, in a neofunctionalist fashion, what works for different ethnocultural groups, a trend that is beginning to appear in some textbooks. Unfortunately, educational psychology theories have not been culturally inclined. The field continues to be chiefly the application of psychological models to educational practice.

One conclusion drawn in this chapter is that much of the past and present research in educational psychology remains relevant and is useful in mapping specific aspects of school and other cultural settings. However, the research landscape is fragmented, and concerns about the future of the discipline are frequently raised (Pintrich, 1994). A cultural-historical framework connects different lines of current research in educational psychology. Process–product, instructional design, student and teacher cognitions, classroom process, and content area research all may be analyzed in terms of their relation to particular features of the social context in which humans develop. In effect, the framework advanced in the chapter builds on the educational psychology by James, Thorndike, and Dewey (S. White, 1991), and extends educational psychology toward a cultural context perspective. Yet the need for educational psychology to integrate culture within many of its research areas a priori is rarely reflected in the main of the literature.

The Thorndike tradition, which, like its founder, is still deeply engrained in educational psychology, seems to have

travelled light theoretically . . . [with] a collection of research programs addressed to a set of operational issues in education . . . adding and subtracting programs as (research) issues and technological possibilities change. . . . (S. White, 1991, p. 35)

White's observation rings true, particularly as one examines the bulk of past educational psychology research and its present and future directions (Ash & Love-Clark, 1985; Ball, 1984; Hilgard, 1988; Jones, 1985; Ronning & Glover, 1987; Tobias, 1985).

Two interrelated points merit comment. First, ethnicity as a mediating factor in academic achievement and in school learning and teaching is a problem that has drawn increased research attention for both pluralistic and demographic reasons. How-

ever, this chapter argued that the main, overriding motive remains scientific and that the inclusion of culture in psychological research inescapably benefits all. An important question remains as to how the discipline will address this topic, and on whose social knowledge basis.

A second concern is the fitting of a cultural, developmental model into a field that has recently experienced the cognitive psychology paradigm shift. If cognition is to be studied in its social context, a merging of both traditions seems inevitable. However, as long as educational psychology follows a cognitive psychology model that situates cognition in the head and fails to consider how it is propelled and distributed socially, it may be some time before a cultural-historical shift is felt in the core of educational psychology. This concern responds, in part, to the second question raised earlier concerning whether educational psychology has anything to offer in the eradication of group-based inequality or in the integration of culture within the discipline as a whole.

Educational psychology does have something to offer, particularly because the issues related to learning and teaching fall squarely on the path of the discipline. In fact, the intertwining of a cultural perspective in educational psychology seems unavoidable and has partially begun. It concerns not only ethnicity and the group-based inequality problem but also the larger question of cognition and development. Hence, a primary challenge for educational psychology is that of exploiting its unique field position in steering the discipline toward a "cultural psychology" (Bruner, 1990) or a "second psychology" (Cahan & White, 1992), both of which may be understood within the cultural-historical framework advanced in this chapter.

Another conclusion to be drawn from this chapter is that a new set of operational issues lies before educational psychology today, and that these issues have yet to become an integral part of educational psychology research and the preparation of future educational psychologists and educators. Many of us have had to become self-taught interdisciplinary educational psychologists. The future education of our graduate students will benefit from having an interdisciplinary base and flexibility in choosing methods of inquiry. This conclusion cannot be emphasized enough.

Educational psychology may also be understood as an activity setting with its own operations, beliefs, scripts, and goals. The study of culture ought not to be reserved for ethnic persons. Nonethnic persons also have culture. The study of culture, via combinations of context and individual indicators, allows it to become a most interesting factor within an experimental design. The functionalist model's emphasis on "what works" according to the criteria of effectiveness (i.e., achievement) may be regarded as a particularly important strategy that is employed in educational psychology in organizing culturally compatible school settings. It provides useful feedback to the system. As educational psychology broadens its theoretical foundations and retains a functionalist approach to the study of ethnicity, it will continue to uncover important principles for teaching and development. The criteria of effectiveness employed in the past may need to be re-mediated in order to target strategic variables in students' learning environments and optimize their development. Learning and teaching in classrooms may be improved by tuning in to different learning environments, both in and out of the school (Heath & McLaughlin, 1994), that maximize students' development.

This chapter addressed the question of whether teaching and learning are generally different for students from dissimilar cultures. The question may be addressed in the following way. As long as teaching is regarded as separate from learning, it may be argued that learning is not different for individuals regardless of origin but rather that teaching is experienced differently. This, of course, may influence learning. On the other hand, if teaching and learning are regarded as a single unitary process, then it may be argued that the process is, in fact, different for students from diverse cultures. The difference is not necessarily because of fixed, intrapersonal characteristics of students, such as so-called learning styles, but rather *learned* styles, identities, and relations. The educational process may be experienced differently depending on any number of intercultural and developmental factors. At one level, the difference may be analyzed by examining teaching and learning processes in the school and other settings in relation to the learning potential of students and in relation to their own agency. At another level, the difference may be examined in terms of cultural compatibility. By taking into account both objective and subjective variables in contexts for learning and teaching, educational psychology stands to improve its understanding of the larger matrix in which much current educational psychology research can be situated.

In conclusion, the forging of an interdisciplinary, cultural foundation in educational psychology remains a difficult challenge in a *Zeitgeist* that is marked by research specialization. It is precisely through such a foundation, however, that current educational psychology can address group-based inequalities, become again relevant in educational reform, and provide excellence in education. Educational psychology's strategic field position for the study of culture in relation to cognition, and for the study of development in general, can also serve to advance psychology. Bruner (1990) addressed the prospect of incorporating new goals and motives in the field by noting, "The program of a cultural psychology is not to deny biology or economics, but to show how human minds and lives are reflections of culture and history as well as of biology and physical resources" (p. 138). It would seem, then, that the study of culture and ethnicity in educational psychology is not only justified but is an essential part of this program.

## References

Alschuler, A. S. (1972). *Motivating achievement in high school students: Education for human growth.* Englewood Cliffs, NJ: Educational Technology Publications.

Apple, M. W. (1982). *Cultural and economic reproduction in education: Essays on class, ideology, and the state.* Boston: Routledge & Kegan Paul.

Ash, M. J., & Love-Clark, P. (1985). A historical analysis of the content of educational psychology textbooks 1954–1983. *Educational Psychologist, 20,* 47–55.

Ball, S. (1984). Educational psychology as an academic chameleon: An editorial assessment after 75 years. *Journal of Educational Psychology, 76*(6), 933–999.

Banks, J. A. (1987). *Teaching strategies for ethnic studies* (4th ed.). Boston: Allyn & Bacon.

Banks, J. A. (1995). *Handbook of multicultural education.* New York: Macmillan.

Banks, J. A., & McGee Banks, C. A. (Eds.). (1989). *Multicultural education.* Boston: Allyn & Bacon.

Baratz-Snowden, J. C. (1988). The educational progress of language minority children: Findings from the NAEP 1985-1986 special study. ERIC document from series: The Nation's Report Card. (May 1988).

Belmont, J. M. (1995). Discussion: A view from the empiricist's window. *Educational Psychologist, 30*(2), 99–102.

Bereiter, C. (1970). Educational implications of Kohlberg's cognitive-developmental view. *Interchange, 1*(1), 25–32.

Berliner, D. C. (1990). The place of process-product research in developing the agenda for research on teacher thinking. *Educational Psychologist, 24,* 325–344.

Berliner, D. C., & Biddle, B. J. (1995). The manufactured crisis, Reading, MA: Addison-Wesley.

Bernstein, Basil. (1961). Social structure, language and learning. *Educational Research, 3,* 163–176.

Bernstein, B. (1971). *Class codes and control: Vol. 1. Theoretical studies toward a sociology of language.* London: Routledge & Kegan Paul.

Bernstein, B. (1973). *Class, codes and control: Vol. 3. Toward a theory of educational transmissions.* London: Routledge & Kegan Paul.

Berry, J. W. (1980). Acculturation as varieties of adaptation. In A. M. Padilla (Ed.), *Acculturation: Theory, model, and some new findings* (pp. 9–25). Boulder, CO: Westview Press.

Berry, J. W. (1983). Acculturation: A comparative analysis of alternative forms. In R. J. Samuda & S. L. Woods (Eds.), *Perspectives in immigrant and minority education* (pp. 65–78). Lanham, MD: University Press of America.

Bevan, W. (1991). Contemporary psychology: A tour inside the onion. *American Psychologist, 46*(5), 475–483.

Bourdieu, P., & Passeron, J. (1977). *Reproduction in education, society and culture.* London: Sage.

Bowles, S., & Gintis, H. (1977). *Schooling in capitalist America: Educational reform and the contradictions of economic life.* New York: Basic Books.

Bowles, S., & Gintis, H. (1988). Schooling in capitalist America: A reply to our critics. In M. Cole (Ed.), *Bowles and Gintis revisited.* London: Falmer Press.

Bronfenbrenner, U. (1979). *The ecology of human development.* Cambridge, MA: Harvard University Press.

Brookover, W. B., Brady, N. V., & Warfield, M. (1981). *Educational policies and equitable education: A report of studies of two desegregated school systems.* East Lansing: Michigan State University, College of Urban Development, Center for Urban Affairs.

Brophy, J. (1988). Research linking teacher behavior to student achievement: Potential implications for instruction of Chapter 1 students. *Educational Psychologist, 23,* 235–286.

Brophy, J., & Good, T. (1974). *Teacher-student relationships.* New York: Holt, Rinehart & Winston.

Brophy, J., & Good, T. (1986). Teacher behavior and student achievement. In M. C. Wittrock (Ed.), *Handbook of research on teaching* (3rd ed., pp. 328–375). New York: Macmillan.

Brown, A. L., & Ferrara, R. A. (1985). Diagnosing zones of proximal development. In J. Wertsch (Ed.), *Culture, communication, and cognition: Vygotskian perspectives* (pp. 273–305). New York: Cambridge University Press.

Bruer, J. T. (1993). *Schools for thought.* Cambridge, MA: MIT Press.

Bruner, J. (1990). *Acts of meaning*. Cambridge, MA: Harvard University Press.

Cahan, E. D., & White, S. H. (1992). Proposals for a second psychology. *American Psychologist, 47*(2), 224–235.

Cazden, C. B. (1986). Classroom discourse. In M. Wittrock (Ed.), *Handbook of research on teaching* (3rd ed, pp. 432–463). New York: Macmillan.

Charles, D. C. (1988). Early research in educational psychology. *Educational Psychologist, 23*(3), 221–233.

Clark, C. A., & Walberg, H. J. (1969). The use of secondary reinforcement in teaching inner-city school children. *Journal of Special Education, 3*(2), 177–185.

Clark, R. (1983). *Family life and school achievement: Why poor black children succeed or fail*. Chicago: University of Chicago Press.

Cole, M. (1985). The zone of proximal development: Where culture and cognition create each other. In J. Wertsch (Ed.), *Culture, communication, and cognition: Vygotskian perspectives* (pp. 146–161). New York: Cambridge University Press.

Cole, M., & Bruner, J. (1971). Cultural differences and inferences about psychological processes. *American Psychologist, 26*, 867–876.

Cole, M., & Cole, S. (1989). *The development of children*. New York: Scientific American Books.

Cole, M., Gay, J., Glick, J. A., & Sharp, D. W. (1971). *The cultural context of learning and thinking*. New York: Basic Books.

Cole, M., & Scribner, S. (1973). Cognitive consequences of formal and informal education. *Science, 182*, 553–559.

Coleman, J. S. (1966). *Equality of educational opportunity*. Washington, DC: U.S. Government Printing Office.

Coleman, J. S. (1973). Equality of opportunity and equality of results. *Harvard Educational Review, 43*(1), 129–137.

Coleman, J. S. (1990). *Equality and achievement in education*. Boulder, CO: Westview Press.

Collier, W. (1987). *Project LIVE: A literacy and dropout prevention program that works*. New York: Children's Aid Society.

Comer, J. P. (1991). Home, school and academic learning. In J. Goodlad & P. Keating (Eds.), *Access to knowledge: An agenda for our nation's schools* (pp. 23–42). New York: College Entrance Examination Board.

Comer, J. P., Haynes, N. M., & Hamilton-Lee, M. (1989). *School power; A model for improving black student achievement*. New Haven, CT: Yale University, Child Study Center.

Cooper, H. M., & Good, T. L. (1983). *Pygmalion grows up*. New York: Longman.

D'Amato, J. (1988). "Acting": Hawaiian children's resistance to teachers. *Elementary School Journal, 88*, 529–544.

Darling-Hammond, L., & Green, J. (1990). Teacher quality and equality. In J. I. Goodlad & P. Keating (Eds.), *Access to knowledge: An agenda for our nation's schools*. New York: College Entrance Examination Board.

Das, J. P. (1995). Some thoughts on two aspects of Vygotsky's work. *Educational Psychologist, 30*(2), 93–97.

Dasen, P. R. (1977). *Piagetian psychology: Cross cultural contributions*. New York: Gardner Press.

Davis, D. G. (1986). *A pilot study to assess equity in selected curricular offerings across three diverse schools in a large urban school district: A search for methodology*. Paper presented at the annual meeting of the American Educational Research Association, San Francisco.

Delgado-Gaitan, C. (1990). *Literacy for empowerment: The role of parents in children's education*. London: Falmer Press.

Delpit, L. (1986). Skills and other dilemmas of a progressive black educator. *Harvard Educational Review, 56*(4), 379–385.

Dominguez, V. R. (1986). *White by definition: Social classification in Creole Louisiana*. New Brunswick, NJ: Rutgers University Press.

Dunham, R. M. (1973). *Toward a public concern for the family: The family as a unit in the study of social problems*. Tallahassee: Florida State University.

Dunham, R. M., Portes, P. R., & Williams, S. (1984). Identification of mother-child interaction patterns: A longitudinal evaluation of early age intervention. *Children and Youth Services Review, 6*(1), 19–37.

Durkin, D. (1979). What classroom observations reveal about reading comprehension instruction. *Reading Research Quarterly, 14*, 481–533.

Dweck, C. S. (1986). Motivational processes affecting learning. *American Psychologist, 41*(10), 1040–1048.

Edmonds, R. (1979). Effective schools for the urban poor. *Educational Leadership, 37*(1), 15–24.

Erickson, F. (1986). Qualitative methods in research on teaching. In M. C. Wittrock (Ed.), *Handbook of research on teacher education*. (3rd ed.) New York: Macmillan.

Evertson, C. (1982). Differences in instructional activities in higher- and lower-achieving junior high English and math classes. *Elementary School Journal, 82*(4), 329–350.

Feuerstein, R. (1990). The theory of structural cognitive modifiability. In B. Z. Presseisen (Ed.), *Learning and thinking styles: Classroom interaction* (pp. 68–134). Washington, DC: National Education Association.

Feuerstein, R. (1991). Cultural difference and cultural deprivation. In N. Bleichrodt & P. Drenth (Eds.), *Contemporary issues in cross-cultural psychology* (pp. 21–33). Amsterdam: Swets & Zeitlinger.

Foley, D. (1991). Reconsidering anthropological explanations of ethnic school failure. *Anthropology and Education Quarterly, 22*(1), 60–86.

Forgotten Half (The). (1988). *Pathways to success for America's youth and young families: Final report*. Washington, DC: William T. Grant Foundation Commission on Work, Family and Citizenship.

Foster, S. (1989). *Respecting differences: The hope for a global community*. Presented at the Annual Bilingual Multicultural Education Conference, Anchorage, AK.

Gagné, R. M. (1987). Peaks and valleys in educational psychology. In R. R. Ronning & J. A. Glover (Eds.), *Perspectives on educational psychology* (pp. 395–402). New York: Plenum Press.

Gallimore, R., & Goldenberg, C. (1993). Activity settings of early literacy: Home and school factors in children's emergent literacy. In E. Forman, N. Minick, & C. A. Stone (Eds.), *Context for learning* (pp. 315–335). Oxford: Oxford University Press.

Garmezy, N. (1991). Resilience and vulnerability to adverse development outcomes associated with poverty. *American Behavior Scientist, 34*(4), 416–430.

Gay, G. (1969). *The enlightenment: An interpretation: Vol. 2. The Science of Freedom*. New York: Norton.

Gay, G. (1977). Curriculum for multicultural education. In F. H. Klassen & D. M. Gollnick (Eds.), *Pluralism and the American teacher: Issues and case studies* (pp. 31–62). Washington, DC: American Association of Colleges for Teacher Education.

Gay, G. (1979). Changing conceptions of multicultural education. In H. P. Baptiste & M. L. Baptiste (Eds.), *Developing multicultural process in classroom instructions: Competencies for teachers* (pp. 18–27). Washington, DC: University Press of America.

Gibson, E. J. (1994). Has psychology a future? *Psychological Science, 5*(2), 69–76.

Gibson, M. A., & Ogbu, J. U. (Eds.). (1991). *Minority status and schooling: A comparative study of immigrants and involuntary minorities*. New York: Garland Press.

Ginsberg, M. (1972). *Mind and belief: Psychological ascription and the concept of belief*. New York: Humanities Press.

Glasman, N. S. (1984). Student achievement and the school principal. *Educational Evaluation and Policy Analysis, 6*(3), 283–296.

Gollnick, D. M., & Chinn, P. C. (1986). *Multicultural education in a pluralistic society* (2nd ed.). Columbus, OH: Merrill.

Good, T. L., & Marshall, S. (1984). Do students learn more in heterogeneous or homogeneous groups? In P. Peterson, L. C. Wilkinson, & M. Hallinan (Eds.), *The social context of instruction: Group organization and group processes* (pp. 15–38). New York: Academic Press.

Good, T. L., & Weinstein, R. S. (1986, October). Schools make a difference: Evidence, criticisms, and new directions. *American Psychologist, 41,* 1090–1097.

Goodlad, J. (1983). *A place called school: Prospects for the future.* New York: McGraw-Hill.

Goodlad, J. I., & Keating, P. (Eds.). (1990). *Access to knowledge: An agenda for our nation's schools.* New York: College Entrance Examination Board.

Gould, S. J. (1981) *The mismeasure of man.* New York: Norton.

Greenfield, P. M. (1983). Ontogenesis, use, and representation of cultural categories: A psychological perspective. In B. Bain (Ed.), *The sociogenesis of language and human conduct* (pp. 109–133). New York: Plenum Press.

Greenfield, P. M. (1993). International roots of minority child development. *International Journal of Behavioral Development, 16*(3), 385–394.

Hall, G. S. (1911). *Adolescence, its psychology and its reactions to physiology, anthropology, sociology, sex, crime, religion and education* (Vol. 2). New York: D. Appleton.

Heath, S. B. (1982). Questioning at home and at school: A comparative study. In G. D. Spindler (Ed.), *Doing the ethnography of schooling* (pp. 102–131). New York: Holt, Rinehart & Winston.

Heath, S. B. (1986). Sociocultural contexts of language development. In C. Cortes (Ed.), *Beyond language: Social and cultural factors in schooling language minority students* (pp. 143–186). Washington, DC: Evaluation, Dissemination and Assessment Center.

Heath, S. B., & McLaughlin, M. W. (1994). *Identity and inner-city youth: Beyond ethnicity and gender.* New York: Teachers College, Columbia University.

Herrnstein, R. J., & Murray, C. A. (1994). *The bell curve: Intelligence and class structure in American life.* New York: Free Press.

Hess, R. D., & Shipman V. (1968). Early experience and the socialization of cognitive modes in children. *Child Development, 36,* 377–388.

Hilgard, E. (1988). *Psychology in America: A historical survey.* New York: Harcourt Brace Jovanovich.

Hodgkinson, H. (1991). Reform versus reality. *Kappan, 73*(1), 8–16.

Hunt, J. (1961). *Intelligence and Experience.* New York: Ronald Press.

Jahoda, G. (1980). Sex and ethnic differences on a spatial-perceptual task: Some hypotheses tested. *British Journal of Psychology, 71*(3), 425–431.

Jencks, C. S., Smith, M., Ackland, H., Bane, M. J., Cohen, D., Gintis, H., Heyns, B., & Michelson, S. (1972). *Inequality.* New York: Basic Books.

Jensen, A. R. (1969). How much can we boost IQ and scholastic achievement? *Harvard Educational Review, 39,* 1–123.

Jones, B. F. (1985). Educational psychologists—where are you? Reflections of an educational psychologist. *Educational Psychologist, 20,* 83–95.

Kagan, D. M. (1990). How schools alienate students at risk: A model for examining proximal classroom variables. *Educational Psychologist, 25,* 105–125.

Kagan, S. (1986). Cooperative learning and sociocultural factors in schooling. In *Beyond language: Social and cultural factors in schooling language minority students.* Los Angeles: California State University, Evaluation, Dissemination and Assessment Center.

Kamii, C., & Radin, N. (1967). *The Ypsilanti Early Education Program.* Ypsilanti, MI: Ypsilanti Early Education Program.

Karabel, J., & Halsey, A. H. (1977). *Power and ideology in education.* New York: Oxford University Press.

Karpov, Y. V. & Bransford, J. D. (1995). L. S. Vygotsky and the doctrine of empirical theoretical learning. *Educational Psychologist, 30,* 61–66.

Kessen, W. (1979). The American child and other cultural inventions. *American Psychologist, 34*(10), 815–20.

Kleinfeld, J. S. (1973). Intellectual strengths in culturally different groups: An Eskimo illustration. *Review of Educational Research, 43,* 341–359.

Kounin J. (1970). *Discipline and group management in classrooms.* New York: Holt, Rinehart & Winston.

Kozulin, A., & Presseisen, B. Z. (1995). Mediated learning experience and psychological tools: Vygotsky's and Feuerstein's perspectives in a study of student learning. *Educational Psychologist, 30*(2), 67–75.

Krewer, B., & Jahoda, G. (1990). On the scope of Lazarus and Steinthal's "Völkerpsychologie" as reflected in the *Zeitschrift für Völkerpsychologie und Sprachwissenschaft 1860–1890. Quarterly Newsletter of the Laboratory of Comparative Human Cognition, 12,* 4–12.

Laosa, L. M. (1979). Social competence in childhood: Toward a developmental, socioculturally relativistic paradigm. In M. W. Kent & J. E. Rolf (Eds.), *Primary prevention of psychopathology: Vol. III. Social competence in children.* Hanover, NH: University Press of New England.

Laosa, L. M. (1981). *Parent-child interaction: Theory, research and prospects.* Edited by R. W. Henderson. New York: Academic Press.

Lazar, I., & Darlington, R. (1982). Lasting effects of early education: A report from the consortium for longitudinal studies. *Monographs of the Society for Research in Child Development, 47*(2–3, Serial No. 195).

Leontiev, A. N. (1981). The problem of activity in psychology. In J. V. Wertsch (Ed.), *The concept of activity in Soviet psychology* (pp. 37–71). Armonk, NY: Sharpe.

Levin, H. M. (1988). Changing the schools. In G. W. Albee, J. M. Joffe, & L. A. Dusenbury (Eds.), *Prevention, powerlessness, and politics: Readings on social change* (pp. 441–460). Newbury Park, CA: Sage.

Levy-Bruhl, L. (1923). *Primitive mentality.* London: Allen & Unwin.

Lewontin, R., Rose, R., & Kamin, L. (1984). *Not in our genes.* New York: Pantheon.

Lorenz, K. (1952). *King Solomon's ring.* London: Methuen.

Luria, A. R. (1979). *The making of the mind.* Cambridge, MA: Harvard University Press.

MacLeod, J. (1987). *Ain't no makin' it.* Boulder, CO: Westview Press.

Marshall, H. H., & Weinstein, R. S. (1984). Classroom factors affecting students' self-evaluations: An interactional model. *Review of Educational Research, 54,* 301–325.

Martin, D. C. (1995). The choices of identity. *Social Identities, 1*(1), 5–20.

Maslow, A. H. (1970). *Motivation and personality* (2nd ed.). New York: Harper & Row.

Matute-Bianchi, M. E. (1986). Ethnic identities and patterns of school success and failure among Mexican-descent and Japanese-American students in a California high school: An ethnographic analysis. *American Journal of Education, 95,* 233–255.

McDermott, R. P., Goldman, S. V., & Herve, V. (1984). When school goes home: Some problems in the organization of homework. *Teachers College Record, 85,* 391–410.

Mehan, H. (1987). Language and power in organizational process. *Discourse Processes, 10,* 291–301.

Mehan, H. (1992, January). Understanding inequality in schools: The contribution of interpretive studies. *Sociology of Education, 65,* 1–20.

Mercer, J. (1974). *Labeling the mentally retarded.* Berkeley: University of California Press.

Miller, S. K. (1985). Research on exemplary schools: An historical perspective. In G. Austin & H. Gatber (Eds.), *Research on exemplary schools* (pp. 3–30). New York: Academic Press.

Minick, N. (1987). *Implications of Vygotsky's theories for dynamic assessment.* Chicago: University of Chicago, Center of Psychosocial Studies.

Moll, L. C. (Ed.). (1990). *Vygotsky and education: Instructional implications and applications of sociohistorical psychology.* Cambridge, England: Cambridge University Press.

Moll, L. C. (1991). *Community knowledge and classroom practice: Combining resources for literacy instruction.* (Technical Report). Tucson: University of Arizona, Tuscon, College of Education.

Moll, L. C. (1992). Funds of knowledge for teaching: Using a qualitative approach to connect homes and classrooms. *Theory into Practice, 31*(1), 132–141.

Morgan, E. P. (1977). *Inequality in classroom learning: Schooling and democratic citizenship.* New York: Praeger.

Munsterberg, H. (1915). *Psychology: General and applied.* New York: Appleton.

Murphy, J. (1988). Equity as student opportunity to learn. *Theory Into Practice, 27*(2), 145–151.

Murphy, J., & Hallinger, P. (1989). Equity as access to learning: Curricular and instructional treatment differences. *Journal of Curriculum Studies, 21*(2), 129–149.

Murphy, J., Weil, M., Hallinger, P., & Mitman, A. (1985). School effectiveness: A conceptual framework. *Educational Forum, 49*(3), 361–374.

Neisser, U. (1986). *The school achievement of minority children: New perspectives.* Hillsdale, NJ: Lawrence Erlbaum Associates.

Newman, D., Griffin, P., & Cole, M. (1989). *The construction zone: Working for cognitive change in school.* Cambridge, MA: Cambridge University Press.

Oakes, J. (1985). *Keeping track: How schools structure inequality.* New Haven, CT: Yale University Press.

Oakes, J. (1991). *Multiplying inequalities: The effects of race, social class, and tracking on opportunities to learn math and science.* Santa Monica, CA: Rand Corporation.

O'Donnell, C. R., & Tharp, R. G. (1990). A theoretical model for community intervention. In A. S., Bellack, M. Hersen, & A. E. Kazdin (Eds.), *International handbook of behavior modification and therapy* (2nd ed., pp. 251–266). New York: Plenum Press.

Ogbu, J. U. (1974). *The next generation: An ethnography of education in an urban neighborhood.* New York: Academic Press.

Ogbu, J. U. (1977). Racial stratification and education: The case of Stockton, California. *ICRD Bulletin, 12*(3), 1–26.

Ogbu, J. U. (1978). *Minority education and caste: The American system in cross-cultural perspective.* New York: Academic Press.

Ogbu, J. U. (1989). The individual in collective adaptation: A framework for focusing on academic underperformance and dropping out among involuntary minorities. In L. Weis, E. Farrar, & H. Petrie, (Eds.), *Issues, dilemmas, and solutions* (pp. 181–204). Albany: State University of New York Press.

Ogbu, J. U. (1991). Low school performance as an adaptation: The case of blacks in Stockton, California. In M. A. Gibson & J. U. Ogbu (Eds.), *Minority status and schooling: A comparative study of immigrants and involuntary minorities* (pp. 249–285). New York: Garland Press.

Ogbu, J. U. (1992). Understanding cultural diversity and learning. *Educational Researcher, 21*(8), 5–14.

Ornstein, A. C., & Levine, D. U. (1989). Social class, race, and school achievement: Problems and prospects. *Journal of Teacher Education, 40*(5), 17–22.

Pai, Y. (1990). *Cultural foundations of education.* Columbus, OH: Merrill.

Paton, S. M., Walberg, H. J., & Yeh, E. G. (1973). Ethnicity, environmental control, and academic self-concept in Chicago. *American Educational Research Journal, 10,* 85–99.

Peal, E., & Lambert, W. E. (1962). The relation of bilingualism to intelligence. *Psychological Monographs, 76*(27, Whole No. 546).

Penuel, W. R., & Wertsch, J. V. (1995). Vygotsky and identity formation: A sociocultural approach. *Educational Psychologist, 30,* 57–59.

Persell, C. H. (1977). *Education and inequality: A theoretical and empirical synthesis.* New York: Free Press.

Piestrup, A. (1973). *Black dialect interference and accommodation of reading instruction in first grade* (Monograph No. 4). Berkeley: University of California, Language Behavior Research Laboratory.

Pintrich, P. R. (1994). Continuities and discontinuities: Future directions for research in educational psychology. *Educational Psychologist, 29,* 137–148.

Phillips, S. (1983). *The invisible culture: Communication in classroom and community on the Warm Springs Indian Reservation.* New York: Longman.

Portes, A., & Rumbaut, R. G. (1990). *Immigrant America.* Berkeley: University of California Press.

Portes, A., & Stepick, A. (1993). *City on the edge: The transformation of Miami.* Berkeley: University of California Press.

Portes, P. R. (1982). The effects of environmental processes on children's intellectual development: Longitudinal effects on family interaction through early intervention. *Dissertation Abstracts International,* The Florida State University, Tallahassee, FL.

Portes, P. R. (1991). Assessing children's cognitive environment through parent-child interactions. *Journal of Research and Development in Education, 24*(3), 30–37.

Purkey, S. D., & Smith, M. S. (1983). Effective schools: A review. *Elementary School Journal, 83*(4), 427–452.

Ramirez, M., & Castaneda, A. (1974). *Cultural democracy, bicognitive development and education.* New York: Academic Press.

Rizo, F. M. (1991). The controversy about quantification in social research: An extension of Gage's "'Historical' Sketch." *Educational Researcher, 20*(9), 9–12.

Rogoff, B. (1982). Integrating context and cognitive development. In M. E. Brown & A. L. Brown (Eds.), *Advances in developmental psychology* (vol. 2, pp. 125–170). Hillsdale, NJ: Lawrence Erlbaum Associates.

Ronning, R. R., & Glover, J. A. (1987). *Perspectives on educational psychology.* New York: Plenum Press.

Roosens, E. (1989). *Creating ethnicity: The process of ethnogenesis.* Newbury Park, CA: Sage.

Rosenshine, B. (1983). Teaching functions in instructional programs. *Elementary School Journal, 83*(4), 335–351.

Rutter, M. (1979) Protective factors in children's responses to stress and disadvantage. In M. W. Kent & J. E. Rolf (Eds.), *Primary prevention of psychopathology: Vol. III. Social competence in children* (pp. 49–74). Hanover, NH: University Press of New England.

Salomon, G. (1995). Reflections on the field of educational psychology by the outgoing journal editor. *Educational Psychologist, 30,* 105–108.

Sarason, S. B. (1981a). An asocial psychology and a misdirected clinical psychology. *American Psychologist, 36,* 827–836.

Sarason, S. B. (1981b). *Psychology misdirected.* New York: Free Press.

Scribner, S., & Cole, M. (1981). *The psychology of literacy.* Cambridge, MA: Harvard University Press.

Sewell, W. H., Hauser, R. M., & Wolf, W. C. (1980). Sex, schooling, and occupational status. *American Journal of Sociology, 86,* 551–583.

Shulman, D. G. (1987). Female subordination and male vulnerability: An integration of psychological and anthropological data. *Journal of Social Behavior and Personality 2*(1), 49–61.

Sigel, I. (1986). Reflections on the belief-behavior connection: Lessons learned from a research program on parental belief systems and teaching systems. In R. D. Ashmore & D. M. Brodzinsky (Eds.), *Thinking about the family: Views of parent and children* (pp. 35–65). Hillsdale, NJ: Lawrence Erlbaum Associates.

Sirotnik, K. A. (1990). Equal access to quality in public schooling: Issues in the assessment of equity and excellence. In J. Goodlad & P. Keating (Eds.), *Access to knowledge: An agenda for our nation's schools* (pp. 159–185). New York: College Entrance Examination Board.

Slavin, R. E. (1983). *Student team learning: An overview and practical guide.* Washington, DC: National Education Association.

Stanfield, J. H. (1985). The ethnocentric basis of social science knowledge production. *Review of Research in Education, 12,* 387–415.

Steinberg, L., Dornbusch, S. M., & Brown, B. B. (1992). Ethnic differences in adolescent achievement: An ecological perspective. *American Psychologist, 47,* 723–729.

Stevenson, H. W., & Stigler, J. W. (1992). *The learning gap: Why our schools are failing and what we can learn from Japanese and Chinese children.* New York: Summit Books.

Suarez-Orozco, M. M. (1987). Becoming somebody: Central American immigrants in U.S. inner-city schools. *Anthropology and Education Quarterly, 18,* 287–299.

Suarez-Orozco, M. M. (1991). Migration, minority status, and education: European dilemmas and responses in the 1990s. *Anthropology & Education Quarterly, 22,* 99–115.

Super, C., & Harkness, S. (Eds.). (1980). *Anthropological perspectives on child development: New directions for child development, No. 8.* San Francisco: Jossey-Bass.

Super, C., & Harkness, S. (1986). The development niche: A conceptualization at the interface of child and culture. *International Journal of Behavior Development, 9,* 1–25.

Tharp, R. G., Jordan, C., Speidel, G. E., Au, K. H., Klein, T. W., Calkins, R. P., Sloat, K. C. M., & Gallimore, R. (1984). Product and process in applied developmental research: Education and the children of a minority. In M. E. Lamb, A. L. Brown, J. B. Rogoff (Eds.), *Advances in developmental psychology, Vol. 3.* (pp. 91–141). Hillsdale, NJ: Lawrence Erlbaum & Associates.

Tharp, R., & Gallimore, R. (1988). *Rousing minds to life: Teaching, learning, and schooling in social context.* Cambridge, England: Cambridge University Press.

Thompson, L., Detterman, D., & Plomin, R. (1991). Association between cognitive abilities and scholastic achievement: Genetic overlap but environmental differences. *Psychological Science, 2,* 158–165.

Tobias, S. (1985). New directions for educational psychologists. *Educational Psychologist, 20,* 96–101.

Timble, K., & Sinclair, R. L. (1986). *Ability grouping and differing conditions for learning: An analysis of content and instruction in ability-grouped classes.* Paper presented at the annual meeting of the American Educational Research Association, San Francisco.

Trueba, H. T. (1987). *Success or failure? Learning and the language minority student.* New York: Newbury House.

Trueba, H. T. (1988). Culturally based explanations of minority students' academic achievement. *Anthropology and Education Quarterly, 19,* 270–287.

United States Bureau of the Census. (1983). Current population reports. Series P-6 No. 183. *Income, poverty and wealth in the U.S.A. chartbook.* Washington, DC: U.S. Government Printing Office.

Valsiner, J. (1985). Parental organization of children's cognitive development within home environment. *Psychologia, 28,* 131–143.

Valsiner, J. (1989). *Human development and culture: The social nature of personality and its study.* Lexington, MA: Lexington Books.

van der Veer, R., & Valsiner, J. (1991). *A quest for synthesis: Life and work of Lev Vygotsky.* London: Routledge.

Vogt, L. A., Jordan, C., & Tharp, R. G. (1987). Explaining school failure, producing school success: Two cases. *Anthropology and Education Quarterly, 18*(4), 276–286.

Vygotsky, L. (1986). *Thought and language.* Cambridge, MA: MIT Press.

Vygotsky, L. S. (1962). *Thought and language.* Cambridge, MA: MIT Press.

Vygotsky, L. S. (1978). *Mind in society: The development of higher psychological processes.* (M. Cole, V. John-Steiner, S. Scribner, & E. Souberman, (Eds.). Cambridge, MA: Harvard University Press.

Vygotsky, L. S. (1982). The historical meaning of the crisis in psychology. In A. R. Luria & M. G. Iaroshevski (Eds.), *L. S. Vygotsky: Collected works.* Moscow: Pedagogika.

Vygotsky, L. S. (1993). *The collected works of L. S. Vygotsky: Vol. 2. The fundamentals of defectology* (J. E. Knox & C. B. Stevens, Trans.). New York: Plenum Press.

Walberg, H. J., & Keefe, J. (1986). *Rethinking reform: The principal's dilemma. A special report of the NASSP Curriculum Council.* Reston, VA: National Association of Secondary School Principals.

Wertsch, J. V. (1985a) *Culture, communication, and cognition: Vygotskyan perspectives.* New York: Cambridge University Press.

Wertsch, J. V. (1985b). *Vygotsky and the social formation of mind.* Cambridge, MA: Harvard University Press.

Wertsch, J. V. (1991). *Voices of the mind: A sociocultural approach to mediated action.* Cambridge, MA: Harvard University Press.

Wertsch, J. V., Minick, N., & Arns, F. A. (1984). The creation of context in joint problem-solving. In B. Rogoff & J. Lave (Eds.), *Everyday cognition: Its development in social contexts* (pp. 151–171). Cambridge, MA: Harvard University Press.

Wertsch, J. V., & Tulviste, P. (1992). L. S. Vygotsky and contemporary developmental psychology. *Developmental Psychology, 28*(4), 548–557.

Wertsch, J. V., Tulviste, P., & Hagstrom, F. (in press). A sociocultural approach to agency. In E. Forman, N. Minick, & C. A. Stone (Eds.), *Knowledge construction and social practice: Institutional and interpersonal contexts of human development.* New York: Oxford University Press.

White, K. R. (1982). The relation between socioeconomic status and academic achievement. *Psychological Bulletin, 91*(3), 461–481.

Whiting, B. (1976). The problem of the packaged variable. In K. Riegel & Meacham (Eds.), *The developing individual in a changing world: Vol. 1. Historical and cultural issues.* The Hague: Mouton.

Whiting, B. (1980). Culture and social behavior: A model for the development of social behavior. *Ethos, 8,* 95–116.

Willis, P. E. (1977). *Learning to labor.* New York: Columbia University Press.

Wise, A. E., Darling-Hammond, L., & Berry, B. (1987). *Effective teacher selection: From recruitment to retention.* Santa Monica, CA: Rand Corporation.

Wittrock, M. C. (Ed.). (1986). *Handbook of research on teaching* (3rd ed.). New York: Macmillan.

Wong-Rieger, D., & Quintana, D. (1987). Comparative acculturation of Southeast Asian and Hispanic immigrants and sojourners. *Journal of Cross-Cultural Psychology, 18,* 345–362.

Zady, M. F. (1994). Home and school interactions in the zone of proximal development: Their relation to science achievement. *Dissertation Abstracts International, 55,* 1819A University of Louisville Kentucky.

Zuckerman, M. (1990). Some dubious premises in research and theory on racial differences. *American Psychologist, 45*(12), 1297–1303.

# ·12·

# GENDER DEVELOPMENT AND GENDER EFFECTS

Nancy Eisenberg                    Carol Lynn Martin

Richard A. Fabes

ARIZONA STATE UNIVERSITY, TEMPE, ARIZONA

How do children learn to perceive and label themselves as boys or girls? Why do boys play with other boys and avoid girls? Do girls and boys differ in their mathematical and verbal skills? In psychological and educational theory and research, these questions are representative of the many and diverse issues concerning gender development and gender effects. One large set of issues concerns the origins and development of children's gender identity, gender stereotypes, and gender-related behaviors and personality characteristics. Another, larger body of research pertains to issues regarding differences between males and females in behaviors, characteristics, and psychological processes (e.g., preferences, attributional biases). A third set of issues concerns the constructs of masculinity, femininity, and androgyny and their relation to behavior and mental health (see Huston, 1983).

Because of the wide range of behaviors, beliefs, self-perceptions, preferences, and behaviors that could potentially differ between females and males in occurrence and in the process or pattern of development, it was impossible to cover in one chapter all or even most of the potential topics in the area of gender typing and gender differences. Gender-related issues in regard to educationally relevant processes and skills are covered in some of the other chapters in this book. Moreover, gender differences in various academic capabilities (e.g., verbal and math skills) frequently have been discussed and reviewed in educational psychology and education journals. For these reasons, our review of many of the traditional gender-related topics in educational psychology (e.g., gender differences in math and verbal abilities, attributions about the causes of one's successes and failures) is relatively brief. Instead we focus considerable attention on issues that are sometimes neglected in the educational psychology journals, such as the development of gender identity, knowledge, preferences and behaviors, and

gender differences in social behaviors and emotional responses that are relevant to children's functioning in and out of school. In addition, our emphasis is primarily on normal development; issues such as learning disabilities, mental disabilities, psychopathology, and delinquency are not discussed or are mentioned only very briefly.

Although problems in learning and psychopathology are of particular interest to many educational and school psychologists, gender differences in normal development are also of importance to the field. In general, an understanding of the existence and causes of gender-stereotypic behavior and gender differences can be used to promote psychological health and constructive social behavior in both sexes. For example, if more women are to enter the sciences and engineering, information about possible gender differences in spatial and mathematical skills, as well as information about factors that might promote or eliminate any existing differences, is of interest. Similarly, knowledge about factors that might be related to aggression and positive social behaviors in boys versus girls, and even the effects of puberty on boys versus girls, could be useful to psychologists and educators who are seeking to understand and deal with the typical array of behavioral problems encountered in school settings. With an understanding of the role of gender in learning and behavior, one can avoid the trap of limiting children's growth by making and acting on stereotypic assumptions about individual children's abilities and development. Moreover, researchers can use information about actual gender differences in competencies and behavior to learn more about the biological and social factors that contribute to the given competencies and behavior. Because of limited space, we have tried to emphasize general issues and patterns of findings (particularly those in recent work) and to provide references for readers who desire more detailed information.

Partial support for the preparation of this chapter was provided by grants from the National Science Foundation (BNS-8807784 and DBS-9208375) to Nancy Eisenberg and Richard A. Fabes, by a Research Scientist Development award from the National Institute of Mental Health (K02 MN00903) to Nancy Eisenberg, and by an Arts, Sciences, and Humanities Faculty Research grant from Arizona State University (RWR-C311) to Richard A. Fabes.

A note of caution is necessary here. Gender differences and gender typing are topics of considerable social and political relevance and engender heated debate and much emotion. Thus, it must be recognized that any discussion of these topics reflects individuals' social values and the values of the historical era. For example, in the 1950s, raising children to adopt traditional gender roles was considered a desirable goal, one that socializers should strive to achieve. More recently, however, primarily because of the women's movement, many people assert that the socialization of only traditionally gender-typed behaviors limits both males' and females' development and potential.

Similarly, researchers do not work in a vacuum. The available data base and theories are influenced not only by the values of individual researchers but also by the values and beliefs of the larger culture. Findings that fit the dominant beliefs of a culture are more readily accepted by the scientific community and by the lay public than those that do not (Bleier, 1990). In addition, the sex of the experimenter, familiarity with the procedures in a study, the content of questionnaires and tests, and subjects' interest in the tasks in a study are all aspects of research that can influence the degree to which gender differences are obtained (Pedersen, Shinedling, & D. L. Johnson, 1968; Rumenik, Capasso, & Hendrick, 1977; Spence, Deaux, & Helmreich, 1985). For example, gender differences in studies of conformity tend to be smaller if the experimenters are women than if they are men (Eagly & Carli, 1981), boys report more prosocial behavior if asked about helping with stereotypically male tasks (Zarbatany, Hartmann, Gelfand, & Vinciguerra, 1985), and children appear to score higher on certain tests of empathy if interviewed by same-sex experimenters (Eisenberg & Lennon, 1983; Lennon, Eisenberg, & Carroll, 1986). Further, because females tend to prefer to engage in experiments with feminine topics whereas males prefer those with masculine topics, self-selection biases may occur in research on gender differences (Signorella & Vegaga, 1984). Moreover, in situations such as the experimental laboratory, people sometimes may present themselves in ways that are consistent with the experimenter's expectations or with cultural stereotypes (D. N. Ruble, 1988). For example, individuals' self-reports of empathy and related emotional reactions seem to be affected by their desire to appear in a socially desirable, stereotypic manner to both others and themselves (Eisenberg & Fabes, 1995; Eisenberg, Miller, et al., 1989).

In addition, in research as in real life, observers' perceptions of what they see and report may be tainted by gender stereotypes (Gurwitz & Dodge, 1975). For example, adults, and especially children, rate an infant's characteristics differently, depending on whether they believe it to be a boy or a girl. In studies of ratings of infants, infants labeled as boys tend to be rated as bigger, stronger, louder, faster, meaner, and harder than the same infants labeled as girls (Stern & Karraker, 1989). There is some evidence that men tend to attribute more differences based on labeling than women, and stereotypic attributions vary somewhat with the ambiguity of the stimulus situation (J. Condry & S. Condry, 1976). Experience with infants may diminish women's tendency to stereotype, although findings in this regard are not consistent, particularly for men (J. Condry & S. Condry, 1976; Meyer & Sobieszek, 1972; see Stern & Karraker, 1989, for a review).

Caution must also be used when interpreting data and drawing conclusions about the meaning of patterns found in the research literature. Nonsignificant results often are not published, with the consequence that findings of no gender difference may not be reported or may not be made salient in papers. When a gender difference is reported, its meaning may be misinterpreted if it is assumed to have a biological basis (Unger, 1979) or that it implies a deficiency for one sex, usually female (Crawford, 1989). Moreover, although males and females may differ on some measure in terms of statistical means, the distribution of the characteristic usually is overlapping, and the modal female and male may be very similar. Indeed, the amount of variance accounted for by gender in a given behavior, preference, or belief frequently is less than 5 percent (D. N. Ruble, 1988), and often an observed gender difference may be due to a small but extreme group of one sex or the other. Nonetheless, small gender differences, particularly if consistent with gender stereotypes, may reinforce patterns of interaction among people, including how parents and teachers deal with girls and boys. Moreover, stereotypes that arise from even small gender differences may affect individuals' self-perceptions, beliefs, aspirations, and behaviors (Deaux & Major, 1987).

A final concern in the study of gender is the weighting of biological and environmental factors as influences on behavior—in other words, the nature–nurture debate. Historically, the study of biological influences has been used to justify social policy and has reflected the political climate of the time (Bleier, 1990). For instance, early research on gender differences in the brain was used to strengthen and maintain existing gender inequalities in social and occupational roles (Shields, 1975). The recent emphasis on environmental factors may be partially in response to fears that results will be used inappropriately (Halpern, 1992). Furthermore, assumptions about the changeability of behavior are made inaccurately in accordance with whether a behavior is seen as having a strong biological or a strong environmental origin (Martin & Parker, 1989). Specifically, behaviors with a strong biological component are believed to be unchangeable, whereas behaviors with a strong environmental component are believed to be changeable, although these assumptions are faulty. Despite the controversy surrounding the nature–nurture issue, most scientists believe that gender effects can be understood only when all the relevant factors are considered.

The aforementioned problems are not confined to research on gender differences but arise in the interpretation of data in many areas in the social and behavioral sciences. Research in many areas of study traditionally was biased by the use of only male subjects and experimenters, by failure to test for gender differences in the data, by theories that eliminated data on females that did not correspond with data on males, and by ignoring important experimental and situational influences, such as the use of male-biased tasks (see Frieze, J. E. Parsons, P. B. Johnson, D. N. Ruble, & Zellman, 1978; McKugh, Koeske, & Frieze, 1986). These limitations in the larger body of research make it difficult to accurately assess gender differences in beliefs, behaviors, and abilities.

Finally, a few words need to be said about terminology. First, although some writers distinguish between "sex" for biologically based characteristics and "gender" for socially based characteristics, we believe, as do others (e.g., Maccoby &

Jacklin, 1987), that it is important not to prejudge the bases of differences. Thus, we do not distinguish between these terms. Second, the terms "sex consistent" and "sex-inconsistent" are used as a convenient shorthand to refer to stereotypic beliefs traditionally associated with one's own sex versus the other sex and are not meant to connote value judgments.

# THEORIES OF GENDER DEVELOPMENT

Within psychology, there have been three major approaches to the study of gender—biological, learning-based, and cognitive. Learning-based and cognitive approaches have been the most influential and have spawned the two major theories of the past 25 years, social learning theory and cognitive-developmental theory. Although these two theories have become much more similar in recent years, their roots and some of their basic assumptions differ considerably. For example, although social learning theory now includes a variety of cognitive processes that are used to process and interpret information and guide behavior, the origin of change is generally viewed as external to the individual. In contrast, in cognitive-developmental theories, cognitive processes are central not only in processing information and in guiding behavior, but also in constructing change within the individual (Overton & Reese, 1973; Reese & Overton, 1970).

In the past decade, the cognitive approach has been expanded by the emergence of schema theories. These theories are based on the idea that individuals form cognitive schemas that organize information about the world and guide their behavioral choices; however, these theories differ from cognitive-developmental theory in some assumptions regarding developmental processes.

We will briefly review each of these approaches and their related theories. Psychoanalytic theory, although still influential, has had relatively little impact on recent gender-related research and, consequently, its coverage is brief. Frieze and colleagues (1978) and Huston (1983) have provided more extensive discussions of gender-related issues in psychoanalytic theory and critiques of the theory.

## Learning-Based Approaches

Learning-based approaches emphasize the role of the environment in gender development. These theories developed from operant conditioning principles, but over the past 15 years they changed considerably in regard to the role played by cognitive factors. As such, there are several variations of learning theories. Nonetheless, the mechanistic metaphor underlies learning theories, implying that change in individuals is assumed to occur in response to changes in the environment.

*Social Learning Theory.* The classic social learning view of gender typing was presented by Mischel (1966, 1970). In this view, gender-typed behavior, like all other behavior, is shaped by environmental contingencies and observational learning (i.e., imitation). Boys are punished for displaying feminine behaviors and rewarded for masculine behaviors; the reverse is true for girls. However, gender-typed behaviors are situationally specific because children also learn when certain behaviors are

appropriate to enact. For example, boys may learn to display aggression at school but not at home. Nonetheless, boys learn to display masculine behaviors in more contexts than do girls, whereas girls learn to enact feminine behaviors in more situations than do boys.

*Cognitive Social Learning Theory.* Bandura (1977, 1986) and Mischel (1979) have developed more cognitively oriented versions of social learning theory. Both emphasize the role of the individual's expectancies regarding likely consequences of behaviors and the notion that reinforcement and punishment convey information regarding the expected consequences of behaviors. People manipulate information gained from experience and observations, generate new knowledge, and can use cognition to guide and regulate their behavior (Bandura, 1986).

In cognitive social learning theory, observational learning involves four component processes all of which involve cognition to varying degrees: attention, retention, motoric reproduction, and motivation. Whether or not children display gender-typed behavior varies depending on these processes. For example, attention is affected by expectancies gained from earlier experiences and by motivational variables. Thus, children may be more motivated to attend to same-sex than other-sex models because of reinforcement for doing so in the past. Retention of observed behaviors is believed to vary as a function of the child's level of cognitive development and existing cognitive schema. As a consequence, children exposed to stereotypic concepts or who are particularly aware of gender stereotypes are expected to be more likely to retain gender-relevant information than other children. Motivation to perform an observed behavior varies as a function of expectancies regarding the consequences associated with the behavior. For example, once children realize the consequences of cross-sex behavior, they will refrain from engaging in these behaviors (Bussey & Bandura, 1992). Children also are likely to imitate the behaviors of same-sex models if they expect rewards for doing so and if they perceive a model to be exhibiting behaviors consistent with the norm for their sex (Bussey & D. G. Perry, 1982; Bussey & Bandura, 1984; D. G. Perry & Bussey, 1979).

Social learning theories have been important for elaborating the role of socialization agents in gender development and for emphasizing situational variability in behavior. The theories have been less effective in explaining developmental changes in children's gender roles.

## Cognitive Approaches

One basic assumption underlying cognitive approaches is that individuals take an active role in perceiving and interpreting information from their environments. Because an active organism model underlies cognitive theories, the locus of change is in the individual. Within cognitive theories, the most influential theory has been Kohlberg's (1966) theory. Recently, however, the emergence of schema theories has helped elaborate the role of cognition in gender development.

*Cognitive-Developmental Theory.* Kohlberg's cognitive-developmental theory is based on the notion that the child's understanding of gender is the foundation for the acquisition of gender roles (Kohlberg, 1966; Kohlberg & Ullian, 1974). Once children acquire an understanding of gender, they have a basis for organizing and regulating their social functioning. Children then actively seek out information about what is appropriate for their sex by observing the actions of those around them. Given that the predominant theories of Kohlberg's time were based on learning principles, Kohlberg's ideas were revolutionary, particularly the idea that self-socialization is involved in gender-role development (Maccoby, 1990b; Maccoby & Jacklin, 1974).

Understanding gender, like other concepts, depends on the child's stage of intellectual development. Gender understanding—recognizing that males and females differ from one another—is believed to occur gradually between 2 and 7 years of age, and becomes irreversible during the concrete operational period. Kohlberg (1966) argued that young children base their gender understanding on differences in size, clothing, and hairstyles, not on genital differences.

Children pass through a series of three stages in acquiring a fully formed gender concept (Kohlberg, 1966; Slaby & Frey, 1975). In the first stage, gender identity or gender labeling, children label males and females according to their gender category. In the second stage, gender stability, children recognize that gender remains constant over time (e.g., a boy realizes that he will grow up to be a man, not a woman). In the third stage, gender constancy, children recognize that gender is a fixed and immutable characteristic that is not altered by situational changes (e.g., a boy dressed up as a girl remains a boy). The sequence of stages of gender understanding has been confirmed in a number of studies in the United States, Great Britain (Leonard & Archer, 1989), Argentina (DeLisi & Gallagher, 1991), and in Belize, Kenya, and American Samoa (R. H. Munroe, Shimmin, & R. L. Munroe, 1984).

There has been much controversy about how to interpret Kohlberg's ideas about gender constancy (see Huston, 1983; Martin & Little, 1990). On the one hand, he argued that children's understanding of the unchangeability of gender was an essential element in gender-role acquisition. For instance, he stated that "the growing cognitive constancy or irreversibility of gender identity in early childhood is the bedrock of later sexual and sex-role attitudes" (Kohlberg & Ullian, 1974, p. 210). On the other hand, Kohlberg argued that children learn gender roles prior to attaining gender constancy. He was not clear about the ages at which gender understanding occurs (Maccoby, 1990b) or about the correlates of different types of understanding. Nonetheless, Kohlberg's writings have generally been interpreted to mean that gender constancy is necessary to provide the motivation for children to attend more to same-sex than other-sex models and to enact sex-consistent activities.

Although Kohlberg's ideas about gender constancy are controversial, many of his ideas are now taken for granted (Maccoby, 1990b). Today, one of the cornerstones of cognitive approaches to gender-role development is Kohlberg's idea that children deal with information in a concept- rather than a data-driven way (Slaby, 1990). Furthermore, Kohlberg's ideas have been integrated into many different theoretical approaches and have sparked interest in gender as a viable area of research.

*Gender Schema Theories.* Three gender schema theories have been proposed in recent years (Bem, 1981; Markus, Crane, Bernstein, & Siladi, 1982; Martin & Halverson, 1981). These models share the assumption that gender schemas influence memory and behavior, but they differ in emphasis. Martin and Halverson (1981, 1987) emphasize developmental changes in schemas and their functions and resulting biases, whereas other approaches emphasize individual differences in gender schemas, particularly in adults (see Roopnarine & Mounts, 1987).

Gender schemas are organized knowledge structures containing information about the sexes that develop from the child's innate tendency to classify and simplify information. Because gender is salient in our society, children recognize its functional significance and use it as a classification strategy (Bem, 1981; Martin & Halverson, 1981).

Gender schemas influence what perceivers notice as well as what they learn and do. The predominant pattern is schematic consistency: Perceivers generally notice, remember, and behave in ways that are consistent with their gender schemas (Martin & Halverson, 1981). Like other schemas, gender schemas provide cognitive economy, that is, they facilitate the processing of complex social information.

Gender schemas are thought to guide behavior, and research supports this contention. Children who have been given novel objects with experimenter-supplied gender-typed labels ("for boys") tend to play more with toys labeled as being for their own sex than with toys labeled as being for the other sex (Bradbard & Endsley, 1983; Bradbard, Martin, Endsley, & Halverson, 1986). Similarly, children's performance is affected by gender-typed labels: Children try harder if a novel game is labeled for their sex than for the other (Montemayor, 1974).

Gender schemas also provide the structure for organizing and attending to information. Generally, schema-consistent information is attended to more, and remembered better, than information that is schema-inconsistent (e.g., Carter & Levy, 1988; Liben & Signorella, 1980), although sometimes schema-inconsistent information is better remembered (Stangor & Ruble, 1989; Trepanier-Street & Kropp, 1986). Similarly, children know more about the sequencing of own-sex activities (Boston & Levy, 1991; Levy, 1989; Levy & Fivush, 1993) and learn more about the functions of novel own-sex objects (Bradbard et al., 1986) than other-sex activities and objects. Furthermore, gender schemas provide an information base that may be used to make inferences when a situation is unclear or information is missing (Berndt & Heller, 1986; Carter & Levy, 1988; Haugh, C. D. Hoffman, & Cowan, 1980; Levy & Carter, 1989; Martin, 1991).

Because schematic processing involves selective attention, encoding, and retrieval, information loss and distortion also occur. Martin and Halverson (1981, 1983a; Martin, 1991) described how children distort information that is inconsistent or neutral, thus making it fit their schema. For instance, a child who sees a boy cooking at a stove may later remember a *girl* cooking rather than a boy, or remember a boy *fixing* the stove, both of which are consistent with gender schemas. Researchers have shown that children distort information about activities and occupations (Cann & Newbern, 1984; Carter & Levy, 1988; Cordua, McGraw, & Drabman, 1979; Martin & Halverson, 1983; Signorella & Liben, 1984) and emotions (Martin, Fabes, Eisenbud, Karbon, & Rose, 1990). These distortions may explain why stereotypes are maintained. Every time schema-inconsistent information is converted into consistent information, the child is *confirming* the stereotype rather than using the information to disconfirm it (Martin & Halverson, 1983a). Because of these distortions, simply showing children counterstereotypic information will not induce change; more active types of intervention strategies may be necessary (Bigler & Liben, 1992; Liben & Bigler, 1987).

Schema theories have been useful for providing new insights into the powerful nature of gender knowledge and have been effective in explaining how gender knowledge is maintained. The theories have been less effective in explaining very early gender-related behavior and the inconsistent relation between behavior and knowledge.

## Biological Approaches

Researchers who apply biological approaches have examined a broad array of issues concerning gender, ranging from sexual differentiation, to chromosomal and hormonal influences on behavior and cognition, to gender differences in the brain. One message from the research is that even the biological categories of male and female are unclear. There are many different biological indicators of sex. For most people, these markers coincide; however, for some people, biological markers provide mixed messages. These "intersex" individuals have been studied because they provide important information about how various biological aspects of gender relate to behavior and thinking. Furthermore, biological approaches have been important because they emphasize that research on variability within the sexes is of vital importance in understanding biological influences on gender roles.

The course of sex differentiation is generally smooth. The 23rd pair of chromosomes (the sex chromosomes) indicates whether the fetus will differentiate into a female (XX) or a male (XY). The main role of the Y chromosome is to carry information about genetic sex: Without its influence, development proceeds in the female direction. The sex chromosomes also carry sex-linked characteristics and diseases. During the sixth prenatal week, under the direction of the chromosomes, the fetal gonads develop and secrete hormones that organize later prenatal development of the internal and external genitalia. Based on animal research, it is believed that these hormones also organize the development of the brain and central nervous system. Prenatally secreted testosterone masculinizes and defeminizes cellular structures throughout the reproductive organs and the brain. These kinds of "organizational" effects alter the central nervous system such that males and females may begin life with subtle structural differences in their brains (Halpern, 1992). Hormones may continue to play an organizational role after birth since the brain continues to develop. Hormone levels are low and similar for both sexes until puberty, when increased levels of hormones and differences in ratios of hormones lead to the development of secondary sexual characteristics. Furthermore, at various ages, circulating hormones may result in "activational" effects, meaning that they activate behavior preorganized during development (see Ehrhardt, 1984).

Using both clinical and normative samples, researchers have illustrated the important role of hormones in behavior. For example, individuals with androgen-insensitivity disorder are genetically males, but because of a rare genetic disorder, their bodies are unable to use androgens. These individuals are typically raised as females because of their feminine appearance. Despite their genetic sex and male gonads, these individuals are typically feminine in their gender identity and gender role.

Thus, because of the body's failure to use androgens (male hormones), feminine patterns result (Money & Ehrhardt, 1972).

When androgens are available and are used by the body, they appear to have some influence on the adoption of masculine gender roles in girls. For instance, if adrenogenital syndrome genetic females are exposed to androgens in utero, their external genitalia may become masculinized and they may require hormone therapy throughout life to avoid further masculinization. Compared to matched controls, these genetic girls, who are raised as girls, nevertheless show masculine interest in toys, some prefer boys as playmates, and parents describe them as "tomboys" (Berenbaum & Snyder, 1995; Huston, 1983; Money & Ehrhardt, 1972). These findings are consistent with animal research on hormones and behavior; but, alternative explanations of these findings and the problems associated with this research must also be considered (Huston, 1983). There is little evidence that prenatal exposure to progesterone or estrogen (viewed as female hormones) influences behavior or personality development (Huston, 1983).

Although few investigators have proposed a direct genetic basis for most gender differences, some have suggested that gender differences in visual-spatial skills result from a sex-linked recessive trait on the X chromosome. Some early research supported this hypothesis; however, more recent work has not (Boles, 1980; Huston, 1983).

Biological approaches have also focused on gender differences in brain structure and function. The arguments for brain differences as explanations for gender differences vary greatly in their focus. Some investigators focus on very specific areas of difference, such as the size of the corpus callosum, the band of fibers that connects the two halves of the brain. Others focus on more global differences such as differences in brain laterality due to prenatal hormones (Geschwind & Galaburda, 1987), or differences in maturation rate at puberty (Waber, 1976). These theories are presently controversial and the supporting evidence is mixed (see Halpern, 1992). In general, males and females have brains that are more alike than different (see Hood, Draper, Crockett, & Petersen, 1987). Furthermore, recent research has challenged the common assumption that the brain is relatively invulnerable to experience. Instead, we now know that the brain is very plastic and that its growth is influenced by the environment (R. M. Lerner, 1984).

Few researchers focus only on biological factors. Instead, interactional views are common. For example, Ehrhardt (1984) proposed a dynamic interactional model to understand gender-related behavior. This model assumes that environmental and biological factors influence behavior in a transactional process, with both factors participating as equal partners. Such an interactional view is consistent with the increasing tendency of researchers to draw on a variety of theoretical approaches when examining gender differences and gender-related development (see Hood et al., 1987).

## Psychoanalytic Theory and Feminist Reformulations and Reactions

In traditional psychoanalytic theory, children become sex typed as a result of the process of identification with their same-sex parent. Identification occurs primarily at ages 4 to 6 years and, for boys, is due to fear of castration by the father in retaliation for the boy's desire for his mother. Explanations of identification for girls are less clear, although girls are viewed as identifying with their mother as a way of symbolically possessing their father once they discover the apparent castration of their own penis and develop penis envy.

Such explanations of gender-related development have been frequently criticized and reformulated. For example, some theorists have proposed that males envy and fear women because of their capacity to bear children (Horney, 1932; Klein, 1957), and as a consequence they devalue and try to dominate women (H. E. Lerner, 1978). Moreover, decades ago some female psychoanalysts pointed out the role of economic and social factors in gender differences (C. M. Thompson, 1964).

More recently, theorists influenced by neopsychoanalytic perspectives have emphasized gender differences in object relations and in ways of knowing (e.g., Chodorow, 1989; Gilligan, N. P. Lyons, & Hanmer, 1990). There has been considerable discussion of women's emphasis on caring and on interrelatedness, which contrasts with the more masculine emphasis on autonomy (Gilligan, 1977; Noddings, 1984). For example, Chodorow (1978, 1989) argued that women's self is "more in relation and involved with boundary negotiations, separation, and connection, men's self more distanced and based on defensively firm boundaries and denials of self-other connection" (1989, p. 2). According to Gilligan, girls, more than boys, are interested in relationships and gain knowledge through relationships. Gilligan and her colleagues have emphasized "girls' knowledge of the human social world, a knowledge gleaned by seeing and listening, by piecing together thoughts and feelings, sounds and glances, responses and reactions until they compose a pattern, compelling in its explanatory power and often intricate in its psychological knowledge" (Gilligan, 1990, p. 14). This connected mode of experiencing self and others is viewed as influencing ways of perceiving oneself and the world and interactions with others (including perceptions of morality and methods of dealing with interpersonal conflict; see Gilligan et al., 1990). Thus, in contrast to theoretical approaches based on data primarily from males (for example, Freud's and Kohlberg's theories), Gilligan and others have focused on women's experiences and psychological development and have argued that connections with others are central in women's psychological development.

# CHILDREN'S GENDER-RELATED DEVELOPMENT

Theories of children's gender development have stimulated research on a variety of topics. The first part of this section reviews the findings concerning how children come to understand gender categories and gender stereotypes. The second part reviews the evidence concerning the development of children's interest in gender-typed activities and in same-sex peers, and briefly discusses children's self-perceptions of their own masculinity and femininity. The final part of this section reviews the research concerning how various types of gender knowledge relate to other aspects of behavior and thinking.

## Understanding Gender Categories

*Discriminating the Sexes.* From birth, infants are surrounded by cues signifying gender. They are given gender labels based on their external genitalia and are wrapped in color-coded blankets and diapers. Parents may also use adornment, hairstyles, and clothing to indicate the sex of their infants (M. Shakin, D. Shakin, & Sternglanz, 1985; B. B. Whiting & Edward, 1988). Even if the appearance of males and females is not exaggerated within a culture, there remain many other types of differences that infants and children can use to identify gender, such as height, smell, skin texture, voice, and softness (Fagot & Leinbach, 1993; Katz, 1983).

Given the abundance of gender cues in the child's social world, it is not surprising that they learn to discriminate gender categories at an early age. At 10 months, infants are able to learn to associate gender with other attributes (Levy, Haaf, & Summer, 1991). About 75% of 1-year-olds can discriminate male and female faces, largely on the basis of hair length (Leinbach & Fagot, 1993). By 12 months, infants have intermodal gender knowledge, that is, they are able to integrate their knowledge of faces and voices (Poulin-Dubois, Serbin, Kenyon, & Derbyshire, 1994).

In addition to examining categorical perception of males and females, researchers have also been interested in whether infants show same-sex preferences for pictures. At this point, the evidence is conflicting. M. Lewis and Brooks-Gunn (1975) found that 10- to 18-month-olds looked longer at same-sex pictures than at opposite-sex pictures, whereas others found no such pattern (Poulin-Dubois et al., 1994).

*Gender Identity and Gender Labeling.* Children must not only be able to identify the sex of others, they must also recognize their own sex. To understand what being a male or female means, children must accurately self-label (Maccoby, 1980). *Gender identity* implies this type of labeling of one's own gender group, although there has been ambiguity in the use of the term (Fagot & Leinbach, 1985; Green, 1974; Money & Ehrhardt, 1972).

The importance of gender identity is particularly emphasized in cognitive approaches to gender-role development. In these approaches, the assumption is that gender identity and gender labeling of others are related and that they influence the child's building of gender knowledge structures (Constantinople, 1979; Fagot, 1985; Kohlberg, 1966; Martin & Halverson, 1981).

The research on gender identity has been conducted primarily by medical clinicians and developmental psychologists. Clinical work has focused on children with mismatches between biological sex and their sex of rearing, and on problems of adjustment for individuals with atypical gender roles or sexual orientation (see Zucker & Green, 1992). Developmental psychologists have focused on how typical children develop knowledge about gender (see Fagot & Leinbach, 1985).

Clinical researchers have demonstrated that gender identity largely depends on the label the child is given by others. In studies on "intersex" children (where there is a mismatch between biological sex and the sex of rearing), self-labeling matches sex of assignment and is resistant to change after toddlerhood as long as the child is reared unambiguously as a boy or girl (Money & Ehrhardt, 1972). Sex of assignment may greatly influence the children's self-labeling, but other factors, such as the value of being male or female in a culture, and biology, have been found to play a role as well (see Ehrhardt, 1984).

For most children, there is no discrepancy between the biological and social indicators of their sex. Developmental psychologists have examined patterns of gender identity development in these children. One approach has been to explore children's understanding of gender constancy for themselves and for others. In these studies, researchers have found that children's understanding of their own gender precedes understanding of gender for others (Eaton, Von Bargen & Keats, 1981; Gouze & Nadelman, 1980; Marcus & Overton, 1978). The other approach has been to investigate when and how children come to understand gender labels for themselves and for others (Fagot, 1985; Fagot & Leinbach, 1985).

The ability to label males and females is considered fundamental in the development of gender identity. One of the earliest studies of gender labeling found that most children could use gender labels accurately by about 30 months of age (S. K. Thompson, 1975). In more recent studies, children's labels for children and adults were assessed separately (Fagot & Leinbach, 1993; Leinbach & Fagot, 1986). This distinction is important: nearly all of the children pass the adult discrimination task (at about 24 months) before they are able to pass the child discrimination task (27 to 36 months; Leinbach & Fagot, 1986; Weinraub et al., 1984). Although little research has focused on socialization influences, individual differences in gender labeling ability appear to be due in part to differences in the salience of gender within families (Fagot & Leinbach, 1993).

Gender labeling is largely based on differences in appearance (S. K. Thompson & Bentler, 1971). Intons-Peterson (1988) analyzed child-generated gender cues and found that hair cues were particularly important for determining gender. Figures with long, curly, blonde hair were believed to be females and those with short, dark, and straight hair were believed to be males. Three- and 8-year-olds could not use dynamic gender cues (e.g., running and sitting) when other cues were obscured, although adolescents could (Intons-Peterson, 1988).

One of the most salient markers of gender is genital information, and understanding of the biological "essence" of maleness and femaleness underlies gender constancy (Bem, 1989). Despite its importance, few researchers have assessed children's knowledge of genital information. In a Swedish study, McConaghy (1979) found that only about one third of 8-year-olds used genital information to make gender judgments. In a recent study, Bem (1989) found that even preschool children could recognize genital differences when more realistic pictures rather than schematic drawings were used.

## Gender Stereotypes

Children learn more about gender than how to identify females and males; they also learn gender stereotypes. For instance, even 3-year-olds believe that "boys hit people" and "girls cry a lot" (Kuhn, Nash, & Brucken, 1978). Gender stereotypes are organized knowledge structures containing category labels (i.e., females, males) and gender-related attributes, which are organized into content domains (e.g., appearance, occupations) (Deaux & L. L. Lewis, 1984; Huston, 1983; Martin, 1993). Particularly among cognitively oriented theorists, gender stereo-

types are believed to provide the knowledge base to which children's behavior is matched, and its appropriateness is evaluated.

*Developmental Changes in Gender Stereotype Knowledge.* Generally, studies on stereotypes show monotonic increases in knowledge of gender stereotypes with age, although the timing of acquisition depends on the content domain and on the types of tasks used (see Huston, 1983; D. N. Ruble & T. L. Ruble, 1982). Children learn about role-related behaviors very early. At 2 years of age, there is little evidence of children understanding stereotypes concerning toys or activities, but by age 3, stereotype knowledge is clearly evident (Blakemore, LaRue, & Olejnic, 1979; S. K. Thompson, 1975; Weinraub et al., 1984). Role-related knowledge continues to increase throughout young childhood (Edelbrock & Sugawara, 1978; Nadelman, 1974; Serbin & Sprafkin, 1986; Serbin, Powlishta, & Gulko, 1992; Trautner, Helbing, Sahm, & Lohaus, 1989). Children learn the stereotypes about some occupations at a young age, and their knowledge increases with age (Kuhn et al., 1978; O'Keefe & Hyde, 1983; Papalia & Tennent, 1975). Gender stereotypes about personality traits seem to be acquired later than other stereotype information. Typically, preschoolers know the gender typing of some traits when simple tasks are used (Reis & Wright, 1982), although trait stereotypes do not match adult stereotypes until around age 10 (Best et al., 1977; Williams, Bennett, & Best, 1975). Trait learning may lag other types because the information is abstract and gender differences are not as readily observed (Huston, 1983).

Recent findings suggest that stereotypes continue to develop in complexity throughout childhood. After children learn to make the simple associations between gender labels and attributes (e.g., "boys play with cars"), they begin to develop more indirect and complex associations within and between the various content domains (e.g., interests and appearance; see Martin, Wood, & Little, 1990). Not until children are around 8 years of age do they acquire a complete understanding of the gender concepts of masculinity and femininity that link information within and between various content domains (Martin, Wood, & Little, 1990; Ullian, 1976).

Two other developmental trends have been found. One is that children's gender-stereotypic judgments become more extreme as they grow older (Martin, Wood, & Little, 1990; Biernat, 1991). For instance, when asked to predict toy preferences, children believe that boys would like masculine toys more than girls, but older children predict greater differences between girls' and boys' preferences than do younger children (Martin, 1989b). Similarly, perceived masculinity and femininity become more negatively correlated with age (Biernat, 1991). These developmental changes may be due to increased breadth of gender-related information. The more information children associate with gender, the more they may differentiate the sexes or gender concepts when given no other information (Martin, 1989b).

Another developmental trend concerns gender-role flexibility. Children's knowledge of gender stereotypes increases with age, but their acceptance of the inflexibility of stereotypes decreases with age (Carter & Patterson, 1982; Huston, 1983; Serbin & Sprafkin, 1986; Signorella, Bigler, & Liben, 1993). For instance, in a large-scale study, Serbin and colleagues (Serbin,

Powlishta, & Gulko, 1993) found that sixth graders knew more about stereotypes than kindergartners but were also more aware of gender-role exceptions. A similar pattern was found in a study of German children. For these children, knowledge and flexibility increased with age, and the height of rigidity in gender roles was found for 6-year-olds (Trautner et al., 1989). When children's concepts regarding cross-gender occupations (e.g., a male nurse), dress (e.g., a boy wearing a skirt), or behaviors of others have been assessed, 5- to 7-year-olds have been found to be less accepting of crossing gender boundaries than 8- to 10-year-olds (Carter & McCloskey, 1984; Damon, 1977; Turiel, 1978).

Changes in gender-role flexibility may be due to increased cognitive flexibility in middle childhood. Children who use multiple classification dimensions are more likely to acknowledge variability within gender groups (e.g., some boys play with dolls) and to be more flexible in their gender-role beliefs (Bigler & Liben, 1993; Leahy & Shirk, 1984). Reasoning about gender roles also changes. Older children treat gender roles as social conventions; in other words, they are seen to be flexible normative expectations (Carter & Patterson, 1982; Smetana, 1983; Stoddard & Turiel, 1985). Recent research, however, suggests that reasoning about gender roles varies depending on the target (male or female) and on the type of information assessed (e.g., appearance versus activities; Smetana, 1986). Another influence on children's flexibility is the family (see Huston, 1983). For instance, children whose mothers work outside the home have more flexible gender-role conceptions than do other children (Katz, 1987; Levy, 1989; Signorella et al., 1993; Weisner & Wilson-Mitchell, 1990).

*Applying Gender Stereotype Knowledge.* Children's applications of gender stereotypes vary when drawing inferences about others' personalities and preferences (Berndt & Heller, 1986; Biernat, 1991; Martin, 1989b). Children also use their stereotype knowledge to generalize beyond their stereotypes. For instance, even very young children will apply stereotypic knowledge to gender-labeled animals and infants (Cowan & C. D. Hoffman, 1986; Haugh et al., 1980). Further, children generalize unfamiliar information on the basis of gender category membership: When told unfamiliar characteristics about a boy, for instance, they assume that other boys will also have the same characteristics (Gelman, Collman, & Maccoby, 1986). Children also generalize expectations about occupational competence based on gender stereotype knowledge. When a male and a female are both described as being in the same job, children will rate the one who fits the gender typing of the position (e.g., a female nurse) as more competent than the other person (Cann & Garrett, 1984).

Researchers have examined whether children rely on stereotypes to make judgments when they have other available information. For example, Cann and Palmer (1986) found that children did not believe that past competence in performance overrode stereotypic expectations when rating competence on a related task. A number of studies have shown that the use of stereotypes remains fairly stable over time but the use of available information increases with age: Young children rely on gender stereotypes and fail to use other kinds of available information (e.g., someone's past interests), whereas older children and adults consider other information (Berndt & Heller, 1986; Biernat, 1991; Martin, 1989b).

Children also apply gender stereotypes in abstract ways. For example, children predict others' preferences for unfamiliar toys based on abstract beliefs about similarity within gender groups and differences between gender groups (i.e., the belief that same-sex peers like the same things as oneself whereas other-sex peers do not; Martin, Eisenbud, & Rose, 1995). In addition, children appear to have some understanding of abstract dimensions underlying masculinity and femininity. Subtle characteristics such as the angularity of a shape can be "metaphorically" related to gender categories, resulting in a "sprawling network" of gender-related associations (Bem, 1981). Leinbach and Hort (1981) confirmed that such a sprawling associative network exists even in 4-year-olds. When asked to sort objects into groups, children assigned bears and fire to males and hearts and flowers to females. Further research has suggested that underlying masculinity are the concepts of dangerous, rough, and hard, whereas underlying femininity are the concepts of soft, light, and warm. These metaphorical dimensions of gender may have their origins in children's first experiences with how men and women feel, how they play, and how they interact with them (Fagot & Leinbach, 1993).

## The Development of Gender Roles

Although the use of the term "gender roles" has been popular, its meaning is not entirely clear (Fagot & Leinbach, 1985). Here we use the phrase broadly to refer to children's enactment of gender-related activities and their adoption of characteristics culturally defined as masculine or feminine (see Huston, 1983; Zucker & Green, 1992).

*Gender-Related Activities and Interests.* One of the earliest signs of gender roles is children's tendency to play with toys traditionally stereotyped as being appropriate for their sex. In one study, 10-month-old girls showed preferences for dolls, but boys and girls did not differ in liking to play with trucks, blocks, and kitchen utensils (Roopnarine, 1986). By 18 months of age, children begin showing a broader range of gender-related activities and interests (Fagot, 1974; Fein, D. Johnson, Kosson, Stork, & Wasserman, 1975; O'Brien & Huston, 1985). By 3 years, in both free play and laboratory settings, children consistently show gender-typed toy choices (see Huston, 1983; Eisenberg-Berg, Boothby, & Matson, 1979; Etaugh, 1983). By 4 to 5 years, children select gender-typed toys when given choices of pictures of toys (Blakemore et al., 1979; Edelbrock & Sugawara, 1978). Children request stereotypic toys for Christmas (Bradbard, 1985; Bradbard & Parkman, 1983; Robinson & Morris, 1986). Also, children avoid inappropriate toys, even when they are appealing (Hartup, Moore, & Sager, 1963). Furthermore, usually by age 5, children have developed stereotypic occupational preferences (see Huston, 1983).

Because of their preferences, boys and girls experience very different play environments. Boys spend time manipulating objects, playing with transportation toys, construction toys, and weapons; and their play tends to be active, not very structured, aggressive, and conducted out-of-doors. Girls prefer playing with dolls, domestic equipment, and soft toys; they enjoy art projects, dressing up, singing, and music; and their play tends to be sedentary, highly structured, and nurturant (see Etaugh, 1983; Huston, Carpenter, Atwater, & L. M. Johnson, 1986; Liss,

1981, 1983; Maccoby, 1988). The experiences that children acquire in their toy play may well contribute to the development of cognitive and social skills (Connor & Serbin, 1977; C. L. Miller, 1987; Peretti & Sydney, 1984; Serbin, Connor, & Iller, 1979). As such, girls and boys may develop different competencies.

There are many external factors that influence children's toy choices. Parents believe that boys and girls have different toy preferences (Fagot, 1978a), and they provide their children with gender-typed toys (Bradbard, 1985; Rheingold & Cook, 1975). Parents encourage gender-typed play by selecting different toys for their sons and daughters, even before children can express their own preferences. For instance, in a study of infants, even 5-month-old children were given toys based on their sex (Pomerleau, Bolduc, Malcuit, & Cossette, 1990). When children request gender-atypical toys, they are less likely to receive them than when they request gender-typical toys. Thus, providing children with gender-typed toys channels their behavior into stereotypic lines (J. H. Block, 1979; Eisenberg, Wolchik, Hernandez, & Pasternack, 1985).

Parents structure children's environments in other ways as well. A consistent pattern across many cultures is that parents assign chores based on gender, with daughters more likely than sons to be involved in home-based activities such as child care and domestic chores (Lackey, 1989). Researchers in the West (M. N. Bloch, 1987; Caldera, Huston, & O'Brien, 1989; Langlois & Downs, 1980; Lytton & Rommey, 1991; Maccoby & Jacklin, 1974) and in other communities around the world (B. B. Whiting & Edwards, 1988) find consistent parental encouragement of gender-typed activities and play. Chore assignments and encouragement of gender-typed activities may influence children's behavior in a number of ways. In a recent study, children who were assigned masculine chores were more likely to have masculine career aspirations, whereas children assigned feminine chores were more likely to have feminine career aspirations, but the causal direction is as yet unclear (Etaugh & Liss, 1992). Further, parents often disapprove of cross-sex play or toy choices (Fagot, 1978b; O'Brien & Huston, 1985; Roopnarine, 1986). Fagot and Hagan (1991) suggested that parental socialization of gender-typed play and activities may be particularly powerful before the age of 5, when children are still rapidly learning about gender roles, rather than when children are older.

Peers may exert even stronger pressures on children to adopt gender-typed activities than parents (see Carter, 1987). One powerful type of influence is the feedback peers provide about activity choices. As predicted by social learning theorists, peer reinforcement and punishment have been found consistently to influence children's activity and toy preferences (e.g., Fagot, 1977; Langlois & Downs, 1980; Roopnarine, 1984; Serbin, Connor, Burchardt, & Citron, 1979). Children modify their behavior to conform to the patterns their peers reinforce (e.g., Lamb & Roopnarine, 1979). Further, peer presence, even with only minimal interaction, inhibits sex-inappropriate play (Serbin et al., 1979). Opportunities for social interaction with same-sex others also influence activity choices: Children's initial engagement with toys depends in part on the number of same-sex peers who are also interested in the toy (Eisenberg, Tryon, & Cameron, 1984; Shell & Eisenberg, 1990). For older children, knowledge of the consequences associated with cross-sex play may

take on a larger role in influencing their behavior. Although older children are more knowledgeable about gender role exceptions, they respond more negatively to gender-role violations than do younger children (Bussey & Bandura, 1992; Carter & McCloskey, 1984).

The acquisition of gender-typed behaviors is also influenced by peer modeling. As noted previously, children are likely to adopt novel activities when they are modeled by a same-sex peer and when the behavior is consistent with gender-typed expectations (Bussey & D. G. Perry, 1982; D. G. Perry & Bussey, 1979). A child who sees a same-sex child demonstrate a new toy is more likely to use the toy than other children (Serbin et al., 1979).

Children's motivation to act consistently with their own sex influences their toy choices. The most compelling evidence for this idea comes from studies using unfamiliar toys. Children tend to play with and remember more about novel toys given experimenter-supplied labels for their own sex ("for girls") than toys given labels for the other sex (Bradbard & Endsley, 1983; Bradbard et al., 1986). Even very attractive novel toys are considered undesirable if given other-sex labels (Martin et al., in press).

Children's motivation to conform to gender stereotypes may be less influential in situations with familiar toys. Eisenberg, Murray, and Hite (1982) found that even when preschoolers selected gender-typed toys they seldom gave gender-related reasons for their choices, although they used this reasoning about other's choices. Preferences for familiar toys may be based on characteristics of the toys, or children may simply make these selections automatically, without conscious awareness of the basis for their choices (Eisenberg et al., 1982). Because of the many influences on children's toy choices, they should not be used as the sole indicator of children's gender roles (Eisenberg, 1983).

***Gender Segregation.*** The fact that children play primarily in same-sex groups is well documented (see Carter, 1987; Maccoby & Jacklin, 1987, for reviews). The implication of this gender-segregated pattern of peer interaction is that boys and girls are socialized in virtually nonoverlapping peer groups by same-sex peers.

Children's same-sex play preferences are relatively resistant to change (Lockheed & Harris, 1984). The magnitude of gender segregation also is quite large and increases in strength as children move into the elementary school period. For example, Luria and Herzog (1985) found that two thirds of preschoolers' play occurred in same-sex groups, and that 80% of public schoolchildren's play was in same-sex groups, although the degree of gender segregation varied by contexts. In addition, Lockheed (1985) reported that gender segregation was less in classroom settings than in the lunchroom. Thus, when left on their own, children seem to adopt gender-segregated patterns of peer interaction, whereas the presence of adults may serve to reduce the degree of gender segregation.

Although children's same-sex preferences have been firmly established, the reasons for this preference are not well understood. Maccoby (1990a) pointed to two factors that seem to be important in producing same-sex preferences and other-sex avoidance. The first is the rough-and-tumble play style of boys and their orientation toward dominance and competition. The second is that girls find it hard to influence boys (e.g., Serbin,

Sprafkin, Elman, & Doyle, 1984). Thus, girls may find it aversive to play with boys because boys are unresponsive to, and unaffected by, girls' influence attempts. Boys, in turn, may find girls less interesting because they do not respond to their rough-and-tumble, hierarchical forms of play.

Fabes (1994) argued that there may be a physiological basis for gender segregation. According to Fabes's model, boys are more easily aroused within evocative social interactions than are girls, and boys have more difficulty regulating their arousal. Moreover, the conditions and contexts that boys and girls find physiologically arousing are different. These differences in arousal may contribute to the differences noted by Maccoby (1990a) in boys' and girls' play styles and the degree to which they are able to influence one another. Thus, biological and physiological differences may set the stage for boys and girls to find various types of interactions pleasurable or aversive. Subsequently, social and cognitive processes influence the degree to which gender segregation is maintained and reinforced.

*Gender-Related Personality.* One of the most popular research topics has been the study of individuals' perceptions of masculinity and femininity (see Huston, 1983). The early bipolar view of masculinity and femininity as being ends of one dimension has given way to the idea that they are independent dimensions. Research has confirmed the separability of the dimensions: For children and for adults, correlations between self-rated masculinity and femininity are quite low (Bem, 1974; J. A. Hall & Halberstadt, 1980; Spence, Helmreich, & Stapp, 1974). Furthermore, each of these concepts is considered to be multidimensional. Along with these changes came a new concept, *psychological androgyny,* which is considered to be a combination of both dimensions within one individual (see Bem, 1974; Spence et al., 1974). Androgynous individuals are those who have both masculine (instrumental) and feminine (expressive) characteristics within their behavioral repertoires. Androgyny is argued to be advantageous because it increases individuals' adaptiveness to new situations (Bem, 1975; see Paulhus & Martin, 1988, for a discussion of interpersonal flexibility). A number of researchers have been interested in exploring the factors that increase children's flexibility about their own gender-related behavior (see Carpenter, Huston, & Holt, 1986; Katz, 1986; Katz & Boswell, 1986).

By middle childhood, girls and boys perceive themselves differently (Davis, Williams, & Best, 1982; J. A. Hall & Halberstadt, 1980). J. A. Hall and Halberstadt (1980) found that over time both boys and girls became more masculine and girls became less feminine. Girls may not endorse feminine characteristics as they grow older, because they realize that the feminine role is less valued by the culture. Researchers have only begun to examine the relation between children's adjustment and their endorsement of feminine and masculine traits, and the results are mixed (J. A. Hall & Halberstadt, 1980; Lobel & Winch, 1992; Silvern & Katz, 1986).

In contrast to the sparse literature on children's self-reported masculinity and femininity, there are numerous studies of children's adoption of masculine and feminine personality characteristics. In their extensive review of the literature, Maccoby and Jacklin (1974) concluded that many fewer personality differences exist than previously believed. However, J. H. Block (1976) suggested that Maccoby and Jacklin may have underesti-

mated the degree of personality differences because they only appear in older children (see J. H. Block, 1976, for review). More recent evidence suggests that gender differences in personality and social behavior are less pronounced than differences in activities and toy choices (see Huston, 1983).

## Interrelations Among Types of Gender Knowledge and Their Relation to Gender-Role Behavior

Much controversy has arisen over the relations among different types of gender knowledge and their correlation with the adoption of gender roles. A consistent theme in cognitive approaches is that behavior, thinking, and memory are all influenced by gender knowledge structures. Learning-based theorists have also become more concerned about the relations among different aspects of gender. The development of gender-typed preferences, however, may be distinct from the development of gender-typed knowledge (Huston, 1983; D. G. Perry, White, & L. C. Perry, 1984). Because of the implications of the idea that there is a cognitive underpinning for action and thought, it is important to evaluate the extent to which this assumption is true (Huston, 1985; Martin, 1993).

*Gender Constancy as a Predictor.* The controversy concerning the issue of coherence in gender knowledge began with Kohlberg's (1966) suggestion that gender constancy was the bedrock for the development of gender roles. The evidence concerning the predictive value of gender constancy has been mixed. In a few studies, attainment of gender constancy was found to be related to children's gender-typed preferences (Downs & Langlois, 1988; Kuhn et al., 1978; Smetana & Letourneau, 1984), whereas in other studies it was not (Carter & Levy, 1988; Emmerich & Shepard, 1984; Fagot, 1985; Marcus & Overton, 1978; Martin & Little, 1990). In one study, children who had attained gender constancy had more gender stereotype knowledge than other children (Kuhn et al., 1978), but in most other studies no such relation was found (Bussey & Bandura, 1992; Levy & Carter, 1989; Lobel & Menashri, 1993; Martin & Little, 1990). The evidence does suggest, however, that gender constancy is related to selective attention to same-sex models, especially for boys (D. N. Ruble, Balaban, & Cooper, 1981; Slaby & Frey, 1975). Overall, however, the preponderance of evidence suggests that children need not acquire gender constancy before they learn other aspects of gender (Carter, 1989; Carter & Levy, 1988; Huston, 1983; Levy & Carter, 1989; Martin & Little, 1990).

The inconsistencies in the literature may be due to methodological differences among studies (Bem, 1989; Intons-Peterson, 1988; Martin & Halverson, 1983; Stangor & D. N. Ruble, 1987). For instance, the outcomes of gender constancy studies are affected by the use of verbal versus pictorial measures (Intons-Peterson, 1988), the wording of questions (Beal & Lockhart, 1989), the procedure of assessing children's explanations for their answers (Emmerich, Goldman, Kirsh, & Sharabany, 1977; Wehren & DeLisi, 1983), and the way children are classified on their level of gender understanding (Martin & Little, 1990). Another concern is that children may misinterpret the meaning of gender constancy questions, with the consequence that the age of acquisition has been underestimated (Leonard &

Archer, 1989; Martin & Halverson, 1983b; also see Trautner, 1985).

An alternative explanation for the mixed evidence is that gender constancy increases children's responsiveness to gender information, rather than acting to *initiate* their responsiveness (Stangor & D. N. Ruble, 1987). According to this approach, gender-constant children are more motivated than pre-gender-constant children to adhere to gender-appropriate standards (D. N. Ruble, 1991). As a consequence, they should be more likely to engage in unpleasant behaviors, as long as those behaviors are sex-appropriate, because it is more important to be "correct" than to do something that is attractive. Frey and D. N. Ruble (1992) found support for this "conflict" hypothesis with 5- to 10-year olds, but only for boys. Because girls' gender roles are more flexible than those of boys, they may not need to adhere to them so strictly.

The verdict is still out concerning the role of gender constancy in gender-role development; thus, it may be premature to abandon the concept (Emmerich, 1982). Nonetheless, there is little empirical support for the idea that gender constancy is a particularly important aspect of early gender-role development (Carter, 1989; Carter & Levy, 1988; Huston, 1983; Levy & Carter, 1989).

*Gender Labeling as a Predictor.* Children may not need to have sophisticated levels of gender knowledge for them to develop gender-typed preferences and gender stereotypic knowledge. Constantinople (1979) and Fagot (1985) argued that merely labeling the sexes is sufficient for children to begin to form rules concerning gender. Serbin and Sprafkin (1986) proposed and found supportive evidence for the idea that gender should be particularly salient for children just before gender roles are learned, thereby enabling the child to learn the properties of gender categories. Maccoby (1980) and Martin and Halverson (1981) adopted a similar view; however, they believe that the major motivator of gender-typed preferences is children's recognition of their own membership in a gender group.

Even before they can label the sexes, children may acquire information about the sexes through the social transmission of gender stereotypes. For instance, children may hear that "boys don't cry" before they can identify a boy. However, when the sexes are recognized, this ability would be expected to enhance learning by facilitating the organization of information in memory and, more important, by providing children with the opportunity to learn by directly observing males and females (Fagot, 1985; Martin, 1993).

Empirical evidence generally confirms the importance of gender labeling. Gender labeling affects peer preferences: Children who can reliably label the sexes spend about 80% of their time in same-sex groups, versus about 50% of the time for those who cannot label the sexes (Fagot, 1985). Children who can distinguish between females and males at a very young age are more likely to adopt gender-typed behavior than those children who cannot distinguish the sexes, although the pattern is not always consistent (Fagot & Leinbach, 1989; Fagot, Leinbach, & Hagan, 1986; Fagot, Leinbach, & O'Boyle, 1992). In longitudinal studies, early gender labelers have been found to be higher in gender stereotype knowledge at age 4 than those children who acquire labels later (Fagot & Leinbach, 1989).

Also, children who are better able to distinguish the sexes have stronger gender-typed preferences and know more about gender stereotypes than those who do not (Fagot et al., 1992; Martin & Little, 1990), although this finding did not hold in another study (Hort, Leinbach, & Fagot, 1991).

*Gender Stereotype Knowledge as a Predictor.* Although gender stereotypes are seen by most theorists as the standards by which children evaluate their behavior, few studies have directly examined the relation of gender stereotype knowledge to other sorts of gender-related behavior or thinking (see Huston, 1983, 1985; Signorella, 1987; Signorella et al., 1993). The concurrent increases in gender stereotype knowledge, behavior, and thinking with age suggest some relation among these aspects of gender typing. The onset of gender-related behaviors, however, generally appears earlier than the onset of gender stereotype knowledge. Gender-typed preferences for activities and toys often are apparent about 6 months before children can demonstrate high levels of gender stereotype knowledge about toys and activities (Blakemore et al., 1979; D. G. Perry et al., 1984; Roopnarine, 1986; Weinraub et al., 1984, see Huston, 1985). To date, however, no studies have compared the onset of gender stereotype knowledge with concurrent gender-related thinking or memory.

Individual differences in gender stereotype knowledge have not been found to map onto individual differences in gender-related behavior or thinking. In one study, boys' but not girls' stereotype knowledge was related to gender-typed choices (Edelbrock & Sugawara, 1978), whereas in other studies no relation was found (Hort et al., 1991; Weinraub et al., 1984). Moreover, the relation between gender stereotypes and gender-related memory effects also is weak (Signorella, 1987).

The failure to find relations between knowledge and behavior may be due to the use of simple stereotype assessments on which most children have very high levels of knowledge by age 5 (i.e., the range of responding is restricted). More sophisticated methods of assessing gender knowledge are needed to adequately test the role of stereotype knowledge in gender-role behavior and other sorts of gender-related thinking (see Martin, 1993; Signorella et al., 1993). Also, flexibility in gender norms may be the predictor of children's behavior, more so than their knowledge about gender stereotypes (see Lobel & Menashri, 1993; Signorella et al., 1993).

## Conceptual Integration

Huston (1983) provided a strong case for considering that gender typing is multidimensional. Her proposal motivated researchers to explore interrelations rather than assume coherence among the different aspects of gender typing. Recent research indicates some coherence, but the overall picture suggests that a multidimensional view is needed.

Two basic patterns are apparent in the literature. One concerns interrelations among measures of the same construct. Studies using multiple measures of preferences or knowledge, both for gender categories (e.g., gender labeling, gender identity) and for gender stereotypes, tend to find coherence among measures (e.g., Downs & Langlois, 1988; Martin & Little, 1990; Serbin et al., 1993). The second pattern, which has more theoretical import, concerns whether there are cognitive underpinnings for children's gender preferences and behaviors (Martin, 1993). One type of gender knowledge, the ability to identify the sexes, appears to relate significantly to the ways children behave and think about gender (Fagot, 1985; Martin & Little, 1990; Weinraub et al., 1984), although these patterns are not always evident (e.g., Bussey & Bandura, 1992). In contrast, the case is not so clear for knowledge about gender stereotypes because seldom is a relation found between this type of knowledge and behavioral preferences (Serbin et al., 1993; Signorella et al., 1993; Weinraub et al., 1984).

In addition to examining interrelations among gender measures, researchers are now adopting a different approach to this issue; namely, they are examining conditions that influence the likelihood of applying gender cognitions. Motivation to adhere to gender cognitions may be influenced by a variety of factors. For instance, a recent study suggested that once children develop ideas about the consequences of their behavior, they refrain from behaving in ways that violate their cognition, thereby avoiding self-censure (Bussey & Bandura, 1992). Children's and adults' beliefs about the origins of gender differences (e.g., biological and socialization influences) may have an impact on behavior and interactions with others (Antill, 1987; Martin & Parker, 1995; see also J. Smith & Russell, 1984; and Taylor & Gelman, 1991, for research on developmental changes in these beliefs). The degree to which children understand about variability in gender groups may also influence the adherence to gender cognitions: Children with flexible gender norms show less gender-typed behavior than children with rigid gender norms (Lobel & Menashiri, 1993). Further, it is unlikely that children will adhere to gender cognitions unless gender knowledge is salient (Serbin & Sprafkin, 1986; Carter & Levy, 1988; Levy & Carter, 1989). Finally, situational demands also may influence the use of gender cognitions: Knowledge may be used automatically in some situations, such as when time is constrained or when one is aroused (Paulhus, Martin, & Murphy, 1992), and more consciously in other situations (Devine, 1989; Martin, 1989a). When situations allow conscious information processing, then the potential consequences of actions and one's values may influence the likelihood that gender knowledge will be applied (Martin, 1989a).

## GENDER DIFFERENCES IN ACADEMICALLY RELEVANT CAPABILITIES

This section reviews the research evidence regarding gender differences in academic achievement and performance. As mentioned previously, owing to space limitations we do not propose to conduct a comprehensive review of this extensive body of literature. Rather, we briefly review the current status of the research on gender differences in academic skills and performance. We begin with a review of gender differences in mathematics, verbal abilities, spatial skills, and physical performance. We then discuss evidence regarding the processes that may influence the degree to which females and males differ in achievement and performance.

## Gender Differences in Ability, by Academic Area

Gender differences in academic performance and achievement have been the focus of considerable attention in the past two decades (Jacklin, 1989). In their seminal work, Maccoby and Jacklin (1974) concluded that gender differences existed for mathematical abilities, verbal abilities, and spatial abilities. However, in recent reviews of the literature, researchers have concluded that gender differences in these areas have declined and are not uniform within these domains (e.g., Linn & Hyde, 1989).

*Mathematical Ability.* Discrepancies between male and female students' mathematical performance have long been noted and have long been a source of concern. By high school, boys outperform girls on math tests, especially those involving problem solving (Eccles, 1985; Hyde, Fennema, & Lamon, 1990). Females also take fewer math courses than males and are underrepresented in math and science professions (Koshland, 1988).

Many researchers have attempted to explain these discrepancies in math ability on the basis of gender differences in cognitive abilities (e.g., Benbow & Stanley, 1980; Halpern, 1986). Recent evidence now challenges these assumptions. Hyde et al. (1990) reviewed 100 studies that yielded 254 independent effect sizes representing over 3,000,000 subjects. When examining samples of the general population, the authors reported an average effect size of −.05 (indicating greater *female* superiority). They also reported that the magnitude of gender differences across all populations (general and select samples) has declined since 1974; for studies published in 1973 or earlier, the effect size was .31, whereas it was .14 for studies published in 1974 or later. Concern however has been raised about the precise degree and cause of these changes over time (Knight, Fabes, & Higgins, in press). No gender differences on computation or mathematical concepts emerged, nor were there significant gender differences for different types of mathematics (e.g., no gender differences in arithmetic or algebra, slight differences favoring males in geometry and calculus). However, differences favoring males emerged on problem-solving tests in high school and college and when highly selected or precocious samples were used.

Some researchers have found that gender differences in math are not consistent across content domains (Linn & Hyde, 1989). Generally, males outperform females on math related to measurement, science, and sports, whereas females outperform males on applications of math to aesthetics, interpersonal relationships, and traditional female tasks such as cooking or sewing. Moreover, gender differences in math appear to vary with age and with the type of skill required. For example, Marshall and J. D. Smith (1987) found that girls in the third grade performed better than boys in almost every mathematics area evaluated (e.g., counting, computations, measurement). This strong performance by girls relative to boys declined by sixth grade. Girls had lost ground in counting and nontraditional problem items (e.g., story problems requiring noncomputational responses such as identifying relevant and irrelevant information or recognition of a similar problem) and had fallen behind in word problems and measurement items. Marshall and Smith (1987) also found that boys and girls made different mathematical errors. For example, girls were more likely than boys to make association errors (e.g., making incorrect associations between words and operations), whereas boys were more likely to err in their use of mathematical rules (e.g., in executing "borrowing" or "carrying" algorithms).

*Verbal Ability.* Hyde and Linn (1988) recently synthesized the extant research on gender differences in verbal ability. They concluded that any differences that once existed are so small that they no longer exist. The average effect size in their meta-analytic review was .11 (slightly favoring females). Moreover, Hyde and Linn reported no systematic variation with age and that gender differences have declined over time to almost zero. For example, the combined effect size for studies conducted prior to 1974 was .23, compared to an average effect size of .10 in studies published during and since 1974. Feingold (1988) reported similar declines in gender differences in studies published between 1966 and 1973.

Thus, gender differences are not evident in general indices of language competence. Process analyses, however, have revealed that females outperform males on questions about aesthetics, whereas males outperform females on questions in which the verbal content is about science and practical affairs (see Linn & Hyde, 1989). Moreover, gender differences favoring females have been consistently reported in vocabulary growth in children under 2 years of age, after which they disappear (Maccoby & Jacklin, 1974). These differences in early vocabulary do not simply reflect differences in talkativeness but appear to reflect true early gender differences in vocabulary growth (Huttenlocher, Haight, Bryk, Seltzer, & T. Lyons, 1991).

The gender differences favoring females prior to 2 years of age do not appear to be due to the popular belief that mothers speak significantly more often to daughters than to sons. Huttenlocher et al. (1991) argued that some aspects of language, such as acquiring phonological dimensions of the language, may be most dependent on maturation (and may require only minimal language input), and that girls may be more advanced than boys early in life in the relevant aspects of maturation. In contrast, after 2 years of age, the acquisition of large numbers of words may depend more on the number of presentations of particular words and, consequently, on parent speech. Therefore, given that the quantity of parental speech to boys and girls is comparable, boys catch up in their language development by the third year of life.

*Spatial Ability.* Many scholars have asserted that gender differences in spatial ability contribute to gender differences in math and science performance (e.g., Benbow & Stanley, 1980; Maccoby & Jacklin, 1974). The relevant data, however, are primarily correlational (Fennema & Sherman, 1978). Moreover, meta-analyses of gender differences in spatial abilities provide little evidence for this assertion. Rather, the findings suggest that gender differences in spatial ability are dependent on the nature of the measure chosen for study (Linn & Petersen, 1985). For example, gender differences in spatial ability favoring males are large only for mental rotation; they are medium for spatial perception and small for spatial visualization. In addition, similar to the findings for math and verbal abilities, gender differences in spatial ability appear to be declining. Studies conducted before 1974 yield an effect size of .30 (favoring males), whereas

studies conducted since 1974 yield an effect size of −.13 (Hyde, 1981; Linn & Petersen, 1985).

Debate regarding gender differences in spatial ability also centers on when these differences first occur. Several researchers have reported differences appearing in early adolescence and have linked the differences to pubertal changes (Petersen, 1976; Waber, 1976). However, recent meta-analyses (Linn & Petersen, 1985) contradict this assertion. For spatial perception, differences are detected in individual studies at about age 8 and, in grouped studies, emerge statistically only at age 18. For mental rotation, gender differences are detected whenever measurement is possible (often this is not possible before the age of 13), whereas there are no age-related findings for spatial visualization. Thus, gender differences in spatial ability, if they emerge at all, emerge before adolescence for some types of spatial skills (see Linn & Peterson, 1985).

The relatively large gender differences in mental rotation may result from the propensity of females to select and consistently use less efficient strategies than do boys (e.g., gender differences occur on speed but not on accuracy; Kail, Carter, & Pellegrino, 1979). Linn and Hyde (1989) suggested that these gender differences in spatial strategies are responsive to training; gender differences on mental rotation are reduced or eliminated when training is employed.

*Physical Performance.* Because physical education is an integral part of schooling, and because gender differences in academic performance may arise from differential participation in physical activities (Baenninger & Newcombe, 1989), evidence regarding gender differences in physical performance is of interest to educational psychologists.

J. R. Thomas and French (1985) examined the degree to which males and females differ in physical performance during childhood and adolescence (data were taken from 64 studies yielding 702 independent effect sizes for 31,444 subjects). Of the 20 motor tasks included their analyses, age-related gender differences were found for 12 tasks (e.g., balance, catching, throwing, vertical jump). Effect sizes for the differences (favoring males) during childhood generally were small to moderate (less than .50). At puberty, the effect sizes for several of these motor tasks rapidly increased until they were between 1.5 to 2.0 standard deviation units. However, the fact that this age-related pattern occurred for only some of the motor tasks does not support the notion of uniform development of gender differences in motor performance. Based on the moderate differences between boys' and girls' motor performance prior to puberty, Thomas and French (1985) suggested that, with the exception of throwing (in which the difference was 1.5 SD at age 3), childhood gender differences more likely reflect environmental than biological influences.

Smoll and Schutz (1990) also found that boys exhibit progressively greater physical performance than girls from Grade 3 to Grade 11. When they averaged across several motor tasks (e.g., long jump, arm hang, running), the variance accounted for by gender increased dramatically with age (particularly from Grades 7 to 11), whereas the variance associated with anthropometric indexes (e.g., percentage body fat, fat-free body weight, etc.) decreased with age. These data suggest that with greater age, gender differences on some physical performance tasks increasingly are a function of the environment.

Around puberty, biology plays an important role in the development of gender differences in physical performance as hormonal changes result in increased muscle mass for boys and increased essential fat for girls. Thus, boys have an advantage in activities involving strength, size, and power. However, gender differences in physical performance after puberty are still influenced by environmental factors because girls are less likely to participate in activities that promote the development of motor skills associated with sports (J. R. Thomas & K. T. Thomas, 1988).

Activity level is another motor-related characteristic that is thought to vary for males and females. Stereotypically, it is widely believed that males have higher motor activity levels (defined as an individual's customary level of energy expenditure through movement) than females. However, Maccoby and Jacklin (1974) failed to find evidence to support this conclusion. More recently, Eaton and Enns (1986) summarized the results of 127 studies and found that males generally are more active than females (mean effect size = .49). The magnitude of the difference between males and females, however, was found to vary with age and situational characteristics. The average effect generally increased with development; the mean effect sizes for prenatal, infant (0 to 11 months), preschool (12 to 72 months), and older (73 to 360 months; 90 percent of the subjects were less than 15 years old) age groups were .33, .29, .44, and .64, respectively. Moreover, greater effect sizes tended to be found in low- rather than high-stress situations and in familiar rather than novel settings. Such findings suggest that maximal gender differences in activity level occur during the school years and in familiar, nonthreatening social settings (such as at home or in some school settings).

*Summary.* Many of the meta-analytic reviews have provided evidence that gender differences related to mathematical, verbal, and spatial abilities, but not some motor skills, generally have disappeared (or nearly so) in recent years. Caution must be used, however, in determining the precise reason for these changes over time (see Halpern, 1989; Knight et al., in press). In any case, the gender differences in career access in science and math are much larger than any of the differences found for cognitive skills. For example, female participation in math and science careers has increased but remains low: from 8.6% women in 1975 to 13.4% women in 1986 (Linn & Hyde, 1989; National Science Board, 1987). Thus, general cognitive differences do not adequately account for the sizable discrepancies between males and females in math and science careers.

Sherman (1967) has argued that gender differences in academic performance may be due to the fact that males and females have differential experiences related to such tasks. For example, boys are given toys that require manipulation and spatial creativity (such as blocks and erector sets; Etaugh, 1983) and are provided with more mathematically oriented toys than girls (Serbin, Zelkowitz, Doyle, Gold, & Wheaton, 1990).

Baenninger and Newcombe (1989) tested Sherman's hypothesis by examining the relation between spatial experiences and ability. In this meta-analysis, Baenninger and Newcombe found that for both males and females, spatial activity participation was related to spatial ability. These data are similar to those presented by Connor and Serbin (1977). In this study, preschoolers' observed play patterns were characterized as to

their gender-typed nature and examined in relation to performance on Block Design (BD) and Embedded Figures (EF). For boys, masculine activity preferences were highly significantly related to EF but not BD performance. Feminine activity preferences, however, were inversely related to BD performance. For females, none of the correlations were significant, although masculine activity preferences were positively, nonsignificantly associated with EF performance and feminine activity preferences were inversely related to EF performance.

Although these data provide evidence that differential experiences are related to academic test performance, the magnitudes of these effects are small. Thus, factors other than cognitive differences may play an important role in influencing male and female academic behavior and achievement. For example, Lubinski and Benbow (1992) suggested that among the mathematically talented, more males than females chose math and science mostly because of their preferences. Gifted females were found to have stronger competing interests in areas other than math or science and appeared to choose to develop their abilities in other areas.

We now turn our attention to factors other than cognitive differences that may account for the limited gender differences in academic skills and achievement.

## Familial Socialization Influence on Boys' and Girls' Achievement

*Parental Beliefs, Attitudes, and Expectations.* A growing body of literature has established the importance of parents' beliefs in influencing their children's achievement attitudes and academic performance (e.g., Hess, Holloway, Dickson, & Price, 1984; Jacobs, 1991; McGillicudy-De Lisi, 1985). In fact, parents' beliefs about children's abilities have been found to have a greater influence on children's achievement and attitudes than does children's previous performance (Coleman et al., 1966).

Eccles and her colleagues (see Eccles-Parsons et al., 1983) have proposed a model of parental influence in which parents play an "expectancy socialization role." Specifically, parents convey their expectations to their child by providing messages concerning their beliefs about the child's abilities. These messages are thought to differ depending on the sex of the child.

Jacobs (1991) tested this model and found support for the gender-specific influence of parental stereotypes on children's achievement attitudes and performance. The influence of the child's gender on parents' beliefs about their child's math abilities and future success depended on the level of parental stereotyping. Stronger parental gender stereotypes were related to greater expectations of children's success and a stronger belief in children's ability for parents of sons (relative to parents of daughters). Moreover, parents' gender stereotypes had an influence on children's beliefs, which then affected their math performance. Thus, boys had consistently higher beliefs about their mathematics abilities and future expectancies than did girls, despite the fact that girls had consistently higher math grades than boys. Jacobs (1991) suggested that this incongruity may be due to the possibility that children form their self-perceptions based on more than just their own performance and that parental beliefs may account, in part, for their non-data-based beliefs.

Additional support for the contention that parental attitudes and expectations affect children's achievement-related beliefs and behaviors is provided by Jacobs and Eccles (1985). Briefly, these researchers found that parents whose gender stereotypes for math ability had been confirmed by reading a media report about math abilities were more likely to change their beliefs about their own children's math abilities (in stereotypic directions) than were parents who had not been exposed to the report. These effects were deleterious to girls. As parents came to believe that math was more difficult for daughters than for sons, their daughters were less likely to take additional math courses.

***Familial Interaction Patterns and Children's Academic Achievement and Performance.*** Researchers have begun to examine the link between parent–child interactions and children's academic performance and achievement. For instance, investigators have found that affective tone, parental involvement, and parenting styles predict a variety of intellectual and academic outcomes (e.g., Baumrind, 1973; Feldman & Wentzel, 1990; Grolnick & Ryan, 1989; Hess et al., 1984). In general, nurturant, didactic, and authoritative styles have been found to be positively related to children's cognitive competence. In contrast, critical, hostile, authoritarian interactions have been found to be related to less advanced cognitive development.

The degree to which parents differentially socialize boys' and girls' behaviors and attitudes continues to be debated. In their extensive review, Maccoby and Jacklin (1974) examined differential socialization of boys and girls and found that after infancy there was a clear pattern that boys received more punishment, particularly physical punishment, than did girls. Similarly, Huston (1983) concluded that parents encouraged boys' participation in active, gross motor activities more often than they did so for girls, and that girls received more encouragement to show dependency and to express affectionate behavior. In achievement domains, Huston (1983) concluded that parents expected and demanded more of boys than they do of girls. In addition, J. Newson and E. Newson (1976) found that boys were given more opportunities to play away from home and away from adult supervision than were girls. These differences in restrictions did not appear to be based on differences in levels of maturity. As such, girls may miss opportunities to develop a sense of autonomous competence and are likely to come under greater pressure to conform to adult standards and expectations, including achievement-related standards and expectations.

Lytton and Romney (1991) conducted a meta-analysis of 172 studies to examine whether parents treat boys and girls differently. Their findings were quite different from the conclusions of Huston (1983) and others (e.g., J. H. Block, 1979, 1983). Of the 19 major socialization areas examined, several have important implications for children's academic achievement (e.g., amount of verbal interaction, encouragement of math achievement, encouragement of dependency). For North American studies, the only one of these socialization areas with a significant effect size was encouragement of gender-typed activities. Thus, at least according to Lytton and Romney's (1991) data, one cannot speak of parents consistently treating boys and girls differently.

Caution must be used, however, in interpreting Lytton and Romney's (1991) findings. In their review they relied on existing literature, which contains few studies of older children, adolescents, and adults. Thus, the findings may be limited by possible age-of-sample biases. For example, J. H. Block (1976) argued that socialization of gender differences frequently may not occur until children approach adolescence. The fact that parents consistently encourage boys and girls in regard to gender-typed activities and interests may act as a filter for children's differential experiences with materials and activities related to academic areas. Moreover, even if parents do not consistently differentiate their child-rearing behaviors toward sons and daughters, the same child-directed behaviors may affect boys and girls differently. For example, Basow (1990) found that boys and girls reacted differently to teachers' expressiveness: Boys performed better with expressive teachers (who were perceived as relatively masculine) in comparison to nonexpressive teachers, whereas the reverse was true for girls. Girls and boys also may respond in different ways to the same parental behavior.

Parents may influence outcomes in children in many ways that are more subtle than have been measured in earlier research. In addition, some existing studies on subtle means of influence were not included in Lytton and Romney's (1991) meta-analysis.

## School-Related Factors

Researchers and educators have long been interested in the school's contributions to gender differences in academic performance and achievement (see Minuchin & Shapiro, 1983). This literature suggests that schools make major contributions to the underrepresentation of women in science and math careers. These school-related effects occur as a function of children's encounters with school personnel and with the structure of the school itself.

***Teachers' Beliefs and Attitudes.*** That teachers treat boys and girls differently has been well documented. For example, several researchers (Fagot, 1977; Serbin, O'Leary, Kent, & Tonick, 1973) have observed that when boys are engaged in task-relevant behaviors, teachers give them more positive attention than they give girls engaged in similar activities. Moreover, the kind of attention teachers give to boys in the classroom may be different from the attention given to girls. For example, Dweck, Davidson, Nelson, and Enna (1978) found that boys received a higher proportion of their positive feedback from teachers based on the intellectual content of their work than did girls. These findings, however, have not been consistently replicated (e.g., J. E. Parsons, Kaczala, & Meece, 1982). Additionally, teachers appear to use praise differently for boys and girls. J. E. Parsons et al. (1982) found that teachers' use of praise was more indiscriminant for girls than it was for boys. Thus, praise may have less informative value for girls than it does for boys.

Research on teachers' attitudes suggests that gender-typed biases and perceptions underlie these differential interactions. For example, Gold, Crombie, and Noble (1987) found that girls whose behaviors were in accordance with the traditional stereotype of girls as good, acquiescing students were perceived by teachers as being more capable than girls who did not match the acquiescent gender stereotype. Evaluations of boys, however, were not affected by teachers' perceptions of their compliant nature. Importantly, compliance was *not* statistically associated with either girls' or boys' performance on objective problem-solving and intelligence tests. Thus, teachers' judgments of the relations between school-related characteristics and performance were erroneous, and these errors may have been due to teachers' gender-stereotyped attitudes and expectations.

*Differential Access to Math and Science Instruction.* Differential experience with materials begins during preschool, where gender differences in the provision and encouragement of play materials have repeatedly been documented (see Huston, 1983; Liss, 1983, for reviews). Upon entrance into the school system, students' academic experiences with math and science continue to be shaped along gender-stereotyped lines. For example, both male and female counselors tend to give conventional, gender-typed advice to students and do not give students materials relevant to, or encouragement for, exploring new fields (Eccles & Jacobs, 1986). Moreover, even when boys and girls are enrolled in the same math course, access to instruction often may not be equal. For example, Leinhardt, Seewald, and Engel (1979) found that teachers spent relatively more time teaching math to boys than to girls; boys received as much as 36 more hours of math instruction than did girls by the time they reached the seventh grade.

The fact that there are more men than women who teach math and science courses may contribute to the differential math and science experiences of females and males (Stockard et al., 1980). Because females may have fewer teachers to serve as role models, they may be less likely to enroll in such courses. Moreover, because females may find classes with male instructors a less positive experience than if they had a female instructor (e.g., they participate less and are less assertive; Crawford & MacLeod, 1990; R. M. Hall & Sandler, 1982), they may avoid these classes. Additional support for this notion is found in studies that show that single-sex educational experiences appear to enable females to overcome certain social and psychological barriers to their academic and professional achievement (Lee & Bryk, 1986; Lee & Marks, 1990).

*Curriculum and Course Content.* Researchers examining gender stereotyping in learning materials have demonstrated gender biases in children's school readers, curriculum materials, items on standardized tests, and textbooks across a wide array of topics from math to social studies (e.g., Pottker & Fishel, 1977; Purcell & Stewart, 1990; Women on Words and Images, 1972). For example, few women are depicted in occupational roles associated with math and science. Although some progress has been made in bringing forth more realistic and balanced portrayals of females and males in children's readers (Purcell & Stewart, 1990), females still are not shown in as wide a range of careers as are males. In addition, analyses of curriculum texts revealed that women's historical contributions and biographies are inadequately represented. Trecker's (1977) analysis of history texts showed that the length of women's skirts received more attention than the contributions of female intellectuals who worked for social reform.

It should also be recognized that educational institutions have made great strides in recent decades in attempting to remedy sexism and sex stereotyping. Educational institutions

are obliged to conform to particular provisions and guidelines ensuring equal treatment for males and females under the law (e.g., Title IX of the Educational Amendment of 1972). Such landmark legislative acts were designed to ensure educational opportunities regardless of gender at every educational level. Schools now offer girls and women substantially more opportunities to participate in vocational educational courses and sports programs. School districts can no longer eliminate school services to pregnant students, and school counselors have begun to test and advise all students using the same standards and criteria. Finally, class materials and curricula have been developed and implemented that are designed to eliminate sex bias and stereotyping.

For all the sex equity adjustments that have occurred, sex stereotyping and sexism have not been eradicated from educational institutions. The infrequency of school text adoptions and the lag time in publishing textbooks limit the availability of up-to-date sex-equitable materials (Keating, 1990). Budgetary restrictions, public attitudes, and the organization and structure of teacher education programs also contribute to these problems (D. Sadker & M. Sadker, 1985). Thus, there is still a long way to go to overcome the sex-based barriers that exist in educational institutions.

## Self-System Processes and Gender Differences in Academic Achievement and Performance

Another possible source of differences in males' and females' academic and occupational achievement and performance may be found in self-system variables (e.g., self-evaluation, anxiety, and self-concept). The following discussion briefly examines some of the more dominant themes in research on this topic.

*Attributions of Academic Competence and Ability.* A commonly held assumption about gender differences in academic achievement and performance is that females underestimate their academic abilities more than males (Eccles, 1985; Maccoby & Jacklin, 1974). Males' and females' expectancies for success generally have been found to be greater in domains stereotyped as appropriate for their gender than in stereotypically inappropriate domains (Huston, 1983). Thus, girls perceive math as more difficult than boys do and have lower expectations for success, even when their performance is not objectively poorer than boys' (Entwistle & Baker, 1983; Ilardi & Bridges, 1988). Girls, in comparison to boys, generally have lower expectancies of success, lower aspirations, greater anxiety about failure, and greater tendencies to attribute their failure to lack of ability and their successes to unstable factors (see Huston, 1983). These gender differences appear in some studies as early as age 4 (Crandell, 1978). Importantly, these achievement-related beliefs have been found to influence academic choices and behaviors (Eccles, 1985; Stipek & Gralinski, 1991).

*Academic Self-Concept.* Marsh and colleagues (e.g., Marsh, 1986; Marsh, Byrne, & Shavelson, 1988; Marsh, Smith, & Barnes, 1985) have proposed that children's academic self-concepts are based on their self-perceptions of their academic ability. Researchers have begun to examine whether the structure of students' academic self-concept is similar for males and females.

For example, Byrne and Shavelson (1987) found that boys' general academic self-concept correlated higher with math self-concept than with verbal self-concept, whereas the reverse was true for girls. Similarly, Skaalvik and Rankin (1990) found that a positive math self-concept had a direct and positive relation to general academic self-concept for boys but was negatively related to girls' general academic self-concept. These results indicate that the structure of boys' and girls' academic self-concept may be different. As a result, boys and girls may come to differentially value academic curricula and professions according to their relevancy to their academic self-concepts (e.g., boys value math and girls value courses emphasizing verbal skills).

Males' and females' academic self-concepts also may vary as a function of differences in the ways that they respond to evaluative feedback in achievement settings. Roberts (1991) suggested that because of their lower status in society, females may have a more limited range of action than males and spend more time monitoring their social environment than acting autonomously. As such, women may be more dependent on feedback and more responsive to the valence of the evaluative feedback they receive than are males. Such findings may explain why males are more likely than females to believe that academic success is a function of ability (e.g., Stipek & Gralinski, 1991).

### Biological Explanations

No strong evidence for genetic influences on gender differences in academic performance has been found. Some evidence suggests that certain aspects of visual-spatial abilities are heritable and may be X-linked (Bock & Kolakowski, 1973; Spuhler & Vandenberg, 1980); however, the majority of the research evidence does not consistently support these explanations (Boles, 1980; Linn & Petersen, 1985; Vandenberg & Kuse, 1979).

Other researchers have postulated that sex hormones affect intellectual performance by differentially interacting with neurotransmitters (e.g., Broverman, Klaiber, Kobayshi, & Vogel, 1968). This differential interaction is hypothesized to predispose the nervous system toward different neural and behavioral activation. Once again, however, evidence in support of the link between hormones and cognitive performance is weak and inconsistent (Maccoby & Jacklin, 1974; Parlee, 1972).

A final biological explanation for gender differences in cognitive and academic performance focuses on gender differences in brain organization. For example, J. Levy (1976) proposed that male superiority on spatial tasks is due to greater hemispheric lateralization of spatial skills among men than among women. Although some studies of brain anatomy have reported small differences between male and female brains (e.g., de Lacoste-Utamsing & Holloway, 1982), the evidence is not yet conclusive or overwhelming, nor has it been definitively linked to cognitive abilities (Huston, 1983). Furthermore, Kimura (1987) has suggested that gender differences in brain anatomy may vary with age, indicating that gender differences in brain organization may be dynamic rather than static. Finally, brain lateralization may be affected by environmental factors; in fact, the lateralization of children's verbal skills appears to be influenced by the quality and quantity of exposure to language (Borowy & Goebel, 1976). Thus, the evidence for gender differences in brain organization is equivocal, and even when evidence has been found, the causes of these differences have not been conclusively determined.

## GENDER DIFFERENCES IN SOCIALLY AND MORALLY RELEVANT CAPABILITIES AND BEHAVIORS

This section reviews gender differences in a variety of sociocognitive abilities and behaviors relevant to children's social, psychological, and moral functioning. We start with a discussion of several sociocognitive skills relevant to social and moral behavior (perspective taking, decoding of others' emotions, and moral reasoning) and then examine gender differences in children's emotional responding, regulation of emotional expression, depression, and vicarious emotional responding (e.g., empathy). Next, gender differences in morally relevant behaviors (i.e., prosocial and aggressive behavior) are reviewed. Finally, gender differences in social competence, friendships, and help seeking are discussed. We selected aspects of sociocognitive, socioemotional, and moral development that have been deemed central in children's social development.

### Gender Differences in Sociocognitive Capabilities

An understanding of others' perspectives and emotions, as well as one's own moral reasoning, has been considered central to the development of social competence and morality (e.g., Feshbach, 1978; M. L. Hoffman, 1982; Kohlberg, 1966; Shantz, 1975; Underwood & Moore, 1982). Thus, any gender differences in these abilities are relevant to an understanding of social and moral functioning.

***Gender Differences in Moral Reasoning.*** The issue of gender differences in moral reasoning has been hotly debated in the past decade. This debate was fueled by Carol Gilligan's (1977, 1982) assertion that Kohlberg's (1984) schema of moral reasoning was biased toward males and her contention that males use a justice-oriented mode of moral reasoning, whereas females' moral reasoning is more care oriented. In her view, Kohlberg's highest stages—stages that stress individuality and autonomy of moral standards—seem incompatible with society's emphasis on the desirability of nurturance and interconnectedness for females. Although Gilligan now acknowledges that both sexes use both types of reasoning, she argues that there is still a gender difference in the predominance of one or the other type of moral reasoning (Brown, Tappan, Gilligan, Miller, & Argyris, 1989).

The research has not supported Gilligan's assertion that males score higher on Kohlberg's rights- and justice-oriented scheme of moral judgment. According to several reviews, boys and men have not scored higher on Kohlberg's schema of moral reasoning (Walker, 1984; see also Ford & Lowery, 1986; Pratt, Golding, & Kerig, 1987); indeed, women score slightly higher than men on Rest's (1979) pencil-and-paper version of Kohlberg's measure (the Defining Issues Test; Thoma, 1986). Moreover, males' and females' justice-related reasoning appears to follow similar developmental trajectories (Colby, L. Kohlberg,

Gibbs, & Lieberman, 1983). Thus, although there is still some debate on this issue (e.g., Baumrind, 1986), there is little evidence of a consistent bias toward males, particularly among children (Walker, 1989; Walker, de Vries, & Trevethan, 1987).

In regard to Gilligan's second point—that women use more reasoning pertaining to a care orientation whereas men use more reasoning pertaining to a rights orientation—the findings are mixed. There is some evidence that adolescent girls and women are somewhat more likely than their male peers to use a care orientation in their moral reasoning (Gibbs, Arnold, & Burkhart, 1984; Gilligan & Attanucci, 1988; Pratt, Golding, Hunter, & Sampson, 1988; Rothbart, Hanley, & Albert, 1986; Walker et al., 1987) and to describe moral conflicts in the context of a relationship (Johnston, L. M. Brown, & Christopherson, 1990). In addition, Eisenberg found that preadolescent and adolescent girls more than boys used certain other-oriented modes of moral reasoning when discussing moral dilemmas about helping (Eisenberg, 1977; Eisenberg et al., 1987); however, there was no such gender difference in children's prosocial reasoning, and gender differences in adolescence were ephemeral (Eisenberg, P. A. Miller, Shell, McNalley, & Shea, 1991). In general, then, it appears that the gender difference in relational and care-related concerns does not emerge until adolescence and is fairly weak (also see Archer & Waterman, 1988; Ford & Lowery, 1986; Galotti, Kozberg, & Farmer, 1991; Garrod, Beal, & Shin, 1990; Walker et al., 1987).

*Gender Differences in Perspective Taking and Decoding Information About Others' Emotional States.* Information about gender differences in understanding others' cognitive and emotional states is embedded primarily in two bodies of literature: work on children's cognitive and affective perspective taking and research on children's and adults' abilities to decode others' emotional states. Research on cognitive and affective perspective taking usually involves providing a child with information about another's situation and, sometimes, a picture of the other person's face, and then asking the child what the other person is thinking or feeling. Alternatively, researchers have assessed children's ability to understand another person's thoughts. In studies of people's ability to decode others' emotional states, the ability to interpret facial, vocal, and gestural cues is examined.

In general, few differences in boys' and girls' ability to understand what another person is thinking or feeling are evident in research reviews (Brody, 1985; Eisenberg & Lennon, 1983; Gross & Ballif, 1991; M. L. Hoffman, 1977). In many studies of perspective-taking skills, gender differences are not reported, presumably in many cases because they did not occur. Moreover, in recent studies of children's abilities to infer others' emotions and cognitions and to understand attempts to control feelings, few gender differences have been found (e.g., Carroll & Steward, 1984; Fabes, Eisenberg, McCormick, & Wilson, 1988; LeMare & Rubin, 1987; Nannis & Cowan, 1987; Taylor, 1988).

An exception to this general pattern may be for children's and adolescents' decoding of another's emotional state from visual and auditory stimuli such as films; females may be more accurate decoders than males of such stimuli (J. A. Hall, 1978). This is significant because by high school age, level of decoding skills has been associated with learning (Bernieri, 1991). Moreover, as adults, women seem to be better at decoding others'

emotional states from a wide variety of stimuli (e.g., including static stimuli; Eisenberg & Lennon, 1983; J. A. Hall, 1978; N. G. Rotter & G. S. Rotter, 1988; Soppe, 1988), although women have little advantage over men at decoding deceptive cues (Blanck, Rosenthal, Snodgrass, DePaulo, & Zuckerman, 1981) and may be worse than men at decoding males' anger (N. G. Rotter & G. S. Rotter, 1988).

It is possible that girls have a better understanding of emotions than do boys. Researchers have found that 24-month-old girls discuss emotions more than do boys (Dunn, Bretherton, & Munn, 1987) and at 40 months are more advanced in affective perspective taking (Dunn, J. Brown, Slomkowski, Tesla, & Youngblade, 1991). However, the findings are not entirely consistent (Dunn, J. Brown, & Beardsall, 1991). Thus, any early gender difference in affective understanding may be limited and short-lived.

Although girls and boys in general may be equally accurate in their ability to infer others' emotions, they sometimes, but not always (Russell, 1990), may attribute others' emotions to different causes. For example, Fabes et al. (1988) and Strayer (1986) found that girls were more likely than boys to attribute emotional reactions to interpersonal causes. In contrast, preschool-aged boys may be more likely than girls to attribute others' naturally occurring emotional reactions to internal causes (e.g., feeling sick or someone's mood; Fabes et al., 1988). Thus, consistent with some of the literature on moral reasoning reviewed above, it is possible that females are more likely than males to emphasize interpersonal aspects of situations, including emotion-evoking circumstances.

Finally, there is a difference between the *ability* to understand another's thoughts or feelings and the *tendency* to use the perspective-taking or decoding skills in one's repertoire. The tendency to perspective take has been assessed in adolescence and adulthood, and fairly consistently favors females (e.g., M. H. Davis, 1980; M. H. Davis & Franzoi, 1991; Eisenberg, P. A. Miller, et al., 1989, 1991). Thus, females appear to be more likely to try to put themselves in another's shoes in social contexts—a tendency that might, over time, improve their decoding and perspective-taking skills (perspective-taking ability has seldom been examined in adulthood).

## Gender Differences in Emotional Reactions

Some of the most prevalent gender stereotypes concern emotionality and the expression of emotion. The commonly held stereotype is that females are more emotional than males, with the exception that males express more anger (e.g., Allen & Haccoun, 1976; Birnbaum, Nosanchuk, & Croll, 1980; I. K. Broverman, Vogel, D. M. Broverman, Clarkson, & Rosenkrantz, 1972; Martin, 1987; Noddings, 1984; Spence & Helmreich, 1978). Although there may be a kernel of truth to these stereotypes, the patterns of findings regarding individuals' beliefs about emotions are more subtle and complex than previously thought. For example, Fabes and Martin (1991; Karbon, Fabes, Carlo, & Martin, 1992) have found that children's and adults' beliefs about gender differences in emotion vary as a function of the age of the target person. Given the centrality of emotion and beliefs about emotions in social, moral, and psychological development, it is important to understand any gender differences in children's emotionally related experience and behavior.

*Gender Differences in Emotional Expression and Reactivity.* Partial support exists for stereotypes of gender differences in emotionality, but the research is not programmatic or very consistent. In addition, this research must be interpreted cautiously because observers in most studies are not blind to the sex of the child and their interpretation of children's emotional reactions may be affected by that knowledge.

In infancy, there is little evidence of consistent gender differences in the expression of positive or negative emotion (see Brody, 1985; Rothbart & Derryberry, 1981; Zahn-Waxler, Cummings, & Cooperman, 1984, for reviews). For example, in a review of studies in infants, Korner (1973) found no consistent differences between newborn boys' and girls' crying. In addition, those gender differences in infants' reactions that are found seem to vary with the context. In two of the few studies in which observers were blind to the sex of the infants, girls showed more interest in social interactions (but there were no differences in anger, pain, joy, surprise; Malatesta & Haviland, 1982), whereas boys were higher in wakefulness, facial grimacing, low-intensity motor activity, and oral activity (viewed as signs of irritability; Phillips, King, & DuBois, 1978). In an additional study in which raters were deceived as to the correct sex of the infant, males were rated as more frequently angry, less frequently sad, and as showing more intense expressions of happiness, anger, sadness, and fear than were females (Cunningham & Shapiro, 1984). Thus, there are some data suggesting that male infants are more irritable and reactive than female infants, although gender differences in infants' emotional responding often are subtle and situationally variable.

Findings in the toddler and preschool years also are not highly consistent (see Brody, 1985). Girls seem to display more anger in some contexts until about 2 years of age (Goodenough, 1931; Malatesta, Culver, Tesman, & Shepard, 1989), but angry outbursts by girls appear to drop off after about age 2 (Goodenough, 1931). In observational research, older preschool boys have exhibited proportionally more anger and less sadness than girls (Fabes, Eisenberg, Nyman, & Michealieu, 1991; cf. Camras, 1977). In studies of temperament, boys generally are rated as more angry than girls, whereas girls are rated as more fearful (Buss, 1989; also see Lewis & Michalson, 1983). Similarly, when watching an emotionally arousing television show, 2- to 4-year-old girls showed more facial fear and happiness, whereas boys showed more anger; there were no differences in sadness (Birnbaum & Croll, 1984). Other findings suggest that young girls show more shame (e.g., Lewis, Alessandri, & Sullivan, 1992), and boys sometimes report more anger (particularly by age 6 to 7 years) and exhibit more aggression (as toddlers) in response to exposure to adults' anger (E. M. Cummings, Iannotti, & Zahn-Waxler, 1985; E. M. Cummings, Vogel, J. S. Cummings, & El-Sheikh, 1989).

By early elementary school, girls show more positive affect in a variety of contexts (see Zahn-Waxler et al., 1984) and girls generally report experiencing more fear and sadness but somewhat less anger than do boys (Brody, 1985). Boys seem to start hiding negative expressions such as sadness and pain (Eisenberg, Schaller, Miller, Fultz, Fabes, & Shell, 1988; Fuchs & Thelen, 1988; Shennum & Bugental, 1982; Strayer, 1983; Zeman & Garber, 1991). In contrast, girls express less anger than boys (Fuchs & Thelen, 1988; Karniol & Heiman, 1987; c.f. Zea-

man & Garber, 1991), and seem to be better than boys at hiding negative emotions such as disappointment that might hurt others' feelings (Cole, 1986; Saarni, 1984).

In late elementary school and high school, girls report more (i.e., greater frequency, intensity, or duration) surprise, sadness, shame, shyness, and guilt; boys report more contempt and are more likely to deny experiencing surprise, sadness, guilt, and disgust (D. G. Perry, L. C. Perry, & Weiss, 1989; Stapley & Haviland, 1989; also see Zahn-Waxler, Cole, & Barrett, 1991). In addition, adolescent girls report greater intensity of experiencing negative and positive emotions when they occur (Diener, Sandvik, & Larsen, 1985; Wintre, Polivy, & Murray, 1990). Among adults, women report more intense emotions (Allen & Haccoun, 1976; Diener et al., 1985; Fujita, Diener, & Sandvik, 1991) and more nonverbal (facial, vocal, gestural) reactions to some emotions (Scherer, Wallbott, & Summerfield, 1986), sometimes report more sadness, joy, and fear (Allen & Haccoun, 1976), display more positive emotion (J. A. Hall, 1984; Halberstadt, Hayes, & Pike, 1988) and slightly more negative emotion (J. A. Hall, 1984), and are perceived as displaying more of most emotions except anger (Fabes & Martin, 1991; Slevin & Balswick, 1980). Adults view women as displaying more communal and socially desirable feelings and fewer self-oriented, undesirable feelings, although women are viewed as experiencing both types of feelings more intensely than men (J. T. Johnson & Shulman, 1988).

The gender differences in emotional displays are not surprising, given our understanding, however limited, of the socialization of emotion. Parents report greater acceptance of boys' anger and girls' fear (Birnbaum & Croll, 1984) and seem to disapprove of girls' anger, even in infancy (Malatesta & Haviland, 1982). Clearly, anger is not consistent with the communal feminine role, whereas the expression of positive affect is. Even in infancy, parents seem to spend more time getting their daughters to smile (Moss, 1974). Also, mothers of 2-year-olds show greater expressivity toward girls than boys (Malatesta et al., 1989), a pattern that may encourage more smiling and reports of emotional intensity by females.

Buck (1984) has argued that the association of sanctions with emotional expression eventually results in males' expressing their emotions internally but not externally (i.e., with nonverbal cues). Consistent with this notion, parental emphasis on controlling negative emotions has been correlated with boys' denial of experiencing vicarious negative emotions, accompanied by physiological signs of emotional reactivity (Eisenberg, Fabes, Schaller, P. A. Miller et al., 1991). Indeed, boys seem to have learned by elementary school not to express emotions such as sadness, fear, and pain. Not only do boys start to hide emotions such as sadness and pain (see above), but they expect more negative consequences for the expression of sadness than do girls (Fuchs & Thelen, 1988).

Mothers talk more about emotions with their daughters (Dunn et al., 1987; Kuebil & Krieger, 1991; Moss, 1974), although they emphasize anger and negative emotions more frequently with boys and positive emotions more with girls (Fivush, 1989). Their willingness and tendency to discuss emotions, particularly positive emotions, with girls may encourage girls to attend to and express emotions. Consistent with this notion, Block (1979) found that parents reported greater insistence on the control of feelings and their expression for sons, but tended to emphasize maintenance of close emotional relationships and verbal discussion of emotions with daughters.

The apparent cultural emphasis on males' avoidance of sadness and fear may be relevant to findings in the literature on anxiety and depression. Although there are no gender differences in elementary schoolchildren diagnosed as having anxiety disorder, a variety of findings suggest that girls worry and are anxious more than are boys (Nolen-Hoeksema, 1987). Zahn-Waxler et al. (1984) suggested that chronic feelings of anxiety about oneself and one's competence may contribute to learned feelings of helplessness and hopelessness, and that such feelings partially account for the greater incidence of depression among women. We now turn to the issue of gender differences in depression.

*Gender Differences in Depression.* In adulthood, women are about twice as likely as men to report significant depression on self-report questionnaires and are approximately one and one-half times as likely to be diagnosed as depressed (Nolen-Hoeksema, 1987, 1991). This gender difference seems to emerge around eighth grade (Horwitz & White, 1987; Petersen, Sarigiani, & Kennedy, 1991; Webb & VanDevere, 1985; see Nolen-Hoeksema, 1991; Nolen-Hoeksema, Girgus, & Seligman, 1991); indeed, in elementary school boys exhibit higher levels of some depressive symptoms (anhedonia and behavioral disturbance, self-derogation, or physiological complaints; Nolen-Hoeksema et al., 1991).

The gender difference in depression in adults does not seem to be solely due to differential reporting of depression, willingness to display depressive symptoms, differences in income, or a greater genetic predisposition to depression in females (Nolen-Hoeksema, 1987). Findings related to hormonal and other biochemical explanations for the gender difference are mixed but do not appear to explain gender differences with certain subgroups (Nolen-Hoeksema, 1987). Nolen-Hoeksema (1987, 1991) has argued that gender differences in how people respond to their own depressed state may contribute to its severity, chronicity, and recurrence. "Specifically, it is argued that the men's responses to their dysphoria are more behavioral and dampen their depressive episodes, whereas women's responses to their depressive episodes are more ruminative and amplify them" (1987, p. 274). Consistent with her argument, there is evidence that an internal focus (i.e., self-focused attention) is associated with negative affect and depression (e.g., Ingram, 1990; Wood, Saltzberg, Neale, Stone, & Rachmiel, 1990; also see Pyszczynski, Greenberg, Hamilton, & Nix, 1991) and that women (and feminine people) have greater propensities to self-focus and ruminate than do men (Conway, Giannopoulos, & Stiefenhofer, 1990; Ingram, Cruet, B. R. Johnson, & Wisnicki, 1988; Nolen-Hoeksema, 1987, 1991).

This gender difference in style of coping with negative events and affect may begin in adolescence. For example, in adolescence (i.e., at ages 14 to 19), boys appear to be higher on ego defenses that externalize (e.g., projection and aggressive-outward defense), and girls may be higher on turning against the self (Levit, 1991) and other internalizing defense mechanisms (Cramer, 1979; also see Vingerhoets & Van Heck, 1990). Among elementary schoolchildren, the finding that boys display more of some depressive symptoms may be due to boys having a more maladaptive explanatory style for negative events (except

academic events) than do girls. That is, boys have been found to explain negative events in terms that are stable, internal, and global (Nolen-Hoeksema et al., 1991). It is unclear, however, why girls exhibit more depression in adolescence; Nolen-Hoeksema et al. (1991) suggested that changes in girls' self-esteem and increasing social pressure on girls with age to act in feminine ways (e.g., to be nonassertive) may account for the greater vulnerability of females to depression with age. However, it has also been argued that girls have more challenges to cope with in adolescence and that the gender difference in adolescents' depression is not significant when early adolescent challenges are controlled for (Petersen et al., 1991). Perhaps issues pertaining to separation are particularly distressing to adolescent females (Gilligan et al., 1990); further work is needed to determine the reasons underlying observed gender differences in depression.

In any case, it seems that the developmental correlates of depression for girls and boys differ. Girls that are depressed in late adolescence tend to have been intropunitive, oversocialized, and overcontrolled in the early school years (J. H. Block, Gjerde, & J. Block, 1991; also see Zahn-Waxler et al., 1991). In contrast, males' depression at age 18 has been associated with aggression, self-aggrandizing, and undercontrolled behavior in childhood (J. H. Block et al., 1991). Thus, it seems likely that the mechanisms underlying the development of males' and females' depression differ, with females' and males' depression being associated with internalizing and externalizing behaviors, respectively. Of course, it is quite possible that low self-esteem and maladaptive coping styles engender depression for both sexes but that the sexes differ in how they express and cope with low self-esteem.

*Gender Differences in Empathy and Related Emotional Responses.* The degree to which males and females have been found to differ in empathy varies with the definition of empathy and the methods used to assess empathy. In early reviews of gender differences in empathy, J. H. Block (1976) and Maccoby and Jacklin (1974) concluded that there was no evidence of a gender difference. However, these reviewers used a broad definition of empathy and did not differentiate among various related emotional and cognitive capacities (e.g., role taking, social sensitivity, vicarious responding). Moreover, they compared studies in which empathy was assessed in a number of different ways.

In another review, M. L. Hoffman (1977) differentiated between studies in which empathy was defined as an emotional response and those in which empathy was defined as role taking or social sensitivity. Hoffman (1977) concluded that girls are more affectively empathic than are boys. However, most of the data Hoffman reviewed were obtained from studies involving a picture-story measure of empathy (a measure in which children hear stories about others in emotionally evocative situations and then are asked how they themselves feel), and more recent studies have cast doubt on the validity of such measures of empathy. For example, Lennon, Eisenberg, and Carroll (1986) found that children's scores on picture-story measures of empathy were significantly higher when the experimenter was the same sex as the child. Because female experimenters have been used in most research on children's empathy involving picture-story measures, the higher scores of girls may be a function of their responsiveness to a same-sex experimenter. Indeed, Eisenberg and Lennon (1983) found a very large association between the effect size of the gender difference in such studies and sex of the experimenter.

In other reviews of gender differences in empathy, Eisenberg and Lennon (1983; Lennon & Eisenberg, 1987) found that the pattern of results varied as a function of the methods used to assess empathy. In Eisenberg and Lennon's reviews, empathy was defined as emotional matching with another's emotional state or condition or sympathetic concern. There were large differences favoring females for self-report measures of empathy, especially questionnaire indices. However, no gender differences were found when the measure of empathy was either physiological or unobtrusive observations of nonverbal behavior. Eisenberg and Lennon suggested that this pattern of results was due to differences among measures in the degree to which both the intent of the measure was obvious and individuals could control their responses. Differences were greatest when demand characteristics were high (i.e., it was clear what was being assessed) and participants had conscious control over their responses (i.e., self-report indices were used); gender differences were virtually nonexistent when demand characteristics were subtle *and* subjects were unlikely to exercise much conscious control over their responding (i.e., physiological indices). Thus, when gender-related stereotypes are activated and people can easily control their responses, they may try to project a socially desirable image to others or to themselves (see Eisenberg & Fabes, 1995).

Investigators have attempted to differentiate between two responses that are likely to stem from empathic processes; sympathy (other-oriented concern) and personal distress (self-focused feelings of anxiety or discomfort in reaction to another's emotional state or condition; Eisenberg, 1986). In this work, investigators frequently have found modest self-reported gender differences in sympathy and personal distress in reaction to empathy-inducing stimuli (females tend to report more), occasional differences in facial reactions (generally favoring females), and virtually no gender differences in heart rate findings (see Eisenberg, Fabes, Schaller, & P. A. Miller, 1989; Eisenberg, Fabes, & Shea, 1989). Additionally, skin conductance (viewed as a marker of personal distress) in response to empathy-inducing films appears to be higher for third- and sixth-grade girls and women (Eisenberg, Fabes, Schaller, Carlo, & P. A. Miller, 1991; Eisenberg, Fabes, Schaller, P. A. Miller, et al., 1991) than for their male peers, but gender differences in skin conductance slightly favored males when participants viewed a film that elicited more personal distress than sympathy (Fabes et al., 1994). Overall, the pattern of findings suggests that females are slightly more likely than males to evince sympathy, but the differences are quite weak (except for questionnaire measures) and dependent on method of measurement and context.

What might be the origins of any gender difference in vicarious emotional responding? Gender differences in empathy-related behaviors have been noted at an early age (M. L. Hoffman, 1977) and may in part be biologically based (Matthews, Batson, Horn, & Rosenman, 1981). Zahn-Waxler, Robinson, and Emde (1992) found a significant gender difference in children's empathy (favoring girls) at both 14 and 20 months of life. Greater concordance between monozygotic than dizygotic

twins for empathic concern and for unresponsive behavior was evident at both 14 and 20 months of age; for self-related distress reactions, heritability seemed somewhat weaker at 20 months than at 14 months of age.

In addition, there is evidence that parents socialize their daughters to be more emotionally responsive than their sons. As noted previously, J. H. Block (1973, 1979) found that parents reported greater insistence on the control of feelings and their expression for their sons, whereas they tended to emphasize maintenance of closer emotional relationships, emotional responsivity, verbal discussion of emotions, and physical displays of affection for their daughters. These and related findings may account in part for gender differences in empathy and related vicarious emotional responses.

Interestingly, parental practices associated with girls' and boy's sympathy also may differ. For boys, parental emphasis on controlling emotion seems to be associated with high levels of personal distress and low levels of sympathy, whereas an emphasis on instrumentally dealing with situations that cause the child's negative emotions has been associated with sympathy in response to another's distress (Eisenberg, Fabes, Schaller, Carlo, et al., 1991). For girls, however, the degree to which soft, submissive negative emotions (e.g., feelings of loss, apologizing) are expressed in the home and sympathetic feelings and behaviors are reinforced has been correlated with sympathy (Eisenberg, Fabes, Schaller, P. A. Miller, et al., 1991; Eisenberg et al., 1992). Thus, parental practices that do not inhibit empathy and that teach sons how to regulate their emotion seem to be associated with sons' sympathy, whereas encouragement to be expressive may promote girls' sympathy.

## Gender Differences in Prosocial and Aggressive Behavior

Aggression and prosocial behavior are two socially relevant behaviors that have been of great interest to psychologists in the past two decades. Interestingly, both have been gender typed, with females viewed as more prosocial and less aggressive. However, the gender differences in these behaviors, especially the former, are not as great as many believe.

*Gender Differences in Prosocial Behavior.* Because empathy or sympathy generally is viewed as a determinant of prosocial behavior (i.e., voluntary behaviors intended to benefit others, such as helping, comforting, and sharing), it is not surprising that females frequently are characterized as more nurturant, supportive, and helpful than are males. Such a stereotype is consistent with the view that females play a more communal and expressive role in the family and society (J. H. Block, 1973; T. Parsons & Bales, 1955), especially in the role of mother.

Despite the stereotype, no gender differences in prosocial responding have been found in the majority of studies of children. However, when gender differences in childhood have been observed, they are somewhat more likely to favor girls (see Radke-Yarrow, Zahn-Waxler, & Chapman, 1983; Underwood & Moore, 1982), particularly when children are explicitly given responsibility for caretaking of infants (Berman, 1980, 1987).

It is likely that, to some extent, the results favoring girls are artifactual. The stereotype that females are more altruistic than boys is widely accepted; girls tend to be viewed as much more prosocial than boys by peers and teachers, even if they are only moderately more prosocial in their actual behavior (Shigetomi, Hartmann, & Gelfand, 1981). Thus, reports by socializers and peers regarding children's prosocial and sympathetic tendencies may be biased in a stereotype-consistent direction (Fabes, Eisenberg, & Eisenbud, 1993). In addition, some research techniques used with children include reports or ratings of behaviors or traits that are more characteristic of girls than boys (such as comforting a younger, injured child), with the consequence that girls score higher. When more masculine modes of prosocial behavior are included in such measures, boys are likely to report more prosocial behavior than are girls (Zarabatany et al., 1985).

Indeed, in research concerning adults' helping behaviors in laboratory or natural settings, males have been found to be more helpful than females (Eagly & Crowley, 1986). This probably is because these studies frequently have involved instrumental, rescuing actions such as helping to change tires, potential danger (for example, picking up hitchhikers), or chivalrous behavior. In situations involving psychological assistance and helping friends and acquaintances, women may be more likely to assist (Aries & F. L. Johnson, 1983; Bem, Martyna, & Watson, 1976; F. Johnson & Aries, 1983), perhaps because of the association between expressivity or femininity and helping in nonemergency situations (Eisenberg, Schaller, et al., 1988).

The aforementioned gender differences may be due to several different factors. For example, child-rearing techniques used with girls (e.g., greater affection and reasoning, and less power-assertive discipline from mothers; M. L. Hoffman, 1975; Lytton & Romney, 1991) may promote sympathetic and supportive behaviors. Furthermore, in many cultures helpfulness and nurturance of known others are considered more appropriate for girls than for boys (B. B. Whiting and J. W. M. Whiting, 1975), and girls are more frequently and more strongly rewarded for such behavior by socializers (Fagot, 1978b; Power & Shanks, 1989; Power & Parke, 1986). In contrast, it is likely that boys are more frequently reinforced for instrumental helping behaviors, especially those that involve some risk or helping females. The masculine role is viewed as more instrumental (T. Parsons & Bales, 1955; J. H. Block, 1983; Spence, 1984), and parents seem to be more concerned with socializing their sons to be autonomous than prosocial (Power & Shanks, 1989).

*Gender Differences in Aggression.* It is commonly believed that males are more aggressive than females (e.g., I. K. Broverman et al., 1972; Cione & Ruble, 1978; Spence & Helmreich, 1978). This perception has been supported in numerous reviews of children's (J. H. Block, 1983; Hyde, 1986; Maccoby & Jacklin, 1974, 1980) and adults' (Eagly & Steffen, 1986; Frodi, Macaulay, & Thome, 1977; Macaulay, 1985) aggression, as well as by data on conduct disorders (Offord, Boyle, & Racine, 1991). The gender difference is particularly strong for children's provoked aggression (B. B. Whiting & Edwards, 1973; see Parke & Slaby, 1983). Inconsistent findings have been reported regarding age differences in the degree to which males and females differ in aggression. Hyde (1984, 1986) reported that gender differences in aggression *decreased* with age. In contrast, Knight et al. (in press), using more complex analyses, found a *positive* relation between age and gender differences in aggression. Thus, caution should be used in drawing

firm conclusions about the nature of gender differences across age.

Despite the consistency of findings indicating that males are more aggressive than females, the amount of variance in aggression accounted for by gender is small. For example, Hyde (1984) found that gender accounted for about 7 percent of the variance in young children and only about 1 percent in adults. Further, it is possible that part of the gender difference in aggression obtained in research is due to observer biases. Lyons and Serbin (1986) found that some adults (a minority) tended to rate children in drawings as more aggressive if they were depicted as boys rather than girls. In another study, adults who saw two children playing roughly viewed the play as relatively nonaggressive if they were told the children were both boys, suggesting that although people expect boys to be more aggressive, they are likely to view boys' aggression during play as simply "roughhousing" (J. C. Condry & Ross, 1985). If people minimize boys' aggression, it is possible that the gender difference is underestimated if the aggression occurs during play.

Indeed, the size of gender differences in aggression may vary as a function of whether the behavior observed is real aggression or play aggression, such as rough-and-tumble play. Among mammals, males frequently engage in more play fighting (aggression characterized by lack of seriousness), and this gender difference seems to be affected by perinatal androgens (Meaney, Hood, & Draper, 1985). However, such play fighting does not seem to be directly associated with a gender difference in real aggression; rather, gender differences in play aggression seem to be linked with gender differences in dominance-related behaviors (Meaney et al., 1985). Thus, both the frequency and origins of rough-and-tumble play and hostile aggression may differ. Because of the rarity of true aggression at any age, it is likely that much of the observed gender difference in children's aggression is due to a difference in play aggression.

In addition, the degree to which gender differences in aggression have been found varies with method of study as well as context. For example, Hyde (1984) found that gender differences tended to be larger in naturalistic correlational studies than in experimental studies and when the measure was direct observation, a projective test, or peer report. Differences were smaller when self-reports, parent reports, or teacher reports were obtained. In studies with adults, Eagly and Steffen (1986) found that men were more aggressive than women, particularly when aggression produced pain or physical injury rather than psychological or social harm. Gender differences were also larger to the extent that women, more than men, believed their aggression would produce harm to the target, guilt, anxiety in oneself, or danger to oneself. The belief by females that aggression is likely to result in guilt and negative consequences to self and others appears to develop fairly easily; among fourth to seventh graders, girls expect more guilt, more peer and parental disapproval, more harm to the victim, and fewer material gains for aggression than do boys (D. G. Perry, L. C. Perry, & Rasmussen, 1986; D. G. Perry, L. C. Perry, & Weiss, 1989). Indeed, by mid- to late elementary school, boys are more concerned than girls with controlling the victim of aggression and less concerned with the victim's suffering, retaliation, peer rejection, or negative self-evaluations (Boldizar, D. G. Perry, & L. C. Perry, 1989). They also are more likely than girls to believe that aggression increases self-esteem (Slaby & Guerra, 1988).

Boys seek and process information related to aggressive contexts differently than girls. For example, elementary school and adolescent males are somewhat more likely than their female peers to focus on perceived hostility and attribute hostility to others (Slaby & Guerra, 1988; M. Steinberg & Dodge, 1983), although this difference may be due to there being a disproportionate number of males among extremely aggressive children. Moreover, when problem solving about situations involving potential conflict, adolescent girls are more likely than boys to ask for more facts and to choose effective solutions to the problem (Slaby & Guerra, 1988; also see Rabiner, Lenhart, & Lochman, 1990).

The origins of the gender difference in aggression probably are both biological and environmental (see Ghodsian-Carpey & Baker, 1987; Lytton, 1990). As argued by Maccoby and Jacklin (1974); the finding of greater aggression among men is consistent across most (if not all) cultures. Moreover, although the research is inconclusive in humans (see Olweus, 1986; Tieger, 1980), there seems to be some evidence of a role for hormones in animal aggression (Maccoby & Jacklin, 1980; see, however, Tieger, 1980). Lytton (1990), citing data on autonomic nervous system and biochemical influences, drug treatment, and behavioral genetics, has argued that conduct disorders (which show a 4:1 male/female ratio [American Psychiatric Association, 1987]), are at least partially due to biological factors. The biological roots of gender differences in aggression could contribute to gender differences in empathy in the early years (Zahn-Waxler et al., 1992), which could result in young males being less inhibited in their aggression by vicarious feedback (see P. A. Miller & Eisenberg, 1988). Additionally, gender differences in strength, reactivity to pain (Lipsitt & N. Levy, 1959; see Lytton, 1990), or temperamental characteristics such as activity level could contribute to gender differences in aggression. For example, given the higher activity level of males than females in infancy and childhood (Eaton & Enns, 1986), boys may be more likely than girls to provoke conflict and may prefer activities in which aggression is relatively likely to occur (indeed, boys do seem to prefer aggression-conducive activities more than do girls; Bullock & Merrill, 1980).

It is doubtful, however, that biological differences account for most of the gender differences in aggression. As noted previously, girls and boys expect different psychological, material, and social consequences for aggression (D. G. Perry et al., 1986, 1989). Thus, boys and girls perceive differences in how their parents and peers react to their aggression. Moreover, it appears that teachers and peers are more likely to ignore toddler girls' assertive and aggressive behaviors, and ignoring girls' aggression serves to terminate the behavior more quickly (Fagot & Hagan, 1985; Fagot, Hagan, Leinbach, & Kronsberg, 1985). Thus, at a young age, girls may learn to expect fewer aggressive outcomes. Further, the greater availability of aggressive males may promote higher levels of aggression among boys.

In a recent review, Lytton and Romney (1991) did not find that parents discouraged girls' aggression significantly more than boys' aggression. However, this review may be biased by the fact that most of the studies reviewed involved relatively young children; thus, it is likely that the parental reactions assessed in these studies frequently were to play aggression rather than hostile aggression. It is also possible that aggression is shaped in large part by peers, siblings, and nonfamilial adults, or is influenced in subtle ways (e.g., by ignoring) rather than by direct discouragement. Further, it is likely that parental emphasis on ladylike behavior counteracts aggression in girls (J. H. Block, 1983). In addition, parents discourage some types of boys' aggression (e.g., that directed toward the parent; J. H. Block, 1979), and many investigators who have examined socialization of aggression have not differentiated among various modes, such as play and real aggression, and the targets of boys' and girls' aggression. Moreover, parental encouragement of boys' physical play or the use of gender-typed toys such as guns (Lytton & Romney, 1991; Maccoby & Jacklin, 1974) may promote aggression (Parke & Slaby, 1983).

Finally, the potential role of the child in his or her own socialization should be noted. As discussed previously, children frequently try to behave in gender-consistent ways; boys would be expected to actively select masculine models and masculine activities, many of which may facilitate aggressive responding.

## Social Competence and Friendships

Given the greater tendency of boys to aggress, it perhaps is not surprising that girls often are viewed as more socially competent than boys (Cohn, 1990; Eisenberg et al., 1992), although children tend to prefer and trust same-sex peers more than other-sex peers (e.g., Feltham, Doyle, Schwartzman, Serbin, & Ledingham, 1985; Hallinan, 1981; Rotenberg, 1984; Singleton & Asher, 1977, 1979). Boys may be viewed as less socially competent than girls because of the nature of children's social interactions. In comparison to girls, boys generally tend to have more disagreements and to be more controlling and less cooperative in peer interactions and in their discourse with peers (Berndt, T. B. Perry, & K. E. Miller, 1988; Cohn, 1990; Gavin & Furman, 1989; Leaper, 1991). Also, boys' play tends to be more aggressive, rough, and oriented toward dominance (De-Pietro, 1981; Maccoby, 1986; Schofield, 1981), and their friendships with other boys involve more conflict and competition than do same-sex female friendships (Berndt & T. B. Perry, 1986; Fabes, Eisenberg, Smith, & Murphy, in press; Hartup, 1989). These findings are consistent with those for adults indicating that men are less concerned than women with interpersonal harmony and more concerned with obtaining personal rewards in games and contests (Kahn, Nelson, & Gaeddert, 1980).

The nature of girls' and boys' friendships and social interactions appears to differ in additional ways. Girls' friendships are more likely than boys' to be characterized by a relatively high level of intimacy (Crockett, Losoff, & Petersen, 1984; Foot, Chapman, & J. R. Smith, 1977; Furman & Buhrmester, 1985; Hunter & Youniss, 1982; Lempers & Clark-Lempers, 1993; Papini, Farmer, Clark, Micka, & Barnett, 1990). For example, girls seek intimate disclosure in their friendships at younger ages than do boys and place more value on companionship (Buhrmester & Furman, 1987). Further, lower-class girls (but not middle-class girls; Pellegrini, 1985, 1986; Selman, 1980) may reason in a more sophisticated manner than their male peers about friendship (Keller & Wood, 1989).

The structural nature of boys' and girls' peer networks also may differ. As noted previously, girls are observed in pairs more often than boys, whereas boys tend more often to congregate in larger groups (see Maccoby & Jacklin, 1974). Studies on the size of girls' and boys' networks of friends (i.e., number of friends) are inconsistent; researchers generally find either no difference or more friends for girls (e.g., Benenson, 1990; Blyth, Hill, & Thiel, 1982; Feiring & M. Lewis, 1991b).

Social status (or the lack thereof) may have different behavioral and sociocognitive correlates for boys and girls. For example, aggressive behavior is more highly related to peer rejection for boys than girls, whereas social withdrawal and low levels of social participation are more closely linked to peer rejection for girls (Coie, Dodge, & Kupersmidt, 1990; Dodge & Feldman, 1990). For boys, position in the peer group or dominance seems to be linked to acceptance by peers (Benenson, 1990; Maccoby, 1986), whereas for girls, characteristics of the social network, including the friendship network (e.g., number of friends and frequency of contact), have been correlated with social competence (Feiring & M. Lewis, 1991a, 1991b). Dodge and Feldman (1990) hypothesized that sociocognitive skills related to aggression (e.g., attributional biases in regard to perceived hostility) discriminate social status more strongly among boys, whereas sociocognitive skills related to cooperativeness and helpfulness (e.g., perspective taking) more strongly differentiate girls. Consistent with this prediction, Custrini and Feldman (1989) found that the ability to decode and encode facial expressions was associated with girls', but not boys', social competence. Thus, different social behaviors and sociocognitive skills appear to be linked to boys' and girls' social status.

## Gender Differences in Help Seeking and Reactions to Aid

Given the gender stereotypes regarding dependency, it is not surprising that girls generally are more comfortable seeking help and have been more likely than boys to report feeling that it was important to seek help (DePaulo, 1978; Northman, 1978). This pattern of findings is consistent with the adult data: Women are more often the recipients of help (Eagly & Crowley, 1986) and are more likely to accept help (DePaulo, 1978; McMullen & Gross, 1983; Searcy & Eisenberg, 1992). However, the tendency of females to seek more help may be confined primarily to assistance with personal or emotional problems, with men being willing to seek help of an instrumental or informational nature (Nadler, 1991).

Although elementary schoolgirls generally are perceived by their peers as more competent academically, children prefer help from same-sex peers (Nelson-Le Gall & De Cooke, 1987). Moreover, girls, more than boys, prefer advice on non-academic problems from a familiar peer, at least until age 17, whereas 8-year-old boys, in comparison to girls, prefer advice from a peer they do not know well but who has had the same problem. In addition, boys cite knowledge as a reason for their choice of consultant, whereas girls cite familiarity (Wintre, Hicks, McVey, & Fox, 1988).

In a study of academic help seeking, Newman and Goldin (1990) found that girls were more concerned than boys that a teacher, in comparison with a classmate, would think they were dumb when they asked a question. This gender difference occurred only in regard to math class, not reading. If girls are more reluctant to ask their teacher for assistance with math, they may not perform as well as males in math in the future. More generally, gender differences in seeking help in academic settings may have important long-term implications

because some modes of instrumental help may foster children's skills and independence by facilitating future successes (see Nelson-Le Gall, 1981; Shell & Eisenberg, 1992). Thus, gender differences in help seeking, which have not been frequently examined, are an important topic of further study.

## The Complex Dynamics of Gender Differences and Gender Influences: The Case of Puberty

Based on the evidence reviewed to this point regarding gender differences, it is clear that whatever differences do exist often are subtle and that their causes are complex. Indeed, it is unlikely that a simplistic, unidimensional explanatory model of gender differences, whether biological, social, or psychological, will be adequate. It also is likely that developmental processes influence males and females in different ways. Because of space limitations, we have not specifically focused on differential patterns of development or the origins of the developmental course of various social, emotional, or academic abilities or behaviors. As a way of illustrating these dynamic and complex influences, we now turn to a discussion of puberty, focusing particularly on how pubertal timing may be related to social, familial, and psychological changes that could differentially affect males and females. We chose to focus on puberty and the period of early adolescence because of the evidence that boys and girls diverge in development during early adolescence (Hill & Holmbeck, 1986; Maccoby & Jacklin, 1974), and because changes related to puberty can impact boys' and girls' educational achievement and performance (e.g., pregnancy is one of the primary reasons adolescents drop out of school; Alan Guttmacher Institute, 1981). Moreover, the differential impact of pubertal timing on males and females has been a popular theme in adolescent research (e.g., Brooks-Gunn & Petersen, 1983; Hill & Lynch, 1983).

Because males and females differ in their rates of pubertal changes, with girls developing earlier than boys by approximately 2 years (Tanner, 1972), and because of the lack of parallel pubertal changes (especially females' experience of menarche and subsequent concerns regarding pregnancy; see Strouse & Fabes, 1988), the dynamics associated with puberty may differ by gender. For example, researchers (e.g., L. Steinberg, 1981; Papini & Sebby, 1987) have examined familial adaptations to biological changes at adolescence and have found that family interactions change during the early period of pubertal growth. Mothers and sons interrupted each other more often and explained themselves less often during this period. These differences increased as the son moved toward pubertal apex. Influence within the family also shifted, with the mother losing influence and the son gaining influence. For daughters, in the first few months after menarche, there is less equalitarian treatment and less participation in family activities (Hill, Holmbeck, Marlow, Green, & Lynch, 1985), and these stresses and strains are particularly likely to persist in families with early-maturing girls. Thus, when menarche occurs around the modal time, changes in parent–child relations appear to be the result of temporary adaptational perturbations. However, when menarche occurs early, the perturbations persist and there is more parent–daughter conflict (Hill et al., 1985).

Generally, it is hypothesized that because girls who mature

early do so *much* earlier than most of their peers, and boys who mature later do so *much* later, these two groups are likely to be at risk for difficulties in social and psychological adjustment. Some empirical support for this hypothesis has been found. For example, some researchers have found that later maturing males and early-maturing females are more likely to receive negative peer and adult evaluations than are early-maturing males or maturationally on-time females (e.g., Peskin, 1973; Tobin-Richards, Boxer, & Petersen, 1983). Moreover, early maturation in males has been found to be positively correlated with sociability, popularity, and athletic ability (e.g., Rutter, 1980; Tanner, 1972). In contrast, early maturation for girls has been associated with undue self-consciousness, introversion, anxiety, and embarrassment (e.g., Peskin, 1975; Tanner, 1972). However, other researchers have failed to find that pubertal status interacts with gender (Simmons, Blyth, & McKinney, 1983; Udry & Talbert, 1988), and findings from recent studies suggest that gender-differentiated effects of pubertal timing are specific rather than global (Petersen & Crockett, 1985) and are influenced by a variety of processes (e.g., sociocultural factors; R. M. Lerner, 1981, 1985).

Importantly, the onset of sexual activity in adolescence is closely linked to pubertal timing, and adolescents who mature early initiate sexual activity at younger ages than their peers (Aro & Taipale, 1987; E. Smith, Udry, & Morris, 1985). The hormonal changes at puberty increase an adolescent's sex drive, interest in sex, and sexual arousal (Udry, 1987; Udry, Talbert, & Morris, 1986). Early sexual activity has also been linked to various problem-related behaviors such as delinquency, truancy, and substance abuse (R. Jessor, Costa, L. Jessor, & Donovan, 1983; Newcomer & Udry, 1987). Moreover, because younger adolescents are less likely than older adolescents to use contraception or to use it efficiently (Zelnik & Kantner, 1977), they are more at risk for an unintentional pregnancy. Thus, young adolescents who are sexually active are more likely to have problems with school or to drop out than are their peers.

Differences in rates of physical maturation and puberty may interact with gender roles. That is, girls who mature early may be viewed by peers (and others) as potentially sexually active or promiscuous, and the increased anxiety and shyness associated with early maturation for girls may be the result of the increased attention they receive as the objects of male sexual and romantic interests. Thus, there exists a negative stereotype that carries potentially detrimental effects on the social status and self-esteem for girls who achieve puberty at relatively early ages. In contrast, boys who mature early are taller and stronger than late-maturing boys. Early-maturing boys also are likely to be better at sports than late-maturing boys (Rutter, 1980), bolstering their popularity and self-esteem. It is plausible that the stereotyped bias in favor of the mature appearance of boys and the prejudicial bias against the overt sexual appearance of girls have powerful and differential effects for each sex.

The picture painted by these findings regarding pubertal timing and psychosocial development for male and female adolescents is a complex one. As a consequence of changes in the physical maturity of the adolescent, they receive differential reactions from socializing agents (parents, teachers, peers). This feedback varies as a function of the gender of the adolescent, the timing of puberty, the attitudes, values, and stereotypes held by social agents, and contextual demands (e.g., home versus school). In turn, this feedback provides a basis for further development and social interaction. Such a model suggests that by bringing different physical characteristics with them into a situation (such as those associated with puberty or other characteristics such as physical attractiveness), adolescents affect how others react to them, which then is linked to different psychosocial outcomes (including educationally related outcomes). The bidirectional nature of this interactional model is useful for understanding how diverse characteristics of a child or adolescent may help to create a unique or distinctive developmental milieu, which in turn provides a basis for greater interindividual differences and outcomes (R. M. Lerner, 1985).

## SUMMARY AND FUTURE DIRECTIONS

In this chapter, we have reviewed a variety of seemingly disparate topics, including the development of gender identity, knowledge, and gender-role behavior, gender differences in academic skills, and gender differences in social behavior, socioemotional, and sociocognitive responding. Although these topics may seem unconnected, there are many links among them. As children spend time with same-sex peers and develop gender-role behaviors, they may be increasingly likely to behave in a manner consistent with some of the gender differences noted previously in the academic and social domains. For example, a girl with a feminine identity and a clear understanding of what is considered feminine behavior in the culture may be relatively likely to learn from female models, shy away from math courses, avoid aggressive encounters, and express emotions such as sadness and fear. Such a child might dress in a more feminine manner and thus be treated differently than less feminine girls by adults, with the consequence that stereotypically feminine patterns of behavior may be reinforced. In general, then, the development of children's early gender-related conceptions and behaviors may serve as a foundation, although not a determinant, for a variety of gender-related preferences and behaviors.

As is evident from this review, there is still much that we do not know about gender-related development and gender differences in academic and social functioning. For example, frequently there are questions regarding the contexts in which observed gender differences are most likely to be displayed and the factors that might inhibit gender-linked behavior. Moreover, there is considerable controversy about the "facts" in regard to many gender differences and the origins (e.g., biological or environmental) of even the few well-established differences. Nonetheless, it is clear that children's gender-related development is multifaceted and complex, and that it influences a variety of children's social, emotional, moral, and academic behaviors. It is equally obvious that ignoring the variable of gender in research often merely creates an illusion of simplicity; frequently the process of development, if not the final outcome, differs for males and females (see our previous discussion of puberty). Given the many questions that remain to be answered, what are some of the more interesting and pressing issues in the area of sex and gender?

## Gender Differences: The Question of Variability

Several important questions have to do with the issue of variability. For example, most of the analyses regarding differences between males and females in cognitive, educational, and social abilities have been focused on gender differences in measures of central tendency (e.g., means). However, the possibility that males and females differ in variability remains an unanswered and debated topic (e.g., Feingold, 1992; Noddings, 1992; Shields, 1975). If males and females differ in variability, the more variable gender might be overrepresented at both the high and low levels of performance where the average scores of males and females are the same. Maccoby and Jacklin (1974) compared males and females for variability and concluded that males were more variable than females in mathematical and spatial abilities, but there were no differences in variability in verbal ability. Feingold (1992) recently confirmed Maccoby and Jacklin's conclusions. Thus, gender differences may vary in magnitude as the level of performance changes (e.g., greater gender differences at the extremes). As such, gender differences in both central tendency and in variability may need to be considered together to fully understand the differences between male and female distributions in cognitive and social abilities.

When a gender difference is found, it may become dichotomized and universalized; that is, it may come to be seen as characteristic of most (if not all) members of one gender group and not a characteristic of the other group (Crawford, 1989). To counteract this tendency, it is important to remember that variability within gender groups is typically *much* larger than variability between gender groups. Further, it is important to acknowledge that characteristics may be attributed to groups even when very few members of a group actually have the characteristic. For example, most studies show a mean difference in aggression, with boys on the average being more aggressive than girls (Maccoby & Jacklin, 1974). There is probably a relatively small group of boys who operate at a high level of aggression that is practically never seen in girls. This behavior then comes to be labeled as "boylike" even though it does not characterize a majority of boys. Characteristics such as aggression may be highly diagnostic and differentiating of the sexes, thereby providing some kernel of truth to gender stereotypes, and yet they may not be present in even most of the members of one sex (Martin & Halverson, 1981).

Rather than limiting their focus to identifying gender differences, researchers are beginning to search in more depth for the causes of these differences, with particular emphasis on defining some of the smaller subgroups within (and across) gender groups that may contribute to findings of a gender difference. For example, Halverson (pers. comm., June 1990) found that young girls and boys differed on several major dimensions such as activity level and impulsivity. Closer examination of his findings, however, revealed that only a small subset of children contributed to the gender difference. Children with a high number of congenital markers of anomalous central nervous system functioning accounted for the gender differences. That is, boys with high numbers of minor physical anomalies were extremely active, whereas girls with high numbers of minor anomalies were extremely inactive. No gender differences were found for children with low numbers of these con-

genital markers. Future researchers need to continue to explore issues of variability to better understand the meaning of gender differences as well as variations within the sexes.

## Gender and Self-Regulation

A construct of particular relevance to many of the gender issues raised in the data presented above is self-regulation, particularly emotional and behavioral regulation. Males frequently score lower than females in regulation, delay of gratification, and related measures (perhaps more so for elementary than preschool children; e.g., J. H. Block & J. Block, 1980; Olson, 1989; Weinberger, 1991; Zuckerman, Kuhlman, & Camac, 1988). Further, individual differences in regulatory capabilities or styles have been linked with a variety of socially and academically relevant behaviors. For example, J. H. Block and J. Block (1980) found that younger children's undercontrol was associated with a rapid personal tempo and restlessness; aggression; teasing of others, low delay of gratification, and overreactivity to frustration; sociability and low levels of shyness; low levels of prosocial and cooperative behavior; jealousy and crying; lack of obedience, compliance, and planfulness; regression under stress; and inattentiveness and inability to concentrate. In other studies, lack of impulse control and low self-regulation also have been associated with aggression, anger, and inability to delay behavior (e.g., Olson, 1989; Olweus, 1980; Pierce & Campbell, 1991; Pulkkinen, 1986; Silverman & Ragusa, 1990), negative self-perceptions (Wagner, Rohrbeck, & Tangney, 1991; Weinberger, 1991; Wentzel, Feldman, & Weinberger, 1991), and low social competence (Eisenberg, Fabes, Bernzweig, et al., 1993; Olson, 1989; Wagner et al., 1991), although some of these associations may be weaker for adolescents than younger children (particularly for girls; J. H. Block & Gjerde, 1986). In addition, high self-restraint and self-control have been correlated with positive academic outcomes such as high test scores, grades, and school motivation (Wagner et al., 1991; Wentzel et al., 1991; Wentzel, Weinberger, Ford, & Feldman, 1990).

There currently seems to be renewed interest in constructs related to regulation in developmental, personality, and clinical psychology (e.g., in the work on coping, emotion, temperament, and behavior problems; see Eisenberg & Fabes, 1992). Based on the findings just reviewed and on the assumed role of regulation in many important capabilities, it seems quite possible that many of the gender differences in social and academic outcomes discussed in this chapter are due in part to gender differences in the regulation of emotion and behavior. For example, Fabes (1994) has discussed the role that gender differences in arousability and regulation may play in influencing boys' and girls' peer preferences. In addition, the gender differences in rates of depression noted previously may be due in part to differences in males' and females' *styles* of regulating emotion (as well as amount of regulation). Thus, the topic of regulation appears to be a fruitful one for researchers who wish to understand better a variety of gender differences.

## Changing Gender Roles

Over the last 20 years, the attitudes of social scientists and, to some extent, of the lay public toward traditional gender roles have changed drastically. Rather than the ideal goal of socialization being to raise a feminine daughter and a masculine son, the emergence of the concept of androgyny has suggested that the ideal goal of socialization should be to raise a child with a wide repertoire of behavioral competencies. Psychologists have embraced the androgyny ideal with greater fervor than the lay public. Some researchers have outlined suggestions to parents to help them raise children who are not bound by gender-related standards (see Bem, 1983). Nonetheless, many adults still believe that traditional roles are better for children, particularly for their sons. Also, many adults are apprehensive about encouraging any type of gender-atypical behavior. For instance, university students report that they fear that boys, but not girls, who engage in cross-sex behaviors will grow up to be psychologically maladjusted and are more likely to be homosexual (Martin, 1990). Researchers need to further address what individuals believe the consequences of gender-atypical upbringing to be, how these beliefs develop, and how they affect people's behaviors and interactions with children. Additionally, we know very little about the effects of nontraditional gender-typed child rearing on children and their families.

Another controversial topic worthy of additional attention is the question as to the specific type of desired change in gender roles (Huston, 1983). One suggestion is that we reduce gender differences by striving for the androgynous ideal. Another suggestion is to encourage balance by changing the ways in which the sexes and their corresponding traditional roles are valued. For instance, if we could increase the value associated with the feminine role, perhaps both males and females would be more accepting and more encouraging of feminine behaviors such as nurturance. Others have suggested that a much more dramatic shift must occur such that gender becomes an irrelevant dimension, not just balanced, in our society (Lorber, 1986).

In addition to practical concerns over how changes in gender roles might occur, there are also ethical issues about encouraging any type of gender-related change. Most of the ethical concerns have been raised in regard to intervention with "gender-deviant" children. The controversy centers on whether individuals who deviate from social norms should be blamed when instead it may be the norms that are faulty (see Huston, 1983). Concerns also can be raised in regard to trying to socialize children to fit gender-atypical patterns when those patterns are not accepted by society at large. Researchers and practitioners need to be aware of these ethical concerns when considering how change can be accomplished within a culture.

## A Final Note

The research on gender differences and gender effects summarized in this chapter is neither uniform in its focus nor easily summarized. In many areas findings are inconclusive, reflecting differences across studies in the types of measures, designs, and the sheer number of relevant variables included in the studies. Moreover, as noted previously, often the studies were not specifically designed to examine questions related to gender, and many have lacked a theoretical basis (Brody, 1985). Nevertheless, it appears fair to say that contemporary researchers are making progress in providing greater insight into the complex nature of gender-related development and sex differences, and how these processes and differences might influence school-related behaviors. Thus, the many roles of gender and gender-related processes in and out of school represent important areas for continued research and development of theory.

## References

Alan Guttmacher Institute. (1981). *Teenage pregnancy: The problem that hasn't gone away.* New York: Planned Parenthood Federation of America.

Allen, J. G., & Haccoun, D. M. (1976). Sex differences in emotionality: A multi-dimensional approach. *Human Relations, 29,* 711–720.

American Psychiatric Association. (1987). *Diagnostic and statistical manual of mental disorders* (3rd ed., rev.). Washington, DC: American Psychiatric Association.

Antill, J. K. (1987). Parents' beliefs and values about sex roles, sex differences, and sexuality: Their sources and implications. In P. Shaver & C. Hendrick (Eds.), *Review of personality and social psychology: Sex and gender* (Vol. 7, pp. 294–328). Newbury Park, CA: Sage.

Archer, S. L., & Waterman, A. S. (1988). Psychological individualism: Gender differences or gender neutrality? *Human Development, 31,* 65–81.

Aries, E. J., & Johnson, F. L. (1983). Close friendship in adulthood: Conversational content between same-sex friends. *Sex Roles, 9,* 1183–1196.

Aro, H., & Taipale, V. (1987). The impact of timing of puberty on psychosomatic symptoms among fourteen- to sixteen-year-old Finnish girls. *Child Development, 58,* 261–268.

Baenninger, M., & Newcombe, N. (1989). The role of experience in spatial test performance: A meta-analysis. *Sex Roles, 20,* 327–344.

Bandura, A. (1977). *Social learning theory.* Englewood Cliffs, NJ: Prentice Hall.

Bandura, A. (1986). *Social foundations of thought and action: A social cognitive theory.* Englewood Cliffs, NJ: Prentice Hall.

Basow, S. A. (1990). Effects of teacher expressiveness: Mediated by teacher sex-typing? *Journal of Educational Psychology, 82,* 599–602.

Baumrind, D. (1973). The development of instrumental competence through socialization. In A. Pick (Ed.), *Minnesota Symposium on Child Development* (Vol. 7, pp. 3–45). Minneapolis: University of Minnesota Press.

Baumrind, D. (1986). Sex differences in moral reasoning: Response to Walker's (1984) conclusion that there are none. *Child Development, 57,* 511–521.

Beal, C. R., & Lockhart, M. E. (1989). The effect of proper name and appearance changes on children's reasoning about gender constancy. *International Journal of Behavioral Development, 12,* 195–205.

Bem, S. L. (1974). The measurement of psychological androgyny. *Journal of Consulting and Clinical Psychology, 42,* 155–162.

Bem, S. L. (1975). Sex role adaptability: One consequence of psychological androgyny. *Journal of Personality and Social Psychology, 31,* 634–643.

Bem, S. L. (1981). Gender schema theory: A cognitive account of sex typing. *Psychological Review, 88,* 354–364.

Bem, S. L. (1983). Gender schema theory and its implications on child development: Raising gender-aschematic children in a gender-schematic society. *Signs, 8,* 598–616.

Bem, S. L. (1989). Genital knowledge and gender constancy in preschool children. *Child Development, 60,* 649–662.

Bem, S. L., Martyna, W., & Watson, C. (1976). Sex typing and androgyny: Further explorations of the expressive domain. *Journal of Personality and Social Psychology, 34,* 1016–1023.

Benbow, C. P., & Stanley, J. C. (1980). Sex differences in mathematical ability: Fact or artifact? *Science, 210,* 1262–1264.

Benenson, J. F. (1990). Gender differences in social networks. *Journal of Early Adolescence, 10,* 472–495.

Berenbaum, S. A., & Snyder, E. (1995). Early hormonal influences on childhood sex-typed activity and playmate preferences: Implications for the development of sexual orientation. *Developmental Psychology, 31,* 31–42.

Berman, P. W. (1980). Are women more responsive than men to the young? A review of developmental and situational variables. *Psychological Bulletin, 88,* 668–695.

Berman, P. W. (1987). Children caring for babies: Age and sex differences in response to infant signals and to the social context. In N. Eisenberg (Ed.), *Contemporary topics on development psychology* (pp. 141–164). New York: Wiley.

Berndt, T. J., Perry, T. B., & Miller, K. E. (1988). Friends' and classmates' interactions on academic tasks. *Journal of Educational Psychology, 80,* 506–513.

Berndt, T. J., & Perry, T. B. (1986). Children's perceptions of friendships as supportive relationships. *Developmental Psychology, 22,* 640–648.

Berndt, T. J., & Heller, K. A. (1986). Gender stereotypes and social inferences: A developmental study. *Journal of Personality and Social Psychology, 50,* 889–898.

Bernieri, F. (1991). Interpersonal sensitivity in teaching interactions. *Personality and Social Psychology Bulletin, 17,* 98–103.

Best, D. L., Williams, J. E., Cloud, J. M., Davis, S. W., Robertson, L. S., Edwards, J. R., Giles, H., & Fowles, J. (1977). The development of sex-trait stereotypes. *Child Development, 48,* 1375–1384.

Biernat, M. (1991). Gender stereotypes and the relationship between masculinity and femininity: A developmental analysis. *Journal of Personality and Social Psychology, 61,* 351–365.

Bigler, R. S., & Liben, L. S. (1992). Cognitive mechanisms in children's gender stereotyping: Theoretical and educational implications of a cognitive-based intervention. *Child Development, 63,* 1351–1363.

Birnbaum, D. W., & Croll, W. L. (1984). The etiology of children's stereotypes about sex differences in emotionality. *Sex Roles, 10,* 677–691.

Birnbaum, D. W., Nosanchuk, T. A., & Croll, W. L. (1980). Children's stereotypes about sex differences in emotionality. *Sex Roles, 6,* 435–443.

Blakemore, J. E., LaRue, A. A., & Olejnik, A. B. (1979). Sex appropriate toy preference and the ability to conceptualize toys as sex-role related. *Developmental Psychology, 15,* 339–340.

Blanck, P. D., Rosenthal, R., Snodgrass, S. E., DePaulo, B. M., & Zuckerman, M. (1981). Sex differences in eavesdropping on nonverbal cues: Developmental changes. *Journal of Personality and Social Psychology, 41,* 391–396.

Bleier, R. (1990). Gender ideology and the brain: Sex differences research. In M. T. Notman & C. C. Nadelson (Eds.), *Women and men: New perspectives on gender differences* (pp. 63–73). Washington, DC: American Psychiatric Press.

Bloch, M. N. (1987). The development of sex differences in young children's activities at home: The effect of social context. *Sex Roles, 16,* 279–301.

Block, J. H. (1973). Conceptions of sex role: Some cross-cultural and longitudinal perspectives. *American Psychologist, 28,* 512–526.

Block, J. H. (1976). Issues, problems, and pitfalls in assessing sex differences: A critical review. *Merrill-Palmer Quarterly, 22,* 285–308.

Block, J. H. (1979). Another look at sex differentiation in the socialization behaviors of mothers and fathers. In J. Sherman & F. L. Denmark (Eds.), *Psychology of women: Future of research* (pp. 29–87). New York: Psychological Dimensions.

Block, J. H. (1983). Differential premises arising from differential socialization of the sexes: Some conjectures. *Child Development, 54,* 1335–1354.

Block, J. H., & Block, J. (1980). The role of ego-control and ego-resiliency in the organization of behavior. In W. Andrew Collins (Ed.), *Development of cognition, affect, and social relations. The Minnesota Symposia on Child Psychology* (Vol. 13, pp. 39–101). Hillsdale, NJ: Lawrence Erlbaum Associates.

Block, J. H., & Gjerde, P. F. (1986). Distinguishing between antisocial behavior and undercontrol. In D. Olweus, J. Block, & M. Radke-Yarrow (Eds.), *Development of antisocial and prosocial behavior: Research, theories, and issues* (pp. 177–206). Orlando, FL: Academic Press.

Block, J. H., Gjerde, P. F., & Block, J. (1991). Personality antecedents of depressive tendencies in 18-year-olds: A prospective study. *Journal of Personality and Social Psychology, 60,* 726–738.

Blyth, D. A., Hill, J. P., & Thiel, K. S. (1982). Early adolescents' significant others: Grade and gender differences in perceived relationships with familial and nonfamilial adults and young people. *Journal of Youth and Adolescence, 11,* 425–450.

Bock, D. R., & Kolakowski, D. (1973). Further evidence of a sex-linked major-gene influence on human spatial visualizing ability. *American Journal of Human Genetics, 25,* 1–14.

Boldizar, J. P., Perry, D. G., & Perry, L. C. (1989). Outcome values and aggression. *Child Development, 60,* 571–579.

Boles, D. B. (1980). X-linkage of spatial ability: A critical review. *Child Development, 51,* 625–635.

Borowy, T., & Goebel, R. (1976). Cerebral lateralization of speech: The effects of age, sex, race, and socioeconomic class. *Neuropsychologia, 14,* 363–370.

Boston, M. B., & Levy, G. D. (1991). Changes and differences in preschoolers' understanding of gender scripts. *Cognitive Development, 6,* 417–432.

Bradbard, M. R. (1985). Sex differences in adults' gifts and children's toy requests at Christmas. *Psychological Reports, 56,* 969–970.

Bradbard, M. R., & Endsley, R. C. (1983). The effects of sex-typed labeling on preschool children's information seeking and retention. *Sex Roles, 9,* 247–260.

Bradbard, M. R., Martin, C. L., Endsley, R. C., & Halverson, C. F. (1986). Influence of sex stereotypes on children's exploration and memory: A competence versus performance distinction. *Developmental Psychology, 22,* 481–486.

Bradbard, M. R., & Parkman, S. A. (1983). Gender differences in preschool children's toy requests. *Journal of Genetic Psychology, 145,* 283–285.

Brody, L. R. (1985). Gender differences in emotional development: A review of theories and research. *Journal of Personality, 53,* 102–149.

Brooks-Gunn, J., & Petersen, A. C. (1983). *Girls at puberty: Biological and psychosocial perspectives.* New York: Plenum Press.

Broverman, I. K., Klaiber, E. L., Kobayashi, Y., & Vogel, W. (1968). Roles of activation and inhibition in sex differences in cognitive abilities. *Psychological Review, 75,* 23–50.

Broverman, I. K., Vogel, S. R., Broverman, D. M., Clarkson, F. E., & Rosenkrantz, P. S. (1972). Sex-role stereotypes: A current appraisal. *Journal of Social Issues, 28,* 59–78.

Brown, L. M., Tappan, M. B., Gilligan, C., Miller, B. A., & Argyris, D. E. (1989). Reading for self and moral voice: A method for interpreting narratives of real-life moral conflict and choice. In M. J. Packer & R. B. Addison (Eds.), *Entering the circle: Hermeneutic investigation in psychology* (pp. 142–164). Albany: State University of New York Press.

Buck, R. (1984). *The communication of emotion*. New York: Guilford Press.

Buhrmester, D., & Furman, W. (1987). The development of companionship and intimacy. *Child Development, 58,* 1101–1113.

Bullock, D., & Merrill, L. (1980). The impact of personal preference on consistency through time: The case of childhood aggression. *Child Development, 51,* 808–814.

Buss, A. (1989). Temperament as personality traits. In G. A. Kohnstamm, J. E. Bates, & M. K. Rothbart (Eds.), *Temperament in childhood* (pp. 49–58). New York: Wiley.

Bussey, K., & Bandura, A. (1984). Gender constancy, social power, and sex-linked modeling. *Journal of Personality and Social Psychology, 47,* 1242–1302.

Bussey, K., & Bandura, A. (1992). Self-regulatory mechanisms governing gender development. *Child Development, 63,* 1236–1250.

Bussey, K., & Perry, D. G. (1982). Same-sex imitation: The avoidance of cross-sex models or the acceptance of same-sex models? *Sex Roles, 8,* 773–784.

Byrne, B. M., & Shavelson, R. J. (1987). Adolescent self-concept: The assumption of equivalent structure across gender. *American Educational Research Journal, 24,* 365–385.

Caldera, Y. M., Huston, A. C., & O'Brien, M. (1989). Social interactions and play patterns of parents and toddlers with feminine, masculine, and neutral toys. *Child Development, 60,* 70–76.

Camras, L. A. (1977). Facial expressions used by children in a conflict situation. *Child Development, 48,* 1431–1435.

Cann, A., & Garrett, A. G. (1984). Sex stereotype impacts on competence ratings by children. *Sex Roles, 11,* 333–343.

Cann, A., & Newbern, S. R. (1984). Sex stereotype effects in children's picture recognition. *Child Development, 55,* 1085–1090.

Cann, A., & Palmer, S. (1986). Children's assumptions about the generalizability of sex-typed abilities. *Sex Roles, 15,* 551–558.

Carpenter, C. J., Huston, A. C., & Holt, W. (1986). Modification of preschool sex-typed behaviors by participation in adult-structured activities. *Sex Roles, 14,* 603–615.

Carroll, J. J., & Steward, M. S. (1984). The role of cognitive development in children's understanding of their own feelings. *Child Development, 55,* 1486–1492.

Carter, D. B. (1987). The roles of peers in sex role socialization. In D. B. Carter (Ed.), *Current conceptions of sex roles and sex typing: Theory & research* (pp. 101–121). New York: Praeger.

Carter, D. B. (1989, April). *Gender identity and gender constancy: The roles of cognitive constancies in early gender-role development.* Paper presented at the biennial meeting of the Society for Research in Child Development, Kansas City, MO.

Carter, D. B., & Levy, G. D. (1988). Cognitive aspects of children's early sex-role development: The influence of gender schemas on preschoolers' memories and preferences for sex-typed toys and activities. *Child Development, 59,* 782–793.

Carter, D. B., & McCloskey, L. A. (1984). Peers and the maintenance of sex-typed behavior: The development of children's conceptions of cross-gender behavior in their peers. *Social Cognition, 2,* 294–314.

Carter, D. B., & Patterson, C. J. (1982). Sex-roles as social conventions: The development of children's conceptions of sex-role stereotypes. *Developmental Psychology, 18,* 812–824.

Chodorow, N. J. (1978). *The reproduction of mothering: Psychoanalysis and the sociology of gender.* Berkeley: University of California Press.

Chodorow, N. J. (1989). *Feminism and psychoanalytic theory.* New Haven: Yale University Press.

Cione, M., & Ruble, D. N. (1978). Beliefs about males. *Journal of Social Issues, 34,* 5–16.

Cohn, D. A. (1990). Child-mother attachment of six-year-olds and social competence at school. *Child Development, 61,* 152–162.

Coie, J. D., Dodge, K. A., & Kupersmidt, J. B. (1990). Peer group behavior and social status. In S. R. Asher & J. D. Coie (Eds.), *Peer rejection in childhood* (pp. 17–59). Cambridge, England: Cambridge University Press.

Colby, A., Kohlberg, L., Gibbs, J., & Lieberman, M. (1983). A longitudinal study of moral judgment. *Monographs of the Society for Research in Child Development, 48* (Serial No. 200), 1–124.

Cole, P. M. (1986). Children's spontaneous control of facial expression. *Child Development, 57,* 1309–1321.

Coleman, J. S., Campbell, H. Q., Hobson, C. J., McPartland, J., Mood, A. M., Weinfeld, F. D., & York, R. L. (1966). *Equality of educational opportunity.* Washington DC: U.S. Office of Education.

Condry, J. C., & Condry, S. (1976). Sex differences: A study of the eye of the beholder. *Child Development, 47,* 812–819.

Condry, J. C., & Ross, D. F. (1985). Sex and aggression: The influence of gender label on the perception of aggression in children. *Child Development, 56,* 225–233.

Connor, J. M., & Serbin, L. A. (1977). Behaviorally based masculine and feminine activity preference scales for preschoolers: Correlates with other classroom behaviors and cognitive tests. *Child Development, 48,* 1411–1416.

Constantinople, A. (1979). Sex-role acquisition: In search of the elephant. *Sex Roles, 5,* 121–132.

Conway, M., Giannopoulos, C., & Stiefenhofer, K. (1990). Response styles to sadness are related to sex and sex-role orientation. *Sex Roles, 22,* 579–587.

Cordua, G. D., McGraw, K. O., & Drabman, R. S. (1979). Doctor or nurse: Children's perception of sex typed occupations. *Child Development, 50,* 590–593.

Cowan, G., & Hoffman, C. D. (1986). Gender stereotyping in young children: Evidence to support a concept-learning approach. *Sex Roles, 14,* 211–224.

Cramer, P. (1979). Defense mechanisms in adolescence. *Developmental Psychology, 15,* 476–477.

Crandall, V. C. (1978, August). *Expecting sex differences and sex differences in expectancies.* Paper presented at a meeting of the American Psychological Association, Toronto.

Crawford, M. (1989). Agreeing to differ: Feminist epistemologies and women's ways of knowing. In M. Crawford & M. Gentry (Eds.), *Gender and thought. Psychological perspectives* (pp. 128–145). New York: Springer.

Crawford, M., & MacLeod, M. (1990). Gender in the college classroom: An assessment of the "chilly climate" for women. *Sex Roles, 23,* 101–122.

Crockett, L., Losoff, M., & Petersen, A. C. (1984). Perceptions of the peer group and friendship in early adolescence. *Journal of Early Adolescence, 4,* 155–181.

Cummings, E. M., Iannotti, R. J., & Zahn-Waxler, C. (1985). Influence of conflict between adults on the emotions and aggression of young children. *Developmental Psychology, 21,* 495–507.

Cummings, E. M., Vogel, D., Cummings, J. S., & El-Sheikh, M. (1989). Children's responses to different forms of expression of anger between adults. *Child Development, 60,* 1392–1405.

Cunningham, J., & Shapiro, L. (1984). *Infant affective expression as a function of infant and adult gender.* Unpublished manuscript. Brandeis University, Waltham, MA.

Custrini, R. J., & Feldman, R. S. (1989). Children's social competence and nonverbal encoding and decoding of emotion. *Journal of Clinical Child Psychology, 18,* 336–342.

Damon, W. (1977). *The social world of the child.* San Francisco: Jossey-Bass.

Davis, M. H. (1980). A multidimensional approach to individual differences in empathy. JSAS: *Catalog of Selected Documents in Psychology, 10,* 85.

Davis, M. H., & Franzoi, S. (1991). Stability and change in adolescent self-consciousness and empathy. *Journal of Research in Personality, 25,* 70–87.

Davis, S. W., Williams, J. E., & Best, D. L. (1982). Sex-trait stereotypes in the self- and peer descriptions of third grade children. *Sex Roles, 8*, 315–331.

Deaux, K., & Lewis, L. L. (1984). Structure of gender stereotypes: Interrelationships among components and gender label. *Journal of Personality and Social Psychology, 46*, 991–1004.

Deaux, K., & Major, B. (1987). Putting gender into context: An interactive model of gender-related behavior. *Psychological Review, 94*, 369–389.

de Lacoste-Utamsing, C., & Holloway, R. L. (1982). Sex dimorphism in the human corpus callosum. *Science, 216*, 1431–1432.

DeLisi, R., & Gallagher, A. M. (1991). Understanding of gender stability and constancy in Argentinean children. *Merrill Palmer Quarterly, 37*, 483–402.

DePaulo, B. M. (1978). Help-seeking from the recipient's point of view. JSAS: *Catalog of Selected Documents in Psychology, 8*, 62. (Ms. No. 1721)

DePietro, J. (1981). Rough and tumble play: A function of gender. *Developmental Psychology, 17*, 50–58.

Devine, P. G. (1989). Stereotypes and prejudice: Their automatic and controlled components. *Journal of Personality and Social Psychology, 56*, 5–18.

Diener, E., Sandvik, E., & Larsen, R. J. (1985). Age and sex effects for emotional intensity. *Developmental Psychology, 21*, 542–546.

Dodge, K. A., & Feldman, E. (1990). Issues in social cognition and sociometric status. In S. R. Asher & J. D. Coie (Eds.), *Peer rejection in childhood* (pp. 119–155). Cambridge, England: Cambridge University Press.

Downs, A. C., & Langlois, J. H. (1988). Sex typing: Construct and measurement issues. *Sex Roles, 18*, 87–100.

Dweck, C. S., Davidson, W., Nelson, S., & Enna, B. (1978). Sex differences in learned helplessness: II. The contingencies of evaluative feedback in the classroom. III. An experimental analysis. *Developmental Psychology, 14*, 268–276.

Dunn, J., Bretherton, I., & Munn, P. (1987). Conversations about feeling states between mothers and their young children. *Developmental Psychology, 23*, 132–139.

Dunn, J., Brown, J., & Beardsall, L. (1991). Family talk about feeling states and children's later understanding of others' emotions. *Developmental Psychology, 27*, 448–455.

Dunn, J., Brown, J., Slomkowski, C., Tesla, C., & Youngblade, L. (1991). Young children's understanding of other people's feelings and beliefs: Individual differences and their antecedents. *Child Development, 62*, 1352–1366.

Eagly, A. H., & Carli, L. L. (1981). Sex of researchers and sex-typed communication as determinants of sex difference in influenceability: A meta-analysis of social influence studies. *Psychological Bulletin, 90*, 1–20.

Eagly, A. H., & Crowley, M. (1986). Gender and helping behavior: A meta-analytic review of the social psychological literature. *Psychological Bulletin, 100*, 283–308.

Eagly, A. H., & Steffen, V. J. (1986). Gender and aggressive behavior: A meta-analytic review of the social psychological literature. *Psychological Bulletin, 100*, 309–330.

Eaton, W. O., & Enns, L. R. (1986). Sex differences in human motor activity level. *Psychological Bulletin, 100*, 19–28.

Eaton, W. O., Von Bargen, D., & Keats, J. G. (1981). Gender understanding and dimensions of preschooler toy choice: Sex stereotype versus activity level. *Canadian Journal of Behavioral Science, 13*, 203–209.

Eccles, J. S. (1985). Sex differences in achievement patterns. In T. B. Sonderegger (Ed.), *Nebraska Symposium on Motivation: Psychology and gender* (Vol. 2, pp. 97–132). Lincoln: University of Nebraska Press.

Eccles, J. S., & Jacobs, J. E. (1986). Social forces shape math attitudes and performance. *Signs, 11*, 367–380.

Eccles-Parsons, J. E., Adler, T. F., Futterman, R., Goff, S. B., Kaczala, C. M., Meece, J. L., & Midgley, C. (1983). Expectancies, values, and academic behaviors. In J. T. Spence (Ed.), *Perspectives on achievement and achievement motivation* (pp. 75–146). San Francisco: Freeman.

Edelbrock, C., & Sugawara, A. I. (1978). Acquisition of sex-typed preferences in preschool children. *Developmental Psychology, 14*, 614–623.

Ehrhardt, A. (1984). Gender differences: A biosocial perspective. In T. B. Sonderegger (Ed.), *Nebraska Symposium on Motivation: Psychology and gender* (pp. 37–57). Lincoln: University of Nebraska Press.

Eisenberg, N. (1977). The development of prosocial moral judgment and its correlates (Doctoral dissertation, University of California, Berkeley). *Dissertation Abstracts International, 37*, 4753B. (University Microfilms No. 77-444).

Eisenberg, N. (1983). Sex-typed toy choices: What do they signify? In M. B. Liss (Ed.), *Social and cognitive skills: Sex roles and children's play* (pp. 45–70). New York: Academic Press.

Eisenberg, N. (1986). *Altruistic emotion, cognition and behavior*. Hillsdale, NJ: Lawrence Erlbaum Associates.

Eisenberg, N., & Fabes, R. A. (1992). Emotion, regulation, and the development of social competence. In M. S. Clark (Ed.), *Emotion and social behavior* (Vol. 14, pp. 119–150). Newbury Park, CA: Sage.

Eisenberg, N., & Fabes, R. A. (1995). Children's disclosure of vicariously induced emotions. In K. Rotenberg (Ed.), *Disclosure processes in children and adolescents* (pp. 111–134). Cambridge: Cambridge University Press.

Eisenberg, N. Fabes, R. A., Bernzweig, J., Karbon, M., Poulin, R., & Hanish, L. (1993). The relations of emotionality and regulation to preschoolers' social skills and sociometric status. *Child Development, 64*, 1418–1438.

Eisenberg, N., Fabes, R. A., Carlo, G., Troyer, D., Speer, A. L., Karbon, M., & Switzer, G. (1992). The relations of maternal practices and characteristics to children's vicarious emotional responsiveness. *Child Development, 63*, 583–602.

Eisenberg, N., Fabes, R. A., Schaller, M., Carlo, G., & Miller, P. A. (1991). The relations of parental characteristics and practices to children's vicarious emotional responding. *Child Development, 62*, 1393–1408.

Eisenberg, N., Fabes, R. A., Schaller, M., & Miller, P. A. (1989). Sympathy and personal distress: Development, gender differences, and interrelations of indexes. *New Directions in Child Development, 44*, 107–126.

Eisenberg, N., Fabes, R. A., Schaller, M., Miller, P. A., Carlo, G., Poulin, R., Shea, C., & Shell, R. (1991). Personality and socialization correlates of vicarious emotional responding. *Journal of Personality and Social Psychology, 61*, 459–471.

Eisenberg, N., Fabes, R. A., & Shea, C. (1989). Gender differences in empathy and prosocial moral reasoning: Empirical investigations. In M. M. Brabeck (Ed.), *Who cares? Theory, research, and educational implications of the ethic of care* (pp. 127–143). New York: Praeger.

Eisenberg, N., & Lennon, R. (1983). Sex differences in empathy and related capacities. *Psychological Bulletin, 94*, 100–131.

Eisenberg, N., Miller, P. A., Schaller, M., Fabes, R. A., Fultz, J., Shell, R., & Shea, C. (1989). The role of sympathy and altruistic personality traits in helping: A re-examination. *Journal of Personality, 57*, 41–67.

Eisenberg, N., Miller, P. A., Shell, R., McNalley, S., & Shea, C. (1991). Prosocial development in adolescence: A longitudinal study. *Developmental Psychology, 27*, 849–857.

Eisenberg, N., Murray, E., & Hite, T. (1982). Children's reasoning regarding sex-typed toy choices. *Child Development, 53*, 81–86.

Eisenberg, N., Shell, R., Pasternack, J., Lennon, R., Beller, R., & Mathy, R. M. (1987). Prosocial development in middle childhood: A longitudinal study. *Developmental Psychology, 24*, 712–718.

Eisenberg, N., Tryon, K., & Cameron, E. (1984). The relation of preschoolers' peer interaction to their sex-typed toy choices. *Child Development, 55*, 1044–1050.

Eisenberg, N., Wolchik, S. A., Hernandez, R., & Pasternack, J. (1985). Parental socialization of young children's play: A short-term longitudinal study. *Child Development, 56,* 1506–1513.

Eisenberg-Berg, N., Boothby, R., & Matson, T. (1979). Correlates of preschool girls' feminine and masculine toy preferences. *Developmental Psychology, 15,* 354–355.

Emmerich, W. (1982). Nonmonotonic developmental trends in social cognition: The case of gender identity. In S. Strauss (Ed.), *U-Shaped behavioral growth* (pp. 249–269). New York: Academic Press.

Emmerich, W., Goldman, K. S., Kirsh, B., & Sharabany, R. (1977). Evidence for a transitional phase in the development of gender constancy. *Child Development, 48,* 930–936.

Emmerich, W., & Shepard, K. (1984). Cognitive factors in the development of sex-typed preferences. *Sex Roles, 11,* 997–1007.

Entwisle, D. R., & Baker, D. P. (1983). Gender and young children's expectations for performance in arithmetic. *Developmental Psychology, 19,* 200–209.

Etaugh, C. (1983). The influence of environmental factors on sex differences in children's play. In M. B. Liss (Ed.), *Social and cognitive skills: Sex roles and children's play* (pp. 1–21). New York: Academic Press.

Etaugh, C., & Liss, M. B. (1992). Home, school, and playroom: Training ground for adult gender roles. *Sex Roles, 26,* 129–147.

Fabes, R. A. (1994). Physiological and behavioral correlates of gender segregation. In C. Leaper (Ed.), *New directions in child development: Childhood gender segregation: Causes and consequences* (pp. 19–34). San Francisco: Jossey-Bass.

Fabes, R. A., Eisenberg, N., & Eisenbud, L. (1993). Behavioral and physiological correlates of children's reactions to others in distress. *Developmental Psychology, 29,* 655–663.

Fabes, R. A., Eisenberg, N., Karbon, M., Bernzweig, J., Speer, A. L., & Carlo, G. (1993). Socialization of children's vicarious emotional responding and prosocial behavior: Relations with mothers' perceptions of children's emotional reactivity. *Developmental Psychology, 30,* 44–55.

Fabes, R. A., Eisenberg, N., McCormick, S. E., & Wilson, M. S. (1988). Preschoolers' attributions of the situational determinants of others' naturally occurring emotions. *Developmental Psychology, 24,* 376–385.

Fabes, R. A., Eisenberg, N., Nyman, M., & Michealieu, Q. (1991). Young children's appraisals of others' spontaneous emotional reactions. *Developmental Psychology, 27,* 858–866.

Fabes, R. A., Eisenberg, N., Smith, M., & Murphy, B. (in press). Getting angry at others: Associations with liking of the provocateur. *Child Development.*

Fabes, R. A., & Martin, C. L. (1991). Gender and age stereotypes of emotionality. *Personality and Social Psychology Bulletin, 17,* 532–540.

Fagot, B. I. (1974). Sex differences in toddlers' behavior and parental reaction. *Developmental Psychology, 10,* 554–558.

Fagot, B. I. (1977). Consequences of moderate cross gender behavior in preschool children. *Child Development, 48,* 902–907.

Fagot, B. I. (1978a). The influence of sex of child on parental reactions to toddler children. *Child Development, 49,* 459–465.

Fagot, B. I. (1978b). Reinforcing contingencies for sex-role behaviors: Effect of experience with children. *Child Development, 49,* 30–36.

Fagot, B. I. (1985). Changes in thinking about early sex role development. *Developmental Review, 5,* 83–98.

Fagot, B. I., & Hagan, R. (1985). Aggression in toddlers: Responses to the assertive acts of boys and girls. *Sex Roles, 12,* 341–351.

Fagot, B. I., & Hagan, R. (1991). Observations of parent reactions to sex-stereotyped behaviors: Age and sex effects. *Child Development, 62,* 617–628.

Fagot, B. I., Hagan, R., Leinbach, M. D., & Kronsberg, S. (1985). Differential reactions to assertive and communicative acts of toddler boys and girls. *Child Development, 56,* 1499–1505.

Fagot, B. I., & Leinbach, M. D. (1985). Gender identity: Some thoughts on an old concept. *Journal of the American Academy of Child Psychiatry, 24,* 684–688.

Fagot, B. I., & Leinbach, M. D. (1989). The young child's gender schema: Environmental input, internal organization. *Child Development, 60,* 663–672.

Fagot, B. I., & Leinbach, M. D. (1993). Gender-role development in young children: From discrimination to labeling. *Developmental Review, 13,* 205–224.

Fagot, B. I., Leinbach, M. D., & Hagan, R. (1986). Gender labeling and the adoption of sex-typed behaviors. *Developmental Psychology, 22,* 440–443. *19,* 200–209.

Fagot, B. I., Leinbach, M. D., & O'Boyle, C. (1992). Gender labeling, gender stereotyping, and parenting behaviors. *Developmental Psychology, 28,* 225–230.

Fein, G., Johnson, D., Kosson, N., Stork, L., & Wasserman, L. (1975). Sex stereotypes and preferences in the toy choices of 20-month-old boys and girls. *Developmental Psychology, 11,* 527–528.

Feingold, A. (1988). Cognitive gender differences are disappearing. *American Psychologist, 43,* 95–103.

Feingold, A. (1992). Sex differences in variability in intellectual abilities: A new look at an old controversy. *Review of Educational Research, 62,* 61–84.

Feiring, C., & Lewis, M. (1991a). The development of social networks from early to middle childhood: Gender differences and the relation to school competence. *Sex Roles, 25,* 237–253.

Feiring, C., & Lewis, M. (1991b). The transition from middle childhood to early adolescence: Sex differences in the social network and perceived self-competence. *Sex Roles, 24,* 489–509.

Feldman, S. S., & Wentzel, K. R. (1990). Relations among family interaction patterns, classroom self-restraint, and academic achievement in preadolescent boys. *Journal of Educational Psychology, 82,* 813–819.

Feltham, R. F., Doyle, A. B., Schwartzman, A. E., Serbin, L. A., & Ledingham, J. E. (1985). Friendship in normal and socially deviant children. *Journal of Early Adolescence, 5,* 371–382.

Fennema, E., & Sherman, J. A. (1978). Sex-related differences in mathematics achievement, spatial visualization, and sociocultural factors. *American Educational Research Journal, 14,* 51–71.

Feshbach, N. D. (1978). Studies of empathic behavior in children. In B. A. Maher (Ed.), *Progress in experimental personality research* (Vol. 8, pp. 1–47). New York: Academic Press.

Fivush, R. (1989). Exploring sex differences in the emotional content of mother-child conversations about the past. *Sex Roles, 20,* 675–691.

Foot, H. C., Chapman, A. J., & Smith, J. R. (1977). Friendship and social responsiveness in boys and girls. *Journal of Personality and Social Psychology, 35,* 401–411.

Ford, M. R., & Lowery, C. R. (1986). Gender differences in moral reasoning: A comparison of the use of justice and care orientations. *Journal of Personality and Social Psychology, 50,* 777–783.

Frey, K. S., & Ruble, D. N. (1992). Gender constancy and the "cost" of sex-typed behavior: A test of the conflict hypothesis. *Developmental Psychology, 28,* 714–721.

Frieze, I. H., Parsons, J. E., Johnson, P. B., Ruble, D. N., & Zellman, G. L. (1978). *Women and sex roles: A social psychological perspective.* New York: Norton.

Frodi, A., Macaulay, J., & Thome, P. R. (1977). Are women always less aggressive than men? A review of the experimental literature. *Psychological Bulletin, 84,* 634–660.

Fuchs, D., & Thelen, M. H. (1988). Children's expected interpersonal consequences of communicating their affective state and reported likelihood of expression. *Child Development, 58,* 1314–1322.

Fujita, F., Diener, E., & Sandvik, E. (1991). Gender differences in negative affect and well-being: The case for emotional intensity. *Journal of Personality and Social Psychology, 61,* 427–434.

Furman, W., & Buhrmester, D. (1985). Children's perceptions of the personal relationships in their social networks. *Developmental Psychology, 21,* 1016–1024.

Galotti, K. M., Kozberg, S. F., & Farmer, M. C. (1991). Gender and developmental differences in adolescents' conceptions of moral reasoning. *Journal of Youth and Adolescence, 20,* 13–29.

Garrod, A., Beal, C., & Shin, P. (1990). The development of moral orientation in elementary school children. *Sex Roles, 22,* 13–27.

Gavin, L. A., & Furman, W. (1989). Age differences in adolescents' perceptions of their peer groups. *Developmental Psychology, 25,* 827–834.

Gelman, S. A., Collman, P., & Maccoby, E. E. (1986). Inferring properties from categories versus inferring categories from properties: The case of gender. *Child Development, 57,* 396–404.

Geschwind, N., & Galaburda, A. M. (1987). *Cerebral lateralization: Biological mechanisms, associations, and pathology.* Cambridge, MA: MIT Press.

Ghodsian-Carpey, J., & Baker, L. A. (1987). Genetic and environmental influences on aggression in 4- to 7-year-old twins. *Aggressive Behavior, 13,* 173–186.

Gibbs, J. C., Arnold, K. D., & Burkhart, J. E. (1984). Sex differences in the expression of moral judgment. *Child Development, 55,* 1040–1043.

Gilligan, C. (1977). In a different voice: Women's conceptions of self and morality. *Harvard Educational Review, 47,* 481–517.

Gilligan, C. (1982). *In a different voice: Psychological theory and women's development.* Cambridge, MA: Harvard University Press.

Gilligan, C. (1990). Preface. In C. Gilligan, N. P. Lyons, & T. J. Hanmer (Eds.), *Making connections: The relational worlds of adolescent girls at Emma Willard School* (pp. 111–134). Cambridge, MA: Harvard University Press.

Gilligan, C., & Attanucci, J. (1988). Two moral orientations: Gender differences and similarities. *Merrill Palmer Quarterly, 34,* 223–238.

Gilligan, C., Lyons, N. P., & Hanmer, T. J., Eds. (1990). *Making connections: The relational worlds of adolescent girls at Emma Willard School.* Cambridge, MA: Harvard University Press.

Gold, D., Crombie, G., & Noble, S. (1987). Relations between teachers' judgments of girls' and boys' compliance and intellectual competence. *Sex Roles, 16,* 351–358.

Goodenough, F. L. (1931). *Anger in young children.* Minneapolis: University of Minnesota Press.

Gouze, K. R., & Nadelman, L. (1980). Constancy of gender identity for self and others in children between the ages of three and seven. *Child Development, 51,* 275–278.

Green, R. (1974). *Sexual identity conflict in children and adults.* New York: Basic Books.

Grolnick, W. S., & Ryan, R. M. (1989). Parent styles associated with children's self-regulation and competence in school. *Journal of Educational Psychology, 81,* 143–154.

Gross, A. L., & Ballif, B. (1991). Children's understanding of emotion from facial expressions and situations: A review. *Developmental Review, 11,* 368–398.

Gurwitz, S. B., & Dodge, D. A. (1975). Adults' evaluations of a child as a function of sex of adults and sex of child. *Journal of Personality and Social Psychology, 32,* 822–828.

Halberstadt, A. G., Hayes, C. W., & Pike, K. M. (1988). Gender and gender role differences in smiling and communication consistency. *Sex Roles, 19,* 589–604.

Hall, J. A. (1978). Gender effects in decoding nonverbal cues. *Psychological Bulletin, 85,* 845–858.

Hall, J. A. (1984). *Nonverbal sex differences: Communication accuracy and expressive style.* Baltimore: Johns Hopkins University Press.

Hall, J. A., & Halberstadt, A. G. (1980). Masculinity and femininity in children: Development of the Children's Personal Attribute Questionnaire. *Developmental Psychology, 16,* 270–280.

Hall, R. M., & Sandler, B. R. (1982). *The classroom climate: A chilly one for women?* (Project on the Status and Education of Women). Washington, DC: Association for American Colleges.

Hallinan, M. T. (1981). Recent advances in sociometry. In S. R. Asher & J. M. Gottman (Eds.), *The development of children's friendships* (pp. 91–115). Cambridge, England: Cambridge University Press.

Halpern, D. F. (1986). *Sex differences in cognitive abilities.* Hillsdale, NJ: Lawrence Erlbaum Associates.

Halpern, D. F. (1989). The disappearance of cognitive gender differences: What you see depends on where you look. *American Psychologist, 44,* 1156–1158.

Halpern, D. F. (1992). *Sex differences in cognitive abilities* (2nd ed.). Hillsdale, NJ: Lawrence Erlbaum Associates.

Hartup, W. W. (1989). Behavioral manifestations of children's friendships. In T. J. Berndt & G. W. Ladd (Eds.), *Peer relationships in child development* (pp. 46–70). New York: Wiley.

Hartup, W. W., Moore, S. G., & Sager, G. (1963). Avoidance of inappropriate sex-typing in young children. *Journal of Consulting Psychology, 27,* 467–473.

Haugh, S. S., Hoffman, C. D., & Cowan, G. (1980). The eye of the very young beholder: Sex typing of infants by young children. *Child Development, 51,* 598–600.

Hess, R. D., Holloway, S. D., Dickson, W. P., & Price, G. G. (1984). Maternal variables as predictors of children's school readiness and later achievement in vocabulary and mathematics. *Child Development, 55,* 1902–1912.

Hill, J. P., Holmbeck, G. N., Marlow, L., Green, T., & Lynch, M. E. (1985). Menarcheal status of parent-child relations in families of seventh-grade girls. *Journal of Youth and Adolescence, 14,* 301–316.

Hill, J. P., & Lynch, M. E. (1983). The intensification of gender-related role expectations during early adolescence. In J. Brooks-Gunn & A. Petersen (Eds.), *Girls at puberty: Biological and psychosocial perspectives* (pp. 201–228). New York: Plenum Press.

Hill, J. P., & Holmbeck, G. N. (1986). Attachment and autonomy during adolescence. *Annals of Child Development, 3,* 145–189.

Hoffman, M. L. (1975). Altruistic behavior and the parent-child relationship. *Journal of Personality and Social Psychology, 31,* 937–943.

Hoffman, M. L. (1977). Sex differences in empathy and related behaviors. *Psychological Bulletin, 84,* 712–722.

Hoffman, M. L. (1982). Development of prosocial motivation: Empathy and guilt. In N. Eisenberg (Ed.), *The development of prosocial behavior* (pp. 281–313). New York: Academic Press.

Hood, K. E., Draper, P., Crockett, L. J., & Petersen, A. C. (1987). The ontogeny and phylogeny of sex differences in development: A biopsychosocial synthesis. In D. B. Carter (Ed.), *Current conceptions of sex roles and sex typing: Theory and research* (pp. 49–77). New York: Praeger.

Horney, K. (1932). The dread of women. *International Journal of Psychoanalysis, 13,* 348–360.

Hort, B. E., Leinbach, M. D., & Fagot, B. I. (1991). Is there coherence among components of gender acquisition? *Sex Roles, 24,* 195–208.

Horwitz, A. V., & White, H. R. (1987). Gender role orientations and styles of pathology among adolescents. *Journal of Health and Social Behavior, 28,* 158–170.

Hunter, F. T., & Youniss, J. (1982). Changes in functions of three relationships during adolescence. *Developmental Psychology, 18,* 806–811.

Huston, A. C. (1983). Sex-typing. In P. H. Mussen (Ed.), *Handbook of child psychology: Vol. 4. Socialization, personality, and social development* (E. M. Hetherington, Ed., pp. 387–467). New York: Wiley.

Huston, A. C. (1985). The development of sex typing: Themes from recent research. *Development Review, 5,* 1–17.

Huston, A. C., Carpenter, C. J., Atwater, J. B., & Johnson, L. M. (1986). Gender, adult structuring of activities, and social behavior in middle childhood. *Child Development, 57,* 1200–1209.

Huttenlocher, J., Haight, W., Bryk, A., Seltzer, M., & Lyons, T. (1991). Early vocabulary growth: Relation to language input and gender. *Developmental Psychology, 27,* 236–248.

Hyde, J. S. (1981). How large are cognitive gender differences? A meta-analysis using w and d. *American Psychologist, 36,* 892–901.

Hyde, J. S. (1984). How large are gender differences in aggression? A developmental meta-analysis. *Developmental Psychology, 20,* 722–736.

Hyde, J. S. (1986). Gender differences in aggression. In J. S. Hyde & M. C. Linn (Eds.), *The psychology of gender: Advances through meta-analysis* (pp. 51–66). Baltimore: Johns Hopkins University Press.

Hyde, J. S., Fennema, E., & Lamon, S. J. (1990). Gender differences in mathematics performance: A meta-analysis. *Psychological Bulletin, 107,* 139–155.

Hyde, J. S., & Linn, M. C. (1988). Gender differences in verbal ability: A meta-analysis. *Psychological Bulletin, 104,* 53–69.

Ilardi, B. C., & Bridges, L. J. (1988). Gender differences in self-system processes as rated by teachers and students. *Sex Roles, 18,* 333–342.

Ingram, R. E. (1990). Self-focused attention in clinical disorders: Review and a conceptual model. *Psychological Bulletin, 107,* 156–176.

Ingram, R. E., Cruet, D., Johnson, B. R., & Wisnicki, K. S. (1988). Self-focused attention, gender, gender role, and vulnerability to negative affect. *Journal of Personality and Social Psychology, 55,* 967–978.

Intons-Peterson, M. J. (1988). *Children's concepts of gender.* Norwood, NJ: Ablex.

Jacklin, C. N. (1989). Female and male: Issues of gender. *American Psychologist, 44,* 127–133.

Jacobs, J. E. (1991). Influence of gender stereotypes on parent and child mathematics attitudes. *Journal of Educational Psychology, 83,* 518–527.

Jacobs, J. E., & Eccles, J. E. (1985). Gender differences in math ability: The impact of media reports on parents. *Educational Researcher, 14,* 20–25.

Jessor, R., Costa, F., Jessor, L., & Donovon, J. (1983). Time of first intercourse: A prospective study. *Journal of Personality and Social Psychology, 44,* 608–626.

Johnson, F., & Aries, E. (1983). Conversational patterns among same-sex pairs of late adolescent close friends. *Journal of Genetic Psychology, 142,* 225–238.

Johnson, J. T., & Shulman, G. A. (1988). More alike than meets the eye: Perceived gender differences in subjective experience and its display. *Sex Roles, 19,* 67–79.

Johnston, D. K., Brown, L. M., & Christopherson, S. B. (1990). Adolescents' moral dilemmas: The context. *Journal of Youth and Adolescence, 19,* 615–622.

Kahn, A., Nelson, R. E., & Gaeddert, W. P. (1980). Sex of subject and sex composition of the group as determinants of reward allocations. *Journal of Personality and Social Psychology, 38,* 737–750.

Kail, R., Carter, P., & Pellegrino, J. (1979). The locus of sex differences in spatial ability. *Perception and Psychophysics, 26,* 182–186.

Karbon, M., Fabes, R. A., Carlo, G., & Martin, C. L. (1992). Preschoolers' beliefs about sex and age differences in emotionality. *Sex Roles, 27,* 377–380.

Katz, P. A. (1983). Developmental foundations of gender and racial attitudes. In R. L. Leahy (Ed.), *The child's construction of social inequality* (pp. 41–78). New York: Academic Press.

Katz, P. A. (1986). Modifications of children's gender-stereotyped behavior: General issues and research considerations. *Sex Roles, 14,* 591–602.

Katz, P. A. (1987). Variations in family constellation: Effects on gender schema. In L. S. Liben & M. L. Signorella (Eds.), *Children's gender schemata.* San Francisco: Jossey-Bass.

Katz, P. A., & Boswell, S. (1986). Flexibility and traditionality in children's gender roles. *Genetic, Social, and General Psychology Monographs, 112,* 105–147.

Keller, M., & Wood, P. (1989). Development of friendship reasoning: A study of interindividual differences in intraindividual change. *Developmental Psychology, 25,* 820–826.

Keating, P. (1990). Striving for sex equity in schools. In J. I. Goodlad & P. Keating (Eds.), *Access to knowledge* (pp. 91–106). New York: College Entrance Examination Board.

Kimura, D. (1987). Are men's and women's brains really different? *Canadian Psychology, 28,* 133–147.

Karniol, R., & Heiman, T. (1987). Situational antecedents of children's anger experiences and subsequent responses to adult versus peer provokers. *Aggressive Behavior, 13,* 109–118.

Klein, M. (1957). *Envy and gratitude.* New York: Basic Books.

Knight, G. P., Fabes, R. A., & Higgins, D. A. (in press). Concerns about drawing causal conclusions from meta-analyses: An example in the study of gender differences in aggression. *Psychological Bulletin.*

Kohlberg, L. A., & Ullian, D. Z. (1974). Stages in the development of psychosexual concepts and attitudes. In R. C. Friedman, R. M. Richart, & R. L. Varde Wiete (Eds.), *Sex differences in behavior* (pp. 209–222). New York: Wiley.

Kohlberg, L. A. (1966). A cognitive-developmental analysis of children's sex role concepts and attitudes. In E. E. Maccoby (Ed.), *The development of sex differences* (pp. 82–173). Stanford, CA: Stanford University Press.

Korner, A. F. (1973). Sex differences in newborns with special reference to differences in the organization of oral behavior. *Journal of Child Psychology and Psychiatry, 14,* 19–29.

Koshland, D. E., Jr. (1988). Women in science. *Science, 239,* 1473.

Kuebil, J., & Krieger, E. (1991, April). *Emotion and gender in parent-child conversations about the past.* Paper presented at the biennial meeting of the Society for Research in Child Development, Seattle.

Kuhn, D., Nash, S. C., & Brucken, L. (1978). Sex role concepts of two- and three-year-old children. *Child Development, 49,* 445–451.

Lackey, P. N. (1989). Adults' attitudes about assignments of household chores to male and female children. *Sex Roles, 20,* 271–281.

Lamb, M. E., & Roopnarine, J. L. (1979). Peer influences on sex-role development in preschoolers. *Child Development, 50,* 1219–1222.

Langlois, J. H., & Downs, A. C. (1980). Mothers, fathers, and peers as socialization agents of sex-typed play behaviors in young children. *Child Development, 51,* 1237–1247.

Leahy, R. L., & Shirk, S. R. (1984). The development of classificatory skills and sex-trait stereotypes in young children. *Sex Roles, 10,* 281–292.

Leaper, C. (1991). Influence and involvement in children's discourse: Age, gender, and partner effects. *Child Development, 62,* 797–811.

Lee, V. E., & Bryk, A. K. (1986). Effects of single-sex secondary schools on student achievement and attitudes. *Journal of Educational Psychology, 78,* 381–396.

Lee, V. E., & Marks, H. M. (1990). Sustained effects of the single-sex secondary school experience on attitudes, behaviors, and values in college. *Journal of Educational Psychology, 82,* 578–592.

Leinbach, M. D., & Fagot, B. I. (1986). Acquisition of gender labeling: A test for toddlers. *Sex Roles, 15,* 655–666.

Leinbach, M. D., & Fagot, B. I. (1993). Categorical habitation to male and female faces: Gender-schematic processing in infancy. *Infant Behavior and Development, 16,* 317–332.

Leinbach, M. D., & Hort, B. E. (1991). *Bears are for boys: "Metaphorical" associations in the young child's gender schemas.* Paper presented at the meetings of the Society for Research in Child Development, Kansas City, MO.

Leinhardt, G., Seewald, A., & Engel, M. (1979). Learning what's taught: Sex differences in instruction. *Journal of Educational Psychology, 71,* 432–439.

LeMare, L. J., & Rubin, K. H. (1987). Perspective taking and peer interaction: Structural and developmental analyses. *Child Development, 58,* 306–315.

Lempers, J. D., & Clark-Lempers, D. S. (1993). A functional comparison of same-sex and opposite-sex friendships during adolescence. *Journal of Adolescent Research, 8,* 89–108.

Lennon, R., & Eisenberg, N. (1987). Gender and age differences in empathy and sympathy. In N. Eisenberg & J. Strayer (Eds.), *Empathy and its development* (pp. 195–217). Cambridge, England: Cambridge University Press.

Lennon, R., Eisenberg, N., & Carroll, J. (1986). The relation between empathy and prosocial behavior in the preschool years. *Journal of Applied Developmental Psychology, 7,* 219–224.

Leonard, S. P., & Archer, J. (1989). A naturalistic investigation of gender constancy in three- to four-year-old children. *British Journal of Developmental Psychology, 7,* 341–346.

Lerner, H. E. (1978). Adaptive and pathogenic aspects of sex-role stereotypes: Implications of parenting and psychotherapy. *American Journal of Psychiatry, 135,* 48–52.

Lerner, R. M. (1981). Adolescent development: Scientific study in the 1980s. *Youth and Society, 12,* 251–275.

Lerner, R. M. (1984). *On the nature of human plasticity.* New York: Cambridge University Press.

Lerner, R. M. (1985). Adolescent maturational changes and psychosocial development: A dynamic interactional perspective. *Journal of Youth and Adolescence, 14,* 355–372.

Levit, D. B. (1991). Gender differences in ego defenses in adolescence: Sex roles as one way to understand the differences. *Journal of Personality and Social Psychology, 61,* 992–999.

Levy, G. D. (1989). Relations among aspects of children's social environments, gender schematization, gender role knowledge, and flexibility. *Sex Roles, 21,* 803–823.

Levy, G. D., & Carter, D. B. (1989). Gender schema, gender constancy, and gender-role knowledge: The roles of cognitive factors in preschoolers' gender-role stereotype attributions. *Developmental Psychology, 25,* 444–449.

Levy, G. D., & Fivush, R. (1993). Scripts and gender: A new approach for examining sex-role development. *Developmental Review, 13,* 126–146.

Levy, G. D., Haaf, R. A., & Sommer, K. L. (1991, April). *Infants' detection of correlated features among social stimuli: A precursor to stereotyping?* Paper presented at the biennial meeting of the Society for Research in Child Development, Seattle.

Levy, J. (1976). Cerebral lateralization and spatial ability. *Behavior Genetics, 6,* 171–188.

Lewis, M., Alessandri, S. M., & Sullivan, M. W. (1992). Individual differences in shame and pride as a function of children's gender, task difficulty, and parental attribution. *Child Development, 63,* 630–638.

Lewis, M., & Brooks-Gunn, J. (1979). *Social cognition and the acquisition of self.* New York: Plenum Press.

Lewis, M., & Michalson, L. (1983). *Children's emotions and moods.* New York: Plenum Press.

Liben, L. S., & Bigler, R. S. (1987). Reformulating children's gender schemata. In L. S. Liben & M. L. Signorella (Eds.), *Children's gender schemata* (pp. 89–194). San Francisco: Jossey-Bass.

Liben, L. S., & Signorella, M. L. (1980). Gender-related schemata and constructive memory in children. *Child Development, 51,* 11–18.

Linn, M. C., & Hyde, J. S. (1989). Gender, mathematics, and science. *Educational Researcher, 18,* 17–19, 22–27.

Linn, M. C., & Petersen, A. C. (1985). Emergence and characterization of sex differences in spatial ability: A meta-analysis. *Child Development, 56,* 1479–1498.

Lipsitt, L. P., & Levy, N. (1959). Electroactual threshold in the neonate. *Child Development, 30,* 547–554.

Liss, M. B. (1981). Patterns of toy play: An analysis of sex differences. *Sex Roles, 7,* 1143–1150.

Liss, M. B. (1983). Learning gender-related skills through play. In M. B. Liss (Ed.), *Social and cognitive skills: Sex roles and children's play* (pp. 147–167). New York: Academic Press.

Lobel, T. E., & Menashri, J. (1993). The relations of conceptions of gender-role transgressions and gender constancy to gender-typed toy preferences. *Developmental Psychology, 29,* 150–155.

Lobel, T. E., & Winch, G. (1992). *Masculinity, popularity and self-esteem among elementary-school girls.* Unpublished manuscript.

Lockheed, M. (1985). Sex equity in classroom organization and climate. In S. Klein (Ed.), *Handbook for achieving sex equity through education* (pp. 189–217). Baltimore: Johns Hopkins University Press.

Lockheed, M., & Harris, A. (1984). Cross-sex collaborative learning in elementary classrooms. *American Educational Research Journal, 21,* 275–294.

Lorber, J. (1986). Dismantling Noah's ark. *Sex Roles, 14,* 567–580.

Lubinski, D., & Benbow, C. P. (1992). Gender differences in abilities and preferences among the gifted: Implications for the math-science pipeline. *Current Directions in Psychological Science, 1,* 63–66.

Luria, Z., & Herzog, E. (1985, April). *Gender segregation across and within settings.* Paper presented at the biennial meeting of the Society for Research in Child Development, Toronto.

Lyons, J. A., & Serbin, L. A. (1986). Observer bias in scoring boys' and girls' aggression. *Sex Roles, 14,* 301–313.

Lytton, H. (1990). Child and parent effects in boys' conduct disorder: A reinterpretation. *Developmental Psychology, 26,* 683–697.

Lytton, H., & Romney, D. M. (1991). Parents' differential socialization of boys and girls: A meta-analysis. *Psychological Bulletin, 109,* 267–296.

Macaulay, J. (1985). Adding gender to aggression research: Incremental or revolutionary change. In V. E. O'Leary, R. K. Unger, & B. S. Wallston (Eds.), *Women, gender, and social psychology* (pp. 191–224). Hillsdale, NJ: Lawrence Erlbaum Associates.

Maccoby, E. E. (1980). *Social development.* San Diego: Harcourt.

Maccoby, E. E. (1988). Gender as a social category. *Developmental Psychology, 24,* 755–765.

Maccoby, E. E. (1990a). Gender and relationships: A developmental account. *American Psychologist, 45,* 513–520.

Maccoby, E. E. (1990b). The role of gender identity and gender constancy in sex-differentiated development. In D. Schroder (Ed.), *New directions for child development* (pp. 5–20). San Francisco: Jossey-Bass.

Maccoby, E. E., & Jacklin, C. N. (1974). *The psychology of sex differences.* Stanford, CA: Stanford University Press.

Maccoby. E. E., & Jacklin, C. N. (1980). Sex differences in aggression: A rejoinder and reprise. *Child Development, 51,* 964–980.

Maccoby, E. E., & Jacklin, C. N. (1987). Gender segregation in childhood. In H. W. Reese (Ed.), *Advances in child development and behavior* (Vol. 20, pp. 239–288). New York: Academic Press.

Malatesta, C. Z., Culver, C., Tesman, J. R., & Shepard, B. (1989). The development of emotional expression during the first two years of life. *Monographs of the Society for Research in Child Development, 54* (Serial No. 219), 1–113.

Malatesta, C. Z., & Haviland, J. M. (1982). Learning display rules: The socialization of emotion expression in infancy. *Child Development 53,* 991–1003.

Marcus, D. E., & Overton, W. F. (1978). The development of cognitive gender constancy and sex role preferences. *Child Development, 49,* 434–444.

Markus, H., Crane, M., Bernstein, S., & Siladi, M. (1982). Self-schemas and gender. *Journal of Personality and Social Psychology, 42,* 38–50.

Marsh, H. W. (1986). Verbal and math self-concepts: An internal/external frame of reference model. *American Educational Research Journal, 23,* 129–149.

Marsh, H. W., Byrne, B. M., & Shavelson, R. J. (1988). A multifaceted academic self-concept: Its hierarchical structure and its relation to academic achievement. *Journal of Educational Psychology, 80,* 366–380.

Marsh, H. W., Smith, M. D., & Barnes, J. (1985). Multidimensional self-concepts: Relations with sex and academic achievement. *Journal of Educational Psychology, 77,* 581–596.

Marshall, S. P., & Smith, J. D. (1987). Sex differences in learning mathematics: A longitudinal study with item and error analyses. *Journal of Educational Psychology, 79,* 372–383.

Martin, C. L. (1987). A ratio measure of sex stereotyping. *Journal of Personality and Social Psychology, 52,* 489–499.

Martin, C. L. (1989a, April). *Beyond knowledge-based conceptions of gender schematic processing.* Paper presented at the biennial meeting of the Society for Research in Child Development, Kansas City, MO.

Martin, C. L. (1989b). Children's use of gender-related information in making social judgments. *Developmental Psychology, 25,* 80–88.

Martin, C. L. (1990). Attitudes and expectations about children with nontraditional and traditional gender roles. *Sex Roles, 22,* 151–165.

Martin, C. L. (1991). The role of cognition in understanding gender effects. In H. Reese (Ed.), *Advances in child development and behavior* (Vol. 23, pp. 113–149). New York: Academic Press.

Martin, C. L. (1993). New directions for assessing children's gender knowledge. *Developmental Review, 13,* 184–204.

Martin, C. L., Eisenbud, L., & Rose, H. (1995). Children's gender-based reasoning about toys. *Child Development, 66,* 1453–1471.

Martin, C. L., Fabes, R. A., Eisenbud, L., Karbon, M. M., & Rose, H. A. (1990, March). *Boys don't cry: Children's distortions of others' emotions.* Paper presented at the biennial meeting of the Southwestern Society for Research in Human Development, Dallas.

Martin, C. L., & Halverson, C. F. (1981). A schematic processing model of sex typing stereotyping in children. *Child Development, 52,* 1119–1134.

Martin, C. L., & Halverson, C. F. (1983a). The effects of sex-typing schemas on young children's memory. *Child Development, 54,* 563–574.

Martin, C. L., & Halverson, C. F. (1983b). Gender constancy: A methodological and theoretical analysis. *Sex Roles, 9,* 775–790.

Martin, C. L., & Halverson, C. F. (1987). The roles of cognition in sex role acquisition. In D. B. Carter (Ed.), *Current conceptions of sex roles and sex typing: Theory and research.* New York: Praeger.

Martin, C. L., & Little, J. K. (1990). The relation of gender understanding to children's sex-typed preferences and gender stereotypes. *Child Development, 61,* 1427–1439.

Martin, C. L., & Parker, S. (1995). Folk theories about sex and race differences. *Personality and Social Psychology Bulletin, 21,* 45–57.

Martin, C. L. K., Wood, C. H., & Little, J. K. (1990). The development of gender stereotype components. *Child Development, 61,* 1891–1904.

Matthews, K. A., Batson, C. D., Horn, J., & Rosenman, R. H. (1981). Principles in his nature which interest him in the fortune of others: The heritability of empathic concern for others. *Journal of Personality, 49,* 237–247.

McConaghy, M. J. (1979). Gender permanence and the genital basis of gender: Stages in the development of constancy of gender identity. *Child Development, 50,* 1223–1226.

McGillicuddy-De Lisi, A. V. (1985). The relationship between parental beliefs and children's cognitive level. In I. E. Sigel (Ed.), *Parental belief systems* (pp. 7–24). Hillsdale, NJ: Lawrence Erlbaum Associates.

McKugh, M. C., Koeske, R. D., & Frieze, I. H. (1986). Issues to consider in conducting nonsexist psychological research. *American Psychologist, 41,* 879–890.

McMullen, P. A., & Gross, A. E. (1983). Sex differences, sex roles, and health-related help-seeking. In B. M. DePaulo, A. Nadler, & J. D. Fisher (Eds.), *New directions in helping: Vol. 2. Help seeking* (pp. 233–263). New York: Academic Press.

Meaney, M. J., Stewart, J., & Beatty, W. W. (1985). Sex differences in social play: The socialization of sex roles. In J. S. Rosenblatt, C. Beer, C. M. Bushnell, & P. Slater (Eds.), *Advances in the Study of Behavior* (Vol. 15, pp. 1–58). Orlando, FL: Academic Press.

Meyer, J. W., & Sobieszek, B. I. (1972). Effect of a child's sex on adult interpretations of its behavior. *Developmental Psychology, 6,* 42–48.

Miller, C. L. (1987). Qualitative differences among gender-stereotyped toys: Implications for cognitive and social development in girls and boys. *Sex Roles, 16,* 473–487.

Miller, P. A., & Eisenberg, N. (1988). The relation of empathy to aggression and externalizing/antisocial behavior. *Psychological Bulletin, 103,* 324–344.

Minuchin, P. P., & Shapiro, E. K. (1983). The school as a context for social development. In P. Mussen (Series Ed.), *Handbook of child psychology* (Vol. IV, pp. 197–274). New York: Wiley.

Mischel, W. (1966). A socio-learning view of sex differences in behavior. In E. E. Maccoby (Ed.), *The development of sex differences* (pp. 57–81). Stanford, CA: Stanford University Press.

Mischel, W. (1970). Sex typing and socialization. In P. H. Mussen (Ed.), *Carmichael's Handbook of Child Psychology* (Vol. 2, pp. 3–72). New York: Wiley.

Mischel, W. (1979). On the interface of cognition and personality: Beyond the person-situation debate. *American Psychologist, 34,* 740–754.

Money, J., & Ehrhardt, A. A. (1972). *Man & woman. Boy & girl.* Baltimore: Johns Hopkins University Press.

Montemayor, R. (1974). Children's performance in a game and their attraction to it as a function of sex-typed labels. *Child Development, 45,* 152–156.

Moss, H. A. (1974). Early sex differences in mother-infant interaction. In R. C. Riedman, R. M. Riehart, & R. L. Vande Wiele (Eds.), *Sex differences in behavior* (pp. 149–164). New York: Wiley.

Munroe, R. H., Shimmin, H. S., & Munroe, R. L. (1984). Gender understanding and sex role preference in four cultures. *Developmental psychology, 20,* 673–682.

Nadelman, L. (1974). Sex identity in American children: Memory, knowledge, and preference tests. *Developmental Psychology, 10,* 413–417.

Nadler, A. (1991). Help-seeking behavior: Psychological costs and instrumental benefits. In M. Clark (Ed.), *Review of personality and social psychology* (Vol. 12, pp. 290–311). Newbury, CA: Sage.

Nannis, E. D., & Cowan, P. A. (1987). Emotional understanding: A matter of age, dimension, and point of view. *Journal of Applied Developmental Psychology, 8,* 289–304.

National Science Board. (1987). *Science and engineering indicators–1987.* Washington, DC: U.S. Government Printing Office.

Nelson-Le Gall, S. A. (1981). Help-seeking: An understudied problem-solving skill in children. *Developmental Review, 1,* 224–246.

Nelson-Le Gall, S. A., & De Cooke, P. A. (1987). Same-sex and cross-sex help exchanges in the classroom. *Journal of Educational Psychology, 79,* 67–71.

Newcomer, S., & Udry, J. (1987). Parental marital status effects on adolescent sexual behavior. *Journal of Marriage and the Family, 49,* 235–240.

Newman, R. S., & Goldin, L. (1990). Children's reluctance to seek help with schoolwork. *Journal of Educational Psychology, 82,* 92–100.

Newson, J., & Newson, E. (1976). *Seven years old in the home environment.* London: Allen & Unwin.

Noddings, N. (1984). *Caring: A feminine approach to ethics and moral education.* Berkeley: University of California Press.

Noddings, N. (1992). Variability: A pernicious hypothesis. *Journal of Educational Research, 62,* 85–88.

Nolen-Hoeksema, S. (1987). Sex differences in unipolar depression: Evidence and theory. *Journal of Personality and Social Psychology, 101,* 259–282.

Nolen-Hoeksema, S. (1991, August). *Sex differences in responses to depression.* Paper presented at the annual meeting of the American Psychological Association, San Francisco.

Northman, J. (1978). Development changes in preferences for help. *Journal of Clinical Child Psychology, 7,* 129–132.

O'Brien, M., & Huston, A. C. (1985). Development of sex-typed play behavior in toddlers. *Developmental Psychology, 21,* 866–871.

Offord, D. R., Boyle, M. C., & Racine, Y. A. (1991). The epidemiology of antisocial behavior in childhood and adolescence. In D. J. Pepler & K. H. Rubin (Eds.), *The development and treatment of childhood aggression* (pp. 31–54). Hillsdale, NJ: Lawrence Erlbaum Associates.

O'Keefe, E. S., & Hyde, J. S. (1983). The development of occupational sex-role stereotypes: The effects of gender stability and age. *Sex Roles, 9,* 481–492.

Olson, S. L. (1989). Assessment of impulsivity in preschoolers: Cross-measure convergences, longitudinal stability, and relevance to social competence. *Journal of Clinical Child Psychology, 18,* 176–183.

Olweus, D. (1980). Familial and temperamental determinants of aggressive behavior in adolescent boys: A causal analysis. *Developmental Psychology, 16,* 644–660.

Olweus, D. (1986). Aggression and hormones: Behavioral relationship with testosterone and adrenaline. In D. Olweus, J. Block, & M. Radke-Yarrow (Eds.), *Development of antisocial and prosocial behavior: Research theories, and issues* (pp. 51–72). Orlando, FL: Academic Press.

Overton, W. F., & Reese, H. W. (1973). Models of development: Methodological implications. In J. R. Nesselroade & H. W. Reese (Eds.), *Life-span developmental psychology: Methodological issues* (pp. 65–86). New York: Academic Press.

Papalia, D. E., & Tennent, S. S. (1975). Vocational aspirations in preschoolers. *Sex Roles, 1,* 197–199.

Papini, D. R., Farmer, F. F., Clark, S. M., Micka, J. C., & Barnett, J. K. (1990). Early adolescent age and gender differences in patterns of emotional self-disclosure to parents and friends. *Adolescence, 25,* 959–976.

Papini, D. R., & Sebby, R. A. (1987). Adolescent pubertal status and affective family relationships: A multivariate assessment. *Journal of Youth and Adolescence, 16,* 1–15.

Parke, R. D., & Slaby, R. G. (1983). The development of aggression. In P. H. Mussen (Ed.), *Handbook of child psychology: Vol. 4: Socialization personality, and social development* (pp. 547–641; E. M. Hetherington, Ed.). New York: Wiley.

Parlee, M. B. (1972). Comments on D. M. Broverman, E. L. Klaiber, Y. Kobayashi, and W. Vogel: Roles of activation and inhibition in sex differences in cognitive abilities. *Psychological Review, 79,* 180–184.

Parsons, J. E., & Kaczala, C. M., & Meece, J. L. (1982). Socialization of achievement attitudes and beliefs: Classroom influences. *Child Development, 53,* 322–329.

Parsons, T., & Bales, R. F. (1955). *Family, socialization, and interaction processes.* New York: Academic Press.

Paulhus, D. L., & Martin, C. L. (1988). Functional flexibility: A new conception of interpersonal flexibility. *Journal of Personality and Social Psychology, 55,* 88–101.

Paulhus, D. L., Martin, C. L., & Murphy, G. (1992). Some effects of arousal on sex stereotyping. *Personality and Social Psychology Bulletin, 18,* 325–330.

Pedersen, D. M., Shinedling, M. M., & Johnson, D. L. (1968). Effects of sex of examiner and subject on children's quantitative test performance. *Journal of Personality and Social Psychology, 10,* 251–254.

Pellegrini, D. S. (1985). Social cognition and competence in middle childhood. *Child Development, 56,* 253–264.

Pellegrini, D. S. (1986). Variability in children's level of reasoning about friendship. *Journal of Applied Developmental Psychology, 7,* 341–354.

Peretti, P. O., & Sydney, T. M. (1984). Parental toy choice stereotyping and its effects on child toy preference and sex-role typing. *Social Behavior and Personality, 12,* 213–216.

Perry, D. G., & Bussy, K. (1979). The social learning theory of sex differences: Imitation is alive and well. *Journal of Personality and Social Psychology, 37,* 1699–1712.

Perry, D. G., Perry, L. C., & Rasmussen, P. (1986). Cognitive social learning mediators of aggression. *Child Development, 57,* 700–711.

Perry, D. G., Perry, L. C., & Weiss, R. J. (1989). Sex differences in the consequences that children anticipate for aggression. *Developmental Psychology, 25,* 312–319.

Perry, D. G., White, A. J., & Perry, L. C. (1984). Does early sex typing result from children's attempts to match their behavior to sex role stereotypes? *Child Development, 55,* 2114–2121.

Peskin, H. (1973). Influence of the developmental schedule of puberty on learning and ego functioning. *Journal of Youth and Adolescence, 4,* 273–290.

Petersen, A. C. (1976). Physical androgyny and cognitive functioning in adolescence. *Developmental Psychology, 12,* 524–533.

Petersen, A. C., & Crockett, L. (1985). Pubertal timing and grade effects on adjustment. *Journal of Youth and Adolescence, 14,* 191–206.

Petersen, A. C., Sarigiani, P. A., & Kennedy, R. F. (1991). Adolescent depression: Why more girls? *Journal of Youth and Adolescence, 20,* 247–271.

Phillips, S., King, S., & DuBois, L. (1978). Spontaneous activities of female versus male newborns. *Child Development, 49,* 590–597.

Pierce, E. W., & Campbell, S. (1991, April). *Impulsivity as a component of behavior problems in preschool boys.* Paper presented at the biennial meeting of the Society for Research in Child Development, Seattle.

Pomerleau, A., Bolduc, D., Malcuit, G., & Cossette, L. (1990). Pink or blue: Environmental gender stereotypes in the first two years of life. *Sex Roles, 22,* 359–367.

Pottker, J., & Fishel, A. (1977). *Sex bias in the schools: The research evidence.* Cranbury, NJ: Associated University Presses.

Poulin-Dubois, D., Serbin, L. A., Kenyon, B., & Derbyshire, A. (1994). Infants' intermodal knowledge about gender. *Developmental Psychology, 30,* 436–442.

Power, T. G., & Parke, R. D. (1986). Patterns of early socialization: Mother- and father-infant interaction in the home. *International Journal of Behavioral Development, 9,* 331–341.

Power, T. G., & Shanks, J. A. (1989). Parents as socializers: Maternal and paternal views. *Journal of Youth and Adolescence, 18,* 203–220.

Pratt, M. W., Golding, G., Hunter, W., & Sampson, R. (1988). Sex differences in adult moral orientations. *Journal of Personality, 56,* 373–391.

Pratt, M. W., Golding, G., & Kerig, P. (1987). Lifespan differences in adult thinking about hypothetical and personal moral issues: Reflection or regression? *International Journal of Behavioral Development, 10,* 359–375.

Pulkkinen, L. (1986). The role of impulse control in the development of antisocial and prosocial behavior. In D. Olweus, J. Block, & M. Radke-Yarrow (eds.), *Development of antisocial and prosocial behavior: Research, theories, and issues* (pp. 149–206). Orlando, FL: Academic Press.

Purcell, P., & Stewart, L. (1990). Dick and Jane in 1989. *Sex Roles, 22,* 177–185.

Pyszczynski, T., Greenberg, J., Hamilton, J., & Nix, G. (1991). On the relationship between self-focused attention and psychological disorder: A critical reappraisal. *Psychological Bulletin, 110,* 538–543.

Radke-Yarrow, M., Zahn-Waxler, C., & Chapman, M. (1983). Prosocial dispositions and behavior. In P. Mussen (Ed.), *Manual of child psychology: Vol. 4. Socialization, personality, and social development* (pp. 469–545; E. M. Hetherington, Ed.). New York: Wiley.

Rabiner, D. L., Lenhart, L., & Lochman, J. E. (1990). Automatic versus reflective social problem solving in relation to children's sociometric status. *Developmental Psychology, 26,* 1010–1016.

Reese, H. W., & Overton, W. F. (1970). Models of development and theories of development. In L. R. Goulet & P. B. Baltes (ed.), *Life-span developmental psychology. Research and theory* (pp. 115–145). New York: Academic Press.

Reis, H. T., & Wright, S. (1982). Knowledge of sex-role stereotyping in children aged 3 to 5. *Sex Roles, 8,* 1049–1056.

Rest, J. R. (1979). *Development in judging moral issues.* Minneapolis: University of Minnesota Press.

Rheingold, H. L., & Cook, K. V. (1975). The contents of boys' and girls' rooms as an index of parents' behavior. *Child Development, 46,* 445–463.

Roberts, T. (1991). Gender and the influence of evaluations on self-assessments in achievement settings. *Psychological Bulletin, 109,* 297–308.

Robinson, C. C., & Morris, J. T. (1986). The gender-stereotyped nature of Christmas toys received by 36-, 48-, and 60-month old children: A comparison between nonrequested vs. requested toys. *Sex Roles, 15,* 21–32.

Roopnarine, J. L. (1984). Sex-typed socialization in mixed-aged preschool classrooms. *Child Development, 55,* 1078–1084.

Roopnarine, J. L. (1986). Mothers' and fathers' behaviors toward the toy play of their infant sons and daughters. *Sex Roles, 14,* 59–68.

Roopnarine, J. L., & Mounts, N. S. (1987). Current theoretical issues in sex roles and sex typing. In D. B. Carter (Ed.), *Current conceptions of sex roles and sex typing* (pp. 7–32). New York: Praeger.

Rotenberg, K. J. (1984). Sex differences in children's trust in peers. *Sex Roles, 11,* 954–957.

Rothbart, M. K., & Derryberry, D. (1981). Development of individual differences in temperament. In M. E. Lamb & A. L. Brown (Eds.), *Advances in developmental psychology* (Vol. 1, pp. 37–86). Hillsdale, NJ: Lawrence Erlbaum Associates.

Rothbart, M. K., Hanley, D., & Albert, M. (1986). Gender differences in moral reasoning. *Sex Roles, 15,* 645–653.

Rotter, N. G., & Rotter, G. S. (1988). Sex differences in the encoding and decoding of negative facial emotions. *Journal of Nonverbal Behavior, 12,* 139–148.

Ruble, D. N. (1988). Sex-role development. In M. H. Bornstein & M. E. Lamb (Eds.), *Developmental psychology: An advanced textbook* (2nd ed., pp. 411–460). Hillsdale, NJ: Lawrence Erlbaum Associates.

Ruble, D. N. (1991, August). *Motivational consequences of social-cognitive transitions.* Paper presented at the annual meeting of the American Psychological Association, San Francisco.

Ruble, D. N., Balaban, T., & Cooper, J. (1981). Gender constancy and the effect of televised toy commercials. *Child Development, 52,* 667–673.

Ruble, D. N., & Ruble, T. L. (1982). Sex stereotypes. In A. G. Miller (Ed.), *In the eye of the beholder: Contemporary issues in stereotyping* (pp. 188–252). New York: Holt, Rinehart, & Winston.

Rumenik, D. K., Capasso, D. R., & Hendrick, C. (1977). Experimenter sex effects in behavioral research. *Psychological Bulletin, 84,* 852–877.

Russell, J. A. (1990). The preschooler's understanding of the causes and consequences of emotions. *Child Development, 61,* 1872–1881.

Rutter, M. (1980). *Changing youth in a changing society: Patterns of adolescent development and disorder.* Cambridge, MA: Harvard University Press.

Saarni, C. (1984). An observational study of children's attempts to monitor their expressive behavior. *Child Development, 55,* 1504–1513.

Sadker, D., & Sadker, M. (1985). The treatment of sex equity in teacher education. In S. S. Klein (Ed.), *Handbook for achieving sex equity through education* (pp. 145–162). Baltimore: Johns Hopkins University Press.

Scherer, K. R., Wallbott, H. G., & Summerfield, A. B. (1986). *Experiencing emotion: A cross-cultural study.* Cambridge, England: Cambridge University Press.

Schofield, J. W. (1981). Complementary and conflicting identities: Images and interaction in an interracial school. In S. R. Asher & J. M. Gottman (Eds.), *The development of children's friendships* (pp. 53–90). Cambridge, England: Cambridge University Press.

Searcy, E. B., & Eisenberg, N. (1992). Defensiveness in response to aid from a sibling. *Journal of Personality and Social Psychology, 62,* 422–433.

Selman, R. L. (1980). *The growth of interpersonal understanding: Developmental and clinical analysis.* New York: Academic Press.

Serbin, L. A., Connor, J. M., Burchardt, C. J., & Citron, C. C. (1979).

Effects of peer presence on sex-typing of children's play behavior. *Journal of Experimental Child Psychology, 27,* 303–309.

Serbin, L. A., Conner, J. M., & Iler, I. (1979). Sex stereotyped and nonstereotyped introductions of new toys in the preschool classroom: An observational study of teacher behavior and its effects. *Psychology of Women Quarterly, 4,* 261–265.

Serbin, L. A., O'Leary, K. D., Kent, R. N., & Tonick, I. J. (1973). A comparison of teacher response to the preacademic and problem behavior of boys and girls. *Child Development, 44,* 796–804.

Serbin, L. A., Powlishta, K. K., & Gulko, J. (1993). The development of sex-typing in middle childhood. *Monographs of the Society for Research in Child Development.*

Serbin, L. A., & Sprafkin, C. (1986). The salience of gender and the process of sex typing in three- to seven-year-old children. *Child Development 57,* 1188–1199.

Serbin, L. A., Sprafkin, C., Elman, M., & Doyle, A. B. (1984). The early development of sex differentiated patterns of social influence. *Canadian Journal of Social Science, 14,* 350–363.

Serbin, L. A., Zelkowitz, P., Doyle, A., Gold, D., & Wheaton, B. (1990). The socialization of sex-differentiated skills and academic performance: A mediational model. *Sex Roles, 23,* 613–628.

Shakin, M., Shakin, D., & Sternglanz, S. H. (1985). Infant clothing: Sex labeling for strangers. *Sex Roles, 12,* 955–963.

Shantz, C. V. (1975). The development of social cognition. In E. M. Hetherington (Ed.), *Review of child development research* (Vol. 5, pp. 257–323). Chicago: University of Chicago Press.

Shell, R., & Eisenberg, N. (1992). A developmental model of recipients' reactions to aid. *Psychological Bulletin, 111,* 413–433.

Shell, R., & Eisenberg, N. (1990). The role of peers' gender in children's naturally occurring interest in toys. *International Journal of Behavioral Development, 13,* 373–388.

Shennum, W. A., & Bugental, D. B. (1982). The development of control over affective expression in nonverbal behavior. In R. S. Feldman (Ed.), *Development of nonverbal behavior in children* (pp. 101–121). New York: Springer.

Sherman, J. A. (1967). Problem of sex differences in space perception and aspects of intellectual functioning. *Psychological Review, 74,* 290–299.

Shields, S. A. (1975). Functionalism, Darwinism, and the psychology of women. *American Psychologist, 30,* 739–754.

Shigetomi, C. C., Hartmann, D. P., & Gelfand, D. M. (1981). Sex differences in children's altruistic behaviors and reputations for helpfulness. *Developmental Psychology, 17,* 434–437.

Signorella, M. L. (1987). Gender schemata: Individual differences and context effects. In L. S. Liben & M. L. Signorella (Eds.), *Children's gender schemata* (pp. 23–38). San Francisco: Jossey-Bass.

Signorella, M. L., Bigler, R. S., & Liben, L. S. (1993). Developmental differences in children's gender schemata about others: A meta-analytic review. *Developmental Review, 13,* 147–183.

Signorella, M. L., & Liben, L. S. (1984). Recall and reconstruction of gender-related pictures: Effects of attitude, task difficulty, and age. *Child Development, 55,* 393–405.

Signorella, M. L., & Vegaga, M. E. (1984). A note on gender stereotyping in research topics. *Personality and Social Psychology Bulletin, 10,* 107–109.

Silverman, I. W., & Ragusa, D. M. (1990). Child and maternal correlates of impulse control in 24-month-old children. *Genetic, Social, and General Psychology Monographs, 116,* 435–473.

Silvern, L. E., & Katz, P. A. (1986). Gender roles and adjustment in elementary-school children: A multi-dimensional approach. *Sex Roles, 14,* 181–202.

Simmons, R., Blyth, D., & McKinney, K. (1983). The social and psychological effects of puberty on white females. In J. Brooks-Gunn & A. Petersen (Eds.), *Girls at puberty: Biological and psychosocial perspectives* (pp. 111–140). New York: Plenum Press.

Singleton, L. C., & Asher, S. R. (1977). Peer preferences and social interaction among third-grade children in an integrated school district. *Journal of Educational Psychology, 69,* 330–336.

Singleton, L. C., & Asher, S. R. (1979). Racial integration and children's peer preferences: An investigation of developmental and cohort differences. *Child Development, 50,* 936–941.

Skaalvik, E. M., & Rankin, R. J. (1900). Math, verbal, and general academic self-concept: The internal/external frame of reference model and gender differences in self-concept structure. *Journal of Educational Psychology, 82,* 546–554.

Slaby, R. G. (1990). The gender concept development legacy. In D. Schrader (Ed.). *New directions for child development* (pp. 21–29). San Francisco: Jossey-Bass.

Slaby, R. G., & Frey, K. S. (1975). Development of gender constancy and selective attention to same-sex models. *Child Development, 52,* 849–856.

Slaby, R. G., & Guerra, N. G. (1988). Cognitive mediators of aggression in adolescent offenders: 1. *Developmental Psychology, 24,* 580–588.

Sleven, K. F., & Balswick, J. (1980). Children's perceptions of parental expressiveness. *Sex Roles, 6,* 293–299.

Smetana, J. G. (1983). Social-cognitive development: Domain distinctions and coordinations. *Developmental Review, 3,* 131–147.

Smetana, J. G. (1986). Preschool children's conceptions of sex-role transgressions. *Child Development, 57,* 862–871.

Smetana, J. G., & Letourneau, K. J. (1984). Development of gender constancy and children's sex-typed free play behavior. *Developmental Psychology, 20,* 691–695.

Smith, E., Udry, J., & Morris, N. (1985). Pubertal development and friends: A biosocial explanation of adolescent sexual behavior. *Journal of Health and Social Behavior, 26,* 183–192.

Smith, J., & Russell, G. (1984). Why do males and females differ? Children's beliefs about sex differences. *Sex Roles, 11,* 1111–1120.

Smoll, F. L., & Schutz, R. W. (1990). Quantifying gender differences in physical performance: A developmental perspective. *Developmental Psychology, 26,* 360–369.

Soppe, H. J. G. (1988). Age differences in the decoding of affect authenticity and intensity. *Journal of Nonverbal Behavior, 12,* 107–119.

Spence, J. T. (1984). Masculinity, femininity, and gender-related traits: A conceptual analysis and critique of current research. In B. A. Maher & W. B. Maher (Eds.), *Progress in experimental research* (Vol. 13, pp. 1–97). New York: Academic Press.

Spence, J. T., Deaux, K., & Helmreich, R. L. (1985). Sex roles in contemporary American society. In G. Lindzey & E. Aronson (Eds.), *Handbook of social psychology* (3rd ed., Vol. 2, pp. 149–178). New York: Random House.

Spence, J. T., Helmreich, R., & Stapp, J. (1974). The Personal Attributes Questionnaire: A measure of sex role stereotypes and masculinity-femininity. *Journal of Supplemental Abstract Service Catalog of Selected Documents in Psychology, 4,* 43.

Spence, J. T., & Helmreich, R. L. (1978). *Masculinity and femininity: Their psychological dimensions, correlates, and antecedents.* Austin: University of Texas Press.

Spuhler, K. P., & Vandenberg, S. G. (1980). Comparison of parent-offspring resemblance in specific cognitive abilities. *Behavior Genetics, 10,* 413–418.

Stangor, C., Ruble, D. N. (1987). Development of gender role knowledge and gender constancy. In L. S. Liben & M. L. Signorella (Eds.), *Children's gender schemata* (pp. 5–22). San Francisco: Jossey-Bass.

Stangor, C., & Ruble, D. N. (1989). Differential influences of gender schemata and gender constancy on children's information processing and behavior. *Social Cognition, 7,* 353–372.

Stapley, J. C., & Haviland, J. M. (1989). Beyond depression: Gender differences in normal adolescents' emotional experiences. *Sex Roles, 20,* 295–308.

Steinberg, L. (1981). Transformations in family relations at puberty. *Developmental Psychology, 17,* 833–840.

Steinberg, M., & Dodge, K. A. (1983). Attributional bias in aggressive

adolescent boys and girls. *Journal of Social and Clinical Psychology, 4,* 312–321.

Stern, M., & Karracker, K. H. (1989). Sex stereotyping of infants: A review of gender labeling studies. *Sex Roles, 20,* 501–522.

Stipek, D. J., & Gralinski, J. H. (1991). Gender differences in children's achievement-related beliefs and emotional responses to success and failure in mathematics. *Journal of Educational Psychology, 83,* 361–371.

Stockard, J., Schmuck, P., Kempner, K., Williams, P., Edson, S., & Smith, M. A. (1980). *Sex equity in education.* New York: Academic Press.

Stoddard, T., & Turiel, E. (1985). Children's concepts of cross-gender activities. *Child Development, 56,* 1241–1252.

Strayer, J. (1983, April). *Developmental changes in nonverbal affect expression.* Paper presented at the biennial meeting of the Society for Research in Child Development, Toronto.

Strayer, J. (1986). Children's attributions regarding the situational determinants of emotion in self and others. *Developmental Psychology, 22,* 649–654.

Strouse, J., & Fabes, R. A. (1988). A conceptualization of transition to nonvirginity in adolescent females. *Journal of Adolescent Research, 2,* 331–348.

Tanner, J. M. (1972). Sequence, tempo, and individual variation in growth and development of boys and girls aged 12 and 16. *Daedalus, 100,* 907–930.

Taylor, M. (1988). Conceptual perspective taking: Children's ability to distinguish what they know from what they see. *Child Development, 59,* 703–718.

Taylor, M., & Gelman, S. A. (1991, April). *Children's beliefs about sex differences: The role of nature vs. nurture.* Paper presented at a meeting of the Society for Research in Child Development, Seattle.

Thoma, S. J. (1986). Estimating gender differences in the comprehension and preference of moral issues. *Developmental Review, 6,* 165–180.

Thomas, J. R., & French, K. E. (1985). Gender differences across age in motor performance: A meta-analysis. *Psychological Bulletin, 98,* 260–282.

Thomas, J. R., & Thomas, K. T. (1988). Development of gender differences in physical activity. *Quest, 40,* 219–229.

Thompson, C. M. (1964). *Interpersonal psychoanalysis: The selected papers of Clara M. Thompson.* New York: Basic Books.

Thompson, S. K. (1975). Gender labels and early sex-role development. *Child development, 46,* 339–347.

Thompson, S. K., & Bentler, P. M. (1971). The priority of cues in sex discrimination by children and adults. *Developmental Psychology, 5,* 181–185.

Tieger, T. (1980). On the biological basis of sex differences in aggression. *Child Development, 51,* 943–963.

Tobin-Richards, M. H., Boxer, A. M., & Petersen, A. C. (1983). The psychological significance of pubertal change: Sex differences in perceptions of self during early adolescence. In J. Brooks-Gunn & A. C. Petersen (Eds.), *Girls at puberty: Biological and psychosocial perspectives* (pp. 127–154). New York: Plenum Press.

Trautner, H. M. (1985, April). *The significance of the appearance-reality distinction for the development of gender constancy.* Paper presented at the biennial meeting of the Society for Research in Child Development, Toronto.

Trautner, H. M., Helbing, N., Sahm, W. B., Lohaus, A. (1989, April). *Beginning awareness-rigidity-flexibility: A longitudinal analysis of sex-role stereotyping in four- to ten-year-old children.* Paper presented at the biennial meeting of the Society for Research in Child Development, Kansas City, MO.

Trecker, J. L. (1977). Women in U.S. history high-school textbooks. In J. Pottker & A. Fishel (Eds.), *Sex bias in the schools: The research evidence* (pp. 110–132). Cranbury, N. J.: Associated University Presses.

Trepanier-Street, M. L., & Kropp, J. J. (1986). Children's recall and recognition of sex role stereotyped and discrepant information. *Sex Roles, 16,* 237–249.

Turiel, E. (1978). The development of concepts of social structure. In J. Glizk & A. Clarke-Stewart (Eds.), *The development of social understanding* (pp. 25–107). New York: Gardner.

Turiel, E. (1983). *The development of social knowledge: Morality and convention.* Cambridge, England: Cambridge University Press.

Udry, J. (1987). Hormonal and social determinants of adolescent sexual initiation. In J. Bancroft (Ed.), *Adolescence and puberty* (pp. 147–163). New York: Oxford University Press.

Udry, J., & Talbert, L. (1988). Sex hormone effects on personality at puberty. *Journal of Personality and Social Psychology, 54,* 291–295.

Udry, J., Talbert, L., & Morris, N. (1986). Biosocial foundations for adolescent female sexuality. *Demography, 23,* 217–230.

Ullian, D. A. (1976). The development of conceptions of masculinity and femininity. In B. Lloyd & J. Archer (Eds.), *Exploring sex differences* (pp. 25–48). London: Academic Press.

Underwood, B., & Moore, B. (1982). Perspective-taking and altruism. *Psychological Bulletin, 91,* 143–173.

Unger, R. K. (1979). Toward a redefinition of sex and gender. *American Psychologist, 34,* 1085–1094.

Vandenberg, S. G., & Kuse, A. R. (1979). Spatial ability: A critical review of the sex-linked major gene hypothesis. In M. A. Wittig & A. C. Petersen (Eds.), *Sex-related differences in cognitive functioning: Developmental issues* (pp. 67–95). New York: Academic Press.

Vingerhoets, A. J. J. M., & Van Heck, G. L. (1990). Gender, coping and psychosomatic symptoms. *Psychological Medicine, 20,* 125–135.

Waber, D. P. (1976). Sex differences in cognition: A function of maturation rate? *Science, 192,* 572–574.

Wagner, P. E., Rohrbeck, C. A., & Tangney, J. P. (1991, April). *Children's self-control and their social emotional adjustment.* Paper presented at the biennial meeting of the Society for Research in Child Development, Seattle.

Walker, L. J. (1984). Sex differences in the development of moral reasoning: A critical review. *Child Development, 55,* 677–691.

Walker, L. J. (1989). A longitudinal study of moral orientation. *Child Development, 60,* 157–166.

Walker, L. J., de Vries, B., & Trevethan, S. D. (1987). Moral stages and moral orientations in real life and hypothetical dilemmas. *Child Development, 58,* 842–858.

Webb, T. E., & VanDevere, C. A. (1985). Sex differences in the expression of depression: A developmental interaction effect. *Sex Roles, 12,* 91–95.

Wehren, A., & DeLisi, R. (1983). The development of gender understanding: Judgments and explanations. *Child Development, 54,* 1568–1578.

Weinberger, D. A. (1991). *Social-emotional adjustment in older children and adults: i. Psychometric properties of the Weinberger Adjustment Inventory.* Unpublished manuscript. Case Western Reserve University.

Weinraub, M., Clemens, L. P., Sockloff, A., Etheridge, R., Gracely, E., & Myers, B. (1984). The development of sex role stereotypes in the third year: Relationships to gender labeling, gender identity, sex-typed toy preferences, and family characteristics. *Child Development, 55,* 1493–1503.

Weisner, T. S., & Wilson-Mitchell, J. E. (1990). Nonconventional family life-styles and sex typing in six-year-olds. *Child Development, 61,* 1915–1933.

Wentzel, K. R., Feldman, S. S., & Weinberger, D. A. (1991). Parental child rearing and academic achievement in boys: The mediational role of socio-emotional adjustment *Journal of Early Adolescence, 11,* 321–339.

Wentzel, K. R., Weinberger, D. A., Ford, M. E., & Feldman, S. S. (1990). Academic achievement in preadolescence: The role of motivational, affective, and self-regulatory processes. *Journal of Applied Developmental Psychology, 11,* 179–193.

Whiting, B. B., & Edwards, C. P. (1973). A cross-cultural analysis of the behavior of children aged 3–11. *Journal of Social Psychology, 91,* 171–188.

Whiting, B. B., & Edwards, C. P. (1988). *Children of different worlds.* Cambridge, MA: Harvard University Press.

Whiting, B. B., & Whiting, J. W. M. (1975). Children of six cultures: A psychocultural analysis. Cambridge, MA: Harvard University Press.

Williams, J. E., Bennett, S. M., & Best, D. L. (1975). Awareness and expression of sex stereotypes in young children. *Developmental Psychology, 11,* 635–642.

Wintre, M. G., Hicks, R., McVey, G., & Fox, J. (1988). Age and sex differences in choice of consultant for various types of problems. *Child Development, 59,* 1046–1055.

Wintre, M. G., Polivy, J., & Murray, M. A. (1990). Self-predictions of emotional response patterns: Age, sex, and situational determinants. *Child Development, 61,* 1124–1133.

Women on Words and Images. (1972). *Dick and Jane as victims: Sex stereotyping in children's readers.* Princeton, NJ.

Wood, J. V., Saltzberg, J. A., Neale, J. N., Stone, A. A., & Rachmiel, T. B. (1990). Self-focused attention, coping responses, and distressed mood in everyday life. *Journal of Personality and Social Psychology, 58,* 1027–1036.

Zahn-Waxler, C., Cole, P. M., & Barrett, K. C. (1991). Guilt and empathy: Sex differences and implications for the development of depression. In J. Garber & K. A. Dodge (Eds.), *The development of emotion regulation and dysregulation* (pp. 243–272). Cambridge, England: Cambridge University Press.

Zahn-Waxler, C., Cummings, E. M., & Cooperman, G. (1984). Emotional development in childhood. In G. J. Whitehurst (Eds.), *Annals of child development* (Vol. 1, pp. 45–106). Greenwich, CN: JAI Press.

Zahn-Waxler, C., Robinson, J. L., & Emde, R. N. (1992). The development and heritability of empathy. *Developmental Psychology, 28,* 1038–1047.

Zarbatany, L., Hartmann, D. P., Gelfand, D. M., & Vinciguerra, P. (1985). Gender differences in altruistic reputation: Are they artifactual? *Developmental Psychology, 21,* 97–101.

Zelnik, M., & Kantner, J. F. (1977). Sexual and contraceptive experience of young unmarried women in the United States, 1987 and 1971. *Family Planning Perspectives, 9,* 55–71.

Zeman, J., & Garber, J. (1991, April). *Children's use of display rules as a function of age, gender, observer, and type of affect.* Paper presented at the biennial meeting of the Society for Research in Child Development, Seattle.

Zucker, K. J., & Green, R. (1992). Psychosexual disorders in children and adolescents. *Journal of Child Psychology and Psychiatry, 33,* 107–151.

Zuckerman, M., Kuhlman, D. M., & Camac, C. (1988). What lies beyond E and N? Factor analyses of scales believed to measure basic dimensions of personality. *Journal of Personality and Social Psychology, 54,* 96–107.

# SCHOOL CURRICULUM AND PSYCHOLOGY

# · 13 ·

# THE COMPARATIVE PSYCHOLOGY OF
# SCHOOL SUBJECTS

## Lee S. Shulman
STANFORD UNIVERSITY

## Kathleen M. Quinlan
STANFORD UNIVERSITY

## THE ARGUMENT

Had the *Handbook of Educational Psychology* been published in 1980, it is unlikely that a section on the curriculum and knowledge, or on the psychology of school subject matters, would have been included. Educational psychology has had an on-again, off-again relationship with subject matter during the past century. At one time, it might have been predicted that school subjects would form the central framework for organizing educational psychology. At other times, subject matters faded into obscurity as relevant dimensions of the discipline of educational psychology, to be replaced by a concern for general mental, developmental, and emotional processes. This chapter reviews the history of the psychology of school subjects from its prominence during the first two decades of the 20th century, when it served to define the essential character of educational psychology, through its extended periods of obscurity during the decades when psychologists sought general theories of learning, teaching, and problem solving, and into the more recent period when the psychology of school subjects appears to be undergoing a renaissance, but in forms not foreseeable during its earlier incarnation. The discussion frequently returns to a set of interlocking questions: What does it mean to know a school subject? In what ways have disciplines been transformed into school subjects? How have psychologists studied the processes of learning and knowing such subjects? What kinds of connection can be made between what it means to know a school subject and how to teach and learn the subject?

What counts as knowing a subject is pivotal to how we theorize about it, how we study it, and how we attempt to influence its development. It matters a great deal whether we consider, for example, that knowing history means being able to restate its major facts and ideas, or being able to apply key historical principles to analyzing the actions and motives of important historical figures, or critically examining the soundness of a politician's argument that purports to employ historical evidence in support of a piece of legislation, or even being able to comprehend and interpret original historical sources in order to write our own historical treatise. Thus, conditions of teaching and learning are treated quite differently as a function of how knowledge and knowing are defined in the particular disciplines to be taught and learned. Moreover, it is likely that a variety of choices exist for converting a discipline or an interdisciplinary domain into a school subject. For example, "knowing art" can mean having a critical appreciation of artistic performances or objects, but it can also mean becoming capable of performing or creating the artistic object.

We begin our account with a return to the roots of educational psychology in the work of John Dewey, Edward L. Thorndike, and Charles Hubbard Judd during the end of the 19th century and the first decades of the 20th century. We describe the kinds of research and writing that characterized the field at that time, and the central (although already somewhat ambivalent) role that school subjects played. We will look carefully at the writings of those pioneers, examining their conception of educational psychology and the ways in which their debates continue to frame many of the conversations in our field. Prominent among those debates, and directly concerned with our questions about knowledge, is a central concept in educational psychology—the concept of *transfer*. When psychologists addressed the problem of transfer, they confronted a critical educational issue. To what extent is knowledge portable? That is, how readily can a learner take knowledge that has been acquired in one situation and make it useful in another? Schools are settings for acquiring knowledge, but it is generally conceded that the sites for application of knowledge are located elsewhere—in laboratories, offices, factories, homes, playgrounds, or other extrascholastic settings. Under what conditions does knowledge *transfer* from one setting to another?

Transfer rapidly became (and has remained) a strategic battleground of learning theory. Theorists argued whether transfer was possible; if so, under what conditions it was possible; and what mechanism accounted for transfer on those occasions when one could find evidence of it. Is it possible to learn *A* in a manner that subsequently helps us learn *B* more rapidly, thoroughly, or effectively? How much could learning in one domain strengthen the capacity to learn in a different one? Certainly, the claims of faculty psychology that the mind is like an organ or a muscle that could be strengthened by exercise, such that logical reasoning could be enhanced through the study of geometry or memory strengthened by drilling to recall nonsense syllables, were grossly overblown. But could study of any subject in some way facilitate the learning of another? Moreover, what of "negative transfer," the condition wherein learning one skill or idea actually inhibits the subsequent learning of new ones?

Although negative transfer has largely disappeared from discussions of contemporary educational psychologists, a variation of the concept is quite contemporary. When modern educational psychologists study the inhibitory impact of prior knowledge on new learning, as in the role of preconceptions, prior dispositions, or habits of mind on learning and problem solving, they are addressing a new (and, as we shall see later in this chapter, a "high-road") version of that old concept, negative transfer.

An aspect of the transfer question occupied Plato in his dialogue *Meno* (1961), and subsequently led him to the conclusion that there must be *innate* ideas. It beset the philosopher Alfred North Whitehead (1929/1967) as the central question in education, and stimulated him to utter his famous lament about the dangers of inert ideas, referring to ideas that had merely been acquired and then lay dormant and useless in the mind. The challenge of learning for transfer motivated Jerome Bruner (1960) to explore the generative virtue of teaching the structure of subject matter in an intellectually honest way. Contemplation of transfer made Thorndike and his followers into pessimists, Judd and his students (such as William Brownell and Ralph Tyler) into optimists, and most contemporary psychologists of school subjects into more moderate realists.

The early prominence of school subjects for educational psychology faded by the mid-1920s. During the heyday of psychological theories of learning in the 1930s, 1940s, and 1950s, the psychology of school subjects faded into the background, a casualty of the vigorous search for the most simple and powerful mechanisms of learning that could claim some universality. In the wake of vigorous debates about fundamental mechanisms of connection and reward, or of Gestalt perceptions and stimulus–response bonds, the particular questions of the psychology of school subjects must have seemed prosaic indeed.

Educational psychologists responded to these challenges not only with general theories, but with a commitment to particular kinds of method as well. Psychologists sought experimental tasks that would be functionally representative of the intellectual work of learning and memory, but would bear no resemblance to the real work of school and occupation, lest some "subjects" hold the inappropriate advantage of familiarity over their peers. The familiarity of the everyday assignments of school subjects became a problem for such designs, where the more exotic and unusual the task, the more likely that it could qualify for the claim of generalizability. This trend is exemplified by J. S. Bruner, Goodnow, and Austin's (1956) work on concept attainment, which used abstract figures to represent the conceptual complexity of ideas. There is an irony to these two aspects of Bruner's work in the late 1950s: He pursued his psychological studies of concept attainment using highly artificial, utterly non-

representative experimental tasks while simultaneously arguing for the centrality of the disciplinary structures of subject matters as the essential features of what should be learned in schools, if students were to have an opportunity "to go beyond the information given." The juxtaposition of these incompatible orientations exemplifies the ambivalence of even the most thoughtful psychologists in that era.

This obsession with identifying the ideal experimental task rather than the most representative school subject also obscured the central questions for any educational psychology of learning and instruction: What counts as a subject matter? In what ways should school subject matters be moderately modified versions of academic disciplines? To what extent should they be radical transformations of the disciplines into interdisciplinary curricular entities such as "the social studies"? Should "understanding" be based on how scholars hold knowledge in a domain or be defined by how ordinary people use knowledge in everyday life? For example, who is a better model for mathematical understanding, a professor of mathematics or a gambler estimating the odds on a football game? For many decades, psychologists avoided these questions. In the contemporary educational psychology of school subjects, they have become central and unavoidable.

Ironically, in discussions of transfer of learning, the apparent weight of the evidence appeared to lean toward the more modest claims of domain specificity, and, one would imagine, should have cast serious doubt on claims for the efficacy of general processes. But the quest for a science of psychology, replete with powerful generalizations about learning, memory, problem solving, and transfer (amid the vigorous battles of the learning theory wars), reduced the attractiveness of the psychology of school subjects.

As psychologists passed into the modern era of information processing, cognition, and higher order reasoning, two different phases of emphasis emerged. At first, the new cognitivists were as generic as their ancestors in learning theory. They, too, sought broad general models using experimental tasks that bore formal resemblance to thinking in general, but no connection to schools or curricula. As we have observed, Bruner used abstract figures in his studies of concept attainment ( J. S. Bruner et al., 1956) even as he admonished educators to focus on the structure of subject matters when they thought about teaching and learning (J. S. Bruner, 1960). Newell and Simon (1972) modeled thinking through puzzles like the Towers of Hanoi and cryptarithmetic and offered models like the General Problem Solver (Newell, Shaw, & Simon, 1958). The prevailing question was how people solved problems *in general*. But a strong challenge to that orientation was looming.

The challenge came from several directions. As information-processing models of reasoning moved into artificial intelligence systems, the claims for broad, general effects weakened. General problem-solving models just did not work very well. Adeptness at the Towers of Hanoi problem did not generalize to other problems, even those that seemed structurally quite similar. Learning to write complex computer programs did not appear to transfer to other strategic planning tasks. Even medical diagnosis, which Arthur Conan Doyle had used as the prototype for general logical reasoning in his wonderful characterization of Sherlock Holmes, appeared to be highly domain specific (Elstein, Shulman, & Sprafka, 1978). Attempts to develop general medical diagnostic systems, for example, progressively narrowed to more specialized domains, eventually resulting in systems for the diagnosis and management of specific symptoms or specific diagnoses.

Similarly, attempts to develop broad programs for teaching general processes of critical reasoning and problem solving met with only modest success (Resnick, 1987). The key to accomplished reasoning seemed to depend on linking the general processes with rich domain-specific knowledge. Interest in human thought became invested in *situated cognition* rather than in highly general, context-independent mental processes (see chapter 2). Research on science learning focused on principle-specific preconceptions within domains, such as how children developed concepts of the Earth, of light and vision, or of geological time, hardly reflecting a generic perspective. Even research on teaching, which had hithero taken a predominantly generic approach to discerning the features of effective teaching, discovered the importance of subject-specific perspectives (Rosenshine & Stevens, 1986; Shulman, 1986/1990).

One of the hallmarks of this renewed commitment to the subject matter was the concept of intellectual honesty, the notion that any act of instruction must give equal attention to the integrity with which the instructional representation is a faithful rendering of the subject matter while also being sensitive to the minds and motives of the learners. The measurement stream of early educational psychology has become much more sensitive to individual differences among learners than to features of content and context, leading Shulman (1970b) to observe that educational research measured individual differences with micrometers and contexts with divining rods.

The current generation of educational psychology takes the psychology of school subjects seriously but goes beyond the narrow particularism of some early 20th century psychology. As we examine the newest exemplars of the genre, we will see an incipient return to John Dewey's vision of full parity and reciprocity between a psychology for subject matter and a subject matter that frames the psychology. We shall conclude our chapter with a discussion of these perspectives and their likely prospects.

## Dimensions of the Analysis

As we examine the evolution of an educational psychology of school subjects during the past century, we shall see that significant changes have occurred along several key dimensions. These dimensions define the essential features of educational psychology, substantively and methodologically. Our purpose in this chapter is to offer one perspective (among the many possible) on where the field has been, where it currently can be located, and where it is likely to go in the coming decades.

There are at least four dimensions that define the research agenda of educational psychology: research problems, research settings, research investigators, and research methods. First, there are the *problems, topics,* or *issues* that constitute its subject matter. These include learning, transfer, problem solving, and child development. For many years, this set of core problems and topics did not include the subjects of the school curriculum. In that sense, the psychology of school subjects lay dormant for a long period. Morever, during much of that time, the topics

of educational psychology centered on issues of *learning,* but did not include *teaching* (Gage, 1963).

Second, a field of study is defined by the *settings* in which the research is conducted. For many years, the settings for educational psychology were psychological laboratories that could be carefully controlled, or classrooms that had been made over to resemble laboratories as closely as possible. The learning of a school subject within a highly controlled setting in which nothing else goes on is likely to be quite different from its comprehension (or noncomprehension) within the buzzing, blooming confusion of an ordinary classroom.

A third element is the background and training of the *investigators* who conduct the research. Typically these scholars have been psychologists who study students and teachers. In the modern era, the scholars increasingly include psychologists who collaboratively study classroom life in partnership with active classroom teachers, as well as teachers who study their own work in their own classrooms.

A fourth element is the *methods* of research. Traditionally these methods were experimental or correlational (Cronbach, 1956). Increasingly in the modern era, these are being augmented by a variety of qualitative or field research methods, often reported in the form of case studies. Taken together, the topics, settings, methods, and investigators define a field of study. As these combinations have changed over the past century, the study of a psychology of school subjects has evolved.

We are now ready to render an account of the zig-zag path through which the educational psychology of school subjects has reached its current condition. We begin by examining the roots of this field in the pioneering work of John Dewey, for whom the psychology and philosophy of education were inextricably bound together. We will examine how the Deweyan vision was dramatically revised in the contrasting ways by which Thorndike, Judd, and their students attempted to invent an authentically scientific educational psychology on which to erect a serious profession of education. We will also examine the substantive losses—to curriculum and pedagogical practice—incurred by the field in this quest for scientific respectability. We shall then discusss the manner in which contemporary educational psychology is attempting to combine rigor and relevance as it reinvents a psychology of school subjects.

## DEWEY: PSYCHOLOGIZING THE SUBJECT MATTER

Psychologizing the subject matter probably began with Dewey. Most modern educational ideas did. Pioneer in both the philosophy and the psychology of education, Dewey argued that psychology lay at the heart of the responsibilities of the teacher and, by implication, the curriculum maker. While the University of Chicago was still in its infancy, Dewey laid out the argument for establishing a school of pedagogy in that newly invested institutional form, the American research university (Dewey, 1896/1972). He distinguished the mission of the traditional teacher training institution, the normal school, and its investment in its "demonstration school," from the research university's development of a "laboratory school" associated with a research university's professional school of pedagogy.

For Dewey, the school of pedagogy of a university would engage in experiments and other studies designed to elucidate the deepest principles of educational practice. As with any other science, education needed its own laboratory for discovering and testing its new theories and practices. Whereas the normal schools used their demonstration schools to model the commonly accepted best practices of the day (hence the "norm" of normal school) so that their future teachers could emulate them, the research universities would treat current practices with a studied skepticism, subjecting them to careful philosophical and empirical analysis. That the scientific discipline upon which most of this work would rest was psychology seemed perfectly obvious to Dewey and his contemporaries. Education was about improving the quality of mind, and the new science of mind was psychology.

The psychology that Dewey had in mind had many facets, including principles of child development, motivation, and interest. But central to his educational psychology was a psychology of school subjects, that science through which the disciplines of the mature mind would be transformed into teachable subjects. In a footnote to his 1897 essay, "The Psychological Aspect of the School Curriculum," Dewey observed:

I note that many critics have objected to the title of the book, *The Psychology of Number,* on the ground that, as one objector put it, "Psychology is the science of the mind, and hence this title virtually reads, "The science of the mind of number" which is absurd." Do these critics mean that quantity, number, etc. are not modes of experience? That they are not specific intellectual attitudes and operations? Do they deny that from the educational, as distinct from the scientific standpoint, the consideration of number as a mode of experience, as a mental attitude and process of functioning, is more important than the definition of number from a purely objective standpoint? (Dewey, 1897/1972, p. 168)

Thus, quite early in his work, Dewey had begun to make two observations that define the role of an educational psychology in his approach. He distinguished between the *logical* and the *psychological* aspects of a subject (a distinction made in many forms by philosophers as early as Aristotle), and he began to think about the bridge between the subject matter in the mind of the mature expert and the subject matter as it is prepared for the pupil, to which he would refer with the now famous phrase, "psychologizing the subject matter." For Dewey, the subject matter was not something *other than* what human beings learn, think, and explore; it was precisely the record and result of human voyages of intellectual discovery.

In *The Child and the Curriculum,* Dewey (1902/1956) explicated the distinction between the logical and the psychological. He argued that we need to understand

the logical and the psychological aspects of experience—the former standing for the subject matter in itself, the latter for it in relation to the child. . . . We may compare the difference between the logical and psychological to the difference between the notes which an explorer makes in a new country, blazing a trail and finding his way along as best he may, and the finished map that is constructed after the country has been thoroughly explored. (p. 283)

Hence the need of reinstating the subject matter of the studies, or branches of learning. It must be restored to the experience from which it has been abstracted. It needs to be *psychologized:* turned over, trans-

lated into the immediate and individual experiencing within which it has its origin and significance (p. 285).

Psychologizing the subject matter has two interacting apects. It reconnects the subject matter to the psychological processes of discovery and deliberation pursued by mature scholars. It also involves the transformation of its mature and crystallized forms into representations that will be meaningful and educative to the child. The psychologized subject matter is faithful to both of its constituents—the child and the curriculum—and that fidelity defines its intellectual honesty.

What, then, is the role of the teacher in this enterprise? According to Dewey,

a teacher . . . is concerned with the subject matter of the science as *representing a given stage and phase of the development of experience;* . . . [W]hat concerns him, as a teacher, is the ways in which that subject may become a part of experience; what there is in the child's present that is usable with reference to it; how such elements are to be used; how his own knowledge of the subject-matter may assist in interpreting the child's needs and doings, and determine the medium in which the child should be placed in order that his growth may be properly directed. He is concerned, not with the subject-matter as such, but with the subject-matter as a related factor in a total and growing experience. Thus, *to see it is to psychologize it* [our italics]. (1902/1956, pp. 285–286)

Dewey's theoretical program rested heavily on elaborating that concept of psychologizing the subject matter. It lay at the heart of his conception of curriculum, of the work of teachers, and of the research agenda for a new educational psychology. For Dewey, to psychologize the subject matter was not to transform an inert body of text into pedagogical representations. Subject matter, like students, is the changing history of human inquiry and invention. Disciplines and school subjects represent experiences of wonder, discovery, conjecture, and assertion conducted by human beings in their own quests for certainty and understanding. Therefore, as he earlier asserted regarding the psychology of number, when we psychologize the subject matter, we are operating on a body of inquiry and understanding that is already deeply experiential and psychological. For Dewey, both the concept of psychologizing and that of subject matter are problematic. Both the process of transforming subject matter into pedagogical forms that are meaningful to pupils and the analysis of the subject matter to find its essential features that can be rendered experientially meaningful to pupils are central to the educator's work.

We shall observe in this chapter how approaches to conducting research in education are inextricably bound up with underlying conceptions of subject matter, learning, and teaching. This was also true for Dewey. His conception of educational research—though it would lie dormant for nearly a century—prefigured contemporary developments in quite remarkable ways. It will be instructive, therefore, to examine how a Deweyan conception of educational investigation was connected with his perspectives on psychologizing the subject matter. We shall now examine the most salient features of Dewey's vision of research in education, and how this vision connects with his conception of psychologizing the subject matter.

## Dewey's Conception of Educational Research

The historian Ellen Lagemann argues that Dewey's conception of educational research rested on three essential tenets. These tenets were a commitment to naturalistic experimentation, the need to link scientific and social innovation, and the necessary connection between schools and the broader world of social and community institutions. By 1896, when the doors of his Laboratory School opened with 16 pupils and two teachers (the Dewey School enrollment would peak at 140 students, 23 teachers, and 10 graduate student assistants in 1902), his thinking and writing about the psychology, philosophy, and pedagogy of school subjects was well under way (Lagemann, 1988).

His first principle was that educational research is essentially experimental and that these experiments must be carried out within the naturalistic settings of schools qua laboratories. This claim, that educational research is both experimental and naturalistic, was rejected by educational psychologists during most of this century. Real science occurred in laboratories, they would claim, not in nature. Only when natural processes could be manipulated under strictly controlled conditions could the power of experimental methods be realized. Nevertheless, Dewey claimed that educational research could and should combine both the experimental and the natural, and this claim, though rejected for many decades, prefigured the recent development of commitments to design experiments conducted collaboratively between researchers and teachers in school sites (e.g., Brown, 1992, 1994; Collins, 1992; chapter 2), which we will discuss in the final sections of this chapter.

The second principle was that educational research should serve as a testing ground of the link between scientific and social innovation. Lagemann quotes Dewey's claim that a laboratory school's special function was to "create new standards and ideals and thus to lead to a gradual change in conditions." Thus, the laboratory school does not serve solely as a setting for testing research hypotheses and discovering psychological principles, though that is a significant role. The laboratory school is also a site for "existence proofs." If we can create and sustain a particular instructional innovation in a real school, we have demonstrated the possibility that it can exist. Once its existence has been demonstrated, we can study its characteristics and the conditions that either foster or inhibit its development. Thus, the laboratory school becomes a setting for creating and documenting visions of the possible.

In these senses, Dewey's vision of a psychology of school subjects was inseparable from developmental efforts in curriculum design and school reform. One studied the learning and teaching of school subjects through the development of innovative curricula in a radically redesigned school context. The notion that one could achieve understanding of the principles of school learning in settings far removed from schools and their curriculum materials was absurd for Dewey.

The third principle reflected Dewey's belief that even the schools were insufficiently broad contexts for educational reform and research. Schools were not separate institutions; they were in and of the surrounding social order. One had to discover ways to increase educational efficiency via creation of social systems in which teaching and learning could be pursued across a variety of institutions, in and out of school. This last principle doubtless owed much to Dewey's long-standing involvement

with and admiration for Jane Addams and her famous Chicago settlement house project, Hull House. (We owe much of this analysis of Dewey's thought and its contrast with the later work of Thorndike and Judd to Ellen Lagemann's [1988] pioneering studies of the history of educational research during this period.) Though Dewey would have had a difficult time imagining the impact of educational television, home computers, and international telecommunications on children's education, he would likely have been quite comfortable with modern psychological theories of situated cognition and cognitive apprenticeships. Psychological studies of "Sesame Street" (e.g., Salomon, 1974, 1976), the experiments of Michael Cole and his colleagues with after-school clubs (e.g., Newman, Griffin, & Cole, 1989) and considerations of "learning in school and out" (Resnick, 1987), would have made supreme sense to John Dewey as manifestations of a new educational psychology.

Although Dewey dubbed his school the laboratory school and continued to compare its function in the university to that of the chemistry laboratory for the department of chemistry, the psychology of school subjects that Dewey envisioned was not a laboratory science in the now conventional sense. Rather than create a laboratory setting in which to study processes abstracted from their real world context, the Deweyan conception called for transformation of a real school into a setting for discovery and inquiry. But in 1904 the Deweyan research program was abruptly aborted when a disagreement between Dewey and the university's first president, William Rainey Harper, led Dewey to leave Chicago for Columbia University, where he joined the philosophy department and ended his active career as school-based educator and educational researcher. Although he would continue to write about education for the remaining years of a long and productive life, most of these writings were based on his reminiscences from that active 8-year period at Chicago.

The mantle of leadership for educational psychology and the psychology of school subjects would transfer to two psychologists, about 15 years his junior, who had been undergraduates together at Wesleyan and would bring a very different set of ideas to the field. One of these men, Edward Lee Thorndike, would spend his career at Teachers College, within a stone's throw of Dewey's office in Columbia's philosophy department. The other, Charles Hubbard Judd, succeeded to Dewey's responsibilities at Chicago 5 years after his departure. Together they represented a dramatic departure from the principles Dewey espoused. Between them, they would define an educational psychology whose methods were decidedly scientific and systematic and decreasingly school based. They each took the psychology of the school subjects quite seriously, but in quite different ways. Their relationship was best known for a decades-long dispute about transfer, a debate whose echoes continue to resound in the halls of educational psychology today, in the confrontation between what Salomon and Perkins (1987) have come to call "low-road" and "high-road" approaches to transfer. Thorndike and Judd maintained an interest in the psychology of school subjects, each publishing widely on the topic with respect to several curriculum areas, including mathematics. Both represented a scientific approach to educational psychology that rejected several of Dewey's tenets. But their contrasting approaches to transfer, to meaningfulness, and to the role of consciousness in educational psychology set them on two distinctive paths, neither one particularly Deweyan.

## THORNDIKE, JUDD, AND DEWEY

In her 1988 presidential address to the History of Education Society, "The Plural Worlds of Educational Research," Ellen Lagemann offered the following characterization of educational research during the present century. "[O]ne cannot understand the history of education in the United States during the twentieth century unless one realizes that Edward L. Thorndike won and John Dewey lost. . . . Thorndike's thought has been more influential within education. It helped to shape public school practice as well as scholarship about education" (p. 185). Although Lagemann's claim does not focus specifically on contrasting positions regarding the psychology of school subjects per se, it is nevertheless interesting to examine her claim in relation to the thesis of this chapter, namely, that a psychology of school subjects, which had been the centerpiece of educational psychology during the first several decades of the 20th century, effectively disappeared from view for half a century, before returning robustly during the past decade.

### Thorndike's Program

What was Thorndike's conception of a psychology of school subjects, and how did it contrast with that of Dewey? Thorndike (1922) laid out his conception clearly in the Introduction to *The Psychology of Arithmetic*:

The psychology of the elementary school subjects is concerned with the connections whereby a child is able to respond to the sight of printed words by thoughts of their meanings, to the thought of "six and eight" by thinking "fourteen," to certain sorts of stories, poems, songs, and pictures by appreciation thereof, to certain situations by acts of skill, to certain others by acts of courtesy and justice, and so on and on through the series of situations and responses which are provided by the systematic training of the school subjects and the less systematic training of school life during their study. The aims of elementary education, when fully defined, will be found to be the production of changes in human nature represented by an almost countless list of connections or bonds whereby the pupil thinks or feels or acts in certain ways in response to the situations the school has organized and is influenced to think and feel and act similarly to similar situations when life outside of school confronts him with them. (p. xi)

Having stipulated that a psychology of school subjects will investigate the connections or bonds that determine all thinking, feeling or action, Thorndike proceeded to outline the research program for his educational psychology. He focused on educators' need to understand the workings of those psychological "functions," that is, those basic processes of learning, believing, feeling, and behaving that are the objects of instructional interventions:

The psychology of school subjects begins where our common sense knowledge of these functions leaves off and tries *to define the knowledge, interest, power, skill, or ideal in question more adequately*, to

measure improvement in it, to analyze it into its constituent bonds, to decide what bonds need to be formed and in what order as means to the most economical attainment of the desired improvement, to survey the original tendencies and the tendencies already acquired before entrance to school which help or hinder progress in the elementary school subjects, to examine the motives that are or may be used to make the desired connections satisfying, to examine any other special conditions of improvement, and to note any facts concerning individual differences that are of special importance to the conduct of elementary work [emphasis added]. (Thorndike, 1922, p. xii)

We have italicized Thorndike's characterization of the role of a psychology of school subjects "to define the knowledge, interest, power, skill or ideal in question more adequately" because in this formulation we find one of the major distinctions between the emerging modern psychology of school subjects with its return to Deweyan principles and the Thorndikean program that educational psychology pursued so assiduously during the early decades of this century. When Thorndike defines the role of educational psychology, he asks, What is the function? For example, just what is "ability to read"? Just what does "the understanding of decimal notation" mean? Just what are "the moral effects to be sought from the teaching of literature"?

There are several strategies for attempting to define the function sought in the education of students within a particular subject matter. The Thorndikean tradition has been to work with practitioners or curriculum specialists to provide task descriptions in behavioral or at least observable terms. These task descriptions are then translated into the particular language of a favored psychological theory through some form of task analysis. For Thorndike, the task descriptions would be translated into the language of connections or bonds. The translated version of the task stands as the psychologically legitimate definition for subsequent purposes of instructional design, curriculum development, and assessment. Thus, Thorndike follows up his questions about defining the function with the following query: "How can we reduce the function to the terms of particular situation–response connections, whose formation can be more surely and easily controlled?" These connections, for Thorndike, are phrased as "sets of bonds." Thorndike's version of "psychologizing the subject matter" is to translate any subject matter into the universal terms of his connectionist theory of learning. For Thorndike, all learning involves situation–response connections, and the role of psychology is to understand those connections well enough to permit their formation to be controlled through curriculum and teaching.

The Thorndikean program was impressively comprehensive. The great virtue of a system that can reduce all simple and complex processes to a common denominator, a behavioral "atom," as it were, is that a variety of different functions can be addressed with the same intellectual tools. Thus, given the notion of bonds or connections as the fundamental building blocks of all learning, and a limited set of laws that explain how bonds are strengthened and weakened, a variety of educational functions can be deduced. Thorndike offered the field a powerful concept of task analysis, of readiness for learning, and of motivation, as well as systematic approaches to the measurement of both prior individual differences and acquired knowledge. He did not limit himself to simple achievements but included acts of understanding, interest, and commitment in his system. A concept of instruction is also derived from these psychological principles.

This comprehensive program integrates curriculum, individual differences, learning principles, and measurement, all economically subsumed under a single comprehensive conception of learning in all organisms. The psychological laboratory becomes the ideal setting for investigating these processes, since it permits the scholar to focus on the functions and their components without the intrusion of extraneous elements of content or context. If successful, such a formulation places psychology on the same footing as those sciences that have made the most dramatic progress. A developmental biology that reduces all of life to the building blocks of RNA and DNA, or a physics that accounts for the features of materials and motions through the interactions of elementary particles, exemplifies the explanatory power of science.

Not surprisingly, given the centrality of connections as the building blocks of learning, Thorndike's conception of transfer is a modest one. For Thorndike, transfer rested on the availability of "identical elements" between the original learning and the transfer situations, connections that could be reinstated in the new setting. The combination of a psychology of particular school subjects and a narrow conception of transfer fit comfortably in Thorndike's system. Although there are particular strategies of teaching, learning, and assessment for each subject matter, they all rest on the same theoretical foundation, on asking the same questions about each subject, and by pursuing answers to those questions in parallel ways. The elegant simplicity of the system attracted Thorndike and his followers. It did not, however, satisfy Judd.

## Judd's Program and the Challenge of Transfer

Charles Hubbard Judd became professor of education at the University of Chicago in 1909, 5 years after Dewey's departure. For the next 30 years he developed a comprehensive approach to the psychology of school subjects, and also contributed significantly to the development of a profession of education. Like Thorndike, he focused heavily on the psychologies of school subjects, but with a much greater emphasis on the development of higher level understandings and broad transfers. Reluctant to reduce all learning to a single and simple set of principles, Judd devoted much more serious attention to the disciplinary particularities of the school subjects, such as questions of what makes history different from mathematics as disciplines (Judd, 1915).

Although Thorndike and Judd were seen as competitors in psychological theory, they were more alike than different when contrasted with Dewey and his conceptions of educational research and theory. Like Thorndike, Judd had deep faith in the psychological laboratory as a context for the discovery and testing of psychological principles which could then be applied to the school setting. For Judd, the school itself was no longer the laboratory it constituted for Dewey. Although Judd pioneered in the use of school surveys, these were not sources for new psychological principles or sites for testing hypotheses. Their function was local; they formed the basis for making administrative and organizational decisions about local problems. Thus, Judd shared with Thorndike the vision of a science

of education, rooted in a scientific psychology, whose investigations could be conducted in the laboratory and applied to educational practice.

The two parents of educational psychology differed dramatically, however, in their conceptions of the fundamental behavioral and cognitive building blocks of a psychology of school subjects. They clashed most directly regarding the respective conceptions of transfer around which they constructed their psychologies of school subjects. Whereas Thorndike, consistent with his fundamental principles, saw broad transfer as a rare and uncommon phenomenon, for Judd, general transfer was a goal worth pursuing vigorously in education. Education was an enterprise of the "higher mental processes," and a broad conception of transfer was essential to such a view.

> The psychology which concludes that transfer is uncommon or of slight degree is the psychology of animal consciousness, the psychology of particular experiences. The psychology of the higher mental processes teaches that the end and goal of all education is the development of systems of ideas which can be carried over from the situations in which they were acquired to other situations. Systems of general ideas illuminate and clarify human experiences by raising them to the level of abstract, generalized, conceptual understanding. (Judd, 1936, p. 201)

Judd thus rejected Thorndike's atomistic reductionism in his commitment to an educational psychology of higher mental processes. The paradox for Judd's psychology of school subjects lay in the simultaneous commitment to domain-specific understandings, as represented by the subject matter disciplines themselves, and a belief in the transfer of learning within those disciplines (but across situations that certainly did not reflect identical elements), and even across disciplinary boundaries. Could he effectively hold fast to both commitments? As Kilpatrick (1992) expresses it:

> Judd tried to relate the learning of complex subject matter to basic psychological processes in a way that would avoid Thorndike's reductionism. To Judd, each subject had its own facts and generalizations that needed to be understood before that knowledge could be used. (p. 10)

The essence of Judd's argument was that transfer occurred because of *what* was transferred, namely, principles, and *how* instruction in principles was undertaken, namely, intentionally, self-consciously, and reflectively. Transfer does not occur effortlessly, mindlessly, and reflexively. The contrast between learning as *reflection* and learning as *reflex* identifies the fundamental differences between Thorndike and Judd. For Judd, teachers must actively and purposively teach for transfer and pupils must thoughtfully learn for transfer if the feat is to be accomplished. Judd stated (quoted in Kilpatrick, p. 11):

> The real problem of transfer is a problem of so organizing training that it will carry over in the minds of students into other fields. There is a method of teaching a subject so that it will transfer, and there are other methods of teaching the subject so that the transfer will be very small. Mathematics as a subject cannot be described in my judgment as sure to transfer. All depends upon the way in which the subject is handled.

Judd's observation that transfer was not a natural process that simply happened reflexively, but rather had to be intentionally taught and learned in an organized manner, is an insight that the field seemed to have lost for many years. As we shall see when we discuss the recent work of Perkins and Salomon (1989), this perspective may be quite central to an effective psychology of school subjects.

## A Middle Path?

Other psychologists, whether allied with Thorndike or with Judd, often tried to navigate an intermediate path between the two extreme positions. Libraries were filled with books on the psychology of school subjects, or its close relative, the psychology of the common branches. Frank Freeman, one of Judd's students and disciples, later to be a prominent member of the Chicago faculty, published a book under the latter title in 1916, with an introduction by the series editor, Stanford's Elwood Patterson Cubberley. In the editor's introduction, Cubberley observed that the psychology of the common branches occupied the territory between the "two extremes of psychology on the one hand and special or general methods on the other" (p. vi). He claimed that, instead of viewing all subject matters through the lens of a single set of psychological principles, we might instead view the different subjects as occupying different levels of a coherent collection of psychological theories that spanned the simple as well as the more complex forms of learning.

Thus, even with his argument that the psychology of school subjects, of learning to write, read, spell, calculate, and so forth, was a special area of applied psychology, Freeman also strove to reduce the psychologies of school subjects to a coherent, underlying psychological model, although in a manner slightly different from Thorndike's. As he wrote, "The different school subjects taken together furnish a pretty comprehensive set of examples of the *various kinds of learning* of which the human mind is capable. The subjects are so arranged that the simpler, more elementary, and less intellectual forms of learning come first, and the higher types in their order" (emphasis added) (1916, p. 5). Thus, handwriting is the simplest school subject, requiring merely sensorimotor learning. It is followed by drawing, reading, and music, which are considered examples of perceptual learning. Spelling follows as an example of the "fixing of associations," and in turn is followed by history and geography, which require the "organization and extension of experience through the use of imagination." Mathematics follows, exemplified by algebra and geometry as well as by arithmetic, as studies that involve abstract thinking. The highest level of thought is exemplified by learning and teaching in the natural sciences, which involve "the ability to generalize upon the basis of accumulated experience" (later quotations are taken from Cubberley's introduction, pp. vi–vii).

The tension between a monistic system, in which all learning is explained by a single set of underlying constructs, and a pluralistic system, in which varieties of learning types are posited, has historical roots and has continued to characterize educational psychology to this day. The British associationist philosophers, such as Locke and Hume, attempted to account for all human knowledge through the combining of fundamental mental connections, or associations. In some cases, the conflict between the two positions is reflected in the evolution of a single scholar's work. Thus, Robert M. Gagné, an eminent instructional psychologist, began his career distinctly in the Thorndikean camp. In the first edition of his book, *The Conditions of Learning,* published in 1965, he offered a model he had been developing for more than 20 years, in which all school learning could be understood in terms of "learning hierarchies," simple to complex sequences of learning tasks with essentially universal features. By the second edition of the same book, published 5 years later, Gagné had given up this unitary model. He now stipulated the existence of five "varieties of learning," of which learning hierarchies were but one genre, that applied to "intellectual skills." But other kinds of learning, he now asserted, such as cognitive strategies, organized bodies of verbal knowledge, attitudes, and motor skills, followed distinctly different principles, which were not sequential and hierarchical (see Shulman, 1970a, for a more detailed account of this change in Gagné's thought and its connections to the more cognitive orientations of Jerome Bruner [1960] and David P. Ausubel [1968]). Although the current scene appears to favor the pluralistic notions of Judd regarding both the nature of learning and the scope of transfer, there remain powerful advocates of a more fundamental, connectionist approach (e.g., Rumelhart, McLelland, & PDP Research Group, 1986).

Although both Thorndike and Judd pursued their contrasting psychologies of school subjects, both viewed the subject matter through the lens of their respective psychology. For Thorndike, the subject matter became a potential system of connections that could be aggregated into ever more complex "knowledge, interest, power, skill, or ideals"; for Judd, the subject matter was constituted of a network of general ideas organized into forms of conceptual understanding. Unlike Dewey, for whom the subject matter and the psychology were equal partners in the processes of education, for both Thorndike and Judd the subject matter was subordinated to the psychology. Each analyzed the subject matter into its psychological constituents, be they bonds or principles, and each understood the pedagogy in terms of those psychological constructs. Most of the intellectual descendants of these two psychologists not only pursued the psychological theories of their forebears, they also proceeded to set aside the centrality of school subject matters altogether and to devote their attention to explicating the powerful psychological ideas that animated their theories.

Although the mainstream of educational psychology lost sight for nearly 50 years of the central role of school subjects, the influence of Judd continued in the work of some of his students. Continuing his emphasis on the importance of higher order thinking and understanding of principles as the fundamental building blocks of educational psychology, some psychologists even sustained an interest in school subjects. Those who came to psychology from a background in educational practice had read Dewey's work, and continued to find it relevant. Like Dewey, some were also influenced by the writings of the Gestalt psychologists, who emphasized the importance of structure and of more holistic, complex features of the learning process. So, although for the moment, Thorndike won and Dewey lost, some followers of Judd followed a different path and kept alive the foundations of a cognitive psychology of school subjects. One of the best examples of this orientation is the research program of William Brownell.

## WILLIAM BROWNELL'S RESEARCH PROGRAM

Each generation of scholars tends to forget the contributions of its predecessors, thereby magnifying the inventiveness of its own discoveries. It is therefore important to recall in this chapter the research activity of an educational psychologist of the period 1928–1950, whose contributions to the psychology of school subjects prefigured many aspects of today's efforts: William A. Brownell. Brownell took his Ph.D. with Judd at Chicago in 1925, after working several years as a schoolteacher. He conducted a series of classic investigations into arithmetic learning that remain significant contributions to that research literature. We shall provide a detailed account of one of these studies to serve as an example for our analysis.

Brownell (1939) designed an extensive study to examine the efficacy of a highly controversial method for teaching "borrowing" in subtraction to elementary school students, the "subtraction crutch." This method of calculation can be employed when confronted by a subtraction problem like the following:

$$
\begin{array}{r}
86 \\
-37 \\
\hline
\end{array}
$$

where the lower number in the units column is a larger integer than the one above it. Most arithmetic texts in 1930s eschewed the "crutch," (essentially a technique of visibly borrowing), which involved changing the numbers in the problem, as shown here:

$$
\begin{array}{r}
{}^{7}\!\!\not{8}{}^{1}\!\!\not{6} \\
-37 \\
\hline
49
\end{array}
$$

Most mathematics educators claimed that the crutch was unnecessary, inconsistent with the practices of adult learners, and likely to result in a permanent impediment to the learner's subtraction skills. But Brownell thought their concerns were groundless and likely to be based on misguided conceptions of mathematical learning.

Brownell designed an experimental study contrasting four scripted treatments that classroom teachers were to enact: a no-crutch treatment; a treatment in which the crutch was used throughout; a treatment in which the crutch was taught, used, and then systematically forbidden; and a treatment in which the crutch was taught and then could be used optionally by the students. The instruction was carried out over an 8-month period, with 2 months of instruction followed by 6 months of follow-up. The research was conducted in 16 classrooms across four cities in North Carolina. In each city, four different classrooms deployed the four treatments.

In addition to pretests of ability and achievement to ascertain comparability of groups, multiple outcome measures were employed. These included accuracy of calculations, speed of calculations, number of practice pages completed, and teacher logs or diaries describing qualitative aspects of the instruction. Because Brownell was particularly interested in student understanding of subtraction, he made special use of patterns of errors in the pupils' practice pages and carefully analyzed the teachers' diaries regarding student understanding and difficul-

ties. There were no conferences or interviews with pupils or teachers and there were no direct classroom observations.

We are not presenting the study because of the findings. They generally confirmed that the students in the crutch treatments learned to subtract quite successfully, did not persist in using the crutch in a mechanical way when it was no longer useful, but did return to using the crutch in the face of unusually difficult math problems. Instead, we wish to review how Brownell approached the questions of the subject matter and its understanding, the research questions being studied, and the methods of research.

The first matter that becomes clear is that Brownell's conception of arithmetic and of mathematical knowledge is heavily weighted with notions of understanding and of representation. To study arithmetic is not merely to master a set of skills:

For years we have been accustomed to think of arithmetic as a "tool" subject, in which skill is acquired by relatively unvaried practice. [Brownell's footnote at this point states, "One person who, consistently and almost alone, has opposed the 'tool' conception of arithmetic is Charles H. Judd."] . . . Of late we have begun to suspect that there is something wrong in our instruction. The pupils who have been subjected to it do not seem to show the expected proficiency. Some item appears to have been missing in our teaching, and that item, we are coming to believe is, *understanding*. Furthermore, we are coming to see that this element of understanding was neglected in our teaching because it escaped observation when we analyzed adult performance . . . [emphasis added]. (Brownell, 1939, p. 72)

On occasion, the advance step to be learned in the conceptual system calls for an understanding which the learner does not possess. In such circumstances what is needed is some kind of *tangible or perceptual representation which will reveal concretely the intrinsic character of what is to be learned* [emphasis added]. (Brownell, 1939, p. 87)

Even when the psychologist of school subjects like Brownell conducted his studies in the particulars of arithmetic learning, he intended the fruits of his labors to extend beyond the study of subtraction. He regularly asserted that the value of his studies lay not only in their contributions to the learning of the particular topic in a specific school subject, but that through such research one could build toward a more general psychology of learning with understanding. In Brownell's words:

In the study reported in this monograph a typical center of disagreement has been isolated for investigation. That this center of disagreement lies in the field of arithmetic is more or less beside the point. . . . Other subject matter fields would certainly have yielded other instructional devices susceptible to quantitative research; but the arithmetic device [the use of a crutch to facilitate borrowing in subtraction] was ready at hand and seemed to promise much for the kind of study proposed.

All of this is but another way of saying that the significance of the data to be reported is by no means limited to the particular arithmetic device under investigation, or even to the particular field of arithmetic as such. It is true that the data afford a test of a certain arithmetic device, and so may contribute to improved arithmetic instruction. But the data, it is thought, should do more than this: they should add to our understanding of the nature of learning. (Brownell, 1939, p. 3)

Brownell then offered a rather revolutionary claim. He argued that this goal of generalizing beyond the school arithmetic task to a more general understanding of the nature of learning is more likely to take place through a classroom-based study of a particular substantive curriculum unit than in a classic psychological laboratory:

> The laboratory psychologist who has his subjects memorize nonsense syllables or learn mazes does not do so primarily to discover how best to memorize nonsense syllables or to learn mazes. On the contrary, his studies are for purposes quite beyond these: he seeks to secure light on the learning process as such. The situation need not be different in the case of the educational psychologist who investigates the learning of the school subjects. . . . [T]here are excellent reasons why his contribution may well transcend the purely "practical" end. This is so because both the learning contents (the school subjects and analogous matter) and the mental processes (the so-called "higher" mental processes) which he studies are of large importance in our culture. It is also because he investigates these processes under conditions which permit them to function in the ways in which they prevail in life, exposed to all the distracting influences which commonly affect and complicate them. . . . [T]he educational psychologist has the opportunity, whether or not he realizes it, to advance significantly our understanding of human learning. (Brownell, 1939, pp. 74–75)

Thus, unlike his contemporaries (and even his mentor), Brownell did not see the classroom as a confounding setting and the laboratory as an opportunity to investigate processes in their pure form. He made the opposite claim, one that would not be made vigorously by most others for another 40 years. He claimed that there is a theoretical advantage to studying basic processes "in the ways in which they prevail in life, exposed to all the distracting influences." This was both a courageous and an unpopular assertion for its time.

Although Brownell pursued a psychology of school subjects, his gaze extends beyond the immediate subject matter toward the elaboration of general models of learning with understanding. Methodologically, Brownell was prepared to use qualitative measures of process gleaned from teachers' diaries, and he also employed careful analyses of error patterns among students, both precursors to more modern methods, in order to pursue his interests in *how* students learn and what they come to understand. He neither interviewed participants nor observed classroom processes. In comparison with the mainstream of educational psychology during this period, Brownell was the exceptional investigator. By the late 1930s the mainstream of the field was decidedly generic rather than subject-specific in its work.

The underlying conception of the subject matter itself, however, remained quite unproblematic for Brownell and his generation. While joining with Judd in attacking the notion that arithmetic was a "tool subject," and asserting that it should be understood and not merely used, what counts as mathematics was rarely engaged. How does subtraction with borrowing fit within a broader conception of mathematics? Does this unquestioned piece of school mathematics have an authentic place within mathematics as a discipline? Although the crutch was examined as an element of later understanding of the processes of school mathematics, it was never scrutinized for its legitimacy as a part of the overall mathematics curriculum.

Similarly, the teachers remained shadowy figures in all this work, as did their central role, teaching itself. While learning, and learning with understanding, become central

constructs, teaching remained merely the prescribed "treatment," and its agents were those who—more or less faithfully—follow the instructional scripts. Even the classroom settings, which Brownell argued afforded educational psychology a greater claim to theoretical generalizability (or what we would now call "ecological validity"), were not examined directly, nor were their variations subjected to careful qualitative analyses.

In the next sections, we shall move to the modern era and review several bodies of work that exemplify more recent developments in the psychology of school subjects, broadly construed. We shall see in the evolution of research on teaching how a hitherto ignored problem of education—teaching—became a central topic of research, although with essentially no reference to subject matter at all. Only since the mid-1980s has the study of teaching begun to focus on both content and cognition. We shall visit two of the most vigorous new fields of revived psychology of school subjects—mathematics and history—and examine the ways in which these two fields are simultaneously quite new manifestations of such a psychology and also a significant return to the tenets of educational research that Dewey espoused nearly a century earlier (and never accomplished in his own work). Chapters 14 and 16 in this *Handbook* offer detailed accounts and analyses of these developments. We conclude this chapter by revisiting the problems of transfer, and review how a psychology of school subjects can be woven into modern conceptions of transfer. We conclude with a set of general propositions about a contemporary psychology of school subjects.

## RESEARCH ON TEACHING

The recent history of research on teaching clearly illustrates the conformation of generic and subject-specific conceptions of educational psychology. The systematic study of classroom teaching is a relatively new enterprise within educational psychology, a field that has long been dominated by a post-Thorndikean concern for "learning" as its central construct. When research on teaching began to develop as a field (Gage, 1963; Shulman, 1986/1990), it incorporated most of the characteristics of the then dominant paradigms of educational psychology, namely, behaviorism, experimental or correlational quantitative analyses, and generic models of pedagogy. The prototypical study was a correlational analysis of the relation between observed patterns of teacher classroom behavior and student performances on tests of achievement or attitude (Gage, 1978). The purpose of the research was to identify general characteristics of teacher behavior that were systematically related to significant improvements in student knowledge and understanding. The assumption, rarely challenged, was that investigators could identify general properties of teacher behavior, such as questioning styles, wait time, turn allocations, patterns of praise and criticism, structuring moves, and the like, that would predict effectiveness. These attributes, in turn, could become the bases for teacher training programs that would yield more effective teachers. Scholars in the field referred to this program of research as the "descriptive-correlational-experimental loop," wherein the relationships between teacher behavior and student outcomes that had been qualitatively described would then be more systematically studied in correlational studies, and the most promising variables from those studies would be verified in well-controlled classroom experiments.

The most widely used conceptual framework from that era was Dunkin and Biddle's (1974) model, which distinguished among four kinds of variables in the study of teaching: *presage, context, process,* and *product. Presage* variables included those attributes of teachers that might influence their effectiveness, such as background, training, verbal ability, sex, race, and so forth. *Context* variables were those aspects of the settings in which teaching occurred that might influence effectiveness. The subject matters being taught were embedded within the concept of context. *Process* variables defined the observable classroom interactions between teachers and students. The emphasis of process was entirely on observable behavior. Teachers' cognitive processes as they planned, taught, or reflected on their teaching were generally ignored. *Product* variables were the measures of student outcome, most typically scores on standardized tests but, in principle, any outcome measures of either intellectual or affective consequences of instruction. Using that language as a conceptual framework, the most widely practiced approach to the study of teaching was dubbed "process–product," seeking to document the connections between teachers' behavior (process) and student academic outcomes (product).

This research shared several characteristics with the foundational field of educational psychology, such as essentially ignoring the role of subject matter as a central feature of teaching and learning, a focus on quantitative analyses of observable behavior, and a concomitant avoidance of concern for teachers' thoughts and judgments. In those senses, it further confirmed Lagemann's observation that Thorndike had won and Dewey had lost. The process–product paradigm was an application of Thorndike's models of learning and measurement to the study of teaching. However, the process–product approach also struck out in significant new ways. Most important, this research took place almost exclusively in real classrooms rather than in laboratories. Observations were made of intact classrooms and the teacher–student interactions that occurred within them. The investigators emphasized the importance of the real classroom context. They claimed that documenting the relationships between teacher behavior and student learning would sustain the claim that variations in teaching behavior accounted for significant amounts of the differences among schools and their effects.

From the perspective of this chapter, the element absent from all these studies was appropriate attention to the centrality of subject matter, not as just another context variable, like class size or student social class, but as a central and pivotal construct in any studies of classroom teaching. Shulman (1986, 1986/1990, 1987) dubbed this problem "the missing paradigm" and argued that subject matter must return to its proper place in research programs on teaching. He argued that teaching and its effectiveness function differently in different content areas. The teaching of mathematics to young children is dramatically different from the teaching of literature to adolescents or adults. One set of pedagogical principles was inadequate to account for both the teaching of physics and the teaching of history. The subject matter needed to be included as a central feature of any studies of teaching.

In this context, a series of studies was conducted that documented the ways in which the subject matter taught influenced the kinds of representations teachers used in their teaching. Variations in teachers' knowledge of their subject matter and how to teach it significantly influenced the quality of pedagogy. Studies by P. L. Grossman (1990), Wilson (1992), Wineburg (1991a, 1991b), Hashweh (1985), Carlsen (1988), Marks (1989, 1990) and others contributed to this research program's explication of the role of *pedagogical content knowledge* in the process of subject matter teaching.

The central feature of this research program was the argument that excellent teachers transform their own content knowledge into pedagogical representations that connect with the prior knowledge and dispositions of learners. The effectiveness of these representations depends on their fidelity to the essential features of the subject matter and to the prior knowledge of the learners. The capacity to teach, therefore, is not composed of a generic set of pedagogical skills; indeed, teaching effectiveness is highly dependent on both content knowledge and pedagogical content knowledge, on how well one understands the subject matter and on how well one understands ways of transforming the subject matter into pedagogically powerful representations.

For example, Hashweh (1985) showed the subject matter background of science teachers influenced their abilities to plan lessons, develop analogies and examples, and respond to questions in biology and physics. The very same teacher who was highly adept at designing and improvising instruction in his deeply understood subject of biology became much more limited when he shifted to physics. P. L. Grossman (1985) documented a similar contrast within a single teacher as she alternated between teaching literature (which she understood deeply) and grammar (which she grasped in a loose, intuitive fashion). P. L. Grossman (1990) also conducted a series of case studies that documented the impact of excellent subject-specific teacher education on the ability to adapt instruction to the backgrounds and interests of students. Carlsen (1988) analyzed the ways in which teachers of biology altered their planning, their teaching behavior, and their discourse as they moved from topics they understood deeply to others in which they held their knowledge more tenuously *within the same discipline.*

These and other studies conducted at this time also highlighted the importance, not only of how well teachers understood the subject matter and had developed pedagogical strategies for "psychologizing" it, but also of how teachers construed their subject and its comprehension by students. Teachers of mathematics or history might be equally knowledgeable about their disciplines but might hold quite different conceptions of what constituted authentic knowing in their discipline. In a field like mathematics, they might hold different views of the role of computation in mathematical knowing, or of the importance of "thinking like a mathematician." Even mathematics educators who agreed that thinking like a mathematician was a key goal of mathematical teaching were likely to disagree sharply on what was meant by mathematical thinking. Was it the work of mathematicians in academic university settings wrestling with the mysteries of Fermat's last theorem? Actuaries attempting to estimate the life expectancies of particular populations? Or bookmakers who recalculated betting odds in their heads as they accepted wagers from their clients? This approach to research on teaching contributed to a reconsideration of the role of subject matter and its conceptualization as a key topic for the research and practice communities.

In a similar manner, Susan Stodolosky (1988) conducted studies of elementary school teachers who taught both mathematics and social studies. She reported that one cannot understand the variations in classroom teaching at the elementary level unless one recognizes that teachers teach differently, organize their classrooms differently, and think differently as they teach these quite different subjects. "The subject matters," she asserted, and she brought forward classroom process data to confirm the assertion. For example, mathematics teaching is much more routinized and selects from a much narrower band of pedagogical methods than does the teaching of social studies. There are many more opportunities for students to discover a "fit" with their own approaches to learning when studying social studies, with its diverse approaches and materials, than when studying mathematics. The experiences of teaching and of learning in these two domains are vastly different. Therefore, attempts to characterize those processes *in general,* while certainly identifying some useful broad general principles, would necessarily miss critical features of the specific pedagogies of each subject matter.

The studies of Shulman and his colleagues tended to focus most heavily on the teachers and how their understandings shaped the ways in which they addressed the challenges of planning units of instruction, conducting classroom discourse, and responding to student difficulties. But these studies rarely took on challenges of the sort issued by process–product researchers: to discern relationships between teachers' understandings, thoughts, judgments, and actions and the academic achievements of their students. Pioneering in such an effort was Gaea Leinhardt, whose work since the early to mid-1980s has served to bridge between aspects of the process–product paradigm and the contemporary rebirth of a psychology of school subjects.

## Leinhardt's Program

The evolution of Gaea Leinhardt's exquisite studies of mathematics teaching further supported the contention that teachers' strategies for organizing and managing the complexities of classroom life were highly subject-specific (e.g., Leinhardt, 1989; Leinhardt & Greeno, 1986; Leinhardt & Smith, 1985). Leinhardt documented and analyzed the ways in which highly effective teachers organized the recurring routines of subject matter teaching, ways that contrasted sharply with the methods of their less effective peers. Concerned with the connections between teaching and measured academic achievement, Leinhardt selected for study teachers whose students had recorded consistently high patterns of achievement as measured by standardized mathematics achievement tests. For example, she demonstrated how the skilled mathematics teacher carried out the daily homework check with which nearly every math class begins. She showed how and why the math teaching was carried out smoothly and with substantial information transmission to the effective teacher, while the less effective teacher tended to stumble through the activity and to learn much less from it as well.

Leinhardt conducted her studies in a consistent manner. She would carefully select the teachers for her inquiries, attempting to ensure that they could be accurately characterized as consistently effective in teaching elementary school mathematics. She would, for example, select teachers for study whose students had exceeded expected achievement gain scores for 3 consecutive years. These would be the "experts" to whom she would contrast less effective "novice" teachers. She would conduct meticulous observational studies in the classrooms of these teachers, recording everything they said and did over long periods of time, in order to establish the rhythms of routine and repeated strategies they employed in their teaching. These longer periods of time were not arbitrary; they corresponded to meaningful "chunks" of curriculum, such as extended instructional units that were conceptually coherent. She would interview the teachers regarding their mathematical knowledge and their observed strategies. She would subject those observations to careful analysis of behavioral patterns or routines, using such analytic methods as "semantic nets" to plot those patterns. In this manner she was able to document the ways in which expert mathematics teachers differed from their less accomplished colleagues—in their mathematical knowledge, their classroom organizational skills for mathematics teaching, their understanding of their students' understandings and misunderstandings, the quality of their explanations, and other aspects of their competence in mathematical pedagogy.

During this first phase of her research program, Leinhardt retained some of the characteristics of the process–product paradigm, even as she initiated her work on the psychology of mathematics teaching. The process–product researchers had built on two important insights. First, researchers should look at the most effective teachers in practice as the best source for understanding the kinds of teacher behavior likely to yield student achievement, rather than deduce principles of good teaching from learning theories. Leinhardt applied this insight in her selection of expert teachers as the focus for her inquiries. Second, she recognized the importance of connecting measures of teaching with indicators of student learning. Leinhardt employed measured student achievement as the basis for selecting her experts. However, although Leinhardt conducted her investigations within mathematics teaching and was cognizant of the importance of the subject matter, she did not critically examine "what counts" as mathematical understanding during this phase of her work. She accepted the traditional mathematics achievement tests as adequate indicators of student performance and hence of teacher expertise. Like Brownell, she pioneered in many aspects of method and research focus, but was content to live with the conventional definition of mathematical learning and its measurement. Nevertheless, unlike the process–product researchers, she studied those longer, connected, coherent curriculum units rather than randomly sampling teaching episodes across time periods. Because she studied the longer units, she was increasingly able to focus her attention away from discrete units of teacher behavior and on the central feature of mathematics teaching, instructional explanations. Unlike aspects of classroom management and organization, instructional explanations are almost entirely shaped by the subject matter—as understood by the teacher, as represented in the text materials, and as apprehended (or misconceived) by the participating students.

Leinhardt next extended her studies to analyses of particular core concepts in mathematics. She was quite self-conscious in recognizing the revolutionary character of her insistence on studying subject-specific and even topic-specific aspects of teaching and learning. Leinhardt and her colleagues introduced a comprehensive review of the research on the teaching and learning of functions, graphs, and graphing (Leinhardt, Zaslavsky, & Stein, 1990) with observations that eloquently resonate with the argument of this chapter even as they echo the sentiments William Brownell had expressed more than 50 years earlier:

> This paper is a review of research and theory related to teaching and learning in a particular subject, mathematics; in a particular domain, functions, graphs, and graphing; at a particular age level, 9–14. Major reviews in education are rarely so embedded. Indeed, since 1970, there has been no subject topic–specific review in the *Review of Educational Research*. Recent theoretical thinking and research in cognitive psychology, cognitive anthropology, educational psychology, and philosophy, however, suggest that there are aspects of learning and teaching specific content that are unique to or more salient to the particular topic than to the field of teaching and learning as a whole. . . . Clearly, if each specific situation is totally unique, then one cannot hope to build a body of accumulated knowledge, let alone science. There is a tension between the specific and the general (Schwab, 1964). It appears at this point, however, that the cumulated study of the specific may enrich our conceptualization of the general. It is from this perspective that we offer this review. (Leinhardt et al., 1990, pp. 2–3)

Unlike her earlier studies, when she was willing to accept conventional definitions of achievement, Leinhardt showed how important it could be to identify the concepts and principles that were critical to the structure of a subject and to study how the most effective teachers organize them for instruction. More recently, to highlight the ways in which variations among subject matters affect the nature of instructional explanations, Leinhardt has been extending her research into comparative studies of teacher explanations in mathematics and history, helping to clarify how the subject matter interacts with the character of more and less useful teacher explanations in those two quite different fields of study.

Leinhardt has also pioneered in highlighting the ways in which psychological and epistemological questions interact in the development of a proper psychology of school subjects. That is, she asserts that we must not only be concerned with how a subject is taught and learned, we must attend to the more fundamental question of what counts as the substance of the subject itself. As we shall see in our explications of the work of Wineburg, Lampert, and Ball, psychologists had for too long accepted uncritically conventional representations of school subjects. The contents of an arithmetic textbook were sufficient to define the tasks of school mathematics; the accounts and chronologies in a history textbook represented historical knowledge. In "Mapping out geography: An example of epistemology and education," Leinhardt and her collaborator (Gregg & Leinhardt, 1994) present an analysis of how epistemic questions in geography help to focus educators on the understandings that are worth seeking for teachers and students. For example, they show how the same topic—volcanoes—takes on quite different emphases when presented as part of geography and as part of earth science. Different kinds of relationships

count as knowledge in each field. Therefore, the forms of pedagogical representations, the academic tasks, the most authentic assessments, will all differ for the two fields. Without a proper epistemological analysis, the work of the educational psychologist could be misguided and even misleading.

Leinhardt began her studies of mathematics teaching looking at organizational routines in the classroom, and subsequently broadened her purview to emphasize the more substantive aspects of explanation and curriculum definition in the domain. By conducting comparative studies of explanation in mathematics and history, she has begun to identify those aspects of instructional explanation that are particularly sensitive to the unique properties of particular disciplines. Samuel Wineburg's work in history begins with the substantive questions and rarely strays from them. He is particularly concerned with how we can come to understand the essential character of historians' learning, thinking, and problem solving and how those insights can inform the teaching and learning of history. To answer these questions he draws on two major sources: empirical studies of historians and history students, and contributions to the philosophy of history and historiography. We turn next to Wineburg's research program, described also in chapter 14.

## Wineburg's Program

Samuel Wineburg has combined aspects of the expert–novice paradigm from cognitive science with a perspective from the analysis of history to initiate a new line of work in the psychology of learning and teaching history. Although historians have written extensively about how they do their work, in a manner not all that different from the self-descriptive writings of mathematicians and scientists, Wineburg began with the assumption that it would be important to combine careful reading in the philosophy and sociology of history with research in which he studied historians at work empirically to develop a conceptual model of historians' thinking. He enriched his understanding of historians by also drawing from research on other knowledge-using professions, such as physicians. Elstein, Shulman, and Sprafka (1978), who studied the thinking of experienced physicians, found that the general lore about how physicians made medical diagnoses bore little resemblance to the processes they employed when their work was carefully studied empirically. Wineburg suspected that the same might be true of historians as well; hence the need to combine empirical research with historiographic writings.

Wineburg (1991a) gave historians sets of original source materials similar to the kinds they might confront in their research, and had them think aloud as they worked their ways through the materials. He then compared their knowledge, strategies, and procedures with those of highly successful high school history students. The differences between the two groups were striking, and not only in the depth of knowledge exhibited by the working historians. Indeed, what most distinguished the two groups were the working heuristics employed by the historians in approaching the evaluation of historical sources. High school students had no sense of how historians evaluated sources and worked with them to make inferences about events and their causes, historical figures, and their motivations. For example, historians reading the expositions of other historians immediately assumed that the writers were writing from a particular point of view or stance and began to engage in a conversation with the text regarding the ways in which the historian's stance must necessarily color his or her interpretation of the material. They approached every historical account with the assumption that it reflected selective use of information and interpretive reconstructions of actions and motives. They imposed their conceptions of history on their readings, seeking motives, causes, and explanations rather than merely reciting chronologies or genealogies, whether political or biological. For the historian, reading history was a special kind of active criticism and construction, quite different from reading a novel or reading an instruction manual. Even the most academically accomplished high school students rarely exhibited the historian's frame of mind in reading historical texts. For them, reading for understanding was a matter of recollection, recitation, and relating one set of facts to another.

Another contrast was observed in how historians and students examined source materials, such as diaries, letters, contemporaneous newspaper accounts, and the like. Even when reading original sources, as yet uninterpreted by an intervening historian, the experienced historians employed critical heuristics unique to history, such as the "sourcing heuristic." They would examine an original source and immediately ask, "Who wrote this? What was that person's special interest, stake, or perspective? How credible a source is this? How might the source be interested in slanting the account in a particular direction?" Here, again, excellent high school students rarely employed the sourcing heuristic in reviewing the same original sources. No one had taught them to read and think historically, and they therefore did not address these materials any differently from the way they approached other texts.

In his work, Wineburg has demonstrated that general domain-independent conceptions of reading comprehension and problem solving do not apply equally well to all fields. History has its own substantive and methodological logic. It encourages certain dispositions and orientations toward texts and their interpretation that are quite different from the orientations needed to understand literary texts or natural science materials. Although philosophers of history, such as Collingwood (1946), have written eloquently about these differences, they become much more helpful to educators when an educational psychologist who has become deeply knowledgeable about history and historiography can investigate those processes and explicate them in terms that are relevant to the design of instruction and the education of teachers. The work of educational psychologists who are knowledgeable about the subject matters whose teaching and learning they study lends credence to the argument that psychologists can no longer conduct credible research on the educational process in a domain with which they have only passing acquaintance. Wineburg's work serves as a powerful reminder that those who would pursue an educational psychology of school subjects must possess (or responsibly acquire) critical understanding of both the substance and the epistemology of the subjects themselves.

Leinhardt echoes Wineburg's perspective, as she also expresses strong views regarding the question of *who* can conduct deep studies of subject-specific learning and teaching:

Many authors . . . have called for both research and reexaminations based on a subject matter perspective. The implications of doing this type of research or review of research, however, are not trivial. Educational psychologists, and perhaps policy analysts as well, must immerse themselves in a discipline and join up with subject matter experts to do the initial research and to integrate strands of research. (Leinhardt, Zaslavsby, & Stein, 1990, p. 54)

The subject-specific studies of teaching that we have been discussing share certain investigative characteristics. In all cases, an investigator observes interviews, and documents the thinking and actions of teachers and students in particular subject matter domains in order to offer an analysis of their work. In the work of Leinhardt and Wineburg, those studies also carefully examine the ways in which knowledge and knowing are defined normatively in those fields. (A "normative" proposition is formulated on theoretical or moral grounds to describe the most desirable state of affairs. To call something normative is not to claim that it is average, normal, typical, or commonplace. Rather, it is claimed as a norm, or a value, in principle. Thus, if a group of historians come together to define, in principle, what is meant by historical understanding, they are rendering a normative judgment, regardless of whether their view is that held by most other people.) That is, they not only emphasize the importance of placing the school subject at the center of the inquiry. They also highlight the need to examine critically how the school subject is defined in relation to the many possible ways in which the discipline itself might be construed. Although some educators may assert that anyone can stipulate what it means to "know history" or "understand mathematics," scholars like Leinhardt and Wineburg document the critical complexity of just such questions.

Nevertheless, that is not the whole story of a renewed psychology of school subjects. A new approach under development offers yet another version of research into the teaching and learning of school subjects. In these studies, the investigators are themselves the teachers under study. The scholars in question not only investigate teaching, they are the teachers under investigation. Not since the earliest days of modern psychology, when Hermann Ebbinghaus (1885/1913) used himself as a subject in his own laboratory experiments on memory, have scholars made themselves the objects of study. Even then, the conditions of the research were far more controlled and artificial, and the function under investigation—memory for a list of nonsense syllables—was hardly an arena for special expertise. The research on classroom mathematics teaching of Magdalene Lampert and Deborah Ball, to which we now turn, provides vivid examples of the attempt to introduce disciplined self-study into a psychology of school subjects. This work serves as a bridge between the psychological study of the learning and teaching of school subjects and the long-neglected tenets of the Dewey school: to study education by designing new practices of teaching and learning school subjects and examining the conditions and consequences of their implementation.

## STUDIES OF ONE'S OWN PRACTICE: THE WORK OF LAMPERT AND BALL

For a number of years, Magdalene Lampert taught mathematics to a fifth-grade class in a Michigan public elementary school.

She would assume responsibility for math teaching from the classroom's full-time teacher, teach the mathematics lessons for each day, collect abundant examples of student work, videotape many of the classroom interactions, maintain detailed journals recounting and reflecting on her own practice, periodically examine the children using both standardized and custom-designed assessments, plan the next day's lessons, and then begin the process anew. Using her own thinking, acting, and reflecting as the data base, she analyzed the practice of teaching. She attempted to document her plans, goals, and strategies, to reconstruct the recurring dilemmas and decisions she faced, and to analyze and classify those in systematic terms. Here was reflective teaching in nearly prototypical form.

In her published papers, Lampert attempted to characterize the routine dilemmas of mathematics teaching, employing extensive case materials from her own practice to support her arguments. She asked what it meant to teach and learn mathematics with understanding, and used detailed descriptions of her interactions with students to illustrate her points. Reading Lampert's articles, one begins to develop a clearer sense of the complexities of teachers' thinking, judgments, and decisions as well as their actions and their consequences, when they actively pursue the goals of higher order mathematical thinking with their students. In this work, Lampert exemplified several aspects of a new approach to the psychology of school subjects: most specifically, renewed analysis of the nature of mathematical knowing, and the development of a research methodology for teachers conducting reflective case studies of their own practice.

With the opening paragraphs of her paper, "When the problem is not the question and the solution is not the answer: Mathematical knowing and teaching," Lampert (1990) signaled the sea change in the approach to the psychology of school subjects. It is not only in the process of self-study that Lampert defined a new form of research. She also approached the subject matter of instruction itself in important new ways. She is squarely in a tradition of educational reform that includes Dewey, Bruner, and Schwab.

Lampert, like Wineburg, believes that any discourse on the learning and teaching of mathematics must first attend to the nature of mathematics itself. Lampert looks to the writings of leading mathematicians and philosophers of mathematics to ask several questions: What is mathematical understanding? What does it mean to *do* mathematics, and how might doing mathematics be different from knowing mathematics? How does someone learn to do mathematics? In what kind of setting do the knowing and doing of mathematics proceed and flourish? Note that Lampert, in the spirit of Dewey and of Whitehead, recognizes that knowing a subject and understanding how to create, test, and reconstruct knowledge in that domain are not the same thing. Like Jerome Bruner (1960) and Joseph Schwab (1962), she is concerned with both the *substance* of mathematics—the skills, concepts, and strategies that constitute the "stuff" of the discipline—and the *syntax* of mathematics—the rules and procedures that mathematicians use to test, critique, and extend their knowledge. Just as Wineburg's definition of historical understanding includes both those aspects of "knowing history," Lampert argues that knowing mathematics must include the ability to engage in mathematical thinking as a member of a disciplinary community. As we indicated earlier,

this is neither a novel nor an outlandish claim. The highly visible and widely admired standards of the National Council of Teachers of Mathematics (1991) are quite consistent with these ideas.

Where does Lampert look to define the nature of mathematical knowing? She begins with an analysis of the nature of mathematics articulated by two of the great thinkers in the discipline, Imre Lakatos (1976) and George Polya (1957):

In the midst of an argument among his students about a theorem in geometry, the teacher in Lakatos's *Proofs and Refutations* (1976) finds it appropriate to announce, "I respect conscious guessing, because it comes from the best human qualities: courage and modesty" (p. 30). Why does the teacher of mathematics think it appropriate to encourage conscious guessing and to celebrate the human virtues of courage and modesty? The answer is to be found in Lakatos's analysis of what it means to know mathematics and his ideas about how new knowledge develops in the discipline. In *Proofs and Refutations*, Lakatos portrays historical debates within mathematics about what the "proof" of a theorem represents by constructing a conversation among a group of students—fictional characters who voice the disagreements among mathematicians through the last several centuries, often using the mathematicians' own words. Lakatos's argument, which comes through in the person of the teacher, is that mathematics develops as a process of "conscious guessing" about relationships among quantities and shapes, with proof following a "zig-zag" path starting from conjectures and moving to the examination of premises through the use of counterexamples or "refutations." This activity of doing mathematics is different from what is recorded once it is done: "Naive conjecture and counterexamples do not appear in the fully fledged deductive structure: The zig-zag of discovery cannot be discerned in the end product" (Lakatos, 1976, p. 42). The product of mathematical activity might be justified with a deductive proof, but the product does not represent the process of coming to know. Nor is knowing final or certain, even with a proof, for the assumptions on which the proof is based—which mathematicians call axioms—continue to be open to reexamination in the mathematical community of discourse. It is this vulnerability to reexamination that allows mathematics to grow and develop. (Lampert, 1990, pp. 29–63)

How is this approach different from the conventional strategies of educational psychology? In the traditions of educational psychology from Thorndike to the present, the starting point for a psychology of school subjects has been the processes of learning as understood by psychology. These processes, whether bonds, schemata, generalizations, or preconceptions, were the terms in which the learning of school subjects was defined. Subject matters were filtered through the prism of psychology, which imbued each of them with its constituent parts. When Dewey, Judd, and Brownell argued for *psychologizing the subject matter,* they were asking that the content of the discipline be transformed into pedagogical and curricular material through an analysis of relevant principles of student learning, development, and motivation. Although both Dewey and Judd gave much closer attention to the disciplinary soundness and distinctiveness of the various subject matters, most of their disciples (including Brownell) treated the subject matter as a given that can be readily psychologized rather than first submitting the discipline to careful analysis and asking how its characteristics might dictate what kind of psychology needs to be deployed or constructed in the service of that kind of discipline. Thus, most educators construed "psychologizing the subject matter" as the challenge of taking nearly any subject and applying the universal principles of instructional psychology to it.

In contrast to this version of psychologizing the subject matter, we might refer to our second alternative as permitting the subject matter to *substantiate the psychology*. That is, we first analyze the subject matter and then ask what kind of psychology would suit it.

How does this strategy unfold for Lampert? She begins her account of mathematical learning by defining how representatives of the discipline stipulate what counts as mathematics. She begins with the syntax of the discipline, with the observations of Lakatos and Polya regarding the manner in which new knowledge is developed in the discipline. She then argues that this perspective on mathematics emphasizes the uncertainty and indeterminacy of the field, rather than the certainty stereotypically associated with this field. As she continues to describe the nature of mathematics, Lampert emphasizes the concepts that compose its major ideas, the rules of conjecture and proof that define its discourse, and the kind of mathematical community within which such interactions take place. Attention to the character of the mathematical community provides the framework for defining a classroom setting that can mirror the contexts for mathematical argumentation and discourse. This account of mathematics—as a logical, epistemological, and socially constructed enterprise—then serves as the template for determining the kind of learning, teaching, and classroom organization needed to conduct mathematical education. The argument begins with the qualities of mathematics as a discipline and a community, and only then stipulates the needed principles of psychology and pedagogy in terms of the disciplinary standard.

Formal structure of the discipline is not the only legitimate starting point for such an analysis. Under the influence of cognitive anthropology, psychologists and educators are often using the way in which laypersons employ disciplinary knowledge in their everyday lives as workers or consumers to define the knowledge of the field that is of most worth. Yet other educators, rather than beginning with either an everyday or a disciplinary definition of a particular subject matter, begin instead with the kinds of problems that characterize everyday life and end up with *inter*disciplinary or thematic conceptions of subject matter. We will discuss both these alternatives in a subsequent section of the chapter.

The work of Lampert and of Wineburg are quite similar in this respect: They emphasize the broad principles of the discipline, both conceptually and procedurally, in their respective definitions of what counts as deep disciplinary understanding. In this sense, they are clearly in the traditions of both Dewey and Judd, who insisted on defining the most important goals of education in terms of broad and powerful concepts and principles. An interesting contrast between the work of Wineburg and that of Lampert is the manner in which each arrives at a conception of the discipline and then moves to studies of its implications for practice. Lampert develops her vision of mathematical pedagogy from a *normative* conception of mathematical knowledge, reasoning, and community. That is, she derives a conception of pedagogy from an analysis and interpretation of the writings of mathematicians and philosophers of mathematics. Thus, Lampert bases her emphasis on

the importance of student conjectures and refutations in the context of a classroom-based microcosm of a mathematical community on her readings of Lakatos, Polya, and other leading mathematicians. She accepts their accounts as reasonable, then designs classroom environments to reflect them. Her research, based heavily on her own teaching, attempts to translate their normative visions into classroom realities. She writes detailed case studies of her classrooms and uses them to explicate the principles and practices of her mathematical pedagogy as well as to create an "existence proof" of her image of ideal mathematical teaching and learning, to identify its critical features in practice, and to investigate its consequences for herself and her pupils.

Wineburg also begins with philosophical and historiographic accounts of historical reasoning, but he goes beyond them to study the actual thinking and problem solving of scholars (and students) engaged in working with historical materials. Hence, much of Wineburg's psychological research involves the study of historians' thinking, in order to provide empirical evidence to support his normative claims about the proper engagement in historical thinking.

## Deborah Ball's Program

Lampert's colleague and close collaborator, Deborah Ball, also studies her own practice as a teacher of elementary mathematics. She follows a daily teaching regimen similar to Lampert's teaching of third-grade mathematics in the same elementary school. In two of her recent case studies, she demonstrates how this kind of research creates a new version of the psychology of school subjects. Ball (1993) begins by reminding her readers of Jerome Bruner's famous epigraph from *The Process of Education*: "We begin with the hypothesis that any subject can be taught effectively in some intellectually honest form to any child at any stage of development." She suggests that teaching that meets the standard of intellectual honesty must exhibit two forms of fidelity: It must be faithful to the essential ideas and processes of the subject matter to be learned, and it must be faithful to the mind and motives of the learners, including their prior knowledge, skills, and dispositions, both cultural and intellectual.

Ball (1993) first presents a case in which she reports on her teaching of the concept of signed numbers to a third-grade classroom. She describes how she began the instruction by offering the analogy of a tall building which has an elevator that goes to as many floors above the ground as below the ground. She explores how well that representation works to clarify positive and negative integers for her students. She then proceeds through accounts of several other analogical representations and discusses them both from the perspective of their effectiveness in enhancing the children's understanding and in terms of their fidelity to the underlying concepts in mathematics. The case beautifully exemplifies the subject specificity of math teaching, not only because the mathematical representations are unique to that content domain, but because the students' understandings and misunderstandings are also content-specific.

In a second case, Ball (1993) reports on an episode in which Sean, a young boy who is normally quiet in class, offers the conjecture that the integer 6 is both positive and negative. The class had been studying the concepts of positive and negative for a while, and Ball was quite sure that everyone had the ideas clearly in mind. Sean's conjecture, however, was interesting because of his explanation. He argued that 6 was a number made up of an odd number of even factors, that is, three groups of two. As such, it was both odd ("three groups") and even ("of twos"). Even as other students point out the flaws in his argument, Sean remains steadfast. Finally, Ball and the students agree to taking seriously Sean's conjecture that there exist numbers that may be both odd and even because they are composed of an odd number of even factors. This conjecture, although eventually rejected by everyone in the class (including Sean), provides a lovely opportunity for students to explore the properties of numbers.

Ball describes her own thought processes during this episode, as well as the attempts by other pupils to refute Sean's conjecture in mathematical terms. Among the interesting facets of the case are the ways in which Ball and the pupils employ a number of different analogical representations from which to argue. They call on the number line that is prominently displayed on the classroom wall above the blackboard, they give examples of the distribution of gifts among a small number of children, they count abstract tallies on the chalkboard, and so on. Here again, the self-investigation yields valuable case data on the role of representation in the teaching and learning of mathematics, conveyed in ways not possible in conventional research methods. Moreover, the case also provides Ball with an opportunity to explore one of the persistent dilemmas of mathematics (and probably other subject matter) teaching: How does a teacher respond to a student idea that is probably incorrect, yet reflects interesting thinking on the student's part? The case of "Sean numbers" is memorable in that sense.

This case, like so many others written by Ball and by Lampert, also exemplifies the dynamism of a Deweyan perspective that argues for conducting psychological research that is rooted in the particularities of practice. We might well be able to offer propositions regarding what it means to "know mathematics" in general and for the most part. However, cases like "Sean numbers" require that we test any abstract formulation against the complexities of situated practice. What does Sean know mathematically? What is he ignorant of? On balance, has he displayed mathematical understanding, the ability to think and reason like a mathematician? Without this kind of case literature in educational psychology, it will be quite difficult to address such questions, much less propose to answer them.

While this form of research is unlikely to replace traditional experimental studies, it offers a new approach that promises quite novel insights into the dynamics of classroom teaching in the content areas. Collaborative design experiments, to be discussed below, represent a fascinating middle ground between teacher research and classic experiments. Other scholars, such as Roth (1987) in science and Wilson (1990) in social studies, are employing a similar method of self-investigation. Here is a research method that substantially erodes the time-honored distinction between subject and object, between the researcher and the researched. Although Lampert and Ball are indeed university professors who spend part of their days in classrooms, we are also witnessing an upsurge in the study of teaching by ordinary classroom teachers (Cochran-Smith & Lytle, 1993). We anticipate that this development will grow

sufficiently in strength to provide yet another new paradigm for the reviving psychology of school subjects, although it has its own serious problems.

Let no one be deceived regarding the complexity of such work and the demands it places on its practitioners. Lampert, Ball, and their colleagues are quite unusual scholar-practitioners. They are not only experienced classroom teachers with the skills and dispositions to conduct disciplined inquiries into their own practice, they are also deeply knowledgeable about their subject matter and the principles of its pedagogy. The admonition that researchers must be well versed in the substance of the subject matters whose pedagogy they study is not limited to university personnel. If teacher researchers wish to pursue investigations of the psychology or pedagogy of particular school subjects, they will need the kind of substantive sophistication displayed by Lampert and Ball. The legitimacy of being "insiders" and speaking with the "teacher's voice" does not in itself establish a warrant for the claims of teacher research.

We began this chapter with a discussion of the central role of the concept of transfer in any psychology of school subjects. Where has this concept gone in the developments we have been examining? How does the return of the subject matter to a central role in the educational psychology of school subjects affect the concept of transfer and its interpretation?

## TRANSFER REDUX

"The first object of any act of learning, over and beyond the pleasure it may give, is that it should serve us in the future. Learning should not only take us somewhere; it should allow us later to go further more easily." In those simple yet eloquent words, Jerome Bruner (1960, p. 17) opened the chapter titled "The Importance of Structure" in his classic work, *The Process of Education*, and declared the question of transfer to be the central challenge for the educational process. As he analyzed, he revisited the issues that divided Thorndike from Dewey and Judd, and cast his lot unambiguously with the latter:

There are two ways in which learning serves us in the future. One is through its specific applicability to tasks that are highly similar to those we originally learned to perform. Psychologists refer to this phenomenon as specific transfer of training; perhaps it should be called the extension of habits and associations. Its utility appears to be limited in the main to what we usually speak of as skills. . . . A second way in which earlier learning renders later performance more efficient is through what is conveniently called nonspecific transfer or, more accurately, the transfer of principles and attitudes. In essence, it consists of learning initially not a skill but a general idea, which can be used as a basis for recognizing subsequent problems as special cases of the idea originally mastered. This type of transfer is at the heart of the educational process—the continual broadening and deepening of knowledge in terms of basic and general ideas. (J. Bruner, 1960, p. 17)

Bruner based his argument in favor of teaching the structures of the various subject matters on the assertion that in this manner educators could maximize the likelihood of successful transfer of the second kind, a broad nonspecific transfer that is "at the heart of the educational process." But is there evidence that this kind of broad transfer exists, in spite of the long-standing support for Thorndike's more modest claims?

Gavriel Salomon and David Perkins (1987; Perkins & Salomon, 1989) have devoted a number of years to examining the competing claims regarding transfer and have developed a formulation that is quite helpful in sorting out the many sides of this question. They distinguish between "high-road" and "low-road" transfer, arguing that both kinds of transfer exist but have different characteristics, obtain under different conditions, and thus have different implications for education. In fact, both types are necessary for learning. They have formulated a "synthesis theory" in which they relate the two types of transfer and stipulate the conditions for their attainment. Their synthesis position is in fact closer to Judd's formulation, since Judd never denied that identical-elements transfer existed, only that it was far too narrow and modest a conception on which to erect a system of education whose goal was the cultivation of the higher mental processes. Transfer is also the subject of chapter 3.

Perkins and Salomon characterize the more modest type of specific transfer as "low-road transfer" and the broad, principle-based transfer as "high-road transfer." They then offer two pairs of concepts that clarify the problems of transfer and their connections to the issues surrounding a psychology of school subjects. Their first concept is the distinction between "strong methods" and "weak methods" of transfer. Strong methods are the stuff of low-road transfer, analogous in some ways to the role of algorithms in problem solving. They work reflexively and directly. But there is a "power-generality" trade-off to be reckoned with. The more power vested in a strong method, the more limited its generality to other situations or domains. Conversely, the more general a strategy, the weaker its transfer to other situations or disciplines. This is analogous to the role of heuristics, those general strategies or rules of thumb we often use in problem solving. See also chapters 2 and 3.

Theorists also distinguish between "general" and "contextualized" rules when they discuss transfer. They imply that broad transfer can be achieved only when a rule or principle applies in general and is not limited by particular contexts. Salomon and Perkins (1987) also point out that general and contextualized are not mutually exclusive. They argue that "there *are* general cognitive skills; but they always function in contextualized ways." As an example they discuss the philosopher's strategic move of seeking counterexamples when testing an argument. At one level, the strategy of seeking counterexamples is broad and general, operating whatever the situation or domain. On the other hand, the choice of particular counterexamples is always specific to the domain from which the examples and counterexamples must be drawn. Thus, these principles (somewhat like Deborah Ball's Sean numbers, which are both odd and even) are both general and contextualized. Many of the principles of effective teaching share those characteristics. The principle of selecting an explanation that articulates with the prior knowledge or preconceptions of the learners is general and broad. Selecting the most fitting explanation, choosing which analogy, metaphor, or narrative will be most apt under the circumstances, is highly domain- and context-specific.

Salomon and Perkins cite Ann Brown and her associates (e.g., Brown & Kane, 1988a, 1988b; Brown & Palincsar, 1989) who argue that transfer does take place when (a) *learners are shown how* problems resemble one another; (b) *learners' attention is directed to the underlying goal structure* of comparable problems; (c) the learners are familiar with the problem domains; (d) examples are accompanied by rules, especially those generated by the learners themselves; and (e) learning takes place in a social context (e.g., reciprocal teaching) whereby justifications, principles, and explanations are socially fostered, generated, and contrasted (quoted from Perkins & Salomon, 1989, p. 22). We would call particular attention to Brown's emphasis (italicized above) on the *metacognitive* conditions that accompany successful transfer. Transfer does not simply happen to a learner who waits passively for it to occur or whose teacher expects that some instructional technique will magically foster the elusive transfer process. Indeed, learners are more likely to transfer when they are helped to become deeply conscious of their own strategies, actively engaged in seeking ways to generalize their understandings, and reflective about their own learning processes and the conditions under which they work.

This principle is reminiscent of Judd's argument, cited earlier, that transfer is most likely to occur if both the teacher and the students have the goal of generalization actively in mind while learning. But "mindfulness" on the part of the learner, while necessary, is not the only essential ingredient in the recipe for transfer. One needs the right kind of menu, a curriculum that promotes transfer in the hands of a teacher who understands how to arrange those conditions and to model those processes. In this regard, we return to John Dewey for one last time.

Dewey appears to have felt that part of the problem of transfer (although he did not use the term) lay in the boundless array of topics and subjects that students confronted in the schools. Like Bruner many years later, he felt that the curriculum had to be simplified if deep and complex learning were to take place. He proposed a strategy of simplification that highlighted the important *structures* of subject matter. As he observed in his monograph, *How We Think* (1902/1956):

Our schools are troubled with multiplication of studies. . . . Our teachers find their tasks made heavier in that they have come to deal with pupils individually and not merely in mass. . . . Some clue of unity, some principle that makes for simplification must be found. This book represents the conviction that the needed steadying and centralizing factor is found in adopting as the end of endeavor that attitude of mind, that habit of thought, which we call scientific. (*John Dewey: The Middle Works,* Vol. 6, p. 179)

Thus Dewey placed his bets on transfer of methods and dispositions associated with scientific reasoning, which he believed would generalize across many domains and conditions. Indeed, Dewey's own philosophical work exemplifies that principle, since he employed the same principles of scientific reasoning, cloaked in a dialectical mode of discourse, whether he was discussing education, ethics, logic, aesthetics, politics, or science. Dewey's call for a curriculum simplified around a few basic ideas, methods, and dispositions also anticipated the contemporary dictum of Sizer (1984) and his Coalition of Essential Schools, that "less is more."

How does this discussion of transfer and context-boundedness relate to a psychology of school subjects? Perkins and Salomon conclude their insightful analysis by observing:

To be sure, general heuristics that fail to make contact with a rich domain-specific knowledge base are *weak*. But when a domain-specific knowledge base operates without general heuristics, it is brittle—it serves mostly in handling formulaic problems. Although we don't want the weak results of the kind of attention to general heuristics that neglects the knowledge base, we also don't want the brittle competency forged by exclusive attention to particularized knowledge! We would hope for more from education. And, according to the synthesis theory, we can get more. (1989, p. 23)

They conclude with an assertion that speaks to the promise of a psychology of school subjects: "We forecast that *wider scale efforts to join subject matter instruction and the teaching of thinking* will be one of the exciting stories of the next decade of research and educational innovation" (emphasis added).

The work of L. B. Resnick (1987) supports that position. She reported on her analysis of a raft of programs oriented toward "learning to think" that promised to teach broad strategies of critical or higher order thinking. She concluded that most failed to deliver on their promise.

We need to identify and closely examine the aspects of education that are most likely to produce ability to adapt in the face of transitions and breakdowns. Rather than training people for particular jobs—a task better left to revised forms of on-the-job training—school should focus its efforts on preparing people to be good *adaptive learners,* so that they can perform effectively when situations are unpredictable and task demands change. (1987, pp. 18)

She went on to describe the results of her survey of programs and their evaluations that had been designed to achieve those ends of adaptive learning:

[T]he most successful programs are organized around particular bodies of knowledge and interpretation—subject matters, if you will—rather than general abilities. The treatment of the subject matter is tailored to engage students in processes of meaning construction and interpretation (e.g., Palinscar & Brown, 1984) that can block the symbol-detached-from-referent thinking that I have noted is a major problem in school. Just such self-conscious meaning construction and interpretation skills are likely to be needed in conditions of breakdown and transition outside school, when one must use powers of reflection and analysis to craft sensible responses to new situations. (1987, pp. 18–19)

An adequate educational psychology cannot limit itself to the elucidation of general principles. As Stodolsky (1988) observed about the title of her book, *This Subject Matters*: "The subject matters" is both an empirical statement of findings and a normative judgment regarding research focus. We seek a psychology of school subjects for which the subject matter substantiates the psychology as much as the social scientist psychologizes the subject matter.

## THE NEW LOOK IN THE PSYCHOLOGY OF SCHOOL SUBJECTS

One of the most important developments in psychology in the early 1960s was dubbed "the new look in perception." The new look (e.g., Bruner & Goodman, 1947) was a turning point in the history of the field because it introduced experimental study of the influence of motives, values, and other forms of thought on that purest of psychological (almost physiological) processes, perception. The new look was a harbinger of the

future even as it became a watershed for the past. What individuals believed, valued, feared, or imagined could reliably influence what they perceived. One's prior knowledge could strongly influence what one was capable of experiencing and, hence, of learning. Although no great surprise to psychodynamic theorists of post-Freudian persuasion, this was apparently a newer insight for those engaged in the experimental study of perception, a field that was moving from its physiological roots to include a more constructivist cognitive future.

We believe that we are similarly observing the emergence of a "new look" in the psychology of school subjects, a Copernican revolution in the role of each discipline, or interdisciplinary subject matter, in fashioning the parameters of its own psychology of learning, teaching, and assessment. In contrast to the earlier forms of the psychology of school subjects, where either general or specific psychological principles of learning or development were applied to subject-specific questions, we are witnessing the emergence of a new field where the analysis begins with an examination of the source discipline in its own terms— what is the thinking, wondering, feeling, reasoning, and collaborating that characterizes the work of history, mathematics or literature? The school subject is then defined through a consideration of the connections between the disciplinary matter and the minds and situations of children, as well as between the subject matter at hand and the more general curriculum and school organization in which it might be embedded; the psychological analysis then moves to consideration of the particular forms of school learning, school teaching, curriculum and materials development, school-based assessment, and teacher preparation that would be faithful to both the essential features of the subject matter and the qualities of mind and motivation characteristic of the children.

Bruner was also responsible for a similar Copernican-style revolution in the concept of educational readiness. In his classic *The Process of Education* (1960), he stated that any subject could be learned in an intellectually honest form by children at any stage of development. The key to this claim lay in the assertion that key ideas in a subject matter could be transformed via multiple modes of representation. Thus, subject matter could be adapted into different stages of readiness instead of treating the subject matter as fixed and then waiting for students to exhibit readiness. Anticipating the "new look" in the psychology of school subjects, Bruner therefore called for the analysis of subject matters into their core structures, those key ideas that were so worth understanding that they would warrant revisiting under different representations in a spiral curriculum.

We have offered several examples of this new look in work on the psychology of school subjects by Leinhardt, Wineburg, Lampert, and Ball. They differ in their choice of discipline— history, geography, or mathematics—and in the strategies they employ to analyze the discipline's features and to operationalize its activities. Yet both research programs exemplify the distinctive character of the new psychology of school subjects with its emphasis on the discipline as starting point rather than as ultimate locus of application.

The new look begins with an in-depth analysis of the *syntax* (using J. J. Schwab's [1962] term) of the discipline itself, the system of rules and protocols by which a discipline tests claims of truth against one another and against reality. Such an analysis can begin with several strategies. One approach, exemplified by the work of Lampert in mathematics, begins with a careful examination of normative conceptions of the discipline and its pursuit. The work of philosophers of mathematics such as Lakatos (1976), reflective mathematicians such as Polya (1957), and an evolving consensus among contemporary mathematics educators are combined into a normative definition of mathematics learning, teaching, and the conditions for fostering both. Once the normative and analytic work has been completed and a working instructional model has been made operational, the empirical work of a psychology of school subjects can begin.

Wineburg's work in history combines a careful study of the philosophical and historiographic sources with more familiar psychological methods. To define the syntax of historical thinking and learning, Wineburg creates a situation in which historians and students of history can engage in doing historical work. Using think-aloud and stimulated recall procedures, he then traces the processes employed by the professional historians and combines his findings with readings in the philosophy of history and historiography.

Both Lampert and Wineburg combine theoretical/normative with empirical approaches in fashioning their working models of disciplinary learning and teaching. Although both draw on psychological and other social science constructs to conduct their studies, their analyses bear no resemblance to the classic Thorndikean analysis of bonds or to the more contemporary Gagnéan analysis of learning varieties. They conduct a more sophisticated, eclectic, and cross-disciplinary form of "task analysis" than is characteristic of expert–novice studies or of typical task analyses.

This "new look" in the psychology of school subjects may finally effect a Deweyan equilibrium between psychologizing the subject matter and substantiating the psychology. If the work of Lampert and Ball in mathematics, of Wineburg in history, and of Leinhardt in both are harbingers of educational psychology's future, then the careful analysis of the intellectual and social processes that comprise the conduct of the discipline or the accomplishment of the practice will take on a central position in the psychologist's activities.

Earlier we asserted that an educational psychology could be identified by how it treated four facets of its work: its core problems and topics, the settings in which it conducted its investigations, the investigators who conducted its studies, and the methods of inquiry they employed. We shall now revisit these four perspectives as we examine the paths that a contemporary educational psychology of school subjects has begun to pursue.

## The Subject Matter: Problems, Topics, and Issues

Increasingly, contemporary psychologists of the school subjects are treating the definition of the subject matter as a significant problem for their research, and are using deliberations on the subject matter as a starting point for their inquiries. Thus, discussions of what counts as authentic mathematics, history, or biology, while a serious topic for the curriculum reformers of the 1960s, has now also become a central issue for the psychologists of school subjects.

There are four general strategies for addressing the question of how to define the subject matter:

1. Using a normative definition of the discipline and its practices, as reflected in Lampert's work or Leinhardt's writings on geography;
2. Using empirical research on how mature scholars in a discipline actually do their scholarly work (often in combination with analysis of normative principles), as reflected in Wineburg's studies;
3. Studying how the ideas of the discipline are actually employed in everyday life, an approach that generally employs the methods of anthropology or ethnomethodology to document the uses of quantitative reasoning among merchants or the forms of written or oral literacy actually practiced in a given community; and
4. Formulating ways in which real-world problems of social interaction, social or political policy, technology applications, urban planning, and the like typically create problems that cross and erode disciplinary lines and project truly interdisciplinary problems.

The normative disciplinary approach uses the testimony of leading scholars in a discipline to define the "authenticity" of a curricular representation. Lampert's references to Polya and Lakatos in her definitions of mathematics, Schoenfeld's (1985) characterizations of mathematical problem solving, or Clement's (1993) stipulations regarding mature thinking among physicists are all examples of a normative disciplinary approach to defining the subject matter. To the extent that there is reasonable consensus in a field, as is claimed for mathematics, this serves as a useful source. If there is substantial disagreement among the experts, as in the social studies, this approach can become quite arbitrary.

It is not only the substantive structure of the discipline to which these scholars refer, or even the formal methods of reasoning and refutation employed to test competing truth claims. Another aspect of the discipline that both Lampert and Ball take quite seriously is the *social organization or community structure* within which members of the discipline pursue their research and interact with one another regarding the methods and findings of the discipline. They attempt to replicate in their classrooms the processes of collaboration, confrontation, and consensus that characterize these disciplines as intellectual and social communities. Neither of these aspects of the discipline received much attention from even the most sophisticated earlier researchers.

When Wineburg studies the actual inquiry processes of historians confronted with original source materials as a basis for defining historiographic expertise, or when Elstein, Shulman, and Sprafka do the same for internal medicine, we encounter a contrasting strategy. While surely informed by normative perspectives on the respective disciplines, the systematic empirical study of both exemplary and developing disciplinary scholars or practitioners forms a central feature of the research. These researchers claim that the most reasonable way for educators to define the essential features of a discipline for instructional purposes is through study of what its practitioners really know and do, not on the basis of what experts in the discipline assert as the essential character of its work. There is ample evidence that skilled practitioners are often in a poor position to attest to the very work they regularly do.

Proponents of a third strategy reject the scholarship of the discipline as an adequate basis for defining the school subject. They argue that elementary and secondary education (even undergraduate liberal education) is a preparation for life rather than a preparation for an academic vocation. Therefore, the proper question is how do ordinary members of communities hold their knowledge and employ it for both use and enjoyment in everyday life. Educators who rest their cases regarding subject matter on the work of anthropologically oriented scholars such as Jean Lave (1988) or Sylvia Scribner and Michael Cole (1981) insist that the proper source for such judgments is how ordinary people in the world use disciplinary information and skills in their everyday lives. Using the methods of anthropology or ethnomethodology, scholars study the ways in which mathematical or scientific principles are applied in the workplace or other informal situations such as supermarkets or organized games. The perspective of this approach is that contexts of use are much more relevant as sources of subject matter than are contexts of formal scholarship. These studies of everyday cognition (Lave, 1988; Scribner & Cole, 1981) are growing rapidly in prominence and influence, helping to redirect scholarship in educational psychology with new concepts such as situated cognition and cognitive apprenticeships (see chapter 2). They are also serving as the natural points of entry for new disciplinary influences on educational psychology, from fields such as anthropology (including general ethnographic methods, ethnographies of communication and conversation, discourse analysis, and the like), linguistics, and computer science.

The fourth orientation finds fault with any attempt to identify school subject matter with academic disciplines. These reformers argue, as did many progressive educators, that the most important problems of living do not respect disciplinary boundaries. Indeed, when social or political policies are made, or when new technologies are deployed, or when communities attempt to solve their problems, these quandaries are never formulated as pure problems of economics, history, mathematics, or government. Instead, the principles and methods of many disciplines must be brought to bear in the service of these deliberations and inquiries. In a similar manner, the proper starting point for school curriculum should be problems and projects, not disciplines, and the disciplines should be interrelated and integrated in connection to the problems. If this approach is taken seriously, the consequences for an educational psychology of school subjects are profound.

The research of Suzanne M. Wilson (1990) exemplifies the value of a multidisciplinary approach, as well as its frequent inevitability when teaching and learning for understanding are pursued by teachers and students. In her paper "Mastodons, maps and Michigan," Wilson describes her own teaching of a third-grade social studies curriculum on the geography and history of Lansing, the capital of Michigan. As the students began to debate the reasons why Lansing was made the capital city, one student speculated that Lansing bacame the capital because it was "in the middle" of the state. Disagreements about the meaning of "middle" in geographical, political, and social terms rapidly spilled over the boundaries of any one discipline into everything from history to the mathematics of ratios and proportions, as students struggled with the uses of scales on their own maps as well as those in their books. The questions they were asking were quite real and highly motivating, but could be contained by no single discipline.

In all these cases of orientations toward defining the problems, topics, and issues of the subject, in spite of their differences in approach and emphasis, scholars agree on the importance of educational psychologists giving careful attention to the question of what counts as the subject matter. The educational researcher does not simply accept a textbook author or curriculum developer's version of the subject matter unquestioningly. Both empirical research and active deliberation on the proper character of subject matter actively occupy the scholarly efforts of the psychologist of school subjects. Moreover, in many cases they have become the central question for the scholar, not merely a preliminary stage to the important questions of instructional technique or student assessment. The subject matter has returned as a core topic, a problem of fundamental analysis.

Each of these four approaches to defining the subject matter can claim John Dewey (and Jerome Bruner) as a central source of its grounding and inspiration. Those who examine the subject matter as understood by its leading authorities can cite Dewey's respect for the disciplines as a starting point for the process of psychologizing the subject matter. Those who focus on what the disciplinary scholars do rather than what they say can remind us of Dewey's emphasis on a discipline as a journey on which scholars embark, not as a static body of facts and theories. Those who place their emphasis on the everyday enactments of disciplinary knowledge can surely draw on Dewey's repeated observations that the ways in which knowledge is actually used and enjoyed become the basis for the instructional situations that will be most meaningful in connecting education with experience. And the scholars who emphasize the importance of transcending individual disciplines and addressing interdisciplinary curriculum can certainly remind us of Dewey's emphasis on broad integrative projects as the ultimate instantiation of his principles. This broad range of Deweyan influence attests either to the universal power of his ideas or to the danger that he has become too many things to too many educators.

## Research Settings

We observed earlier that Dewey's tenet that educational research should be both experimental and naturalistic was regularly ignored or actively rejected by laboratory-based educational psychologists from Thorndike and Judd onward. Even when psychologists like Brownell conducted their experiments within intact classrooms instead of in pull-out groups or under such controlled conditions that the classroom might just as well have been a laboratory, one could hardly declare those classrooms natural learning environments. Perhaps we should distinguish the "naturalistic" from the "natural" in these cases. A laboratory study conducted in a classroom may be naturalistic, but it is hardly natural.

Alan Collins (1992; chapter 2) and Ann L. Brown (1992) have begun to advocate a new form of theory-oriented action research in classrooms that they call "design experiments." These are curriculum-specific in classroom interventions that are theoretically driven, collaboratively designed, and progressively adapted with the classroom teachers. They are documented and assessed using combinations of quantitative and qualitative methods (conjunctions of ethnography and measurement), and willfully confound multiple independent variables in ways that would make most traditional methodologists blanch. As we observed earlier, they are both experimental and naturalistic. Yet if Brownell was correct in his claim that only in a natural classroom learning environment can educational psychologists study real subject matter learning, then they may have no choice but to pursue the new psychology of school subjects in such settings, at least a good deal of the time. Brown insists that there remain good reasons to explore some psychological processes under more pristine and controlled laboratory conditions, and we certainly have no cause to disagree. The alternation between natural sites and highly controlled settings may characterize the future dance steps of educational psychologists. And the other needed form of flexibility may well be a methodological versatility that will include much more vigorous uses of field research methods and case studies in the pursuit of understanding (see also chapter 30). Along with their design characteristics, another feature of these approaches is the frequency with which the investigators either do their own teaching or, more frequently, collaborate actively and interactively with classroom teachers, who participate as partners in both the design and adaptation of the interventions.

## Teachers as Collaborators and Investigators

The work of Lampert, Ball, and their colleagues is likely to signal the entry of many more teachers into the world of school-based research. Once we privilege the natural classroom and school site as the proper setting for research on the psychology of school subjects, and proceed to relax our methodological orthodoxies and offer legitimacy to narrative forms of inquiry such as case studies and investigations of one's own practice, we invite classroom teachers to join us as investigators. Interestingly, John Dewey argued that the teachers in the Laboratory School should be co-investigators with the professors and graduate students. When Lagemann (1988) characterized the relationship that Dewey and his close colleague George Herbert Mead had with the remarkable Jane Addams, she observed that "her most characteristic medium was the anecdote and [Dewey and Mead's] was the theoretical hypothesis." Narrative may be a much more natural form of discourse for schoolteachers than are the more paradigmatic forms favored by social scientists. The new language of a collaborative form of inquiry may well evolve into a kind of narrative-paradigmatic pidgin.

On the other hand, there is a danger that any study undertaken by a practitioner is treated with deference and any investigation pursued by an outside investigator is greeted with suspicion. The "worry over warrant" should never wane (Phillips, 1987). The identity, role, experience, and skill of the investigator are important aspects of a work's validity, especially in those research methods (such as ethnography) where separation of the method from the investigator is difficult. Nevertheless, validity can never be reduced to identifying the investigator, whether in teacher research or in any other form of inquiry.

## Research Methods and Their Disciplines

Taken together, the observations we have made lead to the conclusion that the research methods of educational psychology have undergone a radical change in recent years. There has been a decided qualitative turn reflecting the influence of cognitive science, anthropology, and linguistics. Interpretive

and hermeneutic approaches have become more widespread. This turn has been further amplified by the interest in everyday life as a basis for both disciplinary and interdisciplinary curriculum. Serious contemplation of the nature of school subjects as progeny (or at least close cousins) of disciplines requires that educational psychologists become serious students not only of those disciplines but of the philosophy, history, and sociology of ideas as well. Yet regular use of more formal experiments and methods of inferential statistics remains quite central to our enterprise, appropriately so. In fact, the norm for research into the psychology of school subjects has become an eclectic combining of approaches that were once considered noncommensurable. A lovely example can be found in the conducting of design experiments.

Design experiments in natural settings conducted collaboratively with practitioners produce a set of research methods unimagined by the educational psychologist of the 1940s and 1950s, not to mention a set of approaches that makes many contemporary educational psychologists profoundly uncomfortable. Pre- and posttest measures are regularly employed (along with midcourse monitoring) to establish the direction and degree of changes in students' knowledge, understandings, and attitudes. These include multiple-choice examinations, essays, project reports, and analyses of discourse during lessons. Ethnographers, videographers, and discourse analysts collect data in many forms to document the patterns of interaction and engagement, of self-regulation and conversation, characteristic of teachers and students in the classroom under different circumstances. Teacher journals are compared with the participant observer's notes, and student portfolios provide evidence of how the pupils made sense of the instruction.

The methods have changed, and will continue to change, because the questions we ask are evolving and because the boundaries between psychology and its neighbor disciplines have eroded. It remains unclear whether the new psychology of school subjects requires a different kind of psychology, both substantively and methodologically, or whether psychology alone is no longer sufficient and we must think of ourselves as a new generation of disciplinary and methodological hybrids if we are to pursue a useful study of school subjects. What is clear is that the rules of the game have changed.

The necessary investigations will no longer be exclusively psychological. They have already begun to extend into and to merge with the constructs and methods of other disciplines. It appears to be significant that Dewey's failure to influence educational research during the long Thorndike–Judd era was offset by his influence, after he moved to the philosophy department at Columbia University, on many of the other social sciences, especially public policy and anthropology. There is no escaping the irony that Dewey's reappearance in the recent reconstruction of educational research parallels the end of psychology's long period of disciplinary reclusiveness, at least with respect to the more molar social sciences such as anthropology and sociology.

## THE SUBJECT MATTER MATTERS

As we approach the 21st century, we can anticipate the return of the psychology of school subjects to its former centrality in educational psychology. But it will be with a different psychology, a different sense of school subjects, and a decidedly different conception of the relationships between the two.

It is not only the subject qua discipline that matters. The subject *matter,* which is the subject transformed, interpreted, and arranged for purposes of teaching and learning, matters. Much of the educational psychologist's work will involve inquiries into the advantages of different strategies for transforming subject into subject matter.

The psychology will have blurred its boundaries with other social sciences such as anthropology, sociology, and linguistics; it will be primarily a classroom- and community-based empirical science, using laboratory research to test specific hypotheses or explore particular processes rather than as the major source for new ideas and their verification. Educational psychology's practitioners will not only be professional psychologists, but will include many working teachers who employ social science methods and principles to investigate and reflect on their own practice.

The school subjects will have undergone radical change as well. The modifier *school* will be carefully critiqued, as both the work of scholars in creating the knowledge and of citizens and professional practitioners who use and enjoy the knowledge in the real world play a significant role in defining what counts as subject matter. The social contexts or communities within which the knowledge is discovered and used will become part of the definition of how classrooms are organized for its study. And epistemological questions will finally reach parity with questions of substance in characterizing the curriculum.

The relationship between psychology and school subjects will also change. Greater reciprocity will be achieved between the two, with the principles of psychology no longer exclusively defining the terms of the liaison. Dewey's vision of the subject matters understood as inventions of the human mind, as psychological accomplishments sharing certain characteristics with the intellectual journeys of students struggling to understand them, will flourish as it never did during Dewey's own time. We will appreciate the influence of Judd's formulations, with powerful principles, general strategies, compelling cases, and pivotal facts all interacting in the service of broad transfer. We will not forget Thorndike's emphasis on experimental precision, on careful design, and on the quest for simplification in both theory and method. But we will not permit the quest for parsimony of method or theory to outweigh the need for elegant and powerful theories paired with compelling cases to provide educational relevance and practical utility. The long deferred Dewey era in educational research may now be upon us, in the form of a reinvented psychology of school subjects.

## References

Ausubel, D. P. (1968). *Educational psychology.* New York: Holt, Rinehart & Winston.

Ball, D. (1993). With an eye on the mathematical horizon: Dilemmas of teaching elementary school mathematics. *Elementary School Journal, 93*(4), 373–397.

Brown, A. L. (1992). Design experiments: Theoretical and methodological challenges in creating complex interventions in classroom settings. *Journal of the Learning Sciences, 2*(2), 141–178.

Brown, A. L. (1994). The advancement of learning. *Educational Researcher, 23*(8), 4–12.

Brown, A. L., & Kane, M. J. (1988a, April). *Cognitive flexibility in young children: The case for transfer.* Paper presented at the annual meeting of the American Educational Research Association, New Orleans.

Brown, A. L., & Kane, M. J. (1988b). Preschool children can learn to transfer: Learning to learn and learning from example. *Cognitive Psychology, 20,* 493–523.

Brown, A. L., & Palincsar, A. S. (1989). Guided, cooperative learning and individual knowledge acquisition. In L. B. Resnick (Ed.), *Knowing, learning, and instruction: Essays in honor of Robert Glaser* (pp. 393–451). Hillsdale, NJ: Lawrence Erlbaum Associates.

Brownell, W. A. (1939). *Learning as reorganization: An experimental study in third grade arithmetic.* Durham, NC: Duke University Press.

Bruner, J. (1960). *The process of education.* Cambridge, MA: Harvard University Press.

Bruner, J. S., & Goodman, C. C. (1947). Value and need as organizing factors in perception. *Journal of Abnormal and Social Psychology, 42,* 33–44.

Bruner, J. S., Goodnow, J. J., & Austin, G. A. (1956). *A study of thinking.* New York: Science Editions.

Carlsen, W. S. (1988). *The effects of science teacher subject-matter knowledge on teacher questioning and classroom discourse.* Unpublished doctoral dissertation, Stanford University, Palo Alto, CA.

Clement, J. (1993). Using bridging analogies and anchoring intuitions to deal with students' preconceptions in physics. *Journal of Research in Science Education, 30*(10), 1241–1257.

Cochran-Smith, M., & Lytle, S. L. (1993). *Inside—outside: Teacher research and knowledge.* New York: Teachers College Press.

Collingwood, R. G. (1946). *The idea of history.* New York: Oxford University Press.

Collins, A. (1992). Toward a design science of education. In E. Scanlon & T. O'Shea (Eds.), *New directions in educational technology.* New York: Springer.

Cronbach, L. J. (1975). Beyond the two disciplines of scientific psychology. *American Psychologist, 30*(2), 116–127.

Dewey, J. (1896/1972). Pedagogy as university discipline. In J. A. Boydston & F. Bowers (Eds.), *The early works of John Dewey 1882–1898: Vol. 5. 1895–1898.* Carbondale, IL: Southern Illinois University Press.

Dewey, J. (1897/1972). The psychological aspect of the school curriculum. In J. A. Boydston & F. Bowers (Eds.), *The early works of John Dewey 1882–1898: Vol. 5. 1895–1898.* Carbondale, IL: Southern Illinois University Press.

Dewey, J. (1902/1956). *The child and the curriculum.* In J. A. Boydston (Ed.), *John Dewey. The Middle Works 1899–1924: Vol. 2: 1902–1903.* Carbondale, IL: Southern Illinois University Press.

Dunkin, M. J., & Biddle, B. J. (1974). *The study of teaching.* New York: Holt, Rinehart & Winston.

Ebbinghaus, H. (1885/1913). *Memory: A contribution to experimental psychology.* New York: Teachers College Press.

Elstein, A. S., Shulman, L. S., & Sprafka, S. (1978). *Medical problem solving: An analysis of clinical reasoning.* Cambridge, MA: Harvard University Press.

Freeman, F. N. (1916). *The psychology of the common branches.* Boston: Houghton Mifflin.

Gage, N. L. (1963). Paradigms for research on teaching. In N. L. Gage (Ed.), *Handbook of research on teaching* (pp. 94–144). Chicago: Rand McNally.

Gage, N. L. (1978). *The scientific basis of the art of teaching*. New York: Teachers College Press, Columbia University.

Gagné, R. M. (1965). *The conditions of learning*. New York: Rinehard & Winston.

Gagné, R. M. (1970). *The conditions of learning* (2nd ed.). New York: Holt, Rinehart & Winston.

Gregg, S. M., & Leinhardt, G. (1994). Mapping out geography: An example of epistemology and education. *Review of Educational Research, 64*(2), 311–361.

Grossman, P. L. (1985). *A passion for language: From text to teaching*. Stanford: School of Education, Teacher Knowledge Project, Stanford University.

Grossman, P. L. (1990). *The making of a teacher*. New York: Teachers College Press, Columbia University.

Hashweh, M. Z. (1985). *An exploratory study of teacher knowledge and teaching*. Unpublished doctoral dissertation, Stanford University, Palo Alto, CA.

Judd, C. H. (1915). *The psychology of high school subjects*. Boston: Ginn.

Judd, C. H. (1936). *Education as the cultivation of the higher mental processes*. New York: Macmillan.

Kilpatrick, J. (1992). A history of research in mathematics education. In D. A. Grouws (Ed.), *Handbook of research on mathematics teaching and learning* (pp. 3–38). New York: Macmillan.

Lagemann, E. (1988). The plural worlds of educational research. *History of Education Quarterly, 29*(2), 184–214.

Lakatos, I. (1976). *Proofs and refutations*. Cambridge, England: Cambridge University Press.

Lampert, M. (1990). When the problem is not the question and the solution is not the answer. *American Educational Research Journal, 27*(1), 29–63.

Lave, J. (1988). *Cognition in practice: Mind, mathematics and culture in everyday life*. Cambridge, England: Cambridge University Press.

Leinhardt, G. (1989). Math lessons: A contrast of novice and expert competence. *Journal for Research in Mathematics Education, 20*(1), 52–75.

Leinhardt, G., & Greeno, J. G. (1986). The cognitive skill of teaching. *Journal of Educational Psychology, 78*(2), 75–95.

Leinhardt, G., & Smith, D. A. (1985). Expertise in mathematics instruction: Subject matter knowledge. *Journal of Educational Psychology, 77*, 247–271.

Leinhardt, G., Zaslavsky, O., & Stein, M. K. (1990). Functions, graphs, and graphing: Tasks, learning and teaching. *Review of Educational Research, 60*(1), 1–64.

Marks, R. (1989). *Pedagogical content knowledge in elementary mathematics*. Unpublished doctoral dissertation, Stanford University, Palo Alto, CA.

Marks, R. (1990). Pedagogical content knowledge: From a mathematical case to a modified conception. *Journal of Teacher Education, 41*(3), 3–11.

National Council of Teachers of Mathematics (1991). *Professional standards for teaching mathematics*. Reston, VA: National Council of Teachers of Mathematics.

Newell, A., Shaw, J. C., & Simon, H. A. (1958). Elements of a theory of human problem solving. *Psychological Review, 65*, 151–166.

Newell, A., & Simon, H. A. (1972). *Human problem solving*. Englewood Cliffs, NJ: Prentice Hall.

Newman, D., Griffin, P., & Cole, M. (1989). *The construction zone: Working for cognitive change in school*. Cambridge, England: Cambridge University Press.

Palincsar, A. S., & Brown, A. L. (1984). Reciprocal teaching of comprehension-fostering and comprehension-monitoring activities. *Cognition and Instruction, 1*, 117–175.

Perkins, D. N., & Salomon, G. (1989). Are cognitive skills context-bound? *Educational Researcher, 18*(1), 16–25.

Phillips, D. C. (1987). Validity in qualitative research: Why the worry about warrant will not wane. *Education and Urban Society, 20*(1), 9–24.

Plato. (1961). *Meno*. Cambridge, England: Cambridge University Press.

Polya, G. (1957). *How to solve it*. Garden City, NY: Doubleday.

Resnick, L. B. (1987). *Education and learning to think*. Washington, DC: National Academy Press.

Resnick, L. B. (1987). The 1987 presidential address: Learning in school and out. *Educational Researcher, 16*(9), 13–20.

Rosenshine, B., & Stevens, R. (1986). Teaching functions. In M. C. Wittrock (Ed.), *Handbook of research on teaching* (pp. 376–391). New York: Macmillan.

Roth, K. J. (1987). Curriculum materials, teacher talk and student learning: Case studies in fifth grade science teaching. *Journal of Curriculum Studies, 19*(6), 527–548.

Rumelhart, D. E., McClelland, J. L., & PDP Research Group. (1986). *Parallel distributed processing: Explorations in the microstructure of cognition*. Cambridge, MA: MIT Press.

Salomon, G. (1974). *Sesame Street in Israel: Its instructional and psychological effects on children*. New York: Children's Television Workshop.

Salomon, G. (1976). Sesame Street around the world: Cognitive skill learning across cultures. *Journal of Communication, 26*, 138–145.

Salomon, G., & Perkins, D. N. (1987). Rocky roads to transfer: Rethinking mechanisms of a neglected phenomenon. *Educational Psychologist, 24*(2), 113–142.

Schoenfeld, A. H. (1985). *Mathematical problem-solving*. New York: Academic Press.

Schwab, J. (1969). The practical: A language for curriculum. *School Review, 78*, 1–23.

Schwab, J. J. (1962). The concept of the structure of a discipline. *Educational Record, 43*, 197–205.

Scribner, S., & Cole, M. (1981). *The psychology of literacy*. Cambridge, MA: Harvard University Press.

Shulman, L. S. (1970a). Psychology and mathematics education. In E. G. Begle (Ed.), *Mathematics education: The sixty-ninth yearbook of the National Society for the Study of Education*. Chicago: University of Chicago Press.

Shulman, L. S. (1970b). Reconstruction of educational research. *Review of Educational Research, 40*, 371–396.

Shulman, L. S. (1986). Those who understand: Knowledge growth in teaching. *Educational Researcher, 15*(2), 4–14.

Shulman, L. S. (1986/1990). Paradigms and programs. In M. C. Wittrock (Ed.), *Handbook of research on teaching* (pp. 3–36). New York: Macmillan.

Shulman, L. S. (1987). Knowledge and teaching: Foundations of the new reform. *Harvard Educational Review, 57*(1), 1–22.

Sizer, T. R. (1984). *Horace's compromise: The dilemma of the American high school*. Boston: Houghton Mifflin.

Stodolsky, S. (1988). *The subject matters: Classroom activity in math and social studies*. Chicago: University of Chicago Press.

Thorndike, E. L. (1922). *The psychology of arithmetic*. New York: Macmillan.

Whitehead, A. N. (1929/1967). *The aims of education*. New York: Free Press.

Wilson, S. M. (1990). *Mastodons, maps and Michigan: Exploring uncharted territory while teaching elementary school social studies* (report No. 24). Elementary Subjects Center Series, Michigan State University.

Wilson, S. M. (1992). A case concerning content: Using cases to teach about subject matter. In J. H. Shulman (Ed.), *Case methods in teacher education* (pp. 64–89). New York: Teachers College Press.

Wineburg, S. S. (1991a). Historical problem solving: A study of the cognitive processes used in the evaluation of documentary and pictorial evidence. *Journal of Educational Psychology, 83*(1), 73–87.

Wineburg, S. S. (1991b). On the reading of historical texts: Notes on the breach between school and academy. *American Educational Research Journal, 28*(3), 495–519.

# ·14·

# THE PSYCHOLOGY OF LEARNING AND TEACHING HISTORY

## Samuel S. Wineburg

UNIVERSITY OF WASHINGTON, SEATTLE

It was a politician, not a historian, who offered the most persuasive rationale for studying history. Addressing the Roman Senate nearly a century before the birth of Christ, Cicero proclaimed: "Not to know what happened before one was born is always to be a child." Cicero's dictum provides a challenge to the modern psychologist, who must possess boundless energy merely to keep up with psychology's current developments, not to mention the effort required to gain an awareness of the past. Psychology's progress breeds an ineluctable presentism, a condition that blurs work older than a decade and nearly obliterates everything before that.

My goal in this chapter is to provide some redress for this problem with special reference to psychological work on history. I shall not venture to write a history of research on history, as that would exceed my purview. My hope, more modest, is to shed light on present research efforts by sketching out some historical antecedents and providing some sense of context. Space limitations require that I focus on work in history, leaving the larger body of research on the social studies to others (e.g., Voss, Greene, Post, & Penner, 1983, in political science; Thorton & Wenger, 1990, in geography; and Berti & Bombi, 1988, in economics). My scope is also limited to work in English, although key studies on history have appeared in other languages (e.g., Pozo & Carretero, 1983; von Borries, 1987; cf. Kol'tsova, 1978).

To view the body of psychological work on history as a cohesive undertaking would be to commit the error of the novices in Chi, Feltovich, and Glaser's (1981) classic study: the tendency to group elements by surface similarity, not deep structure. In reality, the studies described in this chapter are united more by common keywords and ERIC searches than by a shared conceptual focus. Research on history may be thought of as the counterpoise to Shakespeare's rose: History, though bearing the same name in these reports, is rarely the same thing. Historical understanding can mean anything from memorizing a list of dates to mastering a set of logical relations, from being able to recite an agreed-upon story to contending with ill-structured problems resistant to single interpretations. These *histories* and the empirical studies done in their name tell as much about the psychologists who did them as the subjects who participated in them. In this sense, the body of psychological research on history constitutes a fascinating historical record in its own right, a landscape of mixed forms attesting to the multiplicity of ways the study of the past can be understood.

My review is organized into three sections. First, I discuss history's treatment by early educational psychologists working in the United States. I spend more time than usual on this work since its accomplishments and shortcomings, its goals achieved and those left unfulfilled, disclose much about our present condition. In the second section I examine research conducted in Great Britain. Although this work goes back to the beginning of the 20th century (e.g., Collie, 1911; cf. Aldrich, 1984), I pick up the story with the programs of British psychologists working in the Piagetian tradition. In the final section I review contemporary research programs that have arisen in the wake of the "cognitive revolution" (Gardner, 1985). I conclude with some speculations about future directions in this research area, and thoughts about the role that educational psychologists might play in shaping it.

## RESEARCH ON HISTORY: SOME EARLY INVESTIGATIONS

For the founders of educational psychology, history was a topic more of theoretical than empirical concern. In the 442

Editorial consultants for this chapter were Gaea Leinhardt and Suzanne M. Wilson. Thanks also to Martin Booth, Pam Grossman, and Peter Seixas for comments on a previous draft. Part of the writing of this chapter was supported by a grant from the Spencer Foundation.

423

pages of Thorndike's *Educational Psychology—Briefer Course* (1923), history goes unmentioned save for a single reference (p. 345) about sex differences in historical achievement (which favored boys). Only in *Education, A First Book* (1912) does history receive more than fleeting attention. Here Thorndike paused to speculate on the burning question of his day: Should history be taught "backwards," that is, beginning with the present and tracing events back in time, or was the traditional chronological treatment best suited to the abilities and dispositions of youngsters? Despite the absence of data, Thorndike did not equivocate:

> The educational value of finding the causes of what is, and then the causes of these causes, is so very much superior to the spurious reasoning which comes from explaining a record already known . . . that the arrangement of the . . . course in history in the inverse temporal order . . . deserves serious consideration. (1912, p. 144)

G. Stanley Hall shared Thorndike's speculative interest in history. Not surprisingly, Hall (1911, p. 285) saw history as a means for helping students place events in a "temporal perspective as products of growth and development," a subject that especially during adolescence should be infused with lessons that "inspire to the greatest degree ideals of social service and unselfishness" (p. 286). Not a contentious battleground of competing interpretations, a conundrum of ill-structured and ill-defined problems, or even a site for critical thinking, Hall's history would be a unifying moralizing force, "a thesaurus of inspiring ethical examples to show how all got their deserts in the end" (p. 296).

Among the founders of educational psychology, only Charles Hubbard Judd dealt incisively with history. Judd's chapter in the *Psychology of High-School Subjects* (1915) was a treatment impressive in scope, embracing in 29 pages the nature of chronological thinking, the difficulties of causal judgment ("much more complicated" in history than in science [p. 384]), the dangers of dramatic reenactments, the psychological difficulties presented by historical evidence, and the motivational role of social (then called "industrial") history. While drawing on the work of others, including the work of the Committee of Seven (American Historical Association, 1899) and the Committee of Five (American Historical Association, 1911), Judd's discussion contains flourishes of insight in its own right. One example comes in a section titled the "Intricacy of Moral Judgments" in which Judd dealt with the psychological push toward presentism, the difficulty—perhaps even the impossibility—of understanding the past on its own terms:

> The modern student is . . . guided in all of his judgments by an established mode of thought . . . peculiar to his own generation. We have certain notions . . . that are wholly different from the notions that obtained at the time that England was in controversy with her American colonies. When . . . [the student] is suddenly carried back in his historical studies to situations that differ altogether from the situations that now confront him, he is likely to carry back, without being fully aware of the fallacy of his procedure, those standards of judgment and canons of ethical thought which constitute his present inheritance. (p. 379)

In this short comment, Judd anticipated issues that would occupy psychologists' attention well into the final decades of the 20th century.

It was not until 1917, the year the United States entered World War I, that history made it into the pages of the fledgling *Journal of Educational Psychology.* J. Carleton Bell, managing editor of the *Journal* and professor at the Brooklyn Training School for Teachers, began Volume VIII with an editorial titled "The Historic Sense." (A timely second editorial examined the relation of psychology to military problems.) Bell claimed that the study of history provided an opportunity for thinking and reflection, the opposite of what went on in much instruction. However, to teachers who would aim at these lofty goals, Bell put two questions: "What is the historic sense?" and "How can it be developed?" (1917, p. 317). Such questions, he continued, did not only concern the history teacher but were ones "in which the educational psychologist is interested, and which it is incumbent upon him to attempt to answer" (p. 317).

Bell offered clues about where to locate the "historic sense." Presented with a set of primary documents, one student produces a coherent account while another assembles "a hodge-podge of miscellaneous facts" (p. 318). What accounts for this discrepancy? Similarly, some college freshmen "show great skill in the orderly arrangement of their historical data," while others "take all statements with equal emphasis . . . and become hopelessly confused in the multiplicity of details" (p. 318). Do such findings reflect "native differences in historic ability," Bell wondered, or are they the "effects of specific courses of training"? Such questions opened up "a fascinating field for investigation" (p. 318) for the new field of educational psychology.

Bell put his finger on questions that continue to occupy our attention: What is the essence of understanding? What determines success on tasks that have more than one right answer? What role might instruction play in improving students' ability to think historically? In light of this forward-looking research agenda, it is instructive to examine how it unfolded in practice. In a companion piece to his editorial, Bell and his associate D. F. McCollum presented an empirical study (Bell & McCollum, 1917) that began by sketching out the various ways historical understanding might be operationalized:

1. "[T]he ability to understand present events in light of the past" (p. 257).
2. The ability to sift through the documentary record— newspaper accounts, hearsay, partisan attacks, contemporary accounts—and construct "from this confused tangle a straightforward and probable account" of what happened. This is important, especially, because it is the goal of many "able and earnest college teachers of history" (p. 257).
3. The ability to appreciate a historical narrative.
4. "[R]eflective and discriminating replies to 'thought questions' on a given historical situation" (p. 258).
5. The ability to answer factual questions about historical personalities and events.

Bell and McCollum conceded that this last aspect was "the narrowest, and in the estimation of some writers, the least important type of historical ability" but it was also the one "most readily tested" (p. 258). In a fateful move, the authors announced that the ability to answer factual questions was therefore "chosen for study in the present investigation" (p. 258). While perhaps the first instance, this was not the last in which ease of measurement, not priority of subject matter understanding, determined the course of a research program.

Bell and McCollum composed a test of names (e.g., John Burgoyne, Alexander Hamilton, Cyrus H. McCormick), dates (e.g., 1492, 1776, 1861), and events (e.g., the Sherman Antitrust Law, the Fugitive Slave Law, the Dred Scott decision) believed by teachers to be important facts every student should know. They gave their test to 1,500 students at the upper elementary (fifth through seventh grades), secondary, and college levels. In the upper elementary grades, students answered 16% of the questions correctly, in high school (after a year of U.S. history), 33%, and in college, after a third exposure to history, 49%. Taking a stand customarily reserved for country preachers, and more recently secretaries of education, Bell and McCollum indicted the educational system and its charges: "Surely a grade of 33 in 100 on the simplest and most obvious facts of American history is not a record in which any high school can take pride" (pp. 268–269).

Five years later Eikenberry (1923) replicated these findings, though on a smaller scale. He found that not one of 34 university seniors could remember who was president during the Mexican War (James K. Polk), and less than half could remember the president of the Confederacy (Jefferson Davis). Similar patterns emerged from a *New York Times* survey of historical knowledge given to 7,000 students in the 1940s (Nevins, 1942; cf. DeVoto, 1943), and little has changed with the recent findings from the National Assessment of Educational Progress examination in American history (Ravitch & Finn, 1987). Viewed in historical perspective, these recent results, rather than providing evidence for a "gradual disintegration of cultural memory" (Finn & Ravitch, 1987, p. 32), instead testify to a peculiar American pastime: the practice by each generation of testing its young, only to discover—and rediscover—their "shameful" ignorance. (The characterization as "shameful" comes from Ravitch and Finn, 1987, p. 201.) However, as Whittington (1991) has shown, when test results from the early part of the 20th century are equated with the most recent findings, we learn that there has been little appreciable change in students' historical knowledge over time. This is remarkable when we consider the expansion of high school enrollments in this century, with only a small elite attending school when Bell and McCollum did their study in 1917 to nearly universal enrollment today. If anything, the consistency of these results casts doubt on a presumed golden age of fact retention in American schools. Appeals to such an age are more the stuff of national lore than national history.

J. Carleton Bell's colleague at the Brooklyn Training School, Garry C. Myers, took a different route in exploring historical knowledge, for Myers (1917b) was more interested in students' wrong answers than in their correct ones. He asked 107 college women to name one fact about each of 50 historical figures. He found that less than 50 percent of the names were recalled accurately, with 40 percent "lost between the time of mastery and that of recall" (p. 277). But this loss was not an erasure. Wrong answers, Myers found, were often statements of fact wrongly connected (p. 282), systematic efforts that followed a discernible pattern. For example, Philip John Schuyler, one of four major generals commissioned by Congress during the Revolutionary War, was connected to wars ranging from the French and Indian War to the Civil War, but his status as general remained unchanged. Names like that of the abolitionist William Lloyd Garrison were confused with names that sounded similar, like that of President William Henry Harrison. And people with common last names, like Cyrus McCormick, the inventor of the reaper, were confused with others bearing a homonymous name, in this case with John McCormack, the Irish crooner whose ballads were popular favorites. "Wrong answers deserve more careful study," urged Myers, anticipating future researchers' concern with error analysis, "and may give the teacher more and better information about his teaching than can be obtained from the traditional study of correct answers" (p. 282).

Myers's study resists easy classification. On one hand, his recognition of the human tendency to "make some kind of response to a situation" (1917a, p. 174) foreshadowed Bartlett's (1932) "effort after meaning" some 15 years later. On the other hand, he struck an Ebbinghausian chord when telling teachers that they need to "exercise the greatest care . . . to insure correct recitations" so that the learner keeps "each element of his knowledge eternally associated with his mate" (1917a, p. 175). But the recitation Myers had in mind was not a mindless drill. Rather, children would "perceive facts in proper relation during study" using "hitching posts," or slots in memory, that the learner "needs to keep constantly in view" (p. 175). Here Myers's appeal to mental hierarchies with major and minor points recalls the earlier Herbartian tradition and anticipates later notions of cognitive organizers popularized by Ausubel (1960) and others.

Not all psychologists shared Myers's fascination with wrong answers or Bell's fascination with the historic sense. B. R. Buckingham, then editor of the *Journal of Educational Research* and professor of education at the University of Illinois, reacted strongly to those who claimed that tests of factual knowledge missed the most important aspects of historical knowing. "The case against memory has been vastly overstated," he wrote. "Even when we think we are appealing to a supposedly higher process, we may really be dealing only with a somewhat higher form of memory" (1920, p. 164). To support his claim, Buckingham administered questions from the Van Wagenen Test of Historical Information and Judgment (Van Wagenen, 1919) to elementary and high school students and found a correlation of .4 between the factual items of this instrument and its "thought" items. Rather than concluding that factual knowledge and historical reasoning went hand-in-hand, Buckingham made a bolder claim: What people called historical reasoning was really nothing more than knowledge of facts! Buckingham argued his case by subjecting Van Wagenen's thought items to an early form of task analysis:

The first [question on the Thought Scale] reads as follows: "Before the steamboats were made people used to travel on the ocean in sail boats. Steamboats were not made until a long, long time after the European people came to make their homes in America. How do you think these early European settlers came to America?" The acceptable answer is "in sail boats" and it is a fact. Therefore the question is a fact question although introduced by the words, "How do you think?" (1920, p. 168)

Buckingham believed that higher forms of historical understanding may be inferred "with substantial accuracy *without giving any other test*" than the factual component of the Van Wagenen (emphasis in original, p. 170). Moreover, claimed Buckingham, because of the relationship between factual tests and higher mental abilities in history, we actually "encour[age] the training of these higher abilities" when we administer tests of facts (p. 171).

Buckingham's logic did not escape his contemporaries. The next issue of the *Journal of Educational Research* carried a short but stinging reponse by F. S. Camp, superintendent of schools in Stamford, Connecticut, who wryly identified himself as a "member of the [research] laity" but "not of the laity so far as teaching history is concerned" (1920, p. 517). Camp pointed to what his successors might have called problems of construct validity in Van Wagenen's scale. His own experience as history teacher told him that it was possible to construct questions that tapped students' ability to think deeply in history: For example, "Suppose Champlain in 1608 had chanced to befriend the Mohawks (Iroquois). What would probably have been the results of the New York campaign of the French in 1758?" (p. 518). The answers to such questions, argued Camp, drew on factual knowledge, but in formulating a response, the student "must examine, weigh and accept or reject facts; he must then organize them. And that requires staunch thinking" (p. 518).

Camp's concerns, while persuasive perhaps to other history teachers, seemed to have little effect on test developers. As research efforts turned increasingly to scale development and refinement (e.g., Harlan, 1920; Odell, 1922; Sackett, 1919), historical knowledge, viewed as a menu of possibilities by Bell and McCollum, moved perilously close to only one of their entrees—the ability to answer factual questions about historical personalities and events. These advances carried with them a certain antipathy to traditional forms of assessment in history classes, like essay writing (cf. Weaver & Traxler, 1931). According to one study (Gorman & Morgan, 1930), essays were "distasteful" not only to students but also to teachers, because the "scrutinizing, marking, and correcting of the student products is the teacher's greatest bugbear" (p. 80). What if it could be shown that written work, in addition to being laborious, produced little benefit? Worse, what if the essay produced "as much harm as it does good" (p. 90)? This was precisely the claim of Gorman and Morgan's study, conducted in three U.S. history classrooms.

These classes, all taught by the same teacher, were assigned different amounts of written homework. Class I was assigned "three units," Class II "one unit," and Class III none at all. Class III indeed did best on the factual outcome measure (181 points vs. 175 for Class I, $n = 31$ and $n = 29$, respectively), but the authors failed to account for the wide disparity in the entering achievement levels of the three classes. Moreover, the researchers' homework assignments often looked more like directions for drawing up lists than for composing thoughtful written responses (e.g., "List Lincoln's cabinet with the offices held by each"; "List the states which seceded in order, with the dates of secession" [p. 81]). When Gorman and Morgan concluded that "the popularity of written work with teachers may result from a confusion of busy work with valid learning procedures" (p. 90), one wonders where the confusion truly lay: with muddled teachers or with researchers hell-bent on demonstrating the ineffectiveness of written assignments?

Advances in psychometrics fueled the movement toward objective testing, as did the spirit of Taylorism that swept American schools between the world wars (Callahan, 1962). The fact-based image of historical knowledge was not an educational invention but fit cozily with prevailing views of knowledge in the discipline of history. As educational psychologists worked to produce reliable and objective history scales, university historians tried to extricate themselves from their humanistic roots to emerge as scientists who would, as the saying went, "cross an ocean to verify a comma" (Novick, 1988, p. 23). This doggedly factualist approach, as Peter Novick (1988) has argued, helped distinguish professional historians from their amateur colleagues, a distinction necessary if history was to become a full-fledged member of the academic community. It is no coincidence, then, that at nearly the same time L. W. Sackett was presenting his refinement of a world history scale in the pages of the *Journal of Educational Psychology,* a scale that would "nearly eliminate the subjective factor in grading history" (1919, p. 348), the *American Historical Review's* editorial policy was being formulated so as to exclude from its pages "matters of opinion" in favor of "matters of fact capable of determination one way or another" (cited in Novick, 1988, p. 200). This was not an age characterized by a breach between school and academy (cf. Wineburg, 1991b) but by a tightly woven nexus.

As behaviorism came to limit the topics studied by educational psychologists following World War I, the concerns of a J. Carleton Bell or an F. S. Camp were all but abandoned, except for some scattered and short-lived exceptions (e.g., Clark, 1934). Even in the odd investigation that took up history (Arnold, 1942), the focus rarely veered from how to apportion facts so that they could be easily committed to memory. The earlier concerns of Charles Judd with history's distinctive psychological features were overshadowed by learning theories that applied equally to all domains. Well into the 1970s, Robert Gagné could write confidently that learning was not unique to subject matter and that there was "no sound rational basis for such entities as 'mathematics learning,' 'science learning,' 'language learning' or 'history learning,' except as divisions of time devoted to these subjects during a school day or term" (1976, p. 30). Not until a decade later would this position meet serious challengers among mainstream educational psychologists.

Ironically, some of the features of history that Judd identified may have contributed to the subject's neglect by researchers. The lack of consensus about right answers in history complicated the measurement of outcomes, for if researchers deemed tests of facts trivial and term papers (often the product of historical understanding at the college level) unwieldy, they were faced with the prospect of creating wholly new measures, a forbidding task for many. Other factors came into play. The rise of social studies on American soil presented new challenges to researchers because of the conceptual and epistemological differences in the disciplines brought under its umbrella. Moreover, unlike in mathematics, where an active research community of subject matter and curriculum experts borrowed from and contributed to psychological theorizing, there was no parallel group among social studies educators. When research was conducted by this group, the street usually ran one-way: Psychological concepts were borrowed, but little was offered in return. These factors—and doubtless others—contributed to a period of relative neglect in research on history from the end of World War I to the advent of the cognitive revolution.

## DEVELOPMENTS IN GREAT BRITAIN: PIAGET, PEEL, AND BEYOND

While American researchers focused their attention on paired associates and serial learning, psychologists in Great Britain followed a different lead. From the late 1950s to well into the 1970s, the theories of Jean Piaget provided the framework for understanding the school curriculum. In a 28-year span beginning in 1955, no fewer than two dozen theses and dissertations on historical learning from a Piagetian perspective were conducted in Great Britain (Booth, 1983). Although recent British work on history has ventured into different areas, it is impossible to conceive of it apart from its Piagetian roots.

Among the most ambitious research programs was that associated with E. A. Peel, a past president of the British Psychological Society and a professor of educational psychology at the University of Birmingham. For Peel, Piaget's theory was the key to understanding children's school performance, a means of classifying and systematizing the types of thinking required by different school subjects. Noting that Piaget's work had direct bearing on math and science, Peel set out to extend the theory to children's textual reasoning, particularly their comprehension of written materials in English and history. The essence of understanding in the latter subject, according to Peel, was not to be found in lists of facts but in sweeping forms of thought, like the ability to grasp "cause and effect, a capacity to follow a sustained argument and a power to evaluate" (1972, p. 164).

Although Peel often addressed history in his theoretical writings (e.g., 1967a, 1967b), it was his student, Roy N. Hallam (1967), who gave historical research in the Piagetian tradition its biggest push. Hallam gave 100 British high school students, ranging in age from 11 to nearly 17, three textbook passages, one on Mary Tudor, another on the Norman conquest, and the third on the civil wars in Ireland. After each, students answered a series of questions. For example, after reading the passage about the Norman conquest, students were asked whether it was right for William to destroy northern England. Not relating the question to the information provided was scored as "pre-operational thinking," a well-organized answer that did not go beyond the text was classified as "concrete operational," and going beyond the text by stating hypotheses and checking them against the text as "formal operational." One student, for example, called William cruel, justifying his characterization by saying that William "carried out massacres for no set reasons . . . but he had a reason to gain revenge. Just ruthless in gaining revenge. He carried it to an extreme" (1967, p. 197). This answer was classified as preoperational because information in the text described a situation of war with provocations on both sides.

Of Hallam's 100 adolescent subjects, only two answered questions consistently at the level of formal operations. Such findings, and similar results from Peel's other colleagues (e.g., Case & Collinson, 1962; Lodwick, 1958, cited in Peel, 1959), led Hallam to conclude that systematic thinking appeared later in history than in math or science. Hallam speculated that this is because history confronts the child "with an 'environment' which envelops the inner motives of adults living probably in another century with mores markedly different from those of the twentieth century" (1967, p. 195). The abstract nature of

history, argued Hallam, "can perplex the most intelligent of adults" (1967, p. 195).

Several features of Hallam's study may have contributed to students' poor performance. First, students were asked questions that had little connection to what they were studying in class. How students might have performed had their instruction stressed the formal aspects of historical reasoning remained an open question. Second, students may have been confused by Hallam's questions (cf. Booth, 1987). Consider, for example, the questions that accompanied the passage on Mary Tudor: "Mary Tudor thought that God wanted her to take England back to the Catholic church. (a) What would God have thought of her methods? (b) Can you think of any reasons why Mary Tudor should use such methods to make people follow her religion?" (quoted in Booth, 1983, p. 104). What were students to answer in response? For his part, Hallam was anything but tentative about the implications of his findings: History, for children younger than 14, "should not be too abstract in form, nor should it contain too many variables" (Hallam, 1970, p. 168).

The desire to isolate basic psychological processes embedded in learning history created challenges for Piagetian workers. One problem was how to minimize the effects of students' prior knowledge, which was viewed as introducing unwanted variation to experimental results. Jurd (1973, 1978) tried to solve this problem by writing "historical" scenarios about three imaginary countries, Adza, Mulba, and Nocha. Students were presented with a chart showing parallel events in two of these countries and had to predict what would happen in the third. In Mulba, for example, "Richard became dictator" after "having led his people to victory against invaders," while in Adza, Henry became king after his father's death (1978, p. 322). Students were then given a list of five events in Nocha's history, from a build-up in military spending to a decline in the standard of living, and asked to order events in the correct sequence using comparative data from Adza and Mulba. Jurd interpreted students' performance in Piagetian terms. Success hinged on "identifying . . . one or more variables and the kinds of relations which might be thought to exist between them" (1978, p. 322). Students who identified only one variable and made no classification of it were judged "preoperational," while those who coordinated multiple variables while holding others constant were judged as exhibiting formal operational thought.

By creating imaginary countries or by restricting historical information to short textbook passages, Jurd, Hallam, and others attempted to control for students' prior knowledge. But there was something odd about decontextualizing historical events (or inventing fictional history) in a field that stressed the centrality of context (cf. Davidson & Lytle, 1982; Hexter, 1971). Filtered through Piagetian lenses, historical reasoning came to resemble the textbook version of hypotheticodeductive reasoning in the natural sciences, complete with formalized techniques for induction and deduction and strategies for the coordination and classification of variables. It was a depiction of historical reasoning, in the final result, that held more sway among psychologists than among historians (cf. Bailyn, 1963; Mink, 1987). Reduced to sets of logical relations and tests of hypotheses, the history in such studies bore only a partial resemblance to the hybrid of narration, exposition, and imaginative reconstruction familiar in the discipline.

Perhaps it is easy to find fault with efforts to strip away

historical context to get at historical cognition. But such criticism should not obscure the fact that Peel, Hallam, Jurd, and others were the first psychologists since J. Carleton Bell to reopen the question of the "historic sense." Their efforts reminded researchers that the best indication of historical reasoning was not children's selection of a right answer, the "mere repetition of learnt facts" (Hallam, 1967, p. 198), but the nature of children's reasoning, their ability to connect ideas, and the justifications they offered for their conclusions. Although these researchers may have gone farther in drawing conclusions than their data allowed, they are to be credited with invigorating a field and lauching projects whose influence is felt today.

One question remaining from Piagetian research was its impact on practice. According to Henry G. Macintosh, the past secretary of the British Southern Regional Examinations Board, Piagetian studies caused many history teachers "to undervalue the capacities of their own students and [helped] to ensure that their own teaching methods [made] it a self-fulfilling prophesy" (1987, p. 184). Similar observations came from history educator John Fines, who claimed that a whole generation of teachers had been "cowed by Piagetian analysis" (1980, p. iii). While it is difficult to assess the accuracy of these claims, it is clear that Piagetian research lent support to historian G. R. Elton's claim (1970) that serious work in history could not begin until students entered university. It is also clear that these findings spurred on other research efforts, particularly those intent on illuminating a brighter side to students' historical capabilities.

This was precisely the challenge before the members of the School's Council History 13–16 Project. Founded at the University of Leeds in 1973 with approximately 60 participating schools, it grew 10 years later to include 20% of all British high schools (H. Dawson, cited in Rosenzweig & Weinland, 1986). Its original mission was a reconsideration of the nature of history and its relevance in secondary schools (Shemilt, 1980), but in its totality, the project offered nothing less than a comprehensive model of the psychology of the subject matter.

The project drew heavily on Paul Hirst's (1973) theory of academic disciplines as forms of knowledge. Hirst believed that the disciplines were more than groupings of related topics but constituted fundamentally different ways of knowing. Accordingly, all knowledge forms exhibited four characteristics: (a) a body of concepts and key ideas—a common vocabulary; (b) distinctive ways of relating these concepts and ideas—a "syntax" for this vocabulary; (c) characteristic ways of establishing warrant for truth claims, such as the psychologist's appeal to the laboratory, the historian's to the documentary record; and (d) distinctive forms of inquiry, such as the chemist's use of X-ray spectroscopy, the historian's use of paleography or diplomatics.

Project founders argued that traditional history instruction constituted a form of information, not a form of knowledge. Students might master an agreed-upon narrative but they lacked any way of evaluating it, of deciding whether it, or any other narrative, was compelling or true. Denis Shemilt, the evaluator of the project and later its director, compared students from traditional history classes to drama students who could talk "sensibly about the separate scenes and characters of *King Lear,* but do not know what a play is" (1983, p. 15). Put differently, such students possessed copious amounts of historical information but had no idea where this information came from.

The School's Council 3-year curriculum began in the eighth grade. It took a nonchronological approach to history, beginning with a course called "What Is History?" that introduced students to the nature of historical evidence, the nature of reasoning from evidence, and problems of reconstruction from partial and mixed evidence. Other parts of the curriculum engaged students in historical research projects and thrust them into intensive inquiries on selected topics (e.g., Elizabethan England, Britain in the years 1815–1851, the American West, the rise of communist China, the Arab–Israeli conflict). Still other topics, like the history of medicine, were included in the curriculum because they exposed students to practices, beliefs, and ways of thinking radically different from their own.

An evaluation of the project was conducted in the late 1970s (Shemilt, 1980). It contained three components: (a) a comparison of 500 project and 500 control students on a series of historical concept tests; (b) a matched-pairs comparison of 75 project and control students on other concept tests (subjects were matched on sex, IQ, and SES); and (c) a matched-pairs study ($n = 78$ pairs) in which researchers engaged students in clinical interviews about the nature of historical inquiry. But before comparisons could be made between project students and control students, project staff first had to invent measures and coding schemes to capture the "form of knowledge" approach to history. For example, students' responses about the nature of history from the matched-pair interviews were coded using one of four levels spanning the range of historical conceptualization. Level I responses were characterized by a "just because" quality. Events happened because they happened, with no inner logic other than their arrangement in temporal sequence. Level II responses viewed history with "an austere, Calvinistic logic" (Shemilt, 1983, p. 7), equating historical reconstruction with slotting pieces of a puzzle into a preexisting form. At Level III, adolescents had a dawning awareness of a disjuncture between historical narratives and "the past," recognizing that the former involved selectivity and judgment and could never reflect the latter in all its complexity. At Level IV, students transcended the search for overarching historical laws and came to understand historical explanation as context bound and context sensitive.

The two highest levels of this typology were attained by 68% of project students versus 29% of the controls. The lowest level was occupied by 15% of control students versus 1% of project students. In each of the three evaluation components, project students outperformed their counterparts from traditional classrooms. For example, 50% of control students were unable to differentiate between historical and scientific knowledge, versus only 10% of project students. And when students were asked to compare history to mathematics, 83% of control students saw math as more difficult than history, versus 25% of project students. As one control student put it, "In history you just look it up, math you work it out"; another control student added, "From one formula in Maths you get three or four others following, but History has no pattern" (Shemilt, 1980, p. 20).

The overall picture emerging from the evaluation supported the idea that adolescents could be taught to understand history as a sophisticated form of knowledge different from other forms in the school curriculum. Yet Shemilt's evaluation is not the story of unqualified success, for, as he noted, the difference between control students and project students could be compared "to the difference between stony, derelict ground barely able to support a few straggling weeds and a cultivated but undisciplined garden in which a few splendid blossoms struggle to show through" (Shemilt, 1980, p. 14).

Even so, the portraits of adolescent reasoning offered by project students contrasted sharply with the images of adolescent reasoning offered by the Piagetians. This contrast was not lost on John Fines, who in his introduction to the evaluation report noted that project students "seem to be performing much more hopefully that the Piagetians first thought" (Fines, 1980, p. ii). Yet, while Shemilt was careful to distinguish the School's Council effort from the Piagetians, the School's Council Project—from the nature of its measures, to its levels of attainment, to even the graphic layout of its results—is impossible to conceptualize apart from that research tradition. One feels Piaget's presence throughout, acting sometimes as touchstone, at other times as provocateur, at yet other times as nodding observer, always present if not always acknowledged.

To be sure, the debt to Piaget is recognized by Shemilt in several places. Shemilt even signaled a certain optimism about applicability of Piagetian constructs provided they were first "specifically tailored" to the exigencies of history (1980, pp. 50–52). Left unacknowledged, however, was a certain similarity in research approach between the evaluation study and what has been called the Piaget–Peel–Hallam tradition (cf. Downey & Levstik, 1991), a shared tendency by both to thrust children into the role of mini-philosopher, with questions more germane to a discussion in metaphysics than one in history (e.g., "Does the fact that things are inevitable mean that we have no control over them?" "If an event can be altered, if it can be changed, how can it be inevitable?" [Shemilt, 1980, p. 14]). No doubt such questions have a bearing on historical understanding. But there is danger in equating students' responses to abstract queries with how they might respond when dealing with concrete historical materials. As the psycholinguists have taught us, it is one thing to use the pluperfect flawlessly and quite another to explain how we do it.

In its totality, the evaluation study of the History 13–16 Project yielded the most in-depth look at adolescent reasoning in history to date. Given the complexity of this portrait, one might expect similar attention to be devoted to the other half of the equation—the knowledge, understanding, and practices of the teachers who participated in the project. Here the evaluation study offered fewer insights. Like the traditional field experiment, this study provides some sense of where students begin and provides evidence that they differ at the end. But beyond an appeal to written curricular materials, it is at a loss to explain change. What did teachers *do* in classes filled with Level I students? How did sophisticated notions of historical understanding get translated into classroom activities, explanations by teachers, or homework assignments for students? What were the key way stations, the cognitive bridges, along the path to higher understanding?

The History 13–16 Project provided few answers to these questions. Moreover, the question of what teachers needed to know in order to enact this curriculum was not addressed. In fact, there are indications that some project teachers may have had more in common with students functioning at Levels I and II than with those at Level IV. Responding to questionnaire

items, nearly half of project teachers believed that primary sources were "necessarily more reliable than secondary sources," and 16% agreed with the statement that "people in the past thought and behaved in exactly the same way as people today, and that only the setting was different" (Shemilt, 1980, p. 76). Shemilt's disclaimer that "teachers need to familiarize themselves with Project philosophy and objectives" (1980, p. 76) surely misses the point. The key question is this: How do we alter adults' deeply held beliefs about history, if at all?

## THE COGNITIVE REVOLUTION: DEVELOPMENTS AND POSSIBILITIES

Every revolution inspires new hopes, and the "cognitive revolution" (Gardner, 1985) was no exception. New images of school learning promised to answer questions that had riddled researchers not only since the beginning of scientific psychology but since humankind began asking itself what it meant to know and learn. During the 1970s and 1980s, cognitive researchers illuminated students' thinking in an array of school subjects, from traditional subjects like arithmetic, biology, physics, and geometry to newer additions to the curriculum such as computer science and economics. But amid this efflorescence of research, the subject matter of history was ignored. Indeed, one of the first attempts to draw together the new work on school learning, Ellen Gagné's (1985) *The Cognitive Psychology of School Learning*, contained over 400 references, but not a single one applied to history.

The past several years have witnessed a dramatic change. Cognitive researchers have made up for lost time by launching investigations that addressed a multiplicity of historical topics, from children's historical misconceptions to the processing of history textbooks, from teachers' subject matter knowledge to the assessment of expertise in history teaching. The following discussion, organized into sections on learning, teaching, and assessment, surveys these and other developments.

### Learning

One of the core insights of the cognitive approach to learning is that the learner brings to instruction a mixture of beliefs and conceptions, some true and others stubbornly false, through which new information is filtered. Although prior research mapped out some aspects of children's historical beliefs, particularly in the area of time and chronology (Jahoda, 1963; Smith & Tomlinson, 1977; cf. Downey & Levstik, 1991), recent studies have explored children's thinking on a range of topics and ideas.

Sinatra, Beck, and McKeown (1992) provided a sketch of the background knowledge the typical fifth grader brings to history instruction. In interviews with 35 fifth graders prior to instruction in American history and 37 sixth graders following instruction, students were asked questions such as "Why do we celebrate the Fourth of July?" "How did our country become a country?" and "Once there was a saying 'no taxation without representation.' What do you think that means?" Sparse understanding characterized students' responses, even after a year of instruction in American history. Seventy-four percent of fifth graders and 57% of sixth graders did not mention the war between Great Britain and the colonies in their responses, and

60% of all students could provide no information about the motivation of the Revolutionary War. But students were hardly blank slates. Questions about the Fourth of July often elicited responses about memorials of "deaths of people who were in wars," indicative of an emerging "holiday schema." Similarly, questions about the Declaration of Independence elicited responses ranging from the freeing of slaves to the Mayflower Compact. Like cognitive explorations in other subjects, and Myers's (1917a, 1917b) earlier work, the study of Sinatra et al. went beyond a right/wrong answer approach to explore systematic patterns in students' responses.

Recent work by VanSledright and Brophy (1992) also examined elementary school children's beliefs about history. Using a qualitative methodology, they interviewed 10 fourth graders about key topics in American history. Although they also found knowledge of these topics to be sparse, they found that some children were willing to construct narratives about events for which they possessed little knowledge. One gifted storyteller, 10-year-old Helen, spun tales about Pilgrims who sailed on a boat called the Mayflower (adding, "that's how we got 'April showers bring May flowers' " [p. 846]) and settled at Plymouth Rock, located somewhere in Michigan's "upper peninsula." To construct these stories, some children conflated information about different historical events learned in school, and then combined this mixture with snippets of information gleaned from cartoon shows or cultural celebrations such as Thanksgiving. VanSledright and Brophy (1992) concluded that children were not only able to construct imaginative stories about the past but were able to see patterns in these stories, overarching themes of tragedy and suspense. In this sense, young children's narrative reconstructions may be viewed as partially formed precursors of the "emplotments" used by academic historians to narrate their stories of the past (White, 1973).

The fanciful elaborations explored in these studies can be classified under Perkins and Simmons's (1988) "content frame," or misunderstandings about specific facts and events in American history. Ashby and Lee (1987) addressed Perkins and Simmons's "epistemic frame," more general and sweeping beliefs children use to interpret the past. Rather than engaging children in interviews, the strategy used in their prior work (cf. Dickinson & Lee, 1978, 1984), they grouped adolescents into trios and videotaped their interactions as they worked through documents about Anglo-Saxon oath-helping and the ordeal. Based on hundreds of hours of videotape, Ashby and Lee created a set of categories to characterize children's "historical empathy," the "intellectual achievement" of "entertain[ing] a set of beliefs and values . . . not necessarily their own" (1987, p. 63). Students least able to do this saw history as a "*Divi* past" (from the British slang for "thick, dumb, or mentally defective"), regarding the subject with "irritated incomprehension and contempt" (p. 68). Students occupying the middle levels of the typology began to view history as an explanatory system but made little attempt to understand the past on its own terms. Only at the highest levels did children start to recognize differences between past and present mind-sets, or historical changes in *Zeitgeist* and *mentalité*. Although Ashby and Lee viewed their typology as a way of characterizing children's thinking about the past, it may also capture aspects of adults' thinking as well. Indeed, some evidence suggests (Wineburg & Fournier, 1992) that the notion of the "timeless past" (Lowenthal, 1989), the

idea that concepts from the present can be easily transported back in time, is embraced by some university students—history majors and nonmajors alike.

***Reading History Textbooks.*** Recent efforts have also focused on students' understanding of history textbooks. The earliest work in this area applied principles of text design and coherence (e.g., Meyer, 1975; van Dijk & Kintsch, 1983) to the writing of textbooks. Armbruster and Anderson (1984) found that typical history books failed to offer readers "considerate" treatments, or ones in which explanations allowed the reader to determine (a) the goal of an action or event, (b) the plan for attaining that goal, (c) the action that was taken in response, and (d) the outcome. If a text failed to answer these questions, according to Armbruster and Anderson, it failed "as a historical explanation" (1984, p. 249). Beck, McKeown, and Gromoll (1989) reached similar conclusions in a more extensive study. They found that fifth-grade textbooks presumed background knowledge most children lacked. Like Armbruster and Anderson, Beck et al. proposed rewriting history textbooks, using, in their words, "causal/explanatory" linkages, or linkages that connect a cause to an event and an event to a consequence.

Beck and her colleagues built on their work in text analysis to design passages that conformed to principles of cognitive text design. Beck, McKeown, Sinatra, and Loxterman (1991) conducted an experiment in which original text passages were compared with their rewritten counterparts. For example, a textbook explanation about the French and Indian War that began, "In 1763 Britain and the colonies ended a 7 year war with the French and Indians," was rewritten to include material that established context and provided linkages between sentences. The new passage began, "About 250 years ago, Britain and France both claimed to own some piece of land, here, in North America" (1991, p. 257).

Eighty-five fourth- and fifth-grade students were assigned to original and revised text conditions and compared in their ability to recall core idea units present in both forms of the text. There was a statistically significant difference in recall (17 of 124 units in the original text condition vs. 24 of 124 in the revised condition), providing support for the notion that textbooks can be revised so that students retain more information in them. An extension of this work (McKeown, Beck, Sinatra & Loxterman, 1992) further showed that 48 fifth graders who were "provided with background knowledge" (p. 84) in an experimenter-led presentation were able to process revised texts better than originals. This finding supported the notion that background knowledge helps most when readers are given well-structured texts.

The work on text design and analysis demonstrates that cognitive principles can be used to make history textbooks more "considerate." A different approach to improving students' understanding might teach students to deal with texts that are, by nature, *inconsiderate*. In a comparison of history textbooks with academic and popular historical writing, Crismore (1984) found that "metadiscourse," or indications of judgment, emphasis, and uncertainty, were used frequently in historical writing but typically edited out of textbooks. For example, historians rely on "hedges" to indicate the indeterminacy of history, using such devices as modals (may, might), certain verbs (suggest, appear, seem) and qualifiers (possibly, perhaps) to convey the uncertainty of historical knowledge. But Crismore found that most textbooks eliminated hedges, providing no indication that interpretation had anything to do with the words on the page. Such writing, she suggested, may be more "considerate," but it also may contribute to the finding that students typically equate knowing history with "knowing the facts" (Berkhofer, 1988; Degler, 1980; Lorence, 1983) and approach their textbook with that goal in mind (McNeil, 1989). As Crismore observed:

What happens to critical reading (learning to evaluate and make judgments about truth conditions) when hedges . . . are absent? When bias is not overt (as it is *not* in most textbooks) are young readers being deceived? . . . What happens to critical reading when attitudinal metadiscourse is delayed until adulthood and readers are not encouraged to become active participants in the reading process? . . . Young readers need to see author biases and evaluate them at an early age; textbooks and teachers need to teach them how to do this. (p. 296)

*Reading Sources.* These different approaches to reading history textbooks point to competing notions about the nature of historical understanding. Is understanding history a case of getting the story straight—knowing that the French and Indian War preceded the Sugar Act, which preceded the Stamp Act, and so on—or is it something more diffuse, perhaps an understanding that "the story," to paraphrase the title of a recent book, must always be crooked (cf. Kellner, 1989)? Little attention has been paid to such questions despite their centrality to any research effort.

Wineburg (1991a, 1991b) explored how historians think about the past as they read a series of primary and secondary sources. Using the think-aloud procedure and protocol analysis (cf. Ericsson & Simon, 1984), he explored how eight historians constructed an understanding of historical events from a group of fragmented and contradictory documents about the Battle of Lexington, the opening of hostilities in the American Revolution. He compared historians' responses to those of eight high school seniors with above-average SAT scores, high grades, and high scores on tests of factual knowledge. Data analyses focused on the ongoing processes of cognition, the intermediate steps in understanding that might provide clues about how historical interpretations develop.

Historians employed three main heuristics to make sense of the documents they evaluated: *corroboration,* in which the details of one document were compared with those of another before being taken as trustworthy or probable; *contextualization,* in which events were situated in concrete temporal and spatial contexts; and *sourcing,* in which readers first looked to a document's source, constructing hypotheses about the author's probity and rhetorical intent, before proceeding to the body of the document.

Historians used this last heuristic in nearly every case, students in less than a third. Although this finding might be cast as a difference in strategy use, it may also indicate different epistemological stances each group brought to the text. In reading texts from top to bottom, students seemed to view texts as vehicles for conveying information in which the attribution was simply another piece of information to be added to the other facts that had been gathered. But for historians, who used the

attribution to erect elaborate scenarios about authors and the circumstances of document generation, the attribution was the fact from which all else emanated. Viewed in this light, the sourcing heuristic was less a problem-solving strategy than it was the manifestation of a belief system in which texts are defined by their authors (Wineburg, 1992).

Like other work in the expert/novice tradition, this work begs the question of how expertise develops or even, more modestly, how to alter students' historical beliefs to bring them closer to mature disciplinary conceptions. One of the few attempts to do this (Greene, 1993) focused on university students' historical understanding. Greene randomly assigned 15 juniors and seniors in the same college seminar on European recovery to a "report" or a "problem-based" writing condition. Students who wrote problem-based essays drew more on prior knowledge, looked more often to themselves as sources of authority, and structured their essays with greater complexity than students in the report condition. Although all students sat in the same class listening to the instructor tell them to go beyond sources to form historical arguments, students in the report condition seemed to access a prior "school schema" in which summarizing sources took precedence over their critical examination. On the other hand, the writing prompt in the problem condition seemed to endow students with the authority to question and challenge sources. Greene's work shows the promise of using writing as a tool both to shape—and reshape—students' conceptions of historical knowledge.

## Teaching

At the core of the "process–product" approach to teaching was an assumption about the fundamental similarity among the subjects taught in school. Variations in content were cast as "context variables" and emerged, if at all, in discussions of error variance or the limitations of research findings. Throughout the 1960s and 1970s, research on teaching witnessed its greatest successes in the teaching of discrete skills, in which a teacher checks for understanding on a concrete outcome and then guides students in doing similar problems or exercises. But as Rosenshine (1986) noted in his analysis of a history lesson on *Federalist #10*, taught by then secretary of education William Bennett, research on skill teaching had relatively little to say about the teaching of content: "We do not even have a good name for it. . . . How does one teach this content and these ideas? The skill model does not help us much" (pp. 303–304).

Shulman (1986a) called the lack of research on teaching content a "missing paradigm" and went on to develop a research program to address it. The Knowledge Growth in Teaching Project at Stanford University was a longitudinal study that tracked changes in teachers' content knowledge from the beginning of their teacher education programs into the first and second years of full-time teaching. An examination of the knowledge growth of four history/social studies teachers was one of the first research reports to emerge from this project.

Wilson and Wineburg (1988) charted the relationship between these four teachers' subject matter knowledge and their instructional decision making. Using extensive interviews and sustained classroom observation, they found that the materials supposed to regulate instruction—textbooks, teachers' guides, films, and the like—were filtered through teachers' preexisting beliefs about subject matter. For example, one teacher, whose background was in political science, equated historical knowledge with knowledge of facts, such as knowing "when the conference in Vienna was held or what were the terms of this agreement" (1988, p. 527). For this teacher, interpretation was the province of the political scientist, not the historian. Another teacher, with a background in physical anthropology, was an environmental determinist; others, with different disciplinary training, believed that historical events had multiple causes and multiple layers of meaning.

Work on the relationship between subject matter knowledge and teaching was extended in a series of Wisdom of Practice studies in which 11 accomplished teachers were observed teaching a unit on the American Revolution. Teachers also engaged in a series of interviews, ranging from an "intellectual autobiography," in which they reconstructed the high points of their high school and college education, to modified think-alouds, in which teachers verbalized their thoughts as they read Washington's farewell address, *Federalist #84* (Hamilton's argument against a bill of rights), and other primary documents.

Wineburg and Wilson (1988, 1991) compared two of these teachers on the basis of their *pedagogical content knowledge* (Shulman, 1986b), or the knowledge they used to transform their content knowledge into instructional representations—examples, metaphors, analogies, stories, demonstrations, and activities—that bridged the gap between their own understanding of subject matter and the emerging understandings of their students. These instructional representations differed dramatically for each teacher. One teacher planned a weeklong debate on the legitimacy of British taxation in the American colonies, saying little as her students thrashed out pros and cons, while another teacher covered similar ground in a more traditional, teacher-directed lecture. Yet despite dramatic differences in the outward appearance of this instruction, there was a fundamental similarity in the history students sense were being taught. In both classrooms, students encountered a vision of the subject matter that challenged them to consider alternatives, forced them to grapple with uncertainty, and invited them to consider how interpretative frameworks colored their perception of the past.

Gaea Leinhardt, one of the first researchers to apply cognitive principles to research on teaching (Leinhardt & Greeno, 1986; Leinhardt, 1986), has extended her work to the teaching of history. Leinhardt (1993) provided a case study of an experienced history teacher based on over 76 sessions in an advanced placement U.S. history class. Leinhardt focused her analysis on the nature of the teacher's historical explanations, distinguishing between two main types of explanations. In "blocked explanations," the teacher provided a self-contained, relatively modular explanation. In "ikat explanations," the teacher gave an abbreviated account or passing reference to something that was later extended and elaborated. At the beginning of the school year, the teacher provided nearly all explanations, as students struggled with notions of multiple causation in the ratification of the Constitution or the conflicting interpretations of a Beard or a Hofstadter. As the year progressed, the teacher progressively drew students into the process of formulating explanations. One measure of her success was the ratio of student to teacher talk, which went from about 40% at the beginning of the year to over 150% by the 13th week.

This incease had an important qualitative dimension as well. Students were not simply saying more in response to the teacher's explanations, but *what* they were saying was characterized by an ever-increasing complexity. By January, Paul, one of the students analyzed by Leinhardt, linked the fall of a cotton-based economy to British trade policy and colonial ventures in Asia as well as to the failure of southern leaders to read public opinion in Great Britain. Students were learning not only a body of factual material but also how to use this material to craft their own interconnected historical explanations.

The work on teacher knowledge in history represents a significant departure from the research on teaching that characterized the 1970s and early 1980s. Researchers abandoned low-inference observation schedules and large samples for intensive interviews and focused observations of a small number of *unrepresentative* teachers. Rather than brief time samples taken every 6 months, observations in these classes tried to preserve the flow of instruction, usually over a unit, but in Leinhardt's case, extending nearly half a year. This work also ventured into new methodological territory, borrowing and modifying methods more commonly found in the anthropologist's or sociolinguist's toolbox than in the psychologist's laboratory. Rather than attempting to formulate a theory of instruction that would hold for all subjects, these investigations aimed at generating theories of the middle range (Merton, 1968), narrower and more provisional theories that applied to the teaching of a particular subject, theories that may or may not have implications for teaching physics or physical education. The focus of this work was not teacher behavior isolated from teacher thought, but the deep and fundamental nexus between what teachers know and what they do.

This research offers compelling portraits of exemplary teaching. But the strength of this work—its finely etched accounts of knowledge use in action—may also be its weakness, for, like museum pieces that arrest the attention and focus it on the here and now, these images tell us more about what is than how it came to be. Was the subject matter knowledge of these teachers a consequence of their undergraduate training or a covariate of it? How did these teachers learn to socialize students into history as a way of knowing? What did their failures look like, and how did they learn from them? Since no teacher is going to become a master by taking a 2-day workshop on historical explanations or pedagogical content knowledge, how do we alter teachers' deep-seated epistemic beliefs about the nature of history? This last question has special meaning, for at the core of this new work on teaching is the assumption that the lessons learned from experts can be used to teach novices. But how, exactly, do we turn portraits of excellence into programs that develop it? These are just some of the unanswered questions that arise from this work on teachers' subject matter knowledge in history.

## Assessment

History has been a fertile site for the development of new forms of student and teacher assessment. What characterizes these approaches is a shift from separating historical knowledge into discrete items on a multiple-choice test to the assessment of complex forms of historical reasoning that requires the orchestration of bodies of knowledge and skill.

Eva Baker and her colleagues at UCLA's Center for the Study of Evaluation (Baker, Freeman, & Clayton, 1991) have focused their efforts on large-scale student assessments. These researchers have sought to develop assessments that would capture "a deeper understanding of history," one that would "map directly on significant features of learning" (1991, p. 135). To do this, they have developed essay tasks asking students to read, interpret, synthesize, and critique primary source documents about events like the Lincoln–Douglas debates and the Great Depression. Rather than establishing a priori scoring criteria, researchers developed criteria on the basis of think-aloud protocols of experts who engaged in the task, a strategy more common to work in artificial intelligence than to traditional forms of test development.

Several aspects of this effort show the promise of combining cognitive theory with advances in measurement (cf. Snow & Lohman, 1989). Instead of pursuing an assessment strategy that maximizes the spread of scores in the distribution, this program set out to modify the assessment context to help all students perform their best. Based on research about the beneficial role of background knowledge in writing performance (e.g., McCutchen, 1986), Baker et al. constructed a prewriting activity intended to instantiate students' prior knowledge before they engaged in the assessment. For example, students who wrote an essay about the Lincoln–Douglas debates first imagined themselves living during the 1850s and "making a special trip to hear Abraham Lincoln and Stephen Douglas debating during their campaigns for the Senate seat representing Illinois" (p. 146). Subsequent prewriting prompts asked students to spend several minutes listing laws, court decisions, and governmental principles relevant to the debate. Only at this point were students asked to write the essay.

In building this assessment, Baker et al. selected texts that "allow for multiple interpretations and inferences . . . which transcend immediate events and allow students to find relationships to other historical and contemporary events" (p. 139). This criterion reached beyond traditional psychometric criteria to make a normative statement about what was most important about knowing history. A similar normative stance was taken by Lee Shulman's Teacher Assessment Project (Shulman, 1988). For nearly a half century, the National Teacher Examination dominated teacher testing with an examination that separated pedagogy from subject matter, despite the fusion of these spheres in the work of teaching. In contrast, the Teacher Assessment Project set out to develop assessments that would reflect the interactive and interconnected nature of knowledge and skill that characterizes many current approaches to cognition. In history, nine performance exercises were developed and pilot tested.

Wilson and Wineburg (1993) analyzed two teachers' responses on three of the exercises: (a) Evaluation of Student Papers, (b) Use of Documentary Materials, and (c) Textbook Analysis. The three exercises took 6 hours to complete and included interactive interview components and written essays. (The full battery of nine exercises extended over a 3-day period in an assessment center context.) Each of these exercises was intended to fuse content and pedagogy. For example, in the Evaluation of Student Papers exercise, teachers not only evaluated papers for students' historical understanding but provided written feedback to students that would help them write better

essays in the future. Likewise, in the Use of Documentary Materials exercise, teachers first had to grapple with a set of dense primary sources before they could formulate a plan for using documents to teach adolescents about the American Revolution. In the Textbook Analysis, teachers first had to evaluate the content of a textbook before they could gauge the text's impact on student understanding.

Several themes unite the Stanford and UCLA research efforts. Both initiatives developed assessments that defied the single-right-answer approach, and both made parallel claims about the nature of deep understanding in learning and teaching history. Perhaps most important, while both projects were informed by psychometric theory, they both began with the nature of understanding in the domain and asked measurement theory to accommodate issues of subject matter, not vice versa (cf. Haertel, 1991).

## CONCLUSION

Current research on history is characterized by diverse investigations that reflect the vigor of cognitive approaches to teaching, learning, and assessment. In several areas, history has not been the final beneficiary of insights gleaned from other subject matters, but the site where these insights first germinated and took root.

There are several reasons to think that the new interest in history is more than a passing fancy. There is a growing recognition by educators and policymakers (e.g., Bradley Commission on History in the Schools, 1988; California State Department of Education, 1988; Gifford, 1988) that questions of historical reasoning carry implications that go well beyond the curricular borders of history. History offers a storehouse of ill-structured, indeterminate, and partial (in both senses of the word) problems, not unlike those that confront us daily in the social world. Examining these problems requires an interpretive acumen that extends beyond the "locate information in the text" skills that dominate many school tasks. Understanding how students succeed in dealing with such complexity, and how teachers aid them in doing so, would not only provide a knowledge base for improving school history but also would inform theories of reading comprehension, which are surprisingly mute about the processes used to form interpretations of complex written texts (cf. Athey & Singer, 1987; Kintsch, 1986).

Three additional developments promise to keep the spotlight on history. First, recent attention to narrative, which sees the formation of narrative as a "cognitive achievement" (cf. Olson, 1994), stands to gain much by extending its scope to the formation of historical narratives (cf. Freeman & Levstik, 1988; Levstik & Pappas, 1987). This topic is already being taken up with increasing self-awareness by professional historians (e.g., Holt, 1990; Cronon, 1992), and psychologists would have much to contribute to this effort. Second, new technologies such as hypermedia and computer data bases have created possibilities in history that were unimaginable a few years ago. A variety of efforts (e.g., Nichol & Dean, 1986; Salomon, 1991; Spoehr & Spoehr, 1994) are under way that explore technology's role in enhancing historical understanding. Finally, history has already been the site of new developments in student and teacher assessment and promises to continue to be a rich development site in the future (cf. Booth, 1980).

Psychologists interested in history have traditionally looked to the extensive body of historiographic writings for clues to the nature of historical thinking. This storehouse of essays and monographs, composed largely by historians (e.g., Becker, 1966; Berkhofer, 1988; Bloch, 1954; Cronon, 1992; Davidson & Lytle, 1982; Degler, 1980; Fischer, 1970; Gottschalk, 1958; Hexter, 1971; Megill, 1989; Novick, 1988) and philosophers of history (e.g., Dibble, 1963; Dray, 1966; Fain, 1970; Mandelbaum, 1938; Mink, 1987; Rüsen, 1993; Skinner, 1985; Stanford, 1986), looks at historical works not for what they disclose about the War of 1812, daily life in the Middle Ages, or the demise of French Indochina but for what they say about historical knowing more generally. The strategy of looking carefully at written histories and inferring from them the processes used in their composition offers many insights to the interested psychologist. However, the problem with using this approach to build a theory of teaching and learning is that final products can be explained by appealing to wholly different intermediate processes (cf. Ericsson & Simon, 1984; Larkin, 1980). Historiography teaches us how to recognize skilled cognition but gives us scant advice for how to achieve it.

There is a second way to understand what it means to think historically. Less developed than the historiographic tradition, this approach examines the steps and missteps that lead to the formation of historical interpretations and conclusions. This work is carried out by psychologists (and increasingly historians, e.g., Frisch, 1989; Miller & Stearns, 1995; Seixas, 1993) who conduct empirical studies into how students, teachers, and historians come to understand history. It asks questions about what people know and how they come to know it. In doing so, this approach wrests questions of epistemology from the clouds and turns them into objects of psychological and historical inquiry (cf. Strike & Posner, 1976).

The pursuit of such research would return us to the beginning of the century when the American Psychological Association and the American Philosophical Society held joint meetings because the psychologist and the philosopher were often one and the same. As a research strategy, this approach would claim intellectual ancestry not from E. L. Thorndike, who displayed little patience with questions philosophical (cf. Joncich, 1968), but from Wilhelm Wundt. Contrary to the popular image of Wundt as a hard-nosed experimentalist singularly determined to establish psychology as an empirical science (e.g., Boring, 1929), the lesser known Wundt was a man whose empirical investigations informed and were informed by his writings on epistemology, logic, and ethics, a man who argued that psychology and philosophy were so interdependent that, separated from one another, both would atrophy (Ash, 1980; Toulmin & Leary, 1985).

What is being advocated here is a research strategy that can best be termed applied epistemology. Taking it seriously would mean a dramatic reorientation in our discipline, not only in how we design our research but in the very way we socialize our young. For as Calfee has noted, "Graduate training for educational psychology seldom entails a deep engagement in mastery of a curriculum domain, and so psychological research on curriculum issues tends to be poorly conceptualized" (1992, p. 166).

There are limitations to this approach as well. We can no longer claim to being the jack-of-all-trades learning specialist whose expertise soars above the particularities of subject matter. Further, before we can function well in this new role, we will have to attend to issues of epistemology and subject matter with the same acuity we have paid to the canons of validity and reliability. But what we forfeit in versatility we gain in potential. Instead of looking to others for our definitions of historical, mathematical, or scientific understanding, we can contribute to these definitions and ultimately transform them.

## References

Aldrich, R. E. (1984). New history: An historical perspective. In A. K. Dickinson, P. J. Lee, & P. J. Rogers (Eds.), *Learning history* (pp. 210–224). London: Heinemann.

American Historical Association, Committee of Five (1911). *The study of history in secondary schools.* New York: Macmillan.

American Historical Association, Committee of Seven (1899). *The study of history in schools.* New York: Macmillan.

Armbruster, B. B., & Anderson, T. H. (1984). Structures of explanations in history textbooks or so what if Governor Stanford missed the spike and hit the rail? *Journal of Curriculum Studies, 16,* 247–274.

Arnold, H. F. (1942). The comparative effectiveness of certain study techniques in the field of history. *Journal of Educational Psychology, 33,* 449–457.

Ash, M. G. (1980). Wilhelm Wundt and Oswald Kulpe on the institutional status of psychology: An academic controversy in historical context. In W. G. Bringmann & R. D. Tweney (Eds.), *Wundt studies* (pp. 396–421). Toronto: Hogrefe.

Ashby, R., & Lee, P. (1987). Children's concepts of empathy and understanding in history. In C. Portal (Ed.), *The history curriculum for teachers* (pp. 62–88). London: Falmer Press.

Athey, I., & Singer, H. (1987). Developing the nation's reading potential for a technological era. *Harvard Educational Review, 57,* 84–93.

Ausubel, D. P. (1960). The use of advance organizers in the learning and retention of meaningful verbal material. *Journal of Educational Psychology, 51,* 267–272.

Bailyn, B. (1963). The problems of the working historian: A comment. In S. Hook (Ed.), *Philosophy and history* (pp. 93–101). New York: New York University Press.

Baker, E. L., Freeman, M., & Clayton, S. (1991). Cognitive assessment of history for large-scale testing. In M. C. Wittrock & E. L. Baker (Eds.), *Testing and cognition* (pp. 131–153). Englewood Cliffs, NJ: Prentice Hall.

Bartlett, F. C. (1932). *Remembering: A study in experimental and social psychology.* New York: Cambridge University Press.

Beck, I. L., McKeown, M. G., & Gromoll, E. W. (1989). Learning from social studies texts. *Cognition and Instruction, 6,* 99–158.

Beck, I. L., McKeown, M. G., Sinatra, G. M., & Loxterman, J. A. (1991). Revising social studies text from a text-processing perspective: Evidence of improved comprehensibility. *Reading Research Quarterly, 26,* 251–276.

Becker, C. (1935/1966). *Everyman his own historian.* Chicago: Quadrangle.

Bell, J. C. (1917). The historic sense. *Journal of Educational Psychology, 8,* 317–318.

Bell, J. C., & McCollum, D. F. (1917). A study of the attainments of pupils in United States history. *Journal of Educational Psychology, 8,* 257–274.

Berkhofer, R. (1988). Demystifying historical authority: Critical textual analysis in the classroom. *Perspectives: Newsletter of the American Historical Association, 26,* 13–16.

Berti, A. E., & Bombi, A. S. (1988). *The child's construction of economics.* Cambridge, England: Cambridge University Press.

Bloch, M. (1954). *The historian's craft.* Manchester, England: Manchester University Press.

Booth, M. B. (1980). A modern world history course and the thinking of adolescent pupils. *Educational Review, 32,* 245–257.

Booth, M. B. (1983). Skills, concepts, and attitudes: The development of adolescent children's historical thinking. *History and Theory, 22,* 101–117.

Booth, M. B. (1987). Ages and concepts: A critique of the Piagetian approach to history teaching. In C. Portal (Ed.), *The history curriculum for teachers* (pp. 22–38). London: Falmer Press.

Boring, E. G. (1929). *A history of experimental psychology.* New York: D. Appleton-Century.

Bradley Commission on History in the Schools (1988). *Building a history curriculum.* New York: Educational Excellence Network.

Buckingham, B. R. (1920). A proposed index in efficiency in teaching United States history. *Journal of Educational Research, 1,* 161–171.

Calfee, R. (1992). Refining educational psychology: The case of the missing links. *Educational Psychologist, 27,* 163–176.

California State Department of Education (1988). *History-social science framework for public schools, K–12.* Sacramento, CA.

Callahan, R. (1962). *Education and the cult of efficiency.* Chicago: University of Chicago Press.

Camp, F. S. (1920). Wanted: A history scale maker. *Journal of Educational Research, 2,* 517–518.

Case, D., & Collinson, J. M. (1962). The development of formal thinking in verbal comprehension. *British Journal of Educational Psychology, 32,* 103–111.

Chi, M. T. H., Feltovich, P. J., & Glaser, R. (1981). Categorization and representation of physics problems by experts and novices. *Cognitive Science, 5,* 121–152.

Clark, M. (1934). The construction of exercises in the use of historical evidence. In T. L. Kelly & A. C. Krey (Eds.), *Tests and measurements in the social sciences* (pp. 302–339). New York: Charles Scribner's Sons.

Collie, F. (1911). The problem method in the history courses of the elementary school. *Journal of Experimental Pedagogy and Training College Record, 1,* 236–239.

Crismore, A. (1984). The rhetoric of textbooks: Metadiscourse. *Journal of Curriculum Studies, 16,* 279–296.

Cronon, W. (1992). A place for stories: Nature, history, and narrative. *Journal of American History, 78,* 1347–1376.

Davidson, J. W., & Lytle, M. H. (1982). *After the fact: The art of historical detection.* New York: Knopf.

Degler, C. N. (1980). Remaking American history. *Journal of American History, 67,* 7–25.

DeVoto, B. (1943, June). The easy chair. *Harper's Magazine,* pp. 129–132.

Dibble, W. J. (1963). Four types of inferences from documents to event. *History and Theory, 3,* 203–221.

Dickinson, A. K., & Lee, P. J. (1978). *History teaching and historical understanding.* London: Heinemann.

Dickinson, A. K., & Lee, P. J. (1984). Making sense of history. In A. K. Dickinson, P. J. Lee, & P. J. Rogers (Eds.), *Learning history* (pp. 117–154). London: Heinemann.

Downey, M. T., & Levstik, L. S. (1991). Teaching and learning history. In J. P. Shaver (Ed.), *Handbook of research on social studies* (pp. 400–410). New York: Macmillan.

Dray, W. H. (1966). *Philosophical analysis and history.* New York: Knopf.

Eikenberry, D. H. (1923). Permanence of high school learning. *Journal of Educational Psychology, 14,* 463–481.

Elton, G. R. (1970). What sort of history should we teach? In M. Ballard (Ed.), *New movements in the study and teaching of history.* London: Temple Smith.

Ericsson, K. A., & Simon, H. A. (1984). *Verbal reports as data.* Cambridge, MA: MIT Press.

Fain, H. (1970). *Between philosophy and history: The resurrection of speculative philosophy of history within the analytic tradition.* Princeton, NJ: Princeton University Press.

Fines, J. (1980). Introduction. In D. Shemilt (Ed.), *School's Council History 13–16 Project* (pp. i–iii). Edinburgh: Holmes McDougall.

Finn, C. E., & Ravitch, D. (1987). Survey results: U.S. 17-year-olds know shockingly little about history and literature. *American School Board Journal, 174,* 31–33.

Fisher, D. H. (1970). *Historians' fallacies.* New York: Harper & Row.

Freeman, E. B., & Levstik, L. (1988). Recreating the past: Historical fiction in the social studies curriculum. *Elementary School Journal, 88,* 329–337.

Frisch, M. (1989). American history and the structure of collective memory: A modest exercise in empirical iconography. *Journal of American History, 75,* 1130–1155.

Gagné, E. D. (1985). *The cognitive psychology of school learning.* Boston: Little, Brown.

Gagné, R. M. (1976). The learning basis of teaching methods. In N. L. Gage (Ed.), *The psychology of teaching methods: Seventy-fifth yearbook of the National Society for the Study of Education* (pp. 21–43). Chicago: University of Chicago Press.

Gardner, H. (1985). *The mind's new science: A history of the cognitive revolution.* New York: Basic Books.

Gifford, B. R. (1988). *History in the schools.* New York: Macmillan.

Gorman, F. R., & Morgan, D. S. (1930). A study of the effect of definite written exercises upon learning in a course in American history. *Indiana School of Education Bulletin, 6,* 80–90.

Gottschalk, L. (1958). *Understanding history: A primer of historical method.* Chicago: University of Chicago Press.

Greene, S. (1993). The role of task in the development of academic thinking through reading and writing in a college history course. *Research in the Teaching of English, 27,* 46–75.

Haertel, E. H. (1991). New forms of teacher assessment. In G. Grant (Ed.), *Review of research in education* (Vol. 17, pp. 3–29). Washington, DC: American Educational Research Association.

Hall, G. S. (1911). *Educational problems* (Vol. II). New York: Appleton.

Hallam, R. N. (1967). Logical thinking in history. *Educational Review, 19,* 183–202.

Hallam, R. N. (1970). Piaget and thinking in history. In M. Ballard (Ed.), *New movements in the study and teaching of history.* London: Temple Smith.

Harlan, C. L. (1920). Educational measurement in the field of history. *Journal of Educational Research, 2,* 849–853.

Hexter, J. H. (1971). *The history primer.* New York: Basic Books.

Hirst, R. H. (1973). Liberal education and the nature of knowledge. In R. S. Peters (Ed.), *Philosophy of education* (pp. 87–101). Oxford: Oxford University Press.

Holt, T. (1990). *Thinking historically: Narrative, imagination, and understanding.* Princeton, NJ: Educational Testing Service.

Jahoda, G. (1963). Children's concepts of time and history. *Educational Review, 15,* 87–104.

Joncich, G. (1968). *The sane positivist: A biography of Edward L. Thorndike.* Middletown, CT: Wesleyan University Press.

Judd, C. H. (1915). *Psychology of high-school subjects.* Boston: Ginn.

Jurd, M. F. (1973). Adolescent thinking in history-type material. *Australian Journal of Education, 17,* 2–17.

Jurd, M. F. (1978). An empirical study of operational thinking in history-type material. In J. A. Keats, K. F. Collis, & G. S. Halford (Eds.), *Cognitive development: Research based on a neo-Piagetian approach* (pp. 315–348). New York: Wiley.

Kellner, H. (1989). *Language and historical representation: Getting the story crooked.* Madison: University of Wisconsin.

Kintsch, W. (1986). Learning from text. *Cognition and Instruction, 3,* 87–108.

Kol'tsova, V. A. (1978). Experimental study of cognitive activity in communication (with specific reference to concept formation). *Soviet Psychology, 17,* 23–38.

Larkin, J. (1980). Teaching problem solving in physics: The psychological laboratory and the practical classroom. In D. T. Tuma & F. Reif (Eds.), *Problem solving and education: Issues in teaching and research* (pp. 111–125). Hillsdale, NJ: Lawrence Erlbaum Associates.

Leinhardt, G. (1986). Expertise in mathematics teaching. *Educational Leadership, 43,* 28–33.

Leinhardt, G. (1993). Weaving instructional explanations in history. *British Journal of Educational Psychology, 63,* 46–74.

Leinhardt, G., & Greeno, J. G. (1986). The cognitive skill of teaching. *Journal of Educational Psychology, 78,* 75–95.

Levstik, L. S., & Pappas, C. C. (1987). Exploring the development of historical understanding. *Journal of Research and Development in Education, 21,* 1–15.

Lorence, J. L. (1983). The critical analysis of documentary evidence: Basic skills in the history classroom. *History Teaching: A Journal of Methods, 8,* 77–84.

Lowenthal, D. (1989). The timeless past: Some Anglo-American historical preconceptions. *Journal of American History, 75,* 1263–1280.

Macintosh, H. G. (1987). Testing skills in history. In C. Portal (Ed.), *The history curriculum for teachers* (pp. 183–219). London: Falmer Press.

Mandelbaum, M. (1938). *The problem of historical knowledge.* New York: Liveright.

McCutchen, D. (1986). Domain knowledge and linguistic knowledge in the development of writing ability. *Journal of Memory and Language, 25,* 431–444.

McKeown, M. G., Beck, I. L., Sinatra, G. M., & Loxterman, J. A. (1992). The contribution of prior knowledge and coherent text to comprehension. *Reading Research Quarterly, 27,* 79–93.

McNeil, J. D. (1989). Personal meanings versus test-driven responses to social studies texts. *Reading Psychology, 10,* 311–319.

Megill, A. (1989). Recounting the past: "Description," explanation, and narrative in historiography. *American Historical Review, 94,* 627–653.

Merton, R. K. (1968). *Social theory and social structure* (3rd ed.). New York: Free Press.

Meyer, B. J. F. (1975). *The organization of prose and its effects on memory.* New York: Elsevier.

Miller, M. M., & Stearns, P. N. (1995). Applying cognitive learning approaches in history teaching: An experiment in a world history course. *The History Teacher, 28,* 183–204.

Mink, L. O. (1987). *Historical understanding.* Edited by B. Fay, E. O. Golob, & R. Vann. Ithaca, New York: Cornell University Press.

Myers, G. C. (1917a). Confusion in recall. *Journal of Educational Psychology, 8,* 166–175.

Myers, G. C. (1917b). Delayed recall in history. *Journal of Educational Psychology, 8,* 275–283.

Nevins, A. (1942, May 3). American history for Americans. *New York Times Magazine,* pp. 6, 28–29.

Nichol, J., & Dean, J. (1986). Computers and children's historical thinking and understanding. In R. Ennals, R. Gwyn, & L. Zdravchev (Eds.), *Information technology and education: The changing school* (pp. 160–176). West Sussex, England: Ellis Horwood.

Novick, P. (1988). *That noble dream: The "objectivity question" and the American historical profession.* Chicago: University of Chicago Press.

Odell, C. W. (1922). The Barr diagnostic tests in American History. *School and Society, 16,* 501–503.

Olson, D. R. (1994). *The world on paper.* New York: Cambridge.

Olson, D. R. (1990). Thinking about narrative. In B. K. Britton & A. D. Pellegrini (Eds.), *Narrative thought and narrative language* (pp. 99–112). Hillsdale, NJ: Lawrence Erlbaum Associates.

Peel, E. A. (1959). Experimental examination of some of Piaget's schemata concerning children's perception and thinking, and a discussion of their educational significance. *British Journal of Educational Psychology, 29,* 89–103.

Peel, E. A. (1967a). Some problems in the psychology of history teaching: Historical ideas and concepts. In W. H. Burston & D. Thompson (Eds.), *Studies in the nature and teaching of history* (pp. 159–172). London: Routledge & Kegan Paul.

Peel, E. A. (1967b). Some problems in the psychology of history teaching: The pupil's thinking and inference. In W. H. Burston & D. Thompson (Eds.), *Studies in the nature and teaching of history* (pp. 173–190). London: Routledge & Kegan Paul.

Peel, E. A. (1972). Understanding school material. *Educational Review, 24,* 163–173.

Perkins, D. N., & Simmons, R. (1988). Patterns of misunderstanding: An integrative model for science, math, and programming. *Review of Educational Research, 58,* 303–326.

Pozo, J., & Carretero, M. (1983). El adolescente como historiador [The adolescent as historian]. *Infancia y Aprendizaje, 23,* 75–90.

Ravitch, D., & Finn, C. E. (1987). *What do our 17-year-olds know?* New York: Harper & Row.

Rosenshine, B. (1986). Unsolved issues in teaching content: A critique of a lesson on Federalist Paper No. 10. *Teaching and Teacher Education, 2,* 301–308.

Rosenzweig, L. W., & Weinland, T. P. (1986). New directions of the history curriculum: A challenge for the 1980s. *The History Teacher, 19,* 263–277.

Rüsen, J. (1993). *Studies in metahistory.* Pretoria, South Africa: Human Sciences Research Council.

Sackett, L. W. (1919). A scale in United States history. *Journal of Educational Psychology, 10,* 345–348.

Salomon, G. (1991). Transcending the qualitative-quantitative debate: The analytic and systemic approaches to educational research. *Educational Researcher, 20,* 10–18.

Seixas, P. (1993). Historical understanding among adolescents in a multicultural setting. *Curriculum Inquiry, 23,* 301–327.

Shemilt, D. J. (1980). *History 13–16: Evaluation study.* Edinburgh: Holmes McDougall.

Shemilt, D. J. (1983). The devil's locomotive. *History and Theory, 22,* 1–18.

Shulman, L. S. (1986a). Paradigms and research programs in the study of teaching: A contemporary perspective. In M. Wittrock (Ed.), *Handbook of research on teaching* (3rd ed., pp. 3–36). New York: Macmillan.

Shulman, L. S. (1986b). Those who understand teach: Knowledge growth in teaching. *Educational Researcher, 15,* 4–14.

Shulman, L. S. (1988). A union of insufficiencies: Strategies for teacher assessment in a period of educational reform. *Educational Leadership, 46,* 36–41.

Sinatra, G. M., Beck, I. L., & McKeown, M. G. (1992). A longitudinal characterization of young students' knowledge of their country's government. *American Educational Research Journal, 29,* 633–662.

Skinner, Q. (1985). *The return of grand theory in the human sciences.* Cambridge, MA: Harvard University Press.

Smith, R. N., & Tomlinson P. (1977). The development of children's construction of historical duration. *Educational Research, 19,* 163–170.

Snow, R. E., & Lohman, D. F. (1989). Implications of cognitive psychology for psychological measurement. In R. L. Linn (Ed.), *Educational measurement* (3rd ed., pp. 263–332). New York: Macmillan.

Spoehr, K. T., & Spoehr, L. W. (1994). Learning to think historically. *Educational Psychologist, 29,* 71–77.

Stanford, M. (1986). *The nature of historical knowledge.* New York: Basil Blackwell.

Strike, K. A., & Posner, G. J. (1976). Epistemological perspectives on conceptions of curriculum organization and learning. In L. S. Shulman (Ed.), *Review of research in education* (pp. 106–141). Itasca, IL: F. E. Peacock.

Thorndike, E. L. (1912). *Education, a first book.* New York: Macmillan.

Thorndike, E. L. (1923). *Educational psychology—briefer course.* New York: Teachers College Press.

Thornton, S. J., & Wenger, R. N. (1990). Geography curriculum and instruction in three 4th-grade classrooms. *Elementary School Journal, 90,* 515–531.

Toulmin, S., & Leary, D. E. (1985). The cult of empiricism in psychology, and beyond. In D. E. Leary & S. Koch (Eds.), *A century of psychology as science* (pp. 594–617). New York: McGraw-Hill.

van Dijk, T. A., & Kintsch, W. (1983). *Strategies of discourse comprehension.* New York: Academic Press.

VanSledright, B., & Brophy, J. (1992). Storytelling, imagination, and fanciful elaboration in children's historical reconstructions. *American Educational Research Journal, 29,* 837–861.

Van Wagenen, M. J. (1919). *Historical information and judgment in pupils of elementary schools.* New York: Teachers College Press.

von Borries, B. (1987). *Geschichtslernen und Persönlichkeits-entwicklung* [The learning of history and the development of self]. *Geschichts-Didaktic, 12,* 1–14.

Voss, J. F., Greene, T. R., Post, T. A., & Penner, B. C. (1983). Problem-solving skill in the social sciences. In G. H. Bower (Ed.), *The psychology of learning and motivation: Advances in research and theory* (Vol. 17, pp. 165–213). New York: Academic Press.

Weaver, R. B., & Traxler, A. E. (1931). Essay examination and objective tests in United States history in the junior high school. *School Review, 39,* 689–695.

White, H. (1973). *Metahistory: The historical imagination in nineteenth-century Europe.* Baltimore: Johns Hopkins University Press.

Whittington, D. (1991). What have 17-year-olds known in the past? *American Educational Research Journal, 28,* 759–780.

Wilson, S. M., & Wineburg, S. S. (1988). Peering at history through different lenses: The role of disciplinary perspectives in teaching history. *Teachers College Record, 89,* 525–539.

Wilson, S. M., & Wineburg, S. S. (1993). Wrinkles in time: Using performance assessments to understand the knowledge of history teachers. *American Educational Research Journal, 30,* 729–769.

Wineburg, S. S. (1991a). Historical problem solving: A study of the cognitive processes used in the evaluation of documentary and pictorial evidence. *Journal of Educational Psychology, 83,* 73–87.

Wineburg, S. S. (1991b). On the reading of historical texts: Notes on the breach between school and academy. *American Educational Research Journal, 28,* 495–519.

Wineburg, S. S. (1992). Probing the depths of students' historical knowledge. *Perspectives: Newsletter of the American Historical Association, 30,* 20–24.

Wineburg, S. S., & Fournier, J. E. (1993). Thinking in time. *History News, 48,* 26–27.

Wineburg, S. S., & Wilson, S. M. (1988). Models of wisdom in the teaching of history. *Phi Delta Kappan, 70,* 50–58.

Wineburg, S. S., & Wilson, S. M. (1991). Subject matter knowledge in the teaching of history. In J. E. Brophy (Ed.), *Advances in research on teaching* (pp. 303–345). Greenwich, CT: JAI.

# · 15 ·

# SHIFTS AND CONVERGENCES IN SCIENCE
# LEARNING AND INSTRUCTION

## Marcia C. Linn
UNIVERSITY OF CALIFORNIA, BERKELEY

## Nancy B. Songer
UNIVERSITY OF COLORADO, BOULDER

## Bat-Sheva Eylon
WEIZMANN INSTITUTE OF SCIENCE, ISRAEL

In this chapter, we examine science learning and instruction historically, identifying shifts in the perspectives of those involved in science education as well as convergences that combine diverse perspectives. For example, natural scientists and precollege science teachers draw on largely distinct experiential bases and commonly hold different perspectives on learning and instruction. These groups often have difficulty establishing common ground, yet the shifts within the views of each group are leading to a convergence.

We define three historical periods and describe convergences during each period as well as shifts from one period to another. We refer to the period prior to the reforms of science education in the 1950s as the *separation* period because groups such as science instructors, natural scientists, or psychologists tended to work separately. The reforms of the 1950s were initiated by natural scientists but included interactions with both developmental psychologists and precollege science instructors. We call this period the *interaction* period. The period starting in the late 1970s we identify as one of *partnerships* between groups, including cognitive researchers, natural scientists, technology experts, and science instructors. These periods capture major trends; there are also historical activities that do not fit this pattern of separation, interaction, and partnership.

In this chapter we highlight the contribution of psychologists to science education. To this end, we distinguish *disposition to learn* from *the nature of instruction*. Psychological studies of

the abilities, interests, and aptitudes of learners—their dispositions—involve distinguishing one student from another. Studies of the nature of instruction, in contrast, involve comparing one science curriculum or activity with another. Partnership projects generally combine the investigations of learning and instruction, seeking to design instruction that elicits a disposition to learn science or that meets the needs of diverse students. In this chapter we discuss disposition to learn in all three historical periods and then discuss the nature of instruction in all three historical periods.

To illustrate the advantages of multidisciplinary collaborations, we start the chapter with two case studies. One case describes a 10-year-long partnership. The other describes historical changes in science education. These case studies show how groups concerned with science education are collaborating and seeking mutually defined goals. We hope that this chapter will help foster a broader convergence among the various groups involved in science education. Thus, we start with concrete case studies, describe historical examples of interdisciplinary interactions that have moved the field ahead, and close with promising directions for the future.

This is not a review but rather an analysis of the events leading to current views of science learning and instruction. By synthesizing the progression of research in science education, we hope to encourage those concerned with science education and especially psychologists to join forces and undertake

This material is based in part on research supported by National Science Foundation grant No. MDR-9155744. Any opinions, findings, and conclusions or recommendations expressed in this publication are those of the authors and do not necessarily reflect the views of the National Science Foundation.

The Fulbright International Exchange of Scholars Program provided partial support for Bat-Sheva Eylon's visit to the University of California, Berkeley.

research to address current and future questions and concerns. Our examples are selective rather than comprehensive: We found many compelling examples, but we were obliged to choose only one in any given category. We selected examples primarily from the physical sciences to enhance coherence. We sought international examples and examples from a broad range of research programs. We sought to frame the trends in a way that would inspire further reflection and investigation. And we looked for the seeds that led to future insights, hoping, in so doing, to model the process of building on research experience to improve overall understanding.

The perspectives of the following groups have shaped our understanding of the disposition and opportunity to learn science: (a) researchers in science education and educational psychology; (b) cognitive scientists; (c) science curriculum developers; (d) college faculty preparing precollege instructors in science; (e) natural scientists, including both college and university faculty in the sciences and researchers in the natural sciences and computer science; (f) precollege science instructors and administrators; (g) educational technologists, including software designers, networking experts, and hardware designers; and (h) policymakers, including community leaders, legislators, industry leaders, and government leaders. We examine shifts and convergences in the views of these groups in the following sections.

## CASE STUDIES

These case studies of collaborations among natural scientists, cognitive scientists, psychologists, precollege instructors, and science educators introduce the themes of this chapter. They characterize the complexity of science education reform and the value of partnerships. They demonstrate the role of trial and reformulation in curricular reform and show how social science research contributes to the process. They introduce disposition to learn and the nature of instruction and show how the two interact. The first case study illustrates the use of trial and refinement to improve middle school physical science learning. The second case study illustrates reform of a national chemistry curriculum.

### The Computer as Learning Partner Project: Scaffolded Knowledge Integration

The Computer as Learning Partner (CLP) project has successfully modified an eighth-grade physical science program with the goal of ensuring that *all* students acquire integrated understanding of thermal events. The curriculum takes advantage of the active, constructing nature of the learner to guide integration and understanding of scientific ideas and experiences. The curriculum features an electronic laboratory notebook and takes advantage of real-time data collection using temperature-sensitive probes connected to computers.

CLP has two broad goals: (a) to support the development of robust, integrated ideas about scientific phenomena, and (b) to help students develop a disposition to understand scientific phenomena, resolve inconsistencies, and apply scientific ideas as citizens or scientists. The challenge has been to support students while still expecting them to be responsible for their own learning. Too much support stands in the way of responsibility, and too little leaves students to flounder endlessly.

Over the past 10 years, this collaborative group has integrated research findings, observations of precollege instructors, classroom trials, software advances, observations of natural scientists, studies of individual learners, and investigations of assessment to create a framework called *scaffolded knowledge integration,* discussed below.

To understand the nature of instruction, the CLP group engaged in trial and refinement of instructional materials, drawing on work in psychology, science education, cognitive science, the history of science, and other disciplines. The group developed a one-semester middle school physical science curriculum and regularly reformulated the materials based on feedback from classroom trials. The computer software is implemented in HyperCard, making revisions relatively straightforward. Studies of group and individual responses to the instruction are regularly conducted and analyzed by natural scientists, psychologists, precollege instructors, technology experts, and others.

The CLP group initially viewed learners as disposed to make sense of science, and instruction as providing opportunities for students to investigate scientific ideas, much as scientists do (e.g., Inhelder & Piaget, 1958). After 10 years, the CLP perspective on instruction, called *scaffolded knowledge integration,* is far more detailed and complex.

In seeking to balance support for students and opportunity for autonomous investigations, CLP built on the investigations of student reasoning carried out by many research teams (e.g., Champagne, Klopfer, & Gunstone, 1982; A. diSessa, 1982; McDermott, 1984). Linn, starting from a Piagetian perspective and inspired by Vygotsky (Linn, 1970; Vygotsky, 1962), developed interviews to elicit the thinking of students as they confront everyday problems (Linn, Clement, & Pulos, 1983; Linn & Thier, 1975), and studied how students learn in project-centered science courses (Linn, 1980, 1985).

The CLP framework evolved in five main cycles (Linn, 1992a; Linn & Songer, 1991, 1993). These address (a) the goals of the curriculum, (b) the application of scientific ideas to everyday problems, (c) the nature of alternative views of scientific events held by students, (d) the strategies for knowledge integration, and (e) the abstraction of scientific ideas.

*Goals of the Curriculum.* Before the partnership period, goals for science courses were generally set by natural scientists advising textbook writers or writing the books themselves. CLP started with goals found in science textbooks for middle school students. In thermodynamics, a typical eighth-grade textbook features kinetic theory—an atomic, mathematically formal, and quantitative view. Historically, molecular kinetic theory had been added to the science curriculum in an effort to "modernize" the goals of the curriculum, but with little reflection on the implications of this modernization (Welch, 1979). These ideas appealed to the natural scientists in the CLP collaboration.

Classroom investigations, however, revealed that students did not understand kinetic theory, even after 13 weeks of instruction (Linn & Songer, 1991, 1993). The classroom teacher suggested that CLP revise the curricular goals.

The cognitive researchers interviewed students and found that students typically believe that heat is the higher level of temperature and that heating and cooling are disconnected processes. This finding is collaborated by the research of Wiser and Carey (Wiser, 1988; Wiser & Carey, 1983). The CLP group concluded that the gap between student knowledge and kinetic theory was too broad to bridge in middle school science. CLP sought an alternative model for thermal events that would be accessible to more students. The researchers interviewed natural scientists to determine the models they used for thermal events. Many scientists use qualitative reasoning based on rate of heat flow to explain everyday thermal events. For example, when asked to explain phenomena such as why a wooden spoon is better than a stainless steel spoon for stirring a hot liquid, scientists regularly describe the process in terms of heat flow (E. L. Lewis & Linn, 1994). The heat flow model is generally among the repertoire of models of thermal phenomena used by scientists and engineers.

Review of research suggested that students unable to make sense of molecular kinetic theory may resort to memorizing information about that topic (Flavell, 1976; Novak & Gowin, 1984). For example, when instruction in mechanics begins by describing frictionless universes, often students, whose total prior experience has been in a friction-filled environment, cannot see the relevance of their experience to the goal of instruction. To solve this problem, they may simply declare these two different topics rather than trying to integrate them (diSessa, 1988).

The CLP group met to negotiate new goals for the curriculum featuring a qualitative model of heat and temperature. CLP adopted the term "heat energy" to refer to the total kinetic energy available for transfer in a substance. As such, heat energy depends on the nature of a substance, its amount, and its temperature. The CLP group sought principles based on heat flow. These principles are called pragmatic principles, because they are often applied by natural scientists to practical problems. Of course, some physicists object to the term "heat flow," since the term "heat" refers to something that exists only under conditions of transfer and flow does not represent the mechanism for heat transfer (instead suggesting that heat is a substance).

Examples of pragmatic principles used in CLP include (a) the direction of heat flow principle (heat energy flows only from objects at higher temperature to objects at lower temperature), and (b) the temperature difference principle (the greater the temperature difference between objects and their surroundings, the faster heat energy flows). CLP activities help students understand and apply these principles. Thus, after conducting several experiments, students create a principle to summarize their conclusions. The CLP computer interface interprets the principle constructed and provides feedback.

Before adopting the heat flow model, CLP conducted empirical studies to compare the version of the curriculum with atomic principles and the version with pragmatic principles. Many students found pragmatic principles appropriate for summarizing classroom experiments as well as their own experiences. In general, the atomic principles were less successful, and, if combined with activities involving computation of changes in calories, often seemed to place a "veil of numbers" over the process of understanding (Linn & Songer, 1991, 1993).

To illustrate how students viewed pragmatic principles, we contrast two interviews. One student who is struggling to understand the principles comments that pragmatic heat flow principles are useful but would be difficult to create:

**Interviewer [I]:** What is a principle, and does it help you understand the experiment?

**Student [S]:** The principle is like I guess, just harder words that we don't quite understand [at first]. . . . Some people might not understand the words [in scientific principles] but they may understand the idea of it. . . . They could understand the concept of it but not how to word it.

Another student who finds the principles accessible describes how they help generalize ideas:

**S:** Yes it does [help understand] because when we first learned about principles, I didn't know what it was about at all and really actually it is just a definition of what we are all trying to figure out and about the results and experiments, it is just a whole big definition.

**I:** How did that help you understand the experiment?

**S:** It helps me a lot because if I don't understand the experiment or what we are trying to look for, it is all explained in the principle. It is something that I can refer back to.

As illustrated, most students could integrate their ideas with pragmatic principles. Pragmatic principles were more accessible to students than atomic principles.

These results show how the goals of the curriculum contribute to the success of science learners. As will be discussed in subsequent sections, the shift in interactions between natural scientists and cognitive psychologists characteristic of the partnership period made it possible to consider goals from more perspectives (e.g., A. diSessa, 1993; Linn, diSessa, Pea, & Songer, 1994; B. Y. White & Frederiksen, 1990).

These results point out some of the issues governing goal selection in science courses. The atomic principles describe a model similar to the one used by research scientists, thus introducing ideas necessary in advanced courses. The pragmatic principles describe a model that applies to many practical problems. Middle school students can use pragmatic principles to explain many everyday problems, thus engaging in the sort of reasoning valued by natural scientists. And middle school students are much more likely to understand pragmatic principles than to understand atomic principles. Nevertheless, if the purpose of the science course is to prepare future scientists, some will argue that the curriculum should teach atomic principles to students who can understand them.

Those arguing for atomic principles often point out that these principles are elegant and parsimonious. These principles depict the beauty of science. In addition, pragmatic principles may stand in the way of understanding atomic principles, thus placing an additional burden on teachers of advanced courses.

Those arguing for pragmatic principles often point out that these principles help students understand the relevance of science to their lives, respect students by building on student observations of the natural world, and motivate students to take advanced courses because the value of science is more apparent. In addition, by teaching students pragmatic principles in middle school and atomic principles later, science courses can help students understand both the competing models available to explain scientific phenomena and the role of models in making sense of the natural world. Students can contrast the atomic model with the heat flow model and learn when to use one or the other. Thus, students can potentially reason as scientists do, selecting models matched to the problem.

*Context of the Problems.* As the discussion of goals suggests, to make science meaningful to students, CLP researchers emphasized problems from everyday life and developed pragmatic principles. Making this change raised some complex issues.

In the early versions of CLP, students used temperature probes connected to a computer to conduct all their experiments. Graphical representations of the experimental results appeared as the experiment progressed. Students were able to focus their attention on observing the experimental situation and interpreting the results, rather than on tediously recording and graphing scientific information (Friedler, Nachmias, & Linn, 1990). CLP involved students in making sense of their scientific investigations with activities where students made predictions, conducted experiments, and explained the relationship between predictions and results consistent with the "predict–observe–explain" framework of Gunstone (Gunstone, White, & Fensham, 1988). Students gained understanding of the pragmatic principles using this curriculum but had difficulty extending their understanding to naturally occurring problems (Songer, 1989).

In reviewing these results, the CLP group noticed that everyday problems were much more complex and ambiguous than situations investigated in classroom science laboratories. In the next version of CLP, the electronic notebook allowed students to conduct both experimental, real-time investigations with classroom apparatus and experimental, simulated investigations of everyday problems (Stern, 1990).

The simulated experiments were selected to reflect the students' interests and activities. Thus, one experiment investigated various ways to keep a drink cold for lunch. Another experiment involved keeping potatoes warm. These experiments provided an opportunity for students to identify parallels between heating and cooling and made complex everyday problems accessible to experimentation.

Comparisons of the curriculum with and without simulations revealed that simulations helped students interpret everyday problems. Students using simulations also gained a more robust understanding of the pragmatic principles (Linn, 1992a; Songer, 1989). As will be discussed in subsequent sections, emphasis on everyday aspects of science, neglected during the interaction period, is now reemerging in the partnership period as the audience for science is broadened to include all citizens.

Adding everyday problems and simulations to the CLP curriculum spurred debate in the group. How should students evaluate simulated experiments? Should they question or accept the assumptions of the simulation? Should they verify the results empirically, or should they check them against the principles they established empirically? The decision was to encourage the latter, but the natural scientists in the group remained somewhat uneasy. Students using the simulations treated the results just like their empirical results, suggesting that they had difficulty distinguishing a simulation from an empirical study. This issue comes up again in the discussion of the nature of science.

*Alternative Conceptions of Scientific Phenomena.* CLP studies and others identify intuitive ideas or alternative conceptions

that guide student thinking and are often more appealing than pragmatic principles (e.g., Driver, Guesne, & Tiberghien, 1985; Linn & Songer, 1991). Students often synthesize ideas about insulation and conduction and other phenomena from observations (Linn & Songer, 1991). For example, students believe that wool keeps things warm, and therefore, wrapping a cold drink in wool would heat it up much more quickly than wrapping the drink in some other material such as aluminum foil. Students have strong intuitions about metals, believing that metals can impart cold to objects. Almost all the students believe that aluminum foil is the best thing to wrap a soft drink in, to keep it cold (E. L. Lewis & Linn, 1994).

This evidence led the CLP researchers to two conclusions. First, students try to make sense of their observations even though their ideas differ from those of experts. Second, students develop a repertoire of ideas, some of which are difficult to reconcile with pragmatic principles. The CLP group sought a way to guide students to build on their predictive ideas, distinguishing among their repertoire of ideas about thermal phenomena (Linn & Songer, 1991). CLP created opportunities for students to contrast their views and select the most explanatory ones.

For example, students generally believe that the polystyrene plastic Styrofoam is effective in insulating cold objects and have evidence that Styrofoam is also effective in insulating warm objects. Building on this intuition helps students identify a situation where heating and cooling are related rather than distinct. Students can gather evidence that Styrofoam insulates both hot and cold materials and then perform additional experiments to determine whether wool has a similar property.

CLP developed a model of conceptual change based on these investigations (Linn & Songer, 1991). Interviews revealed three main categories of student explanations. Action knowledge is tied to a specific activity and describes the action that occurs, such as "the stove burned me" or "my sweater warms me up." Intuitions combine action knowledge from several situations, resulting in generalizations that describe a class of events, such as "wool warms things up" or "stoves produce heat." Principles rely on some mechanisms or causal models such as heat flow or molecular kinetic theory. These categories of knowledge are consistent with the views of Case (1985) and A. diSessa (1988). Rather than labeling action knowledge or intuitions as misconceptions, CLP researchers concluded that intuitions are attempts at generalization that should be encouraged (Linn, Songer, Lewis, & Stern, 1993), and action knowledge is an attempt to identify salient information in a complex situation.

Instructional materials were designed to incorporate prototypes to support the process of generalization. *Prototypes* are events for which students have accurate predictions, although they may lack explanations. For example, students have accurate predictions about whether soup will cool more rapidly if left in a large tureen or distributed into small bowls. They conclude that when the soup is distributed into many small bowls it will cool faster. Most go on to say that the small bowls have collectively more surface area exposed to the air than the large bowl. Some explain that the ratio of surface area to volume is greater for the small bowls. The work of Clement (Clement, Brown, & Zietsman, 1989) on anchoring ideas, and of Minstrell (1982) on benchmarks, inspired CLP's use of prototypes. Activities helped students use prototypes to build accurate intuitions.

Comparing the effectiveness of the CLP curriculum with and without the new focus on distinguishing alternatives revealed improved understanding of the pragmatic principles (E. L. Lewis & Linn, 1994; Linn, 1992a). Respecting the ideas of the student and building on them helps students learn science. This approach is much more successful than Piagetian studies, where instruction consists of contradicting student ideas (e.g., Eylon & Linn, 1988; Linn, 1986).

*Social Context of Science Learning.* CLP encountered difficulty in encouraging students to generate alternatives and distinguish among them because in school, students often seek the right answer rather than knowledge integration (e.g., Cohen, 1986; Lave & Wenger, 1991; Palincsar & Brown, 1984). In particular, students view the teacher as an authority and distrust their own efforts to make sense of science concepts. The CLP classroom teacher sought to renegotiate the authority structure, placing emphasis on evidence from observations and experiments rather than on teacher pronouncements. The software environment monitored many mundane aspects of the class, including keeping track of which activities were completed and which could be attempted, freeing the teacher to tutor individuals and small groups. Analysis of student–teacher interactions revealed that brief tutoring can help students integrate ideas but must direct students to the evidence rather than giving answers.

By combining an analysis of the scientific ideas held by students with observations of how students formed their ideas, CLP describes science learners as struggling to make sense of complex information. This view is in sharp contrast to research during the interaction period that emphasized misconceptions held by students (Eylon & Linn, 1988). Because of their multidisciplinary perspective, the partnership projects tend to examine the origin and persistence of student views, and to find ways to help students integrate their knowledge.

Based on these studies, the CLP curriculum was modified to encourage students to gather evidence and form generalizations. The classroom teacher found that many students were reluctant to come to conclusions on their own, motivating some changes in the social context of instruction. Very effective discussion of alternative scientific perspectives often arose in small groups, motivating CLP to design group activities to foster understanding. The sustained problem solving necessary for projects and complex problems resulted in serious discussion and personalized investigations. Other researchers were also exploring this direction (A. L. Brown & Campione, 1990a; Carver, Lehrer, Connell, & Erickson, 1992; Scardamalia & Bereiter, 1992).

CLP also analyzed how students worked in small groups and found some of the same problems with authority structure that had already been documented in teacher–student interactions (Burbules & Linn, 1991). Often students reinforced stereotypes about who could succeed in science, telling female students that science was for males, interrupting students perceived to be nontraditional, and paying more attention to students who fit the stereotype. A primary outcome of CLP students studying the group learning was to increase the number of computers so that students could work in groups of

two. This group size had the fewest drawbacks and the most advantages (Madhok, 1992).

Thus, the partnership team participation of classroom teachers and sociologists increased attention to the social context of learning. The team reviewed trade-offs between the advantages of group negotiation of meaning and the disadvantages of stereotyping of students. Surveys were formed to maximize learning outcomes.

*Disposition Toward Knowledge Integration.* In spite of these modifications of the curriculum, however, many students retained a limited repertoire of ideas that did not work very well in practice, were not compatible with the pragmatic principles, and were not integrated with their other knowledge. CLP explored the disposition to integrate science knowledge in a longitudinal study.

Representative students were interviewed at six points during the semester, and followed up in subsequent years (E. L. Lewis, 1991). Some of these students converged on a powerful repertoire of ideas about thermal events quite quickly. Other students progressed toward a powerful repertoire during the semester. A third group oscillated among sophisticated and isolated ideas and made no discernible progress. These groups differed in their views of themselves as learners and in their ability to monitor their progress.

*Converging* students expected to make sense of their prior experiences with thermal phenomena and expected to integrate those experiences with their classroom activities. They comprised about 15 percent of the students. They utilized evidence from experiments as well as from observations. They linked their experiments and their observations and sought a coherent view. Finally, these students sought abstract explanations for the phenomena they observed. As a result, they embraced the heat flow model for thermal events.

*Progressing* students (about 70 percent of the students) were similar to converging students in that they were disposed to integrate ideas. However, they differed from converging students in that they focused their integration activities primarily on local rather than global events, and they relied on authority figures for evidence as well as on their own observations and experiments. These students refined intuitive views but rarely sought principles. They often accepted ideas that did not mesh with their prior knowledge. Reliance on local coherence is consistent with the performance of many students in studies of statistical reasoning (Tversky & Kahneman, 1992) and quantity comparison (e.g., Markman, 1978).

Students with *oscillating* ideas failed to integrate new information, occasionally applying new ideas but mostly relying on action knowledge to explain scientific events. They comprised about 15 percent of the students. Oscillating students, like progressing students, relied on information that came from authority figures even when it conflicted with their observations. Often oscillating students failed to see contradictions apparent to others.

To encourage knowledge integration, some longitudinal subjects were asked to reflect on their own ideas. Students compared experiments and experiences and described the similarities and differences. They were asked to rely on their own ideas and view authorities with some skepticism. Students in this group were more likely to integrate their knowledge. This investigation illustrates how instruction can modify students' disposition to integrate ideas. It also demonstrates how partnership projects connect characteristics such as disposition to oscillate or to progress and the nature of instruction.

*Views of Scientific Knowledge and Learning.* The CLP studies suggest the view that students have of science learning, their metacognition (Schoenfeld, 1983; R. T. White, 1988), is a primary component of disposition to learn. Students who view science as a dynamic field and view themselves as integrating and making sense of science are disposed to learn science (Linn & Songer, 1993). Songer (1989) identified students with static, relative, and dynamic views of science and science learning and showed how these interact with learning outcomes.

Students with *static* views regard science as a collection of facts to be memorized rather than as a set of principles that are warranted by evidence. These students say that science is best learned by rote, that science learned in school does not apply to everyday experiences, and that everything in the science book will always be true. One student qualified a response about the truth of information in a textbook by saying that everything is true except the true/false questions, some of which are false.

Students with *dynamic* views of science believe that science proceeds by fits and starts, that scientists seek to explain diverse phenomena with broad principles, that conclusions are based on evidence, and that the way to learn science is to make an effort to understand complicated ideas.

Students who take a *relative* stance toward science argue that "scientists all have different opinions," "science is constantly changing," and "no one is sure about anything." These students expect scientific principles to vary depending on the scientist and the situation. They cannot distinguish among conjecture, opinion, and assertions warranted by evidence. They lack criteria to select among principles. They recommend that scientists repeat their experiments if they do not like the results. As one student asserted, "$E = mc^2$ may change with technology, etc."

National assessments suggest that static and relative views of science persist into adulthood (National Assessment of Educational Progress, 1988). Static and relative views of scientific knowledge, perhaps fostered by students' reliance on authority rather than on their own ideas, stand in the way of integrated understanding of scientific phenomena.

The CLP project found several ways to help students gain a more dynamic view of science and of themselves as science learners. Changing the authority structure in the class by placing more responsibility on groups of students is helpful. Encouraging students to compare explanations or theories and reflect on these also contributes. CLP added activities where students could compare scientific theories such as competing explanations for dinosaur extinction. Communicating a dynamic, progressing view of science remains a challenge to partnership projects. Yet partnerships are better prepared to address this challenge than are investigators working in isolation.

*Summary.* In summary, the multidisciplinary CLP project illustrates both the complexity of teaching science and the advantages of partnerships for solving complex educational problems. The CLP group has abstracted its approach in a framework

called scaffolded knowledge integration. The framework has four components. First, select accessible, relevant goals for students. CLP addresses this with pragmatic principles. Second, make thinking skills visible by supporting both the process of scientific investigation and the product of this work. CLP guides students to explore simulations, models, and experiments, ensuring that they get both the details and the big picture. Third, provide as much social support as necessary to foster knowledge integration and sustained problem solving. Both renegotiating the class authority structure and fostering group learning in a context of mutual respect address this aspect of the framework in CLP. Projects also provide opportunities for knowledge integration. Fourth, engage students as both investigators and critics. To foster understanding of the nature of science, students can reflect on their own ideas and compare them with the ideas of other scholars. CLP includes regular opportunities to critique results and conclusions and reflect on anomalous findings to foster metacognitive skills and responsibility for learning. The CLP framework is closely related to a number of views of instruction emerging in the partnership period (e.g., Bruer, 1993; Collins, Brown, & Holum, 1991). All these projects share a common goal of fostering in students a disposition to view themselves as knowledge integrators and to view science as a dynamic, advancing repertoire of explanations, evidence, and methods. In addition, these projects share a perspective on the nature of instruction as guiding rather than informing students.

### Chemistry Education in Israel

This case study illustrates how the three historical periods in the development of science education unfolded in Israel. In the separation period, science textbooks were either translated into Hebrew from other languages or were written by individuals, rather than by groups or coalitions. For example, the most popular high school physics textbook was a translation of *College Physics,* by Sears and Zemansky (1949).

In the mid-1960s the Amos De Shalit Science Teaching Center was established as a cooperation between academic institutions and the Israeli Ministry of Education and Culture. From its inception, this center featured teams consisting of scientists and experienced teachers who prepared curriculum materials for grades kindergarten through 12, similar to the teams established in America. The teachers continued to work part time in their schools; thus, close ties with the field were maintained. The first secondary curricula involved translation and adaptation of the new American programs—Physical Science Study Committee (PSSC) in physics, Chemistry Study (CHEMStudy) in chemistry, and Biological Science Curriculum Study (BSCS) in biology. Soon after, new programs emerged that were more tailored to local students. In general, the programs were designed for a homogeneous audience consisting mainly of science-oriented, high-ability students.

After an initial phase of curriculum production and implementation, these teams added evaluation and research. As the field of science education in Israel developed, additional constituencies became involved. Also, graduate programs in science education were established, and research became a component of reform. Eventually these natural scientist–led teams were replaced by partnerships.

In the Israeli Science Teaching Center, projects differed from the U.S. projects in several ways. During the interaction period in the United States, teams of experts worked together to design curriculum materials and then dispersed. Sometimes a subteam was established to disseminate and implement the program. When a need arose for changes, very often a new team was set up to accomplish the task. As a result, discontinuity in the improvement of the curriculum was common. The new team rarely possessed the experience accumulated from implementation and evaluation of the previous curriculum, so it could not build on the experiences of previous developers. In addition, most projects lacked systematic research, and therefore it was difficult to formulate recommendations for improvement. This lack of continuity meant that changes in the curriculum were not always improvements and that classroom teachers were regularly asked to make major alterations in their teaching.

In contrast, the Israeli Science Teaching Center began an ongoing effort in the interaction period (Bruckheimer, 1979). Each stage in the development process was based on experience accumulated in the previous stages and formed the basis for future improvement. Revisions built on informal observations and feedback from research. This "evolutionary" approach of the Israeli Science Teaching Center resulted in ongoing change in the national curriculum. To illustrate this process, we describe the evolution of the introductory chemistry course for Israeli high schools.

***Introductory Chemistry.*** Starting in the 1970s, a CHEMStudy-like curriculum called *Chemistry for High School* (1972)—appropriate for a small group of scientifically oriented students—was reformulated into a new curriculum, sensitive to students' scientific ideas and accessible to a large, heterogeneous audience. This reformulation was informed by research on how students develop understanding of basic chemistry concepts (Ben-Zvi, Eylon, & Silberstein, 1986a, 1986b, 1987; Eylon, Ben-Zvi, & Silberstein, 1987). A new curriculum, *Chemistry—A Challenge* (1982), that built on students' ideas emerged from this process. Details on three cycles of the reformulation clarify the approach.

***Diagnosing Student Ideas About Atoms.*** Since students need to understand "atoms" starting with the first lesson in high school chemistry, one question is, What picture of the atom do they have in mind? The ancient view of atoms is manifested, for example, in the words of the Greek philosopher Anaxagoras: "for as gold is made up from gold dust, so all the world is an aggregation of minute bodies, the parts of which are like the whole" (Sambursky, 1975). This is the most intuitive view of the atom. In this view, each piece of a substance, no matter how small, has all the properties of the substance.

Studies of students who completed *Chemistry for High School* (1972) show that many hold this intuitive model of the Greeks: They do not distinguish an atom from an aggregate of atoms, and they assume that each atom has the properties of the aggregate. In addition, one third of the students represented the structure of a molecule of a compound differently from experts. The most prevalent representation of the molecule $N_2O_4$, for example, was two connected or disconnected fragments—one denoting $N_2$ and the other $O_4$. Most represented the gas $O_3$ as three disconnected oxygen atoms. Many students had the intuition that molecules changed when gases were

moved to containers with larger volumes. Based on the view that the chemical unit is an atom, students concluded that increasing the available volume changes the distance between the atoms within the molecules rather than the distance between the molecules.

Furthermore, many aspects of the traditional chemistry curriculum reinforce these intuitive views. Chemical models in textbooks often depict single units. For example, the representation of a chemical reaction, such as the synthesis of HCl, includes one molecule of hydrogen, one molecule of chlorine, and two molecules of hydrogen chloride. Thus, chemical equations are often interpreted as representing single units and not moles of units. Based on these results, versions of the curriculum designed to help students gain a more robust view of the atomic model were designed and evaluated.

***Adding Historical Views of the Atomic Model.*** To respond to student ideas about atoms, the first version of a new program, *Chemistry—A Challenge* (1982), described the historical views of atoms. It illustrated how and why scientists developed new models of the atom.

For example, students studied the Daltonian atom, a view put forth in the 19th century. The curriculum explained that the Daltonian view of the atom could account for how compounds were formed but did not explain some properties of compounds such as electrical conductivity. Students then reviewed the evidence that led scientists to revise their views of the atom. Finally they were introduced to the current model, learning that it is so abstract it can be expressed only by a complicated mathematical equation. Thus, students were introduced to a repertoire of models of the atom.

This version of the curriculum was taught to 540 students in 18 10th-grade classes in five high schools. A comparison group of 538 students (17 classes in five high schools) studied the traditional textbook *Chemistry for High School*. The results showed that about 32 percent of the students using the revised curriculum gained a robust understanding of the atom, compared to 7 percent in the comparison group.

Analysis of student views revealed that intuitions about single atoms still differed from those of experts. The text still reinforced student views of the atom by illustrating ideas using single atoms or molecules. As a result, students applied properties such as electrical conductivity to single atoms rather than to the collective behavior of an aggregate of atoms or molecules. Furthermore, use of the expert model on simple tasks did not guarantee use of this model on complex tasks (Eylon et al., 1987). The demands of the task often overloaded students' working memory so that they abandoned their integrated model and reverted to a simple, less comprehensive model. In response to these findings, the curriculum was further reformulated to include more comprehensive examples.

***Expanding Examples of the Atomic Model to Multiple Particles.*** To respond to student intuitions, the next version of the curriculum took the historical perspective but included examples with many particles rather than single particles. When the authors believed that the representation of many particles might obscure the point under discussion, the new version clarified why only one set of particles was represented. Students compared a representation of a single molecule to representations of many molecules. These decisions were motivated by research suggesting that experience connecting ideas results in "chunking" those ideas into manageable units and reducing memory load (e.g., Simon, 1974).

To evaluate students' understanding of chemical structure resulting from the revised curriculum, another comparative study was carried out. Participants were 1,078 students (average age, 15 years) from 10 high schools all over Israel (35 classes). About half studied the established course, *Chemistry for High School*. The rest studied the new course, *Chemistry—A Challenge*. Students were tested at the beginning of the academic year (pretest), in the middle (midtest), and at the end (posttest).

At both the midtest and the posttest the new curriculum was more effective than the established curriculum in teaching a robust view of the atom. Furthermore, the new curriculum benefited those with average or low pretest scores the most. Students who earned high pretest scores performed similarly in both programs.

Nevertheless, many students lacked integrated understanding. The third version of the curriculum addressed knowledge integration. Here there are some parallels between chemistry curriculum reform and the CLP reforms intended to foster knowledge integration.

*Teaching for Knowledge Integration.* Informal comparisons of teaching practices suggested that classes emphasizing knowledge integration achieved better performance. Thus, a third version of the new curriculum included a systematic effort to increase the opportunity to integrate knowledge by offering integration aids. The curriculum was augmented with: (a) compact summaries with hierarchical maps for each topic, (b) exercises requiring students to construct and use maps, (c) explicit links between phenomenological and explanatory models (e.g., Eylon & Linn, 1994), and (d) an emphasis on relationships between the maps for each topic.

Eylon, Ben-Zvi, and Silberstein (1988) investigated the effect of these enhancements to the curriculum. In this study, the comparison group studied interesting historical accounts of the topics while the integration group used the enhancements. Seven teachers, each teaching two 10th-grade classes, participated. Teachers each taught one class with the knowledge integration enhancements (complete data for 168 students) and one class with the historical accounts (complete data for 195 students). All classes took the same tests. Tests given immediately after the course examined both the understanding of relationships (diagnostic items, summary items) and more standard achievement. A delayed achievement test was given a few months later.

To evaluate integrated understanding, researchers asked students to summarize the important ideas in the program. There was a considerable difference between the groups in amount, content, and structure of the summaries. More than 50 percent of the comparison group wrote a list of chapter titles or a list of concept names, versus 25 percent of the knowledge integration group. The knowledge integration group was significantly more likely to (a) recall more concepts, (b) write sentences linking at least two concepts, and (c) mention more concepts in each sentence. About 39 percent of the students in the integration group provided summaries with an underlying hierarchical structure, versus about 12 percent of the compari-

son group. Students in the integration group referred more frequently to explanatory models and wrote more sentences relating phenomenological and explanatory models (70 percent vs. 45 percent). The use of models in answering the diagnostic items was also significantly greater in the integration group than in the comparison group (40 percent vs. 15 percent). There was also a statistically significant difference on standard achievement tests (immediate and delayed).

This evaluation shows the importance of instruction that fosters knowledge organization. First, the curriculum developers revised the course goals to include an emphasis on a repertoire of historical views of the atom. Second, the developers specifically designed activities to foster knowledge integration. They found that when students actively master an organization of the subject matter, they can both solve standard problems and apply the concepts to nonstandard problems. These reforms suggest that students' disposition to integrate science knowledge benefits where instruction provides appropriate aids to integration.

The revisions to the chemistry curriculum illustrate the advantages of (a) research and curriculum refinement to respond to students' intuitions and (b) specific solutions to knowledge integration problems targeted to the discipline. The cumulative improvement in students' understanding of the atomic theory in this case study illustrates the advantages of combining research on disposition to learn with studies of the nature of instruction to improve science learning.

## HISTORICAL PERIODS: SEPARATION, INTEGRATION, AND PARTNERSHIP

We have introduced three historical periods in science education based on the degree of interaction between groups concerned with science education. In this section we characterize the periods, show how Dewey anticipated the path from separation to partnership, and introduce three themes from Dewey's work.

The three historical periods are the *separation period* (from about 1870 to 1950), the *interaction period* (from about 1950 to 1975), and the *partnership period* (from about 1975 to the present). In the separation period, responsibility for science education was divided: Natural scientists designed curriculum materials, science instructors determined how to teach science, psychologists sought general principles of learning, and researchers in science education described the outcomes. During the interaction period, some of these groups joined forces. For example, the leaders of the science curriculum reform movement (natural scientists) enlisted science instructors to test materials in classrooms and science education researchers to conduct evaluations. Evaluators used psychological constructs to explain outcomes. Science educators led summer workshops to introduce science instructors to the new materials. During the partnership period, collaborations among experts from several perspectives, including experts in computer technology, have emerged. These groups of experts often work in a context of mutual respect.

### From Separation to Partnership: Dewey's Perspective

The path from separation to partnership in science education was anticipated by Dewey, whose influence is evident in many science education projects today. To anchor our discussion of the historical shifts and convergences in views about disposition and opportunity to learn, we highlight Dewey's views, linking them to the case studies discussed above. In his presidential address to the American Psychological Association (Dewey, 1901) and in *The Sources of a Science of Education* (1929), Dewey analyzed the process of educational reform and warned of difficulties that were likely to arise, given the diverse groups concerned about education. Three themes emerged.

First, Dewey called for a "linking science" of instruction that would combine insights from psychology and educational practice. He compared this linking science of instruction to the disciplines of medicine and engineering. In medicine and engineering, researchers develop a systematic understanding of disease and design by drawing on insights from biology and physics. In the anticipated linking science Dewey envisioned, researchers would develop a systematic understanding of instruction by drawing on research and experience in a variety of disciplines, including psychology.

Because little systematic information was available, Dewey concluded that "intuitive" theories of instruction based on synthesis of experience would be the starting point for this linking science. Dewey's view of intuition is consistent with the use of the term in the CLP case study. There we defined intuitive views as based on the integration of observations and examples. Dewey suggested that improved understanding of instruction would result from systematic analysis of educational practice. New methods of research would be needed for these studies. Dewey laid out the progression of understanding in education in a way that is still relevant today.

Dewey argued that models of instruction must be inferred from "*analysis* of what the gifted teacher does intuitively" (Dewey, 1929, pp. 10–11). Dewey identified a number of dangers that apply today as much as they did at the turn of the century. He warned against transforming isolated scientific findings into "*rules* of action" that would give "unquestionable authenticity and authority to a specific procedure to be carried out in the school room" (p. 15). He pointed out that using the techniques of more established sciences is not sufficient to confer generality on isolated educational investigations. He urged educators to analyze educational practice to find abstractions that would *link* phenomena (p. 20) together, forming a relatively coherent system. This process of trial of innovations in classrooms and refinement of instruction characterizes the CLP approach. Dewey argued that developing a linking science would take time and require reflection and synthesis, but would eventually yield principles and laws.

Second, Dewey called for contributions from other disciplines to education. Dewey analyzed the relationship between education and other disciplines such as biology, psychology, and sociology and called for intellectual partnerships among experts in education and experts in related disciplines. He pointed out the need for contributions from many disciplines, yet warned against attempts "to extract from psychology and sociology definite solutions which it is beyond their present power to give" (p. 42). He also warned against developing instructional theories without the active participation of those directly involved in teaching. He noted that precollege instructors were often viewed by natural scientists as "channels of reception and transmission" (p. 47). He lamented that "[t]he

human desire to be an 'authority' and to control the activities of others does not, alas, disappear when a man becomes a scientist" (p. 47). Finally, he pointed out that many who interact with educators fail to recognize the discipline of education and therefore fail to acknowledge the existence of research on instruction. Thus, Dewey called for multidisciplinary projects and research methods suited to these collaborations.

Third, Dewey identified the need for broad, comprehensive goals of education. As a source of ideas or hypotheses about the goals of education, Dewey (a philosopher by training) emphasized the role of philosophy. He identified two advantages to placing hypothetical ideas in the discipline of philosophy. First, philosophers typically focus broadly on the role of education in society. As Dewey argued, "When one begins to extend the range, the scope, of thought to consider obscure collateral consequences that show themselves in a more extensive time-span or in reference to an enduring development, then one begins to philosophize whether the process is given that name or not" (Dewey, 1929, p. 57). Second, philosophical ideas are informed speculations, not established laws. These ideas guide synthesis of experience and suggest innovations to be tested, thus ensuring a place for insights from educational practice.

These themes put forth in 1900 foreshadowed subsequent instructional perspectives. For example, in calling for partnerships Dewey warned about the danger of separating the means of education from the ends and specifically cautioned against separating "psychology" from "subject matter," as follows: "We want a method that will select subject-matter that aids psychological development, and we want a subject-matter that will secure the use of methods psychologically correct" (Dewey, 1929, p. 61). The current focus on developing expertise in science topics reflects this view (e.g., L. B. Resnick, 1987). Dewey also said, "We cannot begin by dividing the field between the psychology of individual activity and growth and studies of subject matters that are socially desirable, and then expect that at the end in practical operation the two things will balance each other" (Dewey, 1901; Dewey, 1929, p. 61). He illustrated this point by describing stimulus-response psychology, arguing that the stimulus-response approach leads to neglect of the longitudinal span of development, not to mention the broader system of human behavior.

For science education, Dewey's themes have some specific entailments. First, whereas Dewey was primarily concerned about struggles for authority between educators and psychologists in setting the educational agenda, in science, the natural scientists often dominated both educators and psychologists in establishing the agenda. Furthermore, the methods of natural science were especially compelling to natural scientists, and, as a result, many discounted or ignored insights from educational practice, either because they appeared mundane or because they lacked statistical power. Second, whereas Dewey focused on broad versus narrow goals and took as examples reading and mathematics, in science the distinction between the goal of preparing citizens and the goal of preparing scientists was also an issue in goal setting.

In light of Dewey's observations, it is interesting to note that the knowledge integration required for researchers seeking a theory of instruction for science education resembles the conceptual change required for students in the CLP project to make sense of science. A repertoire of intuitions from personal observations, evidence from a broad range of contexts, linking of ideas, and reflection on alternative explanations are key components of both processes.

In both cases, there is a tension between accepting authoritative accounts of phenomena and taking responsibility for forming a personal perspective. In both cases, the shift is from natural scientists as the focus of authority for science instruction and science knowledge to partnerships in which natural scientists, psychologists, cognitive scientists, precollege professionals, and other experts collaborate from a position of mutual respect. In both cases the shift is from seeking a single model for scientific concepts to identifying a repertoire of models, each useful for some problems.

In summary, three main themes emerge from Dewey's writing on instructional theory:

1. The need for a linking science arrived at by philosophical speculation combined with synthesis of promising ideas from educational practice, guided by research in related fields like psychology. Dewey expected this linking science to feature informed intuitions drawn from practice and refined as the result of empirical work. This refinement must draw on a repertoire of research methods, including investigations in educational settings and thoughtful reflection on educational experiences.
2. The importance of partnerships among experts in a broad range of disciplines, including at least education, psychology, sociology, and psychiatry. Partners must respect each other to ensure that diverse insights are integrated.
3. The centrality of broad goals for instruction that include both societal and individual outcomes. These goals should incorporate a perspective on learners as members of a community and include a sense of social responsibility.

These three themes will guide discussion of historical trends in subsequent sections. We preview these sections with brief discussions of (a) achieving a linking science, (b) negotiating partnerships, and (c) setting broad goals for science courses.

## Achieving a Linking Science

By the turn of the century, science education had started to emerge as a field in the United States. Science was a topic of the 3rd, 21st, and 31st yearbooks of the National Society for the Scientific Study of Education (NSSE) (Holmes, 1904; McMurry, 1904; Whipple, 1922, 1932). The earliest research on science education was summarized by Francis Curtis (1926). Organizations of science educators were formed starting in the 1930s.

Researchers in science education used the methods of natural science and experimental psychology to conduct comparisons of one teaching method to another. For example, they studied whether teacher demonstrations or student-conducted laboratory exercises were better for transmitting science knowledge. Following Thorndike's (1927) lead, they analyzed the vocabulary in science texts and found that it was complex and demanding.

During the interaction period, the focus was on the science learner. One goal of the reform was to attract more talented students to science. The reformers intuitively believed that students would choose science if they understood the excitement

of scientific discovery. Thus, the reformers sought to add *scientific inquiry skills* to the curriculum. By inquiry skills, they meant the methods used in science to design and interpret experiments.

This inquiry view resonated with the view of the learner that was described by Bruner (1960) at a conference on science education sponsored by the National Research Council. Bruner described the Piagetian view of the learner as developing logical reasoning skill and as benefiting from concrete scientific experiences at least until late adolescence. This made sense to many natural scientists, and guided thinking about the elementary curriculum and the secondary science laboratory.

During the partnership period, the emphasis was on the science instructor working with the student. Dewey's discussion of the social nature of learning foreshadowed the emphasis on social cognition. Dewey suggested that educational practice was ahead of theory in that "those engaged in the act of teaching know that the social tools are best acquired in a social context and for the sake of some social application" (Dewey, 1929, p. 72). This perspective was reinforced by Vygotsky (1978) and is a growing focus in science education research (e.g., Linn & Burbules, 1993; Newman, Griffin, & Cole, 1989; Palincsar, Anderson, & David, 1993; L. Resnick, 1981; J. P. Smith, diSessa, & Roschelle, 1994).

Research bringing together disposition and opportunity to learn emerged in the partnership period. Those studying disposition found that students often develop views of science knowledge and of themselves as science learners that dispose them to memorize rather than to integrate science knowledge, and to believe that science is a male domain. Those studying instruction sought to shape the student's disposition to learn science. One approach was to make science relevant to the lives of students. This required some changes in the course goals. Another approach was to emphasize *metacognition,* or reflection on one's own learning (R. T. White, 1988). Researchers analyzing the participation of women and minorities argued that science courses neglected the social nature of science learning and communicated that future scientists should come from the same sex and ethnic groups as scientists have come from in the past (e.g., Gilligan, 1982; E. F. Keller, 1985).

Researchers building on the evaluation studies of the interaction period have developed methods for studying science curriculum reforms in science classrooms, drawing on successful approaches in anthropology, sociology, and other disciplines. Multiple cycles of trial and refinement have proved beneficial, as illustrated in the case studies. In summary, the work in science education is forming the basis for what Dewey described as a "linking science."

*Negotiating Partnerships.* Science educators and psychologists had little in common during the separation period. While science educators sought to identify successful teaching practices and characterize which students would succeed in science, psychologists sought general laws for learning. Dewey (1901) identified this disconnection and warned educators against expecting too much from psychology.

The reforms of the 1950s and 1960s began with Jerrold Zacharias convening a group of leaders in natural science to address the science education "problem," just as they had addressed other scientific challenges (Goldstein, 1992). Eventually, the National Science Foundation (NSF) contributed $130 million to reforming the precollege curriculum and $565 million for teacher training (W. W. Welch, 1979). A stunning, diverse set of science materials was produced (Swartz, 1991).

The role of the precollege science instructor also shifted during the interaction period. Science instructors were involved in the reform projects to try the new materials and give feedback, yet their comments that materials were too difficult went unheeded. In addition, the reformers set out to transmit information about how to teach science to instructors, thus encroaching on the autonomy common in the separation period.

Researchers expanded studies to include information about the learner, such as developmental level, and introduced the use of correlational methods common in studies of individual differences, often in conjunction with two-group comparisons. Researchers analyzed science tasks to ascertain the information-processing demands on students.

In addition, science educators were included in the reform projects as evaluators. Often, evaluation was postponed until the end of the development process. In these cases, results were gathered too late to be used to improve the curriculum (W. W. Welch, 1979).

Nonetheless, these evaluation studies suggested the potential for involving science researchers earlier in the development process. Many groups reviewing the research base for science education recommended partnerships for reform in which science education researchers and specialists in the various scientific disciplines would work together in an atmosphere of mutual respect (M. Gardner et al., 1990; Greeno, 1983; Linn, 1987). These suggestions resonated with recommendations made more generally by Dewey (1901) in the separation period.

Calls for partnerships were heard by NSF and other foundations, and supported in grant programs. In addition, policymakers at the local, state, and national level began to call for science courses to meet the needs of all students, not just future scientists.

To design instruction that fosters expertise in science, researchers in the partnership period have welcomed precollege science instructors as partners, analyzed expert tutoring to identify successful practices, contrasted expert and novice reasoning about topics such as mechanics, and utilized trial and refinement in science classrooms to develop models of instruction. Apprenticeship (Collins et al., 1991), scaffolded knowledge integration (Linn, in press), and intelligent computer tutoring (J. R. Anderson, Boyle, & Reiser, 1985; J. H. Larkin, 1983) are among the approaches to instruction that emerged from these investigations.

*Setting Broad Goals for Science Courses.* Early work in science education centered on which science topics should be taught. The goal was to teach students the science used by experts, but there were questions about which topics to introduce before secondary school and about whether elementary students should memorize science information or do science projects. There was general agreement that science is difficult to learn.

Most high school courses and many courses for middle school were designed to prepare future scientists. Early texts for high school courses were written by natural scientists. Natural scientists generally held the intuition that students would absorb the science they were taught. It was assumed that students would enroll in science courses if they were interested and

would succeed if they had the necessary ability. Very few women or minority students persisted in science.

During the separation period, efforts to establish the content of the science curriculum did not converge. Many texts became disorganized as chapters were added to address scientific breakthroughs. Eventually, a series of commissions and groups concluded that courses either neglected modern science or treated it haphazardly, and called for reform (Science Manpower Project [Frederick L. Fitzpatrick: Director], 1959). At the same time, a shortage of trained scientists, growing interest in science education by natural scientists (Goldstein, 1992), the establishment of the NSF, and the perception that the United States was behind the Soviet Union in the race for space spurred a reform movement.

The audience for science courses shifted subtly from those who selected science to those who could succeed in science. Some reform projects sought to attract a broader group of students, including women.

The shift to a focus on inquiry skills was accompanied by a shift in the purpose of the science laboratory and in the view of science learning. The view of the learner as absorbing information was expanded to include potential developmental constraints. In response, guided discovery activities were added to science laboratories. At the same time, some curriculum reformers addressed information-processing constraints. The Thorndike word lists of the separation period initiated this approach to making science easier. Gagné's task analysis of science continued the trend (Commission on Science Education, 1964).

The focus during the partnership period has been on improving science instruction, especially by making science accessible to all students. Extensive evidence that precollege, college, and adult students have scientific notions that differ from those of scientific experts defined a challenge: As a result, researchers in science education have shifted their attention from general inquiry skills to a broader emphasis on the development of expertise in specific science topics and disciplines (Driver, 1983; Hestenes, 1992; National Commission on Excellence in Education, 1983; Pfundt & Duit, 1991; Schneps & Sadler, 1989).

Partnership projects clarified the origins of student intuitions about scientific phenonema and the mechanisms that might govern learning. Recall that the CLP project found that students had intuitions about metals based on the observation that metals feel colder than other materials in the same room. A. diSessa (1988) and others observed that students' models were often descriptive. Thus, students observed that "objects in motion come to rest" and "some surfaces slow objects down more than others." In addition, students typically have a repertoire of models for scientific events and invoke the one they find useful. Over time, students expand their repertoire of models and refine these methods for selecting among models. New goals for science courses in the partnership period included supporting this process of building a repertoire of models and refining methods for selecting among them.

## Charting the Contributions of Psychology: Disposition to Learn and the Nature of Instruction

We address contributions of psychology to science education by distinguishing disposition to learn and the nature of instruction and discussing these for each historical period. Disposition to learn refers to both the capability and the motivation to understand science. Historically, factors that have contributed to the disposition to learn science have included (a) the learner's general abilities and developmental accomplishments, (b) the learner's interests and inclination to participate in science, and (c) the mechanisms governing application of scientific ideas in problem solving.

The second broad category is the nature of instruction. We examine how instruction communicates scientific understanding. We purposely place the agent of instruction outside the learner. We employ the term "instruction" in its broadest sense. We analyze (a) the goals of instruction found in the science curriculum and (b) the activities used to achieve these goals.

Under the most favorable conditions, the student is disposed to learn, and instruction makes it easy to achieve the goal of learning. College-bound students from families that value education and who attend safe schools with well-prepared teachers are often in this situation. In the worst case, the student has no inclination to learn and no access to instruction. Inner city students whose primary concern is survival, whose schools are dangerous, and whose teachers lack the materials for teaching science are often in this situation. We will illustrate that, between these extremes, there are conditions in which an excellent disposition to learn can overcome poor instruction and in which excellent instruction can motivate students with little disposition to learn. We will stress the importance of both disposition and instruction in the ultimate success of science courses. Although we distinguish instruction from disposition and treat these conditions somewhat separately, they are compensatory. A high level of disposition to learn can make up for limited instructional opportunities, and vice versa.

In the following two main sections we discuss historical trends in disposition to learn science and in the nature of instruction. We address shifts and convergences in the separation, interaction, and partnership periods. We conclude each main section by returning to the themes of Dewey.

## DISPOSITION TO LEARN SCIENCE

What factors dispose individuals to learn science? In what sense are these factors unique to science? How do science educators form and refine ideas about disposition to learn?

To answer these questions, we examine disposition to learn in the separation, interaction, and partnership periods. For each period we describe the perspectives of science educators, how their views shift, and how disparate views eventually start to converge.

In each section, we discuss three aspects of the disposition to learn science: (a) the role of a student's ability and developmental level, (b) the factors governing inclination and motivation to participate in science courses and careers, and (c) the mechanisms posited to guide the application of scientific ideas in problem solving.

We examine how ability and developmental accomplishments contribute to science learning. Research on the role of ability has shifted from investigation of a single, general ability to studies of a repertoire of abilities, including practical and creative abilities. Research on development has shifted from

study of general learning readiness to analysis of the development of logical reasoning abilities, scientific concepts, and integrated understanding, as illustrated in the case studies.

Views of inclination and motivation to participate in science courses and careers need to account for the predominance of white males in these endeavors. The belief that students would participate if they had an inherent interest in science has shifted to the perspective that interest in science is influenced by a broad range of social factors, including the normative perceptions of the society in which one lives. Consequently, researchers and educators have broadened their focus to take into account students' interests in specific scientific activities and fields as well as the role that factors such as anxiety, confidence, and societal perceptions play in one's motivation to participate in science courses and careers.

Perspectives on how students apply scientific information and ideas to solve problems derive from two perspectives: One originates in psychology and focuses on transfer, the other originates in science education and focuses on instruction. Through small, controlled investigations, psychologists concerned with problem solving have progressively refined their ideas about how concepts are applied to new problems. At the same time, those studying science education have developed and refined intuitions about how instructional practice can improve problem solving. Consistent with the observations of Dewey discussed earlier, these intuitions incorporate experience in science classrooms and guide the design of educational programs. By the partnership period, those concerned with learning to solve problems and those concerned with instruction in problem solving joined forces. Of course, each perspective also influenced the other during earlier periods.

### Disposition in the Separation Period

The predominant belief during the separation period was that students would enroll in science courses if they were interested in science and would succeed if they had the necessary ability. By 1950, about 5 percent of all high school students were learning physics, and most students took courses in general science (Salinger, 1991). This belief about students applied in all three of the areas we address: ability and development, motivation and inclination, and application and problem solving.

***Ability and Development in the Separation Period.*** In the separation period, most researchers believed that students' general ability disposed to their success in science. This view justified instructional practices designed for students who absorbed scientific information and was reflected in research studies that identified the topics in science that were most difficult for students (Curtis, 1926). As a result, precollege teachers often chose to postpone difficult topics, assuming that they would be taught in college courses to the students who persisted in science. An alternative perspective, often taken by natural scientists developing materials for science courses, was that students should be exposed to the most difficult topics and would acquire understanding based on their ability.

Based on the belief that only the most able would succeed in science, designers of elective science courses targeted this audience. The intuition that only a portion of the students would have the ability necessary to learn the material in advanced courses justified the practice of tracking students in science by self-selection. Indeed, large numbers of research investigations revealed that students of higher ability were more likely to succeed in advanced science courses (Curtis, 1926, 1931). These courses were chosen by males far more than females (Whipple, 1932). The preponderance of males in these classes was also attributed to science being of greater interest to males.

This belief about ability was reflected in educators' confidence in using achievement and ability tests to determine who could succeed in science. For example, the 21st yearbook of the NSSE (Whipple, 1922, p. 210) reported that educators had greater confidence in test scores than in school grades. This confidence reflected an intuition that the test scores were more objective. Indeed, tests often involved multiple-choice questions, whereas school grades were generally assigned based on performance in laboratories, written essays, teacher-designed tests, and class recitations.

Confidence in achievement test scores may have stemmed in part from evidence that female students earned higher grades in science courses, while males earned higher test scores (Whipple, 1932). The higher test scores earned by males were consistent with the greater participation of males in science courses and careers and with the intuition that science was a male rather than a female domain. Reliance on test scores rather than school grades was consistent with the views of psychologists that test scores were more indicative of accomplishments than were school grades—again, due to the objectivity of test scores. For example, Tyler in 1938 called achievement tests a "scientific breakthrough" (Tyler, 1938, p. 342) and applauded researchers, including science education researchers, for using achievement tests to evaluate educational innovations.

We note that male superiority on measures of intellectual ability was not seen as a threat to the objectivity of these measures, but female superiority led to test revisions. Thus, early mental tests, designed to establish retardation (Binet, 1908; Binet & Simon, 1916; Yerkes, 1921), yielded the opposite result of the results for achievement tests in science. On the Binet test, when girls outperformed boys, the tests were revised to equalize performance (Maccoby & Jacklin, 1974). In contrast, the Thorndike intelligence examination that was frequently used in science education was known to be biased against women. Thorndike himself pointed out that the test "perhaps slightly penalizes girls in comparison with boys, having been designed primarily for the latter" (quoted in Gambrill, 1922, p. 232). In his study, Gambrill noted that standards may be set five points lower for girls than for boys (p. 232). In spite of identifying potential bias in this achievement test, Gambrill argued that the test provided an objective basis for sectioning students according to their intellectual ability (p. 237). The debate concerning which information is objective, especially in the context of the performance of males and females, has continued up to the present day (Linn, 1992b).

The debate about the objectivity of standardized tests is consistent with Dewey's warnings about relying on "scientific" information. In science education, achievement and intellectual ability tests were used to assign students to courses and assess educational innovations, even when they were not demonstrated to be valid. Indeed, researchers often recommended against new curricular innovations because they were less suc-

cessful than traditional methods in influencing achievement test performance. Later, researchers recognized the importance of matching the outcome measure to the course goals (e.g., Cronbach, 1982).

Intuitions about how students develop intellectual abilities shifted during the separation period. Advocates of the nature study curriculum embraced the developmental perspective put forth by G. Stanley Hall, called the saltatory theory. This perspective indicated that mental abilities appear in serial order and develop one after another as the child matures (Whipple, 1932). Since memory and observation are the first mental traits to appear, it is appropriate to design instruction matched to these developmental accomplishments. The nature study curriculum emphasized memorization and observation (Underhill, 1941). Later in this period, G. Stanley Hall's theory was rejected and development was minimized in curriculum planning (Freeman, 1938; Whipple, 1932). A new, more complex curriculum was introduced. We will return to this topic in discussing the nature of instruction in the separation period.

***Motivation and Inclination in the Separation Period.*** Views of motivation and inclination to participate in science courses and careers developed in a context in which most scientific advances were the work of men and most scientists were male. The intuitions characteristic of the separation period were consistent with the view that individuals interested in participating in a scientific field were likely to resemble those who are already members of the community. Furthermore, these expectations influenced students selecting elective science courses. Many female students reported being told they could not enroll in science courses (Solomon, 1985).

Research studies supported the view that individuals entering science courses and careers would resemble those who already followed such careers. Many concluded that males and females had different backgrounds and goals and should be taught differently. For example, in 1924 Herriott concluded that "physics as a whole enters to the greatest extent into the life of boys, second into the life of men, third into the life of girls, and least into the life of women" (Curtis, 1926, p. 299; Herriott, 1924).

During the wars, this pattern of participation changed. Women were pressed into service in scientific careers and were admitted to science courses in larger numbers. For example, in 1949 women comprised 12 percent of medical school graduates, whereas in 1955 they comprised 5 percent (Solomon, 1985). At war's end, societal pressures for women to marry and take full responsibility for the success of their children and their husbands thwarted their participation in scientific training. In addition, women were often faced with a very difficult choice between having a career or having a family. Even traditional female jobs such as school teaching were open only to single women. And more prestigious jobs were dominated by men who did not welcome women (Solomon, 1985). Furthermore, women were most accepted in fields traditionally assumed to be aligned with their interests, including botany, home economics, and child development. And there was fear that women might displace talented men who needed education more (Rossiter, 1982; Solomon, 1985). Nevertheless, a small group of reformers came to believe that women and minorities failed to participate in science because courses were designed for white males and because leaders preferred white males when selecting students and employees (Solomon, 1985). This situation set the stage for the examination of issues of anxiety and confidence that predominated in the next period.

Work by psychologists on intrinsic motivation was consistent with the intuitions of science educators concerning motivation to participate in science (Thurstone & Chave, 1929). Initially, intrinsic motivation was based primarily on basic biological needs like hunger. Later, however, the drive states that might motivate learning were expanded to include such aspects of science as problem solving. Thus, the intuition that those who chose to participate in science did so because they were motivated to engage in scientific problem solving was consistent with the view that individuals should be left to their own inclinations in determining whether to select science courses.

The psychologists' refinement of intrinsic motivation was consistent with the efforts of scientists to increase the emphasis on problem solving in the science curriculum. Nevertheless, there was some confusion concerning the nature of a problem. Underhill (1941) noted that textbooks featured such problems as "study the life history of a frog" (p. 254).

In summary, the greater participation of males in science courses and careers was consistent with intuitions concerning who was motivated to participate in science. And this motivation was tied to the intrinsic nature of scientific problem solving. Conflicting evidence concerning participation came when women gained opportunities during the world wars, setting the stage for the next period.

*Mechanisms for Reasoning and Problem Solving in the Separation Period.* Mechanisms governing the application of scientific ideas to problems were conceptualized from two perspectives during the separation period. On the one hand, science educators following the observations of Dewey sought to generalize and synthesize promising classroom practices for teaching problem solving. On the other hand, psychologists concerned with learning sought to distinguish the elements of problem solving and describe conditions for problem solving.

Science educators observed that solving problems is difficult and that only those with the necessary ability and motivation would succeed. The role of development in problem solving was unresolved during this period. Some believed that students were ready to learn certain concepts only in the middle school years, while others believed such learning was possible in elementary school.

The difficulties of problem solving were eloquently described by a natural scientist serving as a school principal in 1905: "I studied and taught both chemistry and physics for years without ever asking whether the facts in these sciences showed the same adaptation of means to ends that is exhibited by organic nature. I did not learn that if water in its various forms had merely the average capacity for absorbing heat without change of temperature, the best part of the earth would be a barren wilderness" (Beggs, 1905, p. 101). Beggs went on to argue that "science itself is nothing more" than the process of organizing information. This intuition about knowledge organization is central to thinking about application of scientific ideas. For example, in 1932 the science education reformers argued that "[t]hings that belong together should be brought together" (Whipple, 1932, p. 57).

During the separation period, mechanisms governing the application of scientific ideas to problems emphasized information about scientific phenomena rather than the logical thinking skills involved in problem solving. This perspective stems in part from the belief that general ability is inherent and therefore not amenable to instruction, and in part from the belief that, if it is possible to influence general logical reasoning, such influences will arise in courses focused on formal logic or Euclidean geometry, not in science courses. This separation of scientific reasoning skills and knowledge about scientific phenomena in problem solving persisted into the interaction period.

The most common technique for guiding problem solving was to select related topics from science and to sequence them based on instructional experience. For example, Millikan and Gale (1906), in a textbook entitled *A Laboratory Course in Physics for Secondary Schools,* sought "a systematic, carefully chosen, and well-tested *course* as distinct from an encyclopedic array of homogeneous facts" (Millikan & Gale, 1927, p. v).

Other science educators approached the challenge of helping students organize scientific information for problem solving by identifying the "big ideas" in science and teaching these ideas. Educators believed that identifying generalizations and presenting them would result in learning, consistent with the general view during the separation period that students learn what they are told. A major focus then, as is still apparent in many standard-setting efforts today, was to select the 20 "big ideas" in science and assume that students would learn to use them to solve problems. For example, starting with the principle that "energy for vital and physical processes comes from the sun," the educators redesigning the curriculum in 1932 generated a set of 20 ideas to guide textbook design (Whipple, 1932, p. 49). The view that identifying the main scientific ideas and telling them to students is sufficient for problem solving is still held implicitly by many natural scientists today (Hazen & Trefil, 1991).

Research investigating the conjecture that students will learn the material that they are presented was disappointing. Research studies indicated that students learned only a portion of the material taught, and often connected the information in ways unanticipated by the instructors, or learned isolated pieces of science rather than gaining an ability to solve problems (Curtis, 1926, 1931, 1939). This research had only limited impact on science education practice, however, in part because the methods of investigation lacked power and validity (Watson, 1963).

Another approach to problem solving was promulgated by social philosophers, especially John Dewey, who seeded the progressive education movement (Cremin, 1964). They advocated placing the child at the center of the learning process and emphasized projects that helped students solve problems involving school and community. The progressive education movement embraced nature study because students could conduct their own investigations and observations in neighboring fields and woods. Cremin pointed out that Dewey recognized the difficulty of implementing a child-centered, project-based approach to instruction. In particular, teachers needed considerable subject matter knowledge in order to identify student activities and guide students in appropriate directions. These guiding and directing activities of teachers were key to the application of scientific ideas to problems but were not consistently implemented in schools following the progressive education perspective (Raizen, 1991a, 1991b). Nevertheless, the progressive education movement drew attention to the view of the learner as a participant in a social context, working cooperatively with other students to conduct scientific investigations. This movement emphasized a view of science education as serving all segments of society rather than providing scientific knowledge for an elite group.

Research conducted by psychologists during this same period was narrower and more controlled. Whereas science educators tended to study learning in classrooms, psychologists following the stimulus-response theory were generally studying simple tasks. At the turn of the century, Pavlov, investigating the relationship between stimuli and responses, succeeded in conditioning dogs to salivate at the sound of a bell (Pavlov, 1927). American psychologists, including Thorndike (1910), investigated the relationship between stimuli and responses by studying simple recall problems. For example, a study in 1934 (Bedell, 1934) differentiated recall and inference. Bedell concluded that ability to recall is different from the ability to infer (Bedell, 1934; Curtis, 1939, p. 71). Another study, conducted by Ralph Tyler (Curtis, 1939, p. 307; Tyler, 1933), examined relative rates of retention of information from a zoology course. Tyler reported that specific information was forgotten but the ability to apply information and interpret data persisted. Psychologists assumed that principles governing performance on such problems as shape recognition, nonsense syllable learning, or maze solving would generalize to performance on all problems (Hilgard, 1956). Toward the end of the period, psychologists had developed relatively good understanding of such factors as conditioning, fading, rewards, and punishments.

In general, research on problem solving had limited impact on science education practice. However, psychological studies of learning were consistent with some intuitions about science instruction. In those areas where instructional intuitions and psychological research overlapped, research had some influence. This was particularly apparent in the selection of words in science textbooks.

Thus, Thorndike's (1927) identification of word lists appropriate to specific age groups resulted in analysis of the words introduced in typical science courses, and led to a call for curriculum designers to limit the number of words introduced in the text. For example, Powers (Curtis, 1931, p. 348; Powers, 1925) reported that about one word in 20 in the textbooks of the time was not on Thorndike's list of the 10,000 most common words. Powers also reported that over half of the uncommon words appeared only once. This led Powers to conclude that the books treated science problems superficially, introducing mainly vocabulary. Efforts to reduce the breadth and complexity of science vocabulary were initiated during this period and are still common in textbook analysis today.

We can draw three lessons from the study of mechanisms governing application of scientific ideas and problem solving during the separation period: First, synthesizing mechanisms from effective instructional practice offers promise; second, research on learning can assist (or confuse) science educators in designing materials that communicate to students; and third, since science learning, like all learning, takes place in a social context, understanding the contribution of the social context to scientific outcomes can help students understand how scientific ideas are acquired and applied. During the separation period, these themes emerged but were often ignored.

***Summary of Shifts and Convergences During the Separation Period.*** During the separation period, intuitions about disposition to learn science emphasized the student's inherent characteristics, including ability and development. Conceptualization of the limitations of development on science understanding changed, motivated by the desire of science educators to increase the amount of science material introduced in the elementary years.

Motivation and inclination to learn science were viewed as inherent characteristics. Expectations concerning who would participate were consistent with existing patterns of participation. Since most scientists were males from the majority culture, it was expected that future scientists would have similar backgrounds. This perspective shifted somewhat as a result of increased participation of women in science during the world wars.

Psychologists refined intuitions about disposition to learn in general, while science educators refined intuitions about disposition to learn science. Contact beween learning and instruction was infrequent, and research findings in general had little impact on science education practice. The progressive education movement introduced the notion that science learning occurred in a social context and raised issues that would demand more and more attention as the audience for science courses expanded.

## Disposition in the Interaction Period

During the interaction period researchers expanded and refined the factors that contribute to the disposition to learn science. They showed that ability involves many different components, such as verbal, mathematical, and spatial skills. Similarly, they broke development into two components: logical reasoning and understanding of science concepts. In addition, they showed that inclination and motivation to participate in science courses and careers depends on a broad range of expectations, aptitudes, and interests. Also, they explored the application of scientific ideas arid problem solving in terms of ability, development, and motivation. Better understanding of the aspects influencing disposition to learn science accompanied a broadening of the audience for science courses and a reform of the science curriculum led by natural scientists, drawing on the work of the psychologist Jerome Bruner and others.

***Ability and Development in the Interaction Period.*** During the interaction period, science educators examined the abilities of students more carefully and developed intuitions about those who succeeded and those who were less successful in science courses. In an effort to serve a broader audience, researchers explored the characteristics of students who did not succeed in traditional courses.

For example, the distinction between verbal ability and mathematical ability guided the design of some of the materials developed during this period. Harvard Project Physics (HPP) emphasized connections between science and the humanities in an effort to draw on verbal abilities, which were thought to be more developed in students who were underrepresented in science. In particular, the connections of scientific discoveries to advances in literature and art were included in the curriculum to attract women to science and to make science more appealing to students who did not participate in traditional courses.

In addition, researchers reanalyzed the distinction between scientific reasoning and knowledge of scientific phenomena that had already been recognized during the separation period, incorporating developmental theories to clarify scientific reasoning. Natural scientists reforming the curriculum emphasized the scientific reasoning skills in their field, and, inspired by the developmental theories popularized by Bruner (1960), distinguished between inquiry skills and discipline-specific information. They assumed that inquiry skills cut across all scientific disciplines, whereas students need to acquire specific information within a given discipline.

This perception of ability as being multifaceted is congruent with the work of educational psychologists of the period (see also chapter 8). Thus, Cattell (1963) distinguished between fluid ability and crystallized ability, defining fluid ability as the ability to reason abstractly (as measured by such tasks as Raven's progressive matrices) and crystallized ability as the ability to store and recall pieces of information (as measured by such tasks as vocabulary tests or knowledge tests). The ability to learn, store, and retrieve science knowledge can be seen as a specialized aspect of crystallized ability. Some psychologists went even further to distinguish verbal ability, quantitative ability, and spatial ability, as well as up to 120 different abilities (Guilford & Hoepfner, 1971).

These perspectives on the decomposition of general ability allowed the exploration of several relationships between science learning and ability. For example, one conjecture was that the participation of women in science might be reflected in differential patterns of ability between men and women. Thus, researchers studied whether the underrepresentation of women in science was explained by skill in verbal ability and interest in science topics.

Research on the development on scientific reasoning was spurred by a conference convened by the National Academy of Sciences at Woods Hole in 1959 and chaired by Jerome Bruner of Harvard. The book that emerged from this conference, titled *The Process of Education* (Bruner, 1960), refocused thinking about intellectual development (see also Shulman & Tamir, 1973). In this book Bruner asserted, "We begin with a hypothesis that any subject can be taught effectively in some intellectually honest form to any child at any stage of development. It is a bold hypothesis and an essential one in thinking about the nature of the curriculum. No evidence exists to contradict it; considerable evidence is being amassed that supports it" (Bruner, 1960, p. 33). Bruner went on to describe Piagetian developmental theory and to interpret understanding of intellectual development as an active process involving exploration and discovery. To teach science responsibly to students at any age, he argued, an important component is to actively engage them in investigating scientific phenomena.

The perspective on Piagetian developmental theory emphasized in the Woods Hole Conference stressed the development of logical reasoning and the importance of concrete exploration of scientific phenomena. Piagetian theory (Inhelder & Piaget, 1958; Piaget, 1972a) described how the logical reasoning structures of the child changed with age. Piaget described elementary

school children as capable of organizing observations and experiences, but not of thinking abstractly about possibilities and formal mathematical relationships. The investigations reported by Inhelder and Piaget (1958) illustrated the nature of concrete reasoning and provided specific examples of how students approach an assortment of scientific tasks. Inhelder and Piaget studied tasks such as predicting the projection of shadows at different distances from the light source, explaining the operation of a balance beam, investigating the variables influencing the flexibility of rods, and investigating the operation of the pendulum. The results demonstrated that students had much more difficulty explaining scientific events than many had expected. Most adolescents based conclusions on faulty data and were unable to design experiments that led to consistent and scientifically defensible conclusions. In addition, students displayed specific intuitions about scientific phenomena that were contrary to observation. For example, students predicted that the weight of the bob would influence the frequency of the pendulum and maintained this belief even after seeing experimental evidence contradicting their assertions.

Piaget's theory postulated that elementary-school-aged students would need concrete experiences in order to gain understanding of scientific phenomena. In addition, Piaget argued that the development of logical reasoning strategies was constrained by a biological process, but fostered by experience in investigating the natural world. Furthermore, Piaget suggested that the experience that students needed was general: students' interactions with the world would foster the development of general logical reasoning strategies, which would then allow students to explore new scientific phenomena systematically and, therefore, make inferences about those phenomena. Science materials were designed based on this developmental perspective. Essentially, these materials engaged students in the concrete investigation of scientific phenomena, with the objective of fostering the development of logical reasoning skills (Karplus, 1975).

This developmental perspective reinforced some of natural scientists' intuitions about inquiry skills. If students develop logical reasoning skills from general interactions with scientific phenomena, then opportunities to discover information about scientific systems should foster the development of inquiry skills. As a result of these beliefs, guided discovery activities were added to the secondary curriculum. Both the intuitions of natural scientists concerning the value of discovery learning experiences and the developmental justifications for these experiences contributed to this decision. Scientists were interested in including discovery activities in the curriculum to motivate students to participate in science as well as to foster scientific understanding.

The Piagetian studies of scientific reasoning raised interest in student ideas about specific scientific tasks as well. As mentioned, researchers noted that students' understanding of phenomena such as the operation of the pendulum was guided not only by their observations of the natural world, but also by their intuitions. These specific ideas about scientific phenomena were labeled "misconceptions" or alternative frameworks (Driver, 1973; Driver & Easley, 1978). This work began a series of investigations chronicling the kinds of specific ideas that students develop about scientific phenomena (Eylon & Linn, 1988).

Efforts to understand the development of scientific ideas

spurred research on scientific reasoning. Researchers designed tests to measure scientific understanding (Lawson, 1985; Shayer, Adey, & Wylam, 1981). Interviews following the clinical method of Piaget (1929, 1972b) revealed alternative frameworks for a wide range of phenomena. Interviews of students reasoning about scientific phenomena set the stage for events that occurred during the partnership period as well. Looking closely at the ideas that students have about scientific phenomena provided useful insights into the relationship between ability and development, on the one hand, and science understanding, on the other.

These studies of the specific ideas students hold about scientific phenomena led some researchers to reexamine the relationship between logical reasoning and understanding of specific scientific events. The Piagetian view that logical reasoning guides the development of scientific understanding was distinguished from a view that understanding of scientific concepts guides logical reasoning. The "situated cognition" view becomes important in the partnership period, emphasizing the development of understanding of scientific concepts (J. S. Brown, Collins, & Duguid, 1989; L. Resnick, 1981).

***Motivation and Inclination in the Interaction Period.*** During the interaction period, there was an increase in the participation of women in science but very little change in the participation of other underrepresented groups in science (National Science Board, 1990; National Science Foundation, 1990). As noted in the separation period discussions, the decision to participate in a scientific career is more difficult for women than men, since women generally have to decide between family and career. Such a decision is likely to increase anxiety about science participation. In addition, the normative view that women are less able to succeed in science may have the accompanying consequence of threatening the confidence of women in scientific activities. Indeed, examination of advertisements and movies common during the interaction period revealed that, in general, women's attempts to engage in scientific activities were often ridiculed and rarely viewed seriously.

The intuition that males are more likely than females to succeed in science is consistent with evidence gathered by psychologists that women are more anxious and less confident about science than men (e.g., Ausubel, 1963). Observations in science classes confirmed the conjecture that women participated less in discussions and activities but earned grades equivalent to or higher than those of men (Shulman & Tamir, 1973).

In summary, beliefs that males had succeeded in science in the past and would continue to do so were prevalent during the interaction period. Those beliefs led researchers to search for abilities that might explain differential participation, and also for aspects of interest and inclination to participate in science that might explain participation patterns. At the same time, a small but growing group of women worked to change the conditions of underrepresentation of women in science, disparate salaries between women and men in science careers, and the difficulties of admission to advanced programs in science for women compared to men (Rossiter, 1982; Solomon, 1985).

***Mechanisms for Reasoning and Problem Solving in the Interaction Period.*** During the interaction period, the intuitions about learning and instruction that were developed during the separation period were refined and extended. In particular, researchers shifted their focus to logical reasoning and information-processing capacity.

Intuitions concerning the role of ability in science achievement were explored using new methodological procedures referred to as aptitude–treatment interaction (ATI) studies (Cronbach & Snow, 1977). These studies examined, for example, whether modifying instruction in science to emphasize verbal skills rather than quantitative skills might improve the performance of students who had better verbal skills. The goal of these studies was to identify ideas that would guide the development of instructional procedures to maximize learning outcomes for all students. This approach was investigated by a number of research groups. No consistent findings emerged (Cronbach & Snow, 1977; Peterson & Wilkinson, 1984), and it became clear that the situation was extremely complex (Snow, 1980, 1989). For example, for some problems instruction matched to the learner's abilities leads to success, while in others instruction that helps learners improve weak skills leads to success (Ausubel & Fitzgerald, 1961; Wasik, 1971; W. W. Welch & Walberg, 1972).

A broad array of investigations explored the relationship between developmental accomplishments and scientific understanding. These investigations typically contrasted one form of science laboratory experience with another. Thus, the conjecture that discovery learning experiences could foster logical reasoning was examined by teaching one science course with a discovery laboratory and another with a more didactic laboratory, and examining gains in student understanding on measures of critical thinking or logical reasoning. The results of these studies were uniformly disappointing, in that students given discovery opportunities were not advantaged on measures of logical reasoning (D. I. Levine & Linn, 1977; Shulman & Tamir, 1973).

Studies revealing students' misconceptions or alternative frameworks for scientific phenomena motivated a series of studies that contradicted students' ideas to foster scientific problem solving. These studies were consistent with research conducted in Geneva, Switzerland, by followers of Piaget on cognitive conflict (Flavell, 1976); see also Linn (1986). These studies were similarly unsuccessful in modifying students' understanding of scientific phenomena and in motivating advances in scientific inquiry skills (Case, 1985; Lawson, 1985; Linn, 1986).

Another approach drew on beliefs about knowledge organization as a factor in problem solving. In the separation period, organization was often around scientific principles. In the interaction period, researchers considered a wide range of organizing ideas and principles for students, encouraged students to organize information autonomously, and tried to reduce the amount of information that students needed to organize. For example, to support knowledge organization, Ausubel, working with science educator Joe Novak, studied "advanced organizers" for scientific knowledge (Ausubel, Novak, & Hanesian, 1978). Advanced organizers were narrative descriptions and concept maps that helped students see the relationships among scientific ideas. A series of studies conducted by Novak illustrated the value of these organizing principles for fostering scientific understanding (Novak, 1990; Novak & Gowin, 1984; Novak, Gowin, & Johannsen, 1983; Novak & Musonda, 1991).

Novak, using concept maps, showed that supporting students as they seek integrated understanding of scientific phenomena is extremely advantageous for learning (Novak & Musonda, 1991). When students draw maps to link their ideas and then interact with their teachers to refine their maps, they gain a more integrated and robust understanding of scientific phenomena. Novak advocated concept maps as a tool to help students organize their own ideas. By the partnership period, interest in fostering autonomous knowledge organization, called *metacognition,* was substantial.

A promising line of research on knowledge organization was initiated by psychologists studying information processing. Psychologists studying memory processes demonstrated that students were limited in the amount of information that they could process at a given time. Miller (1956) found that individuals could process, at most, seven pieces of information in working memory. Since Miller conducted this research in a psychological paradigm, the definition of a piece of information was relatively straightforward, generally comprising a nonsense syllable or a number. In contrast, the definition of a piece of information in science was far more complicated.

Those studying knowledge organization compared the ways experts and novices structured their knowledge (Chi, Feltovich, & Smith, 1981; J. Larkin, McDermott, Simon, & Simon, 1980; J. J. Larkin & Reif, 1979). Novices tended to rely on concrete elements such as formulas, whereas experts used more abstract and hierarchical organizations. Several researchers linked work in processing capacity to work on scientific understanding. Case (1974), following the theoretical perspective of Pascual-Leone (Pascual-Leone, Goodman, Ammon, & Subelman, 1978), demonstrated that students could perform tasks far beyond their supposed Piagetian developmental level when the processing demands of those tasks were appropriately reduced.

Siegler (1976) analyzed explanations that students generated for the action of a balance beam and was able to show that young children's performance could be explained with a set of simple rules. Some students focused solely on the distance of the weight from the fulcrum. Others relied solely on the relative mass of the weights. As students increased their understanding of the situation and their ability to combine more information, they progressed from one rule to another and eventually "muddled through," combining these rules concerning the action of the balance beam. Older students used the computational rule for predicting balance beam results.

Explanations of student behavior based on the development of logical reasoning were not successful in predicting which scientific concepts would be easy and which would be difficult. In contrast, studies of information processing conducted by psychologists offered some useful findings that would guide workers during the partnership period.

Science educators also sought to reduce the processing demands of science learning. Gagné analyzed the behaviors necessary for performing a particular scientific task, taught students each of the behaviors separately, and sequenced the behaviors so that they built on each other, culminating in ability to perform the complex task. A major contribution of this hierarchical task analysis to science instruction was the emphasis on careful decomposition of scientific reasoning. In order to identify the behaviors that students needed to exhibit, researchers analyzed each of the behaviors that contributed to a scientific task. These analyses yielded a broad array of components of scientific reasoning and problem solving, including observing, clarifying, and predicting. This approach to acquisition and application of scientific ideas was implemented in the *Science—A Process Approach* curriculum (Commission on Science Education, 1964). Gagné's (1968) approach to sequencing and organizing information to reduce demands on processing capacity revealed several difficulties with this line of investigation. Often, the skills that were identified at the bottom of the learning hierarchy, such as controlling variables, were difficult for students to learn, making it complicated to implement the approach.

During the interaction period, psychologists used information-processing theories to clarify mechanisms governing the acquisition and application of scientific ideas. Two main perspectives on the application of ideas were prevalent during this period. One was a common elements approach, whereby students were thought to learn the various elements necessary to perform a task and were therefore able to reuse those elements on a related task. This approach was taken by Gagné and the *Science—A Process Approach* curriculum materials. Another view of problem solving distinguished task-specific information and powerful reasoning strategies. Here, transfer was presumed to occur as students applied powerful reasoning strategies using the new knowledge. This approach distinguished procedural knowledge from declarative knowledge. Procedural knowledge is represented in condition–action pairs like the rules studied by Siegler. For example, the rule about the distance could be represented as, "If one weight is farther from the fulcrum than the other weight, predict that the arm will go down on the side with a weight at a greater distance." Declarative knowledge, in contrast, consists of information necessary to implement the rule such as a definition of weight. In summary, the information-processing theorists, the developmental researchers following Piaget, and those studying advance organizers suggested by Ausubel all sought to explain how students apply ideas to new problems. In spite of the common goal, science education researchers rarely linked their investigations to studies by information-processing theorists, since the psychological studies tended to focus on very simple concepts and situations such as maze learning or the learning of concepts based on shape and size (Hilgard & Bower, 1966), whereas science educators studied learning in science classrooms.

During the interaction period the progressive education movement's emphasis on the social nature of learning was reflected in studies featuring project work and emphasizing relationships between science and society. Thus, the Unified Science and Mathematics Educational Study extended the progressive education notions of Dewey and encouraged students to conduct community projects with scientific themes. Those using the curriculum identified the advantages of group investigation of scientific phenomena. The student projects conducted following this curriculum definitely demonstrated the motivational effects of project work. Evaluation revealed that students participating in these curricula were as successful overall as students following the traditional curriculum in understanding scientific ideas measured by traditional achievement tests (Shymansky, Kyle, & Alport, 1983).

*Summary of Shifts and Convergences During the Interaction Period.* During the interaction period, most researchers held the view that ability and motivation determined inclination to learn science, but the dimensions of ability and motivation were expanded to include a range of abilities contributing to disposition to learn, new factors in knowledge development, and a broader set of motivational factors, such as anxiety and confidence. In addition, a vocal group became more and more concerned about factors that might shut out individuals who were different from those already involved in science.

Both intuitions from science education practices and findings from psychological research on information processing contributed perspectives on how students organize information and apply scientific ideas to new problems. No consensus emerged. The social context of science learning remained of interest but also separate from studies of reasoning.

## Disposition in the Partnership Period

During the partnership period, intuitions concerning the disposition to learn were expanded in two primary directions. First, insights came from studies of how students solve specific scientific problems, revealing both how knowledge develops and how students regulate their own learning. Second, insights came from studies of how social contexts contribute to scientific understanding, both in science classes and in science laboratories.

*Ability and Development in the Partnership Period.* During the partnership period natural scientists as well as science educators have agreed that citizens need more scientific understanding (Rutherford & Ahlgren, 1990). One response has been an increase in science course requirements. Another has been to identify skills needed by students who do not plan to major in science. In studying ability, researchers are turning to analysis of the skills used by experts such as metacognition. In studying development, students' reasoning about specific problems has become more pronounced.

Metacognition and Knowledge Integration.   Continuing the pattern from the interaction period of attempting to explain why some students succeed and others fail, researchers have identified aspects of expert scientific reasoning appropriate for students. In particular, skills in autonomous processing and synthesizing of information such as metacognition and knowledge integration have been studied. Metacognition involves such activities as planning, evaluating, reflecting, and anticipating personal weaknesses. Encouraging metacognitive activities runs counter to the emphasis on the objective nature of scientific knowledge in most textbooks. The textbooks often imply that science concepts are universal truths. Students taking this view might be inclined to memorize scientific ideas rather than to evaluate and reflect on scientific understanding. The shift to including metacognition in considerations of ability has been accompanied by a shift from communicating science information to communicating the nature of science knowledge.

Research investigations suggest that beliefs about the nature of scientific knowledge vary considerably. For example, students in the CLP case study reported static or dynamic beliefs (see Linn, Songer, & Lewis, 1991). In addition, Chi and Bassok

(1989) reported that students who spontaneously explained connections to themselves achieved a better understanding of physics. Further, individuals who monitored their ideas and reflected on the information they encountered were more likely to revise their ideas and to identify robust explanations for scientific phenomena (R. T. White, 1987, 1988, 1992).

This focus on how reasoners autonomously process information and make connections is consistent with contemporary research in psychology. For example, Sternberg gathered evidence to support a triarchic theory of intelligence (R. J. Sternberg, 1985; chapter 8). He described three aspects of intelligence, one having to do with understanding concepts and ideas, a second having to do with practical tasks such as planning, working with others, or evaluating one's skills, and a third having to do with creativity, such as would be exemplified in an essay or independent investigation. Sternberg's practical intelligence includes aspects of metacognition such as self-monitoring or meta-reasoning. The research of H. Gardner (1983) on multiple intelligences is also consistent with this new view of ability. H. Gardner identifies a repertoire of forms of intelligence, as well as some guidelines concerning how the repertoire is utilized.

Development of Scientific Explanations.   In this period researchers continue to differentiate between the development of logical reasoning skills and the development of understanding of scientific concepts. A changed view about how students acquire knowledge is supported by a vast array of studies documenting the misconceptions, alternative frameworks, or intuitions that students have about scientific phenomena (Pfundt & Duit, 1991). This research strongly indicates that students' ideas about science are developed within specific disciplinary contexts.

Students have a wide range of coherent scientific ideas (e.g., McCloskey, Caramazza, & Green, 1980), many of which are consistent with notions once held by scientists (Clement, 1991, 1992; Clement et al., 1989; Viennot, 1979; Wiser & Carey, 1983). For example, students believe that sound dies out, heat and temperature are the same, and the earth is round like a pancake.

As mentioned in the CLP case study, these views of scientific phenomena are characterized as misconceptions because they differ from the views held by scientists. Examination of these ideas, however, suggests that they might be viewed more reasonably as alternative frameworks or intuitions. Labeling them misconceptions implies that both the reasoning used to achieve these ideas and the ideas themselves are problematic (Nersessian, 1991). Such a perspective reinforces views of scientific phenomena as fixed and immutable, rather than as open to research and refinement.

A. diSessa (1982, 1988, 1993) characterizes student ideas as "phenomenological primitives" because they represent descriptive models of the world as seen through the eyes of the student. Viewing intuitions as phenomenological primitives casts the learner as struggling to make sense of the world, rather than as reaching erroneous conclusions about scientific phenomena. By casting these ideas as primitive, diSessa captures the explanatory characteristics of student reasoning compared with scientists' reasoning.

Analysis of the factors that contribute to students' intuitions about the nature of the world reveals some common influences on student thinking. In particular, students generally base their inferences on observations, focusing on salient but often inessential characteristics of phenomena. For example, in the CLP classroom students observe that metals feel colder than plastic and infer that metals can impart cold to objects. Here students are focusing on an accurate observation, and making an inaccurate conjecture about the underlying explanation.

One interpretation of students' efforts to make sense of the world and form phenomenological primitives is that students engage in reasoning processes that resemble those of scientists but reach conclusions that differ substantially from scientific views, because they focus on different information. If this is the case, then supporting students as they develop their reasoning processes is beneficial.

Another interpretation is that students' efforts to make sense of scientific phenomena also differ from those of scientists. In this view, students' standards of evidence and expectations about the nature of science also contribute to intuitive ideas (D. Kuhn, Amsel, & O'Loughlin, with the assistance of Schauble, 1988; Schauble, Klopfer, & Raghavan, 1991). If this is the case, then students need guidance concerning how to use evidence, in addition to guidance concerning what to reason about.

The shift in intuitions about the role of ability in science learning has been underscored by mounting evidence that even the best students have views of science that differ from those of scientific experts. Tests administered to those completing science courses at universities have revealed a common array of intuitions that differ from those of scientists (Hestenes, 1992). It appears that even the best students have difficulty monitoring their own understanding and frequently achieve an illusion of comprehension that contradicts the actual situation. Other studies have shown that students with similar intellectual abilities may draw different scientific conclusions based on metacognition and beliefs about the nature of science (Chi & Bassok, 1989; Songer, 1989).

These shifts in the view of ability and development have encouraged partnerships to explore two main directions during the partnership period. One group of investigators has focused on conceptual change and the mechanisms that might foster students' reformulations of scientific ideas. Another group has focused on knowledge organization and structure. We turn to these topics in the section on mechanisms governing reasoning.

In summary, views of ability and development have expanded during the partnership period. In particular, contemporary researchers see ability and development as less of a constraint and more of a component of the learning environment. A key realization has been that conceptual change in science is concept specific and that mechanisms for conceptual change need to account for the repertoire of views that students have about scientific phenomena. These conceptual change mechanisms offer very specific guidance to those designing curricula. As discussed in the opportunity section, distinctions between disposition and opportunity lessen with a focus on conceptual change.

*Motivation and Inclination in the Partnership Period.* Intuitions concerning motivation and inclination to participate in science have shifted dramatically during the partnership period. Individuals underrepresented in the scientific enterprise have argued that this underrepresentation constitutes discrimination

rather than selection, pointing, among other examples, to evidence that women earn equal or higher grades in science courses and perform equally as well as or better than men in science careers, yet earn lower salaries. Evidence has mounted that opportunities for women and minorities to participate in science are limited. For example, opportunities to pursue advanced degrees frequently are less available to women and minorities than to majority males. Even when women have equal training and equal experience, their salaries are less than three-quarters those of men (American Association for the Advancement of Science, 1992).

As a result, there has been a shift from the ability model for participation in science to an opportunity model, and a change in traditional views about students' motivation for science courses and careers. Whereas in the past, many believed that women were uninterested in science and therefore chose not to participate, E. F. Keller (1985) and Gilligan (1982) have suggested that the situation is more complex. By favoring a view of science as interrogation of nature, those in power create an environment in science that is incompatible with the perspectives and cultural experiences of many women. In addition, those in power have favored questions of interest to men shaping the research agenda in science. For example, research on heart disease has been carried out primarily in males. Conclusions from studies of males cannot be generalized to females. In some cases, recommendations for treatment based on this research are harmful to women (Henig, 1993).

Other studies have reinforced this shift in perspective. Researchers examining interactions in science classrooms have found that the experiences of male and female students are different. Building on questions raised during the interaction period, a broad array of studies have revealed that, in science classes, teachers treat male and female students differently. They provide more feedback to male students than to female students; they call on male students more often than female students; and they condone the process of interrupting the class and giving out the answers when the perpetrator is a male but not when the perpetrator is a female (Wellesley College Center for Research on Women, 1992). In spite of convincing evidence about these phenomena, the intuitions of science instructors are that they treat males and females equally. Instructors are continuously surprised when confronted with data demonstrating that their behavior toward male and female students differs. Thus, subtle as well as more public processes for interacting with male and female science students and setting the agenda for science research continue to contribute to the normative view that science is a male domain.

*Mechanisms of Reasoning and Problem Solving in the Partnership Period.* Studies of mechanisms for reasoning and problem solving in this period have revealed strong interactions between the activities to which students are exposed in science classes and their disposition to learn science, thus increasing links between disposition and opportunity. Both the broader range of abilities identified during this period and the increased emphasis on knowledge integration and metacognition reinforce the belief that outcomes from science instruction reflect a broad range of influences, of which ability is only one.

Recent intuitions about reasoning and problem solving benefit from partnerships between developmental psychologists and science educators. These groups study specific scientific ideas and determine how ideas might be linked and combined, and examine how students understand scientific phenomena and organize related scientific ideas. Examples include the CLP case study, the Israeli chemistry case study, the electricity curriculum developed by B. Y. White and Frederiksen (1990), and the statistical reasoning instruction of Rubin, Bruce, Rosebery, and DuMouchel, (1988). We discuss mechanisms of conceptual change and knowledge organization.

One major shift during this period has involved methods for fostering conceptual change. Piagetian theory promoted discovery learning and cognitive conflict as mechanisms for fostering scientific understanding. Over the past decade, a new range of studies has focused specifically on fostering conceptual change.

Mechanisms of conceptual change studied in the partnership period build on the cognitive conflict approach described for the interaction period. In addition, models from history and philosophy of science have influenced thinking about conceptual change. One approach put forth by Strike and Posner identified the conditions that motivate students to adopt a new perspective on scientific phenomena. Strike and Posner's work is consistent with the philosophical perspectives of Lakatos (1970) and Toulmin (1972). The intuitions enunciated by Strike and Posner were that students need disquieting evidence about their concepts as well as clear alternatives in order to come up with new perspectives. The primary contribution over the cognitive conflict perspective is the emphasis on alternatives. Another approach, developed by Carey (1985), stemmed from investigations of how students develop understanding of the nature of plants and animals. Carey likened the individual development of understanding to the evolutionary versus revolutionary knowledge reorganization characteristic of the history of science (see T. S. Kuhn, 1970). A third view of conceptual change suggested that students expand their repertoire of scientific ideas and distinguish among them rather than replace one scientific idea with another (A. diSessa, 1993). A fourth view emphasizes the social nature of science learning, suggesting that students appropriate ideas in group discussion (Vygotsky, 1987). A fifth view focuses on metacognition as a mechanism for change (e.g., Collins et al., 1991; R. T. White, 1988).

Taken together, these studies suggest the importance of providing a structure for guiding students as they investigate scientific phenomena, while fostering understanding of the nature of scientific knowledge and imparting skill in metacognition (Champagne et al., 1982; Gunstone, Gray, & Searle, 1992; R. T. White, in press).

Thus, views concerning the nature of conceptual change and the instructional activities that foster conceptual change now focus on supporting students as they make sense of scientific phenomena, rather than on contradicting the conclusions students reach, questioning the reasoning skills students use, or providing students with investigative opportunities but little guidance. This represents a substantial shift from the previous focus on fostering general inquiry skills in guided reasoning activities. We return to the characteristics of this supporting process in the section on the nature of instruction in the partnership period.

Another major shift concerns mechanisms for knowledge organization. Partnerships suggest three main approaches to fostering knowledge organization: (a) provide representations or mental models as organizers for scientific information, (b) identify patterns, procedures, schemes, or templates as the chunks of information to be organized, and (c) encourage the autonomous organization of information by providing integration aids such as concept maps. By studying mechanisms of conceptual change in instructional settings, these projects link disposition to learn to the nature of instruction. We discuss these three approaches below and in the partnership section on the nature of instruction.

Representations and Models.   Research on mental models as organizers draws on intuitions about the representations used by experts. J. Larkin et al. (1980) found that experts solving physics problems organized their information using free-body diagrams and other mental models that increased the effectiveness of their understanding. Studies comparing qualitative models to quantitative representations of scientific phenomena revealed that students were successful in understanding material when it was presented in a qualitative model (Gentner & Stevens, 1983; Greeno, 1989; Vosniadou & Brewer, 1992; B. Y. White & Frederiksen, 1990; Wiser & Carey, 1983).

Patterns.   The pattern acquisition approach grew out of interactions between psychologists with an information-processing perspective and cognitive scientists studying science problem solving. Early work on expertise in complex domains revealed that experts "chunked" knowledge into useful, reusable patterns (Chase & Simon, 1973a, 1973b). Various approaches to the representation of patterns have been explored (J. R. Anderson, 1983; Minsky, 1986; Schank & Abelson, 1977). Researchers have studied knowledge acquisition in complex domains, such as geometry and computer programming (J. R. Anderson, 1983). These studies have explicitly identified the patterns students use to solve problems and illustrate how they form patterns or templates of compiled information about specific problems. Researchers from this perspective argue that the basic element of knowledge is the production rule, which is an extension of the stimulus–response bond. A production rule is a condition–action pair, such as, "If objects in contact have different temperatures, then they will tend toward equilibrium." Researchers point out that one can view learning as the acquisition of a repertoire of production rules, that production rules can be combined into more complex productions governing a sequence of tasks, and that, in general, experts recycle these compiled productions rather than generating new patterns when they encounter problems. Greeno and Simon describe the strategies and reasoning skills that are used when encountering a novel problem as "weak methods" (Greeno & Simon, 1986). They point out that these weak methods are less powerful than using a compiled pattern to solve a problem. Thus, instructors can help students learn to perform well in complex tasks by helping them acquire the repertoire of production rules appropriate for the domain. This approach has proven successful in a number of disciplines (J. R. Anderson, Conrad, & Corbett, 1989; J. R. Anderson & Jeffries, 1985; J. R. Anderson, Pirolli, & Farrell, 1988; C. Smith, Carey, & Wiser, 1985).

A similar approach, but based on entities larger than production rules, has been followed by teams of science instructors, science educators, and psychologists. For example, Clement

(1991) identified what he called "anchoring conceptions" (Clement et al., 1989) as appropriate starting points for science instruction. In this approach, anchoring conceptions are reinforced as patterns that can be applied in a broad range of situations. Students are then guided to use these anchoring conceptions to make sense of more complex scientific phenomena. Ultimately, the anchoring conceptions become templates that can be used in a broad range of situations. Thus, to help students understand the forces affecting a stack of books on a table, Clement and co-workers chose as an anchoring situation the forces acting on a stack of books if the books were placed on a spring. The prototypes in the CLP curriculum, as noted, implement this approach.

Minstrell (A. A. diSessa & Minstrell, in press; Minstrell, 1982) takes a similar perspective in identifying benchmark experiments. Once students have understood these benchmarks, then the additional activities and problems that they solve are interpreted in terms of the benchmarks. In Minstrell's approach, students examine a somewhat complex situation and make predictions concerning the outcome. After gathering evidence about the situation, students whose predictions have been contradicted discuss how they generated their ideas and decide which are more reasonable. The class then compares students' ideas and the outcome. As the instruction continues, students are encouraged to refer back to the benchmark to make sense of new problems. Linn and Clancy (1992a) take a similar approach for computer science. They identified "templates" or abstract representations of code patterns that could be recycled, and implemented these ideas in a Pascal curriculum (Clancy & Linn, 1992).

Autonomous Reflection.    Encouraging autonomous reflection to achieve knowledge organization is an extension of the advance organizer tradition in the interaction period. Research on metacognition and beliefs about the nature of science, combined with information demonstrating the effectiveness of guided reflection, reinforces the intuition that appropriate experiences can motivate students to build more robust and cohesive understanding of scientific phenomena (A. L. Brown & Palincsar, 1987; Palincsar & Brown, 1984). Finally, research analyzing the social nature of learning illustrates how students can contribute to each other's knowledge organization (R. D. Pea, 1985; Scardamalia & Bereiter, 1992, 1993).

During the partnership period, research on the social construction of scientific understanding has investigated tutoring and group interaction. In particular, science educators have built on evidence that tutoring is an effective mechanism for fostering scientific understanding (Bloom, 1984). Further, a major component of tutoring is the interaction between students and an instructor. One question that has been raised is whether students might interact with each other as tutor and tutee in order to take advantage of the strengths of tutoring.

Intuitions concerning the advantages of cooperative group learning have guided interest in the social environment for learning (A. L. Brown & Campione, 1990a, in press; Cohen, 1986; Lave & Wenger, 1991). Many science educators believe that cooperative group learning is an effective mechanism for fostering understanding. Research during the partnership period has clarified how this mechanism might work (see also chapter 26).

Studies of the effect of the peer culture on student understanding have suggested some disadvantages of cooperative group learning (Cohen, 1994; Linn & Burbules, 1993). Eckert (1990) illustrated how peer cultures in precollege settings could shape the expectations and ideas that adolescents have about the nature of science and the nature of learning. In some high schools the peer culture rewards success in sports and disparages scholastic endeavors. Students are in conflict with peer standards if they seek integrated understanding and demonstrate success in difficult academic subjects.

In contrast, there are situations where learners working together might foster each other's understanding. Students working together to make sense of scientific phenomena may contribute diverse ideas, refine each other's ideas, and compare the power of alternative ideas (Klahr & Dunbar, 1988; Klahr, Dunbar, & Fay, 1990). Ultimately, by negotiating with others in the classroom, students may gain a more robust and comprehensive understanding of scientific phenomena. D. Newman (1990), for example, studied group interaction in scientific classes. Inspired by the work of Vygotsky (1962, 1978), D. Newman sought to create "zones of proximal development" that would allow students to explore their own ideas, incorporate appropriate alternative ideas, and ultimately build a more robust understanding of scientific phenomena. The zone of proximal development refers to the range of ideas available to the learner when supported by others who contribute by providing ideas that can be appropriated, by helping keep track of all the information, and by monitoring each other's ideas.

A number of researchers and group partnership projects have investigated what educators have referred to as legitimate peripheral participation (Lave & Wenger, 1991), or apprenticeship (Collins, Brown, & Newman, 1989), and its contribution to scientific understanding. Scientists often gain understanding of scientific phenomena by participating in scientific research communities. Creating a similar atmosphere in a science classroom could foster understanding of scientific phenomena as well as a healthy disposition toward scientific knowledge. Vygotsky (1978), for example, suggested that groups working together create multiple zones of proximal development. If the zone is too broad, students abandon knowledge integration. If the zone is too narrow, students are not sufficiently challenged. A number of research projects have built on this intuition during the partnership period (A. L. Brown & Campione, 1990a, 1990b; A. diSessa, 1992; R. D. Pea, 1992; Scardamalia & Bereiter, 1991; R. T. White, in press). In these projects, an environment for intellectual discussion of scientific phenomena is created, and students jointly interact to address scientific problems. A factor in students' acquisition of scientific ideas and application of ideas to new situations is the support they receive from others in the social environment.

In contrast, others studying interaction in science classrooms (Forman, 1989; Forman & McPhail, 1993) have found that science courses may reinforce the idea of the teacher and text as authority, and the student as either right or wrong. They may also reify undesirable aspects of scientific collaborations, such as status-based access to information (Burbules & Linn, 1991). If the teacher and textbook are viewed by groups of learners as the ultimate source of information, then students may simply consult an authority and reach conclusions without jointly considering alternative solutions to a problem. Under these circumstances group learning is less likely to be effective.

Exploring these mechanisms for knowledge organization and integration has led partnership projects to assess the goals and objectives for science courses. That is, should students develop a single, robust model of scientific phenomena, or is it more appropriate to view knowledge development as culminating in a repertoire of models? What models should be emphasized for citizens who do not plan careers in science?

Examination of the appropriate goals for science understanding has taken several forms. One approach is to examine the behavior of experts and novices, in order to infer goals for science instruction. Initial studies of experts (J. Larkin et al., 1980) suggested uniform views of scientific phenomena that might be the goals for science courses. Subsequent studies, however, suggest that in fact, experts have a broad range of models, depending on the type of problem they are called on to solve (Reif & Larkin, 1991). The realization that experts develop a repertoire of models for scientific phenomena is consistent with conclusions reached by some science educators concerning the goals for science courses.

In particular, Linn and co-workers (1994) propose that the goal of a science course should be to teach students a repertoire of models for scientific phenomena, as well as mechanisms for selecting among the repertoire. The repertoire that students might develop could include rules, strategies, hunches, models, and principles, along with information concerning when each of these perspectives on a scientific phenomenon is most appropriate.

Given these new objectives and goals for science courses, new approaches to assessment are also needed. Recent interest in performance evaluations, where students are assessed on the execution of scientific tasks more similar to those carried out by expert scientists, is compatible with the new goals for instruction. Having students carry out sustained reasoning tasks reflected in projects or other samples of student work not only promotes knowledge integration, but also aligns assessment with classroom activity (Duschl & Gitomer, 1991).

Many partnership projects encourage scientific knowledge integration by defining "cognitive goals," creating social environments for learning, encouraging effective beliefs about the scientific enterprise, and encouraging metacognitive reasoning. These projects establish goals by identifying templates, patterns, anchoring conceptions, or benchmark experiments and by cognitive analysis of scientific tasks. Activities that encourage autonomous organization of information, including reflection, self-monitoring, and concept maps, all stimulate cognitive activity and can be seen as creating broader zones of proximal development (from the Vygotskian perspective), thus enabling students to gain more integrated ideas. Projects implementing the concept of legitimate peripheral participation (Lave & Wenger, 1991) include, in addition, the goal of helping students select the expertise they wish to develop. These cognitive approaches to science knowledge acquisition and knowledge integration can be combined into a coherent view of science instruction that has been variously called scaffolded knowledge integration (Linn, in press), apprenticeship learning (Bruer, 1993; Collins et al., 1991; Scardamalia & Bereiter, 1992), or guided discovery (A. diSessa, 1993; A. diSessa & Abelson, 1986; Tinker & Papert, 1989).

Contrasting partnership projects led by psychologists working with experts in artificial intelligence take a more explicit approach to guiding and tutoring students on the production rules necessary for performing a complex task (J. R. Anderson, 1983). These projects represent knowledge integration in production rules. This approach grows out of information processing and artificial intelligence research and is implemented by tutors that guide students to acquire the production rules that govern a given situation. In this approach students are guided to display a particular form of expert behavior and prevented from dwelling on errors. The apprenticeship approach and the tutoring approach each represent perspectives on science knowledge acquisition and application that are currently under investigation and will be discussed further in the section on the nature of instruction.

***Summary of Shifts and Convergences During the Partnership Period.*** During the partnership period there has been a primary shift toward the view that the social environment plays an important role in science learning and instruction and that minority groups and women have been excluded from participation. Feminists, among others, have called for new conceptions of science education and social programs to broaden the community of participants in the scientific enterprise. In addition, during this period researchers identified a broader repertoire of intellectual abilities that contribute to science learning. These views stem from studies of how students develop specific scientific concepts and specific inquiry skills.

There has been a shift during this period from a view of science learning as the process of uncovering truths to a view of science learning as a process of integrating ideas. Viewing science learning as knowledge integration reveals that students and scientists have many characteristics of reasoning in common. In addition, taking knowledge integration as an aspect of disposition to learn science has illustrated the connection between disposition and opportunity. At the same time, information-processing theorists studying production rules and production systems have turned their attention to the acquisition of more complex productions governing such tasks as computer programming and problem solving in mechanics. The tension between researchers favoring explicit tutoring and those favoring design of environments where students work jointly to gain understanding has sparked a continuing dialogue in the field.

## Disposition to Learn: Shifts

Views concerning disposition to learn science have shifted substantially during the three periods described here, in keeping with many of the themes enunciated by Dewey. First, contrasting the focus on behavior at the beginning of the separation period with the focus on societal influences at the end of the partnership period illustrates the need for a science that links psychology, sociology, and science education and demonstrates that progress is being made toward the development of such a science.

Second, the advantage of partnerships in science education is apparent when one contrasts the investigations of the separation period with those of the partnership period. In the separation period, disposition as studied by psychologists was distinct from disposition studied by science educators or natural scientists. In the partnership period psychologists and natural scientists are working together to analyze disposition to learn science.

The expanding audience for science education helps researchers redefine disposition to learn science. In the separation period, the audience for science was primarily future scientists, and it was assumed that those who succeeded would do so as a result of a combination of interest and ability. During the interaction period, researchers expanded the repertoire of abilities that supposedly contributed to scientific success, but the perspective remained that those who participate and succeed in science do so because of interest and ability. In the partnership period, social perspectives about science knowledge, the role of meta-reasoning, and the contribution of students' views of science as a body of knowledge redefine the nature of disposition. This new view of disposition places responsibility on leaders in science education to provide opportunities for all students to succeed in science.

In addition, during the partnership period, researchers have identified links between disposition and opportunity that contribute to understanding. Approaches to science knowledge acquisition, such as apprenticeship learning and authentic scientific investigation, bridge the gap between disposition and opportunity and reinforce the view of scientific knowledge as a social construct. We elaborate these issues in the section on the nature of science instruction.

## NATURE OF SCIENCE INSTRUCTION

In this section we discuss the nature of science instruction, looking for convergences between the instructional materials developed for science courses and the theories and models of instruction. Natural scientists and classroom teachers have designed and redesigned the science curriculum since the early 20th century. Social scientists have contributed more and more to reframing the questions, to offering theories and models of instruction, to examining specific techniques for improving instruction, and to initiating partnerships that produce instructional materials.

In our analysis we focus on two questions: Which science topics should be taught and what should students learn? and, Which activities communicate the scientific information desired? To characterize the topics and goals for science courses, we analyze science textbooks, science standards or frameworks, as well as policy statements made by those involved in instruction. Textbooks probably have the most impact on what is taught, while remaining the least responsive to the influence of social scientists. Science textbooks have generally been designed by natural scientists, science instructors, or publishers, either alone or in groups. We describe illustrative science curricula to explore this influence.

To characterize the activities believed effective for instruction, we examine research comparing alternative curricula as well as the activities in laboratories and classrooms. At first, social scientists were involved as evaluators. Over time, they began to conduct research studies and establish partnerships with experts in technology and natural science. To ensure comparability, we discuss physical science curricula at the secondary level and general science at the elementary level.

## Interaction in the Separation Period

During the separation period the number of secondary schools expanded, and more science courses were offered. In addition, research on science instruction was initiated (Boenig, 1969; Curtis, 1926, 1931, 1939; Lawlor, 1970; Swift, 1969).

*Goals of the Science Curriculum in the Separation Period.* By 1900, elementary school students followed courses in "nature study," and general science was introduced in the middle grades. Advanced courses were electives offered in secondary schools.

Elementary Science. The nature study curriculum involved the memorization of plant and animal names and the observation of natural behavior (Underhill, 1941). The teaching of nature study in the elementary years was justified by intuitions concerning development. G. Stanley Hall's saltatory theory asserted that students could use memory and observation in elementary school and that more complex abilities emerged in the middle and later years. No doubt nature study was also chosen to be compatible with the science training of individuals who taught elementary school students.

In the 1930s, science educators, recognizing that the amount of material that was needed to be taught during the general science courses in middle school exceeded the available instructional time, sought to add more complex information about scientific phenomena to the elementary curriculum. A new set of curricular goals for elementary education, reported in the NSSE yearbook published in 1932 (Whipple, 1932), was proposed by a commission of science educators and natural scientists. To justify this new curriculum, the commission rejected the developmental perspective of the nature study enthusiasts by arguing that both John Dewey and Robert Thorndike had criticized Hall's saltatory theory. This group argued that nature study was a waste of the elementary years and called for introducing more complex material earlier in the curriculum. For example, the group recommended that elementary science teach that "the properties of the different elements depend on the number and arrangement of the electrons and protons contained in their atoms" (Whipple, 1932, p. 141). The group outlined a spiral curriculum in which topics would be introduced in early years and revisited with more complex perspectives in later years. They described this as a "continuous and correlated program of study" (Whipple, 1932, p. 5). This spiraling remains in widespread use in science textbooks today and has a modern counterpart in the repertoire of models approach described in the CLP case study.

The views of the commission were criticized by psychologists. For example, Freeman (1938), commenting on the description of the curriculum offered in the NSSE yearbook, criticized the proposed spiral curriculum and the assignment of topics to grades by drawing attention to the work of Binet (1908). Freeman noted that Binet offered insights into the development of general ability by identifying tasks appropriate for each age group. He reminded the commission that Binet had identified general ability as an innate, stable characteristic, but had also distinguished the tasks that students can accomplish at each age of their development. Freeman accused science educators of neglecting this developmental progression and of assuming that students' development would proceed more rapidly than Binet had suggested (Freeman, 1938).

Freeman's accusations underscore the lack of connection between the proposals of the science education community and the views of psychologists in the separation period. The proposals in the NSSE yearbook reflected a view of students as receiving scientific information and incorporating it into their understanding. These leaders thought of science learning as a matter of recall and assumed that students who failed lacked the ability or interest to learn science. In contrast, Freeman and other psychologists emphasized the distinction between recall and application of ideas and suggested that the research of Binet indicated the kinds of reasoning characteristic of students at each age.

General Science. General science was most commonly taught in Grades 7 through 10, and, by 1925, over 25 textbooks were available. A study of the most widely used textbooks in general science concluded, "there is no consensus of opinion as to what should be treated in a text in general science and . . . there has been no increase in the unanimity of opinion in this manner" (Klopp, 1927). General science textbooks took a practical approach. They discussed common scientific tools such as barometers and electromagnets, and inventions such as steam engines, oil wells, water purification systems, soap making, and food preservation. In addition, scientific phenomena such as heat transfer, photosynthesis, humidity, and combustion were included in the curriculum (Curtis, 1931; Noll, 1939). Fewer than 5 percent of the pages in texts were devoted to scientific principles (Noll, 1939), consistent with the view described in the discussion of disposition to learn science that science consists of telling students information.

Secondary Courses. Advanced courses were in biology, botany, physics, and chemistry. These courses, like those in general science, included topics of interest and utility to students, rather than scientific principles. A survey of physics texts in 1925 revealed that 31 percent of a typical physics course was devoted to mechanics, 20 percent to heat, 17 percent to electricity, 17 percent to light, and 15 percent to sound (Curtis, 1926, p. 238). Chemistry courses were organized by substance (oxygen, air, sulfur). The primary goal in 1924 was "to show the service of chemistry to the home, to health, to medicine, to agriculture, to industry" (Curtis, 1926, p. 282). The methods of science were predicated on the observation of scientific phenomena and followed the tenets of positivism (Duschl, 1990).

Nobel laureate Robert Millikan, with co-author H. G. Gale (1906), produced one of the early texts. The book features 21 chapters with topics like "pressure in air." The chapter on transference of heat has sections on conduction, convection, radiation, and the heating and ventilation of buildings, all covered in 11 pages. Each topic in a section is introduced with an experimental observation followed by an assortment of details and explanations. After each section there are questions that require recall of information. To illustrate, the topic "conductivity and sensation" is introduced with the observation, "It is a fact of common observation that on a cold day in winter a piece of metal feels much colder to the hand than a piece of wood, notwithstanding the fact that the temperature of the

wood must be the same as that of the metal" (Millikan & Gale, 1927, p. 219). To explain this observation, the books says, "the iron being a much better conductor removes heat from the hand much more rapidly" (p. 219). At the end of the section, the problem asks, "Why will a moistened finger freeze instantly to a piece of iron on a cold winter's day, but not to a piece of wood?" (p. 221). Thus, textbooks described the outcomes of scientific investigations thought to be appropriate for precollege students. They were scientifically accurate, described factual information, and featured practical details. The processes leading to experimental findings, the implications of these findings for problem solving, and the general principles of science were less emphasized. Problems required students to (a) recall information and (b) combine complex information without much guidance.

Thus, in general, texts emphasized scientific information, not scientific reasoning, and absorption of ideas, not understanding. This was consistent with the belief that the logic of science was either developed without instruction or learned by studying some other topic such as Euclidean geometry.

Learning from the Curriculum. Studies of learning outcomes from these textbook materials foreshadow the commentaries on science understanding that are common today. For example, a study of students learning mechanics in an introductory physics course reached this conclusion:

The extent of the lack of comprehension shown therein of the numerical relations of the simplest and most fundamental principles of physics is certainly startling, and lends support to the criticism often heard that the average high school student of physics acquires merely a mass of disconnected facts, with little notion of the underlying and unifying principles. It is clear that the present method of teaching physics fails in its object in so far as it attempts to give the pupil any knowledge of principles which lie back of the common numerical problems. Haziness and guesswork in the realm of the exact are forerunners of lack of appreciation of, or even contempt for scientific method. (Curtis, 1926, p. 41; Randall, Chapman, & Sutton, 1918)

In contrast, science teachers during the separation period had legitimate and ambitious goals for their courses. Harvey in 1901 described his goals as the head of the science department at the Chicago Normal School:

In the determination of the laws of falling bodies, if my classes fail to perceive the continual activity of a constant force by means of the effects, if they do not recognize the uniformity in the apparent diversity, if they do not recognize that here is a law, and how to perceive that law, if all that my students get out of the exercise is a knowledge that $s = \frac{1}{2} gt^2$, or even worse, if they only learn that, in the laboratory, they can get the results that the textbook says they can get, that the book has told the truth, and they have verified the statement, then I am not only a failure as a teacher, but I am a sham and a fraud, and my laboratory is part of a juggler's outfit, the principal purpose of which is to dazzle the pupil and the public. (Harvey, 1901, p. 182)

Harvey clearly wished students to gain the kind of understanding that involves not only memorization but also recognition of the relationship between ideas and their applications to complex problems.

At the same time, many precollege instructors complained that the textbooks produced by scientists were too difficult for their students, and joined with publishers to produce their own textbooks. These textbooks were similar to the scientist-designed texts except that topics deemed too difficult for students were ignored or treated superficially.

Thus, during the separation period, both natural scientists and science instructors found science difficult to teach. This concern about the teachability of science contributed to the establishment of science education as a field. By around 1920, universities were offering doctoral degrees in science education to students who had earned a master's degree in a field of natural science. The impact of precollege instructors and science educators on curriculum materials during the separation period is apparent. Whereas in 1915, more than 50 percent of the authors of the available high school science textbooks were listed in the roster of American Men of Science, by 1955 fewer than 10 percent of the authors were listed (Swartz, 1991). Over time, more and more science texts were written by textbook publishers with contributions from precollege instructors.

As mentioned in the disposition section, psychologists contributed to reducing the difficulty of science by analyzing the vocabulary in science textbooks. Although texts written by publishers were often modified to use fewer complex words, the effects were inconclusive. These efforts to reduce the complexity of the words used in science instruction created controversy. Some instructors felt that this effort to make science more learnable was successful. Others, such as Schwab (Biological Sciences Curriculum Study, 1963), commented that, rather than making science more learnable, changes in vocabulary had simply reinforced the idea that science was incoherent and difficult to understand.

By 1950, a report on the state of science education materials concluded that science textbooks were often unintegrated and incohesive, and remarked that "factual detail has sometimes been regarded, at least by students, as something to be committed to memory as the primary goal of instruction" (Science Manpower Project [Frederick L. Fitzpatrick: Director], 1959). There was a growing consensus that natural scientists and high school science instructors should be involved in the development of science curriculum materials. In addition, the rapid expansion of scientific knowledge convinced curriculum reformers that students needed to learn not just the results of scientific investigation, but also the inquiry skills used by natural scientists to acquire scientific understanding. We return to discussion of the curriculum in the interaction period.

*Science Activities in the Separation Period.* Selecting activities for science classes that contribute to scientific understanding has generated debate and research. Social scientists have contrasted activities in research studies and recommended activities based on theories of learning. Activities include listening to lectures, participating in laboratories, watching films and demonstrations, solving problems, and reflecting on explanations. One reason for studying science activities was to determine how best to teach each science topic. During the separation period, this linkage was often determined on the basis of difficulty. Either difficult topics were omitted, as noted earlier, or they were reinforced with extra activities to increase understanding.

During the separation period, researchers studied the relative difficulty of science topics, selecting teachable topics. They also compared science laboratories to alternatives for teaching about scientific experimentation. Consistent with the warnings of Dewey, researchers sometimes placed too much reliance on single studies and reached insupportable conclusions.

Teachable Topics.  Early studies of science activities were taxonomic, listing the topics covered in different textbooks (e.g., Curtis, 1926, p. 222). Subsequent investigations augmented the taxonomy with information on easy and difficult aspects of science. These reported examination results. In general, the examinations emphasized memorizing information, and students recalled less than expected. Vocabulary definitions, the names of scientists who discovered laws, scientific terms, or formulas were less well remembered than anticipated. Later studies described student responses more completely. One published in 1940 reported, for example, that students (a) confused the terms cyclone and tornado, (b) did not know that "wrigglers" are a stage in the life history of mosquitoes, and (c) thought that $CO_2$ stands for company number 2 (Boenig, 1969, p. 153; Matteson & Kambley, 1940). These studies of specific student responses foreshadow the cognitive analysis of students' thinking about science that occurred in the next period. In general, these studies helped clarify why science is difficult to learn.

Laboratories or Demonstrations?  During the separation period, researchers compared alternative activities for teaching about scientific experiments. Many compared teacher demonstrations to student demonstrations to student-conducted experiments. Varied goals for offering laboratories were specified. The science laboratory was sometimes intended to illustrate facts and principles, sometimes emphasized to increase understanding of difficult topics, and sometimes used to provide career training in science methods. For example, Cureton (1927; Curtis, 1931) reviewed all available textbooks, teachers' guides, and pamphlets on the teaching of junior high science and found widespread support for the view that the purpose of the science laboratory was to develop specific skills and methods useful either at present or in the future real life. A review article in 1946 reported little progress in understanding the benefits of the science laboratory (Cunningham, 1946). Results of these comparison studies were contradictory, prompting some to complain that "no very great benefit can be gained by more group studies" (Cunningham, 1924; Curtis, 1926, p. 103). Instead, more analysis of students' entering level and progress was desired. Other studies, also inconclusive, examined the roles of charts and graphs, films, practical applications, and other teaching activities.

These comparison studies were inconclusive for a number of reasons. First, the treatments were described very generally as laboratories, lectures, textbooks, or demonstrations. Variability within these categories was neglected. Second, outcome measures consisted almost exclusively of paper and pencil achievement tests that were often poorly linked to the treatment. For example, laboratory science was evaluated by recall of the technique and outcome, information likely to be communicated by a demonstration just as well as a hands-on-laboratory. Third, although methods of statistical analysis were tedious to implement and lacked the power needed to infer subtle effects, they were accorded great status and often led to acceptance of reliable differences without sufficient reflection on the validity of the study.

In addition, despite the warnings of Dewey, observations of successful science teachers were not often used to guide interpretation of results. For example, in 1900 Perry, in the preface to an elementary book on practical mechanics, said,

I am inclined to believe that if, instead of forcing the workman to study like a schoolboy, we were to teach the boy as if he had already acquired some of the experience of a workman, and made it our business to give him this experience, we should do better than at present. That is, let the boy work in wood and metal, let him gain experience in the use of machines, let him use drawing instruments and scales, and you put him in a condition to understand and appreciate the truth of the fundamental laws of nature, such a condition as boys usually arrive at only after years of study" (Perry, 1900, p. 111).

Perry questioned reading books and listening to lectures and advocated performing commonsense experiments instead, anticipating the apprenticeship views of the partnership period. Perry believed that students doing the work of science would learn the principles of science.

Pella (1976), summarizing the history of the journal *Science Education,* reinforced the lack of coherence in science education. Up to 1950, Pella reported, research investigations in science instruction were largely descriptive. Science educators described promising practices. Science teachers described their successes and occasionally their failures. Faculty in schools of education described procedures for training teachers. Pella complained that the field had not advanced, in part, because researchers did not agree on the definition of educational terms, and further, that research studies confused facts, concepts, laws, scientific methods, and regulative principles. He suggested that researchers took a disorganized and incoherent view of science instruction. He commented, "Ignorance, vagueness, and mere good intention are of no more virtue in science education than in any other human enterprise" (Pella, 1976, p. 439).

*Shifts During the Separation Period.* During the separation period, one emphasis was on what should be taught in science. The goals of the science curriculum varied depending on the text and the instructor. Although many agreed on the general problem of making science easier to learn, responses were uncoordinated because groups worked separately. For example, precollege instructors asked publishers to create texts that eliminated difficult topics, natural scientists called for adding modern topics, science educators advocated adding laboratories, and social scientists recommended that vocabulary in textbooks be simplified.

Already during the separation period, the trade-off between depth and breadth of coverage was apparent to some. Science instructors, observing their students, reported problems with knowledge integration and advocated apprenticelike learning to help students link ideas. This issue has become more and more important as the curriculum has been refined (for discussion, see Eylon & Linn, 1988).

In the separation period, those who studied disposition to learn and the nature of instruction required little interaction because, as noted in the disposition section, most assumed that students who were interested in science would enroll and

students with the necessary ability would succeed. In addition, the view that exposure to science information was sufficient to teach those who could learn was compatible with studies comparing forms of exposure and measuring general achievement. Looking back, one can see why Dewey advocated a broader role for precollege science teachers. Of all the groups, the teachers had first-hand experience concerning the links between the nature of instruction in specific science topics and the likely student understanding of those topics. Most other groups relied on texts and tests for evidence about instruction and learning.

## Instruction in the Interaction Period

Commissions reviewing the available science curriculum materials in the 1950s found them unsatisfactory (Michaels, 1957). Numerous committees noted that textbooks had not integrated new scientific findings effectively. The report of the Science Manpower Project, commenting on the shortcomings of physics curricula available in 1953, concluded, "They have retained the framework of the classical physics, but have incorporated a few modern concepts here and there, in a sort of afterthought unit at the end of the course" (Science Manpower Project [Frederick L. Fitzpatrick: Director], 1959, p. 3). Similarly, in biology, Schwab reported, "The gulf between scientific knowledge and the content of our textbooks grew wider and wider" (Biological Sciences Curriculum Study, 1963, p. 7).

Natural scientists led an effort funded by the NSF to reform the curriculum. Natural scientists initiated several types of interactions during this period. First, natural scientists leading the curriculum reform effort involved precollege instructors to test the materials. Second, the reformers enlisted experts in pedagogy to conduct evaluations after the materials had been developed. These evaluations, mandated by the NSF, resulted in a number of interactions between reformers and experts on learning and instruction. For example, advances in statistical techniques made it possible to identify methods for analyzing complex instruction more effectively. Social scientists, using statistical expertise and computing machinery, interacted with the curriculum reform projects to examine subtle interactions between students and learning outcomes. Nevertheless, the group tests employed by the evaluators provided some evidence of the effects of instruction but limited insights into the arts of teaching and the processes of understanding that contributed to learning.

*Goals of the Science Curriculum in the Interaction Period.* The curriculum reform projects were led by a group of respected natural scientists, including Uri Haber-Schaim, Gerald Holton, Robert Karplus, Phillip Morrison, George Pimentel, Glenn Seaborg, and Jerrold Zacharias. At the time, there was general agreement that natural scientists could solve almost any problem, including the problem of determining what to teach and how to teach it to precollege students. Novak commented, "The National Science Foundation held to the precedent established with the support of PSSC [Physical Science Study Committee] that curriculum projects in science must be under the leadership of outstanding scientists. So stringently was this criterion applied that almost no NSF support went to projects where major leadership did not reside with natural scientists" (Novak, 1968, p. 376).

Modernizing the curriculum meant that the science in the textbooks was more complex and abstract than the science that had been taught in the past. During the separation period, the primary source of scientific information had been observation. The new curriculum included descriptions of scientific phenomena that could not be observed. For example, emphasis on the atomic model was widespread. In addition, modern physics relied far more on mathematical evidence for scientific conclusions than had been the case in the past. The new texts incorporated abstract principles, such as energy conservation, as unifying themes. Incorporating these themes addressed the important issue of fostering organization of scientific information but was not always successful, since students had difficulty understanding the themes.

Furthermore, since refinement of the curriculum materials occurred primarily in the context of discussions between the curriculum developers and precollege science instructors, it was difficult to achieve modifications that might have made the science materials more learnable. In these interactions, the natural scientists retained control, and the precollege instructors were involved in pilot testing the materials and providing feedback. Precollege instructors were eager to participate, even though their ideas were often ignored. Novak (1968) reported, for example, "The scientists called the shots" (p. 376). W. W. Welch described the reform efforts as follows: "Scientists were usually hesitant to accept the criticism of their 'science' from science teachers, unless very convincing substantiating data were provided. More often than not, decisions on revisions were based on debates and arguments among the project staffs" (W. W. Welch, 1979, p. 288). In retrospect, many science educators thought that the high difficulty level of the middle school and high school curriculum materials stemmed from this tension between science teachers and natural scientists. Thus, although the reformers wished students to understand science, they were unwilling to modify the curriculum to accomplish this goal, and instead left it to precollege instructors.

The reformers viewed modern science as elegant and parsimonious. There is little evidence that they expected it to increase the difficulty of science. On the contrary, many reformers believed the modern ideas would ease the burden on students. Thus, the reformers ignored precollege teachers who complained that the material was too difficult, expecting them to figure out how to communicate the material in the textbook.

For example, in the laboratory guide for the Physical Science Study Committee, the authors address the difficulty of reading the texts by commenting, "The most important point to remember is to adjust your assignments to the reading ability of your pupils" (Physical Science Study Committee, 1966, p. ii). It is not clear how this would occur, since it was not possible to modify the text.

To illustrate the strengths and limitations of the reform movement, we consider one elementary and two secondary curriculum projects in detail. A number of exciting elementary school curricula were developed during the reform movement. These materials were generally guided by the theories of student knowledge development or learning discussed in the disposition section, more than were the secondary school materials. Two science curricula for elementary students illustrate this

situation. The Science Curriculum Improvement Study (Karplus & Thier, 1967) developed by Robert Karplus at the University of California, Berkeley, was inspired by Piagetian theory and focused on identifying patterns of reasoning and encouraging students to develop more powerful scientific reasoning strategies. The *Science—A Process Approach* (Commission on Science Education, 1964) curriculum discussed in the disposition section was inspired by the information-processing theory of Robert Gagné. Careful task analyses were a feature of this work.

Science Curriculum Improvement Study. Robert Karplus, a professor of physics at UC Berkeley, designed a reform of the elementary science program called, revealingly, the Science Curriculum Improvement Study (SCIS) (Karplus & Thier, 1967). Karplus's ideas were compatible with Bruner's admonition that science could be taught responsibly at any age, and were guided by Piaget's emphasis on concrete experience, as described in the disposition section. SCIS abandoned the textbook of the separation period in favor of a kit of materials, a teacher's guide, and a few student worksheets, reflecting the emphasis on concrete materials. The kit was essential, according to the developers, to motivate teachers to engage students in hands-on work.

Topics were selected to illustrate important scientific ideas using hands-on experiments. Some activities came directly from Piagetian experiments, such as (a) a density experiment involving determining which objects float and which objects sink, (b) a balance beam experiment aimed at both proportional reasoning and separation of variables, and (c) sorting activities involving leaves, shells, and other natural materials. Other activities extended Piagetian work. For example, a clever approach to relative position and motion was based on "Mr. O" (where O stands for observer). Students placed plastic models of Mr. O in various locations and described the location of objects relative to themselves and to Mr. O. For example, Mr. O, handily fitted with magnets, could be attached to the side of a swing set or to the swing itself. Students on the swing might say, "I am below Mr. O, moving left to right." Some activities, such as building and observing an aquarium, were reformulations of activities common in elementary school classrooms.

The overall organizing scheme of SCIS was the learning cycle—exploration, invention, discovery—inspired by Dewey (1938). Following this view, students should "explore" an idea without guidance, then the teacher should "invent" the concept of interest in a class discussion, and finally students should "discover" relationships by systematic investigations. A film from the project, titled "Don't tell me, I'll find out," illustrates how successful this approach can be. In the exploration lessons students constructed aquaria with water, sand, plants, and fish. In a few days the sides of the aquaria were green. In the invention lesson, a question these first-grade students raised was, "How did the sides of the aquarium get green?" This invention lesson concluded with a set of conjectures. Students decided the green sides might come from such things as (a) green paper someone dropped in the aquarium, (b) too much fish food, or (c) the plants on the bottom of the aquarium. In their discovery activities, these ideas were tested. As is apparent, success depended on the skills of the elementary teacher.

The SCIS curriculum featured a few carefully chosen topics, rather than covering all the topics in the text curriculum. This decision came from trial and refinement in the classroom, and from the intuitions of natural scientists who endorsed the hands-on notion. Morrison (Apelman, Hawkins, & Morrison, 1985) encouraged this approach, arguing that often less is more. Essentially by studying fewer topics, students would learn linked and coherent scientific ideas.

The SCIS curriculum, like the nature study of the 1900s and the spiral curriculum of the 1930s, was compatible with a developmental perspective on elementary-school-aged students, yet little or no interaction between developmental theorists and curriculum designers took place. Rather, natural scientists designed the activities and classroom teachers tried them out. Reformulations based on feedback were common, but the structure of the curriculum was retained. The SCIS curriculum revealed the value of creative activities as well as the limitations of discovery learning. It was common for students to enjoy the activities yet not change their ideas about science. SCIS provided overarching themes for the curriculum but focused student activity on individual experiments. As a result, knowledge integration was left to individual students, augmented by class discussion. This succeeded in some classes and for some students (Bowyer & Linn, 1978; Linn & Thier, 1975).

Although many precollege instructors resist hands-on science and find the "move from foreground to background" difficult, a group of enthusiastic elementary schoolteachers and school districts endorsed SCIS. Results from meta-analysis suggest that the curriculum, perhaps by increasing emphasis on science, was just as successful as the traditional text in preparing students for achievement tests (Shymansky et al., 1983). And versions of the curriculum remain in use today in the United States and many other countries.

Physical Science Study Committee. The Physical Science Study Committee (PSSC) was the first secondary reform project. Jerrold Zacharias at the Massachusetts Institute of Technology attracted a group of distinguished natural scientists, including Phillip Morrison and Edward Purcell, to help with this effort, which began in 1957 (Goldstein, 1992; Swartz, 1991). The participants included Uri Haber-Schaim of MIT, who was in charge of the high school laboratory and the team leader for the materials prepared for middle school students; Francis Friedman of MIT, who coordinated the texts; Gilbert Finlay, from the University of Illinois, who produced the teacher materials; and Steve White, who coordinated the films (Goldstein, 1992).

Examination of the teacher's resource book (Haber-Schaim, Cross, Dodge, & Walter, 1976) provides a perspective on this curriculum. The course was aimed at the "top fifth of students academically" (Swartz, 1991, p. 24). These students were already enrolled in physics courses, so the curriculum was not designed to attract students to physics, and it acknowledged tracking as appropriate for advanced courses. The developers described the course as follows: "We feel that a course in physics must contribute its share to the general intellectual development of the student. That is, it has to give the students the opportunity—or better yet, require him—to reason, to learn to express his thoughts clearly, and to be able to follow the development of ideas presented by others, whether orally or from the written page" (Haber-Schaim et al., 1976, p. i).

The view toward physics knowledge was one of taming nature. According to the authors, physics could be described as "the purposeful interrogation of nature" (Haber-Schaim et al., 1976, p. i). The authors also emphasized appreciation of science. They stressed the ability to recognize uncertainty and to distinguish between essential and peripheral findings. They noted that opinion and dogma must be separated from evidence. The authors also pointed out, "We would like the course to develop the student's aesthetic sense . . . learning to appreciate the beauty of . . . a concise mathematical formulation of a natural law" (Haber-Schaim et al., 1976, p. i).

In the teacher's resource book, the needs of classroom teachers are addressed from the standpoint of logistic arrangements and teaching style. The authors suggested that instructors "learn to guide your students by raising questions rather than by providing answers" (Haber-Schaim et al., 1976, p. ii). The authors noted that laboratory write-ups could be a chore to write and read, instead saying, "We recommend that each student keep a legible record of what he does at the time he does it. His notebook should contain answers to the questions raised in the Laboratory Guide" (Haber-Schaim et al., 1976, p. ii). They also commented on the chore of grading homework and recommended instead that students present their results at the blackboard.

To simplify assessment, PSSC developed multiple-choice achievement tests. Assessment measures were developed with help from expert test developers, including Henry Chauncey, the first president of the Educational Testing Service (ETS). The authors encouraged high school science teachers to use both the tests and other indicators such as ability to handle experiments. The PSSC developers pointed out that students who achieved at a high level at the end should not be penalized for their slow start, based on the view that learning is cumulative. They expected assessments to tap understanding of broad principles but not to help diagnose weaknesses.

A major contribution of PSSC is a series of films developed by Zacharias. The films show experiments that cannot be done in the classroom, provide difficult demonstrations, and illustrate the thinking of physicists other than the teacher. "The films are an integral part of the course and when used properly save time in adequately studying a topic" (Haber-Schaim et al., 1976, p. iii).

The difficulty of the material was apparent even to the casual observer. After considering alternatives, the PSSC team chose to include all major theoretical ideas. The text covered 27 topics and featured 47 experiments. For example, the introduction addressed light; chapter 1 explored refraction. Chapter 2 introduced a particle model of light, chapter 6 introduced the ripple tank, chapter 7 did interference. At the end of each chapter were questions about the material. These questions were closely related to the topics covered. For example, some questions concerned the size of an image depending on its location relative to the principal focus of the lens. There were no extensions to everyday or practical situations, based on the decision of the developers to omit applications because of time constraints (Goldstein, 1992).

The PSSC curriculum emphasized an abstract, quantitative view of science. This is reflected in the films and the text. The approach is illustrated by the emphasis on ripple tanks and air tracks. The developers believed that these devices would really help students. Thus, PSSC teachers were warned to spend time preparing for these lessons. For example, the following statement appeared in the teacher's resource book:

ADVANCE WARNING: In Chapter 6, your students begin to work with ripple tanks, one of the most interesting and instructive parts of the course. But, YOU NEED TO GET YOUR RIPPLE TANKS OPERATING NOW TO GAIN SOME EXPERIENCE BEFORE YOUR STUDENTS START TO USE THEM! No matter how busy you are, it is essential that you check your ripple tanks soon. (Haber-Schaim et al., 1976, p. 7, emphasis in the original)

Then, when ripple tanks were introduced, the guide pointed out, "Here is a real opportunity to drive home some of the aspects of 'the scientific method.' Experience with quantitative and careful observation of wave motion—isolating events, correlating phenomena, generalizing results—can teach students more science than hundreds of pages in books" (Haber-Schaim et al., 1976, p. 38).

The knowledge required to explore the ideas in PSSC is quite sophisticated. It is not surprising that only a portion of the top 20 percent academically found the materials accessible. Zacharias seemed to have developed a course he would have enjoyed as a student. At least in retrospect, Zacharias wished to prepare students better, not to attract more students (Swartz, 1991). Thus, enthusiasm for the air track and the ripple tank reflected the view that students would be able to incorporate the implications of these experiments into their own views of motion and light. Students who were struggling with the particle model of light and friction-free motion might simply be confused, as later studies suggested (Pfundt & Duit, 1991). Yet the seventh edition of PSSC appeared in 1991 and, for a segment of the student population, remains appropriate (Swartz, 1991). For the best students the experiences in PSSC build on their intuitions. And for these students, the problems are challenging and interesting. Students who enjoy the curriculum prefer exploring challenging ideas because they are there, rather than applying ideas to current scientific problems (French, 1986; W. W. Welch, 1979). These students resemble the "converging" students identified in the CLP case study.

The legacy of PSSC is most apparent in the films and apparatus that were inspired by Zacharias, an experimentalist. The first films designed and executed by physicists came from PSSC. These pioneering efforts laid the groundwork for a wealth of later materials, including the Mechanical Universe, a series of college physics lectures illustrated with computer graphics (Goodstein, 1990).

Harvard Project Physics.  Harvard Project Physics represented an interaction between a professor of physics who was an expert in the history of science, Jerrold Holton; a high school physics teacher, Jim Rutherford; and a science educator, Fletcher Watson. They received 8 years of NSF funding and trained hundreds of precollege instructors to use the materials. Feedback from students and teachers using the material guided refinement of the program. But, as in PSSC, the input from trials was filtered by the project leadership.

The project goals were "to design a humanistically oriented physics course, to attract more students to the study of introductory physics, and to find out more about the factors that influence the learning of science in schools" (Rutherford, Holton, & Watson, 1970, p. 1). Unlike PSSC, HPP was intended to expand the audience for science courses and to appeal to a broader portion of high school students than the traditional course. The view of physics advocated by the authors was also subtly different from PSSC. Here the focus was on the beauty of nature. The authors noted that laboratory physicists "cannot force new phenomena on nature, they can only show more clearly what nature is like" (Rutherford et al., 1970, p. 1). And applications of physics concepts were emphasized.

Specifically, the goals of HPP were (a) to communicate ideas that characterize physics at its best rather than as an assortment of isolated bits, (b) to present ideas in historical and cultural perspective and show that physics is a many-sided human activity, (c) to give students immediately rewarding experiences in physics as well as knowledge useful in the long run, (d) to make it possible for precollege professionals to adapt to interests and abilities of their students, and (e) to take account of the importance of the precollege professional and the vast spectrum of teaching situations. The goal of knowledge integration (as defined in the CLP case study) is apparent (Holton, 1978).

How were these goals achieved in practice? We examine the discussion of heat and temperature. The notion of heat energy was introduced in the context of the steam engine. The text pointed out that the steam engine was invented by engineers before the physics of heat was understood. The evolution of the modern steam engine was detailed and the creativity of engineers was emphasized. The role of heat in doing work as investigated by Joule was used to introduce the notion of heat energy and to distinguish this view from the caloric. Leading up to the notion that energy is conserved in the universe, the next section dealt with energy in biological systems.

The concept of energy conservation was addressed historically from a philosophical as well as scientific perspective. HPP pointed out that the nature philosophers believed that the universe could be understood by direct observation and criticized the mechanistic scientists for analyzing nature, mathematizing it into abstraction, "torturing her with experiments." They felt this gave the wrong idea of science, just as a dissected flower gives the wrong idea of a living wild flower. These same scientists pushed along the idea of conservation of energy by holding the philosophical idea that there is a unity of natural phenomena (Rutherford et al., 1970, p. 60). The text returned to the topic of heat in the chapter on the kinetic theory of gases, introduced internal energy, and went on to measurement of the speed of molecules. Thus, science was placed in a social context. The philosphical perspective was emphasized, compared to other available texts, and the text told a story about physics. A broad range of complex scientific ideas was introduced, and the ideas were related to each other at an abstract level.

Problems for students to solve focused on conservation of energy and on the definition of work. Problems probed the limits of the information supplied. Complex, everyday problems were neglected, but problems like estimating the kinetic energy of a pitched baseball were presented.

Overall, HPP described an integrated view of physics as a historian of science would understand it. The arguments were complex and required substantial knowledge of related topics. For example, appreciating that the Watt steam engine was an improvement over the Newcomen steam engine required understanding of heat transfer, insulation, and specific heat. In addition, students had to keep many ideas in mind until those ideas were revisited in subsequent chapters.

The view that science is done by individuals was well established in the text. Examples of art and poetry were used to suggest the intellectual culture of the times. Precursors to today's emphasis on equity and diversity were apparent in the discussions of inventors and other historical figures. If students could construct a view that mirrored the one in the text, they would be very well informed indeed. Making all the integrations could be difficult. This knowledge integration task was left largely to the student. The overarching discipline-specific themes, such as "energy is conserved across biological and physical systems," were powerful and appealing to experts but too abstract for many students.

The letter to students at the end of the text clarified the goals of HPP. The authors pointed out that advances in physics were rarely achieved for the practical purposes that they accomplished. They argued for the unforeseen advantages of basic research. They also acknowledged the need to diligently examine the possible uses of science to control for inappropriate uses. Basically, they described the course as providing an induction into the world of the research natural scientist.

Fundamentally, HPP described the social components of scientific advance in the context of demanding scientific concepts. Because it was so demanding, HPP did not succeed in expanding the audience for science courses (Swartz, 1991; W. W. Welch, 1979). Research on HPP suggests, however, that the curriculum was more appealing to women students than traditional courses (Cronbach, 1982; W. W. Welch, 1973). Today, HPP and PSSC serve about one-third of the precollege market (Goldstein, 1992).

In summary, the curriculum reform projects shifted the goals of science courses to more up-to-date scientific ideas and introduced more complicated models of scientific concepts, including models from molecular biology, kinetic theory, and nuclear physics. In addition, the reform projects introduced more complicated mathematical analyses of scientific information, and emphasized themes such as "total energy is conserved."

Following the scaffolded knowledge integration framework articulated in the CLP case study, we analyze the impact of the reform curricula on (a) integrated science knowledge and (b) ability to solve everyday science problems. The reformers seemed to believe that principles, theories, and themes would motivate students to integrate their knowledge; however, evaluation studies revealed that students had many difficulties linking science information (e.g., W. W. Welch, 1973). In addition, students had difficulty when they attempted to connect science instruction with their everyday experiences. These difficulties became especially apparent as researchers examined the specific ideas that students held about scientific phenomena (e.g., Driver & Easley, 1978).

***Science Activities in the Interaction Period.*** The reform projects employed discovery learning activities to foster inquiry skills. As discussed in the disposition section, this emphasis on inquiry skills stemmed from new views of the development of scientific understanding popularized at the Woods Hole Conference (Bruner, 1960). Rather than leaving inquiry skills to general courses in reasoning, to teach reasoning in science the reformers incorporated opportunities for guided discovery learning into the science curriculum. The science laboratory featured guided discovery learning, replacing the conflict between demonstration and hands-on experience that arose during the separation period.

Many in science education embraced discovery learning (Apelman et al., 1985). Although the reformers realized that adding discovery to the science curriculum would increase the amount of time needed to study a topic, this information was never fully integrated into thinking about the secondary reform effort. Recall that the SCIS elementary curriculum did reduce the number of topics dramatically. As mentioned, Morrison, one of the originators of PSSC, popularized the idea that "less is more," meaning that students understand more when the total number of topics that they study is less. Yet Morrison was overruled, and the secondary curriculum materials developed during the interaction period tended to increase the number of topics in the curriculum, and to result in teachers rushing through science topics.

Discovery laboratory activities were added to the curriculum to reinforce the intuitions of the reformers that students needed experience engaging in scientific inquiry, both to understand the nature of inquiry and to gain enthusiasm for science learning. There were several problems with implementation of the discovery learning activities. In some cases, students and instructors alike complained that the activities were extremely constrained, and that students had very limited opportunities for discovery. In other situations, students had extensive opportunities for discovery, and the science instructors complained that students might not learn anything from the experience and would instead engage in mindless investigation (Bredderman, 1983; Shulman & Tamir, 1973). Research comparing discovery and traditional instruction suffered the same fate as the studies of laboratories and demonstrations in the separation period. Results were inconclusive, owing to the complexity of the question (Linn, 1986; L. Resnick, 1981; Shulman & Tamir, 1973; Shymansky et al., 1983). Ultimately, discovery activities could empower students to become lifelong learners, but often such activities served primarily to entertain students and frustrate teachers. Identifying an appropriate balance between guidance and discovery continued to trouble researchers and educators during the interaction period and remains a focus of the partnership period.

Besides discovery learning, a variety of technologically motivated activities were explored during the interaction period. All of the reform projects took some advantage of the modern technology, finding ways to use films and creating new apparatus. Building on the demonstrations of the separation period, these innovations were designed to illustrate concepts more effectively. As mentioned previously, air tracks and ripple tanks provided students with the opportunity to use laboratory equipment that had guided research scientists in the past. These materials also helped make thinking about mechanics and about wave motion visible, just as simulations made thinking about heat and temperature visible in the CLP case study. Often, however, the materials failed because they implemented the absorption approach to instruction. In some cases students passively observed the demonstrations but did not change their scientific ideas. In others, students extracted the solution to a scientific problem but not the process leading to the solution, so the thinking process was not visible.

In addition, there were some interactions between psychologists and discipline specialists to design technology-based stand-alone curricula. Typically, these materials were intended to deliver instruction augmented by the science teacher. For example, computer-assisted instruction, championed by Skinner (1958), was investigated in several studies (Schramm, 1964). Recent reviews of the work of Skinner suggest that the programmed instruction approach had limited applicability beyond tasks learned by drill (Delprato & Midgley, 1992; Greenwood et al., 1992; S. C. Hayes & Hayes, 1992; Lattal, 1992; Palmer & Donahoe, 1992). The drill approach was not widely adopted in science.

However, scientists found the Keller plan appealing (F. S. Keller, 1954), and embraced the PLATO project (S. G. Smith & Sherwood, 1976). Both of these projects incorporate task analysis, as discussed in the disposition to learn section, and involve (a) breaking the curriculum into manageable units, (b) assigning these units to students to learn on their own, (c) assessing understanding of each unit, and (d) tutoring students who do not succeed on the assessment. Keller plan courses implemented in science were reasonably successful (J. A. Kulik, Kulik, & Carmichael, 1974). Examination of these courses suggests that they were guided less by task analysis than by personalized instruction. Instruction was personalized in that students were tutored on the material that they had not learned. Personalization was also possible in pacing. Students in Keller plan courses set their own pace; they took examinations when they were ready; there were no lectures or other instructional activities.

PLATO courses resembled the Keller plan in being self-paced but followed the inquiry approach to instruction using computers and distance learning. Developed at the University of Illinois, these courses were delivered by computers. They featured many innovative approaches to learning with computer technologies that are apparent in materials developed during the partnership period (Jones & Smith, 1990; B. A. Sherwood & Sherwood, 1986; S. G. Smith & Sherwood, 1976).

In spite of philosophical differences, both of these approaches to teaching science had useful features. First, they encouraged autonomous knowledge integration by providing students with material and asking them to learn it on their own. Second, they took advantage of the tutoring capability of science teachers by providing interaction with instructors only when students had difficulties. Third, these courses featured clearly stated goals and easy to analyze assessment procedures. Although some complain that computer-assisted instruction takes responsibility away from the learner and may be detrimental to creative work (Jaynes, 1975), examination of these courses suggested that they actually encouraged students to behave autonomously.

Psychologists became more interested in instructional activities during the interaction period. For example, in the 1966 edition of *Theories of Learning*, Ernest Hilgard and Gordon Bower discuss "Learning and the Technology of Instruction." In his chapter, Hilgard discusses the potential applications of theories of learning to instruction. Hilgard substantiates the conjectures put forth by Dewey at the turn of the 20th century by calling for an engineering of science education. Hilgard

states, "It is by now commonly recognized that it is not possible to move from basic science directly to applied science without a number of intervening steps, some of which require all the ingenuity and scientific acumen of the basic research itself," (Hilgard, 1964, p. 413). L. Resnick (1981) summarized preliminary evidence about the unique characteristics of science learning, calling for more research on science instruction. By the end of the interaction period, however, as Greeno noted, progress on learning and instruction had been slow: "Serious analyses of tasks used in school instruction have not played an important part in the recent psychological studies of learning" (Greeno, 1980, p. 726).

*Shifts During the Interaction Period.* During the interaction period the goals of the curriculum shifted. Natural scientists incorporated science knowledge developed after 1900 and emphasized more abstract themes and principles rather than the practical ideas of the separation period. Although the reform projects sought to provide an integrated, sophisticated view of science close to that of experts, the results fell short of expectations. Science remained difficult to learn and advanced courses continued to attract only the best students. From the standpoint of the scaffolded knowledge integration framework, the goals of integrated, linked ideas and of ability to solve relevant, everyday problems were neglected. By seeking to teach an abstract, principled view of science, the reformers neglected the progress in teaching practical science during the separation period. This theme is revisited in the partnership period.

Exploration of promising new scientific activities, especially those associated with discovery learning, reinforced the conclusions of the separation period about the limits of comparison studies. The shift in the goals of science courses toward a more socially oriented view of science knowledge construction was pioneered in HPP. It is interesting to contrast the perspectives on science knowledge in PSSC and HPP. PSSC described science as the purposeful interrogation of nature and emphasized how scientists refute ideas. In contrast, HPP encouraged a reflective and constructive process by emphasizing how views of scientific phenomena developed historically. The HPP authors concluded, "Physics is the study of what makes the world go. We think it is too beautiful to be kept secret from anyone, no matter what his eventual career plans will be" (Rutherford et al., 1970). Here the emphasis was more on appreciating the implications of physics than on interrogating natural phenomena.

Research on instruction was not yet well enough developed to help improve science learning, but interactions in disposition to learn and instruction offered promise. In particular, during the interaction period, the focus was on the learner, and aspects of disposition to learn science were incorporated into the curriculum. The elementary school curriculum emphasized concrete experience compatible with developmental theories. The secondary school curriculum emphasized abstract ideas and cross-cutting themes consistent with Piaget's stage of formal operations. Research on how students learn science revealed, however, that these general developmental stages did not adequately capture the nature of student understanding of science concepts. Rather, as discussed in the disposition section, students of all ages relied on observations and personal experiences to make sense of science and developed reasoning skills in the context of specific problems rather than in an abstract sense.

Links between disposition to learn and instruction were also apparent in efforts to design science materials to meet the needs of a broader range of students. HPP emphasized the social nature of scientific advance. SCIS engaged students in inquiries relevant to their own lives. Yet, many reform curriculum materials and activities reinforced stereotypes about who can learn science and sent the message that science is abstract, impersonal, and not relevant to the lives of individuals. These issues became more prominent in the partnership period.

## Instruction in the Partnership Period

In the partnership period, science education researchers and developers face the challenge of preparing future scientists while also educating all students, with a special emphasis on groups that have traditionally been underrepresented. This requires new goals aligned with the needs of citizens and new activities that connect science and society.

Motivation for a new direction comes from evaluation of the reform projects of the interaction period showing weaknesses in science. For example, in 1983, *A Nation at Risk: The Imperative for Education Reform* brought together a vast array of national and cross-national studies that illustrate weaknesses in student understanding of science and reinforced the importance of teaching science to all students (National Commission on Excellence in Education, 1983).

In addition, mechanisms for conceptual change and knowledge integration described in the disposition section provide a new perspective on how students develop scientific ideas, and opportunities to incorporate technology into the science curriculum allow new teams of reformers to take advantage of these mechanisms.

During this period, these new teams conducting research on instruction often feature partnerships between psychologists and science education experts. These partnerships are starting to shape a model of instruction that encompasses both disciplines. Partnership projects are characterized by a community of mutual respect. Individuals with diverse forms of expertise come together to address science education reform. They value each other's contribution to all aspects of the process. Important parallels between the mutual respect characteristic of partnership projects and the goals of mutual respect in the science classroom are emerging. In both cases, the objective is to create an atmosphere where participants draw on the expertise of each other to gain understanding.

Experts in cognition have catalyzed many of these partnerships, drawing attention to how cognitive analysis of science understanding sheds light on student learning. This analysis points to new forms of instruction, and also helps explain why some innovations have failed.

In addition, the intuitions about instruction that guided curriculum reform during the interaction and separation period are now more substantially represented as partnership projects broaden the role of teachers from precollege settings. Precollege teachers have contributed firsthand understanding of instruction and have helped partnership projects refine practices. Whereas during the interaction period many observers complained that the leaders of the reform projects were reluctant to incorporate information from practicing teachers, during the partnership period the intuitions of practicing teachers have contributed to effective instructional provisions.

Another group of individuals who have contributed to partnership projects are experts in technology. As is illustrated in the CLP case study, many interesting technological innovations are components of these projects. Bringing the tools of experts such as real-time data collection to the classroom is one contribution of technology experts.

Partnership projects have used two innovative methodologies. One has been to gather information that is more precise and detailed than has been used in previous investigations. Thus, researchers gather (a) videotapes of students working in small groups to solve problems, (b) audiotapes or videotapes of students talking aloud as they solve problems or make sense of phenomena, (c) observations of classrooms where students interact to solve problems or better understand scientific ideas, and (d) videotapes of students synthesizing, analyzing, critiquing, or integrating information about science. Furthermore, partnership projects rely on integration of evidence from a multitude of methods, some labor intensive and based on a small sample, such as protocol analysis, and some more generalizable, such as essays, student solutions to complex problems, and projects generated by all students.

Second, partnership projects have been innovative in testing new instructional approaches in regular science education settings. The primary mechanism for investigating the effectiveness of intuitions concerning science instruction has been trial and refinement, as illustrated in the CLP and chemistry case studies described at the beginning of the chapter. Essentially, partnership projects implement their ideas in classroom settings and refine their intuitions as a result of feedback from these experiences.

Whereas many studies provide multiple forms of evidence for the success of an innovation, of course, there remain two-group comparisons and their modern counterparts, meta-analyses, that are also used to characterize the effects of science innovation. For example, J. A. Kulik and Kulik (1989) used meta-analyses to show that courses with computers are more successful than typical courses in imparting an understanding of science. This finding has parallels to the earlier comparisons between laboratories and demonstrations. The results need contextual interpretation before they can have policy impact. In addition, during the partnership period, a meta-analysis comparing the reform curricula of the interaction period with typical courses revealed that, when the reform activities are judged by outcome measures designed to assess their goals, they are effective. However, when traditional achievement tests are used, the reform projects and the traditional curricula are equally effective (Shymansky & Kyle, 1992; Shymansky et al., 1983). This meta-analysis suffered from the same drawbacks as were identified for the two-group comparisons of the separation period: The studies are only as informative as their outcome measures.

*Goals in the Partnership Period.* Goal setting during the partnership period has included both defining new standards for science learning and reanalyzing the nature of science education goals. The new standards efforts build on activities started in the 1930s to identify the topics that students should study.

The reanalysis of goals for science education stems largely from the broadening of the audience for science instruction and also reflects contributions from cognitive science to our understanding of student response to instruction.

New Standards. Efforts to set standards stem from frustration about science performance combined with growing understanding of the importance of rich, complex goals. Many assert that a better list of science topics is needed, that ordering of the topics needs further refinement, and that accountability of students needs to be improved. This decoupling of the goals from the curriculum creates a gap that might be impossible to fill or, worse, might be filled with memorizing rather than understanding.

Several projects embody this perspective, including Project 2061 (Rutherford & Ahlgren, 1990), the National Research Council Standards (National Committee on Science Education Standards and Assessment, 1992; 1993a; 1993b), and the National Science Teachers Association Scope and Sequence and Coordination of Secondary School Science (National Science Teachers Association, 1991).

Project 2061 is sponsored by the American Association for the Advancement of Science (AAAS), with collaboration from the National Science Teachers Association. Some leaders of Project 2061 previously participated in the design of HPP and sought to build on the success of this program. Project 2061 has worked with science teachers and natural scientists to identify a common core of ideas and to narrow the curriculum. The common core of ideas describes the goals for science courses of the future, but not the methods to achieve them (American Association for the Advancement of Science, 1993). This emphasis on goals but not methods reflects the view that methods are best devised by teachers and publishers. Reviewing the materials from this group, however, suggests that the goals might be unteachable—like the goals of the separation period—without attention to the activities and modes of learning necessary to achieve them. In addition, Project 2061 has failed to narrow the curriculum. The project developers have defined over 1,000 separate benchmarks and indicated many thousands of links between these benchmarks.

Defining a common core of ideas bears resemblance to efforts during both the separation and interaction period to identify 20 or so main ideas that would guide the curriculum, and has examples today (Hazen & Trefil, 1991). In Project 2061 this common core of ideas includes (a) being familiar with the natural world and recognizing both its diversity and its unity; (b) understanding key concepts and principles of science; (c) being aware of some of the important ways in which science and technology depend on one another; (d) knowing that science, mathematics, and technology are human enterprises, and knowing what that implies about their strengths and limitations; and (e) using scientific knowledge and ways of thinking for individual and social purposes. The Project 2061 framework goes on to examine each discipline and identify key ideas that students should know at elementary, middle school, and high school levels.

Whereas during the separation period it was assumed that students would do nature study during the elementary school years and then begin to learn the scientific ideas of expert scientists, in Project 2061 students are expected to do discovery activities based on concrete operations up to the end of the fifth grade, and then in sixth grade start to learn the scientific ideas and principles of expert scientists. A spiral approach is advocated. Thus, starting in sixth grade, students are introduced to viruses, the atomic model, molecular kinetic theory, and other unobservable phenomena. They are not expected to understand microscopic phenomena until later. This approach has a discontinuity between the concrete experiences of the first five grades and the sophisticated scientific ideas introduced starting in the sixth grade. The view of learning inherent in this approach is based on "readiness" to learn more advanced ideas. This project interprets research on student understanding of complex distinctions like heat and temperature, mass and weight, power and energy, and speed and acceleration in terms of constraints on student reasoning and concludes that these distinctions "are not worth the extraordinary time required to learn them" (American Association for the Advancement of Science, 1993, p. 81). This view is compatible with the view of disposition from the interaction period but neglects analysis of knowledge integration raised in the partnership period and seems destined to produce students with disconnected, incohesive ideas.

Another approach to goal setting is an undertaking of the National Research Council to establish science education standards and assessment (National Committee on Science Education Standards and Assessment, 1992). This group is also led by natural scientists with the participation of classroom teachers and cognitive scientists. The goals in the reports that have emerged thus far are similar to those of the reforms of the 1960s. The committee will identify the concepts and principles of science that students need to learn at each age and the inquiry skills that students need in order to manipulate the information in the science principles. These reformers seek to narrow the curriculum, acknowledging the difficulty of dealing with all of the current science topics. Commentators on the standards-setting effort have suggested that progress to date is not fully responsive to research on students' understanding of science and the development of science concepts (Linn et al., 1994). This project has an added objective of designing assessments to determine how well students are achieving the goals.

A third approach to reformulating the goals for science instruction is the *National Science Teachers Association Scope and Sequence and Coordination of Secondary School Science* (National Science Teachers Association, 1991). This group is seeking to cut across the traditional "layer cake" approach to science instruction in the United States and achieve a more integrated understanding. The argument is that the sequence of biology, chemistry and physics works against knowledge integration, because students do not see connections across the scientific fields that they study. In addition, many students drop out of the sequence before they take physics, thereby limiting study of physical science.

All of these goal-setting projects represent serious efforts to respond to the difficulties that numerous national and international comparison studies have revealed. Yet these reform efforts often rely on models of disposition to learn science and on instruction from the interaction or separation period. In particular, many of these projects view the learner as constrained by development and not ready for advanced work, absorbing knowledge, and learning science ideas in isolation.

These projects often see technology as a topic in the curriculum but neglect its use in instruction. They neglect the process of knowledge organization and knowledge integration, listing the elements of understanding instead. They focus more on abstract principles than on how these ideas will be applied. Finally, although all these projects acknowledge the difficulty of selecting information from among the vast array of scientific knowledge that has been accumulated and continues to be accumulated, none of the projects has yet taken an approach that is likely to narrow the curriculum.

New Partnership Goals.   The new goals for science instruction of the partnership period are closely tied to new science learning activities. Partnership projects have developed new goals for science instruction by incorporating a new view of disposition to learn and a more precise analysis of the process of learning. Projects focus on knowledge integration and emphasize linkages among topics far more than has been the case in the past. For example, in CLP, specific research studies that characterized the sorts of links that students were forming are used to reformulate the activities. Similarly, the Israeli chemistry program has undergone regular reformulations based on studies of students' understanding. Furthermore, in contrast to earlier reform projects, partnership projects feature a regular process of trial and reformulation. In the past, evaluation studies took place after the project had been finalized, and consequently only a small amount of information could be incorporated into the instructional approach. As discussed below, recent reformulations of projects from the interaction period offer an opportunity to rectify this problem.

In defining new curricular goals, the impact of computer technology has been particularly strong. The new technology has created modeling environments, networked communication, and other approaches to science learning that were not previously available, making new goals possible.

The real question concerning science curricula and technology during the partnership period is not a comparison of approaches, as occurred in the separation and interaction periods, but rather how an approach such as computer simulation might be used to help students gain an understanding of science concepts, distinguish among a repertoire of models, and comprehend scientific phenomena in an integrated manner. Methods for exploring science activities are more and more matched to the goals of the curriculum and incorporate the innovative methodologies described earlier for the partnership period.

Identifying goals that lay a firm foundation for future learning while proving accessible and interesting to students has proved challenging. One promising approach, developing and distinguishing a repertoire of models, extends the notion of the spiral curriculum. Rather than labeling early ideas as incomplete, this approach helps students identify their models, heuristics, rules of thumb, and other explanatory mechanisms. Instruction then encourages students to learn how to determine when to use the various models. The ability to cultivate an appreciation of science in everyday phenomena is compatible with Einstein's view of science as the "refinement of everyday thinking" (Einstein, 1954). This approach incorporates a view of disposition to learn based on making sense of scientific events.

The goal of understanding everyday scientific problems is very compatible with a goal of emphasizing the social nature of scientific learning. Students are far more interested in discussing problems relevant to their lives than in discussing abstract theories. When science is viewed not so much as a body of knowledge or skills but as a social process involving modes of interaction between experts and novices, methods of investigation, and techniques for determining the truth value of assertions, then the goals of the curriculum that are emerging from partnership projects become convincing (see Driver, 1988, for a similar discussion).

*Science Activities in the Partnership Period.*   One response to recent calls for reform is to build on the reforms of the interaction period. Another has been to establish new partnerships based on new goals for science courses to help students link ideas, develop a repertoire of models, and connect science and society. Both approaches have contributed new views of science activities.

Reformulating Earlier Science Curriculum Materials.   The NSF is funding many collaborations to reformulate materials from the reforms of the 1960s, drawing on the experiences of curriculum users. These projects involve curriculum developers, publishers, and equipment experts and are called Triad projects. Each project is required to establish a relationship with a publisher to ensure that the materials will be marketed effectively.

An example of a Triad project is Science for Life and Living (SLL), a commercially available, elementary-level curriculum (Biological Sciences Curriculum Study, 1989, 1990; Bybee & Landes, 1990). SLL encourages students to build on existing concepts and to develop ideas relevant to their personal experiences, incorporating recent work on disposition to learn. Discovery-based learning activities are guided and scaffolded by teachers. This project takes advantage of the social nature of science learning by providing well-structured group activities.

SLL has goals close to those of the projects of the interaction period. In particular, one can see relationships between the SCIS program and the SLL program. In both of these programs, inquiry activities are emphasized, as are realistic scientific investigations. An exciting feature of the SLL curriculum is the emphasis on technology. Students investigate technological tools like screwdrivers and technological innovations like modern insulation materials. Observers of the SLL curriculum raise some of the concerns reflected in the goal-setting activities discussed earlier. Many complain that the content of SLL is limited in comparison to that of traditional textbooks. These complaints draw attention to the tension between those setting standards for science education who create long lists of topics and those devising curricula who base the pace of instruction on classroom experience (e.g., American Association for the Advancement of Science, 1993).

In addition, trial and refinement of the SLL materials revealed that methods for scaffolding learning to develop integrated understanding were often unsuccessful, and many teachers found the group activities chaotic. One difference between SLL and more modest partnership projects is that SLL immediately tried materials in many classrooms instead of refining them in a few classrooms before expanding the program. Incorporating all this feedback proved difficult, especially in the available time.

Activities That Help Students Link Ideas by Encouraging Metacognitive Skills. A broad set of new partnership projects generally led by individuals who have training in both natural science and cognition (e.g., A. diSessa, 1992; Linn, 1992a; Linn & Clancy, 1992b; Minstrell, 1982; R. D. Pea & Gomez, 1992; R. D. Pea, 1992; Reif & Larkin, 1991; Scardamalia & Bereiter, 1992; Songer, 1993; B. Y. White, 1993; Wiser & Carey, 1983), are defining new activities that help students link ideas to address the new goals discussed above.

In discussing disposition to learn during the partnership period, we characterized students and groups of students as struggling to make sense of scientific phenomena and evaluating rather than absorbing information. We emphasized metacognition as a dispositional characteristic and conceptual change as well as knowledge organization as problem-solving mechanisms. In addition, those studying instruction have sought to take advantage of the social nature of the learner as originally emphasized by Dewey and elaborated by Vygotsky (1978). Partnership projects incorporate the view of disposition to learn science that is emerging in the partnership period and also contribute to understanding of the mechanisms governing learning.

As already noted, individuals involved in examining how students understand scientific phenomena first developed models of instruction based on the view that students have misconceptions that need to be replaced. This replacement view is no more than an elaboration of the absorption model from the separation period. Research in the partnership period demonstrated that students reformulate the ideas they encounter in keeping with their intuitions. The challenge, then, for science education is to design instruction to support students as they reformulate their ideas.

A model of how students link ideas has emerged from studies examining how students solve scientific problems (Pfundt & Duit, 1991) and from studies examining the development of students' scientific concepts (A. diSessa, 1988; E. L. Lewis, 1991; Linn & Songer, 1991). Researchers analyzing students making sense of scientific information find that students struggle when everyday vocabulary is used in scientific ways. For example, students asked to explain temperature remark that "Babies have a temperature when they are sick." In addition, students rely on their observations of the world, remarking that, for example, "Objects in motion come to rest." Students also find scientific explanations difficult to connect to their practical experiences. For example, students expect wool to make things warm and do not believe it will insulate cold things. In addition, these studies suggest that students often miss connections between examples that are evident to experts and frequently cannot follow the supposedly straightforward examples provided in science textbooks (Clement, 1983). For example, many students have no experience with how cars move on icy roads, a common example of a low-friction system. Further, students regularly contort new information to align it with their practical experiences and often link examples and observations based on superficial rather than substantive information (J. H. Larkin & Reif, 1979). In addition, students often resort to memorization and other rote practices because they cannot make sense of the instructional materials available (Songer, 1989). This rich, complex data base is difficult to analyze but compelling in its primary message: Making sense of scientific information is a

process of trial and refinement, and students who succeed take responsibility for this process.

To foster the process of understanding scientific concepts and taking responsibility for learning, the partnership projects have designed activities that help students refine ideas from other students in the process of making sense of scientific phenomena. These projects look to research collaborations for models of the social nature of science learning (Lave & Wenger, 1991). They engage students as investigators and critics. One important challenge of this effort has been to renegotiate the authority structure in the classroom. Analyses of students' reasoning reveal that many students rely heavily on the textbook and teacher as authorities instead of taking responsibility for their own understanding and discussing their ideas with their peers (Linn, in press). Thus, activities in the partnership projects encourage and support students as they become responsible for making sense of information for themselves. This approach entails helping students distinguish evidence from hearsay and innuendo, encouraging them to seek links and monitor their own processes of knowledge integration, and helping them identify appropriate models and knowledge organizations for the information that they encounter. When performed by groups of peers guided by an instructor, the process of understanding science, reformulating ideas, and appropriating information from others contributes to understanding (Burbules & Linn, 1991).

A primary reformulation of the view of instruction in the partnership projects is the entwining of inquiry skills with discipline-specific information. This is perhaps the major distinction between the activities in the Triad projects, mentioned above, that continue the traditions of the interaction period and the projects that focus on cognitive task analysis and understanding how students struggle to make sense of scientific information. Evidence suggests that inquiry skills do not generally exist in the abstract but are in fact closely entwined with the information to which they are applied. This characteristic of student knowledge organization has been referred to as "situated cognition" (J. S. Brown et al., 1989; Collins et al., 1989). There are ways in which this view of knowledge development is consistent with the ideas put forth by Bruner in *The Process of Education* (1960). In particular, Bruner discussed aspects of the spiral curriculum that harkened back to the reforms of 1932, and also stressed the importance of the development of context-specific scientific reasoning rather than reliance on inquiry skills as separated from concept understanding. The partnership projects reflect a shift from viewing scientific reasoning as a general skill to viewing scientific reasoning as connected to problems students solve. Following this view, linking scientific notions to the problems students need to solve rather than to the general skills they need to learn are the goals of the course. And, since knowledge integration proceeds slowly, instructional design requires careful analysis of the links among specific scientific ideas as well as the identification of intermediate forms of understanding of scientific events that contribute to more complex understanding (A. diSessa, 1988; 1993). Focusing on the development of scientific concepts also draws attention to the metacognitive skills necessary for organizing this information and for applying it to new problems.

Students' epistemological perspectives about scientific knowledge fundamentally determine how they respond to efforts to support them as they make sense of scientific information. If, as mentioned earlier, students seek authoritative sources and prefer to accept these sources without reflection, then it will be difficult to foster the knowledge integration process. If, instead, students view science knowledge as progressing by fits and starts, subject to reformulation both historically and in the future, then their efforts to understand science will be fundamentally different. The HPP curriculum, with its emphasis on the historical organization of scientific knowledge, emphasizes the epistemological aspects of science that the partnership projects have embraced. One can see the partnership projects as seeking to refine the perspective of HPP, which, although fascinating, frequently motivated students to absorb information rather than actively engaging students as investigators and critics.

Even if the authority structure in the classroom is renegotiated, and students feel more responsibility for learning, they may still believe that there are only two kinds of scientific ideas: those that are true and those that are false. To redirect students' attention to the process of acquiring scientific knowledge and the mechanisms by which truth values are assigned to information, we must reformulate the curriculum (Schoenfeld, 1983; Songer & Linn, 1991) to emphasize metacognition and responsibility for one's own learning. To foster metacognition, specific activities aimed at self-monitoring, reflection, planning, and other cognitive skills are essential.

Psychological research demonstrates the importance of metacognition in knowledge integration (Corno, 1992; Flavell, 1976). In science, a variety of partnerships have included metacognitive skills in instruction. Among the most influential is Novak (Novak et al., 1983) in biology education. Novak used the concept mapping tool to help students become more reflective about their own ideas. Concept maps represent in visual form the relationship between concepts and ideas. These maps can be used to help students clarify the links among their ideas. Special computerized tools have also been designed to help students construct concept maps (Fisher, 1987). Novak and his associates have designed curriculum materials that help students construct concept maps and engage them in appropriate reflective activities to analyze their understanding of concepts as represented by the maps (Kahle, 1990). Ultimately students use the maps to keep a record of their progress and knowledge integration, as illustrated in the chemistry case study.

R. T. White and Gunstone (1989) also have demonstrated the benefits of activities intended to help students develop metacognition and to integrate information. These researchers have focused on distinguishing among alternative scientific models for problems that are relevant and meaningful to students. To foster metacognition, White and Gunstone advocate teaching procedures that help students engage in sustained reflection. R. T. White (1992) claims that "the main implication for curriculum is that it must be flexible and allow room for the teacher to exercise judgment." Metacognitive skill is best developed when learners feel independent of the teacher, rather than viewing the teacher as an authority. Clearly, students are less likely to examine their own ideas flexibly if they are primarily comparing their ideas with those of the teacher or the textbook. White argues, "If quality learning is the goal, the curriculum must not be narrowly specified." White points out

that efforts to establish national curriculum standards and goals may threaten the quality of education because they produce uniform and shallow learning and establish authority structures that stand in the way of students developing skills as investigators and critics.

The Project to Enhance Effective Learning (PEEL) in Australia illustrates how metacognitive strategies can be enhanced in science programs as well as other disciplines (Baird & Northfield, 1992). Initiated by science teachers, this project enlists natural scientists and psychologists to help identify promising metacognitive strategies and design instruction to emphasize these strategies in the classroom. Trial and refinement characterize the classroom investigations. Initiated in 1985, PEEL is now used in many schools in Australia.

This shift to activities that support students as they make sense of scientific phenomena and monitor their own learning, rather than activities that encourage students to develop inquiry skills and use those to learn the ideas of scientists, reflects a distinct shift in the science curriculum. During the interaction period, activities were designed for learners viewed as constrained by development and ability, whereas during the partnership period activities take advantage of the intellectual capabilities of the learner, including especially the learner's ability to reflect on her or his own learning processes. Partnerships design these activities by including experts in the discipline and in psychology. These activities are more likely to succeed if students have appropriate models and case studies to guide knowledge integration.

Activities That Make Thinking Visible. Knowledge integration has been the goal of projects, starting with the progressive education movement's emphasis on student-initiated investigations. Yet it has been far easier to describe failure than to instill success. Whitehead (1929) noted that inert, unconnected knowledge is the outcome of most instruction. In the partnership period progress has been made in changing this situation by making thinking more visible. A. diSessa (1992) and B. Y. White and Frederiksen (1990) have explored models in science and studied how students compare and contrast models as well as develop models consistent with those of experts. diSessa advocates creating "microworlds" where students can explore their ideas and test conjectures. Linn and Clancy (1992a) advocate case studies that make the floundering and reflection of experts visible.

It is possible for students to engage in the design of scientific models using new technologies (R. Tinker & S. Papert, 1989). Powerful computer modeling environments have been developed to support novice science learners (A. Goldberg, 1984; Richards, Barowy, & Levin, 1992; Rubin et al., 1988). For example, A. diSessa (A. diSessa & Abelson, 1986) created the BOXER environment to support individuals and groups as they explore interesting problems or projects. He found that successful groups could achieve breakthroughs comparable to those of research scientists. In one class guided by an expert teacher, a group of students invented a representation for motion in space that, after several trials and refinements, resembled graphing (A. diSessa, 1992). In addition, a variety of researchers inspired by Papert (1980) have designed microworlds that allow students to explore and test models autonomously (A. diSessa, 1982). Under ideal discovery conditions, students could build and refine sophisticated models that were personally meaningful and integrative. Finding ways to guide learners while allowing some autonomy, given the broad range of alternatives available, has challenged instructional designers.

Other partnership projects have made tools of research scientists available to students using off-the-shelf products like STELLA (Mandinach & Cline, in press; Mandinach & Thorpe, 1987). Mandinach (Mandinach & Thorpe, 1987) used the STELLA modeling environment to allow students the opportunity to model scientific phenomena and compare their models to natural experiments. Similarly, in the CLP project, expert tools for real-time data collection were made available to students.

All of these environments support students as they visualize models for scientific phenomena. However, for students to understand the nature of a model and of the science it models, these activities need to be a part of the curriculum. Many alternative approaches have been explored in curriculum projects. One approach was to identify effective representations for scientific phenomena (Reif & Larkin, 1991; Wiser & Carey, 1983). Clearly, such representations could help students understand scientific models and serve as a focus for knowledge integration. Another approach is to help students understand a progression of models. In HPP, as mentioned, students were encouraged to look historically at the models used by scientists. Other projects build on students' intuitive models and refine them to the expert perspective (B. Y. White & Frederiksen, 1990). Generally, having opportunities to experiment with models has helped students develop a repertoire of models and understand the relationships among them. Several studies have demonstrated that by learning a progression of models, students are more successful in understanding the target model than when they are taught the target model alone (F. Goldberg & Bendall, 1992; B. Y. White & Frederiksen, 1990).

A variety of partnership projects have sought models to help students integrate knowledge about difficult science topics. Driver (1988) has worked closely with teachers to incorporate her research on alternative frameworks. Project STAR (Science Teaching through Astronomical Roots) (Schneps & Sadler, 1989) uses astronomy as a foundation to teach a few physics principles that can organize ideas in the physical sciences. A number of researchers have focused on reformulating instruction in mechanics, especially by identifying procedures and mental models that help students make sense of complex ideas (Redish & Wilson, 1993). Projects initiated by Nussbaum (Novick & Nussbaum, 1978) have taken the tack of finding creative ways to help young students understand the particulate model of matter. Nussbaum used early examples of what have later come to be called benchmark experiments or anchoring conceptions, and also encouraged students to refine their ideas in a social context (Nussbaum, 1989). This approach was remarkably successful for the small group of students studied, and suggests the advantages of scaffolding knowledge integration.

Overall, efforts to foster knowledge integration are less successful than efforts to describe how students respond to scientific problems. Being able to describe the process of knowledge integration is far from sufficient for designing instruction to change the process. Curriculum designers have tried explicit instruction as well as guided discovery using computer models.

Guided discovery reaches more students and helps students develop autonomous learning skills. In order for this approach to work reliably, however, more research and reflection is needed. This approach depends, in part, on students developing a repertoire of scientific models that they can apply to their own experiences.

Activities That Help Students Develop a Repertoire of Models for Their Own Scientific Experiences. Partnership projects have re-opened the question of activities for science courses and have dramatically shifted the focus away from the earlier quest for the most central and advanced views of science concepts. These projects illustrate the possibility of modifying the activities of science courses to emphasize relevant, everyday experiences and problems. Indeed, a large number of research studies have demonstrated that students may have excellent understanding of the problems and principles in science textbooks and yet be unable to apply their ideas to everyday problems (A. L. Brown, Kane, & Echols, 1986; Songer, 1989). For example, Kuhn and her colleagues found that students' standards of evidence and forms of inference were different when they confronted everyday problems than when they confronted abstract, decontextualized problems (D. Kuhn et al., 1988). By expanding the curriculum to everyday problems, the partnership projects have increased the challenge of knowledge integration but also improved the prospects for training lifelong learners.

Everyday problems are the emphasis of some projects following the cognitive view of the learner. Recall that during the interaction period, Zacharias decided to leave applications of scientific ideas out of PSSC because of the time that it would take away from learning science principles. In contrast, during the partnership period, the broadening of the audience for science, along with the increased relevance of science and policymaking and voter decision-making, has led to the realization that science curriculum materials, especially those for middle school students, are most effective if they address relevant, everyday problems. If, as suggested in the disposition section, learners develop reasoning skills linked to problem solving, then selecting the problem is the central issue.

Incorporating everyday problems into the curriculum has raised new questions. For example, some projects have discovered that the models in the reform textbooks are too abstract to be useful for everyday problems. This was illustrated in the CLP project. Another difficulty is that there are sensible alternative frameworks for viewing scientific problems that are not represented in textbooks but are particularly effective for certain practical and everyday problems. Often these models are, in fact, utilized in engineering and design courses. Drawing on insights from engineering has broad implications for problem solving. Engineers emphasize design and approximate solutions to complex problems in ways that could enhance precollege instruction. These views have only recently been considered, since engineers were not primarily involved in any of the reforms of the interaction period.

Taken together, these explorations of alternative models, combined with the research described earlier about model progressions and the experience of HPP in providing historical models of scientific phenomena, have resulted in a reexamination of the goals of the curriculum and, in particular, an analysis of the models that students might find most useful for learning science. Finding a single model that would help students answer textbook questions as well as explain phenomena such as the distance required to stop a car, the thermal properties of modern fabrics such as Gore-Tex, or the aerodynamics of dance, has proved impossible. Instead, it has become apparent that, just as scientists have a repertoire of models for scientific phenomena, so might students. Programs designed to foster in students not only a repertoire of models but also techniques for distinguishing among the models have been explored during the partnership period. This is one of the goals of the CLP curriculum as well as a focus of B. Y. White and Frederiksen (1990) and A. diSessa (1992). A similar distinction could be made for models of learning, where mathematical approaches generally are parsimonious but narrow, whereas qualitative models are broader but complex.

One dimension that has continuously arisen in these investigations involves the contrast between mathematically formal models and qualitative models (Reif & Larkin, 1991). In many cases, qualitative models have been more explanatory and useful for dealing with complex and ambiguous problems. In contrast, mathematical models have the advantage that they allow parsimonious and efficient solutions to the problems to which they are applied. An added benefit of qualitative models is that they often help students focus on the essential features of the problem rather than throw a veil of numbers over the situation.

Activities that support learners as they acquire a repertoire of models emphasize that the learner acquires scientific understanding in a social context and that the context in which one learns might dispose one to have particular views about scientific phenomena. This context might also dispose one to have particular views about who can participate in the scientific enterprise. We discussed these issues of participation in the disposition section and mention them again here because they represent links that have emerged during the partnership period between the concepts of disposition and opportunity to learn. We turn now to activities that emphasize the social nature of science and contribute to broader views of science and participants in science.

One approach to emphasizing relevant problems by taking a broad perspective on science is often referred to as science and technology in society, or STS. Reformulations of curricular goals both nationally and internationally reflect a worldwide trend toward greater emphasis on the societal implications of science (Fensham, 1988; Rosier & Keeves, 1991). In general, these curriculum reforms seem inspired by current views of disposition to learn yet are so ambitious that they are likely to sacrifice breadth for depth.

A variety of approaches to STS has emerged. One approach adds emphasis on science and society to existing programs (Association for Science Education, 1986; J. Lewis, 1980). These projects, carried out in the United Kingdom, introduce science topics by identifying a particular social problem and its technological aspects.

In contrast to adding units on STS to the curriculum, the Dutch national reform effort incorporates these themes in all aspects of instruction, thus increasing the probability that students will gain an integrated understanding of the relationships (Eijkelhof & Kortland, 1988). This project, called PLON, has a goal of providing a balance between preparing students to cope

with their future roles as consumers and citizens and preparing students for careers in science. The curriculum emphasizes physics as a tool for decision-making at the personal and societal level, and also includes opportunities for students to master scientific concepts and develop scientific reasoning skills in the context of relevant problems.

Another curriculum that integrates STS issues into the program is Chemistry Study in Victoria (Sanders, 1992). This Australian science curriculum has as a goal imparting all the essential knowledge theories and concepts of traditional chemistry while studying chemistry in a social and technological framework. Thus, decision-making associated with the economic and environmental impact of chemistry is emphasized. For example, in the 11th and 12th grades, the following units are studied: (a) materials, (b) chemistry in everyday life, (c) chemistry in the marketplace, and (d) energy and matter. The integrated approach is reflected not only in the topics of the syllabus but also in the principles of instruction and in the assessment. The Science Technology and Communication Chemistry project in Canada ("Canada," 1984) takes a similar approach. These programs draw on pupil's everyday experiences to develop chemical ideas and ensure that these ideas have direct relevance to students' lives.

Thus, a broad range of national and international projects are defining more relevant and integrated activities for science and are directly engaging students in linking scientific studies with everyday experience. The activities take into account recent research on disposition to learn yet seem to add these emphases to an already packed curriculum. The problem of what to omit may be neglected.

Activities That Take Advantage of Social Support for Learning. Dewey emphasized that all learning is social. Nevertheless, the social component of knowledge construction was generally neglected until the partnership period. In fact, in the 1930s, researchers compared students learning in groups with those learning alone and concluded that group work was inadvisable and should be discontinued (Curtis, 1932, p. 107; Whipple, 1932).

As mentioned earlier, the most compelling justification for social learning environments is their similarity to communities of practice for expert scientists. Lave and Wenger (1991) discussed how old-timers or experts socialize newcomers or novices, and suggested that learning environments that involved novices learning from experts could be beneficial. This is the basic premise of the Communities of Learning in Science project (described below) and has been a feature of other curriculum innovations.

To illustrate how partnership projects have incorporated social aspects of learning into the elementary school curriculum, we discuss a partnership project undertaken by Ann Brown and Joe Campione that we refer to as Communities of Learning in Science (CLS) (A. L. Brown & Campione, 1990a). This project applies important work in reading comprehension to the problems and issues involved in science knowledge acquisition. The team includes elementary science teachers with expertise in biology, cognitive researchers, and technology experts. The group pioneered reciprocal teaching (A. S. Palinscar & Brown, 1984) and found that it fostered knowledge integration and understanding of complex ideas. This cognitive research inspired the design of the CLS curriculum.

A major theme of this work is to create classroom communities where thinking and "learning how to learn" are common. In such communities, teachers and students practice and model varied approaches to learning, including (a) collaborative coaching and tutoring inspired by the reciprocal teaching approach (A. S. Palincsar & Brown, 1984), (b) "ownership" of knowledge useful to the collective community inspired by research on expertise (Lave & Wenger, 1991), and (c) group responsibility through the distribution of knowledge across all community members, inspired by the work of Vygotsky (1978). In this program, students investigate environmental science questions, create group or individual reports, and provide support for each other in their investigative activities. This approach to science learning can be seen as a refinement and extension of the projects from the progressive education movement, which were in turn refined by the integrated physical science approach.

In this approach to project-oriented science, students develop expertise in some aspect of science or technology. They may become experts on topics such as peacocks or computer graphics. The approach encourages teachers and students to create multiple zones of proximal development, thus fostering knowledge development in all students. A feature of this approach is the idea of "majoring," whereby each student selects a particular area of expertise. The idea is that students can teach their expertise to others using approaches similar to reciprocal teaching. By empowering every child to be an expert in some area, all children, even those who normally do not see themselves as classroom leaders, have expertise and knowledge to share. Students select their own majors, thus giving students practice in determining information that is necessary for completing projects and also information that is likely to be valuable to the group as a whole. Research to date demonstrates that this distributed expertise approach successfully fosters knowledge development in classrooms with learners of varied interests and abilities (Campione, A. L. Brown, & Jay, 1992).

The curricular goals for the CLS project focus on the recurrence of content themes, similar to the spiral curriculum described in 1932 and refined by Bruner in the '60s (Bruner, 1966). Investigatory activities take place in 10-week research cycles. Each unit begins with an introductory activity on adaptation that engages the students and captures a major idea of the upcoming unit. This activity is viewed as a benchmark, following the perspectives of Minstrell described above. Then, students and teachers generate questions, categorize the questions, and identify subtopics for further investigation. Each student selects one of these subtopics in conjunction with his or her peers. Students then conduct research to investigate their question and communicate this information to others using a jigsaw approach. By researching a question in a group context and then communicating that information to another group, students have an opportunity to integrate the information more than they would in a typical project-based course. For example, students might investigate the adaptation of a peacock in one group and the adaptation of a garter snake in another, and then get together to compare their perspectives.

Students and teachers change their roles with regard to authority in these classrooms. Often students become more expert on topics than their teachers. Furthermore, rather than always referring to the teacher for assistance, students frequently get help from more experienced students. Students can be experts in writing and editing, as well as in a particular science topic. In addition, this model is extended to cross-age grouping, where students in more advanced classes might be tutors for students in the lower grades.

The primary objective of this program is to ensure that all students feel that they are seriously investigating scientific questions and that other members of the community are interested in their findings. By creating community values and standards for evidence and conclusions, it is possible to have students conduct projects that are more responsible than was often the case in previous project-based undertakings. Furthermore, the emphasis on distributed expertise in the CLS program means that projects are not completed and discarded but instead become a part of the classroom resources.

The CLS project illustrates how partnership activities link instruction and disposition to learn. By allowing students to major in topics that they can master, the project matches the activities to the student's interests and inclinations. By using a group process to decide on activities and to communicate information about findings, the CLS project ensures that students discuss a broad range of scientific information and experience firsthand how social interactions about science can contribute to understanding.

As illustrated by the CLS project, social learning environments can communicate important information about the nature of science and foster understanding of science concepts. A variety of projects have sought ways to harness social interactions such that they lead to better understanding of scientific concepts and more integrated knowledge.

Many of these projects use computer technology. Some projects have focused on the social construction of science knowledge and drawn on technological tools such as networking. These include R. F. Tinker's KidNet (R. F. Tinker, 1987), Pea's Collaborative Visualization Project (R. D. Pea & Gomez, 1993), and Songer's Kids as Global Scientists project (Songer, 1993). Scardamalia and Bereiter in the CSILE project (1992) implement a networked communication methodology that allows students to send and receive messages about models of scientific phenomena, to gather information and provide it to the group, and to contrast alternative perspectives on scientific events. Scardamalia and Bereiter report that the sorts of interactions students engage in are similar to those one might find in a productive scientific community.

Pea (1992) seeks a similar kind of community process in a project designed to foster understanding of concepts in optics. Pea has now extended this work to a new project investigating global climate (R. D. Pea & Gomez, 1992). In these projects, students not only send messages to each other but also can contact experts in atmospheric science in the networked environment and have both a television and computer link. Thus, they can see each other while having a conversation and can also jointly examine data.

Songer's (1993) Kids as Global Scientists project similarly emphasizes networked communication, here incorporating the perspectives of students in different countries on issues having to do with climate change. Songer finds that students' perspectives on science are broadened and deepened as a result of the opportunity for networked communication about global climate.

What we have learned about inclination and motivation to participate in the scientific enterprise suggests that there may be some potential drawbacks to group learning experiences. In particular, rather than interacting in a community of mutual respect, students in group situations may reinforce norms of the society, thus communicating to other students information about whether or not they are welcome in the scientific community. Agogino and Linn (1992) describe how undergraduate engineers can ostracize lone female participants in cooperative groups. Clearly, the social nature of learning is a complex influence on science knowledge integration (Cohen, 1986; de Bono, 1973; Heller & Hollabaugh, 1992; Heller, Keith, & S. Anderson, 1992; J. M. Levine, L. B. Resnick, & Higgins, 1993; Linn & Burbules, 1993; Webb, 1989; and chapter 26). Groups may suppress ideas of individuals, discourage nontraditional students, and accept superficial conclusions.

Like any other science learning activity, group learning requires careful, judicious implementation in order to be effective. Unmonitored and unguided group learning experiences may reinforce societal norms. In contrast, carefully managed group learning experiences may increase respect and communication among groups that have difficulty interacting in other situations. When groups share perspectives and elaborate each other's ideas, they can reach understandings that go beyond the knowledge of each participant.

***Shifts During the Partnership Period: Scaffolded Knowledge Integration Revisited.*** The partnership period has marked a shift from a focus on helping individual students absorb abstract concepts deemed important by scientists to a focus on collaborative design of curricula that helps communities of learners explore real-world problems and phenomena. This shift reflects both the limited success in achieving the first agenda and a recognition of the increased importance of science in our everyday lives. It also represents real steps toward the linking science called for by Dewey and reinforced by Hilgard at the end of the interaction period. Individuals concerned with science education are working in concert to develop a model of science curriculum materials and science activities that foster the sort of knowledge integration deemed appropriate for lifelong science learners.

Examination of the specific ideas that students have about science, and study of the process of knowledge integration and conceptual change, have informed this perspective on science learning and instruction. This shift represents a change from focusing on absorption of ideas, to focusing on inquiry skills, to focusing on discipline-based cognitive goals. Many questions remain: How can we best encourage knowledge integration? What are the ultimate goals for the science curriculum? The most radical view suggests that students should be provided with the opportunity to make sense of scientific phenomena and that the goals that the students achieve should be deemed the ones that were appropriate. A more didactic approach makes the goals explicit and seeks scaffolding or more explicit instruction to achieve these goals.

No matter how one goes about answering these questions, a fundamental dilemma remains: the trade-off between breadth of coverage and depth of understanding. To meet this challenge, we need to create lifelong learners who can learn new material "just in time" to use it. Given the rapid advance of science knowledge today, combined with unprecedented change in employment opportunities, learners will need to master new fields regularly.

Another important shift during the partnership period has been in the direction of respecting the ideas and contributions of people other than expert scientists—not only members of partnership projects, but also students in science classrooms.

Finally, the view has emerged during the partnership period that students are constructing understanding of themselves as learners and that these metacognitive strategies are crucial not only for knowledge integration but for lifelong science learning. Finding mechanisms that foster this kind of understanding remains challenging, but evidence of successful practices is beginning to emerge.

## Nature of Instruction: Shifts

The findings of the partnership period hark back to the scaffolded knowledge integration approach suggested in the CLP case study. The four main elements of this approach are reflected in all the partnership projects, although each project emphasizes different aspects of the framework.

The first aspect of scaffolded knowledge integration is to select a repertoire of goals for students that make science accessible and relevant to everyday experience. This involves grounding learning in a relevant, everyday context, since students need to juxtapose and blend the ideas they find in textbooks and classes with their life experiences. They will not integrate this information successfully unless they understand everyday as well as scientific models and can distinguish one from the other. Learning that is tied exclusively to the domain of the abstract or formal models used in advanced research frequently motivates students to memorize rather than understand and sends the wrong message about the nature of science. In these cases, students might learn the formal model but lack the skill for applying it to naturally occurring problems, where the connections between the model and the problem may be complicated. Developing a repertoire of models, including pragmatic and descriptive models, expands the audience for science and also makes the nature of science more apparent.

The second aspect of scaffolded knowledge integration is to help students develop a repertoire of effective models by representing those models in many different ways and illustrating how they are used. Collins et al. (1991) refer to this as "making thinking visible." Essentially, the representations for scientific phenomena need to be available to and manipulable by students. Activities involving microworlds and other models can help accomplish this. Modeling activities help students consider alternative representations for scientific phenomena. Clement's example of anchoring conceptions (Clement, 1991) is another example of a program that provides structure for knowledge integration. Minstrell takes a similar approach, emphasizing benchmark experiments that encourage students to distinguish and verify their own and others' models for scientific phenomena.

The third aspect of scaffolded knowledge integration involves supporting students as they jointly link ideas. Students regularly come to believe that there are "three Ohm's laws," or that objects come to rest at home but remain in motion at school. To help students construct links among their ideas, instruction needs to engage them in the process of identifying similarities and combining related ideas. A number of examples in partnership projects suggest how renegotiating the authority structure in classrooms and creating communities of scholars can help students link ideas. In addition, students need opportunities for sustained, monitored problem solving that result in complex products. Students link ideas and make connections between experiences as they conduct self-directed investigations.

A fourth aspect of scaffolded knowledge integration is empowering students to reflect on the learning process, to develop metacognitive skills, and to take responsibility for their own learning. This approach gives students the role of both investigator and critic in the science curriculum. By comparing ideas, students gain experience in monitoring their own comprehension and integration processes. Often, students are satisfied with their first product and are reluctant to revise it. When they have the opportunity to compare their ideas to those of other students, then revision and review are more common. By critiquing other ideas, students can deepen and elaborate on their own understanding. Students can develop this skill in a realistic context by critiquing each other's progress. This is a fundamental aspect of communities of practice and offers promise for science classroom communities as well.

A repertoire of approaches to scaffolded knowledge integration has been identified. The most successful instruction is probably best developed through trial and refinement in the social context of the classroom. In this way, all partners can contribute.

Our understanding of the nature of science instruction has improved in the course of the 20th century, resulting in considerable innovation in selecting goals and activities. Dewey's call for partnerships that operate in an atmosphere of mutual respect has emerged as a positive force in establishing science education reforms. The arguments of the progressive education era, that sustained investigations to help students understand scientific ideas, have been expanded to include a more realistic view of the ways experts gain understanding. Researchers now combine multiple methods and rely on diverse forms of evidence to decide among promising classroom activities. Dewey's vision of a linking science, echoed by Hilgard, is beginning to be realized as partnership projects develop a repertoire of promising instructional models.

## CONCLUSIONS

Since the turn of the century, the number of disciplines involved in improving science education has greatly expanded, and the various groups concerned have begun to appreciate the benefits of collaboration.

Perhaps the major advance in science education has been the recognition that improving science learning and instruction is a far broader and more difficult problem than the one science educators initially set out to solve. Rather than transmitting scientific ideas to future scientists, science educators now seek to foster a lifelong quest for integrated scientific understanding in all citizens. Curriculum reformers, pedagogy experts, and natural scientists have elucidated the complexity of science

learning. Natural scientists, while continuing to argue that scientific principles are elegant and "simple," have come to acknowledge also that even students completing the most sophisticated courses at the best universities lack fundamental understanding of scientific phenomena.

The complexity of scientific understanding is reflected in the comments of leading natural scientists. For example, Barbara McClintock argues that understanding in biology means achieving "a feeling for the organism," and she recommends that future scientists "listen to the organism" (quoted in Keller, 1983). Einstein's argument that "science is the refinement of everyday thinking" (1954) accurately characterizes the process that students follow to achieve sophisticated scientific understanding. Fostering the efforts of students to develop their everyday thinking so as to gain a deeper understanding of scientific principles offers an exciting direction for science instruction and helps frame the much more difficult problem that we now define as science education. Thus, the current challenge in science education is to foster students' abilities to refine their everyday thinking, to achieve "a feeling for the organism," and to integrate their observations and experiences with more sophisticated models of scientific phenomena.

To meet this challenge we need a rich repertoire of explanatory models that link instruction and disposition. In addition, we need to refine and elaborate these models by conducting investigations in classrooms, schools, and groups of schools.

This section (a) characterizes changing views of science education, (b) synthesizes shifts in the disposition to learn science and the nature of instruction, (c) highlights current issues in science education, and (d) forecasts features of future periods in science education.

## What Leads to Changed Views of Science Education?

We anticipated that conceptual change in science education could be described in terms of expanding the repertoire of models of science learning and instruction and distinguishing among them. We support this conjecture below by discussing the repertoire of models for the science learner and the goals of science courses.

*Repertoire of Models of the Science Learner.* The most prevalent intuitive model of the science learner is based on absorption: Students learn what they are taught. In the separation period, the audience for science instruction consisted of students who learned what they were told. During the interaction period, one justification for reform was the desire to attract more students to science courses. To accomplish this, natural scientists expanded the repertoire of models for science learning and embraced the view that students learn by deploying processing capacity and developing scientific inquiry skills. This developmental model was consistent with observations and intuitions that natural scientists had about their own learning; it also reflected the views of science instructors who collaborated on reform projects.

This model justified curricula that emphasized concrete experience with scientific phenomena and chronicled historical scientific ideas. It also explained why reducing information-processing demands improved learning outcomes. Nevertheless, embracing the developmental model did not attract future scientists, although it probably increased the satisfaction of those who succeeded. Many students abandoned science, finding the courses inaccessible. This approach—that of taking account of students' views of scientific phenomena and beliefs about science—was more successful later when reinterpreted by partnership projects.

Reform in the partnership period has been strongly influenced by the desire to expand the audience of science courses to all students and by extensive evidence that, in general, students lack scientific understanding. When it became evident that science courses were not succeeding—even for the best students—reformers turned attention to cognition, reflecting on how students organize and integrate knowledge. This effort has generated a model of the learner that emphasizes metacognition (self-monitoring, reflection, planning, and knowledge integration) and the social aspects of learning. The partnership investigators seek to help students emulate the way in which scientific experts integrate information, monitor their ideas, build on ideas of others, and develop a personal perspective.

To encourage metacognition, science courses need to help students (a) understand the nature of science knowledge, (b) see themselves as responsible for developing explanations, (c) build on the ideas of others while retaining a healthy skepticism about "authorities" and science texts, and (d) integrate ideas by comparing and contrasting, and by determining the conditions under which they apply. The metacognitive model, which has guided the work of many partnership projects, resonates with cognitive research on how students respond to scientific information. It also implies the need to be alert to and sensitive about the social context of science learning, which includes cultural expectations about who can and should succeed in science activities.

These three models of the science learner—as absorbing information, as constrained by development, and as guided by metacognition—each apply to some learners and some topics. The metacognitive model can be seen as subsuming the others, and applying most broadly. Expanding the repertoire of models promises to help all learners increase their understanding of science. Further refinements may involve additional models of the learner and better understanding of when each model applies. New models of the learner that explain how metacognition occurs in a particular discipline and social context are on the horizon.

*Repertoire of Models of Science Course Goals.* In the history of science, a wealth of goals for science courses have been developed and refined. Until very recently, science courses focused on the most sophisticated view of scientific phenomena, even attempting to eradicate other views and labeling them as "misconceptions." Often these sophisticated views came across as "watered down" or "schoolish" rather than as powerful or useful. As scientific models have become more abstract and mathematical and as the audience for science courses has broadened, the promise of this approach has diminished. Teaching based on a single model of a scientific phenomenon contradicts the view that learners are guided by metacognition. The meta-reasoning process requires contrasting and integrating multiple perspectives. Just as different models of the learner apply under certain circumstances, so different models of scientific phenomena are useful under certain conditions.

Already partnerships, especially those including representatives from engineering and technology, are moving toward defining a range of *useful* models of scientific phenomena. These partnerships are designing courses to teach a repertoire of relevant ideas, even including models that are less sophisticated than those held by experts, and approximate or heuristic models that are incomplete but predictive under special conditions.

*Implications.* To foster conceptual change in science education for all learners, and especially underrepresented learners, we need to encourage alternative views, nurture those alternatives that arise, and ultimately distinguish among them. To select wisely among the alternatives, we must study the utility and effectiveness of each view and develop criteria for evaluating them. We must, as McClintock counsels, "listen to the organism" to refine our intuitions about how students learn and what they should understand.

## Synthesizing Learning and Instruction

By the partnership period, the distinction between disposition to learn and the nature of instruction was blurring. In the quest to explain why some students learn science and others do not, there have been shifts from an emphasis on one's general ability to absorb established ideas held by experts to an emphasis on conceptual understanding, metacognition, and social roles as they contribute to the learning of an integrated repertoire of scientific models. At the same time, science educators have identified inherent complexities in learning science as well as impediments to scientific understanding that result from curricular decisions. For example, the relentless increases in the breadth of the science curriculum make it more and more difficult for students to achieve integrated understanding. In addition, the daunting task of organizing diverse scientific experiences requires identification of mechanisms that foster coherence. We synthesize the shifts in disposition to learn and the nature of instruction that have led to the current perspective, discussed below.

*Disposition to Learn.* The perception of disposition to learn has shifted from that of a characteristic of the student to that of a dimension influenced by individual, social, and curricular factors. In the separation period, "general" ability was viewed as a primary determinant of scientific understanding. In the interaction period, researchers differentiated quantitative, verbal, and spatial ability, as well as refining developmental constraints, yet much of the variability in science learning remained unexplained. During the partnership period, science educators have found that metacognition and the social context of learning are primary determinants of scientific understanding. There has been a shift from the view that disposition is immutable and unresponsive to instruction to a growing realization that ability to learn science is culturally determined, responsive to instruction, and linked to the goals selected for science courses.

This trend is reflected in views of how students develop scientific knowledge. During the interaction period, there was a shift from viewing development as a general constraint on understanding to viewing development as a constraint on logical reasoning. Thus, young students were viewed as able to reason about concrete but not abstract materials. During the interaction period, evidence mounted to support a distinction between the development of general inquiry skills and the development of the understanding of science concepts. By the partnership period, the emphasis had shifted from developing inquiry skills to developing scientific expertise. Learners are now regularly viewed as making sense of scientific phenomena rather than as separately developing inquiry skills and models of scientific phenomena. This raises the issue of how best to support students as they organize their knowledge.

Partnership projects, themselves, have identified several views of this sense-making process. In a prevalent view, students develop a repertoire of models of scientific phenomena along with the skills necessary to distinguish among them. Questions concern (a) whether this repertoire consists of coherent or fragmented models and (b) whether the skills for distinguishing models are general, concerned with evidence, epistemology, and coherence, or specific to the discipline. Partnership projects have sought to expand the repertoire of alternative models and to emphasize a view of science as model construction.

The current blurring between disposition and opportunity arises since courses often focus on determining the repertoire of models that students can be disposed to learn, and science educators seek to cultivate a disposition toward knowledge integration. Supporting students in the process of knowledge integration is both a primary concern and a considerable challenge to science educators.

*The Nature of Instruction.* The shift in the disposition to learn has been spurred by changes in the audience for science and the goals of science courses. Instead of merely providing information, instructional programs have begun to encourage students to integrate information.

During the separation period, the emphasis on providing information led to disputes about whether demonstrations or hands-on laboratories were most useful for teaching scientific ideas. Given that the primary goal was to provide information, demonstrations were found to be both more efficient and more cost-effective. The emphasis on inquiry skills in the interaction period justified laboratories as an important component of the science curriculum, although without supporting evidence.

In the partnership period, science educators have analyzed hands-on learning and identified ways to ensure that hands-on experiences lead to knowledge integration. This involves identifying promising qualitative, heuristic, or approximate models for scientific phenomena and devising activities to motivate students to organize their information in patterns, hierarchies, visualizations, or prototypes. In this effort, computer models of scientific phenomena are becoming particularly helpful. A dynamic model often motivates students to move from a phenomenological to a more mechanistic understanding of scientific events.

Fostering knowledge integration also requires effective communication among students and authorities. Scientific understanding typically progresses in a climate of active debate. To this end, one goal is to encourage students to struggle with scientific ideas and grapple with observations versus principles. Creating communities of scholars among science learners is a key aspect of many partnerships. A challenge is to incorporate authoritative views of science into the community discourse without stifling debate.

To increase opportunities to learn science, researchers have shifted their focus from those students who quickly master scientific ideas to those who struggle to make sense of scientific ideas and from those students who come from the same social group, as most scientists did in the past, to all students including those underrepresented in the past. The accomplishments of the most talented students have in the past sometimes lulled science educators into complacency. The new focus has forged links between opportunity and disposition to learn.

## Current Issues in Science Education

Since the turn of the century, major improvements in the science curriculum have been achieved, yet the goal of effective science instruction remains elusive. Today, impatience with current science teaching is reflected in (a) calls for standards for science achievement (National Committee on Science Education Standards and Assessment, 1993a; 1993b), (b) reformulations of national science curricula ("Canada," 1984; Committee on Science and Technology Education, 1992; Department of Education and Science, 1988), and (c) widespread enthusiasm for international comparisons of student progress in scientific understanding.

Below, we discuss current concerns related to science courses: (a) the social nature of learning, (b) the role of computer technology in instruction, (c) the repertoire of goals, (d) the scope of science courses, (e) views of the science teacher, (f) coherence of assessment and curricular goals, and (g) methods of research in science education.

*Social Nature of Science Learning.* How to harness social processes to foster science knowledge integration remains a key and crucial question for the future. The benefits of effective group learning are substantial, but simply organizing students into groups is not sufficient to deal with this complex and difficult area. Because communities of scholars can be derailed easily, the process of social interaction needs to be managed carefully and sensitively. Social interaction in science classes often contributes to and reinforces stereotypes of who can succeed in science. For example, asking male students more scientifically complex questions than are asked of female students sends the message that science is a male domain.

*Role of Computer Technology in Instruction and Learning.* Modern electronic technologies offer tremendous opportunities to improve scientific learning and understanding, but there are potential pitfalls. Dynamic models of scientific phenomena can help students develop their repertoire and distinguish views of scientific phenomena. Communication technologies, including networking and video conferencing, permit greater communication, involving a wider range of expertise, but also require that students have powerful strategies for integrating the evidence they gather.

*Repertoire of Science Course Goals.* To fully utilize the repertoire of models approach to conceptual change, we need (a) helpful models and (b) realistic beliefs about science. In addition, we need to develop in the field of science education a realistic, generative view of science knowledge. Often science educators see only a choice between positivism and relativism because they lack a philosophically rich understanding of scientific advance. One challenge is to obtain models that students find familiar, plausible, and useful, especially those that will evolve naturally into powerful, intellectually sophisticated models. As we identify these models, we need to help those involved in science education understand that, although early models may appear more descriptive than explanatory, too limited in scope, and even incorrect in contrast to sophisticated models, this appearance may be deceptive. By providing such intermediate models, we can help students develop a disposition to make sense of the science they experience. This will help set students on a trajectory that does not culminate with the last formal science lesson, but rather continues as they identify new scientific problems.

*The Scope of the Curriculum.* As scientific knowledge has expanded, the science curriculum has become more and more crowded. Many have called for deeper coverage of scientific concepts rather than fleeting coverage of every topic that currently exists (Eylon & Linn, 1988; Minstrell, 1982; Rutherford & Ahlgren, 1990). During the interaction period, Phillip Morrison, a primary contributor to PSSC, argued that "less is more," i.e., that covering fewer topics in the curriculum ultimately results in greater understanding. Yet we have not answered the question of what constitutes "less." Until this question is answered in an intellectually defensible fashion, we will continue to see curriculum materials that demand far too much and achieve far too little.

*Realistic View of the Science Teacher.* Many complain that science teachers know far too little science. Instead, we might wonder whether we are providing science teachers with perspectives on science that can be taught. Starting in the separation period, science teachers have complained that the science in the textbooks is unteachable; however, up to the present day, little has been done to address this problem. Science teachers are building models of scientific phenomena, of the curriculum, and of how students gain scientific understanding. They have accepted a complex, lifelong challenge and need to be supported and encouraged in this endeavor.

*Coherence Between Assessment and Curricular Goals.* Frequently, educators complain that the science that they are expected to teach differs from the science that their students are expected to learn. Science assessments often conflict with modern curricular goals. This is particularly problematic for the alternative models advocated in this chapter. However, this problem is not new. During the separation period, one reason why science demonstrations were chosen over science laboratories was that general achievement tests were used to assess proficiency in science. Demonstrations were more efficient for communicating the information on the assessment, even though laboratories communicated other, perhaps more useful, information to students. There has been a shift in the focus of assessment from general achievement to more sophisticated problem solving, to a current emphasis on performance evaluation portfolio and reasoning in context. These topics require further investigation.

*Methods of Research in Science Education.* Research has shifted from straightforward group comparisons to more interpretive investigations of science learning and instruction. This shift has led to a debate about the relative strengths of qualitative and quantitative approaches to research in science education. We call on science educators to expand their repertoire of research methods. Just as we ask students to build integrated and cohesive knowledge of scientific phenomena, so must we build integrated and cohesive understanding of science methods. This cohesive understanding requires that we accumulate and integrate information from a broad range of sources. Creating false dichotomies between different methodologies, and even disparaging one or another, is less fruitful than looking for the contributions from each. Quantitative research investigations have sometimes yielded false and irrelevant comparisons that, as Dewey mentioned at the turn of the century, mislead thoughtful educators. On the other hand, qualitative investigations using small numbers of unrepresentative individuals sometimes lack validity as well. Our goal is to build an integrated perspective that draws on a broad range of evidence.

## Future Periods in Science Education

We have identified three periods in the history of science education. In these periods we have focused on the nature of the participation of individuals from diverse constituencies. In the first period, we emphasized the separation among research programs. In the second period, we noted instances in which researchers from different perspectives interacted. In the third period, we focused on partnerships in which researchers from a broad range of constituencies have worked jointly in a context of mutual respect to improve science education. Here we discuss the mechanisms governing patterns of communication in science education and forecast future trends.

*Patterns of Communication.* Looking historically at science education, we see important contributions from experts in natural science, social science, technology, and other fields. To characterize the mechanisms governing these contributions, we identify several key collaborations in each period and then describe similarities. We also note difficulties in communication across fields.

In the separation period, the emphasis was on topics for the curriculum. Researchers in science education borrowed methods from natural science to conduct comparisons focused on labs, teamwork and other issues. Those designing instruction looked to social science for ways to make science easier to learn; they adopted Thorndike's view that complex vocabulary should be reduced in science texts. In addition, the progressive education movement spurred some schools and teachers to adopt a project-oriented approach to science instruction.

In the interaction period, the focus shifted to the learner. Science instructors tried out materials for curriculum developers, pioneering the trial and refinement approach to curriculum reform. Curriculum designers incorporated the views of Bruner, Piaget, Cronbach, Cattell, and others who suggested why students had difficulty learning science. These interactions resulted in guided discovery techniques, compatible with natural scientists' desire to communicate inquiry skills to students. Science education researchers adopted the individual differences paradigm from educational psychology and conducted research reinforcing the notion that only some can learn science. Policymakers and researchers concerned about those who were excluded from science also applied this paradigm, but used it instead to identify the influence of social norms and expectations on participation in science.

The partnership period has shifted the focus to instruction. College physics instructors, still perplexed about why science is so hard to learn, have studied their own students, borrowing methods of cognitive psychology. These natural scientists have discovered that their students hold unanticipated models of physical phenomena. Some have been motivated to seek training in learning and instruction, while others have entered into partnerships with experts in these areas. In addition, natural scientists have collaborated with psychologists and anthropologists to identify successful relationships between students, peers, and instructors. Low-cost, widely available, new computer technologies have spurred experts in computer technology to collaborate with curriculum developers to develop scientific tools for students. The methods of cognitive psychology have been widely used to analyze how students learn from these materials.

***Shifts in Communication Patterns.*** Several themes typify patterns of communication in each period. First, groups borrow methods from each other, often without much additional communication. For example, science educators have appropriated and refined the two-group comparison, the correlational study of individual differences, and protocol analysis. In all these efforts the warnings of Dewey concerning overreliance on scientific methods are relevant. At times, the methods of investigation have conferred status on the results that is unjustified.

Second, science curriculum designers consulted psychologists such as Bruner, Piaget, and Vygotsky, primarily to help explain why students had difficulty learning science. Natural scientists incorporated ideas from psychology such as the emphasis on inquiry that were consistent with their intuitions. Many groups used trial and refinement to tailor ideas from social science to the needs of science education. This form of collaboration has laid the groundwork for the linking science envisioned by Dewey. Syntheses of these efforts at trial and refinement can be seen as models for instruction. One such synthesis is the repertoire-of-models view of conceptual change. In this view, students add scientific perspectives to their repertoire of models rather than replacing one view with another. Conceptual change involves helping students distinguish among models and select the most comprehensive or robust model for specific situations (Linn et al., 1994). Another is the scaffolding or apprenticeship approach to knowledge integration—that is, supporting students as they make sense of scientific phenomena and analyzing the process they use to learn.

Third, individuals have sought training in several fields related to science education, such as natural science and cognition, science instruction and cognition, or computer science and curriculum design. Those with cross-training have coordinated partnership projects and facilitated communication among diverse groups. The NSF program on Teaching and Learning Science and the McDonnell Cognitive Studies Program (Bruer, 1993) have been especially influential. These projects, involving a range of experts, are a realization of the partnerships called for by Dewey, yet they represent perspectives on learning and instruction that are quite diverse.

What exists today are many models of learning and instruction, each in the process of refinement and each offering useful insights for one situation or another. Thus, inspired by behaviorism and information processing, we have intelligent tutors aimed at teaching students a set of production rules. Inspired by Vygotsky and Piaget, we have guided discovery environments aimed at supporting learners in their efforts to make sense of topics they select. The CLP case study describes an environment that helps learners explore a repertoire of models of scientific phenomena. The chemistry case study describes a curriculum tailored to how students develop knowledge. An important if perhaps unanticipated outcome of these collaborations has been a broadening of the curriculum in psychology to include study of learning in complex domains like science.

Thus, a number of mechanisms have facilitated communication across constituencies concerned with science education and fostered a useful set of perspectives in science learning and instruction. This process mirrors in many ways the repertoire-of-models approach to conceptual change that we envision students using to gain scientific understanding. And the repertoire of models has expanded in both psychology and science education.

***The Next Period.*** We imagine two alternatives for future patterns of interaction in science education. One is a regression to previous practice. The partnership period is still new. There is danger of regression to the interaction mode, especially if effective communication between natural scientists and social scientists is not sustained. Fostering communication across diverse constituencies is always problematic. The difficulties are intensified when there are perceived differences in status. Although the partnership projects mentioned in this chapter seem by and large to reduce or eliminate problems in communication based on status differences, this is less true in the broader community concerned with science instruction. Fostering effective communication will remain a considerable challenge, one that we must address in order to be successful in improving science learning and instruction in our society. These communication patterns are particularly crucial as science education focuses more and more on educating all citizens and including students of diverse backgrounds rather than primarily on preparing future scientists.

Another alternative is a new, broader consensus about science education, probably spurred by "renaissance scholars" trained in natural science and either (a) cognition, (b) science teaching, or (c) computer technology. We believe that science education could be advanced if those concerned made efforts to synthesize the curriculum reforms that have been carried out in a variety of partnership projects. This would necessitate focusing on the process of reform as well as on outcomes. By synthesizing the processes that have contributed to effective reform, we might be able to identify more principles, heuristics, approximate models, and rules of thumb to guide future curriculum reformers.

Perhaps the greatest challenge for the future involves incorporating new approaches to learning and instruction into courses for all learners. How can we support young children in their efforts to build descriptive and phenomenological models of scientific phenomena and to use evidence to warrant their conclusions? How can we reach students who see no relevance of science in their lives? This is a challenge that will definitely engage science educators in the future. And the effort will be enhanced by those who choose dual specialization in scientific fields and early childhood education, sociology, or psychology.

We call on everyone concerned with improving science learning and instruction to seek modes of communication that lead to successful synthesis of the many promising approaches that have already been developed. We are at an important juncture. Through further productive collaboration, we can make great strides in science education for all people in all countries of the world.

# References

(1972). *Chemistry for high-school* [in Hebrew]. Rehovot, Israel: Weizmann Institute of Science.

(1982). *Chemistry—a challenge* [in Hebrew]. Rehovot, Israel: Weizmann Institute of Science.

"Canada." (1984, April). Science for every student: Educating Canadians for tomorrow's world. *Canada.*

Agogino, A. M., & Linn, M. C. (1992, May–June). Retaining female engineering students: Will early design experiences help? [Editorial]. In M. Wilson (Ed.), *NSF Directions, 5*(2), 8–9.

American Association for the Advancement of Science. (1992). *Science, 255,* pp. 1363–1389.

American Association for the Advancement of Science. (1993). *Benchmarks for science literacy: Project 2061.* New York: Oxford University Press.

Anderson, J. R. (1983). *The architecture of cognition.* Cambridge, MA: Harvard University Press.

Anderson, J. R., Boyle, C. F., & Reiser, B. J. (1985). Intelligent tutoring systems. *Science, 228,* 456–467.

Anderson, J. R., Conrad, F. G., & Corbett, A. T. (1989). Skill acquisition and the LISP tutor. *Cognitive Science, 13*(4), 467–505.

Anderson, J. R., & Jeffries, R. (1985). Novice LISP errors: Undetected losses of information from working memory. *Human-Computer Interaction, 1*(2), 107–131.

Anderson, J. R., Pirolli, P. L., & Farrell, R. (1988). Learning to program recursive functions. In M. T. H. Chi, R. Glaser, & M. Farr (Eds.), *The nature of expertise* (pp. 153–183). Hillsdale, NJ: Lawrence Erlbaum Associates.

Apelman, M., Hawkins, D., & Morrison, P. (1985). *Critical barriers phenomenon in elementary science.* Grand Forks, ND: University of North Dakota, Center for Teaching and Learning.

Association for Science Education. (1986). *Science and Technology in Society.* Association for Science Education.

Ausubel, D. P. (1963). *The psychology of meaningful verbal learning: An introduction to school learning.* New York: Grune & Stratton.

Ausubel, D. P., & Fitzgerald, D. (1961). The role of discriminability in meaningful verbal learning and retention. *Journal of Educational Psychology, 52,* 266–274.

Ausubel, D. P., Novak, J. D., & Hanesian, H. (1978). *Educational psychology: A cognitive view* (2nd ed.). New York: Holt, Rinehart, & Winston.

Baird, J. R., & Northfield, J. R. (Eds.). (1992). *Learning from the PEEL experience.* Melbourne, Australia: Monash University Printing Services.

Bedell, R. C. (1934). The relationship between the ability to recall and the ability to infer in specific learning situations. In F. D. Curtis (Ed.) *Science Education XVIII* (pp. 158–162). York, PA: Maple Press.

Beggs (1905). *The third yearbook of the National Society for the Scientific Study of Education.* Chicago: University of Chicago Press.

Ben-Zvi, R., Eylon, B., & Silberstein, J. (1986a). Is an atom of copper malleable? *Journal of Chemical Education, 63*(1), 64–66.

Ben-Zvi, R., Eylon, B., & Silberstein, J. (1986b). Revision of course materials on the basis of research on conceptual difficulties. *Studies in Educational Evaluation, 12,* 213–223.

Ben-Zvi, R., Eylon, B., & Silberstein, J. (1987). Students' visualisation of a chemical reaction. *Education in Chemistry, 24*(4), 117–120.

Binet, A. (1908). The development of intelligence in the child. *L'Annee psychologique, 14,* 1–94.

Binet, A., & Simon, T. (1916). *The development of intelligence in children.* Baltimore: Williams & Wilkins.

Biological Sciences Curriculum Study. (1963). *Biology teachers' handbook.* New York: Wiley.

Biological Sciences Curriculum Study. (1989). *Science for life and living: Integrating science, technology, and health.* Dubuque, IA: Kendall/Hunt.

Biological Sciences Curriculum Study. (1990). *Science for life and living: Integrating science, technology, and health. Third Annual Progress Report.* Colorado Springs, CO: Biological Sciences and Curriculum Study, Elementary Science and Health Education Project.

Bloom, B. S. (1984). The 2 sigma problem: The search for methods of group instruction as effective as one-to-one tutoring. *Educational Researcher, 13,* 4–16.

Boenig, R. W. (1969). *Research in science education: 1938 through 1947.* New York: Teachers College Press.

Bowyer, J. B., & Linn, M. C. (1978). The effect of six years of experience with the Science Curriculum Improvement Study. *Journal of Research in Science Teaching, 15,* 209–216.

Bredderman, T. (1983). Effects of activity-based elementary science on student outcomes: A quantitative synthesis. *Review of Educational Research, 53,* 499–518.

Brown, A. L., & Campione, J. C. (1990a). Communities of learning and thinking, or, a context by any other name. *Contributions to Human Development, 21,* 108–126.

Brown, A. L., & Campione, J. C. (1990b). Interactive learning environments and the teaching of science and mathematics. In M. Gardner, J. G. Greeno, F. Reif, A. H. Schoenfeld, A. DiSessa, & E. Stage (Eds.), *Toward a scientific practice of science education* (pp. 111–140). Hillsdale, NJ: Lawrence Erlbaum Associates.

Brown, A. L. & Campione, J. C. (in press). Guided discovery in a community of learners. In K. McGilly (Ed.), *Classroom lessons: Integrating cognitive theory and classroom practice.* Cambridge, MA: MIT Press/Bradford Books.

Brown, A. L., Kane, M. J., & Echols, K. (1986). Young children's mental models determine analogical transfer across problems with a common goal structure. *Cognitive Development, 1*(2), 103–122.

Brown, A. L., & Palincsar, A. S. (1987). Reciprocal teaching of comprehension strategies: A natural history of one program for enhancing learning. In J. G. Borkowski & J. D. Day (Eds.), *Cognition in special children: Comparative approaches to retardation, learning disabilities, and giftedness* (pp. 81–132). Norwood, NJ: Ablex.

Brown, J. S., Collins, A., & Duguid, P. (1989). Situated cognition and the culture of learning. *Educational Researcher, 18*(1), 32–41.

Bruckheimer, M. (1979). Creative implementation. In *Proceedings of the Bat-Sheva Seminar on Curriculum Implementation and*

*Its Relationship to Curriculum Development* (pp. 43–49). Tel Aviv, Israel: The Weitzmann Institute of Science.

Bruer, J. T. (1993). *Schools for thought: A science of learning in the classroom.* Cambridge, MA: MIT Press.

Bruner, J. S. (1960). *The process of education.* Cambridge, MA: Harvard University Press.

Bruner, J. S. (1966). *Toward a theory of instruction.* New York: Norton.

Burbules, N. C., & Linn, M. C. (1991). Science education and the philosophy of science: Congruence or contradiction? *International Journal of Science Education, 13*(3), 227–241.

Bybee, R. W., & Landes, N. M. (1990). Science for life and living: An elementary school science program from Biological Sciences Curriculum Study. *American Biology Teacher, 52*(2), 92–98.

Campione, J. C., Brown, A. L., & Jay, M. (1992). Computers in a community of learners. In E. De Corte, M. C. Linn, H. Mandl, & L. Verschaffel (Eds.), *Computer-based learning environments and problem solving.* Berlin: Springer.

Carey, S. (1985). *Conceptual change in childhood.* Cambridge, MA: MIT Press.

Carver, S. M., Lehrer, R., Connell, T., & Erickson, J. (1992). Learning by hypermedia design: Issues of assessment and implementation. *Educational Psychologist, 27*(3), 385–404.

Case, R. (1974). Structures and strictures: Some functional limitations on the course of cognitive growth. *Cognitive Psychology, 6,* 544–573.

Case, R. (1985). *Intellectual development: Birth to adulthood* (Developmental Psychology series, H. Beilin, series Ed.). Orlando, FL: Academic Press.

Cattell, R. B. (1963). Theory of fluid and crystallized intelligence: A critical experiment. *Journal of Educational Psychology, 54,* 1–22.

Champagne, A. B., Klopfer, L. E., & Gunstone, R. F. (1982). Cognitive research and the design of science instruction. *Educational Psychologist, 17*(1), 31–53.

Chase, W., & Simon, H. A. (1973a). The mind's eye in chess. In W. G. Chase (Ed.), *Visual information processing.* New York: Academic Press.

Chase, W., & Simon, H. A. (1973b). Perception in chess. *Cognitive Psychology, 4,* 55–81.

Chi, M. T. H., & Bassok, M. (1989). Learning from examples via self-explanations. In L. B. Resnick (Ed.), *Knowing, learning, and instruction: Essays in honor of Robert Glaser* (pp. 251–282). Hillsdale, NJ: Lawrence Erlbaum Associates.

Chi, M. T. H., Feltovich, P., & Smith, E. L. (1981). Categorization and representation of physics problems by experts and novices. *Cognitive Science, 5*(2), 121–152.

Clancy, M. J., & Linn, M. C. (1992). *Designing Pascal solutions: A case study approach* (1st ed.) (Principles of Computer Science, A. V. Aho & J. D. Ullman, series Eds.). New York: Freeman.

Clement, J. (1983). A conceptual model discussed by Galileo and used intuitively by physics students. In D. Gentner & A. L. Stevens (Eds.), *Mental models.* Hillsdale, NJ: Lawrence Erlbaum Associates.

Clement, J. (1991). Non-formal reasoning in science: The use of analogies, extreme cases, and physical intuition. In J. F. Voss, D. N. Perkins, & J. Siegel (Eds.), *Informal reasoning and education.* Hillsdale, NJ: Lawrence Erlbaum Associates.

Clement, J. (1992). Students' preconceptions in introductory mechanics. *American Journal of Physics, 50,* 66–71.

Clement, J., Brown, D., & Zietsman, A. (1989). Not all preconceptions are misconceptions: Finding "anchoring conceptions" for grounding instruction on students' intuitions. *International Journal of Science Education, 11,* 554–565.

Cohen, E. G. (1986). *Designing groupwork: Strategies for the heterogeneous classroom.* New York: Teachers College Press.

Cohen, E. G. (1994). Restructuring the classroom: Conditions for productive small groups. *Review of Educational Research, 64*(1), 1–35.

Collins, A., Brown, J. S., & Holum, A. (1991). Cognitive apprenticeship: Making thinking visible. *American Educator, 15*(3), 6–11, 38–39.

Collins, A., Brown, J. S., & Newman, S. E. (1989). Cognitive apprenticeship: Teaching the craft of reading, writing, and mathematics. In L. B. Resnick (Ed.), *Cognition and instruction: Issues and agendas* (pp. 453–494). Hillsdale, NJ: Lawrence Erlbaum Associates.

Commission on Science Education. (1964). *Science—a process approach: Commentary for teachers.* Washington, DC: American Association for the Advancement of Science.

Committee on Science and Technology Education. (1992). *Tomorrow 98.* Tel Aviv, Israel: Ministry of Education.

Corno, L. (1992). Encouraging students to take responsibility for learning and performance. *Elementary School Journal, 93*(1), 69–83.

Cremin, L. A. (1964). *The transformation of the school: Progressivism in American education 1876–1957.* New York: Random House.

Cronbach, L. J. (1982). *Designing evaluations of educational and social programs.* San Francisco: Jossey-Bass.

Cronbach, L. J., & Snow, R. E. (1977). *Aptitudes and instructional methods: A handbook for research on interactions.* New York: Irvington.

Cunningham, H. A. (1924). Laboratory methods in natural science teaching. *School Science and Mathematics, 24,* 709–715, 848–851.

Cunningham, H. A. (1946). Lecture method versus individual laboratory method in science teaching: A summary. *Science Education, 30,* 70–82.

Cureton, E. E. (1927). Junior high school science. *School Review, 35,* 767–775.

Curtis, F. D. (1926). *A digest of investigations in the teaching of science in the elementary and secondary schools.* York, PA: Maple Press.

Curtis, F. D. (1931). *Second digest of investigations in the teaching of science.* York, PA: Maple Press.

Curtis, F. D. (1932). Some contributions of educational research to the solution of teaching problems in the science classroom. In G. M. Whipple (Ed.), *The thirty-first yearbook of the National Society for the Study of Education: A program for teaching science* (Pt. I) (pp. 91–108). Bloomington, IL: Public School Publishing Co.

Curtis, F. D. (1939). *Third digest of investigations in the teaching of science.* York, PA: Maple Press.

de Bono, E. (1973). *Lateral thinking: Creativity step by step.* New York: Harper & Row.

Delprato, D. J., & Midgley, B. D. (1992). Some fundamentals of B. F. Skinner's behaviorism. *American Psychologist, 47*(11), 1507–1520.

Department of Education and Science. (1988). *The national curriculum: Science Working Party, Final Report.* London: Her Majesty's Stationery Office.

Dewey, J. (1901). *Psychology and social practice* (Contributions to education). Chicago: University of Chicago Press.

Dewey, J. (1929). *The sources of a science of education.* New York: Horace Liveright.

Dewey, J. (1938). *Experience and education.* New York: Macmillan.

diSessa, A. (1982). Unlearning Aristotelian physics: A study of knowledge-based learning. *Cognitive Science, 6,* 37–75.

diSessa, A. (1988). Knowledge in pieces. In G. Forman & P. Pufall (Eds.), *Constructivism in the computer age* (pp. 49–70). Hillsdale, NJ: Lawrence Erlbaum Associates.

diSessa, A. (1992). Images of learning. In E. De Corte, M. C. Linn, H. Mandl, & L. Verschaffel (Eds.), *Computer-based learning environments and problem solving.* Berlin: Springer.

diSessa, A. (1993). Toward an epistemology of physics. *Cognition and Instruction, 10*(2–3), 105–225.

diSessa, A., & Abelson, A. (1986). Boxer: A reconstructible computational medium. *Communications of the ACM, 29*(9), 859–868.

diSessa, A. A., & Minstrell, J. (in press). Cultivating conceptual change with benchmark lessons. In J. G. Greeno (Ed.), *Thinking practices.* Hillsdale, NJ: Lawrence Erlbaum Associates.

Driver, R. (1973). *The representation of conceptual frameworks in young adolescent science students.* Unpublished doctoral dissertation, University of Illinois, Urbana-Champaign.

Driver, R. (1983). *The pupil as scientist?* London: Open University Press.

Driver, R. (1988). Theory into practice: I. A constructivist approach to curriculum development. In P. Fensham (Ed.), *Development and dilemmas in science education.* London: Falmer Press.

Driver, R., & Easley, J. (1978). Pupils and paradigms: A review of literature related to concept development in adolescent science. *Studies in Science Education, 5,* 61–84.

Driver, R., Guesne, E., & Tiberghien, A. (Eds.) (1985). *Children's ideas in science.* Philadelphia: Open University Press.

Duschl, R. A. (1990). *Restructuring science education: The importance of theories and their development.* New York: Teachers College Press.

Duschl, R. A., & Gitomer, D. H. (1991). Epistemological perspectives on conceptual change: Implications for educational practice. *Journal of Research in Science Teaching 28*(9), 839–858.

Eckert, P. (1990). Adolescent social categories: Information and science learning. In M. Gardner, J. G. Greeno, F. Reif, A. H. Schoenfeld, A. DiSessa, & E. Stage (Eds.), *Toward a scientific practice of science education* (pp. 203–218). Hillsdale, NJ: Lawrence Erlbaum Associates.

Eijkelhof, H., & Kortland, K. (1988). Broadening the aims of physics education. In P. Fensham (Ed.), *Developments and dilemmas in science education.* London: Falmer Press.

Einstein, A. (1954). *Ideas and opinions* [Based on C. Seelig (Ed.), *Mein weltbild*]. New York: Crown.

Eylon, B., Ben-Zvi, R., & Silberstein, J. (1987). Hierarchical task analysis: An approach for diagnosing students' conceptual difficulties. *International Journal of Science Education, 9*(2), 187–196.

Eylon, B., Ben-Zvi, R., & Silberstein, J. (1988). *Active hierarchical organization: A vehicle for promoting recall and problem-solving in introductory chemistry.* Rehovot, Israel: Weizmann Institute of Science.

Eylon, B., & Linn, M. C. (1988). Learning and instruction: An examination of four research perspectives in science education. *Review of Educational Research, 58*(3), 251–301.

Eylon, B., & Linn, M. C. (1994). Models and integration activities in science education. In E. Bar-On, Z. Scherz, & B. Eylon (Eds.), *Designing intelligent learning environments.* Norwood, NJ: Ablex.

Fensham, P. (Ed.). (1988). *Development and dilemmas in science education.* New York: Falmer Press.

Fischer, C. (1987) Advancing the study of programming with computer-aided protocol analysis. In G. M. Olson (Ed.), *Empirical studies of programmers: Second workshop* (pp. 198–216). Norwood, NJ: Ablex.

Flavell, J. H. (1976). Metacognitive analysis of problem solving. In L. B. Resnick (Ed.), *The nature of intelligence* (pp. 231–235). Hillsdale, NJ: Lawrence Erlbaum Associates.

Forman, E. A. (1989). The role of peer interaction in the social construction of mathematical knowledge. *International Journal of Educational Research, 13*(1), 55–77.

Forman, E. A., & McPhail, J. (1993). A Vygotskian perspective on children's collaborative problem-solving activities. In E. A. Forman, N. Minick, & C. A. Stone (Eds.), *Contexts for learning: Sociocultural dynamics in children's development.* New York: Oxford University Press.

Freeman, F. S. (1938). Contributions to education of scientific knowledge about individual differences. In G. M. Whipple (Ed.), *The thirty-seventh yearbook of the National Society for the Study of Education: Part II: The scientific movement in education.* Bloomington, IL: Public School Publishing Co.

French, A. P. (1986). Setting new directions in physics teaching: PSSC 30 years later. *Physics Today, 39*(9), 30–34.

Friedler, Y., Nachmias, R., & Linn, M. C. (1990). Learning scientific reasoning skills in microcomputer-based laboratories. *Journal of Research in Science Teaching, 27*(2), 173–191.

Gagné, R. (1968). *Instructional variables and learning outcomes.* Los Angeles: University of California Press.

Gambrill, B. L. (1922). Some administrative uses of intelligence tests in the normal school. In G. M. Whipple (Ed.), *The twenty-first yearbook of the National Society for the Study of Education: Intelligence tests and their use* (pp. 223–244). Bloomington, IL: Public School Publishing Co.

Gardner, H. (1983). *Frames of mind: The theory of multiple intelligences.* New York: Basic Books.

Gardner, M., Greeno, J. G., Reif, F., Schoenfeld, A. H., diSessa, A., & Stage, E. (Eds.). (1990). *Toward a scientific practice of science education.* Hillsdale, NJ: Lawrence Erlbaum Associates.

Gentner, D., & Stevens, A. L. (1983). *Mental models.* Hillsdale, NJ: Lawrence Erlbaum Associates.

Gilligan, C. (1982). In a different voice: Psychological theory and women's development. *Harvard Educational Review, 47*(7), 481–517.

Goldberg, A. (1984). The influence of object-oriented language on the programming environment. In D. Barstow, E. Shrobe, & E. Sandewall (Eds.), *Interactive programming environments* (pp. 141–174). New York: McGraw-Hill.

Goldberg, F., & Bendall, S. (1992). Computer-video-based tutorials in geometrical optics. In R. Duit, F. Goldberg, & H. Niedderer (Eds.), *Research in physics learning: Theoretical issues and empirical studies* [Proceedings of an international workshop held at the University of Bremen] (pp. 356–379). Kiel, Germany: Institut für die Pädagogik der Naturwissenschaften an der Universität.

Goldstein, J. S. (1992). *A different sort of time: The life of Jerrold R. Zacharias, scientist, engineer, educator.* Cambridge, MA: MIT Press.

Goodstein, D. L. (1990). The mechanical universe and beyond: Physics teaching enters the 20th century. In M. Gardner, J. G. Greeno, F. Reif, A. H. Schoenfeld, A. diSessa, & E. Stage (Eds.), *Toward a scientific practice of science education* (pp. 267–280). Hillsdale, NJ: Lawrence Erlbaum Associates.

Greeno, J. G. (1980). Psychology of learning, 1960–1980: One participant's observations. *American Psychologist, 35*(8), 713–728.

Greeno, J. G. (1983). *Research on cognition and behavior relevant to education in mathematics, science, and technology* (Chapter 6, Educating Americans for the 21st century). Washington, DC: National Science Board Commission on Precollege Education in Mathematics, Science and Technology, National Science Foundation.

Greeno, J. G. (1989). Situations, mental models, and generative knowledge. In D. Klahr & K. Kotovsky (Eds.), *Complex information processing: The impact of Herbert A. Simon.* Hillsdale, NJ: Lawrence Erlbaum Associates.

Greeno, J. G., & Simon, H. A. (1986). Problem solving and reasoning. In R. C. Atkinson, R. Herrnstein, G. Lindzey, & R. D. Luce (Eds.), *Steven's handbook of experimental psychology* (revised ed.). New York: Wiley.

Greenwood, C. R., Carta, J. J. & Hart, B. (1992). Out of the laboratory and into the community: 26 years of applied behavior analysis at the Juniper Gardens Children's Project. *American Psychologist, 47*(11), 1464–1474.

Guilford, J. P., & Hoepfner, R. (1971). *The analysis of intelligence.* New York: McGraw-Hill.

Gunstone, R. F., Gray, C. M. R., & Searle, P. (1992). Some long-term effects of uninformed conceptual change. *Science Education, 76*(2), 175–197.

Gunstone, R. F., White, R. T., & Fensham, P. J. (1988). Developments in style and purpose of research on the learning of science. *Journal of Research in Science Teaching, 25*(7), 513–529.

Haber-Schaim, U., Cross, J. B., Dodge, J. H., & Walter, J. A. (1976). *PSSC physics: Teacher's resource book* (4th ed.). Lexington, MA: Heath.

Harvey, N. (1901). A plea for the study of educational philosophy on the part of teachers of science. *School Science, 1*(4).

Hayes, S. C., & Hayes, L. J. (1992). Verbal relations and the evolution of behavior analysis. *American Psychologist, 47*(11), 1383–1395.

Hazen, R. M., & Trefil, J. (1991). *Science matters: Achieving scientific literacy.* New York: Doubleday.

Heller, P., & Hollabaugh, M. (1992). Teaching problem solving through cooperative grouping: 2. Designing problems and structuring groups. *American Journal of Physics, 60*(7), 637–644.

Heller, P., Keith, R., & Anderson, S. (1992). Teaching problem solving through cooperative grouping: 1. Group versus individual problem solving. *American Journal of Physics, 60*(7), 627–636.

Henig, R. M. (1993, October 3). Are women's hearts different? *The New York Times Magazine*, pp. 58–61, 68–9, 82, 86.

Herriott, M. E. (1924). Life activities and the physics curriculum. *School Science and Mathematics, 24,* 631–634.

Hestenes, D. (1992). Modeling games in the Newtonian world. *American Journal of Physics, 60*(8), 732–748.

Hilgard, E. R. (1956). *Theories of learning* (2nd ed.). New York: Appleton-Century-Crofts.

Hilgard, E. R. (1964). A perspective on the relationship between learning theory and educational practices. In E. R. Hilgard (Ed.), *Theories of learning and instruction* (pp. 402–415). Chicago: University of Chicago Press.

Hilgard, E. R., & Bower, G. H. (1966). *Theories of learning* (3rd ed.). New York: Appleton-Century-Crofts.

Holmes, M. J. (Ed.). (1904). *The third yearbook of the National Society for the Scientific Study of Education: Nature-Study (Pt. II)*. Chicago: University of Chicago Press.

Holton, G. (1978). On the educational philosophy of the Project Physics Course. In G. Holton (Ed.), *The scientific imagination: Case studies*. New York: Cambridge University Press.

Inhelder, B., & Piaget, J. (1958). *The growth of logical thinking from childhood to adolescence: An essay on the construction of formal operational structures*. New York: Basic Books.

Jaynes, J. (1975). Hello, teacher . . . [Review of *The history of psychology: A personalized system of instruction course*, and *Selected readings in the history of psychology: A PSI companion*]. *Contemporary Psychology, 20,* 629–631.

Jones, L., & Smith, S. (1990). Case study: Exploring chemistry. In W. H. Graves (Ed.), *Computing across the curriculum: Academic perspectives* (pp. 27–33). Academic Computing Publications.

Kahle, J. B. (1990). Real students take chemistry and physics: Gender issues. In K. Tobin, J. B. Kahle, & B. J. Fraser (Eds.), *Windows into science classrooms: Problems associated with higher-level cognitive learning* (pp. 92–134). London: Falmer Press.

Karplus, R. (1975). Strategies in curriculum development: The SCIS Project. In J. Schaffarzick & D. H. Hampson (Eds.), *Strategies for curriculum development*. Berkeley, CA: McCutchan Publishing.

Karplus, R., & Thier, H. D. (1967). *A new look at elementary school science: Science Curriculum Improvement Study*. Chicago: Rand McNally.

Keller, E. F. (1983). *A feeling for the organism: The life and work of Barbara McClintock*. San Francisco: Freeman.

Keller, E. F. (1985). *Reflections on gender and science*. New Haven: Yale University Press.

Keller, F. S. (1954). *Learning: Reinforcement theory*. New York: Random House.

Klahr, D., & Dunbar, K. (1988). Dual space search during scientific reasoning. *Cognitive Science, 12*(1), 1–55.

Klahr, D., Dunbar, K., & Fay, A. L. (1990). Designing good experiments to test bad hypotheses. In J. Shrager & P. Langley (Eds.), *Computational models of scientific discovery and theory formation* (pp. 355–402). Palo Alto, CA: Morgan Kaufmann Publishers.

Klopp, W. J. (1927). A study of the offerings of general science texts. *General Science Quarterly, 11,* 236–246.

Kuhn, D., Amsel, E., & O'Loughlin, M., with the assistance of Schauble, L. (1988). *The development of scientific thinking skills* (Developmental Psychology series). Orlando, FL: Academic Press.

Kuhn, T. S. (1970). *The structure of scientific revolutions* (2nd ed.). Chicago: University of Chicago Press.

Kulik, J. A., & Kulik, C-L. C. (1989). Meta-analysis in education. *International Journal of Educational Research, 13,* 221–340.

Kulik, J. A., Kulik, C-L. C., & Carmichael, K. (1974). The Keller plan in science teaching. *Science, 183,* 379–383.

Lakatos, I. (1970). Falsification and the methodology of scientific research programs. In I. Lakatos & A. Musgrave (Eds.), *Criticism and the growth of knowledge* (Vol. 4, pp. 91–196). Cambridge, England: Cambridge University Press.

Larkin, J., McDermott, J., Simon, D. P., & Simon, H. A. (1980). Expert and novice performance in solving physics problems. *Science, 208*(20), 1335–1342.

Larkin, J. H. (1983). A general knowledge structure for learning or teaching science. In A. C. Wilkinson (Ed.), *Computers and cognition*. New York: Academic Press.

Larkin, J. H., & Reif, F. (1979). Understanding and teaching problem solving in physics. *European Journal of Science Education, 1,* 191–203.

Lattal, K. A. (Ed.). (1992). Reflections on B. F. Skinner and psychology [Special issue]. *American Psychologist, 47*(11).

Lave, J., & Wenger, E. (1991). *Situated learning: Legitimate peripheral participation*. Cambridge, MA: Cambridge University Press.

Lawlor, E. P. (1970). *Research in science education: 1953 through 1957*. New York: Teachers College Press.

Lawson, A. E. (1985). A review of research on formal reasoning and science teaching. *Journal of Research in Science Teaching, 22,* 569–617.

Levine, D. I., & Linn, M. C. (1977). Scientific reasoning ability in adolescence: Theoretical viewpoints and educational implications. *Journal of Research in Science Teaching, 14,* 371–384.

Levine, J. M., Resnick, L. B., & Higgins, E. T. (1993). Social foundations of cognition. *Annual Review of Psychology, 44,* 585–612.

Lewis, E. L. (1991). *The process of scientific knowledge acquisition among middle school students learning thermodynamics*. Unpublished doctoral dissertation, University of California, Berkeley.

Lewis, E. L., & Linn, M. C. (1994). Heat energy and temperature concepts of adolescents, naïve adults, and experts: Implications for curricular improvements. *Journal of Research in Science Teaching, 31*(4), 657–677.

Lewis, J. (1980). *Science in Society: Readers' and Teachers' Guide*. London: Heinemann.

Linn, M. C. (1970). *Effects of a training procedure on matrix performance and on transfer tasks*. Unpublished doctoral dissertation, Stanford University, Stanford, CA.

Linn, M. C. (1980). Teaching children to control variables: Some investigations using free choice experiences. In S. Modgil & C. Modgil (Eds.), *Toward a theory of psychological development within the Piagetian framework*. Windsor, England: National Foundation for Educational Research Publishing Co.

Linn, M. C. (1985). The cognitive consequences of programming instruction in classrooms. *Educational Researcher, 14*(5), 14–16, 25–29.

Linn, M. C. (1986). Science. In R. Dillon & R. J. Sternberg (Eds.), *Cognition and instruction* (pp. 155–204). New York: Academic Press.

Linn, M. C. (1987). Establishing a research base for science education: Challenges, trends, and recommendations. *Journal of Research in Science Teaching, 24*(5), 191–216.

Linn, M. C. (1992a). The computer as learning partner: Can computer tools teach science? In K. Sheingold, L. G. Roberts, & S. M. Malcolm (Eds.), *This year in school science 1991: Technology for teaching and learning*. Washington, DC: American Association for the Advancement of Science.

Linn, M. C. (1992b). Gender differences in educational achievement. In J. Pfleiderer (Ed.), *Sex equity in educational opportunity, achievement, and testing: Proceedings of 1991 Educational Testing Service Invitational Conference* (pp. 11–50). Princeton, NJ: Educational Testing Service.

Linn, M. C. (in press). From separation to partnership in science education: Students, laboratories, and the curriculum. In R. Tinker & T. Ellermeijer (Eds.), *NATO advanced research workshop on microcomputer based labs: Educational research and standards*. Belgium: Springer.

Linn, M. C., & Burbules, N. C. (1993). Construction of knowledge and group learning. In K. Tobin (Ed.), *The practice of constructivism in science education* (pp. 91–119). Washington, DC: American Association for the Advancement of Science.

Linn, M. C., & Clancy, M. J. (1992a). Can experts' explanations help students develop program design skills? *International Journal of Man-Machine Studies, 36*(4), 511–551.

Linn, M C., & Clancy, M. J. (1992b). The case for case studies of programming problems. *Communications of the ACM, 35*(3), 121–132.

Linn, M. C., Clement, C., & Pulos, S. (1983). Is it formal if it's not physics? *Journal of Research in Science Teaching, 20*(8), 755–770.

Linn, M. C., diSessa, A., Pea, R. D., & Songer, N. B. (1994, March). Can research on science learning and instruction inform standards for science education? *Journal of Science Education and Technology, 3*(1), 7–15.

Linn, M. C., & Songer, N. B. (1991). Cognitive and conceptual change in adolescence. *American Journal of Education, 99*(4), 379–417.

Linn, M. C., & Songer, N. B. (1993). How do students make sense of science? *Merrill-Palmer Quarterly, 39*(1), 47–73.

Linn, M. C., Songer, N. B., & Lewis, E. L. (Eds.). (1991). Students' models and epistemologies of science [Special issue]. *Journal of Research in Science Teaching, 28*(9).

Linn, M. C., Songer, N. B., Lewis, E. L., & Stern, J. (1993). Using technology to teach thermodynamics: Achieving integrated understanding. In D. L. Ferguson (Ed.), *Advanced educational technologies for mathematics and science* (Vol. 107, pp. 5–60). Berlin: Springer.

Linn, M. C., & Thier, H. D. (1975). The effect of experiential science on the development of logical thinking in children. *Journal of Research in Science Teaching, 12*, 49–62.

Maccoby, E. E., & Jacklin, C. N. (1974). *The psychology of sex differences*. Stanford, CA: Stanford University Press.

Madhok, J. J. (1992). Group size and gender composition influences on discussion. In *1992 Berkeley Women and Language Conference: Locating power*. Berkeley: University of California.

Mandinach, E. B., & Cline, H. F. (in press). The STACI$^N$ Project as a design experiment. In J. Hawkins & A. Collins (Eds.), *Design experiments*.

Mandinach, E. B., & Thorpe, M. E. (1987). The systems thinking and curriculum innovation project. *Technology and Learning, 1*(2), 1, 10–11.

Markman, E. M. (1978). Empirical versus logical solutions to part-whole comparison problems concerning classes and collections. *Child Development, 79*, 168–177.

Matteson, H. D., & Kambley, P. E. (1940). Knowledge of science possessed by pupils entering the seventh grade. *School Science and Mathematics, 40*, 244–247.

McCloskey, M., Caramazza, A., & Green, B. (1980). Curvilinear motion in the absence of external forces: Naive beliefs about the motion of objects. *Science, 210*, 1139–1141.

McDermott, L. C. (1984). Research on conceptual understanding in mechanics. *Physics Today, 37*, 24–32.

McMurry, C. A. (Ed.). (1904). *The third yearbook of the National Society for the Scientific Study of Education: The relation of theory to practice in the education of teachers (Pt. I)*. Chicago: University of Chicago Press.

Michaels, W. C. (1957). High school physics. *Physics Today, 10*(1), 20–21.

Miller, G. A. (1956). The magical number seven, plus or minus two: Some limits on our capacity for processing information. *Psychological Review, 63*, 81–97.

Millikan, R. A., & Gale, H. G. (1906). *A laboratory course in physics for secondary schools*. Boston: Ginn.

Millikan, R. A., & Gale, H. G. (1927). *Elements of physics*. Boston: Ginn.

Minsky, M. L. (1986). *The society of mind*. New York: Simon & Schuster.

Minstrell, J. (1982). Explaining the 'at rest' condition of an object. *Physics Teacher, 20*, 10–14.

National Assessment of Educational Progress. (1988). *The science report card: Elements of risk and recovery: Trends and achievement based on the 1986 national assessment*. Princeton: Educational Testing Service.

National Commission on Excellence in Education. (1983). *A nation at risk: The imperative for educational reform*. Washington, DC: US Government Printing Office.

National Committee on Science Education Standards and Assessment. (1992). *National Science Education Standards sampler (Nov. '92)*. Washington, DC: National Research Council.

National Committee on Science Education Standards and Assessment. (1993a). *National Science Education Standards sampler (Feb. '93)*. Washington, DC: National Research Council.

National Committee on Science Education Standards and Assessment. (1993b). *National Science Education Standards: July '93 progress report*. Washington, DC: National Research Council.

National Science Board. (1990). *Science and engineering indicators—1989*. Washington, DC: National Science Foundation.

National Science Foundation. (1990). *Women and minorities in science and engineering*. Washington, DC: National Science Foundation.

National Science Teachers Association. Scope & Sequence Committee. (1991). *Scope and Sequence curriculum*. Washington, DC: National Science Teachers Association.

Nersessian, N. J. (1991). Conceptual change in science and in science education. In M. R. Matthews (Ed.), *History, philosophy, and science teaching* (pp. 133–148). New York: Teachers College Press.

Newman, D. (1990). Using social context for science teaching. In M. Gardner, J. G. Greeno, F. Reif, A. H. Schoenfeld, A. diSessa, & E. Stage (Eds.), *Toward a scientific practice of science education* (pp. 187–202). Hillsdale, NJ: Lawrence Erlbaum Associates.

Newman, D., Griffin, P., & Cole, M. (1989). *The construction zone: Working for cognitive change in school*. London: Cambridge University Press.

Noll, V. H. (1939). *The teaching of science in elementary and secondary schools*. New York: Longman, Green.

Novak, J. D. (1968). A case study of curriculum change: Science since PSSC. *School Science and Mathematics*, 374–384.

Novak, J. D. (1990). Concept mapping: A useful tool for science education. *Journal of Research in Science Teaching, 27*(10), 937–949.

Novak, J. D., & Gowin, D. B. (1984). *Learning how to learn*. New York: Cambridge University Press.

Novak, J. D., Gowin, D. F., & Johannsen, G. T. (1983). The use of concept mapping with junior high school science students. *Science Education, 67*, 625–645.

Novak, J. D., & Musonda, D. (1991). A twelve-year longitudinal study of science concept learning. *American Educational Research Journal, 28*(1), 117–153.

Novick, S., & Nussbaum, J. (1978). Junior high school pupils' understanding of the particulate nature of matter: An interview study. *Science Education, 62*, 273–281.

Nussbaum, J. (1989). Classroom conceptual change: Philosophical perspectives. In D. E. Herget (Ed.), *First International Conference of the History and Philosophy of Science in Science Teaching*. Tallahassee: Florida State University.

Palincsar, A. S., Anderson, C., & David, Y. M. (1993). Pursuing scientific literacy in the middle grades through collaborative problem solving. *Elementary School Journal, 93*(5), 643–658.

Palincsar, A. S., & Brown, A. L. (1984). Reciprocal teaching of comprehension-fostering and comprehension-monitoring activities. *Cognition and Instruction, 1*, 117–175.

Palmer, D. C., & Donohoe, J. W. (1992). Essentialism and selectionism in cognitive science and behavior analysis. *American Psychologist, 47*(11), 1344–1358.

Papert, S. A. (1980). *Mindstorms: Children, computers, and powerful ideas*. New York: Basic Books.

Pascual-Leone, J., Goodman, D., Ammon, P., & Subelman, I. (1978). Piagetian theory and neo-Piagetian analysis as psychological guides in education. In J. M. Gallagher & J. A. Easley (Eds.), *Knowledge and development* (Vol. 2). New York: Plenum.

Pavlov, I. P. (1927). *Conditioned reflexes* (G. V. Anrep, Trans.). London: Oxford University Press.

Pea, R. D. (1985). Beyond amplification: Using the computer to recognize mental functioning. *Educational Psychologist, 20,* 167–182.

Pea, R. D. (1992). Augmenting the discourse of learning with computer-based learning environments. In E. De Corte, M. C. Linn, H. Mandl, & L. Verschaffel (Eds.), *Computer-based learning environments and problem solving*. Berlin: Springer.

Pea, R. D., & Gomez, L. (1992). Distributed multimedia learning environments: Why and how? *Interactive Learning Environments, 2,* 73–109.

Pea, R. D., & Gomez, L. (1993). Distributed multimedia learning environments: The Collaborative Visualization Project. *Communications of the ACM, 36*(5), 60–63.

Pella, M. O. (1976). Sixty years of science education [Editorial]. *Science Education, 60*(4), 433–439.

Perry, J. (1900). England's neglect of science [Preface to an Elementary Book on Practical Mechanics]. London: Unwin.

Peterson, P., & Wilkinson, L. C. (1984). Instructional groups in the classroom: Organization and processes. In L. C. Wilkinson, P. Peterson & M. Hallinan (Eds.), *The social context of instruction: Group organization and group processes* (pp. 3–11). Orlando, FL: Academic Press.

Pfundt, H., & Duit, R. (1991). *Students' alternative frameworks* (3rd ed.). Kiel, Germany: Institut für die Pädagogik der Naturwissenschaften [Institute for Science Education at the University of Kiel].

Physical Science Study Committee (1966). *Introductory physical science* (Preliminary ed.). Englewood Cliffs, NJ: Prentice Hall.

Piaget, J. (1929). *The child's conception of the world*. London: Routledge & Kegan Paul.

Piaget, J. (1972a). Intellectual evolution from adolescence to adulthood. *Human Development, 15,* 1–12.

Piaget, J. (1972b). *Science of education and the psychology of the child*. New York: Viking Press.

Powers, S. R. (1925). The vocabularies of high school science textbooks. *Teachers College Record, 26,* 368–392.

Raizen, S. A. (1991a). The reform of science education in the U.S.A.: Déjà vu or de novo? *Studies in Science Education, 19,* 1–41.

Raizen, S. A. (1991b). The state of science education. In S. K. Majumdar, L. M. Rosenfeld, P. A. Rubba, E. W. Miller, & R. F. Schmalz (Eds.), *Science education in the United States: Issues, crises and priorities* (pp. 25–45). Philadelphia: Pennsylvania Academy of Science.

Randall, D. P., Chapman, J. C., & Sutton, C. W. (1918). The place of numerical problems in high school physics. *School Review, 26,* 39–43.

Redish, E. F., & Wilson, J. M. (1993). Student programming in the introductory physics course—Muppet. *American Journal of Physics, 61*(3), 222–232.

Reif, F., & Larkin, J. H. (1991). Cognition in scientific and everyday domains: Comparison and learning implications. *Journal of Research in Science Teaching, 28*(9), 733–760.

Resnick, L. (1981). Instructional psychology. *Annual Review of Psychology, 32,* 659–704.

Resnick, L. B. (1987). Learning in school and out. *Educational Researcher, 16*(9), 13–20.

Richards, J., Barowy, W., & Levin, D. (1992). Computer simulations in the science classroom. *Journal of Science Education and Technology, 1,* 67–79.

Rosier, M. J., & Keeves, J. P. (1991). *The International Studies in Educational Achievement (IEA) Study of Science I: Science education and curricula in twenty-three countries*. Oxford, England: Pergamon Press.

Rossiter, M. W. (1982). *Women scientists in America: Struggles and strategies to 1940*. Baltimore: Johns Hopkins University Press.

Rubin, A., Bruce, B., Rosebery, A., & DuMouchel, W. (1988). *Getting an early start: Using interactive graphics to teach statistical concepts in high school,* (Proceedings of the Statistical Education Section). Washington, DC: American Statistical Association.

Rutherford, F. J., & Ahlgren, A. (1990). *Science for all Americans*. New York: Oxford University Press.

Rutherford, F. J., Holton, G., & Watson, F. G. (1970). *The Project Physics course handbook*. New York: Holt, Rinehart & Winston.

Salinger, G. L. (1991). The materials of physics instruction. *Physics Today, 44*(9), 39–45.

Sambursky, S. (Ed.). (1975). *Physical thought from the Presocratics to the quantum physicists: An anthology*. New York: Pica Press.

Sanders, R. (1992, March). Chemistry in context: Victorian chemistry. *Chemistry in Australia, 9,* 112–113.

Scardamalia, M., & Bereiter, C. (1991). Higher levels of agency for children in knowledge building: A challenge for the design of new knowledge media. *The Journal of the Learning Sciences, 1,* 37–68.

Scardamalia, M., & Bereiter, C. (1992). A knowledge building architecture for computer supported learning. In E. De Corte, M. C. Linn, H. Mandl, & L. Verschaffel (Eds.), *Computer-based learning environments and problem solving*. Berlin: Springer.

Scardamalia, M., & Bereiter, C. (1993). Technologies for knowledge-building discourse. *Communications of the ACM, 36*(5), 37–41.

Schank, R. C., & Abelson, R. P. (1977). *Scripts, plans, goals, and understanding: An inquiry into human knowledge structures*. Hillsdale, NJ: Lawrence Erlbaum Associates.

Schauble, L., Klopfer, L. E., & Raghavan, K. (1991). Students' transition from an engineering model to a science model of experimentation. *Journal of Research in Science Teaching, 28*(9), 859–882.

Schneps, M. H., & Sadler, P. M. (1989). *A private universe*. [Video]. Cambridge, MA: Harvard–Smithsonian Center for Astrophysics.

Schoenfeld, A. H. (1983). Beyond the purely cognitive: Belief systems, social cognitions, and metacognitions as driving forces in intellectual performance. *Cognitive Science, 7*(4), 329–363.

Schramm, W. (Ed.). (1964). *Four case studies of programmed instruction*. New York: Fund for the Advancement of Education.

Science Manpower Project (Frederick L. Fitzpatrick: Director). (1959). *Modern high school physics: A recommended course of study* (2nd ed.). New York: Bureau of Publications, Columbia University Teacher's College.

Sears, F. W., & Zemansky, M. W. (1949). *College physics*. Cambridge, MA: Addison-Wesley.

Shayer, M., Adey, P., & Wylam, H. (1981). Group tests of cognitive development ideals and a realization. *Journal of Research in Science Teaching, 18,* 157–168.

Sherwood, B. A., & Sherwood, J. N. (1986). *The CMU tutor language*. Champaign, IL: Stipes Publishing Co.

Shulman, L. S., & Tamir, P. (1973). Research on teaching in the natural sciences. In R. M. W. Travers (Ed.), *Second handbook of research on teaching* (pp. 1098–1148). Chicago: Rand McNally.

Shymansky, J. A., & Kyle, W. C., Jr. (Eds.). (1992). *Journal of Research in Science Teaching, 29*(8).

Shymansky, J. A., Kyle, W. C., Jr., & Alport, J. M. (1983). The effects of new science curricula on student performance. *Journal of Research in Science Teaching, 20,* 387–404.

Siegler, R. S. (1976). Three aspects of cognitive development. *Cognitive Psychology, 8,* 481–520.

Simon, H. A. (1974). How big is a chunk? *Science, 183,* 482–488.

Skinner, B. F (1958). Teaching machines. *Science, 128,* 969–977.

Smith, C., Carey, S., & Wiser, M. (1985). On differentiation: A case study of development of the concepts of size, weight, and density. *Cognition, 21,* 177–237.

Smith, J. P., diSessa, A. A., & Roschelle, J. (1994). Misconceptions reconceived: A constructivist analysis of knowledge in transition. *Journal of the Learning Sciences.*

Smith, S. G., & Sherwood, B. A. (1976). Educational uses of the PLATO computer system. *Science, 192,* 334–352.

Snow, R. E. (1980). Aptitude, learner control, and adaptive instruction. *Educational Psychologist, 15*(3), 151–158.

Snow, R. E. (1989). Toward assessment of cognitive and conative structures in learning. *Educational Researcher, 18*(9), 8–14.

Solomon, B. M. (1985). *In the company of educated women.* New Haven: Yale University Press.

Songer, N. B. (1989). *Promoting integration of instructed and natural world knowledge in thermodynamics.* Unpublished doctoral dissertation, University of California, Berkeley.

Songer, N. B. (1993). Learning science with a child-focused resource: A case study of Kids as Global Scientists. In *Proceedings of the fifteenth annual meeting of the Cognitive Science Society* (pp. 935–940). Hillsdale, NJ: Lawrence Erlbaum Associates.

Songer, N. B., & Linn, M. C. (1991). How do students' views of science influence knowledge integration? *Journal of Research in Science Teaching, 28*(9), 761–784.

Stern, J. L. (1990). *E-LabBook.* Berkeley: UC Regents.

Sternberg, R. J. (1985). *Beyond IQ: The triarchic theory of human intelligence.* Cambridge, England: Cambridge University Press.

Swartz, C. (Ed.). (1991). Pre-college education [Special issue]. *Physics Today, 44*(9).

Swift, J. N. (1969). *Research in science education: 1948 through 1952.* New York: Teachers College Press.

Thorndike, E. L. (1910). The contribution of psychology to education. *Journal of Educational Psychology, 1,* 1–14.

Thorndike, E. L. (1927). *The teacher's word book.* New York: Bureau of Publications, Teachers College, Columbia University.

Thurstone, L. L., & Chave, E. J. (1929). *The measurement of attitude.* Chicago: University of Chicago Press.

Tinker, R., & Papert, S. (1989). Tools for science education. In J. Ellis (Ed.), *1988 AETS yearbook: Information technology and science education.* Columbus, OH: ERIC Clearinghouse for Science, Mathematics, and Environmental Education.

Tinker, R. F. (1987). Network science arrives. *Hands On!, 10*(1), 1, 10–11.

Toulmin, S. (1972). *Human understanding: An inquiry into the aims of science.* Princeton: Princeton University Press.

Tversky, A., & Kahneman, D. (1992). Advances in prospect theory: Cumulative representation of uncertainty. *Journal of Risk and Uncertainty, 5*(4), 297–323.

Tyler, R. W. (1933). Permanence of learning. *Journal of Higher Education, 4,* 203–204.

Tyler, R. W. (1938). The specific techniques of investigation: Examining and testing acquired knowledge, skill, and ability. In G. M. Whipple (Ed.), *The thirty-seventh yearbook of the National Society for the Study of Education: The scientific movement in education (Pt. II).* Bloomington, IL: Public School Publishing Co.

Underhill, O. E. (1941). *The origins and development of elementary-school science.* Chicago, IL: Scott, Foresman.

Viennot, L. (1979). Spontaneous reasoning in elementary dynamics. *European Journal of Science Education, 1*(2), 205–221.

Vosniadou, S., & Brewer, W. (1992). Mental models of the earth: A study of conceptual change in childhood. *Cognitive Psychology, 24,* 535–558.

Vygotsky, L. S. (1962). *Thought and language.* Cambridge, MA: MIT Press.

Vygotsky, L. S. (1978). *Mind in society: The development of higher psychological processes* (M. Cole & et al., series Eds.). Cambridge, MA: Harvard University Press.

Vygotsky, L. S. (1987). *The collected works of L. S. Vygotsky: Vol. 1. Problems of general psychology* (R. W. Rieber & A. S. Carton, series Eds.). New York: Plenum Press.

Wasik, J. L. (1971). A comparison of cognitive performance of PSSC and non-PSSC physics students. *Journal of Research in Science Teaching, 8,* 85–90.

Watson, F. G. (1963). Research on teaching science. In N. L. Gage (Ed.), *Handbook of research on teaching* (pp. 1031–1059). Chicago: Rand McNally.

Webb, N. M. (1989). Peer interaction and learning in small groups. *International Journal of Educational Research, 13*(1), 21–39.

Welch, W., & Walberg, H. J. (1972). A national experiment in curriculum evaluation. *American Educational Research Journal, 9,* 373–383.

Welch, W. W. (1973). Review of the research and evaluation program of Harvard Project Physics. *Journal of Research in Science Teaching, 10*(4), 365–378.

Welch, W. W. (1979). Twenty years of science curriculum development: A look back. In D. C. Berliner (Ed.), *Review of research in education* (pp. 282–308). Washington, DC: American Educational Research Association.

Wellesley College Center for Research on Women. (1992). *How schools shortchange girls.* Washington, DC: American Association of University Women Educational Foundation.

Whipple, G. M. (Ed.). (1922). *The twenty-first yearbook of the National Society for the Study of Education: Intelligence tests and their use. (Pt. I)* Bloomington, IL: Public School Publishing Co.

Whipple, G. M. (Ed.). (1932). *The thirty-first yearbook of the National Society for the Study of Education: A program for teaching science.* Bloomington, IL: Public School Publishing Co.

White, B. Y. (1993). ThinkerTools: Causal models, conceptual change, and science education. *Cognition and Instruction, 10*(1), 1–100.

White, B. Y., & Frederiksen, J. R. (1990). Causal model progressions as a foundation for intelligent learning environments. *Artificial Intelligence, 24*(1), 99–157.

White, R. T. (1987). Trends in science education research. In I. Lowe (Ed.), *Teaching the interactions of science, technology and society* (pp. 294–304). Cheshire, England: Longman.

White, R. T. (1988). Metacognition. In J. P. Keeves (Ed.), *Educational research, methodology and measurement: An international handbook* (pp. 70–75). Oxford, England: Pergamon Press.

White, R. T. (1992). Implications of recent research on learning for curriculum and assessment. *Journal of Curriculum Studies, 24*(2), 153–164.

White, R. T. (in press). Improving the teaching and learning of science in the post-compulsory years. In P. J. Fensham (Ed.), *Science and technological education in Australia.* Melbourne: Australian Council for Educational Research.

White, R. T., & Gunstone, R. F. (1989). Metalearning and conceptual change. *International Journal of Science Education, 11,* 577–586.

Whitehead, A. N. (1929). *The aims of education.* New York: Macmillan.

Wiser, M. (1988). The differentiation of heat and temperature: History of science and novice-expert shift. In S. Strauss (Ed.), *Ontogeny, phylogeny, and historical development.* Norwood, NJ: Ablex.

Wiser, M., & Carey, S. (1983). When heat and temperature were one. In D. Gentner & A. L. Stevens (Eds.), *Mental models* (pp. 267–298). Hillsdale, NJ: Lawrence Erlbaum Associates.

Yerkes, R. M. (1921). Psychological examining in the United States army. *Memoirs of the National Academy of Science, 15,* pp. 11–27.

# · 16 ·

# MATHEMATICS TEACHING AND LEARNING

## Erik De Corte
UNIVERSITY OF LEUVEN, BELGIUM

## Brian Greer
QUEEN'S UNIVERSITY, BELFAST, NORTHERN IRELAND

## Lieven Verschaffel
UNIVERSITY OF LEUVEN, BELGIUM

The domain of mathematics learning and teaching is arguably the clearest example of the subject matter orientation in research on learning and instruction. Particularly in the 1980s and 1990s, this domain has produced a vast body of investigations, reviewed and synthesized in the *Handbook of Research on Mathematics Teaching and Learning* (Grouws, 1992). A few years earlier, the Research Agenda for Mathematics Education project (J. Sowder, 1989), initiated by the National Council of Teachers of Mathematics, generated conferences (in 1987) and subsequent edited volumes relating to four major themes, namely teaching and assessing problem solving (Charles & Silver, 1988), effective mathematics teaching (Grouws & Cooney, 1988), the learning and teaching of algebra (Wagner & Kieran, 1988), and middle school number concepts (Behr & Hiebert, 1988). More internationally balanced overviews are provided in *Mathematics and Cognition,* the research synthesis of the International Group for the Psychology of Mathematics Education (Nesher & Kilpatrick, 1990) and in the forthcoming *International Handbook of Mathematics Education* (Bishop, in press) and a book based on a Working Group at the 7th International Congress of Mathematical Education, *Theories of Mathematical Learning* (Steffe, Nesher, Cobb, Goldin, & Greer, in press).

Taking into account the impressive amount of scholarly literature, we do not attempt in this chapter to summarize what has been achieved so far, nor to provide a comprehensive overview of this vast domain. Rather, our aim is to highlight and selectively illustrate a number of major developments that have occurred recently in the field of research on mathematics teaching and learning.

Romberg and Carpenter (1986) described the state of the art from complementary perspectives, namely the study of mathematical learning and thinking as a domain of psychology, and the analysis of classroom teaching. They concluded that the task for the next decade was "to bring the variety of constructs from both disciplines together and relate them to an appropriate view of the mathematics to be taught" (p. 868). To a considerable extent, the message of this chapter is that substantial progress has been made in this direction.

The perspectives taken by Romberg and Carpenter reflect the two major groups that have contributed to this domain of research since it began to emerge as a fully fledged field of study in the early 1970s (Fischbein, 1990a; Kilpatrick, 1992). These are psychologists who work with mathematics as a domain for studying fundamental issues of cognition and instructional psychology, and educationalists with a specific interest in mathematics who draw on the theoretical frameworks and methodological tools of cognitive and developmental psychology. The increasingly symbiotic relationship between these two groups has both benefited from and contributed to major identifiable shifts of balance—from a focus on general to a focus on domain-specific knowledge, processes, and expertise; from a concentration on the individual to a concern for social and cultural factors; from "cold" to "hot" cognition; from the laboratory to the classroom as the arena for research; and from technically to humanistically grounded methodologies and interpretative approaches. The growing and productive interaction between the two groups, enriched by contributions from many other perspectives, has revitalized the view of mathematics learning as the construction of meaning and understanding based on the modeling of reality, the analysis of pattern, and the acquisition of a mathematical disposition.

Throughout the international community of mathematics educators, there is now a strong consensus about how mathematics education needs to be reformed. This reform is envisioned in documents such as the *Curriculum and Evaluation Standards for School Mathematics* (National Council of Teachers of

The authors gratefully acknowledge the helpful comments provided by Jeremy Kilpatrick, University of Georgia, Tom Romberg, University of Wisconsin, and Alan Schoenfeld, University of California, Berkeley.

Mathematics, 1989) and the *Professional Standards for Teaching Mathematics* (National Council of Teachers of Mathematics, 1991), the *Mathematics Framework for California* (California Board of Education, 1991), the United Kingdom's *Mathematics Counts* (Cockcroft, 1982), the Dutch *Proeve van een Nationaal Programma* (Treffers, De Moor, & Feijs, 1989), and the Australian *A National Statement on Mathematics for Australian Schools* (Australian Education Council, 1990). To what extent the aspirations embodied in these documents can be effectively realized is another matter. Nevertheless, in this chapter we document the growth of the conception of mathematics as a human activity embedded in historical, cultural, social, and experiential contexts, a correspondingly rich and complex view of the nature of mathematical cognition, a vision of what mathematics education might be, and evidence of the concerted efforts being made to realize that vision.

The first section of the chapter establishes a relevant background to current activity in terms of theoretical developments within psychology and in research on mathematics education, with particular attention to the broadening of the methods of inquiry and the emergence of mathematics education as an independent field of study for a clearly identifiable community of researchers and scholars. In the remaining sections, we delineate the current state of the field under four organizing themes. First, we identify fundamental characteristics of mathematics and their implications for research related to this domain. Second, we discuss the learner of mathematics, concentrating on the fundamental themes of effective problem solving, the complexity of knowledge construction, and the fostering of a mathematical disposition. Third, we analyze the cultural and social contexts within which the learner constructs mathematical knowledge, elaborating on the conception of mathematics as a human activity that takes place both in and out of school. Fourth, we delineate important components of instructional environments, namely teachers' knowledge and beliefs, the characteristics of some effective teaching/learning programs, the potential contribution of computers, and the design and implementation of richer forms of assessment as an integral part of instruction.

## THE DEVELOPING PARTNERSHIP BETWEEN PSYCHOLOGY AND MATHEMATICS EDUCATION

To set the scene, we very briefly outline relevant developments in psychology during the 20th century. (For an overview organized under the themes of mathematics as computation and mathematics as conceptual understanding and problem solving, see L. B. Resnick & Ford, 1981.) Throughout the century, mathematics has been an important testing ground for the application of general psychological theories, and it is important to trace the impact of these theories on mathematics education and to recognize their continuing influence on current practice and their conceptual relationship to contemporary theoretical developments.

The more recent history of cognitive psychology has been dominated by what has come to be called the cognitive revolution. We argue here that the first wave in this paradigm shift has been succeeded by a second that relocates intellectual functioning within a broader human framework and takes into account social, cultural, and affective factors (see chapter 2).

Research and theoretical developments in mathematics education have both benefited from and contributed to the successive waves of the cognitive revolution. To a considerable extent, the past 20 years have seen the emergence of research in mathematics education as a field of study in its own right, even as it maintains strong symbiotic links with psychology and other disciplines.

## Contributions from Psychology

*Divergent Aims.* Historically, psychologists who paid attention to the learning of mathematics often exploited selected aspects of mathematics for their own theoretical ends. For example, Kilpatrick (1981, p. 25) said of Thorndike that "His theory was his hammer; he looked around and saw the arithmetic curriculum as something to pound." Freudenthal (1991, p. 149) was highly critical of educational psychology research relating to mathematics "as long as, for the researcher, mathematics is no more than an easily available and easily handled subject matter, chosen to test and apply general ideas and methods, with no regard for the specific nature of mathematics and mathematics instruction." Kilpatrick (1992, p. 5) commented that "mathematics educators have often been wary of psychological researchers because of what they have seen as an indifference to or ignorance of the academic discipline of mathematics, but they have never hesitated to borrow ideas and techniques freely from psychology." Elaborating on this theme, Fischbein (1990a, p. 10) stated that:

Mathematics education raises its own psychological problems, which a professional psychologist would never encounter in his own area. . . . The relationships between abstract and concrete, between formal and intuitive, between algorithmic and heuristic present such a variety of novel facets in the light of mathematics that no deductive endeavor can predict them from general psychological concepts. . . . Further, the research methodology should also be adapted to the specificity of the domain. . . .

A further source of tension between mathematics educators and psychological researchers is the balance among, in Bishop's words, "what is," "what might be," and "what should be" (Bishop, 1992, p. 714). Psychologists who take mathematics as an area of application tend to investigate the situation as they find it or perceive it, to take mathematics as an "uncontroversial 'given'" (Wheeler, 1989, p. 279). In the course of their research they may identify problems and make suggestions for improvement within the existing framework, but without questioning fundamental goals. Mathematics educators, by contrast, are more likely to call for radical change, as expressed by R. B. Davis (1989, p. 159): "We need to encourage research studies that focus on what matters, rather than studies that legitimize practices that need to be changed."

In the following discussion, we offer brief sketches of some of the key figures and movements in the evolving relationship between psychological theory and mathematics education.

*Behaviorism and Its Legacy.* The central tenet of behaviorism was that psychological theory should be built only on the basis of observations of behavior; mental processes such as thoughts, feelings, and intentions, being unobservable, were thereby excluded. To illustrate the extremes to which this principle could be taken, Watson (1913) wrote a paper in which images were reduced to implicit language responses and affect to slight vascular changes in the genitalia. For a full-blown treatment of the learning of mathematics as the reinforcement of verbal behavior, the interested reader is referred to Staats and Staats (1963).

Behaviorism enjoyed a dominant position (more so in the United States than elsewhere) from early in the 20th century until the cognitive revolution acquired momentum in the late 1950s. In historical context, behaviorism may be seen as part of a general quest for scientific objectivity and precision, whose manifestations also included logical positivism and attempts to secure unshakable logical foundations for mathematics. The desire to establish the scientific credentials of psychology was reflected in methodological rigor and the technical elaboration of procedures for quantifying and measuring psychological variables, notably in psychometrics.

There were, of course, opposing theoretical systems and numerous critics of behaviorism throughout its period of dominance. Nevertheless, the influence of behaviorist methodology was considerable in establishing what Bishop (1992, p. 712) called the "empirical scientist tradition" in research on mathematics education. Kilpatrick (1992, p. 11) commented on "the ambivalence that researchers in mathematics education often felt during the first half of this century as they borrowed the research methods of behaviorist psychology while generally disdaining the behaviorist view of school mathematics."

A specific application of behaviorist principles to education was the development by Skinner of programmed learning, the precursor of computer-based drill-and-practice systems such as those constructed by Suppes (Solomon, 1986), and ultimately of intelligent tutoring systems.

Despite behaviorism's loss of status in academic circles as a theoretical and philosophical system, its influence lingers on in the educational system and in the consciousness of people in general (including those responsible for political and administrative decisions). R. B. Davis (1990, pp. 93–94) suggested that at the most important level, that of schools and teachers, one of the two approaches currently dominant in the United States is that of direct teaching, which "argues for a highly-explicit identification of what you want students to learn, a very clear exposition of this information, considerable drill and practice on exactly this information, and testing for the same information." Conceptions of learning as incremental (with errors to be avoided or immediately stamped out), of assessment as appropriately implemented by reference to atomistic behavioral objectives, of teaching as the reinforcement of behavior, of motivation as directly mediated by rewards and punishments, and of mathematics as precise, unambiguous, and yielding uniquely correct answers through the application of specific procedures remain prevalent in folk psychology and, as such, represent the legacy of behaviorism. Moreover, the developments of behaviorism led to persisting views of learning hierarchies within mathematics, with harmful effects, according to L. B. Resnick (1987a, pp. 48–49).

The idea that knowledge must be acquired first and that its application to reasoning and problem solving can be delayed is a persistent one in educational thinking. "Hierarchies" of educational objectives, although

intended to promote attention to higher order skills, paradoxically feed this belief by suggesting that knowledge acquisition is a first stage in a sequence of educational goals. The relative ease of assessing people's knowledge, as opposed to their thought processes, further feeds this tendency in educational practice.

*Thorndike's Connectionism and Its Critics.* Thorndike's theory may be seen within the long-standing tradition of associationism, the central principle of which is that complex ideas are built up from the association of simpler ones. On the basis of laboratory experiments with animals, Thorndike postulated that in any situation, the action performed by an animal depended on the strenghts of the "bonds" between the situation and the various actions possible. Learning took place through the differential strengthening of bonds, by reinforcement.

Thorndike extended this theory to human behavior, including education in general, and mathematics education in particular, notably arithmetic (Thorndike, 1922). From this perspective, the teaching of arithmetic became the scientific design of a program of stimulus-response associations with appropriate rewards to act as reinforcement. This view of mathematics was opposed by many educators. For example, Judd (1928, p. 8; cited in Kilpatrick, 1992, p. 10) offered a very different view of mathematics education:

It is the business of the school to transmit to the pupils the intellectual methods of arrangement by which the complexities of the world may be unravelled and a new pattern made of experience. The most comprehensive and flexible patterns for the rearrangement of experiences are those supplied by the mathematical sciences.

Although Thorndike stressed, for example, that "the school should favor real situations" (Thorndike, 1992, p. 12), and that "only a small part of drill work in arithmetic should be the formation of isolated bonds" (p. 138), one of the main effects of his work, as put into practice by his successors, was to sanction drill as the main method of instruction. Prominent among researchers opposed to this form of teaching was Brownell, who "was noted for his use of a variety of techniques for gathering data, including extended interviews with individual children and teachers, and for his careful, extensive, and penetrating analyses of these data" (Kilpatrick, 1992, p. 20). Based on a series of experiments carried out between 1935 and 1949, he put forward a theory of what he called "meaningful" arithmetic (e.g., Brownell, 1945), emphasizing the understanding of mathematical relationships and the ability to think quantitatively (see L. B. Resnick & Ford, 1981, chap. 2, for a detailed summary, and chapter 13 as well).

Kilpatrick (1992, p. 20) has suggested that meaningful arithmetic, in a sense, was a precursor of the New Mathematics movement of the 1950s. Echoes of the debate continue to this day, for example in discussions of the interaction and proper balance between procedural and conceptual knowledge (Hiebert, 1986).

*Piaget and the Complexity of Children's Cognition.* Piaget made contributions throughout a career spanning some 60 years, and his theory was still evolving in the 1970s (for an overview, see Chapman, 1988). His empirical work and theoretical analysis relating to all the major subdomains of mathematics were foundational and continue to stimulate elaboration, criticism, and reaction.

From a contemporary perspective, Piaget's main contribution to mathematics education was his demonstration of the complexity of children's thinking and the qualitative differences in thinking at various stages of development. He is acknowledged as a major inspiration of the radical shift to the conception of the child as an active constructor of knowledge. Moreover, he pioneered methodological innovations, in particular the use of clinical interviews, thereby foreshadowing the broadening of methods of inquiry characteristic of recent research in cognitive development and in mathematics education.

A general criticism of Piaget is that he underemphasized social and cultural factors, and more specifically that he paid little attention to educational aspects (but see, e.g., Piaget, 1971). According to Vergnaud (1990, pp. 18–19), "he never studied the teaching–learning process, either in the classroom or in the home." Youniss and Damon (1992), while arguing that ideas about social construction are integral to Piaget's genetic epistemology, acknowledged that there are grounds for the caricature of a Piagetian "apocryphal child who discovers formal properties of things, such as number, while playing alone with pebbles on the beach" (p. 268).

The modeling of developmental stages has been another target for theoretical and empirical criticisms of Piagetian theory. Much of this criticism evaporates if it is recognized that, as Chapman (1988, p. 33) argued, these stages were intended as a classification of forms of thinking, not of individual children. The belief that cognitive development can be usefully characterized as a series of hierarchical skill structures grouped into stages has been carried on by theorists synthesizing aspects of information-processing and Piagetian theories (e.g., Biggs & Collis, 1982; Case, 1985)

At many points in his career, Piaget posited parallels between ontological and cultural development. Toward the end of his life, he returned to this theme in collaboration with Garcia (Piaget & Garcia, 1983/1989). Such analyses of parallels between the construction of mathematical knowledge in the individual child and on the historical/cultural plane are becoming increasingly prominent in theorizing about the development of mathematical cognition (e.g., Damerow, 1988).

***Vygotsky and Enculturation.*** The work of Vygotsky, who died in 1934, just after the publication of his major work, *Thought and Language* (Vygotsky, 1934/1962), has been central to the development of Russian psychology in general and theories of mathematical education in particular (e.g., Davydov, 1990; Kruetskii, 1976). Theoretical ideas in this tradition have recently been gaining in prominence in Western psychological and educational research (e.g., Newman, Griffin, & Cole 1989; van Oers, 1990; Wertsch, 1985). Many of Vygotsky's ideas are, as seen through various interpretational lenses, influential in contemporary thinking about the psychology of mathematics education. His theory stands in stark contrast to Piaget's in that, as expressed by Bruner (1962, p. v) "[his] conception of development is at the same time a theory of education."

Vygotsky conceived of an interaction between biological and cultural development whereby naturally developing mental functions are transformed into higher mental functions through interaction with more experienced members of a culture and through the use of culturally designed intellectual tools. As will be seen later, this has echoes in current characterizations of mathematics education as the enculturation of children into a community of mathematicians, and in interest in the relationship between everyday cognition and formal mathematics. Bruner (1962, p. viii) characterized Vygotsky's conception of intelligence as "a capacity to benefit from instruction." This is embodied in the familiar concept of the zone of proximal development, which was introduced with a very practical object in mind, namely, the assessment of children's cognitive abilities. This approach has been recently elaborated by A. L. Brown and colleagues (e.g., A. L. Brown & Ferrara, 1985; Campione & Brown, 1990).

Inseparable from Vygotsky's profound theoretical analyses and critiques of other psychological schools were his radical methodological innovations. He conceived of experimental methods that would make it possible to observe development as it occurred under instruction (if necessary, having been provoked). This methodology is used in work with individual students by current mathematics education researchers such as Steffe (1991). In the classroom context, the approach translates into the teaching experiments which now play a prominent role in mathematics education research (e.g., Cobb, Wood, & Yackel, 1991; Cobb, Wood, Yackel, & McNeal, 1992; Lampert, 1986; Maher, Davis, & Alston, 1991b).

***Structure and Insight in Mathematical Problem Solving: The Gestalt Psychologists, and Polya.*** Problem solving is an obvious area of overlap between cognitive psychology and mathematics education. For reasons of both relevance and convenience, a great deal of the psychological investigation of problem solving has related to mathematical problems.

The Gestalt school of psychology was a major contributor to psychological research and theorizing on problem solving. The key idea of this school, which was originally concerned mainly with perception, was that the mind interprets sense data according to organizing principles whereby humans perceive whole forms (Gestalts) rather than collections of atomistic perceptions. This idea was later extended to thinking and problem solving, with a corresponding emphasis on structure. Given this emphasis, it was natural that much of the Gestaltists' work on problem solving was concerned with mathematical topics.

In *Productive Thinking*, Wertheimer (1945), for example, cited the historical example of how the great mathematician Gauss, as a young pupil, simplified through structural insight the computation involved in adding numbers in arithmetical progression. The anecdote is taken as the starting point for a lengthy analysis of the difference between blind following of procedures and the detection and exploitation of structure. This distinction was illustrated in a classroom in which the children had been taught to find the area of a parallelogram by multiplying the length of the base by the length of the altitude (perpendicular distance between base and opposite side). In the course of teaching, one side of the parallelogram was always parallel to the bottom of the page, and an altitude could always be constructed by "dropping a perpendicular" from one vertex of the parallelogram onto a point on the base (Figure 16–1, top). When Wertheimer posed problems that did not conform to these (irrelevant) restrictions, the pupils were at a loss (Figure 16–1, bottom). His interpretation was that they were blindly following rules, whereas an understanding of the structural properties of the parallelogram would have enabled them to

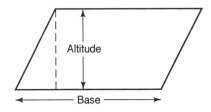

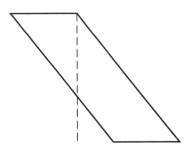

FIGURE 16-1. Finding the Area of a Parallelogram
Children learned a standard procedure from examples for which it was always possible to draw an altitude from one vertex to the base (top). When faced with Wertheimer's variation (bottom), they did not know what to do.

find the area for any parallelogram. (For a fuller discussion of this example and of the Gestalt theorists' contribution in general, see L. B. Resnick & Ford, 1981.)

In recent times, the most important source of ideas about mathematical problem solving has been the work of George Polya (1945, 1954a, 1954b, 1962, 1965). Although he was a mathematician rather than a psychologist, he was influenced by Gestalt theory, and his deep analyses of structural insight and the processes of discovery in mathematical problem solving make it appropriate to discuss his work here.

Polya, as Tymoczko (1986a, p. 96) commented, aimed to present "mathematics as it is actually done." He believed that "in order to understand a theorem really, you must know how it was discovered" (Albers & Alexanderson, 1985, p. 251). In *How to Solve It* (1945), he set out a number of general guidelines (heuristics) for problem solving (Table 16–1). Many attempts were made to employ those guidelines, more or less directly, to teach generalizable problem-solving skills. Stanic and Kilpatrick (1980, p. 17) argued against the sort of distortion whereby "a heuristic becomes a skill, a technique, even, paradoxically, an algorithm." Polya argued that there is no shortcut to learning the art of problem solving; like other practical arts, it is learned by doing it, and reflecting on the doing of it, under the guidance of an expert teacher.

The final major psychological work on problem solving that needs to be summarized is that based on computer simulation, and more generally the computer-related conception of thinking as information processing. This approach forms part of the cognitive revolution, to which we now turn.

## The Cognitive Revolution

*The First Wave.* It is now widely recognized that there was a paradigm shift in psychology at the end of the 1950s (Gardner,

1985); Newell and Simon (1972, p. 882) nominated 1954–1958 as the critical period. Subsequent changes over the next two decades were very positive in many respects. The richness and complexity of mathematical and other tasks used in problem-solving research increased (e.g., Newell & Simon, 1972). Theoretical means for dealing with complex knowledge structures were devised. A far-reaching consequence was that, as expressed by Greeno (1980, p. 726),

> A pleasant prospect in the new study of learning that is now emerging is the revival of strong connections between the psychology of learning and the practice of instruction in schools. . . . A deep theoretical understanding of the psychological processes involved in school learning could become the keystone of a significant new psychological theory of learning.

Computers played a key role in all of this. George Miller (quoted by Jonathan Miller, 1983, p. 26) suggested that "the mind came in on the back of the machine," in that experiences with computers made it respectable to reintroduce the idea of internal representations. Computer simulation became the standard methodology for many of those working within the family of information-processing theories (Rabinowitz, 1988). The paramount virtue of this approach is that specifying a theory in sufficient detail to embody it in a running program enforces rigor in the construction of the theory and in the generation of hypotheses for empirical testing. The performance of such a program can be compared in detail with that of human subjects tackling the same problems. If the match is close, there is support for the theory embodied in the program; if not, the program can be revised and tested again.

Newell and Simon (1972) used protocols, both behavioral and verbal, as the source of evidence in support of the theories embodied in their programs. In the General Problem Solver, they characterized problem solving as a heuristic search through a problem space containing all the possible problem states, with a specification of the operators applicable to these states. The central heuristic is means-end analysis, the key idea of which is to analyze differences between the goal state and the current state within the problem space and to strategically apply operators to reduce the difference. Those interested in mathematical problem solving from an educational point of view find this approach limited in several respects. In particular, it works well only with a restricted subset of problems, namely those that have well-defined problem spaces, such as the Tower of Hanoi and Missionaries and Cannibals, which are semantically lean puzzles. In time, the concentration on general processes independent of domain-specific knowledge came to be seen as fatally restrictive. Moreover, there has been very limited success in simulating visually mediated thinking, which is often critical in problem solving—most obviously, but by no means exclusively, in geometrical problems.

The influence of computers extended well beyond their specific use in simulation, through the core conceptualization of thinking as the processing of information, and associated metaphors (see especially R. B. Davis, 1984, 1990).

*"Buggy" Algorithms and Word Problem Schemata: Prototypes of Information-Processing Analysis.* We present two examples, in some detail, to typify applications of information-processing analyses to mathematics education. The accompanying

TABLE 16–1. Stages of Problem Solving

| | |
|---|---|
| | UNDERSTANDING THE PROBLEM |
| **First.** You have to *understand* the problem. | *What is the unknown? What are the data? What is the condition?* Is it possible to satisfy the condition? Is the condition sufficient to determine the unknown? Or is it insufficient? Or redundant? Or contradictory? Draw a figure. Introduce suitable notation. Separate the various parts of the condition. Can you write them down? |
| | DEVISING A PLAN |
| **Second.** Find the connection between the data and the unknown. You may be obliged to consider auxiliary problems if an immediate connection cannot be found. You should obtain eventually a *plan* of the solution. | Have you seen it before? Or have you seen the same problem in a slightly different form? *Do you know a related problem?* Do you know a theorem that could be useful? *Look at the unknown!* And try to think of a familiar problem having the same or a similar unknown. *Here is a problem related to yours and solved before.* Could you use it? Could you use its result? Could you use its method? Should you introduce some auxiliary element in order to make its use possible? Could you restate the problem? Could you restate it still differently? Go back to definitions. If you cannot solve the proposed problem, try to solve first some related problem. Could you imagine a more accessible related problem? A more general problem? A more special problem? An analogous problem? Could you solve a part of the problem? Keep only a part of the condition, drop the other part; how far is the unknown then determined, how can it vary? Could you derive something useful from the data? Could you think of other data appropriate to determine the unknown? Could you change the unknown or the data, or both if necessary, so that the new unknown and the new data are nearer to each other? Did you use all the data? Did you use the whole condition? Have you taken into account all essential notions involved in the problem? |
| | CARRYING OUT THE PLAN |
| **Third.** *Carry out* your plan. | Carrying out your plan of the solution, *check each step.* Can you see clearly that the step is correct? Can you prove that it is correct? |
| | LOOKING BACK |
| **Fourth.** *Examine* the solution obtained. | Can you *check the result?* Can you check the argument? Can you derive the result differently? Can you see it at a glance? Can you use the result, or the method, for some other problem? |

Note: From *How to Solve It* by G. Polya, 1945, Princeton, NJ: Princeton University Press. Reprinted by permission.

critiques illustrate both the potential for fruitful interaction and the tensions that can exist between cognitive scientists' goals, aims, and perspectives and those of mathematics educators.

The first example is the extensive work on "buggy" algorithms for multidigit subtraction. A theory to explain systematic errors in children's performance of multidigit subtraction was developed by J. S. Brown, Burton, and VanLehn (e.g., J. S. Brown & Burton, 1978; J. S. Brown & VanLehn, 1982; Burton, 1982; VanLehn, 1990). The starting point of this theory was the long familiar observation that children's errors on multidigit subtraction are often systematic; for example, a student may subtract the smaller digit from the larger within each column, regardless of position. Drawing on computer-based metaphors, the theory formalizes observed patterns of errors as "bugs" within correct procedures for the computations. These procedures and bugs are defined in detail on the basis of task analysis, and the analysis shows how bugs can be predicted as constructions of the child faced with an impasse when conditions are encountered beyond the scope of currently mastered procedures. A finite collection of such bugs, often operating in combinations, has been shown to account for many of the errors made by pupils. An educational application based on this work has been to train diagnostic skills in student teachers. The computer is programmed to perform like a child with a particular bug, and the challenge to the student teacher is to identify the bug by presenting the simulated child with new calculations

and analyzing the answers (De Corte, Verschaffel, & Schrooten, 1991).

This example certainly seems to qualify as prototypical, being cited by Boden (1988, p. 263) as one of the few examples of a domain modeled in enough detail to be useful to pupils or teachers, by Rissland (1985) as a good example of "principled" modeling of human mathematical behavior, and by Newell (1990, p. 368) as a rare case in which cognitive theory can predict long stretches of behavior. Mathematics educators, by contrast, are much less enthusiastic (Cobb, 1990; Fischbein, 1990b; Ridgway, 1988; P. W. Thompson, 1989). A fundamental basis of their criticism is that skill in computation—let alone skill in mathematics—involves much more than procedural competence. Local repair of bugs in children's procedures amounts to treating symptoms rather than the underlying causes of imperfect understanding.

The second example is the body of work on addition and subtraction word problems. Throughout the 1980s, and continuing in the 1990s, there has been concerted research on how children learn how to do addition and subtraction word problems involving small collections of discrete objects (for overviews, see Carpenter, Moser, & Romberg, 1982; Fuson, 1992; Verschaffel & De Corte, 1993). A basic distinction emerged that distinguished three classes of situations modeled by addition and subtraction: situations involving *change* of a set of objects from an initial state to a final state through the application of a transformation (increase or decrease), situations involving the *combination* or splitting up of two discrete sets, and situations involving the quantified *comparison* of two discrete sets of objects.

In parallel with empirical studies, simulations of the understanding and solution of such problems were developed by Briars and Larkin (1984) and by Riley, Greeno, Kintsch, and others (Dellarosa, Kintsch, Reusser, & Weimer, 1988; Kintsch & Greeno, 1984; Riley & Greeno, 1988; Riley, Greeno, & Heller, 1983). The consequent interaction between empirical studies and the development of computer models was particularly productive, with benefits in both directions; this body of research is therefore an excellent example of the strengths and weaknesses of the computer simulation approach (see De Corte & Verschaffel, 1988, for a detailed discussion).

The basis of the simulation implemented by Riley et al. (1983) is that the competent problem solver first constructs a network representation of the quantities and semantic relationships in the text in terms of a change, combine, or compare schema. Based on the information in this representation, solution processes operate on sets of imagined blocks as counterparts of the sets of objects implicated in the situation. A range of computational models corresponding to different levels of skill in solving change, combine, and compare problems generate performances comparable with those observed empirically.

From the point of view of mathematics education, these efforts collectively constitute one of the most impressive demonstrations of the potential of the computer simulation approach. As pointed out by Greeno (1987), they have the virtue of making explicit descriptions of knowledge and processes that are normally implicit and often vague. Moreover, they are potentially useful in guiding the design of instructional materials and interventions. However, not all empirical findings have been consistent with the models (e.g., Carpenter & Moser, 1984; De Corte & Verschaffel, 1988), the range of their application is limited, and they do not address psychologically important aspects, such as the influence of textual variables on the construction of an initial internal representation of the problem. Significant discrepancies have been revealed when the comparison of the performance of the programs with empirical evidence has been taken beyond performance data (problem difficulty, solution time, typical errors) to address details of underlying representations, cognitive manipulations, and solution strategies (De Corte & Verschaffel, 1988).

Another limitation is that attempts at computer simulation have been almost entirely confined to word problems unproblematically modeled by addition and subtraction of small, positive, whole numbers. This may be construed as a recognition that the difficulties of the enterprise would mount enormously if the domain were expanded, or as reflecting an attitude that it is the demonstration of the feasibility of the approach that matters, rather than the target tasks. In either case, the application of the methodology to a restricted range of problems limits the educational relevance and applicability of the work.

***The Second Wave.*** Gardner (1985, p. 41) included as one characteristic of cognitive science, as it emerged in the first wave of the cognitive revolution, a "de-emphasis on affect, context, culture and history." We suggest that, in reaction to this limita-

tion, the second wave of the cognitive revolution is under way (Greer & Verschaffel, 1990).

One stimulus for this reaction has been what Gardner (1985, p. 44) termed the "computational paradox," that is, that "the kind of systematic, logical, rational view of human cognition that pervaded the early literature of cognitive science does not adequately describe much of human thought and behavior." Gardner's point is even more paradoxical when mathematical thinking is considered, since mathematics tends to be seen as the epitome of systematic, logical, and rational thought (for a critique of this position, see L. B. Resnick, 1989). What is becoming more and more clear is that a comprehensive theory of mathematical thought and behavior needs to encompass aspects that are not rational in a narrow sense, such as intuition (Fischbein, 1987), beliefs, attitudes, and emotions (McLeod & Adams, 1989), and visually mediated thinking (Dreyfus, 1991; Zimmermann & Cunningham, 1991).

Much of the pressure to relocate cognitive functioning within its social, cultural, and historical contexts has come from mathematics educators, who have pointed out limitations of information-processing psychology, such as its failure to provide an account of conceptual development (Vergnaud, 1990). Cobb (1990) has discerned indications of rapprochement between such points of view and those of some cognitive scientists. These signs include the notion of situated knowledge, the metaphor of cognitive apprenticeship, emphasis on enculturation within a mathematical community (J. S. Brown, Collins, & Duguid, 1989), and recognition of a need for a broader research agenda (e.g., Greeno, 1991b).

## Research in Mathematics Education: A Community Defining Itself

Against the background of the radical changes in psychology from the late 1950s onward, research in mathematics education has been emerging as a field of study in its own right. The major shifts within psychology outlined above have both facilitated this emergence and enhanced the eligibility of psychology as a contributory discipline.

Bishop (1992, p. 712 et seq.) proposed that there were three identifiable traditions reflecting the state of research in mathematics education around 1970: the empirical-scientist tradition, the pedagogue tradition, and the scholastic-philosopher tradition. Within educational psychology in general, the empirical-scientific tradition enjoyed a dominant position for most of the period from 1920 to 1970. It was compatible with methodological behaviorism, with goals of scientific precision and objectivity, and with the belief that curriculum issues could be solved by research (Kilpatrick, 1992, p. 20). Reliance on statistical methods and carefully prescribed designs, the technical apparatus of psychometrics, objectively defined instructional objectives, and an "engineering model" of evaluation were among its characteristics.

To a considerable extent, research in mathematics education was conducted within the empirical-scientific tradition. However, the limited perspective of such research was open to criticism from the perspectives of the other two traditions identified by Bishop. As Kilpatrick (1992, p. 5) pointed out, "mathematicians have a long, if sporadic, history of interest in studying the teaching and learning of their subject." Examples of eminent mathematicians with a highly elaborated and strongly held view of the nature of mathematics and a vision of how mathematics education should be include Polya, Dienes, and Freudenthal. There have been notable, albeit few and isolated, examples of mathematicians who reflected on their own activites (e.g., Poincaré) or on the nature of mathematics learning and thinking (e.g., de Morgan); psychologists (e.g., Wertheimer, 1945) and mathematicians (e.g., Hadamard, 1945) who studied cognitive processes of eminent mathematicians; and historians of mathematical concepts (e.g., Cajori, 1917). Moreover, scholars are increasingly seeking insights through the reconstruction of historical conceptual developments (e.g., Kaput, 1994; Piaget & Garcia, 1989). All of these perspectives contribute to our understanding of mathematical cognition and to a rich conception of the nature of mathematical activity. Increasingly, the scope of research on mathematics education is being widened to include advanced mathematical thinking (Dreyfus, 1990; Tall, 1991).

Given the deep philosophical differences between the traditions, it is not surprising that criticisms have been made of work within the empirical-scientific tradition. A sustained campaign was waged by Freudenthal, notably in *Weeding and Sowing* (1978), among the targets of which were Bloom's taxonomy, educational objectives, atomistic approaches to assessment, the technical "rituals" of psychometrics and statistics in general, and the assumption that a theory of mathematics education could be derived from a domain-independent theory of education.

Perhaps the single feature that best captures the essence of the empirical-scientific tradition is the methodological device of characterizing all aspects of interest as "variables" that can be defined, measured, and subjected to statistical analysis. Within this all-embracing methodological framework, for example, "teaching is taken as a treatment and learning as an effect" (Kilpatrick, 1992, p. 9). The ultimate manifestation of this approach within mathematics education was Begle's program to catalogue the "critical variables in mathematics education" (Begle, 1979). In his address to the first International Congress on Mathematical Education at Lyon, in 1969, Begle explicitly recommended the empirical-scientific approach, modeled on the procedures of physics, chemistry, and biology, to build up a theory of mathematics education. However, in the conclusion of the survey published in 1979, Begle confessed to feeling depressed by the reflection that a decade's accumulation of experimental work had brought about little if any progress toward a theory of mathematics education. Kilpatrick (1992, p. 30) commented:

Research in mathematics education seemed poised to become the experimental science Begle and others envisioned. Yet as the 1970s ended, increasing doubts were being expressed about the contribution research was making to the educational process, and some people eventually began to wonder whether educational research could become a science at all.

From today's perspective, Begle's aim of making educational research into a science similar to physics, chemistry, or biology was ill-conceived. Mathematics education is not an appropriate domain for the type of research that characterizes those sciences; rather, a much broader conception of research, paying due attention to the human and practical aspects of mathematics education, is needed.

Increasing interactions between researchers and scholars working within different perspectives led to the first intimations of the idea that mathematics education could be delineated as a field of study in its own right while retaining strong links with other disciplines (e.g., Vergnaud, 1982). Of these other disciplines, psychology and mathematics itself remain preeminent, but increasingly interest is being taken in the work of sociologists, linguists, anthropologists, and historians, reflecting the increasing recognition of mathematics education's situation in social, cultural, and historical contexts.

An important precursor to the emergence of an identifiable community of mathematics education researchers was the New Mathematics movement. The label is a misnomer insofar as it suggests a unified phenomenon rather than the disparate, loosely connected, and variegated collection of initiatives that it was (Moon, 1986). Nevertheless, it did stimulate international contact and exchange of ideas. During the 1960s, mathematicians and psychologists began to "get acquainted" (Kilpatrick, 1992, p. 24) at a number of meetings in the United States. In international terms, the first International Congress of Mathematical Education (ICME) held at Lyon in 1969, attended by over 600 people from 42 countries, was an early landmark (the seventh ICME in Quebec City in 1992 had nearly 3000 participants from 88 countries). At Lyon, Hans Freudenthal, who was president of the congress, asked Efraim Fischbein and Lee Shulman to organize a roundtable on the psychology of mathematics education. At the second ICME, held in Exeter in 1972, the most popular working group was that on the psychology of mathematics education, initiated by Efraim Fischbein. At the third ICME, this group became a permanent association, the International Group for the Psychology of Mathematics Education (IGPME), which has met annually since its first conference in Utrecht in 1977. In 1980 it adopted a constitution in which the major goals are stated as follows:

1. To promote international contacts and exchange of scientific information in the psychology of mathematics education.
2. To promote and stimulate interdisciplinary research in the aforesaid area with the cooperation of psychologists, mathematicians, and mathematics teachers.
3. To further a deeper and better understanding of the psychological aspects of teaching and learning mathematics and the implications thereof.

A synthesis of IGPME research in its first decade was published in 1990 (Nesher & Kilpatrick, 1990).

Another reflection of, and a stimulus for, the crystallization of the mathematics education research community was the formation of research institutes in several countries. Among the currently active research institutes are the National Center for Research in Mathematical Sciences Education at the University of Wisconsin–Madison; the Shell Centre for Mathematical Education at Nottingham University, England; the Freudenthal Institute at the University of Utrecht, the Netherlands; the Instituts de Recherche pour l'Enseignement de Mathématiques at various places in France; and the Institute für Didaktik der Mathematik in Bielefeld, Germany. The establishment of several domain-specific journals has been a further indication of growing independence.

The emergence of this research community has been characterized by a diversification of methods of inquiry and analysis well beyond the narrow range of the empirical-scientific approach. The range includes:

1. Clinical interviews and analyses of protocols, pioneered by Piaget and later used by Newell and Simon (1972). An overview of their use in studying children's mathematical thinking was provided by Ginsburg, Kossan, Schwartz, and Swanson (1983). Video recording has facilitated such analyses and provided rich records of interactions.
2. Vygotskian methodologies, with observers attempting to observe development as it happens under instruction, either working with individual children or small groups (e.g., Steffe, 1991), or with whole classes in teaching experiments (e.g., Cobb, Wood, & Yackel, 1991; Cobb et al., 1992; Lampert, 1986; Maher et al., 1991b; Newman et al., 1989).
3. Ethnomethodology, applied to the mathematics of cultural groups (Eisenhart, 1988; Gerdes, 1988; Lancey, 1983; Pinxten, 1991; Saxe, 1981).
4. Microgenetic analysis, that is, detailed analysis of the development of mathematical concepts in a single student over a considerable period of time (e.g., Maher, Davis, & Alston, 1991a; Schoenfeld, Smith, & Arcavi, 1993; Siegler & Crowley, 1991).
5. Computer simulation (Briars & Larkin, 1984; Riley et al., 1983; Rissland, 1985; VanLehn, 1990).
6. Methods made possible or enhanced by technological advances, such as on-line computer experimentation and improved equipment for eye-movement analysis (Verschaffel, De Corte, Gielen, & Struyf, 1994).

In a far-sighted paper, R. B. Davis (1967) issued a plea, as appropriate today as it was then, that we should continue to question our choice of methodologies for studying and improving teaching. Davis pointed to the variety of methods available:

There is introspection, autobiography, criticism (as in music and architecture), logical implication, recall under hypnosis, stimulated recall using videotape, the use of observers focussing on supposedly clearly discriminable events and noting their frequency, the use of automatic recording machinery, there is the process of demonstration and imitation, and there is the use of something called intuition. There are methods related to psychology, methods related to anthropology, methods related to psychoanalysis, and methods related to playing the piano. There are methods described as scientific and methods described as art. (p. 2)

In the pursuit of understanding and improving mathematics learning and teaching, researchers in the field are prepared to draw on the methodological and interpretational resources of many disciplines, including mathematics, psychology, anthropology, sociology, linguistics, the brain sciences, and artificial intelligence. Such pragmatic eclecticism may be seen as an appropriate response to the complexity of the task of understanding human behavior in complex settings.

In a thematic issue of the *Journal of the Learning Sciences*, three researchers (A. L. Brown, 1992; Saxe, 1992; Schoenfeld,

1992b) discussed their personal development as researchers and the need they felt to go beyond the methods of their early training in experimental psychology, developmental psychology, and mathematics, respectively. In his editorial comments, Schoenfeld (1992d) stated that they had all found it necessary to invent new methods. Doing so, however, raises many questions about the validity of such methods and the interpretation, dissemination, and evaluation of the evidence they generate.

Given this situation, which one could characterize as liberated or anarchic, depending on one's point of view, it is not surprising that there has been a call for clarification of what is meant by research in mathematics education (Sierpinska et al., 1993); the planned debate promises to be lively.

A further important development is the importance that the international dimension in mathematics education has come to assume in the last 20 years (Bishop, 1992). Among the manifestations of this trend may be listed the growth of contact, collaboration, and international institutions; the carrying out of international comparisons of children's mathematical performance; and a more balanced recognition of the mathematical achievements of all cultures (e.g., Joseph, 1992). In summary, as stated by Kilpatrick (1992, p. 3):

[R]esearch in mathematics education has struggled to achieve its own identity. It has tried to formulate its own issues and its own ways of addressing them. It has tried to define itself and to develop a cadre of people who identify themselves as researchers in mathematics education.

During the last two decades, that task of self-definition has largely been accomplished.

## THE DOMAIN

The emergence of research in mathematics education as a coherent field, as described in the previous section, has both contributed to and been facilitated by the marked shift within educational, cognitive, and developmental psychology toward a greater emphasis on domain specificity, exemplified by Gardner's (1984) suggestion that multiple forms of intelligence may be distinguished, of which one is logico-mathematical intelligence.

As mentioned at the outset, mathematics has become a prime example of the domain-specific approach to research on cognition. One reason for this is that many of the concerns central to cognitive psychology are strongly implicated in mathematical activity, including problem solving, the role of symbols and representations, the interplay between procedural and conceptual knowledge, visually mediated cognition, and the interaction between intellectual and affective factors.

The argument can be taken a step further by pointing out that mathematics may be considered not simply as a single domain, but as a federation of subdomains that differ in terms of their most characteristic methods, styles of thinking, and forms of representation. These subdomains typically are represented in compilations such as that edited by Grouws (1992), which includes chapters on arithmetic, algebra, geometry, and statistics and probability. Of these, probability is arguably the clearest case of a branch of mathematics demanding fundamentally different styles of conceptualization.

Despite these differences between subdomains, it is generally unquestioned that mathematics retains integrity as an intellectual domain. As pointed out by P. J. Davis and Hersh (1981, pp. 6–8), the answer to the question, "What is mathematics?" has changed throughout history and will continue to change. Very broadly, the answer may be said during the 20th century to have evolved from something like "the science of number and space" to a more abstract characterization such as "the science of patterns" (Steen, 1988). However, others would give more weight to problem solving, or the modeling of aspects of the real world, and the quest for a single phrase that could encapsulate an intellectual enterprise with so many facets seems pointless.

Some recent, still somewhat controversial writings on the philosophy of mathematics have argued for a shift away from the view of mathematics as the epitome of certain knowledge and toward its conceptualization as an activity grounded in human practices (Ernest, 1991; Restivo, Van Bendegem, & Fischer, 1993; Tymoczko, 1986c). Tymoczko (1986b) proposed the abandonment of attempts to find absolutely secure foundations for mathematics and suggested instead that

The philosophy of mathematics can be begun anew by reexamining the actual practices of mathematicians and those who use mathematics. If we look at mathematics without prejudice, many features will stand out as relevant that were ignored by the foundationalists: informal proofs, historical development, the possibility of mathematical error, mathematical explanations (in contrast to proofs), communication among mathematicians, the use of computers in modern mathematics, and many more. (p. xvi)

The effects of the increasing use of computers in mathematical research include greater emphasis on mathematics as an experimental science (particularly through technological advances in the generation and manipulation of images) and a forced reconsideration of the nature of proof.

From the many aspects that could be adduced to support the contention that mathematical activity, as a domain for psychological research, differs significantly from other domains, three of the most characteristic are selected for attention here: the dual nature of mathematics as descriptions of perceived reality and as autonomous abstract constructions, its hierarchically structured development on both the cultural and individual planes, and its dependence on external and internal representational systems. Each of these three aspects is related to the central mathematical activity of problem solving, which is treated in detail in the next section.

## Dual Nature of Mathematics

On the one hand, mathematics is rooted in the perception and description of the ordering of events in time and the arrangement of objects in space, and so on ("common sense—only better organized," as Freudenthal [1991, p. 9] put it), and in the solution of practical problems. On the other hand, out of this activity emerge symbolically represented structures that can become objects of reflection and elaboration, independent of their real-world roots. In the process, common sense is soon transcended, yet time and again, the results of such elaborations have proved (often after a considerable lag in time) useful in theoretical descriptions of real-world phenomena and the solution of real-world problems.

The duality is acknowledged in the distinction between pure and applied mathematics. Pure mathematicians may take patterns grounded in descriptions of reality and work with them on a formal basis. A major collective effort of pure mathematics, epitomized in the work of the Bourbaki group and in Klein's systematization of geometry, consists in the systematic organization of abstract patterns. Applied mathematics, on the other hand, is concerned with the construction of models of reality that can be "run" to generate useful results. The "unreasonable effectiveness of mathematics" (Wigner, 1960) raises a fundamental question. As Hersh (1986, p. 23) put it: "We may ask how these objects, which are our own creations, so often turn out to be useful in describing aspects of nature." Hersh suggested that while the working out of the answer in detail is a major task for the psychology of mathematical cognition, the general answer is obvious within an evolutionary perspective: "Our mathematical ideas fit the world for the same reason that our lungs are suited to the atmosphere of this planet." In a similar vein, Rav (1993, p. 89) proposed that cognitive mechanisms have evolved like other biological mechanisms by confrontation with reality, and have become genetically fixed.

The link between the two faces of mathematics is the activity of modeling. Typically, the modeling of a real-world situation leads to a range of solutions, none of which is uniquely "right," but which need to be judged in terms of human criteria such as utility, purpose, and complexity. Introducing pupils early to this perspective may be considered part of the process of enculturation into the practices of mathematicians. However, as R. B. Davis (1992, p. 727) lamented:

we have come (unwisely) to focus nearly *all* of our pedagogical efforts and our testing programs on . . . computations—*and we have come to take for granted the truly mathematical task of modeling the reality in an appropriate way.* (emphasis in original)

(See also P. J. Davis & Hersh, 1981 [especially, pp. 68–79]; Greer, 1993; Reusser, 1988; Silver & Shapiro, 1992.)

The effects of excessive concentration on computational proficiency have been documented in numerous "disaster stories." The following is a particularly striking example:

An army bus holds 36 soldiers. If 1,128 soldiers are being bused to their training site, how many buses are needed?

In a survey carried out in 1982 (National Assessment of Educational Progress, 1983), about 70 percent of a national sample of 13-year-olds in the United States calculated $1128 \div 36$ as $31\frac{1}{3}$, but only about one third of these students gave the answer *appropriate to the situation being modeled,* namely, 32; about one third gave $31\frac{1}{3}$ as the answer, and another one third gave 31 as the answer (see Silver, 1986, and Silver, Shapiro, & Deutsch, 1993, for analysis and discussion of such responses).

## Hierarchically Structured Development

The history of mathematics is essentially coextensive with the history of civilization. With proper acknowledgment of the contribution of non-European civilizations (Joseph, 1992) and of the distribution of mathematical activity across all cultures, there is an identifiable mainstream of mathematical development converging from many sources toward the present Golden Age of mathematics (P. J. Davis & Hersh, 1981; Stewart, 1987), and flowing into the future.

A familiar and instructive example is the development of number concepts, starting from the revealingly termed "natural numbers" 1, 2, 3, . . . that emerge from the practical activity of counting. Situations calling for sharing $n$ objects among $m$ people when $m$ is not a divisor of $n$, and other practical problems, motivate extension to the rational numbers ⅓, 5⁄7 . . . (though the Greeks approached rational numbers through the theory of commensurability in a geometric context, and in the process came to recognize irrational numbers, notably $\sqrt{2}$). The systematization of negative numbers $-3$, $-\frac{7}{4}$ . . . came much later, reflecting the fact that practical problems that can be used to model (such as bank balances) can be handled without recourse to a formal system. Further extensions to complex numbers (alternatively, and significantly, referred to as "imaginary") and beyond have increasingly been driven by abstract and formal considerations.

From a formal point of view, the natural numbers engender addition, subtraction, multiplication, and division. Generative mechanisms characteristic of mathematics are implicated: Addition is a curtailment of counting operations (which themselves develop through progressively efficient stages); one source of multiplication is as a curtailment of repeated addition, and likewise division can arise from repeated subtraction. Operations afford inverting, so addition gives rise to subtraction and multiplication to division. The natural number system is not closed under subtraction or multiplication—that is to say, there is not always a solution for $a - b$ or $a/b$. To achieve closure, the system must be extended to include negative numbers and rational numbers, respectively. Further extensions also have the property of restoring closure; for example, the extension to complex numbers produces a system within which every polynomial of degree $n$ has $n$ roots (allowing for repetitions).

There is a suggestive parallel between the extensions of the number system to achieve closures and Piaget's concept of disequilibrium as a driving force in development leading to a conceptual restructuring at a higher level. Piaget characterized individual cognitive growth as self-organizing; similarly, Freudenthal (1991, p. 15) stated that "mathematics grows . . . by its self-organizing momentum."

Extension of mathematical concepts, definitions, functions, and so on to more general domains is a mode of development characteristic of mathematics. A host of empirical findings and observations, and analyses of the historical record, testify to the difficulties, at both cultural and individual levels, of the radical conceptual restructuring required in the course of this growth, particularly in the domain of number concepts (Greer, 1994). A particularly fascinating and instructive example is the struggle to come to terms with negative numbers and arithmetical operations on them, a struggle that spanned many centuries (Fischbein, 1987; Hefendehl-Hebeker, 1991; Vergnaud, 1990).

Indeed, it is a noticeable trend of recent years that theorists are increasingly turning to the historical record as a source of insight into the development of mathematical conceptualizations. This by no means implies a simplistic view of ontogeny recapitulating phylogeny; nevertheless, certain structural parallels have been suggested, most notably by Piaget and Garcia (1989), who postulated general mechanisms underlying both psychogenesis and the history of the sciences.

Sinclair (1991, p. 19) related the historical and ontogenetic aspects in defining the central problem as follows:

The difficulty of studying learning—and teaching—lies . . . in the fact that it demands the study of the processes by which children come to know in a short time basic principles (in mathematics, but also in other scientific disciplines) that took humanity thousands of years to construct.

The solution recommended by Freudenthal is that the child should have the opportunity to partially retrace the course of historical/cultural development. What he had in mind was the reinvention of processes, not products:

the learner should reinvent mathematising rather than mathematics; abstracting rather than abstractions; schematising rather than schemes; formalising rather than formulae; algorithmising rather than algorithms; verbalising rather than language. . . . (Freudenthal, 1991, p. 49)

Mathematical knowledge structures of individual learners are complex, rich in connections, and develop over long periods. Vergnaud (1990) introduced the term "conceptual fields," defined as

large sets of situations whose analysis and treatment require several kinds of concepts, procedures, and symbolic representations that are connected with one another. Examples of conceptual fields are additive structures, multiplicative structures, projective and Euclidean geometry, logic of classes, and elementary algebra. (p. 23)

Such knowledge structures are not only complex, but also hierarchical. Piaget believed that logico-mathematical knowledge derives from reflective abstraction, that is, reflection not on objects, but on the subject's systems of actions. This process can be repeated at any level, as Freudenthal (1991, p. 123) put it, by "dealing with one's own activity as a subject matter of reflection in order to reach a higher level." It is this hierarchy that enables a structure to be progressively built linking the most mundane activities of everyday life to the rarefied abstractions of mathematics:

Common sense experiences, as it were, coalesced into rules (such as the commutativity of addition), and these rules again become common sense, . . . as a basis of even higher order mathematics—a tremendous hierarchy, built thanks to a remarkable interplay of forces. (Freudenthal, 1991, p. 9)

Locally, progress is achieved by the construction of "conceptual entities," as when a function becomes cognitively accessible as a single object (G. Harel & Kaput, 1991). Globally, as is familiar from Piagetian theory, mental growth is considered to occur in stages, with each stage building on the preceding one but transcending it (Kilpatrick, 1986, p. 11). Effective mathematical cognition involves being able to move flexibly between levels, returning to lower levels when necessary, as well as moving to higher levels for a change of perspective.

## Central Role of External and Internal Representations

The development of mathematics is inextricably dependent on systems of symbols and graphical means for envisioning information, and on physical artifacts and recording media (Cajori, 1917; Kaput, 1987). A powerful illustration of this observation is the familiar computational effectiveness of the Arabic place-value number system relative to the systems used by the Greeks and Romans. At a higher level in the development of number, complex numbers became more accessible and acceptable to mathematicians when they were represented as points in a plane; as Kaput (1986) put it, "they could now see them and also their actions on them" (see also Stewart, 1987, chap. 11, for a discussion of the history and significance of this development). The interaction with cultural artifacts can be illustrated by differences in computational procedures for arithmetic. Indian methods, for example, were adapted to a recording medium that has a premium on space, and in which overwriting is easy (Cajori, 1917, p. 97); conversely, the conventional methods that we are familiar with are adapted to the use of paper and pencil, with space not a problem but erasure difficult. In Japan, the use of the abacus, whether actual or mental, is a major determining factor in computational processes (e.g., Hatano, Miyake, & Binks, 1977).

Recently, these issues have been sharply focused through the opening of "new representational windows" (Kaput, 1986) by the computer and through revolutionary advances in visual technology (Friedhoff & Benzon, 1991). In particular, translations between systems of representations (Janvier, 1987b) can be embodied in software displaying dynamically linked multiple representations (Kaput, 1992).

The visibility and tangibility of external representations contribute to a tendency to define mathematics in terms of its products and mathematical activity in terms of facility in the production and manipulation of such products. Clearly, however, the processes of mathematical thinking occur through an exceedingly complex interplay between external representations (symbols, natural language, graphical representations on pages and computer screens, physical objects, and situations in which people act) and internal mental processes. Such processes, including internal representations, cannot be directly observed, of course. Rather, we build theoretical models to account for observable behavior (Goldin & Kaput, 1992), exploiting a wide range of methodological resources (Mulhern, 1989). The complexity of this task is well illustrated in the collection of contributions edited by Janvier (1987a).

For illustrative purpose, we refer here to Goldin's (1992b) model (Figure 16–2), which extends and elaborates Bruner's (1966) classification of representations as enactive, iconic, and symbolic in postulating complex processes of interaction between five types of internal representational systems, namely:

1. A verbal syntactic system
2. Imagistic systems (visual/spatial, auditory/rhythmic, tactile/kinesthetic)
3. Formal notational systems
4. An executive/heuristic system
5. An affective system

Thus, the model extends well beyond the verbal syntactic and formal notational systems that embody the most salient external manifestations of verbal and written mathematics, respectively. With respect to nonverbal systems for imagistic processing, there has been a long history of introspective accounts by mathematicians testifying to the importance of nonverbal imagery. Increasing attention and importance have been accorded to such ideas within cognitive psychology (e.g., Johnson, 1987), and there are strong signs of renewed interest in visually mediated thinking in mathematics (Dreyfus, 1991; Zimmermann & Cunningham, 1991). Likewise, the crucial role of the system for executive control and heuristic planning has been increasingly emphasized in recent theories of problem solving (e.g., Schoenfeld, 1985).

Whether an affective system should be considered as a form of representation is debatable. At any rate, its inclusion in the model reflects growing awareness of the need to take account of affective factors in intellectual functioning in general and mathematics learning in particular (McLeod & Adams, 1989). Goldin (1992a) included within this system both global aspects of affect—relatively stable beliefs and attitudes, and local aspects—the changing feelings in the course of problem solving or other mathematical activity. Moreover, he suggested (p. 251) that the development of effective affect is an important goal for mathematics education; indeed, a theory of "meta-affect," by analogy with "metacognition," would be appropriate (De Bellis-Kramer & Goldin, 1993).

Goldin and Kaput (1992) present an initial analysis of ways in which mathematical thinking is permeated by interactions between external and internal representations. In some cases, processes of internalization (as stressed by Vygotsky) can be traced, as in the example of the "mental abacus" (Hatano et al., 1977). In other cases we may posit a fairly direct visualization—of transformations of geometrical figures, for example.

In general, however, internal representations are much more elaborated within conceptual structures, networks of meanings, and affective personal associations specific to the individual. Skemp (1979) characterized the distinction as being between surface structures (syntax) of external representations and deep structures (semantics) of mathematical schemata. The task of mathematics education may be seen, to a very considerable extent, as the fostering in the student of powerful, richly connected internal representations and of the ability to move flexibly, in both directions, between these and culturally defined external representations (Mason, 1987).

The fundamental insight that meaning does not inhere in any external representation but only in some individual's construal is not confined to constructivist theorists, although they have certainly rendered a service in hammering home the point (e.g., Cobb, 1990). Much of the recent research on children's learning of mathematics serves to demonstrate the danger of assuming that the construal by the learner will approximate that envisaged by the teacher, and there has been plentiful documentation of misconceptions (Confrey, 1990; Perkins & Simmons, 1988) and other manifestations of individual constructions of knowledge. The implication for teaching is clear, namely, that the teacher needs to adopt a diagnostic rather than punitive stance toward such alternative representations. At the same time, the educational agenda requires convergence on conventional external representations. A rapprochement of

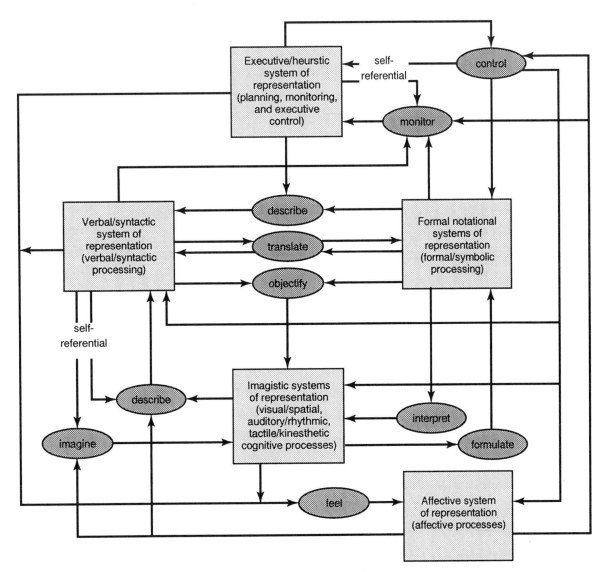

FIGURE 16-2. Goldin's Model of Internal Representational Systems
*Source*: From "Toward an Assessment Framework for School Mathematics" by
G. A. Goldin, 1992, in R. Lesh and S. J. Lamon (Eds.), *Assessments of Authentic
Performance in Elementary Mathematics* (pp. 63–88), Washington, DC: American
Association for the Advancement of Science. Reprinted by permission.

what might broadly be termed Piagetian and Vygotskian perspectives leads to the balanced view that mathematical knowledge develops through the individual's construction of personal construals *within* social and cultural contexts requiring culturally shared means of expression (Salomon, 1993b); this is elaborated in the next section.

## THE LEARNER

In this section we focus on the learner mainly from the following points of view:

1. The aptitudes and disposition required to become a competent learner and problem solver in the domain of mathematics.
2. The conception of the learner as a constructor of knowledge and competence.

We have chosen problem solving as a focus for the discussion of the aptitudes involved in mathematical activity for several reasons. First, although mathematics involves much more, it is generally recognized that solving problems is an activity at the heart of doing mathematics (see, e.g., Dreyfus, 1990). A problem in this context may be broadly defined as a situation in which a person is trying to attain a goal but no solution is immediately accessible. Second, there is today a clear consensus that the acquisition of problem-solving skills is a major objective of mathematics education. In the United States, for example, the National Council of Teachers of Mathematics (NCTM) stated in its *Agenda for Action,* published in 1980, that "problem solving must be the focus of school mathematics" (p. 1). Likewise, in *Curriculum and Evaluation Standards for School Mathematics* (National Council of Teachers of Mathematics, 1989), problem solving is strongly emphasized. Third, mathematical problem solving has been studied very extensively over the past 15 years, as is illustrated by the extensive literature (e.g., Charles & Silver, 1988; Goldin & McClintock, 1984; Schoenfeld, 1985, 1994; Silver, 1985). Recently, attention has also turned to problem posing (S. I. Brown & Walter, 1993; Kilpatrick, 1987; Silver, 1994).

One focus of this work has been an analysis of expertise in problem solving in mathematics, as well as in other domains (for a general review, see Chi, Glaser, & Farr, 1988). This analysis has led to the identification and more precise definition of the crucial aptitudes involved in competent learning and problem solving.

## Aptitudes Involved in Skilled Mathematical Problem Solving

We use the term *aptitude* here in a broad sense to refer to any characteristic of the student that can influence his or her learning and problem-solving activity and achievement. With respect to mathematics, there is today a rather broad consensus that major categories of aptitudes underlying skilled problem solving are domain-specific knowledge, heuristic methods, metacognitive knowledge and skills, and affective components, especially beliefs and emotions (see, e.g., Schoenfeld, 1992a). As such, the topic of problem solving allows us to show clearly that good performance in mathematics requires more than the acquisition of a repertoire of computational and procedural skills. We review each of the four above-mentioned categories of aptitudes in turn, and then discuss their interrelationships (see also De Corte, 1995b).

*Domain-Specific Knowledge.* Domain-specific knowledge involves facts, symbols, conventions, definitions, formulas, algorithms, concepts, and rules that constitute the substance or the content of a subject matter field. A major finding of the analysis of expertise is that expert problem solvers master a large, well-organized, and flexibly accessible domain-specific knowledge base (Chi et al., 1988). Similar observations have been made about students. For example, Silver (1979) studied junior high school students' perceptions of relatedness among word problems. He found that skilled problem solvers categorized tasks in terms of their underlying mathematical structure, such as the equation structure; weak students, on the contrary, based their categorization on surface characteristics of the problem statement or context. Similar differences in the initial problem representation were observed by Krutetskii (1976) and reflected differences of content as well as organization in the knowledge bases of the two groups.

It has been observed in a different way that conceptual domain-specific knowledge already strongly affects the solution processes of young children working on the one-step addition and subtraction word problems discussed previously. For example, De Corte and Verschaffel (1987a) found substantial variation in difficulty level among word problems that can be solved by the same arithmetic operation but have different structures (see also Fuson, 1992). Thus, understanding and solving even those simple word problems requires more than mastering the arithmetic operations of addition and subtraction; in addition, children must apply a conceptual knowledge of the structure underlying these word problems. This conclusion does not, of course, imply that procedural knowledge is unimportant. Indeed, as is argued by Carpenter (1986) and by Riley et al. (1983) with respect to simple word problems, improvement of performance depends on both the use of more sophisticated procedures and on the availability of strong conceptual schemata (see also Hiebert, 1986).

The importance of domain-specific knowledge is also evidenced in a negative way by numerous research findings showing the occurrence of misconceptions and defective skills in many learners. For instance, the so-called "multiplication makes bigger" misconception has been observed in students of different ages and in various countries (see Greer, 1992). De Corte, Verschaffel, and Van Coillie (1988), for example, administered to 116 Flemish sixth graders (12-year-olds) a series of multiplication word problems in which the nature of the multiplicand and of the multiplier was varied systematically: integer, decimal larger than 1, or decimal smaller than 1. They found that a decimal multiplier smaller than 1 had a very strong negative effect on the proportion of correct responses. Almost all errors consisted of choosing division instead of multiplication. This multiplier effect is explained in terms of the misconception that the result of a multiplication is always bigger than the multiplicand (see Fischbein, Deri, Nello, & Marino, 1985, for a theoretical interpretation of this misconception based on the conceptualization of multiplication as repeated addition).

As a result of the seminal work of J. S. Brown, Burton, and VanLehn (J. S. Brown & Burton, 1978; VanLehn, 1990), the best-documented category of defective procedural skills is the set of buggy algorithms, also discussed earlier. (For detailed reviews of the literature on misconceptions and defective skills, see Confrey, 1990, and Perkins & Simmons, 1988.)

The previous examples illustrate the role of knowledge by referring to isolated concepts and skills (see Grouws, 1992, for reviews relating to other mathematical topics). However, even more crucial than mastering separate pieces of subject matter content is the availability and accessibility of a well-organized knowledge base. Indeed, it has been shown that experts differ from novices in that their knowledge base is better and more dynamically structured, and as a consequence more flexibly accessible (Chi et al., 1988). With respect to mathematics learning and teaching this is stressed, for example, by Vergnaud's (1990) notion of conceptual fields, introduced and defined in the preceding section. Research has shown that full mastery of such conceptual fields takes a long period of cognitive development. For example, although some aspects of addition and subtraction are readily grasped by 4-year-olds, one-step addition problems of the type $a + x = b$, where $b$ and $a$ have different signs, are still difficult for the majority of 15-year-olds (Vergnaud, 1990).

Starting from a different theoretical framework, namely, the situated cognition paradigm, Greeno (1991a) introduced the notion of a "conceptual domain" conceived of as an environment involving a range of resources that one can learn to use for understanding and reasoning. An example of a conceptual environment is the domain of numbers and quantities, including different kinds of numbers, such as integers, rationals, and reals; different quantitative domains, such as commercial transactions, cooking, and motions of objects; and different operations on numbers and on quantities.

Besides the more formal elements such as concepts, formulas, and algorithms, students' informal and intuitive knowledge (Fischbein, 1987; Schoenfeld, 1985) and real-world knowledge also influence their learning and problem-solving activities. This is indirectly illustrated by the difficulties that are encountered when one tries to develop intelligent tutoring systems for algebra word problems; indeed, it seems almost impossible to simulate the real-world knowledge involved in understanding and solving such problems (Kintsch, 1991). However, recent research has shown that traditional teaching tends to divorce mathematical problem solving from children's real-world knowledge by using an impoverished and stereotyped diet of standard word problems that can always be modeled and solved by the straightforward application of one or more arithmetic operations with the given numbers (Greer, 1993; Verschaffel, De Corte, & Lasure, 1994; see also the section below, SOCIAL AND CULTURAL CONTEXTS).

*Heuristic Methods.* Polya's analysis of heuristic processes in problem solving was introduced earlier (Table 16–1). Heuristic methods do not guarantee that one will find the solution of a given problem; however, because they induce a systematic and planned approach to the task—in contrast to a trial-and-error strategy—they substantially increase the probability of success. Examples of heuristic methods are carefully analyzing a problem, specifying the knowns and the unknowns; decomposing the problem into subgoals; finding an easier related or analogous problem; visualizing the problem using a drawing or a diagram; and working backward from the intended goal or solution.

One major way in which heuristics can be helpful in solving a problem is as tools or resources that the problem solver uses in transforming the original problem until a familiar routine task emerges for which he or she has a ready-made solution. As remarked by Silver (1994), such reformulations of a problem aimed at making it more accessible for solution can be considered a kind of problem posing. As an illustration of this function of heuristics, let us consider the task given in Figure 16–3 (after Polya, 1965). We assume that this task is perceived by the learner as a genuine problem; this means that she realizes she cannot immediately give the answer and does not have a ready-made solution available, but at the same time she assumes that the task contains the information necessary to find the solution. Transforming the problem to a routine task using one of the heuristics mentioned above might proceed as follows:

> Is there a related problem for which I can find the solution easily?
> *Yes, I can calculate the volume of a right pyramid.*
> Taking this into account, can I restate or transform the initial task?
> *Yes, when I consider the frustrum as part of a complete pyramid*

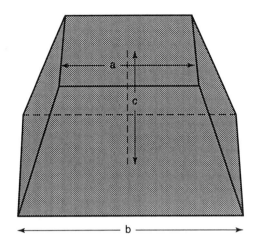

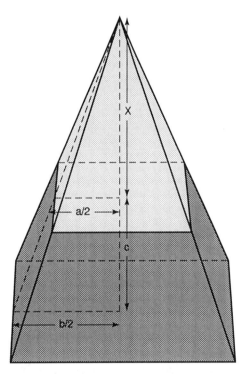

**FIGURE 16–3. Finding the Volume of a Frustrum of a Pyramid with Given Dimensions**
Assuming that it is known how to find the volume of a pyramid, the key insight is that the frustrum can be seen as the difference between two pyramids, as indicated by the lower figure. It is also necessary to know how to calculate x from the given information.
*Source*: After *Mathematical Discovery* (Vol. 2, p. 9) by G. Polya, 1965, New York: Wiley. Adapted by permission.

[see Figure 16–3], *I can find its volume by calculating the difference between the large and the small pyramid.*

Although the importance of heuristics in problem solving has face validity and was rather broadly recognized, throughout the 1970s there was only weak empirical evidence supporting its relationship with success in problem solving, and initial attempts to teach those strategies were not very successful

(Schoenfeld, 1992a). At least two closely related reasons can account for these observations. First, teaching students isolated heuristics does not substantially improve performance on new problems, because they often are unable to decide which method is appropriate for the problem at hand. Second, as noted by Schoenfeld (1992a), Polya's descriptions of the heuristics were not sufficiently detailed to enable students not yet familiar with them to implement the strategies. For example, using the heuristic "finding an easier related or analogous problem" can take very different forms for distinct kinds of problems; indeed, as will be argued below, heuristic strategies and content knowledge interact during the problem-solving process.

Meanwhile, substantial progress has been made in specifying and delineating heuristic strategies in such a way that they become teachable and learnable within a comprehensive approach to the teaching of problem solving. One good example discussed in more detail in a later section is Schoenfeld's (1985, 1987, 1992a) approach, in which specific heuristic strategies are inculcated in conjunction with metacognitive executive control skills. Another illustration is Van Streun's (1989) heuristic mathematics education at the secondary school level.

The necessity to delineate problem-solving strategies, taking into account the type of problems at hand, also accounts largely for the finding that, contrary to what has often been claimed and expected, general heuristic methods do not transfer spontaneously to a variety of problems within the same domain or across domains (see, e.g., Nickerson, Perkins, & Smith, 1985).

*Metacognitive Knowledge and Skills.* Since the 1980s, researchers in the fields of instructional and developmental psychology have shown an intensified interest in metacognition (von Wright, 1992). Although there is still quite a bit of confusion about what the term means and about its usefulness as a scientific construct (Campione, Brown, & Connell, 1988), most scholars in the domain of learning and instruction in general, and in mathematics education in particular (e.g., Garofalo & Lester, 1985), seem to agree that metacognition involves two main aspects, namely, knowledge concerning one's own cognitive functioning, and activities relating to the self-monitoring of one's cognitive processes (A. L. Brown, Bransford, Ferrara, & Campione, 1983).

Metacognitive knowledge includes knowing about the strengths as well as the weaknesses of one's cognitive capacities. Examples are being aware of the limits of short-term memory, and knowing that our memory is fallible but that one can use aids (such as mnemonics) for retaining information. Also involved are beliefs about cognition and ability—for instance, believing that one's mathematical ability is strong.

The self-monitoring or self-regulating mechanisms that constitute the second component of metacognition can be defined as the executive control structure that organizes and guides our learning and thinking processes. This control structure includes skills such as planning a solution process; monitoring an ongoing solution process; evaluating and, if necessary, debugging an answer or a solution; and reflecting on one's learning and problem-solving activities (see also Figure 16–2).

Evidence supporting the crucial role of metacognition for learning and problem solving has been obtained in comparative studies of skilled and weak problem solvers of different ages and in a variety of content domains, including mathematics.

For example, as early as 1959, Gurova (1985) compared the problem-solving approaches of 11-year-old low and high performers on a series of difficult word problems. She reported that the high performers were more aware of their problem-solving activity. They could explain their problem-solving methods better, they could justify their solution strategies more appropriately, and they were more accurate in predicting which problems they had solved correctly. Lester and Garofalo (1982), Krutetskii (1976), and Nelissen (1987) also reported differences between more and less able elementary and secondary pupils with respect to self-monitoring and self-control. Overtoom (1991) observed similar differences between gifted and average students at the primary and secondary level. At the college level, Schoenfeld (1985) found that in comparison with an expert problem solver, students lacked essential metacognitive monitoring, assessing, and decision-making skills. In terms of Kuhl's (1985) theory of self-regulation, one could say that skilled thinkers and problem solvers are characterized by a high level of action control, that is, a systematic and persistent orientation toward a preconceived objective; this implies that they constantly monitor their activity and, whenever necessary, make the required corrections. Taking this into account, it is not surprising that more and more voices are heard demanding more explicit attention to metacognitive skills instruction (see, e.g., Perkins, 1992). Evidence that metacognitive skills can be taught successfully in mathematics will be discussed in a later section (see, e.g., Lester, 1988; Schoenfeld, 1985). However, much theoretical and empirical work remains to be done to achieve a better understanding of metacognition that can guide the design of powerful learning environments for the acquisition of self-regulatory skills. By way of illustration we mention two issues that need further clarification. The first is the degree of consciousness or unconsciousness of metacognitive activities. The second echoes a major topic mentioned with respect to heuristic strategies, namely, the question of generality versus domain-embeddedness of reflection and self-regulation (see, e.g., Nelissen, 1987).

*Affective Components.* It has been recognized for some time that affective factors play an important role in mathematics teaching and learning. For example, the study of positive and negative attitudes toward mathematics and mathematics teaching has a long tradition (see Leder, 1987, for a review). However, as remarked by Lester, Garofalo, and Kroll (1989), most of the work is correlational in nature and has a rather weak theoretical basis. Recently there has been a resurgence of interest accompanied by a substantive and methodological broadening in the study of the relationships between affective factors and mathematics learning. This trend is clearly marked in the 1989 volume edited by McLeod and Adams (see also McLeod, 1990) and is also reflected in Goldin's model of the kinds of representations involved in mathematical problem solving (Figure 16–2).

As is the case for metacognition, the affective domain suffers from a lack of conceptual clarity (Hart, 1989). We follow here the framework proposed by McLeod (1990), according to which beliefs, attitudes, and emotions constitute the range of affective reactions involved in mathematics learning. These terms refer to responses that vary in the intensity of affect involved, from rather cold for beliefs to hot for emotions. They also differ in terms of stability: While beliefs and attitudes are rather stable and resistant to change, emotions alter quickly. Finally, the cognitive component is very strong for beliefs, less so for attitudes, and least for emotions. Although cognition and affect are interwoven in all reactions, beliefs constitute the most obvious interface. Indeed, some authors characterize beliefs as an aspect of metacognition (see, e.g., Schoenfeld, 1987).

McLeod (1990) distinguished between beliefs about mathematics and about self. As beliefs about self can be more or less identified with knowledge of one's cognitive capacities and limitations, we consider them as part of metacognition. As defined by Schoenfeld (1985), beliefs about the domain correspond to

one's mathematical world view, the perspective with which one approaches mathematics and mathematical tasks. One's beliefs about mathematics can determine how one chooses to approach a problem, which techniques will be used or avoided, how long and how hard one will work on it, and so on. (p. 45)

Schoenfeld's view on the impact of beliefs on mathematics learning is echoed in *Curriculum and Evaluation Standards for School Mathematics* (National Council of Teachers of Mathematics, 1989):

These beliefs exert a powerful influence on students' evaluation of their own ability, on their willingness to engage in mathematical tasks, and on their ultimate mathematical disposition. (p. 233)

Research has already identified many beliefs about mathematics, induced by instruction, that have a negative or inhibitory influence on students' learning activities and approaches to mathematics problems (Greeno, 1991b). For example, Schoenfeld (1988) has shown that in high school classes where mathematics is taught in a way that would generally be considered good teaching, students nevertheless acquire debilitating beliefs about the domain, such as "solving a mathematical problem should not take more than just a few minutes," or "being able to solve a mathematical problem is a mere question of luck." It is obvious that such misconceptions will not promote a mindful and persistent approach to new and challenging problems. Similar beliefs are that mathematics consists mainly of a set of rules and procedures that one has to memorize and use in a rather mechanical way, that there is only one correct way to solve a mathematics problem, and that the goal of doing mathematics is to obtain the correct answer (see Frank, 1988; Lampert, 1990; Schoenfeld, 1992a). Major factors influencing the design of instructional environments that produce such misconceptions in students are the beliefs of the teachers themselves about doing and learning mathematics, and societal opinions about the importance and the nature of mathematics.

As argued by McLeod (1990), Mandler's (1989) theory of emotions, developed from an information-processing perspective, offers a promising framework for describing and explaining students' emotional reactions to mathematical tasks and for unraveling the interaction between cognitive processes and affective responses in problem solving. Until now, only initial steps have been taken, suggesting a number of interesting hypotheses, such as that different cognitive processes may be differentially sensitive to affect—more specifically, that metacognitive activities are especially susceptible to emotions,

whereas storage and retrieval processes are not strongly affected, and that the nature of the affective responses may vary, depending on the phase in the problem-solving process (McLeod, 1989). Apart from Mandler's theory, DeBellis-Kramer and Goldin (1993) reported a preliminary attempt to analyze the interactions between cognition and affect in elementary schoolchildren during mathematical problem solving. Using video recording of task-based interviews, they registered the child's solution activities and dialogue with the interviewer, but also recorded facial expressions using a separate camera set up some distance from the student. Interactions were identified by relating cognitive activities and representations generated by the student with affective states inferred from the facial expressions using a standardized coding system.

***Interaction Between the Different Categories of Aptitudes: Toward a Dispositional View of Mathematics Learning.*** So far we have mainly discussed separately the different aptitudes involved in problem solving. However, it is obvious that in expert problem solving those aptitudes, and their subcategories, are applied integratively and interactively. An indication of the complexity of these interactions is conveyed by Goldin's (1992b) model for modes of internal representations involved in mathematical problem solving and thinking (Figure 16–2).

We have already mentioned that solving even one-step addition and subtraction word problems requires mastery of two subcategories of domain-specific knowledge, namely, procedural skills for counting and computing and conceptual knowledge in the form of problem schemata. The major theoretical models with respect to children's solution processes of such problems, developed by Briars and Larkin (1984) and by Riley et al. (1983), assume that improved procedural skill depends on more sophisticated problem schemata. This represents only one example of the more general argument put forward by Hiebert and Lefevre (1986) that conceptually based procedures become more meaningful, and can be used more effectively, when the formal language and action patterns involved in procedures enhance the applicability of conceptual knowledge (see also Silver, 1986). In other words, the benefits are reciprocal.

The relationships between the different categories of aptitudes are also very prominent in skilled problem solving, as illustrated by the following examples. First, in solving the frustrum problem (Figure 16–3), discovering the applicability of the heuristic "finding an easier related or analogous problem" is partially based on one's conceptual knowledge about the pyramid, such as the formula for computing its volume; this exemplifies the interaction between heuristic strategies and domain-specific knowledge referred to earlier. The second example relates to the problem about busing soldiers, mentioned in a previous section. The robust finding that a substantial number of students answer this kind of problem with "$x$, remainder $y$" (see also Carpenter, Lindquist, Matthews, & Silver, 1983) is symptomatic of the belief mentioned above, namely, that mathematics consists of a set of rules and procedures that one has to use in a rather mechanical way. This answer clearly indicates that students apply the algorithm taught without any "sense" of what the numbers mean in this context (Greeno, 1991a), and can, as was argued earlier, be attributed to the lack of mathematical modeling of problem situations in much current teaching. This example also shows that beliefs about mathematics inhibit the application of metacognitive activities such as looking back and evaluating one's solution to the problem (see also Frank, 1988). In sum, this example provides evidence of a negative kind about the importance of the integrated acquisition of the different aptitudes discussed above. The outcomes of more recent studies relating to multiplication (Greer, 1993) and division problems (Silver et al., 1993) confirm this conclusion; both studies convincingly show the dissociation between students' sense making of problems, on the one hand, and their calculations, on the other.

The preceding examples also illustrate that misconceptions and defective skills, discussed earlier under the category of domain-specific knowledge, are intertwined with elements of the other categories. This is in accordance with the multiple-frame interpretation of misconceptions put forward by Perkins and Simmons (1988). These authors distinguish between four frames or levels of knowledge involved in deep understanding in domains like science, mathematics, and computer programming; in some respect these frames cut across our four categories of aptitudes (Perkins & Simmons, 1988, pp. 313–314). The four frames are:

1. The content frame—containing the facts, definitions, and algorithms of a subject matter field, along with metacognitive knowledge for monitoring their use.
2. The problem-solving frame—consisting of the domain-specific and general problem-solving strategies, beliefs about problem solving, and self-regulatory processes.
3. The epistemic frame—incorporating domain-specific as well as general strategies and criteria for the validation of knowledge.
4. The inquiry frame—involving domain-specific and general strategies for extending and challenging work in a domain.

Perkins and Simmons (1988) recognized that misconceptions in a particular domain depended mostly on shortcomings in the content frame, such as naive and incomplete concepts. But they argued, in particular, that misunderstandings are aggravated by weaknesses in the other frames, such as blind trial and error (problem-solving frame), intuitions that mask contrary observation (epistemic frame), and context-encapsulated knowledge (inquiry frame). This integrative view of misconceptions can shed some new light on the frequently reported finding that misconceptions are very resistant to modification through traditional teaching (Confrey, 1990). Indeed, conventional instruction has been characterized by a one-sided emphasis on the content frame and pays hardly any attention to the epistemic and inquiry frames. Elaborating on the preceding discussion, one can conclude that expertise in mathematical problem solving involves more than just the sum of the four categories of aptitudes we described. In this respect, the notion of a mathematical disposition introduced in *Curriculum and Evaluation Standards for School Mathematics* (National Council of Teachers of Mathematics, 1989) is useful as a reference for thinking about the integrated availability and application of those aptitudes:

Learning mathematics extends beyond learning concepts, procedures, and their applications. It also includes developing a disposition toward mathematics and seeing mathematics as a powerful way for looking at situations. Disposition refers not simply to attitudes but to a tendency to think and to act in positive ways. Students' mathematical dispositions are manifested in the way they approach tasks—whether with confidence, willingness to explore alternatives, perseverance, and interest—and in their tendency to reflect on their own thinking. (p. 233)

This view of expertise in mathematics (see also L. B. Resnick, 1989, for a related view) is in accordance with recent ideas in the more general literature on learning and instruction, such as the dispositional approach to thinking and creativity proposed by Perkins, Jay, and Tishman (1993). Important in this respect is that, according to Perkins et al., the notion of disposition involves more than ability and motivation, although both are important aspects of a disposition. They distinguish three components of a disposition: inclination, sensitivity, and ability. Inclination is defined as the tendency to engage in a given behavior because of motivation, habits, and possibly other factors. Sensitivity refers to the feeling for, and alertness to, opportunities for implementing the appropriate behavior. Ability, then, constitutes the actual skill to deploy the behavior. Implied in this view is that students often have the ability to perform certain tasks or solve certain problems but do not exercise that ability because of lack of spontaneous inclination and sensitivity.

How do such aspects as sensitivity and inclination relate to the aptitudes? Should they not be considered as an additional category of aptitudes that also has to be pursued as a direct goal of instruction? Although continued research on this issue is needed, the most plausible perspective seems to be, in line with the view of Perkins et al. (1993) of the components of thinking, that ability, sensitivity, and inclination are characteristics or dimensions of the categories of aptitudes described before. This means that it is not sufficient that students acquire certain concepts, skills, and heuristics, such as estimation skills, but that they also should get a feeling for situations and opportunities to use those skills, and should become inclined to do so whenever appropriate. The acquisition of this disposition—especially the sensitivity and inclination aspects of it—requires extensive experience with the different categories of aptitudes in a large variety of situations. As such, the disposition cannot be directly taught but has to develop over an extended period of time; this implies that the organization of teaching cannot be restricted to a set of discrete goals. For example, what Greeno (1991a) calls number sense includes estimation skills, flexible numerical computation, and quantitative judgment and inference. Although each of these aspects can be taught directly, we agree with Greeno (1991a, p. 173) that the development of number sense results "from the whole range of activities of mathematics education, rather than a designated subset of specially designed activities."

However, students' inclination and sensitivity to apply acquired knowledge and skills can be hindered by emotional blocks. To account for emotions, the preceding theoretical framework of a mathematical disposition can be complemented by Boekaert's (1993) heuristic model of the affective learning process. This model states that, confronted with a learning task, students develop either a learning or a coping intention, depending on their perception of the task demands and the context. Positive expectations and feeling induce a learning intention: Students are primarily oriented toward learning, and this elicits activity in the so-called mastery mode. Negative feelings, by contrast, generate a coping intention: Not learning but restoring their well-being is the primary concern, and this evokes coping activity. It is only after feelings of well-being have been regained that a reappraisal of the task situation can result in a learning intention. Linking the concept of a mathematical disposition to this model involves an attempt to integrate the cognitive and affective aspects of learning processes—a major challenge for modern research on learning and instruction (Shuell, 1992).

## The Learner: From Isolated Information Absorber to Constructor of Knowledge and Competence in a Mathematical Community

If one accepts the preceding view of problem solving as requiring the integration of different categories of aptitudes, culminating, over time, in the development of a mathematical disposition, the question arises as to what kinds of learning processes are conducive to attaining this intended disposition.

The negative answer seems to be that this disposition cannot be achieved through the kind of learning that occurs predominantly in today's classrooms. Indeed, the international literature bulges with data showing that students are not equipped with the necessary knowledge, skills, beliefs, and motivation to approach new problems and learning tasks in an efficient and successful way (see, e.g., De Corte, 1995a). This can be accounted for by the prevailing learning activities in today's schools, which are summarized by Greeno (1991b) as follows:

In most schools, what students mostly do is listen, watch, and mimic things that the teacher and textbook tell them and show them. If students' epistemologies are influenced at all by the experiences they have, then most students probably learn that mathematical knowledge is a form of received knowledge, not something that is constructed either personally or socially. (pp. 81–82)

In other words, the prevailing view of learning in educational practice today is still the information-transmission model, implying that the mathematical knowledge acquired and institutionalized by past generations has to be transmitted as accurately as possible to the next generation (Lave, 1988; Romberg & Carpenter, 1986). But, as argued by Cobb (1990), this conception also underlies what Cobb calls the strong program of information-processing psychology of mathematics education, in which students are considered isolated, environmentally driven systems that have to absorb a collection of prespecified mathematical facts, rules, and procedures. It is not surprising that many intelligent tutoring systems derived from mainstream cognitive science also consider learning, at least implicitly, to be the acquisition of formally taught, explicit knowledge (J. S. Brown, 1990).

An additional aspect of current mathematics education, one that is related to the inappropriate view of learning as information absorption, is that knowledge is often taught and acquired independently from the social and physical contexts from which it derives its meaning and usefulness. This characteristic is illustrated, for example, by a substantial amount of research on so-called street mathematics showing that there often exists a gap between (formal) school mathematics and the (informal) mathematics used to solve tasks in everyday life. It is also illustrated by anthropological work focusing on the analysis of cognitive activities and learning processes in a variety of nonschool settings, showing that knowledge and skill acquisition in those authentic, real-life situations are much more intimately context embedded than is typical classroom learning, which is often decontextualized (Nunes, Schliemann, & Carraher, 1993; L. B. Resnick, 1987b).

The conception of the learner as a decontextualized knowledge absorber and consumer contrasts sharply with the conception that derives from theoretical and empirical studies on learning and instruction in general, and on mathematics learning in particular. First, a substantial amount of evidence shows that learning is, as implied by Greeno, an active and constructive process. Learners are not passive recipients of information; rather, they actively construct their knowledge and skills through interaction with the physical and social environment and through reorganization of their own mental structures. For example, De Corte and Verschaffel (1987a) found, even in the simple domain of one-step addition and subtraction word problems, evidence supporting the constructive nature of children's learning. They observed in first graders a large variety of solution strategies for solving these types of problems, and many of these strategies were not taught in school; in other words, they constituted "inventions" (L. B. Resnick, 1983; see also Ginsburg, 1977), that is, more or less sophisticated solution procedures constructed by the children themselves on the basis of prior knowledge acquired in school as well as in everyday experience. This is illustrated by the sort of trial-and-error strategy applied by a number of the 30 first graders in solving the change problem, "Pete had some apples; he gave 5 apples to Ann; now Pete has 7 apples; how many apples did he have in the beginning?" They estimated the size of the initial amount and checked their guess by decrementing it by 5 to see if there were 7 elements left. Evidence for the constructive nature of learning also comes from the misconceptions and defective skills discussed earlier. For example, buggy algorithms are mostly invented variants of a correct procedure constructed by learners at the moment when they reach an impasse during the execution of a computation.

The constructive conception of mathematics learning has its roots in the work of Piaget (1954), although similar views were held in the United States by Brownell (1945) (for extensive discussions of constructivism, see R. B. Davis, Maher, & Noddings, 1990, and the plenary papers given at the 11th International Conference for the Psychology of Mathematics Education [Bergeron, Herscovics, & Kieran, 1987]). Among the major contemporary theorists of constructivism influenced by Piaget are Bauersfeld (1988), Confrey (1985), and Steffe, Cobb, and von Glasersfeld (1988; see also Cobb, 1990; Steffe & Gale, 1995; von Glasersfeld, 1987). These scholars represent "radical constructivism," according to which all knowledge is a subjective cognitive construction of the learner and not at all the reflection of an objective reality (von Glasersfeld, 1991). As stated by von Glasersfeld (1989, p. 162), "the function of cognition is adaptive and serves the organization of the experiential world, not the discovery of the ontological reality." It is not surprising that this extreme position has elicited criticisms (see, e.g., the paper by Suchting, 1992, with the striking title, "Constructivism Deconstructed"). One important question raised by radical constructivism is, as remarked by Putnam, Lampert, and Peterson (1990), how the individual, almost idiosyncratic processes of knowledge construction can lead to common mathematical concepts and skills among learners. The solution of this problem derives from another basic assumption that has received progressively more attention in constructivism and that goes back to the work of scholars like Mead (1934) and Vygotsky (1978)—namely, that learning is a social process. For example, Sinclair (1991) has defined learning as the interactive re-creation of knowledge. In other words, social interaction is considered essential for learning, with individual knowledge construction occurring through the processes of interaction, negotiation, and collaboration, through which learners become acculturated members of a mathematical community and culture (see, e.g., Cobb, 1994b; Wood, Cobb, & Yackel, 1991). As a result, common meanings, knowledge, and practices are developed by the community members.

This social-constructivist perspective is today broadly shared by constructivists, notwithstanding the existence of obvious conceptual differences along the continuum from radical to more realistic constructivism (Bauersfeld, 1995; Cobb, 1994a; see also the section on the contribution of constructivism in Steffe et al., in press; and chapter 2). Moreover, although social interaction is considered to be a primary source of opportunities for learning, there is wide agreement that the acquisition of mathematical knowledge and skills can also be mediated by cultural artifacts such as educational media, an assumption underlying the so-called cultural-constructivist approach (Scott, Cole, & Engel, 1992). However, stressing the importance for learning of social interaction and mediation by cultural artifacts does not, in our opinion, exclude the possibility that students also individually develop new knowledge (see also Clemens, 1993).

As mentioned above, information-processing psychology, especially the strong version that draws heavily on computer simulation for understanding mathematical cognition, involves a view of learning that contrasts with constructivism. The shift initiated in the late 1980s in cognitive science by former representatives of the strong information-processing approach such as J. S. Brown, Collins, and Greeno (J. S. Brown et al., 1989; Collins, Brown, & Newman, 1989; Greeno, 1989) toward the so-called situated cognition paradigm may herald a rapprochement not only with social and cultural constructivism, but also with activity theory (Cobb, 1990; see also De Corte, 1990; for a comparison of activity theory and information-processing psychology, see van Oers, 1990). The emergence of this paradigm has been strongly influenced by anthropological research on everyday learning and cognition and related analyses of differences between learning in school and in nonschool settings. In this paradigm, learning and thinking are conceived of as interactive activities between the individual and the situation, and knowledge is situated, "being in part a product of the activity, context, and culture in which it is developed and used" (J. S. Brown et al., 1989). Starting from these ideas, Brown and his colleagues propose cognitive apprenticeship as the most promising model for learning and instruction. The convergence with social constructivism becomes obvious from their definition:

Cognitive apprenticeship methods try to enculturate students into authentic practices through activity and social interaction in a way similar to that evident—and evidently successful—in craft apprenticeship. (J. S. Brown et al., 1989, p. 37)

The preceding discussion allows us to answer the question raised in the first paragraph of this subsection. Pursuing the intended mathematical disposition requires the initiation and mediation of constructive acquisition processes in students. Passive learners deserve special attention in this respect, because they should be helped to develop more active learning strategies. Students' constructive learning activities should, moreover, be embedded in contexts that are rich in resources and learning materials, that offer ample opportunity for social interaction in a mathematical community and culture, and that are representative of the kinds of tasks and problems to which the learners will have to apply their knowledge and skills in the future. This conception of mathematics learning has sweeping implications for instructional practice, but represents also a challenge for the interested research community. Indeed, it is obvious that the elicitation of the intended learning processes requires drastic, research-based modifications in current teaching practices. Methods for developing such powerful instructional environments are elaborated in a later section.

## SOCIAL AND CULTURAL CONTEXTS

Mathematics learning and problem solving do not take place in a social and cultural vacuum. The social and cultural aspects of learning and cognition have been neglected not only in the information-processing approach, but also in early constructivist approaches to mathematics learning. Today, mathematics learning and problem solving are viewed as socially and culturally embedded constructive activities. This section highlights three important lines of research contributing to an understanding of this sociocultural dimension of mathematical learning and thinking.

The first subsection reviews research on the ethnomathematics of non-Western indigenous societies as well as work that aims at describing the informal, culturally embedded mathematics used in contemporary Western cultures. Cross-cultural comparative studies of educational systems are discussed next. In the final subsection the typical culture of a mathematics classroom is considered.

Of course, those topics do not cover the entirety of the sociocultural context of mathematical learning and thinking. Other aspects that have also come to the fore and are currently being addressed in interesting ways, such as the computer as a cultural tool, are treated elsewhere in this chapter, while still others, such as mathematics learning and teaching in ethnic minority groups and small-group learning and problem-solving processes, are discussed in other chapters.

### Ethnomathematics

For a long time, it was not questioned that mathematics was universal and culture-free knowledge. During the 1980s people became more aware of historical and anthropological research evidence that demonstrated convincingly that mathematics is not culture-free but culture-bound, and that different sociocultural groups have produced and are practicing different mathematics (Bishop, 1988).

d'Ambrosio (1985) introduced the term *ethnomathematics* to refer to mathematics as practiced, expressed, and transmitted within identifiable sociocultural groups. Both parts of this term should be taken in a broad sense (Borba, 1990). "Ethno" should be understood as referring to all possible kinds of sociocultural groups, such as national-tribal societies, labor groups, professional classes, and even children of a certain age bracket; and "mathematics" should be understood as encompassing a broad range of human activities, such as ciphering, measuring, classifying, ordering, inferring, and modeling. As such, ethnomathematics is a set of knowledge, skills, tools, beliefs, and attitudes that is intrinsically linked to a sociocultural group and to its goals, its values and interests, its language, its reality—its "ethnos" (Borba, 1990).

According to the ethnomathematical approach, mathematics is a pancultural phenomenon: It is considered a cultural product that has evolved in all societies through universal environmental activities like counting, locating, measuring, designing, playing, and explaining (Bishop, 1988). Moreover, underlying the distinct ethnomathematics are basic invariant principles (Nunes, 1992a, 1992b). But at the same time there are remarkable intercultural differences as a result of the fact that the mathematical tools, practices, and beliefs of distinct sociocultural groups are created in response to circumstances, needs, and views unique to each group (Borba, 1990). In this sense, Western professional or academic mathematics as it is internationally known, practiced, and taught today can be considered also a form of ethnomathematics (Bishop, 1988; Borba, 1990), although a very special form because of its degree of sophistication, self-reflectivity, and ubiquity.

*Ethnomathematics of Non-Western Indigenous Cultures.* A first and very important perspective on the ethnomathematics issue comes from research that has analyzed the mathematical values, concepts, and skills existing in remote, indigenous, non-Western cultures where no systematic transmission in school prevails. The decodification of those indigenous mathematics is done using a diversity of ethnographic methodologies, such as carefully analyzing typical behaviors and objects, children's games, mythical stories, the language system, and so forth, eventually in combination with traditional psychological techniques like questionnaires and tests (Eisenhart, 1988). Most of this research has been done within Vygotsky's (1978) theory about the role of culturally elaborated systems of signs in the development of higher forms of human cognition.

As a first example, we refer to Luria's (1976) famous work comparing the performance of nonliterate and literate adults on a series of cognitive tasks like categorization, arithmetic problem solving, and syllogistic reasoning. These studies, conducted in the 1920s and early 1930s in a remote part of Soviet Central Asia, included nonliterate adults who were still engaged in traditional modes of production and a second group of adults that had already been exposed to a radical restructuring of the socioeconomic system (e.g., collectivization) and culture (e.g., literacy). On all tasks, Luria found considerable differences between these two groups. Whereas nonliterates displayed a mode of thinking that relied heavily on personal and practical

experiences, literate subjects demonstrated a more abstract or theoretical attitude that allowed them to disregard particular daily life experiences. For example, on an arithmetic word problem, subjects were asked to calculate the distance between two towns (A and C), given information about the distance between each town and an intermediary town (AB and BC) that deviated from or contradicted subjects' practical knowledge about the actual distances between these three towns. Although literate subjects were able to proceed without concern about the accuracy of the information provided, nonliterates refused to reason within the conditions given in the problem and slipped back into arguments and reasonings based on their everyday concrete experiences. In line with Vygotsky's (1978) theory, Luria (1976) interpreted these qualitative differences between literate and nonliterate subjects as evidence for the hypothesis that culturally elaborated systems of signs like literacy affect psychological functions in a fundamental and general way. However, this conclusion was later subjected to criticisms and alternative interpretations (Nunes, 1992b).

Relying on the same Vygotskian perspective, Gay and Cole (1967) set up a study of the indigenous mathematical knowledge, skills, values, and practices of the Kpelle in Liberia, and of the relationship between the Kpelle's ethnomathematics and a new mathematics curriculum transplanted from the West. As in Luria's (1976) study, they found that the Kpelle were arithmetically skilled as far as that skill belonged to their everyday practice and had to be demonstrated in a context that was concrete and culturally meaningful to them, but failed to apply their skills on problems presented in an unfamiliar or decontextualized format. Moreover, Gay and Cole (1967) found that a lot of learning difficulties occurring in the classrooms were due to the fact that the contents and teaching methods transplanted from the West did not make any sense from the point of view of Kpelle culture.

Since the pioneering studies of Luria (1976) and Gay and Cole (1967), a lot of work has been done, mostly focusing on a particular aspect of the ethnomathematics of a particular society. The most intensively studied aspect is undoubtedly the numeration system, in both its oral and written manifestations (see, e.g., Lancey, 1983; Saxe, 1981, 1982; Zaslavsky, 1973). This research documents the invariant logical principles involved in counting (i.e., one-to-one correspondence between things to be counted and counting labels, fixed order of counting labels, irrelevance of order of to-be-counted objects, cardinality principle), but also the great cultural variations in applying these counting principles (Nunes, 1992a). For example, it shows that a verbal numeration system in which arbitrary number names are used to signify the units and the base 10 principle to generate higher numbers—like the numeration system currently employed in Western societies—is only one among many others. In Papua New Guinea, for example, there are groups that apply a numeration system based on the systematic enumeration of body parts (Saxe, 1981). Other societies apply systems that resemble more the current Western base-structured verbal numeration system but use a base 15 or base 20 instead of the base 10 system (Lancey, 1983). Furthermore, it has been documented how changing socioeconomic conditions (such as increased participation economic exchanges involving currency) may lead to important and inventive adaptations in a society's existing numeration system (Saxe, 1982).

Like oral counting, written numeration systems vary across time and culture, and some systems are more efficient for certain purposes than others. For example, a comparison of ancient systems for representing numbers (such as the Roman system) with the Hindu-Arabic system, which is used throughout the world today, shows that the latter system is a superior vehicle for computing, largely because of the compactness and extensibility of its notation (Nickerson, 1988). The Western adoption of the Hindu-Arabic system can be considered another example of how changing sociocultural circumstances and needs necessitated adaptations of the numeration system (Nunes, 1992a).

Research on ethnomathematics among non-Western people is not restricted to counting and arithmetic problem solving. Another topic that has yielded interesting findings documenting the widely varying and culturally embedded forms of mathematics in different cultures is geometry. Among the growing list of studies in this domain, we mention Gerdes's (1988) fascinating analysis of geometrical patterns and properties in traditional Mozambiquan objects (e.g., baskets, mats, pots) and production techniques (weaving, house building), as well as Pinxten's (1991) in-depth cognitive-anthropological investigation of the spatial and geometrical knowledge of the Navajo Indians, which is closely related to their cosmology, epistemology, and language. These authors have worked out alternative culture-specific curricula for geometry teaching in which problems, concepts, and terms belonging to the experiential world of these people are taken as the principal source of mathematical problematization.

***Informal Mathematics in Western Cultures.*** The term "ethnomathematics" refers also to informal mathematical practices in Western cultures that are embedded in specific out-of-school activities and contexts and that may be contrasted with "school mathematics" (Borba, 1990; Nunes et al., 1993; L. B. Resnick, 1987b).

A substantial portion of work has focused on the early number concepts, counting strategies, and elementary arithmetic skills developed and used by young children who have not yet been taught formal mathematics in school (see, e.g., Carpenter & Moser, 1984; De Corte & Verschaffel, 1987b; Fuson, 1982; Gelman & Gallistel, 1978; Hughes, 1986). This work demonstrated that early in their development and before formal schooling, children have a rich variety of material counting strategies (based on the use of concrete manipulatives) and verbal counting strategies (based on forward or backward counting) for successfully solving addition and subtraction problems. Of course, at that age these informal solution strategies can be used only for solving simple arithmetic tasks given in the context of real or verbally described problem situations that have "real meaning" for children; they cannot be used for solving problems stated in a purely symbolic format (e.g., $2 + 5 = x$ or $2 + x = 7$). Another important finding is that the situational structure of the problem significantly affects the nature of children's informal solution strategies. Specifically, they tend to solve each problem with the material or verbal counting strategy that corresponds most closely to its situational structure. For example, a problem such as "Pete had 6 apples; he gave 2 apples to Ann; how many apples does Pete have now?" is typically solved by taking away two blocks from a set of six or by counting backward two units from 6 ("6 . . . 5, 4"). But most children solve a problem like "Pete had 2 apples; Ann

gave him some more; now Pete has 6 apples; how many apples did Ann give him?" by adding blocks to a set of two until there are six and by counting the number of blocks added, or by counting forward from 2 until 6 and giving the number of words spoken as the answer ("2 . . . 3 is 1, 4 is 2, 5 is 3, 6 is 4 . . . so the answer is 4"). A problem such as "Pete has 2 apples; Ann has 6 apples; how many apples does Pete have more than Ann?" elicits still another material strategy, involving matching a set of two and a set of six blocks and counting the number of unmatched blocks. Children who apply these informal strategies successfully frequently are not aware of their interchangeability, and are unable to link them to the same formal arithmetic operation, namely subtraction. Only over time and after being instructed in formal addition and subtraction are they able to loosen the ties between the situational structure of the problem, on the one hand, and their solution strategy, on the other, and to start using integrated concepts and procedures for solving all kinds of problem situations involving the same operation. However, the above-mentioned research also has shown convincingly that a considerable number of pupils keep using these informal methods to solve problems—especially out of school, but also in school—long after they have been introduced to the more formal solution procedures.

Informal, contextually based strategies are not found only among preschool and beginning elementary schoolchildren. Another group of studies on informal mathematics in Western cultures focuses on the everyday learning and problem-solving practices of particular groups of children and adults (with different grades of formal schooling) who are intensively involved in specific everyday cultural practices like commercial transactions, tailoring, weaving, carpentry, grocery packing, cooking, and the like. Many of these studies involve a contrast between the informal, everyday context and the formal school context, to allow for a systematic analysis of the similarities and differences between both types of mathematical practices. Typical examples of this second group of investigations are:

- Scribner's (1984) study of the arithmetic strategies employed by dairy workers who must make quick and efficient decisions about prices and quantities of dairy goods in the course of their daily work
- Lave, Murtaugh, and de la Rocha's (1984) study of recruits to a Weight Watchers dieting program carrying out activities of shopping and planning and preparing diet meals in their kitchen
- Investigations by Carraher, Carraher, and Schliemann (1985) and by Saxe (1988) on the arithmetic skills and processes of young street vendors in Brazil, both on practice-linked and on standard school arithmetic problems
- Studies by Nunes et al. (1993) contrasting proportional reasoning by foremen and fishermen whose knowledge of proportion developed outside of school and by students in school

A first major outcome of those studies on everyday cognition is that people are remarkably efficient in dealing with quantitative problems encountered in their everyday professional and social activities as compared with the school mathematics context. In the Carraher et al. (1985) study, for example, young street vendors performed very well on the problems in the street-vending context, while on isomorphic school mathematical tasks the rates of correct responses were much lower. Similarly, Lave et al. (1984) noted as the most puzzling outcome of their study "the virtually error-free arithmetic performance by shoppers who made frequent errors in parallel problems in the formal testing situation" (p. 83).

Second, these studies show how the goal and the conditions of the practical activity lead to the use of informal mathematical reasoning and computation processes that differ considerably from the formal, standardized procedures typically transmitted in school. In the Carraher et al. (1985) study, the arithmetic problems in the street-vending context were solved mainly using oral calculation strategies that took into account the meaning of the problem situation and the particularities of the quantities dealt with (i.e., currencies): decomposition (in the case of addition and subtraction problems) and repeated grouping (in the case of multiplication and division problems). On the isomorphic school-like problems, on the other hand, the same youngsters used—frequently without success—generalized, formal written computation procedures, applying the prescribed algorithms learned in school. The impact of the use of these two different systems of representation and calculation on the youngsters' computational skills was reflected not only in their probability of success (see above), but also in the types of errors they made. Errors in written arithmetic were the typical buggy algorithms (see previous sections) and had a higher probability of being far off the correct answer than oral answers. However, despite these important differences, both types of mathematical practice rely on the same implicit invariant logico-mathematical principles, namely, associativity (in the case of addition and subtraction) and distributivity (in the case of multiplication and division) (Nunes, 1992b).

Third, this research has convincingly documented the lack of transfer from one learning context to another. Subjects in the above-mentioned studies did not seem to apply spontaneously and efficiently their formal mathematical knowledge and skills learned at school in out-of-school contexts. This indicates that schooling does not contribute in a direct and obvious way to performance outside of school. Until recently it was taken more or less for granted that people would apply knowledge and skills acquired in formal school settings to relevant situations in everyday life (Säljö & Wyndhamn, 1987). Further, this research documents the limits of the contextualized mathematical knowledge and strategies acquired and used in these practice-linked situations (J. S. Brown et al., 1989; Hatano, in press; L. B. Resnick, 1987b). Indeed, the ability to solve practice-linked tasks does not seem to generalize easily or transfer to the ability to solve new problems—either novel problems presented in the familiar, practice-linked context or problems given in a school mathematics context—although analogical transfer or generalization of everyday knowledge may sometimes occur. For example, Saxe (1988) contrasted the performances on standard school arithmetic problems of young candysellers who attended school with those of nonsellers with the same age and schooling experience, and found some evidence for the transfer of knowledge and skills generated in the selling practice to school mathematics tasks. Similarly, in their studies of the proportional knowledge of foremen and fishermen, Nunes et al. (1993) found that most of them were able to solve proportion problems with numbers and variables that did not belong to

their everyday practice. Based on these and other examples of moderate transfer, Nunes et al. (1993) argue against a simple polarization of forms of knowledge into "general" and "particular."

Finally, the research on informal mathematics has revealed some typical features of the environment that are responsible for the striking ease and smoothness with which these context-bound and practice-linked mathematical competencies are acquired and mastered. They essentially develop through apprenticeship, an informal learning environment in which knowledge and skills are acquired in the context of authentic and situated activity through observation, scaffolding, coaching, and practice (J. S. Brown et al., 1989; Lave, 1977).

Partly drawing on these demonstrations of successful mathematical learning and problem solving outside school, L. B. Resnick (1987b) highlighted the following four broad characteristics of (mathematical) thinking and learning outside school. These characteristics stand in contrast to classical school mathematics work.

1. The domains of learning and performance in the school are individual. Outside of school, many more activities are undertaken in a group.
2. In school, "pure thought" activities without the use of tools prevail. In contrast, the use of tools (materials, books, calculators, etc.) is common in cognitive activities outside of school.
3. The school stresses symbol-based learning and thinking independent of concrete objects and events, whereas out-of-school activities interact with and depend on the features of the situation in which they happen.
4. The school focuses on the teaching of general, widely applicable knowledge and skills. Outside of school, however, situation-specific skills are emphasized.

One could add another important difference relating to the goal of cognitive activity in both contexts. Outside of school, mathematics is a means at the service of some other goal—it is embedded in some other activity that gives meaning to the situation as a whole—whereas in the typical mathematics class the subject's activity is not a means but an end in itself, that is, to solve the problem or to demonstrate competence to oneself or others (R. B. Davis, 1989; Nunes et al., 1993).

Of course, these statements point to extremes, and much current school practice lies between the implied poles. Moreover, as discussed later under INSTRUCTIONAL ENVIRONMENTS, the ongoing school reform of mathematics education can to some extent be characterized as the adoption of some of the above-mentioned features of practical mathematics (L. B. Resnick, 1987b).

***Theoretical and Instructional Implications.*** To finish this section on ethnomathematics, we discuss from a more theoretical perspective some issues that were raised and illustrated in the preceding subsections, and we draw some lessons for mathematics education.

From a theoretical point of view, research on ethnomathematics first of all convincingly demonstrates the importance of considering the physical as well as the mental manifestations of the broader sociocultural context in which mathematics learning and cognition take place. Knowledge acquisition and knowledge application occur in particular contexts; they are coconstituted between a person and a context, and acquired knowledge reflects how it was used and learned in that context (Hatano, in press; Säljö, 1991). As such, the work on ethnomathematics has contributed to the growing criticism of the strong program of cognitive psychology and to the development of a new conceptualization of human learning and cognition that recognizes social, cultural, and historical embedding, as envisioned in the so-called situated-cognition paradigm.

Second, the research on ethnomathematics is compatible with and supportive of the constructivist view on learning. Indeed, just like the evidence on children's and students' appropriate as well as inappropriate inventions in *school* mathematics learning, the findings about different forms of *out-of-school* mathematics being created and developed by societies, professional groups, and individuals to deal with specific circumstances and needs are additional evidence supporting the view of learning as an active and constructive process. A major theoretical contribution of the "ethnomathematicians" in this respect is the demonstration that this construction process is constrained not only by internal cognitive factors, such as the individual's prior knowledge, but also by sociocultural constraints, that is, by cultural artifacts, including the language and notation system, and by other persons (Hatano, in press; Säljö, 1991).

Besides theoretical contributions, ethnomathematics research has provided important lessons for mathematics education. First, this work has contributed to the growing awareness among mathematics educators and teachers that curriculum reforms cannot succeed if cultural notions are not seriously considered and effectively used. Among other things, this implies that the mathematical knowledge teachers possess, and want students to possess, is one particular kind of mathematics, which differs from that known and understood at other times in history or in other sociocultural groups today. So, it helps them beware of adopting and transmitting assumptions of universality or absoluteness of their mathematical knowledge (Bishop, 1988). New mathematics curricula are picking up aspects of the sociology and history of mathematics, even at the elementary school level (see, e.g., California Board of Education, 1991).

Second, the evidently successful problem-solving and learning activities in informal out-of-school settings have inspired people to construct new instructional environments that take advantage of some features of these contexts. A basic characteristic of these new instructional environments is that they start from interesting problems that are placed in pragmatic contexts that are experientially real for children, making it possible for the children to immediately engage in informal mathematical activity (R. B. Davis, 1989; Nunes et al., 1993). However, these new instructional environments also include activities and materials that support children's transition from informal, pragmatic problem solving to more formal and abstract mathematical activity. As discussed above, an important problem with the knowledge acquired in out-of-school contexts is that it is by itself very situation specific and limited, whereas school learning should result in generalized and broadly applicable learning outcomes (J. S. Brown, et al., 1989; L. B. Resnick, 1987b).

## Comparative Studies of Mathematics Learning and Teaching

The role of the cultural context of mathematics learning has been highlighted and investigated also through systematic comparisons of mathematical cognitions and achievements between different countries, as well as through comparisons of the tools, the traditions, the beliefs, the attitudes, and the practices, both in school and out, that support the learning of mathematics in those countries (for more detailed and systematic reviews of these international studies, see Robitaille & Donn, 1993; Robitaille & Travers, 1992; Romberg, 1992c; Stigler & Baranes, 1988; Stigler & Perry, 1988).

*Large-Scale International Comparisons of Mathematics Achievement.* The first major cross-cultural study of mathematics achievement was initiated in 1960 by the International Association for the Evaluation of Education Achievement (IEA) (Husén, 1967). This study measured student performance in various mathematical topics in 12 different countries at two grade levels, one at the bottom and one at the top of secondary level education. In 1980–1982, a second study was carried out that compared student performance in 20 countries (Robitaille & Garden, 1989). One of the most remarkable findings of these studies was the superior mathematical achievement of students from Eastern countries like Japan and Hong Kong, as compared with countries such as the United States, Canada, and New Zealand. This result has led to a growing body of research aimed at unraveling the cultural and instructional factors that explain why children in certain countries (especially Japan) so dramatically outperform their counterparts in other countries (especially the United States). Also, systematic efforts have been undertaken in these latter countries to raise mathematical performance as a response.

Already in the first two IEA studies a serious attempt was made to go beyond collecting overall student achievement data and to explore the reasons for the possible differences in achievement. For example, although class size was found to have no considerable effect on student achievement, the content of the curriculum that is presented to the students ("opportunity to learn") turned out to be of utmost importance (Robitaille & Travers, 1992).

Meanwhile, the feasibility of using those international comparative data to set achievement levels has been questioned. Indeed, some scholars have pointed to the mismatch between the tests' focus on computational skills, on the one hand, and the higher order goals of solving nonroutine problems, making connections between different mathematical topics, and communicating mathematically as envisaged in the new mathematics curricula in these countries, on the other hand (see, e.g., Robitaille & Donn, 1993; Romberg, Smith, Smith, & Wilson, 1992).

The IEA is carrying out a third international study involving more than 50 countries, the major data collection phase of which was scheduled for the 1993–1994 school year (Robitaille & Donn, 1993). Compared to the two previous studies, this third study is characterized by:

• the inclusion of younger, elementary-school-aged populations of students (i.e., 9-year-olds)

- a broader perspective on student learning outcomes, including students' attitudes and beliefs and their capacity to apply their knowledge and skills in nonroutine problem situations
- the study of the comparative efficacy of microlevel aspects of the teaching of mathematics, such as the textbook and the teaching approach, on student outcomes

***Smaller-Scaled Comparative Studies: School Factors.*** Since the IEA studies, a number of researchers have conducted more focused international studies on a more modest scale. The examples we use draw heavily on contrasts between Japan and the United States, because researchers have been very active on this issue. Specifically, we discuss the research project of the University of Michigan comparing mathematics learning and teaching in Japan, Taiwan, and the United States (Stevenson & Stigler, 1992; Stigler & Perry, 1988). This project illustrates two important developments within international comparative research. First, it demonstrates the increasing effort to go beyond achievement data and to break down the independent (country) as well as dependent (achievement) variables into more meaningful, manageable units. Second, it illustrates the growing interest in an age level that has been neglected in previous comparative research—the younger, elementary-school-aged populations of students.

The Michigan project involved two stages of data collection. A first cycle of data collection, carried out in 1979–1980, involved large samples of Grade 1 and Grade 5 children, their teachers, principals, and parents from three cities of the three countries. The second investigation, in 1985–1986, involved the same two Asian cities and another (more representative) American city. In both studies a rich variety of data-gathering techniques was used, including standard tests of mathematics achievement, individually administered tests and interviews, and classroom observations.

The Michigan studies confirmed the pronounced superiority of Japanese and, to a somewhat lesser extent, Taiwanese students over U.S. pupils. These differences showed up as early as the first grade and were larger by the fifth grade. Moreover, the data from the second study suggested that in both Grade 1 and Grade 5, Japanese pupils outscored U.S. pupils not only on computational proficiency, but also on tests measuring a wide variety of other, higher level mathematical concepts and skills. The Taiwanese results were similar to the Japanese data for the fifth grade, but were mixed for the first grade.

Analyses of the interview and classroom observation data indicated dramatic differences in instructional aspects, including the following:

1. Time spent on the teaching and learning of mathematics. Pupils in Japan and Taiwan spent significantly more time learning mathematics in school than pupils in the United States.
2. The level of organization in the classroom. Japanese and Taiwanese pupils spent the vast majority of their time working, watching, and listening together as a whole class under the supervision of the teacher, whereas U.S. pupils mostly worked on their own without being systematically taught or led by the teacher.
3. Coherence from the student's point of view. Both Taiwanese and Japanese teachers seemed to provide more opportunities than U.S. teachers for pupils to construct a coherent representation of the sequence of events that make up a typical mathematics class, and to understand the goal of the activities in which they were engaged.
4. Reflectivity. This dimension refers to the degree to which one emphasizes performance and practice, on the one hand, versus reflective thinking and verbalization, on the other. Based on the available data, this dimension appears to differentiate Taiwanese from Japanese classrooms, with the former being more performance oriented and the latter more reflective. U.S. classrooms do not seem to take a definitive stand on this dimension. The Japanese emphasis on verbalization and reflectivity was evidenced by the high incidence of verbal explanation in the Japanese classrooms, as well as by the focus in those verbalizations on the process by which a problem is solved.

Meanwhile, a new data-gathering phase, involving the same Chinese, Japanese, and American schools as in the original Michigan project, revealed that American elementary schoolchildren in 1990 lagged behind their Chinese and Japanese peers to the same degree as they had 10 years before (Stevenson, Chen, & Lee, 1993). Other collaborative studies involving American and Japanese scholars have yielded further evidence of the superior level of mathematical achievement and thinking among Japanese students (Silver, Leung, & Cai, 1992) and of the above-mentioned salient differences in the content and organization of the mathematics lessons in both countries, especially with respect to the degree to which student thinking, verbalization, and reflection are stressed (Stigler, Fernandez, & Yoshida, 1992). Among the reasons for this qualitative difference between Japanese and American mathematics classes, Stigler et al. stress especially the fact that U.S. teachers—like the rest of the U.S. population—are less mathematically competent themselves than are Japanese teachers; but they also point to the relative lack of resources available to U.S. teachers (as compared with Japanese teachers) containing detailed information on students' correct and incorrect conceptions and strategies with respect to all of the topics in the mathematics curriculum on which one can rely when making a lesson plan.

Other investigations have looked at other aspects of instructional practices that may contribute to differences in performance outcomes between students from different countries, such as textbooks, instructional materials, and so on. Although many of these studies have not directly linked these differences in instructional practices and materials to mathematical achievement, they might help to complete the explanation of the observed international differences in performance. Fuson, Stigler, and Bartch (1988) investigated grade placement of topics on addition and subtraction in textbooks from the United States, Japan, China, Taiwan, and the former Soviet Union, and reported that several topics are introduced 1 to 3 years later in U.S. textbooks as compared with most other countries. Stigler, Fuson, Ham, and Kim (1986) reported considerably less variety and less challenge in the word problems about addition and subtraction in U.S. textbooks than in textbooks used in the former Soviet Union.

***Smaller-Scaled Comparative Studies: Environmental Factors.*** Of course, the sociocultural impact on mathematics learning is not restricted to the school; it extends to support from the student's home and the wider society. These differences in societal and cultural factors may also contribute to differences in mathematical achievement among countries.

Several studies have examined cross-cultural differences in parental beliefs about mathematics learning and teaching, as well as in parents' involvement in their children's mathematical learning. As part of the Michigan project, Stevenson, Lee, and Stigler (1986) found that U.S. mothers were more likely to believe that innate ability underlies children's success in mathematics, whereas Japanese and Taiwanese mothers believed more in effort as a determiner of success in mathematics. Further, although U.S. elementary schools spend far less time teaching mathematics than do schools in Japan and Taiwan, parents in the United States believed that reading rather than mathematics should receive more emphasis in the curriculum. Also as part of the Michigan project, Crystal and Stevenson (1991) asked mothers in Taiwan, Japan, and the United States whether they believed that their child had problems in mathematics, the kind of problems that their child had experienced, and what they had done about the problems. It was found that U.S. mothers evaluated their children's mathematics skills less critically and held lower standards of mathematics achievement for their children than did Asian parents. American mothers seemed also more reluctant to provide assistance when their children experience difficulties.

The environment's role in school mathematics learning is not restricted to what occurs within the child's home. Environmental mathematical experiences that surpass the home culture and that may affect mathematical learning and performance are also influential, such as involvement in the market economy, participating in ceremonies, playing games, and so on (for an overview and a discussion of the available literature, see Balfantz, 1988).

To summarize, while the picture about the differences in what mathematics is taught at school in different countries, how it is taught, and what the results are is far from complete, the available international comparative research evidence indicates that the content and the instructional practices of school mathematics vary widely across countries, and that this variation is reflected in considerable differences in learning outcomes. Moreover, while the role of differences in the content and organization of school mathematics is indisputable, many other cultural factors out of school, such as explicit and implicit learning experiences at home as well as experiences within the broader community, seem important too.

These cross-cultural comparisons of mathematical performance in different countries, and especially the attempts to explore the underlying causes for these performance differences, are not only theoretically interesting. They also provide valuable information for those responsible for mathematics education in the different countries (Robitaille & Donn, 1993). However, as Stigler and Perry (1988) put it, these comparisons do not provide them with blueprints for mathematics education in their own country, but rather with a mirror that they can use to examine themselves.

## The Culture of the Mathematics Classroom

Another way of looking at how sociocultural factors influence mathematical learning and cognition is to consider aspects of culture and socialization within the microcosm of the typical mathematics classroom and to investigate how students' knowledge, perspectives, beliefs, and values are shaped as a function of their involvement with mathematics in school (Nickson, 1992). In other words, some researchers have started to look at the typical mathematics classroom culture from an anthropological point of view.

In this subsection the focus is on how the classroom culture may negatively affect students' mathematical behavior, learning, and thinking. In a later subsection on designing powerful teaching–learning environments, we will illustrate how the culture of the mathematics classroom can be used positively as a vehicle for realizing authentic mathematical learning experiences and valuable learning outcomes.

*Contributions from Interactional Theory.* An interesting, largely (though not exclusively) European approach to the culture of the mathematics classroom and its influence on social interaction and individual thought has come from interactional theory, a perspective that is strongly influenced by sociology, social psychology, and anthropology (such as symbolic interactionism and ethnomethodology). Using microethnographical studies, this research aims at reconstructing the patterns of interaction and sense making between teachers and students during mathematical instruction or testing, mainly based on videotapes, transcripts, and teachers' retrospective data (Bauersfeld, 1988; Brousseau, 1984; Cobb, Wood, Yackel, & McNeal, 1992; Schubauer-Leoni, Bell, Grossen, & Perret-Clermont, 1989; Voigt, 1989).

The basic idea behind the interactional approach is that there is a fundamental tension between the teacher's and the students' definition of the situation. Teachers and students interpret the classroom situation under different perspectives, as a result of different backgrounds of understandings. Despite these different backgrounds, the smooth functioning of classroom discourse succeeds. How is this possible? Because teacher/student behavior in the mathematics lessons is directed by scholastic norms and routines. These norms and routines function implicitly most of the time, as they are usually constructed in day-to-day classroom interactions. Teachers and students jointly produce and elaborate such a repertoire of mutually acceptable behaviors that evolve into reciprocal expectations. This system of hidden norms, rules, and expectations is called the "didactical contract." For example, according to the didactical contract, the teacher is authorized to ask the students to enter into the task as she envisaged it; students have to respond to the questions asked by the teacher rather than asking questions in return; a repeated question by the teacher signals an erroneous response; and so on (Schubauer-Leoni et al., 1989). Thus, the didactical contract has a function of regulating teacher and student habits and reciprocal expectations concerning specific knowledge, and of producing orthodox behavior conforming to its implicit rules. These routines of the teacher and the students reduce the complexity of classroom discourse. The routines restrict the participants' actions and make these actions mutually reliable and predictable.

Using this theoretical and methodological approach, Schubauer-Leoni and colleagues have been able to show how apparently successful interactions between the students and the mathematics teacher do not reflect genuine communication about a mathematical topic but are in fact nothing more than a denaturalized, impoverished ritual. A typical example is the "funnel pattern of interaction," in which the quality of the discussion between the teacher and the student whom the teacher wants to help gradually decreases and deteriorates to a ridiculously low level where the student simply recites a number or completes one single catchword and the teacher has, in fact, done all the important mathematical thinking herself, without the teacher's or the pupil's having been aware of it (for examples, see Bauersfeld, 1988; Voigt, 1989).

This interactional approach also has been used to demonstrate how students can be effective in evaluative contexts—that is, get the correct answer to a given question—not by way of the expected mathematical reasoning, but simply through an interpretation or decoding of the didactical conventions (Brousseau, 1984; Schubauer-Leoni et al., 1989).

***Other Evidence of the Scholastic/Cultural Origins of Undesirable Mathematical Learning Outcomes.*** Although not explicitly starting from the same theoretical framework, several scholars have recently discussed strong cases of unintended and undesirable student learning behavior and learning outcomes resulting directly from characteristics of mathematically negative aspects of the classroom culture (R. B. Davis, 1989; De Corte & Verschaffel, 1985; Nickson, 1992; Säljö, 1991; Säljö & Wyndhamn, 1987; Schoenfeld, 1988, 1991; L. Sowder, 1988). Some illustrative cases are discussed. They concern, respectively, elementary schoolchildren's beliefs about the (un)realistic nature of school arithmetic word problems, children's superficial strategies for coping with such problems, and students' beliefs about construction and proof in geometry.

First, after some years of traditional mathematics education, many pupils seem to have developed incorrect beliefs about school mathematics, such as the view that mathematics consists of a set of rules and procedures that one has to use in a mechanical way, and that have little or no relation to reality. R. B. Davis (1989) reported the following remarkable observation. In an introductory lesson about division, pairs of children were given five balloons that had to be shared. One boy took scissors and cut in half the fifth balloon. R. B. Davis (1989, p. 144) asked, "Was this boy really thinking about solving the actual problem (i.e., effectively sharing the five balloons) or was he trying to accommodate himself to the peculiar tribal culture of the American classroom?" The finding about students responding meaninglessly to the earlier picnic problem from Silver's (1986) study can be considered another example of the fact that students typically do not allow considerations about the realities of the problem situation in their representation and solution of arithmetic word problems. (For additional examples, see Greer, 1993; Nesher, 1980; Säljö, 1991; Schoenfeld, 1988; Verschaffel & De Corte, in press; Verschaffel, De Corte, & Lasure, 1994.) One could ask, Why did these students react according to the belief that solving a school word problem is something completely different from solving a real problem situation? There is no doubt that this belief was not directly taught by the teacher. Rather, it was derived by the pupils, albeit probably implicitly and unconsciously, in response to the meaningless or unrealistic nature of the problems given in the mathematics lessons and to the way the problems were analyzed and solved in those lessons. These aspects of the classroom didactics contained the hidden message that making realistic considerations and elaborations about the situation described in school arithmetic word problems is harmful rather than helpful for arriving at the correct answer as anticipated by the teacher or textbook writer (De Corte & Verschaffel, 1985; Kilpatrick, 1987; Nesher, 1980; Säljö, 1991; Schoenfeld, 1991).

A second example, which can be interpreted in a similar way, is the well-documented finding that, after some years of experience with traditional school arithmetic word problems, many pupils have developed a set of superficial strategies for coping with these problems. These strategies are characterized by lack of a careful semantic analysis of the problem situation and lack of a semantically based choice of operation (Reusser, 1988; Säljö & Wyndhamn, 1987; Schoenfeld, 1991; L. Sowder, 1988; Verschaffel & De Corte, in press). Typical examples of such superficial coping strategies are:

- Looking at cues in the chapter headings or in the environment in which the problem appears (e.g., if the heading is Multiplication, then choose that operation).
- Selecting all the numbers contained in the problem and performing either the operation that was most recently taught in the classroom or the operation on which you feel most competent (e.g., adding).
- Looking for key words in the problem statement that will tell which operations to perform (e.g., if the problem contains the word "altogether," then add).
- Looking at the numbers: They will tell you which operation to use.

As a typical case of the last superficial coping strategy, consider the following response given by a first grader when asked to explain how he arrived at his correct solution of an elementary arithmetic word problem: "I wasn't sure whether to add or to subtract, but finally I decided to subtract because addition would have led to a result larger than 20." Indeed, at the time this protocol was collected, the number 20 was generally considered the upper limit of the number domain for the first grade of the elementary school in Belgium (Verschaffel, 1984). The important message from this and the other examples of superficial coping strategies is, that the student's choice of operation was not based on the intended mathematical reasoning but on the interpretation and application of subtle didactical conventions shared by those involved with the "game of solving school word problems" (De Corte & Verschaffel, 1985). Among the aspects of current teaching practice contributing to the construction of these superficial coping strategies in students, we first of all mention the restricted and stereotyped nature of the problems used in the mathematics lessons, which makes the application of these superficial coping strategies undeservedly successful (Schoenfeld, 1991). Säljö and Wyndhamn (1987) note that Swedish textbooks often contain headings that clearly spell out the nature of the tasks to be performed, so that pupils "know" what operation to perform before they have even begun to read the problem itself. A second important cause is the product-oriented nature of mathematics instruction, which is also reflected in teachers' misbelief that correct answers are a safe indicator of good thinking (L. Sowder, 1988).

Third, we refer to Schoenfeld's (1988) remarkable study of

how a group of students acquired a lot of negative beliefs as a result of a typical "well-taught" geometry course. For example, they learned that proof is ritual activity in which they confirm results that were already known to be true and that were intuitively obvious to begin with; that proof has nothing to do with discovery or invention; that when they work a construction problem in geometry, what really counts is whether the construction looks right; and so on. Once again, the issue is not that these students were taught those wrong perspectives and beliefs by their teacher; rather, the important point is that they extracted them from their day-by-day mathematics classroom activities and experiences.

In sum, this research documents the hidden rules and conventions of the mathematics classroom's sociocultural life, as well as how these hidden rules and conventions govern processes of interaction, meaning construction, problem solving, and learning that take place in the classroom. The major lesson to be derived from it is that researchers as well as practitioners need to be more aware of the unique social and cultural characteristics of the typical mathematics classroom. School mathematics itself is a cultural practice, and students' school mathematics learning occurs essentially through being immersed in that particular culture (R. B. Davis, 1989; Nickson, 1992; Säljö & Wyndhamn, 1987; Schoenfeld, 1991). What they learn as a result of their involvement with these everyday rituals and cultural practices does not always correspond to the explicitly intended learning effects.

The reported evidence for how these subtle, invisible sociocultural aspects of the mathematics classroom can lead to the repression of authentic classroom interaction and of valuable individual mathematical learning and thinking was rather anecdotal and therefore not very compelling. Together with Schoenfeld (1991), we make a plea for more work aimed at unraveling and explaining what students actually learn about mathematics (in a broad sense) by focusing on the lessons they extract as a result of their involvement with the culture of the mathematics classroom.

The interactional approach described above may provide a useful framework for more vigorous theoretical and empirical work on these scholastic/cultural origins of unwanted mathematical behavior and learning outcomes. This is important because it not only can lead to a better understanding of the negative effects of classroom daily rituals and practices on students' mathematical behavior and thinking (as described in this section), but it could help to clarify ways in which the culture of the mathematics classroom can be used as a powerful vehicle for realizing authentic mathematical communication, sense-making, problem-solving processes in line with the constructive and dispositional view of mathematics learning described earlier (Schoenfeld, 1991; see also the later discussion under *Designing Powerful Teaching–Learning Environments*).

## INSTRUCTIONAL ENVIRONMENTS

In this section we focus on the instructional environments in which mathematics learning takes place, and discuss the following aspects of these environments:

1. Teachers' cognitions about mathematics, mathematics learning, and teaching, and the impact of teachers' cognitions on teaching behavior and students' learning outcomes.
2. Examples of powerful teaching–learning environments that embody some major ideas that have emerged from recent theoretical and empirical studies discussed in previous sections.
3. The potential contribution of computers to the realization of such powerful teaching–learning environments.
4. The reform of assessment as an integral part of instruction.

### Teachers' Cognitions

Until the early 1980s, research on teaching mainly focused on domain-independent aspects of teaching. This is certainly true for the vast amount of process–product studies in which the object of study was teachers' external behaviors and skills, but it is also true for the mainstream research on teachers' thinking and decision-making of the 1970s and early 1980s (Shulman, 1986). The obvious neglect of the content of what is taught is all the more remarkable because in research on children's learning and problem solving, the focus since the late 1970s had already shifted toward subject matter concerns.

Since the second half of the 1980s, researchers have started analyzing teachers' cognitions with a focus on the specific content being taught (see chapter 13). As has been the case for research on students' cognition, mathematics has become an attractive area for this new approach to the investigation of teaching.

We first present a brief overview of the research on teachers' cognitions about mathematics, mathematics learning, and teaching, and the impact of those cognitions on how they teach and on students' learning outcomes. Having made a distinction between teachers' knowledge and beliefs, we review attempts to increase the former and to change the latter.

*Teachers' Knowledge.* Like students' knowledge, teachers' knowledge is not monolithic, but consists of various components. In most theoretical frameworks three major categories of subject matter–related teacher knowledge are distinguished, namely mathematical knowledge, pedagogical knowledge, and knowledge of learners' cognitions (Berliner et al., 1988; Cooney, 1994; Fennema & Loef, 1992; Shulman, 1986). These three different types of knowledge will be discussed separately, but, as argued convincingly by Fennema and Loef (1992), they should be considered parts of a larger integrated functioning system, with each part difficult to isolate from the others.

A first category of teacher knowledge includes the concepts, procedures, and problem-solving strategies within the domain of instruction, as well as in related fields. Crucial in this respect also is teachers' understanding of the interrelatedness of these concepts, procedures, and strategies (Fennema & Loef, 1992).

It is generally acknowledged that skillful teaching of a specific topic in mathematics requires that the teacher sufficiently master that specific topic, as well as closely related topics. However, it is also generally questioned whether this basic requirement is fulfilled, especially among elementary and middle school teachers (see, e.g., Lampert, 1986). There is empirical evidence to support this alarming statement, especially in the domain of multiplicative structures. Graeber and Tirosh (1988) studied preservice elementary teachers' knowledge and skills with respect to multiplication and division involving decimals larger and smaller than 1, and found that a considerable number of preservice teachers made the same errors and shared the same misconceptions as observed in 10- to 12-year-olds (see earlier discussion under THE LEARNER). Similar disconcerting results have been reported by Post, Harel, Behr, and Lesh (1988). In a study that focused on the connectedness, rather than the correctness, of prospective teachers' knowledge of division, M. A. Simon (1993) found that their knowledge base was weak with respect to several types of connections, such as the conceptual underpinnings of the familiar algorithm for division, the relationship between partitive and quotitive division (e.g., "what is one-fourth of 24?" as opposed to "how many 4's are there in 24?") and between division and subtraction, and the connection between symbolic division and real-world situations to which it is applicable.

Other studies have focused on the effects of teachers' (insufficient) mathematical knowledge on students' learning outcomes. In a number of correlational studies, no strong relationship was found. However, this could be attributed to the fact that only global and superficial measures of teachers' mathematical knowledge were used, such as the number of college mathematics courses completed or scores on standardized mathematics tests (Fennema & Loef, 1992; Romberg & Carpenter, 1986). Taking into account this methodological criticism, researchers have started to provide detailed descriptions of individual teachers' content knowledge of particular mathematical topics and to relate these descriptions to their instructional actions on these topics. As an example, we refer to a case study by Fennema and Loef (1992) that shows how differences in one elementary schoolteacher's knowledge and understanding of two mathematical topics (elementary addition and subtraction, and fractions) could at least partly account for remarkable differences in the richness of the problem types she gave to her students as well as in the quality of the classroom discourse. The importance of knowledge of subject matter content in skilled mathematics teaching is also evident in the work of Leinhardt (1988; see also Leinhardt & Greeno, 1986).

Being an expert mathematics teacher involves far more than being a skilled problem solver in that particular subject matter domain. Good mathematics teaching requires also pedagogical knowledge and skills. Part of this pedagogical knowledge is general or domain independent (see chapter 21), but another part of this pedagogical knowledge, which is of interest here, is specifically related to the domain of mathematics. It includes several subsystems, such as:

- knowledge of mathematics lesson scripts and mathematics teaching routines
- knowledge about the kinds of problem types, graphical representations, and the like that are best suited to introduce particular mathematical notions or skills to pupils
- knowledge of instructional materials available for teaching various mathematical topics, such as textbooks, program materials, manipulatives, computer software, tests, and so on, together with knowledge about their applicability

For most of these aspects of pedagogical content knowledge, there is empirical evidence of the existence of differences among mathematics teachers, as well as of the impact of these differences on teachers' behavior and student outcomes (for illustrative studies, see Carpenter, Fennema, Peterson, & Carey, 1988; Fennema & Loef, 1992; Leinhardt, 1988).

Finally, there is teacher knowledge of how students think and learn in general, and how this occurs within mathematics in particular. This third component consists of teacher knowledge of the mathematical concepts and procedures that students bring to the learning of a topic, the misconceptions and erroneous procedures they may have developed, and the stages of understanding and skill that they are likely to pass through in the course of gaining mastery of it. Included in this component is also the teacher's knowledge of the individual student's mathematical competence and understanding.

Several researchers have investigated teacher knowledge of students' mathematical processes and skills and tried to relate it to pupil outcomes (for a review, see Fennema & Loef, 1992). The issue of knowledge of individual students' cognitions, in particular, has attracted a lot of research.

As part of their study on beginning elementary schoolteachers' knowledge of pedagogical content and student cognitions about addition and subtraction word problems, Carpenter et al. (1988) investigated the teachers' knowledge of their own students' abilities to solve different types of problems and the typical strategies students used to solve problems. Although teachers were quite good in predicting the performance of individual students, they had great difficulty in anticipating an individual student's preferred solution strategies. Moreover, although teachers' ability to predict student performance correlated significantly with student performance, there was no correlation between teachers' success in anticipating the solution strategies and any measure of student performance. These findings seem to suggest that (experienced) teachers do not base their instructional decisions on a careful, individualized, process-oriented assessment of their pupil's knowledge. This conclusion is also supported by Putnam's (1987) study. He analyzed the thoughts and actions of experienced elementary schoolteachers and preservice teachers as they tutored individual children in whole-number addition, both in a live and a simulated situation. Putnam showed that experienced teachers did not try to construct highly detailed models of the pupil's wrong procedures before attempting remedial instruction. Instead, in most cases they appeared to move through a predetermined set of skills and concepts that they expected the child to know (the so-called lesson script). However, some problematic features of this study (such as the equating of teaching *experience* with teaching *expertise*) make Putnam's evidence against the importance of knowledge of learners' cognitions in expert mathematics teaching far from conclusive (De Corte et al., 1991).

*Teachers' Beliefs.* Since 1980 there has been growing interest in teachers' beliefs about mathematics and mathematics teaching and learning. As in the domain of student cognition, it is difficult, if not impossible, to make a clear distinction between teachers' knowledge and teachers' beliefs (Fennema & Loef, 1992; A. G. Thompson, 1992). As discussed earlier under THE LEARNER, beliefs can be considered the twilight zone between cognitive and affective aspects.

A. G. Thompson (1992) reviewed the studies documenting how teachers differ greatly in their beliefs of the nature and meaning of mathematics, as well as in their views on the important goals of the school mathematics program, the role of the teacher and the student in the mathematics lesson, appropriate learning materials and testing procedures, and so forth. This research has also shown that there exists a relationship between teachers' beliefs and conceptions of mathematics, on the one hand, and their views about mathematics learning and teaching as well as their teaching behavior, on the other.

In a study on the beliefs about mathematics and mathematics teaching of three junior high school teachers, A. G. Thompson (1982) found great differences in the teachers' views on the nature and meaning of mathematics, ranging from mathematics as a static, unified body of absolute and infallible knowledge to mathematics as a continuously expanding field of human creation and invention. These differences in teacher views of mathematics were found to be related to differences in the teachers' beliefs and preferences about important issues of mathematics education, such as the appropriate locus of control in teaching, what constitutes evidence of mathematical understanding in students, the purpose of planning mathematics lessons, and so on. Thompson's research further suggested that teachers' beliefs, views, and preferences about mathematics and its teaching, regardless of whether they are consciously or unconsciously held, play a significant role in shaping teachers' characteristic patterns of instructional behavior. For example, one of the most striking differences observed by Thompson was in teachers' practices regarding the role of problem solving in mathematics teaching. One of the teachers almost totally neglected this activity, and this was accounted for by that teacher's view of her major role, which was to transmit contents, as well as by her limited self-confidence with respect to mathematical ability. However, for other teachers, Thompson reported sharp discrepancies between professed beliefs and instructional practice, suggesting that mathematics teachers' beliefs are not related in a simple way to their teaching behavior. Among the possible sources that might complicate this relationship, she mentioned:

- The social context in which mathematics teaching takes place (expectations of parents, fellow teachers, administrators, students).
- The fact that some beliefs professed by teachers are more manifestations of verbal commitment to abstract ideas and slogans than of an operative theory of instruction.
- Teachers' lack of a strong mathematical knowledge base, which prevented them from being able to recognize and capitalize on opportunities for applying mathematical ideas and procedures.

Cooney's (1985) case study of how a beginning mathematics teacher's idealistic beliefs about the importance of problem solving in mathematics (education) melted away under the pressure of the reality of classroom practice during his first three months of teaching is another good illustration of the complex relationship between teachers' views about mathematics teaching and their actual teaching behavior.

***Modifying Teachers' Knowledge and Beliefs.*** Researchers have begun to address the question of whether and how (pre-service) teachers' cognitions and conceptions can be influenced, taking into account the results from the available studies (see, e.g., Carpenter, Fennema, Peterson, Chiang, & Loef, 1989; Cobb et al., 1991; Cooney, 1994; De Corte et al., 1991; Graeber & Tirosh, 1988; Middleton, Pitman, & Webb, 1993). These intervention studies differ widely in:

- the aspects of (preservice) teachers' cognition addressed (e.g., mathematical content knowledge, pedagogical content knowledge, beliefs about mathematics and mathematics teaching)
- the amount and kind of training provided (e.g., short interventions, interactive video, intensive workshops, workshops followed by classroom visits and afterschool working sessions)
- the number of (preservice) teachers involved
- the way training effects were determined (e.g., teacher cognitions, teaching behavior, student outcomes)

For example, Carpenter et al. (1989; see also Carpenter & Fennema, 1992) investigated whether it is possible to improve teachers' instructional practice and their students' learning outcomes by confronting them with the available research-based knowledge of the development of children's skills and processes for solving addition and subtraction problems. They called their approach cognitively guided instruction (CGI). Basic ideas underlying the CGI approach are that the teaching–learning process is too complex to specify in advance, and that teaching as problem solving is mediated by teachers' thinking and decision-making. Consequently, significant changes in educational practice can best be pursued "by helping teachers to make informed decisions rather than by attempting to train them to perform in a specified way" (Carpenter & Fennema, 1992, p. 460).

Twenty first-grade teachers participated in a one-month-long workshop that attempted to familiarize them with the available research findings on learning and the development of addition and subtraction concepts and skills. Teachers learned to classify problems, to distinguish different levels of mastery, to identify strategies that young children use to solve different problem types, and to relate those strategies to the mastery levels and problem types in which they are commonly used by children. Afterward teachers discussed principles of instruction derived from research and designed their own programs of instruction based on those principles. Based on a large set of data-gathering techniques, including classroom observations, measurements of teachers' cognitions and beliefs, and tests of student learning outcomes, the following findings were obtained:

- CGI teachers taught problem solving significantly more and number facts significantly less than control teachers
- CGI teachers encouraged pupils to use a variety of strategies, and they listened to the processes their students used significantly more than did control teachers
- CGI teachers believed that mathematics instruction should build on students' existing knowledge more than did control teachers, and they knew more about individual students' problem-solving processes
- Pupils of CGI teachers exceeded control pupils in number fact knowledge, problem solving, reported understanding, and reported confidence in problem solving

It is an open question whether CGI would work as effectively at other age levels and with other contents. According to Carpenter and Fennema (1992), there may be some unique characteristics about first-grade teachers and about the domain of addition and subtraction that may not generalize well. However, the positive results of the CGI approach have to some extent already been replicated in several other research projects dealing with different grade levels or different mathematical contents (see, e.g., Cobb et al., 1991).

Notwithstanding that several unanswered questions remain, these studies demonstrate that sharing with teachers research-based knowledge about students' thinking and problem solving can profoundly affect teachers' cognitions and beliefs about mathematics learning and instruction, their classroom practices, and, most important, their students' learning outcomes and beliefs. As such, these positive findings provide evidence for the relevance of the constructive conception and the dispositional view of mathematics learning and teaching, which is complementary to the evidence to be presented in the next subsection. At the same time, these studies demonstrate the feasibility of this new conception in the setting of a typical elementary mathematics classroom. In light of the extremely time-consuming nature of the knowledge-sharing approach followed in CGI and other similar projects (from the point of view of both researchers and teachers), the question remains whether such an approach can be applied on a large scale. New informational technology, such as simulation programs and interactive video, can probably play an important role in helping in-service and preservice teachers interact with CGI or related ideas (see, e.g., De Corte et al., 1991; Van Galen & Feijs, 1990).

At the end of this discussion of the major components of teachers' cognitions, some concluding remarks can be made. First, complementary with the changing view on the learner, there has been a change in the view of the teacher from a transmitter of knowledge to a facilitator whose job it is to support, promote, and encourage the construction of knowledge by students (Romberg, 1992c). This new job assumes a rich knowledge base, including mathematical knowledge and skills, domain-specific pedagogical knowledge, knowledge of students' cognitions about mathematics, and appropriate beliefs about mathematics and mathematics education. As convincingly argued by Fennema and Loef (1992) and by A. G. Thompson (1992), these necessary components of teachers' cognitions cannot be sharply isolated. Just as for student cognitions, they overlap and influence each other in complex ways. More research is needed to establish the exact nature of these interactions among the different aspects of teachers' cognitions.

Second, the available research has shown that there is no simple and straightforward effect of teacher knowledge and beliefs on student learning. Rather, the effect is mediated by the teacher's teaching behavior, which is affected by a lot of factors other than teacher knowledge and beliefs, such as the social and material contexts in which mathematics teaching and learning take place. Future research should include careful analyses of teachers' behavior in the classroom as a factor mediating between their cognitions and student learning (A. G. Thompson, 1992).

Third, teachers' knowledge and beliefs are not static. They originated during the teachers' own years as a mathematics student, were shaped during their preservice training, and evolve further through their own teaching experiences (Fennema & Loef, 1992). Future research should document this evolution in teachers' knowledge and beliefs and investigate further how to modify the latter.

Finally, recent studies suggest that it is possible to help teachers develop richer knowledge bases and more productive beliefs about mathematical learning and teaching and to make better-informed instructional decisions, resulting in significant improvements in student knowledge, skills, and beliefs. However, these studies also show that these changes do not occur quickly or easily.

## Designing Powerful Teaching–Learning Environments

The preceding ideas and research findings concerning the domain of mathematics, the nature of learning processes, the goal of mathematics education as the acquisition of a mathematical disposition involving different categories of aptitudes, and the social and cultural contexts of mathematics learning and teaching confront us with a challenge. We now face the task of elaborating a framework consisting of coherent research-based principles for the design of powerful learning environments, that is, situations and contexts that can elicit in students the learning processes that are conducive to the intended mathematical disposition. This section discusses some examples of mathematics teaching–learning environments that embody to some degree key ideas that have emerged from recent theoretical and empirical studies. More specifically, the major principles underlying the development of those environments are the constructivist view of learning, the conception of mathematics as human activity, the crucial role of students' prior informal and formal knowledge for future learning, the orientation toward understanding and problem solving, the importance of social interaction and collaboration in doing and learning mathematics, and the need to embed mathematics learning in authentic and meaningful contexts. This implies that these examples represent a radical departure from traditional, weak classroom environments based on the view that mathematics learning is a highly individual activity consisting mainly in absorbing and memorizing a fixed body of decontextualized and fragmented knowledge and procedural skills transmitted by the teacher (see also Romberg, 1992c).

The following examples will be discussed: Schoenfeld's heuristic teaching of problem solving (1985, 1987, 1992a), anchored instruction of mathematical problem solving designed by the Cognition and Technology Group at the Vanderbilt Learning Technology Center (1990), and realistic mathematics education developed at the Freudenthal Institute in The Netherlands (Gravemeijer, 1994; Streefland, 1991b; Treffers, 1987). This selection of examples represents both a variety of subject matter content and age levels and a diversity in theoretical perspective and background.

*Schoenfeld's Heuristic Teaching of Problem Solving.* The most representative example of teaching heuristic methods and metacognitive skills is probably the work of Schoenfeld with respect to mathematics problem solving at the college level (1985, 1987, 1992a). A starting point of his approach to teaching problem solving is the well-documented finding that using a set of heuristics embedded in an executive or control strategy for their application is an essential feature of expert problem solving.

This latter finding is in sharp contrast to the typical problem-solving behavior of most students. Schoenfeld collected a set of more than 100 videotapes of college and high school students solving unfamiliar geometry problems in pairs during 20-minute sessions. The problem-solving protocols were analyzed by parsing them in so-called macroscopic chunks or episodes, defined as periods of time during which the problem solvers were involved in essentially the same activity. Six different categories of activities were distinguished: read, analyze, explore, plan, implement, and verify (for a detailed explanation and discussion of the method for data analysis, see Schoenfeld, 1985, 1992b). Schoenfeld observed that in about 60% of the solution attempts, self-regulatory activities such as analyzing the problem and monitoring the solution process, which are characteristic of an expert approach, were totally absent. The typical strategy used in these cases can be summarized as follows: reading the problem, deciding quickly about an approach, and then keeping at it without considering any alternative, even if no progress at all is made. Taking this observation into account, Schoenfeld developed a teaching method that focuses on the strategic aspects of problem solving. In this respect, it is important to remember that according to Schoenfeld, it is not sufficient to teach students isolated heuristics, because then they often are unable to decide which method is appropriate for the problem at hand. That is why it is necessary to teach heuristics within the context of a control strategy that helps the learner select the right heuristic to solve a given problem. Schoenfeld (1985) has proposed such a strategy, which consists of five stages:

1. Analysis oriented toward understanding the problem by constructing an adequate representation.
2. Design of global solution plan.
3. Exploration oriented toward transforming the problem into a routine task. This stage constitutes the heuristic heart of the strategy.
4. Implementation or carrying out the solution plan.
5. Verification of the solution.

Schoenfeld paid a lot of attention to the elaboration of a powerful teaching–learning environment. From the beginning, he orients his students toward the control strategy as a whole, although in a schematic form. Thereafter the different stages of the strategy—analysis, design, exploration, implementation, and verification—are discussed consecutively, and the corresponding heuristics are explained and practiced. In this respect, modeling is extensively used to demonstrate how an expert selects and applies heuristic methods. Afterward, the students themselves are given ample opportunities to apply those methods under the guidance of the teacher, who encourages them to use certain heuristics, gives hints, provides immediate feedback, and, if necessary, helps with the execution of some parts of the task which the student cannot yet carry out autonomously.

Besides modeling and whole-class discussion and teaching, Schoenfeld also frequently uses small-group problem solving. Acting himself as a consultant, he regularly asks three questions during group activities:

1. What are you doing?
2. Why are you doing this?
3. If what you are doing now is successful, how will it help to find the solution?

Asking these questions serves the dual purpose of encouraging students to articulate their problem-solving strategies and to reflect on those activities. Schoenfeld's ultimate goal is that students spontaneously ask the three questions themselves, and in doing so regulate and monitor their own thinking processes.

The results of Schoenfeld's approach are very positive. Indeed, he observed that as an outcome of instruction, students' problem-solving behavior became more expertlike, and that less than 20% of the solution processes were still of the kind that dominated before instruction. The number of correct solutions increased accordingly.

As shown by Collins et al. (1989), Schoenfeld's approach to teaching mathematics problem solving is in accordance with the apprenticeship view of learning and instruction that derives from the situated cognition paradigm. Indeed, Schoenfeld makes ample use of such techniques as modeling, coaching, scaffolding, articulation of and reflection on problem-solving strategies, and social interaction and collaborative learning in small groups that are at the core of apprenticeship. Although explicit teaching of heuristic and self-regulatory skills is involved, the approach is essentially constructivist in nature; indeed, the guidance provided does not give problem solutions or impose solution strategies, but supports students in their attempts at understanding problems, in articulating and discussing their beliefs about problem solving, in reflecting on their solution strategies, and in interiorizing valuable self-monitoring skills. In fact, a major development in Schoenfeld's approach is that at present, the five stages of the control strategy delineated above are less frequently taught in a structured way than was originally the case, but their importance is highlighted when relevant and appropriate in classroom discussions. In this way students are not learning about mathematics, they are doing mathematics, which involves learning to use the tools of mathematics, which leads to the acquisition not only of mathematical concepts but also of a mathematical view of the world and to a sense of mathematical practice and culture (see also Schoenfeld, 1992a). In other words, a mathematical disposition is fostered.

***Vanderbilt University Learning Technology Center's Anchored Instruction.*** Anchored instruction has been developed by the Cognition and Technology Group (1990, 1994) at the Learning Technology Center of Vanderbilt University (CTGV) in response to the well-known problem of inert knowledge observed in many students. Inert knowledge, first described by Whitehead in 1929, is knowledge that is available and can be recalled on request, but is not spontaneously applied in situations where it is relevant to solve new problems. According to H. A. Simon (1980), a major cause of this phenomenon is that students' knowledge is not conditionalized; that is, students do not know under what conditions their knowledge can be applied. H. A. Simon (1980), and likewise the CTGV (Van Haneghan et al., 1992), have argued that instruction itself is largely responsible for making students' knowledge inert. For example, word problem solving by schoolchildren mostly consists of choosing the arithmetic operation to figure the answer; this is far removed from problem solving in the real world, in which posing and defining problems—involving sense making, goal setting, planning, and decision-making—are the major activities, while arithmetic operations serve largely as tools that can be used to carry out a plan or achieve a goal put forward by the problem solver.

Anchored instruction has been designed as an attempt to help students acquire useful instead of inert knowledge. The essence of the approach is described by Bransford, Sherwood, Hasselbring, Kinzer, and Williams (1990) as follows:

At the heart of the model is an emphasis on the importance of creating an anchor or focus that generates interest and enables students to identify and define problems and to pay attention to their own perception and comprehension of these problems. They can then be introduced to information that is relevant to their anchored perceptions. The major goal of anchored instruction is to enable students to notice critical features of problem situations and to experience the changes in their perception and understanding of the anchor as they view the situation from new points of view. (p. 123)

With this goal in mind, the starting point of anchored instruction is the creation of rich, authentic, and interesting problem-solving contexts that can serve as the basis for the development of generative learning environments offering students ample opportunities for problem posing, exploration, and discovery. It is obvious that this has important implications for the role of the teacher, changing it from providing information to guiding and coaching students, and often becoming a fellow, if more advanced, learner (Cognition and Technology Group at Vanderbilt, 1993).

Although the Vanderbilt group indicates that the application of anchored instruction does not necessarily require the use of technology, they nevertheless argue that a technology-based implementation makes the model more powerful (Bransford et al., 1990). Accordingly, they have developed videodisc-based complex problem spaces called macrocontexts because they are broad-based and enable learners to explore and model a problem space involving mathematical problems for extended periods of time from a diversity of perspectives. The Vanderbilt group prefers to situate instruction in video-based anchors, mainly because the medium allows a richer, more realistic, and more dynamic presentation of information than textual material. The macrocontexts provide environments for cooperative learning and discussion in small groups, as well as for individual and whole-class problem solving. However, because applying anchored instruction requires substantial changes in the role of the teacher, the research team has stressed the importance of explicitly addressing the culture of the classroom in which they situate the video-based anchors (Cognition and Technology Group at Vanderbilt, 1993).

Anchored instruction can be applied in a variety of subject matter domains and with students of different ages. However, until now the Vanderbilt group has focused on mathematics instruction with fifth and sixth graders. For example, a videodisc series called *The Adventures of Jasper Woodbury* for mathematical problem solving has been developed, relating to trip planning based on a set of design principles derived from previous research and chosen because they facilitate the elicitation of specific kinds of problem-solving activities in students (Van Haneghan et al., 1992). The major principles are:

1. Video-based presentation format
2. Narrative format (presentation in the form of a story helps to create a meaningful context)

3. Generative structure. (By having the students themselves generate the resolution of the story, which involves identifying problems and collecting relevant information, their active involvement in the learning process is stimulated.)
4. Embedded data design (all the information necessary to solve the problems is included in the story)
5. Problem complexity (the problems are intentionally made complex so that students learn to deal with complexity)

Initial studies with the Jasper series have produced encouraging results. A baseline study confirmed that even above-average sixth graders were very poor in their approach to the macrocontext problems without instruction and mediation, but a 4-day intervention study showed that anchored instruction could substantially improve fifth-graders' problem-solving skills. In this study an experimental group was compared to a control group that received traditional word problem instruction. In line with the basic idea of anchored instruction the experimental group engaged in problem analysis, problem detection, and solution planning to check Jasper's trip-planning decision. Although substantial and significant gains were observed from pretest to posttest in the experimental group, the results of the control group did not improve. Moreover, the analysis of interview protocols relating to children's problem solving with respect to a video near-transfer problem showed significant transfer in the experimental group but not in the control group (for more details see Van Haneghan et al., 1992; results of additional studies are summarized in Cognition and Technology Group at Vanderbilt, 1993).

Anchored instruction is also in line with prevailing key ideas on mathematics learning and teaching. Indeed, it stresses the importance of active and constructive learning embedded in authentic contexts that are rich in resources and learning materials, that engage learners in doing mathematics, and that offer ample opportunities for social interaction. Thus, it is not surprising that the CTGV considers anchored instruction as a model that embodies major features of the apprenticeship view of learning and teaching. Moreover, the group claims that anchored instruction contributes to the solution of a major problem faced by the apprenticeship model, namely, making the transformation of traditional schooling into apprenticeship more feasible (Cognition and Technology Group at Vanderbilt, 1990). Continued research is necessary both to validate this claim and to see whether the initial encouraging findings with respect to the potential of anchored instruction can be replicated in other samples and with other anchors. With respect to a possible large-scale implementation, a number of other important questions need to be addressed, such as how technology dependent anchored instruction is and how easily it can be fitted into the mathematics curriculum.

*The Freudenthal Institute's Realistic Mathematics Education.* Some major epistemological and theoretical ideas implemented in the preceding attempts to design more powerful learning environments for mathematics learning also underlie the so-called Realistic Mathematics Education (RME) evolved by the Research Group on Mathematics Education of what since 1991 has been called the Freudenthal Institute at the University of Utrecht, The Netherlands. This is in some respects remarkable, not only because of the rather different theoretical framework behind RME, but also because Freudenthal founded RME in the early 1970s, many years before the projects discussed were started, and before constructivist and Vygotskian conceptions had had a major impact on mathematics education. This can be explained at least partly by the fact that The Netherlands escaped the New Mathematics wave. Starting in the 1960s the New Mathematics swamped mathematics education in most Western countries, whereas in The Netherlands there was a group of researchers, guided since 1971 by Freudenthal, which was developing an innovative program for mathematics education in the primary school in reaction to the then-dominant mechanistic approach to mathematics instruction (Streefland, 1993; Treffers, 1991b).

In contrast to the view of mathematics as a given formal system of concepts and rules that one has to adopt through learning, RME conceives mathematics as a human activity, so that learning mathematics is essentially doing mathematics or mathematizing. Underlying this view is Freudenthal's (1983, 1991) didactical phenomenology. This epistemological position involves a reaction against the traditional idea that students should first acquire the formal system of mathematics, with the applications to come afterward. According to Freudenthal, this is contrary to the way in which mathematical knowledge has been gathered and developed, that is, starting from the study of phenomena in the real world. Therefore, the basic idea of Freudenthal's realistic approach is

to put the pupils in touch with the phenomena for which the mathematical structure is the organizing tool in order to let them shape these tools themselves in a process of re-invention, and learn to handle and use these mathematical tools in concept formation. (Treffers, 1991a, p. 22)

This means that reality serves not only as a domain of application of knowledge but, in the first place, as a source of mathematical modeling that enables the learners to constitute mental objects, that is, the intuitive notions that precede concept attainment (Freudenthal, 1983). This also implies that the learning environment has to be adaptive to the learners in order to facilitate the intended process of reinvention of mathematics knowledge.

Starting from this fundamental conception of doing mathematics, the design of "realistic" learning environments is guided by a set of interrelated principles, which we now briefly discuss and illustrate (see De Lange, 1987; Gravemeijer, 1994; Treffers, 1987, 1991a, for further details).

1. Learning mathematics is a constructive activity. Students construct their knowledge starting from the exploration and modeling of real situations, and using their own informal knowledge and working methods. In RME, real situations are presented, mostly in the form of context problems that serve a kind of anchoring function as in anchored instruction; they are real-life mathematical problems presented in a broader context such as a story, a game, a press cutting, a drawing, and so forth. For example, it has been shown that third graders can discover a procedure for long division that comes close to the standard division algorithm, starting from exploring context problems relating to the organization of a PTA meeting in the school for which the number of tables and coffeepots has to be figured. To calculate how many tables would be needed,

```
6) 81
    60        10 tables
   ___
    21
    18         3 tables
   ___
     3
     3        (1 table)
   ___
     0        14 tables
```

**FIGURE 16–4. Example of Progressive Schematization in the Realistic Mathematics Education Approach**
This long division scheme is a curtailed form of repeated subtraction for solving the problem, "How many tables are needed for 81 people if 6 can sit at a table?"
*Source:* From Treffers, A. (1991a). Didactical background of a mathematics program for primary education. In L. Streefland (Ed.), *Realistic mathematics education in primary school: On the occasion of the opening of the Freudenthal Institute* (pp. 21–56). Utrecht, The Netherlands: Freudenthal Institute, University of Utrecht.

knowing that 81 parents will attend the meeting and that one table seats 6 persons, a variety of solutions were produced, ranging from very simple (e.g., repeated addition) to more sophisticated ones (e.g., using $10 \times 6$ as a starting point). After discussion of the different methods in class, most children switched to the more efficient 10 strategy to calculate the number of coffeepots needed. Through progressive schematization the class subsequently invented the long division scheme shown in Figure 16–4, which starts from the 10 strategy.

2. Progressing toward higher levels of abstraction. The progressive schematization—in learning long division, for example—implies an increase in the level of abstraction of the procedures used by the students. RME exploits, as much as possible, mathematical tools and models to support the transition from the concrete, intuitive level to the formal system of mathematics. Manipulatives, visual models, schemes, and diagrams can fulfill this bridging function; examples are the number line, the arrow diagram, the rectangle model, and the abacus.

3. Encouraging students' free productions and reflection. This principle derives from the constructive view of the learning process. For example, in the lessons on long division referred to above, children's own productions and inventions played a crucial role in the process of progressive schematization. Considering and discussing these productions led to reflection, which is an important vehicle for attaining higher levels of abstraction. The example shown in Figure 16–5 (dividing 6,394 by 12) illustrates the kind of productions, involving schematization and abbreviation, that a class invented for long division with bigger numbers after a series of 15 lessons with a variety of contexts (for example, a proportion division: translation of months into years) (Treffers, 1987, p. 204; see also Gravemeijer, van den Heuvel, & Streefland, 1990).

The example shows at the same time that at this point in the course the children had reached different levels of schematization. Some children were using a more efficient 500 strategy while others were still applying the more cumbersome 100 strategy. This is an important observation from a diagnostic point of view. Indeed, the nature of children's productions—also in inventing new problems themselves—reflects their progress in doing mathematics.

4. Learning through social interaction and cooperation. In explaining the preceding principles, the role of discussion in

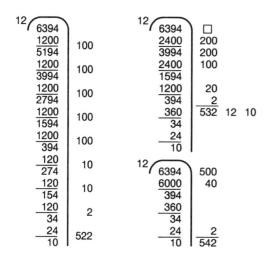

**FIGURE 16–5. Students' Inventions of Ways to Divide 6,394 by 12**

In each case the student is repeatedly subtracting multiples of 12, and keeping a record of how many 12s have been subtracted. The solutions show different levels of curtailment of this method, with the final solution (lower right) approximating the standard algorithm for long division.

*Source:* From *Three Dimensions: A Model of Goal and Theory Description in Mathematics Education. The Wiskobas Project* (p. 204) by A. Treffers, 1987, Dordrecht, The Netherlands: Reidel. Reprinted by permission.

learning and teaching long division has already been mentioned. In RME, whole-class teaching and individual work are combined with cooperative learning in small groups and classroom discussion. Social interaction is considered essential because of the importance in learning and doing mathematics of exchanging ideas, comparing solution strategies, and discussing arguments. Of special significance in this regard is that interaction and collaboration mobilize reflection.

5. Interconnecting knowledge components and skills. This principle derives from the phenomenological basis of RME; indeed, the real phenomena underlying the mathematical concepts are interrelated in manifold ways and constitute a structured whole. Therefore, learning environments must promote in learners the acquisition of a coherent and well-organized knowledge base; for example, instruction should explicitly connect division to the other basic operations. A major advantage of this interconnectedness is that it enhances the accessibility as well as the broad applicability of knowledge elements and skills.

Experimental work in the traditional sense that provides evidence in favor of RME is scarce. One investigation has shown that the RME approach to long division produces better results than traditional instruction. As compared to a control group, an experimental class achieved a result almost twice as good in only half the time (Treffers, 1987). Streefland (1991a) also reported promising comparative results in favor of his realistic approach to the teaching of fractions. In addition, a number of anecdotal studies describe positive outcomes (see, e.g., Streefland, 1991b; van den Brink, 1991). Further, the results of a large-scale assessment in The Netherlands indicate that pupils in schools that use RME-based textbooks do better in several

areas of the mathematics curriculum than pupils in schools that do not (Treffers, 1991b.) But the major achievement of RME is probably its impact on educational practice in The Netherlands, where in 1990 textbooks based on the realistic approach had conquered a 75 percent share of the primary school market (as compared to 5 percent in 1980). Probably this can be largely accounted for by the use of the developmental research strategy, which is characterized by ongoing interaction between theory construction and product development (Treffers, 1991b). It is a creative and constructive process that takes place in the context of a partnership between researchers and practitioners. Interestingly, since 1991, the basic ideas of RME are being tried in an American setting (De Lange, 1993, 1995).

The preceding description of projects attempting a theory-based design of powerful mathematics learning environments could be extended with other examples, such as the work of Cobb and his co-workers (see, e.g., Cobb, Wood, & Yackel, 1991; Cobb et al., 1988; Wood, Cobb, & Yackel, 1995) and of Lampert (1986, 1990), which share major characteristics with those projects. The three examples suffice, however, to clarify and illustrate current efforts to implement in innovative educational settings the new conception of mathematics as a meaningful human activity and of mathematics learning as socially embedded meaning construction in authentic and realistic contexts. As such, these projects aim at fostering in students a mathematical perspective and disposition, and their approach resembles to a variable degree the apprenticeship model of learning. The results reported so far are certainly promising, as they demonstrate that the kind of learning environments described can lead to fundamental changes in the sort of mathematics knowledge, skills, and beliefs that children acquire, and can help make children more autonomous learners. However, these projects also raise some problems and issues for further consideration and research. For example, we need a more fine-grained analysis of the constructive acquisition processes that the kind of learning environments described above elicit in students. But the question also arises as to whether it is realistic to expect that in such environments the majority of the students will indeed develop the intended mathematical disposition. One can even question the feasibility of apprenticeship-like teaching–learning situations in today's schools. These problems are discussed in the final section of this chapter, together with a number of other critical issues needing further study.

## Integrating Computers into Instruction

The high expectations that the introduction of microcomputers into classrooms in the 1980s would have a radical effect on the learning of mathematics remain largely unfulfilled as yet. In the course of the ensuing reappraisal, it became apparent that educators need to consider ways of using computers that are consistent with the enriched conception of mathematics delineated in this chapter, to carry out theoretical analyses and empirical explorations of what the computer can do to transform mathematics learning, and to address practical problems facing the integration of computers within instructional environments.

***Reappraisal Following Unfulfilled Expectations.*** The impact of computers on school mathematics has been limited by problems of implementation and by more deep-seated problems reflecting the general difficulty of innovation in educational systems (Kilpatrick & Davis, 1993). Among the factors identified by Kaput (1992) are limited numbers of high-performance computers in schools, limited access to high-quality software, and limited preparation of teachers. Most of the early programs were of the drill-and-practice variety, which still forms the bulk of commercially produced software (Kaput, 1992) and is the form of software that has predominantly been used in classrooms (Olive, 1993). The role of such software in facilitating practice of routine knowledge and procedures is useful but limited. As De Corte (1994, p. 20) argued:

If, in addition, one takes into account the traditional resistance of the school system to change, the spontaneous reluctance of many educational practitioners to the introduction of any technological device in schools, and the tendency of the school system to neutralize potential effects of innovations through absorption and adaptation to the current situation, it is probably not surprising that computers have not affected education in a substantial way during the past decade.

A major line of development in reaction to the limitations of routine applications has been the attempt to create intelligent tutoring systems, alternatively referred to as intelligent computer-assisted instruction (ICAI). At its most ambitious, the aim of this approach is to have the computer function "as an intelligent, dynamically adaptive substitute for a human teacher, who is capable of performing sensitive cognitive diagnoses, which means to infer, on the basis of a constantly-retuned student model, a person's cognitive states—what the person knows, how she thinks and learns—on the basis of her overt behavior" (Reusser, 1992). A massive, multidisciplinary effort has gone into this effort, but increasingly its feasibility is being questioned. In a review entitled "Intelligent Tutoring, But Not Intelligent Enough," Suppes (1990) doubted whether the approach could ever cope adequately with complex problem-solving domains, and Kintsch (1991, p. 244) argued that an intelligent tutoring system for algebra word problems was impossible, since "the real world situations described in college algebra problems are so numerous and so varied, that only a system that knows essentially as much about the world as college students do could cope with these problems."

In general, mathematics educators are even more critical of the enterprise. Ridgway (1988), for example, argued that ICAI is not only impossible but seditious in many respects. Kaput (1992, p. 545) concluded that:

Typical ICAI systems were applied to teach the syntax of formal notations. . . . [They] did not, because they could not, deal with what the formalisms are used to represent and what they evolved to do in the first place.

. . . But this competence has come to be pedagogically inappropriate and curricularly superfluous. . . .

In short, it appears that intelligent tutoring systems do not offer the answer (De Corte, 1994).

Partly in reaction to these criticisms of intelligent tutoring systems, an approach based on a different conception of, and different goals for, mathematics education is gaining in strength. This approach is based on two broad principles: (a) that computer software should provide flexible tools to help the learner in the process of constructing mathematical knowledge, and (b) that the use of computers to aid learning should be embedded within a learning environment that includes the supportive role of the teacher and social interactions with other students. Kintsch (1991, p. 245), for example, proposed the alternative of "unintelligent tutoring":

A tutor should not provide the intelligence to guide learning, it should not do the planning and monitoring of the student's progress, because these are the very activities the students must perform themselves in order to learn.

To illustrate the potential of software developed in line with this philosophy, we next consider some examples.

*Examples of Innovative Software.* LOGO was a conspicuous exception to the general trend in educational software during the 1970s and 1980s. It fits more naturally into the cultural climate of the 1990s, as "many currents are coming together to favor a period of transformation of the culture of mathematics education" (Papert, 1992, p. xvi).

LOGO embodies the vision of Seymour Papert that children can construct mathematics through linking systems of actions and representations of those systems, and reflecting on the linkages. Thus, LOGO could be thought of as a "Mathland" in which mathematics would be learned as naturally as a foreign language by a child living in the appropriate culture (Papert, 1980). In Papert's exposition of his philosophy (strongly influenced by Piagetian constructivist principles), there is a heavy emphasis on personal involvement, affect, and social interaction. At the same time, the language makes accessible "powerful ideas" of mathematics, in particular the hierarchical construction of more and more complex structures through the use of procedures; other "powerful ideas" relate to such cognitive and metacognitive skills as heuristic problem solving, planning, debugging, and reflection. In short, all of the components in Goldin's model (Figure 16–2) and the interactions among them are implicated. To the extent that this vision can be realized, it represents an ideal instructional environment for the fostering of a mathematical disposition—teaching children to be mathematicians rather than teaching about mathematics (Papert, 1972).

LOGO is widely used in schools, though mainly restricted to on-screen turtle geometry (M. Resnick, 1988). It must be assumed that the impact is attenuated by the institutionalization of LOGO and its transformation into part of the canonical curriculum (Kilpatrick & Davis, 1993). There have been numerous variants, adaptations, and extensions, such as the integration of LOGO with LEGO (M. Resnick, 1988; Weir, 1992), and innovative pedagogical applications, such as involving children as software designers (I. Harel, 1990). However, the use of such enhancements, and the use of LOGO in accordance with Papert's intentions, is probably rather limited.

The very considerable amount of research relating to LOGO is well represented in Hoyles and Noss (1992). Much of this research has documented the difficulty of realizing Papert's vision. Early optimism that experience with LOGO would lead to major changes in general problem-solving skills such as planning and monitoring, the so-called cognitive-effects hypothesis, was not supported in a series of experiments carried out in the early 1980s. However, following reassessment, more recent investigations with more focused aims have produced more positive results (De Corte & Verschaffel, 1989).

Other studies have shown that children, left to themselves, do not, in general, construct the powerful mathematical ideas latent in the LOGO environment. As reported by Noss and Hoyles (1992), they tend to use the available tools unreflectively or to bypass them, to use perceptual rather than analytic strategies, and to avoid mathematical analysis. As would be predicted from a constructivist perspective, they perceive situations in ways unintended by teachers, and they set their own pragmatic goals.

Such results led to a tempering of vision by reality among LOGO enthusiasts, even Papert (1992, p. xv) acknowledging that it was appropriate to put "the dream on the back burner and . . . look for things to do with Logo that have a better chance in the short run than recreating mathematics." One manifestation of this trend has been the greater attention paid to integrating Logo with more standard curricular topics (Gurtner, 1992; Noss, 1987).

A second example of innovative software is the series of tools for exploring geometry, initiated by the Geometric Supposers (Schwartz, Yerushalmy, & Wilson, 1993) and followed by CABRI Geometry (Laborde, 1990) and the Geometer's Sketchpad (Jackiw, 1991). As well as making constructions and measurements easy, these tools for the posing and investigation of conjectures exploit fundamentally new modes of representation. For example, it is a simple matter to construct a quadrilateral figure, then the midpoints of its sides, and the quadrilateral formed by joining those midpoints (Figure 16–6). Now, a vertex of the original quadrilateral can be dragged with the mouse, whereupon the whole *construction* moves as a continuous transformation, affording new insight into the invariance whereby the figure formed by joining the midpoints is always a parallelogram. Another major innovation is that series of constructions can be recorded, repeated on different examples, built up hierarchically, and edited. Procedures become mathematical objects for reflection and modification (Kaput, 1992).

An interesting further development is the GEO-LOGO project in which a LOGO environment has been designed that also includes features of the exploratory tools just described (Clements & Meredith, 1993). It is based on the following five principles (pp. 6–7):

1. Encourage construction of the abstract from the visual
2. Maintain close ties between representations—LOGO code, the action of the turtle, and the resultant figure
3. Facilitate examination and modification of code—ease of editing and repeating constructions and operations
4. Encourage procedural thinking
5. Provide freedom within constraints

This hybrid design enriches LOGO in a way that makes it more easily embeddable within a standard geometry curriculum (De Corte, 1993).

A third example is MathCars, briefly described by its designer in Kaput (1992). By contrast with the first two examples, this is a simulation rather than an exploratory tool. An example of a screen display is shown in Figure 16–7. The driving of a car along a road, from the driver's point of view, is simulated. The user controls its velocity by means of the accelerator shown at the bottom right. Continuous information is provided in the following forms:

- a digital clock and odometer (which can be scrolled to generate a table of time/distance pairs of values)
- visual feedback from passing posts
- auditory feedback, either as echoes from passing posts or as variable-pitch engine sounds
- an analog speedometer, which in this example is vertical—as it moves to the right, it leaves a trace of velocity as a function of time

Perhaps the most central feature of this software is the provision of multiple representations providing dynamic "hot linkages" among formal mathematical representations and between these representations and actions. By hot linkages is meant the capability to reflect actions taken in one system in another system, which is where "the computer contribution becomes most apparent in creating a dynamic, interactive medium" (Kaput, 1992, p. 530).

***Potential for Transforming the Learning of Mathematics.*** Despite the limited effective impact of computers thus far, and although history reminds us of many cases where technological innovations have failed to fulfill their promise in classrooms (Cuban, 1986), there remains widespread conviction that the potential of computers for transforming the learning of mathematics is real and realizable.

A first point to make is that computers are changing the nature of how mathematics is done and conceptualized (Kilpatrick & Davis, 1993). The power of the computer for crunching numbers and for graphical display is obvious, but the availability of this power leads to more fundamental changes. One is the spur given to experimentation in mathematics (Dreyfus, 1993). Another is the accessibility to the building and running of complex mathematical models, and easy exploration of "what if" questions through parametric variation. A third is the shift in balance toward image manipulation as opposed to symbol manipulation (Dreyfus, 1991), which will be increasingly supported by new forms of computer-related visual technologies (Friedhoff & Benzon, 1991). Perhaps the most dramatic change has been in statistics, the practice of which has been revolutionized by computing (Biehler, 1993). According to Biehler:

Statistics is a good case in point where we can very clearly observe *qualitative changes* related to the use of new tools. The reorganisation of thinking and practice . . . is already a cultural reality in some circles of statistical practice. A key notion is *Exploratory Data Analysis* . . . or *interactive, graphical data analysis.* . . .

Dörfler (1993) argues, in line with the situated cognition point of view, that cognition is distributed within a system that includes the individual, representational and computational tools, and other people within a social context. He further argues that interacting with computers within such a system does not merely amplify cognitive capacities, but brings about

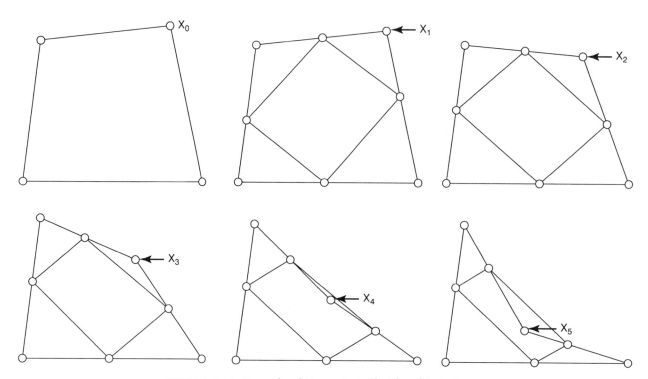

FIGURE 16–6. Example of Geometer's Sketchpad in Action
A quadrilateral figure is constructed from four line segments (first diagram). The midpoints of each side are constructed and joined by line segments (second diagram); the resulting figure is a parallelogram. Now a vertex can be dragged continuously by the mouse (positions $X_1$ to $X_5$ are illustrated in sequence) and the whole configuration moves continuously.

*Source:* From *The Geometer's Sketchpad* by N. Jackiw, 1991, Berkeley, CA: Key Curriculum Press. Reprinted by permission.

a reorganization of cognitive activity (cf. Pea, 1987). Here, by reference to the examples cited above, we consider two of the far-reaching effects that are possible.

The first is that computers offer new ways of promoting links between actions and perceptions and formal mathematical representations (which are located at the beginning and end of cognitive development in Piagetian theory). Papert (1980) saw turtle geometry as having a strong link with children's knowledge of their own bodies. The innovative software for geometrical exploration described above allows direct connection between the action of dynamically transforming a construction and the perception of the effects of this transformation.

MathCars is specifically designed to map the visual and auditory perception of the motion of a vehicle onto graphical and other mathematical representations; the display and related activities can be varied very widely. An example of an activity would be a student's reproducing a given distance/time graph by "driving" appropriately, while getting only feedback for velocity; as Kaput (1992, p. 540) points out, such a student would be "enacting" the fundamental theorem of calculus. As an example of an even more direct connection between bodily experience and mathematical representation, Mokros & Tinker (1987) used a motion sensor interfaced with a computer that can track and represent graphically the movement of a student,

so that the student could be asked, for example, to reproduce a distance/time or speed/time graph by moving appropriately.

Our second example of a way in which cognition can be radically affected is through the creation of mental mathematical objects, to which mental operations can then be applied. One of the "powerful ideas" in LOGO is that procedures defined by the individual can be added to the language and can then become objects of reflection, debugging, or enhancement, and can be hierarchically combined. The facility to record and edit procedures is likewise a powerful feature of the Geometric Supposers and their successors. Such procedure-capturing systems "in a sense, . . . map temporal events onto space and freeze them so that they can be inspected and perhaps manipulated" (Kaput, 1992, p. 543). By way of a rather different example, in MathCars the history of speed variation, as reflected over time by a sliding vertical analog speedometer, can be objectified as a graph in a very direct way (Figure 16–7).

Continuing progress needs to be underpinned by stronger theoretical foundations. This is not an easy undertaking, given the pace of change and the creativity of software designers. The task is magnified insofar as it involves reconstructing theories of representation, symbol use, imagery, and other aspects of cognition to take account of the changing landscape sketched above.

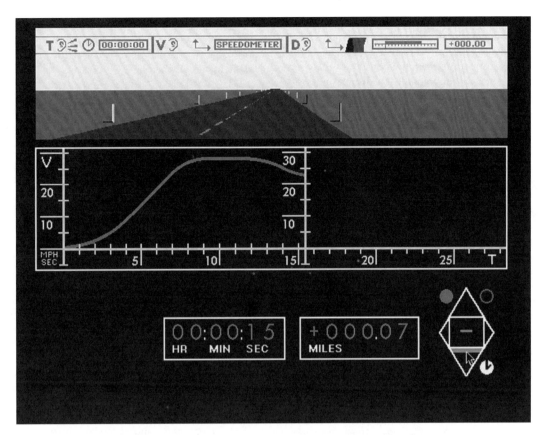

FIGURE 16–7. Example of a Screen Display from MathCars
Source: From "Technology and Mathematics Education" by J. J. Kaput, 1992, in D. A. Grouws (Ed.), *Handbook of Research on Mathematics Teaching and Learning* (pp. 515–556), New York: Macmillan. Reprinted by permission.

***Toward Effective Implementation.*** Concurrently with empirical and theoretical efforts, effective implementation depends on embedding computer use within instructional environments. According to De Corte (1994), there has been a tendency to see the introduction of computers as an add-on enhancement of learning, leaving other aspects unchanged. The contrary point of view, as put by Salomon (1992, p. 251), is that "with its proper introduction *everything* in the classroom, possibly in the school as a whole, changes." A methodological point that arises in this context was made by Papert (1985) and also by Salomon (1990). The standard experimental design whereby the effect of computers is considered as a single isolable variable—either computer use is included or it is not—is invalid if one accepts that the introduction of computers entails changes in the whole system. Accordingly, Salomon advocates the use of "systemic" methodologies to complement the analytic approach that evaluates variables in isolation.

Beyond the carefully planned integration of computer-based work into curricula (Olive, 1993), it is essential to consider how the computer as a resource for the reorganization of cognitive activity implies a radical reappraisal and redesign of the curriculum itself. For example, software such as MathCars raises fundamental questions about the positioning of, and relationship between, algebra and calculus in the curriculum.

Far from computers being able to replace teachers in any

sense, the teacher is crucial in mediating children's interactions with software. For example, on the basis of their project investigating the implementation of LOGO in classrooms, Hoyles and Sutherland (1989) concluded that "the teacher is the pivotal mediator of the technicalities of the language, the mathematics embedded in the computer activity, the problem-solving processes and the connections between LOGO and paper and pencil work." Olive (1993) expressed the belief that

a technology-driven reform effort will have little effect on the classroom curriculum until teachers are given the opportunities, support and training to take charge of the technology and use it to transform their own teaching environments.

The fundamental nature of such a transformation can be illustrated by reference to Lampert's (1988) study of the effect of introducing the Geometric Supposer. After a study in which teachers in a number of classrooms began to work with the Geometric Supposer, Lampert (1988) reported that the program "has the potential to change the way teachers think about what it means to know geometry, to affect what they believe about how that knowledge can be acquired in classrooms, and to change their teaching practice."

A further group of issues relates to the effect of computers on social interaction and classroom culture. Work with LOGO has been the focus of a growing body of research on cooperative learning and social interaction in computer environments (e.g., Hoyles, Healy, & Pozzi, 1992; Mevarech & Kramarski, 1992). Concurrent with the shift away from the concept of the computer as a tutor, there has been a shift toward computers as components of cooperative learning environments (Mevarech & Light, 1992). Although a combination of Vygotskian and Piagetian perspectives offers a starting point for general theoretical frameworks, there is a clear need for more focused theories that would take into account domain specificity and specific learning objectives (Mandl & Renkl, 1992). Communication between children and teachers on a wider scale, through the networking of schools, is another increasingly important means of enhancing collaborative learning (e.g., Newman, 1992, 1993).

On the broadest scale, strategies of innovation are needed to overcome the inertia of old habits, institutional structures, and the practices of education (Kilpatrick & Davis, 1993). Indeed, Kilpatrick and Davis cite the conclusion of Walker (1986) that "the impact of computers on schools will depend more on the difficulties of institutional change than on any other set of factors" (p. 23).

## Reassessing Assessment

In the course of recent reformulations of the goals of mathematics education, it has become increasingly recognized that enrichment of assessment methods is an essential component of attempts to fashion more effective teaching–learning environments (Lesh & Lamon, 1992b; Niss, 1993a, 1993b; Romberg, 1992b, 1995; Silver, 1993; Stephens & Izard, 1992).

In reassessing assessment, it is necessary to keep in mind divergent aims and conflicting interests. Webb (1992, p. 663) enumerated the purposes of assessment as follows:

1. To provide evidence for teachers on what students know and can do
2. To convey to students what it is important to know, do, and believe
3. To inform decision-making within educational systems
4. To monitor performance of the educational system as a whole

We can make a distinction between *student assessment* (yielding information on the mathematical understanding of individual students that will help to guide further instruction) and *evaluation* (judgment of the performance of students, schools, instructional programs, and educational systems); both are important for the development and implementation of effective teaching–learning environments.

According to Clarke (1993b, p. 1), there is a coherent international "assessment agenda," the key elements of which include:

- the replacement of "measurement" by "portrayal" as the underlying metaphor for the purpose of assessment
- the reconciliation of assessment and instruction through the deliberate use of tasks that legitimately serve both purposes and through the requirement that assessment both mirror and constructively inform educational practice
- the development of a new language of assessment by which the goals, practices, products, and consequences of the curric-

ulum might be rendered coherently in both instructional and assessment contexts
- the use of assessment as a catalyst for systemic reform in mathematics education

*The Need for Change.* Romberg, Zarinnia, and Collis (1990, p. 24) referred to the "old world framework" within which assessment has been embedded for many years. Often tests have been constructed by combining classification of content with classification of behaviors, resulting in content-by-behavior matrix schemes. Behaviorism contributed a conception of learning "through the mastery of simple steps, the development of learning hierarchies, explicit directions, daily lesson plans, frequent quizzes, objective testing of the smallest steps, and scope-and-sequence curricula" (Romberg et al., 1990, p. 26). Behaviorist principles thereby served an engineering approach to educational management, epitomized in Bloom's (1956) taxonomy of educational objectives.

Over many years, mathematics educators reacted against standardized methods for the assessment of mathematics and the limited conception of the nature of mathematics education on which they were based; a particularly powerful critique was sustained by Freudenthal (1978).

The consequences of relying on multiple-choice and other forms of standardized tests that primarily assess recall of facts, computation, and standard procedures have been extensively described (e.g., Silver & Kenney, 1995). Such tests can be used to rank students and compare the performance of schools. They cannot yield useful information on problem solving, modeling of complex situations, ability to communicate mathematical ideas, and other higher-order components of mathematical activity. Nor can they provide the detailed diagnostic feedback for the teacher appropriate to the view of the learner as an individual constructor of knowledge. A major concern is the influence that assessment has on the implemented curriculum, dubbed the WYTIWYG (What You Test Is What You Get) principle (Bell, Burkhardt, & Swan, 1992b). As indicated in Webb's (1992) list of purposes of assessment, given above, conceptually limited forms of testing convey an implicit message to students and teachers that only low-level skills are valued in mathematics education.

The concern of mathematics educators to devise forms of assessment more compatible with an enhanced vision of mathematics education has stimulated developments in psychometrics. In the wake of the cognitive revolution there has been increasing recognition of the need for new forms of assessment underpinned by appropriate theoretical frameworks and methodological innovations to reflect radical changes in theories of cognition (Collins, 1990; N. Frederiksen, Mislevy, & Bejar, 1993; Glaser, 1990; Snow, 1990; Snow & Mandinach, 1991).

However, the effects of these radical shifts have been slow to filter through to testing practices in schools and into the consciousness of teachers and others involved in education. With regard to tests constructed by teachers, Silver and Kenney (1995) summed up several surveys as showing that in such tests "the vast preponderance of questions requires low-level knowledge and performance on the part of the students." Romberg, Wilson, Khaketla, and Chavarria (1992) analyzed six commonly used standardized tests and concluded that they failed to assess aspects of mathematical activity stressed in the *Curric-*

ulum and Evaluation Standards for School Mathematics (National Council of Teachers of Mathematics, 1989). By way of contrast, Romberg, Wilson, Khaketla, and Chavarria then cited examples from other tests that were capable of assessing higher-order competencies; similar illustrative examples are provided in the following section.

***Enriched Forms of Assessment.*** Several major projects are under way throughout the world (Niss, 1993a) to develop and implement forms of performance assessment based on sampling of students' mathematical work, compatible with an enriched conception of mathematics education. Examples include the Balanced Assessment Project and the New Standards Project (L. B. Resnick, Briars, & Lesgold, 1992). Assessment is integrated within the QUASAR curriculum project (Silver & Lane, 1993). The National Center for Research in Mathematical Sciences Education in Madison, Wisconsin, has coordinated several projects. Important European centers include the Shell Centre for Mathematical Education in Nottingham, England (a partner in the Balanced Assessment Project), and the Freudenthal Institute in Utrecht, The Netherlands, which has links with Madison and other U.S. centers (e.g., De Lange, van Reeuwijk, Burrill, & Romberg, 1993). The National Council of Teachers of Mathematics (1995) has produced *Assessment Standards for School Mathematics* to complement its earlier standards documents (National Council of Teachers of Mathematics, 1989, 1991).

In reviewing alternative forms of testing, we use four broad categories: enhanced written tests, assessment of students' work, teacher–student interactions, and assessment of mathematical disposition (for similar surveys, see De Lange, 1995; Silver & Kenney, 1995).

Removing the multiple-choice format straightjacket allows open-endedness even within short items testing relatively low-level skills. A further enhancement is the opportunity to ask for judgments and justifications (Figure 16–8). A more elaborate item is shown in Figure 16–9. Such items are designed to elicit many higher-order skills and, in particular, often place heavy emphasis on communication of mathematical ideas.

A radically different form of paper that has been used in advanced level examinations in the United Kingdom (Little, 1993) is the comprehension paper, in which candidates study authentic mathematical papers and answer questions testing comprehension of the mathematics and asking for development of the ideas involved.

Moving on to the second category, there has been a major shift of emphasis toward assessing the work that students do outside of formal, timed tests. In the United States, much attention has recently been given to the compilation of portfolios of students' work (Mumme, 1990; Vermont Department of Education, 1991). Although such an approach can be justified on account of the many educational payoffs it offers, De Lange (1995) suggests that more structured, reliable, and direct alternatives are preferable for strictly assessment purposes. Silver and Kenney (1995) focus on the usefulness of portfolios as a source of information for instructional guidance, for example by documenting the growth of concepts over time, and as a component in self-assessment.

Students' work may be assessed through extended tasks lasting many hours, often spread over several weeks. The range of such tasks include investigations in pure mathematics, exercises in mathematical modeling, statistical investigations, and

The chart below shows the cost for different bus fares.

---
**BUSY BUS COMPANY FARES**

| | |
|---|---|
| One Way | $1.00 |
| Weekly Pass | $9.00 |
---

Yvonne is trying to decide whether she should buy a weekly bus pass. On Monday, Wednesday, and Friday she rides the bus to and from work. On Tuesday and Thursday she rides the bus to work, but gets a ride home with her friends.

Should Yvonne buy a weekly bus pass?_____

Explain your answer.

FIGURE 16–8. Example of an Assessment Item from the QUASAR Project
The student has to make and justify a judgment based on information extracted from the table and the text. Assessment is based on the justification for the answer as well as correct interpretation and compution.
Source: From "Assessment in the Context of Mathematics Instruction Reform: The Design of Assessment in the QUASAR Project" by E. A. Silver and S. Lane, in M. Niss (Ed.), *Cases of Assessment in Mathematics Education: An ICMI Study* (pp. 59–69), Dordrecht, The Netherlands: Kluwer. Reprinted by permission.

design/construction tasks. Examples include the modules developed for the Numeracy Through Problem Solving project in England (Bell, Burkhardt, & Swan, 1992a), such as "Be a Paper Engineer," in which students design, make, and evaluate three-dimensional paper products, and "Be a Shrewd Chooser," in which students research and provide expert consumer advice for fellow students. An example from the Mathematics Framework for California Public Schools is shown in Figure 16–10. Another illustrative example is the Aquarium Problem, in which students provided with appropriate (and authentic) information are asked to make a plan to stock a class aquarium (L. B. Resnick et al., 1992). Many of these tasks are "authentic mathematical activities" in the sense of Lesh and Lamon (1992a): they "are not just surrogates for activities that are important in 'real life' situations, they directly involve actual 'work samples' taken from a representative sample of activities that are meaningful and important in their own rights."

Another form of extended task, particularly developed at the Freudenthal Institute, is termed a "production task" (De Lange, 1995; Streefland, 1990). Such tasks are characterized by open-endedness, as in this example:

Think out as many sums as you can with the result 3.

An especially interesting variant is when students are asked to write tests or teaching materials for other students at varying levels; an example with a ninth-grade U.S. class is discussed by De Lange (1995).

The third category to be considered is the variety of methods depending on student–teacher interactions. Ginsburg has extensively analyzed and developed the use of clinical interviews, as pioneered by Piaget, in mathematics (Ginsburg et al., 1983).

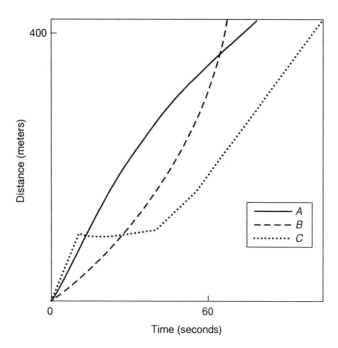

The rough sketch graph shown above describes what happens when three athletes, A, B, and C, enter a 400-meter hurdles race.

Imagine that you are the race commentator. Describe what is happening as carefully as you can. You do not need to measure anything accurately.

FIGURE 16–9. Assessment Item Developed by the Shell Centre for Mathematical Education, Nottingham
A detailed scoring rubric assigns marks for identification of key incidents in the race as indicated by features of the graph, such as runner C stopping after about 10 seconds, probably because of hitting a hurdle.
*Source*: From "Balanced Assessment of Mathematical Reform" by A. Bell, H. Burkhardt, and M. Swan, 1992, in R. Lesh and J. Lamon (Eds.), *Assessments of Authentic Performance in School Mathematics* (pp. 119–144), Washington, DC: American Association for the Advancement of Science. Reprinted by permission.

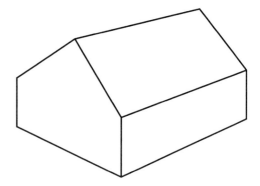

Build a house with paper and tape having about the same shape as the house drawn above, but not necessarily the same size.

Build two more houses, each similar to your first house. That is, make them exactly the same shape—but different sizes.

Prepare a report describing how you made your houses "similar." What can you say, in general, about the relationships among the dimensions, areas, and volumes of similar houses? Glue the three houses to a piece of paper and turn them in with your written report.

Your report will be graded according to these questions:

• How well did you explore the relationships among the three houses? How well did you formulate your generalizations?

• How do we know your houses are similar? Was your approach to making the houses similar a sound one?

• How well did you present your thinking? Are your ideas understandable to the reader? Did you use mathematical representations such as graphs, formulae, diagrams, and tables effectively?

• Are your measurements and calculations appropriate and correct?

FIGURE 16–10. Assessment Item from the California Assessment Project
*Source*: From *Mathematics Framework for California Public Schools* (Preview edition) by California Board of Education, 1991, Sacramento: California State Department of Education. Reprinted by permission.

The use of such methods in assessment of mathematics follows from his stated principles that instruction and assessment are inseparable and that the core of education is the fostering of thinking (Ginsburg, Jacobs, & Lopez, 1993).

In The Netherlands, oral examinations have a long tradition and oral tasks are still extensively used in several different forms (De Lange, 1995). De Lange reports that a survey in Dutch schools during the 1980s showed that oral tasks were primarily used to evaluate students' understanding of processes. Another type of oral task used is when the student prepares a presentation about a subject to be discussed with the teacher. Oral assessment has also been used in the School Mathematics Project in England (Little, 1993).

In the United Kingdom, national monitoring surveys were carried out during the period 1978–1987 by the National Foundation for Educational Research on behalf of the Assessment of Performance Unit (APU) (Foxman, 1993). A particularly innovative aspect of these surveys was the inclusion of practical tests administered by trained testers. These included one-

to-one sessions in which the emphasis was largely but not entirely on working with materials; assessors worked from a script that allowed considerable flexibility. In the 1987 surveys, sessions with groups of three students working together on problem-solving tasks were also used. The problems included "everyday" tasks requiring planning, and investigations of mathematical patterns, and were designed to encourage a variety of solution methods and discussion among the students.

Finally, beyond the assessment of higher-order skills and processes lies the even more complex undertaking of assessing mathematical disposition, the importance of which was highlighted by *Curriculum and Evaluation Standards for School Mathematics* (National Council of Teachers of Mathematics, 1989). According to Webb (1992, p. 667): "If developing a positive disposition towards mathematics is a goal for instruction, then disposition . . . should be assessed."

Clarke and Wallbridge (1992) reported that the effects of a problem-based curriculum, the Interactive Mathematics Project, at three high schools in California went beyond differences in achievement. The students who participated in the project showed differences in "perceptions of the discipline of mathematics, of mathematical activity and the origins of mathematical ideas, of the mathematical nature of everyday activities, and of school mathematics and themselves as mathematicians" (p. 2). Moreover, "[they] appear to be more confident than their peers in conventional classes; to subscribe to a view of mathematics as having risen to meet the needs of society, rather than as a set of arbitrary rules; to value communication in mathematics learning more highly than students in conventional classes; and to be more likely . . . to see a mathematical element in everyday activity." At the same time these students performed on standardized tests at or above the level of students in control classes. A broadly similar study was reported by Nicholls, Cobb, Yackel, Wood, and Wheatley (1990).

These examples testify to the possibility of achieving one of the goals set in the NCTM's *Curriculum and Evaluation Standards for School Mathematics* (1989), namely, for students to gain mathematical power. Another way of furthering this objective is to develop student self-assessment (Kenney & Silver, 1993; Swan, 1993).

As the above overview indicates, there is now an extensive repertoire of modes of assessment available to the teacher. In regard to the contrasting aims of student assessment and system evaluation, the balance has shifted substantially to the former, with assessment as informative, embedded in the ongoing instructional environment, and based on sampling of mathematical performance, as opposed to evaluative, terminal, and based on indirect indicators of competence. The shift in the underlying metaphor from measurement to portrayal necessitates a new language of assessment and more complex forms of documentation of student achievement (Clarke, 1993b). Given the increase in complexity, the question of an appropriate balance must be faced. This and other problems of securing the foundations of new approaches to assessment are considered in the next two subsections.

*Theoretical and Methodological Underpinnings.* Psychometricians, in collaboration with cognitive psychologists, have begun a major program of constructing "test theory for a new generation of tests" (N. Frederiksen, Mislevy, & Bejar, 1993). At the same time, the psychometric characteristics of the innovative assessment methods being introduced into mathematics education need to be considered. In this section we consider these parallel lines of development.

A first general theme that emerges very clearly from commentaries on developments in psychometrics is the need for integration of psychometric theory with current theories of cognitive psychology. New forms of tests are being developed that allow the assessment of qualitatively different levels of understanding (De Corte, 1992), reflecting post-Piagetian models of cognitive development. By way of example, we outline here an approach suggested by Mislevy and his colleagues (Masters & Mislevy, 1991; Mislevy, Yamamoto, & Anacker, 1991). Their starting point is the recognition that assessment needs to reflect the shift from the view of the learner as a passive absorber of knowledge to the view of the learner as an active constructor of meanings, representations, models, strategies, and misconceptions. Accordingly, it is necessary to build cognitive models of key conceptual subfields within the target domain, within which qualitatively different forms of understanding are defined. Classes of responses that interactively have diagnostic value for differentiating these forms of understanding must be constructed and combined with appropriate statistical models. The process is analogous to medical diagnosis, in which patterns of symptoms (syndromes) are linked to diseases through a network of connections derived from medical theory, which may be statistically modeled. Various technical advances contributing to this approach are summarized by Masters and Mislevy (1991) and by Mislevy et al. (1991).

One advantage of a shift to describing mental processes qualitatively is that any output will be information rich in potential for informing future decision-making and guiding future learning and teaching. Another is that the implementation of assessment methods based on cognitive modeling will provide useful information to feed back into theory construction. However, apart from the fact that no implementation of the approach has yet been developed, a very major limitation, as acknowledged by Mislevy et al. (1991, p. 7), is that "what is lacking from the point of view of the educator is the fact that meaningful real world tasks are rarely segregated into these neat little sets."

A second major theme, totally consistent with the views of mathematics educators (e.g., Clarke, 1993b), is the need for assessment to be integrated with teaching (Nitko, 1989). Stated bluntly by Snow and Mandanich (1991, p. 1): "If assessment and instruction can be integrated, education will improve." This implies a shift of emphasis from assessment as providing terminal measures of performance to assessment as providing diagnostic information to the teacher as part of the ongoing stream of education. However, Snow and Mandinach (1991, p. 1) commented that "coordinated theories of learning progress and of diagnostic assessment for adaptive teaching in an instructional domain" are not available at present. They suggest that assessment might be more closely tied to theories of cognitive development. One such approach is the development of "learning potential tests," with an obvious influence from the Vygotskian notion of a zone of proximal development (A. L. Brown & Ferrara, 1985; Hamers, Sijtsma, & Ruijssenaars, 1993). For example, Campione and Brown (1990) have devised a tutoring procedure for diagnosing and promoting mathematical reasoning that yields a learning efficiency score based on the level of hints required to solve problems, and a transfer propensity score derived from performance on transfer tasks varying on the near–far dimension.

Despite these developments, Snow and Lohman (1989, p. 320) admitted that "cognitive psychology has no ready answers for the educational measurement problems of yesterday, today, or tomorrow." Models of assessment, as exemplified by the approach of Mislevy described above, are often applicable only to selected aspects of the mathematics curriculum, and accordingly do not promise, at least in the foreseeable future, a practical solution to the ongoing task of across-the-board assessment. Moreover, the cognitive psychology invoked in this work is predominantly that of the first wave of the cognitive revolution as identified in an earlier section, with little reflection of the second wave.

The other side of the coin is that as innovations in assessment continue, they should be evaluated against appropriate criteria. According to Linn, Baker, and Dunbar (1991, p. 16): "With disparate and influential support for alternatives to large-scale assessments as they are presently conceived and implemented, it is not premature to pose questions about the standards of quality that alternative assessments ought to satisfy." Mehrens (1992) commented that attention has predominantly been given to the advantages of performance assessment for individual diagnosis, with little consideration of the implications for accountability purposes (see also Frechtling, 1991).

Tests that produce open-ended responses introduce judgment into the rating of those responses, inevitably making reliability an issue. For example, the scoring rubric for the investigation shown in Figure 16–10 (California Board of Education, 1991, p. 25) is based on four levels of performance, such as the following (the second highest):

Acceptable. Your report does what it needs to do. It includes an adequate description of your method, learning, and conclusions. This report may be less orderly than a *well done* report, or the relationship between surface area and volume may be less well explained, but you have done the correct mathematics with sufficient accuracy. Yet it is not as clear in its thinking, in the ideas you explored, or in its use of charts, graphs, or models—as a *well done* report.

Likewise, a scoring scheme for the task shown in Figure 16–9 is given by Bell et al. (1992b), and the scoring of the Aquarium Task from the New Standards Project (L. B. Resnick et al., 1992) has received considerable attention. Further, the training of raters to interpret such schemes obviously becomes critical (Kenney & Tang, 1992). A further issue is that of generalizability (Mehrens, 1992): If a small number of performance tasks are used, is it possible to generalize to a domain from such a limited sample? Various concerns were summarized by Clarke (1993a), who juxtaposed a list of eight reasons why open-ended tasks should be used for assessment purposes with a list of ten reasons why they should not. The debate needs to be informed by more research such as that reported by Clarke and Sullivan (1992).

Beyond the question of traditional psychometric criteria, there is the need to extend such criteria (Linn et al., 1991). A very clear example is the concept of validity, which has evolved and broadened very considerably during its long history (Messick, 1989; Shepard, 1993). In particular, there has been a major shift from the restricted notion of validity as defined by consistency with other measures, and the search for indirect indicators which show this consistency statistically, to the view of validity as construct validity and the direct sampling of the target capabilities. Moreover, a much broader concept of validity relates it to relevance and utility, values, and social consequences, as detailed in Messick (1989) and elaborated in Shepard (1993). Consistent with this view is the notion of "systemic validity" introduced by J. R. Frederiksen and Collins (1989):

A systemically valid test . . . is one that induces in the education system curricular and instructional changes that foster the development of the cognitive traits that the test is designed to measure. . . . Evidence for systematic validity would be an improvement in those traits after the test had been in place within the educational system for a period of time.

In other words, the WYTIWYG effect, referred to earlier, could be positive rather than negative (see also Clarke, 1993b).

***Problems of Implementation: Balancing Vision with Practicality.***   In addition to the technical aspects outlined in the previous section, there are many practical problems of implementation of new assessment methods (Bell, Burkhardt, & Swan, 1992c). As De Lange (1995) puts it, there is no change without problems.

Snow (1990) issued a plea for research on teacher understanding and use of assessment, on the grounds that no improvements are possible without such research. The importance of teachers' cognitions and beliefs was discussed in an earlier section, and it has already been pointed out that teachers tend to construct tests that measure predominantly low-level aspects. Thus, teachers need to be dislodged from the "old world framework" described by Romberg et al. (1990). Silver and Kilpatrick (1988, p. 185) have further argued that

[w]hat is needed are serious efforts to re-skill teachers, to provide them with not only the tools such as sample problems and scoring procedures that they can use to construct their own assessment instruments but also with the confidence that they so often lack in their own ability to determine what and how their students are doing in solving mathematical problems.

Performance assessment tasks are substantially more demanding for teachers, as are recommendations that teachers become diagnostic experts, orchestrators of classroom discussions, and compilers of student portfolios, for example. To produce a cohort of teachers with these changed conceptions and enhanced skills implies a major support operation.

Testing is a political issue, as it has been for centuries (Kilpatrick, 1993). Today, as Silver (1993) commented, "the world of educational assessment, especially standardized testing, [is] one of the major battle grounds for educational reform." National prestige (fueled by international comparisons) and the perceived need to raise standards are involved to an unprecedented extent. There is a dangerous gap between the perspectives of mathematics educators and those of political decision-makers. As Romberg (1992a, p. 35) points out, governmental policies tend to be based on "the scientific-experimental notions of the past: behavioral objectives, norm-referenced scores, Bloom's *Taxonomy*." Perhaps the enlightenment of political decision-makers, and other groups such as parents, administrators, and the public in general (De Lange, 1995), is the biggest educational challenge facing reformers.

## CONCLUSIONS AND PERSPECTIVES

### Mathematics Education: A Maturing and Innovating Field of Research

In this chapter, we have presented our view of the current state of the field. Given the vast body of work to be reviewed, we have of necessity been selective, and inevitably a number of topics have been relatively underemphasized, including theories of cognitive development, aspects of abstract mathematics such as proof, and the relationship between mathematics and language. We also have not attempted to review in detail research studies in the various subdomains of mathematics, for which comprehensive coverage is available in Grouws (1992) and Bishop (in press).

At the outset, we stated that a major message of the chapter is that substantial progress has been made toward integrating the two disciplines of research on teaching and learning mathematics (Romberg & Carpenter, 1986). The preceding sections show a clear trend toward linking available knowledge on mathematical learning, thinking, and problem solving to new conceptions of teaching and assessment. Ongoing research efforts, on a worldwide scale, have been aimed at the design of more powerful instructional environments, at the effective application and integration of computers and other media within those environments, and at the development of new forms of assessment. This research effort has been paralleled and to some degree driven by changing conceptions of mathematics and mathematical cognition, resulting in a rethinking and enlarging of the goal of mathematics education as the acquisition of a mathematical disposition.

An important factor contributing to all of these developments has been the increasing collaboration and interaction between scholars from numerous disciplinary backgrounds who share a common interest in mathematics education (Balacheff, 1990; Kilpatrick, 1992; Sierpinska et al., 1993; Vergnaud, 1982). As a result, research on mathematics learning and teaching has emerged as a field of study at the crossroads of a variety of established and relevant disciplines; as such, it is arguably the prime example of the growing domain-specific orientation in instructional psychology. Radical reformulation of the goal of mathematics education as the acquisition of a mathematical disposition has been accompanied by a shift to a conception of mathematics learning as a contextualized, and collaborative, process of knowledge and meaning construction. A correspondingly broader view of mathematical cognition is emerging in which the emphasis has shifted from the conception of cognition as being situated within individual minds to a view of cognition as socially shared and culturally situated.

Notwithstanding these evolving fundamental and positive developments, substantial theoretical and methodological issues for continued study remain to be addressed for the further elaboration of mathematics education as a field of research and inquiry (Balacheff, 1990; Sierpinska et al., 1993).

## Theoretical Issues

The following list of topics for further study is not intended to provide an exhaustive research agenda but to identify some of the most important theoretical issues researchers will face in the coming years.

*Needed: A More Elaborated Constructivist Theory of Learning and Instruction.* There is now substantial evidence for the constructive nature of mathematics learning. Accordingly, we have endorsed the view that learning is an active and constructive process. Moreover, the constructivist philosophy has helped to motivate a marked shift in research efforts toward the design and evaluation of the kind of more powerful teaching–learning environments described in a previous section.

Nevertheless, as argued by Fischbein (1990a, p. 12), there is an obvious need for "a more specific definition of constructivism as a psychological model for mathematical education" (see also Greer, in press). Indeed, the success stories we have described call for additional theoretical and empirical research aimed at a much deeper understanding and fine-grained analysis of the acquisition processes that such kinds of learning environments elicit in students, and of the precise nature of the knowledge, strategies, and beliefs they acquire thereby. These issues are well summarized in Schoenfeld's (1992c) review of *Radical Constructivism in Mathematics Education,* edited by von Glasersfeld (1991).

The trend toward social constructivism represents a rapprochement between an earlier constructivist emphasis on the individual as the constructor of knowledge (for which Piaget has been a major inspiration) and the more recent emphasis on the socially and culturally situatedness of knowledge construction (with the corresponding influence of Vygotsky). An important factor in this development has been the challenge of applying constructivist theories in the context of classroom instruction (e.g., Bauersfeld, 1995; Cobb, 1994b; Cobb & Bauersfeld, 1995; Cobb, Wood, & Yackel, 1991).

*Clarifying the Theoretical Concept of Representation.* With the general acceptance of constructivism (of whatever variety) has come a view of mental processes as much more complex and individualistic than is implied by a transmission-of-knowledge view of learning or an information-processing view of thinking (Cobb, 1990). Recognition of the limitations of formal modes of thought and of the importance of such aspects as intuition, imagery, bodily based experience, metacognition, and affect have considerably widened our conception of what constitutes cognitive activity. This wider conception is embodied, for example, in Goldin's (1992b) model for systems of internal representations (Figure 16–2).

In this chapter, we have elected to use the term "representations" to refer to internal processes as well as external embodiments in order to discuss mathematical thinking and problem solving. This usage is problematic for many constructivists (e.g., Cobb, Yackel, & Wood, 1992; Mason, 1987; von Glasersfeld, 1987), but irrespective of these terminological disagreements, it is clear that much more detailed analysis is required of the development and use of symbol systems and physical artifacts in mathematics, of the mental processes involved in doing mathematics, of the complex interplay between the internal and the external, and of the interaction between individual and distributed cognition (Salomon, 1993a). This is particularly the case when we consider the potential for enhancing and transforming mathematical cognition made possible by technological advances (Dörfler, 1993; Kaput, 1992).

The notion of representation has also come under fire from a very different direction, namely, connectionist models of learning and information processing that propose that knowledge and mental operations are distributed across neural networks. As yet, the forms of information-processing modeled by such approaches have been predominantly low level. As Holyoak (1991) has commented, there are as yet no serious connectionist models of expertise in domains involving high-level cognition. A potentially interesting development, from the perspective of expert performance in mathematics, is the hybridization of traditional artificial intelligence approaches based on symbolic representation with connectionist approaches (Holyoak, 1991).

### Acquiring a Mathematical Disposition: An Attainable Goal?

Is it realistic to expect that the construction of effective instructional environments can result in the acquisition of a mathematical disposition by the majority of students (Steen, 1992)? Further, does it make sense to talk of *a* desirable disposition, given the variation in abilities, needs, and goals of students? Are the characteristics of this disposition the same for a student who will become a mathematician, one who will apply mathematics in another subject, and one who will become a responsible citizen with no specific technical needs for mathematics (Kilpatrick & Davis, 1993)?

From our understanding of expertise, we can infer that the acquisition of an appropriate mathematical disposition requires a large amount of experience and sustained effort over a long period of time. Continued intervention research is needed to clarify under what conditions an intended disposition can be nurtured. Such research should aim at a fine-grained description to provide better understanding of what goes on in powerful environments such as those described earlier in this chapter.

### Questioning Apprenticeship as THE Model for Mathematics Education.

As illustrated in this chapter, innovative learning environments are often convergent with, or modeled on, the cognitive apprenticeship view of learning, which derives from the situated cognition perspective. However, the question arises as to whether mathematics education in our schools can easily be transformed into apprenticeship-like environments. Indeed, such environments would require a radical change of traditional classroom practices. Apart from the fact that such a pendulum swing would necessitate profound changes in preservice and in-service teacher training, some caution is in order, for "pendulums make poor compasses" (Elshout, 1992). Apprenticeship-like environments mainly result from activity in product- or profit-oriented real-life settings (De Corte, 1992; Palincsar, 1989), whereas schools for general education have been deliberately created as self-contained and somewhat artificial settings that are not directly product-oriented and do not serve purposes of immediate utility. Moreover, they often aim at the learning and teaching of (mathematical) knowledge and skills that are not easily encountered or exemplified in everyday life, the more so as one proceeds to higher levels in the educational system. Certain mathematical topics that have to be taught do not lend themselves easily to a realistic or an apprenticeship-like approach. In short, although mathematics instruction can certainly benefit from the basic ideas and the specific methods of apprenticeship, it is questionable whether this model represents an educational panacea for the design of powerful learning environments.

In fact, certain activities that seem to be highly motivating for children and elicit high levels of involvement, such as programming in LOGO, are not necessarily apprenticeship-like. On the other hand, there is recent evidence from research in cultural psychology showing that under certain conditions the apprenticeship model elicits acquisition processes that are at odds with the constructivist view of learning, in the sense that they merely lead to learning outcomes that reflect reproduction and preservation of the status quo. In a well-controlled historical behavioral study of the learning and teaching of weaving in a Mayan people in Mexico, Greenfield (1993) observed that the apprenticeship approach that was common in 1970 resulted in the intergenerational replication of tradition, namely, a very limited and stable repertoire of woven patterns. However, 20 years later, as a consequence of economic and societal changes, apprenticeship had been replaced by a more independent trial-and-error type of learning, allowing for discovery and exploration by the learner and resulting in a large variety of innovative figurative and geometric patterns.

Taking all this into account, one might consider alternatives such as the hobbyist model as at least a complementary metaphor to apprenticeship. This metaphor preserves major features of apprenticeship, such as meaningful, task-oriented activity through legitimate peripheral participation (Lave & Wenger, 1991), the use of informal prior knowledge, and the significance of social interaction and cooperation. However, it differs from apprenticeship by its recreational character, its tolerance for trial-and-error activity, its acceptance of less authentic contexts, and its lower threshold with respect to expertise. Accordingly, transforming mathematics education into hobbyist-like environments may be worthy of consideration as one of the perspectives that can complement the apprenticeship metaphor.

### Situated Cognition and Transfer of Mathematical Knowledge.

Emphasis on the situated character of learning and cognition has led correlatively to deemphasizing the importance and even the possibility of transfer of knowledge. Yet it is characteristic of mathematicians that they can perceive and exploit structural parallels underlying situations with very different surface characteristics (Greer, in press). In the future, theoretical analysis and empirical research should be aimed at a more balanced view of transfer, taking into account the contrast between the specificity of everyday cognition and the generality of mathematical abstraction. Hatano and Inagaki (1992) argued that acquiring expertise is a process of decontextualizing or "desituating" knowledge; as a result, knowledge becomes less context bound and can be applied over a wider range of situations and problems. In a more elaborated analysis, Kang and Kilpatrick (1992, p. 6) proposed that "knowledge is depersonalized and decontextualized when represented for communication, personalized and contextualized when first encountered, depersonalized and decontextualized again as it becomes part of the learner's codified knowledge."

Investigating the conditions under which transfer of knowledge and skills can be achieved is in accordance with the dispositional view elaborated in this chapter. Major aspects of this disposition are that students should develop the ability to recognize opportunities to use their knowledge, and should become inclined to do so whenever appropriate. Future research to unravel the processes underlying desituating and transfer of knowledge could take into account the perspective on transfer in terms of situated cognition proposed by Greeno, Smith, and Moore (1992).

### Cultural Embeddedness and Mathematics Learning in School.

A substantial amount of research reviewed briefly in this chapter has documented the cultural embeddedness of mathematical activity and cognition. Although there is no doubt that these findings are interesting in their own right, their significance and relevance for the future of learning and teaching in mathematics classrooms are far from clear. In this regard, a cautionary note is in order. One has to be rather skeptical about the variety of informal contexts of mathematical practice as a panacea for the problems of current school mathematics, simply because of the fundamentally different nature of the goals of mathematics learning in and out of school, namely, more abstract versus situated. Taking into account the available theoretical analysis and empirical evidence, it is a mistake to believe that simply by working with a great diversity of pragmatic or realistic problems students will by themselves be able to make the transition from informal, context-bound mathematics to formal, abstract mathematics. Although informal and context-bound mathematical activity is extremely important during the initial stages of a teaching–learning process, it constitutes only the starting point from which pupils and students can reflectively abstract, and thereby make the transition to more formal mathematical activity. In this process of progressive schematization, abbreviation, internalization, and generalization of informal and context-bound mathematics, a crucial role is played by carefully chosen problems, models, schemes, and instructional activities that stimulate students to reflect on their mathematical thinking; the contexts should help the students develop richly interconnected mathematics, and the mathematics should provide insight into the contexts. This basic principle is exemplified in all of the illustrations of powerful learning environments presented in this chapter, but especially in the RME approach of the Freudenthal Institute (e.g., Treffers, 1987, 1991a; see also Nunes et al., 1993).

Taking into account the teacher as the third element in the ternary relationship that constitutes education, Chevallard's (1985) theory of didactic transposition is pertinent. Chevallard asserted that bodies of knowledge develop mostly to be used rather than to be taught; didactic transposition is the transposition from knowledge as a tool to be used to knowledge as something to be taught and learned (Kang & Kilpatrick, 1992).

These comments imply the necessity of complementing research on practical, situated mathematics with work focusing on the psychology of abstract, advanced mathematical learning and thinking (Tall, 1991). Our treatment in this chapter reflects the view that many of the recent developments summarized may be subsumed under the general theme that mathematics is a human activity, situated in historical, cultural, and social contexts and influenced by human problems and goals; however, it should not be forgotten that intellectual activity is also part of being human. We may therefore echo the remark made by P. W. Thompson (1993, p. 283), in reviewing Tall's (1991) book, that he considers it "imperative that the mathematics education community regain the sense that mathematics is a deep and abstract intellectual achievement" (and see Greer, in press).

***Rethinking Assessment as an Integral Part of Instruction.*** A number of parallel developments have contributed to the sea change (Shepard, 1993, p. 444) currently taking place in psychological and educational testing. In the psychometric community, the need to devise new approaches and techniques compatible with contemporary cognitive, developmental, and educational theories has been accepted. The development of methods for assessing qualitatively distinct levels of understanding, for iden-

tifying differences in problem-solving strategies, and for assessing learning potential in line with the Vygotskian notion of a zone of proximal development represent some of the responses to this challenge. The need to integrate assessment with instruction and the importance of assessment yielding information to guide further instruction have been emphasized (Snow & Mandinach, 1991), in line with Clarke's (1993b) suggestion that the underlying metaphor has shifted from measurement to portrayal.

These developments have occurred partly in response to criticisms from within mathematics education of the pejorative effects of traditional assessment methods (e.g., Romberg, Wilson, Khaketla, & Chavarria, 1992; Silver, 1993), together with pressure to introduce performance-based modes of assessment compatible with a richer vision of mathematics education. There has been an upsurge of creative activity on a worldwide scale (Niss, 1993a), including major new projects that are generating many examples of innovative assessment materials and procedures and, according to Clarke (1993b), constituting a coherent "assessment agenda." However, in the course of this activity, enthusiasm has outstripped firm evidence for the effectiveness of the new methods (Linn et al., 1991). Accordingly, there is need for converging efforts: On the one hand, continuing refinement of psychometric theory and techniques in close collaboration with cognitive and educational psychology, and, on the other, consolidation and evaluation of innovative assessment programs as they are implemented. To enable this convergence to take place, a new language of assessment needs to be developed to reflect the radical change in conception of what is to be assessed, and why (Clarke, 1993b).

***The Problems of Change.*** At many points in the chapter we have pointed to the constraints of reality that limit the effectiveness of the most rational and carefully considered attempts to improve mathematics education. There are phenomena at the level of the classroom, such as the functioning of the mathematics classroom as a cultural setting (Nickson, 1992), that require further study. In the context of effective instructional environments, we included as an important component teacher cognitions; moreover, in discussing both the embedding of computers within instruction and the rethinking of assessment, we made it clear that support both of and from teachers is a vital element. At the level of educational systems, forces for inertia are recognized, but there are few firm principles to contribute to a theory of innovation at the system level; this is another crucial challenge for the future that psychologists and mathematics educators can scarcely ignore.

## Methodological Issues

Addressing the key research issues listed above also demands changes in the methods of research. In this respect, we endorse Fischbein's (1990a, p. 11) declaration of the necessity of elaborating "a comprehensive, systematic theory of research methodology in mathematics education." Starting from the principle that the methodology should be adapted to the specificity of the domain, Fischbein (1990a, pp. 10–11) advocated that:

Psychological research related to mathematics education must combine a large variety of research methods including classroom observation, dialogues with teachers, clinical methods, interviews, questionnaires, case studies, experimental lessons, and historical analyses. Pure statistics based on laboratory-like investigations will always yield only incomplete, superficial information.

Most of the techniques listed by Fischbein, but also some others that can be added, such as computer simulations, eye-movement registration, and ethnomethodological studies, have been used more or less extensively over the past decade. In addition, new techniques and approaches, such as microgenetic analysis and design experiments, are under development or further elaboration, as illustrated by a thematic issue of the *Journal of the Learning Sciences*, entitled *Research Methods in and for the Learning Sciences* (Schoenfeld, 1992d). There is, however, a need for continued refinement and systematization of the methods in terms of their appropriateness for fine-grained investigation of the processes involved in mathematics learning, and of the multiple interactions occurring in the complex classroom environments in which this learning takes place.

We need a much more detailed analysis of the nature, reliability, and validity of the data collected by the variety of techniques mentioned above. For example, the microgenetic method—characterized by a high density of observations of individual students over a longer period of time—has the potential to yield the kind of data that are necessary to grasp and infer changes in children's understanding and problem solving during mathematics learning (see, e.g., Saxe, Guberman, & Gearhart, 1987; Schoenfeld et al., 1993; Siegler & Crowley, 1991). Further, we need to explore how triangulation—the combined application of several research techniques in studying the same phenomena—can help us to get a more complete understanding of mathematics learning and teaching. Triangulation is also useful for the cross-validation of data gathered through different techniques (see, e.g., Schoenfeld, 1992b; Verschaffel, De Corte, Gielen, & Struyf, 1994).

It is also essential to continue to complement descriptive investigations with intervention-based research attempting to construct powerful learning environments similar to those described earlier in this chapter. Of course, the idea of intervention-based research is by no means new in educational psychology. For instance, within the Vygotskian school, teaching experiments have been the major research method for several decades (Kalmykova, 1970). However, the new conception of the goals and processes of mathematics learning and teaching, as well as newly available educational media and tools, open new perspectives for the application of intervention-based research. This is illustrated by the so-called developmental research strategy used by the Freudenthal Institute (Treffers, 1991b; see the section on designing powerful instructional environments), but also by the idea of design experiments introduced by scholars who explicitly aim at the development and methodological underpinning of a design science of (mathematics) education (A. Brown, 1992; Collins, 1992).

According to Collins (1992, p. 15), "a design science of education must determine how different designs of learning environments contribute to learning, cooperation, and motivation." As a result, a design theory should emerge that can guide the implementation of educational innovations by specifying the variables influencing their success or failure. The major strategy consists of attempts to create in real classrooms—in close cooperation with practitioners as co-investigators—complex instructional interventions that embody the characteristics of effective learning processes (see, e.g., A. Brown, 1992). In this respect, design experiments are an illustration of Salomon's (1990) systemic approach to educational research (as opposed to the traditional analytic approach that focuses on the effects of single variables).

Although this intervention research is intended to contribute to the optimization of educational practice, the primary goal is nevertheless to advance theory building. However, this orientation toward theory building requires the elaboration of an appropriate methodology for designing experiments in complex classroom settings in such a way that the empirical data allow us to draw theoretically valid conclusions concerning the critical dimensions that can account for the power of powerful learning environments (see Collins, 1992, for a number of guiding principles for the development of such a methodology). Indeed, until now most of the work reported is in line with the strategy that "if you want to understand something, try to change it." As argued earlier in this chapter, it is undeniable that some understanding has been achieved; however, so far this has been only at a rather molar level. As remarked by Palincsar (1992), the statement also holds the other way around, namely, "if you want to try to change something, understand it." Especially in view of a more widespread change of educational practice through large-scale implementation of the new approach to mathematics learning and teaching, a more molecular analysis and understanding will be required of the instructional and contextual factors that elicit the productive psychological and social processes involved in doing mathematics.

With the methodological refinement and conceptual elaboration of this integrated activity of situated research and theory building, we can look forward to further progress toward the goal set by Romberg and Carpenter (1986), namely, to bring together the constructs from cognitive research on mathematics learning and the analysis of classroom teaching, and to relate them to an enriched conception of mathematical education.

## References

Albers, D. J., & Alexanderson, G. L. (1985). *Mathematical people: Profiles and interviews*. Boston: Birkhauser.

Australian Education Council. (1990). *A national statement on mathematics for Australian schools*. Carlton, Victoria, Australia: Curriculum Corporation.

Balacheff, N. (1990). Future perspectives for research in the psychology of mathematics education. In P. Nesher & J. Kilpatrick (Eds.), *Mathematics and cognition: A research synthesis by the International Group for the Psychology of Mathematics Education* (pp. 135–148) (ICMI Study Series). Cambridge, England: Cambridge University Press.

Balfantz, R.(1988). The role of environmental knowledge in early mathematical performance. *Cultural Dynamics, 1,* 158–179.

Bauersfeld, H. (1988). Interaction, construction, and knowledge: Alternative perspectives for mathematics education. In D.A. Grouws, T. J. Cooney, & D. Jones (Eds.), *Perspectives on research on effective mathematics teaching* (pp. 27–46). Hillsdale, NJ: Lawrence Erlbaum Associates/Reston, VA: National Council of Teachers of Mathematics.

Bauersfeld, H. (1995). The structuring of structures: Development and function of mathematizing as a social practice. In L. P. Steffe & J. Gale (Eds.), *Constructivism in education* (pp. 137–158). Hillsdale, NJ: Lawrence Erlbaum Associates.

Begle, E.G. (1979). *Critical variables in mathematics education.* Washington, DC: Mathematical Association of America.

Behr, M., & Hiebert, J. (Eds.). (1988). *Number concepts and operations in the middle grades.* Hillsdale, NJ: Lawrence Erlbaum Associates.

Bell, A., Burkhardt, H., & Swan, M. (1992a). Assessment of extended tasks. In R. Lesh & S. J. Lamon (Eds.), *Assessments of authentic performance in school mathematics* (pp. 145–176). Washington, DC: American Association for the Advancement of Science.

Bell, A., Burkhardt, H., & Swan, M. (1992b). Balanced assessment of mathematical performance. In R. Lesh & S. J. Lamon (Eds.), *Assessments of authentic performance in school mathematics* (pp. 119–144).Washington DC: American Association for the Advancement of Science.

Bell, A., Burkhardt, H., & Swan, M. (1992c). Moving the system: The contributions of assessment. In R. Lesh & S. J. Lamon (Eds.), *Assessments of authentic performance in school mathematics* (pp. 177–194). Washington, DC: American Association for the Advancement of Science.

Bergeron, J. C., Herscovics, N., & Kieran, C. (Eds.). (1987). *Proceedings of the 11th International Conference for the Psychology of Mathematics Education.* Montreal, Canada: University of Montreal.

Berliner, D. C., Stein, P., Sabers, D., Clarridge, P., Cushing, K., & Pinnegar, S. (1988). Implications of research on pedagogical expertise and experience for mathematics teaching. In D. A. Grouws, T. J. Cooney, & D. Jones (Eds.), *Perspectives on research on effective mathematics teaching* (pp. 67–95). Reston, VA: National Council of Teachers of Mathematics; Hillsdale, NJ: Lawrence Erlbaum Associates.

Biehler, R. (1993). Software tools and mathematics education: The case of statistics. In C. Keitel & K. Ruthven (Eds.), *Learning from computers: Mathematics education and technology* (NATO ASI Series F, Computers and Systems Sciences, Vol. 121, pp. 68–100). Berlin: Springer.

Biggs, J. B., & Collis, K. F. (1982). *Evaluating the quality of learning: The SOLO taxonomy.* New York: Academic Press.

Bishop, A. J. (1988). The interactions of mathematics education with culture. *Cultural Dynamics, 1,* 145–157.

Bishop, A. J. (1992). International perspectives on research in mathematics education. In D. A. Grouws (Ed.), *Handbook of research on mathematics teaching and learning* (pp. 710–723). New York: Macmillan.

Bishop, A. J. (Ed.). (in press). *International handbook of mathematics education.* Dordrecht, The Netherlands: Kluwer.

Bloom, B.S. (Ed.). (1956). *Taxonomy of educational objectives: The classification of educational goals: Handbook I: Cognitive domain.* New York: McKay.

Boden, M. A. (1988). *Computer models of mind.* New York: Cambridge University Press.

Boekaerts, M. (1993). Being concerned with well-being and with learning. *Educational Psychologist, 28,* 149–167.

Borba, M. C. (1990). Ethnomathematics and education. *For the Learning of Mathematics, 10,* 39–42.

Bransford, J. D., Sherwood, R. S., Hasselbring, T. S., Kinzer, C. K., & Williams, S. M. (1990). Anchored instruction: Why we need it and how technology can help. In D. Nix & R. Spiro (Eds.), *Cognition, education, and multimedia: Exploring ideas in high technology* (pp. 115–141). Hillsdale, NJ: Lawrence Erlbaum Associates.

Briars, D. J., & Larkin, J. H. (1984). An integrated model of skill in solving elementary word problems. *Cognition and Instruction, 1,* 245–296.

Brousseau, G. (1984). The crucial role of the didactical contract in the analysis and construction of situations in teaching and learning mathematics. In H. G. Steiner (Ed.), *Theory of mathematics education* (pp. 110–119) (Occasional paper 54). Bielefeld: IDM.

Brown, A. L. (1992). Design experiments: Theoretical and methodological challenges in creating complex interventions in classroom settings. *Journal of the Learning Sciences, 2,* 141–178.

Brown, A. L., Bransford, J. D., Ferrera, R. A., & Campione, J. C. (1983). Learning, remembering, and understanding. In P. H. Musssen, J. H. Flavell, & E. M. Markman (Eds.), *Child psychology: Vol. III. Cognitive development* (pp. 77–166). New York: Wiley.

Brown, A. L., & Ferrara, R. A. (1985). Diagnosing zones of proximal development. In J. V. Wertsch (Ed.), *Culture, communication and cognition: Vygotskian perspectives* (pp. 273–305). Cambridge, England: Cambridge University Press.

Brown, J. S. (1990). Toward a new epistemology for learning. In C. Frasson & J. Gauthiar (Eds.), *Intelligent tutoring systems: At the crossroads of artificial intelligence and education* (pp. 266–282). Norwood, NJ: Ablex.

Brown, J. S., & Burton, R. R. (1978). Diagnostic models for procedural bugs in basic mathematical skills. *Cognitive Science, 2,* 155–192.

Brown, J. S., Collins, A., & Duguid, P. (1989). Situated cognition and the culture of learning. *Educational Researcher, 18*(1), 32–42.

Brown, J. S., & VanLehn, K. (1982). Towards a generative theory of "bugs." In T. P. Carpenter, J. M. Moser, & T. Romberg (Eds.), *Addition and subtraction: A cognitive perspective* (pp. 117–135). Hillsdale, NJ: Lawrence Erlbaum.

Brown, S. I., & Walter, M. I. (1993). *Problem posing: Reflections and applications.* Hillsdale, NJ: Lawrence Erlbaum Associates.

Brownell, W. A. (1945). When is arithmetic meaningful? *Journal of Educational Research, 38,* 481–498.

Bruner, J. S. (1962). Introduction. In L. S. Vygotsky, *Thought and language.* Cambridge, MA: MIT Press.

Bruner, J. S. (1966). *The process of education.* Cambridge, MA: Harvard University Press.

Burton, R. B. (1982). Diagnosing bugs in a simple procedural skill. In D. H. Sleeman & J. S. Brown (Eds.), *Intelligent tutoring systems* (pp. 157–183). New York: Academic Press.

Cajori, F. (1917). *A history of elementary mathematics.* New York: Macmillan.

California Board of Education. (1991). *Mathematics framework for California public schools* (Preview edition). Sacramento, CA: California State Department of Education.

Campione, J. C., & Brown, A. L. (1990). Guided learning and transfer: Implications for approaches to assessment. In N. Frederiksen, R. Glaser, A. Lesgold, & M. Shafto (Eds.), *Diagnostic monitoring of skill and knowledge acquisition* (pp. 141–172). Hillsdale, NJ: Lawrence Erlbaum Associates.

Campione, J. C., Brown, A. L., & Connell, M. L. (1988). Metacognition: On the importance of understanding what you are doing. In R.A. Charles & E. A. Silver (Eds.), *The teaching and assessment of mathematical problem solving* (pp. 93–114). Reston, VA: National Council of Teachers of Mathematics/Hillsdale, NJ: Lawrence Erlbaum Associates.

Carpenter, T. P. (1986). Conceptual knowledge as a foundation for procedural knowledge. In J. Hiebert (Ed.), *Conceptual and procedural knowledge: The case of mathematics* (pp. 113–132). Hillsdale, NJ: Lawrence Erlbaum Associates.

Carpenter, T. P., & Fennema, E. (1992). Cognitively guided instruction: Building on the knowledge of students and teachers. *International Journal of Educational Research, 17,* 457–470.

Carpenter, T. P., Fennema, E., Peterson, P. L., & Carey, D. A. (1988). Teachers' pedagogical content knowledge of students' problem solving in elementary arithmetic. *Journal for Research in Mathematics Education, 19,* 385–401.

Carpenter, T. P., Fennema, E., Peterson, P. L., Chiang, C. P., & Loef, M. (1989). Using knowledge of children's mathematical thinking in classroom teaching: An experimental study. *American Educational Research Journal, 26,* 499–532.

Carpenter, T. P., Lindquist, M. M., Matthews, W., & Silver, E. A. (1983). Results of the Third NAEP Mathematics Assessment: Secondary school. *Mathematics Teacher, 76*(9), 652–659.

Carpenter, T. P., & Moser, J. M. (1984). The acquisition of addition and subtraction concepts in grades one through three. *Journal for Research in Mathematics Education, 15,* 179–202.

Carpenter, T. P., Moser, J. M., & Romberg, T. A. (Eds.). (1982). *Addition and subtraction: A cognitive perspective.* Hillsdale, NJ: Lawrence Erlbaum Associates.

Carraher, T. N., Carraher, D. W., & Schliemann, A. D. (1985). Mathematics in streets and schools. *British Journal of Developmental Psychology, 3,* 21–29.

Case, R. (1985). *Cognitive development.* New York: Academic Press.

Chapman, M. (1988). *Constructive evolution: Origins and development of Piaget's thought.* Cambridge, England: Cambridge University Press.

Charles, R. I., & Silver, E.A. (Eds.). (1988). *The teaching and assessing of mathematical problem solving.* Hillsdale, NJ: Lawrence Erlbaum Associates.

Chevallard, Y. (1985). *La transposition didactique* [The didactical transposition]. Grenoble, France: La Pensée Sauvage.

Chi, M. T., Glaser, R., & Farr, M. J. (Eds.). (1988). *The nature of expertise.* Hillsdale, NJ: Lawrence Erlbaum Associates.

Clarke, D. J. (1993a, March). *Open-ended tasks and assessment: The nettle or the rose.* Paper presented to the Research Pre-session of the 71st Annual Meeting of the National Council of Teachers of Mathematics, Seattle, WA.

Clarke, D. J. (1993b, September). *The assessment agenda.* Paper presented at a conference of the European Association for Research on Learning and Instruction, Aix-en-Provence, France.

Clarke, D. J., & Sullivan, P. (1992). The assessment implications of open-ended tasks in mathematics. In M. Stephens & J. Izard (Eds.), *Reshaping assessment practice: Assessment in the mathematical sciences under challenge* (pp. 161–179). Hawthorn, Victoria, Australia: Australian Council for Educational Research.

Clarke, D. J., & Wallbridge, M. (1992). *The other consequences of a problem-based mathematics curriculum.* Oakleigh, Victoria, Australia: Australian Catholic University (Victoria).

Clemens, H. (1993). The Standards: A roadmap for following the math. *Educational Researcher, 22*(4), 28–30.

Clements, D. H., & Meredith, J. S. (1993). *Design of a Logo environment for elementary geometry.* Buffalo: State University of New York at Buffalo.

Cobb, P. (1990). A constructivist perspective on information-processing theories of mathematical activity. *International Journal of Educational Research, 14*(1), 67–92.

Cobb, P. (1994a). Constructivism. In T. Husén & T. N. Postlethwaite (Eds.), *International encyclopedia of education* (2nd ed., pp. 1049–1052). Oxford, U.K.: Pergamon Press.

Cobb, P. (1994b). Where is the mind? Constructivist and sociocultural perspectives on mathematical development. *Educational Researcher, 23*(7), 13–20.

Cobb, P., & Bauersfeld, H. (Eds.). (1995). *The emergence of mathematical meaning: Interaction in classroom cultures.* Hillsdale, NJ: Lawrence Erlbaum Associates.

Cobb, P., Wood, T., & Yackel, E. (1991). A constructivist approach to second grade mathematics. In E. von Glasersfeld (Ed.), *Constructivism in mathematics education* (pp. 157–176). Dordrecht, The Netherlands: Kluwer.

Cobb, P., Wood, T., Yackel, E., & McNeal, G. (1992). Characteristics of classroom mathematics traditions: An interactional analysis. *American Educational Research Journal, 29,* 573–602.

Cobb, P., Wood, T., Yackel, E., McNeal, G., Merkel, G., Preston, M., & Wheatley, G. (1988). *The Purdue problem-centered mathematics curriculum: Revised.* West Lafayette, IN: School Mathematics and Science Center, Purdue University.

Cobb, P., Wood, T., Yackel, E., Nicholls, J., Wheatley, G., Trigatti, B., & Perlwitz, M. (1991). Assessment of a problem-centered second-grade mathematics project. *Journal for Research in Mathematics Education, 22,* 3–29.

Cobb, P., Yackel, E., & Wood, T. (1992). A constructivist alternative to the representational view of mind in mathematics education. *Journal for Research in Mathematics Education, 23,* 2–33.

Cockcroft, W. H. (1982). *Mathematics counts* (Report of the Committee of Inquiry into the Teaching of Mathematics in Schools). London: Her Majesty's Stationery Office.

Cognition and Technology Group at Vanderbilt. (1990). Anchored instruction and its relationship to situated cognition. *Educational Researcher, 19*(6), 2–10.

Cognition and Technology Group at Vanderbilt. (1993). Anchored instruction and situated cognition revisited. *Educational Technology, 33*(3), 52–70.

Cognition and Technology Group at Vanderbilt. (1994). Multimedia environments for enhancing student learning in mathematics. In S. Vosniadou, E. De Corte, & H. Mandl (Eds.), *Technology-based learning environments: Psychological and educational foundations* (NATO ASI Series F: Computers and Systems Sciences, Vol. 137, pp. 167–173). Berlin: Springer.

Collins, A. (1990). Reformulating testing to measure learning and thinking. In N. Frederiksen, R. Glaser, A. Lesgold, & M. G. Shafto (Eds.), *Diagnostic monitoring of skill and knowledge acquisition* (pp. 75–87). Hillsdale, NJ: Lawrence Erlbaum Associates.

Collins, A. (1992). Toward a design science of education. In E. Scanlon & T. O'Shea (Eds.), *New directions in educational technology* (NATO ASI Series F: Computers and Systems Sciences, Vol. 96, pp. 167–173). Berlin: Springer.

Collins, A., Brown, J. S., & Newman, S. E. (1989). Cognitive apprenticeship: Teaching the crafts of reading, writing, and mathematics. In L. B. Resnick (Ed.), *Knowing, learning and instruction: Essays in honor of Robert Glaser* (pp. 453–494). Hillsdale, NJ: Lawrence Erlbaum Associates.

Confrey, J. (1985). Towards a framework for constructivist instruction. In L. Streefland (Ed.), *Proceedings of the Ninth International Conference for the Psychology of Mathematics Education* (Vol. 1, pp. 477–483). Noordwijkerhout, The Netherlands: Psychology of Mathematics Education.

Confrey, J. (1990). A review of the research on student conceptions in mathematics, science, and programming. In C. B. Cazden (Ed.), *Review of research in education* (Vol. 16, pp. 3–55). Washington, DC: American Educational Research Association.

Cooney, T. J. (1985). A beginning teacher's view of problem solving. *Journal for Research in Mathematics Education, 16,* 324–336.

Cooney, T. J. (1994). Research and teacher education: In search of common ground. *Journal for Research in Mathematics Education, 25,* 608–636.

Crystal, D. S., & Stevenson, H. W. (1991). Mothers' perceptions of children's problems with mathematics: A cross-national comparison. *Journal of Educational Psychology, 83,* 372–376.

Cuban, L. (1986). *Teachers and machines: The classroom use of technology since 1920.* New York: Teachers College Press.

d'Ambrosio, U. (1985). Ethnomathematics and its place in the history and pedagogy of mathematics. *For the Learning of Mathematics, 5,* 44–48.

Damerow, P. (1988). Individual development and cultural evolution of arithmetical thinking. In S. Strauss (Ed.), *Ontogeny, phylogeny and historical development* (pp. 125–152). Norwood, NJ: Ablex.

Davis, P. J., & Hersh, R. (1981). *The mathematical experience.* Boston: Birkhauser.

Davis, R. B. (1967, Fall). Mathematics teaching: With special reference to epistemological problems. *Journal of Research and Development in Education, Monograph, 1* (1).

Davis, R. B. (1984). *Learning mathematics: The cognitive science approach to mathematics education.* Norwood, NJ: Ablex.

Davis, R. B. (1989). The culture of mathematics and the culture of schools. *Journal of Mathematical Behavior, 8,* 143–160.

Davis, R. B. (1990). How computers help us understand people. *International Journal of Educational Research, 14* (1), 93–100.

Davis, R. B. (1992). Reflections on where mathematics education now stands and on where it may be going. In D. A. Grouws (Ed.), *Handbook of research on mathematics teaching and learning* (pp. 724–734). New York: Macmillan.

Davis, R. B., Maher, C. A., & Noddings, N. (Eds.). (1990). *Constructivist views on the teaching and learning of mathematics. Journal for Research in Mathematics Education, Monograph 1* (4). Reston, VA: National Council of Teachers of Mathematics.

Davydov, V. V. (1990). *Types of generalization in instruction: Logical and psychological problems in the structuring of school curricula.* (Soviet Studies in Mathematics Education, Vol. 2). Reston, VA: National Council of Teachers of Mathematics.

DeBellis-Kramer, V. A., & Goldin, G. A. (1993). Analysis of interactions between affect and cognition in elementary school children during problem solving. In J. R. Becker & B. J. Pence (Eds.), *Proceedings of the Fifteenth Annual Meeting of the North American Chapter of the International Group for the Psychology of Mathematics Education* (Vol. 2, pp. 56–62). San Jose, CA: San Jose State University Center for Mathematics and Computer Science Education.

De Corte, E. (1990). Acquiring and teaching cognitive skills: A state-of-the-art of theory and research. In P. J. Drenth, J. A. Sergeant, & R. J. Takens (Eds.), *European perspectives in psychology* (Vol. 1, pp. 237–263). Chichester, England: Wiley.

De Corte, E. (1992). Design and evaluation of powerful learning environments. In B. P. H. Creemers & G. J. Reezipt (Eds.), *Evaluation of educational effectiveness* (pp. 5–27). Groningen, The Netherlands: Interuniversitair Centrum voor Onderwijsonderzoek.

De Corte, E. (1993). Toward embedding enriched Logo-based learning environments in the school curriculum: Retrospect and prospect. In P. Georgiadis, G. Gyftodimos, Y. Kotsanis, & C. Kynigos (Eds.), *Proceedings of the 4th European Logo Conference.* Athens, Greece: Doukas School.

De Corte, E. (1994). Toward the integration of computers in powerful learning environments. In S. Vosniadou, E. De Corte, & H. Mandl (Eds.), *Technology-based learning environments: Psychological and educational foundations* (NATO ASI Series F: Computers and Systems Sciences, Vol. 137, pp. 19–25). Berlin: Springer.

De Corte, E. (1995a). Designing powerful teaching-learning environments conducive to the acquisition of cognitive skills. In R. Olechowski & G. Khan-Svik (Eds.), *Experimental research on teaching and learning* (pp. 67–82). Frankfurt, Germany: Peter Lang.

De Corte, E. (1995b). Fostering cognitive growth: A perspective from research on mathematics learning and instruction. *Educational Psychologist, 30,* 37–46.

De Corte, E., & Verschaffel, L. (1985). Beginning first graders' initial representation of arithmetic word problems. *Journal of Mathematical Behavior, 4,* 3–21.

De Corte, E., & Verschaffel, L. (1987a). Children's problem solving skills and processes with respect to elementary arithmetic word problems. In E. De Corte, H. Lodewijks, R. Parmentier, & P. Span (Eds.), *Learning and instruction: European research in an international context* (Vol. 1, pp. 297–308). Leuven, Belgium: Leuven University Press/Oxford, U.K.: Pergamon.

De Corte, E., & Verschaffel, L. (1987b). The effect of semantic structure on first graders' strategies for solving addition and subtraction word problems. *Journal for Research in Mathematics Education, 18,* 363–381.

De Corte, E., & Verschaffel, L. (1988). Computer simulation as a tool in research in problem solving in subject-matter domains. *International Journal of Educational Research, 12,* 49–69.

De Corte, E., & Verschaffel, L. (1989). Logo: A vehicle for learning. In B. Greer & G. Mulhern (Eds.), *New directions in mathematics education* (pp. 63–81). London: Routledge.

De Corte, E., Verschaffel, L., & Schrooten, H. (1991). Computer simulation as a tool in studying teachers' cognitive activities during error diagnosis in arithmetic. In P. Goodyear (Ed.), *Teaching knowledge and intelligent tutoring* (pp. 267–278). Norwood, NJ: Ablex.

De Corte, E., Verschaffel, L., & Van Coillie, V. (1988). Influence of number size, problem structure, and response mode on children's solutions of multiplication problems. *Journal of Mathematical Behavior, 7,* 197–216.

De Lange, J. (1987). *Mathematics, insight, and meaning.* Utrecht, The Netherlands: University of Utrecht.

De Lange, J. (1993). Real tasks and real assessment. In R. B. Davis & C. A. Maher (Eds.), *Schools, mathematics, and the world of reality* (pp. 263–287). New York: Allyn & Bacon.

De Lange, J. (1995). Assessment: No change without problems. In T. Romberg (Ed.), *Reform in school mathematics and authentic assessment* (pp. 86–172). Albany: State University of New York Press.

De Lange, J., van Reeuwijk, M., Burrill, G., & Romberg, T. (1993). *Learning and testing mathematics in context. The case: Data visualization.* Madison, WI: National Center for Research in Mathematical Sciences Education.

Dellarosa, D., Kintsch, W., Reusser, K., & Weimer, R. (1988). The role of understanding in solving word problems. *Cognitive Psychology, 20,* 405–438.

Dörfler, W. (1993). Computer use and views of the mind. In C. Keitel & K. Ruthven (Eds.), *Learning from computers: Mathematics education and technology* (NATO ASI Series F: Computers and Systems Sciences, Vol. 121, pp. 159–186). Berlin: Springer.

Dreyfus, T. (1990). Advanced mathematical thinking. In P. Nesher & J. Kilpatrick (Eds.), *Mathematics and cognition: A research synthesis by the International Group for the Psychology of Mathematics Education* (pp. 113–134). Cambridge, England: Cambridge University Press.

Dreyfus, T. (1991). On the status of visual reasoning in mathematics and mathematics education. In F. Furinghetti (Ed.), *Proceedings of the 15th International Conference for the Psychology of Mathematics Education* (Vol. 1, pp. 33–48). Genoa: University of Genoa.

Dreyfus, T. (1993). Didactic design of computer-based learning environments. In C. Keitel & K. Ruthven (Eds.), *Learning from computers: Mathematics education and technology* (NATO ASI Series F: Computers and Systems Science, Vol. 121, pp. 101–130). Berlin: Springer.

Eisenhart, M. A. (1988). The ethnographic research tradition and mathematics education research. *Journal for Research in Mathematics Education, 19,* 99–114.

Elshout, J. (1992). Formal education versus everyday learning. In E. De Corte, M. Linn, H. Mandl, & L. Verschaffel (Eds.), *Computer-based learning environments and problem solving* (NATO ASI Series F: Computers and Systems Sciences, Vol. 84, pp. 5–17). Berlin: Springer.

Ernest, P. (1991). *The philosophy of mathematics education.* London: Falmer.

Fennema, E., & Loef, M. (1992). Teachers' knowledge and its impact. In D. A. Grouws (Ed.), *Handbook of research on mathematics teaching and learning* (pp. 147–164). New York: Macmillan.

Fischbein, E. (1987). *Intuition in science and mathematics: An educational approach.* Dordrecht, The Netherlands: Reidel.

Fischbein, E. (1990a). Introduction. In P. Nesher & J. Kilpatrick (Eds.), *Mathematics and cognition: A research synthesis by the International Group for the Psychology of Mathematics Education* (pp. 1–13) (ICMI Study Series). Cambridge, England: Cambridge University Press.

Fischbein, E. (1990b). Intuition and information processing in mathematical activity. *International Journal of Educational Research, 14*(1), 31–50.

Fischbein, E., Deri, M., Nello, M. S., & Marino, M. S. (1985). The role of implicit models in solving verbal problems in multiplication and division. *Journal for Research in Mathematics Education, 16,* 3–17.

Foxman, D. (1993). The Assessment of Performance Unit's monitoring surveys 1978–1987. In M. Niss (Ed.), *Investigations into assessment in mathematics education* (pp. 217–228). Dordrecht, The Netherlands: Kluwer.

Frank, M. L. (1988). Problem solving and mathematical beliefs. *Arithmetic Teacher, 35*(5), 32–34.

Frechtling, J. A. (1991, Winter). Performance assessment: Moonstruck or the real thing? *Educational Measurement: Issues and Practice,* 23–25.

Frederiksen, J. R., & Collins, A. (1989). A systems approach to educational testing. *Educational Researcher, 18*(9), 27–32.

Frederiksen, N., Mislevy, R., & Bejar, I. (1993). *Test theory for a new generation of tests.* Hillsdale, NJ: Lawrence Erlbaum Associates.

Freudenthal, H. (1978). *Weeding and sowing.* Dordrecht, The Netherlands: Reidel.

Freudenthal, H. (1983). *Didactical phenomenology of mathematical structures.* Dordrecht, The Netherlands: Reidel.

Freudenthal, H. (1991). *Revisiting mathematics education.* Dordrecht, The Netherlands: Kluwer.

Friedhoff, R. M., & Benzon, W. (1991). *Visualization.* New York: Freeman.

Fuson, K. C. (1982). An analysis of the counting-on solution procedure in addition. In T. P. Carpenter, J. M. Moser, & T. A. Romberg (Eds.), *Addition and subtraction: A cognitive perspective* (pp. 67–81). Hillsdale, NJ: Lawrence Erlbaum Associates.

Fuson, K. C. (1992). Research on whole number addition and subtraction. In D. A. Grouws (Ed.), *Handbook of research on mathematics teaching and learning* (pp. 243–275). New York: Macmillan.

Fuson, K. C., Stigler, J. W., & Bartch, K. (1988). Grade placement of addition and subtraction topics in Japan, mainland China, the Soviet Union, Taiwan, and the United States. *Journal for Research in Mathematics Education, 19,* 449–456.

Gardner, H. (1984). *Frames of mind: The theory of multiple intelligences.* London: Heinemann.

Gardner, H. (1985). *The mind's new science.* New York: Basic Books.

Garofalo, J., & Lester, F. K. (1985). Metacognition, cognitive monitoring, and mathematical performance. *Journal for Research in Mathematics Education, 16,* 163–176.

Gay, J., & Cole, M. (1967). *The new mathematics and an old culture.* New York: Holt, Rinehart & Winston.

Gelman, R., & Gallistel, C. R. (1978). *The child's understanding of number.* Cambridge, MA: Harvard University Press.

Gerdes, P. (1988). On culture, geometrical thinking and mathematics education. *Educational Studies in Mathematics, 19,* 137–162.

Ginsburg, H. P. (1977). *Children's arithmetic: The learning process.* New York: Van Nostrand.

Ginsburg, H. P., Jacobs, S. F., & Lopez, L. S. (1993). Assessing mathematical thinking and learning potential. In R. B. Davis & C. A. Maher (Eds.), *Schools, mathematics, and the world of reality* (pp. 237–262). New York: Allyn & Bacon.

Ginsburg, H. P., Kossan, N. E., Schwartz, R., & Swanson, D. (1983). Protocol methods in research on mathematical thinking. In H. P. Ginsburg (Ed.), *The development of mathematical thinking* (pp. 7–47). New York: Academic Press.

Glaser, R. (1990). Toward new models for assessment. *International Journal of Educational Research, 14,* 475–483.

Goldin, G. A. (1992a). On developing a unified model for the psychology of mathematical learning and problem solving. In W. Geeslin & K. Graham (Eds.), *Proceedings of the Sixteenth Annual Meeting of the International Group for the Psychology of Mathematics Education* (Vol. 3, pp. 235–261). Durham: University of New Hampshire.

Goldin, G. A. (1992b). Toward an assessment framework for school mathematics. In R. Lesh & S. J. Lamon (Eds.), *Assessments of authentic performance in elementary mathematics* (pp. 63–88). Washington, DC: American Association for the Advancement of Science.

Goldin, G. A., & Kaput, J. J. (1992). *A joint perspective on the idea of representation in learning and doing mathematics.* Paper presented at ICME-7, Quebec City, Canada. [To be revised for publication; cited by permission of the authors]

Goldin, G. A., & McClintock, C. E. (Eds.). (1984). *Task variables in mathematical problem solving.* Philadelphia: Franklin Institute Press.

Graeber, A., & Tirosh, D. (1988). Multiplication and division involving decimals: Preservice elementary teachers' performance and beliefs. *Journal of Mathematical Behavior, 7,* 263–280.

Gravemeijer, K. (1994). *Developing realistic mathematics education.* Utrecht, The Netherlands: Freudenthal Institute, University of Utrecht.

Gravemeijer, K., van den Heuvel, M., & Streefland, L. (1990). *Context, free production, tests and geometry in realistic mathematics education.* Utrecht, The Netherlands: Research Group for Mathematical Education and Educational Computer Centre, University of Utrecht.

Greenfield, P. (1993, July). *Cultural historical studies in cognition.* Paper presented at a Workshop on Culture and Mathematical Cognition, Maragogi, Brazil.

Greeno, J. G. (1980). Psychology of learning, 1960–1980: One participant's observations. *American Psychologist, 35,* 713–728.

Greeno, J. G. (1987). Instructional representations based on research about understanding. In A. H. Schoenfeld (Ed.), *Cognitive science and mathematics education* (pp. 61–88). Hillsdale, NJ: Lawrence Erlbaum Associates.

Greeno, J. G. (1989). A perspective on thinking. *American Psychologist, 44,* 134–141.

Greeno, J. G. (1991a). Number sense as situated knowing in a conceptual domain. *Journal for Research in Mathematics Education, 22,* 170–218.

Greeno, J. G. (1991b). A view of mathematical problem solving in school. In M. U. Smith (Ed.), *Toward a unified theory of problem solving: Views from the content domains* (pp. 69–98). Hillsdale, NJ: Lawrence Erlbaum Associates.

Greeno, J. G., Smith, D. R., & Moore, J. L. (1992). Transfer of situated learning. In D. Detterman & R. Sternberg (Eds.), *Transfer on trial: Intelligence, cognition, and instruction* (pp. 99–167). Norwood, NJ: Ablex.

Greer, B. (1992). Multiplication and division as models of situations. In D. A. Grouws (Ed.), *Handbook of research on mathematics teaching and learning* (pp. 276–295). New York: Macmillan.

Greer, B. (1993). The mathematical modeling perspective on wor(l)d problems. *Journal of Mathematical Behavior, 12,* 239–250.

Greer, B. (1994). Extending the meaning of multiplication and division. In G. Harel & J. Confrey (Eds.), *The development of multiplicative reasoning in the learning of mathematics* (pp. 61–85). Albany: State University of New York Press.

Greer, B. (in press). Theories of mathematics education: The role of cognitive analyses. In L. P. Steffe, P. Nesher, P. Cobb, G. A. Goldin, & B. Greer (Eds.), *Theories of mathematical learning.* Hillsdale, NJ: Lawrence Erlbaum Associates.

Greer, B., & Verschaffel, L. (Eds.). (1990). Mathematics education as a proving-ground for information-processing theories. *International Journal of Educational Research, 14,* 1–100.

Grouws, D. A. (Ed.). (1992). *Handbook of research on mathematics teaching and learning.* New York: Macmillan.

Grouws, D. A., & Cooney, T. J. (Eds.). (1988). *Perspectives on research on effective mathematics teaching.* Hillsdale, NJ: Lawrence Erlbaum Associates.

Gurova, L. L. (1985). De reflectie op het eigen handelen tijdens het oplossen van rekenopgaven bij schoolkinderen [Reflection on one's own activity during the solution of arithmetic tasks]. In. L. Verschaffel & M. Wolters (Eds.), *Zes Sovjetrussische bijdragen over vraagstukkenonderwijs en cognitieve ontwikkeling* [Six Soviet contributions about word problem instruction and cognitive development] (Internal Report No. 30, pp. 15–30). Leuven, Belgium: K. U. Leuven, Afdeling Didactiek.

Gurtner, J.-L. (1992). Between Logo and mathematics: A road of tunnels and bridges. In C. Hoyles & R. Noss (Eds.), *Learning mathematics and Logo* (pp. 247–268). Cambridge, MA: MIT Press.

Hadamard, J. (1945). *The psychology of invention in the mathematical field*. Princeton, NJ: Princeton University Press.

Hamers, J. H. M., Sijtsma, K., & Ruijssenaars, A. J. J. M. (1993). *Learning potential assessment: Theoretical, methodological and practical issues*. Amsterdam/Lisse, The Netherlands: Swets & Zeitlinger.

Harel, G., & Kaput, J. (1991). The role of conceptual entities and their symbols in building advanced mathematical concepts. In D. Tall (Ed.), *Advanced mathematical thinking* (pp. 82–94). Dordrecht, The Netherlands: Kluwer.

Harel, I. (1990). Children as software designers: A constructionist approach for learning mathematics. *Journal of Mathematical Behavior, 9*, 3–93.

Hart, L. E. (1989). Describing the affective domain: Saying what we mean. In D. B. McLeod & V. M. Adams (Eds.), *Affect and mathematical problem solving: A new perspective* (pp. 37–48). New York: Springer.

Hatano, G. (in press). A conception of knowledge acquisition and its implications for mathematics education. In L. E. Steffe, P. Nesher, P. Cobb, G. A. Goldin, & B. Greer (Eds.), *Theories of mathematical learning*. Hillsdale, NJ: Lawrence Erlbaum Associates.

Hatano, G., & Inagaki, K. (1992). Desituating cognition through the construction of conceptual knowledge. In P. Light & G. Butterworth (Eds.), *Context and cognition: Ways of learning and knowing* (pp. 115–133). Hemel Hempstead, England: Harvester-Wheatsheaf.

Hatano, G., Miyake, Y., & Binks, M. G. (1977). Performance of expert abacus operators. *Cognition, 5*, 57–71.

Hefendehl-Hebeker, L. (1991). Negative numbers: Obstacles in their evolution from intuitive to intellectual constructs. *For the Learning of Mathematics, 11*(1), 26–32.

Hersh, R. (1986). Some proposals for reviving the philosophy of mathematics. In T. Tymoczko (Ed.), *New directions in the philosophy of mathematics* (pp. 9–28). Boston: Birkhauser.

Hiebert, J. (Ed.). (1986). *Conceptual and procedural knowledge: The case of mathematics*. Hillsdale, NJ: Lawrence Erlbaum Associates.

Hiebert, J., & Lefevre, P. (1986). Conceptual and procedural knowledge in mathematics: An introductory analysis. In J. Hiebert (Ed.), *Conceptual and procedural knowledge: The case of mathematics* (pp. 1–27). Hillsdale, NJ: Lawrence Erlbaum Associates.

Holyoak, K. J. (1991). Symbolic connectionism: Toward third-generation theories of expertise. In K. A. Ericsson & J. Smith (Eds.), *Toward a general theory of expertise* (pp. 301–335). Cambridge, England: Cambridge University Press.

Hoyles, C., Healey, L., & Pozzi, S. (1992). Interdependence and autonomy: Aspects of groupwork with computers. *Learning and Instruction, 2*, 239–257.

Hoyles, C., & Noss, R. (Eds.). (1992). *Learning mathematics and Logo*. Cambridge, MA: MIT Press.

Hoyles, C., & Sutherland, R. (1989). *Logo mathematics in the classroom*. London: Routledge.

Husén, T. (1967). *International study of achievement in mathematics: A comparison of twelve countries* (Vol. 1). New York: Wiley.

Hughes, M. (1986). *Children and number*. Oxford, U.K.: Blackwell.

Jackiw, N. (1991). *The geometer's sketchpad* [Software]. Berkeley, CA: Key Curriculum Press.

Janvier, C. (Ed.). (1987a). *Problems of representation in the teaching and learning of mathematics*. Hillsdale, NJ: Lawrence Erlbaum Associates.

Janvier, C. (1987b). Translation processes in mathematics education. In C. Janvier (Ed.), *Problems of representation in the teaching and learning of mathematics* (pp. 27–32). Hillsdale, NJ: Lawrence Erlbaum Associates.

Johnson, M. (1987). *The body in the mind: The bodily basis of meaning, imagination, and reason*. Chicago: University of Chicago Press.

Joseph, G. G. (1992). *The crest of the peacock: Non-European roots of mathematics*. London: Penguin.

Judd, C. H. (1928). The fallacy of treating school subjects as "tool subjects." In J. R. Clark & W. D. Reeve (Eds.), *Selected topics in the teaching of mathematics* (3rd Yearbook of the National Council of Teachers of Mathematics (pp. 1–10). New York: Columbia University, Teachers College.

Kalmykova, Z. I. (1970). Methods of scientific research in the psychology of instruction. In E. Stones (Ed.), *Readings in educational psychology: Learning and teaching* (pp. 125–142). London: Methuen.

Kang, W., & Kilpatrick, J. (1992). Didactic transposition in mathematics textbooks. *For the Learning of Mathematics, 12*(1), 2–7.

Kaput, J. J. (1986). Information technology and mathematics: Opening new representational windows. *Journal of Mathematical Behavior, 5*, 187–208.

Kaput, J. J. (1987). Toward a theory of symbol use in mathematics. In C. Janvier (Ed.), *Problems of representation in the teaching and learning of mathematics* (pp. 159–196). Hillsdale, NJ: Lawrence Erlbaum Associates.

Kaput, J. J. (1992). Technology and mathematics education. In D. A. Grouws (Ed.), *Handbook of research on mathematics teaching and learning* (pp. 515–556). New York: Macmillan.

Kaput, J. J. (1994). Democratizing access to calculus: New routes using old roots. In A. H. Schoenfeld (Ed.), *Mathematical thinking and problem solving* (pp. 77–156). Hillsdale, NJ: Lawrence Erlbaum Associates.

Kenney, P. A., & Silver, E. A. (1993). Student self-assessment in mathematics. In N. L. Webb (Ed.), *Assessment in the mathematics classroom: 1993 yearbook* (pp. 229–238). Reston, VA: National Council of Teachers of Mathematics.

Kenney, P. A., & Tang, H. (1992, April). *Conceptual and operational aspects of rating student responses to performance assessment*. Paper presented at the annual meeting of the American Educational Research Association, San Francisco.

Kilpatrick, J. (1981). The reasonable ineffectiveness of research in mathematics education. *For the Learning of Mathematics, 2*(2), 22–29.

Kilpatrick, J. (1986). Reflection and recursion. In M. Carss (Ed.), *Proceedings of the Fifth International Congress on Mathematical Education* (pp. 7–29). Boston: Birkhauser.

Kilpatrick, J. (1987). Problem formulating: Where do good problems come from? In A. H. Schoenfeld (Ed.), *Cognitive science and mathematics education* (pp. 123–147). Hillsdale, NJ: Lawrence Erlbaum Associates.

Kilpatrick, J. (1992). A history of research in mathematics education. In D. A. Grouws (Ed.), *Handbook of research on mathematics teaching and learning* (pp. 3–38). New York: Macmillan.

Kilpatrick, J. (1993). The chain and the arrow: From the history of mathematics assessment. In M. Niss (Ed.), *Investigations into assessment in mathematics education* (pp. 31–46). Dordrecht, The Netherlands: Kluwer.

Kilpatrick, J., & Davis, R. B. (1993). Computers and curriculum change in mathematics. In C. Keitel & K. Ruthven (Eds.), *Learning from computers: Mathematics education and technology* (NATO ASI Series F: Computers and Systems Sciences, Vol. 121, pp. 203–221). Berlin: Springer.

Kintsch, W. (1991). A theory of discourse comprehension: Implications for a tutor for word algebra problems. In M. Carretero, M. Pope,

R. J. Simons, & J. I. Pozo (Eds.), *Learning and instruction: European research in an international context* (Vol. 3, pp. 235–253). Oxford, U.K.: Pergamon Press.

Kintsch, W., & Greeno, J. G. (1984). Understanding and solving arithmetic word problems. *Psychological Review, 92,* 109–129.

Krutetskii, V. A. (1976). *The psychology of mathematical abilities in school children.* Chicago: University of Chicago Press.

Kuhl, J. (1985). Volitional mediators of cognition-behavior consistency: Self-regulatory processes and action versus state orientation. In J. Kuhl & J. Beckman (Eds.), *Action control: From cognition to behavior* (pp. 101–128). Berlin: Springer.

Laborde, J.-M. (1990). *CABRI geometry* [Software]. France: University of Grenoble 1.

Lampert, M. (1986). Knowing, doing, and teaching multiplication. *Cognition and Instruction, 3,* 305–342.

Lampert, M. (1988). *Teachers' thinking about students' thinking about geometry: The effects of new teaching tools* (Technical Report). Cambridge, MA: Harvard Graduate School of Education, Educational Technology Center.

Lampert, M. (1990). When the problem is not the question and the solution is not the answer: Mathematical knowing and teaching. *American Educational Research Journal, 27,* 29–63.

Lancey, D. F. (1983). *Cross-cultural studies in cognition and mathematics.* New York: Academic Press.

Lave, J. (1977). Cognitive consequences of traditional apprenticeship training in West Africa. *Anthropology and Education Quarterly, 7,* 177–180.

Lave, J. (1988). *Cognition in practice: Mind, mathematics, and culture in everyday life.* Cambridge: Cambridge University Press.

Lave, J., Murtaugh, M., & de la Rocha, O. (1984). The dialectic of arithmetic in grocery shopping. In B. Rogoff & J. Lave (Eds.), *Everyday cognition: Its development in social context* (pp. 67–94). Cambridge, MA: Harvard University Press.

Lave, J., & Wenger, E. (1991). *Situated learning: Legitimate peripheral participation.* Cambridge, England: Cambridge University Press.

Leder, G. C. (1987). Attitudes towards mathematics. In. T. A. Romberg & D. M. Stewart (Eds.), *The monitoring of school mathematics* (Vol. 2, pp. 261–277). Madison: Wisconsin Center for Education Research.

Leinhardt, G. (1988). Expertise in instructional lessons: An example from fractions. In D. A. Grouws, T. J. Cooney, & D. Jones (Eds.), *Perspectives on research on effective mathematics teaching* (pp. 47–66). Reston, VA: National Council of Teachers of Mathematics/Hillsdale, NJ: Lawrence Erlbaum Associates.

Leinhardt, G., & Greeno, J. G. (1986). The cognitive skill of teaching. *Journal of Educational Psychology, 2,* 75–95.

Lesh, R., & Lamon, S. J. (1992a). Assessing authentic mathematical performance. In R. Lesh & S. J. Lamon (Eds.), *Assessments of authentic performance in school mathematics* (pp. 17–63). Washington, DC: American Association for the Advancement of Science.

Lesh, R., & Lamon, S. J. (Eds.). (1992b). *Assessments of authentic performance in elementary mathematics.* Washington, DC: American Association for the Advancement of Science.

Lester, F. K. (1988). Reflections about mathematical problem-solving research. In R. A. Charles & E. A. Silver (Eds.), *The teaching and assessment of mathematical problem solving* (pp. 115–124). Reston, VA: National Council of Teachers of Mathematics/Hillsdale, NJ: Lawrence Erlbaum Associates.

Lester, F. K., & Garofalo, J. (1982, March). *Metacognitive aspects of elementary school students' performance on arithmetic tasks.* Paper presented at the annual meeting of the American Educational Research Association, New York.

Lester, F. K., Garofalo, J., & Kroll, D. L. (1989). Self-confidence, interest, beliefs, and metacognition: Key influences on problem-solving behavior. In D. B. McLeod & V. M. Adams (Eds.), *Affect and mathematical problem solving: A new perspective* (pp. 75–88). New York: Springer.

Linn, R. L., Baker, E. L., & Dunbar, S. B. (1991). Complex, performance-based assessment: Expectations and validation criteria. *Educational Researcher, 20*(8), 15–21.

Little, C. (1993). The School Mathematics Project: Some secondary school assessment initiatives in England. In M. Niss (Ed.), *Cases of assessment in mathematics education* (pp. 85–98). Dordrecht, The Netherlands: Kluwer.

Luria, A. R. (1976). *Cognitive development: Its cultural and social foundations.* Cambridge, MA: Harvard University Press.

Maher, C. A., Davis, R. B., & Alston, A. (1991a). Brian's representation and development of mathematical knowledge: A 4-year study. *Journal of Mathematical Behavior, 10,* 163–210.

Maher, C. A., Davis, R. B., & Alston, A. (1991b). Implementing a "thinking curriculum" in mathematics. *Journal of Mathematical Behavior, 10,* 219–224.

Mandl, H., & Renkl, A. (1992). A plea for "more local" theories of cooperative learning. *Learning and Instruction, 2,* 281–285.

Mandler, G. (1989). Affect and learning: Causes and consequences of emotional interaction. In D. B. McLeod & V. M. Adams (Eds.), *Affect and mathematical problem solving: A new perspective* (pp. 3–19). New York: Springer.

Mason, J. (1987). What do symbols represent? In C. Janvier (Ed.), *Problems of representation in the teaching and learning of mathematics,* (pp. 73–82). Hillsdale, NJ: Lawrence Erlbaum Associates.

Masters, G. H., & Mislevy, R. J. (1991). New views of student learning: Implications for educational measurement. In N. Frederiksen, R. J. Mislevy, & I. I. Bejar (Eds.), *Test theory for a new generation of tests* (pp. 219–242). Hillsdale, NJ: Lawrence Erlbaum Associates.

McLeod, D. B. (1989). The role of affect in mathematical problem solving. In D. B. McLeod & V. M. Adams (Eds.), *Affect and mathematical problem solving: A new perspective* (pp. 20–36). New York: Springer.

McLeod, D. B. (1990). Information-processing theories and mathematics learning: The role of affect. *International Journal of Educational Research, 14,* 13–29.

McLeod, D. B., & Adams, V. M. (1989). *Affect and mathematical problem solving: A new perspective.* New York: Springer.

Mcad, G. H. (1934). *Mind, self, and society.* Chicago: University of Chicago Press.

Mehrens, W. A. (1992, Spring). Using performance assessment for accountability purposes. *Educational Measurement: Issues and Practice,* 3–9, 20.

Messick, S. (1989). Validity. In R. L. Linn (Ed.), *Educational measurement* (3rd ed., pp. 13–103). New York: American Council on Education/Macmillan.

Mevarech, Z. R., & Kramarski, B. (1992). How and how much can cooperative Logo environments enhance creativity and social relationships? *Learning and Instruction, 2,* 259–274.

Mevarech, Z. R., & Light, P. H. (Eds.). (1992). Cooperative learning with computers. *Learning and Instruction, 2,* 155–285.

Middleton, J. A., Pitman, A., & Webb, N. L. (1993, April). *Collaboration and change in mathematics teachers' professional beliefs: A report of a four-year longitudinal study.* Paper presented at the annual meeting of the American Educational Research Association, Atlanta, GA.

Miller, J. (Ed.). (1983). *States of mind: Conversations with psychological investigators.* London: British Broadcasting Corporation.

Mislevy, R. J., Yamamoto, K., & Anacker, S. (1991). *Toward a test theory for assessing student understanding.* Princeton, NJ: Educational Testing Service.

Mokros, J., & Tinker, R. (1987). The impact of microcomputer-based labs on children's ability to interpret graphs. *Journal of Research in Science Teaching, 24,* 369–383.

Moon, B. (1986). *The "New Maths" curriculum controversy: An international study.* London: Falmer.

Mulhern, G. (1989). Between the ears: Making inferences about internal processes. In B. Greer & G. Mulhern (Eds.), *New directions in mathematics education* (pp. 29–62). London: Routledge.

Mumme, J. (1990). *Portfolio assessment in mathematics*. Santa Barbara, CA: University of California, Santa Barbara, California Mathematics Project.

National Assessment of Educational Progress. (1983). *The third national mathematics assessment: Results, trends, and issues*. Denver, CO: Education Commission of the States.

National Council of Teachers of Mathematics. (1980). *Agenda for action*. Reston, VA: National Council of Teachers of Mathematics.

National Council of Teachers of Mathematics. (1989). *Curriculum and evaluation standards for school mathematics*. Reston, VA: National Council of Teachers of Mathematics.

National Council of Teachers of Mathematics. (1991). *Professional standards for teaching mathematics*. Reston, VA: National Council of Teachers of Mathematics.

National Council of Teachers of Mathematics. (1995). *Assessment standards for school mathematics*. Reston, VA: National Council of Teachers of Mathematics.

Nelissen, J. M. C. (1987). *Kinderen leren wiskunde: Een studie over constructie en reflectie in het basisonderwijs* [Children learning mathematics: A study on construction and reflection in elementary school children]. Gorinchem, The Netherlands: Uitgeverij De Ruiter.

Nesher, P. (1980). The stereotyped nature of school word problems. *For the Learning of Mathematics, 1*(1), 41–48.

Nesher, P., & Kilpatrick, J. (Eds.). (1990). *Mathematics and cognition: A research synthesis by the International Group for the Psychology of Mathematics Education*. Cambridge, England: Cambridge University Press.

Newell, A. (1990). *Unified theories of cognition*. Cambridge, MA: Harvard University Press.

Newell, A., & Simon, H. A. (1972). *Human problem solving*. Englewood Cliffs, NJ: Prentice Hall.

Newman, D. (1992, December). Technology as support for school structure and school restructuring. *Phi Delta Kappan,* 308–315.

Newman, D. (1993). School networks: Delivery or access. *Communications of the ACM, 36*(5), 49–51.

Newman, D., Griffin, P., & Cole, M. (1989). *The construction zone: Working for cognitive change in school*. Cambridge, England: Cambridge University Press.

Nicholls, J. G., Cobb, P., Yackel, E., Wood, T., & Wheatley, G. (1990). Students' theories about mathematics and their mathematical knowledge: Multiple dimensions of assessment. In G. Kulm (Ed.), *Assessing higher order thinking in mathematics* (pp. 137–154). Washington, DC: American Association for the Advancement of Science.

Nickerson, R. S. (1988). Counting, computing, and the representation of numbers. *Human Factors, 30,* 181–199.

Nickerson, R. S., Perkins, D. N., & Smith, E. E. (1985). *The teaching of thinking*. Hillsdale, NJ: Lawrence Erlbaum Associates.

Nickson, M. (1992). The culture of the mathematics classroom: An unknown quantity? In D. A. Grouws (Ed.), *Handbook of research on mathematics teaching and learning* (pp. 101–114). New York: Macmillan.

Niss, M. (Ed.). (1993a). *Cases of assessment in mathematics education*. Dordrecht, The Netherlands: Kluwer.

Niss, M. (Ed.). (1993b). *Investigations into assessment in mathematics education*. Dordrecht, The Netherlands: Kluwer.

Nitko, A. J. (1989). Designing tests that are integrated with instruction. In R. L. Linn (Ed.), *Educational measurement* (3rd ed., pp. 447–474). New York: American Council on Education/Macmillan.

Noss, R. (1987). How do children do mathematics with Logo? *Journal of Computer Assisted Learning, 3,* 2–12.

Noss, R., & Hoyles, C. (1992). Looking back and looking forward. In C. Hoyles & R. Noss (Eds.), *Learning mathematics and Logo* (pp. 431–468). Cambridge, MA: MIT Press.

Nunes, T. (1992a). Cognitive invariants and cultural variation in mathematical concepts. *International Journal of Behavioral Development, 15,* 433–453.

Nunes, T. (1992b). Ethnomathematics and everyday cognition. In D. A. Grouws (Ed.), *Handbook of research on mathematics teaching and learning* (pp. 557–574). New York: Macmillan.

Nunes, T., Schliemann, A. D., & Carraher, D. W. (1993). *Street mathematics and school mathematics*. Cambridge, U.K.: Cambridge University Press.

Olive, J. (1993). Technology and school mathematics. *International Journal of Educational Research, 17,* 503–516.

Overtoom, R. (1991). *Informatieverwerking door hoogbegaafde leerlingen bij het oplossen van wiskundeproblemen* [Information processing by gifted students in solving mathematical problems]. De Lier, The Netherlands: Academisch Boeken Centrum.

Palinscar, A. S. (1989). Less charted waters. *Educational Researcher, 18*(4), 5–7.

Palincsar, A. S. (1992, April). *Beyond reciprocal teaching: A retrospection and prospective view*. Invited address presented at the annual meeting of the American Educational Research Association, San Francisco.

Papert, S. (1972). Teaching children to be mathematicians vs. teaching about mathematics. *International Journal of Mathematics Education and Science Technology, 3,* 249–262.

Papert, S. (1980). *Mindstorms: Children, computers, and powerful ideas*. New York: Basic Books.

Papert, S. (1985). Computer criticism vs. technocentric thinking. *Logo 85: Theoretical papers*. Cambridge, MA: MIT.

Papert, S. (1992). Foreword. In C. Hoyles & R. Noss (Eds.), *Learning mathematics and Logo* (pp. xi–xvi). Cambridge, MA: MIT Press.

Pea, R. D. (1987). Cognitive technologies for mathematics education. In A. H. Schoenfeld (Ed.), *Cognitive science and mathematics education* (pp. 89–122). Hillsdale, NJ: Lawrence Erlbaum Associates.

Perkins, D. N. (1992). *Smart schools: From educating memories to educating minds*. New York: Free Press.

Perkins, D. N., Jay, E., & Tishman, S. (1993). Beyond abilities: A dispositional theory of thinking. *Merrill Palmer Quarterly, 39,* 1–21.

Perkins, D. N., & Simmons, R. (1988). Patterns of misunderstanding: An integrative model for science, math, and programming. *Review of Educational Research, 58,* 303–326.

Piaget, J. (1954). *The construction of reality in the child*. New York: Ballantine Books.

Piaget, J. (1971). *Science of education and the psychology of the child*. London: Longman.

Piaget, J., & Garcia, R. (1989). *Psychogenesis and the history of science*. New York: Columbia University Press. (Original work published 1983)

Pinxten, R. (1991). Geometry education and culture. *Learning and Instruction, 1,* 217–228.

Polya, G. (1945). *How to solve it*. Princeton, NJ: Princeton University Press.

Polya, G. (1954a). *Induction and analogy in mathematics*. Princeton, NJ: Princeton University Press.

Polya, G. (1954b). *Patterns of plausible inference*. Princeton, NJ: Princeton University Press.

Polya, G. (1962). *Mathematical discovery* (Vol. 1). New York: Wiley.

Polya, G. (1965). *Mathematical discovery* (Vol. 2). New York: Wiley.

Post, T. R., Harel, G., Behr, M., & Lesh, R. (1988). Intermediate teachers' knowledge of rational number concepts. In E. Fennema, T. P. Carpenter, & S. J. Lamon (Eds.), *Integrating research on teaching and learning mathematics* (pp. 92–131). Madison: University of Wisconsin, Wisconsin Center for Education Research.

Putnam, R. T. (1987). Structuring and adjusting content for students: A study of live and simulated tutoring of addition. *American Educational Research Journal, 24,* 13–48.

Putnam, R. T., Lampert, M., & Peterson, P. L. (1990). Alternative perspectives on knowing mathematics in the elementary school. In C. B.

Cazden (Ed.), *Review of research in education* (Vol. 16, pp. 57–150). Washington, DC: American Educational Research Association.

Rabinowitz, M. (Ed.). (1988). Computer simulations as research tools. *International Journal of Educational Research, 12,* 1–102.

Rav, Y. (1993). Philosophical problems of mathematics in the light of evolutionary epistemology. In S. Restivo, J. P. Van Bendegem, & R. Fischer (Eds.), *Math worlds: Philosophical and social studies of mathematics and mathematics education* (pp. 80–109). Albany: State University of New York Press.

Resnick, L. B. (1983). Toward a cognitive theory of instruction. In S. G. Paris, G. M. Olson, & H. W. Stevenson (Eds.), *Learning and motivation in the classroom* (pp. 5–38). Hillsdale, NJ: Lawrence Erlbaum Associates.

Resnick, L. B. (1987a). *Education and learning to think.* Washington, DC: National Academy Press.

Resnick, L. B. (1987b). Learning in school and out. *Educational Researcher, 16*(9), 13–20.

Resnick, L. B. (1989). Treating mathematics as an ill-structured discipline. In R. A. Charles & E. A. Silver (Eds.), *The teaching and assessment of mathematical problem solving* (pp. 32–60). Reston, VA: National Council of Teachers of Mathematics/Hillsdale, NJ: Lawrence Erlbaum Associates.

Resnick, L. B., Briars, D., & Lesgold, S. (1992). Certifying accomplishments in mathematics: The New Standards examining system. In I. Wirszup & R. Streit (Eds.), *Developments in school mathematics education around the world* (Vol. 3, pp. 186–207). Reston, VA: National Council of Teachers of Mathematics.

Resnick, L. B., & Ford, W. W. (1981). *The psychology of mathematics for instruction.* Hillsdale, NJ: Lawrence Erlbaum Associates.

Resnick, M. (1988). Lego, Logo, and life. In C. Langton (Ed.), *Artificial life* (pp. 397–406). Menlo Park, CA: Addison-Wesley.

Restivo, S., Van Bendegem, J. P., & Fischer, R. (Eds.). (1993). *Math worlds: Philosophical and social studies of mathematics and mathematics education.* Albany: State University of New York Press.

Reusser, K. (1988). Problem solving beyond the logic of things: Contextual effects on understanding and solving word problems. *Instructional Science, 17,* 309–338.

Reusser, K. (1992). Tutoring systems and pedagogical theory: Representational tools for understanding, planning, and reflections in problem-solving. In S. Lajoie & S. Derry (Eds.), *Computers as cognitive tools* (pp. 143–177). Hillsdale, NJ: Lawrence Erlbaum Associates.

Ridgway, J. (1988). Of course ICAI is impossible . . . worse, though, it might be seditious. In J. Self (Ed.), *Artificial intelligence and human learning* (pp. 28–48). London: Chapman & Hall.

Riley, M. S., & Greeno, J. G. (1988). Developmental analysis of understanding language about quantities and of solving problems. *Cognition and Instruction, 5,* 49–101.

Riley, M. S., Greeno, J. G., & Heller, J. I. (1983). Development of children's problem-solving ability in arithmetic. In J. P. Ginsburg (Ed.), *The development of mathematical thinking* (pp. 153–196). New York: Academic Press.

Rissland, E. L. (1985). Artificial intelligence and the learning of mathematics: A tutorial sampling. In E. A. Silver (Ed.), *Teaching and learning mathematical problem solving: Multiple research perspectives* (pp. 147–176). Hillsdale, NJ: Lawrence Erlbaum Associates.

Robitaille, D. F., & Donn, S. (1993). TIMSS: The Third International Mathematics and Science Study. In M. Niss (Ed.), *Investigations into assessment in mathematics education* (pp. 229–244). Dordrecht, The Netherlands: Kluwer.

Robitaille, D. F., & Garden, R. A. (1989). *The IEA studies of mathematics: II. Contexts and outcomes of school mathematics.* Oxford, U.K.: Pergamon Press.

Robitaille, D. F., & Travers, K. J. (1992). International studies of achievement in mathematics. In D. A. Grouws (Ed.), *Handbook of research on mathematics teaching and learning* (pp. 687–709). New York: Macmillan.

Romberg, T. A. (1992a). Evaluation: A coat of many colours. In T. A. Romberg (Ed.), *Mathematics assessment and evaluation* (pp. 10–36). Albany: State University of New York Press.

Romberg, T. A. (Ed.). (1992b). *Mathematics assessment and evaluation: Imperatives for mathematics educators.* Albany: State University of New York Press.

Romberg, T. A. (1992c). Mathematics learning and teaching: What we have learned in ten years. In C. Collins & J. N. Mangieri (Eds.), *Teaching thinking: An agenda for the 21st century* (pp. 43–64). Hillsdale, NJ: Lawrence Erlbaum Associates.

Romberg, T. A. (Ed.). (1995). *Reform in school mathematics and authentic assessment.* Albany: State University of New York Press.

Romberg, T. A., & Carpenter, T. P. (1986). Research on teaching and learning mathematics: Two disciplines of scientific inquiry. In M. C. Wittrock (Ed.), *Handbook of research on teaching* (3rd ed., pp. 850–873). New York: Macmillan.

Romberg, T. A., Smith, M., Smith, S., & Wilson, L. (1992). *The feasibility of using international data to set achievement levels for the national assessment of educational progress* [Internal report]. Madison, WI: National Center for Research in Mathematical Sciences Education.

Romberg, T. A., Wilson, L., Khaketla, M., & Chavarria, S. (1992). Curriculum and test alignment. In T. A. Romberg (Ed.), *Mathematics assessment and evaluation: Imperatives for mathematics educators* (pp. 37–60). Albany: State University of New York Press.

Romberg, T. A., Zarinnia, E. A., & Collis, K. F. (1990). A new world view of assessment in mathematics. In G. Kulm (Ed.), *Assessing higher order thinking in mathematics* (pp. 21–38). Washington, DC: American Association for the Advancement of Science.

Säljö, R. (1991). Learning and mediation: Fitting reality into a table. *Learning and Instruction, 1,* 261–272.

Säljö, R., & Wyndhamn, J. (1987). The formal setting as context for cognitive activities. An empirical study of arithmetic operations under conflicting premises for communication. *European Journal of Psychology of Education, 2,* 233–245.

Salomon, G. (1990). Studying the flute *and* the orchestra: Controlled experimentation vs. whole classroom research on computers. *International Journal of Educational Research, 14,* 521–532.

Salomon, G. (1992). Effects *with* and *of* computers and the study of computer-based learning environments. In E. De Corte, M. C. Linn, H. Mandl, & L. Verschaffel (Eds.), *Computer-based learning environments and problem solving* (pp. 249–263). Berlin: Springer.

Salomon, G. (Ed.). (1993a). *Distributed cognitions: Psychological and educational considerations.* New York: Cambridge University Press.

Salomon, G. (1993b). No distribution without individual's cognition: A dynamic interactional view. In G. Salomon (Ed.), *Distributed cognitions: Psychological and educational considerations* (pp. 111–138). New York: Cambridge University Press.

Saxe, G. B. (1981). Body parts as numerals: A developmental analysis of numeration among remote Oksapmin populations in Papua New Guinea. *Child Development, 52,* 306–316.

Saxe, G. B. (1982). Developing forms of arithmetic operations among the Oksapmin of Papua, New Guinea. *Developmental Psychology, 18,* 583–594.

Saxe, G. B. (1988). Candy selling and math learning. *Educational Researcher, 17*(6), 14–21.

Saxe, G. B. (1992). Studying children's learning in context: Problems and prospects. *Journal of the Learning Sciences, 2,* 215–234.

Saxe, G. B., Guberman, S. R., & Gearhart, M. (1987). Social processes in early number development. *Monographs of the Society for Research in Child Development, 52*(2, Whole No. 216).

Schoenfeld, A. H. (1985). *Mathematical problem solving.* New York: Academic Press.

Schoenfeld, A. H. (1987). What's all the fuss about metacognition? In A. H. Schoenfeld (Ed.), *Cognitive science and mathematics education* (pp. 61–88). Hillsdale, NJ: Lawrence Erlbaum Associates.

Schoenfeld, A. H. (1988). When good teaching leads to bad results: The disasters of "well-taught" mathematics courses. *Educational Psychologist, 23,* 145–166.

Schoenfeld, A. H. (1991). On mathematics as sense-making: An informal attack on the unfortunate divorce of formal and informal mathematics. In J. F. Voss, D. N. Perkins, & J. W. Segal (Eds.), *Informal reasoning and education* (pp. 311–343). Hillsdale, NJ: Lawrence Erlbaum Associates.

Schoenfeld, A. H. (1992a). Learning to think mathematically: Problem solving, metacognition, and sense-making in mathematics. In D. A. Grouws (Ed.), *Handbook of research on mathematics teaching and learning* (pp. 334–370). New York: Macmillan.

Schoenfeld, A. H. (1992b). On paradigms and methods: What do you do when the ones you know don't do what you want them to? Issues in the analysis of data in the form of videotapes. *Journal of the Learning Sciences, 2,* 179–214.

Schoenfeld, A. H. (1992c). Radical constructivism and the pragmatics of instruction [Review of *Radical constructivism in mathematics education*]. *Journal for Research in Mathematics Education, 23,* 290–295.

Schoenfeld, A. H. (1992d). Research methods in and for the learning sciences. *Journal of the Learning Sciences, 2,* 137–139.

Schoenfeld, A. H. (1994). *Mathematics thinking and problem solving.* Hillsdale, NJ: Lawrence Erlbaum Associates.

Schoenfeld, A. H., Smith, J. P., & Arcavi, A. A. (1993). Learning: The microgenetic analysis of one student's evolving understanding of a complex subject-matter domain. In R. Glaser (Ed.), *Advances in instructional psychology* (Vol. 4, pp. 55–175). Hillsdale, NJ: Lawrence Erlbaum Associates.

Schubauer-Leoni, M-L., Bell, N., Grossen, M., & Perret-Clermont, A-N. (1989). Problems in assessment of learning: The social construction of questions and answers in the scholastic context. *International Journal of Educational Research, 13,* 671–683.

Schwartz, J. L., Yerushalmy, M., & Wilson, B. (Eds.). (1993). *The Geometric Supposer: What is it a case of?* Hillsdale, NJ: Lawrence Erlbaum Associates.

Scott, T., Cole, M., & Engel, M. (1992). Computers and education: A cultural constructivist perspective. In C. Grant (Ed.), *Review of research in education* (Vol. 18, pp. 191–251). Washington, DC: American Educational Research Association.

Scribner, S. (1984). Studying working intelligence. In B. Rogoff & J. Lave (Eds.), *Everyday cognition: Its development in social context* (pp. 9–40). Cambridge, MA: Harvard University Press.

Shepard, L. A. (1993). Evaluating test validity. In L. Darling-Hammond (Ed.), *Review of research in education* (Vol. 19, pp. 405–450). Washington, DC: American Educational Research Association.

Shuell, T. J. (1992). Designing instructional computing systems for meaningful learning. In M. Jones & P. H. Winne (Eds.), *Adaptive learning environments: Foundations and frontiers* (NATO ASI Series F: Computers and Systems Sciences, Vol. 85, pp. 19–54). Berlin: Springer.

Shulman, L. S. (1986). Paradigms and research programs in the study of teaching: A contemporary perspective. In M. C. Wittrock (Ed.), *Handbook of research on teaching* (3rd ed., pp. 3–36). New York: Macmillan.

Siegler, R. S., & Crowley, K. (1991). The microgenetic method: A direct means for studying cognitive development. *American Psychologist, 46,* 606–620.

Sierpinska, A., Kilpatrick, J., Balacheff, N., Howson, A. G., Sfard, A., & Steinbring, H. (1993). What is research in mathematics education and what are its results? *Journal for Research in Mathematics Education, 24,* 274–278.

Silver, E. A. (1979). Student perceptions of relatedness among mathematical verbal problems. *Journal for Research in Mathematics Education, 10,* 195–210.

Silver, E. A. (Ed.). (1985). *Teaching and learning mathematical problem solving: Multiple research perspectives.* Hillsdale, NJ: Lawrence Erlbaum Associates.

Silver, E. A. (1986). Using conceptual and procedural knowledge: A focus on relationships. In J. Hiebert (Ed.), *Conceptual and procedural knowledge: The case of mathematics* (pp. 181–198). Hillsdale, NJ: Lawrence Erlbaum Associates.

Silver, E. A. (1993). Assessment and mathematics education reform in the United States. *International Journal of Educational Research, 17,* 489–502.

Silver, E. A. (1994). On mathematical problem posing. *For the Learning of Mathematics, 14*(1), 19–28.

Silver, E. A., & Kenney, P. A. (1995). Sources of assessment information for instructional guidance in mathematics. In T. Romberg (Ed.), *Reform in school mathematics and authentic assessment* (pp. 38–86). Albany: State University of New York Press.

Silver, E. A., & Kilpatrick, J. (1988). Testing mathematical problem solving. In R. I. Charles & E. A. Silver (Eds.), *The teaching and assessing of mathematical problem solving* (pp. 178–186). Reston, VA: National Council of Teachers of Mathematics.

Silver, E. A., & Lane, S. (1993). Assessment in the context of mathematics instruction reform: The design of assessment in the QUASAR project. In M. Niss (Ed.), *Cases of assessment in mathematics education: An ICMI study* (pp. 59–69). Dordrecht, The Netherlands: Kluwer.

Silver, E. A., Leung, S. S., & Cai, J. (1992). Solving a nonroutine mathematics problem: An analysis of U.S. students' solution strategies and modes of explanation and a comparison with Japanese students. In J. P. Becker (Ed.), *Report of US-Japan cross-national research on students' problem-solving behaviors* (pp. 3–23). Carbondale: Southern Illinois University.

Silver, E. A., & Shapiro, L. J. (1992). Examinations of situation-based reasoning and sense-making in students' interpretations of solutions to a mathematics story problem. In J. P. Ponte, J. F. Matos, & D. Fernandes (Eds.), *Mathematical problem solving and new information techniques* (pp. 113–123). Berlin: Springer.

Silver, E. A., Shapiro, L. J., & Deutsch, A. (1993). Sense making and the solution of division problems involving remainders: An examination of middle school students' solution processes and their interpretations of solutions. *Journal for Research in Mathematics Education, 24,* 117–135.

Simon, H. A. (1980). Problem solving and education. In D. T. Tuma & R. Reif (Eds.), *Problem solving and education: Issues in teaching and research* (pp. 81–96). Hillsdale, NJ: Lawrence Erlbaum Associates.

Simon, M. A. (1993). Prospective elementary teachers' knowledge of division. *Journal for Research in Mathematics Education, 24,* 233–254.

Sinclair, H. (1991). Learning: The interactive recreation of knowledge. In L. P. Steffe & T. Wood (Eds.), *Transforming children's mathematics education* (pp. 19–29). Hillsdale, NJ: Lawrence Erlbaum Associates.

Skemp, R. R. (1979). *Intelligence, learning, and action.* Chichester, England: Wiley.

Snow, R. E. (1990). New approaches to cognitive and conative assessment in education. *International Journal of Educational Research, 14,* 455–473.

Snow, R. E., & Lohman, D. F. (1989). Implications of cognitive psychology for educational measurement. In R. L. Linn (Ed.), *Educational measurement* (3rd ed., pp. 263–331). New York: American Council on Education/Macmillan.

Snow, R. E., & Mandinach, E. B. (1991). *Integrating assessment and instruction: A research and development agenda.* Princeton, NJ: Educational Testing Service.

Solomon, C. (1986). *Computer environments for children.* Cambridge, MA: MIT Press.

Sowder, J. (1989). *Setting a research agenda* (Research Agenda for Mathematics Education, Vol. 5). Hillsdale, NJ: Lawrence Erlbaum Associates.

Sowder, L. (1988). Children's solutions of story problems. *Journal of Mathematical Behavior, 7,* 227–238.

Staats, A. W., & Staats, C. K. (1963). *Complex human behavior.* New York: Holt, Rinehart & Winston.

Stanic, G. M. A., & Kilpatrick, J. (1980). Historical perspectives on problem solving in the mathematics curriculum. In R. Charles & E. A. Silver (Eds.), *The teaching and assessing of mathematical problem solving.* Hillsdale, NJ: Lawrence Erlbaum Associates.

Steen, L. A. (1988). The science of patterns. *Science, 240,* 611–616.

Steen, L. A. (1992). Will everybody ever count? In I. Wirszup & R. Streit (Eds.), *Developments in school mathematics education around the world* (Vol. 3, pp. 3–13). Reston, VA: National Council of Teachers of Mathematics.

Steffe, L. P. (1991). The constructivist teaching experiment: Illustrations and implications. In E. von Glasersfeld (Ed.), *Radical constructivism in mathematics education* (pp. 177–194). Dordrecht, The Netherlands: Kluwer.

Steffe, L. P., Nesher, P., Cobb, P., Goldin, G. A., & Greer, B. (Eds.). (in press). *Theories of mathematical learning.* Hillsdale, NJ: Lawrence Erlbaum Associates.

Steffe, L. P., Cobb, P., & von Glasersfeld, E. (1988). *Construction of arithmetical meanings and strategies.* New York: Springer.

Steffe, L. P., & Gale, J. (1995). *Constructivism in education.* Hillsdale, NJ: Lawrence Erlbaum Associates.

Stephens, M., & Izard, J. (Eds.). (1992). *Reshaping assessment practice: Assessment in the mathematical sciences under challenge.* Hawthorn, Victoria, Australia: Australian Council for Educational Research.

Stevenson, H. W., Chen, C., & Lee, S-Y. (1993). Mathematics achievement of Chinese, Japanese, and American children: Ten years later. *Science, 259,* 53–58.

Stevenson, H. W., Lee, S-Y., & Stigler, J. W. (1986). Mathematics achievement of Chinese, Japanese, and American children. *Science, 231,* 693–699.

Stevenson, H. W., & Stigler, J. W. (1992). *The learning gap: Why our schools are failing and what we can learn from Japanese and Chinese education.* New York: Summit Books.

Stewart, I. (1987). *The problems of mathematics.* Oxford: Oxford University Press.

Stigler, J. W., & Baranes, R. (1988). Culture and mathematics learning. In E. Z. Rothkopf (Ed.), *Review of research in education* (Vol. 15, pp. 253–306). Washington, DC: American Educational Research Association.

Stigler, J. W., Fernandez, C., & Yoshida, M. (1992, August). *Children's thinking during mathematics instruction in Japanese and American elementary school classrooms.* Paper presented at the Seventh International Congress on Mathematical Education, Quebec City, Canada.

Stigler, J. W., Fuson, K. C., Ham, M., & Kim, M. (1986). An analysis of addition and subtraction word problems in U.S. and Soviet elementary mathematics textbooks. *Cognition and Instruction, 3,* 153–171.

Stigler, J. W., & Perry, M. (1988). Cross cultural studies of mathematics teaching and learning: Recent findings and new directions. In D. A. Grouws, T. J. Cooney, & D. Jones (Eds.), *Perspectives on research on effective mathematics teaching* (pp. 194–223). Hillsdale, NJ: Lawrence Erlbaum Associates.

Streefland, L. (1990). Free productions in teaching and learning mathematics. In K. Gravemeijer, M. van den Heuvel-Panhuizen, & L. Streefland (Eds.), *Contexts, free productions, tests and geometry in realistic mathematics education* (pp. 33–52). Utrecht, The Netherlands: State University of Utrecht, Research Group for Mathematical Education and Educational Computer Centre.

Streefland, L. (1991a). *Fractions in realistic mathematics education: A paradigm of developmental research.* Dordrecht, The Netherlands: Kluwer.

Streefland, L. (Ed.). (1991b). *Realistic mathematics education in primary school: On the occasion of the opening of the Freudenthal Institute.* Utrecht, The Netherlands: Freudenthal Institute, University of Utrecht.

Streefland, L. (Ed.). (1993). *The legacy of Hans Freudenthal. Educational Studies in Mathematics, 25,* 1–164.

Suchting, W. A. (1992). Constructivism deconstructed. *Science & Education, 1,* 223–254.

Suppes, P. (1990). Intelligent tutoring, but not intelligent enough. *Contemporary Psychology, 35,* 648–650.

Swan, M. (1993). Assessing a wider range of students' abilities. In N. L. Webb (Ed.), *Assessment in the mathematics classroom: 1993 yearbook* (pp. 26–39). Reston, VA: National Council of Teachers of Mathematics.

Tall, D. (Ed.). (1991). *Advanced mathematical thinking.* Dordrecht, The Netherlands: Kluwer.

Thompson, A. G. (1982). *Teachers' conceptions of mathematics and mathematics teaching: Three case studies.* Unpublished doctoral dissertation, University of Georgia, Athens.

Thompson, A. G. (1992). Teachers' beliefs and conceptions: A synthesis of the research. In D. A. Grouws (Ed.), *Handbook of research on mathematics teaching and learning* (pp. 127–146). New York: Macmillan.

Thompson, P. W. (1989). Artificial Intelligence, advanced technology, and learning and teaching algebra. In S. Wagner & C. Kieran (Eds.), *Research issues in the learning and teaching of algebra* (pp. 135–161). Hillsdale, NJ: Lawrence Erlbaum Associates; Reston, VA: National Council of Teachers of Mathematics.

Thompson, P. W. (1993). Yes, Virginia, some children do grow up to be mathematicians [Review of *Advanced Mathematical Thinking*.] *Journal for Research in Mathematics Education, 24,* 279–284.

Thorndike, E. L. (1922). *The psychology of arithmetic.* New York: Macmillan.

Treffers, A. (1987). *Three dimensions: A model of goal and theory description in mathematics education. The Wiskobas project.* Dordrecht, The Netherlands: Reidel.

Treffers, A. (1991a). Didactical background of a mathematics program for primary education. In L. Streefland (Ed.), *Realistic mathematics education in primary school. On the occasion of the opening of the Freudenthal Institute* (pp. 21–56). Utrecht, The Netherlands: Freudenthal Institute, University of Utrecht.

Treffers, A. (1991b). Realistic mathematics education in The Netherlands 1980–1990. In L. Streefland (Ed.), *Realistic mathematics education in primary school: On the occasion of the opening of the Freudenthal Institute* (pp. 11–20). Utrecht, The Netherlands: Freudenthal Institute, University of Utrecht.

Treffers, A., De Moor, E., & Feijs, E. (1989). *Proeve van een nationaal programma voor het reken/wiskunde-onderwijs op de basisschool: Deel 1. Overzicht einddoelen* [Towards a national curriculum for mathematics education in the elementary school: Part 1. Overview of the goals]. Tilburg, The Netherlands: Zwijsen.

Tymoczko, T. (1986a). Interlude. In T. Tymoczko (Ed.), *New directions in the philosophy of mathematics* (pp. 95–98). Boston: Birkhauser.

Tymoczko, T. (1986b). Introduction. In T. Tymoczko (Ed.), *New directions in the philosophy of mathematics* (pp. xiii–xvii). Boston: Birkhauser.

Tymoczko, T. (Ed.). (1986c). *New directions in the philosophy of mathematics.* Boston: Birkhauser.

Van den Brink, J. (1991). Didactic constructivism. In E. von Glasersfeld (Ed.), *Radical constructivism in mathematics education* (pp. 195–227). Dordrecht, The Netherlands: Kluwer.

Van Galen, F., & Feijs, E. (1990). Interactive video in teacher training. In L. Streefland (Ed.), *Realistic mathematics education in primary school: On the occasion of the opening of the Freudenthal Institute* (pp. 183–208). Utrecht, The Netherlands: Freudenthal Institute, University of Utrecht.

Van Haneghan, J., Barron, L., Young, M., Williams, S., Vye, N., & Bransford, J. (1992). The *Jasper* series: An experiment with new ways to enhance mathematical thinking. In D. F. Halpern (Ed.), *Enhancing thinking skills in the sciences and mathematics* (pp. 15–38). Hillsdale, NJ: Lawrence Erlbaum Associates.

VanLehn, K. (1990). *Mind bugs: The origins of procedural misconceptions.* Cambridge, MA: MIT Press.

Van Oers, B. (1990). The development of mathematical thinking in school: A comparison of the action-psychological and information-processing approaches. *International Journal of Educational Research, 14,* 51–66.

Van Streun, A. (1989). *Heuristisch wiskunde-onderwijs: Verslag van een onderwijsexperiment* [Heuristic mathematics education: Report of a teaching experiment]. Unpublished doctoral dissertation, Rijksuniversiteit Groningen, Groningen, The Netherlands.

Vergnaud, G. (1982). Cognitive and developmental psychology and research in mathematics education: Some theoretical and methodological issues. *For the Learning of Mathematics, 3*(2), 31–41.

Vergnaud, G. (1990). Epistemology and psychology of mathematics education. In P. Nesher & J. Kilpatrick (Eds.), *Mathematics and cognition: A research synthesis by the International Group for the Psychology of Mathematics Education* (pp. 14–30). Cambridge, U.K.: Cambridge University Press.

Vermont Department of Education. (1991). *Looking beyond "The answer": Report of Vermont's Mathematics Portfolio Assessment Program.* Montpelier: Vermont Department of Education.

Verschaffel, L. (1984). *Representatie-en oplossingsprocessen van eersteklassers bij aanvankelijke redactie-opgaven over optellen en aftrekken* [First graders' representation and solution processes on elementary addition and substraction word problems]. Unpublished doctoral dissertation, University of Leuven, Belgium.

Verschaffel, L., & De Corte, E. (1993). A decade of research on word-problem solving in Leuven: Theoretical, methodological, and practical outcomes. *Educational Psychology Review, 5*(3), 1–18.

Verschaffel, L., & De Corte, E. (in press). Word problems: A vehicle for promoting mathematical understanding and problem solving in school? In P. Bryant & T. Nunes (Eds.), *How do children learn mathematics?* Hillsdale, NJ: Lawrence Erlbaum Associates.

Verschaffel, L., De Corte, E., Gielen, I., & Struyf, E. (1994). Clever rearrangement strategies in children's mental arithmetic: A confrontation of eye-movement data and verbal protocols. In J. E. H. Van Luit (Ed.), *Research on learning and instruction of mathematics in kindergarten and primary school* (pp. 153–180). Doetinchem, The Netherlands/Rapallo, Italy: Graviant.

Verschaffel, L., De Corte, E., & Lasure, S. (1994). Realistic considerations in mathematical modeling of school arithmetic word problems. *Learning and Instruction, 4,* 273–294.

Voigt, J. (1989). Social functions of routines and consequences for subject matter learning. *International Journal for Educational Psychology, 13,* 647–656.

von Glasersfeld, E. (1987). Learning as a constructive activity. In C. Janvier (Ed.), *Problems of representation in the teaching and learning of mathematics* (pp. 3–17). Hillsdale, NJ: Lawrence Erlbaum Associates.

von Glasersfeld, E. (1989). Constructivism in education. In T. Husén & T. N. Postlethwaite (Eds.), *International encyclopedia of education: Supplementary Vol. 1. Research and studies* (pp. 162–163). Oxford, U.K.: Pergamon Press.

von Glasersfeld, E. (Ed.). (1991). *Radical constructivism in mathematics education.* Dordrecht, The Netherlands: Kluwer.

von Wright, J. (1992). Reflections on reflection. *Learning and Instruction, 2,* 59–68.

Vygotsky, L. S. (1962). *Thought and language* (A. Kozulin, Ed.). Cambridge, MA: MIT Press. (Original work published 1934)

Vygotsky, L. S. (1978). *Mind in society: The development of higher psychological processes.* Cambridge, MA: Harvard University Press.

Wagner, S., & Kieran, C. (Eds.). (1988). *Research issues in the learning and teaching of algebra.* Hillsdale, NJ: Lawrence Erlbaum Associates.

Walker, D. F. (1986). Computers and the curriculum. In K. J. Rehage (Ed.), *Microcomputers and education* (85th Yearbook of the National Society for the Study of Education, Pt. 1, pp. 22–39). Chicago: National Society for the Study of Education.

Watson, J. B. (1913). Image and affect in behavior. *Journal of Philosophy, 10,* 421–428.

Webb, N. L. (1992). Assessment of students' knowledge of mathematics: Steps toward a theory. In D. A. Grouws (Ed.), *Handbook of research on mathematics teaching and learning* (pp. 661–683). Reston, VA: National Council of Teachers of Mathematics/New York: Macmillan.

Weir, S. (1992). LEGO-Logo: A vehicle for learning. In C. Hoyles & R. Noss (Eds.), *Learning mathematics and Logo* (pp. 165–190). Cambridge, MA: MIT Press.

Wertheimer, M. (1945). *Productive thinking.* London: Tavistock.

Wertsch, J. V. (1985). *Vygotsky and the social foundation of mind.* Cambridge, MA: Harvard University Press.

Wheeler, D. (1989). Contexts for research on the teaching and learning of algebra. In S. Wagner & C. Kieran (Eds.), *Research issues in the learning and teaching of algebra* (pp. 278–287). Hillsdale, NJ: Lawrence Erlbaum Associates/Reston, VA: National Council of Teachers of Mathematics.

Whitehead, A. N. (1929). *The aims of education.* New York: Macmillan.

Wigner, E. P. (1960). The unreasonable effectiveness of mathematics in the natural sciences. *Communications in Pure and Applied Mathematics, 13,* 1–14.

Wood, T., Cobb, P., & Yackel, E. (1991). Change in teaching mathematics. *American Educational Research Journal, 28,* 587–616.

Wood, T., Cobb, P., & Yackel, E. (1995). Reflections on learning and teaching in elementary school. In L. P. Steffe & J. Gale (Eds.), *Constructivism in education* (pp. 401–422). Hillsdale, NJ: Lawrence Erlbaum Associates.

Youniss, J., & Damon, W. (1992). Social construction in Piaget's theory. In H. Beilin & P. B. Pufall (Eds.), *Piaget's theory: Prospects and possibilities* (pp. 267–286). Hillsdale, NJ: Lawrence Erlbaum Associates.

Zaslavsky, C. (1973). *Africa counts.* Boston: Prindle, Weber & Schmidt.

Zimmermann, W., & Cunningham, S. (Eds.). (1991). *Visualization in teaching and learning mathematics* (MAA Notes, No. 19). Washington: Mathematical Association of America.

# ·17·

# PSYCHOLOGICAL PERSPECTIVES ON LITERACY AND EXTENSIONS TO EDUCATIONAL PRACTICE

## Elfrieda H. Hiebert
### UNIVERSITY OF MICHIGAN, ANN ARBOR

## Taffy E. Raphael
### MICHIGAN STATE UNIVERSITY, EAST LANSING

To review the relationship of educational psychology to research in literacy and literacy instruction is to review educational psychology itself. Almost since the start of the 20th century, reading and writing have been the primary foci of study for educational psychologists. In turn, educational psychology has dominated views on reading and writing and on their instruction in the elementary school. It is no coincidence that Nila Banton Smith (1934/1965), in her history of American reading instruction, identified 1910, the year in which the *Journal of Educational Psychology* was launched, as the first great breakthrough in American reading instruction:

The dramatic period beginning within the year of 1910 ushered in the first truly great break-through in American reading instruction. While there was no strong nationalistic aim for education or for reading at this time a new development suddenly shaped up which had startling effects in changing reading methods and materials. This era in the history of reading was marked by the birth of the scientific movement in education. In 1909 Thorndike made the initial presentation of his handwriting scale before a meeting of the American Association for the Advancement of Science, and in 1910 (Thorndike, 1910) it was published. Generally speaking, the publication of the Thorndike scale has been recognized as the beginning of the contemporary movement for measuring educational products scientifically. (p. 157).

Smith suggests that Thorndike's work introduced the field of literacy education to the idea of scientific bases for its practices. Not surprisingly, practices of interest centered on the foundation of work in elementary schools—students' abilities to read and write text. The connection between educational psychology and literacy was firmly established.

Even a fraction of the studies that have been conducted since this "first truly great break-through" cannot be captured within a single chapter. Authors of chapters in volumes devoted to literacy research such as the *Handbook of Reading Research* (Barr, Kamil, Mosenthal, & P. D. Pearson, 1991). *Theoretical Models and Processes of Reading* (R. B. Ruddell, M. R. Ruddell, & Singer, 1994), or the *Handbook of Research on Teaching the English Language Arts* (Flood, Jensen, Lapp, & Squire, 1991) have the license to focus on particular topics and recently published studies. Insofar as this *Handbook of Educational Psychology* is a first volume, we viewed our task to be one of presenting the primary perspectives from educational psychology on literacy learning and the extensions of these perspectives to school literacy practice.

Much of educational psychology has been consumed with describing theories of learning, and literacy has been a primary content arena for studying these theories. Theories from educational psychology have been critical in defining the views of literacy held by educators and the public. A grounding in the primary theoretical perspectives on literacy and literacy learning in educational psychology seemed an appropriate point of departure for this chapter. Two perspectives—behaviorism and cognitive science—have been particularly influential in past and current views of literacy and literacy learning. A third perspective, social constructivism, which has currency among a growing number of educational psychologists, was included because its focus on the nature of knowledge and learning is consonant with the questions and issues that have defined educational psychology (see Chapter 2, this volume).

The second aim of this chapter was to study the extensions of these views to school practice. While many (including the authors of chapters in this volume) identify different events and dates as the initiating points of educational psychology, the founding of the *Journal of Educational Psychology* in 1910 is

We wish to thank Donna Alvermann, Richard C. Anderson and Edys S. Quellmalz for their thoughtful reviews of this chapter. We are also thankful for the comments of Kathy Au, Charles Fisher, Susan Florio-Ruane, James Gavelek, Virginia Goatley and Connie Juel.

evidence of a distinct field. Numerous studies of reading processes were published before that year, (see Huey, 1908/1968) but the influence of this research on educational practice was less direct. Thorndike's aim of establishing "instructional practices grounded in science" (Walberg & Haertel, 1992, p. 8) marked a different kind of involvement by psychologists in education. While early educational psychologist themselves did not enter classrooms and teach children (although W. S. Gray had been a teacher prior to taking a master's degree with Thorndike at Teachers College and a doctorate at the University of Chicago [Guthrie, 1984]), they taught teachers (Thorndike, 1906), they designed textbook materials (Thorndike, 1921), and they created tests (Gates, 1921; Gray, 1915; Thorndike, 1917, 1918). They viewed the classroom as an important laboratory in which to act. To examine the manifestations of the theoretical perspectives in school practice is consonant with the underlying aims of educational psychology.

We focus on three constructs that fall within the intersection of the field of education, studies of the nature of literacy, and the lens of the educational psychologist: tests, texts, and teaching. Education, literacy, and educational psychology each consider a range of phenomena, but each area concerns itself with how students' progress is evaluated, the nature of the texts that are read and written, and the nature of teaching that supports and encourages student learning. Each of the three constructs of tests, texts, and teaching has a unique role in literacy education which occurs apart from the research of educational psychologists. Tests and texts have been developed by separate industries, industries that have operated in isolation from the academic institutions where teachers participate in preparatory or in-service course work. In fact, these three constructs draw on a different set of community members who are responsible for the decisions and policies that lead to the formats and content that ultimately form the tests, are found in the texts, or are the basis for teacher education curricula. Although links across these communities, such as the involvement of educational psychologists in textbook programs, as illustrated by Gray's (Elson & Gray, 1930; Gray, Arbuthnot, Artley, & Monroe, 1957) sustained efforts with Scott Foresman and by the presence within the same corporations of textbook and test divisions, such as Harcourt Brace Jovanovich (a textbook publisher) and Psychological Corporation (a test publisher), have long existed, the size of the community that spans these three constructs is and has been comparatively small relative to the community of educational psychologists and curriculum and instruction scholars who work with teachers. In the decades following Cattell (1890) and Thorndike (1918), the educational psychologists who became the mainstays of the test publishing business were specialists in testing, measurement, and evaluation; that is, they were psychometricians with increasingly tenuous connections to educational psychology as a whole (Shepard, 1991). The text publishing field became the domain of literacy educators, some of whom serve as consultants for or authors of commercially prepared materials used to teach reading or the language arts (see, e.g., Farr et al., 1993; P. D. Pearson et al., 1989). In teacher education programs, students continue to take a course in educational psychology, but in many institutions educational psychologists rarely play primary roles in the overall teacher education curriculum. Thus, the three constructs exist outside the field of educational psychology

to include scholarship in general and literacy education, yet appear to be viable spheres of influence within educational psychology.

The purpose of this chapter, then is twofold: (a) to describe the views of literacy and its learning that emanate from educational psychology and (b) to summarize the extensions of these views to three central constructs of school literacy practice—tests, texts, and teaching. We believe that within the task parameters we have set, we provide readers with points of departure for continued examination of the relationships between educational psychology and literacy research.

# PERSPECTIVES ON LITERACY AND LITERACY LEARNING

Perspectives on literacy and the literacy learner have shaped the ways in which literacy has been defined, the models that have been adopted to guide literacy research and instruction, and the legacies that are apparent in today's schools. In this section we consider the changing definitions of literacy, then discuss three perspectives on learning—behaviorism, cognitive science, and social constructivism—that have relevance to literacy educational research and practices today.

## Changing Definitions of Literacy

Many historians, linguists, educational psychologists, and philosophers have attempted to describe what literacy is, the criteria by which it is evaluated, and the role that it plays in individuals' and societies' development. The range of definitions is not unrelated to the way in which the field of educational psychology has chosen to study literacy acts or events and the way in which research has influenced pedagogical approaches to literacy instruction, from elementary schools through college study skill courses. The definitions of literacy have ranged from those focusing on the decoding and encoding of print, or as Spache (1964) said, "a series of word perceptions," to those more broadly focused on comprehension, interpretation, and political power, as reflected in the writings of scholars such as Scribner and Cole (1981). The definition of literacy has been the source of debate among researchers (Aaron, Chall, Durkin, K. Goodman, & Strickland, 1990) as well as policymakers (Wixson, Peters, Weber, & Roeber, 1987). The acceptance of particular definitions shapes research agendas as well as instructional foci and accountability activities for teachers and students.

Literacy has been defined as: (a) "the ability to decode and comprehend written language at a rudimentary level, that is, the ability to look at written words corresponding to ordinary oral discourse, to say them, and to understand them" (Kaestle, Damon-Moore, Stedman, Tinsley, & Trollinger, 1991, p. 3); (b) a psycholinguistic process (F. Smith, 1982); (c) a psycholinguistic guessing game (K. S. Goodman, 1976); (d) "a cognitive skill" (Venezky, 1991, p. 49); (e) "the capacity to employ language as a tool for thinking and communicating" (Calfee & Nelson-Barber, 1991, p. 44); (f) the ability to read and write, decode and encode (the minimalist definition) to being well-read, learned, and thus, well-educated (the maximal meaning) (Hawkins, 1991, p. 1); (g) "adaptation," "power," and "state of grace" (Scribner & Cole, 1981); (h) a set of cultural practices in which people engage (L. B. Resnick, 1991); (i) a way of thinking, acting, or speaking, defined in terms of differential power relationships and structures within society (Gee, 1988); (j) not one literacy but a plurality of literacies, each responding to a particular social need (e.g., literacy for recitation of religious text, literacy to encourage creative thinking and interpretation) (Damon, 1991); and so forth. Several scholars distinguish between those who are "literate" and those "who have used reading and writing merely as tools to achieve somewhat limited ends within narrow occupational roles" (Heath, 1991, p. 4), arguing that to be literate implies one is also learned, beyond attention to daily sustenance, labor, and knowledge derived from direct experiences.

Bruner (1991) perhaps best summarizes the issue, arguing that "'literacy' is an issue that far transcends the mere mastery of reading and writing, one that has deep roots in our national history" (p. vii), that it is a "first step in the empowerment of mind, albeit a crucial one. For what we learn from history, from anthropology, and from studies of human development is that literacy not only provides access to the culture's written record, it also shapes the way in which mind is used" (p. vii). Although the focus of educational psychologists on the acquisition of literacy skills could be interpreted to define such skills as cognitive in scope, to do so would limit the substantive contributions of the field to understanding literacy acquisition, since such learning may be understood only within its social and historical contexts, and as it relates to issues of power, authority, and culture.

The separation of reading from other language processes, the emphasis on component skills and subskills of reading, and neglect of the cultural and social contexts in which literacy occurs have led some to question the value of the knowledge generated by educational psychologists. Merritt (1986), for example, argues that "the idea that teachers need courses packed with linguistics and the esoterica of reading research seems increasingly hard to justify" (p. 185). Such attitudes toward research develop when the research is decontextualized from the broader community to which the work is relevant and should apply. Educational psychologists who wish to influence the field through research must contextualize their work within broad, pressing questions. L. B. Resnick (1991) proposes that "instead of asking what constitutes literacy competency or ability, terms that invite efforts to list the skills and knowledge possessed by individual who are judged literate, [we should] examine literacy as a set of cultural practices that people engage in," and in turn "shift [our] perspective from personal skill to cultural practice, with implications for a changed view of teaching and instruction" (pp. 170–171), and, by implication, research focus.

The evolving emphasis on what educational psychologists should study to enhance understanding of literacy learning can also be understood within the social and historical contexts of the multidisciplinary field called literacy. The scholarship on literacy is closely linked to the paradigms and rhetorical structures of psychology and of the "hard" sciences. It is only recently that educational psychologists have begun to draw direct connections to the fields of linguistics, anthropology, literary criticism, and sociology.

Interconnections across literacy areas have been as conspicuously absent as multidisciplinary connections. When we began

this chapter, our intent was to provide an integrative review of research on reading and writing from the perspectives of educational psychology. Although the topic of reading–writing connections has been popular in recent years (Dyson, 1989; Irwin & Doyle, 1992), the model building for this integration is in its initial stages (Tierney & Shanahan, 1991). Clifford's (1989) historical analysis of the separation of reading and writing indicates that it is not only educational psychologists who have treated aspects of literacy (and language) separately but that such separation is endemic to theory, research, and practice across disciplines in which scholars study literacy. Even in a climate of calls for integration, the separate treatment of literacy areas continues. In the *Handbook of Research on Teaching,* where extensive reviews of reading and writing instruction can be found, chapters on writing and reading appear next to one another (Calfee & Drum, 1986; Scardamalia & Bereiter, 1986), but with few shared references or themes. A similar pattern is evident in the recent *Handbook of Research on Teaching the English Language Arts* (Flood et al., 1991) where, despite the inclusion of literacy in many chapter titles, most authors focused on aspects of reading or writing.

Although the literatures could not be integrated completely, similar themes run through reading and writing research in earlier decades when views of educational psychology dominated. The fields are moving together, as the subsequent discussions illustrate. The evolution of the field of literacy studies from a focus on discrete behaviors to the examination of multiple literacies is reflected in the shifting paradigms that have guided literacy research conducted by educational psychologists over time. We turn now to an examination of the three dominant theoretical lenses that have guided and shaped current school literacy practices: behaviorism, cognitive science, and social constructivism. In the discussion that follows, we use the terms *perspective, theory,* and *field* to describe behaviorism, cognitive science, and social constructivism. Although we have attempted to characterize these views as carefully as possible, our aim was not to provide a historical or comprehensive review of these perspectives. We recognize that each of these perspectives that we present as unitary is characterized by long-standing divisions, debates, and unresolved issues. Other chapters in this volume provide the needed background for readers who wish to trace the shared premises and differences within particular perspectives. Readers interested in historical background for perspectives on literacy can refer to sources such as Kaestle et al. (1991). To set the record straight, we have attempted to use perspective rather than theory, recognizing that behaviorism represents a single theory, cognitive science represents a field based on a set of theories, and social constructivism represents a set of related theories (R. C. Anderson, personal communication, April 1994).

## Behaviorist Views of Literacy and Literacy Learning

Behaviorism is a perspective that has long influenced both research and practice. Its legacies are evident today in such school practices as seatwork and criterion-referenced tests. Behaviorism's emphasis on the study of observable behavior limited the aspects of literacy that could be examined. Not unexpectedly, studies of handwriting, grammar, word recognition, and knowledge of sound–symbol correspondences were common.

From the late 1800s through the early 1900s, psychologists focused on reading as a perceptual process, primarily measuring perception of print (i.e., single letters, words) through reaction time studies, or focused on areas such as eye–voice span, speed of reading, and lip movements during silent reading (see Venezky, 1984, for a review of this research). Within these lines of research, virtually no attention was paid to whether or not the readers had comprehended the text—either because connected text was not used or because meaning construction was beyond the purview of the study. Thus, despite research reflecting what Venezky termed "the golden years" (1984, p. 7), in hindsight, psychology had little to say about the complex processes of literacy that must be understood to influence the development of literate youngsters through formal education.

The first generation of educational psychologists and their students drew to some degree on this research, but their overriding point of agreement was on behaviors. It was no accident that handwriting, with a clear-cut artifact, received initial attention from educational psychologists. The study of reading and writing (handwriting, spelling, and grammar, but not composing) was limited to behaviors that were observable and measurable. Consistent with the focus on observable behaviors, Venezky (1984) noted that while there were occasional studies of comprehension, the study of reading generally referred to studies of oral reading. Comprehension was assumed to have occurred if readers were able to pronounce words correctly. Where meaning was of concern, it tended to focus on vocabulary development, something that could be more cleanly defined and measured. Thus, for the first 50 years of research by educational psychologists on literacy, little concern existed for understanding the construction of meaning, since it was beyond the purview of the research.

The notable exceptions to this trend were found in research that examined meaning construction in terms of memory for text and problem solving. Both foreshadowed more extensive lines of research conducted in the 1970s through 1980s. Bartlett's (1932) work, often cited as the basis of schema-theoretic views of reading, inferred individual's processes for meaning construction from their recalls of texts read. In his book, *Remembering,* Bartlett describes the role of schemata, the way of organizing past experiences and reactions, in the memory that readers have for text they have read. His methods, still used today, consisted of asking readers to recall previously read text over successive periods of time, then examining the content recalled (e.g., topics, details, words). From the readers' recall protocols, the researchers then inferred what had been salient and memorable aspects of texts for that reader. From Bartlett's view, meaning construction was an individual process reflected in the individual's abilities to recall original forms and ideas from the text, influenced by the texts read, the amount of time that passed between the reading and the recall activities, and the readers' own knowledge.

Other notable exceptions to the deemphasis of meaning construction as integral to reading are found in Thorndike's (1917) research, in which Thorndike examined the incorrect responses readers gave to open-ended questions following reading, and in Reed's (1938/1992) review of the role of meaning in learning. Like Bartlett, meaning construction for Thorn-

dike involved an individual interaction with text, but Thorndike assumed that this occurred during the reading process: not a result of memory or organizational strategies, but as a result of problem-solving activities as one reads. For example, he suggested that failure to understand could be attributed to vocabulary difficulties, assigning the wrong levels of importance to particular words or ideas, or not monitoring one's reading.

Reed (1938/1992) raised concerns that researchers of the time had "oversimplified the learning process, covered too narrow a field, favored mechanistic interpretations, and kept the principal field of human learning, that of meaningful materials, largely untouched" (Reed, 1938/1992, p. 395). Reed reviewed studies of memory for text that contrasted list versus sentence versus prose learning (e.g., English & Welborn, 1937; English, Welborn, & Killian, 1934) and concluded that "it is clear that memory for prose substance does not depend so much on the fact of repetition as on other factors, the most important of which is probably comprehension" (1938/1992, p. 397). Although comprehension was understood to be critical, the research of the time did not provide adequate means for understanding comprehension processes. The examples do suggest that scholars at the time assumed there is meaning inherent in materials being read, and that the job of the active individual reader is to uncover that meaning.

Thus, until the end of the 1950s, issues related to the nature of comprehension or constructing meaning tended to be ignored or deemphasized. When given attention, meaning construction was assumed to involve memory for, or identification of, information presented in the text. Since the simplistic view that behaviorists took of reading (reading was reading words and writing was writing words) emphasized word recognition, one might have expected understandings of word recognition to have been furthered by behaviorists, yet little was added to the work of previous decades. Work on perceptual processes and eye-span movements, which Huey's (1908/1968) review indicated had been extensive during the late 19th and early 20th centuries, virtually ceased as the dominant perspective of educational psychology became behaviorism. The associationism of Thorndike, the respondent conditioning of Watson (1919), and the operant conditioning of Skinner (1954) differed in important ways (Glover & Ronning, 1987; Kratochwill & Bijou, 1987) but they shared an emphasis on observable behavior.

Behaviorists took a fairly straightforward view of literacy. Thorndike began his 1917 article in the *Journal of Educational Psychology* by describing the accepted definition of reading:

It seems to be a common opinion that reading (understanding of printed words) is a rather simple compounding of habits. Each word or phrase is supposed, if known to the reader, to call up its sound and meaning and the series of word or phrase meanings is supposed to be, or be easily transmuted into the total thought. (p. 323)

Despite Thorndike's description of "reading as reasoning" in this article (and even here the reading task involved a single sentence), neither Thorndike's attention nor that of his colleagues focused on the underlying processes of reading or writing. By concentrating on the visible acts of reading and writing, these early educational psychologists did not pursue the research on reading processes such as the research on time taken to see and name letters and words conducted by Thorndike's mentor, Cattell (1886). Instead, Thorndike and colleagues directed their efforts in applying the laws of learning to the subject areas of the school curriculum. The same laws of learning—effect, exercise, readiness, and identical elements (Thorndike, 1903)—were applied across subject areas but, because of the place of reading and writing in the 3 Rs, considerable attention was paid to the pedagogy of reading and writing. The law of readiness meant that the critical behaviors of reading, which were viewed as recognizing the most frequently used words, needed to be sequenced. The laws of identical elements and exercise dictated that students practice repeatedly on specific sets of target words (or, prior to that, letters) to ensure a connection between stimulus and response. The law of effect meant that correct responses such as the reading of a story made up of the target words or filling in a target word within a workbook exercise should be praised. Since the early decades of the 20th century, when these laws were applied to reading and writing learning and its instruction, the fads and fashions in literacy education have come and gone (Feitelson, 1988). Although theories of literacy have also been many (Graubard, 1991), manifestations of the laws of behaviorists can be seen in such activities as the ubiquitous workbook exercises where students practice one reading element, then the next, and so on.

Skinner's (1954, 1965) view of operant conditioning gave behaviorism new life in the middle of the 20th century, especially as it pertained to school reading instruction. With this view of learning, a content area such as reading could be broken into steps, each of which could be the basis for exercises in text or on a machine. Each element of an exercise required an overt response, which was followed by immediate feedback. When a student's response was correct, the feedback was reinforcing. When the student responded incorrectly, the student was told to give another response until he or she got it right. Learning to read became the center of activity, as researchers devised hierarchies of seemingly endless skills that were made up of subskills that themselves had subskills, and so forth, such as the Wisconsin Design for Reading Skill Development (Otto, 1977) and Individually Prescribed Instruction (Glaser, 1963).

Historical events intervened to influence the particular translation of curriculum or what was to be learned. Russia's success with *Sputnik* focused U.S. attention on the skill levels of U.S. schoolchildren. Solutions for improving skills in reading were often simplistic, such as Flesch's (1957) thesis that lack of phonics instruction caused children to fail to learn to read. As a result, the curriculum of skills and subordinate skills focused on easily defined and measured skills such as phonics and structural analysis. Although comprehension skills were also demarcated, it was with less specificity and quantity.

Although some of the work of the behaviorists provides a historical outlook on literacy, to dismiss behaviorism as a historical artifact is to ignore current practices so embedded in the culture of schools as to appear to be givens. As a recent national study of academic instruction for low-income students showed (Knapp, Shields, & Turnbull, 1992), workbook exercises that reinforce isolated skills continue to be a prominent part of the school lives of many students.

## Cognitive Science Perspectives on Literacy and Literacy Learning

The cognitive science revolution shifted the focus from the study of observable behaviors to attempts to describe unobservable mental processes. Because reading is an unobservable mental process, educational psychologists in the late 1960s and 1970s began to focus extensively on describing the underlying cognitive processes involved in reading. As Bruner (1990) suggests, cognitive science reflected "an effort to establish meaning as the central concept of psychology—not stimuli and responses, not overtly observable behavior" (p. 2). Although this represented a major shift from the influence of behaviorism, it still focused on the more easily defined and measurable aspects of reading. Much of this work harkened back to the early 20th-century definition of reading as a perceptual process (e.g., P. B. Gough, 1972; LaBerge & Samuels, 1974; Gibson & Levin, 1975) and the tradition of developing models and studying perceptual skills such as letter recognition and letter–sound correspondences. Although the act of constructing meaning was not deemphasized in the same way as it had been at the turn of the 20th century, it nonetheless did not receive direct attention. Rather, it was characterized as a mysterious process beyond description—for example, a process controlled by "Merlin" the magician of the King Arthur myths—and represented as an outcome, "The Place Where Sentences Go When They Are Understood," or TPWSGWTAU (P. B. Gough, 1972). As limited as these models were in defining literacy, they represented an important departure from the lack of attention to reading processes in the preceding decades.

Meaning construction came into prominence in the late 1970s. The work of Bartlett (1932) laid the foundation for schema theory, which focused attention on what it meant to comprehend in the history of educational psychologists' work in literacy. Studies of the process of meaning construction conducted through the lens of cognitive science assumed that text had meaning and that the task of a reader was to use all available strategies and skills to construct that meaning. Thus, readers were not in the passive role of merely pulling information rotely from the printed page. Rather, readers were active as they drew on their background knowledge, knowledge of text structures, and knowledge of relationships among words to determine the meaning of the text.

Cognitive scientists conducting research at this time included two groups of scholars. Although both groups were clearly interested in the invisible processes of cognition and thinking, some can be characterized within information-processing traditions in model building (e.g., P. B. Gough, 1972; A. M. Lesgold & Perfetti, 1981) and learning text information (e.g., Frase & Schwartz, 1975; Rothkopf & Bisbicos, 1967), while others reflected constructivist perspectives within cognitive science (e.g., R. C. Anderson, 1977; Bransford, 1979; A. L. Brown, 1978; Collins, J. S. Brown, & Larkin, 1980). These scholars represented different ends of a continuum, at one end of which meaning was seen as being transported from author to reader, while at the other, meaning was seen as being constructed by the reader based on information provided by the author.

Research within the domain of cognitive science spawned numerous studies of writers' activities in creating text and the nature of readers' activities in determining the author's message, as well as insights into word recognition processes. We discuss representative work below in terms of (a) readers' background knowledge and knowledge associated with cultural and religious background, (b) metacognitive strategy knowledge, and (c) word learning.

*Background Knowledge.* Studies of the role of background knowledge proliferated during this period as educational psychologists attempted to understand the nature of readers' schemata, how information was organized in memory, problems related to background knowledge, and the effects of activating this knowledge at different points in the reading process. Studies in these areas analyzed the potential role of background knowledge in readers' abilities to recall, retell, and summarize expository and narrative text. One of the major lines of research was conducted by R. C. Anderson and his colleagues at the Center for the Study of Reading (for summaries of this work, see R. C. Anderson & P. D. Pearson, 1984; R. C. Anderson, Spiro, & Montague, 1977). The studies in this research used two different types of texts. In the first, the text content was potentially of differential importance to similar readers (e.g., college undergraduates) assumed to have different perspectives or backgrounds. In the second, the text was purposely ambiguous so that readers had to create or invoke a context to make sense of the material. Both methods revealed that the readers' background knowledge or perspective was critical to how they constructed the meaning intended by the authors.

For instance, in one now well-known text, two boys skip a day of school and spend it at the home of one of the boys. As they move through the house, the boy who lives there tells his friend pieces of information (e.g., where his father's coin collection is located, the day his mother is not home, which door is unlocked, the newly painted basement), while the authors provide descriptions of the setting (e.g., the distance of the house from its neighbors). Readers who were asked to take the perspective of either a burglar or a home buyer recalled information differently. Generally, "burglars" remembered facts that would support their ability to break into the home and items worth stealing, while "home buyers" recalled items related to the care of the house and its potential retail value. Interestingly, when asked to shift perspectives after reading and recalling information, readers were able to recall additional factors related to their newly adopted perspective. Such research provided insights into the processes of constructing meaning, suggesting that mental predisposition influences what is deemed important but that a new task may allow readers to recall previously "forgotten" information.

A second major line of research into how readers use their background knowledge, or schemata, to interpret text was conducted by Bransford and his colleagues (Bransford & Johnson, 1972; see Bransford, 1979, for review). These researchers used ambiguous texts to study how readers draw on schemata differently and the effects of these differences on comprehension. One text used in these studies remained untitled but described the well-known activity of washing clothes. The passage began with the statements, "The procedure is actually quite simple. First, you arrange the items into different groups. Of course one pile may be sufficient depending on how much there is to do." The text was purposely constructed so that it would be vague and difficult to understand. For example, had the word

"clothes" been used in the second sentence instead of the word "items," readers would have been immediately signaled as to the content of the text. This passage was designed to explore what happens when readers have the background knowledge necessary to understand the text but do not use it, and what happens when readers invoke background knowledge that the writers had not intended. In the former case, readers displayed difficulties recalling information, and thus, it was inferred, comprehending. In the latter case of invoking an inappropriate schema, readers lacked comprehension and actually misunderstood the content of the passage.

As studies of adult readers' activation of background knowledge established the existence of and need for schemata as part of effective comprehension, this line of study was extended to the nature of comprehension in younger students and to the role of identity such as religious (Lipson, 1983) or ethnic identity (Reynolds, Taylor, Steffensen, Shirey, & Anderson, 1982) as well as knowledge. P. D. Pearson and his colleagues (see P. D. Pearson & Fielding, 1991; P. D. Pearson & Gallagher, 1983, for reviews) demonstrated that the influence of background knowledge was critical for both children's and adults' comprehension, and that children used their knowledge to advantage. For example, P. D. Pearson, Hansen, and Gordon (1979) asked second-grade students questions designed to reveal their knowledge about spiders before the students read about the animals. They showed that students with greater knowledge were able to answer questions designed to tap their understanding of the passage better than those with less knowledge prior to reading.

*Metacognition.* As more aspects of meaning construction were revealed, issues of how readers maintain control over processes related to meaning construction were explored. Initial descriptions of such control processes were offered by J. H. Flavell (1970, 1979) relative to control of memory processes as "metacognition" and later extended by Brown (see L. Baker & A. Brown, 1984) to control of comprehension processes as "metacomprehension." The notion of metacognition quickly achieved currency with researchers and teachers, resulting in criticisms that it was a "fuzzy concept" (J. Flavell, 1981, p. 37), an "abused concept" (Garner, 1987, p. 15), or a "buzzword" (Gavelek & Raphael, 1985, p. 107). Yet the very fact that it has attained such notoriety as a concept attests to its ability to resonate with two fundamental issues of concern to educational psychologists: how learners come to control their own learning processes, and how learning in one domain may generalize or transfer to those of others.

*Metacognition* has been defined as knowing about one's own cognitive processes and the control of that knowledge as one engages in a cognitive event such as reading or writing (Garner, 1987; Garner & Alexander, 1989; Paris, Wasik, & Turner, 1991). Two components of metacognitive knowledge were consistently included in these descriptions of metacognition: declarative knowledge, which captures knowing *that,* and procedural knowledge, which captures knowing *how.* To these, Paris, Lipson, & Wixson (1983) added the component of conditional knowledge, knowing *when* and *why.* Declarative knowledge is defined in terms of knowledge of task structures and task goals. In writing, this knowledge includes knowing that writing may involve more than the act of putting pen to paper, and in fact involves active engagement in prewriting events such as topic consideration, activation of relevant experiences, consideration of audience, and the intent of the written piece. However, declarative knowledge does not assume a writer's ability to actually engage in such activity. Procedural knowledge includes the repertoire of possible behaviors or strategies open to the learner to meet his or her goals. In writing, procedural knowledge includes strategies for inviting the reader into the text, such as by asking a rhetorical question, and it includes knowing ways for editing and revising text to ensure clarity of presentation and coherence of ideas presented. However, such knowledge does not necessarily indicate the learners' awareness of when to use such strategies or why they may help enhance a written piece of work. Conditional knowledge pertains to knowing how a particular strategy might be used, under what circumstances, or for what purposes.

Researchers within a cognitive science tradition have conducted numerous studies and reviews of metacognitive knowledge about reading and writing. For purposes of illustration, research on metacognitive knowledge about writing is used, including work on writers' declarative (e.g., Raphael, Englert, & Kirschner, 1989), procedural, and conditional knowledge (Bereiter & Scardamalia, 1987; Englert, Raphael, L. M. Anderson, Anthony, & Stevens, 1991). This research provided the foundation for extended lines of research on text and text structure and strategy instruction, both of which are discussed later in the chapter.

The cognitive science perspective brought about a radical change of views on writing. As Hull (1989) describes it, writing came to be considered "a process with an identifiable set of behaviors and cognitions. . . . [T]o think of writing as an activity that can be studied, analyzed, and understood, that can, in short be demystified—this indeed is revolutionary, for it turns writing into something that can be acquired rather than something that one possesses or lacks" (p. 105). The concept of demystification is at the root of much of the research on metacognition about writing. For example, Flower & Hayes (1981) described writing as a problem-solving process, constrained by the writer's need for integrated knowledge of the subject of the paper, general linguistic knowledge of how the language system works, and the rhetorical problem itself, or the purpose, audience, and projected role of the writer in the piece to be produced. Research into writers' knowledge about how to address these constraints is research into the role of metacognitive knowledge in writing.

Scardamalia (1981) examined the procedural knowledge of students ages 10 through 14 in producing narrative and expository text by asking students to produce essays on assigned topics assumed to be of interest to students at this grade level—e.g., "Should students be able to choose what they study in school?" Based on students' performance on such tasks, Scardamalia identified areas in which lack of metacognitive knowledge might impede students' ability to create text. These areas included knowledge about and ability to initiate plans as well as to record ideas in notes for later use, and ability to monitor the success of one's writing through rereading and revising.

Flower and Hayes (1980, 1981) examined the role of metacognitive knowledge in successful writing with college students. Specifically, procedural knowledge related to planning (e.g., pursuing an interesting feature, finding contradiction or conflict, making an outline) was critical to successful writing. They suggest that a writer's awareness of the writing process is important and that this awareness is less likely to be nurtured by reading anthologies or other models because they do not "give a hint of the intellectual process the writer went through to produce it—the methods and the decisions as well as the false starts and frustrations" (1981, p. 56).

Cognitive science provided a lens for studying readers' and writers' underlying processes in a way that had not been considered possible in earlier years. Such a perspective opened the door for a virtual avalanche of research on strategies for reading and writing from early grades through college. It pushed the instructional curriculum from its emphasis on products (e.g., the five-paragraph essay; oral reading fluency) to that of process, and by doing so helped teachers and students demystify literacy. Although such a lens may have shortcomings with regard to the routinization of complex processes, its privileging of a particular text interpretation, or its naïveté with regard to the importance of social interaction and context, it moved educational psychologists away from a long-standing focus on product to a consideration of process.

*Learning Words.* The emphasis on processes within cognitive psychology provided insight into both what successful readers need to learn to decode and comprehend what they read, and what less able readers seem to have difficulty learning, which ultimately impedes their ability to read successfully (Wixson & Lipson, 1991). The metacognitive stance that was described as characterizing proficient readers is a critical part of the effective beginner's repertoire, even though the strategies and knowledge relevant to the effective beginning reader may not be precisely the same as those of the proficient literacy user. For example, children learning to read require cryptanalytic intent, the disposition to decipher letter-to-sound codes, and the disposition to attend to a task that, initially, young readers may not entirely understand (P. B. Gough & Hillinger, 1980). Cognitive scientists have contributed extensively to our knowledge of two key processes for successful reading acquisition—automaticity and phonemic awareness.

Identifying Critical Processes That Influence Acquisition. The construct of *automaticity* refers to the ability to automatically process lower level perceptual information critical to the efficient decoding of print, ultimately freeing the attention of the reader to concentrate on higher level and more complex cognitive processes such as comprehension. Automaticity was not a new construct; psychologists of "the golden age" such as Huey (1908/1968) had identified automaticity as characteristic of the proficient reader (Stanovich, 1991). Further, behaviorists have held dear the principles of accuracy and speed. However, the description by LaBerge and Samuels in 1974 of automaticity of processing came at a time when cognitive psychologists were beginning to describe in depth the processes that had to be coordinated. LaBerge and Samuels, using the metaphor of the computer, noted that human information processors are limited in the amount of attention they can direct to any one mental process at a time. They explored the notion of how efficient readers distributed their attention across the various processes required in proficient reading, including perceptual processes (e.g., identifying letters, connecting to sounds, identifying spelling patterns) and meaning-making processes in comprehension (e.g., lexical access for identifying the meaning of the words they have read). They proposed that, as limited information processors, proficient readers learned to distribute their attention effectively, processing print automatically and using their conscious cognitive processing for comprehension. Arguably, if young learners are just beginning to decode print, it would take much of their attention to figure out letters and letter patterns and to recognize phonemes and connect them into meaningful units; thus, little attention would remain to be devoted to constructing meaning. Similarly, poor readers struggling with the lower level processes of reading would also be diverting attention from the high-level processes of comprehension.

The construct of automaticity thus gave rise to numerous examinations of the relative roles of accuracy and speed of processing and the connection of rapid and accurate processing of words to comprehension (Lesgold, Resnick, & Hammond, 1985). When word recognition occurs rapidly (and the words are ones which are in the readers' lexicon), meaning occurs immediately (Bruer, 1993; Stanovich, 1994). For many poor readers and many young children, word recognition is not automatic; while they can "figure words out," it takes time. Thus, their processing capacity is consumed by the demands of word recognition, leaving less to devote to comprehension. Reexaminations of the construct of automaticity, including one by Samuels and LaBerge (1983), emphasize that automaticity in processing does not mean that readers are free from devoting *any* attention to a particular process; further, automaticity need not develop incrementally (Stanovich, 1991). Juel (1991) noted that precisely what becomes automatic—phonetic elements, spelling patterns, whole words, or something else—has yet to be established.

Although questions remain about automaticity, the rate and accuracy with which readers recognize words are important. For example, when a measure of oral reading rate for a passage was obtained for a sample of fourth graders who took the 1992 National Assessment of Educational Progress (NAEP), both rate and accuracy of oral reading were highly related to students' comprehension of the passage (Campbell & Ashworth, 1995). Students who read slowly and with frequent errors on the oral reading task had had low comprehension scores on a previous silent reading of the same passage, while those who had the highest comprehension scores had read the passage rapidly and accurately. Thus, an outcome of the research on automaticity has been recognition of its potential for providing insight into contributions to learners' successful entry into literacy use.

Another contribution of cognitive science to the study of reading acquisition has been the identification of phonemic awareness as present in children who learn to read and lacking in children who do not. Phonemic awareness is the label given to a set of processes that involve the ability to analyze words into phonemes (basic units of speech sounds) or the knowledge that words are made up of phonemes. During the behaviorist era, phonics had received the lion's share of attention as the critical set of skills for the beginner. While a hodgepodge of skills constituted the phonics components of commercial reading programs (I. A. Beck & McCaslin, 1978), phonics was most typically equated with matching

letters and sounds. Although phonics batteries included tasks that could be classified as increasing phonemic awareness, the preponderance of instructional time was devoted to matching letters and sounds.

The U.S. Office of Education study had established children's awareness of and ability to distinguish among phonemes as the second best predictor of reading success (G. Bond & Dykstra, 1967). However, the work of linguists and cognitive psychologists clarified the processes of phonemic awareness, establishing that it was the ability to manipulate and think about sounds that was critical to literacy acquisition (Adams, 1990). Many dimensions of phonemic awareness have been identified, eventually serving as the basis for instructional interventions. Although some of these dimensions may in fact be artifacts of reading and writing (Ehri, 1991), the processes of phonemic segmentation and blending have consistently been found to be part of the repertoire of children who are successful at becoming literate, while these same processes are missing from those of children who are unsuccessful (Bradley & Bryant, 1983; Juel, 1988; Juel, Griffith, & P. B. Gough, 1986; Perfetti, I. L. Beck, Bell, & Hughes, 1987).

Since cognitive scientists often studied the processes of expert readers, their models left unaddressed critical questions related to the acquisition or development of these processes. Do these processes manifest themselves in full form? Are there different stages through which a successful beginner progresses? If the latter, are there critical constituents of particular stages? What are the mechanisms that facilitate acquisition? Several researchers within the cognitive science tradition, notably Juel and Ehri, have focused their attention on just such issues.

The Developmental Progression of Processes. Juel (1991) has distinguished between nonstage and stage models of reading acquisition. In nonstage models, exemplified by the natural language model of K. S. Goodman and Y. M. Goodman (1979), proficiency is seen as a matter of degree. Stage models of reading acquisition see children's proficiencies and tasks changing qualitatively over time, bringing young readers to the point of proficient reading (and writing). Examples of stage models are those of Ehri (1991) and Juel (1991). A brief historical sketch of perspectives on the acquisition of literacy underscores the contribution of Juel and Ehri in developing models of literacy acquisition.

There is a history in the United States of separation in the research programs and even theoretical orientations of those who work with young children and those who work with elementary-school-aged children. The child study movement, emanating from the work of Hall (1894), had roots as early as those of educational psychology. Remnants of this perspective remained, even when the work of Thorndike, Cattell, and others outshone those of Hall (Davidson & Benjamin, 1987). In literacy, the child study movement was apparent in the reading readiness perspective (National Society for the Study of Education, 1925), a belief that children would come to literacy when they had achieved a level of developmental preparedness: They would bloom when ready. This perspective remains strong in American education, although its current manifestation—developmental appropriateness—has been transformed to fit the times (McGill-Franzen, 1993).

This need for different theoretical sources to explain early development or acquisition processes is understandable when it becomes apparent that American psychologists and educational psychologists, whatever their perspective, have focused on the proficient reader. Behaviorists viewed novice and mature reading as fundamentally the same–connections are made between particular stimuli and responses—but differing in degree (the novice makes fewer of these connections). While differing in significant ways in their explanation of learning, cognitive scientists similarly emphasized the expert. A theory of learning does not necessarily make a theory of development and acquisition (L. B. Resnick, 1981). Not surprisingly, those interested in the very earliest stages of literacy responded to the cognitive revolution by examining other perspectives for explanations of development and acquisition. Drawing on the work of Piaget (1959), Vygotsky (1962, 1978), and Chomsky and Halle (1968), a group of scholars came to describe the nature of literacy in its earliest form and the processes of development and learning as emergent literacy (see Mason, 1984; Sulzby & Teale, 1991; for reviews). If asked to choose from among the three perspectives laid out in this chapter, most scholars within the emergent literacy perspective would prefer the label of social constructivism to that of cognitive science. We raise the emergent literacy perspective here, however, because of Ehri and Juel's efforts to bridge the emergent literacy perspective and work on beginning reading within a cognitive science perspective.

The three stages that characterize young children's word recognition strategies, according to Juel (1991), are selective-cue, spelling–sound, and automatic word recognition. Children at the selective-cue stage identify words by relying maximally on contextual information (e.g., a thumbprint on a card, distinctive letters, placement of a word on a page) and minimally on graphic information. During the spelling–sound stage, children have become aware of the graphic features to a fault, attending maximally to graphic information. Children's entry into the automatic stage, according to Juel, is marked by a qualitative change in how words are recognized, in that children now see words holistically through automatic processing of their visual orthographic features.

Ehri (1991) bases a stage model on Frith's (1985) three phases: logographic, alphabetic, and orthographic. Prereaders, as Ehri refers to children at the logographic stage, depend on environmental and visual cues for recognizing words, such as use of the golden arches to recognize the word "McDonald's." When children enter the alphabetic stage, they attain the status of "novice" and are characterized by phonologically recoding of spellings into pronunciations according to grapheme-phoneme correspondence rules. The final stage of veteran early reading is the orthographic phase, in which children have accumulated enough knowledge of spelling patterns that recur in words that their phonological recoding of letter sequences becomes automatic or, with sight words, they have stored enough alphabetic information about words in memory that they can read similarly spelled sight words (e.g., *look* and *book*).

There are differences in these two stage models in how they define which information is most salient and accessible to young children and what children access in memory. However, these models represent efforts by cognitive psychologists to describe developmental processes, not just the processes of the expert, and as such provide perspectives that can begin to inform

school practice. Also significant is the attention that these scholars give to the role of writing words, not just reading them, in a model of literacy acquisition. Juel describes children's interest in writing, once they have some phonemic awareness and knowledge of letter names. These efforts, especially when children are given the opportunity to attempt their own representations of phoneme-grapheme relationships in "invented spelling" (Read, 1975), can facilitate spelling–sound knowledge. Although few cognitive psychologists have engaged in efforts to build models of word production parallel to those of word recognition, Juel's attention to the role of invented spelling in a model of word recognition acquisition demonstrates the connection that is increasingly being made between learning to read and learning to write.

Using lenses from cognitive science, psychologists returned to examining word recognition processes initially explored at the beginning of the 20th century. The metaphor of mind as computer gave rise to numerous model-building efforts as psychologists worked to define and explain the many processes in which proficient readers engage (P. B. Gough, 1972). Such model-building efforts continue, with descriptions of word recognition maintaining a central role (see, e.g., P. Gough, 1984; Just & Carpenter, 1987; Stanovich, 1991). Teachers, curriculum planners, test makers, and textbook publishers require knowledge about processes underlying reading and writing, but most models are sufficiently complex and too focused on the processes of the expert literacy user to guide the design of appropriate instructional interactions, instructional materials, or assessments.

Although contributions to our understanding of beginning reading through concepts such as automaticity and phonemic awareness, and through models of literacy acquisition, were important, these studies did not lead to the explosion of training studies that were typical within the areas of comprehension and composition. Although some training studies have been conducted, among them Dahl's (1979) and Herman's (1985) studies of repeated reading, which grew out of the research on automaticity, and Lundberg, Frost, and Petersen's (1988) and Lie's (1991) training studies, which grew out of research on phonemic awareness, the range and quantity have been less extensive than was characteristic of studies of comprehension and composition. However, with the publication of Adams' (1990) landmark book, *Beginning to Read,* more attention has been focused on this body of work, and implications for school practice are likely to occur.

Since our major focus in this section has been to describe cognitive psychologists' contributions to understanding critical processes of literacy acquisition and the developmental progression of these processes, we must note the considerable contributions of cognitive psychologists to explaining word-level processes of another sort: those related to semantics. Cognitive psychologists' contributions to understandings of lexical or semantic access—or the role of word-level meanings in comprehending and composing—have been as rich and extensive as those related to word recognition (Beck & McKeown, 1991). Research contributions by cognitive psychologists to our understanding of vocabulary have been extensive and well-documented and space does not permit us to do justice to this work, which has been reviewed in numerous other sources. Beck and McKeown (1991) provide a comprehensive review of research on vocabulary (see also Graves, 1986). The work of R. C. Anderson, Nagy, and other researchers at the Center for the Study of Reading has elucidated the ways in which readers build vocabularies through reading (Anderson, Wilson, & Fielding, 1988) and through knowledge of morphology (Nagy, Anderson, Schommer, Scott, & Stallman, 1989). A recent study by Nagy, Garcia, Durgunoğlu, and Hancin-Bhatt (1993) in which knowledge of Spanish cognates was extended to the English reading of Spanish–English bilingual students promises to bridge work on vocabulary learning and biliteracy.

## Social-Constructivist Perspectives on Literacy and Literacy Learning

Just as cognitive science reestablished the primacy of mind in the research of psychology by replacing behaviorism and its tenets with alternative models, social constructivism brings the social dimensions of learning to the forefront (see chapter 2, this volume). Although insights from cognitive science on the processes and knowledge of expert readers and writers were extensive, cognitive science left open the question of how such knowledge is acquired. Scholars within a social-constructivist tradition raise questions about the nature of the knowledge to be acquired and how such acquisition occurs (Bruffee, 1986; Wertsch, 1991). In this section, we describe social constructivism and contrast it with the assumptions of cognitive science, and then examine basic constructs within the perspective of social constructivism that shape questions about school literacy acquisition and learning. We end with a discussion of the treatment of issues involving literacy learning in schools within a social-constructivist perspective.

*Social Constructivism in Relation to Previous Perspectives.* Much current scholarship in literacy learning traces its theoretical position to social constructivism, which emphasizes literacy in relation to culture, context, and authentic activity (see Bruner, 1990; Harré, 1984; Wertsch, 1985, 1991). Although behaviorism and cognitive science continue to leave their mark on literacy practices in schools, they are being challenged by the view that literacy acquisition and the construction of meaning have a social basis. At the heart of the challenge is an alternative epistomology that rejects the visual metaphors that have been used to describe literacy acquisition. In a cognitive science paradigm, human beings "view," "get the picture," "see," and have "insights" (Bruffee, 1986). The language of vision has been used to describe the working of the mind, which has been described as both a mirror reflecting what is "out there" in nature and as an inner eye contemplating the reflection. This visual stance is consistent with the behavioral and cognitive perspectives of objectivity, or something "out there," and subjectivity, or something "inside." The search for how an individual came to understand the "world out there" guided much of the practice within the behavioral and cognitive science traditions.

The social-constructivist position stresses instead the symbolic nature of knowledge and thought. Bruffee (1986), for example, has argued that social constructivism and its views on knowledge, thinking, and individual versus social dimensions eliminate any idea of a knowledge foundation. Instead, there is "only an agreement, a consensus arrived at for the time being

by communities of knowledgeable peers" (Bruffee, 1986, p. 777). While there is a physical world, to be sure, knowledge derives from agreed-upon beliefs about that physical world and human beings' interactions within that world.

Cognitive scientists suggest that thinking occurs through objectifiable and measurable entities such as "higher order reasoning," "cognitive processes," or "intellectual development." Although some cognitive psychologists (e.g., R. C. Anderson, 1977; Bransford, 1979; Kintsch & van Dijk, 1978) discussed meaning as being constructed, they tended to emphasize the individual nature of the construction. Social aspects such as culture were treated as variables that contributed to meaning construction, rather than as the fabric within which meaning construction occurs (e.g., Reynolds, M. A. Taylor, Steffensen, Shirey, & R. C. Anderson, 1982). Although cognitive scientists were relatively mute with respect to the social interactions from which meaning develops, it is this social aspect that distinguishes social constructivism from the constructivist line of work within cognitive science.

Social constructivists suggest that thinking is an internalized version of conversation. Terms such as "higher order reasoning" are not objective entities but rather, a specific form of language that has a mutually agreed-upon meaning within a particular social community. Cognitive scientists stress the individual as the center of all thought, emphasizing individual minds rather than the social. Social constructivists propose that the center of thought lies in the community of knowledgeable peers who share a particular language within the community.

Finally, cognitive scientists see knowledge as being inherently problematic because of the gap between the inner eye and the inner mirror and the fact that knowledge of the natural world is, in fact, inaccessible except through inference. In contrast, social constructivism argues that the inaccessibility exists only because of the adoption of a visual metaphor. Instead, if knowledge is a social construct, it is identical to the language and symbol systems used to describe it. Thus, those who study the symbol systems and how human beings are initiated into these systems are particularly well suited to shed light on both knowledge and the process of knowing or coming to know.

*Assumptions of Social Constructivism.* Social constructivism has become more widely adopted as a theoretical lens for studying literacy education, though many of the implications of its theoretical position have yet to be explored. For example, if all knowledge is socially constructed by a particular community, what are the boundaries to the interpretations of a given community as they read and discuss a text? What constructs provide coherence to those exploring literacy development within this perspective? Although responses to questions such as these may not be entirely fleshed out at this point, a set of concepts that underlie this perspective have been used to understand and explain various aspects of literacy and literacy learning in various social contexts. From the writing of scholars who have described learning in general (Harré, 1984) and literacy specifically (see chapters in Moll, 1991), three assumptions underlying social constructivism can be established: (a) higher mental functions (e.g., reading, writing) derive from social life; (b) human action, both social and individual, is mediated by tools and signs; and (c) knowledgeable members of the culture assist others in learning.

For Vygotsky (1978), learning occurs on two planes: the social ↔ individual and the public ↔ private. Learning happens first on the social plane where, through interactions with more knowledgeable others, learners come to understand new concepts and strategies. Individuals eventually use and extend these concepts and strategies to other contexts but meanings and interpretations have been initiated in social interaction rather than in solitary action. Similarly, what is learned transpires first in the public domain, where it is used by more knowledgeable members of the culture and made visible to learners. Through such interactions within a public domain, individuals adopt and adapt what has been observed and begin to use it privately.

Harré (1984) has developed what he calls the "Vygotsky space" to describe this process of internalization. The Vygotsky space is a quadrant formed by the planes of public/private and social/individual (see Gavelek, 1992). As students move through the quadrant (i.e., from public/social to private/individual), they engage in processes of appropriation, transformation, publication, and conventionalization. Within the quadrant formed by the intersection of the public/social planes, higher mental processes such as reading and writing are introduced to new learners and begin to develop. As students move from the public/social to the private/individual, appropriation occurs as students adopt and adapt the public disclosure and visible strategies introduced within this setting. Reciprocal teaching (Palincsar & A. L. Brown, 1984) is an example of how teachers working with small groups of students model the interrelationship of four strategies—questioning, summarizing, clarifying, and predicting—that are often treated separately in various developmental reading programs. Through modeling, thinking aloud, and prompting students, teachers and more experienced peers help those less experienced begin to use these strategies in the context of learning from a text within a public domain such as a small group. Initially, learners may appropriate the strategies exactly as modeled, using them in various contexts as they work individually. Even in situations such as this, there are opportunities for feedback from more experienced others, be they teachers or peers.

As students move toward the private/individual, they begin to individualize or tailor strategies and concepts to their own purposes. Thus, as they adopt strategies or concepts they have observed in a public domain, they begin to transform the strategies to make them meaningful for their own learning contexts. For example, after students have learned the four strategies of reciprocal teaching, they might decide that they prefer generating questions as a way to review what has been read, rather than creating a simple summary. Eventually, the learned abilities become tools to be used individually and privately for the achievement of personal goals. When students begin to control such knowledge, they have internalized the convention and may begin to use it as individuals in a more public domain such as through classroom interactions, work with peers, or in large groups. Eventually, they are in a position to move back toward the first quadrant, with the conventionalized knowledge of particular strategies and their use, perhaps working with other peers. Thus, social constructivism with its focus on the process of acquisition begins to provide a lens that extends

and magnifies definitions of literacy as well as how literacy is acquired through social interactions across the life span.

*Social Constructivism and Tensions in Literacy Education.* As important as the currency that the social-constructivist perspective has had in the educational research community, this perspective has been associated with a range of instructional practices and philosophies that many teachers in English-speaking countries have adopted. These practices and philosophies that emphasize the social contexts of learning and define literacy as a diverse and varied array of strategies and responses are often described as whole language, although other labels such as literature-based literacy or natural language are used by proponents. While writers within the whole language tradition are only beginning to connect their work to the social constructivist perspective (Clay & Cazden, 1991; Goodman, 1989), many of the applications that will be described in the subsequent sections on tests, texts, and teaching have been labeled as whole language efforts but have drawn heavily on social constructivist principles.

Because of the recency of this perspective, several aspects of a social-constructivist perspective merit discussion before the applications of this perspective to educational problems are reviewed. First, while not within the traditional confines of educational psychology, social constructivism is consistent with the aims and methods of educational psychologists and their continuing efforts to understand literacy learning in schools. Second, this perspective of learning has been the basis for a generation of projects that aim to solve educational problems—an underlying objective of educational psychology from its inception (Glover & Ronning, 1987). Many of these projects are multidisciplinary in nature, but educational psychologists are central players as they examine learning within and across social-instructional contexts. Thus, one reality within a social-constructivist perspective is that the background and methods that inform its research are interdisciplinary, drawing on disciplines beyond those traditionally reflected in educational psychologists' research.

Third, despite its promise, a social-constructivist stance has yet to be explicated for some aspects of literacy: (a) how literacy is acquired by all students, (b) how successful students are as a result of participating in instructional programs based on social-constructivist principles, and (c) how single areas of research such as that on text, tests, and teaching can be studied from a perspective that emphasizes their interaction. For example, how is literacy acquired in contexts where there are large groups of students who come to school without some of the background that contributes to successful early reading? Cazden (1983) has suggested that early parent–child language interactions serve as one basis for an instructional model for literacy acquisition. Through interactions with parents while lap-reading or talking about environmental print such as the name of a breakfast cereal, children begin to participate in literacy events. The perspective that young children acquire valuable knowledge about literacy and that contexts such as these work best for young children's literacy acquisition has been the basis for what we describe in this chapter as a subset of the social-constructivist perspective: emergent literacy (Clay, 1975; Teale & Sulzby, 1986). Although proponents of this view emphasize what it is that many children know about literacy (see, e.g., K. S. Goodman & Y. M. Goodman, 1979), emergent literacy does not necessarily result in conventional literacy without direction and focus on print from adults in the environment (Cazden, 1991). For children who have participated extensively in print-related interactions in their homes and communities, conventional literacy comes quickly in school. Many children, however, have not participated extensively in lap reading and similar literacy events as preschoolers.

We feel that the question, "How well are children reading as a result of participating in these contexts?" is a critical one to ask, although it may be interpreted as reflecting a reductionistic paradigm. Yet this question has ecological validity, asked by parents and other groups, as well as individuals who have "completed" school yet lack sufficient literacy abilities. Some projects within a social-constructivist or emergent literacy perspective have drawn on interactive patterns at home as a basis for creating school contexts such as the Kindergarten Early Literacy Project (Martinez, Cheyney, McBroom, Hemmeter, & Teale, 1989). Other researchers from this perspective have examined the conversations that occur between children as they write, documenting a rich network of talk that elucidates literacy for young children (Dyson, 1987). Although some of these research projects provide descriptions of the accomplishments of case study students (e.g., Martinez et al., 1989), often the literacy accomplishments are assumed. As Cazden (1991) states, "[T]here is still no research evidence that immersion in rich experience is sufficient for all children" (p. 421).

We also raise the question of whether it is appropriate, from a social-constructivist perspective, to examine applications of this perspective separately to tests, text, and teaching. It can be legitimately argued that a construct such as text cannot be examined in isolation from the reader and the literacy context. The intention here is not to treat text (or teaching or tests) as an isolated variable. In the world of public schools, business, and universities, however, tests, texts, and teaching each have a reality, regardless of the learning theory that underlies the form of each. A social-constructivist perspective extends the view of text, for example, to include conversations or other funds of knowledge (Moll, Amanti, Neff, & Gonzalez, 1992) as texts. The studies that are reviewed here as representative of a social-constructivist perspective examine a construct such as texts with lenses that move beyond straight text analysis. The studies that will be reviewed as examples of social-constructivist perspectives toward text may place interactions around text in the foreground (e.g., Eeds & Wells, 1989) since the text itself is not the sole focus of attention.

A final comment addresses the reality that any review reflects the perspective of its authors. We place ourselves currently within the perspective of social constructivism, as reflected in the description of our own work in those sections. However, we are each influenced by our individual and collective histories as scholars within an educational psychology tradition, and predictably, strong influences of cognitive science can be traced within our projects, such as an emphasis on phonemic awareness (Hiebert, Colt, Catto, & Gury, 1992) or on strategic guidance (Raphael et al., 1992). We are not behaviorists, although we recognize that our careers as teachers, graduate students in educational psychology, teacher educators, and researchers have been spent in the United States, where strong residuals of behaviorism remain.

Cazden, in writing about the contributions of different perspectives to understanding literacy learning, proposes that the

design of optimal literacy learning should be the focus of discussions of teachers and university researchers rather than "arguments between one extreme and the other" (p. 422). In a similar vein, our aim in writing this chapter has been to focus on the contributions of educational psychology to views of tests, texts, and teaching rather than to promote or impugn a particular perspective.

## EXTENSIONS OF PERSPECTIVES ON LITERACY AND LITERACY LEARNING TO SCHOOL PRACTICE

To the first and most subsequent generations of educational psychologists, the distinction between psychology and educational psychology involved the extension of theories and perspectives on learning to school practice, not simply descriptions of learning and development. Since these extensions to literacy practices in schools have been far reaching, choices were necessary to make our task manageable. Our selection for the organization of this section parallels three dominant directions educational psychologists took in working on literacy learning in schools: tests, texts, and teaching. These three constructs exist in school literacy practices, each with histories and traditions as extensive as any theoretical perspective. Although the perspectives of behaviorism, cognitive science, and social constructivism have been extended to the three constructs, the influence of the perspective has differed within each one. Consequently, we discuss the extension within each construct, rather than describing the impact of a particular theoretical perspective on literacy education in general.

Ever since the first major breakthrough in literacy research was marked by the introduction of a test (N. B. Smith, 1934/1965), tests have influenced other aspects of literacy practice considerably. Thus, a discussion of testing serves as our point of departure. We next examine educational psychologists' study of textbooks, described by some as external to instruction (see, e.g., K. S. Goodman, Shannon, Y. Freeman, & Murphy, 1988). Since, ultimately, tests and texts are used by teachers within instructional contexts, we explore ways in which educational psychologists—and others on whose work we have built— have studied teaching (i.e., instruction and curriculum) from the three theoretical perspectives. For each construct (tests, text, and teaching), the primary themes in educational psychologists' work are identified. Since theory or research do not necessarily impact school practice according to the visions of educational psychologists, the influence of these themes on current practice is summarized in a concluding section of each discussion.

### Extensions of Perspectives on Literacy Learning to Tests and Testing

The central concern of educational psychologists with the literacy behaviors and dispositions of individuals has meant a focus on measuring literacy outcomes at different age levels and for different individual characteristics. Educational psychologists have developed many literacy measures, using a variety of formats and measuring various aspects of literacy. One type of literacy assessment, however, has dominated all others—the norm-referenced test. Reflecting the stronghold of behaviorism, norm-referenced tests were joined by criterion-referenced tests in the 1960s. If the creation and refinement of norm- and criterion-referenced reading and language arts tests are viewed as a first stage, critiques of these tests from the perspectives of cognitive science and social constructivism as a second stage, and the development of new measures from the perspectives of cognitive science and social constructivism as a third stage, educational psychologists have had a central role in theory and research at each juncture of the road.

*The Creation of Literacy Tests.* Due to a series of historical events and social, cultural, and political patterns in American society which are not within the purview of this chapter to review, a particular set of measures became, and remain, the dominant form of assessment in American schools. Educational psychologists created these assessments and contributed to their use through an extensive body of technical research. Insofar as literacy has been of primary concern in elementary schools, literacy tests are central to the testing industry. The number of literacy tests is even greater because of accountability requirements of Chapter 1, the largest and longest running federally funded program for schools.

Combined with the higher stakes that have been increasingly placed on tests for accountability purposes, the choices of the early educational psychologists about content and formats have influenced strongly the literacy experiences of subsequent generations of schoolchildren. The major development in literacy tests from the early part of the 20th century to the early 1980s was the initiation of criterion-referenced tests. The goal of establishing criteria (or standards, to use the current term) could have meant a new direction, but the currency of hierarchical learning at the time meant that even more minute behaviors were tested. This section provides an overview of the origins of norm- and criterion-referenced tests, decisions that were made about their content, and the research base underlying these tests. More extended histories and descriptions of norm- and criterion-referenced literacy tests are available (e.g., P. H. Johnston, 1984; D. P. Resnick, 1982).

Origins, Content, and Research on Norm-Referenced Literacy Tests. During the initial decades of educational psychology, work on testing showed considerable diversity. For example, Thorndike's (1910) handwriting scale consisted of "prototypes" against which students' performances could be matched, a concept quite similar to the use of "anchors" or examples of student responses that were used in scoring the open-ended responses to reading on the 1992 NAEP test (Mullis, Campbell, & Farstrup, 1993). Gray (1915) identified oral reading passages that could be used as prototypes, and Thorndike (1917) examined the nature of the "incorrect" responses that readers provided in short, open-ended responses to comprehension questions. Historical events cut short the experimentation and supported the emphasis on a particular form of assessment, silent reading tests. World War I served as an impetus for organizing and standardizing silent reading tests and conducting research related to that effort (Gray, 1938). Such tests met the needs of the time in that they were easy to administer and score and had straightforward and uniform content. Subsequent historical events contributed to the spreading use of these tests, specifically the invention of the IBM 805, in 1935, which made scoring

inexpensive and thus secured the multiple-choice format as a fixture of norm-referenced tests (P. H. Johnston, 1984). In 1933, Hildreth observed that silent reading tests were the most frequently used assessments in schools, and the basic content and formats have remained relatively unchanged to the present (Farr & Carey, 1986).

Two features of norm-referenced tests manifest themselves uniquely (and consequentially) in literacy: grade equivalents for norms and the content and weighing of discrete subtests. The assumptions underlying the norming procedure had particular implications for reading where norms were extrapolated to grade equivalents. Unlike mathematics, where the meaning of "fourth-grade proficiency" in mathematics requires description of the curriculum (e.g., algorithms to be learned), the assignment of readability levels to graded passages based on the frequency counts of words by early test developers (Thorndike, 1921) meant that grade designations could easily be assigned to students' reading performances on norm-referenced tests. For example, a particular percentile would be equated with reading at mid-third-grade level. Since a prototype of a "first-semester Grade 3" text could easily be identified through readability formulas, grade equivalents influenced practice. Reading groups were formed on the basis of test performances, and test performances were used to assign particular levels of text for reading groups. A perspective based on these grade-level designations of students as on, below, or above grade level became an impenetrable part of reading pedagogy, with materials, instructional groups, and even class assignment based on these scores. The use of grade equivalents has been discouraged by professional organizations (International Reading Association, 1981), but norm-referenced tests have long served as an endorsement of a scientifically based grading system of text and a deep-seated perception that many children—the half that score below the norm—are poor readers.

The answer of behaviorists to the question, "What is reading?" was a tripartite perspective of comprehension, vocabulary, and word analysis, with each weighted equally in the composite or total score of the reading test. The comprehension subtest of most silent reading tests over the past 60 years has consisted of numerous (8 to 10) short paragraphs, each with a handful of questions that require students to select a single answer from a set of multiple choices (Farr & Beck, 1991). Most silent reading tests contain word analysis and vocabulary subtests as well, although the word analysis component typically is eliminated from intermediate forms on some tests. The presence of the subtests substantiated a view of literacy as comprising discrete skills, a view that was reinforced by the equal weight given to subtests in composite test scores. Subtests for word analysis that outnumber subtests for comprehension on a reading test imply to teachers, parents, and students that these skills have importance in their own right, rather than as processes that aid meaning making (Stallman & Pearson, 1990).

Although awareness that selecting the correctly spelled word or the correctly punctuated sentence from among several choices did not equate with producing a coherent and well-reasoned composition, the low costs of scoring and fears of "subjectivity" in scoring meant a parallel development between language arts and reading tests, both using subtests and multiple-choice formats. Language arts tests typically consist of subtests of spelling (where students choose the correctly spelled word from a group of distractors), usage (possessives, plurals), mechanics (punctuation, capitalization), and grammar (identification of parts of speech and tenses of verbs). Language arts tests have begun to include writing samples (Hoover, Hiernyomus, Frisbie, & Dunbar, 1992) that resemble the tasks that have been used for NAEP writing assessments (Applebee, Langer, & Mullis, 1986), where students are given a topic and a period of time (15 to 30 minutes) to write. However, the mainstays of norm-referenced language arts tests continue to be multiple-choice tests of mechanics and usage.

Numerous studies of the psychometric features of literacy tests have been conducted, but many remain in-house technical reports of publishing companies that examine content validity, verifying that the items on a subtest of, for example, auditory discrimination pertain to sound–symbol correspondences, or that examine concurrent validity, corroborating that the content of a test closely matches that of other available tests (Shepard, 1993). Until recently, scholarship that addressed how well these tests indicated that an individual would be able to read and write in the contexts of a technology-driven workplace or the voting booth was missing. For example, a review of measures used with kindergartners and first graders, which are often the basis for important decisions (retaining children in kindergarten, placing them in Chapter 1, recommending to parents that students start school a year later than age peers), indicates that information on predictive validity is relatively limited in scope (Shepard & Graue, 1992). When Ellwein, Walsh, Eads, and A. Miller (1991) considered the ability of a group of readiness tests used in Virginia to guide decisions about children's initial reading experiences, they found that none of the four assessments was a strong predictor of future test performance. The accuracy of beginning-of-kindergarten test performance in predicting end-of-kindergarten test performance was in the vicinity of 40 to 50 percent, or, as Ellwein et al. (1991) concluded, "no more accurate than the toss of a fair coin" (p. 171).

Although norm-referenced tests have not changed considerably over the past decades, a perusal of the Buros Institute's mental measurement yearbooks (Conoley, 1989) confirms the existence of many different tests using alternative formats. The most notable of these is the Degrees of Reading Power (DRP) test (College Board, 1983), which has been adopted as the primary test in New York state (C. Freeman, 1987). The DRP employs the cloze technique, which requires students to pick the best of five choices for each of the key words that have been deleted from a series of passages judged to be progressively more difficult by a readability formula. If the same readability scale is applied to tests and books, the publishers of the DRP argue (College Board, 1983), the results of this test can allow a "perfect match" between students' reading levels and texts. Many arguments have been raised against the use of readability formulas, which provide the underlying foundation for the DRP. Further, the processes in which readers engage during a cloze test seem to differ significantly enough from those of proficient reading to call into question assessments based exclusively on this format (C. Freeman, 1987; Powell, 1988).

Other scholars have proposed alternative interpretative systems or test formats but their proposals have not been integrated into policy and practice as extensively as the DRP (Carver, 1992;

Royer & Cunningham, 1981). Carver, for example, studied the use of mathematical formulas devised to predict the amount of a passage that a student will comprehend from measures of general reading ability, the time allowed to read, the reading rate of the individual (i.e., the ordinary reading rate of the individual—involves no studying), and the relative difficulty of the material. Carver argues that such a formula allows a measure of "pure" reading ability without considering processes such as predicting, the type of text, or the reader's prior knowledge of the passage's topic.

Origins, Content, and Research on Criterion-Referenced Literacy Tests.  The culmination of behaviorist thinking in assessment was the criterion-referenced test (Popham, 1978, 1987). The use of criteria rather than norms for describing student performances is not itself behaviorist. Indeed, the current concept of standard bares a striking resemblance to the notion of criterion in that both encompass identification of levels of attainment and educational goals. Whereas current standard-setting efforts (P. D. Pearson, 1993a) have tried to articulate broad-based goals such as "critically responding to text," the criterion-referenced systems were absorbed by behaviorist notions such as skills hierarchies (Gagné, 1968), mastery learning (Bloom, 1971), and behavioral objectives (Mager, 1962). Unlike the broader standards of today, these tended to be "micro" instantiations of reading activities. For example, an objective that emanates from this process might state that the student will be able to identify words with a vowel plus *l* (Level C, Delta, 1974). Because literacy initiatives were high on the agenda of the federal and state government at the same time (see Carroll & Chall, 1975), reading and, to a much lesser degree, language arts became the primary content area for criterion-referenced systems.

Through state tests such as Texas's Assessment of Academic Skills (Texas Education Agency, 1994), criterion-referenced instructional and assessment programs like the Wisconsin Design for Reading Skill Development (Otto, 1977) and the University of Pittsburgh's Individually Prescribed Instruction (IPI) (I. L. Beck & Mitroff, 1972; Glaser, 1966; L. B. Resnick, Wang, & Kaplan, 1973), and the unit and book tests with correlated worksheet and workbook pages for objectives that were added to textbook series in the 1970s, criterion-referenced tests became an integral part of reading instruction and assessment (see Glaser, 1963, 1971). Although criterion-referenced systems such as the Wisconsin Design and IPI have fallen by the wayside, the mandated reading tests of many states are skill-driven, criterion-referenced tests. Since the most recent textbook series were created for Texas (Texas Education Agency, 1990) with its mandated criterion-referenced test, the cycle of unit and book tests and correlated worksheets undoubtedly continues.

According to Venezky (1974), norm- and criterion-referenced tests were fundamentally different in content and use. Whereas the goal of developers of norm-referenced tests is to identify a set of items that is neither too hard nor too easy for the majority of the norming group, criterion-referenced tests begin with the set of desired behaviors and then derive the test items. However, once the criterion-referenced notion entered mainstream practice as part of textbook programs, the two forms of assessment became relatively indistinguishable. In analyzing the content and forms of reading readiness and first-grade assessment components of textbook programs and of norm-referenced tests, Stallman and P. D. Pearson (1990) found the basal tests to be remarkably like one another, and all bore a close resemblance to widely used norm-referenced tests. Although a comparable analysis has not been conducted on the worksheets and workbook pages of the textbook programs, publishers promise that these exercises provide practice for the skills tests, implying a match to the content and formats of norm-referenced tests.

The criterion-referenced tests of state assessment programs and textbook companies have been studied even less than norm-referenced tests, yet these tests are often the ones that teachers use to plan instruction or to evaluate student capability (Dorr-Bremme & Herman, 1986; Stiggins, Conklin, & Bridgeford, 1986). Psychometric features such as reliability have been found to be poor (Tindal et al., 1985). Bangert-Drowns, J. A. Kulik, and C. C. Kulik (1983) have used findings from a meta-analysis to argue that the increase in test taking in criterion-referenced programs is related to higher test scores. However, this finding could also be interpreted to demonstrate another potential problem with criterion-referenced tests: that students' performances reflect practice on tasks similar to those on the tests (if not the actual tests) rather than real learning.

One of the few studies of textbook-embedded tests suggests that, as these tests became part of conventional practices, one of the argued benefits of these tests—the use of these assessments to identify problem areas—may have been lost. In an intervention that B. Taylor, Frye, and Gaetz (1990) initiated, students were released from worksheets and workbooks if they could pass the end-of-unit test at the beginning of the unit within the textbook program. Until Taylor et al. initiated their intervention, all of the students did all of the worksheets for each objective, regardless of pretest performance. Taylor et al. found that most students were able to pass pretests on reading skills before the skills were covered in the basal reader program. When students spent the time reading rather than doing worksheets, their performances on end-of-book skill tests remained high. This finding applied to below-average students as well, who were able to pass the basal skills tests on the first round in approximately 76 percent to 88 percent of the time, with no negative effects on the end-of-unit skills tests. The results of the study are encouraging in suggesting that these tests may be unnecessary, but, at the same time, the contexts prior to the intervention suggest that teachers were no longer using criterion-referenced systems to emphasize students' problem areas but were assigning everything to everyone, regardless of need. The uses and even forms of criterion-referenced tests seem to have changed beyond their intended aims, with an apparent test-practice function (Stallman and P. D. Pearson, 1990).

### Critiques of Literacy Tests from Cognitive Science and Social Constructivism.

Until the past 15 years, there was little exchange between educational psychologists and psychometricians about the content of norm-referenced tests. Educational psychologists studied learning processes; psychometricians verified the psychometric characteristics of new tests and new editions of old tests against old tests. Although norm-referenced tests have had their critics in every generation (see Mercer's

[1989] review), cognitive science supplied a conceptual framework that previous generations had not had for evaluations of literacy tests and for empirical examinations of the interactions between reader and the text (i.e., passages, questions, multiple choices) of tests. The critiques of tests by educational psychologists, initially from the perspective of cognitive science (Glaser, 1981) and, more recently, from a social-constructivist perspective (Garcia & P. D. Pearson, 1994; Quellmalz, 1985; L. B. Resnick & D. P. Resnick, 1992), focused on the content and format of tests, processes that these engender in readers, or influences of test content and events on curriculum and learning. Although many of the analyses that follow are directed specifically at norm-referenced reading tests, the same criticisms apply to criterion-referenced reading tests because of their close correlation to the content and formats of norm-referenced tests (Stallman & P. D. Pearson, 1990) and to norm- and criterion-referenced language arts tests.

In relation to language arts tests, the performance and portfolio assessments that cognitive scientists advocate for reading began in writing almost 20 years ago with collections of students' writing samples as part of large-scale assessments such as the NAEP (Diederich, 1974). Unlike reading, where cognitive and social-constructivist perspectives are used to critique norm-referenced tests, cognitive and social-constructivist perspectives are used to criticize performance assessments or direct writing assessments (e.g., Freedman, 1993; Huot, 1990; Purves, 1992). Even though performance assessments have a more extended history in writing than in reading, norm-referenced language arts tests remain relatively intact and, although analyses are few, influential in the language arts curricula and assessment programs of many states, districts, and schools. The three primary areas in which tests have been criticized are (a) in features of norm- and criterion-referenced tests that mitigate the processes of proficient readers and writers, (b) in the authenticity of passages and tasks, and (c) in the influence of the tests on the larger contexts of literacy.

### Test Features that Mitigate the Processes of Proficient Readers and Writers.

Questions about reading tests were among the first to be raised as cognitive models were applied to existing literacy constructs and practices (Bormuth, 1970). Through theoretical proofs and empirical investigations, two aspects of comprehension subtests of norm-referenced tests were identified as particularly conspicuous problems in measuring proficient reading—the treatment of prior knowledge and the nature of passages, questions, and responses. Because the focus was on reading comprehension, little time was spent on critiques of subtests of word meaning and word analysis. In almost all cases, these subtests have been eliminated in the new performance assessments (Kapinus, Collier, & Kruglanski, 1994; Simmons & Resnick, 1993; Weiss, 1994).

A consistent feature of an interactive model of reading is active involvement of the readers as they access knowledge related to the topic, structure, and genre of the text. Educational psychologists within a cognitive tradition argued that norm-referenced tests had been developed to "wash out" the effects of prior knowledge (N. Frederiksen, 1984; P. H. Johnston, 1984). That is, those passages on which the majority of students have a rich store of background knowledge are unlikely to remain on tests because everyone gets a high score on these items. As a consequence, performances on norm-referenced tests may reflect students' access to particular cultural phenomena or knowledge rather than their reading proficiency. The test that Garcia (1991) designed to examine the contribution of background knowledge to Hispanic students' test scores included passages about which Hispanic students might have more extended background knowledge or at least as much background knowledge as their Anglo peers (piñatas and polar bears) as well as the expository passages from norm-referenced tests on typical topics (water erosion and chimpanzees). On the topics for which Hispanic students had limited background knowledge, they frequently chose distractors that, according to follow-up interviews, reflected inappropriate or poorly developed schemata. On passages for which Hispanic students had better developed schemata, they performed comparably to Anglo students. Other reports show how tests, especially when presented in English, limit the representations of language-minority-students' literacy (O'Connor, 1989).

A handful of studies can be identified in which changes have been made to norm-referenced tests to build on principles from cognitive science. For example, Rowe and Rayford (1987) restructured the norm-referenced Metropolitan Achievement Test to include purpose-setting questions that required students to make predictions about passages before reading. The students, who were tested in Grades 1, 6, and 10, produced responses that were related to the information in the purpose question or to unstated story schema categories. Rowe and Rayford concluded that students over an extended age range can use purpose-setting questions as cues to activate background knowledge, and suggested that topic familiarity, amount of information presented, and the presence of genre clues could all be used to activate readers' schemata on tests.

The Authenticity of the Texts, Tasks, and Contexts of Standardized Tests. Two features of standardized tests have been studied from a social-constructivist perspective in relation to the literacy events of schools and communities: (a) the texts and tasks of tests and (b) the context in which students are tested. The primary task of the norm- and criterion-referenced silent reading test requires students to read short paragraphs (usually of 150 to 300 words) and to answer questions about these passages by selecting the best response from the available choices. These paragraphs form a unique genre that appears on tests or in workbook exercises designed to improve test performance (Pearson & Valencia, 1987). The selections that make up trade (library) books that students get from their school or community libraries, magazines like *Ranger Rick* or *Cricket* that are written for an elementary-school-age audience, and the passages in the anthologies that are part of textbook programs are usually longer. There is a mismatch between the passages of "authentic" text that students read and the text upon which evaluations of students' reading are based.

Research paradigms from cognitive science were used to demonstrate further structural problems with the short-paragraph passages that were usually the only basis for making judgments of students' reading. Short paragraphs often lack structural and topical integrity, making it difficult to create questions that tap higher level literacy processes such as inferencing (Pearson & Valencia, 1987). Further, many of the connections that allow the reader to make meaning may have been elimi-

nated, creating a similar kind of confusion for readers as the ambiguous passages used by Bransford and his colleagues (Bransford, 1979). When researchers such as Langer (1987) and Drum, Calfee, and Cook (1981) have studied students' thinking about passages as well as analyzed the test passages, they have found that the wording of passages, questions, and response choices can create ambiguity for even the best students. For example, the short paragraphs tend to leave out the context and motivations of characters, leaving students mulling over issues that cannot be connected. Different tasks in a testing context can elicit different reader processes as well. Sixth-grade students who were observed in testing contexts with a range of tasks by Powell (1988) were less involved cognitively on a cloze task (text with deleted words for which students identify the best choice) than on a multiple-choice test, written retellings of a text, or a nonassessed reading task, on which student processes were not appreciably different.

The typical testing context can also render a less than typical representation of students' reading. Although usually tasks are scaffolded by adults or peers, the tasks of reading tests are mysterious in intent and form for many students, especially those from linguistically and culturally diverse backgrounds (Hill & Wigfield, 1984). Studies that compare readers' processes in testing contexts to those in more typical instructional contexts have found that readers are more actively involved and give more complex responses under typical instructional contexts than in evaluative contexts (Mosenthal & Na, 1980) and benefit from elements of text and context that scaffold the task (Braun, Rennie, & Gordon, 1987).

Influence of Tests on the Larger Contexts of Learning. Because of their interest in the sociohistorical contributions to learning and development, researchers from a social-constructivist perspective have studied ways in which the definitions and contexts of literacy have been influenced by norm- and criterion-referenced tests. Reading and language arts curriculum and instruction have not been isolated from the effects of high-stakes testing (see, e.g., M. L. Smith, 1991), since the reading test is the most publicized and emphasized of tests given in elementary schools (Andelin et al., 1992). The conclusions of these studies suggest that the higher stakes placed on such test scores lead to more time being spent on testlike exercises, particularly in the areas of reading and language arts. Descriptions of the activities that are displaced by the "100-hour bite" taken out of the curriculum by test preparation are limited, but the available evidence indicates that the largest bite comes out of meaningful reading and writing activities (M. L. Smith, 1991). For example, Smith cites a case in one of the two schools that she and her colleagues observed over an 18-month period. Because students had shown a month less than a year's progress on the language arts test the previous year, the principal mandated that some time be spent each day on exercises of mechanics and usage. Teachers cut activities such as writing stories and journals from the writing workshop so that they would have time available for the mandated exercises.

Glimpses can be gained of the effects of high-stakes testing on student learning. Students' scores on reading tests are consistently high, a phenomenon first made public by a physician (Cannell, 1988), but the basic pattern has been confirmed in more systematic analyses (Linn, Graue, & Sanders, 1990). Although it is periodically argued that the higher scores reflect real gains in literacy attainments, the NAEP results, which constitute the long-term American data base, suggest otherwise. Evaluations of reading performances on the NAEP test over the past 20 years indicate that, after an initial rise in performance in the early 1970s, patterns have been maintained (Applebee, Langer, & Mullis, 1989). Although students perform adequately on low-level literacy tasks, the majority struggle with higher level literacy tasks such as writing a description of a character's motives or identifying the underlying theme of a poem (Kirsch & Jungeblut, 1986; Mullis et al., 1993). The differences in domains measured by the NAEP and the literacy assessments of the International Evaluation Association (IEA) and norm-referenced tests make comparisons difficult. Obtaining data to substantiate the results of standardized tests is a catch-22. Assessments are needed to establish reading and writing patterns of large groups of students. When such assessments are based on a cognitive model of literacy, they take different forms and use different scoring schemes than norm-referenced tests, which makes it difficult to compare results to those of norm-referenced tests. This is not the context to argue whether gains on reading tests and declines on verbal college entry examinations are real. When reading tests take on high stakes in communities and federal agencies and become the focal point of educational accomplishments, curriculum, instruction, and instructional materials appear to be sufficiently influenced that testlike exercises consume considerable chunks of students' time in reading and language arts periods.

Further, high-stakes testing appears to influence the school literacy experiences of some students more than others. Schools where a high percentage of students come from low-income homes devote more time to testing (Dorr-Bremme & Herman, 1986), partly due to Chapter 1 policies. McGill-Franzen and Allington (1993) describe the increase in retentions and special education placements in schools with high stakes placed on tests, with reading performance a primary criterion for these choices. Exemptions from testing were obtained for special education students, while other students were retained with the hope that their scores would be better the following year, practices that encourage special education placements and retentions. The consistent finding that testlike exercises consume more time in Chapter 1 reading classes than in other classes is further evidence of the influence of tests on the curriculum for low-income students (P. Johnston & Allington, 1991).

*Development and Study of Authentic Assessments.* Although norm-referenced reading tests are often included in a battery of measures, researchers frequently use alternative measures such as retellings and think-alouds in studies of literacy. Further, the assessments designed for classroom use have been many and varied, such as the use of oral reading samples (Gray, 1920) and miscue analyses (K. S. Goodman, 1968). Interviews of students by teachers in regular conferences have been encouraged as the context for assessing students' writing (DiPardo & Freedman, 1988). However, it is rare to find the use of performance or portfolio assessments for purposes usually associated with large-scale assessment, such as reporting students' accomplishments on critical literacy goals to policymakers. The critiques by scholars from cognitive science and social-constructivist perspectives have led to increased attention to two types of assessments for purposes beyond classroom use: performance and portfolio assessments.

Frameworks for and Research on Performance Assessments. Performance assessments have been described as tasks on which "students are required to demonstrate their level of competence or knowledge by creating a product or a response" (Valencia, Hiebert, & Afflerbach, 1994, p. 11). The label "performance" assessment originated in content areas such as science where assessments involved hands-on tasks rather than the recognition tasks of standardized tests. The tasks of the assessment would require students to be involved in the processes in which scientists engage, rather than in selecting the best answer from a set of choices. In writing, performance assessments have meant that students produce compositions rather than marking the best choice for a question about mechanics or usage. Because students are writing rather than recognizing features of writing, these assessments have also been called "direct writing" assessments.

With reading, critics have been quick to point out that the typical task of standardized reading tests—selection of multiple-choice items after silently reading short passages—does not parallel the requisite performances of proficient readers in real-world contexts. These criticisms have been attended to in performance assessments by requiring students to read long passages that come from already existing sources such as trade books or magazines and by requiring them to answer questions with phrase, sentence, and paragraph responses. Some performance assessments include events that are modeled after typical literacy events such as brainstorming about background knowledge prior to reading and group discussions after reading. Even when group interactions are part of the assessment events, the current literacy performance assessments continue to focus on the products of individuals. There are differences, though, between performance and norm- and criterion-referenced tests on at least three features: standards, content, and format.

A basic difference between performance assessments and norm- and criterion-referenced tests has to do with what is measured. Standards, more like criteria than norms, are broadly conceived descriptions of students' performances on holistic exercises such as creating a persuasive essay or recognizing the needs of the intended audience. Students' performances are described in terms of the degree to which their work matches or departs from benchmark levels within the standard, with "rubrics" or examples of student work defining the specific benchmark levels (P. D. Pearson, 1993b).

Performance assessments and traditional tests also differ in typical formats (Farr & M. D. Beck, 1991). The passages of performance assessments are longer than those on norm- and criterion-referenced tests. Students read one or two passages, each of which averages 900 to 1,800 words, rather than the 8 to 10 passages of 150 to 300 words on norm-referenced tests. Although some of the earliest performance assessments in reading (Wixson et al., 1987; P. D. Pearson & Valencia, 1987) continued to use multiple-choice formats, responses on more recent performance assessments have been entirely open-ended (Kapinus et al., 1994; B. Weiss, 1994).

A third difference between the performance assessments and norm- and criterion-referenced tests is perhaps the most striking departure: the nature of the content. The tripartite sub-test structure of the norm-referenced tests (comprehension, vocabulary, and word analysis) is gone with assessments exclusively devoted to comprehension. In the place of word analysis and vocabulary are, on occasion, assessments of metacognition/reading strategies, topic familiarity/prior knowledge, and attitudes/self-perceptions/literacy experiences.

Performance assessments have a more extensive history in writing (Freedman, 1993). Many districts include writing samples as part of their annual assessment. In these assessments, the writing task typically specifies the audience, the purpose to be served by the writing, and often the writing format (Farr & Beck, 1991). In the national efforts, writing assessment has been central to the rhetoric and advocacy of the new assessments (Brewer, 1989; Wolf, Bixby, Glenn, & Gardner, 1991). Although writing performances may seem easier to define than reading performances, a number of critical issues, such as designation of topic and opportunities for revision, remain unresolved (Freedman, 1993; Huot, 1990; Purves, 1992).

In the past several years, a second generation of performance assessments was initiated, exemplified by the New Standards Project (Simmons & Resnick, 1993) and the state assessments of Maryland (Kapinus et al., 1994) and California (B. Weiss, 1994). These assessments continue to emphasize constructing and comprehending text, with one or more extended texts, but feature at least two unique aspects relative to previous efforts. A first is the creation of contexts that resemble those of typical instructional events. For example, assessments may span a several-day period and involve discussion before and after students' reading or writing. A second is the integration of reading and writing assessments. The composition task typically comes at the end of the 3- to 5-day assessment event so that students can use what they learned from reading in their compositions.

Not unlike the studies that were conducted in the early decades of norm-referenced tests, studies on scoring procedures have been more frequent than studies of the impact of these assessments on literacy practices or students' literacy processes. Linn, Baker, and Dunbar (1991) have outlined a "new generation" of criteria for this new generation of assessments, but these criteria, while applicable to literacy, have not been applied to the current waves of literacy assessments. Are these assessments truly more cognitively complex? Do they capture the processes that their proponents suggest? At this point, the primary concern has been the establishment of those indices associated with a psychometric model. For example, the interrelationships between scores on writing assignments where topic is prescribed and those where students select their own samples for evaluation are not necessarily high (e.g., Koretz, Stecher, Klein, McCaffrey & Deibert, 1993). This is not surprising in light of reports that different writing tasks and contexts, even different aspects of the same composition, can produce considerably different ratings (Freedman, 1983). For example, the rating for mechanics of a composition may be quite separate from students' development of an argument or the quality of their message (Freedman, 1983). ›

In tracing the history of multiple-choice formats, Mercer (1989) notes that the original aim of "objective" measures was to promote equal access to higher education. Performance and portfolio assessments have the same intent. But evidence has not been forthcoming to indicate that the new literacy assessments support the low-income students about whom consequential and frequent judgments are made from assessments. Those performance assessments on which data have been reported to the public indicate that the majority of students are performing poorly (see, e.g., Kapinus et al., 1994, or Mullis et al., 1993). Some argue that delivery standards, that is, access to good school environments and instruction, may explain these results (E. Baker, 1989). However, there have been no research efforts to describe the particular aspects of the assessments that create problems for students. The number of variables that have changed include text difficulty, task difficulty, and response demands. One preliminary analysis of text difficulty on the new assessments indicates that text difficulty has not been specified (Hiebert & Shepard, 1994). Teachers reported the passages to be difficult for many of their students, but assessment developers failed to say how passages had been determined to be appropriate for particular levels.

Frameworks for and Research on Portfolio Assessments. Portfolios have been defined as "collections of artifacts of students' learning experiences assembled over time" (Valencia et al., 1994, p. 14). Unlike performance assessments, which involve events that maintain elements of consistency across students, portfolios vary as a function of the events in classrooms and the choices of teachers and students. Portfolio components have been part of several large-scale efforts such as the writing portion of the NAEP (Freedman, 1993) and, most notably, for a widely publicized state assessment—Vermont's (Brewer, 1989). Despite extensive rhetoric, however, the portfolio efforts at the national and state levels have been limited (Calfee & Hiebert, 1991). Although portfolio assessments are more likely to be manifested at the district or school levels, such assessments have been difficult to obtain. Existing reports indicate that a range of measures are used (Valencia et al., 1994).

Anecdotal accounts of portfolio and performance assessment implementation are full of descriptions of goodwill and professional growth on the part of teachers (Snider, Lima, & DeVito, 1994). However, projects that have documented more closely the processes and the outcomes of teachers' involvement with portfolios shed a more pessimistic light on teachers' initiative in portfolio gathering without extensive support systems. Even with systematic support, research suggests that the process takes considerable time (Au, 1994; Valencia & Place, 1994). The direction taken by England and Wales, when a national assessment was mandated, relied more heavily on an oral reading strategy model that drew on efforts like the Primary Language Record (Barrs, Ellis, Tester, & Thomas, 1989). Even when this assessment was tied directly in to classroom routines, teachers found it difficult to integrate this assessment into their classroom instruction (Gipps, 1993).

Whereas teacher expectations have a long history, teachers' assessments of student literacy proficiency that are part of routine classroom events, such as teacher-made tests and placement into materials and groups, are comparatively untapped. Furthermore, staff development efforts have not attempted to refine teachers' developing skills in these areas. Although teachers create many of their own assessments (Stiggins et al., 1986), their ability to articulate descriptions of their students' proficiencies in reading trade books differs as a function of school context, with teachers in well-to-do suburban schools describing their students' knowledge base more fully than inner-city teachers (Johnston, Weiss, & Afflerbach, 1990). Johnston et al. (1990) tie this differential knowledge base of teachers to constraints placed on teachers by their districts in terms of teacher versus curricular "authority." Teachers in urban districts are more likely to be constrained by required adherence to basal readers and standardized tests. In suburban districts, teachers have greater autonomy. The situation is undoubtedly more complicated, however, in that teachers typically are given little information about test construction and interpretation in teacher education programs (Schafer & Lissitz, 1987). Without extensive knowledge, teachers' beliefs become a critical factor. In examining teachers' beliefs about their students' capabilities on the new assessments, Rueda and Garcia (1992) found a substantial gap between teachers' beliefs and the new practices. In particular, Latino students in special education programs were viewed as least capable. Portfolios were used but contained worksheets and spelling lists. These results are all the more troubling in that teachers came from districts that were regarded as progressive in supporting holistic curriculum and assessment. As portfolio projects proliferate, analyses of classroom uses of portfolios indicate that these projects involve extensive staff development for teachers to learn about portfolios and require increased autonomy for teachers (Athanases, 1994; N. W. Baker, 1993).

*Current Test Practices and Themes From Educational Psychology.* A survey by the General Accounting Office (1993) identified three test publishers as dominating the production of criterion-referenced and state assessments as well as norm-referenced tests. Despite such dominance by a small set of tests, the major reading and language arts tests have not been subjected to the same kind of scrutiny that textbook programs have received (e.g., Durkin, 1981). A search of archival journals produced no analyses of current editions of literacy tests and the views of literacy they manifest. Although educational psychologists were not the ones who mandated the yearly administration of norm-referenced or criterion-referenced tests or matched the content of tests with workbook exercises, the influence of the first generation of educational psychologists is manifest daily in the literacy curricula of most schools and districts through the role that norm-referenced tests have come to have. Accelerated by the reform movement of the 1980s, which made educational excellence synonymous with high performances on tests, test content and test format have become a major influence (some would say *the* major influence) on literacy curriculum.

U.S. schools have never had a legislated national reading and language arts curriculum, but the similarity across textbooks and tests suggests that these represent a de facto national curriculum. The two developed together, informed and acted upon by the same educational psychologists (Gray, 1915; Thorndike, 1918). Precisely how the increasing demands of tests have resulted in new components to textbooks, however, is unclear, for available historical analyses of the reading textbook (Shannon, 1989) treat the textbook as the primary source and leave tests in the background. Despite the lack of research on tests, accountability demands from federal programs such as Chapter 1 and from state reform efforts in the 1980s now give scores from reading tests a high-stakes status, where decisions about funding, personnel, and students' placements in special programs are based primarily on test scores and where such scores are disseminated to the public.

Perspectives from educational psychologists underlie the achievement tests of reading and language arts. These tests have played an important role in determining views of critical literacy knowledge and also of children's abilities to learn. As the paradigms have shifted, educational psychologists have been instrumental in demonstrating the impact of reductionist tests on student learning and on teaching. They have been responsible for exploring alternatives as well, although at this point the directions that will be taken are not clear. The development and use of tests on a large-scale basis have been less of an empirical process than a pragmatic and philosophical one—the *Zeitgeist*. Once a test becomes part of the institutional machinery, it becomes very difficult to change the format, even when the *Zeitgeist* changes.

## Extensions of Perspectives on Literacy Learning to School Texts

Similar to research on testing, research on texts has changed as different theoretical perspectives have been favored within the discipline. Behavioral theories of the first half of the 20th century characterized literacy as an observable product (i.e., decoding and fluency) in which readers' goals were to decode the print and recall the text. Cognitive science shifted the focus from primarily recognizing words to examining narrative and expository texts. Definitions during this period focused on literacy as a meaning-construction process and research was concerned with how texts were structured, as well as with individual differences in processing and remembering text information. With the influence of social-constructivist theories and an emphasis on multiple literacies and the social construction of meaning, a third shift occurred. Research within this perspective focused on the contributions of the social context and the individuals within it, on the authenticity of the text within a literacy event, and on related changes in the nature of literacy instruction.

*Creating Materials to Teach Children to Read.* Textbooks had a long history in U.S. schools before the heyday of the behaviorists, with over 120 million copies of the McGuffey Readers sold from 1836 to 1920 (Shannon, 1989). The McGuffey Readers represented a departure from previous reading materials in the grading of books, the gradual introduction of vocabulary, and the use of word repetition and control of sentence length (Bohning, 1986) but the Readers and their competitors maintained the emphasis on reading material dealing with moral values and truths, a tradition that had roots in the *New England Primer* (Venezky, 1987). The direction taken by the behaviorists was a different one. The year 1920 marked the end of the era in which the McGuffey Readers dominated American reading instruction (Shannon, 1989); the following year saw the publication of Thorndike's *The Teacher's Word Book*. The new era that was ushered in by the behaviorists was marked by efforts to apply the science of learning to the creation of text that would provide the best learning experiences for children. Text was one arena in which the laws of learning could be carefully applied with an assurance that, while a teacher might deviate from the instructions given in a guidebook, the content of a text remained intact in a classroom. Once the critical content had been identified through word frequency counts such as offered in *The Teacher's Word Book* (Thorndike, 1921), text could be created that allowed the sequencing (readiness) and repetition of particular content (exercise) with different stories and books progressing in this same content (identical elements). Further, the task could be a gratifying one for children, allowing pleasure and reinforcement.

The design of reading materials was also of interest to educational psychologists working from an operant conditioning perspective. But the forms that materials took were somewhat different within the two forms of behaviorism. Within the associationism of Thorndike (1906, 1921) and colleagues, high-frequency words and short, simple sentences were emphasized in the design of text. The design of text became even more intricate within operant conditioning as guidelines for size of stimuli, pacing, and feedback were defined (Skinner, 1954). The extensions of associationism and operant conditioning perspectives to school text are, respectively, identifying and controlling factors of text difficulty within school text, and creating comprehensive programs with the right conditions for literacy learning.

Identifying and Controlling Factors of Text Difficulty.    The stereotype of "Run, Spot, run" as the language of reading textbooks has its basis in the choices made by the first generation of educational psychologists. Thorndike's (1903) laws of learning said little specifically about what the mind processed as students learned to read and write. As Venezky's (1984) review demonstrated (and as was summarized in the earlier discussion of perspectives on literacy and literacy learning), the psychology literature from the first decade of the 20th century is quite rich. Gestalt psychology's explanations of perception were used by educational psychologists as the basis for applying the laws of learning. As interpreted by educational psychologists, what needed to be learned (i.e., the stimulus) was the whole word. Words that held high interest for students or those that represent frequently occurring patterns in English (*e.g., cat, cake*) could have become the focus. Instead, the direction mapped out by Thorndike in *The Teacher's Word Book* was a focus on high-frequency words. This emphasis was to direct the field until the mid-1960s. High-frequency words were identified through word counts of the texts that students might read. The words that occurred the most frequently needed to be taught first. Thus, the priority of a word in text and curriculum became a function of its appearance in existing texts. The machinery of the laws of learning was applied to high-frequency words in designating school text for both beginning and more proficient readers but, because of the differences of students' reading proficiency, their manifestations took slightly different forms.

For beginning readers, textbook publishers did not turn to already existing books. To initiate beginners into reading, the behaviorists identified the most frequently occurring words (heavily dominated by articles, prepositions, and conjunctions) and devised little stories that used these words in a formulaic way. We could find no records of these rules in research or pedagogical articles. Although specific formulas based on behaviorist principles are discussed in vague terms (Gray & Leary, 1935), an examination of a passage in a 1989 textbook series (P. D. Pearson et al., 1989) suggests that frequency, spacing, and repetition were applied according to an algorithm. The first passage of the first preprimer, entitled "Look for the Dog," included words presented in the earlier readiness level as well as the following eight new words (with repetitions for each word given in parentheses): find (7), for (4), you (5), did (6), see (4), puppies (7), and (3), tan (3). The six new words and their repetitions in the next passage, "Bingo, the Naughty Dog," followed a similar pattern: Bingo (8), naughty (9), come (10), here (17), am (4), was (4). Counts of new words in the remaining four passages in this preprimer confirm a pattern of no fewer than three repetitions of a new word within a passage. Except for those words that presumably are thought to meet the criterion of high interest for young children (e.g., truck, puppies, naughty), a "new" word appears again at least three times within one of the subsequent passages. Flipping through a series such as this one indicates that this contrived text based on word frequency does not continue beyond the first-grade. However, "primerese" (Amsterman, Ammon, & Simons, 1990) characterized the text for first graders.

With the advent of educational psychology, primerese quickly came to dominate school text. Gray had a strong and extended influence on the Scott-Foresman readers that featured Dick and Jane (Elson & Gray, 1930; Gray et al. 1957). In the 1930s through 1950s, Gray's role was duplicated at other publishing houses by other educational psychologists and reading educators such as Gates, Bond, and Betts (N. B. Smith, 1934/1965). Constraints of high-frequency vocabulary and sentence length and a view that the content of stories should reflect the everyday experiences of a cast of typical characters meant that the ensuing passages were limited in scope. Dick, Jane, and Sally (and similar casts of characters in other textbook series) went to the store, chased their runaway pets, or baked cookies with mother. The case for attending to high-regularity words such as *ran, can,* and *pan* would not be made forcibly until Chall's (1967/1982) *Learning to Read: The Great Debate.* It was a position that linguists assumed as well (Fries, 1963). Further, children's books by authors who had intriguing stories to tell or who used rhyming and rhythmical text (e.g., Dr. Seuss, Bill Martin) fell within the purview of the trade book divisions of publishing houses, which operated separately from the school textbook divisions (Chall & Squire, 1991).

Had an emphasis on high-frequency words as the unit of importance in creating school text remained as a focus solely for beginning reading materials, the character of American reading books used with students in Grades 3 through 6 might have taken a very different form. Although high-frequency words could have been emphasized in texts for the early part of first-grade instruction, other criteria (e.g., interesting story lines and information) could have been used as the basis for selection of additional reading material for beginning readers and for higher grade levels. This did not happen because of the continued emphasis on high-frequency words in the texts developed for older readers, with development guided by readability formulas.

The motivation behind readability formulas was, and continues to be, an entirely legitimate one: an interest in factors that contribute to making texts comprehensible for readers. The problem lies in the concentration on one approach to judging readability over decades and a commensurate lack of attention to any other approaches. Thorndike's (1921) *Teacher's Word Book* was used as the basis by the first generation of educational psychologists, and this approach remained popular for decades. Words were designated as "unfamiliar" if they occurred infrequently according to Thorndike's high-frequency word list or the lists that subsequently followed. Since simplicity of sentences was seen as the other major contributor to difficulty, indices soon sprang up that allowed a calculation of relative complexity of sentences (measured by sentence length or syllables within a particular corpus of words) and number of infrequent or unfamiliar words (Klare, 1984). Lively and Pressey's (1923) readability formula is often cited as the first, and numerous formulas followed (e.g., Dale and Chall, 1948, Fry, 1968). By the early 1980s, well over a thousand studies had been conducted on text readability (Klare, 1984). These studies considered potential factors that, when varied, contributed to making texts easier or more difficult to read. Formulas weighed these factors in some measurable way and were validated by empirical investigations of the degree to which readers of different abilities could fluently read a graded set of texts. Students of different ages usually read manipulated text, since designs that included other forms of text were rare. Using this somewhat limited form of text, the line of research verified the thinking of the time that texts with short sentences and familiar words were easier to comprehend than text with longer sentences and more difficult words.

Criticisms of readability formulas came soon after their development (Moore, 1935). Although cautions about the misuses of these formulas were raised by their developers (Chall, 1984), and alternatives were proposed (Bormuth, 1966), the use of readability formulas was unbridled. Readability formulas became part of the institutional machinery as states established acceptable readability levels for their textbook adoption lists. In these mandates, readability requirements were stipulated across the grades, influencing the text for students in higher grades in at least two ways. First, publishers began to manipulate texts to fit the requirements of formulas. Even if the passages from a popular children's book were included in a textbook, the text might be altered to satisfy the requirements of the readability formulas, with multisyllabic words changed to monosyllabic ones, conjunctions or other connections removed to create shorter, less complex sentences, and so forth. Such manipulations occurred without serious attention to subtle changes in meaning or to the removal of information about causal relationships.

Second, Davison and Kantor's (1982) analyses suggested that the impact of readability formulas went beyond manipulation of existing text to the creation of texts. It was not only the preprimers and the primers that were the creation of textbook writers attempting to apply particular formulas. Davison and Kantor demonstrated similar influences for textbooks created for the students in Grades 8 through 12. By the early 1980s it was recognized that readability formulas had influenced school texts, and not only those used to teach young children to read, but also those used to teach secondary students biology, chemistry, and physics.

*Creating Programs with the Right Conditions for Literacy Learning.* The principles of operant conditioning (Skinner, 1954) had a profound effect on forms of text as well. Ideas such as breaking a skill or body of knowledge into its logical and hierarchical steps, the pacing of the learning of these steps, and quick and consistent feedback for negative or positive behavior often resulted in numerous worksheets rather than stories or books. Attention moved away from the passage as a whole to lists of words, groups of phrases, or short paragraphs. Further, passages could as easily consist of nonsensical text (but consistent according to the linguistic principle being reinforced) as a text with profound or informative ideas.

A number of programs were developed, including IPI—Individually Prescribed Instruction—at the University of Pittsburgh's Learning Research and Development Center (Beck & Mitroff, 1972; Glaser, 1963, 1966) and the Wisconsin Design at the Wisconsin Research and Development Center for Cognitive Science (Otto, 1977). These programs contributed to a long-term, large-scale change when commercial textbook programs integrated similar features such as more practice exercises. Although textbook series previously had included workbooks and ancillary worksheets, the sequencing and pacing of literacy components advocated within an operant conditioning perspective meant that the "practice" components of these series became even more prominent. The pretest, worksheets for objectives which a pretest showed students unable to meet, and the follow-up worksheets and posttest meant ever smaller pieces of text. The Wisconsin Design for Reading Skill Development (Otto, 1977) illustrates a readng program based on this philosophy. Six readng skills were identified: word attack, comprehension, study skills, self-directed reading, interpretive reading, and creative reading. For word attack, there were an additional three levels (A through C), which in turn had additional components. For example, A had seven components: rhyming words, rhyming phrases, shapes, letters/numbers, words/phrases, colors, and initial consonants. For initial consonants, a set of lessons was devoted to each consonant, with periodic review lessons of groups of consonants. Aukerman (1984), in a compendium of approaches to beginning reading, describes another of these efforts, Developmental Reading, (Amidon, 1975), as having 800 specific reading subskills in its fundamental program. In cases like the Wisconsin Reading Design and Developmental Reading, materials consisted primarily of worksheets with pretests and posttests. But there were also instances of "reading books" based on this philosophy, such as the Sullivan reading program (Buchanan & Sullivan, 1963/1980). These books are better characterized as workbooks than as trade or library books or even as typical school reading books. A page in a Sullivan Reader had a two-column format, with the child instructed to pull a tab down the column on which the correct responses were given. After reading a sentence such as "Is this an ant?" (accompanying a picture of a boy), the student was to pull the tab down the second column to see if his or her response of "no" was correct.

Observations of classrooms in the 1970s showed that students spent considerably more time on workbook and worksheet tasks than they did on reading text (Fisher et al., 1978; Leinhardt, Zigmond, & Cooley, 1981). Although the observational studies in the late 1980s were not as extensive, the notion of "practice" through filling out worksheets and workbook pages continues to dominate the reading experiences of many students, especially those perceived to be problem readers (P. Johnston & Allington, 1991).

Despite massive implementation efforts such as the IPI and the Wisconsin Design by educational psychologists and the hundreds of studies on verbal learning that are published annually, there is little research that describes the learning processes, outcomes, or the content of the worksheets that millions of children spend several hours completing each day of their school careers. Two lines of research constitute the research literature on this prolific text in elementary classrooms. L. M. Anderson, Brubaker, Alleman-Brooks, and G. Duffy (1985) examined the amount of time students spent completing worksheets and the students' perceptions of the purpose, activities, and procedures for doing so. They found that most students viewed worksheets, their most common text experience, as tasks to complete. They often competed to see who could complete the tasks most quickly, and they saw the goal as having the task behind them so that they could move on to more interesting activities such as recess or activity centers. Osborn's (1984) study of the content of the worksheets indicated that students' perceptions are entirely justified. The categories that Osborn examined raised questions about the type of text in worksheets, a mismatch between their instructional intent and their content, and the ostensible purposes of the lessons. For example, many worksheets that purport to provide practice in reading related words are actually matching tasks rather than reading events. Students frequently practice filling in blanks rather than reading, generating, and thinking about ideas and information.

This handful of studies gives a dismal view of the content of worksheet exercises and the consequences of participating in these activities over an extended period of time. An additional research base to support the use of such texts in elementary classrooms is probably not advisable, necessary, or appropriate. However, the legacy of behaviorism in the texts known as worksheets, added to their presence in the test-taking programs aimed at raising performances on standardized tests (Mehrens & Kaminski, 1989), suggests that the school literacy experiences of students are dominated by microlevel activities that bear little resemblance to literacy processes in mature and nonschool reading. Although the theory and research of educational psychologists at one point provided the rationale for these activities, educational psychologists have been remarkably uncritical as a group when it comes to questioning the status quo of reading and writing instruction. This remains a problem despite progress in studies of text within a cognitive science perspective.

***Establishing the Complexity of Text and its Influence on Reader-Writer Processes.*** Cognitive science perspectives have raised important questions about the nature of text, focusing on the big question of how text "works." Research within those perspectives has been directed toward uncovering the rules that guide text production and comprehension and identifying optimal ways to convey these rules to students across age and ability levels. This focus resulted from two important shifts as educational psychology moved from behavioral to cognitive science perspectives. Whereas behavioral psychologists restricted themselves to studying what is observable, such as frequency counts of words, cognitive scientists were concerned

with the invisible processes that underlie successful reading (Anderson & Pearson, 1984) and writing (Flower & Hayes, 1980, 1981; Scardamalia & Bereiter, 1986). Second, in contrast to behaviorists' focus on words as a measure of literacy performance levels, cognitive scientists focused on comprehension and production of more extended texts, initially sentences and paragraphs, later connections between ideas in different sentences, across paragraphs, and within book chapters.

As a result of these shifts, educational psychologists tackled the difficult challenge of explaining the nature of texts (Mandler & Johnson, 1977; Meyer, 1975; Stein & Glenn, 1979), students' metacognitive knowledge related to text (e.g., Garner & Gillingham, 1987; Gordon, 1990; Flower & Hayes, 1981), and factors that contribute to readers' and writers' ease or difficulty in processing text (e.g., Armbruster & Anderson, 1985), with related questions about traditional measures of readability (Amsterman et al., 1990; Green & Davison, 1988).

*Understanding How Text Works.* Studies of the nature of text have focused on identifying the broad macrostructures that characterize narrative and expository text forms, identifying factors that contribute to text coherence, and developing an understanding of text memorability (see Barthes, 1975; Brewer & Lichtenstein, 1982; Moffett & Wagner, 1983). As Fitzgerald (1989) notes, factors that make text work include content, style, force, affect, point of view, and other ways in which the ideas are transmitted. The largest body of research by far has focused on descriptions of the structure or organizational patterns of text. Although many of the initial studies on the workings of text focused on text structures, an extensive body of research that preceded this research grew out of work in mathemagenic behaviors (Rothkopf, 1965), or behaviors that give rise to learning.

One of the primary concentrations of research on mathemagenic behaviors was on the role of adjunct questions—questions that were inserted at different positions in text to facilitate readers' selective attention to upcoming information or to promote their review of preceding information (Reynolds, Standiford, & Anderson, 1978). For example, Rothkopf (1966) conducted a study that was typical of those within this research tradition. He divided a 5,200-word passage from *The Sea Around Us*, by Rachel Carson, into 20 equal segments, then inserted questions requiring one- or two-word answers at the intervals created by each segment. The influence of the questions on readers' recall of information that preceded or followed the questions was examined. This research line represented an initial movement away from the focus on reading as a decoding process to one of learning from text, and away from the use of words and sentences as the basic textual materials to using longer passages of connected text. But with few exceptions, the studies were conducted with mature readers rather than children and with limited attention to likely interactive effects of the structure of the text, the level of readers' knowledge on the topic of the selection, or the kinds of questions that were asked. However, this research represented a redirection to the ways in which texts are structured and how structures related to understanding text.

Many of the earliest studies of text structure examined young children's development in understanding the structure of narratives (Mandler & Johnson, 1977; Rumelhart, 1977; Stein & Glenn,

1979), but within a few years, similar lines of research were conducted on the structures of expository text (Kintsch & van Dijk, 1978; Meyer & Rice, 1984). The research on text structures complemented the growing work by schema theorists on knowledge structures (e.g., Anderson & Pearson, 1984; Bransford, 1979). After patterns of organization had been identified and researched in terms of their impact on memory for text, instructional research was designed to make these text structures apparent to students and to create strategies for using this knowledge as tools (e.g., Fitzgerald & Teasley, 1986; Raphael et al., 1989). The study of text structures, then, provided a window into one aspect of how text worked: the overarching models or frames that characterize texts found in stories from a range of cultures and in textbooks that pervade U.S. classrooms.

While this research on narrative and expository text structure continues (see Graesser, Golding, & Long, 1991; Weaver & Kintsch, 1991), the level of activity on text structure research was at its peak in the late 1970s and early 1980s. Classic studies on narrative text structures and children's developing understandings were conducted by Mandler and Johnson (1977) and by Stein and Glenn (1979), both defining a story grammar as analogous to the linguistic grammars that underlie sentences. The search for this generic pattern of narrative structure is traceable to folklorists' efforts to describe the range of tales within the folktale tradition (Meyer & Rice, 1984). In short, story grammar research is characterized by the search for a generic pattern that constitutes stories and the study of when and how children develop this schema as visible in their telling/writing and understanding/remembering the various components that characterize a fully developed narrative. Story grammars describe the hierarchical organization of story constituents (e.g., setting, episodes) and, in turn, the properties of constituents (e.g., initiating event, internal response of an episode). For example, Stein and colleagues (e.g., Stein & Glenn, 1979; Stein & Trabasso, 1982) detailed the constituents of a story through asking readers of different developmental levels to retell a range of stories. From their retellings, the researchers deduced the generic or basic constituents that made a story meaningful, as well as preschool through elementary aged children's developing conceptions of story. Stein suggested that simple stories consist of the following components: setting, initiating event, internal response, attempt, consequence, and reaction. The extensive body of research on narrative structure (see reviews by Bruce, 1984; Just & Carpenter, 1987; Meyer & Rice, 1984) provided the basis for instructional studies designed to enhance students' understanding of story structure and their ability to use this knowledge to more successfully comprehend and compose stories of their own (Fitzgerald, 1992).

Like research within a cognitive science tradition on narrative text, research on expository text has focused to a large degree on identifying elements of sructure, though unlike narrative text, expository text research has defined a variety of text structures that characterize its means of conveying ideas and information (e.g., Armbruster & Anderson, 1985; Meyer, 1975). Most of this research, however, examined structures of relatively small units of text, such as the paragraph or short passage. In large texts, such as chapters and books, text structures are found typically in combinations rather than in any pure form (Calfee & Chambliss, 1987). Despite this limitation in scope of text, research on text structures has provided insights into facilitators and barriers to both text production and comprehension.

Meyer (1975; Meyer & Rice, 1984) approached the study of prose with an interest in what makes some information in text more memorable than other information. She weighed the relative impact of text structure, serial position of information, and the relative importance of the information as measured by readers' ratings. Her fndings suggested that structure was the variable that most influenced memory. She identified five organizational patterns common to content area text, then examined how these different patterns influenced readers' memory for text. The patterns identified included cause/effect, comparison/contrast, problem/solution, description, and collection. Findings from a series of studies she conducted suggested that the higher the level of information in the text structure, the more memorable it was, and that some structures (e.g., cause/effect) facilitate information recall more than others (e.g., simple description).

Reviews of the theoretical schemes of expository text can be found in Meyer and Rice (1984) and Weaver and Kintsch (1991), and reviews of the research conducted on the use of knowledge about expository text in comprehending and composing expository text are available as well (e.g., Britton & Black, 1985; Roller, 1990; Slater & Graves, 1989). In most of the reviews of models of expository text, a feature of the theoretical framework that is often overlooked is the limited array of texts used in the theoretical constructs and also the empirical evaluations. Most frequently, the texts used were written or identified because of their compliance with a specific structure (e.g., enumeration, description, compare-contrast, sequence). However, some (e.g., Armbruster & Anderson, 1985) suggest that the structures that are used within particular disciplines in presenting their work require attention, while efforts to create frameworks for large texts, such as textbooks that might be used in a college survey course, have been initiated (Calfee & Chambliss, 1987).

Some research on the nature of text has broadened beyond specific attention to structure to tackle questions about specific forms of text (e.g., journal introductions, documents, journalistic text) used within different disciplines or in nonschool settings. For example, Swales (1990) examined the structure of introductions to academic journal articles in physics and educational psychology, specifically in terms of the presence of antcipated findings in the introduction. Swales found differences in expectations within the disciplines, with introductions to educational psychology articles containing far fewer references to their findings than either the physics journal articles or the recommendations of journal publishers.

Guthrie, Britten, and Barker (1991) explored another form of text, documents, and the influence of document structure on readers' ability to locate and remember information. They presented information in a table, a directory, and in prose form on a series of computer screens, then asked readers questions that required them to successfully use at least two categories of information. The computer program was able to track how the readers spent their time in reading and responding to the questions, specifically where they went in the documents to seek information. Like other researchers on text structure, these researchers found that text structure influenced the way in which readers spent their time in responding to the questions and the strategies they used to search and select information. The researchers concluded that to be selective in inspecting the documents, readers had to be able to grasp the overall organizational structure and be aware of ways to enter that structure.

These two studies reflect current concerns about text structure that move the research beyond identifying generic patterns and outside the range of traditional school texts. Yet their findings are consistent with those of more traditional studies of text structure: Readers and writers benefit from an awareness of such structures in their ability to identify relevant information and in their ability to participate as writers of a particular genre. However, these two studies suggest that there may be unique features of real-world texts that must be understood, outside the narrow focus of stories and school texts. A logical extension of much of the research on text structure was to examine students' knowledge about structure and the relationship of this knowledge to their ability to compose and comprehend stories and exposition. This research was conducted as part of the large body of work within the area of metacognition.

Exploring Students' Metacognitive Knowledge About Text Structure. An extensive body of research exists documenting students' knowledge of text structures as one important step toward understanding the role of text structure in comprehension of narrative and expository text. Developed within the research tradition of studies of metacognition, text structure knowledge reflected one aspect of metacognitive knowledge related to text. Questions about students' metacognitive knowledge focus on the problem-solving aspects of both writing and reading, taking as part of the process the importance of understanding the task variables that contribute to the challenges of solving problems. This has been identified explicitly within writing research through the research of Flower and Hayes (1980, 1981), and implicitly in much of the research exploring text structure knowledge and reading. Specifically, research on metacognitive knowledge related to text has taken the form of three types of studies: (a) examinations of students' knowledge about structure as a function of text types, (b) examinations of students' knowledge about structure as revealed through different tasks, and (c) examination of student's knowledge about structure within intervention studies that emphasize structure of text.

McGee and colleagues (McGee, 1982; Richgels, McGee, Lomax, & Sheard, 1987) have studied students' knowledge of text structure as a function of text type. For example, McGee (1982) examined adults' and students' (sixth and ninth graders') ability to use a problem/solution text structure to organize ideas when recalling previously read text and when composing original text. This study showed that metacognition about problem/solution structures varied developmentally, with more mature readers and writers using a more fully developed problem/solution structure in their recall and composition than less mature readers. The latter group, however, was capable of using text structure for recalling information from text but not for composing. Although a follow-up study (Richgels et al., 1987) indicated that a problem/solution text structure was found to be less accessible to sixth graders than structures such as compare/contrast, such differences have not been found reliably across

studies (Gordon, 1990). Studies such as these suggest that readers' and writers' metacognitive knowledge of text structures varies and that this difference in knowledge appears to influence the reading and writing of readers of different ages and abilities.

Others have examined students' knowledge of text structure to uncover ways in which text contributes to comprehension difficulties across various tasks. For example, Garner and Gillingham (1987) examined fifth- and seventh-grade students' ability to construct a coherent paragraph, based on the elements of topic relatedness (i.e., parts belong together), superordination (i.e., details relate to the main idea), and cohesion (ideas linked across sentences). Students created their paragraphs using a computer program that guided them to unscramble two sets of sentences, one describing earthworms, the other quilts. Not surprisingly, the researchers were able to document that the students' ability to relate what they knew about structural properties was linked to the ways in which such information was assessed, suggesting that students' verbal reports of their knowledge of these factors may not always correlate with their actual performance. Students were able to identify when a text "worked," although they were not always able to construct one. Further, they were sometimes unable to articulate what made a text work, yet were able to construct a coherent text based on the sentences provided.

A third approach to examining students' knowledge of how text works has been through instructional studies in narrative and expository text structures. One such study has been part of a line of research by Fitzgerald (1989, 1992) on students' composition and comprehension of narrative texts. Fitzgerald and Teasley (1986) worked with fourth graders to examine their knowledge of narrative structure followed by instruction that emphasized coherence, temporal and causal connection, and creativity. Over a period of 7 weeks, with three 30- to 45-minute sessions for the first 2 weeks and two sessions thereafter, students were introduced to how narratives were structured and factors that constitute effective narratives. The instruction in narrative structure enhanced students' ability to organize the narratives they were constructing and improved the overall quality of their compositions.

Similarly, Englert and Raphael (1989) examined students' metacognitive knowledge about the structures of texts as part of a line of instructional research designed to enhance their reading and writing of informational text. Using a combination of group questionnaires, individual interviews, writing samples, and observations, they analyzed regular and special education upper elementary students' ability to articulate differences between narrative and expository text and to identify specific questions addressed within different types of expository texts. They then examined the impact of teaching students about text structures and their use in composing and comprehending text on levels of metacognitive knowledge about writing. In one study, fifth- and sixth-grade students were placed in one of four experimental conditions: instruction in text structure, a writing process environment, a combination of these two, or a control condition (Raphael et al., 1989). While students across interventions were able to detail the broad differences in purposes between narrative and expository texts, students who had been directly taught about text structure were more able to articulate the kinds of questions one might expect to be addressed in texts of different structures. Extending this research to students identified as learning disabled, Englert et al. (1988) documented the difficulty these students had in analyzing the organizational patterns of text such as using conceptual categories to generate related ideas or using text structures as a way of organizing ideas. Based on these results, Englert et al. (1991) designed a yearlong intervention for learning-disabled students in which instruction in text structures was embedded within the context of a process writing classroom. Findings from this study were encouraging in that participants in the intervention were more able to talk about strategies for organizing ideas they had generated and to use text structure–related questions to monitor the effectiveness of their writing than were learning-disabled students who had not had the opportunity to participate in the intervention.

The line of research within a cognitive science tradition exploring text structures suggests that students are aware of and use their knowledge of text structure in their reading and writing of narrative and expository text. However, such knowledge is not simply a matter of "have it, use it." Rather, the use of such knowledge for understanding text seems to be part of a larger process that is influenced by the purpose of the text-related activity, the amount of teacher guidance, whether the task involves composing or comprehending, and factors such as the learner's ability or developmental level. However, despite such qualifications, the findings related to the existence of text structure knowledge and its amenability to instruction have helped provide a basis for curriculum and instruction with regard to both narrative and expository text.

Re-examining Text Difficulty.    Like the earlier studies of text, many of the texts in studies on readers' story and topic schemata were contrived, some more than those found in school textbooks. However, these new perspectives on text did inspire examinations of school texts and proved to be an entrée for examining a much more fundamental issue than the compliance of texts with story grammars—the impact of the pervasive readability formulas, as was discussed previously. These new conceptual frameworks on text and discourse provided the basis for empirical investigations that could demonstrate, in ways that the critiques of readability formulas during the previous decades of behaviorism had been unable to do, the effects of simplistic applications of readability formulas on the comprehensibility, cohesiveness, and interestingness of school texts. The bulk of these studies took a broader view of school text than simply examining the story grammars and critiquing the stories themselves, drawing on rhetorical, literary, and discourse analytic frameworks (Green & Davison, 1988). These studies showed that in complying with the requirements of readability formulas (e.g., high-frequency words, shorter sentences), roadblocks to comprehension were inadvertently created. By substituting high-frequency words for those descriptive and ostensibly more difficult ones based on word frequency counts, meanings were often changed or made more obscure. By eliminating conjunctions, shorter choppy sentences were created, often without the causal connections that had helped make the ideas comprehensible. Bland or missing descriptive language creates primerese (Amsterman et al., 1990), which many children find unfamiliar and even nonsensical, while connections

between characters' motives and actions may become implicit and more difficult to understand (Green & Davison, 1988).

Findings such as these were used to create better stories and became the basis for comparing students' comprehension between well and poorly structured texts (Amsterman et al., 1990; Brennan, Bridge, & Winograd, 1986; Feldman, 1985). The patterns of these studies were fairly consistent, confirming the support for comprehension that well-constructed passages provide. For example, when Brennan et al. (1986) asked second graders to read an intact textbook passage that failed to adhere to story grammar conventions and a passage based on the same content but adapted to form a coherent story (and judged to be more difficult according to readability formulas), they recalled more explicit (but not implicit) information from the well-formed study in the right sequence and with less text-erroneous information than with the original sentence. Beck, McKeown, Omanson, & Pople (1984) conducted a comprehensive redesign of stories in school text, attending to elements of text beyond the compliance with story grammars. The comprehension of third-grade students was facilitated by what Armbruster (1984) has called "considerate" text, that is, text written to take into account the reader's need for coherence and clarity.

Cognitive scientists were more apt to implement instructional studies aimed at improving text strategies of readers or writers than they were to create or identify specific texts that support literacy processes. However, findings from studies about the contribution of well-structured text to readers' comprehension and the impediments to comprehension as a result of indiscriminate application of readability formulas have had the most immediate extension to and influence on practice since the first decade of research in educational psychology. This influence is described in the next section as research on text from a social-constructivist perspective is explored, raising questions about the basis for the texts that had been used for decades in educational settings.

***Understanding the Authenticity and Purposes of Text in Literacy Events.***    Social constructivism has raised new questions on definitions of text, views of how meaning is negotiated, and the role of text in literacy learning. These shifts have required changes in research methodologies and metrics for assessing students' growth and change. As Kuhn (1962) observed in *The Structure of Scientific Revolutions*, it is often difficult to assess the impact of the research while in the midst of changing perspectives and criteria. Thus, in this section, without the benefit of hindsight, we offer an interpretation of the critical studies, their potential for impact, and the questions these studies raise. After providing background on what a social-constructivist perspective means for the study of text, we describe three research areas that have benefited from the redefinition of text and its study within literacy contexts: (a) negotiating the meanings of text within school contexts, (b) producing text within school contexts, and (c) understanding teachers' roles in enhancing students' interactions with text.

Redefining the Meaning of Text and Its Relation to Context. Definitions of text have broadened within a social-constructivist perspective, building from earlier views of reasoning and problem solving about print. One of the reasons for the broader view of text is that what is important about reading and writing as intellectual development goes beyond the language use which occurs with printed materials. For example, Wells (1990) suggests that text should be defined as

any artifact that is constructed as a representation of meaning using a conventional symbolic system since, by virtue of its permanence and the symbolic mode in which it is created, such an artifact performs the essential function of allowing us to create an external, fixed representation of the sense we make of our experience so that we may reflect upon and manipulate it. (p. 378)

Within such a definition of text, it becomes possible that, while literate thinking may occur and be encouraged with written print, it does not depend solely on it. As such, encouraging such literate thinking can occur with the use of written text, but is not dependent on it. Dyson and Freedman (1991) write that written language "figures into particular kinds of communicative events" (p. 756), using the term "communicative event" to reflect a broader conception of what counts as text and moving beyond print as the basis for literate activity. Further, Michaels and O'Connor (1990) suggest that "reading and writing may be part of the picture, but only a part. Becoming literate in any particular domain involves learning a specific discourse—particular ways of thinking, acting, and valuing." They argue that this means that literacy is "about ways of being in the world and ways of making meaning with and around text" (p. 11). Finally, working within the tradition of literary theory, DeFabio (1989) describes a high school literature class as "a literary text which I must read, interpret, and criticize as I would any literary text" (p. 1). In short, for those working within a social-constructivist tradition, texts include print, certainly, but also include conversation, media, and the broader social discourse.

A second change that has influenced research about text has been a shift in views of the relationship between text and context. For most of the history of educational psychology, text has been an object of study, as reflected first in the study of words and perception and later in the study of how readers' knowledge structures relate to understanding texts with different structures. A social-constructivist perspective draws attention to how readers' negotiation of meaning is influenced by the context in which reading occurs. A focus on text within context has made the limitations of traditional research methodologies in studying such complex and interconnected phenomena apparent. Thus, educational psychologists have turned to the research of ethnographers of communication (Florio-Ruane, 1994), sociolinguistics (e.g., Gee, 1988; Michaels & O'Connor, 1990), and educational anthropologists (e.g., Cazden, 1991, 1992). These researchers have made the study of context their focus but often without specific attention to the contribution of text. It is the merging of these perspectives and methods that holds promise for understanding text as part of the broader picture.

In sum, the study of text within a social-constructivist perspective differs from past work on text in two related and critical levels. First, text has been refined in a manner such that research on print medium is a smaller piece of the pie defined as "text." Second, even where a focus on print medium is a primary interest, studies consider the influences of the broader context

on meaning making, with text only one of many sources contributing to the larger picture. A final aspect that has influenced the nature of the specific research questions is a subtle distinction that has major ramifications for research across test, text, and teaching: the distinction between constructing and negotiating meaning.

When the perspective is one of constructing meaning, as it has been within the cognitive tradition, text plays a major role in determining the nature of that meaning. Readers are responsible for bringing their knowledge to bear to make sense of the text, but writers are responsible for providing enough detail—but not more than necessary—to convey their message and to signal readers to fill in any gaps. However, when social constructivists describe meaning as negotiated, the relative contributions of reader, author, text, and context change. The reader's contribution, the context in which the text is read, and the purposes for reading all serve to reduce the contribution of the text as the chief source of meaning. Thus, the three lines of research we now discuss focus on the context in which text interactions occur.

Understanding Context Factors and Readers' and Writers' Meaning Negotiations.   Researchers from a range of disciplines have examined text/context interactions that contribute to meaning negotiation consistent with a social-constructivist perspective. Drawing on ethnographic traditions, Florio-Ruane (1994) offered a model of writing conferences that underscored the complexity of any classroom literacy event. She noted contextual factors acting upon and being interpreted by the teachers as including their beliefs, attitudes, and so forth (i.e., teacher attributes), cultural and societal expectations, and the district-mandated curriculum. Influencing the students' interpretation of text are personal attributes, knowledge of the norms of classroom communication, use of learning strategies, and family and cultural expectations. The text itself, then, is one small part of the overall picture of meaning creation.

Extending these notions to a study of the genre of autobiography, Florio-Ruane (1994) explored how the context in which readers (in this case, preservice teachers) read and responded to text, interacted with the genre itself, and influenced the way in which they interpreted the texts they read. With these student teachers, Florio-Ruane created the Autobiography Club, a monthly discussion of a different autobiography, with authors from a range of cultures represented. Based on a combination of interviews, participants' response journals, and field notes of the meetings of the Autobiography Club, Florio-Ruane found that the meanings negotiated among the groups were reflected in the participants' ability to link events from the autobiographies to their own lives, the informal setting in which the discussions occurred (her home), and the unobtrusive role she played in promoting the discussion. Speaking for the participants, one participant noted that initially they had assumed that Florio-Ruane would expect them to relate each of the texts to their concurrent student teaching experiences, despite the fact that few of the books dealt directly with issues of teaching or teacher education, and that there were certain points to be correctly identified in their sketch books and discussions. Over time, they redefined the goal as understanding themselves as learners and teachers, especially the role of their own culture in shaping their beliefs about teaching and learning. Unlike a cognitive science experiment, in which the focus would have been on structure of autobiographies and how memorable events from the text related to the background knowledge and experiences of the reader, this study demonstrates another tradition in which the broader influences on readers' negotiation of meaning are considered, leaving open the issue of whether the readers' interpretations are "correct."

Although cognitive scientists have explicated many aspects of the writing process, from early drafting through going public with one's work, and the importance of scaffolding young writers' attempts to write within a range of genres (see Bereiter & Scardamalia, 1987), they have remained relatively mute with respect to what factors outside knowledge of the writing process contribute to the ability of teachers and peers to engage successfully around students' text. Denyer's (1993) ethnographic account of a writing conference between a student teacher, Maureen, and a third-grade student, Katy, who had written a poem, demonstrates the manner in which issues such as these can be addressed by research from a social-constructivist perspective. In a 14-minute conference, Maureen asked Katy more than 60 questions about her poem. These questions, designed to scaffold Katy's poetry writing, not surprisingly had the opposite effect. Though Katy had indicated that her poem did not have to rhyme, several questions focused on the absence of rhyme. When Katy indicated that she was not happy with her final line, Maureen was at a loss to guide her. This student teacher's lack of knowledge about the genre, the emphasis on revision, and the traditional power hierarchy of "teacher as expert" created a complex context that affected Katy's ability to move her poem forward. Studying Katy's text, even across revisions, would provide little in the ways of insights into how the text was created. The projects of Florio-Ruane (1994) and Denyer (1993) illustrate the insights on text and their negotiation and production when researchers take a social-constructivist perspective. It would not be sufficient merely to add context as a factor and attempt to identify interactions among reader, text, and context. The context itself is the fabric of which meanings are made and cannot be treated as a separate piece in which text can be embedded.

Restructuring the context in which students use text is a second line of research, one that has engaged scholars identified within educational psychology's traditions. Eeds and Wells (1989) and McGee (1992) have studied shifts in meaning making when the context shifts from traditional reading groups directed by the teacher to one in which the teacher leads "grand conversations" about text. Others (e.g., McMahon, Raphael, & Goatley, 1995; O'Flahavan, 1989) have explored student-led discussions about text instead of traditional reading group organizations. Finally, Thornburg (1993) studied a context in which parents of children from nonmainstream cultures were included in the school storybook reading period, as well as encouraged to engage in storybook reading at home. These lines of research draw on discourse analysis procedures, qualitative methodologies, and literary theory as a supplement to long-standing approaches to the study of meaning making from text.

In attempts to create "grand conversations" about literature among students (Eeds & Wells, 1989; McGee, 1992), restructuring the context involves moving teachers from asking comprehension questions with known answers (or "efferent responses," to use Rosenblatt's [1978] terminology), to raising questions that invoke more personal, or aesthetic, responses. Eeds and Wells examined what happened when a small group of upper elementary students met with a student teacher to discuss a novel. The teachers in training were participating in a practicum experience that stressed Rosenblatt's concept of transaction, which emphasizes reading as a process of change—that is, both reader and text are changed by the interaction. Part of the practicum instruction also stressed the importance of the teachable moment, points during the discussion which lend themselves to teaching students particular literary features, text processing activities, and possibilities for interpretive response. Such conversatons shift the focus from the "road to comprehension to a river of interpretation" (McMahon, 1994, p. 109).

Eeds and Wells discovered that even within the grand conversations that occurred when teachers encouraged dialogue rather than merely question-answer-evaluation patterns, students did not ignore comprehension-oriented responses. Students indicated through retellings that they understood the story, and could draw and support inferences from their reading. Finally, they related the texts to their own lives, and critiqued aspects of the books they had read. The researchers concluded that "it is not necessary to carry on even a gentle inquisition if the goal is to have children practice what has traditionally been called reading comprehension skills" (p. 14). Further, such traditional emphases occur within contexts in which the students and their teacher in training had built a sense of community where students offered interpretations that the teacher and peers recognized as valued, yet ones that the teacher may not have thought about prior to the students' contribution. Further, students across ability levels were active participants, using the group as a means of support as well as contributing unique and interesting ideas. McGee (1992), in extending the work of Eeds and Wells to first-grade students, found that these young students were capable of interpretative and personal responses to text that were much more sophisticated than generally presumed within a model that emphasizes literal comprehension.

McMahon and Raphael (McMahon, 1994; McMahon et al., in press) have created a classroom context that is centered on student-led discussions of novels and informational books—in other words, a book club. Over a 3-year period, these researchers examined the influence of participation in the book club on students' comprehension, interpretation, and personal response, their evolving abilities to engage in written response to different types of texts, and the abilities of special-needs students to participate in meaningful student-led discussions about text (see McMahon et al., 1995, for a summary of this work; see also Raphael et al., 1992). One part of this project examined students' understanding, interpretation, and synthesis of historical fiction set in Japan and Europe during World War II. Like the students in Eeds and Wells' (1989) project, students discussed texts in a range of ways: making connections from the text to their own lives, clarifying points of confusion in the texts, drawing inferences to fill in gaps left by the text, and critiquing the quality of the texts read (McMahon, 1994; McMahon, Pardo, & Raphael, 1991). With the genre of folktales (Raphael et al., 1992), students' responses were also diverse. These results suggest that, when students are given more control over the way in which text discussions evolve and receive guidance from their teachers on ways to respond to literature and to peers, they engage in a range of text responses that include, but are not limited to, text comprehension.

A similar aim of creating alternative contexts for responding to text but in a secondary literature context rather than the elementary classrooms of a book club motivated Rogers's (1991) collaboration with a high school English teacher. After observations revealed a context typical of many high school classrooms, where talk about text is lackluster or lacking altogether, Rogers created an environment similar to those described above: Students first engaged in individual personal interpretation of text, shared these interpretations with peers for response and critique, and constructed a final interpretive essay. Like other work within a social-constructivist tradition, the context emphasized the social construction of meaning and the instructional environment created opportunities for the negotiation of interpretation among peers. Such opportunities lead students to make more intertextual connections, though Rogers's case study profiles show that the degree of intertextual connections varied markedly across students.

What emerges from the line of studies described is a complex process of meaning negotiation around texts read and heard, one that is enhanced when students have greater opportunity to engage in meaningful dialogue about the books they have read. However, most studies within this vein have not directly examined the influence of types of texts read. One exception is Leal's (1992) examination of the role of text type in students' interactions. Leal worked with one group each of six first, third, and fifth graders as they listened to and discussed three different texts: an illustrated storybook, an illustrated informational book, and an informational storybook. Group interactions were examined for topics, how talk was influenced by age and text type, and the range of sources of prior knowledge invoked by the students across grades and text. Leal's findings suggest that all three types of text evoked rich discussions for students across the grades, but that older students tended to draw on a wider range of prior knowledge sources (e.g., peers, own prior knowledge, and combinations of the two), and this was enhanced when discussing the informational texts more than with the storybook.

Social constructivism has begun to influence the nature of research on text, shifting our focus away from how text features shape the ease or difficulty of text comprehension to how the social context in which the text exists influences the way in which meaning and interpretations are negotiated. Such negotiations do not come without cost, however, as students and teachers must learn new ways of interacting to support their text construction and interpretation.

Uncovering the Constraints on Students' Text Production. Research on writing within a social-constructivist perspective has focused on the context in which students engage in the writing process (see Dyson & Freedman, 1991; Nystrand, 1989). These discussions have centered on the critical contribution of students' participation as members of a writing community as a way of understanding author/reader relationships, taking perspectives outside oneself, and so forth.

Researchers who have studied the initiation of these events in classrooms and students' negotiation of their own voices as writers and readers describe a complex system of interactions for teachers and students (Applebee, 1981; Florio & Clark, 1982). In McCarthey's (1994) examination of the interactions between two sixth-grade students and their teacher in a process writing classroom patterned after Calkins's (1991), the case study students experienced the context for constructing text in different ways—one quite positive and one quite difficult–raising questions about the emphasis on writing personal experience accounts and about students' perceptions about the place of personal journals and notebooks in the process writing classroom. One of McCarthey's case studies, Anthony, was a 9-year-old Latino student who had lived in Manhattan his whole life. He read and wrote a great deal, kept scientific journals of his own discoveries, and had participated in process writing classrooms prior to entering this sixth-grade classroom. He was enthusiastic about his writing topic—a tribute to his grandmother who had recently died. His teacher encouraged his writing on this topic, supporting him within the writing conference and helping him with organization and description. His final piece, a moving account of his grandmother, was valued as an important writing contribution to the classroom. He is a success story in creating text within a process writing classroom emphasizing personal experience stories.

Anita, in contrast, had a less positive experience. At the time of the study, Anita, an 11-year-old African American who commuted to the school by train from the Bronx. She had had limited experience with process writing until this class, rarely contributed to whole class discussions, and chose not to share her writing in the whole class setting. Her notebook contained many incidents from her life, including good times at the swimming pool and with her grandfather, poignant descriptions of a bullying brother, and some reference to negative feelings about and abusiveness from her father. She had created a narrative about her time spent at Lenox Hill Camp when she met with her teacher for her writing conference. Within the conference, the teacher conveyed a very different message to her than she had to Anthony. Her teacher felt her story "did not 'get to the bottom' of something" (McCarthey, 1994, p. 187), nor did it share any of her emotions that arose from her camp experiences. The teacher's valuing of text as a way to convey and explore emotions was reflected throughout the conference. She encouraged Anita to write about something else, specifically to write about her father, despite Anita's obvious resistance to the idea. Her message to Anita was that the Lenox Hill narrative was not worthy of development, creating a dilemma for Anita: the need to please her teacher while wanting to avoid writing about this particular topic. As a compromise, Anita eventually wrote a poem about her grandfather.

McCarthey's study brings to the surface underlying tensions within these new settings. As Denyer (1993) suggests, the power relationships associated with schools do not go away instantaneously with the advent of collaborative structures, and Anita's experiences underscore such tensions. The teacher is continually faced with the tensions between the instructional goals (producing a public text to share with peers from a personal notebook) and the agency of students who may, within these alternative contexts, choose a path that does not meet the teachers' implicit agenda. How to balance between such competing goals is an issue in both writing and reading. As students have more control over their topics for writing and for text discussion, teachers face a loss of control over their instructional curriculum and plans.

Lensmire's (1994) ethnography of a third-grade writing classroom suggests another source of tension within the more collaborative environments of the process writing classrooms. In tracing the difficulty of bringing students into the world of peer collaboration, Lensmire found that students unknowingly hurt one another when they based their personal experience stories on classroom events, making up names for the individuals involved but only thinly veiling their actual identities. Thus, through the writing workshop, otherwise silenced conflicts related to gender, socioeconomic status, ethnicity, and race were made visible within the classroom. This research can be interpreted as underscoring the tensions that potentially arise when the personal experiences that are highly valued as the seed of the texts students create lead to negative consequences. Yet, despite the challenges such a situation presents, it also creates opportunities for the teacher of literacy, opportunities that remain invisible in classrooms in which silenced conflicts remain silent.

Identifying Alternative Roles for Teachers in Enhancing Students' Interactions with Text. The research within a social-constructivist tradition on creating alternative contexts for text comprehension, interpretation, and construction shares a long-standing goal of educational psychologists' research on text over time, from the behaviorists' attempts to design instructional curriculum through the cognitive scientists' attempt to restructure text so that it is more readable to the attempts to develop more collaborative contexts in which students' voices are highly valued. The implications from a social-constructivist perspective, however, shift from trying to change the curriculum materials and texts themselves to rethinking the teachers' role in literacy contexts in which authenticity of text dominates. Students read "real" materials, including trade books, informational texts, media, and so forth. They create "real" texts in the sense that the topics about which they write are personally meaningful. Such a model suggests that teachers need to be more flexible and perhaps more knowledgeable about the range of texts and features of texts that contribute to understanding.

For example, Denyer's (1993, p. 74) study of the teacher-student writing conference on the student's poem about the cat revealed how constrained the teacher was by her lack of knowledge of the genre of poetry. As a result of participating in the study, the student teacher elected to take a course about poetry. Following the course, she returned to watch the videotape of her conference with the student about her poem and articulated different ways she would currently approach the same situation. Her knowledge of poetry provided her with a broader entrée to define the teachable moment and to embed instruction in a more meaningful way for the student.

A social-constructivist perspective on text leads to the realization that teachers need a broad understanding of text, genre, and features, as well as how these understandings relate to instructional approaches for helping students understand how text works. To do so within the teachable moments of the process writing classrooms or the discussion-centered literature-based reading programs requires more of teachers and more flexibility in the texts and curricular support provided. Such a view extends our knowledge of the complexity of text

beyond that of genre and structure to the ways in which text operates in the broader context of the classroom, school, and students' lives beyond school.

***Current School Texts and Themes from Educational Psychology.*** Text is one area where the extensions of cognitive scientists to school practice have had an influence. Critiques of the passages in school texts, including the role of readability formulas in creating or manipulating these texts, were communicated to practitioners through documents such as *Becoming a Nation of Readers* (Anderson, Hiebert, Scott, & Wilkinson, 1985) and *Learning to Read in American Schools* (Anderson, Osborn, & Tierney, 1984). The conclusion of these documents—that reliance on readability formulas may actually make text more difficult for readers—hit a responsive chord with teachers. This work led to calls for a halt in the use of readability formulas; the calls came in state documents that influence textbook publishers, such as California's *Framework for English/Language Arts* (California English/Language Arts Committee, 1987). The translation of research into practice went a step further than simply using guidelines for text comprehensibility (e.g., Beck et al., 1984). The California textbook guidelines and a similar set that was subsequently issued by Texas (Texas Education Agency, 1990), another influential textbook adoption state, mandated authentic (i.e., not adapted) text in the textbooks that would be listed on their state-endorsed textbook lists. An analysis of the textbook series that were adopted in California in 1988 and in Texas in 1993 confirms that the contrived genre of primerese is gone (Hoffman et al., 1994). Textbooks now consist of either entire pieces of literature or chapters from trade books. However, our perusal of studies on text comprehension in the most prominent journals that publish studies on literacy from a psychological perspective (Walberg & Haertel, 1992) uncovered another critical pattern. Although textbook publishers have heeded the call for selections from trade books, cognitive scientists continue to use contrived texts in their studies. As a result of the work of cognitive scientists during the 1970s and 1980s, school practice has changed. To continue to have an influence on practice, researchers must use authentic, meaningful texts in their inquiries. As long as such text forms the basis for reading instruction, there is still much to learn. In the move to emphasizing high-quality materials, insights into and understanding of what makes such text comprehensible may be gained.

## Extensions of Perspectives on Literacy Learning to Literacy Teaching

It is more difficult to describe extensions of learning perspectives to literacy instruction than to describe literacy learning and its extension to text and tests, since the manifestations of literacy teaching occur in thousands of classrooms daily, year after year. Educational psychologists have made innumerable recommendations for school practices over the past century. The research relevant to this section pertains to instructional studies in which educational psychologists have been concerned not merely to study learning in a controlled laboratory setting but to study the influence of teaching on learning, which typically occurs in school contexts. For information on literacy learning beyond the scope of the present review, interested readers should examine relevant chapters from both editions of the *Handbook of Reading Research* (Barr et al., 1991; P. D. Pearson, Barr, Kamil, & Mosenthal, 1984), as well as existing reviews of reading (e.g., Calfee & Drum, 1986) and writing instruction (e.g., Dyson & Freedman, 1991; Scardamalia & Bereiter, 1986). In this chapter, we focus on describing the stances of educational psychologists and related researchers over the past 75 years, the nature of research conducted within these stances, and the influence of these stances on the instruction and learning of students. The three perspectives—behaviorism, cognitive science, and social constructivism—are distinct from one another in instructional content, instructional methodology, and research methodology.

*Identifying Universal Teaching Methods.* Like many educational psychologists from a range of perspectives, behaviorists were interested in identifying general principles underlying good instruction. These general principles, it was hoped, could then be applied to provide efficacious instruction for all children (Thorndike, 1903, 1906). The belief in a set of universals meant that literacy educators began looking for the "best" approach that exemplified these principles in practice. This approach saw a second life in the 1980s with the use of meta-analytic techniques (see, e.g., Slavin, 1987; Stahl & Miller, 1989). Once identified, this best method could be communicated to all teachers so that they could provide the proper instruction. Thus, educational psychologists conducted research that sought to establish optimal instructional conditions, focusing at the local level of individual lesson plans as well as the more global level of attempting to determine the best instructional method.

The local focus on the individual lesson plan closely parallels the value placed by educational psychologists on standardized instructional procedures. Scripted lessons, often in the form of standard protocols, exist in the directions for administering standardized tests and in the guidelines for teachers in manuals that accompany curriculum materials. These standard protocols, which came into vogue in the 1930s, still exist today in commercially developed curriculum materials used to teach reading. Within the manuals are page reproductions of the students' text, along with the words that the teacher can use to frame the lesson, ask questions, and generally guide students. Within the script are listed answers that the teacher can expect from the students. Since the universe of student response was felt to be identifiable, it made sense to make clear to the teacher both what those responses should be and how they could be elicited from the students.

The long-standing influence of scripted lessons can be seen in the following example that comes from a teacher's manual for a 1993 textbook:

*Expanding the Literature* Where does this story take place? (It takes place in a city by the sea). When does the story take place? How do you know? (You can tell that the story takes place sometime in the past by looking carefully at the clothes people are wearing.) (Farr et al., 1993, p. T22)

It may surprise the reader to learn that these questions refer to a well-known children's book, *Miss Rumphius* (Cooney, 1982), but the scripting of directions (down to the appropriate student

responses) and the sense that there is a single path for both teacher and student remain, even in the "new literature-based" textbook programs.

More precise views of behaviorism that held sway in the 1950s and 1960s went a step further. The extension of Skinner's (1954) programmed learning to criterion-referenced systems (e.g., Glaser, 1966; Otto, 1977) aimed to create "teacher-proof" programs. Teachers might serve a pacing function (i.e., using the test data to determine if students had "mastered" one objective and were ready to go on to the next); however, even that role could be circumvented by using teachers' aides or computers. Even with the participation of leading educational psychologists in the criterion-referenced systems of the 1960s, research on learning and instruction within these highly prescriptive programs was rare. Presumably, educational psychologists believed that their understanding of learning principles translated into teaching principles, thus making the empirical examination of what children learned and how their learning progressed in these programs a less than pressing question. As will be seen shortly, researchers at the same time were attempting to identify "ideal" instruction—whether an instructional method, age to begin reading instruction, or mode of reading, silent or oral. Creators of textbook programs have claimed to integrate these findings into their teachers' guides, but with varying degrees of success (Beck & McCaslin, 1978). There has been, and continues to be, a substantial amount of pedagogical design based on findings from educational psychology that is presented to teachers as an ideal or optimal form of literacy instruction, the implementation of which is rarely investigated.

If the assumption during the behaviorist era was that students needed to learn the foundations of reading and writing, it is not surprising that little research was conducted on comprehension and composition processes. The key question of the time focused on the optimal methods for teaching students to read, especially at the beginning levels. Approaches were pitted against each other—natural language (e.g., whole language/language experience) versus basic skills (e.g., phonics)—to determine the universally best approach. Virtually no attention was paid to the ways in which teachers implemented each approach, the characteristics of the students involved, the values and beliefs of teachers and students, and so forth. Rather, teaching was believed to fall within the category of a "treatment" that could be "controlled" through experimental design.

The research prompted by the search for best methods took a range of forms. For example, in a small-scale study within a single school district, Morphett and Washburne (1931) attempted to identify the best age at which to begin instruction. Despite their small sample, the skewed nature of their population (upper middle-class, Caucasian suburban students), and the short time frame of the study (one semester), their finding of the optimal mental age for initial reading instruction as 6 years, 6 months was quickly translated into the "best age to begin reading instruction is 6 years." The ongoing popularity of this view can be seen as policymakers and others in positions of determining directions of education continue to draw on and create studies within this tradition.

Efforts aimed at finding the best age to begin reading instruction illustrated one interest in early studies from a behaviorist perspective. Even more attention was paid by early educational psychologists to instructional methods, whether language based or skills instruction. Although debates over the best methods for the initial stages of literacy learning continue (Chall, 1989; Edelsky, 1990), the search for the best method of teaching children to read reached its pinnacle in the early 1960s with the U.S. Office of Education's First-Grade Studies and the publication of Chall's *Learning to Read: The Great Debate*. Reflective of that era's concern for establishing a definitive role for phonics, the U.S. Department of Education funded an ambitious research program, the Cooperative First-Grade Project. This project consisted of 27 studies that employed the same design and analyses, each of which contrasted first-grade children's learning in an innovative program (basal plus phonics, linguistic, Initial Teaching Alphabet [ITA], language experience, phonics-linguistic) relative to a traditional textbook program. Bond and Dykstra's (1967) synthesis of the findings of these studies was that programs that stressed systematic instruction of sound–symbol relationships tended to produce higher achievement, approximately 1 to 2 months' grade-equivalence difference, than basal programs. Dykstra's (1968) analysis of the second-year extensions of these programs found that ITA, phonic-linguistic, and linguistic approaches were associated with higher achievement on word recognition and spelling than the basal or basal-plus-phonics programs. Subsequent analyses and reanalyses of the data produced differing interpretations, with Lohnes and Gray (1972) concluding that the variance in achievement could be accounted for by general intelligence, and Guthrie and Tyler (1978) concluding that application of a different covariance model showed that the structural linguistics and supplementary phonics-plus-basal method produced higher achievement than the basal program and that sound–symbol approaches produced higher achievement than the language experience method.

The various analyses and reviews of the U.S. Office of Education's studies characterize the interpretations and reinterpretations that often occur with attempts to establish the "right method." The search for universals assumed that the practices of a particular method occurred similarly across classrooms. The obscuring within these comparisons of crucial aspects of instruction and of learner processes created a fundamental problem for interpretation. If teachers were implementing the phonics method or the language experience method, a particular set of procedures was assumed to be in place in all classrooms using that method. Since learner processes and teacher processes were viewed to be prescribed by the instructional method, only the outcomes of the methods were studied. By not considering the nature of learner processes as a function of instructional elements, these studies invariably resulted in ambiguous findings that continue to be rehashed. Interestingly, just prior to publishing the seminal review of phonics instruction, in 1967, Chall (Chall & S. Feldman, 1966) published a contribution to the Cooperative First-Grade Project which concluded that as much variation existed within a particular approach as across approaches. Although Chall (1967/1982) discussed the processes of proficient reading that phonics instruction facilitates, critics interpreted Chall's work as a call for a single best method.

As Chall's efforts indicate, there were researchers who persistently attempted to direct attention to issues of literacy processes and their relation to instruction despite the domination of be-

haviorism. Further examples of efforts that attempted to direct attention to children's strategies and away from a single best method can be found in Barr's (1984) review of instructional research in literacy. Barr's (1974–1975) own work described student strategies as a function of the kind of reading instruction they received, while MacKinnon (1959) also observed the nature of student responses as they learned to read. But, as Barr (1984) concluded in her review, the prominent stance toward beginning reading instruction prior to the efforts of cognitive scientists and even extending beyond it was the "quest to establish the best method" (p. 574).

*Strategy Instruction for Enhancing Comprehension and Composition.* After a decades-long search for the best method for reading and writing instruction, the advent of cognitive science brought with it a shift in focus from finding best methods to a concern for underlying processes. Although behaviorism limited itself to outcomes, and thus a focus on the outward benefits of participation in a particular instructional approach, cognitive scientists explored ways of making invisible processes visible. Initial research tended to identify specific strategies that appeared to be part of the repertoire of skilled readers and writers (e.g., summarization, prediction). Then, differences in the way more and less successful readers and writers used the strategies were documented. Next, instructional strategies were developed to enhance learners' reading and writing abilities, tested under controlled conditions by the researcher, and, often, then tested in classrooms with the cooperation and teaching of the classroom teacher. Research by educational psychologists and others within a cognitive science perspective shared a number of features that are described below: (a) instructional vision of guiding the practice of the naive learner, (b) a model of learning relying on expert/novice distinctions, (c) continued scripting of lessons, though with a focus different from that of the behaviorist tradition, and (d) an emphasis on teaching students strategies rather than skills (see Duffy, 1993, for a discussion of the difference between the two). A popular metaphor for teaching and learning within the strategy instruction movement was that of cognitive apprenticeship (Brown, Collins, & Duguid, 1989). Other terms to characterize the nature of the teacher–student relationship were "direct explanation" (Duffy et al., 1987), "explicit instruction" (Dole, Duffy, Roehler, & Pearson, 1991), "guided participation" (Pearson & Gallagher, 1983), and "procedural facilitation" (Bereiter & Scardamalia, 1987). These visions of instruction shared an emphasis on thinking aloud, modeling, and some form of explicit instruction.

The content of this modeling and thinking aloud, whether in an instructional experiment or program, was derived from the studies of experts. Once the strategies of experts had been established, this information was used to design instruction for novice and poor readers and writers. In these instructional experiments and programs, researchers typically served as experts who transmitted what they knew to teachers, who in turn served as experts to their students, transmitting what they knew to them. Thus, while cognitive science did foreshadow the social or interactive nature of learning, its purpose was not to jointly construct new understandings but to help enlist the learner into more expert ways of processing or creating text.

Most of the strategy research within the cognitive science

tradition was conducted within the constraints of traditional quantitative research methods, dictating experimental and control groups, meeting the assumptions of analysis of variance, and with great attention to the veracity of the strategies to be taught. Thus, for reasons of experimental purity, scripts were often created to guide or direct the teachers' interactions with their students. The scripts served a second function as well. Within the perspective of expert/novices, there was an assumption of expertise residing in the researchers who developed the strategy being tested. Thus, the script, produced with care by the researchers, was also seen as a way of ensuring an equating of teachers within and across treatment groups. Teachers were expected to follow the script developed by the expert and remain true to the experimental condition, ensuring that they had the necessary knowledge to conduct the lesson effectively.

A growing research literature that described the strategies of experts (and often a deficiency of these strategies by novices or poor readers) and the findings of an observational study that showed that typical comprehension instruction in American classrooms in the mid-1970s gave students few occasions for exposure to comprehension strategies (Durkin, 1978–1979) led to numerous studies on comprehension instruction. Similar criticisms of writing instruction (see Hairston, 1982; Shaughnessy, 1977) provided bases for studies identifying effective instruction about the writing process. The comprehension instruction studies began with attention to single strategy identification, instructional approach development, and implementation by researchers, then teachers, with students of different age and ability levels (e.g., Beck, McKeown, & McCaslin, 1983; Brown & Day, 1983; Pearson et al., 1979; Taylor & Beach, 1984). These studies of single strategies were followed by those exploring multiple strategy use (e.g., Beck, McKeown, & Gromoll, 1989; Langer, 1985; Palincsar & Brown, 1984; Paris & Oka, 1986; Schuder, 1993). Studies of instruction in the writing process similarly attempted to identify "strategy-teaching approaches . . . ranging from those that work at the algorithmic level to those that work at the very general levels of description" (Scardamalia & Bereiter, 1985, p. 565). All of these studies shared a focus on the nature of the strategies first and, secondarily, on the role of teachers in transmitting knowledge about the strategies to their students. Research by Pressley and his colleagues is presented to illustrate recent efforts in the area of reading comprehension instruction within this tradition (Pressley & El-Dinary, 1993), while Scardamalia and Bereiter's (1986) research on procedural facilitation in writing illustrates attempts to enhance students' strategic knowledge about writing. We begin, however, with a line of research focused primarily on the teacher's role within the area of comprehension instruction, research illustrated below by the work of Duffy, Roehler, and their colleagues, and guiding the work of those such as Pressley and his colleagues interested in strategy instruction.

Teachers' Talk in Building Strategic Readers. Drawing on the literature on metacognition, G. G. Duffy and Roehler and colleagues on the Teacher Explanation Project (G. G. Duffy et al., 1987; G. G. Duffy et al., 1986) emphasized the importance of teachers' explanations to students of what a strategy or skill is, how it works, and when and why it would be used, paralleling the concepts of declarative, procedural, and conditional

knowledge. These studies examined how the types of explanations that teachers provide influence students' learning and use of strategies. For example, G. G. Duffy et al. (1986) used a research design typical of the cognitive science tradition, assigning fifth-grade teachers and low-performing students to treatment or control groups based on stratified random procedures (management indices for teachers, standardized test scores for students). Teachers in the intervention group participated in in-service activities that were designed to increase their talk about the strategic nature of skills. Control group teachers participated in an in-service activity focusing strictly on classroom management but which supported their perception that they were part of an experimental group as well. Lessons were observed and a sample of students was interviewed following each observed lesson. The intervention led to enhanced explicit explanations about strategy use and related increases in students' awareness of what was learned during lessons, when they might use the strategies, and how they would apply them. However, the findings on standardized test performances showed no significant differences between students in treatment or control groups. As Duffy et al. noted, several explanations are possible for the lack of difference such as the inappropriateness of standardized measures for capturing strategic reading. But additional explanations surfaced as a result of follow-up interviews and observations of teachers that showed that teachers did not consistently employ the explicit instruction techniques and that teachers' lessons varied considerably in their levels of explicit instruction.

This research on the role of teachers' talk in the development of strategic readers was extended in a qualitative study of 11 teachers as they taught reading to their at-risk students (G. G. Duffy, 1993). Through extensive interviews with the teachers and twice monthly observations as well as interviews with the teachers' five lowest scoring students, Duffy identified nine stages in teachers' implementations of strategy instruction. The first four stages began with confusion and rejection, for example, moving back to the teachers' manuals of their reading program. Then come attempts at teaching the strategies but not giving students explicit information. Later on there is the inclusion of details, strategy names, and procedures. Finally, there is the initiation of strategy modeling with specific student texts. At the fifth phase, which was described as "hitting a wall," teachers realized that despite their good feelings about moving toward modeling and explicit instruction, it was not enough to help their lowest achieving readers. As they moved toward the sixth phase, they made it "over the hump" with the realization that the point of strategy instruction was to assist learners in understanding that reading was supposed to make sense and realize there were ways to facilitate this. The final three phases involved growing sophistication in conveying strategy information to the students, moving toward emphasizing creating meaning for authentic purposes, and releasing control of the process over to students.

These findings have led Duffy (1993) to suggest that prior projects (e.g., Duffy et al., 1986) may have stopped too soon and that more complex models of teacher education are needed. According to Duffy (1993), "the real challenge of strategy instruction research is getting teachers themselves to be exemplars of 'higher-level thinking' who deal strategically with the complexities and dilemmas of effective strategy instruction"

(p. 119). In short, the teachers remain at the center of the learning process, orchestrating the learner's development of strategy knowledge. In this role, it is critical for them to develop more sophisticated levels of expertise to be able to impart that knowledge appropriately to their students. Like Pressley and his colleagues, Duffy underscores the value of strategic behavior on the part of the student and the importance of the teacher in guiding the students' development (see also Calfee, 1992, in describing the Inquiring School project).

Teaching Strategic Reading and Writing to Elementary Students.    Enhancing strategy use in reading and writing has been the focus of research within a cognitive science tradition, as illustrated by two lines of work: "transactional strategy instruction," conducted by Pressley and his colleagues (e.g., Pressley, Schuder, SAIL Faculty and Administration, Bergman, & El-Dinary, 1992; Schuder, 1993) and strategy instruction in writing, designed to enhance learners' self-regulatory abilities (e.g., Scardamalia & Bereiter, 1985, 1986).

Current research within the tradition of strategy instruction has been conducted by Pressley and his colleagues, who characterize their work as "transactional strategy instruction" (e.g., Pressley et al., 1992). Like many cognitive scientists, Pressley and his colleagues (e.g., Pressley, Goodchild, Fleet, Zajchowski, & Evans, 1989) use the computer metaphor to develop a rationale for strategy use. The mind is like a computer with short-term and long-term storage areas and various storage and retrieval mechanisms for the knowledge that has been acquired. Strategies are what control knowledge storage and retrieval, and strategy use is influenced by the components themselves, learners' styles, their metacognitive knowledge about strategies, task awareness, motivational beliefs, and so forth. Designers of teachers' manuals are expected to include such teacher guides as: "(a) directions as to how and when to teach particular strategies as part of materials covered in texts, (b) prompts to encourage all of the elements of good strategy use, and (c) explanations as to how particular types of instruction facilitate competent performance" (p. 310). Such suggestions are consistent with the transmission model of learning that undergirds cognitive science. Implicit within the suggestions is the assumption that teachers will receive the information conveyed by the experts who developed the manuals and will in turn transmit this knowledge to their students.

Transactional strategy instruction extends Pressley's earlier writings to explore strategy instruction in school settings where "meaning develops through teacher-student-text transactions involving cognitive strategies" (El-Dinary & Schuder, 1993, p. 207). El-Dinary and Schuder explored teachers' responses to such an approach through interviews and classroom observations of seven different elementary teachers using a school-generated strategy program called Students Achieving Independent Learning (SAIL). Borrowing from the tradition illustrated by the discussion above of Duffy and Roehler's research, SAIL teachers used direct explanation about strategies such as predicting, summarizing, visualizing, and thinking aloud. Similar to G. G. Duffy's (1993) project, the teachers in this program sought to apply strategy instruction to the reading of authentic text.

Training of teachers occurred over four half-day sessions in which they were introduced to samples of materials to use with their students, but no specific scripts to follow. The authors noted that some of the training was less than ideal in that the style of presentation was didactic (i.e., transmission) rather than growing out of the teachers' knowledge base, and teachers' commitment may have been minimal because attendance was required of them by their principals, rather than something in which they had expressed an interest. Not surprisingly, only two of seven target teachers seemed to endorse the SAIL curriculum and adopt it as their own. The researchers concluded that more intensive training was needed, as well as support within their school environment, more voice in identifying methods of teaching to fit their own styles, more explanation and modeling of effective teaching, and more coaching and in-class problem solving. In short, the training model suggested is parallel to the strategy instruction model suggested with students: teacher/trainer control in the beginning, with gradual release of responsibility to the learner over time.

Scardamalia and Bereiter (1985) were concerned with enhancing students' self-regulatory mechanisms, each mechanism "representing an information-processing skill or executive function amenable to improvement in its own right, a function that involves its own goal setting knowledge retrieval, processing, and storage operations" (p. 565). They argue that introducing students to self-regulatory functions is critical because they serve as "change-inducing agents that will have the effect of altering the rules by which the system operates" (p. 566). Their point is that if teachers provide students with knowledge about and means for using these functions, the students will be in a better position to continue their development as writers, since use of each mechanism raises their level of performance and opens the door for their achievement of more complex goals. However, they note that introducing students to new self-regulatory mechanisms creates two potential problems. First, using the metaphor of a computer, they note that attention must be directed back and forth from the overall writing activity to the use of the new mechanism, creating the need for increased amounts of attention and perhaps leading to the learner simply forgetting to use a newly acquired strategy. Second, new mechanisms simply require more processing capacity and take away processing capacity from other parts of the process, leading to writers who forget what they are doing, lose sight of their goals, and so forth.

To address these two potential problems, Scardamalia and Bereiter offer a technique they identify as "procedural facilitation." This technique serves to provide cues or routines related to new self-regulatory skills and to reduce the resource demands that one would expect if using the newly learned skill. Procedural facilitation involves four steps: (a) identifying the function that expert performances seem to use but that is lacking in the performance of novices, (b) describe the function as explicitly as possible (e.g., revision reduced to comparing, diagnosing, choosing a revision tactic, and generating alternatives), (c) design a cue system for reminding learners of the subprocesses and how they might be addressed, and (d) designing external supports or aids (e.g., cue cards with revision strategies).

Like much of the research in this area, greater attention has been paid to the identification of strategies and the development of the support (i.e., procedural facilitation), with less attention to how teachers might initiate such instruction within the constraints of today's classrooms or within the overall curricular goals of their programs. Given the complexity of strategy instruction suggested by G. G. Duffy (1993) and others, many questions have yet to be addressed regarding widespread adoption of such instruction within school settings.

Facilitating the Processes of Beginning Literacy. Similar to processes of comprehending and composing, the interest of cognitive scientists was also drawn to beginning literacy processes. Unlike the research on comprehending and composing, many of the studies on beginning literacy processes were conducted in laboratory settings. By laboratory settings, we mean settings where an experimenter asks a student to complete a task in a context which, while it may occur in the school library, nurse's office, or even a back corner of the classroom, has been created solely for the purposes of the experiment and where interaction between adult and child is one-to-one. Any teaching that takes place in the experiment is in the form of "training" where the student is involved in the task repeatedly until a criterion level or specified number of trials is reached.

We chose to focus this review on studies that have been conducted in the contexts of typical primary-level classrooms where a single adult (the teacher) is juggling the learning experiences for the 24 students who make up the average U.S. first-grade classroom (National Education Association, 1992). We made this choice deliberately because we believe that recent reviews by Adams (1990), Juel (1991), Ehri (1991), and Stanovich (1991) summarize well and comprehensively the laboratory research of cognitive scientists over the past two decades. We focused on studies in which, as in laboratory studies, children's learning is at the forefront but where the instruction that supports this learning is also part of the design or analysis of the research.

Within the parameters for instruction on beginning literacy processes, we identified three groups of studies: (a) instructional experiments, (b) investigations of intact instruction, and (c) interventionist school programs. We provide a sampling of each type of study to convey the tenor of the work.

Unlike the instructional studies used with older, less proficient readers and writers, which have aimed to make students aware of the "how, why, and when" of strategies (e.g., Englert et al., 1991; Paris et al., 1983), the instructional studies with young readers and writers have concentrated on developing the processes associated with expert reading. Most studies aimed to develop phonemic awareness or automaticity in either young children in the initial stages of reading instruction or in students who had not become successful readers after several years of school. Throughout the 1970s and 1980s, a considerable body of research was amassed indicating that the presence of phonemic awareness in the early grades distinguished students who would become expert readers from those who would not (see Juel, 1991, for a review of this literature). These studies were primarily descriptive in nature and, as already described, derived from laboratory contexts. In recent years, these findings have become the basis for classroom experiments. One such study was conducted by Ball and Blachman (1991) with kindergartners. Members of the research team went into kindergarten classrooms on a daily basis for a 7-week period, with children receiving one of three conditions: (a) phoneme segmentation, letter naming, and letter–sounding matching, (b) letter naming and letter–sound matching only, or (c) no intervention. The group

receiving the phoneme awareness training performed best on reading and spelling tasks after the 7-week intervention, with students in the letter naming plus letter–sound matching group showing no appreciable gains over children who received no focused instruction. Over a similar period of time, Uhry and Shepherd (1993) found that first graders in whole language classrooms who received supplemental instruction twice weekly in segmenting and spelling phonetically regular words did better on most tasks (but not comprehension) than children who spent a similar amount of time learning to read words and text.

Research teams such as those of Ball and Blachman (1991) and Uhry and Shepherd (1993) instructed small groups of students in classrooms, but the design of the instruction or the fidelity of instruction to particular guidelines was not a priority in their analysis. A study that draws more directly on the "strategic guidance" studies (Paris et al., 1983) that have been prominent with older students was conducted by Cunningham (1990). She applied a strategic guidance model in teaching phonemic awareness to kindergartners and first graders. A metacognitive instructional format was compared with a skill-and-drill format and a control format. In the metacognitive training format, the researcher talked with children about the application, value, and utility of phonemic awareness for reading, as well as about procedural knowledge about segmenting and blending phonemes. For example, children might be told to think about a story about a baseball game they were reading and to decide if a word that they were learning to segment and blend (/b/ a/t/) might be found in the story. Or they would be told that, when they came to words that they didn't know, a good strategy would be to "cut the word up" into its smallest pieces, thinking about what that word sounds like, and then thinking of any words they knew that resembled that set of sounds. The skill-and-drill group received only the procedural information and practice in segmenting and blending phonemes, while students in the control situation listened to and discussed stories. Both experimental groups performed at a higher level on a standardized reading measure than did the control group. First-grade children in the metacognitive group did better than those in the skill-and-drill group on a transfer reading task. This pattern did not extend to kindergarten, where children were not "learning to read," leading Cunningham to conclude that the benefits of metacognitive training depend on children's active involvement in learning to read.

Whether the strategy or skill is recognizing common rimes—vowels and subsequent consonants) within a syllable—across words or increasing phonemic abilities, the reason for teaching young children strategies and skills is to set the stage for automatic reading. In another group of instructional studies, automaticity has been attended to directly through instruction that focuses on repeated reading of text. The technique of reading along with others has had a long history in reading pedagogy, with forms of choral or echoic reading dating back to colonial times (Allington, 1984). Samuels's (LaBerge & Samuels, 1974) interest in automaticity led to a reexamination of repeated readings of text. In a dissertation that extended Samuels's work on automaticity, Dahl (1979) had second graders begin a session by reading a text with an adult (a member of a research team). Reading with the adult was followed by repeated reading of the passage by the student independently, with the student noting each iteration of the passage on a chart. The session ended with the student reading the passage to the adult. Students continued this cycle with a passage until they reached a criterion of 100 words per minute. Although this study is frequently cited to substantiate the value of repeated reading, it should be noted that a second treatment labeled "hypothesis/ test" produced results as positive as the repeated reading condition. In this second experimental condition (which, in a later era, would be termed metacognitive), students were required to provide responses to questions about words, including predicting words as part of cloze exercises.

Subsequent instructional experiments designed to increase readers' automaticity have proved successful with younger (Dowhower, 1987; Reutzel, Hollingsworth, & Eldredge, 1994) and older readers (Herman, 1985). Dowhower's project compared Dahl's (1979) independent practice model with a read-along procedure, finding that second graders with good decoding ability but below-average reading rate benefited from either procedure. However, prosodic reading, as Dowhower called reading in meaningful phrases, was facilitated most by the read-along procedure. An extension of the repeated reading technique that has generated interest is the repeated reading of text using a computer (Rashotte & Torgensen, 1985).

The insights gained from cognitive science also led to examinations of intact instruction in classrooms where teachers pursued their typical methods. These studies differed from those that had been conducted by behaviorists in the particular processes that were studied in students (e.g., phonemic awareness, automaticity). Often, these studies were longitudinal in nature, with researchers studying the development of particular processes as a function of instruction over an extended period of time. In the first wave of studies (A. Lesgold et al., 1985; Juel, Griffith, & P. B. Gough, 1986), researchers selected classrooms in which conventional pedagogies were in effect. There was little expectation from researchers that the findings of cognitive scientists had filtered down to teachers and informed their practices.

In a longitudinal study of this type, A. Lesgold et al. (1985) followed children's reading development in two curricula (code, with an emphasis on word analysis, and global, with an emphasis on comprehension of text), and found that automaticity (characterized not just by accuracy but by speed as well) in Grades 1 and 2 predicted reading comprehension performance in Grades 3 and 4. The trajectories in the two approaches were different (i.e., children in the code approach were slower initially to recognize words). Neither approach, the investigators concluded, provided strong support for developing automaticity. A substantial number of children from both approaches left first grade reading so slowly as to interfere with comprehension even with easy material.

The measures that Juel et al. (1986) gathered on their longitudinal sample focused on phonemic awareness acquisition more than automaticity. Without phonemic awareness, Juel et al. concluded, extensive exposure to text does not foster the types of strategies and processes that children will need to perform the literacy tasks of later grades. Reports of students' performances in subsequent years are even more sobering (Juel, 1988). In examining the students' performances at the end of Grade 4, Juel (1988) reported a correlation of .88 between their status in first grade and fourth grade. If a child did not learn

to read well in first grade, chances were high that he or she would not be reading well in fourth grade.

Clarke's (1988) examination focused on an aspect of the beginning literacy curriculum that has been suggested as an ideal context for developing phonemic awareness as part of an authentic task for young children—writing with invented spelling. She investigated children's progress in first-grade classrooms with teachers who either encouraged the use of invented spelling during writing periods or who specified conventional spelling. Clarke studied children as they wrote, their written productions, and their performances on a set of reading and spelling measures. The children in the "invented spelling" classrooms wrote more earlier in the school year and produced longer productions later during the same year (although with more spelling errors than children in the traditional spelling classrooms). Of particular interest was the finding that children in the invented spelling classrooms performed at a higher level on measures of word analysis than did children in the traditional classrooms, although not in flash word recognition. Initially, low-performing students particularly benefited in their spelling and reading performances from participating in the invented spelling classrooms.

We have labeled the third group of studies as "interventionist" school programs where teachers, rather than members of the research team, implement the instruction. In the area of early literacy, there has not been a parallel set of the school-implementation research projects in which researchers worked with teachers similar to the comprehension and/or composition projects of Englert and Raphael, Paris, Pressley, and others. Several projects that are closest in their attention to staff development and extended involvement by researchers have been conducted in Scandinavia (Lie, 1991; Lundberg, Frost, & Petersen, 1988). Lundberg and colleagues' year-long work with preschool teachers showed that when teachers consistently integrated phonemic awareness activities into their curricula, students gained appreciably in their phoneme segmentation ability, an understanding that persisted into Grade 2. In Lie's project, first-grade teachers were guided in teaching their students in one of three ways over the school year: (a) phoneme isolation, where teachers taught students to attend to individual phonemes and to identify those phonemes in initial, medial, or final position in target words, (b) phoneme segmentation, where teachers taught students to identify the phonemes in a word sequentially and to blend them, or (c) discussion, where teachers devoted a comparable amount of time to students' examination and discussion of illustrations. By the end of second grade, it mattered less which phoneme awareness instruction a student's teacher had provided in first grade, so long as the teacher had provided some phoneme awareness guidance. Further, this effect was greatest for students of lower ability.

Perhaps because of the urgency with which beginning literacy acquisition is viewed by teachers and the public in the United States, the scope of the early literacy projects in which cognitive scientists have worked with teachers in changing instruction has been much more extensive than the projects of Lie (1991) and Lundberg et al. (1988), encompassing entire schools and even school systems. A number of prominent cognitive scientists have been involved in these efforts, which include the design of the decoding program of the Benchmark School (see, e.g., I. W. Gaskins et al., 1988) and the Project

READ model, which includes a strong decoding component (Henry, 1988) and has been implemented in large urban districts such as the Los Angeles Unified and New York City schools (Calfee, 1981, 1992). These programs have involved changes along numerous dimensions, making it difficult to extract the influence of particular changes in teachers' instruction on particular dimensions of student learning (e.g., phonemic awareness or automaticity). The continued involvement and extension of such programs, however, attest to the differences that teachers and principals are seeing in their students' literacy levels (Calfee, 1992).

The instructional studies and interventionist school implementation projects are a start in describing the long-term effects of many of the practices that have been advocated for teachers as a result of the cognitive revolution. There remains a wealth of information from cognitive science that has yet to be translated into teaching or the instructional curricula. Because many teachers of beginning readers are confused by the current debates and wonder if they should "interfere" at all (McKenna, Stahl, & Reinking, 1994), researchers need to work on translating findings on beginning literacy acquisition into instructional contexts.

*Defining New Roles for Teachers and Learners.* Just as social-constructivist theory invited alternative models of testing and changes in research on text, so it has led to a rethinking of the role of teachers in reading and writing instruction. Behaviorism downplayed the role of the teacher from instructional leader to system manager. Cognitive science placed the teacher at the center of children's literacy learning as the expert whose goal was to create expertise in the novice literacy user. Within social constructivism the teacher remains an important participant in students' learning, but in the role of mediating learners' interactions. The shift in perspective to social constructivism has led to numerous projects in various contexts and with various participants, including teachers acting as researchers in their own classrooms (Burton, 1991). The proliferation of work within this research paradigm required a way of parsing the field. The four topics that follow provide a comprehensive sampling of the nature and foci of research: (a) rethinking the role of the teacher in literacy instruction, (b) changing the roles of teachers and researchers, (c) changing the relationship of literacy learning in school and the community, and (d) designing early school contexts to prevent literacy failure.

Rethinking the Roles of Teachers and Learners During Literacy Instruction.   Within a social-constructivist perspective, the teacher's role shifts from transmitting knowledge to helping learners restructure their own knowledge (A. L. Brown & Palincsar, 1990). The implications of this approach are broad, in that new relationships are possible among learners and teachers. For example, either teachers or students may serve in the capacity of a "more knowledgeable other" (Wood, Bruner, & Ross, 1976) in some contexts, while all may act as learners in others. Fundamental to understanding the nature of learning within a social-constructivist perspective is an understanding of the context in which facilitating experiences occur for restructuring learners' knowledge. As A. L. Brown and Palincsar note, "the key explanatory concept in [theories of Vygotsky, Piaget, Binet, and Dewey] is some form of internalization; that which is witnessed

in social settings becomes harnessed as individual cognition" (1990, p. 397). Yet they also note that specific learning and instruction activities aimed at restructuring aspects of learners' strategies or knowledge will be needed, because not everything that is witnessed is internalized by students.

Three related concepts help guide research that examines and explains the teacher's role in promoting internalization of ideas: proleptic teaching (B. Rogoff, 1990; R. Rogoff & Gardner, 1984), the Zone of Proximal Development (ZPD) (Vygotsky, 1978), and scaffolded instruction (Greenfield, 1984; Wertsch, 1984; Wood et al., 1976). The ZPD describes the disparity between what learners are able to accomplish with support and what they are able to accomplish when working independently. The nature of support a teacher offers within the ZPD to facilitate students' performances has been described as proleptic teaching or scaffolded instruction (B. Rogoff, 1990; Wood et al., 1976). Several researchers have examined the nature of proleptic teaching or scaffolded instruction during reading and writing instruction as a way of rethinking the teacher's role during instruction.

Au and Kawakami (1986), for example, explored Vygotsky's (1978) concept of ZPD when applied to teacher–student interactions in a second-grade classroom during a series of small teacher-led discussions of a narrative text, *Annie and the Old One* (Miles, 1971). The narrative tells the story of a young girl, Annie, who takes literally her grandmother's statement that she will return to Mother Earth when Annie's mother completes the weaving on the loom. Annie tries several schemes to prevent this, until her grandmother helps her understand the cycle of life, death, and rebirth. The researchers analyzed 84 interchanges over a 4-day study of this book to explore the nature of the teacher's work within students' ZPDs through the teacher's questions, studying the 21 percent of exchanges in which the teacher's opening question received an incorrect or incomplete response from students.

Analyses showed that this teacher's responses were quite consistent across exchanges, with questioning used to elicit more elaborated responses from students until their responses showed deeply thought-out reasoning for conclusions and were more consistent with evidence available in the text. The teacher was able to help students develop elaborated responses from their existing statements, which were often cursory. In one such exchange, the teacher took the two-word response ("the sun") of one student, Rachel, and involved her and her peers in using the text to establish the metaphorical meaning that the author was giving to the rising and setting of the sun (birth and death).

The teacher worked with the group to create the metaphorical interpretation, building on Rachel's initial response and guiding them to think in terms of the life cycle. While an opening question on the life cycle may have been beyond the ability of any individual second-grade student, working within their ZPD through questions, comments, and access to text provided a meaningful experience and an introduction to the author's craft of symbolism.

Scaffolded instruction is another feature that can be part of the ZPD or examined as a separate teacher approach consistent with social-constructivist principles. Wood et al. (1976) characterized a scaffold as something that is temporary, adjustable, and provides support. Applied to the role of the teacher, it is consistent with the idea of proleptic teaching and the ZPD as it details the way in which teachers lead students who are faced with challenges beyond their individual abilities. Greenfield (1984) detailed the actual structure of scaffolded instruction in language acquisition and weaving, identifying six features of these interactions such as "if difficulty level rises, more scaffolding is provided" and "the teacher appears to be unaware of the teaching going on." Though Greenfield suggested that such scaffolds are not within the scaffolders' awareness, such teaching functions may need to be made explicit for teachers if they are to adapt their instruction consistent with this perspective. In fact, the teacher in Au and Kawakami's work described above may not have been aware of specific scaffolding strategies, but she was providing just such support for her learners as she worked within their ZPDs. Palincsar and A. L. Brown's (1984) work in reciprocal teaching, described in an earlier section, provides an example of scaffolded instruction made explicit to teachers for guiding students in comprehending informational text.

The three concepts described above place the teacher at the center of the learning environment, although in a different role from that of an "inquisitor" who asks questions, elicits responses, and evaluates these responses. Other researchers have explored another aspect of teachers' roles within this paradigm—creating and supporting instructional environments in which students work cooperatively to create text, study topics of interest, or discuss literature.

Enhancing the peer collaboration within literacy events was examined by Daiute (1986) with an added component—the use of computers as the primary writing tool. Using a two-group intervention design, Daiute asked students in both groups to create six texts: two written individually, one before and one at the end of the intervention, and four texts in between. For the intervention group, the four texts were produced by pairs of students who had chosen to work together; for the nonintervention group, these were written individually. Students in both groups were provided with a book about animal facts, and the task for both groups was to write a series of stories about how animals' lives can be difficult. The students who worked in pairs wrote compositions that were more positively evaluated for features such as length, linguistic complexity, and use of language conventions than students who wrote individually. A case analysis of one pair produced examples of students learning about writing conventions such as dialogue from one another as well as more complex text features such as alternative story structures. In cases where pairs did not work as effectively as the case study pair, Daiute described the critical role of the teacher in facilitating interactions and highlighting points of partners' discussions. Such a function for the teacher is a far cry from the traditional transmission model of instruction, and from more nativist traditions that assume that reading and writing develop naturally.

Another format that drew heavily on the interactions around computers was the writing environment created by Bruce and Rubin (1993), called QUILL. The tools included a component for planning and organizing text and a text editor. Students used these tools on an information management system comparable to a classroom library and an electronic bulletin board. Bruce et al. explored changes in the ways teachers defined their role during writing instruction as a result of initiating use of the QUILL program, identifying three areas of impact:

(a) changes in the nature of teachers' feedback for revision, (b) changes to more meaningful writing activities within the classroom into which instruction was embedded, and (c) changes in the social structure of the classroom to facilitate more collaborative writing (see also Cochran-Smith, 1991).

Chang, Wells, and Maher (1990) were interested in bringing a social-constructivist perspective to the study of students' learning in collaborative settings and the role of the teacher in orchestrating such an environment. The project took place in Maher's fourth-grade classroom during a study unit on animals. The focus was on students' discourse in small collaborative groups where first-hand observations, library research, and displays of learning by individuals were shared. In studying students' discussions of first-hand observations of crayfish, Wells et al. described the role played by the teacher in listening to discussions, a venue where students' difficulties and successes became apparent. Unlike a lecture format, where difficulties arise but often remain undetected, the teacher was able to identify misconceptions and provide subsequent guidance. Another teacher role involved monitoring students' topic choice selections and using them as a basis for conferences with individuals and groups. In doing so, the teacher was able to model the acceptability of revising goals and plans and helped make visible the reasons for doing so. Finally, the teacher helped students recognize the range of possible learning activities and types of learning that had occurred in their interactions. As the authors note, "the construction of knowledge requires goal-directed engagement with new information through direct experience and exposition, through discussion and deliberation with others, and through communing with self in writing and reading" (p. 118).

Changing the Roles of Teachers and Researchers. Concomitant with the research on teacher–student interactions just described has been research on university researcher–classroom teacher interactions. This work aims to define alternative models of interaction between teachers and researchers and the impact of these alternative models on teachers' curriculum and instruction. Studies span changes in the curriculum and teaching of undergraduate preservice education programs, staff development efforts, and advanced degree programs for teachers. Characterizing all of these studies is the emphasis on working with teachers within their ZPDs. In each study, the university participant has found ways of connecting to teachers' incoming beliefs, philosophies, biases, and understandings, then working from those positions in a collaborative model that encourages reflection, rethinking, and reconstructing such beliefs. Further, learning is a two-way street, with university participants also changing their instructional practices and views.

Richardson (1994) characterizes such research efforts as reflecting a fundamental change in our views of research on teaching. She suggests that traditional research in this area has fallen within the realm of formal research, or research conducted by members outside the teaching community for the purpose of creating knowledge to be generalized to the broader research community. Richardson argues that research by teachers, work she characterizes as "practical inquiry," is undertaken by practitioners to "understand their contexts, practices, and in the case of teachers, their students. The outcome of the inquiry may be . . . new ways of looking at the context and the problem and/or possibilities for changes in practice" (p. 7). In the studies described here, the research falls into formal research as well as practical inquiry, as university and school researchers conduct studies to add to the knowledge base of the field, as well as to change the contexts in which they act as teacher educators, staff developers, and teachers. In so doing, these researchers reflect the assumptions of a social-constructivist perspective, particularly in terms of how knowledge is constructed within the particular community of literacy educators.

We return to Florio-Ruane's (1994) study, which was discussed earlier as an example of new interpretations of text as a function of context. We chose this study because it illustrates the numerous threads that run through research from a social-constructivist perspective. Here we emphasize the design of this project in extending the understandings of student teachers' views of cultures and their cultural identities as a necessary foundation for supporting their students' learning. Florio-Ruane's underlying argument was that until teachers, usually European-American, middle-class women, can understand personally the role of culture in their own lives as literacy learners, they will have difficulty understanding its impact on the literacy learning of their students. Traditional teacher education courses treat issues related to culture and diverse students within a course called "multicultural education," reflecting the belief that knowledge about culture can be defined and transmitted to teachers, eventually guiding their practice. Cazden (1991), among others, has argued that such courses may have the opposite effect by inadvertently conveying stereotypes or simplistic views of culture. Florio-Ruane's choice of the genre of autobiography was deliberate, for scholarship on narrative, literary theory, and autobiography had led her to believe that the Autobiography Club, which combined elements of each, would serve as a safe context in which to heighten student teachers' awareness of culture and their cultural identities. This context did encourage student teachers to reflect on their own cultures and how their interpretations of text had been influenced by their cultural identities, and it had an effect on the university professor as well, leading Florio-Ruane to revisit choices about curriculum and activities in courses. Studies such as this one within a social-constructivist tradition demonstrate the potential for changing the role between university professor and student as well as changing teachers' views of text and interpretation of text, reflecting both formal research and practical inquiry.

The potential for changing roles is further demonstrated in the projects of Hunsaker and M. Johnston (1992) and Zellermayer (1993). The projects shared the following features: (a) involvement of inservice teachers in advanced university degree programs, (b) exploration of the role of narrative in promoting teachers' changes in instruction in reading and writing, (c) emphasis on the potential for changing roles of teachers and researchers, and (d) illustrations of the bi-directional aspects of change in both classroom practices and in researchers' ways of conceptualizing their work with in-service teachers. Hunsaker and Johnston, respectively a classroom teacher and a university researcher, were participants in a cooperative master's degree program designed by the school district, the university, and the teachers' association. Through their interactions within this program, the two agreed to collaborate on a research project supporting changes in Hunsaker's language arts instruction from a "direct instruction, authoritarian management, and textbook-focused curriculum" (p. 352) to holistic, literature-based instruction. The researchers describe the complex process of working through differential power relationships, theoretical perspectives, social and educational philosophies, personalities, and conceptions of research as they co-constructed the research project and its related curriculum and as they analyzed findings. Johnston spent time in Hunsaker's classroom; they maintained an interactive reflective journal; and they talked extensively about teaching and learning.

Projects such as this one indicate that the suggestion that "more time is needed for change" (G. G. Duffy, 1993) may be only part of the answer. In reflecting on the major changes that Hunsaker initiated in her language arts instruction, both Hunsaker and Johnston argue that Hunsaker's changes in curriculum, materials, structure, and discourse patterns would have been far less likely to occur within the more "efficient" model of transmitting information from expert (i.e., Johnston) to novice (i.e., Hunsaker). Although it may not be realistic to assume that such interactions are possible on a wide scale, we cannot ignore the reality of how difficult fundamental change can be and how unlikely it is that within a transmission model, sustained changes in classroom practices could occur.

Like Hunsaker and M. Johnston (1992), Zellermayer (1993) was interested in how sustained conversations about classroom practices influence teachers' understanding of curriculum and instruction. The project focused on teachers' movement from traditional writing instruction with an emphasis on conventions and usage to a process writing approach. Teachers wrote narratives about their instruction which provided insights into the constraints they felt and the moments that created the tensions and insights that led to substantive changes in teaching. Consistent with the findings of Hunsaker and M. Johnston, an important part of the five case-study teachers' ability to grow and evolve in their teaching was rooted in their ability to let go of control, take the perspectives of others (e.g., students, members of the teachers' group), and create a classroom environment in which authentic conversations among students and between teacher and students occurred. Like Florio-Ruane's findings, another important aspect of their growth was traced to making connections between their own and students' school and home lives.

Finally, Richardson, Anders, Tidwell, and Lloyd (1991) initiated a research program within the context of a staff development effort that supported the finding that changes in teaching occur when teachers have the time and support for engaging in different ways of thinking about their own practices, as well as the staff development to support using new approaches that are consistent with changing ways of thinking about literacy instruction. The staff development effort reflected both formal research examining the relationship between teachers' beliefs and practice and practical inquiry in which they examined their roles and effectiveness within the staff development program.

The findings of Richardson et al., together with those of Florio-Ruane, Hunsaker and M. Johnston, and Zellermeyer, illustrate the influence of a social-constructivist perspective on the nature of the research questions that are asked, the means for addressing these questions, and the findings that emerge from these efforts. The aims of the newly funded National Reading Research Center (Alvermann & Guthrie, 1993) are further evidence of the movement in literacy research to collaborative ventures between researchers and teachers. Results of the projects are only beginning to be disseminated at conferences but, according to Alvermann and Guthrie (1993), more than 30% of the investigators on current projects are classroom teachers, district-level curriculum coordinators, administrators, or members of state boards of education. This change in relationship between researchers and practitioners shows a growing recognition of the complexity of the change process. As Richardson (1994) points out, change dictated from without (e.g., through policymakers, administrators, or school district officials) has created an image that change hurts and that teachers are reluctant to change. Current conceptions create a distinctly different picture of teachers—one of professionals who are likely to engage voluntarily in change processes and who change frequently and with good reason, but who do so from professional goals, not because of external mandates.

Changing the Relationship Between School and Community. From a social-constructivist perspective, understanding the nature of literacy interactions in the home is critical for the design of literacy contexts in schools. At the most fundamental level, children's knowledge about literacy and their ways of approaching literacy grow out of their home literacy interactions. With few exceptions, literacy events exist in the environments of almost all children, there is an abundance of print, and children are familiar with print (e.g., A. A. Anderson & Stokes, 1984, Lavine, 1977), although adults may not comment on the nature or use of literacy or engage children in literacy events in the same ways (Heath, 1983). Yet rarely are the ordinary literacy events of homes or the print of the environment integrated into school contexts (Clay, 1991).

When the literacies of community, home, and school are viewed as complementary, students' participation in literacy can be greatly enhanced. The use of literacy in homes, stores, and other community contexts is a form of the "everyday concepts" that Vygotsky (1987) described as living knowledge. In most school contexts, literacy use often requires reflection or strategy use—or scientific knowledge. When the two forms of knowledge—academic and social—build on one another, connections are made for students. Moll and his colleagues (Moll et al., 1992; Moll, Tapia, & Whitmore, 1993) work with teachers both to recognize the existence and richness of the literacies and knowledge of communities and then to integrate this knowledge into school contexts. Their project has three interrelated components: (a) an ethnographic analysis of the nature of knowledge and its transmission within households of the Latino community, (b) an after-school laboratory in which teachers and students interact with one another, using literacy in ways that are not typical of the classroom but resemble to a greater degree the literacies of their community, and (c) classroom connections that integrate activities from the after-school laboratory. The aim is to integrate the three components. For example, students employ ethnographic methods to document ways of writing in their community (e.g., letters to relatives in other countries, account books) as part of the after-school laboratory. Then, working with their peers, they create modules on topics that reflect the expertise of members of their commu-

nity (e.g., knowledge about mechanics and repair work). To gather information to include in their module, students inteview members of their communities, communicating with one another and, through electronic mail, with students in classrooms in other parts of the country who are engaged in similar module activities. The knowledge and ways of knowing within communities or "funds of knowledge" that contribute to school learning extend beyond literacy-specific knowledge to include knowledge such as that of mechanics and repair, which one student applied to the real-world task of fixing bicycles.

In some home contexts, the literacies of the home may be adapted to become more school-like as children near school entry (Heath, 1983), which helps to ease the children's transition to school literacy learning. However, for children whose community and school literacies may differ, educators' conscious recognition of home literacy patterns and efforts to make connections are needed. School literacy activities, when imposed on homes and without thought to the interaction patterns of homes, can create disjunctures in students' literacies. In the homework of the six children whom Delgado-Gaitan (1992) studied, a preponderance of the reading homework consisted of worksheets that they had not finished at school. Whether children were novice or advanced readers, parents supported their children's homework completion, often sitting with and trying to help their children complete the exercises. Unfortunately, such support may not be reflected in what the student brings back to school, as illustrated in the following example. Norma's homework, like that of many students who were reading below the grade level, consisted primarily of worksheets reflecting drill-and-practice exercises. In one case, she needed to know what "characters" in a story were. Her mother, who was working with her on the homework, first identified the illustrator's name as the character and then changed it to the book title, which Norma wrote down on her worksheet. Not surprisingly, her answers were marked incorrect by the teacher, frustrating the student, who had had adult help, and frustrating the parents, whose inadequate "school knowledge" base was underscored. Such situations discourage students from engaging in doing homework, leading to stereotypes of the poor reader who doesn't work and of parents who don't care. If homework more closely approximated "real reading" instead of the decontextualized skill practice that characterizes school curricula, both parents and students would benefit (Goldenberg, Reese, & Gallimore, 1992). A social-constructivist lens focused on instruction emphasizes the importance of making stronger the connections between home and school literacy.

The case studies of Delgado-Gaitan (1992) demonstrate the efforts of low-income parents as supporting their children's learning. Goldenberg et al. (1992) explored how the materials that teachers send home are filtered through the prior experiences and beliefs of the parents. Goldenberg et al. (1992) conducted case studies with Hispanic kindergarten children to determine the effects of school and home literacy events with either photocopied storybooks (*libros*) or worksheets. In school, students in the *libros* classes performed significantly better than children in the control classrooms (worksheets) on the Bilingual Syntax measure (used as a proxy for literacy) and on a set of early literacy skill and knowledge measures that included letter recognition, concepts about print, and comprehension of a story read aloud. The opposite pattern occurred as a result of home experiences. There, worksheets but not the storybooks were significantly related to literacy outcomes at the end of kindergarten. Parents of children who were in the storybook group at home tended to use the books for drill. Correct pronunciation of each word on a page was emphasized, with relatively little focus on meaning of the stories. The worksheets were more consistent with parents' views of reading development, which was sequential (letters, sounds, syllables, words, and, finally, extended text) and skill oriented. The nature of the interaction around the books, Goldenberg et al. suggest, was what made the books successful in school but less so at home. Further, these interactions at home were influenced strongly by parents' beliefs about literacy and development.

A number of projects build on parents' interest in supporting their children's literacy, guiding the parents' interactions with their children around books (Edwards, 1991). For example, Project Family Literacy—Aprendiendo, Mejorando, Educando (FLAME), or Learning, Bettering, Educating, in Chicago's Latino communities involves literacy training and support for Hispanic, limited-English-proficient parents. The aim is to guide parents who speak another language and have limited proficiency in English in providing more literacy opportunities in their homes, increasing literacy interactions with their children, serving as literacy models for their children, and increasing school–home relationships (Shanahan & Rodriguez-Brown, 1993). Parents attend twice weekly English as a second language (ESL) classes; participate in Parents as Teacher classes twice a month; and attend a summer institute. ESL sessions include parents making books for their children or sharing books in English. From the participating families, a cadre is selected annually to receive training as parent leaders. Twice monthly the parent leaders hold family literacy seminars at neighborhood schools. By the end of the third year of the project, Owen and Shanahan (1993) reported literacy growth in children whose parents were involved in the project, differences that were attributable to project participation rather than development, maturation, learning, or normal exposure.

Designing Early School Contexts to Prevent Literacy Failure.   What makes the projects in this section distinct from other interventions we have described to this point is their application of a social-constructivist perspective to instructional contexts in which most students have not attained conventional literacy. In the projects described previously, either the students have basic literacy proficiencies (e.g., the Book Club Project, Moll's community/school extensions), or, when they cannot read, instructional contexts are adapted so that students can hear the text through read-alongs or read-alouds (e.g., McGee, 1992).

The extensions of social-constructivist thinking to literacy instruction have been many and have transformed visions of what is possible in school contexts. The question of what this philosophy means when large groups of children are not independently literate continues to generate controversy (see Chall, 1989; Edelsky, 1990). Increasingly this question is being addressed from a social-constructivist perspective, although the past traditions in early childhood that have already been described in this chapter mean that most projects of this type are described as emergent literacy rather than social-constructivist. Whatever the label, the focus of these projects has been on low-income students who are most likely to depend on school

contexts to acquire school literacy, with the underlying belief that successful participation in literacy from the start can prevent students from entering the cycle of failure that characterizes the literacy experiences of many low-income students.

The initial set of projects from an emergent literacy or social-constructivist perspective tended to focus on a single element, such as the nature of children's writing within writing centers (Dyson, 1987) or children's renditions of text after repeated reading of predictable text (McCormick & Mason, 1989). A tendency in some, although not all, of these studies was to assume that activities from an emergent literacy perspective would facilitate movement from context-dependent to independent or conventional reading and writing (Martinez et al., 1989). Consequently, children's processes might be described but their independent control of literacy was not always documented in this first wave of studies from an emergent literacy perspective. With increasing efforts to extend emergent literacy notions into classrooms, projects in the second wave of research on emergent literacy have increasingly attended to multiple aspects of the literacy curriculum as students move from context-dependent to conventional literacy. These early literacy projects have built on the work of cognitive scientists. For example, activities aimed at fostering phonemic awareness and automaticity have been central to these projects (see, e.g., Clay, 1985; Hiebert et al., 1992; B. M. Taylor, Strait, & Medo, 1994). But these instructional projects differ from the experiments of most cognitive scientists during the 1970s and 1980s in at least three important ways: (a) the features of the literacy instruction; (b) the connections of this instruction to literacy contexts across the school day, children's school careers, and their home communities; and (c) the role of teachers in implementing and sustaining the instruction.

In examining the features of literacy events that are put into place as part of these interventions, the embedding of skill instruction within reading and writing of connected texts reflects the influence of a social-constructivist perspective. In the Early Literacy Project (Englert, Raphael, & Mariage, 1994), for example, many of the special education students for whom the project is designed have not acquired independent or conventional literacy. Many experiences are provided that will ensure proficiency in independent literacy but, unlike the reductionistic exercises that have often dominated special education classrooms (Poplin, 1988), these strategies and skills are taught within the context of reading of books and writing stories, journals, and other compositions. To involve students who were not yet reading independently in literacy events that were not skill-and-drill exercises, teachers recognized the need for adaptations of activities such as the use of a wordless picturebook in a book-sharing arrangement. Similarly, in the first- and second-grade intervention of Hiebert and colleagues (Hiebert et al., 1992), skills and strategies that are part of independent reading and writing are developed through repeated reading of predictable text and extensive writing by students. For example, after repeated reading of a book with a predictable pattern, such as *Brown Bear, Brown Bear, What Do You See?* (Martin, 1967), the teacher might guide children in making words with the rime *og*, using the word *frog*, one of the characters in the book.

The influence of social-constructivist thinking on literacy events can be seen in the scaffolding of tasks for students

(Clay & Cazden, 1991). In describing this feature of Reading Recovery—the tutorial program that has been implemented most widely of any intervention in English-speaking countries—Clay and Cazden (1991) state that it is "a system of social interaction organized around the comprehension and production of texts that demonstrably creates new forms of cognitive activity in the child" (p. 206). Tasks are scaffolded by the tutors in Reading Recovery so that their tutees develop a self-extending system that allows them to implement appropriate strategies in new literacy tasks in regular classroom contexts. In other projects such as the Early Literacy Project of Englert et al. (1994), the social interaction surrounding literacy tasks, too, has been carefully designed and studied.

Another manifestation of social constructivism in these early literacy projects is the connection of the instructional events to other literacy contexts, including those in classrooms, homes, and other grades (see Hiebert & Taylor, 1994). Although connections across literacy contexts are an emphasis of these projects, differences are extensive as to what connections are in the foreground. Some projects such as Reading Recovery (Clay & Cazden, 1991; Clay, 1985) are aimed at one grade level—first grade—and involve specially trained teachers who tutor students. Other projects, such as the Early Literacy Project (Englert et al., 1994), are focused on special education students and their instruction across resource and mainstreamed classrooms and across the primary grades. One project that began as an early literacy intervention for Grade 1 students and was provided by Chapter 1 teachers (Hiebert et al., 1992) has been extended to Grade 1 classrooms (Hiebert & Almanza, 1993) and to Grade 2 Chapter 1 and classroom contexts (Catto, 1993). As students who received the literacy interventionist instruction as first and second graders have moved to the middle grades, third- and fourth-grade teachers have been adapting their instruction of reading and writing in content areas to accommodate the changes in overall literacy levels of their students (Hiebert, 1994).

The influence of social constructivism is also evident in roles that teachers and researchers assume in these projects. A foundation in classroom settings with instructional practices integrated into the routines of teachers and long-term collaborations between school- and university-based educators (see, e.g., Hiebert & Taylor, 1994) characterize these projects. Systematic interactions between university- and school-based educators where they can learn from one another and, subsequently, influence the learning of children are integral as well. For example, Gaffney and R. C. Anderson (1991) have described the learning process of Reading Recovery teachers within a Vygotskian perspective, citing two tiers of scaffolding. In the first, the teacher scaffolds the learning process for students in tutorials. According to Gaffney and R. C. Anderson, experience in the first tier creates consciousness of children, their capabilities and development, and of instructional processes. These experiences in scaffolding tasks for children are drawn on in the second tier of scaffolding, where the learning events of the training sessions are scaffolded by teacher leaders so that teachers gain new insights into their tutees' strategies and needs.

Although these collaborative projects in early literacy between researchers and teachers repeatedly report high levels of literacy in participating students, the number of children and teachers who have been influenced by such projects is small.

The widescale involvement of teachers and the support that is required for projects to be sustained over extended periods of time are issues that will continue to challenge educators and educational psychologists.

***Current Instructional Practices in Literacy and Themes from Educational Psychology.*** In addition to the three themes related to teaching and curriculum in literacy—identifying universal teaching methods, teaching strategies, and changing instructional contexts—our review revealed at least as many subthemes evident in the work of educational psychologists related to teaching. A critical question to raise, then, is, "What evidence is there for the impact of this work on the literacy experiences of students?" Advocates from different paradigms may face off and one side may "win" in the research literature (McKenna et al., 1994; Stanovich, 1990), or curriculum policies may "mandate" the activities from newer paradigms (e.g., California English Language Arts Committee, 1987), but ultimately, students' literacy experiences can remain unscathed by these debates.

Unlike in the test and textbook publishing industries, there is no denouement in the paradigm wars where all of the teachers from one paradigm are replaced by teachers from the next paradigm. New ideas are added to the repertoires of teachers, sometimes replacing, sometimes transforming, sometimes juxtaposed with existing activities. It is much more difficult to find evidence of these themes in teaching than to find their manifestations in texts and tests. It does appear, however, that the influence on American literacy instruction of a behaviorist perspective has endured for a number of generations. Massive surveys like those of Austin and Morrison (1963) showed that the universals of teaching had been communicated to teachers. The overwhelming majority of reading periods in American classrooms consisted of division of activity into three ability groups that had similar lessons but at a different pace. Students who were not working with the teacher did workbook exercises independently at their desks.

According to I. L. Beck (1993), information about strategic literacy instruction has filtered down to teachers, while Bruer (1993) sees cognitive science as the source for transforming schools into settings that promote thinking. Scholars have provided to practitioners various translations and frameworks of research based on cognitive science (R. C. Anderson et al., 1985; Pressley et al., 1989). Partly because a "universal" teaching method is not expected, survey research such as Austin and Morrison's (1963) summary of literacy instruction in an earlier era has not been conducted, so typical practices in American classrooms in the late 1980s and early 1990s must be interpreted from a handful of descriptive studies, few of which have been conducted within the past 5 years. The few observational studies that have been conducted in recent years show little evidence of change in the patterns reported a decade ago (Alvermann et al., 1990; Armbruster et al., 1991). Substantial amounts of time were, and apparently still are, spent on seatwork activities, while occasions for silent reading were, and apparently still are, limited to short periods per the day (L. M. Anderson et al., 1985; Fisher et al., 1978).

Classrooms and schools where children are most in need of outstanding literacy instruction may well be those that have been least impacted by the shifts supported by cognitive science. In Chapter 1, the program to assist low-income students (P. Johnston & Allington, 1991), special education (Haynes & Jenkins, 1986), and bilingual students (Rueda, 1991), literacy periods are likely to emphasize worksheets and skill sheets, with less time spent on extended reading of stories, magazines, and books (see also Knapp et al., 1992). It is little wonder that the effects of Chapter 1 have been transitory (Kennedy, Birman, & Demaline, 1986).

Although the level and quality of implementation of the wealth of knowledge on strategic guidance from cognitive science are difficult to determine, the discussion and interest in literacy instruction that cognitive science spawned may have served as an impetus for whole language (P. D. Pearson, 1993b). As we have mentioned previously in this review, whole language cannot be equated with social-constructivist thinking, although whole language proponents are increasingly acknowledging commonalities between their philosophy and social-constructivist principles (K. S. Goodman, 1989). Whole language appears to have been widely accepted by teachers even to the point where basal textbooks now call themselves "whole language" series (Hoffman et al., 1994). The degree to which there have been substantive changes in literacy instruction that reflect social-constructivist principles, such as scaffolding of tasks and conversations by teachers for different students, is uncertain. It is too soon to establish the influence of the flurry of research activity currently conducted from a social-constructivist perspective. Since most of these projects are intensive collaborative efforts among researchers, teachers, parents, or members of the broader community, critical thought must be given to how these projects can influence more than the classrooms or other sites in which they occur.

Because the social-constructivist paradigm is only now gaining momentum within educational psychology, there is not the hindsight provided when a paradigm has begun to shift or been in place for a decade or more. There are a number of unresolved tensions within this paradigm that set the stage for future research. One such tension is that between "received views" or knowledge that is accepted in current culture. What are the boundaries to what a child can construct? How can the processes by which received views are learned be described, then transformed through construction? How can the learner be assisted in understanding that current knowledge, the received view, was socially constructed and will change? A second tension relates to the parameters of instruction. If meaning is socially constructed, what are the limits to what a teacher can or should accept as a child constructs meaning? When should teachers intervene and say that a construction is wrong or doesn't make sense?

## EPILOGUE

As we worked on this chapter, we received many comments from our colleagues, especially those who have recently entered the profession. "Does educational psychology have a future as a basis for our instructional practices in literacy?" asked one. When we consider current perspectives on the study of classrooms, we believe that educational psychology has a critical role in solving some of the problems related to literacy learning and instruction that confront students, teachers, parents, and

producers of curricula for schools. The concerns of the educational psychologist—the nature and caliber of thinking processes with text, ways in which contexts can be designed so that these thinking processes can be enhanced, and the means for making these contexts available to the students who need them—are at the very heart of current issues related to literacy learning and instruction.

As this review has shown, school literacy practices in the form of tests, texts, and teaching have been heavily influenced by the perspectives of educational psychologists and their research on learning in general as well as their specific study of literacy processes. Although many of these influences have provided useful guidance and have been strong and lasting, the outcomes—especially for school practices—have not always been the ones that educational psychologists anticipated or desired. One unanticipated consequence of some research has been to see what were intended as solutions by educational psychologists of one generation (e.g., making the complex processes of literacy more accessible by breaking them into smaller units for extensive practice) become the problems that plague subsequent ones (e.g., extensive and often meaningless drill-and-practice routines on decontextualized skill sheets for Chapter 1 students). As P. Johnston & Allington (1991) have described, the experiences of Chapter 1 students are often devoid of meaning-focused activities, surely not the anticipated consequences of the psychologists of an earlier era. We have also seen unintended consequences of research grow out of perhaps misguided applications of findings from educational psychology without regard to the changing demographics within our schools. An underemphasis on the importance of language and culture for students' learning may have contributed to the disproportionate placement of students from linguistically and culturally diverse backgrounds in special education (McGill-Franzen & Allington, 1993). Both established practices and perspectives militate against full access to literacy for all students. Further, the classrooms that teachers face at the end of the 20th century and the beginning of the 21st are increasingly diverse and complex. The mix of languages and cultures in North American classrooms can be seen as a source of strength for creating readers and writers with the flexible viewpoints and rich repertoires required for full participation in a technological society. However, this mix creates challenges in designing meaningful literacy instruction. The need for well-designed solutions that are built on strong scholarship is particularly pressing at a time when social policies and historical patterns have left many children living in poverty. For the children of poverty, the degree to which their literacy is developed in school contexts will critically influence their access within society and the workplace (Scribner, 1984).

The majority of U.S. students are not attaining the levels of literacy needed for full participation in society (Kirsch & Jungeblut, 1986; Mullis et al., 1993). Meeting the challenges of the complex and diverse contexts of 21st-century classrooms requires both concerted efforts and inventive solutions. We believe that educational psychologists have a critical role to play in creating and initiating solutions. In this concluding section, we outline the contribution that educational psychologists can make to improving literacy practices in and beyond school by continuing to address prominent areas of concern within traditional lines of educational psychological research, and by shifting directions to pursue key questions that must be addressed if our contributions are to be realized.

With calls for changes in the social context and mandates for equity, the potential role to be played by educational psychologists becomes a key one. Descriptions that focus only on the social context and mandates for equity that provide no insight as to how this equity might be achieved will be insufficient to guide teachers in initiating changes in their literacy instructional practices. Goals of access to high-quality instruction require descriptions of the nature of this instruction and the manner in which it supports the development of higher and multiple literacies. The nature of literacy learning, the manner in which literacy learning can be enhanced by text and through teaching, and the means by which literacy learning can be appropriately assessed are the traditional concerns of educational psychologists and ones that must continue to be emphasized. Educational psychologists bring to the study of literacy learning a much-needed stance without which commitments to equity and access for all students will be difficult to realize.

However, to make this contribution requires a shift in direction on the part of many in our community of scholars. As present-day educational psychologists have observed in reflecting on our predecessors (Glover & Ronning, 1987; J. Levin, 1992; Walberg & Haertel, 1992), the first generation of educational psychologists saw the attention to questions of practice as distinguishing and justifying their discipline. Today, we have important research questions to address with regard to practice, expanded methodologies for doing so, and, through rapid communication and easier access, the possibility for drawing on a range of disciplines to enhance the practices in literacy education in schools, homes, communities, and the workplace. Unfortunately, many of today's educational psychologists who focus their research on literacy learning have moved away from their grounding in the problems of practice. Although we value and encourage work within the category of "basic research" in reading and writing, we stress the importance of work that aims to extend models and perspectives into practice and, with it, the importance of critiquing that work for its relevance to the problems to literacy learning and use in the homes, schools, and workplaces of today.

As part of this review, we studied many journals that publish the scholarship of educational psychologists in literacy. We found many studies that pertain to lines of work where it is no longer clear whether the fundamental problem exists in practice, where we question the relevance of the research for helping us understand text, tests, or teaching, broadly defined. In our survey of the premiere journals in educational psychology, there were only a handful of studies in which the literacy learners had languages or cultures that were not English and middle class. We were surprised to find a preponderance of studies whose sole subjects were the stereotypic "college sophomore," rather than children, even when investigators claimed extensions of their findings to school-age populations. Studies provided answers to questions that do not seem to match the questions of today's test or text publisher, teacher, or teacher educator. For example, research on text structures continues for rather limited genres and length of text, while current questions about text pertain to large pieces of text (chapter books, informational books) and its appropriate use for students of differing abilities and ages.

There are many questions about literacy in the diverse educational contexts of the late 20th century that could benefit from the lenses of educational psychologists. To answer these questions, however, educational psychologists will once again need to become immersed in the issues of practice. We do not mean that every educational psychologist should visit a classroom. Rather, whether the learning site is the school or the workplace, the home or community, educational psychologists must turn attention to the pressing questions of the field, defining our role and our contributions as part of the unique field that we have been. Calls for integration within language and literacy and between literacy and content areas have left unanswered many questions about effective literacy instruction in new contexts. To make the impact that we can, we must immerse ourselves in the questions that underlie our work and to examine the relevancy and centrality of our questions.

By bringing our readers through a progression of perspectives that have guided literacy research, extensions of this literacy research to practice, and the consequences of these extensions, we hoped to pique our readers' interest in examining particular aspects of educational practices that involve and focus on reading and writing. Commitment and belief in support of good practice characterized educational psychology at the outset. What is needed by the current and next generation of educational psychologists is a return to our roots—to a clear focus on the problems that practitioners face. When problems are clear, the multiple perspectives of educational psychology can be applied to create inventive solutions.

## *References*

Aaron, I. E., Chall, J. S., Durkin, D., Goodman, K., & Strickland, D. S. (1990). The past, present, and future of literacy education: Comments from a panel of distinguished educators. Parts I and II. *Reading Teacher, 43,* 302–311, 370–380.

Adams, M. J. (1990). *Beginning to read: Thinking and learning about print.* Cambridge, MA: MIT Press.

Allington, R. L. (1984). Oral reading. In P. D. Pearson, R. Barr, M. L. Kamil, & P. Mosenthal (Eds.), *Handbook of reading research* (Vol. 1, pp. 829–864). New York: Longman.

Alvermann, D. E., & Guthrie, J. T. (1993). *Themes and directions of the National Reading Research Center* (Perspectives in Reading Research No. 1). Athens, GA, College Park, MD: Universities of Georgia and Maryland, National Reading Research Center.

Alvermann, D. E., O'Brien, D. G., & Dillon, D. R. (1990). What teachers do when they say they're having discussions of content reading assignments: A qualitative analysis. *Reading Research Quarterly, 25,* 296–322.

Amidon, P. S. (1975). *Developmental Reading.* St. Paul, MN: Paul S. Amidon & Associates.

Amsterman, L., Ammon, P., & Simons, H. (1990). Children's elicited imitations of controlled and rewritten reading texts. *Journal of Educational Psychology, 82,* 486–490.

Andelin, J., & staff (1992). *Testing in American schools: Asking the right questions.* Washington, DC: Congress of the United States, Office of Technology Assessment.

Anderson, A. A., & Stokes, S. J. (1984). Social and institutional influences on the development and practice of literacy. In H. Goelman, A. Oberg, & F. Smith (Eds.), *Awakening to literacy* (pp. 24–37). Portsmouth, NH: Heinemann.

Anderson, L. M., Brubaker, N. L., Alleman-Brooks, J., & Duffy, G. (1985). A qualitative study of seatwork in first-grade classrooms. *Elementary School Journal, 86,* 123–140.

Anderson, R. C. (1977). The notion of schemata and the educational enterprise. In R. C. Anderson, R. J. Spiro, & W. E. Montague (Eds.), *Schooling and the acquisition of knowledge* (pp. 415–431). Hillsdale, NJ: Lawrence Erlbaum Associates.

Anderson, R. C., Hiebert, E. H., Scott, J. A., & Wilkinson, I. A. G. (1985). *Becoming a nation of readers.* Urbana-Champaign, IL: Center for the Study of Reading.

Anderson, R. C., Osborn, J., & Tierney, R. J. (Eds.). (1984). *Learning to read in American schools: Basal readers and content texts.* Hillsdale, NJ: Lawrence Erlbaum Associates.

Anderson, R. C., & Pearson, P. D. (1984). A schema-theoretic view of basic processes in reading comprehension. In P. D. Pearson, R. Barr, M. Kamil, & P. Mosenthal (Eds.), *Handbook of reading research* (Vol. 1, pp. 255–293). New York: Longman.

Anderson, R. C., Spiro, R. J., & Montague, W. E. (Eds.). (1977). *Schooling and the acquisition of knowledge.* Hillsdale, NJ: Lawrence Erlbaum Associates.

Anderson, R. C., Wilson, P. T., & Fielding, L. G. (1988). Growth in reading and how children spend their time outside of school. *Reading Research Quarterly, 23,* 285–303.

Applebee, A. N. (1981). *Writing in the secondary school.* Urbana, IL: National Council of Teachers of English.

Applebee, A. N., Langer, J. A., & Mullis, I. V. S. (1986). *The writing report card: Writing achievement in American schools* (Report No. 15-W-02). Princeton, NJ: National Assessment of Educational Progress, Educational Testing Service.

Applebee, A. N., Langer, J. A., & Mullis, I. V. S. (1989). *Crossroads in American education: A summary of findings* (Report No. 17-OV-01). Princeton, NJ: Educational Testing Service.

Armbruster, B. B. (1984). The problem of "inconsiderate" text. In G. G. Duffy, L. R. Roehler, & J. Mason (Eds.), *Comprehension instruction* (pp. 202–217). New York: Longman.

Armbruster, B. B., Anderson, T., Armstrong, J., Wise, M., Janisch, C., & Meyer, L. (1991). Reading and questioning in content area lessons. *Journal of Reading Behavior, 23,* 35–59.

Armbruster, B. B., & Anderson, T. H. (1985). Frames: Structures for informative text. In D. H. Jonassen (Ed.), *The technology of text* (Vol. 2, pp. 90–104). Englewood Cliffs, NJ: Educational Technology Publications.

Athanases, S. Z. (1994). Teachers' reports of the effects of preparing portfolios of literacy instruction. *Elementary School Journal, 94,* 421–440.

Au, K. H. (1994). Portfolio assessment: Experiences at the Kamehameha Elementary Education Program. In S. W. Valencia, E. H. Hiebert, & P. Afflerbach (Eds.), *Authentic reading assessment: Practices and possibilities* (pp. 103–126). Newark, DE: International Reading Association.

Au, K. H., & Kawakami, A. J. (1986). The influence of the social organization of instruction on children's text comprehension ability: A Vygotskian perspective. In T. Raphael (Ed.), *The contexts of school-based literacy* (pp. 63–78). New York: Random House.

Aukerman, R. C. (1984). *Approaches to beginning reading* (2nd ed.). New York: Wiley.

Austin, M. C., & Morrison, C. (1963). *The first R.* New York: Macmillan.

Baker, E. (1989). Mandated tests: Educational reform or quality indicator? In B. Gifford (Ed.), *Future assessments: Changing views of aptitude, achievement, and instruction* (pp. 3–23). Boston: Kluwer Academic.

Baker, L., & Brown, A. L. (1984). Metacognitive skills and reading. In P. D. Pearson, R. Barr, M. Kamil, & P. Mosenthal (Eds.), *Handbook of reading research* (Vol. 1, pp. 353–394). New York: Longman.

Baker, N. W. (1993). The effect of portfolio-based instruction on composition students' final examination scores, course grades, and attitudes toward writing. *Research in the Teaching of English, 27,* 155–174.

Ball, E. W., & Blachman, B. A. (1991). Does phoneme segmentation training in kindergarten make a difference in early word recognition and developmental spelling? *Reading Research Quarterly, 26,* 49–66.

Bangert-Drowns, R. L., Kulik, J. A., & Kulik, C. C. (1983). Effects of coaching programs on achievement test performance. *Review of Educational Research, 53,* 571–585.

Barr, R. (1974–1975). The effect of instruction on pupil reading strategies. *Reading Research Quarterly, 10,* 555–582.

Barr, R. (1984). Beginning reading instruction. In P. D. Pearson, R. Barr, M. Kamil, & P. Mosenthal (Eds.), *Handbook of reading research* (Vol. 1, pp. 545–581). New York: Longman.

Barr, R., Kamil, M., Mosenthal, P., & Pearson, P. D. (Eds.). (1991). *Handbook of reading research* (Vol. 2). New York: Longman.

Barrs, M., Ellis, S., Tester, H., & Thomas, A. (1989). *The primary language record: Handbook for teachers.* London: London Education Authority.

Barthes, R. (1975). An introduction to the structural analysis of narrative. *New Literary History, 6,* 559–572.

Bartlett, F. C. (1932). *Remembering: A study in experimental and social psychology.* Cambridge, England: Cambridge University Press.

Beck, I. L. (1993). On reading: A survey of recent research and proposals for the future. In A. P. Sweet & J. I. Anderson (Eds.), *Reading research into the year 2000* (pp. 65–87). Hillsdale, NJ: Lawrence Erlbaum Associates.

Beck, I. L., & McCaslin, E. S. (1978). *An analysis of dimensions that affect the development of code-breaking in eight beginning reading programs.* Pittsburgh: University of Pittsburgh, Learning Research and Development Center.

Beck, I. L., & McKeown, M. (1991). Conditions of vocabulary acquisition. In R. Barr, M. Kamil, P. Mosenthal, & P. D. Pearson (Eds.), *Handbook of reading research* (Vol. 2, pp. 789–814). New York: Longman.

Beck, I. L., McKeown, M., & Gromoll, E. W. (1989). Learning from social studies texts. *Cognition and Instruction, 6,* 99–158.

Beck, I. L., McKeown, M. G., & McCaslin, E. S. (1983). Vocabulary development: All contexts are not created equal. *Elementary School Journal, 83,* 177–181.

Beck, I. L., McKeown, M., Omanson, R., & Pople, M. (1984). Improving the comprehensibility of stories: The effects of revisions that improve coherence. *Reading Research Quarterly, 19,* 263–277.

Beck, I. L., & Mitroff, D. D. (1972). *The rationale and design of a primary grades reading system for an individualized classroom.* Pittsburgh, PA: University of Pittsburgh, Learning Research & Development Center.

Bereiter, C., & Scardamalia, M. (1987). *The psychology of written composition.* Hillsdale, NJ: Lawrence Erlbaum Associates.

Bloom, B. S. (1971). Mastery learning. In J. H. Block (Ed.), *Mastery learning: Theory and practice* (pp. 47–63). New York: Holt, Rinehart & Winston.

Bohning, G. (1986). The McGuffey Eclectic Readers: 1836–1986. *Reading Teacher, 40,* 263–269.

Bond, G., & Dykstra, R. (1967). The Cooperative Research Program in first-grade reading instruction. *Reading Research Quarterly, 2,* 5–141.

Bormuth, J. R. (1966). Readability: A new approach. *Reading Research Quarterly, 1,* 79–132.

Bormuth, J. R. (1970). *On the theory of achievement test items.* Chicago: University of Chicago Press.

Bradley, L., & Bryant, P. E. (1983). Categorizing sounds and learning to read: A causal connection. *Nature, 301,* 419–421.

Bransford, J. D. (1979). *Human cognition: Learning, understanding, remembering*. Belmont, CA: Wadsworth.

Bransford, J. D., & Johnson, M. K. (1972). Contextual prerequisites for understanding: Some investigations of comprehension and recall. *Journal of Verbal Learning and Verbal Behavior, 11,* 717–726.

Braun, C., Rennie, B. J., & Gordon, C. J. (1987). An examination of contexts for reading assessment. *Journal of Educational Research, 80,* 283–289.

Brennan, A., Bridge, C., & Winograd, P. (1986). The effects of structural variation on children's recall of basal reader stories. *Reading Research Quarterly, 21,* 91–104.

Brewer, R. (1989, June). *State assessments of student performance: Vermont.* Paper presented at the annual meeting of the Education Commission of the States, Colorado Department of Education, Boulder, CO.

Brewer, W. F., & Lichtenstein, E. H. (1982). Stories are to entertain: A structural-affect theory of stories. *Journal of Pragmatics, 6,* 473–486.

Britton, B. K., & Black, J. B. (Eds.). (1985). *Understanding expository text: A theoretical and practical handbook for analyzing explanatory text.* Hillsdale, NJ: Lawrence Erlbaum Associates.

Brown, A. L. (1978). Knowing when, where, and how to remember: A problem of metacognition. In R. Glaser (Ed.), *Advances in instructional psychology* (Vol. 1, pp. 77–165). Hillsdale, NJ: Lawrence Erlbaum Associates.

Brown, A. L., & Day, J. D. (1983). Macrorules for summarizing texts: The development of expertise. *Journal of Verbal Learning and Verbal Behavior, 22,* 1–14.

Brown, A. L., & Palincsar, A. S. (1990). Guided cooperative learning and individual knowledge acquisition. In L. B. Resnick (Ed.), *Knowing, learning, and instruction: Essays in honor of Robert Glaser* (pp. 393–452). Hillsdale, NJ: Lawrence Erlbaum Associates.

Brown, J. S., Collins, A., & Duguid, P. (1989). Situated cognition and the culture of learning. *Educational Researcher, 18,* 32–42.

Bruce, B. (1984). A new point of view on children's stories. In R. C. Anderson, J. Osborn, & R. J. Tierney (Eds.), *Learning to read in American schools: Basal readers and content texts* (pp. 153–174). Hillsdale, NJ: Lawrence Erlbaum Associates.

Bruce, B., & Rubin, A. (1993). *Electronic quills.* Hillsdale, NJ: Lawrence Erlbaum Associates.

Bruer, J. T. (1993). *Schools for thought: A science of learning in the classroom.* Cambridge, MA: MIT Press.

Bruffee, K. A. (1986). Social construction, language, and the authority of knowledge: A bibliographic essay. *College English, 48,* 773–790.

Bruner, J. (1990). *Acts of meaning.* Cambridge, MA: Harvard University Press.

Bruner, J. (1991). Introduction. In S. Graubard (Ed.), *Literacy: An overview by fourteen experts* (pp. vii–xi). New York: Farrar, Straus & Giroux.

Buchanan, C. D., & Sullivan, M. W. (1980). *Sullivan Reading.* Palo Alto, CA: Learning Line. (Original work published 1963.)

Burton, F. R. (1991). Teacher-researcher projects: An elementary school teacher's perspective. In J. Flood, J. M. Jensen, D. Lapp, & J. R. Squire (Eds.), *Handbook of research on teaching the English language arts* (pp. 226–230). New York: Macmillan.

Calfee, R. C. (1981). Cognitive psychology and educational practice. In D. C. Berliner (Ed.), *Review of Research in Education* (Vol. 9, pp. 3–74). Washington, DC: American Educational Research Association.

Calfee, R. C. (1992). The Inquiring School: Literacy for the year 2000. In C. Collins & J. N. Mangieri (Eds.), *Teaching thinking: An agenda for the twenty-first century* (pp. 147–166). Hillsdale, NJ: Lawrence Erlbaum Associates.

Calfee, R. C., & Chambliss, M. J. (1987). The structural design features of large texts. *Educational Psychologist, 22,* 357–378.

Calfee, R. C., & Drum, P. (1986). Research on teaching reading. In M. C. Wittrock (Ed.), *Handbook of research on teaching* (3rd ed., pp. 804–849). New York: Macmillan.

Calfee, R. C., & Hiebert, E. H. (1991). Classroom assessment of literacy. In R. Barr, M. Kamil, P. Mosenthal, & P. D. Pearson (Eds.), *Handbook of reading research* (Vol. 2, pp. 281–309). New York: Longman.

Calfee, R. C., & Nelson-Barber, S. (1991). Diversity and constancy in human thinking: Critical literacy as amplifier of intellect and experience. In E. H. Hiebert (Ed.), *Literacy for a diverse society: Perspectives, practices, and policies* (pp. 44–57). New York: Teachers College Press.

California English/Language Arts Committee (1987). *English-language arts framework for California public schools (kindergarten through grade twelve).* Sacramento: California Department of Education.

Calkins, L. M. (1991). *Living between the lines.* Portsmouth, NH: Heinemann.

Campbell, J. R., & Ashworth, K. P. (1995) (Eds.). *A synthesis of data from NAEP's 1992 Integrated Reading Performance Record at Grade 4.* Washington, DC: Office of Educational Research & Improvement, US Department of Education.

Cannell, J. J. (1988). Nationally normed elementary achievement testing in America's public schools: How all 50 states are above the national average. *Educational Measurement: Issues and Practice, 7,* 5–9.

Carroll, J. B., & Chall, J. S. (Eds.). (1975). *Toward a literate society.* New York: McGraw-Hill.

Carver, R. P. (1992). What do standardized tests of reading comprehension measure in terms of efficiency, accuracy, and rate? *Reading Research Quarterly, 27,* 346–359.

Cattell, J. M. (1886). The time it takes to see and name objects. *Mind, 11,* 63–65.

Cattell, J. M. (1890). Mental tests and measurements. *Mind, 15,* 373–380.

Catto, S. L. (1993). *An examination of a second-grade literacy intervention: Patterns of student performance and the relationship of selected factors.* Unpublished doctoral dissertation. University of Colorado–Boulder.

Cazden, C. B. (1983). Peekaboo as an instructional model: Discourse development at school and at home. In B. Bain (Ed.), *The sociogenesis of language and human conduct: A multidisciplinary book of readings* (pp. 33–58). New York: Plenum Press.

Cazden, C. B. (1991). Contemporary issues and future directions: Active learners and active teachers. In J. Flood, J. M. Jensen, D. Lapp, & J. R. Squire (Eds.), *Handbook of research on teaching the English language arts* (pp. 418–422). New York: Macmillan.

Cazden, C. B. (1992). *Whole language plus: Essays on literacy in the United States and New Zealand.* New York: Teachers College Press.

Chall, J. S. (1982). *Learning to read: The great debate* (2nd ed.). New York: McGraw-Hill. (Original work published 1967).

Chall, J. S. (1984). Readability and prose comprehension: Continuities and discontinuities. In J. Flood (Ed.), *Understanding reading comprehension: Cognition, language, and the structure of prose* (pp. 233–246). Newark, DE: International Reading Association.

Chall, J. S. (1989). Learning to read: The great debate 20 years later: A response to 'Debunking the great phonics myth.' *Phi Delta Kappan, 70,* 521–538.

Chall, J. S., & Feldmann, S. (1966). First grade reading: An analysis of the interactions of professed methods, teacher implementation, and child background. *Reading Teacher, 19,* 56–575.

Chall, J. S., & Squire, J. R. (1991). The publishing industry and textbooks. In R. Barr, M. Kamil, P. Mosenthal, & P. D. Pearson (Eds.), *Handbook of reading research* (Vol. 2, pp. 120–146). New York: Longman.

Chang, G. L. M., Wells, G., & Maher, A. (1990). Creating classroom communities of literate thinkers. In S. Sharan (Ed.), *Cooperative learning* (pp. 95–121). New York: Praeger.

Clarke, L. S. (1988). Invented versus traditional spelling in first graders' writings: Effects on learning to spell and read. *Research in the Teaching of English, 22,* 281–309.

Clay, M. M. (1975). *What did I write?* Portsmouth, NH: Heinemann.

Clay, M. M. (1985). *The early detection of reading difficulties.* Portsmouth, NH: Heinemann.

Clay, M. M. (1991). *Becoming literate: The construction of inner control.* Portsmouth, NH: Heinemann.

Clay, M. M., & Cazden, C. (1991). A Vygotskian interpretation of Reading Recovery. In L. C. Moll (Ed.), *Vygotsky and education: Instructional implications and applications of socio-historical psychology* (pp. 206–222). New York: Cambridge University Press.

Chomsky, N., & Halle, M. (1968). *The sound pattern of English.* New York: Harper & Row.

Clifford, G. J. (1989). A Sisyphean task: Historical perspectives on writing and reading instruction. In A. Dyson (Ed.), *Collaboration through writing and reading: Exploring possibilities* (pp. 25–84). Urbana, IL: National Council of Teachers of English.

Cochran-Smith, M. (1991). Word processing and writing in elementary classrooms: A critical review of related literature. *Review of Educational Research, 61,* 107–155.

College Board. (1983). *Degrees of reading power: User's guide. PA series.* New York: College Entrance Examination Board.

Collins, A., Brown, J. S., & Larkin, K. M. (1980). Inference in text understanding. In R. Spiro, B. Bruce, & W. F. Brewer (Eds.), *Theoretical issues in reading comprehension* (pp. 385–407). Hillsdale, NJ: Lawrence Erlbaum Associates.

Conoley, J. C. (Ed.). (1989). *The tenth mental measurements yearbook.* Lincoln, NE: Buros Institute.

Cooney, B. (1982). *Miss Rumphius.* New York: Viking.

Cunningham, A. E. (1990). Explicit versus implicit instruction in phonemic awareness. *Journal of Experimental Child Psychology, 50,* 429–444.

Dahl, P. R. (1979). An experimental program for teaching high-speed word recognition and comprehension skills. In J. E. Button, T. Lovitt, & T. Rowland (Eds.), *Communications research in learning disabilities and mental retardation* (pp. 33–65). Baltimore: University Park Press.

Daiute, C. (1986). Do 1 and 1 make 2? *Written Communication, 3,* 382–408.

Dale, E., & Chall, J. S. (1948). A formula for predicting readability. *Educational Research Bulletin 27,* 11–20, 37–54.

Damon, W. (1991). Reconciling the literacies of generations. In S. Graubard (Ed.), *Literacy: An overview by fourteen experts* (pp. 33–53). New York: Farrar, Straus & Giroux.

Davidson, E. S., & Benjamin, L. T., Jr. (1987). A history of the child study movement in America. In J. A. Glover & R. R. Ronning (Eds.), *Historical foundations of educational psychology* (pp. 41–60). New York: Plenum Press.

Davison, A., & Kantor, R. N. (1982). On the failure of readability formulas to define readable texts: A case study from adaptations. *Reading Research Quarterly, 17,* 187–209.

DeFabio, R. (1989). *Classroom as text: Reading, interpreting, and critiquing a literature class* (Tech. Rep. No. 2.7). Albany: State University of New York, Center for the Learning and Teaching of Literature.

Delgado-Gaitan, C. (1992). School matters in the Mexican-American home: Socializing children to education. *American Educational Research Journal, 29,* 495–513.

*Delta: Design for Word-Attack Growth.* (1974). Tulsa, OK: Educational Development Corporation.

Denyer, J. E. (1993). *Teaching by talking, teaching by listening: The conversation complexity of learning to engage children in educative conversations about text in writing conferences.* Unpublished doctoral dissertation, Michigan State University, East Lansing, MI.

Diederich, P. (1974). *Measuring growth in English.* Urbana, IL: National Council of Teachers of English.

DiPardo, A., & Freedman, S. W. (1988). Peer response groups in the writing classroom: Theoretic foundations and new directions. *Review of Educational Research, 58,* 119–150.

Dole, J. A., Duffy, G. G., Roehler, L. R., & Pearson, P. D. (1991). Moving from the old to the new: Research on reading comprehension instruction. *Review of Educational Research, 61,* 239–264.

Dorr-Bremme, D. W., & Herman, J. L. (1986). *Assessing student achievement: A profile of classroom practices.* Los Angeles: UCLA, Center for the Study of Evaluation.

Dowhower, S. S. (1987). Effects of repeated reading on second-grade transitional readers' fluency and comprehension. *Reading Research Quarterly, 22,* 389–406.

Drum, P. A., Calfee, R. C., & Cook, L. K. (1981). The effects of surface structure variations on performance in reading comprehension tests. *Reading Research Quarterly, 16,* 486–514.

Duffy, G. G. (1993). Teachers' progress toward becoming expert strategy teachers. *Elementary School Journal, 94,* 109–120.

Duffy, G. G., Roehler, L., Meloth, M., Vavrus, L., Book, C., et al. (1986). The relationship between explicit verbal explanations during reading skill instruction and student awareness and achievement: A study of reading teacher effects. *Reading Research Quarterly, 21,* 237–252.

Duffy, G. G., Roehler, L., Sivan, E., Rackliffe, G., Book, C., Meloth, M., Vavrus, L. G., Wesselman, R., Putnam, J., & Bassiri, D. (1987). The effects of explaining the reasoning associated with using reading strategies. *Reading Research Quarterly, 22,* 347–368.

Durkin, D. (1981). Reading comprehension instruction in five basal reader series. *Reading Research Quarterly, 16,* 515–544.

Durkin, D. (1978–1979). What classroom observations reveal about reading comprehension instruction. *Reading Research Quarterly, 15,* 481–533.

Dyson, A. H. (1987). The value of "time off task": Young children's spontaneous talk and deliberate text. *Harvard Educational Review, 57,* 396–420.

Dyson, A. H. (1989). (Ed.). *Collaboration through writing and reading: Exploring possibilities.* Urbana, IL: National Council of Teachers of English.

Dyson, A. H., & Freedman, S. W. (1991). Writing. In J. Flood, J. M. Jensen, D. Lapp, & J. R. Squire (Eds.), *Handbook of research on teaching the English language arts* (pp. 754–774). New York: Macmillan.

Dykstra, R. (1968). Summary of the second-grade phase of the cooperative research program in reading instruction. *Reading Research Quarterly, 4,* 49–70.

Edelsky, C. (1990). Whose agenda is this anyway? A response to McKenna, Robinson, & Miller. *Educational Researcher, 19,* 7–11.

Edwards, P. A. (1991). Fostering early literacy through parent coaching. In E. Hiebert (Ed.), *Literacy for a diverse society: Perspectives, practices, and policies* (pp. 199–213). New York: Teachers College Press.

Eeds, M., & Wells, D. (1989). Grand conversations: An explanation of meaning construction in literature study groups. *Research in the Teaching of English, 23,* 4–29.

Ehri, L. C. (1991). Development of the ability to read words. In R. Barr, M. Kamil, P. Mosenthal & P. D. Pearson (Eds.), *Handbook of reading research* (Vol. 2, pp. 383–417). New York: Longman.

El-Dinary, P. B., & Schuder, T. (1993). Seven teachers' acceptance of transactional strategies instruction during their first year using it. *Elementary School Journal, 94,* 207–219.

Ellwein, M. C., Walsh, D. J., Eads, G. M. I., & Miller, A. (1991). Using readiness tests to route kindergarten students: The snarled intersection of psychometrics, policy, and practice. *Educational Evaluation and Policy Analysis, 13,* 159–175.

Elson, W. H., & Gray, W. S. (1930). *Elson Basic Readers.* Chicago, IL: Scott, Foresman & Company.

Englert, C. S., & Raphael, T. E. (1989). Developing successful writers through cognitive strategy instruction. In C. Greenwich (Ed.), *Advances in research on teaching* (Vol. 1, pp. 105–151). Greenwich, CT: JAI Press.

Englert, C. S., Raphael, T. E., Anderson, L. M., Anthony, H. M., Fear,

K. L., & Gregg, S. L. (1988). A case for writing intervention: Strategies for writing informational text. *Learning Disabilities Focus, 3,* 98–113.

Englert, C. S., Raphael, T. E., Anderson, L. M., Anthony, H. M., & Stevens, D. D. (1991). Making writing strategies and self-talk visible: Cognitive strategy instruction in regular and special education classrooms. *American Educational Research Journal, 28,* 337–372.

Englert, C. S., Raphael, T. E., & Mariage, T. V. (1994). Developing a school-based discourse for literacy learning: A principled search for understanding. *Learning Disability Quarterly, 17,* 2–32.

English, H. B., & Welborn, E. L. (1937). Logical learning: A general review of experiments with meaningful verbal materials. *Psychological Bulletin, 34,* 1–20.

English, H. B., Welborn, E. L., & Killian, C. D. (1934). Studies in substance memorization. *Journal of General Psychology, 9,* 233–260.

Farr, R., & Beck, M. D. (1991). Formal methods of evaluation. In J. Flood, J. Jensen, D. Lapp, & J. Squire (Eds.), *Handbook of research on teaching the English language arts* (pp. 489–501). New York: Macmillan.

Farr, R., & Carey, R. F. (1986). *Reading: What can be measured?* Newark, DE: International Reading Association.

Farr, R., Strickland, D. S., Abrahamson, R. F., Booth-Church, E., Bowen-Coulter, B., Gallego, M. A., Irwin, J. L., Cutiper, K., Wokota, J., Ogle, D. M., Shanahan, T., & Smith, P. (1993). *Treasury of literature: Like a thousand diamonds* (Grade 3). Dallas, TX: Harcourt Brace Jovanovich.

Feitelson, D. (1988). *Facts and fads in beginning reading: A cross-language perspective.* Norwood, NJ: Ablex.

Feldman, M. (1985). Evaluating pre-primer basal readers using story grammar. *American Educational Research Journal, 22,* 527–547.

Fisher, C. W., Filby, N. N., Marliave, R. S., Cahen, L. S., Dishaw, M. M., Moore, J. E., & Berliner, D. C. (1978). Teaching behaviors, academic learning time, and student achievement. In *Beginning teacher evaluation study* (Tech. Rep. No. V-1). San Francisco: Far West Regional Laboratory.

Fisher, C. W., & Hiebert, E. H. (1990). Characteristics of tasks in two approaches to literacy instruction. *Elementary School Journal, 91,* 3–18.

Fitzgerald, J. (1989). Research on stories: Implications for teachers. In K. D. Muth (Ed.), *Children's comprehension of text* (pp. 2–36). Newark, DE: International Reading Association.

Fitzgerald, J. (1992). Reading and writing stories. In J. W. Irwin & M. A. Doyle (Eds.), *Reading/writing connections: Learning from research* (pp. 81–93). Newark, DE: International Reading Association.

Fitzgerald, J., & Teasley, A. (1986). Effects of instruction in narrative structure on children's writing. *Journal of Educational Psychology, 78,* 424–433.

Flavell, J. (1981). Cognitive monitoring. In W. P. Dickson (Ed.), *Children's oral communication skills* (pp. 35–60). New York: Academic Press.

Flavell, J. H. (1970). Developmental studies of mediated memory. In H. W. Reese & L. P. Lipsitt (Eds.), *Advances in child development and behavior* (Vol. 5, pp. 181–211). New York: Academic Press.

Flavell, J. H. (1979). Metacognition and cognitive monitoring: A new area of cognitive-developmental inquiry. *American Psychologist, 34,* 906–911.

Flesch, R. (1957). *Why Johnny can't read.* New York: Random House.

Flood, J., Jensen, J. M., Lapp, D., & Squire, J. R. (Eds.). (1991). *Handbook of research on teaching the English language arts.* New York: Macmillan.

Florio, S., & Clark, C. M. (1982). The functions of writing in an elementary classroom. *Research in the Teaching of English, 16,* 115–130.

Florio-Ruane, S. (1994). The future teachers' autobiography club: Preparing educators to support literacy learning in culturally diverse classrooms. *English Education, 26,* 52–66.

Flower, L. S., & Hayes, J. R. (1980). The dynamics of composing: Making plans and juggling constraints. In L. Gregg & E. Steinberg (Eds.), *Cognitive processes in writing* (pp. 31–50). Hillsdale, NJ: Lawrence Erlbaum Associates.

Flower, L. S., & Hayes, J. R. (1981). Problem-solving and the cognitive processes in writing. In C. Frederiksen & J. F. Dominic (Eds.), *Writing: The nature, development, and teaching of written communication* (pp. 39–58). Hillsdale, NJ: Lawrence Erlbaum Associates.

Frase, L. T., & Schwartz, B. J. (1975). The effect of question production and answering on prose recall. *Journal of Educational Psychology, 67,* 628–635.

Frederiksen, N. (1984). The real test bias: Influences of testing on teaching and learning. *American Psychologist, 39,* 193–202.

Freedman, S. W. (1983). Student characteristics and essay test writing performance. *Research in the Teaching of English, 17,* 313–325.

Freedman, S. W. (1993). Linking large-scale testing and classroom portfolio assessments of student writing. *Educational Assessment, 1,* 27–52.

Freeman, C. (1987). A study of the Degrees of Reading Power test. In R. Freedle & R. Duran (Eds.), *Cognitive and linguistic analyses of test performance* (pp. 245–297). Norwood, NJ: Ablex.

Fries, C. C. (1963). *Linguistics and reading.* New York: Holt, Rinehart & Winston.

Frith, U. (1985). Beneath the surface of developmental dyslexia. In K. E. Patterson, J. C. Marshall, & M. Coltheart (Eds.), *Surface dyslexia* (pp. 301–330). Hillsdale, NJ: Lawrence Erlbaum Associates.

Fry, E. B. (1968). A readability formula that saves time. *Journal of Reading, 11,* 513–516, 575–578.

Gaffney, J. S., & Anderson, R. C. (1991). Two-tiered scaffolding: Congruent processes of teaching and learning. In E. H. Hiebert (Ed.), *Literacy for a diverse society: Perspectives, practices, and policies* (pp. 184–198). New York: Teachers College Press.

Gagné, R. M. (1968). Learning hierarchies. *Educational Psychologist, 6,* 1–9.

Garcia, G. E. (1991). Factors influencing the English reading test performance of Spanish-speaking Hispanic students. *Reading Research Quarterly, 26,* 371–392.

Garcia, G. E., & Pearson, P. D. (1994). Assessment and diversity. In L. Darlington-Hammond (Ed.), *Review of Research in Education, 20,* 337–391. Washington, DC: American Educational Research Association.

Garner, R. (1987). *Metacognition and reading comprehension.* Norwood, NJ: Ablex.

Garner, R., & Alexander, P. A. (1989). Metacognition: Answered and unanswered questions. *Educational Psychologist, 24,* 143–158.

Garner, R., & Gillingham, M. G. (1987). Students' knowledge of text structure. *Journal of Reading Behavior, 19,* 247–259.

Gaskins, I. W., Downer, M. A., Anderson, R. C., Cunningham, P. M., Gaskins, R. W., Schommer, M., & the Teachers of Benchmark School (1988). A metacognitive approach to phonics: Using what you know to decode what you don't know. *Remedial and Special Education, 9,* 36–41, 66.

Gates, A. I. (1921). An experimental and statistical study of reading and reading tests [in three parts]. *Journal of Educational Psychology, 12,* 303–314, 378–391, 445–465.

Gavelek, J. R. (1992). *A sociocultural perspective in early literacy instruction: A theoretical framework.* Paper presented at the National Reading Conference, Palm Springs, CA.

Gavelek, J. R., & Raphael, T. E. (1985). Metacognition, instruction, and the role of questioning activities. In D. L. Forrest-Pressley, G. E. MacKinnon, & T. G. Waller (Eds.), *Metacognition, cognition, and human performance* (pp. 103–136). New York: Academic Press, Inc.

Gee, J. P. (1988). The legacies of literacy: From Plato to Freire through Harvey Graff. *Harvard Educational Review, 58,* 195–212.

General Accounting Office. (1993). *Student testing: Current extent and expenditures, with cost estimates for national examination.* Washington, DC: United States General Accounting Office, Program Evaluations and Methodology Division.

Gibson, E. J., & Levin, H. (1975). *The psychology of reading.* Cambridge, MA: The MIT Press.

Gipps, C. (1993, April). *Emerging models of teacher assessment in the classroom.* Paper presented at the annual meeting of the American Educational Research Association, Atlanta, GA.

Glaser, R. (1963). Instructional technology and the measurement of learning outcomes: Some questions. *American Psychologist, 18,* 519–521.

Glaser, R. (1966). *The program for Individually Prescribed Instruction.* Pittsburgh, PA: University of Pittsburgh, Learning Research and Development Center.

Glaser, R. (1971). A criterion-referenced test. In W. Popham (Ed.), *Criterion-referenced measurement: An introduction.* Englewood Cliffs, NJ: Educational Technology Publications.

Glaser, R. (1981). The future of testing: A research agenda for cognitive psychology and psychometrics. *American Psychologist, 36,* 923–936.

Glover, J. A., & Ronning, R. R. (1987). Introduction. In J. Glover & R. Ronning (Eds.), *Historical foundations of educational psychology* (pp. 5–15). New York: Plenum Press.

Goldenberg, C. N., Reese, L., & Gallimore, R. (1992). Effects of literacy materials from school on Latino children's home experiences and early reading achievement. *American Journal of Education, 100,* 497–536.

Goodman, K. S. (1968). The psycholinguistic nature of the reading process. In K. S. Goodman (Ed.), *The psycholinguistic nature of the reading process* (pp. 13–26). Detroit: Wayne State University.

Goodman, K. S. (1976). Reading: A psycholinguistic guessing game. In H. Singer & R. Ruddell (Eds.), *Theoretical models and processes in reading* (pp. 497–508). Newark, DE: International Reading Association.

Goodman, K.S. (1989). Whole-language research: Foundations and development. *Elementary School Journal, 90,* 207–222.

Goodman, K. S., & Goodman, Y. M. (1979). Learning to read is natural. In L. B. Resnick & P. A. Weaver (Eds.), *Theory and practice of early reading* (Vol. 1, pp. 137–154). Hillsdale, NJ: Lawrence Erlbaum Associates.

Goodman, K. S., Shannon, P., Freeman, Y., & Murphy, S. (1988). *Report card on basal readers.* Katonah, NY: Richard C. Owen.

Gordon, C. J. (1990). Contexts for expository text structure use. *Reading Research and Instruction, 29,* 55–72.

Gough, P. (1984). Word recognition. In P. D. Pearson, R. Barr, M. Kamil, & P. Mosenthal (Eds.), *Handbook of reading research* (Vol. 1, pp. 225–254). New York: Longman.

Gough, P. B. (1972). One second of reading. In J. F. Kavanagh & I. G. Mattingly (Eds.), *Language by ear and by eye* (pp. 331–365). Cambridge, MA: MIT Press.

Gough, P. B., & Hillinger, M. L. (1980). Learning to read: An unnatural act. *Bulletin of the Orton Society, 30,* 179–196.

Graesser, A., Golding, J. M., & Long, D. L. (1991). Narrative representation and comprehension. In R. Barr, M. Kamil, P. Mosenthal, & P. D. Pearson (Eds.), *Handbook of reading research* (Vol. 2, pp. 171–205). New York: Longman.

Graubard, S. (Ed.). (1991). *Literacy: An overview by fourteen experts.* New York: Farrar, Straus & Giroux.

Graves, M. F. (1986). Vocabulary learning and instruction. In E. Z. Rothkopf (Ed.), *Review of Research in Education, 13,* 91–128.

Gray, W. S. (1915). *Oral reading paragraph test.* Bloomington, IN: Public School Publishing.

Gray, W. S. (1920). The value of informal tests of reading accomplishment. *Journal of Educational Research, 1,* 103–111.

Gray, W. S. (1938). Contributions of research to special methods: Reading. In G. M. Whipple (Ed.), *The scientific movement in education* (37th yearbook of the National Society for the Study of Education, Part 1, pp. 99–106.) Bloomington, IN: Public School Publishing.

Gray, W. S., Arbuthnot, M. H., Artley, A. S., & Monroe, M. (1957). *The New Basic Readers.* Chicago, IL: Scott, Foresman & Company.

Gray, W. S., & Leary, B. E. (1935). *What makes a book readable?* Chicago: University of Chicago Press.

Green, G., & Davison, A. (Eds.). (1988). *Linguistic complexity and text comprehension: Readability issues reconsidered.* Hillsdale, NJ: Lawrence Erlbaum Associates.

Greenfield, P. M. (Ed.). (1984). *A theory of the teacher in the learning activities of everyday life.* Cambridge, MA: Harvard University Press.

Guthrie, J. T. (Ed.). (1984). *Reading—William S. Gray: A research retrospective, 1988–1941.* Newark, DE: International Reading Association.

Guthrie, J. T., Britten, T., & Barker, K. G. (1991). Role of document structure and metacognitive awareness in the cognitive process of searching for information. *Reading Research Quarterly, 26,* 300–324.

Guthrie, J. T., & Tyler, S. J. (1978). Cognition and instruction of poor readers. *Journal of Reading Behavior, 10,* 57–78.

Hairston, M. (1982). The winds of change: Thomas Kuhn and the revolution in the teaching of writing. *College Composition and Communication, 33,* 76–88.

Hall, G. S. (1894). The new psychology as a basis of education. *Forum, 17,* 710–720.

Harré, R. (1984). *Personal being: A theory for individual psychology.* Cambridge, MA: Harvard University Press.

Hawkins, D. (1991). The roots of literacy. In S. Graubard (Ed.), *Literacy: An overview by fourteen experts* (pp. 1–14). New York: Farrar, Straus & Giroux.

Haynes, M. C., & Jenkins, J. C. (1986). Reading instruction in special education resource rooms. *American Educational Research Journal, 23,* 161–190.

Heath, S. B. (1983). *Ways with words: Language, life, and work in communities and classrooms.* Cambridge, MA: Harvard University Press.

Heath, S. B. (1991). The sense of being literate: Historical and cross-cultural features. In R. Barr, M. Kamil, P. Mosenthal, & P. D. Pearson (Eds.), *Handbook of reading research* (Vol. 2, pp. 3–25). New York: Longman.

Henry, M. K. (1988). Beyond phonics: Integrated decoding and spelling instruction based on word origin and structure. *Annals of Dyslexia, 38,* 258–275.

Herman, P. A. (1985). The effect of repeated readings on reading rate, speech pauses, and word recognition accuracy. *Reading Research Quarterly, 20,* 553–564.

Hiebert, E. H. (1994, April). *Performing the tasks of third grade as a function of school context and an early intervention (George Graham Lecture).* Charlottesville, VA: University of Virginia.

Hiebert, E. H., & Almanza, E. (1993, May). *Extending an early literacy intervention to classroom contexts.* Paper presented at the annual meeting of the International Reading Association, San Antonio, TX.

Hiebert, E. H., Colt, J. M., Catto, S., & Gury, E. (1992). Reading and writing of first-grade students in a restructured Chapter 1 program. *American Educational Research Journal, 29,* 545–572.

Hiebert, E. H., & Shepard, L. A. (1994, August). *The treatment of text difficulty in large-scale assessments.* Paper presented at the annual meeting of the American Psychological Association, Los Angeles.

Hiebert, E. H., & Taylor, B. M. (Eds.) (1994). *Getting reading right from the start: Effective early literacy interventions.* Boston: Allyn & Bacon, Inc.

Hildreth, G. H. (1933). *A bibliography of mental tests and rating scales.* New York: Psychological Corporation.

Hill, K. T., & Wigfield, A. (1984). Test anxiety: A major educational problem and what can be done about it. *Elementary School Journal, 85,* 106–126.

Hoffman, J. V., McCarthey, S. J., Abbott, J., Christian, C., Corman, L., Curry, C., Dressman, M., Elliot, B., Matherne, D., & Stahle, D. (1994). So what's new in the "new" basals. *Journal of Reading Behavior, 26,* 47–73.

Hoover, H. D., Hieronyomus, A. N., Frisbie, D. A., & Dunbar, S. B. (1992). *Iowa Test of Basic Skills.* Chicago: Riverside.

Huey, E. B. (1968). *The psychology and pedagogy of reading.* Cambridge, MA: MIT Press. (Original work published 1908)

Hull, G. (1989). Research on writing: Building a cognitive and social understanding of composing. In L. B. Resnick & L. E. Klopfer (Eds.), *Toward the thinking curriculum: Current cognitive research* (pp. 104–128). Washington, DC: Association for Supervision and Curriculum Development.

Hunsaker, L., & Johnston, M. (1992). Teacher under construction: A collaborative case study of teacher change. *American Educational Research Journal, 29,* 350–372.

Huot, B. (1990). The literature of direct writing assessment: Major concerns and prevailing trends. *Review of Educational Research, 60,* 237–263.

International Reading Association. (1981). Resolution on grade equivalents. *Reading Research Quarterly, 16,* 615.

Irwin, J. W., & Doyle, M. A. (Eds.). (1992). *Reading/writing connections: Learning from research.* Newark, DE: International Reading Association.

Johnston, P., & Allington, R. L. (1991). Remediation. In R. Barr, M. Kamil, P. Mosenthal, & P. D. Pearson (Eds.), *Handbook of reading research* (Vol. 2, pp. 984–1012). New York: Longman.

Johnston, P., Weiss, P., & Afflerbach, P. (1990). *Teachers' evaluations of teaching and learning in literacy and literature* (Tech. Rep. No. 3.4). Albany: SUNY–Albany, Center for the Study of Literature.

Johnston, P. H. (1984). Assessment in reading. In P. D. Pearson, R. Barr, M. Kamil, & P. Mosenthal (Eds.). *Handbook of reading research* (Vol. 1, pp. 147–184). New York: Longman.

Juel, C. (1988). Learning to read and write: A longitudinal study of fifty-four children from first through fourth grades. *Journal of Educational Psychology, 80,* 437–447.

Juel, C. (1991). Beginning reading. In R. Barr, M. Kamil, P. Mosenthal, & P. D. Pearson (Eds.), *Handbook of reading research* (Vol. 2, pp. 759–788). New York: Longman.

Juel, C., Griffith, P. L., & Gough, P. B. (1986). The acquisition of literacy: A longitudinal study of children in first and second grade. *Journal of Educational Psychology, 78,* 243–255.

Just, M. A., & Carpenter, P. A. (1987). *The psychology of reading and language comprehension.* Boston, MA: Allyn & Bacon.

Kaestle, C. F., Damon-Moore, H., Stedman, L. C., Tinsley, K., & Trollinger, W. V., Jr. (1991). *Literacy in the United States: Readers and reading since 1880.* New Haven: Yale University Press.

Kapinus, B. A., Collier, G. V., & Kruglanski, H. (1994). The Maryland School Performance Assessment Program: A new view of assessment. In S. Valencia, E. Hiebert, & P. Afflerbach (Eds.), *Authentic reading assessment: Practices and possibilities* (pp. 255–276). Newark, DE: International Reading Association.

Kennedy, M. M., Birman, B. F., & Demaline, R. E. (1986). *The effectiveness of Chapter 1 services.* Washington, DC: Office of Educational Research & Improvement, U.S. Department of Education.

Kintsch, W., & van Dijk, T. (1978). Toward a model of text comprehension and production. *Psychological Review, 85,* 363–394.

Kirsch, I. S., & Jungeblut, A. (1986). *Literacy: Profiles of America's young adults.* Princeton, NJ: Educational Testing Service.

Klare, G. (1984). Readability. In P. D. Pearson, R. Barr, M. Kamil, & P. Mosenthal (Eds.), *Handbook of reading research* (Vol. 1, pp. 681–744.). New York: Longman.

Knapp, M. S., Shields, P. M., & Turnbull, B. J. (1992). *Academic challenge for the children of poverty: Summary report.* Menlo Park, CA: SRI International.

Koretz, D., Stecher, B., Klein, S., McCaffrey, D., & Deibert, E. (1993). Can portfolios assess student performance and influence instruction? The 1991–92 Vermont experience (CSE Tech. Rep. No. 371). Los Angeles, CA: National Center for Research on Evaluation, Standards, & Student Testing, University of California, Los Angeles.

Kratochwill, T., & Bijou, S. (1987). The impact of behaviorism on educational psychology. In J. Glover & R. Ronning (Eds.), *Historical foundations of educational psychology* (pp. 131–158). New York: Plenum Press.

Kuhn, T. S. (1962). *The structure of scientific revolutions.* Chicago: University of Chicago Press.

LaBerge, D., & Samuels, S. (1974). Toward a theory of automatic information processing in reading. *Cognitive Psychology, 6,* 293–323.

Langer, J. (1985). Levels of questioning: An alternative view. *Reading Research Quarterly, 20,* 586–602.

Langer, J. (1987). The construction of meaning and the assessment of comprehension: An analysis of reader performance on standardized test items. In R. Freedle & R. Duran (Eds.), *Cognitive and linguistic analyses of test performance* (pp. 225–244). Norwood, NJ: Ablex.

Lavine, L. (1977). Differentiation of letterlike forms in prereading children. *Developmental Psychology, 13,* 89–94.

Leal, D. J. (1992). The nature of talk about three types of text during peer group discussions. *Journal of Reading Behavior, 24,* 313–338.

Leinhardt, G., Zigmond, N., & Cooley, W. (1981). Reading instruction and its effects. *American Educational Research Journal, 18,* 343–361.

Lensmire, T. (1994). *When children write: Critical re-visions of the writing workshop.* New York: Teachers College Press.

Lesgold, A. M., Resnick, L. B., & Hammond, L. (1985). Learning to read: A longitudinal study of work skill development in two curricula. In G. MacKinnon & T. Waller (Eds.), *Reading research advances in theory and practice* (pp. 107–137). Orlando, FL: Academic Press.

Lesgold, A. M., & Perfetti, C. (1981). *Interactive processes in reading.* Hillsdale, NJ: Lawrence Erlbaum Associates.

Levin, J. (1992). Editorial. *Journal of Educational Psychology, 85,* 3–5.

Lie, A. (1991). Effects of a training program for stimulating skills in word analysis in first-grade children. *Reading Research Quarterly, 26,* 234–250.

Linn, R., Graue, M., & Sanders, N. (1990). Comparing state and district test results to national norms: The validity of claims that 'Everyone is above average.' *Educational Measurement, 9,* 5–14.

Linn, R., Baker, E., & Dunbar, S. (1991). Complex, performance-based assessment: Expectations and validation criteria. *Educational Researcher, 20,* 15–21.

Lipson, M. Y. (1983). The influence of religious affiliation on children's memory for text information. *Reading Research Quarterly, 18,* 448–457.

Lively, B., & Pressey, S. (1923). A method for measuring the "vocabulary burden" of textbooks. *Educational Administration and Supervision, 9,* 389–398.

Lohnes, P. R., & Gray, M. M. (1972). Intelligence and the cooperative reading studies. *Reading Research Quarterly, 7,* 466–476.

Lundberg, I., Frost, J., & Peterson, P. (1988). Effects of an extensive program for stimulating phonological awareness in preschool children. *Reading Research Quarterly, 23,* 263–284.

Mager, R. (1962). *Preparing instructional objectives.* Belmont, CA: Pitman Learning.

MacKinnon, A. (1959). *How do children learn to read?* Vancouver, BC: Copp Clark.

Mandler, J., & Johnson, N. (1977). Remembrance of things parsed: Story structure and recall. *Cognitive Psychology, 9,* 111–151.

Martin, B., Jr. (1967). *Brown bear, brown bear, what do you see?* New York: Holt, Rinehart & Winston.

Martinez, M., Cheyney, M., McBroom, C., Hemmeter, A., & Teale, W. (1989). No-risk kindergarten literacy environments for at-risk children. In J. Allen & J. Mason (Eds.), *Risk-makers, risk takers, risk breakers: Reducing the risks for young literacy learners* (pp. 93–124). Portsmouth, NH: Heinemann.

Mason, J. M. (1984). Early reading from a developmental perspective. In P. D. Pearson, R. Barr, M. Kamil, & P. Mosenthal (Eds.), *Handbook of reading research* (Vol. 1, pp. 505–543). New York: Longman.

McCarthey, S. (1994). Opportunities and risks of writing from personal experience. *Language Arts, 71,* 182–191.

McCormick, C., & Mason, J. (1989). Fostering reading for Head Start children with little books. In J. Allen & J. Mason (Eds.), *Risk makers, risk takers, risk breakers: Reducing the risks for young literacy learners* (pp. 154–177). Portsmouth, NH: Heinemann.

McGee, L. M. (1982). Awareness of text structure: Effects of children's recall of expository text. *Reading Research Quarterly, 17,* 581–590.

McGee, L. M. (1992). An exploration of meaning construction in first graders' grand conversations. In C. K. Kinzer & D. J. Leu (Eds.), *Literacy research, theory, and practice: Views from many perspectives* (pp. 177–186). Chicago: National Reading Conference.

McGee, L. M., & Lomax, R. G. (1990). On combining apples and oranges: A response to Stahl and Miller. *Review of Educational Research, 60,* 133–140.

McGill-Franzen, A. (1993). Literacy for all children. *Reading Teacher, 46,* 424–427.

McGill-Franzen, A., & Allington, R. (1993). Flunk 'em or get them classified: The contamination of primary grade accountability data. *Educational Researcher, 22,* 19–22.

McKenna, M. C., Stahl, S. A., & Reinking, D. (1994). Critical issues: A critical commentary on research, politics, and whole language. *Journal of Reading Behavior, 26,* 211–233.

McMahon, S. I. (1994). Student-led book clubs: Traversing a river of interpretation. *New Advocate, 7,* 109–125.

McMahon, S. I., Pardo, L. S., & Raphael, T. E. (1991). Bart: A case study of discourse about text. In S. McCormick & J. Zutell (Eds.), *Learner factors/teacher factors: Issues in literary research and instruction* (pp. 285–295). Chicago: National Reading Conference.

McMahon, S. I., Raphael, T. E., & Goatley, V. J. (1995). Changing the context for classroom reading instruction: The Book Club project. In J. Brophy (Ed.), *Advances in Research on Teaching* (pp. 123–166). Greenwich, CT: JAI Press.

Mehrens, W. A., & Kaminski, J. (1989). Methods for improving standardized test scores: Fruitful, fruitless, or fraudulent? *Educational Measurement: Issues and Practices, 8,* 14–22.

Mercer, J. (1989). Alternative paradigms for assessment in a pluralistic society. In J. Banks & C. Banks (Eds.), *Multicultural education: Issues and perspectives* (pp. 289–304). Boston: Allyn & Bacon.

Merritt, J. (1986). What's wrong with teaching reading. In A. Cashdan (Ed.), *Literacy: Teaching and learning language skills* (pp. 180–192). Oxford, England: Basil Blackwell.

Meyer, B. J. F. (1975). *The organization of prose and its effect on memory.* Amsterdam: North-Holland.

Meyer, B. J. F., & Rice, G. E. (1984). The structure of text. In P. D. Pearson, R. Barr, M. Kamil, & P. Mosenthal (Eds.), *Handbook of reading research* (Vol. 1, pp. 319–352). New York: Longman.

Michaels, S., & O'Connor, M. (1990). Literacy as reasoning within multiple discourses: Implications for policy and education reform. Paper presented at the Summer Institute of the Council of Chief State School Officers, Newton, MA.

Miles, M. (1971). *Annie and the old one.* Boston: Little, Brown.

Moffett, J., & Wagner, B. J. (1983). *Student-centered language arts and reading, K-13* (3rd ed). Boston: Houghton Mifflin.

Moll, L. (Ed.). (1991). *Vygotsky and education.* New York: Cambridge University Press.

Moll, L., Amanti, C., Neff, D., & Gonzalez, N. (1992). Funds of knowledge for teaching: Using a qualitative approach to connect homes and classrooms. *Theory into Practice, 31,* 132–141.

Moll, L., Tapia, J., & Whitmore, K. (1993). Living knowledge: The social distribution of cultural resources for thinking. In G. Salomon (Ed.),

*Distributed cognitions: Psychological and educational considerations* (pp. 139–163). Cambridge, England: Cambridge University Press.

Moore, A. C. (1935). Recoiling from reading: A consideration of the Thorndike Library. *Library Journal, 60,* 419–422.

Morphett, M. V., & Washburne, C. (1931). When should children begin to read? *Elementary School Journal, 31,* 496–503.

Mosenthal, P., & Na, T. J. (1980). Quality of children's recall under two classroom testing tasks: Towards a socio-psycholinguistic model of reading comprehension. *Reading Research Quarterly, 15,* 504–528.

Mullis, I. V. S., Campbell, J. R., & Farstrup, A. E. (1993). *NAEP 1992 reading report card for the nation and the states.* Washington, DC: U.S. Government Printing Office.

Nagy, W. E., Anderson, R. C., Schommer, M., Scott, J. A., & Stallman, A. C. (1989). Morphological families and word recognition. *Reading Research Quarterly, 24,* 262–282.

Nagy, W. E., Garcia, G. E., Durgunoğlu, A. Y., & Hancin-Bhatt, B. (1993). Spanish-English bilingual students' use of cognates in English reading. *Journal of Reading Behavior, 25,* 241–260.

National Education Association. (1992). *Status of the America Public School Teacher, 1990–1991.* Washington, DC: National Education Association.

National Society for the Study of Education. (1925). *Report of the National Committee on Reading* (24th yearbook of the National Society for the Study of Education). Bloomington, IN: Public School Publishing.

Nystrand, M. (1989). A social-interactive model of writing. *Written Communication, 6,* 66–85.

O'Connor, M. (1989). Aspects of differential performance by minorities on standardized tests: Linguistic and sociocultural factors. In B. Gifford (Ed.), *Test policy and test performance: Education, language, and culture* (pp. 129–181). Boston: Kluwer Academic.

O'Flahavan, J. O. (1989). *Second graders' social, intellectual, and affective development in varied group discussions about narrative texts: An explanation of participation structures.* Unpublished doctoral dissertation, University of Illinois, Urbana-Champaign.

Osborn, J. (1984). The purposes, uses and content of workbooks and some guidelines for publishers. In R. Anderson, J. Osborn, & R. Tierney (Eds.), *Learning to read in American schools* (pp. 45–112), Hillsdale, NJ: Lawrence Erlbaum Associates.

Otto, W. (1977). *Wisconsin Design for Reading Skill Development*, Minneapolis: National Computer Systems.

Owen, V., & Shanahan, T. (1993, April). *Validating success: A three-year evaluation of the children's literacy gains.* Paper presented at the annual meeting of the American Educational Research Association, Atlanta, GA.

Palincsar, A. S., & Brown, A. L. (1984). Reciprocal teaching of comprehension-fostering and comprehension-monitoring activities. *Cognition and Instruction, 1,* 117–175.

Paris, S. G., Lipson, M. Y., & Wixson, K. K. (1983). Becoming a strategic reader. *Contemporary Educational Psychology, 8,* 293–316.

Paris, S. G., & Oka, E. R. (1986). Children's reading strategies, metacognition, and motivation. *Developmental Review, 6,* 25–56.

Paris, S. G., Wasik, B. A., & Turner, J. C. (1991). The development of strategic readers. In R. Barr, M. Kamil, P. Mosenthal, & P. D. Pearson (Eds.), *Handbook of reading research.* (Vol. 2, pp. 609–640). New York: Longman.

Pearson, P. D. (1993a). Standards for the English Language Arts: A policy perspective. *Journal of Reading Behavior, 25,* 457–476.

Pearson, P. D. (1993b). Teaching and learning reading: A research perspective. *Language Arts, 70,* 502–511.

Pearson, P. D., Barr, R., Kamil, M., & Mosenthal, P. (Eds.). (1984). *Handbook of reading research* (Vol. 1). New York: Longman.

Pearson, P. D., & Fielding, L. (1991). Comprehension instruction. In R. Barr, M. Kamil, P. Mosenthal, & P. D. Pearson (Eds.), *Handbook of reading research* (Vol. 2, pp. 815–860), New York: Longman.

Pearson, P. D., & Gallagher, M. C. (1983). The instruction of reading comprehension. *Contemporary Educational Psychology, 8,* 317–344.

Pearson, P. D., Hansen, J., & Gordon, C. (1979). The effect of background knowledge on young children's comprehension of explicit and implicit information. *Journal of Reading Behavior, 11,* 201–210.

Pearson, P. D., Johnson, D. D., Clymer, T., Indrisano, R., Venezky, R. L., Baumann, J.F., Hiebert, E. H., Toth, M., Grant, C., & Paratore, J. R. (1989). *All through the town.* Needham, MA: Silver Burdett & Ginn.

Pearson, P. D., & Valencia, S. (1987). Assessment, accountability, and professional prerogative. In J. Readence & R. Baldwin (Eds.), *Research in literacy: Merging perspectives* (pp. 3–16). Rochester, NY: National Reading Conference.

Perfetti, C. A., Beck, I. L., Bell, L. C., & Hughes, C. (1987). Phonemic knowledge and learning to read are reciprocal: A longitudinal study of first-grade children. *Merrill-Palmer Quarterly, 33,* 283–319.

Piaget, J. (1959). *The language and thought of the child* (3rd ed.). London: Routledge & Kegan Paul.

Popham, W. (1978). *Criterion-referenced measurement.* Englewood Cliffs, NJ: Prentice Hall.

Popham, W. (1987). The merits of measurement-driven instruction. *Phi Delta Kappan, 68,* 679–682.

Poplin, M. S. (1988). Holistic-constructivist principles: Implications for the field of learning disabilities. *Journal of Learning Disabilities,* 401–416.

Powell, J. (1988). *An examination of comprehension processes used by readers as they engage in different forms of assessment.* Unpublished doctoral dissertation, Bloomington, IN: Indiana University.

Pressley, M., & El-Dinary, P. B. (1993). Introduction. *Elementary School Journal, 94,* 105–108.

Pressley, M., Goodchild, F., Fleet, J., Zajchowski, R., & Evans, E. D. (1989). The challenges of classroom strategy instruction. *Elementary School Journal, 89,* 301–342.

Pressley, M., Schuder, T., SAIL Faculty & Administration, German, J., & El-Dinary, P. B. (1992). A researcher-educator collaborative interview study of transactional comprehension strategies instruction. *Journal of Educational Psychology, 84,* 231–246.

Purves, A. (1992). Reflections on research and assessment in written composition. *Research in the Teaching of English, 26,* 108–122.

Quellmalz, E. S. (1985). Needed: Better methods for testing higher-order thinking skills. *Educational Leadership, 43,* 29–35.

Raphael, T. E., Englert, C. S., & Kirschner, B. W. (1989). Students' metacognitive knowledge about writing. *Research in the Teaching of English, 23,* 343–379.

Raphael, T. E., McMahon, S., Goatley, V., Bentley, J. L., Boyd, F. B., Pardo, L. S., & Woodman, D. A. (1992). Research directions: Literature and discussion in the reading program. *Language Arts, 69,* 55–61.

Rashotte, C. A., & Torgensen, J. K. (1985). Repeated reading and reading fluency in learning disabled children. *Reading Research Quarterly, 20,* 180–188.

Read, C. (1975). *Children's categorization of speech sounds in English.* Urbana, IL: National Council of Teachers of English.

Reed, H. B. (1992). Meaning as a factor in learning. *Journal of Educational Psychology, 84,* 395–399. (Originally printed, *29,* 419–430).

Resnick, D. P. (1982). History of educational testing. In A. Wigdor & W. Garner (Eds.), *Ability testing: Uses, consequences and controversies* (pp. 173–194). Washington, DC: National Academy of Education.

Resnick, L. B. (1981). Social assumptions as a context for science: Some reflections on psychology and education. *Educational Psychologist, 16,* 1–10.

Resnick, L. B. (1987). Learning in school and out. *Educational Researcher, 16,* 13–20.

Resnick, L. B., & Resnick, D. P. (1992). Assessing the thinking curriculum: New tools for educational reform. In B. Gifford & M. O'Connor (Eds.), *Future assessments: Changing views of aptitude, achievement, and instruction* (pp. 37–75). Boston: Kluwer.

Resnick, L. B., Wang, M. C., & Kaplan, J. (1973). Task analysis in curriculum design: A hierarchically sequenced introductory mathematics curriculum. *Journal of Applied Behavior Analysis, 6,* 679–710.

Reutzel, D. R., Hollingsworth, P. M., & Eldredge, J. L. (1994). Oral reading instruction: The impact on student reading development. *Reading Research Quarterly, 29,* 41–62.

Reynolds, R. E., Standiford, S. N., & Anderson, R. C. (1978). *Distribution of reading time when questions are asked about a restricted category of text information* (Tech. Rep. No. 83). Urbana, IL: University of Illinois, Center for the Study of Reading.

Reynolds, R. E., Taylor, M. A., Steffensen, M. S., Shirey, L. L., & Anderson, R. C. (1982). Cultural schemata and reading comprehension. *Reading Research Quarterly, 17,* 353–366.

Richardson, V. (1994). Conducting research on practice. *Educational Researcher, 23,* 5–10.

Richardson, V., Anders, P., Tidwell, D., & Lloyd, C. (1991). The relationship between teachers' beliefs and practices in reading comprehension instruction. *American Educational Research Journal, 28,* 559–586.

Richgels, D. J., McGee, L. M., Lomax, R. G., & Sheard, C. (1987). Awareness of four text structures: Effects on recall of expository text. *Reading Research Quarterly, 22,* 177–196.

Rogers, T. (1991). Students are literary critics: The interpretive experiences, beliefs, and processes of ninth-grade students. *Journal of Reading Behavior, 23,* 391–424.

Rogoff, B. (1990). *Apprenticeship in thinking: Cognitive development in social context.* New York: Oxford University Press.

Rogoff, R., & Gardner, W. (1984). Adult guides of cognitive development. In B. Rogoff & J. Love (Eds.), *Everyday cognition* (pp. 95–116). Cambridge, MA: Harvard University Press.

Roller, C. M. (1990). The interaction of knowledge and structure variables in the processing of expository prose. *Reading Research Quarterly, 25,* 79–89.

Rosenblatt, L. M. (1978). *The reader, the text, and the poem: The transactional theory of the literacy work.* Carbondale, IL: Southern Illinois University Press.

Rothkopf, E. Z. (1965). Some theoretical and experimental approaches to problems in written instruction. In J. D. Krumboltz (Ed.), *Learning and the educational process* (pp. 193–221). Chicago: Rand-McNally.

Rothkopf, E. Z. (1966). Learning from written instructive materials: An exploration of the control of inspection behavior by test-like events. *American Educational Research Journal, 3,* 241–249.

Rothkopf, E. Z., & Bisbicos, E. E. (1967). Selective facilitative effects of interspersed questions on learning from written materials. *Journal of Educational Psychology, 58,* 56–61.

Rowe, D., & Rayford, L. (1987). Activating background knowledge in reading comprehension assessment. *Reading Research Quarterly, 2,* 160–176.

Royer, J. M., & Cunningham, D. J. (1981). On the theory and measurement of reading comprehension. *Contemporary Educational Psychology, 6,* 187–216.

Ruddell, R. B., Ruddell, M. R., & Singer, H. (Eds.). (1994). *Theoretical models and processes of reading* (4th ed). Newark, DE: International Reading Association.

Rueda, R. (1991). Characteristics of literacy programs for language-minority students. In E. H. Hiebert (Ed.), *Literacy for a diverse society: Perspectives, practices, and policies* (pp. 93–107). New York: Teachers College Press.

Rueda, R., & Garcia, E. (1992). *A comparative study of teachers' beliefs about reading assessment with Latino language minority students* (Technical Report). Santa Cruz, CA: National Center for Cultural Diversity and Second Language Learning, University of California–Santa Cruz.

Rumelhart, D. E. (1977). Toward an interactive model of reading. In S. Dornic (Ed.), *Attention and performance VI* (pp. 573–603). Hillsdale, NJ: Lawrence Erlbaum Associates.

Samuels, S. J., & LaBerge, D. (1983). A critique of a theory of automaticity in reading: Looking back. In L. Gentile, M. Kamil, & J. Blanchard (Eds.), *Reading research revisited* (pp. 39–55). Columbus, OH: Merrill.

Sawyer, D. J. (1992). Language abilities, reading acquisition, and developmental dyslexia: A discussion of hypothetical and observed relationships. *Journal of Learning Disabilities, 25,* 82–95.

Scardamalia, M. (1981). How children cope with the cognitive demands of writing. In C. H. Frederiksen, M. S. Whiteman, & J. T. Dominic (Eds.), *Writing: The nature, development, and teaching of written communication* (Vol. 1, pp. 81–103). Hillsdale, NJ: Lawrence Erlbaum Associates.

Scardamalia, M., & Bereiter, C. (1985). Fostering the development of self-regulation in children's knowledge processing. In S. S. Chipman, J. W. Segal, & R. Glaser (Eds.), *Thinking and learning skills: Current research and open questions* (Vol. 2, pp. 563–577). Hillsdale, NJ: Lawrence Erlbaum Associates.

Scardamalia, M., & Bereiter, C. (1986). Research on written composition. In M. C. Wittrock (Ed.), *Handbook of research on teaching* (3rd ed., pp. 778–803). New York: Macmillan.

Schafer, W. D., & Lissitz, R. W. (1987). Measurement training for school personnel: Recommendations and reality. *Journal of Teacher Education, 38,* 57–63.

Schuder, T. (1993). The genesis of transactional strategies instruction in a reading program for at-risk students. *Elementary School Journal, 94,* 183–200.

Scribner, S. (1984). Literacy in three metaphors. *American Journal of Education, 93,* 7–22.

Scribner, S., & Cole, M. (1981). *The psychology of literacy.* Cambridge, MA: Harvard University Press.

Shanahan, T., & Rodriguez-Brown, F. V. (1993, April). *Project FLAME: The theory and structure of a family literacy program for the Latino community.* Paper presented at the annual meeting of the American Educational Research Association, Atlanta, GA.

Shannon, P. (1989). *Broken promises: Reading instruction in twentieth-century America.* Granby, MA: Bergin & Garvey.

Shaughnessy, M. (1977). *Errors and expectations.* New York: Oxford University Press.

Shepard, L. A. (1991). Psychometricians' beliefs about learning. *Educational Researcher, 20,* 2–9.

Shepard, L. A. (1993). Evaluating test validity. In L. Darling-Hammond (Ed.), *Review of Research in Education* (pp. 405–450). Washington, DC: American Educational Research Association.

Shepard, L. A., & Graue, M. E. (1992). The morass of school readiness screening: Research on test use and test validity. In B. Spodek (Ed.), *Handbook of research on the education of young children* (pp. 293–305). New York: Macmillan.

Simmons, W., & Resnick, L. B. (1993). Assessment as the catalyst of school reform. *Educational Leadership, 50,* 11–15.

Skinner, B. F. (1954). The science of learning and the art of teaching. *Harvard Educational Review, 24,* 86–97.

Skinner, B. F. (1965). Reflections on a decade of teaching machines. In R. Glaser (Ed.), *Teaching machines and programmed learning: II. Data and directions* (pp. 5–20). Washington, DC: National Education Association.

Slater, W. H., & Graves, M. F. (1989). Research on expository text: Implications for teachers. In K. D. Muth (Ed.), *Children's comprehension of text* (pp. 140–166). Newark, DE: International Reading Association.

Slavin, R. E. (1987). Ability grouping: A best-evidence synthesis. *Review of Educational Research, 57,* 293–336.

Smith, F. (1982). *Understanding reading: A psycholinguistic analysis of reading and learning to read.* New York: Holt, Rinehart and Winston.

Smith, M. L. (1991). Put to the test: The effects of external testing on teachers. *Educational Researcher, 20,* 8–11.

Smith, N. B. (1965). *American reading instruction.* Newark, DE: International Reading Association. (Original work published 1934)

Snider, M. A., Lima, S. S., & DeVito, P. J. (1994). Rhode Island's literacy portfolio assessment project. In S. W. Valencia, E. H. Hiebert & P. P. Afflerbach (Eds.), *Authentic reading assessment: Practices and possibilities* (pp. 71–88). Newark, DE: International Reading Association.

Spache, G. (1964). *Reading in the elementary school.* Boston: Allyn & Bacon.

Stahl, S. A., & Miller, P. D. (1989). Whole language and language experience approaches for beginning reading: A quantitative research synthesis. *Review of Educational Research, 59,* 87–116.

Stallings, J. (1975). Implementation and child effects of teaching practices in Follow Through classrooms. *Monographs of the Society for Research in Child Development, 40*(7–8).

Stallman, A. C., & Pearson, P. D. (1990). Formal measures of early literacy. In L. Morrow & J. Smith (Eds.), *Assessment for instruction in early literacy* (pp. 7–44). Englewood Cliffs, NJ: Prentice Hall.

Stanovich, K. E. (1990). A call for an end to the paradigm wars in reading research. *Journal for Reading Behavior, 22,* 221–232.

Stanovich, K. E. (1991). Word recognition: Changing perspectives. In R. Barr, M. Kamil, P. Mosenthal, & P. D. Pearson (Eds.), *Handbook of reading research* (Vol. 2, pp. 418–452). New York: Longman.

Stanovich, K. E. (1994). Romance and reality. *Reading Teacher, 47,* 280–291.

Stein, N. L., & Glenn, C. G. (1979). An analysis of story comprehension in elementary children. In R. Freedle (Ed.), *New directions in discourse processing* (Vol. 2, pp. 53–120). Norwood, NJ: Ablex.

Stein, N. L., & Trabasso, T. (1982). What's in a story: An approach to comprehension and instruction. In R. Glaser (Ed.), *Advances in the psychology of instruction* (Vol. 2, pp. 213–267). Hillsdale, NJ: Lawrence Erlbaum Associates.

Stiggins, R. J., Conklin, N. F., & Bridgeford, N. J. (1986). Classroom assessment: A key to effective education. *Educational Measurement: Issues and Practice, 5,* 5–17.

Sulzby, E., & Teale, W. H. (1991). Emergent literacy. In R. Barr, M. Kamil, P. Mosenthal, & P. D. Pearson (Eds.), *Handbook of reading research* (Vol. 2, pp. 727–757). New York: Longman.

Swales, J. M. (1990). *Genre analysis: English in academic and research settings.* Cambridge, England: Cambridge University Press.

Taylor, B., Frye, B., & Gaetz, T. (1990). Reducing the number of reading skill activities in the elementary classroom. *Journal of Reading Behavior, 22,* 167–180.

Taylor, B. M., & Beach, R. W. (1984). Effects of text structure instruction on middle grade students' comprehension and production of expository text. *Reading Research Quarterly, 19,* 134–146.

Taylor, B. M., Strait, J., & Medo, M. (1994). Early intervention in reading: Supplemental instruction for groups for low-achieving students provided by first-grade teachers. In E. Hiebert & B. Taylor (Eds.), *Getting reading right from the start: Effective early literacy interventions* (pp. 107–121). Boston: Allyn & Bacon.

Teale, W. H., & Sulzby, E. (Eds.). (1986). *Emergent literacy: Writing and reading.* Norwood, NJ: Ablex.

Texas Education Agency. (1990). *Proclamation of the state board of education: Advertising for bids on textbooks.* Austin: Texas State Department of Education.

Texas Education Agency. (1994). *Texas Assessment of Academic Skills.* Austin: Texas State Department of Education.

Thornburg, D. G. (1993). Intergenerational literacy with bilingual families: A context for the analysis of social mediation of thought. *Journal of Reading Behavior, 25,* 323–352.

Thorndike, E. L. (1903). *Educational psychology*. New York: Lemcke & Buechner.

Thorndike, E. L. (1906). *The principles of teaching based on psychology*. New York: A. G. Seiler.

Thorndike, E. L. (1910). *Handwriting*. New York: Columbia University Press.

Thorndike, E. L. (1917). Reading as reasoning: A study of mistakes in paragraph reading. *Journal of Educational Psychology, 8,* 323–332.

Thorndike, E. L. (1918). The nature, purposes, and general method of measurements of educational products. In S. Courtis (Ed.), *The measurement of educational products* (17th yearbook of the National Society for the Study of Education, Part 2, pp. 16–24). Bloomington, IL: Public School Publishing.

Thorndike, E. L. (1921). *The teacher's word book*. New York: Columbia University Press.

Tierney, R. J., & Shanahan, T. (1991). Research on the reading-writing relationship: Interactions, transactions, and outcomes. In R. Barr, M. Kamil, P. Mosenthal, & P. D. Pearson (Eds.), *Handbook of reading research* (Vol. 2, pp. 246–280). New York: Longman.

Tindal, G., Fuchs, L. S., Fuchs, D., Shinn, M. R., Deno, S. L., & Germann, G. (1985). Empirical validation of criterion-referenced tests. *Journal of Educational Research, 78,* 203–209.

Uhry, J. K., & Shepherd, M. J. (1993). Segmentation/spelling instruction as part of a first-grade reading program: Effects on several measures of reading. *Reading Research Quarterly, 28,* 218–233.

Valencia, S. W., Hiebert, E. H., & Afflerbach, P. P. (Eds.). (1994). *Authentic reading assessment: Practices and possibilities*. Newark, DE: International Reading Association.

Valencia, S. W., & Place, N. A. (1994). Literacy portfolios for teaching, learning, and accountability: The Bellevue Literacy assessment project. In S. W. Valencia, E. H. Hiebert, & P. P. Afflerbach (Eds.), *Authentic reading assessment: Practices and possibilities* (pp. 134–156). Newark, DE: International Reading Association.

Venezky, R. L. (1974). *Testing in reading: Assessment and instructional decision making*. Urbana, IL: National Council of Teachers of English.

Venezky, R. L. (1984). The history of reading research. In P. D. Pearson, R. Barr, M. Kamil, & P. Mosenthal (Eds.), *Handbook of reading research* (Vol. 1, pp. 3–39). New York: Longman.

Venezky, R. L. (1987). A history of the American reading textbook. *Elementary School Journal, 87,* 247–265.

Venezky, R. L. (1991). The development of literacy in the industrialized nations of the west. In R. Barr, M. L. Kamil, P. B. Mosenthal, & P. D. Pearson (Eds.), *Handbook of reading research* (Vol. 2, pp. 46–67). New York: Longman.

Vygotsky, L. S. (1962). *Thought and language*. Cambridge, MA: MIT Press.

Vygotsky, L. S. (1978). *Mind in society: The development of higher psychological processes*. Cambridge, MA: Harvard University Press.

Vygotsky, L. S. (1987). Speech and thinking (N. Minick, Trans.). In R. Rieber & A. Carton (Eds.), *The collected works of L. S. Vygotsky* (Vol. 1, pp. 39–285). New York: Plenum Press.

Walberg, H. J., & Haertel, G. D. (1992). Educational psychology's first century. *Journal of Educational Psychology, 84,* 6–19.

Watson, J. B. (1919). *Psychology from the standpoint of a behaviorist*. Philadelphia: Lippincott.

Weaver, C. A. I., & Kintsch, W. (1991). Expository text. In R. Barr, M. Kamil, P. Mosenthal, & P. D. Pearson (Eds.), *Handbook of reading research* (Vol. 2, pp. 230–245). New York: Longman.

Weiss, B. (1994). California's new English-language arts assessment. In S. Valencia, E. Hiebert, & P. Afflerbach (Eds.), *Authentic reading assessment: Practices and possibilities* (pp. 197–217). Newark, DE: International Reading Association.

Wells, G. (1990). Talk about text: Where literacy is learned and taught. *Curriculum Inquiry, 20,* 369–405.

Wertsch, J. V. (1984). The zone of proximal development: Some conceptual issues. In B. Rogoff & J. Wertsch (Eds.), *Children's learning in the "zone of proximal development"* (pp. 7–18). San Francisco: Jossey-Bass.

Wertsch, J. V. (1985). *Vygotsky and the social formation of mind*. Cambridge, MA: Harvard University Press.

Wertsch, J. V. (1991). *Voices of the mind: A sociocultural approach to mediated action*. Cambridge, MA: Harvard University Press.

Wixson, K. K., & Lipson, M. Y. (1991). Perspectives on reading disability research. In R. Barr, M. Kamil, P. Mosenthal, & P. D. Pearson (Eds.), *Handbook of reading research* (Vol. 2, pp. 539–570). New York: Longman.

Wixson, K. K., Peters, C. W., Weber, E. M., & Roeber, E. D. (1987). New directions in statewide reading assessment. *Reading Teacher, 40,* 749–754.

Wolf, D., Bixby, J., Glenn, J., III, & Gardner, H. (1991). To use their minds well: Investigating new forms of student assessment. In G. Grant (Ed.), *Review of Research in Education* (Vol. 17, pp. 31–74). Washington, DC: American Educational Research Association.

Wood, B., Bruner, J. S., & Ross, G. (1976). The role of tutoring in problem solving. *Journal of Child Psychology and Psychiatry, 17,* 89–100.

Zellermayer, M. (1993, July). *When we talk about collaborative curriculum-making, what are we talking about?* Paper presented at the meeting of the International Society for the Study of Teacher Thinking, Gothenborg, Sweden.

# · 18 ·

# BILINGUALISM AND SECOND LANGUAGE LEARNING: SEVEN TENSIONS THAT DEFINE THE RESEARCH

## Kenji Hakuta
STANFORD UNIVERSITY

## Barry McLaughlin
UNIVERSITY OF CALIFORNIA, SANTA CRUZ

## INTRODUCTION

The roots of the study of bilingualism and second language acquisition can be traced to activities in multiple disciplines as well as to catalytic forces from the practice of language education. The primary disciplines involved are linguistics, psychology, anthropology, and sociology, with additional contributions from biology. The catalytic forces of practice might be differentiated into foreign language education (e.g., the teaching of German in the United States), second language education (e.g., the teaching of English as a second language to immigrants to the United States, or in areas of the world where English serves important societal functions such as commerce), and bilingual education (the use of two languages as a medium of instruction).

At least five major moments in the 20th century can be identified when, either because of disciplinary changes or because of practical needs, attention was intensely focused on bilingualism and second language acquisition. The first phase, which we call the psychometrics phase, came in the 1920s during the height of interest in psychometrics and concern about the intellectual character of the "new immigration" (see Hakuta, 1986). Because most of the new immigrants came from non-English-speaking backgrounds, questions arose about the possible effects of bilingualism on performance on intelligence tests; related questions concerned whether the new immigrants were learning English and becoming American rapidly enough. Although much of the research from this period is discredited because of unsound sampling and measurement practices, the debate reflected many of the themes that continue to the present day about the nature of language, whether it (and other human abilities) are biologically based, and the effects of bilingualism on these capacities.

The second phase, called here the foreign language phase, began in the late 1950s, stimulated by the Soviet launching of *Sputnik* and a growing American anxiety over national security and the poor preparedness of the nation in foreign languages. The field of linguistics provided the technical backbone to this movement and gave rise to a field known as contrastive analysis, in which careful comparisons were made between the grammatical structures of the native and foreign language, with the goal of targeting instruction to those areas where difficulties were predicted (Lado, 1964). This movement resulted in the proliferation of the "audiolingual" method for teaching foreign languages, which was focused on drilling problematic grammatical patterns, often aided by language laboratory exercises. The audiolingual method, as Rivers (1964) noted in review of the field, was grounded in the psychology of learning based on the formation and interaction of learned habits. As this theory of learning became less acceptable with the advent of cognitive theories, starting in the 1960s, the movement ground to a halt.

The third phase, called here the language acquisition phase, came in the 1960s on the heels of a revolution in the understanding of language acquisition by children, which in turn was influenced by a revolution in theoretical linguistics that started with Chomsky's (1957) *Syntactic Structures*. Applied linguists such as Pit Corder (1967) who were trying to understand the sources of learner errors in second language learning found many similarities with errors being reported in the child language literature: Both seemed to be driven by an attempt to make sense of the target language, rather than being driven by slavish adherence to the structures of the native language, as contrastive analysis might lead one to believe. Since that time, although the research in first and second language acquisition has tended to be conducted by different groups of researchers in different academic departments, the questions have come to be intertwined: whether the capacity to learn language is best defined as specific to language or reflects general learning mechanisms, and whether there are maturational constraints on language-learning capacity.

The fourth phase, called the Canadian immersion phase, also started in the 1960s but stemmed from innovations in French immersion education in Canada. French immersion programs were a radical way of responding to the needs of the English speakers of bilingual Montreal who wanted to ensure that their children had access to the benefits of bilingualism. In these programs, native English-speaking children were instructed exclusively in French from their first day of school (Lambert & Tucker, 1972). This innovation has become very popular in Canada, even in its English-dominant areas, and has generated considerable research on its effectiveness and the conditions under which the native language and academic achievement are maintained even as the student becomes proficient in a second language.

Finally, beginning in the 1980s, there appeared another wave of interest in bilingualism and second language acquisition. This wave, called the language-minority phase, was driven by educational needs. This time, however, the needs stemmed from population changes in the immigrant population, especially in industrialized nations (Organisation for Economic Cooperation and Development [OECD], 1989; Padilla, 1990). As a result, there has been intense scrutiny of language and educational policies in many nations, including an evaluation of the emphasis to be placed on the native language of the students. In comparison to the "additive" bilingual policies pursued in French immersion programs, in which the second language learning is an increment to the native language base, the policies pursued in general for immigrant, language-minority students are replacive in nature. In the United States, for example, most of the official program evaluation research has focused on whether the students in bilingual education programs are learning English fast enough, and under what conditions this process can be optimized. Many basic researchers, on the other hand, have tended to focus on what happens to the native language and the ethnic community, often within disciplinary frameworks (e.g., Fishman & Gertner, 1985; Extra & Verhoeven, 1993).

Given this rather complex history of the field of bilingualism and second language acquisition, we have decided to organize our review of the field by outlining key tensions that we believe capture the field's character. These tensions are (a) empiricism versus nativism, (b) linguistics versus psychology, (c) psycholinguistics versus sociolinguistics, (d) cognitive skills versus whole language, (e) elite versus folk bilingualism, (f) basic versus applied research, and (g) theory versus methodology. This list of tensions does not exhaust the issues, nor do we claim that they are orthogonally related. However, they are historically embedded within these phases and therefore are the legends of this century of research in the area.

## EMPIRICISM VERSUS NATIVISM

The tension between empiricism and nativism is not restricted to the field of second language acquisition. It is, however, a deeply ingrained issue in the field, which

underscores the point that the acquisition of a second language is related to a central problem in human learning and development.

## Bilingualism and Intelligence

The earliest manifestation of the tension came during the psychometrics phase, when there was concern that immigrant children were handicapped in their language growth, as measured by standardized tests of language development, because of their bilingualism (e.g., Smith, 1931). The handicap would be predicted—as the empiricists did predict it—if there were a direct relation between energy spent on learning and the outcome, for bilingual learners would have to distribute their learning energy across two languages. This assumption led to the advice commonly given to immigrant parents not to use the native language at home because it might lead to linguistic retardation (Thompson, 1952).

Interestingly, radical nativists during this early period were content with the conclusion that the poor performance of immigrant children on tests of language was not caused by their diffused learning experience. They favored the explanation that these children came from inferior genetic stock (e.g., Goodenough, 1926; see Hakuta, 1986, for a review).

This line of controversy has continued to the present day, but in two different forms. On the one hand, the nature–nurture question with regard to intelligence continues, with minimal attention to the question of the role of bilingualism (Jensen, 1980). On the other hand, the issue of the relationship of bilingualism and cognitive development continues to be explored as an empirical question, but with no implication as to the nature of development. This literature generally indicates a mildly positive effect of bilingualism, especially in areas related to metalinguistic awareness (e.g., Bialystok, 1988).

## The Linguistic Abstractness Argument

Another instance of the empiricism–nativism tension can be found in assumptions about what it is that is learned in second language acquisition. This problem received attention especially during the language acquisition phase, which went through a period of intense appreciation for both the logical linguistic arguments as well as the behavioral and neurological evidence about the special status of language (a characteristic that Chomsky [1965] called "task-specificity" and the philosopher Jerry Fodor [1983] calls "modularity").

The logical linguistic argument is covered in greater detail in the next section on linguistics and psychology. Briefly, the argument posits that all mature speakers of a language have knowledge about their language that is highly abstract. This can be proved by showing that people are able to distinguish between grammatical and ungrammatical sentences that differ only along this abstract dimension. The logical argument is that this ability could not have been induced from simple exposure to the surface patterns of the language. The only way in which mature speakers could have gotten to their present state is if they had a critical a priori knowledge about language. When this deduction is combined with the observation that children display mature knowledge of most aspects of language by age 5, the conclusion is that many aspects of language must be innate. For second language acquisition, the extension is that if learners successfully make similar distinctions, they must also do so following their innate knowledge.

## Language as Specialized Behavior

The behavioral evidence on the special status of language comes from a variety of areas.

One area is the perception of speech sounds. Studies of infant speech perception since the 1971 publication of Eimas, Siqueland, Jusczyk, and Vigorito have suggested that very young infants actively segment sounds into phonemic categories even when the acoustic properties of these sounds vary along continuous dimensions. Recent comparative research on infants exposed to Swedish and English showed that these infants had already segmented the vowel continuum in ways that corresponded to the language of exposure (Kuhl, Williams, Lacerda, Stevens, & Lindblom, 1992).

For second language learners, the evidence suggests that the phonemic categories of the native language serve as a starting point, but that adjustments are made in the course of second language acquisition. Williams (1974) made good use of a difference between Spanish and English in the voice onset time (VOT) speech parameter that distinguishes, for example, between the sounds /ba/ and /pa/. In distinguishing between these sounds, the VOT is the time period between the initial release of air from the lips and the vibration of the vocal cords. For English, native speakers categorize sounds at a VOT of less than 25 milliseconds as /ba/ and anything above that as /pa/. For Spanish, the boundary is at about 10 milliseconds. Williams studied both speech perception and production among Puerto Rican native speakers of Spanish who were learning English, and found that they shifted from the Spanish boundary to the English boundary both as a function of length of exposure to English and as a function of the initial age at which they were exposed to the second language. Even though the boundary shifted, the subjects preserved the categorical nature of their perception.

Another clear example of the special nature of language can be found in the variables that seem to affect the course of development. Brown (1973) found no effects of parental frequency of usage of forms, reinforcement, or correction on the course of grammatical development. Recently, Marcus et al. (1993) found that the course of development of regular and irregular past tense marking on verbs is remarkably similar between children learning English and German, despite the fact that irregular verbs are far more common in English, whereas regular verbs are far more common in German. Such evidence indicates that humans are highly prepared to learn language, and this preparedness is relatively immune to variations in the input language.

Interestingly, there is some evidence to indicate that input frequency is more important in second language acquisition than might be supposed from first language acquisition. Larsen-Freeman (1976) found that the relative frequencies of grammatical morphemes (such as the noun and verb inflections, prepositions, the verb to be, and articles) successfully predicted the overall order in which they were mastered by second language learners across a wide range of ages and native language backgrounds. First language learners of English master these same

structures in a different order, an order that is not related to the input frequency but rather is predicted by the syntactic and semantic complexity of the structures (Brown, 1973). The greater sensitivity of second language learners to input frequency, however, does not explain persistent differences between second language learning by native speakers of different languages, such as the great difficulty that native speakers of Japanese have with the English article system, despite the very frequent occurrence of these forms in the English language (Hakuta, 1983).

## Age Constraints on Second Language Acquisition

One area that has witnessed considerable empirical activity is the question of whether there are age constraints on language acquisition. This question was first raised by Penfield and Roberts (1959) when they reported dramatic results of stimulation of language areas of the brain of patients during surgery. These hardware explanations of language, in conjunction with the known plasticity of the brain in childhood, were forwarded as arguments for foreign language education in the elementary grades during the foreign language phase of the field.

The hypothesis about the age constraints on second language acquisition took shape with the publication of Lenneberg's (1967) *Biological Foundations of Language*. Lenneberg brought together the Chomsky-inspired logical linguistic arguments about the necessary abstractness and complexity of language with a review of the evidence on recovery from childhood traumatic aphasia and other disorders that affect language development. The amassed evidence indicated that the potential for language learning existed through childhood but disappeared at around puberty. Lenneberg suggested that the period between birth and puberty constituted a critical period, much like the time-bounded and highly prepared period for learning specific information that is observed in other species, such as greylag geese (Lorenz, 1958).

The idea of extending the critical period for second language learning was subjected to empirical testing by a number of researchers. The earliest convincing demonstration of an age effect was reported by Oyama (1976), who rated the pronunciation of Italians who had immigrated to the United States at various ages. She found a strong negative effect of age at arrival, and no effect for length of exposure once age at arrival was controlled for. Patkowski (1980) compared ratings of syntax in the transcribed speech of adult learners who had learned English before or after puberty and found differences in favor of prepubescent learners. More recently, Johnson and Newport (1989) looked at the ability to judge the grammaticality of English sentences by native speakers of Chinese and Korean who had learned English at ages ranging from 3 to 39. Their data suggest the following: (a) there is a decline in judgment across the age span that begins as early as age 5 and continues through adulthood; (b) there was greater individual variation among subjects who had arrived after puberty than those who arrived at a younger age; and (c) the decline in performance was steeper among those who had arrived before puberty than among those who had arrived after puberty.

It should be noted that all of these studies have considerable difficulty in controlling for length of exposure to English when they look at age at arrival, especially because the age of the subject at the time of testing can become a factor for younger and older subjects. Since these three factors are necessarily related (i.e., current age is the sum of age at arrival and length of exposure), the designs of these studies are never fully satisfactory.

Aside from the inherent empirical blemishes that mark these studies, the results indicate that the question is much more complicated than it appeared at first blush. One complication is that the age-related decline is better characterized as monotonic in nature, rather than categorical. The ability to learn a second language does not seem to suddenly disappear, as might be expected of an ability that is bounded by a critical period, such as the development of the visual system (Hubel, 1988). Even proponents of the biological view readily concede that second language learning might better be described as having a "sensitive period." Perhaps the overall decline in performance as a function of age is not the withering away of a specific innate capacity.

A second complication arises from the fact that there are many similarities between child and adult acquisition of a second language. For example, the types of grammatical errors as well as the order of acquisition of grammatical morphemes are not different with respect to age. Indeed, we are not aware of any reported qualitative differences by age in the process of second language acquisition. To paraphrase the sage observation: if they look like one another, quack like one another, and walk like one another, then they are probably learning to talk in the second language in the same way. The question might be rephrased as what is lost (or gained) in specific language-learning ability as one gets older. White and Genesee (1992) recently demonstrated that many advanced adult second language learners master highly abstract grammatical patterns that are thought to be innately determined by the human language capacity.

A final theoretical complication arises from a consideration of whether the process of second language acquisition is at all relevant to the question of a critical or sensitive period for language acquisition. All second language learners, by definition, have already acquired a first language. So the notion of a critical period applies to second language acquisition only under certain theoretical views about what happens in the process of language acquisition.

According to one view, second language acquisition is like reinventing the wheel, and thus it is a rerun of first language acquisition. Such a view might be held by theorists who see language acquisition as an essentially concrete, close-to-the-surface event. This interpretation of language acquisition would also be generally compatible with empiricist accounts of language acquisition (e.g., Moerk, 1983). Extending this scenario, one might argue that the tools necessary to invent the wheel might be available only during a critical period, and thus second language acquisition would decline accordingly.

According to another view, acquiring a second language might be regarded as only moderately incremental to what the learner has already accomplished in first language acquisition. Maybe it is more like recycling—learning new terminology for old concepts, as may happen to a Californian who moves to Boston and learns that "regular coffee" comes served with cream and sugar rather than "black" as at home. The view that second language learning is incremental can be derived from

the theory that language acquisition is a highly abstract process, that can be explained only by rationalist accounts of learning. According to this view, because the language acquisition ability was already capacitated in the course of first language acquisition, there may be no age implications for second language acquisition, even if a critical period effect for first language acquisition existed (see Newport, 1991). Curiously, however, the critical period hypothesis has found its most ardent support among researchers with strong rationalist orientations (e.g., Johnson & Newport, 1989; Long, 1985; Patkowski, 1980).

In sum, there are a number of complications in interpreting the data on age effects on second language acquisition, especially as they might bear on the question of empiricism versus rationalism. It may well be that until there is better elaboration of the theoretical predictions, the primary reasons for investigating the question are simple curiosity and perhaps the need to answer educational policy questions such as the optimum age to begin foreign language instruction.

## LINGUISTICS VERSUS PSYCHOLOGY

The tension between linguistics and psychology has existed since the language acquisition phase of research, which began in the 1960s. Prior to the Chomskyan revolution in linguistics, there was a fundamental compatibility between linguistics and psychology, both of which were solidly empiricist in their orientation. Even during the early stages of paradigm change in linguistics, psychologists were enthralled by the possibilities of the new and more powerful linguistics. But efforts to test predictions from linguistic theory failed miserably and psychologists and psycholinguists became disillusioned with the new linguistics. As the distinction between competence and performance became more clearly understood on each side, it became apparent that linguists and psychologists were in pursuit of two different holy grails. Linguists were concerned with the linguistic intuitions of an idealized speaker; psychologists were concerned with the behavior of their all-too-real subjects. Nonetheless, researchers investigating bilingualism and second language acquisition have drawn on both linguistics and psychology.

### The Linguistics Perspective

On the linguistics side, the dominant current influence is Chomskyan generative grammar. This approach assumes that the first language learner comes to the acquisition task with innate, specifically linguistic, knowledge, or universal grammar. The claim is that certain principles of the human mind are, to a degree, biologically determined and specialized for language learning. As Chomsky put it: "Universal grammar is taken to be the set of properties, conditions, or whatever, that constitute the 'initial' state of the language learner, hence the basis on which knowledge of language develops" (1980, p. 69). These abstract and linguistically significant principles are thought to underlie all natural languages and to constitute the essential faculty for language with which all humans are uniformly and equally endowed.

According to this theory, the ability to acquire a human language is genetically determined. The theory postulates that the child faces a "projection problem" in that the language-learning task must be accomplished with deficient input data. The only way to explain how children succeed is to assume that they approach the task endowed with a universal grammar that comprises a rich set of innate principles that govern the emergence of language. The universal grammar constrains the hypotheses that children make, and the child's language environment determines which principles of the universal grammar will be accessed. Acquisition involves setting the parameters of a particular language in a specific way.

As a linguistic theory, universal grammar does not concern itself with second language acquisition. Nonetheless, a number of second language researchers have applied the theory in their work, motivated by the need for a sufficiently sophisticated linguistic theory to describe the complex structural characteristics of interlanguages. The concept of a universal grammar, its proponents argue, provides a detailed linguistic theory to account for second language phenomena.'

Second language learners are thought to face the same "projection problem" (White, 1985); that is, they, like first language learners, have to work out a complex grammar on the basis of deficient data. The learner's grammatical knowledge cannot be explained by the input data alone. Felix (1984) listed three limitations. First, some structures are so rare and marginal that it would not be possible for learners to obtain sufficient exposure to them. Second, incorrect hypotheses require negative feedback (correction, identification of errors, etc.) if they are to be discarded, but such feedback usually does not occur. Finally, the rules of any grammar are highly abstract and so do not reflect the surface properties of the language.

Universal grammar theory provides a conceptual framework for accounting for language variation, including variation between native and target languages. The development of parameter theory, in particular, is seen as providing a coherent account of how language properties inherent in the human mind provide a set of general principles that apply to all grammars— including the intermediate grammars of the second language learner's interlanguage.

According to universal grammar theory, the principles of universal grammar involve a set of properties with certain parameters. These parameters remain "open" until they are set by experience with the environment. For Chomsky, language acquisition is not so much a problem of acquiring grammatical rules, but rather a process whereby the learner sets the values of the parameters of the principles of the universal grammar. The grammar of a language is the set of values the learner assigns to various parameters. As Chomsky put it, "Experience is required to set the switches. Once they are set, the system functions" (1984, p. 25).

An oft cited example of such a parameter is the pro-drop parameter. Languages vary with regard to whether they allow the deletion of pronouns in subject positions, and also differ in related phenomena such as inversion of subject and verb. English does not have pro-drop because a subject is required for every sentence and the positions of subject and verb cannot be inverted in declarative sentences. However, this is not true of Spanish, a pro-drop language that allows empty subjects and subject–verb inversion in declarative sentences.

Another example is the principle of adjacency, according to which noun phrases must be next to the verb or preposition that gives them case. Hence in English an adverb cannot intervene between a verb and its direct object. Sentences such as "Mary ate quickly her dinner" are not allowed, whereas in French such sentences are permitted: "Marie a mange rapidement le diner" (White, 1989). The French option is assumed to be "set" for the child learning French as a first language on the basis of positive evidence in the form of such sentences.

The crucial issue in much linguistically based second language research is how the parameters that have been set in the first language need to be reset or readjusted for the second language. Some investigators argue that the principles of universal grammar are fully available to the learner and the task of second language learning involves resetting the first language parameters in line with those of the second. The relative similarity or difference of specific parameters across the learner's first and second languages would then constrain this resetting process (Flynn, 1984).

Other researchers maintain that the principles of universal grammar are available but that they interact with and are highly constrained by other factors, among them cognitive strategies and processing considerations (Bley-Vroman, Felix, & Ioup, 1988). Bley-Vroman (1990) argued that the child language learner possesses a language acquisition system that contains the following two subcomponents: (a) a definition of possible grammar: a universal grammar; and (b) a way of arriving at a grammar based on available data: a learning procedure (or set of procedures). The adult second language learner, Bley-Vroman argued, does not have access to universal grammar but instead constructs a kind of surrogate for universal grammar from knowledge of the native language. This knowledge, plus general cognitive abilities that enable adult learners to deal with abstract formal systems, enables adult learners to acquire imperfect knowledge of target languages.

## The Psychological Perspective

Bley-Vroman's position accords well with what most psychologists and psycholinguists would maintain about second language learning. The contention is that there may be some access to universal grammar through knowledge of the first language and that adult second language learning is the result of this knowledge and general cognitive abilities. From this perspective second language learning, like all adult cognitive problem solving, is goal-oriented, and involves analysis, hypothesis formation and testing, and analogy. The learner is thought to proceed with practice from attention-demanding, controlled processing to more automatic processing.

Second language theorists and researchers have drawn from cognitive psychological work in general problem solving, schema theory, and production models. For example, O'Malley and Chamot (1989) used Anderson's (1983) notions of declarative and procedural knowledge to express the manner in which information about language is represented in memory. Kennedy (1988) made a similar distinction based on Gagné's (1985) information-processing model. Both approaches stress the difference between knowing concepts, propositions, and schemas (declarative knowledge) and knowing how to perceive and classify patterns and how to follow specific steps until a goal is reached (procedural knowledge). A related distinction is made by Bialystok (1981), who uses the concepts "analysis" and "control" to distinguish between the cognitive skills involved in the learner's linguistic knowledge and the skills involved in control of processing.

Procedural knowledge is thought to be acquired through extensive practice and feedback and, once learned, to be more easily activated in memory than declarative knowledge. Initially, the learning of procedures requires conscious attention, but as the learner becomes more and more skilled at a task, less conscious work is required. McLaughlin, Rossman, and McLeod (1983) used Shiffrin and Schneider's (1977) distinction between controlled and automatic processing to account for this progression from a more cognitively demanding to an autonomous stage of learning.

As performance becomes more automatic, elements of the task become unitized (Gagné, 1985). That is, there is an integration of skills into larger and more efficient units. This unitization process involves a progressive reorganization of information as an increasing number of procedures become automatic and controlled processes are freed for new tasks. In the case of second language learning there is a constant restructuring as learners simplify, unify, and gain increasing control over the procedures involved in processing the language (McLaughlin, 1990).

Another area of cognitive psychology that has had an impact on second language research concerns expert versus novice systems. The literature suggests that "experts" use different information-processing strategies than do "novice" learners. Differences between experts and novices have been found in research on learning mechanisms in physics, arithmetic, algebra, geometry, computer programming, and chess. For the most part, research indicates that experts restructure the elements of a learning task into abstract schemas that are not available to novices, who focus principally on the surface elements of a task. Thus experts replace complex subelements with single schemas that allow more abstract processing.

In the realm of language learning, experts are those individuals who have learned a number of languages. There is considerable anecdotal evidence (though little empirical research) that suggests that once a person has learned a few languages, subsequent language learning is greatly facilitated. In a study using a miniature artificial linguistic system, Nayak, Hansen, Krueger, and McLaughlin (1989) found that multilingual subjects showed more flexibility in switching strategies than did monolingual subjects. This is consistent with the research of Nation and McLaughlin (1986), who found that multilingual subjects were able to avoid perseveration errors more than were other subjects in their experiment. Similarly, Ramsey (1980) reported that multilingual subjects demonstrated greater flexibility in "restructuring mental frameworks" than did monolingual subjects. Thus there is some evidence to suggest that more expert language learners show greater plasticity in restructuring their internal representations of the rules governing linguistic input.

In other research within an "expert systems" framework, Faerch and Kasper (1983), McGroarty (1989), Oxford (1986), and O'Malley and Chamot (1989) have attempted to specify strategies that good language learners use. The ultimate goal of much of this research has been to expand and refine the repertoire of strategies of poor learners so that they may benefit from strategies used to good effect by expert learners. Wenden (1987) noted that intervention research on training learners in cognitive strategies in other skill areas has demonstrated that the appropriate selection and use of strategies in a variety of situations requires metacognition. It is not enough for learners to be trained to use a particular strategy; they must also understand the significance of the strategy and be able to monitor and evaluate its use.

The research on learner strategies and the cognitive approach generally fit well with the needs of classroom teachers. Contemporary linguistic theory with its concern with pro-drop and subjacency parameters is arcane and inaccessible to teachers. Most teachers are more comfortable with an approach that sees language learning as a process of internalization, through practice, of various rules and representations. Teachers are at home with a theory that is concerned with learning, production, and communication strategies. Nonetheless, the insights of contemporary linguistics have had a powerful effect on thinking about how languages are acquired. It remains to be seen whether these insights will be communicated to classroom teachers.

## PSYCHOLINGUISTICS VERSUS SOCIOLINGUISTICS

The psycholinguistic perspective dates back to the language acquisition phase, especially early work on error analysis and the morpheme studies (Ellis, 1985; Hatch, 1983). Here we will focus on two contemporary manifestations—work on the "competition model" and work using miniature artificial languages. The sociolinguistic perspective stresses the social nature of language and its use in varying contexts, and in many ways defined itself as a reaction to the dominance of psycholinguistics. According to the sociolinguistic perspective, the psycholinguistic experiment is only one of many possible contexts in which language is used, and consequently does not tell the whole story. The speaker's competence is multifaceted: How a person uses the language will depend on what is understood to be appropriate in a given social setting, and as such, linguistic knowledge is situated not in the individual psyche but in a group's collective linguistic norms.

### The Psycholinguistic Perspective

One of the ways to study how individuals learn a second language is to examine how grammatical forms are acquired in a manner consistent with the ways in which the language is used. This is the question of "form–function mappings" that is central to a popular research paradigm developed by Bates, MacWhinney, and their colleagues (Bates & MacWhinney, 1982; MacWhinney, Bates, & Kliegl, 1984). Their model, called the *competition model*, assumes that the structural principles of language are represented not in terms of rules (explicit or otherwise), but rather by mappings between surface linguistic forms and underlying functions. In any given language, a particular instantiation of a form-function mapping is assigned a weight depending on how often and how reliably a given form is used to perform a given function. The information a learner uses to decide which function is meant to be expressed by a particular form is referred to as a *cue*, and cues vary in their reliability and availability.

In the second language context, the task facing the learner is to discover how specific forms are used for specific functions in the new language. Typical experiments testing this model use bilingual subjects in a within-subjects, cross-language design. Subjects are given a sentence interpretation task designed to produce "competitions" among a restricted set of grammatical cues (e.g., word order, animacy relations, subject–verb agreement, and case inflections). The task is to say which noun is the agent of the action. For example, subjects may hear, "The apple is eating the man." In this example the canonical subject–verb–object pattern of English is in competition with the animacy cue. Studies comparing different groups of bilingual subjects suggest that during the initial period of second language acquisition, subjects rely on the transfer of first language strategies to aid sentence competition. Thus, Italian and Japanese subjects learning English tend to rely on the animacy cue rather than use the word order cue, which is the processing strategy employed by native English speakers (Gass, 1987; Harrington, 1987).

From experiments using various combinations of competing cues, advocates of this approach argue that it is possible to examine which cues are most important in sentence comprehension in a language, and how certain cues come under strategic control as fluency increases. This would have important pedagogical implications, as it is those cues that would be critical for learners coming from particular background languages, and teachers could attend to such cues in teaching these learners.

Recently, however, Gibson (1992) has questioned the adequacy of the definitions of key concepts in the competition model, especially the notion of cue and cue reliability and validity. Gibson argues that insufficient attention has been paid to how cues are identified and used by learners. He also argues that the experimental paradigm used to support the model may tap into different processing mechanisms—specifically, if a given stimulus string is grammatical in a language, it may be processed differently than ungrammatical strings.

One wonders, moreover, about the "ecological validity" of an experimental procedure in which subjects have to make decisions about sentences that are as deviant as "The apple is eating the man" (McLaughlin & Harrington, 1989). Perhaps subjects are not processing such sentences as they would in actual communicative situations but are settling on a particular problem-solving strategy to get them through the many judgments of this nature they have to make. One particularly disturbing finding from the competition model is that there is a great deal of first language transfer, whereas most naturalistic research reveals surprisingly little first language transfer (McLaughlin, 1986). As MacWhinney and Bates (1989) have noted, it is important for testing the adequacy of the competition model to develop more on-line measures of sentence processing, with respect to both comprehension and production.

Another psycholinguistic research method that is widely used in current second language research involves the use of *miniature artificial languages* (MALs). Because natural language learning takes place in an environment where it is impossible to control the input the learner receives, researchers have not been able to specify as accurately and exhaustively as possi-

ble those features of the environment that causally influence learning. By clearly specifying the input and output characteristics of the language acquisition task through the use of MALs, it becomes possible to make systematic inferences about the structures and processes within the organism that make learning a language possible.

Artificial linguistic systems resemble natural languages in that they contain a set of verbal symbols and a set of rules for combining these symbols into sentences. Like natural languages, the set of rules can specify class membership, order, and co-occurrence constraints on the linguistic structure of the artificial language. Unlike natural languages, this set of rules is fairly limited in scope, thus making it possible to observe a language-learning situation wherein various language features can be studied in isolation from the complex interactions found in natural systems. It is this ability to manipulate systematically all features that might influence language-learning mechanisms that makes the study of artificial linguistic systems an important tool in psycholinguistic research (Moeser, 1977; Morgan & Newport, 1981).

Subjects in an experiment using an artificial linguistic system are exposed to a limited subset of permissible strings. The question of interest is whether they can apply generalizations derived from the learned subset to novel strings, and if so, what is the nature of these generalizations. In a number of papers based on MAL research, Reber and his associates (e.g., A. Reber, 1976; A. S. Reber & Allen, 1978) have argued for what they have called "implicit learning." In this research, subjects were exposed to finite-state grammars made up of letter strings and were found to be significantly accurate when they subsequently had an opportunity to judge the grammaticality of novel grammatical and nongrammatical strings. Because subjects seemed to be learning these rules without being able to articulate their knowledge, Reber concluded that the learning was implicit and unconscious.

This conclusion has been challenged by Dulany and his associates (Dulany, Carlson, & Dewey, 1984), who questioned the degree to which the knowledge of subjects in these experiments is properly characterized as abstract and the degree to which it is truly unconsciously held. Their research indicated that subjects developed personal and idiosyncratic sets of rules and that these sets of rules correlated with the finite-state grammar in the sense that both sets of rules resulted in the same grammatical classifications. The subjects' idiosyncratic rules were of imperfect validity and of limited scope, but were accessible to consciousness. This is an important pedagogical point, as there are some (e.g., Krashen, 1982) who argue that second language learning is largely an unconscious process, and others (e.g., Schmidt, 1990) who maintain that what is learned has to be "noticed."

The critics of research with MALs question whether the abilities recruited in such experiments are the same as those engaged in natural language learning, specifically those recruited when a child is acquiring a first language. McLaughlin (1980) has argued that because subjects learning artificial linguistic systems are not linguistically naive, research on artificial linguistic systems, is viewed as a better method for furthering our knowledge of the process of second language learning, rather than a method for understanding the nature of first language acquisition. In fact, as some research suggests (Nation & McLaughlin,

1986; Nayak et al., 1990), the amount of exposure that subjects have had to various natural language systems may be a critical factor in how they go about learning a new linguistic system.

## The Sociolinguistic Perspective

One of the axioms of the sociolinguistic perspective is that speakers have several "styles" that they use according to the demands of the social context. The "vernacular" style is associated with informal, everyday speech. It requires minimal attention and is at the opposite end of the continuum from language used in formal situations, where speech is highly monitored. It is not possible to tap the vernacular style of the speaker by experimentation in a psycholinguistic laboratory; instead, the only way to obtain good data on speech is through systematic observation in various settings.

The classic research is Labov's (1970) study of the speech patterns of New Yorkers. He sampled speech styles that ranged from casual speech to carefully monitored speech. It was possible to characterize different styles of speaking in terms of the variable use of such sounds as the *th* in "thing." In more casual speech, he found a greater use of nonprestige variants of *th*, such as /t/.

Similar research with second language learners (Dickerson, 1975; Schmidt, 1977; Tarone, 1983) indicates that language learners also show contextual variability according to linguistic setting. There is a continuum of usage, with one end represented by the *vernacular style*, which is seen when the learner is not attending to speech. At the other end is the *careful style*, which involves close attention to speech. Tarone called this the "interlanguage continuum." It reflects the fact that differing degrees of attention are required for different performance tasks.

Tarone (1983) argued that second language learners have variable capability and that this is a better theoretical description than a Chomskyan competence model. This variable capability underlies all interlanguage behavior and is due, ultimately, to the differential attention given to language in different tasks. Ellis (1985), like Tarone, maintained that interlanguage output occupies a continuum ranging from planned discourse to unplanned discourse, but he differed from Tarone in distinguishing nonsystematic and systematic variability. The first includes free variation or unpredictable variability; the second is similar to the variability described by Labov and Tarone.

The views of Tarone and Ellis have been criticized on theoretical grounds by Gregg (1990), who argued that variation models of second language acquisition are inherently incapable of accounting for the phenomena they are invoked to explain. Gregg's views reflect what Preston (1993) called the "dominant paradigm" (the principles and parameters or government and binding model of linguistic competence). For Gregg, variation exists, but it is not interesting; indeed, it is not something that a theory of acquisition need be concerned with. It is a pesky mosquito that is best ignored.

Preston (1993) took a different tact. He is uncomfortable with free or unpredictable variation and argues that all variation is systematic. For him, the task for sociolinguistics is to determine the probabilistic weightings of influences on varying forms that occur in language change. Preston's approach requires multivariate analysis of factors that affect the occurrence of one

form or another. This work is especially promising as a way of linking sociolinguistic and psycholinguistic concerns. As Preston argued, it provides quantifiable features that make a storage–production psycholinguistic model possible—at least in principle. Thus, to some extent there is a converging of interests, as both psycholinguists and sociolinguists such as Preston are concerned with determining the important features influencing language use and how these features get added in a predictive equation.

---

# COGNITIVE SKILLS VERSUS WHOLE LANGUAGE

---

For many researchers working within the framework of contemporary cognitive psychology, second language learning is one of many complex cognitive skills that can be learned as practice leads to automaticity. Initially the learner is overwhelmed by the sheer number of tasks that have to be performed in speaking a second language—correct articulation of sounds, correct lexical choice, correct grammar. But with practice, it becomes easier to pronounce the sounds of the language correctly, and more attention can be given to correct word choice and grammar.

For advocates of the whole language approach, this view of learning is overly simplistic and leads to a fragmentation of the learning process into discrete, isolated tasks. It leads to a deadening pedagogy that focuses on skills rather than engaging the learner. Focusing on skills is especially detrimental to the education of language-minority children learning English in America's schools. In the whole language approach, meaning is essential and the learning of skills is subordinated to the task of making learning meaningful to the student.

## The Cognitive Skills Approach

In what follows, we will focus on a particular task, that of learning to read in a second language. Reading can be viewed as a cognitive skill—indeed, as the most complex and difficult of all the cognitive skills that the child must master in school. The child who translates a string of printed letters accurately and efficiently into meaningful communication may appear to be accomplishing that task with little mental effort. In fact, from a cognitive skills perspective, the child is engaging in complex interactive processes that are dependent on multiple subskills and an enormous amount of coded information. The fluent reader must have automated language skills, intact visual and auditory memory, the ability to associate and integrate intra- and intermodal stimuli, and the ability to abstract and generalize patterned or rule-generated information (Vellutino & Scanlon, 1982).

More specifically, to become an accomplished reader, the child must have mastered three important tasks (Table 18–1). These three tasks are developmentally linked to each other. Only after the child has automated word-decoding operations is it possible to acquire more sophisticated reading and comprehension skills. Similarly, the automation of word-decoding skills is dependent on mastery of symbol–sound correspondence rules.

Research by cognitive psychologists with good and poor

TABLE 18-1. Developmental Progression of Reading Tasks

1. First, the child must master the rules governing symbol–sound correspondences in English.
2. The child must be able to use those rules in learning words and must progressively refine and automate word-decoding operations.
3. Building on automated decoding skills, the child must acquire and perfect a complex set of processing skills that allows rapid processing of incoming material and the extraction of meaning.

readers has indicated that certain components of the reading process are more advanced in good than in poor readers. Specifically, good readers are distinguished from poor readers by the following:

*Bottom-up skills:*
- superior ability to store information in short-term memory
- superiority in visual discrimination
- superior phonological analysis skills
- superior attentional abilities

*Top-down skills:*
- superior ability to use syntactic knowledge
- superior semantic knowledge and ability to use context
- superior ability to go beyond the single sentence in drawing inferences about the story line

It seems reasonable to argue that the cognitive skills required in reading are difficult tasks for second language learners to master and often lead to frustration and school failure.

A crucial period is the late elementary grades. It is at this time that children typically read reasonably smoothly in units larger than individual words but are not yet fully mature and skilled readers (Gibson & Levin, 1975). The jump to mastery in reading requires that the child learn how to extract meaning quickly from text—a task that assumes that words are decoded quickly enough to allow space in working memory for retaining the evolving meanings (LaBerge & Samuels, 1974; Perfetti & Hogaboam, 1975). Hence, poor readers may be hampered in achieving comprehension by their inability to achieve automatic word decoding or even by nonautomatic symbol–sound matching.

Reading in a second language requires all these "bottom-up" decoding skills. Further, children who are learning to read in a second language may have more problems than monolingual children because of their lack of familiarity with the semantic and syntactic constraints of the target language. If children are not able to identify spontaneously and exploit syntactic relations and are not flexible in their use of semantic context as a guide to prediction, their reading comprehension and speed decline (Carr, 1981).

In addition, children who are learning to read in English as a second language may receive instruction in English that focuses on the mechanical process of reading, even when their skills in "going for meaning" are fairly advanced in their first language. Teachers may assume that because a child cannot pronounce English correctly, more time must be spent on symbol–sound correspondences, when in fact the child has automated decoding skills and needs more skill at extracting mean-

ing from text. Often these children received a sparse literacy diet, one that is excessively weighted toward lower level phonics and decoding skills, when they are capable of more advanced work.

Second language readers who are reading literary texts that are appropriate for their age and abilities may need special help in three areas: (a) vocabulary development, (b) syntactic development, and (c) cultural knowledge. Failure to comprehend text may often be the result of lack of appropriate vocabulary knowledge. Studies have shown that a strong relationship exists between knowledge of word meaning and ability to comprehend passages containing those words. The more difficult the words of a passage are for a reader, the more difficulty the reader will have in making sense of the text. Research has also shown that student comprehension of the gist of a text is increased by teaching the meanings of a few key words during each lesson, and explicitly drawing the semantic and topical relations of the words to students' background knowledge. Such training has also been shown to enhance their inferencing abilities.

Research also shows that a strong relation exists between knowledge of syntax and reading comprehension. The better a reader is at understanding how syntax can constrain meaning, the more able that reader will be to predict the information contained in oncoming text. Being able to predict and verify the prediction with continued reading is a crucial part of the reading process. Because poor readers often misunderstand the gist of a text, bolstering their syntactic knowledge may greatly enhance their comprehension. This is especially important for poor readers for whom English is a second language, as it provides the explicit information that often is implicitly known by the native English speaker.

Strong evidence has been found for the existence of a causal relationship between background knowledge and reading comprehension. Intervention techniques that improve children's background knowledge have been found to lead to significant improvements in reading. Inadequacies in background knowledge have been thought to play a large role in producing comprehension difficulties for children from language-minority backgrounds. After the level of background information has been determined through questioning, poor readers from linguistic minorities can be exposed to an appropriate level of cultural information by use of analogy and indirect, inductive techniques. Analogy allows these readers to compare sets of familiar information developed through their native culture to new, less familiar information sets they are attempting to learn.

## The Whole Language Approach

The intervention techniques described above for developing vocabulary knowledge, knowledge of syntax, and background knowledge would be anathema to advocates of the whole language approach. They would view such efforts as fragmentary and reductionistic. The emphasis in the whole language approach is on making reading meaningful and on involving students personally. Language should not be taught piecemeal, but as the essential focus of the entire curriculum. Thematic instruction makes reading an integral part of instruction, not a subject matter of its own.

Whereas the traditional cognitive approach discussed in this

TABLE 18–2. A Comparison of the Cognitive Approach and the Whole Language Approach

| Parameter Compared | Cognitive Approach | Whole Language |
|---|---|---|
| Orientation | Teacher as expert | Teacher as facilitator |
| Students' role | Apprentice | Define tasks |
| Literacy skills | Separate | Interrelated |
| Materials | Specially developed | Authentic |
| Progress | Oral before reading | No sequence |
| Mistakes | Corrected | Not corrected |
| Focus | On skills | On functional literacy |

chapter views the teacher as an expert and the students as apprentices, the whole language approach sees the teacher as a facilitator and the student as defining the task of making meanings. The traditional approach tends to view the skills involved in reading as developmentally sequenced, whereas in the whole language approach a skill is taught when a particular child needs it for something that the child is working on. Literacy skills are seen as interrelated in the whole language approach; oral skills need not be fully developed before reading, nor does reading necessarily precede writing. Table 18–2 summarizes critical differences between the cognitive and the whole language approaches.

The whole language movement is more than a theory of language learning; it represents a philosophical stance on education and makes a political statement regarding the distribution of power (Edelsky, 1990). It sees education as a socially and culturally shared activity and asks how literacy is socially constructed in the classroom. Students need to be empowered so that they value their own experiences, communities, and cultures.

The whole language movement has impacted more traditional views of literacy instruction. For example, Means and Knapp (1991), in a discussion of how the cognitive approach applies to children from culturally diverse backgrounds, argue that curricular changes need to have a focus on complex, meaningful problems and that connections should be made with students' out-of-school experience and culture. While stressing the importance of modeling powerful thinking strategies and providing scaffolding to enable students to accomplish complex tasks, these authors also note the importance of encouraging multiple approaches and solutions and making dialogue the central medium for teaching and learning. Similarly, in a recent discussion of methods of teaching comprehension strategies, Harris and Graham (1992) noted that such instruction must take place in appropriately meaningful contexts and environments.

In the area of writing, similar efforts have been made to place the construction of meaning at the center of the curriculum and to make writing integral to all instruction. This movement views writing as a process, and has been brought into the classroom by the National Writing Project and the Writing Project of the University of California. The writing process approach is used widely with mainstream children and has been applied in some contexts to language-minority children (Gutierrez, 1992).

In a review of the research base of the whole language approach, Pearson and Raphael (1991) noted that several features of the whole language model have been positively associated with successful literacy instruction. For example, there is considerable evidence that reading literature results in better reading comprehension than does isolated skill practice. Similarly, research has indicated that the quality and quantity of children's writing improve when they are encouraged to participate in wide-ranging, unfettered writing activities from the outset of schooling. In addition, reliance on authentic functional literacy tasks has been shown to develop a more realistic view of the uses of reading and writing.

There is also evidence that the whole language approach reduces the cultural mismatch that frequently occurs in classrooms with children from linguistically and culturally diverse backgrounds because the students, not the teacher, define the context of the learning situation. However, there are also unanswered questions about the effectiveness of reform efforts in teaching literacy skills to ethnic and language-minority children. Delpit (1986) and others have been critical of the effects of writing process instruction on minority children. The concern is that such methods do not allow students to learn and produce the type of discourse on which assessment is based—that is, standard academic discourse.

A number of authors have recently attempted to reconcile whole language and more traditional cognitive approaches (e.g., Garcia & Pearson, 1990; McKenna, Robinson, & Miller, 1990). However, Edelsky (1990) and others have argued that such attempts are futile and that the whole language approach represents a paradigm shift. Attempts, for example, to use traditional assessment instruments as outcome measures to determine instructional effectiveness are regarded by whole language advocates as instances of paradigm blindness. Reliance on test score data is seen by whole language advocates as reinforcing mechanisms for stratifying society—that is, test score–based tracking.

Whether these conflicting views can be reconciled remains to be seen. However, regardless of whether researchers use the more qualitative methods of the whole language paradigm or more traditional quantitative methods, it is important to determine under what conditions innovative instructions are effective with language-minority students. Especially in the late elementary grades, where literacy skills are central to academic success for these children, there are few more important educational challenges.

## ELITE VERSUS FOLK BILINGUALISM

Fishman (1977) draws a key distinction between situations where bilingualism is a goal for the elite and those where bilingualism is the predicament of the common folk. Other terminology that had been offered includes additive versus subtractive bilingualism (Lambert, 1975) and elective versus circumstantial bilingualism (Valdes, 1992). The distinction between different situations of bilingualism, especially as it pertains to the status of the groups, is useful in understanding the orientation of researchers working in the different phases, and in sorting through conflicting findings and conclusions (Hakuta, 1986).

The teaching of a second language to the elite has been the main preoccupation of the foreign language phase and the

Canadian immersion phase of research. In these situations, the problem to be solved was how to most creatively or most aggressively teach the second language because of the needs of the middle and upper classes. During the foreign language phase, the need was international competitiveness. In the case of Canadian immersion programs, the main proponents were middle-class Anglophone parents who sensed opportunities for their children learning French in a society that is officially bilingual. In either event, the status of the native language is never questioned, and the desired goal is bilingualism.

During the psychometric phase and language-minority phase, on the other hand, attention has been focused on the population of students who are usually immigrants and from less educated ("folk") backgrounds. The main social question—whether the immigrants are assimilating fast enough—is often propelled by a fear of unrelenting and impermeable ethnolinguistic ghettos that could lead to social fragmentation. In the psychometric phase, during the early part of the 20th century, researchers used the yardstick of standardized intelligence tests to see whether the new immigrants were sizing up to the old (Hakuta, 1986). In the current period of interest in language minorities, researchers tend to measure assimilation by the speed of English proficiency development and measures of school achievement. In these settings, the status of the native language is marginal, and while the native language might be acceptable in the home, bilingualism is not a desirable goal (Imhoff, 1990).

As Hakuta (1986) has documented, the social status of the subjects and the values of the researcher have led to very different conclusions about the effects of bilingualism on intelligence. Bilingualism among the elite is associated with positive psychological outcomes, whereas bilingualism among immigrants is associated with problems. A key question is the locus of the difference.

Cummins (1976) surveyed the research on bilingualism and intelligence and hypothesized that the key mediator was whether a threshold level of bilingualism had been attained. The threshold hypothesis states that positive outcomes result only when children have attained a high level of functioning in two languages. Furthermore, in situations of folk bilingualism in which the first language is compromised, such as that found in immigrants who replace their native language with the second language, negative consequences would result. An appropriate question that arises is whether the appropriate explanatory factor is a cognitive one, that is, the level of bilingualism attained, which is in turn determined by the sociological circumstances of language status, or a sociological one, that is, social status affects both linguistic and psychological conclusions. The threshold hypothesis places the locus at the cognitive level.

The theoretical perspective on language implied by the threshold hypothesis has been attacked for implicitly legitimizing the notion of "semilingualism" (Cummins & Swain, 1983; Edelsky et al., 1983), a condition in which the child develops full proficiency in neither language (Skutnabb-Kangas & Toukomaa, 1976; see Romaine, 1989). Whether semilingualism actually exists as a cognitive condition has been a matter of great controversy (Paulston, 1982).

The roots of this controversy go back to the fundamental issue of whether certain linguistic codes related to social class can be inherently limited in their functioning—distinctions such as orality versus literacy (Ong, 1982) and restricted versus elaborated code (Bernstein, 1961; see Snow, 1987, for a good review of these and other distinctions). The controversy parallels the debate over Black English in the 1960s, when it was debated whether the vernacular was simply a degraded version of standard English or possessed its own integrity as a linguistic system (Labov, 1972). The controversy also parallels the debate over code switching in bilingual speakers and whether the phenomenon demonstrates linguistic confusion or a controlled form of expression (Zentella, 1981). In the view of some critics of the concept of semilingualism, there is nothing deficient in the language of folk bilinguals, and insisting on its existence merely reflects middle-class bias (Brent-Palmer, 1979). Thus, the locus of explanation, in their view, is social bias against lower-class immigrants and the acceptance of linguistic and cognitive measures that are not valid.

## Bridges Between Elite and Folk Bilingualism

It is our view that basic psychological and linguistic processes are not fundamentally different between elite and folk bilingual speakers. Error and performance analyses of the acquisition of second language grammar, for example, do not point to systematic differences as a function of social status. We subscribe to what John Macnamara (1976) once said about language acquisition: "[W]hen an infant, a ten-year-old child, and an adult learn Russian, the most remarkable outcome is Russian" (p. 175). The cognitive and linguistic mechanisms for learning language are universally available and are unlikely to be incapacitated in most circumstances of bilingualism.

In addition to similarities in the process of second language acquisition, the literature suggests other important bridges between elite and folk bilingual speakers. There are positive correlations between bilingualism and measures of cognitive performance even among folk bilingual subjects when proper methodological controls are employed (Duncan & De Avila, 1979; Hakuta, 1987). There appears to be nothing about the sociological situation that causes the results to be different from what has been found with elite bilinguals. Likewise, studies of "natural" translation among children not formally trained in the task show a high level of functioning among both elite bilinguals in Geneva (Malakoff, 1991) and Puerto Rican bilingual speakers of low socioeconomic status in New Haven, Connecticut (Malakoff & Hakuta, 1991).

A final example of a bridge between elite and folk bilingual speakers is found in two-way bilingual education programs, which are rapidly gaining in popularity in the United States (Christian & Mahrer, 1992). These programs begin in elementary school and serve an equal number of language-minority and language-majority children, with the goal of bilingualism for both groups. In effect, they combine the characteristics of traditional bilingual education programs for language-minority students with immersion education for language-majority students. They address one of the major concerns about these programs in that they address the sociolinguistic needs of language development. A prime concern has been that language-minority students in bilingual education are not sufficiently exposed to English models. That concern, however, is alleviated by the fact that English is spoken everywhere in the United States. A more serious problem is that traditional immersion programs have tended to create their own sociolinguistic situation because of the lack of native speakers of the language (Selinker, Swain, & Dumas, 1975). This elite–folk combinant experiment deserves to be followed with special interest because it directly addresses the major sociological tension in the field of second language acquisition.

## BASIC VERSUS APPLIED RESEARCH

Both first and second language acquisition are exciting fields because they hold promise to help answer important fundamental theoretical questions on the nature of language, mind, and culture. Yet one striking characteristic about research in second language acquisition is the extent to which it is motivated by the need to answer real-world problems. The activity of second language acquisition researchers is far more clearly shaped by societal concerns than is the work of their first language acquisition counterparts.

For example, an impressive and productive body of research has accumulated on the Canadian French immersion experience, in which Anglophone students are placed in French-only classes from kindergarten (Lambert, 1984; Lambert & Tucker, 1972). The main question that is asked is whether they are able to maintain pace in English language arts and subject matter with Anglophone students schooled only in English. This question takes priority over the one about how well the students are progressing in French (which is taken for granted), because that is the primary concern of parents who send their children to immersion programs. The parents want their children to become functional in French, but they also want strong reassurance that the children are not losing ground in the dominant language of the country. The research further responds to the effectiveness of variations in immersion adapted to the clientele, using different configurations of grade and language mixtures (see Genesee, 1984).

The questions that motivate second language acquisition researchers fall along the entire spectrum from basic to applied. On the more theoretical end of questions asked by second language acquisition researchers are the following: Are there any negative or positive consequences, either in terms of language or cognitive development, of developing bilingualism (e.g., Diaz, 1983)? Is there an optimum age for second language learning/teaching (e.g., Long, 1990)? What are the differences between the cognitive and social characterizations of language when it comes to second language acquisition (e.g., Snow, 1987).

Somewhat more program oriented are questions such as: What should be the expected rate of second language acquisition (e.g., Collier, 1987)? How can bilingual children best be assessed in terms of their language proficiency and academic achievement (e.g., Cummins, 1981)?

Many applied research questions concern program evaluation: What are the characteristics of effective bilingual education classes (e.g., Tikunoff, 1983)? Does immersion in French impede the academic and English language development of Canadian Anglophone students (e.g., Lambert & Tucker, 1972)? What is the relative effectiveness of various approaches to the education of language-minority students (e.g., Ramirez, Yuen, Ramey, & Pasta, 1991).

Perhaps not surprisingly, it is the applied, policy-oriented questions that tend to generate the greatest amount of political controversy. At times, the political heat obstructs the ability to conduct objective research, or unnecessarily constrains the way in which the questions are framed. In our view, such a situation must be balanced by good, theoretically sound research. This need is most dramatically demonstrated in the case of the pursuit of a single policy point: the *Lau* question.

### The *Lau* Question

The *Lau* question refers to whether there is sufficient evidence to support a prescription of transitional bilingual education (providing content instruction in the native language until the child becomes proficient in English) for school districts with large numbers of students of limited English proficiency. The name *Lau* comes from the 1974 Supreme Court ruling, *Lau v. Nichols*, which ruled that the San Francisco school district had violated Title VI of the Civil Rights Act of 1964 by failing to provide specialized programs to meet the needs of Chinese-American students who were limited in English proficiency. In response to this ruling, the Department of Health, Education and Welfare (DHEW) issued a set of proposed remedies (known as the *Lau* remedies) to be used by the Office for Civil Rights to negotiate compliance plans with school districts that did not provide special programs for limited-English-proficient students, and thus were in violation of federal law. These proposed remedies, and a proposed federal regulation issued in 1980, required the provision of transitional bilingual education in most instances (see Baker & de Kanter, 1983a, Appendices A, B, and C).

In addition to the proposed remedies, the Bilingual Education Act (Title VII of the Elementary and Secondary Education Act) authorized competitive grants to local school districts to develop their capacity to provide bilingual education. This law required that most grants be used to provide funds that used native language instruction. Combined with the *Lau* remedies, these federal actions could be viewed as the affirmation and prescription of bilingual education for limited-English-proficient students (Birman & Ginsburg, 1983).

The *Lau* question has been controversial from the beginning, especially during the conservative presidency of Ronald Reagan (1981–1988). The political character of the problem stemmed from the perception that this amounted to a federal sanction of ethnolinguistic diversity as well as the intrusion of the federal government on local governance (Epstein, 1977). These are questions that speak to the heart of American identity. The *Lau* question has inevitably come to define the research in this area, especially those funded by the government.

A number of major attempts have been made to see if bilingual education is more effective than alternatives, such as the provision of ESL (English as a Second Language) only. All of them were conducted at the elementary school level, in most cases focusing on the attainment of English proficiency and achievement scores measured in English. A study by American Institutes for Research (Danoff, Coles, McLaughlin, & Reynolds, 1977, 1978) compared a large sample of students in Title VII–funded transitional bilingual education programs with those who were not. Baker and de Kanter (1983b) summarized available individual evaluations of Title VII projects that reported data from control groups that did not have bilingual education. In the 1980s, the Department of Education commissioned a pair of longitudinal studies. One study (Development Associates, 1986) attempted to follow a nationally representative sample of limited-English-proficient students who varied in the types of services they received, and to conduct causal modeling of the data to determine the effectiveness of the service types. Another (Ramirez et al., 1991) used a more traditional comparison model to look at three existing models—transitional bilingual education, structured immersion in English only, and bilingual education with a native language maintenance orientation—in a selected number of schools.

These studies, many of them rather expensive, failed to provide conclusive evidence. Is the null hypothesis correct? Or have we a case of Type II error? Many have speculated. Critics of bilingual education prefer the interpretation that the evidence is accurate, and there is indeed no effect (Rossell & Ross, 1986). Supporters claim the evidence foul, pointing out the flaws (not a difficult task) in the studies (e.g., Gray, 1981), or becoming philosophical about whether the positivistic approach toward program evaluation is appropriate (Cziko, 1992). Other supporters look at the evidence and find solace in the fact that the more honest comparisons yield data in favor of bilingual education (Willig, 1985).

These evaluation studies seem to point to the limits of an approach that compares one program type with another. A National Academy of Sciences panel conducted a thorough review of the two major national longitudinal studies (Fienberg & Meyer, 1992). Aside from documenting the fatal design flaws in the studies, the panel was critical of the general atheoretical orientation of the research program, essentially arguing that large studies cannot serve as theoretical prostheses. Rather, the panel recommended a model of knowledge development based on smaller scale, targeted studies that would test and refine the basic theoretical premises of bilingual education.

Many of the theoretical questions, it turns out, have been asked by second language acquisition researchers whose work leans toward the basic research end of the spectrum. For example, in answering the question of whether bilingual education is effective, much of the fear is based on the belief that second language acquisition is a zero-sum process in which instruction in the native language detracts from rapid and efficient learning of English. Yet the basic research suggests that if anything, there is a positive correlation between first and second language proficiency, and that the cognitive consequences of bilingualism are probably positive (Cummins, 1976). These findings should allay the concern that bilingual education comes at the expense of English language development.

Another important finding is the rate of second language acquisition, which suggests that most children do not attain the asymptotic levels of English proficiency for anywhere between 5 to 7 years, considerably less than the time frame (usually 2 years) required by federal and state legislation (Collier, 1987). Setting more realistic expectations of the rate of English development is critical in ensuring that bilingual education programs not be evaluated solely on the speed with which students exit from the programs.

Perhaps the most important contribution of the perspective provided by basic research has been its ability to offer insights into the processes involved in the maintenance and loss of bilingualism. This effort is a multidisciplinary one, ranging from sociology (e.g., Fishman, Nahirny, Hofman, & Hayden, 1966; Veltman, 1983) to ethnography of communication (e.g., Gal, 1979; Gumperz, 1982; Trueba, 1989) to linguistics (e.g., Extra & Verhoeven, 1993), and to psychology (e.g., Hakuta, Diaz, & Ferdman, 1987; Hakuta & D'Andrea, 1992). These perspectives amply demonstrate the complexity of the factors involved in bilingualism and point to the barren nature of the ways in which the questions have been addressed in the evaluation studies. In a nutshell, they extend the perspective on bilingual proficiency from the psycholinguistic to the sociolinguistic, and from the individual to the speech community as the unit of concern. Under the sociolinguistic view, what is learned is not just the ability to speak the second language and maintain the native language, but rather the ability and the social capacity to become active participants in two speech communities. In addition, maintenance of bilingual proficiency is viewed not just as the question of an individual who, in the course of the lifetime, might retain or lose proficiency in the ethnic language. Rather, the additional question is whether the ethnic language gets transmitted to the next generation of the speech community, or whether the speech community withers away.

It is likely that the community of policymakers would have little patience for what they would see as social science gibberish on bilingualism. From their perspective, they are interested in the bottom line, whether the programs that are funded work or do not work. They are not interested in fantasizing about what is possible. To use Cziko's (1992) words, they are interested in the probable outcome of the programs, not in what is possible. Basic and applied research must meet somewhere in between if they are to have any impact. The ideas generated from basic research need to be woven into the culture of policy and program and become an integral part of the evaluation designs.

## THEORY VERSUS METHODOLOGY

One of the enduring tensions in any field of inquiry concerns theory and methodology. This is no less the case in second language research. There are those who argue that theory should drive research and others who feel that one should work from the bottom up, building theory piece by piece on the basis of research findings.

### Where to Begin

This issue has been addressed by Long (1985), who distinguished what he called a "theory-then-research" strategy from a "research-then-theory" strategy. No research is entirely atheoretical, but some research is more theory driven than other research. Long noted that there are advantages and disadvantages to both the theory-then-research and the research-then-theory orientations.

The theory-then-research strategy has the advantage of providing an approximate answer until the "final truth" is known. Such theories serve a useful heuristic, assuming that they generate testable hypotheses that can confirm or disconfirm the theory. The disadvantage of a theory-driven approach is what social psychologists call "confirmation bias" (Greenwald, Pratkanis, Leippe, & Baumgardner, 1986): The preliminary hypotheses have a decided advantage in the judgment process.

The advantage of the research-then-theory approach is that the researcher is closer to the empirical evidence at hand and makes only limited claims. The likelihood of a confirmation bias is not ruled out because all research tests implicit theory, but there is less investment in a theoretical point of view. The disadvantage is that such an approach may be too limited and lacks the heuristic power of a more developed theoretical approach.

Long (1985) argued that the theory-then-research strategy allows for more efficient research. He maintained that the theory governing the research at any point in time tells the investigator what the relevant data are and what the critical experiment is to run. Such a research strategy leads to explanatory accounts of the processes at work in a given domain. In contrast, Greenwald and his associates (1986) have argued that the researcher who sets out to test a theory is likely to become ego-involved with a theoretical prediction, to select procedures that lead eventually to prediction-confirming data, and thereby to produce overgeneralized conclusions.

The debate has a long history in the philosophy of science. Kuhn (1960), who favored the theory-then-research strategy, argued that ordinary scientific activity thrives on theory confirmation—solving puzzles within the existing paradigm. He pointed out, however, that theory confirmation does not succeed indefinitely. Anomalous results accumulate only until a major theoretical reorganization (scientific revolution) can accommodate them. Popper (1959), on the other hand, regarded the exclusive use of confirmation-seeking methods as nonscientific. In his view, empirical knowledge in a scientific domain grows only by the use of critical, falsification-seeking methods.

The difficulty is that falsification seeking is given more lip service than practiced. If, as many have argued, all research has an implicit theory, it is impossible to escape confirmation bias. Even researchers who stay within a limited domain and deal with only certain issues are likely to have definite expectations about their data. Nonetheless, many agree with Popper that

we start our investigation with problems. We always find ourselves in a certain problem situation; and we choose a problem which we hope we may be able to solve. The solution, always tentative, consists in a theory, a hypothesis, a conjecture. (1976, p. 86)

Because we approach problems with an implicit theory, the process is an interactive one: We test our conjectures, we modify our theory, and as the theory withstands tests we are less tentative in accepting the original hypothesis.

In second language research, many investigators are currently working with a research-then-theory strategy, looking first at what the data tell them descriptively and then moving upward toward theoretical claims. Thus there were numerous empirical studies of acquisitional sequences in second language learning before theoretical arguments were made about "natural" developmental sequences. Similarly, the data from transfer studies have only begun to be incorporated theoretically as the predictions of markedness theory are tested.

On the other hand, universal grammar research can be described as a theory-then-research approach. Many present-day second language researchers—perhaps the majority—accept the Chomskyan framework of principles and parameters and test the predictions of the theory with second language learners. As Schachter (1993) has pointed out, however, current universal grammar theoretical speculations are quite limiting when applied to second language research. We do not even know whether the knowledge of universal grammar necessary to reset the parameters is available for adult second language acquisition. It may turn out that mature second language learners exhibit only those characteristics of universal grammar instantiated in their first language and are not able to access the innate knowledge of universal grammar they once possessed.

## Theory and Method

The philosopher of science, Abraham Kaplan (1964), defined what he called the *law of the instrument* with the example of the boy and the hammer: Give a boy a hammer and he will find that everything needs pounding. Second language research has had its instruments, its ways of doing research, and these have set limits to the questions that could be answered.

One example was the "morpheme addiction" that characterized early work in the field. Roger Brown (1973) had determined that children learning English as a first language follow a common "invariant" sequence of acquisition for 14 functors—function words in English that help to convey sentence meaning, such as noun and verb inflections, articles, auxiliaries, copulas, and prepositions such as *in* and *on*. Morpheme studies in second language research were the rage in the 1970s, based on the assumption that if all learners of English showed a similar "invariant" sequence of acquisition, one could conclude that there existed a "natural" order based on a putative innate language-learning mechanism. The results of this line of research were inconsistent. There were numerous methodological problems (Hakuta & Cancino, 1977; McLaughlin, 1986), and eventually this line of research was abandoned.

Another, more contemporary fad has been the use of sentence interpretation tasks designed to produce "competitions" among a restricted set of grammatical cues (e.g., word order, animacy relations, subject–verb agreement, case inflections). As we have seen, the subject's task is to say which noun is the agent of the action in sentences like "The apple is eating the man." As we have seen, this popular technique is open to a number of criticisms, including the criticism that this task requires problem-solving strategies that may be part of second language learning but are not central to the learner's task.

Research on universal grammar relies almost exclusively on one technique, grammatical judgments. One classic example is Ritchie's (1978) study in which adult learners of English correctly judged as grammatical sentences such as "That a boat had sunk that John had built was obvious." However, sentences such as "That a boat had sunk was obvious that John had built" were judged to be ungrammatical. Ritchie saw this to be evidence that the learners had access to the universal grammar principle called the "right roof constraint," which limits the movement of elements in a sentence across certain types of boundaries.

However, as we have seen, other studies using the same

method are not so clear on whether adult language learners have access to universal grammar. As the studies multiply and the debate rages, a more central question is ignored. Even if it can be shown through grammaticality judgment tasks that adults have full access to the conditions of universal grammar, there is still the question of how second language theory is to explain what Preston (1993) has referred to as the aspects of language that do not "fall out of" the principles and parameters. Preston gives the example of English embedded questions that undo auxiliary movement:

1. Why did George leave?
2. I know why did George leave.
3. I know why George left.

Preston argues that, whereas universal grammar principles can describe the difference in structure between statements 2 and 3, there is nothing in the theory that predicts that statement 3 succeeds while statement 2 does not. In fact, he argues, there are many areas of the grammar where one form or the other cannot be predicted on the basis of the principles and parameters model. Grammaticality judgment studies have been restricted to a very small set of principles, and the larger question of the adequacy of the theory has been ignored.

## Theory and Truth

In recent years there has been considerable discussion in the field of second-language research concerning the role of theory. This is reflected in the debate over the question of whether to proceed from theory to data or from data to theory. It is also reflected in the concern that the methods used in second language research limit the question that can be answered.

One of the issues in this discussion concerns the Kuhnian notion of a paradigm. As has been pointed out repeatedly (e.g., Phillips, 1987), the Kuhnian notion of a paradigm has many different meanings. Kuhn himself was said to have used the term in 21 different meanings (Masterman, 1970) in his classic book, *The Structure of Scientific Revolutions* (1962). Nonetheless, it is clear that Kuhn was talking of a paradigm as a framework that determines the key concepts and methods, the problems that are significant, and the criteria for assessing the validity of scientific findings. The choice of a paradigm cannot be made on rational grounds because "[such a choice] is not and cannot be determined merely by the evaluative procedures characteristic of normal science, for these depend in part upon a particular paradigm, and that paradigm is at issue" (1962, p. 93). Once a scientist is working within a paradigm, rules of argument and evidence put forward by those working in another paradigm are bound to be suspect.

But does this not lead to the position that the arguments advanced by a scientist from one framework are no better or truer than those put forward by someone working within another paradigm? Is not a particular argument or a particular knowledge claim relative to a given framework or paradigm? This is a view that has been advanced in the second language field by Schumann (1983), who argued that all theories are social constructions based on metaphorical systems and that it is fruitful at this stage of our knowledge to approach second

language learning from as many perspectives as possible. The dominant theories in the field—universal grammar, cognitive theory, and sociolinguistic theory—all have something to offer in increasing our knowledge. Schumann argued that it is possible to choose between theories on an aesthetic basis, because each theoretical position is simply an alternate construction of reality. For Schumann, no approach is unimportant; every one has something to offer.

This is the issue of *incommensurability*. As Phillips (1987) notes, the Kuhnian notion of paradigms leads to the conclusion that rival paradigms are incommensurable and that scientists from different paradigms are not able to engage in rational dialogue across the boundary. If Kuhn is correct and scientists working in different paradigms live and work "in different worlds," then there is no way to make interparadigmatic judgments, and rational discourse is impossible across paradigms.

Certainly, truth can never be known directly and in its totality. All knowledge is mediated by the symbol systems used by scientists and by the constraints of time and culture. The symbol system or metaphor used by a particular scientific approach may help us see more clearly, but it does not constitute ultimate truth. Nor does the combination of all partial representations of truth add up to ultimate truth. Ultimate truth is only approximated by the shadows cast by the metaphors of our theories.

How, then, is one to avoid theoretical solipsism? The answer that most second language researchers give is to invoke the notion of falsifiability. Theories that are self-contained cannot be tested. The theory may survive, though at best it will survive as an impervious fortress, perhaps invincible but in splendid isolation. The theory needs to be tested, though the results of the research "probe" do not "prove" a theory. A theory may repeatedly survive such probing—but may always be displaced by a new probe. In practice, this means that a theory is either disconfirmed or escapes being disconfirmed. But it is never confirmed. This is the logic of statistical inference as well: The null hypothesis is never accepted, it can only be rejected or fail to be rejected.

This is not to say that Popper's criterion of falsifiability leads to ex cathedra statements and infallibility. Negative evidence may not in fact undermine a theoretical position because such findings can be absorbed without invalidating the whole theory. Indeed, some theories have survived continual refutation (Feyerabend, 1978). While pointing out the limitations of programs of research based on the criterion of falsifiability, second language researchers nonetheless acknowledge that this criterion is critical to theoretical development (Beretta, 1993; McLaughlin, 1993). Thus, for example, the argument that it is possible to learn second languages subliminally—say, as one is falling asleep—is a hypothesis that can be empirically tested, falsified, and put to rest as a viable theory of second language learning.

It may turn out to be the case that a theory of second language learning needs revision as negative results are found. It may be that the theory holds in some conditions (say, with some languages and not with others). Such complexities do not invalidate the enterprise. Research is not carried out in a theoretical vacuum. Theory dictates where the researcher looks; not everything is meaningful and worth exploring.

## CONCLUSION

We have surveyed nearly a century's worth of research on bilingualism and second language acquisition from the dual lenses of historical phases and defining tensions. Besides providing a useful narrative structure that served as a good opportunity in which to embed empirical nuggets, has this exercise produced anything that might be of lasting value for the future researcher? From our vantage point, here is what we think are going to be the sturdy markers for what lies ahead:

• The field will continue to be driven primarily by needs generated by practice and policy rather than by theory. Demographics of international migration that were prominent during the psychometrics phase and the language-minority phase will continue to be the main force underlying interest in folk bilingualism, and will probably continue to dominate the attention over the issues of elite bilingualism.

• Key theoretical chestnuts, such as empiricism versus rational-ism and the psycholinguistic versus sociolinguistic distinctions, will become increasingly salient concepts in the thinking of practitioners and policymakers once they emerge from the myopic focus on English acquisition. Researchers will have to play a role as catalysts in this process.

• The most influential research will be that which successfully incorporates these theoretical chestnuts and provides guidance on the correctness or incorrectness of the positions as they are applied to practice, professional development, and policy.

• It is unlikely that researchers who work in the basic disciplines will become terribly excited about attending to the problems of bilingualism and second language acquisition, even though these problems are filled with opportunities for testing their theories. This prospect might be a source of frustration for some second language researchers because it means that they will always bear the mark of being derivative researchers asking questions that other people decide are either relevant or outmoded in the disciplines. The comforting news here is that the really good research questions have a tendency to come back around quite frequently, at least within a century.

## References

Anderson, J. R. (1983). *The architecture of cognition*. Cambridge, MA: Harvard University Press.

Baker, K., & de Kanter, A. (Eds.). (1983a). *Bilingual education: A reappraisal of federal policy*. Lexington, MA: Lexington Books.

Baker, K., & de Kanter, A. (1983b). Federal policy and the effectiveness of bilingual education. In K. Baker & A. de Kanter (Eds.), *Bilingual education: A reappraisal of federal policy* (pp. 33–86). Lexington, MA: Lexington Books.

Bates, E., & MacWhinney, B. (1982). Functional approaches to grammar. In E. Wanner & L. Gleitman (Eds.), *Language acquisition: The state of the art*. New York: Cambridge University Press.

Beretta, A. (1993). "As God said, and I think, rightly. . . ." Perspectives on theory construction in SLA: An introduction. *Applied Linguistics, 14*, 221–224.

Bernstein, B. (1961). Social class and linguistic development: A theory of social learning. In A. H. Halsey, J. Floud, & C. Anderson (Eds.), *Education, economy and society* (pp. 288–314). Glencoe, IL: Free Press.

Bialystok, E. (1981). Some evidence for the integrity and interaction of two knowledge sources. In R. Anderson (Ed.), *New dimensions in second language acquisition research*. Rowley, MA: Newbury House.

Bialystok, E. (1988). Levels of bilingualism and levels of linguistic awareness. *Developmental Psychology, 24*, 560–567.

Birman, B., & Ginsburg, A. (1983). Introduction: Addressing the needs of language-minority children. In K. Baker & A. de Kanter (Eds.), *Bilingual education: A reappraisal of federal policy* (pp. ix–xxi). Lexington, MA: Lexington Books.

Bley-Vroman, R. (1990). The logical problem of foreign language learning. *Linguistic Analysis, 20*, 3–49.

Bley-Vroman, R., Felix, S., & Ioup, G. (1988). The accessibility of universal grammar in adult language learning. *Second Language Research, 4*, 1–32.

Brent-Palmer, C. (1979). A sociolinguistic assessment of the notion 'immigrant semilingualism' from a social conflict perspective. *Working Papers on Bilingualism, 9*, 1–43.

Brown, R. (1973). *A first language: The early stages*. Cambridge, MA: Harvard University Press.

Carr, T. (1981). Building theories of reading ability: On the relation between individual differences in cognitive skills and reading. *Cognition, 9*, 73–114.

Chomsky, N. (1957). *Syntactic structures*. The Hague: Mouton.

Chomsky, N. (1965). *Aspects of the theory of syntax*. Cambridge, MA: MIT Press.

Chomsky, N. (1980). *Rules and explanations*. New York: Columbia University Press.

Chomsky, N. (1984). *Changing perspectives on knowledge and use of language*. Unpublished manuscript. Cambridge, MA: MIT Department of Linguistics. Cited in Flynn (1984).

Christian, D., & Mahrer, C. (1992). *Two-way bilingual programs in the United States: 1991–1992*. Washington, DC: National Center for Research in Cultural Diversity and Second Language Learning, Center for Applied Linguistics.

Collier, V. (1987). Age and rate of acquisition of second language for academic purposes. *TESOL Quarterly, 21*, 617–641.

Corder, S. P. (1967). The significance of learners' errors. *International Review of Applied Linguistics, 5*, 161–170.

Cummins, J. (1976). The influence of bilingualism on cognitive growth: A synthesis of research findings and explanatory hypothesis. *Working Papers on Bilingualism, 9*, 1–43.

Cummins, J. (1981). The role of primary language development in promoting educational success for language minority students. In *Schooling and language minority students: A theoretical framework* (pp. 3–49). Sacramento: California State Department of Education.

Cummins, J., & Swain, M. (1983). Analysis-by-rhetoric: Reading the text or the reader's own projections? A reply to Edelsky et al. Applied Linguistics, 4, 23–41.

Cziko, G. (1992). The evaluation of bilingual education: From necessity and probability to possibility. *Educational Researcher, 21*, 10–15.

Danoff, M., Coles, G., McLaughlin, D., & Reynolds, D. (1977, 1978). *Evaluation of the impact of ESEA Title VII Spanish/English bilingual education programs* (3 vols.). Palo Alto, CA: American Institutes for Research.

Delpit, L. (1986). Skills and other dilemmas of a progressive black educator. *Harvard Educational Review, 56,* 379–385.

Development Associates. (1986). Year 1 report of the longitudinal phase (Tech. Rep.). Arlington, VA: Development Associates.

Diaz, R. M. (1983). Thought and two languages: The impact of bilingualism on cognitive development. *Review of Research in Education, 10,* 23–54.

Dickerson, L. (1975). Interlanguage as a system of variable rules. *TESOL Quarterly, 9,* 401–407.

Dulany, D. E., Carlson, R. A., & Dewey, G. I. (1984). A case of syntactical learning and judgment: How conscious and how abstract? *Journal of Experimental Psychology: General, 113,* 541–555.

Duncan, S., & De Avila, E. (1979). Bilingualism and cognition: Some recent findings. *NABE Journal, 4,* 15–50.

Edelsky, C. (1990). Whose agenda is this anyway? A response to McKenna, Robinson, and Miller. *Educational Researcher, 19,* 7–11.

Edelsky, C., Altwerger, F., Barkin, B., Flores, S., Hudelson, S. & Jilbert, K. (1983). Semilingualism and language deficit. *Applied Linguistics, 4,* 1–22.

Eimas, P., Siqueland, E., Jusczyk, P., & Vigorito, J. (1971). Speech perception in infants. *Science, 171,* 303–306.

Ellis, R. (1985). *Understanding second language acquisition.* Oxford: Oxford University Press.

Epstein, N. (1977). *Language, ethnicity, and the schools: Policy alternatives for bilingual-bicultural education.* Washington, DC: Institute for Educational Leadership, George Washington University.

Extra, G., & Verhoeven, L. (Eds.). (1993). *Immigrant languages in Europe.* Clevedon, England: Multilingual Matters.

Faerch, C., & Kasper, G. (Eds.). (1983). *Strategies in interlanguage communication.* London: Longman.

Felix, S. (1984). Two problems of language acquisition: The relevance of grammatical studies in the theory of interlanguage. In A. Davies & C. Criper (Eds.), *Interlanguage: Proceedings of the seminar in honor of Pit Corder.* Edinburgh: Edinburgh University Press.

Feyerabend, P. (1978). *Against method.* London: Verso.

Fienberg, S., & Meyer, M. (Eds.). (1992). *Assessing education studies: The case of bilingual education strategies.* Washington, DC: National Academy Press.

Fishman, J. (1977). The social science perspective. In *Bilingual education: Current perspectives. Social science* (pp. 1–49). Arlington, VA: Center for Applied Linguistics.

Fishman, J., & Gertner, M. (1985). *The rise and fall of the ethnic revival: Perspectives on language and ethnicity.* Berlin: Mouton.

Fishman, J., Nahirny, V., Hofman, J., & Hayden, R. (1966). *Language loyalty in the United States.* The Hague: Mouton.

Flynn, S. (1984). A universal in L2 acquisition based on a PBD typology. In F. Eckman (Ed.), *Universals in second language acquisition.* Rowley, MA: Newbury House.

Gagné, E. (1985). *The cognitive psychology of school learning.* Boston: Little, Brown.

Fodor, J. A. (1983). *Modularity of mind.* Cambridge, MA: MIT Press.

Gal, S. (1979). *Language shift: Social determinants of linguistic change in bilingual Austria.* New York: Academic Press.

Garcia, G. E., & Pearson, P. D. (1990). Modifying reading instruction to maximize its effectiveness for "disadvantaged" students. In *Better schooling for the children of poverty: Alternatives to conventional wisdom.* Washington, DC: U.S. Department of Education, Office of Planning, Budget and Evaluation.

Gass, S. M. (1987). The resolution of conflicts among competing systems: A bidirectional perspective. *Applied Psycholinguistics, 8,* 329–350.

Genesee, F. (1984). Historical and theoretical foundations of immersion education. In *Studies on immersion education* (pp. 32–57). Sacramento: California State Department of Education.

Gibson, E. (1992). The crosslinguistic study of sentence processing, by MacWhinney and Bates. *Language, 68,* 812–830.

Gibson, E., & Levin, H. (1975). *The psychology of reading.* Cambridge, MA: MIT Press.

Goodenough, F. (1926). Racial differences in the intelligence of school children. *Journal of Experimental Psychology, 9,* 388–397.

Gray, T. (1981). *Challenge to USOE "Final Evaluation of the Impact of ESEA Title VII Spanish/English Bilingual Education Programs."* Arlington, VA: Center for Applied Linguistics.

Greenwald, A. G., Pratkanis, A. R., Leippe, M. R., & Baumgardner, M. H. (1986). Under what conditions does theory obstruct research progress? *Psychological Review, 9,* 216–229.

Gregg, K. R. (1990). The variable competence model of second language and why it isn't. *Applied Linguistics, 11,* 364–383.

Gumperz, J. (1982). *Discourse strategies.* New York: Cambridge University Press.

Gutierrez, K. (1992). A comparison of instructional contexts in writing process classrooms with Latino children. *Education and Urban Society, 24,* 244–262.

Hakuta, K. (1986). *Mirror of language: The debate on bilingualism.* New York: Basic Books.

Hakuta, K. (1987). Degree of bilingualism and cognitive ability in mainland Puerto Rican children. *Child Development, 58,* 1372–1388.

Hakuta, K., & Cancino, H. (1977). Trends in second-language acquisition research. *Harvard Educational Review, 47,* 294–316.

Hakuta, K., & D'Andrea (1992). Some properties of bilingual maintenance and loss in Mexican background high-school students. *Applied Linguistics, 13,* 72–99.

Hakuta, K., Diaz, R., & Ferdman, B. (1987). Bilingualism and cognitive development: Three perspectives. In S. Rosenberg (Ed.), *Advances in applied psycholinguistics: Vol. II. Reading, writing and language learning* (pp. 284–319). Cambridge, England: Cambridge University Press.

Harrington, M. (1987). Processing transfer: Language-specific processing strategies as a source of interlanguage variation. *Applied Psycholinguistics, 8,* 351–378.

Harris, K. R., & Graham, S. (1992). Self-regulated strategy development: A part of the writing process. In M. Pressley, K. W. Harris, & J. T. Guthrie (Eds.), *Promoting academic competence and literacy in schools.* New York: Academic Press.

Hatch, E. (1983). *Psycholinguistics: A second language perspective.* Rowley, MA: Newbury House.

Hubel, D. (1988). *Eye, brain, and vision.* New York: Scientific American Library.

Imhoff, G. (1990). The position of U.S. English on bilingual education. *Annals of the American Academy of Political Science, 508,* 48–61.

Jensen, A. R. (1980). *Bias in mental testing.* New York: Free Press.

Johnson, J., & Newport, E. (1989). Critical period effects in second language learning: The influence of maturational state on the acquisition of English as a second language. *Cognitive Psychology, 21,* 60–99.

Kaplan, A. (1964). *The conduct of inquiry: Methodology for the behavioral sciences.* San Francisco: Chandler.

Kennedy, B. L. (1988). Adult versus child L2 acquisition: An information-processing approach. *Language Learning, 38,* 477–495.

Krashen, S. (1982). *Principles and practices of second language acquisition.* Oxford: Pergamon Press.

Kuhl, P., Williams, K., Lacerda, F., Stevens, K., & Lindblom, B. (1992). Linguistic experience alters phonetic perception in infants by 6 months of age. *Science, 255,* 606–608.

Kuhn, T. S. (1962). *The structure of scientific revolutions.* Chicago: University of Chicago Press.

LaBerge, D., & Samuels, S. J. (1974). Towards a theory of automatic information processing in reading. *Cognitive Psychology, 6,* 293–323.

Labov, W. (1970). The study of language in its social context. *Studium Generale, 23,* 30–87.

Labov, W. (1972). *Language in the inner city.* Philadelphia: University of Pennsylvania Press.

Lado, R. (1964). *Language teaching: A scientific approach.* New York: McGraw-Hill.

Lambert, W. E. (1975). Culture and language as factors in learning and education. In A. Wolfgang (Ed.), *Education of immigrant students* (pp. 55–83). Toronto: Ontario Institute for Studies in Education.

Lambert, W. E. (1984). An overview of issues in immersion education. In *Studies on immersion education* (pp. 8–30). Sacramento: California State Department of Education.

Lambert, W. E., & Tucker, G. R. (1972). *Bilingual education of children: The St. Lambert experiment.* Rowley, MA: Newbury House.

Larsen-Freeman, D. (1976). An explanation for the morpheme acquisition order of second language learners. *Language Learning, 26,* 125–134.

Lenneberg, E. H. (1967). *Biological foundations of language.* New York: Wiley.

Long, M. (1985). *Theory construction in second language acquisition.* Paper presented at the Second Language Research Forum, University of California, Los Angeles.

Long, M. (1990). Maturational constraints on language development. *Studies in Second Language Acquisition, 12,* 251–285.

Lorenz, K. (1958, December). The evolution of behavior. *Scientific American, 119*(6), 67–78.

MacNamara, J. (1976). Comparison between first and second language learning. *Die Neueren Sprachen, 2,* 175–188.

MacWhinney, B., & Bates, E. (Eds.). (1989). *The crosslinguistic study of sentence processing.* Cambridge, England: Cambridge University Press.

MacWhinney, B., Bates, E., & Kliegl, R. (1984). Cue validity and sentence interpretation in English, German and Italian. *Journal of Verbal Learning and Verbal Behavior, 23,* 127–150.

Malakoff, M. E., & Hakuta, K. (1991). Translation skill and metalinguistic awareness in bilinguals. In E. Bialystok (Ed.), *Language processing and language awareness in bilingual children* (pp. 141–166). Oxford: Oxford University Press.

Marcus, G., Brinkmann, U., Clahsen, H., Wiese, R., Woest, A., & Pinker, S. (1993). *German inflection: The exception that proves the rule* (Occasional Paper 47). Cambridge, MA: Center for Cognitive Science, MIT.

Masterman, M. (1970). The nature of a paradigm. In I. Lakatos & A. Musgrave (Eds.), *Criticism and the growth of knowledge.* Cambridge, England: Cambridge University Press.

McGroarty, M. (1989). *The "good learner" of English in two settings.* (Tech. Rep. No. 12). Los Angeles: University of California, Center for Language Education and Research.

McKenna, M. C., Robinson, R. D., & Miller, J. W. (1990). Whole language: A research agenda for the nineties. *Educational Researcher, 19,* 3–6.

McLaughlin, B. (1980). On the use of miniature artificial languages in second-language research. *Applied Psycholinguistics, 1,* 353–365.

McLaughlin, B. (1986). *Theories of second-language learning.* London: Arnold.

McLaughlin, B. (1990). Restructuring. *Applied Linguistics, 11,* 1–16.

McLaughlin, B. (1993). *Paradigms lost: The evolution of knowledge in the search for truth.* Paper presented at the working meeting, Second Language Acquisition Theory Construction, Washington, DC.

McLaughlin, B., & Harrington, M. (1989). Second-language acquisition. *Annual Review of Applied Linguistics, 10,* 122–134.

McLaughlin, B., Rossman, T., & McLeod, B. (1983). Second-language learning: An information-processing perspective. *Language Learning, 33,* 135–158.

Means, B., & Knapp, M. S. (1991). Models for teaching advanced skills to educationally disadvantaged children. In *Teaching advanced skills to educationally disadvantaged children.* Washington, DC:

U.S. Department of Education, Office of Planning, Budget, and Evaluation.

Moerk, E. (1983). *The mother of Eve—as a first language teacher.* Norwood, NJ: Ablex.

Moeser, S. D. (1977). Semantics and miniature artificial languages. In J. MacNamara (Ed.), *Language learning and thought.* New York: Academic Press.

Morgan, J. L., & Newport, E. L. (1981). The role of constituent structure in the induction of an artificial language. *Journal of Verbal Learning and Verbal Behavior, 20,* 67–85.

Nation, R., & McLaughlin, B. (1986). Experts and novices: An information-processing approach to the "good language learner" problem. *Applied Psycholinguistics, 7,* 41–56.

Nayak, N., Hansen, N., Krueger, N., & McLaughlin, B. (1989). Language-learning strategies in monolingual and multilingual subjects. *Language Learning, 40,* 221–244.

Newport, E. (1991). Contrasting conceptions of the critical period for language. In S. Carey & R. Gelman (Eds.), *The epigenesis of mind: Essays in biology and cognition* (pp. 111–130). Hillsdale, NJ: Lawrence Earlbaum Associates.

OECD. (1989). *One school, many cultures.* Paris: Centre for Educational Research and Innovation, Organisation for Economic Co-operation and Development.

O'Malley, J. M., & Chamot, A. U. (1989). *Learning strategies in second language acquisition.* New York: Cambridge University Press.

Ong, W. (1982). *Orality and literacy: The technologizing of the word.* London: Methuen.

Oxford, R. L. (1986). *Second language learning strategies: Current research and implications for practice* (Tech. Rep. No. 3). Los Angeles: University of California, Center for Language Education and Research.

Oyama, S. (1976). A sensitive period for the acquisition of a nonnative phonological system. *Journal of Psycholinguistic Research, 5,* 261–285.

Padilla, A. (1990). Bilingual education: Issues and perspectives. In A. Padilla, H. Fairchild, & C. Valadez (Eds.), *Bilingual education: Issues and strategies* (pp. 15–26). Newbury Park, CA: Sage.

Patkowski, M. (1980). The sensitive period for the acquisition of syntax in a second language. *Language Learning, 30,* 449–472.

Paulston, C. (1982). *Swedish research and debate about bilingualism: A report to the National Swedish Board of Education.* Stockholm: National Swedish Board of Education.

Pearson, P. D., & Raphael, T. E. (1991). Reading comprehension as a dimension of thinking. In B. F. Jones & L. Idol (Eds.), *Dimensions of thinking and cognitive instruction: Implications for educational change.* Hillsdale, NJ: Lawrence Erlbaum Associates.

Penfield, W., & Roberts, L. (1959). *Speech and brain mechanisms.* Princeton, NJ: Princeton University Press.

Perfetti, C. A., & Hogaboam, T. W. (1975). The relationship between single word decoding and reading comprehension skill. *Journal of Educational Psychology, 67,* 461–469.

Phillips, D. C. (1987). *Philosophy, science, and social inquiry.* New York: Pergamon Press.

Popper, K. (1959). *The logic of scientific discovery.* New York: Basic Books.

Popper, K. (1976). *Unended quest.* LaSalle, IL: Open Court.

Preston, D. (1993). Variation linguistics and SLA. *Second Language Research, 9,* 153–172.

Ramirez, D. J., Yuen, S. D., Ramey, D. R., & Pasta, D. J. (1991). *Longitudinal study of structured-English immersion strategy: Early-exit and late-exit transitional bilingual education programs for language-minority children* (2 vols.). San Mateo, CA: Aguirre International.

Ramsey, R. M. G. (1980). Language-learning approach styles of adult multilinguals and successful language learners. *Annals of the New York Academy of Sciences, 345,* 73–96.

Reber, A. (1976). Implicit learning of synthetic languages: The role of instructional set. *Journal of Experimental Psychology: Human Learning and Memory, 2,* 88–94.

Reber, A. S., & Allen, R. (1978). Analogic and abstraction strategies in syntactic grammar learning: A functionalist interpretation. *Cognition, 6,* 189–221.

Ritchie, W. (1978). The right-roof constraint in an adult acquired language. In Ritchie, W. (Ed.), *Second language acquisition research: Issues and implications.* New York: Academic Press.

Rivers, W. (1964). *The psychologist and the foreign language teacher.* Chicago: University of Chicago Press.

Romaine, S. (1989). *Bilingualism.* Oxford: Basil Blackwell.

Rossell, C., & Ross, J. M. (1986). The social science evidence on bilingual education. *Journal of Law and Education, 15,* 385–419.

Schachter, J. (1993). Second language acquisition: Perceptions and possibilities. *Second Language Research, 8,* 173–187.

Schmidt, R. (1977). Sociolinguistic variation and language transfer in phonology. *Working Papers on Bilingualism, 12,* 79–95.

Schmidt, R. (1990). The role of consciousness in second language learning. *Applied Linguistics, 11,* 129–158.

Schumann, J. (1983). Art and science in second language acquisition research. *Language Learning, 33,* 49–75.

Selinker, L., Swain, M., & Dumas, G. (1975). The interlanguage hypothesis extended to children. *Language Learning, 25,* 139–152.

Shiffrin, R. M., & Schneider, W. (1977). Controlled and automatic human information processing: II. Perceptual learning, automatic attending, and a general theory. *Psychological Review, 84,* 27–190.

Skutnabb-Kangas, T., & Toukomaa, P. (1976). *Teaching migrant children's mother tongue and learning the language of the host country in the context of the socio-cultural situation of the migrant family.* Helsinki: Finnish National Commission for UNESCO.

Smith, M. (1931). Some light on the problem of bilingualism as found from a study of the progress in mastery of English among pre-school children of non-American ancestry in Hawaii. *Genetic Psychology Monographs, 21,* 119–284.

Snow, C. E. (1987). Beyond conversation: Second language learners' acquisition of description and explanation. In J. P. Lantolf & A. Labarca (Eds.), *Research in second language learning: Focus on the classroom* (pp. 3–16). Norwood, NJ: Ablex.

Tarone, E. (1983). On the variability of interlanguage systems. *Applied Linguistics, 4,* 143–163.

Thompson, G. G. (1952). *Child psychology.* Boston: Houghton Mifflin.

Trueba, H. (1989). *Raising silent voices.* Rowley, MA: Newbury House.

Tikunoff, W. J. (1983). *Significant Bilingual Instructional Features Study.* San Francisco: Far West Laboratory.

Valdes, G. (1992). Bilingual minorities and language issues in writing. *Written Communication, 9,* 85–136.

Vellutino, F. R., & Scanlon, D. M. (1982). Verbal processing in poor and normal readers. In C. J. Brainerd & M. Pressley (Eds.), *Verbal processes in children: Progress in cognitive development research.* New York: Springer.

Veltman, C. (1983). *Language shift in the United States.* Berlin: Mouton.

Wenden, A. L. (1987). Metacognition: An expanded view on the cognitive abilities of L2 learners. *Language Learning, 37,* 573–598.

White, L. (1985). The acquisition of parameterized grammars: Subjacency in second language acquisition. *Second Language Research, 1,* 1–17.

White, L. (1989). *Universal grammar and second language acquisition.* Amsterdam: John Benjamins.

White, L., & Genesee, F. (1992, October). How native is a near-native speaker? Paper presented at the Boston University Conference on Language Development, Boston, MA.

Williams, L. (1974). *Speech perception and production as a function of exposure to a second language.* Unpublished doctoral dissertation, Department of Psychology and Social Relations, Harvard University, Cambridge, MA.

Willig, A. (1985). A meta-analysis of selected studies on the effectiveness of bilingual education. *Review of Educational Research, 55,* 269–317.

Zentella, A. C. (1981). Language variety among Puerto Ricans. In C. A. Ferguson & S. B. Heath (Eds.), *Language in the USA* (pp. 218–238). New York: Cambridge University Press.

# · 19 ·

# THE INFORMAL CURRICULUM

## Mary McCaslin
### UNIVERSITY OF ARIZONA

## Thomas L. Good
### UNIVERSITY OF ARIZONA

In this chapter we discuss what we term the *informal curriculum,* that course of study which, although not deliberately offered in U.S. schools, nonetheless permeates the school context and is learned in some fashion by most students. The informal curriculum is not official; it is not prescribed, orchestrated, or monitored. Yet, we argue, it is the stuff of schooling—the continuous, albeit uncoordinated, stream of momentary experiences that students aggregate and internalize with varying degrees of awareness, protest, and satisfaction.

The informal curriculum is not a particularly new concern in education (e.g., Dewey, 1938), although those who have contributed to our understanding of the unstated/understated implications of schooling typically do not hail from educational psychology (e.g., Metz, 1978). Our purpose is to present an additional viewpoint on the informal curriculum, a viewpoint derived from educational psychology. We maintain that the linkages among society's expectations of schools, the enactment of these expectations in classrooms, and students' mediation of classroom experiences can be viewed profitably from a psychological perspective that explores the social origins of students' intrapersonal processes.

The approach we have suggested, namely, that social influences both in society and in the classroom affect the inter- and intrapersonal processes that compose the informal curriculum, meshes with Doyle's (1992) analysis of the formal curriculum. The informal curriculum as we envision it is influenced, in Doyle's language, by two levels of the formal curriculum: the abstract curriculum, which embodies societal expectations of schooling, and the analytical curriculum, which represents the enactment of the abstract curriculum through classroom teaching. We begin our analysis with a brief discussion of the abstract curriculum, specifically certain features of societal expectations of schooling that embed generic conceptions of students and particular beliefs about gender, race/ethnicity, and economic opportunity, within differential traditions of instruction.

Second, we examine how societal expectations—the abstract curriculum—are manifested in the structural features of classroom teaching—the analytical curriculum—such as tasks, assessments, opportunities for student autonomy, and criteria for accountability. Throughout our analysis we consider the potential impact of different experiences with each of these structural features on students, differences that reflect (and, we will argue, reify) societal beliefs about and expectations of students.

Third, we attempt to delineate the inter- and intrapersonal processes of the informal curriculum. Our discussion of informal curriculum processes links the structural and interpersonal features of the abstract and the analytical curricula. We focus in particular on how different expectations, and thus opportunities, within the abstract and analytical curricula can affect student intrapersonal dynamics of learning, motivation, volition, and affect.

Fourth, we assert that current conceptions of the individual or the task as the basic *unit* of classrooms, and achievement or work as the basic *goal* of classrooms are too discrete and limit the potential contributions of the informal curriculum. We argue that a view of intrapersonal dynamics within the context of interpersonal influence calls for the design of and research on *co-regulation* as fundamental to an explicit informal curriculum. Co-regulation is based on the concepts of (a) *relationship* (with individuals and with objects) as the basic unit of classrooms; (b) *goal coordination* (Dodge, Asher, & Parkhurst, 1989) (of multiple goals within classrooms and between classroom and nonclassroom settings) as the student's basic task; and (c) *provision of supportive scaffolding and affording opportunities* to promote student mediation processes (of motivation, enactment, and self-evaluation) as the teacher's basic task. We delineate areas of potential research on co-regulated learning, the dynamics of student goal coordination (including the possibility of goal modification or abandonment), and the effects of chang-

Preparation of this chapter was supported, in part, by grant No. TPE-8955171 from the National Science Foundation.

ing relationships on teacher supportive scaffolding across the school years.

Fifth, we present selective reviews of two interdependent research themes—the dynamics of help seeking and small-group learning—that, taken together, illustrate the power of an explicit, socially situated integration of the abstract and analytical curricula within the informal curriculum. The relative emphasis within each review differs. We begin with a focus on the setting, then move to interpersonal dynamics and, finally, to intrapersonal processes. As will become apparent, the two research strands are mutually informative and connote reciprocal phenomena.

A social-constructivist/cultural psychology theoretical perspective (e.g., J. Brown, Collins, & Duguid, 1989; Bruner, 1990; Vygotsky, 1962, 1978; Wertsch, 1985) guides our discussion. This perspective highlights the social origins and situated enactment of higher psychological processes; intrapersonal dynamics are related to former and ongoing interpersonal influences and activity. We envision students in emergent interaction (Wertsch & Stone, 1985) with their social world, which consists of the multiple and sometimes non-compatible contexts of school, home, and work. In this perspective, evolving social contexts interact with a developing person whose biology also is part of mind. Biological development and determinants, although important considerations within an emergent interactive perspective, are not pursued in our analysis. We stress socialization processes, affording opportunities, and the dynamics of internalization as features of the informal curriculum that are experienced by students whose need for, perception of, and ability to profit from a given experience differ across the school years (see McCaslin Rohrkemper, 1989, for an extended discussion).

Throughout, we argue that deliberate attention to the informal curriculum is fundamental if schools are to play (and we maintain that they must play) a role that enhances the lives of students within and beyond the schoolyard. Others have also argued for deliberate study of nonacademic outcomes of schooling. Berliner (1992), for example, notes that the primary reason workers are fired is because of poor interpersonal skills and failure to take personal responsibility. Noddings (1992) states:

Teenage pregnancies nearly doubled between 1965 and 1985; the teen suicide rate has doubled in the same period of time; teenage drinking takes a horrible toll in drunk driving accidents and dulled sensibilities; children take guns to school, and homicide is the leading cause of death among minority teens; a disgraceful number of children live in poverty. And still many school people and public officials insist that the job of the schools is to increase academic rigor. In direct opposition, I will argue that the first job of the schools is to care for our children. We should educate all our children not only for competence but also for caring. (p. xiv)

The informal curriculum has enormous power, in part because of its cumulative effects on the "nonability determinants" (Bandura, 1990) of self-esteem and competence and thus on the development of adaptive learning. In this chapter we take the position that classrooms ought to enhance the development of students' adaptive learning, including their hardiness, capacity for self-regulation, sense of personal agency, and valuing of self, community, and the learning process. It seems important to consider how the social/instructional environments of classrooms prepare students for adaptive learning in the 21st century.

## THE ABSTRACT CURRICULUM: SOCIETAL BELIEFS ABOUT EDUCATION, EXPECTATIONS OF STUDENTS, AND CONCEPTIONS OF INSTRUCTION

The term "curriculum" has several definitions. The distinction proposed by Doyle (1992) between the abstract curriculum and the analytical curriculum provides an organizational scheme for our analysis of the precursors of (and reciprocal influences on) what we term the informal curriculum. In Doyle's terms, the abstract curriculum defines the connection between schooling and society, and the analytical curriculum translates curriculum policy into actual curriculum events. Thus, the abstract curriculum essentially defines what schooling is by and to the larger culture at a particular time. In our analysis, the abstract curriculum defines what and who "students" are, the educational expectations of the culture, and the standards by which students and schools are to be judged as U.S. society approaches the 21st century.

## CONCEPTIONS OF EDUCATION

The public's understanding of educational issues is relatively superficial. This is, in large part, because most information about education is based on personal experience, which is limited, and media reports, which are replete with expedient analyses of the causes of educational failure and the failure of educational reforms. And both sources—the individual and the media—adhere to the societal myth about the power of individual effort.

In the 1980s, policymakers and citizens linked U.S. economic failures with poorly motivated and poorly educated students who did not (would not) perform well on standardized tests and in cross-national comparisons (House, 1991). Hence, students, their families, and educators were blamed for the failure of schools to produce students who competed successfully for their country. Reforms within this formula were designed to make teachers and students work harder (Hamilton, 1990; McCaslin & Good, 1992). They involved simplistic and punitive increases in accountability that directly intruded into the analytical curriculum (longer school days, more tests) and the home (more homework).

Society's unquestioning belief in test scores is especially problematic—and expensive. For example, Paris, Lawton, Turner, and Roth (1991) estimate that approximately half a billion dollars *a year* is spent testing students. Smith (1991) notes that time spent on testing is time not spent on instruction, at the rate of approximately 100 hours *a year*. Not only do such accountability tactics fail to measure what they claim (see, e.g., Haladyna, Nolan, & Haas, 1991), but they increasingly force schools to offer a narrow, "measurable," and outdated curriculum, a point to which we will return (see McCaslin & Good, 1992, for an extended discussion).

One reason society seeks testing as an avenue of reform

(although a punitive one) is because students can be held accountable for their test performance in terms of their effort. Effort is synonymous with motivation. Society promotes the rewards of effort: Effort brings success, and failure is due to lack of effort. Rose (1989), in examining his own escape from poverty through education, expresses the effort myth in this way:

We live, in America, with so many platitudes about motivation and self-reliance and individualism—and myths spun from them like Horatio Alger—that we find it hard to accept the fact that they are serious nonsense. (p. 47)

Rose maintains, and we agree (see McCaslin & Good, 1992, 1993), that individual effort, although typically necessary for meaningful achievement, is insufficient. Effort is not merely an individual variable, and education is not merely a student outcome.

## CONCEPTIONS OF STUDENTS

In U.S. culture there is considerable ambivalence about children. The popular culture is replete with discordant messages about children, their culpability and vulnerability, what they are responsible for, and who is responsible for them. Conceptions of "student" are also conflicted and reflect confusion about responsibility, even though there is an easy readiness to assign blame for lack of student attainment of societal goals. Commitment to education in the popular culture vacillates. As we have noted, students are expected to do well on standardized tests, but they are also expected to participate in extracurricular activities (e.g., sport, volunteerism) and to purchase their own "got-to-have-its" with money earned from part-time jobs that vary in quality and in reasonableness of hours (see McCaslin & Good, 1992, for an extended discussion). Ironically, who works, and for what purposes, has changed significantly in recent years. The prototype of urban and rural lower- and working-class students employed in part-time jobs to aid family finances has been replaced by the image of suburban, middle-class students working for self-gratification (Hamilton, 1990). Hamilton (1990) notes that the sheer number of students combining school and work has increased dramatically: 16-year-old males in school are 5 times more likely to work today than in 1940; 16-year-old females in school are 16 times more likely to combine work with school (p. 20).

In short, students are supposed to do it all. This is the time of their lives. But, even though the larger culture does not prioritize its expectations for them, students are expected to detect a priority in the disarray and plan their time and allocate their resources accordingly. When students do not succeed, they are blamed for their failures. Student failure in this scenario resides in their opposition, lack of motivation, and absence of personal responsibility (e.g., U.S. Department of Education, 1990), not in their lack of understanding of societal messages or of ability to organize and pursue them.

The construct "student," then, is fairly generic (and often pejorative) in the larger culture; however, there are identifiable subcategories of students in the cultural repertoire. We briefly note the subcategories of gender, race, and socioeconomic status because (a) individually they represent differentiated perception and treatment of students based on prejudicial knowledge, and (b) collectively they illustrate the pernicious effects of subtle and overt discrimination in the larger culture that pervade the schools by way of the analytical curriculum.

### Different Kinds of Discrimination

Some would argue that incidents of subtle bias are more damaging than overt discrimination because they typically occur without the full awareness of the participants. They constitute what Rowe (1977, in Hall, 1982) described as

small differential behaviors that often occur in the course of everyday interchanges . . . micro-inequities. . . . Each instance may in and of itself seem trivial and may even go unnoticed. However, when taken together throughout the experience of an individual, the small differences in treatment can create an environment which maintain[s] unequal opportunity, because they are the air we breathe . . . and because we cannot change the personal characteristic that leads to this inequity. (p. 5)

Overt discrimination and subtle differentiation are of central concern in the study of the informal curriculum. We attend especially to characteristics of subtle discrimination because they involve the unexamined transfer of cultural biases about gender, race, and socioeconomic status (and other human characteristics)—the "blind spots" that permeate classrooms.

### Different Kinds of Students

*Gender.* Debate continues over what it means to be female or male and over the roles of women and men in our society. The ratio of overt to subtle discrimination toward women has likely changed in the past 25 years; nonetheless, discrimination on the basis of sex endures. For instance, it is illegal to pay women less than men for equal work, but the law does not address differences among jobs. Occupations traditionally dominated by women, such as nursing, teaching, and social work, are paid less and structured with a lower pay ceiling, independent of the work being done. The Associated Press's analysis of the 1991 U.S. Bureau of the Census data found that at every educational level, women make less money than men with the same amount of schooling. Unequal pay for equal education becomes even more marked over the life span. Women's relative earnings drop steadily so that by the time they are in their mid-50s, women earn approximately half the money earned by similarly educated men (54% if college educated; 53% if a high school graduate). Gender inequality pervades societal expectations for schooling.

In the not too distant past, schools were created only for men; when women eventually gained access to schooling, the school climate was structured more for male than for female students, at all levels of schooling. Society does not call for deliberate stratification of schooling to create gender differences as explicitly as it once did. However, expectations about gender that students bring to school are inadvertently sustained through more subtle mechanisms of hierarchical instruction in gender-based skills (Frey & Slaby, 1979), goals (Dweck, Davidson, Nelson, & Enna, 1978), and dispositions (Fennema, 1987). Fennema (1987) summarizes the effects of this maintenance system:

W]hat inequities in educational outcomes exist? Males do not develop their verbal skills to the same level as females, and females achieve at lower levels than males in mathematics and science. Perhaps more important, fewer females than males develop leadership skills, but more demonstrate lowered self-esteem in their ability to learn, negative attributional styles, and habits of dependency. (pp. 335–336)

In short, the result of this silent acquiescence is the loss of human talent. As Hall (1982) underscores:

Whether overt or subtle, differential treatment based on sex is far from innocuous. Its cumulative effects can be damaging not only to individual women and men students but also to the educational process itself. (p. 3)

It is beyond the scope of this chapter to review in depth gender-related societal expectations and their intrusion into schooling. We refer interested readers to several recent comprehensive reviews and studies on issues of gender and schooling (American Association of University Women [AAUW], 1992, 1993; Noddings, 1992; M. Sadker, D. Sadker, & Klein, 1991). Systematic attempts to change cultural beliefs about gender, however, are virtually nonexistent (M. Sadker et al., 1991; Tetreault & Schmuck, 1985).

*Race/Ethnicity.* In a better world it would go without saying that the differential—detrimental—treatment of human beings as a function of race or ethnicity would be deplorable. But this is not a better world, and prejudice based on race or ethnicity is pervasive in U.S. society.

Separate Education; Unequal Education. Schools in the United States remain largely segregated; 63.3% of black students attend racially segregated schools, and in some states the figure is 80% (Hacker, 1992). Hispanic and other language-minority children also attend segregated schools or are segregated because of language barriers within a given school. Romero, Mercado, and Vázquez-Faria (1987) report that the non-English language background population in the United States is expected to increase from 30 million in 1980 to 39.5 million in 2000. These authors estimate that 2.5 million school-age children live in homes where a language other than English is spoken. Separate schools are not equal schools. Formulas for school funding ensure an inverse relationship between need and receipt: The rich get richer (see also Berliner, 1992; McCaslin & Good, 1992; Natriello, McDill, & Pallas, 1990). In our society the correlation between income and race or ethnicity ensures that the majority of minority students attend underfunded schools. We will return to the dynamics of personal status and economic funding.

Assimilation Demands. Federal support for bilingual education is declining and society's belief in language assimilation is on the rise. One manifestation of society's intolerant attitude toward immigrants, refugees, and resident minorities in the 1980s was the English-only movements of that decade, which resulted in legislation making English the "official" state language in 17 states. Indeed, societal attitudes about the heritage of limited-English speakers vis-à-vis "what it means to be Ameri-can" mediate second language instruction and learning (Snow, 1992).

Since the enactment of Title VII, which provided for federally funded bilingual education, in the early 1970s, little consensus about the effectiveness of these programs and how to measure it has emerged (see, for an extended discussion, special issues of the *American Journal of Education* [Arias, 1986] and *Educational Researcher* [Editors, Hakuta & Pease-Alvarez 1992]). Cziko (1992), for example, has argued that the effectiveness of such programs cannot be known and that emphasis is more appropriately placed on their possibilities rather than on their probable outcome (see also Romero et al., 1987).

Minority Identity. Minority communities do not seem to be successful in mediating the inappropriate expectations for minority youth harbored by the majority culture. Regrettably, prejudicial attitudes and behavior are part of our analysis of the informal curriculum. Ogbu (1992) makes a compelling case for understanding the nature of the relationship between a given minority group and the majority, white culture. He maintains that minority groups fundamentally differ in that relationship and, thus, confront fundamentally different problems in attaining success in school. We disagree with Ogbu's analysis and categorization of minority subgroups because our concern is with any minority student who is differently, prejudicially treated because of her or his race or ethnicity. For example, we consider both the low, undifferentiated expectations of African-American and Native American students because of their race or ethnicity and the high, differentiated expectations of Asian and Jewish students solely because of theirs, to be inappropriate.

Ogbu (1992) maintains that minority group members share difficulty in school that is due to differing preconceptions about schooling or approaches to learning, English language limitation, and so on. They are also limited by the insensitivity of the analytical curriculum to these differences in expectation (e.g., S. Phillips, 1983), prior experience (e.g., Rodriguez, 1982), cultural heritage (e.g., Au, 1980), and community life (e.g., Moll, 1992).

Ogbu further argues that, in certain situations, minority persons do not believe that they will have access to the rewards that effort, hard work, and persistence are expected to bring. Similar to Erikson's (1964) analysis of the dynamics of negative identity and Steele's (1988) description of "disidentification," Ogbu argues that the very boundaries used to exclude minorities can be transformed by them, changing obstacles to opportunities; features to resist can become features to embrace (e.g., dress, language, communication style). In contrast to Ogbu, we maintain that the dynamics of negative identity are not restricted to a particular subset of minority (i.e., involuntary minorities, such as black Americans), nor are they necessarily the purview of a particular stage of life (Erikson, 1964). Rather, we suspect this process can be found whenever and wherever an individual is at a disadvantage because of prejudice, when the requirement is to "trade ethnicity for school learning" (Secada & Lightfoot, 1993, p. 53).

Role of Schools. Not all the problems that minorities confront in society can be dealt with by schooling. As we and many others have argued, minority students, especially if they are also economically disadvantaged, need many forms of structural support if they are to succeed in school and beyond (see McCaslin & Good, 1992). These structures need to include support from minority communities for the academic success of their youth (see also Ogbu, 1992; Rose, 1989). The fundamental obligation of schools may be to provide youth with unbiased information about race and minority experience in America and to confront the inherent tensions of the "melting pot" metaphor.

*Socioeconomics and Aptitude.* A Natural Experiment. Kaufman and Rosenbaum (1992) explored the effects on black youth of family relocation from urban housing projects. In 1976 the U.S. government was held accountable for segregated housing in Chicago; the results were the Gautreaux program, which required government financial assistance for family relocation, and a natural experiment as black families moved to another urban location (with few resources for schools) or to the suburbs (with available resources for schools and community, e.g., opportunities for afterschool work).

Some of the black youths whose families chose the suburbs evinced initial adjustment difficulties (e.g., academic expectations) relative to youths whose families remained in an urban setting. Seven years later, however, suburban youths were more likely than those who had stayed in the city to be in high school, in college preparatory classes, attending college, or employed in jobs with benefits. Kaufman and Rosenbaum (1992) attributed these differences in quality of life opportunities to increased community resources available to the young black people whose families had moved to the suburbs. As one parent in the suburban group noted, those effects included higher expectations and a change in personal disposition. She stated that her daughter "wouldn't have the drive, the challenge, the desire to advance that's needed to get ahead in life . . . if we hadn't moved. She wouldn't be in college now" (p. 237).

Comparisons with the beliefs of parents who relocated to other urban (financially stressed) areas underscore the importance of intrapersonal effects of tangible resources: "The housing project environment brings you down . . . makes you not care about the future . . . living in the type of environment where nobody wants nothing, nobody does nothing, nobody gets up and tries to have nothing" (p. 237). These data are in stark contrast to societal beliefs about economic status and aptitude, to which we now turn.

Societal Beliefs. The abstract curriculum embodies societal beliefs about and expectations for the education of its citizenry. It is useful to consider how these beliefs differ as a function of broad economic categories as well as individual characteristics like gender and race or ethnicity. One of the more obvious of these societal categories concerns resources. It is naive to consider gender, race/ethnicity, and economics as independent contributors to societal expectations for schooling as these characteristics are correlated. Nonetheless, it seems useful to consider each factor in relative isolation. Here we stress economic resources and the relation between wealth and aptitude.

School financing formulas that rely on local funding of schools reinforce societal beliefs about economic differentiation and quality of student learning. Schools that differ in economic resources tend to differ in notions of what works for their students. Similarly, within a given setting, students who are perceived to differ in personal resources (e.g., realized ability) are believed to profit from different educational opportunities. As others have noted (e.g., Oakes, 1992), economic status and ability ranking, as measured by normative, standardized tests, covary. The skills, knowledge, and, we argue as most essential, *dispositions* that economically (and educationally) advantaged families afford their children are those same domains labeled "intelligent," measured by traditional aptitude tests, and valued as (some would argue *because* they are) scarce resources. These resources are also the ticket to advantaged classrooms.

Thus, the traditional definition of intelligence that undergirds the educational system accentuates the role of wealth in the manifestation of what many persist in viewing as innate, fixed, and normally distributed. Such reasoning supports a differential curriculum for differentiated learners as necessary (Raudenbush, Rowan, & Cheong, 1993). One result is a two-tiered system of American education that, although no longer considered appropriate by many educators (e.g., National Council of Teachers of Mathematics, 1990), nonetheless endures.

Indeed, the ramifications of the relationship between economics and the definition and measurement of ability are pronounced in the distribution of educational opportunity. According to Oakes (1992), race, social class, and track assignments correlate for both elementary and secondary grades such that children of low-income and non-Asian minority families are overrepresented in low track classes compared with children of affluent or white families. Similarly, schools that enroll children of primarily low-income and non-Asian minority families offer relatively more remedial and vocational tracks and fewer academic options in their curriculum. The reverse pattern characterizes schools that enroll children of predominantly white or affluent families. Differential offerings continue in afterschool care programs: More affluent schools offer a range of educationally stimulating activities, such as computer courses, while the less affluent provide opportunities for homework completion (Perrault, 1983, reported in Tangri & Moles, 1987).

*Summary.* Bifurcation of educational opportunity for students due to gender, race, differential economic resource, or perceived ability or need to learn has been the focus of heated debate for decades (e.g., Berliner, 1992; Goodlad, 1984; Oakes, 1992). Our purpose is to demonstrate how societal beliefs can permeate schooling through the enactment of curricular opportunities in the classroom, which in turn filters student experience of the informal curriculum. Any analysis of this sort, by necessity, engages in prototypes. In so doing, much variation within and overlap between types of schooling experience is omitted from discussion (e.g., Page, 1992). We recognize this limitation but believe there is much to be gained in understanding the potential of the informal curriculum to differentially envelop students.

## CONCEPTIONS OF INSTRUCTION

Ironically, two instructional traditions that have been at the center of debate within the educational community since the time of Socrates coincide with popular societal beliefs about the kinds of educational opportunities differing students ought to receive. We use the framework suggested by Jackson (1986) to describe briefly each of these traditions, the transformative and the mimetic, attending to the general goals, teaching styles, and indicators of success that characterize each. Both traditions have a legitimate history and defensible claims; in practice, however, each is associated with a differentiation among learners that elevates one at the expense of the other.

We then distinguish between the conceptions of curricular goals and appropriate instruction that are typically held for the more advantaged students, that is, those who are advantaged by their enrollment in financially more able schools and/or by their perceived (higher) realized ability (or gender or race), and the curricular goals typically held for the less advantaged students, that is, those who are less advantaged because of their enrollment in poorly financed schools and/or because of their perceived (lower) potential (or gender or race). For more advantaged students, the curricular goal typically centers on problem solving and the elaboration of meaning. For less advantaged students, the curriculum typically focuses on drill and memorization of facts (see McCaslin & Good, 1992; Raudenbush et al., 1993). It is important to note that, at the level of the abstract curriculum, "differential" implies "hierarchical and compatible." As we will see, however, at the level of the analytical curriculum, "differential" often simply means "detrimental."

## Instructional Traditions

In *The Practice of Teaching*, Philip Jackson (1986) describes what he terms the *transformative tradition* in instruction and compares it with the *mimetic tradition*. The essential goal of the transformative tradition in educational practice is to foster a fundamental, qualitative change in the learner that goes beyond incremental changes in quantity of knowledge or skill. Successful teaching in the transformative tradition includes changes in learner dispositions and character that endure; it seeks to modify core values and attitudes. Transformative educators' teaching styles are as difficult to specify as are their attainments. However, Jackson (1986, pp. 124–125) describes personal modeling, "soft" suasion, and the use of narrative (especially stories with a moral nature) as common elements. Transformative teachers' classrooms are noteworthy for their discussion, demonstration, and argumentation; they are viewed as the arena for the development of "fuller participants in an evolving moral order" (Jackson, 1986, p. 127). We argue as well that, in practice, these are participants whose traits are valued by that order. Importantly, the relationship between teacher and student within this tradition appears personal and intense, with greater opportunity and demand placed on learners to process and share information.

The second tradition in educational practice discussed by Jackson (1986), the mimetic tradition, focuses on the transmission from teacher to student of knowledge and skills that are considered essential. In this tradition, learning is imitative, so that knowledge can be predictably acquired and measured; more is better. Correct answers are the measure of teaching success. Teaching styles are often formulaic in this tradition. Mimetic approaches typically include the language of "basic skills" (Rosenshine & Stevens, 1986), the procedures of direct instruction, broadly defined (Rosenshine, 1993), the goals of

mastery learning (Bloom, 1976), and the outcomes of competency testing (e.g., Popham, 1987). Teaching reduces the information-processing opportunities and demands on students, and with them the burden of initiative-based participation. We add that the likely relationship between teacher and student is more professional than personal, more efficient than intense (although, as we later discuss, these environments can be intensely efficient, to the further detriment of some learners). Indeed, in practice, students needing more personal and extensive teacher contact (those defined as needing remediation) are typically sent out of the classroom to be dealt with by a specialist.

In the current vernacular, in the mimetic tradition the teacher presents, in the transformative tradition the learner discovers. As Jackson persuasively argues, however, the mimetic and transformative traditions are complementary: Reality is a "vision of teaching as both a noble and a prosaic undertaking" (1986, p. 128). Teachers likely do both; the issue is one of proportion and, within that, quality.

## Form versus Quality

Instructional tradition is independent of quality. One can imagine transformative teaching that is impersonal and formulaic, and mimetic teaching that is engaging and coconstructed by teacher and students. The confounding of value with tradition is common in the educational literature (see also Rosenshine, 1993), as is the confounding of type of student learning with instructional tradition (e.g., Ausubel, 1968; Ausubel, Novak, & Hanesian, 1978). Thus, our concern is not with the instructional traditions of the abstract curriculum per se. We maintain that education involves both acquisition and integration; thus, in our view students benefit from a blend of the traditions. We are troubled, however, that the proportion and quality of the mix short-circuits some students' educational opportunity.

We would hope that all students would have the opportunity to engage in the sort of meaningful integration that characterizes transformative teaching. Opportunities for this type of instruction may well diminish for all learners, however, because problem solving and meaningful elaboration are not predictable outcomes of instruction, whether that instruction is in the transformative or mimetic tradition (Gagné, 1985; Blumenfeld, 1992b), and therefore are not apt to translate into enhanced standardized achievement scores. Indeed, it seems uncomfortably safe to predict that current calls for problem-solving, process-oriented curricula will become even more rare in practice (see also Bruner, 1985; Jackson, 1986) because the accountability pressures that drive the educational system are more congruent with mimetic instruction and the concomitant assumptions about objectivity, precision in measurement, and the normal distribution. Perhaps a more complicating issue is that politicians typically are not aware of the gap between problem-solving capacity and accountability measures. Thus, they fail to recognize that their demands for increased accountability have historically pushed the curriculum farther away from a problem-solving orientation.

## Differential Instruction for Differentiated Learners

In practice, then, teaching is at best a blend of traditions: the transformative—the teaching for understanding, problem solving, and elaboration that we call "meaningful integration"—and the mimetic—the teaching for acquisition of facts and skills that we call "intellectual skills" (after Gagné, 1985). Within this blend, however, different opportunities for meaningful integration and level of skill acquisition exist among students (Raudenbush et al., 1993).

*Advantaged Learners.* Our concern here is with the opportunities afforded and demanded of the advantaged learner, especially the opportunity to discover. We maintain that learning through discovery in U.S. schools is a privilege of the advantaged that is particularly important to explore because it evokes a view of the learner that, in turn, promotes a self-system of motivational goal setting and attainment within a social system of high status and reward. Hence, we examine an important conduit between the abstract curriculum and personal reality.

In *The Process of Education,* Jerome Bruner (1960) called for a contemporary approach to education within the transformative tradition: an appreciation of organization rather than discrete fact, a preference for problem definition over problem solution, and a search for questions more than answers. Using a compelling extension of Piagetian (1983) conceptions of development and the processes of learning, Bruner advocated discovery learning through a "spiral curriculum" organized from the top down (see also Shulman, 1970). He provided educators with specific examples of discovery learning curricula in math, science, and social studies. In each of these subject areas, Bruner argued for a spiral curriculum predicated on the learner's continuous discovery of incongruity and similarity among concepts and problems. Bruner's learners, like Piaget's, were actively seeking to understand the laws of the natural; unlike Piaget's learners, Bruner's learners also sought to understand the artificial (e.g., culture).

Bruner's disentangling of Piagetian constructs of mental representations and operations from the strict confines of stage theory empowered educators well beyond the early childhood classroom. Indeed, much research in the ensuing decades pointed to the fruitfulness of distinguishing these constructs from the functions of prior knowledge (e.g., Case, 1985; Chi, 1987; Glaser & Pellegrino, 1987). Much debate also accompanied the enactment of discovery learning (e.g., Ausubel, 1968; Ausubel et al., 1978; Shulman, 1970). Issues of content (e.g., the role of values in MACOS: Man—A Course of Study, the Brunerian social studies curriculum) and issues of learner ability to profit from this instructional approach recurred. An uneasy consensus emerged among educators that (a) more advantaged learners would likely profit from a curriculum predicated on the processes of equilibration and (b) asking less advantaged learners to "discover" or self-instruct could be detrimental to their performance (see, e.g., Cronbach & Snow, 1977) and motivation.

Thus, in practice, when instruction has been framed by a spiral curriculum, it typically has been confined to advantaged students in mathematics and science. Indeed, the base metaphor of discovery learning, the learner-as-scientist who acts on objects, is evident in current research on student error in meaningful integration of math and science (e.g., Eaton, Anderson, & Smith, 1984), the learning goal set for the advantaged. Long established Piagetian-based concepts, such as "misconception," have been powerful tools for understanding enduring and generalized difficulties that students encounter in meaningful learning in these subjects.

The current adaptation of discovery learning changes instructional tasks for teachers in important ways. Namely, it shifts the burden from the learner to the *teacher* to discover and illuminate prior and present (mis)understandings that impede each student's meaningful integration of the subject matter. Student misconceptions are targeted because they are believed fundamentally to impair student ability to elaborate on and profit from present instructional experiences. Apparently, even advantaged learners need help recognizing that they should be experiencing Piaget's "disequilibrium" and engaging in relatively more accommodation than assimilation processes. This conception of student thinking and learning has much in common with current information-processing models that distinguish metacognitive from cognitive strategies (e.g., Chipman, Segal, & Glaser, 1985; Segal, Chipman, & Glaser, 1985).

Embedded within the abstract curriculum of meaningful integration is a conception of student who, although apparently not as self-aware as educators wish, is, nonetheless, an abstraction of a learner that is highly valued in this culture: one who seeks to understand, to explore, to integrate. A learner who, like Socrates, knows what is not known, what to ask, and how to seek it (see also Jackson, 1986): an individual who is known by disposition and capability rather than by accumulated facts.

Thus, the abstract curriculum includes and promotes a vision of learner that enjoys special status in our society. Advantaged status is enhanced by a curriculum that supports the elaboration of knowledge even as it challenges what is known. In short, the advantaged student-as-learner is cast as an information processor in the Piagetian mold: an individual acting on objects, struggling to achieve equilibrium between her or his current understanding and the challenges of the task, with an arsenal of generalized and domain-specific cognitive strategies and metacognitive supports (see also McCaslin, 1989). Further, when learning goals do require factual or skill acquisition, these students are more apt to approach such intellectual skill learning within a larger framework of "meaningful subsumption" (Ausubel, 1968).

*Disadvantaged Learners.* The situation is quite different in schools that are characterized by less economic opportunity or in classes for disadvantaged students. Typically, these settings adhere to the curricular goals within the mimetic tradition—intellectual skill acquisition—and, within this tradition, from a bottom-up perspective (Shulman, 1970) that contrasts with the top-down approach more typical of the instruction of the advantaged. Thus, disadvantaged learners are more apt to learn the "basics" as discrete and isolated bits. Ironically, the students who are believed to possess fewer resources for learning are presented with the more difficult integrative task (Good, 1981). We maintain that this is because, at the abstract level, curriculum goals are hierarchical. Disadvantaged learners are not believed to need the insights and aspirations of the advantaged; their lot is to fill in the fact, perform the skill.

In effect, the differing instructional traditions have further deepened the fissures in our society. Disadvantaged learners are not only exposed to more intellectual skill instruction than are advantaged learners, they are also exposed to its worst manifestation (see also Goodlad, 1984). One also could convincingly argue that it is the disadvantaged learner who is in need of an intense and personal relationship with the teacher (e.g., Dyson, 1987). As we have noted, however, each instructional tradition embodies a teaching style that differs in the nature of the teacher–student relationship. The instructional tradition that informs intellectual skill acquisition is relatively more efficient, bureaucratic, and impersonal than is the tradition that seeks meaningful integration. Thus, disadvantaged students may also have a more difficult interpersonal task in the classroom than their advantaged peers. They may not be as able to identify with the teacher as an adult who knows and cares about them, who seeks to influence them in fundamental ways, and as someone who will simply look out for them. There are teachers who do meaningfully intervene in disadvantaged students' lives within the intellectual skill acquisition tradition (see Dyson, 1987; Rose, 1989); however, this reflects more the commitment of the individual teacher than the intent of the instructional tradition.

Externally imposed accountability mandates would seem to help the situation, given the linkages between mimetic instruction and "objective" tests. However, disadvantaged schools and learners are severely limited in the arenas within which they can "successfully" compete, often only against each other in locally mandated criterion-based yet ultimately norm-referenced tests. Drill and practice of basic skills in the hope of producing marketable skills in the workplace (Berliner, 1992) has not paid off in standardized test performance, although there is mounting evidence that preparation for such tests does much to interfere with instruction (M. L. Smith, 1991) and, we add, damage student motivation.

It is sobering to note that "second chances" within these settings or with disadvantaged students do not necessarily bring about desired effects in student learning or disposition. In a comparative ethnographic study of learning- and non-learning-disabled students in regular and vocational education tracks in a blue-collar community junior high school, S. E. Miller, Leinhardt, and Zigmond (1988) found that accommodating disadvantaged students by limiting demands made on them or providing alternatives may keep them in school, but graduation per se may not represent a desired outcome. They state (p. 485):

Our sense is that accommodation, although it may keep students in school, may not only limit adolescents' acquisition of formal knowledge, but may also be a poor model for preparing adolescents for the world beyond school. Believing that there will always be a second chance, learning that you can get through school without challenge and hard work, and being bored may teach students to look for second chances. . . . [The challenge] is not simply to keep students in school until graduation, but to provide them with educationally worthwhile experiences while they are there.

Apparently a second chance at the same thing does not ameliorate the effects of the system; it simply exacerbates it. Indeed, the literature on grade retention (Mantzicopoulos & Morrison, 1992) supports this conclusion.

Embedded within the abstract curriculum of intellectual skills is a conception of student that is an abstraction of the "worker": one who is known for skill rather than character, who is valued for punctuality more than initiative, volition rather than motivation. This is the learner we expect to "bear down" not "dream up"; to reproduce, not create. Thus, disadvantaged

students in this instructional system are typically *not* perceived as a function of their cognitive development and enduring preconceptions in interaction with the instructional goal of meaningful integration. Rather, these students are known by their specific prior information and skills. They make mistakes rather than entertain misconceptions and, thus, are more likely to "review and practice" than to "experience incongruity." In short, the disadvantaged student-as-worker is cast as an information processor in a narrow behavioral mold: an individual who masters discrete facts and skills through repetition and rehearsal and who is reinforced by quick, frequent, and correct answers and the rewards they elicit (see also Rohrkemper & Corno, 1988).

## Summary

The abstract curriculum represents societal expectations of what schooling is for whom. Expectations of and goals for students embodied in the abstract curriculum are differentiated and divergent. We have specifically discussed gender, race/ ethnicity, and socioeconomic status as dimensions along which society categorizes its citizens. We have used the terms advantaged and disadvantaged to describe learners for whom societal expectations are more and less empowering. The implications of the differentiated societal vision of the purposes of schooling for the quality of education that students experience are considerable. We now turn to the daily enactment of these societal expectations in classrooms through the analytical curriculum. First, however, we note that there are obviously other learners differentiated within the abstract curricular vision (e.g., learners with physical disabilities, emotional disorders) whom we have not discussed. Their very labels connote their relative status.

## THE ANALYTICAL CURRICULUM: CURRICULUM ENACTMENT AND CLASSROOM DYNAMICS

The abstract curriculum includes differentiated and divergent goals for students as one way of coping with diversity and meeting societal needs. It is not necessarily the case, however, that the *enactment* of societal expectations through the analytical curriculum is also knowingly differential. As we will see, much of the variation in students' daily experiences of the analytical curriculum is due to unexpected and unexamined effects of the management of instruction and the management of students.

In aggregation, however, students' steady diet of uncoordinated strands of classroom experience likely *results* in student attainment of the divergent societal goals set for them. We do not believe, however, that this is necessarily the conscious intent of individual educators. Rather, we hypothesize that much of the differentiated (and debilitating) aspects of the analytical curriculum experienced by students is a function of the interplay of (a) unexamined permeation of societal beliefs into classroom processes through its participants (e.g., administrators, teachers, students, parents); (b) uncritical acceptance of institutional demands on curriculum and instruction; (c) the pressing immediacy and multidimensionality of classroom teaching and learning, which considerably strain human judgment and decision-making (Doyle, 1986; T. Good & Brophy, 1994; Jackson, 1968);

(d) unexamined ramifications of particular definitions of and orientations toward teaching dilemmas (Ball, 1993; Lampert, 1985); and (e) implicit theories of learning, motivation, and individual differences that may impede the realization of curricular goals or be differentially appropriate for particular instructional strategies.

We generate a list of hypothesized sources of differentiated or detrimental treatment of students via the analytical curriculum because there is a relative paucity of informative research on these processes within the context of classroom and school settings to which teachers can turn to inform their practice. Indeed, one goal of this chapter is to call persuasively for more informed research on the structure and functions of the analytical curriculum and on the role of the analytical curriculum in the dynamics of the informal curriculum. We begin our analysis of the differential features of the analytical curriculum with what others have argued is its basic unit: task (e.g., Blumenfeld, 1992a; Doyle, 1983; Mergendoller, 1988).

## TASK AFFORDANCE

The idea that classrooms are workplaces (Marx & Walsh, 1988, p. 207) has functioned as a powerful metaphor for classroom processes since the 1980s, reflecting in large part the impact of arguments by Doyle (1983), who maintained that teacher behavior (the dominant focus of research in the previous decade) was not the most direct way to understand what students learn. Doyle argued that it was more efficacious to consider that what students do in classrooms is work (as compared with "learn" or "play," for example); thus, what students *work on* is a critical feature of classrooms.

According to Doyle (1983), academic work consists of three major features: the products expected, the operations that generate them, and the resources available to support completion. In short, academic tasks "are defined by answers students are required to produce and the routes that can be used to obtain these answers" (p. 161). The decade since publication of "Academic Work" (Doyle, 1983) has been characterized by a recognition of the role of task in addition to teacher and student behavior and thought processes in the dynamics of classrooms. We will return to the student-as-worker metaphor when we consider the relative significance of motivation and volition in student intrapersonal processes in the informal curriculum. Here our concern is with the elevation of task in classroom research.

Importantly, the focus on task has been consistent with an information-processing (e.g., Simon, 1969) and with a coconstructive (e.g., Vygotsky, 1978) or "activity" (e.g., Zinchenko, 1985) theory of thinking, learning, and change. For example, much of the recent research on tasks has examined as well the interplay of student motivation, affect, and thinking processes in task involvement (e.g., Blumenfeld, 1992b; Corno, 1992; McCaslin Rohrkemper, 1989). It is critical that task research be broadened to include the social world of students, including the relations between teacher and students (e.g., Blumenfeld & Meece, 1988; Marx & Walsh, 1988) and among students (e.g., Blumenfeld, 1992; Good, McCaslin, & Reys, 1992).

Our purpose here is not to review the task literature but to consider the general issue of task affordance in the analytical curriculum and its potential for the intrapersonal processes of the informal curriculum. We focus on three features of task affordance—task complexity, task difficulty, and individual preference for task difficulty—each of which informs the potential relationship between learners and tasks.

### Task Complexity

The match between task complexity and individual motivation has received uneven attention in classroom research. Rohrkemper and Corno (1988) have argued that educators' nearly exclusive focus on student task success as an indicator of student learning has led to the engineering of tasks that ensure success rather than promote (and perhaps at the expense of) learning. They argue that designing such tasks obviates the need for and student potential to undertake meaningful learning.

This is, in part, because of the dynamic relationship between task complexity and the development and refinement of metacognitive and cognitive strategies. Meaningful learning opportunities—complex tasks—allow the use, expansion, and refinement of one's learning tools (McCaslin Rohrkemper, 1989; Rohrkemper, Slavin, & McCauley, 1983). Thus, in this perspective, task complexity is an essential feature of the level of learning per se *and* the development of "self-regulated" learning; the absence of task complexity limits learning *and* the potential to learn.

Atkinson (1964) posited a task-specific motivational relationship between task complexity and learner competence, a relationship he termed "individual motivation strength." He argued that the more complex a task, the relatively lower is the learner's optimal level of motivation. Conversely, the less complex the task, the relatively higher is the optimal motivation level. For example, if a student is highly motivated to engage in a complex task but finds the task frustrating and her performance wanting, reducing motivation strength is predicted to increase performance. If the task is relatively simple, however, and performance is insufficient, then an increase in motivation level is predicted to enhance performance. Exactly how one might go about modifying one's own motivation level was not specifically researched by Atkinson, but his notion of learner malleability is consistent with strategies for task and self-modification as a function of adaptive learning (McCaslin & Good, 1996; McCaslin & Murdock, 1991; McCaslin Rohrkemper, 1989; Rohrkemper & Bershon, 1984; Rohrkemper & Corno, 1988) and volitional control strategies in particular (Corno, 1992, 1993).

The latter case described by Atkinson (1964), which is essentially a case of understimulation, wherein the task per se is not complex enough to engage meaningful thought and requires extra motivation (or, in the current vernacular, "volition"), is of particular concern in any discussion of differential task affordance in the analytical curriculum. All students likely experience the boredom that is the "stress of tedium" (Rohrkemper & Corno, 1988, p. 299); however, it is likely the less advantaged students, who are exposed to the "coverage curriculum" with extensive repetition of intellectual skills (e.g., Porter, 1989) and receive little intellectual demand from the teacher (Good & Brophy, 1994), who typically have the more difficult motivational task. Ironically, instruction as inculcation appears to require, in Atkinson's framework, relatively more motivation on students' part to engage tasks in the first place. Ach's (1910, cited in Heckhausen, 1991; in Kuhl & Beckmann, 1985) "difficulty law of motivation," wherein level of effort was found to adjust automatically to the difficulty of the task, also suggests that an extra motivational burden ("volitional" burden) is placed on students if tasks are not sufficiently stimulating. Not only are they required to overcome a lack of task stimulation to see through required tasks and to meet expectations for effortful performance, but their performance, even if objectively successful, does not involve the refinement of their learning tools or an expansion of their "tool kit" (McCaslin Rohrkemper, 1989). In these task situations, then, students may be learning how to stay with a boring task, an important volitional skill, but we would hope this intrapersonal knowledge was not the lesson objective.

## Task Difficulty

Task difficulty and task complexity are typically correlated in research, but they are not necessarily comparable in classrooms. As Doyle (1983, 1986) has noted, classroom accountability systems are an essential feature of tasks. And in classrooms, task complexity (a function of task features and learner competence) and task difficulty (based on the accountability criteria) may actually be inversely related. Consider, for example, the distinction between "higher order" (believed more complex) and "lower order" (believed relatively easy) questions. As Good and Brophy (1994) note, it is often easier to "do well enough" in response to a complex question than it is to a simple one. This is because the assessment criteria for each typically differ.

For example, a student may be asked to discuss the putative relationship among theory, research, and practice in education (theoretically a complex and difficult question) or the correct location for the Nebraska Symposium on Motivation (theoretically a less complex and less difficult question). The questions differ in two important ways. First, because they differ in (objective) complexity, the interpretation of student behavior in response to each question may also differ. A halting response to the first, more complex question may signal a "considered" opinion; delay or hesitation in answering the second, less complex question, however, signals failure. Second, the ultimate assessment criterion also differs for each: There is a much broader bandwidth of acceptable response to the first question than to the second ("Kansas" isn't close enough). Thus, when asked a complex question, students are given more time and more room than when they are asked a less complex question. In effect, it is often the case that the more complex the question, the less difficult is the task. Research by Fields (1990) illustrates these dynamics. Elementary students selected and reportedly preferred complex and ambiguous tasks because ambiguous tasks were perceived as the *least* risky. These students' mediation of accountability criteria was the opposite of that proposed by Doyle (1983, 1986): More ambiguity meant less risk, not more.

Further, the effects of each type of question on subsequent expectations for comprehension likely differ. Consider the possible modification of your strategies for comprehension monitoring of this chapter if, at this juncture, you were asked to discuss the validity of the asserted relationship among the abstract, analytical, and informal curricula for different types of learners. What if the assigned task was to identify three types

of curricula? The point is that anticipation of performance opportunities may alter learning and comprehension strategies in ways not necessarily congruent with the apparent complexity of the task (reading this chapter).

It does not take much imagination to predict which type of student is asked (at best proportionately) more of which level of question as he or she attempts to master the analytical curriculum. Once again, the advantaged are likely advantaged, not only through the curriculum established for them, but also through more fluid response criteria for the tasks and questions they engage. Their performance opportunities also are more apt to be sufficiently structured to arouse optimum motivation and cognitive engagement, and thus more likely to afford and promote the development of self-regulation and self-evaluation of learning progress. Simple questions, like simple tasks, do not enhance arousal (except, perhaps, fear of evaluation), nor do they enable meaningful self-evaluation of emergent competence. Too often, less advantaged students are restricted to either/or judgments (their own or others') rather than the more enabling self-assessments of incomplete learning or partial understandings that are features of the education of their more advantaged peers.

In short, task difficulty is not objective. It is constructed by the learner as a function of learner competence, motivation, and expectations for performance criteria in emergent interaction with task affordance and accountability features, in a given instance and within the context of aggregated previous instances. We will argue that, in terms of the informal curriculum, task difficulty is also a function of the *social* nature of classrooms, which yields even more idiosyncratic task difficulty experiences as students attempt to coordinate multiple presses toward different goals (e.g., as social comparison processes enter the achievement equation [McCaslin & Murdock, 1991]).

## Task Difficulty Preference

In contrast to educational research, "moderate difficulty" has been a constant theme in motivational and risk-taking research (e.g., Clifford, 1991; Rohrkemper, 1986b). Moderate difficulty is typically defined by a match between task demands and learner competence that is associated with an approximately 50:50 chance of successful learner performance. Research on task difficulty preference integrates risk with motivation (see Clifford, 1991, for a review of these traditions). Preference for level of difficulty has been hypothesized as a function of (a) individual affect (e.g., Atkinson, 1964); (b) a need for information about self-competence (e.g., Weiner, 1986), be it protective (e.g., Covington, 1992) or realistic (e.g., Trope & Brickman, 1975); (c) a desire to learn or perform (e.g., C. Ames, 1992; Clifford, 1991); and (d) a need to feel in control of one's own learning (e.g., Deci, 1975; Deci, Vallerand, Pelletier, & Ryan, 1991) and of oneself (e.g., Csikszentmihalyi, 1990; deCharms, 1976).

Research on preferred task difficulty also typically integrates task choice with task preference; thus, distinctions among complexity, difficulty, preference, and choice often can be blurred. And, unfortunately for those who would apply task preference research to the study of the analytical curriculum, choice is not an essential feature of classroom learning. Many motivational researchers, however, call for task choice if learners are ever to become intrinsically motivated or at least experience moments of intrinsic motivation (e.g., Clifford, 1991; Deci & Ryan, 1985; Nolen, 1988).

Research on gender mediation of task choice, however, cautions endorsement of choice as the vehicle to intrinsic motivation. Nash (1979, as reported in Fennema, 1987) found that from Grades 2 through 12, students perceive certain intellectual skills as feminine (e.g., social, verbal) and others as masculine (e.g., spatial, mechanical). At the onset of puberty, students add mathematics and science to the "masculine" list. These beliefs are all the more troubling because students *choose* tasks they identify as *sex-appropriate*, persist at them longer, and value their performance on perceived sex-appropriate tasks more than their successes on non-sex-appropriate tasks— intrinsic motivation, to be sure, but also silent acquiescence. Intrinsic motivation can substitute for meaningful pursuit of meaningful learning goals. And pursuit of intrinsic motivation may further exacerbate gender inequities in the classroom.

Further, even within a controlled choice paradigm where complexity and difficulty co-occur, Atkinson's data on the dynamics of experienced task difficulty and the approach–avoidance orientation of learners indicate that simply allowing students a choice of curriculum tasks will not necessarily result in increased quality of learning or enhancement of learner dispositions (Atkinson, 1981, 1987; Atkinson & Raynor, 1974). Even if student dispositions toward the task are enhanced—even if students are "intrinsically motivated" or are "motivated to learn"—they are not, by that fact alone, engaged in meaningful integration or improved performance (Blumenfeld, 1992b).

Decisions about the opportunity for student choice among tasks that differ in complexity, difficulty, and personal cost also involve decisions about the proportion and sequence of experienced task difficulty to optimize student learning and motivation. Such curriculum task decisions certainly are complex but are important parameters to consider if a curriculum is to include educative student choice, which we believe is essential for student empowerment and should be available to all learners. Three additional potential venues for student empowerment in the analytical curriculum that we explore are (a) opportunities for autonomy within the constraints of assigned classroom tasks and procedures, (b) assessment procedures, and (c) motivation and accountability beliefs in classroom management.

## AUTONOMY

Opportunities for meaningful and educative task choice, largely absent in classrooms, should be available to all learners because they are essential for personal knowledge of emergent competence and interpersonal power. Unfortunately, these opportunities are differently available to students, even though such self-knowledge influences quality of learning, motivation, and volitional processes and, hence, the realization of analytical curriculum goals.

Opportunities for meaningful and educative task choice also directly influence the informal curriculum because they affect the dynamics of interpersonal relationships and intrapersonal knowledge. We consider the relationship between affording opportunities and intrapersonal processes to be one of "emergent interaction" (Wertsch & Stone, 1985), with reciprocal influences between the developing student and the social/instructional environment. Thus, meaningful and educative task choice in the analytical curriculum is one vehicle toward the enhancement of those intrapersonal processes that we term "adaptive learning." We agree with deCharms (1976) that the opportunity to choose, to intentionally select a goal ("motivation," after Heckhausen, 1991) and to maintain the intention to achieve it ("volition," after Heckhausen, 1991), is fundamental to feeling responsible for goal attainment and its consequences. "Personal causation," the recognition of a relationship between responsibility and intention, is conceived as both a motivational goal and a motivational process that influences the quality of learning of the task and of the self (deCharms, 1976). We hypothesize personal causation as one link mediating between the structural features of the analytical curriculum and the intrapersonal dynamics of the informal curriculum.

DeCharms's influence can be seen in much of the last two decades of research on the interactive nature of consequences (e.g., rewards), motivation (e.g., intrinsic), and quality of learning (distinct from performance) (e.g., Lepper & Greene, 1978)— work that directly informs the management of motivated learners (McCaslin & Good, 1992), a feature of the analytical curriculum. Here we stress the critical role of opportunities for choice in the learning of personal causation. Later we examine the role of choice in learning how to assess one's progress, and we posit self-assessment as a basic construct for motivated classroom learning. We have already noted that, in the abstract curriculum, advantaged students are expected to have more of the types of opportunities (through curricular goals and instructional features) that promote a sense of personal causation than are disadvantaged students.

The extensive data on teacher expectation effects also document differential teacher treatment of students (e.g., Good & Brophy, 1994) and differential opportunities afforded students on the basis of their realized ability (e.g., Weinstein, 1993) and gender (AAUW, 1992) *within* classrooms. Inequity within classrooms, in which students are exposed to the same or considerably overlapping curricular goals, can only underestimate the inequities of within-class ability grouping, tracking, or differential resources among schools (e.g., Mason & Good, 1993). In these situations, students are exposed to different and fixed curricula (meaningful integration or intellectual skill acquisition) that likely also differ in quality (e.g., Goodlad, 1984; Oakes, 1992). Raudenbush, Rowan, and Cheong (1993), for example, found significant differences in curricular goals, opportunities, and instructional strategies associated with tracking levels even when the various levels were taught by the same teacher.

### Opportunity for Choice

Weinstein and colleagues examined students' perceptions of teacher treatment of students who differed in gender and achievement (relatively high or low) in Grades 4, 5, and 6 (Brattesani, Weinstein, & Marshall, 1984; Weinstein, Marshall, Brattesani, & Middlestadt, 1982). Their purpose was to examine a potentially mediating link between the differential teacher treatment of high and low achievers typically found in observational research (e.g., Brophy & Good, 1974; Cooper, 1979; Good, 1980; Weinstein & Middlestadt, 1979) and subsequent student performance. Weinstein and colleagues were among the first investigators to assess if students' perceptions of teacher behavior might influence students' personal expectations and self-concepts as learners. Weinstein modified the expectation construct from a social-psychological perspective to a more clinical one.

Participating teachers differed in instructional setting features that allowed comparison between "open" classrooms (believed to allow students more choice in task selection and to provide more flexible and individualized evaluation) and "traditional" classrooms (believed to restrict student choice and employ normative and public evaluation). The hypothesis of divergent setting affordances defined by these criteria was not supported, however. Students in both types of classroom structures described their teacher as treating students differently based on achievement (but not gender). Students reported that, compared with low achievers, high achievers had more opportunities ("the teacher lets [him/her] do as he/she likes as long as he/she finishes his/her work") and choice ("the teacher lets him/her decide things"). Students believed that their teacher held higher expectations for high-achieving students.

In contrast, low achievers were perceived to receive more teacher direction ("the teacher chooses the books [he/she] will read"), negative feedback ("the teacher scolds [her/him] for not listening"), and a general rule and "worker" orientation ("when [he/she] is working on a project, the teacher tells him/her what to do"; "when the teacher asks [him/her] a question, [he/she] needs to know the facts to answer it"). Students of both sexes and all ability levels reported the same patterns of perceived teacher response; however, perceived teacher treatment of low achievers was more varied than perceived treatment of high achievers. Advantaged (high ability) students in each type of classroom apparently also received more coherent teacher treatment than did less advantaged (low ability) students. Thus, less advantaged students experienced restricted opportunities, limited quality of expectations, and negative feedback—features of control that limit a sense of personal causation and establish a sense of oneself as a "pawn" in another's agenda (deCharms, 1976). Nonetheless these less-advantaged students were required to think harder to make sense of their classroom experiences. Their social cognitive task can only be compounded when we consider that these students are often exposed to multiple teachers with potentially conflicting expectations (Good, 1981).

Students perceive teachers to differentiate students, then, not only in terms of positive or negative quality of feedback (as repeatedly found by observational researchers), but also in terms of *structural autonomy*. We hypothesize that lack of opportunity for individual autonomy that is informed by experience with meaningful task choice and self-evaluation undermines the attainment of the prescribed analytical curriculum. We suggest that restricted opportunity for this type of self-knowledge also undermines fundamental intrapersonal processes and attenuates the development of self-competence, a point to which we return. Once again, it is the more advantaged learner within the classroom who benefits from differential task opportunity and socialization and, thus, differential opportunity for self-knowledge that informs one's place—in the classroom and in the community. More advantaged students learn leader-ship—setting and seeing through goals for oneself and others—through privilege and self-direction; less advantaged students learn, at best, to find and follow the direction in the disarray.

This is not a small difference in opportunity. Differential opportunity for choice in classrooms means that some students (especially those who are less advantaged) are not learning and refining motivational (e.g., goal-setting) strategies. Instead, they are learning that their motives and wishes do not matter, hence, their motivation is a moot point. Less advantaged students' opportunities are typically restricted to learning and refining volitional processes—to stay with and follow through on tasks that are set for them (the "work and rule orientation" of Weinstein et al., 1982). Approach and avoidance as motivational dispositions take on new meaning when we consider if the learner is choosing or avoiding his own goals or tasks set by others. What is a display of initiative for Atkinson's (1964, 1981, 1987) subjects and advantaged learners may simply be a demonstration of compliance for the less advantaged learner. Initiative for the less advantaged learner may instead be displayed by noncompliance; an example is the oppositional stance of certain minority youth as described by Ogbu (1992).

## Emergent Competence

We hypothesize that differential opportunity for task choice reverberates such that a classroom caste system is instantiated that includes interpersonal status and intrapersonal dynamics. Advantaged students have more opportunities to learn about decision-making and goal setting; thus, their achievements are multiplex. These students have the opportunity for learning more than the task under scrutiny and engaging in post hoc explanations (attributions) for their performance; they also learn how to envision the future in present decisions and plans. And, even when the tasks have been assigned, they are likely to be understood as part of a larger structure.

Thus, when advantaged students finish a task, they can make informed decisions about subsequent action, perhaps within the task (e.g., elaboration), or exercise their general power to choose (e.g., select a book to read, prepare for the next day). In contrast, less advantaged students have more opportunities to learn about adhering to imposed standards. When they finish a task, if time allows, they await another. In a fundamental sense, different and divergent curricular opportunities are shaping the personal dispositions of "origin" (the originator of one's goals) and "pawn" (the follower of others' goals) discussed by deCharms (1976). Opportunities to learn motivational *and* volitional intrapersonal strategies, knowledge, and dispositions (see also Sockett, 1988) promote "origin" characteristics; opportunities to practice volition without motivational power promote "pawn."

Finally, we hypothesize that opportunities for meaningful choice and goal setting also are important conditions for acquiring a time orientation that extends beyond the present. Goals are set and decisions are made in the present moment, but they involve a more comprehensive temporal perspective (Barker, Dembo, & Lewin, 1943; Lewin, 1935). Thus, appropriate goal setting integrates an appreciation of the past with a vision of the future, in the present moment. Opportunities to incorporate these time frames, to learn "presence of mind," seem an important feature of realistic proximal and distal goal setting. Goal setting is developmentally mediated (H. N. Mischel & W. Mischel, 1987) and learned (Bandura, 1986; Schunk, 1991). It is common, for example, for young students to have unrealistic goals, especially if they are temporally distant. Thus, a third grader may report that he wants "to be a surgeon and a truck driver" when he grows up (Rohrkemper, 1983).

Young students' lack of distal goal–proximal path clarity is developmentally appropriate. Older students' aspirations that lack integration of a time perspective with competence in goal setting, however, are not developmentally appropriate. They reflect a lack of supportive socialization and opportunities to select goals and evaluate one's attempts to meet them that promote an integration of motivation, enactment, and evaluation processes, which we call co-regulated learning (and subsequently discuss in detail).

The inability to set meaningful distal goals is yet one more example of the unexamined effects of the analytical curriculum on the informal curriculum. The analytical—enacted—curriculum denies some students the opportunity to learn fundamental intrapersonal processes for planning for the future and thus also limits their ability to successfully marshal needed support to help realize *any* future. Thus, differential opportunity for meaningful choice in classrooms can deny opportunity in a fundamental sense. This is a harmful and dangerous potential outcome of different and divergent conceptions of learners. So it is distressing, but not surprising, that it is the less advantaged adolescent who is more apt to claim that he wants "to be a lawyer, an eye surgeon, and a professional basketball player" (*New York Times*, March 7, 1992, p. 16) when he graduates from high school.

## ASSESSMENT

As we have noted, many educators are concerned about the pervasiveness and interpretation of measures of student performance (e.g., special issue of *Educational Researcher*, 1991); assessment, however, is the mainstay of classroom learning. Assessment of student performance is a critical feature of the analytical curriculum. Through assessment, whether it is in the form of standardized achievement tests, report card grades, or teacher comments, students learn about their learning progress and their learning potential. Our concern here is with approaches to assessment that enhance student self-knowledge of emergent competence. We hypothesize that assessment procedures imposed by others (e.g., teachers, administrators) that align with opportunities for student *self*-assessment of learning progress are the crux of the analytical and informal curricula. We envision the opportunity for self-evaluation as the opportunity to learn important motivational, enactment, and evaluation skills that, in their *integration*, enhance the development of students' adaptive learning.

Briefly we hypothesize that in isolation, these processes are incomplete. That is, motivation without the facility to follow through (volitional control, which is part of what we term "enactment strategies") is insufficient to realize desired (and attainable) goals (see Corno, 1992, 1993; Corno & Kanfer, 1993 for extended discussion of modern conceptions of volition). Volition without motivation (the opportunity and the ability to set goals) places the individual in the position of a pawn (de-

Charms, 1976)—one who satisfies others' goals, a means to another's end. Self-evaluation involves taking stock about one's progress toward a goal, recognition of incompleteness, or realization of the goal's attainment. Self-evaluation also includes reconsideration of the appropriateness of a goal and the costs of its pursuit (and therefore its possible abandonment), independent of the level of success (or failure) attained. Thus, motivation and volition without self-evaluation can leave the individual running in place in a frenzied loop of unexamined behavior and unrealized consequences. Finally, self-evaluation without knowledge of its relationship to motivation and volitional and other enactment strategies can compartmentalize self-concept and achievement so that the relationship between self-regard and personal attainment is weakly correlated, if at all. We will return to these hypotheses in our analysis of the informal curriculum and model of co-regulation.

Unfortunately, typical approaches to assessment do not attend to opportunities for self-evaluation and, indeed, often focus on trivial aspects and disconnected facts (Lohman, 1993). Currently, there are notable attempts to design portfoliolike alternatives of students' completed work or work in progress in place of or in addition to traditional testing procedures (e.g., Mitchell, 1992; Moss et al., 1992). The dominant assessment of student performance, however, leaves most opportunities for self-evaluation up to the resources of the learner, through incidental or discovery learning stimulated by a task or social comparison. Self-evaluation is a critical part of the learning process that requires deliberate promotion through modeling, guided demonstration, and, most important, *opportunities* for practice and refinement in everyday classroom learning (Zuckerman, 1994). One essential component of self-evaluation is affording tasks. As we have discussed, tasks differ in the degree to which they allow for sufficient levels of motivation and thinking. Tasks that consist of subgoals and meaningful units permit a taking stock and assessment of progress toward a standard of performance. Another important component of self-evaluation, to which we now turn, is *time*.

### Instructional Management and Self-Assessment Opportunities

Self-evaluation takes time. Unfortunately, current conceptions of classroom management typically include quickly paced transitions and instruction to prevent lulls or delays in which students might get off task, or misbehave (e.g., Evertson, Emmer, Clements, Sanford, & Worsham, 1983; Kounin, 1970). Fast-paced instructional environments, however, rather than obviating potential deficits in student motivation to perform (as intended), have been found to exacerbate deleterious effects of student motivation on performance due to increased test anxiety (Weinert & Helmke, 1987). As Weinert and Helmke note, however, the increased predictive power of test anxiety on student performance (in this research, fifth-grade mathematics) in classrooms that place a premium on instructional time may be a function of multiple factors. For example, students may interpret the continuous focus on task achievement as evidence that they are valued only for their achievement, to the exclusion of other potential goals (e.g., getting along with peers). Important to this discussion, fast-paced instruction also provides fewer opportunities and less time for students to check on their errors and misunderstandings—in short, fewer opportunities for what we call self-evaluation. Lack of opportunity for self-evaluation in these settings may leave students feeling less aware and less in control of their own learning, and may thereby increase anxiety.

Instructional and managerial systems based on time management are typically designed to compensate for the motivational deficiencies of the less advantaged learner. Indeed, there is some evidence (see Rosenshine & Stevens, 1986) that this teaching strategy is effective in bringing about the intended curriculum for what Weinert and Helmke (1987) term "the less talented and socially disadvantaged student" (p. 237). It appears, however, that these students' attainments in the analytical curriculum can co-occur with increased performance anxiety and decreased opportunity for reflective self-evaluation, features of the informal curriculum.

Lack of deliberate attention to self-evaluation through instruction and practice (with appropriate questions and tasks) also can leave many students essentially nonreflective about their own role in learning. To educators' chagrin, many students go through schooling blithely accepting of their performance; they feel fine and they are doing "well enough" (McCaslin & Good, 1992). For other students, however, there is near paralysis as they are unable to bring self-evaluation to any resolution. Unmet performance goals function as a sort of mischievous Zeigarnik (1927, in Heckhausen, 1991; in Weiner, 1992) effect: an open wound of failure or incompletion that makes new task aspiration difficult (see also Heckhausen & Kuhl, 1985). For both types of student there is little relationship between competence and self-esteem.

There are data to indicate that focusing students on the "next task" to restrict self-incrimination and keep students forward-looking can attenuate the effects of undeveloped or detrimental self-evaluation processes (C. Ames, 1984; Beckmann & Heckhausen, 1988, in Heckhausen, 1991; Rohrkemper, 1986b). However, as noted above, the difference between "forward-looking" and "forward-pushing" is not easily established in instructional management. Our goals for the informal curriculum include the deliberate development of self-evaluation processes that facilitate students' realistic assessment of their learning progress and promote their commitment to seek needed resources that help them meet their goals. Thus, our concern is with how to cultivate adaptive self-evaluation, not how to circumvent self-evaluation altogether.

## Student Mediation of Teacher Evaluation

There is evidence that students can profit from exposure to consistent assessment procedures and instructional environments that help them focus on the self in relation to the subject matter, as compared with a focus on self in relation to others (social comparison or normative assessment) or a focus on subject matter acquisition per se (criterion-referenced assessment). One study is particularly informative. We describe it in detail as an example of informative research on the power of feedback and evaluation structures in student learning of subject matter and self (see also, e.g., C. Ames, 1992; E. Cohen, 1986; Covington, 1992; Elawar & Corno, 1985; Rosenholtz & Simpson, 1984).

*Functions of Feedback.* Krampen (1987) examined the effects of teacher comments on student examinations on subsequent student learning and motivation. Krampen adhered to an expectancy-value theory of motivation; the study used an aptitude–treatment interaction design. Thirteen fifth-grade mathematics classes were randomly assigned to one of four treatment conditions defined by the type of teacher comment made on student examinations (comments were provided in addition to grades). The first treatment condition consisted of socially oriented teacher comments that, in essence, exacerbated norm-referenced grading ("in comparison with the other pupils . . ."). The second treatment condition consisted of subject matter–related comments based on absolute standards of understanding (similar to criterion-referenced feedback). The third consisted of individually oriented personalized feedback in which the student's present performance was compared with past performance. The fourth treatment condition served as a control so that the students received only their examination grades (with no teacher comment).

Dependent variables included repeated measures of (a) student achievement and (b) an array of cognitive-motivational and personality-oriented instruments. The treatment phase continued for one semester; dependent measures were administered throughout the treatment phase and for one semester after treatment was discontinued. Thus, student self-report and achievement data could be analyzed for immediate and long-term effects and for different patterns associated with treatment condition (checked for fidelity of implementation) and student achievement level (defined by prior performance in math).

Analyses of obtained *achievement* indicated that individually oriented feedback was associated with improved performance for all levels of learners. High-achieving students' performance was also enhanced by socially oriented (comparative) feedback; in contrast, low- and moderately low-achieving students' performance was seriously undermined by socially oriented feedback. Student-reported *expectancy of improvement* continued these trends, even though the highest achieving students' reports were omitted from this analysis because of the (assumed) inherent ceiling effects in their ability to improve on similar tasks. Expectancy results indicated a general positive effect of individually oriented (and to a lesser extent, subject matter–oriented) feedback on expectations for improvement for each level of student ability (students who [now] ranged from "high-moderate" to "low" ability in math). Socially oriented feedback, however, affected students differently and, for many, detrimentally. Specifically, low- and moderately low-achieving students' expectations for improvement were seriously undermined by comparative feedback; in contrast, moderately high-achieving students appeared to (intrapersonally) thrive under such information.

Krampen cautions that feedback differences associated with increased student performance were not maintained beyond the treatment phase of the study; however, some long-term effects were associated with two attitude clusters. First, there were long-term increases in negative attitude toward school and authority in students exposed to socially oriented feedback. Second, students who received individually oriented feedback increased in internality and decreased in test anxiety.

Taken together, these results make a strong case for the deliberate examination of assessment procedures used in the analytical curriculum, as they may affect manifest (e.g., student achievement of subject matter) and implicit (informal) curriculum goals (e.g., learner dispositions toward self, school, and authority). Individually oriented feedback improves performance and it improves evaluation of the self as learner. Socially oriented feedback, based on competitive interindividual comparisons, is problematic. Socially oriented feedback (compared with individually oriented feedback) increases variation in achievement among students but without increasing the attainments of the high-achieving students. Rather, increased dispersion among learners appears located in the steep slopes associated with the *decreased* performance of relatively lower achieving students—who also are intrapersonally undermined by this type of feedback.

Thus, although the relatively higher achieving students appear more personally self-enhanced by socially oriented feedback than by the other types of feedback, their performance is not. The putative gains associated with competition among learners, such as increased striving for excellence, are not supported by these data. Instead, increases appear in the *variation* in achievement (due to the lowered performance of less capable students) and in distorted self-regard (of both more and less capable students).

In sum, individually oriented feedback and, to a lesser extent, subject matter (criterion) feedback that foster enabling self-evaluation appear the only defensible approaches to evaluation of student performance: Students learn the set curriculum, and it does not cost them their beliefs about personal striving. Individually oriented feedback is differential without being detrimental; it is the most equitable form of learner assessment. Learners of all achievement levels profit.

In contrast, social comparison feedback further advantages the advantaged learner because it depresses others' performance and aspirations. It costs too much and apparently is not what many think they are buying (i.e., higher attainment by the highly able). Nonetheless, the notion of interpersonal comparison (competition) is a standard feature of varied conceptions of achievement motivation that guide the analytical curriculum, a point to which we return. It appears to exacerbate even further the relative standing of the advantaged and the less advantaged (see also C. Ames, 1985; Rosenholtz & Simpson, 1984).

*Functions of Teacher Beliefs.* Research by Rheinberg (1980, as discussed in Heckhausen, 1991) further supports the importance of individually referenced evaluation norms. In a longitudinal, field-based study Rheinberg examined teacher commitment to different evaluation systems and explored the relationship between instruction and evaluation strategies embedded in their beliefs. Specifically, Rheinberg was interested in the stability of teachers' "reference norm orientation," its relationship to adaptive teaching strategies (see Corno & Snow, 1986), and the motivational effect on students. He found that teachers with an individual-reference-norm orientation (IRN) were more flexible and adaptive in their evaluation strategies than were teachers who adhered to a social-reference-norm orientation (SRN). SRN teachers consistently preferred the same evaluation standard.

Teachers' evaluation orientation also covaried with their beliefs about achievement. Teachers with an SRN orientation viewed student achievement in terms of stable and internal student factors. That is, SRN teachers believed that student achievement was the result of student ability, and that student ability was fixed and not open to modification (also called an "entity" theory of intelligence by Dweck [1986]). In contrast, IRN teachers were more apt to consider unstable, and therefore changeable, factors in their theories of student achievement. IRN teachers' beliefs included aspects of the instructional setting, which they attempted to adapt to student factors.

Teachers responded differently to student performance as a function of their beliefs. IRN teachers encouraged students; they supported student struggling. SRN teachers rewarded students; they reinforced achievement outcomes. Data indicated that longitudinal exposure to teacher reference norm orientation modified student motivation.

*Promotion of Realistic Self-Evaluation.* There is evidence that an individual reference norm, and the self-evaluation processes it affords, can be taught to even very young students. Russian educators (Zuckerman, 1994), for example, teach self-evaluation in first grade to promote students' active participation in their own learning.

Zuckerman (1994) defines self-evaluation, termed "self-appraisal," as the ability to differentiate one's knowledge, partial knowledge, and ignorance in a "manner that is as optimistic as possible, perceiving in the areas of ignorance and inability not evidence of his or her weakness and helplessness, but a prospect of further improvement" (p. 410). "Introduction to school life" is a deliberate attempt to change private, intrapersonal perceptions of deficiency into active interpersonal opportunities, to replace "why can't I do this" self-recrimination with "what help do I need" action. In Kuhl's terms, the student is learning to replace a "state orientation" with an "action (volitional) orientation" (Kuhl, 1985, 1987a, 1987b). We note as well that the action orientation expands the learner's personal boundaries to include the social/instructional environment. Self-evaluation in this program deliberately links intrapersonal processes with the analytical curriculum, thereby enhancing the efficacy of each.

Self-appraisal, as we have discussed previously, is not necessarily realistic or enabling. Zuckerman (1994) attends to the match between teacher and student appraisal to promote realistic student self-evaluation. If teacher and student evaluations coincide (independent of level of attainment), the child is praised for appropriate self-evaluation. Over- or underestimation is confronted. Evaluations that do not involve an objective criterion are considered opinions, which are individual rights, neither correct nor incorrect.

Zuckerman's work seems a promising introduction to school life when student over- and underestimation of performance occurs throughout the school years. Realistic self-evaluation, for example, is especially problematic for talented females (e.g., D. A. Phillips & M. Zimmerman, 1990). We hypothesize that realistic self-evaluation functions as a powerful *motivational tool* available to the learner because it fosters the integration of realistic goal setting (motivation), protection of intentions (volition), and analysis of level of attainment (or nonattainment) and its consequences. Motivational systems believed to undergird the analytical curriculum are a bit different from this conception, however.

## MOTIVATION AND ACCOUNTABILITY

Achievement is a function of realized ability; thus, it is a culturally mediated and an inherently motivational construct. Motivation has become a dominant theme in societal and educational discourse in the 1990s; the rhetoric of motivation (as in "lack of") permeates discussion of "just what is wrong with our schools and their graduates." Success in the international economic arena is believed to be directly tied to student achievement, which in turn is believed to be linked to student motivation.

When students do not "do what it takes," the explanatory net is flung a bit wider than the students themselves to include those who are believed responsible for them. For example, Cross (1990), writing for the United States Department of Education's Office of Educational Research and Improvement (OERI), called for more research on motivation at *all* extant government-funded research centers and in all individually proposed research because the "question of *teacher, student, and parent* motivation is one of the single most important questions we face" (emphasis added) (p. 22).

Ironically, motivation may well predict success in the work force and international economic markets, but not because of its link with innovative achievement. Rather, motivation predicts success in the workplace because of its link with volition and personal qualities like dependability, responsibility, and patience (see also Corno & Kanfer, 1993; Sockett, 1988). Berliner (1992) reports that "it is the affective and motivational characteristics of workers that our employers worry most about. They depend on employees to show up on time, to get along with others, to care about doing well on the job, and so forth. *They do not find the technical ability of the work force to be a problem for them*" (emphasis added) (pp. 33–34).

Two recent surveys of desired skills in the workplace support Berliner's claim. In one survey, the five least important skills for employment were math, social sciences, natural sciences, computer programming, and foreign languages. In the second survey, the five least important areas were natural science, calculus, computers, art, and foreign language (Berliner, 1992). It appears that societal concerns about student achievement of the curriculum (e.g., Hirsch, 1987; U.S. Department of Education, 1990) do not mesh with the typical experiences of the work force. Concerns with student achievement appear relevant only to the accomplishments of the more advantaged students, whose future work is believed more professional and managerial than "labor." Apparently volitional skills, like any other, however, are only useful to the extent they are used (Bandura, 1986); hence, we return to the problem of motivation.

Direct linkages between the functions of schooling and the goals of business are typically assumed in society. Participants in the analytical curriculum, however, are less certain about the role of business in public schooling in general and student employment in particular (see also McCaslin & Good, 1992). They are also more conflicted about what is meant by motivation, how it relates to productivity and quality, and how to hold students accountable for it. The tensions among what is achieved, who achieves it, and with how much effort are evident in evolving conceptions of student motivation in the analytical curriculum.

## Achievement Motivation as Concern with Excellence

It is telling that, in U.S. culture, achievement motivation is arguably the most studied human motive. The motive to achieve subsumes the purposes of classroom processes, although not necessarily our understanding of them. Murray's (1938) definition of "n(eed) Achievement" set the fundamental criterion for achievement motivation in the psychological literature—the concern with a standard of excellence:

To accomplish something difficult. To master, manipulate or organize physical objects, human beings, or ideas. To do this as rapidly and as independently as possible. To overcome obstacles and attain a high standard. To excel one's self. To rival and surpass others. To increase self-regard by the successful exercise of talent. (p. 164)

The standard definition of achievement motivation is all about the promotion of self in and through mastery over difficulty which, by definition, is not readily available—to oneself or others. Successful striving in this formula enhances self-regard in one's own mind and in the eyes of others. Each facet of the achievement motive as defined by Murray requires affording and informative experiences, particularly appropriate tasks, for its development. As we have seen, however, affording and informative classroom experiences—curricula, tasks, and teacher treatment—are differentially available to students. We have also seen that rivaling and surpassing others does not necessarily translate into increased excellence on the part of winners and can further burden the majority, who lose (e.g., C. Ames, 1992; Covington, 1992; Krampen, 1987).

One problem with the presumption of the motive to achieve as the energy source for classroom dynamics—as the force that drives the system—is that it is amoral. Achievement motivation as concern with excellence defines a conquering relationship between the individual and the world of "physical objects, human beings, or ideas" as if all were equal and interchangeable features of the task. Achievement in classrooms involves more than relationships with objects; relationships with people ethically cannot be reduced to object relationships.

Further, excellence that rests on individual salience is incompatible with the purported value system of the analytical curriculum, which is all about individuals striving and fair play. The need to achieve reduces the inherently social nature of classroom learning to a sort of social Darwinism. We have already noted where this stance is congruent with differential societal expectations. Its deliberate enactment in the analytical curriculum is a different matter, however. Independent of ethical debate, students who can't win won't play.

Schools recognize this basic cost of a social-comparative excellence criterion; thus, the "bandwidth" (A. L. Brown & Reeve, 1987) of what is to be called excellent is broadened to encompass the nonacademic, including personal character and volitional predisposition (Maker, 1987). For example, definitions of giftedness have been broadened to include "task commitment" in addition to ability and creativity (Renzulli, 1978). "Honors society" membership requirements often include good citizenship and perfect attendance categories to offset less than excellent achievement of potential recruits. The result, although more inclusive, has been an uneven transformation of achievement motivation away from a standard of excellence—based on a relationship with objects—and toward personal disposition and an ethic of responsibility—based on interpersonal relationships and individual commitment, independent of excellence.

## Motivation as Personal Resource

Motivation as personal resource is believed to locate motivation more fairly because it places motivation under individual (versus competitive) control. In so doing, however, it also makes individuals more accountable. Motivation becomes something that one possesses and dispenses in varying amounts; typically, more of it is better. Motivation is believed necessary for success; indeed, an important American myth is that a motivated person, one who strives, will succeed. As we have noted, however, this is not necessarily the case, especially for those whose "lives [are] on the boundary" (Rose, 1989), whom we have called disadvantaged students.

In one sense, then, motivation as personal resource is more equitable than motivation as concern with excellence because it does not require besting others, only oneself. In another sense, though, motivation as personal resource is inherently inequitable because it locates motivation intrapersonally rather than contextually. Thus, the Horatio Alger myth of self-reliance and individualism (Rose, 1989) permeates classroom accountability systems, even though individual effort is insufficient without an infrastructure that can support individual goal setting and goal-directed behavior (see also Kaufman & Rosenbaum, 1992; McCaslin & Good, 1992; Weinstein, 1990).

Motivation as personal resource does not attend to these constraints. Motivation is quantified, not qualified; its believed relationship to achievement is direct and incremental. In this conception, failure to put one's motivational resources to work is known by the *outcome* (of the alleged effort) because lack of success is a function of lack of motivation, thereby necessitating a reactive (i.e., blaming) versus proactive (i.e., influential) stance. Lack of motivation, then, is a culpable act, for oneself and those "who should know better"; students and those who are responsible for them share the responsibility of student motivation and blame for its absence.

The focus on achievement motivation as personal resource leads to unidimensional traitlike conceptions of students, who are construed as more or less willing to learn the curriculum. It also fosters the design of motivational and accountability strategies that adults in students' lives (teachers and parents) are expected to use to obtain compliance (or identification) with societal expectations. Thus, when student motivation is deficient (i.e., students are withholding their motivation), remediation strategies typically revolve around a hedonic core. That is, students are believed to change their motivation (have more or less) as a function of reinforcement, lack of reinforcement, or punishment for their performance (or lack thereof). Importantly, although the student may be seen as the source of the motivational problem, he or she typically is not required to organize the solution; that is the place of the adults and institutions in the student's life. Even so, the focus tends to be on the product rather than the process, on achievement rather than achieving.

*Differentially Motivated Learners.* Although remediation strategies are based on a hedonic model of student (e.g., one

who seeks pleasure and avoids pain), the vehicles believed to propel student pleasure-seeking (pain-avoiding) behavior typically differ for students who differ in relative advantage. Consistent with the differential conceptions of learner characteristics in the abstract curriculum, advantaged students' motivation is more apt to be encouraged and disadvantaged students' lack of motivation is more apt to be discouraged. Thus, challenging tasks with "optimal incongruity" (e.g., Hunt, 1961, 1965), competitive reward structures and grading systems, honor societies, and realization of long-term goals (e.g., college preparation and professional status) are presumed to be key inspirational sources for advantaged students. These strategies bear striking resemblance to features of Murray's (1938) need achievement.

In contrast, disadvantaged students are more apt to be prodded with carrots and sticks. They are the more likely recipients of token reinforcement programs, threats of "no pass no play" (Covington, 1992; F. R. Webb, Covington, & Guthrie, 1993), and the looming realities of the workplace. Disadvantaged students' parents have even been threatened with warrants and loss of (and have actually lost) federal assistance money if their children did not manifest motivation through school attendance and appropriate behavior (F. R. Webb et al., 1993). In Kelman's (1958) terms, socialization goals for disadvantaged students appear confined to *compliance*, wherein attitude or behavior is exchanged for reward or prevention of punishment. In contrast, socialization goals for more advantaged students appear to include as well *identification* with salient school participants (e.g., teachers) and *internalization* of their norms and expectations. The advantaged students are the continuous link between present and future expectations for schooling.

*When Business Comes to School.* Motivation is the overarching construct in the abstract and the analytical curricula that provides the direction and goal of classroom processes for students. It is the adhesive that bonds students and tasks. The focus on individuals and interpersonal "persuasion" to understand or bolster achievement motivation, however, distracts from a more fundamental question about the functional role of the educational setting, which includes societal expectations and opportunities, in curriculum enactment.

The interaction of the setting with student dispositions seems critical in understanding (and possibly enhancing) student motivation in a given situation. Rather than entertaining the complexity of setting and dispositional factors in a given situation of achievement motivation (see, e.g., C. Ames, 1992), however, the conception of motivation as personal resource provides generic "solutions," as we have described. Thus, remediation strategies steeped in (typically misapplied) theories of reinforcement are straightforward, even if unsuccessful, attempts to enhance student achievement motivation and subsequent achievement.

For example, the programs spawned by the business community to increase student achievement motivation, like that underwritten by Pizza Hut, often undermine the very achievement they were designed to support. They also favor the advantaged student (whose motivation to read is probably not a cause for concern in the first place). Rewarding students for numbers of books read is consistent with societal reasoning about motivation that is represented in the analytical curriculum. Reinforcing students will increase their achievement motivation and, therefore, their achievement. What actually happens is a bit different.

The enactment of the Pizza Hut program in the analytical curriculum, like other reward-for-products programs, typically results in detrimental student competition and the replacement of quality of reading experience with sheer quantity of books read. It should not be surprising that, once students (and their teacher and parents) adopt the goal "win pizza," the formula: short books + easy books = fast books = more books = more pizza (for me) would be worked out and the strategy implemented by some (i.e., advantaged) students, while others, who realized they do not have the skills to win, would simply quit (see also Maehr & Midgley, 1991; Weinstein, 1990). Reinforcement apparently does not transform motivation as personal resource into motivation as concern for excellence; rather, the response appears to be mere expansion of relatively superficial personal resources (e.g., pizza).

Business is not the only sector of society attempting to demonstrate the utility of the personal resource metaphor in manipulating motivation. Government rewards that recognize "excellent schools" for their students' achievements have also been found to undermine faculty and student achievement motivation by replacing a concern with more thoughtful learning with worries about continued "excellent" (i.e., "correct") performance (Fetterman, 1990). Similarly, inconsistent criteria within schools between principal and teachers (C. Ames, 1990; Maehr & Midgley, 1991; McCaslin Rohrkemper, 1989) and among teachers (Fetterman, 1990) for the enhancement of student achievement motivation through rewards for performance have been found to undermine classroom attempts to engage students in meaningful learning rather than mere completion rates (seen by many students as proxies for ability).

*Compliant Cognition.* None of the results of these programs are unpredictable. For some time there has been a coherent body of literature in social psychology on the "hidden costs of rewards" (Lepper & Greene, 1978) that has repeatedly demonstrated that simplistic notions of reinforcement fail to instill motivation (however defined) or increase performance, and that mindless use of reinforcement can actually undermine extant intrinsic motivation, hamper quality of learning, and detrimentally mediate student covert processing (e.g., C. Ames, 1992; Lepper, 1983b; Lepper & Greene, 1978).

Sheer manipulation of motivation without concern for a standard of excellence does not promote meaningful learning. The assumption that one can elicit "compliant cognition" is simply not supported. Integrative learning and meaningful problem solving are not compatible with obedience by demand or persuasion (McCaslin & Good, 1992). Further, "more" motivation is not necessarily better; rejection of the excellence criterion has not in itself resulted in equitable classroom motivation and enhanced achievement. Perhaps this is one reason why the analytical curriculum vacillates between motivation as personal resource (that is open to influence through interpersonal relationships and consequences) and motivation as personal responsibility (independent of any relationships, whether interpersonal or with objects) when holding students accountable for their learning.

## Motivation as Personal Responsibility

Achievement motivation resides in students and schools. Schools are achievement settings, "signal systems" that cue achievement behavior (R. Barker, 1968). Thus, students who are not motivated not only resist interpersonal efforts to enhance their motivation, they also violate the norms of the institution. Failure to influence student motivation to achieve in places designed for achievement is frustrating and unexpected. In situations in which individual behavior (a) is unexpected and (b) conflicts with setting expectations, the individual (vs. the setting) is perceived as the cause of the discrepancy (e.g., E. E. Jones & Nisbett, 1972). This general rule of "naive psychology" (e.g., Heider, 1958) holds for students in schools as well. Students, rather than features of instruction (e.g., tasks, performance expectations, accountability criteria) or management systems (e.g., rules, form of reward/punishment, schedule of consequences), are held accountable for lack of student motivation. In contrast, when student motivation is realized, credit is shared.

In effect, lack of achievement motivation is ultimately located within the individual; achievement motivation is a synonym for *individual responsibility*. Students are accountable if their performance falls short or if they do not (will not) profit from instruction. Motivation as personal responsibility alleviates the roles of the culture, the community, and the school in the dynamics of student motivation and, thus, student achievement. Hence, motivation as personal responsibility further increases the burden of individual culpability. It allows a motivational policy of benign neglect in the abstract and analytical curriculum. It assumes that students should be motivated (whether or not they can envision a future in which they can meaningfully participate).

Unquestioning acceptance of achievement motivation as the primary vehicle for classroom phenomena and its simultaneous devolution to the level of "excuse" (should achievement goals we set for students remain unattained) dominate the enactment of the analytical curriculum. It is not surprising, for example, that the U.S. Department of Education's (1990) call for research on (the lack of) student motivation followed nearly a decade of student failure to benefit from the policies and reform efforts (e.g., longer and more school days, more homework) embedded in *A Nation at Risk* (National Commission on Excellence in Education, 1983).

In short, the movement in classrooms from capability to motivation to value (the "could–would–should" loop of classroom accountability) is swift. Thus students, not classroom settings, are understood by and held accountable for their deficient achievement motivation (e.g., Ericson & Ellett, 1990), in spite of compelling research that addresses the complexity of their interaction (e.g., C. Ames, 1984; Covington, 1992; McCaslin & Good, 1992; Pepitone, 1985; Rosenholtz & Simpson, 1984; Weinstein, 1990). In this conception of student motivation, other participants in the analytical curriculum may choose to facilitate student motivation, but they are not required to do so. The student is both the source of the problem and the source of the solution.

*Attributional Judgment.* Judgments about personal responsibility—one's own and others'—are common exchange in the social world. Much research has explored the regularities of "naive" or "folk" psychology, the study of how people understand and order the complexities of everyday events and interpersonal relationships (e.g., Heider, 1958; Kelley, 1967; Weiner, 1986). Considerations such as personal consistency over time, consensus over individuals, and distinctiveness over tasks have been hypothesized to guide the processing of information by the naive (rational) decision-maker (Kelley, 1967).

Weiner (1986) and colleagues maintain that interpretations of the locus of events (internal or external to the individual) (Lefcourt, 1976; Rotter, 1966) and their constancy (stability over time and across situations) enhance individuals' predictions of their future recurrence. In addition, the naive psychologist judges responsibility for an act or event through assessments of individual control and intention (Abramson, Seligman, & Teasdale, 1978; Carroll & Payne, 1976, 1977; Weiner, 1986, 1991). The three causal domains explicated by Weiner (1986, 1991)—locus, constancy, and (especially) responsibility— provide a useful framework for understanding the implications of student achievement motivation as personal responsibility.

Rules of naive psychology for interpersonal understanding can inform an array of interpretations of student lack of achievement. Consider as an example that a student, Giulia, fails a math exam. One interpretation of Giulia's failure might be, "Giulia did poorly because she didn't care"; another might be, "Guilia failed because she still doesn't understand the material." The first interpretation might attributionally parse: internal locus of control (Giulia is the source of the behavior); unstable over time (she used to care, perhaps she will again) and uneven across tasks (Giulia continues to do well in her other subjects); and controllable (Giulia could have performed better had she prepared or tried). In this analysis, the fluctuation of student effort (intensity and/or duration) is understood as the cause of nonachievement; effort is believed the responsibility of the student. Thus, the student is to blame for her nonachievement.

The second interpretation parses differently. Giulia does not understand the material. The locus may be internal to Giulia (she is not very capable in math) or external (the material was not presented meaningfully; the test does not tap Giulia's knowledge). Constancy attributions also might differ. Perhaps it has always taken Gulia longer than the allotted time to learn material (stable) and it seems to be this way for most subjects (global). Importantly, responsibility attributions do differ. Giulia is not in control of her misunderstandings; she did not intentionally fail to perform. Giulia is not to blame for her failure.

A third, contrasting, interpretation of Giulia's experience is based on Covington's (1992) self-worth theory, which holds that the need for self-justification is primary and universal (in contrast to the attributional claim that understanding is the primary need). In the self-worth perspective, Giulia may be self-handicapping (e.g., not trying, procrastinating) to ensure a ready excuse in the event of failure. Giulia knows that effort is a "double-edged sword" (Covington & Omelich, 1979). Optimal effort leaves the learner most vulnerable in the event of failure. There are no excuses.

How events are attributionally interpreted matters because attributional knowledge informs emotion (toward other and self) and interpersonal behavior (Weiner, 1986). An attributional analysis can be "objectively" incorrect. "Correctness" is not part of the attributional claim; rather, the point is that once

perceptions and attributional judgments are rendered, predictable patterns of emotion and behavior are expressed (see Weiner, 1986). This is especially the case for interpretations of unexpected or unacceptable behavior. There is considerable literature on the dynamics of helping, both in emergencies (e.g., J. A. Piliavin & I. M. Piliavin, 1972; I. M. Piliavin, Rodin, & J. A. Piliavin, 1969) and in the everydayness of the classroom between teachers and students (e.g., Brophy & McCaslin, 1992; Brophy & Rohrkemper, 1981; Rohrkemper & Brophy, 1983) and among students (Rohrkemper, 1984, 1985; Segal-Andrews, 1994), that support this assertion.

Recall the first attributional profile of Giulia, where she is determined responsible for her failure because of her lack of effort (judged as internal, unstable, and controllable). Attribution theory would predict, and research has found, that her teacher's response, given this interpretation and the teacher's perceived role vis-à-vis that interpretation, is apt to be brief, to the point, and punitive. Lack of effort is a punishable offense when motivation is one's personal responsibility. In contrast, in the second attributional analysis Giulia has met her personal responsibility; she deserves and receives instructional support. In the third, self-handicapping analysis, Giulia is likely to receive supportive counseling to promote self-insight and taught strategies for coping with anxiety (Brophy & McCaslin, 1992; Brophy & Rohrkemper, 1981; Rohrkemper & Brophy, 1983). Of these three response scenarios the first, punishment for lack of effort perceived as controllable/intentional, is the dominant teacher response pattern.

Whether these ascription patterns are the result of the individual's spontaneous attributional problem solving in situ or the manifestation of acquired cultural knowledge (e.g., justification scripts for experienced affect or behavior) is an open question; however, an attributional framework appears to dominate the conception of motivation as personal responsibility. Students are judged and held accountable for their lack of motivation to achieve the curriculum.

Unfortunately, participants in the analytical curriculum (teachers and students) engage these attributional rules with no more sophistication than do nonprofessionals (Rohrkemper, 1984, 1985). Punishment for perceived lack of effort, for example, does little to promote a more appropriate attitude toward tasks found difficult, threatening, or tedious. Inhibiting behavior (through punishment) is not to be confused with instilling attitudes (Lepper, 1983b). Student obedience does not equal student motivation (see also McCaslin & Good, 1992).

*Autobiography and Aspiration.* It appears that the permeation of naive psychology of interpersonal relations into the classroom setting does not notably enhance the understanding of student achievement motivation. Important interpersonal rules of the social world that help students function personally and socially are modeled and learned (Rohrkemper, 1984, 1985), but classrooms are more than interpersonal settings; they also are places of enduring societal expectations for and curricular demands on students. Thus, understanding student motivation to engage in tasks of varying quality—the curriculum—in the context of a social world known by its continuous accountability demands and ambiguous (and potentially conflicting) feedback from multiple sources—the classroom—is not promoted (see also Blumenfeld, 1992a, 1992b; Corno & Rohrkemper, 1985;

Doyle, 1983; Good et al., 1992; Goodenow, 1992; Rohrkemper & Corno, 1988).

In addition, the attributional focus on motive and biography, the looking back focused on "why," for understanding student mediation of the curriculum is limited. Students may not be engaged in asking retrospective questions when confronting tasks, particularly when there is no end to the stream of requirements and the outcomes are often vague (C. Ames, 1984; Blumenfeld, Hamilton, Bossert, Wessels, & Meece, 1983; Rohrkemper, 1986b).

Students appear to have a valid question when they ask, "What for?" It seems that a more future-oriented motivational question concerning goals and instrumentality (e.g., C. Ames, 1992) is a promising focus for understanding student willingness to assume personal responsibility for their learning. The analytical curriculum conveys more than reasons for past and present achievement; it alludes to the future, to goals and possibilities and their relation to the present. Achievement motivation as personal responsibility for extant motivation is inadequate if educators are to harness the power of the analytical curriculum to enhance (a) student motive, (b) motivation to learn, and (c) volitional strategies to protect the enactment of that motivation in the analytical curriculum and beyond.

Finally, the laissez-faire stance of motivation as personal responsibility also yields inequities among students. A policy of benign neglect further legitimates and empowers the different tasks and instructional opportunities that are presented to students who differ in relative advantage in the first place. Thus advantaged students, by virtue of their curricular and instructional exposure, are provided with more opportunities to experience the personal satisfaction of and reward for effortful behavior that leads to meaningful learning that is also open to self-evaluation. In contrast, less advantaged students engage in tasks that may structurally require more effort, yet they do not receive supplemental motivational supports. Theirs, ironically, is the more difficult motivational burden. Benign neglect in this case is more apt to function as motivational extinction.

## Summary

In brief, achievement motivation is the assumed adhesive that bonds the abstract curriculum, societal expectations for schooling, the analytical curriculum, the enactment of those expectations, and student achievement of that curriculum. Reasons believed to underlie student motivation have evolved with each failure to enhance student achievement. Thus, the perceived dynamics of student motivation have ranged from conquering tasks and people (motivation as concern with excellence), to pleasing authority (motivation as personal resource), to self-reliance (motivation as personal responsibility). As we will see, most recent analytical curriculum innovations include students in small groups. Apparently, current wisdom predicts that, even though many students will not achieve for standards, adults, or themselves, they just might for peers.

The considerable limitations of achievement motivation, however defined, as *the* adhesive of learners who are held accountable for performance on assigned tasks of varying (objective and subjective) demands, difficulty, and coherence within a social setting remain largely unexamined. Attempts to manipulate—that is, to increase—student motivation through

the administration of consequences have largely been ineffective and may even have been detrimental. Doing nothing is not necessarily better than doing something, however. Failure to enhance student motivation to learn or achieve gives even more power to the features of the analytical curriculum—tasks, opportunities for autonomy, and assessment procedures—that result in nonreflective but nonetheless differential treatment of students.

We hypothesize that one way to enhance student motivation to learn the analytical curriculum is to recognize that students are confronted with multiple goals whose interrelationship may well undermine (a) student motivation to achieve and (b) the utility of achievement motivation as the backdrop for the analytical curriculum. We predict that how students mediate their classroom experiences is more complicated than allowed by current dispositional approaches that classify students according to global individual difference variables in relation to achievement motivation such as "performance" or "mastery oriented" (e.g., C. Ames, 1992; see also Blumenfeld, 1992a).

Even so, these more recent approaches are a considerable advance in understanding students situated in classrooms over earlier work that did not attend to classrooms as places, let alone contexts. Differentiations of students at the level of gross classifications like sex, age, and ability have provided important information about differences between and variations within groups of students. It is now time to understand more fully the dynamics of the socially situated student. We look to research in the narrative tradition as one promising vehicle both to understand these dynamics and to convey that understanding in ways that participants in the analytical curriculum can understand and thereby effectively engage.

## THE INFORMAL CURRICULUM: CURRICULUM ENACTMENT AND INTRAPERSONAL PROCESSES

Thus far we have attempted to trace the transformation of societal beliefs about the functions of schooling—what for, and for whom—represented in the abstract curriculum through selected features of the analytical curriculum—task affordance, opportunities for autonomy, assessment procedures, and motivation and accountability beliefs. We have demonstrated that, intentionally or not, the effects of the analytical curriculum may powerfully fulfill differential societal expectations for students and schools. One problem with the current narrow focus on subject matter acquisition as *the* unit of instructional concern is that it keeps the dynamics of human relationships with objects and persons that we have examined out of the problem space. Value judgments aside, this omission is not practical, as it interferes with student achievement of the goals we set for them.

We now address the implications of extant curricula for the dynamics of the informal curriculum. We call for explication of and research on an informal curriculum that will directly address the promotion of adaptive learning for all students. As noted by Griffin (1993), recent advances in technology, cognitive science, educational psychology, and curriculum theory make it possible to realize the integration of individual and social responsibility as articulated by Dewey and participants in the progressive education movement.

Our vision of the informal curriculum includes three basic assertions. First, classrooms are about more than achievement (however defined); thus, students are more than their achievement motivation (however defined). Second, a socially situated conception of students and their relationships within classrooms is a useful framework within which to promote student achievement as one aspect of what occurs in that context. Tasks, teachers, peers, and individual students are more than features of classrooms that can be manipulated in relative isolation. Learning is socially situated; the relationship among classroom features—and, hence, their coordination—is an integral part of student learning and motivation. One task of the informal curriculum as we see it is to consider the various possible relationships among goals and help students learn to identify and coordinate them.

Third, students are more than what they do. Another task of the informal curriculum is to legitimize the intrapersonal dynamics–motivation, enactment, self-evaluation–involved in adaptive student learning. We hypothesize that helping students to (a) distinguish among these processes (e.g., strategies for setting a goal vs. attaining it) and (b) understand their interrelation (e.g., self-evaluation and periodic, critical goal review) will enhance students' understanding of self in relation to context and thereby increase their facility for adaptive learning. Adaptive learning includes the internalization of goals, the motivation to commit, challenge, or reform them, and the competence to enact and evaluate those commitments (McCaslin & Murdock, 1991, pp. 217). Adaptive learning begins in the social world.

## CLASSROOMS AS SOCIAL RESOURCES FOR ACHIEVEMENT

Student motivation and learning are typically conceptualized as individual variables; assessments locate their presence or absence within students. The inherently social nature of classroom learning challenges this notion of individualism, however. The need for student "belongingness" (e.g., Maslow, 1968) or "affiliation" (e.g., French, 1958a, 1958b) has been articulated by educators for some time. The power of a social identity construct in understanding both individual students and the types of relationships among them (e.g., norms and status perceptions that support complementary dominant/submissive relationships), however, is just beginning to be realized in classroom research and theoretical development (see also Goodenow, 1992).

We now briefly review two aspects of "resource management" (Corno & Mandinach, 1983) that involve students learning with and through peers: help seeking and cooperative learning. It will become evident that what we know about students' use of the social resources in classrooms is restricted to the level of reciprocal exchange in pursuit of a teacher-defined achievement goal. Nonetheless, this work represents an important step in researchers' recognition of the social fabric of classrooms.

Instances of student failure to seek assistance and cooperate

in the pursuit of achievement are particularly informative. Identification of the multiple goals that students juggle, and their interrelation, is necessary to inform strategies for effective goal coordination. We hypothesize that, until such coordination strategies are known, students will be unwilling or unable to profit from much of the support available in the social/instructional environments of classrooms.

## Social Resources and Individual Achievement: Help Seeking

In general, students fail to become adept at seeking and using information from others to enhance their personal learning. Home and school social/instructional environments may differently prepare students to engage in these behaviors. For example, students who come to school "classroom literate" are more able to perceive and deal with classroom demands than are students who do not possess such information and skills (Corno, 1989). These students may also be more able to seek help when they need it.

***Mismatch Between Home and School Expectations.*** Home factors are likely important predictors of student preparation for and predisposition to use resources adaptively in school settings. For example, student question-asking behavior is a proxy for student initiative in the classroom. However, students come to school differently prepared to participate in questioning exchanges with peers and teachers. In schools, adults often ask students to answer questions whose answers the adults already know. Parents from upper- and middle-class homes also are more likely to ask such questions of their children than are other parents (Heath, 1982).

Romero et al. (1987) describe the adjustment to school problems faced by language-minority students. They note two major areas in which cultural differences can create dissonance for language-minority students in school: child-rearing practices in the home and the child's language and the ways in which it mediates experience. Casanova (1987) describes how ethnic and cultural differences in parents' perceived relationship with the school can affect student adjustment. She notes that Puerto Rican parents tend to give the school control of their children's education and discipline (when in the school), but do not give the school control over matters of child attendance. In comparison, Anglo parents tend to do the opposite: Schools can demand attendance, but parents expect a say in curriculum decisions and discipline strategies. Not surprisingly, when students come to school with varied understandings of social norms related to classroom learning, behavior, and verbal and nonverbal communication patterns, it is likely the more advantaged student who possesses the informative prior experience (Corno, 1989).

Present intrapersonal dynamics (e.g., *I know I do not understand, and I feel comfortable asking a question now*) can be related to former and continuing interpersonal influences (how teachers, parents, coaches, peers, and the like react to question asking). Students' home learning (e.g., whether effort is more important than ability, how responsibility is defined, dynamics of pride, response to curiosity) influences their understanding of and attitudes toward using resources to promote their own achievement. Certain aspects of school and home can be mutually supportive, whereas others may conflict. For example, teachers and parents may agree or disagree on such fundamental issues as whether seeking help is valued and, indeed, what it indicates—initiative or dependence.

Although educators are becoming more sensitive to differences between home and school cultures (e.g., E. Hiebert, 1991; Hoffman, 1991), especially when the contrasts are striking, subtle variations in expectations for self-management and self-regulated learning between home and school can have important effects on students' approaches to learning (see also McCaslin & Murdock, 1991). And we know that differences between home and school are bridged more easily by some students than by others.

*Mismatch Within Educational Expectations.* Nelson-Le Gall (1981) notes that, although scholars differ about whether help seeking reflects initiative or dependency, the strong tendency for most educators is to conceive of help seeking as a form of dependency. Her analysis challenges this assumption and provides a compelling argument that help seeking and question asking should not be included as part of a cluster of characteristics indicating dependency. For example, Nelson-Le Gall noted that empirical evidence is often weak. She reports that Beller (1957) found a correlation between help seeking and achievement striving of $-.17$, and notes that students seek help for multiple reasons (to gain mastery, to avoid a task, etc.).

We concur that an examination of the help-seeking literature suggests a pervasive tendency to interpret help seeking as undesirable or as a sign of weakness. For example, Wilson and Shantz (1977) found help-seeking and role-taking ability to be highly correlated, especially for older children. These researchers suggested that seeking help places the burden on the child to take the viewpoint of the prospective helper in order to *manipulate* him or her. This interpretation reflects both a value judgment (you treat a person as an object or as instrumental to a competitive advantage by using her information, insights, etc.) and a unidimensional interpretation of a correlation (role taking leads to help seeking vs. help seeking teaches about others).

Researchers in other areas also frequently view using interpersonal resources pejoratively. For example, Sternberg (1990) seems to accept only begrudgingly the adaptiveness of a graduate student (who did better than expected in the psychology program at Yale University) who sought needed human resources for assistance. He wrote, "At least some of Celia's skills are necessary if one is to use one's intelligence and have an impact on the world" (p. 136). This conception of help seeking is especially problematic because Sternberg is trying to communicate respect for different types of competence. We maintain that seeking resources to facilitate one's learning and the pursuit and realization of one's goals is an important feature of personal competence and what we call adaptive learning.

*Differential Instructional Opportunities.* A student's decision to seek help or information is affected not only by specific home learning and general attitudes within the educational community. It is also affected by the student's perception of the teacher's and peers' beliefs about question asking. One way teachers communicate these beliefs is through instructional procedures and tasks. Recall, for example, that several studies have shown that students (e.g., low and high achievers, males

and females) are not always afforded equal opportunity for classroom participation (AAUW, 1992; Bank, Biddle, & Good, 1980; Brophy & Good, 1974; Cooper & Good, 1983).

Differential curriculum assignments and task requirements, described previously, may also affect certain students' development of academic curiosity and assertiveness, which in turn affect help seeking. Students in lower ability groups, for example, receive less academic stimulation from peers, partly because of the type of tasks they engage in (e.g., Allington, 1983, 1991; E. Hiebert, 1991; E. H. Hiebert & Fisher, 1992; Mergendoller, 1989) and when they engage in them (after everyone else). We suspect that repeated low-level assignments (especially if they include tasks that other students in the class may have done weeks earlier) may inadvertently create a social learning environment in which it is difficult for some students to ask questions of their teacher. That is, the timing and type of task may create a situation in which teachers interpret question asking as indicative of inattention or low ability. It may also create social learning environments that make it difficult to ask questions of more capable peers.

Students who struggle with how to learn and how to function in school often have restricted opportunities for interaction with more mature students who have well-developed social and resource management skills. Often the least mature learners are grouped with other immature students. Eder (1981), for example, studied the learning environments of students assigned to high and low reading groups in a first-grade class of a school attended primarily by middle-class students. Despite the similarity among students, the teacher formed reading ability groups according to kindergarten teachers' recommendations, which were based on students' maturity as well as perceived ability.

Eder found that the low reading group moved slowly through the curriculum, largely because it contained several immature, inattentive students who frequently created managerial problems. Compared with students in the high reading group, those in the low reading group spent almost twice as much time in off-task behavior. Thus, the academic initiative of low-group students may decline over time partly because they are often placed in "ragged" and boring social learning contexts in which there are few academic or social peer role models. The lack of such peer leadership also means that low-group students seldom finish a task smoothly or quickly and thus seldom have the opportunity to reflect on a task (to consider what they have done and why). There seems to be a growing consensus that homogeneous grouping of lower ability students for instruction does not promote the goals we set for them, such as content mastery, interpersonal skills, and resource management (e.g., Dunne & Bennett, 1990). One instructional format that has received much support from researchers and educators, however, is heterogeneous ability grouping, both in whole-class and in small-group formats (e.g., NCTM, 1991).

*Instructional Grouping.* There is ample evidence that certain students are often reluctant to raise questions in public whole-class recitation settings (e.g., Dillon, 1988, 1990; van der Meij, 1988, 1990). It could be argued that in a smaller, more intimate setting and with less evaluation, the problem would dissipate. However, research has suggested that heterogeneous small-group settings also lead to passivity among some students. For example, Mulryan (1989) found that the work conditions in small groups provided a learning context in which students could remain passive if they wished. This is because students tolerated others' lack of task involvement as long as those off task did not disrupt the students who were working (see also Rohrkemper, 1985). If students withdrew from the group, other students did not typically encourage them to become involved.

Mulryan also argued that the roles of helper and helped that emerged in many small groups may have created a hierarchical social system that restricted both question asking and information giving. Lower ability group members ask; higher ability members answer (see also King, 1993). Such typecasting inhibits the initiative of *all* group members; apparently it also promotes differential interpersonal perception. Mulryan found considerable variation in how students perceived the same peer behavior in small group.

For example, students tended to view "verbal domination" differentially as a function of achievement. During interviews about student behavior in small groups, low achievers explained frequent peer verbalizations with phrases like "[they] think they know more than others," "[they] want to control the group," or "[they] don't want to give others a chance." In contrast, high achievers explained others' frequent verbal behavior with comments like "because they are depended upon and like the people in the group," or "[they] understand the task well."

Simple placement of students into small groups does not necessarily stimulate more active thinking, intelligent information seeking, or interpersonal understanding (e.g., Blumenfeld, 1992b; Good et al., 1992; Mulryan, 1989, 1992). Some grouping patterns appear to attenuate the hierarchical and exclusionary relationships among students that Mulryan found, however. McCaslin and colleagues (1994) found that restricting the range of student achievement differences within small groups to a difference of one level (e.g., relatively highs with moderates, moderates with lows) appeared to both promote and equalize (across relative ability levels and gender) reported giving and getting help among fourth graders learning math. Earlier, N. M. Webb and Kenderski (1984) had found that seventh and eighth graders learned more math if they were placed in such two-ability-level groups. Perhaps equitable exchange of resources was a contributing factor.

***Student Perception About Seeking Help.*** Classrooms are complex environments. Aspects of classroom structure and climate other than grouping significantly affect students' willingness to seek help. Students also contribute to the development and maintenance of classroom norms. There is an emerging literature on students' perceptions of seeking help or, in our framework, using social resources. R. S. Newman and Schwager (1992) interviewed 177 students in Grades 3, 5, and 7. They examined (a) students' preference of helper (teacher or peer), (b) students' interest in seeking help (as predicted by students' perception of teacher support for question-asking behavior and students' perceived relationship with the teacher), and (c) students' perception of normative comparisons as facilitating or inhibiting help seeking.

Students consistently reported that if they had problems with assigned mathematics work, they preferred to obtain help from a teacher. Students both liked asking the teacher and believed

they learned more than when they asked peers. A similar pattern was reported by Rohrkemper and Bershon (1984), who found that students (Grades 3 through 5) reportedly first ascertained the extent of their misunderstanding in math before seeking help: The more lost, the greater the reliance on the teacher than on a cooperative group member or other classmate. Concurrently, students grouped in cooperative teams for rewards yet working on individualized tasks claimed to assess their own knowledge before venturing to help another; this was especially the case with relatively low-achieving students.

R. S. Newman and Schwager (1992) found that upper-grade students' decisions to seek help involved more social comparison with peers and concern with teacher approval than younger students' decisions. First, older students were more likely to report asking for help if they thought that peers also needed assistance; second, the more seventh graders were bothered that the teacher would think they were "dumb," the less likely were they to report that they asked the teacher for assistance. Even so, in general, students' beliefs that asking questions in class helps them to learn are positively related to students' reporting that they do ask questions.

In response to questions about who asks the teacher more questions, "smart" or "dumb" students, interesting results were obtained. In third grade, 70% of students named "dumb" students as asking more questions and in Grade 5, 54% nominated "dumb" students as question askers. In contrast to both, in seventh grade, 66% of the students identified the "smart" students as question askers. Earlier research by R. Newman and Goldin (1990) with students in Grades 2, 4, and 6 yielded similar results; among sixth graders, the lowest achievers reportedly had both the greatest perceived need for help and the greatest resistance to asking for help. Taken together, these data are consistent with Good's (1981) passivity model, in which some students (especially low-achieving students) learn to reduce their question-asking behavior over the school years.

***Who Seeks Help?*** Students' perceptions about who seeks help correspond with observational research on student question asking, particularly the evolution of student passivity, conducted by Good, Slavings, Harel, and Emerson (1987). Various writers have decried the number of passive learners in U.S. schools (Boyer, 1984; Goodlad, 1984; Sizer, 1984). Good and colleagues sought to test a passivity model (Good, 1981) in which certain students may actually learn to become passive in classrooms.

For example, teachers may implicitly encourage students to become passive by calling on students they believe to be low achievers less often, giving them less time to respond, providing them with answers rather than trying to help them improve their responses when they answer incorrectly, praising them less for their successes, and criticizing them more for their failures. Because low achievers are less likely to answer correctly and because many of their mistakes occur in public, these students have to deal with high levels of personal risk when they respond. Good et al. (1987) maintain that, although there is pressure on all students, there is considerably more pressure on disadvantaged learners because these students are less apt to develop skills for identifying when and how to use classroom resources (e.g., when it is okay to approach the teacher). Recall also that Weinstein and colleagues (1982) found that students perceived teacher treatment of low achieving students to be more varied and inconsistent than their treatment of high-achieving students. Thus, the instructional environment for disadvantaged learners, in addition to risky instructional tasks, is inherently ambiguous. These students are more likely to be criticized for behavior they believe is desirable, such as asking the teacher for information, because they engage in the behavior at the wrong time (from the teacher's perspective). Under the circumstances, a good strategy for them is to remain passive—to not volunteer, not to respond when called on, not to seek assistance from teachers or peers. Thus, passivity can be an adaptive short-term response to classroom tasks and instructional opportunities.

Good et al. (1987) tested this model using student-initiated questions as the dependent measure in a cross-sectional study in classrooms in kindergarten and Grades 1, 3, 6, 7, 9, and 12. They argued that if schooling helps students to become progressively more self-regulated, older students should ask more and different types of questions than younger students (e.g., more mature learners should ask questions calling for explanations rather than mere diversion). Participation rates were also expected to differ for different types of students.

In general, data supported the passivity hypothesis. Low-achieving elementary students became less active question askers with increasing age. Within a classroom, however, some students have more and better resources than others (e.g., some low achievers are better liked and receive more peer support). Thus, students who fail to seek information likely do so for various reasons, not only instructional opportunity (Segal-Andrews, 1991). But they didn't start school that way.

Low achievers enter school expressing as much interest in participating as do other students, at least as can be inferred from their willingness to ask questions. Over time, and with experience, many of these students' willingness to ask questions—that is, the actual question rate—declines. Good et al. argue that students who are relatively immature when they begin school (e.g., have not attended preschool, have short attention spans) appear to learn in the early grades that question asking sometimes yields teacher criticism (for asking at the wrong time, for not having listened carefully, etc.) or causes peers and teachers to infer that they are not intelligent.

Observation data (Good et al., 1987) indicate a change in question asking over the grades; student perception data (R. S. Newman & Schwager, 1992) indicate that students' beliefs about the types of students who ask questions also change over the grades. The data are complementary. Briefly, in the early years, students believe that less able students ask more questions. As students get older (Grades 6 and 7), they are more likely to report that more talented students ask the most questions. It appears that the student reports in Newman and colleagues' data represent veridical perception of who seeks help in the classroom and why.

Taken together, these studies suggest that as students move through the grades there is a gradual but irrevocable shift in who "owns" the social resources of the classroom. High-achieving, more advantaged students occupy center stage. Lower achieving students are on the sidelines and are engaged in anything but "legitimate peripheral participation" (Lave & Wenger, 1991). As these students move through the grades, the ramifications of their status are multiplicative: They learn not to ask their

questions; perhaps they learn not to formulate them at all. They become marginalized.

Ironically, social resources available in heterogeneous small-group learning typically press less advantaged students to instantiate further the differences between the advantaged and the not: Their role is to seek and *appreciate* help from their more advantaged peers. They are expected to display dependency and gratitude. By asking their peers for help, but not their teacher, these students reify their disadvantaged status. Their more advantaged peers are the gatekeepers to their success. Clearly, small-group learning per se is not a panacea for the potentially detrimental dynamics of the interpersonal world of the classroom. Equally clear is the need for informative research; group ability configuration (e.g., McCaslin et al., 1994) seems an important construct to explore.

***Why Students Seek Help.*** Students ask questions for various reasons. For example, questions are useful tools for testing the teacher, distracting from the learning process, preventing a pop quiz, expressing curiosity, and obtaining needed information. Students may also ask questions because teacher presentation is stimulating or vague or incomplete, or because the task is boring. There is evidence that seeking help tends to increase with age (van Hekken & Roelofsen, 1982), but that a subset of children—perhaps a third—appear to lack the ability to use human resources.

Myers and Paris (1978) found sixth graders more likely than second graders to report seeking help as a strategy for resolving difficulties they had with a reading task. Nelson-Le Gall (1987) found similar age differences between third and fifth graders, with high-ability fifth graders requesting more unnecessary help than their low-ability peers. Apparently, older students of higher ability learn to act on their environment even if the goal is simply to make tasks more interesting (Rohrkemper & Corno, 1988).

Nelson-Le Gall (1981, 1985) has hypothesized that some students may seek help to avoid thinking, whereas others seek assistance to gain mastery. Nelson-Le Gall and E. Jones (1990) noted that seeking help can often be adaptive and argued that researchers tend to study primarily the cost of seeking assistance rather than the cost of *not* seeking help. They hypothesized that to seek help requires that the student actively identify problems and assume responsibility for overcoming them. Further, Nelson-Le Gall and E. Jones (1990) contended that *self-assessment* can serve as a basis for a student to establish his need to seek help. Finally, they also considered individual predisposition by elaborating the dichotomous mastery versus performance goal orientation used by some to describe student motivation in classrooms (e.g., C. Ames, 1992; Dweck, 1986). Nelson-Le Gall and E. Jones (1990) reasoned that students who are *mastery oriented* (who want to learn, who like challenging tasks) are more likely to seek help than students who are *performance oriented* (e.g., prefer less challenging tasks).

Seventy-nine third- and fifth-grade black American students from working-class and lower-class backgrounds were studied (Nelson-Le Gall & E. Jones, 1990). On a test of words of similar meaning, students were given 16 words, one at a time, and told that they had two chances to choose a correct answer. They were to write down a tentative response and to fill out a rating that indicated how certain they were that the response was correct. Students had the opportunity to give their initial response to the experimenter as the final solution or to seek help before giving their final response. Two types of help were offered: direct help (a chance to look at the paper of another student of the same grade level who did well and left his/her paper) or indirect help (the student left some hints).

As predicted, students' self-assessments of performance were an important determinant of their decisions to seek help: Self-assessed performance accounted for one-half of the variation in help seeking. In contrast, objective correctness of performance accounted for one-fourth of the variation. Students characterized by high intrinsic orientation toward mastery showed a clear preference for help that allowed them to figure out solutions rather than a preference for ready-made answers. Older students (fifth graders) perceived the need for help more often and sought help more, and they preferred to overcome difficulties in performing the task rather than to obtain the correct answer.

Extrapolation from laboratory studies to classrooms is always fraught with difficulty. For example, the sanctioned chance to look at a peer's work before completing an assigned task is atypical in classrooms. And, as we have noted, the different types of tasks and instructional opportunities that different learners face make it questionable to locate motivational orientation as a stable, internal, learner disposition. How students mediate the opportunity for help is an issue that deserves further study (Do some see it as cheating? Do some see it as a way of comparing their performance to others'?). As we try to conceptualize students' ability to use resources, we need to understand better why students make certain decisions (e.g., when the older or higher achieving students asked to examine a peer's paper, were they competing, assessing comparative advantage?). Although factors associated with student mediation have largely gone unexplained, the work by Nelson-Le Gall and colleagues demonstrates that both individual differences in students' orientations to learning (in a given situation) as well as developmental variables (in interaction with experience), explain, in part, differences in students' help-seeking behavior.

R. S. Newman (1991) also argues that adaptive help seeking (i.e., for the purpose of learning) is predicted by motivational and developmental characteristics of students as well as by characteristics of the classroom. In particular, he maintains that the relation between independence and help seeking changes with age. For example, R. Newman (1990) found that in elementary school, a student with higher dependence on the teacher was more likely to seek help. In contrast, in middle school, a student higher in *in*dependence was more apt to seek help from the teacher. Newman noted that asking for help can serve multiple and even contradictory purposes and contended that to understand help seeking, one must know what motivates a student to seek help. According to Newman, the relative importance of different goals can and does vary over the school years.

In addition to goals and motives, students' self-perceptions of ability also appear to influence their help seeking. Students who perceive themselves as competent view help seeking as instrumental for classroom learning, and therefore are more likely to seek help when they need it (R. Ames, 1983). Further, students who are high in domain-specific knowledge and do not need help as often are more likely to seek it capably when they do need it (Karobenik & Knapp, 1991). The student who sees her- and himself as weak academically and who has less domain-specific information is relatively unlikely to seek assistance from the teacher. The stockpile of the advantaged learner continues to accrue.

***Why Students Should Seek Help.*** We have described serious inequities in which students participate. At a minimum, research is needed to identify an array of help-seeking strategies for specific and global needs without the concomitant status that now accompanies them. Teacher participation in the instantiation of student norms regarding help seeking might encourage students to exchange information more comfortably and competently. Among other things, the language used to describe help (e.g., "information exchange") is apt to become more functional as it becomes more value free and differentiated, as concepts like sharing (which imply when one should use attributional rules of personal responsibility to give aid, etc.) are replaced with more forceful and descriptive taxonomies of resource exchange.

Although some students develop a greater capacity to use human resources than do other students, in both whole-class and small-group settings, most students could become more active learners. Dey, Astin, and Korn (1991) have found large declines (about one-fifth or greater) over the past 25 years in the number of high school students who initiated an academic argument with a teacher in class or who checked out books from or studied in the library. It is likely that this decline is primarily represented in the advantaged strata, with passivity and compliance replacing earlier initiative and assertion.

Students' ability to identify and utilize needed resources, especially human resources, is a critical set of dispositions and skills to be developed and sustained in school settings. To be active, adaptive learners, students must develop the capacity to use the insights and knowledge of others in pursuit of intellectual issues of personal interest. Students need to be able to find and solve problems on their own, but they must also challenge and possibly integrate their own knowledge and opinions with the resources of others (e.g., knowledge, perspectives). If students are to function and flourish in an interdependent world they must also learn how to participate in groups whose members collectively define problems and integrate their talents to develop solution strategies. We refer, of course, to opportunities for small-group learning, an instructional format that explicitly manipulates the social and interdependent character of classroom learning. Thus far, we have examined small-group contexts in terms of the dynamics of student help seeking and individual achievement; we now consider existing practice and its implication for the intrapersonal dynamics of the informal curriculum.

## Social Resources and Group Achievement: Small-Group Learning

Societal beliefs about the value of cooperative work are ambiguous and contradictory. It is often difficult to determine whether individual effort is marshaled to improve the firm, team, or college or to strengthen one's personal résumé or value in the marketplace. Companies refer to their employees as "family," while complex laws such as those pertaining to patents and copyrights encourage individual effort and competition and discourage cooperative enterprises. Thus, social norms regarding the virtues of cooperation are tangled and often quite contradictory.

Society envisions the family as a cooperative, interdependent unit, although there tends to be little agreement on just what constitutes the boundaries of a family unit (see also McCaslin & Good, 1992). What families teach their members about cooperation (independent of family size) is largely unknown. With some exceptions, such as work by S. Phillips (1983) on the role of Hispanic and Indian cultures in the transmission of cooperative values, and by Pepitone (1985) on urban and rural differences in children's cooperation in the eastern United States, little is known about the preconceptions about cooperation that children bring to their roles as students. It is likely, however, that families mirror the complex messages about cooperation found in society. Children enter school with varying (and potentially conflicting) knowledge and appreciation of and capacity for cooperative work.

*School Contexts and Classroom Norms.* Classroom norms exist within school contexts and schools differ in the extent to which cooperation among students (e.g., how awards are defined) and among teachers (e.g., team teaching) is promoted. Much communication among teachers occurs in some schools, so that students frequently see cooperative learning being modeled (e.g., collaborative curriculum development). In other schools, however, even to ask another teacher for help is seen as a sign of weakness (Rosenholtz, 1989). Thus, school social context likely affects the implementation of cooperative learning in classrooms.

Teachers' beliefs and experiences will mediate when and how they use cooperative learning structures (e.g., for teaching core topics, or only for review or enrichment, when they know a lot about the topic or relatively little [see Carlson, 1991]) and whether they use cooperative learning to influence social or academic goals. Teachers' conceptions of cooperative learning likely affect and are affected by students' conceptions in complex ways. Unfortunately, research is lacking on attempts to differentiate among cooperative models and to detail how those models might interact with students' conceptions of cooperation (that have evolved developmentally and through experience) and teachers' histories and expectations, within the broader school context.

*Uneven Implementation and Unrealistic Expectations.* As we have noted elsewhere (McCaslin & Good, 1992), most policymakers offer simplistic strategies for improving student learning (and its assessment). For example, in a *Newsweek* article, "A Dismal Report Card" (Kantrowitz & Wingert, 1991), Bill Honig, then California Superintendent of Schools, is quoted as saying this about small-group instruction: "It's like we have a cure for polio, but we're not giving the inoculation" (pp. 64–65). The *Newsweek* article indicated that the mathematics achievement of American youth would improve if students spent more time learning problem solving in small groups.

In some circumstances (certain content or types of students), students would benefit from more small-group instruction. However, Honig's advice is not easily enacted in classrooms. Without resources for basic research and subsequent staff development, it is unreasonable to expect teachers to dispense the

"cure" for low achievement. Indeed, in a study of California teachers, Prawat (1992) and Putnam (1992) found that some teachers had not even been given copies of the standards for mathematics teaching that they were asked to implement.

It is no surprise, then, that small-group instruction is often problematic. As we have discussed, this type of instruction allows many students to become even more passive and more dependent learners than they are in whole-class settings (Good et al., 1992). Blumenfeld (1992b) found that, although cooperative small-group work was more motivating than whole-class work, students' active learning declined in such settings. When small-group curriculum tasks are poorly designed, students often are swamped by procedural problems (they spend more time carrying out superficial procedures than thinking about the meaning of tasks) (Good et al., 1992; Good, Reys, Grouws, & Mulryan, 1989–1990). Further, small-group learning often focuses on drill and the mastery of discrete concepts. This is especially the case for less advantaged learners.

There is at least some evidence that competent teachers do not use small-group strategies frequently in their classrooms (Battistich, Solomon, & Delucchi, 1993). Involving experienced teachers in small-group instruction does not necessarily lead them to develop high-quality small-group learning activities (Good & McCaslin, in press). Further, teachers who are trained in managing cooperative groups are not necessarily successful in promoting cooperative exchanges among students; negative interactions among students are common (Cohen, Lotan, & Catanzarite, 1990; Huber & Eppler, 1990). Finally, Battistich et al. (1993) found that frequent use of small groups that have low-quality interactions resulted in negative student outcomes.

Small-group learning processes are poorly conceptualized. We maintain that this is in part because those who study small-group learning compartmentalize its features. For example, too often cooperative learning enthusiasts readily lapse into moral imperatives, instructional theorists overlook affective realities, and motivational researchers slight the task for the success rate (see also Rohrkemper, 1986a). One reason cooperative learning is popular among reformers (but not necessarily among classroom teachers; see, e.g., Good, Grouws, & Mason, 1990; Good, Grouws, Mason, Slavings, & Cramer, 1990) is because it is defined in vague, positive terms. It is a mistake, however, to believe that a simple change in grouping format around the same learning task will enable students to achieve both the goals of the analytical curriculum (e.g., subject matter learning, achievement motivation) and the informal curriculum (e.g., enhancing sense of personal competence and interpersonal value).

*Potential Advantages and Disadvantages of Small-Group Learning.* Small-group learning has advantages as well as disadvantages. Building on the research on D. Johnson and R. Johnson (1985), Bossert (1988–1989) noted that four major mediating (process) explanations could account for the success of cooperative methods: (a) reasoning strategies (exchange in cooperative groups may stimulate students to engage in more higher order thinking); (b) constructive controversy (heterogeneous cooperative groups force the accommodation of the opinions of various members, and students must therefore search, engage in problem solving and take another's perspective); (c) cognitive processing (cooperative methods increase opportunities for students to rehearse information orally and to integrate it, especially explanations of how to approach a particular task); and (d) peer encouragement and involvement in learning (students help one another during group work). These positive interactions increase friendship, acceptance, and cognitive information processing.

Possible Advantages.    There are various additional reasons why cooperative groups may enhance students' achievement and social relations. For example, Good et al. (1992) hypothesize the following:

1. School tasks are similar to those outside school. Tasks done in small work groups tend to be more like work done at home (and in many jobs), where everyone pitches in (or does his part) to get a job done. The give and take and sharing that characterize work in small groups are much more like the models that students have seen outside school.

2. Subject matter knowledge is increased. When students work together it is more likely that someone will know how to begin the problem-solving process or will recognize or construct a key formula that applies to the process. The knowledge of procedures and content that the group possesses is almost always greater than the knowledge of any individual student. Thus, with more knowledge, group problem-solving strategies can be more varied, fine-tuned, and powerful.

3. Students develop appropriate dispositions toward challenging work on shared tasks. Because academic work is done with others, challenging tasks are more malleable, approachable, or more doable because of shared expertise and students' increased willingness to take risks.

4. Group members serve as models for one another. Students have the chance to learn important learning-to-learn skills from other students: for example, how to ask questions, how to stay on task. Further, when tasks are appropriately chosen, group work is a natural way of learning in which students can bring varied ways of knowing to bear on a task.

5. Students learn to manage others' resources. Experience in group work increases individual students' ability to use other group members' time and talents. Students learn how to coordinate work with others, how to obtain information from peers, which peers to ask for what type of help, and so forth.

6. Students value shared academic work. It is likely that students will understand mathematics better in small groups because proportionately more group time is spent on conceptual understanding, in comparison to individual time, which tends to be spent on products. Thus, students may value shared academic work more because of the increased emphasis on understanding during small-group instruction. This argument assumes that appropriate small-group learning experiences allow more student understanding of mathematical ideas, which in turn enhances students' attitudes about the work.

7. Students develop an expanded understanding of self and others. The opportunity to work with others helps students to identify and appreciate individual differences in performance and motivation. Students learn that other students are not just "smart" or "dumb"; they develop a sense that others as well as they possess both weaknesses and strengths. This profile awareness of social and cognitive aptitude may allow students to be more creative, to view errors as acceptable, and to learn from failure.

8. Students can regulate their own resources. Individual work pace can be more flexible in a group setting. For example, individual students are more in control of their time and energy; a student can work intensively for a while and then allow others in the group to be active leaders.

Possible Disadvantages.    Despite these ways in which small groups can provide useful learning experiences for students, problems that develop in some group situations may prevent or minimize constructive learning. Good et al. (1992) argue that the following problems may occur during small-group instruction:

1. Students value the product more than the process. If group members focus too narrowly on the group product, the criterion for success can become the answer. Under these conditions, students are unlikely to attempt to understand or explore mathematical tasks. Further, when groups are pitted against other groups, speed may take precedence over the problem-solving process, and groups may pay more attention to the rate of production than to the process of problem solution. In some groups, the rewards for task completion may undermine the process of achieving understanding.

2. Students' misconceptions are reinforced. There is increasing evidence that students often have misconceptions about academic content that are difficult to change even with direct, explicit instruction. These misconceptions may simply be reinforced during small-group interactions if other group members also hold common misconceptions.

3. Students value group processes more than the academic product. In some classrooms, attention to group processes and "learning to learn with others" may take precedence over subject matter learning so that much time is spent teaching students elaborate and potentially artificial procedures for dealing with controversy, group conflict, and the like.

4. Students shift dependency from teacher to peers. In some groups, the fact that the teacher is not an active participant may mean that certain students assume the role of authority figure or expert in their groups. Hence, the shift from whole-class to small-group instruction may be a superficial change (i.e., student as teacher) rather than an actual structural change (i.e., collaborative learning).

5. Students receive differential attention and status. In heterogeneous groups, students do not have equal abilities. Some group situations may present little more than an opportunity for high-achieving students to perform for other students. In other groups, high achievers may feel excessive pressure to do the work for the group.

6. Some students may learn that they do not need to contribute. Social comparison may exacerbate social loafing. In groups, students constantly see how they perform in comparison to others and evaluate how their ideas are accepted or rejected by peers. Some students may consistently receive feedback suggesting that their skills are not valued as much as those of some of their peers. Students of both high and low ability may recognize that their group makes progress whether or not they contribute actively. These students may learn to engage in social loafing: They do relatively little thinking or participating during group work either because they do not value the work or the group, or because they do not excel and, thus, are trying to protect their self-esteem.

7. Some students believe they are not able to contribute. Some students will perceive themselves as having little to contribute to their peers during group learning. These students may become indebted to group members who consistently help them do most of the work. They may even feel shame and develop various self-protection strategies.

8. Group accountability may mediate failure-avoiding and success-enhancing behavior. For example, students who have reputations as know-it-alls may withhold information so as not to enhance their (unwanted) reputations. Other students may withhold information in an attempt to be fair and to let other students contribute more. Such altruistic behavior may come at the expense of learning. Further, the classroom accountability system may convince students in some classes that cooperative work is not important material. The work assigned to cooperative groups often does not appear on classroom tests, and this may indicate to students that group work is not an important part of the curriculum.

*Reservations About Findings on Small-Group Learning.* Despite the fact that past research on cooperative learning has helped practitioners to conceptualize alternative instructional models that appear to have merit (Bossert, 1988–1989; Davidson, 1985; D. Johnson & R. Johnson, 1974; D. Johnson, R. Johnson, & Maruyame, 1983; D. Johnson, Maruyame, R. Johnson, Nelson, & Skon, 1981; Sharan, 1980; Slavin et al., 1985; Slavin, 1990; N. Webb, 1989), many issues about small-group learning have not been resolved. One concern is the level of content that is emphasized during small-group learning. For example, Davidson (1985) has argued that achievement comparisons have largely been made in reference to computational skills, simple concepts, and simple application problems—a narrow range of dependent measures. According to Davidson, more information is needed about how higher order skills are affected by small-group mathematics learning, especially since educators are concerned that instruction should emphasize understanding rather than impart isolated skills (see also, Good et al. 1992).

Cooperative learning research may be questioned on other theoretical grounds. Following the research of Stipek (1986) and others who have explored intrinsic motivation, future research needs to examine what happens to students when cooperative behavior is maintained by the use of external incentives over an extended period. Pepitone (1985) has argued that to study cooperative interaction, it is theoretically essential that students have some choice about curriculum tasks. She contends that unless group goals are chosen by members, it makes little sense to explore issues like group cohesion.

Some theorists have pointed out that cooperative groups may not lead to enhanced participation for low-status students. E. Cohen (1986) provided a theoretical framework, based on expectation states theory (Berger, Cohen, & Zelditch, 1972), that suggests that cooperative small-group structures make status differences among students more salient. Because students work closely together during small-group activities, achievement differences are likely to become more evident (especially on certain types of tasks) and status differences may increase. Because of these status differences, high achievers will dominate, and low-status students will remain relatively passive. Lockheed (1984, in Fennema, 1987) reported differential partici-pation in small groups associated with sex. Boys assumed or were assigned leadership roles more often than girls, a pattern that paralleled whole-class activities. Student beliefs about male leadership are well entrenched: In one study, although no gender differences in contribution to group process were observed, boys were voted their group's leader by 94% of the students.

*Need for Observational Data.* Only a paucity of process research has described student interaction and teacher behavior during cooperative learning. Bossert (1988–1989) noted that most researchers have employed a "black box" approach. That is, students are assigned to one or two treatments, outcomes are measured, and effects are compared. When effects are found, post hoc rationales are used to explain the results. According to Bossert, mediating factors that explain why cooperative procedures work or fail to work must be examined in observational research, and assumptions about desirable learning processes during small-group work need to be verified and modified on the basis of such research. We also have expressed the need for observational studies of small-group learning (Good, et al., 1992; Good et al., 1992).

Bossert pointed out that researchers often fail to verify whether students have even engaged in cooperative interactions, and he noted that when researchers observe instructional processes directly, the results have not always supported theories of cooperative learning. In recent work, Good (1990) examined several types of process studies of cooperative learning. In many studies the hoped-for effects did not occur when students were allowed to work cooperatively. Rather, detrimental effects on student learning and interpersonal relations were evident, particularly for the low-achieving students (Good et al., 1989–1990; King, 1992; Mulryan, 1989; 1992).

*Need for Student Perception Data.* Small groups also can be problematic for students whose personal dispositions are not oriented toward *esprit de corps*. Mulryan (1989) found that norms for personal (and group) responsibility change with small-group experience. For example, in the beginning of her study most students reportedly viewed passive behavior in small groups as due to personal traits or conditions beyond the control of the passive students (e.g., shy, does not understand). At the end of the study, however, all students were more likely to view passivity as intentional. We have already discussed the relations among attribution, affect, and behavior. This change in basic attributional norm regarding student passivity likely affects as well students' interpersonal affect and the likelihood of their extending or withholding help (e.g., Rohrkemper, 1984, 1985). The predicted cycle is also self-fulfilling. Ignoring, withholding assistance, or exhibiting hostility toward passive students likely increases their passivity and withdrawal.

### Conceptualization of Small-Group Work

Academic Tasks. Just as the poor performance of U.S. schools has been overstated (Berliner, 1992), so too has the success of small-group instruction. Observational research consistently illustrates that both the normative structure that surrounds group participation and the interactive process itself seldom match the high aspirations that many educators hold for the model. Trade-offs will likely always occur when this method is used, as is the case in any instructional setting for any method. Any learning activity has more value for some students than for others. At present, much of the potential of small-group instruction probably goes unrealized because educators have not carefully conceptualized various factors related to grouping (group composition, group stability, curriculum tasks, appropriate assessment). Small-group models tend to be used explicitly to increase students' achievement motivation and, therefore, achievement; but these efforts to increase achievement motivation often are unsuccessful and sometimes self-defeating. Direct transfer of (ineffective) beliefs about and strategies for individual learning to small-group learning is apt to be equally disappointing. Socially situated learning in small groups begins with the *task* students are asked to engage in and the *structure* that defines how they are to engage one another around and through the task.

Despite the growing consensus that school assignments should stress students' understanding and in-depth coverage of fewer topics (rather than superficial coverage of numerous topics), studies of the structure of school tasks indicate that teachers tend to assign tasks involving isolated, discrete concepts that encourage students to memorize—not to understand, integrate, or attempt to apply concepts (Blumenfeld, 1992b; Doyle, 1983; Fisher & E. Hiebert, 1990; E. H. Hiebert & Fisher, 1992; Mergendoller, Marchman, Mitman, & Packer, 1988; Porter, 1989). It is also how they design tests (Lohman, 1993). It is unlikely that many teachers will develop new curriculum tasks or assessment opportunities for small-group learning unless they are given the time, resources, and support necessary to do so. And even then the results are not clear. Recent work by Blumenfeld (1992b) shows that simply making tasks more complex and more challenging does not automatically lead to more student thinking.

Assessment Criteria. Assessing processes and progress (e.g., artifacts) in small-group learning is likely more informative than assessing final products. Good et al. (1992) have hypothesized four initial criteria by which it might be possible to assess small-group progress when mathematical problem solving is of primary interest. First, the task should engage all group members. Group engagement does not mean learning mathematics quickly or efficiently. Rather, the focus is on students' valuing mathematical processes, or the reasoning involved in solving a problem, more than products (correct answers). Students' responses and artifacts should be reasonable (e.g., internally consistent arguments, models that characterize the problem) but not necessarily optimal (the most correct, fastest, or efficient response). Further, engagement implies two steps: (a) each student thinks about the problem in a meaningful way, trying to understand the problem, and (b) each student participates in other students' problem-solving thinking. That is, students listen to other students' ideas and attempt to understand them, not correct them.

Second, an appropriate work-group task is sufficiently challenging that it requires collective group interaction on possible solution strategies but not so challenging that it causes the group to give up prematurely or regress in interpersonal behavior. This sensitive balance between a task that is challenging yet attainable likely varies according to the particular group of students and instructional model (e.g., is the teacher expected to lead or clarify).

Third, work-group tasks that involve the use of manipulatives (graph paper, geoboards, calculators, and so forth) often encourage members to work together to organize or use the materials. It is not assumed that individual students understand the relationship of manipulatives to the problem under investigation, however. The belief that action improves thinking— learning by doing—is not always supported in observations of small-group learning (Good & McCaslin, in press).

Fourth, work-group tasks that introduce a concept are often more productive than ones that review a mathematical idea. In other words, the task should evoke an idea that may surprise the learners. This element of surprise often encourages group members to accommodate new information through additional exploration or discussion. In this way, small-group work can be creative and socially constructed learning rather than overt performance of prior learning. Good et al. argue that these four task criteria may, on occasion, afford group learning that no single student in the group could experience if working alone. Academic tasks, then, are essential features of small-group learning. When small-group learning goals include the features of the informal curriculum (e.g., constructive conflict), however, other process dimensions become more salient for assessment (e.g., student identification and management of conflict [e.g., Shantz & Hartup, 1993]). In either case, pursuit of analytical or informal curricular goals, the cooperative task structure that governs group processes is a fundamental concern.

Task Structures. Learners can cooperate in different ways. The three task structures described by Dunne and Bennett (1990) are a useful starting point: independent students in a group, interdependent students in a group, and students as a group. In the independent-students-in-a-group structure, students work individually on identical tasks. Each student has her own materials and works on her own task. Students are encouraged to seek and give help as needed.

In contrast, in the second task structure, interdependent students in a group, students work individually on different tasks that, when completed, form one shared group outcome (this is often called the "jigsaw" method, after Aronson, Blaney, Stephan, Sikes, & Snapp, 1978). Each student works with material that is informative in its own right and that also contributes to the larger group project. Finally, in the task structure of students as a group, students work together on the same task for a shared outcome. Students share materials and help each other produce a single product.

Tasks that require different degrees of cooperation probably have different effects, depending on the type of content and the amount and type of previous experience students have had with cooperative learning. It seems important to explore the effects of various task structures on students' language, cooperation in groups, and subject matter learning, and how these effects differ for particular types of learners (e.g., socially anxious or high-ability learners). There is some evidence that task structures differentially affect the quality of student cooperation and task engagement so that the same task may be significantly transformed by differing task structures (McCaslin & Good, in press). Learners confront the task *and* each other when they learn in small groups. Teachers need to make explicit decisions regarding the type and degree of cooperation (e.g., tutorial help vs. collaboration) expected of students because in so doing they are simultaneously determining the level and nature of student achievement of the analytical curriculum. To ignore the interface between academic task and task structure is to undermine student achievement of subject matter goals and to underemploy and thus thwart the development of important features of the informal curriculum.

### Conceptualization of Small-Group Composition

Group Composition.   Elsewhere we have identified several areas in which extensive programmatic research on composition and student interpersonal dynamics in small groups is needed (Good, Mulryan, & McCaslin, 1992). Here we mention only a few topics to illustrate both the complexity of group composition and the type of research that may inform the emergent interaction of small-group experience and intrapersonal processes.

Typically, small groups are understood by the characteristics of the learners assigned to them. Usually this means level of achievement (perhaps mediated by considerations of gender, personality, and race or ethnicity). Most current models about how to place students in small groups involve compensatory relationships (e.g., low achievers need the expertise of brighter students, shy students need the gregarious, leaders need followers). We have already noted the typical effects of this type of grouping decision rule, intended or not, in the informal curriculum: caste systems among students that reify the hierarchies of the abstract and analytical curricula.

There are other ways to view group membership; however, grouping decisions should co-occur with explicit informal curricular goals. For example, decisions to form groups based on social relationships (e.g., friends) should coincide with an instructional goal of providing students meaningful experience in friendship, perhaps the opportunity to disentangle affiliation and competence (e.g., French, 1958a, 1958b). Similarly, if students are grouped such that a student is salient in personal characteristics (e.g., gender, race or ethnicity, ability), the instructional goal of the informal curriculum should be congruent, perhaps to afford students the opportunity to discern relevant from irrelevant personal characteristics within a group context.

Finally, complementary relationships wherein both parties are enhanced by each other's strengths are another viable strategy to enhance the goals of the informal curriculum. For example, consider a student quite capable in goal-setting strategies, but with less volitional skill to realize them, paired with a student opposite in relative strength (i.e., low in goal-setting skill but high in volitional strategies). This pairing may well meet analytical goals of subject matter learning and task completion and informal curriculum goals of peer modeling of intrapersonal strength.

Group Stability.   Group composition is one thing; the stability of group membership is another. How long groups stay together may affect the quality of the subject matter learning and the quality of the interpersonal/intrapersonal learning of the informal curriculum. For example, if the instructional goal is simply to use cooperative methods as a way for students to practice academic content or to improve social graces (e.g.,

listening, politeness, turn taking), both fairly superficial goals, then stability of group membership may not emerge as a concern. Depending on the instructional goal and the reality of implementation, however, the impact of group stability on the informal curriculum may be enormous.

Teachers might change group membership frequently because of classroom management concerns. For example, if two students are truly difficult to interact with (e.g., a class bully, a student who is extremely hyperactive or withdrawn), a teacher may want to rotate these students in and out of various groups to minimize other students' contact with them and to keep all groups functioning more smoothly much of the time. By changing group membership frequently (and these students in particular), the teacher is able to maintain "fair" and satisfactory conditions for learning for most students. In short, changing group membership after one or two periods may occasionally benefit individual students and groups by allowing them to work with a wider range of students and perhaps to avoid the negative consequences of personal conflicts and disagreement that could characterize more stable groups.

Group rotation may also obviate the development of important interpersonal knowledge, however. For example, if group membership changes frequently and during a lesson one student dominates the group, it is unlikely that other group members would attempt to alter the behavior of the dominating student unless it were especially irritating and disrupted the group's ability to complete the task. Similarly, if a talented student were passive and did not contribute, group members would have little need to develop strategies to draw the student into the group if the likelihood of future interaction was random.

Obviously, there are advantages and disadvantages in having students work together in the same group for a relatively long period. Group stability allows students to become familiar with the working styles, competencies, and personal characteristics of other group members and allows group norms for student behavior to develop. Students who work in relatively permanent groups might be more likely to work out their differences than students in groups whose membership changes frequently (e.g., a withdrawn student may become more participatory).

Other concerns about stability of group membership are perhaps even more fundamental to the informal curriculum. For example, when group membership changes frequently, students may well be learning strategies for manipulation more than cooperation, fine-tuning strategies for engaging others in "my" goals rather than in legitimate coparticipation. Students also may become more narrowly defined as a result of small-group rotation. Cohen (1986) has predicted greater social comparative knowledge of interpersonal competence. We would add that students may be reduced to their particular skill (e.g., the notetaker, the question asker, the reporter).

We suspect that one reason students report liking small-group more than whole-class learning formats (e.g., Mulryan, 1989, 1992; Rohrkemper & Bershon, 1984) is partly because group membership typically is relatively unstable. Thus, the more interesting tasks usually associated with small-group work and the opportunity to work with a variety of peers provide stimulation without requiring students to learn to deal with others in a meaningful and potentially difficult way (e.g., management of conflict). Small-group learning under these conditions also can be quite efficient. Even though students know they are expected to work together, subdivision of tasks is common, with consequent individualized work. Indeed, many students think task division is a primary asset of small-group work. Speed of task completion is mentioned as a criterion of group success by both high- and low-achieving students (Mulryan, 1989).

*Conceptualization of Small-Group Learning.* Learning is different from performance, cooperation is differentiated in kind and degree, students are more than their achievement and learn more than subject matter in small groups. Thus, we call for research on small-group learning that involves the integration of three "considerations" (after Blumenfeld, 1992b) if the goals of the analytical and the informal curricula are to be mutually informative and taken seriously. First, the task must be amenable to group learning and assessed by process and change; second, the task structure that governs how group members are to engage one another through the task must be mindful (rather than determined, for example, by the number of available manipulatives); and third, the composition and maintenance of group membership must be deliberate and deliberately monitored. These considerations allow for the exploration of the texture of meaningful group learning. We provide one possible taxonomy of small-group learning experience to illustrate our point.

At least five levels of learning experience relevant to the attainment of analytical curriculum goals are possible for individual learners in a small work group. We suggest that type of learning experience is a more viable conceptualization of student ability than is mere achievement level when considering the effects of group membership on student learning. Obviously, a group of four learners could and likely would have various configurations. An examination of a possible task experience for each learner provides a starting point for considering the meaning of a problem-solving context for each learner and for the four students as a group. We discuss these task experiences in terms of hypothesized complexity of engagement, beginning with the most complex form of engagement (see also Good et al., 1992).

We hypothesize that the most complex task engagement experience for a learner is what is currently labeled a misconception in the literature. In this situation a learner can objectively "understand" a task only if his previous misconceptions are altered, because the student's past subject matter knowledge or life experience is inconsistent with the knowledge demands of the present task. We call this Level 1 task engagement experience *disequilibrium and accommodation,* after Piaget (1983) (i.e., the "reconstruction" of concepts that are no longer appropriate).

A second task engagement experience involves the confrontation of a task that is so new to a learner that previous experiences do not inform the task in any meaningful way. Thus, the learner is unable to assess what is "reasonable" within the task or in his responses to it. In this situation, like a novice learner, novel or salient task features likely dominate student construction. Preoperational children's construction of conservation tasks are an example of this type of task engagement; their attention is decontextualized (e.g., height independent of width). We call this Level 2 task experience *new learning.* "New

learning" is obviously a relative concept; learning situations for constructivist learners are not absolutely, objectively, new.

We assume that some learners will find a curriculum task assigned to their work group to be meaningful in that it allows them to bring their subject matter knowledge and life experiences to bear on the task. These learners can integrate new material with their previous knowledge. We call this Level 3 task engagement experience *integrative learning* because, although the task has a new dimension for the learners, it connects with their previous understanding and experience. The elaboration and integration of new knowledge are thus facilitated.

A fourth possible task engagement experience is one in which the learner is not thoughtfully engaged by a task but simply responds routinely or mechanically to it. Indeed, in such cases the student is simply performing, not learning. For example, a student may apply a memorized formula or a rote procedure automatically, without thinking about the task requirements. We call this Level 4 learning experience *algorithmic responding.* We hypothesize that, as in Level 2 learning experience, task features dominate student engagement.

A fifth potential task experience is *disengagement.* Here the student depends on others to process the information and to generate appropriate solution paths, owing to either inability to generate his own learning scaffold or a more dispositionally based passivity. Disengagement may be either overt or covert. For example, a student may actively misbehave or may appear to attend but may be thinking about something other than the assigned group task.

It seems helpful to recognize that the same task may simultaneously create five different task engagement experiences for work-group learners: disequilibrium/accommodation, new learning, integrative learning, algorithmic responding, or disengagement. It is important to learn more about the effects of small-group learning on, and as a function of, the array of task engagement experiences of individual group members—if instructional goals include achievement of the analytical curriculum. Clearly, the dynamics of socially situated learning will differ between a work group composed of two students for whom a task represents an integrative learning experience and two students for whom the task is a new learning experience, and a work group composed of four students who are all experiencing disequilibrium (and potentially for different reasons).

The interpersonal and intrapersonal affective processes accompanying these task engagement experiences are also part of the small-group experience (e.g., McCaslin et al., 1994; McCaslin, in press). Consider the interpersonal perception and intrapersonal dynamics when one student is frustrated, unable to ascertain the meaning in her disequilibrium experience, yet she notes that two group members are excited and insightful (their learning experience is integrative—and shared) and the third peer has already completed the task and complains that she is bored.

In sum, small-group learning is a complicated instructional format that fuses task with task structure. Students' experiences within these learning contexts are not microcosms of their experiences in whole-class or individual settings. Much more research is needed on the social/instructional processes that are involved in small groups (defined by composition and stability). Deliberate attention to the type of learning experience a given task affords, the type of interpersonal press of the given task structure, and the concomitant opportunities for interpersonal and intrapersonal learning that emerge seems a useful start. Research on the integration of these affective and intellectual features is likely to enhance the mutual attainment of goals of the analytical and informal curricula.

## FORMALIZATION OF THE INFORMAL CURRICULUM

Students do not appear to profit from social resources available in classrooms even when instructional formats are explicitly designed to enhance social learning opportunities. We suggest that the social stratification associated with seeking help—from whom and by whom—and students' hesitancy to actively promote their learning through social resources are, in part, symptoms of the tensions inherent in classroom learning. Educators may think of the student as "one who learns the curriculum," but it is doubtful that students' intentions are as focused.

Students are coordinating more than analytical curriculum goals (e.g., allocating relatively more time to a science project, less to English composition) within the classroom. The social nature of classroom learning makes curriculum goal realization even more difficult because interaction with people is more complicated and less predictable than is interaction with objects (e.g., the science project is with a small group, the essay is to be shared with the class) (see also Vandenberg, 1991). Just as tasks vary in difficulty and complexity, so too do social interactions. The inability to understand and respond to a peer's explanation or affect is at least as frustrating as not being able to understand the textbook example, especially as students move through the grades.

Students also are coordinating more than the classroom within the context of their lives. Students live complicated lives in a world that challenges their ability to cope daily (Garbarino, Dubrow, Kostelny, & Pardo, 1992; Natriello, McDill, & Pallas, 1990). At a minimum, students juggle expectations from home and school. As students age, the sources of expectations for their time and energy expand. Many students, for example, work for employers who subject them to long and unpredictable hours. Pulls on students away from achievement of the analytical curriculum are not just from without the system, however. School-sponsored activities can be equally divisive. For example, students in sport are expected to bear down and give it their all; students working for the school paper and yearbook are ruled by deadlines; band members practice daily at 6:30 a.m. for Saturday performances, no matter what the weather.

As we have described, for many students, especially disadvantaged students, classroom experience—be it through tasks, opportunity for autonomy, or relations with peers—does not help them understand themselves as active participants in their own classroom community, in their own destiny. Unfortunately, for many of these students, there also is no reason to expect that successful performance in the classroom (however defined) will enhance their quality of life (see also McCaslin & Good, 1992; Ogbu, 1992).

In this chapter we have used a framework wherein the expectations of society regarding the function and value of schooling—what for and for whom—flow into the daily enactment of the analytical curriculum. We have located the informal curriculum in the everydayness of curriculum enactment. The informal curriculum is in reciprocal relation to the analytical and abstract curricula: students participate in the cycle of events that results in the realization of the different and divergent societal goals set for them.

We believe that to break this cycle of fulfilled expectation, educators must formalize the informal curriculum so that students can—must—recognize and act on their learning within it. We offer three premises as part of this formalization. First, *relationship* is a useful conception of students engaged in learning and performance tasks (relations with objects) within the social/instructional environment (relations with others) of classrooms. Second, students must learn to *coordinate* multiple goals while occupying the role of "student" (e.g., enhance social relationships *and* strive for a standard of excellence) if they are to profit from, rather than be undone by, the array of opportunities available in schools. It is not enough to be "popular *or* smart" (Kunjufu, 1988). Third, teachers through their relationships with students and the opportunities they provide them, support and scaffold adaptive student learning. We term this process *"co-regulation."*

Given these premises, we call for deliberate and meaningful instruction in (a) the identification of goals, their interrelationships, and strategies for coordination (sketched in Table 19–1 and (b) intrapersonal dynamics that influence and are influenced by interpersonal relationships and setting features that we term co-regulated learning (outlined in Table 19–2). We hypothesize that such instruction will provide students with the tools to understand themselves as learners and members of the educational community. We now outline each feature of a proposed informal curriculum—goal coordination and co-regulated learning—that may be useful in stimulating a research agenda on its formalization.

### Goal Coordination

It is useful to distinguish among (a) goals, (b) motivation to engage them, (c) strategies to meet them, and (d) strategies to coordinate among them. A fundamental point is that learner-adopted goals are not apparent. The observer cannot assume the adoption of a particular goal, especially a goal prescribed by others, even if manifest behavior appears congruent with it. If nothing else, for example, educators have come to realize that they cannot assume that students' goal is to "do their best" on achievement tests.

*Motivated Goal Engagement.* Students also may undertake a common prescribed goal for differing reasons that likely involve some combination of endogenous and exogenous reasons (after Kruglanski, 1978). That is, a student may complete an assignment because doing so increases her understanding (an endogenous reason) or because completing it is instrumental to going out with friends (an exogenous reason). A host of other possibilities may apply, perhaps simultaneously. For example, the task might be moderately interesting, the student expects to succeed and looks forward to feeling good about completed performance, peers might notice that she is doing well and ask for help, maybe phone after school, the teacher will be pleased, and, once the assignment is done, the student will not have to do it again. If students have multiple goals it

TABLE 19–1. Classroom Goal Coordination: Potential Sources of, Relationships Among, and Realization of Goals

ANALYTICAL CURRICULUM PRESS ⟶ *Potential Student Goal Engagement*

INFORMAL CURRICULUM PRESS ↓ *Potential Student Goal Engagement*

| | RESOURCE MANAGEMENT | | GOAL COORDINATION | | | INTRAPERSONAL AND INTERPERSONAL DYNAMICS | |
|---|---|---|---|---|---|---|---|
| | Social (teacher, peer, family, etc.) | Object (manipulatives, text, technology, etc.) | Identification (interpersonal/intrapersonal, proximal/distal, etc.) | Relationships[a]: Compatible (compensatory, complementary, instrumental), incompatible (interference, negation), independent | Coordination strategies[a] (single, integrative; multiple, simultaneous; deferment; modification; substitution; abandonment) | Competence (global self, academic, athletic, job, personal, physical, social, etc.) | Affiliation (general belongingness; relations within classroom: teacher, peers; friends, chums; compassion, helpfulness, etc.) |
| INSTRUCTION Performance learning, etc. | | | | | | | |
| MANAGEMENT Compliance, self-regulation, etc. | | | | | | | |
| ASSESSMENT Reproduction, integration, etc. | | | | | | | |

Note: It is hypothesized that relations within and between all components are reciprocal, and that differentiation within various types of potential student goal engagement covaries with development and opportunities for learning.

[a]Adapted from Argyle, Furnham & Graham, 1981; Dodge, Asher, & Parkhurst, 1989.

TABLE 19–2. Co-regulated Learning: A Heuristic Model of Intrapersonal Processes Afforded by the Social/Instructional Environment (SIE) of Classrooms

| | MOTIVATION | ENACTMENT | | EVALUATION | |
| | | Overt and Covert Strategies | | assessment ←→ congruence | |
| Motive | Goal Setting | SIE-Directed | Intrapersonally Directed | Self-Evaluation of Progress — Assessment TOTE—Interim, Final | Teacher Evaluation of Student Progress — Assessment of Progress, Product |
|---|---|---|---|---|---|
| Needs/wishes/desires Interests | Individual goal(s): difficulty, level of attainment, specificity, timing, etc. | Other-involved (e.g., assistance, assertion, equity) | Self-involved (e.g., affect, volition, goal, motive reconsideration) | Affect Attributions | Affect Attributions |
| Knowledge about/relations among self, task, situation | Goal relationships (e.g., instrumentality of proximal/distal goals) Goal coordination strategies (e.g., integration, modification) Periodic goal review (e.g., recommitment, reformulation, rejection) | Setting-involved (e.g., transform objects, control setting features) | Task-involved (e.g., cognitive, metacognitive strategies, goal refinement) | Decision re persistence: (e.g., continue, modify, or cease) | Decision re instruction: (e.g., continue, modify, or cease) |
| Attributions Efficacy Expectations | | | | Attributional interpretation, immediate and delayed (for future related: goals, tasks, self) | Attributional consequences, immediate and delayed (e.g., opportunities, tasks, assessment, accountability) |

→Artifacts

follows that they can be multimotivated. Thus, we assert that it is more useful to consider the coordination of student motives and goals than only to abstract and dichotomize them (e.g., "intrinsically" or "extrinsically" motivated [e.g., Harter, 1981]; "learning" or "performance" orientation [e.g., C. Ames, 1992]).

Similarly, it is risky to infer a goal from an apparent strategy. Take, for example, effort. Student manifestation of effort is often equated with student interest, learning, or desire to learn. Students can adjust their effort, however (a point to which we return), and do so for various reasons. For example, effort is a useful impression management strategy that can function independent of ability; one can "be smart and virtuous too" (Covington, 1985). Expended effort can also compensate for quality of performance; manifest effort is a viable strategy to increase the evaluation (independent of quality) of performance that is low ("but I really worked hard on this . . . "). Effort can also serve as an effective task-avoidance strategy. For example, as long as I approach (or endure) the present task I can avoid another, potentially even more stressful one. Text revision may be preferable to text generation; perseveration on this task precludes the adoption of another. In short, effort— persistence—can be complicated. It is not only about the "why" but also the "what for" and, as we will see, the "how."

Individual goals can be understood by dimensional characteristics, such as their locus (e.g., self, other), specificity, temporal boundaries, and difficulty of attainment; thus, goal coordination strategies are also multifaceted. Dodge, Asher, and Parkhurst (1989) predict that complexity among goals increases to the extent that the goals are equally specific (and therefore generally more difficult to overlap), difficult (and thus occupy considerable personal resources), occur within a limited time (making sequential goal pursuit a less viable strategy), and clash with others' needs and interests (e.g., continued personal goal pursuit threatens interpersonal relationships). Dodge et al. (1989) stress that personal competence should not be equated with successfully meeting one's original goals. Original goals themselves may be more or less appropriate, but often personal and environmental constraints can be insurmountable, or the relationships among the goals (e.g., conflicting vs. compatible) may be inhibitory. And sometimes, on reflection, original goals are no longer judged worthy of personal pursuit.

Thus, if the individual is to coordinate goals, then she must be empowered to make proactive, interactive, and reactive decisions that recognize and modify goals that are no longer desired, important, or possible. We consider *periodic, critical goal review* for the purpose of (a) reassessing the value and feasibility of one's goals and (b) deciding to recommit, reformulate, or reject them, fundamental to goal coordination. We also hypothesize periodic, critical goal review as an essential feature of co-regulation and intrapersonal dynamics, a point to which we return. Unfortunately, the ability to change one's mind after thoughtful reflection is a form of intelligence seldom encouraged in school.

### Task Features and Goal Coordination Strategies.

Dodge et al. (1989) define competence in goal coordination as "the greatest possible satisfaction of needs and desires, given the circumstances" (p. 122). They conceive of goal coordination as a task in the information-processing (e.g., Simon, 1969) tradition. Using an information-processing framework, they delineate five sequential steps—encode, interpret, generate possible responses, evaluate and select response, enact and monitor selected responses—that may be somewhat offset or totally derailed by emotion.

Of special interest here, Dodge et al. also posit four strategies to promote goal coordination in the interpersonal realm: (a) a single, integrative strategy, which is the most efficient but requires that goals be compatible and the individual have a certain amount of skill; (b) multiple simultaneous strategies, which are useful when certain goals are less difficult so that the individual can, in effect, "overlap" (Kounin, 1970) varied strategies in the pursuit of multiple goals; (c) deferment strategies, which involve both individual recognition that she can't "have it all" and prioritizing, while keeping some goals on the "back burner" (vs. abandoning them); and (d) modification strategies, which may involve changing the goal or the criteria for satisfaction along the lines of "satisficing" strategies discussed by Simon (1969).

To this list, we add two strategies that seem generally important but particularly problematic in classroom goal coordination. These additional strategies are (e) goal substitution (that goes beyond goal modification in that the learner engages an alternate goal that does not promote progress toward the original) and (f) goal abandonment without pursuit of an alternate; for example, sheer withdrawal and passivity. In the specific instance, these strategies may well be appropriate (e.g., giving up the goal to be best) or bring temporary relief (e.g., from embarrassment) but in aggregation and the long run they may restrict important opportunities (e.g., venture into new learning) or prohibit the development of adaptive strategies (e.g., development of a degree of hardiness; with a few extreme exceptions, withdrawal as a life strategy is untenable and maladaptive).

These six goal coordination strategies appear to have face validity for the coordination of multiple classroom goals. We envision them in *decreasing* levels of inclusiveness, with the "single, integrative" strategy allowing the simultaneous pursuit of the most goals and "abandonment" the most restrictive and exclusive goal coordination strategy. In our framework, the six goal coordination strategies—single integrative, multiple simultaneous, deferment, modification, substitution, and abandonment—are reciprocally related to situated opportunity and emergent competence. That is, differing opportunities (defined, e.g., by the number, timing, instrumentality, and difficulty of goals) *require and promote* differing knowledge, skill, and goal coordination strategies (personal competence). We hypothesize that differing goal coordination strategies affect quality of learning and integration of experience and, thus, inform future goal opportunities (and, hence, learning and experience). If research supports these hypothesized relationships, then goal coordination strategies would appear to be a critical feature of the informal and the analytical curricula.

Finally, we conceptualize student goal coordination tasks in classrooms (and, although it is not our purpose, a case could easily be made for teachers as well [see Spencer, 1984]) to include the integration of proximal and distal goals in the interrelation of social, self, and academic goals. Further, students juggle the expectations of parents, peers, principals, teachers (McCaslin & Murdock, 1991; McCaslin Rohrkemper, 1989) and others involved in their social/instructional worlds (e.g., coaches, employers). As we have noted throughout, this sizable goal coordination task exists within a context of accountability and societal expectations for student performance.

***Classroom Enactment.*** The likely distribution of goal coordination strategies required of and therefore experienced by students is apparent. We have seen, for example, that it is the more advantaged learner who has developed the more future-oriented presence of mind and whose goals and daily classroom experiences are more apt to be instrumental and congruent with educational structures. Thus, it is reasonable to hypothesize that these students are engaged in a single, integrative strategy with respect to proximal and distal goals (e.g., academic excellence now informs future educational and professional opportunities) more often than are their less advantaged peers. When required, advantaged students also can employ multiple simultaneous strategies ("overlapping") in the more proximal interpersonal sphere. For example, in small-group learning they can meet academic demands while engaging in small talk with peers; their work doesn't suffer, nor do their friendships. These students are also more apt to be "classroom literate" (Corno, 1989); thus they are more apt to know how to time their off-task behavior so that their relationship with the teacher is unimpaired (Spencer-Hall, 1981).

In contrast, it is more likely the disadvantaged student who is required to coordinate multiple goals by modifying, substituting, or abandoning them all together, which is the case of the "negative identity" adolescent described by Erikson (1964) and the "involuntary minority" student hypothesized by Ogbu (1992). Our purpose at this juncture, however, is not so much to continue to describe differences in the type of goal coordination strategy *required* of students because of the differential opportunities provided them in the analytical curriculum. These differences should be obvious. Further, the differences in the sheer difficulty of the goal coordination task as a function of the type of goal relationship, which typically differs for advantaged and disadvantaged students, should be equally apparent. Being able to "have it all" (by having compatible and instrumental goals) is certainly easier than having to decide where to cut one's losses (because of incompatible and negated goals). In reality, however, both types of goal coordination tasks, in appropriate proportion, are important learning opportunities.

Instead, our purpose is to provide one lens for organizing the features of a goal coordination task that any student may confront at any given time. We believe that understanding goals, their sources, and their possible interrelation will help students identify when to use and how to implement particular goal strategies. We hypothesize that such knowledge will empower students within their social/instructional environment and promote the enhancement of their adaptive learning by enabling them to make decisions among goals (which may well include goal abandonment) and maintain the pursuit of multiple goals. We argue that coordination of multiple goals is an essential feature of adaptive learning and general mental health. Single-mindedness (even if in academic pursuit) is not a viable strategy in a continuously changing interdependent world (see also Dodge et al., 1989).

***A Proposed Framework for Classroom Goals.*** Table 19–1 outlines parameters that we believe are useful for understanding possible (a) sources of multiple goals that students juggle and (b) the relationships among them, which may well require (c) different strategies for goal coordination. We have already discussed the point that individual goal characteristics (e.g., difficulty, timing) may increase the difficulty of a goal coordination task. Here we note as well that the type of relationship between goals (e.g., degree of compatibility) influences potential coordination strategies and, hence, the probability of goal realization (adapted from Argyle, Furnham, & Graham, 1981, and Dodge et al., 1989).

Potential Sources of Classroom Goals. As Table 19–1 illustrates, the press of the analytical curriculum is communicated through instruction, management systems, and assessment procedures. We advocate that the press of the informal curriculum include deliberate attention to resource management, goal coordination, and inter- and intrapersonal outcomes.

Student potential engagement of these curricular presses is represented in the adjacent column (analytical) and subsequent rows (informal). Thus, student potential response to the demands of instruction, management, and assessment in the analytical curriculum may include differing levels of learning, degree of internalization of social norms, and type of performance in assessment opportunities. Student potential engagement of the informal curriculum is hypothesized to include different sources of resource management (Corno & Mandinach, 1983), opportunities for goal coordination tasks, and multiple inter- and intrapersonal outcomes. By resource management we mean both social and physical resources, which include other participants and objects in the classroom setting (e.g., teachers, peers; texts, computers) and beyond (e.g., parent, employer; library, television). We conceptualize goal coordination as a three-pronged task (described more fully shortly): identification of individual goals, understanding of their interrelation, and strategies for optimizing realization of multiple goals within the given constraints. As we have already noted, periodic critical review of goals is considered an important overarching component of goal coordination.

Finally, we briefly note the mutually informative and interdependent inter- and intrapersonal dynamics of competence and affiliation as placeholders for the dynamics of student mediation and co-regulation more fully explicated and hypothesized in Table 19–2. Student differentiation between and within competence and affiliation domains increases with development (e.g., Harter, 1990). Even young students, however, are apt to consider both competence (although likely confounded with conduct) and affiliation (more likely with the teacher than a peer) in their pursuit of the expectations of the analytical curriculum. Indeed, we hypothesize that this interface is a source of much conflict for students—a conflict that increases with development—because the result is multiple goals that are difficult to identify and coordinate.

Potential Relationships Among Goals. Classroom goals may stem from multiple presses simultaneously. For example, a student attends to instruction to do well on a test (what others term "performance-oriented" [e.g., C. Ames, 1992]). He complies with instructional, management, and assessment expectations: pays attention, attempts to do the work, and ultimately performs as best he can on the examination. In this example, the student apparently has successfully mediated the press of the analytical curriculum, yet we have not considered the possible goals he may pursue that are embedded in the informal curriculum. For example, perhaps student performance on the examination is tied to a "no pass—no play" rule for school sports and, for this student, not letting down his coach and teammates is the ultimate goal and "reason" for curriculum engagement.

In this example, abiding by the expectations of the analytical curriculum was compatible with the student's interpersonal goal of commitment to others and intrapersonal goal of pursuing sports. As shown in Figure 19–1, goals can be considered by the nature of their interrelationship (Argyle, Furnham, & Graham, 1981). Compatible relationships among goals include: (a) compensatory, wherein achieving A offsets B (e.g., to a considerable degree, more effort can compensate for less talent); (b) complementary, wherein A completes B (e.g., model behavior to complement model achievement); and (c) instrumental, wherein A facilitates B (e.g., high performance on this examination exempts the student from taking the course, allowing him opportunity to take an elective). In the no pass—no play example, course performance was instrumental to other goals.

Goals can be independent of one another. They also can be incompatible. Incompatible goals are those that (a) interfere with one another (e.g., if I study for the examination tonight I cannot go to the party) and (b) negate one another, that is, pursuit of A invalidates B (e.g., cheating on an examination invalidates all preparation for it). Identification of goals and the nature of their interrelationship affords strategic planning and proactive coordination. Thus, goal coordination results in more empowering and less emotional experiences for students. Indeed, this reasoning underlies our call for explicit attention to goal identification and coordination in the informal curriculum.

*Goal Coordination Tasks in Everyday Classroom Events.* It also is useful to consider goal coordination as a function of differing contexts likely associated with students across the school years. For example, particular developmental tasks (Havinghurst, 1972) may differ for students as they proceed through school. Younger students may be more concerned with gaining teacher approval and being a good student (as we noted), whereas preadolescent students may focus on peer approval rather than, and perhaps at the expense of, teacher approval and good student status. In contrast to both, many adolescent students may be more engaged in negotiating individual relationships and the world of work rather than, and perhaps at the expense of, attainments of the analytical curriculum and teacher or generic peer endorsement.

In general, then, students are likely juggling different, developmentally appropriate goals across schooling, often as they wrestle with the same expectations and enactments of the analytical curriculum. We provide one illustration. Consider the seemingly universal teacher response to an incorrect student answer in recitation: "No, that's not it. Mike (Maria), can you help Jeff (Jill) with the correct answer?"

We would expect that student negotiation of this "opportunity" differs such that most younger elementary students, eager to please the teacher and be "smart" too, and who typically are willing to compete with friends (Berndt & Perry, 1990), likely experience goal compatibility and readily respond. In contrast, many preadolescent students may well perceive basic goal incompatibility. For example, if they respond correctly to the teacher, they fulfill the expectations of the analytical curriculum in general and the teacher in particular (they are attending, performing, compliant), but they may do so at the expense of interpersonal goals that evolve through relations with peers. To provide the correct answer may seem in one's own eyes and in the eyes of peers to be engaging in competitive one-upmanship, playing to authority, or flaunting one's ability. Thus, preadolescent students may feign lack of knowledge to maintain a friendship (Berndt & Perry, 1990) or to save face with peers. They may also do so altruistically, to soften a peer's embarrassment of not knowing by not making them salient, demonstrating that others don't understand it either. In either case, they do not answer or do not answer correctly. The teacher likely moves on to the next student.

Adolescents may consider yet a third scenario. Given their more advanced capacity for abstract and metacognitive reasoning and their greater accumulation of experience in the social/instructional world of the classroom, these students may well bring the attributional rules of naive psychology (e.g., Weiner, 1986) to the goal coordination task. In this framework, a decision to "help" a peer understand material involves attributional judgments of responsibility. If the peer does not understand through no fault of his own (because of illness, late working hours, or lack of ability) then help—giving the correct answer—is due. However, if the cause is internal and stable as well, such as low ability, the student may consider whether help is truly help (i.e., if it can be reciprocated) or if it is potentially detrimental and status building (i.e., conveys pity, demands gratitude).

In contrast, if the adolescent student perceives that the peer does not know because he went to a party instead of studying, then attributional judgments regarding the appropriateness of help differ considerably. In this case the student may withhold help because the peer is judged responsible for not knowing and does not deserve help; therefore, helping would be actually detrimental and lack of help is justified because the student must learn to take responsibility for his own learning.

Withholding help invites possible conflict with the teacher, however. Thus, the student may decide to "punish" a negligent peer by providing the correct answer and thereby reinforcing teacher judgment that students ought to understand this material—at the possible expense of smooth future relations with this particular peer. Resentment is not considered an appropriate response to help; however, it is an appropriate response to manipulation and control—in this example by both teacher and "helping" peer. Hence, by helping, the student also risks the negative collective judgment of classmates who may not understand the particulars of this event, but witnessed and vicariously experienced student alliance with authority rather than with peers.

Student goal coordination, then, is no small matter. Imagine the changing complexities if the previous example had involved cross-gender dynamics as well! Students confront such interpersonal dilemmas daily *because* they attempt to engage in the goals of the analytical curriculum. In addition to the give-and-take of whole-class recitation, we expect the identification of multiple goals, their relationships, and their coordination are essential features of small-group learning. Giving help is often a complicated goal coordination task for students that likely changes across the school years to become more complicated, not less, with experience.

These examples illustrate the lived experience of classrooms. Students learn about interpersonal relationships and, through these, about the self as a member of a group and as an individual who relates to subject matter and to others, and thus, as one who must learn to coordinate multiple goals. One limitation of an analytical curriculum that focuses solely on subject matter acquisition is the lack of attention to fundamental relationships and the social learning that undergirds classroom processes. Student core beliefs about things that matter—personal implications of knowing or not, of helping or not—and their complex understandings and emotions in relationships with others are not part of the analytical curriculum. (Others have also voiced concern about the narrow focus of subject matter as the stuff of schooling; see, e.g., Jackson, Boostrom, & Hansen, 1993, on the moral influence of schools.) As long as classrooms are not tutorial contexts, learning is not only social in theory (e.g., Bruner, 1990; Vygotsky, 1962, 1978; Wertsch, 1985), it is social in reality (e.g., Corno & Rohrkemper, 1985). The setting and coordination of multiple goals are important considerations for adaptively negotiating this context.

*Student Goal Coordination and Intrapersonal Dynamics.* The promotion of student goal coordination is intricately related to co-regulation and intrapersonal processes. We have called for the deliberate promotion of—instruction in—each of these features of the informal curriculum. Before we turn to a possible model of co-regulation processes that may facilitate instruction, however, we note that we have not discussed the socialization of student goals.

It seems reasonable to predict that, as educators, we wish to do more than help students acquire strategies to coordinate multiple goals. We also wish to influence the goals students seek. Indeed, a strong case could be made that strategic knowledge, in the absence of appropriate goals, can be destructive (for example, multiple simultaneous strategies are an effective goal coordination tool for a drug dealer) (see also May, 1972). Nonetheless, some research has suggested that the social/moral domain, including norms of commission and omission, receives the least emphasis in classrooms, even though it plays a prominent role in student conceptions of self and others in relation to classroom expectations (Blumenfeld et al., 1983).

There is a research literature relevant to the question of socialization/internalization of goals and values that we briefly noted in our previous discussion of the general futility of behavior modification programs that attempt to inculcate students by consequating their behavior (or lack thereof). Research on internalization of social norms, however, likely informs a research agenda on goal coordination that asks not only "how" but "why" and "what for." We briefly review three points derived from the work of Kelman (1958, 1961) which are consistent with work by Lepper (1981, 1983a, 1983b; Lepper & Greene, 1978) and Hoffman (1983); and are discussed in McCaslin & T. Good (1992). Kelman distinguished among three goals of interpersonal influence: (a) compliance, which occurs when an attitude and a behavior are expressed only when the individual expects to get a reward or avoid punishment (i.e., the behavior, or goal, is instrumental to the consequence); (b) identification, in which the atti-

tude and congruent behavior occur as long as the person whom the individual wishes to emulate is salient; and (c) internalization, in which the attitude and behavior endure across a variety of settings in the absence of external constraints. Internalization goals involve a shift from initially external forms of control to internalized social control. In the language of social constructivism, in internalization the personal value or goal is a function of the emergent interaction of the individual with her or his social/instructional environment.

It seems reasonable to predict that, for some student goals, educators may settle for simple compliance with (vs. internalization of) cultural norms. For example, teachers may not care if students internalize beliefs about procedures for lining up, turn-taking, or hand-raising for recognition; they just want students to comply with classroom rules that promote a smooth and predictable environment. Compliance is promoted with judicious use of consequences (e.g., informative rewards that are sufficient to obtain compliance [e.g., Deci and colleagues, 1975; 1985; 1991]). As we have discussed, however, this strategy tends to be generally ineffective for the types of student goals that seem to matter to educators and the culture at large, i.e., meaningful engagement of the analytical curriculum.

We offer two hypotheses for this outcome. First, perhaps the unilateral preconception of student motivation as "unwilling" or "resistant" to learning is wrong; thus, the believed motivational status we wish to influence is incorrect. Rather than instilling student motivation for learning, then, perhaps our task is to help students maintain their motivation. Research by Lepper and colleagues (Lepper, 1981, 1983a, 1983b; Lepper & Greene, 1978) predicts that the provision of external rewards for the maintenance of intrinsic motivation is more likely to undermine than enhance existing motivation *and* learning, which can only compound the perceived problem. A second hypothesis targets errors in remediation rather than diagnosis. Hypothesis two assumes that the presumed need to instill motivation is correct but questions the efficacy of the imposed consequences intended to instill and promote student motivation. Research indicates that rewards are most effective when subtle and informative. Further, rewards that are salient and obvious attempts to control (e.g., E. Deci, 1975; E. L. Deci & Ryan, 1985), distract the learner from an internal focus on the self, which is required for internalization. Rewards-to-control can breed resentment rather then gratitude or identification with authority. Internalization of goals and values requires internal dialogue (Meichenbaum, 1977), not external reasons for behavior (e.g., Hoffman, 1983; Lepper, 1983a).

We assert that a principal feature of co-regulation in the informal curriculum is the promotion of student internalization of the goals we wish them to seek. Informative research on these socialization/internalization processes is an essential part of any research program on student goal coordination and intrapersonal dynamics. We conceptualize the adoption (or acceptance) of a goal as a fundamental component of co-regulation and intrapersonal dynamics.

## Co-Regulation: Structural Support, Affording Opportunity, and Intrapersonal Dynamics

In recent years, much has been written about and much energy has been expended delineating theoretical features of intrapersonal knowledge, their function, interrelation, origin, and mechanisms for change. The interested reader can find ample literature on, for example, attribution theory (e.g., Weiner, 1986, 1991), cognitive and metacognitive strategies (e.g., Bereiter & A. Scardamalia, 1987; Brown, 1974, 1978; Deshler & Schumaker, 1993; Paris, Wasik, & Turner, 1991; Perkins & Salomon, 1989), efficacy and goal setting (e.g., Bandura, 1986; D. H. Schunk, 1991; B. J. Zimmerman, Bandura, & Martinez-Pons, 1992), emotion and interest (e.g., Izard, 1977; Renninger, Hidi, & Krapp, 1992; Segal-Andrews, 1991, 1994; Weiner, 1986), expectancy value (e.g., Eccles, 1983), inner speech dynamics (e.g., D'Amico, 1986; McCaslin, 1990; McCaslin Rohrkemper, 1989; Segal-Andrews, 1991), instruction in cognitive and metacognitive strategies (e.g., Palincsar, 1986; Palincsar & Brown, 1984; Pressley & El-Dinary, 1993), self-regulated learning (e.g., Pintrich & Schrauben, 1992; B. Zimmerman & D. Schunk, 1989), and volition (e.g., Corno, 1989, 1992; Corno & Kanfer, 1993; Kuhl, 1985, 1987a, 1987b; Pervin, 1991).

Our purpose is not to reproduce these literatures but to offer instead an integrative model that may prove a useful heuristic for research on and instruction in intrapersonal dynamics within the social context of the classroom. The overarching construct we propose for this model is *co-regulated learning*. We propose co-regulated learning because this construct can take into consideration much of the advances in research on the various component processes referenced above as it integrates the social/instructional environment with the learner in mutual pursuit of a standard of excellence, within a setting of accountability. Co-regulated learning conveys a sense of we-ness. Learning is not merely an individual struggle, nor is motivation.

***Structural Support.*** Co-regulated learning socially situates the learner. Co-regulated learning integrates the changing learner with changes in features of the social/instructional environment that provide appropriate structures that support and require motivated student learning (e.g., tasks, opportunity for autonomy, assessment procedures). When the student has internalized the social structural supports, she is capable of relatively self-regulated learning in that particular domain. Thus, although the ultimate goal may be relatively self-regulation, co-regulation is the process by which the social/instructional environment supports or *scaffolds* (Palincsar & Brown, 1984) the individual via her *relationships* within the classroom, relationships with teacher and peers, objects and setting, and, ultimately, the self. Internalization of these supportive relationships empowers the individual to seek new challenges within co-regulated support.

This conception of co-regulation is the opposite of that hypothesized by *self*-regulated learning theorists, who posit a learner whose task is to *compensate for inadequacies* of the social/instructional environment. Where the foci of the co-regulated learning construct are the relationship, social structural supports, opportunity, and emergent interaction, the focus of the self-regulated learning construct is the individual, who is expected to make tasks and teaching more meaningful. As stated by John W. Gardner, former Secretary of Health, Education, and Welfare, and quoted by B. Zimmerman and D. Schunk (1989, dedication page), "The ultimate goal of the educational system is to *shift to the individual* the *burden* of pursuing his own education" [emphasis added].

Thus, co-regulated learning replaces an exclusive focus on

students who are more or less willing (in protest or in self-protection) and able (because of degree of prior knowledge or cognitive or metacognitive strategies) to learn the analytical curriculum. It also replaces an exclusive focus on societal expectations and prejudicial opportunities that promote a conception of student as beneficiary or victim that distracts those who would seek change from the emergent interaction of student characteristics with the educational context. Co-regulation connotes shared responsibility.

***Affording Opportunities.*** Opportunities are fundamental to co-regulated learning. The role of opportunities in the integration of affective and cognitive processes and their enhancement is a basic tenet of present-day extensions of Vygotskian theory, termed "activity theory" (Wertsch, 1985; Zinchenko, 1985). Indeed, Wertsch (1985) posits "tool-mediated, goal-directed action," the individual engaged with objects, as the basic unit of psychological analysis. The integration of intrapersonal affective and cognitive processes, defined by reported self-involved and task-involved inner speech, and how it is differently afforded by varied classroom tasks (defined by their subjective difficulty and familiarity), has been the focus of a research program with elementary schoolchildren (Bershon, 1987; Fields, 1990; McCaslin & Murdock, 1991; McCaslin Rohrkemper, 1989; Rohrkemper, 1986a; Rohrkemper & Bershon, 1984; Rohrkemper et al., 1983; Segal-Andrews, 1991, 1994).

Tasks that appear to promote the most efficacious integration of affective and cognitive processes (i.e., require and challenge both self-involved and task-involved inner speech) are those that are subjectively of moderate difficulty. Tasks that are too easy do not require effortful cognition and therefore do not promote the refinement of cognitive strategies. Tasks perceived as too difficult and therefore beyond personal expectations do not engage the learner because she does not possess (or cannot use) strategies to make these tasks accessible and thereby hold the self accountable. One implication of this research is the design of classroom tasks, opportunities, and assessment procedures that afford the integration of the "affective with the intellectual" (Vygotsky, 1978), variously defined as "interest and learning" (Renninger et al., 1992), "motivated learning" (Corno & Rohrkemper, 1985), and "will with skill" (Paris, 1988), to further the refinement of one's "tool kit."

Previously we described features of the analytical curriculum that differed in the kinds of demands placed on students to invest in classroom learning. We detailed, for example, how tasks could differ in the motivational and volitional burdens required of learners to engage in them. We also examined assessment procedures, focusing in particular on opportunities for student self-evaluation within the context of accountability systems, instructional management, and tasks. To review briefly, the most educative and empowering intrapersonal dynamics appeared to be afforded by individually referenced assessment, time to reflect on one's learning, and tasks that were constructed to allow assessment of learning in part and learning in progress. We noted that self-evaluation under these conditions was characterized by a concern with self-referent achievement of the task—self-referent progress toward the desired standard of excellence—without the distraction/derailment of invidious social comparisons.

In these conditions, concern with the task—the standard of

excellence—is less apt to be sacrificed to an exclusive (and detrimental) concern with student self; thus, they afford an enabling integration of the affective with the intellectual. Protective self-concern often is necessitated by other forms of assessment, tasks, and instructional management. Many students are undone by these. Self-concern replaces concern for the task. Opportunities for enabling self-evaluation integrate the learner and what is to be learned; students are more than their achievement but they are not dissociated from it. We argue that opportunities for enabling self-evaluation afford not only student learning of the subject matter and knowledge about oneself as a learner, but also keep the student focused on *self in relation to* subject matter. Thus, self-evaluation is also apt to inform the desire and the goals for subject matter engagement, key motivational features of co-regulated learning.

The maintenance of self in relation to subject matter and self in relation to others need not be adversarial (competitive). Indeed, one benefit of the co-regulated learning construct for intrapersonal dynamics in the social world of classroom learning would be an increased facility in students' legitimate and reciprocal use of social resources for the promotion of academic and social goals.

*Intrapersonal Dynamics.* Table 19–2 delineates a proposed sequence of intrapersonal involved in co-regulated learning that begins and ends with attributional judgments. We view attributional self-knowledge as the stuff of autobiography; present experiences are understood within the context of reconstructed prior experiences, in particular and in aggregation.

The dynamics of intrapersonal processes are sequentially arrayed in Table 19–2 because we suspect they ideally are, although circumstances may allow or require one to "enter" at various points in the process. For example, if a student is not allowed to choose a task or set a goal, then her motives and goal-setting strategies are a moot point. However, she certainly can determine the level of goal attainment by deciding, for example, to do "well enough" rather than to optimize personal performance. We suggest that this is not an uncommon motivational strategy in response to classroom tasks.

Motivation. Attribution theory (Weiner, 1986) is one approach to understanding motivation. It focuses on the "look back," the "why" behind my own or another's performance. Another approach that informs motivation is efficacy theory (Bandura, 1977). Its primary focus is on the "look forward," the "what next" that influences how we understand ourselves in relation to a future task. Motivation, as we mean it here, incorporates both aspects. One's present is understood in relation to prior self-knowledge (including desires and interests) and future expectation; motivation informs decisions for action (see Table 19–2). Intrapersonal motivation, in this perspective, is enhanced by individual self-evaluation of where one is in relation to where one wants to be—a sort of taking stock of oneself and one's goals—and, if not one's own goals, then those inescapably imposed by another (see Table 19–2). Evaluation opportunities, by self and other, inform motivation, a point to which we return.

Enactment. If the Motivation column in Table 19–2 is conceptualized as the individual's "reality orientation" (e.g., reason-

able goals set for the individual's present capabilities and situation), then the Enactment column can be considered the arena of "reality testing." As indicated in Table 19–2, we think it is useful to disentangle strategies (overt and covert) for control of the social/instructional environment and strategies for control over the self. Extending work by McCaslin and colleagues (Bershon, 1987; Fields, 1990; McCaslin & Murdock, 1991; McCaslin Rohrkemper, 1989; Rohrkemper & Bershon, 1984; Rohrkemper & Corno, 1988; Segal-Andrews, 1991, 1994), we delineate attempts to influence fellow participants in the social/instructional world from attempts to control the objects of that world (e.g., task and setting features). Both are distinguished from (and related to) attempts to direct the self (through self-involved and task-involved inner speech).

Thus, in our view, the various literatures on cognitive and metacognitive strategies, volitional control strategies, dynamics of inner speech in the integration of the affective and intellectual, and the work on interpersonal relationships like help seeking, power, and so forth, can inform and facilitate the enactment phase. We hypothesize that *overt* strategies such as (a) asking a peer for advice on an essay (participant other modification), (b) changing seats to avoid an intrusion (setting modification), (c) starting from the back of the problem if found difficult or introducing time constraints if too easy (task modification [after Rohrkemper & Corno, 1988]), and (d) getting a drink of water to break a cycle of frustration (self-modification) are useful beginnings for intervention research aimed at increasing students' facility to realize (their own or another's) goals. Indeed, transfer of training in *covert* strategies has proved difficult even when learners are developmentally able (e.g., Pintrich & Schrauben, 1992).

Recall, however, that apparent enactment is not isomorphic with prescribed goals. Enactment strategies do not ensure the socialization/internalization of a given goal, they simply indicate strategic behavior. For instance, one way to avoid a self-evaluation of failure is to remain volitional, thereby avoiding task closure and subsequent evaluation of lack of progress toward the goal (McCaslin, in press). Students may also covertly resist a cognitive strategy that would, if implemented, promote goal attainment (especially if the goal is set by others). For example, decreased time needed to learn is often the "hook" of cognitive strategy training programs aimed at getting students to think "smarter," that is, more efficiently and effectively. But students know they can try "less" for longer and still get there. Much to the chagrin of cognitive strategy reformers, this is often the path students take. Rather than focus our attention on why students only seem capable of or prefer rehearsal strategies, however, we may want to enlarge our focus to include student motivation and goal coordination. If students cannot select achievement goals or have not prioritized the present one, rehearsal may well be an optimal strategy: impressions are managed and other tasks (equally or less valued) are at least delayed.

As we have already discussed, we believe learners are best served by the opportunity to set *and* pursue goals—to be motivational *and* volitional. An optimal agenda for intrapersonal learning in the informal curriculum, then, includes instruction in and opportunities for both motivation (e.g., strategies for reasoned proximal and distal goal setting, determining goal relationships and their coordination) and volitional enactment (e.g., postdecisional overt and covert strategies to protect the intention to pursue and coordinate goals, whatever their source).

Feedback loops are also possible, indeed desirable. For example, continuous engagement in volitional enactment strategies to enhance goal attainment may be disrupted as the learner reconsiders whether or not the goal is worth the investment, what other potential goals are not being pursued in its place, and whether or not goal attainment is even under learner control. We argue that volitional striving is not isomorphic with adaptive behavior. Indeed a case could be made that much of midlife crisis is all about the cessation of the unexamined volitional pursuit of previous goals (set or accepted) that are finally reconsidered and accepted, modified, or abandoned. The effects of unexamined volition can be especially detrimental if the pursuit was a single-minded one. This process of periodic critical goal review, wherein striving is examined in relation to its goal and goals are examined in terms of their continued value and interrelationships (described previously in the context of goal coordination), is represented as part of the motivation/goal-setting processes in Table 19–2.

Briefly, in our view, although an essential component of conscious and, in some conditions, unconscious (Corno & Kanfer, 1993) goal pursuit and enactment, volition (a) cannot be mistaken for motivation and (b) can be counterproductive. We expect that much future research will explore the relation among motivational and volitional processes; clearly, life is not just "pluck and will" (James, 1890, 1983), but neither is it the "pluck and luck" frequently espoused by disenfranchised adolescents.

Evaluation. A third critical feature of co-regulated learning is the opportunity for (and instruction in) self-evaluation. Self-evaluation processes usually start after completing a given task (if time allows), although they may also occur along the way, especially if the task affords it (i.e., it is comprised of subgoals). The process can be thought of as a TOTE unit (test–operate–test–exit) in the information-processing tradition (G. A. Miller, Galanter, & Pribram, 1960), wherein the individual compares present performance with a standard. If the standard has been met, the cycle is complete. The learner can "exit," or as Heckhausen (1991) notes, "linger a while with the pleasant feeling" (p. 187).

If the performance standard is not met, however, then (at least) three things can happen, although only one is commonly acceptable in the classroom. The learner can (a) keep trying (yes), (b) modify the task, or (c) abandon the task. Finally (optimally), in self-evaluation, the learner pulls up and, taking the long view, determines what can be learned from the present task experience that is relevant for future goal setting. The TOTE unit is admittedly not an ideal model of self-evaluation by individuals who feel, as well as think, about what they do (Vygotsky, 1978). Self-evaluation is as much about *affect* as it is about progress toward standards. In our analysis it also involves *realism*.

Co-regulated learning includes as well evaluation of student performance by other participants in the classroom, especially the teacher. Evaluation is the arena of "reality feedback." Table 19–2 illustrates the self- and teacher evaluation of student artifacts, which we hypothesize are mutually supportive. The *con-*gruence of student and teacher assessment is an essential feature of self-evaluation that is learned through affording opportunities and structural support by the teacher. Student self-evaluations need to be realistic in order to be useful in the service of learning and mental health. Self- and teacher evaluation set in motion affective and attributional processes that inform co-regulation of learning and instruction decisions, both in the present and in implication for the future. Derived attributional knowledge informs future motivation, strategic progress informs future enactment, and so on.

*Summary.* In brief, co-regulated learning is a useful construct for understanding student participation in the informal and analytical curricula. The dynamics of co-regulated learning encompass student intrapersonal processes of motivation, enactment, and evaluation within the context of a relationship with other participants, structural supports, and affording opportunities in the social/instructional environment. Motivation includes (a) predecisional wishes (desires, needs), attributions, beliefs, and expectations about the situated self, and (b) decisions about goal setting, goal relationships, and their coordination. Enactment involves postdecisional overt and covert strategies to advance a goal that coordinates the demands of the goal with (a) the emotions and capabilities of the self (intrapersonally directed strategies) and (b) the participant and setting resources of the social/instructional environment (SIE-directed strategies). Artifacts, in progress or in completion, that result from strategic enactment are subject to evaluation. Evaluation involves self- and other (especially teacher) evaluation and, fundamentally, their congruence. Self-evaluation is the process by which the learner takes stock of where he or she is in relation to where he or she is going and determines whether to continue, modify, or cease enactment or goal-setting strategies. The relationship between self- and teacher-evaluation informs subsequent co-regulation of learning and instruction. Ultimately, self-evaluation of degree of goal attainment or nonattainment becomes part of the autobiographical record that informs motivation.

Finally, our intent is not to overdirect the focus on potential inner workings of the individual or to disassociate intrapersonal processes of the learner from the affordances of the social/instructional environment. Rather, our goal is to stress the fundamental and reciprocal relationship between the social/instructional environment and individual cognitive and affective processes in the moment to moment of classroom life and in aggregation. We have labeled this reciprocal relationship the arena of co-regulation. The arena of co-regulation includes higher psychological processes that teachers and students share in emergent interaction; "emergent interaction" indicates the evolving dynamics within and between participants.

Co-regulation involves supportive relationships and affording opportunities. The goals of co-regulation we have discussed reflect our priority for the informal curriculum; the enhancement of adaptive learning. Adaptive learning includes student internalization of the goals we wish them to seek, the motivation to commit, challenge or reform them, and the competence to enact and evaluate those commitments (McCaslin & Murdock, 1991). Thus, we have discussed how teachers might co-regulate the (a) socialization of student motivational goals (e.g., through task selection, periodic critical goal review); (b) internalization of enactment strategies (e.g., through overt and covert strategy instruction); and (c) congruence of self- and other evaluation (e.g., through individually-referenced assessments).

Student mediational processes are interdependent, as are scaffolding opportunities and emergent interaction dynamics. For example, student motivation, enactment, and evaluation processes are each influenced by opportunity to engage a range of task difficulty. Students cannot learn to set appropriate goals, refine enactment strategies, or recognize instances of not knowing, incomplete understanding, and mastery, without confronting a full array of task challenge, with primary exposure to tasks of moderate difficulty. Thus, task selection, represented as a feature of socialization of student motivation, also affects strategic internalization and realistic self-evaluation.

Further, we suggest that a heuristic model of co-regulated psychological processes may have considerable potential for teachers and students as they engage the informal and analytical curricula. Finally, in our view, only an integrative approach that attends to the emergent interaction of the developing individual within the social/instructional environment represented in the abstract and analytical curricula will facilitate the realization of the powerful role that we believe the informal curriculum plays in the educational process.

## CONCLUSION

This chapter attempts to define the informal curriculum, the ubiquitous but uncoordinated stream of momentary experiences in classrooms, which students currently experience and aggregate with varying degrees of awareness. The framework we posit asserts a linkage between societal expectations, classroom enactment, and intrapersonal dynamics through the interrelationships among the abstract, analytical, and informal curricula, respectively. We argue that deliberate attention to the informal curriculum is critical if schools are to enhance the lives of students by promoting their competence and adaptive learning.

Unfortunately, our analysis suggests that it is more likely that the analytical and informal curricula impede rather than foster the development of adaptive learning. Further, our analysis indicates that opportunities for meaningful educative experiences are differentially available to students so that the divergent societal expectations for them are (intentionally or not) often realized. We maintain that, at a minimum, the types of learning experiences afforded advantaged learners must be available for all learners.

During the past 50 years, individual motivation has been heralded as the prescription for school and life success. The revolving door of remediation strategies to enhance student motivation, however, has been largely ineffective. Students apparently will not perform for the sheer attainment of excellence, approval of authority or the consequences they control, or self-reliance. Current instructional formats incorporate peer relationships to enhance student motivation for performance. Our review has convinced us that small-group instructional formats are not a panacea for improving student motivation, interpersonal relationships, or meaningful learning. Indeed, if careful attention is not given to the curriculum task, the structure of cooperation, and the composition and stability of group membership, small-group instructional formats may actually undermine them.

We believe that the analytical curriculum fails to the extent that it fulfills prejudicial societal expectations for students. We argue that this occurs, in part, because of a lack of deliberate attention to the dynamics of the informal curriculum. We maintain that if we are to break from traditional practices that fulfill low and needlessly differential expectations, it is time for educators to formalize the informal curriculum. This is an incredibly complex undertaking and we have consistently argued that much research and development needs to focus on this task.

As a starting point, we suggest that the informal curriculum involves official recognition that students are more than their achievement and achievement motivation. Further, we assert that psychological conceptions that locate learning and motivation solely within individual students are incomplete and thus inappropriate constructs for understanding the achievement of the analytical curriculum (defined as the enactment of the abstract curriculum) within the context of classrooms. Instead, we posit that conceptions of learning and motivation that attend to the *relationships* students engage in, both with objects, defined in part by setting and task features, and with other participants in the social/instructional environment of classrooms, are more useful for advancing student achievement of the analytical curriculum and promotion of student adaptive learning in the informal curriculum.

We have outlined a research agenda for an informal curriculum based on relationship as the basic unit of classrooms, goal coordination as a basic task for students, and supportive co-regulation as the basic task for teachers. First, we have asserted that students must learn to set and coordinate multiple goals, among which we include individually referenced striving for excellence. Second, we suggest co-regulated learning as a viable construct for research on the mutual relations between intrapersonal processes and (a) interpersonal relationships and (b) task and setting features. We hypothesize that co-regulation rather than self-regulation will aid the establishment of classroom norms whereby students learn how to use, and do use, their own resources and those of other participants in (e.g., peers) and features of (e.g., opportunities for challenge) the setting adaptively.

These are just two considerations in the articulation of an informal curriculum to enhance student adaptive learning and attainment of the analytical curriculum. For example, beyond the consideration of this chapter are integrative dimensions that require changing structures (e.g., longer class periods for certain types of academic tasks, such as project-based science), the complex use of existing resources (e.g., math and science teachers working together), or methods of communication to parents (e.g., report card mediation to prevent child abuse). As we expand definitions of curriculum tasks (e.g., opportunities for meaningful integration for all students) and of motivation to engage them, we will also need to expand structural and temporal dimensions of school settings (e.g., integration of school and community services, extension of building hours and use to include parent goal pursuit).

We have called for more research throughout our analysis. Extensive conceptualization and research is required to understand the informal curriculum more adequately. It is our hope that this chapter has successfully argued the importance of the informal curriculum and its potential power for fostering the development of adaptive learning so that other researchers and funding agencies will commit to systematic, sustained inquiry in this area.

Finally, we close with the observation that as we approach the 21st century, it is time for educators to actively address issues of equity and opportunity in the analytical and informal curricula. A pressing challenge for education continues to be the creation of meaningful educational opportunities for an increasingly diverse culture. We believe that deliberate attention to the informal curriculum is one part of that challenge.

# References

Abramson, L., Seligman, M., & Teasdale, J. (1978). Learned helplessness in humans: Critique and reformulation. *Journal of Abnormal Psychology, 87,* 49–74.

Allington, R. (1983). The reading instruction provided readers of differing reading ability. *Elementary School Journal, 83,* 548–559.

Allington, R. (1991). Children who find learning to read difficult: School responses to diversity. In E. Hiebert (Ed.), *Literacy for a diverse society: Perspectives, practices, and policies* (pp. 237–252). New York: Teachers College Press.

American Association of University Women. (1992). *AAUW Report: How schools shortchange girls: A study of major findings on girls in education.* Washington, DC: American Association of University Women Educational Foundation.

American Association of University Women. (1993). *Hostile hallways: The AAUW survey of sexual harassment in American schools.* Washington, DC: American Association of University Women Educational Foundation.

Ames, C. (1984). Competitive, cooperative, and individualistic goal structures: A cognitive-motivational analysis. In R. Ames, & C. Ames (Eds.), *Research on motivation in education* (Vol. 1, pp. 177–208). Orlando, FL: Academic Press.

Ames, C. (1990). Motivation: What teachers need to know. *Teachers College Record, 91,* 409–421.

Ames, C. (1992). Classrooms: Goals, structures, and student motivation. *Journal of Educational Psychology, 84,* 261–271.

Ames, R. (1983). Help-seeking and achievement orientation: Perspectives from attribution theory. In B. DePaulo, A. Nadler, & J. Fisher (Eds.), *New directions in helping: Vol. 2. Help-seeking* (pp. 165–186). New York: Academic Press.

Argyle, M., Furnham, A., & Graham, J. A. (1981). *Social situations.* New York: Cambridge University Press.

Arias, M. B. (Ed.) (1986). *The education of Hispanic Americans: A challenge for the future* [Special issue]. *American Journal of Education, 95*(1).

Aronson, E., Blaney, N., Stephan, C., Sikes, J., & Snapp, M. (1978). *The Jigsaw classroom.* Beverly Hills, CA: Sage.

Atkinson, J. W. (1964). *An introduction to motivation.* Princeton, NJ: Van Nostrand.

Atkinson, J. W. (1981). Studying personality in the context of an advanced motivational psychology. *American Psychologist, 36,* 117–128.

Atkinson, J. W. (1987). Michigan studies of fear of failure. In F. Halisch & J. Kuhl (Eds.), *Motivation, intention, and volition* (pp. 47–60). Berlin: Springer.

Atkinson, J. W., & Raynor, J. O. (1974). *Motivation and achievement.* New York: Wiley.

Au, K. (1980). Participant structures in a reading lesson with Hawaiian children. *Anthropology and Education Quarterly, 11,* 91–115.

Ausubel, D. (1968). *Educational psychology: A cognitive view.* New York: Holt, Rinehart & Winston.

Ausubel, D., Novak, J., & Hanesian, H. (1978). *Educational psychology: A cognitive view.* New York: Holt, Rinehart & Winston.

Ball, D. L. (1993). With an eye on the mathematical horizon: Dilemmas of teaching elementary school mathematics. *Elementary School Journal, 93,* 373–397.

Bandura, A. (1977). *Social learning theory.* Englewood Cliffs, NJ: Prentice Hall.

Bandura, A. (1986). *Social foundations of thought and action: A social cognitive theory.* Englewood Cliffs, NJ: Prentice Hall.

Bandura, A. (1990). Conclusion: Reflections on nonability determinants of competence. In R. J. Sternberg & J. Kolligian, Jr. (Eds.), *Competence considered* (pp. 315–408). New Haven, CT: Yale University Press.

Bank, B. J., Biddle, B. J., & Good, T. (1980). Sex roles, classroom instruction, and reading achievement. *Journal of Educational Psychology, 72,* 119–132.

Barker, R. (1968). *Ecological psychology.* Stanford, CA: Stanford University Press.

Barker, R. G., Denbo, T., & Lewin, K. (1943). Frustration and regression. In R. G. Barker, J. S. Kounin, & H. F. Wright (Eds.), *Child behavior and development.* New York: McGraw-Hill.

Battistich, V., Solomon, D., & Delucchi, K. (1993). Interaction processes and student outcomes in cooperative learning groups. *Elementary School Journal, 94,* 19–32.

Bereiter, C., & Scardamalia, M. (1987). An attainable version of high literacy: Approaches to teaching higher-order skills in reading and writing. *Curriculum Inquiry, 17,* 9–30.

Berliner, D. C. (1992, February). *Educational reform in an era of disinformation.* Paper presented at a meeting of the American Association of Colleges for Teacher Education, San Antonio, TX.

Berger, J., Cohen, B., & Zelditch, M., Jr. (1972). Status characteristics and social interaction. *American Sociological Review, 6,* 479–508.

Berndt, T., & Perry, T. (1990). Distinctive features and effects of early adolescent friendships. In R. Montemayor, G. Adams, & T. Gullotta (Eds.), *From childhood to adolescence: A transitional period?* (pp. 269–287). Newbury Park, CA: Sage.

Bershon, B. L. (1987). *Elementary school students' reported inner speech during a cooperative problem-solving task.* Unpublished doctoral dissertation. Maryland: University of Maryland-College Park.

Bloom, B. (1976). *Human characteristics and school learning.* New York: McGraw-Hill.

Blumenfeld, P. (1992a). Classroom learning and motivation: Clarifying and expanding goal theory. *Journal of Educational Psychology, 84,* 272–281.

Blumenfeld, P. (1992b). The task and the teacher: Enhancing student thoughtfulness in science. In J. Brophy (Ed.), *Advances in research on teaching: Vol. 3. Planning and managing learning tasks and activities* (pp. 81–114). Greenwich, CT: JAI Press.

Blumenfeld, P., Hamilton, L., Bossert, S., Wessels, K., & Meece, J. (1983). Teacher talk and student thought: Socialization into the student role. In J. Levine & M. Wang (Eds.), *Teacher and student perceptions: Implications for learning* (pp. 143–192). Hillsdale, NJ: Lawrence Erlbaum Associates.

Blumenfeld, P., & Meece J. (1988). Task factors, teacher behavior, and students' involvement and use of learning strategies in science. *Elementary School Journal, 88,* 235–250.

Bossert, S. (1988–1989). Cooperative activities in the classroom. In E. Rothkopf (Ed.), *Review of research in education* (Vol. 15, pp. 225–250). Washington, DC: American Educational Research Association.

Boyer, E. (1984). *High school: A report on secondary education in America.* New York: Harper & Row.

Brattesani, K., Weinstein, R., & Marshall, H. (1984). Student perceptions of differential teacher treatment as moderators of teacher expectation effects. *Journal of Educational Psychology, 76,* 236–247.

Brophy, J., & Good, T. L. (1974). *Teacher-student relationships: Causes and consequences.* New York: Holt, Rinehart & Winston.

Brophy, J., & McCaslin, M. (1992). Teachers' reports of how they perceive and cope with problem students. *Elementary School Journal, 93,* 3–68.

Brophy, J., & Rohrkemper, M. (1981). The influence of problem ownership on teachers' perceptions of and strategies for coping with problem students. *Journal of Educational Psychology, 73,* 295–311.

Brown, A. L. (1987). Metacognition, executive control, self-regulation, and other more mysterious mechanisms. In F. E. Weinert & R. H. Kluwe (Eds.), *Metacognition, motivation, and understanding* (pp. 65–116). Hillsdale, NJ: Lawrence Erlbaum Associates.

Brown, A. L. (1974). The development of memory: Knowing, knowing about knowing, and knowing how to know. In H. W. Reese (Ed.), *Advances in child development and behavior* (Vol. 10, pp. 103–152). New York: Academic Press.

Brown, A. L. (1978). Knowing when, where, and how to remember: A problem of metacognition. In R. Glaser (Ed.), *Advances in instructional psychology* (Vol. 1, pp. 77–165). Hillsdale, NJ: Lawrence Erlbaum Associates.

Brown, A. L., & Reeve, R. A. (1987). Bandwidths of competence: The role of supportive context in learning and development. In L. S. Liben (Ed.), *Development and learning: Conflict or congruence?* (pp. 173–223). Hillsdale, NJ: Lawrence Erlbaum Associates.

Brown, J. S., Collins, A., & Duguid, P. (1989). Situated cognition and the culture of learning. *Educational Researcher, 18*(1), 32–42.

Bruner, J. (1960). *The process of education.* Cambridge, MA: Harvard University Press.

Bruner, J. (1985). Narrative and paradigmatic modes of thought. In E. Eisner (Ed.), *Learning and teaching the ways of knowing* (84th Yearbook of the National Society for the Study of Education, Pt. 2, pp. 97–115). Chicago: University of Chicago Press.

Bruner, J. (1990). *Acts of Meaning.* Cambridge, MA: Harvard University Press.

Carlson, W. (1991). Subject-matter knowledge and science teaching: A pragmatic perspective. In J. Brophy (Ed.), *Advances in research on teaching* (Vol. 2, pp. 115–144). Greenwich, CT: JAI Press.

Carroll, J. S., & Payne, J. W. (1976). The psychology of the parole decision process: A joint application of attribution theory and information processing psychology. In J. S. Carroll & J. W. Payne (Eds.), *Cognition and social behavior.* Hillsdale, NJ: Lawrence Erlbaum Associates.

Carroll, J. S., & Payne, J. W. (1977). Judgments about crime and the criminal: A model and method for investigating parole decisions. In B. D. Sales (Ed.), *Perspectives in law and psychology: Vol. 1. The criminal justice system.* New York: Plenum Press.

Carter, K., & Doyle, W. (1982). *Variations in academic tasks in high- and average-ability classes.* Paper presented at the annual meeting of the American Educational Research Association, New York.

Casanova, U. (1987). Ethnic and cultural differences. In V. Richardson-Koehler (Ed.), *Educators' handbook: A research perspective* (pp. 370–393). New York: Longman.

Case, R. (1985). *Intellectual development: Birth to adulthood.* New York: Academic Press.

Chi, M. T. H. (1987). Representing knowledge and metaknowledge: Implications for interpreting metamemory research. In F. E. Weinert & R. H. Kluwe (Eds.), *Metacognition, motivation, and understanding* (pp. 239–266). Hillsdale, NJ: Lawrence Erlbaum Associates.

Chipman, S. F., Segal, J. W., & Glaser, R. (Eds.). (1985). *Thinking and learning skills: Vol. 2. Research and open questions.* Hillsdale, NJ: Lawrence Erlbaum Associates.

Clifford, M. M. (1991). Risk-taking: Theoretical, empirical, and educational considerations. *Educational Psychologist, 26,* 263–297.

Cohen, E. (1986). *Designing group work: Strategies for the heterogenous classroom.* New York: Teachers College Press.

Cohen, E., Lotan, R., & Catanzarite, L. (1990). Treating status problems in the cooperative classroom. In S. Sharan (Ed.), *Cooperative learning: Theory and research* (pp. 203–229). New York: Praeger.

Cooper, H. (1979). Pygmalion grows up: A model for teacher expectation communication and performance influence. *Review of Educational Research, 49,* 389–410.

Cooper, H., & Good, T. (1983). *Pygmalion grows up: Studies in the expectation communication process.* New York: Longman.

Corno, L. (1989). What it means to be literate about classrooms. In D. Bloome (Ed.), *Learning to use literacy in educational settings* (pp. 29–52). New York: Ablex.

Corno, L. (1992). Encouraging students to take responsibility for learning and performance. *Elementary School Journal, 93,* 69–83.

Corno, L. (1993). The best-laid plans: Modern conceptions of volition and educational research. *Educational Researcher, 22,* 14–22.

Corno L., & Kanfer, R. (1993). The role of volition in learning and performance. In L. Darling-Hammond (Ed.), *Review of research in education* (Vol. 19, pp. 3–43). Washington, DC: American Educational Research Association.

Corno, L., & Mandinach. E. (1983). The role of cognitive engagement in classroom learning and motivation. *Educational Psychologist, 18,* 88–108.

Corno, L., & Rohrkemper, M. (1985). Self-regulated learning. In R. Ames & C. Ames (Eds.), *Research on motivation in education* (Vol. 2, pp. 53–90). Orlando, FL: Academic Press.

Corno, L., & Snow, R. E. (1986). Adapting teaching to individual differences among learners. In M. C. Wittrock (Ed.), *Third handbook of research on teaching* (pp. 605–629). New York: Macmillan.

Covington, M. V. (1985). Strategic thinking and the fear of failure. In N. J. Segal, S. Chipman, R. Glaser (Eds.), *Thinking and learning skills: Vol. 1. Relating instruction to basic research* (pp. 389–416). Hillsdale, NJ: Lawrence Erlbaum Associates.

Covington, M. V. (1992). *Making the grade: A self-worth perspective on motivation and school reform.* New York: Cambridge University Press.

Covington, M. V., & Omelich, C. L. (1979). Effort: The double-edged sword in school achievement. *Journal of Educational Psychology, 71,* 169–182.

Cronbach, L., & Snow, R. (1977). *Aptitudes and instructional methods.* New York: Irvington.

Cross, C. T. (1990). National goals: Four priorities for educational researchers. *Educational Researcher, 19,* 21–24.

Cziko, G. A. (1992). The evaluation of bilingual education. *Educational Researcher, 21,* 10–15.

Csikszentmihalyi, M. (1990). *Flow: The psychology of optimal experience.* New York: Harper & Row.

D'Amico, A. J. (1986). *Individual differences in adolescents' classroom behavior and reported problem solving inner speech.* Unpublished doctoral dissertation, Bryn Mawr College, Bryn Mawr, PA.

Davidson, N. (1985). Small-group learning and teaching in mathematics: A selective review of the literature. In R. Slavin, S. Sharan, S. Kagan, R. Lazarowitz, C. Webb, & R. Schmuck (Eds.), *Learning to cooperate, cooperating to learn* (pp. 211–230). New York: Plenum Press.

deCharms, R. (1976). *Enhancing motivation: Change in the classroom.* New York: Irvington.

Deci, E. L. (1975). *Intrinsic motivation.* New York: Plenum Press.

Deci, E. L., & Ryan, R. M. (1985). *Intrinsic motivation in self-determination in human behavior.* New York: Plenum Press.

Deci, E. L., Vallerand, R. J., Pelletier, L. G., & Ryan, R. M. (1991). Motivation and education: The self-determination perspective. *Educational Psychologist, 26,* 325–346.

Deshler, D. D., & Schumaker, J. B. (1993). Strategy mastery by at-risk students: Not a simple matter. *Elementary School Journal, 94,* 153–167.

Dewey, J. (1938). *Experience and education.* New York: Collier Books.

Dey, E., Astin, A., & Korn, W. (1991). *The American freshman: Twenty-five year trends.* Los Angeles: University of California, Graduate School of Education.

Dillon, J. (Ed.). (1990). *The practice of questioning.* New York: Rutledge.

Dillon, J. T. (1988). The remedial status of student questioning. *Journal of Curriculum Studies, 20,* 197–210.

Dodge, K. A., Asher, F. R., & Parkhurst, J. T. (1989). Social life as a goal-coordination task. In C. Ames & R. Ames (Eds.), *Research on motivation in education: Vol. 3. Goals and cognition* (pp. 107–135). New York: Academic Press.

Doyle, W. (1983). Academic work. *Review of Educational Research, 53,* 159–200.

Doyle, W. (1986). Classroom organization and management. In M. Wittrock, (Ed.), *Handbook of research on teaching* (3rd ed., pp. 392–431). New York: Macmillan.

Doyle, W. (1992). Curriculum and pedagogy. In P. Jackson (Ed.), *Handbook of research on curriculum* (pp. 486–516). New York: Macmillan.

Dunne, E., & Bennett, N. (1990). *Talking and learning in groups.* London: Macmillan.

Dweck, C. (1986). Motivational processes affecting learning. *American Psychologist, 41,* 1040–1048.

Dweck, C., Davidson, W., Nelson, S., & Enna, B. (1978). Sex differences in learned helplessness: II. The contingencies of evaluative feedback in the classroom. III. An experimental analysis. *Developmental Psychology, 14,* 268–276.

Dyson, A. H. (1987). The value of "time off task": Young children's spontaneous talk and deliberate text. *Harvard Educational Review, 57,* 396–419.

Eaton, J. F., Anderson, C. W., & Smith, E. L. (1984). Students' misconceptions interfere with science learning: Case studies of fifth-grade students. *Elementary School Journal, 84,* 365–379.

Eccles, J. (1983). Expectancies, values, and academic behaviors. In J. T. Spence (Ed.), *Achievement and achievement motives* (pp. 75–146). San Francisco: Freeman.

Eder, D. (1981). Ability grouping as a self-fulfilling prophecy: A microanalysis of teacher-student interaction. *Sociology of Education, 54,* 151–161.

Elawar, M. C., & Corno, L. (1985). A factorial experiment in teachers' written feedback on student homework: Changing teacher behavior a little rather than a lot. *Journal of Educational Psychology, 77,* 162–173.

Ericson, D. P., & Ellett, F. S., Jr. (1990). Taking student responsibility seriously. *Educational Researcher, 19,* 3–10.

Erikson, E. H. (1964). *Childhood and society.* New York: Norton.

Evertson, C., Emmer, E., Sanford, J., & Clements, B. (1983). Improving classroom management: An experiment in elementary school classrooms. *Elementary School Journal, 84, 173–188.*

Fennema, E. (1987). Sex-related differences in education: Myths, realities, and interventions. In V. Richardson-Koehler (Ed.), *Educators' handbook: A research perspective* (pp. 329–347). New York: Longman.

Fetterman, N. (1990). *The meaning of success and failure: A look at the social instructional environments of four elementary school classrooms.* Unpublished doctoral dissertation, Bryn Mawr College, Bryn Mawr, PA.

Fields, R. D. (1990). *Classroom tasks, children's control perceptions,*

*and their relation to inner speech.* Unpublished doctoral dissertation, Bryn Mawr College, Bryn Mawr, PA.

Fisher, C., & Hiebert, E. (1990). Characteristics of tasks in two approaches to literacy instruction. *Elementary School Journal, 91,* 3–17.

French, E. G. (1958a). Development of a measure of complex motivation. In J. W. Atkinson (Ed.), *Motives in fantasy, action, and society* (pp. 242–248). Princeton, NJ: Van Nostrand.

French, E. G. (1958b). Effects of the interaction of motivation and feedback on task performance. In J. W. Atkinson (Ed.), *Motives in fantasy, action, and society* (pp. 400–408). Princeton, NJ: Van Nostrand.

Frey, K. S., & Slaby, R. G. (1979, March). *Differential teaching methods used with girls and boys of moderate and high achievement levels.* Paper presented at a meeting of the American Educational Research Association, San Francisco.

Gagné, R. M. (1985). *The conditions of learning and theory of instruction.* New York: Holt, Rinehart & Winston.

Garbarino, J., Dobrow, N., Kostelny, K., & Pardo, C. (1992). *Children in danger: Coping with the consequences of community violence.* San Francisco: Jossey-Bass.

Glaser, R., & Pellegrino, J. W. (1987). Aptitudes for learning and cognitive processes. In F. E. Weinert & R. H. Kluwe (Eds.), *Metacognition, motivation, and understanding* (pp. 267–288). Hillsdale, NJ: Lawrence Erlbaum Associates.

Good, T. (1980). Classroom expectations: Teacher-pupil interactions. In J. McMillan (Ed.), *The social psychology of learning.* New York: Academic Press.

Good, T. (1981). Teacher expectations and student perceptions: A decade of research. *Educational Leadership, 38,* 415–423.

Good, T., & Brophy, J. (1994). *Looking in classrooms* (6th ed.). New York: HarperCollins.

Good, T., Grouws, D., & Mason, D. (1990). Teachers' beliefs about small-group instruction in elementary school mathematics. *Journal for Research in Mathematics Education, 21,* 2–15.

Good, T., Grouws, D., Mason, D., Slavings, R., Cramer, K. (1990). An observational study of small-group mathematics instruction in elementary schools. *American Educational Research Journal, 27,* 755–782.

Good, T., McCaslin, M., & Reys, B. J. (1992). Investigating work groups to promote problem solving in mathematics. In J. Brophy (Ed.), *Advances in research on teaching* (pp. 115–160). Greenwich, CT: JAI Press.

Good, T., Reys, B., Grouws, D., & Mulryan, C. (1989–1990). Using work groups in mathematics instruction. *Educational Leadership, 47,* 56–62.

Good, T., Slavings, R., Harel, K., & Emerson, H. (1987). Student passivity: A study of question asking in K–12 classrooms. *Sociology of Education, 60,* 181–199.

Good, T. L., Mulryan, C., & McCaslin, M. (1992). Grouping for instruction in mathematics: A call for programming research on small-group processes. In D. A. Grouws (Ed.), *Handbook of research on mathematics teaching and learning* (pp. 165–196). New York: Macmillan.

Goodenow, C. (1992). Strengthening the links between educational psychology and the study of social contexts. *Educational Psychologist, 27,* 177–196.

Goodlad, J. (1984). *A place called school.* New York: McGraw-Hill.

Griffin, G. (1993, April). *Slicing through the system: Necessary conditions for teaching for understanding.* Paper presented at the annual meeting of the American Educational Research Association, Atlanta.

Hacker, A. (1992). *Two nations: Black and white, separate, hostile, unequal.* New York: Scribners.

Hakuta, K., & Pease-Alvarez, L. (Eds.). (1992). *Educational Researcher* (Special issue), *21,* 2.

Haladyna, T., Nolan, S., & Haas, N. (1991). Raising standardized achievement test scores and the origins of test score pollution. *Educational Researcher, 20,* 2–7.

Halisch, F., & Kuhl, J. (1987). *Motivation, intention, and volition.* Berlin: Springer.

Hall, R. M. (with Sandler, B. R.). (1982). The classroom climate: A chilly one for women? *Project on the status of education of women.* Washington, DC: Association of American Colleges.

Hamilton, S. F. (1990). *Apprenticeship for adulthood: Preparing youth for the future.* New York: Free Press.

Harter, S. (1981). A new self-report scale of intrinsic versus extrinsic orientation in the classroom: Motivational and informational components. *Developmental Psychology, 17,* 300–312.

Harter, S. (1990). Causes, correlates and the functional role of a global self-worth: A life-span perspective. In R. J. Sternberg & J. Kolligian, Jr. (Eds.), *Competence considered* (pp. 67–97). New Haven, CT: Yale University Press.

Havinghurst, R. (1972). *Human development and education.* New York: Longman.

Heath, S. B. (1982). Questioning at home and at school: A comparative study. In G. Spindler (Ed.), *Doing the ethnography of schooling* (pp. 102–131). New York: Holt, Rinehart & Winston.

Heckhausen, H. (1991). *Motivation and action* (P. Leppmann, Trans.). Berlin: Springer.

Heckhausen, H., & Kuhl, J. (1985). From wishes to action: The dead-ends and shortcuts on the long way to action. In M. Frese & J. Sabini (Eds.), *Goal-directed behavior: Psychological theory and research on action* (pp. 134–160). Hillsdale, NJ: Lawrence Erlbaum Associates.

Heider, F. (1958). *The psychology of interpersonal relations.* New York: Wiley.

Hiebert, E. (1991). Introduction. In E. Hiebert (Ed.), *Literacy for a diverse society: Perspectives, practices, and policies* (pp. 1–6). New York: Teachers College Press.

Hiebert, E. H., & Fisher, C. W. (1992). The tasks of school literacy: Trends and issues. In J. Brophy (Ed.), *Advances in research on teaching* (pp. 191–223). Greenwich, CT: JAI Press.

Hirsch, E. D., Jr. (1987). *Cultural literacy: What every American needs to know.* Boston: Houghton Mifflin.

Hoffman, M. L. (1983). Affective and cognitive processes in moral internalization. In E. T. Higgins, D. Rubel, & W. Hartup (Eds.), *Social cognition and social development: A sociocultural perspective* (pp. 236–274). New York: Cambridge University Press.

Hoffman, S. (Ed.). (1991). *Educational partnerships: Home-school-community* [Special issue]. *Elementary School Journal, 91*(3).

House, E. (1991). Big policy, little policy. *Educational Researcher, 20,* 21–26.

Huber, G., & Eppler, R. (1990). Team learning in German classrooms: Process and outcomes. In S. Sharan (Ed.), *Cooperative learning: Theory and research* (pp. 151–171). New York: Praeger.

Hunt, J. McV. (1961). *Intelligence and experience.* New York: Ronald.

Hunt, J. McV. (1965). Intrinsic motivation and its role in psychological development. In D. Levine (Ed.), *Nebraska Symposium on Motivation* (Vol. 13). Lincoln: University of Nebraska Press.

Izard, C. E. (1977). *Human emotions.* New York: Plenum Press.

Jackson, P. (1968). *Life in classrooms.* New York: Holt, Rinehart, & Winston.

Jackson, P. W. (1986). *The practice of teaching.* New York: Teachers College Press.

Jackson, P. W., Boostrom, R. E., & Hansen, D. T. (1993). *The moral life of schools.* San Francisco: Jossey-Bass.

James, W. (1890). *Principles of psychology.* New York: Henry Holt.

James, W. (1983). *Talks to teachers on psychology and to students on some of life's ideals* (F. Burkhardt & F. Bowers, Eds.). Cambridge, MA: Harvard University Press.

Johnson, D., & Johnson, R. (1974). Instructional goal structure: Cooperative, competitive, or individualistic. *Review of Educational Research, 44,* 213–240.

Johnson, D., & Johnson, R. (1985). The internal dynamics of cooperative learning groups. In R. Slavin, S. Sharan, S. Kagan, R. Hertz-Lazarowitz, C. Webb, & R. Schmuck (Eds.), *Learning to cooperate, cooperating to learn* (pp. 103–124). New York: Plenum Press.

Johnson, D., Johnson, R., & Maruyame, G. (1983). Interdependence and interpersonal attraction among heterogeneous and homogeneous individuals: A theoretical formulation and a meta-analysis of the research. *Review of Educational Research, 53,* 5–54.

Johnson, D., Maruyame, G., Johnson, R., Nelson, D., & Skon, L. (1981). Effects of cooperative, competitive, and individualistic goal structures on achievement: A meta-analysis. *Psychological Bulletin, 89,* 47–62.

Jones, E. E., & Nisbett, R. E. (1972). The actor and the observer: Divergent perceptions of the causes of behavior. In E. E. Jones, D. E. Kanouse, H. H. Kelley, R. E. Nisbett, S. Valins, & B. Weiner (Eds.), *Attribution: Perceiving the causes of behavior.* Morristown, NJ: General Learning.

Kantrowitz, B., & Wingert, P. (1991, June 17). A dismal report card: Rich and poor, north and south, black, brown, and white, eighth graders flunked the national math test. What can be done about this scandal? *Newsweek,* pp. 64–65.

Karobenick, S., & Knapp, J. (1991). Relationship of academic help-seeking to the use of learning strategies and other instrumental achievement behavior in college students. *Journal of Educational Psychology, 83,* 221–230.

Kaufman, J. E., & Rosenbaum, J. E. (1992). The education and employment of low-income black youth in white suburbs. *Educational Evaluation and Policy Analysis, 14,* 229–240.

Kelley, H. H. (1967). Attribution theory in social psychology. In D. Levine (Ed.), *Nebraska Symposium on Motivation* (pp. 192–238). Lincoln: University of Nebraska Press.

Kelman, H. C. (1958). Compliance, identification, and internalization: Three processes of opinion change. *Journal of Conflict Resolution, 2,* 51–60.

Kelman, H. C. (1961). Processes of attitude change. *Public Opinion Quarterly, 25,* 57–78.

King, L. H. (1993). High and low achievers' perceptions and cooperative learning in two small groups. *Elementary School Journal, 93,* 399–416.

Kounin, J. (1970). *Discipline and group management in classrooms.* New York: Holt, Rinehart & Winston.

Krampen, G. (1987). Differential effects of teacher comments. *Journal of Educational Psychology, 79,* 137–146.

Kruglanski, A. W. (1978). Endogenous attribution and intrinsic motivation. In M. Lepper & D. Greene (Eds.), *The hidden costs of reward: New perspectives on the psychology of human motivation* (pp. 85–108). Hillsdale, NJ: Lawrence Erlbaum Associates.

Kuhl, J. (1985). Volitional mediators of cognition-behavior consistency: Self-regulatory processes and action versus state orientation. In J. Kuhl & J. Beckmann (Eds.), *Action control: From cognition to behavior* (pp. 101–128). Berlin: Springer.

Kuhl, J. (1987a). Action control: The maintenance of motivational states. (pp. 279–292). In F. Halisch & J. Kuhl (Eds.), *Motivation, intention, and volition* (pp. 279–292). Berlin: Springer.

Kuhl, J. (1987b). Feeling versus being helpless: Metacognitive mediation of failure-induced performance deficits. In F. E. Weinert & R. H. Kluwe (Eds.), *Metacognition, motivation, and understanding* (pp. 217–238). Hillsdale, NJ: Lawrence Erlbaum Associates.

Kuhl, J., & Beckmann, J. (1985). Historical perspectives in the study of action control. In J. Kuhl & J. Beckmann (Eds.), *Action control: From cognition to behavior* (pp. 89–100). Berlin: Springer.

Kunjufu, J. (1988). *To be popular or smart: The blacks' peer group.* Chicago: African American Images.

Lampert, M. (1985). How do teachers manage to teach? Perspectives on problems in practice. *Harvard Education Review, 55,* 178–194.

Lave, J., & Wenger, E. (1991). *Situated learning: Legitimate peripheral participation.* Cambridge, England: Cambridge University Press.

Lefcourt, H. M. (1976). *Locus of control*. Hillsdale, NJ: Lawrence Erlbaum Associates.

Lepper, M. (1981). Intrinsic and extrinsic motivation in children: Detrimental effects of superfluous social controls. In W. A. Collins (Ed.), *Minnesota Symposium on Child Psychology* (Vol. 14). Hillsdale, NJ: Lawrence Erlbaum Associates.

Lepper, M. (1983a). Extrinsic reward and intrinsic motivation: Implications for the classroom. In J. Levine & M. Wang (Eds.), *Teacher and student perceptions: Implications for learning* (pp. 281–318). Hillsdale, NJ: Lawrence Erlbaum Associates.

Lepper, M. (1983b). Social-control processes and the internalization of social values: An attributional perspective. In E. T. Higgins, D. N. Ruble, & W. W. Hartup (Eds.), *Social cognition and social development* (pp. 294–330). New York: Cambridge University Press.

Lepper, M., & Greene, D. (Eds.). (1978). *The hidden costs of reward: New perspectives on the psychology of human motivation*. Hillsdale, NJ: Lawrence Erlbaum Associates.

Lewin, K. (1935). *A dynamic theory of personality*. New York: McGraw-Hill.

Lohman, D. (1993). Teaching and testing to develop fluid abilities. *Educational Researcher, 22*, 12–23.

Maehr, M. L., & Midgley, C. (1991). Enhancing student motivation: A schoolwide approach. *Educational Psychologist, 26*, 399–427.

Maker, C. J. (1987). Gifted and talented. In V. Richardson-Koehler (Ed.), *Educators' handbook: A research perspective* (pp. 420–456). New York: Longman.

Mantzicopoulos, P., & Morrison, D. (1992). Kindergarten retention: Academic and behavioral outcomes through the end of second grade. *American Educational Research Journal, 29*, 182–198.

Marx, R. W., & Walsh, J. (1988). Learning from academic tasks. *Elementary School Journal, 88*, 207–220.

Maslow, A. H. (1968). *Toward a psychology of being*. New York: Van Nostrand.

Mason, D., & Good, T. (1993). Effects of two-group and whole-class teaching on regrouped elementary students' mathematics achievement. *American Educational Research Journal, 30*, 328–360.

May, R. (1972). *Power and innocence: A search for the sources of violence*. New York: Norton.

McCaslin, M. (1989). Whole language: Theory, instruction, and future implementation. *Elementary School Journal (Special Issue on Whole Language Instruction), 90*, 223–229.

McCaslin, M. (1990). Motivated literacy. In J. Zutell & S. McCormick (Eds.), *Literacy theory and research: Analyses for multiple paradigms* (39th Yearbook of the National Society for the Study of Education, pp. 35–50). Rochester, NY: National Reading Conference.

McCaslin, M., & Good, T. (1992). Compliant cognition: The misalliance of management and instructional goals in current school reform. *Educational Researcher, 21*, 4–17.

McCaslin, M., & Good, T. (1993). Classroom management and motivated student learning. In T. M. Tomlinson (Ed.), *Motivating students to learn: Overcoming barriers to high achievement* (pp. 245–261). Berkeley, CA: McCutchan.

McCaslin, M., & Good, T. (1996). *Listening to students*. New York: HarperCollins.

McCaslin, M., & Murdock, T. B. (1991). The emergent interaction of home and school in the development of students' adaptive learning. In M. L. Maehr & P. R. Pintrich (Eds.), *Advances in motivation and achievement* (pp. 213–259). Greenwich, CT: JAI Press.

McCaslin, M., Tuck, D., Wiard, A., Brown, B., LaPage, J., & Pyle, J. (1994). Gender composition in small-group learning in fourth-grade mathematics. *Elementary School Journal, 94*, 467–482.

McCaslin Rohrkemper, M. (1989). Self-regulated learning and academic achievement: A Vygotskian view. In B. Zimmerman & D. Schunk (Eds.), *Self-regulated learning and academic achievement: Theory, research, and practice* (pp. 143–168). New York: Springer.

Mergendoller, J., Marchman, V., Mitman, A., & Packer, M. (1988). Task demands and accountability in middle-grade science classes. *Elementary School Journal, 88*, 251–265.

Mergendoller, J. R. (Ed.). (1988). *Schoolwork and academic tasks* [Special issue]. *Elementary School Journal, 88*.

Metz, M. (1978). *Classrooms and corridors: The crisis of authority in desegregated secondary schools*. Berkeley: University of California Press.

Miller, G. A., Galanter, E., & Pribram, K. H. (1960). *Plans and the structure of behavior*. New York: Holt.

Miller, S. E., Leinhardt, G., & Zigmond, N. (1988). Influencing engagement through accommodation: An ethnographic study of at-risk students. *American Educational Research Journal, 25*, 465–487.

Mischel, H. N., & Mischel, W. (1987). The development of children's knowledge and self-control strategies. In F. Halisch & J. Kuhl (Eds.), *Motivation, intention, and volition* (pp. 321–336). Berlin: Springer.

Mitchell, R. (1992). *Testing for learning: How new approaches to evaluation can improve American schools*. New York: Free Press.

Moll, L. C. (1992). Bilingual classroom studies and community analysis. *Educational Researcher, 21*, 20–24.

Mulryan, C. (1989). *A study of intermediate-grade students' involvement and participation in cooperative small groups in mathematics*. Unpublished doctoral dissertation, University of Missouri–Columbia.

Mulryan, C. (1992). Student passivity during cooperative small groups in mathematics. *Journal of Educational Research, 85*, 261–273.

Murray, H. (1938). *Explorations in personality*. New York: Oxford University Press.

Myers, M., & Paris, S. G. (1978). Children's metacognitive knowledge about reading. *Journal of Educational Psychology, 70*, 680–690.

National Commission on Excellence in Education. (1983). *A nation at risk: The imperative for educational reform*. Washington, DC: Department of Education.

National Council of Teachers of Mathematics, Commission of Standards for School Mathematics. (1990). *Curriculum and evaluation standards for school mathematics*. Reston, VA: Author.

National Council of Teachers of Mathematics. (1991). *Professional standards for teaching mathematics*. Reston, VA: Author.

Natriello, G., McDill, F., & Pallas, A. (1990). *Schooling disadvantaged children: Racing against catastrophe*. New York: Teachers College Press.

Nelson-Le Gall, S. (1981). Help-seeking: An understudied problem-solving skill in children. *Developmental Review, 1*, 224–246.

Nelson-Le Gall, S. (1985). Help-seeking behavior in learning. In E. Gordon (Ed.), *Review of research in education* (Vol. 12, pp. 55–90). Washington, DC: American Educational Research Association.

Nelson-Le Gall, S. (1987). Necessary and unnecessary help-seeking in children. *Journal of Genetic Psychology, 148*, 53–62.

Nelson-Le Gall, S., & Jones, E. (1990). Cognitive-motivational influences on children's help-seeking. *Child Development, 61*, 581–589.

Newman, R. (1990). Children's help-seeking in the classroom: The role of motivational factors and attitudes. *Journal of Educational Psychology, 82*, 71–80.

Newman, R., & Goldin, L. (1990). Children's reluctance to seek help with school work. *Journal of Educational Psychology, 82*, 92–100.

Newman, R. S. (1991). Goals and self-regulated learning: What motivates children to seek academic help? In M. L. Maehr & P. R. Pintrich (Eds.), *Advances in motivation and achievement* (Vol. 7, pp. 151–183). Greenwich, CT: JAI Press.

Newman, R. S., & Schwager, M. T. (1992). Student perceptions and academic help seeking. In D. Schunk & J. Meece (Eds.), *Student perceptions in the classroom* (pp. 123–146). Hillsdale, NJ: Lawrence Erlbaum Associates.

Noddings, N. (1992). *The challenge to care in schools*. New York: Teachers College Press.

Nolen, S. B. (1988). Reasons for studying: Motivational orientations and study strategies. *Cognition and Instruction, 5*, 269–287.

Oakes, J. (1992). Can tracking research inform practice? Technical, normative, and political considerations. *Educational Researcher, 21,* 12–21.

Ogbu, J. G. (1992). Understanding cultural diversity and learning. *Educational Researcher, 21,* 4–14.

Page, R. (1992). *Lower track classrooms: A curricular and cultural perspective.* New York: Teachers College Press.

Palincsar, A. (1986). Metacognitive strategy instruction. *Exceptional Children, 53,* 118–124.

Palincsar, A., & Brown, A. (1984). Reciprocal teaching of comprehension-fostering and comprehension-monitoring activities. *Cognition and Instruction, 1,* 117–175.

Paris, S., Wasik, B., & Turner, J. (1991). The development of strategic readers. In R. Barr, M. Kamil, P. Mosenthal, P. D. Pearson (Eds.), *Handbook of reading research* (Vol. 2, pp. 609–640). New York: Longman.

Paris, S. G. (1988, April). *Fusing skill and will in children's learning and schooling.* Paper presented at the annual meeting of the American Educational Research Association, New Orleans, LA.

Paris, S. G., Lawton, T. A., Turner, J. C., & Roth, J. L. (1991). A developmental perspective on standardized achievement testing. *Educational Researcher, 20,* 12–20, 40.

Pepitone, E. (1985). Children in cooperation and competition: Antecedents and consequences of self-orientation. In R. Slavin, S. Sharan, S. Kagan, R. Lazarowitz, C. Webb, & R. Schmuck (Eds.), *Learning to cooperate, cooperating to learn* (pp. 17–67). New York: Plenum Press.

Perkins, D. N., & Salomon, G. (1989, January–February). Are cognitive skills context-bound? *Educational Researcher, 18,* 16–25.

Pervin, L. A. (1991). Self-regulation and the problem of volition. In M. Maehr & P. Pintrich (Eds.), *Advances in motivation and achievement* (Vol. 7, pp. 1–20). Greenwich, CT: JAI Press.

Phillips, D. A., & Zimmerman, M. (1990). The developmental course of perceived competence and incompetence among competent children. In R. Sternberg & J. Kolligian, Jr. (Eds.), *Competence considered* (pp. 41–66). New Haven, CT: Yale University Press.

Phillips, S. (1983). *The invisible culture: Communication in the classroom and the community on the Warm Springs Indian Reservation.* New York: Longman.

Piaget, J. (1983). Piaget's theory. In P. Mussen (Ed.), *Handbook of child psychology: Vol. 1. History, theory, and methods* (W. Kessen, Ed.) (pp. 103–128). New York: Wiley.

Piliavin, I. M., Rodin, J., & Piliavin, J. A. (1969). Good samaritanism: An underground phenomenon? *Journal of Personality and Social Psychology, 13,* 289–299.

Piliavin, J. A., & Piliavin, I. M. (1972). The effect of blood on reaction to a victim. *Journal of Personality and Social Psychology, 23,* 253–261.

Pintrich, P. R., & Schrauben, B. (1992). Students' motivational beliefs and their cognitive engagement in classroom academic tasks. In D. Schunk & J. Meece (Eds.), *Student perceptions in the classroom: Causes and consequences* (pp. 149–183). Hillsdale, NJ: Lawrence Erlbaum Associates.

Popham, W. J. (1987). The merits of measurement-driven instruction. *Phi Delta Kappan, 68,* 679–682.

Porter, A. (1989). A curriculum out of balance: The case of elementary school mathematics. *Educational Researcher, 18,* 9–15.

Prawat, R. (1992). Are changes and views about mathematics teaching sufficient? The case of a fifth-grade teacher. *Elementary School Journal, 93,* 195–212.

Pressley, M., & El-Dinary, P. B. (Eds.). (1993). Strategies instruction. (Special issue) *Elementary School Journal, 94* (2).

Putnam, R. (1992). Teaching the "hows" of mathematics for everyday life: A case study of a fifth-grade teacher. *Elementary School Journal, 93,* 163–178.

Raudenbush, S. W., Rowan, B., & Cheong, Y. F. (1993). Higher-order instructional goals in secondary schools: Class, teacher, and school influences. *American Educational Research Journal, 30,* 523–553.

Renninger, K., Hidi, S., & Krapp, A. (Eds.). (1992). *The role of interest in learning and development.* Hillsdale, NJ: Lawrence Erlbaum Associates.

Renzulli, J. S. (1978). What makes giftedness? Re-examining a definition. *Phi Delta Kappan, 60,* 180–184.

Rodriguez, R. (1982). *Hunger of memory.* Boston: David Godine.

Rohrkemper, M. (1983). *Student cognition study: II. Myths about motivated learning.* Unpublished manuscript.

Rohrkemper, M. (1984). The influence of teachers' socialization style on students' social cognition and reported interpersonal classroom behavior. *Elementary School Journal, 85,* 245–275.

Rohrkemper, M. (1985). Individual differences in students' perceptions of routine classroom events. *Journal of Educational Psychology, 77,* 29–44.

Rohrkemper, M. (1986a). Education and cooperation. *Review of Education, 12,* 19–22.

Rohrkemper, M. (1986b). The functions of inner speech in elementary school students' problem-solving behavior. *American Educational Research Journal, 23,* 303–313.

Rohrkemper, M., & Bershon, B. L. (1984). The quality of student task engagement: Elementary school students' reports of the causes and effects of problem difficulty. *Elementary School Journal, 85,* 127–147.

Rohrkemper, M., & Brophy, J. (1983). Teachers' thinking about problem students. In J. Levine & M. C. Wang (Eds.), *Teacher and student perceptions: Implications for learning.* Hillsdale, NJ: Lawrence Erlbaum Associates.

Rohrkemper, M., & Corno, L. (1988). Success and failure on classroom tasks: Adaptive learning and classroom teaching. *Elementary School Journal, 88,* 299–312.

Rohrkemper, M., Slavin, R., & McCauley, K. (1983, April). Investigating students' perceptions of cognitive strategies as learning tools. Paper presented at the annual meeting of the American Educational Research Association, Montreal.

Romero, M., Mercado, C., & Vázquez-Faria, J. (1987). Students of limited English proficiency. In V. Richardson-Koehler (Ed.), *Educators' handbook: A research perspective* (pp. 348–369). New York: Longman.

Rose, M. (1989). *Lives on the boundary: The struggles and achievements of America's underprepared.* New York: Free Press.

Rosenholtz, S. (1989). *Teachers' workplace: The social organization of schools.* White Plains, NY: Longman.

Rosenholtz, S., & Simpson, C. (1984). The formation of ability conceptions: Developmental trend or social construction. *Review of Educational Research, 54,* 31–63.

Rosenshine, B. (1993, April). *Is direct instruction different from expert scaffolding?* Paper presented at the annual meeting of the American Educational Research Association, Atlanta.

Rosenshine, B., & Stevens, R. (1986). Teaching functions. In M. C. Wittrock (Ed.), *Handbook of research on teaching* (3rd ed., pp. 376–391). New York: Macmillan.

Rotter, J. (1966). Generalized expectancies for internal versus external control of reinforcement. *Psychology Monographs, 80,* 1–28.

Sadker, M., Sadker, D., & Klein, S. (1991). The issue of gender in elementary and secondary education. In G. Grant (Ed.), *Review of research in education* (Vol. 17, pp. 269–334). Washington, DC: American Educational Research Association.

Schunk, D. H. (1989). Social cognitive learning. In B. Zimmerman & D. Schunk (Eds.), *Self-regulated learning and academic achievement: Theory, research and practice* (pp. 83–110). New York: Springer.

Schunk, D. H. (1991). Goal setting and self-evaluation: A social cognitive perspective on self-regulation. In M. L. Maehr & P. R. Pintrich (Eds.), *Advances in Motivation and Achievement* (pp. 85–113). Greenwich, CT: JAI Press.

Secada, W. G., & Lightfoot, T. (1993). Symbols and the political context of bilingual education in the United States. *Bilingual Education: Politics, Practice, and Research.* Chicago: University of Chicago Press.

Segal, J. W., Chipman, S. F., & Glaser, R. (Eds.). (1985). *Thinking and learning skills: Vol. 1. Relating instruction to research.* Hillsdale, NJ: Lawrence Erlbaum Associates.

Segal-Andrews, A. M. (1991). *Intrapersonal functioning and interpersonal context: A proposed model of interaction from a Vygotskian perspective.* Unpublished doctoral dissertation, Bryn Mawr College, Bryn Mawr, PA.

Segal-Andrews, A. M. (1994). Understanding student behavior in one fifth-grade classroom as contextually defined. *Elementary School Journal, 95,* 183–197.

Shantz, C. U., & Hartup, W. W. (1993). *Conflict in child and adolescent development.* New York: University Press.

Sharan, S. (1980). Cooperative learning in small groups: Recent methods and effects on achievements, attitudes, and ethnic relations. *Review of Educational Research, 50,* 241–271.

Shulman, L. S. (1970). Psychology and mathematics education. In E. G. Begle (Eds.), *Mathematics education* (69th Yearbook of the National Society for the Study of Education, pp. 23–71). Chicago: National Society for the Study of Education.

Simon, H. (1969). *The sciences of the artificial.* Cambridge, MA: MIT Press.

Sizer, T. (1984). *Horace's compromise: The dilemma of the American school.* Boston: Houghton Mifflin.

Slavin, R., Sharan, S., Kagan, S., Lazarowitz, R., Webb, C., & Schmuck, R. (Eds.). (1985). *Learning to cooperate, cooperating to learn.* New York: Plenum.

Slavin, R. E. (1990). *Cooperative learning: Theory, research, and practice.* Englewood Cliffs, NJ: Prentice Hall.

Smith, M. L. (1991). Put to the test: The effects of external testing of teachers. *Educational Researcher, 20,* 8–11.

Snow, C. E. (1992). Perspectives on second-language development: Implications for bilingual education. *Educational Researcher, 21,* 16–19.

Sockett, H. (1988). Education and will: Aspects of personal capability. *American Journal of Education, 96,* 195–214.

Spencer, D. (1984). The home and school lives of women teachers: Implications for staff development. *Elementary School Journal, 84,* 299–314.

Spencer-Hall, D. (1981). Looking behind the teacher's back. *Elementary School Journal, 81,* 281–290.

Steele, C. M. (1988). The psychology of self-affirmation: Sustaining the integrity of the self. In L. Berkowitz (Ed.), *Advances in experimental social psychology* (Vol. 21, pp. 261–302). New York: Academic Press.

Sternberg, R. (1990). Prototypes of competence and incompetence. In R. Sternberg & J. Kolligian, Jr. (Eds.), *Competence considered* (pp. 117–145). New Haven, CT: Yale University Press.

Stipek, D. (1986). Children's motivation to learn. In T. Tomlinson & H. Walberg (Eds.), *Academic work and educational excellence* (pp. 197–221). Berkeley, CA: McCutchan.

Tangri, S., & Moles, O. (1987). Parents and the community. In V. Richardson-Koehler (Ed.), *Educators' handbook: A research perspective* (pp. 519–550). New York: Longman.

Tetreault, M., & Schmuck, P. (1985). Equity, education reform, and gender. *Issues in Education, 3,* 45–67.

Trope, Y., & Brickman, P. (1975). Difficulty and diagnosticity as determinants of choice among tasks. *Journal of Personality and Social Psychology, 31,* 218–226.

U.S. Department of Education. (1990, November). *Hard work and higher expectations: A conference on student motivation.* Arlington, VA: Office of Educational Research and Improvement.

Vandenberg, B. (1991). Is epistemology enough? An existential consideration of development. *American Psychologist, 46,* 1278–1286.

van der Meij, H. (1988). Constraints on question-asking in classrooms. *Journal of Educational Psychology, 80,* 401–405.

van der Meij, H. (1990). Question asking: To know that you do not know is not enough. *Journal of Educational Psychology, 82,* 505–512.

van Hekken, S., & Roelofsen, W. (1982). More questions than answers. *Journal of Child Language, 9,* 445–460.

Vygotsky, L. (1962). *Thought and language.* Cambridge, MA: MIT Press.

Vygotsky, L. (1978). *Mind in society: The development of higher psychological processes.* Cambridge, MA: Harvard University Press.

Webb, F. R., Covington, M. V., & Guthrie, J. W. (1993). Carrots and sticks: Can school policy influence student motivation? In T. M. Tomlinson (Ed.), *Motivating students to learn: Overcoming barriers to high achievement* (pp. 99–124). Berkeley, CA: McCutchan.

Webb, N. (1989). Peer interaction and learning in small groups. *International Journal of Educational Research, 13,* 21–39.

Webb, N. M., & Kenderski, C. M. (1984). Student interaction and learning in small-group and whole-class settings. In P. Peterson, L. C. Wilkinson, & M. Hallinan (Eds.), *The social context of instruction: Group organization and group processes* (pp. 153–170). Orlando, FL: Academic Press.

Weiner, B. (1986). *An attributional theory of motivation and emotion.* New York: Springer.

Weiner, B. (1991). Metaphors in motivation and attribution. *American Psychologist, 46,* 921–930.

Weiner, B. (1992). *Human motivation: Metaphors, theory, and research.* Newbury Park, CA: Sage.

Weinert, F. E., & Helmke, A. (1987). Compensatory effects of student self-concept and instructional quality on academic achievement. In F. Halisch & J. Kuhl (Eds.), *Motivation, intention, and volition* (pp. 233–248). Berlin: Springer.

Weinert, F. E., & Kluwe, R. H. (1987). *Metacognition, motivation, and understanding.* Hillsdale, NJ: Lawrence Erlbaum Associates.

Weinstein, R., Marshall, H., Brattesani, K., & Middlestadt, S. (1982). Student perceptions of differential teacher treatment in open and traditional classrooms. *Journal of Educational Psychology, 74,* 678–692.

Weinstein, R., & Middlestadt, S. (1979). Student perceptions of teacher interactions with high and low achievers. *Journal of Educational Psychology, 71,* 421–431.

Weinstein, R. (1990, November). *Different lives within the classroom and the school: Children make sense of ability differences.* Paper presented at Hard Work and Higher Expectations: A Conference on Student Motivation. Arlington, VA: U.S. Department of Education.

Weinstein, R. S. (1993). Children's knowledge of differential treatment in school: Implications for motivation. In T. M. Tomlinson (Ed.), *Motivating students to learn: Overcoming barriers to high achievement* (pp. 197–224). Berkeley, CA: McCutchan.

Wertsch, J. (1985). *Vygotsky and the social formation of mind.* Cambridge, MA: Harvard University Press.

Wertsch, J., & Stone, C. (1985). The concept of internalization in Vygotsky's account of the genesis of higher mental functions. In J. Wertsch (Ed.), *Culture, communication, and cognition: Vygotskian perspectives* (pp. 162–182). New York: Cambridge University Press.

Wilson, K., & Shantz, C. (1977). Perceptual role-taking and dependency behavior in preschool children. *Merrill-Palmer Quarterly, 23,* 207–211.

Zimmerman, B., & Schunk, D. (Eds.). (1989). *Self-regulated learning and academic achievement: Theory, research, and practice.* New York: Springer.

Zimmerman, B. J., Bandura, A., & Martinez-Pons, M. (1992). Self-motivation for academic attainment: The role of self-efficacy beliefs in personal goal setting. *American Educational Research Journal, 29,* 663–676.

Zinchenko, V. P. (1985). Vygotsky's ideas about units for analysis of mind. In J. Wertsch (Ed.), *Culture, communication, and cognition: Vygotsky in perspectives* (pp. 94–118). New York: Cambridge University Press.

Zuckerman, G. (1994). A pilot study of a 10-day course in cooperative learning for beginning Russian first graders. *Elementary School Journal, 94,* 405–420.

*Part*

## ·IV·

# TEACHING AND INSTRUCTION

# LEARNING TO TEACH

## Hilda Borko

UNIVERSITY OF COLORADO, BOULDER

## Ralph T. Putnam

MICHIGAN STATE UNIVERSITY

Much has been written about learning to teach. Researchers and scholars have examined teachers' learning—changes in what they know, what they believe, how they think, how they act, and how they think of themselves as professionals and people—from a variety of perspectives (e.g., Carter, 1990; Feiman-Nemser, 1983; Richardson, 1990). The greatest challenge we faced in writing this chapter was deciding what to include and what to omit. Which of the many perspectives on learning to teach are reasonably thought of as psychological? Of those perspectives that are psychological, which are most in keeping with this *Handbook*'s focus—as described in Chapter 1—on cognition as the prevailing theoretical framework in contemporary educational psychology and on the renewed engagement of educational psychology in issues of practice? To answer these questions for ourselves, and decide what to include in the chapter, we took cognitive psychology as our starting point.

The central focus of cognitive psychology is the mental life of the individual. As Lauren Resnick (1985) noted, "The heart of cognitive psychology is the centrality given to the human mind and the treatment of thinking processes as concrete phenomena that can be studied scientifically" (p. 124). Because of cognitive psychology's emphasis on the content and process of thought—on how knowledge is organized and used by individuals—we have made the primary emphasis of this chapter the knowledge and beliefs of teachers. The major question we address is how knowledge and beliefs change over time as novice teachers learn to teach and experienced teachers attempt to make changes in their teaching practices.

This question served as our guide for choosing research studies and programs to include in this review. We therefore excluded consideration of entire areas of research on various aspects of teacher learning and development that are important but not directly related to teachers' knowledge and beliefs. Such areas include, for example, research on teacher socialization

and career development. Further, rather than trying to be exhaustive in covering a research literature that has mushroomed in the past few years, we selected studies to be representative of research approaches and of various aspects of our conceptual framework. We discuss these issues in more detail after presenting the conceptual framework for the chapter. That framework incorporates key assumptions underlying a cognitive psychological perspective on learning to teach, and a model of domains of teachers' knowledge and beliefs. Using the framework as an organizer, we then review research on how preservice and in-service teachers learn to teach. We conclude with a set of recommendations for helping novice and experienced teachers expand and elaborate their professional knowledge base.

## CONCEPTUAL FRAMEWORK

### Assumptions from Cognitive Psychology

There are numerous cognitive psychological perspectives on learning or thinking that could be applied to studies of learning to teach (Eisenhart & Borko, 1993; Putnam, Lampert, & Peterson, 1990; Resnick, 1989). Several assumptions and themes are central to most perspectives. Among the shared themes are: (a) the central role of knowledge in thinking, acting, and learning, (b) learning as an active, constructive process, and (c) knowledge and learning as situated in contexts and cultures. We first consider these themes individually and then explore how they come together to demonstrate the critical role of prior knowledge in learning to teach.

***The Central Role of Knowledge.*** Cognitive psychologists assume that an individual's knowledge structures and mental

Ralph Putnam's work on this chapter was supported in part by grants from the Pew Charitable Trust (grant No. 91-04343-000), Carnegie Corporation of New York (grant No. B 5638), and the National Science Foundation (grant No. ESI-9153834). The views expressed in this chapter are those of the individual authors and are not necessarily shared by the grantors. The two authors contributed equally to the conceptualization and writing of this chapter. The order of authorship is alphabetical. The authors were helped by reviews from P. Grossman, V. Richardson, R. Cliff, M. Simon, M. K. Stein, S. Guberman, J. Bisanz, and the Educational Policy and Practice research group at Michigan State University.

representations of the world play a central role in thinking, acting, and learning. The most significant shift away from the behaviorist perspectives that dominated American psychology and educational psychology for the first half of the 20th century was the willingness of psychologists to hypothesize mental structures and mental events as meaningful objects of study. This willingness has resulted in a multitude of ways of characterizing how knowledge might be structured in the minds of individuals (e.g., schemata, scripts, production systems, procedural and declarative knowledge) and the nature of that knowledge in particular domains of expertise. From studies of expert performance and problem solving in various domains outside of education, psychologists have learned that knowledge plays a central role in expert performance (Glaser, 1984). The accumulation of richly structured and accessible bodies of knowledge allows individuals to engage in expert thinking and action. In studies of teaching, this understanding of expertise has led researchers to devote increased attention to teachers' knowledge and how it is organized. Much of this interest was catalyzed by Shulman's (1986a) call for students of teaching to attend more carefully to teachers' knowledge, especially their knowledge of the content they teach.

***Learning Is an Active Constructive Process.*** "Cognitive theories tell us that learning occurs not by recording information but by interpreting it" (Resnick, 1989, p. 2). The learning of individuals, including teachers, is a constructive and iterative process in which the person interprets events on the basis of existing knowledge, beliefs, and dispositions. Learning outcomes are the changes in mental organization, structures, and processes that result from this active, constructive process. These changes in turn influence the individual's actions in various settings. Teaching from this perspective is less a matter of presenting knowledge and ready-made understandings to learners and more a matter of creating environments that supports learners' efforts to construct meanings. Although learning can be heavily influenced by instruction, how and what individuals learn is always shaped and filtered by their existing knowledge and beliefs. It can therefore never be completely determined by instruction (Norman, 1980; Putnam, 1992b).

***Knowledge and Learning Are Situated in Physical and Cultural Contexts.*** Early cognitive theories, especially information-processing theories, typically treated knowledge and cognitive processes rather mechanistically, as the manipulation of symbols inside the mind of the individual. In contrast, many current cognitive theorists, influenced by the confluence of ideas from disciplines such as anthropology, linguistics, and philosophy (Bruner, 1990; Gardner, 1985), are concerned with the relationship between knowledge as it exists in the mind of the individual and the situations in which that knowledge is acquired and used (J. S. Brown, Collins, & Duguid, 1989; Bruner, 1990). Rather than thinking of knowledge as abstract and detached from the external world, these theorists emphasize the situated nature of cognition. Knowledge, they argue, cannot be thought of as independent from the contexts or situations in which individuals acquire and use it. (See chapter 2.)

For instruction, this perspective implies that students should learn valued knowledge, skills, and dispositions as they occur in meaningful contexts. This view contrasts with traditional instructional theories grounded in behaviorist and early information-processing perspectives, which assume that learning is facilitated by breaking complex tasks into component parts that can be taught and practiced in isolation (e.g., Gagné, 1985). According to these traditional theories, students acquire the component parts one by one, ultimately putting them together into complex performances. School curricula based on these theories have too often consisted of discrete facts and skills removed from any meaningful context or sense of purpose. Students spend inordinate hours memorizing and practicing letter–sound correspondences, rules for subject–verb agreement, or computational algorithms, with few opportunities to read, write, or solve mathematical problems as complete and meaningful tasks. In preservice and in-service teacher education, this reductionist perspective has been associated with teaching teachers about relatively disembodied educational theories and training them in various component skills of teaching. For example, preservice teachers often enroll in "foundations" courses (e.g., philosophy, sociology, and psychology of education) and "methods" courses (e.g., in reading and mathematics), with few opportunities to integrate or coordinate content across courses. They are then expected to put these theories and skills together into an instructional program for their classrooms.

Increasingly, educators have rejected such disembodied bits-and-pieces approaches to schooling by proposing alternative instructional models that are compatible with cognitive theorists' emphasis on the situated nature of learning. These alternatives, including reciprocal teaching (Palincsar & A. L. Brown, 1984), cognitive apprenticeships (Collins, J. S. Brown, & Newman, 1989), and instructional conversations (Saunders, Goldenberg, & Hamann, 1992; Tharp & Gallimore, 1988), are all attempts to situate students' learning in more complete and meaningful contexts. In addition, reformers in various subject matter domains are calling for curricula and teaching that emphasize understanding, reasoning, and connections among important ideas, all intertwined with the settings in which this knowledge will be used (e.g., National Council of Teachers of Mathematics, 1989; National Research Council, 1993). Attempts to educate teachers, both preservice and in-service, have seen similar shifts in both the way knowledge is conceptualized and how it is thought to be acquired by novice and experienced teachers (e.g., Carter, 1990).

***The Role of Prior Knowledge and Beliefs in Learning to Teach.*** Thus, contemporary cognitive theories view learning as an active, constructive process that is heavily influenced by an individual's existing knowledge and beliefs and is situated in particular contexts. Just as cognitively oriented studies of learning have demonstrated the central role that students' existing conceptions play in determining how they interpret instruction and what they learn (Garner, 1987; Resnick, 1985), research on learning to teach shows that teachers' existing knowledge and beliefs are critical in shaping what and how they learn from teacher education experiences. Just as many fundamental conceptions of students about science and mathematics are resistant to change through instruction (Confrey, 1990), teachers' knowledge and beliefs about teaching and learning are difficult to change. And just as students seem better able to make use of knowledge acquired in the context of meaningful tasks (J. S. Brown et al., 1989), research on teachers' learning suggests that for knowledge to be useful for teaching, it must be integrally linked to, or situated in, the contexts in which it is to be used.

In thinking about learning to teach, we focus on two important and interrelated aspects of teachers' knowledge and beliefs. On the one hand, the knowledge and beliefs that prospective and experienced teachers hold serve as filters through which their learning takes place. It is through these existing conceptions that teachers come to understand recommended new practices. On the other hand, knowledge and beliefs themselves are critical targets of change. Because teachers' knowledge and beliefs—about teaching, about subject matter, about learners—are major determinants of what they do in the classroom, any efforts to help teachers make significant changes in their teaching practices must help them to acquire new knowledge and beliefs. Thus, a teacher's knowledge and beliefs are both the *objects* or *targets* of change and important *influences* on change (Cohen & Ball, 1990b; Putnam, Heaton, Prawat, & Remillard, 1992).

## A Framework for Organizing Research on Teachers' Knowledge and Beliefs

We organize our discussion of learning to teach around three domains of knowledge that are particularly relevant to teachers' instructional practices: (a) general pedagogical knowledge and beliefs, (b) subject matter knowledge and beliefs, and (c) pedagogical content knowledge and beliefs. These domains are taken loosely from the categories proposed by Shulman (1986b, 1987) when he first argued for the importance of attending seriously to teachers' knowledge in studies of teaching. Knowledge about students may seem glaringly absent from the categories we use. Shulman (1987) included knowledge of learners as a category and Peterson (1988) highlighted the importance of teachers' knowing about the thinking of their students. We agree that knowledge about students is critically important—arguably the most important knowledge a teacher can have. It is so intertwined with general pedagogical knowledge and pedagogical content knowledge, however, that we decided to embed our discussion of knowledge about students within these categories. Organizationally, that makes it easier to discuss teachers' general knowledge and beliefs about students and how they learn, and their knowledge about subject-specific understandings and misunderstandings that students might have.

Before describing our category scheme, it is important to note that any categorization of teacher knowledge and beliefs is somewhat arbitrary. There is no single system for characterizing the organization of teachers' knowledge. In fact, with the increased attention to teacher knowledge in recent years, schemes for categorizing and describing different types of knowledge have proliferated (e.g., Ball, 1988b; Carter & Doyle, 1987; Clandinin, 1986; Connelly & Clandinin, 1985; Elbaz, 1983; Grossman, 1990; Leinhardt & D. Smith, 1985; Shulman, 1986b). Further, because all knowledge is highly interrelated, the categories of teacher knowledge within a particular system are not discrete entities, and boundaries between them are necessarily blurred (Marks, 1990). Another concern is that there is no agreed-upon distinction between knowledge and beliefs (Fen-

stermacher, 1994). Despite the difficulties inherent in delineating categories of knowledge and beliefs for teaching, such a delineation can serve as a useful analytic tool for thinking about teacher learning.

***General Pedagogical Knowledge and Beliefs.*** The domain of general pedagogical knowledge encompasses a teacher's knowledge and beliefs about teaching, learning, and learners that transcend particular subject matter domains. It includes knowledge of various strategies and arrangements for effective classroom management, instructional strategies for conducting lessons and creating learning environments, and more fundamental knowledge and beliefs about learners, how they learn, and how that learning can be fostered by teaching.

Classroom Management. One large component of general pedagogical knowledge and beliefs is the teachers' knowledge of classroom management—how to keep a group of 20 to 35 students working together and oriented toward classroom tasks. This component of teaching was an important focus in the process–product studies that dominated the 1970s, with their emphasis on teacher behaviors that are effective at keeping students highly engaged. The knowledge underlying these management behaviors was thus a natural place for researchers to turn when they first began studying teachers' cognitions, and it became the focus of a number of studies of teacher thinking, planning, decision-making, and judgment (for reviews, see Borko & Shavelson, 1990; Clark & Peterson, 1986; chapter 21).

Doyle (1986) offered a conception of classroom management that is compatible with a cognitive psychological perspective on teaching in that it focuses on teachers' decisions rather than behaviors. According to Doyle, classroom teaching has two major tasks—promoting order and learning. The task of promoting order is primarily one of establishing and maintaining an environment in which learning can occur. To accomplish this task, teachers must have repertoires of strategies for establishing rules and procedures, organizing groups, monitoring and pacing classroom events, and reacting to misbehavior. With the recent emphasis of many researchers on subject matter knowledge of teachers and on aspects of instruction that are subject specific, general pedagogical knowledge of classroom management has sometimes received short shrift. This domain of knowledge, however, remains indispensable for successful teaching.

Instructional Strategies. Teachers also continually draw on knowledge of strategies for conducting lessons and creating learning environments. Regardless of the instructional approaches they take, teachers need knowledge of how to structure classroom activities, as well as repertoires of strategies and routines for interacting with students, for ensuring student participation and engagement, and for keeping lessons running smoothly (Leinhardt & Greeno, 1986). Although much of the recent research on teaching for understanding has focused on teaching in particular subject matter domains, the instructional approaches described in this research share a number of common elements (L. M. Anderson, 1989a, 1989b, 1989c; Brophy, 1989). Knowledge of these elements—the teacher's role as a mediator of meaningful student learning, instructional strategies that promote active cognitive processing of academic content, classroom environments that foster learning for understanding and self-regulation, and methods of assessment that reveal students' thinking—constitutes a major component of the general pedagogical knowledge that teachers must have in order to teach for students' active construction of meaning and self-regulated learning.

Learners, Learning, and Teaching. Teachers' knowledge and beliefs about how to manage classrooms and create learning environments are supported by, and intertwined with, knowledge and beliefs about how children think and learn, and about how teachers can foster that learning. As we noted earlier, recent cognitive psychological research and theory characterize learning as a student-mediated process, one that occurs when the learner imposes meaning and organization on experience by relating it to existing knowledge, and monitors his or her understanding throughout the learning process. In this *cognitive-mediational* conception of learning, learners are characterized as active problem solvers who construct their own knowledge. The teacher is considered to be responsible for stimulating students' cognitive processes that are necessary for learning (L. M. Anderson, 1989c). This conception is very different from the view of learners often implicit in direct instruction models of teaching—a *receptive-accrual* view (L. M. Anderson, 1989c) in which the learner's role is to receive and practice information and skills presented by the teacher. To adopt a cognitive-mediational view, then, represents a substantial shift in beliefs for many experienced teachers.

*Subject Matter Knowledge and Beliefs.* Few people would disagree with the statement that having a flexible, thoughtful, conceptual understanding of subject matter is critical to effective teaching for understanding. Yet, just as subject matter was once the "missing paradigm" in research on teaching (Shulman, 1986a), it has only recently become a central focus in research on learning to teach. Several important distinctions within knowledge of subject matter have been made by researchers studying teachers' knowledge and learning. In initiating the recent wave of interest in teachers' content knowledge, Shulman (1986a, 1986b) distinguished between subject matter knowledge—the knowledge of a subject or discipline per se, which is not unique to teaching, and pedagogical content knowledge—knowledge of a subject that is specifically related to teaching that subject. (We treat pedagogical content knowledge as a separate category in the next section.) Shulman also emphasized Schwab's (1964) distinction between *substantive* and *syntactic* structures of a discipline. Substantive structures are the ways in which the ideas, concepts, and facts of a discipline are organized—the key principles, theories and explanatory frameworks of the discipline. Syntactic structures are rules of evidence and proof that guide inquiry in a discipline—the ways of establishing new knowledge and determining the validity of claims. As the work of Shulman and his colleagues evolved, they came to distinguish four categories of subject matter knowledge: knowledge of content (facts, concepts, and procedures), knowledge of substantive structures, knowledge of syntactic structures, and beliefs about the discipline (Grossman, 1989). They argued that all four components influence both what teachers choose to teach and how they choose to teach it.

Writing about mathematics, Ball (1990a, 1991) made similar distinctions between knowledge *of* mathematics and knowledge *about* mathematics. She defined knowledge of mathematics to include an understanding of particular topics, procedures, and concepts, as well as the organizing structures and connections within mathematics. Knowledge about mathematics includes an understanding of the nature of mathematical knowledge—where it comes from, how it changes, how truth is established, and what it means to know and do mathematics.

The particular model of subject matter knowledge that one adopts does not seem to us to be crucial. What is essential to recognize is the argument that teachers need to know more than just the facts, terms, and concepts of a discipline. Their knowledge of the organizing ideas, connections among ideas, ways of thinking and arguing, and knowledge growth within the discipline is an important factor in how they will teach the subject. These understandings of subject matter become especially important when students' conceptual understanding is a central goal.

*Pedagogical Content Knowledge and Beliefs.* The construct *pedagogical content knowledge* (Shulman, 1986a, 1986b) has served as an important catalyst for considering the ways in which teachers need to think about the subjects they teach. As first described by Shulman (1986b), pedagogical content knowledge includes "the ways of representing and formulating the subject that make it comprehensible to others," and "an understanding of what makes the learning of specific topics easy or difficult: the conceptions and preconceptions that students of different ages and backgrounds bring with them to the learning of those most frequently taught topics and lessons" (p. 9). As this definition implies, pedagogical content knowledge is an integration of knowledge from several domains, and its boundaries with those domains—for example, subject matter knowledge and general pedagogical knowledge—are fuzzy. Yet it is an important domain, for it focuses explicitly on the subject-specific knowledge and skills that are unique to the teaching profession.

Grossman (1990) expanded on Shulman's definition, characterizing pedagogical content knowledge as including four central components. Together, these components constitute the focus of many of the studies reviewed in this chapter. The first component Grossman identified is the teacher's overarching conception of the purposes for teaching a subject matter—what he or she knows and believes about the nature of the subject and what is important for students to learn. This overarching conception serves as a conceptual map for instructional decision-making; it serves as the basis for judgments about classroom objectives, appropriate instructional strategies and student assignments, textbooks and curricular materials, and the evaluation of student learning.

Grossman's (1990) second category is knowledge of students' understandings and potential misunderstandings of a subject area. We also include in this category knowledge and beliefs about how students learn in a particular content domain. This component of pedagogical content knowledge differs from general knowledge of learners by virtue of its focus on specific content. In the subject areas of science and mathematics, for example, researchers have identified preconceptions, misconceptions, and alternative conceptions commonly held by learners about topics such as division of fractions, negative numbers, heat energy and temperature, and photosynthesis (for a review, see Confrey, 1990). Knowing the understandings and misunderstandings about particular topics that both students in general and specific individuals bring to class is important for teachers, especially when their emphasis is on teaching for understanding rather than on mechanical or rote learning.

Grossman's third category is knowledge of curriculum and curricular materials. This component of pedagogical content knowledge includes familiarity with the range of textbooks and other instructional materials in various media that are available for teaching particular topics. It also includes knowledge of how the topics and ideas in a subject are organized and structured both horizontally (within a grade level or course) and vertically (across the kindergarten through Grade 12 curriculum).

The fourth category is the teacher's knowledge of strategies and representations for teaching particular topics. This component was the starting point for Shulman's (1986b) definition of pedagogical content knowledge and the one addressed most extensively in his work. It is also the component that has been discussed and researched to the greatest degree. The pedagogical tool that has probably received the most attention from educational researchers is the instructional representation—the model, example, metaphor, simulation, demonstration, or illustration a teacher uses to foster students' understanding of a specific topic (McDiarmid, Ball, & Anderson, 1989). Researchers have examined the extent of teachers' repertoires of powerful representations and their ability to adapt these representations in multiple ways to meet specific instructional goals for particular learners.

This framework of knowledge and beliefs for teaching provides the structure for our review of the research literature on learning to teach. Before turning to that review, however, we suggest two cautionary notes.

*Forms of Teacher Knowledge: Alternative Frames.* A potential danger inherent in any description of categories of knowledge is that people may come to see the categories as representing an actual storage system in the human mind rather than a heuristic device for helping us think about teacher knowledge. That is, we may find ourselves thinking that teachers' knowledge is organized into abstract, isolated, discrete categories, whereas in fact, what teachers know and believe is complexly intertwined, both among domains and with actions and contexts. Numerous researchers have posed alternative constructs to capture the rich contextualized nature of teachers' knowledge (see Chapter 21, this volume). Some of these ideas grow out of the movement in cognitive science toward thinking of knowledge as situated in physical and social contexts (J. S. Brown et al., 1989), or out of the movement toward acknowledging narrative forms of knowing (Bruner, 1986). This search for alternative conceptions of knowledge has led educational researchers to write about *situated knowledge* (Leinhardt, 1988), *event-structured knowledge* (Carter & Doyle, 1987), *personal practical knowledge* (Connelly & Clandinin, 1985; Elbaz, 1983), *images* (Calderhead, 1988; Clandinin, 1986), and *knowledge in action* (Schön, 1982). All of these constructs are attempts to depict teachers' knowledge about teaching in ways that pre-

serve its close connection to the practice from which it arose and in which it is used.

Although the organizational structure of this chapter does not reflect these alternative representations of knowledge, we incorporate relevant research based on these constructs into our discussions of the various domains of teacher knowledge. By doing so, we assume a certain compatibility among the different ways of representing knowledge—that it makes sense in all of them to talk about various domains or categories of teachers' knowledge and beliefs.

*Other Perspectives on Teachers' Learning and Development.* Because we chose in this chapter to focus on the role of teachers' knowledge and beliefs in learning to teach, there are other perspectives that do not receive much attention. In cognitively oriented research on teaching, some researchers have focused on the thought *processes* entailed in teaching— for example, teacher planning, judgment, decision-making, reflection, and reasoning (Borko & Shavelson, 1990; Clark & Peterson, 1986). Such processes clearly are related to teachers' knowledge and beliefs, and our discussions incorporate consideration of these thinking processes where appropriate. We do not, however, give separate attention to how teachers learn these cognitive processes or how their use of them changes over time.

Researchers in scholarly communities other than those grounded in cognitive psychology also have examined how teachers learn and change over time from a number of valuable perspectives. For example, researchers have studied how teachers' careers develop over time and the issues that teachers address in various stages of their careers (Burden, 1990; Fuller, 1969; Huberman, 1989; Oja, 1991), teachers' personal biographies and the meanings that they construct for themselves (e.g., Butt & Raymond, 1989; Trumbull, 1990), and the socialization of teachers into the cultures of schools and teaching (Zeichner & Gore, 1990). Although this work makes important contributions to our understanding of teacher change, we do not address it because of our emphasis on a cognitive psychological perspective.

## A Note on Research Methods

In writing this chapter, we attended very little to methodological issues, focusing instead on the ideas and conceptual constructs of the research. The studies we review employ a wide variety of research perspectives and methods; considering these in any detail is beyond the scope of the chapter. We do, however, want to make a few comments about research methods here.

Other published works reviewing various aspects of teachers' cognitive lives dealt more directly with research methods. For example, when Clark and Peterson (1986) reviewed research on teachers' thought processes several years ago, they described a handful of fairly specific techniques that researchers had used to study teachers' thinking, such as thinking aloud, stimulated recall, and policy capturing. At that time, the research on teaching community had just begun to move away from the quantitative research methods that dominated process–product studies of teaching, by exploring ways to incorporate more qualitative research methods while still maintaining the "objectivity" that had become the norm in research on teaching.

Since that time, researchers studying teachers' thinking, knowledge, and learning have greatly expanded both the settings of their research and the research techniques they use. Many researchers have moved toward interpretive perspectives and qualitative methods, in order to capture the richness and complexity of teachers' knowledge and belief systems and how they change. The contexts in which research is conducted have expanded to include collaborative research and research in which teachers and teacher educators study their own practice. Included in this review, for example, are a number of studies focusing on individual professors studying their own teacher education courses—courses designed to address particular problems or issues of teacher learning. Also prominent in the research we review are several large-scale education programs for practicing teachers—programs in which researchers work with teachers to support their learning and simultaneously document and study changes in the teachers' knowledge, beliefs, and practices.

Within these diverse settings, researchers have drawn on a rich array of observation and interview techniques to study teachers' knowledge, beliefs, and practices. In attempting to look at teachers' learning in new ways, many individual researchers and research groups have constructed their research techniques as part of their work, often borrowing from ethnography and other interpretive research perspectives. The result has been a number of refreshingly innovative and complex views of the learning of teachers in particular settings. In light of these trends, and in contrast to the situation that existed when Clark and Peterson (1986) wrote their review of teacher cognition, it is no longer possible to identify a set of commonly used and accepted research techniques.

The next three sections of this chapter review the research literature on learning to teach, organized around the three domains of teachers' knowledge and beliefs described earlier in this section: general pedagogical knowledge and beliefs, subject matter knowledge and beliefs, and pedagogical content knowledge and beliefs. Within each domain we examine the knowledge, beliefs, and learning of preservice teachers and then consider the same topics for experienced teachers.

# GENERAL PEDAGOGICAL KNOWLEDGE AND BELIEFS

In examining the general pedagogical knowledge and beliefs of novice teachers, we consider the general beliefs about teaching that prospective teachers bring to teacher education experiences, their conceptions of themselves as teachers, their knowledge and beliefs about learners and learning, and their knowledge and beliefs about classroom management. We also look at studies that examined the impact of courses and experiences specifically designed to change novice teachers' general pedagogical knowledge and beliefs. Because experienced teachers typically have acquired considerable expertise in general aspects of teaching, we focus primarily on resistance of their pedagogical knowledge and beliefs to change, and on efforts to help teachers rethink their general pedagogical beliefs.

## General Pedagogical Knowledge and Beliefs of Novice Teachers

Prospective teachers experience more than 10,000 hours of an "apprenticeship of observation" through their own experiences as students before entering formal teacher preparation programs (Lortie, 1975). As a result, they come to these programs equipped with sets of knowledge and beliefs about teaching and learning, teachers, and students. Such knowledge and beliefs play powerful roles in shaping what prospective teachers learn through various teacher education experiences.

*General Beliefs About Teaching.* At the most general level, a number of studies have examined prospective teachers' beliefs and expectations about teaching. In reviewing these studies, Brookhart and Freeman (1992) found that "entering teachers view the nurturing and interpersonal aspects of a teacher's role as more important than academic aspects" (p. 51). Prospective teachers report being confident and self-assured in their teaching ability, although they also express concern about how they will perform as teachers. For example, in one of a series of studies of preservice teachers' beliefs and expectations about teaching, Weinstein (1988) had elementary teacher education students who were about to begin student teaching rate various aspects of teaching for how problematic they would be for the average first-year teacher and for themselves personally. The prospective teachers consistently expected teaching tasks to be less problematic for themselves than for others, particularly in the areas of organization and management. Weinstein suggested that preservice teachers may be unrealistically optimistic about their future teaching performance, a posture that could translate into a lack of motivation to become seriously engaged in teacher preparation (see also Weinstein, 1989, 1990).

An investigation by Hoy and Woolfolk (1990) began where Weinstein left off, examining the effect of the student teaching experience on preservice teachers' orientations toward control, social problem solving, and sense of efficacy. From questionnaire data they found that student teachers became more custodial in their orientation toward pupil control and more controlling in their orientation toward social problem solving. They became less confident that teachers in general could overcome the limitations of home environments and family background. In contrast, and similar to Weinstein's findings, the student teachers became more confident in their own abilities to motivate and be effective with difficult students. A comparison group of students who were preparing to teach but had not yet enrolled in student teaching did not experience these changes in perspective.

In another series of studies on the influence of prospective teachers' knowledge and beliefs on their learning in teacher education programs, Ross and colleagues (Ross, Johnson, & Smith, 1991) examined students' experiences in the PROTEACH teacher education program. Two central goals of PROTEACH were the development of reflective judgment and mastery of the knowledge base about teaching. Activities and strategies designed to promote program goals included reflective writing, development and analysis of personal theories of teaching and learning, curriculum development and analysis, inquiry-oriented supervision, action research projects, and faculty modeling of the reflective process. Based on several studies of

PROTEACH's impact on students' reflections and actions, Ross and colleagues concluded that learning to teach is influenced by a complex array of factors, one of the most significant of which is the entering perspective of the student. Entering perspective serves as a filter that determines how experiences within the teacher education program are interpreted.

*Conceptions of Self and Teaching.* A number of researchers have studied beliefs and general orientations toward teaching by examining teachers' images of teaching and conceptions of themselves as teachers. Whereas the researchers in the work described above speak of teachers' expectations or beliefs, these researchers write about teachers' biographies, conceptions of self, and images of teaching. Their work is grounded primarily in theoretical frameworks and constructs from sociology rather than psychology, and the findings are typically interpreted within the context of the literature on teacher socialization rather than learning to teach. We include a brief examination of the work in this chapter, however, because we see the constructs of biography and image as important alternative conceptions for thinking about the knowledge and beliefs of teachers. Further, as Calderhead and Robson (1991) noted, "the notion of images has also attracted a growing interest in cognitive psychology over the past decade" (p. 3). Cognitive psychologists have increasingly turned their attention to the mental models (Gentner & Stevens, 1982), images, or metaphors (Lakoff & Johnson, 1980) that persons use to shape their thinking and action.

Bullough and Knowles (1990, 1991; Knowles, 1992) conducted a yearlong study of seven first-year teachers in which they traced changes in participants' personal identities as teachers—the metaphors and images they used to understand and describe themselves as teachers. Drawing on data from five case studies, Knowles (1992) concluded that teachers early in the participants' educational experiences were the most important role models in the formation of their images of self as teacher. In no case was the university teacher preparation experience strongly evident in the individuals' role identities as teachers or their classroom behaviors. In contrast, Knowles and Bullough found evidence to suggest that teachers' role identities can be modified by their initial teaching experiences, while at the same time affecting those experiences. The case of Barbara (Bullough & Knowles, 1991) is illustrative. Barbara began her first year of teaching with the metaphor of teacher as nurturer. She found herself spending more and more time with, and energy on, the students. By November, she was having a hard time balancing being the kind of teacher that fit her image of teacher as nurturer and a single parent to five children. As the personal costs continued to grow and become more apparent, she realized that she had to become less involved with her students, and she began to modify her image of herself as teacher. Although she did not abandon the metaphor of teacher as nurturer, "her conception of nurturing changed in subtle but significant ways, reflecting a change in her own needs and expectations for teaching" (p. 136). Like the researchers discussed earlier who found that prospective teachers' expectations and beliefs play an important role in determining how they experience teacher education, Bullough and Knowles (1991) concluded that metaphors and images of self as teacher form lenses through which prospective teachers

interpret teacher education and teaching, and help to determine their classroom practices. They suggested that teacher education programs designed to assist novice teachers make explicit, carefully analyze, and thoughtfully explore and critique the metaphors and images they bring to teaching might make initial teaching experiences easier.

A study by Calderhead and Robson (1991) of 12 primary student teachers during their first teacher preparation course confirmed the findings of Bullough, Knowles, and colleagues that prospective teachers enter preservice preparation programs with preexisting images of teaching. Calderhead and Robson, like Bullough and Knowles, also found individual differences among prospective teachers' images. The images of teaching held by some participants seemed to provide powerful organizing frameworks for their thinking about teaching. In contrast, one participant had few images. His talk about classroom practice centered on principles without a clear conception of how those principles might be put into place in a classroom.

Drawing on Calderhead's conception of images of teaching, as well as Clandinin's (1986) definition of images of teaching as one aspect of teachers' personal practical knowledge, Johnston (1992) explored the ways in which two student teachers thought about themselves as teachers and how their thinking related to their classroom practices. Both student teachers entered practice teaching with well-articulated images of teaching. Their images were highly personal in nature and were based primarily on past personal and professional experiences (both had had other careers before entering teaching). These images were linked to their classroom practices and were persistent themes in their discussions of teaching. The practice teaching experience provided an opportunity for both teachers to refine and clarify their images of teaching, and both teachers' images were modified during the course of that experience.

These three research programs suggest that novice teachers' conceptions of themselves as teachers, as represented in their images of teaching, influence the way they teach. In many cases these images can be modified by teachers' initial teaching experiences. Images of teaching can be useful in teacher preparation programs as a tool for helping novice teachers understand themselves as teachers, and scrutinize, clarify, and challenge their knowledge of teaching (Calderhead & Robson, 1991; Johnston, 1992). They can also provide teacher educators with some understanding of the nature of novice teachers' professional knowledge base (Calderhead & Robson, 1991).

Thus far, we have focused on research that shows how prospective teachers' general beliefs, expectations, and images influence their learning to teach. Other research has examined more specific aspects of new teachers' general pedagogical knowledge, particularly their knowledge and beliefs about learners and learning, and about classroom management.

*Learners and Learning.* Teachers' knowledge and beliefs about learners and how they learn are critical components of general pedagogical knowledge. Two aspects of novice teachers' knowledge and beliefs about learners and learning emerge as especially important. First, the beliefs about learners and learning promoted in many teacher education programs and reform agendas differ, sometimes markedly, from those prevalent in the schools and characteristic of many entering teachers. Because existing knowledge and beliefs exert such a strong influence on learning, and because prospective teachers often experience traditional forms of teaching during their field experiences, helping new teachers change their beliefs about how students learn so that these beliefs are more consistent with current thinking in the field can be a daunting task. Second, even though it seems difficult for new teachers to change their orientations toward learners, they do learn a lot about the children they teach, particularly during their first teaching experiences.

A number of researchers have examined preservice teachers' knowledge and beliefs about learners and learning and how these knowledge and beliefs change—or do not change—through teacher education experiences. For example, Holt-Reynolds (1992) found through interviews with nine students in a content area reading course that the beliefs they brought to teacher education, based on their personal histories, influenced their receptiveness to ideas encountered in the course. Whereas the professor promoted a student-centered, process-focused approach to classroom teaching and questioned the value of teacher telling as an instructional tool, the preservice teachers rejected his ideas based on their existing conceptions of "good" teaching, "good" subject matter classrooms, and "good" student capabilities derived largely from their own personal histories. Holt-Reynolds found the preservice teachers' arguments for rejecting their professor's ideas to be coherent, cohesive, and clearly grounded in their personal histories. She cautioned teacher educators about the apparent primacy of preservice teachers' personal history-based beliefs when they encounter new ways of teaching and thinking, and about the relative impotence of experiences in a single course to affect those beliefs.

Hollingsworth (1989) also found that prospective teachers' prior beliefs about the nature of learning influenced their learning during a fifth-year teacher education program that emphasized a constructivist or participatory view of learning. Half of the 14 participants in her study entered the program believing that student learning is accomplished primarily through teacher-directed instruction, with little active student involvement. By the end of the program, every participant believed that students actively construct their own knowledge. However, the depth of their beliefs differed, with variations corresponding to the students' previously held beliefs about how students learn in school settings. Bird (1991) made a similar point about the effects that entering preservice teachers' knowledge and beliefs can have on what they learn in teacher education programs.

These studies demonstrate both that preservice teachers' beliefs about learners and learning can change and that their existing knowledge and beliefs can influence what they learn. Other research has focused on the kinds of knowledge about learners that preservice teachers do acquire, especially through their student teaching experiences. This research highlights the important role that novice teachers' initial teaching experiences can play in learning about students. For example, Calderhead (1988) followed 10 students in the United Kingdom through a 1-year professional training course for middle school teachers. Participants reported learning a great deal about children during their field experience. Based primarily on watching the children and interacting with them, the preservice teachers could readily cite examples of new discoveries about children. They learned about children's general behavior and their responses to partic-

ular tasks, and they formulated ideas about how to present these tasks in the future to avoid confusion and misunderstanding. In an analysis of profiles of pupils written by elementary and secondary student teachers, Kagan and Tippins (1991) found that student teachers who experienced the most professional growth during the semester tended to see pupils in multifaceted terms, respond affectively to pupils, and attempt to account for pupil behavior in terms of cause-and-effect relationships. They concluded that learning about pupils is a major component of novices' learning to teach.

Ammon and his colleagues (Ammon, 1991; Levin & Ammon, 1992) argued that new teachers' thinking about how students learn and about pedagogy progresses through developmental stages. These researchers examined changes in preservice teachers' thinking about learning as they progressed through a teacher education program designed around a view of learning and development grounded in Piagetian theory. Their interview data suggest that participants' thinking about learning became more complex and integrated and more consistent with constructivist theory over the course of the program. This development continued into the teachers' initial years of classroom teaching (Levin & Ammon, 1992).

Focusing on the next phase of learning to teach, Bullough, Knowles, and Crow (1989) examined first-year teachers' learning about students. The teachers started the year with little knowledge of their students. Their initial images were formed by drawing on personal experiences with children and recalling images of themselves as young people. These images were fleshed out as they gained knowledge of the particular individuals and groups in their classes and then began to notice commonalities in their interests, concerns, and learning patterns. Bullough and colleagues argued that once teachers begin teaching, their interactions with students shape the images they form. A key developmental factor is the teachers' recognition of commonalities among students. This recognition, and the overall process of image formation, are closely linked to teachers' self-perceptions and their instructional purposes. That is, they notice characteristics of individuals and groups and respond to students in ways that are consistent with their self-perceptions as teachers.

The Teacher Education and Learning to Teach (TELT) research program, conducted by Michigan State University's National Center for Research on Teacher Education, investigated one aspect of knowledge of students—learning to teach diverse learners (Feiman-Nemser, 1990; National Center for Research on Teacher Education, 1988; 1991). An extensive study of learning to teach in teacher education programs, TELT combined case studies of teacher education programs with longitudinal studies of teachers' learning. At each of 11 sites (including preservice, induction, in-service, and alternative-route teacher education programs), researchers followed a sample of teachers as they moved through teacher education, tracking changes in their knowledge, skills, and dispositions. They focused on two subject areas—mathematics and writing—on the assumption that the contrast between the two areas would help them understand the role of subject matter in the process of learning to teach. A central intention of the study was to identify differences among learners that teachers thought they should attend to in their classrooms and teachers' ideas about how these differences influence children's learning. Although the researchers had some reservations about the reliability and validity of their data on these issues, they did identify some trends. Preservice teachers claimed that categorical differences among students—race, social class, gender—did not matter in teaching. The only differences that did matter (i.e., have a role in teaching), they thought, were individual differences such as personality characteristics. Most preservice teachers saw student diversity as a problem to be overcome or solved, rather than a feature of all classrooms. They saw individualized instruction as a solution to the problem, and they appeared uncritical of that solution. There was no evidence of substantial changes in knowledge or beliefs about diversity among student teachers in the sample. One induction program, however, did suggest some promising approaches to influencing teachers' thinking about diverse learners. In that program, learner diversity was examined within the context of teachers' own classrooms, and participants had the opportunity to think and talk about issues arising from their practice in forums with others who faced similar situations. The program seemed to strengthen participants' convictions regarding teachers' responsibility for students' failure in school, and to heighten their commitment to attending to students' uniqueness.

Across these research programs, there is evidence that prospective teachers do acquire important knowledge about students. However, limitations remain in their knowledge and beliefs about learners, at least from the perspective of current educational scholarship. These limitations often seem resistant to change through instruction and experiences in teacher education programs.

*Classroom Management.* Acquiring the knowledge and skills for managing a classroom is an especially salient task for the new teacher; many war stories of first-year teachers involve their learning how to orchestrate activities and get and keep students engaged. Research examining novice teachers' learning about classroom management supports the importance of this domain.

Student teachers in the study by Calderhead (1988) reported that they learned a great deal about classroom management during the first half of their field experience, particularly the first 2 weeks. For example, student teachers could readily cite examples of managerial tactics that they had found to work. They saw their task primarily as one of fitting into the supervising teacher's routines. They adopted timetables worked out by these teachers, as well as their procedures for carrying out different classroom activities.

Hollingsworth (1989) also found that novice teachers' learning about classroom management was influenced by their cooperating teachers, as well as their prior beliefs. Thirteen of the 14 participants in her study came into the program with the belief that classroom management is synonymous with relating equally with pupils. They shared prior beliefs about management, such as the importance of being liked by students and not being too firm with them, and the desire to be more consistent in their approach to management. Half of the participants were able to reach a more balanced managerial style; they developed cognitive scripts for management that appeared to free cognitive space for them to consider other issues such as subject matter content, the design of classroom activities, and pupil learning. Several of the other participants were unsuccessful in learning

routines for classroom management; they were also unable to concentrate on transforming subject matter knowledge for student understanding. Factors associated with successful learning included an image of self as learner and critic of teaching, an awareness of the need to change initial beliefs, a cooperating teacher or university supervisor who served as a role model and facilitator of change, and a notion of having something worth teaching.

Some researchers (Berliner, 1989; Hollingsworth, 1989; Kagan, 1992) have suggested that novice teachers need to become competent in the skills of classroom management before they can successfully turn their attention to other aspects of their teaching. Although the studies we reviewed clearly point to the importance of new teachers acquiring management skills and routines, when viewed from the perspective of current reform efforts, they also suggest some cautions. In both studies new teachers acquired the management strategies of the experienced teachers with whom they were working. To the extent that we think of the learning of new teachers as gaining the competence of the status quo—of learning to teach in traditional classrooms—this situation might be justified. If, however, we think about new teachers learning to teach in new ways, the kinds of management routines and knowledge they acquire may conflict or interfere with their instructional efforts. To understand this potential conflict, we need more systematic research on the relationship between the ways in which teachers organize and manage their classrooms and the instructional/learning aspects of their teaching.

*Teaching General Pedagogical Knowledge and Beliefs.* Drawing on their research on prospective teachers' experiences in teacher education courses, Holt-Reynolds, Hollingsworth, Bird, and Ross all suggested characteristics of teacher education experiences that might be successful in affecting preservice teachers' beliefs. Such experiences should encourage preservice teachers to share the beliefs that guide their thinking and action, identify differences between those beliefs and the principles that teacher educators want them to explore, examine the strengths and limitations of using their personal beliefs as a data source, and respect and utilize their beliefs as standards against which to judge research-based principles (Holt-Reynolds, 1992). Ross and colleagues (Ross et al., 1991) cautioned that change in beliefs or perspectives is difficult to achieve. Preservice teachers may be more likely to confront their preexisting beliefs after experiencing the disequilibrium that results from a mismatch between their beliefs and those of their cooperating teachers (Hollingsworth, 1989).

One message common to many of these studies is that, because of their prior beliefs, prospective teachers may not see the relevance of their pedagogy courses to the process of learning to teach, and they may not attend closely to the information or experiences offered by those courses. Three researchers have studied the impact of their own courses on preservice teachers' beliefs. McDiarmid (1990) and Ball (1988c) both taught sections of "Exploring Teaching," a course in Michigan State University's teacher preparation program designed specifically to challenge prospective teachers to examine their "web of beliefs" about the teacher's role, pedagogy, learning, diverse learners, subject matter, context, and learning to teach. The core of McDiarmid's section was a field experience in which students observed an experienced teacher, Deborah Ball, who taught in ways likely to challenge their beliefs, interviewed her before and after each class session, and responded in writing to questions about what they had observed. A key component of Ball's (1988c) section was a curriculum unit in which prospective teachers learned about permutations, watched a teacher (Ball) help a young child explore the concept, and then tried to help someone else (either child or adult) learn about permutations. Goals for Comeaux's (1992) "Social Foundations of Education" course included challenging students to examine their views of teaching and learning and supporting them to shift from a more positivistic to a more constructivist world view. Data collected by all three researchers suggest that when courses in pedagogy explicitly attempt to challenge preservice teachers' beliefs, changes in those beliefs can and do take place. Despite positive evidence of change, however, McDiarmid remained skeptical about the effects of such courses. He cautioned that students who are willing to reexamine their understandings and beliefs may not be prepared to transfer the lessons they learn to their own teaching. Further research is needed to address that issue.

## General Pedagogical Knowledge of Experienced Teachers

Most teachers who have spent several years in classrooms have acquired considerable general pedagogical knowledge. Research comparing experienced or expert teachers with novices (e.g., Berliner, 1988; Leinhardt & Greeno, 1986) shows that experienced teachers have developed expertise in managing their classrooms and conducting smoothly running and effective lessons. As with expertise in other fields, much of this knowledge has become automatic and intuitive. For example, Berliner and his colleagues (Berliner, 1988; Carter, Cushing, Sabers, Stein, & Berliner, 1988; Carter, Sabers, Cushing, Pinnegar, & Berliner, 1987; Sabers, Cushing, & Berliner, 1991) compared the performance of teachers identified as experts, advanced beginners (student teachers and first-year teachers who received excellent evaluations during student teaching), and novice teachers (professionals from other fields with an expressed interest in teaching but no pedagogical training) on a series of tasks simulating various aspects of teaching. One of the tasks involved watching a lesson displayed simultaneously on three video screens that showed the lesson from different camera angles. Whereas the advanced beginners and novices found the videotapes confusing and made inconsistent interpretations about what was going on, the expert teachers were quickly able to discern, interpret, and make hypotheses about such things as the motivation of the students and the nature of the ongoing activity. The expert teachers had developed the extensive and situated knowledge of classroom activities needed to interpret what they saw.

Well-practiced routines also play an important role for expert teachers, just as they do for expert surgeons, ice skaters, and other highly skilled professionals (Bloom, 1985). For example, in comparing elementary school mathematics lessons taught by an expert and by a novice teacher, Leinhardt and Greeno (1986) found that the expert had efficient routines for checking homework, hand-raising to get attention, signaling the beginning and end of various segments of lessons, and more. These well-rehearsed routines allowed lessons to flow fluidly and provided teacher and students with a framework of expectations for their actions. In contrast, the novice teacher lacked established routines, resulting in difficulties maintaining students' attention, maintaining a flow to the lesson, and getting a sense about which students were having trouble with lesson content. In the research by Berliner and colleagues (Berliner, 1988), the importance of routines was revealed both by experts' recognition of routines being used on the videotaped lessons they observed and by the difficulty and frustration they faced when teaching a short lesson on probability to a group of students they had never taught before. The expert teachers were unhappy with their lessons, in part because they did not have time to establish clear routines with students in this brief teaching encounter. As one expert said, "[T]hese kids didn't know me, and they didn't know the way that I operate, that all are supposed to participate, and why, and that they're all supposed to be on task [constantly]" (Berliner, 1988).

These studies comparing expert and novice teachers highlight the importance of having rich knowledge and well-rehearsed routines for managing the classroom and conducting lessons, and being able quickly and automatically to interpret classroom events and act accordingly. Berliner (1988) argued that teachers acquiring this expertise progress through five stages paralleling the development of expertise in other domains: novice, advanced beginner, competent, proficient, and expert. Berliner emphasized the importance of classroom experience and practice in gaining the automaticity that characterizes the knowledge and skill of teachers at the higher stages. His model is an important reminder that expertise is not acquired overnight and that becoming proficient in teaching requires large amounts of practice and experience.

Berliner has used his model primarily to describe expertise in fairly generic aspects of classroom teaching such as classroom management. Pedagogical knowledge and skills of this sort are indisputably important aspects of teaching. Much of the research on effective teaching conducted within the process–product paradigm focused on identifying and improving the generic teaching skills and behaviors of experienced teachers (see Brophy & Good, 1986, and Rosenshine & Stevens, 1986, for reviews).

Most process–product research, expert–novice studies, and other research examining teachers' acquisition of general pedagogical skills—especially the routines of classroom management—have taken expert traditional teaching as their vision of good teaching. These investigations help show what skills and knowledge new teachers must acquire to be proficient at teaching in the traditional modes that currently predominate in schools. Berliner's (1988) model can be seen as proposing stages in moving toward this kind of expertise. This learning on the part of teachers is supported by their long "apprenticeships of observation," discussed earlier in the context of novice teachers: New teachers form their initial routines and ways of perceiving classroom events based largely on their past experiences in classrooms, and they practice and refine these skills and routines until they become fluid and automatic. Recently, however, researchers and reformers have been calling for changes away from these traditional modes of teaching. Much of the recent research on teachers' learning has focused on how teachers can be supported in changing the way they teach.

There are two important things to note here. First, much of the research on teaching and teacher learning has shifted away from the generic knowledge and skills that make up general pedagogical knowledge, especially the management aspects of classroom teaching, and toward subject matter–specific aspects of teaching. Hence, most of the research on experienced teachers learning to teach in new ways that we discuss in this chapter focuses on subject matter–specific aspects of knowledge and beliefs and is addressed in subsequent sections of the chapter.

The second point concerns the routines and other automatic knowledge that make up much of experienced teachers' general pedagogical knowledge. Although this situated and largely implicit knowledge is indisputably important for skilled teaching, the same well-rehearsed routines and ways of interpreting classroom events that allow the efficient and fluid performance of expert teachers can serve as impediments to changes in teaching. When routines have become automatic, teachers may continue to use them even if they conflict or interfere with other changes they are trying to make. For example, an important part of changing instruction to make it more intellectually challenging is changing the kinds of interactions teachers and students have around subject matter content. Because classroom interactions, like all conversations, are partly determined by routines and conventions for interacting (Cazden, 1986), changing some of these routines is an important part of changing the nature of instruction (e.g., National Council of Teachers of Mathematics, 1991). It may be important for experienced teachers seeking major changes in their teaching practices to find ways to step back and consider their existing routines and the knowledge and beliefs that underlie them. In the remainder of this section on the general pedagogical knowledge and beliefs of experienced teachers, we consider some of the attempts to encourage teachers to reconsider their general approaches to teaching.

*Reconsidering Existing Knowledge, Beliefs, and Practices.* Researchers studying teachers' use of new curricula and instructional practices have long been concerned that teachers often adapt and change these recommended practices as they implement them (e.g., McLaughlin, 1987; Richardson, 1990). Although policymakers and curriculum developers are likely to view these changes as distortions of the intent of the new practices or curriculum, they can just as well be viewed as adaptations by teachers to the particular context of the classroom and students being taught. What is increasingly clear is that whenever teachers set out to adopt a new curriculum or instructional technique, they learn about and use the innovation through the lenses of their existing knowledge, beliefs, and practices (Cohen & Ball, 1990b; Putnam et al., 1992; Richardson, 1990). Vivid examples of this filtering of new ideas through existing knowledge, beliefs, and practices—the interplay between innovative practices and teachers' current practices and contexts—are provided by a set of case studies of teachers responding to California's recent efforts to encourage major changes in the way mathematics is taught in elementary schools (Cohen & Ball, 1990a; Prawat, Remillard, Putnam, & Heaton, 1992). The cases are part of the California Study of Elementary Mathematics, a program of research exploring relationships among state-level policies, district-level activities, and the thinking and classroom practices of elementary schoolteachers (Co-

hen & Ball, 1990a, 1990b; Peterson, 1990). One of the teachers studied arranged her second-grade students into small groups in response to calls by her state and district to make more use of cooperative learning (Cohen, 1990). Although the physical arrangement of students changed, however, instructional discourse in the classroom continued to consist of exchanges between the teacher and individual students or between the teacher and the whole class. Students were discouraged from interacting directly with one another, and the small groups played no distinctive instructional role. This teacher's use of cooperative groups thus was shaped by her existing beliefs and practices for interacting with students.

Schreiter and Ammon (1989) similarly found that for experienced teachers learning about and beginning to use literature contracts in their elementary classrooms, the teachers' existing ways of thinking about learners and pedagogy strongly influenced the ways in which they adapted the new instructional techniques. The teachers, who learned about literature contracts in an in-service workshop, transformed the concept and techniques of literature contracts to match their current teaching practices. Schreiter and Ammon, using language from a Piagetian developmental framework, referred to this adaptation of instructional practices in terms of the teacher's existing perspectives as *assimilation*, with *accommodation* referring to the accompanying changes in the teachers' thinking.

Researchers, teacher educators, and policymakers are increasingly arguing that for teachers to make meaningful changes in their instructional practices, they must become more reflective about their practices in ways that make their knowledge and beliefs about pedagogy and learners more explicit, and they must be more willing to reconsider their practices on the basis of these reflections (e.g., Clift, Houston, & Pugach, 1990; Schön, 1991). Fenstermacher and Richardson (1993) proposed that one way to encourage teachers to reconsider their existing practices in light of new ideas, particularly ideas from the research literature, is to engage them in reconstructing the *practical arguments* for their pedagogical actions. Practical arguments are formal statements of a person's reasoning about actions; they describe the rationales, empirical support, and situational contexts that serve as premises for actions. Using practical argument as the basis for staff development entails having teachers make explicit their reasons for various instructional actions (i.e., their premises). Teachers then reconsider these premises through interaction with knowledgeable others. This approach values teachers' practical knowledge; at the same time, it helps teachers make more explicit and reconsider their knowledge, beliefs, and practices.

Teachers who participated in a practical argument-based staff development program as part of the Reading Improvement Study (Richardson & Anders, 1994; Richardson, Anders, Tidwell, & Lloyd, 1991) exhibited changes in their theories of reading, learning to read, and teaching reading; in their beliefs about reading comprehension; and in their reading instructional practices. For example, many teachers moved toward a broader, deeper, and more cognitively oriented definition of reading comprehension. Changes in practice included less reliance on basal readers, use of more prereading practices, and integration of literature into other subjects.

In our consideration of preservice teachers' general pedagogical knowledge and beliefs we pointed out that their knowledge and beliefs about learners and learning seemed critically important in efforts to help them teach in ways that break from tradition to focus more on student understanding. Knowledge and beliefs about learners and learning have also emerged as critically important in efforts to help experienced teachers learn to teach in new ways. A growing body of research suggests that lasting and meaningful changes in teaching practices must be accompanied by changes in the fairly fundamental beliefs that teachers hold about the nature of learners and the learning process. Whereas traditional pedagogies are grounded in a view of learning as a process of mastering presented information and skills through practice, most current reform efforts are grounded in a *cognitive-mediational* conception of learning as a student-mediated process and learners as active problem solvers who construct their own knowledge (L. M. Anderson, 1989c).

Work with teachers that has been successful in changing their views about learners and learning has entailed helping them rethink their teaching in particular subject matter domains (e.g., Carpenter, Fennema, Peterson, Chiang, & Loef, 1989; D. C. Smith & Neale, 1991; Wood, Cobb, & Yackel, 1991). Although there are similarities in the views of learning being promoted for the teaching of various subject matter domains (e.g., viewing students as actively determining their own learning, the importance of attending carefully to students' thinking), it is not clear whether changes in teachers' beliefs about learners and learning generalize across domains.

Wood, Cobb, and Yackel (1990) explored this issue in a case study of a second-grade teacher with whom they worked collaboratively to make fundamental changes in the nature of her mathematics instruction. The researchers began working with this teacher to create a classroom environment where instruction would be compatible with constructivist views of knowledge, in order to study children's construction of mathematical knowledge in a classroom setting. They did not intend to explore the teacher's learning (Cobb, Wood, & Yackel, 1990). As the collaborative team worked together, however, the teacher experienced profound changes in her thinking about students' learning of mathematics and her role as a facilitator of that learning. She came to view students as possessing much richer mathematical knowledge and being more capable of solving problems on their own than she had previously assumed. And she reconceptualized her role in teaching mathematics away from being an authority transmitting mathematical knowledge to one of being "actively involved with students' learning by negotiating mathematical meanings with them" (Wood et al., 1990, p. 502). Wood et al. found virtually no evidence of similar changes in the teacher's views and practices in the teaching of reading. Despite the fairly profound changes taking place in how she viewed learners and her role in teaching mathematics, the teacher continued to view the learning of reading primarily as a matter of practicing skills and knowledge modeled and presented by the teacher. The changes in her views of learners and learning in mathematics apparently did not generalize to her teaching of reading.

Wood and colleagues offered three potential reasons for the lack of change in the teacher's belief and practices in reading. First, they argued that significant changes in a teacher's knowledge or beliefs will occur only when the teacher sees something problematic in his or her own practices. Working collaboratively with the researchers in mathematics gave rise to the teacher's realization that her students were not understanding mathematics in the ways that she had assumed, giving her reason to try to change her mathematics teaching. There was no similar event in reading to cause the teacher to question the effectiveness of her pedagogical beliefs and practices. Wood et al.'s second explanation was that the instructional activities they developed together for teaching mathematics gave rise to multiple learning opportunities for the teacher because the activities encouraged students to express rich and varied mathematical thinking. The instructional activities in the basal reading textbook provided few such opportunities for students to express their thinking, and hence few opportunities for teacher questioning and learning. Third, the goals of instruction dictated by the prevailing school practices and culture (including testing and accountability) reinforced the teacher's traditional views of learning to read, whereas in mathematics, the collaborative research project, with its emphasis on the meanings of mathematics that children were constructing, removed most of the external press to cover particular material in prescribed ways and at a particular pace.

In contrast to the teacher with whom Wood and colleagues worked, Ball and Rundquist (1993) reported that Rundquist's teaching changed in subject areas beyond mathematics as a result of her collaborative work with Ball. Ball taught mathematics on a regular basis for several years in Rundquist's third-grade classroom, and the two educators developed a collaborative relationship that included extensive discussions about students, content, curriculum, learning, and teaching. In addition, Rundquist watched Ball's teaching, keeping notes and questions about the mathematics learning and teaching she observed. In the course of these years of collaboration Rundquist

found herself changing the way she interacted with students in other subject areas, especially science and language arts. She began questioning her reliance on the basal reading text and turned increasingly to children's literature. She found herself asking students about their thinking more often, and she noticed that she often followed their ideas rather than sticking to what she had planned. (p. 28)

Thus, in Rundquist's case, changes in beliefs about learners and learning in one subject area—mathematics—did lead to related shifts in other domains. As more teachers attempt changes in how they teach various subjects, we will have additional opportunities to explore the generalizability across domains of changes in teachers' knowledge, beliefs, and practices.

## Summary: General Pedagogical Knowledge and Beliefs

In this section we have considered a number of aspects of the general pedagogical knowledge and beliefs of novice and experienced teachers. Prospective teachers' knowledge and beliefs about teaching, learning, and learners are shaped by years of their own school experience and can be highly resistant to change. The ways in which prospective teachers make sense of and value their teacher education experiences are considerably influenced by the preexisting beliefs, expectations, and images they bring to their classes and field experiences. Experienced teachers' attempts to learn to teach in new ways also are highly influenced by what they already know and believe about teaching, learning, and learners. For example, experienced teachers have much routinized knowledge about how to conduct lessons and manage classrooms that can, at times, impede their efforts to reflect on their own practices, to see things in new ways, or to learn new instructional approaches. And although some efforts to help teachers change their beliefs about learners and how they learn have been successful in particular subject matter domains, there is mixed evidence as to whether these changes in perspective are likely to spread to other domains.

## KNOWLEDGE AND BELIEFS ABOUT SUBJECT MATTER

Early studies of teaching failed to establish systematic relationships between teachers' subject matter knowledge and their students' learning (Byrne, 1983; General Accounting Office, 1984; School Mathematics Study Group, 1972). These studies, however, have been criticized for their limited definitions of teachers' knowledge (e.g., number of university-level courses taken, college grade point average, teacher test scores; see Fennema & Franke, 1992). In contrast, recent research, which includes more in-depth analysis of subject matter knowledge, has documented some of the important ways that teachers' knowledge of the subjects they teach shapes their instructional practices. Numerous studies have revealed differences in the focus and style of instruction associated with differences in the depth and character of content knowledge of both beginning and experienced teachers. After reviewing several of these studies, particularly ones dealing with novice teachers' subject matter knowledge, we examine research on what preservice and novice teachers know of the subjects they are preparing to teach and what they appear to learn from teacher education experiences. We then examine research on the role of experienced teachers' subject matter knowledge in learning to teach in new ways.

### Role of Subject Matter Knowledge in Teaching

Numerous teacher educators have argued that teaching in accord with current reform efforts' emphasis on understanding and use of knowledge requires teachers to have rich and flexible knowledge of the subjects they teach. To help students come to understand important ideas in a discipline, teachers need to understand not only the facts, procedures, and concepts they teach, but also something about how these ideas are related to other ideas in the discipline—in other words the substantive structure of the discipline (C. W. Anderson, 1989; McDiarmid et al., 1989). Schifter and Fosnot (1993), for example, have argued that to teach mathematics for understanding, "teachers must have an understanding of the mathematical concepts they are charged with teaching, including a sense of the connections that link these concepts to one another and to relevant physical contexts" (p. 13). Others have emphasized the importance of teachers knowing *about* the disciplines they are teaching (i.e., syntactic structure) to help prepare students for learning on their own, and for critically judging the knowledge claims of others (e.g., Ball, 1991; McDiarmid, 1994). To the extent that teachers teach by trying to build on the current thinking and problem-solving efforts of individual students or groups of stu-

dents, an even richer knowledge of subject matter may be required, for teachers must be prepared to see connections between what students are thinking and important ideas within the discipline—to know which ideas to follow up on and how to guide students' thinking in productive directions (Schifter & Fosnot, 1993; Simon & Brobeck, 1989).

A number of studies have suggested that, in general, teachers with greater subject matter knowledge tend to emphasize the conceptual, problem-solving, and inquiry aspects of their subjects. Less knowledgeable teachers tend to emphasize facts, rules, and procedures and to stick closely to detailed lesson plans or the text, sometimes missing opportunities to focus on important ideas or connections among ideas. Ball (1988a) and Wilson (1988), for example, found that student teachers with deeper knowledge of their subjects (math and history) placed more emphasis on conceptual explanations and more often drew connections among topics within the curriculum than did their colleagues with less deep knowledge. The Knowledge Growth in a Profession project, conducted by Shulman and colleagues at Stanford University (Grossman, Wilson, & Shulman, 1989; Shulman & Grossman, 1987), focused on preservice teachers' subject matter knowledge and how they learned to transform that knowledge into representations and forms of presentation that make sense to students. The participants were 20 student teachers representing the subject areas of English, social studies, biology, and mathematics. Twelve of the participants were followed into their first year of full-time teaching. In-depth interviews addressing the preservice teachers' knowledge of their subject areas, combined with observations of lessons during student teaching, revealed relationships between the teachers' subject matter knowledge and teaching practices similar to patterns reported by Ball and Wilson. For example, novice mathematics teachers with greater subject matter knowledge were more likely to see problem solving as central to mathematics instruction and to emphasize a conceptual approach to teaching. In comparison with teachers with much less mathematical knowledge, they gave more explanations about why certain procedures do or do not work, conveyed the nature of mathematics to students by addressing the relationships among concepts and showing applications of the material studied, presented material in a more abstract form, and engaged students more in problem-solving activities (Steinberg, Haymore, & Marks, 1985). Similarly, science teachers with greater subject matter knowledge were more likely to stress the importance of scientific inquiry in their teaching. Their personal knowledge of the scientific method, gained through research experience, was reflected in their beliefs that teaching science means teaching inquiry (Baxter, Richert, & Saylor, 1985). Stein, Baxter, and Leinhardt (1990) found similar influences of subject matter knowledge in an analysis of a sequence of lessons on functions and graphing taught by an experienced fifth-grade teacher. The teacher's knowledge was organized in a superficial way that did not include deep connections among ideas and was missing several key mathematical ideas. These limitations led to an overemphasis on rules and procedures and missed opportunities for fostering meaningful connections among key concepts and representations.

Looking across subject areas in the Knowledge Growth in a Profession project, Grossman et al. (1989) noted that novice teachers sometimes try to avoid teaching materials they do not know well. When they cannot avoid teaching the unfamiliar, they may rely heavily on the textbook and stick closely to detailed lesson plans. Hashweh (1987) found that student teachers teaching outside areas of their own expertise tended to treat material in science textbooks mechanically and missed errors in the text.

Carlsen (1987, 1989, 1991) analyzed the classroom discourse during lessons on topics for which student teachers had high versus low subject matter knowledge. When teaching topics on which they had high knowledge, teachers asked fewer questions but a greater proportion of higher order questions. They tended to talk less of the time and for shorter periods of time. Students talked more, asked more questions, volunteered to speak more, and spoke in longer discourse sequences. With respect to the substance of their discourse, teachers devoted less time to anecdotes, stories, and announcements unrelated to the scientific content of the lesson when teaching topics on which their knowledge was high. They were more likely to talk about aspects of the topic that were not discussed in the textbook, and they drew more connections among topics. Instructional strategies also varied with level of subject matter knowledge. A comparison of lesson plans from the three highest knowledge and three lowest knowledge units revealed that teachers were more likely to conduct whole-class recitations when teaching units on which they had high knowledge. They were more likely to use activity types such as laboratory activities and group projects when teaching units on which their knowledge was low. Carlsen (1989) characterized the former instructional strategies as "conversationally risky" and the latter as "conversationally safe."

The disciplinary perspectives and prior knowledge that novices bring to teaching also affect their instructional practices. Wilson and Wineburg (1988) found that the disciplinary perspectives associated with novice social studies teachers' academic majors influenced their conceptions of history and the ways in which they organized both their own knowledge and the classes they taught. Jane, a history major, and Bill, an American Studies major, used historical frameworks to organize their knowledge. In contrast, Fred's knowledge of political science and Cathy's knowledge of anthropology dominated the organization and structure of both their own knowledge and their respective classes.

Taken together, these studies support the claim that teachers must have rich and flexible subject matter knowledge to teach in ways compatible with educational reform efforts (e.g., in ways that emphasize understanding, reasoning, and connections among ideas). We now turn to research exploring the nature of novice teachers' subject matter knowledge and the extent to which it achieves this goal.

## Novice Teachers' Subject Matter Knowledge and Beliefs

In considering novice teachers' knowledge and beliefs about subject matter, we first examine what they typically know of the content and substantive structures of the disciplines. We then consider what they know and believe *about* the subjects they teach—their syntactic knowledge of the disciplines. Finally, we look at how the knowledge and beliefs of novice

teachers do and do not change as a result of various learning opportunities in their teacher preparation programs.

*Content and Substantive Structures.* Much of the research on prospective teachers' subject matter knowledge has focused on their knowledge of content and substantive structures—what they know of the central facts, concepts, and principles within a discipline and the relationships among them, as well as the discipline's key explanatory frameworks and paradigms. Results are not particularly optimistic: "Unfortunately, considerable evidence suggests that many prospective teachers, both elementary and secondary, do not understand their subjects in depth" (McDiarmid et al., 1989, p. 199).

The most extensive set of evidence comes from the TELT—Teacher Education and Learning to Teach—research program. In the area of mathematics, TELT researchers (Ball, 1988b, 1990a, 1990b; National Center for Research on Teacher Education, 1991) found that incoming students in teacher education had weak understandings of several elementary mathematics topics (e.g., place value, division, fractions, zero, relationship between area and perimeter). For example, their knowledge of division seemed to be founded more on memorization than on conceptual understanding. Although most entering preservice teachers were able to perform the algorithm for division of fractions correctly, only 20 percent of the elementary school teaching candidates and 38 percent of the secondary school teaching candidates were able to identify a correct meaning of division of fractions. Even fewer were able to generate an appropriate representation illustrating what it might mean to divide by a fraction. The entering preservice teachers' responses also showed almost no evidence of an understanding of the connectedness of topics in mathematics. Based on these findings, Ball argued that prospective teachers' understanding of the principles underlying mathematical procedures is not adequate for teaching. Also, their knowledge of mathematics is not sufficiently connected to enable them to break away from the common approach to teaching and learning mathematics by compartmentalizing topics. These findings and conclusions are supported by Simon's (1993) study of prospective elementary teachers' knowledge of division.

Simon and Blume (1994a, 1994b, in press) also found limitations in prospective teachers' mathematical understandings in their Construction of Elementary Mathematics (CEM) project. The project was a 3-year study of the mathematical and pedagogical development of 26 prospective elementary schoolteachers. Participants were enrolled in an experimental teacher preparation program based on social-constructivist views of mathematics learning and designed to increase their mathematical knowledge and foster their development of views of mathematics, learning, and teaching consistent with current reform efforts. They began the program with poor conceptual understandings of mathematical ideas such as ratio and area of rectangular regions. In addition to these projects focusing on mathematics, similar findings have been reported in the subject areas of physics (Clement, 1982) and history (Wilson, 1988).

*Syntactic Structures.* Researchers have also studied prospective teachers' knowledge of the syntactical structures of their disciplines, the canons of evidence and proof used to guide inquiry in a field. Ball (1988a, 1990a) found that prospective teachers often enter teacher preparation with naive conceptions of mathematics as an abstract, mechanical, and meaningless series of symbols and rules to be memorized. They understand little about mathematical reasoning, and they look to experts (e.g., the teacher and text) as authorities for establishing mathematical truth. Simon and Blume (in press) similarly found that several students in the CEM mathematics course relied on external authority to justify responses to mathematical problems. Others relied on inductive empirical justification (e.g., identifying patterns in concrete examples without asking why the patterns existed). Few provided deductive justifications based on mathematical knowledge shared within their learning community.

In the Knowledge Growth in a Profession project, Grossman et al. (1989) noted tremendous variation in beginning teachers' knowledge of the syntactic structures of their disciplines. For example, participants' disciplinary perspectives influenced their views of the roles of factual knowledge, evidence, and interpretation in history (Wilson & Wineburg, 1988). Cathy (anthropology) saw interpretation and evidence as fused, viewed understanding and interpreting the past primarily as a search for archaeological evidence, and believed that interpretation should stick closely to physical evidence. In contrast, Jane (history) saw history as both narrative and interpretation and viewed interpretation as central to the processes of historical inquiry. From her perspective, interpretation went far beyond evidence. As she explained, "The making of history, the task of the historian, involves very clear thinking about argument and logic, about evidence, about how to split hairs sensibly" (p. 528). In contrast to both Cathy and Jane, Fred (political science), although he recognized the importance of interpretation in social science, viewed history as limited to facts and interpretation as the purview of political scientists. "I think knowing history is the basic facts of what happened. . . . [Y]ou don't ask how it happened. You just ask, 'What are the events?' " (p. 529). He looked to politics and economics for evidence to support interpretations of historical events.

Grossman (1991b) similarly reported differences in the views regarding evidence and interpretation held by novice English teachers in the Knowledge Growth in a Profession project. Colleen, who held bachelor's and master's degrees in English and entered teaching because of her love of the subject matter, saw the text as central to the interpretation of literature. Evidence for one's interpretation must lie within the text and students should provide details from the text to support their explanations and opinions. Although Martha also held a bachelor's degree in English, she came to it by way of engineering and then political science. She entered teaching because of her love of students. Martha encouraged students to draw connections between the text, their own experiences, and their ideas about human nature. From her perspective, the meaning of a text was based on the reader's personal and subjective interpretation. Comparable variations were observed in novice science teachers' views of the nature and role of scientific inquiry (Baxter et al., 1985).

*Learning and Teaching of Subject Matter Knowledge.* Research evidence on the extent to which subject matter knowledge is or can be learned during preservice teacher preparation programs is mixed. At one extreme, researchers in the TELT project found that few of the prospective teachers in the teacher education programs they studied—either elementary or secondary—increased or deepened their understanding of mathematics or their beliefs about the nature of mathematics during preservice teacher education (National Center for Research on Teacher Education, 1991). Many prospective teachers completed their programs still seeing mathematics as a body of rules and having difficulty with ideas such as place value and division of fractions.

A similar lack of change in preservice teachers' knowledge of mathematics was found in the Learning to Teach Mathematics project. This research program examined the process of becoming a middle school mathematics teacher by following a small number of novice teachers through their final year of teacher preparation and first year of teaching (Borko et al., 1992; Eisenhart et al., 1993). The primary goal of the project was to understand and describe participants' knowledge, beliefs, thinking and actions related to the teaching of mathematics over the 2-year course of the study. Additional goals were to describe and explain the contexts for learning to teach created by the novice teachers' university teacher education experiences and their experiences in the public schools where they student-taught and held their first teaching jobs. Ms. Daniels, the prospective teacher who was the focus of the project's initial case study analysis, demonstrated only superficial understanding of division of fractions throughout her final year of teacher preparation. Although she appeared to gain some additional understanding of division during her mathematics methods course, she remained unable to construct coherent explanations or powerful representations, even away from the pressures of the classroom. At the same time, Daniels believed that her knowledge of mathematics was adequate for teaching. This belief interfered with a recognition that she did not have the content knowledge necessary to teach for student understanding, at least for some topics (Borko et al., 1992).

There is also evidence, however, that preservice teachers can learn about the subjects they are preparing to teach. Shulman and colleagues (Grossman et al., 1989; Shulman & Grossman, 1987) reported that almost all of the participants in their Knowledge Growth in a Profession project experienced growth in their subject matter knowledge as a result of teaching and preparing to teach. Participants noted that they often needed to review content as they prepared to teach so that they could understand particular topics well enough to explain them to students. Further, because the match between a college major and the secondary school curriculum is far from perfect, on many occasions the novice teachers learned new content as they prepared to teach. English teachers taught works of literature that were new to them. Mathematics teachers taught topics they had not studied since high school. And, in science and social studies, where the match between college major and secondary school curriculum is likely to be poorest, participants found themselves preparing to teach material they had never studied themselves.

Lederman and Gess-Newsome (1991) also reported some amount of change in preservice secondary biology teachers' knowledge of biology during their final year of teacher preparation. Lists and diagrams of biology topics, generated four times during the year, indicated that participants did not have a coherent structure for thinking about the discipline, even by the conclusion of their university course work. Although the format of their diagrams remained relatively constant, changes such as an increase in the number of terms included and better integration were observed. In addition, participants reported that their conceptions of the meaning of the structures changed.

A few studies of specific courses or series of courses about mathematics and mathematics teaching have demonstrated that prospective teachers can be supported in changing their beliefs about the nature of mathematics and in learning more mathematics for teaching. One of the teacher education programs studied by TELT—Learning to Teach Mathematics in Innovative Mathematics and Methods Courses—made a significant difference in participants' subject matter knowledge. This preservice program for elementary schoolteachers focused specifically on mathematics teaching (Schram, Wilcox, Lappan, & Lanier, 1989; Wilcox, Schram, Lappan, & Lanier, 1990). The program emphasized helping prospective teachers rethink the nature of mathematics and how it is learned, and facilitated their learning of particular mathematical content. The program was successful in getting the prospective teachers to change their views about mathematics. Students entered the first course with a traditional view of mathematics as an abstract, mechanical, and meaningless series of symbols and rules. By the end of the course, most students were beginning to question that view and to appreciate the value of a conceptual understanding of mathematics. For their own learning, they were beginning to value a learning environment organized around problem solving, group work, and opportunities to talk about mathematics. By the end of the second year, there were significant changes in participants' beliefs about themselves as learners of mathematics, what it means to know mathematics, and how mathematics is learned. For example, the prospective teachers showed a growing conceptual orientation to the study of mathematics (Schram & Wilcox, 1988; Wilcox et al., 1990).

Similarly, Civil (1992) taught a course that was successful in changing novice teachers' knowledge and beliefs about mathematics. Eight preservice elementary teachers were enrolled in the summer course. Civil's goals were to develop the students' beliefs that they could do mathematics and that they could develop their own ways of tackling mathematics tasks. Students spent most of their time in class engaged in doing mathematics tasks in small groups. They made progress in the ways they went about doing mathematics. They also showed growth as reflective learners about what it means to do mathematics, gave clear signs of enjoying doing mathematics, and were insightful in their comments, contrasting their experience in the course with their previous experiences learning mathematics.

Simon and Blume (1994a) also reported changes in the mathematical understandings of participants in the CEM project, such as more complete understandings of the area of a rectangular region as a multiplicative relationship between the lengths of its sides. Their research suggests that as preservice teachers study a small number of mathematical topics in depth, their understanding of the nature of mathematics and their mathematical problem-solving strategies increase, and they may become able to learn new mathematical content more quickly. These studies of prospective teachers' learning in courses about mathematics and mathematics teaching suggest that organizing such courses around problem solving, group work, and opportunities to talk about mathematics can result in changes in the participants' understandings of what it means to know mathematics and how mathematics is learned, as well as improving their substantive knowledge of mathematics content.

Thus far in this section we have focused on what prospective teachers learn about subject matter in courses intended specifically for teachers. It is widely assumed, however, that it is in courses outside of schools of education–disciplinary courses in university humanities and science departments—that teachers can and should gain the subject matter knowledge they need to teach successfully. Evidence for what prospective teachers (and other undergraduates) actually learn in such disciplinary courses is sketchy. McDiarmid (1994) has argued that, despite evidence that undergraduates accumulate knowledge as they take courses in those disciplines (Pascarella & Terenzini, 1991), we know very little about the sorts of understandings of central ideas in the discipline and knowledge *about* the discipline (i.e., syntactic knowledge) that students develop in academic course work. C. W. Anderson (1989) has argued that there is a mismatch between the goals of the professors in many academic courses—to explain facts and concepts and to socialize students into particular disciplines—and the need for prospective teachers to develop richer knowledge of the structure and functions of disciplinary knowledge and how it typically develops in individuals. It appears that prospective teachers typically have few opportunities to gain, either in education courses or in humanities and science courses, the sorts of rich and flexible knowledge *of* and *about* subject matter they need to teach successfully for understanding.

This set of studies of novice teachers' subject matter knowledge suggests that prospective teachers enter teacher preparation programs with widely different subject matter backgrounds and leave the programs with different degrees of content knowledge, substantive knowledge, and syntactic knowledge of their disciplines. These differences influence how they represent their disciplines to students, what and how they teach, and how they use textbooks and other instructional tools. There is limited evidence that the components of subject matter knowledge change as the result of participation in some teacher preparation programs.

## Experienced Teachers' Subject Matter Knowledge

For experienced teachers, the issue of subject matter knowledge comes up frequently in the context of discussions about improving the quality of instruction. Numerous writers have argued that the ambitious teaching being sought in current reform efforts requires richer and more flexible understandings of subject matter than many teachers have (C. A. Brown & Borko, 1992; Cohen, 1989; Roth, Anderson, & Smith, 1986). For example, teaching that emphasizes student understanding, reasoning, and problem solving often entails moving away from preestablished instructional activities in textbooks and being more responsive to the thinking of students. As we suggested earlier, these sorts of changes require that teachers be prepared to make connections between students' diverse ideas and important ideas in the discipline, and to help nurture and guide the development of students' thinking. Fennema and Franke (1992) found that a primary schoolteacher's instruction on addition and subtraction—a domain the teacher understood well—was more responsive to students' thinking, more oriented toward problem solving, and facilitated greater student learning than the same teacher's instruction on fractions, which she understood less well. Case studies by Heaton (1992) and Putnam (1992a) documented difficulties resulting from teachers' weak knowledge of the mathematics they and their students encountered as they attempted to move away from textbook-based activities and toward more situated and meaningful problems and activities.

Although many writers have argued for the importance of rich subject matter knowledge, surprisingly little research has focused on efforts to improve practicing teachers' subject matter knowledge per se. The lack of explicit studies of teachers' subject matter knowledge may be due in part to the sensitive nature of this issue. Because it is implicitly assumed that teachers should understand the content they teach, asking questions that may reveal weaknesses in their knowledge can be quite threatening. Few researchers want to put teachers, especially those with whom they have developed collaborative working relationships, on the spot by asking them questions that might make them feel inadequate. Nor do they want to cast teachers, whose work and grounded knowledge they respect deeply, in a negative light. As a result, questions directly assessing subject matter knowledge often are not asked. Or researchers cast their questions about subject matter in terms of students' understandings or instructional representations—aspects of pedagogical content knowledge that are highly interrelated with subject matter knowledge per se. We review research that has taken this approach later in the chapter.

Three studies that did look explicitly at experienced teachers' subject matter knowledge were conducted by D. C. Smith and Neale (1991), Krajcik, Layman, Starr, and Magnusson (1991), and Schifter and Simon (1992; Simon & Schifter, 1991; see also Schifter & Fosnot, 1993). These researchers assumed that improving teachers' ability to teach science and mathematics with an emphasis on understanding requires deepening the teachers' knowledge of these subject areas. All three studies looked at changes in teachers' subject matter knowledge and pedagogical content knowledge that occurred during intensive summer professional development experiences.

In the University of Maryland Middle School Probeware Project, conducted by Krajcik and colleagues (Krajcik et al., 1991), middle school teachers participated in two intensive 3-week workshops on using microcomputer-based laboratory equipment and procedures to teach temperature and heat energy concepts to middle school students. The workshops were held during two consecutive summers. Their primary goals were to strengthen the participating teachers' understanding of temperature and heat energy (content knowledge) and their pedagogical content knowledge for teaching these concepts. Krajcik et al. assessed the teachers' subject matter knowledge and pedagogical content knowledge through a series of semistructured interviews before and after the workshops. They analyzed each teacher's responses by forming them into propositions and concept maps (Novak & Gowin, 1984; Pines & Novak, 1985) with which they could represent change in the teacher's understanding over time. The concept maps revealed that, before the workshop, the teachers held partial or alternative (incorrect) conceptions of temperature and heat energy. For example, they tended to view temperature as a measure of heat energy instead of a measure of hotness or coldness. As a result of their participa-

tion in the workshops, most of the teachers gained more accepted understandings of temperature, distinguishing it from heat energy. Most of the teachers, however, failed to develop richer understandings of the more difficult heat energy concept. Krajcik et al. interpreted these findings as supporting the value of intensive work focused on teachers' own conceptual understanding, as well as their belief that relatively complete scientific understanding, although desirable, will be developed by teachers only over long periods of time.

D. C. Smith and Neale (1991) similarly found teachers to have weak understandings of scientific concepts they were being asked to teach and met with mixed success in increasing teachers' understandings through intensive workshops. These researchers studied changes in primary schoolteachers' knowledge in a project centered around a four-week summer program on teaching about light and shadows from a conceptual change perspective. They focused on changes in the teachers' substantive knowledge about light and shadow (subject matter knowledge), as well as their knowledge and beliefs about teaching science and their knowledge of children's ideas (pedagogical content knowledge). During the summer program, teachers read literature on children's misconceptions about light and shadow, conducted clinical interviews with students, participated in activities organized around their own knowledge about light and shadows, and taught small groups of children in a morning summer camp. They also planned units on light and shadow that they taught in their own classrooms the following school year. During that school year, the teachers met monthly with researchers.

Smith and Neale collected a variety of data for this study, including videotapes of lessons taught before and after the summer program and interviews about content and teaching practices. They found that, before the summer program, the teachers' content knowledge, both of science in general and of light and shadows in particular, was limited. Participants exhibited many of the same misconceptions about light and shadow as children often have, and they lacked coherent conceptual models for understanding and talking about light. Through their participation in the summer workshops and teaching experiences, the teachers' substantive knowledge improved considerably. They exhibited fewer misconceptions and were accurate in their treatment of content about light and shadows in their summer lessons. Smith and Neale attributed these changes, however, largely to the fact that the teachers stuck closely to the activities they had done themselves in the previous week of the workshop. Further, despite these improvements, most teachers still held a number of weak or faulty conceptions about light and shadows, and they continued to struggle to understand the difficult ideas during the monthly seminars throughout the school year. As Smith and Neale pointed out, "For teachers who began with naive conceptions of the nature of light, one week's activities were obviously not enough" (p. 206). Only one of the teachers, who already had a good conceptual model of light before the workshop, exhibited no misconceptions in the fall content interview.

Schifter and Simon (1992; Simon & Schifter, 1991; see also Schifter & Fosnot, 1993) reported on SummerMath for Teachers, an in-service program for elementary and secondary teachers of mathematics that was also based on an assumption that fundamental change in teaching requires growth or change in teachers' conceptions about subject matter and learning. More specifically, Schifter and colleagues believed that to achieve a successful practice grounded in constructivist principles of learning requires, in part, a qualitatively different and richer understanding of mathematics than most teachers possess. Teachers participated in a 2-week summer institute followed by extensive support and supervision through the subsequent year. The institute was designed to give teachers opportunities to learn mathematics in a setting where construction of meaning was valued and encouraged, to reflect on these experiences and on the roles of teachers and students, to focus on children's learning, and then to design instructional sequences that would provide their own students with similar opportunities. During the year following the summer institute, staff members visited the teachers' classrooms on a weekly basis and provided feedback, demonstration teaching, and opportunities for reflection. The teachers also attended workshops that provided opportunities for sharing their efforts to change their teaching; for further exploring issues related to mathematics, learning, and teaching; and for participating in small-group planning sessions. As a result of these experiences, many of the teachers began to develop different conceptions of the nature of mathematics and deeper understandings of mathematical learning. These changes often evolved slowly and were accompanied by feelings of discomfort and disequilibrium as their habits and assumptions about mathematics were called into question.

These three studies address a number of important issues regarding experienced teachers' subject matter knowledge. First, they support the finding that teachers may have limited conceptual understandings of topics they are asked to teach. Second, they show that, with explicit attention to increasing teachers' subject matter understanding, intensive professional development experiences can help teachers develop more powerful understandings of these topics. At the same time, they provide evidence that meaningful learning is a slow and uncertain process for teachers, just as it is for students. Intensive and ongoing interaction around important subject matter content seems just as necessary for the learning of teachers as it is for the learning of students.

### Summary: Subject Matter Knowledge and Beliefs

In this section we argued that the subject matter knowledge of teachers does make a difference in how they teach, and that novice and experienced teachers alike often lack the rich and flexible understanding of the subject matter they need in order to teach in ways that are responsive to students' thinking and that foster learning with understanding. But research in this area also shows that with focused and sustained instruction, in either preservice courses or in-service workshops, teachers can develop richer and more powerful understandings of subject matter content and transform their beliefs about the nature of the subjects they teach.

## PEDAGOGICAL CONTENT KNOWLEDGE AND BELIEFS

Our discussion of teachers' pedagogical content knowledge is organized according to the four central components of this knowledge domain identified by Grossman (1989, 1990): (a) an overarching conception of what it means to teach a particular subject, (b) knowledge of instructional strategies and representations for teaching particular topics, (c) knowledge of students' understanding and potential misunderstandings of a subject area, and (d) knowledge of curriculum and curricular materials.

### Novice Teachers' Pedagogical Content Knowledge and Beliefs

Pedagogical content knowledge is relatively undeveloped in novice teachers. Further, like pedagogical knowledge, it is clearly under the purview of teacher education programs and has received explicit attention from teacher educators and researchers. In this section we review studies that gave it this attention, focusing first on novice teachers' knowledge of and beliefs about the four central components of pedagogical content knowledge, and then on efforts to address prospective teachers' pedagogical content knowledge and beliefs through specific courses.

*Overarching Conception of Teaching a Subject.* As defined by Grossman (1989, 1990), a teacher's overarching conception of a subject for teaching is closely related to the teacher's beliefs about the nature of the subject itself. The overarching conception for teaching, however, is related more specifically to how the teacher thinks about the subject matter domain for *students*—what it is that students should learn about mathematics, history, or English, and the nature of those subjects. There is considerable evidence, across educational levels and subject areas, that prospective teachers enter teacher preparation programs with limited overarching conceptions of what it means to teach particular subjects. At least in some cases, however, these conceptions are modified during teacher education. In this section we discuss a number of studies that examined prospective teachers' overarching conceptions, how they change during teacher education experiences, and how they influence teaching practice.

Researchers with the TELT project found prospective teachers to have limiting overarching conceptions for teaching writing, and limited evidence that teacher education experiences were successful in changing those conceptions. College juniors entering teacher education programs held a set of beliefs that emphasized only one side of writing—the side having to do with writing conventions. They tended to believe that students need to learn writing conventions before they can generate texts of their own, and that it is important for students to learn such things as the parts of speech and the terms people use to describe writing conventions. They also tended to agree that the teacher's role in teaching writing is to evaluate the texts that students produce. Prospective teachers in all of the teacher education programs, however, moved toward a more expanded view of teaching and learning writing. For example, they tended to move from agreement toward neutrality regarding whether a piece of writing should be judged for how well it conveys the writer's message, and from neutrality to disagreement regarding the importance of technical correctness in evaluations of students' papers. In many cases these changes were slight. The only programs that yielded substantial changes in teaching practices combined a strong orientation to a process approach to writing instruction with intensive, ongoing classroom assistance. Both programs were for practicing rather than preservice teachers. The TELT researchers concluded that teacher education programs desiring to promote an expanded view of writing and learning to write must, in addition to teaching pedagogical techniques, help prospective teachers implement these ideas in their classrooms.

A dissertation study related to the Knowledge Growth in a Profession project, Grossman (1989, 1990) provided evidence that participation in teacher preparation programs can influence novice teachers' conceptions of the teaching of writing and other components of the secondary English curriculum, and that these conceptions have an impact on teaching practices. Grossman conducted case studies and a cross-case analysis of six beginning English teachers, all of whom, while undergraduates, had strong preparation in their subject matter. Three of the teachers graduated from the same teacher education program at a research university that emphasized strong subject-specific preparation. The other three elected to enter teaching without formal pedagogical preparation. These six teachers differed in their conceptions of the purposes for teaching English and their ideas about what to teach in secondary English classes. Two of the teachers with no professional preparation made little distinction between English as an intellectual discipline and English as a subject for high school students. For them, the central goal of studying English was learning literary criticism and textual analysis. The other four teachers saw secondary English more as an opportunity to encourage self-expression and understanding through reading and writing. For them, the major purpose of high school English was teaching students how to express themselves in writing. The three teachers who graduated from a teacher preparation program attributed many of their ideas about the purposes of secondary English to their curriculum and instruction courses. Kate, the fourth teacher, was a discrepant case. She acquired much of her pedagogical content knowledge through her own experiences as a student, particularly in high school. Her lack of pedagogical course work was apparent in the disjunction between her conception of secondary English and her practice; in observations, Kate focused primarily on the literary text.

Once the teachers in Grossman's (1989, 1990) study were in the classroom, their overarching conceptions influenced their instructional decisions about class goals and objectives, curricular materials, activities and assignments for students, and evaluations of student learning. Units on *Hamlet* taught by Jake and Stephen illustrate this relationship. The teachers differed in their views on the role of textual analysis and student experience in literary interpretation. Jake, who did not participate in a teacher preparation program, placed primary emphasis on the text itself. He spent 7 weeks on *Hamlet*, leading the students through the play word by word and stressing the learning of textual analysis skills. His assignments included an analysis of a soliloquy, memorization and recitation of a soliloquy, a five-page paper on any theme in the play, and a final examination. In contrast, Stephen, who went through a teacher preparation program, saw the text as a springboard for broadening students' perspectives. He spent only 2½ weeks on the play; his goals were to interest the students in the play and to help them see connections between Hamlet's dilemmas and dilemmas they might face in their own lives. Students never read the play; instead, they watched parts of a videotape of the play and read summaries prior to watching. In class discussions, Stephen moved back and forth between the play and the students' own experiences. In lieu of a final examination, students wrote an essay about one of Hamlet's characteristics that exist in people today, using evidence from the play to support their arguments.

Clift (1987) noted differences in the overarching conceptions of English majors with no intention to teach and no course work in education and English majors at the same institution who were obtaining certification in secondary teaching and had completed their student teaching. The two groups of students varied in their granting of "authority" regarding the interpretation of literature and evaluation of writing. The English majors who did not intend to teach viewed literature as something to be understood, and they defined understanding as seeing things in the same way as the instructor. According to the prospective teachers, in contrast, students should be encouraged to interpret literature actively and to construct personal understandings of text.

In mathematics, prospective teachers' overarching conceptions for teaching the subject seem resistant to change through teacher education programs. In the Learning to Teach Mathematics project, almost all of Ms. Daniels's ideas about good mathematics teaching were verbalized in interviews conducted at the beginning of her final year of teacher preparation (i.e., before her mathematics methods course and her student teaching experiences). These ideas, which focused primarily on making mathematics relevant and meaningful for students (Borko et al., 1992), did not change substantially over the year. In the section below on teaching pedagogical content knowledge to novice teachers, we review several additional studies that found limited changes in prospective teachers' overarching conceptions for teaching mathematics resulting from specific courses designed to help prospective teachers rethink their views of mathematics teaching.

Overall, the studies of novice teachers' overarching conceptions for teaching particular subjects provide inconsistent evidence for whether these conceptions can be changed significantly as a result of teacher education experiences. They also provide at least some evidence that such overarching conceptions do influence the instructional decisions and approaches of novice teachers in the classroom.

*Instructional Strategies and Representations.* When writing about pedagogical content knowledge, many researchers emphasize the role of representations in teaching. Indeed, Shulman's classic definition of pedagogical content knowledge, presented earlier in the chapter, focuses primarily on "ways of representing and formulating the subject that make it comprehensible for others" (Shulman, 1986b, p. 9). Despite the theoretical prominence of this component of pedagogical content knowledge, we found limited research evidence regarding its role in novices' learning to teach. One reason may be the difficulty, in theory and even more so in practice, of distinguishing the pedagogical content knowledge of instructional strategies and representations from subject matter knowledge. Findings that researchers have interpreted as indicating limited subject matter knowledge can often be viewed as evidence for limited pedagogical content knowledge of instructional representations, and vice versa. A good example is the research that reveals novice teachers' inability to produce appropriate representations for division of fractions, discussed in the section on novice teachers' subject matter knowledge (D. L. Ball, 1990a, 1990b; Borko et al., 1992; National Center for Research on Teacher Education, 1991). Ball interpreted fndings from the TELT project as indicative of limitations in prospective teachers' subject matter knowledge. Borko and colleagues interpreted similar findings in the Learning to Teach Mathematics project as evidence that Daniels's pedagogical content knowledge (as well as subject matter knowledge) was limited. Regardless of how the knowledge is labeled, there is a growing body of evidence that novice teachers lack adequate repertoires of powerful representations for teaching in their subject matter areas (McDiarmid et al., 1989).

There is also evidence that limitations in student teachers' repertoires of instructional strategies and representations are associated with problems in teaching for student understanding. In the Learning to Teach Mathematics project, Daniels's representation of a factor tree to illustrate prime factors and counting oranges on a table to explain why zero is not a counting number left her students confused (Eisenhart et al., 1993). Similarly, in the Knowledge Growth in a Profession project, one novice English teacher experimented with three different metaphors for "theme" in his teaching of literature. He felt that none of them was ultimately successful in helping his students understand the concept of theme (Shulman & Grossman, 1987). Findings such as these support the recommendation that developing novice teachers' repertoires of instructional strategies and representations should be a major component of preservice teacher education (Borko et al., 1992; Wilson, Shulman, & Richert, 1987).

***Students' Understandings, Thinking, and Learning in a Subject.*** As we discussed in the section on general pedagogical knowledge, novices frequently report that they do not know what their students know or are capable of learning. This lack of knowledge also extends to particular subject areas: Novices cannot predict where in the curriculum the students are likely to run into problems. Limitations in this component of pedagogical content knowledge can lead to difficulties in planning and implementing appropriate instructional activities. For example, Borko, Livingston, McCaleb, and Mauro (1988) examined the planning and postlesson reflections of elementary and secondary student teachers. Several student teachers discussed problems they encountered trying to present content in ways that would be appropriate for their students. Jack's comments are typical; he noted that he began student teaching by covering too much content, "not realizing that I'm teaching it to people who are learning it for the first time" (p. 72). He began slowing his pace as he learned more about what his students did and did not know.

Civil (1992) also found limitations in prospective teachers' knowledge of student understanding. Students in her mathematics content course for preservice elementary schoolteachers seemed to lack an awareness or appreciation of children's unique ways of looking at problems or their mathematical creativity. They also did not seem to believe that children enjoy working with difficult or confusing ideas. Civil attributed these limitations to the fact that the prospective teachers had practi-

cally no experience teaching children, or probably even listening to them.

All six teachers in Grossman's (1989, 1990) research reported learning most of what they knew about student understanding of English from their teaching experience. They differed, however, in the content and nature of their knowledge. The three teachers without formal teacher preparation seemed to have difficulty learning from experience or incorporating their developing awareness of student understanding into their instructional planning. They seemed to have few frameworks for interpreting and organizing their insights about students, and they lacked a repertoire of instructional strategies that support student learning. The three teachers who graduated from a teacher preparation program were better able to learn about students from their initial teaching experiences, to see the instructional implications of their knowledge of student understanding, and to incorporate that knowledge into their instructional goals and plans. The teacher education program seemed to provide a framework that shaped what they subsequently learned from their classroom experience.

The two groups of students in Clift's (1987) research also differed in their implicit models of learners and teachers in English classrooms. English majors had a "still-life portrait" of learners as persons who understand English through the information brought to them by knowledgeable teachers. Prospective teachers seemed to have a more "kinetic" view of learners. They believed that students understand literature by relating it to their prior experience, and that the teacher's role is to facilitate communication between author and reader. They saw themselves as educators first and subject matter specialists second.

Findings from these research programs suggest that novice teachers' pedagogical content knowledge about students parallels their general pedagogical knowledge. That is, they enter the classroom as a teacher for the first time with little information about who their students are or what they know about the subject matter being taught. This lack of information affects their ability to design appropriate instruction. Many novice teachers in the research we reviewed, however, moved toward a conception of students as active learners in both their general and subject-specific views of learners. There is little research evidence concerning novice teachers' knowledge of specific understandings and misunderstandings that children have about particular subject matter content. Additional research is needed to explore how novice (and experienced) teachers can be helped to acquire such knowledge.

***Curriculum and Curricular Materials.*** Researchers have not focused much attention on what novice teachers know and learn about curriculum and curricular materials. Grossman (1989, 1990) found new teachers to have limited knowledge of curriculum, with these limitations varying across individuals and their preservice preparation. For example, the six teachers in her study differed in their knowledge and beliefs about the selection and organization of content for secondary English. The three teachers who participated in a teacher education program planned to organize a hypothetical ninth-grade English class around writing; the three without teacher education planned to organize it around literature. Differences in the teachers' choices of texts for the class were also associated with teacher education. In part, these curricular choices reflected the different grounds on which the novice teachers made their decisions: knowledge of students' interests in the case of the teachers with teacher education, and knowledge of literature in the case of the teachers without it. They also paralleled the teachers' conceptions of teaching English.

***Teaching Pedagogical Content Knowledge to Novice Teachers.*** The literature cited above suggests that teachers can, at least in some cases, increase their pedagogical content knowledge through participation in teacher preparation programs. We now review several studies that focused on specific courses or series of courses and their impact on prospective teachers' pedagogical content knowledge and beliefs.

Descriptions of the "Exploring Teaching" courses taught by Ball and McDiarmid (Ball, 1988c; McDiarmid, 1990; see also the section *General Pedagogical Knowledge and Beliefs,* earlier in this chapter) suggest that, as early as their introductory courses in teacher preparation programs, prospective teachers can be helped to reconsider their views about teaching and learning of subject matter. For example, students in Ball's course became aware that subject matter knowledge for teaching might be different from knowledge needed for personal functioning, and they learned that mathematical concepts can be explained in more than one way. Students in McDiarmid's course learned the importance of considering the value and appropriateness of various representations of subject matter.

Grossman (1991a) analyzed how the secondary English methods course helped prospective teachers in her study overcome their apprenticeships of observation. The course instructor used modeling and overcorrection to introduce prospective teachers to new models for the teaching of English. His strategies included making his own goals, intentions, strategies, and reflections about the course transparent; encouraging students to rethink English teaching from the perspective of theoretical frameworks he introduced; providing examples of student work and teaching strategies oriented toward students who find writing difficult; modeling "extreme" activities; providing a common technical language; and alternating between theoretical and practical concerns. He provided a "new apprenticeship of observation" in which class members were both students who participated in activities and prospective teachers who analyzed the activities from their perspectives as teachers. Grossman claimed that the instructor's strategies for fostering innovative classroom practices within the context of teacher education course work were likely to generalize across subject areas. Thus, this case study provides an "image of the possible" for policymakers and practitioners.

A number of studies of particular courses intended to promote change in prospective teachers' pedagogical content knowledge in mathematics have reported mixed success. For example, although the teacher education program studied by Wilcox, Schram, and colleagues (Wilcox et al., 1990; see also the section *Novice Teachers' Subject Matter Knowledge and Beliefs,* earlier in this chapter) seemed to be a powerful influence on prospective teachers' thinking about mathematics for themselves, its impact did not seem to carry over to how they thought about mathematics for young children. By the end of their first year in the program, nearly half of the participants continued to associate elementary mathematics with basics—number facts and whole-number operations, hierarchically or-

dered content, a need to master computational skills before problem solving, and a belief that skills at one level must be mastered before proceeding to the next. (Note that these beliefs are intertwined with what we referred to earlier as general pedagogical knowledge and beliefs.)

Even after the second and third year of data collection, despite dramatic changes in their beliefs about mathematics and about themselves as learners of mathematics, participants were inclined to teach in traditional ways in their elementary school classrooms. The researchers offered various explanations for this outcome. Although the preservice teachers' experiences in the program led them to revise their own attitudes toward mathematics and gave them images of alternative pedagogy, these experiences may not have been sufficient to convince them that the approaches they were learning were feasible with elementary students or in public school classrooms. Second, what was encouraged and supported in the public schools was discrepant with what they had learned in their program; these contextual constraints may have interfered with the novice teachers' efforts to teach differently. A third possibility is that, although the novice teachers held changed ideas about mathematics and mathematics teaching, they needed help translating these ideas into actual classroom practice.

Civil (1992) reported a similar pattern of findings. By the end of her mathematics content course for preservice elementary teachers, participants' comments differed depending on whether they were focusing on themselves as teachers or as learners of mathematics. Their ideas about how and what to teach did not appear to change substantially during the course. Participants placed a high priority on the teaching of mathematics skills, and they seemed to have difficulty seeing the point of lengthy explorations of the meanings of rules. They believed that mathematics should be taught linearly, one topic at a time, efficiently, and with a great deal of practice. These novice teachers also seemed to want to conform to teaching the way they had been taught, despite the fact that most of them had had negative experiences with school mathematics.

Ball (1989) reported some success at challenging preservice elementary teachers' knowledge and beliefs about mathematics and the teaching of mathematics in a mathematics methods course that she taught. Like the instructor in the course Grossman (1991a) studied, Ball intended her course to challenge the prospective teachers' knowledge and beliefs about mathematics, about themselves in relation to mathematics, and about the roles of teachers and students in learning mathematics. Also like that instructor, she asked students to be both students of mathematics and prospective teachers who analyzed their experiences as she introduced them to new models for teaching and learning mathematics. They worked in two learning communities: the methods class itself, and the public school third-grade classroom in which Ball taught mathematics daily. In both classes Ball posed mathematical tasks, and she encouraged students to collaborate, to generate solutions and supporting justifications. This double experience with learning mathematics provoked some prospective teachers to reinterpret their own past experiences with mathematics (i.e., their apprenticeship of observation) and to develop a new sense of what it means to understand something in mathematics. It also persuaded many of them that representations such as pictures, stories, and concrete materials play an important role in learning to understand mathematics. However, Ball questioned the extent to which her course, or any single course, can redirect prospective teachers' learning to teach.

Simon and colleagues raised a similar question based on case studies of two prospective elementary teachers who participated in the CEM project (Simon & Brobeck, 1993; Simon & Mazza, 1993). By participating in the mathematics course and the course on mathematics learning and teaching (both taught by Simon), Toni experienced a shift in her relationship to mathematics. She approached student teaching with a commitment to incorporate opportunities for students to develop their own ideas and strategies, to work with manipulatives and diagrams, and to participate in discussions of mathematical ideas. However, although Toni used teaching strategies such as cooperative groups and manipulatives to create these opportunities, she did not focus on student understanding of the mathematics she was teaching. Simon and Mazza (1993) suggested that limitations in Toni's teaching were due to factors such as a lack of ability to identify key mathematical ideas in what she was teaching and the absence of a theory of how children learn mathematics. Another teacher, Georgia, also experienced a dramatic shift in her conception of mathematics learning through participation in the CEM courses, toward a conception more compatible with current reform efforts. Her understanding of mathematics, however, improved only slightly (Simon & Brobeck, 1993), and she was less far along than Toni in her development as a mathematics teacher by the time of student teaching. Simon and colleagues concluded that programs such as theirs (two-semester courses combined with 5-week and 15-week classroom-based experiences) are insufficient to facilitate the learning required for prospective mathematics teachers to teach in ways compatible with reform visions.

Ball (1989) suggested, based on her experience teaching elementary mathematics methods, that teacher educators consider how to extend the duration and form of such courses in ways that make it more likely that we can prepare teachers to learn from their own practice. Ball's cautions are reminiscent of McDiarmid's (1990) concerns about the impact of teacher education courses on students' general pedagogical knowledge, and they receive additional support from studies such as those by Wilcox et al. (1990), Civil (1992), and Simon and colleagues (Simon & Brobeck, 1993; Simon & Mazza, 1993). Her suggestions seem to be an excellent guideline for teacher education reform efforts.

## Pedagogical Content Knowledge and Beliefs of Experienced Teachers

A growing body of research on experienced teachers' efforts to learn to teach in new ways points to the importance of pedagogical content knowledge and beliefs in shaping teachers' classroom practices and their learning of new instructional approaches and strategies. This theme emerges clearly in several of the California Study of Elementary Mathematics case studies of teachers responding to state efforts to reform elementary school mathematics teaching (Prawat et al., 1992; Putnam et al., 1992). These case studies focused on the role of teachers' knowledge and beliefs—about teaching and learning and about mathematics—in their reponses to calls for change in the form of the state-level mathematics framework and new mathematics

textbooks. One of the important themes in the case studies concerned the influence of teachers' overarching conceptions of mathematics and how it should be taught on their interpretations of various messages for changing their mathematics instruction. For example, in using new textbooks, teachers sometimes skipped lessons that did not involve clear right answers because they thought mathematics should be presented in a clear and straightforward manner. At other times they skipped questions that were intended to promote open-ended discussions about mathematical ideas because they thought of mathematics as primarily the learning of arithmetic facts and algorithms. The case studies clearly demonstrate that changing one's mathematics teaching is a complex enterprise that entails, at times, rethinking fairly fundamental assumptions about the nature of the mathematics students are learning in school and teachers' roles in facilitating mathematics learning.

Recognizing the importance of what teachers know and believe about teaching and learning in particular subject matter domains, a number of researchers have worked directly with teachers to change their pedagogical content knowledge and beliefs and have studied the impact of these professional development efforts. In contrast to earlier sections of the chapter in which we included numerous small-scale studies in addition to large-scale research projects, in this section we focus almost exclusively on five major staff development and research efforts: the Second-Grade Mathematics project (Cobb et al., 1990), SummerMath for Teachers (Schifter & Simon, 1992), a conceptual change science teaching project (D. C. Smith & Neale, 1991), the Cognitively Guided Instruction project (CGI; Carpenter et al., 1989), and the University of Maryland Middle School Probeware Project (Krajcik & Layman, 1989). We use this approach because research on experienced teachers' learning of pedagogical content knowledge has been dominated by a small number of large-scale research programs.

In contrast to previous staff development efforts that focused on improving general strategies or approaches to teaching (e.g., L. M. Anderson, Evertson & Brophy, 1979; Evertson, Anderson, Anderson, & Brophy, 1980; Evertson, Emmer, Sandford, & Clements, 1983; Stallings, 1980), the five projects we highlight are situated in the teaching of particular subject matter domains. Further, all five have explicitly sought to help teachers change their instruction by supporting them in learning new pedagogical content knowledge and beliefs (as well as subject matter knowledge, in several cases). Although the different projects have emphasized and attended to different aspects of teachers' knowledge, beliefs, and practices, each has assumed that meaningful changes in teachers' practices require changes in their pedagogical content knowledge and beliefs.

Our discussion of the projects is organized around three of the components of pedagogical content knowledge identified by Grossman (1989, 1990): overarching conception of teaching a subject; instructional strategies and representations; and students' understanding, thinking, and learning. Grossman's fourth component, curriculum and curricular materials, is not addressed separately as it was not a central focus in any of the projects.

*Overarching Conception of Teaching a Subject.* Four of the staff development/research projects highlight the important role that teachers' overarching conceptions of teaching a subject play in their efforts to change their classroom practice. We begin with the two projects in which teachers' overarching conceptions were the primary focus of both the professional development effort and the reported research, continuing with projects in which overarching conceptions were examined along with other aspects of teachers' pedagogical content knowledge and beliefs.

In writing about the learning of the teacher in the Second-Grade Mathematics Project, Wood, Cobb, and Yackel (1991; Cobb et al., 1990) focused on changes in the teacher's knowledge and beliefs about learning and teaching mathematics—her overarching conception of teaching mathematics and her beliefs about learners and learning in the context of mathematics. As we noted earlier in the chapter, the original research focus of the project was to create an environment in which to study children's construction of mathematical meaning. Key components of that environment included a set of problem-centered instructional activities for all areas of mathematics developed by the research team during the course of the year, opportunities for children to work collaboratively to solve the instructional activities, and whole-class discussions to enable children to explain and justify their answers and listen to others' explanations. The researchers discovered that the classroom environment was also a significant source for teacher learning. In particular, the teacher realized, through clinical interviews with her students, that students did not understand concepts she had been teaching. This realization provided a powerful motivation for the teacher to seek changes in her practices.

Two things stand out in Wood and colleagues' analysis of the teacher's learning. First, creating a classroom environment that was based on constructivist views of learning, and in which children's efforts to construct mathematical meaning played a central role, required fairly fundamental changes in the teacher's beliefs about mathematics, teaching, and learning and in her knowledge of ways to interact with students. Wood and colleagues described the teacher as going through three major reconceptualizations over the year of working together with researchers and students: (a) recognizing a shift in her role as teacher from one of presenting information to one of listening to students' ideas and encouraging their mathematical thinking, (b) recognizing that her role was not to impose her methods and ways of thinking but to create opportunities for negotiating meanings and resolving conflicts, and (c) recognizing that she could play an active role in helping students construct expected mathematical meanings without imposing her thinking on them. Second, these changes came about, the authors argue, primarily as a result of trying to solve problems of teaching practice. That is, changes occurred only when the teacher saw problems with what and how her students were learning and then worked together with the project researchers to make changes in her practice.

Unlike Wood and colleagues, Simon and Schifter (1991; Schifter & Simon, 1992; see also Schifter & Fosnot, 1993) set out explicitly to help teachers change. Their efforts in SummerMath for Teachers (described earlier in this chapter) centered on "helping teachers to construct an epistemological perspective informed by the principles of constructivism, offering them opportunities for new and deeper understandings of the mathematics they teach, and supporting them as they develop a classroom practice guided by these epistemological and math-

ematical conceptions" (Schifter & Fosnot, 1993, p. 195). Simon and Schifter assessed changes in teachers' beliefs and classroom practices through analysis of synthesis papers that participating teachers wrote during the program, an instrument to assess their adoption of a constructivist epistemological perspective, and structured interviews in which the teachers described how they implemented what they had learned from the SummerMath program, its strengths and weaknesses, and their plans for further changes. The researchers concluded that the intervention had a substantial impact on teachers' beliefs about mathematics learning and teaching, and that the changes in their beliefs affected their classroom teaching of mathematics, as reported by the teachers. For example, many teachers' views changed in the direction of seeing students as more active and responsible for their own learning. Participants expressed an increased commitment to teaching for student thinking and understanding. They also reported listening more to students and focusing on their ideas and understandings. Almost all the teachers who completed the summer institute and classroom follow-up component reported implementing strategies such as group problem solving, use of manipulatives, and nonroutine problems.

Earlier in this chapter we also described Smith and Neale's (1989, 1991; Neale, Smith, & Johnson, 1990) summer program for primary grade teachers on the teaching of light and shadows. The goal of this staff development program was to help primary teachers use conceptual change strategies for teaching science. Smith and Neale assumed that using these strategies would require the teachers to have greater knowledge in several domains. Therefore, in addition to substantive content knowledge about light and shadow, they sought to help teachers acquire or construct general pedagogical knowledge and pedagogical content knowledge to support conceptual change teaching strategies.

One component of pedagogical content knowledge that Smith and Neale examined was teachers' orientations toward science teaching and learning—in other words, their overarching conceptions of teaching science. Their staff development goal was to help teachers move toward a conceptual change orientation, one that assumes that students bring previous conceptions and understandings to instruction and emphasizes "children's explanations for phenomena, the predictive adequacy of alternative explanations, the use of evidence in supporting and justifying claims, and the role of discussion and debate in establishing knowledge and making progress in understanding" (D. C. Smith & Neale, 1991, p. 194). Through analysis of interviews and videotaped lessons taught before the summer workshop, Smith and Neale found that the teachers' predominant orientation toward teaching and learning science before the summer program was a hands-on discovery approach; which assumed that students' natural curiosity would lead them to discover scientific truths if they were provided with direct experiences watching, experiencing, and manipulating. Some teachers were also concerned about content mastery. During their classroom lessons, these teachers combined a discovery orientation with their concern for content mastery by incorporating more didactic teaching in addition to, but separate from, their discovery-oriented activities. These overall conceptions of teaching science influenced how teachers responded to and learned from the various activities in the summer program. Although many of the teachers made progress in terms of using more conceptual change teaching strategies after the summer workshops (we discuss these changes below), Smith and Neale did not report on changes in the teachers' overall conceptions of teaching science.

In contrast to Smith and Neale (1991), who began with a clearly specified model of conceptual change science teaching and presented teachers with particular instructional strategies and activities, researchers on the CGI project (Carpenter, Fennema, Peterson, & Carey, 1988; Carpenter et al., 1989) worked from a somewhat different perspective, one in which teachers' pedagogical content knowledge also was central, but in which teachers were not presented with specific instructional strategies. CGI is a multiyear, multiphased program of curriculum development, professional development, and research. The professional development component was based on the premises that teaching is essentially a problem-solving process, and that teachers will be most effective if their problem solving is informed by in-depth knowledge of their students and the subject matter they are teaching (in this case, mathematics). CGI professional development efforts focused on providing opportunities for teachers to learn specific subject matter knowledge (the nature of addition and subtraction) and how children typically learn it (pedagogical content knowledge), and to reflect on that knowledge and how it might shape instructional strategies. Just as Smith and Neale (1991) wanted teachers to adopt a conceptual change orientation to teaching and learning science, CGI researchers hoped to foster the perspective that "instruction should build on children's existing knowledge and that teachers should help students to construct mathematical knowledge rather than passively absorb it" (Carpenter et al., 1989, p. 502). In the organizational framework of this chapter, these beliefs fall mainly within the overarching conception of teaching a subject, but they are highly interrelated with general and subject-specific beliefs about learners and learning.

In a 4-week summer workshop, CGI researchers introduced first-grade teachers to research and ideas about children's learning of addition and subtraction, provided them with opportunities to plan how to use that knowledge in their classrooms, and gave them time to reflect on what happened as a result. During the year following the workshop researchers collected data in CGI and control classes through classroom observations, interviews and questionnaires with teachers and students, and several assessments of students' mathematical understandings and attitudes. Six teachers continued to work with CGI researchers during the second year following the workshop. One project assistant worked with each teacher, spending at least 2 hours per week in the teacher's classroom observing mathematics and talking with her about how she used children's thinking. In addition, project staff and the six participating teachers met monthly to discuss the teachers' mathematics instruction. Case studies of these teachers have been reported by Fennema, Carpenter, Franke, & Carey (1992) and by Fennema, Franke, Carpenter, & Carey (1993).

Questionnaires and interviews administered the year following the summer workshop revealed that the CGI teachers changed their overall beliefs about teaching mathematics, responding to a greater extent than control teachers that instruction should build on students' existing knowledge. Classroom observations indicated that the CGI teachers, in comparison to control teachers, taught problem solving more and number

facts less, encouraged students to use a variety of problem-solving strategies, and more frequently listened to students as they solved mathematical problems. An important aspect of the CGI research is that along with increased specific knowledge—subject matter knowledge of the various kinds of addition and subtraction problems, and pedagogical content knowledge of the kinds of problems students find difficult, the solution strategies students use, and different ways to pose problems—changes in teachers' more fundamental beliefs about teaching and learning mathematics were critical to their success in making changes in their mathematics teaching.

Patterns in the Role of Overarching Conceptions.   The four projects that addressed overarching conceptions revealed the importance of teachers' views of the nature of the subject and how it is taught and learned. In Smith and Neale's (1991) study, the teachers' views that children learn science through discovery of content residing outside the individual led to a lack of attention to students' ideas, predictions, and explanations as possible starting points for meaningful conceptual change. In the Second-Grade Mathematics, SummerMath for Teachers, and CGI projects, teachers' fundamental beliefs about how mathematics is taught and learned were both difficult to change and centrally important to the changes that participants made in their classroom practices.

The researchers in these projects agreed about the importance of creating situations in which teachers confronted limitations in their belief systems. They differed, however, in their views about how to facilitate teachers' reconsidering their beliefs about school subjects and how those subjects are taught and learned. The SummerMath program, for example, focused on changing teachers' beliefs about mathematics and learning directly, then supporting teachers' efforts to adapt their classroom practices to be consistent with these new beliefs. In contrast, Wood and colleagues (1991) argued that the overall conceptions and beliefs of the teacher in their case study changed as a result of that teacher's attempts to implement new classroom strategies and in response to problems she perceived in her instruction.

***Instructional Strategies and Representations.*** Although all five staff development/research projects were interested in changes in teachers' use of instructional strategies and representations, they differed in the extent to which staff development efforts focused explicitly on this component of pedagogical content knowledge. We begin our discussion with the work of Krajcik and colleagues and Smith and Neale; in both projects, specific instructional strategies and representations were a central focus.

In the University of Maryland's Probeware Project, discussed earlier with respect to teachers' learning about temperature and heat energy, Krajcik et al. (1991) examined teachers' pedagogical content knowledge and how it changed. Teachers' knowledge of specific instructional strategies for teaching students about concepts of temperature and heat energy was a primary focus of both the workshops on microcomputer-based laboratory activities and the project's research component. Most teachers who participated in the workshops became more knowledgable about activities to help students learn temperature and heat energy concepts, with the largest knowledge gains being made by teachers who actually performed the laboratory activities with their students during the school year.

In a similar investigation, Clermont, Krajcik, and Borko (1993) studied middle school science teachers' repertoires of demonstrations for teaching chemistry. Again, the focus was on teachers acquiring knowledge of specific strategies and representations for teaching particular science concepts. Clermont and colleagues reported on a 2-week summer institute whose purpose was to increase teachers' use of chemical demonstrations in their teaching of chemistry and physical science. Teachers observed and discussed demonstrations by workshop instructors, conducted demonstrations for their peers, received feedback from colleagues and workshop instructors, and planned and conducted demonstrations for groups of middle school students. The researchers assessed participating teachers' conceptions of effective chemical demonstration teaching through interviews before and after the workshop. Their responses demonstrated growth in pedagogical content knowledge—especially their repertoires for demonstrating fundamental topics in chemistry—and an increased awareness of chemical demonstration teaching.

These studies by Krajcik et al. (1991) and Clermont et al. (1993) were grounded on the assumption that knowledge of specific instructional strategies and representations is important in teaching for understanding. The studies support claims that teachers often lack the knowledge of specific instructional strategies and representations to help students learn scientific concepts with anything more than a superficial understanding. Further, both studies show that teachers can enhance their repertoires of instructional strategies through intensive workshop experiences. This research, however, stops short of examining whether and how teachers make use of their newly acquired knowledge when they return to their classrooms.

Smith and Neale's (1989, 1991) efforts to help primary teachers change their teaching of light and shadow went beyond the projects by Krajcik et al. and Clermont et al. by observing participating teachers' classrooms the year following the summer institute. Smith and Neale were particularly interested in teachers' knowledge of general strategies that are thought to be important in facilitating students' conceptual change, among them such strategies as "eliciting students' preconceptions and predictions about phenomena," "providing discrepant events," and "clearly presenting alternative scientific explanations" (D. C. Smith & Neale, 1991, p. 191). In addition, they examined participants' knowledge for shaping and elaborating the content, especially specific examples, explanations, and representations for supporting the learning of particular concepts.

Before the summer program, the teachers used few of the strategies associated with conceptual change teaching. In the summer lessons, three of the five teachers who were studied in detail made substantial changes in their teaching strategies. For example, they focused on scientific content, elicited students' ideas, predictions, and explanations, and asked children to test ideas. Two teachers who began with a strong discovery orientation made few changes. The focus of their summer lessons continued to be on having fun, not challenging and changing students' ideas. Analysis of videotapes of light and shadow lessons taught during the subsequent school year revealed that all of the teachers made progress over the previous year in their use of conceptual change teaching strategies (Neale et al.,

1990). Within this overall improvement, however, researchers found substantial variations among teachers with respect to the aspects of conceptual change teaching they were successful in implementing. For example, one teacher, who began the program with considerable dissatisfaction with her science teaching, embraced the conceptual change orientation, making dramatic changes in her own knowledge of physics and in the strategies she used in the classroom. Another teacher, despite interest and effort, had difficulty implementing the light and shadows unit and the various conceptual change strategies. In terms of more specific strategies and representations for specific content, during the summer lessons the teachers used appropriate examples and representations and dealt with the physics content accurately, largely because they used activities that they themselves had just done in the workshop. They did not, however, make use of other examples, analogies, or representations that might help students understand. Smith and Neale argued that because the teachers' own understanding of light and shadow was still being constructed, they lacked the familiarity and flexibility with the content needed to generate or modify appropriate activities, representations, and explanations for students. The one exception was a teacher who began the program with a fairly solid conceptual understanding of light and shadow, an understanding that was strengthened during the summer program. This teacher generated new activities and representations to help her students understand the physics concepts being taught.

Patterns in Teachers' Knowledge and Beliefs About Instructional Strategies and Representations. Although researchers in all five projects assumed the importance of teachers' knowledge of specific strategies and representations for teaching particular subject matter content, they had very different perspectives on how this knowledge can be acquired in ways that will result in changes in classroom practice. Specific representations and instructional activities constituted the major focus of the summer workshops studied by Krajcik et al. (1991) and Clermont et al. (1993), serving as sites for teachers to learn both the science concepts themselves and how to use these representations and activities in their classrooms to facilitate students' concept learning. Smith and Neale (1989, 1991) also presented teachers with particular instructional activities and representations, and they supported the teachers in adapting them for their own classrooms. Wood and colleagues developed instructional activities that they shared with the teacher in project meetings. These activities were not, however, the major focus of the meetings or the teacher's change process. The SummerMath and CGI projects, in contrast, did not present teachers with particular instructional strategies or representations to implement in their classrooms. Instead they supported teachers in developing and selecting their own strategies and representations based on their changing ideas and knowledge about mathematics, teaching, and learning. Despite these differences in focus, teachers in all five projects appeared to change in their pedagogical content knowledge of instructional strategies and representations.

*Students' Understandings, Thinking, and Learning in a Subject.* As was the case with the other two components of pedagogical content knowledge, the projects differed in the extent to which they focused explicitly on students' understandings and potential misconceptions of science or mathematics. Again, we begin our discussion with the two projects in which this component was most centrally featured.

Because student thinking and how it changes is such a critical element of a conceptual change orientation to science teaching, it is not surprising that this component of pedagogical content knowledge pervaded both the summer program and the research agenda in Smith and Neale's project. The researchers investigated teachers' knowledge of students' understandings and misconceptions related to light and shadow and their ability to predict student performance on various light and shadows tasks. They also considered the extent to which the teachers paid attention to students' ideas, predictions, and explanations when they talked about science teaching and during their actual teaching of science lessons. Before the summer program, the teachers had limited knowledge of likely student misconceptions about light and shadow, although they generally were able to predict what the children would have trouble doing or find hard to understand. In some cases the teachers' predictions about how students would answer various questions were right because the teachers held the same alternative conceptions about light and shadows as do young children. Only one teacher expressed awareness that children's own ideas might affect how they come to understand scientific concepts, and teachers rarely focused on students' ideas, predictions, or explanations during their lessons.

Through the activities in the summer program, especially the clinical interviews with individual children and readings about children's conceptions of light and shadows and how they change, the teachers learned about children's typical misconceptions and the role that children's ideas play in learning. The lessons that teachers planned and taught to children during the summer program were sometimes intended to dispel certain misconceptions. Although the teachers paid more attention to students' ideas, procedures and activities nevertheless continued to predominate their lessons. As Smith and Neale (1991) concluded, "It appeared that teachers knew about children's misconceptions, elicited them by asking for predictions, recognized them when they occurred in lessons, but then were unsure how to use them to contrast alternatives or to move the lesson and children's understanding along" (p. 215). In follow-up interviews a year after the summer program, all teachers said that the biggest change they experienced as a result of the program was the increased attention they gave to students' thinking. Teachers expressed a new awareness of the depth of children's thinking, even if not "correct," and the importance of listening carefully to children and what they are thinking.

As was the case with the conceptual change science teaching project, a central goal of the CGI workshop was to help teachers understand children's thinking. Thus, videotapes of children solving various kinds of addition and subtraction problems and research-based readings on how children typically solve problems were made available for the teachers' consideration. Interacting with these materials appeared to have an impact on this component of the teachers' pedagogical content knowledge. After the summer workshop CGI teachers knew more about the strategies individual students used to solve number facts and problems than did control teachers. During the year following the workshop, they more frequently listened to the processes their students used to solve problems.

The case studies conducted the second year following the workshop revealed that teachers' listening to their students and building on what the students already knew were key elements in CGI classrooms (Fennema et al., 1992; Fennema et al., 1993). The researchers speculated that the specific knowledge about children's thinking in a clearly defined content domain was critical to the success of the program. The taxonomy of addition and subtraction problem types and children's solution strategies provided a rationale for teachers' selection of problems, guidance regarding what to listen for, and a context for interpreting students' responses. Using the taxonomy as an organizing framework, teachers built on their students' informal knowledge by starting with problems they could solve. Drawing on their understanding of what their students knew, they were able to select and adapt problems so that individual students worked on problems at an appropriate level of challenge.

Patterns in Teachers' Knowledge and Beliefs About Students' Understandings, Thinking, and Learning.   Teachers' attending more to the ways students think and learn about particular subject matter content emerges across all of the projects as critically important, both as a goal for change and as a starting point for other changes in knowledge, beliefs, and practices. For example, in addition to the two projects discussed in detail above, Simon and Schifter (1991) noted that the most commonly reported impact of SummerMath for Teachers on participants' teaching was that they listened more to students, focusing on their ideas and understandings. Clermont and colleagues (1993) reported that participants in the summer workshop became more aware of how the complexity of some chemical demonstrations can foster confusion and misconceptions among students, and of ways of simplifying or adapting complex demonstrations in order to promote science learning for understanding.

Taken together, these projects suggest that it is important for teachers to acquire knowledge of students' ways of thinking and common misconceptions in particular domains (e.g., how they think of light and shadow, or the strategies they typically use to solve addition and subtraction problems). Perhaps even more important, they suggest that teachers be helped to recognize the importance of children's thinking in the learning process, and that they learn to listen more closely to students. The ideas and ways of thinking that students bring to instruction are critically important in shaping what those students learn. Only by listening to students are teachers able to build on what the students already know and can do, in order to design appropriate learning activities.

## Summary: Pedagogical Content Knowledge

In this section we saw that the pedagogical content knowledge of novice teachers is often insufficient for thoughtful and powerful teaching of subject matter content. And although experienced teachers have generally acquired a good deal of pedagogical content knowledge, their knowledge often is not sufficient or appropriate for supporting teaching that emphasizes student understanding and flexible use of knowledge. Teachers' overarching conceptions of teaching a subject can limit their efforts to learn to teach in new ways and can be resistant to changes through preservice courses or in-service workshops. Novices have limited knowledge of subject-specific instructional strategies and representations, and of the understandings and thinking of their students about particular subject matter content. Experienced teachers typically have more knowledge of instructional strategies and of their students, but they often do not have appropriate knowledge and beliefs in the areas to support successful teaching for understanding.

The various studies of efforts to help novice and experienced teachers acquire richer and more appropriate pedagogical content knowledge and beliefs suggest that teachers can learn to teach in new ways, but that they require considerable and sustained support to do so. In particular, both novice and experienced teachers need support and opportunities to integrate their new pedagogical content knowledge and beliefs into their current teaching practices, an idea that echoes the theme from cognitive psychology on the importance of situating knowledge and learning in the contexts in which they will be used.

## CONCLUSIONS AND IMPLICATIONS

Learning to teach is a complex process. Novice teachers must learn multiple sets of knowledge, skills, and understandings to be well prepared to enter the teaching profession. They must learn enough classroom management skills and routines to maintain order in a classroom, keeping students motivated and productively engaged; they must learn about the subject matter they will teach, their students and how they learn, and the myriad other issues to which teachers must attend.

In addition to encompassing many domains of knowledge, belief, and skill, the learning-to-teach process itself is complex. It involves, as Calderhead (1988) has argued,

complex interactions amongst student teachers' cognitive/metacognitive processes, their knowledge structures, affective predispositions, and their classroom practice. . . . Ensuring that student teachers are engaged in practical tasks in which they have the requisite knowledge, skills, interest, and motivation to take part, and in which their knowledge, skills, and attitudes may also be enhanced as a result is an exceptionally difficult challenge for teacher education. (p. 48)

For novice teachers the complex process of learning to teach is made even more daunting by conflicting messages and supports for the kind of teaching they are learning. Advocates of educational reform, including many teacher educators, often see teacher education as a site for changing the teaching and learning taking place in public schools, and they try to support novice teachers to teach in new ways—ways that are different from what they experienced in their own education and different from the teaching they observe in many of their classroom-based field experiences. Much of the research we have examined in this chapter has focused on this problem: How can new teachers be supported in learning to teach in new ways?

Experienced teachers seeking to change the way they teach also face major challenges. Current reform efforts advocate

instructional programs, curricula, and approaches that involve thinking about students and how they learn, as well as the subject matter, in new and sometimes fundamentally different ways. Experienced teachers often must try to learn about new approaches while simultaneously continuing to juggle the many demands of classroom life, and in the face of long-established knowledge and beliefs that may conflict in subtle but important ways with the changes they are trying to make.

In closing this chapter, we address the challenge of supporting novice and experienced teachers in their efforts to learn to teach in new ways. We focus first on several impediments to teachers' learning and then on ways of constructing teacher education experiences to facilitate the learning process. Along the way we offer our suggestions for how research from a cognitive psychological perspective might better inform teacher education.

### Impediments to Learning to Teach

*Personal Factors.* A central theme in this chapter has been that teachers' existing knowledge and beliefs serve as filters through which they, like people in general, view and interpret their experiences. Just as the orientations, expectations, and understandings that a student brings to the classroom are important determinants of what that student learns from instruction, a teacher's expectations, knowledge, and beliefs shape what he or she learns about teaching. This shaping or filtering of learning experiences occurs from the very general level of what teachers expect to learn from various educational opportunities to much more specific aspects of their beliefs about the teaching and learning of particular topics within a subject area.

At the most general level, several studies we reviewed suggest that prospective teachers' beliefs about the sufficiency of their knowledge for teaching and their unrealistic optimism about their future teaching performance may make them unreceptive to learning from teacher education experiences (e.g., Brookhart & Freeman, 1992; Weinstein, 1990). Further, prospective teachers can influence the nature of the teacher education program itself, by molding the program to conform to their personal perspectives about teaching (Ross et al., 1991). Experienced teachers, too, may be more or less receptive to opportunities to learn about various aspects of teaching, depending on the expectations and concerns that they bring to these learning opportunities. Research on how teachers and their concerns develop and change over time suggests that teachers may be more receptive to calls for change in their teaching at particular phases in their careers (e.g., Fuller, 1969; Oja, 1991; see Burden, 1990, and Oja, 1989, for reviews of the literature on teacher development).

Much of the research we reviewed in this chapter focused on the role that more specific knowledge and beliefs play in the learning of novice and experienced teachers. We saw, for example, that new teachers are likely to bring to their initial teaching experiences a host of assumptions about the nature of learners and learning, assumptions that shape the instructional skills and routines they learn. In many cases, these beliefs about how students learn and the teacher's role in facilitating learning—beliefs acquired over years of experience as students in traditional educational settings—are incompatible with the views of learning underlying the instructional approaches advocated by teacher education programs. These beliefs often remain implicit, serving as filters that help to shape how novice teachers interpret and learn new instructional strategies and approaches. Because existing knowledge and beliefs do serve as filters, they are highly resistant to change (Ball, 1989; Borko et al., 1992; Holt-Reynolds, 1992; McDiarmid et al., 1989). Experienced teachers' assumptions about learners and the learning process similarly shape their attempts to learn new instructional strategies and approaches. For them, there is an additional concern: Because much of their knowledge has become routinized and automatic, it is even less accessible to scrutiny and conscious change than the knowledge of novice teachers.

Limitations in teachers' subject matter knowledge and beliefs can also impede their efforts to learn to teach in new ways. Both novice and experienced teachers sometimes lack the rich and flexible knowledge of subject matter required for teaching for understanding in ways currently advocated in the educational community. Without adequate subject matter knowledge, it is difficult or impossible for teachers to learn powerful strategies and techniques for representing the subject to students and for attending and responding to students' thinking about the subject in ways that help support their meaningful learning. Perhaps even more important is that new and experienced teachers' beliefs about the nature of the subjects they teach—their overarching conceptions of the subject and how it is best taught and learned—may conflict with the assumptions underlying new instructional practices they are being asked to adopt.

*Contextual Factors.* Numerous factors in the university and public school settings in which teachers work and learn can also impede learning to teach. For novice teachers, the teacher education programs through which they first learn to teach sometimes fail to support acquisition of the knowledge base needed to teach for understanding. Many discipline-based courses in universities do not stress meaningful learning (McDiarmid, 1994). Instead, students are often expected to reproduce a body of knowledge presented by the professor (C. W. Anderson, 1989). For example, mathematics courses taken by majors during the first 2 years of university study typically emphasize rote learning of computational techniques rather than meaningful learning of mathematics. Courses that do stress conceptual topics typically treat them at high levels of abstraction, and they do not focus on concepts that are central to the kindergarten through Grade 12 mathematics curriculum (Committee on Mathematics Education for Teachers, 1991; National Research Council, 1991). Such courses do little to help prospective teachers develop the strong and flexible knowledge they need to interact meaningfully with students around important subject matter content.

The overall demands and pressures of the teacher education program are sometimes not conducive to the reflection and thoughtfulness needed for meaningful learning and examination of the assumptions and beliefs that shape one's teaching. Pressures to teach every day compel student teachers to think ahead to the next lesson rather than reflect on the one they have just taught. The common perception of student teaching as a test to be passed rather than a learning experience colors participants' views of their relationships with program personnel. In addition, novices often confront incon-

sistent messages and demands from university personnel. They may be asked both to teach for conceptual understanding and to meet the public schools' demands that procedures be mastered (Calderhead, 1988; Eisenhart, Behm, & Romagnano, 1991).

The public school settings in which prospective teachers first try their hands at classroom teaching may do little to support or reinforce ideas presented in their university teacher education programs. These teachers may have few opportunities to observe teaching for meaningful learning and little encouragement to develop the kinds of teaching styles and strategies stressed by university instructors. When they do experiment with novel ideas, their opportunities to learn from these experiments are often limited. University supervisors are rarely present, and cooperating teachers typically remain uninvolved in the planning or evaluation of these lessons (Calderhead, 1988; Eisenhart et al., 1991).

For experienced teachers, too, contextual factors may work against learning to teach in new ways. For example, the working conditions in most public schools are often not conducive to promoting teacher reflection and learning. Most teachers use the scarce planning time that is available to prepare for the many students and subjects they must teach every day. There are few opportunities for meaningful collaboration with other teachers.

In addition, many of the beliefs about teaching, learning, learners, and subject matter that pervade the schools are personal impediments to change. Such views are widely held by other teachers, school administrators, students, and parents. They underlie many existing school practices and policies such as grading of students, evaluation of teachers, and commitments to standardized testing. Teachers struggling to adopt a view of students as active learners and to think through and try the implications of this view in their classrooms may bump up against countervailing beliefs held by students, their parents, and other teachers, making it that much more difficult to change their beliefs and practices (McLaughlin & Talbert, 1993).

## Facilitating Teachers' Learning

Despite the many potential impediments to teachers' learning, there is reason for optimism. Our review revealed a number of success stories—experiences that resulted in positive and significant changes in preservice and experienced teachers' knowledge, beliefs, thinking, and practices. Here, we offer suggestions for promoting such changes, based on our analysis of the literature—filtered, of course, through our own knowledge and beliefs. Our emphasis is on facilitating teachers' learning to teach in ways that promote student understanding—teaching that places special demands on teachers to be knowledgeable and thoughtful in their practice. We organize our discussion around five features that contribute to successful learning opportunities for teachers, whether the teachers are novices just learning to teach, or experienced teachers attempting to teach in new ways. These features should have a familiar ring, as they are directly related to the themes from cognitive psychology with which we began the chapter. They are:

1. addressing teachers' preexisting knowledge and beliefs about teaching, learning, learners, and subject matter

2. providing teachers with sustained opportunities to deepen and expand their knowledge of subject matter
3. treating teachers as learners in a manner consistent with the program's vision of how teachers should treat students as learners
4. grounding teachers' learning and reflection in classroom practice
5. offering ample time and support for reflection, collaboration, and continued learning

In the final sections of this chapter we elaborate on these features, first in the context of preservice teacher education programs and then with respect to learning opportunities for experienced teachers.

*Preservice Teacher Education.* New teachers must develop and draw on a number of different knowledge bases simultaneously as they learn to teach. In addition, they have the special problem of having to learn for the first time how to get along in a classroom as a teacher while they also learn about myriad other aspects of teaching. We believe that successful teacher education programs will help novice teachers simultaneously gain the experience and skills they need to survive in classroom settings and reflect on and reconsider the various assumptions and beliefs underlying their practices.

Addressing Existing Knowledge and Beliefs. Because the knowledge and beliefs that prospective teachers bring to their teacher education programs exert such a powerful influence on what and how they learn about teaching, programs that hope to help novices think and teach in new ways must challenge participants' preexisting beliefs about teaching, learning, subject matter, self as teacher, and learning to teach (Ball, 1988c; Bullough & Knowles, 1990; Comeaux, 1992; Holt-Reynolds, 1992; Kagan, 1992; McDiarmid, 1990; Weinstein, 1990). They must help prospective teachers make their implicit beliefs explicit and create opportunities for them to confront the potential inadequacy of those beliefs. They should also provide opportunities for prospective teachers to examine, elaborate, and integrate new information into their existing systems of knowledge and beliefs.

Learning Subject Matter. Novices must have the opportunity to strengthen their subject matter knowledge and pedagogical content knowledge throughout the teacher education experience. Learning to teach a subject well entails learning the discipline's different ways of knowing, as well as integrating new information into one's existing knowledge systems (Wilson & Wineburg, 1988). Ideally, perhaps, prospective teachers should acquire this knowledge in undergraduate (upper division) and graduate courses in disciplinary departments. This assumption underlies the push in many states and universities toward requiring more disciplinary course work of prospective teachers. As McDiarmid (1994) and C. W. Anderson (1989) have argued, however, such courses in departments of humanities and sciences often do not deal with the subject matter in ways that will help prospective teachers develop the knowledge they need to teach for understanding. They emphasize instead the accumulation of facts and skills, without considerable reflection on relationships among key ideas (substantive structure of the disci-

pline) or how knowledge is developed (syntactic structure of the discipline). Thus, simply increasing the number of disciplinary courses is unlikely to prepare teachers with the richer understandings *of* and *about* the disciplines they need for teaching.

Grossman et al. (1989) argued for the importance of systematically incorporating discussions of substantive and syntactic knowledge of disciplines into programs of teacher education to ensure that prospective teachers consider these issues in relation to the tasks of teaching. One approach to accomplishing this goal, supported by both McDiarmid (1994) and C. W. Anderson (1989), is ongoing dialogue between faculty in education and the academic disciplines about what prospective teachers should be learning about subject matter and how various courses are or are not supporting that learning. Another approach is having subject matter courses taught in schools of education or by faculty with joint appointments in schools of education and discipline-based departments. This approach was used in the teacher education programs by Schram, Wilcox, and colleagues (Schram et al., 1989) and Simon (1995; Simon & Blume, in press) described earlier in the chapter.

In addition to disciplinary knowledge, learning to teach entails learning to create appropriate pedagogical representations of the subject matter—representations that incorporate an understanding of how students learn particular topics and where they are likely to encounter difficulty (Ball, 1993; Grossman, 1989, 1990). For such complex learning to occur, novices must confront problems of subject matter teaching and learning continually, with guidance and support from teacher education faculty.

Subject-specific course work can be a powerful influence on how novice teachers think about and teach their subjects. "Subject-specific teacher education course work can help teachers construct conceptions of what it means to teach a subject, conceptions grounded in current knowledge about teaching and learning specific content areas in secondary school" (Grossman, 1990, p. 143). By providing frameworks for thinking about teaching the subject matter of a discipline and strategies for putting these ideas into practice, such courses can make a difference in novice teachers' pedagogical content knowledge (Clift, 1987; Grossman, 1990).

Consideration of issues related to the teaching of subject matter, however, should not be the exclusive domain of methods courses and student teaching (Roth et al., 1988). It should be integrated into all phases of preservice preparation, including pre-education undergraduate courses and foundations courses. Novice teachers should begin developing and using interpretive lenses for making sense of subject matter content, learning processes, and teaching for conceptual understanding of subject matter early in their teacher education experience so that they will have the opportunity to revisit, rethink, and repeatedly struggle with these important issues while receiving guidance and support from teacher education faculty.

Teachers as Learners. One strategy that seems to be successful in promoting novice teachers' learning of subject matter knowledge and pedagogical content knowledge is to have them engage in experiences that mirror the experiences we would like them to create in their own classrooms. The community of learners that Wilcox, Schram, and colleagues (Wilcox et al., 1990) created in their preservice mathematics and methods courses, in which prospective teachers engaged in doing mathematics in small-group and whole-class settings, is one example. Civil (1992) and Simon (1995) used similar approaches in their mathematics courses for preservice elementary teachers.

Grounding Learning in Classroom Practice: Public School Experiences.   Most researchers on learning to teach agree that it is important to place novice teachers in classroom settings that provide opportunities and support for them to teach in ways that are compatible with the goals and vision of the university teacher education program. Such a classroom-based component of teacher education explicitly addresses the messages from cognitive psychology to create environments that support learners' efforts to construct meaning and learning experiences that are situated in meaningful contexts. Novices should be able to observe experienced teachers model alternative teaching strategies, should have the time and incentives to prepare lessons that focus on conceptual knowledge, and should receive feedback on the lessons they teach (Civil, 1992; Eisenhart et al., 1993). Hollingsworth (1989) offers a different perspective. Based on her case studies of learning to teach, she suggests that there may be a value to creating disequilibrium within the student teaching experience. Placing preservice teachers with cooperating teachers whose ideas differ from theirs or from the teacher education program philosophy may challenge the preservice teachers to confront their ideas in a way that fosters knowledge growth. Research is needed to determine under which conditions each of these two approaches is better in facilitating learning to teach in new ways.

Time and Support.   In either case, it is important that student teachers have the time and opportunity to think about their teaching. Initial responsibilities during student teaching should be minimal. Responsibilities should be added gradually, in order to provide student teachers with a more realistic opportunity to develop their skills of planning and reflection (Borko & Livingston, 1989; Lederman & Gess-Newsome, 1991).

To help foster these attributes of a preservice teacher education program, better coordination is needed between the universities in which teacher education programs are housed and the public schools in which new teachers get their practical experiences. For example, Roth, Rosaen, and Lanier (1988) stress the importance of coordination between field assignments and university experiences during early professional studies. From the beginning of their teacher education programs, novices should have the opportunity to ground their theoretical study in the reality of classroom practice and to explore how disciplinary knowledge is planned, taught, and interpreted in school settings.

Similar coordination is important during the student teaching experience. At this stage, an added consideration is that support and feedback from university supervisors and cooperating teachers should be compatible and mutually reinforcing. Eisenhart and colleagues (Eisenhart et al., 1993) provide one model for such coordination. They suggest that university personnel (e.g., methods course instructors) and school personnel (e.g., cooperating teachers) share conceptions of teaching and learn-

ing and work together to identify the kinds of experiences, support, and feedback to provide to novice teachers. Such collaborative efforts will enable the development of a coherent set of learning-to-teach opportunities.

*Learning Opportunities for Experienced Teachers.* Experienced teachers are often presented with mandates for changing the way they teach, through national standards, new textbooks, or school, district, or state policies. Despite these expectations or demands for change, teachers are not typically treated as learners. In-service programs often seem to harbor an implicit assumption that when teachers have finished their education, they have learned most of what they need to know; continued professional development is primarily a matter of fine-tuning, usually by learning new instructional techniques. In-service programs often are designed to help teachers comply with new district mandates or to meet specific certification requirements. Given this situation, it is not surprising that Feiman-Nemser (1983) wrote in her analysis of the in-service phase of learning to teach, "In short, improving the practice of experienced teachers has not been taken seriously as a legitimate inservice priority" (p. 164).

If we truly expect teachers to learn to teach in new ways, then this situation must change. We must begin to view schools as places for teachers, as well as their students, to learn (Little, 1982; McLaughlin & Talbert, 1993; Sarason, 1990). Further, in-service or staff development programs must be designed to take advantage of what we know about the process of learning to teach. In the remainder of this section we suggest some characteristics of staff development programs that address these concerns.

Addressing Existing Knowledge and Beliefs.   To be successful, efforts to support teachers' learning must recognize that teachers' knowledge and beliefs about teaching, learning, learners, and subject matter will play a critical role in determining whether and how they implement new instructional ideas. Virtually all the projects we examined in this chapter that were successful in facilitating meaningful change in experienced teachers' instructional practices explicitly addressed the teachers' preexisting knowledge and beliefs and supported participants in examining and changing them.

The best way to provide such support is not clear. Some researchers have tried to promote meaningful change in pedagogical practices by helping teachers reexamine their beliefs (e.g., Carpenter et al., 1989; Richardson et al., 1991; Schifter & Simon, 1992). Other researchers have argued that the changes in beliefs will come only after teachers have made changes in their practices and seen them to be successful (e.g., Guskey, 1986). We believe, like Richardson (1994), that the order in which beliefs and practices are addressed in staff development programs may not be that important. What is critical is that both practices and beliefs become the object of reflection and scrutiny. Meaningful change in one requires change in the other as well.

Learning Subject Matter.   Learning opportunities for teachers should be grounded in the teaching of particular subject matter domains and should provide opportunities for teachers to enhance their own subject matter knowledge and beliefs. This recommendation has taken on particular importance in recent years, because the vision of learning and teaching called for by current educational reform efforts demands strong conceptual understanding of subject matter on the part of teachers. Not surprisingly, all of the successful programs we reviewed supported teachers in deepening and broadening their understanding of the particular content domains they taught, for example addition and subtraction (Carpenter et al., 1989) or the physics of light and shadow (D. C. Smith & Neale, 1991).

Teachers as Learners.   Each successful in-service project we reviewed in this chapter also treated teachers as learners in ways that were consistent with the project's perspective on student learning. If teachers are to be successful in creating classroom learning environments in which subject matter and learners are treated in new ways, they need to experience such learning environments themselves. For example, if mathematics teachers are to support their students in participating in a learning community and in making sense of mathematics as something more than a collection of predetermined computational rules, then the teachers themselves need to experience what it means to actively participate in a community of learners striving to make sense of a particular mathematical domain. Simply telling them that they should help students make explicit their current conceptions and articulate their problem-solving strategies is unlikely to engage the teachers in meaningful change.

Grounding Learning in Classroom Practice.   Teachers must have the opportunity to learn and reflect about new instructional strategies and ideas in the context of their own classroom practice. Several of the projects we described found that the teachers benefited greatly from support and supervision provided by members of the research and staff development team as they attempted to incorporate new ideas developed during summer workshops into their ongoing classroom practices. Observations by workshop personnel, and opportunities to receive feedback on their experiences, helped the teachers adapt their existing instructional strategies and routines and solidify changes in their knowledge and beliefs (e.g., Fennema et al., 1992; Schifter & Simon, 1992). Although intensive out-of-classroom experiences such as summer workshops may play an important role in teachers' learning, without classroom-based opportunities such as these, teachers are unlikely to make meaningful changes in their teaching.

Time and Support.   Finally, teachers must be provided with sustained time and support for reflection, collaboration, and continued learning. Again, the ongoing support systems in the projects we described are revealing. Teachers continued to grow and change in the years after the intensive interventions when they were provided with the opportunity for continued collaboration among teachers and between teachers and researchers/staff developers. The success stories in Little's (1982) study of workplace conditions of school success provide additional evidence. Little concluded that two critical features of schools that are conducive to continued learning by teachers are norms of collegiality and experimentation: that teachers expect to work collaboratively on the planning, implementation, and evaluation of various teaching activities,

and that they view improvements in their knowledge, beliefs, and practices as never ending. In schools where these norms existed, time was organized, both formally and informally, to support frequent and varied professional interactions among teachers.

McLaughlin and Talbert (1993) reported similar conclusions in the longitudinal study of professional contexts for high school teaching conducted by the Center for Research on the Context of Secondary School Teaching. As they noted, teachers' ability to successfully adapt their practices to meet the national reform agenda depended on "participation in a professional community that discusses new teaching materials and strategies and that supports the risk taking and struggle entailed in transforming practice" (p. 15).

## Studying the Learning Process

Our CONCLUSIONS AND IMPLICATIONS section has focused primarily on implications for practice, although we have offered some ideas for research as well. We have also suggested areas for future research throughout the chapter when unresolved issues were addressed. In these final paragraphs we provide a few additional thoughts about characteristics of research efforts that are likely to provide insights into learning to teach, and about the relationship between research and practice (see Richardson & Anders, 1994, for a more indepth consideration of the study of teacher change). Just as successful teacher education programs take into account the complexity of learning to teach, research that is likely to enhance our understanding of learning to teach must also address this complexity. One way of approaching this issue is to continue to expand the contexts in which we study the learning of teachers. Beginning teachers learn in individual university courses and in their student teaching placements. But they also learn from other teachers during their initial teaching experiences and from a multitude of other sources, such as their interactions with students, the professional reading they do, and various in-service workshops and other professional development activities they experience during their initial years of teaching. Experienced teachers, too, can learn in a variety of settings, only a few of which have been studied systematically. Because the change process is a slow one, researchers must be prepared to study teachers over time, certainly for more than 1 year, and preferably for several years after their participation in teacher education.

It is also important for researchers to capture the complexity of changes in teachers' knowledge, beliefs, and practices across domains of the professional knowledge base. Doing so entails the use of multiple data sources such as observations of teachers in workshop and classroom settings; interviews about knowledge, beliefs, and practices; and teachers' reflective writings. This triangulation to support claims with data from a number of sources is important because of the fairly high levels of interpretation and inference involved in understanding changes in the mental lives of teachers—what they know and believe and how they think about what they do.

A key aspect of the change process is its unpredictability. To accommodate this unpredictability, teacher education programs often are open-ended, evolving to meet the needs of participants. The Second-Grade Mathematics project (Cobb et al., 1990) is one example. The researchers/staff developers modified their approach to working with the teacher collaborator when they realized that she was not participating as an equal partner in the project. Studies of teacher change must similarly remain open-ended, evolving along with teacher education programs to accommodate the unpredictability of change. One way to facilitate flexibility in both research and teacher education is for researchers and teacher educators (who are often the same people) to conceive of the two components of a project as mutually interactive. Research questions, data collection, and analysis are modified to accommodate changes in the teacher education process; at the same time, research findings are systematically drawn on to revise the change process. This recommendation is in keeping with a growing recognition by educational psychologists of the need to interweave systematic research with attempts to facilitate change in existing educational settings at all levels (A. L. Brown, 1992).

# References

Ammon, P. (1991, April). *Expertise in teaching from a developmental perspective: The developmental teacher education program at Berkeley*. Paper presented at the annual meeting of the American Educational Research Association, Chicago.

Anderson, C. W. (1989). The role of education in the academic disciplines in teacher education. In A. E. Woolfolk (Ed.), *Research perspectives on the graduate preparation of teachers* (pp. 88–107). Englewood Cliffs, NJ: Prentice Hall.

Anderson, L. M. (1989a). Classroom instruction. In M. C. Reynolds (Ed.), *Knowledge base for the beginning teacher* (pp. 101–116). Oxford: Pergamon Press.

Anderson, L. M. (1989b). Implementing instructional programs to promote meaningful, self-regulated learning. In J. Brophy (Ed.), *Advances in research on teaching: Vol. 1. Teaching for meaningful understanding and self-regulated learning* (pp. 311–343). Greenwich, CT: JAI Press.

Anderson, L. M. (1989c). Learners and learning. In M. C. Reynolds (Ed.), *Knowledge base for the beginning teacher* (pp. 85–99). Oxford: Pergamon Press.

Anderson, L. M., Evertson, C. M., & Brophy, J. E. (1979). An experimental study of effective teaching in first-grade reading groups. *Elementary School Journal, 79,* 193–223.

Ball, D. L. (1988a). *Knowledge and reasoning in mathematical pedagogy: Examining what prospective teachers bring to teacher education*. Unpublished doctoral dissertation, Michigan State University, East Lansing.

Ball, D. L. (1988b, April). *Prospective teachers' understandings of mathematics: What do they bring with them to teacher education?* Paper presented at the annual meeting of the American Educational Research Association, New Orleans, LA.

Ball, D. L. (1988c). Unlearning to teach mathematics. *For the Learning of Mathematics, 8,* 40–48.

Ball, D. L. (1989, March). *Breaking with experience in learning to teach mathematics: The role of a preservice methods course*. Paper presented at the annual meeting of the American Educational Research Association, San Francisco.

Ball, D. L. (1990a). The mathematical understandings that prospective teachers bring to teacher education. *Elementary School Journal, 90,* 449–466.

Ball, D. L. (1990b). Prospective elementary and secondary teachers' understanding of division. *Journal for Research in Mathematics Education, 21,* 132–144.

Ball, D. L. (1991). Research on teaching mathematics: Making subject-matter knowledge part of the equation. In J. Brophy (Ed.), *Advances in research on teaching: Vol. 2. Teachers' knowledge of subject matter as it relates to their teaching practice* (pp. 1–48). Greenwich, CT: JAI Press.

Ball, D. L. (1993). Halves, pieces, and twoths: Constructing and using representational contexts in teaching fractions. In T. P. Carpenter, E. Fennema, & T. Romberg (Eds.), *Rational numbers: An integration of research* (pp. 157–196). Hillsdale, NJ: Lawrence Erlbaum Associates.

Ball, D. L., & Rundquist, S. S. (1993). Collaboration as a context for joining teacher learning with learning about teaching. In D. K. Cohen, M. W. McLaughlin, & J. E. Talbert (Eds.), *Teaching for understanding: Challenges for policy and practice* (pp. 13–42). San Francisco: Jossey-Bass.

Baxter, J., Richert, A., & Saylor, C. (1985). *Content and process in biology* (Knowledge Growth in a Profession Technical Report). Stanford, CA: School of Education, Stanford University.

Berliner, D. C. (1988, February). *The development of expertise in pedagogy*. Paper presented at the annual meeting of the American Association of Colleges for Teacher Education, New Orleans, LA.

Berliner, D. C. (1989). Implications of studies of expertise in pedagogy for teacher education and evaluation. In *Proceedings of the 1988 Educational Testing Service Invitational Conference: New directions for teacher assessment* (pp. 39–65). Princeton, NJ: Educational Testing Service.

Bird, T. (1991, April). *Making conversations about teaching and learning in an introductory teacher education course*. Paper presented at the annual meeting of the American Educational Research Association, Chicago.

Bloom, B. S. (1985). *Developing talent in young people*. New York: Ballantine.

Borko, H., Eisenhart, M., Brown, C. A., Underhill, R. G., Jones, D., & Agard, P. C. (1992). Learning to teach hard mathematics: Do novice teachers and their instructors give up too easily? *Journal for Research in Mathematics Education, 23,* 194–222.

Borko, H., & Livingston, C. (1989). Cognition and improvisation: Differences in mathematics instruction by expert and novice teachers. *American Educational Research Journal, 26,* 473–498.

Borko, H., Livingston, C., McCaleb, J., & Mauro, L. (1988). Student teachers' planning and post-lesson reflections: Patterns and implications for teacher preparation. In J. Calderhead (Ed.), *Teachers' professional learning* (pp. 65–83). New York: Falmer.

Borko, H., & Shavelson, R. J. (1990). Teachers' decision making. In B. Jones & L. Idol (Eds.), *Dimensions of thinking and cognitive instruction* (pp. 311–346). Hillsdale, NJ: Lawrence Erlbaum Associates.

Brookhart, S. M., & Freeman, D. J. (1992). Characteristics of entering teacher candidates. *Review of Educational Research, 62,* 37–60.

Brophy, J. (1989). Conclusion: Toward a theory of teaching. In J. Brophy (Ed.), *Advances in research on teaching: Vol. 1. Teaching for meaningful understanding and self-regulated learning* (pp. 345–355). Greenwich, CT: JAI Press.

Brophy, J., & Good, T. L. (1986). Teacher behavior and student achievement. In M. C. Wittrock (Ed.), *Handbook of research on teaching* (3rd ed., pp. 328–375). New York: Macmillan.

Brown, A. L. (1992). Design experiments: Theoretical and methodological challenges in creating complex interventions in classroom settings. *Journal of the Learning Sciences, 2,* 141–178.

Brown, C. A., & Borko, H. (1992). Becoming a mathematics teacher. In D. A. Grouws (Ed.), *Handbook of research on mathematics teaching and learning* (pp. 209–239). New York: Macmillian.

Brown, J. S., Collins, A., & Duguid, P. (1989). Situated cognition and the culture of learning. *Educational Researcher, 18*(1), 32–42.

Bruner, J. (1986). *Actual minds, possible worlds.* Cambridge, MA: Harvard University Press.

Bruner, J. (1990). *Acts of meaning.* Cambridge, MA: Harvard University Press.

Bullough, R. V. J., & Knowles, J. G. (1990). Becoming a teacher: Struggles of a second-career beginning teacher. *Qualitative Studies in Education, 3,* 101–112.

Bullough, R. V. J., & Knowles, J. G. (1991). Teaching and nurturing: Changing conceptions of self as teacher in a case study of becoming a teacher. *Qualitative Studies in Education, 2,* 121–140.

Bullough, R. V. J., Knowles, J. G., & Crow, N. A. (1989). Teacher self-concept and student culture in the first year of teaching. *Teachers College Record, 91,* 209–233.

Burden, P. R. (1990). Teacher development. In W. R. Houston, M. Haberman, & J. Sikula (Eds.), *Handbook of research on teacher education* (pp. 311–328). New York: Macmillan.

Butt, R. L., & Raymond, D. (1989). Studying the nature and development of teachers' knowledge using collaborative autobiography. *International Journal of Educational Research, 13,* 403–419.

Byrne, C. J. (1983, October). *Teacher knowledge and teacher effectiveness: A literature review, theoretical analysis, and discussion of research strategy.* Paper presented at the 14th Annual Convention of the Northeastern Educational Research Association, Ellenville, NY.

Calderhead, J. (1988). The development of knowledge structures in learning to teach. In J. Calderhead (Ed.), *Teachers' professional learning* (pp. 51–64). London: Falmer.

Calderhead, J., & Robson, M. (1991). Images of teaching: Student teachers' early conceptions of classroom practice. *Teaching and Teacher Education, 7,* 1–8.

Carlsen, W. (1987, April). *Why do you ask? The effects of science teacher subject-matter knowledge on teacher questioning and classroom discourse.* Paper presented at the annual meeting of the American Educational Research Association, Washington, DC.

Carlsen, W. (1989, April). *Teacher knowledge and teacher planning: The impact of subject-matter knowledge on the biology curriculum.* Paper presented at the annual meeting of the National Association for Research in Science Teaching, San Francisco.

Carlsen, W. (1991). Subject-matter knowledge and science teaching: A pragmatic perspective. In J. E. Brophy (Ed.), *Advances in research on teaching: Vol. 2. Teachers' subject matter knowledge and classroom instruction* (pp. 115–143). Greenwich, CT: JAI Press.

Carpenter, T. P., Fennema, E., Peterson, P. L., & Carey, D. A. (1988). Teachers' pedagogical content knowledge of students' problem solving in elementary arithmetic. *Journal for Research in Mathematics Education, 19,* 385–401.

Carpenter, T. P., Fennema, E., Peterson, P. L., Chiang, C., & Loef, M. (1989). Using knowledge of children's mathematical thinking in classroom teaching: An experimental study. *American Educational Research Journal, 26,* 499–532.

Carter, K. (1990). Teachers' knowledge and learning to teach. In W. R. Houston, M. Haberman, & J. Silkula (Eds.), *The handbook of research on teacher education* (pp. 291–310). New York: Macmillan.

Carter, D., Cushing, K., Sabers, D., Stein, P., & Berliner, D. (1988). Expert-novice differences in perceiving and processing visual classroom information. *Journal of Teacher Education, 39,* 25–31.

Carter, K., & Doyle, W. (1987). Teachers' knowledge structures and comprehension processes. In J. Calderhead (Ed.), *Exploring teachers' thinking* (pp. 147–160). London: Cassell.

Carter, K., Sabers, D., Cushing, D., Pinnegar, S., & Berliner, D. C. (1987).

Processing and using information about students: A study of expert, novice, and postulant teachers. *Teaching and Teacher Education, 3,* 145–157.

Cazden, C. B. (1986). Classroom discourse. In M. C. Wittrock (Ed.), *Handbook of research on teaching* (3rd ed., pp. 432–463). New York: Macmillan.

Civil, M. (1992, April). *Prospective elementary teachers' thinking about mathematics.* Paper presented at the annual meeting of the American Educational Research Association, San Francisco.

Clandinin, D. J. (1986). *Classroom practice: Teacher images in action.* Philadelphia: Falmer Press.

Clark, C. M., & Peterson, P. L. (1986). Teachers' thought processes. In M. C. Wittrock (Ed.), *Handbook of research on teaching* (3rd ed., pp. 255–296). New York: Macmillan.

Clement, J. (1982). Students' preconceptions in introductory mechanics. *American Journal of Physics, 50,* 66–71.

Clermont, C. P., Krajcik, J. S., & Borko, H. (1993). The influence of an intensive inservice workshop on pedagogical content knowledge growth among novice chemical demonstrators. *Journal of Research in Science Teaching, 30,* 21–43.

Clift, R. T. (1987). English teacher or English major: Epistemological differences in the teaching of English. *English Education, 19,* 229–236.

Clift, R. T., Houston, W. R., & Pugach, M. C. (Eds.). (1990). *Encouraging reflective practice in education.* New York: Teachers College Press.

Cobb, P., Wood, T., & Yackel, E. (1990). Classrooms as learning environments for teachers and researchers. In R. Davis, C. Maher, & N. Noddings (Eds.), *Constructivist views on the teaching and learning of mathematics* (pp. 125–146). Reston, VA: National Council of Teachers of Mathematics.

Cohen, D. K. (1989). Teaching practice: Plus ça change. . . . In P. W. Jackson (Ed.), *Contributing to educational change: Perspectives on research and practice* (pp. 27–84). Berkeley: McCutchan.

Cohen, D. K. (1990). A revolution in one classroom: The case of Mrs. Oublier. *Educational Evaluation and Policy Analysis, 12,* 311–329.

Cohen, D. K., & Ball, D. L. (1990a). Policy and practice: An overview. *Educational Evaluation and Policy Analysis, 12,* 233–239.

Cohen, D. K., & Ball, D. L. (1990b). Relations between policy and practice: A commentary. *Educational Evaluation and Policy Analysis, 12,* 330–338.

Collins, A., Brown, J. S., & Newman, S. E. (1989). Cognitive apprenticeship: Teaching the craft of reading, writing and mathematics. In L. B. Resnick (Ed.), *Knowing, learning, and instruction: Essays in honor of Robert Glaser* (pp. 453–494). Hillsdale, NJ: Lawrence Erlbaum Associates.

Comeaux, M. (1992, April). *Challenging students' views about teaching and learning: Constructivism in the Social Foundations Classroom.* Paper presented at the annual meeting of the American Educational Research Association, San Francisco.

Committee on Mathematics Education for Teachers. (1991). *A call for change: Recommendations for the mathematical preparation of teachers of mathematics.* Washington, DC: Mathematical Association of America.

Confrey, J. (1990). A review of the research on student conceptions in mathematics, science, and programming. In C. B. Cazden (Ed.), *Review of Research in Education* (Vol. 16, pp. 3–56). Washington, DC: American Educational Research Association.

Connelly, F. M., & Clandinin, D. J. (1985). Personal practical knowledge and the modes of knowing: Relevance for teaching and learning. In E. Eisner (Ed.), *Learning and teaching the ways of knowing* (84th Yearbook of the National Society for the Study of Education, Pt. II, pp. 174–198). Chicago: University of Chicago Press.

Doyle, W. (1986). Classroom organization and management. In M. C. Wittrock (Ed.), *Handbook of research on teaching* (3rd ed., pp. 392–431). New York: Macmillan.

Eisenhart, M., Behm, L., & Romagnano, L. (1991). Learning to teach: Developing expertise or rite of passage? *Journal of Education for Teaching, 17,* 51–71.

Eisenhart, M., & Borko, H. (1993). *Designing classroom research: Themes, issues and struggles.* Needham, MA: Allyn & Bacon.

Eisenhart, M., Borko, H., Underhill, R., Brown, C., Jones, D., & Agard, P. (1993). Conceptual knowledge falls through the cracks: Complexities of learning to teach mathematics for understanding. *Journal for Research in Mathematics Education, 24,* 8–40.

Elbaz, F. (1983). *Teacher thinking: A study of practical knowledge.* New York: Nichols.

Evertson, C., Anderson, C. M., Anderson, L. M. & Brophy, J. (1980). Relationships between classroom behaviors and student outcomes in junior high mathematics and English classes. *American Educational Research Journal, 17,* 43–60.

Evertson, E., Emmer, E., Sanford, J., & Clements, B. (1983). Improving classroom management: An experiment in elementary school classrooms. *Elementary School Journal, 84,* 173–188.

Feiman-Nemser, S. (1983). Learning to teach. In L. Shulman & G. Sykes (Eds.), *Handbook of teaching and policy* (pp. 150–170). New York: Longman.

Feiman-Nemser, S. (1990). Teacher preparation: Structural and conceptual alternatives. In W. R. Houston (Ed.), *Handbook for research on teacher education* (pp. 212–233). New York: Macmillan.

Fennema, E., Carpenter, T. P., Franke, M. L., & Carey, D. (1992). Learning to use children's mathematics thinking: A case study. In R. Davis & C. Maher (Eds.), *Schools, mathematics, and the world of reality* (pp. 93–117). Needham Heights, MA: Allyn & Bacon.

Fennema, E., & Franke, M. L. (1992). Teachers' knowledge and its impact. In D. A. Grouws (Ed.), *Handbook of research on mathematics teaching and learning* (pp. 147–164). New York: Macmillan.

Fennema, E., Franke, M. L., Carpenter, T. P., & Carey, D. A. (1993). Using children's mathematical knowledge in instruction. *American Educational Research Journal, 30,* 555–583.

Fenstermacher, G. D. (1994). The knower and the known in teacher knowledge research. In L. Darling-Hammond (Ed.), *Review of research in education* (Vol. 20, pp. 3–56). Washington, DC: American Educational Research Association.

Fenstermacher, G. D., & Richardson, V. (1993). The elicitation and reconstruction of practical arguments in teaching. *Journal of Curriculum Studies, 25,* 101–114.

Fuller, F. F. (1969). Concerns for teachers: A developmental conceptualization. *American Educational Research Journal, 6,* 207–226.

Gagné, R. (1985). *The conditions of learning* (4th ed.). New York: Holt, Rinehart & Winston.

Gardner, H. (1985). *The mind's new science.* New York: Basic Books.

Garner, R. (1987). *Metacognition and reading comprehension.* Norwood, NJ: Ablex.

General Accounting Office. (1984). *New directions for federal programs to aid math and science teaching* (GAO-PEMO-85-5). Washington, DC: Author.

Gentner, D., & Stevens, A. L. (Eds.). (1982). *Mental models.* Hillsdale, NJ: Lawrence Erlbaum Associates.

Glaser, R. (1984). Education and thinking: The role of knowledge. *American Psychologist, 39,* 93–104.

Grossman, P. L. (1989). A study in contrast: Sources of pedagogical content knowledge for secondary English. *Journal of Teacher Education, 40*(5), 24–31.

Grossman, P. L. (1990). *The making of a teacher: Teacher knowledge and teacher education.* New York: Teachers College Press.

Grossman, P. L. (1991a). Overcoming the apprenticeship of observation in teacher education coursework. *Teaching and Teacher Education, 7,* 345–357.

Grossman, P. L. (1991b). What are we talking about anyway? Subject-matter knowledge of secondary English teachers. In J. E. Brophy (Ed.), *Advances in research on teaching: Vol. 2. Teachers' subject matter knowledge and classroom instruction* (pp. 245–264). Greenwich, CT: JAI Press.

Grossman, P. L., Wilson, W. M., & Shulman, L. S. (1989). Teachers of substance: Subject matter knowledge for teaching. In M. Reynolds (Ed.), *Knowledge base for the beginning teacher* (pp. 23–36). New York: Pergamon Press.

Guskey, T. R. (1986). Staff development and the process of teacher change. *Educational Researcher, 15*(5), 5–12.

Hashweh, M. Z. (1987). Effects of subject matter knowledge in teaching biology and physics. *Teaching and Teacher Education, 3,* 109–120.

Heaton, R. M. (1992). Who is minding the mathematics content? A case study of a fifth-grade teacher. *Elementary School Journal, 93,* 151–192.

Hollingsworth, S. (1989). Prior beliefs and cognitive change in learning to teach. *American Educational Research Journal, 26,* 160–189.

Holt-Reynolds, D. (1992). Personal history-based beliefs as relevant prior knowledge in coursework: Can we practice what we teach? *American Educational Research Journal, 29,* 325–349.

Hoy, W., & Woolfolk, A. (1990). Socialization of student teachers. *American Educational Research Journal, 27,* 279–300.

Huberman, M. (1989). On teachers' careers: Once over lightly, with a broad brush. *International Journal of Educational Research, 13,* 347–361.

Johnston, S. (1992). Images: A way of understanding the practical knowledge of student teachers. *Teaching and Teacher Education, 8,* 123–136.

Kagan, D. M. (1992). Professional growth among preservice and beginning teachers. *Review of Educational Research, 62,* 129–169.

Kagan, D. M., & Tippins, D. J. (1991). How student teachers describe their pupils. *Teaching and Teacher Education, 7,* 455–466.

Knowles, J. G. (1992). Models for understanding preservice and beginning teachers' biographies: Illustrations from case studies. In I. Goodson (Ed.), *Studying teachers' lives* (pp. 99–152). London: Routledge.

Krajcik, J. S., & Layman, J. W. (1989, March). *Middle school teachers' conceptions of heat and temperature: Personal and teaching knowledge.* Paper presented at the annual meeting of the American Educational Research Association, San Francisco.

Krajcik, J. S., Layman, J. W., Starr, M. L., & Magnusson, S. (1991, April). *The development of middle school teachers' content knowledge and pedagogical content knowledge of heat energy and temperature.* Paper presented at the annual meeting of the American Educational Research Association, Chicago.

Lakoff, G., & Johnson, M. (1980). *Metaphors we live by.* Chicago: University of Chicago Press.

Lederman, N. G., & Gess-Newsome, J. (1991, April). *Subject matter structures: Abstractions confront the concrete world of teaching.* Paper presented at the annual meeting of the American Educational Research Association, Chicago.

Leinhardt, G. (1988). Situated knowledge and expertise in teaching. In J. Calderhead (Ed.), *Teachers' professional learning* (pp. 146–168). London: Falmer.

Leinhardt, G., & Greeno, J. G. (1986). The cognitive skill of teaching. *Journal of Educational Psychology, 78,* 75–95.

Leinhardt, G., & Smith, D. (1985). Expertise in mathematics instruction: Subject matter knowledge. *Journal of Educational Psychology, 77,* 241–271.

Levin, B. B., & Ammon, P. (1992). The development of beginning teachers' pedagogical thinking: A longitudinal analysis of four case studies. *Teacher Education Quarterly, 19*(4), 19–37.

Little, J. W. (1982). Norms of collegiality and experimentation: Workplace conditions of school success. *American Educational Research Journal, 19,* 325–340.

Lortie, D. (1975). *Schoolteacher.* Chicago: University of Chicago Press.

Marks, R. (1990). Pedagogical content knowledge: From a mathematical case to a modified conception. *Journal of Teacher Education, 41*(3), 3–11.

McDiarmid, G. W. (1990). Challenging prospective teachers' beliefs during early field experience: A quixotic undertaking? *Journal of Teacher Education, 41*(3), 12–20.

McDiarmid, G. W. (1994). The arts and sciences as preparation for teaching. In K. Howey & N. Zympher (Eds.), *Informing faculty development for teacher educators.* Norwood, NJ: Ablex Publishing.

McDiarmid, G. W., Ball, D. L., & Anderson, C. (1989). Why staying ahead one chapter just won't work: Subject-specific pedagogy. In M. C. Reynolds (Ed.), *Knowledge base for the beginning teacher* (pp. 193–205). New York: Pergamon Press.

McLaughlin, M. (1987). Learning from experience: Lessons from policy implementation. *Educational Evaluation and Policy Analysis, 9,* 171–178.

McLaughlin, M., & Talbert, J. E. (1993). *Contexts that matter for teaching and learning: Strategic opportunities for meeting the nation's educational goals.* Stanford, CA: Center for Research on the Context of Secondary School Teaching, Stanford University.

National Center for Research on Teacher Education. (1988). Teacher education and learning to teach: A research agenda. *Journal of Teacher Education, 39*(6), 27–32.

National Center for Research on Teacher Education. (1991). *Final report: The teacher education and learning to teach study.* East Lansing: College of Education, Michigan State University.

National Council of Teachers of Mathematics. (1989). *Curriculum and evaluation standards for school mathematics.* Reston, VA: Author.

National Council of Teachers of Mathematics. (1991). *Professional standards for teaching mathematics.* Reston, VA: Author.

National Research Council. (1991). *Moving beyond myths: revitalizing undergraduate mathematics.* Washington, DC: National Academy Press.

National Research Council. (1993). *National science education standards: An enhanced sampler. A working paper of the National Committee on Science Education Standards and Assessment.* Washington, DC: Author.

Neale, D. C., Smith, D., & Johnson, W. G. (1990). Implementing conceptual change teaching in primary science. *Elementary School Journal, 91,* 109–131.

Norman, D. A. (1980). What goes on in the mind of the learner. In W. J. McKeachie (Ed.), *Learning, cognition, and college teaching: New directions for teaching and learning* (pp. 37–49). San Francisco: Jossey-Bass.

Novak, J. D., & Gowin, D. B. (1984). *Learning how to learn.* Cambridge, England: Cambridge University Press.

Oja, S. N. (1989). Teachers: Ages and stages of adult development. In M. L. Holly & C. S. McLoughlen (Eds.), *Perspectives on teacher professional development* (pp. 119–154). London: Falmer Press.

Oja, S. N. (1991). Adult development: Insights on staff development. In A. Lieberman & L. Miller (Eds.), *Staff development for education in the 90s.* New York: Teachers College Press.

Palincsar, A. S., & Brown, A. L. (1984). Reciprocal teaching of comprehension-fostering and monitoring strategies. *Cognition and Instruction, 1*(2), 117–175.

Pascarella, E. T., & Terenzini, P. (1991). *How college affects students.* San Francisco: Jossey-Bass.

Peterson, P. L. (1988). Teachers' and students' cognitional knowledge for classroom teaching and learning. *Educational Research, 17*(5), 5–14.

Peterson, P. L. (1990). The California study of elementary mathematics. *Educational Evaluation and Policy Analysis, 12,* 241–245.

Pines, A. L., & Novak, J. D. (1985). The interaction of audio-tutorial instruction with student prior knowledge: A proposed qualitative, case-study methodology. *Science Education, 69,* 212–228.

Prawat, R. S., Remillard, J., Putnam, R. T., & Heaton, R. M. (1992).

Teaching mathematics for understanding: Case studies of four fifth-grade teachers. *Elementary School Journal, 93,* 145–152.

Putnam, R. T. (1992a). Teaching the "hows" of mathematics for everyday life: A case study of a fifth-grade teacher. *Elementary School Journal, 93,* 163–177.

Putnam, R. T. (1992b). Thinking and authority in elementary-school mathematics tasks. In J. Brophy (Ed.), *Advances in research on teaching: Vol. 3. Planning and managing learning tasks and activities* (pp. 161–189). Greenwich, CT: JAI Press.

Putnam, R. T., Heaton, R. M., Prawat, R. S., & Remillard, J. (1992). Teaching mathematics for understanding: Discussing case studies of four fifth-grade teachers. *Elementary School Journal, 93,* 213–228.

Putnam, R. T., Lampert, M., & Peterson, P. L. (1990). Alternative perspectives on knowing mathematics in elementary schools. In C. Cazden (Ed.), *Review of research in education* (Vol. 16, pp. 57–150). Washington, DC: American Educational Research Association.

Resnick, L. B. (1989). Introduction. In L. B. Resnick (Eds.), *Knowing, learning, and instruction: Essays in honor of Robert Glaser* (pp. 1–24). Hillsdale, NJ: Lawrence Erlbaum Associates.

Resnick, L. B. (1985). Cognition and instruction: Recent theories of human competence. In B. L. Hammonds (Ed.), *Master lecture series: Vol. 4. Psychology and learning* (pp. 123–186). Washington, DC: American Psychological Association.

Richardson, V. (1990). Significant and worthwhile change in teaching practice. *Educational Researcher, 19*(7), 10–18.

Richardson, V. (1994). The consideration of beliefs in staff development. In V. Richardson (Ed.), *Teacher change and the staff development process: A case of reading instruction* (pp. 90–108). New York: Teachers College Press.

Richardson, V., & Anders, P. (1994). The study of teacher change. In V. Richardson (Ed.), *Teacher change and the staff development process: A case of reading instruction* (pp. 158–180). New York: Teachers College Press.

Richardson, V., Anders, P., Tidwell, D., & Lloyd, C. (1991). The relationship between teachers' beliefs and practices in reading comprehension instruction. *American Educational Research Journal, 28,* 559–586.

Rosenshine, B., & Stevens, R. (1986). Teaching functions. In M. C. Wittrock (Ed.), *Handbook of research on teaching* (3rd ed., pp. 376–391). New York: Macmillan.

Ross, D. D., Johnson, M., & Smith, W. (1991, April). *Developing a professional teacher at the University of Florida.* Paper presented at the annual meeting of the American Educational Research Association, Chicago.

Roth, K., Anderson, C., & Smith, E. (1986). *Curriculum materials, teacher talk and student learning: Case studies in fifth grade science teaching* (Research Series No. 171). East Lansing: Michigan State University, Institute for Research on Teaching.

Roth, K., Rosaen, C., & Lanier, P. (1988). *Learning to teach subject matter: Three cases in English, mathematics, and science.* Paper presented at the Midwest Regional Holmes Groups Conference, Chicago.

Sabers, D. S., Cushing, K. S., & Berliner, D. C. (1991). Differences among teachers in a task characterized by simultaneity, multidimensionality, and immediacy. *American Educational Research Journal, 28,* 63–88.

Sarason, S. (1990). *The predictable failure of educational reform: Can we change course before it's too late?* San Francisco: Jossey-Bass.

Saunders, W., Goldenberg, C., & Hamann, J. (1992). Instructional conversations beget instructional conversations. *Teaching and Teacher Education, 8,* 199–218.

Schifter, D., & Fosnot, C. T. (1993). *Reconstructing mathematics education: Stories of teachers meeting the challenges of reform.* New York: Teachers College Press.

Schifter, D., & Simon, M. A. (1992). Assessing teachers' development of a constructivist view of mathematics learning. *Teaching and Teacher Education, 8,* 187–197.

Schön, D. A. (1982). *The reflective practitioner.* New York: Basic Books.

Schön, D. A. (Ed.). (1991). *The reflective turn: Case studies in and on educational practice.* New York: Teachers College Press.

School Mathematics Study Group. (1972). Correlates of mathematics achievement: Teacher background and opinion variables. In J. W. Wilson & E. A. Begle (Eds.), *NLSMA Reports* (No. 23, Part A). Palo Alto, CA: Author.

Schram, P., & Wilcox, S. K. (1988). Changing preservice teachers' conception of mathematics learning. In M. Behr & C. Lacampagne (Eds.), *Proceedings of the Tenth Annual Meeting of the North American Chapter of the International Group for the Psychology of Mathematics Education.* DeKalb: Northern Illinois University.

Schram, P., Wilcox, S. K., Lappan, G., & Lanier, P. (1989). Changing mathematical conceptions of preservice teachers: A content and pedagogical intervention. In C. Maher, G. Goldin, & R. Davis (Eds.), *Proceedings of the Eleventh Annual Meeting of the North American Chapter of the International Group for the Psychology of Mathematics Education* (pp. 296–302). New Brunswick, NJ: Rutgers University.

Schreiter, B., & Ammon, P. (1989, March). *Teachers' thinking and their use of reading contracts.* Paper presented at the annual meeting of the American Educational Research Association, San Francisco.

Schwab, J. J. (1964). The structure of disciplines: Meanings and significance. In G. W. Ford & L. Pugno (Eds.), *The structure of knowledge and the curriculum.* Chicago: Rand McNally.

Shulman, L. S. (1986a). Paradigms and research programs in the study of teaching: A contemporary perspective. In M. C. Wittrock (Ed.), *Handbook of research on teaching* (3rd ed., pp. 3–36). New York: Macmillan.

Shulman, L. S. (1986b). Those who understand: Knowledge growth in teaching. *Educational Researcher, 15*(2), 4–14.

Shulman, L. S. (1987). Knowledge and teaching: Foundations of the new reform. *Harvard Educational Review, 57,* 1–22.

Shulman, L. S., & Grossman, P. L. (1987). *Final report to the Spencer Foundation* (Knowledge Growth in a Profession Technical Report). Stanford, CA: School of Education, Stanford University.

Simon, M. A. (1993). Prospective elementary teachers' knowledge of division. *Journal for Research in Mathematics Education, 24,* 233–254.

Simon, M. A. (1995). Reconstructing mathematics pedagogy from a constructivist perspective. *Journal of Research in Mathematics Education, 26,* 114–145.

Simon, M. A., & Blume, G. W. (1994a). Building and understanding multiplicative relationships: A study of prospective elementary teachers. *Journal for Research in Mathematics Education, 25,* 472–494.

Simon, M. A., & Blume, G. W. (1994b). Mathematical modeling as a component of understanding ratio-as-measure: A study of prospective elementary teachers. *Journal of Mathematical Behavior, 13,* 183–187.

Simon, M. A., & Blume, G. W. (in press). Mathematical justification in the classroom: A study of prospective elementary teachers. *Journal of Mathematical Behavior.*

Simon, M. A., & Brobeck, S. (1989, March). *Support for and challenges to mathematics reform in classrooms.* Paper presented at the annual meeting of the American Educational Research Association, San Francisco.

Simon, M. A., & Brobeck, S. (1993, October). *Changing views of mathematics learning: A case study of a prospective elementary teacher.* Paper presented at the annual meeting of the North American Chap-

ter of the International Group for the Psychology of Mathematics Education (PME-NA), Monterey, CA.

Simon, M. A., & Mazza, W. (1993, October). *From learning mathematics to teaching mathematics: A case study of a prospective teacher in a reform-oriented program.* Paper presented at the annual meeting of the North American Chapter of the International Group for the Psychology of Mathematics Education (PME-NA), Monterey, CA.

Simon, M. A., & Schifter, D. (1991). Towards a constructivist perspective: An intervention study of mathematics teacher development. *Educational Studies in Mathematics, 22,* 309–331.

Smith, D. C., & Neale, D. C. (1989). The construction of subject matter knowledge in primary science teaching. *Teaching and Teacher Education, 5,* 1–20.

Smith, D. C., & Neale, D. C. (1991). The construction of subject-matter knowledge in primary science teaching. In J. Brophy (Ed.), *Advances in research on teaching: Vol. 2. Teachers' knowledge of subject matter as it relates to their teaching practice* (pp. 187–243). Greenwich, CT: JAI Press.

Stallings, J. (1980). Allocated academic learning time revisited, or beyond time on task. *Educational Researcher, 8*(11), 11–16.

Stein, M. K., Baxter, J. A., & Leinhardt, G. (1990). Subject-matter knowledge and elementary instruction: A case from functions and graphing. *American Educational Research Journal, 27,* 639–663.

Steinberg, R., Haymore, J., & Marks, R. (1985, April). *Teachers' knowledge and structuring content in mathematics.* Paper presented at the annual meeting of the American Educational Research Association, Chicago.

Tharp, R., & Gallimore, R. (1988). *Rousing minds to life: Teaching learning, & schooling in social context.* Cambridge, England: Cambridge University Press.

Trumbull, D. J. (1990). Evolving conceptions of teaching reflections of one teacher. *Curriculum Inquiry, 20,* 161–182.

Weinstein, C. S. (1988). Preservice teachers' expectations about the first year of teaching. *Teaching and Teacher Education, 4,* 31–40.

Weinstein, C. S. (1989). Teacher education students' preconceptions of teaching. *Journal of Teacher Education, 5,* 53–60.

Weinstein, C. S. (1990). Prospective elementary teachers' beliefs about teaching: Implications for teacher education. *Teaching and Teacher Education, 6,* 279–290.

Wilcox, S., Schram, P., Lappan, G., & Lanier, P. (1990, April). *The role of a learning community in changing preservice teachers' knowledge and beliefs about mathematics education.* Paper presented at the annual meeting of the American Educational Research Association, Boston.

Wilson, S. M. (1988). *Understanding historical understanding: Subject matter knowledge and the teaching of history.* Unpublished doctoral dissertation, Stanford University, Stanford, CA.

Wilson, S. M., Shulman, L. S., & Richert, A. E. (1987). "150 different ways" of knowing: Representations of knowledge in teaching. In J. Calderhead (Ed.), *Exploring teachers' thinking* (pp. 104–124). London: Cassell.

Wilson, S. M., & Wineburg, S. S. (1988). Peering at history through different lenses: The role of disciplinary perspectives in teaching history. *Teachers College Record, 84,* 525–539.

Wood, T., Cobb, P., & Yackel, E. (1990). The contextual nature of teaching: Mathematics and reading instruction in one second-grade classroom. *Elementary School Journal, 90,* 497–513.

Wood, T., Cobb, P., & Yackel, E. (1991). Change in mathematics teaching: A case study. *American Educational Research Journal, 28,* 587–616.

Zeichner, K. M., & Gore, J. M. (1990). Teacher socialization. In W. R. Houston, M. Haberman, & J. Sikula (Eds.), *Handbook of research on teacher education* (pp. 329–348). New York: Macmillan.

# · 21 ·

# TEACHERS: BELIEFS AND KNOWLEDGE

## James Calderhead
### UNIVERSITY OF BATH, ENGLAND

Research on teachers' knowledge and beliefs has grown rapidly over the past two decades and now constitutes a substantial area of inquiry in explorations of the nature of teaching. How teachers make sense of their professional world, the knowledge and beliefs they bring with them to the task, and how teachers' understanding of teaching, learning, children, and the subject matter informs their everyday practice are important questions that necessitate an investigation of the cognitive and affective aspects of teachers' professional lives.

The growth of research in this area has instigated new ways of thinking about teaching and about professional and educational development. It has led to a wider repertoire of research techniques in inquiries into teaching. In addition, various implications have been drawn from the research evidence for both policy and practice in teacher education, curriculum development, and educational management.

Research on various aspects of teacher cognitions has been reviewed at different times in the past 15 years, sometimes for particular purposes. Shavelson and Stern (1981) reviewed research on teachers' thoughts, judgments, and decisions. Borko, Livingston, and Shavelson (1990) reviewed research on teacher planning and interactive thinking in relation to a cognitive psychological framework. A review of research on curriculum decision-making was undertaken by Reid (1978). Greta Morine-Dershimer (1991a) reviewed research on teachers' interactive thinking and the models of teachers' knowledge and thought that underpinned it. Kagan (1990) reviewed the methodology of research on teacher thinking. A comprehensive review of research on teachers' planning, interactive thinking, and beliefs was conducted by Clark and Peterson (1986). Research on teachers' knowledge and learning to teach has been reviewed by Carter (1990). Several edited collections of papers have also appeared overviewing the field; among them are works by Halkes and Olson (1984), Ben-Peretz, Bromme, and Halkes (1986), Calderhead (1987b), Lowyck and Clark (1989), and Day, Pope, and Denicolo (1990).

This discussion considers research that has been published since 1985, while also referring to earlier research that was influential in shaping thinking about teachers' cognitions. Research in the period 1985–1992 has been particularly characterized by an emphasis on the content and nature of teachers' knowledge and beliefs and on the processes involved in the growth of professional knowledge in teaching.

This chapter is structured around the key areas of research within the field. It begins with the history of development of the research area. This is followed by an account of the research methodology that has grown up around this topic and a review of empirical inquiries into teacher cognitions, including research on teacher planning, interactive thinking, and postactive reflection. Then, research on teachers' knowledge and beliefs is reviewed, followed by a short discussion of the implications of research in the field for teacher education, curriculum development, and school improvement. The review concludes with a look at possible future directions of research.

## HISTORICAL BACKGROUND

Research on teachers' cognitions has grown mostly since the early 1970s. The research on teaching in the late 1960s was strongly characterized by a behaviorist stance that sought to describe teaching in terms of sequences of behavior, and then to investigate the relationship of that behavior to children's learning. The research in the next two decades, however, became far more concerned with how teachers understand their work and the thought processes, judgments, and decisions that their work involves.

This shift in emphasis of the research on teaching can be explained by three factors. First, an important impetus was the growing dissatisfaction with the narrow focus of behaviorist studies. Attempts to define teaching competencies in terms of behavioral skills (Flanders, 1970) and to relate particular pat-

Acknowledgment: The author would like to thank Virginia Richardson (University of Arizona) for her helpful review of an earlier draft of this chapter.

terns of classroom behavior to learning outcomes (Brophy & Good, 1986; Rosenshine, 1971) left much of the skillfulness of teaching out of the account. A plethora of process–product studies that devised measures of classroom interaction based on the use of systematic observation schedules and that attempted to relate these measures to student learning outcomes seemed to be advancing the field very little. These studies often produced contradictory findings (see Dunkin & Biddle, 1974) or conclusions that some critics asserted were so obvious and trivial as not to have warranted investigation at all (McNamara,1981). Some detailed ethnographic studies of classrooms published in the late 1960s, such as Jackson's (1968) *Life in Classrooms* and L. M. Smith and Geoffrey's (1968) *The Complexities of an Urban Classroom,* were beginning to highlight the complex demands of the teaching role and the important contributions of teachers' own understandings of their work. As Shavelson (1973) later explained, what characterizes the skillful teacher may not be the ability to ask higher order questions, for example, but the ability to ask the right question of the right child at the right time. Such claims shifted attention from what teachers do in classrooms to the ways in which they think. How teachers made sense of classroom activity and the children they were teaching and how these understandings influenced the day-to-day decisions that teachers made became a subsequent focus of research on teaching.

A second factor that influenced the shift in emphasis in research on teaching was cognitive psychology. The view that human beings were capable of constructing their own reality and responding to it in unique and idiosyncratic ways directed psychologists' interests to the interactions of knowledge, thought, and behavior and led to many fruitful areas of inquiry. The rapid growth of research on human mental life in general in the 1970s brought a range of theories and research methods that seemed highly applicable to research on teaching. Winne and Marx (1977) coined the term *cognitive mediational model* to describe a new way of looking at classroom processes in terms of the interrelationships of teachers' and children's cognitions and behaviors. In the model, the cognitions of both teachers and children were acknowledged in a process of continuously interpreting and making sense of classroom life and influencing classroom behavior.

The emergence of cognitive science from the areas of cognitive psychology and artificial intelligence resulted in the development of theories of knowledge structure (e.g., Anderson, 1983), and this also influenced some researchers in the field of teacher cognitions who sought to map out the everyday working knowledge of teachers (e.g., Leinhardt & Greeno, 1986).

A third factor that contributed to the growth of research on teacher cognitions was increasing recognition of the centrality of the teacher in educational processes. Work in the area of curriculum development, for instance, had frequently been pursued by curriculum experts producing packages of ideas and materials to be passed on and implemented by the teacher, and theoretical models of curriculum development were derived from psychological theory or analytical philosophy (Taba, 1962; Wheeler, 1967). The inability of several large-scale development projects in the 1960s and early 1970s to alter teaching and learning processes in classrooms drew attention to the role of the teacher in curriculum development (e.g., Doyle & Ponder, 1977) and to the intrinsic involvement of teachers' own profes-

sional development in the processes of curriculum change (e.g., Stenhouse, 1975). Similarly, researchers examining the social effects of schooling had in the past tended to focus on educational policies and systems and the outcomes of education in terms of the qualifications obtained; in the 1970s they began to devote attention to developing fuller accounts of the educational processes at work in classrooms that resulted in differential patterns of attainment. This research focused on how teachers interpreted and were affected by the political, ideological, and material contexts in which they worked. It also drew attention to the key role of teachers in the educational system, and in particular to the thinking and decision-making that informed their practice (e.g., Eggleston, 1977; Woods, 1980).

Over the past two decades research on teachers' knowledge, thinking, and decision-making has progressed through three distinct stages, each characterized by an emphasis on a particular aspect of teachers' cognitive life or a particular model of teachers' thought and practice. In the 1970s, studies typically focused on teachers' decision-making. Decision-making was seen as the link between thought and action, and, following Jackson's (1968) distinction between preactive and interactive teaching, for a time research explored both the reflective decision-making that occurred in teachers' planning (Morine, 1976) and the spontaneous decision-making that occurred during classroom interactions (Peterson & Clark, 1978). Several experimental studies were conducted using policy-capturing techniques (e.g., Borko, Cone, Atwood Russo, & Shavelson, 1979) or simulations (e.g., Rohrkemper & Brophy, 1983) that aimed to explicate the information that teachers use in decision-making and to identify how different information influenced the outcome of their decisions. It was quickly recognized, however, that the concept of decision-making was quite restricted in accounting for the mental life of teachers. Much of teachers' cognitive activity did not seem to involve the degree of deliberation and choice that is generally associated with decision-making, and in consequence, research diversified to include teachers' perceptions, attributions, thinking, judgments, reflections, evaluations, and routines. This expansion of the research marked the second phase of research on teachers' thinking.

The third phase of research focused on investigating the knowledge and beliefs that lay behind the practice of teaching. L. S. Shulman (1986a) stimulated an interest specifically in the subject matter knowledge of teaching, suggesting that the ways teachers understood subject matter and the knowledge they developed that helped them foster students' learning of a subject was a much neglected area of research (see chapter 13). Also, a large number of biographical studies of teachers explored the knowledge and beliefs that were acquired before and during professional training (Bullough, Knowles, & Crow, 1991). Several studies explored the knowledge that lay behind an individual teacher's classroom practice. Some of these relied on detailed case studies of teachers (e.g., Clandinin, 1986; Elbaz, 1983); others involved more systematic knowledge elicitation procedures with the aim of charting the development of the knowledge base of teachers (Beyerbach, 1988; Leinhardt & Greeno, 1986; Morine-Dershimer, 1991b).

To chart a human knowledge base in any area of professional activity is, however, an ambitious and potentially endless task. Teachers clearly have a vast, somewhat idiosyncratic knowledge base that may be continuously changing and restructuring.

Nevertheless, studies in this area have raised many questions about the nature of teachers' knowledge and about qualitative differences in the types of knowledge teachers hold. Further, several critiques of research on teachers' cognitions have drawn attention to the separation of cognitions and behavior in research on teaching (Berliner, 1989; McNamara, 1990; Yinger, 1986) and raised questions about the fruitfulness of studying teacher cognitions devoid of the behavior associated with them. Other critiques have pointed to the omission of an affective dimension. This has led to several debates on the epistemology of teachers' practice and the interrelationships of knowledge, thought, and action. Stimulated to some extent by Schon's (1983, 1987) work on professional practice, considerable effort recently has been expended on examining such concepts as reflection in action and knowledge in action. Concepts such as situated cognition (Brown, Collins, & Duguid, 1989) in cognitive psychology have also attracted interest in exploring the interrelationship of knowledge and action in the classroom context and developing an understanding that more accurately captures the cognitive, affective, and behavioral aspects of teachers' work.

## METHODOLOGY

The exploration of teachers' cognitions has led to the development of a range of innovative methods for collecting evidence about teaching. Observation alone is of limited value, for the cognitive acts under investigation are normally covert and beyond immediate access to the researcher. Methods of eliciting the knowledge, beliefs, and thinking of teachers have frequently been borrowed from the fields of cognitive psychology, human problem solving, social anthropology, and the humanities. The methods commonly used are described below in five categories. The advantages and limitations of the methods are considered. This is followed by a discussion of general issues concerning the validity and representativeness of the data collected through the use of these methods and the relationship of the methods to theoretical perspectives on teacher cognitions.

### Simulations

Simulation methods include policy capturing, critical incidents, the use of controlled planning tasks, and the use of video taped excerpts of teaching situations. These methods are characterized by the use of a contrived problem, situation, or context that often can be manipulated by the researcher and can be used to elicit teachers' thinking about practical teaching situations. Policy capturing has been used to study teachers' judgments and the factors that influence them (e.g., Borko et al., 1979). It involves a series of descriptions or vignettes of a decision-making situation in which each description covers several features that can be systematically varied. Rohrkemper and Brophy (1983), for example, provided teachers with descriptions or vignettes of different types of difficult children and asked them how they would respond to them in a range of different classroom situations. By examining the relationship between the teachers' judgments or decisions and the factors

varying within the vignettes, it was possible to trace those features of children that influenced teachers' decisions.

Much of this research developed out of earlier work by Tversky and Kahneman (1974) on the heuristics that are adopted in human judgment and the factors that influence their use.

### Commentaries

Attempts to gain access to teachers' thought processes have frequently relied on what teachers report about their thinking. Such commentaries have taken the form of *think-aloud commentaries* (e.g., Yinger, 1980), in which teachers are asked to think aloud while planning a lesson or unit of work; *stimulated recall commentaries* (e.g., Peterson & Clark, 1978), in which teachers watch a video of their own teaching and attempt to recall their thinking at the time; and *structured interviews,* where, for instance, a teacher might be interviewed immediately after a lesson about particular episodes of his interaction with children and the perceptions and judgments that accompanied his action (e.g., Borko & Livingston, 1989; Bromme, 1987). Some researchers have also used *teachers' talk* about their own teaching in an interview context as a source of data for inferring teachers' conceptual models, metaphors, and ways of thinking about teaching (e.g., Munby, 1986).

When teacher commentaries have been used as data concerning teacher cognitions, several issues have emerged concerning the status and significance of the elicited reports. The debate has focused particularly on stimulated recall data (see Calderhead, 1987a; Morine-Dershimer et al., 1992; Yinger, 1986), but several of the issues apply equally to other verbal reporting methods. Researchers using stimulated recall techniques often cite the work of Bloom (1953), who first adopted the technique to explore the thinking of university students, and justify the use of the method by reference to the work of Ericsson and Simon (1980), who suggested, on the basis of observed human problem-solving situations, that recall immediately after the event appears to reflect accurately the problem-solving strategies employed. However, teaching is substantially different from laboratory-based problem-solving situations. When teachers are asked to recall their thinking, what status do such reports have? Early research took these reports to be a reasonable representation of teachers' thinking (e.g., Peterson & Clark, 1978), but several questions have been raised about the various possible influences on teachers' reporting of their thoughts, and also about the adequacy with which words represent thought. It has been suggested, for example, that teachers' thoughts during teaching may at times be more appropriately represented in terms of images, feelings, or metaphors and may be difficult to express in words (Wubbels, 1992). It has also been argued that teachers may not have access to much of their thinking, so that reports may be partial; or the research context may place teachers in situations where they may tend to produce post hoc rationalizations for their behavior (Yinger, 1986).

Other studies have regarded teachers' verbal reports as an amalgam of justifications, explanations, recollections, and partial descriptions and either have sought a more sensitive, qualitative and ethnographic interpretation (Brown & McIntyre, 1993) or have used a linguistic analysis, categorizing the language and concepts used in an attempt to uncover the kinds of conceptual frameworks that are implicit in teachers' talk about their practice (e.g., Mosenthal, 1989; Munby, 1986).

Clearly, care must be taken in the elicitation and analysis of verbal report data and in interpreting the significance of the data. Consideration must be given to what the data represent and the limitations on the extent to which such data can provide an accurate description of teachers' thinking (Leinhardt, 1990).

## Concept Mapping and Repertory Grid

A variety of methods are loosely categorized under concept mapping and repertory gridding. The common feature of these methods is their attempt to systematically elicit and represent conceptual structures. Concept mapping has been used to investigate teachers' understandings of planning (Beyerbach, 1988) and classroom management (Morine-Dershimer, 1991b). It involves a three-stage process in which teachers are first asked to brainstorm on a particular topic, producing a list of concepts; then to indicate how these concepts are interrelated; and finally to name the relationships between concepts. A similar procedure is the ordered tree analysis adopted by Roehler et al. (1988) in which teachers are presented with key concepts concerning reading and reading instruction and asked to organize them into networks of relationships to reflect their own thinking. This method was used to investigate differences in the knowledge structures of expert and novice teachers.

These procedures have been employed in examining the nature of teachers' understandings in particular areas. For example, the teacher who associates classroom management with personal relationships, classroom climate, and an ethos of mutual respect would most likely have quite a different understanding of his or her practice from one who associates classroom management with rules, sanctions, rewards, and praise.

Concept mapping has been found to be particularly useful in examining changes in teachers' conceptions over time, evaluating, for example, the effects of training courses on teachers' conceptions (Morine-Dershimer, 1991b; Morine-Dershimer et al., 1992). However, concept mapping has also been criticized for imposing a particular structure on teachers' thinking, presuming that teachers' understandings are reducible to a set of propositional concepts and relations (Kagan, 1990) rather than a richer amalgam of less easily defined thoughts and feelings.

Repertory grid and card sort techniques have similarly attempted to map out teachers' understandings. Derived largely from Kelly's (1955) personal construct theory, they are based on the assumption that human beings understand their environment in terms of their own construct system, which can be represented in terms of a repertoire of bipolar dimensions. Triadic elicitation is one of the most commonly adopted methods in this area. This was used, for example, by Morine-Dershimer (1979) in investigating teachers' conceptions of their pupils. The names of the pupils in a class were written on individual cards, and the teacher was then given three cards selected at random and asked to say how two of the children were similar and the third different. This procedure was repeated with other selections until the elicited constructs began to be repeated. In the case of a card sort technique, teachers are presented with a series of cards, each one describing the elements (e.g., children, situations) under investigation. The teacher is asked to sort them into groups and then to talk

about the differences between the groups. Again, the process is repeated to form alternative groups until no further significant groups are possible or until the elicited constructs are repeated.

Repertory grid techniques (so called because the elicited constructs and their interrelationships can be represented in grid form) are relatively easy to use and are readily adapted to different contexts, but they also impose a simple bipolar structure on knowledge, which some have argued may misrepresent its nature (Calderhead, 1987a).

## Ethnography and Case Studies

Detailed case studies of teaching using a variety of observational and interview procedures have frequently resulted in well-documented and insightful accounts of teachers' thoughts and practice. The first studies to draw attention to the significance of teachers' thinking were ethnographic in nature (Jackson, 1968; L. M. Smith & Geoffrey, 1968), and ethnographic studies of teachers and beginning teachers have emerged periodically over the past two decades (Lacey, 1977; Tabachnick & Zeichner, 1984). Although the methods employed in ethnographic studies have varied considerably and although studies have drawn variously on precedents in sociology, psychology, and anthropology (see Delamont & Atkinson, 1980), their common aim is to produce a detailed and supported interpretation of the behavior and perspectives of others. By dwelling on one individual teacher, ethnographic studies are able to amass extensive data about a teacher's practice and to offer more detailed accounts of the relationship between thought and action. Ethnographic studies enable the complex network of factors involved in particular classroom actions to be explored, and, because of the sustained relationship between researcher and teacher over a long period, the researcher is often in a suitable position to develop insights into the work of the teacher that can be tested with the data in hand. Leinhardt (1988), for example, after studying several mathematics lessons taught by one teacher and after extensive interviews about both the lessons and the teacher's own past experiences of mathematics, pieced together an account of how the teacher's practice was contextualized within her own past experiences of learning mathematics and was influenced by her own professional training and contact with different curricular materials.

Some of the drawbacks of ethnographic methods, however, are that they require careful and systematic analysis of large amounts of qualitative data, and several writers have drawn attention to the possibility that researchers can extract from this data interpretations to which they are themselves particularly disposed (Miles & Huberman, 1984). The potential of ethnographic research to yield generalizations about teaching has also been debated (e.g., Stenhouse, 1980), some researchers arguing that the merit of the approach lies in the insights about particular aspects of teaching that such detailed studies can provide (e.g., Woods, 1979).

## Narratives

Teachers' own accounts of their teaching, in the form of diaries (Tann, 1993), stories (Clandinin, 1986; Elbaz, 1983), or negotiated biographies in which a researcher works with the teacher to make the teacher's life and experiences of teaching explicit (Bullough, 1991b), have been used increasingly to describe teachers' cognitions. Narrative accounts of teaching aim to describe teaching in teachers' own words and to represent the real-life complexity of teaching. Some narrative researchers view this research as following traditions derived from the humanities rather than the social sciences (Connolly & Clandinin, 1990). Rather than perceiving teaching through the theoretical frameworks of psychology and sociology, the researchers aim to describe teachers' own theories and perspectives. Elbaz (1992) suggests there is a moral issue at stake here in that narrative research allows teachers a voice in how they themselves are portrayed, a voice that, she argues, is denied in much social scientific research. It also raises several ethical issues in that the function of the researcher becomes one of facilitating self-disclosure and in consequence making explicit the beliefs and assumptions of the teacher, raising the teacher's level of consciousness of his or her practice, with potential consequences for affective, cognitive, and behavioral change.

Narrative research has focused both on specific aspects of teaching and on teachers' wider perspectives on their work. Gudmundsdottir (1991) provided a case study of one English teacher in which narrative accounts of the lessons were used to construct a model of how the teacher thought about the teaching and learning of literature. Clandinin (1986), on the other hand, provided accounts of three primary teachers' classroom practices in terms of fundamental images or metaphors that shaped their thinking about practice and that often originated in other life experiences. One teacher, for example, is described as holding an image of "language as the key," so that language was perceived as the basis of all classroom activity. Another held the image of the classroom as a home, and this image manifested itself in her relationships with children and her organization of the classroom. Bullough et al. (1991) provide life history accounts of six beginning teachers, drawing on various key life experiences in an attempt to explain how each teacher's practice develops as it does.

Narrative studies are a source of teachers' perspectives on their own teaching and often take a broader focus, examining teachers' practice in the context of other life experiences. Methods involved in narrative studies have varied somewhat, and in education this approach to research has developed substantially in recent years. Debates over the status of narratives, questions about what teachers are capable of narrating, and debates over the veracity of narratives are ongoing (e.g., Carter, 1993) and will no doubt contribute further to the development of this area of research.

## PURPOSE, VALIDITY, AND RELIABILITY

Research can be pursued for different reasons and within different frameworks of assumptions about the nature of research activity itself and of what counts as appropriate data and valid interpretation. Distinctions have commonly been made between research that is positivist, interpretive, or critical in orientation, carrying different assumptions about the nature and organization of knowledge and the purpose of inquiry (Gibson, 1986).

*Positivist research* derives its principles and procedures from the natural sciences. It assumes an objective reality and aims to develop testable generalizations about human behavior that would enable greater levels of prediction and control. *Interpretive research,* on the other hand, is concerned with describing an individual's experience of reality and aims for highly detailed studies of individuals for the purpose of understanding human action in context. Research within the *critical tradition* has a greater concern with emancipation through understanding, aiming to sensitize people, through a critical analysis of their situation, to the power relations in their own context and the causes and consequences of their own actions.

Research on teachers' cognitions has occurred within each of these traditions, and consequently has been carried out with various purposes in mind, complying with different methodological conventions. This plurality must be borne in mind in any comparison or synthesis of research findings.

## RESEARCH ON TEACHERS' COGNITIONS

Some of the first inquiries into the cognitive aspects of teaching identified qualitative differences in the thinking of teachers before, during, and after classroom interaction (Jackson, 1968). Whereas teachers' thinking before and after teaching seemed to be characterized by some deliberation and evaluation, teachers' thinking in the classroom was by necessity much more immediate and spontaneous. This observation gave rise to the distinctions of preactive, interactive, and postactive phases of teaching. Many studies have since focused on teachers' cognitions in one of these phases, elaborating on our understanding of the processes involved, while a few have examined the interactions among the thinking in two or all three phases.

### Preactive Teaching

Planning and preparing for teaching is an area where student teachers frequently experience difficulty. It is also an aspect of teaching that is typically undervalued, as the time allowed for planning and the support offered to teachers to undertake this work is often inadequate. Conventional models used to instruct teachers in planning techniques frequently have been found to be of limited value; they have been derived from rational analyses of the planning task, focusing on the specification of aims and objectives and how these are to be achieved. Given the difficulties that planning presents in teaching and in learning to teach, it is not surprising that research in this field has attracted considerable interest.

Research on teachers' planning has taken several different methodological approaches but consistently has highlighted six main features of the processes involved. These are discussed below.

1. *Planning occurs at different levels.* Clark and Yinger (1979) found that teachers regularly planned at six different levels—yearly, termly, unit, weekly, daily, and lesson. Teachers' concerns and the focus of their planning were found to differ at different stages. In yearly planning, for instance, teachers might be most concerned about the selection and sequencing of topics, whereas at the weekly level teachers might be more concerned with matters of timing and the organization of particular materials or activities. Research by McCutcheon (1980) with 24 elementary schoolteachers also confirmed that teachers

engage in different types of planning at different times over the course of the school year.

Clark and Yinger (1987) describe planning as a nested process in which decisions taken at different levels frame the decisions made at other levels, and that the plans for a particular day's or lesson's activities may have developed in the context of diverse planning decisions that may have been made some time previously. Teachers' planning, therefore, is rarely an isolated process. It may be seen more realistically as a continuous process of reexamining, refining, and adding to previous decisions.

2. *Planning is mostly informal.* Although teachers do occasionally write formal plans and keep a record of their planning activities, several researchers have suggested that this is frequently only to satisfy administrative requirements, and that teachers generally do not value the writing of formal plans or find such activities too time-consuming. Much of teachers' planning is therefore of an informal variety—"mental planning," as McCutcheon (1980) called it. This frequently occurs at odd times during the day when the teacher reflects on how things have gone and on what needs to be done for the coming activities.

3. *Planning is creative.* Rational planning models tend to emphasize the logical deductive processes involved in translating aims and objectives into classroom activities. Studies of the thinking processes of teachers while planning indicate that planning has a problem-finding as well as problem-solving phase. Planning involves teachers considering alternative ways of looking at situations, identifying problems to analyze and follow up. The planning of a year's work or the planning of an individual lesson involves creating ideas and drawing on one's knowledge about teaching to translate these into workable classroom activities (Sardo-Brown, 1988; Yinger, 1980).

4. *Planning is knowledge based.* The task of planning involves teachers drawing on different areas of knowledge. These areas include knowledge of subject matter; knowledge of classroom activities; knowledge of children—their interests and abilities, and how long it takes them to complete certain tasks; knowledge of teaching, of school conventions, of materials, and of school texts. In fact, planning requires teachers to have a very wide knowledge base and to be able to orchestrate this knowledge in the process of constructing activities. One of the major reasons offered for why planning is a difficult task for beginning teachers is that they lack the extensive knowledge base that is required (Borko & Livingston, 1989; Calderhead, 1987c; Sardo-Brown, 1990). Consequently, their plans may be incomplete, or turn out to be unworkable in the classroom context.

5. *Planning must allow flexibility.* Experienced teachers have been found to possess a large repertoire of plans in memory—clear conceptions of how particular types of lessons are acted out, or of how particular topics are taught. Consequently, for experienced teachers, planning may involve the fine-tuning of existing plans to a particular context, whereas for the beginning teacher the construction of plans may involve much more fundamental thought processes. Because of the repertoire of complex plans that teachers can develop with experience, it may be possible for them to be more adaptable to particular contexts. Whereas beginning teachers have been found to adhere more rigidly to their plans in teaching, even when it might

be inappropriate to do so, the experienced teacher may be better placed to cope with unexpected events and responses. A feature of effective planning may be to prepare teachers to be able to adapt planning activities to suit a variety of situations that might emerge (Borko & Livingston, 1989; Clark & Yinger, 1987).

6. *Planning occurs within a practical and ideological context.* The nature of teachers' planning can be influenced by the expectations that exist within the school (McCutcheon, 1980) or by the subject matter itself. John (1991), for example, found that a sample of student mathematics teachers held a similar view of their subject, namely, that it was a hierarchically structured body of knowledge and skills, which led them to plan in a sequential manner, whereas student geography teachers in the same institution appeared to have no shared definition of their subject and were less homogeneous in their approaches to planning. In another questionnaire study of factors influencing teachers' decisions about the content of their mathematics lessons, teachers generally ranked the textbooks in use and the students' and teachers' own conception of the subject and how it should be taught as influential in their decisions, although teachers seemed to follow different styles of decision-making, some being more influenced by the textbook, others by district objectives or by their own views of mathematics teaching (Schmidt, Porter, Floden, Freeman, & Schwille, 1987).

## Interactive Teaching

Research on teachers' thinking during interactive teaching suggests that teachers make few decisions in the classroom. Much of teachers' thinking focuses on the children and the instructional process and is concerned with implementing the planned activity, or adjusting the activity to the children and context using well-established instructional routines. During interactive teaching, teachers seem to be particularly attentive to cues that have strategic significance in indicating how the activity is progressing and whether children in general understand and are able to complete the activity. Lundgren (1972), for example, found that in whole-class teaching in secondary science lessons, teachers took particular note of the progress of students toward the lower end of ability and paced the lesson accordingly. Bromme (1987) also found that after teaching a lesson, secondary mathematics teachers were able to remember and comment on examples of children's understanding and misunderstanding that represented significant moments in the lesson when they found they had to explain, elaborate a point, or move on. But the teachers did not associate these incidents with the abilities or progress of individual children. Teachers, it seems, rarely act as diagnosticians and remediators of individual children's difficulties, but have developed ways of understanding and responding to difficulties that are more specifically adapted to the complex classroom context.

Putnam (1987) also suggests that the diagnostic/remediation model does not fit the behavior of experienced teachers and suggests an alternative model based on the concepts of curriculum script and agenda. A curriculum script is viewed as a loosely ordered but well-defined set of skills and concepts students are expected to learn, together with the activities and strategies associated with teaching the particular topic. In classroom interaction, the script largely determines the teachers' agenda, a dynamic mental plan for the particular lesson. As the lesson is taught, the teacher notes various performance cues, which are used to add to, revise, or update the agenda. Experienced teachers are seen as having a vast repertoire of curriculum scripts that provide the foundation for individual lesson agendas.

An alternative conceptualization is offered by Clark and Yinger (1987), who suggest that both planning and interactive teaching contain characteristics of a design process. They propose that Schon's (1983) notion of reflection in action captures well some of the creative aspects of teaching. When teachers encounter a novel situation, they draw on their past experience to develop hypotheses about the nature of the problem and possible solutions to it. This reflection in action leads teachers to try certain solutions, to monitor their effects, and to interpret the outcomes to determine future action.

## Postactive Reflection

After teaching, teachers may reflect on classroom events. This reflection, in addition to being a retrospective analysis, may have a prospective dimension. Teachers may be considering what can be learned from recent experience, the significance of the day's or week's events, and what the implications are for future teaching.

In recent years there has been considerable interest in reflection during teacher education and how reflection might be facilitated to improve the quality of teachers' learning (Clift, Houston, & Pugach, 1990; Calderhead, 1987c). Several researchers, drawing on Habermas's distinction of "interests at hand" (see Ewert, 1991), have distinguished three levels of reflection; the technical, the practical, and the critical (e.g., Zeichner & Liston, 1987). At the technical level, teachers' reflections are concerned with whether particular objectives were achieved according to given criteria. For instance, judgments about the effectiveness of one's classroom management might be made in terms of the level of engagement of the children in a specified task. At the practical level, teachers, as well as questioning the effectiveness of their actions, also are questioning the ends to which those actions lead. At this level, ethical and moral considerations about what are appropriate ends and means enter into teachers' thinking. The critical level refers to a much more deliberative form of reflection that questions not only teachers' actions and their effects, but the ideological and material contexts in which those actions take place. Consequently, reflection at the critical level involves questioning the purposes of education and the assumptions that underlie practice.

Achieving these levels of reflection has not proved easy, however. The pressures on teachers, together with a school culture that generally values action above reflection, make it difficult for teachers to find the time and opportunities for reflection. Studies of teachers' reflection tend to indicate fairly superficial levels of analysis and evaluation. Attempts to increase the extent and depth of student teachers' reflection through action research, professional journals, and various reflective tasks have met with limited success (e.g., Tabachnick & Zeichner, 1991; Valli, 1992). McIntyre (1993) suggests that this limited progress might be explained in terms of the lack of analytical frameworks that students themselves possess and the paucity of such frameworks during teacher training for

examining and evaluating practice in detail. He suggests that this helps to identify the vital role of higher educational institutions in teacher education, in identifying, developing, and contributing such frameworks to the professional development process.

Research on teachers' thinking has helped to clarify some of the complex and creative aspects of teaching. It has also highlighted the enormous range of knowledge that the experienced teacher possesses and uses and that has come to be embedded within teachers' practice. Teachers, it seems, hold a vast array of knowledge about teaching, children, the curriculum, and schools. Research on teachers' thinking has raised several questions about how this knowledge is organized, how it is acquired, and how it is used.

## TEACHERS' KNOWLEDGE AND BELIEFS

The terms *knowledge* and *beliefs* have been widely used in reference to teachers' cognitions. Research has focused on many aspects of knowledge and belief, and the two concepts are not always easily distinguishable. Although beliefs generally refer to suppositions, commitments, and ideologies, knowledge is taken to refer to factual propositions and the understandings that inform skillful action. Research, however, has identified a variety of content and forms that teachers' knowledge and beliefs can take.

### Teachers' Knowledge

The attention that research on teachers' knowledge has received in recent years has often been motivated by a concern to explore and map the knowledge base of teaching, providing both a basis for training programs and a demonstration of the complexity of teaching and its right to due recognition as a professional activity (Reynolds, 1989). However, considerable debate has emerged over what constitutes teachers' professional knowledge, how it might be represented, and how knowledge relates to practice. Tom and Valli (1990) have drawn attention to the different conceptions of knowledge that have emerged from the three epistemological positions mentioned earlier. Within the positivist tradition, professional knowledge is viewed as a set of lawlike generalizations that can be identified through classroom research and applied by practitioners. The interpretive tradition, on the other hand, views meaning as context dependent and seeks the meaning that humans attach to the interpersonal and social aspects of their lives. Explicit knowledge exists in the form of case studies and ethnographies and serves to generate ways of viewing situations and solving problems that teachers might be able to interpret within the context of their own classrooms. The critical theory tradition views knowledge as serving particular interests and characterizing certain power relations. A critical theory perspective aims to sensitize teachers to the ways in which knowledge is being used and the values that are implicit within it.

Yinger and Hendricks-Lee (1993) argue that the knowledge and expertise of teachers have been regarded too often as a property of the individual, whereas, they suggest, it may be more appropriate to consider knowledge as lying within the interaction of particular contexts and situations. They suggest that teachers' working knowledge is as much dependent on the environment within which teachers work as on the individuals. They propose that knowledge exists within various systems—cultural, physical, social, historical, and personal—and that learning to teach involves developing ways of interacting within these systems.

Recent discussion of the concept of situated cognition (Brown, Collins, & Duiguid, 1989) has emphasized how knowledge is in part a product of the activity, context, and culture in which it is developed and used. Leinhardt (1988), in an in-depth case study of one teacher, demonstrated how this concept might be applied.

Grimmett, MacKinnon, Erickson, & Riecken (1990) similarly argue that discussions of teachers' knowledge frequently presume that knowledge is of a propositional nature. In their discussion of the nature of reflection and the role of knowledge, they present the possibility that knowledge in teaching is dialectical, arising out of interactions among people in particular situations, where participants constantly reconstruct their understandings of action situations, themselves as teachers, and their assumptions about teaching.

Research has yielded a number of categories that have been applied to the day-to-day working knowledge of teachers, and each has generated its own field of literature. Some typologies of knowledge also have been proposed in an attempt to delineate the types of knowledge that teachers hold and how they might be interrelated (Grossman, 1990; Kremer-Hayon, 1990). Several types of knowledge are discussed below.

*Subject Knowledge.* Much of the research on classroom interaction and the thinking of teachers has focused on the managerial aspects of teaching—how teachers organize the classroom and the children, and general strategies of planning. L. S. Shulman (1986b) suggests that an important omission has been the study of teachers' understandings of their subject and the role this understanding plays in helping children develop their understanding of the subject.

L. S. Shulman (1986a) suggests that teachers' subject knowledge consists of three main categories: subject matter content knowledge, pedagogical content knowledge, and curricular knowledge. Subject matter content knowledge refers not only to the facts of the discipline but to how those facts are organized within the discipline and how they are generated and tested as valid and acceptable. Pedagogical content knowledge refers to the body of knowledge that enables particular content to be taught. Such knowledge includes the analogies, illustrations, examples, anecdotes, explanations, and demonstrations that can be used to represent subject matter to the learner, as well as knowledge of the common misconceptions and areas of difficulty that students encounter that enables teachers to help children understand the subject. Shulman suggests that pedagogical content knowledge is highly specific to particular subject matter and that learning to teach requires not only understanding the subject itself, but also developing a wide repertoire of pedagogical content knowledge so that teachers can help learners of different backgrounds and intuitive understandings appreciate and understand new subject matter. Curricular knowledge refers to the individual materials that are available,

the ideas and issues they contain, and the concepts of organization, coherence, and progression that underlie them.

Several studies have recently explored the nature of teachers' subject knowledge in mathematics (Lampert, 1986), English (Grossman, 1987), language (Freeman, 1991a), history (Wilson & Wineburg, 1988), and social studies (Cornett, 1990; Gudmundsdottir & Shulman, 1989). The specificity of these studies suggests the highly specific content-related areas of knowledge that teachers develop and use in their teaching. Studies of experts and novices have also found that student teachers spend a great deal of time in the first 2 years of full-time teaching developing their own understanding of a subject. Teachers, it seems, require a deep and full understanding of the subject area, an understanding that is characterized by a knowledge of many concepts and their interrelationships. This knowledge is both broad and deep, enabling them to facilitate the building of similar connections in the minds of others. The novice teacher must also develop a large repertoire of pedagogical content knowledge and a curricular knowledge of the materials and resources that are available within the subject area.

In a series of studies of student teachers, Grossman (1990) attached considerable importance to pedagogical content knowledge, which she divided into four categories: conceptions of purposes for teaching subject matter, knowledge of students' understanding (including common misconceptions and difficulties), curricular knowledge, and knowledge of instructional strategies. She argued that much of this knowledge is acquired in the conventional curriculum and instruction courses of college preservice education, although the value of such courses has not always been fully recognized either by student teachers or by teacher educators.

Although Shulman and his colleagues have emphasized the significance and complexity of teachers' subject knowledge, the model underlying much of the work in this area is basically a transmission model. It has been assumed that teachers understand a subject and, through appropriate tasks, explanations, and demonstrations, develop this understanding in children. Researchers adopting a more constructivist conception of teaching and learning processes have questioned whether Shulman's suggested structure of teachers' knowledge is a necessary prerequisite for teaching (e.g., Sockett, 1987). Others have suggested that different approaches to teaching and learning may pose different demands on a pedagogical knowledge base (Wubbels, 1992). The concept of pedagogical content knowledge has also been questioned by some researchers who have suggested that it is not a discrete category of knowledge at all, but inextricable from content knowledge itself (Marks, 1990; McNamara, 1991). Several studies have indicated also that student teachers' understandings of a subject seem to be influenced by a variety of past experiences, which can shape the way in which their understanding of the subject from the perspective of a teacher develops (Wilcox, Schram, Lappen, & Lanvier, 1990; McDiarmid, 1993).

D. L. Ball and McDiarmid (1990) suggest that student teachers' lack of expertise and confidence in subject matter is a serious issue in teacher education, and that the development of subject matter competence needs to be addressed. Similarly, in a survey of student primary teachers in England, Bennett and Carré (1993) found that student teachers' understanding of the subject, particularly of mathematics and science, as revealed in concept attainment tests was frequently weak and improved little during their teacher education course.

***Craft Knowledge.*** The term *craft knowledge* has been used to refer specifically to the knowledge that teachers acquire within their own classroom practice, the knowledge that enables them to employ the strategies, tactics, and routines that they do. It has sometimes been referred to as "the wisdom of practice" (Schwab, 1971; L. S. Shulman, 1987). Brown and McIntyre (1993) refer to craft knowledge as "the professional knowledge which teachers use in their day-to-day classroom teaching, knowledge which is not generally made explicit by teachers and which teachers are not likely always to be conscious of using" (p. 19). Interest in teachers' craft knowledge has grown particularly out of Schon's seminal work on the reflective practitioner (Schon, 1983, 1987), in which Schon contrasted academic propositional knowledge and the craft knowledge or knowledge in action of the practitioner. Schon suggested that professionals rely very little on academic knowledge and that the idea that professionals apply academic knowledge to practical problems is a basic misconception of the nature of professionals' work. Instead, he suggested, professionals have developed an extensive body of highly context-specific craft knowledge that enables them to relate their past experience to current problems, define these problems, and test out possible solutions to them.

Berliner (1988), in a study of expert and novice teachers, drew on the model of human expertise proposed by H. L. Dreyfus and S. E. Dreyfus (1986) to explain the development of craft knowledge in teaching. This mode depicts five stages in the acquisition of expertise, beginning with the novice stage, in which students seek rules and recipes to guide their actions. The novice stage is followed by the advanced beginner stage, in which the teacher seeks contextual and strategic knowledge and begins to understand when rules are appropriate and when they might be broken. The third stage is competence; the teacher is able to make conscious choices about what she is going to do and is able to monitor her own actions in the classroom and adapt them to suit her chosen goals. The fourth stage is proficiency, marked by the use of intuition and know-how. The teacher has come to perceive the classroom and her own actions in more holistic, interconnected terms. She can automatically link her past experiences to present circumstances and has developed an intuitive feel for how things are going and what needs to be done next. Finally, the fifth stage is the stage of the expert. The teacher and the task have become inseparable. The teacher's practice is characterized by a fluency and automaticity in which the teacher is rarely surprised and is fully adapted to and in control of the situation. Although Berliner speculates that the novice stage might last for the first year of teaching, and that most teachers would reach a competent stage after 3 or 4 years, only a modest proportion of teachers, he suggests, move to the proficient stage, and even fewer reach the expert stage.

Several studies have investigated differences between expert and novice teachers in the ways in which they interpret and respond to simulated or real-life teaching situations. Kagan and Tippins (1992) had a group of preservice and in-service teachers observe and comment on three videotaped teaching episodes. A subset of each sample of teachers also observed and evaluated

a real-life teaching situation. In general, preservice teachers defined good teaching in terms of fun, children's involvement, and affective features of classroom interaction. In-service teachers defined good teaching more in terms of lesson structure and teaching strategies. The in-service teachers were better able to take account of context and purpose. Housner and Griffey (1985), comparing the planning and teaching of physical education lessons by eight experienced and eight inexperienced teachers, similarly found that the inexperienced teachers focused on the interest level of the class, whereas the experienced teachers made more strategic decisions and considered individual children's interest and achievement more. Swanson, O'Connor, and Cooney (1990), in a study of expert novice differences in solving hypothetical problems concerning classroom discipline, found that experts spent much more time considering alternative ways of defining and representing the problem than did novices, who focused more on generating possible solutions.

Other studies have demonstrated how experienced teachers are able to bring their past experience to bear on real or simulated problem situations. The experienced teacher is able to make a deeper interpretation of events, interpreting significant contextual cues and generating hypotheses about the situation in question. As a result of experience, teachers seem to have developed rich, well-organized knowledge bases or schemata that enable them to draw readily on their past experiences (Carter, Sabers, Cushing, Pinnegar, & Berliner, 1987; Peterson & Comeaux, 1987). As in studies of human expertise in other fields, it has been found that teachers have a highly developed but domain-specific knowledge base. Borko and Livingston (1989) point out that although differences between expert and novice teachers are now well documented, more needs to be known about the processes of transition so that novices can be helped to develop and use their knowledge in more expert fashion. This point is also made by Leinhardt (1990), who considers how a fuller understanding of the craft knowledge of teachers might lead to more appropriate forms of assessment for both teacher preparation and certification purposes.

Genberg (1992), drawing on a range of expert–novice studies, has proposed a four-stage model of expertise in which each stage is characterized by a particular state of knowledge, an ability to represent situations, a level of personal involvement, and certain behavioral patterns. The novice has a discrete and disorganized knowledge base consisting of isolated facts and rules that are unrelated to each other or to particular contexts; the novice is unable to identify the important elements in a situation, feels little responsibility for the outcome of his or her acts, and behaves in a rule-like manner, judging his or her own performance in terms of how well he or she followed the rules. In the transition through advanced beginner and intermediate to expert stages, facts and rules become integrated into more holistic patterns of thought and action, situations are perceived in context and can be related to other recent events, there is a high level of personal commitment, and action often appears automatic but fine-tuned and undertaken in anticipation of particular outcomes.

***Personal Practical Knowledge.*** Several researchers have pointed out certain distinctive features of teachers' craft knowledge, such as the way that teachers' understandings of and approaches to their work are strongly shaped by the personalities of the teachers themselves, their past experiences, and how they view teaching. Elbaz (1983) provided a case study of a secondary school English teacher, for example, that suggested how the teacher's own ideas about children and English influenced how she saw her work. Claudinin (1986), in a study of three primary schoolteachers, similarly suggested that teachers' past life experiences provide metaphors for thinking about teaching that shape the kind of knowledge they develop and influence how they adapt particular teaching tasks. Several studies have developed narrative accounts of teachers' lives and careers in an attempt to illustrate how teachers' personal and professional lives interact and how past life experiences influence the ways in which teachers make sense of their environment and define their role within it (Bullough et al., 1991; Goodson, 1992).

*Case Knowledge.* Comparisons of teaching with other professions have resulted in several inquiries into the case knowledge of teachers. Just as in the practice of law or medicine, cases have importance in setting precedents and in defining typical and appropriate practice. It has been suggested that teachers build their own case knowledge—a knowledge base of significant incidents, events, and people that enables new situations to be identified and helps guide teachers' practice.

Schon (1983) has suggested that much of the everyday problem-finding and problem-solving in which various professionals engage involves a knowledge base of cases. A new problem situation is viewed as a case and is compared with other cases. The professional questions how it differs from other cases, what its unique properties might be; and this influences how the professional perceives the situation and reasons about an appropriate response. Although this might seem to attribute too great a level of deliberation to teachers' classroom activities, there may be occasions when the reflective use of case knowledge describes well what teachers do. Grimmett and Erickson (1988) provide a number of accounts of teaching in which case knowledge appeared to be an appropriate means of thinking about teachers' work. Studies of case-based reasoning in medicine—a discipline in which case studies are an established part of education—have been used to justify the further development of case work in teacher education (Elstein, 1992; Merseth, 1991; J. H. Shulman, 1991).

*Theoretical Knowledge.* The contention that teaching might be based on a body of theoretical knowledge is a phenomenon that has developed in relatively recent decades (Alexander, 1984). The growth of rich bodies of literature on children's learning and maturation, curriculum development, and the organization of the school, all of which seem highly relevant to the work of the teacher, would seem to be essential elements of a teacher education curriculum that might equip teachers with concepts and theories for thinking about their day-to-day practice. It is often the case, however, that the theoretical elements of a teacher preparation program are not highly valued by student teachers, and theory comes to be viewed as lacking purpose and value (Book, Byers, & Freeman, 1983). The difficulties of transferring theoretical knowledge into practical action are also well documented (Eraut, 1985). Furlong, Hirst, Pocklington, & Miles (1988) suggest a fourfold classification of

activities in teacher education in terms of levels of professional training, including *direct experience* in schools and classrooms; *indirect practice,* focusing on practical matters but in classes or workshops in the college; *practical principles,* involving the critical study of principles concerning practice; and *disciplinary theory,* involving the critical study of practice and principles in the light of theory and research. This is a hierarchical division of professional activities in which theoretical knowledge is seen as serving a critical organizing function in helping to develop practice, although Furlong et al. do stress the importance of integration across these levels in order to develop well-informed, critical and reflective practice. McIntyre (1993), on the other hand, suggests that equally important as the theoretical content of teacher education programs is the theorizing process that enables student teachers to think critically and analytically about a range of ideas from various sources. The student teacher, he argues, might use academic theory to analyze and evaluate practice, but equally use practice to analyze and evaluate theory.

*Metaphors and Images.* Many of the inquiries into teachers' knowlege have assumed that their professional knowledge is largely propositional and capable of being articulated. Several researchers, however, have suggested that some of teachers' knowledge may be better represented in terms of metaphors and images. Through an analysis of teachers' language in talking about their practice, Munby (1986) demonstrated that there are frequently metaphors in teachers' talk that may well indicate how teachers think about their practice. For instance, he noted that teachers often use a vocabulary of motion or travel in talking about lessons, suggesting a conception of a lesson as a moving, developing process. Several narrative studies of teaching have demonstrated how teachers' past experiences can provide ways of thinking about teaching—for instance, as mothering or as managing people. Lakoff and Johnson (1980) have argued that there are deep or structural metaphors, derived from past experience, that shape our understandings and perceptions of social situations. Their concept of structural metaphor has been adopted by several researchers. Bullough (1991b) and Bullough et al. (1991) in a series of narrative case studies identified student teachers' use of metaphors as a means of making sense of experience and identifying their own role as teachers. Grant (1992), in case studies of three teachers. discussed metaphors that teachers use in thinking about the teaching of their subject. A physics teacher adopted a metaphor of magic in thinking about the wonder and excitement of science and the motivation this offers for children's learning. A history teacher appeared to think of his subject as a game in which students come to appreciate multiple perspectives and alternative accounts of historical events. An English teacher saw thinking about the teaching and learning of literature as a journey involving a continual reimagining of outcomes. S. Johnston (1990) uses the term *image* to refer to the ways in which teachers appear to have organized their knowledge. Images, she argues, encapsulate a perspective taken by the teacher and permeate several aspects of teachers' experience. Images are a metaphorical and partly visual way for teachers to conceptualize their work. In a later study of 25 student teachers, Johnston documented the ways in which students' images of teaching captured moral elements of teaching, defining "the right way to teach," and how these images interacted with practical classroom experiences to shape teachers' understandings of, and practice within, classrooms (Johnston, 1992).

Calderhead and Robson (1992) describe how student teachers start their training with images of what teaching is like. They can mentally picture themselves undertaking the task and have a model in mind of what teaching ideally involves, which shapes how they think about their preservice training program. Wubbels (1992) suggests that the propositional and image-based knowledge that teachers hold may be associated with the different ways that the two hemispheres of the brain process information. It has been suggested that the left hemisphere deals more with language and logical operations and the right hemisphere deals more with emotions. Wubbels suggests that current hypotheses on the ways in which the right and left hemispheres process information may help to explain the different types of knowledge that teachers use. Right hemisphere knowledge may have more to do with the feelings, images, and metaphors that teachers have about their work, while the left hemisphere is concerned with theories and reasoning. Wubbels speculates that this dichotomy in ways of thinking about teaching may help to explain the perennial difficulties in teacher education of bridging theory and practice, since each involves different types of knowledge and different types of thinking. Wubbels suggests that the metaphors, models, and analogies that teachers use to think about teaching can have far-reaching effects on how their practice develops. Thinking about the teacher as a lion tamer, a captain of the ship, or a master of ceremonies, for instance, carries different implications for how the teacher might respond in different situations and the behavior the teacher might expect from the children. The influence of prior experience on shaping the constructs and images of student teachers has also been demonstrated, past experience of schooling being particularly influential (Calderhead & Robson, 1991; John, 1991). Powell (1992), however, found that mature entrants' images of teaching were more often influenced by work and family experiences, whereas younger student teachers' ideas about teaching were more influenced by their own experiences of secondary schools and by relatives who were teachers. Korthagen (1993) suggests that student teachers' images, however derived, are quite resistant to change, and that teacher education needs to create innovative means for examining, challenging, and developing this form of knowledge. Korthagen provides several examples of how this might be done by encouraging students to draw or describe their images or to interpret visual presentations of classrooms, thus making their own images more explicit.

## Teachers' Beliefs

The term *beliefs* has been used in research in numerous ways. As Pajares (1992) pointed out, such terms as beliefs, values, attitudes, judgments, opinions, ideologies, perceptions, conceptions, conceptual systems, preconceptions, dispositions, implicit theories, personal theories, and perspectives have frequently been used almost interchangeably, and it is sometimes difficult to identify the distinguishing features of beliefs and how they are to be separated from knowledge.

In a study of teachers' beliefs, Nespor (1987) drew on the work of Abelson (1979) to demonstrate that four features can be used to distinguish beliefs from knowledge. He termed those features existential presumption, alternativity, affective and evaluate loading, and episodic structure. Beliefs, he argues, frequently assert the existence or nonexistence of entities. Teachers, for instance, were found to have beliefs concerning the causes of children's attainment, according to which they often attributed attainment to relatively stable or uncontrollable characteristics such as ability or maturity. Beliefs also often incorporate a view of an ideal or alternative state that contrasts with reality and provides a means of summarizing goals and paths. Third, beliefs are strongly associated with affective and evaluative components. Beliefs among teachers about the nature of history, for example, were found to be associated with strong feelings about what children ought to learn. Finally, beliefs could be distinguished from knowledge by their episodic structure. Beliefs were often found to be associated with particular, well-remembered events. Nespor also suggested that beliefs tend to be organized in terms of larger belief systems, which are loosely bounded networks with highly variable and uncertain linkages to events, situations, and knowledge systems. The larger belief systems may contain inconsistencies and may be quite idiosyncratic. Nespor suggested, however, that they have great value in dealing with complex, ill-defined situations. They help to interpret and simplify classroom life, to identify relevant goals, and to orient teachers to particular problem situations. Because of the complex and multidimensional nature of classroom life, knowledge alone would be inadequate in making sense of classroom situations and prioritizing problems to be tackled and actions to be undertaken.

Pajares (1992) suggests that beliefs serve another important function in the ways in which schools operate. He argues that they help individuals identify with one another and form mutually supportive social groups. Belief systems reduce dissonance and confusion; and teachers, he suggests, are able to gain confidence and clearer conceptions of themselves from belonging to groups that support their particular beliefs.

Teachers hold many untested assumptions that influence how they think about classroom matters and respond to particular situations. Little has been written on qualitative differences in types of belief, although there are five main areas in which teachers have been found to hold significant beliefs. Such areas, however, could well be interconnected, so that beliefs about teaching, for instance, may be closely related to beliefs about learning and the subject. If a teacher believes mathematics to be about the application of techniques, for example, this might itself imply certain beliefs about how the subject is most appropriately taught and learned and what the role of the teacher should be.

*Beliefs About Learners and Learning.* The assumptions teachers make about their students and how their students learn are likely to influence how they approach teaching tasks and how they interact with their students. Anning (1988), in a study of teachers of young children, found that the teachers held various commonsense theories about children's learning that influenced how they structured tasks and how they interpreted information about children. The teachers' conceptions of children's learning focused on the importance of active involvement, for example, or on the need for an emotionally secure environment in which failure was nonthreatening, or on the value of exploration in open-ended activities where learning was through trial and error. Teachers with different beliefs about children's learning tended to provide different types of classroom activity and supported different patterns of classroom interaction. Several experimental studies of teacher attributions have suggested that various features of the learner influence teachers' judgments of children and their behavior toward them (Levine & Wang, 1983). Such features can include the effort children appear to put into their work (Peterson & Barger, 1984), their personal characteristics (Rohrkemper & Brophy, 1983), and even their attractiveness (Ritts, Patterson, & Tubbs, 1992).

*Beliefs About Teaching.* Teachers hold varying beliefs about the nature and purposes of teaching. Some may view teaching as a process of knowledge transmission, others as a process of guiding children's learning. Some teachers may view teaching more in terms of developing social relationships and a classroom community, others may see their task in much more academic terms.

Several studies suggest that student teachers frequently start professional training with views of teaching as telling and learning as remembering (Calderhead, 1988; Russell, 1988), and this presents difficulties when student teachers are encouraged to adopt a more constructivist approach toward teaching and learning in which children's own commonsense thinking is recognized and challenged (Stoddart, 1992).

Attitude scales have been used to assess student teachers' belief systems about teaching (Hoy & Rees, 1977). Such studies have typically found that student teachers start with control-oriented belief systems that emphasize the importance of maintaining order and good discipline and guiding the activities of the children. These attitudes change slightly during training, becoming more liberal and child centered, but when teachers enter full-time teaching they revert to a control-oriented belief system again. Such findings have often been interpreted in terms of a powerful control-oriented ideology that exists within schools and reinforces the beliefs that student teachers have acquired from being students themselves (Lacey, 1977).

*Beliefs About Subject.* Each subject area within the school curriculum tends to be associated with a range of beliefs concerning epistemological issues—what the subject is about, what it means to know the subject or to be able to carry out tasks effectively within that subject domain. Consequently, teachers of history might believe their subject to concern the acquisition of factual knowledge, an ability to empathize with particular historical periods or characters, or an ability to use archival material and to draw appropriate, substantiated conclusions from historical evidence. Studies of teachers' beliefs about their subject have taken place in mathematics (McDiarmid, 1993), science (Cornett, Yeotis, & Terwilliger, 1990), English (Grossman, 1987), foreign languages (Freeman, 1991a), and social studies (M. Johnston, 1990). They have demonstrated that teachers can have very limited to very eclectic views of their subject and that in some cases their ideas about their subject vary from one context to another. Elbaz (1983), for instance, found that an English teacher viewed English as a creative literature-based meaning-making endeavor with one class, but as a system of linguistic rules to be mastered with another.

In a study of science teachers in an in-service course on constructivist approaches to science teaching, D. C. Smith and Neale (1989) distinguished four different orientations to science teaching and learning, which they termed *discovery, process, didactic/content mastery,* and *conceptual change.* Each orientation was associated with particular beliefs about the nature of science, the nature of school science, and the teaching and learning of science. In studying changes in teachers' thinking and practice of science, Smith and Neale emphasized the importance of knowing which orientation the teacher started from. Their study suggested that fundamental changes in beliefs and practices are achieved slowly and only with considerable support in helping teachers understand how particular beliefs and practices relate to each other in the teaching and learning of specific content areas.

*Beliefs About Learning to Teach.* Teachers, particularly student teachers, also have been found to hold beliefs about their own professional development and how one learns to teach. Curiously, experienced teachers, even those considered by their peers to be highly competent, have often been found to hold fairly restricted and simple accounts of the processes involved. They commonly report, for instance, that one learns from one's own experience in the classroom, or that teaching is largely a matter of personality together with a few managerial tactics that can be learned from observing other teachers (Calderhead, 1988). Similar responses have been obtained from student teachers. Classroom experience is usually the most valued part of teacher training, and student teachers emphasize the importance of learning from experience (Book et al., 1983). Some student teachers, however, see becoming a teacher as a process of personal as much as professional growth. The kind of teacher they are to be is very much a reflection of their own personality and how they relate to other people (Bullough et al., 1991). Some student teachers also have been found to take a much more reflective approach to their professional learning, being more fully disposed to analyzing their own experience and the practice of others in order to learn from it (Korthagen, 1988). There is evidence from some case studies of student teachers that the conceptions student teachers have about learning to teach influence how they approach professional learning and the aspects of their preservice programs to which they attach importance (Calderhead & Robson, 1991).

*Beliefs About Self and the Teaching Role.* Teaching, perhaps more than most professions, involves a high level of personal involvement. The act of teaching requires teachers to use their personality to project themselves in particular roles and to establish relationships within the classroom so that children's interest is maintained and a productive working environment is developed. The teacher relies on his personality and his abilities to form personal relationships in order to manage the class and ensure its smooth running.

Several studies have identified beliefs that student teachers hold about themselves, particularly in relation to the teaching role, and have indicated in case descriptions how these may shape the ways in which student teachers come to think about the development of classroom practice (Calderhead & Robson, 1991; S. Johnston, 1992). Biographical research on teachers' lives has also led some researchers to identify the conceptions teachers have of themselves as significant factors in affecting the teaching roles and practices that teachers adopt (S. Ball & Goodson, 1985).

## Relationship of Beliefs to Classroom Practice

Although it is readily acknowledged that teachers hold various beliefs in relation to their work, it has been a contestable issue whether or not such beliefs influence their classroom practice. A number of studies highlight large discrepancies between teachers' espoused beliefs and their observed classroom practices (e.g., Galton, Simon, & Croll, 1980). On the other hand, several studies have identified associations between teachers' beliefs and how they perceive situations in their own classrooms (R. J. Short & P. M. Short, 1989), and numerous case studies have reported consistencies between teachers' beliefs about their subject or about teaching and learning and the ways in which they plan their work and teach in the classroom (Cornett et al., 1990; Wilson & Wineburg, 1991). Teachers' beliefs, however, may well be quite generalized, abstract value commitments, and it has been found that teachers can sometimes hold quite conflicting beliefs that create dilemmas for them in thinking about practice or result in contrasting beliefs being used to justify contradictory actions in different contexts (e.g., Cornett, 1990). Freeman (1991b) argues that an important aspect of teachers' professional development is the process of making implicit belief systems explicit and thereby developing a language for talking and thinking about their own practice, questioning the sometimes contradictory beliefs underpinning their practice, and taking greater control over their own professional growth.

In considering the relationship between teachers' beliefs and teachers' practices in staff development programs, Guskey (1986) found that staff development activities were most effective at changing beliefs when teachers could be helped to adopt a new practice and could see that it was successful. Changes in belief follow rather than precede changes in practice, he argued. This position has been challenged by Richardson (1995), however, on the basis of a study of staff development in reading instruction. Richardson suggests that in the process of change, there is a constant interaction between beliefs and practice, and that professional development may be initiated by a change in either beliefs or practice.

## THE IMPLICATIONS OF RESEARCH ON TEACHERS' COGNITIONS

The relationship between research and practice has been conceptualized in several ways. Fenstermacher (1986), for example, has argued that educational research findings inform practice through practical arguments, where empirical research serves the function of clarifying, testing, and informing the premises on which everyday judgments are based. In discussing the relevance of research on teachers' cognitions in particular, Clark (1988) has argued that research findings serve to sensitize teacher educators to the ways in which they might think about professional education, encouraging them to ask questions of their own practice and thereby guide their efforts to help beginning teachers. Floden and Klinzing (1990), on the other hand,

have suggested that research might not at the moment offer more than sensitization to issues but that, as our understanding of teachers' thinking improves, it has the potential to offer more substantial principles for action in teacher education in the future.

However the research evidence is actually used in practice, there is increasing recognition that the teacher is at the center of any attempt to improve the quality of teaching and learning in schools. Attempts at school reorganization, curriculum development, and improving teacher effectiveness all ultimately rely on the professional development of the teacher—an observation that has been repeatedly articulated in studies of educational innovation (e.g., Stenhouse, 1970). Research on teacher cognitions has helped to identify the nature and complexity of the teacher's work, and helped to provide ways of thinking about the processes of change and support. Learning to teach, for example, clearly involves developing and orchestrating various forms and areas of knowledge that are acquired in different ways and that may necessitate alternative types of training experience (Calderhead, 1991; Carter, 1990; see also chapter 20, this volume). The processes of curriculum change involve teachers as interpreters of ideas and holders of values, influenced by a range of previous experiences, who work within institutions involving complex interactions of ideas and actions. Curriculum change is not easily represented in mechanistic terms; it is more of an organic, interactive process (Day, 1990; Edwards & Brunton, 1993). Similarly, research on the specific diagnostic and instructional interactions of teachers and students, and the thinking that accompanies these interactions, indicates the need to take account of teachers' knowledge and beliefs and the contexts in which they are developed and used in order to understand how teaching and learning occur in classrooms and how they might be improved (Leinhardt, 1988; Putnam, 1987).

In addition to providing ways of thinking about the professional development of teachers, research on teachers' cognitions has provided also a range of methods that have come to be adopted in practical training contexts, and has contributed toward a rationale for their use. The development of reflective journals in teacher education (Tann, 1993) and the introduction of case-based training (J. H. Shulman, 1991), for example, owe much to the conceptual advances offered by research on teacher cognitions as well as the methods that have become evident in the research.

## FUTURE DIRECTIONS IN RESEARCH

Research on teachers' cognitions has highlighted the complex array of factors that interact in the processes of teaching and learning. In particular, research has pointed to the elaborate knowledge and belief structures that teachers hold, to the influence of their past experiences, even experiences outside of teaching, in shaping how teachers think about their work, and to the diverse processes of knowledge growth involved in learning to teach. Research also has begun to unravel some of the pedagogical processes involved in classroom teaching and the different types of knowledge that teachers draw on in their efforts to help children to learn and understand. Current research has adopted a diverse range of methodologies to explore these areas and is making considerable progress in unpacking the nature of teachers' knowledge and expertise. Because of the complexity of the area, diverse methodologies are needed, each contributing its own evidence and perspective to an overall understanding of teaching. Such an eclectic approach may enhance our appreciation of teachers' work and contribute to a fuller recognition of what it means to teach and to learn, and how the quality of such processes might be improved.

# References

Abelson, R. (1979). Differences between belief systems and knowledge systems. *Cognitive Science, 3,* 355–366.

Alexander, R. J. (1984) Innovation and continuity in the initial teacher education curriculum. In R. J. Alexander, M. Craft, & J. Lynch (Eds.), *Changes in teacher education: Context and provision since Robbins* (pp. 103–160). London: Holt, Rinehart & Winston.

Anderson, J. R. (1983). *The architecture of cognition.* Cambridge, MA: Harvard University Press.

Anning, A. (1988). Teachers' theories about children's learning. In J. Calderhead (Ed.), *Teachers' professional learning* (pp. 128–145). London: Falmer Press.

Ball, D. L., & McDiarmid, G. W. (1990). The subject matter preparation of teachers. In W. R. Houston (Ed.), *Handbook of research on teacher education* (pp. 437–449). New York: Macmillan.

Ball, S., & Goodson, I. F. (1985). *Teachers' lives and careers.* London: Falmer Press.

Ben-Peretz, M., Bromme, R., & Halkes, R. (1986). *Advances of research on teacher thinking.* Lisse, Netherlands: Swets & Zeitlinger.

Bennett, N., & Carré, C. (1993). *Learning to teach.* London: Routledge.

Berliner, D. C. (1988, February). *The development of expertise in pedagogy.* Paper presented at the meeting of the American Association of Colleges for Teacher Education, New Orleans, LA.

Berliner, D. C. (1989). The place of process-product research in developing the agenda for research on teacher thinking. In J. Lowyck & C. M. Clark (Eds.), *Teacher thinking and professional action* (pp. 3–21). Leuven, Belgium: Leuven University Press.

Beyerbach, B. A. (1988). Developing a technical vocabulary on teacher planning: Preservice teachers' concept maps. *Teaching and Teacher Education, 4*(4), 339–374.

Bloom, B. S. (1953). Thought processes in lectures and discussions. *Journal of General Education, 7,* 160–169.

Book, C., Byers, J., & Freeman, D. (1983). Student expectations, and teacher education traditions with which we can and cannot live. *Journal of Teacher Education, 34*(13), 9–13.

Borko, H., Cone, R., Atwood Russo, N., & Shavelson, R. J. (1979). Teachers' decision making. In P. L. Peterson, & H. J. Walberg (Eds.), *Research on teaching: Concepts, findings and implications* (pp. 136–160). Berkeley, Ca: McCutchan.

Borko, H., & Livingston, C. (1989). Cognition and improvisation: Differences in mathematics instruction by expert and novice teachers. *American Educational Research Journal, 26*(4), 473–498.

Borko, H., Livingston, C., & Shavelson, R. J. (1990). Teachers' thinking about instruction. *Remedial and Special Education, 11,* 6, 40–49.

Bromme, R. (1987). Teachers' assessment of students' difficulties and progress in understanding in the classroom. In J. Calderhead (Ed.), *Exploring teachers' thinking* (pp. 125–146). London: Cassell.

Brophy, J., & Good, T. L. (1986). Teacher behavior and student achievement. In M. C. Wittrock (Ed.), *Handbook of research on teaching* (3rd ed., pp. 328–375). New York: Macmillan.

Brown, J. S., Collins, A., & Duguid, P. (1989). Situated cognition and the culture of learning. *Educational Researcher, 18*(1), 32–42.

Brown, S., & McIntyre, D. (1993). *Making sense of teaching.* Buckingham, England: Open University Press.

Bullough, R. V. (1991a, April). *Case studies as personal teaching texts.* Paper presented at a meeting of the American Educational Research Association, Chicago.

Bullough, R. V. (1991b). Exploring personal teaching metaphors in preservice teacher education. *Journal of Teacher Education, 42*(1), 43–51.

Bullough, R. V., Knowles, J. G., & Crow, N. A. (1991). *Emerging as a teacher.* London: Routledge.

Calderhead, J. (1987a). Developing a framework for the elicitation and analysis of teachers' verbal reports. *Oxford Review of Education, 13*(2), 183–189.

Calderhead, J. (Ed.). (1987b). *Exploring teachers' thinking.* London: Cassell.

Calderhead, J. (1987c). The quality of reflection in student teachers' professional learning. *European Journal of Teacher Education, 10*(3), 269–278.

Calderhead, J. (1988). The contribution of field experiences to student primary teachers' professional learning. *Research in Education, 40,* 33–49.

Calderhead, J. (1991). The nature and growth of knowledge in student teaching. *Teaching and Teacher Education, 7*(5/6), 531–535.

Calderhead, J., & Robson, M. (1991). Images of teaching: Student teachers' early conceptions of classroom practice. *Teaching and Teacher Education, 7,* 1–8.

Carter, K. (1990). Teachers' knowledge and learning to teach. In W. R. Houston (Ed.), *Handbook of research on teacher education* (pp. 291–310). New York: Macmillan.

Carter, K. (1993). The place of story in the study of teaching and teacher education. *Educational Researcher, 22*(1), 5–12, 18.

Carter, K., Sabers, D., Cushing, K., Pinnegar, S., & Berliner, D. C. (1987). Processing and using information about students: A study of expert, novice and postulant teachers. *Teaching and Teacher Education, 3*(2), 147–157.

Clandinin, D. J. (1986). *Classroom practice: Teacher images in action.* London: Falmer Press.

Clark, C. M. (1988). Asking the right questions about teacher preparation: Contributions of research on teacher thinking. *Educational Researcher, 17*(2), 5–12.

Clark, C. M., & Peterson, P. L. (1986). Teachers' thought processes. In M. C. Wittrock (Ed.), *Handbook of Research on Teaching* (3rd ed., pp. 255–296). New York: Macmillan.

Clark, C. M., & Yinger, R. J. (1979). *Three studies of teacher planning.* Research monograph No. 55. East Lansing, MI: Michigan State University, Institute for Research on Teaching.

Clark, C. M., & Yinger, R. J. (1987). *Teacher planning.* In J. Calderhead (Ed.), *Exploring teachers' thinking* (pp. 84–103). London: Cassell.

Clift, R. T., Houston, W. R., & Pugach, M. C. (1990). *Encouraging reflective practice in education: An analysis of issues and programs.* New York: Teachers College Press.

Connelly, F. M., & Clandinin, D. J. (1990). Stories of experience and narrative enquiry. *Educational Researcher, 19*(5), 2–14.

Cornett, J. W. (1990). Teacher thinking about curriculum and instruction: A case study of a secondary social studies teacher. *Theory and Research in Social Education, 18*(3), 248–273.

Cornett, J. W., Yeotis, C., & Terwilliger, L. (1990). Teacher personal practical theories and their influence upon teacher curricular and instructional actions: A case study of a secondary science teacher. *Science Education, 74*(5), 517–529.

Day, C. (1990). The development of teachers' personal, practical knowledge through school-based curriculum development projects. In C. Day, M. Pope, & P. Denicolo (Eds.), *Insights into teachers' thinking and practice* (pp. 213–239). London: Falmer Press.

Day, C., Pope, M., & Denicolo, P. (Eds.). (1990). *Insights into teachers' thinking and practice*. London: Falmer Press.

Delamont, S., & Atkinson, P. (1980). The two traditions in educational ethnography: Sociology and anthropology compared. *British Journal of Sociology of Education, 1*(2), 139–152.

Doyle, W., & Ponder, G. A. (1977). The practicality ethic and teacher decision-making. *Interchange, 8*, 1–12.

Dreyfus, H. L., & Dreyfus, S. E. (1986). *Mind over machine: The power of human intuition and expertise in the era of the computer*. New York: The Free Press.

Dunkin, M. J., & Biddle, B. J. (1974). *The study of teaching*. New York: Holt, Rinehart and Winston.

Edwards, A., & Brunton, D. (1993). Supporting reflection in teachers' learning. In J. Calderhead & P. Gates (Eds.), *Conceptualizing reflection in teacher development* (pp. 154–166). London: Falmer Press.

Eggleston, J. (Ed.). (1979). *Teacher decision-making in the classroom*. London: Routledge & Kegan Paul.

Elbaz, F. (1983). *Teacher thinking: A study of practical knowledge*. London: Croom Helm.

Elbaz, F. (1992). Hope, attentiveness and caring for difference: The moral voice in teaching. *Teaching and Teacher Education, 8*(5/6), 421–432.

Elstein, A. A. (1992, April). *Research on medical cognitive processes: Implications for education*. Paper presented at a meeting of the American Educational Research Association, San Francisco.

Eraut, M. (1985). Knowledge creation and knowledge use in professional contexts. *Studies in Higher Education, 10*(2), 117–133.

Ericsson, K. A., & Simon, H. A. (1980). Verbal reports as data. *Psychological Review, 87*, 215–251.

Ewert, G. D. (1991). Habermas and education: A comprehensive overview of the influence of Habermas in educational literature. *Review of Educational Research, 61*(3), 345–378.

Fenstermacher, G. D. (1986). Philosophy of research on teaching: Three aspects. In M. C. Wittrock (Ed.), *Handbook of research on teaching* (3rd ed., pp. 37–49). New York: Macmillan.

Flanders, N. A. (1970). *Analyzing teacher behavior*. Reading, MA: Addison-Wesley.

Floden, R. E., & Klinzing, H. G. (1990). What can research on teacher thinking contribute to teacher preparation? A second opinion. *Educational Researcher, 19*(5), 15–20.

Freeman, D. (1991a). *The same things done differently: A study of the development of four foreign language teachers' conceptions of practice through an inservice teacher education program*. Unpublished doctoral dissertation, Graduate School of Education, Harvard University.

Freeman, D. (1991b). To make the tacit explicit: Teacher education, emerging discourse, and conceptions of teaching. *Teaching and Teacher Education, 7*(5/6), 439–454.

Furlong, V. J., Hirst, P. H., Pocklington, K., & Miles, S. (1988). *Initial teacher training and the role of the school*. Milton Keynes: Open University Press.

Galton, M., Simon, B., & Croll, P. (1980). *Inside the primary classroom*. London: Routledge & Kegan Paul.

Genberg, V. (1992). Patterns and organizing perspectives: A view of expertise. *Teaching and Teacher Education, 8*(5/6), 485–495.

Gibson, R. (1976). *Critical theory and education*. London: Hodder & Stoughton.

Goodson, I. (Ed.) (1992). *Studying teachers' lives*. London: Routledge.

Grant, G. E. (1992). The sources of structural metaphors in teacher knowledge: Three cases. *Teaching and Teacher Education, 8*(5/6), 433–440.

Grimmett, P. P., & Erickson, G. L. (Eds.). (1988). *Reflection in teacher education*. New York: Teachers' College Press.

Grimmett, P. P., MacKinnon, A. M., Erickson, G. L., & Riecken, T. J. (1990). Reflective practice in teacher education. In R. T. Clift, W. R. Houston, & M. C. Pugach (Eds.), *Encouraging reflective practice in education: An analysis of issues and programs* (pp. 20–38). New York: Teachers' College Press.

Grossman, P. (1987, April). *A tale of two teachers: The role of subject matter orientation in teaching*. Paper presented at a meeting of the American Educational Research Association, Washington, DC.

Grossman, P. (1990). *The making of a teacher: Teacher knowledge and teacher education*. New York: Teachers College Press.

Gudmundsdottir, S. (1991). Ways of seeing are ways of knowing: The pedagogical content knowledge of an expert English teacher. *Journal of Curriculum Studies, 23*(5), 409–421.

Gudmundsdottir, S., & Shulman, L. S. (1989). Pedagogical knowledge in social studies. In J. Lowyck & C. M. Clark (Eds.), *Teacher thinking and professional action* (pp. 23–34). Leuven, Belgium: Leuven University Press.

Guskey, T. (1986). Staff development and the process of teacher change. *Educational Researcher, 15*, 5–12.

Halkes, R., & Olson, J. K. (Eds.). (1984). *Teacher thinking: A new perspective on persisting problems in education*. Lisse, Netherlands: Swets & Zeitlinger.

Housner, L. D., & Griffey, D. C. (1985). Teacher cognition: Differences in planning and interactive decision-making between experienced and inexperienced teachers. *Research Quarterly for Exercise and Sport, 56*(1), 45–53.

Hoy, W., & Rees, R. (1977). The bureaucratic socialization of student teachers. *Journal of Teacher Education, 28*(1), 23–26.

Jackson, P. W. (1968). *Life in classrooms*. New York: Holt, Rinehart & Winston.

John, P. D. (1991). A qualitative study of British student teachers' lesson planning perspectives. *Journal of Education for Teaching, 17*(3), 301–320.

Johnston, M. (1990). Teachers' backgrounds and beliefs: Influences on learning to teach in the social studies. *Theory and Research in Social Education, 18*(3), 207–233.

Johnston, S. (1990). Understanding curriculum decision-making through teacher images. *Journal of Curriculum Studies, 22*(5), 463–471.

Johnston, S. (1992). Images: A way of understanding the practical knowledge of student teachers. *Teaching and Teacher Education, 8*(2), 123–136.

Kagan, D. M. (1990). Ways of evaluating teacher cognition: Inferences concerning the Goldilocks Principle. *Review of Educational Research, 60*(3), 419–471.

Kagan, D. M., & Tippins, D. J. (1992). How US teachers 'read' classroom performances. *Journal of Education for Teaching, 18*(2), 149–158.

Kelly, G. A. (1955). *The psychology of personal constructs*. New York: Norton.

Korthagen, F. A. J. (1988). The influence of learning orientations on the development of reflective teaching. In J. Calderhead (Ed.), *Teachers' professional learning* (pp. 35–50). London: Falmer Press.

Korthagen, F. A. J. (1993). Two modes of reflection. *Teaching and Teacher Education, 9*(3), 317–326.

Kremer-Hayon, L. (1990). Reflection and professional knowledge. In C. Day, M. Pope, & P. Denicolo (Eds.), *Insight into teachers' thinking and practice* (pp. 57–70). London: Falmer Press.

Lacey, C. (1977). *The socialisation of teachers*. London: Methuen.

Lakoff, G., & Johnson, M. (1980). *Metaphors we live by*. Chicago: University of Chicago Press.

Lampert, M. (1986). Knowing, doing and teaching multiplication. *Cognition and Instruction, 3*, 305–342.

Leinhardt, G. (1988). Situated knowledge and expertise in teaching. In J. Calderhead (Ed.), *Teachers' Professional Learning* (pp. 146–168). London: Falmer Press.

Leinhardt, G. (1990). Capturing craft knowledge in teaching. *Educational Researcher, 19*(2), 18–25.

Leinhardt, G., & Greeno, J. G. (1986). The cognitive skill of teaching. *Journal of Educational Psychology, 78*(2), 75–95.

Levine, J. M., & Wang, M. C. (Eds.). (1983). *Teacher and student perceptions: Implications for learning.* Hillsdale, NJ: Lawrence Erlbaum Associates.

Lowyck, J., & Clark, C. M. (1989). *Teacher thinking and professional action.* Leuven, Belgium: Leuven University Press.

Lundgren, U. P. (1972). *Frame factors and the teaching process.* Stockholm: Elmquist & Wiksell.

Marks, R. (1990). Pedagogical content knowledge from a mathematical case to a modified conception. *Journal of Teacher Education, 41*(3), 3–11.

McCutcheon, G. (1980). How do elementary school teachers plan? The nature of planning and influences on it. *Elementary School Journal, 81,* 4–23.

McDiarmid, G. W. (1993). Changes in beliefs about learners among participants in eleven teacher education programs. In J. Calderhead & P. Gates (Eds.), *Conceptualizing reflection in teacher development* (pp. 113–143). London: Falmer Press.

McIntyre, D. (1993). Theory, theorizing and reflection in initial teacher education. In J. Calderhead & P. Gates (Eds.), *Conceptualizing reflection in teacher development* (pp. 39–52). London: Falmer Press.

McNamara, D. R. (1981). Attention, time-on-task and children's learning: Research or ideology? *Journal of Education for Teaching, 7*(3) 284–297.

McNamara, D. R. (1990). Research on teachers' thinking: Its contribution to educating student teachers to think critically. *Journal of Education for Teaching, 16*(2), pp. 147–160.

McNamara, D. R. (1991). Subject knowledge and its application: Problems and possibilities for teacher educators. *Journal of Education for Teaching, 17*(2), 113–128.

Merseth, K. K. (1991). The early history of case-based instruction: Insights for teacher education for today. *Journal of Teacher Education, 42*(4), 243–249.

Miles, M. B., & Huberman, A. M. (1984). *Qualitative data analysis.* Newbury Park, Ca: Sage.

Morine, G. (1976) *A study of teacher planning* (Research report). San Francisco: Far West Laboratory for Educational Research and Development.

Morine-Dershimer, G. (1979). *Teacher plan and classroom reality: The South Bay study: Part 4* (Research Series No. 60). East Lansing: Institute for Research on Teaching.

Morine-Dershimer, G. (1991a). Learning to think like a teacher. *Teaching and Teacher Education, 7*(2), 159–168.

Morine-Dershimer, G. (1991b, April). *Tracing conceptual change in preservice teachers.* Paper presented at a meeting of the American Educational Research Association, Chicago.

Morine-Dershimer, G., Saunders, S., Artiles, A. J., Mostert, M. A., Tankersley, M., Trent, S. C., & Nuttycombe, D. G. (1992). Choosing among alternatives for tracing conceptual change. *Teaching and Teacher Education, 8*(5/6), 471–484.

Mosenthal, J. H. (1989, April). *Towards a method for representing and documenting change in teacher thinking.* Paper presented at the meeting of the American Educational Research Association, San Francisco.

Munby, H. (1986). Metaphor in the thinking of teachers: An exploratory study. *Journal of American Studies, 18*(2), 197–209.

Nespor, J. (1987). The role of beliefs in the practice of teaching. *Journal of Curriculum Studies, 19*(4), 317–328.

Pajares, M. F. (1992). Teachers' beliefs and educational research: Cleaning up a messy construct. *Review of Educational Research, 62*(3), 307–332.

Peterson, P. L., & Barger, S. A. (1984). Attribution theory and teacher expectancy. In J. B. Dusek (Ed.), *Teacher Expectancies* (pp. 159–184). Hillsdale, NJ: Lawrence Erlbaum Associates.

Peterson, P. L., & Clark, C. M. (1978). Teachers' reports of their cognitive processes during teaching. *American Educational Research Journal, 15,* 555–565.

Peterson, P. L., & Comeaux, M. A. (1987). Teachers' schemata for classroom events: The mental scaffolding of teachers' thinking during classroom instruction. *Teaching and Teacher Education, 3*(4), 319–331.

Powell, R. P. (1992). The influence of prior experiences on pedagogical constructs of traditional and nontraditional preservice teachers. *Teaching and Teacher Education, 8*(3), 225–238.

Putnam, R. T. (1987). Structuring and adjusting content for students: A study of live and simulated tutoring of addition. *American Educational Research Journal, 24*(1), 13–48.

Reid, W. A. (1978). *Thinking about the curriculum.* London: Routledge & Kegan Paul.

Reynolds, M. C. (1989). *Knowledge base for the beginning teacher.* Oxford: Pergamon.

Richardson, V. (1995). The consideration of beliefs in staff development. In V. Richardson (Ed.), *A theory of teacher change and the practice of staff development: A case in reading instruction.* New York: Teachers College Press.

Ritts, V., Patterson, M. L., & Tubbs, M. E. (1992). Expectations, impressions and judgments of physically attractive students: A review. *Review of Educational Research, 62*(4), 413–426.

Roehler, L. R., Duffy, G. G., Hermann, B. A., Conley, M., & Johnson, J. (1988). Knowledge structures as evidence of the 'Personal': Bridging the gap from thought to practice. *Journal of Curriculum Studies, 20*(2), 159–165.

Rohrkemper, M. M., & Brophy, J. E. (1983). Teachers' thinking about problem students. In J. M. Levine & M. C. Wang (Eds.), *Teacher and student perceptions: Implications for learning* (pp. 75–104). Hillsdale, NJ: Lawrence Erlbaum Associates.

Rosenshine, B. (1971). *Teaching behaviours and student achievement.* London: National Foundation for Educational Research.

Russell, T. (1988). From preservice teacher education to first year of teaching: A study of theory and practice. In J. Calderhead (Ed.), *Teachers' Professional Learning* (pp. 13–34). London: Falmer Press.

Sardo-Brown, D. (1988). Twelve middle-school teachers' planning. *The Elementary School Journal, 89*(1), 69–87.

Sardo-Brown, D. (1990). Experienced teachers' planning practices: A US survey. *Journal of Education for Teaching, 16*(1), 57–71.

Schon, D. (1983). *The reflective practitioner: How professionals think in action.* New York: Basic Books.

Schon, D. (1987). *Educating the reflective practitioner.* San Francisco: Jossey-Bass.

Schmidt, W. H., Porter, A. C., Floden, R. E., Freeman, D. J., & Schwille, J. R. (1987). Four patterns of teacher content decision-making. *Journal of Curriculum Studies, 19*(5), 439–455.

Schwab, J. J. (1971). The practical: Arts of the eclectic. *School Review, 79*(4), 493–542.

Shavelson, R. J. (1973). What is the basic teaching skill? *Journal of Teacher Education, 24,* 144–151.

Shavelson, R. J., & Stern, P. (1981). Research on teachers' pedagogical thoughts, judgments, decisions and behavior. *Review of Educational Research, 51,* 455–498.

Short, R. J., & Short, P. M. (1989). Teacher beliefs, perceptions of behavior problems and intervention preferences. *Journal of Social Studies Research, 13*(2), 28–33.

Shulman, J. H. (1991). Revealing the mysteries of teacher written cases: Opening the black box. *Journal of Teacher Education, 42*(4), 250–262.

Shulman, L. S. (1986a). Paradigms and research programs in the study of teaching: A contemporary perspective. In M. C. Wittrock (Ed.),

*Handbook of Research on Teaching* (3rd ed., pp. 3–36). New York: Macmillan.

Shulman, L. S. (1986b). Those who understand: Knowledge growth in teaching. *Educational Researcher, 14*(2), 4–14.

Shulman, L. S. (1987). Knowledge and teaching: Foundations of the new reform. *Harvard Educational Review, 57*(1), 1–22.

Smith, D. C., & Neale, D. C. (1989). The construction of subject matter knowledge in primary science teaching. *Teaching and Teacher Education, 5*(1), 1–20.

Smith L. M., & Geoffrey, W. (1968). *The complexities of an urban classroom: An analysis toward a general theory of teaching.* New York: Holt, Rinehart & Winston.

Sockett, H. (1987). Has Shulman got the strategy right?. *Harvard Educational Review, 52*(2), 208–219.

Stenhouse, L. (1975). *An introduction to curriculum research and development.* London: Heineman.

Stenhouse, L. (1980). The study of samples and the study of cases. *British Educational Research Journal, 6*(1), 1–6.

Stoddart, T. (1992, April). *Conceptual change in teacher education.* Paper presented at the annual meeting of the American Educational Research Association, San Francisco.

Swanson, H. L., O'Connor, J. E., & Cooney, J. B. (1990). An information processing analysis of expert and novice teachers' problem solving. *American Educational Research Journal, 27*(3), 533–556.

Taba, H. (1962). *Curriculum development: Theory and practice.* New York: Harcourt, Brace & World.

Tabachnick, B. R., & Zeichner, K. (1984). The impact of the student teaching experience on the development of teacher perspectives. *Journal of Teacher Education, 35*(6), 28–36.

Tabachnick, B. R., & Zeichner, K. (Eds.). (1991). *Issues and practices in inquiry-oriented teacher education.* London: Falmer Press.

Tann, S. (1993). Eliciting student teachers' personal theories. In J. Calderhead & P. Gates (Eds.), *Conceptualizing reflection in teacher development* (pp. 53–69). London: Falmer Press.

Tom, A. R., & Valli, L. (1990). Professional knowledge for teachers. In W. R. Houston (Ed.), *Handbook of research on teacher education* (pp. 373–392). New York: Macmillan.

Tversky, A., & Kahneman, D. (1974). Judgment under uncertainty: Heuristics and biases. *Science, 185,* 1124–1131.

Valli, L. (Ed.). (1992). *Reflective teacher education: Cases and critiques.* New York: State University of New York Press.

Wheeler, D. K. (1967). *Curriculum process.* London: University of London Press.

Wilcox, S. K., Schram, P., Lappen, G., & Lanvier, P. (1990, April). *The role of a learning community in changing preservice teachers' knowledge and beliefs about mathematics education.* Paper presented at the meeting of the American Educational Research Association, Boston.

Wilson, S. M., & Wineburg, S. (1988). Peering at history through different lenses: The role of disciplinary perspectives in teaching history. *Teachers College Record, 89,* 525–539.

Wilson, S. M., & Wineburg, S. (1991, April). *Using performance-based exercises to assess the knowledge of history teachers: A cross-case analysis.* Paper presented at the annual meeting of the American Educational Research Association, Chicago.

Winne, P. H., & Marx, R. W. (1977). Reconceptualizing research on teaching. *Journal of Educational Psychology, 69,* 668–678.

Woods, P. (1979). *The divided school.* London: Routledge & Kegan Paul.

Woods, P. (Ed.). (1980). *Teacher strategies: Explorations in the sociology of the school.* London: Croom Helm.

Wubbels, T. (1992). Taking account of student teachers' preconceptions. *Teaching and Teacher Education, 8*(2), 137–149.

Yinger, R. J. (1980). A study of teacher planning. *Elementary School Journal, 80,* 107–127.

Yinger, R. J. (1986). Examining thought in action: A theoretical and methodological critique of research on interactive teaching. *Teaching and Teacher Education, 2*(3), 263–282.

Yinger, R., & Hendricks-Lee, M. (1993). Working knowledge in teaching. In C. Day, J. Calderhead & P. Denicolo (Eds.), *Research on teacher thinking: Understanding professional development* (pp. 100–123). London: Falmer Press.

Zeichner, K. M., & Liston, D. (1987). Teaching student teachers to reflect. *Harvard Educational Review, 57*(1), 23–48.

# TEACHING AND LEARNING IN A CLASSROOM CONTEXT

## Thomas J. Shuell

STATE UNIVERSITY OF NEW YORK AT BUFFALO

Educational psychology has been concerned with teacher effects and student learning for more than 100 years. During this period, a substantial body of knowledge on these topics has accumulated, and we know far more about effective teaching than is often acknowledged. Nevertheless, most of our knowledge about teaching and learning is fragmented, narrowly focused, and limited in the psychological understanding it can shed on the important problems of education. Teaching and learning have typically been studied as separate entities (Shuell, 1993), and complexities of the teaching–learning exchange have usually been ignored.

In recent years, a number of significant changes have occurred in the way psychologists and educators think about teaching, learning, and the schooling process. Changes have also occurred in the methodologies and theoretical approaches used to investigate these topics and in the assumptions underlying educational research in general. These changes present important challenges to educational psychology and its efforts to understand the teaching–learning process as it occurs in the context of various classroom activities.

Teachers do many things as they help students acquire the knowledge, understanding, skills, and attitudes that are the goals of education. The way in which these activities are carried out by the teacher strongly influences the way students go about the task of learning and the substance of what they ultimately acquire. Yet teaching is neither the unidirectional (teacher-to-student) nor strictly cognitive process it is often thought to be. Teachers and students work together in the rich psychological soup of a classroom, a soup comprised of cognitive, social, cultural, affective, emotional, motivational, and curricular factors. The common image of a teacher standing in front of a class, giving information to 25 or 30 students who are sitting more or less passively at their desks (i.e., teaching by telling and learning by remembering) is simply archaic, according to current thinking in psychology and education.

Educational psychology has long sought to be scientific in its quest for an understanding of educational processes. The scientific approach has many advantages, but it is important to realize that there is not a single scientific paradigm. Certain fundamental principles are involved in all scientific inquiry, but these principles can be satisfied in various ways. Each of the legitimate scientific paradigms has its own profile of strengths and weaknesses, and each is most appropriate for answering a particular type of research question.

For many years, educational psychologists adhered to an interpretation of science (logical positivism) well suited for the natural sciences. As a result, the validity of other scientific paradigms, especially those used in the social sciences, were typically overlooked or disparaged. In order to make the problem being studied manageable and to achieve scientific precision, many educational psychologists selected a relatively narrow or simplified aspect of the problem to investigate, especially from an educational perspective. Such a limited approach, however, often resulted in blindness to other aspects of the problem and the way in which the various parts of the problem fit together. Today, it seems clear that a variety of methodological tools are needed if an adequate understanding of the complex nature of the relationship between teaching and learning is to be achieved.

Thus, any discussion of psychological research and theory concerned with the way teachers affect student learning must consider a variety of issues germane to this research. These issues provide a context for interpreting the research presently available and for identifying an appropriate agenda for future research. The present chapter addresses these issues and the relevant research in the following major sections:

- Changing conceptions and new assumptions related to teaching, learning, and scientific research, including an overview of traditional conceptions of teaching and models of instruction.

- The nature of "psychological" inquiry and research.
- Current models of teaching and learning.
- A summary of what is currently known (and not known) about teacher effects.
- Steps that might be taken to obtain a better understanding of the teaching–learning process.

The following discussion is predicated on several realizations about the nature of teacher effects. First, teacher effects and instructional methods that would be equally applicable across all situations, or even a wide range of situations, simply do not exist. General principles of teaching and learning undoubtedly exist, and although these principles can inform both our understanding of the teaching–learning process and the selection of appropriate instructional methods, these principles often operate in substantially different ways with different students, in different content areas, and in different instructional settings. The long search by some individuals for a single best method of teaching will never be realized. Although aptitude–treatment interactions have proved elusive in the research literature, they do exist (Snow, 1989). The effect that a teacher has on his or her students is limited by a variety of factors, including the developmental level and prior knowledge of the students, the cultural context in which the instruction occurs, the specific content being taught, and the academic goals being pursued.

Second, teacher effects are multidimensional. Although cognitive processes typically receive the most attention, cognition neither occurs in isolation nor is it the only psychological system that influences both the content and noncognitive outcomes that students acquire from an educational experience. Emotional, motivational, attitudinal, cultural, and other affective and social factors operate simultaneously with cognitive factors and play a critical role in determining what is learned. In fact, it is impossible for a student to acquire subject matter content without simultaneously acquiring or reaffirming a variety of noncognitive outcomes associated with his or her prior knowledge and affective predispositions and with the instructional experience within which the learning occurs. A student does not merely learn facts about the Civil War, for example; he or she also learns whether the study of history is enjoyable or boring, acquires attitudes about Southerners and Yankees and whether certain individuals are to be trusted, obtains information about the horrors (or glory) of war, and discovers whether he or she is a good student with good ideas and the ability to learn history (or school subjects in general), *regardless of whether or not these issues were an explicit part of the lesson.* Contrary to common belief, it is impossible for teachers to present a lesson in such a way that only cognitive information is acquired.

Third, in the final analysis, it is the psychological response of the student that determines the exact nature of whatever teacher effects are obtained, and teachers are only part of the psychological and social context that affect what students learn. The manner in which the student perceives, interprets, and processes information from the various things that happen during a lesson (and at other times) is the primary determiner of the educational outcomes acquired by students. This issue will be discussed more fully in a subsequent section of this chapter on student mediation of instruction.

Fourth, teachers affect students in indirect and subtle ways as well as in the more direct ways that typically come to mind when one thinks about teaching. For example, the assignment of certain topics and tasks rather than others influences both what students learn and how they learn it. The teacher might structure a given learning experience in a particular way (e.g., by using a learning group), anticipating that the exchange of information, the necessity for students to articulate their ideas, and peer feedback will result in the desired learning. From a psychological perspective, it is the exchanges among the students in each group, not the action of the teacher in forming the group or the silent monitoring of group activities, that produce the desired learning. Nevertheless, the teacher clearly has had an effect on the students, although in an indirect manner. Other sources of indirect effects include classroom management procedures and the form of language used by the teacher in carrying out instruction (e.g., Wertsch, 1991). Indirect effects are discussed further in a subsequent section of this chapter.

Finally, every individual has an implicit model or conceptualization of teaching, knowledge, and learning that determines the way that person thinks about the instructional process. These models, often implicit, are so ingrained in our thinking that usually we are not even aware of the extent to which they influence our beliefs, theories, and actions (e.g., see Lakoff & Johnson, 1980). It seems clear that the instructional practices of a teacher and the research questions pursued by an investigator are determined largely by the conceptual model of teaching and learning that he or she holds. If a person, for example, conceives of knowledge as a static entity, learning as a process that consists of the repeated practice of factual information, and teaching as a process of transmitting to students a body of preestablished knowledge (i.e., the existing knowledge of a discipline), then he or she is more likely to employ a lecture–discussion mode of teaching (perhaps losing opportunities for students to engage in exploratory activities) than is a teacher who conceives of teaching as an activity in which students are encouraged to construct their own knowledge. In a similar manner, a researcher who holds the latter conception is more likely to conduct studies concerned with instructional techniques that foster self-regulated learning than studies concerned with the effectiveness of didactic methods of teaching. A more detailed discussion of ways in which our conceptions of teaching and learning have been changing in recent years is presented in the next section.

## CHANGING CONCEPTIONS AND NEW ASSUMPTIONS

Neither research nor practice occurs in a vacuum. A variety of social and intellectual factors influence the manner in which these activities are carried out. It is common, at least among researchers, to think that scientific research determines our conceptions of the world and the various practices utilized by professionals. Although this type of influence does occur, it is clear that the relationship between scientific research and the world views and professional practices of a particular culture is not unidirectional. The social philosophy and intellectual conceptions held by individuals at a given time and place in history play an extremely important role in determining the kind of research that is conducted and the scientific theories that are suggested. Such a realization, of course, is not new, for *Zeitgeist* is an old term in psychology.

Thus, our conceptions and understandings of phenomena change over the years, reflecting both new knowledge accumulated through research and changes in the prevailing social, intellectual, and political philosophies. As these factors interact, new understandings evolve that permit us to think about relevant issues in new and hopefully more productive ways. Nearly always, however, these new ways of thinking are based on assumptions that are different from those involved in earlier conceptions, and it is wise to remember that the new conceptions and assumptions have limitations as well as advantages. New is not always better; sometimes new is merely different.

For instance, different theoretical perspectives often focus on different aspects of the same phenomenon, and each may provide a critical part of a truly comprehensive understanding of the phenomenon. Thus, different theoretical perspectives need to be evaluated with regard to their respective strengths and weaknesses and the extent to which the strengths and weaknesses of different perspectives complement one another, rather than with regard to one being correct and another being incorrect.

Conceptions of teaching, of course, have been influenced by a centuries-old philosophical debate about the nature of education that is unlikely to be settled in the foreseeable future. Contrast, for example, the factory model of schooling, which has dominated education in the United States for most of the 20th century, with the views of Thoreau, Dewey, and other individuals who argued that education should emphasize discovery, social reform, and freedom. The former model, along with its related methods of teaching and management, is based on a social philosophy and world outlook that is consistent with the Industrial Revolution that proved so successful in business and industry during the 1800s and early 1900s. The latter views, on the other hand, are based on a more humanistic perspective of society, and for many years these views had a relatively minor impact on education. During the past 10 years, however, these concerns have been receiving more and more attention, and their influence is clearly evident in current thinking about cooperative learning, cognitive apprenticeship, self-regulated learning, and authentic learning experiences.

Before further elaboration on how conceptions of teaching have changed in recent years, it may be helpful to consider the nature of the phenomenon we are trying to understand, namely, the classroom setting in which most teaching occurs. Although it is appropriate for one to study only part of this complex process, an awareness that the various pieces must ultimately fit together into an overall whole helps one to maintain a healthy empirical and theoretical perspective. Other forms of instruction (e.g., textbooks, computer-aided instruction, tutoring, seatwork) involve issues similar to those encountered in a live classroom, although these issues often need to be addressed in different ways. This chapter focuses on classroom teaching, with the realization that similar issues need to be addressed when other forms of instruction are considered.

## Teaching and Learning in a Classroom Environment

Classrooms are not the neat, orderly places we sometimes imagine them to be. The typical classroom is an active place in which many things are happening. Friends, strangers, adversaries, and dating partners (current, future, and imagined) find themselves together for long periods of time, and as Jackson (1968) noted, "In the small but crowded world of the classroom, events come and go with astonishing rapidity. There is evidence [for instance] . . . to show that the elementary school teacher typically engages in 200 to 300 interpersonal interchanges *every hour* of her working day" (p. 149, emphasis added).

These events, many of which are occurring simultaneously, evoke a variety of psychological reactions in the teacher and students as they try to keep pace with the ever-changing nature of classroom life and the instructional process. It is not uncommon, however, for research-oriented educational psychologists to think of these activities and psychological processes in limited ways, most often in terms of one or two factors closely related to the acquisition of subject matter content (e.g., learning, motivation, etc.). Few would deny that the main purpose of school is for students to acquire the skills and knowledge necessary for them to function productively as adults, but much more is involved than merely learning the day's lesson!

Gump (1967), for example, observed teachers in six third-grade classrooms for 2 days and found that only about half (51%) of a teacher's acts (the shortest meaningful unit of behavior directed toward students) were related to instruction. The other half involved the structuring of behavior, including the movement of props and pupils (23%), dealing with deviant behavior (14%), dealing with individual problems (8%), and amenities and miscellaneous (4%). Unfortunately, comparable data are not available for the upper grades. Although it would be reasonable to expect that in high school a higher percentage of a teacher's acts would be directed toward instruction, common sense suggests that this percentage would not approach unity.

Although the acquisition of academic content by individual students is clearly the major focus of most classroom activities, it is equally clear that "formal education is essentially a social process" (C. S. Weinstein, 1991, p. 495). Many psychological factors (e.g., emotional, developmental, cultural, and motivational, as well as cognitive and social factors) work together, often simultaneously and interactively, on many different levels. In order to understand the instructional process and the manner in which teachers affect students, one must be aware of this complexity, and of the fact that students in real classrooms are whole organisms and not just a collection of psychological processes that operate independently of one another.

***Characteristics of Classroom Environments.*** The characteristics of classroom environments have been summarized in several different ways, and it is significant that most of these characteristics are already in place before instruction even begins (L. M. Anderson, 1989; Doyle, 1986). For example, Doyle (1986) suggests that classroom settings have six distinctive properties that transcend the particular way in which students are organized for learning and the educational philosophy of the teacher, namely:

1. *Multidimensionality*—Classrooms are crowded settings with a large number of events and tasks occurring and a limited supply of resources that compete for the attention of both the teacher and the students.

2. *Simultaneity*—Many things happen at the same time.
3. *Immediacy*—A large number of interpersonal exchanges and events progress at a rapid pace with little time for reflection.
4. *Unpredictability*—Since classrooms involve social interactions that are jointly produced, it is difficult to predict how a particular activity will turn out on any given day, and unexpected turns of events are common.
5. *Publicness*—Classrooms are public places in which events such as those involving the teacher or disruptive students are witnessed by a large portion of the class. There are few places for either the teacher or students to hide.
6. *History*—Any group that remains together for a period of time accumulates a common history of experiences, norms, and routines that provide a context in which current activities are conducted. Former experiences and their outcomes, both good and bad, are not easily modified.

Linda Anderson (1989) has proposed that classroom environments and teachers differ along the following five dimensions, which have implications for the way in which instruction is delivered and the effects that teachers have on student learning:

1. *The academic goals of schooling.* The academic goals, both implicit and explicit, pursued in a school and classroom can vary from the recall of facts and the acquisition of context-specific skills to problem solving, critical thinking and creativity. This dimension might include various types of social goals for some teachers and classrooms.
2. *Perceptions of the teacher's instructional roles.* Teachers, students, and administrators differ in their views about the teacher's instructional role, and these views/conceptions range from the teacher as a disseminator of information (i.e., teaching by telling) to the teacher as a mediator in students' construction of knowledge.
3. *Students' roles in promoting their own learning.* Closely related to the perceived instructional role of teachers are beliefs about the nature of learning and students' participation in their own learning. These beliefs vary from students being passive receptors of information in a process closely controlled by the teacher to students being the discoverers or constructors of new knowledge in a self-regulated manner.
4. *The nature of academic tasks.* Academic tasks used in classrooms vary from those that call for the recall of specific information to those that require students to solve problems or produce creative products such as papers, artifacts, or art work. Instructional tasks also vary along a continuum from "academic" to "authentic" and "real-world" activities.
5. *The social environment as the context for individual learning.* Classroom social environments vary in a number of ways that have consequences for instructional programs. For example, failure may have negative social consequences or may be viewed as a natural and accepted part of the learning process that provides opportunity for constructive feedback; other students may be seen either as a hindrance to learning (e.g., someone who wastes your time or is a competitor for a limited number of good grades); and so forth.

Another factor, *characteristics of the students*, might reasonably be added to the above list. The social class, ethnicity, and race of the students in a class, as well as their prior knowledge and academic ability, influence both the teacher's and the students' perceptions of what can be accomplished in the classroom. The extent to which students in a class deviate from cultural and academic norms affects both the expectations that a teacher has for the class and the manner in which he or she behaves toward the students.

Factors such as the ones identified by Doyle (1986) and Anderson (1989) serve to define the academic/instructional and social milieu of the classroom. This milieu, in turn, influences (a) the content presented for learning (i.e., the curriculum), (b) the expectations of the teacher and students, and (c) the ways in which the teacher teaches. In conjunction with these general characteristics of classrooms, the more specific types of instructional activities that occur in classrooms also influence the effects that teachers have on students. Several of these activities will be discussed next.

***Toward a Structure of Classroom Activities.*** Within the complex social environment of the classroom, teachers and students engage in a variety of activities as they work together to accomplish tasks that have academic, social, and personal consequences. The subenvironments or subsettings in which these activities occur are probably the most meaningful units of analysis for studying the ways in which teachers and students affect one another. Ecological psychologists refer to these subenvironments or subsettings as "activity segments" (Berliner, 1983; Gump, 1967; C. S. Weinstein, 1991). These activity segments, which typically last between 10 and 20 minutes, differ in the social, cognitive, curricular, emotional, and communicative demands they place on both teacher and students, as well as in the responses they elicit from the various participants. They also pose constraints or norms, such as who can talk to whom, where things are to occur (e.g., individually at one's desk, in a small group of students, in a whole-class setting), the type of learning that is expected (e.g., memorization of facts, explanation of concepts), and so forth. Although there is a tendency to think of activity segments in terms of lessons, one should be cautious about making such a comparison, since either can extend beyond the other. Activity segments provide a powerful conceptual tool for studying the teaching–learning process in the context of an actual classroom, although they should be psychologically (as well as socially) meaningful and possess psychological validity.

A number of studies have sought to identify the subenvironments or subsettings that are meaningful with regard to teaching and learning in classroom settings. It appears that a relatively few activity segments can describe most of the activities that occur in American elementary schools (research at the secondary level is virtually nonexistent). One of the first studies to investigate activity segments in classrooms was Gump's (1967) observational study of six third-grade classrooms. From the vast amount of data collected, seven "action structures" emerged as accounting for most of the data. These segments were described in terms of four a priori dimensions (teacher leadership pattern, pupil activity, action sequencing, and grouping arrangements) rather than more commonly used labels such as seatwork, recitation, and so forth. For example, one of these segments is described in terms of the teacher not being directly involved in the segment and the students working on their own

TABLE 22–1. Classroom Activities Found in Studies by Berliner (1983) and Stodolsky et al. (1981)

| Berliner (1983) | Stodolsky et al. (1981) |
| --- | --- |
| Seatwork | Seatwork |
| | Diverse seatwork |
| | Individualized seatwork |
| Two-way presentation | Discussion |
| | Recitation |
| | Tutorial |
| One-way presentation | Lecture |
| | Demonstration |
| | Giving instructions |
| Mediated presentation (film, audio tapes, etc.) | Film/audiovisual |
| Reading circle | |
| Silent reading | |
| Construction (student creates a product from a set of materials) | |
| Games | Contest |
| Play | |
| Transition | |
| Housekeeping | |
| | Checking work |
| | Tests |
| | Group work |
| | Student reports |
| | Preparation |
| | Other |

materials in a self-paced, private manner, an arrangement many would refer to as seatwork. Among the seven action structures identified, two represent variations of what would normally be called seatwork, three represent variations of recitations, and one involves readying the students for another activity (usually getting ready to leave).

Other investigators have identified varying numbers of classroom activities. The 11 activities proposed by Berliner (1983) and the 17 activities proposed by Stodolsky, Ferguson, and Wimpelberg (1981) are listed in Table 22–1. Yinger (1977), however, found that the primary grade teacher he studied used a total of 53 activities over a 12-week period. Table 22–1 is arranged in a manner that highlights the overlap and similarities between the two sets of findings that are presented. It may be noted, for example, that in certain instances, the categories found by one investigator represent subcategories of those found by the other (e.g., Berliner's seatwork and Stodolsky et al.'s seatwork, diverse seatwork, and individualized seatwork). In some cases, however, it is difficult to determine the extent of overlap, for with the exception of recitation, which was the focus of this particular study, Stodolsky et al. did not describe, define, or provide examples of the various segments. In any case, it should be noted that it is difficult, if not impossible, to determine an appropriate level of specificity for activity segments, since the types of activities needed to describe the events in a particular study depend on the characteristics of that study, including the subject matter being taught (Stodolsky et al., 1981) and the sample that participated in the study.

Generally speaking, activity segments constitute the basic unit of classroom organization. As noted previously, they involve several different dimensions. The social, academic, and conversational aspects of these segments have received the most attention in the literature, although, Brophy and Alleman (1991) recently discussed a variety of issues related to the design, selection, and evaluation of classroom activities, primarily from a curriculum perspective. Typically each aspect has been studied separately, although Erickson (1982) discussed the characteristic of both "academic task structures" and "social participation structures." For a good introduction to some of the relevant issues and research, the reader is referred to C. S. Weinstein's (1991) review of research concerned with the social structure of five activity segments: (a) recitation, (b) teacher-directed small groups, (c) sharing time, (d) seatwork, and (e) student-directed small groups.

The use of activity segments to investigate the teaching–learning process has a number of advantages, although they need to be related to psychological issues and mechanisms if a comprehensive understanding of how students learn in classroom settings and how teachers and students affect one another is to be accomplished. These concerns are reflected, for example, in Gump's (1967) raising the following questions in his discussion of how motivation is or might be related to various activity segments:

[W]hat sort of action structures stimulate interest in a subject matter, create a desire [for the pupil] to do more with the area? There must be segmental arrangements which enhance or retard various kinds of learning. For example, reading circles usually produce high pupil involvement. Are children also learning better because of this small, interdependent, close-to-teacher externally-paced segment? Or would a different arrangement yield faster learning? (p. 85)

## Some Characteristics of Teaching and Its Relationship to Learning

Within this context of classroom life, the teacher does many things. Few would question that the teacher's primary responsibility is to help students achieve appropriate educational goals, but this task involves far more than the simple dissemination of subject matter content. Teachers affect students in many ways and on many different levels as they orchestrate and manage the complex and multidimensional activities that form the basis for students' acquisition of the academic and social goals of education. We typically think of this process as a unidirectional one, but as any experienced teacher knows, students affect teachers and what they do, as well as the other way around (Fiedler, 1975).

How does the teacher navigate this complex environment, successfully performing the various things that must be done if students are to acquire appropriate educational outcomes? The knowledge needed to accomplish this task certainly includes knowledge of the subject matter being taught and the curriculum in which that subject matter is embedded, in addition to an understanding of the psychological nature of human learning and cognition. However, the type of professional knowledge needed to manage the complexity of the classroom transcends these more traditional psychological domains of relevant knowledge (see, e.g., Schön, 1983). The teacher must know, for example, how to manage the various instructional events and behavioral problems that occur in the classroom (Doyle,

1986). He or she also must know how to relate to and work with a variety of individuals, including parents, other teachers, the principal, and students with a variety of backgrounds and extracurricular interests. It is within this context of classroom activity that teachers have an opportunity to influence students and what they learn.

In understanding how teacher effects operate, it may be helpful to consider several issues regarding the nature of the teaching–learning process. These issues include concerns for teaching as intervention in student learning, the multiple levels (affective and motivational as well as cognitive) on which teachers affect students, the direct and indirect nature of these effects, and the role of student mediation in the teaching–learning process. These issues are considered next.

***Teaching as Intervention.*** As noted previously, various conceptions of education differ with regard to the teacher's role in providing instruction. At one end of the continuum is the didactic, teacher-centered view in which the teacher's role is to present the knowledge to be learned and to direct, in a rather explicit manner, the learning process of the students. At the other end of the continuum is the exploratory, discovery view which emphasizes that students should be left free to discover and to construct knowledge on their own. According to this latter view, intervention by the teacher should be kept to an absolute minimum, for such intervention only interferes with or prevents meaningful learning from occurring.

Nevertheless, it is difficult to deny that teaching, by its very nature, involves some sort of intervention in the learning processes of students in an attempt to facilitate their acquisition of desired educational outcomes. Few would deny that the reason we have schools is to help students understand hard to learn material that probably would not be acquired were it not for schools (Bereiter, 1989). Gradations certainly exist between the two extremes identified above, and a guided-construction or guided-discovery view of teaching and learning probably is most consistent with current psychological thinking.

Thus, intervention is an important aspect of learning from instruction, and the goal of psychological research on teaching and classroom learning is to understand the psychological nature and appropriateness of this intervention. The kind of intervention that is appropriate for one instructional situation may be inappropriate for a different instructional situation. For example, identifying the instructional goals of a particular learning experience may be appropriate for both a lesson in which the teacher is trying to help students learn certain basic knowledge about a topic through didactic presentation or class discussion, and a lesson in which the teacher is trying to help students acquire problem-solving or critical thinking skills by using a discovery lesson in which the students work on their own (or in small groups) to explore a series of objects, phenomena, or examples. In the first case, it may be most appropriate for the teacher to identify the goals for the students. In the second case, however, it may be most appropriate for the teacher, at various phases of the lesson, to have students articulate (as best they can) the instructional goals being pursued. In both cases there is instructional intervention, but it is accomplished in very different ways.

The educational benefit of open-ended explorations by students can be greatly enhanced if the explorations are accompa-

nied by appropriate instructional intervention and structuring. These activities might include, for example, discussions between the teacher and students about (a) various features of the learning activity to which the students should attend, (b) observations made by different students about the learning experience, or (c) what students believe they have learned from engaging in the activity. These discussions might occur either before, during, or after the students have engaged in the exploration/discovery experience. The teacher might also set up similar discussions among the students, but in all of these cases, intervention by the teacher plays a critical role in determining if and what the students learn.

Instructional intervention can take several different forms. For example, it can involve (a) providing appropriate subject matter content, including specific knowledge and learning tasks; (b) eliciting various psychological processes in the student, both cognitive and affective; (c) providing cues as to which information in the material being studied is most important and the manner in which students might process that information; (d) doing things to encourage motivation in the students (e.g., setting attainable goals, creating suspense and curiosity, using unique and unexpected contexts when applying concepts and principles); and (e) providing affective and personal support such as encouragement. In each of these cases, the teacher is intervening in the learning processes of the students in the hope that desirable educational goals will be accomplished.

***The Multiple Facets of Teacher Effects.*** There is a tendency to think of teacher effects only in terms of cognitive factors, especially those factors directly concerned with the acquisition of subject matter content. Thus, it is not surprising to find that most research on ways in which teachers influence student learning has focused on cognitive and behavioral processes, with little concern for the social, affective, and motivational factors that are equally important in determining how teachers affect student learning. Typically, these latter factors are studied independently, with little concern for specific ways in which teachers might modify their instruction (Blumenfeld, Puro, & Mergendoller, 1992).

It is increasingly recognized, however, that thinking and learning do not occur in a cognitive vacuum and that "thinking must be understood as a form of social interaction" (Levine, Resnick, & Higgins, 1993, p. 588). As Levine et al. note,

In the messy "real world" it is difficult to imagine any situation that is purely cognitive—devoid of emotions, social meanings, social intentions, and social residues in the form of inherited roles and tools. (p. 604)

The various things that teachers do in the classroom affect students on many levels. Noncognitive factors such as beliefs, attitudes, emotions, and social relationships, as well as a variety of motivational factors, influence students and what they learn in ways that are as important as the more widely recognized cognitive factors. Some of these effects, although certainly not all, are indirect in nature (direct versus indirect effects are discussed in the next section), but they play a critical role nevertheless.

Although much has been written about the importance of noncognitive factors in classroom learning, surprisingly few studies have investigated the specific ways in which noncognitive aspects of the teacher's behavior or classroom procedures influence student learning. There is some evidence, however, that teacher support and the quality of a student's relationship with the teacher can determine whether the student remains engaged in the learning process or mentally and emotionally withdraws (Batcher, 1981; Goodenow, 1992; Kramer, 1991). Perhaps the best evidence in support of noncognitive teacher effects is related to the ways in which teachers communicate expectations and goals to students and the ways in which teachers enhance motivation (C. Ames, 1992; Blumenfeld et al., 1992; Marshall & Weinstein, 1984). Although these latter factors are not directly concerned with the acquisition of subject matter content, they are closely related. Further, it is interesting to note that the teacher behaviors that communicate high expectations and serve to keep the students engaged in the instructional task (i.e., motivated) are quite similar to the more strictly cognitive factors associated with subject matter learning. For example, Blumenfeld et al. (1992) suggest that

teachers can communicate high expectations by choosing varied tasks that are at appropriate levels of difficulty, by scaffolding student learning, and by teaching learning strategies to enable students to accomplish tasks. (p. 209)

Blumenfeld et al. (1992, p. 213) go on to report a study comparing experienced teachers whose classes reported different levels of motivation and cognitive engagement. Students in fifth- and sixth-grade science classes reported higher levels of motivation to learn when their teacher:

- "stressed ideas rather than facts,
- "highlighted the value of science through stories about scientists or about how science was related to everyday events,
- "related their own excitement by telling personal stories of their scientific experiences . . . ,
- "made conceptual material more concrete and interesting by providing examples and by relating it to their own students and their experience or to current events . . . ,
- "assigned tasks that were more varied, and
- "encouraged student cooperation in small groups."

The teachers in those classrooms where students reported lower levels of motivation, on the other hand, tended to focus on quizzes, grades, and correct answers. More generally, Blumenfeld et al. (1992) identify four factors that characterize the practice of teachers in those classrooms where students reported high levels of cognitive engagement (i.e., motivation):

1. *Opportunities to learn*—Opportunities for students to learn were created in various ways that focused on substantive tasks at a level appropriate for the student. Lessons were tightly organized around a main idea and included concrete examples, demonstrations, and discussions that encouraged students to make connections between the new material and other experiences and information, and students were encouraged to become actively involved by responding to high-level questions, being asked to summarize, and so forth.
2. *Press*—By means of the teachers' feedback and participation

techniques, students were pressed to explain and justify their answers. The teachers also reframed questions about which students were unsure and broke them into smaller parts, monitored for student understanding rather than procedural correctness, and encouraged answers from all students.
3. *Support*—The teachers provided instructional support to students in their attempts to understand through the use of scaffolding, modeling thinking and suggesting strategies rather than merely providing students with the correct answer, encouraging collaborative efforts among students, and so forth.
4. *Evaluation*—The evaluation and accountability systems used by the teachers emphasized understanding and learning rather than work completion and right answers. Mistakes were used as a way for students to check their thinking. Students were encouraged to take risks; and students who had done poorly on quizzes and assignments were allowed to redo them.

R. Ames and C. Ames (1991) suggest the following set of guidelines for teacher actions that are likely to enhance student motivation in the classroom:

- *Reduce social comparison.* The tendency of students to compare themselves with one another, especially with regard to their performance on classroom tasks, tests, and report cards, should be minimized by (a) reducing public evaluation and the emphasis on success and grades, (b) communicating performance expectations in advance, and (c) using a variety of grading practices.
- *Increase involvement in learning.* Student involvement should be increased through such things as the use of cooperative learning methods, peer tutoring, and the use of games and simulations, as well as by allowing the student real choices with regard to method, pace, and specific content.
- *Focus on effort.* The teacher can focus on effort by emphasizing student progress, by reinforcing students' learning and effort, by telling students that mistakes and errors are a normal part of the learning process, and by requiring reasonable effort from the students.
- *Promote beliefs in competence.* Teachers can help students realize the importance of effort and the use of various learning strategies in achieving their goal, including the teaching of problem-solving skills; making grades contingent on students achieving their goals; communicating positive expectations; and making plans with students for improving their performance, including an explicit example of the strategic thinking that is needed for making improvements.
- *Increase chances for success.* Teachers should teach students strategic thinking and give them practice in using strategic thinking on different academic tasks. Instructional methods that are likely to increase students' chances for success should be used, such as peer tutoring, cooperative learning, and individualized instruction.

The close relationship between cognitive and noncognitive factors is evident, although more studies concerned with the affective dimension of teacher effects are clearly needed. Classroom activities, goals, and structures are multidimensional in nature (C. Ames, 1992; Wentzel, 1989), and the various facets of the teaching–learning process need to be studied in a more integrated manner (Shuell, 1993).

*Direct versus Indirect Teacher Effects.* Teachers affect the instructional process in both direct and indirect ways. Direct effects are those that involve the presentation of specific content in a particular manner, as when a science teacher begins a lesson on the water cycle by having students recall and briefly discuss relevant information in yesterday's lesson, using a diagram as an advance organizer in presenting the information in today's lesson, and then having students explain their understanding of the new information to a partner. In these cases, the teacher influences the students' learning of the desired content by the nature of his or her actions. These direct effects are the ones that normally come to mind when teacher effects are considered, and they are the ones that have received the most attention in research on teaching and learning.

Teachers also affect student learning in a variety of ways that can be characterized as indirect. These indirect effects often appear subtle in terms of traditional conceptions of teaching and learning, and consequently they typically have been overlooked in research on teacher effects. It is now clear, however, that the way in which a classroom is structured, the instructional and managerial procedures that are employed, the social norms that are established, and the nature of the instructional task that is assigned (e.g., one that calls for rote memory versus one that calls for a demonstration of understanding) all play an extremely important role in determining what students learn (e.g., Brophy & Alleman, 1991; Doyle, 1983, 1986; Morine-Dershimer, 1983; C. S. Weinstein, 1991).

When a teacher establishes cooperative learning groups, for example, he or she has little direct control over the specific learning experiences that occur in the groups. These experiences determine what the students learn, but it is virtually impossible to predict exactly what will happen. In most cases, what occurs in a group is determined more by the students than by the teacher. Nevertheless, the teacher influences the students' learning by arranging for a particular type of learning environment in which there is a high probability that certain kinds of psychological processes essential for the acquisition of desired educational goals will occur. Typically, the teacher also structures the group activities in certain ways (by establishing guidelines for the way in which the groups are to function, assigning tasks, etc.) and usually monitors and intervenes when necessary to ensure that the group functions in a reasonably productive manner. Most of the pedagogical experiences that occur in the group, however, cannot be attributed to the direct influence of the teacher. Nevertheless, the teacher has had an important, albeit indirect, effect on the students' learning.

Other types of indirect effects also occur. For example, the instructional and questioning strategies used by a teacher can have substantial effects on (a) which students participate in classroom activities, (b) which students are listened to (i.e., their comments remembered) by other students during classroom discussions, (c) the cognitive level of comments to which students attend, and (d) how much is learned (Morine-Dershimer, 1983). Morine-Dershimer observed teachers who used one of three different types of instructional strategies: textbook based, student experience based, and model based (i.e., the types of

instructional models discussed by Joyce, Weil, & Showers [1992]). Each instructional strategy involved the assignment of different kinds of classroom tasks, the asking of different types of questions, differing patterns of teacher praise and feedback, and different patterns of academic and social status among students in the various classrooms. These different styles of teaching probably represent different world views of the teachers involved—that is, different conceptions of the learning process and the role of students, different beliefs about the nature of knowledge (at least the knowledge that is important for students to learn), and so forth. The teachers may not be able to articulate these differences, but their actions in the classroom do have differential effects on the students.

Student learning is also affected by the nature of the discourse in which the teacher and students engage. Although most sociolinguistic researchers recognize that classroom discourse "affects the thought processes of each of the participants and thereby the nature of what is learned" (Cazden, 1986, p. 451), most sociolinguistic research to date has focused on social rather than instructional functions of language (see Cazden, 1986). Several recent studies, however, have investigated the instructional function of classroom talk (e.g., Orsolini & Pontecorvo, 1992; Wertsch, 1991). Through the use of language, for example, the teacher can focus on relevant rather than irrelevant (for purposes of instruction) aspects of the material being studied, thereby indicating in subtle ways the information to which the student should pay attention. This shift in focus is nicely illustrated in the following show-and-tell discussion involving a piece of lava brought in by a student:

S: I've had it [the piece of lava] ever since I was . . . I've always . . .
T: (*In a low voice to another student*): Careful.
S: I've always been, um, taking care of it.
T: Uh hum.
S: It's never fallen down and broken.
T: Uh hum. Okay. Is it rough or smooth?
S: Real rough and it's . . . and it's . . . and it's sharp.
T: Okay. Why don't you go around and let the children touch it. Okay? (*S takes it around the group, which is sitting on the floor.*) Is it heavy or light?
S: It's heavy.
T: It's heavy.
S: A little bit heavy.
T: In fact, maybe [the other students] could touch it and hold it for a minute. (Wertsch, 1991, pp. 113–114)

This type of instructional exchange is so common that it is easy to overlook the instructional significance of the teacher shifting the discussion from nonacademic to academic characteristics of the lava. It is through linguistic exchanges of this sort that students learn, without being explicitly told, that certain types of questions and ways of thinking are more valued than others and that they must adopt these "accepted" ways as their own if they are to be successful in school (Goodnow, 1992). In the face of such evidence on the indirect effects of various instructional methods, it is wise to avoid an oversimplified view of the manner in which teachers affect the behavior and learning of students.

*Student Mediation of Instruction.* Most of the early research on teaching focused on teacher behaviors and their relationship to a variety of criteria, including but not limited to student achievement. Even in those cases when student outcomes were assessed, there typically was little concern for the psychological functioning or characteristics of the learner. Most process–product research, for instance, correlated teacher behaviors directly with student outcomes, paying little if any attention to how students reacted to the teacher's behaviors or how they processed the information presented by the teacher in ways that resulted in the outcomes observed. This almost exclusive focus on the teacher's behavior, it might be noted, is consistent with the didactic, factory models of teaching prevalent at the time. According to these models, the teacher is almost totally responsible for what the students learn. The students must be sufficiently motivated, of course, but aside from that requirement, it is the teacher who determines what students learn (much as the factory worker is responsible for the quality of the product produced, as long as the raw materials are of sufficient quality).

The relationship between teacher behaviors and student outcomes, however, is never a direct one, regardless of whether the outcomes are cognitive, affective, motivational, or attitudinal. Students perceive instructional stimuli and the environmental context in which they occur in idiosyncratic ways, interpreting and processing the information in ways that are consistent with their prior experiences and personal goals. Further, they commonly ignore what the teacher wants them to do, focusing instead on what they perceive to be the purpose of the assigned activity or what they find most interesting (L. Anderson, 1984; Gelman & Greeno, 1989). For many students, especially the middle and low achievers, this involves the pursuit of social goals such as "having fun" and "making or keeping friendships" (Wentzel, 1989).

Consequently, the effect that teachers have on students is determined ultimately by the students' psychological response to what the teacher does (Doyle, 1978; Shulman, 1986; Wittrock, 1986), and to a very large extent, it is this student mediation of the teacher's instructional behavior that makes the study of teacher effects a psychological endeavor. As Doyle (1978) notes:

It is conceivable that a student would fail to learn from a particular instructional setting, regardless of its "quality," because of an inability to recognize and interpret cues that signal which performances are being taught. (p. 185)

In a very real sense, the manner in which the learner perceives, interprets, and processes information in the instructional situation (including the content being learned and the social context in which the instruction occurs) is more important than the actions of the teacher in determining what the student will learn. This statement does not mean that the teacher plays only a minor or inconsequential role in student learning. Far from it—for the manner in which the teacher relates to the student and intervenes in the learning process plays an essential and critical role in determining what and if the student learns. What it does mean is that teacher effects cannot be determined merely by observing how the teacher behaves in the classroom. In order to understand teacher effects on student learning, it is necessary to consider the student's prior knowledge, perception of the teacher's expectations, learning strategies, self-efficacy, interpersonal relationships, and other student factors that affect learning from instruction.

Student mediation of instruction occurs on a social as well as a cognitive level (Shulman, 1986). Students simultaneously attend to the many cognitive, affective, and social cues present in the composite instructional setting, continuously interpreting them on the basis of their prior knowledge and experiences, self-perceptions, personal goals, and expectations, as well as on the basis of the social history of the classroom and other relevant groups (peer, family, etc.) to which the student belongs.

For example, praise is widely regarded as something that enhances the learning process, and teachers are often encouraged to make liberal use of praise in their teaching practices. Teacher praise, however, can be interpreted by students in many different ways, some of which can be debilitating to the learning process. A student who is fighting a teacher's pet image among his peers, for instance, might interpret praise from the teacher in a manner that would cause the teacher's comment to function psychologically as punishment for that student, reducing the frequency of responses appropriate for successful learning (Brophy, 1981). Praise also can carry hidden (perhaps unintended) messages about the student's ability, as when praise (or even, perhaps, a lack of criticism) for performance on an easy task, or on a task that most other students can perform, is interpreted by the student as a low-ability message (Weiner, Graham, Taylor, & Meyer, 1983). Ultimately, it is the perception of the student, not the intent of the teacher, that determines the effect that an instructional act has on the student's learning.

The realization that students' psychological responses mediate the effects that teachers have on students has a number of important implications for the teaching–learning process. Acknowledging that learning is self-regulated (e.g., Corno, 1987; Zimmerman, 1989; Zimmerman & Schunk, 1989) changes, for instance, the emphasis placed on student decision-making during the instructional process. As the learning process unfolds, the student makes a variety of decisions about what to do next. These decisions include which part of the material to pay attention to (or whether to gaze out the window instead), whether to rehearse a particular piece of information, to relate one piece of information to another, and whether to seek an answer to a question that just came to mind. Traditional conceptions of teaching often portray the teacher as the primary person performing or determining these types of activities. Although the teacher plays a critical role in assisting the student to engage in these activities, current theories of teaching and learning recognize the necessity for them to be performed by the student.

Student mediation of instruction also places an increased emphasis on studying (e.g., McClintock, 1971; Rohwer, 1984; Thomas, 1988). This emphasis on self-regulation and studying provides a viable alternative to traditional conceptions that focus on didactic teaching (teaching by telling; learning by remembering). For purposes of understanding the teaching–learning process, however, especially the nature and role of teacher effects, more emphasis needs to be placed on the instructional variables and teacher behaviors that influence learning; the concern for learning functions discussed elsewhere in this chapter is one step in that direction.

## Traditional Conceptions of Teaching

Diverse conceptions of education have existed for centuries, and there is a long history of tension between teacher-directed (didactic) and pupil-centered (discovery) views of education. For most of the 20th century, American education has been dominated by a factory model of schooling based on a world view associated with the Industrial Revolution. This model is consistent with the traditional view of a teacher as an authority whose role is to disseminate knowledge to students, largely through lectures and verbal exchanges. Knowledge, according to this traditional conception, is an entity that exists in some tangible form (in books, the minds of authorities, etc.), and this entity is capable of being transferred to students in a more or less intact form. This view of knowledge and teaching is consistent with the functional, pragmatic nature of early American social philosophy and the focus of early American psychology on behavior rather than knowledge. It also provided, to varying degrees, the theoretical rationale for conducting research on teaching.

For example, the question of effectiveness (e.g., "How well does it work?") is a natural one in this type of social milieu, and it should be no surprise that the question of teacher effectiveness was one of the first to be addressed by educational researchers in the United States. In one of the earliest studies, for example, Kratz (1896) questioned over 2,000 children in Grades 2 through 8 about the characteristics of their best teachers. The characteristics mentioned most frequently by the pupils were: "helped in studies," "personal appearance," "good and kind," "patient," "polite," and "neat." Dunkin and Biddle (1974) claim that by the early 1970s, over 10,000 such studies on teacher effectiveness had been published.

One major difficulty with these early studies of teacher effectiveness was an almost total lack of concern for what occurred in the classroom. The actual teaching–learning process, including the role played by the student and the psychological impact that the teacher and the classroom environment have on the learner, was of little or no interest to these researchers. Their conception of teaching focused on the teacher as the deliverer of a product (knowledge) or as a worker on an assembly line (remember that the factory model of teaching was a common way for individuals during this period to look at schooling). Consequently, it was the behavior of the teacher that was considered to be important rather than the behavior of the learner, who typically was viewed as the passive recipient of the knowledge or an object to be manipulated.

This situation began to change during the 1960s and early 1970s when researchers began to observe interactions between pupils and teacher in actual classroom settings (e.g., Amidon & Hough, 1967; Flanders, 1970). During this period, research on teaching began to flourish. The appearance in 1963 of the first *Handbook of Research on Teaching*, edited by Nathaniel L. Gage (1963a), identified the field as a legitimate area of scientific investigation. During the 1970s and 1980s, process–product research added greatly to our understanding and empirical knowledge base about teaching (e.g., Brophy & Good, 1986). Nevertheless, this research focused primarily on student outcomes rather than student learning. Although the role of student mediation was emphasized by a number of investigators (e.g., Doyle, 1978; Winne & Marx, 1980; Wittrock, 1986), the psycho-

logical processes of students responsible for the acquisition of these outcomes received little attention in process–product research. Given that these researchers were interested in teaching rather than learning, a paradigm that focused almost exclusively on teaching did not appear unreasonable to them, especially since teaching was generally viewed as a unidirectional, top-down, knowledge-dispensing process in which teaching by telling was the predominant mode of instruction.

Other researchers during this period conducted research on the teaching–learning process from the perspective of student learning, arguing that teaching methods should be based on psychological research on human learning (e.g., Gagné, 1962a, 1965; Glaser, 1976, 1978a; Stolurow, 1965). In a similar manner, Carroll's (1963) model of school learning, which defined student aptitude in terms of the time required for a student to achieve an instructional outcome rather than in terms of the likelihood that he or she would ever achieve it, provided the theoretical foundation for Bloom's (e.g., 1971, 1976) work on mastery learning. Although this research tended to ignore the details of teaching in much the same way that the research on teacher effects ignored the details of student learning, it has important implications for teaching, and in many ways the two approaches complement one another very nicely.

Then, during the 1980s, alternative conceptions of teaching and learning began to gain prominence. The largely functional (does a relationship exist?) orientation of behavioral psychology and the factory model of schooling were challenged by the concern of cognitive psychology for mental process explanations and more egalitarian views of social interactions, including education. The metaphor of schooling as work, and the work for work's sake orientation that often accompanied it (see, e.g., L. Anderson, 1984), began to be replaced by a learning metaphor (Marshall, 1988, 1990). Conceptions of the teacher's role also began to change from one in which an authority disseminates knowledge to one in which the teacher creates and orchestrates complex learning environments, engaging students in appropriate instructional activities so that the students can construct their own understanding of the material being studied, and working with students as partners in the learning process.

Some of the earlier research will be discussed in the next few sections, including (a) the criterion-of-effectiveness paradigm and early research on teacher effects, (b) Carroll's model of school learning and the mastery learning movement, (c) the research of Gagné, Glaser, and others that evolved from research on air force training during and shortly after World War II, and (d) the achievements and limitations of the process–product research that brought to culmination an important era in research on teacher effects. These various research efforts provided a knowledge base that is still useful for understanding the instructional process, even though they provide only part of the picture needed for an adequate understanding of teaching and learning in classroom settings. The newer conceptions of the teaching–learning process also have had a significant impact on research concerned with teacher effects, and they will be discussed further in subsequent sections.

***The Criterion-of-Effectiveness Paradigm and Early Research on Teacher Effects.*** The vast majority of the early research on teaching utilized the criterion-of-effectiveness paradigm (Gage,

FIGURE 22–1. The Criterion-of-Effectiveness Paradigm

*Source*: From "Paradigms for Research on Teaching" by N. L. Gage, 1963, in N. L. Gage (Ed.), *Handbook of Research on Teaching* (pp. 94–141), Chicago: Rand McNally. Reprinted by permission.

1963b), illustrated in Figure 22–1. This commonsense approach to research on teaching involves identifying a criterion (or a set of criteria) to serve as a benchmark for determining the extent to which teachers are successful in performing their job—for example, student achievement, ratings of principals, composite scores on paper-and-pencil tests thought to measure teacher effectiveness, practice teaching grades, and so forth. These criteria are then measured and become the dependent variables used in the study for investigating teacher effects. Next, variables that might be related to these criteria are identified and measured. These potential correlates of teacher effectiveness might include a variety of teacher characteristics and behaviors. Finally, correlation coefficients are calculated between these two categories of variables in an effort to describe the nature of effective teaching.

Few of the criteria used in the early studies involved student achievement or learning. For example, two studies on teacher effectiveness (Boyce, 1912; Ruediger & Strayer, 1910) appeared in the first three volumes of the *Journal of Educational Psychology*, and both studies involved principals' and supervisors' rank ordering of teachers on general merit (the criterion variable) and various other factors such as voice, teaching skill, personal appearance, initiative or originality, strength of personality, energy and endurance, and other similar factors (the potential correlates). None of the 11 factors in the Ruediger and Strayer study and only one of the 21 factors in the Boyce study ("success of pupils (results)") was related to student learning or achievement. Likewise, in the large number of studies on teacher effectiveness carried out at the University of Wisconsin over a period of several decades, 39% of the studies used in-service ratings of teaching by the superintendent, principal, teacher educators, and other similar individuals, while only 21% of the studies used criteria involving pupil gain scores (Beecher, 1961).

This early research on teacher effectiveness suffered from several serious limitations that prevented it from producing useful findings, especially for those interested in the ways teachers influence student learning. Dunkin and Biddle (1974) suggest four reasons for the failure of this early research:

1. The failure to observe teaching activities. Research utilizing the criterion-of-effectiveness paradigm seldom, if ever, considered the actual processes involved in classroom teaching, and "if teachers do vary in their effectiveness, then it must be because they vary in the behaviors they exhibit in the classroom" (p. 13).
2. Theoretical impoverishment. Typically, variables and batteries of test scores were included in the analyses with little, if any, rationale provided as to why they might be important. Consequently, any attempt to understand teacher effectiveness was severely limited.

3. The use of inadequate criteria of effectiveness. Variables other than ones related to student learning were typically used.
4. A lack of concern for contextual effects. Universal qualities of effective teachers were sought, and virtually no attention was paid to the fact that effective teaching most likely varies from situation to situation.

During the 1960s and early 1970s, research that involved the direct observation of teaching in classroom settings became more popular. This research was concerned with a variety of issues related to teaching (Dunkin & Biddle, 1974; Rosenshine & Furst, 1973), and Rosenshine and Furst's review of 50-odd observational studies that investigated the relationship between naturally occurring teacher behaviors and student achievement is directly relevant to the present discussion. These studies used a variety of observational instruments and rating scales to measure various teacher behaviors, and measures of student achievement ordinarily were adjusted statistically for differences in relevant pretest measures. According to Rosenshine and Furst, the following nine teacher variables appear to yield the most significant and/or consistent results:

1. *Clarity*—A variable that is hard to define objectively, but one that can be judged without too much difficulty. The concern here is for cognitive clarity, and factors such as organization of the material presented for learning are most likely involved. Clarity, of course, must be from the perspective of the learner and obviously depends on his or her prior knowledge. Something that is clear and well organized from the perspective of the teacher and/or observer may not be clear or well organized from the student's vantage point, and vice versa.
2. *Variability*—Includes variables labeled "flexibility" as well as "variability." Involves using a variety of instructional methods, types of tests, types of teaching devices, number of different activities and materials, etc.; also involves such things as "flexible in procedure" and "adaptable versus inflexible."
3. *Enthusiasm*—Includes variables such as ratings on factors like "dull versus stimulating," observer estimations of the teacher's "vigor and power," student ratings of the teacher's involvement or excitement in the lesson, and frequency counts of the teacher's movements, gestures, and voice inflections. Enthusiasm is the only variable on the present list supported by at least some experimental, rather than correlational, data.
4. *Task-oriented and/or businesslike*—Does not imply that the teacher should be cold, distant, or aloof, only that it is best to stay focused on the material and skills being learned.
5. *Criticism*—Twelve of 17 studies yielded negative correlations, with six being statistically significant ($r = -.38$ to $-.61$). Ten were statistically significant when only seemingly harsher forms of criticism were involved. No significant correlations with achievement were obtained with milder forms of criticism, such as telling a student that his or her answer was wrong or providing academic directions.
6. *Teacher indirectness*—Significant results were seldom obtained with most measures of teacher indirectness, although 7 of 8 studies obtained positive correlations ($r = .17$ to .40)

for "use of student ideas," and 11 of 13 studies obtained positive correlations ($r = .12$ to $.51$) favoring a higher indirect/direct ratio.

7. *Student opportunity to learn criterion material*—The extent to which the student has a chance to learn, study, or be taught the material that will be assessed; the extent to which the assessment instrument or procedures are relevant to the instruction that was provided (e.g., sometimes a teacher will test for information that has not been covered in class); the extent to which sufficient time has been spent on the material considered important enough to assess.

8. *Use of structuring comments*—Two small groups of studies (one with four studies, the other with three studies) using considerably different procedures for defining "structuring comments" obtained positive results, suggesting to Rosenshine and Furst that the topic merits further investigation.

9. *Multiple levels of questions or cognitive discourse*—Significant results were obtained in three studies in which questions or cognitive discourse were classified into three or more levels and these classifications were retained in the statistical analysis. Given the problems in doing research on this topic (see, e.g., Redfield & Rousseau, 1981; Winne, 1979), it is wise to be cautious in the interpretation of these findings.

These findings are limited by the vagueness of the teacher variables and the correlational nature of the data (e.g., high achievement may cause students to be more enthusiastic about their teacher rather than the teacher's enthusiasm being the cause of student achievement), but they provide useful data in attempts to gain an empirically based understanding of the teaching–learning process. These studies also represent some of the earliest examples of process–product research, an approach to research on teaching that evolved out of research on teacher effectiveness. Both of these approaches involve a style of research that reflects the best tradition of pragmatism, the philosophical underpinning for the psychological school known as functionalism (Berliner, 1989). In this case, the pragmatic concern is for identifying the characteristics of individuals (teachers) who perform well in classroom settings.

*Process-Product Research: Achievements and Limitations.* The term *process–product* comes from a model developed by Dunkin and Biddle (1974) to summarize the general factors that influence classroom learning. Following terminology suggested earlier by Mitzel (1960), the model identifies four main classes of relevant variables: (a) *presage* variables (characteristics of teachers such as social class, type of teacher preparation program, intelligence, personality, etc.), (b) *context* variables (student characteristics and characteristics of the school and classroom environment), (c) *process* variables (the actual activities of classroom teaching and learning), and (d) *product* variables (the outcomes of teaching, i.e., what the students learn, although affective outcomes such as attitudes and social adjustment are not excluded).

Various combinations of these classes of variables may form different paradigms for studying teaching. One of these paradigms, process–product, is concerned with the relationship between various types of teacher behavior and measures of student achievement or other types of student outcomes. Although process–product research typically focuses on classroom activities, the paradigm, at least in principle, could involve a surrogate teacher (such as a prose passage, computer, etc.) as well as a live teacher. A historical overview of process–product research is presented by Brophy and Good (1986).

Three types of process–product studies were conducted. The first type involved the observation of teachers in natural classroom settings. A large variety of observation schedules and rating scales were used to record specific teacher behaviors that had been selected on the basis of philosophical beliefs, educational theory, or psychological principles of learning (Dunkin & Biddle, 1974; Rosenshine & Furst, 1973). The observed frequency or rated value of the teacher behavior being investigated was then correlated with measures of student achievement to determine the relationship between the two.

In the second type of study, most notably a series of studies conducted by Brophy, Evertson, and their colleagues (for a summary of these studies, most of which were published only as technical reports, see Brophy & Good, 1986), achievement data for the students of 165 experienced second- and third-grade teachers were collected for 3 consecutive years. On the basis of these data, adjusted gain scores of their students were calculated for each teacher for each of the 3 years. In these carefully conducted studies, teachers who consistently produced better student learning were identified, as were teachers who consistently produced less favorable results. Forty teachers who were consistent in their effects on students—roughly distributed across the full range of student achievement—were subsequently observed over a 1- to 2-year period, and the data obtained from these observations were then correlated with student achievement.

The third type of study involved training teachers how to increase their students' academic achievement by engaging in behaviors that previous process–product research had found to be correlated with student learning. These experimental studies took place in regular classrooms. One group of teachers was instructed in specific instructional procedures, while teachers in another group continued to teach in their regular manner (Rosenshine & Stevens, 1986). A number of successful studies found that the students of teachers who implemented the instructional procedures that were taught had higher achievement or higher academically engaged time.

Process–product research produced a number of important findings about the relationship between teacher behavior and student learning, for as Shulman (1986) pointed out:

Teachers who consistently were associated with higher achievement gains tended to behave differently from those who were not. The data accumulated across correlational studies and survived experimental field tests. Teachers seemed capable of learning to perform in the manners suggested by the research program and the performances tended to produce higher achievement among their pupils. Within the limits of whatever activities standardized achievement tests were measuring, the program was palpably successful. Not only were the proposed interventions effective, they were typically acceptable and credible to experienced teachers. (p. 11)

A summary of process–product findings, based on Brophy and Good's (1986) summary and integration, is presented in Table 22–2. Although these findings make an important contribution to the existing knowledge base on effective teaching, their interpretation should be tempered with an understanding

TABLE 22-2. Summary of Findings from Process–Product Research

*Quantity and Pacing of Instruction*

1. Opportunity to Learn/Content Covered. Student learning is directly related to the opportunities students have to acquire the desired content or skills—e.g., number of pages covered, the extent to which information and skills on the assessment instrument were taught in class, duration of the school day/year (assuming appropriate instruction), etc.
2. Role Definition/Expectations/Time Allocation. Students learn more when teachers emphasize the importance of academic instruction, expect their students to master the curriculum, and allocate the majority of class time to curriculum-related activities.
3. Classroom Management/Student Engaged Time. The amount of time students spend actually engaged in academic activities depends on the teacher's ability to organize and manage the classroom in a manner consistent with effective academic learning.
4. Consistent Success/Academic Learning Time. Although it is important for students to move through the curriculum at a brisk pace in order to maximize content coverage, the teacher must also ensure that they are making progress in understanding the material, experiencing moderate to high levels of success, and avoiding high levels of frustration that inhibit learning.
5. Active Teaching. Students learn more in classes in which they spend most of their time being taught or supervised by their teacher rather than working on their own (or not at all), although this finding undoubtedly depends on the nature of the material/skill being learned, the nature of the teacher's supervision, and the extent to which the students are actively engaged in the instructional task.

*Giving Information*

6. Structuring. Students achieve more when teachers structure the material to be learned through the use of overviews, advance organizers, outlines, periodic summarizations, and other means of making the organizational structure of the material clear to students.
7. Redundancy/Sequencing. Achievement is higher when a degree of redundancy is present in the lesson, especially by repeating and reviewing general rules and key concepts.
8. Clarity. There is a consistent correlation between lesson clarity, measured in a variety of different ways, and student achievement.
9. Enthusiasm. Enthusiasm often correlates more with affective than with cognitive outcome, although it is often related to achievement, especially for older students.
10. Pacing/Wait Time. Especially at higher grade levels, sufficient time must be allowed for students to assimilate the new information and process it in meaningful ways.

*Questioning the Students*

11. Difficulty Level of Questions. Although the data yield mixed results, it appears that approximately three-fourths of teachers' questions should elicit correct answers and most of the remainder should elicit a substantive response (incorrect or incomplete answer) rather than no response at all.
12. Cognitive Level of Questions. The findings are inconsistent, although it does not appear that higher order questions are necessarily better; lower order questions often result in higher achievement, but this finding may be dependent on the type of assessment instrument employed and the extent to which students are adequately prepared to respond to higher order questions (see J. Brophy & Good, 1986; Redfield & Rousseau, 1981; Winne, 1979).
13. Clarity of Question. Students sometimes are unable to respond to a teacher's question (which is desirable, even if their answer is incorrect) because the question is vague or ambiguous, or the teacher asked another question without waiting for a response.
14. Postquestion Wait Time. Students achieve more (both in terms of accuracy and quality) if the teacher pauses for about 3 seconds after a question before calling on a student so that all students have an opportunity to think about the question before a response is given.
15. Selecting the Respondent. Findings with regard to this issue depend on grade level, socioeconomic status, and whole-class versus small-group setting. In general, especially in the early grades and during small-group lessons, learning is best when all students participate overtly on a roughly equal basis. Various methods can be used for accomplishing this goal, including the use of "patterned turns" in small-group reading lessons and calling on nonvolunteers as well as volunteers.
16. Waiting for the Student to Respond. In general, when a teacher calls on a student, especially nonvolunteers, the teacher should wait for some type of substantive response from the student, a request for help or clarification, or "I don't know."

*Reacting to Student Responses*

17. Reactions to Correct Responses. Although praise does not appear to be necessary, feedback does. Correct responses should be acknowledged as such (in some cases, a mere nod of the head will suffice), for even if the respondent knows that the answer is correct, some of the other students may not.
18. Reacting to Incomplete or Partly Correct Responses. For these types of responses, the teacher should normally affirm the correct part and then follow up by giving clues or rephrasing the question. If this is not successful, the teacher can give the correct answer or call on another student.
19. Reacting to Incorrect Responses. After indicating that the answer was incorrect, the teacher in most cases should try to elicit an improved response by either rephrasing the question or giving clues. In some cases, the teacher should provide an explanation as to why the correct answer is correct or how it can be determined from the information given.
20. Reacting to "No Response." Students should be trained to respond overtly to questions, even if the only thing they say is "I don't know." Thus, after an appropriate period of silence, the teacher should probe ("Do you know?"), elicit an overt response, and then follow up by providing feedback, giving the correct answer, or calling on another student.
21. Reacting to Student Questions and Comments. The importance of using students' ideas appears to increase with grade level. Teachers should answer relevant questions or redirect them to the class, and incorporate relevant comments into the lesson.

*Other Findings*

22. Handling Seatwork and Homework Assignments. These activities should be varied and interesting enough to keep students engaged, provide worthwhile learning experiences rather than mere busywork, and at a level of difficulty that allows success with reasonable effort. Students should know what they are expected to do and how to get help if needed. Work should be monitored for completion and accuracy, and feedback should be provided.
23. Context-Specific Findings. Virtually all of the process–product findings need to be qualified with regard to the context of instruction, and J. N. Brophy and Good (1986) specifically identify three factors that need to be considered: grade level, student SES/ability/affect, and the teacher's intentions/objectives.

Note: Based on "Teacher Behavior and Student Achievement" by J. Brophy and T. L. Good, 1986, in M. C. Wittrock (Ed.), *Handbook of Research on Teaching* (3rd ed., pp. 328–375), New York: Macmillan. Adapted by permission.

of their limitations with regard to both theoretical significance and practical application. Many of these limitations are summarized by Brophy (1988) and Brophy and Good (1986), and Gage (1989) provides a thoughtful critique of various criticisms of process–product research.

Virtually all process–product studies observed the frequency with which various teacher behaviors occurred. These frequencies were then correlated, in one manner or another, with measures of student achievement, typically standardized achievement tests. One must avoid, however, becoming overly concerned with how frequently a teacher engages in a particular behavior, for frequency alone can be a very misleading characteristic of effective teaching. For example, it does not follow from these data that good teachers engage in certain behaviors not observed in weaker teachers. Most teachers are capable of performing, and actually exhibit, behaviors related to high levels of student achievement; the better teachers, however, appear to engage in these behaviors more often.

In a study by L. M. Anderson, Evertson, and Brophy (1979), for instance, teachers in the treatment group were asked to follow a set of instructional principles while teaching their regular classroom reading groups, although no attempt was made to specify exactly what a teacher should do or say in a particular situation. These guidelines were derived from an integration of research on classroom teaching and learning. Teachers in the control group received no information about these principles or their use. Teachers in both groups were observed 10 times over a 6-month period, and various teacher behaviors were recorded and correlated with the reading achievement of their students. At the end of the year, reading achievement was significantly higher for students in the treatment group than for those in the control group. With regard to one of the teacher behaviors (instructional principles) that was observed (the use of sustaining feedback to elicit some response from a student who initially fails to respond), teachers in the treatment group were twice as likely as teachers in the control group to exhibit this behavior. For both groups, however, the frequency with which teachers exhibited this behavior was strongly correlated with student reading achievement.

Several other considerations also must be taken into account when analyzing the frequency of a teacher's behavior. For example, the extent to which the behavior is appropriate for a particular instructional setting is just as important as its frequency in determining its effectiveness (Berliner, 1976, 1977). In order to be effective in promoting student learning, a teacher must possess more than a repertoire of effective teaching behaviors; he or she also must know when each one should and should not be used. Another consideration involves the fact that the sequence in which various behaviors occur, not merely their frequency, is important in determining how effective those behaviors will be (Gage, 1989).

From the perspective of modern-day educational psychology, one of the more serious limitations of process–product research is its failure to investigate the cognitive (and other psychological) processes of students that mediate the teacher's behavior and its effect on student outcomes (e.g., Winne, 1987). An adequate understanding of the psychological mechanisms involved in learning from instruction is needed in order to explain how teachers affect student learning. Very little is known about the way in which specific instructional practices influence the cognitive, affective, and motivational processes of students (but see Wittrock, 1986), and more psychological research on these issues is clearly needed.

Overall, the findings from process–product research provide a sound body of knowledge about the way teachers affect student learning, but various factors limit their generalizability across settings, contexts, and students (see Brophy & Good, 1986). Many of the process–product research findings deal with classroom management rather than the instructional process per se (Gage, 1989), although management and instruction are closely interrelated (Doyle, 1986). In a number of instances, there have been attempts to evaluate teachers on the basis of process–product findings, but this practice is questionable and must be done with extreme caution. Merely exhibiting the indicated behaviors does not necessarily mean that a person is a good teacher, and in any case, if the concern is for student learning, then measures of student learning (not achievement) should be considered (see Brophy, 1988; Brophy & Good, 1986).

The functional view of teaching provided by process–product research (Berliner, 1989) provides a useful way of studying what many consider to be a major role of teachers, namely, to facilitate the academic achievement of their students. Consequently, process–product research, in one form or another, is likely to continue, and the ways in which the field is evolving will be discussed in a subsequent section of this chapter.

***Carroll's Model of School Learning and the Mastery-Learning Movement.*** Although Carroll's (1963, 1989) model of school learning did not deal with the effect of specific teacher behaviors on student learning, it had such a major impact on the way educational psychologists think about classroom practices that it would be a serious omission if it were not included in this chapter. The model probably is best known for its influence on Bloom's (e.g., 1971, 1976; Bloom, Hastings, & Madaus, 1971) work on mastery learning, but its importance extends beyond the mastery learning model, especially with respect to its efforts to redefine student aptitude in terms of time required to learn, rather than in terms of a person's ability to achieve a particular level of performance. Technically, Carroll's model is not a model of teaching or learning in the traditional sense; "rather, [it] may be thought of as a description of the 'economics' of the school learning process; it takes the fact of learning for granted" (Carroll, 1963, p. 725). Nevertheless, the model summarizes the major factors affecting success in school learning from a psychological perspective and assumes "that the learner will succeed in learning a given task to the extent that he spends the amount of time that he *needs* to learn the task" (Carroll, 1963, p. 725; emphasis in the original).

Carroll (1963) suggested that the extent to which a student learned the instructional material could be expressed as a ratio of the amount of time the student actually spent in trying to learn to the total amount of time he or she needed to learn the task to the desired level. This relationship can be depicted as follows:

$$\text{Degree of learning} = f\left(\frac{\text{Time actually spent}}{\text{Time needed}}\right).$$

The time that the student actually spends in learning depends on two factors:

1. opportunity to learn—the amount of time allowed for learning; and
2. perseverance—the amount of time the learner is willing to spend in trying to learn the material or skill being taught.

Carroll also suggested that the time needed to learn depended on three factors:

1. *Aptitude*—The amount of time that the learner needs to learn a given task, unit of instruction, or curriculum to an acceptable level under optimal instructional conditions of instruction and student motivation.
2. *Ability of the learner to understand the instruction provided.*
3. *Quality of instruction*—The extent to which the instruction provided enables the student to learn the task as rapidly and as effectively as he or she is capable. Included are such characteristics as teacher performance, characteristics of textbooks and workbooks, characteristics of films, and the like.

It should be noted that three of the factors—aptitude, perseverance, and the ability to understand instruction—involve characteristics of the learner, while two of the factors—opportunity to learn and quality of instruction—are characteristics of the environment. The two latter factors involve things that theoretically are under the control of the teacher, although as Carroll (1989) noted:

The model is not very specific about the characteristics of high quality instruction, but it mentions that learners must be clearly told what they are to learn, that they must be put into adequate contact with learning materials, and that steps in learning must be carefully planned and ordered. (p. 26)

In addition, Carroll (1963) mentioned the importance of using words that the learner can understand and adapting the instruction to the special needs and characteristics of the learner. In any case, Carroll's reconceptualization of aptitude in terms of time fit the growing mood of egalitarianism in American education and provided the theoretical foundation for Bloom's (1971, 1976; Bloom et al., 1971) model of learning for mastery and the subsequent mastery learning movement.

The concept of mastery learning dates back to the 1920s (e.g., Morrison, 1926; Washburne, 1922), although research on effective mastery learning procedures did not appear until the 1970s. Mastery learning involves more than a psychological model of teaching, for as Block and Burns (1977) note:

Underlying mastery learning theory and practice is an explicit philosophy about learning and teaching. . . . Essentially this philosophy asserts that under appropriate instructional conditions virtually all students can learn well, that is, can "master" most of what they are taught. Moreover, it proposes that teachers can teach so that all students *do* learn well. (p. 4, emphasis in the original)

Although mastery learning represents a system of teaching, it is concerned primarily with administrating the evaluation and assessment aspects of teaching. Consequently, as is the case with other models of teaching to be discussed later in this chapter, specific instructional procedures such as lecture, group discussion, review, structuring comments, and so on are not specified. In fact,

There are many feasible strategies for mastery learning. Each must incorporate some way of dealing with individual differences in learners by relating the instruction to their needs and characteristics. Each strategy must find some way of dealing with the five variables discussed [in Carroll's model of school learning]. (Bloom et al., 1971, p. 51)

Bloom's learning-for-mastery (LFM) model is the best-known system of mastery learning, especially at the elementary and high school levels, where it is most widely used. Another approach to mastery learning, known as the Personalized System of Instruction (PSI) or the Keller Plan (Keller, 1968; Keller & Sherman, 1974), has been used almost exclusively at the college level. The PSI system is based on principles of operant conditioning rather than on Carroll's model of school learning, and although there are many similarities between PSI and LFM, there are also some notable differences. With LFM, for example, mastery tests are ungraded and used only for diagnostic purposes, instruction is primarily teacher paced, and traditional methods of instruction are typically used to teach the material. With PSI, on the other hand, students must achieve mastery on each test before going on to the next topic or unit, studying for the mastery tests is done individually (or sometimes in pairs) with little if any group instruction, and therefore instruction is primarily student paced.

Many variations of mastery learning are in use at all levels of education, although these systems share, to varying degrees, certain common features that can be summarized as follows:

1. Mastery is defined in terms of particular educational outcomes that may reflect the acquisition of factual information, higher order thinking skills, attitudes, problem solving, or virtually any outcome that the teacher would normally expect students to achieve. Appropriate means of assessing these outcomes are developed, and every student is expected to achieve the outcomes during the course.
2. Instruction is organized into well-defined learning units, although these units do not necessarily have to be either classroom based (e.g., they can be used on field trips as well) or consist entirely of drill-and-practice sessions.
3. Mastery of each unit is expected of students before they proceed to the next unit, although this expectation is necessary only when the next unit requires the skills and knowledge of the previous unit as a strict prerequisite.
4. Depending on the particular mastery system being used, an ungraded or a graded diagnostic-progress test is administered at the completion of each unit to provide feedback on the adequacy of the student's learning. Typically, mastery is defined as performance in the range of 80 to 90 percent accuracy.
5. On the basis of this diagnostic information, especially if the student does not achieve mastery, the original instruction is supplemented with appropriate learning correctives so that the student has the opportunity to complete the learning unit successfully. These correctives might consist of tutoring, small-group sessions, review of the material, alternative instructional activities, and so forth.
6. For those students who do not achieve mastery on the first

test, a parallel form of the formative or summative test is administered, and the cycle may be repeated several times. In most but not all cases, the student is given the same credit if mastery is achieved on one of these subsequent tests as he or she would have received if mastery had been achieved on the first attempt.

7. Time is used as a variable in individualizing instruction and in fostering student achievement; that is, students are allowed, at least in theory, sufficient time for achieving the desired outcomes. The emphasis is on mastering the material rather than on how well students do in comparison with one another.

Considerable controversy has surrounded the use of mastery learning, a controversy that involves a variety of philosophical, theoretical, and methodological issues, as well as several dilemmas inherent in the mastery learning approach, such as coverage versus mastery of the content being covered, and equity in the allocation of time to good and poor learners. (The flavor of this controversy is evident in the recent exchange among L. W. Anderson and Burns [1987], Guskey [1987], C. C. Kulik, J. A. Kulik, and Bangert-Drowns [1990], J. A. Kulik, C. C. Kulik, and Bangert-Drowns [1990], and Slavin [1987a, 1987b, 1990].) A detailed consideration of the issues involved in this debate is beyond the scope of this chapter, although some discussion of the empirical research on mastery learning and its effects on student learning must be included.

A number of reviews and meta-analyses of studies on mastery learning have been published in recent years (Block & Burns, 1977; Guskey & Gates, 1986; Guskey & Pigott, 1988; C. C. Kulik, J. A. Kulik, & Bangert-Drowns, 1990; Slavin, 1987a). In general, these reviews have found that students in mastery programs do better on classroom tests and have more favorable attitudes toward course content and instructional method than students in conventionally taught classes, although additional time is usually required in mastery programs. Differences on standardized tests are very small or nonexistent, although the extent to which teacher-made tests or standardized tests are the most appropriate measures of student achievement can be debated. Although the achievement differences obtained with classroom tests are less than what mastery learning advocates such as Bloom (1984) suggest are to be expected (0.5–0.8 SD, vs. 1.0–2.0 SD), they are impressive nevertheless and deserve serious consideration in discussions of effective classroom teaching and learning.

Mastery learning, however, represents a different approach to concerns for teacher effects. Although quality of instruction, and the various teacher behaviors that it represents, is an integral part of the mastery learning model (Bloom, 1976; Carroll, 1963, 1989), the primary emphasis is on more macro aspects of the teaching–learning process, especially the organization, specification, and sequence of the curriculum and the diagnostic and summative assessment of learning. These activities represent more the indirect types of effects discussed previously, and it is clear from the empirical evidence on mastery learning that these effects influence student learning.

The reaction to implementing mastery learning programs in schools has been mixed, everything from extreme enthusiasm to outright hostility. The latter reaction comes from individuals, including some well-known educational researchers, who see mastery learning as being so behavioristic that it is counterproductive to the attainment of the real goals of education, goals that involve meaningful understanding rather than rote memory. Although the mastery learning model is not a rigid system of instruction inherently limited to low-level outcomes, it is perceived that way by many, and it could be used in that manner by those who are so inclined. As Carroll (1989) points out:

Mastery learning does not necessarily require breaking down the learning task into highly specific stages and skills, nor does it demand attending to those skills one by one in isolation from the total learning task. Sometimes it may be useful to look at specific skills, but they must be taught in the context of the broader final task and in relation to each other. (p. 28)

The mastery learning model and its associated research provide a number of useful insights into classroom teaching practices, although as with all teaching practices, trade-offs are involved. In addition, when any approach runs counter to existing beliefs and practices, resistance to its acceptance is to be expected, for neither world views nor behaviors are easily changed. Berliner (1989) probably is correct when he speculates that one of the main reasons mastery learning has not been successfully implemented by more schools is that it challenges the teacher's conceptions about student behavior (by suggesting that ability is a time variable and that virtually all students are capable of learning the material if given sufficient time) and by taxing the teacher's capability of managing a heterogeneous class of 30 students each working at his or her own pace.

*Gagné's and Glaser's Research on Learning and Instruction.* Another approach to teaching that has greatly influenced the thinking of educational psychologists is represented by the work of Robert Gagné and Robert Glaser. This approach to instruction is based on psychological research on learning, test construction, and the related field of instructional design. Although the contributions made by Gagné and Glaser grew out of research on military training conducted during and shortly after World War II, the general approach it represents has a long and distinguished history in educational psychology, dating back to the work of E. L. Thorndike and John Dewey (see Glaser, 1978b, 1982b). This perspective on teaching and learning presumes that instructional practices should be based on psychological principles of learning, although current approaches recognized very early that these principles are neither the only nor necessarily the most important ones to consider in designing a unit of instruction (e.g., Gagné, 1962b). A theory of instruction (or instructional design) is needed to supplement more traditional principles of learning. For example, Gagné (1962b) suggests that:

The basic principles of [instructional] design consist of: (a) identifying the component tasks of a final performance; (b) insuring that each of these component tasks is fully achieved; and (c) arranging the total learning situation in a sequence which will insure optimal mediational effects from one component to another. (p. 88)

Gagné (1962b) goes on to point out that there is a set of principles concerned with instructional design that has very different names from the principles of learning with which most people are familiar, a set of principles

concerned with such things as *task analysis, intratask transfer, component task achievement*, and *sequencing.* . . . These principles are not set in opposition to the traditional principles of learning, such as reinforcement, differentiation of task elements, familiarity, and so on, and do not deny their relevance, only their *relative importance*. They are, however, in complete opposition to the previously mentioned assumption [that] "the best way to learn a task is to practice the task." (p. 88, emphasis in the original)

Thus, concern for a task analysis of the desired performance and the establishment of a learning hierarchy that identifies the subordinate knowledge and skills (including intellectual skills) needed to achieve the desired performance became an important part of the planning for and design of an instructional unit (Gagné, 1962a, 1965). Gagné (1965, 1984) also emphasized that there are different types of learning outcomes, each requiring its own combination of internal (e.g., prerequisite knowledge) and external (e.g., practice, reinforcement) that must be present in order for that type of learning to occur. Although the types of learning identified by Gagné have changed somewhat over the years, most recently he has suggested that there are five varieties of learning outcomes or learned capabilities: (a) intellectual skills (procedural knowledge); (b) verbal information (declarative knowledge); (c) cognitive strategies (executive control processes or strategic knowledge); (d) motor skills; and (e) attitudes. In addition, Gagné (1977) proposes four basic types of learning: (a) signal learning (or classical conditioning); (b) stimulus-response learning (or operant conditioning); (c) chaining; and (d) verbal associations.

Glaser (e.g., 1962, 1970, 1982b, 1990; Glaser & Bassok, 1989) has proposed a model of instruction that represents the same basic perspective on the planning and delivery of instruction and that complements the work of Gagné just described. The labels used to describe the various components of the model have changed somewhat over the years, but the conceptual framework is basically the same as when the model was first proposed some 30 years ago. The four major components of the model consist of:

1. Analysis and description of the competent performances (knowledge and skill) that we want students to acquire, including intermediate performances
2. Identification and description of the learner's knowledge, ability, and other goal-relevant states prior to instruction
3. Explication of the processes and conditions that can be implemented in instructional settings to assist the learner in moving from his or her initial state to the desired state of competence
4. Monitoring and assessment of the learners' performance and both the short-term (e.g., classroom performance) and long-term (e.g., transfer, generalization, ability for further learning) effects of the instructional implementation

Much like the mastery learning model discussed in the preceding section, the Glaser model represents an overall approach to the planning and delivery of instruction and does not address in any direct manner the specific instructional procedures that

might be utilized in the third component of the model. Gagné (1970; Gagné & Driscoll, 1988), however, proposes that the instructional process is comprised of nine separate psychological events, and given the similarity in theoretical approach, these nine instructional events could easily form the basis for the third component in Glaser's model. These nine events consist of the following: (a) gaining attention, (b) informing the learner of the objectives, (c) stimulating recall of prior learning, (d) presenting the stimulus, (e) providing learning guidance, (f) eliciting performance, (g) providing feedback, (h) assessing performance, and (i) enhancing retention and transfer.

Thus, this general approach combines an analysis of the competency (or task) that the student is to acquire with a concern for establishing the conditions necessary for the learner to acquire the competency. (For a good discussion of task analysis, its history, and its use in the teaching of mathematics, see Resnick [1976b].) For approximately the past 15 years, the approach has been heavily influenced by cognitive psychology and has become known as instructional psychology (e.g., Glaser, 1978a, 1978b, 1982a; Resnick, 1981). Within this context, a large variety of instructional issues have been studied, including reading and the comprehension of text, mathematical skill and understanding, aptitude and intelligence, writing, science, and social studies (Dillon & Sternberg, 1986; Glaser, 1978a, 1982a, 1982b, 1987; Glaser & Bassok, 1989).

Although most of the recent research in instructional psychology retains a concern for the analysis of competent performance, the corresponding theories of learning that address the manner in which that competence is acquired reflect the active, constructive, and self-regulated views of learning and the cognitive apprenticeship model of teaching that will be discussed in subsequent sections of this chapter (e.g., see Glaser, 1990, 1991; Glaser & Bassok, 1989). Glaser and Bassok (1989) discuss a variety of instructional principles consistent with recent research in instructional psychology that include (a) learning by problem solving (i.e., "Learning occurs by doing, by interpretation of declarative knowledge via problem solving" [p. 637]); (b) problem specification and immediate error correction; (c) minimization of working memory load; (d) enabling student use of strategies for monitoring comprehension; (e) teacher serving as model and coach; (f) shared responsibility for task performance; (g) an articulated expert model as an object of study; (h) explication of the reasoning process; (i) construction of a situation-specific model; (j) sequencing and selection of appropriate models and problems; (k) causal explanation; (l) teaching and supporting multiple learning strategies; and (m) minimization of error.

The rational, technical approach to teaching represented by the research discussed in the preceding few sections has diminished in popularity among educational researchers in recent years. It is seen as being too mechanistic, didactic, and structured by those individuals who feel that *all* learning should be exploratory and consist of self-discovery. Once again, the tension between two perennial philosophies of education becomes evident! To some extent, the above criticisms have merit and represent legitimate limitations of these approaches. Nevertheless, some teaching does, and probably should, occur in the manner described by these approaches, for some legitimate school learning involves the acquisition of factual information and skill-like abilities. In addition, most of the research in instructional psychology is clearly concerned with the understanding of meaningful material and self-regulated learning—instructional goals that are quite similar to the goals of those who advocate exploration and self discovery. The view that there is only one type of learning, or one best way to teach or engage the student in meaningful instructional tasks, is extremely shortsighted. A number of different approaches to teaching and learning provide useful insights into teacher effects and the instructional process, and as older conceptions and findings yield to new ones, the process is likely to involve evolution as much as revolution. In any case, the advantages of each approach—especially when they address the limitations of one another, for each possesses both strengths and weaknesses—needs to be considered. In trying to understand a process as complex and multifaceted as teaching and learning, in all likelihood each approach is capable of explaining only part of the overall problem.

## Changing Conceptions of Learning and Teaching

Teaching and learning are closely interrelated, so closely that for purposes of educational research one could argue that the two should be studied jointly, as an integrated whole, rather than as separate phenomena (Shuell, 1993). Psychological theories of learning have long influenced our instructional theories and educational practices, and this relationship is obvious in current thinking about teaching and learning (see Mayer, 1992). During the 1980s, however, new ways of thinking about both teaching and learning began to emerge and gain prominence. These new views tended to be less mechanistic with regard to the roles of both the teacher and the students, and they coincided with evolving theories about the social nature of teaching and learning and the active, constructive, and self-regulated nature of meaningful learning.

Psychological theories of learning have changed dramatically in recent years (see chapter 2, this volume), as behavioral theories have given way to mental models, constructivism, and situated cognition. Teaching is now viewed more as a task of orchestrating a complex environment of learners and activities rather than an assembly line in which knowledge is transferred (disseminated) from someone who knows (the teacher) to individuals who don't (the students) by means of a monologue (teaching by telling). A growing number of investigators now argue that teaching and learning are essentially a social and linguistic process (a process of communication) rather than merely a cognitive ones. A comparison among some of the assumptions about teaching and learning underlying behavioral, cognitive-constructive, and social-constructive theoretical perspectives is presented in Table 22–3.

Generally speaking, current conceptions of learning are influenced by two major beliefs: (a) that learning is constructive rather than reproductive, and (b) that learning is primarily a social, cultural, and interpersonal process governed as much by social and situational factors as by cognitive ones. Current conceptions of teaching and teacher effects reflect these themes to a large extent. The "work" metaphor that dominated classroom life for such a long period of time (a metaphor consistent with the factory model discussed previously) is being challenged by a "learning" metaphor (Marshall, 1988). Influenced by theorists such as Vygotsky (1962, 1978) and the changing

*Zeitgeist*, several common themes pervade most current thinking about teaching and learning from instruction, namely: (a) the social and sociolinguistic nature of learning; (b) a focus on understanding, problem solving, and conceptual change rather than on the memorization of "inert" knowledge; (c) a belief that learning is an active, constructive, and self-regulated process; (d) a belief that classroom activities should consist of "authentic," real-world learning tasks rather than the traditional academic tasks used in most classrooms; and (e) the situation (context)-specific nature of learning, cognition, and knowledge. Changes also have occurred in the way people think about competence (i.e., the source and nature of individual and developmental differences), as traditional conceptions of "intelligence" gave way to a concern for difference between expert and novice performance.

The remainder of this section will address some of these theoretical issues related to teaching that were not discussed in the preceding section, namely: (a) the active, constructive, cumulative nature of learning, (b) teaching and learning as a social process of communication, (c) the situated nature of teaching and learning and the call for more authentic learning experiences, and (d) changing conceptions of competence. Research associated with several specific models of teaching will be discussed in a subsequent section.

*The Active, Constructive, Cumulative Nature of Learning.* Traditional conceptions of learning tend to view learning in a stimulus-response framework, as something that happens to the learner from the outside in. A stimulus occurs in the environment (perhaps something the teacher does or says), the student responds (perhaps by raising a hand to answer the teacher's question or by looking out the window), and, depending on what happens next (the occurrence of reinforcement or punishment), the likelihood that the learner will make the response again either increases or decreases (e.g., the frequency of hand raising either increases due to the teacher's positive statement following a correct response or decreases due to the teacher consistently calling on other students or the embarrassment that results from providing an incorrect answer). Generally speaking, it was assumed that the learner acquired associations between stimuli and responses and that general laws of learning were applicable to all, or nearly all, situations. Given this perspective, the instructional procedures and educational policies of the time did not appear unreasonable to educators and researchers of the day.

During the so-called cognitive revolution that occurred during the 1970s, conceptions of learning and teaching began to change. Most current theories of learning assume that learning arises out of the internal conditions or states of the learner (from the inside out rather than from the outside in), and that these internal factors are more important than external environmental factors. The learner does not merely record or remember the material to be learned. Rather, he or she constructs a unique mental representation of the material to be learned and the task to be performed, selects information perceived to be relevant, and interprets that information on the basis of his or her existing knowledge and current needs. In the process, the learner adds information not explicitly provided by the teacher whenever such information is needed to make sense of the material being studied (e.g., Shuell, 1986a, 1988, 1992). This process is an

TABLE 22–3. Some Assumptions About Teaching and Learning from Three Different
Theoretical Perspectives

| | Behaviorist-Derived | Constructivist-Derived | |
| --- | --- | --- | --- |
| | | Cognitive | Social |
| Learning | Acquisition of facts, skills, and concepts | Active construction and the restructuring of prior knowledge | Collaborative construction of socially defined knowledge and values |
| | Occurs through drill and practice | Occurs through multiple opportunities and diverse processes to connect new knowledge to what is already known | Occurs through socially constructed opportunities |
| | Occurs within the individual's head | Occurs through interaction with others and the environment | Occurs through interaction with others and the environment |
| | Involves surface processing and procedural display | Involves deep processing | Involves multiple processing of content, procedures (how to learn), and interpretations (what it means to learn, which knowledge is of value) |
| Teaching | Transmission presentation (telling) | Challenge, guide thinking toward more complete understanding | Coconstruct knowledge (with students) |
| | | | Expand repertoire of options (of how to go about learning) |
| Role of teacher | Predefined as an adult | Self or anyone with greater expertise | Self or anyone with greater expertise |
| | Primary source of knowledge | A source of knowledge (along with student, materials, and the environment) | A source of knowledge (along with others, materials, social artifacts, and the environment) |
| | Manager or supervisor | Facilitator or guide | Facilitator or guide |
| | | | Coparticipant |
| | Encourage on-time task completion | Create opportunities for interacting with meaningful ideas, materials, others | Construct with students opportunities for interacting with meaningful ideas, materials, others |
| | Correct wrong answers | Listen for ideas, misconceptions | Coconstruct different interpretations of knowledge; listen to socially constructed conceptions |
| Role of peers | Not usually considered | Not necessary, but can stimulate thinking, raise questions | Ordinary part of process of knowledge construction |
| | | | Contribute to definition of knowledge (in intersubjective space of groups) |
| | | | Help define opportunities for learning |
| Role of student | Passive reception of information | Active construction (within mind) | Active coconstruction with others and self |
| | | Source of knowledge (individual and group) | Source of knowledge (group and individual within group) |
| | Worker | Generator, constructor | Cogenerator, coconstructor |
| | Active listener, direction-follower | Active thinker, explainer, interpreter, questioner | Active thinker, explainer, interpreter, questioner |
| | Complete work on time | Understand, question, explain | Understand, question, explain |
| | | | Coconstruct, interpret social context |

Note: Based on "Reconceptualizing Learning for Restructured Schools" by H. H. Marshall, 1992, in R. F. Elmore (Chair), "Restructuring Schools for Learning: Extending the Dialogue," a symposium conducted at a meeting of the American Educational Research Association, San Francisco. Adapted by permission.

active one in which the learner must carry out various cognitive operations on the new materials in order for it to be acquired in a meaningful manner.

Although the theme of constructivism is evident in virtually all current discussions of learning, there is considerable variation in the philosophical and theoretical underpinnings of the perspective taken by individual investigators (Derry, 1992; Marshall, 1992b). The constructive nature of meaningful learning implies that no two students have exactly the same perception of the instructional situation or end up with exactly the same

understanding of the material being learned. Thus, when all is said and done, the way in which the learner processes new material and the type of cognitive processing in which he or she engages is the single most important determiner of what is learned—more important than even the activities of the teacher. The teacher's role, however, is far from trivial, for teachers have the extremely important job of ensuring that students are engaged in meaningful and appropriate ways with the material to be learned. This conception of learning as an active, constructive process has important implications for teaching and the nature of teacher effects. Many of these implications will be discussed in subsequent sections of this chapter, although they are nicely summarized by Wood, Cobb, and Yackel (1992) as follows:

- Teachers should provide instructional activities that will give rise to problematic situations for children.
- Children's actions are rational to them, and teachers should attempt to view students' solutions from their perspective.
- Teachers should recognize that what seem like errors and confusions from an adult['s] point of view are children's expressions of their current understanding.
- Teachers should realize that substantive learning occurs in periods of conflict, confusion, [and] surprise, over long periods of time, and during social interactions in which negotiation of taken-as-shared-meaning is essential. (p. 182)

It should be noted, however, that much of the empirical work needed to support these suggestions and understand the nature of the psychological relationships through which they operate remains to be accomplished.

All learning is cumulative in that new learning always builds on and is influenced by the learner's prior knowledge. Prior knowledge is a major determiner of what and how much a student learns, and this effect can be either facilitating or inhibiting. One example of this powerful influence is evident in the large body of empirical evidence on the way prior conceptions (many of which are misconceptions, according to the content knowledge presented in school) affect learning and the difficulty students have in trying to overcome previous misconceptions (e.g., Champagne, Klopfer, & Gunstone, 1982; Perkins & Simmons, 1988). Research on instructional programs that address concerns for misconceptions and prior knowledge will be discussed in a later section of this chapter.

In addition, meaningful learning is most likely to be successful when the learner is aware (at least generally) of the learning goal toward which he or she is working and holds appropriate expectations for achieving the desired outcomes. Appropriate goals and expectations can be established in many ways, but according to prevailing views of learning from instruction, it is the student's goals and expectations, not the teacher's, that determine what the student will learn. Statements about goals or objectives by the teacher may be helpful but will not guarantee that the desired learning will occur. Unless the learner understands and adopts the instructional goals as his or her own, they will have little, if any, impact on the student's learning.

**_Teaching and Learning as a Social Process of Communication._** The typical classroom consists of 20 to 30 individuals working together in a relatively small room for long periods of time. In such an environment, it is inevitable that the individuals involved (both students and teacher) and what they learn are influenced by a variety of social, emotional, interpersonal, and cultural factors, in addition to the cognitive factors typically associated with classroom learning. Together, the teacher and students create a social, cultural environment that includes the establishment of social norms, permissible roles, a range of interpersonal relationships, and personal feelings of self-efficacy. In this context of social interaction, opportunities for

learning are created and new knowledge is constructed (e.g., E. Collins & Green, 1992).

> From their first encounters, the human participants in this [classroom] environment (e.g., students *and* teacher) join together to construct and conduct the events and activities and the routines and rituals that define their daily lives. As individuals interact, they observe, monitor, and interpret the behaviors and actions of others. . . .
>
> The structure and meaning of an evolving academic discourse is embedded within an evolving social structure. Simply put, the social structure mediates who can talk to (or act toward) whom, when, where, in what ways, for what purposes, under what conditions, and with what tangible or imagined outcomes. (Weade, 1992, pp. 94–95, emphasis in the original)

A growing number of educational researchers are looking at classroom events and the teaching–learning process from a sociolinguistic, cultural, and ethnographic perspective, with many suggesting that learning is first and foremost a social process of communication. Variations, of course, are evident in the approaches taken by different investigators. For example, some of those concerned with the social nature of teaching and learning emphasize sociopsychological issues (see Goodenow, 1992), others emphasize sociolinguistic and sociocultural issues (E. Collins & Green, 1992; Weinstein, 1991), and Levine, Resnick, and Higgins (1993) have recently suggested that a new field concerned with sociocognition is beginning to emerge. These new conceptions of teaching and learning have important implications for research on teaching and teacher effects.

Studies on the social nature of teaching and learning have added greatly to our understanding of the richness and complexity of the teaching–learning process. Most existing studies, however, have focused on descriptions of the teaching–learning environments to which students are exposed rather than on the ways in which students learn in these environments or the specific ways in which teachers' actions and behaviors influence student learning (so, for example, they might know how to change the way they teach a specific lesson). Some investigators would argue that such concerns are of little interest, if not misguided, since teaching does not "cause" learning (e.g., see Fenstermacher, 1986; Weade, 1992); rather, teachers and students join together in an active collaboration in which "they co-construct and co-investigate the questions, dilemmas, issues, and concerns that mark the substantive, topical character of these interactions" (Weade, 1992, p. 93). Although this argument is a compelling one, it does not negate the concern for teacher effects, and the issues associated with "teaching as intervention," discussed earlier in this chapter, must be considered at some point.

Three secondary analyses of Judith Green's (1977) dissertation data (Golden, 1988; Green, Weade, & Graham, 1988; Harker, 1988) provided an illustration of sociolinguistic research consistent with more traditional conceptions of teacher effects. Nevertheless, these analyses are more reminiscent of the process–product paradigm than the mediation paradigm. The original data set was drawn from a study of 11 teachers teaching the same reading comprehension lesson to a group of six students in the teacher's own primary classroom. The teachers were told that the children would be asked to recall the story after the lesson, but they were free to teach the lesson in any way they wished. Since the teachers were involved in an 18-month, in-service program, they were at least exposed to the same discussions of teaching comprehension.

Following the lesson during which the story was read and discussed, each child met individually with the investigator and was asked to retell the story, pretending that he or she was telling the story to other children in the classroom who had not heard the story. Transcriptions of the retellings were scored for the number of story episodes and the number of episode elements recalled by the students. Each teacher's lesson was videotaped, and the three secondary analyses discussed here were conducted on transcripts of the lesson taught by two teachers, one whose students performed very well on the retelling task (Teacher G), and one whose students performed poorly on the task (Teacher S).

Although all three analyses are sociolinguistic in nature, each represents a different methodological perspective. The results of the first analysis (Green et al., 1988) indicate that (a) the two lessons were constructed differently, with Teacher G's lesson consisting of two phases and Teacher S's lesson consisting of four phases; (b) Teacher G talked less, had fewer divergences, but covered more content in her conversations than Teacher S; (c) different patterns of turn allocation were used (Teacher G asked more questions that were open for any student to answer; Teacher S asked more questions targeted to specific students); and (d) different types of questions were asked by the two teachers.

The propositional analysis used by Harker (1988) revealed that (a) the lesson taught by Teacher G contained twice as much story-related discussion as the one taught by Teacher S; (b) although Teacher G's lesson was shorter, it was more tightly woven around the story content; and (c) different themes are apparent in the questions asked by the two teachers. Golden (1988) used a more literary-based analysis that compared similarities among the structure of the story being studied, the lesson taught by each teacher, and the structure of the story recalled by the students. This analysis shows that (a) Teacher G made more references to information in specific episodes in the story; (b) Teacher G made more references across episodes; and (c) Teacher G's students recalled more episodes and more episode elements than was the case with Teacher S.

These three analyses complement one another and demonstrate some of the ways in which sociolinguistic research adds to our understanding of the social interactions that compose the teaching–learning process. Hopefully, future research will combine this perspective with some of the psychological concerns for teaching, learning, and teacher effects discussed in this chapter.

The emphasis on dialogue (or instructional conversations) by many educational researchers, rather than the more traditional emphasis on teacher monologues, represents another aspect of concern for the social nature of teaching and learning. The instructional role of dialogue is well portrayed in the following statement that Palincsar and A. L. Brown (1989) attribute to Jerome Bruner:

One of the most crucial ways in which culture provides aid in intellectual development is through a dialogue between the more experienced and the less experienced.

The importance of dialogue in the instructional process also is

consistent with Vygotsky's (1962, 1978) theory of the role played by inner and external speech and social exchanges in a child's acquisition of new knowledge, and sociolinguists have long used discourse analysis in their explorations of the classroom as a social system and the way in which teaching and learning are accomplished through face-to-face interactions among those involved (Palincsar & Brown, 1989; Weade, 1992).

*Situated Cognition and "Authentic Learning."* Traditional research on learning sought to identify general laws of learning applicable to all, or nearly all, situations. The assumption was made that these laws would hold across various situations and subject matter areas. Although different types of learning might exist, each occurring according to its own set of conditions or principles, a concept (or verbal association) in any domain (e.g., chemistry, mathematics, social studies, art) would be learned in the same manner (e.g., Gagné, 1965).

The school curriculum often was established on similar assumptions. It was common to distinguish between general (or academic) education and vocational training, but for the most part, schools taught general knowledge that presumably would transfer to the large variety of situations that students encountered outside of school, especially when they became adults. Discussion, even debate, was heard about the best way to prepare students for these future situations, but in general, the unique environment of the school was highly valued, sometimes (in the long tradition of classical education) for its own sake. In general, research on teaching and school learning was separated from the range of situations outside of school in which students would be using the knowledge and skills they acquired in school.

This traditional view of schooling, learning, and reasoning began to be challenged in a serious way by educational and cognitive science researchers during the 1980s. Influenced by the work of anthropologists like Lave (e.g., 1988; Lave & Wenger, 1991), sociolinguists like those discussed in the preceding section, and educational psychologists like Resnick (1987) and Glaser (1984), the view that knowledge, learning, and cognition are situated within a particular context began to gain ascendancy. As J. S. Brown, Collins, and Duguid (1989) note:

The activity in which knowledge is developed and deployed . . . is not separable from or ancillary to learning and cognition. Nor is it neutral. Rather, it is an integral part of what is learned. (p. 32)

The socially shared cognitive activities in which students engage and the context in which those activities occur (and which enables and supports those activities as they evolve) determine what students learn and the extent to which these outcomes are likely to prove useful in real-life situations outside the classroom. According to this perspective, students do not learn generalizable knowledge that is free of the context within which it is acquired, and the activities through which it is acquired. Rather, what they learn depends heavily on the cues and cognitive support inherent in that context and in those activities (see chapter 2 this volume).

A number of prominent researchers (e.g., J. S. Brown et al., 1989; Lave, 1988; Resnick, 1987) have argued that the type of learning that occurs in the typical classroom is very different from the type of learning and expectations for performance that

TABLE 22–4. Similarities and Differences Among the Learning Activities of Just Plain Folks (JPFs), Expert Practitioners, and Students

| Activity | JPFs | Students | Expert Practitioners |
|---|---|---|---|
| Reasoning with: | Causal stories | Laws | Causal models |
| Acting on: | Situations | Symbols | Conceptual situations |
| Resolving: | Emergent problems | Well-defined problems | Ill-defined problems and dilemmas |
| Producing: | Negotiable meaning and socially constructed understanding | Fixed meaning and immutable concepts | Negotiable meaning and socially constructed understanding |
| Goals: | Sense making | Good grades | Sense making |

Note: Based on "Situated Cognition and the Culture of Learning" by J. S. Brown, A. Collins, and P. Duguid, 1989, *Educational Researcher*, 18(1), 32–42; "Situated Cognition and the Culture of Learning" by J. S. Brown, 1989, presented at a meeting of the American Educational Research Association, San Francisco; and "Toward a New Epistemology for Learning" by J. S. Brown, 1990, in C. Frasson and G. Gauthier (Eds.), *Intelligent Tutoring Systems: At the Crossroads of Artificial Intelligence and Education* (pp. 266–282), Norwood, NJ: Ablex. Adapted by permission.

occur outside of schools. Consequently, classroom instruction should consist of authentic activities that reflect the type of cognitive activities that occur in real life, rather than the abstract, declarative knowledge, and artificial type of instructional activities found in most classrooms. For example, based on Lave's (1988) ethnographic studies of learning and everyday activities, J. S. Brown (1990; J. S. Brown et al., 1989) suggests that there are more similarities between the way in which expert practitioners and everyday people ("just plain folks," or JPFs) go about learning something than there is between either of these groups and the way students go about learning. For example, ordinary persons (JPFs) and expert practitioners

[b]oth have their activities situated in the cultures in which they work, within which they negotiate meanings and construct understanding. The issues and problems that they face arise out of, are defined by, and are resolved within the constraints of the activity they are pursuing. (J. S. Brown et al., 1989, p. 35)

Some of the similarities and differences that characterize the three groups are presented in Table 22–4.

Even if this portrayal of learning activities is accurate, however, the significance of the differences is not clear. For instance, do they reflect legitimate differences (e.g., that schools should be engendering a more analytical type of thinking), or do they imply that school learning would be more effective (and perhaps reach more children) if it more closely resembled learning in real-life situations? Other issues, such as the following, also need to be addressed more fully: (a) What is the nature of knowledge and of learning if knowledge resides in a particular situation or interpersonal interaction? Does not some residue have to remain in the mind of each individual? (b) If all knowledge is situated, how is it ever possible for an individual to use it in a different situation? (c) What is the relationship between mediated learning (in which students acquire knowledge already discovered by other individuals) and situated learning?

Although many questions remain to be answered, the notions of situated learning, authentic activities, and shared cognitions have a number of implications for instruction. A. Collins (1991), for example, suggests that

[t]he benefits of situated learning include: (a) students learn conditions for applying knowledge . . . ; (b) situations foster invention . . . ; (c) students see the implications of the knowledge . . . ; and (d) context structures knowledge appropriate to its uses. (pp. 122–123)

Most educational researchers who support the theory of situated cognition and authentic learning activities consider cognitive apprenticeships (discussed in a subsequent section of this chapter) to be most consistent with the notion of situated learning (e.g., J. S. Brown et al., 1989; Cognition and Technology Group at Vanderbilt, 1990; Glaser, 1991). In addition, the closely related notion of distributed or shared cognitive activities can be seen in the learning activities of many instructional groups and one-on-one situations, such as when a father helps his daughter learn to read by saying words with which she is unfamiliar (see, e.g., Resnick & Johnson, 1988). Nevertheless, considerably more needs to be learned about the effects of these types of instructional interventions on the psychological processes responsible for learning in students.

*Changing Conceptions of Competence.* During the late 1970s, traditional conceptions of competence and how it is acquired began to change. Prior to that time, competence tended to be viewed in one or both of two ways: (a) in terms of intelligence (one either has it or one doesn't, and it is difficult, if not impossible, to acquire it if you don't), and (b) in terms of factual knowledge (not only is it relatively easy to measure factual knowledge on a multiple-choice test, but we tend to value it for its own sake, as evidenced, for example, by the continuing popularity of game shows such as "Jeopardy"). Although lip service frequently was given to the attainment of higher order thinking and creativity, the instructional methods, assessment instruments, and grading practices that were employed (as well as the research focus that was adopted) often belied these factors.

During the late 1970s and 1980s, increasing attention was focused on the acquisition of higher order thinking skills, learning strategies, and problem-solving ability. Theories of individual differences in ability began to be influenced by research on expert–novice differences, by changing conceptions of intelligence, and by more egalitarian views on competence and ability (e.g., Chi, Glaser, & Farr, 1988; Resnick, 1976a; Shuell, 1986b). This research, heavily influenced by cognitive psychology, led many investigators to conclude that competence is something that is acquired rather than something with which an individual is endowed.

This changing perspective on the nature of competence has a number of important implications for research on teacher effects, and its relationship to several, rather different approaches to instructional research can be readily identified. For example, two general findings of research on expert–novice differences are that the knowledge possessed by experts is qualitatively different from the knowledge possessed by novices (i.e., experts don't merely know more, their knowledge is organized in different ways), and expertise is largely limited to a particular domain. These findings are clearly reflected in both the rather structured approach involved in cognitive task analysis and the more ill-defined goals involved in the cognitive apprenticeship models to be discussed in a subsequent section of this chapter.

Although considerable effort has been spent in analyzing the differences in competence between experts and novices, little attention has been paid to the manner in which expertise is acquired—that is, how the novice acquires the competence of the expert. The notion that competence and ability can be learned has important implications for teaching and learning, but until we understand better the specific learning processes that are involved in the acquisition of the type of complex performance and understanding characteristic of competence as we normally think of it, and the instructional procedures appropriate for helping students to acquire such competence, our understanding of teacher effects in these situations will be limited.

## WHAT MAKES INQUIRY PSYCHOLOGICAL?

The history of research on teaching and teacher effects is a lengthy one, and a large body of literature has accumulated on the ways in which teaching is or should be conducted. Many different perspectives are represented in this literature, including philosophical, sociological, linguistic, cultural, practical, narrative, and, of course, psychological. Each perspective provides a unique and complementary understanding of teaching and the manner in which teachers affect students. Nevertheless, for a handbook on educational psychology, it is appropriate to ask what makes psychological research on teaching different from other approaches concerned with the same fundamental issues. What evidence, insights, and understandings are provided by psychological inquiry, analysis, and theory that cannot be culled from thoughtful inquiry in other disciplines?

The various disciplines, of course, are not enclaves with rigid, exclusionary boundaries, although they sometimes are treated that way. Fields of inquiry often involve overlapping disciplines, as in the case of social psychology and psycholinguistics. In addition, different aspects of the same problem can be and often are investigated by different disciplines, although unfortunately, there often is little awareness and little respect for disciplined inquiry outside of one's own field. The world views, methodologies, and theories that characterize a particular discipline often change over the years, and even at a given

time, considerable variability can often be found in the theoretical and methodological paradigms used in a discipline. Nevertheless, a field of inquiry presumably contains certain common elements, if it is indeed a discipline.

Psychology is generally considered to be the science or the study of behavior and the factors that influence behavior. Beyond that level of generality, however, disagreement can be found with regard to what constitutes behavior and the types of processes (e.g., mental, emotional, psychodynamic, motivational) considered appropriate for psychological inquiry. Must all "behavior," for example, be external and observable? Or can implicit and internal activities such as thinking be considered a form of behavior worthy of psychological investigation? If the latter definition is appropriate, how can these internal processes be measured or observed in a scientific manner?

During the first half of the 20th century, the mainstream of psychological thinking considered external, observable behavior to be the primary, if not the only, legitimate object of psychological inquiry. With the advent of the cognitive revolution in the 1960s and 1970s, mental processes became the main topic of psychological inquiry, as the psychological mainstream shifted from a behavioral to a cognitive orientation. With only a few exceptions, however, affective, emotional, and motivational factors were not among those addressed by cognitive psychologists. For a variety of reasons, the holistic nature of human behavior continued to be ignored by most investigators, even though a synthesis of cognitive and noncognitive factors is needed for an adequate and comprehensive understanding of how humans function in real-world environments such as classrooms.

For research and inquiry (on either a scholarly or professional level) to be "psychological," it must in some manner be concerned with or focus on the behavior, thoughts, or feelings of individuals. These activities, however, occur neither in isolation nor wholly on the basis of current factors. Contextual and social factors contribute heavily to the psychological functioning of the individual, and what an individual does is strongly influenced by his or her prior experiences, goals, and expectations about the likely outcome of the actions performed. As Altman (1988) puts it:

I begin with the assumption that all psychological phenomena consist of *psychological processes* (perception, cognition, performance and other behaviours) that are performed by holistic *social units* (individuals, groups, organizations) in *physical and social settings* (homes, offices, laboratories, organizations). (p. 263, emphasis in original)

During the past several decades, much educational and psychological research has shifted away from a relatively narrow focus on individuals functioning on their own toward greater concern for the social and cultural context in which the behavior occurs. Consequently, there has been less emphasis on precisely controlled laboratory experiments and more emphasis on naturalistic settings such as a regularly functioning classroom. Although in many cases this research has been very informative with regard to issues that concern educational psychologists (such as teacher effectiveness, the nature of learning in classroom settings, cognitive development, etc.), in the strictest sense, it has not always been *psychological* research, at least in those cases when it has not focused on the psychological functioning of the individuals involved.

Each of the disciplined approaches contributes something important to an adequate understanding of a phenomenon as complex as classroom teaching and learning, although the boundaries among various approaches are often blurred. Part of the differences among the various approaches involves a difference in the level of analysis. Sociological research, for example, tends to focus on differences among various social groups (e.g., teachers and certain groups of students, such as white males, have more say than other groups in determining what occurs in the classroom and which values are enforced; teachers interact differently with students from different social, ethnic, and gender groups). In the strictest sense, sociological research does not consider in any detail how these factors affect the way the individuals involved react to the social factors being considered or how these factors affect the behavior of these individuals. Psychological (or social psychological) research concerned with these same issues would be interested in the way these sociocultural factors are interpreted by students, how these interpretations affect their self-efficacy and motivation, and the way in which these social factors influence how students process the content and social information with which they are presented.

A comparison of psychological and nonpsychological research more germane to the concerns of this chapter is afforded by considering the parallel research on teaching functions (Rosenshine & Stevens, 1986) and learning functions (Shuell, 1988, 1992). Rosenshine's (1983; Rosenshine & Stevens, 1986) consolidation of findings from studies on teacher effects was a major step toward establishing an empirical knowledge base for teaching. The six teaching functions identified by Rosenshine focus on what effective teachers do in the classroom, and although teaching effectiveness is defined in terms of student achievement, little attention is paid to the way students process the instructional behavior of the teacher.

Building on Rosenshine's conception of functions, Shuell (1988, 1992) identified 12 learning functions, or psychological processes, that must be engaged in students if they are to learn from the instruction provided. Various ways in which these processes can be elicited by the teacher or the learner are also discussed. Perhaps the biggest difference between the functions proposed by Rosenshine and those proposed by Shuell is that Rosenshine's teaching functions focus primarily on what teachers do, whereas Shuell's learning functions focus primarily on what students do. Consequently, learning functions provide a basis for a psychological explanation of why various instructional behaviors affect student learning and achievement. Given the importance and complementary nature of the two approaches to the concerns of this chapter, each will be discussed at greater length.

## Teaching Functions

Rosenshine and Stevens (1986) summarized the findings from a large number of studies on effective teaching in terms of the six teaching functions listed in Table 22–5. The validity of these findings is strengthened by the field-based nature of the studies and the possibility for causative interpretations due to the experimental nature of the training studies. Thus, the procedures presented in Table 22–5 provide useful guidelines for effective teaching, especially in well-structured content areas

for which they are most appropriate. Nevertheless, the general principles which they represent are applicable in most teaching situations and for most students, although the manner in which the principles are implemented will vary considerably in these other instructional settings. The importance of these teaching functions for our understanding of the teaching–learning process will be discussed in a subsequent section of this chapter. In the present section, they are discussed in the context of understanding the nature of psychological inquiry.

For the most part, the various studies summarized by the six teaching functions were designed to identify successful teaching practices by examining the relationship between specific instructional procedures and the academic achievement of the students experiencing those practices. Used for this purpose, the teaching functions are very useful in helping us determine those characteristics of effective instruction that are related to successful student learning. Unfortunately, they provide few insights into the psychological processes that are responsible for some instructional procedures being more effective than others.

Nevertheless, three of Rosenshine and Stevens' (1986) teaching functions—guided practice, independent practice, and feedback—are clearly related to established principles of learning. These teaching functions are also reflected in Shuell's (1988, 1992) learning functions based on research concerned with psychological principles of learning rather than on research on teaching. Further, as Rosenshine and Stevens (1986) point out in a section of their chapter titled "Information Processing and Instruction," "there is good correspondence between the results of [recent research on human information processing] and the research on effective teaching" (p. 378). However, the discussion of the psychological research which supports the various teaching functions and informs their use, and the psychological analysis of how the behavior of the teacher affects student learning are conducted at a relatively general level, as illustrated in the following example:

> When teachers present new information, they should be concerned with not presenting too much information at one time. Current information-processing theories suggest that . . . there are limits to the amount of information learners can attend to and process effectively. (p. 378)

## Learning Functions

Learning functions differ from teaching functions in that learning functions focus on various psychological principles of learning involved in learning from instruction (Shuell, 1988, 1992). They are based on a large body of psychological theory and research on learning, in much the same way as Rosenshine and Stevens' (1986) teaching functions are based on a large body of empirical data on teacher effects. In contrast to teaching functions, however, learning functions involve a psychological analysis of factors involved in effective teaching. They also are based on psychological theory and research on learning independent of teaching, a fact that has both strengths and weaknesses. Learning functions provide a useful way of relating instructional practices to learning theory, and they are based on the premise that various psychological processes (attention,

TABLE 22–5. Six Teaching Functions

1. Daily review and checking homework
   a. Checking homework (routines for students to check each other's papers).
   b. Reteaching when necessary.
   c. Reviewing relevant past learning (may include questioning).
   d. Review prerequisite skills (if applicable).
2. Presentation
   a. Provide short statement of objectives.
   b. Provide overview and structuring.
   c. Proceed in small steps but at a rapid rate.
   d. Intersperse questions within demonstration to check for understanding.
   e. Highlight main points.
   f. Provide sufficient illustrations and concrete examples.
   g. Provide demonstrations and models.
   h. When necessary, give detailed and redundant instructions and examples.
3. Guided practice
   a. Initial student practice takes place with teacher guidance.
   b. High frequency of questions and overt student practice (from teacher and/or materials).
   c. Questions are directly relevant to the new content or skill.
   d. Teacher checks for understanding (CFU) by evaluating student responses.
   e. During CFU, teacher gives additional explanation, process feedback, or repeats explanation, where necessary.
   f. ALL students have a chance to respond and receive feedback; teacher insures that all students participate.
   g. Prompts are provided during guided practice (where appropriate).
   h. Initial student practice is sufficient so that students can work independently.
   i. Guided practice continues until students are firm.
   j. Guided practice is continued (usually) until success rate of 80% is achieved.
4. Correctives and feedback
   a. Quick, firm, and correct responses can be followed by another question or a short acknowledgment of correctness (i.e., "That's right").
   b. Hesitant correct answers might be followed by process feedback (i.e., "Yes, Linda, that's right because . . .").
   c. Student errors indicate a need for more practice.
   d. Monitor students for systematic errors.
   e. Try to obtain a substantive response to each question.
   f. Corrections can include sustaining feedback (i.e., simplifying the question, giving clues), explaining or reviewing steps, giving process feedback, or reteaching the last steps.
   g. Try to elicit an improved response when the first one is incorrect.
   h. Guided practice and corrections continue until the teacher feels that the group can meet the objectives of the lesson.
   i. Praise should be used in moderation, and specific praise is more effective than general praise.
5. Independent practice (seatwork/homework, etc.)
   a. Sufficient practice.
   b. Practice is directly relevant to skills/content taught.
   c. Practice to overlearning.
   d. Practice until responses are firm, quick, and automatic.
   e. Ninety-five percent correct rate during independent practice.
   f. Students alerted that seatwork will be checked.
   g. Students held accountable for seatwork.
   h. Actively supervise students, when possible.
6. Weekly and monthly reviews
   a. Systematic review of previously learned material.
   b. Include review in homework.
   c. Frequent tests.
   d. Reteaching of material missed in tests.

Note: From "Teaching Functions" by B. Rosenshine and R. Stevens, 1986, in M. C. Wittrock (Ed.), *Handbook of Research on Teaching* (3rd ed., p. 379), New York: Macmillan. Reprinted by permission.

motivation, comparison of similarities and differences, etc.) must occur in the pupil if he or she is to learn anything of consequence from the instruction being provided.

These learning functions, as conceptualized by Shuell (1988, 1992), possess two characteristics that make them powerful tools for thinking about teaching and for planning appropriate learning experiences. First, each function can be performed in a number of equally valid and effective ways. Thus, in contrast to some of the other recommendations for effective teaching methods, this approach suggests that there is not a single best way to teach effectively, a comment that is heard frequently in discussions of how research-on-teaching data can be applied to the improvement of classroom instruction. Rather, the professional judgment of the teacher plays a critical role in the application of psychological theory and research to the solution of instructional problems.

According to Shuell (1988, 1992), the learner must perform each function for meaningful learning from instruction to occur in an optimal manner. However, it is possible (even desirable) to elicit each function in a variety of equally appropriate and effective ways, depending on the nature of the particular instructional situation involved (the content being learning, the types of students in the class, etc.). For instance, attention might be elicited by (a) highlighting in some way (by using a boldface or italic font, putting a border or circle around part of a picture or diagram, etc.) that part of the material to which the learner should pay attention, (b) using a matrix to reveal the organizational structure of the material being learned, or (c) verbally stating that the next point is important or will be on the next test, as well as a variety of other techniques. The important thing is not *how* the function (attention) was performed, but *whether* the learner paid attention to relevant aspects of the material being acquired.

The second important characteristic of learning functions is that they can be initiated by either the teacher (or other instructional agent, such as a textbook, computer, etc.) or the learner. This characteristic acknowledges the joint and interactive nature of the teaching–learning process. The teacher (or author, etc.) should ensure that the learner performs the various functions in an appropriate manner.

The effective teacher, however, also realizes that in the real world people frequently find themselves in situations in which they must learn or perform a task with less than optimal instructional support (e.g., trying to understand the main ideas in a book or movie, putting together an item purchased with "some assembly required"). In these cases, as in classrooms that provide less than adequate instructional support, the functions must be initiated by the learner if the desired outcome is to be achieved. It is easy for those interested in the teacher side of the coin to lose sight of the fact that students can become overly dependent on the teacher providing adequate instructional support and fail to learn how to initiate the functions on their own when it is necessary or helpful to do so. Even in situations that provide good instruction, students will benefit by initiating various functions on their own as needed to help them understand the material being considered.

The 12 learning functions identified in Table 22–6 are neither exhaustive nor mutually exclusive. They represent the various psychological processes that current psychological theory and research indicate need to be elicited in students if the teaching–learning process is to be successful, especially when meaningful learning is involved. Examples of how each function might be elicited by the teacher or the students are also presented in Table 22–6.

A. L. Brown, Palincsar, and Armbruster (1984) identify six reading comprehension skills mentioned frequently in that literature as relevant to the teaching of comprehension skills. The similarity of these skills, listed below, to the learning functions discussed above is obvious:

1. understanding the purpose of the reading, both explicit and implicit
2. activating relevant background knowledge
3. allocating attention so that concentration can be focused on the major content at the expense of trivia

4. evaluating content critically for internal consistency, and compatibility with prior knowledge and common sense
5. monitoring ongoing activities to see if comprehension is occurring, by engaging in such activities as periodic review and self-interrogation
6. drawing and testing inferences of many kinds, including interpretations, predictions, and conclusions (Brown et al., 1984, p. 263)

# CURRENT MODELS OF TEACHING AND LEARNING

Current models of teaching and teacher effects tend to share certain concerns about the nature of classroom teaching and learning. For the most part, these models assume that (a) learning is a social process, (b) competence involves expertise rather than native ability, (c) learning, at least meaningful learning, is constructive and self-regulating rather than reproductive, and (d) classroom activities should reflect real-world learning rather than traditional academic tasks. To a large extent, the models of teaching currently receiving the most attention are based on psychological and other theories developed outside the classroom context. Although a growing number of studies are investigating these models in classroom settings, with promising results, many unanswered questions remain about the applicability of these theories in normal classroom environments such as those described earlier (i.e., classrooms inhabited by average teachers and typical students).

The role of the teacher varies, depending on the particular model being discussed. In each case, however, the teacher's role is considered to be important, and the present discussion focuses on the nature of that role and the behaviors in which the teacher is expected to engage. Among the models of teaching and classroom learning discussed in this section are (a) several cognitive apprenticeship models (including reciprocal teaching), (b) teaching for conceptual change, (c) a series of studies by Nuthall and Alton-Lee that may serve as a prototype for the next generation of process–product research, and (d) the teaching of learning strategies, self-regulation, and metacognitive skills.

## Cognitive Apprenticeship

Apprenticeship is the way we learn most naturally. It characterized learning before there were schools, from learning one's language to learning how to run an empire. (A. Collins, Brown, & Newman, 1989, p. 491)

Learning is a natural process that often occurs with the assistance of another individual or an artifact created by another individual (e.g., a book [fiction or nonfiction], movie, instructional manual, video). There is a tendency to associate teaching with schools, but a great deal of our learning from instruction occurs outside of school from parents, friends, and other individuals with whom we come in contact. The way in which we learn outside of school, however, often is very different from the way students are expected to learn in school.

TABLE 22–6. Examples of Ways in Which Learning Functions Can Be Engaged by the Instructional Agent and by the Learner

| Function | Teacher Initiated | Learner Initiated |
|---|---|---|
| Expectations | Specify goal/purpose of lesson; provide overview of the material to be studied, etc. | Identify the purpose for doing an assigned project or homework, reading a chapter, etc. |
| Motivation | Provide opportunities for student interaction; use interesting material | Look for ways to make material, lesson, or project personally relevant |
| Prior knowledge activation | Remind students of prerequisite information, relevant information in previous lessons, etc. | Ask self what is already known about the topic and what information is needed to complete the assignment |
| Attention | Highlight important information and/or characteristics; use verbal emphasis | Identify key features of material being studied; underline key information; take notes |
| Encoding | Provide diagrams and/or multiple examples/contexts; suggest mnemonics, etc. | Generate mnemonics, images, and/or multiple examples in multiple contexts |
| Comparison | Encourage comparison through the use of questions, diagrams, or charts | Look for similarities; draw diagrams or charts that compare the material being studied |
| Hypothesis generation | Ask "What if?" questions; encourage students to think of alternative courses of action | Generate possible alternatives and corresponding solutions |
| Repetition | Guide practice and/or reflection; multiple perspectives and/or examples | Systematically review and reflect on the material being studied |
| Feedback | Provide instructionally relevant feedback and correctives | Seek answers and/or reactions to self-posed questions |
| Evaluation | Encourage students to evaluate their performance and point of view on the basis of the feedback received | Ask "What do I currently know about what I am studying?" "What do I need to know and/or find out?" |
| Monitoring | Check for understanding | Monitor performance; self-testing |
| Combination, integration, synthesis | Suggest ways of combining and integrating information (e.g., by constructing diagrams, graphs, etc.) | Establish categories; construct tables; seek higher order relationships |

Note: Based on "The Role of the Student in Learning from Instruction" by T. J. Shuell, 1988, Contemporary Educational Psychology, 13, 276–295; and "Designing Instructional Computing Systems for Meaningful Learning" by T. J. Shuell, 1992, in M. Jones and P. H. Winne (Eds.), Adaptive Learning Environments: Foundations and Frontiers (pp. 19–54), New York: Springer. Adapted by permission.

Resnick (1987), for example, suggests that mental activities required by the academic tasks typically used in schools differ in four ways from the type of thinking that occurs in more natural settings outside of schools:

• First, school learning is largely an individual effort, with each student being evaluated almost exclusively on his or her own performance; outside of school, learning is more likely to be a team effort, with contributions from each member of the group.

• Second, the focus in school learning is typically on activities that require "pure thought," and the use of tools such as books, notes, and calculators is usually minimized, especially during examinations; in learning that occurs outside of school, however, most mental activities involve the use of tools rather than pure thought.

• Third, school learning typically involves the manipulation of symbols, while learning outside of school usually involves contextualized reasoning.

• Finally, school learning stresses general, widely used skills and theoretical principles, while much of the reasoning that occurs outside of school involves situation-specific learning. In a similar manner, John Sealy Brown (1990; J. S. Brown et al., 1989) identifies various similarities and differences among the way in which "just plain folks," students, and experts go about the task of learning something.

It is reasonable to ask which method of learning is most likely to achieve our educational goals and prepare students to cope with real-life situations. A simple, straightforward answer to that question, however, is not readily available. One might argue, for example, that, as is the case with most of the models discussed in this section, school learning should be consistent with the kind of learning in which humans engage most naturally (i.e., the type of out-of-school learning described above). On the other hand, however, it can be argued that the unique characteristics of school learning (i.e., the acquisition of academic knowledge and skills) is what separates education from training. The two perspectives involve, at least to some extent, differences in the perceived nature of schooling ("education" in the classic sense versus "preparation for life"). Most investigators probably would agree that both perspectives need to be considered, but a detailed discussion of the relevant issues is beyond the scope of this chapter.

The educational value of apprenticeships has long been recognized in many nonschool situations. When an individual wishes to establish expertise in a particular field, for instance, he or she becomes an apprentice to an established expert in that field who helps that individual acquire the knowledge and skills characteristic of experts in that field. The person initially learns by observing and performing tasks that represent only a small part of the overall task. Through these and subsequent observations (modeling), coaching from the mentor, practice on increasingly more complex tasks, and progressive fading of instructional support, the apprentice gradually develops the competence of the mentor. These characteristics are evident in the various apprenticeship models that have been suggested for use in the schools.

Although there are a number of differences between traditional models of apprenticeship and cognitive apprenticeship models of teaching, the latter is proposed in the belief that knowledge and skills learned in school have become too abstracted from their use in the world outside of school (see A. Collins et al., 1989). In their consideration of apprenticeship-like approaches to teaching, Collins et al. (1989) discuss four characteristics of ideal learning environments: (a) content, (b) methods, (c) sequence, and (d) sociology. For purposes of this chapter, however, the discussion will focus on only the second and third of these characteristics.

Generally speaking, cognitive apprenticeship models of teaching involve the following six teaching methods, according to Collins et al.:

1. Students observe an expert (usually the teacher) *model* the desired performance in an environment similar to the ones in which the performance is to occur.
2. External support is provided in the form of *coaching* by a tutor or expert (hints, feedback, modeling, reminders, etc.).
3. Conceptual *scaffolding* is provided as the teacher and student work together on the task, with the explicit understanding that the student is to assume as much of the task as possible, as soon as possible, and the teacher is to gradually *fade* the external support as the student gains proficiency.
4. Students *articulate* their knowledge, understanding, and reasoning of the material being learned.
5. Students *reflect* on their understanding and reasoning in the domain being studied by, for instance, comparing their problem-solving processes with those of an expert, another student, and ultimately their own cognitive model of expertise in the subject matter area.
6. Students are required to *explore* new ways in which the knowledge or skill can be used.

The first three methods (modeling, coaching, and scaffolding), according to Collins et al., are designed to help students acquire an integrated set of cognitive and metacognitive skills through processes of observation and of guided and supported practice. The next two (articulation and reflection) are methods designed to help students both focus their observations of expert problem solving and gain conscious access to (and control of) their own problem-solving strategies. The final method (exploration) is aimed at encouraging learner autonomy, not only in carrying out expert problem-solving processes, but also in defining or formulating the problems to be solved. (p. 481)

With regard to the sequencing of instruction, A. Collins et al. (1989) suggest that learning experiences should be sequenced with regard to:

1. *increasing complexity*, so that more and more of the concepts and skills involved in expert performance are required by the instructional task
2. *increasing diversity* of the skills and strategies required to perform the instructional task, so that students can learn to tell the conditions under which the skills and strategies do and do not apply

3. focusing on the acquisition of *global before local skills*

Any instructional program consistent with the above principles constitutes a cognitive apprenticeship. Thus, there is not a single cognitive apprenticeship model of teaching, for a variety of instructional programs can be so classified. A. Collins et al. (1989), for example, identify three successful cognitive apprenticeship programs: Palincsar and Brown's reciprocal teaching of reading comprehension (discussed in the next section), Scardamalia and Bereiter's (Bereiter & Scardamalia, 1987; Scardamalia & Bereiter, 1985) procedural facilitation of writing, and Schoenfeld's (1985) method for teaching mathematical problem solving. Reciprocal teaching, the best known of these programs, will be discussed at greater length in the next section. In addition, Anderson and Roth (1989) consider the instructional procedures and materials they have developed for teaching conceptual change in science (discussed in a subsequent section) to be a form of cognitive apprenticeship.

## Reciprocal Teaching

Palincsar and A. L. Brown (1984, 1989; A. L. Brown & Palincsar, 1989) have developed a procedure for teaching reading comprehension known as reciprocal teaching. The procedure involves a structured dialogue in which the teacher and students take turns (hence the name) leading a discussion about a segment of text that each group member has just read silently. The procedure focuses on one of four factors commonly accepted as determiners of successful learning from text, namely, the strategies used by the student to enhance understanding and retention and circumvent comprehension failures (Palincsar & Brown, 1984). (The other three factors are decoding fluency, considerate text, and compatible content.) The discussion involves four types of strategic activities: predicting, questioning (making up a question on the main idea), summarizing (self-review), and clarifying.

Reciprocal teaching occurs in a cooperative learning group with the intention of providing an introduction to group discussion techniques, as well as an opportunity for guided practice in applying concrete strategies useful in comprehending text. Before the group reads or listens to a portion of text (usually a paragraph or so), the adult teacher assigns a "teacher" for that segment. The discussion typically begins with the group generating *predictions* about the content of the segment based on the title, the prior knowledge of group members concerning information suggested by the title, or their expectations, based on questions they have about the topic or experiences they have had with similar kinds of text. Next, the group reads the text segment, and the designated leader begins the discussion by asking *questions* on the content of the passage. The other members of the group respond to these questions and suggest additional questions, which the group also answers. The leader then *summarizes* the passage, and other members of the group are encouraged to comment or elaborate on this summary.

Throughout the instructional session, the adult teacher provides guidance and feedback (scaffolding) tailored to the needs of the current discussion leader in an attempt to improve the level of his or her performance. A. L. Brown and Palincsar (1989) indicate that in reciprocal teaching, the adult teacher plays a number of different roles:

First, she provides a model of expert behavior. . . . Second, the teacher has a *clear instructional goal.* . . . Third, the adult teacher closely monitors the learning leaders, giving them room to control the discussions when they can. But she is always ready to provide feedback and, if necessary, to take back the leader role when things go awry. The adult teacher provides *feedback that is tailored to the students' existing levels,* encouraging them to progress gradually toward full competence. . . . The idea is for the teacher to take control only when needed and to hand over the responsibility to the students whenever they are ready. (pp. 417–418, emphasis in the original)

Reciprocal teaching engages a number of psychological mechanisms in the learner. For example, when students ask questions about and summarize the passage they have just read, they must pay *attention* to the content in the passage and check to see how well they understand it (i.e., *monitor* their comprehension). Asking students to clarify forces them to engage in *critical evaluation* of what they have read and heard, and asking students to make predictions about future content induces them to draw and test inferences. All four strategic activities involve the *activation of prior knowledge*, and the fact that the instructional activities are embedded in a context of reading for the purpose of answering questions about the passage encourages the establishment of appropriate *expectations* (Palincsar & Brown, 1984). In addition, reciprocal teaching involves *modeling (observation)* of desired performance, and the use of conceptual scaffolding encourages *organization*. A. Collins et al. (1989) also suggest that having students serve as both producers and critics (producing summaries and questions of their own, as well as evaluating the summaries and questions of others) forces students to *articulate* their knowledge about the nature of good questions, predictions, and summaries, thereby making their knowledge more available for application.

As Rosenshine and Meister (1994) point out in their review of reciprocal teaching, the exact procedures that one should follow when using this model in the classroom have not been clearly specified. One advantage of this diversity, of course, is that the different approaches serve to increase the generality of the findings across instructional contexts, thereby providing a more comprehensive evaluation of the strengths and weakness of using reciprocal teaching in various situations. Such evaluations can also assist in refining our psychological understanding of this teaching model.

The major difference in how reciprocal teaching is implemented appears to be in the manner in which the students are taught to use the four strategies (predicting, questioning, summarizing, and clarifying). Nine of the 19 studies reviewed by Rosenshine and Meister followed the general procedures used in the initial studies on reciprocal teaching (Palincsar & Brown, 1984). In these studies, students were not provided with explicit instruction on the strategies prior to the dialogues; rather, the adult teacher provided prompts, models, cues, and feedback on the use of the strategies as the reciprocal teaching session evolved. Ten of the 19 studies, however, did provide explicit instruction on use of the cognitive strategies before the reciprocal teaching session began.

The initial investigation of reciprocal teaching by Palincsar and Brown (1984) involved carefully designed studies in which a variety of dependent variables were used, and a number of substantial differences in favor of the reciprocal teaching group

were found. In the meta-analysis of 19 studies on reciprocal teaching conducted by Rosenshine and Meister (1994), however, experimental–control group differences were evenly distributed between significant and nonsignificant results, although an overall median effect size of .57 was obtained. The effects of reciprocal teaching, however, were greater when the comprehension strategies were explicitly taught prior to the reciprocal teaching dialogues rather than in conjunction with them (median effect size = .60 and .34, respectively). The results were mostly nonsignificant when below-average students (e.g., those poor at decoding) were involved (median effect size = .48) and usually significant when all other students were involved (median effect size = .57). Differences between the use of experimenter-developed tests and standardized tests were large (median effect size = .87 and .32, respectively), with the results usually being statistically significant in the former case and nonsignificant in the latter.

Thus, reciprocal teaching appears to be a reasonably effective method of teaching reading comprehension, at least under certain conditions and for certain types of students. The psychological processes and the theory on which the approach is based have been discussed by Palincsar and Brown (1984) and by Rosenshine and Meister (1994). Nevertheless, reciprocal teaching does not represent a rigid or fixed model. As previously noted, it is one of several cognitive apprenticeship models. In addition, it seems likely that reciprocal teaching could incorporate strategies other than the four identified initially, and this possibility needs to be investigated. An adequate understanding of why reciprocal teaching seems to work best under certain conditions requires additional research on how and why various components of the instructional model affect the psychological processes of the learner.

## Conceptual Change Teaching

During the past 10 or 15 years, a large body of literature has evolved, primarily in science and mathematics education, on overcoming the misconceptions that many students have prior to the start of classroom instruction (e.g., Anderson & Roth, 1989; Anderson & Smith, 1987; Champagne et al., 1982; Resnick & Omanson, 1987). For example, in order to understand photosynthesis, many students must overcome the incomplete and often erroneous conceptions about food they have developed on the basis of their experience with food for people. They "must abandon their assumptions about the metabolic similarities between plants and humans and restructure their thinking about the nature of food. . . . [In this regard, they must] learn that [certain of their] beliefs about food do not generalize from humans to plants while [other beliefs must] be clarified, expanded, and given new prominence" (Anderson & Roth, 1989, p. 278).

As it turns out, the initial, usually intuitive conceptions that students have about the world are extremely resistant to change, even in the face of clear evidence to the contrary (Champagne et al., 1982; Driver & Easley, 1978; Nissani & Hoefler-Nissani, 1992). The process of conceptual change through which students must pass in order to have an adequate understanding of the issues and phenomena they are studying is extremely complex. Posner, Strike, Hewson, and Gertzog (1982) have suggested that four conditions must be fulfilled in order for accommodation or conceptual change to occur in students. These conditions, which follow, have received considerable attention, especially in science education, from individuals concerned with conceptual change teaching:

1. *The student must become dissatisfied with his or her existing conceptions.* Individuals are unlikely to make major changes in the way they conceptualize or think about something unless they believe that their prior conceptions are no longer functional and that less radical changes will not work.
2. *The new conception must be intelligible.* The student must acquire a minimal initial understanding of the new conceptual structure in order to explore the possibilities that exist within it. Posner et al. suggest that "writers often stress the importance of analogies and metaphors in lending initial meaning and intelligibility to new concepts" (p. 214).
3. *The new conception must appear initially plausible.* Any new conceptual system must appear capable of solving the problems generated by its predecessor for an individual to consider it as having sufficient plausibility to warrant an attempt to establish its validity.
4. *The student must see the new conception as a fruitful or useful one for purposes of understanding a variety of situations.* New possibilities for understanding and explaining things must be apparent to the student.

In a somewhat similar manner, Nissani and Hoefler-Nissani (1992) suggest that individuals go through several stages as their initial conceptions change into more appropriate ones. These stages include (a) initial discomfort, (b) ad hoc explanations, (c) adjustment of observations and measurements to fit one's expectations, (d) doubt, (e) vacillation, and finally (f) conceptual shift. It seems inevitable that students have prior conceptions (or stereotypes) in domains other than science, although little research has been done on the nature of students' prior conceptions in these other content areas.

The most extensive research on instructional methods suitable for conceptual change teaching has been conducted in science education. To a large extent, these methods share many similarities with those proposed in models of cognitive apprenticeship, most notably reciprocal teaching (Anderson & Roth, 1989). In any case, concern for conceptual change teaching (or teaching for understanding in general) involves more than merely concern for specific teaching methods. Although it is possible to identify instructional guidelines consistent with the approach, *specific* teaching methods cannot be articulated since the complexity and unpredictability of the instructional situation, along with a need to adapt instruction to the needs of individual students, means that considerable teacher judgment is involved in effective teaching for conceptual change. Discussions of various features designed to enhance conceptual change learning are available in two doctoral dissertations (Roth, 1985; D. Smith, 1989). Concern for how students are thinking and processing the information in the lesson is also involved (see Anderson & Smith, 1987).

Anderson and Roth (1989) suggest that the key to successful conceptual change teaching is getting students to use their evolving understanding of the phenomenon being studied (e.g., photosynthesis) "to describe, predict, and explain how plants get their food" (p. 280). Notice the emphasis on getting students

to actively use their existing knowledge and—through interactions with the teacher, the instructional materials, and other students—probe the adequacy of their understanding. As Anderson and Smith (1987) note:

For phenomena to be useful in promoting conceptual change, students must not only encounter them but must also become actively involved in trying to *explain* them. (p. 97, emphasis in the original)

In fact, a series of studies by Anderson and Roth (1989) suggest that the success of their instructional procedures is due primarily to students adopting what they call a "conceptual-change sense-making" strategy for learning; students exposed to traditional teaching strategies overwhelmingly used a variety of less effective learning strategies (e.g., avoiding learning by using strategies that enabled them to perform at least some of the instructional tasks without actually learning anything, learning lists of facts and definitions, and egocentric sense making).

According to Anderson and Roth (1989), both the successful instructional materials they developed and the practices of the most effective conceptual change teachers they have observed share two general characteristics:

First, there is a curricular commitment to teaching for understanding rather than to covering a wide range of content superficially . . . [that] enables teachers to focus students' attention on sense-making rather than on memorization of long lists of facts and terms.

Second, . . . there is a need for an array of teaching strategies that can be used flexibly in response to students' needs. However, these strategies share an important characteristic: They all engage students in conceptual change sense-making, involving them in actively struggling with ideas rather than simply witnessing the teacher's performance. (p. 288)

In the most successful science classroom, Anderson and Roth go on to note, three kinds of activities generally occur (presumably, similar activities would characterize successful conceptual change teaching in other content areas):

1. At the onset of instruction, the teacher establishes problems and asks questions that engage the students in thinking about the topics they will be studying, taking into account the students' naive conceptions. In addition, the teacher listens to what the students say. "This process activates prior student knowledge and helps make them aware of its limitations, serves an important diagnostic function for the teacher, and engages teacher and students in dialogue about commonly understood issues" (p. 293).
2. The use of modeling and coaching through scaffold tasks and dialogue. The procedures suggested here are similar to those used in models of cognitive apprenticeship and reciprocal teaching.
3. Independent student work and the use of ideas in other contexts are used to encourage the independent use of scientific knowledge and integration with other scientific knowledge.

A similar set of criteria for conceptual change teaching in elementary school science has been suggested by Neale, Smith, and Johnson (1990). The main finding of the Neale et al. study is that 8 out of 10 teachers were able to successfully implement a

2-week conceptual change science unit in their own classrooms during the year following their attendance at a 4-week summer institute.

## Toward the Next Generation of Process–Product Research

Process–product research, in one form or another, is likely to continue, despite the limitations of earlier research employing this paradigm. Two ways in which this research might evolve will be discussed in this section. The first involves research that would investigate the extent to which the earlier findings could be extended to a type of instructional content not considered in that research; the second involves a major new research methodology that would enable researchers to investigate entirely new aspects of the teaching–learning process.

Process–product research conducted during the 1970s and 1980s involved, for the most part, the teaching of various skills, such as those in mathematics, for which a large number of examples exist. However, a large amount of what is taught in schools, especially at the secondary level, involves knowledge about and understandings of issues, events, and conceptions that consist of declarative rather than procedural knowledge. Examples of declarative knowledge include the learning of the water cycle, the significance of the Declaration of Independence, the structure of the atom, and the meaning of Jack London's *The Call of the Wild*. Presently, we know little about teacher effects for this type of subject matter (Rosenshine, 1986). Research on teacher effects for academic content areas such as these may well constitute the next generation of process–product research.

Although current process–product findings probably are relevant to teaching in these situations, at least to some extent, the various factors would be implemented in very different ways. In order to see this relevance, however, it may be necessary to set aside certain preconceptions. For many individuals, for example, the term "guided practice" carries a connotation that is antithetical to current theories of teaching and learning. These individuals often feel that the term represents a particular theoretical orientation and that the term implies a single correct answer or one right way of doing things. In light of the historical context in which process–product research developed, such a connotation is understandable. It is not uncommon for the word *practice* to be used in reference to situations in which repetition occurs for the purpose of memorization or perfecting a given skill.

It is possible, however, to conceptualize the underlying psychological variables and the way in which they are applicable to meaningful learning in less restrictive ways. For example, practice also can be thought of in terms of multiple exposures (perhaps from different perspectives) to the material being learned, or in terms of the events that occur during the time an individual is exploring various exhibits in a museum or a computer microworld, and so forth. It is not unreasonable to suggest that the concept of practice and its psychological validity refer as much to an individual's continued engagement in the learning process as to the more limited definition of repeating the exact same act over and over. Repetition is only one of several ways in which a learner is exposed to the same content on several occasions during learning.

Conceptualized in this manner, guided practice represents the process of assisting the learner during multiple exposures to the content so that the experience is as productive and meaningful as possible. Such a conception is not inherently inconsistent with a constructivist theory of learning. Understanding does not occur with the first exposure to the content.

Nevertheless, the way in which guided practice should occur is quite different for teaching factual information and for teaching about the Federalist Papers (Rosenshine, 1986, 1989). In the latter situation, for example, guided practice might be accomplished by asking students to explain the relevance of the Federalist Papers for the present time, or the view of human nature and human rights embodied in the ideas of the authors. Feedback could be provided by the teacher or other students, with the student providing the original explanation being asked to respond to these comments. Such feedback or guidance would not lead to a single correct answer. Rather, the instructional goal might be multiple understandings of the relevant ideas, as reflected in the students' explanations of, questions about, and commentary on the Federalist Papers. The extent to which the original process–product findings can be generalized to other situations, and the validity of the above analysis, remain to be determined, but the possibility deserves further consideration.

The second way in which process–product research may evolve involves a series of studies conducted by Graham Nuthall and Adrienne Alton-Lee (1990, 1991) at the University of Canterbury in New Zealand. The research methodology employed in these studies may serve as a model for the next generation of research on classroom teaching and learning that focuses on the relationship between teacher behavior and student outcomes. This methodology makes it possible to identify the specific learning experiences and instructional activities responsible for a student's performance on a subsequent test, either one taken at the end of a unit or a follow-up test administered 12 months later. In other words, these studies permit a determination of when and how students acquire the information needed to answer a given item on the test or other type of assessment instrument.

During the various instructional units that were studied during the year, data on the learning/instructional experiences of selected target students were collected by using one observer for each target child; these assignments were rotated daily to avoid bias. Audio recordings also were obtained from microphones suspended around the classroom in two studies and from individual broadcast microphones worn by selected student in two other studies. In addition, the classroom activities were videotaped. Pre- and posttesting and interviewing were conducted to determine what students had learned during the lesson and were able to remember a year later. In addition, copies and records of the pupils' work and the visual and other instructional resources used in the class were collected.

The relationships between teaching and learning that can be studied in this rich collection of data is illustrated by the analysis of a test item for one pupil, Mia. The test item compares the crime rate in Christchurch, New Zealand, and New York City. On the pretest Mia indicated that she did not know the answer to the question, but on both the unit and the 1-year follow-up tests, she indicated that New York had the higher crime rate. During class, Mia was exposed to many examples of crime in New York City.

On Day 1, for example, Mia's hand was semiraised as she watched the teacher add "crime" to a list on the overhead projector that the teacher was creating from responses to the following probe question: "Without thinking hard, what does the word New York make you think of?" On Day 3, Mia rested her head on the desk while another pupil read a poem about violence. On Day 4, Mia silently read a story filled with violence about a Puerto Rican boy living in New York; while reading silently, she fiddled with her hair, glanced at the teacher, and talked to herself: "Ooh, ooh, yuk . . . unhygienic! . . ." Although Mia was never told that New York has a higher crime rate than Christchurch, by Day 5 she had apparently made up her mind on the matter, for on an activity sheet comparing New York and Christchurch with regard to 48 descriptors, she indicated that "violence by gangs" and "gang warfare" accurately described New York City but not Christchurch.

One important finding from these studies is that individual students learn different things from what an observer might conclude are the same classroom activities. Every instructional activity is experienced in an idiosyncratic manner by the various students. In one of the studies, for example, 84% of the items answered correctly on the end-of-unit test were correctly answered by only one or two of the four pupils tracked in the study, and only 4% of the items were answered correctly by all four students. Consequently, average test scores of the students in a class are likely to misrepresent the learning of individual students.

It also was found that the relationships between the students' behavior and what they learned differed for the three major types of context observed in the studies (teacher-directed activities, group tasks, and individual tasks), making it clear that the classroom should not be studied as a single context. Another finding was the discovery that students often have a rather clear understanding of their own learning and memory processes. In a number of instances, for example, students could remember specific class discussions, overhead transparencies, and printed worksheets associated with the learning of specific content, even 12 months after these events occurred. Some pupils even recalled specific confusions they had experienced during class; "It got a bit confused, you know, with subway and Broadway. . . . I think that one reason why I might be a bit confused is it came up [in the unit] all at once, the street signs, Broadway and subway, and I think it didn't sort of register which each were" (Nuthall & Alton-Lee, 1990, p. 564).

Through the use of both quantitative and qualitative data, these studies provide useful insights into the way individual students acquire knowledge about specific content during classroom instruction. Not only do they capture the dynamic nature of classroom learning, but they suggest why certain classroom activities are either effective or ineffective and why particular students remember some things about the lesson but not other things.

## The Teaching of Learning Strategies, Self-Regulation, and Metacognitive Skills

According to the active, constructive, self-regulated conception of learning discussed earlier in this chapter, students are not passive recipients of knowledge. Rather, in order to learn and understand the large variety of information, conceptualizations, and skills they are expected to acquire in school, they must engage in a largely self-regulated process that involves various learning strategies and metacognitive skills. The students' ability to perform these psychological activities is extremely important, for the extent to which appropriate learning strategies are implemented in a given situation determines the extent to which they will acquire the desired knowledge, understanding, or skill, both in the classroom and outside of school.

It seems likely, for example, that the job market of the future will require learning-to-learn skills as much as, perhaps even more than, specific knowledge per se. Although the individual will need to have a basic repertoire of knowledge and understanding about the field he or she is entering—say physics, or physiology, or teaching—it will be equally important for students to know how to learn physics, physiology, or knowledge relevant to teaching. The teaching of such learning strategies and metacognitive skills, however, is often considered to be appropriate only for remedial students. Students in regular classrooms are seldom provided with explicit instruction on how to learn and reason effectively. However, there is a growing belief among educators and educational researchers that "good teaching includes teaching students how to learn, how to remember, how to think, and how to motivate themselves" (Weinstein & Mayer, 1986, p. 315).

Several current models of teaching incorporate the teaching of learning strategies and metacognitive skills in one way or another. It may be recalled, for example, that reciprocal teaching involves students acquiring and using four types of learning strategies. Other programs and guidelines for teaching learning strategies, metacognitive skills, reasoning, and problem solving also have been suggested (Baron & Sternberg, 1987; Chipman, Segal, & Glaser, 1985; Levin, 1986; McKeachie, Pintrich, & Lin, 1985; Segal, Chipman, & Glaser, 1985; Weinstein, Goetz, & Alexander, 1988; Weinstein & Mayer, 1986). There is considerable agreement, however, that the teaching of these strategies and skills cannot be accomplished in either a short period of time or as something separate from the total, ongoing curriculum (e.g., Derry & Murphy, 1986; Pressley & Associates, 1990; Pressley, Goodchild, Fleet, Zajchowski, & Evans, 1989).

Although it is difficult to summarize briefly the research on how the teaching of learning and metacognitive skills should proceed, Pressley et al. (1989; Pressley & Associates, 1990) have suggested the following guidelines for teaching such strategies:

- Select a few strategies with which to begin, and teach these strategies across the various content areas as part of the on-going curriculum. Additional strategies should be introduced only after the initial strategies have been fairly well established.

- Describe the strategies being taught and model their use for the students, commenting aloud on how the strategies should be performed.

- Model the strategies again, reexplaining those aspects of using the strategies that are not well understood.

- Explain why the strategies should be used, what they accomplish, and the specific situations in which they should be used.

- Provide plenty of guided practice by having students use the strategies for as many appropriate tasks as possible, providing reinforcement and feedback on how the students can improve their execution of the strategies.
- Encourage students to monitor their performance when using the strategies.
- Encourage generalization of the strategies by having students use them with different types of materials in the various content areas, as well as their continued use.
- "Increase students' motivation to use strategies by heightening student awareness that they are acquiring valuable skills that are at the heart of competent functioning.
- "Emphasize reflective processing rather than speedy processing; do all possible to eliminate high anxiety in students; encourage students to shield themselves from distraction so they can attend to academic tasks" (Pressley & Associates, 1990, p. 18).

One might notice that the model suggested by Pressley is quite consistent with the research on teacher effects discussed earlier in this chapter, especially the findings of process–product research (Brophy & Good, 1986; Rosenshine & Stevens, 1986). In fact, it is possible that research on the teaching of learning strategies could become a new form of process–product research in which the outcomes are now learning strategies, metacognitive skills, and the ability to reason.

The concern for learning strategies, however, has not been limited to the cognitive aspects of using such strategies. A number of investigators (e.g., R. Ames & C. Ames, 1991; C. Ames & Archer, 1988; Pressley & Associates, 1990; Pressley et al., 1989; Weinstein & Mayer, 1986) have stressed the importance of motivational factors in the effective use of learning strategies by students. For example, C. Ames and Archer (1988) found that students were more likely to use effective learning strategies when they perceived that their classrooms emphasized mastery rather than performance goals.

When considering the teaching of learning, metacognitive, and reasoning strategies, it is helpful to be aware of the difference between instructional strategies and the generic category of learning strategies (Shuell, 1988). An *instructional* strategy is performed by the teacher in an attempt to help students learn something; examples are providing an organizational structure for the day's lesson or suggesting a mnemonic to help students learn specific information. A *learning* strategy, on the other hand, is performed by the student on his or her own without the aid of the teacher or instructional agent (e.g., textbook), such as the spontaneous development of an outline or other scheme for organizing the material being learned. In teaching learning strategies, it is important to realize that the goal of the instruction is to enable students to carry out these strategies autonomously in other situations. Care must be taken to avoid students becoming dependent on the instructional strategies employed by the teacher for learning new material and skills, for as Rohwer (1970) noted:

the child cannot always count upon the world to offer up information in optimal ways; therefore, he should be equipped to transform information himself into a form that renders it maximally memorable. (p. 402)

## WHAT CURRENTLY IS KNOWN (AND NOT KNOWN) ABOUT TEACHER EFFECTS

Teaching and learning in a classroom setting are, as we have seen, an extremely complex process that involves a number of interrelated factors. A considerable body of reliable knowledge on teacher effects and the nature of effective teaching is currently available, although a great deal still remains to be discovered. But is enough known for us to base educational policy or instructional practices on that knowledge base? That issue is a legitimate one for a discipline concerned with the application or relevance of psychological theory and research to the practice of education. There is, however, a wide disparity of views on this matter, even among educational psychologists. Many factors contribute to this disparity. A comprehensive analysis of these factors is beyond the scope of this chapter, but some discussion of the issue is necessary in order to summarize the findings on teacher effects in an adequate manner.

Part of the problem appears to be preconceived notions about the poor quality of educational data. Classroom teaching and learning are a far more complex process than most of those studied in the physical and biological sciences. In many cases, however, data on teaching and learning are of the same magnitude (e.g., effect size) and consistency (e.g., likelihood that the same findings would be obtained if the study was to be conducted again) as data in physics and medicine (Berliner, 1987; Gage, 1985, 1993; Hedges, 1987). Yet it is not uncommon for public policy and ethical decisions to be made with considerable confidence in the latter areas even as policymakers argue that comparable data from educational research are not worth considering.

An overall summary of the broad and diverse range of data considered in this chapter is difficult to accomplish. Various attempts to summarize and integrate certain subareas of the research have already been discussed, and these provide a reasonable starting point for establishing a viable knowledge base on teacher effects. These efforts include Brophy and Good's (1986) summary and integration of the findings of process–product research (see Table 22–2), Rosenshine and Stevens' (1986) teaching functions, distilled from large-scale training studies on teacher effectiveness (see Table 22–5), and Shuell's learning functions (1988, 1992), distilled from research on learning from instruction (see Table 22–6). Brophy and Good (1986) note that two common themes cut across the various process–product findings. The first involves academic learning time, while the second theme involves the structuring of the information being presented. In addition, it should be noted that many of the findings involve classroom management as much as they do specific instructional behaviors per se, although the two are closely interrelated (Doyle, 1986; Gage, 1989).

There is considerable agreement among these various findings, although, as already indicated, they also have a number of limitations. Nevertheless, they provide a reliable body of knowledge about teacher effects that is relevant to a large portion of classroom teaching. However, they provide only part of the total picture. Other considerations must be taken into account in trying to gain a comprehensive understanding of classroom teaching and learning. For example, research on the social context of the classroom is beginning to provide us with important findings. In addition, the newer models of teaching, such as cognitive apprenticeships, provide new ways of thinking about and carrying out the teaching–learning process that are useful for many types of learning outcomes. Although it seems likely that the types of teaching variables identified by the earlier research on teacher effects are also relevant to teaching in these newer types of learning environments, research on this relationship remains to be accomplished. Finally, although certainly not of least importance, it seems clear that various noncognitive factors, such as motivation and interest, play an extremely important role in deterring the effects that teachers have on students, and these factors should not be ignored (e.g., see R. Ames & Ames, 1991; Pintrich, Marx, & Boyle, 1993; Pressley et al., 1989).

In applying these findings to actual teaching situations, however, it is helpful to remember that

neither teacher-effects data nor any other scientific data can directly prescribe guidelines for practice. . . . Research findings do not translate directly into guidelines for practice. Instead, the meanings and implications of the findings must be *interpreted*. (Brophy, 1988, pp. 7–11, emphasis in the original)

This interpretation constitutes the "art" of teaching involved in Gage's (1978, 1985) references to the scientific knowledge that forms the basis for the art of teaching and the professional judgment involved in Shuell's (1988, 1992) discussions of learning functions.

There are a number of equally valid ways of teaching that are consistent with the findings presented in this chapter, and even in ideal teaching, trade-offs are involved that prevent optimization in an absolute sense (Brophy & Good, 1986). In some cases, these findings have been used as the basis of teacher evaluation, often without taking into account the types of limitations discussed above. The rigid use of these findings (e.g., as a checklist) for teacher evaluation is simply inappropriate. The context in which a teacher carries out a particular action must be taken into account; otherwise, knowing that a teacher either performs or does not perform a particular act has little meaning.

Another factor that limits our knowledge about teacher effects is the fragmented nature of the findings and the substantially different perspectives of educational researchers with regard to classroom teaching and learning. Diversity can be healthy, but attempts to integrate existing knowledge about teacher effects would add greatly to our knowledge about effective teaching and learning.

Another limiting factor is that most of the existing research has been conducted at the elementary level. We know little about the extent to which the current findings are applicable to teaching at the secondary level. It seems likely that similar principles are involved in the two situations, but substantial differences exist between the two levels, including differences in the type of expected outcomes, the instructional methods most commonly employed, the prior knowledge and developmental level of the students, and the students' outside interests. Given these differences and the paucity of research at the secondary level, it is wise to be cautious about generalizing the findings to these situations. Research on teacher effects at the secondary level is clearly needed.

## TOWARD A BETTER UNDERSTANDING OF THE TEACHING–LEARNING PROCESS: NEXT STEPS

Our current understanding of the teaching–learning process can be expanded in a variety of ways. Some of these ways involve a particular focus, such as the need for more research at the secondary level and the need to simultaneously consider the cognitive, affective, social, motivational, and developmental factors that contribute to both the direct and indirect effects that teachers have on student learning. Other ways involve methodological issues such as the need to recognize the complementary nature of different research paradigms (e.g., quantitative and qualitative) and the need to consider innovative methods of data collection (e.g., those employed by Nuthall & Alton-Lee, 1990, 1991).

Concern for appropriate methodology, of course, is closely related to the research question being asked. Actually, the selection of the research question should precede the choice of what methodology is to be employed, a sequence that is sometimes reversed in practice. The changing and evolving conceptions of teaching and learning discussed in this chapter give rise to new types of research questions. These new questions present researchers with a challenge to rethink a variety of methodological issues that must be addressed if the field is to advance.

New ways of looking at some of the methodological issues involved in research on teacher effects need to be considered. Among these issues are the reality that the contextualized nature of our understanding of teaching and learning makes local knowledge just as important—if not more important, at least for purposes of implementation—than the general type of knowledge to which educational psychology has become accustomed (Goldenberg & Gallimore, 1991). The complexity of the interactions that occur in a classroom suggest that ways of capturing these interactions are required. Distinctions between quantitative and qualitative and between basic and applied research may be oversimplified. Salomon (1991) proposes that a distinction between analytic and systematic approaches to educational research is more appropriate than either of the former distinctions for studying the interdependent factors that influence classroom activities. Along with Gibbs (1979), Altman (1988), and other researchers, Salomon argues that a combination of methodological approaches is needed, for as Gibbs (1979) points out, the real need in this type of research is for "the cross-fertilization of deductive rigor with inductive relevance" (p. 129).

Finally, research on teacher effects needs to expand its concern for the psychological mechanisms that are responsible for students learning from instruction. Within the context of this handbook, that concern is probably the major challenge facing educational psychologists interested in the teaching–learning process. Many individuals believe that concern for psychological theory is an esoteric exercise with little practical consequence, and in many cases educational psychologists have played into that belief by conducting studies that are far removed from issues related to classroom teaching and learning or by inadequately explaining how such studies contribute to an understanding of classroom activities.

Psychological theory and knowledge about the psychological mechanisms responsible for learning have considerable practical importance. For example, Brophy and Alleman (1991) note that

[c]urriculum planners can prescribe activities but cannot guarantee that these activities will result in the desired learning experiences (e.g., requiring students to answer questions about the Declaration of Independence will not guarantee that they think critically about the issues involved). (p. 10)

The learning experiences that determine what students do learn consist of the students' psychological reactions to the learning activities that are presented, as well as a variety of contextual and social issues. Understanding how these psychological mechanisms operate permits teachers and other educational designers to solve the practical problems confronting education in a more adequate manner than would be the case if such theoretical understanding were not available.

One of the challenges facing educational psychology, if it is to be perceived as being relevant to educational practice, is for more researchers to investigate problems closer to practice. This involves, in part, studies that investigate the relationship among cognitive, affective, social, and motivational aspects of learning from instruction (R. Ames & Ames, 1991; Levine et al., 1993; Pintrich et al., 1993; Pressley et al., 1989). It also might involve the study of new types of relevant variables, such as the indirect effect that teachers can have through working with parents to improve the home learning environment. We know a great deal about the way teachers affect student learning, but there is a vast amount of uncharted territory that remains to be explored and understood.

# References

Altman, I. (1988). Process, transactional/contextual, and outcome research: An alternative to the traditional distinction between basic and applied research. *Social Behaviour, 3,* 259–280.

Ames, C. (1992). Classrooms: Goals, structures, and student motivation. *Journal of Educational Psychology, 84,* 261–271.

Ames, C., & Archer, J. (1988). Achievement goals in the classroom: Students' learning strategies and motivational processes. *Journal of Educational Psychology, 80,* 260–267.

Ames, R., & Ames, C. (1991). Motivation and effective teaching. In L. Idol & B. F. Jones (Eds.), *Educational values and cognitive instruction: Implications for education* (pp. 247–271). Hillsdale, NJ: Lawrence Erlbaum Associates.

Amidon, E. J., & Hough, J. B. (Eds.). (1967). *Interaction analysis: Theory, research and application.* Reading, MA: Addison-Wesley.

Anderson, C. W., & Roth, K. J. (1989). Teaching for meaningful and self-regulated learning of science. In J. Brophy (Ed.), *Advances in research on teaching* (Vol. 1, pp. 265–306). Greenwich, CT: JAI Press.

Anderson, C. W., & Smith, E. L. (1987). *Teaching science.* New York: Longman.

Anderson, L. M. (1984). The environment of instruction: The function of seatwork in a commercially developed curriculum. In G. G. Duffy, L. R. Roehler, & J. Mason (Eds.), *Comprehension instruction: Perspectives and suggestions* (pp. 93–103). New York: Longman.

Anderson, L. M. (1989). Implementing instructional programs to promote meaningful, self-regulated learning. In J. Brophy (Ed.), *Advances in research on teaching* (Vol. 1, pp. 311–341). Greenwich, CT: JAI Press.

Anderson, L. M., Evertson, C. M., & Brophy, J. E. (1979). An experimental study of effective teaching in first-grade reading groups. *Elementary School Journal, 79,* 193–223.

Anderson, L. W., & Burns, R. B. (1987). Values, evidence, and mastery learning. *Review of Educational Research, 57,* 215–223.

Baron, J. B., & Sternberg, R. J. (Eds.). (1987). *Teaching thinking skills: Theory and practice.* New York: Freeman.

Batcher, E. (1981). *Emotions in the classroom: A study of children's experience.* New York: Praeger.

Beecher, C. (1961). Data-gathering devices employed in the Wisconsin studies. *Journal of Experimental Education, 30,* 30–47.

Bereiter, C. (1989, March). The role of an educational learning theory: Explaining difficult learning. In W. J. McKeachie (Chair), *Toward a unified approach to learning as a multi-source phenomenon.* Symposium conducted at a meeting of the American Educational Research Association, San Francisco.

Bereiter, C., & Scardamalia, M. (1987). *The psychology of written composition.* Hillsdale, NJ: Lawrence Erlbaum Associates.

Berliner, D. C. (1976). Impediments to the study of teacher effectiveness. *Journal of Teacher Education, 27,* 5–13.

Berliner, D. C. (1977). Impediments to measuring teacher effectiveness. In G. D. Borich & K. S. Fenton (Eds.), *The appraisal of teaching: Concepts and process* (pp. 146–161). Reading, MA: Addison-Wesley.

Berliner, D. C. (1983). Developing conceptions of classroom environments: Some light on the T in classroom studies of ATI. *Educational Psychologist, 18,* 1–13.

Berliner, D. C. (1987). Knowledge is power: A talk to teachers about a revolution in the teaching profession. In D. C. Berliner & B. V. Rosenshine (Eds.), *Talks to teachers: A festschrift for N. L. Gage* (pp. 3–33). New York: Random House.

Berliner, D. C. (1989). The place of process-product research in developing the agenda for research on teacher thinking. *Educational Psychologist, 24,* 325–344.

Block, J. H., & Burns, R. B. (1977). Mastery learning. In L. S. Shulman (Ed.), *Review of research in education* (Vol. 4, pp. 3–49). Itasca, IL: Peacock.

Bloom, B. S. (1971). Mastery learning. In J. H. Block (Ed.), *Mastery learning: Theory and practice* (pp. 47–63). New York: Holt, Rinehart and Winston.

Bloom, B. S. (1976). *Human characteristics and school learning.* New York: McGraw-Hill.

Bloom, B. S. (1984). The 2 sigma problem: The search for methods of instruction as effective as one-to-one tutoring. *Educational Researcher, 13*(6), 4–16.

Bloom, B. S., Hastings, J. T., & Madaus, G. F. (1971). *Handbook on formative and summative evaluation of student learning.* New York: McGraw-Hill.

Blumenfeld, P. C., Puro, P., & Mergendoller, J. R. (1992). Translating motivation into thoughtfulness. In H. H. Marshall (Ed.), *Redefining student learning: Roots of educational change* (pp. 207–239). Norwood, NJ: Ablex.

Boyce, A. C. (1912). Qualities of merit in secondary school teachers. *Journal of Educational Psychology, 3,* 144–157.

Brophy, J. (1988). Research on teacher effects: Uses and abuses. *Elementary School Journal, 89,* 3–21.

Brophy, J., & Alleman, J. (1991). Activities as instructional tools: A framework for analysis and evaluation. *Educational Researcher, 20*(4), 9–23.

Brophy, J., & Good, T. L. (1986). Teacher behavior and student achievement. In M. C. Wittrock (Ed.), *Handbook of research on teaching* (3rd ed., pp. 328–375). New York: Macmillan.

Brophy, J. (1981). Teacher praise: A functional analysis. *Review of Educational Research, 51,* 5–32.

Brown, A. L., & Palincsar, A. S. (1989). Guided, cooperative learning and individual knowledge acquisition. In L. B. Resnick (Ed.), *Knowing, learning, and instructions: Essays in honor of Robert Glaser* (pp. 393–451). Hillsdale, NJ: Lawrence Erlbaum Associates.

Brown, A. L., Palincsar, A. S., & Armbruster, B. B. (1984). Instructing comprehension-fostering activities in interactive learning situations. In H. Mandl, N. L. Stein, & T. Trabasso (Eds.), *Learning and comprehension of text* (pp. 255–286). Hillsdale, NJ: Lawrence Erlbaum Associates.

Brown, J. S. (1989, March). *Situated cognition and the culture of learning.* Paper presented at a meeting of the American Educational Research Association, San Francisco.

Brown, J. S. (1990). Toward a new epistemology for learning. In C. Frasson & G. Gauthier (Eds.), *Intelligent tutoring systems: At the crossroads of artificial intelligence and education* (pp. 266–282). Norwood, NJ: Ablex.

Brown, J. S., Collins, A., & Duguid, P. (1989). Situated cognition and the culture of learning. *Educational Researcher, 18*(1), 32–42.

Carroll, J. B. (1963). A model of school learning. *Teachers College Record, 64,* 723–733.

Carroll, J. B. (1989). The Carroll model: A 25-year retrospective and prospective view. *Educational Researcher, 18*(1), 26–31.

Cazden, C. B. (1986). Classroom discourse. In M. C. Wittrock (Ed.), *Handbook of research on teaching* (3rd ed., pp. 432–463). New York: Macmillan.

Champagne, A. B., Klopfer, L. E., & Gunstone, R. F. (1982). Cognitive research and the design of science instruction. *Educational Psychologist, 17,* 31–53.

Chi, M. T. H., Glaser, R., & Farr, M. J. (Eds.). (1988). *The nature of expertise.* Hillsdale, NJ: Lawrence Erlbaum Associates.

Chipman, S. F., Segal, J. W., & Glaser, R. (Eds.). (1985). *Thinking and learning skills: Vol. 2. Research and open questions.* Hillsdale, NJ: Lawrence Erlbaum Associates.

Cognition and Technology Group at Vanderbilt. (1990). Anchored instruction and its relationship to situated cognition. *Educational Researcher, 19*(6), 2–10.

Collins, A. (1991). Cognitive apprenticeship and instructional technology. In L. Idol & B. F. Jones (Eds.), *Educational values and cognitive instruction: Implications for education* (pp. 121–138). Hillsdale, NJ: Lawrence Erlbaum Associates.

Collins, A., Brown, J. S., & Newman, S. E. (1989). Cognitive apprenticeship: Teaching the crafts of reading, writing, and mathematics. In L. B. Resnick (Ed.), *Knowing, learning, and instruction: Essays in honor of Robert Glaser* (pp. 453–494). Hillsdale, NJ: Lawrence Erlbaum Associates.

Collins, E., & Green, J. L. (1992). Learning in classroom settings: Making or breaking a culture. In H. H. Marshall (Ed.), *Redefining student learning: Roots of educational change* (pp. 59–85). Norwood, NJ: Ablex.

Corno, L. (1987). Teaching and self-regulated learning. In D. C. Berliner & B. V. Rosenshine (Eds.), *Talks to teachers: A festschrift for N. L. Gage* (pp. 249–266). New York: Random House.

Derry, S. J. (1992). Beyond symbolic processing: Expanding horizons for educational psychology. *Journal of Educational Psychology, 84,* 413–418.

Derry, S. J., & Murphy, D. A. (1986). Designing systems that train learning ability: From theory to practice. *Review of Educational Research, 56,* 1–39.

Dillon, R. F., & Sternberg, R. J. (Eds.). (1986). *Cognition and instruction.* Orlando, FL: Academic Press.

Doyle, W. (1978). Paradigms for research on teacher effectiveness. In L. S. Shulman (Ed.), *Review of research in education* (Vol. 5, pp. 163–198). Itasca, IL: Peacock.

Doyle, W. (1983). Academic work. *Review of Educational Research, 53,* 159–199.

Doyle, W. (1986). Classroom organization and management. In M. C. Wittrock (Ed.), *Handbook of research on teaching* (3rd ed. pp. 392–431). New York: Macmillan.

Driver, R., & Easley, J. (1978). Pupils and paradigms: A review of literature related to concept development in adolescent science students. *Studies in Science Education, 5,* 61–84.

Dunkin, M. J., & Biddle, B. J. (1974). *The study of teaching.* New York: Holt, Rinehart and Winston.

Erickson, F. (1982). Classroom discourse as improvisation: Relationships between academic task structure and social participation structure in lessons. In L. C. Wilkinson (Ed.), *Communicating in the classroom* (pp. 153–181). New York: Academic Press.

Fenstermacher, G. D. (1986). Philosophy of research on teaching: Three aspects. In M. C. Wittrock (Ed.), *Handbook of research on teaching* (3rd ed., pp. 37–49). New York: Macmillan.

Fiedler, M. (1975). Bidirectionality of influence in classroom interaction. *Journal of Educational Psychology, 67,* 735–744.

Flanders, N. A. (1970). *Analyzing teacher behavior.* Reading, MA: Addison-Wesley.

Gage, N. L. (Ed.). (1963a). *Handbook of research on teaching.* Chicago: Rand McNally.

Gage, N. L. (1963b). Paradigms for research on teaching. In N. L. Gage (Ed.), *Handbook of research on teaching* (pp. 94–141). Chicago: Rand McNally.

Gage, N. L. (1978). *The scientific basis for the art of teaching.* New York: Teachers College Press.

Gage, N. L. (1985). *Hard gains in the soft sciences: The case of pedagogy.* Bloomington, IN: Phi Delta Kappa.

Gage, N. L. (1989). Process-product research on teaching: A review of criticisms. *Elementary School Journal, 90,* 253–300.

Gage, N. L. (1993, July). *Research implying the effectiveness of the Educational Research and Development Program of the American Federation of Teachers.* Paper presented to the local site coordinators of the Educational Research and Dissemination Program, American Federation of Teachers, Washington, DC.

Gagné, R. M. (1962a). The acquisition of knowledge. *Psychological Review, 69,* 355–365.

Gagné, R. M. (1962b). Military training and principles of learning. *American Psychologist, 17,* 83–91.

Gagné, R. M. (1965). *The conditions of learning.* New York: Holt, Rinehart and Winston.

Gagné, R. M. (1970). *The conditions of learning* (2nd ed.). New York: Holt, Rinehart and Winston.

Gagné, R. M. (1977). *The conditions of learning* (3rd ed.). New York: Holt, Rinehart and Winston.

Gagné, R. M. (1984). Learning outcomes and their effects: Useful categories of human performance. *American Psychologist, 39,* 377–385.

Gagné, R. M., & Driscoll, M. P. (1988). *Essentials of learning for instruction* (2nd ed.). Englewood Cliffs, NJ: Prentice Hall.

Gelman, R., & Greeno, J. G. (1989). On the nature of competence: Principles for understanding in a domain. In L. B. Resnick (Ed.), *Knowing, learning, and instruction: Essays in honor of Robert Glaser* (pp. 125–186). Hillsdale, NJ: Lawrence Erlbaum Associates.

Gibbs, J. C. (1979). The meaning of ecologically oriented inquiry in contemporary psychology. *American Psychologist, 34,* 127–140.

Glaser, R. (1962). Psychology and instructional technology. In R. Glaser (Ed.), *Training research and education* (pp. 1–30). Pittsburgh: University of Pittsburgh Press.

Glaser, R. (1970). Evaluation of instruction and changing educational models. In M. C. Wittrock & D. E. Wiley (Eds.), *The evaluation of instruction: Issues and problems* (pp. 70–86). New York: Holt, Rinehart and Winston.

Glaser, R. (1976). Components of a psychology of instruction: Toward a science of design. *Review of Educational Research, 46,* 1–24.

Glaser, R. (Ed.). (1978a). *Advances in instructional psychology* (Vol. 1). Hillsdale, NJ: Lawrence Erlbaum Associates.

Glaser, R. (1978b). Introduction: Toward a psychology of instruction. In R. Glaser (Ed.), *Advances in instructional psychology* (Vol. 1, pp. 1–12). Hillsdale, NJ: Lawrence Erlbaum Associates.

Glaser, R. (Ed.). (1982a). *Advances in instructional psychology* (Vol. 2). Hillsdale, NJ: Lawrence Erlbaum Associates.

Glaser, R. (1982b). Instructional psychology: Past, present, and future. *American Psychologist, 37,* 292–305.

Glaser, R. (1984). Education and thinking: The role of knowledge. *American Psychologist, 39,* 93–104.

Glaser, R. (Ed.). (1987). *Advances in instructional psychology* (Vol. 3). Hillsdale, NJ: Lawrence Erlbaum Associates.

Glaser, R. (1990). The reemergence of learning theory within instructional research. *American Psychologist, 45,* 29–39.

Glaser, R. (1991). The maturing of the relationship between the science of learning and cognition and educational practice. *Learning and Instruction, 1,* 129–144.

Glaser, R., & Bassok, M. (1989). Learning theory and the study of instruction. *Annual Review of Psychology, 40,* 631–666.

Golden, J. M. (1988). The construction of a literary text in a story-reading lesson. In J. L. Green & J. O. Harker (Eds.), *Multiple perspective analyses of classroom discourse* (pp. 71–106). Norwood, NJ: Ablex.

Goldenberg, C., & Gallimore, R. (1991). Local knowledge, research knowledge, and educational change: A case study of early Spanish reading improvement. *Educational Researcher, 20*(8), 2–14.

Goodenow, C. (1992). Strengthening the links between educational psychology and the study of social contexts. *Educational Psychologist, 27,* 177–196.

Goodnow, J. J. (1992). Putting persons and culture back together [Review of *Voices of the mind: A sociocultural approach to mediated action* by J. V. Wertsch and *Thinking through cultures: Expeditions in cultural psychology* by R. A. Shweder]. *Educational Researcher, 21*(7), 33–35.

Green, J. L. (1977). *Pedagogical style differences as related to comprehension performance: Grades one through three.* Unpublished doctoral dissertation, University of California at Berkeley.

Green, J. L., Weade, R., & Graham, K. (1988). Lesson construction and student participation: A sociolinguistic analysis. In J. L. Green & J. O. Harker (Eds.), *Multiple perspective analyses of classroom discourse* (pp. 11–47). Norwood, NJ: Ablex.

Gump, P. V. (1967). *The classroom behavior setting: Its nature and relation to student behavior* (U.S. Office of Education, Bureau of Research [U.S. Office of Education, Project No. 2453, Contract No. OE-4-10-107]). (ERIC Document Reproduction Service No. ED 015 515)

Guskey, T. R. (1987). Rethinking mastery learning reconsidered. *Review of Educational Research, 57,* 225–229.

Guskey, T. R., & Gates, S. L. (1986). Synthesis of research on the effects of mastery learning in elementary and secondary classrooms. *Educational Leadership, 43*(8), 73–80.

Guskey, T. R., & Pigott, T. D. (1988). Research on group-based mastery learning programs: A meta-analysis. *Journal of Educational Research, 81,* 197–216.

Harker, J. O. (1988). Contrasting the content of two story-reading lessons: A propositional analysis. In J. L. Green & J. O. Harker (Eds.), *Multiple perspective analyses of classroom discourse* (pp. 49–70). Norwood, NJ: Ablex.

Hedges, L. V. (1987). How hard is hard science, how soft is soft science? The empirical cumulativeness of research. *American Psychologist, 42,* 443–455.

Jackson, P. W. (1968). *Life in classrooms.* New York: Holt, Rinehart and Winston.

Joyce, B., Weil, M., & Showers, B. (1992). *Models of teaching* (4th ed.). Boston: Allyn & Bacon.

Keller, F. S. (1968). Goodbye, teacher. . . . *Journal of Applied Behavior Analysis, 1,* 79–89.

Keller, F. S., & Sherman, J. G. (1974). *The Keller Plan handbook.* Menlo Park, CA: Benjamin.

Kramer, L. (1991). The social construction of ability perceptions: An ethnographic study of gifted adolescent girls. *Journal of Early Adolescence, 11,* 340–362.

Kratz, H. E. (1896). Characteristics of the best teachers as recognized by children. *Pedagogical Seminary, 3,* 413–419.

Kulik, C. C., Kulik, J. A., & Bangert-Drowns, R. L. (1990). Effectiveness of mastery learning programs: A meta-analysis. *Review of Educational Research, 60,* 265–299.

Kulik, J. A., Kulik, C. C., & Bangert-Drowns, R. L. (1990). Is there better evidence on mastery learning? A response to Slavin. *Review of Educational Research, 60,* 303–307.

Lakoff, G., & Johnson, M. (1980). *Metaphors we live by.* Chicago: University of Chicago Press.

Lave, J. (1988). *Cognition in practice: Mind, mathematics, and culture in everyday life.* Cambridge, England: Cambridge University Press.

Lave, J., & Wenger, E. (1991). *Situated learning: Legitimate peripheral participation.* Cambridge, England: Cambridge University Press.

Levin, J. R. (1986). Four cognitive principles of learning-strategy instruction. *Educational Psychologist, 21,* 3–17.

Levine, J. M., Resnick, L. B., & Higgins, E. T. (1993). Social foundations of cognition. *Annual Review of Psychology, 44,* 585–612.

Marshall, H. H. (1988). Work or learning: Implications of classroom metaphors. *Educational Researcher, 17*(9), 9–16.

Marshall, H. H. (1990). Beyond the workplace metaphor: The classroom as a learning setting. *Theory into Practice, 29*(2), 94–101.

Marshall, H. H. (1992a, April). Reconceptualizing learning for restructured schools. In R. F. Elmore (Chair), *Restructuring schools for learning: Extending the dialogue.* Symposium conducted at a meeting of the American Educational Research Association, San Francisco.

Marshall, H. H. (1992b). Seeing, redefining, and supporting student learning. In H. H. Marshall (Ed.), *Redefining student learning: Roots of educational change* (pp. 1–32). Norwood, NJ: Ablex.

Marshall, H. H., & Weinstein, R. S. (1984). Classroom factors affecting students' self-evaluations: An interactional model. *Review of Educational Research, 54,* 301–325.

Mayer, R. E. (1992). Cognition and instruction: Their historic meeting within educational psychology. *Journal of Educational Psychology, 84,* 405–412.

McClintock, R. (1971). The place of study in a world of instruction. *Teachers College Record, 73,* 161–205.

McKeachie, W. J., Pintrich, P. R., & Lin, Y.-G. (1985). Teaching learning strategies. *Educational Psychologist, 20,* 153–160.

Mitzel, H. E. (1960). Teacher effectiveness. In C. W. Harris (Ed.), *Encyclopedia of educational research* (3rd ed., pp. 1481–1486). New York: Macmillan.

Morine-Dershimer, G. (1983). Instructional strategy and the "creation" of classroom status. *American Educational Research Journal, 20,* 645–661.

Morrison, H. C. (1926). *The practice of teaching in the secondary school.* Chicago: University of Chicago Press.

Neale, D. C., Smith, D., & Johnson, V. G. (1990). Implementing conceptual change teaching in primary science. *Elementary School Journal, 91,* 109–131.

Nissani, M., & Hoefler-Nissani, D. M. (1992). Experimental studies of belief dependence of observations and of resistance to conceptual change. *Cognition and Instruction, 9,* 97–111.

Nuthall, G., & Alton-Lee, A. (1990). Research on teaching and learning: Thirty years of change. *Elementary School Journal, 90,* 547–570.

Nuthall, G., & Alton-Lee, A. (1991, April). *Determining how pupils learn from the information they are exposed to in the classroom.* Paper presented at a meeting of the American Educational Research Association, Chicago.

Orsolini, M., & Pontecorvo, C. (1992). Children's talk in classroom discussions. *Cognition and Instruction, 9,* 113–136.

Palincsar, A. S., & Brown, A. L. (1984). Reciprocal teaching of comprehension-fostering and comprehension-monitoring activities. *Cognition and Instruction, 1,* 117–175.

Palincsar, A. S., & Brown, A. L. (1989). Classroom dialogues to promote self-regulated comprehension. In J. Brophy (Ed.), *Advances in research on teaching* (Vol. 1, pp. 35–67). Greenwich, CT: JAI Press.

Perkins, D. N., & Simmons, R. (1988). Patterns of misunderstanding: An integrative model for science, math, and programming. *Review of Educational Research, 58,* 303–326.

Pintrich, P. R., Marx, R. W., & Boyle, R. A. (1993). Beyond cold conceptual change: The role of motivational beliefs and classroom contextual factors in the process of conceptual change. *Review of Educational Research, 63,* 167–199.

Posner, G. J., Strike, K. A., Hewson, P. W., & Gertzog, W. A. (1982). Accommodation of a scientific conception: Toward a theory of conceptual change. *Science Education, 66,* 211–227.

Pressley, M., & Associates. (1990). *Cognitive strategy instruction that really improves children's academic performance.* Cambridge, MA: Brookline Books.

Pressley, M., Goodchild, F., Fleet, J., Zajchowski, R., & Evans, E. D. (1989). The challenges of classroom strategy instruction. *Elementary School Journal, 89,* 301–342.

Redfield, D., & Rousseau, E. (1981). A meta-analysis of experimental research on teacher questioning behavior. *Review of Educational Research, 51,* 237–245.

Resnick, L. B. (1976a). Introduction: Changing conceptions of intelligence. In L. B. Resnick (Ed.), *The nature of intelligence* (pp. 1–10). Hillsdale, NJ: Lawrence Erlbaum Associates.

Resnick, L. B. (1976b). Task analysis in instructional design: Some cases from mathematics. In D. Klahr (Ed.), *Cognition and instruction* (pp. 51–80). Hillsdale, NJ: Lawrence Erlbaum Associates.

Resnick, L. B. (1981). *Instructional psychology.* Palo Alto, CA: Annual Reviews.

Resnick, L. B. (1987). Learning in school and out. *Educational Researcher, 16*(9), 13–20.

Resnick, L. B., & Johnson, A. (1988). Intelligent machines for intelligent people: Cognitive theory and the future of computer-assisted learning. In R. S. Nickerson & P. P. Zodhiates (Eds.), *Technology in education: Looking toward 2020* (pp. 139–168). Hillsdale, NJ: Lawrence Erlbaum Associates.

Resnick, L. B., & Omanson, S. F. (1987). Learning to understand arithmetic. In R. Glaser (Ed.), *Advances in instructional psychology* (Vol. 3, pp. 41–95). Hillsdale, NJ: Lawrence Erlbaum Associates.

Rohwer, W. D., Jr. (1970). Images and pictures in children's learning. *Psychological Bulletin, 73,* 393–403.

Rohwer, W. D., Jr. (1984). An invitation to an educational psychology of studying. *Educational Psychologist, 19,* 1–14.

Rosenshine, B. (1983). Teaching functions in instructional programs. *Elementary School Journal, 83,* 335–351.

Rosenshine, B. (1986). Unsolved issues in teaching content: A critique of a lesson on Federalist Paper No. 10. *Teaching and Teacher Education, 2,* 301–308.

Rosenshine, B. (1989, October). *Three academic tasks and how to teach them.* Paper presented at a meeting of the Northeastern Educational Research Association, Ellenville, NY.

Rosenshine, B., & Furst, N. (1973). The use of direct observation to study teaching. In R. M. W. Travers (Ed.), *Second handbook of research on teaching* (pp. 122–183). Chicago: Rand McNally.

Rosenshine, B., & Meister, C. (1994). Reciprocal teaching: A review of the research. *Review of Educational Research, 64,* 479–530.

Rosenshine, B., & Stevens, R. (1986). Teaching functions. In M. C. Wittrock (Ed.), *Handbook of research on teaching* (3rd ed., pp. 376–391). New York: Macmillan.

Roth, K. J. (1985). *The effects of science texts on students' misconceptions about food for plants.* Unpublished doctoral dissertation, Michigan State University, East Lansing.

Ruediger, W. C., & Strayer, G. D. (1910). The qualities of merit in teachers. *Journal of Educational Psychology, 1,* 272–278.

Salomon, G. (1991). Transcending the qualitative-quantitative debate: The analytic and systemic approaches to educational research. *Educational Researcher, 20*(6), 10–18.

Scardamalia, M., & Bereiter, C. (1985). Fostering the development of self-regulation in children's knowledge processing. In S. F. Chipman, J. W. Segal, & R. Glaser (Eds.), *Thinking and learning skills: Vol. 2. Research and open questions* (pp. 563–577). Hillsdale, NJ: Lawrence Erlbaum Associates.

Schoenfeld, A. H. (1985). *Mathematical problem solving.* New York: Academic Press.

Schön, D. A. (1983). *The reflective practitioner: How professionals think in action.* New York: Basic Books.

Segal, J. W., Chipman, S. F., & Glaser, R. (Eds.). (1985). *Thinking and learning skills: Vol. 1. Relating instruction to research.* Hillsdale, NJ: Lawrence Erlbaum Associates.

Shuell, T. J. (1986a). Cognitive conceptions of learning. *Review of Educational Research, 56,* 411–436.

Shuell, T. J. (1986b). Individual differences: Changing conceptions in research and practice. *American Journal of Education, 94,* 356–377.

Shuell, T. J. (1988). The role of the student in learning from instruction. *Contemporary Educational Psychology, 13,* 276–295.

Shuell, T. J. (1992). Designing instructional computing systems for meaningful learning. In M. Jones & P. H. Winne (Eds.), *Adaptive learning environments: Foundations and frontiers* (pp. 19–54). New York: Springer.

Shuell, T. J. (1993). Toward an integrated theory of teaching and learning. *Educational Psychologist, 28,* 291–311.

Shulman, L. S. (1986). Paradigms and research programs in the study of teaching: A contemporary perspective. In M. C. Wittrock (Ed.), *Handbook of research on teaching* (3rd ed., pp. 3–36). New York: Macmillan.

Slavin, R. E. (1987a). Mastery learning reconsidered. *Review of Educational Research, 57,* 175–213.

Slavin, R. E. (1987b). Taking the mystery out of mastery: A response to Guskey, Anderson, and Burns. *Review of Educational Research, 57,* 231–235.

Slavin, R. E. (1990). Mastery learning re-reconsidered. *Review of Educational Research, 60,* 300–302.

Smith, D. (1989). *The role of teacher knowledge in teaching conceptual change science lessons.* Unpublished doctoral dissertation, University of Delaware, Newark.

Snow, R. E. (1989). Aptitude-treatment interaction as a framework for research on individual differences in learning. In P. L. Ackerman, R. J. Sternberg, & R. Glaser (Eds.), *Learning and individual differences: Advances in theory and research* (pp. 13–59). New York: Freeman.

Stodolsky, S. S., Ferguson, T. L., & Wimpelberg, K. (1981). The recitation persists, but what does it look like? *Journal of Curriculum Studies, 13,* 121–130.

Stolurow, L. M. (1965). Model the master teacher or master the teaching model. In J. D. Krumboltz (Ed.), *Learning and the educational process* (pp. 223–247). Chicago: Rand McNally.

Thomas, J. W. (1988). Proficiency at academic studying. *Contemporary Educational Psychology, 13,* 265–275.

Vygotsky, L. S. (1962). *Thought and language.* Cambridge, MA: MIT Press.

Vygotsky, L. S. (1978). *Mind in society: The development of higher psychological processes.* Cambridge, MA: Harvard University Press.

Washburne, C. W. (1922). Educational measurements as a key to individualizing instruction and promotions. *Journal of Educational Research, 5,* 195–206.

Weade, G. (1992). Locating learning in the times and spaces of teaching. In H. H. Marshall (Ed.), *Redefining student learning: Roots of educational change* (pp. 87–118). Norwood, NJ: Ablex.

Weiner, B., Graham, S., Taylor, S. E., & Meyer, W.-U. (1983). Social cognition in the classroom. *Educational Psychologist, 18,* 109–124.

Weinstein, C. E., Goetz, E. T., & Alexander, A. P. (Eds.). (1988). *Learning and study strategies: Issues in assessment, instruction, and evaluation.* New York: Academic Press.

Weinstein, C. E., & Mayer, R. E. (1986). The teaching of learning strategies. In M. C. Wittrock (Ed.), *Handbook of research on teaching* (3rd ed., pp. 315–327). New York: Macmillan.

Weinstein, C. S. (1991). The classroom as a social context for learning. *Annual Review of Psychology, 42,* 493–525.

Wentzel, K. R. (1989). Adolescent classroom goals, standards for performance, and academic achievement: An interactionist perspective. *Journal of Educational Psychology, 81,* 131–142.

Wertsch, J. V. (1991). *Voices of the mind: A sociocultural approach to mediated action.* Cambridge, MA: Harvard University Press.

Winne, P. (1979). Experiments relating teachers' use of higher cognitive questions to student achievement. *Review of Educational Research, 49,* 13–50.

Winne, P. H. (1987). Why process-product research cannot explain process-product findings and a proposed remedy: The cognitive mediational paradigm. *Teaching and Teacher Education, 3,* 333–356.

Winne, P. H., & Marx, R. W. (1980). Matching students' cognitive responses to teaching skills. *Journal of Educational Psychology, 72,* 257–264.

Wittrock, M. C. (1986). Students' thought processes. In M. C. Wittrock (Ed.), *Handbook of research on teaching* (3rd ed., pp. 297–314). New York: Macmillan.

Wood, T., Cobb, P., & Yackel, E. (1992). Change in learning mathematics: Change in teaching mathematics. In H. H. Marshall (Ed.), *Redefining student learning: Roots of educational change* (pp. 177–205). Norwood, NJ: Ablex.

Yinger, R. J. (1977). *A study of teacher planning: Description and theory development using ethnographic and information-processing methods.* Unpublished doctoral dissertation, Michigan State University, East Lansing.

Zimmerman, B. J. (1989). A social cognitive view of self-regulated academic learning. *Journal of Educational Psychology, 81,* 329–339.

Zimmerman, B. J., & Schunk, D. H. (Eds.). (1989). *Self-regulated learning and academic achievement: Theory, research, and practice.* New York: Springer.

# TEACHER EVALUATION

## Carol Anne Dwyer
EDUCATIONAL TESTING SERVICE, PRINCETON, NEW JERSEY

## Daniel Stufflebeam
WESTERN MICHIGAN UNIVERSITY

## INTRODUCTION

This chapter examines the role of evaluation in efforts to improve elementary and secondary school teaching, with particular attention to the decisions that occur throughout a teacher's career. The chapter reviews and examines alternative evaluation methods that pertain to teacher education evaluation, teacher licensing evaluation, teacher employment evaluation, and teacher advancement and national certification evaluation. The chapter reviews recent criticisms and pressures for reform of teacher evaluation practice, summarizes the professional standards of sound educational personnel evaluation, and describes a range of research and development responses to the problems of teacher evaluation. Specifically considered are recent developments in teacher evaluation, including the National Board for Professional Teaching Standards, the development of the Praxis licensing examination, and recent projects to use measures of student achievement gains for evaluating teacher effectiveness. Considering the state of the art of teacher evaluation, the chapter directs the research attention of educational psychologists to a wide range of technical, legal, substantive, and practice issues in teacher evaluation. The basic aim of the chapter is to provide analyses and recommendations that will assist the personnel of schools, state education departments, universities, research and development organizations, and professional education societies to develop and implement more effective teacher evaluations and thereby help improve teaching and learning in the schools.

## A CONCEPTUAL FRAMEWORK FOR TEACHER EVALUATION

Often, evaluation and assessment activities involved in educating, licensing, appointing, supervising, promoting, and dis-

missing teachers have been viewed in isolation from each other. This practice has served to fragment teacher evaluation practices. This chapter is keyed to a framework for holistic and systematic analysis of teacher evaluation.

Table 23-1 portrays teacher evaluation as an integral part of efforts by higher education, government, schools, school districts, and professional organizations to prepare, license, engage, and develop teachers. The first breakdown on the main horizontal dimension includes four career stages: preparation, licensing, practice, and professional development/advancement. The vertical dimension divides each career stage into entry activities (i.e., selection of a candidate for entry into one of the four stages shown on the main horizontal dimension, such as a teacher preparation program), participation (preparation to become a teacher or actual teaching in a school), and exit (e.g., advancement to the next career stage or termination). The second breakdown on the horizontal dimension shows evaluations and decisions that are involved in the entry, participation, and exit activities of each of the four career stages.

Overall, this matrix is designed to encompass all the decisions and associated evaluations involved from the beginning of a teacher's preparation throughout the teacher's career. As such, it helps to identify the range of evaluation methods needed to meet all requirements of teacher evaluation. The full range of evaluations shown in the matrix is important to staffing schools successfully with qualified and effective teachers. It needs to be stressed that the totality of teacher evaluation activity requires careful attention if evaluation is to realize its full potential for affecting the quality of teaching and helping to ensure that teachers effectively assist all students in learning and developing their capacities. Paying attention to all the evaluations and decisions referenced in the matrix should help educators address a range of important concerns. Specifically, it should help them:

The authors' efforts in developing this chapter were partially supported by the Educational Testing Service; the Office of Educational Research and Improvement, U.S. Department of Education (grant No. R117Q00047); and the Western Michigan University Evaluation Center. The opinions expressed are those of the authors, and no official endorsements by the Educational Testing Service or the U.S. Department of Education are intended or should be inferred.

TABLE 23–1. Types of Evaluations and Decisions Involved in Preparation, Licensing, Employment, and Professionalization of Teachers

| Activities in Each Career Stage | Stages in the Career of a Teacher | | | | | | | |
| --- | --- | --- | --- | --- | --- | --- | --- | --- |
| | Preparation | | Licensing | | Practice | | Professionalization | |
| | Evaluations | Decisions | Evaluations | Decisions | Evaluations | Decisions | Evaluations | Decisions |
| **Entry** | Evaluations of supply & demand<br>Evaluations of recruitment programs<br>Assessment of applicants | Ranking & funding training programs<br>Redesign of the programs<br>Selection of students | Review of credentials | Approval to enter the certifications process | Evaluation of staffing needs<br>Evaluation of recruitment program<br>Evaluation of applicants | Job definitions, job search<br>Program redesign<br>Selection of staff members | Examination of staff needs and institutional needs<br>Assessment of needs & achievements of teachers<br>Assessment of basic qualifications for national certification | Continuing education opportunities<br>Approval of study leaves & special grants<br>Participation in a national certification program |
| Participation | Intake evaluations<br>Evaluations of students' mastery of course requirements<br>Cumulative progress reviews | Planning student programs<br>Grades<br>Counseling<br>Remediation<br>Counseling<br>Revising student programs<br>Termination | Induction evaluation during a probationary year<br>Licensing | Provisional state license<br>Partial qualification for a license | Comparison of job requirements & teacher competencies<br>Performance review<br>Investigation of charges | Assignment<br>End of probation<br>Promotion<br>Tenure<br>Merit pay<br>Staff development<br>Honors<br>Rulings on grievances | Intake evaluations<br>Examination of competence | Designing individual education programs<br>National certification |
| **Exit** | Final evaluation of students' fulfillment of graduation requirements<br>Exit interviews<br>Follow-up survey | Graduation<br>Program review & improvement<br>Program review & improvement | Review of success in teaching for a designated period | Permanent or long-term license | Comparison of resources, staff needs, & staff seniority<br>Performance review | Reduction in force<br>Termination or sanctions | Participant achievement in continuing education<br>Examination of competence & aptitude | Qualification for future leaves<br>New assignments |

- Ensure that the strongest possible efforts are made to select promising teacher education students.
- Systematically prepare those students for teaching service.
- Thoroughly assess their fulfillment of preservice education requirements before certifying them for long service.
- Carefully examine their qualifications for particular teaching assignments. Monitor their progress as teachers, and provide feedback for improvement and professional growth.
- Make appropriate decisions concerning their retention, promotion, and recognition in the teaching field.

The cell entries in the matrix show that the evaluations and decisions involved are of three different types. A few are program evaluations, such as evaluation of recruitment programs. Others, such as evaluations of teacher education students' mastery of college courses, are student evaluations. Finally, the majority of the evaluations identified in the matrix fit the common view of teacher evaluation, that is, assessments of the qualifications, competence, or performance of individual teachers for licensing, selection, continuation, promotion, tenure, professional growth, merit pay, or national certification. This chapter encompasses the full range of teacher evaluations extending across the teacher's career.

# CRITICISM AND PRESSURES FOR REFORM OF TRADITIONAL TEACHER EVALUATION PRACTICES

## The Reform Context

During the 1980s there was a great deal of pressure for educational reform. Reports urging reform came from many quarters and were highly influential in changing public opinion and in leading to a broad array of changes in educational practice, including the evaluation of teachers. Highly visible reports included *A Nation at Risk* (National Commission on Excellence in Education, 1983), *Who Will Teach Our Children?* (California Commission on the Teaching Profession, 1985), *A Nation Prepared* (Task Force on Teaching as a Profession, 1986), and *Tomorrow's Schools* (Holmes Group, 1990). The general thrust of these and other reports was summarized in *The Educational Reform Decade* (Educational Testing Service, Policy Information Center, 1990). These reports indicate the depth of public concern over the quality of teaching and learning in America, and also indicate the ongoing enthusiasm for educational reform. Demands for teacher accountability and student assessment have always been an integral part of the reform phenomenon, and they continue to be so today, in the form of national education goals and standards and calls for national testing.

The reform reports and the activities they spawned cover a broad range of topics. These include desired levels of student achievement; what qualifications teachers should have; how to ensure the availability of good teachers of all races; the proper locus of responsibility for school management; what qualifications school administrators should have; the need for research on teaching and teacher education; the need for curriculum reform for students, particularly in the areas of mathematics and science; and the need for more rigorous and relevant teacher evaluation. It is useful to focus on those topics specific to teaching and teacher evaluation.

## Reform Efforts Specific to Teaching

The quality of teaching plays a central part in reform debates. Improvements in individual teachers' levels of education and classroom performance, the perception and reality of teaching as a profession, and the content and quality of the education of teachers are all key issues that recur in discussions of educational reform. Some specific themes common to the reform conversation include:

- Improving the quality of teaching in order to improve student performance
- The need to professionalize teaching, and to elevate the status and responsibilities of those who teach
- Improving the supply of teachers, particularly teachers of mathematics and science, special education teachers, and minority teachers
- The need to remove incompetent practitioners from the teaching force
- The need to develop a better understanding of the process of teaching

All of these reform themes have implications for teacher evaluation and have been influential in evaluation practice in various ways. They do, however, represent competing goals and interests. For example, the struggle for power over educational decision-making is evident in debates over accountability. Calls for higher standards for teacher licensing, for teachers to be held accountable for student performance, for elimination of teacher tenure, and for the recertification of practicing teachers all reflect a press for accountability through the external control of teachers. It is often proposed that this be accomplished through some form of summative testing.

In contrast to the external accountability point of view, calls for increased participation of teachers in school and district decision-making, in assessment, and in research on teaching all reflect the desire to establish accountability and control of teaching and teacher evaluation through the teaching profession and through individual teachers themselves. With respect to testing, the focus of this point of view is an assessment for purposes of instruction, self-development, or formative evaluation. Such differences in basic orientation reflect the competing values and interests of regulatory groups such as state and national governments, on the one hand, and of teachers themselves on the other.

## Criticisms of Teacher Evaluation Practice

In this broad context of reform of teaching, there have also emerged a number of specific criticisms of the way teacher evaluations are currently carried out for entry into teacher preparation programs, for licensing, for employment selection and retention, and for professional advancement. Virtually no segment of the educational system has been left uncriticized in the professional literature, the public media, and the courts.

Given the extent and complexity of teacher evaluation, a complete discussion of the criticisms of teacher evaluation is beyond the scope of this chapter, but we will provide an overview of major criticisms in this section and a discussion of legal issues in a later section.

Teacher evaluation is a highly controversial area, with myriad stakeholders and a wealth of technical, psychological, political, ethical, and educational complexities. Teacher evaluation is relevant to every segment of the educational system, and society at large has an intense interest in how it is carried out and what its impact on education and on individuals' lives will be. Thus, the criticisms of theory and practice are strongly held, and how (or whether) these criticisms are resolved has direct implications for the quality of American schooling.

In general, recent criticisms of the evaluation of beginning teachers have heavily stressed the fairness of instruments and procedures, especially with respect to the performance of minority group members (e.g., Darling-Hammond, 1986; Garcia, 1985; Haney, Madaus, & Kreitzer, 1987; Hood & Parker, 1989, 1991). A specific subtheme of this criticism is often that teacher evaluation practices are carried out in inconsistent ways, thus violating individuals' constitutionally protected rights to due process.

Criticisms in the professional literature also have raised concerns about the actual or potential impact of teacher evaluation practices on prospective teachers' rights to teaching licenses or access to employment (Haney et al., 1987; Madaus & Pullin, 1987), on teacher education institutions' curricula (Milner, 1991), and on the profession of teaching itself (Darling-Hammond, 1986).The majority of this criticism concerns the use of multiple-choice tests of knowledge rather than performance evaluations, but this distinction often is not clearly drawn. Indeed, an important issue in itself is the fact that little distinction is made among the wide variety of types of teacher evaluations: Assessments of basic enabling skills (reading, writing, mathematics), subject matter knowledge, pedagogical content knowledge, pedagogical skill, and classroom performance are all too frequently treated in the literature as if they were interchangeable for the purposes of making inferences and predictions about teachers. Failure to recognize this simple but critical point clouds many discussions of teacher evaluation.

Stufflebeam et al. (1990) have identified eight major issues in teacher evaluation that relate primarily to the use of evaluations for teacher selection and employment:

1. Use of unvalidated evaluation systems
2. Insufficient use of professional standards for planning and improving evaluation systems
3. Ineffectual choices of clear, valid, applicable criteria for assessing performance of educators and schools
4. Need for techniques and materials to carry out the generic steps for evaluation
5. Lack of evaluation training
6. Failure to consider context in evaluations of personnel and schools
7. Lack of guidelines for evaluating personnel providing service to special populations
8. Inadequate theoretical basis for personnel and school evaluation

Many of these issues take on a different character in different evaluation settings. For example, school districts are often criticized for failing to carry out validation and cut-score studies, while states are likely to be taken to task for more technical issues such as how their validation and cut-score studies are carried out. Although the importance of validation for legal and professional reasons is taken for granted in most professional and technical settings (Linn et al., 1989; Madaus, 1987; *United States v. South Carolina*, 1977), for the most part evaluation systems used by school districts or recommended in the literature to evaluate the in-school performance of teachers and administrators have not been rigorously studied or validated (Burry, Chissom, & Shaw, 1990; French, Holdzkom, & Kuligowski, 1990; Scriven, 1987; Streifer & Iwanicki, 1987).

Some of the criticisms of teacher evaluations clearly can be tied to lack of appropriate resources, such as lack of training for assessors, lack of appropriate instruments, and lack of information from validation studies. Other criticisms are tied more closely to the current state of the art of teacher evaluation. For example, many critics of performance-based teacher evaluations have pointed to the failure of most systems to take the classroom context into account as part of the assessment (Darling-Hammond, Wise, & Pease, 1983; Evertson & Green, 1986; Shulman, 1989, 1988; Stodolsky, 1988; Stufflebeam et al., 1990). While recognizing the importance of the content being taught and the characteristics of the students, very few evaluation systems have been able to devise credible means of taking these factors into account as part of the assessment (but see Dwyer, 1993b, 1993c; Dwyer & Villegas, 1993; Webster, Mendro, & Almaguer, 1993). Similarly, lack of theoretical grounding is clearly a problem for many teacher evaluation systems (Scriven, 1988a, 1988b; Wise, Darling-Hammond, McLaughlin, & Bernstein, 1984b), but the field of research on teaching offers little guidance even on how to approach this problem, much less specific advice on how school districts and states can use theory to devise better teacher assessments.

## PROFESSIONAL STANDARDS FOR EDUCATIONAL PERSONNEL EVALUATIONS

As one means of addressing the deficiencies in teacher evaluation, researchers and practitioners need to invoke principles of sound professional practice of evaluation. This is crucial to help protect students, educators, and other constituents from harmful, corrupt, or incompetent evaluations and to ensure that evaluation improvement efforts are not misdirected. Educators need standards to design sound evaluation systems and to demonstrate the worth and merit of evaluation services (Herbert & McNergney, 1989). Evaluation funders and clients need standards to assess evaluation plans and reports and sometimes to avoid expensive litigation. The courts need standards to help settle legal disputes over evaluation (Rebell, 1988, 1989, 1990). For example, as this chapter was being completed there was a flurry of court cases in Michigan concerning demands by community members and parents that school districts publicly release records of past evaluations given to teachers. As one of us said in depositions for three of the cases, release of such records to persons not previously authorized to receive them and for uses other than those previously defined would violate the Personnel Evaluation Standards (Joint Committee on Standards for Educational Evaluation 1988), particularly the Access to Evaluation Information standard. Evaluators need standards to examine and improve their evaluation systems (American Educational Research Association, American Psychological Association, & National Council on Measurement in Education, 1985; Joint Committee, 1988).

As one response to the severe criticisms of teacher evaluation that were being heard in the early 1980s, and the need for professional standards to help upgrade and control the quality of educator evaluations, the Joint Committee on Standards for Educational Evaluation (1988) launched the project to develop standards for educational personnel evaluation, with the focal objective of improving teacher evaluation. The Joint Committee was formed in 1975 by the American Educational Research Association, the American Psychological Association, and the National Council on Measurement in Education for the purpose of developing the Standards for Evaluations of Educational Programs, Projects, and Materials (Joint Committee, 1981). The committee now includes representatives of those groups and 12 additional professional associations.

In 1989, the Joint Committee became the first educational group to be accredited by the American National Standards Institute. This is the major U.S. group that promotes voluntary standards for public services and consumer products; it accredits standard-setting bodies and specific standards and cooperates extensively with the U.S. Bureau of Standards. Although educational agencies have used the program and the Personnel Evaluation Standards to assess and improve their evaluation systems (see, e.g., Herbert & McNergney, 1989; Reineke, Willeke, Walsh, & Sawin, 1988), much greater dissemination and use are needed. These standards have been validated and must also be periodically reviewed and updated (Linn et al., 1989). Educational psychologists are encouraged to conduct research related to the standards, and also to help with their dissemination. For example, they might examine certain teacher evaluation policies and practices and compare them with the standards to identify priorities for development of new evaluation techniques and to help policymakers examine and strengthen both school district and state systems of teacher evaluation. Also the standards are appropriate for coverage in assessment and evaluation courses.

## LEGAL DEVELOPMENTS AND OTHER PRESSURES FOR CHANGE IN TEACHER EVALUATION

### General Background

An in-depth review of all of the legal aspects of teacher evaluation is well beyond the scope of this chapter. The interested reader may wish to review summaries by the Educational Testing Service (1988), Hood and Parker (1991), McDonough and Wolfe (1988), Rebell (1986, 1988, 1990), and Strike and Bull (1981) for more complete analyses and references. Fischer, Schimmel, and Kelly (1991) also address these issues in a format addressed directly to the teacher. This section focuses on general themes and highlights related to legal issues in teacher evaluation.

Trends in the law and in the education, psychology, and measurement professions have converged in ways that have shaped the practice of teacher evaluation in all segments of the educational system, but have been particularly dramatic in the area of teacher licensing.

During the 1980s, in the midst of the climate of educational reform, there was a greatly increased interest in the individual's right to exert control over all forms of assessment at all levels (local, state, and national). For example, one teachers' union brought litigation specifically designed to obtain more valid evaluation criteria and evaluation forms (*Saydel Education Association v. Perb*, 1983). Not surprisingly, teachers' interest in controlling teacher evaluation, combined with the interest in educational reform, spawned a number of legal developments in teacher evaluation. The relationship between the courts and teacher evaluation practice is important for several reasons. As Rebell (1990) has noted, the impact of legislation and lawsuits on teacher evaluation practice is potentially great: "Because the state of the art concerning teacher evaluation practices is at a sensitive developmental stage, extensive court intervention at this point can substantially influence—for better or worse—the future direction of basic practice in the field" (p. 339).

Social factors that have contributed to the increased interest in the legal defensibility of teacher evaluations include a heightened awareness of consumer or individual interests vis-à-vis "establishment" or institutional interests, and a concomitant skepticism on the part of the general public about the actions and intentions of institutions that were previously impervious to criticism or pressures for change. The concept of individuals' rights in evaluation situations in general (including teacher evaluations) became much more highly developed during the 1980s. During this period there was also continued interest in supporting the rights of women and minorities. In teacher evaluation, this interest was expressed in the form of challenges to the fairness and due process rights of teacher evaluations. It is also widely reported that there was a nationwide increase in the litigiousness of American society during this period. Rebell (1988) noted that "It has become virtually a truism in contemporary America that disgruntled individuals and, in fact, society at large bring their grievances and their public policy disputes to the courthouse door" (p. 59). Within the legal system itself, Rebell (1990) noted that the increase in significant judicial attention to issues of teacher testing was related to a broadened notion of jurisdiction, especially of the federal courts, to consider social reform issues such as testing, and to judges' increasing experience with technical issues encountered in areas such as job discrimination and school desegregation that provide insights into teacher evaluation cases (pp. 338–339).

Education, psychology, and the measurement professions also participated in these changes in attitudes and practice pertaining to evaluation. These professions may, in part, have been responding to the social and legal pressures about evaluation issues, but they were also responding to separate and consistent trends within their own professions. The American Psychological Association's Division of Industrial and Organizational Psychology published the second edition of *Principles for the Validation and Use of Personnel Selection Procedures* in 1980. This set of principles provides standards that were applied to teacher evaluations during the 1980s, but the principles themselves are clearly conceptual extensions of the preceding edition. As another example of the intersection of larger professional trends with legal and social trends related to teacher evaluation, the American Educational Research Association, the American Psychological Association, and the National Council on Measurement in Education published the fourth edition of their *Standards for Educational and Psychological Testing* in 1985. This edition of the *Standards* signaled some important changes in professional opinions that have had a large impact on legal and professional issues related to teacher evaluation. These changes were not short-term responses to public and professional criticism, however; they stemmed from technical debates with a long history in the fields of education, measurement, and psychology. For example, these *Standards* gave increased attention to the consequences of measurement, both for individuals and for the educational systems in which they are situated. This emphasis has already had a significant effect on evaluation practices of states and localities, for it clearly defines such concerns as adverse impact on minority groups and influences of testing on curricula as legitimate validation concerns. This emphasis on consequences signals the effective culmination of a long psychometric debate about the nature of validity. These *Standards* also conveyed some important changes in professional and technical views of how assessments should be evaluated, and they clearly differentiated between assessment for licensing and assessment for selection.

## Specific Legal Issues Related to Teacher Evaluation

The threat as much as the actual occurrence of lawsuits has strongly influenced the development of teacher evaluation instruments and how they are used. As is the case in the practice of medicine, many in teacher evaluation today are practicing defensive evaluation. Although research on this point is rare, anecdotal information abounds, and inspection of the practices of states in teacher licensing evaluation reveals a consistently high level of concern for the legal defensibility of their instruments. For example, the Educational Testing Service has developed guidelines that are intended to ensure, among other things, the legal defensibility of their Praxis Series teacher and licensing assessments (Educational Testing Service, 1988, 1992). In general, developers and users of teacher evaluations take great care to defend themselves against such charges as violations of constitutional rights, bias, and lack of due process.

In keeping with the conceptual framework of this chapter, court cases related to teacher evaluation can be divided into four categories by type of teacher evaluation: cases related to (a) preparing teachers, (b) licensing teachers, (c) selecting and monitoring teachers, and (d) fostering and certifying the professionalization of teachers. One also can further subdivide these categories into state and federal legal cases and trends.

*Teacher Education.* During the 1980s there was a strong trend toward states' involvement in setting entrance requirements for teacher education programs, and a corresponding increase in legal actions on the part of those who did not meet these requirements. Rudner (1988) reported that 27 states required testing for admission to teacher education programs. Prospective teachers who were members of minority groups were heavily affected by these requirements, and the role of possible test bias was a central issue in their legal complaints.

*Licensing.* McDonough and Wolfe (1988) have provided an excellent background and summary of early decisions related to teacher assessment for the licensing of teachers. Licensing is the area of teacher assessment that has seen the most intensive federal involvement. McDonough and Wolfe relate this involvement to federal judiciary involvement in civil rights issues and other broad social concerns, particularly those that relate to the rights of minority groups. A case argued in the U.S. Supreme Court (*United States v. South Carolina,* 1978) has been extremely influential in teacher evaluation validation practices and is cited in nearly every technical discussion of the validity of teacher assessments. This case established firmly that, with acceptable content validation procedures, assessment for teacher licensing would be supported.

*Selecting and Monitoring.* As is the case with court actions related to assessment for teacher licensing, assessment for selecting and monitoring teachers has been judged primarily on the basis of whether a rational process has been carefully followed, rather than on the content of the assessments or other professional and technical grounds. This has tended to be the case even when the substance of the assessment has been highly controversial among education and measurement professionals. In the case of *Scheelhaase v. Woodbury Central Community School District,* teacher evaluation was carried out using student standardized achievement test scores as the primary criterion for judging teacher competence. This practice, although widely criticized in the professional literature, was upheld by the courts based on the regularity of the process that was used to carry out the evaluation.

Usually, the substance of the assessment is easily agreed upon in principle but more difficult to operationalize in specific cases. Bridges (1986) notes that schools currently tend to evaluate teachers on five major criteria—knowledge of subject matter, ability to impart knowledge, ability to maintain classroom discipline, ability to maintain a suitable classroom climate, ability to establish rapport with parents and students—but that school supervisory staff lack specific guidance in defining these criteria, and that teachers are vague about what is expected of them. According to Bridges, although most states have laws permitting schools to fire teachers for incompetence, only Alaska and Tennessee have attempted to define the term, and even those two states provide no specific criteria. Bridges also cites a 1979 judgment of the Michigan Court of Appeals that supported school boards' right to dismiss teachers for lacking: knowledge of the subject, ability to impart it, ability to discipline students, rapport with parents and other teachers, or the physical and mental ability to withstand the strain of teaching.

Such determinations of competence are usually made on the basis of principals' observations, although complaints from parents and other teachers and student test results are also frequently used as evidence. It is much more rare that passing a standardized test is proposed as one of the criteria for continued employment, but this has been done in Arkansas, Georgia, and Texas. In Arkansas and Texas, experienced teachers were faced with the prospect of passing tests of subject and pedagogical knowledge or being denied renewal of their teaching licenses.

The Educational Testing Service withdrew permission for Arkansas's use of the NTE for this purpose, saying that it did not constitute proper use of the NTE. (Texas and Georgia use custom-made tests for recertification decisions.)

*Professional Development.* Some interesting cases have been brought against states for their teacher evaluation practices. During the 1980s suits were brought against Alabama for its teacher licensing practices and against Texas for its practices concerning induction into teacher training and the evaluation of experienced teachers (Shepard & Kreitzer, 1987). In both states there was significant concern about minority teachers' performance and the possibility of test bias. More recently, the states of Arkansas and Georgia have been the targets of suits related to their teacher observation systems. In Georgia, which used the Teacher Proficiency Assessment Instrument, the plaintiff challenged the validity of the evaluation criteria, charging that they were excessively subjective. The case was settled on other grounds, without a judgment being made as to the validity of this claim.

It is difficult to make an absolute differentiation between the threat of litigation and changes in public values, expectations, and mores. More Americans, particularly educators, are now sensitive to discrimination issues and feel that the burden of proof in discrimination disputes should be on institutions rather than on individuals. Institutions should show that they have given due and careful consideration to the rights of individuals.

Rebell (1990) also has noted that both state and federal courts have tended strongly to emphasize principles of objectivity and procedural regularity in their decisions, especially in areas where there is significant potential for practices the courts might view as subjective or biased. This presents a significant challenge for the assessment of teaching, where the activity is inherently complex and objectivity is both an elusive concept and a dubious goal. With few exceptions, courts have also tended not to probe the substance of the evaluative criteria or methods used to assess inservice teachers. The courts' decisions consistently emphasize good record keeping and the appearance of objectivity, rather than substantive matters such as technical or scientific standards of validity. In recent years there has been increased delving into technical matters by the courts, but such explorations still have not been the basis of decisions or settlements. In the 1985 case of *Allen v. The State of Alabama,* for example, many expert witnesses were marshalled to debate the smallest details of Alabama's test development process and other highly technical issues. Significantly, however, this information was part of an attempt to determine whether appropriate professional standards had been adhered to and was not used directly to debate the quality of those standards themselves. The case was eventually settled out of court, and the terms of the settlement stipulated that the state would construct a new test according to a predetermined set of statistical rules designed to minimize score differences between black and white test takers.

Rebell (1990) has also expressed concern that court involvement, or simply the fear of it, may actually already have resulted in states lowering their standards for teacher licensing in order to forestall complaints from prospective teachers that they have been treated unfairly. Popham and Kirby (1987), Millman

(1989), and Mehrens (1991) have expressed concern that this stance inevitably works to the detriment of students.

## IMPORTANT RECENT DEVELOPMENTS IN TEACHER EVALUATION

Current topics of research relating to teacher performance assessment instrumentation deal with content-specific assessment (Shulman, 1987b), context of the classroom observation (Evertson & Burry, 1989, Evertson & Green, 1986), and multiple perspectives (Burry & Shaw, 1988; Green & Harker, 1987). Other salient issues include a new generation of tests for licensing beginning teachers (Dwyer, 1989, 1993b, 1993c; Dwyer & Villegas,1993), national certification for the teaching profession (Kelly, 1989), differences in teachers' professional development (Joyce & McKibbin, 1982), multiple measures of teacher performance assessment (Burry, 1990), movement from one developmental growth stage to another (Sprinthall & Thies-Sprinthall, 1983), and teaching in a developmental sequence of skill building (Berliner, 1989). These topics provide substantive direction for the development of teacher evaluation instruments.

Emerging innovative evaluation models employing "authentic assessment" or applied performance examinations, in situ examination of teachers' performances in professional development or "teaching schools" (Holmes Group, 1990), simulations, duties-based evaluation (Scriven, 1990), and video portfolios (Kelly, 1989) have not yet been tested sufficiently as to purpose, cost, ease of use, validity, and long-range significance (Bird, 1990; Haertel, 1986, 1990; Hambleton, 1990; Holmes Group, 1990). For example, it would be useful to assess the evaluation development projects of the National Board for Professional Teaching Standards (1990; Kelly, 1989, the Educational Testing Service's new Praxis Series: Professional Assessments for Beginning Teachers, and Michael Scriven's duties-based teacher evaluation model (1988a, 1988b) against the requirements of the Joint Committee's 1988 Personnel Evaluation Standards. Each of these projects has a different purpose directed toward the evaluation of teachers at different stages of professional development.

### The National Board for Professional Teaching Standards for Conferring National Certification on Outstanding Teachers

The National Board for Professional Teaching Standards (NBPTS) was established in 1987 to create a system for certifying experienced teachers. "Certification" refers to a means of bestowing distinction on those teachers who meet high and rigorous standards. This voluntary process is controlled by the profession. The first assessments became operational in 1995. The NBPTS has devoted a great deal of effort to defining standards for teachers of specific grade levels or disciplines and to attempting to secure a broad consensus on these standards. The NBPTS also has done pioneering research in a number of areas related to the use of simulations for teacher assessment, including videotaped performances, the use of portfolios, and assessment center exercises of varying types. The NBPTS has recently turned its attention to the inclusion of development of materials to assist experienced teachers in skill development.

## The Praxis Series

A second major effort, conducted by the Educational Testing Service, is the development of a replacement for the NTE. The Praxis Series: Professional Assessments for Beginning Teachers is a three-stage set of licensure examinations for beginning teachers. The first stage is computerized assessment of basic academic skills of reading, writing, and mathematics, the second stage is paper-and-pencil assessment of subject matter knowledge and pedagogical principles, and the third stage is assessment of teaching performance through observation and interviews. This process regulates entry into practice for beginning teachers, is controlled by each state, and is usually mandatory for state licensure in states that have adopted it. Similar to the efforts of the NBPTS, described above, developers of the Praxis Series have devoted considerable effort to research such as defining and operationalizing criteria for good teaching; seeking national consensus on assessment goals, content, and methodology; use of technology; and equity-oriented topics such as the infusion of culturally responsive pedagogy into the classroom performance assessments.

## NEEDS FOR RESEARCH AND DEVELOPMENT TO ADVANCE THE PRACTICE OF TEACHER EVALUATION

School districts and state education departments have struggled to clarify, choose, and apply appropriate performance criteria, and it is widely acknowledged that there is no consensus on what criteria should be used to evaluate the performance of educators (French et al., 1990; Johnson, 1980; Osborne & Wiggins, 1989; Travers, 1981; Wise et al.,1984a, 1984b). Many critics observe that the "law of the instrument" (Kaplan, 1963) prevails; that is, the criteria of effective job performance are merely those of some conveniently available measurement instrument.

Also, there is the problem of the work environment, which can significantly influence how well an educator or school performs (Darling-Hammond et al., 1983; Evertson & Burry, 1989; Evertson & Green, 1986; McKenna, 1973, 1981; Shulman, 1988; Shulman, Bird, & Haertel, 1988).Work environment conditions include community resources and support of schools; state standards, mandates, and support programs; court and union involvement in education; school district philosophy, priorities, climate, calendar, schedule, and resources; student characteristics; competence of the evaluators, administrators, and teachers; and the prescribed curriculum. Classroom factors include number of students, student ability levels, proportion of at-risk students, supervision, administrative support, parent involvement, and equipment and materials (J. Brophy & Evertson, 1978).

Still another issue is that the evaluation of teachers is inescapably prone to political influences that can corrupt or impede evaluations (Chance, 1987; Darling-Hammond & Berry, 1988).

The "get accountable quickly" approaches mandated and instituted by several states and school districts have often proved to be illogical, legally vulnerable, costly, and counterproductive, as shown by several court cases (e.g., *St. Louis Teachers Union v. Board of Education,* 1987; *Georgia Association of Educators v. Nix,* 1976; *Texas State Teachers Association v. State of Texas,* 1986; *Walston v. County School Board of Nansemond County,* 1973).

Adding to the complexity of the issues in teacher evaluation are the problems associated with evaluating the performance of teachers who work with special populations of students. These include handicapped, at-risk, vocational education, limited-English-proficient, and underserved students. There is a need for focused research and development concerned with performance evaluations for teachers who work with such groups.

Another issue requiring work concerns evaluation theory. Teacher evaluation has been largely atheoretical, apart from some pioneering work (Berliner, 1989; Brookover, 1979; Schmitt & Doherty, 1988; Scriven, 1988b). Ongoing theory development could benefit the practice of teacher evaluation by helping practitioners to think more holistically and analytically about the role of teacher evaluation in education, by providing educators with pragmatic leads to improving evaluation practices, and by providing researchers with questions and hypotheses for rigorous examination. It seems clear that teacher evaluation could be greatly improved were practice to become grounded in ongoing theory development.

## RESPONSES TO PRESSURE FOR REFORM

### State-Level Responses

The response of state teacher licensing organizations to pressures for educational reform was swift and dramatic. In 1993, 34 states used some part of the NTE for teacher licensing or initial certification, and during the 1980s a number of other states chose to develop their own teacher assessments. By contrast, only 7 states used NTE services at the beginning of the 1980s. Lehman and Phillips (1987) and Rudner (1988) have provided good overview updates on states' testing practices for the licensing of beginning teachers that illustrate their rapid expansion. With respect to performance assessment for the licensing of beginning teachers, the Educational Testing Service (1991) gathered detailed information on performance assessment practices of the states. The National Association of State Directors of Teacher Education and Certification (NASDTEC). NASDTEC also publishes a detailed annual state-by-state *Manual on Certification and Preparation of Education Personnel in the United States* (1991).

In the early years of evaluation for teacher licensing, activity was largely restricted to the Southeast. As mentioned earlier, a lawsuit against the state of South Carolina's teacher evaluation practices was taken to the United States Supreme Court in 1974 (*United States v. South Carolina,* 1978). At that time the issues raised in that case were largely perceived by others as a regional concern, linked to racial struggles in the Southeast. In recent years, however, these issues have come to be seen as a national concern.

In response to the educational reform pressures of the 1980s, and with the backing of the courts through the South Carolina case, states moved quickly and virtually unanimously to formal external evaluation of teachers for licensing purposes. The states did not, however, all move in the same direction, owing to differences in philosophy, funding, and a host of practical factors such as a state's size and population dispersion.

Most of these state efforts focused on the control of teacher qualifications before full or permanent licensing. Today, no states allow teachers to obtain full or permanent licensing status without first having gone through a period of provisional licensing. Although the duration of the provisional licenses and the structures of the subsequent licenses vary greatly from state to state, the process always consists of at least a two-step licensing procedure.

Note that the use of the terms "licensing" and "certification" has been somewhat confusing. In this chapter we use "licensing" in the sense defined by Shimberg (1985) and the *Standards for Educational and Psychological Testing* (American Educational Research Association, American Psychological Association, National Council for Measurement in Education, 1985) to mean a process controlled by state governments in order to protect the public from potential harm that could be caused by incompetent practitioners. Thus, in teacher evaluation, "licensing" refers to state activities directed at enabling teachers to practice within that state, but unrelated to their ability to obtain employment in the state. We use the word "licensure" in contrast to "certification," which we reserve for use in situations related to processes usually controlled by professional groups for the purposes of authenticating or documenting the accomplishments of members of that profession. Licensure is characteristically a mandatory process; certification is characteristically a voluntary process.

Even before the point of teacher licensing, however, a number of states now use paper-and-pencil testing as part of their requirements for entry to teacher education. Although the concept of ability to benefit from teacher education is occasionally invoked, testing for entry into teacher education is done primarily on the premise that the state expects beginning teachers to have certain literacy and numeracy skills when they begin to teach, but that the acquisition of these skills is not properly part of the mission of teacher education. Therefore, states require that prospective teacher education students demonstrate an appropriate level of these skills before entry into teacher education. Such entry requirements are very common (Rudner, 1988). Reading, writing, and mathematics are the skills most frequently tested. The Educational Testing Service offers the Pre-Professional Skills Test, which is currently used by 12 states for entry into teacher education. In other cases, such as California's CBEST tests, states have developed their own assessments for the same purpose. According to Rudner (1988), three states use college admissions tests (the SAT or the ACT) for this purpose.

Formal evaluations are used as part of the licensing of beginning teachers in addition to experience requirements and educational program requirements. During the 1980s, most states added such requirements for formal assessment. As is usual in bureaucracies of any size, new requirements were generally added to the existing requirements rather than substituted for them. These requirements took many forms. Increasingly, it is understood by states and others that paper-and-pencil testing and performance testing are complementary, not competing, models. Some states, such as Alabama, New York, and Pennsylvania, have developed their own paper-and-pencil knowledge tests for licensing purposes. Many others use the national knowledge and skill tests offered by ETS.

Seventeen states have developed classroom performance assessment tests as part of the teacher induction and licensing process. These performance assessments generally consist of classroom observations by administrators or others. There are two distinct generations of these classroom performance assessments, the first built on the basis of the process–product research (see Wittrock, 1986, for comprehensive summaries), and the second with a more cognitive orientation added. At present, the second generation of state classroom performance assessment tests consist primarily of those developed by Connecticut and Louisiana. The Educational Testing Service has developed also nationally available classroom performance assessment tests for the Praxis Series that have a heavily cognitive orientation.

Far fewer states have used teacher evaluations for decision-making about permanently licensed teachers. Those that have done so have generally sought one of two goals: removal of incompetent teachers, or the establishment of career ladder programs that provide monetary and other incentives for increasing knowledge and skills or for producing documented increments in student learning. Shepard and Kreitzer (1987) provide an interesting analysis of the procedures and consequences of this form of teacher testing in Texas, documenting a widespread and largely negative impact on the educational system as a whole.

State teacher assessment programs are frequently linked, at least conceptually, to other induction or staff development activities such as mentoring programs. Unfortunately, however, there is seldom any formal connection between the testing requirement set by the states and the induction programs that they have concurrently set in place.

## Responses of the Education Profession

Teachers, through their professional organizations, have also been active participants in response to the calls for educational reform. Both the American Federation of Teachers and the National Education Association initiated projects responsive to the reform themes, and were active participants in the planning of many of the reform efforts. In-service education for both novice and experienced teachers is a strong theme in teacher organization efforts.

Within the world of research and assessment development, the standards development activities referred to earlier formed part of the climate of educational reform. Parallel theoretical concerns in the measurement world, such as changes in the dominant research paradigm from behavioristic to cognitive, had earlier roots (see, for example, Berliner [1990], who traces the current research trends in teacher education to the early part of this century) but were influential in enabling change in teacher evaluation (Dwyer, 1991, 1993b). The funding by the U.S. Department of Education of the National Center for Research on Educational Accountability and Teacher Evaluation, the development of the Praxis Series by the Educational Testing

Service, the development in Tennessee and in Dallas, Texas, of sophisticated systems for evaluating teacher effectiveness based on analysis of student characteristics and gains in achievement measures, and the work of the NBPTS are other examples of research-based activity responding to themes in the reform literature.

The development of new forms of assessment such as "authentic" assessment, the use of student and teacher portfolios, and the more widespread use of constructed-response questions have been part of the response of the measurement and education professions to the calls for reform. Some often cited projects include Arts Propel, the portfolio-based assessments carried out in the Pittsburgh public schools; the Teacher Assessment Project at Stanford University, initiated by Lee Shulman; and the College Board's Advanced Placement tests. There has, of course, been a long history of non-multiple-choice educational measurement, particularly in writing and the arts, but these forms of measurement are now often characterized as "new."

There have been important changes also in educational research orientations, priorities, and activities that are related to teacher evaluation issues. These include heightened attention to defining the nature of teaching and the characteristics of teachers (Kagan, 1990; Shavelson, Webb, & Burstein, 1986; Shulman, 1986).

With respect to more technical issues related to teacher evaluation, Popham (1991) has provided a good interpretive summary of content validation efforts for teacher licensure tests. A great deal of methodological criticism has been directed toward such validation efforts and toward the related issue of standard setting (see, e.g., Haney et al., 1987, for critiques of current practice). It is probably fair to say that currently there does not exist a professional consensus on a single model of validation for teacher assessments.

Educational research has increasingly turned its attention to the relationship between teacher evaluation and other parts of the educational process. This research is primarily policy oriented and includes such topics as the impact of teacher evaluation on teacher education and teacher supply issues, particularly for teachers of mathematics and science and for minority teachers. Interestingly, there has been relatively little attention to the impact of teacher evaluations on students, their achievements, or their rights (see Millman, 1989; Mehrens, 1991; and Popham & Kirby, 1987, for discussions of this point of view).

A related topic, and one that is relatively unexamined, is the question of the actual rate of incompetence among teachers. The public perception is that teacher incompetence is a significant problem in public education today, and this is one of the primary motivations for states' instituting teacher assessment programs. Mehrens (1991) and others accept that widespread teacher incompetence is a problem, but Haney and colleagues (1987) disagree with this view and emphasize the need to protect the employment rights of these presumably competent teachers. Bridges (1986) makes the point that even if the percentage of incompetent teachers is small, the number of students affected is large and will tend to consist disproportionately of students of low socioeconomic status.

Another kind of response to pressures for educational reform has come in part from teachers themselves, and in part from the educational and research and development world through the creation of the National Board for Professional Teaching Standards. This organization, created in 1988, is dedicated to articulating the standards that should prevail for experienced teachers and to designing a voluntary system of certification of these experienced teachers by other teaching professionals. The NBPTS has devoted considerable time and resources to clarifying the meaning of professional standards for teachers, both for the profession as a whole and within specific educational disciplines. The assessment development efforts are still very much in their infancy, so little can be said of their final shape, except to note that the NBPTS is strongly committed to performance assessments and emphasizes the need for assessments to have a positive impact on education, or "systemic validity."

## Responses in the Form of Different Teacher Performance Evaluation Rationales and Associated Models

A range of rationales and associated models and general approaches for teacher performance evaluation are evident both in the evaluation literature and actual evaluation practice. Table 23–2 lists and classifies 32 evaluation models and general approaches according to six different rationales: improvement of classroom teaching, professional accountability and development, administrative supervision, research-based indicators, consumer protection and community responsiveness, and merit pay.

***Models Oriented to Instructional Improvement.*** Evaluations oriented toward improving classroom teaching tend to see teaching as a profession with a theory base and emphasize regular constructive observation of teaching practice as an aid to improvement. Such evaluations assume a continuum from novice to accomplished teacher, plus basic principles of sound teaching that can be taught, learned, and assessed. Trained evaluators observe and record whether teachers are effectively employing the desired teaching methods and provide them with feedback for improving teaching skills and performance. Regular staff development is stressed. Some of the evaluation models in this category are mainly formative, as advocated by Hunter (1988a, 1988b), and some are also summative (Manatt, 1988; Manatt & Stowe, 1984). Other models in this group have been presented by Duke and Stiggins (1990), Flanders (1970), Iwanicki (1981), McGreal (1983), and Shulman (1986).

***Models Oriented to Professional Accountability.*** Evaluations oriented to professional accountability engage teachers to strive continually to improve their service to students and to police their own ranks. This orientation views teaching as a profession that requires teachers and their professional associations to engage in self-referent evaluation. Teachers are expected to compile evidence of the extent and quality of their service, to present it to education authorities, and to use the evaluation to improve their competence and performance. Thus, the emphasis is on both accountability and improvement. For example, in the Toledo public schools, tenured teachers apply peer evaluation to assess the performance of probationary teachers (Wise et al., 1984a, 1984b). Based on this peer assessment, they recom-

TABLE 23–2. Rationales and Models for Teacher Performance Evaluations

| Aspects of Rationales | Rationales | | | | | |
|---|---|---|---|---|---|---|
| | Improvement of Classroom Teaching | Professional Accountability and Development | Administrative Control | Research-Based Indicators for Improving Student Outcomes | Consumer Protection and Public Responsiveness | Merit Pay |
| Description of the rationale | Views teaching as a craft or profession with a theory base. The practice continuum ranges from novice to expert. Trained observers provide teachers with feedback for improving teaching skills and performance. Regular staff development is stressed. Evaluations are mainly formative, but sometimes summative. | Views teaching as a profession that requires teachers to present evidence of the extent and quality of their service and to engage in ongoing self-assessment for improvement. The teachers or their professional societies compile relevant evidence and present it to education authorities. The emphasis is on both accountability and improvement. Under this rationale, teachers police their own ranks and strive continually to improve their service to students. | Views teaching as a job in a bureaucracy that must be regularly supervised and monitored. Principals assess teacher performance to assure that annual accountabilities are fulfilled. Evaluations often are based on classroom visits and informal observations. The emphasis is on ensuring that the teacher is not negligent. Evaluations subscribing to the rationale can provide a legally viable basis for terminating poor teachers. | Views teaching as a set of independent variables that impact on student achievement. Evaluations are focused on promoting and assessing those teaching behaviors that research shows to correlate positively with student achievement. Tends to identify and emphasize style variables over job responsibilities. Teaching correlates of student learning are often assessed by means of low-inference observations. | Views teaching as a vital public service and advocates effective teaching plus protection of students' welfare. Requires independent evaluations. Focuses on student achievement and teaching responsibility. Emphasizes employability and college readiness. Obtains feedback from students and parents and expects teachers to maintain evidence of effective execution of teaching responsibilities. Emphasizes the importance of setting high standards for teacher performance. | Views teachers as needing recognition and rewards. Posits that pay for performance will beget better teaching. Assessments are based on student achievement and supervisors' judgments. Teacher may be required to provide a portfolio of evidence on performance and achievement. Some writers advocate merit schools instead of merit teachers as a means of reducing unproductive competition. |
| Main proponents | Instructional leaders and curriculum and instruction specialists | Teachers and their professional societies | School administrators | University-based educational researchers | The public, business, higher education; a basic rationale for teacher licensing | The public, and state and local officials who must maintain credibility with the public |
| Models and general approaches used to implement the rationale | Hunter's ITIP model<br>Manatt's "clinical supervision" model<br>Iwanicki's professional growth-oriented model<br>McGreal's professional development approach<br>Flanders' classroom interaction model<br>EPIC model with videotape feedback<br>Assessment centers<br>Microteaching<br>Deming's team problem solving | Good's teacher self-evaluation approach<br>Higher education-type portfolio evaluations<br>Toledo, Ohio, Peer Evaluation model<br>Résumé updates and reviews<br>Professional specialty boards, e.g., National Board for Professional Teaching Standards | Andrews' comprehensive administrative summative evaluation<br>Job description-based performance review by principal/supervisor<br>Unstructured classroom visits by principal<br>Interview/discussion by principal/supervisor or evaluation team<br>Redfern's management by objectives | Medley, Coker, and Soar: measurement-based teacher performance evaluations<br>Georgia teacher evaluation system<br>(Many state systems are derivatives of the above two approaches) | Scriven's duties-based evaluation<br>Student ratings of instruction<br>Student test scores/work products<br>Inspector visits<br>Team visits managed by school, school district, or other authority<br>Survey of parents and/or students<br>Praxis Series: Professional Assessments for Beginning Teachers (ETS) | Career ladder<br>Merit increments only, added to base<br>Merit increment added to annual regular increment<br>Merit 1-year bonus<br>Merit schools |

mend tenure for those teachers who are performing effectively. The work of the NBPTS also illustrates the teacher accountability orientation.

***Models Oriented to Administrative Supervision.*** Teacher performance evaluators who follow the administrative control orientation view teaching as a job within a bureaucracy that must be regularly monitored and supervised. Principals assess teacher performance to ensure that annual accountabilities are fulfilled. Evaluations often are based on classroom visits and informal observations. Their evaluations are intended to provide regular checks to ensure that teachers are not grossly neglecting their responsibilities. The evaluators might use a standard form or define more specific criteria for individual teachers. In general, they observe teaching performance, possibly in a very structured, systematic manner but usually informally, then report and discuss the observation results in teacher–principal conferences. Optimally, administratively oriented evaluations give skillful principals opportunities to help teachers strengthen their performance. Such evaluations may be used also to recommend and provide legally defensible evidence for terminating ineffective teachers. The administrative orientation to teacher performance evaluation has been discussed by Andrews (1985), Dunkin and Biddle (1974), Good and Mulryan (1990), and Redfern (1963, 1980).

***Evaluations Designed to Implement the Findings of Process-Product Research.*** Evaluations that subscribe to indicators based on correlational research promote and assess those teaching behaviors that research shows to correlate positively with student achievement. Teaching is viewed as a set of independent variables that affect student achievement. The rationale for this approach is that teaching behaviors that cause improved student learning would show positive correlations with measures of student achievement. Moreover, by identifying and promoting the high correlates of student achievement measures, schools can direct teachers to perform teaching behaviors that, on the average, should pay off in higher student tests scores and other indicators of school achievement. Evaluations following this rationale tend to emphasize teaching style behaviors, such as enthusiasm and inquiry method. Teaching correlates of student achievement measures are often assessed by means of low-inference indicators. Early research in search of effective teaching behaviors by Barr (1950) and Ryans (1960) found somewhat disappointing results. The Coleman report (Coleman et al., 1966) and reanalysis (Jencks et al., 1972) prepared the way for the process–product studies of the 1970s and 1980s (see, e.g., Medley, Coker, & Soar, 1984). These studies then laid the foundation for many large-scale evaluation development endeavors, including the Texas teacher effectiveness project, the Texas teacher effectiveness study, and the California beginning teacher evaluation study (McDonald, 1976; McDonald & Elias, 1976). Numerous statewide and district evaluation assessment procedures and instruments have emerged from these studies and developmental projects.

There is division in the education profession over the value of the research-based indicators approach. Scriven (1988a, 1988b) argued that variables for assessing a teacher's performance should never be selected for the reason that in past research they correlated positively with students' test scores.

He sees this rationale for choosing personnel evaluation variables as illicit on grounds of both invalidity and unfairness. He emphasizes that variables chosen for such reasons especially should not be used as the basis for personnel decisions, lest one be guided to choose or terminate teachers based on such possible high correlates with student achievement as race, gender, or certain teaching style variables.

***Evaluations Designed to Protect Student Interests.*** Evaluations focused on protecting student interests view teaching as a vital public service. They place highest priority on delivering effective teaching to students and on protecting their welfare. This rationale requires independent perspectives. For example, teacher evaluations are overseen by school boards and state education departments. The criteria of effective teaching include teacher responsibilities, school goals, student achievement, and vital societal interests. Especially, teachers are expected to help all students master basic skills, become well qualified for the next level of education, meet the school's achievement goals, become employable, and become competitive in the world economy. Data for assessing teacher effectiveness include feedback from students and parents, student achievement results, and assessment by a supervisor of the teacher's fulfillment of teaching responsibilities. There is an emphasis on setting high standards for teacher performance, and teachers are expected to maintain evidence of effective execution of teaching responsibilities. Scriven (1987, 1988a, 1988b), Sanders and McLean (1984), and Webster et al. (1993) have proposed methods for implementing this form of evaluation.

***Evaluations for Determining Merit Pay.*** A long-standing rationale for teacher performance evaluation is to provide a basis for awarding merit pay. According to this rationale, teachers want to be recognized for their efforts and achievements, and if they are paid extra for exemplary performance they will teach better. The rationale also assumes that competition among teachers will motivate them to teach better and promote better learning. Often merit assessments are based on student achievement as well as supervisor judgments and recommendations. Teachers may be required to provide a portfolio of evidence of their performance and the achievements of their students. There has been a trend toward providing salary schedules that consider both length of teaching service and meritorious performance.

A variation of merit pay for teachers is merit pay for individual schools as a means of reducing unproductive competition. For example, the Dallas Independent School District pits the faculties of different schools against each other. The prize is bonuses for all the teachers in the schools that most accelerate the achievement gains of their students. It is argued that the merit schools approach encourages teachers to cooperate rather than compete (Webster et al., 1993).

## SUBSTANTIVE ISSUES IN TEACHER EVALUATION

### The Knowledge Base

The major substantive issue still unresolved for teacher evaluation is the issue of the content of assessments: What can or should be measured about teachers? This has historically been a very difficult area that has not yielded entirely to solutions, even today. There are, of course, many views on what constitutes the appropriate knowledge base for teaching, but many of these views are incomplete or are pitched at a level that is not helpful for such practical purposes as constructing teacher assessments. Many fundamental theoretical disagreements contribute to this lack of resolution concerning a knowledge base. Kagan (1990) has provided some interesting insights into the conflicts that still exist between behavioral and cognitive views of teaching. These conflicts contribute directly to the difficulties in resolving knowledge base questions. Kagan concludes that the research on teacher cognition is not yet mature, and he argues that cognitively oriented research on teaching currently largely serves a heuristic function because not enough is known about the underlying constructs. Enumerating important obstacles to assessing teacher cognition, Kagan points out that the notion of teacher cognition is in itself somewhat ambiguous, that teachers' cognitions cannot generally be assessed directly, that the methods used to elicit and assess teachers' thoughts are extremely time-consuming, and that it is difficult to determine appropriate methods for rendering comparative judgments about teachers' cognitions (what constitutes good or bad reflection, for example). Kagan concludes, concurring with Howey and Zimpher (1989, 1990), that cognitive views of teaching have thus far largely failed to affect the nature of teacher education.

The world of teacher evaluation is nonetheless currently debating the role of teacher cognition in teacher evaluation and the feasibility of assessing such cognitions. Researchers on teacher cognition themselves hold greatly divergent opinions about the appropriate role of their research as a basis for evaluation. Eminent researchers such as Richardson (1990), while acknowledging the importance of such questions as how teacher reflection can be measured and how effective it is in producing learning in students, counsel extreme caution in pursuing these questions for practical purposes. At present, Richardson argues, we need to examine the concept of reflection itself and resist the premature formulation of questions that might erroneously imply that this line of research can provide answers to questions posed from a positivist research approach. Others, stressing political realities, are concerned with such issues as the ability of researchers and universities to maintain control over their research and teaching, and are eager to see the results of their research put into action in teacher evaluation programs and elsewhere, under the proper circumstances (Goodman, 1988; Shavelson, 1988).

Despite the many still unresolved theoretical and practical issues, teacher evaluations being developed today are greatly influenced by research on teacher cognition. Evaluations based on the process–product research paradigm are increasingly being criticized for their inability to deal with the complexities of classroom life (e.g., Berliner, 1990).

In a greatly differing view, Scriven (1988a, 1988b, 1990, 1991) has propounded a duties-based view of teaching as the appropriate underpinning for teacher evaluation. This view rejects the notion of a knowledge base for teaching that is derived from empirical research linking teacher behavior to student outcomes and couches the central question in moral and values terms, addressing such questions as what parents and students have a right to expect from teachers. Scriven thinks that teachers should be evaluated in the following categories of duties: knowledge of subject matter (including field of special competence and pervasive curriculum subjects), instructional competence (including skills in communication, classroom management, and course development and evaluation), assessment (including testing, grading, and reporting), professionalism (including ethics, attitudes, professional development, service, knowledge of duties, and knowledge of the school and its context), and other individualized services to the school and community. Focusing on generic teaching duties, such as those advocated by Scriven, is a constructive response to school administrators who seek commonality in teacher evaluations. To supplement this approach, we believe that teacher evaluations should be grounded not only in such generic duties but also in the particular responsibilities and performance objectives from the teacher's up-to-date job description.

There have been a number of attempts to address the knowledge base for teaching from a variety of perspectives and for a variety of purposes. The American Association of Colleges of Teacher Education sponsored the publication of *Knowledge Base for the Beginning Teacher* (Reynolds, 1989), and groups of scholars have tackled this problem (e.g., Dill, 1990, *What Teachers Need to Know: The Knowledge, Skills, and Values Essential to Good Teaching*). Using the methodology of job analysis, Rosenfeld and his colleagues (Rosenfeld, Freeberg, & Bukatko, 1992; Rosenfeld, Reynolds, & Bukatko, 1992; Rosenfeld & Tannenbaum, 1991; Rosenfeld, Thornton, & Skurnik, 1986; Rosenfeld, Wilder, & Bukatko, 1992), as part of the underpinnings of the NTE and of the Praxis Series, carried out a series of survey-based analyses of the job of beginning teachers. A number of states, in developing their own teacher evaluations, also have pursued state-level job analyses and conducted their own reviews of the effective teaching literature in support of their assessments.

At the national level, the Praxis Series has approached this problem using a variety of methodologies in addition to job analysis, including literature reviews and descriptive syntheses of the state instruments and procedures, in an effort to represent the differing points of view that contribute to a knowledge base of teaching for the purposes of assessment for licensing (Dwyer, 1991, 1993a, 1993c). This effort has led to a conceptual framework that organizes 19 specific teaching criteria into four major areas concerned with subject matter content, delivery of instruction, classroom environment and teacher professionalism.

Despite these efforts, an important and difficult problem that remains largely unsolved for many assessment systems is the link between the knowledge base and the instruments and procedures that will enable effective evaluation to occur. In order to make this link, it is necessary to determine what teachers need to know and what teachers need to be able to do, as well as what role teacher decision-making will play in the evaluation system. Effective resolution of these issues presupposes the existence of a guiding conception of teaching and of learning. This conception is seldom made explicit but is critically important to the development of teacher evaluations. An example of such a guiding conception and its implications for performance assessment is provided in Dwyer and Villegas (1993).

The above elements that translate a knowledge base into practice can result in a set of desiderata that may well be beyond the bounds of the practically feasible for a given situation. At some point it must be determined which, among all the things that are important about teaching, can be measured with the available techniques and resources.

Another critical issue in the conceptualization and implementation of teacher evaluation systems is how the classroom context will be dealt with. It is generally conceded that in any set of important principles of effective teaching, not all of these will be appropriate in a particular context (that is, with a particular subject matter to be taught, and with a particular group of individuals). This question of context in teacher evaluation has been addresssed from a variety of perspectives (Dwyer & Villegas, 1993; McKenna, in Millman, 1981; Shulman, 1987, 1988; Stodolsky, 1988). The large body of process–product research notwithstanding, few would argue against the importance of context. Rather, the debate is generally about the degree to which given teacher behaviors can generalize across situations, or even the degree to which it is appropriate to search for such generalizations.

A particularly interesting part of the context problem concerns the cultural backgrounds of students. Villegas (1991) and others have argued persuasively that the growing mismatch between the cultural backgrounds of teachers and the cultural backgrounds of their students will require specific teacher skills to cope with students of different cultural backgrounds. Deficit models of cultural differences do not provide an adequate basis for teacher actions in this area.

## Consequences of Teacher Evaluation for Teacher Education

A great many people are concerned about the effects that teacher evaluation will, sooner or later, have on teacher education. Little research exists on the effects of large-scale testing on teacher education and what there is tends to be done rather informally (e.g., Milner, 1991). Popham (1987) takes a positive view of the power of assessments to influence curricula and teaching practice, but little hard data exist on the influence of teacher evaluation practices on teacher education. It would be logical to draw the conclusion, however, that teacher educators look closely at the requirements of the state licenses for which they are preparing their students, and then adjust their curricula as necessary to ensure their students' attainment of these requirements. Although teacher educators are frequently deeply involved in setting states' requirements in the first place, they still need to be concerned about their ability to maintain control over their own institutions' curricula and to influence the state's teacher education requirements.

## TECHNICAL ISSUES IN TEACHER EVALUATION

Technical issues in teacher evaluation are no longer of interest only to measurement specialists. These issues have direct ramifications for local, state, and national teacher evaluation practices in that they relate directly to the educational and professional practices of administrators, teachers, and teacher educators. Increasingly, they relate to legal concerns as well. There has been a great increase in the technical sophistication of the methods and research available for teacher evaluation, but there has been some lag in utilizing this sophisticated knowledge base at the state and local levels. Teacher assessment trends are also part of larger measurement and educational trends such as paradigm shifts from behavioral to cognitive orientations and reconceptualizations of validity (Dwyer, 1991, 1993b).

## Validity of Teacher Assessments

Validation is currently conceptualized as a broad, nearly all-encompassing concept (Cronbach, 1990; Messick, 1989; Tittle, 1989). Lawsuits and less formal complaints about teacher evaluation usually involve some aspect of validity. In addition to "validity" being a broad concept, there is not much agreement on its precise meaning. (This is, of course, a problem shared by the general public with the measurement specialists themselves.) Some validity issues that are frequently raised by critics about paper-and-pencil (particularly multiple-choice) testing include the charge that teacher evaluations fail to get at the heart of teaching. Critics assert that teacher evaluations in their present form focus on knowledge and behaviors that may not relate to good teaching. Such evaluations, they charge, encourage behaviors that may not lead to student learning at all and that may not be appropriate for teaching all students, especially minority students, the handicapped, and others who are traditionally disadvantaged by the education system. There is a consistent theme in the teacher evaluation literature of the inability of paper-and-pencil tests to demonstrate high correlations with later measures of good teaching, although most of the studies in this area are not recent and suffer from a number of technical defects, often related to the inability to define a substantively and technically adequate criterion of good teaching. Haney et al. (1987) provide a commentary on these studies from a point of view highly critical of current teacher assessment practices.

Critics of teacher assessment also point to the deleterious effects of testing on curriculum. This is a rather broad criticism, applying in principle both to the curriculum for elementary and high school students and to the curriculum for teacher education. Concern over this issue is consistent with the emerging technical views of validity, including construct validity (Cronbach, 1990; Messick, 1989) and its more specific offshoot, systemic aspects of validity (Frederiksen & Collins, 1989).

Other important technical issues related to paper-and-pencil testing include how questions are asked in validation studies, how data are combined and reported, and how many judges are asked to render opinions on such questions as the importance of the various elements of the test questions (Educational Testing Service, 1989; Lawshe, 1975).

Validity issues are also raised by critics about performance assessments, which, as noted earlier, primarily consist of classroom observations. Milner (1991) has summarized these criticisms and assigns them to three categories. The first criticism is that the research base drawn on for teacher performance assessments is inadequate. It is inadequate in that it is based too heavily on research carried out in Grades 1 through 3; that it is based too often on mathematics and other subjects in which "simple answers" were sought; and that use of this research base implies an unwarranted reliance on meta-analysis, which is intrinsically flawed by combining studies disparate in design and concept.

Milner's second general complaint is the failure of evaluation systems to evaluate the "dynamic interplay" between content knowledge and teaching method. The general form of this criticism is that a teacher could spout gibberish while using the approved teaching method or, conversely, could be penalized for innovative teaching, or for not using the manner or sequence prescribed by the evaluation instrument. A further concern related to this category of criticism is that an objective instrument cannot measure the subjective dimension of the classroom.

Milner's third criticism is that teacher performance evaluations stem from a top-down orientation that threatens teachers' professionalism and forces them to adopt restrictive and trivialized techniques for the evaluation procedure.

Another validity-related criticism of great practical and theoretical significance that might be added to Milner's list is that of test bias. Although this criticism is not unique to teacher evaluation, there is a great deal of concern in teacher evaluation about preventing bias against minorities (women are seldom mentioned in this context, perhaps because many still assume that teaching is a woman's field). Most large-scale teacher evaluations continue to show considerably lower test scores for racial and ethnic minorities than for majority candidates (Coley & Goertz, 1991), although it has not been demonstrated that these are testing effects rather than preparation effects.

## Testers' Views of Validation Problems

In contrast to the critics' views on problems with teacher evaluation, testers themselves and others involved in teacher evaluation are concerned about a number of conceptual and policy issues related to the validity of teacher evaluation. Among these is the fact that many purposes exist for testing teachers. That no single test can address all of the important things about teaching is an accepted truth among measurement specialists, but one that is often lost sight of in critical debates among educators about teacher testing.

There is also nearly unanimous agreement among measurement specialists that test scores, whether of the paper-and-pencil kind or the performance kind, should not be used as the sole criterion for making important decisions about teachers.

Perhaps the major unresolved validation issue from the testing specialists' point of view is the absence of a technically, logically, and ethically defensible criterion for good teaching. Many critics have asked that tests of teacher knowledge and skills be shown to correlate with good teaching in the classroom. Many measurement specialists have retorted, "Yes, but what *is* good teaching?" Some studies have attempted to use supervisors' ratings as a definition of good teaching. Principals' ratings of the teachers they supervise, however, consistently lack variability. In practice, most principals tend to rate most teachers as being satisfactory or better. Thus, their ratings show almost no variability and cannot be meaningfully correlated with other measures. Ethical and practical obstacles also exist in carrying out the classic predictive validity paradigm that attempts to associate test scores with the acceptability of teachers' performance. This could be called a failure-group problem: Letting teachers thought to have poor skills actually teach children for the purpose of demonstrating the test's validity is ethically

unacceptable as well as infeasible in practical terms. In the teacher licensing context, where the fundamental aim is to protect the public from the harm caused by poor professional practice, assessment results should logically indicate that poor assessment results are related to harmful levels of practice; it is not logically required to demonstrate for licensing purposes that higher levels of assessment results necessarily produce better teaching.

Another validation issue that is of concern to testers is how to take the classroom context into account. As mentioned earlier, it is generally thought that there are few principles of good teaching that hold for all teaching contexts. The first definitive large-scale study to conclude this was carried out in the early 1970s (McDonald, 1976; McDonald & Elias, 1976). This effort foreshadowed a new wave of research on teaching.

Based on considerable work around the United States, we predict that state education departments and large school districts will increase the use of student outcome measures to assess teacher effectiveness. This development is sure to raise questions about the validity of the student outcome measures employed. The main criticism against such work in Tennessee is that the measure used so far, the Tennessee version of the California Achievement Test, is too narrow to serve as a criterion of student achievement and teacher effectiveness. In response to this criticism, Tennessee will soon add course content tests. In a similar effort, the Dallas Independent School District has strongly addressed the validity issue (Webster et al., 1993). This district appointed a large representative districtwide accountability panel and charged it to define a sufficient set of student outcome measures for use in assessing teacher effectiveness. They defined, and the district's research and evaluation department operationalized, approximately 40 outcome measures across the 12 grades. These measures go far beyond standardized tests and include course content tests, student attendance, and a wide range of other variables.

## Current Validation Practices

Local school districts use teacher evaluation instruments for both teacher selection and annual evaluation. Such uses often rely on indirect evidence of validation from studies carried out by others. The validation methodology used is largely restricted to content validation. Lawsuits in this area pose a constant threat but, as noted earlier, are usually decided on procedural grounds rather than on more technical validation grounds.

State validation practices can be divided into two groups: (a) the licensing of beginning teachers and (b) career ladder and other programs for practicing teachers. It should also be noted that a number of states develop and carry out their own testing programs, while others rely on national tests or tests developed for them by independent contractors. A further differentiation is that some state teacher evaluations consist of paper-and-pencil-based knowledge tests, whereas others are classroom performance tests.

With respect to the validation of paper-and-pencil teacher assessments, for national tests (primarily Praxis) states rely to some extent on validity evidence gathered by other states, but they always do supplemental local studies. The Praxis Series has provided comprehensive guides (Educational Testing Service, 1992, 1993), that provide states with information on understanding what a validation study is, on understanding what a standard-setting study is, and on who should conduct such studies, why they are needed, when they must be done, and how they should be carried out. In these validation studies there has been, and continues to be, a strong emphasis on content validation. This is in part because of its strong support in legal precedents, including *United States v. South Carolina* (1978), although there has been surprisingly little actual litigation (McDonough & Wole, 1988). As noted earlier with respect to validation, state and federal courts continue to rest their decisions more heavily on developers' and users' intentions and conformity to generally accepted professional practice, documentation, and orderly processes than on technical or professional issues.

State teacher evaluation performance assessments have been carried out by 17 states. The validation processes associated with each of these systems vary widely. Relative to paper-and-pencil testing, there is little litigation in this area. A recent exception is a case brought against the state of Georgia for the implementation of the Teacher Proficiency Assessment Instrument, in which the plaintiff argued that a number of the evaluation criteria were inappropriate. As in paper-and-pencil knowledge testing, performance assessments tend to be validated primarily in terms of their content validity. There is considerable interest on the part of the states in generalizability studies, especially among those states that have been doing performance assessments for many years and have thus accumulated the necessary data, such as the state of Georgia. In classroom performance assessments as in other performance assessments, the adequacy of the training of the evaluators is a very important issue (which is also related to the clarity of the criteria to be assessed). The adequacy of this training forms an important part of the basis for drawing inferences about the validity of classroom performance assessments.

## Future Trends

The prediction of future trends in an area as fluid as teacher assessment is a highly speculative endeavor, but certain themes already evident seem unlikely to disappear in the near term. One such theme is the broad-based technical and lay interest in improving the validity of teacher evaluation, which has led to both methodological and content-related changes that seem to be gathering momentum. With respect to methodology, there is intense interest at present in the use of performance assessments for teacher evaluation, and increasing interest in Tennessee's and Dallas's use of measures of student gains in achievement to assess teacher effectiveness. Despite the high likelihood that such assessments will be more costly in terms of effort and money, states and localities are pursuing many innovative efforts with the express hope that performance assessment methods will make a positive contribution to the validity of teacher assessments and to the relationship of these assessments to the larger educational system. The educational and measurement literature also reflects interest in performance assessments and their promise for enhanced construct and systemic validity. A great deal of research related to this area is under way and likely to continue.

A related theme is the interest in identifying means of using teaching assessment data in a predictive paradigm. The common-sense appeal of using teacher assessments to predict who will eventually prove to be good teachers is powerful, and the lack of practically or conceptually sound criteria for good teaching is becoming increasingly problematic for researchers and practitioners in this area. Well-constructed performance assessments based on direct samples of teaching may hold promise for progress in this historically very difficult area of research and practice. However, given the problems noted earlier with respect to selecting teachers based on predictor variables that have been chosen for their correlations with some measure of teaching success (Scriven, 1991), the utility of such correlational research, other than for career counseling purposes, is not clear.

The strong move toward reconceptualizing teaching and learning from a constructivist position is also likely to continue and has direct implications for teacher assessment. For example, if teaching is considered to be a complex activity involving both actions and decision-making, assessments faithful to this view must take into account the context in which teaching and learning occur. This view then implies that appropriate assessment must be context sensitive, and thus cannot depend on "cookbook" rules for good teaching or checklists. More sophisticated judgments by other education professionals and careful study of the particular teaching contexts are required if the promise of this point of view is to be fulfilled. Present work in this area seems likely to continue into the foreseeable future.

## Performance Standards

The arbitrary method of setting standards for test performance of teachers and other educators, although still popular, is increasingly coming under fire from assessment specialists. The commonly used methods of standard setting are logical but not statistically sophisticated. Their main aim is to provide a rational structure for decisions based on professional judgment. Underlying this aim is a desire to clarify and provide a basis for defending these judgments. These procedures are usually carried out as separate studies by states or their subcontractors. Studies using Praxis tend to use some variation on the Angoff method (Angoff, 1971; Livingston & Zieky, 1982). In practice, it should be noted, many states take the results of such studies and lower the cut-scores in order to reduce the risk of false-negative decisions and to ensure an adequate supply of teachers.

One of the main criticisms of all standard-setting methods is that they are fundamentally judgmental processes. Critics of standard setting tend to call such judgments arbitrary and capricious. There is, however, no escaping the fact that standards must be set, and that all standards must be set in terms of value judgments. Legitimate questions thus include who is qualified to make such judgments, how their judgments ought to be combined, what issues they ought to address, and what information they should take into account. Ultimately, however, professional judgments (involving many factors drawn from the experiences of those doing the judging) will determine the standards, and thus who passes and who fails the examinations. Criteria can, should be, and usually are applied to the collection of these professional judgments, and a high value is placed on the process and data being open to critical examination.

In observation systems, decision rules rather than the simpler cut-scores are typically developed. In such circumstances the role played by professional judgment is much more obvious. Developers of observation systems usually specify rules governing determination of the presence or absence of criteria for acceptable teaching, then determine "metarules" for combining these judgments into a single yes/no decision about performance.

## Determining the Appropriate Assessment Methods

As we grow more sophisticated about the nature of teaching, determining appropriate assessment methods is increasingly recognized as a significant issue in teacher evaluation. The need to match the assessment method to the aspect of teaching that is of interest is also being increasingly recognized. As noted earlier, there are three main classes of teacher assessment methods in use today: (a) paper-and-pencil knowledge tests, usually involving multiple-choice questions and sometimes written essays or problem sets or other constructed responses, (b) performance assessments (which usually consist of classroom observation), and (c) interviews, used especially in the selection of new teachers. Other methods such as assessment centers have been used only experimentally for decision-making about teachers, although they have been widely used for evaluating principals, foreign service officers, and business executives. Despite continuing optimism and a great deal of progress, realistic computer simulations for the purposes of teacher evaluations still seem quite far in the future.

Evaluation of teacher performance in schools consists primarily of classroom observations, usually carried out by the principal or his or her direct designee, but sometimes by peer teachers. Important issues in determining whether this is an appropriate method in a given situation include the adequacy of training provided for the evaluators, the clarity and scope of the evaluation criteria, and the consistency with which the evaluations can be carried out in their natural setting. Although classroom observations can contribute appropriately to evaluating teacher performance, additional methods, such as teacher-prepared portfolios, examination of student work products, examination of teacher-made tests and other assessment devices, examination of teacher grading practices, and feedback from students and their next year's teachers, are needed to assess the full range of teaching duties.

With respect to state testing of teachers, paper-and-pencil assessments are not generally seen as competitive to performance testing but as complementary. States are becoming increasingly aware of the differences between knowledge and performance, and of the utility of different kinds of assessment for each circumstance.

## Formative versus Summative Assessments

Most teacher assessment today is carried out for the purposes of decision-making, and summative uses thus predominate. However, there is growing concern that this has some undesirable potential effects on the educational system and on individual teachers (e.g., Frederiksen & Collins, 1989).

There has been a large upturn in the number and quality of staff development programs provided for beginning teachers. Mentoring programs of various sorts, aimed at the induction,

development, and retention of beginning teachers, figure prominently in this upturn (Wilder & Ashare, 1990). The American Federation of Teachers and the National Education Association have also made staff development a priority. One of the strong rationales for such programs from the point of view of local districts and states is increased retention of beginning teachers, whereas the AFT and the NEA tend to emphasize the upgrading of professional standards. Some state activities emphasize both these aspects. For example, the Minnesota Board of Teaching has developed a comprehensive licensing plan that includes professional development schools for all new teachers.

States are just beginning to make explicit connections between these teacher induction programs for beginning teachers and a need for formal assessment of what is learned in them. Conventional paper-and-pencil testing is not considered an attractive alternative in this context. Observations, interviews, and, to a limited degree, simulations seem to be today's preferred paths.

A number of state observation systems incorporate formative elements into their system through feedback to teachers, either directly from the evaluators or in the form of written reports to the teacher. Again, however, there is little systematic connection between this feedback and the curricula of the mentoring programs themselves. Most local systems provide little or no formal feedback, although there are conspicuous exceptions, such as the systems used in Toledo, Ohio; Northfield, Minnesota; and Rochester, New York. The Educational Testing Service's Praxis Series Classroom Performance Assessments is another example of a system that is designed for instructional as well as assessment purposes.

## Using Student Work for Teacher Evaluation

This is a highly controversial area that involves a great many technical issues such as the use of gain scores, taking context and resources into account, and so on. Those opposed to using student work to evaluate teachers are more vocal and more numerous than those in favor of it at the current time, although much of the general public believes strongly that using student work to evaluate teachers is desirable. In fact, Kagan (1990) notes that "for the most part, the public knows but one sign of good teaching—student achievement" (p. 458).

The state of Oregon has incorporated student work into evaluations of teachers at all levels; for initial licensing, for tenure decisions, for career ladders, and for job placements (D. Shalock & M. Shalock, 1990). The main opposition to the concept appears to be feasibility, both technical and practical. Practical concerns heavily stress fairness to the teacher, with such issues as how to take account of difficult-to-teach classrooms in the forefront (Berk, 1988; Glass, 1990; Millman, 1981b).

Large teacher assessment projects in Texas and Tennessee seem to be having more success. They are using computer power and advanced statistical techniques to assess the effectiveness of individual teachers and groups of teachers (Webster et al., 1993) based on measures of student outcomes. The findings of their studies refute the previously published conclusions that the effects of teachers on assessed student performance cannot be separated from the effects of family background, student ability, past student achievement, and many other variables (Berk, 1988; Glass, 1990). Given sufficient information about the extent of a teacher's contact with given students, the achievement gains of those students over a period of years, the extent of the students' contact with other teachers, and student background variables, these researchers found that a teacher's unique contributions to students' achievement gains can be reliably determined. The Tennessee and Dallas studies independently reached this conclusion using somewhat different statistical approaches. Their main disagreements are philosophical and not technical. The Tennessee researchers are working with the Tennessee Department of Education toward the goal of holding each teacher accountable for student achievement. The Dallas team disagrees with this approach because they believe it would result in counterproductive competition between teachers in the same school. Instead, the Dallas team assesses the collective contributions of all the teachers in a school to student outcomes. Their aim is to engender collaboration among a school's teachers while also promoting healthy competition between schools. Both the Tennessee and the Dallas teacher accountability systems are designed to provide teachers with information they can use to assess why they were or were not successful in effecting student gains.

## SPECIFIC RECOMMENDATIONS TO EDUCATIONAL PSYCHOLOGISTS

We have noted the limitations and deficiencies attendant on the use of research correlating specific teaching behaviors with indicators of student outcomes as a basis for constructing general-purpose forms for evaluating the performance of individual teachers. Clearly, there is room for productive research and development of appropriate observation approaches and forms. Such work should aim to produce forms that define and directly address each teacher's particular responsibilities and take into account the particular work setting. We also believe that for evaluating practicing teachers such forms can be grounded in core duties, such as those that have held up in litigation on teacher evaluation—knowledge of subject matter, ability to communicate the subject matter, classroom management, and student achievement (provided it correlates with one of the first three variables) (see Andrews, 1985; Strike & Bull, 1981). In pursuing work on classroom observation, it will be important to consider that only students have a daily opportunity to observe the teacher's performance of duties. It could be very important to find ways to engage students in producing valid and reliable information in a way acceptable to teachers on the teacher's performance of duties.

Major problems that have to be considered in research on classroom observation concern who should do the observing and evaluation, when it is best to use a high- versus a low-inference approach, and whether the observations should be announced or unannounced. Relatedly, it is important to consider whether and under what circumstances one group (such as students) should do the observing and recording of observations, while another (such as a principal or group of peer reviewers) uses the data to arrive at interpretation and evaluation. Among the possible observers of classroom performance

are students, peers, administrators, state inspectors, other external evaluators, and parents. We recommend that the full set of variables identified in this section (duties, job responsibilities, observers, evaluators, high- vs. low-inference approach, announced vs. unannounced classroom visits) be considered in research and development that is aimed at obtaining valid and reliable evaluative information from the classroom observation approach to teacher evaluation.

Other topics for needed research, development, and professional leadership related to teacher evaluation include the following:

- Improving the evaluative aspects of student teaching.
- Strengthening schools' use of sound job descriptions in teacher evaluations.
- Closely examining the consequences of the different rationales for teacher performance evaluation.
- Field testing existing teacher evaluation models, and developing better ones.
- Increasing the dissemination and use of professional standards for personnel evaluation.
- Increasing and improving educators' preparation to conduct program and personnel evaluation.
- Developing and researching new ways of considering student achievement and learning environments in the evaluation of teaching.
- Developing guidelines for evaluating teachers who work with special populations.
- Developing a sound theory base for teacher evaluation, including the creation of professionally and technically acceptable criteria for what constitutes good teaching, including the complexities attendant on adopting a constructivist view of teaching.
- Setting levels for acceptable performance. Methods for setting levels for acceptable performance on new forms of teacher assessment need to be developed and evaluated in both technical terms and in terms of application to diverse settings.
- Examining the outcomes of teacher assessment in light of equity concerns. The assessment development process and the use of assessments provide a number of critical points at which equity concerns arise. At this point in time, little is known of the impact that various new types of assessments, particularly performance-based assessments, will have on minorities and women.
- Effectiveness of simulations of teaching. In certain circumstances it may be highly desirable to evaluate teachers using simulations of teaching situations rather than naturalistic settings and direct interaction with the assessor. Although some work has been done in this area, many questions remain about the relationship between simulations and naturalistic assessments.
- Interventions for improving teacher skill. Based on the results of various sorts of teacher assessments, areas for improvement can be identified. What interventions (e.g., mentors, internship curricula, self-study, video clubs) are effective in improving teaching skill? How do teachers make use of assessment information, and how do they change over time in response to it?

# References

American Educational Research Association, American Psychological Association, National Council on Measurement in Education. (1985). *Standards for educational and psychological testing*. Washington, DC: American Educational Association.

American Psychological Association, Division of Industrial and Organizational Psychology. (1980). *Principles for the validation and use of personnel selection procedures* (2nd ed.). Berkeley, CA: Author.

Andrews, H. A. (1985). *Evaluating for excellence: Addressing the need for responsible and effective faculty evaluation*. Stillwater, OK: New Forums Press.

Angoff, W. H. (1971). Scales, norms, and equivalent scores. In R. L. Thorndike (Ed.), *Educational measurement* (2nd ed., pp. 508–600). Washington, DC: American Council on Education.

Barr, A. (1950). Teaching competencies. In W. Monroe (Ed.), *Encyclopedia of educational research* (rev. ed., pp. 1446–1454). New York: Macmillan.

Berk, R. A. (1988). Fifty reasons why student achievement gain does not mean teacher effectiveness. *Journal of Personnel Evaluation in Education, 1*, 345–363.

Berliner, D. C. (1989). Implications of studies of expertise in pedagogy for teacher education and evaluation. In *New directions for teacher assessment: Proceedings of the 1988 ETS Invitational Conference* (pp. 39–68). Princeton, NJ: Educational Testing Service.

Berliner, D. C. (1990). The place of process-product research in developing the agenda for research on teacher thinking. *Educational Psychologist, 24*, 325–344.

Bird, T. (1990). The schoolteacher's portfolio: An essay on possibilities. In J. Millman & L. Darling-Hammond (Eds.), *The new handbook of teacher evaluation* (pp. 241–256). Newbury Park, CA: Sage.

Bridges, E. (1986). *The incompetent teacher: The challenge and the response*. Philadelphia: Falmer Press.

Brookover, W. B. (1979). *School social systems and student achievement: Schools can make a difference*. New York: Praeger.

Brophy, J., & Evertson, C. (1978). Context variables in teaching. *Educational Psychologist, 12*, 310–316.

Brophy, J. E., & Good, T. L. (1988). Teacher behavior and student achievement. In M. Wittrock (Ed.), *Handbook of research on teaching* (3rd ed., pp. 328–375). New York: Macmillan.

Burry, J. A. (1990). Multiple methods of data collection for beginning teacher assessment. In *Compendium of papers presented at the statewide Colloquium on Instructional Personnel*. Tallahassee: Florida State Department of Education.

Burry, J. A., Chissom, B. S., & Shaw, D. G. (1990, March). *Validity and reliability of classroom observations: A paradox*. Paper presented at a meeting of the National Council on Measurement in Education, Boston.

Burry, J. A., & Shaw, D. G. (1988). Teachers and administrators differ in assessing teacher effectiveness. *Journal of Personnel Evaluation in Education, 2*, 33–41.

California Commission on the Teaching Profession. (1985). *Who will teach our children? A strategy for improving California's schools*. Sacramento, CA: California Commission on the Teaching Profession.

Chance, W. (1987). *Reforming America's public schools in the 1980s*. Chicago: John D. and Catherine T. MacArthur Foundation.

Coker, H., Medley, D., & Soar, R. (1980). How valid are expert opinions about effective teaching? *Phi Delta Kappan, 62*, 131–134.

Coleman, J. A., Campbell, E. Q., Hobson, C. J., McPartland, J. Mood, A. M. Weinfeld, F. D., & York, R. L. (1966). *Equality of educational opportunity*. Washington, DC: U.S. Government Printing Office.

Coley, R. J., & Goertz, M. E. (1991). *Characteristics of minority NTE test-takers* (Teacher Programs Council Research Report Series No. 91-1). Princeton, NJ: Educational Testing Service.

Cronbach, L. J. (1990). *Essentials of psychological testing* (5th ed., pp. 150–189). New York: Harper Collins.

Darling-Hammond, L. (1986). A proposal for evaluating in the teaching profession. *Elementary School Journal, 86*, 531–569.

Darling-Hammond, L., & Berry, B. (1988). *The evolution of teacher policy*. Santa Monica, CA: Rand Corporation.

Darling-Hammond, L., Wise, A. E., & Pease, S. R. (1983). Teacher evaluation in the organizational context: A review of the literature. *Review of Educational Research, 53*, 285–328.

Deming, W. E. (1986). *Out of crisis*. Cambridge: MIT Press.

Dill, D. D. (Ed.). (1990). *What teachers need to know: The knowledge, skills, and values essential to good teaching*. San Francisco: Jossey-Bass.

Duke, D. L., & Stiggins, R. J. (1990). Beyond minimum competence: Evaluation for professional development. In J. Millman & L. Darling-Hammond (Eds.), *The new handbook of teacher evaluation: Assessing elementary and secondary school teachers* (pp. 116–132). Newbury Park, CA: Sage.

Dunkin, M. J., & Biddle, B. J. (1974). *The study of teaching*. New York: Holt, Rinehart and Winston.

Dwyer, C. A. (1989). A new generation of tests for licensing beginning teachers. In *New directions for teacher assessment: Proceedings of the 1988 ETS Invitational Conference* (pp. 29–37). Princeton, NJ: Educational Testing Service.

Dwyer, C. A. (1991). Measurement and research issues in teacher assessment. *Educational Psychologist, 26*, 3–22.

Dwyer, C. A. (1993a). *Development of the knowledge base for the Praxis III: Classroom Performance Assessments assessment criteria*. Princeton, NJ: Educational Testing Service.

Dwyer, C. A. (1993b). Innovation and reform: Examples from teacher assessment. In R. E. Bennett & W. C. Ward (Eds.), *Construction versus choice in cognitive measurement* (pp. 265–289). Hillsdale, NJ: Lawrence Erlbaum.

Dwyer, C. A. (1993c). Teaching and diversity: Meeting the challenges for innovative teacher assessments. *Journal of Teacher Education, 44*(2), 119–129.

Dwyer, C. A., & Villegas, A. M. (1993). *Guiding conceptions and assessment principles for "The Praxis Series: Professional Assessments for Beginning Teachers."* Princeton, NJ: Educational Testing Service.

Educational Testing Service. (1989). *Validity: Using NTE tests*. Princeton, NJ.

Educational Testing Service. (1990). *The educational reform decade*. Princeton, NJ: Author (Policy Information Center).

Educational Testing Service. (1991). *CHART*. Princeton, NJ.

Educational Testing Service. (1992). *Guidelines for proper use of "The Praxis Series: Professional Assessments for Beginning Teachers."* Princeton, NJ.

Educational Testing Service. (1993). *Validity: Q & A*. Princeton, NJ.

Evertson, C., & Burry, J. (1989). Capturing classroom context: The observation system as a lens for assessment. *Journal of Personnel Evaluation in Education, 2*, 297–320.

Evertson, C., & Green, J. (1986). Observation as method and inquiry. In M. Wittrock (Ed.), *Handbook of research on teaching* (3rd ed., pp. 162–213). New York: Macmillan.

Fischer, L., Schimmel, D., & Kelly, C. (1991). *Teachers and the law* (3rd ed.). New York: Longman.

Flanders, N. (1970). *Analyzing teacher behavior*. Reading, MA: Addison-Wesley.

Frederiksen, J. R., & Collins, A. (1989). A systems approach to educational testing. *Educational Researcher, 18*(9), 27–32.

French, R. L., Holdzkom, D., & Kuligowski, B. (1990). *Teacher evaluation in SREB states (Stage 1)*. Unpublished manuscript, Atlanta, GA: Southern Regional Education Board.

Garcia, P. A. (1985). *A study of teacher competency testing and tests validity with implications for minorities: Final report.* (NIE Grant No. NIE-G-85-0004). Edinburgh, TX: Pan American University.

Georgia Association of Educators v. Nix, 407 F. Supp. 1102 (N.D. Ga. 1976).

Ghorpade, J., & Atchison, T. J. (1980, Fall). The concept of job analysis: A review and some suggestions. *Public Personnel Management Journal,* 134–144.

Glass, G. V (1990). Using student test scores to evaluate teachers. In J. Millman & L. Darling-Hammond (Eds.), *The new handbook of teacher evaluation* (pp. 191–215). Newbury Park, CA: Sage.

Good, T. L., & Mulryan, C. (1990). Teacher ratings: A call for teacher control and self-evaluation. In J. Millman & L. Darling-Hammond (Eds.), *The new handbook of teacher evaluation* (pp. 191–215). Newbury Park, CA: Sage.

Goodman, J. (1988). The political tactics and teaching strategies of reflective, active preservice teachers. *Elementary School Journal, 89,* 23–41.

Green, J., & Harker, J. (1987). *Multiple perspective analysis of classroom discourse.* Norwood, NJ: Ablex.

Haertel, E. (1986). The valid use of student performance measures for teacher evaluation. *Educational Evaluation and Policy Analysis, 8,* 45–60.

Haertel, E. (1990). Performance tests, simulations, and other methods. In J. Millman & L. Darling-Hammond (Eds.), *The new handbook of teacher evaluation* (pp. 278–294). Newbury Park, CA: Sage.

Hambleton, R. K. (1990). Boston, MA: Presidential address at the National Council on Measurement in Education.

Haney, W., Madaus, G., & Kreitzer, A. (1987). Charms talismanic: Testing teachers for the improvement of American education. In E. Z. Rothkopf (Ed.), *Review of research in education* (Vol. 14, pp. 169–238). Washington, DC: American Educational Research Association.

Herbert, J., & McNergney, R. (1989). Evaluating teacher evaluators using a set of public standards. *Journal of Personnel Evaluation in Education, 2,* 321–334.

Holmes Group. (1990). *Tomorrow's schools: Principles for the design of professional development schools.* East Lansing, MI: Author.

Hood, S., & Parker, L. (1989). Minority bias review panels and teacher testing for initial certification: A comparison of two states' results. *Journal of Negro Education, 58,* 511–519.

Hood, S., & Parker, L. (1991). Minorities, teacher testing, and recent U.S. Supreme Court holdings: A regressive step. *Teachers College Record, 92,* 603–618.

Howey, K. R., & Zimpher, N. L. (1989) Pre-service teacher educators' role in programs for beginning teachers. *Elementary School Journal, 89,* 451–470.

Howey, K. R., & Zimpher, N. L. (1990). *Profiles of preservice teacher education: Inquiry into the nature of programs.* Albany: State University of New York Press.

Hunter, M. (1988a). Create rather than await your fate in teacher evaluation. In S. Stanley & W. J. Popham (Eds.), *Teacher evaluation: Six prescriptions for success* (pp. 32–54). Alexandria, VA: Association for Supervision and Curriculum Development.

Hunter, M. (1988b). Effecting a reconciliation between supervision and evaluation. *Journal of Personnel Evaluation in Education, 1,* 275–279.

Iwanicki, E. F. (1981). Contract plans: A professional growth-oriented approach to evaluating teacher performance. In J. Millman (Ed.), *Handbook of teacher evaluation* (pp. 203–228). Beverly Hills, CA: Sage.

Jencks, C. (1972). *Inequality: A reassessment of the effect of family and schooling in America.* New York: Basic Books.

Johnson, S. (1980). Performance based staff lay-offs in the public schools: Implementation and outcomes. *Harvard Education Review, 50,* 214–233.

Joint Committee on Standards for Educational Evaluation. (1981). *Standards for evaluations of educational programs, projects, and materials.* New York: McGraw-Hill.

Joint Committee on Standards for Educational Evaluation. (1988). *The personnel evaluation standards.* Newbury Park, CA: Sage.

Joyce, B., & McKibbin, M. (1982). Teacher growth states and school environments. *Educational Leadership, 47,* 70–77.

Kagan, D. M. (1990). Ways of evaluating teacher cognition: Inferences concerning the Goldilocks principle. *Review of Educational Research, 60,* 419–469.

Kaplan, A. (1963). *The conduct of inquiry.* San Francisco: Chandler.

Kelly, J. (1989). Strengthening the teaching profession through national certification. *New Directions for Teacher Assessment: Proceedings of the 1988 ETS Invitational Conference* (pp. 1–11). Princeton, NJ: Educational Testing Service.

Lawshe, C. H. (1975). A quantitative approach to content validity. *Personnel Psychology, 28,* 563–575.

Lehman, I. J., & Phillips, S. E. (1987). A survey of state teacher-competency examination programs. *Educational Measurement: Issues and Practice, 6*(1), 14–18.

Linn, R., Buchmann, M., Gould, B., Kellaghan, T., Lawrence, D., Robinson, P., & Zirkel, P. (1989). The development, validation, and applicability of The Personnel Evaluation Standards. *Journal of Personnel Evaluation in Education, 2,* 199–214.

Livingston, S. A., & Zieky, M. J. (1982). *Passing scores: A manual for setting standards of performance on educational and occupational tests.* Princeton, NJ: Educational Testing Service.

Madaus, G. F. (1990). *Legal and professional issues in teacher certification testing: A psychometric snark hunt.* In J. V. Mitchell, S. L. Wise, and B. S. Plake (Eds.), *Assessment of teaching: Purposes, practices, and implications for the Profession* (pp. 209–259). Hillsdale, NJ: Lawrence Erlbaum.

Madaus, G. F., & Pullin, D. (1987, September). Teacher certification tests: Do they really measure what we need to know? *Phi Delta Kappan, 69*(1), 31–38.

Manatt, R. P. (1988). Teacher performance evaluation: A total systems approach. In S. J. Stanley & W. J. Popham (Eds.), *Teacher evaluation: Six prescriptions for success* (pp. 79–108). Alexandria, VA: Association for Supervision and Curriculum Development.

Manatt, R. P., & Stow, S. (1984). *The clinical manual for teacher performance evaluation.* Ames: Iowa State University Research Foundation.

McDonald, F. (1976). Report on Phase II of the Beginning Teacher Evaluation Study. *Journal of Teacher Education, 27*(1), 39–42.

McDonald, F., & Elias, P. (1976). *The effects of teaching performance on pupil learning: Beginning Teacher Evaluation Study, Phase II, 1974–76. Final report* (5 vols.). Princeton, NJ: Educational Testing Service.

McDonough, M. W., & Wolfe, W. C., Jr. (1988). Court actions which helped define the direction of the competency-based testing movement. *Journal of Research and Development in Education, 21,* 37–43.

McGreal, T. (1983). *Successful teacher evaluation.* Alexandria, VA: Association for Supervision and Curriculum Development.

McKenna, B. H. (1973). A context for teacher evaluation. *National Elementary Principal, 52,* 18–23.

McKenna, B. H. (1981). Context/environment effects in teacher evaluation. In J. Millman (Ed.), *Handbook of teacher evaluation* (pp. 23–37). Beverly Hills, Ca: Sage.

Medley, D. M., Coker, H., & Soar, R. S. (1984). *Measurement-based evaluation of teacher performance: An empirical approach.* New York: Longman.

Mehrens, W. A. (1991). Social issues in teacher testing. *Journal of Personnel Evaluation in Education, 4,* 317–319.

Messick, S. (1989). Validity. In R. L. Linn (Ed.), *Educational measurement* (3rd ed., pp. 13–103). New York: Macmillan.

Millman, J. (1981a). *Handbook of teacher evaluation*. Beverly Hills, CA: Sage.

Millman, J. (1981b). Student achievement as a measure of teacher competence. In J. Millman (Ed.), *Handbook of teacher evaluation* (pp. 146–166). Beverly Hills, CA: Sage.

Millman, J. (1989). If at first you don't succeed: Setting passing scores when more than one attempt is permitted. *Educational Researcher, 18*(6), 5–9.

Milner, J. O. (1991). Suppositional style and teacher evaluation. *Phi Delta Kappan, 72*, 464–467.

National Association of State Directors of Teacher Education and Certification. (1991). *Manual on certification and preparation of education personnel in the United States*. Seattle, WA: Author.

National Commission on Excellence in Education. (1983). *A nation at risk: The imperative for educational reform*. Washington, DC: U.S. Government Printing Office.

Osborne, W. D., & Wiggins, T. (1989). Perceptions of tasks in the school principalship. *Journal of Personnel Evaluation in Education, 2*, 367–376.

Popham, W. J. (1987). The shortcomings of champagne teacher evaluation. *Journal of Personnel Evaluation in Education, 1*(1), 25–28.

Popham, W. J. (1991, June). *Judging the content of teacher licensure tests: How good is good enough?* Preliminary draft presented at the annual conference of National Association of State Directors of Teacher Education and Certification, Bellevue, WA.

Popham, W. J., & Kirby, W. N. (1987). Recertification tests for teachers: A defensible safeguard for society. *Phi Delta Kappan, 69*, 45–48.

Rebell, M. A. (1986). Disparate impact of teacher competency testing on minorities: Don't blame the test takers—or the tests. *Yale Law and Policy Review, 4*, 375–403.

Rebell, M. A. (1988). Legal issues concerning bias in testing. In R. Allan, P. Nassif, & M. Elliot (Eds.), *Bias issues in teacher certification issues* (pp. 59–73). Hillsdale, NJ: Lawrence Erlbaum Associates.

Rebell, M. A. (1989). Testing, public policy and the courts. In B. R. Gifford (Ed.), *Testing and the allocation of opportunity*. Boston: Kluwer-Nijhoff.

Rebell, M. A. (1990). Legal issues concerning teacher evaluation. In J. Millman & L. Darling-Hammond (Eds.), *The new handbook of teacher evaluation* (pp. 337–355). Newbury Park, CA: Sage.

Redfern, G. B. (1963). *How to appraise teaching performance*. Columbus, OH: School Management Institute.

Redfern, G. B. (1980). *Evaluating teachers and administrators: A performance objectives approach*. Boulder, CO: Westview Press.

Reineke, R., Willeke, M., Walsh, L., & Sawin, C. (1988). Review of personnel evaluation systems: A local application of the Standards. *Journal of Personnel Evaluation in Education, 1*, 373–378.

Reynolds, M. C. (1989). *Knowledge base for the beginning teacher*. Elmsford, NY: Pergamon Press.

Richardson, V. (1990). The evolution of reflective teaching and teacher education. In R. T. Clift, W. R. Houston, & M. C. Pugach (Eds.), *Encouraging reflective practice in education* (pp. 3–19). New York: Teachers College Press.

Rosenfeld, M., Freeberg, N. E., & Bukatko, P. (1992). *The professional functions of secondary school teachers*. Princeton, NJ: Educational Testing Service.

Rosenfeld, M., Reynolds, A., & Bukatko, P. (1992). *The professional functions of elementary school teachers*. Princeton, NJ: Educational Testing Service.

Rosenfeld, M., & Tannenbaum, R. T. (1991). *Identification of a core of important enabling skills for the NTE Successor Stage I examination* (RR-91-37). Princeton, NJ: Educational Testing Service.

Rosenfeld, M., Thornton, R. F., & Skurnik, L. S. (1986). *Analysis of the professional function of teachers: Relationships between job functions and the NTE core battery* (Report No. 86-8). Princeton, NJ: Educational Testing Service.

Rosenfeld, M., Wilder, G., & Bukatko, P. (1992). *The professional functions of middle school teachers*. Princeton, NJ: Educational Testing Service.

Rudner, L. M. (1988). Teacher testing: An update. *Educational Measurement: Issues and Practice, 7*(1), 16–19.

Ryans, D. G. (1960). *Characteristics of teachers*. Washington, DC: American Council on Education.

Sanders, W. L., & McLean, R. A. (1984). *Objective component of teacher evaluation—a feasibility study*. Knoxville: University of Tennessee, College of Business Administration Working Paper Series.

Saydel Education Association v. PERB, 333 N.W. 26486, Iowa (1983).

Schmitt, N., & Doherty, M. (1988). NASSP study of measurement and model linkage issues for the comprehensive assessment of school environments. Unpublished technical report (available from NASSP), East Lansing: Michigan State University.

Scriven, M. (1987). Validity in personnel evaluation. *Journal of Personnel Evaluation in Education, 1*, 9–23.

Scriven, M. (1988a). Duties-based teacher evaluation. *Journal of Personnel Evaluation in Education, 1*, 319–334.

Scriven, M. (1988b). Evaluating teachers as professionals: The duties-based approach. In S. J. Stanley & W. J. Popham (Eds.), *Teacher evaluation: Six prescriptions for success* (pp. 110–142). Alexandria, VA: Association for Supervision and Curriculum Development.

Scriven, M. (1990). Teacher selection. In J. Millman & L. Darling-Hammond (Eds.), *The new handbook of teacher evaluation* (pp. 76–103). Newbury Park, CA: Sage.

Scriven, M. (1991). *Teacher evaluation models* (TEMP memos, Teacher Evaluation Models Project). Kalamazoo, MI: Center for Research on Educational Accountability and Teacher Evaluation.

Shalock, D., & Shalock, M. (1990, September). Extending teacher assessment beyond knowledge and skills: An emerging focus on teacher accomplishments. *Issues and Practices in Performance Assessment, 2*, 81–126.

Shavelson, R. J., Webb, N., & Burstein, L. (1986). Measurement of teaching. In M. Wittrock (Ed.), *Handbook of research on teaching* (3rd ed., pp. 50–91). New York: Macmillan.

Shavelson, R. J. (1988). Contributions of educational research to policy and practice: Constructing, challenging, changing cognition. *Educational Researcher, 17*(7), 4–11, 22.

Shepard, L. A., & Kreitzer, A. E. (1987). The Texas Teacher Test. *Educational Researcher, 16*(6), 22–31.

Shimberg, B. (1985). Testing for licensure and certification. *American Psychologist, 36*, 1138–1146.

Shulman, L. S. (1986). Those who understand: Knowledge growth in teaching. *Educational Researcher, 15*, 4–14.

Shulman, L. S. (1987a). Assessment for teaching: An initiative for the profession. *Phi Delta Kappan, 69*, 38–44.

Shulman, L. S. (1987b). Knowledge and teaching: Foundations of the new reform. *Harvard Educational Review, 57*, 1–22.

Shulman, L. S. (1988). A union of insufficiencies: Strategies for teacher assessment in a period of educational reform. *Educational Leadership, 46*, 36–41.

Shulman, L. S. (1989). The paradox of teacher assessment. In *New directions for teacher assessment: Proceedings of the 1988 ETS Invitational Conference* (pp. 13–27). Princeton, NJ: Educational Testing Service.

Shulman, L. S., Bird, T., & Haertel, E. (1988). *Toward alternative assessments of teaching: A report of work in progress*. Stanford, CA: Stanford University School of Education, Teacher Assessment Project.

Sprinthall, N. A., & Thies-Sprinthall, L. (1983). The teacher as an adult learner: A cognitive-developmental view. In G. Griffin (Ed.), *Staff development*. 82nd Yearbook of the National Society for the Study of Education, Part II, (pp. 13–35). Chicago: University of Chicago Press.

St. Louis Teachers Union, Local 420 v. Board of Education of the City of St. Louis, 652 F. Supp. 425 (E.D. Mo. 1987).

Stodolsky, S. S. (1988). *The subject matters*. Chicago: University of Chicago Press.

Streifer, P., & Iwanicki, E. (1987). The validation of beginning teacher competencies in Connecticut. *Journal of Personnel Evaluation in Education, 1,* 33–55.

Strike, K., & Bull, B. (1981). Fairness and the legal context of teacher evaluation. In J. Millman (Ed.), *Handbook of teacher evaluation*. Beverly Hills, CA: Sage.

Stufflebeam, D. L. (1990). *Research and development center on teacher performance evaluation and educational accountability*. Technical proposal submitted to the Office of Educational Research and Improvement, U.S. Department of Education. Kalamazoo: Western Michigan University Evaluation Center.

Task Force on Teaching as a Profession. (1986). *A nation prepared: Teachers for the 21st century*. New York: Carnegie Forum on Education and the Economy.

Texas State Teachers Association v. State of Texas, 711 SW. 2nd 421 (Texas 1986).

Tittle, C. K. (1989). Validity: Whose construction is it in the teaching and learning context? *Educational Measurement: Issues and Practice, 8,* 5–13, 34.

Travers, R. M. W. (1981). Criteria of good teaching. In J. Millman (Ed.), *Handbook of teacher evaluation* (pp. 14–22). Beverly Hills, CA: Sage.

United States v. South Carolina, 445 F. Supp. 1094 (D.S.C. 1977), aff'd 434 U.S. 1026 (1978).

Villegas, A. M. (1991). *Culturally responsive teaching*. Princeton, NJ: Educational Testing Service.

Walston v. County School Board of Nansemond County, 492 F. 2d 919 (4th Cir. 1973).

Webster, W. J., Mendro, R. L., & Almaguer, T. O. (1993). *Effectiveness indices: The major component of an equitable accountability system*. Paper presented at the annual meeting of the American Educational Research Association, Atlanta, GA.

Wilder, G. Z., & Ashare, C. J. (1990). *A study of mentoring programs: Phase 2*. Princeton, NJ: Educational Testing Service.

Wise, A. E., Darling-Hammond, L., McLaughlin, M. W., & Bernstein, H. T. (1984a). *Case studies for teacher evaluation: A study of effective practices*. Santa Monica, CA: Rand Corporation.

Wise, A. E., Darling-Hammond, L., McLaughlin, M. W., & Bernstein, H. T. (1984b). *Teacher evaluation: A study of effective practices*. Santa Monica, CA: Rand Corporation.

Wittrock, M. C. (Ed.). (1986). *Handbook of research on teaching* (3rd ed.). New York: Macmillan.

---

# · 24 ·

---

# TOWARD A SITUATED SOCIAL PRACTICE MODEL

# FOR INSTRUCTIONAL DESIGN

## Sharon Derry

UNIVERSITY OF WISCONSIN–MADISON

## Alan Lesgold

UNIVERSITY OF PITTSBURGH

The discipline of instructional design is in a state of transition. An extensive technology is now being challenged. Although the challengers have yet to offer a fully systematic, well-grounded replacement, they have shown weaknesses in the current approach and have begun to demonstrate alternative schemes. This chapter summarizes the current technology and discusses the changes now occurring. The goal is to point in the direction of ongoing instructional design research, stating principles where possible and showing the direction of new work when it is too early to distill principles.

After several decades of research into verbal learning and the beginnings of a cognitive psychology reacting to it, educational psychologists and training designers developed an extensive prescriptive technology for the systematic design of instruction. This technology, called instructional design or instructional systems design, is taught in graduate programs that prepare instructional designers and training managers for positions in industrial, military, and some educational organizations. The intellectual base for instructional design consists of a body of knowledge, terminology, and procedures that are generally accepted by professionals within the instructional design culture and that are described in a number of widely used texts (e.g., Dick & Carey, 1985; R. M. Gagné, Briggs, & Wager, 1988; Reigeluth, 1983). This base reflects an extensive body of experimental learning studies.

Although existing instructional design technology has been extremely valuable, bringing system to an otherwise chaotic activity, today the instructional design field is in transition. In this chapter we discuss aspects of traditional and existing practice, as well as an emerging situated cognition paradigm that emphasizes the role of cognitive apprenticeship. We begin with a brief historical overview of traditional instructional design theory, focusing particularly on the concept of task analysis. Then, because changes in instructional design practice reflect changes in basic psychological understanding about knowledge and the learning process, we give some attention to new outlooks regarding the content and processes of instruction. We

then illustrate the application of these ideas, describing in detail a case study based on Sherlock, an intelligent, coached, cognitive apprenticeship environment for training a complex military job task. Finally, we revisit the issue of task analysis from an object-oriented design perspective, which appears to carry promise for supporting situated cognition approaches to instructional design.

---

## INSTRUCTIONAL DESIGN:
## A HISTORICAL PERSPECTIVE

---

Robert M. Gagné is generally acknowledged as the founder and most influential theorist of instructional design. An experimental psychologist, Gagné served with the Army Aviation Psychology Program during the war, and in positions as research and technical director of major air force laboratories from 1949 to 1957. In a 1962 American Psychological Association address to the Military Training Division, Gagné set forth psychological principles for training that established roots for the instructional design field. Recognizing that people learn to do very complex cognitive work, Gagné proposed an instructional approach based on recursive decomposition of knowledge. The basic idea is that complex competence is built by adding coordination and other structure to simpler pieces of knowledge. Further, Gagné argued, instruction is most likely to be effective if severe constraints are placed on the amount of new structure that must be added to already known atoms to yield each new knowledge unit. The idea was to make the amount of learning required at any one time manageably small. Instructional design, then, should consist of several steps:

- analyze the domain knowledge into a hierarchy of atoms, each of which is either a very small piece of knowledge or a relatively simple combination of previously specified atoms;
- sequence the atoms for instruction so that a combination atom is not taught until its component atoms are taught; and

787

• design an instructional approach for each atom in the sequence.

Ideas pertaining to task analysis and instructional sequencing were unique within the context of experimental paradigms of the time, which included paired associate learning, operant conditioning, serial learning, and concept formation. Gagné characterized his stance as opposed to the prevailing assumption that the best way to learn a task is to practice it. He acknowledged that while his principles were not yet supported by empirical evidence, he was stating them so that experimental work could begin.

An early major strand of this work was research on learning hierarchies. A learning hierarchy is a decomposition of a complex task into a progression of increasingly complex capabilities leading to the performance of that task. An example of a learning hierarchy for the target task, "finding formulas for the sum of $n$ terms in a number series," is depicted in Figure 24–1 (see R. M. Gagné, 1962a;b). As shown, the target task is analyzed into simpler components, with these in turn further analyzed into still simpler ones. For a number of such tasks and hierarchies, including developmental tasks such as Piaget's conservation of volume, Gagné (1985) and others demonstrated that successively higher level skills (at the top of the hierarchy) were more readily learned when their subordinate skills (lower in the hierarchy) were well learned first. "This suggested a principle of instructional sequencing that went beyond the frame-by-frame organization of programmed instruction, which I called 'cumulative learning' " (R. M. Gagné, 1989, p. 171).

Gagné also wrote about attempts to validate the cumulative learning hypothesis that did not meet with success (Gagné, 1985). This, as well as a growing body of literature on verbal learning that favored a top-down superordinate learning model over a bottom-up cumulative one, eventually led him to conclude that learning hierarchies applied primarily to one particular class of learning outcome, intellectual skills (Gagné, 1985). Intellectual skills were defined as operations representing what people are able to *do*, and were differentiated from verbal knowledge, the information that people retrieve from memory. Later Gagné (e.g., 1985) wrote about additional classes of learning outcomes to which the cumulative learning model did not apply: motor skills, attitudes, and cognitive strategies, the latter being equated with higher order thinking skills. Throughout his career, however, Gagné appeared to favor intellectual skills as the most important and trainable learning goals for work and school, suggesting at one point that verbal information was less important because it could be looked up if needed (Gagné, 1968). Cognitive strategies also were regarded as less important as targets for instruction because the state of knowledge pertaining to them was primitive. Further, Gagné (R. M. Gagné, personal communication, 1984; Gagné, 1985) suspected that strategic capabilities could not be trained directly but evolved over time as by-products of problem solving in many situations.

From about 1969, Gagné and his associates at Florida State University developed and evolved what is now widely regarded as "traditional" instructional design theory. Called Instructional Systems Design, or ISD, it consisted of guidelines and procedures for the rational decomposition of complex tasks into learning hierarchies and detailed prescriptions for the design of instructional programs based on such hierarchies. A theme in this body of work was the use of taxonomies representing different levels of complexity in learning outcomes. For example, different levels of intellectual skills were identified: discriminations, identified concepts, defined concepts, rules, and higher order rules. The significance of such taxonomies was that different types of learning outcomes were associated with different "conditions of learning" and thus were paired with particular prescriptions for training. Although ISD acknowledged and dealt with various forms of learning, it was best known and most powerful as a technology for the efficient training of intellectual skills.

This emphasis on intellectual skills had a major impact on the field of instructional design. For example, it helps explain why instructional design today is perceived as better serving the training needs of business and industry than the more general educational needs of public schools. Although the experimental research on Gagné's instructional theory was conducted primarily with schoolchildren, and although most of Gagné's writings were directed toward public education, American schools favored verbal learning and gave less attention to intellectual skills training.

There have certainly been many exceptions to this broad generalization. It is at least the case that the standardized measures used to index educational success tended not to emphasize the more complex information-processing capabilities (as opposed to specific bits of knowledge), even as industrial and military jobs got more complex and thus involved more complex algorithmic knowledge. Nevertheless, Dick (1992) has argued that "instructional designers cannot be blamed for poor student performance because designers have had almost no part in shaping the American public school curriculum." However, intellectual skills training was embraced as an issue of great significance to the military and industry at the time. ISD technology fit well with corporate and military agendas in an era when the goals of training were conceptualized as the programming of a work force to perform complex, though fairly routinized, duties.

Today, traditional ISD fits less well with the training needs of a society where workers are expected to help solve complex problems and cope with rapidly changing environments and advanced technologies. Based on our combined experience as training engineers and advisors for military and industrial organizations, we know that today's managers are more likely to conceptualize training needs in terms of generalized learning and problem-solving skills that can help employees adapt to such changes. Similarly, many educators now believe that beyond intellectual skills and verbal knowledge, higher order thinking capabilities are the most important goals for schooling. As traditional instructional design theory does not address these types of learning outcome, it is not capable of addressing the challenges associated with the winds of corporate and educational reform that are sweeping our country today.

## CHANGING VIEWS OF KNOWLEDGE AND LEARNING

The field of instructional design is in transition. Traditional practice is supported by an extensive design system that is

**THE ACQUISITION OF KNOWLEDGE**

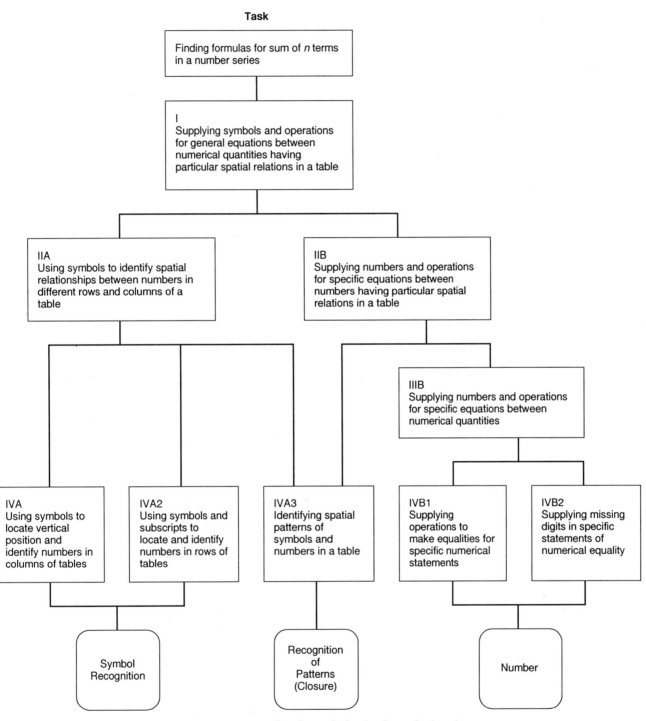

FIGURE 24–1. Hierarchy of Knowledge for the Task of Finding
Formulas for the Sum of *n* Terms in a Number Series.
Source: From R. M. Gagné (1962a). Reproduced with permission.

internally consistent and, within certain constraints, supported by empirical research. On the other hand, new challenges and emerging new theory have called much of that practice into question (e.g., Duffy & Jonassen, 1992). Efforts to modernize the field have led educational psychologists concerned with instructional design to depart from the traditional model in varying ways and degrees (e.g., R. M. Gagné, 1985; Landa, 1974; Merrill, 1987; Merrill, Zhongmin, & Jones, 1990a–c; Reigeluth, 1983; Scandura, 1983). Because these changes in practice reflect changes in basic psychological understanding about knowledge and learning, we need to give some attention to the content and processes of instruction before considering new approaches to instructional design.

For much of the 20th century, two basic views about the nature of knowledge dominated research on learning and prescriptions for teaching. One view was that the units of knowledge are associations between stimulus properties and behaviors. The other view was that the storage of (generally verbal) knowledge in memory was what learning was about. There was, of course, a long line of research in both the behavioral strand and the verbal learning theory strand. Against this theoretical backdrop, educational psychologists involved with instructional design needed to innovate; indeed, much innovation, often inspired by an emerging cognitive psychology, occurred.

Following cognitive psychology, instructional designers, including Gagné himself, embraced the metaphor that the mind is an information-processing system. As described by Vera and Simon (1993), such systems have (a) memories capable of storing symbols and symbol structures; and (b) information processes that form symbol structures as a function of sensory input, produce symbol structures causing motor actions, and modify symbol structures in memory in a variety of ways. Theories of learning based on these premises focus on explaining the processes whereby human symbol systems acquire symbolic knowledge. Thus, theories of instructional design grounded in cognitive psychology are specifications for how to design training that will help individual learners acquire performance capabilities in the form of stored symbol structures. Note that this view of symbolization gives minimal importance to second-order symbolization, the giving of explicit names to objects of the physical or mental environment. Many of the specific arguments against Vera and Simon's view interpret them as having suggested a universality for second-order symbolic processing, whereas the supporting evidence they offer includes many cases where only first-order symbolization is necessarily involved.

Early information-processing views are based largely on the multistore memory model proposed by Atkinson and Shiffrin (1968). This model proposed the existence of separate short-term memory and long-term memory stores and emphasized the role of rehearsal in moving information from temporary to permanent storage. This view was eventually replaced by elaborative constructive models of learning, models in which knowledge was seen as being constructed by the learner rather than stored in the form of its presentation by an instructor or other learning source. Two strands of constructivist thinking were visible by the 1970s: the verbal learning (e.g., R. C. Anderson, Spiro, & Montague, 1977; Spiro, Bruce, & Brewer, 1980) and the skill acquisition (e.g., J. R. Anderson, 1983) traditions. Both strands held that all learning took place within a limited-capacity working memory that represented the span of a person's immediate attention. In the verbal learning strand, meaningful learning was believed to occur when new, incoming data were encoded in the context of prior knowledge structures, called schemata, thereby updating knowledge. In the skill acquisition strand, learning was viewed as the gradual proceduralization, through practice, of rules that govern behavior, which, like any algorithm realizable by a computer, could be expressed as sequences of condition–action pairs. In both strands, it was assumed that limited-capacity short-term memory could process only a few ideas or rules at a time, thus underscoring the view that complex performances or bodies of verbal knowledge must be constructed a step at a time.

Modern instructional projects often represent marriages of cognitive views with borrowings from traditional ISD, as much of Derry's work illustrates (e.g., Derry, 1992b). More central to the theme of this chapter, however, is the observation that advances in cognitive theory are motivating evolution of prescriptive technologies employed within the traditional ISD community. To illustrate, we cite Instructional Design$_2$ (ID$_2$), an approach under development at Utah State University, that combines ideas from both the verbal and skills development strands of cognitive theory (Merrill et al., 1990b, c). ID$_2$ retains Gagné's original assumption that there are different learning outcomes and that different conditions are required to promote each of them. Merrill et al. asserted that instead of teaching specific components of prerequisite knowledge, instruction should help students actively construct more global models, complex symbol structures believed to underlie complex systems of performances, called enterprises. Enterprise-based instruction must explicitly organize and elaborate specific knowledge components so that the necessary semantic interrelationships and structural interdependencies are acquired by the student. Before such instruction can be developed, however, a detailed task analysis must be conducted to derive an explicit representation of the to-be-taught knowledge. To facilitate the process of analysis, Merrill has developed tools to help developers construct knowledge bases that can serve as input to instructional design and software development procedures. Merrill's knowledge bases are structural representations of domain content, made up of frames and relational concepts.

Although ID$_2$ may well represent a desirable move toward holistic instructional design theory, Merrill and colleagues continued to recommend that the components of knowledge that make up enterprises can be taught separately, as individual symbolic abstractions. To some extent, then, ID$_2$ leaves intact an atomistic, analytical view of knowledge. Such analytical approaches ensure that each new atom is relatively easy to learn. However, ID$_2$ has some problems. First, if the functionality being taught consists of composite atoms of knowledge, this functionality is not exercised until all the prerequisite atoms have been taught. For example, a hierarchical analysis scheme might lead designers of reading and literacy curricula to teach all symbol–sound associations and to provide lots of practice in reading trivially simple texts until a learner had fully mastered the word-perception part of reading. Slower learners would therefore miss opportunities to read meaningful materials (i.e., newspapers) while they continued to be drilled on trivial texts. Over the primary years—or even the elementary years—slower children, ironically, would then receive less practice in "reading for meaning." Although some might argue that these children "aren't ready" for more complex reading activities, the reality remains that the time available for education is not totally elastic, and often only the units at the top of the hierarchy, and hence the end of a course sequence, have real external or motivational value.

Another general problem is that the atoms of knowledge resulting from traditional hierarchical analyses were overly abstracted. This problem interacts with the first. Following further on the reading example, students often learn to recognize whole words even before they are facile in making all the symbol–sound associations implied by a word on a page. Indeed, precocious readers sometimes develop rich whole-word recognition capability before "inventing" phonics, even though the hierarchical sequence seems as though it should proceed in the other direction. The abstract relationship between a letter and its corresponding sound does not fully capture what children learn about letters and words as they learn to read—it is too abstracted from the contextual cues that mediate real reading.

## CHALLENGES TO THE INSTRUCTIONAL SYSTEMS DESIGN APPROACH

Although instructional design theory updates itself by appealing to cognitive science, continual movement toward the cognitive science mainstream does not constitute a revolutionary paradigm shift. For like traditional ISD, traditional cognitive psychology also has met with limitations and is itself now being challenged on a number of theoretical fronts (e.g., Derry, 1992a; von Glasersfeld, 1991; Lave, 1991; Wenger, 1990; Wenger & Eckert, 1991; see also chapter 2), as we shall now discuss.

### Knowledge Is Socially Situated

Training typically aims for a behavioral fit to a model that constitutes an acceptable standard of job performance. Virtually all versions of instructional design technology begin with a task analysis intended to delineate the knowledge base that will produce expert performance. The assumption is that this expert knowledge base will be acquired by trainees and later transferred into the workplace. However, a difficulty arises when one attempts to operationalize the expert model through task analysis, even if we address only job tasks for which the expert performance model consists of apparently programmable routines. Of course, real work generally includes a variety of infrequent but important demands for adaptive problem solving: the machinist handling a missing tool or specification, the pilot handling an exceptional condition on an aircraft, the teacher handling a classroom emergency, and so forth. Moreover, jobs are performed in specific work situations, not generic training centers. One major reaction to the instructional design world has been based on the view that all knowledge is fundamentally situated in the environment within which it was acquired. This has been called the *situated cognition* view.

On the one hand, routine and generic job routines are envisioned and perhaps even designed by management to be imposed on employees. On the other hand, the job routines actually performed by expert workers in the field often involve more complex problem solving and more attunement to specific situations (see, for example, J. S. Brown & Duguid, 1991). Even as we were preparing this chapter, one of us (A. L.) had the experience of being asked, while presenting work on training the most complex and emergent aspects of a job, why he considered his work to be related to training when it dealt only with relatively rare, *nonroutine* aspects of the job. The questioner, steeped in the instructional design methodology, seemed to view the rare but critical nonroutine aspects of a job as outside the scope of training because of their statistical infrequency.

An alternative view is that *the ability to cope with the nonroutine is perhaps the only knowledge worthy of instructional design in many cases, since most of the rest can be acquired quickly from on-the-job participation.*

An issue with virtually all forms of work activity is the probable misalignment between the official corporate agenda of the larger organization and what actually evolves as expertise within the working community itself (J. S. Brown & Duguid, 1991). It is true that useful job routines can be acquired through training as symbolic knowledge and carried by trainees into the workplace. But evidence is accruing (e.g., Hamper, 1986; Wenger, 1990) that the routines handed down through training are greatly modified, perhaps even set aside, in favor of practices that evolve in response to the work environment, workers' perception of corporate goals (e.g., "If I follow the rules, the company will be embarrassed, so I'd better come up with a better plan"), and individual workers' personal goals.

For example, Orr (discussed in Brown & Duguid, 1991) found cases in which repair technicians would attempt to fix faults even when official company policy was to declare the machine unrepairable or to claim there was no real problem; their goal was to preserve customer goodwill and faith in the company. A more pathological example is related by Hamper (1986) in his autobiographical account of life on the General Motors assembly line. He describes the practice of "doubling up," whereby one worker would perform the job of two people at the same time while the other took a nap, read a magazine, or even left the plant for half a workday. Such practice is in fact extremely difficult, requiring mastery of two jobs as well as considerable strength and stamina. Some workers become so adept at this performance that they are able to hide their practice from management while at the same time achieving production quotas and producing acceptable indicators of quality. Although such behaviors may not constitute an expert model for instructional design purposes, they do, in fact, reflect the actual practice of experts.

In a lengthy ethnographic study of insurance claims processors at work, Wenger (1990) documented numerous instances of misalignment between the official agenda of corporate management and what was actually learned and practiced within a working community. He argued that actual practices within a work community represent a negotiated response to a complex landscape that incorporates the goals of individuals in the work force, as well as the working community's negotiated and often limited understanding of its meaning and purpose within the corporate organism. One implication of Wenger's work is that the concepts of knowledge and mastery cannot be understood separately from the social environment in which they emerge and evolve. This idea challenges traditional conceptualizations of knowledge, mastery, and transfer typically associated with cognitive psychology and instructional systems design.

The issues raised above are not restricted to the realm of seemingly routinized clerical and blue collar job tasks. While higher level management and professional positions are not often viewed as programmable routines, instructional design theorists nevertheless frame the issues of management and professional training in terms of acquiring relatively specific target knowledge. For example, Reigeluth (personal communication, 1994) has developed a "transfer" instructional design approach applicable to training for nonroutine (adaptive) tasks, such as counseling or teaching, that are never performed exactly the same way twice. The method begins with a task analysis during which designers work with acknowledged experts to uncover and decontextualize the set of underlying causal models, or principles, that govern expert performance. Once uncovered, explicit descriptions of these tasks become targeted objectives for training. Of course, instruction is designed so that principles are presented and practiced in the context of problem-solving situations representing different classes of problems defined by different causal models. The traditionalist instructional designer might therefore argue that the instruction is sufficiently situated in the decision space wherein it is to be demonstrated.

But in exactly the same sense that there is always a degree of misalignment between an official agenda and the job routines that actually evolve within an organization's working communities, there is also misalignment between the operating premises evolved by practicing professional communities and those evolved by other communities with which those professionals interface. For example, the operating principles that evolve to govern the actual performance of a classroom teacher will undoubtedly be quite different from those taught in teacher education courses. They are also likely to differ from those of the students, the principal, the superintendent, the parents, and the school board. The fact that expert teacher performance evolves in response to all of these constituencies is a key to understanding why the expert teacher is unlikely to match the expert model preferred by any one of them.

Our point is that job performance, like all authentic cognitive activity, is socially constituted. It exists and evolves as an integral part of a complex social system that exerts powerful influence on the very structure and meaning of work. It is unlikely that such structure and meaning can be captured by the symbolic skills and principles derived from traditional forms of task analysis, which largely ignore the social landscape in which actual performance will be situated. The message for instructional designers is that relatively little of that entity that we call expertise can be acquired through instruction that is completely removed from the actual social activity of the work itself.

An extremely important part of that social activity is "cognitive apprenticeship" (Collins, Brown, & Newman, 1989). Cognitive apprenticeship denotes the sharing of problem-solving experiences between novices and one or more mentors. In the workplace or educational environment, the mentor may be a teacher or another worker or student with greater experience and expertise.

As novices and mentors work together they negotiate their understandings and actions through dialogue, which publicly exposes knowledge and thinking processes involved in their joint problem solving. According to cognitive apprenticeship views of learning, novices' active participation in and conversation about problem solving, accompanied by assistance, or "scaffolding," from mentors, enables novices to devote limited cognitive resources to internalization of critical new knowledge, to negotiate that knowledge within working and conversational contexts that give it meaning, and to internalize the language and reflective self-regulation that are modeled through a mentor's guidance.

In early stages of learning, good mentors provide overall direction and encouragement, but assume only that portion of the task that currently is too advanced for novices to manage alone. As novice performance improves, the mentor gradually fades support, encouraging novices to work and think more independently. A. L. Brown (1987) has suggested that this process, observed in everyday social settings, be characterized in terms of a three-step model that specifies different roles for the mentor at each stage. In the first stage, the mentor serves as a model problem solver, thinking aloud to demonstrate the forms of executive control involved. Stage two is a complex activity in which the mentor and student work together. Control processes continue to be made public through dialogue, although the mentor guides and prompts only when the student falters or makes a query. In the final stage, the mentor cedes control to the student, functioning primarily as a supportive, empathetic audience. Brown's model represents a class of possible models of social and linguistic processes in natural learning settings, which have been ignored until recently by cognitive psychologists and instructional designers alike. We suggest that the development of such models will play an increasingly important role in newer conceptualizations of both cognitive task analysis and instructional design.

## Performance Is Physically Situated

In addition to being socially situated, job performance as a thinking activity is also physically situated in the sense that it is directly interconnected to and operates in concert with the material world of work. A recent analysis by Greeno (1989a) suggests that new theoretical concepts are needed to help define the nature of physically situated cognitive activity.

This nature is illustrated in an anecdote from Lesgold (in press–b), describing a project at the Learning Research and Development Center (LRDC) to develop a curriculum that would integrate the last two years of high school and two years of junior college with an apprenticeship in the machine tool trade. At the beginning of this project, task-analysis interviews indicated that most machinists felt they needed to know trigonometry in order to perform their jobs. In observing machinists at work, LRDC researcher Martin Nahemow was able to gain an understanding of how trigonometry was a part of the machinists' work activity. These observations were used as a basis for designing model-based tasks that captured the various skills that machinists had lumped under the heading of "trigonometry." Task analysts and the machinists felt that the tasks required only the standard content of trigonometry courses.

At a workshop conducted to engage and prepare teachers involved in this program, project researchers presented teachers with one of the tasks, which involved working from some mechanical drawings to build a complex wheeled device out of cut and folded file-folder paper. An interesting outcome of this exercise was that the mathematics teachers who participated had difficulty with the task, while the vocational education teachers did not. This happened even though the missing knowledge of the mathematics teachers was exactly the knowledge that the machinists believed they acquired in mathematics classes. A formal foundation in trigonometric concepts was not sufficient when an actual job performance incorporating trigonometric concepts was required. Rather, the situated trigonometric and geometric construction knowledge was "buried" by machinists' beliefs that they had acquired this knowledge from mathematics classes when in fact it came partly out of many work situations they had experienced.

Greeno (1989b) has speculated about the range of theoretical concepts needed to explain phenomena such as the observation that vocational teachers but not teachers of mathematics could spontaneously perform practical tasks representing mathematical concepts. These conceptual categories include

- formal symbolic notational systems (e.g., language and mathematics);
- objects, including their arrangements and possible transformations in the real world;
- abstract entities (e.g., concepts) that are embodied in real-world activity and expressed in formal notional systems; and
- models, both of abstract entities and of real-world situations.

Consider that the "trigonometry" task of building the wheeled device involved manipulation of paper objects that modeled relevant aspects of a real-world task. In fact, these manipulations corresponded to mathematical transformations that might be represented in formal symbolic notation. However, drawing a correspondence between mathematical symbol manipulations and object manipulations required the bridging knowledge of abstract entities (e.g., the concepts of trigonometry). This bridging knowledge includes understanding how these concepts are represented and manipulated symbolically (which the math teachers probably understood), as well as how they are embodied in the arrangement and transformations of the actual objects being manipulated (which the math teachers probably did not see). Because the math teachers' conceptual understandings were not tied to object manipulations in the real world, their ability to apply mathematics in a practical task was limited. On the other hand, the vocational education teachers probably possessed a conceptual understanding that was grounded in practical activity but that might not have been linked consciously to symbolic mathematical representations. Possibly, these latter teachers would have been unable to formulate symbolic expressions capturing the mathematical nature of the task.

Note that Greeno's decomposition includes distinctions that are not recognized in many aspects of daily life. Like the old saw about the person who had always wanted to learn to write prose and was surprised to discover that she already knew how, the machinists may not know the labels, or even be able to see the distinctions, among the categories of knowledge just listed. However, these categories are important to instructional design. When we teach only the verbalizations about a body of knowledge, or even the abstracted principles behind situations to which that knowledge applies, we may not be providing the learner with accessible, real-life knowledge, nor may we be taking full advantage of the power of situations to provide an experiential grounding for those abstractions.

Greeno's analysis suggests that practical work is a cognitive activity that incorporates objects from the world. In effective work practice, these objects are restructured and transformed to produce a combination of specifically learned situational instrumentalities and abstracted (e.g., scientific and mathematical) principles. It agrees with Davydov's (Confry, 1991) theoretical position that abstract scientific concepts are anchored in

the transformations and manipulations of physical objects that take place in pursuit of a work goal. Since working communities require tools for communication and thinking, notational systems and language evolve through the social process of "naming" (Confry, 1991), whereby terms come to be associated with objects, activities, and object transformations that characterize the nature of the work. Cognitive knowledge is situated in the experiences that underlie socially shared abstractions, in the terms we use to talk to each other about those experiences and abstractions, and in the social constraints present in those experiences.

That goal-oriented problem solving incorporates objects from the environment and is in turn structured by that environment is an idea that achieved its foothold with a now well-worn story (Lave, 1988) about the unusual way in which a weight watcher measured his cottage cheese. Rather than resorting to computations that would permit the use of an incomplete set of measuring cups, the dieter invented a creative solution that used and incorporated available environmental artifacts, spreading the cheese out on a plate into a rectangle and splitting that rectangle into the appropriate number of equal smaller rectangles. The implication of this observation (and many others like it) is that real-world problem solving is productive, rather than procedural, in nature.

Problem solvers display a natural tendency to draft available pieces of their immediate world and employ them as tools to facilitate and structure their thinking. It is interesting to note that Piaget observed similar forms of concrete activity in what he considered to be the preformal stage of intellectual development. However, recent analyses of authentic work activity seem to indicate that much of it is concretely grounded, productive problem solving. This view of performance is reminiscent of Gibsonian theory (Gibson, 1979), but is at odds with cognitive models supposing that people first acquire abstract symbolic structures during an educational process that is removed from physical activity, and then go out into the world and transfer these structures into various physical settings.

To summarize, we have seen a transition from a view of learning that was very school oriented and assumed a progression from *learn* to *do*. The emerging view is that learning must be grounded in experience, from which abstractions are constructed, largely by the learner. This suggests a cyclical progression from *do* to *learn* (grounded in the past experience) to *do* (trying out the abstractions just learned).

## ROLE FOR INSTRUCTIONAL TECHNOLOGY

Situated cognition theory suggests a number of interesting roles for computer-based instructional technologies. The emphasis on learning through apprenticeship in the context of authentic work activity invokes a vision of computer technologies that function in dual roles, as tools that help workers accomplish the direct tasks at hand and as facilitators that enable workers to develop adequate models of the relevant logical, legal, scientific, or possibly even moral aspects of their work. For example, in addition to using the computer to help structure and organize their daily activities, claims processors (cf. Wenger, 1990) might also be provided with access to information resources containing explanations of corporate policy and scientific concepts relevant to the business of insurance claims processing. In addition, a networking bulletin board system could be implemented to facilitate and encourage the exchange and negotiation of knowledge and meaning that already is so vital to that community's practice. These are rough suggestions, two of many possibilities that exist for enriching the community practice of claims processors in ways that might benefit the corporate whole. It is important to note that such innovations do not suggest the weakening of evaluative systems based on production quotas, quality indicators, turnover analyses, and the like. To the extent that such evaluative indicators remain healthy and relevant, they help evaluate the success of efforts such as those we propose.

This vision of computer-based training is antithetical to the image of students sitting in classrooms removed from the work environment, interacting one-on-one with computers designed to serve as teacher/experts. Rather, it is a vision of workers engaged in intellectual partnerships representing distributed processing that is shared among individuals and tools working together in teams. Routine activity is off-loaded onto the technology. But the technology also facilitates communication within and between community boundaries and provides access to a world of performance-enhancing knowledge and tools beyond that which might otherwise reside within the working community.

However, not all training should take place in the context of daily activity. There are work situations, such as emergencies, that occur only occasionally in natural settings but that require a high state of readiness and expertise on the part of workers when they do occur. Below we describe one example of a learning by doing approach that uses simulated work experience and computer-based coaching to bring the advantages of learning by doing to jobs for which both real-world practice situations and true expert coaches are often in short supply.

## The Sherlock Project

For the past 10 years, a number of LRDC and U.S. Air Force experts have been developing an instructional approach called intelligent coached apprenticeship (Eggan & Lesgold, 1992; Katz & Lesgold, 1991; Katz, Lesgold, Eggan, & Gordin, 1992, 1993; Lajoie & Lesgold, 1989; Lesgold, 1993–1995; Lesgold, Eggan, Katz, & Rao, 1992; Lesgold & Katz, 1992; Lesgold, Katz, Greenberg, Hughes, & Eggan, 1992; Lesgold, Lajoie, Bunzo, & Eggan, 1992). Sherlock II, the current embodiment of the ideas we discuss in this chapter, has been a collaborative effort that has included Daniel Abeshouse, Marilyn Bunzo, Roberta Catizone, Dennis Collins, Richard Eastman, Gary Eggan, Mark Galloway, Maria Gordin, Linda Greenberg, Sherrie Gott, Ellen Hall, Edward Hughes, Ron Kane, Sandra Katz, Dimitra Keffalonitou, Susanne Lajoie, Alan Lesgold, Thomas McGinnis, Johanna Moore, Dan Peters, Bob Pokorny, Rudianto Prabowo, Govinda Rao, Rose Rosenfeld, and Arlene Weiner. Collins, Galloway, Gott, Hall, Kane, and Pokorny are U.S. Air Force uniformed or civilian employees; the others are or were at the University of Pittsburgh. Sherlock II is based on the opportunity to experience the most difficult aspects of cognitively intense jobs in a simulated work environment where assistance in the form of an intelligent computer-based coach is always available and where there are opportunities to reflect on simulated work experi-

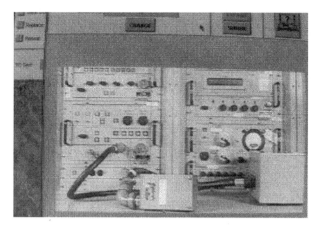

FIGURE 24–2. Partial View of F-15 Manual Avionics Test Station, Showing Sherlock Screen Display

ences. We have developed two generations of tutors for training a specialized electronics maintenance job in the U.S. Air Force, namely, the F-15 manual avionics test station technician specialty (Figure 24–2 shows part of the test station as seen in a Sherlock screen image). The tutor focuses on the hardest part of the job, isolating failures in the test station itself. Both generations of the training system we have built, named Sherlock I and Sherlock II, have worked remarkably well, in that success has fostered high levels of job expertise and, with Sherlock II, promoted transfer to new electronics troubleshooting tasks on novel equipment.

Sherlock trains technicians who work with a test station. This is a tool for diagnosing failures in aircraft parts, specifically navigation electronics from the F-15 tactical fighter plane (for more explanation of the job for which Sherlock trains, see Appendix 1). Technicians have no difficulty learning to use the test station to diagnose parts from the F-15, largely because the process is mainly one of following directions from a troubleshooting guide. The test station is a giant switch, like a telephone exchange, that connects power sources to various contacts on an aircraft part and also connects measurement devices to other contacts on the part. The troubleshooting guide tells exactly which buttons to push on the test station to effect each connection and what action to take as a result of particular measurements made by the station. The problem arises when the test station itself fails. Then, there are no instructions sufficient to avoid having to do some heuristic problem solving. It is test station failure problems that Sherlock provides as a basis of its training regimen, because that is what technicians have trouble learning to do.

Air force colleagues involved in testing the latest version of Sherlock report experimental versus control effects of 2 standard deviations, several times the effects usually found with short-term instructional treatments (S. P. Gott, personal communication, August, 1993). Further, testing was done with a criterion of real-world performance of the hardest parts of the job and with blind scoring of performances, something quite unusual in educational technology development. Earlier tests of Sherlock established that what is learned is retained (6-month retention tests showed losses of no more than 10 percent of what was learned). The first round of field testing showed that 20 to 25 hours of Sherlock training produced learning equivalent to about 4 years of on-the-job experience.

The Sherlock cognitive apprenticeship borrows heavily from everyday learning situations, such as learning to play football. Generally, learning to play football involves a lot of actual football play. There are often special drills, but they are motivated by observations of ongoing play. It would seem quite strange for a prospective player to be told to spend 3 months on tackling and then 3 months on throwing and then 3 months on running before trying to actually play in a game. In contrast, long strings of prerequisites have characterized academic approaches to schooling and training—in formal education, whole performances are often the distant goal rather than the foundation of learning activity. To the extent that current instructional design procedures contribute to this problem of having too many barriers in the way of beginning authentic, real-world practice of target competence, those procedures merit careful reexamination.

A second characteristic of everyday informal learning is that various forms of coaching, assignment within teams, matching of competing teams, and technological supports help ensure some success in holistic practice from the outset. A Little League player just starting to play baseball has about the same rough odds of being in a winning game as a major leaguer. In essence, the trick of informal learning is that it is "sink or swim" but with some engineering to ensure that trainees do not sink. Further, while special talent is recognized, it is assumed that everyone is capable of learning to perform creditably. In contrast, formal schooling often involves norms that index quality of instruction by the number who fail to learn.

A third characteristic of informal learning in domains like football is that while activity is too intense to permit much reflection during performance, reflective opportunities do take place outside of the performance periods and are founded on holistic experience. The best football players and coaches review films of each game they or their opponents play. Suggested drills or improvements are motivated by the specifics of games just played. Fragments of needed knowledge are meaningful because they are acquired in response to impasses reached during holistic, real-world practice. Other needed knowledge is inferred after extensive reflection on recent experience in the task or discussions with others who watched the performance and gained different insights from a different angle.

The primary activity within Sherlock is holistic work, at the highest levels of real-world difficulty. Everyone completes every problem, though often this requires coaching, which is available on demand. The approach has several distinguishing characteristics:

- Learning activity is centered in a simulated work environment.
- Learning activity is centered on problems that exemplify the hardest parts of the job for which one is being trained.
- For each problem, two kinds of activities occur:
  - The student solves the problem, requesting advice from the intelligent tutor as necessary.
  - The student reviews a record of her problem-solving activity.

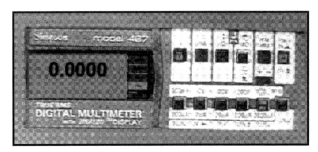

FIGURE 24–3. Partial Screen Display of Hand-held Multimeter, Showing Video with Computer Graphic Overlays (e.g., the 0.000 Reading)

(To enhance readability, we alternate between masculine and feminine pronouns rather than using more cumbersome forms. About 23 percent of the target population of the Sherlock system are women.)

Sherlock provides a simulation of the work environment for the F-15 avionics job, using a combination of video and computer graphic displays (Figure 24–3 shows an example display). Simulated controls can be operated with the computer mouse, and the displays change to reflect an underlying computer simulation of the devices being simulated. Since the fundamental activity of troubleshooting in this job is making tests with meters, this is provided realistically by having icons of meter probes that can be "attached" to video images of device test points (an example screen is shown in Figure 24–4).

*Support for Reflection.* We have developed a collection of tools for reflection. One provides an intelligent replay of the trainee's actions. A trainee can "walk through" the actions he just performed while solving the problem. In addition, he can access information about what can in principle be known about the system given the actions replayed so far (the work of troubleshooting is mostly the making of electrical measurements and then figuring out which possibilities are ruled out and which supported by the pattern of results). Also, he can ask

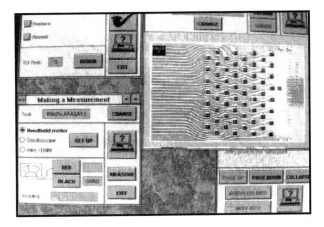

FIGURE 24–4. Sherlock Screen Image Showing Video Image of a Printed Circuit Card with Test Point Numbers Overlaid in Computer Graphics (*middle right*)

what an expert might have done in place of any of his actions, get a critique of his action, and have his action evaluated by the system. In addition, extensive conceptual knowledge about the system's functions is available from intelligent hypergraphic displays of an expert's circuit model schematic drawing. In these drawings, the boxes that stand for circuit components are all mouse-sensitive and can "tell about themselves." We have also built a tool for displaying an expert solution to the problem, again with extensive conceptual information available as appropriate to each step. Further, there is an option for side-by-side listing of an expert solution and the trainee's most recent effort.

The tools we have built are motivated by substantial research on the reflective activities that might foster learning. For example, Chi and VanLehn (1991; VanLehn, Jones, & Chi, 1992) analyzed the activity of more and less effective learners in studying worked-out physics problems. They found that more effective learners showed a different pattern of study, paying more attention to the conditions under which various steps in the solution were taken, to the relations between actions and goals, to the consequences of actions, and to the underlying meanings for formalisms such as equations. Bielaczyc, Pirolli, and Brown (1993, April; Pirolli & Bielaczyc, 1989) demonstrated that students could be taught the following approach to learning from examples and that such metacognitive instruction improved their learning ability:

1. Identify and elaborate the relations between the main ideas discussed in the text.
2. Determine both the form and the meaning of (the content of) the examples.
3. Connect the concepts in the texts and the examples.

Basically, reflecting on a problem after solving it affords about the same learning opportunities as reflecting on examples presented in a textbook or a class. Working from the Chi and the Bielaczyc studies just cited, we can infer several possible roles for postproblem reflection. First, if the trainee reached impasses during his efforts and had to ask for help, then there is some learning work to be done. The trainee must figure out why the suggestions of the intelligent coach were useful and what rules can be inferred. Second, problem-solving experiences afford opportunities for tuning the generality of procedural knowledge and also for elaborating conceptual knowledge. This is especially the case where intuitive guessing was part of the solution process: "I tried doing $x$ because it seemed like it might work; why did I think it should work?"

Problems can often be solved in nonoptimal ways. When this happens, there is no impasse to cue the trainee that her knowledge needs further tuning. So, criticism may be a useful part of the reflection opportunity. Of special relevance are the trade-offs involved in testing hypotheses by swapping parts versus measuring electrical properties of the faulted system. Just as in football, part of what a coach can do is to point out possibilities for improvement that may not be evident to the trainee.

As will be outlined below, while this instructional approach differs radically from the approaches promoted by traditional instructional design schemes, it is equally dependent on good task analysis. What is different is that the structure of learning tasks is more authentic, rooted in the needs of practice (or simulated practice) rather than being derived directly from task analysis structure.

*Intelligent Hyperdisplays.* One important innovation of Sherlock, in addition to the coached apprenticeship approach to training, is the intelligent hyperdisplay (Figure 24–5). When Sherlock constructs a schematic diagram to help illustrate the advice it is providing, that diagram is organized to show expert understanding of the system with which the trainee is working. The structure of the diagram reflects the expert representation of the circuitry involved in carrying out the function that failed. Diagrams are designed by the computer system to suit the specific needs of the trainee at the time they are presented. The displays are "shallow hypertext." What is displayed is approximately what a trainee would want to know at that time, but any piece of information can be used as a portal to more detail or explanation. The part of the system on which the expert would be focusing at a given point in the problem solution process is allocated the most space in the diagram and presented in the most detail. All diagram components are "buttons" that can be pushed to expand their level of detail. Boxes in the diagram are color coded to indicate what is known about them, given the tests carried out so far. Circuit paths are color coded to indicate whether the electrical properties of those paths are known to be appropriate or inappropriate for the function that has failed. Sometimes during problem solving, information is deleted from the display before it is shown, so that the trainee doesn't substitute looking at labels in the displays for inferring what circuitry is involved in the functional failure being diagnosed.

From an instructional design point of view, then, the intelligent hyperdisplay, as a component of instruction, is constructed in response to an emergent task performance situation in which a student needs assistance. The assistance that is assembled reflects three kinds of knowledge:

- the curriculum or goal structure for the instruction;
- an expert's knowledge of how to deal with the task at hand; and
- the known structure of the work environment that is being provided or simulated as part of the task at hand.

Again, we note that this approach depends on the same kinds of task analyses that traditionally have been conducted, with only some subtle modifications. The subtleties have to do with the extent to which the task analyst adds a symbolic processing model to the information being directly gleaned from the subject matter expert. Historically there has been a tendency for task analysts to elaborate models of expert performance in ways that go beyond the information provided by subject matter experts. For example, assumptions were made about what information had to be memorized, about how information would be "retrieved from memory" when needed, and so forth. The analyses we have done to support projects like Sherlock focus on a plan for performance as framed by an expert, including the representations the expert appeals to, but not including explicit representation of basic mental operations such as "retrieve from memory" or "compare."

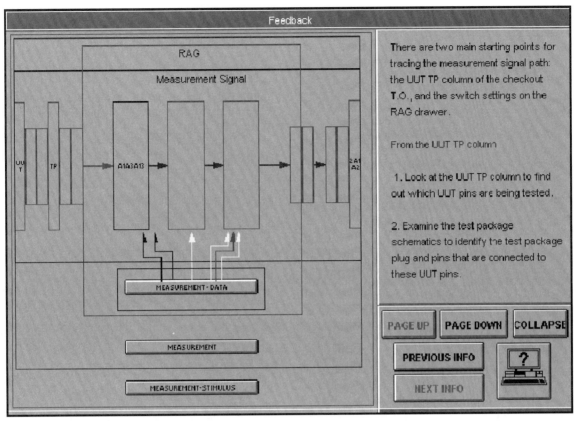

FIGURE 24–5. Example of Intelligent Hyperdisplay Used for Coaching

*How Sherlock Works.* Although the Sherlock system is a complex piece of software (the program is roughly of the scale of the newest versions of major word processors or multimedia presentation systems—20 MB of files needing 12 MB of computer memory or more), its basic design is rather straightforward. In declarative terms, it contains a large data base of "objects." Most of these objects represent components of the work environment and contain descriptions of what the component is, what it does, how it can fail, how it can be tested, and what an expert might know specifically about it (as opposed to any category of which it might be a part). This knowledge base corresponds to the architecture of the test station, that is, the work environment toward which learning is directed. For example, since the test station contains an oscilloscope as a major component, the knowledge base would need to contain an object corresponding to all that needs to be known or represented about an oscilloscope in order to handle all the tasks that arise in that environment.

From a procedural point of view, the organization of Sherlock is better seen as a collection of teams, a design approach developed by Edward Hughes. The teams represent different kinds of expertise that the system must have in order to provide simulated work situations, coaching, assessment, etc. As can be seen from Table 24–1, the four teams deal with the issues of curriculum, circuit diagnosis expertise (both about how the work environment operates and about how to diagnose failures), coaching, and student judging. Further, some teams are

components of others; for example, most teams depend on the expert modeling capability (circuit troubleshooting team) to accomplish their purposes.

From a software design point of view, a team is really a controlled interface between a set of computational routines and the rest of a system. However, as is always the case with a well-evolved design, these top-level components of the system represent the key concerns of the learning methodology embodied in Sherlock. The curriculum planning team represents the decision that some simulated work experiences will afford better learning opportunities than others, that a mapping from the knowledge required to address a problem to the knowledge the student is believed already to have will suggest constraints on the selection of tasks to provide as practice opportunities. The circuit diagnosis team embodies the expertise the system is designed to convey.

That is, the fundamental claim is that if the system can

- accurately represent work situations,
- coach a trainee when she encounters difficulty in a situation, and
- explain how things work and why it advises a particular course of action,

then this support will be sufficient to make practice in a simulated work environment an effective means of learning the

TABLE 24–1. Components of Sherlock System

| Team | Members |
| --- | --- |
| Curriculum Planning | Student Judging Team |
| | Training Manager |
| | Circuit Diagnosis Team |
| | Monitor |
| Circuit Diagnosis | Document Librarian |
| | Document Understander |
| | Device Simulation |
| | Suspect Chooser |
| | Inferencer |
| | Action Taker |
| | Monitor |
| Coaching | Student Judging Team |
| | Circuit Diagnosis Team |
| | Rhetorician |
| | Monitor |
| Student Judging | Circuit Diagnosis Team |
| | Training Manager |
| | Monitor |

work. Other aspects of the system, such as reflection opportunities, are means of amplifying the effects of this basic arrangement. The fundamental determinant of success is hypothesized to be the completeness and accuracy of the domain knowledge that supports the three basic functions of simulating the work environment, coaching practice within the environment, and defending the simulation and coaching via explanations. This is our version of the old saw that "you can't teach what you don't know."

## TASK ANALYSIS

As we have been suggesting, curriculum always begins, explicitly or implicitly, with task analysis, that is, with an analysis of what the student should know, or be able to do, after successfully completing a learning activity. Unfortunately, explicit task analysis often does not take place. Rather, long-standing assumptions about what should be taught simply persevere, with incremental changes made periodically to accommodate new ideas about schooling. This situation occurs in part because we all have everyday wisdom about what students should be taught, and we tend not to invest in new task analyses unless our beliefs are challenged substantially. However, there are serious problems that arise when curriculum evolves without regular analyses of how the to-be-taught knowledge might be used.

Traditional instructional design approaches are analytic. That is, they attempt to decompose complex behaviors into simpler ones, ending up with a set of microprocedures and conditions under which they should be applied. Today, there are tools that can be used to support this analysis. One, called TARGET, was developed at NASA. Another, called CAT, was designed by Kent Williams (now at Virginia Polytechnic Institute). To provide a sense of the basic procedure, suppose we were teaching Alan Lesgold (AL) to dial his mother's phone number. A program like CAT would walk us step by step

through the process of dialing, asking questions along the way to identify procedures (or goals) and the conditions under which they might apply. At a gross level of analysis, the scheme shown in Figure 24–6 shows the result of going through the analysis process. Basically, the analysis revealed that there is a preprogrammed code for that number which can be used on the phone at home, but that the usual dialing process is needed if AL is calling from some other phone. This level of analysis is incomplete, however, because it does not show the level of detail needed to actually do the dialing work. A complete breakdown of what is needed is presented in Figure 24–7. Serious task analysts might go even deeper into this process, if the total amount of material to be taught wasn't too large. And, there appears to be no question that one would know how to dial AL's mother if one had absorbed all of the knowledge adumbrated in Figure 24–7. However, at some level, the specified knowledge remains incomplete.

Suppose that new phones were purchased for the house. Because the knowledge listed contains no explanation of either the possibility of programming a phone or that available programming affords the opportunity for faster dialing, someone who knew only what is shown in Figure 24–7 would either be stuck when the phones were changed or else, more likely, simply revert to the away-from-home procedure. The possibility that the new phone should be programmed is not covered by what is explicitly stated in the task analysis. Unfortunately, task analysis of the kind just illustrated does not deal with the background knowledge needed to recover from environmental changes that render prior knowledge obsolete. Some might argue that this problem is handled because experts often state that there is declarative knowledge one also needs to know, and the task analyst then does an analysis of that declarative knowledge. However, it remains the case that the task analytic procedures generally used today do not result in a knowledge base that includes explicitly within it the knowledge needed

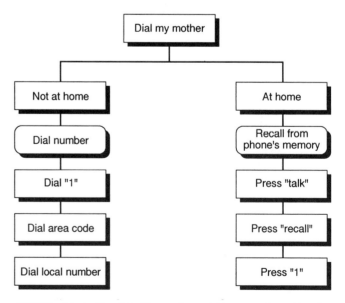

FIGURE 24–6. Graphic Illustration of Top Level of Simple Task Analysis

```
MAIN GOAL "Dial my mother"                          RULE "Dial local number"
                                                      METHOD "Local Number"
RULE "Dial my mother" "Dial a phone call to my mother";     STEP "Dial Exchange"
 METHOD "Dial Number";                                      STEP "Dial Last four digits";
     STEP "Dial "1" ",                                 END;
     STEP :Dial area code",                          END;
     STEP "Dial local number";
 IF "Not at home"                                     RULE "Dial Exchange";
     TRY METHOD "Dial Number";                        METHOD INCOMPLETE "Exchange";
 END;                                                       STEP "Press "5" ",
 METHOD "Recall from phone's memory";                       STEP "Press "5" ",
     STEP "Press "talk" "'                                  STEP "Press "5" ";
     STEP "Press "recall" "'                            END;
     STEP "Press "1" ";                               END;
 IF "At home"
     TRY METHOD "Recall from phone's memory";         RULE "Dial Last four digits";
 END;                                                 METHOD INCOMPLETE "Final Four";
END;                                                        STEP "Press "1" ",
                                                            STEP "Press "3" ",
                                                            STEP "Press "7" ",
RULE "Dial area code";                                      STEP "Press "5" ";
 METHOD "Area Code 414";                                END;
     STEP "Press "4" ",                               END;
     STEP "Press "1" ",
     STEP "Press "4" ",
 END;
END;
```

FIGURE 24–7. Rules Derived from Task Analysis of Schemes
for Calling Home

to understand why procedures are the way they are or the common sense, domain-specific knowledge, and knowledge organization needed to support revisions in one's knowledge in the face of environmental change.

Below, we discuss one small effort toward improved task analysis approaches. However, we caution the reader that there are deep unsolved problems in this area, some of which will require extended computer science and cognitive psychology research. In essence, the efforts in computer science to develop adaptive computer systems have posed the same questions that keep arising in efforts to articulate instructional technology well enough that it might be done partly by machine.

Recall the workshop example discussed earlier in which the role of trigonometry knowledge in machinists' work was examined. Martin Nahemow's experience in that workshop was that mathematics teachers generally could not carry out a "trigonometry task" successfully, while industrial arts teachers often could. Assuming that it is generally not easy to teach what you don't know, we conclude that this is an example of a part of society believing that course titles like geometry and trigonometry denote offerings that provide certain knowledge about laying out and interpreting drawings, when it is actually unlikely that these skills are taught very directly—if at all. Although traditional task analysis approaches might identify aspects of this problem, they suffer in the end from lack of agreement among analysts about what constitutes a sufficient breakdown of knowledge into components. Equally important, they cannot capture the informal and intuitive mechanisms involved in adapting prior knowledge to emergent situations.

When examples such as this are discussed, inevitably someone states, with some piety, that schools are meant to educate, not to train machinists. Our purpose is not to take sides in that debate but rather to suggest that the task analyses behind both job-specific training and educational curriculum planning often lack systematic treatment of the relative abstraction of the material targeted for instruction. Often, an intermediate level of abstraction is considered, without either a mapping onto specific work situations or a systematic exploration of possible abstract connections among different knowledge components. We suggest that a strong curriculum must be based in strong analyses of what is to be taught, and that those analyses must attend to issues of abstraction.

There are two abstraction issues to consider. First, as just suggested, it is important to determine how general a level of knowledge is desired as the outcome of instruction. In spite of various platitudes about "real education" versus "mere training," a basic finding of psychology is that transfer of knowledge is very specific and very limited. Simply knowing an abstraction does not mean that it will be applied when needed. Further, it may be difficult or impossible to acquire some abstractions without being able to anchor them to real-world situations. A second concern is the structuring of abstractions. We suspect that being able to use abstract knowledge comes partly from understanding with some clarity how it derives from specific experience and which of its aspects are important to preserve over situations.

Our strategy in the two major sections that follow is first to introduce some ideas from computer science about computational objects and object-oriented design, and then to return to the issue of representing the target knowledge for a body of instruction.

## THE NATURE OF OBJECTS

We are struck by the similarity between the task of the instructor and the task of a software designer trying to produce an intelligent, maintainable piece of software. As software systems grew larger and lasted longer, it became clear that the very term "programming" failed to capture the work involved in designing software systems. Rather, it has become evident that the knowledge embodied in a complex program needs to be publicly available, at least to the community that maintains the software and partly to those who use it. Absent such an accessible public character, software becomes unaffordable. It takes too long to alter or improve, and it is not possible even to predict how expensive any particular change might be. Just as the analysis of dialing a telephone number was inadequate because it contained no background conceptual support, so most early computer programs were unmaintainable because their purpose was not connected intimately with their content. In such situations making changes is extremely difficult, and the line between "bugs" (failures of the program to perform as advertised) and "features" (properties designed intentionally that may be misunderstood) becomes very fuzzy and permeable.

### States, Behaviors, and Identity

We have found it useful to bring some of the concepts of object-oriented software design into our thinking about task analysis (portions of this section appear in similar form in Lesgold, 1995). Booch (1991) defines an *object* as an entity that has *states, behaviors,* and *identity.* The concept of object is related to the notion of *schema* (Kant, 1794; Minsky, 1986; Schank, 1982; Schank & Abelson, 1977). Every object has associated with it a class of situations for which it is relevant and a means of deciding whether a particular situation is within that class or not. Some objects, such as a stop sign, are defined mostly by perceptual features: When we see a stop sign, we stop the car. Other objects are defined more by features of purpose, such as a scientific paper for publication or a lottery ticket.

Consider what all we know about a stop sign. First, we know how to recognize one. In the terminology of object-oriented design, we have acquired a perceptual capability that "triggers" the stop sign object in our minds when we see stop signs. By trigger, we mean that the stop sign object receives a message stating that a stop sign has been seen. The response to this message is called a method. The *behaviors* of an object

can be captured as a set of methods for dealing with the class of situations for which that object is relevant. So, the stop sign object needs to know what to do when it is notified that a stop sign has been seen. Probably, it needs to determine how far away the stop sign is and then send a message to a car-steering object to stop the car before reaching the sign's location. So, objects like the stop sign object are computational units, or programs, if you prefer (or agents, in the sense of Minsky, 1986).

Objects usually have to store some local data, information meaningful only within the context of the given object, in this case, perhaps the distance from the stop sign to the person perceiving it. We call the pattern of this stored data the object's *state.* Those objects that represent components of the world in which we are active have states corresponding to states in that world. Objects associated with mental models have states corresponding to states of those models when they are "run" mentally. The states of an object are indexed by "local" variables, which function as parameters for its method. Depending on the values of an object's variables, it will do different things. So, altogether, an object represents all that we know about some thing in the world, including state information, how to mentally model that thing (in this case, how to anticipate changes in the distance from the stop sign), and how to act in the context of that thing (e.g., sending a message to another object to stop the car). Finally, an object has *identity:* We can reflect on what it does and whether it could be modified or augmented.

### Inheritance Hierarchies

The traffic light object has an identity. We can think about it. The identity has an extension—all the situations in which we find ourselves encountering a traffic light. It also has meaning, derived from how we can think about a traffic light (its colors, for example) and how we can think about what we do in response to traffic lights.

It is possible to have a *specialized* knowledge object, such as a fast-highway traffic light object. Such an object might know how to respond specially to traffic lights on high-speed highways (e.g., the response must occur earlier and deceleration must be controlled to avoid problems from behind). Similarly, one might have a specialized city traffic light object. Alternatively, one might have only one general traffic light object that keeps track of its locational state (city vs. highway) as the value of a variable.

From these possibilities emerge some important object principles, notably the principles of *abstraction* and of *inheritance.* Abstraction of one object from another involves identification of essential properties of function and state that might apply to a wider range of situations. For example, we might generalize from highway stoplights to stoplights in general. What is essential to all stoplights is that we must stop in front of them when they are red. What is specific to the highway stoplight is that a special stopping plan must be used to ensure that one stops in time but without being hit from behind. What is specific to a Pittsburgh city traffic light is that one should expect the driver opposite to make a quick left turn when the light turns green. And so on.

We can arrange families of objects into *inheritance hierarchies,* which are partial orderings of objects in terms of their degree of abstraction. For example, the general traffic light object is above the city traffic light object in such an inheritance hierarchy, because it is a generalization of the city light, and the Pittsburgh traffic light is even further specialized. Inheritance can also produce lattice structures if we permit multiple inheritance of specialized objects from generalized objects. For example, a flashing red light at an intersection inherits some of its identity from the red light in a regular, three-lens traffic light and part of its identity from a stop sign.

## Usage Networks

Another kind of relationship besides inheritance is usage. In many software situations, objects get work done by delegating it—they *use* other objects. For example, a graphic editor program creates an instance of some object for each element drawn on the screen—each line, curve, box, piece of text, and so on. Sometimes a set of elements is grouped together, as when several drawing elements are combined to make a single complex figure. Such a group is represented by a separate group object. When the group object is sent a message to draw itself on the screen, it accomplishes this by instructing each of its "member" objects to draw themselves (for the deeply interested reader: consider how work is divided when a complex object wants to shrink itself). The psychological concept of learning hierarchies (R. M. Gagné, 1977) is similar to the idea of a usage network, but not all usage relationships are hierarchical. For example, suppose there were a computer program to coach football. It might, in turn, contain two important objects, the defensive coach and the offensive coach. When the defensive coach recognizes that the program's team has just received the ball, it might send a message to the offensive coach to take over. The offensive coach might do the same for the defensive coach. For this level of coordination, a head coach is not needed, yet the coordination is outside of the immediate contents of the two coaching roles.

We suggest that usage hierarchies and inheritance hierarchies have different instructional purposes. In order to explain *why* a particular problem-solving approach is appropriate in a particular situation, for example, we would want to resort to abstracted levels in an inheritance hierarchy, as we will illustrate below. On the other hand, usage networks are like good recipe books. They allow us to keep track of which "basic strokes" are used for which purposes. So, they have an important role to play in helping teach what to do. Relative to the traditional learning hierarchy notion, the object-oriented approach also calls our attention to inheritance hierarchies as distinct from usage hierarchies but at least as important.

## Other Properties of Objects

Object-oriented design has introduced some additional desiderata for objects, and these too have some importance for instructional design. Objects are *modular*. That is, each one responds to messages based only on its own internal state (which of course may represent part of the environment) and the contents of the message. Similarly, it is helpful to think about performance modules that have some real independence. In addition, objects can be *encapsulated*. That is, they can be treated as black boxes that can be counted on for certain

behaviors but that need not be examined internally. In this sense, one can speak of providing a set of encapsulated objects to be used as tools in developing a program for a new application. The new objects to be programmed must be understood deeply by the programmer, but the tool objects can be considered as affordances that need be understood only from the viewpoint of the tool user. For example, many systems have window objects that manage windows on the screen. They respond to messages to display their contents, to shrink into icons, and the like. The programmer need not know exactly how these functions are carried out to use these objects, and most do not. In human cognitive performance, there are some encapsulated performances as well, such as arithmetic computations or symbolic manipulations (algebra or calculus).

On the other hand, we believe that the instructional design world erred in assuming that all knowledge could be recursively decomposed into encapsulated tool modules. Although people do have some basic capabilities they bring to task situations, those capabilities must be tuned to particular circumstances, and that seems to depend not only on having a good stock of modular knowledge on hand but also on having considerable familiarity with the real-world domain in which the task situations arise. The learning by doing view discussed above is particularly strong at providing that aspect of instructional design and perhaps not as strong at ferreting out the modular knowledge that is also needed.

## AN OBJECT-ORIENTED VIEW OF KNOWLEDGE

We now consider more concretely whether we can import the ideas of object-oriented analysis—figuring out how a machine could do a task—into discussions of the education of people. At a superficial level, we might speak of defining the objects that a program would need to perform some function and then teaching the person to carry out each object's function. Further, we might speak of the knowledge a person has that corresponds to the programming content of an object as a *knowledge object*. In this section, we consider some of the implications of this point of view and some of the difficult problems that need to be solved before it can be considered to be a helpful viewpoint on the design of education.

In representing knowledge as a collection of knowledge objects, we must be sensitive to a fundamental problem of knowledge: knowing when to use it. Before the knowledge represented by an object can be used, it must be "triggered" (cf. Feltovich & Barrows, 1984; Feltovich, Johnson, Moller, & Swanson, 1984). In this respect, we see objects as a level above productions (simple associations between situational conditions and relevant actions), perhaps at the level often called *schema* within cognitive psychology. Just as a production has an *if* side and a *then* side, objects, as dispositions to action, also have triggering circumstances, as discussed above. This triggering can occur in two ways, each representing somewhat different viewpoints from which a knowledge object might be seen, namely its *extension* and its *intension*. In extensional terms, an object can be seen as one or more situations and a person's capability for acting in those situations. In intensional terms, an object represents what we know about relating to a class of situations, possibly relative to the requirements of some other object. Thus, an object's intension might be indexed by the messages sent to it by other objects (and perhaps those it sends to other objects), along with the reflective knowledge one has of the object's knowledge (e.g., I know that I know how to solve quadratic equations).

## Inferring Objects
## from Situation-Specific Performances

Task analysis often consists of observing and questioning an expert while the expert handles job-relevant problem situations. The goal is to discover the features common to the problem situations observed and also the commonalities among the actions, cognitive and overt, of the expert in responding to these situations. From this information base, the task analyst must construct a tentative collection of objects that represent the expert's knowledge. Put another way, each expert's pattern of response to each problem represents a candidate knowledge object (which in turn may be decomposable into lower level knowledge objects). From the collection of candidate knowledge objects, the circumstances of each problem, and the comments of the expert about his reasons for actions and expected outcomes of his actions, the task analyst must somehow infer a more efficient set of more powerful objects—objects that "work" in more than one specific situation.

This is the same problem faced by an apprentice when learning by watching an expert demonstrate situation-appropriate behavior. Therefore, in order to be effective instructionally, experts' demonstrations (combined with their advice and comments) must be a sufficient basis for acquiring the expertise of the domain through observation. Because it is difficult to acquire any significant body of expertise solely through observation, task analysis requires an additional phase. Observations of expert performances can be alternated with performances by the task analyst, which are then critiqued by the expert. Allen Newell referred to this approach as the fundamental knowledge engineering approach in remarks made during a panel discussion at the 1988 annual meeting of the Cognitive Science Society.

This process of successive approximation is very similar to ideal apprenticeship. Further, the specific approaches that turn out to be most effective in conducting the task analysis for a given domain may be useful learning heuristics to pass on to trainees, depending on their prior knowledge. That is, *knowledge engineering may recapitulate apprenticeship,* which means that the process of having defined a knowledge object helps prepare for teaching about the knowledge indexed by that object. However, prior knowledge must also be considered. For example, a physicist trying to learn how to maintain a particular piece of electronic equipment might use different techniques to understand the domain than a technical school student would use. From the point of view of task analysis, it is critical that the means whereby knowledge is acquired and described be mappable onto the experience of the student.

Situations can be classified into objects in several ways. The first is feature identification. When the task analyst notices a particular approach or method or entity being mentioned repeatedly in the course of the expert's commented performances,

he can note the features characterizing the application of that method and verify, with the expert, that those features are the ones to attend. We might refer to this approach as *extensional probing.* Another approach, *model probing,* is to start with mental models and then accumulate a list of the variables and methods that go with them. This approach can be very effective, especially when the experts have some sense of the role of mental models in their cognitive activity. Further, by focusing on the mental models that experts use, the task analyst is getting a good head start on specifying important information to drive instruction. A third approach is *intensional probing* of the expert. That is, the expert is asked to give information about the meaning or purpose of her actions in the normal course of the probed problem-solving approach to task analysis (cf. Gott, 1989). This information can be collated and used to define candidate knowledge objects based on the meaning of the methods exhibited during the expert performances. This approach is similar to the model-probing approach, except that the information is derived directly from intensional probing of the expert rather than from the expert's discussions of her mental representations of problems.

## Task Analysis = Knowledge Engineering
## = Negotiation of Meaning

We made a central claim in the last section: A negotiation process is required to acquire knowledge. Recent learning psychology has focused in part on this process, which is sometimes called "negotiation of meaning" (e.g., Hall & Newman, 1991; Roschelle & Behrend, in press; Sipusic, Roschelle, & Pea, 1991). This is a term from the language development literature (e.g., Tudge & Rogoff, 1989) that takes notice of the fact that verbal communication always depends on some level of shared reference. That is, when we talk to each other about a situation, we end up having to negotiate the terms we are using, and that negotiation process forces the development of a useful generality. At the very least, it ensures that the generalizations each speaker makes from her own experiences are not too idiosyncratic and that shared experience is favored in generalization. When two people must interact around a problem-solving task, the meaning negotiation process, anchored in knowledge that is both task relevant and shared, helps ensure that any generalizations they form will be useful in related tasks.

The methods we discussed involve some give and take, a dialectic, between the task analyst and the expert. Further, we assert, following the situated cognition theoretical framework, that knowledge acquisition by the student must also involve this negotiation of meaning. Consequently, it is critically important that the outcome of knowledge engineering be not only the meaning finally understood by the task analyst but also a process for negotiating meaning with the student that can lead to the student's having a functionally similar body of knowledge after learning. This is clearly a tougher assignment than the classic task of specifying the target knowledge independent of the task situation or the student's prior knowledge. This added requirement is what distinguishes traditional instructional design approaches from situated cognition approaches. Further, the need for a rich context in which to anchor the meaning negotiation process lies at the core of our concerns that learning a body of knowledge cannot necessarily be done by acquiring a hierarchy of progressively more complex knowledge fragments. Some meaning may be negotiable only in the context of rich, complex, authentic tasks.

*Analyzing Pre-instructional Knowledge.* There is another way in which the task analyst must be able to view work situations not only from the viewpoint of an expert but also from the viewpoint of a trainee. If there is strong evidence that trainees generally understand certain abstractions and can tie them to specific concrete situations, then those abstractions can be used in knowledge object specifications without further concern. On the other hand, if such evidence is not present, or if counter evidence exists, then a task analysis should include not only the knowledge objects of the expert but also those more concrete, more specifically situated objects that might represent the limits of trainee knowledge during early stages of training.

It is commonplace for experts and instructors to overestimate the abstracted knowledge of trainees. This is because they already have some abstractions that trainees lack. Abstraction is necessarily a process of induction from experiences, and that which is evident to someone who has experienced many cases may not be at all apparent to someone who has experienced only one or two. Consequently, we suggest that inheritance hierarchies and the explanations they can support may be a powerful and direct way of teaching for transfer in technical domains, and perhaps others as well. We turn now to how this might be done.

## Generalizing Objects: The Inheritance Hierarchy

Knowledge objects have varying degrees of similarity. When two objects have a lot in common, it may be productive to consider them to be specializations of a common, more abstracted object. In other cases, one object may be a specialization of another. In addition to common methods and local variables, objects should, if placed in inheritance relationships to one another, also have relationships in terms of the mental model components they represent and/or other aspects of their meaning. That is, there should be some intelligible rationale for the inheritance hierarchy of knowledge objects. This is needed to drive any coaching or commenting that might be aimed at transfer from one object to another.

For example, within the domain taught by our electronics troubleshooting coached apprenticeship system, Sherlock, there are a number of testable components called relay cards. Each has an array of relays that act as a switching tree to connect an information input to one of perhaps a dozen output ports. Control signals to these logic cards control the relays, determining which of the possible paths is configured. Each kind of relay card can be considered to be the referent of a possible expert knowledge object. It is a component of an expert's mental models in the domain of Sherlock, and there are specific methods for dealing with troubleshooting situations in which it becomes the focus of testing. Further, the object has both extensional and intensional definition. Its extension is the set of relay cards of that type. Its intension is its meaning, namely its function (switching to one of a collection of path clusters) and its mechanism (using a control current to energize an electromagnet, or solenoid, which physically switches the signal current by pulling a conductor from one contact to another).

It would be reasonable for training to include explicit mention of such relay cards, to coach the methods for troubleshooting them, and otherwise to encourage trainees to think in terms of relay cards (of this particular kind) when doing troubleshooting of circuits that involve such components.

It could turn out that absent deeper understanding of how relay cards work (i.e., considering them as black boxes), very situation-specific knowledge is involved in deciding which relays' solenoid inputs to check in a particular situation. In that case, from the viewpoint of concrete situated knowledge, two kinds of relay cards might be treated as needing different corresponding knowledge objects. That is, one might know perfectly well how to test one kind but not be sure about the other. If we as task analysts realize how similar two types of cards are, we might choose to define their objects as inheriting most of their knowledge from a more general knowledge object that is generic across all relay cards. This generic relay object would represent expert troubleshooting knowledge in the domain common to the two more specific relay objects.

Having this more abstracted object from which the card-specific objects inherit their core capabilities can be useful in driving coaching that is both situated and mindful of potential loci of generalization. With a card-specific object, an intelligent coaching system can make very situated comments, such as "You know that the path this relay is supposed to be configuring is from *A* to *X*, and that Relay *T* controls this path, so do the following tests."

On the other hand, an intelligent coach can point out interesting generalities by having access to both the more abstracted object and the "sibling" objects for the particular one corresponding to the current situation. This might lead to comments like the following:

This relay card is just like the A1A3A10 card you worked on earlier, except that the configuration of relays is different. In all relay cards, you need to first check to see if the signal is being routed properly by the relays. If not, then you need to test to see whether the problem is in the relays themselves or in the control inputs to their solenoids. This relay card has a linear array of relays, only one of which should be active at any time. Therefore. . . .

We see the design of inheritance hierarchies of knowledge objects as being of central importance in developing a full specification of the knowledge needed to support instruction. By including functional and conceptual abstractions as part of the domain of task analysis, it is possible to achieve analyses that preserve a clear account of the componential breakdown of mental and physical behaviors in the expert repertoire while also providing bases for developing an understanding that goes beyond the snippets of prerequisite skills found in traditional task analyses, which are essentially usage hierarchy analyses.

Although usage hierarchies can be built largely from analyses of individual experts' behaviors, inheritance hierarchies require some analysis of the particular categories and abstractions present in the culture of experts and, if trainees are from a different culture, theirs as well. For example, the idea that two different relay cards are members of the same abstract category must rest on some demonstration that the category exists in the discourse and interactions among experts and between experts and their work environment. In addition, unless it can be demonstrated that the category also has meaning for the community of likely students/trainees, further analyses are required to show how the expert categories can be anchored intensionally in a combination of student prior knowledge and/or extensionally in specific "laboratory" experiences.

Recalling A. L. Brown's (1987) three-stage model for apprenticeship interaction described earlier in the chapter, we now suggest that there are potentially many such models for knowledge negotiation in cognitive apprenticeship settings, and that identifying and describing their features for particular job task settings is a vital part of the task analyst's job.

## CONCLUDING REMARKS

We have described a still evolving set of theoretical constructs about how human thinking and learning occur in the context of authentic work activity that is both socially and physically situated in the real world. We then provided a view, borrowed partly from software engineering, of how expertise might be analyzed to support improved instructional designs. We also indicated the ways in which a learning by doing approach can be highly effective. What is being challenged is the notion undergirding traditional instructional design: that a large amount of prerequisite instruction must take place before a student is ready to practice complex, real-world performance.

Traditional instructional designers tend to make complex performance the reward for successful subskill learning rather than the vehicle whereby learning can take place. In contrast, a theory of instructional design based on situated cognitive apprenticeship would rely much more on the processes of enculturation through which students develop and adopt the tools and conceptual categories of a practice community as they participate in that community. A new prescriptive theory of instructional design will need to address itself to methods for helping corporations and schools move trainees into systems that support apprenticeship in authentic work environments. This new approach will require the design of tools and technologies to facilitate rich, learning communities within which members can negotiate meaningful scientific and conceptual models for understanding their chosen practices, including the connectedness of those practices to broader society. Finally, of major importance is the identification of nonroutine but important tasks that occur irregularly or rarely in the daily work environment and consequently do not lend themselves to training through participation in daily work routines. These tasks might best be addressed by computer-based, coached, simulated apprenticeships.

In summary, we suggest that the new instructional systems approaches will proceed along the lines outlined below:

- Identify communities of practice within the workplace, and identify their membership, as well. Within those communities, identify any respected "old-timers" who may already serve (possibly informally) as mentors.
- Conceptualize a suitable model of apprenticeship that is compatible with the style and form of apprenticeship that already takes place within the work environment.
- Bring management and community mentors together to create understanding and alignment between their respective training goals.
- Facilitate the design of mentorship programs so that teaching expertise becomes part of the community knowledge and is perpetuated as new workers gain experience and gradually assume mentorship responsibilities themselves.
- Design and develop technologies (job aids, communications technologies) to facilitate and afford social interactions associated with cognitive apprenticeship.
- Identify critical job tasks, such as emergency procedures or special troubleshooting skills, that do not occur regularly and thus must be learned outside the daily routine of work.
- Conduct task analyses (including development of both usage and inheritance hierarchies) and develop simulated cognitive apprenticeship training environments (as with Sherlock) for nonroutine aspects of work.

This list differs from the one given at the beginning of the chapter in two important ways. First, it sees the goals of training and education as having both a performative and a conceptual side, and it articulates the connections between these viewpoints as different structures of knowledge objects. Second, it proceeds from the view that learning involves some mixture of novice communities of practice absorbing expert knowledge and expert communities of practice helping the novitiate become full intellectual members of these expert communities.

Throughout this chapter, we have made little distinction between the terms *education* and *training*. When the viewpoint we espouse is taken, these are seen as two viewpoints on a process that, when healthy and complete, provides students with both the ability to participate in new communities of practice and the understanding of what their new performances mean.

## References

Anderson, J. R. (1983). *The architecture of cognition.* Cambridge, MA: Harvard.

Anderson, R. C., Spiro, R. J., & Montague, W. E. (1977). *Schooling and the acquisition of knowledge.* Hillsdale, NJ: Lawrence Erlbaum Associates.

Atkinson, R. C., & Shiffrin, R. M. (1968). Human memory: A proposed system and its control processes. *The psychology of learning and motivation* (Vol. 2). New York: Academic Press.

Bielaczyc, K., Pirolli, P., & Brown, A. L. (1993, April). *Strategy training in self-explanation and self-regulation strategies for learning com-* *puter programming.* Report No. CSM-5. Berkeley, CA: University of California, School of Education.

Booch, G. (1991). *Object-oriented design with applications.* Redwood City, CA: Benjamin/Cummings.

Brown, A. L. (1987). Metacognition, executive control, self-regulation, and other more mysterious mechanisms. In F. Weinert & R. Klewe (Eds.), *Metacognition, motivation and understanding.* Hillsdale, NJ: Lawrence Erlbaum Associates.

Brown, J. S., & Duguid, P. (1991). Organizational learning and communities-of-practice: Toward a unified view of working, learning, and innovation. *Organizational Science, 2,* 40–57.

Chi, M. T. H., & VanLehn, K. (1991). The contents of physics self-explanations. *Journal of the Learning Sciences, 1,* 69–106.

Collins, A., Brown, J. S., & Newman, S. E. (1989). Cognitive apprenticeship: Teaching the craft of reading, writing, and mathematics. In L. B. Resnick (Ed.), *Knowing, learning and instruction: Essays in honor of Robert Glaser* (pp. 453–494). Hillsdale, NJ: Lawrence Erlbaum Associates.

Confry, J. (1991). Steering a course between Vygotsky and Piaget. *Educational Researcher, 20*(8), 28–34.

Derry, S. J. (1992a). Beyond symbolic processing: Expanding horizons for educational psychology. *Journal of Educational Psychology, 84,* 413–418.

Derry, S. J. (1992b). Metacognitive models of learning and instructional systems design. In M. Jones & P. H. Winne (Eds.), *Adaptive learning environments: Foundations and frontiers.* Berlin: Springer.

Dick, W. (1992). An instructional designer's view of constructivism. In T. M. Duffy & D. H. Jonassen (Eds.), *Constructivism and the technology of instruction: A conversation* (pp. 91–98). Hillsdale, NJ: Lawrence Erlbaum Associates.

Dick, W., & Carey, L. (1985). *The systematic design of instruction* (2nd ed.). Glenview, IL: Scott Foresman.

Duffy, T. M., & Jonassen, D. H. (Eds.) (1992). *Constructivism and the technology of instruction: A conversation.* Hillsdale, NJ: Lawrence Erlbaum Associates.

Eggan, G., & Lesgold, A. (1992). Modelling requirements for intelligent training systems. In S. Dijkstra, H. P. M. Krammer, & J. J. G. van Merrienboer (Eds.), *Instructional models in computer-based learning environments* (97–111). Heidelberg: Springer-Verlag.

Feltovich, P. J., & Barrows, H. S. (1984). Issues of generality in medical problem solving. In H. G. Schmidt & M. L. Devolder (Eds.), *Tutorials in problem-based learning.* Ashen, The Netherlands: Van Gorcum.

Feltovich, P. J., Johnson, P. E., Moller, J. H., & Swanson, D. B. (1984). LCS: The role and development of medical knowledge in diagnostic expertise. In W. J. Clancey & E. H. Shortlife (Eds.), *Readings in medical artificial intelligence.* Reading, MA: Addison Wesley.

Gagné, R. M. (1977). *The conditions of learning* (3rd ed.). New York: Holt, Rinehart & Winston.

Gagné, R. M. (1962a). The acquisition of knowledge. *Psychological Review, 69,* 355–365.

Gagné, R. M. (1962b). Military training and principles of learning. *American Psychologist, 17,* 83–91.

Gagné, R. M. (1985). *The conditions of learning* (4th ed.) New York: Holt, Rinehart & Winston.

Gagné, R. M. (1989). *Studies of learning: 50 years of research.* Tallahassee, FL: Learning Systems Institute.

Gagné, R. M., Briggs, L., & Wager, W. (1988). *Principles of instructional design* (3rd ed.). New York: Holt, Rinehart & Winston.

Gibson, J. J. (1979). *The ecological approach to visual perception.* Boston: Houghton Mifflin.

Gott, S. P. (1989). Apprenticeship instruction for real world cognitive tasks. In E. Z. Rothkopf (Ed.), *Review of Research in Education, XV.* Washington, DC: American Educational Research Association.

Greeno, J. G. (1989a). A perspective on thinking. *American Psychologist, 44*(2), 134–141.

Greeno, J. G. (1989b). Situations, mental models, and generative knowledge. In D. Klahr & K. Kotovsky (Eds.), *Complex information processing: The impact of Herbert A. Simon.* Hillsdale, NJ: Lawrence Erlbaum Associates.

Hall, R., & Newman, S. (1991, March). *From motion to marks: The social and material construction of abstraction.* Paper presented at the Third Biannual Workshop on Cognition and Instruction, Pittsburgh, PA.

Hamper, B. (1986). *Rivethead.* New York: Time Warner Books.

Kant, I. (1794). *Kritik der reinen Vernunft* [Critique of pure reason] (4th ed.). Riga, Latvia: J. F. Hartknoch.

Katz, S., & Lesgold, A. (1991). Modeling the student in Sherlock II. In J. Kay & A. Quilici (Eds.), *Proceedings of the IJCAI-91 Workshop W.4: Agent modelling for intelligent interaction* (pp. 93–127). Sydney, Australia.

Katz, S., & Lesgold, A. (1993). The role of the tutor in computer-based collaborative learning situations. In S. Lajoie & S. Derry (Eds.), *Computers as cognitive tools* (pp. 289–317). Hillsdale, NJ: Lawrence Erlbaum Associates.

Katz, S., Lesgold, A., Eggan, G., & Gordin, M. (1992). Self-adjusting curriculum planning in Sherlock II. In *Lecture Notes in Computer Science: Proceedings of the Fourth International Conference on Computers in Learning (ICCAL '92).* Berlin: Springer-Verlag.

Katz, S., Lesgold, A., Eggan, G., & Gordin, M. (1993). Modeling the student in Sherlock II. *Journal of Artificial Intelligence and Education* (Special issue on student modeling, G. McCalla & J. Greer, Eds.) *3,* 495–518.

Lajoie, S., & Lesgold, A. (1989). Apprenticeship training in the workplace: Computer coached practice environment as a new form of apprenticeship. *Machine-Mediated Learning, 3,* 7–28.

Landa, L. N. (1974). *Algorithmization in learning and instruction.* Englewood Cliffs, NJ: Educational Technology Publications.

Lave, J. (1988). *Cognition in practice: Mind, mathematics, and culture in everyday life.* Cambridge, England: Cambridge University Press.

Lave, J. (1991). Situating learning in communities of practice. In L. Resnick, J. Levine, & S. Teasley (Eds.), *Perspectives on socially shared cognition.* Washington, DC: American Psychological Association Press.

Lesgold, A. (1993). Information technology and the future of education. In S. Lajoie & S. Derry (Eds.), *Computers as cognitive tools* (pp. 369–383). Hillsdale, NJ: Lawrence Erlbaum Associates.

Lesgold, A. (1994). Assessment of intelligent training systems. In E. Baker & H. O'Neil, Jr. (Eds.), *Technology assessment in education and training* (Vol. 1) (pp. 97–116). Hillsdale, NJ: Lawrence Erlbaum Associates.

Lesgold, A. (1995). Process control for educating a smart work force. In L. B. Resnick, J. Wirt, & D. Jenkins (Eds.), *Linking school to work: Roles for standards and assessment.* New York: Jossey-Bass.

Lesgold, A. (1995). An object-based situational approach to task analysis. In M. Caillot (Ed.), *Learning electricity and electronics with advanced educational technology* (pp. 291–302). NATO ASI Series F, Vol. 115. Berlin: Springer-Verlag.

Lesgold, A., Eggan, G., Katz, S., & Rao, G. (1992). Possibilities for assessment using computer-based apprenticeship environments. W. Regian & V. Shute (Eds.), *Cognitive approaches to automated instruction* (pp. 49–80). Hillsdale, NJ: Lawrence Erlbaum Associates.

Lesgold, A., & Katz, S. (1992). Models of cognition and educational technologies: Implications for medical training. In D. A. Evans & V. L. Patel (Eds.), *Advanced models of cognition for medical training and practice* (pp. 255–264). NATO ASI Series F, Vol. 97. Berlin: Springer-Verlag.

Lesgold, A., Katz, S., Greenberg, L., Hughes, E., & Eggan, G. (1992). Extensions of intelligent tutoring paradigms to support collaborative learning. In S. Dijkstra, H. P. M. Krammer, & J. J. G. van Merrienboer (Eds.), *Instructional models in computer-based learning environments* (pp. 291–311). Berlin: Springer-Verlag.

Lesgold, A. M., Lajoie, S. P., Bunzo, M., & Eggan, G. (1992). SHERLOCK: A coached practice environment for an electronics troubleshooting job. In J. Larkin & R. Chabay (Eds.), *Computer assisted instruction and intelligent tutoring systems: Shared issues and complementary approaches* (pp. 201–238). Hillsdale, NJ: Lawrence Erlbaum Associates.

Merrill, D. M. (1987, Summer). An expert system for instructional design. *IEEE Expert,* pp. 25–37.

Merrill, D. M., Zhongmin, L., & Jones, M. K. (1990a). Limitations of first generation instructional design. *Educational Technology,* pp. 7–11.

Merrill, D. M., Zhongmin, L., & Jones, M. K. (1990b). Second generation instructional design (ID₂). *Educational Technology,* pp. 7–14.

Merrill, D. M., Zhongmin, L., & Jones, J. K. (1990c). The second generation instructional design research program. *Educational Technology,* pp. 26–31.

Minsky, M. L. (1986). *The society of mind.* New York: Simon & Schuster.

Pirolli, P., & Bielaczyc, L. (1989). Empirical analyses of self-explanation and transfer from learning to program. *Proceedings of the 11th annual conference of the Cognitive Science Society* (pp. 450–457). Hillsdale, NJ: Lawrence Erlbaum Associates.

Reigeluth, C. M. (Ed.) (1983). *Instructional-design theories and models: An overview of their current status.* Hillsdale, NJ: Lawrence Erlbaum Associates.

Roschelle, J., & Behrend, S. D. (in press). The construction of shared knowledge in collaborative problem solving. In C. O'Malley (Ed.), *Computer supported collaborative learning.*

Scandura, J. M. (1983). Instructional strategies based on the structural learning theory. In C. M. Reigeluth (Ed.), *Instructional design theories and models: An overview of their current status.* Hillsdale, NJ: Lawrence Erlbaum Associates.

Schank, R. C. (1982). *Dynamic memory: A theory of reminding and learning.* New York: Cambridge University Press.

Schank, R. C., & Abelson, R. P. (1977). *Scripts, plans, goals, and understanding: An inquiry into human knowledge structures.* Hillsdale, NJ: Lawrence Erlbaum Associates.

Sipusic, M. J., Roschelle, J., & Pea, R. (1991, March). *Talking to learn, learning to talk: Conceptual change in Dynagrams and the Envisioning Machine.* Paper presented at the Third Biannual Workshop on Cognition and Instruction, Pittsburgh, PA.

Spiro, R., Bruce, B., & Brewer, W. (Eds.). (1980). *Theoretical issues in reading comprehension.* Hillsdale, NJ: Lawrence Erlbaum Associates.

Taylor, F. W. (1911). *The principles of scientific management.* New York: Harper.

Tudge, J., & Rogoff, B. (1989). Peer influences on cognitive development: Piagetian and Vygotskian perspectives. In M. H. Bornstein & J. S. Bruner (Eds.), *Interaction in human development* (pp. 17–40). Hillsdale, NJ: Lawrence Erlbaum Associates.

VanLehn, K., Jones, R. M., & Chi, M. T. H. (1992). A model of the self-explanation effect. *Journal of the Learning Sciences, 2,* 1–59.

Vera, A. H., & Simon, H. A. (1993). Situated action: A symbolic interpretation. *Cognitive Science, 17,* 7–48.

von Glasersfeld, E. (1991). An exposition of constructivism: Why some like it radical. In E. von Glasersfeld (Ed.), *Radical constructivism in mathematics education.* The Netherlands: Kluwer.

Wenger, E. (1990). *Toward a theory of cultural transparency.* Unpublished doctoral dissertation, University of California, Irvine.

Wenger, E., & Eckert, P. (1991, March). *Learning and communities of practice.* Presented at the Third Biannual Workshop on Cognition and Instruction, Pittsburgh, PA.

## APPENDIX 1: THE F-15 MANUAL AVIONICS TEST STATION

A test station is a large switch, more or less like a telephone exchange. It also contains instruments for measuring electrical energy patterns, such as a digital multimeter and an oscilloscope, and devices for creating patterned energy inputs to the aircraft component being tested. Each test on a box from an aircraft (called a line-replaceable unit, LRU, or sometimes the unit under test, UUT) involves applying patterned electrical energy to various inputs of the UUT and then connecting various of its outputs to a measurement device. A central section of the test station, called the relay assembly group (RAG), mediates the switching process. The technician sets various switches on the front of the test station to specify a particular test configuration, and then the RAG effects that configuration by energizing relays in giant switching trees. When all the relays are set properly, a signal circuit is created in which electrical inputs go from power supplies and signal generators on the test station, through an active connecting cable array (called the test package, TP), to the UUT, and outputs go from certain pins on the UUT's electrical interface through the switching array to a measurement device. On some test stations, a computer executes a series of tests of the UUT by directly controlling switching relays, but on the F-15 manual station, switching is effected via control settings on the test station's front panel.

When a test station fails, this failure is manifested in some function that the test station does not perform properly. A first requirement in the face of a possible failure is to be sure that the abnormal outcome is not due to a fault in the unit under test, the box from the aircraft. This is the most likely situation—after all, the whole purpose of the test station is to reveal faults in aircraft components. Another possibility that must be ruled out is a failure of the test package, the component that connects the UUT to the test station. If both the UUT and the test package are operating normally, then the problem is in the test station itself.

The top-level diagnostic strategy would first attempt to isolate the problem into one of two main functional areas. Either the patterned energy inputs are not getting to the UUT, or its outputs are not getting to a measurement device successfully. A single test of the inputs of the test station to the UUT will reveal if the problem is on the signal input side or the output measurement side. The next step is to trace the signal through the pathway, ending with an identification of a component that receives good inputs but has faulty outputs. If this component is involved in the switching process, there are two ways it could be failing. Either it is broken itself, or it is receiving wrong control signals from the switches on the front panel of the test station. In the latter case, the control inputs to the component in question will be wrong, and attention should be turned to diagnosing the path from control switches to the component now being addressed. On the other hand, if a component has good signal inputs, bad outputs, and good control inputs, then that component is a candidate for replacement.

This global strategy is really a combination of a weak or general method of space splitting, or "divide and conquer," with a specific model of the test station that provides an understanding of the meaningful units of the system that should be the focus of space splitting. The tactics for testing a particular subset of the test station, on the other hand, represent specific knowledge that can be generalized after appropriate experience and perhaps some expert suggestions.

# LOOKING AT TECHNOLOGY IN CONTEXT: A FRAMEWORK FOR UNDERSTANDING TECHNOLOGY AND EDUCATION RESEARCH

## Cognition and Technology Group at Vanderbilt*

LEARNING TECHNOLOGY CENTER, PEABODY COLLEGE AT VANDERBILT UNIVERSITY

This chapter discusses technology and its role in education. Questions that we raise and attempt to answer are: What do we know about the effects of technology on student learning and educational practice? What will future research on technology look like, and how might it differ from what has been done in the past?

It is extraordinarily challenging to attempt answering these questions. From our perspective, informed answers require a simultaneous exploration of at least three areas: (a) technology, (b) theories of human potential and human learning, and (c) issues of educational practice. These areas, and their intersections, are illustrated schematically in Figure 25–1. The challenge of discussing the areas in Figure 25–1 is increased by the fact that each has undergone major change during the past 10 to 15 years. In particular:

- *Technology.* Computer, video, and telecommunications systems available today were hard to imagine even 10 years ago. Many argue that the rate of change is increasing, making it almost impossible to foresee what will be possible within even a short span of time (e.g., Nickerson & Zodhiates, 1988; Nair, 1994). At the same time, Becker (1994) indicates that much of the latest technology has not reached the schools.

- *Learning Theory.* Visions of technology look very different, depending on the tacit or explicit theories of learning that guide their design and implementation (e.g., Collins, 1996; Duffy, Lowyck, & Jonassen, 1993; Hofmeister, Carnine, & Clark, 1993; Hooper & Hannafin, 1991; Means et al., 1993; Newman, 1990a, 1990b; Nix & Spiro, 1990; R. D. Pea, 1992; Regian & Shute, 1992; Salomon, 1992; Salomon, Perkins, & Globerson, 1991; Spiro & Jehng, 1990; Spiro, Feltovich, Jacobson, & Coulson, 1991; Spiro, Vispoel, Schmitz, Samarapungavan, & Boeger, 1987). Theories of learners and learning have undergone radical change during the past one and a half decades, and this has important implications for how technology-based applications are used and assessed.

- *Educational Practice.* The primary goals of education have changed in the past one and a half decades, and the implications of these changes must be understood by researchers. Perhaps the most important shift involves the assumption that all students, not just a select few, must be prepared to be lifelong learners and hence must learn to think, learn, and reason on their own (Resnick, 1987a). This requires a shift from an exclusive focus on basic skills to one that emphasizes the use of relevant skills and knowledge in the context of pursuing meaningful learning and problem-solving goals

*The Cognition and Technology Group at Vanderbilt (CTGV) refers to an interdisciplinary group of individuals at the Learning Technology Center, Peabody College at Vanderbilt University. The framework discussed in this chapter was developed by the Co-Directors of the Center: John Bransford, Susan Goldman and Ted Hasselbring. Members of the CTGV contributing to this chapter are the following (in alphabetical order): Brigid Barron, Linda Barron, Olin Campbell, Nathalie Coté, Thad Crews, Laura Goin, Elizabeth Goldman, Rachelle Hackett, Daniel Hickey, Cindy Hmelo, Ronald Kantor, Xiadong Lin, Cynthia Mayfield-Stewart, Allison Moore, Joyce Moore, Mitchell Nathan, James W. Pellegrino, Faapio Poe, Anthony Petrosino, Daniel Schwartz, Teresa Secules, Diana Sharp, Robert Sherwood, Carolyn Stalcup, Laura Till, Sashank Varma, Rosa Volpe, Nancy Vye, Susan Williams, and Linda Zech. The comments of Ellen Mandinach and Gavriel Salomon on earlier drafts of this chapter were extremely helpful.

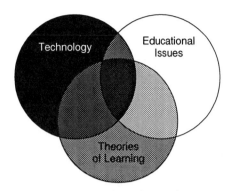

FIGURE 25-1. Three Intersecting Areas of Study that must Be Examined in order to Understand the Effects of Technology on Student Learning and Educational Practice

(e.g., Resnick & Klopfer, 1989). This shift affects curriculum, instruction, and assessment in all subject areas taught in school (J. D. Bransford, Goldman, & Vye, 1991). As we shall see, this shift also requires efforts to connect students and teachers to the broader community (Ramirez & Bell, 1994b).

The challenge of discussing technology, learning theory, and education is increased by the fact that all three areas interact with one another. Changes in theories of leaning affect uses of technology, but new technologies also make new kinds of interactions possible and hence affect theories of learning (e.g., Kozma, 1994; Salomon, 1993b, 1993c). These changes affect issues of assessment as well (e.g., A. L. Brown, Campione, Webber, & McGilly, 1991; Collins, Hawkins, & Frederiksen, 1993–1994; S. R. Goldman, Pellegrino, & Bransford, 1994; Hawkins, Collins, & Frederiksen, 1990; Salomon, 1991). Similarly, changes in technologies affect educational policy, and vice versa. For example, several years ago it appeared that all students needed to learn some type of computer language such as BASIC or COBOL to be prepared for the work force. Today, applications are much more user friendly, and workplace success is less dependent on traditional programming skills.

We agree with Sheingold's (1991) argument that the areas of technology, educational policy, and learning theory need to be considered simultaneously:

The agendas of active learning, technology, and (a push for) restructuring—each a powerful vehicle for changing learning and teaching in schools—need to be pursued concurrently to be maximally effective. If we imagine all three coming together in schools and districts, the potential for synergy is very great indeed. (Sheingold, 1991, p. 27)

The need to consider three areas simultaneously creates interesting challenges for research in education. For example, traditional research in educational psychology has focused on the individual, and often only the cognitive characteristics of the individual. Treatment variables are defined with respect to particular educational practices, and experimental studies examine their effects on individual performance. Under this model of educational research, technology is just another treatment variable. Changes in technologies, theories of human learning, and the goals of education make it quite difficult to

maintain the traditional view of educational psychology research. The simultaneous consideration of practice, theory, and technology implies new learning environments that are much more complicated to study than are traditional research designs (Mandinach & Cline, 1994; Salomon, 1992). This added complexity calls for new ways of thinking about research on technology and education.

## FOCUS OF THE PRESENT CHAPTER

A major goal of this chapter is to present a framework for approaching research that accommodates traditional as well as expanded investigations of learning, technology, and educational practice. However, the need to consider three different subject areas, each of which has undergone major changes, means that we have been forced to make certain choices about what is included in this chapter. Before presenting our framework, we outline what we do *not* attempt to do.

1. We do not attempt an exhaustive review of all literature relevant to technology, education, and theories of learning. If we published nothing more than a bibliography of relevant studies, we would exceed the page limitations for this chapter.

2. We do not attempt to provide detailed information about any particular technology-based application. For example, we do not provide complete descriptions of Anderson and colleagues' geometry tutor (Anderson, Boyle, & Yost, 1985; Koedinger & Anderson, 1993), Papert's LOGO (1980), Bank Street College of Education's *Voyage of the Mimi* (1984), Salomon's Writing Partner (1993c), Scardamalia and Bereiter's CSILE (Scardamalia, Bereiter, McLean, Swallow, & Woodruff, 1989), Bruce and Rubin's QUILL (1993), and so forth. Instead, we provide relevant references that allow readers to read about these programs in more detail.

3. We do not attempt to provide methodological critiques of studies using technology. We discuss *general* methodological issues (e.g., R. Clark, 1983; R. Clark & Salomon, 1986; R. Clark, 1994), but we do not evaluate the methodology of specific studies per se. The field seems to be in transition stage, moving from small, well-defined studies of individual students to classroom-based and school-based "design experiments" (e.g., A. L. Brown, 1992; A. L. Brown et al., 1993; Hawkins & Collins, in press; Mandinach & Cline, 1994). These ventures raise methodological issues that are just beginning to be recognized and understood (Lamon et al., in press; Salomon, 1992).

In this chapter we explore the interplay among technology, educational practice, and theories of learning. Decisions about each of these areas are involved in any attempt to design, implement, and evaluate uses of technology for education. But these decisions are often tacit. As Collins (1996) argues, it is better to make one's decisions explicit so that they can be consciously considered and, when appropriate, subjected to empirical testing.

In the discussion that follows, we limit our scope to electronic technologies that have become available since the 1960s; hence, we do not consider technologies such as the printing press and traditional audiovisual devices such as the overhead projector, slide projector, radio, and closed-circuit television. The framework of our discussion is designed to focus attention on the fact that research questions and methodologies change as a function of changes in technology, theories of learning, and issues of educational practice. It is a framework for looking at technology in the context of learning theories and research settings and is called the LTC framework, for *looking at technology in context*.

## A FRAMEWORK FOR LOOKING AT TECHNOLOGY IN CONTEXT

Our discussion of past and future trends in research will be organized around the framework illustrated In Figure 25–2. The LTC framework—*looking at technology in context*—focuses on the intersection of technology, learning theory, and educational practice. It does so by considering the matrix created by two dimensions of context. The columns in the LTC framework represent issues of educational practice; they have to do with the educational contexts within which research is situated. The rows represent the theoretical context; they highlight issues relevant to learning theory, including theories of human potential, and pedagogy. The LTC framework is discussed in more detail below.

### Educational Contexts in Which Research Is Situated

The columns of the LTC framework represent the *educational contexts* in which various programs are situated and studied—contexts that range from isolated laboratory settings to classrooms to connected sets of schools. The LTC framework includes three categories along the contexts of usage dimension: (a) *in vitro* laboratory settings, (b) *in vivo* settings, involving individual classrooms or sometimes schools, and (c) *connected* settings, involving sets of connected classrooms and schools. When one works in these different settings, different theoretical and practical issues become relevant, as described below.

- *In vitro laboratory settings* include experiments conducted in university-based research laboratories as well as experiments in schools where researchers do the teaching and assessment in order to test particular ideas. The advantages of this context include greater experimental precision and fidelity of implementation; however, many issues that are important for educational success might never be addressed (see below).

- *In vivo classroom settings* include studies conducted in individual classrooms by classroom teachers. A research team may collect the data, but the intervention is managed by the teachers rather than the researchers from the laboratory. This type of arrangement raises a host of important new issues. For example, researchers who have moved from the laboratory to classroom settings have discovered that their programs may require more extensive professional development for administrators and classroom teachers than was anticipated, or may require a restructuring of typical school schedules from 50-minute class periods to larger blocks of time (e.g., see chapters in Hawkins & Collins, in press; Lamon et al., in press; McGilly, 1994).

- *Connected settings* consist of connected classrooms and schools; studies conducted in them explicitly attempt to re-

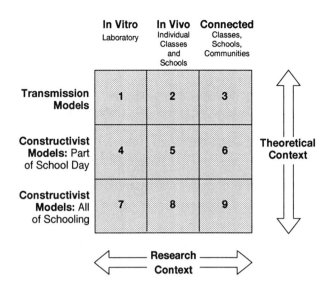

Cell 1: Studies of drill and practice programs in math, spelling, or particular content areas that are administered by research staff.

Cell 2: Studies of drill and practice programs in math, spelling, or particular content areas that are administered by classroom teachers.

Cell 3: Studies of distance learning connecting various classrooms that involve lectures and traditional tests.

Cell 4: Studies of constructivist-oriented programs (e.g., Logo, Voyage of the Mimi, Jasper) where the teaching and assessment are conducted by research staff.

Cell 5: Studies of constructivist-oriented programs (e.g., Logo, Voyage of the Mimi, Jasper) where the teaching and assessment are conducted by regular classroom teachers.

Cell 6: Studies of constructivist-oriented programs (e.g., Logo, Voyage of the Mimi, Jasper) where the teaching and assessment are conducted by regular classroom teachers and the classrooms are linked through telecommunications and interact on the project involved.

Cell 7: Studies of constructivist-oriented programs that fill the entire school day and take place in an experimental school with specially trained staff.

Cell 8: Studies of constructivist-oriented programs that fill the entire school day and take place in normal classrooms; however, the classrooms tend to operate independently of one another.

Cell 9: Studies of constructivist-oriented programs that fill the entire school day and take place in linked classrooms that interact on common problems and projects.

FIGURE 25–2. LTC Framework: A Framework for Looking at Technology in the Context of Learning Theory and Educational Practice

lieve the isolation of classrooms and schools and connect them to form broad-based learning communities. An important reason for creating learning communities is to attempt to deal with issues of equity (e.g., Hawkins, 1991; Hawkins & Sheingold, 1985). Many schools do not have access to teachers of specialized subject matters or to a broad range of reference materials. If classrooms are connected, scarce resources can be shared. A second reason for connecting classrooms is that they provide authentic audiences that allow students to share ideas, data, and opinions (e.g., Bruce, Peyton, & Batson, 1993; Cognition and Technology Group at Vanderbilt [CTGV], 1994a; J. A. Levin, Kim, & M. M. Riel, 1990; J. A. Levin, M. Riel, Miyake, & M. Cohen, 1987; Newman, 1992b; M. Riel, 1990a, 1990b; M. M. Riel & J. A. Levin, 1990). A third reason for connecting classrooms is to facilitate the professional development needed to begin and sustain educational reform. This includes issues of "scaling up" and moving beyond "laboratory" or "hothouse" schools (e.g., CTGV, in press; Hawkins & Collins, in press; Mandinach & Cline, 1994).

As noted earlier, each type of educational research context within the LTC framework has unique advantages and disadvantages. The primary advantage of working in laboratory contexts (cells 1, 4, and 7) is that one can control important sets of variables and ensure high degrees of fidelity of program implementation. The disadvantage of working in these cells is that many issues relevant to real classrooms and real schools are not dealt with, thereby limiting the applicability of the findings to real classroom settings.

Researchers who have moved from laboratories to real classrooms have discovered that their programs may:

- motivate students only when they are special events, not when they are a part of regular classroom practices;
- work well when there is a small researcher-to-student ratio, but not in classrooms with one teacher and 20 or more students;
- require levels of professional development for administrators and classroom teachers that were unanticipated;
- require a restructuring of typical school schedules (e.g., typical 50-minute class periods may not work);
- produce gains that are not measured by the typical achievement tests used for accountability; and
- require research methodologies (e.g., ethnographic analysis) that are new to researchers schooled in traditional laboratory research.

Migrations from laboratory to classroom settings have also raised new issues of research methodology. In laboratory settings, each individual often receives an experimental treatment that is independent of the treatment given to any other individual. In contrast, in classroom-based research, groups of children within a classroom usually receive the same treatment. Therefore, students are not independent of one another, and research conducted in actual classrooms requires one to think of the classroom as a unit. When one works with connected sets of classrooms (cells 3, 6, and 9), one can no longer assume the independence of classrooms. Although there are methods for handling these dependencies, such as hierarchical linear modeling (e.g., Bryk & Raudenbush, 1992), researchers need to be more cognizant of them and, more generally, of the need to employ multiple methodologies and convergent measures (e.g., A. L. Brown, 1992; Lamon et al., in press; Mandinach & Cline, 1994; Salomon, 1991). Discussions of the theoretical, practical, and methodological issues involved in research in real classrooms can be found in a number of articles, including CTGV (1992d, in press), Blumenfeld et al. (1991), A. L. Brown (1992), Hawkins & Collins (in press),

Lamon et al. (in press), Schofield, Evans-Rhodes, & Huber (1990), and Salomon (1991, 1992).

## Theoretical Context of Applications

The rows of the LTC framework represent the *theoretical context* of technology-based applications. The theoretical context affects assumptions about curriculum, instruction, and assessment. These assumptions have important implications for implementation and research efforts.

Especially important is the congruence between the theoretical context of a particular program and the educational context or setting (laboratory, classroom, connected classrooms) in which the program is placed. When the theoretical context and the setting are congruent, it is easy to incorporate one's application into the context of existing practice. When the assumptions of the program and the setting are incongruent, the challenges are greater because of the need to transform traditional classroom practices.

For purposes of the present discussion, we assume that most classroom practices are consistent with transmission models of instruction rather than constructivist-oriented models (these models are discussed in more detail in the second and third sections of this chapter). As Greeno (1991) states: "In most schools, what students mostly do is listen, watch, and mimic things that the teacher and textbook tell them and show them" (p. 81). When technology programs are congruent with transmission models, they can be assimilated quite easily into traditional classroom settings. The first row of the LTC framework reflects implementations of technology that can be assimilated without fundamental change in theoretical perspectives on learning, instruction, and assessment.

Technology implementations that are based on constructivist theories cannot simply be assimilated into traditional classroom practices. Instead, the classrooms must be transformed (e.g., Bereiter, 1994; Bransford et al., 1991; Cobb, 1994; Cobb, Yackel, & Wood, 1992; Collins, 1991b; Pea, 1992; L. B. Resnick & Klopfer, 1989; Savery & Duffy, in press). The LTC framework emphasizes that there are multiple levels at which transformation can be attempted. The challenges increase as one moves from attempts to transform only part of the school day (row 2) to attempts to transform the entire nature of schooling (row 3). These efforts include attempts to transform linkages between schools and the home and community, as well as transform what happens in classrooms.

## Combining the Two Dimensions of Context

Combining the two dimensions of context—the educational and the theoretical—yields nine cells in the LTC framework. These cells can be used to characterize a vast array of possible studies. Examples of the kinds of studies that fit in each cell are provided in Figure 25–2. By situating a study in a particular cell (one cannot do this with 100 percent certainty but one can do it approximately), what emerges is a better picture of what has been learned and how that information can be generalized. In the following discussion we use the LTC framework to organize discussions of the theoretical issues, research findings, and research prospects related to technology. We begin with the first row of the LTC framework, which represents some of the historically earlier work on technology.

## THEORY AND RESEARCH RELEVANT TO TRANSMISSION MODELS OF LEARNING

Our goal in this section is to summarize some of the research relevant to the transmission models of learning (cells 1, 2, and 3, in the LTC framework). This research began in the early 1960s using mainframe computers, with subsequent "downsizing" to mini- and microcomputers as they became available. Most of this research was guided by a transmission theory of the nature of teaching, learning, and assessment. We discuss this theory in more detail below.

### Theoretical Context of Row 1: Transmission Models of Learning

The early pioneers who conducted research on technology and education took existing classroom practice as a given and attempted to use technology to make it more efficient. Most classroom practice was consistent with what has come to be called a *transmission model* of instruction and assessment. Sometimes the work was conducted in laboratory settings (cell 1), and sometimes it was conducted in classroom settings that were either independent of one another (cell 2) or connected (cell 3). Work relevant to cell 3 involved experiments in distance learning whereby multiple classrooms were linked to a single instructor and the instructional design and pedagogy involved "transmission at a distance."

Transmission models are based on assumptions that:

- learning involves the accumulation of particular sets of facts and skills;
- teaching involves the transmission of facts and skills by an expert; and
- assessment involves an accounting of whether the desired facts and skills have been acquired.

These assumptions are consistent with the dominant psychological theory of learning in the United States from the early 1900s until the late 1960s, which was actually a class of theories known as behaviorism, as exemplified in the work of B. F. Skinner (1953; Keller & Schoenfeld, 1950) and James Holland in education (e.g., Holland & Skinner, 1961). The root metaphor of behaviorism was an organism whose behavior was a product of the contingencies that existed in the environment. Learning was the result of a lifetime of accumulating associations between behaviors and their consequences. Rewards for desired behaviors increased their frequency; appropriate responding could be shaped through the reinforcement of behaviors that successively approximated the desired behaviors. For reward mechanisms to operate in the intended manner, discrete sets of target behaviors had to be specified.

Transmission models are also consistent with the metaphor of education as an industrial assembly line, according to which students progressed along a moving assembly line as they proceed from kindergarten through Grade 12 and, for some, college. At particular points in the assembly line, specific sets of skills and knowledge were introduced to the students. Over time, students would accumulate as much knowledge and skill as their capacities allowed.

Classroom environments based on transmission models usually involve students who adopt the role of receivers of wisdom that is dispensed by teachers, textbooks, and other media (A. L. Brown, 1992; Means, 1994). The role of the teacher is to deliver information and manage learning. The role of the student is to engage in "knowledge telling" (Bereiter & Scardamalia, 1989; Scardamalia & Bereiter, 1991) and demonstrate that what has been transmitted has been retained. Usually, everyone is taught the same thing at the same time, although there is some room for individualization with respect to the speed of learning specific sets of skills and competencies. Assessments typically measure how much each student has learned by assessing discrete sets of facts and skills.

### Three Areas of Research Relevant to Transmission Models

Over the past three decades, research on three types of technology implementations has dominated investigations that fit within the first row (transmission models) of the LTC framework. We first provide an overview of these areas; later we discuss the findings from and issues associated with the research.

*Computer as Delivery Mechanism: Computer-Assisted Instruction.* The first type of implementation took traditional curricula and delivered them by computer (initially mainframe computers; subsequently mini- and microcomputers). The purpose of the research on these implementations was to determine if instruction delivered by computer would be as good as or better than instruction delivered by a teacher, either in place of or in addition to traditional instruction. In other words, could technology make knowledge transmission occur more efficiently than it did when delivered by a human? Much of this research occurred in classroom settings (cell 2 of the framework), but some, mostly pilot studies conducted by software developers, occurred in laboratory settings (cell 1). Pedagogy was largely drill and practice of traditional skills, with some emphasis on well-defined tutorials in the style of programmed instruction (e.g., Holland & Skinner, 1961). The bulk of the large-scale evaluation studies conducted on computer-assisted instruction (CAI) focused on technology implementations of this type. Effects were measured by increased accuracy, distinguishing this kind of research from work on component skills, discussed below.

In the late 1970s and early 1980s, new variants of CAI were stimulated by cognitive theories of complex cognitive skill acquisition (Anderson, 1982, 1987; Anderson, Conrad, & Corbett, 1989; Schneider & Shiffrin, 1985). These theories analyzed complex skills into their components and stressed the importance of fluency (not just accuracy) in executing these components (e.g., S. R. Goldman, Pellegrino, & Mertz, 1988; LaBerge & Samuels, 1974). For example, Hasselbring, Goin, and Bransford (1988) showed that, with respect to accuracy in basic math facts, special needs students began to catch up with regular education students between the first and eighth grades. However, with respect to speed of responding (fluency), differences between special needs and regular education students increased over the grades.

***Computer Programming and Literacy.*** The second type of technology implementation treated *computers* as a subject matter area and was conducted in classroom contexts. These implementations were stimulated by the increased availability in the early 1980s of microcomputers (e.g., Commodore 64, Tandy, Apple II and IIe). Computer literacy and computer programming courses appeared more and more frequently (e.g., Luehrmann & Peckham, 1983). Research focused largely on the effects of learning to program computers on students' thinking. It is noteworthy that national surveys of computer usage continue to show that the dominant uses of computers in schools are for programming and drill and practice, reflecting little change over the past 15 years (Becker, 1983, 1984a, 1984b, 1984c, 1991, 1994; Cosden, Gerber, Goldman, D. S. Semmel, & M. I. Semmel, 1986; Cosden, Gerber, D. S. Semmel, Goldman, & M. I. Semmel, 1987).

***Distance Learning.*** The third type of technology implementation is distance learning that delivers traditional, transmission model instruction to multiple sites (cell 3 of the LTC framework). Such education emphasizes student autonomy, independence, and isolation (e.g., Barker, 1991; Barker, Frisbie, & Patrick, 1989; Garrison, 1989, 1993; L. M. Harasim, 1990; Hawkins, 1991; Hiltz, 1986; Holmberg, 1989; Moore, 1989). Research examines the effect of distance learning on student achievement. For the most part, the findings confirm that there is no significant difference in student achievement between one technological delivery system and another when the theoretical basis for instruction is a transmission model (e.g., Barker & Bannon, 1992; Hezel & Associates, 1993; Hiltz, 1986; Hobbs & Osburn, 1988; Hobbs, 1990; Holznagel, 1990; Moore, 1989; Sisung, 1992; Tushnet, Uriarte, Manuel, & Broekhuizen, 1993).

## Evaluation Research on Computer-Assisted Instruction

We consider the evaluation of CAI from a historical perspective. In the late 1960s and early 1970s, several large-scale evaluations of CAI were conducted in which elementary schoolchildren were given 10 to 20 minutes of CAI instruction daily. In almost all cases, researchers reported that, compared to traditional instruction, CAI produced equivalent or superior results on standardized measures of achievement when effects were corrected for time spent in instruction (Atkinson, 1968; Suppes & Morningstar, 1968).

In the late 1970s, the Educational Testing Service (D. Alderman & Mahler, 1973; D. L. Alderman, 1978; Murphy & Rhea-Appel, 1977; Swinton, Amarel, & Morgan, 1978) evaluated the implementation of two major computer-based instructional systems in community colleges, PLATO (Programmed Logic for Automatic Teacher Operations; Alpert & Bitzer, 1970; Eastwood & Ballard, 1975) and TICCIT (Time-shared, Interactive, Computer-Controlled, Information Television; Bunderson, 1975). The two projects differed in several ways. PLATO was a large educational network supporting nearly 1,000 terminals,

each accessing content from a central library. Classroom teachers, coordinated by PLATO central staff, were involved in the preparation of the lessons. TICCIT, on the other hand, was a small, local facility that used minicomputers and television receivers. Teams of specialists, including teachers, produced the courseware. Both systems successfully produced advanced instructional programs capable of serving many students at one time and may be seen as precursors to today's integrated learning systems (ILSs).

Although these early evaluation studies produced some valuable information on the effects of CAI, the results of many studies were inconsistent and the conclusions drawn by the investigators were often unclear. In an attempt to gain a better understanding of the effect of CAI on achievement, reviews were written to bring the separately published studies together to reveal the common findings. These early reviews used a box score technique for integrating the results. These box score reviews generally reported the proportion of studies that were favorable and unfavorable toward CAI, as well as narrative comments on the studies.

***Box Score Reviews.*** In one of the first box score reviews, Vinsonhaler and Bass (1972) summarized the results of 10 major studies conducted from 1967 to 1970 involving CAI drill and practice with more than 10,000 elementary schoolchildren from different sections of the country. The investigators concluded that children who received computerized drill and practice generally showed performance gains of 1 to 8 months over control children who received only traditional instruction.

The Vinsonhaler and Bass conclusions were supported in a later review by Edwards, Norton, Taylor, Weiss, and Dusseldorp (1975), who evaluated the effects of drill-and-practice, problem-solving, simulation, and tutorial computer instruction programs for producing achievement gains in schoolchildren. Based on results from six studies, they concluded that CAI plus traditional instruction was more effective than traditional instruction alone. CAI as a substitute for traditional instruction produced positive effects in nine studies and no difference compared with traditional instruction in eight others. Two studies in this review indicated that CAI drill-and-practice programs were more effective for low-ability students than for children of average ability. These reviewers noted that CAI reduced the time it took students to learn. They concluded that CAI produced better results than did traditional instruction on end-of-course examinations but not on retention examinations.

Similarly, Jamison, Suppes, and Wells (1974) concluded that when CAI was used as a supplement to traditional instruction at the elementary level, achievement scores were improved, especially for disadvantaged students. At the secondary and college level, the investigators concluded that CAI was at least as effective as traditional instruction, and in some cases CAI resulted in substantial savings in student time.

Although the box score reviews provided additional insight into the fundamental questions regarding the effectiveness of CAI, this type of review was shown to have limitations. For example, the box score reviews did not say how much better one method was than another; they simply reported how often a particular method came out on top. Further, they did not use statistics to find the characteristics that distinguished studies with positive results from those with negative findings. In an attempt to overcome the limitations of box score reviews, researchers employed a more sophisticated meta-analysis approach where differences between treatments were reported in effect sizes.

*Meta-analyses.* Several meta-analyses were conducted in the late 1970s and early 1980s that examined the effects of CAI on student achievement (Burns & Bozeman, 1981; Hartley, 1977; J. Kulik, C. Kulik, & Cohen, 1980; J. A. Kulik, Bangert, & Williams, 1983). In each of these meta-analyses, the reviewers reported moderate positive effects for the CAI treatment. Burns and Bozeman (1981) used meta-analysis to integrate findings on CAI in mathematics teaching in elementary and secondary schools. They found that computer-based tutorials raised achievement test results by 0.45 standard deviation (SD) and that computer-based drill and practice raised test scores by 0.34 SD. In a summary of their analysis, Burns & Bozeman (1981) wrote:

While no ultimate answers related to CAI effectiveness can be presented, the analysis and synthesis of many studies do point to a significant enhancement of learning in instructional environments supplemented by CAI, at least in one curricular area—mathematics. (p. 37)

J. A. Kulik et al. (1983) reported that when CAI was used in instruction, student scores on final examinations were raised from the 50th to the 63rd percentile, representing a 0.32 SD increase. In addition, Kulik and colleagues reported that student attitudes toward the subject being learned and student ratings of the quality of instruction were slightly more favorable with CAI. As well, students' attitudes toward computers were significantly more positive as a result of CAI.

***Attempts to Understand the Benefits of Technology.*** As research on technology progressed, researchers began to ask why CAI advantages occurred. One possible explanation for the reported positive effects of CAI on student achievement was presented by Bright (1983). He made a strong argument for explaining the "CAI phenomenon" and its positive effect on student achievement using data from the Beginning Teacher Evaluation Study (Denham & Lieberman, 1980). Bright (1983) argued that when academic learning time (ALT) is increased there is a concomitant gain in student achievement. Academic learning time is defined as the amount of time the student is engaged in a task and is highly successful in completing the task. Bright argued that ALT appeared to be a mediating variable for achievement. That is, the more ALT a student accumulated, the more the student learned.

Bright suggested that the many CAI activities could lead to an increase in ALT. For example, the amount of ALT was often increased by providing the student with an exciting computer-based learning environment through games or adventures while at the same time providing learning tasks in which the student could be highly successful. Bright argued that the combination of high-engagement time and high success rates correlated with student achievement. Hence, the very nature of many CAI activities could lead to an increase in ALT and achievement.

A second but related class of explanations of the positive effects of CAI has to do with the motivational context established by some of the programs. Many drill-and-practice programs include gamelike features that presumably motivate continued use of the software (Lepper & Chabay, 1985; Lepper & Malone, 1987). Although these gamelike features may promote continued use of the software, they are external rewards and do little to help, and may even work against, the development of intrinsic motivation. For some students the motivational "bells and whistles" may create a confusing environment that interferes with task performance (e.g., Christensen & Gerber, 1990).

Researchers who emphasized speed as well as accuracy provided another explanation for the benefits of technology. They examined whether speed of responding increased in the context of drill and practice on such component skills as arithmetic facts (S. R. Goldman et al., 1988; Hasselbring et al., 1988), word recognition (Frederiksen, Warren, & Rosebery, 1985; Roth & Beck, 1987), and spelling (English, Gerber, & Semmel, 1985; Hasselbring, 1984). The bulk of these studies found that speed of responding did increase over time, with no loss of accuracy. Weaker but significant positive effects were shown for the positive impact of increased fluency in the components on the complex cognitive skills of which they were a part. However, these effects were much less consistent across studies than the direct effects of drill and practice on the components, largely owing to the importance of planning and monitoring in the execution of the complex cognitive skill (cf. S. R. Goldman & Pellegrino, 1987; Hasselbring et al., 1987–1988, 1991).

Research also suggests that some design principles for creating skill-based software are especially important for special needs students. For example, beginning with a small set of to-be-learned items, rather than picking randomly from a larger set (e.g., Bjork, 1979; Torgesen, 1984; Torgesen & Young, 1983), has been shown to be very beneficial for students who have trouble mastering basic skills (Hasselbring et al., 1988).

***Methodological Confounds.*** At the same time that Bright was suggesting that a CAI phenomena existed, Clark (1983; Clark & Salomon, 1986) was arguing that studies comparing CAI with traditional classroom instruction were basically meaningless because they were hopelessly confounded. Clark argued that the experimental and comparison groups differed not only with respect to the availability of media (e.g., computers), but also with respect to the exact nature of the instruction provided. Based on a review of the literature, Clark suggested that there was no evidence to support the conclusion that media influenced learning and achievement under any conditions. Clark (1983) stated,

The best current evidence is that media are mere vehicles that deliver instruction but do not influence student achievement any more than the truck that delivers our groceries causes changes in our nutrition. Basically, the choice of vehicle might influence the cost or extent of distributing instruction, but only the content of the vehicle can influence achievement. (p. 445)

Some of our own research supports Clark's claims. We (Hasselbring et al., 1987–1988) conducted a study that compared the use of an overhead projector and a videodisc to present material, with content controlled for. Both groups received direct instruction on fraction and fraction computations using a procedurally oriented approach. The same teacher taught both groups and used the same instructional sequence, which was presented by videodisc to one group and by overhead projector and transparencies to the other. Consistent with Clark's (1983) analysis, the group taught with transparencies displayed on an overhead projector did no better than the group taught with a videodisc, although both did better than two groups taught using the traditional classroom curriculum and methods. However, using the videodisc was definitely easier than handling a huge stack of transparencies, and the same information was covered in less time using the videodisc. The distressing part of this research was that even though two experimental groups did well on a criterion-referenced test over the fractions information, when asked to apply this knowledge to real-life problems, they were unable to do so. Findings such as these have motivated many educators to seek alternatives to transmission models of learning and instruction. These are discussed later, under constructivist models of learning.

## Research on Computer Programming

Research on computers also included a great deal of interest in teaching computer programming and in the effects this might have on students' thinking (Dalbey & Linn, 1985; Linn, 1985). Salomon (1992) provides an excellent discussion of this work. For example, he notes that the goal of helping students become "computer literate" was translated into teaching programming. Luehrmann (1972, cited in Salomon, 1992) stated: "If the computer is so powerful a resource that it can be programmed to simulate the instructional process, shouldn't we be teaching our students mastery of this intellectually powerful tool?" (p. 77).

Early efforts to teach programming focused primarily on BASIC (Beginners All-purpose Symbolic Instruction Code). The emphasis was primarily on languages such as BASIC as curricula to be learned. The publication of Papert's *Mindstorms: Children, Computers, and Powerful Ideas* in 1980 generated a great deal of interest in Logo programming and its potential cognitive benefits. Furthermore, Papert's vision for teaching LOGO was dramatically different from teaching methods consistent with transmission models (cf. Harel & Papert, 1991). We discuss research on Logo programming later, under constructivist models of learning.

## Research on Distance Learning

Very early work on distance learning focused on the effects of one-way instructional television (Chu & Schramm, 1967; Schramm, 1977; Whittington, 1987). Later work included the use of one-way video with two-way audio systems (Cookson, 1989; Moore, 1989). Russell (1993) discusses numerous studies that demonstrate that students learn as well with distance technology as their counterparts who receive on-campus, face-to-face instruction (see also Shavelson, Webb, & Hotta, 1987). It is important to note that most of the early uses of distance learning technologies were based on the transmission model, and most addressed traditional instructional goals.

More recent studies have attempted to compare the effectiveness of different types of distance learning technologies with one another as well as with face-to-face instruction (Beare,

1989; Galvin, 1987; Learmont, 1990; Martin & Rainey, 1993; Pugh, Parchman, & Simpson, 1992; Ritchie & Newby, 1989; Schlosser & Anderson, 1994; J. B. Smith, 1993). Consistent with Clark's argument, these experiments and evaluations found little difference between the effectiveness of delivery systems (Clark, 1983; Clark, 1989). These studies indicate the need to investigate the effects of different instructional designs rather than the effectiveness of various technologies as the means to deliver or transmit content to learners.

## Migration from Laboratories to Classrooms and Connected Classrooms

The LTC framework includes an emphasis on research settings—laboratory, classrooms, connected classrooms—because different issues arise as researchers move from one setting to another. For example, as one moves from laboratory to classroom settings, a simple but extremely important question arises: Where does one find the time in the day for students to work on computer-based applications? Because the time available in a school day is limited, this question is by no means trivial.

In general, technology applications that are consistent with transmission models of learning (cells 1, 2, and 3) are easier to move into classroom settings than are applications consistent with constructivist models. The reason is that most classrooms are consistent with transmission models of learning; hence applications consistent with these models can simply be assimilated into existing classroom practice. When we discuss constructivist models later in the chapter, we will see many more challenges involved in moving from laboratory contexts to real classrooms in real schools.

The use of ILSs in a school computer laboratory setting (cell 2) is a particularly clear example of ease of assimilation. Under this model, classroom teachers do not need additional expertise in technology; they can simply send their students to the school's computer laboratory. It is much easier to train one laboratory technician per school than to train every teacher in a school. Similarly, the use of one-way distance learning technologies (cell 3) does not require much change in traditional classroom practice.

## Summary

Overall, the results of early research on CAI suggested that it sometimes produced results that were superior to traditional classroom instruction. However, Clark's arguments about the confounds of the research conducted cannot be ignored. Equally important is a consideration of the kind of instruction and assumptions about learning made by the majority of CAI programs prior to 1990. In most cases, the technology was used to deliver instruction more efficiently and was consistent with a teaching-is-telling approach. Likewise, traditional approaches to assessment and evaluation of student performance were based on the same set of assumptions. Most present-day ILSs carry on in this tradition (see Means et al., 1993, for some exceptions).

Early research on the effects of computer programming treated the area as a curriculum to be transmitted rather than as a tool to be used to accomplish goals established by students and teachers (Mayer, 1988b; Salomon, 1992). Research on distance learning was also driven by a transmission model of learning and teaching. Its effects were compared with the achievement of students in traditional classrooms where the teacher was present rather than at a remote site.

Since applications based on transmission models are consistent with existing practice in most classrooms, migrations from laboratory to school contexts were relatively smooth. In contrast, migrations are much more challenging when the theory of learning underlying the application requires a transformation of existing classroom practice.

## THEORY AND RESEARCH RELEVANT TO CONSTRUCTIVIST MODELS OF LEARNING

This section explores shifts in thinking about learning and education that have taken place the past 15 to 20 years, and how these shifts have shaped the design, implementation, and study of technology-based applications. In the context of the LTC framework, these changes involve a shift from the first row of the framework (programs based on transmission models of learning) to the second and third rows (programs based on constructivist models of learning). In this section we discuss the second row (cells 4, 5, and 6) of the LTC framework, or constructivist-based applications that transform part, but not all, of the school day. The third row of the LTC framework is discussed in the next section.

### The Need for Change in the Goals of Education

In 1983, the authors of *A Nation at Risk* called attention to the serious problems of schooling in the United States by describing the nation's efforts as "an act of unthinking, unilateral educational disarmament" (National Commission on Excellence in Education, 1983). Spurred by the report, politicians, business leaders, and educators sounded the call for educational reform (e.g., Wise, 1989).

A number of theorists have attempted to better define the nature of the educational crisis identified in *A Nation at Risk* and expressed by so many others (e.g., Resnick, 1987a). As Bruer (1993) suggests: "Consistently, the assessments show that the educational crisis is not one of decline; it is one of stagnation" (p. 2). The major problem is that schools have not kept pace with society's expectations and needs for the rapidly changing world of the 21st century (see also Berryman, 1993; Reich, 1993; U.S. Department of Labor, 1992).

The idea of preparing people for a rapidly changing world is a daunting new challenge. Rapid change requires lifelong learning, and this means that people who enter the work force must be prepared to learn on their own. Resnick (1987a) cites a number of ways in which schools have failed to prepare students for lifelong learning:

Employers today complain that they cannot count on schools and colleges to produce young people who can move easily into more complex kinds of work. They seem to be seeking general skills such as the ability to write and speak effectively, the ability to learn easily on the job, the ability to use quantitative skills needed to apply various tools of production and management, the ability to read

complex materials, and the ability to build and evaluate arguments. These abilities go well beyond the routinized skills of the old mass curriculum. (pp. 6–7)

Resnick emphasizes that the skills required for effective work following high school graduation are now essentially equivalent to those that were required for college-bound students in the 1980s. She states: "It is a new challenge to develop educational programs that assume that all individuals, not just an elite, can become competent thinkers" (Resnick, 1987a, p. 7).

### New Visions of Human Potential and Human Learning

The ability to achieve genuine and dramatic change requires new visions of human learning and human potential. Ideas about learning have been strongly influenced by theoretical developments that have accompanied the cognitive revolution in psychology. Several authors (e.g., Gardner, 1985; Resnick & Klopfer, 1989) provide excellent descriptions of this revolution. One major shift is in the view of learning. Instead of knowledge being viewed as something to be received, accumulated, and stored, it is viewed as being actively constructed by organisms through interaction with their physical and social environments and through the reorganization of their own mental structures (e.g., Cobb, 1994; Cobb, et al., 1992; Collins, 1991a; Greeno, Smith, & Moore, 1993; Harel & Papert, 1991; Papert, 1980; Savery & Duffy, in press; see also chapters 2 and 16). A second major shift has been in a realization of the importance of social contexts for learning. In chapter 16, De Corte and co-authors argue that social considerations are part of the second wave of the cognitive revolution. During the first wave, the primary focus was on individual thinkers and learners, with a deemphasis on affect, context, culture, and history (Gardner, 1985). During the second wave, theorists have attempted to relocate cognitive functioning within its social, cultural, and historical contexts (e.g., Bransford et al., 1991; J. S. Brown, Collins, & Duguid, 1989; Duffy & Jonassen, 1992; Duffy et al., 1993; Padilla, 1991; Pea, 1993a, 1993b; vonGlaserfeld, 1989; Wheatley, 1993, chapter 2).

Taken together, the two phases of the cognitive revolution have led to important changes in thinking about ways to assess and facilitate human intelligence and development.

*Changing Views of Intelligence.* In conjunction with new views of human learning are new visions of human potential and how we might assess it. An important change in thinking involves the concept of human intelligence. Almost a century ago, Binet (Binet & Simon, 1908) developed an assessment instrument whose purpose was to predict school success. And it did that well (see Kail & Pellegrino, 1985, for discussion). Unfortunately, the intelligence test came to define what it meant to be intelligent in general rather than what it meant to be intelligent in an academic sense.

There have been a number of efforts to broaden the concept of intelligence to encompass more and varied kinds of thinking. Neisser (1976) argued that the concept of academic intelligence needed to be supplemented with another concept that he called "practical intelligence" and defined as "intelligent performance in practical settings." Differences between academic and practical intelligence capture the difference between individuals who seem "book smart" but who do not function well in the everyday world. Of course, some individuals do well in both domains. The book *Practical Intelligence* (Sternberg & Wagner, 1986) contains a number of articles that provide evidence of the value of the concept of practical intelligence.

Another criticism of traditional concepts of intelligence is that they overemphasize verbally loaded skills. Gardner (1983) argued persuasively for broadening the concept of intelligence to make room for multiple intelligences, including musical, spatial, and so forth. Expanded views of intelligence are especially important because people's beliefs about the nature of intelligence can affect their assessment of their own capabilities and their actual performance. For example, in studying task performance, Bandura and Dweck (1985; cited in Cain & Dweck, 1989) found that children who believed that intelligence was incremental tended to emphasize developing their skills and improving their abilities. However, children who held an entity view of intelligence were oriented toward demonstrating how smart they were and reacted to the task as a test of ability. In the face of failure, incremental views tended to be associated with "mastery" orientations, whereas entity views tended to be associated with "helplessness" responses (Cain & Dweck, 1989; Dweck, 1989).

Researchers have also argued for the importance of a concept of "distributed intelligence" (e.g., A. L. Brown & Campione, 1990; Hutchins, 1983; Pea, 1993b, 1994; Pea & Gomez, 1992; Salomon, 1993b; Salomon et al., 1991). Rather than being viewed as existing in individual minds, intelligence is viewed as a property of groups of individuals who collaborate to achieve shared goals. The concept of distributed intelligence has important implications for issues of curriculum, instruction and assessment. (See Salomon, 1993a, for an edited volume concerned with the implications of distributed cognition.)

*Explorations of the Nature of Expertise.* An alternative to equating thinking with intelligence as measured by intelligence tests is to examine the characteristics of individuals who are among the very best thinkers in their fields. Classic work on the nature of expertise and expert thinking focused on the area of chess (e.g., Chase & Simon, 1973; deGroot, 1965). Since then, researchers have begun to study the nature and development of expertise in a variety of other areas, including physics, mathematics, computer programming, writing, social studies, and teaching (e.g., Berliner, 1991; Bransford, Sherwood, Vye, & Rieser, 1986; Carter, Cushing, Sabers, Stein, & Berliner, 1988; Chi, Feltovich, & Glaser, 1981; Chi, Glaser, & Farr, 1988; Chi, Glaser, & Reese, 1982; Glaser, 1986, 1991; Hayes, 1990; Larkin, McDermott, D. P. Simon, & H. A. Simon, 1980; Lesgold, 1988; Sabers, Cushing, & Berliner, 1991). A major conclusion from the research is that high-level expertise requires a great deal of domain-specific knowledge. Experts do not simply have more knowledge about an area than novices, they also seem to have organized that knowledge in ways that are qualitatively different. Like the concept of intelligence, the idea of individual expertise has been augmented by a concept of distributed expertise (e.g., A. L. Brown & Campione, 1990; Hutchins, 1983; Pea, 1993b, 1994; Pea & Gomez, 1992; Salomon, 1993b; Salomon et al., 1991).

*Learning in Everyday Settings.* Insights from the work on practical intelligence and the nature of expert performance have been enhanced by work on the learning and problem solving of children and adults performing everyday tasks in everyday settings, such as getting around their house or shopping in a grocery store (e.g., Bransford & Heldmeyer, 1983; T. N. Carraher, D. W. Carraher, & Schliemann, 1985; Lave, 1988; Lave & Wenger, 1991; Nunes, Schliemann, & D. W. Carraher, 1993; Resnick, 1987b; Rogoff, 1990; Rogoff & Lave, 1984; Saxe, 1988; Schliemann & Acioly, 1989). It has become clear that many aspects of everyday cognition differ from the more formal processes emphasized in school and tested on tests. The picture from research on learning in everyday settings is that humans are much more adaptable than one would have imagined from traditional curricula and traditional tests (e.g., CTGV, 1993a; Lave & Wenger, 1991).

*Research on Early Competencies.* Research on the nature of expertise and everyday cognition has been accompanied by a correlative change in conceptions of children's thinking. Increasingly greater emphasis is being placed on the importance of the physical and social context in which thinking occurs and on the interaction of the individual with the objects and events in the environment (Carey, 1985; Donaldson, 1979; Driver, Guesne, & Tiberghien, 1985; Greeno et al., 1993; Pea, 1992, 1993a; L. B. Smith, Sera, & Gattuso, 1988; Wheatley, 1993).

Within appropriate physical and social contexts, "early competencies" have been observed in young children's number, communication, problem-solving, and search behavior (Gelman & Gallistel, 1978; Gelman, Meck, & Merkin, 1986; Klahr, 1978; Shatz, 1982; Wellman & Somerville, 1982). These competencies may profitably be understood in terms of the performances afforded or enabled by the environment. For example, a number of elements have to be properly aligned in order for children's competencies to reveal themselves: The context of the task must be familiar to the children, the amount of information must not exceed their working memory capacity, constraints on the materials may encourage certain behaviors and prevent others, and so forth (e.g., Case, 1985; Klahr 1978; Siegler, 1978). Even analogical transfer and learning-to-learn competencies can be demonstrated in preschoolers under the appropriate scaffolded circumstances (A. L. Brown & Kane, 1988; A. L. Brown, Kane, & Echols, 1986; A. L. Brown, Kane, & Long, 1989).

*Research on Motivation.* Researchers have also begun to clarify the roles of motivation and interest in human learning. Early research on motivation was consistent with transmission models that focused on delivering instruction. As it was delivered, researchers asked about the kinds of consequences (rewards) that might motivate students to continue with the learning task. For example, programs designed to teach math facts might follow a correct answer with a "correct" or with an elaborate set of consequences (e.g., getting to continue with a search through a maze). Several papers describe the results of this type of research (e.g., Lepper, 1985; Lepper & Chabay, 1985; Lepper & Malone, 1987; Parker & Lepper, 1992).

In recent years, there have been new approaches to the study of motivation. For example, Collins (1996) discusses differences between approaches that attempt to make learning fun through fantasy and elaborate reinforcements and those that attempt to enhance motivation by focusing on authentic tasks that students perceive as real work for real audiences. Several investigators report that students are very interested in tasks that, despite requiring a lot of work, are perceived by them as authentic (e.g., Blumenfeld et al., 1991; Bransford et al., in press; A. L. Brown & Campione, 1994; Collins, Hawkins, & Carver, 1991; CTGV, 1992d, 1993b, 1994b; S. R. Goldman et al., in press; Hickey et al., 1993; Lamon et al., in press; Scardamalia, Bereiter, & Lamon, 1994; Sharp et al., 1992a, 1992b).

An emphasis on motivation based on authentic tasks is one example of a promising theoretical shift away from a generalized concept of motivation and interest toward context-specific constructs. For example, Paris and Turner (1994; Paris & Brynes, 1989) have introduced the term *situated motivation* to describe new socioconstructivist conceptualizations of motivation in relation to the particular topic and setting within which motivation is tested. (See Renninger, Hidi, and Krapp [1992] for similar approaches to interest.) Consistent with this approach, motivation researchers are increasingly using descriptive research methods more typical of socioconstructivist research (e.g., McCaslin, 1993; Meece, 1991; Pintrich & DeGroot, 1993; Turner; 1992).

Research by McCombs (1991, 1994) is also highly relevant to constructivist models of learning and instruction. She conceptualizes motivation for lifelong learning as "a natural response to learning opportunities that is the result of three elements: (1) self-constructed evaluations of the meaning and relevance of a particular learning opportunity relative to one's personal interests, needs and goals; (2) an understanding of one's agency and capacities for self-regulation; and (3) contextual conditions that support perceptions of meaningfulness and self-determination, including supportive personal relationships" (1994, pp. 5–6).

An important point about situations that motivate people is the idea that motivation frequently involves a combination of intrinsic and extrinsic factors. For example, in analyzing factors that influence activities in our technology center (B. Barron et al., in press), it became clear to us that, although intrinsic motivation is extremely important, extrinsic motivation in the form of outside challenges and deadlines also plays an extremely important role. In our Jasper Challenge Series we have tried to create conditions in schools that successfully bring both intrinsic and extrinsic motivational factors into play (e.g., B. Barron et al., in press; CTGV, 1994a, in press; S. R. Goldman et al., 1994).

*Summary of New Visions of Learners and Learning.* Overall, research with children, as well as with adult learners acquiring expertise in a particular field, suggests that the development of thinking is limited more by lack of knowledge than by the absence of general logical capacities. One important implication of this finding is that thinking can and should be part of the curriculum from the earliest grades (e.g., Resnick & Klopfer, 1989). A second implication is that traditional modes of assessment, such as intelligence tests, fail to provide an accurate picture of human potential and adaptability (e.g., Ceci & Ruiz, 1993; S. R. Goldman & Pellegrino, 1991). The fact that knowledge and experience play such important roles in thinking also suggests that we should expect significant individual differences

in development and hence in readiness for various types of learning. This argues against "assembly line" schooling where the approach is to instill the same knowledge in each child at the same point in time.

## New Visions of Curriculum, Instruction, and Assessment

New conceptions of human learning and human potential have important implications for curriculum, instruction, and assessment (e.g., Bereiter, 1994; Bransford et al., 1991; Bruer, 1993; Perkins, 1992; Resnick, 1987a; Savery & Duffy, in press). One problem with traditional approaches has been called the "inert knowledge" problem (Whitehead, 1929). Students in traditional classrooms are often able to retrieve specific facts and skills when explicitly prompted to do so. However, they often fail to use potentially relevant knowledge when asked to solve open-ended problems (e.g. Bransford, Franks, Vye, & Sherwood, 1989; Hasselbring et al., 1991). In Whitehead's terms, their knowledge remains inert. Attempts to help students develop usable knowledge require simultaneous changes in curriculum, instruction, and assessment. Each of these areas is discussed below.

*Changes in Curriculum.* Many theorists have begun to search for approaches to curriculum that provide opportunities for sustained thinking about authentic problems that form the basis of authentic inquiry in domains such as science, social studies, and mathematics (e.g., CTGV, 1990; Honebein, Duffy, & Fishman, 1993; Kinzer, Gabella, & Rieth, 1994; Pea, 1993a). This means that materials that attempt to provide a breadth of factual coverage must be replaced by, or supplemented by, ones that involve opportunities for in-depth exploration. As A. L. Brown and colleagues (A. L. Brown et al., 1993) argue, existing curricular guidelines of the scope-and-sequence variety are insufficient. These guidelines, often correlated with standardized test questions, result in disjointed survey courses.

Alternatives to disjointed survey courses include curricula that emphasize case-based and problem-based learning. Results from a number of studies suggest that these approaches are motivating and more likely to produce transfer in complex problem-solving tasks than are fact-based survey courses (e.g., Barrows, 1985; Bransford & Stein, 1993; Clancy & Linn, 1992; CTGV, 1992a, 1992d, 1993b; Duffy, in press; Elstein, Shulman, & Sprafka, 1978; Hmelo, 1994; Hmelo, Gotterer, & Bransford, 1994; Lyon et al., 1991; Mandl & Grasel, 1993; Norman & Schmidt, 1992; Patel & Groen, 1986; Patel, Groen, & Norman, 1993; Schank, Linn, & Clancy, 1993; Schmidt, 1993; Williams, 1992, 1994). Others report similar results when using project-based curricula where students create products (reports, multimedia documents) based on questions they have generated (e.g., A. L. Brown & Campione, 1994; A. L. Brown et al., 1991; Carver, Lehrer, Connell, & Erickson, 1992; Collins et al., 1991).

Several authors report that transfer can be enhanced by beginning with concrete, problem-based curricula (where problems are presented to students in the form of verbal or visual cases) and then proceeding to more student-generated projects that build on the ideas presented in the problem-based curricula (e.g., CTGV, 1994a; Williams, 1994). In addition, data suggest that flexibility of transfer is enhanced when students are prompted to revisit cases from a "what if" perspective (e.g., "What if this part of the problem were changed?") and asked to explore the implications of the change (e.g., CTGV, 1993b; Williams, 1994).

**_Changes in Instruction._** Curricula that emphasize sustained thinking also require a change in the instructional climate of typical classrooms. In most classrooms, students adopt the role of receivers of information that is dispensed by teachers, textbooks, and other media (A. L. Brown, 1992; Means, 1994). The role of the teacher is to deliver information and manage learning. Usually, everyone is taught the same thing at the same time.

In constructivist classrooms, students are usually provided with opportunities to plan and organize their own research and problem solving, plus opportunities to work collaboratively to achieve important goals (e.g., Blumenfeld et al., 1991; A. L. Brown & Campione, 1994; A. L. Brown et al., 1993; Carver et al., 1992; CTGV, 1994a; Collins et al., 1991; Lamon et al., in press; Linn & Clancy, 1992; Savery & Duffy, in press). In addition, many constructivist classrooms are consistent with an emphasis on the importance of distributed expertise (e.g., B. Barron et al., 1995; A. L. Brown et al., 1993; Pea, 1993b, 1994). Students are allowed to specialize in particular areas so that the community can capitalize on diversity. An emphasis on distributed expertise is distinctively different from environments in which all students are asked to learn the same things at the same points in time.

Mitchell Nathan and Sashank Varma provide the following analysis of information flow in transmission versus constructivist classrooms. In transmission models the information flow goes exclusively from teacher ($T$) to each of the students ($S_1$, $S_2$, . . . $S_n$). The flow of question and discussion is exclusively from each student to the teacher. For $n$ students, the number of connects is simply $n$ for either information flow or questions/ discussions. In contrast, in the constructivist classroom information flow and the flow of questions/discussions occur among all members of the group (teacher and students). In the maximally connected graph containing $n$ students and one teacher (i.e., $n + 1 = m$ members or nodes), the number of links is ($m - 1$) + ($m - 2$) + $\cdots$ + 1, which equals $[m(m - 1)]/2$. For 30 students and one teacher this is 465 lines of communications (which operate both ways!). In comparison, only 30 lines exist in the transmission model. Obviously, the transmission model represents a highly restricted form of communication.

**_Changes in Assessment._** A focus on curriculum and instruction inevitably leads to the issue of assessment. What is measured and how is the information used? During the 1980s there was a great deal of discussion of standardized forms of assessment and how they worked against the development of curricula for improving content-relevant thinking skills. Major criticisms have been raised against standardized testing, in part because overly high stakes have been placed on students' performance on these tests and in part because of the kinds of competencies that they test. (See Gifford and O'Connor [1991] for various perspectives on changes in assessment.)

Although there is wide consensus on the problems created by the testing movement, most researchers do not take the view that testing ought to be eliminated. As Frederiksen and Collins (1989) emphasize:

Such an approach, however, would deny to the educational system the ability to capitalize on one of its greatest strengths: to invent, modify, assimilate, and in other ways improve instruction as a result of experience. No school should be enjoined from modifying its practices in response to their perceived success or failure. (p. 28)

The problem, according to these authors, is not that teachers teach to the test. Instead, the problem is the _type_ of instruction that is engendered by standardized tests. Many teachers are teaching concepts and procedures in a superficial way. Schoenfeld (1991) described an extreme case in which the structure of the test items on a state-administered geometry test was such that students who had been taught to rote memorize geometric proofs performed best. The test did not require students to justify the steps in their constructions and thereby demonstrate their mathematical reasoning abilities. It merely required that their constructions contain all of the arcs and lines and that they be accurately drawn.

Researchers (Frederiksen & Collins, 1989; Pellegrino, 1991; Quellmalz, 1985) have suggested that we need to change the types of tests that we use to assess educational outcomes in order to prevent the kind of abuse described above. Standardized tests mostly emphasize low-level skills, factual knowledge, and memorization of procedures. Frederiksen and Collins (1989) propose that we endeavor to develop "direct tests"—others use the term "performance-based assessments"—of students' thinking. Direct tests attempt to evaluate students' performance on high-level cognitive tasks over an extended period of time (e.g., Lesgold, Eggan, Katz, & Rao, 1992). For example, the task might involve writing a piece of persuasive text or conducting a scientific experiment (e.g., Eylon & Linn, in press; Linn & Clark, in press).

Even performance assessments do not ensure that students are developing the foundations for lifelong learning. Lin et al. (in press) argue that most assessments of transfer are static tests; people learn something and then receive a set of transfer problems (e.g., M. Gick & K. Holyoak, 1980; M. L. Gick & K. J. Holyoak, 1983) or perform a specific task. Scores on such problems can be increased by "teaching to the test," which explicitly includes "teaching for transfer." However, high scores on a specific, static transfer test do not guarantee that students have learned to learn on their own. Assessments of learning to learn require tests of dynamic transfer. A. L. Brown, Bransford, Ferrara, and Campione (1983) discuss a situation in which a learner did very poorly on tests of static transfer yet was able to demonstrate a rich variety of learning-to-learn skills when given a dynamic test that provided the opportunity to access resources that could help him _learn_ to solve problems that he needed to solve.

**_Linking Curriculum, Instruction, and Assessment._** The ways in which curriculum, instruction, and assessment are linked reflects the overall climate or community of the classroom. In constructivist classrooms, students working on problem-based and project-based curricula often uncover issues that exceed the immediate expertise of the teacher (e.g., B. Barron et al., 1995; A. L. Brown & Campione, 1994). Therefore, teachers as well as students must be learners. Instructional strategies involve a focus on ways to help students take responsibility for their own learning rather than on ways for teachers or technology to deliver instruction. Assessment is formative and is designed to encourage reflection and subsequent improvement both by students and by teachers (e.g., B. Barron et al., 1995; CTGV, in press; S. R. Goldman et al., 1994). Connections with groups outside the classroom provide opportunities for authentic audiences who can help teachers and students work together to meet outside goals. In the process, students and teachers are also helped to reflect on their thinking and revise their work (e.g., B. Barron et al., 1995; A. L. Brown & Campione, 1994; Scardamalia et al., 1994).

## Technology Research Relevant to Constructivist Models of Learning

The preceding discussion suggested new visions of what classrooms might look like. Technology can support these new visions, but it can support traditional ones as well (e.g., Jones, Valdez, Nowakowski, & Rasmussen, 1994; Newman, 1992b). In this section we discuss technology-based applications that are consistent with constructivist models of learning. We focus on applications designed to transform only part of the school day (cells 4, 5, and 6 of the LTC framework). Attempts to transform all of schooling (cells 7, 8, and 9) are discussed in the next section.

*Types of Technology Applications.* Our discussion in this section is organized around four categories of educational technology that were used in an excellent review by Means et al. (1993): tutorials, exploratory environments, applications (tools), and communication. We also add a fifth category, teaching programming, as a particular type of exploratory environment. For each category we discuss how technology programs that fit classrooms consistent with constructivist models of learning (cells 4, 5, and 6) differ from those that fit classrooms operating according to transmission theories (cells 1, 2, and 3).

Tutorial Environments.    Earlier we noted that the learning systems developed in the 1960s and 1970s were consistent with transmission models of instruction (cells 1, 2, and 3 in the LTC framework). Whether they were ILSs or stand-alone programs, these systems were usually designed to help students acquire discrete sets of facts and skills. Assessment was based on student performance on these facts and skills.

New versions of tutorial programs have changed along a number of dimensions that fit constructivist models of learning. An especially important one is the nature of the information that students are asked to acquire. In geometry, for example, computer tutorial systems can help students memorize facts about points, lines, the measurement of angles, and so forth. The acquisition of these kinds of facts is consistent with research in row 1 of the LTC framework.

In contrast, systems such as those developed by John Anderson, Ken Koedinger, and their colleagues (Anderson, 1987; Anderson et al., 1985; Koedinger & Anderson, 1990, 1993) are designed to support the *process* of geometric reasoning. For example, in the original Geometry Tutor, Anderson and colleagues provided explicit support for search through the space of theorems and axioms that were expected to connect the "given" statements to the "goal" statements (Anderson et al.,

1985). In later versions of geometry tutors such as ANGLE, support included the development of diagram configurations (visual cases, which are essentially pieces of common diagrams) that research indicated were useful to expert geometricians across a wide variety of problems. Overall, tutorial systems designed to support students' reasoning are very different from ones designed to help students memorize sets of discrete facts (e.g., the definitions of a point and a line) and skills (e.g., how to measure angles).

It is noteworthy that the tutorial programs developed by Anderson, Koedinger, and colleagues are based on an elaborate cognitive model of the user. An important aspect of their model-tracing paradigm is that the process data these systems can collect are very informative. For example, they are a projection of a student's process onto the prerecorded paths of experts or of prior students' misconceptions. In general, student modeling approaches to building tutoring systems are very different from simply recording the accuracy of student responses and providing feedback such as "right" or "wrong" (e.g., Anderson, Corbett, Fincham, Hoffman, & Pelletier, 1992). Derry and Lajoie (1993) provide insightful discussions of the roles of student models in computer design. Other examples of student modeling systems can be found in Lajoie and Derry (1993a).

Interestingly, another strategy for building tutors that enhance understanding (rather than the mere memorization of facts or procedural skills) is to provide information that can inform the reflection of the humans who use the programs. Developers of so-called "unintelligent" systems have adopted this strategy (e.g., Derry & Lajoie, 1993; Nathan, 1990; Reusser, 1993). For example, students can be provided with computer simulations that show the implications of their problem solving, and these simulations can allow users to reflect on and refine their own thinking (CTGV, 1994a; Nathan, Kintsch, & Young, 1992). Similarly, tutorial environments can provide methods for scaffolding users' reflections on the problem-solving processes and their experiences with the system (Katz & Lesgold, 1993; Lajoie, 1993; Lesgold, Lajoie, Bunzo, & Eggan, 1992; Lin, 1993). These have been shown to facilitate transfer to subsequent tasks (Lin, 1993; Nathan et al., 1992).

An interesting variation on tutorial environments is provided by Hunt and Minstrell (1994). They have developed a computer-based "diagnoser" that captures students' thinking about key ideas in physics. Through the use of the diagnoser, the instructor is able to assign students problems that help them change their preconceptions and develop new theoretical points of view.

Exploratory Environments.    Exploratory environments allow students to direct their own learning through discovery or guided discovery processes. They are environments in which students construct their own knowledge, usually in the context of complex problems or situations. Therefore, they are particularly appropriate to the second row of the LTC framework and its concern for constructivist classroom settings.

An excellent illustration of an exploratory computer environment is the Geometric Supposer, developed by Schwartz, Yerushalmy, and colleagues (Yerushalmy, 1991; Yerushalmy, Chazan, & Gordon, 1990). It is a powerful environment for making and proving conjectures in geometry. Another dynamic geometry microworld is the Geometer's Sketchpad (Jackiw, 1991). Users can construct and manipulate geometric figures to investigate geometric relationships. Research suggests that both geometry environments require teacher guidance to function well (e.g., Yerushalmy, 1991; Yerushalmy et al., 1990; Wiske, 1990). In the science area, Linn and colleagues (Friedler, Nachmias, & Linn, 1990; Linn, 1992) have developed the Computer as Lab Partner (CLP) curriculum for heat and thermodynamics. Students formulate and design experiments, predict the outcomes and explain the predictions, conduct the experiment, reconcile the results with their predictions, and interpret the results (Linn & Songer, 1991; Songer & Linn, 1991; see also chapter 15). The computer provides simulations and a laboratory notebook for recording the information, thereby scaffolding student understanding.

A more general application for allowing students to explore systems is STELLA (Structural Thinking Experiential Laboratory with Animation) and the hypercard version STELLAStack (Richmond, 1985, 1993; Richmond & Peterson, 1988, 1990). These modeling and simulation applications permit students to build and observe the operation of dynamic systems. STELLA and STELLAStack are important components of the STACI project (Mandinach & Cline, 1994). STACI has been concerned with implementing systems thinking in classroom instruction in history, science, and mathematics. Consistent with constructivist philosophy, systems thinking is a problem-solving strategy for examining the dynamic relationships among the parts of a phenomenon. Systems thinking often emphasizes change over time. STELLA has been a primary mechanism for introducing systems thinking into the classroom culture (Mandinach & Cline, 1994).

The development of computer-based microworlds provides additional examples of exploratory environments. Examples include Smithtown, an economics microworld (Shute, 1993; Shute & Glaser, 1991); ThinkerTools, a world of Newtonian principles of mechanics (White, 1993); Boxer, an environment in which students create their own computational representations of content areas such as physics (diSessa, 1993); and 4MChem, a system for exploring chemical equilibrium (Kozma, Russel, T. Jones, Marx, & Davis, 1993). Software such as Sim City and Rocky's Boots has also been used as a basis for exploratory projects in school (e.g., Bransford & Stein, 1993; Delclos & Kulewicz, 1986). Pogrow (1990a, 1990b) has made ingenious use of computers and computer software as objects that students want to learn about. Students develop reading, comprehension, and problem-solving skills as they consult manuals and collaborate to achieve their learning goals.

Video and multimedia environments have also been used to create exploratory contexts. Programs such as *Palenque* (Wilson, 1987), *Voyage of the Mimi* (Bank Street College of Education, 1984), *The Adventures of Jasper Woodbury* (CTGV, 1990, 1991, 1992a, 1992c, 1993b; Zech et al., 1994), the Young Children's Literacy Series (e.g., Bransford et al., in press; Brophy et al., 1994; Sharp et al., 1992a, 1992b); the Young Sherlock Project (e.g., Bransford et al., 1988; Bransford, Vye, Kinzer, & Risko, 1990; CTGV, 1990; Kinzer, Williams, & Cunningham, 1992; McLarty et al., 1990), Scientists in Action (CTGV, 1992b; S. R. Goldman et al., in press; Sherwood et al., in press), the Adult Literacy Project (CTGV, 1992a), The Great Space Race (Tom Snyder Productions, 1992), and The Math Mystery Series (Human Relations Media, 1992) are all examples of complex, authentic situations in which students use content in mathemat-

ics, science, and social sciences to solve problems. Software extensions to these programs provide additional kinds of learning support.

Interactive multimedia systems such as the ASK systems (Ferguson, Bareiss, Birnbaum, & Osgood, 1992), *Rain Forest* (National Geographic, 1991), and software relevant to modeling ecosystems (Jackson, Stratford, Guzdial, Krajcik, & Soloway 1995) allow the learner to explore various topics from multiple perspectives (see also Spiro & Jehng, 1990; Spiro et al., 1987). Interactive CD products such as *Treasures of the Smithsonian* (Hoekema, 1993) also create potentially rich environments for students to take control of their learning.

A danger in some of the emerging multimedia systems is that they do not engage the learner in active processing and restructuring of information. In some cases there is little opportunity for students to directly explore and manipulate the models that underlie various simulations. Other uses of multimedia function more as "encyclopedias" than as environments in which problems can be posed or solved (CTGV, 1993c). Of particular importance are multimedia resources that allow students to create their own multimedia products that they can show to others. Examples of these kinds of activities include the Thinking Skills Project (Reeves & Hamm 1993), the Discover Rochester Project (Carver et al., 1992; Collins et al., 1991; the Young Children's Literacy Project (Brophy et al., 1994), and the High School Literacy Project (CTGV, 1994b).

Important issues for pedagogy and assessment arise in the context of exploratory environments. Much of the activity in exploratory environments occurs in small groups because students deal with authentic problems that are quite complex. Working on them together facilitates problem solving and capitalizes on distributed expertise (e.g., B. Barron, 1991; A. L. Brown et al., 1993; CTGV, 1992c, 1993b, 1994a; Yackel, Cobb, & Wood, 1991). However, not all collaborations work effectively (S. R. Goldman, Cosden, & Hine, 1992; Linn & Burbules, 1993; Salomon & Globerson, 1989). Procedures for "making students' thinking visible" provide opportunities for formative assessments that can be used to optimize learning (B. Barron et al., 1995; CTGV, 1994a)

Teaching Computer Programming. We noted in our earlier discussion of transmission models of learning that early efforts to teach programming tended to focus on programming languages such as BASIC as a curriculum to be learned. Papert's *Mindstorms* (1980) suggested a vision for teaching programming that makes it into an exploratory environment. Papert argued that, with an appropriately structured language such as LOGO, students would not simply learn to program a computer. They would also discover how to think and learn for themselves. LOGO was designed to provide an exciting environment that had no ceiling and no floor (i.e., that could be used by people who varied from young children to advanced programmers).

Early attempts to assess the cognitive effects of LOGO programming found few cognitive benefits (e.g., Pea & Kurland, 1984). Subsequent studies (see Mayer, 1988b) found cognitive benefits (e.g., better planning), but they required changing the instruction that surrounded LOGO in order to achieve these effects. For example, Littlefield and colleagues (Littlefield et al., 1988) noted that most of the early studies of LOGO had failed to include an assessment of how well students had learned

LOGO programming in the first place. When this was assessed, students' knowledge of LOGO was often found to be weak. Littlefield and colleagues noted that, if there is only a modest amount of initial learning, there is little reason to expect any transfer to new tasks.

Many researchers began to design instruction around Logo that encouraged students to become more planful and take a design stance toward their programming. Without this type of instruction, students' behavior during LOGO programming often fit a pattern of trial and error (Carver, 1988; Hawkins, 1987b; Littlefield et al., 1988). As LOGO began to be taught as a means to other ends (to the acquisition of planning skills, knowledge of geometry, and so forth), cognitive benefits on transfer tests began to show up (e.g., Lehrer, Guckenberg, & Lee, 1988; Lehrer, Lee, & Jeong, 1994; Lehrer, Randle, & Sancilio, 1989).

Salomon (1992) points out that research on LOGO suffers from an interesting paradox. He argues that LOGO taught according to the original vision of Papert (1980) fared poorly in tests of cognitive benefits. However, as uses of LOGO strayed from the original vision, the results began to look more favorable. Salomon believes that LOGO and other programming languages are more successful when they become viewed as tools to help students achieve more specific goals, such as learning to create efficient designs or learning key principles of geometry. We discusss additional computer tools for learning in the section below.

We agree with Salomon's analysis of the evolution of attempts to teach LOGO. We add that, after viewing several tapes of Papert in LOGO classrooms, it seemed to us that Papert was an outstanding teacher who continually helped students reflect on what they were doing and define and evaluate their goals and strategies. He did not simply step back and let students flounder on their own. Papert's *descriptions* of LOGO teaching focused primarily on discovery learning. In contrast, Papert's *actions* as a teacher fit very well with constructivist models of curriculum, assessment, and instruction that advocate scaffolding and mediation by teachers and others rather than discovery learning (e.g., A. L. Brown & Campione, 1994; Lin et al., 1995; Vygotsky, 1978, 1986). As research with LOGO has focused more attention on the teaching that surrounds it, the results on cognitive transfer have been more favorable (e.g., Lehrer et al., 1994; Mayer, 1988a).

Applications (Tools).   Technology in this category refers to software that supports various user activities such as writing (e.g., word-processing systems), calculating (e.g., spreadsheets), and the composition of multimedia documents as in the use of Hypercard (Apple systems), Linkway (MS-DOS systems), ToolBook (Windows systems), or Media Text (Hay et al., in press).

Means et al. (1993) note that many new hypermedia applications support the emergence of novel genre that exploit the capacities of hardware environments. The nonlinear format enables students to engage in different kinds of knowledge construction activities than would be possible with strictly linear applications. The products students create sometimes take advantage of the nonlinear capabilities, although sometimes they do not look much different than a typical report (e.g., Carver

et al., 1992; Duffy & Knuth, 1990; Honebein et al., 1993; Lehrer, 1993; Spoehr, 1994).

As noted earlier, computer applications tend to be treated differently when used in the context of constructivist models of education (cells 4, 5, and 6) compared with transmission models (cells 1, 2, and 3). In many classrooms based on transmission models, the applications *are* the curriculum. In constructivist-inspired classrooms, applications are usually treated as tools for reaching other goals, as in QUILL (Bruce & Rubin, 1993). These goals include solving important problems, building knowledge about new ideas and concepts, or creating text or multimedia documents about specific areas of research (e.g., Collins et al., 1991; Carver et al., 1992; CTGV, 1992a, 1994b; Lehrer, 1993; Scardamalia et al., 1994; Spoehr, 1994).

A second way in which applications are affected by transmission versus constructivist models involves the degree to which they are augmented to provide support for learning. Early computer-based research on writing, conducted within the traditional school-based writing framework, asked whether writing on the computer was easier or better than writing by hand, and did not use the technology to augment the task environment. Results were equivocal regarding benefits, although it appeared that revising was more likely on the computer (e.g., Bradley, 1982; Daiute, 1985b; Gerlach, 1987; Kerchner & Kistinger, 1984; MacArthur & Graham, 1987; Vacc, 1987; Woodruff & Bereiter, 1982). Despite the greater likelihood of revision, many of the revisions dealt with spelling, grammar, and punctuation. Meaning-based revisions such as reorganization, insertion, or deletion of information rarely occurred (Hine, Goldman, & Cosden, 1990).

QUILL is an early example of an augmented environment for writing. It was designed to provide opportunities for children to collaboratively solve problems and to have access to real audiences for their writing (Bruce & Rubin, 1993). The pedagogical goals for QUILL also included an emphasis on the integration of reading and writing, making writing public to establish community and meaningful communication with an audience, and revision. The computer environment consisted of four interrelated programs: Writer's Assistant, for word processing (Levin, Boruta, & Vasconcellos, 1983); Planner, for supporting brainstorming; Library, for sharing written work with other students; and Mailbag, an electronic mail system. The QUILL system was used during a yearlong implementation (1983–1984) in 20 classrooms in Alaska. Results indicated that students appropriated a number of meaningful goals for writing, most notably newspapers and mail. The system had little impact on revisions, however.

Examples of other environments for supporting writing are Salomon's Writing Partner (Salomon, 1993b), Rubin's Story Maker (Rubin, 1980, 1983); and the CTGV's work on reading support to help learning handicapped students develop their own multimedia designs (CTGV, 1994b).

Computer tools have also been developed to help teachers conduct the kinds of performance assessments that are consistent with constructivist curricula (e.g., Gearhart, Herman, Baker, & Novak, 1992; Hawkins et al., 1990; Lesgold, Eggan, et al., 1992; Sheingold & Frederiksen, 1994). For example, electronic portfolios allow teachers easily to capture and store records of student progress that include text, audio, and video (e.g., the Grady Portfolio, developed by Aurbach & Associates,

1991). Bar code readers have also been used by teachers to score performances and send these scores to a computer to be stored (e.g., Victoria Learning Society & Sunburst/Wings for Learning, 1994). Portable computers such as the TYCHO system (Stewart & Watson, 1994; Vecchione, 1994) and systems for the Newton (Victoria Learning Society & Sunburst/Wings for Learning, 1994) are being used for assessment as well.

Work under way as part of the Jasper series is examining the idea of having students learn to construct "SMART Tools" that enable them to solve classes of problems efficiently. For example, in the Jasper adventure *Working Smart*, the challenge is to construct a set of SMART Tools that allows students to qualify for an exciting job opportunity. Initial data indicate that students are motivated to construct SMART Tools and that the process of doing so helps them discover important mathematical patterns and concepts. The construction of SMART Tools also provides an excellent way to make students' thinking visible to themselves, their teachers, and their peers.

Overall, research indicates that an application's or tool's impact on the learner or educational setting depends on how it is implemented (e.g., Daiute, 1985a; Daiute & Kruidenier, 1985), and also on whether the technology leaves a "cognitive residue" (Salomon, 1993b; Salomon et al., 1991). Salomon and colleagues argue that the use of a cognitive tool ought to result in changed understandings on the part of learners. Such changes are effects *of* the technology, not just effects achieved *with* the technology. Effects *of* technology are ones that learners can transfer to new situations. Important research issues concern appropriate methodologies and benchmarks for examining performance in new situations.

Communication and Telecommunication.   Implicit but central to constructivist-based applications is communication. Knowledge is constructed through conversations—whether face-to-face or electronic, whether synchronous or asynchronous, whether spoken or written (see Pea & Gomez, 1992). Technologies for supporting conversations are undergoing rapid change.

An exciting communication technology that supports collaboration is CSILE (Scardamalia et al., 1989, 1992). It is designed to provide opportunities for groups of individuals to collaboratively build new understandings and theories. Because all students on a network share an easily accessible data base, they can collaborate even though they cannot all be in the same place at the same time.

Additional examples of within-school systems that support collaborative learning are the Collaborative Learning Laboratory (Koschmann, Myers, Feltovich, & Barrows, 1994), which is used to facilitate collaboration among team members engaged in medical preclinical education, and EarthLab (Newman, Goldman, Brienne, Jackson, & Magzamen, 1989; S. V. Goldman & Newman, 1992), which provides support for coordinated investigations by small groups of students. (For further discussion of collaborative systems see the *Journal of Learning Sciences*, Vol. 3, No. 3, 1994, a special issue guest edited by Koschmann.)

Bubble dialogue (O'Neill & McMahon, 1992) is another promising tool that promotes conversation and collaboration. It is especially useful for helping students deal with complex emotional issues that they might otherwise have difficulty discussing. It does so by engaging students in computer-based role-playing scenarios structured to allow greater amounts of student reflection as they discuss complex aesthetic issues concerning literature and social themes (Kantor & McMahon, 1994).

The use of communications technology to encourage within-school collaborative knowledge building falls within cell 5 of the LTC framework (individual classrooms). The increased capabilities of networked electronic systems to support interactive information storage and exchange are giving rise to systems that support wide-area communal data bases that may be added to, accessed by, and operated on by communities of learners. With a sufficiently large bandwidth, wide-area systems can also support audio and video messaging in addition to text-based communication. Programs such as these fall within cell 6 (connected classrooms).

There are also numerous examples of wide-area communication systems that provide participants with the ability to share data bases asynchronously. One is the AT&T Learning Circle, in use by teachers (Riel, 1990a, 1990b, 1991b). LabNet is also a tool for teachers and students, particularly with regard to assessment (Ruopp, Gal, Drayton, & Pfister, 1993). Recently, Thought Box (Alexander & Lincoln, 1989), originally designed to support distance learning, has been redesigned to allow for more humanlike interfaces and collective construction of theme or topic-based group knowledge. CSILE (Scardamalia et al., 1994) is also being expanded to TeleCSILE in order to support wide-area communication. Project-based learning in science is supported by systems such as ALICE (Parker, 1991) and the CoVis Collaboratory Notebook (Edelson & O'Neill, 1994). Desktop videoconferencing has been used to support school–community interactions such as tutoring sessions on problem solving held between college students and students in middle schools (CTGV, 1994a).

An important characteristic of the communication technologies discussed above is that they are usually introduced as a means to solve complex problems or engage in collaborative inquiry around authentic problems. Additional well-known projects of this type are National Geographic Society (NGS) Kids Network (Julyan, 1991; Technical Educational Research Center, 1990; Tinker & Papert, 1989), the Technical Educational Research Center's (TERC) Star Schools Project (Berger, 1989), the Jason Project (1993), AT&T's Long Distance Learning Network (Riel, 1991a, 1991b; Riel & Levin, 1990), the CoVis project (Pea, 1994), the Co-NECT Project (Bolt Beranek & Newman, 1994a; Richards, 1993) and the Intercultural Learning Network (J. A. Levin, Riel, Miyake, & Cohen, 1987). In a number of programs, electronic mail has also been used to provide students with access to subject matter experts (Campione, Brown, & Jay, 1992; Newman, 1990b).

There is so much activity over electronic mail that tools for organizing the profusion of messages are beginning to emerge (e.g., J. A. Levin & Jacobson, 1993). Similarly, the need for organizational tools emerges quickly in the context of the CSILE communal data base. Cohen (1994) has developed a set of electronic teacher tools that allow teachers to search data bases to find high-density topics of conversation as well as the individual contributions of particular individuals. Tools such as these are extremely helpful for monitoring group discussions and keeping them on track. Experiences of other projects involving network-based classrooms in a wide variety of settings are reviewed in a recent volume by Bruce et al. (1993).

Issues arising in the context of electronic networks and communal data bases concern fundamental issues in knowledge organization, including search heuristics, psychologically adaptive schematics for supporting users' understanding of the data base landscape, and systematic but psychologically plausible updating mechanisms. When students are free to put in their thoughts and coconstruct knowledge, misconceptions often appear in the data base. What happens to such misconceptions is an important issue for research. As well, general questions about information sharing in electronic environments and communication etiquette (e.g., postulates for electronic conversations) are important for understanding the sociolinguistic implications of technology and the building of discourse communities. For a discussion of these issues see Mason and Kaye (1989) and Sproull and Kiesler (1991).

***Issues that Arise in Moving from Laboratories to Classrooms to Connected Classrooms.*** The preceding discussion focused on the general implications of moving from the first row of the LTC framework (transmission models) to the second row (constructivist models that transform part of the school day). In this section we discuss some of the implications of moving across the second row, that is, moving from laboratories to classrooms to sets of connected classrooms.

Examples from Our Own Research.   First, we reiterate that research in all cells of the LTC framework is valuable. For example, in our own work on the Jasper Woodbury Problem Solving Series, research conducted in laboratory settings (cell 4) has allowed us to compare the effects on transfer of having students work with Jasper versus having students work for the same amount of time with the same subproblems that are found in Jasper, but without the integrated problem context. By using teachers from our own research team in the context of laboratory studies, we were able to ensure a high degree of fidelity of implementation for both our experimental and control conditions. By focusing on a relatively small number of students, we were able to conduct in-depth assessments that asked students to think aloud as they attempted to solve new transfer problems (S. R. Goldman et al., 1991; S. R. Goldman & CTGV, 1991; Van Haneghan et al., 1992). These studies allowed us to document that opportunities to work in integrated problem contexts such as Jasper were very important (e.g. CTGV, 1993b; Van Haneghan et al., 1992).

In contrast to laboratory research, studies of Jasper that involved classrooms (cell 5) revealed a different set of problems and opportunities. The opportunities were that we were able to study the effects of Jasper as it was taught by a variety of classroom teachers in nine different states (CTGV, 1992d, in press; Pellegrino et al., 1991). However, large-scale studies also involve new problems. One was that we were unable to study the fidelity with which Jasper was implemented in each classroom. Another problem was that the best we could do for comparison groups was to find students with similar levels of achievement and economic status who received "regular classroom instruction" in mathematics rather than Jasper. A third problem was that we had to settle for paper-and-pencil assessment rather than in-depth performance assessments.

Overall, it was impossible to be as precise about the Jasper instruction, and the instruction received by comparison classes, as it was when we conducted our studies in laboratory contexts. Nevertheless, the opportunity to study Jasper across a large number of different sites was extremely beneficial (CTGV, 1992d, in press; Pellegrino, 1991).

We have also studied Jasper in the context of connected sets of classrooms (cell 6). The Jasper "SMART Challenge" Series was designed to connect groups of classrooms and teachers so that they could learn from one another (CTGV, 1994a). Data indicate that this increased the achievement of students relative to Jasper-alone instruction, and it also helped change teachers' teaching styles (e.g., B. Barron et al., 1995; CTGV 1994a).

Additional Examples of Migration.   During the past 5 years, an increasing number of researchers have migrated from the laboratory to classrooms and sets of classrooms (e.g., Hawkins & Collins, in press; Mandinach & Cline, 1994; McGilly, 1994; Salomon, 1992). In the process, they have discovered issues with important implications for the design and use of technology. Collins (1996) provides an insightful discussion of some of the design tradeoffs that must be considered in schools.

An extremely important lesson from a number of different projects is that designers must focus simultaneously on issues of curriculum, instruction, assessment, and professional development. If any of these issues is ignored, applications often fall short of their designers' goals.

Means et al. (1993) provided an example of the need to consider assessments in her discussion of a California school system that implemented a constructivist-based technology program that changed the schools' curriculum, instruction, and professional development. However, the assessments were not changed, and they focused on specific skills rather than on more complex performances. Students did poorly on the skills tests, and the system began to question the technology. To be effective, assessment must be aligned with one's educational goals (see also S. R. Goldman et al., 1994).

The need to focus on instruction is illustrated by early efforts to implement LOGO. As noted previously, early implementations of LOGO tended to treat it as a new addition to the curriculum without paying serious attention to the nature of the instruction and formative assessment needed to support the goals of Papert and his colleagues (see Mayer, 1988a). In many classrooms, students were more likely to take a trial-and-error approach to LOGO programming than to approach the task as designers who plan and debug their own work (e.g., Littlefield et al., 1988). Later efforts to teach LOGO have been more successful at demonstrating cognitive benefits, in part because they (a) structured the instruction to encourage planning and reflection and (b) designed assessments that were more sensitive to the thinking processes that students developed (e.g., Lehrer et al., 1994).

Research conducted by Schofield et al. (1990) provides an excellent example of the effects of instructional context on learning. She studied Anderson and colleagues' geometry tutor in classroom contexts and found that a low degree of peer competition was a vital factor in promoting learning. These kinds of insight would be difficult to discover if one worked solely with individual students in the context of research laboratory.

A lesson learned by a number of research groups, ours included, is the need to pay a great deal of attention to the professional development of teachers who will be using the programs (e.g., Hawkins & Collins, in press; Mandinach & Cline, 1994; McGilly, 1994). Initially, many researchers underestimated the importance of this aspect of research, and their results were underwhelming. Several groups have developed technology-based applications that are very promising for strengthening the ability of both preservice and practicing teachers to implement programs in ways that are successful (e.g., Ball, 1994; L. C. Barron & Goldman, 1994; Duffy, in press; Fishman & Duffy, 1992; E. S. Goldman, Barron & Witherspoon, 1992; Kinzer, 1993; Kinzer et al., 1992; Lampert & Ball, 1990; J. A. Levin & Jacobson, 1993; J. A. Levin, Waugh, Brown, & Clift, 1993; Risko, 1992, 1993).

## Summary of Row 2 of the LTC Framework

Changes in the goals of education and in views of human learning and human potential have suggested new visions of curriculum, instruction, and assessment. Technology can support these new visions, although it can support traditional ones as well.

Technology applications that fit within row 2 of the LTC framework (constructivist models of learning) look quite different from those that fit row 1 (applications based on transmission models). It has been challenging to move constructivist-based applications from laboratories (cell 4) into classrooms (cell 5) and connected sets of classrooms (cell 6) because most existing classrooms are based on transmission models of curriculum, instruction, and assessment. Technology researchers who have made the transition from cell 4 to cells 5 and 6 have discovered a number of new issues that did not arise in the laboratory. Issues of professional development—both for the technology and for new approaches to curriculum, instruction, and assessment—are challenging issues faced by virtually every research group we know.

## THEORY AND RESEARCH RELEVANT TO ROW 3 IN THE LTC FRAMEWORK

Studies that fit into row 3 in the LTC framework (cells 7, 8, and 9) are based on the same constructivist principles as those relevant to row 2 (cells 4, 5, and 6). However, there is a difference in the degree of restructuring involved, and this raises new theoretical and practical issues. Studies relevant to row 2 in the framework involve efforts to transform only part of schooling. Further, most of them involve studies of only a single application, such as Quill, CSILE, Thinker Tools, Co Vis, Jasper, and so forth. In contrast, studies relevant to row 3 in the LTC framework (cells 7, 8, and 9) involve efforts to transform all of schooling. This usually involves the need to study the effects of a whole suite of technologies on the overall learning environment that they support.

## Theoretical Issues Relevant to Transforming all of Schooling

An important issue that arises as one moves from the goal of transforming part of the school day (row 2) to transforming

all of schooling (row 3) involves the need to provide a balanced curriculum. In row 3 (cells 7, 8, and 9) it is no longer sufficient to simply be the mathematics advocate or the science advocate or the literacy advocate. Each of these advocates usually wants more time for his or her particular subject, but there is only so much time in a day. Researchers who work in row 3 must acknowledge that students can gain expertise in one area of the curriculum at the expense of losing opportunities to learn about other areas. One approach to this dilemma is to create projects that integrate traditional curricula (e.g., Berger, 1994; Berlin, 1994; CTGV, 1994a; Dossey, 1994; Mandinach & Cline, 1994; Steen, 1994; Tinker, 1994).

The responsibility of thinking about the entire school day also raises issues of compatibility among different classroom cultures as children change classes, issues of restructuring class periods to create blocks of time necessary to pursue problem-based and project-based curricula, and issues of links to the home and community. A number of non-technology-based reform efforts have collected valuable information about issues such as these (e.g., Comer, 1988/1993; Hilliard, 1988; H. M. Levin, 1987/1993; Madden et al., 1991/1993).

Responsibility for transforming all of schooling also requires a new concern with issues of accountability. When working with only a single technology program, it is often easy to finesse requirements for local accountability because of the experimental nature of one's work, and because students' levels of achievement can be measured in other subject areas that are not the focus of experimentation. Accountability issues must be directly addressed when one attempts to restructure the entire school day. Especially challenging are cases in which local tests of accountability are not consistent with the goals of the technology-based programs. Whether or not one believes in the value of these tests, they cannot be ignored (e.g., see example from Means et al., 1993, cited earlier).

We believe that the goal of transforming all of schooling, and of accepting responsibility for local accountability, is likely to encourage a careful examination of the use of "mixing models" of educational reform. For example, the more that we attempt to take responsibility for the student's whole day, the more we find ourselves inclined to combine constructivist-inspired activities such as problem- and project-based learning with more traditional drill-and-practice activities that fall into the laboratory setting row of the LTC framework (cells 1, 2, and 3) (e.g., Bransford et al., 1988; S. R. Goldman et al., 1988; Lin et al., 1995). However, we introduce these practice activities as part of a problem-solving curriculum in which students assess their own needs (e.g., to acquire particular skills) and work collaboratively to find ways to meet them. Under these conditions, there is great promise for well-structured diagnosis and practice software.

## Research Relevant to Transforming all of Schooling

To our knowledge, there are only a few technology-based research projects relevant to row 3 in the LTC framework. There are, of course, a number of projects involving the restructuring of schools (see Backler & Eakin, 1993). However, most of them either (a) fall within cell 2 or 3 of the LTC framework (transmission models in classrooms and connected classrooms) or (b) make almost no use of technology.

One project relevant to row 3 (cells 8 and 9) is the Co-NECT project (e.g., Bolt, Beranek, & Newman, 1994a; Richards, 1993). Co-NECT schools are organized in multiage clusters of approximately 100 students and four to five teachers. Each cluster is responsible for setting its own goals, planning curriculum, and monitoring progress. Technology is used extensively both within classrooms and schools and to connect different schools. Similarly, the STACI[N] project (Mandinach & Cline, 1994) connects teachers in schools across the country as they implement a systems thinking approach in multiple areas of the curriculum. Over the 8-year evolution of the STACI[N] (and its nonnetworked predecessor, STACI), teachers have formed dynamic, cross-disciplinary teams for the purpose of creating more meaningful, integrated curricula.

Another project relevant to row 3 (cells 8 and 9) is the Schools for Thought Project (e.g., Lamon, 1993; Lamon et al., in press; Lin et al., 1995). Named after John Bruer's award-winning book, the project involves close collaboration among A. L. Brown and Campione's (1994) "Fostering a Community of Learners" Project, Scardamalia and Bereiter's CSILE Project (e.g., Scardamalia et al., 1994), the St. Louis Science Center and public schools, and CTGV's Jasper Woodbury Project (e.g., CTGV, 1994a).

Initial work relevant to the Schools for Thought Project involved a restructuring of the entire school day in sixth-grade classrooms in several different cities. During the second year, the number of sixth-grade classrooms increased to four and the program expanded to four seventh-grade classrooms in order to create a corridor for the Year 1 sixth graders and connect different classrooms and schools through networking. The ultimate goal is to expand the program to both upper and lower grades.

The Co-NECT, STACI[N], and Schools for Thought projects are relatively new and have not yet generated a great deal of hard data. What is clear, however, is that multiple methods are needed to understand and evaluate issues of student learning, program implementation, and professional development. Issues of performance assessment and accountability are high priorities for these research groups in the coming years.

## ISSUES FOR THE FUTURE

We believe that future research in technology and education will include work in all cells of the LTC framework, but especially in row 3 (cells 7, 8, and 9). Work in all cells is important because each offers unique strengths and opportunities. Work in row 3 is important because there is a strong need to study entire systems rather than look only at piecemeal effects (see Mandinach & Cline, 1994). Attempts to work in these cells raise a number of new issues that we believe will receive increasing attention. We discuss several of them below.

### Expanding the Scope of the LTC Framework

In our discussion so far, the scope of research within each cell in the LTC framework has been left undefined. For example, when we discussed constructivist approaches that attempt to transform all of schooling in connected classrooms (cell 9), we did not specify whether the scope of analysis was a single grade,

middle school, kindergarten through Grade 12, or kindergarten through college. The scope of most research projects involves only a single grade level or, at most, two or three consecutive grade levels. There are important differences between thinking about changes within a single grade or small set of grades, and thinking about changes from kindergarten through college. These differences are illustrated in Figure 25–3.

A. L. Brown and Campione's (1994) Community of Learners project is a good example of a project with a broad-scope focus. They emphasize the importance of "deep principles" in areas such as biology (deep principles might be "interdependence," "biological diversity," and so forth). Most important for the present discussion, Brown and Campione also explicitly attempt to create curricula and instructional opportunities that enable students to understand deep principles at early ages, and then to have the opportunity to expand their understandings as they progress throughout the grades. One advantage is that students can develop a level of expertise in particular domains that is extraordinary by current standards. Another advantage is that students can engage in cross-age tutoring sessions that include highly sophisticated discussions. To take this approach, one must be willing to rethink existing curricula, instruction, and assessment across multiple grades.

Kaput and Lesh (1994) have discussed the importance of a broad-scope focus in the area of mathematics. Why, they ask, should students suddenly be confronted with *the* course in algebra or geometry or calculus? Similar to Brown and Campione, they argue that there are "big ideas" in mathematics that can be introduced early and gradually refined over the years.

We believe that a broad-scope focus may be necessary for truly profound changes in academic achievement. In addition to helping students acquire more in-depth knowledge, it can provide new avenues to expertise that are denied to many students who are expected to learn an entire subject matter all at once when they receive *the* course in algebra, genetics, and so forth. Ideally, broad-scope approaches to education will attempt to integrate curricula from kindergarten through college so that mathematics, science, literature, and other subjects may be learned synergistically (Bransford, Sherwood, & Hasselbring, 1988). To achieve these ideals, technology-based applications must be designed with broad-scope goals in mind.

### Technology in the Service of Learning Communities

A concept that we believe will be increasingly important for the future thinking about technology is the concept of learning communities. We agree with Senge (1994) that the concepts of learning organizations and learning communities are in danger of becoming meaningless because they are being defined in almost every manner possible. Nevertheless, we think that these concepts are potentially very powerful ones that warrant rigorous research and theoretical articulation. We also believe that they are strongly linked to technology. Indeed, the STACI[N] project (Mandinach & Cline, 1994) has adapted these ideas in the analysis of teacher change in the process of learning to work in a technologically rich classroom environment. In the following discussion we discuss learning organizations and learning communities as they are being explored in both the business community and the education community.

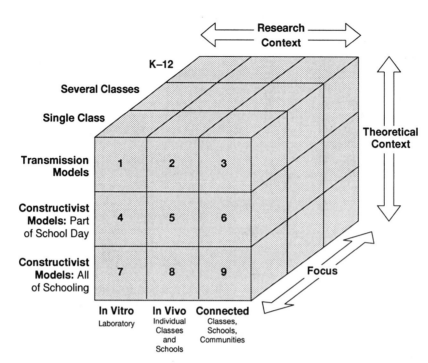

FIGURE 25–3. Expanded LTC Framework: Looking at the Use of Technology in Single Grades, Several Consecutive Grades, or Across Schooling

***Businesses as Learning Organizations.*** A number of insights into learning organizations and learning communities come from business leaders who need to cope with rapid change and reinvention and their implications for human capital (e.g., Knowles, 1983; Senge, 1990); our colleague Neal Nadler helped point us to the relevant literature. Traditional business structures have tended to be relatively inflexible and more likely to support the status quo than to support change. However, to respond to today's economic climate they must transform themselves into learning organizations (Mills & Friesen, 1992).

Mills and Friesen (1992) note that most organizations attempt to ensure learning by hiring good people. But one of the criticisms of current schooling is that it does not develop the kinds of flexible thinkers and problem solvers needed for modern-day organizations. Many businesses have begun their own training programs rather than rely on the schools. Unfortunately, business training programs often produce as much inert knowledge as traditional elementary, secondary, and college education. Authors such as Knowles (1983), Mills and Friesen (1992), and Senge (1990) provide important insights into the nature of the social and organizational structures that can overcome inert knowledge and help employees continue to learn, and to apply and refine what they know.

Mills and Friesen (1992) also emphasize that *organizations* must learn; otherwise nothing is preserved when people leave. Organizations learn by systematizing knowledge into practices, processes, and procedures, relying in part on what they can learn from their employees. We believe that theories of learning communities in elementary and secondary classrooms and preservice educational settings have much to learn from learning communities in business.

***Classrooms as Learning Communities.*** Within the educational research community, much of the interest in learning communities stems from analyses of successful, informal learning environments that exist outside of school (e.g., Bransford & Heldmeyer, 1983; J. S. Brown et al., 1989; CTGV, 1993a; Lave, 1988; Lave & Wenger, 1991; Resnick, 1987b). For example, students who participate in successful informal learning environments typically do not spend most of their time simply memorizing what others teach them. In many settings (e.g., many apprenticeships), there is little formal teaching, yet a great deal of learning occurs (Holt, 1964; Lave & Wenger, 1991; Sternberg & Wagner, 1986).

In classrooms organized into learning communities, students are provided with opportunities to plan and organize their own research and problem solving, and to work collaboratively to achieve important goals (e.g., A. L. Brown & Campione, 1994; A. L. Brown et al., 1993, Carver et al., 1992; Collins et al. 1991; CTGV, 1994a; Lamon et al., in press; Linn & Burbules, 1993; Bolt, Beranek, & Newman, 1994a; Richards, 1993; Savery & Duffy, in press). In addition, learning communities usually emphasize the importance of distributed expertise (e.g., B. Barron et al., in press; A. L. Brown et al., 1993; Pea, 1993, 1994). Students are allowed to specialize in particular areas so that the community can capitalize on diversity. An emphasis on distributed expertise is distinctively different from environments where all students are asked to learn the same things at the same points in time.

***Beyond Classrooms.*** The idea of classrooms as learning communities becomes most powerful when they, in turn, are seen as part of larger communities. The goal is to break the isolation of individual classrooms and allow students, teachers, parents, and community members to interact. This is important for a number of reasons. One is that teachers and students can gain access to expertise that may not be available within the context of their classroom (e.g., B. Barron et al., 1995; A. L. Brown et al., 1993). Another is that opportunities to interact with others can provide important occasions for formative assessment by students and teachers (e.g., B. Barron, 1995, CTGV, 1994a).

Talbert and McLaughlin (1993) point out another reason for the importance of broader definitions of learning communities: Strong professional communities are essential conduits and learning contexts for ideas about new teaching practices. They note that these communities must exist in order to expect long-term change. In addition, they must consistently emphasize and support innovation and reform; otherwise they serve to reinforce the status quo and, in many cases, make teachers less rather than more flexible in adapting to student needs. A number of researchers are creating technology-based programs for building professional communities that look highly promising (e.g., Ball, 1994; L. C. Barron & Goldman, 1994; Duffy, in press; Evertson & Smithey, 1993; Jones, Knuth, & Duffy, 1993; Kinzer, 1993; Lampert & Ball, 1990; Risko, 1992/1993).

## New Research Strategies

In keeping with an interest in learning communities, we believe that work in the future will evolve toward more collaborative research strategies. We do not argue that all research should proceed within the cell in the LTC framework that attempts to transform all of school in connected sets of classrooms (cell 9). Research in every cell is important and has valuable insights to provide. For example, as discussed earlier, some issues that we have been able to study in laboratory contexts (cell 4) would have been practically impossible to study in classroom contexts (cells 5 and 6) (CTGV, 1993), and vice versa.

*Collaborative Testbed Studies.* A relatively recent strategy for evaluating technology programs is the idea of national testbeds (e.g., Bolt, Beranek, & Newman, 1994b; Hunter, 1993). Hunter (1993) notes that testbeds involve collaborative inquiry in networked communities over relatively long periods of time.

A new research strategy that we see emerging involves closely coupled links between research conducted in laboratory contexts (cells 1, 4, and 7) and testbed research that involves constructivist approaches to classrooms and connected classrooms (cells 5, 6, and 8, 9). The interplay between these two types of endeavors can be highly synergistic. As noted earlier, laboratory studies provide the kinds of controlled conditions that allow precise examination of variables. The downside is that many issues of real classrooms and learning communities never emerge in these kinds of settings. Work in classroom contexts (cells 5, 6, 8, and 9) provides opportunities to discover new, important issues that might eventually be capable of more precisely focused research. Note that this research strategy does not necessarily mean that one research group is responsible for everything. Different groups can take on different components of overall research projects. What is important is a tight coupling of projects so that research and practice are closely linked.

We also believe that efforts to transform all of schooling

according to constructivist principles (cells 8 and 9) can breathe new life into the perceived importance of studies conducted in the first row of the LTC framework (research based on transmission models). As noted earlier, the more one begins to take responsibility for the whole child, the more one realizes that part of children's learning is the opportunity to practice skills and develop some degree of fluency. When technology-based skill packages are introduced as part of a problem-solving environment where students define learning goals and attempt to accomplish them, we believe that they can do a lot of good.

*Value-added Studies.* A second research strategy we see emerging is related to the previous one but slightly different. It involves studies that assess the "value-added" of adding technology components to existing efforts at school reform. For example, many of the restructuring projects facilitated by the work of Slavin (Madden et al., 1991/1993), H. M. Levin (1987/1993), Comer (1988/1993), and others (see Backler & Eakin, 1993; Prestine & Bowen, 1993) are quite successful but make very little use of technology. Can the addition of well-motivated, technology-based curricula, tools, assessments, and performance supports for professional development increase the effectiveness of these environments? We believe that the answer is a definite yes. But to our knowledge, such research has not yet been attempted.

## New Roles for Researchers, Developers, Teachers, and Students

We believe that efforts to restructure schools will require new roles for researchers, developers, teachers and students. Usually, researchers and developers study interventions that they develop or which they are particularly knowledgeable about. However, it is unlikely that any researcher or research group can create products necessary to meet the goal of transforming all of schooling. This means that different groups must collaborate. In order to do so, they must give up the role of always being the experts who teach others; they must also adopt the role of novices who attempt to learn about their colleagues' programs.

In implementing the Schools for Thought project (Lamon et al., in press; Lin et al., 1995), the challenge of collaborating with other research groups has been extremely revealing to us. For example, we were very familiar with A. L. Brown and Campione's work (1994) and Scardamalia and Bereiter's work (Scardamalia et al., 1994). However this familiarity was at the level of talking about the programs from a theoretical perspective and discussing their results. We discovered a large gap between this level of knowing and the knowing required to actually implement these ideas in classrooms. It became clear that a several-day or even several-week workshop was insufficient. We needed (and still need) opportunities for frequent interactions with experts in each program as the implementation progresses in the classrooms. Teachers need similar kinds of support.

Constructivist-oriented classrooms also require new roles for teachers and students. Teachers must be able to accept the role of learner rather than always be the expert. Students must learn to work collaboratively rather than always compete.

We are optimistic about the increasing need for different

groups to collaborate. It forces the research community to learn how difficult it can be to understand others' ideas at a level necessary to implement those ideas. As researchers learn to appreciate the challenges faced by novice learners, they should be able to collaborate better with teachers, parents, principals, and other community leaders who, collectively, are necessary for the development of successful learning communities.

## New Appreciation of Realities

Increasing efforts to restructure all of schooling (cells 8 and 9) should also help the research community appreciate some realities of educational reform that become especially salient when one attempts to "scale up" programs and study them on a broad scale.

*Equity.* There is a great deal of concern about equity and technology, in part because equity has such a powerful impact on the life chances of individuals (e.g., Backler & Eakin, 1993; Boruta et al., 1983; Hawkins, 1987a, 1991; Hawkins & Sheingold, 1985; Hollins, King, & Hayman, 1994; Lepper & Gurtner, 1989; Malcolm, 1991; Prestine & Bowen, 1993; Ramirez & Bell, 1994a; Sabelli & Barrett, 1994; Sutton 1991; Warren & Rosebery, 1993). Federal agencies are looking at equity issues from the perspective of a National Information Infrastructure through Internet and other resources (e.g., Clinton & Gore, 1993; National Information Infrastructure, 1994).

The research community can play an important role in achieving equity by demonstrating the value of adding technology to existing educational programs—especially programs for traditionally underserved populations (e.g., Bransford et al., in press). As the added value becomes clear, there should be more pressure for state and federal agencies to provide the technologies necessary for success for all. The research community also needs to help policy makers and others understand that support for helping teachers learn to use technology is extremely important. This brings up lessons of infrastructure.

*Infrastructure.* An interesting session at the 1994 Association for Educational Computing Technology conference was called "Building Planes That Fly." Participants discussed questions such as how engineering principles and theories of physics were combined by the Wright brothers, and how similar approaches might be used to develop technologies that fly. Discussions in the session were fruitful and went in a number of directions. However, one participant noted that the problem of education goes far beyond the challenge of building a single airplane. Instead, it is more analogous to the challenge of creating and maintaining an air transportation system for a nation. To achieve the latter, one needs a vast infrastructure that includes plane manufacturers, airplane mechanics, fueling services, ticketing services, meal services, airports, vehicles and roads to get to and from the airports, places for people to stay once they reach their destinations, continual training programs for pilots and mechanics, and so forth.

The importance of infrastructure is often forgotten when we think about new technologies such as computers for the schools. We tend to dump them into classrooms in a manner analogous to giving a small, isolated town an airplane without

also giving it a pilot, mechanic, fuel service, or runway. One of the important lessons learned by those who have moved from laboratories to schools is that the technology infrastructure in school buildings is virtually nonexistent. In some cases, projects have had to assume responsibility for phone line installation, electrical work, appropriate furniture, and so forth, as well as supply computer hardware and software (see CTGV, in press, and other chapters in Hawkins & Collins, in press). The infrastructure for school personnel to develop the knowledge necessary to function in constructivist and technology-rich environments is a primary concern and one that has begun receiving attention at federal, state, and local levels in both the public and the private sector. The necessity for infrastructures for technology in education needs to be recognized, and funded, so that technology has a chance to contribute to the kind of revolution in learning that many envision.

## SUMMARY

Our goal in this chapter has been to provide a framework for thinking about research on technology and education. We noted the impossibility of attempting an exhaustive review of all relevant research because the area is too massive. At a minimum, an exploration of the potential benefits of technology for education requires a discussion of the three areas illustrated in Figure 25–1—technology, learning theory, and educational issues. Therefore, our goal was to provide an overview of where research has focused in the past and where it might go.

Our discussion of past and future trends in research was organized around the LTC framework that was introduced in the first section and illustrated in Figure 25–2. We call it the LTC framework because it focuses on *l*ooking at *t*echnology in *c*ontext, where context includes the theoretical context for the application (transmission theories vs. constructivist theories) as well as the educational context in which the application is used (e.g., laboratory, classrooms, connected classrooms).

In the second section we discussed research relevant to row 1 of the LTC framework, which involved early research on technology and education. This work took existing classroom practice as a given, and typical practice was usually consistent with a transmission model of curriculum, instruction, and assessment. Because they could be assimilated into existing practice, the technology applications studied by early researchers could move relatively easily from laboratories to classrooms and connected classrooms.

In the third section we focused on row 2 of the LTC framework and noted that research conducted during the past several decades suggests that transmission models of instruction are no longer sufficient because of changes in educational goals in response to new societal needs for lifelong learning. We discussed new visions of human learning and human potential and related them to changes in assumptions about curriculum, instruction, and assessment. These changes reflect a constructivist philosophy of learning rather than a transmission–reception philosophy. Technology developed from a constructivist perspective cannot simply be assimilated into traditional classroom contexts. Therefore, important issues arise as one attempts to migrate from laboratory to classroom contexts. Of particular importance is the fact that professional development involves not only learning about technology, but learning about new philosophies of education as well.

In the fourth section we considered theory and research relevant to the third row (cells 7, 8, and 9) of the LTC framework. Theory and research in this row are also based on constructivist assumptions, but new issues arise when the goal becomes that of restructuring all of schooling rather than restructuring only part of a school day. We know of only a few technology-based research programs that fit into row 3 (cells 7, 8, and 9).

In the fifth section we looked at issues for the future. We noted that the LTC framework can be viewed three dimensionally, where the scope of the analysis (a single grade, a set of grades, kindergarten through grade 12 represents an additional dimension. Serious consideration of broad-scope issues (such as those encompassing all elementary and secondary schoolrooms) seems important because they have the potential to produce considerable change. We also argued that an important

theoretical goal is to encourage further theory and research on the concept of learning communities and roles for technology in fostering and maintaining these communications. To do so requires new kinds of research designs, methodologies, and collaborations.

We ended by noting that research on educational technology needs to contribute to an increased appreciation of important realities such as issues of equity and the need to build an infrastructure that can enable technology to live up to its promise of encouraging extraordinary student achievement. Pursuing that promise on a broad scale is a major challenge for the next 10 years of research. It requires expansions of the issues on the educational psychology plate. Those expansions need to occur at the theoretical, methodological, and pragmatic levels and should apply simultaneously to technology, theories of human learning and potential, and educational practice.

## References

Alderman, D. L. (1978). *Evaluation of the TICCIT computer-assisted instruction system in the community college.* Princeton, NJ: Educational Testing Service.

Alderman, D. L., & Mahler, W. A. (1973). *The evaluation of PLATO and TICCIT: Educational analysis of the community college components* (PR-73-49). Princeton, NJ: Educational Testing Service.

Alexander, G., & Lincoln, C. (1989). The thought box: A computer-based communication system to support distance learning. In A. Kaye & R. Mason (Eds.), *Mindweave: communication, computers, and distance education* (pp. 86–100). Oxford: Pergamon Press.

Alpert, D., & Bitzer, D. L. (1970). Advances in computer-based education. *Science, 167,* 1582–1590.

Anderson, J. R. (1982). Acquisition of cognitive skill. *Psychological Review, 89,* 369–406.

Anderson, J. R. (1987). Skill acquisition: Compilation of weak-method problem solutions. *Psychological Review, 94,* 192–210.

Anderson, J. R., Boyle, C. F., & Yost, G. (1985). The geometry tutor. In *Proceedings of the International Joint Conference on Artificial Intelligence* (pp. 1–7). Los Angeles, CA: IJCAI.

Anderson, J. R., Conrad, F. G., & Corbett, A. T. (1989). Skill acquisition and the LISP Tutor. *Cognitive Science, 13,* 467–506.

Anderson, J. R., Corbett, A. T., Fincham, J. M., Hoffman, D., & Pelletier, R. (1992). General principles for an intelligent tutoring architecture. In J. W. Region & V. J. Shute (Eds.), *Cognitive approaches to automated instruction* (pp. 81–106). Hillsdale, NJ: Lawrence Erlbaum Associates.

Atkinson, R. (1968). Computerized instruction and the learning process. *American Psychologist, 23,* 225–239.

Aurbach & Associates, Inc. (1991). Grady Profile Portfolio Assessment, Version 2. St. Louis, MO: Author.

Backler, A., & Eakin, S. (Eds.). (1993). *Every child can succeed: Readings for school improvement.* Bloomington, IN: Agency for Instructional Technology.

Ball, D. (1994, October). *Inquiry and teaching: Blurring the boundaries between research and practice.* Paper presented at the conference, Constructing Cases for Reflective Practice: Using Story, Narrative, Video, and Hypermedia, Tucson, AZ.

Bank Street College of Education. (1984). *Voyage of the Mimi.* Scotts Valley, CA: Wings for Learning, Sunburst Co.

Barker, B. O. (1991). K-12 distance education in the United States: Technology strengths, weaknesses, and issues. In *1st Annual International Conference on Distance Learning* (pp. 2–11). Washington, DC: Brigham Young University–Hawaii Campus.

Barker, B. O., & Bannon, J. (1992). *The Hawaii teleschool: An evaluation of distance learning for advanced placement calculus instruction in "Paradise."* Paper presented at the annual conference of the National Rural and Small Schools Consortium (p. 20). (ERIC Documentation Reproduction Service No. 334 729).

Barker, B. O., Frisbie, A. G., & Patrick, K. R. (1989). Broadening the definition of distance education in light of the new telecommunications technologies. *American Journal of Distance Education, 3*(1), 20–29.

Barron, B. (1991). *Collaborative problem solving: Is team performance greater than what is expected from the most competent member?* Unpublished doctoral dissertation, Vanderbilt University, Nashville, TN.

Barron, B., Vye, N. J., Zech, L., Schwartz, D., Bransford, J. D., Goldman, S. R., Pellegrino, J., Morris, J., Garrison, S., & Kantor, R. (1995). Creating contexts for community based problem solving: The Jasper Challenge Series. In C. Hedley, P. Antonacci, & M. Rabinowitz (Eds.), *Thinking and literacy: The mind at work* (pp. 47–71). Hillsdale, NJ. Lawrence Erlbaum Associates.

Barron, L. C., & Goldman, E. S. (1994). Integrating technology with teacher preparation. In B. Means (Ed.), *Technology and education reform: The reality behind the promise* (pp. 81–110). San Francisco: Jossey-Bass.

Barrows, H. S. (1985). *How to design a problem-based curriculum for the preclinical years.* New York: Springer.

Beare, P. (1989). The comparative effectiveness of video, audio, and telelecture. *American Journal of Distance Education, 3*(2), 57–66.

Becker, H. J. (1983). *School uses of microcomputers* (No. 3). Baltimore, MD: Johns Hopkins University, Center for Social Organizations of Schools.

Becker, H. J. (1984a). *School uses of microcomputers* (No. 4). Baltimore: Johns Hopkins University, Center for Social Organizations of Schools.

Becker, H. J. (1984b). *School uses of microcomputers* (No. 5). Baltimore: Johns Hopkins University, Center for Social Organizations of Schools.

Becker, H. J. (1984c). *School uses of microcomputers* (No. 6). Baltimore: Johns Hopkins University, Center for Social Organizations of Schools.

Becker, H. J. (1991). How computers are used in United States schools: Basic data from the 1989 I.E.A. computers in education survey. *Journal of Educational Computing Research, 7,* 385–406.

Becker, H. J. (1994). *Conclusion to analysis and trends of school use of new information technologies* (Technical Report, Office of Technology Assessment, U.S. Congress, Contract No. K3-0666.0). Irvine: University of California, Irvine, Department of Education.

Bereiter, C. (1994). Implications of postmodernism for science, or, science as progressive discourse. *Educational Technology, 29,* 3–12.

Bereiter, C., & Scardamalia, M. (1989). Intentional learning as a goal of instruction. In L. B. Resnick (Ed.), *Knowing, learning, and instruction: Essays in honor of Robert Glaser* (pp. 361–392). Hillsdale, NJ: Lawrence Erlbaum Associates.

Berger, C. F. (1994). Breaking *what* barriers between science and mathematics? Six myths from a technological perspective. In D. F. Berlin (Ed.), *NSF/SSMA Wingspread Conference: A network for integrated science and mathematics teaching and learning* (pp. 23–27). Columbus, OH: School Science and Mathematics Association.

Berger, S. (1989). Toward "real science": The TERC Star Schools project. *Hands On!, 12*(2), 1, 12–13.

Berlin, D. F. (Ed.). (1994). *NSF/SSMA Wingspread Conference: A network for integrating science and mathematics teaching and learning.* Columbus, OH: School Science and Mathematics Association.

Berliner, D. C. (1991). Educational psychology and pedagogical expertise: New findings and new opportunities for thinking about training. *Educational Psychologist, 26*(2), 145–155.

Berryman, S. E. (1993). Learning for the workplace. In L. Darling-Hammond (Ed.), *Review of research in education* (pp. 343–401). Washington, DC: American Educational Research Association.

Binet, A., & Simon, T. (1908). Le développement de l'intelligence chez les enfants. *Année Psychologie, 14,* 1–94.

Bjork, R. A. (1979). Information processing analysis of college teaching. *Educational Psychologist, 14,* 15–23.

Blumenfeld, P. C., Soloway, E., Marx, R. W., Krajcik, J. S., Guzdial, M., & Palincsar, A. (1991). Motivating project-based learning: Sustaining the doing, supporting the learning. *Educational Psychologist, 26*(3 & 4), 369–398.

Bolt, Beranek, & Newman, (1994a). The Co-NECT Project. *Connections: Technologies for learning and technology, Spring,* 2–4.

Bolt, Beranek, & Newman, (1994b). The national school network testbed. *Connections: Technologies for learning and technology, Winter,* 3–5.

Boruta, M., Carpenter, C., Harvey, M., Keyser, T., LaBonte, J., Mehan, H., & Rodriguez, D. (1983). Computers in the schools: Stratifier or equalizer? *Quarterly Newsletter of the Laboratory of Comparative Human Cognition, 5,* 51–55.

Bradley, V. N. (1982). Improving students' writing with microcomputers. *Language Arts, 58,* 18–22.

Bransford, J. D., Franks, J. J., Vye, N. J., & Sherwood, R. D. (1989). New approaches to instruction: Because wisdom can't be told. In S. Vosniadou & A. Ortony (Eds.), *Similarity and analogical reasoning* (pp. 470–497). New York: Cambridge University Press.

Bransford, J. D., Goin, L. I., Hasselbring, T. S., Kinzer, C. K., Sherwood, R. D., & Williams, S. M. (1988). Learning with technology: Theoretical and empirical perspectives. *Peabody Journal of Education, 64*(1), 5–26.

Bransford, J. D., Goldman, S. R., & Vye, N. J. (1991). Making a difference in peoples' abilities to think: Reflections on a decade of work and some hopes for the future. In L. Okagaki & R. J. Sternberg (Eds.), *Directors of development: Influences on children* (pp. 147–180). Hillsdale, NJ: Lawrence Erlbaum Associates.

Bransford, J. D., & Heldmeyer, K. (1983). Learning from children learning. In J. Bisanz, G. Bisanz, & R. Kail (Eds.), *Learning in children:*

*Progress in cognitive development research* (pp. 171–190). New York: Springer.

Bransford, J. D., Sharp, D. M., Vye, N. J., Goldman, S. R., Hasselbring, T. S., Goin, L., O'Banion, K., Livernois, J., Saul, E., & the Cognition and Technology Group at Vanderbilt. (1996). MOST environments for accelerating literacy development. In S. Vosniadou, E. De Corte, R. Glaser, & H. Mandl (Eds.), *International perspectives on the psychological foundations of technology-based learning environments* (pp. 223–256). Hillsdale, NJ: Lawrence Erlbaum Associates.

Bransford, J. D., Sherwood, R., & Hasselbring, T. (1988). The video revolution and its effects on development: Some initial thoughts. In G. Foreman & P. Pufall (Eds.), *Constructivism in the computer age* (pp. 173–201). Hillsdale, NJ: Lawrence Erlbaum Associates.

Bransford, J. D., Sherwood, R. S., Vye, N. J., & Rieser, J. (1986). Teaching thinking and problem solving: Research foundations. *American Psychologist, 41,* 1078–1089.

Bransford, J. D., & Stein, B. S. (1993). *The IDEAL problem solver* (2nd ed.). New York: Freeman.

Bransford, J. D., Vye, N., Kinzer, C., & Risko, V. (1990). Teaching thinking and content knowledge: Toward an integrated approach. In B. F. Jones & L. Idol (Eds.), *Dimensions of thinking and cognitive instruction: Implications for educational reform* (Vol. 1, pp. 381–413). Hillsdale, NJ: Lawrence Erlbaum Associates.

Bright, G. (1983). Explaining the efficiency of computer-assisted instruction. *Association for Educational Data Systems Journal, 16*(3), 144–152.

Brooks, D., & Kop, T. W. (1990). Technology and teacher education. In W. B. Huston (Ed.), *Handbook of research on teacher education* (pp. 498–513). New York: Macmillan.

Brooks, J. G., & Brooks, M. G. (1993). *The case for the constructivist classroom.* Alexandria, VA: Association for Supervision and Curriculum Development.

Brophy, S., Goin, L., Bransford, J. D. Sharp, D., Moore, P., Hasselbring, T., & Goldman, S. R. (1994). *Software support for instruction in "deep" comprehension and decoding.* Paper presented at the annual meeting of the American Educational Research Association, New Orleans, LA.

Brown, A. L. (1992). Design experiments: Theoretical and methodological challenges in creating complex interventions in classroom settings. *Journal of the Learning Sciences, 2*(2), 141–178.

Brown, A. L., Ash, D., Rutherford, M., Nakagawa, K., Gordon, A., & Campione, J. C. (1993). Distributed expertise in the classroom. In G. Salomon (Ed.), *Distributed cognitions* (pp. 188–228). New York: Cambridge University Press.

Brown, A. L., Bransford, J. D., Ferrara, R., & Campione, J. (1983). Learning, remembering, and understanding. In J. Flavell & E. Markman (Eds.), *Mussen handbook of child psychology* (2nd ed., Vol. 1, pp. 77–166). New York: Wiley.

Brown, A. L., & Campione, J. C. (1990). Communities of learning and thinking or a context by any other name. *Human Development, 21,* 108–125.

Brown, A. L., & Campione, J. C. (1994). Guided discovery in a community of learners. In K. McGilly (Ed.), *Classroom lessons: Integrating cognitive theory and classroom practice* (pp. 229–272). Cambridge, MA: MIT Press.

Brown, A. L., Campione, J. C., Webber, L. S., & McGilly, K. (1991). Interactive learning environments: A new look at assessment and instruction. In B. R. Gifford & M. C. O'Connor (Eds.), *Changing assessments: Alternative views of aptitude, achievement and instruction* (pp. 121–211). Boston: Kluwer.

Brown, A. L., & Kane, M. J. (1988). Preschool children can learn to transfer: Learning to learn and learning from example. *Cognitive Psychology, 20,* 493–523.

Brown, A. L., Kane, M. J., & Echols, C. H. (1986). Young children's mental models determine analogical transfer across problems with a common goal structure. *Cognitive Development, 1,* 103–121.

Brown, A. L., Kane, M. J., & Long, C. (1989). Analogical transfer in young children: Analogies as tools for communication and exposition. *Applied Cognitive Psychology, 3,* 275–294.

Brown, J. S., Collins, A., & Duguid, P. (1989). Situated cognition and the culture of learning. *Educational Researcher, 18,* 32–41.

Bruce, B. C., Peyton, J. K., & Batson, T. (1993). *Network-based classrooms: Promises and realities.* Cambridge, MA: Cambridge University Press.

Bruce, B. C., & Rubin, A. (1993). *Electronic quills: A situated evaluation of using computers for writing in classrooms.* Hillsdale, NJ: Lawrence Erlbaum Associates.

Bruer, J. T. (1993). *Schools for thought.* Cambridge, MA: MIT Press.

Bryk, A. S., & Raudenbush, S. W. (1992). *Hierarchical linear models: Applications and data analysis methods.* Newbury Park, CA: Sage.

Bunderson, C. V. (1975). The TICCIT project: Design strategy for educational innovation. In S. A. Harrison & L. M. Stolurow (Eds.), *Improving instructional productivity in higher education* (pp. 91–111). Englewood Cliffs, NJ: Educational Technology.

Burns, P., & Bozeman, W. (1981). Computer-assisted instruction and mathematics achievement: Is there a relationship? *Educational Technology, 10*(2), 32–39.

Cain, K. M., & Dweck, C. S. (1989). The development of children's conception of intelligence: A theoretical framework. In R. J. Sternberg (Ed.), *Advances in the psychology of human intelligence* (Vol. 5, pp. 47–82). Hillsdale, NJ: Lawrence Erlbaum Associates.

Campione, J. C., Brown, A. L., & Jay, M. (1992). Computers in a community of learners. In E. De Corte, M. Linn, H. Mandl, & L. Verschaffel, (Eds.), *Computer-based learning environments and problem solving* (NATO ASI Series F: Computer and Systems Science 84, pp. 163–192). Berlin: Springer.

Carey, S. (1985). *Conceptual change in childhood.* Cambridge, MA: MIT Press.

Carraher, T. N., Carraher, D. W., & Schliemann, A. D. (1985). Mathematics in the streets and in schools. *British Journal of Developmental Psychology, 3,* 21–29.

Carter, K., Cushing, K., Sabers, D., Stein, P., & Berliner, D. C. (1988). Expert-novice differences in perceiving and processing visual information. *Journal of Teacher Education, 39*(3), 25–31.

Carver, S. M. (1988). Learning and transfer of debugging skills: Applying task analysis to curriculum design and assessment. In R. E. Mayer (Ed.), *Teaching and learning computer programming: Multiple research perspectives.* (pp. 259–297). Hillsdale, NJ: Lawrence Erlbaum Associates.

Carver, S. M., Lehrer, R., Connell, T., & Erickson, J. (1992). Learning by hypermedia design: Issues of assessment and implementation. *Educational Psychologist, 27,* 385–404.

Case, R. (1985). *Intellectual development: Birth to adulthood.* New York: Academic Press.

Ceci, S. J., & Ruiz, A. I. (1993). Inserting context into our thinking about thinking: Implications for a theory of everyday intelligent behavior. In M. Rabinowitz (Ed.), *Cognitive science foundations of instruction* (pp. 173–188). Hillsdale, NJ: Lawrence Erlbaum Associates.

Chase, W. G., & Simon, H. A. (1973). Perception in chess. *Cognitive Psychology, 1,* 33–81.

Chi, M. T. H., Feltovich, P., & Glaser, R. (1981). Categorization and representation of physics problems by experts and novices. *Cognitive Science, 5,* 121–152.

Chi, M. T. H., Glaser, R., & Farr, M. (1991). *The nature of expertise.* Hillsdale, NJ: Lawrence Erlbaum Associates.

Chi, M. T. H., Glaser, R., & Rees, E. (1982). Expertise in problem solving. In R. J. Sternberg (Ed.), *Advances in the psychology of human intelligence* (Vol. 1). Hillsdale, NJ: Lawrence Erlbaum Associates.

Christensen, C. A., & Gerber, M. M. (1990). Effectiveness of computer-ized drill and practice games in teaching basic math facts. *Exceptionality, 1,* 149–165.

Chu, G., & Schramm, W. (1967). *Learning from television: What the research says.* Washington, DC: National Association of Educational Broadcasters.

Clancy, M. J., & Linn, M. C. (1992). Case studies in the classroom. In C. M. White & J. Hartman (Eds.), *Networking for knowledge: SIGCSE Technical Symposium '92* (pp. 220–224). New York: Association for Computing Machinery.

Clark, R. E. (1983). Reconsidering research on learning from media. *Review of Educational Research, 53,* 445–459.

Clark, R. E. (1989). *Evaluating distance learning technology* (Information Analyses No. ERIC #325097). Paper prepared at the invitation of the United States Congress, Office of Technology Assessment.

Clark, R. E. (1994). Media will never influence learning. *Educational Technology Research and Development, 42,* 21–29.

Clark, R. E., & Salomon, G. (1986). Media in teaching. In M. C. Wittrock (Ed.), *Handbook of research in teaching* (3rd ed., pp. 464–478). New York: Macmillan.

Clinton, W., & Gore, A. (1993). *Technology for America's economic growth: A new direction to build economic strength.* Washington, DC: Office of the President of the United States.

Cobb, P. (1994). Where is the mind? Constructivist and sociocultural perspectives on mathematical development. *Educational Researcher, 23*(7), 13–20.

Cobb, P., Yackel, E., & Wood, T. (1992). A constructivist alternative to the representational view of mind in mathematics education. *Journal for Research in Mathematics Education, 19,* 99–114.

Cognition and Technology Group at Vanderbilt. (1990). Anchored instruction and its relationship to situated cognition. *Educational Researcher, 19*(6), 2–10.

Cognition and Technology Group at Vanderbilt. (1991). Technology and the design of generative learning environments. *Educational Technology, 31,* 34–40.

Cognition and Technology Group at Vanderbilt. (1992a). An anchored instruction approach to cognitive skills acquisition and intelligent tutoring. In J. W. Region & V. J. Shute (Eds.), *Cognitive approaches to automated instruction* (pp. 135–170). Hillsdale, NJ: Lawrence Erlbaum Associates.

Cognition and Technology Group at Vanderbilt. (1992b). Anchored instruction in science and mathematics: Theoretical basis, developmental projects, and initial research findings. In R. A. Duschl & R. J. Hamilton (Eds.), *Philosophy of science, cognitive psychology, and educational theory and practice* (pp. 245–273). New York: State University of New York Press.

Cognition and Technology Group at Vanderbilt. (1992c). The Jasper experiment: An exploration of issues in learning and instructional design. *Educational Technology Research and Development, 40,* 65–80.

Cognition and Technology Group at Vanderbilt. (1992d). The Jasper series as an example of anchored instruction: Theory, program description, and assessment data. *Educational Psychologist, 27,* 291–315.

Cognition and Technology Group at Vanderbilt. (1993a). Integrated media: Toward a theoretical framework for utilizing their potential. *Journal of Special Education Technology, 12*(2), 76–89.

Cognition and Technology Group at Vanderbilt. (1993b). The Jasper series: Theoretical foundations and data on problem solving and transfer. In L. A. Penner, G. M. Batsche, H. M. Knoff, & D. L. Nelson (Eds.), *The challenge in mathematics and science education: Psychology's response* (pp. 113–152). Washington, DC: American Psychological Association.

Cognition and Technology Group at Vanderbilt. (1993c). Toward integrated curricula: Possibilities from anchored instruction. In M. Rabinowitz (Ed.), *Cognitive science foundations of instruction* (pp. 33–55). Hillsdale, NJ: Lawrence Erlbaum Associates.

Cognition and Technology Group at Vanderbilt. (1994a). From visual word problems to learning communities: Changing conceptions of cognitive research. In K. McGilly (Ed.), *Classroom lessons: Integrating cognitive theory and classroom practice* (pp. 157–200). Cambridge, MA: MIT Press.

Cognition and Technology Group at Vanderbilt. (1994b). Multimedia environments for developing literacy in at-risk students. In B. Means (Ed.), *Technology and educational reform: The reality behind the promise* (pp. 23–56). San Francisco: Jossey-Bass.

Cognition and Technology Group at Vanderbilt. (in press). The Jasper series: A design experiment in complex, mathematical problem solving. In J. Hawkins & A. Collins (Eds.), *Design experiments: Integrating technologies into schools.* New York: Cambridge University Press.

Cohen, A. (1994). *The effect of a teacher-designed assessment tool on an instructor's cognitive activity while using CSILE.* Unpublished manuscript. Toronto, Ontario: Institute for the Study of Education.

Collins, A. (1991a). Cognitive apprenticeship and instructional technology. In L. Idol & B. F. Jones (Eds.), *Educational values and cognitive instruction: Implications for reform* (pp. 119–136). Hillsdale, NJ: Lawrence Erlbaum Associates.

Collins, A. (1991b). The role of computer technology in restructuring schools. *Phi Delta Kappan, 73,* 28–36.

Collins, A. (1996). Design issues for learning environments. In S. Vosniadou, E. De Corte, R. Glaser, & H. Mandl (Eds.), *International perspectives on the psychological foundations of technology-based learning environments* (pp. 347–362). Hillsdale, NJ: Lawrence Erlbaum Associates.

Collins, A., Brown, J. S., & Newman, S. E. (1989). Cognitive apprenticeship: Teaching the crafts of reading, writing and mathematics. In L. B. Resnick (Ed.), *Knowing, learning and instruction: Essays in honor of Robert Glaser.* Hillsdale, NJ: Lawrence Erlbaum Associates.

Collins, A., Hawkins, J., & Carver, S. (1991). A cognitive apprenticeship for disadvantaged students. In B. Means, C. Chelemer, & M. S. Knapp (Eds.), *Teaching advanced skills to disadvantaged students* (pp. 216–243). San Francisco: Jossey-Bass.

Collins, A., Hawkins, J., & Frederiksen, J. R. (1993–1994). Three different views of students: The role of technology in assessing student performance. *Journal of the Learning Sciences, 3,* 205–217.

Comer, J. P. (1993). Effective schools: Why they rarely exist for at-risk elementary-school and adolescent students. In A. Backler & S. Eakin (Eds.), *Every child can succeed: Readings for school improvement* (pp. 65–82). Bloomington, IN: Agency for Instructional Technology. (Original work published 1988)

Cookson, P. S. (1989). Research on learners and learning in distance education: A review. *American Journal of Distance Education, 3*(2), 22–34.

Cosden, M. A., Gerber, M. M., Goldman, S. R., Semmel, D. S., & Semmel, M. I. (1986). Survey of microcomputer access and use by mildly handicapped students in southern California. *Journal of Special Education Technology, 7*(4), 5–13.

Cosden, M. A., Gerber, M. M., Semmel, D. S., Goldman, S. R., & Semmel, M. I. (1987). Microcomputer use within micro-educational environments. *Exceptional Children, 53,* 399–409.

Daiute, C. (1985a). Issues in using computers to socialize the writing process. *Educational Communication & Technology Journal, 33,* 41–50.

Daiute, C. (1985b). *Writing and computers.* Reading, MA: Addison-Wesley.

Daiute, C., & Kruidenier, J. (1985). A self-questioning strategy to increase young writers' revising processes. *Psycholinguistics of Writing, 6,* 307–318.

Dalbey, J., & Linn, M. C. (1985). The demands and requirements of computer programming: A review of the literature. *Journal of Educational Computing Research, 1,* 253–274.

deGroot, A. (1965). *Thought and choice in chess.* The Hague: Mouton.

Delclos, V. R., & Kulewicz, S. J. (1986). Improving computer-based problem solving training: The role of the teacher as mediator. *Computers and Human Behavior, 2,* 135–146.

Denham, A., & Lieberman, A. (1980). *Time to learn.* Washington, DC: National Institute of Education.

Derry, S. J., & Lajoie, S. P. (1993). A middle camp for (un)intelligent instructional computing: An introduction. In S. P. Lajoie & S. J. Derry (Eds.), *Computers as cognitive tools* (pp. 1–11). Hillsdale, NJ: Lawrence Erlbaum Associates.

diSessa, A. A. (1993). Toward an epistemology of physics. *Cognition and Instruction, 10,* 105–225.

Donaldson, M. (1979). *Children's minds.* New York: Norton.

Dossey, J. A. (1994). Mathematics and science education: Convergence or divergence? In D. F. Berlin (Ed.), *NSF/SSMA Wingspread Conference: A network for integrated science and mathematics teaching and learning* (pp. 13–22). Columbus, OH: School Science and Mathematics Association.

Driver, R., Guesne, E., & Tiberghien, A. (Eds.). (1985). *Children's ideas in science.* Philadelphia, PA: Open University Press.

Duffy, T. M. (in press). Strategic teaching framework: An instructional model for learning complex interactive skills. In C. Dills & A. Romiszowski (Eds.), *Instructional development state of the art: Vol. 3. Paradigms.* Educational Technology.

Duffy, T. M., & Jonassen, D. (Eds.). (1992). *Constructivism and the technology of instruction: A conversation.* Hillsdale, NJ: Lawrence Erlbaum Associates.

Duffy, T. M., & Knuth, R. A. (1990). Hypermedia and instruction: Where is the match? In D. H. Jonassen & H. Mandl (Eds.), *Designing hypermedia for learning* (pp. 199–225). New York: Springer.

Duffy, T. M., Lowyck, J., & Jonassen, D. (Eds.). (1993). *Designing environments for constructivist learning.* Heidelberg: Springer.

Duschl, R. A., & Gitomer, D. H. (1991). Epistemological perspectives on conceptual change: Implications for educational practice. *Journal of Research in Science Teaching, 28,* 839–858.

Dweck, C. S. (1989). Motivation. In A. Lesgold & R. Glaser (Eds.), *Foundations for a psychology of education* (pp. 87–136). Hillsdale, NJ: Lawrence Erlbaum Associates.

Eastwood, L. F., & Ballard, R. J. (1975). The PLATO IV CAI system: Where is it now? Where can it go? *Journal of Educational Technology Systems, 3,* 267–283.

Edelson, D., & O'Neill, K. (1994, June). *The CoVis collaboratory notebook: Supporting collaborative scientific inquiry* (pp. 1–16). Boston: Proceedings of the National Educational Computing Conference, Eugene, OR: International Society for Technology in Education.

Edwards, J., Norton, S., Taylor, S., Weiss, M., & Dusseldorp, R. (1975). How effective is CAI? A review of the research. *Educational Leadership, 33,* 147–153.

Elstein, A. S., Shulman, L. S., & Sprafka, S. A. (1978). *Medical problem solving: An analysis of clinical reasoning.* Cambridge MA: Harvard University Press.

English, J. P., Gerber, M. M., & Semmel, M. I. (1985). Microcomputer-administered spelling tests: Effects on learning handicapped and normally achieving students. *Journal of Reading, Writing, and Learning Disabilities International, 1*(2), 165–176.

Evertson, C. M., & Smithey, M. W. (1993, April). *Teacher inquiry: Mentor's use of reflective discovery.* Paper presented at the annual meeting of the American Educational Research Association, Atlanta, GA.

Eylon, B., & Linn, M. C. (in press). Models and integration activities in science education. In E. Bar-On, Z. Scherz, & B. Eylon (Eds.), *Designing intelligent learning environments.* Norwood, NJ: Ablex.

Ferguson, W., Bareiss, R., Birnbaum, L., & Osgood, R. (1992). ASK systems: An approach to the realization of story-based teachers. *Journal of the Learning Sciences, 2,* 95–134.

Fishman, B., & Duffy, T. M. (1992). Classroom restructuring: What do teachers really need? *Educational Technology Research and Development, 40,* 221–239.

Frederiksen, J. R., & Collins, A. (1989). A systems approach to educational testing. *Educational Researcher, 18*(9), 27–32.

Frederiksen, J. R., Warren, B. M., & Rosebery, A. S. (1985). A componential approach to training reading skills: Part 1. Perceptual units training. *Cognition and Instruction, 2*(2), 91–130.

Friedler, Y., Nachmias, R., & Linn, M. C. (1990). Learning scientific reasoning skills in microcomputer-based laboratories. *Journal of Research in Science Teaching, 27,* 173–191.

Galvin, P. (1987). *Telelearning and audiographics: Four case studies.* DE: No. Delaware-Chenango BOCES.

Gardner, H. (1983). *Frames of mind.* New York: Basic Books.

Gardner, H. (1985). *The mind's new science: A history of the cognitive revolution.* New York: Basic Books.

Garrison, D. R. (1989). *Understanding distance education: A framework for the future.* London: Routledge.

Garrison, D. R. (1993). A cognitive constructivist view of distance education: An analysis of teaching-learning assumptions. *Distance Education, 14*(2), 199–211.

Gearhart, M., Herman, J. L., Baker, E. L., & Novak, J. (1992). *A new mirror for the classroom: A technology-based tool for documenting the impact of technology on instruction* (Tech. Rep. No. 336). Los Angeles: University of California, Center for the Study of Evaluation.

Gelman, R., & Gallistel, C. R. (1978). *The child's understanding of number.* Cambridge, MA: Harvard University Press.

Gelman, R., Meck, E., & Merkin, S. (1986). Young children's numerical competence. *Cognitive Psychology, 15,* 1–38.

Gerlach, G. J. (1987, April). *The effect of typing skill on using a word processor for composition.* Paper presented at the annual meeting of the American Educational Research Association, Washington, DC.

Gick, M., & Holyoak, K. J. (1980). Analogical problem solving. *Cognitive Psychology, 12,* 306–355.

Gick, M. L., & Holyoak, K. J. (1983). Schema induction and analogical transfer. *Cognitive Psychology, 15,* 1–38.

Gifford, B., & O'Connor, C. (Eds.). (1991). *New approaches to testing: Rethinking aptitude, achievement and assessment.* New York: National Committee on Testing and Public Policy.

Glaser, R. (1986). Intelligence as acquired proficiency. In R. J. Sternberg & D. K. Determan (Eds.), *What is intelligence? Contemporary viewpoints on its nature and definition* (pp. 77–83). Norwood, NJ: Ablex.

Glaser, R. (1991). Intelligence as an expression of acquired knowledge. In H. A. H. Rowe (Ed.), *Intelligence: Reconceptualization and measurement* (pp. 47–56). Hillsdale, NJ: Lawrence Erlbaum Associates.

Goldman, E. S., Barron, L. C., & Witherspoon, M. L. (1992). *Integrated media activities for mathematics teacher education: Design and implementation issues.* Paper presented at the annual meeting of the American Educational Research Association, San Francisco.

Goldman, S. R., & the Cognition and Technology Group at Vanderbilt. (1991, August). *Meaningful learning environments for mathematical problem solving: The Jasper problem solving series.* Paper presented at the Fourth European Conference for Research on Learning and Instruction, Turku, Finland.

Goldman, S. R., Cosden, M. A., & Hine, M. S. (1992). Working alone and working together: Individual differences in the effects of collaboration on learning handicapped students' writing. *Learning and Individual Differences, 4,* 369–393.

Goldman, S. R., & Pellegrino, J. W. (1991). Cognitive developmental perspectives on intelligence. In H. A. H. Rowe (Ed.), *Intelligence: Reconceptualization and measurement* (pp. 77–96). Hillsdale, NJ: Lawrence Erlbaum Associates.

Goldman, S. R., & Pellegrino, J. W. (1987). Information processing and educational microcomputer technology: Where do we go from here? *Journal of Learning Disabilities, 20*(3), 144–154.

Goldman, S. R., Pellegrino, J. W., & Bransford, J. D. (1994). Assessing programs that invite thinking. In E. Baker & H. F. O'Neil, Jr. (Eds.),

*Technology assessment in education and training* (pp. 199–230). Hillsdale, NJ: Lawrence Erlbaum Associates.

Goldman, S. R., Pellegrino, J. W., & Mertz, D. L. (1988). Extended practice of basic addition facts: Strategy changes in learning disabled students. *Cognition & Instruction, 5,* 223–265.

Goldman, S. R., Petrosino, A., Sherwood, R. D., Garrison, S., Hickey, D., Bransford, J. D., & Pellegrino. (in press). Anchoring science instruction in multimedia learning environments. In S. Vosniadou, E. De Corte, R. Glaser, & H. Mandl (Eds.), *International perspectives on the psychological foundations of technology-based learning environments.* Hillsdale, NJ: Lawrence Erlbaum Associates.

Goldman, S. R., Vye, N. J., Williams, S. M., Rewey, K., Pellegrino, J. W., & the Cognition and Technology Group at Vanderbilt. (1991, April). *Solution space analyses of the Jasper problems and students' attempts to solve them.* Paper presented at a meeting of the American Educational Research Association, Chicago, IL.

Goldman, S. V., & Newman, D. (1992). Electronic interactions: How students and teachers organize schooling over the wires. *Interactive Learning Environments, 2,* 31–44.

Greeno, J. G. (1991, November). *Situations for productive learning.* Preprint of paper presented at the University of South Florida Conference on Contributions of Psychology to Science and Math Education, Tampa, FL.

Greeno, J. G., Smith, D. R., & Moore, J. L. (1993). Transfer of situated learning. In D. K. Detterman & R. J. Sternberg (Eds.), *Transfer on trial: Intelligence, cognition, and instruction* (pp. 99–167). Norwood, NJ: Ablex.

Harasim, L. (1993). Collaborating in cyberspace: Using computer conferences as a group learning environment. *Interactive Learning Environments, 3,* 119–130.

Harasim, L. M. (1990). Online education: An environment for collaboration and intellectual amplification. In L. M. Harasim (Ed.), *Online education: Perspectives on a new environment* (pp. 39–64). New York: Praeger.

Harel, I., & Papert, S. (Eds.). (1991). *Constructionism.* Norwood, NJ: Ablex.

Hartley, S. (1977). *Meta-analysis of the effects of individually paced instruction in mathematics. Dissertation Abstracts International, 38,* 7-A, 4003. (University Microfilms No. 77-20, 926)

Hasselbring, T. S., Goin, L., & Bransford, J. D. (1988). Developing math automaticity in learning handicapped children: The role of computerized drill and practice. *Focus on Exceptional Children, 20*(6), 1–7.

Hasselbring, T. S., Sherwood, R. D., Bransford, J. D., Fleenor, K., Griffith, D., & Goin, L. (1987–1988). An evaluation of a level-one videodisc program. *Journal of Educational Technology Systems, 16*(2), 151–169.

Hasselbring, T. S., Sherwood, R. D., Bransford, J. D., Mertz, J., Estes, B., Marsh, J., & Van Haneghan, J. (1991). *An evaluation of specific videodisc courseware on student learning in a rural school environment* (Technical Report). Nashville, TN: Vanderbilt University, Learning Technology Center.

Hawkins, J. (1987a). Computers and girls: Rethinking the issues. In R. Pea & K. Sheingold (Eds.), *Mirrors of minds: Patterns of experience in educational computing* (pp. 242–257). Norwood, NJ: Ablex.

Hawkins, J. (1987b). The interpretation of LOGO in practice. In R. Pea & K. Sheingold (Eds.), *Mirrors of minds: Patterns of experience in educational computing* (pp. 3–34). Norwood, NJ: Ablex.

Hawkins, J. (1991). Technology-mediated communities for learning: Designs and consequences. *Annuals, AAPSS, 514,* 159–174.

Hawkins, J., & Collins, A. (Eds.). (in press). *Design experiments: Integrating technologies into schools.* New York: Cambridge University Press.

Hawkins, J., Collins, A., & Frederiksen, J. (1990). Interactive technologies and the assessment of learning. In *Proceedings of the UCLA*

*Conference on Technology Assessment: Estimating the future.* University of California, Los Angeles.

Hawkins, J., & Pea, R. D. (1987). Tools for bridging the cultures of everyday and scientific thinking. *Journal of Research in Science Teaching, 24,* 291–307.

Hawkins, J., & Sheingold, K. (1986). The beginning of a story: Computers and the organization of learning in classrooms. In *Microcomputers and education* (85th Yearbook of the National Society for the Study of Education). Chicago: National Society for the Study of Education.

Hay, K., Guzdial, M., Jackson, S., Boyle, R., & Soloway, E. (in press). Students as multimedia composers. *Computers and Education Journal.*

Hayes, J. R. (1990). Individuals and environments in writing instruction. In B. F. Jones & L. Idol (Eds.), *Dimensions of thinking and cognitive instruction* (pp. 241–263). Hillsdale, NJ: Lawrence Erlbaum Associates.

Hezel & Associates. (1993). *1992–93 evaluation of SERC: Preliminary report.* No. Satellite Educational Resources Consortium.

Hickey, D. T., Pellegrino, J. W., Goldman, S. R., Vye, N. J., Moore, A. L., & the Cognition and Technology Group at Vanderbilt. (1993). *Interests, attitudes, and anchored instruction: The impact of one interactive learning environment.* Paper presented at the annual meeting of the American Educational Research Association, Atlanta, GA.

Hilliard, A. G. (1993). Public support for successful instructional practices for at-risk students. In A. Backler & S. Eakin (Eds.), *Every child can succeed: Readings for school improvement* (pp. 83–96). Bloomington, IN: Agency for Instructional Technology. (Original work published 1988)

Hiltz, R. (1986). The "virtual classroom": Using computer mediated communication for university teaching. *Journal of Communication, 36*(2), 95–104.

Hine, M. S., Goldman, S. R., & Cosen, M. A. (1990). Error monitoring by learning handicapped students engaged in collaborative microcomputer-based writing. *Journal of Special Education, 23,* 407–422.

Hmelo, C. E. (1994). *Development of independent learning and thinking: A study of medical problem solving and problem-based learning.* Unpublished doctoral dissertation, Vanderbilt University, TN.

Hmelo, C. E., Gotterer, G. S., & Bransford, J. D. (1994, April). *The cognitive effects of problem-based learning: A preliminary study.* Paper presented at the annual meeting of the American Educational Research Association, New Orleans, LA.

Hobbs, V. M., & Osburn, D. (1988). *Distance learning evaluation study report: II. A study of North Dakota and Missouri schools implementing German 1 by satellite.* Denver, CO: Mid-Continent Regional Educational Laboratory. (ERIC Document Reproduction Service No. ED 317 195)

Hobbs, V. M. (1990). *Distance learning in North Dakota: A cross-technology study of the schools, administrators, coordinators, instructors, and students. Two-way interactive television, audiographic tele-learning, and instruction by satellite.* Denver, CO: Mid-Continent Regional Educational Laboratory. (ERIC Document Reproduction Service No. ED 328 225)

Hoekema, J. (1993). Hypercard and CD-I: The "Mutt and Jeff" of multimedia platforms. In D. M. Gayeski (Ed.), *Multimedia for learning* (pp. 51–61). Englewood Cliffs, NJ: Educational Technology.

Hofmeister, A., Carnine, D., & Clark, R. (1993, August). *Blueprint for action: Technology, media, and materials* (Draft report prepared for Project 2061). Washington, DC: American Association for the Advancement of Science.

Holland, J. G., & Skinner, B. F. (1961). *The analysis of behavior: A program for self-instruction.* New York: McGraw-Hill.

Hollins, E. R., King, J. E., & Hayman, W. C. (Eds.). (1994). *Teaching diverse populations: Formulating a knowledge base.* Albany: State University of New York Press.

Holmberg, B. (1989). *Theory and practice of distance education.* London: Routledge.

Holt, J. (1964). *How children fail.* New York: Dell.

Holznagel, D. C. (1990). *A depiction of distance education in the northwest region* (Report No. 143). Portland, OR: Northwest Regional Educational Laboratory.

Honebein, P., Duffy, T. M., & Fishman, B. (1993). Constructivism and the design of learning environments: Context and authentic activities for learning. In T. M. Duffy, J. Lowyck, & D. Jonassen (Eds.), *Designing environments for constructive learning.* Heidelberg: Springer.

Hooper, S., & Hannafin, M. J. (1991). Psychological perspectives on emerging instructional technologies: A critical analysis. *Educational Psychologist, 26,* 69–95.

Human Relations Media. (1992). *Real world problem solvers series.* Pleasantville, NY: Author.

Hunt, E. & Minstrell, J. (1994). A cognitive approach to the teaching of physics. In K. McGilly (Ed.), *Classroom lessons: Integrating cognitive theory and classroom practice* (pp. 51–74), Cambridge, MA: MIT Press.

Hunter, B. (1993). Collaborative inquiry in networked communities. *Hands On!, 16,* 16–18.

Hutchins, E. (1983). Understanding Micronesian navigation. In D. Gentner & A. Stevens (Eds.), *Mental models* (pp. 191–225). Hillsdale, NJ: Lawrence Erlbaum Associates.

Jackiw, N. (1991). The Geometer's Sketchpad [Software]. Berkeley, CA: Key Curriculum Press.

Jackson, S., Stratford, S., Guzdial, M., Krajcik, J., & Soloway, E. (1995, April). *The ScienceWare Modeler: A case study of learner-center software design.* Paper presented at the 1995 annual meeting of the American Educational Research Association, San Francisco.

Jamison, D., Suppes, P., & Wells, S. (1974). The effectiveness of alternative instructional media: A survey. *Review of Educational Research, 44*(1), 19–26.

Jason project. (1993).

Jones, B. F., Knuth, R. M., & Duffy, T. M. (1993). Components of constructivist learning environments for professional training. In T. M. Duffy, J. Lowyck, & D. H. Jonassen (Eds.), *Designing environments for constructive learning* (pp. 125–139). New York: Springer.

Jones, B. F., Valdez, G., Nowakowski, J., & Rasmussen, C. (1994). *Learning, technology, and policy for educational reform.* Oak Brook, IL: North Central Regional Educational Laboratory.

Julyan, C. (1991). Getting connected to science. *Hands On!, 14*(1), 4–7.

Kail, R., & Pellegrino, J. W. (1985). *Human intelligence: Perspectives and prospects.* New York: Freeman.

Kantor, R., & McMahon, H. (1994, April). *Bubbling with great ideas: How innovative software can allow students to co-construct knowledge of the implicit and explicit meanings of ancient Greek drama.* Paper presented at the annual meeting of the American Educational Research Association, New Orleans, LA.

Kaput, J., & Lesh, R. (1994, May). *Rethinking mathematics education.* Presentation at a National Science Foundation conference, Research Using a Cognitive Science Perspective to Facilitate School-Based Innovation in Teaching Science and Mathematics, Sugarloaf Conference Center, Chestnut Hill, PA.

Katz, S., & Lesgold, A. (1993). The role of the tutor in computer-based collaborative learning situations. In S. P. Lajoie & S. J. Derry (Eds.), *Computers as cognitive tools* (pp. 289–317). Hillsdale, NJ: Lawrence Erlbaum Associates.

Keller, F. S., & Schoenfeld, W. N. (1950). *Principles of psychology.* New York: Appleton-Century-Crofts.

Kerchner, L. B., & Kistinger, B. J. (1984). Language processing/word processing: Written expression, computers, and learning disabled students. *Learning Disability Quarterly, 7,* 329–335.

Kinzer, C. K. (1993, October). *What do teachers/administrators learn from video cases?* Research working group at a Working Conference on Case-Based Teaching, University of Nevada, Las Vegas.

Kinzer, C. K., Risko, V., Carson, J. Meltzer, L., & Bigenho, F. (1992, December). *Students' perceptions of instruction and instructional needs: First steps toward implementing case-based instruction.* Paper presented at the 42nd Annual Meeting of the National Reading Conference, San Antonio, TX.

Kinzer, C. K., Gabella, M. S., & Rieth, H. J. (1994). An argument for using multimedia and anchored instruction to facilitate mildly-disabled students' learning of literacy and social studies. *Technology and Disability Quarterly, 3*(2), 117–128.

Kinzer, C. K., Williams, S. M., & Cunningham, J. J. (1992). The Young Sherlock Project: Macrocontexts to enhance learning. *Interface, 1*(2), 1–3.

Kinzie, M. B. (1990). Requirements and benefits of effective interactive instruction: Learner control, self-regulation, and continuing motivation. *Educational Technology, Research, and Development, 38,* 5–21.

Klahr, D. (1978). Goal formulation, planning and learning by pre-school problem solvers. In R. S. Siegler (Ed.), *Children's thinking: What develops?* (pp. 181–212). Hillsdale, NJ: Lawrence Erlbaum Associates.

Knowles, M. S. (1983). *Creating lifelong learning communities.* (A working paper prepared for the UNESCO Institute for Education)

Koedinger, K. R., & Anderson, J. R. (1990). Abstract planning and perceptual chunks: Elements of expertise in geometry. *Cognitive Science, 14,* 511–550.

Koedinger, K. R., & Anderson, J. R. (1993). Reifying implicit planning in geometry: Guidelines for model-based intelligent tutoring system design. In S. P. Lajoie & S. J. Derry (Eds.), *Computers as cognitive tools* (pp. 15–45). Hillsdale, NJ: Lawrence Erlbaum Associates.

Koschmann, T. D., Myers, A. C., Feltovich, P. J., & Barrows, H. S. (1994). Using technology to assist in realizing effective learning and instruction: A principled approach to the use of computers in collaborative learning. *Journal of the Learning Sciences, 3,* 225–262.

Kozma, R. B. (1993, September). *Will media influence learning? Reframing the debate.* Paper presented at the meetings of the European Association for Research on Learning and Instruction, Aix-en-Provence, France.

Kozma, R. B. (1994). Will media influence learning? Reframing the debate. *Educational Technology, Research and Development, 42,* 7–19.

Kozma, R. B., Russell, J., Jones, T., Marx, N., & Davis, J. (1993, September). *The use of multiple, linked representations to facilitate science understanding.* Paper presented at the meetings of the European Association for Research on Learning and Instruction, Aix-En-Provence, France.

Kulik, J. A., Bangert, R. L., & Williams, G. W. (1983). Effects of computer-based teaching on secondary school students. *Journal of Educational Psychology, 75,* 19–26.

Kulik, J. A., Kulik, C., & Cohen, P. (1980). Effectiveness of computer-based college teaching: A meta-analysis of findings. *Review of Educational Research, 50*(1), 525–544.

LaBerge, D., & Samuels, S. J. (1974). Toward a theory of automatic information processing in reading. *Cognitive Psychology, 6,* 293–323.

Lajoie, S. P. (1993). Computer environments as cognitive tools for enhancing learning. In S. P. Lajoie & S. J. Derry (Eds.), *Computers as cognitive tools* (pp. 261–288). Hillsdale, NJ: Lawrence Erlbaum Associates.

Lajoie, S. P., & Derry, S. J. (Eds.). (1993a). *Computers as cognitive tools.* Hillsdale, NJ: Lawrence Erlbaum Associates.

Lajoie, S. P., & Derry, S. J. (1993b). A middle camp for (un)intelligent instructional computing: An introduction. In S. P. Lajoie & S. J. Derry (Eds.), *Computers as cognitive tools* (pp. 1–14). Hillsdale, NJ: Lawrence Erlbaum Associates.

Lamon, M. (1993). *St. Louis Science Center/St. Louis Public Schools:*

*Middle school curriculum collaborative.* Unpublished manuscript. St. Louis, MO: St. Louis Science Center.

Lamon, M., Secules, T. J., Petrosino, T., Hackett, R., Bransford, J. D., & Goldman, S. R. (in press). The Schools for Thought Collaborative. In L. Schauble & R. Glaser (Eds.), *The contributions of instructional innovation to understanding learning.* Hillsdale, NJ: Lawrence Erlbaum Associates.

Lampert, M., & Ball, D. L. (1990). Using hypermedia technology to support a new pedagogy of teacher education (Issue Paper 90-5). East Lansing: Michigan State University, National Center for Research on Teacher Education.

Larkin, J., McDermott, J., Simon, D. P., & Simon, H. A. (1980). Expert and novice performance in solving physics problems. *Science, 208,* 1335–1342.

Lave, J. (1988). *Cognition in practice: Mind, mathematics, and culture in everyday life.* Cambridge, England: Cambridge University Press.

Lave, J., & Wenger, E. (1991). *Situated learning: Legitimate peripheral participation.* Cambridge, England: Cambridge University Press.

Learmont, D. (1990). *Affective differences between host-site and remote-site distance learners participating in two-way interactive television classrooms for high school course credit.* Unpublished doctoral dissertation, Wayne State University, Detroit.

Lehrer, R. (1993). Authors of knowledge: Patterns of hypermedia design. In S. P. Lajoie & S. J. Derry (Eds.), *Computers as cognitive tools* (pp. 197–227). Hillsdale, NJ: Lawrence Erlbaum Associates.

Lehrer, R., Guckenberg, T., & Lee, O. (1988). Comparative study of the cognitive consequences of inquiry-based LOGO instruction. *Journal of Educational Psychology, 80,* 543–553.

Lehrer, R., Lee, M., & Jeong, A. (1994). *Reflective teaching of LOGO.* Unpublished manuscript.

Lehrer, R., Randle, L., & Sancilio, L. (1989). Learning pre-proof geometry with LOGO. *Cognition and Instruction, 6,* 159–184.

Lepper, M. R. (1985). Microcomputers in education: Motivation and social issues. *American Psychologist, 40,* 1–18.

Lepper, M. R., & Chabay, R. W. (1985). Intrinsic motivation and instruction: Conflicting views on the role of motivational processes in computer-based education. *Educational Psychologist, 20,* 217–230.

Lepper, M. R., & Gurtner, J. L. (1989). Children and computers: Approaching the twenty-first century. *American Psychologist, 44*(2), 170–178.

Lepper, M. R., & Malone, T. W. (1987). Intrinsic motivation and instructional effectiveness in computer-based education. In R. E. Snow & M. J. Farr (Eds.), *Aptitude, learning, and instruction: III. Cognitive and affective process analyses* (pp. 255–296). Hillsdale, NJ: Lawrence Erlbaum Associates.

Lesgold, A. (1988). Problem solving. In R. J. Sternberg & E. E. Smith (Eds.), *The psychology of human thought* (pp. 188–213). New York: Cambridge University Press.

Lesgold, A., Eggan, G., Katz, S., & Rao, G. (1992). Possibilities for assessment using computer-based apprenticeship environments. In J. W. Regian & V. J. Shute (Eds.), *Cognitive approaches to automated instruction* (pp. 49–80). Hillsdale, NJ: Lawrence Erlbaum Associates.

Lesgold, A., Lajoie, S. P., Bunzo, M., & Eggan, G. (1992). A coached practice environment for an electronics troubleshooting job. In J. Larkin, R. Chabey, & C. Cheftie (Eds.), *Computer assisted instruction and intelligent tutoring systems: Establishing communication and collaboration* (pp. 201–238). Hillsdale, NJ: Lawrence Erlbaum Associates.

Levin, H. M. (1993). Accelerated schools for disadvantaged students. In A. Backler & S. Eakin (Eds.), *Every child can succeed: Readings for school improvement* (pp. 196–205). Bloomington, IN: Agency for Instructional Technology. (Original work published 1987)

Levin, J. A., Boruta, M. J., & Vasconcellos, M. T. (1983). Microcomputer-based environments for writing: A writer's assistant. In A. C. Wilkinson (Ed.), *Classroom computers and cognitive science* (pp. 219–232). New York: Academic Press.

Levin, J. A., & Jacobson, M. (1993, April). *Educational electronic networks and hypertext: Constructing personal and shared knowledge spaces*. Paper presented at the annual meeting of the American Educational Research Association, Atlanta, GA.

Levin, J. A., Kim, H., & Riel, M. M. (1990). Analyzing instructional interactions on electronic message networks. In L. M. Harasim (Ed.), *Online education: Perspectives on a new environment* (pp. 185–213). New York: Praeger.

Levin, J. A., Riel, M., Miyake, N., & Cohen, M. (1987). Education on the electronic frontier: Teleapprentices in globally distributed educational contexts. *Contemporary Educational Psychology, 12,* 254–260.

Levin, J. A., Waugh, M., Brown, D., & Clift, R. (1993, April). *Teaching teleapprenticeships: A new organizational framework for improving teacher education using electronic networks*. Paper presented at the annual meeting of the American Educational Research Association, Atlanta, GA.

Lin, X. D. (1993). *Far transfer problem-solving in a non-linear computer environment: The role of self-regulated learning processes*. Unpublished dissertation, Purdue University, West Lafayette, IN.

Lin, X. D., Bransford, J. D., Hmelo, C., Kantor, R., Hickey, D., Secules, T., Petrosino, A., Goldman, S. R., & the CTGV. (1995). Instructional design and the development of learning communities: An invitation to a dialogue. *Educational Technology, 35*(5), 53–63.

Linn, M. C. (1985). The cognitive consequences of programming instruction in classrooms. *Educational Researcher, 14,* 14–16, 25–29.

Linn, M. C. (1992). The computer as learning partner: Can computer tools teach science? In L. Roberts, K. Sheingold, & S. Malcolm (Eds.), *This year in school science, 1991*. Washington, DC: American Association for the Advancement of Science.

Linn, M. C., & Burbules, N. C. (1993). Construction of knowledge and group learning. In K. Tobin (Ed.), *The practice of constructivism in science education* (pp. 121–134). Washington, DC: American Association for the Advancement of Science.

Linn, M. C., & Clancy, M. J. (1992). The case for case studies in programming instruction. *Communications of the ACM, 35*(3), 121–132.

Linn, M. C., & Clark, H. C. (in press). How can assessment practices foster problem solving? In D. R. Lavoie (Ed.), *Towards a cognitive-science perspective for scientific problem solving* (No. 2004). Manhattan, KS: National Association for Research on Science Teaching.

Linn, M. C., & Songer, N. B. (1991). Teaching thermodynamics to middle school students: What are appropriate cognitive demands? *Journal of Research in Science Teaching, 28,* 885–918.

Littlefield, J., Delclos, V., Lever, S., Clayton, K., Bransford, J., & Franks, J. (1988). Learning LOGO: Method of teaching, transfer of general skills, and attitudes toward school and computers. In R. E. Mayer (Ed.), *Teaching and learning computer programming* (pp. 111–135). Hillsdale, NJ: Lawrence Erlbaum Associates.

Luehrmann, A., & Peckham, H. (1983). *Computer literacy: A hands-on approach*. New York: McGraw-Hill.

Lyon, H. D., Healy, J. C., Bell, J. R., O'Donnell, J. F., Shultz, E. K., Wigton, R. S., Hirai, F., & Beck, J. R. (1991). Significant efficiency findings from an evaluation of two years of PlanAlyzer's double crossover trials of computer-based, self-paced, cased-based programs in anemia and chest diagnosis. *Journal of Medical Systems, 15,* 117–132.

MacArthur, C., & Graham, S. (1987). Learning disabled students' composing under three methods of text production: Handwriting, word processing and dictation. *Journal of Special Education, 21,* 22–42.

Madden, N. A., Slavin, R. E., Karweit, N. L., Dolan, L., & Wasik, B. A. (1993). Success for *all*. In A. Backler & S. Eakin (Eds.), *Every child can succeed: Readings for school improvement* (pp. 334–346). Bloomington, IN: Agency for Instructional Technology. (Original work published 1991)

Malcolm, S. M. (1991). Equity and excellence through authentic science assessment. In G. Kulm & S. M. Malcolm (Eds.), *Science assessments in the service of reform* (pp. 313–328). Washington, DC: American Association for the Advancement of Science.

Mandl, H., & Grasel, C. (1993). *Case-based learning: Facilitating acquisition of diagnostical reasoning*. Paper presented at the meetings of the European Association for Research on Learning and Instruction, Aix-en-Provence, France.

Mandinach, E. B., & Cline, H. F. (1994). *Classroom dynamics: Implementing a technology-based learning environment*. Hillsdale, NJ: Lawrence Erlbaum Associates.

Martin, E. E., & Rainey, L. (1993). Student achievement and attitude in a satellite-delivered high school science course. *American Journal of Distance Education, 7*(1), 54–61.

Mason, R., & Kaye, A. (Eds.). (1989). *Mindweave: Communication, computers, and distance education*. Oxford: Pergamon Press.

Mayer, R. E. (1988a). Introduction to research on teaching and learning computer programming. In R. E. Mayer (Ed.), *Teaching and learning computer programming: Multiple research perspectives* (pp. 1–12). Hillsdale, NJ: Lawrence Erlbaum Associates.

Mayer, R. E. (Ed.). (1988b). *Teaching and learning computer programming: Multiple research perspectives*. Hillsdale, NJ: Lawrence Erlbaum Associates.

McCaslin, M. (1993, April). *Expanding the study of student motivation through case study methods*. Paper presented at the annual meeting of the American Educational Research Association, Atlanta, GA.

McCombs, B. L. (1991). Motivation and lifelong learning. *Educational Psychologist, 26*(2), 117–127.

McCombs, B. L. (1994, April). *Why students want to self-regulate: Developing the will component*. Paper presented at the American Educational Research Association meetings, New Orleans, LA.

McGilly, K. (Ed.). (1994). *Classroom lessons: Integrating cognitive theory and classroom practice*. Cambridge, MA: MIT Press.

McLarty, K., Goodman, J., Risko, V. J., Kinzer, C. K., Vye, N., Rowe, D. W., & Carlson, J. (1990). Implementing anchored instruction: Guiding principles for curriculum development. In J. Zutell & S. McCormick (Eds.), *Literacy theory and research: Analysis for multiple perspectives* (39th NRC yearbook, pp. 109–120). Chicago: National Reading Conference.

Means, B. (1993). Cognitive task analysis as a basis for instructional design. In M. Rabinowitz (Ed.), *Cognitive science foundations of instruction* (pp. 97–118). Hillsdale, NJ: Lawrence Erlbaum Associates.

Means, B. (1994). Introduction: Using technology to advance educational goals. In B. Means (Ed.), *Technology and education reform* (pp. 1–21). San Francisco: Jossey-Bass.

Means, B., Blando, J., Olson, K., Middleton, T., Morocco, C. C., Remz, A. R., Zorfass, J. (1993). *Using technology to support education reform*. Washington, DC: U.S. Department of Education, Office of Educational Research and Improvement.

Meece, J. (1991). The classroom context and student motivational goals. In M. L. Maehr & P. R. Pintrich (Eds.), *Advances in motivation and achievement* (Vol. 7, pp. 261–285). Greenwich, CT: JAI Press.

Mills, D. Q., & Friesen, B. (1992). The learning organization. *European Management Journal, 10*(2), 146–156.

Moore, M. G. (1989, May). *Effects of distance learning: A summary of the literature* (NTIS Accession No. PB90-125238/XAB; prepared for the Office of Technology Assessment, Washington, DC). University Park, PA: Pennsylvania State University.

Murphy, R. T., & Rhea-Appel, L. R. (1977). *Evaluation of the Plato IV computer-based education system in the community college*. Princeton, NJ: Educational Testing Service.

Nair, G. (1994, November 11). Picking the winners. *Wall Street Journal,* R31.

Nathan, M. J. (1990). Empowering the student: Prospects for an unintelligent tutor for word algebra problem solving. In *Proceedings of computer-human interaction* (pp. 407–414). Association of Computing Machinery.

Nathan, M. J., Kintsch, W., & Young, E. (1992). A theory of algebra word problem comprehension and its implications for the design of computer learning environments. *Cognition and Instruction, 9*(4), 329–389.

National Commission on Excellence in Education. (1983). *A nation at risk: The imperative for educational reform.* Washington, DC: U.S. Government Printing Office.

National Geographic Society. (1991). *Rain forest.* Washington, DC: Author.

National Information Infrastructure. (1994). *Agenda for action.* Washington, DC: Author.

Neisser, U. (1976). General, academic, and artificial intelligence. In L. B. Resnick (Ed.), *The nature of intelligence* (pp. 135–144). Hillsdale, NJ: Lawrence Erlbaum Associates.

Newman, D. (1990a). Opportunities for research on the organizational impact of school computers. *Educational Researcher, 19*(3), 8–13.

Newman, D. (1990b). Telecommunications: Using phone lines in the classroom. In C. Warger (Ed.), *Technology in today's schools* (pp. 57–64). Washington, DC: Association for Supervision and Curriculum Development.

Newman, D. (1992a, April). *Computer support for a sociocultural approach to school work.* Paper presented at the annual meeting of the American Educational Research Association, San Francisco.

Newman, D. (1992b). Technology as support for school structure and school restructuring. *Phi Delta Kappan, 74,* 308–315.

Newman, D., Goldman, S. V., Brienne, D., Jackson, I., & Magzamen, S. (1989). Computer mediation of collaborative science investigations. *Journal of Educational Computing Research, 5,* 151–166.

Nickerson, R. S., & Zodhiates, P. P. (Eds.). (1988). *Technology in education: Looking towards 2020.* Hillsdale, NJ: Lawrence Erlbaum Associates.

Nix, D., & Spiro, R. (Eds.). (1990). *Cognition, education and multimedia: Exploring ideas in high technology.* Hillsdale, NJ: Lawrence Erlbaum Associates.

Norman, G. R., & Schmidt, H. G. (1992). The psychological basis of problem-based learning: A review of the evidence. *Academic Medicine, 67,* 557–565.

Nunes, T., Schliemann, A. D., & Carraher, D. W. (1993). *Street mathematics and school mathematics.* Cambridge, England: Cambridge University Press.

O'Neill, B., & McMahon, H. (1992). *More than just stories.* Unpublished manuscript. Coleraine, Northern Ireland: University of Ulster, Language Development and HyperMedia Resource Group.

Padilla, M. (1991). Science activities, process skills, and thinking. In S. Glynn, R. Yeany, & B. Britton (Eds.), *The psychology of learning science.* Hillsdale, NJ: Lawrence Erlbaum Associates.

Papert, S. (1980). *Mindstorms: Children, computers, and powerful ideas.* New York: Basic Books.

Parker, P. (1991). ALICE: Telecommunications for education. In R. F. Tinker & P. M. Kapisovsky (Eds.), *Consortium for educational telecomputing: Conference proceedings* (pp. 113–121). Cambridge, MA: Technical Education Research Center.

Parker, L. P., & Lepper, M. R. (1992). Effects of fantasy contexts on children's learning and motivation: Making learning more fun. *Journal of Personality and Social Psychology, 92,* 625–633.

Paris, S. G., & Brynes, J. P. (1989). The constructivist approach to self-regulation and learning in the classroom. In B. J. Zimmerman & D. H. Schunk (Eds.), *Self-regulated learning and academic achievement: Theory, research, and practice.* New York: Springer.

Paris, S. G., & Turner, J. C. (1994). Situated motivation. In P. Pintrich, D. Brown, & C. Weinstein (Eds.), *Student motivation, cognition, and learning: Essays in honor of Wilbert J. McKeachie* (pp. 213–238). Hillsdale, NJ: Lawrence Erlbaum Associates.

Patel, V. L., & Groen, G. J. (1986). Knowledge-based solution strategies in medical reasoning. *Cognitive Science, 10,* 91–116.

Patel, V. L., Groen, G. J., & Norman, G. R. (1993). Reasoning and instruction in medical curricula. *Cognition & Instruction, 10,* 335–378.

Pea, R. D. (1992). Augmenting the discourse of learning with computer-based learning environments. In E. De Corte, M. C. Linn, H. Mandl, & L. Verschaffel (Eds.), *Computer-based learning environments and problem solving* (pp. 313–344). New York: Springer.

Pea, R. D. (1993a). Learning scientific concepts through material and social activities: Conversational analysis meets conceptual change. *Educational Psychologist, 28*(3), 265–277.

Pea, R. D. (1993b). Practices of distributed intelligence and designs for education. In G. Salomon (Ed.), *Distributed cognitions: Psychological and educational considerations* (pp. 47–87). New York: Cambridge University Press.

Pea, R. D. (1994). Seeing what we build together: Distributed multimedia learning environments for transformative communications. *Journal of the Learning Sciences, 3,* 285–301.

Pea, R. D., & Gomez, L. M. (1992). Distributed multimedia learning environments: Why and how? *Interactive Learning Environments, 2,* 73–109.

Pea, R. D., & Kurland, D. M. (1984). On the cognitive effects of learning computer programming. *New Ideas in Psychology, 2,* 137–168.

Pellegrino, J. W. (1991). Measuring what we understand and understanding what we measure. In B. Gifford & M. C. O'Connor (Eds.), *Changing assessments: Alternative views of aptitude, achievement and instruction* (pp. 275–300). Boston: Kluwer Academic.

Pellegrino, J. W., Hickey, D., Heath, A., Rewey, K., Vye, N. J., & the Cognition and Technology Group at Vanderbilt (1991). *Assessing the outcomes of an innovative instructional program: The 1990–1991 implementation of the "Adventures of Jasper Woodbury"* (Tech. Rep. No. 91-1). Nashville, TN: Vanderbilt University, Learning Technology Center.

Perkins, D. (1992). *Smart schools: From training memories to educating minds.* New York: Free Press.

Pintrich, P. R., & DeGroot, E. V. (1993, April). *Narrative and paradigmatic perspectives on individual and contextual differences in motivational beliefs.* Paper presented at the annual meeting of the American Educational Research Association, Atlanta, GA.

Pogrow, S. (1990a, January). Challenging at-risk students: Findings from the HOTS program. *Phi Delta Kappan,* 389–397.

Pogrow, S. (1990b). Learning dramas: An alternative curricular approach to using computers with at-risk students. In C. Warger (Ed.), *Technology in today's schools* (pp. 103–118). Alexandria, VA: Association for Supervision and Curriculum Development.

Prestine, N. A., & Bowen, C. (1993). Benchmarks of change: Assessing essential school restructuring efforts. *Educational Evaluation and Policy Analysis, 13*(3), 298–319.

Pugh, H. L., Parchman, S. W., & Simpson, H. (1992). Video telecommunications for distance education: A field survey of systems in US public education, industry and the military. *Distance Education, 13*(1), 46–64.

Quellmalz, E. (1985). Needed: Better methods for testing higher order thinking skills. *Educational Leadership, 43,* 29–36.

Ramirez, R., & Bell, R. (1994a). *Byting back: Policies to support the use of technology in education* (Technical Report). Oak Brook, IL: North Central Regional Educational Laboratory.

Ramirez, R., & Bell, R. (1994b). *Education navigates the highway—finally.* Unpublished manuscript.

Reeves, T., & Harmon, S. (1993, April). *Systematic evaluation procedures for instructional hypermedia/multimedia.* Paper presented at the annual meeting of the American Educational Research Association, Atlanta, GA.

Regian, J. W., & Shute, V. J. (1992). Automated instruction as an approach to individualization. In J. W. Regian & V. J. Shute (Eds.), *Cognitive approaches to automated instruction* (pp. 1–13). Hillsdale, NJ: Lawrence Erlbaum Associates.

Reich, R. B. (1992). *The work of nations*. New York: Vintage.

Renninger, K. A., Hidi, S., & Krapp, A. (Eds.). (1992). *The role of interest in learning and development*. Hillsdale, NJ: Lawrence Erlbaum Associates.

Resnick, L. B. (1987a). *Education and learning to think*. Washington, DC: National Academy Press.

Resnick, L. B. (1987b). Learning in school and out. *Educational Researcher, 16*(9), 13–20.

Resnick, L. B., & Klopfer, L. E. (Eds.). (1989). *Toward the thinking curriculum: Current cognitive research*. Alexandria, VA: Association for Supervision & Curriculum Development.

Reusser, K. (1993). Tutoring systems and pedagogical theory: Representational tools for understanding, planning, and reflection in problem solving. In S. P. Lajoie & S. J. Derry (Eds.), *Computers as cognitive tools* (pp. 143–177). Hillsdale, NJ: Lawrence Erlbaum Associates.

Richards, J. (1993, February). *The Co-NECT School: Design for a new generation of American schools*. Cambridge, MA: Bolt Beranek & Newman.

Richmond, B. (1985). STELLA [Computer program]. Lyme, NH: High Performance Systems.

Richmond, B. (1993). Systems thinking: Critical thinking skills for the 1990's and beyond. *System Dynamics Review, 9*, 113–133.

Richmond, B., & Peterson, S. (1988). STELLAStack [Computer program]. Lyme, NH: High Performance Systems.

Richmond, B., & Peterson, S. (1990). STELLA II [Computer program]. Lyme, NH: High Performance Systems.

Riel, M. (1990a). A model for integrating computer networking with classroom learning. In A. McDougall & C. Dowling (Eds.), *Computers in education* (pp. 1021–1026). North-Holland: Elsevier.

Riel, M. (1990b). Cooperative learning across classrooms in electronic learning circles. *Instructional Science, 9*, 445–466.

Riel, M. (1991a). Computer mediated communication: A tool for reconnecting kids with society. *Interactive Learning Environments, 1*(4), 255–263.

Riel, M. (1991b). Learning circles around the globe. *Writing Notebook, 8*(3), 38.

Riel, M., & Levin, J. A. (1990). Building electronic communities: Success and failure in computer networking. *Instructional Science, 19*(2), 145–169.

Risko, V. J. (1992). Developing problem solving environments to prepare teachers for instruction of diverse learners. In B. Hayes & K. Camperell (Eds.), *Yearbook of the American Reading Forum* (Vol. 12, pp. 1–13). Logan: Utah State University.

Risko, V. J. (1993). *What do teachers/administrators learn from video cases?* Research working group at a working conference on Case-based Teaching, University of Nevada, Las Vegas.

Ritchie, H., & Newby, T. J. (1989). Classroom lecture/discussion vs. live televised instruction: A comparison of effects on student performance, attitude, and interaction. *American Journal of Distance Education, 3*(3), 36–45.

Rogoff, B. (1990). *Apprenticeship in thinking*. New York: Oxford University Press.

Rogoff B., & Lave, J. (Eds.). (1984). *Everyday cognition: Its development in social context*. Cambridge, MA: Harvard University Press.

Roth, S. F., & Beck, I. L. (1987). Theoretical and instructional implications of the assessment of two microcomputer word recognition programs. *Reading Research Quarterly, 22*(2), 197–218.

Rubin, A. D. (1980). Making stories, making sense. *Language Arts, 57*(3), 285–298.

Rubin, A. D. (1983). The computer confronts language arts: Cans and shoulds for education. In A. C. Wilkinson (Ed.), *Classroom computers and cognitive science* (pp. 201–271). New York: Academic Press.

Ruopp, R., Gal, S., Drayton, B., & Pfister, M. (Eds.). (1993). *LabNet: Toward a community of practice*. Hillsdale, NJ: Lawrence Erlbaum Associates.

Russell, T. L. (1993). *The "no significant difference" phenomenon as reported in research reports, summaries, and papers* (Report issued by Office of Instructional Telecommunications). Raleigh: North Carolina State University.

Sabelli, N., & Barrett, L. (1994). *Learning and technology in the future* [Draft]. Summary of proceedings for a National Science Workshop, October 4–6, 1993. Washington, DC: National Science Foundation.

Sabers, D. S., Cushing, K. S., & Berliner, D. C. (1991). Differences among teachers in a task characterized by simultaneity, multidimensionality, and immediacy. *American Educational Research Journal, 28*(1), 63–88.

Salomon, G. (1991). Transcending the qualitative-quantitative debate: The analytic and systemic approaches to education research. *Educational Researcher, 20*(6), 10–18.

Salomon, G. (1992, April). *Computer's first decade: Where were we and where are we going next?* Paper presented at the annual meeting of the American Educational Research Association, San Francisco.

Salomon, G. (Ed.). (1993a). *Distributed cognitions: Psychological and educational considerations*. New York: Cambridge University Press.

Salomon, G. (1993b). No distribution without individuals' cognition: A dynamic interactional view. In G. Salomon (Ed.), *Distributed cognitions: Psychological and educational considerations* (pp. 111–138). New York: Cambridge University Press.

Salomon, G. (1993c). On the nature of pedagogic computer tools: The case of the Writing Partner. In S. P. Lajoie & S. J. Derry (Eds.), *Computers as cognitive tools* (pp. 179–196). Hillsdale, NJ: Lawrence Erlbaum Associates.

Salomon, G., & Globerson, T. (1989). When teams do not function the way they ought to. *International Journal of Educational Research, 13*, 89–99.

Salomon, G., Perkins, D. N., & Globerson, T. (1991). Partners in cognition: Extending human intelligence with intelligent technologies. *Educational Researcher, 20*(3), 2–9.

Saxe, G. B. (1988). Children's mathematical thinking: A developmental framework for preschool, primary, and special education teachers by A. J. Broody, *Contemporary Psychology, 33*, 997.

Scardamalia, M., & Bereiter, C. (1991). Higher levels of agency for children in knowledge building: A challenge for the design of new knowledge media. *Journal of the Learning Sciences, 1*, 37–68.

Scardamalia, M., Bereiter, C., Brett, C., Burtis, P. J., Calhoun, C., & Lea, N. (1992). Educational applications of a networked communal database. *Interactive Learning Environments, 2*, 45–71.

Scardamalia, M., Bereiter, C., & Lamon, M. (1994). The CSILE Project: Trying to bring the classroom into world 3. In K. McGilly (Ed.), *Classroom lessons: Integrating cognitive theory and classroom practice* (pp. 201–228). Cambridge, MA: MIT Press.

Scardamalia, M., Bereiter, C., McLean, R. S., Swallow, J., & Woodruff, E. (1989). Computer-supported intentional learning environments. *Journal of Educational Computing Research, 5*, 51–68.

Schank, P. K., Linn, M. C., & Clancy, M. J. (1993). Supporting Pascal programming with an on-line template library and case studies. *International Journal of Man-Machine Studies, 38*, 1031–1048.

Schliemann, A. D., & Acioly, N. M. (1989). Mathematical knowledge developed at work: The contribution of practice versus the contribution of schooling. *Cognition and Instruction, 6*, 185–222.

Schlosser, C. A., & Anderson, M. L. (1994, February). *Distance education: Review of the literature*. Washington, DC: Association for Educational Communications and Technology (AECT).

Schmidt, H. (1993). Foundations of problem-based learning: Some explanatory notes. *Medical Education, 27*, 422–432.

Schneider, W., & Shiffrin, R. M. (1985). Categorization (restructuring) and automatization: Two separable factors. *Psychological Review, 92*(3), 424–428.

Schoefield, J. W., Evans-Rhodes, D., & Huber, B. R. (1990). Artificial intelligence in the classroom: The impact of a computer-based tutor on teachers and students. *Social Science Computer Review, 8*(1), 24–41.

Schoenfeld, A. H. (1991). On mathematics as sense-making: An informal attack on the unfortunate divorce of formal and informal mathematics. In J. F. Voss, D. N. Perkins, & J. W. Segal (Eds.), *Informal reasoning and education* (pp. 311–344). Hillsdale, NJ: Lawrence Erlbaum Associates.

Schramm, W. (1977). *Big media little media*. Beverly Hills, CA: Sage.

Senge, P. (1994, July). *Learning organizations*. Paper presented at the Sixth International Conference on Thinking, Cambridge, MA.

Senge, P. M. (1990). *The fifth discipline: The art and practice of the learning organization*. New York: Doubleday.

Sharp, D. L. M., Bransford, J. D., Vye, N., Goldman, S. R., Kinzer, C., & Soraci, S., Jr. (1992). Literacy in an age of integrated-media. In M. J. Dreher & W. H. Slater (Eds.), *Elementary school literacy: Critical issues* (pp. 183–210). Norwood, MA: Christopher-Gorden Publishers.

Sharp, D. L. M., Vye, N. J., Bransford, J. D., Goldman, S. R., O'Banion, K., Beaty, J., & Saul, E. (1992, April). *Technology for building literacy skills in young children*. Paper presented at the annual meeting of the American Educational Research Association, San Francisco.

Shatz, M. (1982). On mechanisms of language acquisition: Can features of the communicative environment account for development? In E. Wanner & L. R. Gleitman (Eds.), *Language acquisition: The state of the art* (pp. 102–127). New York: Cambridge University Press.

Shavelson, R. J., Webb, N. M., & Hotta, J. Y. (1987). The concept of exchangeability in designing telecourse evaluations. *Journal of Distance Education, 2*(1), 27–40.

Sheingold, K. (1991). Restructuring for learning with technology: The potential for synergy. *Phi Delta Kappan, 73,* 17–27.

Sheingold, K., & Frederiksen, J. (1994). Using technology to support innovative assessment. In B. Means (Ed.), *Technology and education reform: The reality behind the promise* (pp. 111–132). San Francisco: Jossey-Bass.

Sherwood, R. D., Petrosino, A. J., Lin, X., Lamon, M., & the Cognition and Technology Group at Vanderbilt. (in press). Problem-based macro contexts in science instruction: Theoretical basis, design issues, and the development of applications. In D. Lavoie (Ed.), *Towards a cognitive-science perspective for scientific problem solving.* Manhattan, KS: National Association for Research in Science Teaching.

Shute, V. J. (1993). A comparison of learning environments: All that glitters . . . . In S. P. Lajoie & S. J. Derry (Eds.), *Computers as cognitive tools* (pp. 47–73). Hillsdale, NJ: Lawrence Erlbaum Associates.

Shute, V. J., & Glaser, R. (1991). An intelligent tutoring system for exploring principles of economics. In R. E. Snow & D. E. Wiley (Eds.), *Improving inquiry in social science: A volume in honor of Lee J. Cronbach* (pp. 333–360). Hillsdale, NJ: Lawrence Erlbaum Associates.

Siegler, R. S. (1978). The origins of scientific reasoning. In R. S. Siegler (Ed.), *Children's thinking: What develops?* (pp. 109–149). Hillsdale, NJ: Lawrence Erlbaum Associates.

Sisung, N. J. (1992). *The effects of two modes of instructional delivery: Two-way forward facing interactive television and traditional classroom on attitudes, motivation, on-task/off-task behavior and final exam grades of students enrolled in humanities courses.* Unpublished dissertation, University of Michigan, Ann Arbor, MI.

Skinner, B. F. (1953). *Science and human behavior*. New York: Free Press.

Savery, J. R., & Duffy, T. M. (in press). Problem based learning: An instructional model and its constructivist framework. *Educational Technology.*

Smith, J. B. (1993). *Implementation of satellite distance learning in Illinois rural secondary schools: A descriptive study.* Unpublished doctoral dissertation, Southern Illinois University, Carbondale.

Smith, L. B., Sera, M., & Gattuso, B. (1988). The development of thinking. In R. J. Sternberg & E. E. Smith (Eds.), *The psychology of human thought* (pp. 366–391). Cambridge, England: Cambridge University Press.

Songer, N. B., & Linn, M. C. (1991). How do students' views of science influence knowledge integration: *Journal of Research in Science Teaching, 28,* 761–784.

Spiro, R. J., Feltovich, P. L., Jacobson, M. J., & Coulson, R. L. (1991). Cognitive flexibility, constructivism, and hypertext: Random access instruction for advanced knowledge acquisition in ill-structured domains. *Educational Technology, 31*(5), 24–33.

Spiro, R. J., & Jehng, J. C. (1990). Cognitive flexibility and hypertext: Theory and technology for the nonlinear and multidimensional traversal of complex subject matter. In D. Nix and R. J. Spiro (Eds.), *Cognition, education, and multimedia: Exploring ideas in high technology* (pp. 163–205). Hillsdale, NJ: Lawrence Erlbaum Associates.

Spiro, R. J., Vispoel, W. L., Schmitz, J., Samarapungavan, A., & Boeger, A. (1987). Knowledge acquisition for application: Cognitive flexibility and transfer in complex content domains. In B. C. Britton & S. Glynn (Eds.), *Executive control processes in reading* (pp. 177–199). Hillsdale, NJ: Lawrence Erlbaum Associates.

Spoehr, K. T. (1994). Enhancing the acquisition of conceptual structures through hypermedia. In K. McGilly (Ed.), *Classroom lessons: Integrating cognitive theory and classroom practice* (pp. 75–101). Cambridge, MA: MIT Press.

Sproull, L., & Keisler, S. (1992). *Connections: New ways of working in the networked organization.* Cambridge, MA: MIT Press.

Steen, L. A. (1994). Integrating school science and mathematics: Fad or folly? In D. F. Berlin (Ed.), *NSF/SSMA Wingspread Conference: A network for integrated science and mathematics teaching and learning* (pp. 7–12). Columbus, OH: School Science and Mathematics Association.

Sternberg, R. J., & Wagner, R. K. (1986). *Practical intelligence.* New York: Cambridge University Press.

Stewart, B., & Watson, F. (1994). TYCHO, A schoolyear 2000 initiative. *Ed Tech News, 14*(4), 1.

Suppes, P., & Morningstar, M. (1968). Computer-assisted instruction. *Science, 166,* 343–350.

Sutton, R. E. (1991). Equity and computers in the schools: A decade of research. *Review of Educational Research, 61*(4), 475–503.

Swinton, S. S., Amarel, M. A., & Morgan, J. A. (1978). *The PLATO elementary demonstration educational outcome evaluation* (PR-78-11). Princeton, NJ: Educational Testing Service.

Talbert, J. E., & McLaughlin, M. W. (1993). Understanding teaching in context. In D. K. Cohen, M. W. McLaughlin, & J. E. Talbert (Eds.), *Teaching for understanding: Challenges for policy and practice* (pp. 167–206). San Francisco: Jossey-Bass.

Technical Educational Research Center (TERC). (1990). *The National Geographic kids network, year 4 final annual report.* Cambridge, MA: Author.

Tennyson, R. D. (1990, July). Integrated instructional design theory: Advancements from cognitive science and instructional technology. *Educational Technology,* 9–15.

Tinker, R. F., & Papert, S. (1989). Tools for science education. In J. D. Ellis (Ed.), *1988 AETS yearbook, information technology and science education.* Columbus, OH: Association for the Education of Teachers in Science and ERIC Clearinghouse for Science, Mathematics and Environmental Education.

Tinker, R. F. (1994). Integrating mathematics and science. In D. F. Berlin (Ed.), *NSF/SSMA Wingspread Conference: A network for integrated science and mathematics teaching and learning* (pp. 49–52). Columbus, OH: School Science and Mathematics Association.

Tom Snyder Productions. (1992). *The wonderful problems of Fizz & Martina.* Watertown, MA: Author.

Torgesen, J. K. (1984). Instruction uses of microcomputers and elementary aged mildly handicapped children. *Special Services in the Schools, 1*(1), 37–48.

Torgesen, J. K., & Young, K. A. (1983). Priorities for the use of microcomputers with learning disabled children. *Journal of Learning Disabilities, 16*(4), 234–347.

Turner, J. C. (1992, April). *Identifying motivation for literacy in first grade: An observational study.* Paper presented at the annual meeting of the American Educational Research Association, San Francisco.

Tushnet, N. C., Uriarte, C. B., Manuel, D., & Broekhuizen, D. V. (1993, July). *Star schools evaluation report one.* Los Alamitos, CA: Southwest Regional Laboratory.

U.S. Department of Labor. (1992). *Learning a living: A blueprint for high performance.* Washington, DC: Secretary's Commission on Achieving Necessary Skills.

Vacc, N. N. (1987). Word processor vs. handwriting: A comparative study of writing samples produced by mildly mentally handicapped students. *Exceptional Children, 54,* 156–166.

Van Haneghan, J. P., Barron, L., Young, M. F., Williams, S. M., Vye, N. J., & Bransford, J. D. (1992). The Jasper series: An experiment with new ways to enhance mathematical thinking. In D. F. Halpern (Ed.), *Enhancing thinking skills in the sciences and mathematics* (pp. 15–38). Hillsdale, NJ: Lawrence Erlbaum Associates.

Vecchione, A. (1994, October 3). A lesson in efficiency. *Information Week,* 1.

Victoria Learning Society & Sunburst/Wings for Learning. (1994). *Learner profile.* Pleasantville, NY: Sunburst Communications.

Vinsonhaler, J., & Bass, R. (1972). A summary of ten major studies of CAI drill and practice. *Educational Technology, 12*(7), 29–32.

vonGlaserfeld, E. (1989). Cognition, construction of knowledge, and teaching. *Synthese, 80,* 121–140.

Vygotsky, L. S. (1978). *Mind in society: The development of higher psychological processes.* Cambridge, MA: Harvard University Press.

Vygotsky, L. S. (1986). *Thought and language* (A. Kozulin, Trans.). Cambridge, MA: MIT Press. (Original English translation published 1962)

Warren, B., & Rosebery, A. (1993). Equity in the future tense: Redefining relationships among teachers, students, and science in linguistic minority classrooms. Working paper 1-93. Cambridge, MA: TERC.

Wellman, H. M., & Somerville, S. C. (1982). The development of human search ability. In M. E. Lamb & A. L. Brown (Eds.), *Advances in developmental psychology* (Vol. 2, pp. 41–48). Hillsdale, NJ: Lawrence Erlbaum Associates.

Wheatley, G. (1993). The role of negotiation in mathematics learning. In K. Tobin (Ed.), *The practice of constructivism in science education* (pp. 121–134). Washington, DC: American Association for the Advancement of Science.

White, B. Y. (1993). ThinkerTools: Causal models, conceptual change, and science education. *Cognition & Instruction, 10,* 1–100.

Whitehead, A. N. (1929). *The aims of education.* New York: Macmillan.

Whittington, N. (1987). Is instructional television educationally effective? A research review. *American Journal of Distance Education, 1*(1), 47–57.

Williams, S. M. (1992). Putting case-based instruction into context: Examples from legal and medical education. *Journal of the Learning Sciences, 2*(4), 367–427.

Williams, S. M. (1994). *Anchored simulations: Merging the strengths of formal and informal reasoning in a computer-based learning environment.* Unpublished doctoral dissertation, Vanderbilt University, Nashville, TN.

Wilson, K. S. (1987). *Palenque: An interactive multimedia optical disc prototype for children* (Working Paper No. 2). New York: Bank Street College, Center for Children and Technology.

Wise, A. E. (1989, October 18). Calling for "National Institutes of Education." *Education Week,* 36.

Wiske, M. S. (1990, April). *Teaching geometry through guided inquiry: A case of changing mathematics instruction with new technologies.* Paper presented at the annual meeting of the American Educational Research Association, Boston.

Woodruff, E., & Bereiter, C. (1982). On the road to computer-assisted composition. *Education Technology, Systems, 10,* 133–148.

Yackel, E., Cobb, P., & Wood, T. (1991). Small group interactions as a source of learning opportunities in second grade mathematics. *Journal for Research in Mathematics Education, 22*(5), 390–408.

Yerushalmy, M. (1991). Enhancing acquisition of basic geometric concepts with the use of the Geometric Supposer. *Journal of Educational Computing Research, 7,* 407–420.

Yerushalmy, M., Chazan, D., & Gordon, M. (1990). *Guided inquiry and technology: A yearlong study of children and teachers using the Geometry Supposer.* Newton, MA: Education Development Center, Center for Learning Technology.

# · 26 ·

# GROUP PROCESSES IN THE CLASSROOM

## Noreen M. Webb
UNIVERSITY OF CALIFORNIA, LOS ANGELES

## Annemarie Sullivan Palincsar
UNIVERSITY OF MICHIGAN, ANN ARBOR

It is hard to exaggerate the interest in group learning in today's schools. There are signs everywhere, from state mandates that children participate in cooperative learning experiences, to the commercially available guides designed to assist teachers to plan, implement, and manage cooperative learning, to the representation of group learning in virtually every contemporary educational psychology textbook, to the consistency with which increased use of small-group instruction is included in recommendations for curriculum and instructional reform (e.g., *Everybody Counts*, National Research Council, 1989). At the same time, because of the number and nature of questions about the process of coconstructing knowledge, it is hard to imagine an area richer with research possibilities. In fact, much remains to be learned about how social interaction facilitates cognitive development.

In this chapter, a group is considered to be constituted by persons engaged in a common task who are interdependent in the performance of that task and interact in its pursuit. Hence, we do not consider groups that are principally teacher led, such as reading recitation groups. Similarly, although we draw distinctions between peer tutoring and group learning, we do not elaborate on peer tutoring.

This chapter discusses current research on group processes in the classroom: the processes taking place in peer-led groups that shape learning, and the impact of different group and classroom structures on the group processes that emerge. The first three sections lay the groundwork for the empirical findings to be presented later. The first section provides a historical overview of group processes and group learning in education. The second section details several theories about how learning occurs in group contexts. The third section discusses some contemporary approaches to peer-based learning in the classroom.

The next three sections present and discuss findings from empirical literature about when and how group processes influence learning and other outcomes. Thus, the fourth section describes the outcomes typically investigated in research on group processes, the fifth section describes ways in which group processes have influenced learning outcomes, and the sixth section examines the powerful effects that structuring groups and group work can have on the processes emerging within them. The concluding section summarizes the state of the field and poses a number of questions for further research.

## HISTORICAL PERSPECTIVES

### Group Processes

The history of group processes in Western literature is perhaps best traced by examining the literature on social psychology. This section summarizes this literature and points out ways in which the discussions of group learning prior to the 1950s foreshadowed contemporary discussions.

There are two helpful reviews of the early group process literature. The first, written by Dashiell, can be found in the 1935 edition of *Handbook of Social Psychology*, and the second, written by Kelley and Thibaut, in the 1954 edition of that handbook. As suggested by the title of Dashiell's chapter, "Experimental Studies of the Influence of Social Situations on the Behavior of Individual Human Adults," most of the early investigations focused on the effects of various social contexts on individual thought and work. Typically, investigations were designed to compare individuals working alone with individuals working side by side on identical tasks, and the focus was almost exclusively on the individual products of work and the performance of individuals within the group.

Representative of this research was the study conducted by F. H. Allport (1924) in which Allport investigated individuals working alone on tasks, such as word association tasks, and working on tasks in the presence of others who were completing the same tasks. Anticipating contemporary interest in the

We would like to thank Daniel Solomon and Steven Bossert for their helpful comments on an earlier draft of this paper.

communication process involved in interactive learning (e.g., Stone's discussions of inference), Allport observed that "there appears to be a 'conversationaling' of our thought in the social setting. . . . When working *with* others we respond in a measure as though we were reacting *to* them" (p. 274). Allport concluded from his investigations that while overt responses, such as the number of words offered in a word association task, were facilitated in groups, intellectual responses, such as the arguments tendered in support of the associations, were hampered rather than facilitated by groups. Further, in tests of maintenance of these effects, he determined that social facilitation of even overt responses became less effective as work continued. He interpreted this outcome to mean that increased attentiveness is necessary to overcome the distractions afforded by others.

A study conducted by South in 1927 is one of the first known investigations to focus on genuine group products of individuals working together. This study used activities that the researcher selected as reflective of the "practical life" decision-making in which committees engage, including judging English compositions and judging emotions from photographs. The participants were university undergraduates. Among South's conclusions was the observation that, generally speaking, committees whose members were all male or all female were more efficient than mixed committees, particularly when completing concrete and personal tasks. This effect for gender was more marked when the group size was small (e.g., three as opposed to six). Finally, imposing time limits increased the efficiency of female groups more than the efficiency of male groups.

Given contemporary interest in the motivation of group members in relation to goal structures, it is fascinating to note that as early as 1929, Maller provided evidence that what is referred to today as "cooperative goal structures" (Slavin, 1987) played themselves out differentially, depending on the degree to which the members were concerned about the shared goals rather than their more personal goals. He determined that work performed for a shared prize is sometimes more and sometimes less efficient than working for a prize for oneself, depending on the nature of the group for which the effort is expended. This work led to questions about the circumstances under which individuals accept a group goal. Maller (1929) determined that member acceptance of group goals was heightened by a goal-setting procedure involving discussion and participation in selecting the goal. Certainly this observation is not unlike the argument that M. Miller (1987) has made, namely, that the extent to which there is concurrence and cogeneration of the question influences the activity and outcome of group problem solving.

During the 1930s the number of studies investigating both group and individual products increased. Propelling the work of such researchers as Thorndike (1938) and G. B. Watson (1928) was a question that could be paraphrased as, "Are groups superior to their average individual member?" Indeed, Watson's 1928 article, "Do Groups Think More Efficiently Than Individuals?" is an interesting forerunner of such articles as Daiute's (1986) "Do 1 and 1 Make 2?" and Glachan and P. H. Light's (1982) "Peer Interaction and Learning: Can Two Wrongs Make a Right?" In aggregate, this body of research suggests that early researchers acknowledged the complexity of understanding group processes. For example, Thorndike (1938) included in his analyses discussions of the role of such variables as the heterogeneity of ability among the group members, the degree

of self-reported confidence in the expressed opinions of group members, and the nature of the task at hand.

A study conducted by Bos (1937) provides evidence of the burgeoning interest in the role that communication among group members plays in the outcome of group activity. Bos maintained that the act of formulating an opinion or idea in order to communicate it to the group led to a sharpening and refining of the idea. Bos studied 68 children ranging in age from 11 to 13 years. The children in one group worked individually at first, and then several weeks later worked on the same task in pairs, while children in a second group continued to work individually. Children in a third group began working in pairs and then worked individually. In one task, students identified pictures painted by the same painter. In a second task, students arranged sets of five pictures so that they made a sensible story. The results indicated that the group problem solving resulted in much more accurate responses. Bos's explanation for this outcome was based on informal observations that group members resisted vagueness and, in essence, demanded clarity of evidence before accepting a response. Bos also determined, through observation, that children who had a correct response but were unable to present their insights persuasively were disadvantaged in the group context; their opinions did not prevail, despite their accuracy. Bos's discussion anticipates Grice's (1975) discussion of conversational maxims.

In the 1940s, the study of group problem solving underwent a dramatic shift in focus, influenced in part by the theoretical work of Lewin. Prior to the 1940s, the dominant American theory focused on historical antecedents of individual behavior. Lewin, who emigrated to the United States in 1933, under the auspices of the Emergency Committee on Displaced Scholars, emphasized, in contrast, the direct effect of the present situation and context on a person's behavior. His pursuit of an explanation of "national psychology" (e.g., an understanding of how children reared in Germany and America develop appreciably different types of personalities) led to the articulation of his "field theory," a method of analyzing causal relations (Lewin, 1951). In 1945 he became the first director of the Research Center for Group Dynamics at the Massachusetts Institute of Technology, a laboratory that was founded for the purpose of combining research and action. The themes pursued by the laboratory included racial and religious prejudice, intolerance, and divisive social and cultural differences.

There was now a strong trend away from the end products of group problem-solving activity and toward an emphasis on motivations, emotion, and interactions of individuals within the group. This phase included studies of security, fear, motivation, interpersonal relationships, and communication. With this shift in focus came a shift in methodology, with greater reliance on subjective data arising from the theory suggesting that attitudes mediated individual behavior within the group. Concurrently, there was much greater emphasis on observations of the ongoing stream of activity, the interactions and communications that constitute the problem-solving process. For example, Deutsch (1949), a student of Lewin's, designed seminal investigations of goal structures, examining the behavioral processes that emerged when university students were placed in competitive or cooperative conditions. Deutsch observed no difference in student engagement in the two conditions. However, he did observe more coordinated effort, more helpfulness, and fewer communication problems among participants in the cooperative condition, whereas participants in the competitive condition were obstructive and aggressive in their interactions.

In keeping with the emphasis on the stream of activity, Benne and Sheats (1948) described functional role categories that they observed to emerge "naturally" in the course of group interactions: the "energizer," who prodded the group to action; the information seeker; the information giver; the initiator-contributor, who proposed new ideas; the elaborator, who spelled out suggestions and provided examples; the opinion giver; and the evaluator-critic. Other roles were the harmonizer, the expediter, and the encourager.

Similarly, Bales (1950), observing "normal" adults, described certain patterns that emerged from groups whose interactions he regarded as fruitful. He described a sequence of phases in problem solving, including (a) an orientation phase, which included asking for, giving, repeating, and clarifying information; (b) an evaluation phase, during which members sought and gave opinions, provided analyses, and communicated feelings; and (c) a control phase, which included asking for and giving suggestions regarding directions and lines of action. In keeping with the trend at this time, Benne and Sheats, as well as Bales, examined the group process with little regard for such features as group size or nature of the task, and there was little attention to the outcomes of the group processes.

By 1954 Kelley and Thibaut reported a shift away from research examining group problem solving and toward the study of group discussions with no obvious shared goal. In hand with this trend they observed a move away from group process and toward group product once again. Kelley and Thibaut (1954) criticized the trend to compare the outcomes of individual and group problem solving, believing that this practice would lead to the collection of data that would inform neither individual nor group processes. By studying only end products and not social communication, they argued, it would be impossible to understand the "process of assembling and combining individual contributions to create group solutions."

Kelley and Thibaut specifically identified Bales's research as the kind they were criticizing—that is, research conducted in the absence of "good theory." Yet Bales (1950, p. 62) was very concerned with the effects of social processes on group and individual problem solving:

One can say that the process of problem solving in a group involves a series of social processes. Conversely, those phenomena in social systems referred to as social processes are or should be regarded as problem solving processes. One can go further and say that what we usually regard as individual problem solving or the process of individual thought, is essentially, in form and in genesis, a social process; thinking is a re-enactment by the individual of the problem solving process as he originally went through it with other individuals. It can probably be maintained with considerable success that the best model we have for understanding what goes on inside the individual personality is the model of what goes on between individuals in the problem solving process. The component parts—acts in a system of interaction—are identical. In short, the idea of an interaction system is a key theoretical starting point. From it one can derive the ideas of personality, social system, and culture as particular subtypes.

What is arresting about this quotation is that it characterizes a theoretical perspective that has been a major influence in contemporary discussions of group learning, namely, the work of Vygotsky, which is discussed later in this chapter. Yet this perspective was not acknowledged as a driving theory at the time that Bales was writing, and there are no indications that Bales knew of Vygotsky's work.

## The History of Group Learning in Education

Despite social psychologists' enthusiasm for and research into cooperation and competition, there is very little mention in their writings of the implications of their work for society at large, including the institution of schools. However, independently, there has been considerable interest among educators in examining these implications. In this section we trace the history of competition and cooperation in the educational setting by relating it to sociopolitical and economic trends. An excellent review of this history can be found in Pepitone (1980).

The history of cooperation and competition in U.S. educational settings is particularly interesting insofar as the United States has traditionally been considered the bastion of individualism, where the prescription for success was and is a blend of pioneer spirit, self-assertion, individual ingenuity, and individual effort. Although this "national character" has been challenged over the decades, the Horatio Alger story is still a prominent text in American culture.

One individual who sharply criticized the prevailing competitive tradition was John Dewey. While establishing the Laboratory School at the University of Chicago, and afterwards, Dewey was mindful of a rapidly changing America. He believed the changes undermined the family, and so he advocated recreating for children a meaningful family context by fashioning a cooperative school community. He criticized the use of competition among students as the basis for success, advocating instead cooperation and mutual assistance as a way of promoting the "interchange of thought" and "unity of sympathetic feeling" that hold society together (Dewey, 1966, cited in Pepitone, pp. 9–10). A kindred spirit of Lewin's, Dewey believed that democracy must be learned anew with each generation, and that the key to maintaining democracy was understanding and fidelity to the laws of human nature in group settings. Dewey's ideas were operationalized in publications by William Heard Kilpatrick (1922, 1925), in which Kilpatrick described curricula that were driven by interdisciplinary projects in which each student pursued his or her own interest but contributed to the total group activity.

In response to growing voices against laissez-faire individualism in depression America, an organized campaign was launched by a number of prominent businesses. This movement has been well documented by S. Alexander Rippa (1958, 1964), who detailed the formation of the Liberty League in 1934. This was a consortium of individual business organizations as well as influential industrial interests such as Dupont, General Motors, and United Steel. Using media such as billboards, a radio series ("The American Family Robinson"), and newspapers, including one paper a week that was directed at youth, their message was a defense of "the American way of life," including the freedom to pursue individual and personal interests. Concurrently, organizations such as the American Legion and the New York State Economic Council determined that social science textbooks were too critical of the American way of life, indoctrinating students into thinking that competition was evil while appearing to extol the principles of collectivism. There were public book burnings, and the Daughters of the American Revolution issued a call that all public school books be reviewed and expunged of un-American content. Finally, the National Association of Manufacturers called on educators to achieve a more complete understanding of private enterprise. Schools were called on to provide competitive situations that would mirror the competitive culture of North America and western Europe (May & Doob, 1937).

During the war years, attention in this arena turned to personality assessment and predictions regarding social interactions in deliberately created and controlled conditions. Research focused on developing theories of group dynamics, and little attention was paid to schools. The voices of progressive educators who advocated cooperation and collectivism were submerged. When they attempted to reemerge, they were met with sharp criticism, perhaps best captured in the words of Rickover (1959, cited in Cremin, 1961) responding to the launch of Sputnik:

Our technological supremacy has been called into question and we know that we have to deal with a formidable competitor. . . . Parental objectives no longer coincide with those professed by progressive educationists. (p. 347)

In a foreshadowing of the current challenge to strive for excellence, there was a dramatic increase in the use of competitive norms such as Scholastic Aptitude Tests and the Graduate Record Examination, frequent quizzes, and the use of more standardized assessment.

In the 1960s however, there was once again a swing away from competition and toward individualized instruction and cooperative learning structures. It was during the sixties that open classrooms, peer teaching, cross-age learning, and value clarification programs were introduced into schools. Much of the turbulence during this period centered on civil rights, and schools were identified as fostering inhumanity by socializing students toward competitive interrelations with others (Friedenberg, 1963; Goodman, 1956). Cooperative interactions were identified as one means of reducing prejudice, and many of the procedures that were developed to support cooperative learning were, in fact, rooted in Allport's theory that sheer contact alone, under certain circumstances, may in fact reinforce prejudice. The spirit of this effort is captured in a review by Slavin (1977), in which he summarized the effects of cooperative structures on "social connectedness," observing that there had been impressive effects of cooperative reward structures on such dimensions as interracial friendships, positive interracial attitudes, interracial helping on school tasks, and reductions in interracial tension. Slavin concluded by arguing that "it is particularly the effects of cooperative reward structures on social connectedness that makes the search for effective cooperative structures important, perhaps imperative" (p. 645). In fact, the search for effective cooperative structures and investigations of the differential outcomes of various cooperative structures have assumed a prominent place in contemporary research on peer learning. Interestingly, however, the emphasis in research has shifted from sociometric measures to cognitive and motivational outcomes. Most current research on peer-based instruc-

tion in the classroom focuses on learning outcomes, with attitudinal outcomes receiving secondary attention. The next section discusses the mechanisms by which group contexts are hypothesized to influence these learning-related outcomes.

## THEORETICAL PERSPECTIVES REGARDING THE MECHANISMS BY WHICH LEARNING OCCURS IN GROUP CONTEXTS

The growing interest in group processes among educational and cognitive psychologists is related in part to evolving constructivist views of the learner. Constructivism holds that knowledge or meaning results from individuals' interpretations of their experiences in particular contexts. However, experience refers not only to direct experiences but also to learning that occurs through interactions with others. As instructional theorists turn their attentions to contextualized practice, there is heightened interest in situations where elaboration, interpretation, explanation, and argumentation are integral to the activity of the group and where learning is supported by other individuals. In this sense, constructivism holds that cognition is an outcome of social processes.

How do people jointly construct knowledge? How do our interactions with others shape our understanding and our reasoning processes? At the heart of these questions are issues related to mechanism: What is the mechanism by which we shape one another's knowledge and thinking? In keeping with this focus, this section is organized according to varying perspectives on mechanism. It is not an exhaustive review but rather addresses the most prominent contemporary visions of mechanisms.

### Sociocognitive Conflict as a Mechanism for Learning

Derived principally from the work of Piaget and his followers is the view that the instantiation of cognitive conflict leads to higher levels of reasoning and learning: "Cognitive conflict created by social interaction is the locus at which the power driving intellectual development is generated" (Perret-Clermont, 1980, p. 12). According to this perspective, cognitive conflict arises when there is a perceived contradiction between the learner's existing understanding and what the learner experiences. This contradiction and the disequilibrating effect it has on the learner lead the learner to question his or her beliefs and to try out new ideas (Forman & Cazden, 1985; Gilly, 1990). In Piaget's words, "[disequilibrium] forces the subject to go beyond his current state and strike out in new directions" (1985, p. 10). This perspective is commonly identified as sociocognitive conflict theory, in reference to the fact that the cognitive conflict that occurs results from social exchanges in which it becomes clear that one must reexamine one's ideas.

Piaget (1976) regarded social exchanges between children and adults as unlikely to lead to the kinds of cognitive development that exchanges with child peers promote. Because children and adults do not cooperate as equals and do not exercise mutual control over the interaction, the child cannot really share the adult's point of view.

Damon (1984) has elaborated that a child's age peers are

potentially compelling sources of sociocognitive conflict because (a) the age peers speak at a level that the child can understand; (b) child age peers are more likely to challenge one another than to challenge an adult, whose ideas they are more likely simply to accept; (c) they take feedback from others seriously; (d) they are motivated to reconcile contradictions; and (e) communication between children is less threatening than is corrective advice from adults.

Illustrative of the studies that have explored sociocognitive conflict theory is one conducted by Bell, Grossen, and Perret-Clermont (1985). They determined that children working with peers showed more cognitive growth, as measured by performance on conservation tasks, than children who worked alone. However, this growth did not occur by passively observing one's peer strategically approaching the targeted problem but only when the child was actively engaged in the problem solving as well. Further, if the partner's cognitive level was too much in advance of the child's, the result was similar to what would be expected in an interaction with an adult: The partner's answer was merely accepted and did not stimulate "striking out in different directions."

Clearly there is room for considerable elaboration on this theory. For example, although Piaget claimed that peer interaction provided greater opportunities for learning than adult–child interactions, research such as that conducted by Radziszewska and Rogoff (cited in Rogoff, 1991), provides contrary evidence. Radziszewska and Rogoff compared children's interactions with adults and with peers, using one group of peer partners with no special preparation and another group of peer partners who had been taught to use an optimal strategy for successfully completing an errand-planning task. When the children were later asked to plan without assistance, those who had collaborated with adults performed better than those who had worked with prepared or unprepared peers. Seeking a reconciliation between these apparently conflicting results and the results of Piagetian studies, Damon (1984) called attention to the nature of the shift the learner must make. He suggested that development that requires giving up current understandings to reach a new perspective might best be attained by an exchange of ideas on an equal basis, while learning that does not require a transformation of perspective (such as learning a strategy or skill) might best be attained by working with more skillful partners (in this case, the adults).

E. A. Forman and Kraker (1985) cautioned that cognitive conflict may not be enough if verbal interaction is not permitted or encouraged or if the social structure permits passive compliance. They suggested that verbal interaction is the key to coconstruction and cognitive change.

Even when collaboration with peers is effective, there are additional variables to be considered. For example, Russell, Mills, and Reiff-Musgrove (1990), in another investigation of moving from nonconserving to conserving, observed that social dominance influenced whether a child's conserving answer was adopted by the other child. Having the right answer was not always enough to persuade the other child.

A significant criticism of sociocognitive conflict theory is that it fails to describe how the process of resolving interindividual conflicts leads to the resolution of intraindividual imbalance (as characterized by Doise & Mugny, 1984). Although Forman did attempt to analyze the social interactions and strategies that were employed during collaborative problem solving, there was no clear evidence on how conflicting perspectives are reconciled and lead to enhanced intellectual development (E. A. Forman & Cazden, 1985).

Further, although argumentation is useful for bringing about change and agreement (Gilly, 1990), there are many instances in which agreement is reached without argumentation (Amigues, 1990) and acquiescence occurs merely as a function of a poorly coordinated verbal exchange (S. A. Miller & Brownell, 1975). This may well be a function of the multiple demands involved in argumentation. For example, if conflict is indeed established, there is little evidence that children understand how to reconcile opposing views, how to request or use evidence, or how to support one's own position (A. L. Brown, 1989; Eichinger, 1992).

These criticisms are not to suggest that the sociocognitive conflict theory does not offer considerable potential for guiding investigations of cognitive change in group learning. For example, this theory would support the view of scaffolding students' discussions by teaching them how to use the features of argumentation (e.g., requesting and providing explanations, comparing explanations, and systematically using and evaluating evidence).

In summary, from a conflict perspective, although social interaction is regarded as essential to learning, the social interaction is considered from the perspective of how effective it is in creating conflict within the individual. From this perspective we begin by considering the individual and then move to the social interaction. In the next perspective to be considered, the social interaction is considered primary.

## The Internalization of Social Processes as the Mechanism for Learning

The idea of social processes as a mechanism for learning is usually identified with Vygotsky. In Vygotsky's view, "the social dimension of consciousness is primary in time and in fact. The individual dimension of consciousness is derivative and secondary" (Vygotsky, 1979, p. 30, cited in Wertsch & Bivens, 1992). Vygotsky's most general statement about the social origins of individual mental functioning is represented in his "general genetic law of cultural development":

Any function in the child's cultural development appears twice, or on two planes. First it appears on the social plane, and then on the psychological plane. First it appears between people as an interpsychological category, and then within the child as an intrapsychological category. This is equally true with regard to voluntary attention, logical memory, the formation of concepts, and the development of volition. . . . [I]t goes without saying that internalization transforms the process itself and changes its structure and functions. Social relations or relations among people genetically underlie all high functions and their relationships. (Vygotsky, 1981, p. 163)

As Wertsch (1991) points out, Vygotsky's general genetic law makes a number of claims not widely shared or understood in contemporary psychology. For example, Vygotsky was not merely suggesting that the mental functioning of the individual is derived from participation in social interaction. Rather, he was arguing that the specific structures and processes of intrapsychological functioning can be traced to their genetic precursors on the interpsychological plane. However, this claim was not meant to suggest that higher mental functions are merely direct copies of socially organized processes, for "[i]nternalization transforms the process itself and changes its structure and functions."

Illustrative of empirical research supporting the theory that social processes promote cognitive change is the work of E. A. Forman and Kraker (1985). Investigating seventh graders involved in a task that required students to predict the nature of shadows cast by geometric shapes in different orientations, Forman and Kraker found that new predictions for the problem-solving task emerged as a consequence of peer interactions and that the conceptions of the goals held by the group members changed from being initially incomplete and dissimilar to complete and similar. Further, they observed that "in the process of attempting to solve the task, appropriate strategies are selected and recombined in new ways, feedback from social and nonsocial environment is incorporated into subsequent activities and eventually, new definitions of the task situation emerge. What the child gains are some metacognitive or strategic skills" (p. 34).

As with the social-cognitive conflict perspective, we are left with the question of how social processes give rise to individual cognitive processes. Wertsch and Bivens (1992) provide two interpretations from this perspective: modeling and text mediation. From a modeling perspective, social functioning provides a model that is gradually taken over and internalized on the individual cognitive plane. More specifically, the language that one uses to guide oneself reflects the language that one has experienced in interactions with others. Thus, this view assumes that active participation in dialogue is essential for the transition of self-regulation from the social plane to the intrapersonal plane. An empirical test of this interpretation was conducted by A. L. Brown and Palincsar (1989) in a study, conducted with middle-grade students, in which they compared teacher modeling of four text comprehension strategies (questioning, summarizing, predicting, and clarifying) with reciprocal teaching among students in which students used these same strategies. Although the comprehension assessments indicated some improvement among students who watched the teacher engage in think-alouds in the modeling condition and responded to the teacher-generated questions, the performance of the students in the reciprocal teaching condition was significantly better.

The second interpretation of how social processes give rise to individual cognitive processes is the text mediational view. The assumptions of this view are (a) that social and individual cognitive functioning is fundamentally shaped by mediational means, such as forms of language, and (b) that all participants in social functioning are actively engaged in shaping this functioning. Empirical support for this interpretation is provided in an exploratory study conducted by Bivens (1990). Bivens examined the interchanges among students of various ages (5 to 10 years old) as they observed experiments designed to disclose various properties of water. The instructional activity was adopted from the hypothesis–experiment–instruction procedure commonly used in Japanese classrooms (cf. Hatano & Inagaki, 1991). In this procedure the class is presented with a question and three alternative answers. After independently choosing a response and tallying the groups' responses, the

children are encouraged to explain, defend, and discuss their choices with one another. In the course of these sessions, Bivens observed shifts in children's understandings that were best accounted for in terms of the ways in which children used one another's ideas to assist in restructuring their own explanations. Bivens proposed that children made use of the utterances of others as "thinking devices" that enabled them to reflect on and transform their own thought.

The text mediational interpretation proposed by Wertsch and Bivens seems to have much in common with contemporary approaches that purport to promote conceptual understanding through "mutually shared cognition." According to this approach, responsibility is distributed across members of the group, expertise is shared, and cognition is mutually constructed and negotiated (Roschelle, 1992; see also chapter 15). This perspective intersects with those research programs that have been conducted for the purpose of examining the nature of verbal interactions among peers (cf. Hatano & Inagaki, 1991; King, 1990; Peterson & Janicki, 1979; N. M. Webb, 1989, 1992; N. M. Webb & Farivar, 1994), to be described in detail in later sections.

## Goal Structures as the Mechanism for Learning

As mechanisms for learning, the modeling perspective and the text mediational perspective are informed principally by developmental and cognitive theories. A different perspective on learning is informed by motivational theory. In contrast to an interest in the interactions among students engaged in collaboration, motivationalists are concerned with the reward or goal structures under which group members operate. Generally, there are three goal structures that have been implemented in cooperative learning investigations: *cooperative goal structures*, in which group members can attain their own personal goals only if the group is successful; *competitive structures*, in which each individual's goal-oriented efforts frustrate the attainment of others' goals; and *individualistic structures*, in which each individual's goal-oriented efforts have no consequences for the attainment of others' goals. From a motivational perspective the critical element in group learning is the peer norms and sanctions that support individual efforts when the cooperative reward structure is in place.

The outcomes of research examining this array of goal structures are inconclusive. Slavin (1983b, 1990a, 1990b) argued that cooperative learning methods are useful only if group rewards (such as certificates of recognition for teams that meet a preset criterion) are provided and if both groups and individuals are held accountable. By making the team's success dependent on the individual learning of all members of the team, group rewards based on learning ensure individual accountability, and a feeling of personal responsibility for what happens in the group. Students work hard toward the group goal, encourage others to do the same, and help each other to ensure the group's success (Deutsch, 1949). On the other hand, L. K. Miller and Hamblin (1963) determined that cooperative goal structures were most effective when they were used with interdependent tasks, and that competitive or individualistic goal structures were better suited to independent tasks. But Johnson and Johnson (D. W. Johnson & R. T. Johnson, 1985a, 1985b, 1990; R. T. Johnson, D. W. Johnson, & Stanne, 1985; D. W. Johnson, Maruyama, R. Johnson, Nelson, & Skon, 1983) concluded that cooperative goal structures were better than competitive structures across all tasks, especially when students encouraged and facilitated each other's efforts, used small-group communications skills, and regularly discussed how to improve their group's functioning. Finally, Michaels (1977) concluded that competitive goal structures were more effective than cooperative goal structures on all tasks.

The use of extrinsic rewards, whether group or individual, is a controversial issue among proponents of peer-based learning. Research in child development, most notably that of Lepper (Lepper, 1983; Lepper & Green, 1978), shows that extrinsic rewards can undermine intrinsic motivation and interest in the classroom. In addition to declining interest in the activities that are being rewarded, this research suggests that students may begin to pay more attention to obtaining the reward than to performing the task. Students may invest the least effort necessary to obtain rewards, may choose to perform less challenging tasks, or may even subvert the task entirely: "imposition of an attractive reward system may lead children to find ways of cheating to arrive at answers that will produce the reward without doing the required work" (Lepper, 1983, p. 297). These results have led some advocates of peer-based learning to develop approaches that do not use extrinsic rewards but instead use other means, such as classroom norms, to encourage desired behavior (Yackel, Cobb, & T. Wood, 1991).

## Imitation, Modeling, and Observational Learning: An Addendum

Many developmental researchers have taken great pains to show that cognitive gains made during collaboration are not due only to imitation of a model who gives the correct answer. If social interaction merely gave students opportunities to imitate each other's responses, then the more capable students would imitate the responses of less capable students, thus appearing to regress as a result of the collaboration. Further, collaborative settings would not help generate knowledge, understanding, and beliefs apart from those held by individual group members prior to group work. But repeated evidence shows that more capable students often benefit by working with less capable students, and that students can generate understanding and problem-solving strategies that no group member had prior to collaboration (see Bell et al., 1985; Tudge & Rogoff, 1989).

Although imitation is not the only mechanism to explain how collaboration may foster cognitive growth, few would dispute that students can learn by observing others. A large literature provides evidence that students can learn new skills, beliefs, and behaviors by observing adult and peer models without interacting with them (Bandura, 1986; Schunk, 1987). Bandura (1986) proposed four processes involved in observational learning through modeling:

- *Attention*: The observer pays attention to, and analyzes, the modeled behavior.
- *Retention*: The observer forms a mental representation of the behavior to remember it.
- *Production*: The observer translates the mental representation into overt behavior (practice).

- *Motivation*: By anticipating or receiving reinforcement for performing the behavior, the observer persists at it.

In addition to learning entirely new behavior, students can correct their own misconceptions by observing others. An example is correcting erroneous strategies for adding fractions with unlike denominators (N. M. Webb & Farivar, 1994).

Not only do students learn from observing others, but peers may be more effective models than adults. Schunk (1987) reviewed research showing that when children have doubts about their own capabilities, watching peers successfully perform a task may raise their self-efficacy for performing well. Watching peers similar to themselves accomplish a task, solve a problem, or learn new material gives students hope that they can do it too. Watching more advanced models (e.g., adults, more highly skilled peers) accomplish the task does not have the same effect because they are assumed to be competent already. In peer-directed group settings in the classroom, students have many opportunities to watch their peers learn how to perform new tasks. They can internalize the skills displayed by others and build confidence in their own ability to perform them.

The theoretical perspectives on how collaboration can foster learning and cognitive development have given rise to a great many peer-based approaches to learning in the classroom. Some of these approaches are described in the next section.

## CONTEMPORARY APPROACHES TO PEER LEARNING IN THE CLASSROOM

Contemporary researchers are investigating a wide variety of approaches to peer learning. The following descriptions use the labels that have been applied by the researchers themselves.

### Basic Approaches

*Peer Tutoring.* Peer tutoring has a long history in educational settings (see review by Wagner, 1982) and has been of particular interest to special educators, who have examined the role of both peer and cross-age tutoring in the mainstreaming of students with learning difficulties (cf. Greenwood, Delquadri, & Hall, 1989). These researchers have focused principally on increases in task engagement and academic gains that ensue with the use of peer tutoring arrangements. Even within what has traditionally been described as peer tutoring arrangements, there is considerable variation in the participant structures. For example, Spurlin, Dansereau, Larson, and Brooks (1984) structured the situation so that one member of a peer pair had information and the other had to acquire that knowledge through inquiry. Yager, D. W. Johnson, and R. T. Johnson (1985) had a comparable condition in which there was a learning leader and a learning listener. In general, peer tutoring has not been conducted for the purpose of teaching processes but rather for basic skill instruction.

There has been a resurgence of interest in peer tutoring as educators attend to the increasing diversity of student populations. For example, Cazden (1988) stressed the importance of including peer (both same-age and cross-age) tutoring in classrooms to help build continuity between home and school cultures with culturally and linguistically diverse students. Garcia (1987/1988) recommended peer tutoring as a means of building on culturally relevant socialization factors and providing peer-to-peer communication. Richard-Amato (1992) has referred to peer teachers as the "neglected resource in multicultural classrooms," suggesting that peer tutoring is an effective means of relinquishing traditional teacher authority and getting teachers off center stage.

*Cooperative Learning.* Cooperative learning is a second approach to peer-based instruction. This expression generally refers to alternative ways of organizing classrooms that contrast with individualistic and competitive classroom organization. There are numerous varieties of cooperative learning. For example, Kagan (1985) has described six varieties of cooperative learning which he argues vary across 25 dimensions (such as philosophy of education, nature of learning, student roles and communication, and evaluation). The six varieties of cooperative learning and their associated features are presented next.

The *student teams achievement divisions (STAD)* learning approach, as described by Slavin (1980) has five components: (a) presentation of material to the whole class, (b) team work in a peer tutoring format to master the information presented, (c) quizzes to assess individual achievement, (d) maintenance of an individual student record of achievement, and (e) team recognition for high individual performance.

The *teams games tournaments (TGT)* is identical to STAD, with the exception that quizzes are replaced by academic games in which students demonstrate their knowledge of the material that they have practiced in their teams. Students are seated at "tournament tables" in homogeneous ability groups of three, with the highest scorer earning 6 points for his or her team, the next highest earning 4 points, and the lowest scorer earning 2 points. As the tournament proceeds, students are reassigned so that the highest scorer advances to a higher ability level table and the lowest scorer moves to a lower ability level table. This procedure is designed to ensure that students have an equal opportunity to earn points for their team.

*Jigsaw I* (developed by Aronson et al. 1978) was designed to provide a situation in which peers would experience high interdependence. Each student is provided with only a portion of the materials or information necessary to master a unit of study but is accountable for the entire unit of study. To meet this requirement, students have to learn the unique information that is presented by the other members in the group. Components of Jigsaw include (a) specially designed materials ensuring that each member has unique information, and (b) team building and communication preparation, during which students role play, brainstorm about problem solving in group activity, and engage in preparatory group activities.

*Jigsaw II* was adapted from the original jigsaw and includes some features of STAD (Slavin, 1980). The students in Jigsaw II are assigned to teams as in STAD and are assigned to topics with which they are to become expert. Following study of their topic of expertise, the students return to their teams, meet in expert groups, report to their group members, take an individual quiz (which contributes to a team score), and receive both individual and team recognition. Brown and Campione (1994) employed a version of Jigsaw II in their research on "communi-

ties of learners" investigating the theme of interdependence in nature.

*Group investigation* (see S. Sharan & Hertz-Lazarowitz, 1980) proceeds in the following consecutive stages: (a) identifying the topic and organizing the pupils into research groups, based on shared interest in a topic; (b) planning the learning task, during which the members determine the subtopics for inquiry as well as the tasks appropriate to the inquiry; (c) carrying out the investigation, during which students gather information, analyze and evaluate their data, and reach conclusions; (d) preparing a final report, during which considerable attention is paid to the selection and organization of the information; (e) presenting the final report with the use of alternative presentation formats such as exhibits and skits; and (f) evaluation, which is done in collaboration with the teacher and students and includes evaluation of learning as well as affective outcomes.

In *Co-op Co-op* (described in Kagan, 1985), students work in cooperative groups toward the attainment of a goal that will help the other students in the class. Co-op Co-op begins with student-centered discussions to stimulate students' curiosity regarding an issue or topic. Students then are assigned to heterogeneous teams based on ability, gender, and ethnicity. As in Jigsaw, team-building activities occur, after which the team selects a topic so that each team in the class is responsible for one aspect of the unit. Within each team every student selects a subtopic on which he or she will become an expert. Students individually prepare themselves regarding their topic. The team then meets to prepare the joint presentation to the whole class. The whole-class presentation follows, with groups encouraged to use nondidactic presentation styles. Finally, multipronged evaluation occurs with teammates evaluating the work of their own members, classmates evaluating the presentations of the teams, and teachers (generally) evaluating the work of each individual student.

In subsequent sections of this chapter we will return to these forms of cooperative learning in discussing processes and outcomes.

*Collaboration.* In collaboration, the thinking is distributed among the members of the group. Although certain forms of cooperative learning can occur without collaboration, collaborative learning is generally assumed to subsume cooperation. Considerably less has been written about collaboration than about cooperation; however, the sense emerging from the literature is that the essence of collaboration is convergence—the construction of shared meanings for conversations, concepts, and experiences (A. L. Brown & Palincsar, 1989; Roschelle, 1992; Roth, 1992). Roschelle (1992), for example, argues that convergence is achieved through cycles of displaying, confirming, and repairing shared meanings. The iterative interactions lead to the joint use of meanings, meanings that are progressively constrained. The process of achieving consensus can also be considered the attainment of intersubjectivity, which Trevarthen (1980) defines as "both recognition and control of cooperative intentions and joint patterns of awareness" (p. 330).

The research methodology that has been used to examine collaborative learning is principally microgenetic analysis driven by questions regarding the processes whereby intersubjectivity is achieved or derailed. Examples of this research include the work of A. L. Brown and Campione (1990), Cobb, T. Wood, and Yackel (1991), Cooper, Marquis, and Edward (1986), Palincsar, Anderson, and David (1993), Roschelle (1992), Roth (1992), and Tharp and Gallimore (1988).

***Peer Response Groups in Writing.*** There is a significant history of interest in peer learning in the context of writing response groups—a history nicely captured in the work of DiPardo and Freedman (1987) and Gere (1987). The interest in peer collaboration during writing activity springs from the increased attention that has been paid to the inherently social nature of writing; that is, while working in groups, writers experience the processes of inquiry, clarification, and elaboration (among others) that are essential to successful writing. The assumption is that, in the context of group work, students are willing and able to provide each other with the support and assistance that are helpful to developing writers.

We present a few examples of research on peer writing groups to illustrate the issues and concerns central to this inquiry. Daiute and B. Dalton (1993) have examined the ways in which young children, 7 to 9 years old, bring diverse expertise to bear as they teach each other how to write stories. According to Daiute and Dalton, the peer collaboration process resembles the expert–novice collaboration one might observe between teacher and child, resulting in the generation of new story elements and the growth of mature writing strategies in the absence of formal instruction. In addition, they maintain that the shared perspective children may have (regarding language and life experiences) renders peers better collaborative writers than teachers. A similar observation was made by Parecki and Palincsar (1992) in their study of journal feedback sessions conducted in a special education setting for students with learning disabilities.

Kearney (1991) was interested in the influence that the teacher exerts on the discourse of peer writing groups. Apropos of her observations that (high school) students spent considerable time trying to make sense of the teacher's expectations as they wrote and revised their work, she referred to the teacher as "the absent presence" in writing groups.

In an effort to speak more definitively about the management and results of peer writing groups, Kinsler (1990) assigned college students to one of four conditions in supportive feedback sessions—writer/reader, unity/main idea, thesis support, or organization/coherence. The last three conditions paralleled topics that were part of the writing curriculum. For example, in the unity/main idea condition, the listener would identify the main idea and thesis statement of the essay and verify these with the author. Students listened from the perspective of their scripted roles and then provided the writers/readers with specific oral and written feedback. Kinsler observed that while supportive peer collaboration significantly improved the writers' use of thesis support statements, as well as the unity and organizational coherence of their essays, the collaboration process did not enhance the passing rate on the exit essay examination.

***Book Club.*** Another contemporary context for examining peer learning are student-led discussions regarding literature, referred to as the book club (S. McMahon, 1992; Raphael et al., 1992). Studies of book club indicate that students' interactions change as a consequence of the instructional focus (e.g., personal response, reading strategies), the group composition, and the activities surrounding the reading of the literature. These researchers reported that students adopted an array of roles in their small groups—roles that were fluid, depending on the mix of students. In addition, they found that students needed instruction on new interaction styles and time to allow their responses to develop (through reading, writing, and discussion), and that the quality of interactions was generally enhanced through the use of themes. Further, S. McMahon (1992) observed that when teachers returned to traditional instructional activities, students quickly reverted to their previous interactional styles, suggesting that group discussion norms run counter to those typically encountered in classrooms.

***Peer Learning in Whole-Class Contexts.*** A final form of peer learning that is receiving increased attention is the opportunity for peer learning in whole-class contexts. One example is the research of Hatano and Inagaki (1991), which examined the use of the Japanese science education method called hypothesis–experiment–instruction. The procedure includes the following sequence:

1. Pupils are presented with a question having three of four answer alternatives. The question specifies how to confirm which alternative is right.
2. Pupils are asked to choose one answer by themselves.
3. Pupils' responses, counted by a show of hands, are tabulated on the board.
4. Pupils are encouraged to explain and discuss their choices with one another.
5. Pupils are asked to choose an alternative again, with the invitation to change their choice.
6. Pupils are allowed to test their predictions by reading or conducting an investigation.

Hatano and Inagaki reported free-flowing discussions among groups of 40 to 45 students, especially in Step 4 of this process.

In peer learning in a whole-class context, the teacher assumes the role of moderator, working to encourage the horizontal exchange of information and to establish a norm whereby consensus emerges through peer interaction and not as a consequence of turning to a teacher who is regarded as the authority and source of right answers.

## Structural Approaches versus Forms of Peer Interaction: A Caveat

The terms used to classify approaches to peer learning do not necessarily define or correspond to the kinds of interaction occurring within them. A single classroom setting can give rise to interactions among students that vary in the equality of roles that students adopt (for example, equal influence vs. teacher–learner roles) and the mutuality of interaction (the extent to which students' discourse is extensive and connected; Damon & Phelps, 1989).

A study by Cooper, Marquis, and Edward (1986) illustrates the array of group forms that can arise naturally when collaborative interactions are encouraged as a means of accomplishing school learning. The setting was a Montessori elementary school attended by children ages 5 to 12 years, principally from white, middle-class families. The students were divided into two groups. The younger group consisted of 37 5- to 9-year-olds and the older group consisted of 31 7- to 12-year-olds. Students were grouped based not only on age but also on cognitive and social profiles. Using experimental, observational, and interview methodologies, Cooper et al. concluded that, in such a setting, a wide range of peer learning forms emerge. For example, some children worked alone, allowing others to assume the role of onlookers who made occasional comments. They also observed a parallel-coordinate form of interaction in which two or more children each worked on their own projects, exchanging information and occasionally helping one another concentrate on and accomplish individual goals. These interactions included both brief exchanges regarding task-relevant information as well as extraneous discussion. Cooper et al. used the term "guided" to describe those forms in which one child helped another, generally directing the other in accomplishing some activity. Yet another form of guidance, which they referred to as "executive guidance," was used to describe those situations in which one child directed another in teaching a third child. In collaborative interaction, children shared power in directing the interaction more equally, either through alternating or sharing the teacher role or by not assuming a clear leader–follower pattern. Thematic collaboration occurred when children collaborated in loosely associated projects that accomplished some superordinate goal. Differentiated collaboration referred to those occasions when students collaborated on a project but engaged in different interrelated tasks that accomplish a shared goal. Cooper et al. concluded from the interviews that were conducted along with the observations that an observer had to be well informed to be able to make a determination about the form of peer interaction because the form could not be determined simply by observation.

Although some approaches to peer-based learning may give rise to interaction that is higher in equality and mutuality than others (as argued by Damon & Phelps, 1989), Cooper et al.'s observations show that considerable variation in peer interaction may emerge within a single structure. Moreover, the forms of peer interaction that emerge within a single setting may be due in part to the structural aspects of the approach (e.g., presence or absence of group rewards, designated roles as tutor and tutee), but they may also arise from features of the classroom context that are not defined explicitly in the approach. Some possibilities include physical aspects, such as the resources with which the groups are working (e.g., one computer or multiple computers with community notebooks, a library full of readings or a single text), historical and temporal aspects (e.g., the success with which the learners have worked together in the past and the number of opportunities they have had to do so), situational aspects (e.g., being paired with a friend or foe), linguistic aspects (e.g., the spoken norms about group work and the explicitness with which social norms are part of the classroom discourse), and intraindividual aspects (e.g., individual achievement motivation).

## Comparisons of Peer-Based Approaches

Comparisons across studies of group learning, whether those studies were informed by developmental or motivational perspectives, are impeded by the use of different group structures, different tasks, different outcome measures, and different reward structures. Cooperative learning methods, for example, differ from each other and from traditional instruction in many ways, including opportunities to interact with peers, group goals, type and frequency of rewards, individual accountability, equal opportunities for success, team competition, task specialization, adaptation to individuals, training of teachers, prescriptiveness of instruction, and feedback to students about the functioning of their groups (Bossert, 1988–1989; Slavin, 1990b). Isolating the features of a collaborative setting that account for positive effects, then, is extremely difficult.

Adding to the complexity, a number of studies have found that students of some ability levels, predispositions to cooperate, or racial backgrounds may benefit from collaboration more than others. For example, Peterson, Janicki, & Swing (1981) found that high- and low-achieving students learned best in small-group settings and average achievers learned best working individually (partially confirmed by N. M. Webb & Kenderski, 1984). Others have reported interactions between instructional method and orientation toward working cooperatively with others, with students performing better when their social orientation was consistent with instruction. Students inclined to cooperate did best in cooperative learning, students inclined to work by themselves did best in traditional whole-class or individual settings, and students who preferred to compete with others did best in competitive settings (Dunn et al., 1990; Okebukola, 1986; S. Sharan & Shaulov, 1990). Differences of social orientation among different racial or ethnic groups may explain why some groups (e.g., African-American, Hispanic) often seem to benefit more from cooperative learning than other groups (e.g., European Americans; see review by Slavin, 1983a). Kagan, Zahn, Widaman, Schwarzwald, and Tyrrell (1985) suggest that the cooperative social orientation of Hispanic students, and to some extent African-American students (DeVoe, 1977; Richmond & Weiner, 1973), makes them especially receptive to the structure and requirements of cooperative learning settings, whereas the greater competitive orientation of European-American students (Kagan, 1984; Kagan & Knight, 1981) may enable them to thrive in traditional classroom instruction with individual work and competitive grading.

Still another difficulty in comparing studies of peer-based learning is that the focus of the research varies. Although the focus in research conducted from a motivational perspective has been on the outcomes of group learning, with little consideration for the thinking processes or problem-solving activities in which group members engaged (A. L. Brown & Palincsar, 1989; S. Sharan, 1980), research conducted from a developmental perspective has paid inadequate attention to the conditions under which learners are most likely to engage in the kinds of sustained interaction believed to enhance learning (Slavin, 1987).

Instead of cataloging the differences among peer-based learning approaches, the rest of this chapter will concentrate on features of the classroom context that have been shown in empirical studies to influence the interaction of students. Our

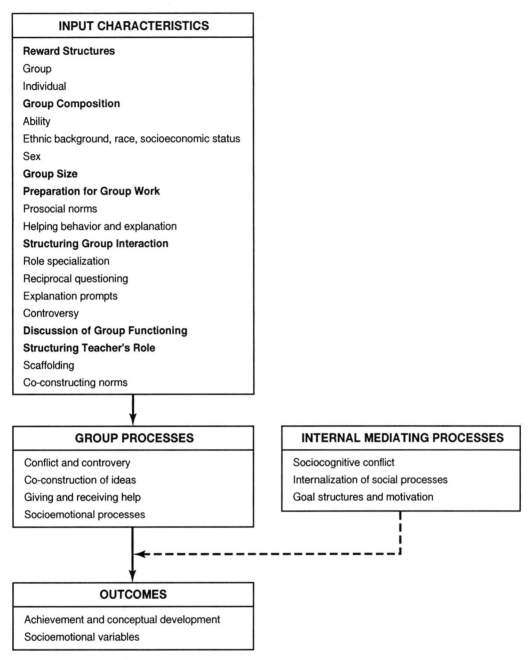

FIGURE 26–1. Input–Process–Outcome model of group processes in the classroom

review assigns equal importance to group processes and conditions that influence them.

## REPRESENTING THE RESEARCH LITERATURE BY AN INPUT–PROCESS–OUTCOME MODEL

Most of the rest of this chapter discusses the findings from empirical studies on group processes and learning in the classroom. A convenient way of representing the factors to be considered is the input–process–outcome model, shown in Figure 26–1. The input characteristics suggest the great variety of ways

in which structuring groups and group work have influenced group processes. The different kinds of group processes in turn influence a variety of outcomes. The figure also includes the internal mediating processes that are hypothesized to explain *how* group processes influence outcomes. These internal mediating processes, the same ones already discussed in this chapter, have only an indirect relation to processes and outcomes in this model because they are not directly observable. However, because these internal processes are essential for understanding how group processes operate in the classroom, they will be included in the discussion of group processes and outcomes.

The relations among input characteristics, group processes, and outcomes are the focus of the remaining sections of this chapter. Rather than follow this model from top to bottom, however, it is easier to describe the empirical research results from the bottom up. A description of outcomes helps delimit the research to be considered, and a description of group processes makes it simpler to present the research that has investigated ways of influencing those processes.

## Outcomes

Collaborating with others in the classroom can have a powerful effect on students' learning, motivation, and attitudes toward themselves and others. This section briefly summarizes the outcomes measured in empirical research of group processes in the classroom.

*Learning-Related Outcomes.* As mentioned earlier in the chapter, most contemporary research on group processes in the classroom focuses on learning-related outcomes. The studies vary in the breadth and depth of subject matter measured. In breadth, the measures range from tests of a specific concept (e.g., conservation of volume or number; Tudge & Rogoff, 1989) to achievement tests of whole curriculum units (e.g., LOGO computer programming; N. M. Webb, 1984a). The depth of measures ranges from automatized skills (e.g., spelling; Kagan et al., 1985) to complex concepts and reasoning (e.g., the processes of photosynthesis; Coleman, 1992).

The topics and subject matters vary widely. Studies of specific cooperative learning methods, for example, have measured vocabulary, spelling, rules of grammar, reading comprehension, listening comprehension and speaking ability in a foreign language, paraphrasing and explaining metaphors, identifying main ideas in reading passages, mathematics computation, knowledge of biology, geology, geography, genetics, and literature, and solving problems in mathematics, geography, chemistry, and computer programming (DeVries & Slavin, 1978; Kagan et al., 1985; R. T. Johnson et al., 1985; Lazarowitz, Baird, Hertz-Lazarowitz, & Jenkins, 1985; S. Sharan et al., 1985; Skon, D. W. Johnson, & R. T. Johnson, 1981; Stevens, Slavin, & Farnish, 1991; Tingle & Good, 1990). Additional concepts and topics measured in studies of collaborative learning include identifying place value in arithmetic (Saxe, 1992), performing arithmetic operations on the abacus (Hatano, 1988), examining relationships between matter and molecules (Palincsar et al., 1993), spatial perspective taking (Bearison, Magzament, & Filardo, 1986; Mugny & Doise, 1978), deducing chemicals in chemical reactions (E. A. Forman & Cazden, 1985), transformational geometry (E. Forman, 1989), deducing relationships between weight and distance from the fulcrum of a balance beam (Damon & Phelps, 1989), logical analysis (Light & Glachan, 1985), classification of forms according to shape and color (Kuhn, 1972), collaborative writing (Daiute, 1986; Gere, 1987), moral reasoning (Damon & Killen, 1982), errand planning (Gauvain & Rogoff, 1989), Lego model building (Azmitia, 1988), and medical procedures (Hythecker, Dansereau, & Rocklin, 1988). This list is by no means exhaustive, yet it shows the tremendous variety of topics and concepts investigated in collaborative learning research.

*Social, Motivational, and Attitudinal Outcomes.* Slavin (1990b) has reviewed the theoretical and research literature demonstrating the positive impact of cooperative learning on a wide variety of noncognitive outcomes, among them:

- Intergroup relations (improved attitudes and greater friendships among students of different race or ethnic backgrounds)
- Acceptance of mainstreamed academically handicapped students (reduced rejection, greater acceptance, and more friendships between handicapped and nonhandicapped students)
- Self-esteem (increased feelings of being liked by peers and greater confidence in students' own academic performance)
- Pro-academic peer norms (more perceived support from classmates)
- Locus of control (greater belief that students can control their own academic success through effort)
- Time on task and classroom behavior (more time spent engaged in academic tasks and increased class attendance)
- Liking of classmates and feeling liked by classmates (positive relationships and friendships among classmates)
- Cooperation, altruism, and the ability to take another's perspective (greater tendency to cooperate with others, make altruistic choices, and improved ability to identify others' viewpoints and understand their feelings)

Slavin also described some of the mechanisms accounting for these positive effects. Cooperative learning settings provide students from different backgrounds or with different characteristics opportunities to work together to achieve common goals, to get to know one another, and to work with each other as equals, conditions hypothesized by G. Allport (1954) to increase liking of others and to reduce prejudice. Most cooperative settings also satisfy the conditions for friendship formation and cohesion: contact, perceived similarity with others, participating in pleasant activities, and working toward common goals (A. J. Lott & B. E. Lott, 1965), all of which promote positive attitudes of students toward others.

The mechanisms accounting for the effects of collaboration on learning, social, motivational, and attitudinal outcomes are largely theoretical. "Black box" studies comparing the effects of different instructional methods on learning outcomes will not explain why effects arise. To understand why cooperative learning works, or works better for some students than for others, it is necessary to examine students' experiences in collaborative group settings. The group processes that may give rise to different outcomes are discussed next.

## Group Processes Promoting Learning and Cognitive Development

The processes operating in groups that influence learning and other outcomes are beginning to be explored systematically. This section describes empirical research that has linked the dynamics of classroom groups to learning outcomes. We focus mainly on observational research that has linked observations of group processes with learning and cognitive development.

*Conflict and Controversy.* As described previously, a leading theoretical perspective regarding the mechanisms by which learning occurs in group contexts is Piaget's model of sociocognitive conflict and learning. Interaction with others may produce discrepancies between a child's views and new information, giving rise to cognitive conflict within the child and leading the child to try out new ideas. One way in which internal cognitive conflict may be manifested in interaction with others is through overt conflict or controversy, during which individuals not only recognize that their beliefs are different from those of others but also confront others about their differences. Overt conflict encourages individuals to explain and justify their own positions, raises uncertainties about their beliefs, encourages individuals to seek new information to help resolve their disagreements and arguments, and helps them understand alternative points of view, all of which can promote learning (A. L. Brown & Palincsar, 1989; D. W. Johnson & R. T. Johnson, 1979).

The few studies that have systematically observed overt conflict and controversy found, however, that conflict does not necessarily promote learning or cognitive development. Two studies found little relationship between conflict and learning. Damon and Killen (1982) videotaped three-person groups of children aged 5 to 9 years as the children debated how to distribute money among members of their class. Conflict was not significantly related to advancement in moral reasoning, although there was some indication that children who exhibited overt conflict (disagreement, contradiction, contrary solutions) were least likely to show gains. Among four-person groups of second- and third-grade children working together to learn how to solve mathematics problems, Lindow, Wilkinson, and Peterson (1985) found that within-group participation in verbal disagreements was only marginally related to achievement. Students who disagreed more often than their teammates performed only marginally better than their teammates on the achievement test. Between-group differences did not occur: Groups with more disagreements and groups with fewer disagreements performed about the same.

Bearison, Magzamen, and Filardo (1986) reported a complex relationship between conflict and learning that may help explain the lack of relationship shown in the previous studies. Bearison et al. found a curvilinear relationship (inverted U-shaped curve) between conflict and cognitive gains among pairs of children aged 5 to 7 who were working collaboratively on spatial perspective problems (reconstructing a model of a house from different spatial perspectives). Students who engaged in infrequent or very frequent verbal disagreements gained less than students who engaged in a moderate amount of verbal disagreement. Infrequent conflict may reflect suppression of disagreements, either from the domination of one group member over the others (A. L. Brown & Palincsar, 1989) or from social pressures not to challenge others (D. W. Johnson & R. T. Johnson, 1979). Or it may reflect pseudoconsensus, another way of avoiding conflict in which students resolve their disagreements in ineffective ways. Brown and Palincsar (1989, p. 407) give an example of pseudoagreement between two students working on a conservation-of-length task: "When you are looking at it, it is bigger, but when I'm looking, they are just the same." Too much conflict, on the other hand, may prevent group members from seeking new information to resolve their disagreements. If they spend all of their time arguing, they may

never develop new insights. To better understand how different degrees of conflict may influence learning, it is important to document whether and how disagreements are resolved.

*Coconstruction of Ideas.* At the heart of Vygotsky's theory of how individuals internalize problem-solving processes initially carried out in social settings is the notion that students can coconstruct knowledge that they did not have prior to collaboration (Damon & Phelps, 1989). Several researchers have documented how coconstruction during peer collaboration improves learning. E. A. Forman and Cazden (1985), for example, described how two 9-year-old children developed sophisticated strategies for testing which chemical in a mixture accounted for a chemical reaction. The problem required the children to consider all possible combinations of a set of chemicals. During collaboration, the children developed a deductive procedure for generating all possible pairs of chemicals using complementary problem-solving roles (one child suggested combinations and the other gave guidance and made corrections). In time, both children internalized the deductive procedure for generating two-element combinations that they had developed collaboratively, and used it successfully to solve problems individually. In another study of mathematics learning using a game called Treasure Hunt, in which students make transactions using gold doubloons that represent denominations of 1, 10, 100, and 1,000, Saxe (1992) observed students coconstructing understanding of place value. By working together to determine how to represent the numerical values in gold doubloons, students came to realize the equivalence of different numbers (e.g., 1,000 is the same as 10 hundreds) and the meaning of the number in each place value. In other studies, researchers have observed instances of internalizing strategies developed during collaboration for a wide variety of tasks, including transformational geometry (determining which shadows could be projected from a given shape; E. Forman, 1989), moral reasoning (deciding how to distribute money among classmates; Damon & Killen, 1982), errand planning (Gauvain & Rogoff, 1989), the Tower of Hanoi problem (using a physical apparatus with three vertical pegs, requiring that three rings be moved from one peg to another with the constraint that a larger ring may not be placed over a smaller one; Glachan & Light, 1982), and multiplication of whole numbers (Yackel et al., 1991).

*Giving and Receiving Help.* Students working interactively can also learn by helping each other. Most research on the relationship between helping behavior and achievement has distinguished between explanations or elaborated help (e.g., detailed step-by-step descriptions of how to solve a problem) and nonelaborated help (e.g., the answer to a problem without any description of how to solve it; N. M. Webb, 1991). From a theoretical perspective, both the help giver and the help receiver stand to benefit from elaborated help. Giving explanations encourages the explainer to clarify and reorganize the material in new ways to make it understandable to others (Bargh & Schul, 1980). This cognitive restructuring may help the explainer to understand the material better, develop new perspectives, and recognize and fill in gaps in his or her understanding. By accommodating explanations to the difficulties of other students, helpers may construct more elaborate conceptualizations than they would when solving the problems for themselves (Benware & Deci, 1984; Yackel et al., 1991). The early work of Zajonc (1960) on "cognitive tuning" also showed that the prospect of having to explain material to someone else leads to more differentiated, complex, unified, and organized cognitive structures than does merely learning the material for oneself. The benefits of giving explanations go beyond the cognitive rehearsal involved in simply verbalizing material. Durling and Schick (1976), for example, found that vocalizing to a peer (presumably with the intent to teach that person) produced greater concept attainment than vocalizing to the experimenter (presumably only to demonstrate mastery of the material). The purpose of the communication, in this case helping others versus summarizing material learned, has more impact on cognitive restructuring than the act of verbalizing material itself.

Receiving explanations can benefit the receiver by filling in gaps in his or her understanding, correcting misconceptions, and strengthening connections between new information and previous learning (Mayer, 1984; Wittrock, 1990). Students may be even more effective explainers than adults because peers share a similar language and can translate difficult vocabulary and expressions into language that fellow students can understand (Noddings, 1985). Learning material at the same time as other students may help them tune into each other's misconceptions, so they may give more relevant explanations than adults can (Vedder, 1985; cf. Ellis & Rogoff, 1982, for a different perspective). Having their errors detected immediately helps make students aware of their misunderstanding. Further, students can control the pace of explanations (as well as the pace of group work) to better understand them.

Giving and receiving nonelaborated help, on the other hand, may have fewer benefits for the help giver and the help receiver. Giving nonelaborated help may not always involve cognitive restructuring or clarifying on the part of the helper, and receiving nonelaborated help will probably not enable students to correct their misconceptions or lack of understanding.

Most of the empirical results on the relationship between helping behavior and learning in small groups confirm the theoretical predictions for giving help. The vast majority of studies have reported significant positive correlations between giving explanations and achievement, and nonsignificant correlations between giving nonelaborated help and achievement (see reviews by N. M. Webb, 1989, 1991).

The results of several recent studies (N. M. Webb, 1992; N. M. Webb & Farivar, 1994; N. M. Webb, Troper, & Fall, 1995), however, raise questions about the relationship between giving nonelaborated help and learning. These studies found a positive relationship between giving correct answers and achievement. Part of the reason for the apparent discrepancies between the recent studies and earlier research may lie in the definition of what constituted giving an answer. In the recent studies, students were coded as giving answers only when they gave clear evidence of having solved the problem themselves or actively coconstructing the entire solution with other students. These students probably carried out reconceptualization and clarification in the process of solving the problem. That is, these students may have spontaneously generated "self-explanations" that helped them to resolve conflicts in their own minds and to construct an understanding of the problem (Chi & Bassock,

1989; Chi, Bassock, Lewis, Reimann, & Glaser, 1989). In at least some of the earlier studies, in contrast, students were coded as giving answers even if they had not participated fully in solving the problem. Repeating solutions that other students had largely carried out probably involved little reconceptualization and little constructive activity (Chan, Burtis, Scardamalia, & Bereiter, 1992), and would account for the near-zero correlations between giving nonelaborated help and achievement in those studies.

To help clarify the effects of giving nonelaborated help, it is important for future studies to be very specific when defining nonelaborated help. Comparing the achievement of students required to explain how they solved problems with that of students required to solve problems and give answers would clarify this issue even further.

Empirical results on the relationship between receiving explanations and achievement are mixed, with many studies reporting no significant relationship (N. M. Webb, 1989, 1991). These results suggest that receiving explanations is not always sufficient for learning. Vedder (1985) proposed a condition that must be met in order for explanations to be effective for learning: Students must be given, and use, opportunities to apply the explanations to solve problems or perform tasks for themselves. Unless they perform the work without assistance, students may not realize that they are still confused, and the group may come to the wrong conclusion about whether students need additional help. Two empirical studies have confirmed Vedder's (1985) prediction. N. M. Webb (1992) and N. M. Webb et al. (1995) reported that students who applied the explanations to the work at hand were much more likely to learn the material than students who merely listened to the explanations without trying to use them to solve the problems or complete the work. Moreover, student application of the explanations received was a much better predictor of learning than the level of elaboration of the explanations themselves.

Finally, most empirical studies have reported nonsignificant correlations between receiving nonelaborated help and achievement, supporting the theoretical predictions (N. M. Webb, 1989, 1991). However, when the nature of the request for help was taken into account, an interesting pattern emerged. When students indicated a need for elaborated help, either by requesting explanations or by making errors, receiving nonelaborated help was detrimental for achievement. The more frequently students asked for elaborated help and failed to receive it, the worse was their achievement. Not only would nonelaborated help leave students with their confusion and misconceptions intact, but it may have had negative motivational effects as well, causing students to stop asking for help and stop trying to understand.

Although research shows that giving and receiving elaborated explanations during collaboration influence learning, albeit in complex ways, an unanswered question concerns the nature of elaboration that students should be encouraged to give others. Some possibilities (Coleman, 1992; King, 1992; Palincsar et al., 1993; Shavelson, N. M. Webb, Stasz, & McArthur, 1988; N. M. Webb, 1991) include:

- Using multiple representations to explain a concept (e.g., geometric figures, pictures, mathematical symbols, algebraic expressions, numerical examples to explain mathematical problems)

- Showing how to coordinate and translate among different representations to solve problems
- Giving specific examples to illustrate general concepts
- Translating unusual or unfamiliar vocabulary into familiar terms
- Creating analogies to relate new ideas to familiar concepts
- Describing the relationship between different concepts
- Providing detailed descriptions of how to perform tasks
- Providing detailed justifications of the reasoning used to solve problems
- Using observations, data, evidence, and background knowledge to support one's opinions and beliefs
- Comparing real-world experiences with information, explanations, and predictions learned in class

Although many researchers are confident that carrying out these elaboration activities will benefit the explainer (a proposal discussed further in a later section), the benefit for students *receiving* them remains untested.

***Social-Emotional Processes.*** Groups are social systems. Students' interaction with others is not only guided by the learning task, it is also shaped by their emotions, perceptions, and attitudes. Some social-emotional processes are beneficial for learning, others are not.

Beneficial Processes. Many cooperative learning methods are based on motivational perspectives. According to the motivational theory of Deutsch (1949), when groups work toward a common goal, students will praise, encourage, and support each other's efforts, resulting in greater effort, and greater liking of the task and other students (see also D. W. Johnson & R. T. Johnson, 1985b). Although some researchers have found that working in cooperative groups increases students' motivation to learn (as measured, for example, by perseverance at the task) and that students who are highly motivated to learn show high achievement (S. Sharan & Shaulov, 1990), the precise link between group processes and motivation is unknown. Finding that receiving praise, encouragement, and support during group work directly affects motivation to learn would constitute powerful support for motivational theory.

Debilitating Processes. Not all groups function in ways that are optimal for learning and cognitive development. Although social and organizational psychologists have documented a great many debilitating processes that inhibit group functioning and performance in out-of-school settings (Hackman, 1990; Hare, 1992), only a few researchers have investigated debilitating processes in educational settings that may be detrimental for learning. Salomon and Globerson (1989) observed four such processes among pairs of students working on reading and writing tasks at the computer. In the "free rider" effect (Kerr & Bruun, 1983), also called "diffusion of responsibility" (Slavin, 1990b), one or more group members sat back and let others do the work. The free rider effect sometimes turned into the "sucker effect" when the group members who were doing all

of the work discovered that they had been taken for a free ride and started to contribute less to group work to avoid being a sucker. The third effect was dominance of some group members over others, with high-status students having undue influence over group functioning and low-status students prevented from making contributions or obtaining the help that they needed (see Dembo & McAuliffe, 1987). By not allowing input from others, domineering members may also lead the group off track, pursuing the wrong task or incorrect solutions to problems. Finally, Salomon and Globerson (1989) observed some pairs deciding to go through the motions without actually performing the assigned task ("ganging up on the task"), such as pretending that they were busy without actually working on the assignment. P. Deering (1989) also observed debilitating processes that may in part be due to group members' personalities or behavior styles, such as aggressiveness and hostility leading to unconstructive and bitter arguments, or passivity and acquiescence leading to premature agreement on answers.

Another debilitating process that may arise in a group setting is failure to seek help when it is needed. Insights into when students do and do not seek help come from Nelson-Le Gall's comprehensive, five-step model of children's help seeking (Nelson-Le Gall, 1981, 1985; Nelson-Le Gall, Gumerman, & Scott-Jones, 1983) (Figure 26–2). First, students must be aware that they need help. Students may fail to realize that they do not understand the material or cannot perform the task if they do not know their own limitations or do not appreciate the complexity of the task (Nelson-Le Gall et al., 1983). They may watch their teammates solve a problem or accomplish a task and assume that they can do it too, without attempting it for themselves (N. M. Webb, 1991).

Second, even if students are aware that they need help, they may decide not to seek it for fear of being judged incompetent and undesirable as a teammate. They may not want to feel indebted to those giving the help or feel obliged to reciprocate the help. Students may believe that help seeking is undesirable (as a result of classroom norms to be quiet and work alone without disturbing others, or sex-typed role norms that view help seeking as more appropriate for females than males) or may have received unsatisfactory responses to previous help-seeking attempts (e.g., rebukes, responses that did not aid understanding). Finally, they may believe that no one in the group has the competence or resources to help or that responses will not be helpful; or they may lack motivation or a sense of responsibility to do the work (Cook, 1986; Graham & Barker, 1990; Nelson-Le Gall et al., 1983; Newman, 1990; N. M. Webb, 1991). The best way to pinpoint why students decide not to seek help may be through introspective or stimulated recall techniques in which students are shown videotapes of their behavior (e.g., appearing to be confused but not asking for help) and are asked what they were thinking at the time.

Third, students must be able to identify someone who can provide help. Students may select helpers who are nice or kind, or have high status, rather than those who have task-relevant skills (Dembo & McAuliffe, 1987; Nelson-Le Gall et al., 1983).

Fourth, students must use effective strategies to elicit help. The nature of the questions that students ask each other has important effects on the kind of response given. Wilkinson and colleagues have repeatedly shown that requests for help that are explicit, precise, and direct will be more likely to elicit

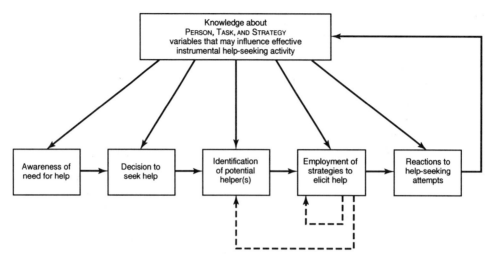

FIGURE 26–2. Nelson-Le Gall's Model of Help-Seeking Processes (Nelson-LeGall et al., 1983. Reprinted by permission)

explanations than vague and indirect questions (Peterson, Wilkinson, Spinelli, & Swing, 1984; Wilkinson, 1985; Wilkinson & Calculator, 1982a, 1982b; Wilkinson & Spinelli, 1983; see also N. M. Webb et al., 1992; Webb & Kenderski, 1984). Of course, the nature of a student's question is not the only factor that will determine the nature of the response. The group's perception of the reason for the request may also influence the response given. Weiner (1980) found that requests attributed to a lack of ability (not under the student's control) were more likely to elicit help than requests attributed to lack of effort (under the student's control). Students who appear to be loafing may be less likely to receive adequate help than those who appear to be working hard.

Finally, students must be able to assess the effectiveness of the help they receive and, if necessary, reevaluate their choice of helper or strategies for obtaining help. If students' efforts to obtain satisfactory explanations continue to fail, however, students may give up because they have lost faith that the group can or is willing to help, or because they do not want to antagonize others (Nelson-Le Gall et al., 1983; N. M. Webb, 1991).

As Salomon and Globerson (1989) point out, most socioemotional effects arise from the evolution of the group as a social system. Group members become interdependent, and individuals' behaviors and cognitions influence those of others in reciprocal fashion. Patterns of communication develop over time, instead of being isolated sets of "unrelated questions and answers, queries and responses," so that beneficial and debilitating processes may not occur within the time frame of most short-term studies (Salomon & Globerson, 1989, p. 93). Now that long-term programs of collaborative work are in place in many classrooms, it should be possible to study the effects of beneficial and debilitating processes on learning and cognitive development.

## Structuring Groups and Group Work

Although the exact mechanisms linking students' experiences in classroom groups to their learning, conceptual development, and social-emotional outcomes are complex and not yet well understood, few would dispute that group interaction and mediating processes have major influences on outcomes of group work. How can we predict the nature of group interaction and mediating processes that will occur in any particular group setting? Even more important, how can we structure groups and group work to produce the kinds of interaction that are advantageous for learning and other desired outcomes? This section describes the features of group work that have been shown to influence group processes: reward or incentive structure, composition of small groups, group size, training in communication skills, structuring the task to require certain kinds of interaction (role specialization, reciprocal questioning, controversy versus concurrence seeking), requiring discussion of group functioning, and structuring the teacher's role.

***Reward or Incentive Structure.*** A controversial way of manipulating group structure is through the use of extrinsic group rewards or incentives. American classrooms have typically rewarded and graded students on the basis of their own individual performance (individual rewards). Individuals may compete against each other as in traditional grading "on the curve" (an individual-competitive reward structure) or individuals may be compared only with their own previous performance (an individualistic reward structure, Johnson & Johnson, 1985a). From a motivational perspective, individual rewards are thought to be counterproductive to cooperative group functioning. Students are discouraged from helping others for two reasons. First, helping others may reduce one's own chance of receiving a good reward or grade. Second, giving help reduces time available to do one's own work (see especially D. W. Johnson & R. T. Johnson, 1975a,b).

To counter these detrimental tendencies, many, although not all, cooperative learning methods use group rewards. Groups are rewarded on the basis of the group's performance and everyone in the group gets the same reward. Group rewards can be based on individual learning or on a group product. With group rewards based on individual learning, students' scores on a learning measure administered individually are combined to form a group score and every member of the group receives that group score. For example, the mean of group members' quiz scores may serve as the basis for special awards, prizes, or privileges for the entire group. Alternatively, groups can be evaluated on the basis of a single product (e.g., worksheet, test, presentation, report). Groups may compete against each other for rewards (intergroup competition) or they may be compared to their own previous performance.

Group rewards (whether competitive or not) are thought to improve group functioning by increasing individual accountability: students hold themselves and each other accountable for their learning and this motivates them to contribute to group work, to work hard, and to help others. These behaviors increase the chance of a favorable group outcome and, consequently, a favorable reward for each group member. In addition to the cognitive benefits of helping each other, mutual help also leads to feelings of mutual support, liking, and acceptance, and continued interest and persistence on the task (D. W. Johnson & R. T. Johnson, 1987).

On the other hand, group rewards may also generate processes that are detrimental for group functioning. One criticism of group rewards, whether based on individual learning or on the group product, is that they may lead students to place extrinsic value on cooperation and learning; students may help each other only as the means to an external reward rather than valuing helping each other and learning for their own sakes (Damon & Phelps, 1989). Others worry about the impact of team failure on interpersonal relations and group functioning. C. Ames (1981), for example, manipulated the performance of otherwise comparable groups so that half would succeed at the task and win a prize and half would fail to reach the goal and thus fail to win the prize. The failing groups showed lower self-perceptions of their ability and lower feelings of satisfaction than groups who succeeded. Ames suggested that, because group failure makes the unequal contributions of team members particularly salient, high performers may blame low performers for the group's failure.

Group rewards based on the quality of the group product are subject to an additional criticism. Slavin (1987) argues that rewarding groups on the basis of a group product (e.g., single report, worksheet, or project) fails to promote individual accountability. Some group members can escape responsibility for contributing to the group by letting others do the work (the "free rider" effect [Kerr & Bruun, 1983], or "diffusion of responsibility" [Slavin, 1990b]). Some cooperative learning methods that use group products counter these detrimental tendencies by requiring all students to assume responsibility for part of the task (e.g., Group Investigation, S. Sharan & Hertz-Lazarowitz, 1980). Recognizing the potential danger that students may master only their part of the task, Maskit (1986; described in Hertz-Lazarowitz, 1992), created an adaptation of Group Investigation called the Circle, in which every group member studied all of the material before selecting a part of it to specialize in for the group product.

Up to this point, the debate has been largely theoretical. Few studies have systematically compared different incentive structures while holding constant other features of group work, such as the content and specific learning task students work on, the responsibility of each student, instructions for interacting

in teams, and the presence or absence of competition among teams. Although the few studies that have controlled other features of the cooperative setting generally find greater achievement with group rewards than with individual rewards (Slavin, 1983b, 1989, 1990b), the reasons for those results are not clear. The little available empirical evidence on group functioning in those studies suggests that cooperative learning with group rewards promotes more peer helping than cooperative learning with individual rewards (e.g., Slavin, 1978a, 1978b, 1978c; Wodarski, Hamblin, Buckholdt, & Ferritor, 1973), but the nature of the helping behavior is unclear.

Only one study has explored how group rewards influence specific kinds of helping behavior, most important, the level of elaboration in students' responses to requests for help. In an 11-week study of seventh-grade mathematics, Chang (1993) compared peer interaction and learning in classes using cooperative learning with group rewards and classes using cooperative learning with individual rewards. Whereas most studies used group scores as the basis of recognition in the class, Chang factored group scores into students' grades in the course: 30% of students' final grades were based on the average of their team's average scores across nine quizzes administered individually during the semester. Classes using these high-stakes group rewards tended to show higher achievement and to engage in more explaining than classes using individual rewards (the students' own grades on the quizzes). However, students in the group reward condition also reported more guilt and shame than students in the individual reward condition, possibly the result of the greater peer pressure they reported feeling. These results suggest that high-stakes group rewards may produce a trade-off between more elaborated explanations and increased learning, on the one hand, and negative socioemotional effects on the other. Whether lower-stakes group rewards, such as recognizing high-performing teams in class newsletters or basing group rewards on the quality of the group product instead of individual learning, would have similar effects on group dynamics, achievement, and socioemotional outcomes has yet to be investigated.

The Chang (1993) study and other research just described focused on extrinsic rewards, both group and individual. In light of many researchers' concerns that extrinsic rewards may undermine intrinsic motivation (e.g., Damon & Phelps, 1989; Lepper, 1983), it is important to compare the nature of group processes across conditions with no extrinsic rewards as well as with different types of extrinsic rewards. Partially in response to this issue, Meloth and P. D. Deering (1992) compared peer group discussions and reading comprehension in two cooperative learning treatments, one with extrinsic group rewards and one with no rewards except verbal praise and feedback from the teacher. In the group reward condition, individuals' scores were summed to form a team score. On a classroom poster, teams were designated as "super," "great," or "good" based on their improvement from week to week. Their study was not designed to constitute a clean comparison of extrinsic group rewards and no extrinsic rewards because the nature of instruction was somewhat different in the two conditions: Teachers in the group reward condition were trained to use direct instruction, whereas teachers in the no-reward condition were trained to direct students' discussions toward substantive task content. Nevertheless, the results were consistent with what critics of extrinsic rewards would have predicted. Students in the no-reward condition focused more on their discussions on concepts and strategies and less on facts, and obtained higher reading comprehension scores, than did the students in the reward condition. To provide a comprehensive picture of the role of extrinsic and intrinsic rewards, further research should manipulate the reward structure separately from other features of instruction, and should include extrinsic individual rewards in the comparisons among reward structures.

### Group Composition: Characteristics of Groups and Group Members.
Teachers often ask how they should assign students to collaborating groups in their classrooms. Many cooperative learning methods recommend that groups be formed heterogeneously to reflect the diversity of ability, gender, and ethnic background in the class. The reasons include maximizing the opportunities for peer tutoring and support, improving cross-race and cross-sex relations, ensuring that every group has at least one student who can do the work (Kagan, 1992), and making groups comparable for fair intergroup competition (Slavin, 1990b). But whether heterogeneous groups optimize student learning has rarely been investigated empirically. The few systematic comparisons of different kinds of group compositions have examined ability, ethnic background, and gender. With few exceptions, these studies show that students' behavior and experiences are shaped by a combination of their own characteristics and those of the group they are in. The same student may behave differently in different groups, making it impossible to separate the effects of individual and group characteristics on behavior and outcomes. The following discussion of the effects of group composition on group processes and learning, then, integrates effects of characteristics of individuals and groups on learning outcomes.

Ability. One of the primary arguments for using heterogeneous ability groups is to benefit low-ability students, who can learn from their more able peers. Theoretical support comes from developmental theories of children's concept development. Vygotsky (1978) argued that social interaction is more likely to be beneficial when the child's partner is more competent and provides assistance within the child's "zone of proximal development," the difference between what the child can achieve independently and what he or she can accomplish with help from an adult or a more capable peer. According to Vygotsky, the help must be at a more advanced level than the child can already perform independently. But the help cannot be too advanced or the child will not be able to understand it or use it to solve the problem. By practicing skills with support during collaboration, the child gradually internalizes them so he or she can perform them without assistance, and they become part of his or her individual repertoire.

Proposing somewhat different processes about the benefits of social interaction, Piaget (1932) theorized that interacting with others forces children to confront perspectives that conflict with their own and helps them to correct their own misconceptions and develop more advanced concepts. Working with more able peers is more likely to produce this "disequilibrium" than working with peers of similar ability or cognitive development.

Research on concept development in children working in collaborative pairs provides empirical evidence of the benefits

of heterogeneous pairing on the cognitive development of low-ability students. Typically, pairs of children work on conservation tasks: They discuss whether some characteristics of objects (e.g., the volume of liquid) remain the same when others (e.g., the width or height of the container) change. When children who have not yet learned the principle of conservation are paired with children who have mastered it to solve tasks requiring conservation, they generally gain in conservation skills, compared to nonconservers paired with other nonconservers (Bell et al., 1985; Doise & Mugny, 1984; Mugny & Doise, 1978; Murray, 1982; Perret-Clermont, 1980), although there are exceptions (G. J. Ames & Murray, 1981; Glachan & P. H. Light, 1982).

Research on nonconservation tasks and in larger groups has also found that low-ability students learn more in heterogeneous groups than in homogeneous groups. Azmitia (1988) reported that novice children paired with expert children learned how to build Lego models better than novices paired with other novices. Using a mathematical balance beam task in which students had to consider simultaneously the number of weights and the distance from the fulcrum, Tudge (1989) found that students with less understanding of the variables influencing balance advanced more when paired with students who had more understanding than when paired with students who had similar understanding. In four-person groups, less able students working with more able students learned how to solve novel mathematical problems (N. M. Webb, 1980) and solved problems using a computer-based fictitious symbol system (Hooper & Hannafin, 1988) better than less able students working with other less able students. Other studies, however, found heterogeneous grouping to be no more effective than homogeneous grouping for low-ability or low-achieving students (e.g., Hooper, Ward, Hannafin, & Clark, 1989).

Some of these studies have systematically observed group interaction to shed light on how low-ability students benefited by working with more capable peers. N. M. Webb (1980) found that low-ability students working on novel mathematics problems received more explanations in heterogeneous groups than in homogeneous groups. In homogeneous groups, low-ability students tended not to exchange correct explanations, probably because they lacked sufficient skills. In Azmitia's (1988) study of Lego model building, novice children paired with expert children also received more explanations and demonstrations than novices paired with other novices. In Tudge's (1989) study of children working with a mathematical balance beam, lower ability students paired with higher ability students were likely to be exposed to reasoning at a higher level than they could generate otherwise.

Other studies have examined group dynamics to explain why low-ability students benefited from some kinds of heterogeneous groups but not others. Mugny and Doise (1978) described group processes occurring in pairs of students learning how to reconstruct models of a village with different spatial orientations; these processes, Mugny and Doise proposed, explained why low-ability students made significant gains when they worked with medium-ability students, but not when they worked with high-ability students. By verbalizing their strategies for solving the problem, as well as their doubts and difficulties, and by allowing low-ability students to participate in the collaboration, medium-ability students gave low-ability students opportunities to learn the strategies. High-ability students, in contrast, dominated group work and rarely explained to low-ability students how they solved the problems, so that low-ability students could not learn their strategies. Even when high-ability students did provide explanations, they may have been outside the zone of proximal development of low-ability students. Low-ability students may have found it easier to understand the explanations given by medium-ability students. Mugny and Doise's (1978) findings show that it is important for the low-ability student to participate in the group's collaboration. They also show that while assigning low-ability students to heterogeneous groups provides opportunities for assistance and shared collaboration, it does not guarantee them.

Although most educators recognize the potential benefits of heterogeneous ability grouping for low-ability students, such groupings are often criticized for "holding back" high-ability students (Oakes, 1990). Empirical evidence about high-ability students' achievement in heterogeneous groups usually does not bear out this fear, however. In most empirical studies, high-ability students have performed equally well on achievement tests after working in heterogeneous and homogeneous groups (e.g., Azmitia, 1988; Hooper & Hannafin, 1988; Hooper et al., 1989; Skon et al., 1981). Moreover, one study found that high-ability students learned *more* in heterogeneous groups than in homogeneous groups (N. M. Webb, 1980). In heterogeneous groups, high-ability students often assumed the role of teacher and explained the material to other group members, typically the low-ability students. Other studies have also demonstrated the tendency of high-ability students to adopt the role of explainer (e.g., Bereiter & Scardamalia, 1989; see also review by N. M. Webb, 1991). In homogeneous groups, in contrast, high-ability students exchanged relatively few explanations, apparently because they assumed that everyone was competent enough to master the material without help.

The tendency for high-ability students to adopt a leadership role in heterogeneous groups is not necessarily based on their competence as measured by ability and achievement tests. Instead, it may be due to perceived competence, which may be related to actual ability weakly or not at all. Webb and Kenderski (1984) found that relative ability within the group was a significant predictor of giving explanations whereas absolute ability was not. Similarly, Cohen et al. (1990, p. 207) reported that students identified by their classmates as "best at math and science" talked more and offered more assistance than students with lower perceived competence. Perceived competence has been shown to predict behavior even when it had no relation at all to actual competence. Dembo & McAuliffe (1987) created an artificial ability variable by assigning students fictitious scores on a pretest. When assigned to heterogeneous groups, "more-able" students initiated more activity and gave more help than did "less-able" students.

Whereas heterogeneous ability grouping may benefit low-ability students and at least not disadvantage high-ability students, it may put medium-ability students at risk. High-ability and low-ability students in such groups often form a teacher–learner relationship, excluding medium-ability students from group interaction, with negative consequences for their achievement (N. M. Webb, 1989). In homogeneous groups and heterogeneous groups with a narrower range of ability than in the whole class (medium-ability and low-ability students in a group; or medium-ability and high-ability students in a group), in contrast, there are no obvious "middle" students, and medium-ability students can participate as teacher, learner, or collaborator. Medium-ability students in wide-range heterogeneous groups (highs, mediums, and lows) have been shown to give and receive fewer explanations than high-ability and low-ability students in these groups, and fewer than medium-ability students in homogeneous groups or in narrow-range heterogeneous groups. Consequently, the achievement of medium-ability students is higher in homogeneous and narrow-range heterogeneous groups than in wide-range heterogeneous groups (see review by N. M. Webb, 1991).

The studies described here show that few group compositions are optimal for all students. Heterogeneous grouping may benefit some students; more homogeneous grouping may benefit others.

Ethnic Background, Race, and Socioeconomic Status. One of the initial goals of cooperative learning theory and research was to promote interethnic integration and improved cross-race relations in multiethnic classrooms and schools (S. Sharan et al., 1985). Specifically, investigators hoped to design social settings that satisfied G. Allport's (1954) three requirements for reducing intergroup prejudice in multiethnic settings: "(1) [that] members of the different groups experience direct and unmediated contact, (2) [that] the interaction occurs under conditions of equal status and cooperative interaction, and (3) [that] the contact receives clear sanction by the people in authority" (Sharan et al., 1985, p. 314). Peer-directed, cooperative heterogeneous groups with respect to ethnic background and race are thought to satisfy these conditions.

Although peer-directed heterogeneous groups may promote face-to-face contact among students from different groups, the condition of equal-status interaction may be very difficult to fulfill. Ethnic background and race may serve as status characteristics that greatly influence interaction in heterogeneous small groups. According to expectations states theory, when group members do not have a clear way to judge each other's competence on the task, they will use other "socially evaluated" characteristics (such as ethnic background, race, and gender), called diffuse status characteristics, to form their judgments. When group members do not know each other, these status characteristics will determine relative influence in the group (Berger, Rosenholtz, & Zelditch, 1980).

There is ample evidence that ethnic background and race operate as status characteristics in multiracial groups in the classroom, especially in laboratory studies where students do not know each other. White students tend to be more active and influential than minority students, while minority students tend to be less assertive and more anxious, to talk less, and to contribute fewer ideas than white students (Cohen, 1982).

Using an approach called expectation training, Elizabeth Cohen and her colleagues were able to reduce the dominance of high-status students in multiracial groups in controlled experiments (Cohen, 1973; Cohen & Roper, 1972; Cohen, Lockheed, & Lohman, 1976). To increase the competence of low-status students and to increase the high-status students' perceptions of the competence of low-status students, low-status students (e.g., black, Mexican-American, Middle Eastern) received special training on academic and nonacademic tasks and then taught high-status students (e.g., white, Western) how to do the tasks. All students then worked on unrelated tasks in multiracial groups. Throughout several weeks of work in multiracial groups, high-status and low-status students showed equal rates of task-related talk. The important feature of this training program was changing high-status students' perceptions of the competence of low-status students. Increasing the competence of low-status students without also manipulating the high-status students' expectations of low-status students' performance did not equalize interaction among students.

Also sensitive to the relationship between status and power in groups, N. Miller and Harrington (1990) caution teachers to be careful about how they form heterogeneous groups. They are particularly critical of assignment procedures that make it obvious that groups were constructed on the basis of social characteristics (such as race), suggesting instead that it would be preferable to use random grouping or to form groups that are diverse in task-relevant skills rather than in social characteristics. When using social characteristics to form groups, they suggest subtle ways of attaining heterogeneity that may help make those characteristics less salient. For example, students could vary on different social characteristics simultaneously, such as a black male, a white male, a black female, and a white female, instead of two black females and two white males. Greater diversity within a group (such as including Asian, Hispanic, white, and black students in a group instead of only Asian and black students) would make that characteristic less salient to group members. And "solo status," such as a single minority student, should be avoided because it calls attention to that social characteristic. By making differences in social characteristics less salient, it may be possible to reduce inequalities in group interaction that would otherwise arise.

Gender. There is considerable evidence that gender also operates as a diffuse status characteristic, particularly among adults, with men being more active and influential than women in mixed-sex groups (Lockheed, Harris, & Nemceff, 1983), although recent work suggests that only men, not women, behave as if sex were a status characteristic (Smith-Lovin & Brody, 1989). Evidence emerging over the past decade suggests that gender also influences children's cross-sex behavior and attitudes, with boys dominating interaction in mixed-sex groups (Hazelwood et al., 1992; Lockheed & Harris, 1984).

Recent studies of interactions in mixed-sex groups suggest, however, that the specific gender composition of the group may influence the behavior of group members. In a comparison of three kinds of mixed-sex groups (two females and two males, three females and one male, and three males and one female), N. M. Webb (1984b) found that group composition influenced both students' behavior and achievement. In groups with an equal number of girls and boys, girls and boys showed similar interaction patterns and similar achievement. In majority-male groups and majority-female groups, however, girls were less successful than boys in obtaining answers to their questions and learned less as a result. The mechanisms producing these results were different in the two group compositions. In majority-male groups, the boys tended to ignore the girl in the group. In majority-female groups, girls directed most of their requests for help to the boy in the group, who tended not to answer their questions.

Interestingly, a similar study in the same school during the same year, but with mostly low-achieving black students instead of relatively high-achieving white students, found no significant differences between males and females on any interaction or achievement measure, and no effect of the gender composition of the group (N. M. Webb & Kenderski, 1985). Corroborating evidence that ethnic background can mediate the effects of gender on interactions in mixed-sex groups comes from Grant (1986). From observations of 15 elementary school classrooms, Grant (1986, p. 27) concluded that sex differentiates peer relationships more for white students than for black students: "Cross-gender interactions among whites more so than blacks encourage white girls to play 'service' roles to white males. Black students' peer interactions are more egalitarian at all grade levels. Even though black girls are insulted and asked to play 'service' roles, they resist." These studies suggest the intriguing notion that the function of gender in peer interactions may not be the same for different ethnic groups.

In summary, the research on the effects of group composition on group processes and learning outcomes shows that the makeup of a collaborating group has profound implications for the experiences of students in it. It also shows that determining the optimal assignment of students to groups is no easy matter. Groups can vary on so many variables simultaneously that it is difficult to unravel the relative impact of each one.

*Group Size.* Most cooperative learning methods advocate using four-person groups. But is one group size better than another for promoting beneficial kinds of peer interaction or for enhancing learning? Very few studies have compared interaction and learning in groups of different sizes. This issue has been of concern mainly in computer learning settings, where group size influences students' access to the computer. Not surprisingly, individual access to the keyboard decreases as the size of the group increases. Further, students in pairs and triads have been shown to interact more than students in quads (Trowbridge & Durnin, 1984a, 1984b). The unequal patterns of participation between quads and other groups did not translate into achievement differences, however. Students showed equal achievement across group sizes. Evidence about differences in behavior between pairs and triads is mixed. Guntermann and Tovar (1987) showed similar patterns of task-related and socioemotional verbal interaction and achievement in two-person and three-person groups learning LOGO. Two other studies suggested a specific difference between interaction in these group sizes: Students in triads learning LOGO often ignored teammates' questions (N. M. Webb, 1984b), but students in dyads learning BASIC rarely did so (N. M. Webb, Ender, & Lewis, 1986). Whether working on a computer or not, larger groups make it possible for students to shirk responsibility for answering questions.

*Preparation for Group Work.* All of the ways to structure groups and group work described above influence group processes, but not necessarily in predictable ways. Researchers have recently designed ways to shape the nature of group interaction more directly by preparing students for group work. One approach focuses mainly on developing norms for prosocial behavior. The other adds instruction in specific helping skills known to influence learning.

Developing Cooperative and Prosocial Norms. In many classroom settings, students are discouraged from interacting with their classmates, or even forbidden to do so, and consequently have little opportunity to develop skills they need to work effectively with others. When given work to do collaboratively, then, students will not necessarily behave in ways that are productive for learning or even for completing the task. Instead of listening to others, allowing everyone to participate, and resolving disagreements in constructive ways, students may try to bully others, dominate group work without listening to others or letting them participate, sit back and let others do all of the work, or criticize others in hurtful ways.

To help prepare students for working with others, many cooperative learning methods have students carry out activities to establish norms for cooperative behavior in the classroom and to help students develop and practice communication skills (e.g., Learning Together, D. W. Johnson, R. T. Johnson, Holubec, & Roy, 1984; Group Investigation, S. Sharan & Y. Sharan, 1976; Co-op Co-op, Kagan, 1992).

Some entire programs are built around prosocial development. For example, the Child Development Program developed in San Ramon, California (D. Solomon et al., 1985; D. Solomon, Watson, Schaps, Battistich, & J. Solomon, 1990) builds classroom instruction around five components designed to strengthen children's prosocial orientation:

1. Helping activities—classroom and schoolwide activities in which children help others
2. Highlighting prosocial values, such as kindness, fairness, consideration, responsibility, and honesty
3. Promoting social understanding through reading and discussion of literature, discussions in class meetings, school assemblies, and other school activities (e.g., cross-cultural fairs) to promote understanding of other people
4. Developmental discipline—techniques for helping children build bonds with others, attain self-control, resolve conflicts with others, achieve optimal opportunities to participate in classroom decision making, and develop intrinsic motivation for both prosocial and intellectual/academic activities
5. Cooperative learning—peer-directed and teacher-directed activities designed to build students' prosocial values and social skills while they work on academic content

The program strives to promote a cooperative orientation in all classroom activities, not only in formal cooperative learning groups. All classroom experiences are designed to develop "autonomy, self-direction, community participation, responsible decision making, being helpful to others, learning to understand and appreciate others, and learning to collaborate with others" (D. Solomon et al., 1990, p. 236).

Cohen, Lotan and Catanzarite's 1990 adaptation of *Finding Out/Descubrimiento* (DeAvila & Duncan, 1980) also emphasizes developing cooperative norms. The original program assigned students to linguistically and academically heterogeneous small groups that carried out complex science and mathematics tasks in learning centers with materials available in English and Spanish. Cohen et al. added three new compo-

nents to the program. First, teachers were prepared in methods of classroom management to increase students' ability to help other people, listen to them, explain and demonstrate how things work, give them what they need, and ask them questions. Second, students were assigned roles to promote participation in the group, such as the role of facilitator, who was responsible for ensuring that all group members obtained the help they needed. Third, to reduce the effects of perceived status on behavior, Cohen et al. trained teachers to modify students' expectations of each other's competence. To help dispel the notion that some students are either competent or incompetent on a range of tasks (which makes them dominant or submissive in group interaction), teachers tried to convince students that academic tasks required multiple abilities and that *all* students would excel at some and not others.

The third component of Cohen and colleagues' program, the multiability intervention, was shown in previous controlled experiments to equalize interaction among students. For example, Rosenholtz (1985) developed a 6-day curriculum to teach students that multiple abilities, such as visual thinking, intuitive thinking, and reasoning, were needed to solve important problems. By performing group tasks that exemplified each ability, students demonstrated their competence with these alternative abilities. This program was successful in reducing the usual dominance of students with high academic status in small group interaction (see also Tammivaara, 1982, for successful results of a similar program).

Kagan's (1992) program of cooperative learning also advocates team building, class building, and development of social skills. To help build enthusiasm, trust, and mutual support in a small group, Kagan designed team-building activities to help students become acquainted with each other, learn each other's names, interests, and aspirations, form a team identity, learn to count on other group members for support, learn to value differences among group members, and experience group accomplishments. Analogous activities at the class level help create a positive classroom context in which students feel empowered and a part of their class: Students become acquainted with their classmates, identify with their class, value differences among classmates, feel that they are supported by their classmates, and experience the power of working together as a class. To help students develop social skills needed for working with others, such as listening, turn taking, helping, praising, polite waiting, encouraging, appreciating, asking for help, staying on task, and resolving conflicts in nonhostile ways, Kagan described roles for students to practice skills, ways of structuring activities to elicit particular social skills, techniques of teacher modeling and reinforcement, and techniques for group reflection and planning.

Comprehensive programs of team-building and prosocial development activities seem to improve students' ability to communicate with one another. D. Solomon, Watson, Delucchi, Schaps, & Battistich (1988), for example, reported a higher incidence of supportive and friendly behavior and spontaneous prosocial behavior in classes participating in the Child Development Project than in classes not receiving the program. Cohen et al. (1990) found more task-related talk and offers of assistance as a result of their modifications of *Finding Out/Descubrimiento*. Cohen et al. also found that their experimental program weakened the relationship between academic status and interaction in heterogeneous groups. Without the intervention, high-status students talked more than low-status students; with the intervention, high-status and low-status students showed equal rates of task-related talk. Even with the intervention, however, high-status students offered more assistance than low-status students, showing that they still held positions of influence in peer interaction. To help increase the influence of low-status students, Cohen et al. (1990) described how teachers might be trained to assign competence to low-status children to increase their beliefs in their own abilities as well as to influence other students' perceptions of them.

The extent to which the effects on student behavior were due to the instruction in communications skills or other features of these programs is unclear, however. In the Solomon et al. (1990) study, because the comparison classes had no formal collaborative group work, the effects of the experimental program could have been due to cooperative learning experiences, the activities designed to promote prosocial behavior, or both. In the Cohen et al. (1990) study, the comparison program permitted, but did not require, students to work together in the learning centers, making it difficult to determine whether the effects of the modified program were due to activities to build cooperative norms, management roles of students in small groups, activities to modify competence expectations, or the requirement that the whole group had to finish the task before students moved on to a new learning center. Systematic comparisons of interaction in peer-directed groups with and without prosocial development activities would help clarify the effects of normbuilding on student behavior.

Instruction in Helping Behavior.  Based on the consistent finding that giving explanations to others is positively related to learning outcomes, two studies instructed students in giving explanations to other students. Premised on the belief that the development of specific explaining skills depends on the prior development of general interpersonal communication skills and social norms conducive to successful collaboration, both studies combined instruction in explaining behavior with development of general communication skills and prosocial norms.

Through a combination of discussion, demonstration, practice, and feedback, Swing and Peterson (1982) taught students interpersonal relationship skills and explaining skills to improve their ability to teach other students in small groups. In two training sessions, students were instructed how to monitor each other's progress, give explanations to each other, and check each other's answers. Compared to groups that did not receive this training prior to group work, trained groups engaged in more task-related interaction, provided more higher order explaining, and checked each other's answers more frequently. The positive effects of instruction in peer interaction did not translate into increased achievement, however. Achievement results favored the trained students but were not statistically significant.

Building on the instructional program designed by Swing and Peterson (1982), N. M. Webb and Farivar (1994) conducted a larger, longer-term study of the effects of instruction in helping behavior on peer interaction and learning in middle school mathematics. In an expanded version of Swing and Peterson's trained group, one set of classrooms received instruction in basic communication skills (e.g., checking for understanding, sharing ideas and information, encouraging, and checking for agreement), norms for group behavior (e.g., attentive listening, no put-downs, moderate voice level, equal participation by everyone), and helping skills (e.g., asking for and giving elaborated explanations instead of only the answer, asking clear and precise questions). Instead of receiving no instruction, however, the comparison classes in this study received instruction in the communication skills and prosocial norms, but not the instruction in helping behavior. The two programs produced significantly different patterns of verbal interaction and achievement. Minority students (Hispanic and black) were more likely to receive elaborated help in classes receiving instruction in communications skills, prosocial norms, and helping behavior than in classes receiving instruction only in the communication skills and prosocial norms, and showed greater mathematics achievement as a result.

*Structuring Group Interaction.* The previous section described ways of preparing students for group work in order to promote behavior that would be beneficial for learning. Instruction generally occurred prior to group work, and the interaction among students following instruction was relatively unstructured. Students made their own decisions about when and how to use the instructed behaviors. Another approach to promoting behavior beneficial for learning structures the task to control the kinds of interaction that students engage in, and sometimes even the sequence of behaviors to be carried out. This kind of approach includes giving students specific roles to play, requiring students to ask each other certain types of questions, requiring students to give specific kinds of explanations, and requiring students to argue with each other or reach consensus.

Role Specialization.  A popular way of managing and facilitating group work is to assign students to different roles, each with different prescribed behavior. Kagan (1992), for example, lists 12 roles corresponding to different social skills:

- Encourager—to "bring out" reluctant students and motivate the group
- Praiser—to show appreciation of others' work and ideas
- Cheerleader—to celebrate others' accomplishments
- Gatekeeper—to equalize participation in the group
- Coach—to help with academic content
- Question commander—to ensure that students ask their questions and the group answers them
- Checker—to check the group's understanding
- Taskmaster—to keep the group on task
- Recorder—to write down ideas and decisions
- Reflector—to reflect group progress
- Quiet captain—to monitor the noise level in the group
- Materials monitor—to obtain and return supplies

The purpose of these management roles is to help groups function smoothly, which ultimately should have positive effects on student learning.

In contrast to management roles are roles requiring students to engage in behavior hypothesized to influence learning directly: *summarizing* and *active listening*. In individual learning settings, summarizing is thought to promote learning because it facilitates cognitive rehearsal, elaboration, and cognitive restructuring of the material, and metacognitive strategies such as self-testing (e.g., Doctorow, Wittrock, & Marks, 1978). Summarizing for others in peer-directed settings can be even more beneficial because it invokes additional cognitive rehearsal, elaboration, and restructuring of the material to make summaries understandable to others and to help decide which ideas are most important to communicate to others (Hythecker et al., 1988; S. M. Ross & DiVesta, 1976; Yager et al., 1985).

To facilitate the active processing of material that is hypothesized to occur during oral summary, students can adopt the roles of summarizer and listener. The summarizer, also called the "learning leader" (Yager et al., 1985) and the "recaller" (Hythecker et al., 1988), summarizes the main points of the material. Only one student in a group can summarize the material at any given time; the others have to listen. To encourage active processing of material by the nonsummarizing students, the "learning listener" or "listener/facilitator" is responsible for detecting errors and omissions in the summary and must ask questions of the summarizer to help clarify the material. Students may rotate roles daily (Yager et al., 1985) or may alternate roles for different portions of the material (Hythecker et al., 1988).

In some cooperative learning methods, the summarizer and listener roles have been incorporated into a complex script for cooperative work. Dansereau and colleagues developed a six-step program for group work which they call "First-Degree MURDER" (the latter an acronym): "(1) setting a proper *Mood* for learning; (2) reading for *Understanding;* (3) *Recalling* the information; (4) *Detecting* errors or omissions in the recall; (5) *Elaborating* to make the material more easily remembered; and (6) a final *Review*" (Rocklin et al., 1985, p. 67). The third and fourth steps require the summarizing and listening roles. The fifth step requires students, without playing specific roles, to carry out additional activities together such as reorganizing the information into outlines or networks, generating pictures, developing mnemonics to help remember the material better, and creating a supersummary of all of the material (Hythecker et al., 1988).

Which role is more beneficial for learning—summarizer or listener—is fairly clear. To study this question, a series of studies on text recall assigned students to a fixed summarizer role or a fixed listener role throughout the material, or to alternating roles. Consistent with the many cognitive processes hypothesized to take place during oral summary, summarizers (whether always summarizing or alternating between roles) consistently outperformed listeners on achievement posttests (Dansereau, 1988; Lambiotte et al., 1987; Spurlin et al., 1984).

A more general question is whether the overall effects of role assignment, combining the effects of summarizing and listening, are greater than group discussion without role assignment. The answer is unclear. Some studies have reported positive effects of roles on initial achievement and retention (Yager et al., 1985), others have found roles to be advantageous for transfer but not for initial learning (Dansereau, 1988), others have found no effects of roles on any learning measure, (O'Donnell, Dansereau, Hall, & Rocklin, 1987), and still others have reported complicated results such as role assignment producing better performance and recall when groups were instructed to

study different kinds of information simultaneously (the procedures and the equipment involved in setting up and starting an intravenous infusion) but not when groups studied different kinds of information sequentially (information about the equipment before information about the procedures [O'Donnell et al., 1990]).

Whether summarizer/listener roles produce greater learning than group discussion without roles surely depends on the quality of summarizing and listening in which students engage. In the studies finding positive effects of role assignment, students may have carried out extensive elaboration and reorganization of the material. In the studies finding no effects, the quality of the summaries and responses to them may have been no better than those in the general discussion groups.

Lambiotte et al. (1987) pointed out some additional detrimental group dynamics that may create less than optimal summarizing and listening in groups assigned summarizer/listener roles. The detrimental processes are most likely to arise when both the summarizer and listener have studied the same material. First are negative processes arising out of social concerns. The listener may be reluctant to point out the summarizer's misunderstanding or confusion for fear of being impolite, or appearing stupid. And the summarizer may worry about how others will evaluate his or her summary. Second, because they have studied the same material, both summarizer and listener may make inferences about what the other is saying and "fill in the gaps" in the summary. By overestimating their own or the other students' level of comprehension, listeners may fail to ask questions for clarification, and summarizers may not work hard to make the summary clear or detailed.

Lambiotte et al. (1987) suggested that one possible solution is to have students teach each other different material. This is the heart of the Jigsaw method of cooperative learning, for example, in which students first learn material in expert groups and then go back to their original group to teach the material to the other group members. In this teacher–learner relationship, the "teacher" covers material to which the rest of the group has not been exposed. Neither the summarizer nor the listener can rely on the other student to use the previously studied information to fill in gaps in what is said. Lambiotte et al. hypothesized that the listener in this situation will be more likely to ask questions for clarification, and the summarizer will be forced to organize the material more effectively and clearly, and to remember it better to present it to others. And both students will worry less about how others will evaluate their questions and summaries, and can focus better on the task. In a controlled study, Lambiotte et al. (1987) did indeed find greater recall of the material when students taught each other different portions of the material than when students read the same material and alternated summarizer and listener roles.

It would be very informative to compare the nature of the summaries and questions asked when students study common material and when they study different material. The possibility that the advantages of teaching are greatest when the material is divided has important implications for structuring cooperative work in the classroom.

Reciprocal Questioning. Summarizing material is not the only learning strategy that has been adapted for use in collaborative groups. Two other learning strategies initially studied in individual settings that have been adapted for use in collabora-tive settings are self-questioning and self-generated elaboration. In self-questioning, students generate comprehension ques-tions during or after reading written text material or listening to lectures. Responding to self-generated questions is more effective than alternative strategies, such as summarizing material, rereading it, and answering instructor-formulated questions, because it encourages learners to actively process and analyze the material, to focus on what is important to learn and remember, to monitor their own comprehension of the material, and, when they realize that they do not understand something, to seek further information and clarifi-cation (Wong, 1985).

In self-generated elaboration, students elaborate on mate-rial to make it clearer and more meaningful to themselves, and because they link the new information to information they already know, the information becomes easier to remember (Pressley et al., 1992; Wittrock, 1990). Specific elaborative activities include adding details to information, paraphrasing, summarizing, clarifying, creating analogies, relating multiple concepts, making inferences, visualizing images, and question answering (King, 1992; C. E. Weinstein & R. F. Mayer, 1985). As an example, one intensively studied question-answering technique, called elaborative interrogation (Pressley et al., 1992, p. 99), improves recall of prose by requiring students to generate elaborations in response to "why" questions about factual material they have read. For example, after reading the statement, "Often the skunk lives alone, but families of skunks sometimes stay together," students may be asked to respond to the question, "Why do families of skunks sometimes stay together?"

Adapting self-questioning and elaborative techniques to the collaborative setting takes the form of reciprocal questioning, in which students ask each other questions about the material (e.g., Fantuzzo, Riggio, Connelly, & Dimeff, 1989; King, 1989, 1990). Reciprocal questioning methods vary in the nature and extent of instruction about generating questions. Students can receive minimal guidance about the questions to ask each other (Fantuzzo et al., 1989), or they can receive general instructions about distinguishing between recall questions (to test memory of previously studied material) and critical thinking questions (to elicit "application, analysis, interpretation, and evaluation of ideas"; King, 1990). Or they may receive specific instructions about generating thought-provoking questions that will pro-mote elaborated discussion. In such fine-tuned reciprocal ques-tioning, King (1989, 1990, 1992) trained students to use generic question stems to create their own high-level questions about the material (Table 26–1).

In addition to the benefits of self-questioning and self-generated elaboration described above, reciprocal questioning has potential benefits that are specific to the peer interaction setting, as described by King (1992). Because different students bring different perspectives to bear on the material, the ques-tions generated in a group and the explanations offered in response can expose students to new insights into the material. Answering each other's questions can encourage students to recognize their own misconceptions and gaps in understanding, recognize different viewpoints, seek new information to clarify what puzzles them, resolve disagreements and differences with others, and reconceptualize and reorganize information to jus-

### TABLE 26–1. King's Generic Question Stems to Guide Student Discussions

What is a new example of . . . ?
How would you use . . . to . . . ?
What would happen if . . . ?
What are the strengths and weaknesses of . . . ?
What do we already know about . . . ?
How does . . . tie in with what we learned before?
Explain why . . .
Explain how . . .
How does . . . affect . . . ?
What is the meaning of . . . ?
Why is . . . important?
What is the difference between . . and . . . ?
How are . . . and . . . similar?
What is the best . . . , and why?
What are some possible solutions for the problem of . . . ?
Compare . . . and . . . with regard to. . . .
How does . . . affect . . . ?
What do you think causes . . . ?
Do you agree or disagree with this statement . . . ? Support your
    answer.

Note: Table from "Facilitating Elaborative Learning Through Guided Student-Generated Questioning," by Alison King, 1992, *Educational Psychologist*, 27, p. 113. Copyright 1992 by Lawrence Erlbaum Associates, Inc. Reprinted by permission.

tify their responses or make them clearer to others. Because they know that other students may evaluate what they say, students may work harder to ask better questions and give more thoughtful answers. These processes, in turn, will increase their understanding and recall of the material.

Not only have empirical studies found reciprocal ques-tioning to be more effective for learning than is group discussion or review of material (Fantuzzo et al., 1989; King, 1989, 1990), but more instruction on how to generate questions is often better than less (King, 1990). King's detailed analyses of verbal interaction in these various conditions provide clues to help explain some of the achievement results. She found that stu-dents trained in the use of "why" and "how" questions asked more critical thinking questions and gave and received more elaborated explanations than students in other group conditions (King, 1990, 1992), providing avenues for the beneficial pro-cesses on learning described above.

Explanation Prompts. Two studies gave students specific prompts to encourage them to give elaborated explanations of scientific information and observations in collaborative small groups. Instead of requiring students to ask each other ques-tions to elicit elaboration, these studies gave students guidelines to use when formulating their own explanations, as well as when responding to others. Palincsar, Anderson, and David (1993) taught middle school students to use scientific explana-tion to support their discussions while collaboratively solving problems related to matter and molecules. Students were told that their explanations should include (a) identification of the substances involved in the problem, (b) descriptions of what was happening to the substances (using observations, data, evidence, and background knowledge), and (c) descriptions of what was happening to the molecules of the substances.

These explanation prompts were combined with guided use of social norms conducive to successful collaboration (contributing to the group's efforts and helping others contribute, supporting one's ideas by giving reasons, working to understand others' ideas, and building on one another's ideas). The combination of explanation prompts and guided use of norms encouraged students to give thoughtful explanations of scientific concepts and promoted their conceptual understanding. Moreover, the effects were more pronounced for open-ended problems than for constrained problems.

Coleman (1992) gave upper elementary school students specific explanation prompts to use while collaboratively constructing a concept map and solving problems related to photosynthesis. Coleman (1992, pp. 47–48) developed nine explanation prompts to encourage students to construct explanations, to use explanations when justifying answers and beliefs, to relate what they learned in class to the task at hand, to distinguish between "scientific" and "everyday" definitions and explanations, and to compare real world experiences to class learning:

- Can you explain this in your own words?
- Can you compare how you used to think about this with how you think about it now?
- Explain why you believe that your answer is correct or wrong.
- How does your answer compare with another person's answer?
- What did we learn in class about this particular topic?
- Can you explain this using the "scientific" information that we learned in class?
- Is that explanation a "scientific" definition or an "everyday" definition?
- How does that explanation compare with the scientific definition that we learned in class?
- Can you compare how things in the world appear to how they differ from the scientific information that we learned in class?

Compared to collaborative groups who did not receive the explanation prompts, groups that received the explanation prompts gave more conceptually advanced explanations during their discussions and attained more accurate scientific and functional understanding of photosynthesis.

Controversy versus Concurrence Seeking.    Still another approach to shaping group interaction is to structure the task to require certain processes and not others, such as controversy versus concurrence seeking. Controversy in a group can increase learning when students seek additional information to resolve conflicting ideas and information (D. W. Johnson & R. T. Johnson, 1979). Further, students can solidify their own understanding of material when they reconceptualize, reorganize, or clarify material to justify their own position to others. To promote these beneficial processes, several studies built controversy into the group's task by subdividing groups into teams and requiring teams to master material on different sides of an issue, to debate the issue with the other team, and then to synthesize the two positions. Compared with groups required

to seek concurrence by working cooperatively and compromising instead of arguing, groups required to debate the issues carried out more high-level discussion of material ("elaboration, synthesis, and rationale") and less description of facts and information (K. A. Smith, D. W. Johnson, & R. T. Johnson, 1984), and showed higher achievement (D. W. Johnson, R. T. Johnson, Pierson, & Lyons, 1985). Interestingly, incorporating controversy into the task did not prove to be divisive or make some students reject others, common fears of many teachers who try to suppress conflicts in their classrooms (D. W. Johnson et al., 1985). Whether the positive effects of controversy apply equally to students arguing assigned positions and to those arguing their own, strongly held positions is not yet known. In any case, the Johnsons' results to date suggest that structuring academic tasks around controversy may be a good way to prepare students to deal with controversy in a wide range of settings inside and outside the classroom.

*Discussion of Group Functioning.*    Some social psychologists maintain that groups will function most effectively if they discuss their group's interaction and how they might improve it, sometimes called "group processing." Such discussions may help groups identify, understand, and solve general communication problems (e.g., lack of student participation, disruptive or bullying behavior) and may reinforce students for collaborating with each other (D. W. Johnson & R. T. Johnson, 1987). When groups resolve these kinds of problems, they should be able to focus more fully on the task at hand. One study did show that engaging in group processing (analyzing positive and negative behaviors of group members) led to improved achievement (Yager, R. T. Johnson, D. W. Johnson, & Snider, 1986). But information is needed about what groups should discuss during group-processing time, how those discussions affect their subsequent task-related interaction, and how these changes in group dynamics affect learning.

Structuring the Teacher's Role.    In the previously described approaches to shaping group interaction, the teacher typically sets up the group context, gives instruction and training, and then lets groups proceed fairly independently, with some observation and monitoring by the teacher but little direct intervention. In two other approaches—teacher scaffolding and coconstruction of norms—the teacher participates actively and continuously to shape the group's dialogue.

Scaffolding.    Scaffolding is a "process that enables a child or novice to solve a problem, carry out a task, or achieve a goal which would be beyond his unassisted efforts" (D. Wood, Bruner, & G. Ross, 1976, p. 90). In teacher scaffolding, the teacher explains and models the behavior that he or she wants students to engage in, gives them opportunities to demonstrate that behavior, provides feedback on their performance, and gradually provides less assistance as students become more competent at displaying the desired behavior (Palincsar & Brown, 1984). Palincsar and Brown (1984) developed teacher-scaffolded instruction, referred to as reciprocal teaching, to help students carry out certain strategies designed to improve comprehension of text: generating questions about the text they have read, clarifying what they do not understand, summarizing the text, and generating predictions. Teachers initially take the

READING:
Cats also "talk" by making other sounds. Some scientists think cats may have as many as 100 different calls. Cats have calls for greeting people, for showing hunger, for making a threat to another cat, and even for scolding their kittens. When a cat is frightened or angry, it may growl, spit, hiss, or scream.

| | | |
|---|---|---|
| 39. | T: | C____, as a teacher, can you ask someone a question about this information? [pause] Sometimes it helps if you're having a hard time to summarize what I just told you. [pause] What was I telling you about, what kind of information? |
| 40. | S2: | About different ways they talk. |
| 41. | T: | You mean there are [sic] more than one way for them to communicate? |
| 42. | S2: | A hundred ways. |
| 43. | T: | I did talk about that. They communicate with a hundred different sounds. Why do they need all those different sounds? |
| 44. | S2: | To tell people stuff. |
| 45. | S6: | To see if their babies are okay. |
| 46. | T: | Possibly. Now, with that information, C ____, knowing that they have all those different ways to talk and to communicate, can you think of a question to ask? You can start your question with the word what ... or when ... or why? |
| 47. | S2: | Why do they purr? |
| 48. | T: | Who is they? |
| 49. | S2: | The cats. |
| 50. | T: | Okay, let's have that information in your sentence. Why ... |
| 51. | S2: | Why do the cats purr? |
| 52. | S5: | To tell them what they want. |
| 53. | T: | Can you tell us a little bit more? |
| 54. | S5: | [not audible] |
| 55. | T: | Would it sound the same way for all those things? |
| 56. | S5: | No. |
| 57. | T: | So that's why it needs a hundred sounds. So, I might say, if I were going to ask a question, why do cats have so many different sounds or calls? |
| 58. | S3: | Because they have so many different colors in their fur. |
| 59. | T: | I said calls, not colors. Why do they have so many different calls, or sounds? [pause] Think of what R ____ told us. Do they always want the same thing? |
| 60. | S3: | No. |
| 61. | T: | Then why do they have so many different ones? Is it so they can communicate what they really want? |

FIGURE 26–3. Example of Teacher Scaffolding During Reading Instruction (Palincsar, 1986. Reprinted by permission)

leadership in explaining the strategies and modeling their use in making sense of text. Then teachers ask students to demonstrate the strategies, but give them considerable support. For example, to help a student generate questions to ask other students, the teacher might probe what information the student gleans from the text, and help the student phrase a specific question using that information. The teacher gradually assumes the less active role of coach, giving students feedback and encouraging them, as shown in the excerpt in Figure 26–3. Using this approach, students learned how to engage in the strategies for reading comprehension with minimal intervention from the teacher and make major gains in reading comprehension (A. L. Brown & Palincsar, 1989; Palincsar, 1986; Palincsar & A. L. Brown, 1984).

Coconstructing Norms. In most training programs designed to promote group cooperation and prosocial behavior, instruction and practice in norms for group behavior take place before students begin participation in work groups, usually in the context of team-building activities unrelated to the academic material to be learned (Cohen, 1986; Cohen et al., 1990; N. B. Graves & T. D. Graves, 1985; D. W. Johnson & R. T. Johnson, 1986; Kagan, 1985, 1992; S. Sharan & Y. Sharan, 1976; Solomon

et al., 1990; N. M. Webb & Farivar, 1994). During group work on the academic material, the teacher assumes a monitoring role, reminding groups about the desired norms for behavior and intervening when group dynamics go awry.

In contrast to the usual monitoring role of the teacher, Yackel, Cobb, and T. Wood (1991; see also T. Wood & Yackel, 1990) developed an approach toward fostering peer interaction in which the teacher and students mutually constructed norms in the context of formal group work. The teacher used several strategies. First, when negative situations arose spontaneously in group work, she intervened to explain her expectations (e.g., that the group ensure that all of its members understand how to solve the problems and are given opportunities to do so) and to give specific directions to students (e.g., to stop a student who is solving all of the problems himself; to make sure that students listen to and understand each other's explanations). Then, she used those negative situations she observed, as well as positive ones, to initiate discussions with the entire class about their obligations in group work. Finally, in whole-class discussions, the teacher invented hypothetical scenarios and asked students to describe their responsibilities in specific cases (e.g., sharing, cooperating, achieving consensus about the answer, justifying one's own work, understanding other students' procedures; Yackel et al., 1991, pp. 398–399). A question for further study is whether active and ongoing participation by the teacher in constructing norms is more likely to generate desired group processes than an initial package of instruction and practice with norms followed by less active teacher monitoring.

*Conclusions.* Many features of groups and classroom settings influence the nature and extent of collaboration among students. On one hand, these features provide evidence, for both researchers and educational practitioners, regarding the complexity of the influences on student collaboration. On the other hand, the long list of group and classroom features provides a menu of possible ways to enhance the quality of collaboration in classrooms.

## CONCLUSIONS AND FUTURE RESEARCH

In concluding this chapter, we note that it is not for lack of history, enthusiasm, good ideas, or sound research that group processes in the classroom remain somewhat enigmatic. It is, rather, the complexities of designing, implementing, and evaluating learning and problem solving in groups that render it difficult to neatly summarize and draw conclusions from this work. Consider the numerous intraindividual factors (e.g., prior knowledge, motivation, language) that influence the learning of one child in "individualistic" activity. Place this learner in a group context, and not only does one have to contend with all the issues that attend the interaction among the group members (from the very mundane resource issues to the more lofty issues of attaining intersubjectivity), but in addition, other intraindividual factors that may have receded into the background when considering individualistic activity now emerge as salient, indeed critical (e.g., the learner's gender and social status).

The most substantive progress that has been made in the area of group processes within the last two decades may be the broad recognition of this complexity and the increasing sophistication with which researchers approach the study of group processes, as reflected in the refinement of theory, the specificity of the research questions, and the methodology used both in data collection and analyses. It is in the spirit of continuing to advance this movement that we offer the following suggestions for future research on group processes.

Typically, the outcomes of small-group learning have been identified in terms of skills and simple concepts. Clearly, we need more evidence regarding how students' thinking and problem solving is influenced by small-group learning. In hand with an interest in the role of collaboration in influencing thinking, understanding, and general problem-solving activity, there is the need for continued exploration of ways of productively scaffolding group interactions, including exploring the extent to which these scaffolds must be domain specific. Research representative of this line of inquiry is the ongoing work of Good and McCaslin and their colleagues (Good et al., 1990), who are investigating the effects of group learning in mathematics on mathematical judgment, the development of number sense, and mathematical reasoning.

Across the literature, there is the need to study more closely the mechanisms that are at work in group processes. Although the literature is rich with speculation about whether cognitive conflict, internalization, or motivation is providing the impetus for learning, there is a need for rigorous studies that systematically investigate the variables that are hypothesized to mediate learning in groups. The observational work of Bivens (1990) is illustrative of this kind of research.

Despite the emphasis on small-group learning in classroom restructuring initiatives, researchers know relatively little about the role that individual differences such as ability, achievement, and motivational orientation play in the outcomes of small-group work. The research of Davidson (1985) regarding the differential outcomes of group work based on achievement, the research of Cohen (1986) examining the role that status differences play in small-group interactions, and the observations of Mulryan (1989) indicating that low achievers experience greater difficulty adapting to small-group learning all suggest the need to proceed more carefully in the use of group learning to redress educational inequities.

Despite the influence of the nature and structure of the learning task on group processes, these factors have not been examined systematically. Dimensions for further study include the level of conceptual understanding involved in the task (e.g., deep versus easily automated skills [Damon & Phelps, 1989]), the dimensionality of the task (e.g., the variety of academic and social skills required [Cohen, 1986, 1994]), the extent to which a task can be completed successfully without contributions by all members (Steiner, 1972), the extent to which the task can be divided into parts and whether division of labor leads to unequal role assignments in the group (Hertz-Lazarowitz, Kirkus, & N. Miller, 1992), and the extent to which the task requires the group to integrate the thinking of its members (Hertz-Lazarowitz, 1992).

As difficult as it is, individual studies need to take into account as many potential predictors of group processes as possible (e.g., group composition, reward structure, nature of the learning task, instructions for interacting in specific ways). Numerous internal group factors that have received very little attention to date might be conjectured to have a powerful influence on learning outcomes. Examples include cohesiveness, role differentiation, and group history. Systematically manipulating or controlling potential predictors will help make the antecedents of group processes in any single study less ambiguous. Even when predictors are not explicitly manipulated, giving detailed descriptions of as many features of the group and classroom context as possible will increase our prospects for making sensible comparisons across studies.

Finally, small-group learning cannot be examined independently of the curriculum, the culture of the classroom, assessment practices, and the instructional climate of the classroom (e.g., other participation structures valued by the teacher). Small-group learning needs to be examined in more systemic ways and in collaboration with teachers. A. L. Brown and Campione (1990) are examining some of these issues in their yearlong schoolwide curriculum implemented around the theme of interdependence in nature. Scardamalia and Bereiter (1991) are examining these issues within a computer-assisted environment. Cobb, Wood, and Yackel (1991) are exploring the multiple demands that are placed on teachers who engage in small-group activity. Such efforts will help us understand how groups operate in the larger social context of the classroom and school.

The past two decades of research on group processes in the classroom have revealed the myriad forces operating in group contexts. Grappling with this complexity will make it possible to offer meaningful recommendations for the improvement of educational practice.

## References

Allport, F. H. (1920). The influence of the group upon association and thought. *Journal of Experimental Psychology, 3,* 159–182.

Allport, F. H. (1924). *Social psychology.* Boston: Houghton Mifflin.

Allport, G. (1954). *The nature of prejudice.* Cambridge, MA: Addison-Wesley.

Ames, C. (1981). Competitive versus cooperative reward structures: The influence of individual and group performance factors on achievement attributions and affect. *American Educational Research Journal, 18,* 273–287.

Ames, G. J., & Murray, F. B. (1981). When two wrongs make a right: Promoting cognitive change by social conflict. *Developmental Psychology, 18,* 894–897.

Amigues, R. (1990). Peer interaction and conceptual change. In H. Mandl, E. De Corte, S. N. Bennett, & H. F. Frederich (Eds.), *Learning and instruction: European research in international context. Vol. 2: 1. Social and cognitive aspects of learning and instruction* (pp. 27–43). Oxford: Pergamon.

Aronson, E., Blaney, N., Stephan, C., Sikes, J., & Snapp, M. (1978). *The Jigsaw classroom.* Beverly Hills, CA: Sage.

Azmitia, M. (1988). Peer interaction and problem solving: When are two heads better than one? *Child Development, 59,* 87–96.

Bales, R. F. (1950). *Interaction process analysis.* Chicago: University of Chicago Press.

Bandura, A. (1986). *Social foundations of thought and action: A social cognitive theory.* Englewood Cliffs, NJ: Prentice Hall.

Bargh, J. A., & Schul, Y. (1980). On the cognitive benefit of teaching. *Journal of Educational Psychology, 72,* 593–604.

Bearison, D. J., Magzamen, S., & Filardo, E. K. (1986). Socio-conflict and cognitive growth in young children. *Merrill-Palmer Quarterly, 32,* 51–72.

Bell, N., Grossen, M., & Perret-Clermont, A.-N. (1985). Sociocognitive conflict and intellectual growth. In M. W. Berkowitz (Ed.), *Peer conflict and psychological growth* (pp. 41–54). San Francisco: Jossey-Bass.

Benne, K., & Sheets, P. (1948). Functional roles of group members. *Journal of Social Issues, 4,* 41–49.

Benware, C. A., & Deci, E. L. (1984). Quality of learning with an active versus passive motivational set. *American Educational Research Journal, 21,* 755–765.

Bereiter, C., & Scardamalia, M. (1989). Intentional learning as a goal of instruction. In L. B. Resnick (Ed.), *Knowing, learning, and instruction: Essays in honor of Robert Glaser* (pp. 361–392). Hillsdale, NJ: Lawrence Erlbaum Associates, Inc.

Berger, J., Rosenholtz, S. J., and Zelditch, M. (1980). Status organizing processes. *Annual Review of Sociology, 6,* 479–508.

Bivens, J. (1990, April). *Children scaffolding children in the classroom: Can this metaphor completely describe the process of group problem solving?* Paper presented at the annual meeting of the American Educational Research Association, Boston, MA.

Bos, M. C. (1937). Experimental study of productive collaboration. *Acta Psychologia, 3,* 315–426.

Bossert, S. T. (1988–1989). Cooperative activities in the classroom. *Review of Research in Education, 15,* 225–252.

Brown, A. L. (1989). Analogical learning and transfer: What develops? In S. Vosniadou & A. Ortony (Eds.), *Similarity and analogical reasoning.* New York: Cambridge University Press.

Brown, A. L., & Campione, J. C. (1990). Communities of learning and thinking, or a context by any other name. *Developmental Perspectives on Teaching and Learning Thinking Skills, 21,* 108–126.

Brown, A. L., & Campione, J. C. (1994). Guided discovery in a community of learners. In K. McGilly (Ed.), *Classroom lessons: Integrating cognitive theory and classroom practice* (pp. 229–270). Cambridge, MA: MIT Press.

Brown, A. L., & Palincsar, A. S. (1989). Guided, cooperative learning and individual knowledge acquisition. In L. B. Resnick (Ed.), *Knowing, learning, and instruction: Essays in honor of Robert Glaser* (pp. 393–451). Hillsdale, NJ: Lawrence Erlbaum Associates.

Cazden, C. B. (1988). *Classroom discourse: The language of teaching and learning.* Portsmouth, NH: Heinemann.

Chan, C. K. K., Burtis, P. J., Scardamalia, M., & Bereiter, C. (1992). Constructive activity in learning from text. *American Educational Research Journal, 29,* 97–118.

Chang, S.-C. (1993). *The effects of group reward on student motivation, interaction, and achievement in cooperative small groups.* Unpublished doctoral dissertation, University of California, Los Angeles.

Chi, M. T. H., & Bassock, M. (1989). Learning from examples via self explanations. In L. B. Resnick (Ed.), *Knowing, learning, and instruction: Essays in honor of Robert Glaser* (pp. 251–282). Hillsdale, NJ: Lawrence Erlbaum Associates.

Chi, M. T. H., Bassock, M., Lewis, M., Reimann, P., & Glaser, R. (1989). Self-explanations: How students study and use examples in learning to solve problems. *Cognitive Science, 13,* 145–182.

Cobb, P., Wood, T., & Yackel, E. (1991). Analogies from the philosophy and sociology of science for understanding classroom life. *Science Education, 75*(1), 23–44.

Cohen, E. G. (1973). Modifying the effects of social structure. *American Behavioral Scientist, 16,* 861–879.

Cohen, E. G. (1982). Expectation states and interracial interaction in school settings. *American Review of Sociology, 8,* 209–235.

Cohen, E. G. (1986). *Designing group work: Strategies for the heterogeneous classroom.* New York: Teachers College Press.

Cohen, E. G. (1994). Restructuring the classroom: Conditions for productive small groups. *Review of Educational Research, 64,* 1–36.

Cohen, E. G., Lockheed, M. E., & Lohman, M. R. (1976). The center for interracial cooperation: A field experiment. *Sociology of Education, 59,* 47–58.

Cohen, E. G., Lotan, R., & Catanzarite, L. (1990). Treating status problems in the cooperative classroom. In S. Sharan (Ed.), *Cooperative learning: Theory and research* (pp. 203–230). New York: Praeger.

Cohen, E. G., & Roper, S. (1972). Modification of interracial interaction disability: An application of status characteristics theory. *American Sociological Review, 37,* 643–657.

Coleman, E. B. (1992). *Facilitating conceptual understanding in science: A collaborative explanation-based approach.* Unpublished doctoral dissertation, University of Toronto.

Cook, S. W. (1986, April). *Reactions to helping and being helped in interracial cooperative groups: Effects on respect and liking for group members.* Paper presented at the annual meeting of the American Educational Research Association, San Francisco.

Cooper, C. R., Marquis, A., & Edward, D. (1986). Four perspectives on peer learning among elementary school children. In E. C. Mueller &

C. R. Cooper (Eds.), *Process and outcome in peer relationships* (pp. 269–298). New York: Academic Press.

Cremin, L. A. (1961). *The transformation of the school: Progressivism in American education: 1876–1957.* New York: Vintage Books.

Daiute, C. (1986). Do 1 and 1 make 2? *Written Communication, 3*(3), 382–408.

Daiute, C., & Dalton, B. (1993). Collaboration between children learning to write: Can novices be masters? *Cognition and Instruction, 10,* 281–333.

Damon, W. (1984). Peer education: The untapped potential. *Journal of Applied Developmental Psychology, 5,* 331–343.

Damon, W., & Killen, M. (1982). Peer interaction and the process of change in children's moral reasoning. *Merrill-Palmer Quarterly, 28,* 347–367.

Damon, W., & Phelps, E. (1989). Critical distinctions among three methods of peer education. *International Journal of Educational Research, 13,* 9–19.

Dansereau, D. F. (1988). Cooperative learning strategies. In C. E. Weinstein, E. T. Goetz, & P. A. Alexander (Eds.), *Learning and study strategies: Issues in assessment, instruction, and evaluation* (pp. 103–120). Orlando, FL: Academic Press.

Dashiell, J. F. (1935). Experimental studies of the influence of social situations on the behavior of individual human adults. In C. Murchison (Ed.), *Handbook of social psychology* (pp. 1097–1158). Worcester, MA: Clark University Press.

Davidson, N. (1985). Small-group learning and teaching in mathematics: A selective review of the literature. In R. Slavin, S. Sharan, S. Kagan, R. Hertz-Lazarowitz, C. Webb, & R. Schmuck (Eds.), *Learning to cooperate, cooperating to learn* (pp. 221–230). New York: Plenum Press.

DeAvila, E. A., & Duncan, S. E. (1980). *Finding Out/Descubrimiento.* Corte Madera, CA: Linguametrics Group.

Deering, P. (1989). An ethnographic approach for examining participants' construction of a cooperative learning classroom culture. Paper presented at the annual meeting of the American Anthropological Association, Washington, DC.

Dembo, M. H., & McAuliffe, T. J. (1987). Effects of perceived ability and grade status on social interaction and influence in cooperative groups. *Journal of Educational Psychology, 79,* 415–423.

Deutsch, M. (1949). An experimental study of the effects of cooperation and competition upon group process. *Human Relations, 2,* 199–231.

DeVoe, M. W. (1977). Cooperation as a function of self-concept, sex, and race. *Educational Research Quarterly, 2,* 3–8.

DeVries, D. L., & Slavin, R. E. (1978). Teams-games-tournaments (TTG): Review of ten classroom experiments. *Journal of Research and Development in Education, 12*(1), 28–38.

Dewey, J. (1966). *The school and society* (8th Phoenix ed.). Chicago: University of Chicago Press.

DiPardo, A., & Freedman, S. W. (1987, May). *Historical overview: Groups in the writing classroom* (Tech. Rep. No. 4). University of California at Berkeley and Carnegie Mellon University, Center for the Study of Women.

Doctorow, M. J., Wittrock, M. C., & Marks, C. B. (1978). Generative processes in reading comprehension. *Journal of Educational Psychology, 70,* 109–118.

Doise, W., & Mugny, G. (1984). *The social development of the intellect.* Oxford: Pergamon Press.

Dunn, R., Giannitti, M. C., Murray, J. B., Rossi, I., Geisert, G., & Quinn, P. (1990). Grouping students for instruction: Effects of learning style on achievement and attitudes. *Journal of Social Psychology, 130,* 485–494.

Durling, R., & Schick, C. (1976). Concept attainment by pairs and individuals as a function of vocalization. *Journal of Educational Psychology, 68,* 83–91.

Eichinger, D. C. (1992). *The roles of content knowledge, scientific argument, and social norms on collaborative problem solving.* Unpublished doctoral dissertation, Michigan State University, East Lansing.

Ellis, S., & Rogoff, B. (1982). The strategies and efficacy of child vs. adult teachers. *Child Development, 53,* 730–735.

Fantuzzo, J. W., Riggio, R. E., Connelly, S., & Dimeff, L. A. (1989). Effects of reciprocal peer tutoring on academic achievement and psychological adjustment: A component analysis. *Journal of Educational Psychology, 81,* 173–177.

Forman, E. (1989). The role of peer interaction in the social construction of mathematical knowledge. *International Journal of Educational Research, 13,* 55–70.

Forman, E. A., & Cazden, C. B. (1985). Exploring Vygotskian perspectives in education: The cognitive value of peer interaction. In J. V. Wertsch (Ed.), *Culture, communication, and cognition: Vygotskian perspectives* (pp. 323–347). New York: Cambridge University Press.

Forman, E. A., & Kraker, M. J. (1985). The social origins of logic: The contributions of Piaget and Vygotsky. In M. W. Berkowitz (Ed.), *Peer conflict and psychological growth* (New Directions for Child Development No. 29, pp. 23–39). San Francisco: Jossey-Bass.

Friedenberg, E. (1963). *Society's children.* New York: Random House.

Garcia, E E. (1987/1988). Effective schooling for language minority students. *New Focus, 1.* Silver Springs, MD: National Clearing House for Bilingual Education.

Gauvain, M., & Rogoff, B. (1989). Collaborative problem solving and children's planning skills. *Developmental Psychology, 25,* 139–151.

Gere, A. R. (1987). *Writing Groups: History, theory, and implications.* Carbondale: Southern Illinois University Press.

Gilly, M. (1990). The psychosocial mechanisms of cognitive constructions: Experimental research and teaching perspectives. In A. N. Perret-Clermont & M. L. Schubauer-Leoni (Eds.), *Social factors in learning and instruction,* 607–621.

Glachan, M., & Light, P. H. (1982). Peer interaction and learning: Can two wrongs make a right? In G. Butterworth & P. H. Light (Eds.), *Social cognition: Studies of the development of understanding* (pp. 238–262). Chicago: University of Chicago Press.

Good, T. L., McCaslin, M. M., & Reys, B. J. (1990). Investigating work groups to promote problem solving in mathematics. In J. Brophy (Ed.), *Advances in research on teaching* (Vol. 3). Greenwich, CT: JAI Press.

Goodman, P. (1956). *Growing up absurd.* New York: Random House.

Graham, S., & Barker, G. (1990). The down side of help: An attributional-developmental analysis of helping behavior as a low-ability cue. *Journal of Educational Psychology, 82,* 7–14.

Grant, L. (1986, April). *Classroom peer relationships of minority and nonminority students.* Paper presented at the annual meeting of the American Educational Research Association, San Francisco.

Graves, N. B., & Graves, T. D. (1985). Creating a cooperative learning environment: An ecological approach. In R. Slavin, S. Sharan, S. Kagan, R. Hertz-Lazarowitz, C. Webb, & R. Schmuck (Eds.), *Learning to cooperate, cooperating to learn* (pp. 403–436). New York: Plenum Press.

Greenwood, C. R., Delquadri, J., & Hall, R. V. (1989). Longitudinal effects of classwide peer tutoring. *Journal of Educational Psychology, 81,* 371–383.

Grice, H. P. (1975). Logic and conversation. In P. Cole & J. L. Morgan (Eds.), *Syntax and semantics: 3. Speech acts* (pp. 41–58). New York: Academic Press.

Guntermann, E., & Tovar, M. (1987). Collaborative problem-solving with Logo: Effects of group size and group composition. *Journal of Educational Computing Research, 3,* 313–334.

Hackman, J. R. (1990). *Groups that work (and those that don't): Creating conditions for effective teamwork.* San Francisco: Jossey-Bass.

Hare, A. P. (1992). *Groups, teams, and social interaction: Theories and applications.* New York: Praeger.

Hatano, G. (1988). Social and motivational bases for mathematical understanding. In G. B. Saxe and M. Gearhart (Eds.), *Children's Mathematics* (pp. 55–70). San Francisco, CA: Jossey-Bass.

Hatano, G., & Inagaki, K. (1991). Sharing cognition through collective comprehension activity. In L. Resnik, J. Levine, & S. Teasley (Eds.), *Perspectives on socially shared cognition*. Washington, DC: American Psychological Association.

Hazelwood, C. C., Roth, K. J., Hasbach, C., Hoekwater, E., Ligett, C., Lindquist, B., Peasley, K., & Rosaen, C. (1992). *Gender and discourse: The unfolding "living text" of a science lesson* (Tech. Rep. No. 60). Michigan State University, East Lansing: Center for the Learning and Teaching of Elementary Subjects.

Hertz-Lazarowitz, R. (1992). Understanding interactive behaviors: Looking at six mirrors of the classroom. In R. Hertz-Lazarowitz & N. Miller (Eds.), *Interaction in cooperative groups: Theoretical anatomy of group learning* (pp. 71–101). New York: Cambridge University Press.

Hertz-Lazarowitz, R., Kirkus, V. B., & Miller, N. (1992). Implications of current research on cooperative interaction for classroom application. In R. Hertz-Lazarowitz & N. Miller (Eds.), *Interaction in cooperative groups: Theoretical anatomy of group learning* (pp. 253–280). New York: Cambridge University Press.

Hooper, S., & Hannafin, M. J. (1988). Cooperative CBI: The effects of heterogeneous versus homogeneous grouping on the learning of progressively complex concepts. *Journal of Educational Computing Research, 4,* 413–424.

Hooper, S., Ward, T. J., Hannafin, M. J., & Clark, H. T. (1989). The effects of aptitude composition on achievement during small group learning. *Journal of Computer-Based Instruction, 16,* 102–109.

Hythecker, V. I., Dansereau, D. F., & Rocklin, T. R. (1988). An analysis of the processes influencing the structured dyadic learning environment. *Educational Psychologist, 23,* 23–27.

Johnson, D. W., & Johnson, R. T. (1975a). *Joining together: Group theory and group skills*. Englewood Cliffs, NJ: Prentice Hall.

Johnson, D. W., & Johnson, R. T. (1975b). *Learning together and alone: Cooperation, competition, and individualization*. Englewood Cliffs, NJ: Prentice Hall.

Johnson, D. W., & Johnson, R. T. (1979). Conflict in the classroom: Controversy and learning. *Review of Educational Research, 49,* 51–70.

Johnson, D. W., & Johnson, R. T. (1985a). Classroom conflict: Controversy versus debate in learning groups. *American Educational Research Journal, 22*(2), 237–256.

Johnson, D. W., & Johnson, R. T. (1985b). The internal dynamics of cooperative learning groups. In R. Slavin, S. Sharan, S. Kagan, R. Hertz-Lazarowitz, C. Webb, & R. Schmuck (Eds.), *Learning to cooperate, cooperating to learn* (pp. 103–124). New York: Plenum Press.

Johnson, D. W., & Johnson, R. T. (1986). *Learning together and alone* (2nd ed.). Englewood Cliffs, NJ: Prentice Hall.

Johnson, D. W., & Johnson, R. T. (1987). *Joining together: Group theory and group skills,* 2ed. Englewood Cliffs, NJ: Prentice Hall.

Johnson, D. W., & Johnson, R. T. (1990). Cooperative learning and achievement. In S. Sharan (Ed.), *Cooperative learning: Theory and research* (pp. 23–38). New York: Praeger.

Johnson, D. W., Johnson, R. T., Holubec, E. J., & Roy, P. (1984). *Circles of learning*. Alexandria, VA: Association for Supervision and Curriculum Development.

Johnson, D. W., Johnson, R. T., Pierson, W. T., & Lyons, V. (1985). Controversy versus concurrence seeking in multi-grade and single-grade learning groups. *Journal of Research in Science Teaching, 22,* 835–848.

Johnson, D. W., Maruyama, G., Johnson, R. T., Nelson, D., & Skon, L. (1983). Effects of cooperative, competitive, and individualistic goal structures on achievement: A meta-analysis. *Psychological Bulletin, 89,* 47–62.

Johnson, R. T., Johnson, D. W., & Stanne, M. B. (1985). Effects of cooperative, competitive, and individualistic goal structures on com-

puter-assisted instruction. *Journal of Educational Psychology, 77,* 668–677.

Kagan, S. (1984). Interpreting Chicano cooperativeness: Methodological and theoretical considerations. In J. L. Martinez & R. H. Mendoza (Eds.), *Chicano psychology* (2nd ed., pp. 289–333). New York: Academic Press.

Kagan, S. (1985). Dimensions of cooperative classroom structures. In R. Slavin, S. Sharan, S. Kagan, R. Hertz-Lazarowitz, C. Webb, & R. Schmuck (Eds.), *Learning to cooperate, cooperating to learn* (pp. 67–96). New York: Plenum Press.

Kagan, S. (1992). *Cooperative Learning*. San Juan Capistrano, CA: Resources for Teachers.

Kagan, S., & Knight, G. P. (1981). Social motives among Anglo American and Mexican American children: Experimental and projective measures. *Journal of Research in Personality, 15,* 93–106.

Kagan, S., Zahn, G. L., Widaman, K., Schwarzwald, J., & Tyrrell, G. (1985). Classroom structural bias: Impact of cooperative and competitive classroom structures on cooperative and competitive individuals and groups. In R. Slavin, S. Sharan, S. Kagan, R. Hertz-Lazarowitz, C. Webb, & R. Schmuck (Eds.), *Learning to cooperate, cooperating to learn* (pp. 277–312). New York: Plenum Press.

Kearney, B. A. (1991, April). *The teacher as absent presence*. Paper presented at the annual meeting of the American Educational Research Association, Chicago.

Kelley, H., & Thibaut, J. W. (1954). Experimental studies of group problem solving and process. In G. Lindzey (Ed.), *Handbook of social psychology* (3rd ed., pp. 735–785). Reading, MA: Addison-Wesley.

Kerr, N. L., & Bruun, S. E. (1983). Dispensability of member effort and group motivation losses: Free-rider effects. *Journal of Personality & Social Psychology, 44,* 78–94.

Kilpatrick, W. H. (1922). *The project method: the use of the purposeful act in the educative process*. New York: Teachers College Press.

Kilpatrick, W. H. (1925). *Foundations of method*. New York: Columbia University Press.

King, A. (1989). Effects of self-questioning training on college students' comprehension of lectures. *Contemporary Educational Psychology, 14,* 366–381.

King, A. (1990). Enhancing peer interaction and learning in the classroom through reciprocal questioning. *American Educational Research Journal, 27,* 664–687.

King, A. (1992). Facilitating elaborative learning through guided student-generated questioning. *Educational Psychologist, 27,* 111–126.

Kinsler, K. (1990). Structured peer collaboration: Teaching essay revision to college students needing writing remediation. *Cognition and Instruction, 7* (4), 303–321.

Kuhn, D. (1972). Mechanisms of change in the development of cognitive structures. *Child Development, 43,* 833–844.

Lambiotte, J. G., Dansereau, D. F., O'Donnell, A. M., Young, M. D., Skaggs, L. P., Hall, R. H., & Rocklin, T. R. (1987). Manipulating cooperative scripts for teaching and learning. *Journal of Educational Psychology, 79,* 424–430.

Lazarowitz, R., Baird, J. H., Hertz-Lazarowitz, R., & Jenkins, J. (1985). The effects of modified Jigsaw on achievement, classroom social climate, and self-esteem in high school science classes. In R. Slavin, S. Sharan, S. Kagan, R. Hertz-Lazarowitz, C. Webb, & R. Schmuck (Eds.), *Learning to cooperate, cooperating to learn* (pp. 231–254). New York: Plenum Press.

Lepper, M. R. (1983). Extrinsic reward and intrinsic motivation. In J. M. Levin & M. C. Wang (Eds.), *Teacher and student perceptions: Implications for learning* (pp. 281–318). Hillsdale, NJ: Lawrence Erlbaum Associates.

Lepper, M. R., & Green, D. (Eds.). (1978). *The hidden costs of reward*. Hillsdale, NJ: Lawrence Erlbaum Associates.

Lewin, K. L. (1951). *Field theory in social science*. New York: Harper & Row.

Light, P., & Glachan, M. (1985). Facilitation of individual problem solving through peer interaction. *Developmental psychology and education* (Special Issue: Educational Psychology), *5*, 217–225.

Lindow, J. A., Wilkinson, L. C., & Peterson, P. L. (1985). Antecedents and consequences of verbal disagreements during small-group learning. *Journal of Educational Psychology, 77*(6), 658–667.

Lockheed, M. E., & Harris, A. M. (1984). Cross-sex collaborative learning in elementary classrooms. *American Educational Research Journal, 21*, 275–294.

Lockheed, M. E., Harris, A. M., & Nemceff, W. P. (1983). Sex and social influence: Does sex function as a status characteristic in mixed-sex groups of children? *Journal of Educational Psychology, 75*(6), 877–888.

Lott, A. J., & Lott, B. E. (1965). Group cohesiveness and individual learning. *Journal of Educational Psychology, 57*(2), 61–73.

Maller, J. B. (1929). *Cooperation and competition: an experimental study in motivation.* New York: Teachers College Press.

Maskit, D. (1986). *Cooperative teaching and learning in adult learning.* Unpublished master's thesis, University of Haifa, School of Education. (In Hebrew.)

May, M., & Doob, L. (1937). *Competition and cooperation.* New York: Social Science Research Council.

Mayer, R. E. (1984). Aids to prose comprehension. *Educational Psychologist, 19*, 30–42.

McMahon, S. (1992). Book club: A case study of a group of fifth graders as they participate in a literature-based reading program. *Reading Research Quarterly, 27*(4), 292–294.

Meloth, M. S., & Deering, P. D. (1992). Effects of two cooperative conditions on peer-group discussions, reading comprehension, and metacognition. *Contemporary Educational Psychology, 17*, 175–193.

Michaels, J. W. (1977). Classroom reward structures and academic performance. *Review of Educational Research, 47*, 87–98.

Miller, L. K., & Hamblin, R. L. (1963). Interdependence, differential rewarding, and productivity. *American Sociological Review, 28*, 763–778.

Miller, M. (1987). Argumentation and cognition. In M. Hickmann (Ed.), *Social and functional approaches to language and thought.* New York: Academic Press.

Miller, N., & Harrington, H. J. (1990). A situational identity perspective on cultural diversity and teamwork in the classroom. In S. Sharan (Ed.), *Cooperative learning: Theory and research* (pp. 39–76). New York: Praeger.

Miller, S. A., & Brownell, C. A. (1975). Peers, persuasion, and Piaget: Dyadic interaction between conservers and nonconservers. *Child Development, 46*, 992–997.

Mugny, G., & Doise, W. (1978). Socio-cognitive conflict and structure of individual and collective performances. *European Journal of Social Psychology, 8*, 181–192.

Mulryan, C. (1989). *A study of intermediate-grade students' involvement and participation in cooperative small groups in mathematics.* Unpublished doctoral dissertation, University of Missouri—Columbia.

Murray, F. B. (1982). Teaching through social conflict. *Contemporary Educational Psychology, 7*, 257–271.

National Research Council. (1989). *Everybody counts: A report to the nation of the future of mathematics education.* Washington, DC: National Academy Press.

Nelson-Le Gall, S. (1981). Help-seeking: An understudied problem-solving skill in children. *Developmental Review, 1*, 224–246.

Nelson-Le Gall, S. (1985). Help-seeking behavior in learning. In E. V. Gordon (Ed.), *Review of research in education* (Vol. 12, pp. 55–90). Washington, DC: American Educational Research Association.

Nelson-Le Gall, S., Gumerman, R. A., & Scott-Jones, D. (1983). Instrumental help-seeking and everyday problem-solving: A developmental perspective. *New directions in helping* (Vol. 2, pp. 265–283). New York: Academic Press.

Newman, R. S. (1990). Children's help-seeking in the classroom: The role of motivational factors and attitudes. *Journal of Educational Psychology, 82*, 71–80.

Noddings, N. (1985). Small groups as a setting for research on mathematical problem solving. In E. A. Silver (Ed.), *Teaching and learning mathematical problem solving.* Hillsdale, NJ: Lawrence Erlbaum Associates.

O'Donnell, A. M., Dansereau, D. F., Hall R. H., & Rocklin, T. R. (1987). Cognitive, social/affective, and metacognitive outcomes of scripted cooperative learning. *Journal of Educational Psychology, 79*, 431–437.

O'Donnell, A. M., Dansereau, D. F., Hall, R. H., Skaggs, L. P., Hythecker, V. I., Peel, J. L., & Rewey, K. L. (1990). Learning concrete procedures: Effects of processing strategies and cooperative learning. *Journal of Educational Psychology, 82*, 171–177.

Oakes, J. (1990). *Multiplying inequalities: The effects of race, social class, and tracking on opportunities to learn mathematics and science* (Report R-3928-NSF). Santa Monica, CA: Rand Corp.

Okebukola, P. A. (1986). The influence of preferred learning styles on cooperative learning in science. *Science Education, 70*, 509–517.

Palincsar, A. S. (1986). The role of dialogue in providing scaffolded instruction. *Educational Psychologist, 21*, 73–98.

Palincsar, A. S., Anderson, C., & David, Y. M. (1993). Pursuing scientific literacy in the middle grades through collaborative problem solving. *Elementary School Journal, 93*(5), 643–658.

Palincsar, A. S., & Brown, A. L. (1984). Reciprocal teaching of comprehension-fostering and comprehension-monitoring activities. *Cognition and Instruction, 1*, 117–175.

Parecki, A., & Palincsar, A. S. (1992, November). *Examining "feedback" as a context for literacy learning among students identified as learning disabled.* Paper presented at the National Reading Conference, San Antonio, TX.

Pepitone, E. A. (1980). *Children in cooperation and competition.* Lexington, MA: Lexington Books.

Perret-Clermont, A.-N. (1980). *Social interaction and cognitive development in children* (European Monographs in Social Psychology No. 19, H. Tajfel, Series Ed.). New York: Academic Press.

Peterson, P. L., & Janicki, T. C. (1979). Individual characteristics and children's approaches. *Journal of Educational Psychology, 71*, 677–687.

Peterson, P. L., Janicki, T. C., & Swing, S. R. (1981). Ability × treatment interaction effects on children's learning in large-group and small-group approaches. *American Educational Research Journal, 18*, 453–473.

Peterson, P. L., Wilkinson, L. C., Spinelli, F., & Swing, S. R. (1984). Merging the process-product and the sociolinguistic paradigms: Research on small-group process. In P. L. Peterson, L. C. Wilkinson, & M. Hallinan (Eds.), *The social context of instruction* (pp. 126–152). Orlando, FL: Academic Press.

Piaget, J. (1932). *The language and thought of the child* (2nd ed.). London: Routledge & Kegan Paul.

Piaget, J. (1976). *The grasp of consciousness: Action and concept in the young child.* Cambridge, MA: Harvard University Press.

Piaget, J. (1985). *The equilibration of cognitive structures: The central problem of intellectual development.* (T. Brown & K. L. Thampy, Trans.). Chicago: University of Chicago Press.

Pressley, M., Wood, E., Woloshyn, V. E., Martin, V., King, A., & Menke, D. (1992). Encouraging mindful use of prior knowledge: Attempting to construct explanatory answers facilitates learning. *Educational Psychologist, 27*, 91–110.

Raphael, T. E., McMahon, S. I., Goatley, V., Bentley, J., Boyd, F. B., Pardo, L. S., & Woodman, D. A. (1992). Literature and discussion in the reading program. *Language Arts, 69*, 54–61.

Richard-Amato, P. A. & Snow, M. A. (Eds.). (1992). *The multicultural classroom: Readings for content-area teachers.* White Plains, NY: Longman.

Richmond, B. O., & Weiner, G. P. (1973). Cooperation and competition among young children as a function of ethnic grouping, grade, sex and reward condition. *Journal of Educational Psychology, 64,* 329–334.

Rickover, H. M. (1959). *Education and freedom.* New York: Dutton.

Rippa, S. A. (1958). The textbook controversy and the free enterprise campaign, 1940–41. *History of Education Journal, 9,* 49–57.

Rippa, S. A. (1964). The business community and the public schools on the eve of the great depression. *History of Education Quarterly, 4,* 1, 33–43.

Rocklin, T., O'Donnell, A., Dansereau, D. F., Lambiotte, J. G., Hythecker, V., & Larson, C. (1985). Training learning strategies with computer-aided cooperative learning. *Computers and Education, 9,* 67–71.

Rogoff, B. (1991). Guidance and participation in spatial planning. In L. Resnick, J. Levine, & S. Teasley (Eds.), *Perspectives on socially shared cognition* (pp. 349–383). Washington, DC: American Psychological Association.

Roschelle, J. (1992). Learning by collaborating: Convergent conceptual change. *Journal of Learning Sciences, 2,* 235–276.

Rosenholtz, S. J. (1985). Modifying status expectations in the traditional classroom. In J. Berger & M. Zelditch (Eds.), *Status, rewards, and influence* (pp. 445–470). San Francisco: Jossey-Bass.

Ross, S. M., & DiVesta, F. J. (1976). Oral summary as a review strategy enhancing recall of textual material. *Journal of Educational Psychology, 68,* 689–695.

Roth, W. M. (1992, April). *Semiotic mediation during the collaborative construction of meaning in a high school science class.* Paper presented at the annual meeting of the American Educational Research Association, San Francisco.

Russell, J., Mills, I., & Reiff-Musgrove, P. (1990). The role of symmetrical and asymmetrical social conflict in cognitive change. *Journal of Experimental Child Psychology, 49,* 58–78.

Salomon, G., & Globerson, T. (1989). When teams do not function the way they ought to. *International Journal of Educational Research, 13,* 89–99.

Saxe, G. B. (1992). Studying children's learning in context: Problems and prospects. *Journal of the Learning Sciences, 2,* 215–234.

Scardamalia, M., & Bereiter, C. (1991). Higher levels of agency for children in knowledge building: A challenge for the design of new knowledge media. *Journal of the Learning Sciences, 1,* 37–68.

Schunk, D. H. (1987). Peer models and children's behavioral change. *Review of Educational Research, 57,* 149–174.

Sharan, S. (1980). Cooperative learning in small groups: Recent methods and effects on achievement, attitudes, and ethnic relations. *Review of Educational Research, 50,* 241–272.

Sharan, S., & Hertz-Lazarowitz, R. (1980). A group-investigation method of cooperative learning in the classroom. In S. Sharan, P. Hare, C. D. Webb, & R. Hertz-Lazarowitz (Eds.), *Cooperation in education* (pp. 14–46). Provo, UT: Brigham Young University Press.

Sharan, S., Kussell, P., Hertz-Lazarowitz, R., Bejarano, Y., Raviv, S., & Sharan, Y. (1985). Cooperative learning effects on ethnic relations and achievement in Israeli junior-high-school classrooms. In R. Slavin, S. Sharan, S. Kagan, R. Hertz-Lazarowitz, C. Webb, & R. Schmuck (Eds.), *Learning to cooperate, cooperating to learn* (pp. 313–344). New York: Plenum Press.

Sharan, S., & Sharan, Y. (1976). *Small-group teaching.* Englewood Cliffs, NJ: Educational Technology Publications.

Sharan, S., & Shaulov, A. (1990). Cooperative learning, motivation to learn, and academic achievement. In S. Sharan (Ed.), *Cooperative learning: Theory and research* (pp. 173–202). New York: Praeger.

Shavelson, R. J., Webb, N. M., Stasz, C., & McArthur, D. (1988). *Teaching mathematical problem solving: Insights from teachers and tutors.* In R. Charles & E. Silver (Eds.), *Teaching and assessing mathematical problem-solving: A research agenda* (pp. 203–231). Hillsdale, NJ: Lawrence Erlbaum Associates.

Skon, L., Johnson, D. W., & Johnson, R. T. (1981). Cooperative peer interaction versus individual competition and individualistic efforts: Effects on the acquisition of cognitive reasoning strategies. *Journal of Educational Psychology, 73,* 83–92.

Slavin, R. E. (1977). Classroom reward structure: An analytical and practical review. *Review of Educational Research, 47,* 633–650.

Slavin, R. E. (1978a). *Student learning teams and scores adjusted for past achievement: A summary of field experiments* (Report No. 227). Baltimore, MD: Johns Hopkins University, Center for Social Organization of Schools.

Slavin, R. E. (1978b). Student teams and achievement divisions. *Journal of Research and Development in Education, 12,* 39–49.

Slavin, R. E. (1978c). Student teams and comparison among equals: Effects on academic performance and student attitudes. *Journal of Educational Psychology, 70,* 532–538.

Slavin, R. E. (1980). Effects of student teams and peer tutoring on academic achievement and time-on-task. *Journal of Experimental Education, 48,* 252–257.

Slavin, R. E. (1983a). *Cooperative learning.* New York: Longman.

Slavin, R. E. (1983b). When does cooperative learning increase student achievement? *Psychological Bulletin, 94,* 429–445.

Slavin, R. E. (1987). Developmental and motivational perspectives on cooperative learning: A reconciliation. *Child Development, 58,* 1161–1167.

Slavin, R. E. (1989). Cooperative learning and student achievement. In R. E. Slavin (Ed.), *School and classroom organization* (pp. 129–156). Hillsdale, NJ: Lawrence Erlbaum Associates.

Slavin, R. E. (1990a). Comprehensive cooperative learning models: Embedding cooperative learning in the curriculum and the school. In S. Sharan (Ed.), *Cooperative learning: Theory and research* (pp. 261–284). New York: Praeger.

Slavin, R. E. (1990b). *Cooperative learning: Theory, research, and practice.* Englewood Cliffs, NJ: Prentice Hall.

Smith, K. A., Johnson, D. W., & Johnson, R. T. (1984). Effects of controversy on learning in cooperative groups. *Journal of Social Psychology, 122,* 199–209.

Smith-Lovin, L., & Brody, C. (1989). Interruptions in group discussions: The effects of gender and group composition. *American Sociological Review, 54,* 424–435.

Solomon, D., Watson, M., Battistich, V., Schaps, E., Tuck, P., Solomon, J., Cooper, C., & Ritchey, W. (1985). A program to promote interpersonal consideration and cooperation in children. In R. Slavin, S. Sharan, S. Kagan, R. Hertz-Lazarowiz, C. Webb, & R. Schmuck (Eds.), *Learning to cooperate, cooperating to learn* (pp. 371–402). New York: Plenum Press.

Solomon, D., Watson, M., Delucchi, K. L., Schaps, E., & Battistich, V. (1988). Enhancing children's prosocial behavior in the classroom. *American Educational Research Journal, 25,* 527–554.

Solomon, D., Watson, M., Schaps, E., Battistich, V., & Solomon, J. (1990). Cooperative learning as part of a comprehensive classroom program designed to promote prosocial development. In S. Sharan (Ed.), *Cooperative learning: Theory and research* (pp. 231–260). New York: Praeger.

South, E. B. (1927). Some psychological aspects of committee work. *Journal of Applied Psychology, 11,* 348–368.

Spurlin, J. E., Dansereau, D. F., Larson, C. O., & Brooks, L. W. (1984). Cooperative learning strategies in processing descriptive text: Effects of role and activity level of the learner. *Cognition and Instruction, 1,* 451–463.

Steiner, I. (1972). *Group process and productivity.* New York: Academic Press.

Stevens, R. J., Slavin, R. E., & Farnish, A. M. (1991). The effects of cooperative learning and direct instruction in reading comprehension strategies and main idea identification. *Journal of Educational Psychology, 83,* 8–16.

Swing, S. R., & Peterson, P. L. (1982). The relationship of student ability and small-group interaction to student achievement. *American Educational Research Journal, 19,* 259–274.

Tammivaara, J. S. (1982). The effects of task structure on beliefs about competence and participation in small groups. *Sociology of Education, 55,* 212–222.

Tharp, R. G., & Gallimore, R. (1988). *Rousing minds to life: Teaching, learning, and schooling in social context.* Cambridge, England: Cambridge University Press.

Thorndike, R. L. (1938). On what type of task will a group do well? *Journal of Abnormal and Social Psychology, 33,* 409–413.

Tingle, J. B., & Good, R. (1990). Effects of cooperative grouping on stoichiometric problem solving in high school chemistry. *Journal of Research in Science Teaching, 27,* 671–683.

Trevarthen, C. (1980). The foundations of intersubjectivity: Development of interpersonal and cooperative understanding in infants. In D. R. Olson (Ed.), *The social foundations of language and thought* (pp. 316–342). New York: Norton.

Trowbridge, D., & Durnin, R. (1984a). *A study of student-computer interactivity.* Unpublished paper, University of California, Irvine.

Trowbridge, D., & Durnin, R. (1984b). *Research from an investigation of groups working together at the computer.* Unpublished paper, University of California, Irvine.

Tudge, J. (1989). When collaboration leads to regression: Some negative consequences of socio-cognitive conflict. *European Journal of Social Psychology, 19,* 123–138.

Tudge, J., & Rogoff, B. (1989). Peer influences on cognitive development: Piagetian and Vygotskian perspectives. In M. H. Bornstein & J. S. Bruner (Eds.), *Interaction in human development* (pp. 17–40). Hillsdale, NJ: Lawrence Erlbaum Associates.

Vedder, P. (1985). *Cooperative learning. A study on processes and effects of cooperation between primary school children.* Westerhaven, Groningen, Netherlands: Rijkuniversiteit Groningen.

Vygotsky, L. S. (1978). *Mind in society: The development of higher psychological processes* (M. Cole, V. John-Steiner, S. Scribner, & E. Souberman, Eds. and Trans.). Cambridge, MA: Harvard University Press.

Vygotsky, L. S. (1979). Consciousness as a problem in the psychology of behavior. *Soviet Psychology, 17*(4), 3–35.

Vygotsky, L. S. (1981). The genesis of higher mental functioning. In J. V. Wertsch (Ed.), *The concept of activity in Soviet psychology* (pp. 144–188). Armonk, NY: Sharpe.

Wagner, L. (1982). *Peer teaching: Historical perspectives.* New York: Greenwood Press.

Watson, G. B. (1928). Do groups think more efficiently than individuals? *Journal of Abnormal and Social Psychology, 23,* 328–336.

Webb, N. M. (1980). A process-outcome analysis of learning in group and individual settings. *Educational Psychologist, 15,* 69–83.

Webb, N. M. (1984a). Microcomputer learning in small groups: Cognitive requirements and group processes. *Journal of Educational Psychology, 76,* 1076–1088.

Webb, N. M. (1984b). Sex differences in interaction and achievement in cooperative small groups. *Journal of Educational Psychology, 76,* 33–34.

Webb, N. M. (1989). Peer interaction and learning in small groups. *International Journal of Educational Research, 13,* 21–40.

Webb, N. M. (1991). Task-related verbal interaction and mathematics learning in small groups. *Journal for Research in Mathematics Education, 22,* 366–389.

Webb, N. M. (1992). Testing a theoretical model of student interaction and learning in small groups. In R. Hertz-Lazarowitz & N. Miller (Eds.), *Interaction in cooperative groups: The theoretical anatomy of group learning* (pp. 102–119). New York: Cambridge University Press.

Webb, N. M., Ender, P., & Lewis, S. (1986). Problem-solving strategies and group processes in small groups learning computer programming. *American Educational Research Journal, 23,* 248–262.

Webb, N. M., & Farivar, S. (1994). Promoting helping behavior in cooperative small groups in middle school mathematics. *American Educational Research Journal, 31,* 369–395.

Webb, N. M., & Kenderski, C. M. (1984). Student interaction and learning in small group and whole class settings. In P. L. Peterson, L. C. Wilkinson, & M. Hallinan (Eds.), *The social content of instruction: Group organization and group processes* (pp. 153–170). New York: Academic Press.

Webb, N. M., & Kenderski, C. M. (1985). Gender differences in small group interaction and achievement in high-achieving and low-achieving classrooms. In L. C. Wilkinson & C. B. Marret (Eds.), *Gender related differences in classroom interaction* (pp. 209–226). New York: Academic Press.

Webb, N. M., Troper, J. D., & Fall, R. (1995). Constructive activity and learning in collaborative small groups. *Journal of Educational Psychology, 87,* 406–423.

Weiner, B. (1980). May I borrow your class notes? An attributional analysis of judgments of help giving in an achievement-related context. *Journal of Educational Psychology, 72,* 676–681.

Weinstein, C. E., & Mayer, R. F. (1986). The teaching of learning strategies. In M. C. Wittrock (Ed.), *Handbook of research on teaching* (3rd ed., pp. 315–327). New York: Macmillan.

Wertsch, J. V. (1991). *Voices of the mind: A sociocultural approach to mediated action.* Cambridge, MA: Harvard University Press.

Wertsch, J. V., & Bivens, J. (1992). The social origins of individual mental functioning: Alternatives and perspectives. *Quarterly Newsletter of the Laboratory of Comparative Human Cognition, 14*(2), 35–44.

Wilkinson, L. C. (1985). Communication in all-student mathematics groups. *Theory into Practice, 24*(1), 8–13.

Wilkinson, L. C., & Calculator, S. (1982a). Effective speakers: Students' use of language to request and obtain information and action in the classroom. In L. C. Wilkinson (Ed.), *Communicating in the classroom.* New York: Academic Press.

Wilkinson, L. C., & Calculator, S. (1982b). Requests and responses in peer-directed reading groups. *American Educational Research Journal, 19,* 107–120.

Wilkinson, L. C., & Spinelli, F. (1983). Using requests effectively in peer-directed instructional groups. *American Educational Research Journal, 20,* 479–502.

Wittrock, M. C. (1990). Generative processes of comprehension. *Educational Psychologist, 24,* 345–376.

Wodarski, J. S., Hamblin, R. L., Buckholdt, D. R., & Ferritor, D. E. (1973). Individual consequences versus different shared consequences contingent on the performance of low-achieving group members. *Journal of Applied Social Psychology, 3,* 276–290.

Wong, B. Y. L. (1985). Self-questioning instructional research: A review. *Review of Educational Research, 55,* 227–268.

Wood, D., Bruner, J. S., & Ross, G. (1976). The role of tutoring in problem solving. *Journal of Child Psychology and Psychiatry, 17,* 89–100.

Wood, T., & Yackel, E. (1990). The development of collaborative dialogue within small group interactions. In L. P. Steffe & T. Wood (Eds.), *Transforming early childhood mathematics education: An international perspective* (pp. 244–252). Hillsdale, NJ: Lawrence Erlbaum Associates.

Yackel, E., Cobb, P., & Wood, T. (1991). Small-group interactions as a source of learning opportunities in second-grade mathematics. *Journal for Research in Mathematics Education, 22,* 390–408.

Yager, S., Johnson, D. W., & Johnson, R. T. (1985). Oral discussion, group-to-individual transfer, and achievement in cooperative learning groups. *Journal of Educational Psychology, 77,* 60–66.

Yager, S., Johnson, R. T., Johnson, D. W., & Snider, B. (1986). The impact of group processing on achievement in cooperative learning groups. *Journal of Social Psychology, 126,* 389–397.

Zajonc, R. B. (1960). The process of cognitive tuning in communication. *Journal of Abnormal and Social Psychology, 61,* 159–167.

# FOUNDATIONS OF THE DISCIPLINE

# · 27 ·

# QUANTITATIVE RESEARCH METHODS AND DESIGN

## Richard M. Jaeger and Lloyd Bond
### UNIVERSITY OF NORTH CAROLINA AT GREENSBORO

## ABOUT THIS CHAPTER

This chapter contains two major sections beyond this introduction. In the first, we examine common threats to the validity of disciplined, quantitative inquiry in education in general, and educational psychology in particular, and suggest remedies. In the second, we focus on quantitative analytic procedures that can be applied to data collected through a variety of techniques and with a variety of research objectives. These two foci omit much of value, even within the bounds of quantitative approaches to research on the psychology of education.

### Our Biases and Their Consequences

Our own research preparation was quantitative, given to description and explanation as much as validation (Krathwohl, 1993). Our research perspective is decidedly positivist; we believe in the existence of objective truth and knowledge even as we acknowledge our obvious subjectivity in selecting problems for study and our ways of studying them. Other researchers in the social and behavioral sciences, including educational psychology, contend that all reality is essentially subjective and that research consisting of rich description, close attention to the meaning of concepts and truth claims, and careful acknowledgment of perspectives and biases should encompass the whole of scholarly inquiry in education, including its psychology. We acknowledge this latter view, recognize its recent ascendancy, and ignore it beyond this acknowledgment. Lest we be accused of the naïveté of the student who said to the astronomer, "I can understand how you scientists figured out the brightness and distance from Earth of the stars, but how did you figure out their *names?*" we fully appreciate that, as scientists, we *impose* our understanding, in the form of models, on objective reality, but this in no way negates the existence of that objective reality. The Earth revolved around the sun, in much the way that Kepler and Newton later conceived it, long before the appearance of *homo sapiens* on the planet.

Quantification is *not* essential to sound, effective, and useful research in educational psychology. For instance, Piaget pro-

vided rich insights into the cognitive development of children by observing, recording, and analyzing the behavior of his own daughters. His insights have, for the most part, stood the test of time and have been validated in countless more formal studies; many are widely accepted even today. Nonetheless, because quantitative research methods have dominated the field of educational psychology since its inception, and have dominated our lives as well, we ignore qualitative inquiry methods entirely beyond this brief acknowledgment. This omission can be remedied by studying chapter 30, on data analysis, by John T. Behrens and Mary Lee Smith in this volume, or one or more of a wide variety of broad-based research texts (e.g., Gay, 1992; Jaeger, 1988; and Krathwohl, 1993).

By far the dominant products of scholarly inquiry in educational psychology would be regarded as focusing on validation rather than on description or explanation (Krathwohl, 1993), or as conclusion oriented rather than decision oriented (Cronbach & Suppes, 1969). Such studies begin with statements of belief (termed hypotheses) and employ well-structured analytic strategies in an attempt to validate the researchers' hypotheses. In disciplines as formally immature as the psychology of education, inquiry that focuses on detailed description of the objects of research and the contexts that surround them, or inquiry that focuses on relationships between antecedent conditions and current characteristics of the objects of research (here termed explanatory research), will often provide rich insights that motivate later attempts at validation. In our selection of content we attempt to deal in a balanced way with research strategies that support rigorous description, attempts at explanation, and quests for validation. We give them nearly equal attention because we consider them to be equally important to scholarly inquiry in the field of educational psychology.

Thus, this chapter provides an overview of important concepts of quantitative, positivist inquiry that have been widely applied by researchers in the field of educational psychology. These concepts are presented at a level that is accessible to graduate students early in their methodological preparation. Others with more formal research background and greater experience should find that this chapter provides a useful review, plus an introduction to some research methods or analytic strategies that entered the lexicon of social science inquiry after the completion of their own methodological training. Both audiences should consider this chapter to be an introduction more than a guide, and certainly not a text that provides background sufficient to apply any of the procedures described.

Our discussion relies largely on the verbal descriptions of research methods and statistical procedures employed by Jaeger (1990). For detailed statistical and computational procedures we refer to texts like those of Winer, Brown, and Michaels (1991), Ferguson and Takane (1989), and Timm (1975). The level of presentation is aimed at readers at the graduate and postgraduate levels of education and psychology who have a basic understanding of the elements of quantitative research methods but desire a review of basic concepts and an introduction to some advanced quantitative analytic techniques.

## What Is Research?

The word "research" has assumed broad meaning in common parlance. Writers of fictional prose and film scripts do research when they strive for authentic description of a story context. Politicians do research when they gather information on the demographic characteristics of their constituents or explore the legislative history of a pending bill. Artists do research when they formulate the composition of an art work.

Educational psychologists do research when they examine the cognitive development of young children; explore relationships between teachers' instructional preferences, educational experiences, and classroom performances; manipulate the structural features of lessons and study resulting student participation levels; or explore issues associated with the interactions of teachers, learners, and learning contexts in situations as they are or as the researcher intervenes in an attempt to influence them. The distinguishing feature of research as defined in this chapter is its disciplinary nature. Cronbach and Suppes (1969) characterized research as "disciplined inquiry," and that is the definition we adopt here. Disciplined inquiry is distinguished from casual examination of conditions or problems by its rigorous structure and its disciplinary grounding. Inquiry that is disciplined adheres to formal rules of procedure for gathering information and testing the truth of claims that derive from the investigation of collected data. In addition, it is firmly grounded in one or more disciplines—such as psychology, sociology, history, or anthropology—that follow well-recognized rules of inquiry.

## Reading Comprehension, an Example

The ability to discern meaning from prose, fundamental to the acquisition of knowledge, has been the subject of volumes of research in the psychology of learning. Among topics examined in studies of language acquisition have been such antecedent factors as support for learning in the home, including the opportunity to practice reading skills by having substantial sources of reading material present in the student's home. In 1992 the Educational Testing Service published a report titled "The Family and Learning" that examined the relationship in 18 nations between students' mean scores on an international assessment of reading comprehension and the percentage of students who reported that their homes contained 25 or more reading sources.

**TABLE 27–1 Results of a Comparison of Reading-Source-Rich and Reading-Source-Poor Children**

| | Mean Reading Comprehension Score | Volunteered Response Frequency | Mean Reading Time |
|---|---|---|---|
| News-Mags children | 26 | 8 | 3.1 hr/wk |
| Control children | 20 | 7 | 1.8 hr/wk |

Imagine a study designed to follow up this report. Assume that a research team identifies two groups of 50 young children in the United States, where a preliminary survey shows that the homes contain no reading materials—no newspapers, magazines, or books. The researchers remedy this perceived deficiency by delivering a daily newspaper and two weekly magazines to the homes of one group of 50 children (the News-Mags group). The control group receives weekly advertisements from local groceries and drug stores. Both groups are surveyed monthly to determine reading and television-viewing activities.

At the end of a year, the researchers compare the performance of the two groups on a 40-item reading comprehension test, assess their willingness to answer questions in class based on assigned reading passages, and survey children's reports of time spent reading outside of class. They find that the average reading comprehension score of the News-Mags children is 26 items correct, while the average for the control group is only 20 items correct. The average frequency of volunteered responses to class-assigned readings is 8 per class period for the News-Mags group and 7 per class period for the control group, and the average time spent reading outside of class is respectively 3.1 hours and 1.8 hours per week for the two groups. The results are shown in Table 27–1.

From these results, the researchers conclude that (a) the effects of having reading materials in the home on the reading comprehension scores of young children are substantial, (b) the presence of reading materials in the home has a negligible influence on children's in-class discussion of reading passages, but (c) these materials have a substantial effect on out-of-school reading behavior.

Do you agree with these conclusions? Are the results trustworthy? Would you be right in advising the parents of young children to purchase a daily newspaper and to subscribe to several magazines based on these results?

Whenever we encounter conclusions drawn from empirical research studies, we must consider their trustworthiness. Fortunately, issues surrounding the trustworthiness of research findings have been codified and enjoy a rich literature developed by thoughtful and insightful pioneers in the field of empirical research methods. In the following section we examine several of the most important issues in some depth. Additional coverage can be found in Campbell and Stanley (1963), Cook and Campbell (1979), Bracht and Glass (1968), and chapter 15 of Borg and Gall (1989).

## THREATS TO VALID RESEARCH

A fundamental dichotomy is traditionally used to classify issues concerning the trustworthiness of conclusions drawn from empirical research: *internal validity* (the trustworthiness of conclusions for the persons and groups observed, and circumstances in which the research was conducted), and *external validity* (the trustworthiness of generalizations from this research to other persons, groups, or circumstances). This distinction is less clear-cut than it appears at first glance. In considering the preceding example, for instance, we will investigate in the next section the degree to which the researchers' conclusions can be justified, based on the particular sample of children and homes used, the particular set of measures applied, and the particular treatment used. But as soon as we use the term "reading comprehension test," we *imply* some degree of conceptual connection to comprehension in general; and as soon as we describe a treatment in which newspapers and magazines are provided to the homes, we *imply* some connection to reading materials in general (Krathwohl, 1993).

The next two sections deal in turn with internal and external validity. Each section is organized into two parts: threats to validity that arise from conditions in the selection of people, groups, and the settings in which they exist, and threats to validity that arise from the conditions of the experiment, including the treatments and the instruments used to assess reactions to the treatments.

## Internal Validity

Let us return to the study involving reading-source-rich homes and reading-source-poor homes. The researchers concluded that the presence of reading sources in the home resulted in substantial increases in children's scores on a reading comprehension test, negligible increases in their in-class participation in reading discussion, and substantial increases in their out-of-school reading time. Although it is indisputably true that differences between the two groups were observed in this study, the researchers run into trouble when they unequivocally attribute these results to differences in amount of reading materials provided to the homes. The researchers are asserting that differences in the amount of reading materials in the children's homes *caused* the differences in reading comprehension test performance, classroom participation, and amount of out-of-school reading observed for these children, and it is this assertion that provokes questions about internal validity.

On what basis can the researchers conclude unequivocally that the differences observed were caused by, or even associated with, the amount of reading materials available in the children's homes? Although it is possible that differences in reading materials produced the observed differences in the variables measured, many other explanations come to mind, and the causes of the observed differences may be entirely unrelated to the reading materials. To support a claim to causal effect, it is necessary to consider, in the words of Cook and Campbell (1979), "plausible rival explanations" and to demonstrate why these alternatives are unlikely.

*Control* is the critical construct in critiquing the internal validity of a study. In research, control means designing a study so that most if not all potentially plausible alternative explanations of the findings are rendered implausible, or far less plausible. In challenging a researcher's conclusions, we are really asking, How adequate is the research design? The counterpart to control is *confounding*. Most threats to internal validity arise

because, in some way, one or more other factors of importance to the conclusions covary with a treatment. A research design is adequate when it allows the researcher to counter alternative explanations. The threats are numerous; the most important to be discussed here are summarized in Table 27–2.

*Persons, Groups, and Settings.* The first set of plausible alternatives that we consider here arise from the way that persons or groups are selected for assignment to different treatment conditions, or the influence of covariations with other predetermined characteristics of these persons. We will use the home reading study for illustration. First, it is possible that only some of the families in the News-Mags group took up the offer to participate in the study; it's a bother to deal with strangers, to submit to interviews, and to handle the extra trash. The home backgrounds and life experiences of the children whose parents agreed to accept newspapers and magazines might differ substantially from those of children whose parents did not agree. Such parents might themselves be better educated and more interested in reading; more of these children might have two parents living in their homes than those children whose parents were unwilling to accept donated reading materials. Both of these factors have been found to be related to children's reading test performances in previous studies. The intrusions for the control group were far less extensive, it would appear, producing possible differences having nothing to do with the reading materials. Confounding might work in other ways to produce the same effect. For example, families who agreed to participate in the News-Mags group might be more assertive than those in the control group.

In both of these examples, it is not the availability of reading materials in the home but differences in family education and family structure or personality differences that promote or inhibit extra school reading among the young. This plausible rival explanation comes under the heading *group selection,* so designated by Cook and Campbell (1979). That is, the members of the two groups being compared in the research were selected in such a way that they were different at the outset. It is these initial differences, not the experience or treatment that occurred between subjects' selection and their assessment, that account for the differences found when the assessment was conducted. We cannot be certain that selection totally explains the differences observed in the reading study, but the claim is plausible and must be countered.

Selection of individuals for the groups to be compared in a research study contributes to many plausible explanations for the results of that study. In this example, if the 50 children in the reading-source-rich homes were of higher socioeconomic status than the 50 children in the reading-source-poor homes, the history of their experience from the time of their selection to the time of their assessment would be different from the history experienced during the same time period by the treatment children. Parents of low socioeconomic status typically live in neighborhoods with a higher incidence of crime and in households that offer fewer of the amenities that facilitate children's academic performance, such as parental support of children's academic pursuits. It is therefore quite plausible that the results observed in the research study—children in the News-Mags group having somewhat higher levels of reading test performance, slightly higher levels of in-class participation,

TABLE 27–2 Threats to the Internal Validity of Empirical Research Studies, Appropriate Control Methods, and Techniques for Detecting the Operation of Such Threats

| Type of Threat | Control Procedure | Detection Method |
|---|---|---|
| Group selection | Random assignment | Examine pretest characteristics of experimental subjects and comparison subjects |
| Selection history | Random assignment | Examine pretest histories of experimental subjects and comparison subjects |
| Selection maturation | Random assignment | Examine pretest characteristics and histories of experimental subjects and comparison subjects |
| Statistical regression | Avoid selection of extreme groups at pretest, or use statistical correction methods | Examine distribution of pretest scores of experimental subjects and, when used, comparison subjects |
| Mortality | Random assignment and incentives to remain in the study | Examine characteristics of those who leave the study compared with those who stay |
| Instrumentation | Use measurement instruments that operate the same way over the entire scale needed | Look for below-chance scores and near-perfect scores on pretest and posttest measures |
| Diffusion of treatment | Use pre-experimental comparison or a comparison group in a different setting | Collect detailed data on experimental treatment and comparison treatment, as delivered |
| Compensatory equalization | Use pre-experimental comparison or a comparison group in a different setting | Collect detailed data on experimental treatment and comparison treatment, as delivered |
| John Henry effect | Use pre-experimental comparison group | Interview providers of comparison treatment, or compare with pre-experimental performance of comparison providers |
| Testing effect | Use Solomon four-group design | Use Solomon four-group design |

and substantially greater time spent in out-of-class reading—could be attributed solely to differences in these children's prior experiences, quite apart from the amount of reading material available in their homes, between the time of their birth and the time their reading comprehension, in-class participation, and out-of-school reading time were assessed. Cook and Campbell (1979) refer to this as *selection history*.

Here is yet another rival explanation. The researchers appear to have paid little attention to the ages of the children in their study other than to note that they were all in elementary school. If the children whose homes were given the newspaper and magazine subscriptions happened to be, on average, a year older than the children whose homes were not given the reading materials, differences in age could, by themselves, explain the findings of the research study. Older children will, on average, earn higher reading comprehension test scores, will be more likely to understand reading passages and therefore to volunteer answers in class, and will be more likely to spend time reading outside of class. Beyond these initial differences, however, children in different age groups mature at different rates, thus enhancing their differences when they are measured, say, a year later. Differential maturity between the two groups, even if the children were comparable on other measures, could be a factor in explaining the results; this is an example of *selection maturation*.

What can be done to address threats due to selection problems? Can one ever trust the results of a research study? The answer to the first question is, a lot can be done, and to the second, most definitely. The key to handling these matters is to take care in designing and documenting the study.

For example, suppose that the News-Mags children performed better because they came from higher socioeconomic status families. The researchers could address this explanation at the outset by obtaining data on the socioeconomic status of the two groups of families. If they could show that the distributions of socioeconomic status of these families were very similar,

the explanation would be implausible. Even better, if the researchers designed the study to intentionally select pairs of children from families with similar socioeconomic status, with one child in each pair being assigned to the News-Mags group and one child to the control group, this rival explanation would have been eliminated. This strategy illustrates the concept of a *matching design*. It is effective in creating groups of subjects who are similar in the characteristics on which they are matched (in this case, socioeconomic status). The researcher needs to be smart in choosing matching factors that really matter. For example, groups of children whose families are similar in socioeconomic status might still differ markedly in other factors. Graduate students often have low incomes, but for purposes of this study that is less important than parents' educational level. Also, as we point out later, matching designs control only for differences on the matching variables. The groups could still differ on other variables.

We suggested earlier that the children assigned to the News-Mags and control treatments might have had different levels of reading ability at the beginning of the study. The same claim could be made concerning propensity to volunteer and propensity to read outside of school. Rival explanations involving preexisting differences often can be refuted by using *pretest-posttest designs*. Here groups of subjects are measured or observed before the treatment and again at the end of the treatment. If the groups are comparable on the pretest, rival explanations involving selection on the variables measured at time of pretest are controlled. The final phrase in the preceding sentence is very important. Just as in matching designs, groups that are comparable on one set of characteristics, in this case, average reading comprehension score, propensity to volunteer in class, and average amount of time spent reading outside of class, are not necessarily comparable in other ways.

Although there is no way to ensure with complete certainty that the groups to be compared in a research study will be comparable to each other at the outset of a study, an excellent method for increasing the likelihood of comparability is through *random assignment* of subjects to groups. If subjects are randomly assigned to groups, we can be certain that these groups will differ from each other on any characteristic that could be measured only to the extent that the luck of the draw might result in some chance differences. Unlike matching designs, in which subjects that are alike with respect to one, two, or three characteristics are assigned to different groups, when random assignment is used, groups of subjects are essentially comparable to each other on all possible characteristics. We emphasize the term "essentially comparable" because random assignment typically does not result in perfect matching of the groups on any characteristic. However, the groups will differ only within the bounds of chance fluctuation.

The power of random assignment of subjects is so profound that researchers consider research designs that incorporate random assignment to be in an entirely different class from those that do not. If random assignment is *not* used in a research design, it is generally termed a *quasi-experimental design*. The power of random assignment in empirical research has been well described by Porter (1988). Although random assignment does not allow a researcher to refute all rival explanations, it renders many of them far less plausible. First, since randomly assigned subjects differ from each other only by chance, rival explanations attributable to selection effects become implausible. For example, had the children in the reading study been assigned at random either to the News-Mags group or to the control group, it would no longer be plausible that their posttest differences in reading comprehension, classroom participation, or extraclass reading time were due to differences in the socioeconomic status of their families or to differences in their ages.

Explanations that depend on selection-maturity effects can also be refuted when subjects are randomly assigned. Recall our earlier conjecture that the average reading comprehension test score of the News-Mags group was higher than that of the control group when the study ended, not because the first group had higher levels of reading comprehension to begin with, but because age differences allowed them to progress at a higher rate during the study. This claim would have no substance if the ages of the News-Mags children differed from those of the control children only by chance. Similarly, rival explanations based on claims of differing prior histories for the groups are not viable when subjects are randomly assigned to groups.

Can we assume that the researchers assigned children in the reading materials study at random? Probably we cannot. As noted at the outset, some parents might refuse to accept the free subscriptions or to allow their children to participate in the study. For a variety of practical or ethical reasons, researchers are often faced with situations in which random assignment of subjects to groups is impossible. In such situations, quasi-experimental designs, rather than experimental designs, become the only possibility. It is in these situations that knowledge of the kinds of rival explanations we have discussed so far becomes essential. A researcher armed with such knowledge can use other elements of research design, such as pretesting, to control plausible threats to internal validity. And a consumer of research with such knowledge can exercise healthy skepticism when the results of a research study are attributed unequi-

vocally by the researcher to the conditions or treatments examined in the study without addressing these concerns.

We have used a controlled experiment to illustrate selection problems and remedies. Educational psychologists often must deal with investigations in which these problems are far more serious and the remedies far less obvious. In the mid-1960s the federal government appropriated funds for students labeled "educationally disadvantaged." With new funding came new requirements for evaluation of the effects of special programs; a veritable army of educational researchers became evaluators.

Evaluation of these programs presented a host of research design problems, not the least of which was the near impossibility of assigning students at random to special programs. The legislation specified that recipients of special programs had to be the neediest children in the school or school district operating the programs, thus ensuring that these students were systematically different from the children assigned to conventional programs with whom they were compared.

It was usual in the federal program to identify students with the lowest achievement test scores as the most educationally disadvantaged. Comparison students were therefore higher achievers at the outset than were the special students. This pretreatment difference made it difficult to explain posttest achievement differences between groups. If program students had larger gains in achievement test scores than the comparison students, could the program take credit for the differences? Perhaps, but not necessarily. All of the threats to internal validity we discussed above for nonrandom groups apply to this example with even greater force. The problem has partly to do with tests, but it has mostly to do with people.

The validity threat arises because achievement tests are not perfectly reliable (see chapter 28), and so an individual student's test score will vary from one occasion to another, even though his or her true achievement is the same. One effect of this unreliability is a systematic shift in average scores between the pre- and posttests of low-scoring students. Students whose initial scores are the lowest of the lot are probably poor achievers, but their performance also reflects a host of short-term factors having little if anything to do with their true achievement levels. They might have been ill or upset on the day they were tested. The specific form of the test used for pretesting may have tapped knowledge that they could not handle. They might have been unusually unlucky in their guesses. These same students, retested a week later on a different form of the test, are likely to do better, a phenomenon known as *statistical regression*. Ask 100 people to rate how they feel on a particular day, and the person with the most complaints is likely to feel relatively better tomorrow. The person who feels absolutely best is also likely to be second or third best in a few days.

Statistical regression is a plausible rival explanation of performance gains whenever people have been selected on the basis of extreme scores. There are formulas for estimating statistical regression, but the best remedy is to use alternatives to selection based on extremes. In the federal program described in this example, this remedy was not always available. To be sure, a few enterprising evaluators managed random assignment of students to special programs and comparison groups while adhering to the principle of serving the most educationally disadvantaged students. Program funds did not always accommodate all needy children in a given semester or school year, and these researchers randomly divided the most needy children into a group served during an initial time period and a group served later in the school year, permitting important comparisons during both of the time periods.

The strategy described above avoids the problem of statistical regression, but other threats are present in this situation. For example, children who are educationally disadvantaged come from families who are economically disadvantaged. Poor children tend to be geographically mobile. Even if an evaluator managed random assignment to treatment and comparison groups, many students present at pretesting were not around for the posttest. Groups that were randomly equivalent at the outset might differ at the end of the study because of a threat commonly referred to as *mortality*. When substantial numbers of people drop out, especially if these individuals differ substantially from those who remain, then the researcher confronts threats to internal validity.

Several procedures diminish the mortality threat. For example, the researcher can compare the pretest scores of children who left the treatment group and those who left the comparison group. Another approach is to compare the children remaining in the program and those in the comparison group on other relevant variables.

*Treatments and Tests.* This section covers threats due to a lack of control over factors that relate directly to the experimental treatments, and to the instruments employed by the investigator to assess the experimental outcomes. Unlike the selection threats discussed in the previous section, the issues described below are all under the experimenter's influence. At the top of the list is *treatment fidelity,* the assurance that the conditions described by the researcher actually prevailed in the study. Most readers of a research report assume that the treatments delivered were the treatments planned. This may not be the case, even when all participants are well-intentioned and conscientious. The only remedy for alleviating this threat to internal validity is rich description of the *actual* treatments delivered. These descriptions can be secured through direct observation, through logs or diaries, or by interviewing participants throughout the study.

Other threats are more subtle and less easy to remedy. For example, when treatments vary within a single school, routine communication can undermine the distinctions between treatments. Teachers talk to each other in the teachers' lounge, in the hallways, and at lunch. If a new instructional method works particularly well, the teachers using that method will describe it to their colleagues, who may then apply it to their comparison-group students. The result is an invalid comparison between the experimental and comparison treatments, *as planned.* The researcher may think she is comparing apples and oranges, but wind up comparing two varieties of apples! This threat to validity is called *diffusion* or *imitation of treatments.* The risk of treatment diffusion can be reduced by constituting experimental groups and comparison groups in different contexts—different schools or other organizations. The cost of this strategy is that the different locations provide different contexts, and the treatment effect must be greater than the resulting between-location variation. This problem can be especially serious if one school is designated as the experimental site and another as the control

site. Treatments and sites will be totally confounded, with no way to tell how serious this confounding might be.

Alternative approaches to reducing the threat of treatment diffusion or imitation include (a) securing agreement by participants to keep details under wraps until the end of the research study, or (b) altering the research context so that on-the-job contact between groups is minimal. The practicality of either of these approaches will depend on the contexts. Practically speaking, it is easy to ensure that university students participating in a verbal learning study do not talk with one another. It is far more difficult to achieve such confidentiality in an elementary school, but more feasible if a study is between departments in a high school.

If the participants in a study do find out about the treatments, several threats can result. One is named after John Henry, the railroad worker who "died with a hammer in this hand." According to the song, John Henry wasn't about to "let that steam drill beat him down," so he worked himself to death in a race to prove that he was better than the new technology of the time. In the *John Henry effect,* the comparison group exerts extra effort in an attempt to minimize the contribution of the experimental treatment. Researchers have also identified instances of the "reverse John Henry effect," in which demoralization of the comparison group leads to diminished performance. Finally, the *Hawthorne effect* refers to situations in which the experimental group, because it is singled out to receive special attention, performs better than is typical only because of the novelty of the treatment. The term derives from a series of studies conducted in the 1930s at the Hawthorne plant of Western Electric in which researchers discovered that, no matter what treatment a group of assembly-line workers received, they outperformed their colleagues who continued working in the factory rather than in the special experimental room.

An important remedy for these threats is documentation. In addition, the researcher can also take steps to make the control group feel special in some way unrelated to the treatment. In the reading study described at the beginning of this chapter, for example, the control families received advertisements and calls from the researchers to control for special-treatment influences. In addition, preassessments allow a check on whether the groups are equal at the outset, but also a check on the degree to which the various groups show gains (a novelty effect) or losses (effects of resentment and demoralization).

Another practical threat to internal validity arises from our democratic desire to promote equality of opportunity. If an experimental treatment is perceived as providing enriched opportunities for recipients, how can those in charge of a school deny any consideration for those in the comparison treatment? Thus, in schools where federal funds provide for teachers' aides in experimental classrooms, principals might appeal to parent–teachers' organizations to provide volunteers to assist teachers in comparison classrooms. The principals' motivation is not a desire to undermine the experiment but a concern that control students are unfairly disadvantaged by having fewer adults in their classrooms. Such *compensatory equalization of treatments* cannot always be avoided, but it can be documented by thorough description of treatments, as noted earlier. In addition, it is often possible to offer the treatment to the control group at the conclusion of the study, as suggested earlier in this chapter.

A final set of threats to internal validity falls under the general

TABLE 27–3. Example of a Solomon Four-Group Design

| Group 1 | Pretest | Reading materials provided | Posttest |
|---------|---------|----------------------------|----------|
| Group 2 |         | Reading materials provided | Posttest |
| Group 3 | Pretest | No reading materials provided | Posttest |
| Group 4 |         | No reading materials provided | Posttest |

heading of *testing effects*. Heisenberg's uncertainty principle holds that the act of measurement may affect the object of measurement. Heisenberg was a physicist, but the principle seems even more applicable when the object is a person and the attribute is a behavior. In the reading study, for example, by asking young children how much time they spend reading outside of class at the beginning of the study, researchers may affect the children's report at the end of the study. Administering a reading comprehension pretest may give all children clues that will help them on the posttest.

A standard remedy to these problems is the *four-group design* shown in Table 27–3. Children are assigned to two groups provided home reading materials and to two control groups. Then, one group of each kind is administered a pretest and the other is not. Analysis of the posttest scores allows the researcher to estimate the effects of pretesting separate from the effects of the treatment factor.

## External Validity

Even in the most practically focused research study, a researcher's interest is seldom confined exclusively to specific subjects, settings, and treatments. A researcher's conclusions invariably carry an implicit if not explicit assumption that the results can be *generalized* to "other times," "subjects like these," "similar settings," and "comparable treatments." External validity is the label attached to the trustworthiness of such generalizations. Analyses of external validity consider factors that limit, and research design features and practices that enhance the trustworthiness of such generalizations.

Even when a researcher interprets his or her results only for the subjects, time period, and context used in a particular study, consumers of the results inevitably engage in generalization. If you are Detroit's director of public housing, why should you care about a study on reduction of vandalism that applies only to 20 housing units observed in Seattle during 1988? If the vandalism-control methods worked well in Seattle, you would presume their applicability to public housing projects in Detroit. You would generalize the results of the study *from* Seattle, *from* 1988, and *from* the 20 housing units studied *to* Detroit, *to* the public housing projects where you have a vandalism problem, and *to* the year when you need to take action.

When the research goal is to contribute to theoretical knowledge, in contrast to application, generalization is of central importance. If generalization is not possible, there can be no contribution to theory. Generalization is also critical in survey research, where the goal is to extrapolate from a sample of respondents (the persons who have been interviewed or asked to complete a questionnaire) to a population of potential respondents (the larger collection of persons who are of central research interest). An example is the Harris Poll, where opinions on such things as "the quality of the job the President is doing," given by about 1,500 carefully selected adults (the sample), are

generalized to the adult population of the United States (the population of interest). Professional survey researchers have refined procedures for selecting respondents that ensure sound bases for generalization and methods for assessing the adequacy of generalization in particular instances. Whatever the goals, however, external validity depends on people and contexts, and on treatments and instruments, parallel to the categories described earlier for internal validity. The two sections that follow are organized according to these categories.

***Persons, Groups, and Settings.*** Two principal threats to external validity in survey research are *bias error* and *random error*. In survey research, these forms of error are readily characterized. Bias error occurs when the persons who have been interviewed or those who have completed questionnaires differ systematically from persons in the population to which generalization is desired. Systematic differences can occur for a variety of reasons, such as the researcher having done a poor or careless job of selection, or because those who actually completed a questionnaire or those actually interviewed were a small, self-selected portion of the persons the researcher selected to complete a questionnaire or be interviewed.

Suppose, for example, that a researcher wanted to draw conclusions about the degree of personal stress experienced by families headed by single mothers, and intended to generalize to the entire population of such families in the state of California. In the researcher's design, data to inform these conclusions are collected by interviewing single women who are heads of households. Ideally, the researcher would obtain a list of all women in California who were single and heads of households, and then randomly select a sample from the list. In this ideal world, all selected women would agree to be interviewed and would provide clear and complete responses to the researcher's questions. In reality, no list of single female heads of households in California exists, so selection of interviewees would have to be accomplished through referrals from such sources as social welfare agencies, churches, women's groups, school systems, and the like. There would be no way of determining with certainty whether the collective characteristics of the women in the sample, including the degree of personal stress experienced by their families, were similar to or systematically different from the characteristics of the population of all such women in California. Therefore, the potential exists for serious bias, and generalization from the sample to the population would be risky. Adding to the problem of external validity is the likelihood that some of the mothers would refuse to be interviewed for any of a variety of reasons, including their personal stress. The latter possibility leads to severe bias by systematically excluding women whose families experienced the highest degree of personal stress.

We mentioned the possibility that some women might refuse to be interviewed or refuse to complete a questionnaire. Refusal to participate is a problem that threatens external validity in all kinds of research studies, not just in surveys. The crux of the problem is that those who agree to be studied are typically different from those who refuse. Because the population that is of real research interest includes both kinds of persons, generalizing from a sample of volunteers to a population containing participants and *non*participants is almost certain to be erroneous.

Although there is no way to compel nonincarcerated individuals to participate in a research study (and even prisoners have the right of nonparticipation), there are ways to encourage participation. Researchers can provide illustrations of the societal benefits that might result from the research, or can offer incentives to those who agree to participate in the research. Because some refusals are inevitable despite the best efforts of the researcher, it is important to keep accurate records on rates of refusal and to compare the known characteristics of those who agree and those who refuse. The critical reader of research reports should look for information on the methods the researchers used to identify and select their research subjects, and on rates of participation and refusal.

Random error means that, even if the survey could be conducted under the ideal conditions described earlier, the sample average on the personal stress indicator is likely to differ somewhat from the average in the population. If two different samples of women were interviewed, the averages computed for each sample would differ from each other. The difference between the sample averages results from *random sampling fluctuation*. There is always some degree of error when the average for a sample is used to estimate the population average and, indeed, when any sample statistic is used to estimate a population parameter.

Unlike bias error, which may be difficult to control, random error can almost always be reduced by using a larger sample. The average personal stress for a sample of 100 single California women selected under ideal conditions will generally be closer to the average for *all* single women in California than would an average based on only 10 women. A researcher can usually reduce random error by selecting a larger sample, but bias error is not reduced merely by increasing sample size. Representing the population well is the key to reducing bias error.

Generalization can differ, depending on the reader's purpose. You might ask, for example, whether the successful results of an innovative reading program conducted in an inner-city elementary school with a low-income, predominantly Hispanic population are likely to be experienced in a school of particular interest to you—perhaps one that is located in a middle-income suburb and enrolls mostly African-American students. The external validity you demand extends *beyond* the bounds of the population that might be represented most immediately by the setting and sample studied. You want to generalize to a population that differs, in ways often associated with reading performance, from the sample used in the research.

You might reason that a reading program that works with children whose primary language is not English should work even better with children who have spoken English all of their lives. However, you would be ignoring the potential influence of nonstandard English. You might also recall that children from low-income families have traditionally experienced greater difficulty with reading than have children from more affluent families. You might therefore suspect that the innovative reading program would be more effective with children in the school of interest to you than with children in the school originally studied.

Clearly, these deductions are fraught with dangers and oversimplifications. Although completely in English, the reading program might take advantage of Spanish language idioms.

The subject matter of reading passages used in the program might be central to the experiences of inner-city children and relatively foreign to children from the suburbs. More detailed study of the program would be essential before decisions were made about extending the conclusions to other situations. But the type of reasoning illustrated here is at the heart of establishing external validity, where the aim is to generalize from the context and sample of a particular research study to a different context and setting.

Researchers can do much to enhance the generalization of their findings from one context to another. An effective strategy involves systematic variation of the conditions under which the research is conducted. Had the study of the innovative reading program been conducted in several school systems that differed in prescribed ways (e.g., one inner-city school system, one in a suburb, one in a rural area, one enrolling mostly African-American children, one enrolling mostly Hispanic children, another enrolling mostly white children, and one that was racially and ethnically balanced), the limits of generalization of the study's results would be far clearer. Consistent findings across all of these contexts would suggest safe generalization to a wide variety of settings that were similar to any of these sites or to contexts that incorporate elements of several of them. For example, if the reading program were found to be successful in an inner-city school system with Hispanic students and in a suburban school system with African-American students, it would more likely be successful in an inner-city school system with African-American students.

If the reading program were substantially more successful in some of the contexts examined than in others, the limits of generalization would be revealed. Consistency of findings is not prerequisite to increased knowledge of the external validity of a study. Even when differences in results are found, researchers and consumers of research are better informed.

***Treatments and Tests.*** The treatment in the home reading study described at the beginning of this chapter provided daily newspapers and weekly magazines, but the researcher probably intended that conclusions apply beyond this particular operationalization to a broader range of treatment possibilities. The basic idea is to ensure that the family has ready access to print materials. What if only newspapers were provided? News magazines? Comic books? A weekly visit by a mobile library? Only logical analysis, based on careful attention to earlier research findings, can provide a basis for answering these questions about external generalization. Many of the recommendations described in the previous section apply to generalization to treatments and tests.

One set of questions has to do with the similarity between the original treatment and proposed variations. Library books, for example, may be more challenging to a family with a low level of literacy than would newspapers and magazines. The latter are written in smaller chunks of prose and deal with more familiar topics. Comic books may be easy to read but may offer little support for the development of literacy skills needed in school.

External generalization can also depend on circumstances that are not part of the official treatment. For example, if the researcher spent some time explaining to the families how to use the printed materials to good advantage with their children, the outcomes may have as much to do with this activity as with the materials per se. A local newspaper, deciding on the basis of the findings to distribute day-old newspapers to poor families, may be disappointed when there are no benefits from sending batches of newspapers to local schools for students to take home with them. Some papers may never reach home, and those that do may not serve the intended purpose. Treatment fidelity, described in previous sections, can be important for establishing external as well as internal validity.

*Replication and Interaction.* Although the distinction between internal and external validity is an important one, some broad considerations cut across both. In particular, the trustworthiness of a particular finding is strengthened when a variety of replications of the finding is available, and the conditions of generalizability are clearer when the evidence clarifies potential interactions between the treatment factor and contextual factors. Replication refers to the "redoing" of a study with different samples and in different contexts. Although there are some advantages to exact replications, in general, the greater the degree of variation, the more informative the replications. If the same findings appear across a wide range of situations and samples, then the conclusions can be considered more trustworthy. In that case, the researcher would be likely to obtain the same result in settings that are of interest to him or her.

Beyond the effects of setting, organizational and physical context, and characteristics of research subjects, time is another element that often limits the external validity of research findings. Consider drawing conclusions about the nature of discipline problems in today's public schools on the basis of research studies conducted in the 1950s or the 1960s. School discipline problems of the 50s are claimed to include such transgressions as chewing gum in class, talking out of turn, fistfights in the halls, writing graffiti on restroom walls, and the like. In today's schools, discipline problems purportedly concern abuse of illegal drugs and alcohol, assault on other students and teachers, rape, teenage pregnancy, destruction of school property, robbery, and so forth. Problems of disruption have turned into problems of crime. Research on school discipline that was accurate in the 1950s and 1960s may have little relevance for today's public schools.

A less dramatic example of time-limited external validity arose in a test of general aptitudes used to predict workers' rated proficiency in a variety of jobs. As noted in Hartigan and Wigdor (1989), the effectiveness of the General Aptitude Test Battery in predicting supervisors' ratings of employees' job proficiencies was found to be substantially lower in studies conducted after 1983 than in studies conducted before that date. Although the reasons for the test's diminished predictive power are not well understood, suspicions include changes in the specific nature of jobs in the U.S. economy, as well as changes in the examinee population that are not well characterized by their test performances. Whatever the reasons, it is clear that the external validity of the pre-1983 studies is limited, and that the predictive validity of the General Aptitude Test Battery today is not well described by studies conducted more than 13 years ago.

The moral of these examples is twofold. First, researchers are advised to replicate earlier research studies to see whether results found today are consistent with results found in earlier periods. If so, generalization of earlier findings is warranted. If not, useful limits of generalization will be established. Second, researchers are advised to be cautious in generalizing the findings of an earlier era to today's social contexts and milieus. In prescribing caution we might be accused of avoiding the issue, in much the same way as the air traffic controller who, when told by two pilots that he had just instructed them to land on the same runway from opposite directions, was heard to reply, "Y'all be careful, now, ya hear!"

It is difficult to be more prescriptive about common sense. The first of our examples, generalizing from school discipline studies of the 1950s to the schools of today, is fraught with threats to internal and external validity. The study of the predictive power of the General Aptitude Test Battery is less obviously time-bound. When considering the results of any research study that is more than a few years old, the informed reader should ask how conditions in the research setting (e.g., schools, factories, cities, colleges, universities) have changed. Are the populations encountered today likely to be different from the sample used in the earlier study in ways that are substantially related to the phenomena studied? If the answer to this question suggests that the phenomena studied are likely to operate differently in current institutions or with current populations, the findings of older studies should be taken with a grain of salt.

Evidence that the results vary across settings in describable ways can also help you to determine the results you would likely find, were you to conduct the study in a setting that is of interest to you. For example, if the reading program mentioned earlier produced consistently positive achievement effects for African-American students and Hispanic students in inner-city schools, but failed to produce positive effects for African-American students in a suburban school, you could reasonably assume that urbanism of school location was related to the program's effectiveness.

When the results of a study vary across settings or types of subjects, we say that an *interaction effect* exists. The preceding example entailed an interaction among three factors: the reading program, urbanism of school location, and the ethnic background of the students served by the program. The detection of interaction effects helps to define the boundaries within which research findings can be generalized, and consequently the limits of external validity. Factorial experimental designs, described later in the chapter, provide systematic control for identifying and describing interactions.

From one perspective, failure to replicate a particular finding may seem to undercut the external validity of the result. Viewed from another perspective, however, these failures take shape as interactions that can be informative in their own right. It is unlikely in a domain as complex as education that any finding is unconditional. Part of the researcher's job is to establish the *boundary conditions,* the limits within which a given finding holds. Finding these limits can be of practical importance, but can also inform theoretical issues.

For example, suppose that in four replications of the home reading study, positive outcomes appear in two cases, but the other two show no internally consistent effects. One possible conclusion is that the treatment lacks external validity: Sometimes it seems to work, at other times it doesn't. At a practical level, educators interested in the program are advised to be cautious about relying on the program. Another strategy is to look for a pattern: What seem to be contrasts between the two sets of conditions that might be producing the interaction? Suppose you discover that there was a home contact person in the two successful implementations of the program. This systematic difference can then be established through a replication in which the home contact factor is systematically varied; families are randomly assigned to the four combinations of reading materials/advertisements and home contact/no home contact. Besides assessing the reading outcomes for children, it would also make sense to study carefully the activities of the home contact person and the relationship of this person to the family. In the meantime, the program might carry a "warning label": Use this program with care. It is likely to work only under certain conditions.

## EXPERIMENTS, EXPERIMENTAL DESIGNS, AND DATA-ANALYTIC PROCEDURES

In this section we reintroduce the notion of an experiment and distinguish experiments from other approaches to the collection of research data. In addition, we describe a variety of analytic methods that can be used in conducting research on the psychology of education. Many of these methods are best applied to data collected in accordance with the rules of experimental research. Others enjoy broader applicability and serve best when the objective of inquiry is the degree of association among variables or the relationship between independent and dependent variables.

We begin with an example. If teachers-to-be learn how to explain concepts to elementary school students, will their students learn concepts more effectively? This research question was explored by Pool and Capie (1977) in a study involving 35 prospective elementary-school teachers in their junior year of a teacher education program. Pool and Capie conducted a true experiment. They randomly assigned 17 of the prospective teachers to a treatment group and the other 18 to a control group. Teachers assigned to the control group received a traditional instructional program on how to teach young children, while teachers assigned to the treatment group completed five self-instructional modules on how to explain concepts: (a) listening, (b) structuring, (c) application/validity/simplicity/clarity, (d) focus/rule–example–rule/vagueness/summarizing, and (e) check yourself. They then taught several lessons to elementary students, who were given a concept attainment test. Question: To what degree was student performance affected by the teachers' participation in the special treatment?

Two features characterized this experiment. First, the researchers imposed a treatment. That is, they intervened in the training of the prospective teachers rather than merely observing their training. Second, the researchers established distinct groups of prospective teachers using a process called *random assignment*. Moreover, prospective teachers were also assigned at random to different "classes"—groups of six to nine students who were randomly grouped for these special lessons. These two features of research design—intervention and randomization—distinguish true experiments from other research approaches, including quasi-experiments, correlational research, and survey research.

### Randomized Groups Designs

The research design used by Pool and Capie is an example of a *randomized groups* design. In such designs, research subjects are assigned to two or more groups through a process that achieves or approximates a purely chance procedure, totally devoid of systematic or purposeful selection. To examine their hypothesis that students would learn more from teachers in the treatment group, Pool and Capie evaluated the students' concept scores by using a statistical procedure called analysis of variance (ANOVA). Formally, Pool and Capie applied a linear model to their data:

$$Y_{ij} = \mu + \alpha_i + \varepsilon_{ij}.$$

This equation can be read as follows. The test score for student $j$ in group $i$, $Y_{ij}$, equals the mean score of all students in the entire population, $\mu$, plus an effect, $\alpha_i$, due to the student's assignment to either a treatment or a control teacher, plus an error element, $\varepsilon_{ij}$, that represents the idiosyncrasies of the particular student. The final term is also called a residual or random error element. In ANOVA, sample data are used to estimate the population parameters in the model. Thus, $\mu$ is estimated by the overall sample mean score, $\alpha_i$ by the difference between the sample mean for condition $i$ and the overall sample mean, and $\varepsilon_{ij}$ by the difference between the condition $i$ mean and the score for individual $j$ in group $i$.

Pool and Capie hoped to find statistical evidence that would allow them to reject the *null hypothesis:* The average test score for the population of students taught by teachers in the "How to Explain" program does *not* differ from the average for the population of students taught by control teachers. The essence of the ANOVA procedure is a comparison of systematic variance and residual variance. Taking the overall mean, $\mu$, as a base level, individual student scores differ from one another partly because of their assignment to one group or the other (the $\alpha$ effect) and partly because of individual idiosyncrasies (the $\varepsilon$ effect). In ANOVA, variance estimates are calculated for each of these sources, and the two variance estimates are compared by a test statistic called the $F$ ratio. This statistic, named after Sir Ronald Fisher, the father of experimental design, is calculated as the ratio of the systematic variance due to the $\alpha_i$ component, plus the residual variance due to the $\varepsilon_{ij}$ component, divided by the residual variance due to the $\varepsilon_{ij}$ component. Variance estimates are referred to in ANOVA parlance as *mean squares* (MS, for short), and so the $F$ ratio in this example is computed as MS(Factor A)/MS(Residual). If the null hypothesis is true (that is, if the $\alpha_i$ values are zero), then, on average, the two mean squares will be roughly equivalent, yielding an $F$ ratio in the neighborhood of 1. If the null hypothesis is *not* true—if the $\alpha_i$ values are *not* zero—then the mean square for factor A (MS (factor A)) will tend to be larger than the mean square residual (MS (Residual)), leading to $F$ ratios larger than 1. The larger the $F$ ratio from a particular study, the greater the likelihood that the null hypothesis is untenable.

Researchers refer to the probability of a *Type I error,* the likelihood of deciding to reject the null hypothesis when it is actually true, in talking about statistical significance. This probability, $p$, springs from statistical decision theory but often serves a descriptive role in educational research. Researchers use a conventional $p$ value of .05 (an outcome that would occur by chance only 5% of the time, or once in 20 tests, on average, if the null hypotheses were true) as a rationale for presenting a finding as trustworthy. Smaller $p$ values of .01 or .001 carry implications of findings that are more trustworthy and quite unusual under the null hypothesis.

When Pool and Capie applied ANOVA to their data, they observed an $F$ ratio of 3.35, a value sufficiently large that it would occur only around once in 20 replications of a similar study. The sample mean for the treatment condition, 17.4 correct answers, was only slightly larger than the sample mean for the control condition, 16.8. Nonetheless, this difference is *statistically significant;* it is unlikely that the difference between the two population means is really zero.

## Randomized Block Designs

Deciding whether a treatment or collection of treatments has a trustworthy influence on performance is influenced by three things: (a) how large an effect the treatments really have, (b) how large the residual variability is, and (c) how much the investigator is willing to risk claiming an effect when it is not there. Large effects are easier to detect than small ones, all other things being equal. Substantial random variability makes it hard to see systematic differences. Caution about crying wolf means that you may fail to spot a wolf when one actually arrives.

Randomized block designs help with the second problem. For example, in the Pool–Capie study, the $\varepsilon_{ij}$ component contains several sources of variability that might be pinned down to good advantage. Some teachers might be more intrigued than others by the concept instruction strategy. Male and female students may vary in how they react to this type of teaching. Teachers and students differ in their propensity for abstract versus hands-on approaches. All of the variability attributable to these factors has been lumped together in the Pool–Capie analysis, so that MS(Residual) is much larger than it might be if these sources were identified and eliminated from the residual variance.

By including background factors in a research design, the researcher's objective is to reduce error variance by applying treatments to samples that are more similar than would likely result from simple random assignment of subjects to treatments. Instead of randomly assigning subjects to treatments without regard to their characteristics, subjects are matched on factors likely to be correlated with the dependent variable, and then are randomly assigned to treatments (typically in equal numbers) from each block of matched subjects. The desired result of this approach is to control for the systematic effect of the variable used for *blocking* or *stratification.*

In a randomized block design, the blocking and treatment factors are assumed to be *strictly additive,* that is, they *do not interact.* The model for this situation is

$$Y_{ijk} = \mu + \alpha_i + \beta_j + \varepsilon_{ijk}.$$

The only new effect in this model is the blocking factor. Although $\varepsilon_{ijk}$ looks the same in this model, it is reduced by the

### TABLE 27–4. Latin Square Design for Efficient Control of Three Factors: Parents' Age, Parents' Marital Status, and Treatment

| Parents' Age (yrs) | Parents' Marital Status | | |
|---|---|---|---|
| | Single | Married | Divorced |
| 20–34 | A | B | C |
| 35–49 | B | C | A |
| 50+ | C | A | B |

Note: Treatment A = home materials and home contact person; Treatment B = home materials only; Treatment C = advertisements.

All three factors are counterbalanced with 9 combinations rather than 27 (3 × 3 × 3) required by a full factorial design.

magnitude of $\beta_j$, the blocking effect. Estimates for all of the elements in the model are obtained by subtraction of appropriate sample means, as in the randomized groups design.

The efficiency of a randomized block design depends on the degree to which the blocking factor affects the dependent variable. The larger the variability in the outcome measure associated with the blocking factor, the greater is the reduction in residual variability, and hence the greater the sensitivity of the study to identifying effects of the treatment factor, given that the latter actually exist.

## Latin Square Designs

One problem with blocking is cost. Suppose the home reading researcher from the beginning of this chapter is interested in designing a follow-up study that compares three conditions: Treatment A provides home reading materials with a home contact person; Treatment B provides home reading materials with no contact person; Treatment C provides advertisements only. The researcher, based on exploratory analyses from the first study, identifies two blocking factors, each at 3 levels: parents' marital status (single, married, divorced), and parents' age range (20–34, 35–49, 50+). With limited resources and a complex question, the researcher confronts the challenge of investigating a design with 3 × 3 × 3 or 27 combinations.

The Latin square design provides an efficient plan for addressing this problem. A Latin square is a symmetric plan in which three factors, each with three levels, are combined in a compact arrangement. Table 27–4 shows the plan for the replication described above, in which the effects of all three factors can be assessed by an in-depth study of only nine families. The cost of this efficiency is the assumption that there are no interaction effects, either between blocking variables or between either blocking variable and the treatment variable. That is, all effects are assumed to be strictly additive. No combination of effects is different from the sum of its parts.

Latin Square designs are used for the same purpose as randomized block designs: to increase the homogeneity of experimental subjects who receive different treatments and thereby control for extraneous variation. A major advantage of the Latin Square technique is its efficient control over multiple variables. Notice that each treatment appears once and only once in each row and column of the design. If the blocking variables are correlated with the dependent variable, the Latin Square design can reduce error variance substantially, thus providing more efficient estimation of the treatment effects and more powerful hypothesis tests. The three-level design used in this example can be extended to larger numbers of levels and to other fractional designs (Winer et al., 1991).

## Fixed versus Random Factors

An important issue in the analysis of experimental data concerns the researcher's conception of the nature of the independent variables (called *factors*). One possibility is that the factor levels in the study exhaust all possible levels of the factor, in which case the experimenter's generalizations are *fixed* or limited to those levels. An example is sex. Since only two levels of sex exist for purposes of biological classification, a finding that sex has a significant effect on some dependent variable covers the entire range of that variable.

When the experimenter has selected levels of a factor at random from a larger population of possible levels, then generalizations about this factor are typically *random*. The persons selected for a study are almost always a random factor, because researchers intend the findings to apply to persons other than those in the study. Classrooms, schools, and families are other examples of typically random factors.

In randomized block designs, the treatment factor is usually a fixed factor (the researcher wants to generalize only to the treatment levels in the design), while the blocking factor may or may not be a random factor. For example, suppose that a researcher plans to investigate the effects of three elementary social studies curricula on students' later interest in civic affairs. The researcher conducts her experiment in five different schools. Based on her assumption that school settings affect students' interest in civic affairs, she employs schools as a random-effect blocking factor, selecting three teacher–class combinations in each school for assignment to each of the social studies curricula. If the researcher is interested *only* in these particular social studies curricula, she will regard the levels of the curriculum factor as fixed, because the three curricula exhaust the entire range of the factor that is of interest. You might imagine a situation in which the three curricula are samples from a larger set of possibilities, in which the curriculum factor now becomes a random factor. Some factors are inherently fixed or random, but others can be interpreted as either fixed or random, depending on the researcher's intention.

In many educational research studies, the settings used to collect data (classrooms, schools, school systems, etc.) are selected on the basis of convenience or availability rather than through a purely random process. Nonetheless, researchers rarely restrict their interest to the settings used for data collection but, more typically, seek to generalize their findings to some larger population of settings. The settings used to collect data are regarded as a representative sample of some larger population that has characteristics somewhat like those of the experimental settings.

The way in which data are collected is not the distinguishing feature of a random versus a fixed-factor experiment. The experimenter would collect data in exactly the same way, whether she wanted to generalize her results only to the curricula and schools represented in her experiment or wanted to consider these levels to be samples from some larger population. It is the intended range of generalization that distinguishes a random factor from a fixed factor. The techniques to test hypotheses associated with the presence or absence of effects do differ, depending on whether the factors are conceived to be fixed or random. For definitive information on the statistical foundation for hypothesis testing in these situations, see Winer et al. (1991) and Cornfield and Tukey (1956).

## Factorial Designs

Factorial designs permit evaluation of the effects of two or more independent variables on a dependent variable, both individually and jointly. Each independent variable is called a *factor*, and each factor is represented in the design at one or more *levels*. Each combination of factors in the design forms a *cell* of the design. For example, in a 2 × 3 factorial design there would be two factors, say Factor A and Factor B, with two levels of Factor A and three levels of Factor B.

Factorial designs have a number of distinctive features:

- The researcher can explore the existence of interactions among the factors and test their statistical significance.
- Since more systematic variation is accounted for in the statistical model, control is increased and random error is decreased.
- Factorial designs are efficient. They permit examination of several statistical hypotheses (significance of main effects and interaction effects) and thus are more efficient than single-factor experiments for the same number of observations.
- They permit examination of the generalizability of the effects of one factor across levels of another factor.

The statistical model for a factorial design assesses main effects, just as in a randomized block design, but also interaction effects. For example, in a 2 × 3 factorial design with Factors A and B, the model is:

$$Y_{ijk} = \mu + \alpha_i + \beta_j + \alpha\beta_{ij} + \varepsilon_{ijk}$$

where $\alpha\beta_{ij}$ represents the combined effects of Factors A and B at levels $i$ and $j$. If the sample sizes in each cell are equal, or at least proportional across rows or columns of the design, then the estimates for each main effect and each set of interactions will be statistically independent. The researcher can assess main effects and interactions confident that these estimates are not confounded with one another. The parameter estimates for the mean, the main effects of each factor, and the residual are each computed by subtraction of appropriate means, as in the previous models. Interaction effects can be most easily understood as the remainder for a given cell mean after all the component main effects have been subtracted. In the present case, each interaction is computed as

$$\widehat{\alpha\beta}_{ij} = \text{mean}_{ij} - \text{overall mean} - a_i - b_j,$$

where $a_i$ and $b_j$ are the estimates for the main effects of condition $A_i$ and $B_j$, respectively. An absence of significant interaction effects means that the data are well described by examining the main effects one at a time. Significant interactions mean that the main effects must be examined in relation to one another. It is therefore traditional to look *first* at test(s) for significant interaction, and then to examine main effects. The interpretation

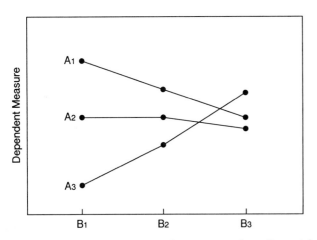

FIGURE 27–1. Two-Way Interaction Patterns from Factorial Design

of significant main effects becomes complicated when statistically significant interaction effects are found.

Interactions in a factorial design are classified as two basic types: *ordinal* and *disordinal*. An ordinal interaction occurs when the rank order of cell means for one factor in a factorial design does not change across levels of another factor. A disordinal interaction occurs when the rank order of cell means for one factor in a factorial design differs across the levels of at least one other factor. For example, Figure 27–1 shows an illustrative data structure for a 3 × 3 design. The two factors interact substantially, in that the differences $A_i$ and $A_j$ are different from one level to the next of the B factor. The interaction of levels $A_1$ and $A_2$ with the B factor exemplifies an *ordinal* interaction. The mean for $A_1$ is larger than the mean for $A_2$ at all levels of factor B. The interaction of level $A_3$ and the other two levels of A with B is *disordinal*. The rank order of means for levels $A_1$, $A_2$ and $A_3$ of factor A changes at different levels of factor B.

Once the primary analyses for a factorial design have been completed, the appropriate type of follow-up analysis depends on whether significant interactions have been found. If no significant interactions have been found, then *multiple comparisons* among levels of main effects are in order. When significant interactions are present, multiple comparisons among levels of main effects are uninterpretable, and the existence of significant *simple main effects* should be investigated within each level of the factors.

Multiple comparisons apply to situations where an experimental factor has three or more levels. With a two-level factor, only a single comparison is possible, and that comparison is assessed as the main effect. First, assume that no significant interaction effects have been found, but that one or more of the main effects are statistically significant. These factors have a trustworthy effect on performance. The purpose of multiple comparisons is to determine which of the three (or more) means in the collection differ significantly from one another. Several techniques have been developed for assessing pairwise differences between means; Winer et al. (1991) and Glass and Hopkins (1984) describe methods developed by Tukey, Scheffé, and Dunn, which are among the most commonly used. The Scheffé procedure permits a posteriori comparisons and is very

conservative. The basic principle is that the more comparisons a researcher makes, the greater becomes the likelihood of failing to detect real differences when they exist—concluding that two population means are equal when they are not. Another approach to multiple comparisons, *planned orthogonal comparisons*, allows the researcher to define important comparisons in advance without the penalty entailed in unplanned comparisons (Kirk, 1968; Winer et al., 1991).

For the 3 × 3 design, suppose that Factor A proves to have significant effects on performance. Three pairwise comparisons are possible: $A_1$ versus $A_2$, $A_1$ versus $A_3$, and $A_2$ versus $A_3$. These comparisons are not independent of one another. If $A_1$ is larger than $A_2$ and $A_2$ is larger than $A_3$, it is certain that $A_1$ is larger than $A_3$. Planned orthogonal contrasts are designed to be independent of one another. For example, one orthogonal set for Factor A would be to compare the average of $A_1$ and $A_2$ with $A_3$, and then compare $A_1$ with $A_2$. These two contrasts exhaust the information contained in the variations among the three means.

If statistically significant interactions are found, the statistical significance of differences for the levels of one factor *within* each level of the other factor must be investigated. This approach is termed the analysis of *simple main effects*. In the 3 × 3 design, for instance, there are three comparisons among the $A_i$ means for each level of the B factor, or nine comparisons in all. In general, the greater the number of contrasts conducted with a collection of means, the less sensitive each contrast will be in detecting significant differences. The cost of asking lots of questions is a more conservative and less powerful assessment of each answer.

## Repeated Measures Designs

In the experimental designs discussed above, each experimental subject is assigned to a single combination of levels of the factors in the design and is measured only once. In repeated measures designs, each subject is assigned to all combinations of levels of the repeated measures factors. This design feature has several advantages, the greatest of which is control of extraneous variation due to differences among experimental subjects. If, in a conventional randomized groups design, Subjects 1 and 2 are assigned to Treatment $A_1$ and Subjects 3 and 4 are assigned to Treatment $A_2$, differences in scores on the dependent variable may be due to differences in the effectiveness of the two treatments or to preexisting differences among the subjects. This is true even when subjects are randomly assigned to treatments. If a repeated measures design is used, all four subjects will be administered both treatments. Measures of the dependent variable are taken following the administration of each treatment. With a repeated measures design, differences between mean scores on the dependent variable following the administration of Treatments $A_1$ and $A_2$ could not be attributed to differences among subjects, because each subject would constitute his or her own control.

The logic of repeated measures designs extends to any number of experiment treatments and to experimental designs involving more than one factor in addition to the subjects factor. In complex designs, repeated measures can be taken for subjects assigned to combinations of several factors, while different random samples of subjects are assigned to combinations of other factors. Statisticians refer to repeated measures designs in a variety of ways. Edwards (1979, chapter 11) and Kirk (1968, chapter 8) called them split-plot designs; Winer et al. (1991) talk about single-factor experiments having repeated measures on the same elements (chapter 4) or multifactor experiments having repeated measures on the same elements (chapter 7), and Lindquist (1953, chapter 14) and Myers (1979, chapter 8) label them mixed designs.

Repeated measures designs with a single factor can be viewed as randomized block designs in which each experimental subject constitutes a block. In fact, the linear model and hypothesis-testing procedures described above for randomized block designs can be used directly with data collected in a single-factor repeated measures design. The hypothesis test for block effects becomes a test of a between-subjects effect. As was true for randomized block designs, control of extraneous variation (in this case, the between-subjects effect) typically results in greater statistical efficiency and, for a fixed sample size, greater statistical power. Or, put another way, to achieve a given level of statistical power usually requires a smaller sample size when a repeated measures design is used than when a corresponding randomized groups design is used.

Repeated measures designs are not without limitations. First, many experimental treatments result in carryover effects (in the case of education, we certainly hope this is the case), so that the administration of alternative treatments to the same subjects produces the risk of treatment contamination. For example, once a student has learned basic statistics in one way, it is impossible to erase that learning so that a second treatment can be administered. Second, experimental subjects can become fatigued and bored. How many different problems from basic statistics can you tolerate in a given session? Third, repeated assessments, regardless of intervening treatments, can be problematic. Persons learn from the administration of almost any outcome measure. Memory effects can be problematic and can unintentionally become part of the treatment. Namboodiri (1972) has discussed these problems at some length. Although these problems must be carefully considered in deciding whether a particular factor should be varied between or within subjects, the increased sensitivity of within-subjects variation always merits consideration.

## CORRELATIONAL TECHNIQUES

In the previous section, discussion centered on research questions that the investigator attempted to answer by randomly assigning subjects to experimental and control or comparison groups. Whether assignment to treatment and comparison groups was fully random or not, in every situation discussed, the experimenter *intervened* in the normal course of events by introducing some treatment or condition that was of theoretical or practical importance (e.g., a new reading program compared with the regular curriculum).

Many questions of great significance to educators and educational psychologists cannot be readily investigated using experimental methods. Consider, for example, the following questions:

• What early child-rearing practices predict school readiness at age 5?

• Of the many home environment variables that affect student achievement, which ones affect achievement directly, and which affect achievement indirectly through other variables?

• What distinct mental abilities underlie performance on standardized tests?

None of these questions involves the assignment of persons to treatments. An important distinction between the research approaches discussed in this section and the experimental and quasi-experimental designs discussed earlier is the *absence of interventions* by the researcher in correlational research studies. In correlational investigations, the researcher seeks to understand relationships among variables just as (s)he finds them. There is no researcher-defined treatment or strategy through which the researcher attempts to draw the causal inferences possible with experimental designs.

### Linear Regression Analysis

Regression analysis is central to all of the correlational research procedures discussed below. Comprehensive and very readable texts on the subject include those by Kerlinger and Pedhazur (1973), Pedhazur (1982), Pedhazur and Schmelkin (1991), and Darlington (1990). A slightly more advanced treatment can be found in Draper and H. Smith (1981). These texts also discuss the relationships between correlational methods and the analysis of variance; the latter procedures can be formulated in the language of regression analysis in most instances.

In Figure 27–2a is a bivariate scatterplot, the data display that is of fundamental importance in understanding a bivariate relationship. This figure shows data that might be obtained in the home reading study from a comparison of the relationship between reading pretests and posttests. As Behrens and Smith note in chapter 30, this volume, a researcher should routinely employ exploratory data-analytic methods like the scatterplot. In the simplest situation, educational psychologists are interested in the nature and degree of relationship between two variables. They might want to know whether extended verbalizations of mothers are associated with larger vocabularies of their children at age 5, say, or whether students from higher socioeconomic status families have higher educational aspirations than do those from lower socioeconomic status families. In the social and behaviorial sciences, the nature of most relationships between two variables is *monotonic* (as one variable increases, the other systematically increases or decreases); in these instances, the degree of correspondence can often be captured by a *linear* or straight-line relation.

A best-fitting straight line has been fit to the data in Figure 27–2a to illustrate the method. The key to interpreting a scatterplot is to examine the pattern of residuals from the statistical model employed in a particular instance. Like the $\varepsilon_{ij}$ in ANOVA, the residuals are the difference between the scores predicted by the model and the individual scores. Correlational methods are generally based on the assumption that the residuals are normally and comparably distributed across the entire range of both variables. An eyeball analysis of the distribution of residuals shows that this distribution is neither normal nor comparable in the present instance, suggesting that the straight-line regression, even if statistically significant, may not be the most appropriate description of the data. Students with lower pretest scores (scores on the left-hand side of the figure) have far more variable posttest scores than do students with higher pretest scores (scores on the right-hand side). The pattern is consistent with the notion that some of the lower performing students gained significant benefit from the treatments, whereas the higher performing students tended to do well on the posttest no matter what.

There can be important exceptions to both monotonicity and linearity. The well-known learning curve investigated by many educational psychologists typically is not straight, and sometimes can be quite curvilinear (Figure 27–2a). During the initial stages of learning, the function is typically linear and fairly steep, but then it levels off and becomes fairly flat. Non-monotonic relationships also can be found in which one variable increases across some ranges of the second variable and then decreases (Figure 27–2c). For example, the relationship between intelligence test performance and job satisfaction is nonmonotonic for many occupations. A person barely able to follow simple instructions is likely to be unhappy with any job that demands average or above intellectual ability. For highly intelligent persons, however, that same job might, because of boredom, be the source of considerable dissatisfaction.

In formal language, the linear regression model consists of two parts: a *deterministic* part and a *stochastic* part. The deterministic part is a mathematical model of the relationship between a dependent variable $Y$ (e.g., school readiness at age 5), and an independent variable $X$ (e.g., mothers' verbalizations). The stochastic part reflects the inability to specify the relationship between $X$ and $Y$ perfectly. The linear regression model assumes that $X$ predicts $Y$ by the equation:

$$Y_i = a + bX_i + e_i.$$

In plain language, $Y$ equals $a$ (the $Y$-intercept) when $X$ equals zero, and a one-unit increase in $X$ leads to a prediction of a change of $b$ units in $Y$. The symbol $b$, the regression coefficient, denotes the amount of change in $Y$ as a function of a unit increase in $X$. Because the model is *linear*, the deterministic part of the model says that increasing $X$ from, say, 21 to 22 has the same effect on $Y$ as increasing $X$ from, say, 1 to 2; that is, $Y$ will increase by amount $b$ in either case.

The stochastic part of the model appears as the collection of $e_i$'s, referred to variously as the error of prediction or the residual. This stochastic term is the portion of the dependent variable $Y$ that is not predicted by the linear relationship between $Y$ and $X$. As noted earlier, regression analysis assumes that the residuals are normally distributed (the familiar bell-shaped curve) across the entire range of the $X$ variable. In particular, the $X$ variable should not be related to any characteristics of the residuals. If you look back at Figure 27–2A you will see that the variability of the residuals is higher for small values of $X$ and decreases as $X$ increases, which raises questions about the interpretation of the regression analysis. Most computer programs for statistical analysis include procedures for the statistical investigation and graphical presentation of residuals (also see Norüsis, 1990). Regrettably, in published research these options are seldom used.

Linear regression is the foundation for a variety of correlational procedures. If a researcher seeks to predict persons' heights from their weights, then the linear regression equation

**(a)**

**(b)**

**(c)**

FIGURE 27–2. Regression Patterns. (a), scatterplot with best-fitting linear model. (b) and (c), curvilinear and nonmonotonic models, respectively.

is the simplest method. More complex nonlinear models are routinely provided in the statistical packages available to anyone with a personal computer. These packages also allow the researcher to assess the adequacy of various models through analyses of residuals.

Regression analysis is idiosyncratic to a particular situation. The *product–moment correlation coefficient* provides a universally interpreted statistical index much like the $F$ ratio. If a researcher reports that systematic variance attributable to a factor is 10 times the error variance, this statement has meaning across all settings. The correlation coefficient serves this same purpose through the use of *standardized scores*, $z_{y_i}$ and $z_{x_i}$, for each of the variables. A variable is standardized by subtracting its mean and dividing by its standard deviation: $z = (X - M)/s$ in statistical terminology. A standardized score has a mean equal to zero and a variance equal to 1; like the meter or the liter, it constitutes a reference point that can be translated into a variety of specific situations. The correlation coefficient predicts the relationship between two variables, $Y_i$ and $X_i$, by the model:

$$z_{y_i} = r_{yx} z_{x_i},$$

where the coefficient $r_{yx}$ is estimated by

$$r_{yx} = 1/n \sum_i z_{y_i} z_{x_i},$$

the mean product of the two sets of standardized scores. No matter what two variables are correlated, once they are standardized, the correlation coefficient provides a standard index of the degree of linear relationship. If $r_{yx} = 1$, then the linear relationship between the two scores is perfect; $z_{y_i} = z_{x_i}$ for all values of $i$. If $r_{yx} = 0$, then $z_{y_i}$ is predicted to be zero (the average for a standardized score) for all values of $z_{y_i}$.

The correlation coefficient also provides an index of the *goodness of fit* of a predictive equation; $s^2_{\text{Residual}}$, the variance of the residuals around the best-fitting straight line, equals the variance of scores on the dependent variable, $s^2_y$, times $1 - r^2_{yx}$. Notice that if $r^2_{yx} = 1$, then the variance of the residuals is zero, while if $r^2_{yx} = 0$, then the variance of the residuals equals the variance of $Y$, and no reduction in uncertainty has been achieved. Most statistics packages generate the correlation or standardized regression coefficient along with the nonstandardized regression coefficient.

## Multiple Regression

The research questions studied by educational psychologists (e.g., how learning occurs, what motivates students to achieve academically) can seldom be answered adequately by using a single independent variable. The ability to read, for example, depends on physiological maturation, social and cognitive readiness, and instruction and practice, among other things. Any attempt to explain the development of reading ability that does not include multiple variables is almost certainly incomplete. Factorial designs are employed in experimental research to control this complexity, and multiple regression methods serve the same purpose in correlational research.

In the multiple regression model, the single predictor in the simple linear regression model we described above is extended to include any number of predictors:

$$Y_i = a + b_1 X_{1_i} + b_2 X_{2_i} + \cdots + b_j X_{j_i} + \cdots + b_p X_{p_i} + e_i.$$

The intercept $a$ and the residual term $e_i$ have the same meaning as in the simple linear regression model. The $b_j$ are partial regression coefficients. The regression coefficients represent the expected change in $Y$ per unit increase in $X$ while all other independent variables are held constant. Multiple regression employs *partial correlations* among collections of predictor factors as the basis for prediction. The partial correlation between two variables $A$ and $B$, with variable $C$ partialed out of both, is calculated as the correlation between the residuals from the regression of variable $A$ on variable $C$ with the residuals from the regression of variable $B$ on variable $C$. If the predictor variables are uncorrelated with one another, then multiple regression is virtually the same as ANOVA, but with continuous rather than categorical independent variables. In place of the *experimental* control from other variables in a true experiment, multiple regression analysis attempts to control *statistically* for effects of other variables. It is even possible to calculate the interaction effects between predictor variables in a regression analysis, although that is not often attempted.

The multiple correlation, $R$, is a standardized measure of the prediction of $Y$ by the entire collection of $X$ predictors, and can be interpreted in much the same way as the bivariate correlation. For example, the squared multiple correlation, $R^2$, gives the proportion of variation in the dependent variable that is predicted or "explained" by the linear combination of predictors.

When several independent variables are included in a study, it is often the case that some sets of these predictors will be correlated. Predictors within such a set can be redundant, in the sense that including all of them will not add significantly to the prediction equation over and above the contribution of the best predictor in the set. This condition is known as *multicollinearity*, and it has a number of troublesome consequences.

For example, most stepwise regression programs, unless directed otherwise by the researcher, will select the predictor with the highest simple correlation with the dependent measure, and then the remaining predictors in the set effectively "fight it out" to enter the prediction. The result can be the "bouncing beta" phenomenon, in which regression coefficients differ dramatically from sample to sample. This phenomenon is an inevitable result of two or more of the independent variables being moderately to highly correlated with each other.

One antidote to multicollinearity is to select from a set of highly correlated predictors the single predictor that is of greatest theoretical or practical importance. Which predictor to select is, of course, a substantive issue that depends on reasoned consideration of the research question. Another, more costly solution is to draw very large samples, which minimizes the influence of random error in estimating regression coefficients.

Multiple regression analysis serves two fundamentally different purposes. On the one hand, a researcher may have a logical, substantively driven theory about how family background variables or instructional practices affect educational achievement. Under these circumstances, multiple regression is intended to *explain* variation in achievement, and such explanatory variables as number of books in the home, the educational level of the parent, or the quality of a teacher's responses to students' queries might be used to explain the causes of variation in students' achievement. In this situation, a study that uses regression can resemble a quasi-experiment. On the other hand, if the researcher's purpose is to achieve the best prediction possible, then no theory need guide the selection of predictors. The market value of a student's family home, for example, might be a workable proxy for number of books in the home or parental educational level, all of which represent an underlying construct of parental influence on a student's academic growth. Any of these variables might work equally well to predict students' achievement, even though no coherent theory relates value of homes per se to students' achievement. Moreover, proxies might be subject to misinterpretation; moving families to more expensive homes might or might not have a beneficial impact on students' achievement. The point is an ancient one, but it bears repeating nevertheless: We cannot say that a phenomenon has been *explained* merely because we can *predict* it, no matter how accurate the prediction may be.

## Analytic Methods That Combine ANOVA and Regression

Methods for design and analysis of experiments and correlational studies spring from different traditions. They employ different language and operate from different philosophies. Specific statistical computer programs tend to be oriented toward one approach or the other. In fact, the same design principles are operative in all settings. Confounding and collinearity are actually different names for the same threat to validity, for example. The analytic models for ANOVA and multiple regression analysis both assume that each observation can be described as the sum of a collection of effects.

Differences in design strategy are probably the most important distinction between these two domains. Experimenters spend a great deal of time planning data collection so that the independent variables are truly independent; the purpose of factorial design techniques is to avoid confounding and collinearity. If an experiment has been well designed, analysis of the data is relatively straightforward. Correlationists are more likely to conduct surveys in which a representative group of persons is assessed on a variety of variables, some of which are viewed as dependent measures and others as independent variables or predictors. The design emphasis is on the sample of informants, not on the orthogonality of the predictors. For example, a representative sample of schoolchildren might include various ethnic groups, parent educational levels, and various socioeconomic strata; in our society, these three predictors are highly correlated, so that in this sample the ethnic minorities are more likely to be from families in which the parents have attained relatively lower levels of formal education and are from lower socioeconomic strata. For correlationists, the big challenge is not design but analysis: Once the data are in hand—how are statistical methods employed to sort out the patterns?

No general solution exists to the design problem, but statisticians have developed a strategy, the *general linear model*, for analyzing data of any character. Most statistical programs include this very powerful general-purpose strategy. The good news is that the researcher has the tools to combine virtually any collection of experimental and correlational factors for analyzing a set of outcome measures. The bad news is that preparing the program to conduct such an analysis requires a great deal of time and sophistication. One application of the general linear model, analysis of covariance (ANCOVA), is described in the next section. It attempts to control for the effects of confounding variables statistically rather than through experimental design. However, it should be used cautiously (Elashoff, 1969).

## Analysis of Covariance (ANCOVA)

As noted earlier, random assignment of subjects to treatment and experimental groups creates a level playing field for administration of experimental treatments only on average across thousands of replications of an experiment. Random assignment in a particular experiment may result in anomalies, in which subjects assigned to one group differ substantially from those assigned to another group on one or more variables that are highly related to the dependent variable. The threat to validity is that between-group differences may be attributed erroneously to treatment effects when the a priori variations are the real cause of variations in the outcome measure. Even if there is no confounding between background variables and the treatment assignment, variations in background variables, if not included in the model, become a source of error in the analysis. Sometimes random assignment to treatment and comparison groups is impractical; the researcher is aware of selection artifacts that introduce confounding but is not in a position to do anything about this problem.

Analysis of covariance is a statistical procedure that addresses a priori differences between groups in an experiment. Unlike the blocking techniques discussed earlier in the chapter, ANCOVA controls extraneous variation through statistical adjustments. When its stringent assumptions are satisfied, ANCOVA adds materially to the power and precision of an experiment, while adding little to the costs of conducting the research. Analysis of covariance adjusts the dependent variable for the effects of one or more continuous independent variables, the *covariates*, which usually are measured prior to the administration of the treatments.

Statistical adjustment for the effects of covariates is effective only when the covariates are correlated with the dependent variable in an experiment, and only when other statistical assumptions are satisfied. The most important assumption is *homogeneity of the variance-covariance matrix*. In essence, the variances and the correlations (covariances) in each cell of the design must be roughly equivalent. If the covariate is highly correlated with the dependent measure in some cells but not in others, then the appropriateness of ANCOVA is undermined.

The ANCOVA procedure works by adjusting posttreatment means on the dependent variable for covariate differences. Rather than assessing the differences between sample means directly, as in the analysis of variance, ANCOVA allows a researcher to examine the significance of these differences after adjustment for covariate effects. Figure 27–3 illustrates the technique for the simplest case—two treatments and a single covariate. The top panel depicts the scatterplots and linear regressions for the two treatment groups. The regression lines are parallel, indicating that the assumption of homogeneous correlations and variances is satisfied. The two treatments differ on the dependent variable, but they also differ on the covariate. The adjustment process moves the two groups along the common-slope regression lines to the same covariate position, and then

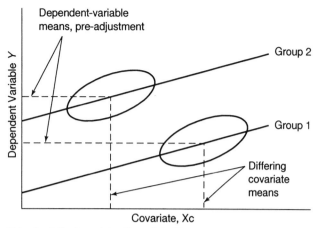

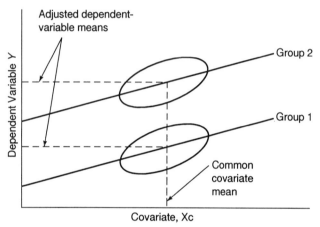

FIGURE 27–3. Analysis of Covariance (ANCOVA) Plot. Plot shows how adjustment to a common covariate level affects estimated differences between treatment groups on outcome measure.

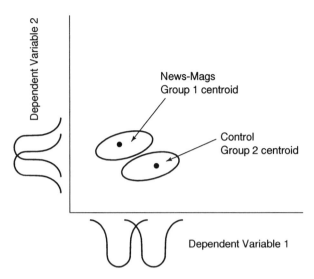

FIGURE 27–4. Multivariate Analysis of Variance Plot with Two Treatment Groups and Two Outcome Measures. Statistical significance of difference between groups is measured by distance between group centroids.

the difference between the adjusted means is assessed for statistical significance. This illustration shows the situation desired by most researchers; the difference between the outcome measures is enhanced by the adjustment. It is equally possible for ANCOVA to reduce the size of this difference; imagine that the covariate placements of Groups 1 and 2 were exchanged in the figure, for example. Then, moving the two groups along their regression lines to the same covariate position would decrease the difference.

## Multivariate Analysis of Variance (MANOVA)

In the examples described above, the investigator assessed the effects of different treatments on a single outcome measure. Research often centers on multiple dependent variables. In the home reading study used as an example at the beginning of this chapter, for instance, the investigators assessed reading comprehension, but also in-class discussion and out-of-school reading activity. One strategy for analyzing the results of this study is to assess the results for each of the outcomes taken one at a time. Multivariate analysis of variance (MANOVA) offers the investigator a technique for assessing the effects of the treatment variations on the complete array of outcomes. An integrated analysis offers at least three advantages over separate ANOVAs. The first is control over experimentwise error rate. As noted above, the more statistical tests a researcher performs, the more likely are false alarms. MANOVA allows the researcher to ask at the outset, "Given this *collection* of outcomes, do the treatment factors matter?"

Second, it can happen that the multivariate *F* test will be statistically significant even though some or all of the separate *F* tests are not. Figure 27–4 illustrates this point for a case involving two treatments and two dependent variables from the home reading study, showing the interplay of experimental and correlational methods. Unlike the situation with ANCOVA, the idea here is not to adjust any of the means; each of the outcomes is important in its own right. Rather, MANOVA assesses the difference between the means in the bivariate space. Neither of the marginal differences is as large as the distance between the two *centroids*, the middle points of the groups in the bivariate space.

A third reason for considering MANOVA is that the dependent variables themselves may be correlated, as is the case in the example above. If so, then separate ANOVAs are misleading; the researcher is not really testing separate hypotheses, but a single complex hypothesis. Consider the home reading study. Suppose, in addition to the three measures of reading comprehension, in-class discussion, and out-of-school reading, the researcher also assessed functional vocabulary, breadth of world knowledge, frequency of visits to the library, and frequency of conversations with older children and adults. The researcher might now be in a position to report seven significant differences. In fact, all of the measures might simply reflect aspects of a more fundamental variable, which one might call general academic ability. MANOVA offers the researcher a way to look at the overall pattern but also to distinguish among specific outcome effects.

MANOVA typically proceeds in two stages. The first is an assessment of the significance of differences among the group centroids. The outcome of this analysis parallels the $F$ ratio for each factor in the design (see Green, 1978; Jones, 1966; Tatsuoka, 1988). The second or follow-up stage depends on the purposes of the investigation. One direction is to explore contrasts among various sets of treatments, akin to the pairwise comparisons or multiple contrasts described for ANOVA. The second direction is to perform separate one-way analyses of variance (Bock, 1975; Cooley & Lohnes, 1971; Cramer & Bock, 1986; Finn, 1974; Tatsuoka, 1988; Wilkinson, 1975). In many instances, researchers are interested in the dynamic relationships among the entire set of dependent variable measures, and in the complex ways that the various treatments affect the experimental groups under study. A particularly useful follow-up analysis when centroids have been shown to differ significantly is discriminant function analysis (Bray & Maxwell, 1985; Tatsuoka, 1988).

## Factor Analysis

With the possible exception of multiple regression analysis, factor analysis has for years been the most popular nonexperimental statistical procedure used by educational psychologists. As an aid to the explication of human cognitive abilities and to our understanding of attitudes, values, and the dimensions of personality, factor analysis has proved to be indispensable.

In the first decade of the 20th century, the English psychologist Charles Spearman (1927) noted that scores on all measures of intellectual performance, from digit span tests to mathematics word problems to reading comprehension tests, were positively correlated. He reasoned that this was so because each measure had something in common; each was tapping to some extent a "general mental ability," which he labeled $g$. Because the correlations varied in size and because all were less than perfect, some measures were tapping more of $g$ than others, and all had something unique about them. Thus, a test of the ability to recite a string of orally presented digits backward and a test of the ability to define words were both indicators of $g$, to some extent, but each also reflected, to some degree, different abilities unique unto themselves. Spearman posited a two-factor theory of intelligence: one general factor and a variety of specific factors. The specific factor in a test may be mechanical ability, spatial ability, mathematical ability, or any number of other cognitive abilities, but each test also measures $g$ to some extent. Spearman proposed a simple mathematical model, factor analysis, that is similar in many respects to the linear regression model discussed earlier, to account for the intercorrelations among tests of different cognitive abilities.

Factor analysis is now a generic term that embraces a wide variety of related techniques for reducing a large number of observable variables to a smaller set of more fundamental "explanatory" variables. Although the origins of factor analysis can be found in mental ability testing, factor-analytic procedures are enormously popular in virtually all of the social and behavioral sciences and in many physical sciences as well, such as biology, geology, and meteorology. In education and psychology, factor analysis is a principal analytic technique for determining the number of distinct abilities underlying cognitive tests or batteries of tests and the number of factors underlying personality and attitude scales.

In this chapter we can give only a brief introduction to factor analysis. Gorsuch (1983) provides a basic, nontechnical and comprehensive introduction to the essentials. Harman's 1976 text, now a classic, is no longer in print, but those interested may wish to consult older editions in libraries. Its clarity and precision remain unsurpassed. A relatively complete, advanced treatment can be found in Mulaik (1972).

Let $z_{ij}$ be the score of individual $i$ on test $j$, standardized to have a mean of zero and a standard deviation of 1. Spearman's two-factor model can be stated simply as

$$z_{ij} = a_j F_i + u_{ij}.$$

The coefficient $a_i$, called a *factor loading*, indicates the extent to which the test measures $g$. This simple factor model states that the test $z_j$ is a function of only two variables, a general factor $F$ and a specific factor $u$. More specifically, individual $i$'s score on test $j (z_{ij})$ is a function of two independent components: the product of the loading $(a_j)$ of test $j$ on the common factor and the individual's score on the common factor $(F_i)$, plus the individual's score on the unique component of the test $(u_{ij})$. A central assumption is that the general factor and the unique component are uncorrelated. The various methods for estimating $a$, $F$, and $u$ are fully explicated in Mulaik (1972) and other texts on factor analysis.

It shortly became apparent that the two-factor model was simply too parsimonious to account for the observable correlations between the burgeoning number of mental tests that appeared in the first quarter of the century. Several psychologists, most notably L. L. Thurstone, argued that there was not a single common factor but several. A more accurate picture of human intelligence would have to include a *verbal* factor, a *spatial/mechanical* factor, a *quantitative* factor, and several others as well, to account for the fact that items on a verbal analogies test, say, correlated significantly more highly among themselves than they did with items on tests of quantitative ability, mechanical comprehension, or spatial relations. The notion of a single factor underlying performance on a battery of tests was replaced with the notion of several factors underlying performance on the tests.

Deciding on the number of factors underlying a test or battery of tests requires judgment and is not a mechanical decision. In addition to selecting a method of estimation, the user of factor analysis must decide how many factors are necessary to explain or account for the observed correlations among the items on a test or among the tests in a battery, whether the factors are best viewed as correlated or uncorrelated in the population of interest, and, most important, how to interpret the factors. Several statistical and graphical indicators, fully explained in the texts mentioned previously, can inform reasoned judgment on this issue.

The versatility of factor-analytic procedures allows the investigator to obtain factors that are correlated as well as factors that are uncorrelated. Whether factors should be viewed as correlated or uncorrelated is a decision of considerable substantive and statistical importance. In the cognitive ability domain, it is likely that factors underlying intellectual performance are positively correlated. Virtually all measures of verbal ability and mathematical ability, for example, have been found to correlate moderately (between +.40 and +.60). Because no such consistently positive correlations have been observed in the personality domain, when such measures are factor analyzed it is more difficult to decide whether to obtain correlated or uncorrelated factors. One's substantive knowledge of the domain in question should ultimately guide the decision, but when in doubt, it is probably best to err on the side of uncorrelated factors because they greatly simplify further research and interpretation.

The interpretation and naming of factors has been described as more art than science. Factor interpretation obviously requires some knowledge of the domain in question, but by simply examining the pattern of correlations between the factors and the original measures (standard output of any factor analysis computer program), one can usually get a good idea of the general nature of a particular factor.

Over the years, a distinction has been made between *exploratory* factor analysis and *confirmatory* factor analysis. When a researcher has developed a new measure or is working in a relatively new area of research, "data snooping" in the form of exploratory factor analysis is common. In exploratory factor analysis, the researcher attempts to discover the structure underlying a test or battery of tests, and to confirm the reality of that structure with additional, independent samples. In confirmatory factor analysis, the factor structure underlying the test or test battery is specified beforehand on the basis of one's substantive knowledge of the domain in question, and the factor solution is appraised for its fit to this structure.

The great appeal and popularity of factor-analytic techniques lie in the reduction of a large number of variables to a smaller set of more fundamental explanatory dimensions, with little loss of information. If, for example, only four factors are necessary to account for the covariation among 20 variables, then any variable (e.g., grades in school) that can be predicted or explained by the 20 original measures can be explained just as well by the four factors. The appeal of this reduction in the number of variables should not be lost on the reader. Newton's status as one of the greatest figures in the history of science stems precisely from his ability to explain a large number of seemingly unrelated phenomena by the universal law of gravitation and three simple laws of motion. So it is, although to a far less dramatic extent, with factor analysis in mental testing, personality theory, and many other disciplines in the social and behavioral sciences. To be sure, every individual, every classroom, and every school is unique in some sense. But if there are no commonalities, no general principles, no underlying explanatory dimensions of variation, then educational psychology is not viable as science.

## Multilevel Analysis

Educational psychologists are often, though not exclusively, interested in the study of students, teachers and classrooms, schools and districts. The focus is typically on matters such as the application of principles of learning and development on curriculum design and instructional pacing. The natural assumption is that the student is the fundamental unit of analysis. From one perspective, learning is fundamentally an individual phenomenon. But school learning does not exist in a social or organizational vacuum. What happens outside the classroom can have dramatic effects on teaching and learning inside the classroom, and student learning is certainly affected by the classroom context. Students and teachers are nested within larger social structures: departments, schools, districts, and states.

Procedures for analyzing data with this nested character are variously called multilevel or hierarchical models (Bryk & Raudenbush, 1992). These procedures sort the data into the various levels of the hierarchy, evaluating treatment factors according to the level at which they have been introduced, and assessing the correlational relations that apply at each of the levels. Several statistical programs include techniques for handling hierarchical data, although these require considerable sophistication. Less attention has been given to design considerations for multilevel systems. The issues are similar to those discussed earlier under the heading of repeated measures designs. In a sense, the key questions are the interplay of treatment variations at different levels of a complex social system.

Correlational patterns also vary from one level to another in a hierarchical system. Individual differences often account for the lion's share of the variation on such important variables as IQ and achievement. But the strength of relationship is not constant across levels. For example, the correlation between socioeconomic status and standardized achievement, when calculated at the student level, typically ranges from .30 to .40. However, when this correlation is calculated from school-level data, the values typically increase to .80 or higher. The reasons for this increase are twofold. First, the within-school variation in achievement due to socioeconomic status is lost. Second, students, schools, and neighborhoods are "assortatively mated" (Cooley & Lohnes, 1976), so that relatively more students from poorer families attend some schools, and relatively more affluent (and higher achieving) students attend other schools. A regression with the student as the unit of analysis based on 1,000 students amounts to no more than three to five schools. The scatterplot for school averages may show stable points that fall close to a straight line; the within-school individual variations are lost. The failure to consider the level of aggregation used to calculate a correlation has occurred often enough in the social sciences that it has a name, the *ecological fallacy* (Robinson, 1950).

## CONCLUDING REMARKS

This chapter has addressed only the basic quantitative, analytic methods used in research on the psychology of education. Many potentially fruitful approaches to disciplined inquiry in this field are beyond the scope of this chapter. Examples of analytic methods not addressed include cross-lagged panel analysis (Kenny, 1975, 1979), canonical analysis (Levine, 1977), and latent class analysis (Bollen, 1989; Hagenaars, 1993; McCutcheon, 1987). Other omissions include meta-analytic research (Hedges & Olkin, 1985), single-subject research designs and their analysis through time-series methodology (Glass, Willson, & Gottman, 1975; McDowall, McCleary, Meidinger & Hay, 1980; Cromwell, Labys, & Terraza, 1994), and survey research methods (Rossi, Wright, & Anderson, 1983; Fowler, 1993).

We believe, as does Lee Shulman (1988), that choice of method in large part governs the nature of inquiry in education. Just as one's conception of the nature of snow is limited by the unitary label the English vocabulary provides (in contrast to the rich and diverse descriptions fostered by the many labels found in Iñupiat), researchers' conceptions of objects and topics of inquiry are limited by their exposure to diverse analytic methods. What one cannot conceive, one is unlikely to investigate. We therefore encourage the reader to go well beyond this chapter in his or her methodological explorations and to tap the sources cited throughout, including those we have listed in this concluding section.

# References

Bock, R. D. (1975). *Multivariate statistical methods in behavioral research*. New York: McGraw-Hill.

Bollen, K. A. (1989). *Structural equations with latent variables*. New York: Wiley.

Borg, W. R., & Gall, M. D. (1989). *Educational research: An introduction* (5th ed.). New York: Longman.

Bracht, G. H., & Glass, G. V (1968). The external validity of experiments. *American Educational Research Journal, 5,* 437–474.

Bray, J. H., & Maxwell, S. E. (1985). *Multivariate analysis of variance*. Beverly Hills, CA: Sage.

Bryk, A. S., & Raudenbush, S. W. (1992). *Hierarchical linear models*. Newbury Park, CA: Sage.

Campbell, D. T., & Stanley, J. C. (1963). Experimental and quasi-experimental designs for research on teaching. In N. L. Gage (Ed.), *Handbook of research on teaching* (pp. 171–246). Chicago: Rand McNally.

Cook, T. D., & Campbell, D. T. (1979). *Quasi-experimentation: Design and analysis issues for field settings*. Chicago: Rand McNally.

Cooley, W. W., & Lohnes, P. R. (1971). *Multivariate data analysis*. New York: Wiley.

Cooley, W. W., & Lohnes, P. R. (1976). *Evaluation research in education*. New York: Irvington.

Cornfield, J., & Tukey, J. W. (1956). Average values of mean squares in factorials. *Annals of Mathematical Statistics, 27,* 907–949.

Cramer, E. M., & Bock, R. D. (1986). Multivariate analysis. *Review of Educational Research, 36,* 604–617.

Cromwell, J. B., Labys, W. C., & Terraza, M. (1994). *Univariate tests for time series models*. Newbury Park, CA: Sage.

Cronbach, L. J., & Suppes, P. (1969). *Research for tomorrow's schools*. New York: Macmillan.

Darlington, R. B. (1990). *Regression and linear models*. New York: McGraw-Hill.

Draper, N. R., & Smith, H. (1981). *Applied regression analysis* (2nd ed.). New York: Wiley.

Educational Testing Service. (1992). *The family and learning*. Princeton, NJ: Author.

Edwards, A. L. (1979). *Multiple regression and the analysis of variance and covariance*. San Francisco: Freeman.

Elashoff, J. D. (1969). Analysis of covariance: a delicate instrument. *American Educational Research Journal, 6,* 383–401.

Ferguson, G. A., & Takane, Y. (1989). *Statistical analysis in psychology and education*. New York: McGraw-Hill.

Finn, J. D. (1974). *A general model for multivariate analysis*. New York: Holt, Rinehart & Winston.

Fowler, F. J., Jr. (1993). *Survey research methods* (2nd ed.). Newbury Park, CA: Sage.

Gay, L. R. (1992). *Educational research: Competencies for analysis and application*. New York: Macmillan.

Glass, G. V, & Hopkins, K. (1984). *Statistical methods in education and psychology* (2nd ed.). Englewood Cliffs, NJ: Prentice Hall.

Glass, G. V, Willson, V. L., & Gottman, J. M. (1975). *Design and analysis of time series experiments*. Boulder: Colorado Associated University Press.

Gorsuch, R. L. (1983). *Factor analysis*. Hillsdale, NJ: Lawrence Erlbaum Associates.

Green, P. E. (1978). *Analyzing multivariate data*. Hinsdale, IL: Dryden Press.

Hagenaars, J. A. (1993). *Log linear models with latent variables*. Newbury Park, CA: Sage.

Harman, H. H. (1976). *Modern factor analysis* (3rd ed). Chicago: University of Chicago Press.

Hartigan, J. A., & Wigdor, A. K. (Eds.). (1989). *Fairness in employment testing: Validity generalization, minority issues, and the General Aptitude Test Battery*. Washington, DC: National Academy Press.

Hedges, L. V., & Olkin, I. (1985). *Statistical methods for meta-analysis*. San Diego, CA: Academic Press.

Jaeger, R. M. (Ed.). (1988). *Complementary methods for research in education*. Washington, DC: American Educational Research Association.

Jaeger, R. M. (1990). *Statistics: A spectator sport*. Newbury Park, CA: Sage.

Jones, L. V. (1966). Analysis of variance in its multivariate developments. In R. B. Cattell (Ed.), *Handbook of multivariate experimental psychology* (pp. 244–266). Chicago, IL: Rand McNally.

Kenny, D. A. (1975). Cross-lagged panel correlation: A test for spuriousness. *Psychological Bulletin, 82,* 887–903.

Kenny, D. A. (1979). *Correlation and causality*. New York: Wiley.

Kerlinger, F. N., & Pedhazur, E. J. (1973). *Multiple regression in behavioral research*. New York: Holt, Rinehart and Winston.

Kirk, R. E. (1968). *Experimental design: Procedures for the behavioral sciences*. Belmont, CA: Brooks/Cole.

Krathwohl, D. R. (1993). *Methods of educational and social science: An integrated approach*. White Plains, NY: Longman.

Levine, M. S. (1977). *Canonical analysis and factor comparison*. Beverly Hills, CA: Sage.

Lindquist, E. F. (1953). *Design and analysis of experiments in psychology and education*. Boston: Houghton Mifflin.

McCutcheon, A. L. (1987). *Latent class analysis*. Newbury Park, CA: Sage.

McDowall, D., McCleary, R., Meidinger, E. E., & Hay, R. A. (1980). *Interrupted time series analysis*. Beverly Hills, CA: Sage.

Mulaik, S. A. (1972). *The foundations of factor analysis*. New York: McGraw-Hill.

Myers, J. L. (1979). *Fundamentals of experimental design* (3rd ed.). Boston: Allyn & Bacon.

Namboodiri, N. K. (1972). Experimental designs in which each subject is used repeatedly. *Psychological Bulletin, 77,* 54–64.

Norūsis, M. J. (1990). *SPSS advanced statistics: Student guide*. Chicago: SPSS.

Pedhazur, E. J. (1982). *Multiple regression in behavioral research* (2nd ed.). New York: Holt, Rinehart & Winston.

Pedhazur, E. J., & Schmelkin, L. P. (1991). *Measurement, design, and analysis: An integrated approach* (Student ed.). Hillsdale, NJ: Lawrence Erlbaum Associates.

Pool, K. W., & Capie, W. R. (1977, April). *The Miltz (1971) How to Explain Program and its effects on preservice elementary teacher explaining ability*. Paper presented at the annual meeting of the American Educational Research Association, Los Angeles, CA. (ERIC Document No. ED 201 780).

Porter, A. (1988). Comparative experiments in educational research. In R. M. Jaeger (Ed.), *Complementary methods for research in education*. Washington, DC: American Educational Research Association.

Robinson, W. S. (1950). Ecological inference and the behavior of individuals. *American Sociological Review, 15,* 351–357.

Rossi, P. H., Wright, J. D., & Anderson, A. B. (Eds.). (1983). *Handbook of survey research*. New York: Academic Press.

Shulman, L. S. (1988). The nature of disciplined inquiry in education. In R. M. Jaeger (Ed.), *Complementary methods for research in education*. Washington, DC: American Educational Research Association.

Spearman, C. E. (1927). *The abilities of man*. New York: Macmillan.

Tatsuoka, M. M. (1988). Multivariate analysis of variance. In J. R. Nesselroade & R. B. Cattell (Eds.), *Perspectives on individual differences* (2nd ed., pp. 399–419). New York: Plenum Press.

Timm, N. H. (1975). *Multivariate analysis with applications in education and psychology*. Monterey, CA: Brooks/Cole.

Wilkinson, L. (1975). Response variable hypothesis in the multivariate analysis of variance. *Psychological Bulletin, 82,* 408–412.

Winer, B. J., Brown, D. R., & Michaels, K. M. (1991). *Statistical principles in experimental design* (3rd ed.). New York: McGraw-Hill.

# ADVANCES IN ASSESSMENT MODELS, METHODS, AND PRACTICES

## Ronald K. Hambleton

UNIVERSITY OF MASSACHUSETTS, AMHERST

Educational assessment in the 1990s looks quite different from the assessment practices of the past couple of decades. In the 1990s, more educational assessments are "performance based"; that is, they require students to complete tasks such as writing essays, conducting experiments, preparing portfolios, or providing written answers to problems. These new assessments are more likely to measure higher level cognitive skills than educational assessments of the past—or at least that is the expectation of many educational reformers. In fact, use of the term "educational assessment" rather than "educational testing" highlights two important shifts in emphasis in testing: (a) the assessment of higher level cognitive skills and (b) the use of a wide variety of item formats (Linn, 1995).

Multiple-choice testing, or objective testing, as it is sometimes called, is not likely to be discontinued in U.S. or Canadian schools, in large-scale assessments, or in credentialing examinations, but objective forms of assessment such as multiple-choice tests most likely will be balanced in school, state or provincial, employment, and national testing programs by more direct measures of assessment such as writing tasks, performance tests, computer simulation exercises, hands-on projects, and portfolios of work.

News about changes in educational assessment practices will hardly come as a surprise to psychologists. Since the late 1980s, education and psychology journals, books, newspapers, and magazines have been filled with reports addressing the validity (or lack of validity) of objective approaches to assessment (Wiggins, 1989a, 1989b) and the strengths and weaknesses of performance assessments (E. L. Baker, O'Neil, & Linn, 1993; Calfee, 1995; Koretz, Stecher, Klein, & McCaffrey, 1994; Linn,

1995; Shavelson, Baxter, & Pine, 1992; Taylor, 1994); and school districts and provincial/state departments of education have been redirecting or "reforming" their testing programs by adding performance assessments and portfolios (e.g., California Assessment Program Staff, 1989; Horvath, 1991; Kentucky Department of Education, 1993; Koretz et al., 1994; Roeber & Dutcher, 1989).

The major test publishers themselves appear to be following recent trends in assessment practices by including more advanced cognitive skills in their standardized achievement tests. The latest technical manual for the Metropolitan Achievement Tests (7th ed.) addresses the change in the following way:

> Furthermore, there has sometimes been an underemphasis on including in these [standardized achievement test] batteries items that assessed the various high-order cognitive processes and instead including a preponderance of knowledge or recall items. As a result [our new battery] was planned . . . to include a greater number of items assessing higher-order thinking skills than has ever been on this kind of test before. (Psychological Corporation, 1993, p. 12)

Important U.S. national assessment programs, such as the National Assessment of Educational Progress (NAEP) and the New Standards Project (New Standards Project, 1993; L. B. Resnick & D. P. Resnick, 1992), are making considerable use of open-ended item formats and exercises and the assessment of higher order skills in the 1990s to fall into line with new curriculum specifications (e.g., Collis & Romberg, 1991; National Assessment Governing Board, 1992; National Council of Teachers of Mathematics, 1989). The direction for assessment practices

The author thanks Ron Berk and Ross Traub for their constructive suggestions on earlier drafts of this chapter.

in the 1990s and into the foreseeable future seem clear: more performance assessments, assessments closely linked to classroom instruction and looking very much like classroom activities, more focus on the assessment of higher level cognitive skills, and reduced use of multiple-choice test items (Frederiksen & Collins, 1989; Nickerson, 1989).

Where is the impetus for change in assessment practices coming from? The main impetus for changes in assessment, as well as for changes in school organization, curricula, teacher training, and so forth, is coming from educational policymakers at the national and state levels who hold the view that schools are not doing the job they should be doing. Results from recent international studies of educational achievement lend some support for this position (Cheney, 1991; Lapointe, Mead, & Askew, 1992; Lapointe, Mead, & Phillips, 1989). For example, U.S. students placed last (among six countries participating in a 1988 study) in mathematics (Lapointe et al., 1989). Some of the headlines from U.S. newspapers that followed were, "Educators Say Public Schools Need Overhaul, Not Reform," "U.S. Youth Fail Math Test," and "American Schools Perpetuate Failure."

On the other hand, there is research or alternative interpretations of existing international comparative data of educational achievement to suggest that the current quality of education is not nearly as poor as some policymakers have made the situation appear (see Berliner, 1993; Jaeger, 1992; Westbury, 1992). For example, several of the international comparative studies of educational achievement appear to have flaws in their design or implementation (e.g., choice of samples, assessment administration conditions), and factors outside a school's control, such as the number of parents in the home and parents' level of education, account for a relatively high proportion of the variability in school achievement (Robinson & Brandon, 1994). But no matter what the true situation is regarding the current quality of education, there is little or no disagreement that major changes are taking place in what schools teach and how students are being taught and assessed.

The six national educational goals prepared by then-president George Bush and the state governors in 1989 are the policymakers' response to the educational problems they identified in the United States at the time, and these goals are intended to improve education substantially by the year 2000. Goals 2000: Educate America Act, which was passed by the Congress in 1993, is the impetus for the educational reform movement throughout the country. It is intended to be a broad federal initiative to encourage and support restructuring, reform, and improvements in public education. The original six comprehensive and far-reaching goals are (a) to prepare preschoolers for learning by improving their health care and nutrition, (b) to increase the high school graduation rate, (c) to make the United States best in the world in science and mathematics, (d) to reduce the adult rate of illiteracy to zero (from the current level of 13%), (e) to make every school free of drugs and violence, and (f) to require students in Grades 4, 8, and 12 to demonstrate competency of higher level cognitive skills in history, math, science, geography, and English. Two additional goals were added in 1993: (g) expand parental involvement, and (h) increase professional development opportunities for educators.

The eight goals in the Educate America Act are ambitious. To assess goals (c) and (f), major changes in assessment will need to take place, and specifically a shift from the assessment of a student's knowledge about a subject to an assessment of a student's ability to reason, think critically, and solve problems. As a result, educational assessment practices in the United States will need to change what is measured (to reflect curriculum changes) and expand the approaches used in assessment to ensure valid educational assessments. Similar changes can be seen in the assessment practices in many Canadian provinces.

The shift from objective to performance assessments in education has been the major change in assessment practices in recent years, but other significant changes are taking place, too. For one, classical test models and procedures (see Gulliksen, 1950; Lord & Novick, 1968), which have provided the technical underpinnings for the development and evaluation of educational assessments (recall, classic test theoretic concepts such as true score, parallel tests, the standard error of measurement, parallel form reliability, the KR-20, the Spearman-Brown formula, the correction for attenuation, and classic item difficulty and item discrimination statistics), are gradually being replaced by models and methods associated with *item response theory* (IRT) (Crocker & Algina, 1986; Hambleton, Swaminathan, & Rogers, 1991; Lord, 1980; Wright & Stone, 1979).

The flexibility and usefulness of these new IRT models in test development and in solving practical measurement problems, such as equating forms of a test (in popular jargon, preparing a conversion table for finding comparable scores on pairs of tests) and identifying biased test items, have stimulated the interest in new psychometric models for assessment. The impetus for new psychometric models came initially with the publication of Lord and Novick's (1968) *Statistical Theories of Mental Test Scores*. Recently, additional IRT models have been developed to accommodate the special requirements of performance assessments such as the need for models that can handle polychotomous scoring and the representation of multidimensional abilities underlying assessment performance (see, e.g., Traub, 1994; van der Linden & Hambleton, in press, for a discussion of 27 IRT models).

Another major change in assessment practices today is the expanding role of computers. Traditionally, computers have been used in scoring, analyzing test results, and reporting scores. Today, computers are being used in the construction and administration of tests, and their capabilities for providing multimedia environments are being capitalized upon to extend the variety of item formats for assessing students. Assessment practices in the 21st century will be very different from today's practices because of the power and flexibility of computers (van der Linden, 1995).

Other changes in assessment practices include an intense concern for fair or unbiased assessments. In measurement jargon, the goal is to construct assessment measures that are free of *differential item functioning* (DIF). Basically, fairness in assessment is present when students from two subgroups of interest, such as females and males, matched on the ability measured by the assessment (i.e., have the same ability), have the same chance of success (i.e., have the same expected score) on an assessment task. When students in the two groups of interest who are matched on ability have unequal chances of success, DIF is said to be present, the assessment material is not used, and attempts to find explanations for the difference in performances are made.

Research on the detection of DIF has been extensive (see, e.g., Camilli & Shepard, 1994; Holland & Wainer, 1993), with the development of many DIF detection methods, the conduct of many comparative studies of these methods, and applications of the methods to a wide variety of assessments. The use of psychometric methods for the detection of DIF has become as common as item analyses in the test development process in many national and state testing agencies, though questions remain about which DIF detection methods are best and how results from applying these methods should be interpreted (Camilli & Shepard, 1994; Hambleton, Clauser, Mazor, & R. W. Jones, 1993).

Also associated with the educational reform movement is the demand for high performance standards, even "world-class performance standards," for interpreting educational assessment results. It has been said that these so-called world-class standards are driving the educational reform movement by providing targets or goals to achieve (Taylor, 1994). But who should set these standards, if they should be set at all, and by what methods? These, too, are current problems being studied, and the solutions will change the ways in which policymakers and educators use educational assessments (e.g., Phillips et al., 1993).

The main goal of this chapter is to describe some of the new directions in educational assessment. The remainder of this chapter is divided into seven sections, with each section devoted to an important advance: assessment competencies for teachers, performance assessment, item formats, computer technology, new psychometric models, differential item functioning, and standard setting. A concluding section summarizes the main points of the chapter and makes suggestions for future research.

## ASSESSMENT COMPETENCIES FOR TEACHERS

An important issue in education today concerns what to teach teachers about assessment (e.g., Schafer, 1991). The issue is important enough that the two largest teacher unions in the United States, the National Education Association (NEA) and the American Federation of Teachers (AFT), joined with the National Council on Measurement in Education (NCME) to produce the Standards for Teacher Competence in Educational Assessment of Students (1990). (A similar set of standards was recently prepared in Canada.) The standards were prepared to serve a number of purposes:

- as a guide for teacher educators who design or approve teacher education programs
- as a basis for teachers conducting a self-evaluation of their educational testing skills
- as a guide for the design of testing workshops for teachers
- as a directive to educational measurement specialists and teacher trainers to broaden their conception of student assessment and convey this broader conception in their research, writing, and teaching

The Standards for Teacher Competence are more powerful and important than other efforts to develop assessment guide-

lines (e.g., Popham & Hambleton, 1990) because they have the full backing of the two national teacher unions, which have a combined membership of over 2 million. Also, unlike some of the past efforts, these standards were widely circulated and reviewed prior to their publication and were comprehensive in the sense that a broad definition of student assessment was adopted to match the goals of the educational reform initiatives in the United States. Also, the standards cover the complete set of teacher activities where student assessments are done. These activities are (a) activities prior to instruction, (b) activities occurring during instruction, (c) activities occurring after the regular segment of instruction, (d) activities with teachers' involvement in school and school district decision-making, and (e) activities associated with teachers' involvement in the wider community of educators.

The assessment competencies for teachers were organized by AFT, NCME, and NEA into seven broad areas, with each area further described by a set of skills that teachers would need to be proficient.

1. Teachers should be skilled in choosing assessment methods appropriate for instructional decisions.
2. Teachers should be skilled in developing assessment methods appropriate for instructional decisions.
3. Teachers should be skilled in administering, scoring, and interpreting the results of both externally produced and teacher-produced assessment methods.
4. Teachers should be skilled in using assessment results when making decisions about individual students, planning teaching, and developing curriculum and school improvement.
5. Teachers should be skilled in developing valid pupil grading procedures that use pupil assessments.
6. Teachers should be skilled in communicating assessment results to students, parents, other lay audiences, and other educators.
7. Teachers should be skilled in recognizing unethical, illegal, and otherwise inappropriate assessment methods and uses of assessment information (AFT, NCME, NEA, 1990).

By starting with what seemed to be a broad, reasonable, and appropriate definition of student assessment,

Assessment is defined as the process of obtaining information that is used to make educational decisions about students, to give feedback to the student about his or her progress, strengths, and weaknesses, to judge instructional effectiveness and curricular adequacy, and to inform policy (AFT, NCME, NEA, 1990, p. 1),

the AFT, NCME, and NEA made a very strong argument for performance assessment and performance assessment training without the usual rhetoric. There was no denigration of norm-referenced testing, no criticisms of current standardized testing practices were offered, and there was no direct challenge to the multiple-choice format or other objective item formats. Still, the case for the use of a broader set of item formats in educational assessment was clearly articulated in the definition of student assessment and the associated assessment competencies for teachers.

Of course, arguing for an expanded set of assessment competencies for teachers is only part of the solution. Training teachers to achieve the competencies is likely to be difficult and time-consuming and will involve substantial changes in the current preservice training of teachers. There is also the need for expanded teacher in-service training in assessment. Next, the topic of performance assessment in classroom setting and other environments will be considered.

## PERFORMANCE ASSESSMENT

The new era in educational assessment practices has been labeled *authentic assessment* by some proponents (Wiggins, 1989b). This term seems less than ideal to describe the changes taking place in assessment because it appears to denigrate 80 years of important advances in psychometric research (see, e.g., Hambleton & Zaal, 1991; Linn, 1989). Other terms to describe the changes taking place in assessment include direct assessment, alternative assessment, performance testing, and performance assessment. The terms *performance testing* or *performance assessment* will be used here because they are descriptive, neutral, and meaningful to psychologists. There is a long tradition of performance testing in industrial psychology, and this tradition has strongly influenced assessments in industry and the military (e.g., assessments for selection, placement, and promotion) (Fitzpatrick & Morrison, 1971). Also, the term "performance testing" has appeared in the classroom testing literature for a long time.

Performance assessments should result in more valid educational assessments for policymakers, school administrators, teachers, students, and parents if problems associated with their development, administration, scoring, and use can be overcome (see, e.g., E. L. Baker, O'Neil, & Linn, 1993), and if concerns about the transfer or generalizability of scores from performance on a small set of performance tasks to larger domains of tasks in the content domains of interest can be adequately addressed (Linn & Burton, 1994). Objective testing, as represented by multiple-choice, matching, and true-false formats, appear to be able to carry a significant part of the assessment requirements today (see, e.g., Farr, Pritchard, & Smitten, 1990), but certainly not all of them.

As more use is made of assessment results in educational accountability (e.g., evaluating teachers, schools, programs, and even states—see, e.g., the 1990 and 1992 NAEP Trial State Assessments at the Grade 8 level [Linn, 1993]), those affected by the results will want to be sure that the assessments themselves are fair and accurately measure what the assessments were intended to measure. Even the most ardent supporters of standardized achievement tests would not claim that these tests measure more than a fraction of what schools expect students to learn or that the tests can measure, with the multiple-choice format, all of the important higher order cognitive outcomes, such as reasoning, problem solving, and critical thinking, which are being highlighted in the new curriculum frameworks (see, e.g., National Assessment Government Board, 1992).

If teachers are going to teach to the skills covered by an assessment (and there is substantial evidence that they do already; this is known as the WYTIWYG principle, or "what you test is what you get"), current thinking is that assessments should measure what is really important in a curriculum (Madaus, 1988) and should look more like instructional activities

than like tests. Then, teaching to the assessment would be constructive and desirable. Shepard (1989) has even argued that educational assessments should approximate the learning tasks of interest, so that, when students practice for the assessment, some useful learning takes place.

A similar argument was made to teachers with criterion-referenced tests in the 1970s and 1980s: Construct tests to measure the skills that students are expected to learn, and then teach to the test (although not to the exact objectives or items that will appear on the test). Teaching to the test becomes equivalent to teaching the curriculum.

The terms performance testing and (equivalently) performance assessment are receiving widespread use in the education literature, although a single definition has not been agreed upon by users. The Office of Technology Assessment of the United States Congress (1992) provided one definition of performance tests that seems clear and descriptive: "testing that requires a student to create an answer or a product that demonstrates his or her knowledge or skills" (reported by Rudner & Boston, 1994). Implicit in the definition and other popular definitions of performance tests or assessments are five features:

1. Performance tests are intended to assess what it is that students know *and* can do, with the emphasis on "doing."
2. Performance tests should use direct methods of assessment (e.g., writing samples to assess writing, and oral presentations to assess speaking skills).
3. Performance tests should have a high degree of realism about them (that is, "fidelity" should be high). In reading assessments, for example, students would be expected to read reasonably lengthy passages (perhaps several pages) prior to answering questions, and in mathematics tests, students would be expected to work with rulers, protractors, calculators, and so forth, in solving mathematics problems. (Such changes, for example, have been incorporated into the new versions of the Scholastic Assessment Test.)
4. Performance tests might involve (a) activities for which there is no correct answer, (b) assessing groups rather than individuals (e.g., a group putting on a play), (c) testing that would continue over an extended period of time, or (d) self-evaluation of performances, projects, and so forth.
5. Performance tests are likely to use open-ended tasks aimed at assessing higher level cognitive skills.

The first feature is not unique to performance testing. In fact, it is a central feature of criterion-referenced testing (see, e.g., Popham, 1978). But it is an important feature of performance testing, and highlights the concern in score interpretation with what students know and can do, and not with how students compare to a norm group. Clearly, performance testing fits within the broad framework of criterion-referenced assessment (Hambleton, 1984, 1990). Certainly performance tests, like other criterion-referenced tests that are constructed to interpret student performance in relation to well-defined instructional outcomes, could be used to rank order examinees (i.e., they could be used to facilitate norm-referenced assessments), but that is rarely their stated purpose, and as a result they are not constructed optimally to distinguish among students. Hambleton (1990) and Popham (1978) offer detailed comparisons between norm-referenced and criterion-referenced assessments.

The second feature is not unique either, although it would be correct to say that performance testing advocates aspire to see a great deal more use of performance tests than has been the norm (see Linn, 1991; Linn, E. L. Baker, & Dunbar, 1991). For example, at the lower grade levels in British Columbia, many of the important objectives or school outcomes are being measured with performance tests. In Kentucky, standardized assessments with multiple-choice items have been replaced almost totally by performance tests, and only the performance test results are used in school and district accountability. Formal and informal observations, qualitative analysis of student performances and products, oral questioning, and analysis of student records are just a few of the other assessment methods that have been suggested in the educational assessment literature.

The third feature is very important: The goal is to make testing more like instructional activities than like highly structured tasks in which answer choices are provided (i.e., "constructed responses" are preferred to "selected responses"). Constructed responses are more valued than selected responses in performance assessments, although one could imagine exceptions. Some changes can be made to multiple-choice testing by providing more realistic stimuli such as longer, more interesting, and thought-provoking passages, and by preparing "application of knowledge" questions, but there are practical limits to what can be done. The use of non-multiple-choice formats appears to hold more promise generally for assessing higher-order thinking skills. Performance tests might require students to prepare a research paper, solve a complex problem, conduct an experiment, participate in a debate, and so on.

The range of assessment possibilities represented by the fourth feature makes it nearly impossible to produce standardized directions, scoring, and interpretations. Standardization may be attainable within classroom testing practices if teachers are fully trained in performance testing methods, but it will be difficult to achieve in school, and certainly in provincial/state and national testing programs, without considerable cost and effort. The feasibility of more performance-based testing at the provincial/state and national level is a hotly debated topic at the moment. Major national assessment initiatives such as NAEP appear to be interested in seeking a balance between objective and performance assessment tasks. States such as California, Kentucky, and Vermont have focused their assessment efforts almost totally on performance materials. A variety of reliability and validity concerns have been raised about this material (see, e.g., Cronbach, Bradburn, & Horvitz, 1994; Koretz et al., 1994). At the same time, performance testing initiatives at the district, state, and national levels are better in quality today because of the knowledge gained from these pioneering state and federal performance testing projects.

The fifth feature is that the tasks themselves assigned to students are often open ended in the sense that students have considerable latitude in preparing their answers. This makes scoring more difficult but often permits a more valid assessment of higher level cognitive skills (Wiggins, 1993). Interestingly, little work has been done on validation of the constructs that are actually being measured by performance tests in educational settings.

Advocates for performance assessment in education appear to want to bring testing methods more in line with instruction. They want assessments to approximate closely what it is students should know and be able to do: complete a science experiment, write a persuasive essay, prepare a report on farming in New England, deliver a speech, and so on. At a philosophical level, it is hard to disagree. Assessment methods are needed to measure these and other skills, and objective testing methods will not always suffice. But it would be incorrect to argue that performance assessment is totally new. Performance testing, which has had a long history in the fields of industrial and organizational psychology (see Cascio, 1987), is well developed, and the concept of an assessment center where performance assessments are or would be administered is well established and accepted (Bray, Campbell, & Grant, 1974). Performance testing, too, was well established years ago in vocational and technical education (Fitzpatrick & Morrison, 1971) and was the predominant form of assessment before the invention of objective approaches to assessment earlier in the 20th century. Finally, performance assessment by teachers at the classroom level has a long tradition. For example, essay tests, class projects, and writing samples have always been popular with teachers.

Performance tests were described earlier in the chapter as one type of criterion-referenced assessment. What distinguishes the current performance testing movement from the earlier one for criterion-referenced testing in the 1970s are two features: (a) policymakers and educators today are arguing for the teaching and assessment of higher level cognitive skills rather than the narrower and lower level discrete skills (i.e., behavioral objectives) that were popular between 1965 and 1985 (see Popham, 1978), and (b) there is more emphasis today on performance testing that directly measures the skills of interest (Hambleton, 1994). But the concepts underlying criterion-referenced testing and performance testing are not at odds. In fact, performance testing is simply one form of criterion-referenced testing. Perhaps if criterion-referenced testing had not become so closely (and inappropriately) associated with the assessment of basic skills with multiple-choice tests, the use of the terms performance assessment or authentic assessment would not have been necessary.

Although support for performance assessment in many parts of the United States and Canada is high, effective implementation is being hindered by several problems. First, experience in constructing and using performance tests is lacking among many educational measurement specialists. Most classroom teachers and administrators know even less about the formal aspects of development, since performance assessment is not typically a part of any preservice or in-service training they have received. (This situation appears to be changing, albeit slowly.) Second, performance tests will, in many instances, take considerably more time to construct, administer, and score than objective tests. And, principles described in the American Educational Research Association (AERA), American Psychological Association (APA), and NCME Standards for Educational and Psychological Testing (1985) for standardization, reliability, and validity will be difficult for many test developers to apply directly to their performance testing work. The texts by Stiggins (1994) and Airasian (1994) are two excellent references for performance test developers and teachers.

Linn, E. L. Baker, and Dunbar (1991) offered a set of eight

guidelines to supplement the Test Standards in the area of performance assessment. One of their main points is that while performance assessments such as writing tasks have face validity for educators and students (i.e., these assessments appear suitable for the intended purposes), substantially more validity evidence is needed to support the use of these assessments for monitoring educational reform and evaluating student progress. The fact that new forms of assessment are appealing and attractive to many educators is not a guarantee that these assessments are valid for their intended purposes. They note too that the nature of the validity evidence required represents an expansion of the types of evidence that might be compiled with more familiar standardized achievement tests (not surprising, since validity evidence should be consistent with the intended purpose of the instrument) and is consistent with the broader definition of validity offered by Messick (1989, 1994).

Linn, E. L. Baker, and Dunbar's list of eight guidelines or criteria, with brief descriptions of the validity evidence that is needed with performance assessments, is as follows:

*Consequences.* It is important to assess the consequences of performance-based assessments. Do teachers teach differently? What do students learn? These and other consequences, both intended and unintended, are part of the validity evidence that must be compiled.

*Fairness.* Fairness is always an issue in validating assessments. In the case of performance assessments, it is important to recognize that the use of performance assessments is no guarantee of fairness for all students. (The argument is sometimes advanced that performance assessments will be less biased against blacks than more objective forms of assessment such as multiple-choice tests.) For example, the expanded use of writing in the assessment of, say, mathematics and science skills may actually increase the unfairness of these assessments for many subgroups of students (whose writing skills may be deficient) over objective forms of assessment. If writing skills are minor in terms of the skills for which the assessment was designed, then differential writing skills across subgroups will serve as a source of bias in the assessment. Another example might be associated with the differential proficiency of subgroups in using calculators in a mathematics assessment. Even scoring guides and their use by scorers from one cultural group with students in another cultural group could introduce some unfairness in an assessment.

*Transfer and Generalizability.* To what extent can performance on a small set of tasks on an assessment be generalized to a larger class of tasks? This is a validity concern that needs to be addressed, since the generalization is often the goal of the assessment. At an absolute minimum, evidence of generalizability of student performance over raters and tasks is needed. When limited generalizability is found, such a finding should be used in interpreting the results. There is also an unstated assumption that students can transfer the skills demonstrated on an assessment to real-life problems. Again, validity evidence to support this type of inference should be compiled.

*Cognitive Complexity.* The main point of this guideline is that the use of complex performance tasks is not a guarantee that higher level cognitive skills are being measured. As Linn et al. (1991) report, even difficult material such as calculus can be memorized, as can proofs to geometry theorems. These tasks could be cognitively challenging or they could be answered by simply recall of facts and procedures that were memorized. It is important to assess exactly the cognitive level that is being assessed so that the correct inferences about student performance can be made. Coaching and practice are at least as relevant on performance assessments as they are on objective forms of assessments such as multiple-choice tests.

*Content Quality.* In view of the limited sampling of content that is possible with performance assessments, evidence needs to be compiled to determine the extent to which the content of the tasks chosen for inclusion on the assessment is important and relevant.

*Content Coverage.* Typically, the number of tasks chosen for an assessment is small in relation to the number of tasks defining the curriculum. For example, in a single yearly assessment, only a small fraction of the important outcomes of instruction can be assessed. This means, therefore, that evidence must be compiled to address the adequacy of the sampling of the tasks on an assessment. If similar tasks are chosen each year, there could be a negative consequence due to a narrowing of the curriculum to avoid teaching the underrepresented areas on the assessment. A narrowing of the content coverage will also enhance the effectiveness of coaching.

*Meaningfulness.* Some evidence pertaining to the meaningfulness of performance assessments to students and teachers is needed. To the extent that the assessments are not meaningful (or consequential), there could be negative consequences such as low student motivation to perform well. This problem has been observed on low-stakes assessments such as NAEP (at the Grade 12 level) and recent international assessments such as the International Assessment of Educational Progress (at the Grade 8 level) (Wainer, 1993). The administration of "a nonmeaningful assessment" can have a major impact on the validity of inferences from district, state, and national assessment results.

*Cost and Efficiency.* Generally, performance assessments are more time-consuming and costly to construct, administer, and score than objective forms of assessments such as multiple-choice tests. Evidence needs to be compiled to show that these additional expenditures of time and money are worthwhile in some important ways. Do the positive consequences (such as what teachers are doing in the classrooms, and what students may be learning) justify any of the negative consequences associated with performance assessments?

The eight guidelines offered by Linn, Baker, and Dunbar should be of considerable value to developers of performance assessments since they provide clear directions for compiling validity evidence. No doubt these guidelines will appear in a similar form in the next edition of the AERA, APA, and NCME Test Standards (see Linn, 1994).

## ITEM FORMATS

The movement toward performance assessment has increased interest considerably in the development of new item

TABLE 28–1. Typical Forms of Performance Assessment

| Form | Description |
|---|---|
| Individual Projects | Completion of projects often requires a comprehensive set of skills; sometimes they are interdisciplinary; often they require organization, initiative, and creativity |
| Group Projects | Group projects permit the assessment/development of additional skills: cooperative behavior, planning, leadership, oral presentations, etc.; often, group projects may be more complex than individual projects, thus permitting the assessment of higher level cognitive skills. |
| Interview/Oral Presentations | Students can develop/demonstrate oral presentation skills |
| Constructed-Response Questions | Students must produce their own answers, thus permitting the assessment of organization and writing skills and knowledge of the subject matter (without the aid of prompts, i.e., answer choices); every format, from filling in a blank, to providing a short answer, to writing a report, is possible |
| Essays | This format provides the opportunity for students to demonstrate their level of understanding of a topic; in the long form (i.e., unrestrictive essay), the assessment of higher level cognitive skills is possible |
| Experiments | Experiments are used, for example, in the sciences to assess ability to apply the scientific method as well as demonstrate an understanding of scientific concepts and principles; hypothesis testing, designing and carrying out studies, and writing up and interpreting results are skills that can be assessed with this format |
| Demonstrations | This format allows students to demonstrate their grasp of skills and knowledge |
| Portfolios | Students compile their work in a subject area over a period of time; in organizing their portfolios, students need to show judgment in their selection of documents as well as skills in preparing documents |

Note: Based on material from Rudner and Boston (1994).

formats to supplement those already in general use. Rudner and Boston (1994) identified several of the popular performance assessment techniques: individual projects, group projects, interview/oral presentations, constructed-response questions, essays, experiments, demonstrations, and portfolios of student work. Table 28–1 contains brief descriptions of these techniques. These forms of assessment are intended to be direct measures of the outcomes or skills of interest in the educational reform movements at the national, state/provincial, and district levels.

The rationale behind performance testing is that if you wish to evaluate how effectively a student can perform a task, then observe and evaluate the student performing that task. Many item formats for assessment from a wide variety of fields including education, medical assessment, and military testing will follow. Several of the examples are from a paper prepared by Hambleton, R. Jones, and Slater (1993) for UNESCO.

It should be emphasized that the new item formats, although more attractive in some respects than the common multiple-choice format, are still required to meet psychometric standards of excellence. This point appears to have been lost by some performance assessment developers. For them, simply for performance assessments to be different in appearance from standard assessment procedures is sufficient to justify their use. In fact, concerns about the validity of these new forms of assessment are especially critical because they are new, because valid assessment of higher level skills can be expected to be more difficult to do generally, and because often there is limited experience in developing, administering, and scoring these new forms of assessment. As has been stated by many measurement specialists, the appearance of validity (i.e., face validity) of an assessment is not sufficient justification for use of that assessment in practice.

The remainder of this section is organized around several item formats that are likely to be used in the future. This discussion includes standard (or conventional) as well as new item formats, and is organized into two categories for discussion purposes: constructed-response and selected-response item formats. A list of item formats available to the performance assessment developer organized by these two categories is presented in Table 28–2. Readers are referred to the edited volume of Bennett and Ward (1993) for an excellent comparison of constructed- and selected-response item formats, and studies such as those by Bennett, Rock, and Wang (1991), Bridgeman (1982), and Traub and Fisher (1977) for samples of research studies on the topic.

## Constructed-Response Item Formats

Many of the recently developed item formats that involve performance assessments do not permit clear-cut objective scoring whereby an examiner can, without judgment, score an item as correct or incorrect. In fact, often the task will not have a correct or incorrect response. These formats involve a greater degree of judgment about the scores to assign to student perfor-

TABLE 28–2. Possible Assessment Formats

| Constructed Response | Selected Response |
|---|---|
| Short-answer (free response) | True-False |
| Short-answer (gridding answers) | Multiple-choice |
| Essay | Multiple-choice with justifications |
| Performance | Multiple-choice with extended stimulus |
| Computer-based problem solving | Audiovisual context setting |
| Standardized patient | Matching |
| Portfolios | Problem sets |
| | Figural response |

mance. Items of this type include short answer (free response), short answer (gridding answers), essay, performance, computer-based problem solving, standardized patient, and portfolios.

*Short Answer.* The short-answer format is a constructed-response item format where students are required to write their responses to a task. Because short-answer items focus on information that can be reported briefly in a few words or sentences, this format has the advantage that a wide range of content can be covered without the use of the prompts (i.e., answer choices) associated with multiple-choice items. The negative aspect is that scoring is more subjective and often needs to be done by scorers. However, even with this limitation, the short-answer format is useful for evaluating areas that require factual recall and problem solving (Osterlind, 1989). Short-answer items have been very popular in state and national assessments because they are performance assessments without the high scoring costs and concerns about scorer reliability.

A minor variation on the short-answer format is the sentence completion format. Here, students demonstrate their knowledge and skills by completing a sentence that poses a problem to the student.

Short answer (gridding) is the format where the student can effectively "bubble in" a short answer to a question. Such a format works well with numerical answers but can be used with verbal responses, also. This format permits machine scoring of short-answer responses. The new Scholastic Assessment Tests, the New Jersey Department of Education, and the American Institute of Certified Public Accountants' Uniform CPA Examination have used this format with success. Still, some problems have been reported owing to students improperly bubbling in their answers. Forgetting to bubble in answers is one type of error. Bubbling in answers incorrectly, or in unreadable forms, is another.

*Essay.* Essay formats, including writing samples and writing exercises (Osterlind, 1989), are valuable for evaluating understanding of subject matter and organizing skills (White, 1985). Perhaps one of the earliest performance assessments to be developed, the essay remains the best item format by which to assess a student's ability to write. A stimulus is usually provided (sometimes called a prompt) and the student is required to respond to the stimulus by writing an essay (or providing a writing sample). The essay may be restrictive, in the sense of requesting a few sentences of the student, or extended, requiring a considerably longer response.

For example, the student might be asked to write an extended essay, stating his or her views about the following statement: "The art of conversation is dead." Usually a choice of several stimuli is offered to students, though problems can arise in comparing student performance when choice is available (Wainer & Thissen, 1994). Stimuli of unequal difficulty is one source of error. Improper choice of a stimulus by students is another.

*Performance.* Performance assessment is increasingly being incorporated into assessments in educational and credentialing situations. Two samples from the Kentucky Instructional Results

### Figure 28–1. Sample Grade 4 Science Performance Task Used in Kentucky

**Learner Outcome**
Students understand the tendency of nature to remain constant or move toward a steady state in closed systems.

**Task**
When plants and animals die, their remains decay as bacteria and other organisms get energy for their cells from the dead material. In what important ways does this action help the environment? Tell what would happen if dead things did not decay.

**Scoring Guide**
4—Student clearly discusses importance of *disposal* of materials to prevent accumulation of dead material *and return* of materials to the environment for use by other living things and/or because of limited resources; *or* student provides in-depth discussion of either *disposal* or *return*, including insightful explanation of important, long-term effects.
3—Student identifies importance of *disposal* and *return* of materials with little discussion or elaboration.
2—Student identifies the importance of either *disposal* or *return*, with little discussion or elaboration.
1—Student does not perceive the effect of dead things not decaying *or* gives irrelevant response (e.g., it would smell).
0—Blank.

**Example of a Student Paper at Each Score Level[a]**
4—This action helps the environment in very many ways. For one thing, it puts minerals back into the ground, and helps trees to grow. If dead things did not decay, we wouldn't have much oxygen because trees wouldn't be able to live, or plants.
3—The other organisms may not be able to get food easily, and I think it helps the environment by getting rid of dead things.
2—If dead things did not decay the earth would look horrible, and nature not take its course. For dead things would just build up little by little.
1—Well pick up the environment and help keep it clean. Water the plants and let the sun give them energy keep your dog away from the road or water.

[a] Student errors have not been corrected.

Note: Released assessment material. From the Kentucky Department of Education. Reproduced with permission.

Information System (KIRIS) are shown in Figures 28–1 and 28–2. Each performance task in KIRIS is organized around four components: the learner outcome, the task itself, the scoring guide, and examples of student papers (called "anchor papers") at each score point. The presence of a detailed scoring guide and anchor papers is intended to standardize the scoring process across scorers. When performance scores are used in student and school accountability, training of scorers is usually extensive, and often the scorers must achieve a high level of score consistency with the trainers before being permitted to score student responses. The goal is to maximize the interrater reliability of scores assigned to student responses. The two examples highlight (a) the typical formats used for performance assessments in many schools, (b) the selection of tasks to assess learner outcomes in science and social studies, and (c) the scoring rubrics used in these assessments.

Other types of tasks included in this category are individual and group projects, interview/oral presentations, experiments,

Figure 28–2. Sample Grade 12 Social Studies Performance
Task Used in Kentucky

**Learner Outcome**
Students understand the structure and function of social
systems.

**Task**
Over the past 50 years, there has been a shift in the population
from rural to urban living. This has had a tremendous impact on
American cultural values, which in turn has had an effect on society, family, and the individual. For each of these three areas (society, family, individual), discuss what these effects are and give
advantages and disadvantages of each.

**Scoring Guide**
4—Student gives more than one advantage and disadvantage
for each effect, using historical or cultural examples.
3—Student gives more than one advantage and/or disadvantage
for each effect.
2—Student gives one advantage or disadvantage for each.
1—Student discusses the effects population shifts have had on
society, the family, and the individual, but is unable to show
any advantages or disadvantages.
0—Blank.

**Example of a Student Paper at Each Score Level**[a]
4—The urbanization of America has irreversibly altered the life-
style of America. No longer are we a nation of farmers. Instead, we are a nation of city dwellers, and values have
shifted with the population. Society now moves at a faster
pace; news, products, and people move quicker than they
did in the past. This can be beneficial or determental. More
can be produced and transported, but are these goods of
the best quality? News travels faster, but it can bring horror
into our living rooms. "Family values", that oft-used phrase,
have indeed changed. Few families have more than seven
children, single-parent families are increasing, and "split"
(stepparent) families are becoming more common. While
these "family values" alter, it is not necessarily wrong. Families change as society changes. Perhaps the greatest result
of urbanization is the adaption of the individual to a fast
paced world. People may not always know their neighbors,
but they learn and experience more in cities. They may not
always be safe, but they have more opportunities to better
themselves. Sacrifice-trading something for something else.
Such is the cost of urbanization.
3—The population shift has drastically altered American cultural
values. American society has become more diverse; in every
city, there are more groups who share unique interests.
More distinctions exist between different classes of people.
Family values have changed, for urban life does not promote
traditional living. Young men and women have a new set of
morals that condone premarital sex and other nontraditional
practices. There are more single, self-supporting mothers,
and a higher rate of divorce due to this population shift. Individuals are more independent in the city, for their cultural
values call for them to be self-reliant above all else.
2—The advantages for society, family, and individual is more
people will be around them and their society will be bigger.
The disadvantage is it will be harder because there is more
people and less jobs.
1—Urban living has had an effect on all of the population. It is
a horrible site. The ural people live in poverty. The families
are effected by the lack of jobs.

[a] Student errors have not been corrected.
Note: Released assessment material. From the Kentucky Department of Education. Reproduced with permission.

and demonstrations. These tasks may be scored using analytic,
holistic, or a combination of scoring methods. Again, subjectivity of scoring can be a problem, especially with the more open-
ended tasks. Training of scorers is often extensive to ensure
comparability of scores over classrooms, schools, districts, and
even states, in the case of national assessments.

*Computer-Based Problem Solving.* One format for assessing
problem solving is the use of computer-based clinical situations
(in an earlier era, items in this format were called "patient
management problems," or PMPs). This format has been used,
for example, in the medical assessment field. This format uses
computers to present a student with information about a hypothetical situation and requires the student to make appropriate
decisions or take appropriate actions. Students are evaluated
on the basis of how well they perform the appropriate tasks
as a consequence of the prompting they receive from the computer-based scenarios.

Perhaps this format is too expensive at the present time for
widespread use in education. Most of the applications of this
format to date can be found in the military and medical assessment areas. For example, a flight simulator can be programmed
with the historically accurate events preceding a known airline
disaster. An airline pilot (either a trainee or an experienced
pilot scheduled for a periodic examination) steps into the flight
simulator, and the computer simulation begins. As the computer
presents the candidate with the computer-generated scenario,
the candidate is required to make the appropriate decisions at
the appropriate time and to take the correct course of action.
One of the many advantages achieved through items such as
this is an extremely high level of face validity.

The examinee's performance may be evaluated by a panel
of examiners who can determine a score by referring to a
standardized form. Alternatively, the use of computers in this
item format offers the additional advantages of increasing objectivity and facilitating scoring by programming the computer to
evaluate and score the candidate's performance. Considerable
judgment is exercised and arbitrary decisions are made in determining the scoring scheme to be programmed in the computer. The validity of the scoring schemes associated with this
type of assessment is a concern and needs to be studied.

These computer-based situations contain all the advantages
of any computer-based assessment system. They include (a)
the potential for computerized adaptive assessment, (b)
greater flexibility regarding when and where candidates take
the assessment (i.e., candidates may no longer need to be
brought together to a central location for the administration,
but instead may be able to report to a regional center), (c)
immediate score reporting, and (d) the creation of computerized item banks for the construction of randomly equivalent
forms of an assessment.

*Standardized Patient.* A promising new performance-based
assessment in medical assessment is the "standardized patient"
format. This is particularly suitable for assessing outcomes that
involve contact with others, such as those commonly occurring
in education, medicine, nursing, clinical and counseling psychology, and dentistry. For example, the outcome might be the
successful resolution of a student's problem during a counseling
session between a teacher and a student.

In this item format, an actor or actress is trained to display specific aspects or symptoms of a particular situation, that is, to become a "standardized patient." The patient is then introduced to the candidate, who must question or interview the patient to determine the nature of the problem and prescribe appropriate treatment or actions. The examiner observes the behavior of the candidate and can score the candidate with regard to interpersonal skills, problem solving, efficiency, and any other factors that may be desired.

The subjectivity of the scoring procedure can be reduced by requiring the examiners to score candidates on a standardized scoring form. This form could contain details of predetermined criteria that the candidate is required to meet and that were established earlier by a panel of suitably qualified and experienced personnel.

The advantages of this format are many and include the concurrent assessment of complex composite skills, and the very practical nature of the assessment, which closely reflects events that the candidate is likely to meet in practice. However, thorough training is required of the actor or actress in all aspects of the simulation, and of those who will score the process. Moreover, careful control must be exerted over the standardized patients to ensure that they always present consistent performances to the candidates and that effects such as fatigue, boredom, or dislike of the candidate do not bias the assessment one way or another (van der Vleuten & Swanson, 1990). Because of the costs associated with the development and administration of assessments in this format, use is probably limited to credentialing examinations for high-level professionals such as physicians, with a fairly low volume of candidates each year.

From a psychometric point of view, this format offers the additional challenge of considering important new concerns of scoring. For example, how should a candidate be scored if his or her performance is totally wrong or if the candidate completes the task correctly except for one fatal error? There is also the matter of the number of tasks a candidate should pass to be credentialed. Many psychometric questions relating to development, scoring, reliability, validity, and standard setting remain with this approach to assessment.

*Portfolios.* A comparatively new item format in educational assessment is the portfolio (Farr & Tone, 1994; Koretz et al., 1994). This format requires that students be provided with file folders into which they may place pertinent information relevant to the task that is to be evaluated. For example, in a portfolio for use in writing assessment, the student might be encouraged to include a poem, a short story, a personal narrative, a writing sample from a subject area such as history or English literature, a persuasive letter, and the like. Portfolio assessments appear to be the equivalent of work samples, which are popular in industrial assessments and the arts.

The portfolio format has the advantage of enhancing realism for the student, thereby increasing face validity. Moreover, this format opens the possibility for the assessment of a variety of higher order thinking skills involving analysis, synthesis, problem solving, organization, and so on. Some states, such as Kentucky and Vermont, currently make extensive use of portfolios in both individual and group (class or school) assessment. On the technical side, numerous questions about portfolio assessments remain to be resolved: What are the criteria for

deciding what to include in portfolios? How can scoring be handled on a consistent basis? (This is especially important when portfolio scores are used for accountability purposes.) How should performance standards be set and applied? How should portfolio results be reported?

Current thinking is that portfolio assessments can provide classroom teachers with valuable information about the performance and progress of their students. The use of portfolios in large-scale school, district, and state assessments is more problematic because of the cost and scoring difficulties (see, e.g., Koretz et al., 1994).

## Selected-Response Item Formats

An objective item format is one that leads to student responses that can be scored with little or no judgment (Osterlind, 1989). A scoring key is developed and can be applied by an examiner or by a computer to score student responses. True-false, multiple-choice, and matching items are the best-known and most popular examples of objective item formats. But there are other formats, developed recently, that can be useful to assessment specialists.

In part, these new objective formats are being developed to accommodate the needs of assessment specialists who are looking for both more item format variety in their assessments and objective item formats that permit the assessment of skills that cannot be measured validly with the better known objective item formats.

Several objective item formats are described next, including true-false, multiple-choice, multiple-choice with justifications, multiple-choice with extended stimulus, audiovisual context setting, matching, problem sets, and figural response.

*True-False.* The true-false item format is the simplest of item formats. As the term implies, a student is presented with a statement and then asked to indicate (usually in writing, but occasionally verbally) whether the statement is true or false. This item format has the obvious advantages of being easy and inexpensive to write and score. Assessment is limited to factual information, and the unreliability of individual item scores is balanced by the capability for including many items in a fairly short testing time.

*Multiple-Choice.* A multiple-choice item may be narrowly defined as a test item consisting of two parts: a stem and several answer choices. The stem describes a problem for the student. Answer choices are usually four or five in number, one of which is correct or best, and the others are incorrect or, at least, less correct than the correct answer. Item stems can be written as sentences, incomplete sentences, or questions, though the question format is often recommended by measurement specialists because it is the easiest format to use to ensure that a problem is presented to students. A validated set of item-writing guidelines was provided by Haladyna and Downing (1989a, 1989b).

An interesting variation that overcomes the problem of guessing is to create a pool of answer choices that is used with all of the items in a multiple-choice test. Thus, with 30 items, perhaps 100 to 150 answer choices might be available. A drawback is the amount of time a student might spend looking for the answer.

Multiple-choice items have received considerable criticism from educational reformers because of a belief that such items send the wrong message to teachers when they are used. That message is that instruction should change, but assessment methods will remain the same. The many criticisms leveled at multiple-choice items, such as that they (a) foster a one-right-answer mentality, (b) narrow the curriculum, (c) focus on discrete skills, (d) underrepresent the performance of lower socioeconomic status students, and (e) lack validity for assessing higher level cognitive skills, make their use problematic for many educational reformers and teachers. That teachers will teach to the assessment is another good reason for deemphasizing the use of multiple-choice items in educational assessments. On the other hand, the psychometric evidence to support the continuing use of multiple-choice items appears strong (Bennett & Ward, 1993; Hambleton & Murphy, 1992). There is substantial evidence to suggest, for example, that multiple-choice items are capable of assessing some higher level cognitive skills, as a review of such documents as the *GRE: Practicing to Take the General Test* (Graduate Record Examination Board, 1994) and Bennett and Ward (1993) attest.

*Multiple-Choice with Justifications.* Not all new formats place a heavy emphasis on the use of modern technology or simulation. One such example is the multiple-choice with justifications format. This item format retains many of the benefits of the multiple-choice format, but additional information is gathered from the student through the requirement that the student provide a brief written justification for his or her answer. This item format is particularly useful for formative assessments because valuable information can be obtained regarding incorrect reasoning, misconceptions, and gaps in the knowledge base of students.

*Multiple True-False.* Items of the multiple true-false format are constructed by preparing multiple-choice items without the restriction of a single correct answer. Again, students are required to indicate whether they consider each of a set of answers to a problem true or false (correct or incorrect). This is a potentially powerful new format in that it permits multiple correct answers. The requirement of a one-correct-answer item format has been a common criticism of multiple-choice items (Hambleton & Murphy, 1992).

*Multiple-Choice with Extended Stimulus.* The only difference between this item format and the multiple-choice format is that the extended-stimulus format incorporates an illustration, table, or other useful documentation into the stem of the item. The extended stimulus often permits the assessment of higher order cognitive skills such as extracting relevant information, locating discrepancies or errors, or using information within an illustration. Other higher order skills involving synthesis, analysis, and evaluation can also be assessed.

*Audiovisual Context Setting.* This is a very realistic item format that creates the performance scenario through the use of audio and/or visual stimuli. Technological advances such as video camera-recorders have made it comparatively easy to film sce-

narios and present them to students as a way to "set the stage" for a performance assessment. Indeed, the responsive ability of videodisc technology, which can provide the operator with a choice of options and immediate feedback, makes it possible for students to be presented with an audiovisual representation of a scenario, from which they are required to make a decision. Feedback regarding the outcome of this decision can be immediately provided to the student in the form of a modified scenario that continues to unfold until the student is required to make another decision, whereupon immediate feedback is again provided.

An assessment can consist of one or several of these realistic scenarios through which the student must work successfully in order to provide a satisfactory performance. The student responds to each problem by making a selection from a set of choices, as with a multiple-choice item.

Not surprisingly, the development of assessments in this format can be time-consuming and expensive. Therefore, use has been limited to important assessments such as teacher certification examinations. A great many teacher certification examinations have been correctly criticized for their inability to simulate the varied and complex environment encountered within the classroom. Through the use of an item incorporating an audiovisual context-setting format, the reality of the examinations can be enhanced.

Teachers applying for certification can be placed in front of a television monitor, where they are shown a classroom scenario recorded on a videodisc. Such a scenario might involve a student conducting a science experiment. At certain intervals during the scenario the presentation stops and the candidate is asked to select a desired course of action in response to what has unfolded in the classroom situation. The candidate is given a series of choices. A candidate enters his or her desired choice of action (possibly by the use of a computer mouse or pen-sensitive monitor) and then is shown the next sequence of events, which in theory could be determined by the course of action selected by the candidate. Branched assessments are a good concept, but the cost could be prohibitive. A linear sequence of tasks, common for all candidates, regardless of the choices they make, is more practical.

Audiovisual context-setting formats offer the potential for increased face validity, compared to traditional assessments, and the possibility of evaluating complex and interacting cognitive skills. The audiovisual apparatus may also be programmed to evaluate the performance of the candidate, thereby increasing objectivity and avoiding the need for an expert examiner to be present for the purposes of scoring (although, of course, a proctor would still be required). The main drawback to this format to date has been the heavy developmental cost.

*Matching.* Particularly useful with younger students, the matching format requires a student to correctly match one group of stimuli with a second group of stimuli. Typically, this can involve the matching of a group of definitions on one side of a page with the appropriate definitions on the other side of the page.

*Problem Sets.* A useful item format capable of being adapted to many achievement, aptitude, and ability tests is the problem set. This format involves the writing of two or more multiple-choice items that are related to a stimulus such as an illustration, graph, passage, or scenario. It has been a popular format for credentialing examinations. Students need to apply their knowledge and skills to arrive at the correct solutions. This item format is particularly attractive because it often seems more realistic to students than a set of discrete, independent items.

*Figural Response.* Another format that builds on the traditional test rather than on recent technology is the figural response format. The items provide stimulus material in the form of graphical, diagrammatic, or pictorial illustrations, and the student is typically required to answer a question or series of questions by recording responses on the illustration itself. These responses may require greater detail than those required by a multiple-choice item and so provide greater insight into the cognitive reasoning behind a student's choices.

This item format can be machine scored. The "machine" may be as simple as an electronic scanner that scores the responses made by a student on a standardized answer sheet or as complex as a computer into which a student enters a response that is evaluated by the testing program such as the program described with the computer-based problem-solving format. Scoring by machine is valuable because of the consistency, objectivity, and speed with which a large number of responses can be scored without the effects of confounding factors such as fatigue, boredom, or inconsistency on the part of scorers.

## Conclusion

The item formats described in this section offer a wide range of formats from which to choose. None is ideal for all situations, but the careful selection of different formats, combined with careful item writing, can enable assessment developers to assess targeted skills and knowledge across all levels of cognitive complexity.

---

## COMPUTERS IN ASSESSMENT

---

The advances in computer technology appear to have considerable potential for improving assessment practices (F. B. Baker, 1989; Bunderson, Inouye, & Olsen, 1989; van der Linden, 1995). The evolution of powerful, fast, and modestly priced personal computers (PCs) offer the assessment specialist the opportunity to conduct many complex analyses that once would have required a mainframe computer. Moreover, the availability of commercially produced testing software packages (such as BILOG, MULTILOG, MICROCAT, OTD, and RASCAL) offers the assessment specialist the opportunity to develop assessments and analyze data at a fraction of the cost that would have been required only a few years ago. Similarly, powerful, readily available statistical packages (such as SPSS/PC+, SAS, STATA, MINITAB, and LISREL) enable the assessment specialist to perform many complex statistical analyses quickly and accurately. Concomitant advances in computer graphics and exploratory data analyses have made it easier for the assessment specialist both to explore results and to communicate findings.

Computer technology has advanced to the point where it can now be used at all stages of the assessment process. And, with the development of PCs, desktop scanners, and associated software, this technology is no longer limited to large-scale test publishers (Linn, 1989). Applications of the microcomputer to assessment now include item writing, item banking, test construction, test administration, test scoring, item and test analysis, and score reporting (F. B. Baker, 1989).

Van der Linden (1995) described a number of computer uses that have produced a new generation of assessment practices. Each of these uses is described briefly below.

1. *Graphics.* The graphics capabilities associated with many computer systems (e.g., Harvard Graphics, WordPerfect Presentations, Excel) will encourage assessment developers to increase the use of graphics. In the past, graphics were used, but they were tedious to draw and had to be inserted into assessments by layout specialists. Errors were common, which discouraged many assessment developers from using graphics. Often graphics are a good way to present information, and their use makes assessment content more diverse and interesting.

2. *Measurement of Response Times.* Psychologists have long been interested in the response time variable (Jensen, 1982) but in paper-and-pencil assessments, it is difficult, if not impossible, to collect response time data. Computer testing changes that situation, and response times (i.e., response latencies) can be routinely collected with many software packages.

   Already research is under way on the Graduate Record Examination and other assessments to study item response times and their relationships to gender, ethnicity, item format, and ability level (O'Neill & Powers, 1993), and psychological models to understand response times are being developed, along with models for combining response times and performance into a single ability measure (see, e.g., an up-to-date review of available response time models by Roskam, in press). All of this research has the potential for improving assessment practices in the future.

3. *Authoring Systems.* Word processing is common among assessment developers, but now software is being developed specifically for assessment developers. This new software facilitates steps in the assessment development process such as preparing item and content specifications and writing and editing assessment materials.

4. *Multiple Media.* The potential to administer assessment material using both audio and visual modalities opens up many exciting new possibilities. Listening comprehension can be conveniently assessed, for example. One could imagine, too, how foreign language comprehension such as in the Test of English as a Foreign Language (TOEFL) might be assessed with the use of audio presentations of stimulus material within an assessment.

5. *Storage of Assessment Material.* With the huge memory capacity of even the smallest computers, assessment material can be stored in the computer to be recalled as needed. Stored with the assessment items or tasks could be a variety of data, including format, content information, difficulty, discriminating power, and more. Twenty or more such features are commonly described for each assessment task. These features are then used in the selection process, either to be presented to a student sitting at a computer terminal or to be presented in an assessment booklet. Assessments can be

constructed quickly and in a flexible way to respond to the needs of particular students or groups of students.

Some software packages allow item statistics to be updated as the items are used (see, e.g., the examination system of the National Association of Security Dealers). This is an especially useful feature when the items have been field tested on relatively small samples and therefore have relatively unstable item statistics.

6. *Optimal Test Design.* Optimal test design, a new application of the computer, involves the use of computer software to select items from a bank of items (with item statistics available) to produce an assessment meeting a set of item and content specifications. With some of the larger software packages, far more options are available than almost certainly would ever be needed by the assessment developer. Even after the assessment is assembled, the developer has the option of making a variety of changes including item substitutions and item edits. Computer-generated assessments are emerging as a viable option for assessment developers. The mathematics (linear programming) for this application are described by van der Linden and Boekkooi-Timminga (1989) and by Stocking, Swanson, and Pearlman (1991a, 1991b).

7. *Computer-Adaptive Testing.* Since the beginning of modern testing in the early 1900s with Binet's test of intelligence, the concept of adaptive testing has been in the psychometric literature. Quite simply, it is more efficient to match test items or tasks to the ability levels of students than it is to administer a fixed-length assessment to the students. Little information is gained from administering easy assessment material to highly able students or hard assessment material to less able students. When the difficulty of assessment material is matched to the student's ability level, the most measurement information is gained about a student's ability level. Of course, in practice the purpose of assessment is to determine the ability level of the student. If it were known, there would be no need for assessment. In computer-adaptive testing, after a few assessment tasks are administered, ability levels can be assessed and then used in the selection of subsequent assessment material for the student. After each task is completed and scored by computer, ability levels can be updated, then used in the selection of additional assessment material. Testing can continue until the estimate of the student's ability level reaches a desired level of precision. Often, the result of computer-adaptive testing is a test half as long as the fixed-length test, or even less, with no loss in precision.

In the United States and Canada there is a movement by some testing agencies toward computer-based testing (e.g., the Graduate Record Examination and the credentialing examinations for nurses and nurse practitioners). This computer-based testing may be as rudimentary as transposing existing paper-and-pencil items into a computer and using the computer to administer and score the items (Linn, 1989). However, the more promising complex computer-based testing development is computer-adaptive testing (Wainer et al., 1990). These computer-adaptive tests are sometimes referred to as second-generation computerized tests, to distinguish them from the first generation of simple computer-administered and -scored tests.

To date, all prominent applications of computer-adaptive testing have been carried out with multiple-choice items, but in principle, items in any machine-scorable format could be used.

Bunderson, Inouye, and Olson (1989) have identified several advantages of computer-adaptive testing:

1. Improved security (each student sees only a small fraction of the available assessment material)
2. Scores equivalent to those on the full-length test, with reduced testing time
3. More accurate collection of responses, compared to paper-and-pencil test administrations
4. Reduced measurement error through matching of assessment materials to ability levels (e.g., less error due to guessing behavior, which seems to be minimized)
5. Recording of response latencies, if desired
6. Immediate scoring and reporting
7. Automation of the administration of assessments designed to be administered on an individual basis

Other advantages include the potential for more complex scoring systems (e.g., pattern scoring) and individualization of the pace of work for students.

As computer technology becomes even more powerful and affordable, and as software packages are developed and refined, the advantages of computerized testing are expected to result in the increased use of computers in educational and psychological assessment. One disadvantage is that student scores (i.e., number of points earned) can no longer serve as a basis for comparing students to each other or to performance standards because, in theory, each student is administered a different assessment, and these assessments will vary in their difficulty. Two students may receive the same score but have very different ability levels. What is needed is a measurement theory that takes into account the difficulty of the assessment material when assessing student proficiency. One such measurement theory, item response theory, is considered in the next section.

## NEW PSYCHOMETRIC MODELS

### Importance of Test Theories and Models

Test theories and related models are important to the practice of educational and psychological assessment because they provide a framework for considering assessment issues and addressing technical topics such as reliability and validity. One of the most important issues is the handling of measurement errors. A useful test theory or model can help in understanding the role that measurement errors play in (a) estimating examinee ability and how the contributions of error might be minimized (e.g., by lengthening a test), (b) correlations between variables (see, e.g., the disattenuation formulas), and (c) reporting true scores or ability scores and associated confidence bands.

How theories and models handle error is one of the ways in which they differ, and often determines their usefulness in practical applications. For example, errors may be assumed to be normally distributed in one model, while no distributional assumptions about errors may be made in another. In one model, the size of the measurement errors might be assumed to be constant (e.g., the standard error of measurement) across the test score scale. In another model, the size of errors might be assumed to be related to examinee true score (e.g., the binomial error model). The assumptions made about error in a model will affect how error scores are estimated and reported.

A useful test theory or model can provide a frame of reference for preparing tests or assessments and solving other practical problems. A useful test model might specify the precise relationships among test items or assessment tasks and ability scores so that careful test design work can be done to produce desired score distributions and errors of the size that are not inconsistent with the intended use of the scores.

Models always provide incomplete representations of the assessment data to which they are fitted; hence, with sufficient amounts of data, they can be falsified—that is, found to be misfitting. Therefore, the meaningful question is not whether a model is correct or incorrect, for all models are incorrect in the sense that they provide incomplete representations of the data to which they are applied. The question instead is whether a model fits the data well enough to be useful in guiding the assessment process. Statistical evidence and judgment play important roles in answering the question.

## Some Psychometric History

Lord (1952, 1953) and psychometricians before him (see, e.g., Gulliksen, 1950) were interested in psychometric models with which to assess examinees independently of the particular choice of items or assessment tasks that were used in the assessment. The basic idea is that there is an ability underlying performance on a test or assessment, and it is the examinee's standing on this latent or underlying ability that is of interest. Test scores have the unfortunate property of being dependent on the difficulty of the test, which compounds the direct comparison of test scores from different forms of a test. Also, psychometricians felt that measurement practices would be enhanced if item and test statistics could be made *sample independent*. The dependency of item and test statistics on the samples from which they are obtained limits their usefulness in practical assessment work.

Although classic test theory and related models provide a sound theoretical basis for constructing and evaluating tests, the limitations of classic test theory are troublesome. The first limitation is that the two primary item statistics of interest, item difficulty and item discrimination, which form the cornerstones of many classic test theoretic analyses, are group dependent. Thus, the $p$ and $r$ values, as they are called, so essential in the application of classic test models, are entirely dependent on the examinee sample from which they are obtained. In terms of the discrimination indices, this means that higher values will tend to be obtained from heterogeneous examinee samples and lower values from homogeneous examinee samples. In terms of difficulty indices, higher values will be obtained from examinee samples of above average ability and lower values from examinee samples of below average ability (Hambleton, 1989).

Another limitation of classic test theory and related models is that scores are entirely test dependent. Consequently, test

difficulty directly affects examinee true scores (i.e., expected test scores over parallel-forms) and the resulting test scores. This is an important shortcoming because the practical constraints of assessment practice frequently necessitate that students be compared on different forms or versions of the same assessment. The construction of equivalent performance assessments is especially problematic because they are often short, and multidimensionality in the tasks is common.

Classic test theory may be described as test based. The true score model does not permit consideration of examinee responses to any specific item. Consequently, no basis exists to predict how an examinee or group of examinees may perform on a particular test item or assessment task. This property of a measurement model is valuable for certain modern testing applications such as computer-adaptive testing.

For measurement specialists who value invariant item and person statistics, one solution lies in the concepts, models, and methods associated with IRT. This was the point made by Lord (1952, 1953), who was the first to develop an item response model for the analysis of dichotomously scored unidimensional achievement and aptitude data. Next came Birnbaum, with a series of technical reports in 1957 and 1958 that introduced logistic test models and model parameter estimation. For an accessible account of this work, see Birnbaum (1968). Georg Rasch (1960) published a book describing several item response models, one of which has become known as the Rasch model (or the one-parameter logistic model), with applications to achievement testing.

Later work in the 1960s by Lord (see Lord, 1968; Lord & Novick, 1968) and Wright (1968) brought considerable attention to IRT. Through the 1970s and 1980s, measurement journals (e.g., *Applied Psychological Measurement*, the *Journal of Educational Measurement*) published numerous papers describing technical advances and applications, and many papers and books for practitioners that described IRT models and their applications were written (see, e.g., Hambleton, 1989; Hambleton & Swaminathan, 1985; Hambleton et al., 1991; Lord, 1980; Wright & Stone, 1979).

## Item Response Theory and Related Models

Unidimensional, dichotomously scored IRT postulates (a) that underlying examinee performance on a test is a single ability or trait, and (b) that the relationship between examinee performance on each item and the ability measured by the test can be described by a monotonically increasing curve. This curve is called an item characteristic curve (ICC) and provides the probability that examinees at various ability levels will answer the item correctly. Examinees with more ability have higher probabilities for giving correct answers to items than lower-ability examinees (Hambleton, 1989).

Figure 28–3 shows the general form of ICCs for the three-parameter logistic model. ICCs (which are always S-shaped curves) are generated for the three-parameter model from the expression:

$$P_i(\theta) = c_i + (1 - c_i)[1 + e^{-Da_i(\theta - b_i)}]^{-1}, \, i = 1, 2, \ldots, n \quad (1)$$

which serves as the mathematical model linking the observable dichotomously scored data (item performance) to the unobserv-

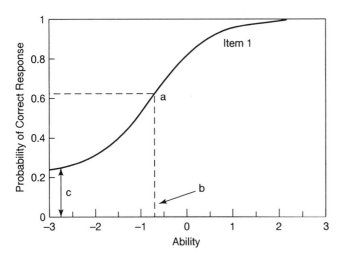

FIGURE 28–3. Typical Item Characteristic Curve

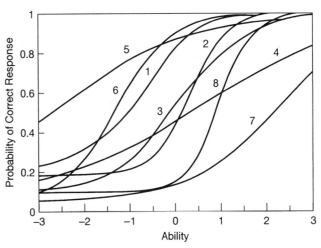

FIGURE 28–4. Set of Characteristic Curves for Eight Typical Dichotomously Scored Items or Assessment Tasks

able data (ability). $P_i(\theta)$ gives the probability of a correct response to item $i$ as a function of ability (denoted $\theta$). The symbol $n$ is the number of items or assessment tasks in the test. The $c$ parameter in the model is the height of the lower asymptote of the ICC and is introduced into the model to account for the performance of low-ability examinees on multiple-choice test items. This parameter is not needed in a model that is applied to performance data.

The $b$ parameter is the point on the ability scale where an examinee has a $(1 + c)/2$ probability of a correct answer. The $a$ parameter is proportional to the slope of the ICC at point $b$ on the ability scale. In general, the steeper the slope, the higher is the $a$ parameter. The item parameters $b$, $a$, and $c$ are correspondingly referred to as the item difficulty, item discrimination, and pseudoguessing parameters. $D$ in the model is a scaling factor. By varying the item parameters, many S-shaped curves or ICCs can be generated to fit actual assessment data. Simpler logistic test models can be obtained by setting $c_i = 0$ (the two-parameter model) or setting $c_i = 0$ and $a_i = 1$ (the one-parameter model). Thus, three different logistic models may be fit to assessment data. A typical set of ICCs is shown in Figure 28–4. For more details on logistic models, see Hambleton (1989) or Harris (1989).

Assessment tasks are often graded or evaluated with scoring rubrics having more than two score points. Figures 28–1 and 28–2 highlight assessment tasks with 4-point grading systems. Polychotomous IRT models such as the partial credit and graded response models are available to handle the polychotomous response data that are produced with many performance assessments (for descriptions of many of these IRT models, see van der Linden & Hambleton, in press).

Figure 28–5 shows an extension of the ICC concept to an assessment task scored on a 4-point scale (the task is scored 0 to 3). The relationship between each score point (0 to 3) and ability is shown. Figure 28–5 shows the most likely or probable scores of students at different locations on the ability scale. With student performance on a set of assessment tasks, each described by score response functions like those shown in Figure 28–5, ability estimation can be carried out.

Within an IRT measurement framework, ability estimates for an examinee obtained from tests or assessments that vary in difficulty will be the same, except for the usual measurement errors. Some samples of items are more useful for assessing ability, and therefore the corresponding errors associated with ability estimation will be smaller. But the ability parameter being estimated is the same across item or assessment task samples, unlike in classic test theory, where the person parameter of interest, true score, is defined with each item sample or test. This invariance feature in the ability parameter is obtained by incorporating information about the items (i.e., their statistics) into the ability estimation process. The ability is simply the label attached to what it is the set of test items or assessment tasks measures. This is determined through validity studies. In performance testing contexts, this ability might be called "proficiency" or "achievement."

Furthermore, item statistics are defined on the same scale

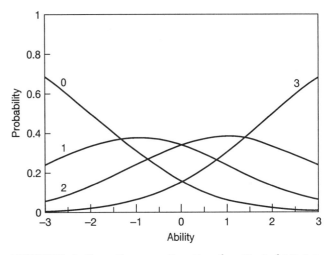

FIGURE 28–5. Score Response Functions for a Typical 4-Point Assessment Task

as examinee ability, and, in theory, item parameters are independent of the particular examinee sample used in obtaining the estimates of the item parameters. Item parameter invariance is accomplished by defining item parameters in such a way that the examinee ability distribution does not influence the item parameters or their interpretations.

Finally, IRT provides a direct way to estimate measurement error at each ability level. This strategy is superior to reporting a single estimate of error (the standard error of measurement) and applying this error to all examinees regardless of ability level (Hambleton, 1989).

IRT models, if correct for the data, provide both invariant item statistics and ability estimates. Both features are of considerable value to test developers because they open new directions for assessment, such as adaptively administered tests and item banking. Presently, in some countries (e.g., the United States and Canada), item response models, especially the one-parameter (often called the Rasch model in the measurement literature) and three-parameter logistic models, are receiving increasing use from testing agencies, certification/licensure testing agencies, government departments, state departments of education, and the uniformed services. This use includes addressing item bias and equating and reporting test scores. Measurement specialists are also exploring the uses of IRT in preparing computerized banks of assessment material and in computer-administered and computer-adaptive tests. Detailed descriptions of IRT procedures and applications are available in Hambleton and Swaminathan (1985) and Hambleton, Swaminathan, and Rogers (1991). At this time, it seems reasonable to predict that IRT will continue to have a growing and substantial influence on many measurement applications.

IRT is a general statistical theory about examinee item and test performance and how performance relates to the abilities that are measured by the items or assessment tasks in the test. Item responses can be discrete or continuous and can be dichotomously or polychotomously scored; item score categories can be ordered or unordered; there can be one ability or many abilities underlying test performance; and there are many ways (i.e., models) in which the relationship between item responses and the underlying ability or abilities can be specified. Within the general IRT framework, many models have been formulated and applied to real test data (see van der Linden & Hambleton, in press). For example, IRT models are available with one-, two-, and three-item parameters to use with dichotomously scored achievement and aptitude data, with the capability of handling graded response data (as well as continuous data) such as data from many performance assessments, with the capability of handling multidimensional tests, and with the capability of handling attitudinal data and psychomotor data (see van der Linden & Hambleton, in press).

Methods for ability and item parameter estimation have been developed over the course of the last 25 years. Variations on maximum likelihood estimation (joint, conditional, and marginal maximum likelihood estimation) are popular and are incorporated into standard model parameter estimation programs such as BILOG and LOGIST (see Hambleton & Swaminathan, 1985; Lord, 1980).

One useful IRT feature is that of the *test characteristic curve* given in Equation 2 and represented in Figure 28–6 for a set of items or assessment tasks. It is the sum of the ICCs that make

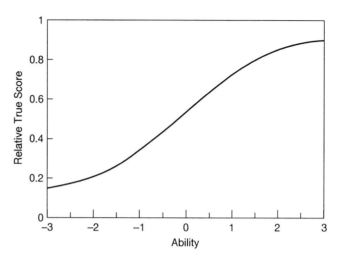

FIGURE 28–6. Example of a Test Characteristic Curve

up a test or assessment and can be used to predict the scores of examinees at given ability levels (or to obtain estimated true scores on the particular sample of items):

$$\text{TCC}(\theta) = \sum_{i=1}^{n} P_i(\theta). \quad (2)$$

The TCC, as it is called, is often scaled by $1/n$ to remove the role of the number of items in the expression. The TCC is the mathematical expression linking true score (or relative true score) on a test to the underlying ability measured by the test. If a test is made up of test items that are relatively difficult, then the TCC is shifted to the right on the ability scale and examinees tend to have lower expected scores on the test than if easier test items are included. Thus, it is possible through the TCC to explain how it is that examinees with a fixed ability can perform differently on two tests, apart from differences due to errors of measurement. The TCC connects ability scores in IRT to true scores in classical test theory, because an examinee's expected test score at a given ability level is by definition the examinee's true score on that set of test items.

Another feature of IRT models is the presence of item information functions. In the case of the simple logistic models, item information functions show the contribution of particular items to the assessment of ability. In general, items with higher discriminating power contribute more to measurement precision than items with lower discriminating power, and items tend to make their best contribution to measurement precision around their *b* value (or a little bit above, if the *c* parameter is greater than zero) on the ability scale. Figure 28–7 shows the item information functions that correspond to the items shown in Figure 28–4. Notice that Item 1 is easier than Item 2, hence the item information function for Item 1 is centered at a lower ability level than the item information function for Item 2. Also, since Items 4 and 5 are less discriminating than Items 2 and 8 (see Figure 28–4), the corresponding item information functions are lower than for Items 2 and 8.

Another special feature of item response models is the concept of a *test information function*, denoted $I(\theta)$, where:

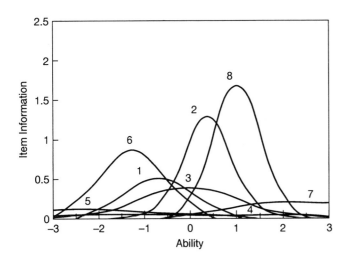

FIGURE 28–7. Item Information Curves for the Corresponding Item or Assessment Tasks in Figure 28–4

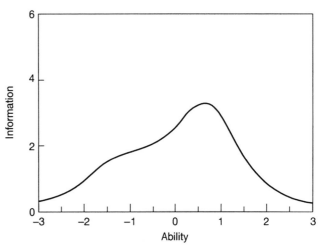

FIGURE 28–8. Sample Test Information Function

$$I(\theta) = \sum_{i=1}^{n} I_i(\theta). \tag{3}$$

It is the sum of item information functions in a test, where

$$I_i(\theta) = \frac{[P'_i(\theta)]^2}{P_i(\theta)Q_i(\theta)} \quad i = 1, 2, \ldots, n. \tag{4}$$

If Equation 1 for the three-parameter logistic model is substituted into Equation 4, then

$$I_i(\theta) = \frac{2.89a_i(1^2 - c_i)}{[c_i + e^{1.7a_i(\theta - b_i)}][1 + e^{-1.7a_i(\theta - b_i)}]^2}. \tag{5}$$

From Equation 5, the role of the $b$, $a$, and $c$ parameters in the item information function can be seen. In general, higher values of the $a$ parameter increase the amount of information an item provides, and in general, the lower the $c$ parameter, the more information an item provides. One advantage of performance assessments is that guessing is minimal, and therefore no information is lost as a result of this source of measurement error.

Equation 3 can be used to obtain estimates of the errors associated with (maximum likelihood) ability estimation, specifically,

$$SE(\theta) = \frac{1}{[I(\theta)]^{1/2}}. \tag{6}$$

This means that the more information provided by an assessment at a particular ability level, the smaller the errors associated with ability estimation. Figure 28–8 provides a sample test information function where the test is doing its best measurement in the region of $\theta = 1$. This might be an especially effective assessment if $\theta = 1$ was a performance standard for sorting students into "mastery" and "nonmastery" categories. The presence of item and test information functions substantially alters the ways in which tests are constructed within an IRT frame-

work. Test information functions also provide an excellent basis for comparing tests measuring the same ability.

Item and test characteristic functions and item and test information functions are integral features of IRT models, and they are very useful. But the essential property of these functions is what is important—that is, model parameter invariance. Figure 28–9 represents the situation highlighting item parameter invariance. Notice that, for Groups 1 and 2, the same ICC applies. For each ability level there is a probability of a correct response. Of course, that probability does not and should not depend on the number of examinees in each group at that ability level. In that sense, the ICC applies equally well to both groups. Were classical item statistics computed, the item would be easier and more discriminating in Group 2. It can also be shown that

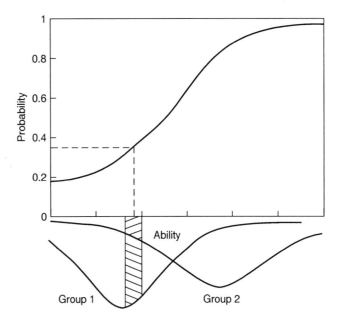

FIGURE 28–9. ICC and Ability Distributions for Two Groups of Examinees

person parameters or abilities are estimated independently of the particular test items, and this is accomplished by incorporating the item statistics into the estimation process. Of course, the property of model parameter invariance is obtained only with models that fit the test data to which they are applied.

IRT models have technical and practical shortcomings, too. On the technical side, IRT models tend to be complex, and model parameter estimation problems can arise in practice, especially when the examinee sample size is small and the test or assessment is short. Model fit, too, can be a problem. It is still not completely clear how problems of model fit should be addressed, especially problems that relate to test dimensionality. Evidence of multidimensionality has been observed in some performance assessments. Also, polychotomous IRT models are less well developed at the present time, and it is these models that are needed with many performance assessments.

On the practical side, almost regardless of application, the technical demands of IRT models tend to be more complex than the demands that arise with the classical models. The one-parameter IRT model certainly is more straightforward to apply than the other IRT models (and the software, in general, is user friendly). On the other hand, questions arise about the fit of the one-parameter model because of the restrictiveness of the model assumptions.

An awareness of the shortcomings of classical test theory and the potential benefits offered by IRT has led some measurement practitioners to choose to work within an IRT framework. The reason for this change of emphasis by the psychometric and measurement community from classical to item response models is as a consequence of the benefits obtained through the application of item response models to measurement problems. These benefits include:

1. Item statistics that are independent of the groups from which they were estimated
2. Scores describing examinee proficiency or ability that are not dependent on test difficulty
3. Test models that provide a basis for matching items or assessment tasks to ability levels
4. Models that do not require strict parallel tests or assessments for assessing reliability

## Test Development

In this section, the use of the three-parameter model in test development is briefly considered to provide a flavor of test development within an IRT framework. An assumption is made, without loss of generality, that all of the items or assessment tasks are dichotomously scored. Additional IRT applications are described in detail by Hambleton et al. (1991).

*Item Analysis.* When IRT is employed, item analysis consists of (a) determining sample-invariant item parameters using relatively complex mathematical techniques and large sample sizes, and (b) utilizing goodness-of-fit criteria to detect items that do not fit the specified response model. The property of sample invariance inherent within IRT means that developers do not need a representative sample of the examinee population to obtain item statistics. They do, however, need a heterogeneous

and large examinee sample to ensure proper (i.e., stable and unbiased) item parameter estimates. As can be seen from Figure 28–9, even when examinee samples differ, the test developer is able to use the principles of IRT to estimate the same ICC, regardless of the examinee sample used in the item calibration process. However, the test developer using IRT is faced with a different problem. Because IRT requires larger sample sizes to obtain good item parameter estimates, the test developer must ensure that the examinee sample is of sufficient size to guarantee accurate item calibration.

The detection of poor items using IRT is not as straightforward as when classic test theory is used. Items are generally evaluated in terms of their goodness of fit to a model using a statistical test or an analysis of residuals. An adequate fit of model to data is essential for successful item analysis; otherwise items may appear poor as an artifact of poor model fit. Readers wishing to learn more about goodness of fit techniques are referred to Hambleton et al. (1991, chap. 4). Poor items are usually identified through a consideration of their discrimination indices (the value of $a_i$ will be a low positive or even negative) and difficulty indices (items should neither be too easy nor too difficult for the group of examinees to be assessed). It is not uncommon in practical test development work to carry out a classic item analysis as well. The information can be valuable in detecting item flaws.

*Item Selection.* As is the case with classic test theory, IRT also bases item selection on the intended purpose of the test. However, the final selection of items will depend on the information the items contribute to the overall information supplied by the test. A particularly useful feature of the item information functions used in IRT test development is that they permit the test developer to determine the contribution of each item or assessment task to the test information function independent of other items in the test. Lord (1980) outlined a procedure, originally conceptualized by Birnbaum (1968), for the use of item information functions in the test-building process. Basically, this procedure entails that a test developer take four steps:

1. Describe the shape of the desired test information function over the desired range of abilities. Lord (1980) calls this the *target information function.*
2. Select items or assessment tasks with information functions that will fill up the hard to fill areas under the target information function.
3. After each item or assessment task is added to the test, calculate the test information function for the selected assessment material.
4. Continue selecting assessment material until the test information function approximates the target information function to a satisfactory degree.

For example, suppose a test developer wished to build a test to fill the target information function shown in Figure 28–8. The first step would be to specify this information function as the target information function. The next step would be to add an item or assessment task to the test, filling up the hard to fill areas first. Item 2 or 8, shown in Figure 28–4, would be a suitable first choice. The test information function should be recalculated after the addition of each item or assessment task so as to identify the specific information required to complete the test. By following this procedure the test developer would create the ideal test to match the target information function shown in Figure 28–8. In practice, statistical considerations are balanced with content specifications to ensure that the resulting test has content validity as well as the desired statistical properties.

This procedure allows the test developer to build a test that will precisely fulfill any set of desired statistical and content specifications. Thus, it is possible to build a test that discriminates well at any particular region on the ability continuum. That is, if the test developer has a good idea of the ability of a group of examinees, assessment material can be selected so as to maximize test information in the region of ability spanned by the examinees being tested. Of course, this optimum selection of assessment material will contribute substantially to the precision with which ability scores are estimated.

Furthermore, with performance tests, it is common to observe lower test performance on a pretest than on a posttest. Given this knowledge, an instructor might select easier items for the pretest and more difficult items for the posttest. Then, for both administrations, measurement precision will have been maximized in the ability region where the examinees would most likely be located. Moreover, because items on both tests measure the same ability and because ability estimates are independent of the particular choice of test items, the instructor can measure growth by subtracting the pretest ability estimate from the posttest ability estimate.

*Item Banking.* Today many assessments are constructed with the aid of an item bank. An item bank, or item pool, as it is often called, is a collection of precalibrated assessment material brought together and stored in a common location. Items can be selected from this bank to build an assessment. The developer is able to access an item bank and select items for an assessment without having to write and determine the psychometric properties of each item for every assessment the developer wishes to create. Information concerning items within the bank enables the developer to be very discerning about the items that he or she selects. The test developer is able to choose assessment material on the basis of such factors as content, difficulty, and discrimination. Therefore, a test developer can build an assessment to fit any desired test information function, so long as the item bank contains sufficient items with the desired properties to build a test.

Item banks, especially those containing items calibrated using item response models, offer considerable aid to the developer of educational assessments (Hambleton & de Gruijter, 1983; Lord, 1980). If the item banks used contain content-related and technically sound items, the quality of educational assessments can be higher than the quality of assessments produced by test developers creating all of the material on their own.

Although the concept of an item bank was first proposed within the framework of classic test theory, it was not until the development of IRT that the maximum benefit of item banks could be achieved. Classic item statistics are of limited value for describing items in an item bank because they are dependent on the particular sample used in the item calibration process. Conversely, item parameter values within the framework of IRT are independent of the sample from which they were obtained.

The theoretical property of invariance within item response models makes it possible for item writers to build large item banks and obtain statistics that are comparable across groups (Hambleton & Swaminathan, 1985). New items or assessment tasks can easily be added to the bank when desired and comparisons can be made across dissimilar samples.

## DIFFERENTIAL ITEM FUNCTIONING

As the uses of tests and performance assessments have become more important in the field of education, additional attention has been focused on the detection of biased assessment material (see, e.g., Camilli & Shepard, 1994; Holland & Wainer, 1993). Today, assessment results are being used to deny high school diplomas to students; to assess the quality of education at the district, state, and national levels; to reward and sanction schools; and to hire and fire teachers. Clearly, then, educational assessments are going to receive very careful scrutiny, and they need to be capable of withstanding technical and legal challenges. To this end, various statistical and judgmental methods for detecting potentially biased assessment material have been proposed in the educational measurement literature (e.g., Camilli & Shepard, 1994; Holland & Thayer, 1988; Shepard, Camilli, & Williams, 1984). Much of the statistical work to date, which has been extensive, has been limited to the assessment of dichotomously scored items or assessment tasks. Currently, extensions to polychotomous data are being developed (e.g., Zwick, Donoghue, & Grima, 1993).

Although no statistical method can detect "bias" as such, many methods are being used to identify assessment material that is functioning differentially in two groups of interest (e.g., males and females). The groups are often referred to as majority and minority groups, or reference and focal groups, and the studies are referred to as studies of differential item functioning. Once a set of items is identified as exhibiting DIF, further study can be carried out to determine the most likely cause or causes of the DIF (see, e.g., Curley & Schmitt, 1993; Scheuneman, 1987). Then, appropriate action can be taken, and when necessary, the defective items can be removed from the assessment or from the item bank used for test development. In some instances, the assessment material can be revised and returned to the item bank. This might be the case if the defect was an improper word or two. On the other hand, if the problem concerned the contents of a passage, then the passage and all associated assessment material would need to be eliminated.

One of the strong arguments for emphasizing performance assessments in education was the belief that this form of assessment would show less bias. Evidence is limited, but it appears that the argument may be incorrect. In fact, as much or more DIF is being detected because of the central role of writing in completing many of the assessments. Even some of the more cognitively challenging assessment material is showing up as DIF because this material is not always being taught, and the opportunity to learn the more advanced material may be confounded with ethnic background.

A widely accepted definition of DIF is that an item or assessment task exhibits DIF (or is potentially biased) if students of equal ability but from different subgroups (for example, males

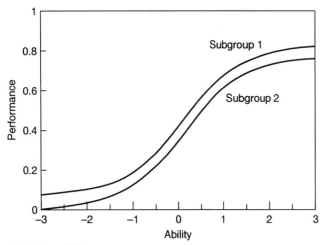

**(a)** Uniform DIF

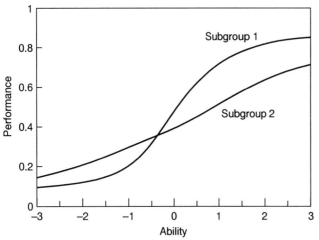

**(b)** Nonuniform DIF

FIGURE 28–10. Illustrations Showing the Difference Between Uniform and Nonuniform DIF

and females) do not have *an equal probability of correctly responding to that item* (or an equal expected score on the assessment task, in the case of polychotomously scored assessment material) (Hambleton et al., 1991). If the discrepancy in item performance between the subgroups of interest is equal across the entire range of abilities, then the DIF is said to be uniform. However, if the difference between the subgroups is not consistent across the entire range of abilities, then the DIF is said to be nonuniform.

Figure 28–10 illustrates these two situations. Basically, the bigger the differences in the performance levels of the two groups, the greater the concern is about the item or assessment task. Of course, in the ideal situation the differences are small and random, and the conclusion is that no DIF is present.

Figure 28–10A shows that on the item in question, the minority group (Subgroup 2) performs consistently (uniformly) lower than the majority group (Subgroup 1) at all ability levels. Figure 28–10B shows that on the item in question, the minority group performs lower than the majority group at the higher end of

the ability scale and performs higher than the majority group at the lower end of the ability scale. Thus the differences are inconsistent (or nonuniform) but still important. The distinction between uniform and nonuniform DIF is important, too, because the effectiveness of some statistical methods in the detection of DIF varies as to the likelihood of detecting nonuniform DIF. For example, the popular Mantel-Haenszel procedure, mentioned below, is not effective in detecting nonuniform DIF in assessment material of medium difficulty (Hambleton & Rogers, 1989).

The most promising statistical methods are discussed next, and then judgmental methods are considered briefly.

## Statistical Methods Using IRT

Statistical methods using IRT entail comparing ICCs obtained in the two groups of interest (e.g., Figure 28–10). This method has the strong advantage that item performance in the two groups is compared at each ability level. In fact, this approach to the identification of DIF is completely consistent with the earlier definition of DIF (Camilli & Shepard, 1994; Hambleton et al., 1991). Comparing ICCs also, in theory, permits the detection of both uniform and nonuniform DIF.

Different researchers have adopted different strategies for comparing ICCs. Lord (1980) proposed a significance test on the item parameter estimates obtained in the two groups. The method is straightforward to apply, although the method appears to have a Type I error rate that is too high (that is, too many acceptable items are flagged as potentially problematic). Rudner, Getson, and Knight (1980) recommended that the area between ICCs over the interval of interest be computed in studying DIF. Then, the area could be used as an indicator of DIF. For example, this interval might be defined over the minority score distribution. Items showing large differences between ICCs are those that are identified as exhibiting DIF and are studied further. It is also possible to weight the differences along the ability continuum by the minority distribution. In this way, a weighted area can be used instead of the total area. This variation has the advantage that large differences between two ICCs are not taken seriously unless the differences occur in a region on the ability scale where there are minority group members.

The IRT-based methods have two problems. One is that IRT-based methods are somewhat difficult to carry out because of the complexities associated with placing the item parameter estimates from the two groups on a common scale. This becomes a problem whenever the score distributions in the two groups are different, and in general, they should be assumed to be different at the outset of the analysis. The second problem is that often the sample size of the minority group is relatively small and therefore IRT item calibrations cannot be done very well. Quite simply, ICCs from the minority group may be too unstable to permit meaningful comparisons with ICCs obtained in the majority group. Linn and Harnisch (1981) produced one solution to the small-minority-group problem that involves estimating ICCs in the majority group and then estimating abilities for examinees in the minority group using ICCs from the majority group. With ability estimates in hand for the minority group, it is possible to determine the extent to which ICCs for the majority group actually match the item-by-item performance of the minority group members. When violations are noted, corresponding items are flagged as exhibiting DIF.

## Mantel-Haenszel Method

The Mantel-Haenszel method has become the DIF detection method of choice (Holland & Wainer, 1993). It is considerably simpler to apply than IRT-based methods, produces results comparable to those achieved with IRT-based methods (Hambleton & Rogers, 1989), requires considerably smaller sample sizes, and has associated statistical tests. Numerous research studies have been conducted detailing the best approaches for applying this method (Hambleton, Clauser, et al., 1993; Holland & Wainer, 1993).

In a few words, the Mantel-Haenszel method matches examiners from the two groups of interest using total test score (or on the adjusted test score by removing potentially biased test items that might be identified by a judgmental review or an initial statistical analysis). Majority and minority group members are assigned to groups based on their total scores (or adjusted scores); that is, examinees are matched on their ability levels, and then item performance of the two groups is compared in each score group. In the ideal situation, with an $n$-item test, $n + 1$ score groups should be formed. In this way, ability differences within the score groups can be minimized, and they will not confound the results of the study.

Differences in item performance in each score group are weighted by the size of the samples and then summed over score groups. If the differences are weighted and summed correctly, it is possible to test the sum for statistical significance with a chi-square test. The Mantel-Haenszel method is being routinely applied in the test development process by many agencies. DIF items are flagged and studied to determine the source of the problem. Sometimes the problem may be due to test speededness (when this is the case, later items show up as exhibiting DIF) or choice of situations and vocabulary. Very often the source of the problem cannot be identified on judgmental review. At that point, a policy decision is made about what to do with the problematic items.

## Judgmental Reviews.

Panels consisting of minority group members, curriculum specialists, and measurement specialists are often formed to review assessment materials for bias (racial, ethnic, gender, regional, age, etc.). Two problems are common. First, panels often fail to distinguish biased items (items that are truly unfair to persons in a minority group) from items merely reflecting stereotyping. Stereotyping is undesirable (e.g., showing males performing physical activities and females working around the home), but it is not likely to influence minority group performance. Panels need to focus their reviews on aspects of assessment material (e.g., situations, vocabulary, assessment format, reading level, time limits) that might negatively influence actual performance by the minority group or groups of interest.

Second, advance identification of items that are likely to show DIF is extremely difficult. Often, the correlation between items identified as exhibiting DIF by judgmental and empirical methods is low, although methodological shortcomings with both empirical and judgmental methods are part of the reason

(Hambleton & Jones, 1994). Another reason is that the basis for biased items is still not well known. More research on this topic is in order.

## Conclusion

Methods for detecting DIF are not without their shortcomings, but they are applied routinely by test developers in their work. Current research is focused on developing a base of knowledge about the sorts of items that are not detected as exhibiting DIF by judgmental methods, and extending current DIF technology to the polychotomously scored items that are common to performance assessments.

# PERFORMANCE STANDARD-SETTING

Policymakers and educators today talk about the need for world-class performance standards for interpreting educational assessment results for individuals and groups (e.g., Pashley & Phillips, 1993). Performance standards are the scores, or profiles of scores across exercises in an assessment, that must be achieved for students to be classified as, say, basic, proficient, or advanced. For example, the performance standard for a student to achieve the advanced level of performance on an assessment might be 90 percent. Another example of a performance standard for advanced-level performance might be that the student performs at an 80 percent level or higher on each of the exercises in the assessment and has an overall average on the assessment of 85 percent. Performance standards, or simply standards, are different from content standards, which lay out the content areas students are responsible for. Performance standards define the amount of or "how much" performance students need to exhibit.

In a typical project to set performance standards on an educational assessment, a group of persons is selected to form a panel, and then the panel meets. The meeting might run about 2 days (or longer, if extensive exposure is given to the exercises and scoring rubrics), with the following agenda:

1. Review of the purpose of the educational assessment.
2. Exposure to the assessment itself and the scoring rubrics (sometimes panelists are administered the assessment under testlike conditions).
3. Development and discussion of the performance categories: e.g., novice, apprentice, proficient, expert; or sometimes simply masters or nonmasters.
4. Training and practice on the standard-setting method.
5. Setting standards–panelists go through the method and set their initial standards.
6. Discussion among the panelists about their standards. Sometimes consequential information is introduced, such as the percentage of students who would be in each proficiency category if the standards were adopted. Other information panelists might receive would be difficulty levels and discriminating powers of the exercises.
7. Setting standards again–panelists repeat the process. Very often, the panelists' standards converge, and remaining differences among panelists are handled by "averaging" the standards of panelists. Several rounds of discussion and stan-

dard setting are usual (that is, steps 5 and 6 may be repeated several times).

The seven steps listed above provide a flavor of the standard-setting process. Of course, the particular method of standard setting influences the nature of the feedback provided to panelists and the number of iterations in the process.

Who should set the performance standards? How high do they need to be to be "world class"? What method or methods should be used in setting these performance standards? These are important questions that must be answered for each educational assessment.

The answer to the first question is a matter of policy. In the case of performance standards on the NAEP test, 70% of the constituency of the standard-setting panels consists of educators and the remaining 30% consists of members of the public. With state educational assessments, there is usually a balance of policymakers and educators, including administrators, curriculum specialists, and teachers, on the panels. With credentialing examinations, usually a balance between senior-level and intermediate-level persons working in the profession is sought in setting standards. However, even after the composition of a panel has been decided on, there remains the difficult task of selecting representatives of the constituent groups.

The second question—How high should standards be?—has not been properly answered at this time. World-class standards are meant to be high standards for interpreting assessment results, but no one seems quite sure how high is high enough. International comparative studies of achievement provide one basis for setting world-class standards (Lapointe et al., 1989, 1992). The Third International Mathematics and Science Study (TIMSS), a study with over 60 participating countries, should provide policymakers in 1996 and again in the year 2000 with valuable data for setting performance standards on state and national assessments.

The fear among policymakers and educators in setting performance standards is that if they are set unreasonably high, many students will appear to perform poorly, and the educational system will be criticized unfairly. On the other hand, if the performance standards are set too low, the results may flatter the educational system and hold back important educational reforms which are needed. It is no surprise, then, that setting performance standards is often controversial, time-consuming, and technically challenging.

The third question concerns the selection of a method. It is perhaps important to note first that all standard-setting methods in use today involve some type of judgment, and so in that sense they are arbitrary. Glass (1978) argued that arbitrary standards are not defensible in educational assessment. Popham (1978) countered with this response:

Unable to avoid reliance on human judgment as the chief ingredient in standard-setting, some individuals have thrown up their hands in dismay and cast aside all efforts to set performance standards as arbitrary, hence unacceptable.

But *Webster's Dictionary* offers us two definitions of arbitrary. The first of these is positive, describing arbitrary as an adjective reflecting choice or discretion, that is, "Determinable by a judge or tribunal." The second definition, pejorative in nature, describes arbitrary as an adjective denoting capriciousness, that is, "selected at random and without reason." In my estimate, when people start knocking the stan-

dard-setting game as arbitrary, they are clearly employing Webster's second, negatively loaded definition.

But the first definition is more accurately reflective of serious standard-setting efforts. They represent genuine attempts to do a good job in deciding what kinds of standards we ought to employ. That they are judgmental is inescapable. But to malign all judgmental operations as capricious is absurd. (Popham, 1978, p. 168)

As judged by the common use of performance standards (a) at the district, state, and national levels in education, and (b) in credential examinations, it seems clear that Popham's representation of the standard-setting process, the second definition, is the one subscribed to by many policymakers and educators.

The available standard-setting methods have been described, compared, and evaluated in the educational assessment literature (Berk, 1986; Jaeger, 1989; Kane, 1994), and steps for applying several of the popular methods are described by Livingston and Zieky (1982). A full review will not be repeated here.

Available methods can be organized into two categories: test-centered and examinee-centered methods. Also, there are several new methods that have not been well researched but that show promise for use with performance assessments. These methods are introduced next.

## Test-Centered Methods

The best example is the Angoff method (e.g., Jaeger, 1989). Panelists develop or are given a definition of borderline competence (e.g., a description of the students at the borderline where the performance standard will be set) and then panelists attempt to simulate that student's performance (and other students' performance at the same performance level) on the assessment. For example, with the 1992 NAEP Mathematics Assessment (Mullis, Dossey, Owen & Phillips, 1993, p. 51), the following descriptions were used in setting eighth-grade performance standards for basic, proficient, and advanced-level performance:

*Basic Level.* Eighth-grade students performing at the basic level should exhibit evidence of conceptual and procedural understanding in the five NAEP content areas. This level of performance signifies an understanding of arithmetic operations—including estimation—on whole numbers, decimals, fractions, and percents.

Eighth graders performing at the basic level should complete problems correctly with the help of structural prompts such as diagrams, charts, and graphs. They should be able to solve problems in all NAEP content areas through the appropriate selection and use of strategies and technological tools—including calculators, computers, and geometric shapes. Students at this level also should be able to use fundamental algebraic and informal geometric concepts in problem solving.

As they approach the proficient level, students at the basic level should be able to determine which of available data are necessary and sufficient for correct solutions and use them in problem solving. However, these 8th graders show limited skills in communicating mathematically.

*Proficient Level.* Eighth-grade students performing at the proficient level should apply mathematical concepts and procedures consistently to complex problems in the five NAEP content areas.

Eighth graders performing at the proficient level should be able to conjecture, defend their ideas, and give supporting examples. They should understand the connections between fractions, percents, decimals, and other mathematical topics such as algebra and functions. Students at this level are expected to have a thorough understanding of basic level arithmetic operations—an understanding sufficient for problem solving in practical situations.

Quantity and spatial relationships in problem solving and reasoning should be familiar to them, and they should be able to convey underlying reasoning skills beyond the level of arithmetic. They should be able to compare and contrast mathematical ideas and generate their own examples. These students should make inferences from data and graphs; apply properties of informal geometry; and accurately use the tools of technology. Students at this level should understand the process of gathering and organizing data and be able to calculate, evaluate, and communicate results within the domain of statistics and probability.

*Advanced Level.* Eighth-grade students performing at the advanced level should be able to reach beyond the recognition, identification, and application of mathematical rules in order to generalize and synthesize concepts and principles in the five NAEP content areas.

Eighth graders performing at the advanced level should be able to probe examples and counterexamples in order to shape generalizations from which they can develop models. Eighth graders performing at the advanced level should use number sense and geometric awareness to consider the reasonableness of an answer. They are expected to use abstract thinking to create unique problem-solving techniques and explain the reasoning processes underlying their conclusions.

With multiple-choice items, panelists are asked to estimate the probability with which the borderline students will answer the item correctly. The sum of the expected item scores is the panelist's standard. These standards can be averaged across panelists to arrive at a group standard. Normally, before the process is finalized, panelists are given some information on actual performance (e.g., item difficulty values, score distributions) to provide a framework for considering their ratings. The basic idea is one of consequential validity. In a typical Angoff standard-setting method, panelists complete the first set of ratings after some training, then they receive some empirical data, which they discuss along with their ratings with other panel members, and finally they provide a second set of ratings. Both intrajudge and interjudge ratings are considered as part of a reliability study on the standards.

Other popular methods with selected-response items include the Nedelsky and Ebel methods (Berk, 1986; Livingston & Zieky, 1982). These methods have received considerably less use than the Angoff method in educational assessment.

## Examinee-Centered Methods

The best known of the examinee-centered methods is the contrasting-groups method. Suppose the task is to set a standard to separate masters from nonmasters on a student assessment. (A similar task can be used to separate novices from apprentices, apprentices from proficient, etc.) Using clear criteria, those who know the students (e.g., teachers) sort the students into masters and nonmasters, or certifiable and not certifiable. Then the score distributions of the two groups are studied (Figure 28–11), and a standard is set to minimize some loss function such as the number of misclassification errors (passing students identified by the judges as not certifiable, or failing students identified by the judges as certifiable).

The point of intersection of the two score distributions is

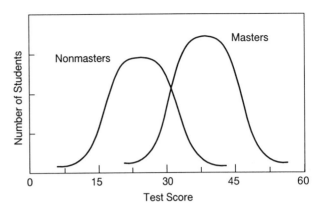

FIGURE 28–11. Contrasting-Groups Method for Setting Standards

often taken as the initial standard. The standard can be moved up to reduce the number of false-positive errors (students identified as masters by the assessment but who were not in the masters group formed by the judges) or down to reduce the number of false-negative errors (students identified as nonmasters by the assessment but who were in the masters group formed by the judges). The direction in which the standard is moved will depend on the relative seriousness of the false-positive and false-negative errors. If the score distributions overlap completely, no mastery–nonmastery decisions can be made reliably. The ideal situation would be one in which the two distributions do not overlap at all. Then the standard could be positioned between the two distributions, and the assignment of students to mastery states would be in complete agreement with the judges' assignments.

The validity of this approach to standard setting depends, in part, on the appropriateness of the classifications of students. If the judges tend to err in their classifications by assigning students to the mastery group who do not belong, the result is that standards from the contrasting-groups method are lower than they should be. On the other hand, the standards tend to be higher if judges err by assigning some masters to the nonmastery group who do not belong. Like the Angoff method, or modified Angoff method, the contrasting-groups method can also be applied to performance assessment data.

A variation on this method includes the borderline group method (Livingston & Zieky, 1982). With the borderline method, only the assessment scores of students judged as "borderline" or who "just meet the expectations outlined for the performance level" are considered. The panel studies this distribution and then sets a performance standard. One consideration is the number of borderline students who should pass the assessment. With this determination, the performance standard can be set.

## New Methods for Performance Assessments

All of the new methods developed to date would be classified as test centered. One method is a simple extension of the Angoff method. Panelists are asked to estimate the expected score of the minimally competent student (i.e., the student or students who are located at the standard being set) on the score scale associated with each performance task or exercise. For example, with a 4-point rating scale, a panelist might indicate that a borderline student performing at the proficient level would obtain a score of 3. These expected scores can be summed over the exercises to arrive at a performance standard for the assessment for a single panelist (see Hambleton & Plake, 1995). Standards from the panelists can be averaged to obtain a standard from the panel.

This extended (or modified) Angoff standard-setting method is called a compensatory method because the standard is a particular score and no attempt is made to dictate how that score is obtained. It is conceivable that a student might do extremely well on a few exercises and poorly on others and still receive a total score that is high enough to pass the assessment.

Jaeger (1995) has developed a method known as "policy capturing." With this method, panelists are invited to sort score profiles (across the assessment tasks) into those that are certifiable and those that are not. For example, suppose an assessment consists of five exercises and each exercise is scored on a 4-point scale (1 = poor, 4 = excellent). Possible score profiles might be (3, 4, 3, 2, 3), (2, 2, 1, 3, 1), and (3, 3, 3, 3, 3); there are 1,021 others. One panelist might certify the first and third. Another panelist might certify only the first. On the basis of the evaluations of many score profiles, it is possible to use mathematical modeling to try to find a standard or standards that are implicit in the panelist's judgments of score profiles.

Thus a standard might be compensatory or conjunctive or a combination, and it would be applied to student score profiles (defined over the assessment exercises). A conjunction standard would be one where a panelist defined a required minimum score for each exercise, and only students who achieved at least that minimum score on each exercise would be certified.

Jaeger's policy-capturing method appears to hold some promise with performance assessments because training is straightforward, there is the capability of aggregating over panelists to arrive at a standard for the group of panelists, and the option exists for standards that are not strictly compensatory. Also, the sorting task is one that the panelists can handle. This method seems to have potential in situations where panelists are not capable of actually stating their preferences directly about the standard. This may be true because the standard is very complex. Panelists' standards are inferred from their evaluations of score profiles.

Putnam, Pence, and Jaeger (1995) described a direct method for standard setting on performance assessments. Panelists work together to reach consensus on a performance standard by considering score profiles and consequential data (e.g., passing rates). In some field-test work, this direct method has followed the policy-capturing method. One of the difficulties of this direct method is that it is not usually clear how differences in the panelists' standards should be handled since often the standards (sometimes called the standard-setting policy with performance assessments) are fairly complex (e.g., the student must have a score of 3 on Exercises 1 and 4, a combined score across the five exercises of at least 14, and have no score of 1 on any of the exercises). Averaging is not possible because of the nature of the policies. In some of the field-test work, the dominant views about the standards have been summarized, and panelists

have shown their preferences by voting on the dominant standard-setting policies among panel members. Consensus, however, on a single standard for classifying students is not guaranteed.

## Conclusions

Many performance standard-setting methods are in the literature and have been found to be practical and to lead to valid results. Still, questions remain about applying some of the methods, and the issue of method effect makes many persons uncomfortable with standards. There is even the important question of replication of standards with new samples of panels. To what extent would the same standard or standards be produced if a "parallel panel" were chosen? Then there is the matter of performance standards for performance assessments. Only a few methods exist in the literature, and none of them has been fully validated at this time. It seems clear that the area of standard setting will remain a technical and political problem for many years to come.

## CONCLUSIONS

This chapter has described advances in assessment models, methods, and practices. The case being made for performance testing in assessment in education was outlined in the first part of the chapter and was followed by some guidelines for validating performance tests. Not addressed in this chapter were new methods for approaching performance test reliability assessment, which are contained within generalizability theory (Brennan, 1992; Shavelson & Webb, 1991). Generalizability theory, which is an extension of classical reliability theory, provides a basis for easily analyzing errors in performance assessments due to raters or graders, the assessment tasks, assessment methods, and the timing of the assessment administrations. Basically, experimental designs can be used to determine the role that various factors such as raters exert on assessment scores.

A comprehensive list of assessment formats was provided in the chapter. It seems clear that considerable progress is being made in this area, and computer technological advances have become especially important. Not only is computer technology opening up possibilities for the use of audio and video components in educational assessments, but sequential assessments, free-form responses, and more complexity in scoring become possible, too.

Item response theory is a broad psychometric framework for analyzing all kinds of data associated with new forms of assessment. Even response times to complete assessment tasks can now be studied within an IRT framework (Roskam, in press). The use of unidimensional as well as multidimensional models is possible, and the latter may become necessary with complex performance assessments. Psychologists, too, are developing new IRT models that can identify cognitive components underlying performance on assessments and facilitate the construction of assessments with cognitive components of special interest (Embretson, in press). This latter feature permits a kind of systematic test construction capable of building construct validity into the assessments. In contrast, it is more common but less satisfactory to design an assessment and then assess construct validity in the hope that what is of interest is actually being measured. The combination of IRT and associated models, in conjunction with new computer technology, has opened up a new era in assessment that includes computer-adaptive assessment and computer-based test construction (van der Linden, 1995).

The last two topics taken up in the chapter are two of the most studied in assessment practice today. Both were intensively studied with objectively based assessments because the presence of bias undermines the credibility of any assessment, and standards are needed for score reporting and decision-making. In performance assessments, the topics are no less important, but the research is far less advanced.

# References

Airasian, P. (1994). *Classroom assessment.* New York: McGraw-Hill.

American Educational Research Association, American Psychological Association, & National Council on Measurement in Education. (1985). *Standards for educational and psychological testing.* Washington, DC: American Psychological Association.

American Federation of Teachers, National Council on Measurement in Education, National Education Association. (1990). Standards for teacher competence in educational assessment of students. *Educational Measurement: Issues and Practice, 9*(4), 30–32.

Baker, F. B. (1989). Computer technology in test construction and processing. In R. L. Linn (Ed.), *Educational measurement* (3rd ed., pp. 409–428). New York: Macmillan.

Baker, E. L., O'Neil, H. F., & Linn, R. L. (1993). Policy and validity prospects for performance-based assessment. *American Psychologist, 48*(12), 1210–1218.

Bennett, R. E., Rock, D. A., & Wang, M. (1991). Equivalence of free-response and multiple-choice items. *Journal of Educational Measurement, 28,* 77–92.

Bennett, R. E., & Ward, W. C. (Eds.). (1993). *Construction versus choice in cognitive measurement: Issues in constructed response, performance testing, and portfolio assessment.* Hillsdale, NJ: Lawrence Erlbaum Associates.

Berk, R. A. (1986). A consumer's guide to setting performance standards on criterion-referenced tests. *Review of Educational Research, 56,* 137–172.

Berliner, D. C. (1993). Mythology and the American system of education. *Phi Delta Kappan, 74*(8), 632–640.

Birnbaum, A. (1968). Some latent trait models and their use in inferring an examinee's ability. In F. M. Lord & M. R. Novick, *Statistical theories of mental test scores* (pp. 397–479). Reading, MA: Addison-Wesley.

Bray, D. W., Campbell, R. J., & Grant, D. L. (1974). *Formative years in business: A long-term AT&T study of managerial lives.* New York: Wiley.

Brennan, R. L. (1992). *Elements of generalizability theory* (2nd ed.). Iowa City, IA: American College Testing Program.

Bridgeman, B. (1992). A comparison of quantitative questions in open-ended and multiple-choice formats. *Journal of Educational Measurement, 29,* 253–271.

Bunderson, C. V., Inouye, D. K., & Olsen, J. B. (1989). The four generations of computerized educational measurement. In R. L. Linn (Ed.), *Educational measurement* (3rd ed., pp. 367–408). New York: Macmillan.

Calfee, R. (1995). Implications of cognitive psychology for authentic assessment and instruction. In T. Oakland & R. K. Hambleton (Eds.), *International perspectives on academic assessment* (pp. 25–48). Boston, MA: Kluwer Academic.

California Assessment Program Staff. (1989). Authentic assessment in California. *Educational Leadership, 46*(7), 6.

Camilli, G., & Shepard, L. A. (1994). *Methods for identifying biased test items.* Newbury Park, CA: Sage.

Cascio, W. F. (1987). *Applied psychology in personnel management.* Englewood Cliffs, NJ: Prentice Hall.

Cheney, L. V. (1991). *National tests: What other countries expect their students to know.* Washington, DC: National Endowment for the Humanities.

Collis, K., & Romberg, T. A. (1991). Assessment of mathematical performance: An analysis of open-ended test items. In M. C. Wittrock & E. L. Baker (Eds.), *Testing and cognition* (pp. 82–130). Englewood Cliffs, NJ: Prentice Hall.

Crocker, L., & Algina, J. (1986). *Introduction to classical and modern test theory.* New York: Holt, Rinehart & Winston.

Cronbach, L. J., Bradburn, N. M., & Horvitz, D. G. (1994, July). *Sampling and statistical procedures used in the California Learning Assessment System* (Final Report). Sacramento: California Department of Education.

Curley, W. E., & Schmitt, A. P. (1993). *Revising SAT-Verbal items to eliminate differential item functioning* (College Board Report No. 93-2). New York: College Board.

Embretson, S. E. (in press). Multi-component response models. In W. J. van der Linden & R. K. Hambleton (Eds.), *Handbook of item response theory.* New York: Springer.

Farr, R., Pritchard, R., & Smitten, B. (1990). A description of what happens when an examinee takes a multiple-choice reading comprehension test. *Journal of Educational Measurement, 27,* 209–226.

Farr, R., & Tone, B. (1994). *Portfolio and performance assessment.* San Antonio: Harcourt Brace.

Fitzpatrick, R., & Morrison, E. J. (1971). Performance and product evaluation. In R. L. Thorndike (Ed.), *Educational measurement* (2nd ed., pp. 237–270). Washington, DC: American Council on Education.

Frederiksen, J. R., & Collins, A. (1989). A systems approach to educational testing. *Educational Researcher, 9*(9), 27–32.

Glass, G. V (1978). Standards and criteria. *Journal of Educational Measurement, 15,* 237–261.

Graduate Record Examination Board. (1994). *GRE: Practicing to take the General Test* (9th ed.). Princeton, NJ: Educational Testing Service.

Gulliksen, H. (1950). *Theory of mental tests.* New York: Wiley.

Haladyna, T. M., & Downing, S. M. (1989a). A taxonomy of multiple-choice item writing rules. *Applied Measurement in Education, 2,* 37–50.

Haladyna, T. M., & Downing, S. M. (1989b). Validity of a taxonomy of multiple choice item writing rules. *Applied Measurement in Education, 2,* 51–78.

Hambleton, R. K. (1984). Validity of test scores. In R. Berk (Ed.), *A guide to criterion-referenced test construction* (pp. 199–230). Baltimore: Johns Hopkins University Press.

Hambleton, R. K. (1989). Principles and selected applications of item response theory. In R. L. Linn (Ed.), *Educational measurement* (3rd ed., pp. 147–200). New York: Macmillan.

Hambleton, R. K. (1990). Criterion-referenced testing methods and practices. In T. B. Gutkin & C. R. Reynolds (Eds.), *The handbook of school psychology* (pp. 388–415). New York: Wiley.

Hambleton, R. K. (1994). The rise and fall of criterion-referenced measurement? *Educational Measurement: Issues and Practice, 13*(4), 21–26.

Hambleton, R. K., Clauser, B. E., Mazor, K. M., & Jones, R. W. (1993). Advances in the detection of differentially functioning test items. *European Journal of Psychological Assessment, 9*(1), 1–18.

Hambleton, R. K., & de Gruijter, D. N. M. (1983). Application of item response models to criterion-referenced test item selection. *Journal of Educational Measurement, 20,* 355–367.

Hambleton, R. K., & Jones, R. (1994). Comparison of empirical and judgmental methods for detecting differential item functioning. *Educational Research Quarterly, 18*(1), 21–36.

Hambleton, R. K., Jones, R., & Slater, S. (1993). *Innovations in testing and evaluation of student competencies in technical and vocational education* (Final Report). Paris: UNESCO.

Hambleton, R. K., & Murphy, E. (1992). A psychometric perspective on authentic assessment. *Applied Measurement in Education, 5*(1), 1–16.

Hambleton, R. K., & Plake, B. S. (1995). Using an extended Angoff procedure to set standards on complex performance assessments. *Applied Measurement in Education, 8,* 41–56.

Hambleton, R. K., & Robers, H. J. (1989). Detecting potentially biased test items: Comparison of IRT and Mantel-Haenszel methods. *Applied Measurement in Education, 2*(4), 313–334.

Hambleton, R. K., & Swaminathan, H. (1985). *Item response theory: Principles and applications.* Boston: Kluwer Academic.

Hambleton, R. K., Swaminathan, H., & Rogers, H. J. (1991). *Fundamentals of item response theory.* Newbury Park, CA: Sage.

Hambleton, R. K., & Zaal, J. N. (Eds.). (1991). *Advances in educational and psychological testing.* Boston: Kluwer Academic.

Harris, D. (1989). Comparison of 1-, 2-, and 3-parameter IRT models. *Educational Measurement: Issues and Practice, 8,* 35–41.

Holland, P. W., & Thayer, D. T. (1988). Differential item performance and the Mantel-Haenszel procedure. In H. Wainer & H. Braun (Eds.), *Test validity* (pp. 129–145). Hillsdale, NJ: Lawrence Erlbaum Associates.

Holland, P. W., & Wainer, H. (Eds.). (1993). *Differential item functioning.* Hillsdale, NJ: Lawrence Erlbaum Associates.

Horvath, F. G. (1991, April). *Assessment in Alberta: Dimensions of authenticity.* Paper presented at the meetings of NATD/NCME, Chicago.

Jaeger, R. M. (1989). Certification of student competence. In R. L. Linn (Ed.), *Educational measurement* (3rd ed., pp. 485–514). New York: Macmillan.

Jaeger, R. M. (1992). World class standards, choice, and privatization: Weak measurement serving presumptive policy. *Phi Delta Kappan, 74*(2), 118–128.

Jaeger, R. M. (1995). Setting performance standards through two-stage judgmental policy capturing. *Applied Measurement in Education, 8,* 15–40.

Jensen, A. R. (1982). Reaction time and psychometric g. In H. J. Eysenck (Ed.), *A model for intelligence* (pp. 93–132). Berlin: Springer.

Kane, M. (1994). Validating the performance standards associated with passing scores. *Review of Educational Research, 64*(3), 425–462.

Kentucky Department of Education. (1993). *Kentucky Instructional Results Information System, 1991–92 Technical Report.* Frankfort, KY: Author.

Koretz, D., Stecher, B., Klein, S., & McCaffrey D. (1994). The Vermont portfolio assessment program: Findings and implications. *Educational measurement: Issues and practice, 13*(3), 5–16.

Lapointe, A. E., Mead, N. A., & Askew, J. M. (1992). *Learning mathematics* (Report No. 22-CAEP-01). Princeton, NJ: Educational Testing Service.

Lapointe, A. E., Mead, N. A., & Phillips, G. W. (1989). *A world of differences: An international assessment of mathematics and science* (Report 19-CAEP-01). Princeton, NJ: Educational Testing Service.

Linn, R. L. (1989). Current perspectives and future directions. In R. L. Linn (Ed.), *Educational measurement* (3rd ed., pp. 1–10). New York: Macmillan.

Linn, R. L. (1991, April). *Alternative forms of assessment.* Paper presented at a meeting of American Educational Research Association, Chicago.

Linn, R. L. (1993). Educational assessment: Expanded expectations and challenges. *Educational Evaluation and Policy Analysis, 15*(1), 1–16.

Linn, R. L. (1994). Performance assessment: Policy promises and technical measurement standards. *Educational Researcher, 24*(10), 4–14.

Linn, R. L. (1995). High-stakes uses of performance-based assessments: Rationale, examples, and problems of comparability. In T. Oakland & R. K. Hambleton (Eds.), *International perspectives on academic assessment* (pp. 49–73). Boston: Kluwer Academic.

Linn, R. L., Baker, E. L., & Dunbar, S. B. (1991). Complex, performance-based assessment: Expectations and validation criteria. *Educational Researcher, 20*(8), 15–21.

Linn, R. L., & Burton, E. (1994). Performance-based assessment: Implications of task specificity. *Educational Measurement: Issues and Practice, 13*(1), 5–8, 15.

Linn, R. L., & Harnisch, D. L. (1981). Interactions between item content and group membership on achievement test items. *Journal of Educational Measurement, 18*(2), 109–118.

Livingston, S. A., & Zieky, M. J. (1982). *Passing scores: A manual for setting standards of performance on educational and occupational tests.* Princeton, NJ: Educational Testing Service.

Lord, F. M. (1952). A theory of test scores. *Psychometric Monographs, 7.*

Lord, F. M. (1953). The relation of test score to the trait underlying the test. *Educational and Psychological Measurement, 13,* 517–548.

Lord, F. M. (1968). An analysis of the *Verbal Scholastic Aptitude Test* using Birnbaum's three-parameter logistic model. *Educational and Psychological Measurement, 28,* 989–1020.

Lord, F. M. (1980). *Applications of item response theory to practical testing problems.* Hillsdale, NJ: Lawrence Erlbaum Associates.

Lord, F. M., & Novick, M. R. (1968). *Statistical theories of mental test scores.* Reading, MA: Addison-Wesley.

Madaus, G. F. (1988). The influence of testing on the curriculum. In I. N. Tanner (Ed.), *Critical issues in curriculum: 87th yearbook of the National Society for the Study of Education* (pp. 83–121). Chicago: University of Chicago Press.

Messick, S. (1989). Validity. In R. L. Linn (Ed.), *Educational measurement* (3rd ed., pp. 13–104). New York: Macmillan.

Psychological Corporation. (1993). *Metropolitan Achievement Tests (Seventh Edition) Technical Manual (Spring Data).* Orlando, FL: Author.

Putnam, S. E., Pence, P., & Jaeger, R. M. (1995). A multistage dominant profile method for setting standards on complex performance assessments. *Applied Measurement in Education, 8.*

Rasch, G. (1960). *Probabilistic models for some intelligence and attainment tests.* Copenhagen: Danish Institute for Educational Research.

Resnick, L. B. & Resnick, D. P. (1992). Assessing the thinking curriculum: New tools for educational reform. In B. R. Gifford & M. C. O'Connor (Eds.), *Changing assessments: Alternative views of aptitude, achievement, and instruction* (pp. 37–75). Boston: Kluwer Academic.

Robinson, G. E. & Brandon, D. P. (1994). *NAEP test scores: Should they be used to compare and rank state educational quality?* Arlington, VA: Educational Research Service.

Roeber, E., & Dutcher, P. (1989). Michigan's innovative assessment of reading. *Educational Leadership, 46*(7), 64–70.

Roskam, E. E. (in press). Models for speed and time-limit tests. In W. J. van der Linden & R. K. Hambleton (Eds.), *Handbook of item response theory.* New York: Springer.

Rudner, L. M., & Boston, C. (1994). Performance assessment. *ERIC Review, 3*(1), 2–12.

Rudner, L. M., Getson, P. R., & Knight, D. L. (1980). A Monte Carlo comparison of seven biased item detection techniques. *Journal of Educational Measurement, 17*, 1–10.

Schafer, W. D. (1991). Essential assessment skills in professional education of teachers. *Educational Measurement: Issues and Practice, 10*, 3–6, 12.

Scheuneman, J. D. (1987). An experimental, exploratory study of causes of bias in test items. *Journal of Educational Measurement, 24*, 97–118.

Shavelson, R. J., Baxter, G. P., & Pine, J. (1992). Performance assessments: Political rhetoric and measurement reality. *Educational Researcher, 21*(5), 22–27.

Shavelson, R. J., & Webb, N. (1991). *Generalizability theory: A primer.* Newbury Park, CA: Sage.

Shepard, L. A. (1989). Why we need better assessments. *Educational Leadership, 46*(7), 4–6.

Messick, S. (1994). Foundations of validity: Meaning and consequences in psychological assessment. *European Journal of Psychological Assessment, 10*(1), 1–9.

Mullis, I. V. S., Dossey, J. A., Owen, E. H., & Phillips, G. W. (1993). *NAEP 1992 mathematics report card for the nation and the states* (Report No. 23-ST02). Washington, DC: National Center for Education Statistics.

National Assessment Governing Board (1992). *Reading framework for the 1992 National Assessment of Educational Progress.* Washington: Author.

National Council of Teachers of Mathematics. (1989). *Curriculum and evaluation standards for school mathematics.* Reston, VA: Author.

New Standards Project (1993). *Harriet Tubman* (4th grade pilot assessment task). Pittsburgh, PA: University of Pittsburgh, Learning Research and Development Center.

Nickerson, R. S. (1989). New directions in educational assessment. *Educational Researcher, 18*(9), 3–7.

Office of Technology Assessment, Congress of the United States (1992). *Testing in American schools: Asking the right questions.* Washington, DC: Government Printing Office.

O'Neill, K., & Powers, D. E. (1993, April). *The performance of examinee subgroups on a computer-administered test of basic academic skills.* Paper presented at a meeting of the National Council on Measurement in Education, Atlanta, GA.

Osterlind, S. J. (1989). *Constructing test items.* Boston: Kluwer Academic.

Pashley, P., & Phillips, G. W. (1993). *Toward world-class standards: A research study linking international and national assessments* (Final Report). Princeton, NJ: Educational Testing Service.

Phillips, G. W., Mullis, I. V., Bourque, M. L., Williams, P. L., Hambleton, R. K., Owen, E. H., & Barton, P. E. (1993). *Interpreting NAEP scales.* Washington, DC: National Center for Education Statistics.

Popham, W. J. (1978). *Criterion-referenced measurement.* Englewood Cliffs, NJ: Prentice Hall.

Popham, W. J., & Hambleton, R. K. (1990). Can you pass the test on testing? *Principal*, 38–39.

Shepard, L. A., Camilli, G., & Williams, D. M. (1984). Accounting for statistical artifacts in item bias research. *Journal of Educational Statistics, 9*, 93–128.

Stiggins, R. J. (1994). *Student-centered classroom assessment.* New York: Macmillan.

Stocking, M. L., Swanson, L., & Pearlman M. (1991a). *Automated item selection (AIS) methods in the ETS testing environment* (Research Memorandum 91-5). Princeton, NJ: Educational Testing Service.

Stocking, M. L., Swanson, L., & Pearlman, M. (1991b). *Automated item selection using item response theory* (Research Report 91-9). Princeton, NJ: Educational Testing Service.

Taylor, C. (1994). Assessment for measurement or standards: The peril and promise of large-scale assessment reform. *American Educational Research Journal, 31*(2), 231–262.

Traub, R. E. (1994, June). *Facing the challenge of multidimensionality in performance assessment.* Invited address at the sixth Ottawa Conference on Medical Education, Toronto.

Traub, R. E., & Fisher, C. W. (1977). On the equivalence of constructed-response and multiple-choice tests. *Applied Psychological Measurement, 1*(3), 355–369.

van der Linden, W. J. (1995). Advances in computer applications. In T. Oakland & R. K. Hambleton (Eds.), *International perspectives on academic assessment* (pp. 105–123). Boston: Kluwer Academic.

van der Linden, W. J., & Boekkooi-Timminga, E. (1989). A maximin model for test design with practical constraints. *Psychometrika, 53*, 237–247.

van der Linden, W. J., & Hambleton, R. K. (Eds.). *Handbook of item response theory.* New York: Springer.

van der Vleuten, C. P. M., & Swanson, D. B. (1990). Assessment of clinical skills with standardized patients: State of the art. *Teaching and Learning in Medicine, 2*, 58–76.

Wainer, H. (1993). Measurement problems. *Journal of Educational Measurement, 30*(1), 1–21.

Wainer, H., Dorans, N. J., Green, B. F., Steinberg, L., Flaugher, R., Mislevy, R. J., & Thissen, D. (Eds.). (1990). *Computerized adaptive testing: A primer.* Hillsdale, NJ: Lawrence Erlbaum Associates.

Wainer, H., & Thissen, D. (1994). On examinee choice in educational testing. *Review of Educational Research, 64*(1), 159–195.

Westbury, I. (1992). Comparing American and Japanese achievement: Is the United States really a low achiever? *Educational Researcher, 21*(5), 18–24.

White, E. M. (1985). *Teaching and assessing writing.* San Francisco: Jossey-Bass.

Wiggins, G. (1989a). A true test: Toward more authentic and equitable assessment. *Phi Delta Kappan, 70*(9), 703–713.

Wiggins, G. (1989b). Teaching to the (authentic) test. *Educational Leadership, 46*(7), 41–47.

Wiggins, G. (1993). Assessment: Authenticity, context, and validity. *Phi Delta Kappan,* November, 200–214.

Wright, B. D. (1968). Sample-free test calibration and person measurement. *Proceedings of the 1967 Invitational Conference on Testing Problems.* Princeton, NJ: Educational Testing Service.

Wright, B. D., & Stone, M. H. (1979). *Best test design.* Chicago: MESA Press.

Zwick, R., Donoghue, J. R., & Grima, A. (1993). Assessment of differential item functioning for performance tasks. *Journal of Educational Measurement, 30*(3), 233–251.

# SCHOOL AND PROGRAM EVALUATION

## Eva L. Baker

UNIVERSITY OF CALIFORNIA, LOS ANGELES

## David Niemi

UNIVERSITY OF MISSOURI, COLUMBIA

Educational evaluation is the process of making systematic judgments about the quality of educational programs, services, products, and personnel. Although approaches to evaluation are derived from a variety of disciplines, a special relationship exists between educational psychology and evaluation. Because they often share objects of study and method, the boundaries between research in educational psychology and evaluation are blurred.

The chapter begins with a discussion of educational psychologists whose work illustrates the integration of research and evaluation or who, as psychologists, have particularly influenced the practice of evaluation. We then turn to the emergence of evaluation as a field of study in its own right and focus on its diverse knowledge base. To illustrate its evolution, we consider formal evaluation approaches and models emanating from different knowledge sources and describe efforts to classify and compare evaluation models.

The discussion then considers ways in which evaluation practices affect schools. We examine characteristics of evaluation in innovative educational programs, in complex, large-scale programs, in educational policy, and in the evaluation of institutions. We also review the role that student assessment plays in educational evaluation. Finally, we offer predictions about the future of educational evaluation.

## EDUCATIONAL PSYCHOLOGY AND EVALUATION

Historically, educational psychology and evaluation have much in common. Both disciplines were originally rooted in practical concerns; they were founded with the intention to improve the quality of education by providing a sound basis for decisions about alternative courses of educational action. Both disciplines moved from an exclusive focus on the student or learner to consider other participants in the teaching and learning process; both relinquished their early concentration on the details of practice in favor of more general formulations of educational principles. In psychology, examples of this evolution can be found in the work of Rice, Thorndike, Binet, and Vygotsky, all of whom were committed to improving learning. Not coincidentally, these psychologists also made contributions to evaluation practice.

Joseph Rice, for example, turned from medical practice to psychology and began research on improving schools, carrying out large-scale comparative studies of U.S. students' proficiency in spelling, arithmetic, and language (Rice, 1893, 1913). Rice's large-scale testing methods and efforts to determine average scores at each grade level deeply influenced the work of Edward Thorndike, who elaborated Rice's techniques and trained a number of measurement specialists, who in turn became test developers.

Thorndike is perhaps best known in psychology and education for his systematic application of learning theory to simple skill instruction, for his fundamental psychological laws, including the law of effect (Thorndike, 1913), and for his extended influence on instruction in arithmetic. But he also taught and wrote about measurement theory, introducing a number of technical innovations. He was one of the earliest to claim that intelligence tests should measure ability to learn (Thorndike, 1926), and one of the first to make a case for the importance of assessing transfer of knowledge (Thorndike & Woodworth, 1901), a key element in much of the evaluation of instruction.

The work reported herein was supported under the Educational Research and Development Center Program, cooperative agreement number R117G10027 and CFDA catalogue number 84.117G, as administered by the Office of Educational Research and Improvement, U.S. Department of Education.

The findings and opinions expressed in this report do not reflect the position or policies of the Office of Educational Research and Improvement or the U.S. Department of Education.

A thank you to Amy Williams, John Joon Lee, Zenaida Aguirre-Muñoz, David Westhoff and to Marvin Alkin for their assistance.

In the first decade of the 20th century, psychologists Alfred Binet and Theophile Simon (1916) took up the pragmatic task of identifying "mentally deficient" schoolchildren in France. In an effort to develop a series of tasks that would effectively differentiate levels of intellectual development, Binet tested hundreds of items. His empirical approach to item analysis, norming, and validation was at odds with the conventional practice of using informal logic to design tests, but eighty years later many of the item design methods he pioneered are still in use.

Another influential psychologist, Lev Vygotsky, undertook a number of studies with significant practical implications. To test the effects of introducing formal schooling in central Asia, Vygotsky and Luria (1993) compared the performance of schooled and unschooled subjects on a battery of psychological tests of perceptual and memory strategies, classification, problem solving, logical deduction, and metacognition. Their work—one of the earliest attempts to investigate systematically the effects of school-based literacy—has influenced developmental and educational psychology in both the United States and Europe. Vygotsky also developed methods for obtaining data on the dynamics of knowledge development by assessing the extent to which subjects could demonstrate assisted and unassisted competencies. He conceptualized the difference in competencies as a "zone of proximal development" (Vygotsky, 1978). This research has been a major stimulus for researchers and evaluators, including Ann Brown and her colleagues (see, e.g., A. L. Brown, Bransford, Ferrara, & Campione, 1983; A. L. Brown & Ferrara, 1985).

Two streams of research, one in public school education and one in the military, further illustrate the intellectual connections between educational psychology and evaluation. The Eight-Year Study (see Madaus & Stufflebeam, 1989; E. R. Smith & R. W. Tyler, 1942), was a landmark effort in which innovations in public school curriculum and teaching practices in the United States were systematically assessed. This study used carefully developed measures as well as qualitative techniques to determine program effects on student performance. With this study, Ralph W. Tyler and his colleagues laid the foundation for thought about school-developed educational achievement and for the domain of action in educational development and improvement. The Eight-Year Study of educational innovation led Tyler (1942), who was trained as an educational psychologist, to organize the tasks and goals of evaluation in a framework that was to be the dominant paradigm for almost half a century. With this paradigm, presented in *Basic Principles of Curriculum and Instruction* (1949), Tyler defined and prescribed key elements in school programs, including the delineation of goals and objectives, opportunity to learn, and the integration of theories of learning in decision-making and assessment. His work was elaborated and extended by his students Bloom and Krathwohl, who emphasized the detailed analysis and classification of goals and objectives and their corresponding assessments (Bloom & Krathwohl, 1956; Krathwohl, Bloom, & Masia, 1964). Tyler, as director of the Examination Staff of the U.S. Armed Forces Institute, also brought his concern for evaluation of outcomes to the military, a sector that has often combined approaches from educational psychology and evaluation. Tyler continued his efforts until 1994, emphasizing the importance of practical thought and sensible application of research in

evaluation, measurement, policy development, and technology-based learning. His work, compiled by Madaus and Stufflebeam (1989), deeply colored many of the studies and programs reported in this chapter.

Psychology and evaluation were eventually integrated to serve the purposes of military training, notably in the work of social and experimental psychologists assigned to training commands during the Second World War. As part of the war effort, expertise in psychology was applied in an attempt to use scientific methods to design efficient training. The science of psychology was applied to three main educational problems: (a) the selection and assignment of individuals to training and to tasks at which they could succeed, (b) the development of systematic training programs for the inculcation of skills, and (c) the social aspects of team development. The first of these areas, the measurement of human abilities, generated a robust branch of educational psychology and provided a key methodological foundation for the field of educational evaluation. The Army General Classification Test, developed in 1940 by the Personnel Testing Section of the Adjutant General's Office, was used to determine the eligibility of trainees for a variety of military roles (Baker & Stites, 1991). Buoyed by the apparent success of selection testing for military training in World War II, psychologists continued to advocate the broad use of similar tests in vocational and educational contexts. An excellent analysis of the intellectual roots of selection testing can be found in the report of the Committee on Educational Research of the National Academy of Education (Cronbach & Suppes, 1969).

The second area in which military programs brought together psychology and evaluation was in the development of training skills, especially those emphasizing the acquisition of procedural knowledge and physical skills. The focus of this training research was twofold: to train the desired skills and to develop a technology of learning. The learning technology research aimed at analyzing and automating the procedures used by students in their acquisition of technical tasks (Skinner, 1954). Not surprisingly, the goal of creating a learning technology was married to the tasks of using tools and technology systems, and the military was the first major user of technology as a teaching and assessment medium. Procedural training in the use of equipment and in the use of technology-based systems created a legacy in the area of educational psychology that can be traced through the influential writings of Gagné (1965), Lumsdaine (1960), and the early works of Glaser (1963, 1965). In their present incarnation, learning technology and concepts of training are central to the design of modern workforce training systems (U.S. Department of Labor, 1991).

World War II also stimulated the application of social psychological principles as means of influencing the opinions and social behavior of military personnel. Through a series of experiments, some of which are reported by Hovland, Lumsdaine, and Sheffield (1949), the film series "Why We Fight" was developed; the history of its development shows how systematic applications and controlled experimentation based on psychological theories were used to influence attitudes and opinions. These studies also illustrate the sophistication of measures and experimental methods employed to evaluate the effectiveness of the interventions. For example, one inquiry investigated ways to enhance and supplement film messages about the valor and suffering of the British and Russian allies (Hovland et al., 1949).

Because the military had access to a large pool of captive subjects, psychologists were able to evaluate the effects of psychological theories of learning on a far grander scale than in other venues.

The integration of educational psychology and evaluation activities persisted in military and industrial training during the 1950s and early 1960s in the form of behaviorally oriented psychological research and development. Early behavioral studies, summarized by Holland and Skinner (1961) and Markle (1965), were based on the integration of psychological theory, Tylerian assessment, and training traditions. Carefully specified instructional outcomes, or desired objectives, served as dependent variables for the design of tightly focused instructional segments. This work was extended in the 1960s to measurement in school environments through the work of applied behaviorists such as Hively and his colleagues (Hively, Patterson, & Page, 1968). Popham (1967) concentrated on its use in teacher education. Schutz (1970) and others applied integrated psychology and evaluation approaches to the development of school curricula in regional educational laboratories supported by the federal government.

During this same period, a national commitment was made to improve the educational status of minority students. Enacted in 1965 as an outgrowth of the civil rights movement and the War on Poverty, new legislation, the Elementary and Secondary Education Act (ESEA), further legitimated the integration of educational psychology and the evaluation of interventions in the service of national goals. Moreover, the scale of application to the civilian educational sector through the enactment of Title I, with its focus on poor and disadvantaged students, kicked educational evaluation into a rapid and unprecedented scale-up process. More attention is given to the evaluation of Title I in a later section.

## THE EVOLUTION OF EDUCATIONAL EVALUATION AND SOURCES OF EVALUATION KNOWLEDGE

Driven in the 1960s by external requirements to report the effectiveness of national educational programs, evaluation developed in a pattern similar to that seen in other hybrid fields. Trailblazers in the new field drew from existing theoretical and practical knowledge in other disciplines. When the 1965 ESEA legislation created strong incentives for conducting evaluation studies, training of evaluators, and codifying and disseminating new evaluation practices, many of those responsible for evaluations looked to the academic community for help. Through a coordinated program of federal grants and contracts supporting key university groups, hotbeds of educational evaluative activity were created throughout the country. Ohio State University, the University of Chicago, the University of Illinois, Stanford University, the University of California at Los Angeles, the University of Wisconsin, and Northwestern University were among the centers of intensive effort. Predictably, academics used what they knew as the basis for their strategies. Researchers in psychology relied on canonical methods in science, particularly experimentation and measurement. Educators with scholarly interests in schooling and administration cleaved to formal orga-

nizational approaches to evaluation. Educators from the humanities promoted evaluation strategies that featured criticism and analysis over empiricism. A discordant chorus of evaluation theorists abstracted these approaches into rough themes based on the priority each theorist placed on evaluation knowledge sources, purposes, and users. Proponents of various models engaged in intense debate about the ideal forms evaluations should take, and pejorative terms, such as "soft" and "reductionist," were traded in public discourse. The intensity of the conflict subsided in the 1980s. But these disputatious origins continue to permeate today's evaluation practices and will undoubtedly reappear in future evaluation practice. Four disparate sources for evaluation thinking are briefly reviewed here: experimentation, measurement, systems analysis, and interpretive approaches. We also present examples of evaluation approaches derived from these sources.

### Experimentation

One technical advance influencing educational evaluation was the development of experimental methodologies to strengthen the quality of inferences drawn from empirical work. One early group of evaluators used social science research methods as their principal referent. If the problem of evaluation was to determine whether an intervention was working, many reasoned that it was essential to have evaluation studies based on research designs, permitting valid inferences. The focus on scientific designs and appropriate inferences was to emerge as a major, persistent theme for proponents and critics of actual evaluation studies.

The development of what was often overgeneralized as "the scientific method"—the creation of experimental designs and statistical tests, as exemplified in Fisher's *The Design of Experiments* (1951)—provided a touchstone for a large segment of educational research and evaluation. The elaboration and clarification of this general line of work in Campbell and Stanley's chapter in the first *Handbook of Research on Teaching* (1963) influenced those responsible for training researchers and evaluators for careers in educational analysis. The underlying purpose of Campbell and Stanley's chapter, the investigation of sources of invalidity in research studies, pushed one flank of evaluation practice into concerns about weak and strong inferences, adequacy of design comparisons, strategies to ensure randomization, and precise implementation of experimental treatments.

Cook and Campbell (1979) extended this work on the validity of designs in a follow-up book based on their and others' experience implementing experimental and quasi-experimental studies. Throughout the 1970s Campbell and his supporters (Lumsdaine & Bennett, 1975) consistently asserted the primacy of experimental over quasi-experimental design and the requirement for internal validity as a precondition for external validity. Experimental purists were concerned not only with random assignment of students, but with issues of unit of assignment and analysis. Classrooms, not students, were identified as the relevant unit for most educational evaluation, a view that increased the difficulty of applying the methodology. In the spirit of avoiding contamination and increasing internal validity, experimentalists argued that educational "treatments" should not be modified during the evaluation period so that clear distinctions could be drawn between experimental and control effects. This stricture limited the practicality of this approach for evolving school programs. As the 1970s wore on, correlational, naturalistic, and qualitative methodologies gradually augmented experimental and quasi-experimental approaches. Yet reliance on the experimental paradigm persists. Many still advocate the use of randomized field experiments, where allowable under legal and ethical constraints, as the best strategy for determining program effectiveness (e.g., Boruch, 1991). In practice, the delivery of educational programs of extended length and variable intensity, as well as ethical standards to provide the best options for all children, has limited the use of the true experiment in educational evaluation.

Tension developed between methodologists who supported the application of experimental designs and analytic techniques based on them and those who argued for a more pragmatic stance. The argument is one of trading internal and external validity, or the validity of the design and the validity of the broader inferences drawn from the results. The pragmatists, as represented by Cronbach (Cronbach, 1982; Cronbach et al., 1981), argued for the relevance and credibility of evaluation findings as standards to be used along with scientific criteria. The development and dissemination of sophisticated regression approaches (Kerlinger & Pedhazur, 1973) provided the analytic support for natural comparisons that appeared to fit better the realities of school program implementation.

## Measurement

A second ready source for evaluation concepts was in educational and psychological measurement. Although most measurement efforts had focused on the assessment of individual differences for the purposes of selection and classification, these approaches were later adapted to the measurement of achievement, conceived by many to be the best criterion of school effectiveness. Such measures reported student performance normatively and for the most part used item development strategies and scoring techniques intended to assess efficiently broad areas of content. It was logical to believe that educational programs should affect student learning, and the use of standardized norm-referenced tests as credible dependent measures defined impact in a way that was rarely challenged. Cost and time constraints of most evaluation studies also required evaluators to use convenient measures and look at immediate rather than delayed or long-range effects of programs. Commercially available standardized tests provided strong psychometric data about their reliability, and their national distribution and generality of content were thought to permit fair comparisons. Yet there were rarely analyses of the validity of their content or formats for the interventions assessed.

Given the salience and low cost of standardized norm-referenced tests, it is not surprising that many early evaluations relied on them to judge program impact. Not everyone interested in assessing the effect of instruction or training was sanguine about the use of these tests, however. Glaser (1963) raised questions about the design and reporting of standardized tests, proposing instead criterion-referenced measurement. Popham and Husek (1969) and Millman (1974) also argued that outcome measures should be more closely related to goals of particular programs. Nonetheless, the ubiquity of standardized tests and their

acceptance by the public as proxies for student achievement seriously constrained the direction of evaluation. Even today, the standardized test is regarded as the single best criterion in much of the public policy sector. The rise or fall of scores on these tests is still used as an indicator of the quality of educational programs. For many, the practice of evaluation is reduced to finding an acceptable test, administering it on a regular schedule, and comparing the scores of students in different programs.

## Emergence of Systems Thinking

A third source of knowledge for evaluation practice came from outside the realm of educational psychology, from the field of systems analysis (Churchman, 1971; Weiner, 1948). In simple terms, systems analysis examined a broad set of variables likely to interact in a complex process or organization. Whereas early model builders had concerned themselves primarily with scientific and measurement models focused on collecting data to assist presumptively rational decision-making processes, later theorists asserted that decision-makers often could not or did not bother to use scientific data (e.g., Weiss, 1972, 1973). New models were then advanced that focused on ensuring the utility of evaluation results. In the early 1960s, systems thinking was everywhere. It was most dramatic in the program, planning, and budgeting approaches taken in industry and by the Department of Defense (Schlesinger, 1963; Wildavsky, 1964, 1972). Cost-benefit analysis (Levin, 1983; Rossi, Freeman, & Wright, 1979) also derived from systems orientations. Systems analysis captivated both educational policymakers and program designers, for the approach was at once technical, congruent with the influential writings of Tyler, and supported intellectually by tenets of the dominant psychological paradigm, behaviorism.

One of the best-known approaches, Stufflebeam's CIPP (context, input, process, product) model, used systems analysis to classify managerial decisions and the information needed to make them (see, e.g., Stufflebeam et al., 1971). Stufflebeam's work was influential in shifting evaluation attention to include background factors and inputs and broadened the relatively narrow approach of most experimentalists. Closely related was Alkin's model (1969, 1991), which stressed the importance of identifying evaluation needs as a basis for evaluation design and reporting. Decision models typically assumed that the primary function of evaluation was to assist decision-makers in determining whether the stated goals of a program had been achieved (Provus, 1969), and that the goals themselves need not be evaluated. Offspring of early decision models included utilization approaches developed by Alkin, Daillak, and White (1979), Patton (1978, 1988), and Wholey (1979, 1983); these approaches attempted to deal with how evaluation information is actually used in the real world. Arguments raised by Weiss (1972, 1973) and others about the diffuse and often unpredictable uses of evaluation results influenced Cronbach's (1982) conception of evaluation as deeply embedded in social and political activity rather than as the product of rational, decontextualized decision-making. Although it is unimaginable that the creators of decision-oriented evaluation models would support this tactic, evaluation practitioners often interpreted the stages of decision models mechanistically, marching in precise steps from needs assessments to impact studies, with little concern for iterative feedback procedures and less understanding of the complex role evaluation plays in program development. Systems approaches were also applied to the design of instructional products and materials (Baker, 1973; Hemphill, 1969). To this day, systems models continue to influence leading formulations of educational reform (M. S. Smith & O'Day, 1991).

## Interpretive Approaches

Interpretive epistemologies provided a fourth general source of knowledge for evaluation. Early methodological debates sometimes took a philosophical turn, as in Scriven's (1967) response to Cronbach's (1963) discussion of the limits of empiricism in evaluative contexts, but for the most part philosophical assumptions stayed implicit and argumentation focused on nontheoretical matters, such as how to maximize the utility of results for achieving socially determined goals.

In the past 20 years, philosophical orientations have become increasingly explicit and have gained prominence as an issue in evaluation design. An example is the recent use of hermeneutical philosophy and interpretive theories of knowledge as grounds for conducting evaluations as exercises in interpretation and judgment (Guba & Lincoln, 1989). Theorists desiring to present a critique of what they regard as the unmerited dominance of positivism in evaluation have argued that any evaluation approach has epistemological implications, and that the types of information conventionally collected imply positivistic, reductionist views of human knowledge.

Interpretive theories differ in detail but generally converge on the point that the purpose of program evaluation, for example, is not to make causal inferences about the relationship between particular educational programs or teacher behaviors and outcome measures of program effectiveness. Rather, the purpose of such evaluation is to generate descriptive interpretations and judgments of the complex processes that influence student and teacher performance, and of relationships among those processes, although this interpretation might well be challenged on practical grounds by the sponsors of particular evaluation studies.

Within the broad framework of interpretive or hermeneutical approaches to evaluation, the type of evidence to be gathered is typically influenced by the belief that there are no absolute standards that can be used to judge a program or individual performance. The overriding aim, therefore, is not to establish what the facts are, but to examine what a situation means to the people involved in it, what their outlook is, and what frames of reference they use to make sense of and evaluate the situation. These models parallel the growth of situated cognition theories in cognitive psychology (J. S. Brown, Collins, & Duguid, 1989). As Stake (1978) put it, the goal is to understand, not explain.

Among the models deriving from the interpretive perspective are judgmental approaches in which the considered opinion of experts or others involved in the evaluation process forms the basis of evaluation. Stake's (1973) early "countenance" model, for example, highlighted the importance of judgments relevant to various stakeholders in the evaluation process. Data to be collected under this influential model included program rationale; information on program antecedents, transactions, and outcomes; specification of standards; and judg-

ments about the quality of the program, blending elements of systems and philosophical thinking. Other approaches advocate evaluation procedures based on connoisseurship (Eisner, 1985, 1991) or critical judgments (e.g., Willis, 1978) of highly trained experts in the subject matters of interest. In these models, the meaning derived by participants presumably benefits from the power of disciplinary standards.

Some recent interpretive models are noteworthy for their commitment to democratic ethics and client-centered methodology. These approaches generally require extensive and repeated interaction with clients and depend to a high degree on intuitive judgments. Exemplars include transaction and responsive models requiring that evaluators respond primarily to audience concerns and values, and participatory models calling for full participation by all audiences for the evaluation (e.g., Lincoln & Guba, 1985).

Critics of stakeholder approaches have argued that stakeholders may be interested only in trivial issues, and that evaluations addressing those issues may be usable but not worthwhile. To cite one example, in an evaluation of community health centers reported by Salasin (1980), information requested by managers centered on billing and public relations, not on the effectiveness of the centers in addressing targeted social problems.

## CLASSIFYING EVALUATION MODELS

At midcentury, few writers other than Tyler and Cronbach had attempted conceptual analyses of the domain of evaluation. By the late 1960s, the effort to produce systematic models was under full steam, and by 1987 at least 50 evaluation models had been developed (Worthen & Sanders, 1987). A handful of these models have significantly influenced both the design of evaluations and the conception of evaluation as a discipline, but most cannot be called scientific models in any deep sense. In most instances, their function has been to explicate a particular evaluation orientation—for example, to focus attention on certain philosophical assumptions, on a methodology, or on a framework for the interpretation and use of evaluation. Such models have been variously tuned to the needs of particular evaluation contexts, and experience shows that extremely diverse practices can be derived from the same model.

To clarify and resolve some of the apparent dissonance across models and to provide heuristic guidance for evaluation practice, a large number of competing classifications have surfaced. A successful classification of existing models could provide obvious theoretical and practical benefits, making it possible, for example, to compare models on the basis of underlying principles, to predict some of the differential effects of employing different models, and to make methodological decisions. Alkin and Ellett (1979) add that classifications encourage the definition and introduction of new concepts and can lead to the formulation of new views about evaluation.

The following review is intended to illustrate the striking range of conceptual schemes that have been turned to the purpose of sorting and comparing evaluation models. House, an influential proponent of evaluation as an instrument for social justice, focused his 1980 categorization scheme on the different ways in which evaluation models make validity claims.

Systems analysis approaches, for instance, claim to be scientific, following rigorous procedures to produce reliable information, but yield findings, according to House (1980), that often are not credible to those evaluated and may be unfair or undemocratic as well. Behavioral objectives approaches base their claims for validity on specification of the domain and behaviors to be observed, holding programs accountable for their stated goals but not including methods for judging the correctness of the goals. Decision-making and goal-free approaches claim validity by virtue of utility to decision-makers and lack of bias, respectively. These four approaches are termed "objectivist" by House. They contrast with the four "subjectivist" approaches, which invoke experience and credibility rather than scientific method as the basis for validity. House's subjectivist approaches are art criticism, professional review, quasi-legal approaches, and case studies. Differences among these approaches stem from the types of experience relied on for validation. Art criticism approaches rely on the experience of an expert judge or connoisseur, professional review on a collective tradition of professional expertise, quasi-legal approaches on the procedural fairness of legal tradition, and case study approaches on the experience of the participants in and audience for a given evaluation.

Another, more parsimonious scheme is Cook and Shadish's (1986) three-category, quasi-chronological analysis. One type of evaluation in this analysis, called "manipulable solutions," uses evaluation to test techniques for solving social problems (e.g., Campbell, 1969, 1971; Scriven, 1983). Advocates of these approaches, which dominated early evaluation research, hold that it is less important to know how or why programs work than to know whether they work. Cook and Shadish argue that these models lost popularity because of the difficulty of using their experimental research-based techniques in educational settings, and because proponents did not have strong plans for disseminating results. These inadequacies led to the development of "generalized explanation" models embodying the notion that the complexity of educational programs can be expressed best in terms of higher order statistical interactions, not simple main effects. Rather than the summative decisions favored by manipulable solutions theorists, generalizable explanation theorists use descriptive and correlational techniques to define the program, how it is implemented, and relations between aspects of implementation and program effects. Models developed by Cronbach (1982), Rossi (Chen & Rossi, 1980, 1983), and Weiss (1977) are cited by Cook and Shadish as exemplifying generalized explanations. Later, according to Cook and Shadish, "stakeholder service" models emerged that subordinated every other component of the evaluation process to the problem of generating information useful to stakeholders, with some disagreement across models about who the relevant stakeholders might be. Two subgroups are identified. In one group of models, program administrators and decision-makers are the essential audience (e.g., Patton, 1978; Wholey, 1983); in another set of models (e.g., Guba & Lincoln, 1981; Stake, 1983; Stake & Easley, 1978), evaluation addresses a broader array of stakeholders, including program managers, program providers such as teachers, service recipients such as students, local boards, parents, and so forth. Regardless of audience, there is agreement in stakeholder models that evaluation should be more concerned with understanding and providing informa-

tion on particular programs than with generalizing findings to other programs or projects.

Cook and Shadish's scheme does not capture the diversity of other classifications such as Stake's 9- and 11-category systems (Stake, 1973, 1991). Stake calls all evaluation models "persuasions," meaning that they essentially represent attempts to sway others to the beliefs of their authors. The persuasions in his 11-category system include and elaborate on headings used by House and by Cook and Shadish, adding (a) accountability, intended to "assure that new promises, previous goal commitments, and community customs are honored" (Stake, 1991, p. 71); (b) case study, focusing on program contexts; (c) democratic, countering authoritarian control; (d) ethnographic, emphasizing cultural relationships and information; (e) experimental, establishing causal effects and influences; (f) illuminative, portraying events in terms that are meaningful to evaluation readers; (g) judicial, pitting optimized versions of program pros and cons against one another; and (h) naturalistic, studying "ordinary events in natural settings" (p. 72).

Popham (1975, 1988) has published two classification systems, his latest involving five categories: goal-attainment models, models judging inputs, models judging outputs, decision-facilitation models, and naturalistic models. Other schemes have addressed the same issues with different emphases. Stufflebeam and Webster (1981) used three categories: political, questions, and values orientation; Worthen and Sanders (1987) proposed six: objectives, management, consumer, expertise, adversary, and participant oriented. Alkin & House (1992) have devised a dimensional system, analyzing evaluation practice in terms of methods, values, and uses, each of which varies on a continuum. Methods range from quantitative to qualitative, values from unitary to plural, and uses from instrumental to enlightenment.

Scriven sees the classification of models as a first step toward establishing a general and distinct discipline of evaluation and in a recent article (Scriven, 1994) delineated six "early" views (passing over those that he referred to as "exotica," e.g., jurisprudential and connoisseurship models). His six headings are (a) strong decision support (exemplified by Tyler and Stufflebeam); (b) weak decision support (Alkin); (c) relativistic (Rossi and Freeman; Provus); (d) rich description (Stake); (e) social process (Cronbach and colleagues); and (f) fourth-generation or constructivist (Guba and Lincoln). Finding serious conceptual limitations in all these views, Scriven advances a "transdisciplinary view," which he sees as providing a comprehensive theoretical and technical framework embracing all types, not just program evaluation.

Despite the considerable agreement on model types across classification schemes and the fact that each of the schemes affords a useful framework for thinking about evaluation, the categories of models within these schemes remain problematic. While clarifying thought in the field, extant model typologies are somewhat limited in their practical applications. In nearly all cases the categories within any given scheme are intended to highlight differences in basic orientation among models. In searching for organizing principles, some model builders have chosen to orient their thinking toward program goals, while others have settled elsewhere, such as on the potential uses of evaluation, notions of causality, data collection methods, or theories of knowledge. Not surprisingly, categories within classification systems reflect the diversity of these orientations and are not necessarily logically equivalent. None of the classification schemes constitutes a true taxonomy, and none addresses comprehensively the problem of comparing approaches on single major dimensions, such as the purpose of an evaluation. For example, if a researcher wanted to know which models and methods were most appropriate for a particular evaluative purpose, a review of existing descriptive classifications would provide only minimal guidance. Neither could the researcher rely on an exhaustive review of model descriptions, because not all models explicitly state the purposes for which they are appropriate, nor do they describe the generality of their methods.

A related practical difficulty springs from the disparity of methods advocated in different models. Many types of models advise extensive initial contact with program designers or overseers to identify the ostensible program objectives, but Scriven's arguments (1967, 1973, 1991) are directed against such contact and against an emphasis on the detailed elicitation of program goals. Shadish, Cook, and Leviton (1991) observe other intermodel contradictions. Decision-oriented models, for example, often describe relatively formal, stepwise procedures for collecting, analyzing, and reporting information to decisionmakers (e.g., Alkin, 1969; Wholey, 1979). Stake (1978), in contrast, spells out a case study approach that requires "descriptions that are complex, holistic, and involving a myriad of not highly isolated variables; data that are likely to be gathered at least partly by personalistic observation; and a writing style that is informal, perhaps narrative, possibly with verbatim quotation, illustration, and even allusion and metaphor" (p. 7). As full implementations of both models, given any reasonable set of practical constraints, would seem to be impractical, questions of picking and choosing are raised. Are these methods logically incompatible, or can they be melded in some way? The most sensible strategy for addressing these and many other evaluation design issues would seem to be pragmatic: What is likely to be the most effective approach to serve particular purposes in a particular context? Example evaluations that attempted to integrate systems and qualitative approaches have been undertaken (Baker, 1976; Shepard & M. L. Smith, 1989). They reflect the realization, forcefully conveyed by Cronbach (1982; Cronbach et al., 1981), that evaluations take place in a world of unending political accommodation where decisions can be shaped but never determined by theory or logic alone.

## TO EVALUATE

Guidance for evaluation practice has recently been provided by the Joint Committee on Standards for Educational Evaluation (1981). Produced by scholars and practitioners from professional organizations, the standards treat topics such as utility, feasibility, propriety, and accuracy (Joint Committee on Standards for Educational Evaluation, 1981; Stufflebeam, 1991). They also include a functional classification of practical issues, such as administering and budgeting evaluations, defining and designing evaluations, and collecting, analyzing, and reporting evaluation information. Systematic attempts to train evaluators in tasks such as these have been widespread (Herman, 1987; Morris, 1978; Worthen & K. R. White, 1987).

To provide guidance in conceiving, organizing, and planning evaluations, we would argue for the practical utility of a scheme organized around dimensions of comparison that could serve as choice points for evaluation design. In addition to identifying key decision points, such a scheme would also permit analysis and comparison of extant models on each of several dimensions, an analysis that only partially exists at present. Dimensions that have consistently emerged as pivotal to evaluation design are characterized below in terms of central issues to be addressed. Note that there is considerable overlap in these questions as well.

1. *Purposes of the evaluation.* It is now commonplace for the purposes of evaluation to be differentiated in terms of the distinction between summative and formative evaluation, terms coined by Scriven (1967) in response to Cronbach's essay on the fundamental importance of using evaluation to improve educational practice. Summative evaluations are generally conducted at the end of a program, with the intention of ascertaining whether the program is worth retaining or adopting; formative evaluations occur during a program for the purpose of modifying a program in use, or perhaps modifying an individual performance (Baker & Alkin, 1973). In many forms of evaluation, Scriven (1991) and others have noted, the two purposes are profoundly intertwined, and it is not necessarily crucial to be able to apply the labels precisely to a given evaluative activity. Questions relevant to evaluation design include: Is the purpose of the evaluation to improve program performance by providing information to guide ongoing management of the program (formative)? Or is it to determine a program's value by comparing it to alternative programs or assessing its impact on relevant problems? Or is the purpose twofold? In reality, because programs develop constituencies, almost all evaluation ultimately serves an improvement purpose.

Long-term or conceptual purposes may also be explicit goals for the study. Will it be useful to infer, for example, *why* a program worked (which is information that might generalize to the design of other programs)?

2. *Scope.* Here it is important to ask, What is the nature and scope of evidence to be gathered? How much information will be collected, and what is the time frame for collecting it?

3. *Clarity of program goals.* How precisely have the goals of the program been formulated? Is the level of precision adequate for design and evaluation purposes? Should the evaluation focus exclusively on whether the program has achieved its aims, or should other important or unanticipated effects also be considered, as in goal-free models (Scriven, 1973)? Should the worth of the goals themselves be evaluated?

4. *Design.* What methods will be used to answer the specified questions? How will program inputs, such as resources, program structure and activities be described? How will the relationship among these entities and outcome measures be modeled? What levels of aggregation will be used? Will outcome measures be derived from program goals, peripheral effects, social science, ethical theories, legislation, or other sources? How will criteria be determined for judging the success of the program or other evaluated entity?

5. *Identity of the evaluator.* Will the program be externally or internally evaluated? What degree of self-interest do the evaluators have? How independent will they be? What role should the evaluators play? (For example, should program goals

be judged, or should evaluators simply provide information to determine whether a program is achieving its stated goals?) What types and levels of expertise do evaluators need? To whom are evaluators primarily responsible—scientific peers? Stakeholder groups? Sponsors?

6. *Participatory nature of the evaluation.* Who will participate, and to what extent? How will participants be recruited, and what will be their roles?

7. *Contextualization.* To what extent should the evaluation process be set apart from or embedded in ongoing program activities?

8. *Reporting.* To whom will results be disseminated, and which methods of reporting will be most useful to them? Should the use of results be facilitated? If so, how?

9. *Political dimensions.* Who has a stake in how the results of the evaluation are determined and reported, and how can the interests of all stakeholders be served? What are the likely consequences for various stakeholders? Should persons being evaluated have a say in how their own evaluation is conducted?

10. *Costs.* Given available resources, what type of evaluation can be done? Will this form of evaluation be worthwhile or significant to anyone? (This question links costs to other dimensions.) Given the expected benefits, would the projected costs be more effectively allocated elsewhere?

From this review of evolving program evaluation approaches and efforts to schematize them, we move to the context of evaluation as it affects schools. This topic covers an astonishingly diverse collection of evaluation endeavors, but we focus on the most paradigmatic, program evaluation.

## EVALUATION AS IT AFFECTS SCHOOLS

Evaluations in schools have historically focused on one of four areas: (a) the evaluation of identifiable programs, (b) the evaluation of policies affecting the schools, (c) the evaluation of student attainment, or (d) the evaluation of the school or institution. Personnel evaluation—the assessment and certification of teachers, administrators, and counselors—is another major line of activity in evaluation, but because its methods are focused on individual decisions, in the interest of coherence, we have chosen to exclude it from this discussion.

### Evaluating School Programs

Of the four evaluation areas, the evaluation of school programs fits most directly into the mainstream of educational evaluation theory and practice. The most commonly evaluated programs are stand-alone, innovative programs. Thousands of evaluations of specific interventions have been conducted, probably accounting for the lion's share of evaluation efforts undertaken in the past 20 years.

*Innovative Programs.* One set of innovative programs and attendant evaluations addresses new forms of school organization, such as magnet schools (Atwood & Baker, 1984; Baker, Alkin, Russo, & Doby, 1981). Another category includes programs seeking to expand services beyond normal school offerings, such as afterschool programs for disadvantaged students

(Brooks & Herman, 1991) or artist-in-residence programs (Redfield, 1990). New curricular or teaching approaches present another relatively coherent set of evaluated programs (Aschbacher, 1991; Brownell, 1964; Kerslake, 1986; Niemi, 1994a; Steffe & Parr, 1968). The proliferation of technology has engendered another category of evaluations, that of examining the effects of new media or technology (Baker, Gearhart, & Herman, 1994; Goldman, Pellegrino, & Bransford, 1994; Leahy, 1991; Slavin, 1991).

These examples of school-based educational programs, although superficially very different, do in fact cluster on a number of dimensions germane to their evaluation. Each program is a special innovation made possible by special funding, often from nongovernmental sources. Each intervention began at a known time and had specific aims, evolving into sets of guidelines, procedures, training components, and explicit expectations, making it possible to assess the degree and success of program implementation. Each of these programs was also generally directed toward improving some component of student outcomes. In most cases the motivation for program evaluation came from outside the sites of implementation and addressed the dual concerns of formative and summative evaluation. In each of the evaluation examples cited above, recommendations were made to the program organizers regarding incremental improvements in the design and operation of programs, as well as the current impact of programs relative to their general goals.

Evaluations of innovative programs share other attributes. They are written for particular clients. They may serve any number of local bureaucratic purposes, such as showing symbolic concern for management, supporting requests to maintain funding, or substantiating plans for program expansion. Evaluations of this sort are almost never conducted for the purpose of constricting or ceasing program activity. Comparisons with current practices may be desired, but because most participating institutions have volunteered their involvement, the difficulty of achieving randomization limits the degree to which generalizable causal inferences can be made. In many ways, the programs are treated by evaluators as design prototypes or demonstrations rather than as interventions to be assessed by comparison with existing programs. Part of the reason for this is that the goals of some of these programs, such as promoting interdisciplinary learning or teaching respect for the arts, may not be among the goals of regular school programs. Cronbach and his colleagues (1981) used the term "superrealization" to characterize a developing program tested under conditions likely to maximize its effectiveness, and the term "prototype" to indicate the phase of development when a program is carefully expanded to new sites under conditions close to those that would apply if the program were adopted as policy.

The evaluators of innovative school programs are often drawn from outside the supporting agency, serve as an external team or as consultants hired for a particular, limited purpose, and, following the conduct and reporting of the study, may have little contact with the program or the initiating agency. Sometimes the evaluation study operates only for a very short period, perhaps less than 6 months; at other times a fixed commitment might be made for evaluation services for as long as 3 or 5 years. In almost every example discussed above, the evaluators were solicited to perform the studies for an agreed-upon sum, rather than participating in a formal, competitive request for proposals. As an aside, such evaluations are almost always underfunded.

Because innovative programs have a self-contained character, they usually do not threaten the educational status quo directly, nor do they immediately impinge on mainstream educational practice. The selection of sites for implementation of innovative programs typically depends on both available financial resources and acceptability to school sites, not on selection criteria that might support generalizability of the results of even a volunteer sample. It is also important in interpreting evaluations of multisite innovations to remember that the programs in question may not have been subjected to painstaking, small-scale development and testing; there may in fact be little prior evidence that a particular program is likely to succeed.

Unhappily, the development of innovative programs often does not follow the precepts of rational educational planning, for example, careful design, formative evaluation, revision, slow expansion, and ultimately dissemination (Baker, 1973; Petry, Mouton, & Reigeluth, 1987). This is particularly true for innovations serving a particular ideological or political agenda, because sponsors of such programs need to build a constituency and cannot risk finding that an ideologically pure innovation did not work as publicly promoted. In fact, the need to oversell the benefits of new programs in order to ensure their funding often raises hopes far beyond what a realistic evaluation is likely to find.

*Instructional Products.*  One variation of stand-alone program evaluation is not necessarily conducted in schools but for school populations. Evaluation of instructional products, media, and curricula at one time accounted for a large number of controlled studies, but the tendency to combine sources of innovation into larger programs has largely overtaken the product evaluation approach. Lumsdaine (1960) summarized early efforts to develop standards for the evaluation of instructional products, particularly the idea that a product could be shown to result in replicable results when employed with students and settings as intended. An early example (Holland, 1967) focused on obtaining quantitative measures of the quality of instructional materials, and L. L. Tyler and Klein (1976) proposed more qualitatively oriented methods. Other examples include Komoski's efforts at the Education Products Information Exchange (EPIE) to formulate specific criteria and a *Consumer Reports*-style service (Komoski, 1975, 1987), and the National Diffusion Network's efforts to subject educational products to some empirical evaluation prior to dissemination. The latter organization has produced replicability and impact criteria for submitted innovations (Crandall, 1983; Taylor, 1982).

*Complex, Large-Scale Programs.*  A second category of commonly evaluated programs includes those sponsored by large agencies outside the school sites, such as school districts, state departments of education, or the federal government. Activities undertaken at the behest of these sponsors sometimes only loosely fit the concept of program. The intervention may have general goals, such as to assist students with special needs. Broad guidelines or restrictive regulations may convey standards of implementation; or programs may simply provide additional financial support to needy sites. Because of their govern-

mental inception, these programs often bring with them strong political elements, advocates who either support the creation or continuation of the program or are ideologically opposed to it. Evaluations of large-scale programs almost always have to serve a combination of needs: to account for the use of public funds, to examine whether the intervention is operating as intended, to shore up or perhaps undermine political and public support, and to determine at the point of reconsideration or reauthorization whether the programs have been successful enough to continue. Such evaluations are often thought to be negative political acts. Given the known conservatism of summative evaluations (Aaron, 1978), the charge is likely true, for it is usually hard to document the success of new approaches, particularly in comparison to comfortable extant practices.

Complex programs of this sort are not designed to stay compartmentalized and work apart from the main intentions of schooling, as in the case of many innovative programs. In some ways, large-scale programs attack the most difficult educational problems, the ones with which educators have been least successful. There have been many such programs at federal and state levels, developed in successive waves of educational reform. Leading the list are compensatory education programs for disadvantaged students such as Chapter 1 (Title I) of the ESEA of 1965, bilingual provisions and programs, programs for migrant children, and Head Start and Follow Through programs. At the state level, mirror-image programs often develop, focused, for example, on mainstreaming special population students or on providing additional instruction in reading and language for disadvantaged students.

These complex programs also share a set of common characteristics. They are usually implemented in all qualifying schools. They typically provide significant financial support. They may have obligations to serve every eligible student, with legal sanctions for failure to do so. Their goals may be diffuse and encourage local interpretation. Their management is often remote from their implementation sites, and therefore they may depend on guidelines and regulations for administrative control. These requirements may inadvertently deform program intent (Rose-Ackerman, 1983).

The methodologies, politics, and impact of evaluation of complex, large-scale programs have been extensively analyzed, and intelligent analysts have come to vastly different conclusions on these issues. Referent investigations of the design and evaluations of early education interventions such as Head Start and Follow Through programs were edited by Rivlin and Timpane (1975) and included thoughtful pieces by Elmore, Datta, M. S. Smith, and Cohen. House, Glass, McLean, and Walker (1978) prepared a critique of federal program evaluation efforts, and House's Follow Through analysis challenged the design and validity of the studies. Cooley and Lohnes (1976) analyzed assumptions underlying the evaluation of Follow Through programs. An excellent volume edited by Raizen and Rossi (1981) reviewed evaluation practices and policies used in large-scale federal programs. These and other volumes emphasize the interaction of policy development and evaluation.

Title I—An Example.  Because we are focusing on school evaluation and educational psychology, we will illustrate continuing evaluation issues by highlighting only a few segments of the vast work undertaken in a major educational program,

Title I of ESEA. Because the Title I (sometimes called Chapter 1) program was central to the expansion of the field of evaluation, we can consider it an archetype of large-scale programs and the evaluations they evoke.

Title I is designed to provide educational services to children who are disadvantaged both economically and educationally. In the mid-1990s more than 70% of American schools received some level of Title I support. Issues that have plagued this program include how students are identified for services, approaches to ensure that resources reach children in need, and the identification and diffusion of successful programs. The details of the administration of this program have varied over the years, but in the mid-1990s, Title I funds were administered through the states, with both federal and state requirements guiding districts and schools. Evaluation requirements have fluctuated in an attempt to balance the competing goals of providing sensible documentation for Congress and Department of Education managers, as well as giving guidance to districts and states. A key issue has been the creation of procedures and reporting mechanisms to help schools internalize and act upon their responsibilities (Cronbach, 1982; McLaughlin, 1975). Because Congress wished to ensure that Title I funds would reach targeted children, certain program purposes were supported. The first of these was to ensure that Title I children received special educational services and that these services were neither diluted nor diverted from the children who needed them. Second, the desire to provide appropriate role models in schools led to the practice of hiring teaching assistants and aides to work with Title I students. Third, evaluations were required at school sites, with measured student achievement to be reported in a nationally comparable form. Operationally, this meant, for the most part, that a fixed number of commercially available standardized tests were used to report student results.

As is well known, Title I has not yet significantly solved the problems of the educationally and economically disadvantaged, although few are prepared to imagine the state of affairs without this program. Because the largest proportion of recipients of the program come from minority groups, the program has developed a strong political constituency, which influences the kinds of changes implemented in the program. Further, even though the program provides only limited resources when compared with the total expenditures on education from all sources, Title I discretionary assets provide flexibility not otherwise available through the assets of the school itself.

Issues Emerging Through Title I Implementation Requirements and Title I Evaluations. The scale and complexity of Title I program implementation make evaluation-based generalizations about its effectiveness difficult to obtain. In an attempt to decentralize evaluation, three evaluation models, varying in the degree to which they approximated scientific standards of experimentation, were promulgated in the mid-1970s (Tallmadge & Wood, 1976); Linn (1980) has summarized critiques of these models, including their measurement assumptions. A key element of these designs was the provision for making achievement tests comparable on a normative basis (Horst, Tallmadge & Wood, 1975), and a careful analysis of the consequences of this strategy was prepared by Jaeger (1980). Because, for most of its history, Title I has been directed toward assisting individual students, one element of the program that has been repeatedly singled out is the practice of separating Title I–eligible students from their regular classmates for special instruction in an effort to ensure that services are given to the students for whom they were intended. "Pull-out" programs, whereby children are assigned to specialist teachers, or the analogous practice of homogeneous grouping with aides assisting only Title I students, have stimulated a raft of criticism. Studies of classroom practices in disadvantaged classrooms, particularly the work on homogeneous grouping, have led to the conclusion that Title I has contributed to the development of a de facto tracked system of education (Oakes, 1985; Slavin & Braddock, 1993). As noted by M. S. Smith and O'Day (1991), tracking of students has resulted in a closing of the achievement gap between white and African-American students, attributable to the simultaneous rise in achievement among African Americans and a small drop in achievement among whites. The basic skills orientation of the achievement measures used in the evaluation of Title I is thought to be partly responsible for this effect.

Policy remedies are once again on the horizon. Two new elements were planned for 1994–1995 Title I implementation. First, in an effort to reduce the imputed negative effects of grouping and pull-out programs, a much greater proportion of resources was to be placed into schoolwide projects. In these projects, resources could be used to benefit all children, for instance, by reducing class size or providing teacher development programs. In a recent study of Chapter 1 schoolwide projects (Schenck & Beckstrom, 1993), 57 percent of respondents in sampled schools reported that they had reduced class size and 48 percent claimed they had introduced or strengthened heterogeneous student grouping, while about 44 percent reportedly engaged in cross-grade grouping strategies for particular subject matter instruction. (It would be interesting to determine if the cross-age groups were homogeneously organized.) Nonetheless, schoolwide project evaluation results suggest that the "following the dollars" approach embedded in previous studies will have a much less pervasive effect with this new model. A second major change is intended to counter negative side effects of evaluation requirements, particularly the basic skills orientation of norm-referenced achievement tests. This change, initiated in 1992 by the National Council on Education Standards and Testing (NCEST, *Raising Standards for American Education*), is embedded in the 1994 reauthorization of the ESEA. Each state will be asked to demonstrate that the same content standards and assessments are used for all its students and that these assessments focus on challenging outcomes. The actual implementation of this policy will strongly influence the course of future school evaluation, particularly the extent to which program practices to reach higher standards can be documented economically.

## Policy Evaluation

A closely related and, to some, indistinguishable type of evaluation is that which focuses on educational policies themselves. These policy evaluations attempt to determine the impact of new legislation or regulations. The series of studies conducted to assess the impact of readiness testing for entry into kindergarten and delayed entry into first grade (Shepard & M. L. Smith, 1989) provides a strong set of examples of this work.

A second illustration is the evaluation of changing curriculum standards, where evaluators assessed whether new course requirements actually affected what was delivered to students, as opposed to merely stimulating a resorting of content and renaming of courses (McDonnell, Burstein, Ormseth, Catterall, & Moody, 1990). A third example of a policy evaluation is the study conducted by Noble and M. L. Smith (1994) assessing the impact of the new state testing system in Arizona.

Policy evaluators have strong influence on educational practice and may drive the research agenda in educational psychology because they have the opportunity to raise fundamental questions about our educational hypotheses. For example, with respect to early intervention projects: Is there a reason to believe in the developmental paradigms that have inspired these interventions and their evaluations? Will state regulatory and incentive policies produce their desired impact on schools, teaching, and learning? Because we are in another tide of educational reform, created by a new and fragile consensus about the merits of constructivist approaches to education, it is likely that evaluators will soon be conceiving deeper ways to assess the early impact of these and other interventions.

Those who have studied the impact of the evaluation of large governmental programs and policies paint a dismal picture and depict evaluation as an essentially conservative process (Aaron, 1978). Some evaluative approaches, especially those set in social science traditions, necessarily result in muffled uncertainty more often than ringing support of new programs. New programs may be supported only superficially by educational practitioners, whose center of gravity may seek the comfort of experience and tradition rather than the tumult and ambiguity of change. Further, lack of trust in the quality of governmental decisions predisposes policymakers themselves to limit the effectiveness of evaluation findings. Aaron (1978) has described the events of the 1960s and 1970s as resulting in a deep cynicism over the ability of government to produce anything of value. The 1990s have seen a continued erosion of confidence in institutional and societal sources of unity and strength. We would expect this erosion to influence the evaluation of large-scale programs. Evaluation-based requirements, such as high standards, may influence school practices, but whether schools are able to act formatively on evaluation results is less certain. Other critics have pointed to a fundamental mismatch in goals and processes between policymakers and researchers (Lindbloom & Cohen, 1979; Rein & White, 1977; Wildavsky, 1972).

## Evaluating Student Performance

The third major strand of inquiry in school evaluation is one that is closely tied to the early roots and current practices of educational psychologists—student evaluation. The following discussion is limited to the evaluation of student achievement and other school outcomes and does not include evaluations undertaken to classify students for special programs or assessments that have a more clinical orientation.

Assessment of student performance is essential for most evaluations of school-based programs, for in the majority of instances interventions are intended to affect either directly or indirectly the success of students in schools. We have briefly noted the strong history of standardized tests and alluded to

their role in evaluation as well as to beliefs that they are partly responsible for the alleged negative state of U.S. educational affairs. Let us provide a quick review of where educational assessment now stands as it operates in schools and how its new shape may influence the direction of future evaluation practices.

Assessment can be used for a number of different purposes. It can be the core of a monitoring system, reporting in general on the nature of American educational programs, such as the National Assessment of Educational Progress (e.g., Mullis, Dossey, Owen, & Phillips, 1991; Wolf, 1993). It can provide the core outcome of program evaluation studies. Assessment can be used either formally or informally to advance students to higher grades or different educational institutions—a summative use. Assessment can also help teachers decide what progress students have made, where they need additional attention, and, in the best case, where the teacher needs to rethink his or her overall instructional strategy—a formative use. In the highest stakes situation, assessment can provide the basis of certification of accomplishment, with graduation and the awarding of diplomas dependent on assessment scores. Assessments can be used to make selection decisions, for college entry, using the Scholastic Aptitude Test or the American College of Testing examination, or for hiring decisions in the work force. Policymakers continue to take the view that one type of performance assessment could and should perform all of these functions (Tucker, 1991).

In the 1990s, educational testing and assessment remain in the middle of a full-blown revolution. Performance assessment has been embraced by many policymakers, educators, and researchers as a way to push the educational system in a direction at once consonant with high standards and our educational psychology knowledge base. Writers such as L. B. Resnick and D. P. Resnick (1989, 1990) have promoted the use of new assessments that embody the best attributes of our conceptions of learning, namely (a) that learning is the process of construction, (b) that it is knowledge dependent, and (c) that it is situated in a context (L. B. Resnick, 1989). Noble and M. L. Smith (1994) label this approach "cognitive-constructivist" and characterize it as a part of a new kind of measurement-driven reform. (The old kind was motivated by now rejected behavioral interpretations of learning; behaviorism and minimum standards somehow became linked, although this connection is obviously not inevitable.) The evaluation of student learning, if it is used as a principal dependent measure of educational reform, will therefore influence the design of educational options. Systemic critiques of educational policy (NCEST, 1992; M. S. Smith & O'Day, 1991) would seem to require this.

Performance assessments have several defining characteristics. They are open-ended, requiring students to create or make products or performances. Although challenging multiple-choice examinations have been available for years, and many depend on the construction of concepts or strategies in order to select the right answer, the format of selected responses has been eschewed by most believers in the new assessments. These new assessments are supposed to present to students tasks that have particular characteristics, one set of which has been described by Linn, Baker, and Dunbar (1992). They include *cognitive complexity*, implying multiple steps, deep processing of information, and problem solving or application of knowledge. The tasks are embedded in situations, to use Resnick's term (J. S. Brown, Collins, & Duguid, 1989), and Linn et al. (1992) claim these situations are supposed to be *meaningful* to the students. Newmann used the term "authentic" to capture the sense that the tasks are motivating to students and have real-world application (Newmann, 1991). A third characteristic of these measures, one that is implied by the cognitive complexity of their tasks, is the requirement that judges, raters, or other experts determine the quality of assessments according to explicit standards. Considerable disagreement exists on the extent to which these standards must be consensually developed, need to survive beyond the particular social setting of their application, and may be applied to various topics and subject matters. Opinions on these issues depend in part on the use of assessment results—that is, how public, how consequential, and how contextualized they will be (Messick, 1989).

Because the tasks require actual performances or their traces, many responses to performance tasks require considerable verbal ability on the part of the student. Students may be expected to tell about or to write a description, a procedure, an explanation, or a justification as a way of demonstrating their mastery of the domain. They may also be asked to read and interpret complex task directions. This language dependence of performance tasks applies to subject areas heretofore reliant primarily on symbolic manipulations, such as some aspects of mathematics and science (Gelman & Greeno, 1989; Niemi, 1994a). Where linguistically complex tasks are used to assess nonlinguistic knowledge, it is anticipated that judges may overestimate the performance of students with good verbal ability. Similarly, as the population of schoolchildren diversifies, the use of linguistically demanding performance tasks may underestimate the abilities of students with less verbal or English language facility. So it is possible that these new techniques, as part of a reform effort intended to promote learning for the most poorly served segment of schoolchildren, may operate against the interests of those students, at least in the short run or where the tasks are used for summative decision-making.

Some alternative techniques are being explored to provide support to students who encounter performance tasks with high verbal demands; these demands may occur at either the input or output end of a task, or both. Some history tasks, for example, require reading primary source materials written in a historical period (Baker, 1994a). Approaches to reduce language difficulty have included the provision of dialogue boxes for help, definition, and other types of support (Ni, 1993). Other approaches have been to provide cognitive strategies emphasizing comprehension to help students cope with new types of tasks (Aguirre-Muñoz, Baker, Wittrock, Niemi, & Lee, 1994). On the output side, to reduce the burden of producing connected discourse, studies of the representation of concepts have been undertaken by Novak and Musonda (1991) and by Baker, Niemi, Novak, and Herl (1992). Indirect methods of assessing knowledge structure have also been proposed by Britton (1991) and Shavelson and Stasz (1980). These methods have low verbal demands but lack the constructivist face validity that seems to be the minimum standard for most new assessments. Ironically, because of the dominance of measurement-driven models and the concomitant belief that teachers will isomorphically model their teaching on assessment strategies, indirect approaches will likely be restricted to research uses.

The validity of performance measures, although widely dis-cussed, has almost never been tested for the variety of policy uses for which the measures have been proposed (Cronbach, 1994). In fact, the same concerns that have plagued the design of evaluation are recapitulated in the assessment area. They include questions of adequate comparisons, reliability, internal validity, and external or consequential validity; the detection of side effects; the optimal degree of participation (by the stakeholders) in development, administration, and analysis of assessments; and issues of public reporting. The revisitation of these topics in the performance assessment area will influence our projection of the future of the field.

## Institutional and System Evaluation

The fourth area of serious interest in evaluation has been the evaluation of institutions and systems. Most evaluation at the institutional level has focused on the development of a set of comprehensive indicators against which the progress of a given institution within a system could be judged. Sometimes these indicators are public, as in the *U.S. News and World Report* rankings of professional and graduate schools (Elfin, September, 1994), and sometimes they are based on more scholarly analyses (Pace, 1986). At the collegiate level, evaluation of institutions in the United States has emphasized accreditation as an approach to make judgments about the standards appropriate for school quality (Association of Independent Colleges and Schools, 1980; Thompson, 1993).

*Accreditation Models.* Institutions in the United States have been evaluated by means of accreditation models that require visitors to spend some time on site, conducting interviews and making informal observations. With these data, the evaluators make judgments about whether a particular school or program meets a set of standards. Such approaches have a longer history in other developed nations, evolving into "inspectorates" staffed by experienced teachers and principals with an independent charter to determine the quality of school programs. Cuttance (1994), for example, has written about quality assurance approaches in Australia that combine accreditation, inspectorates, professional development, and formative evaluation.

Precollegiate institutional evaluation in the United States began in the mid-1980s with consideration of appropriate educational indicators. This approach derived directly from the systems-oriented evaluation models of the late 1960s and 1970s. The difference, of course, is that the indicators of inputs, processes, and outputs were to become institutionalized and periodically reported rather than episodic and created for a transitory evaluation purpose. Design of indicator systems has been advocated by McDonnell et al. (1990), Murnane and Raizen (1988), Oakes (1989), Raizen and Jones (1985), and Shavelson, McDonnell, and Oakes (1989). The tenor of these indicator systems varies as the authors' emphases move across curriculum, subject matter, and classroom concerns. A major international effort in the area of indicators of educational quality was the project of the Organization of Economic Community Development (*Education at a Glance: OECD Indicators*, 1993). With contributions from 26 member countries, this document, released in 1992 and updated in 1993, presents data on 38 indicators. These address demographics, social and economic context, costs, school processes, human resources, program participation and characteristics, decision-making, and governance, in addition to results that include performance, system outcomes such as graduation and retention, and labor market outcomes.

During the debate surrounding the development of a national policy on standards and assessment in the United States (NCEST, 1992), one controversy centered on the need for indicator systems of educational processes. Both indicators of system quality and indicators of school quality were considered, essentially to provide information on the capacity of the delivery system to meet the outcomes implied by the reforms. School and system indicator data, it was argued, were needed to serve as protection from lawsuits (Phillips, 1994) or as a brake against premature implementation of high-stakes applications of new assessments, as well as to provide interim measures of changes in schools thought to predict improvement in student achievement. The proposals for such process indicators were rejected by the NCEST in its final report. Nonetheless, the debate stimulated studies of the development of measures of school process underway by researchers in collaboration with the Council of Chief State School Officers (Burstein & Winters, 1994) and the state of California (Bennett, 1994; Burstein & McDonnell, 1994; Wiley, 1993). Technical approaches to modeling such data have been explored by Muthén (1986) in an attempt to target the strength of the relationship between process indicators and outcome measures. Bottom-up strategies intended to involve parents, administrators, and teachers in deciding on key opportunity-to-learn elements have also been tried (Baker, 1994b; Niemi, 1994b). These efforts are part of a more general interest in involving school communities in the regular assessment of school quality.

Opportunity to Learn. A particular operational construct focusing attention on the most achievement-relevant indicators has been the idea of "opportunity to learn" (Porter, 1991; Schmidt, 1993a, 1993b). This idea entered mainstream educational thought through Ralph Tyler's volume, *Basic Principles of Curriculum and Instruction* (1949), in which Tyler described learning experiences and criteria for their selection. It came into focus again during the period of behaviorism, in the concept of appropriate practice (Popham & Baker, 1970), where it was intended, more narrowly, to convey the opportunity students were given by the teacher to engage in desired outcomes. It was again transformed in the work of Berliner and colleagues in the Beginning Teacher Evaluation Study (Berliner, Fisher, Filby, & Marliave, 1978; Berliner & Tikunoff, 1976) as the idea of engaged learning, which implied relevance to instructional intent. Another variation on the idea emerged from litigation regarding the fairness of competency test results in the 1979 *Debra P.* v. *Turlington* case in Florida (Phillips, 1994; Pullin, 1982). In that case the court held that students and schools needed to be given adequate notice about the general content of outcome measures so that they could provide relevant and effective instruction. Perhaps because of the legal precedent, the idea of opportunity to learn has become synonymous to many with drill-and-practice regimens to reach the minimalist goals of competency-based systems.

Opponents of using opportunity-to-learn data to aid in the interpretation of achievement results also fear that this category of reporting could be used prescriptively and would result in external control of school and classroom instruction by centralized authorities far removed from schools. Their assumption is that less direct controls, through sanctions and incentives associated with high-stakes use of assessments, will be a more efficient and benign approach. One can argue against prescriptive guidelines for instruction for another reason—the paucity of generalizable knowledge about how to teach. But process or opportunity-to-learn models present real problems of design and implementation: (a) manageability problems at sites expected to provide data; (b) the frequency and intrusiveness of data collection, balanced against a desire for formative use of educational improvement; (c) uncertainty about the best logic for the combination of data in order to permit reasonably global reporting categories; (d) the challenge of educating the audience to interpret reports appropriately and act on them sensibly; and (e) problems related to engagement in and ownership of the system by its intended users. Nevertheless, states in the United States and policymakers in the international community continue to pursue the collection of process data, much of it based on constructs from educational psychology, in their institutionalization of evaluation functions.

## EVALUATION PROSPECTS

The history of evaluation, particularly the continuing use of evaluation to judge the quality of educational programs, the impact of evaluation studies, and new developments in performance assessments and indicator systems, all point to significant changes in the future practice of evaluation.

We expect that episodic program evaluations will be supplanted by the institutionalization of data systems at every level of educational authority, from the federal system down to the individual school site. Instead of special-purpose evaluations conducted for discrete special programs, we would expect some efficiencies to be developed with the use of emerging indicator systems as sources for information about inputs, processes, and outcomes associated with particular evaluation questions. As systems engage the school site in the evaluation process, they will encourage the collection and analysis of locally adaptive information in response to particular local goals. The present worldwide movement to restructure school authority and deputize it to local site leadership will also have effects on evaluation. For reasons of efficiency, equity, and quality, school communities will be more centrally involved in the oversight of their own programs. In recent times in the United States, this trend has accelerated with the development of magnet and charter schools and evolving models of private education. Evaluation in these contexts is viewed as a principal and internal responsibility of the local team working under an agreed-upon vision of desired outcomes and reasonable constraints. Such local, adaptive, and systematic evaluation is consonant with approaches promoted throughout the business community by proponents of total quality management (Lozier & Teeter, 1993). But the ability to provide the time and resources necessary for true local engagement in evaluation may be limited in the short term by both will and economics.

Most interesting will be the continuing tension between pressures for individuality and uniqueness in the measurement of student outcomes and the persistent concern of parents, community, and government for comparisons. This issue, of course, may be seen as a variant of the earlier contention by representatives of the experimentalist and the interpretive schools of evaluation design. Considerable effort has been expended to build linear evaluation systems, in which information flows from the top down or, occasionally, from the bottom up. These systems use fundamentally common information that differs only in aggregation level and portrayal. As an alternative, we can imagine the creation of a parallel system that uses evaluation data to drive reform and accountability agendas at multiple levels. This system may have unique elements collected only at particular levels of management or governance. For example, real responsibility could be vested in the school site for instructional design, teacher development, and the assessment of student learning where approaches are used that are especially appropriate to the staff and community context of children (Aschbacher, 1994; Sizer, 1992). In parallel, sampling designs of process and outcome measures could be employed to ensure gross parity of progress made at various schools and to provide broader, comparative system views. Some elements of this sort of system are already in place, but unfortunately they contend with rather than support the functions of reform and accountability. Large-scale comparative samples of student achievement could be developed if agreements were made on a reasonable corpus of prior knowledge for students at different points in their development. Instead of using existing standardized tests of skills, the comparative measurement of the acquisition of prior knowledge (in appropriately contextualized and politically acceptable ways) could provide a productive dimension on which schools were compared. Such knowledge would help schools identify tasks of appropriate complexity for students, tasks on which students were likely to be able to achieve early success, and could assist in decisions to embed unacquired but important declarative and procedural knowledge in instruction. Schools could differ in the way this knowledge was applied in performance assessments, although there might be key commonalities in scoring rubrics in areas such as understanding and problem solving (Baker, 1994a; Baxter, Glaser & Raghavan, 1994; Niemi, 1994a; Sugrue, 1994). The impact of these commonalities might be to move the system toward a structure of deep agreement on fundamental processes. Adopting an approach that emphasizes the deep structure of superficially different tasks could ameliorate the effects of mobility of families and students. Even so, for this new evaluation model to succeed, three key problems remain to be solved.

First, there is the problem of equity and the extent to which it is possible to find legitimate and moral ways to reconcile different needs and different goals into a coherent educational system. The potential impact of court precedent or threat cannot be overestimated. For example, the concept of adverse impact, the differential success rates of students of different ethnic or racial backgrounds, has in the past guided policy and statistical decisions made in selecting cut-scores as well as the evaluations inferred from them. Under a set of relatively common standards, as articulated by a state, for example, we would expect an adverse impact to occur until such time as high-quality instructional systems were in place. To avoid closing the gap between groups by reducing the performance of our highest students, we need to legitimate systems that encourage students to go beyond any core standards that are articulated, and to accomplish this without limiting options or devaluing the accomplishments of those who meet the core standards.

Second, we need to accommodate the need for diverse outcomes for all students without falling into a postmodern morass that legitimates any experience and holds any outcome valid. Nothing will accelerate the losses of the public educational system more than the idea that there is nothing of common value to be learned.

Third, we must find ways to bring into play the broadest range of resources in evaluating the quality of our programs. This chapter has not addressed the issue of cost or the use of technology to energize, simplify, and verify the quality of our educational programs. New approaches involving networking (Burns, 1994), new strategies for data collection, scoring, and aggregation (Bennett, 1993), and more advanced options involving intelligent assistance may help us reconceive and make more practical our efforts to evaluate (Baker & O'Neil, 1994; O'Neil & Baker, 1994). As education itself extends its reliance on technology, we can expect to see more refined and transparent approaches to collecting, managing, summarizing, and reporting evaluation data. And vastly underused resources in communities, in families, and in educational and public institutions will need to be mobilized to assist in the definition, development, and analysis of educational quality.

Yet to be resolved is the perennial argument about the purposes and effects of evaluation. Does it serve primarily an information function and act as a demonstrable instrument in the improvement of education? Is it a process by which visions are clarified and valuable educational processes are developed? Is it a symbolic activity created to rationalize political endeavor? The answers are yes, yes, and yes, but more important questions remain about the balance chosen among values of information, regulation, sanctions, and consensus. The choice of emphasis clearly affects our research and development preferences in educational psychology as well as our picture and projections of the field of educational evaluation.

## References

Aaron, H. J. (1978). *Politics and the professors: The great society in perspective*. Washington, DC: Brookings Institution.

Aguirre-Muñoz, Z., Baker, E. L., Wittrock, M. C., Niemi, D., & Lee, J. J. (1994). *Assessing the effects of instruction of text structure and background knowledge integration on content understanding in high school history*. Los Angeles: University of California, National Center for Research on Evaluation, Standards, and Student Testing.

Alkin, M. C. (1969). Evaluation theory development. *Evaluation Comment, 2*, 2–7.

Alkin, M. C., Daillak, R., & White, P. (1979). *Using evaluations: Does evaluation make a difference?* (Vol. 76). Beverly Hills, CA: Sage.

Alkin, M. C., & Ellett, F. S., Jr. (1979). The importance of category systems in evaluation theory: A personal viewpoint. *CEDR Quarterly, 12*(3), 3–5.

Alkin, M. C., & House, E. R. (1992). Evaluation of programs. In M. C. Alkin (Ed.), *Encyclopedia of educational research* (6th ed., Vol. 2, pp. 462–467). New York: Macmillan.

Aschbacher, P. R. (1991). Humanitas: A thematic curriculum. *Educational Leadership, 49*(2), 16–19.

Aschbacher, P. R. (1994, June). *Bridging the gaps between large and small scale assessment in break-the-mold schools: The Los Angeles Learning Centers approach.* Paper presented at the CCSSO National Conference on Large-Scale Assessment, Albuquerque, NM.

Association of Independent Colleges and Schools. (1980). *Accreditation standards: Policies, procedures, and criteria.* Washington, DC: Accrediting Commission of the Association of Independent Colleges and Schools.

Atwood, N., & Baker, E. L. (1984). *Magnet schools as voluntary desegregation programs: A three-year evaluation perspective* (CSE Tech. Rep. No. 230). Los Angeles: University of California, Center for the Study of Evaluation.

Baker, E. L. (1973). The technology of instructional development. In R. M. W. Travers (Ed.), *Second handbook of research on teaching* (pp. 245–285). Chicago: Rand McNally.

Baker, E. L. (1976). *Evaluation of the California Early Childhood Education Program.* Los Angeles: University of California, Center for the Study of Evaluation.

Baker, E. L. (1994a). Learning-based assessments of history understanding [Special issue]. *Educational Psychologist, 29*(2), 97–106.

Baker, E. L. (1994b, July). *Quality school portfolio assessment.* Paper presented at the AMP LEARN training session at Pepperdine University, Malibu, CA.

Baker, E. L., Alkin, M., Russo, N., & Doby, W. (1981). *Magnet schools evaluation.* Los Angeles: Los Angeles Unified School District.

Baker, E. L., & Alkin, M. C. (1973). ERIC/AVCR annual review paper: Formative evaluation of instructional development. *AV Communication Review, 21*(4), 389–418.

Baker, E. L., Gearhart, M., & Herman, J. L. (1994). *The Apple classrooms of tomorrow: The UCLA evaluation studies* (CSE Tech. Rep. No. 353). Los Angeles: University of California, Center for the Study of Evaluation.

Baker, E. L., Niemi, D., Novak, J., & Herl, H. (1992). Hypertext as a strategy for teaching and assessing knowledge representation. In S. Dijkstra, H. P. M. Drammer, & J. J. G. van Merriënboer (Eds.), *Instructional models in computer-based learning environments* (pp. 365–384). Heidelberg: Springer.

Baker, E. L., & O'Neil, H. F., Jr. (Eds.). (1994). *Technology assessment in education and training.* Hillsdale, NJ: Lawrence Erlbaum Associates.

Baker, E. L., & Stites, R. (1991, April). *Trends in testing in the United States.* Paper presented at the annual meeting of the American Educational Research Association, Chicago.

Baxter, G. P., Glaser, R., & Raghavan, K. (1994). *Analysis of cognitive demand in selected alternative science assessments* (CSE Tech. Rep. No. 382). Los Angeles: University of California, National Center for Research on Evaluation, Standards, and Student Testing.

Bennett, R. E. (1993). On the meanings of constructed response. In R. E. Bennett & W. C. Ward (Eds.), *Construction versus choice in cognitive measurement: Issues in constructed response, performance testing, and portfolio assessment* (pp. 1–27). Hillsdale, NJ: Lawrence Erlbaum Associates.

Bennett, S. (1994, June). *Illustrative strategies for collecting and using data on opportunity to learn from the 1993 California State Assessment in Mathematics.* Paper presented at the Special Workshop on State Use of Opportunity to Learn Data, CCSSO National Conference on Large-Scale Assessment, Albuquerque, NM.

Berliner, D., Fisher, C., Filby, N., & Marliave, R. (1978). *Executive summary of Beginning Teacher Evaluation Study.* San Francisco: Far West Laboratory.

Berliner, D. C., & Tikunoff, W. J. (1976). The California Beginning Teacher Evaluation Study: Overview of the ethnographic study. *Journal of Teacher Education, 27*(1), 24–30.

Binet, A., & Simon, T. (1916). *The development of intelligence in children (the Binet-Simon scale)* (E. S. Kite, Trans.). Baltimore: Williams & Wilkins.

Bloom, B. S., & Krathwohl, D. (Eds.). (1956). *Taxonomy of educational objectives: The classification of educational goals, by a committee of college and university examiners.* New York: Longman, Green.

Boruch, R. F. (1991). The president's mandate: Discovering what works and what works better. In M. W. McLaughlin & D. C. Phillips (Eds.), *Evaluation and education at quarter century* (90th Yearbook of the National Society for the Study of Education, Part II, pp. 147–167). Chicago: National Society for the Study of Education.

Britton, B. (1991, April). *Pushing around mental representations by revising texts.* Paper presented at the annual meeting of the American Educational Research Association, Chicago.

Brooks, P. E., & Herman, J. L. (1991). *LA's BEST: An after school education and enrichment program.* Los Angeles: University of California, Center for the Study of Evaluation. (ERIC Document Reproduction Service No. ED 340 807)

Brown, A. L., Bransford, J. D., Ferrara, A. L., & Campione, J. C. (1983). Learning, remembering, and understanding. In J. H. Flavell & E. M. Markman (Eds.), *Mussen handbook of child psychology* (2nd ed., Vol. 3, Cognitive development, 77–166). New York: Wiley.

Brown, A. L., & Ferrara, R. A. (1985). Diagnosing zones of proximal development. In J. V. Wertsch (Ed.), *Culture communication and cognition* (pp. 273–305). Cambridge, England: Cambridge University Press.

Brown, J. S., Collins, A., & Duguid, P. (1989). Situated cognition and the culture of learning. *Educational Researcher, 18*(1), 32–42.

Brownell, W. A. (1964). *Arithmetical abstractions: The movement toward conceptual maturity under differing systems of instruction.* Berkeley: University of California Press.

Burns, H. (1994). Inventing technology assessments on local area networks: An estimate of the importance of motives and collaborative workplaces. In H. F. O'Neil, Jr., & E. L. Baker (Eds.), *Technology assessment in software applications* (pp. 235–254). Hillsdale, NJ: Lawrence Erlbaum Associates.

Burstein, L., & McDonnell, L. (1994, April). *Validity of opportunity to learn measurements.* Paper presented at the annual meeting of the American Educational Research Association, New Orleans, LA.

Burstein, L., & Winters, L. (1994, June). *Models for collecting and using data on opportunity to learn at the state level: OTL options for the CCSSO SCASS science assessment.* Paper presented at the Workshop on Models for Collecting and Using Opportunity to Learn at the State Level, CCSSO National Conference on Large-Scale Assessment, Albuquerque, NM.

Campbell, D. T. (1969). Reforms as experiments. *American Psychologist, 24,* 409–428.

Campbell, D. T. (1971). *Methods for the experimenting society.* Paper presented at a meeting of the Eastern Psychological Association, New York, and at a meeting of the American Psychological Association, Washington, DC.

Campbell, D. T., & Stanley, J. C. (1963). Experimental and quasi-experimental designs for research. In N. L. Gage (Ed.), *Handbook of research on teaching* (pp. 171–246). Chicago: Rand McNally.

Chen, H., & Rossi, P. H. (1980). The multi-goal, theory driven approach to evaluation: A model linking basic and applied social science. *Social Forces, 59,* 106–122.

Chen, H., & Rossi, P. H. (1983). Evaluating with sense: The theory-driven approach. *Evaluation Review, 7,* 283–302.

Churchman, C. W. (1971). *The design of inquiring systems: Basic concepts of systems and organization.* New York: Basic Books.

Cohen, D. K. (1975). The value of social experiments. In A. M. Rivlin & P. M. Timpane (Eds.), *Planned variation in education: Should we give up or try harder?* (pp. 147–175). Washington, DC: Brookings Institution.

Cook, T. D., & Campbell, D. T. (1979). *Quasi-experimentation: Design and analysis issues for field settings.* Chicago: Rand McNally.

Cook, T. D., & Shadish, W. R., Jr. (1986). Program evaluation: The worldly science. *Annual Review of Psychology, 37,* 193–232.

Cooley, W. W., & Lohnes, P. R. (1976). *Evaluation research in education.* New York: Irvington.

Crandall, D. P. (1983, November). The teacher's role in school improvement. *Educational Leadership, 41*(3), 6–9.

Cronbach, L. J. (1963). Course improvement through evaluation. *Teachers College Record, 64,* 672–683.

Cronbach, L. J. (1982). *Designing evaluations of educational and social programs.* San Francisco: Jossey-Bass.

Cronbach, L. J. (1994, September). *On the uncertainty of assessment results.* Paper presented at the 1994 CRESST Conference, Getting Assessment Right! Los Angeles, CA.

Cronbach, L. J., Ambron, S. R., Dornbusch, S. M., Hess, R. D., Hornik, R. C., Phillips, D. C., Walker, D. F., & Weiner, S. S. (1981). *Toward reform of program evaluation* (2nd ed.). San Francisco: Jossey-Bass.

Cronbach, L. J., & Suppes, P. (Eds.). (1969). *Research for tomorrow's schools: Disciplined inquiry for education.* National Academy of Education, Committee on Educational Research. New York: Macmillan.

Cuttance, P. (1994). Quality assurance in education systems. *Studies in Educational Evaluation, 20,* 99–112.

Datta, L. (1975). Design of the Head Start Planned Variation experiment. In A. M. Rivlin & P. M. Timpane (Eds.), *Planned variation in education: Should we give up or try harder?* (pp. 79–99). Washington, DC: Brookings Institution.

*Education at a glance: OECD Indicators.* (1993). Paris: Centre for Educational Research and Innovation.

Eisner, E. W. (1991). Taking a second look: Educational connoisseurship revisited. In M. W. McLaughlin & D. C. Phillips (Eds.), *Evaluation and education at quarter century* (90th Yearbook of the National Society for the Study of Education, Part II, pp. 169–187). Chicago: National Society for the Study of Education.

Eisner, E. W. (1985). *The educational imagination: On the design and evaluation of school programs* (2nd ed.). New York: Macmillan.

Elementary and Secondary Education Act of 1965: Improving America's Schools Act. Public Law No. 103-227 (1994).

Elfin, M. (Ed.). (1994, September). America's best graduate schools: The latest word on admissions, entrance tests and job prospects [Special issue]. *U.S. News & World Report.*

Elmore, R. (1975). Design of the Follow Through experiment. In A. M. Rivlin & P. M. Timpane (Eds.), *Planned variation in education: Should we give up or try harder?* (pp. 23–45). Washington, DC: Brookings Institution.

Fisher, R. A. (1951). *The design of experiments* (6th ed.). Edinburgh, Scotland: Oliver & Boyd.

Gagné, R. M. (1965). *The conditions of learning.* New York: Rinehart & Winston.

Gelman, R., & Greeno, J. G. (1989). On the nature of competence: Principles for understanding in a domain. In L. B. Resnick (Ed.), *Knowing, learning, and instruction: Essays in honor of Robert Glaser* (pp. 125–186).

Glaser, R. (1963). Instructional technology and the measurement of learning outcomes: Some questions. *American Psychologist, 17,* 519–521.

Glaser, R. (1965). Toward a behavioral science base for instructional design. In R. Glaser (Ed.), *Teaching machines and programmed learning, II. Data and directions* (pp. 771–809). Washington, DC: National Education Association of the United States.

Goldman, S. R., Pellegrino, J. W., & Bransford, J. (1994). Assessing programs that invite thinking. In E. L. Baker & H. F. O'Neil, Jr. (Eds.),

*Technology assessment in education and training* (pp. 199–230). Hillsdale, NJ: Lawrence Erlbaum Associates.

Guba, E. G., & Lincoln, Y. S. (1981). *Effective evaluation: Improving the usefulness of evaluation results through responsive and naturalistic approaches.* San Francisco: Jossey-Bass.

Guba, E. G., & Lincoln, Y. S. (1989). *Fourth generation evaluation.* Newbury Park, CA: Sage Publications.

Hemphill, J. K. (1969). The relationships between research and evaluation studies. In R. W. Tyler (Ed.), *Educational evaluation: New roles, new means* (68th Yearbook of the National Society for the Study of Education, Pt. II, pp. 189–220). Chicago: National Society for the Study of Education.

Herman, J. L. (Ed.). (1987). *CSE program evaluation kit* (2nd ed.). Newbury Park, CA: Sage.

Hively, W., Patterson, H. L., & Page, S. (1968). A universe defined system of arithmetic achievement tests. *Journal of Educational Measurement, 5,* 275–290.

Holland, J. G. (1967). A quantitative measure for programmed instruction. *American Educational Research Journal, 4*(2), 87–102.

Holland, J. G., & Skinner, B. F. (1961). *The analysis of behavior: A program for self-instruction.* New York: McGraw-Hill.

Horst, D. P., Tallmadge, G. K., & Wood, C. T. (1975). *A practical guide to measuring project impact on student achievement* (No. 1 in a series of monographs on evaluation in education). Washington, DC: U.S. Department of Health, Education and Welfare.

House, E. R. (1980). *Evaluating with validity.* Beverly Hills, CA: Sage.

House, E. R., Glass, G. V, McLean, L. D., & Walker, D. F. (1978). No simple answer: Critique of the Follow Through evaluation. In T. D. Cook, M. L. Del Rosario, K. M. Hennigan, M. M. Mark, & W. M. K. Trochim (Eds.), *Evaluation studies: Review annual* (Vol. 3, pp. 611–640). Beverly Hills, CA: Sage.

Hovland, C. I., Lumsdaine, A. A., & Sheffield, F. D. (1949). *Experiments on mass communication.* Princeton, NJ: Princeton University Press.

Jaeger, R. M. (1980). *On combining achievement test data through NCE scaled scores* (USOE Contract No. 300-76-0095). Research Triangle Park, NC: Research Triangle Institute.

Joint Committee on Standards for Educational Evaluation. (1981). *Standards for evaluations of educational programs, projects, and materials.* New York: McGraw-Hill.

Kerlinger, F. M., & Pedhazur, E. J. (1973). *Multiple regression in behavioral research.* New York: Holt, Rinehart, and Winston.

Kerslake, D. (1986). *Fractions: Children's strategies and errors: A report of the Strategies and Errors in Secondary Mathematics project.* Philadelphia: NFER-Nelson.

Komoski, K. (1975). Instructional materials: Do they or don't they? *Learning, 3*(7), 92–93.

Komoski, K. (1987). Beyond innovation: The systemic integration of technology into the curriculum. *Educational Technology, 27*(9), 21–25.

Krathwohl, D. R., Bloom, B. S., & Masia, B. B. (1964). *Taxonomy of educational objectives: Handbook II: Affective domain.* New York: David McKay.

Leahy, P. (1991). A multi-year formative evaluation of IBM's "Writing to Read" program. *Reading Improvement, 28*(4), 257–264.

Levin, H. M. (1983). *Cost-effectiveness: A primer.* Beverly Hills, CA: Sage.

Lincoln, Y. S., & Guba, E. G. (1985). *Naturalistic inquiry.* Newbury Park, CA: Sage.

Lindblom, C. E., & Cohen, D. K. (1979). *Usable knowledge: Social science and social problem solving.* New Haven, CT: Yale University Press.

Linn, R. L. (1980). Evaluation of Title I via the RMC models: A critical review. In E. L. Baker & E. S. Quellmalz (Eds.), *Educational testing and evaluation: Design, analysis, and policy* (pp. 121–142). Beverly Hills, CA: Sage.

Linn, R. L., Baker, E. L., & Dunbar, S. B. (1992, Winter). Complex, performance-based assessment: Expectations and validation criteria. *Evaluation Comment,* pp. 2–9.

Lozier, G. G., & Teeter, D. J. (1993, Summer). Six foundations of total quality management. *New Directions for Institutional Research,* (78), 5–11.

Lumsdaine, A. A. (1960). Teaching machines: An introductory overview. In A. A. Lumsdaine & R. Glaser (Eds.), *Teaching machines and programmed learning: A source book* (pp. 5–22). Washington, DC: National Education Association of the United States.

Lumsdaine, A. A. (1965). Assessing the effectiveness of instructional programs. In A. A. Lumsdaine & R. Glaser (Eds.), *Teaching machines and programmed learning, II: Data and directions* (pp. 267–320). Washington, DC: National Education Association of the United States.

Lumsdaine, A. A., & Bennett, C. A. (Eds.). (1975). *Evaluation and experiment: Some critical issues in assessing social programs.* New York: Academic Press.

Madaus, G. F., & Stufflebeam, D. L. (Eds.). (1989). *Educational evaluation: Classic works of Ralph W. Tyler.* Boston: Kluwer Academic.

Markle, S. M. (1965). Programmed instruction in English. In A. A. Lumsdaine & R. Glaser (Eds.), *Teaching machines and programmed learning: A source book* (pp. 546–583). Washington, DC: National Education Association of the United States.

McDonnell, L. M., Burstein, L., Ormseth, T., Catterall, J. S., & Moody, D. (1990). *Discovering what schools really teach: Designing improved coursework indicators.* Santa Monica, CA: Rand Corp.

McKnight, C. C. (1987). *The underachieving curriculum.* Champaign, IL: Stipes.

McLaughlin, M. W. (1975). *Evaluation and reform: The Elementary and Secondary Education Act of 1965.* Cambridge, MA: Ballinger.

Messick, S. (1989). Validity, In R. L. Linn (Ed.), *Educational measurement* (3rd ed., pp. 13–103). New York: Macmillan.

Millman, J. (1974). Criterion-referenced measurement. In W. J. Popham (Ed.), *Evaluation in education* (pp. 309–397). Berkeley, CA: McCutchan.

Morris, L. L. (Ed.). (1978). *Program evaluation kit.* Beverly Hills, CA: Sage.

Mullis, I. V. S., Dossey, J. A., Owen, E. H., & Phillips, G. W. (1991). *The state of mathematics achievement: NAEP's 1990 assessment of the nation and the trial assessment of the states* (Report No. 21-ST-04, prepared by Educational Testing Service). Washington, DC: National Center for Education Statistics, U.S. Department of Education, Office of Educational Research and Improvement.

Murnane, R. J., & Raizen, S. A. (Eds.). (1988). *Improving indicators of the quality of science and mathematics education in grades K-12* (Committee on Indicators of Precollege Science and Mathematics Education, National Research Council). Washington, DC: National Academy Press.

Muthén, B. (1986). *Some uses of structural equation modeling in validity studies: Extending IRT to external variables using SIMS results.* Los Angeles: University of California, Center for the Study of Evaluation. (ERIC Document Reproduction Service No. ED 293 888)

National Council on Education Standards and Testing. (1992). *Raising standards for American education.* Washington, DC: U.S. Government Printing Office.

Newmann, F. M. (1991). Linking restructuring to authentic student achievement. *Phi Delta Kappan, 72*(6), 458–463.

Ni, Y-J. (1993). *Applying CRESST history assessment specifications and scoring rubrics to upper elementary level history assessment* (Project Report). Los Angeles: University of California, National Center for Research on Evaluation, Standards, and Student Testing.

Niemi, D. (1994a). *Assessing fifth-grade students' fraction understanding.* Unpublished doctoral dissertation, University of California, Los Angeles.

Niemi, D. (1994b). *Teachers' understanding of the link between instruction and assessment.* Paper presented at the annual meeting of the American Educational Research Association, New Orleans, LA.

Noble, A. J., & Smith, M. L. (1994). *Measurement-driven reform: The more things change, the more they stay the same* (CSE Tech. Rep. No. 373). Los Angeles: University of California, National Center for Research on Evaluation, Standards, and Student Testing.

Novak, J. D., & Musonda, D. (1991). A twelve year longitudinal study of science concept learning. *American Educational Research Journal, 28*(1), 117–154.

Oakes, J. (1985). *Keeping track: How schools structure inequality.* New Haven, CT: Yale University Press.

Oakes, J. (1989). What educational indicators? The case for assessing the school context. *Educational Evaluation and Policy Analysis, 11*(2), 181–199.

O'Neil, H. F., Jr., & Baker, E. L. (Eds.). (1994). *Technology assessment in software applications.* Hillsdale, NJ: Lawrence Erlbaum Associates.

Pace, R. C. (1986). *Quality, content, and context in the assessment of student learning and development in college* (CSE Tech. Rep. No. 256). Los Angeles: University of California, National Center for Research on Evaluation, Standards, and Student Testing.

Patton, M. Q. (1978). *Utilization-Focused Evaluation.* Beverly Hills, CA: Sage.

Patton, M. Q. (1988). The evaluator's responsibility for utilization. *Evaluation Practice, 9*(2), 5–24.

Petry, B., Mouton, H., & Reigeluth, C. M. (1987). A lesson based on the Gagné-Briggs theory of instruction. In C. M. Reigeluth (Ed.), *Instructional theories in action: Lessons illustrating selected theories and models* (pp. 11–44). Hillsdale, NJ: Lawrence Erlbaum Associates.

Phillips, S. E. (1994, September). *Legal and political issues surrounding performance assessment.* Symposium conducted at the 1994 CRESST Conference, University of California, Los Angeles.

Popham, W. J. (1967). *Development of a performance test of teaching proficiency.* Los Angeles: University of California.

Popham, W. J. (1975). *Educational evaluation.* Englewood Cliffs, NJ: Prentice Hall.

Popham, W. J. (1988). *Educational evaluation* (2nd ed.). Englewood Cliffs, NJ: Prentice Hall.

Popham, W. J., & Baker, E. L. (1970). *Systematic instruction.* Englewood Cliffs, NJ: Prentice Hall.

Popham, W. J., & Husek, T. R. (1969). Implications of criterion-referenced measurement. *Journal of Educational Measurement, 6*(1), 1–9.

Porter, A. C. (1991). Creating a system of school process indicators. *Educational Evaluation and Policy Analysis, 13*(1), 13–29.

Provus, M. M. (1969). Evaluation of ongoing programs in the public school system. In R. W. Tyler (Ed.), *Educational evaluation: New roles, new means.* (68th Yearbook of the National Society for the Study of Education, Pt. II, pp. 242–283). Chicago: National Society for the Study of Education.

Pullin, P. (1982). *Minimum competency testing, the denied diploma, and the pursuit of educational opportunity and educational adequacy* (CSE Tech. Rep. No. 180). Los Angeles: University of California, Center for the Study of Evaluation.

Raizen, S. A., & Jones, L. V. (Eds.). (1985). *Indicators of precollege education in science and mathematics.* (ERIC Document Reproduction Service No. ED 315 273)

Redfield, D. L. (1990). *Evaluating the broad educational impact of an arts education program: The case of the Music Center of Los Angeles County's Artists-in-Residence program.* Los Angeles: University of California, Center for the Study of Evaluation. (ERIC Document Reproduction Service No. ED 329 578)

Rein, M., & White, S. H. (1977, Fall). Can policy research help policy? *Public Interest, 49,* 119–136.

Resnick, L. B. (1989). *Knowing, learning, and instruction: Essays in honor of Robert Glaser.* Hillsdale, NJ: Lawrence Erlbaum Associates.

Resnick, L. B., & Resnick, D. P. (1989, October). *Tests as standards of achievement in schools.* Pittsburgh, PA: University of Pittsburgh,

Learning and Research Development Center. (ERIC Document Reproduction Service No. ED 335 421)

Resnick, L. B., & Resnick, D. P. (1990). Tests as standards of achievement in schools. *The uses of standardized tests in American education: Proceedings of the 1989 ETS Invitational Conference.* Princeton, NJ: Educational Testing Service.

Rice, J. M. (1893). *The public-school system of the United States.* New York: Century.

Rice, J. M. (1913). *Scientific management in education.* New York: Arno Press.

Rivlin, A. M., & Timpane, P. M. (1975). *Planned variation in education: Should we give up or try harder?* Washington, DC: Brookings Institution.

Rose-Ackerman, S. (1983). Unintended consequences: Regulating the quality of subsidized day care. *Journal of Policy Analysis and Management, 3*(1), 14–30.

Rossi, P. H., Freeman, H. E., & Wright, S. R. (1979). *Evaluation: A systematic approach.* Beverly Hills, CA: Sage.

Salasin, S. (1980). The evaluator as an agent of change. *New Directions for Program Evaluation, 7,* 1–9.

Schenck, E. A., & Beckstrom, S. (1993). *Chapter 1 Schoolwide Project Study* (Contract Nos. LC91027001 & LC91028001). Portsmouth, NH: RMC Research Corp.

Schlesinger, J. R. (1963). Quantitative analysis and national security. In Captain G. F. Smale (Ed.), *National security management: A commentary on defense management: Industrial College of the Armed Forces.* Washington, DC: Industrial College of the Armed Forces.

Schmidt, W. (1993a). *Survey of mathematics and science opportunities* (Research Report Series No. 56, TIMSS: Concepts, Measurements and Analyses. Draft document delivered to the International Coordinating Center). East Lansing: Michigan State University.

Schmidt, W. (1993b). *Survey of mathematics and science opportunities* (Research Report Series No. 57, TIMSS: Curriculum Analysis—A Content Analytic Approach. Draft document delivered to the International Coordinating Center). East Lansing: Michigan State University.

Schutz, R. E. (1970). *Programmatic instructional development.* (ERIC Document Reproduction Service No. ED 055 431)

Scriven, M. (1967). The methodology of evaluation. In R. E. Stake (Ed.), *Curriculum evaluation* (American Educational Research Association monograph series on evaluation, No. 1, pp. 39–83). Chicago: Rand McNally.

Scriven, M. (1973). Goal-free evaluation. In E. R. House (Ed.), *School evaluation: The politics and process* (pp. 319–328). Berkeley, CA: McCutchan.

Scriven, M. (1983). Evaluation ideologies. In G. F. Madaus, M. Scriven, & D. L. Stufflebeam (Eds.), *Evaluation models: Viewpoints on educational and human services evaluation.* Boston: Kluwer-Nijhoff.

Scriven, M. (1991). Beyond formative and summative evaluation. In M. W. McLaughlin & D. C. Phillips (Eds.), *Evaluation and education at quarter century* (90th Yearbook of the National Society for the Study of Education, Pt. II, pp. 19–64). Chicago: National Society for the Study of Education.

Scriven, M. (1994). Evaluation as a discipline. *Studies in Educational Evaluation, 20,* 147–166.

Shadish, R. J., Cook, T. D., & Leviton, R. C. (1991). *Foundations of program evaluation.* Newbury Park, CA: Sage.

Shavelson, R. J., McDonnell, L. M., & Oakes, J. (Eds.). (1989). *Indicators for monitoring mathematics and science education.* Santa Monica, CA: Rand Corp.

Shavelson, R. J., & Stasz, C. (1980). Some methods for representing structure of concepts in prose material. In J. Hartley (Ed.), *The psychology of written communication.* New York: Nichols.

Shepard, L. A., & Smith, M. L. (Eds.). (1989). *Flunking grades: Research and policies on retention.* Bristol, PA: Falmer Press, Taylor & Francis.

Sizer, T. R. (1992). *Horace's School: Redesigning the American high school.* New York: Houghton Mifflin.

Skinner, B. F. (1954, Spring). The science of learning and the art of teaching. *Harvard Educational Review, 24:* 86–97.

Slavin, R. E. (1991). Reading effects of IBM's "Writing to Read" program: A review of evaluations. *Educational Evaluation and Policy Analysis, 13*(1), 1–11.

Slavin, R. E., & Braddock, J. H. I. (1993). Ability grouping: On the wrong track. *College Board Review, 168,* 11–17.

Smith, E. R., & Tyler, R. W. (1942). *Appraising and recording student progress.* New York: Harper.

Smith, M. S. (1975). Evaluation findings in Head Start Planned Variation. In A. M. Rivlin & P. M. Timpane (Eds.), *Planned variation in education: Should we give up or try harder?* (pp. 101–111). Washington, DC: Brookings Institution.

Smith, M. S., & O'Day, J. (1991). Systemic school reform. In S. H. Fuhrman & B. Malen (Eds.), *The politics of curriculum and testing* (pp. 233–267). London: Falmer Press.

Stake, R. E. (1973). Program evaluation, particularly responsive evaluation. In G. F. Madaus, M. S. Scriven, & D. L. Stufflebeam (Eds.), *Evaluation models.* Boston: Kluwer-Nijhoff.

Stake, R. E. (1978). The case study method in social inquiry. *Educational Researcher, 7*(2), 5–8.

Stake, R. E. (1983). Stakeholder influence in the evaluation of Cities-in-Schools. In A. S. Bryk (Ed.), *New directions for program evaluation* (pp. 15–30). San Francisco: Jossey-Bass.

Stake, R. E. (1991). Retrospective on "The countenance of educational evaluation." In M. W. McLaughlin & D. C. Phillips (Eds.), *Evaluation and education at quarter century* (90th Yearbook of the National Society for the Study of Education, Pt. II, pp. 67–88). Chicago: National Society for the Study of Education.

Stake, R. E., & Easley, J. A. (1978). *Case studies in science education.* Champaign: University of Illinois, Center for Instructional Research and Curriculum Evaluation.

Steffe, L. P., & Parr, R. B. (1968). *The development of the concepts of ratio and fraction in the fourth, fifth and sixth years of the elementary school* (Wisconsin Research and Development Center for Cognitive Learning Technical Report No. 49). Madison: University of Wisconsin.

Stufflebeam, D. L. (1991). Professional standards and ethics for evaluators. In M. W. McLaughlin & D. C. Phillips (Eds.), *Evaluation and education at quarter century* (90th Yearbook of the National Society for the Study of Education, Pt. II, pp. 249–282). Chicago: National Society for the Study of Education.

Stufflebeam, D. L., Foley, W. J., Gephart, W. J., Guba, E. G., Hammond, R. L., Merriman, H. O., & Provus, M. M. (1971). *Educational evaluation and decision making.* Itasca, IL: Peacock.

Stufflebeam, D. L., & Webster, W. J. (1981). An analysis of alternatives to evaluation. In H. E. Freeman & M. A. Solomon (Eds.), *Evaluation studies review annual* (6, pp. 70–85). Beverly Hills, CA: Sage.

Sugrue, B. (1994). *Specifications for the design of problem-solving assessments in science* (CSE Tech. Rep. No. 387). Los Angeles: University of California, National Center for Research on Evaluation, Standards, and Student Testing.

Tallmadge, G. K., & Wood, C. T. (1976, October). *Users guide: ESEA Title I evaluation and reporting system.* Mountain View, CA: RMC Research Corp.

Taylor, J. A. (1982). *The infrastructure of innovation: The case of the National Diffusion Network.* Andover, MA: NETWORK.

Thompson, H. L. (1993). Recharting the future of accreditation. *Educational Record, 74*(4), 39–42.

Thorndike, E. L. (1913). *Educational psychology: The psychology of learning* (Vol. 2). New York: Columbia University.

Thorndike, E. L. (1926). *The measure of intelligence.* New York: Columbia University.

Thorndike, E. L., & Woodworth, R. S. (1901). The influence of improvements in one mental function upon the efficiency of other functions. *Psychological Review, 8,* 247–261, 384–395, 553–564.

Tucker, M. (1991, April). Testimony before the Subcommittee on Select Education, Committee on Education and Labor. Hearing on the Office of Educational Research and Improvement, Major R. Owens, Chairperson, U.S. House of Representatives, Washington, DC.

Tyler, L. L., & Klein, M. F. (1976). *Evaluating and choosing curriculum and instructional materials.* Los Angeles: Educational Resource Associates.

Tyler, R. W. (1942, October). Some techniques used in the follow-up study of college success of graduates of the thirty schools participating in the Eight-Year Study of the Progressive Education Association. *Journal of the American Association of Collegiate Registrars, 18,* 23–28.

Tyler, R. W. (1949). *Basic principles of curriculum and instruction.* Chicago: University of Chicago Press.

U.S. Department of Labor. (1991, June). *What work requires of schools: A SCANS report for America 2000.* Washington, DC: U.S. Department of Labor, Secretary's Commission on Achieving Necessary Skills.

Vygotsky, L. S. (1978). *Mind in society: The development of higher psychological processes.* Cambridge, MA: Harvard University Press.

Vygotsky, L. S., & Luria, A. R. (1993). *Studies on the history of behavior: Ape, primitive, and child.* Hillsdale, NJ: Lawrence Erlbaum Associates.

Weiner, N. (1948). *Cybernetics.* New York: Wiley.

Weiss, C. H. (1972). *Evaluation research: Methods for assessing program effectiveness.* Englewood Cliffs, NJ: Prentice Hall.

Weiss, C. H. (1973). Where politics and evaluation research meet. *Evaluation, 1,* 37–45.

Weiss, C. H. (1977). Research for policy's sake: The enlightenment function of social research. *Policy Analysis, 3,* 531–45.

Wholey, J. S. (1979). *Evaluation: Promise and performance.* Washington, DC: Urban Institute.

Wholey, J. S. (1983). *Evaluation and effective public management.* Boston: Little, Brown.

Wildavsky, A. (1964). *The politics of the budgetary process.* Boston: Little, Brown.

Wildavsky, A. (1972). The self-evaluating organization. *Public Administration Review, 32*(5), 509–520.

Wiley, D. (1993). *Opportunity to learn and mathematics achievement: Analyses of the CAP 1992 spring field test.* Evanston, IL: Northwestern University, School of Education.

Willis, G. (Ed.). (1978). *Qualitative education: Concepts and cases in curriculum criticism.* Berkeley, CA: McCutchan.

Wolf, R. M. (1993, November). The National Assessment of Educational Progress: The nation's report card. *NASSP Bulletin, 77*(556), 36–45.

Worthen, B. R., & Sanders, J. R. (1987). *Educational evaluation: Alternative approaches and practical guidelines.* New York: Longman.

Worthen, B. R., & White, K. R. (1987). *Evaluating educational and social programs: Guidelines for proposal review, onsite evaluation, evaluation contracts, and technical assistance.* Boston: Kluwer-Nijhoff.

# DATA AND DATA ANALYSIS

## John T. Behrens
ARIZONA STATE UNIVERSITY

## Mary Lee Smith
ARIZONA STATE UNIVERSITY

Whereas data analysis was once considered synonymous with statistics, a broader view is emerging in educational psychology. In their prescient work, Tukey and Wilk (1966/1986) articulated such a broad view, one we adopt for this chapter: "[T]he science and art of data analysis concerns the process of learning from . . . records of experience" (p. 554). Although Tukey and Wilk wrote about their own quantitative analysis, the definition seems equally appropriate for qualitative work. Good data analysis, regardless of the approach, is a mixture of science and art. Data analysis employs creativity in search of meaning, intelligibility, and pattern while rooted in systematic methods that emphasize open-mindedness and public scrutiny. Regardless of the theoretical emphasis, data analysis seeks revelation—the unveiling of the world around us.

This broad view of data analysis leads to a broad agenda for the chapter. First, the opening section describes several contexts in which data analysis occurs in educational psychology and enumerates aspects of data analysis that are consistent across all approaches to learning from data. The second section discusses quantitative methods, including ways of conceptualizing quantitative data analysis; reviews important schools of thought and techniques; and discusses computer programs for quantitative analysis. The third section, on qualitative methods, identifies the characteristics of qualitative inquiry, reviews three approaches to data analysis in this tradition, and discusses the use of computers in this context. The fourth and final section considers the possibilities and challenges for contemporary data analysts.

Because the quantitative approach continues to provide the primary research tools in educational psychology, this chapter discusses some of the foundational concepts and techniques in quantitative methods and introduces some uncommon methods. At the same time, however, the use of qualitative research methods is growing rapidly and warrants treatment. The section on qualitative methods focuses on introducing these methods to those who may not have worked with these tools. The lengthier discussion of quantitative methods reflects the current emphasis of the educational psychology research community and what we believe educational psychologists, on average, are ready to

hear, rather than weighing either method as more or less important.

Methodologically, educational psychology is at a crisis, the Latin word for crossroads. This chapter is unable to speak a single party line with clear-cut dos and dont's, as may have been possible in the past. As the same time, this crisis leads us to a reexamination of the foundations of our methods and a discussion of what is common and unique to data-analytic endeavors.

## FOUNDATIONS OF DATA ANALYSIS

### The Contexts of Data Analysis

Data analysis is a human activity and should be understood in relation to the contexts that shape that activity. The importance of the social and psychological contexts of the phenomenon educational psychologists examine is well established. We extend this valuing of the social and psychological context of action by discussing four contexts of data-analytic training and practice: the context of history, the context of application, the context of practice, and the context of alternative methods. These contexts impose boundaries on what data-analytic activity is considered acceptable and what activity occurs. An understanding of these contexts is an important part of understanding data analysis itself and should be addressed explicitly in the training of educational psychologists. Insofar as this occurs, the data analyst gains insight that aids the generalization of ideas and practice beyond cookbook recipes for data analysis.

*The Context of History.* Researchers live in many historical contexts. Two contexts most germane to the researcher are the field's intellectual history and the researcher's personal history. Each of these contexts affects the activity of the individual and thereby affects what becomes normative in the research community.

Although most educational psychologists study the historical developments of psychological theories, few are aware of the historical developments in statistical (or interpretivist) methods. An ahistorical presentation of data analysis may give the impression of offering a single, mathematically true version of statistics that implies that all other methods are in error. However, even a cursory view of the developments of statistical theory and practice in the 20th century will uncover a rich diversity that mandates rejection of such a view.

For example, we recognize R. A. Fisher as the father of modern statistics because he was responsible for such mainstays as the proof for the shape of the *t* distribution, the development of analysis of variance (ANOVA) and analysis of covariance (ANCOVA), and adumbration of the logic of the null hypothesis test. Fisher challenged the practices of Karl Pearson, who developed the correlation coefficient and the chi-square tests of independence and fit. Among his many accomplishments, Fisher (1922a) showed that Pearson's chi-square test had for more than 20 years been computed with the improper degrees of freedom. Jerzy Neyman and Egon Pearson, Karl Pearson's son, built on Fisher's work. They introduced the notions of the alternative distribution, Type II error, power, and confidence intervals. These ideas formed the foundation of what is taught in statistics classes. However, Fisher regarded these ideas as completely misguided (e.g., Fisher, 1956).

By neglecting such controversies and differences, statistical texts and teachers suggest a seamless piece of logical development (Gigerenzer, 1993) and promote the current prototypical approach as the single best or only alternative. There is, however, no single statistical method, only the myth of one. The myth functions to give a sense of identity and to sweep unresolved problems under the carpet: In what way is statistical power sensible? In what ways should .05 be considered a cutoff? What information is conveyed by a confidence interval? In what ways is the word *probability* used? These fundamental questions continue to fuel statistical research and discussion. Failure to recognize legitimate differences among statisticians is failure to understand the field.

The data-analytic history of the field also constrains the type of questions educational psychologists ask. When students learn data analysis without regard for historical and theoretical contexts, techniques devised to answer specific questions in the past may become the canonized analyses of the present (Gigerenzer, 1987, 1993). This canonization determines not only what analyses are conducted, but also how research questions are formulated. Insofar as ANOVA dominates statistical thinking in educational research, an early goal for graduate students is learning how to conceive of problems in terms of mean differences. By learning to conceptualize the world as consisting of continuous and discrete variables (the former usually appropriate for dependent variables, the latter for independent variables), the researcher not only facilitates a smooth transition from problem statements to research design and analysis, but also learns to limit the questions asked and the set of appropriate topics for research.

In addition to the larger historical context that drives the methods taught to researchers, the personal history of the researcher affects the data analysis as well. Most researchers inherit their tools of data analysis and employ them on the authority of texts or teachers, rather than as a result of personal evaluation. If researchers are like the subjects used in psychological investigations, data-analytic behavior is greatly affected by their social and educational background. Accordingly, researchers may act not out of thoughtful commitment to a methodology but out of liking or disliking for a dissertation advisor, statistics consultant, or qualitative research teacher. Not all choices of method are rational. As Kendall (1963) wrote in R. A. Fisher's obituary, "a man's attitude toward inference, like his attitude toward religion, is determined by his emotional make-up, not by reason or mathematics" (p. 4).

The examples given above refer to the quantitative tradition of statistical testing. However, the limitations described are based on psychological and social dynamics operating in all approaches to inquiry. Inclusion or omission of a tradition in these examples is not meant as an indictment or exoneration of any particular approach.

*The Context of Application.* Data analysis, when properly implemented, grows out of and serves a substantive question and avoids restricting or leading inquiry. Data analysis is not a set of techniques that can be inserted into or laid over a substantive area. For example, trait theories of mental attributes place individuals on scaled continua along which traits vary in magnitude. Such a conception of the individual is consistent with psychometric data and data-analytic techniques such as ANOVA and linear regression techniques. ANOVA is a technique for comparing the variability of mean scores of different groups against the variability among individual scores within each group. This technique provides an assessment of the amount of overlap that occurs in the scores of different groups placed on a continuous scale. Linear regression is a means for predicting scores on one scale using scores collected on another measure by examining the degree to which differences from the mean of one scale are matched by relatively equal differences from the mean of another scale. In regression analysis the scale being predicted is called the *dependent* or *response* variable and the scale used for prediction is called the *independent* or *explanatory* variable. Both ANOVA and linear regression techniques are consistent with the idea that people have attributes that can be measured and described on the basis of variability along scaled continua.

Information-processing views of cognition, on the other hand, emphasize the presence or absence of specific strategies or component processes and often lead to the collection of binary data indicating the presence or absence of those strategies. To fit such data onto a continuous scale, researchers may add up the number of different strategies used by each individual. However, this transformation of strategy-level data to person-level data obscures differences in strategy use across and within individuals—an important loss for a research endeavor that supposes componential psychological processes (Siegler, 1987).

Fortunately, there are more analyses in this world than any one researcher knows. Researchers in epidemiology developed techniques aimed at predicting the occurrence or absence of a single event using logistic regression techniques. Logistic regression is analogous to common linear regression except that the dependent variable is dichotomous rather than continuous. The dichotomous variable may indicate the presence or absence of a strategy, or success or failure on a specific task. Although slope estimates in linear regression analysis tell the increase expected in the predicted variable for each one-unit change in an explanatory variable, logistic regression slopes indicate the change in the probability of the dependent event occurring for each one-unit change in an explanatory variable. Further, logistic regression does not have restrictions concerning the normality of the distributions, as do common approaches to linear regression.

Dee-Lucas and Larkin (1991), for example, analyzed subjects' responses on a series of tasks, which they scored as correct or incorrect. They appropriately employed logistic regression to identify explanatory variables associated with correct responses. In another study (Dee-Lucas & Larkin, 1990) these authors examined participant changes in ratings (yes/no) of text important as a function of presentation order of different material. In each of these cases the authors understood the binary nature of the dependent variable and employed appropriate techniques for modeling it.

Sometimes the historical carryover of methods leaves investigators with tools ill-suited for research in their discipline. Researchers correct this problem when they pause to reassess their methods in light of current theories, independent of inherited methods. Anderson (1987) presented a good example of such a reassessment in his review of cognitive psychology at experimental and epistemological levels. From this analysis, he concluded that data collection should focus more on the processes revealed in short-term memory, and he recommended the increased use of protocol analysis and other process-oriented procedures. Respondents Seifert and Norman (1987) noted that analysis of protocol data lacks the appearance of objectivity inherent in statistical tests. In turn, Anderson called for improving methods that fit the problem (i.e., better analysis of protocol data) rather than continuing to fit problems to inappropriate methods. Anderson understood that the right answer to the wrong problem is not the right answer. Without evaluations of the relation between substantive questions and data-analytic methods, of the sort provided by Anderson, researchers risk conducting normal science in a mechanized and less informative manner.

***The Context of Practice.*** Many aspects of research instruction are divorced from practice. For example, in the statistical literature, J. Cohen (1990), Rossi (1990), and Sedlmeier and Gigerenzer (1989) have shown that despite almost 30 years of calls for the use of statistical power analysis (and approximately 60 years since its invention), this technique continues to have little impact on applied statistics. Similarly, appeals to recognize the limitations of $p$ values (Rosnow & Rosenthal, 1989), the value of confidence intervals (Stevens, 1990), and the erroneous use of simple statistics (Brewer, 1985) continue, with little effect. Despite many advances in statistical methods over the past several decades, instructional practices (Aiken, West, Sechrest, & Reno, 1990) and publication practices lag far behind. Assessments of typical publication practices have led some researchers to near exasperation (e.g., Olkin, 1990).

All this suggests, unfortunately, that techniques that innovative and thoughtful researchers find most useful upset the status quo and are less likely to be accepted for publication. There is little in the publication process to reward going out on a methodological limb, yet much to reward the appearance of objectivity inherent in the religion of statistics and the $p$ value (see Salsburg, 1985). Although the attitude of editors toward divergent quantitative (Levin, 1991; Loftus, 1993) and qualitative work (Smith, 1987) has warmed recently, reviewers still favor the traditional conventions. Thus, absorbing the message in this chapter may improve your research but not necessarily your résumé.

***The Context of Alternative Methods.*** Along with Campbell (1978), we assume that there is no quantitative knowing without qualitative knowing. Unfortunately, the field of data analysis in general is now divided into qualitative and quantitative methods. Psychology sought to differentiate itself from philosophy, and adherence to the appearance of objectivity and quantification was considered part of the price (Hornstein, 1988). To gain legitimacy, normal psychology reduced its scope to matters that could be studied with numerical precision and the appearance of objectivity (Gigerenzer, 1987; Hornstein, 1988). To use a chapter title from Danziger's (1990) book, *Constructing the Subject,* psychology moved "from quantification to methodolatry." In this movement the sanctification of results sometimes overshadowed critical thinking regarding broader theoretical and substantive issues.

Before one approaches research, a conception of what is important, in what way it is important, and how it should be studied ought to be constructed, explicitly or otherwise. Much valuable quantitative information can be gained following, and in parallel to, deep qualitative analysis of possible areas of inquiry. Using a critical theory perspective (see Popkewitz, 1990), one may analyze the economic and political agenda that makes inquiry valuable to a researcher: "If this research is important to me, what was it about my view of the economic, political, and social world that led me to study this topic rather than something else, and what implications for my research follow?" Ethnographic inquiry may allow an understanding of values, meanings, and interpretations held by those involved in the phenomenon investigated: "In what ways are the values, meanings, actions, and customs of the people involved consonant with my expectations and understandings, and what are the implications for my research?" Such approaches deal seriously with the problems of the context dependence of social behavior.

By failing to address the social context of inquiry or by assuming understanding of the experience of those being observed, the researcher is forced to fill in many gaps in interpreting how the data are collected. In what way did the subject understand the question? Did the subject know how to behave in the experiment? Did the respondent answer honestly on the survey? What did failure to participate indicate? What unintended aspect of the situation did the participants react to (Rosenthal, 1966)? Insofar as some of these gaps can be filled through systematic qualitative inquiry, quantitative analysis should generally build on and work with rigorous qualitative analysis. All quantities are measures of qualities, and the understanding of qualities is no simple matter.

In the past few years, even some hard-core traditionalists have incorporated some aspects of qualitative analysis into their work. Although this can occur in a fruitful and synergistic manner, long experience in one paradigm often makes it difficult to conceptualize problems and analyses in an alternative framework. After one learns to think in terms of variables and means, it is quite difficult to conceive of research without these constructs. Accordingly, the inclusion of qualitative methods in quantitative research can be mishandled in several ways. First, experimental researchers may use the term *naturalistic* to describe any study intervention that takes place outside of the laboratory. From a qualitative perspective, this is an obvious misuse of the term, which should instead connote research conducted *of* the everyday life of participants, as little interfered with as possible, aimed at elucidating participant meaning and action, and approached without preconceived definitions and hypotheses (Lincoln & Guba, 1985). Second, researchers sometimes report that they collect qualitative data when they solicit free-response data at the end of a questionnaire or write short descriptions of the study setting or subjects. However, this may amount to simply adding pictures to statistics, with the qualities of the participants' experiences—the true focus of qualitative inquiry—not contributing to the inferences reached. Third, researchers may relegate qualitative approaches to the discovery phase of a study, as a means to specify a hypothesis or refine a treatment. The "hard data" part of the study then begins with precedence in generating conclusions.

Such incorporation represents a weak and patronizing version of qualitative inquiry that misunderstands the nature of that inquiry. For most researchers, qualitative research is a foreign culture, and these attempts at supposed integration are not unlike the casual tourist who wants to get to know, or act like, a foreign native. Such endeavors are often headed for failure because the real value system of the foreign culture may not be discernible by the outsider or, worse, may be misconstrued.

Another common misunderstanding has to do with the role of qualitative research in the entire research program. From a quantitative viewpoint, qualitative input seems valuable in the variable-defining stages, to be replaced later with quantification. For most reearchers who use qualitative methods, however, the content studied and the processes employed by qualitative methods make those methods appropriate for the exploratory and hypothesis-testing phases of research. Insofar as qualitative methods address questions and offer perspectives that quantitative research cannot or does not care to address, the two systems work in parallel, not in series. As Kvale (1983) argued, quantitative and qualitative analyses are complementary means of understanding a substantive problem, with "no fixed order" of application (p. 437).

These difficulties are not unique to statistical data analysis but are encountered in all research traditions. For example, the Marxist–feminist ethnographer will certainly be familiar with the contexts described above as constraining quantitative data analysts. The researcher who thinks deeply in terms of participant meaning and the semiotics of a social event may have a hard time incorporating substantive quantitative techniques in an investigation. Moreover, all traditions are subject to their own mythology and methodoltry.

In sum, although the merging of qualitative and quantitative approaches is welcome and encouraged, these systems begin with different foundational assumptions and value sets. Interpreting the acts of one group through meanings derived from another group, like "naturalistic" or "positivist," leads to greater division. It is difficult to become an expert in a single paradigm. Working functionally in two is far more difficult. Any attempt to cross over or cross-evaluate needs to be done in the knowledge that "we may not really know what they are talking about."

## What Is Common to All Data Analysis

Quantitative and qualitative researchers hold unique views of what is important to study and how data should be collected and analyzed. Nevertheless, the common goal of learning from the world binds them by five characteristics.

First, the act of analysis is a construction of the researcher. It is neither immaculate perception nor psychological projection. That is, the researcher is not merely a neutral, passive reader of the environment, a faceless replicate disguised by the use of *E* in the research report. Nor is the researcher simply reading his or her own psychological makeup as in an ink blot. A better model of what the researcher does is consistent with a cognitive-constructivist learning theory (see, e.g., Resnick, 1989), which holds that the mind constructs knowledge through transactions with text, research participants, and data. The researcher, like any learner, brings to the episode a set of prior knowledge, experience, capacities, intentions, and interests. This set is unlikely to be precisely the same as the set of another researcher and therefore must be taken into account in examining the validity claims of the knowledge constructed. Both quantitative and qualitative analyses are interpretive, making meaning from data.

It follows, therefore, that all analysis is theory laden (Hanson, 1957). Kant (1781/1969) articulated a similar point at a philosophical level. Kant noted that when information reaches one's senses, it comes in a meaningless form, which he called the "manifold of experience." This manifold would be perceived according to categories that he considered innate and about which cognitive science continues to argue. We accept the notion that observation and analysis cannot be separated from theory, and we argue, with Campbell (1978), that there is no perspective-free stance a researcher can assume, nor is any method free of error. Although objectivity is unattainable, one can pursue a kind of bounded rationality in research efforts, maintain a skeptical stance toward one's accounts, and rigorously examine their warrant. Qualitative analysis is neither more nor less subjective than quantitative analysis, in this scheme. Phillips (1990) noted that

"[O]bjective" seems to be a label that we apply to inquiries that meet certain procedural standards, *but objectivity does not guarantee* that the results have any certainty . . . [but implies] that the inquiries so labeled are free from gross defects. . . . (p. 23; emphasis in the original)

If data analysis is a learning process, then it is essentially a psychological one and tied to all the advantages and disadvantages of cognition. Sadler (1981) used the results of subjective probability experiments to suggest that inferential errors can be made when the analyst's conceptual apparatus meets a wealth of data. These inferential errors include (a) basing inferences on selective subsets of data and ignoring the rest, (b) overweighting first impressions or novel instances, (c) ignoring data contrary to one's hypotheses, and (d) overlooking problems of unreliability, biased sampling of units and instances, missing information, and the like. Although Sadler considered these issues in relation to qualitative analysis, they seem equally likely to apply to all data analysis. For example, Stephen Jay Gould in *The Mismeasure of Man* (1981) gave numerous accounts of how data analyses were mistakenly conducted in the domain of intelligence testing. Almost without exception, errors led to conclusions supporting the cultural and social values of the investigators. Just as our learning is affected by social, cultural, and historical forces, so also is our data analysis.

A second point common to all data analysis is that words and numbers are symbols. Neither can be said to be soft or hard. There is nothing particularly hard about IQ = 125, or soft about "the social loss of dying patients" (a category discovered in the grounded theory analysis of Glaser & Strauss [1967]). Both are symbols that have underlying referents, and in both cases a whole series of inferences and arguments connect the referents to the symbol.

The term *data* is used in two ways that should be clearly delineated. At one level the term refers to presentational aspects of the phenomenon under study. Generally, however, these data of sense experience (which we may call the data of the phenomenon) are recorded and recoded into a second representational level of data that comprises the records of experience—tally marks, field notes, survey responses, tape recordings. It is on the records of this second layer of data that the analysis is performed. This second layer we call the data of the analysis, to distinguish it from the data of the phenomenon.

Clearly, the data of the analysis are not equal to the data of the phenomenon. Instead, the data of the phenomenon are mapped onto words or numbers that serve as the data for analysis. The quality of all analysis, then, hinges on the mapping process. Information is always lost or distorted in the mapping process. The farther an analyst is away from the details of the mapping process, the less able is he or she to extract meaning from the data of analysis. Beveridge (1950) summarized the difference between the data collector who sees all the details of the mapping process and those who see only the final results: "no one believes an hypothesis except its originator but everyone believes an experiment except the experimenter" (p. 65).

In quantitative analysis the mapping is called measurement. Qualitative analysts sometimes argue that quantitative analysts throw too much out when the data of the phenomenon are mapped onto predetermined scales broken up into individual sentences or indications of isolated behaviors. On the other hand, quantitative analysts are likely to argue that the interpretations of the qualitative researcher are too full of the researcher's own views. In these arguments the quantitative researcher is placing high value on precision in the data of analysis and striving to make the mapping meaningful and consistent with the data of the phenomenon. This necessarily entails missing large parts of the data of the phenomenon. The qualitative researcher, on the other hand, is more likely to value inclusiveness of the data of the phenomenon and to strive to rein in the semantic messiness of the data of analysis. Each approach is driven by a different set of values, which makes communication of goals difficult.

The third characteristic common to all data analysis is that the process of analysis is social. The researcher refers backward to transactions with participants or subjects and forward to transactions with colleagues and audiences. The relationship between researcher and subjects (qualitative researchers prefer the term "participant" to the term "subject") provides a social vantage point from which the researcher can view the research unit and the phenomenon of study. In traditional quantitative studies, the nature of this relationship was often obscured and assumed (Kvale, 1983): The researcher defined the problem and found a compliant population, then tried to maintain a suitable social distance from the individuals or worried when this distance was broached. Still, the researcher's access to the data was based on the subjects' compliance with the researcher's design or with the agreements between researcher and the gatekeepers of the institutions where the subjects worked or studied. Qualitative research tends to make these relationships and agreements more visible and acknowledges their significance to the validity of accounts eventually generated. In conducting the analysis and constructing the account, both quantitative and qualitative researchers anticipate the scrutiny of readers and critical audiences (Bazerman, 1988; Signorile, 1989). These ways make analysis social.

Fourth, the aim in both forms of analysis is to reduce large amounts of data to a summary that is comprehensible to the human mind without sacrificing meaning. A set of 10 data points—self-efficacy scores on 10 adolescents, for example—can be readily grasped and held in mind. One hundred such scores, however, must be reduced (Fisher, 1922b). Calculating measures of central tendency, variability, and shape effectively reduces 100 pieces of information to 3, sometimes without losing the essential characteristics of the data as a whole. Various qualitative analysis procedures, as will be described later in this chapter, work the same way, reducing the sheer number of pieces of information (interview or observation segments, as an example) to a set of categories or constructs that are abstracted from the data and preserve the meaning of the whole. Both quantitative and qualitative analyses break the data down and then put them back together in a meaningful way, and construct accounts—conclusions, models, assertions, or even narrative lines (Eisner, 1991). And in both modes of analysis there is a trade-off between precision and richness as particulars are folded into general categories.

Fifth, the results of analysis must be considered provisional and contestable, whether one works with numbers or with text. Because research methods are fallible and subject to the vagaries of "auxiliary assumptions" (Meehl, 1978), reality is complex, and researchers' capacities variable; uncertainty can never be reduced to zero. The more we try to control for certain kinds of inference, the more we lose control over other kinds of inference (Cronbach, Ambron, Dornbusch, Hess, Hornick, Phillips, Walker, & Weiner 1980). "Generalizations decay" (Cronbach, 1975) faster than researchers can tip the ratio of trust to doubt (Campbell, 1978).

## Conclusion: The Many Dimensions of Data Analysis

Meanings are socially negotiated and vary across contexts. Accordingly, the context from which data arise needs to be considered. Using this rule reflexively, we began the section on data analysis by discussing some contexts relevant to current practices and beliefs about data analysis in educational psychology. Second, we laid out what we consider to be key aspects of data analysis. Central to this discussion is the notion that data analysis is about learning from data. As with all learning, the processes and products of the analysis vary with the problem and the learner in complex ways and at many social and psychological levels. Good data analysis has a complexity that defies transcontextual cookbooks for formula or theme extraction. Far from being the most firmly grounded aspect of educational psychology, the appropriate methods of data analysis shift as the field reconceptualizes the nature of learning, the goals of education, and the uses of data analysis. Regardless of the mathematical and philosophical theories available to guide us, data analysis remains a social and psychological act whose humanness cannot be obscured by assent to algorithms.

Having established a framework for considering data analysis in general, we next turn to the specifics of quantitative and qualitative analysis. A discussion of emerging themes from both traditions concludes the chapter.

## QUANTITATIVE DATA ANALYSIS

### Introduction to Quantitative Methods

***What Is Quantitative Data Analysis?*** Quantitative data analysis is so pervasive in Western cultures that it is seldom given explicit definition. Often it is simply considered the breaking down and organizing of quantified phenomena—numbers. Although the use of numbers is certainly central to quantitative data analysis, this definition does not tell the whole story because it has only specified the nature of the data, while remaining silent on the nature of the analysis. Certainly quantitative data are sometimes analyzed in ways that are not rigorously quantitative. Thus, although quantitative data may be necessary for defining quantitative analysis, they are not sufficient. This means that "the analysis of quantitative data" and "the quantitative analysis of data" are not necessarily equivalent. For our purposes, we want to emphasize the quantitative nature *of the analysis,* and we define quantitative data analysis as *the building of models in which relations between conceptual elements of the inquiry are described quantitatively.* The idea here is that the most important aspect of quantitative data analysis is that quantitative descriptions are built. The quantification of phenomena is simply a step along the way to a quantitative analysis.

When properly conducted, quantitative analysis allows parsimonious descriptions of the structure of the world in precise numerical terms that can provide rich descriptions of the phenomena of interest. Quantitative data analysis values mathematics because it is a form of symbolic logic—a means for making relationships explicit and tractable. At the same time, the quantitative researcher recognizes that the precision suggested by quantitative analysis rests entirely on the measurement process, which in turn rests on meanings ascribed to numbers (Velleman & Wilkinson, 1993). Sophisticated data analysis cannot make good on inappropriate research design or measurement.

A good example of the descriptive power available from quantitative analysis is provided by Friedman (1989), who summarized the results of numerous studies of gender differences in achievement. When the data from many studies were grouped together, there appeared to be no practical difference between the achievement of males and of females. The average difference was near zero, as illustrated in Figure 30–1A. In this analysis, the size of the effect is the difference in mean achievement between males and females measured in standard deviations. Positive effect sizes indicate superior female achievement; negative effects reflect a male advantage. Recognizing the complexity of the world, and knowing the importance of considering the world from multiple viewpoints, Friedman then analyzed the data by relating the size of the achievement differences to

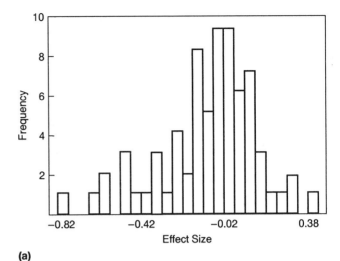

(a)

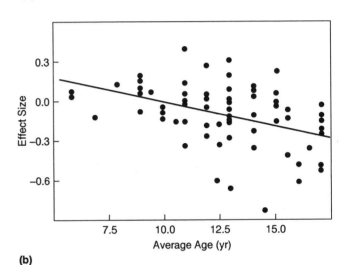

(b)

FIGURE 30–1. One-Dimensional (A) and Two-Dimensional (B) View of Effect Sizes from Investigations of Sex Differences in Mathematics Achievement
*Source*: From "Mathematics and the Gender Gap: A Meta-analysis of Recent Studies on Sex Differences in Mathematical Tasks" by L. Friedman, 1989, *Review of Educational Research*, 59, 185–213. Reprinted by permission.

the year in which the study was conducted and the average age of the participants. It was not sufficient to examine each aspect in isolation; rather, all three variables had to be considered at once.

To accomplish this, Friedman used multiple regression, which is an extension of simple linear regression that leads to a predictive formula in multiple dimensions. Using this approach, she summarized how achievement differences were related to the year of study and participant age by the formula:

Achievement difference (in standard deviations)
= 0.006 * (Years since 1960)
− 0.014 * (Average age of participants).

This formula indicates that the gap between male and females decreases slightly more for each year after 1960 that the study took place. This is balanced against the fact that the male advantage increases more than twice as fast for each year increase in the average age of the individuals studied. This increase in male advantage is illustrated in Figure 30–1B, which includes a line reflecting the change in effect sizes over time. Friedman also examined how research reports differed depending on the type of participant. She found the male advantage to increase by another .348 if gifted children were involved and by another .323 if a college entrance examination was taken. The male advantage was reduced in favor of the females by .223 if the participants were from minority groups.

The formula presented above provides a summary of what to expect, on average, from the results of numerous studies. By describing a published study in terms of the study's year of publication and age of participants, one can estimate the expected achievement difference. This estimation can be improved when participant characteristics are added as well.

Such an analysis provides both a terse model and a rich description of the relation between a number of variables, while illuminating aspects of contemporary social issues. It also illustrates the importance of knowing relevant aspects of the data. If Friedman did not know the variables relevant to her study, she could have simply stopped with the conclusion that no differences existed. Her knowledge of the phenomenon led her to seek a description that was less simple, yet more true to the world. Her description is quantitative and predictive, and therefore testable.

Quantitative data analysis occurs in the broader setting of quantitative research. Quantitative research is not a single entity but rather a set of related traditions and activities that are bound together by the appeal of precision in quantification and the advantages of quantitative data analysis that follow. Quantitative research is sometimes equated with positivist or postpositivist philosophical views. Positivism is a school of thought most notably articulated by August Comte (1830/1974). Comte believed that human knowledge had evolved through phases based first on theology and then on metaphysics, and was entering a new phase based on positive knowledge from observation—a phase he called the positivist era. The term "positivist" is sometimes used derisively to suggest extreme reductionism and naive realism (e.g., Firestone, 1990; Guba, 1990). Reductionism is the idea that the world can be broken down into elementary parts that can be understood in isolation, while realism is the belief that there is a single reality that one can truly come to know.

Contrary to these suggestions, much of Comte's work is quite consistent with contemporary intuitions about knowledge and data analysis held by quantitative and qualitative researchers. Comte (1830/1974) held up mathematics as a model of logic while cautioning against its overuse in other fields. He emphasized both deductive and inductive reasoning in inquiry, and called for both observation and theory as well as "active imagination." His attitude toward realism was also clear:

[E]very investigation of laws of phenomenon is eminently relative, since it presupposes that the progress of thought is dependent on the gradual improvement of observation, exact reality being never, in any subject, perfectly disclosed. (p. 140)

Indeed, Comte rejected the use of statistics, believing that the idea of quantifying uncertainties was too imprecise in statements of what is true and not true, and likely to lead to irrational results (Pickering, 1993).

*Quantitative Analysis and the Process of Inquiry.* Another myth of quantitative data analysis concerns the progression of the entire inquiry process when quantitative data are to be collected. Perhaps as an extension of mythical positivism, the process of inquiry is often portrayed as occurring in a lockstep, linear manner. Gay (1987, p. 5), for example, argued that the steps involved in research are

1. selecting and defining a problem;
2. executing research procedures;
3. analyzing the data; and
4. drawing and stating conclusions.

Gay also argued for the linearity of data analysis:

The research plan must include a description of the statistical technique or techniques that will be used to analyze study data. . . . Once the data are collected, it is too late. . . . The hypothesis of the study determines the design, which in turn determines the statistical analysis. (p. 87)

Gay argued for the fixed ordering of hypothesis development as well when he wrote, "Following the review, and preceding the actual conduct of the study, the hypothesis is refined and finalized" (p. 53).

This common idea, that hypotheses must be generated and refined based almost exclusively on experience in the library, is an idealization that poses pragmatic difficulties for data analysis and hypothesis refinement. The difficulty for data analysis is that hypotheses are often formulated in terms of theoretical constructs that need to be operationalized in measurements and data collection procedures. It is not unusual for researchers to have clear ideas about how abstract variables may be related but to have little idea how this relationship will be borne out in specific measurements. For example, Gelb and Mizokawa (1986) examined the relationship between state-level measures of social stratification and the percentage of students categorized for biologically and nonbiologically based disabilities. These authors found several results consistent with their expectations, but they also failed to find a number of results that should have occurred if their hypothesis was correct.

As will be discussed below, one problem with this analysis is that the authors appeared to have little knowledge of the distributions of the measures employed. The shapes of the distributions of some variables were markedly skewed and therefore violated the assumptions of the statistical tests employed. Their specification of a relationship between social stratification and percentage of students categorized in nonbiological statuses is sufficient for theoretical communication. However, to test such variables empirically, not only must the theory be well specified, but the distributions of the empirical variables must also be known. When a researcher has little knowledge of how the measurements are shaped in the real world, there is great room for error. This error is best avoided by knowing the theoretical constructs well, knowing how they have been borne out in the previous literature, and developing

TABLE 30–1. Types of Quantitative Data Analysis
and Their Goals

| Type of Analysis | Goal |
| --- | --- |
| Exploratory data analysis | Generate and refine hypotheses; provide rich description |
| Confirmatory data analysis | Test hypotheses |
|   Significance tests | Rough guide regarding rejection of null effect |
|   Hypothesis tests | Decision-making regarding presence of specific effect |
| Confidence intervals | Estimate population parameter with admission of range of possibilities |
| Meta-analysis | Relate effect sizes to study characteristics |

a rich understanding of the details of the data collected. When such knowledge and understanding are combined with flexibility in reassessing what is appropriate in light of new knowledge about the form of the data, the researcher is well prepared to think about the complexity of research in dynamic fields such as educational psychology.

***The Goals of Quantitative Methods.*** There are a number of different schemes for considering the myriad tools of quantitative analysis. This presentation is organized according to the goals of data analysis that occur at different points in the research process. These goals are not sequential but should be thought of as forming a web in which several elements may be called at any one time in the long process of research. Table 30–1 enumerates these approaches and their goals. First, we discuss the tradition of exploratory data analysis (EDA), whose goal is to find patterns in data for hypothesis generation and refinement. We will argue for the importance of EDA at all stages of research. Next, statistical tests are discussed under the heading of confirmatory data analysis (CDA). Confirmatory data analysis is concerned with hypothesis testing and making inferences about populations. It forms the majority of what most educational psychologists are taught as quantitative methods or statistics. We attempt to reconcile apparent contradictions in statistical practice by differentiating among the historical traditions of significance testing and hypothesis testing, which are typically considered together. This is followed by a discussion of statistical estimation as it is applied in the frequentist approach to confidence intervals. Although confidence intervals rely heavily on the mechanics of statistical tests, their use represents an entirely different logical application of probability and a different logical goal in research. This is followed by a discussion of research synthesis, with a focus on meta-analysis as the first comprehensive statistical tool for integrating research findings. Our discussion of quantitative analysis concludes with an overview of issues related to statistical computing.

## Exploratory Data Analysis

In contrast to the common emphasis on hypothesis testing, exploratory data analysis, in the Tukey, Mosteller, and Hoaglin tradition (e.g., Hoaglin, Mosteller, & Tukey, 1983, 1985, 1991), aims primarily at model building and hypothesis generation

rather than model testing. These authors, and many who have taken up this approach, have produced a well-established set of principles and techniques that distinguish EDA from the general idea of exploratory statistics (Mulaik, 1984), data exploration (Peshkin, 1993), or the assumption that EDA is what one does when one doesn't know what else to do. EDA was introduced to educational psychology by a number of writers, including G. Leinhardt (G. Leinhardt & Leinhardt, 1980), and Wainer (1984a, 1984b). In addition, most current computer packages are influenced by the EDA tradition and incorporate some tools of this approach. Classic texts in this area include Tukey's (1977) seminal work, *Exploratory Data Analysis,* along with works by Mosteller and Tukey (1977), the three volumes by Hoaglin, Mosteller, and Tukey (1983, 1985, 1991), and the third, fourth, and fifth volumes of Tukey's collected works (1986b, 1986c, 1988). The documentation to Velleman's (1992) Data Desk software is a superb introduction to EDA. It includes previously unpublished techniques and a description of software that is single-mindedly aimed at improving EDA. Excellent introductions to statistical graphics that play an important role in EDA are provided by Cleveland (1985, 1993), Wainer (1992), and Wainer and Thissen (1981).

Although a courtroom metaphor is frequently used to describe the evaluation of hypotheses under CDA (e.g., Kraemer & Thiemann, 1987), the metaphor of data analysis as detective work is a consistent theme in EDA (Tukey, 1969/1986a, 1977). The goal of EDA is to develop a rich description of the quantitative representation of a phenomenon. Such a description may lead to preliminary hypotheses, the refinement of theoretical ideas that have yet to be translated into quantities, an explanation for the failure of confirmatory procedures to match an expectation, or simply a very understandable description of the phenomenon of interest. EDA stresses both ecumenism and skepticism of method—use whatever tool is helpful, but never completely believe what you see or think. In the language of the legal metaphor, the goal of EDA is indictment, whereas the goal of CDA is conviction. Because the goal of each type of analysis is different, the two modes are complementary rather than antagonistic (Tukey, 1980).

Because EDA seeks the unexpected, an algorithmic approach seems contrary to its goals. There are, however, a number of consistent themes in the EDA literature that can be used to guide exploratory analyses. It is important to keep in mind that Tukey (1977) considered EDA not merely a set of tools, but also an attitude toward data analysis. The open-mindedness and skepticism referred to above run through EDA. In terms of analytic tools, EDA is characterized by a contextually sensitive application of graphics, robust methods, and reexpression that occurs through an iterative process of tentative model expression, examination of residuals, and restatement of the tentative model. Each of these aspects is discussed below.

An important first step in EDA is to gather information about the domain under investigation. Far from the characterization of exploratory work as naive empiricism, the EDA tradition has long stressed the importance of the context of the analysis (Bode, Mosteller, Tukey, & Winsor, 1949; Tukey, 1979, 1986d) in a manner consistent with the constructivist-friendly view of data analysis presented here.

After establishing some background regarding the data of interest, the data analyst typically begins by examining numer-

TABLE 30-2. Average Group Intelligence Data Provided by Burt (1961)

| Social Class | Adult Mean IQ | Child Mean IQ |
|---|---|---|
| Higher professional | 139.7 | 120.8 |
| Lower professional | 130.6 | 114.7 |
| Clerical | 115.9 | 107.8 |
| Skilled | 108.2 | 104.6 |
| Semiskilled | 97.8 | 98.9 |
| Unskilled | 84.9 | 92.6 |

Note: From *Elements of Graphing Data* (p. 97) by W. S. Cleveland, 1985, Monterey, CA: Wadsworth Advanced Books and Software, based on data supplied in "Intelligence and Social Mobility" by C. Burt, 1961, *British Journal of Statistical Psychology*, 14, pp. 3–23. Reprinted by permission.

ous graphical representations of the data. Tukey (1977) made graphical analysis a foundation of EDA, arguing that "[t]he greatest value of a picture is when it forces us to notice what we never expected to see" (p. vi). For example, Cleveland (1985; see also Wainer, 1989) presented the data in Table 30–2 that were originally reported by Burt (1961). These data are the mean IQ scores for groups of adults and their children organized by type of profession. As Cleveland explained, "the data . . . look innocent enough until they are graphed" (p. 97), as in Figure 30–2. Here it is clear the trend is remarkably linear. The line overlaid on the data is the line formed from the equation: Child score − 100 = ½(Adult score − 100), which was proposed by Conway (1959). Hearnshaw (1979) made a strong case that Conway was the nom-de-plume of Burt, who was also the editor of the journal in which the Burt and Conway manuscripts were published. The graphic jumps out at the reader as too exact to be above suspicion. This graphic makes us notice what we did not expect, which Tukey suggests is the very goal of graphics.

When dealing with complex data sets, the data analyst usually begins by examining univariate displays, followed by bi- and trivariate displays. Among the most common univariate displays is the box plot. The box plot is a graphical representaton of a five-number summary for a batch of data: the first,

second, and third quartiles, and either the highest and lowest value or an otherwise extreme point beyond which data are considered candidates for further scrutiny. Common variations on this scheme are discussed by Frigge, Hoaglin, and Iglewicz (1989). The panels of Figure 30–3 show the relationship between box plots, density smoothing, and histograms. The top illustration of each panel is a histogram based on 500 observations. Although histograms are useful, they can hide details in the shape of the distribution and can be misleading, since their appearance is arbitrarily tied to the number of bars used (Scott, 1992). To overcome these difficulties, density estimation functions have been developed to construct smooth curves over the data. These graphics can be thought of as the result of constructing histograms with many small columns and averaging the tops of the columns until a smooth line is found to substitute for the big steps of the bars ordinarily used.

The bottom illustration of each panel is a box plot representing the same data on the same scale. The center line of the box represents the location of the median of the distribution, and the left and right edges of the box represent the location of the 25th and 75th percentiles. In these displays, dashed lines extend from the ends of the boxes to the farthest data point up to 1.5 times the length of the box. Observations farther away are considered outliers and are represented by individual symbols. The length of the box is the scale value difference between the 75th and 25th percentiles and is called the interquartile range (IQR). The IQR is a measure of spread or dispersion of the data. It is often substituted for the standard deviation in exploratory work because it is not affected by extreme scores as the standard deviation is.

With some practice, a researcher can easily identify patterns in multiple box plots. Because each box plot represents the shape and location of a batch of data, visual comparisons of groups and variables are greatly facilitated. For example, Figure 30–4A depicts the distribution of scores of students' preintervention attitudes toward several academic subjects (from Stevens, 1990). The plots in panel A suggest either that the students in this sample have more positive attitudes toward mathematics than toward other subjects or that the subscales of the test are not equated. Figures 30–4B and C show the scores when they are separated for female and male students, respectively. It can be seen that some of the moderate responses of the aggregated data are a combination of low and high attitudes from the different gender groups. This is most clear in science attitudes, where half of the females fall below a score of 3, whereas only 25% of the males are in this range. The gender differences in mathematics attitude are notable here because these groups have equivalent scores for the 50th, 75th, and 100th percentiles and differ only in the variability in the bottom half of the scores. Box plots are valuable because they can indicate the central tendency, spread, and shape of several distributions simultaneously.

A plot of the mathematics attitude pretest score for each teacher involved in the study is presented in Figure 30–5. Here the graphic serves Tukey's function of showing us what we did not expect. The single line for Teacher 3 indicates that each value in the five-number summary is the same. This means either that all the students performed the same, or that only one student is represented. Returning to the data, we find that the second case is true. The fact that this single child is found among the set of Teacher 2 participants suggests it is merely a

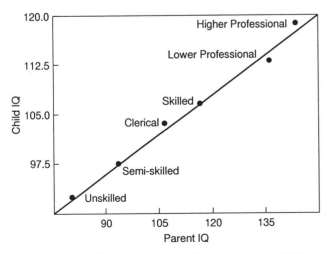

FIGURE 30-2. Plot of Average IQ for Parents and Children from Data Presented by Burt (1961). Graph from Cleveland (p. 98, 1985).

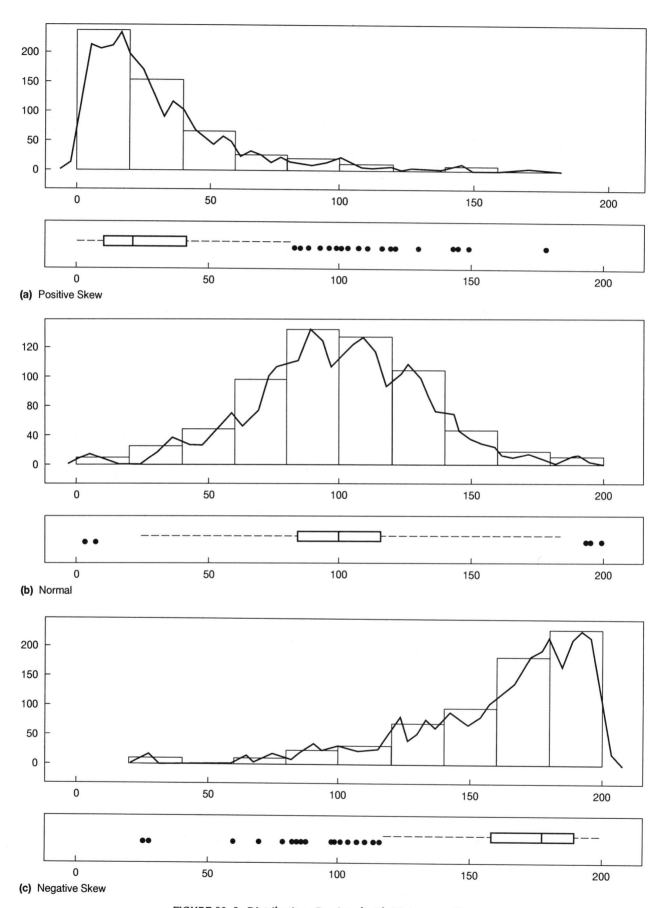

FIGURE 30–3. Distributions Depicted with Histograms, Density Estimates and Box Plots for (A) Positive Skew, (B) Bell-shaped Distribution, and (C) Negative Skew

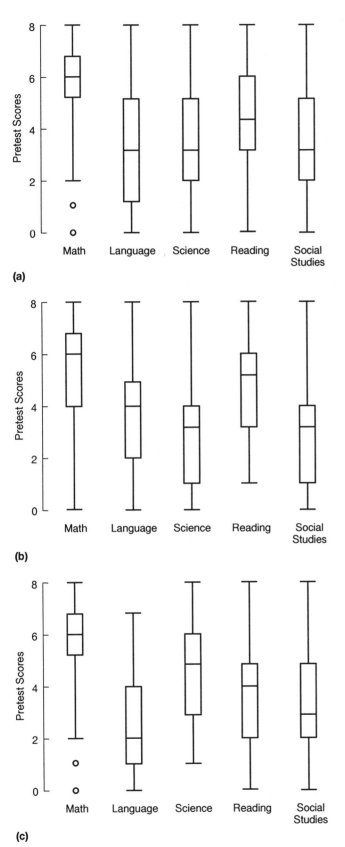

**(a)**

**(b)**

**(c)**

FIGURE 30–4. Pretest Measures of Attitudes Toward Individual Subjects for **(A)** All Students Investigated, **(B)** Female Students Only, and **(C)** Male Students Only

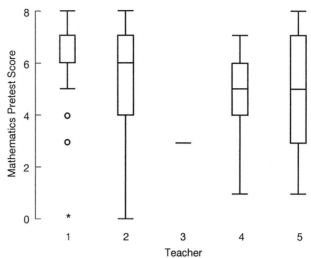

FIGURE 30–5. Box Plots of Mathematics Attitude Pretest Scores, Including Typographical Error Leading to Anomalous Values

typographical error in which Teacher 2 was accidentally indicated with a 3. Stevens (1990) cleverly included this example in his text to accustom the student to the imperfections of data from the field. Because EDA seeks the unexpected, it is quite useful for data cleaning and checking.

Another situation in which box plots can be useful is in the analysis of discrete bivariate data. Many times Likert scales are employed with a fixed number of possible scores. When such variables are plotted against each other in a scatterplot, the symbols stack up on each other and the pattern of multiple responses is obscured. Such a case is presented in Figure 30–6A, which is a failed attempt at communicating the relationship between the science and reading pretest scores. Box plots can be used by constructing a box plot of the science scores at each level of the reading scores, as shown in Figure 30–6B. This figure depicts the distribution of science scores, conditional on each reading score—the basis of regression. The analyst must remember that the box plots each represent a unique set of scores, and often, as in this case, the number of scores varies across groups. Some computer programs can produce box plots with sample sizes indicated.

Another way to overcome the stacking of discrete scores is to change each score by a small random amount so that it moves slightly from its original position. This technique of jittering is illustrated in Figure 30–6C. Figure 30–6D shows a contour plot depicting levels of frequency across the science and reading attitude dimensions. It provides a smoothed (or averaged) count of the points throughout the two dimensions. This is a crude frequency-based technique analogous to methods of multivariate density estimation such as that described in Scott (1992).

Box plots use quartiles to describe the distribution rather than the more common mean and standard deviation. This is based on a desire to employ robust estimators of the position and spread of the data. *Robustness* is the degree to which statistics are insensitive to underlying assumptions (Hoaglin et

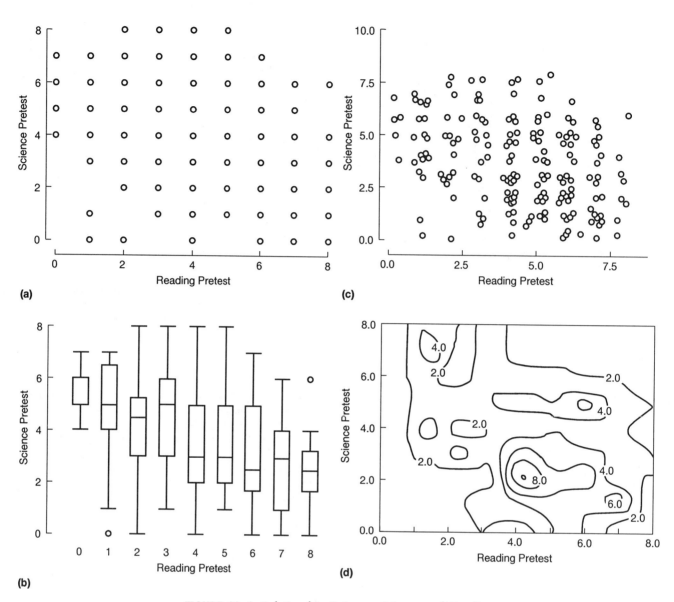

FIGURE 30–6. Relationship Between Science and Reading Attitudes Depicted Using (**A**) a Simple Scatterplot, (**B**) Conditional Box Plots, (**C**) a Jittered Scatterplot, and (**D**) a Contour Plot

al., 1983). When data occur in a form that closely matches the underlying assumptions of a statistic, robustness is not important. For example, when data are normally distributed, the mean and median are equal and IQR is 1.63 times the standard deviation. However, when the data come in an unexpected form, or in an expected but messy form, robustness can be very important. Perhaps the most common aspect of robustness examined is resistance. Resistant statistics are those that are insensitive to minor perturbations in the data. In general, statistics based on averaging, such as the mean and standard deviation, will not be resistant and will be easily affected by extreme scores. Because grading in most schools is accomplished using means, most researchers have long experience with this statistic and may have depended on its being changed by a single

extreme score. It is this sensitivity to extreme scores that allows a high score on the final examination to "pull up" the previously low grades. In other cases, however, extreme scores are not desired to have a large effect on the mean and a more resistant measure is desired. For example, in judging some Olympic events, the highest and lowest scores of a set of judges are thrown out to remove the effect of extremes. A similar strategy is sometimes used in classrooms where the teacher allows a student to drop the lowest quiz grade from the averaging process.

Robustness is first accomplished in EDA by using measures based on an observation's position in the distribution. The median, for example, is in the center of the list of ordered scores and is not affected by the smallest or largest extremes.

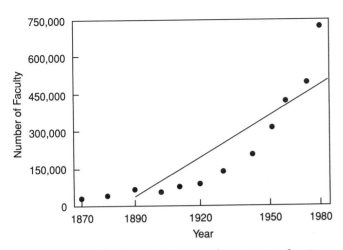

**FIGURE 30–7. Number of Higher Education Faculty Employed in the United States for Each Decennial Year from 1870 to 1980**
The solid line represents the pattern of predicted values obtained using common linear regression.

Other ways of obtaining resistant estimates are available as well. Winsorizing is a process of changing any scores past a certain value (usually the 95th percentile) to equal the value of scores at that percentile. Trimming is the process of simply ignoring observations that fall beyond a preset percentile. Taking the mean of the data in the IQR weighs the inside data and is called the midmean, while averaging the first, second, and third quartiles with the median counting twice is called the trimean. Each of these methods produces more robust measures of the center of distributions than the mean and thereby helps keep the data analyst from being misled by a few extreme points. Of course, as electronic computing power increases, the investigator has the ability to use a number of statistics and compare their performance. Since Tukey's early work, robustness has become a mainstay of statistical research, with extensions of this general principle to regression analysis, ANOVA, and many other common techniques. For a more complete introduction the reader is referred to Lind and Zumbo (1993).

Investigation in EDA is an iterative process of model fitting and assessment. In this framework data are said to consist of modeled and residual aspects, or data = model + residuals. When a graphic analogy is applied to this concept, it is sometimes expressed as data = smooth + rough. The smooth part of any analysis is the part that is modeled or related to a mathematical function. Because the mathematical summary of the data is simpler than the data itself, the model generally produces smooth idealizations of the data that contrast with the rough, unmodeled aspect of the data. Residuals are simply the difference between the smooth that is predicted by a model and what actually occurs in real data. The pattern and magnitude of residuals indicate where and how much the model is different from the data being investigated.

To illustrate the iterative cycle, we examine the higher education faculty employment data presented in Figure 30–7. Here the data form a curved pattern. When the standard linear regression model is used for prediction, predicted values in the depen-

dent variable form a line. Figure 30–7 includes a line marking the pattern of predicted values obtained using linear regression. Because the predicted values fall in a line but the actual values form a curve, application of linear regression techniques is inappropriate in this case. As always, a good start with the data is to examine the univariate data. Histograms of the two variables indicate that the year variable is flat and the faculty variable is quite positively skewed. Because the skew in the faculty variable is the cause of the bend in the line, if we can determine the degree to which there is skew in the data, we can also determine how much bend exists in the line. Knowing the amount of bend that exists in the line means we can describe or model the bend.

When data come in nonsymmetric forms (as in the case of skew), exploratory data analysts generally re-express the variable in a symmetric form. By finding an appropriate re-expression we can assess the departure from normality in the single variable, and hence the departure from linearity in the bivariate relationship. For many simple cases, a transformation can be recommended by using the ladder of re-expression (Mosteller & Tukey, 1977). The ladder of re-expression is a list of exponents that data can be raised to for re-expression. In this analogy there is a rung for each possible exponent. Because an exponent of 1 means no change in the variable, it serves as the starting point for choosing a re-expression. Exponents less than 1 form the lower rungs of the ladder and exponents higher than 1 form the higher rungs of the ladder. Because an exponent of zero always changes a variable to a value of 1, the $\log_{10}$ of the variable is usually taken for this rung. The change produced by a log transformation fits naturally between small positive and negative exponents in terms of the shape of its re-expression (Mosteller & Tukey, 1977). The ladder can be expressed by the sequence:

$$-x^{-3} \quad -x^{-2} \quad -x^{-1} \quad -x^{-1/2} \quad \log_{10} x \quad x^{1/2} \quad x \quad x^2 \quad x^3$$

The analyst decides whether to go up or down the ladder by moving toward the bulk of the distribution. In the present case, the bulk of the data is at the low end of the distribution, so we should examine re-expressions based on the lower rungs of the ladder. Moving from the unchanged variable of faculty[1] we should examine re-expressions based on faculty[1/2] and $\log_{10}$ (faculty) until a roughly bell-shaped distribution is formed.

As we saw above, assessing normality on the basis of histograms is precarious because the shape of the histograms will be largely determined by the number of bins used. One alternative is to use box plots, as shown in Figure 30–8. These plots reveal that as we re-express the original data by moving down the ladder of re-expression, the data become more normal. Returning to the bivariate relationship, we next plot the re-expressed variable against the year of measurement variable in Figure 30–9A. This relatively straight pattern can be well summarized using a linear regression formula that predicts the data to fall in a straight line. Figure 30–9B is a plot of the predicted values from a least squares regression formula that constitutes the smooth form of this data. This plot suggests we have come a long way toward improving our description, an idea substantiated by the size and pattern of the residuals presented in Figure 30–9C. The combination of all these panels illustrates the additive nature of the effects.

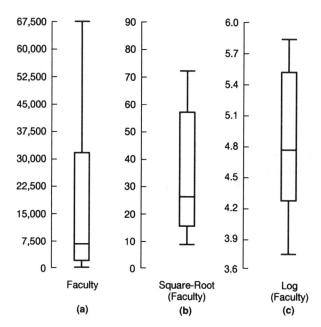

FIGURE 30–8. Multiple Box Plots Illustrating the Move To-ward Normality That Occurs as Transformations Are Computed on Raw Data

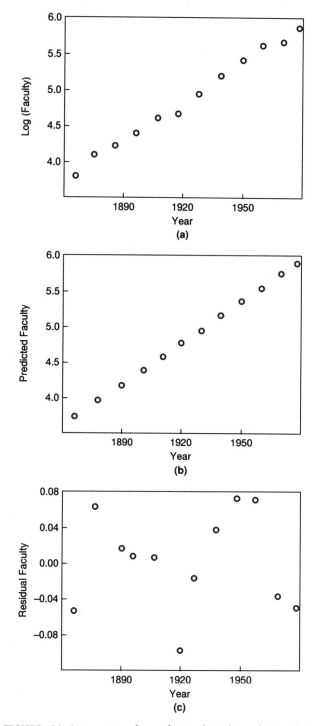

FIGURE 30–9. Log-Transformed, Predicted, and Residual Scores for Faculty Employment Data Plotted Against Year of Data Collection

Although re-expression is common in many areas of the physical and human sciences, some researchers view this technique with suspicion because it can appear that the data are being changed to fit a desired outcome. This is true only insofar as the data are being expressed in a different scale so that an interpretable (usually additive and linear) model can be used. In the present example, graphical analysis makes it clear that a model of the form

$$\text{Faculty} = \text{constant} + \text{slope (years)} + \text{residuals}$$

will not work well. This describes a straight line that misses the bulk of the data (see Figure 30–7). A much better description can be obtained if we use the form

$$\text{Log}_{10}(\text{Faculty}) = -31. + .18 \text{ (years)} + \text{residuals},$$

which is equivalent to:

$$\text{Faculty} = 10^{-31. + 18 \text{ (years)} + \text{residuals}}.$$

The first of these two re-expressions describes a straight line that follows data that have been straightened, and the second describes a curved line that follows curved data. However, the two expressions are identical in their accuracy in describing the data.

Re-expression is essentially about measurement. Original scales do not always produce data in an appropriate form for analysis. Re-expression addresses these difficulties and presents a valuable alternative to conducting data analysis with scales that violate the assumptions of subsequent analysis. Several reexpressions are so common that we do not even consider them such. As examples, percentages consist of multiplying a

score times the reciprocal of the highest reference score, and miles per gallon is the reciprocal of gas used multiplied by the number of miles driven. These are simply re-expressions that allow analysis in an appropriate and interpretable scale. Hoaglin (1988) provides a number of other examples from everyday experiences.

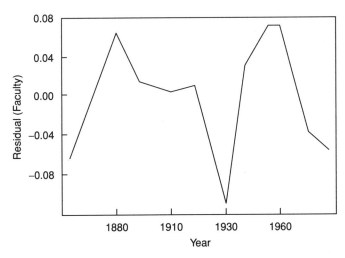

FIGURE 30–10. Pattern of Residuals Remaining After Removal of Pattern Associated with Log(Faculty) Regression

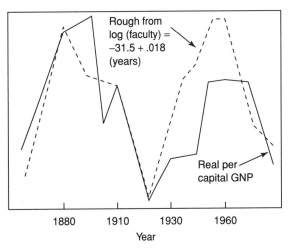

FIGURE 30–11. Correspondence Between Pattern of Residuals Following First Regression and Pattern of Economic Strength Indicated by Real per capita Gross National Product

Up to this point, we have applied re-expression and classic regression computations to form an initial model and residuals. If all detectable pattern has been removed from the residuals, (also called the rough in EDA) then the job is complete. If not, and if the rough still contains a pattern that can be described, the rough from this first pass at the data becomes the data for a second pass, and the process is continued.

Reexamination of the data from this rough (i.e., pattern of residuals) (Figure 30–9C) shows that linear pattern has been removed from the data and the residuals fall sporadically around the plot. However, because the data reflect measurements made over successive time periods, a line plot connecting the points in time may be helpful. In Figure 30–10, simple connection of points brings out a pattern that was not easy to detect in the previous plot. Here we see up and down cycles, with low points following the Civil War (1870), World War I (1920), and in the 1970s and 1980s. Although the first pass through the data led to a logarithmic model suggestive of population growth, this pattern is suggestive of a business cycle. It is only after the layer of population growth is peeled from the data that this pattern becomes visible.

Continuing our analysis with the rough from the previous step as our data, we look for a way to describe the cyclical pattern. One possibility is to use gross national product (GNP), which provides a broad measure of economic strength. Because inflation changes the value of goods measured in GNP, we should probably examine real GNP. Real GNP is GNP adjusted for (or reexpressed for) inflation. Measures of GNP will also be confounded with the size of the population, because larger populations produce more goods and services. Reexpressing real GNP to account for population growth produces real per capita GNP. Plotting this variable against time leads to a pattern very similar to that of the faculty residuals.

When these data are overlaid on the residuals, quite a good match is provided, as seen in Figure 30–11. The plot of the rough from the first pass against real per capita GNP is provided in Figure 30–12A. The smooth, based on linear regression, is shown in Figure 30–12B, and the rough from this pass is shown in Figure 30–12C. No obvious pattern remains in the residuals

of this second step. An economist may detect a pattern we are unaware of, or may suggest a variable more appropriate than real per capita GNP. If this occurred, these leads would be assessed as well. For our purposes, we can conclude that faculty size is primarily a function of population growth and the strength of the economy.

We do not intend here to provide a definitive model of these data but rather use it to illustrate several important aspects of EDA. First, the analysis rests on the graphical display of data and statistical summaries. During prepublication work with this data, all attempts to develop a model led to a consistently large residual for one observation. After a number of techniques were applied without success, the data were rechecked and a typographical error was detected. Such a mistake could easily have been overlooked had detailed analysis of the data, predicted values, and residuals not been employed. Second, the value of re-expression for determining the proper form of a model has been illustrated. Assuming linearity or normality because many other things are linear or normal can lead to very bad descriptions.

Third, the iterative process of tentative model fitting, residual analysis, the model respecification has been illustrated. The process shown here is the EDA equivalent of forward selection in automated linear regression analysis. In this case the pattern of the economic cycle became visible only after the pattern of population growth had been stripped off. The difference between the two approaches is that most automated procedures rely exclusively on the size of correlation coefficients for variable selection without attending to finer details in the shape or pattern of the data. Because correlation coefficients are measures of linear relationships, departures from linearity will lead to the computation of inappropriate coefficients. As Henderson and Velleman (1981) argued, "The fundamental axiom of this philosophy of data analysis is the declaration: The data analyst knows more than the computer" (p. 391). We believe researchers can often improve their advantage over the computer by appropriately applying techniques of EDA.

The techniques described above can be generalized to larger

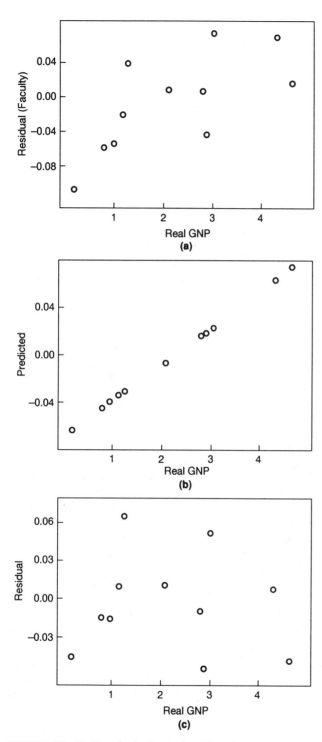

FIGURE 30–12. Residuals from the First Regression, Predicted Values Using Real per capita Gross National Product, and Residuals for Current Analysis, Each Plotted Against Year of Data Collection

data sets with more variables. Gelb and Mizokawa (1986) used simple and multiple regression analysis to examine the relationships between percentage of students placed in special education classes and measures of social and economic strength, as well as racial diversity and educational spending in each state. Special education categories were educable mentally retarded (EMR), severely emotionally disturbed (SED), gifted, or having a specific learning disability (SLD). Socioeconomic factors included number of inmates in the state, percentage of children below the poverty level, infant mortality rate, and percent of blacks, Hispanics, Asian Americans, and Indian Americans living in the state. First the authors examined the simple correlations between each diagnostic category and each of the socioeconomic variables. Diagnostic categories with more than one significant correlation were then examined further with multiple regression analysis.

Although the form of data screening used is not reported, the authors noted that Washington, D.C., was an outlier because 94% of its residents were African Americans and the next highest observation was South Carolina, with only 41% African Americans. In EDA, an outlier is an unusual observation that calls for further examination. Often outliers are set aside and not included in the bulk of the analysis, as was done by Gelb and Mizokawa (1986). Such a move is appropriate when there is reason to believe that the observation represents a different underlying process than the other observations. Including such an observation in the analysis would be mixing apples and oranges, with the risk that neither category is described well. In this case the observation reflected the urban nature of a city, rather than the heterogeneous nature of a state. The authors acted appropriately by conducting the analysis both with and without the questionable observation, by reporting these steps explicitly, and by providing all of the data in the journal article so that others could replicate the analysis.

When working with such large data sets, exploratory analysts are likely to employ a scatterplot matrix. A scatterplot matrix is the graphical analogue to a correlation matrix. A matrix of scatterplots is arranged according to column and row headings that indicate the variables on the top/bottom and left/right side of each scatterplot. The variable plotted on the vertical axis of each scatterplot is the variable named in the leftmost plot of the row. The variable on the horizontal axis of each plot is the variable named in the bottom-most plot of the column. For example, the plot in the upper right-hand corner shows EMR on the vertical axis, and Education Cost on the horizontal axis. Because the plots have been reduced in size to fit the computer screen, the variable labels are partly obscured. Figure 30–13 is a scatterplot matrix of the data, including the offending observation from Washington, D.C., which is indicated by an open circle in contrast to the filled symbols for each state. The third plot from the right on the top row includes a regression line that misses the bulk of the data. This occurs because it is leaning over to try to account for Washington, D.C., and thereby poorly describes most states. The ethnic percentage variables have been excluded from this graphic because individual windows would be prohibitively small if more were added in this space.

In the Data Desk (Velleman, 1992) statistical package used here, normal probability plots are placed along the diagonals of the matrix. Normal probability plots are designed specifically to assess a distribution's match with normality. Matches with other distributions can be assessed using other types of quantile–quantile plots, of which the normal probability plot is a single instance. These plots exploit the fact that when data are normally distributed, then, by knowing the percentile in which

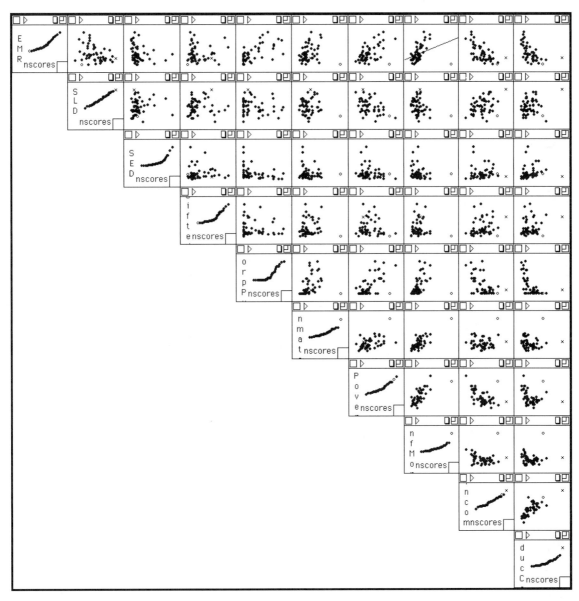

FIGURE 30-13. Scatterplot Matrix of Subset of Variables Presented by Gelb and Mizokawa (1986)

an observation falls, one can obtain the corresponding z score. Plotting the z scores of the raw data against the data of the normal distribution produces a straight line. Deviation from this straight line indicates deviation from normality.

By examining the matrix, the reader may observe that outliers still remain in the data, as does sharp nonlinearity in some variables and scatterplots. Alaska, for example, appears as an outlier in the two columns along the right-hand side of the matrix, which depict per capita income and school expense. In these plots, the point marking Alaska has been changed to an **x** to differentiate it from other expense-related variables because of the high cost of services in that state. All scatterplots associated with either the percent gifted or the percent SED variable have wide bands at the bottom reflecting a floor effect and positive skew for these variables. When Gelb and Mizo-

kawa (1986) published these data they reported that EMR and SLD percentages were significantly related to social and economic indicators, but that gifted and SED categories were not. This matrix and the box plots in Figure 30-14 suggest that the normality of the EMR and SLD variables may allow appropriate use of regression and correlation, whereas the floor effects in the other two variables make correlation inappropriate without reexpression. For example, the scatterplot relating percentage of SED students in each state (with Washington, D.C., omitted) to the infant mortality rate and the residuals from a linear regression of these variables are presented in Figures 30-15A and B, respectively. The floor effects in both variables have led to grossly nonnormal data. The very poor modeling of observations is reflected in the large residuals and non-bell-shaped pattern. Figures 30-15C and D show the scatterplot following

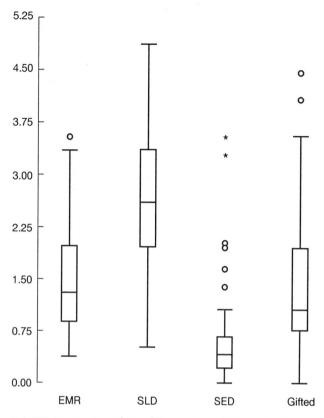

FIGURE 30–14. Box Plots of Percentage of Students Categorized as Educably Mentally Retarded (EMR), Having a Specific Learning Disability (SLD), Being Seriously Emotionally Disturbed (SED), or Gifted in Each of 50 States and District of Columbia

$\log_{10}$ re-expression on both variables. The normality in the re-expressed bivariate data is evident in the normality of the residuals. Figure 30–15C includes a second line that represents the regression line when an extreme observation indicated by a + is removed. This allows quick assessment of the effect of that observation on the slope. Further analysis with this observation set aside may be called for but cannot be pursued here.

The re-expression employed now allows for appropriate use of linear models such as linear regression and Pearson correlation coefficients. In this case the correlation coefficient changes from −.24 when its assumptions are violated to −.34 when linearity is restored. The goal, of course, is not to find a larger or smaller correlation, but rather to find out what the correlation is when it is properly used on variables with a linear relationship. The more appropriate correlation of −.34 is statistically significant, as are at least two other variables re-expressed to linearity. In Gelb and Mizokawa (1986) the SED variable was not analyzed using multiple regression because it was believed to have only one significant correlation. This reanalysis demonstrates that when the marginal and bivariate distributions are not closely examined, conclusions concerning curved relationships measured by linear functions, such as Pearson's correlation, can be misleading. As we noted at the begin-

ning of the quantitative methods section, appropriate analyses cannot always be determined a priori, and there is no substitute for a thorough understanding of the details of the data.

Our final example of EDA techniques illustrates how the idea of data = smooth + rough is used to interpret two-way tables. Two-way tables are common in educational psychology. They are used to report cell means for ANOVA results as well as for presenting information from nearly any type of factorial design. For example, Table 30–3 presents data from Swanson, O'Connor, and Conney (1990) on the percentage of expert and novice teachers who used particular cognitive strategies or heuristics when considering solutions to hypothetical student behavior problems. Participants were considered novice or expert on the basis of their previous experience and were instructed in a manner that directed or did not direct them to attend to problem-solving processes.

From an EDA point of view, each piece of data represents a combination of row and column effects. Without extracting the smooth underlying Table 30–3, it is difficult to make direct comparisons of numbers. What counts as a large difference between numbers across the columns of a particular row will depend on the magnitude of the numbers in that row—something that itself can only be assessed by comparison across rows. The difficulty in making between-row and between-column comparisons simultaneously may lead to a focus on surface features rather than on deep structure. In their discussion of these data, Swanson et al. noted the highest and lowest use categories for experts and novices without mention of the effect of type of direction (the experimental manipulation), nor did they address any anomalies or other patterns of strategy use. This suggests the data as presented were simply too complex to interpret without extracting a smooth.

To extract the smooth for such a table a two-way fit based on median polish is available (Emerson & Hoaglin, 1983). An initial assessment of row effects can be obtained by using the median (or mean) of each row. Because the median will act as the tentative smooth, it is subtracted from each row to leave residuals. Next, the residuals left in the table are analyzed for column effects by subtracting the appropriate column median from each row-corrected observation. With a set of initial row medians and column medians, the medians of these groups of data can be used to form a grand median—which is likewise subtracted from the original row and column medians. This process of subtracting out row and column effects is repeated until further iterations produce no decrease in residuals. What is left then is an estimate of an overall effect (the combination of all row and column effects) as well as row and column effects that exist in addition to the overall effect. For each cell, the sum of these effects (grand, row, and column) forms the smooth of the data and serves as a predicted value. The difference between the smooth and the actual value is the residual.

The smooth and residuals of the two-way fit for the data shown in Table 30–3 are presented in Tables 30–4 and 30–5, respectively. The reader may notice that each cell in the original table is the sum of all smooth effects plus the residuals. Because the smooth removes the row and column effects, large residuals represent an additional nonadditive effect called an interaction.

The two-way plot was developed to portray a two-way fit,

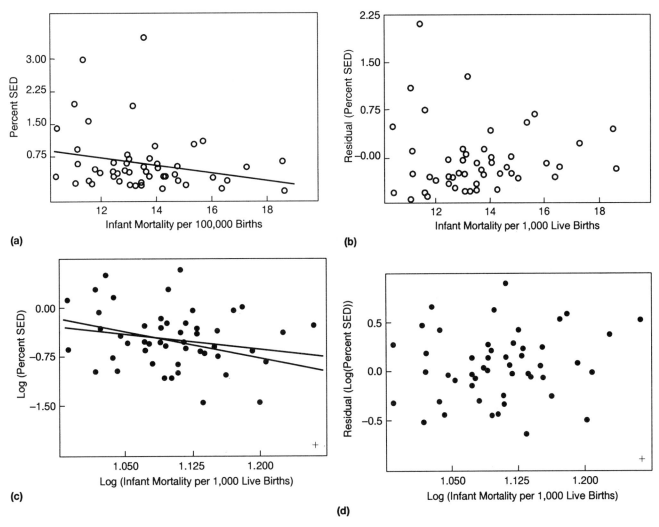

**(a)**

**(b)**

**(c)**

**(d)**

FIGURE 30–15. Scatterplot (**A**) and Residual Plot (**B**) for Regression of Percent SED on Infant Mortality Rate for Untransformed Data; **C** and **D**, Same Plots for Log-Transformed Data

TABLE 30–3. Percentage of Strategy and Heuristic Use Across Groups

| | Group | | | |
|---|---|---|---|---|
| Strategy/Heuristic | Expert Direct | Expert Nondirect | Novice Direct | Novice Nondirect |
| Definition of Problem | 50.1 | 58.2 | 35.5 | 32.1 |
| Data Acquisition | 33.5 | 48.6 | 34.3 | 27.9 |
| Interpretation | 17.5 | 35.3 | 10.8 | 15.3 |
| General Problem Solver | 38.4 | 52.3 | 35.6 | 26.4 |
| Feedback | 13.9 | 35.6 | 2.5 | 8.8 |
| Pattern Extraction | 10.8 | 26.5 | 1.5 | 0.0 |
| Hypothetico-Deductive | 16.7 | 40.3 | 7.4 | 12.2 |
| Evaluation | 48.6 | 52.2 | 21.7 | 33.3 |
| Basic Problem Solving | 44.6 | 52.0 | 43.3 | 36.7 |

Note: From "An Information Processing Analysis of Expert and Novice Teachers Problem Solving" by H. L. Swanson, J. E. O'Conner, and J. B. Cooney, 1990, *American Educational Research Journal*, 27, pp. 533–556. Reprinted by permission.

as shown in Figure 30–16. The scale that indicates the predicted value of each observation is located on the left side of the graphic. Each observation is indicated by intersecting lines with the corresponding row and column labels. Intersecting lines higher in the figure represent effects with higher predicted values. The fact that all intersections of strategies and heuristics with the Expert/Nondirect column occur high in the plot reflects the higher strategy/heuristic use in this group. Strategies and heuristics are also spaced according to their predicted values. The most frequently used strategies and heuristics are higher on the graphic and those used less frequently are lower. For example, the top point of the plot is the intersection of the highest frequency group (Expert/Nondirect) and the highest frequency heuristic or strategy (Definition of Problem). The combination of the row effect (9.81) plus the column effect (17.32) and the overall effect (31.32) sums to 58.45, which is the predicted value. Looking at the intersection of the two lines and then moving the eyes to the left, the reader will recognize that the scale value of that intersection is 58.45. Such a process can be repeated for each observation. Some effects may not total the actual value exactly because of rounding of the effects.

This decomposition reveals the underlying structure of the table. Each predicted value equals the row effect (type of strategy/heuristic), a column effect (group membership), and the grand effect, which is the overall average strategy use independent of strategy or group type. The actual values are simply the predicted values plus the residuals, and, vice versa, the residuals are simply the difference between the predicted and actual values.

Although the value of individual observations can be decomposed in this manner, the purpose of the plot is to communicate numerous aspects of the data simultaneously. The most obvious pattern is that the effects for Novice/Direct and Novice/Nondirect are quite similar, while experts differ according to whether they were in the Direct or Nondirect conditions. Predicted values for strategies/heuristics in the Expert/Nondirect group are 14 percentage points higher than the Expert/Direct group. This indicates an expertise by treatment interaction in which the treatment did not affect the novices but may have had an impact on experts.

A second pattern concerns the grouping of the strategies/heuristics. The Interpretation, Feedback, Hypothetico-Deductive, and Pattern Extraction effects were all low-use strategies. This highest use of this cluster of strategies is about 14% below the lowest frequency of the other set of strategies/heuristics. Several patterns or clusters appear in the high-use group of strategies as well.

The smooth tells only part of the story; the rest is told by the rough. Figure 30–17 is a two-way plot with residuals added. The vertical lines starting at intersecting row and column points

TABLE 30–4. Smooth from Two-Way Analysis of Table 30–3

| Effect | |
|---|---|
| Overall | 31.32 |
| Row | |
| Definition of Problem | 9.81 |
| Data Acquisition | 0.00 |
| Interpretation | −13.99 |
| General Problem Solver | 3.66 |
| Feedback | −19.95 |
| Pattern Extraction | −23.94 |
| Hypothetico-Deductive | −16.85 |
| Evaluation | 4.50 |
| Basic Problem Solving | 9.35 |
| Column | |
| Expert/Direct | 3.42 |
| Expert/Nondirect | 17.32 |
| Novice/Direct | −5.88 |
| Novice/Nondirect | −3.42 |

represent the distance from the predicted to the actual value. For the Basic Problem Solving percentage in the Expert/Nondirect group, the predicted value is $31.32 + 9.35 + 17.32 = 57.99$, but the actual value is 5.99 percent lower, so a line descends from the predicted value of 57.99 down to the actual value of 52. Long vertical lines mean long residuals and an increasingly bad fit. Interaction effects for particular strategies can be easily identified in this plot. Those in the Novice/Direct group used the Basic Problem Solving strategy more than predicted, as indicated by a line extending up from the predicted value of $31.32 + 9.35 - 5.88 = 34.79$ to the actual value of 43.3. The difference between these two values is 8.51, which is the size

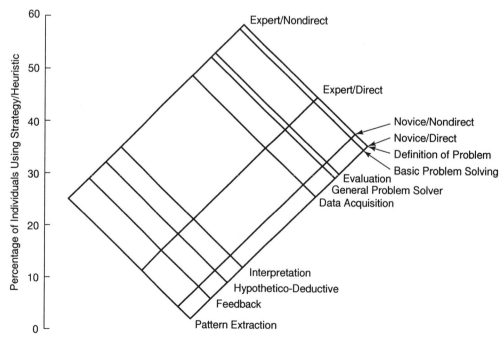

FIGURE 30–16. Two-Way Plot of Data Presented in Table 30–3 Using Smoothing Information Presented in Table 30–4

TABLE 30–5. Rough (Residuals) from Two-Way Analysis of Table 30–3

| Strategy/Heuristic | Group | | | |
|---|---|---|---|---|
| | Expert Direct | Expert Nondirect | Novice Direct | Novice Nondirect |
| Definition of Problem | 5.55 | −0.25 | 0.25 | −5.61 |
| Data Acquisition | −1.24 | −0.04 | 8.86 | 0.00 |
| Interpretation | −3.25 | 0.65 | −0.65 | 1.39 |
| General Problem Solver | 0.00 | 0.00 | 6.50 | −5.16 |
| Feedback | −0.89 | 6.91 | −2.99 | 0.85 |
| Pattern Extraction | 0.00 | 1.80 | 0.00 | −3.96 |
| Hypothetico-Deductive | −1.19 | 8.51 | −1.19 | 1.15 |
| Evaluation | 9.36 | −0.94 | −8.24 | 0.90 |
| Basic Problem Solving | 0.51 | −5.99 | 8.51 | −0.54 |

of the residual and the length of the residual line. This use is higher than one would expect in light of the row and column effects and contrasts with the behavior of the Expert/Nondirect group, which used the strategy less than would be expected in light of their group effect and the overall rate of use of this strategy.

As in the previous examples, an underlying structure of the data has been exposed and graphics have been employed to present the numerous pieces of information in an integrated manner. In addition, residuals were analyzed to improve our understanding of the behavior of the observations relative to their predicted values. The table has revealed the additive two-way effects that are often sought in ANOVA yet often overlooked in favor of more removed summaries.

This section has presented a brief overview of techniques and attitudes data analysts employ when working in the exploratory mode. The analyst is always conscious that the work is not a definitive end, but a tentative beginning. Any hypotheses generated when working in this mode need to be tested using confirmatory methods applied to different data if confirmatory statements about hypotheses are to be used. In this way EDA helps modify the set of plausible hypotheses. The goal is not to replace confirmatory methods, but rather to supplement them. We believe that data exploration is an important part of any data analysis. Even when the researcher has rich previous experience with a domain of data, or an exact hypothesis to test, the unexpected is always possible and EDA should always be used to anticipate this possibility.

## Confirmatory Data Analysis

Confirmatory data analysis remains the mainstay of data analysis for journal publication in educational psychology. When accomplished properly it offers wide benefit. However, important basic assumptions and technical details are often missed in textbooks (Brewer, 1985; Cobb, 1987) as well as by instructors and practitioners. In addition, the wide availability of computer programs for statistics allows anyone to compute statistics regardless of their knowledge of the meaning of statistical results (Searle, 1989). These factors have led to some misuse and myth concerning the proper goal and possible achievements of confirmatory procedures. In this section we review some of the underlying principles of confirmatory procedures and relate the views of the dominant traditions under this approach.

Whereas EDA is focused on hypothesis generation and

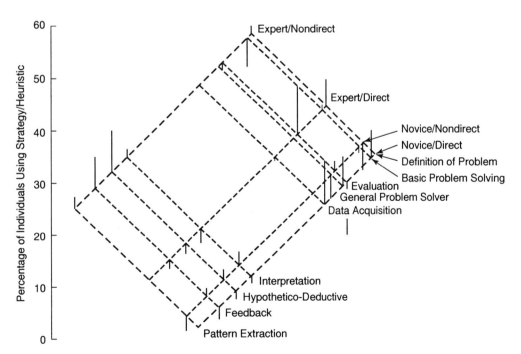

FIGURE 30–17. Two-Way Plot of Data Presented in Table 30–3 Using Smoothing Information from Table 30–4 and Residual Information from Table 30–5

model refinement, CDA is focused on hypothesis testing and inferences extended to populations by using probabilities. Confidence intervals and meta-analysis are extensions of the reasoning discussed in this section and are addressed under separate headings below.

CDA aims to assess a hypothesized quantitative relation by describing what would happen if a hypothesis was true, and then comparing an empirical outcome with the hypothesized outcome. This process rests on the foundations of sampling theory and probability.

*Quantifying Fluctuation: The Sampling Distribution.* Sampling theory is a mathematically precise way to describe what to expect in samples drawn from a larger set of data. The larger set of data is called a population and is generally considered a group about which one wants to make an inference. The sample is any subset of this population. Sometimes populations exist physically, like the set of all special education teachers in a state. At other times populations are theoretical, such as the set of all possible replications of a test. Numeric summaries of populations are called parameters and numeric summaries of samples are called statistics or estimates.

One of the primary goals of sampling theory is to explain the easily observable fact that if we have a population parameter, say a mean, samples drawn from that population will not necessarily have the same mean. Over repeated samples we would expect some sample means to be higher than the population mean and some to be lower. For example, assume we randomly picked individuals from across the country to rate the president of the United States on a scale from 1 to 10. If the population mean is 5, we would expect some samples to have means larger than 5 and some samples to have means lower than 5. This reflects the general idea that sample statistics fluctuate around population parameters.

When asked to explain why this happens many people suggest that an underlying cause affects each sample differently. In this case, perhaps presidential approval is tied to party affiliation and the percentage of Republicans or Democrats varies from sample to sample. Although this may be true, a more fundamental process underlies all sampling of this sort. This process is called, variously, random variation, random sampling variability, or error. Each of these terms refers to the fluctuation from sample to sample that occurs even when there is *no* other cause for the differences between samples. This is the effect of randomly selecting subsets, which leads to different things happening on different occasions simply because random processes lead to random outcomes.

This effect can easily be demonstrated by creating a large set of numbers and randomly pulling numbers out in subsets and calculating the means in each subset. Here the large set serves as an artificial population and the subsets serve as simulated samples. In such a case the means will still vary, even though there is no underlying effect other than random sampling fluctuation. It is this random fluctuation that can be well described mathematically and that serves as the foundation of confirmatory procedures.

To describe this variability in outcomes, statisticians have constructed maps that indicate how far statistics, like means, vary and how often they vary to specific distances. Distributions described by these maps are distributions of statistics that arise from repeated samples from a population, and are therefore called sampling distributions. It is of great importance that one not confuse the notion of a *sampling* distribution with the notion of a *sample* distribution. A sampling distribution is a distribution of summary statistics that occurs over repeated sampling from a population. A sample distribution is the distribution of raw scores in a single sample. It seems unfortunate that words for these very distinct concepts differ by only three letters.

The sampling distribution is central to inferential statistics because it maps out what sample statistics to expect from a hypothesized population. This map of expectation is compared against statistics collected from research. If it is rare to find statistics in the sampling distribution as large as or larger than the empirical outcome, the researcher has reason to consider that the empirical statistic may come from a population other than the one hypothesized. By concluding that a hypothesized population did not generate the empirical statistic, a researcher is indicating the type of population that did generate the empirical statistic. In practice, this typically means rejecting the hypothesis and sampling distribution associated with no treatment effect or relationship. This rejection implies that the true sampling distribution is associated with some unknown (but nonzero) treatment effect or relationship.

*Determining the Shape of the Sampling Distribution.* The shapes of sampling distributions are found in a number of ways. First, mathematical statisticians can sometimes determine the shape of a sampling distribution by using mathematical knowledge of how summaries vary. This leads to formulas that describe the shape of a sampling distribution very precisely. Most statistical computer packages use these formulas to inform researchers where an empirical sample statistic falls in the map of expected sample statistics.

A second method for determining the shape of a sampling distribution has been described already and is called a Monte Carlo simulation. A Monte Carlo simulation begins with the construction of a population with certain characteristics. Typically this is done on a computer, which is then used to repeatedly draw random samples from the population. The sampling distribution is determined by looking at the distribution of statistics that come from calculating a statistic on each random sample. Panel A of Figure 30–18 shows the distribution of raw scores in an artificially constructed population with a mean of 100 and an SD of 15. Panels B, C, D, and E show the distribution of means that occurs when calculated on repeated samples of size 5, 10, 20, and 30, respectively. The reader may note that as the sample size increases with each subsequent panel, the variability in the means decreases. This is a general rule for statistics that matches our intuition that it is better to have more data than less data. As the amount of data in a sample increases, a sample statistic is, on average, more likely to be close to the population parameter. Statistics in larger samples fluctuate less than statistics in smaller samples. Figure 30–19A shows box plots for these distributions, and Figure 30–19B presents the interquartile range for each distribution.

Monte Carlo methods are quite valuable when the exact mathematical form of a sampling distribution cannot be determined. For example, Student (1908) provided the original formulas for the sampling distribution of the *t* test for testing differences between group means. Although he was correct in his mathematics, he was unable to complete one step of the proof. To check his work, he performed an extensive Monte

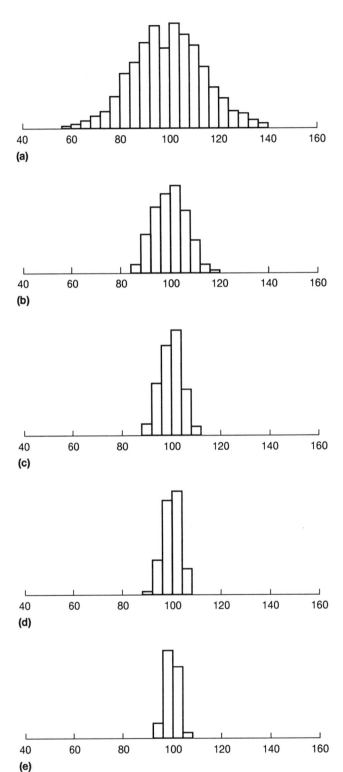

FIGURE 30–18. Sampling Distributions of Means from Population with a Mean of 100 and SD of 15 for Samples of Size (A) 1, (B) 5, (C) 10, (D) 20, and (E) 30

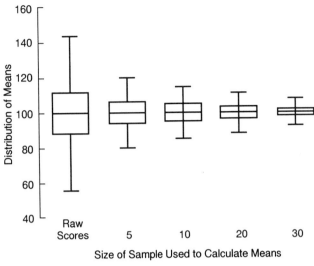

(a)

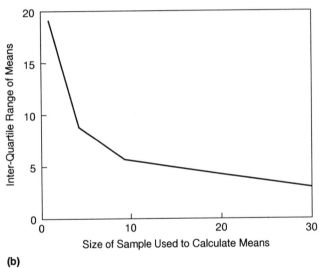

(b)

FIGURE 30–19. **A**, Multiple Box Plots Depicting Sampling Distribution of Means for Varying Sample Sizes; **B**, Line Plot Indicating Relationship Between Interquartile Range of Sampling Distribution of Means and Sample Size When Drawn from a Population with a Mean of 100 and SD of 15

Carlo simulation by drawing numbers out of a bowl. The distribution generated by his simulation closely matched the shape suggested by his formulas. It was another 17 years before R. A. Fisher (1925) provided the complete mathematical proof.

A third method for determining what outcomes one should expect from random sampling fluctuation is based on randomizing the data from the research rather than the hypothetical data of a population. Referred to as either the randomization or the permutation test, this procedure utilizes the set of all possible permutations of the data when random assignment or selection holds. In our previous examples we examined the fluctuation of sample means from a single population mean. For this example we consider the slightly more complex case of examining the fluctuation in mean differences that occur when two groups differ only by random sampling fluctuation. When two populations are exactly the same, they are indistinguishable in terms of their elements, and therefore can be considered a single population. Specifying the set of possible outcomes that could

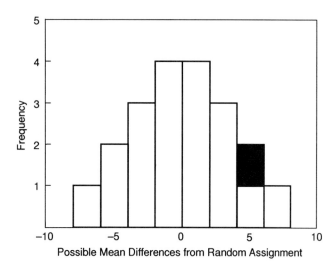

FIGURE 30–20. Histogram of All Possible Mean Differences Obtainable from Example Data Varying only by Random Assignment

occur via random assignment from a single population thereby establishes the outcomes expected from two populations under the condition of sampling fluctuation alone.

The randomization test is well explained with a hypothetical example. Take 6 subjects randomly assigned to groups A or B, exposed to different treatments, and tested on a paper-and-pencil test to produce the following scores:

Group A: Joe—25　Fred—19　Sally—23　　mean = 22.3.
Group B: Sam—12　Tracy—22　Jamie—16　　mean = 16.6.

Difference between mean A and mean B = 5.7.

If these people are all from the same population and have been separated only by the sample-to-sample fluctuation of random assignment, then the following case is equally likely:

Group A: Sam—12　Fred—19　Sally—23　　mean = 18.
Group B: Joe—25　Tracy—22　Jamie—16　　mean = 21.

Difference between mean A and mean B = −3.

With 6 subjects in two groups of 3 there are $\frac{6!}{3!3!} = 20$ possible random ways to form these two groups, and hence 20 possible mean differences—the set of all possible outcomes given only random sample fluctuation when there is no difference in the populations. The set of all possible mean differences consists of the following numbers:

$$-7.7\ -5.7\ -5\ -3.7\ -3.7\ -3\ -1.7\ -1\ -1\ -0.3$$
$$+7.7\ +5.7\ +5\ +3.7\ +3.7\ +3\ +1.7\ +1\ +1\ +0.3.$$

By plotting the distribution of these numbers, one can map out what is expected when the hypothesis of a single population is true, as seen in Figure 30–20. The observed mean difference of 5.7 is marked on the distribution, indicating that it is somewhat high in the set. If we wanted to know how probable is

a mean difference of 5.7 or larger, this could easily be assessed in terms of relative frequency in the set of possible outcomes. Since four of the means are equal to or more extreme (positive and negative) than 5.7, the probability is 4/20, or .25. If our empirical outcome was much less likely to occur under the assumed case of a single population, that assumption would become suspect.

Each of these three approaches to determining the sampling distribution has advantages and disadvantages. The mathematical specification is by far the most widely used in practice because it is built into most statistical packages. In addition, most textbooks rely on this approach and provide tables matching the size of a statistic with the amount of the sampling distribution that falls past it. Because the mathematics begin with certain assumptions about the shape of the population and the way the data were collected, researchers must be very familiar with the assumptions underlying the test and the degree to which they can be violated. Failure to heed the underlying logic of a statistic may lead to reporting results that are quite wrong.

The Monte Carlo method is seldom used in practice, but it is used widely in statistical research to see what shape sampling distributions take under conditions other than those that are well described mathematically. For example, the two-group $t$ test is a common method for testing the hypothesis that two groups have the same population mean—the same question examined in the randomization test above. The mathematics of this procedure assume the variances of the populations are equal for the mathematical sampling distribution to be appropriate. How can we know whether the mathematical sampling distribution is still appropriate when our samples come from populations with different variances? To answer such a question, a statistician may conduct Monte Carlo simulations using artificial populations with different variances. The researcher then compares the match between the mathematical sampling distribution, which is dependent on the assumption of common variances, and the Monte Carlo–created distribution based on different variances. To the degree that the two sampling distributions differ, the mathematical distribution is inappropriate and will give misleading results. This leads to the case that $p$ values provided by standard computer packages and texts are inappropriate in some cases. A good statistics book will address the issue of robustness of a test and provide information concerning the departure from assumptions and the difference between true and assumed $p$ values. The results of a Monte Carlo simulation assessing the violation of the equal variances assumption are reported by Glass, Peckham, and Sanders (1972).

Application of the randomization test has long been deterred by the lack of high-speed computing needed to assess the permutations possible in even moderately sized data sets. Nevertheless, the randomization test forms the logical basis of all statistical tests. Describing the mathematical approach to specifying sampling distributions, Fisher (1936; cited in Kempthorne, 1955) wrote, "[their] conclusions have no justification beyond the fact that they agree with those which could have been arrived at by this elementary method." However, besides the computational difficulty, which is rapidly fading, randomization tests result in lumpy distributions when small samples are used, as illustrated in Figure 30–20. However, they do provide a

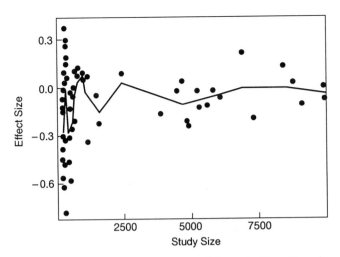

FIGURE 30–21. Plot Indicating Variability of Effect Sizes in the Friedman (1989) Meta-analysis, Related to Sample Size

sampling distribution that is appropriate for the data at hand and thereby remove the concern about the generalizability of mathematical methods to problems when it is unclear whether mathematical assumptions are met (Agresti, 1992). Advances in statistical computing have led to the development of efficient algorithms for computing permutation tests (e.g., Mehta & Patel, 1983) and a renewed interest in randomization tests. The wide applicability of the procedure is evidenced by its recent application to single-subject research (Busk & Marascuilo, 1992). The brevity of the current discussion glosses over some subtle nuances in the interpretation of randomization tests, which are discussed by Edgington (1980), who presents a comprehensive discussion of randomization tests as applied to commonly used psychological statistics, including regression techniques and repeated measures ANOVA.

The idea of sampling distributions leads the statistically minded methodologist or researcher to consider the world in a very specific way. For every event studied there is the consideration of what happened empirically, and what could have happened. What could have happened is determined by a mental extrapolation based on the knowledge that the single experiment uses a sample that is drawn from a larger population. The researcher recognizes that on this sample a certain statistic, such as a mean, was obtained, but this could be a mean either below the true population mean, quite near the true population mean, or above the true population mean. The next study will likewise be a fluctuation around a population mean and is not expected to be the same. This intuitive idea, which was demonstrated by simulation, is played out in the results of real research reports as well. The fluctuation of effects and their relationship to sample size are illustrated in Figure 30–21 for the set of studies investigated by Friedman (1989). The reader may note the wide variability in effect sizes when the sample sizes are small and the less variability in effect sizes as the sample size increases. Also note that studies with many participants generally have effect sizes quite close to the mean effect size for all studies. The wavy line running through the plot is a resistant indicator of the local center of the data at each level of sample size.

To describe how often different outcomes are expected, data analysts use the language of probability. The frequentist definition of probability is the most common. It refers to probability as "relative frequency in the long run." Relative frequency refers to the result of dividing the number of a particular type of outcome by the total number of outcomes. If we ask, "What is the probability that a student chosen at random will be diagnosed as learning disabled?" we would divide the number of learning-disabled students by the number of total students and obtain a result between 0 and 1. If we were to ask, "What is the probability of selecting a sample with mean greater than 105 from a population whose mean is 100 and SD is 15?" we would count the number of means greater than 105 and divide by the number of means in the sampling distribution.

A number of important implications follow from this definition of probability, of which three are central to CDA. First, all probabilities are conditional on the set of total outcomes chosen. In the example concerning the probability of a learning disability diagnosis, the answer will depend on whether the set of total outcomes is the set of all students in the world, my country, my state, my district, or the schools to which I can gain access. In the example concerning the mean of 105, the answer will depend on which sampling distribution is used—the distribution based on samples of size 10, 20, 30, and so on. Because each sampling distribution has a different shape, each sample size will lead to a different probability. For example, in the Monte Carlo experiment shown in Figures 30–18 and 30–19, with samples of size 5, 233 or 1,000 means is greater than 105, so the probability is .23. For samples of size 10, 20, and 30 the probabilities are .14, .06, and .05, respectively.

Second, there is no probability for a single outcome, only for a class of outcomes. The question, "What is the probability that my son will be classified as learning disabled?" is unanswerable in this framework. The question needs to be framed according to sets of outcomes, not an individual outcome. By varying the sets we can specify the probability of a boy (in general) being diagnosed as learning disabled, or a sixth grader, or a sixth-grade boy. However, for an individual the event either happens or does not happen, and so no probability statement is available in the frequentist framework.

Third, relative frequencies only make sense as probabilities when they have been observed over a large number of events. This is well known intuitively. If I wanted to know the proportion of people who say they support the president, is it better to ask a lot of people or just a few people? If I asked a single person, who then responded "yes," then I would have 1/1 relative frequency in favor. Clearly, this does not mean that the probability of meeting someone at random who supports the president is 1. It is only in the long run (using numerous outcomes) that a probability can be trusted as describing the true state of affairs. The reader is encouraged to see von Mises (1928/1957) for a readable and classic treatment of the frequentist position.

***Putting the Pieces Together: R. A. Fisher.*** Putting together the pieces of sampling variability and probability led to much of what is considered modern statistics. Fisher (e.g., 1922b) was one of the first to clearly articulate the logic: If one can show that an empirically obtained outcome is unlikely to occur in a sampling distribution formed from a hypothesized population, then one can conclude the empirical outcome is inconsistent with the hypothesized setup, and reject the hypothesized setup as the source of the empirical result. The more rare the event, the more evidence exists against the hypothesized parameter. The rarity could be quantified in terms of the probability of randomly obtaining a more extreme statistic from the sampling distribution. This quantity is simply the proportion of possible statistics that are more extreme, or farther out in the tails of the distribution, than the location of the empirically determined statistic. The sampling distribution is usually centered on the case that occurs when there is no effect. This allows rejection of the idea of no effect and gives evidence to the contrary position, namely, that there is an effect.

Because this case is the case of no effect, it is called the null distribution and the hypothesized population parameter is the null hypothesis. The proportion of scores in the sampling distribution beyond the position of the empirically obtained statistic is called the $p$ value. The smaller the $p$ value, the greater is the evidence against the null hypothesis. When a sufficiently small $p$ value is obtained to reject the null hypothesis, the outcome is typically considered *statistically significant.*

The nature of null sampling distributions and the nature of probability as it is defined in the frequentist tradition have important implications for what a $p$ value means. First, a $p$ value obtained in a significance test is about the probability of one of a set of theoretically possible outcomes, and not about the probability of the event occurring in the world. This implies that $p$ values offer no direct information about the probability that a conclusion is right, and no information about what will happen in the future. These are aspects of the empirical world, not the theoretical world of the sampling distribution. Sample statistics fluctuate. A small $p$ value and rejection of the null hypothesis give no indication of what will happen in a subsequent investigation, in which the result may fluctuate to either a more or less extreme position.

Second, the $p$ value is only interpretable when an empirical statistic is obtained using randomization procedures that parallel the randomization that occurs in the sampling distribution. If there is no random assignment or random selection in individuals and groups under study, there is no way to know what fluctuation is going on and no way to know what the appropriate sampling distribution is. Any $p$ value provided by a computer will be based on assumptions that are unmet, and will therefore be uninterpretable in the usual sense.

Third, even when randomization occurs, the typical mathematical tables and software for determining $p$ values are accurate only insofar as the assumptions of the test are met. The difference between the assumed $p$ value and the true value can be drastic in some cases. It is the researcher's responsibility to know the assumptions of a test and the degree to which those assumptions can be violated under specific circumstances. The blanket statement that a procedure is robust is never true in all circumstances.

Fourth, what counts as a rare event is closely tied to the sample size, as we saw in the example of finding the probability of obtaining a mean larger than 105 from a population with mean 100 and an SD of 15. As sample sizes increase, the tails of a sampling distribution are pulled in, and slight departures from the population obtain increasingly small $p$ values. When

sample sizes are large, even trivial differences can be shown to be unlikely and obtain the label *significant.*

### Three Approaches to the Logic of Statistical Tests.
While Fisher laid out the basic logic of statistical tests, his approach had a number of nuances that are important to understand. The first is Fisher's recognition that using an extreme deviation to reject the null hypothesis is dangerous because the null distribution itself generates extreme deviations. If a researcher considered statistics in the outer 5 percent of the tail as far enough to reject the null, then 5 percent of the truly null statistics could be erroneously counted to reject the null. Fisher recognized the possibility of this error.

Fisher was a practicing scientist who had to deal with the difficulties of applied research. He did not consider the $p$ value only as "significant" or "not significant," as is commonly done today, but saw $p$ values as a measure of shades or *degrees* of evidence. Following this logic, Fisher (1955, 1956) argued that unwavering prior cutoffs for significance should not be set. In Fisher's (1949) eyes, the method of null hypothesis significance testing was not merely a single statistical technique, but rather the basis for all scientific knowledge: "Inductive inference is the only process known to us by which essentially new knowledge comes into the world" (p. 7).

Fisher was a staunch frequentist who recognized the importance of the long run and believed that evidence must be accumulated over experiments, with the results of any single experiment to be viewed tentatively. Noting the tendency to ignore this view, Fisher argued in *The Design of Experiments* that

we thereby admit that no isolated experiment, however significant itself, can suffice for the experimental demonstration of any natural phenomenon; for the "one chance in a million" undoubtedly occurs, with no less and no more than its appropriate frequency, however surprised we may be that it should occur to *us.* (Fisher, 1949, pp. 13–14)

As reflected here, repeated experimentation was not considered a luxury as it is today, but rather was seen as integral to the logic of the work.

There are many criticisms of significance testing (see, e.g., Hogben, 1957; Howson & Urbach, 1993; Morrison & Henkel, 1970). Here we note that significance testing is limited in use by three points:

1. Error in the determination of significance is always possible. Only in the long run of multiple experiments is the true case clear.
2. The $p$ value does not directly indicate the importance of the departure from the assumed distribution because it is a function both of any difference between populations and of the sample size.
3. As sample size increases, substantively trivial deviations from the assumed distribution are considered significant.

Cox and Hinkley (1974) present an excellent survey of Fisher's work and, while pointing out limitations 2 and 3 above, argue:

These are of course, arguments in favor of a much fuller specification of the problem and the close linking of the significance test with a problem of estimation. It is essentially consideration of intellectual economy that makes the pure significance test of interest. (p. 81)

The fuller specification of the problem and close linking to estimation was brought about by Jerzy Neyman and Egon Pearson (1928). These researchers introduced many familiar concepts that were omitted in the previous discussion, including statistical power, Type II error, selecting alpha to balance these errors, the importance of a priori cutoffs in decision-making, and the idea of the alternate distribution. Examining Fisher's work in the 1920s, Neyman and Pearson reflected on the idea of rejecting the null hypothesis. They held that such a rejection would imply that the observed sample statistic came from a population other than the null. In this view, statistical tests should not simply be a test of the null hypothesis alone, but should be seen as a decision between two alternative distributions. This was a radical change from the Fisherian view of a single null distribution. With two competing distributions, errors of the kind Fisher had specified would still exist, although there would also be "errors of the second kind," as well as the idea of the power of a test—the probability of rejecting the null hypothesis based on the size of the effect. This would also allow choice of a cutoff point for deciding significance that would balance Type I and Type II errors. The introduction of a second kind of error prompted the names Type I and Type II error. Type I error concerns Fisher's original formulation of an error in the null distribution, while Type II error is concerned about missing the second, alternate distribution.

On the surface, the Neyman–Pearson additions may appear as logical extensions of the Fisherian paradigm. However, Neyman and Pearson had a very different conception of sampling and populations than Fisher did. For Neyman and Pearson, acceptance sampling was the sine qua non of sampling. Acceptance sampling is a quality control procedure in which samples are taken repeatedly from a factory and decisions are made regarding whether the sample is acceptable or unacceptable for sale or shipment. In terms of statistical distributions one may consider a machine that works properly when making widgets 10 mm in diameter but improperly when making widgets 12 mm in diameter. One would want to decide whether a particular sample (say, with mean diameter of 11.4) should be considered acceptable or unacceptable. By attaching relative risk or cost to the errors of rejecting a good sample or missing a bad one, one could pick an appropriate cutoff. Further, to make the decision precise and unambiguous, the cutoff would be set prior to data collection and adhered to unwaveringly.

Neyman and Pearson laid out the general idea and the specific computations for these concepts and gave industrial sampling examples to tie them to the empirical world. For Neyman and Pearson the repeated sampling of the machine would allow determination of the two sampling distributions. At the level of interpretation, Neyman and Pearson stressed the behavioristic idea of "acting" according to the yes/no outcome and used the term *inductive behavior,* as opposed to Fisher's degree of evidence concept, which was called *inductive inference.* To signify these differences the Neyman and Pearson approach was called "hypothesis testing" in contrast to Fisher's "significance testing."

Emphasizing the idiosyncratic nature of significance tests in scientific work, Fisher (1956) condemned the Neyman–Pearson approach as "absurdly academic," since, in his view, "no scientific worker has a fixed level of significance at which from year to year, and in all circumstances, he rejects hypotheses" (p. 42). Further, he thought the concept of repeated sampling from a single population would lead to mathematical inconsistencies (Fisher, 1955). Conceiving of only the fluctuation around the null, Fisher (1949, p. 17) attacked any description of the alternate distribution:

The notion of an error of the so-called "second kind," due to accepting the null hypothesis "when it is false" . . . has no meaning with respect to simple test of significance, in which the only available expectations are those which flow from the null hypothesis being true.

Notions of power (rather than sensitivity) and decision-making (rather than accumulating evidence) were likewise summarily rejected.

Neyman and Pearson articulated an approach to making yes/no decisions by being very specific about the distributions of interest, whereas Fisher was arguing for tests whose goal was to send up a flag concerning the general departure of an effect from expectation. Along these lines Fisher (1955) wrote:

In an acceptance procedure, . . . acceptance is irreversible, whether the evidence for it was strong or weak. It is the result of applying mechanically rules laid down in advance. . . . By contrast, the conclusions drawn by a scientific worker from a test of significance are *provisional.* (pp. 73–74; emphasis in the original)

In this way, Fisher's work was much more tentative and can be seen as almost exploratory in modern eyes. As a practicing research scientist Fisher rejected the decision-making approach for much the same reason that power analysis and specification of Type II error are not widely considered today. Fisher argued that in scientific work, as opposed to industrial quality control, the alternate distribution is seldom known, so the power and Type II error cannot be specified, and the alpha level can only be set in terms of his original Type I error.

We find, then, that Fisher's work was mathematically incomplete (failing to take account of power and Type II error) and led to assessments of significant departure from the null hypothesis that were arbitrarily tied to sample size. On the other hand, Neyman and Pearson provided a fuller specification of outcomes and conditions, yet provided it in a scenario that assumed repeated experience with sampling and specification of the alternate distribution, which is typically unknown in scientific inquiry.

It may be clear by now that what is taught in departments of psychology and education is largely what Gigerenzer (1993) calls a hybrid or mishmash of the Fisherian and Neyman–Pearson approaches. Gigerenzer and his colleagues have provided detailed documentation of the progression of the mishmash (Gigerenzer, 1987, 1991, 1993; Gigerenzer & Murray, 1987; Gigerenzer et al., 1989; Sedlmeier & Gigerenzer, 1989) and argued that the mishmash has had highly negative consequences on the field by glossing over controversy and institutionalizing a .05 alpha level (Gigerenzer, 1987), corrupting concepts such as power (Sedlmeier & Gigerenzer, 1989), and distorting psychological notions of reasoning (Gigerenzer, 1991; Gigerenzer & Murray, 1987).

TABLE 30–6. Characteristics of Statistical Procedures Among Frequentist Traditions

| | Tradition | | |
|---|---|---|---|
| Issue | Fisher | Neyman–Pearson | Mishmash, Blend |
| Characterization | Inductive inference | Inductive behavior | Statistics |
| Name | Significance test | Hypothesis tests | Either used interchangeably |
| Distributions | A single null | A null and an alternate | A single null, usually |
| Use of preset cutoffs | Used loosely | Used strictly | Used strictly |
| Type of conclusion | Rough assessment | Make yes/no decision | Make yes/no decision |
| Choice of alpha | Based on Type I error | Need to balance Type I and Type II error | Based on Type I error |
| Role of power | None | Important | Important/seldom used |
| Determine sample size? | Use what you have/sensitivity to null | Calculate power | Important/seldom used |

Table 30–6 summarizes how the proponents of traditional Fisherian and Neyman–Pearson approaches stand on different aspects of statistical inference and how those approaches compare with procedures in common use. Although some of these differences may be easily reconciled, others are not. For example, Huberty (1987) laid out the decision rules of the two approaches (rows 4 and 5 in Table 30–6) and recommended that researchers set cutoffs beforehand but report the additional information regarding degree of significance as well. Reconciling the overt behavior by doing both seems incomplete since it does not reconcile the underlying issues that led to the differences in view and does not address the degree of conclusiveness that is appropriate to a test result.

Other concepts, such as the power of the test, are even less easily reconciled. As noted above, in the Fisherian approach only a null distribution is considered, so an effect size or proportion of the alternate distribution is not even definable. Indeed, it is likely that the failure of many students to understand and use power is a combination of good logic and understanding of the significance tests. To the thoughtful graduate student trained in Fisherian logic, preplanning power calculations for a dissertation may seem illogical and draw objections such as "I want to find any effect"; "My goal is to reject the null"; "The $p$ value is about the null distribution"; "I'm looking for any alternate distribution." Such statements are valid conclusions from the Fisherian point of view.

The common mishmash is not to be avoided simply because it is an incomplete treatment of historical issues, but rather because it presents contradictory suppositions about inference under the guise of a unified approach. This leaves students to question either the contradictions or their own understanding. Given the mathematical aura of statistical work and the myth of a single method, few students are likely to question the logic of the approach.

Perhaps the most dangerous aspect of the mishmash approach concerns the lack of congruence between hypothesis and conclusion specificity. In the Fisherian approach, the hypothesis is vaguely specified in terms of a single null distribution. In practice, the null is often a standard hypothesis that requires little consideration, such as a test that the population correlation is equal to zero. Although this specification of the null alone fails to ensure adequate power, it is well matched with the weak conclusions whose provisional nature is stressed. The Neyman–Pearson approach, on the other hand, establishes specific competing distributions and makes strong and specific conclusions about the outcome of the test. The mishmash ap-

proach generally begins with a vague null hypothesis and concludes with a strong yes/no decision. This practice is contrary to the practice of both traditions and seems a likely way to become unjustifiably sure in one's results. In contrast, researchers should both decrease their confidence in the validity of statements of significance and increase the specificity of their hypotheses by specifying the minimum effect size sought and using a sample size with adequate power for detection of an effect. In this case the true power is not known, but at least it can be calculated for a supposed effect size. By adding the specificity of the effect size and power and increasing the tentativeness of binary decision-making, researchers are less likely to conclude the results of sampling fluctuation are unwavering signs of significance or nonsignificance. At the very least, researchers should recognize, and teach, that the surety of decision-making is not inherent in the null significance test but is based on a probability model whose specifics are seldom obtained in scientific work. Equally important, supposed tests of significance should be prefaced with good exploratory work that suggests whether or not theoretical hypotheses can be empirically tested, given the patterns of data that reflect the theoretical constructs.

***Bayesian Statistics: The Other Approach.*** The traditions described above are based on frequentist notions of probability. For researchers in those camps, probabilities are about frequencies and nothing else. This definition restricts the use of the concept to a small corner of the set of possible uses. In fact, it seems that many times researchers use the term "probability" not in the specific sense of relative frequency but in the sense of degree of evidence or strength of belief. Such a stance would allow probabilities and probabilistic computations about statements and beliefs—an important aspect of Bayesian statistics.

Bayesian statistics differ from the more common frequentist statistics on three major points. First, the definition of probability is not restricted to frequencies but can be mapped onto statements of belief. Second, while the frequentist views described above only use data from the single investigation in assessment of empirical evidence, the Bayesian approach explicitly incorporates prior information or belief about the probable location of the population parameter. That is, the analyst specifies a distribution of what is expected to occur based on prior experience that is combined with the new data collected during the experiment. Third, the outcome of the analysis is a distribution that maps out the probability associated with the population parameter occurring at each point along the scale. This result is quite different from the frequentist approach, which results in a distribution that maps the probability associated with the sample statistic occurring at each point in the scale and uses this distribution for inference about the distribution's own appropriateness for describing the data.

Although the mathematics of the two approaches offer little debate, questions about the appropriateness of considering probability as a wider concept than frequency, and the combination of prior expectations with new data, have led to strong opinions for and against this approach. It is notable that students learning the frequentist view often unknowingly assume the Bayesian interpretation of frequentist computations. A deeper discussion of this important approach is beyond the already broad scope of this chapter, and we encourage the interested reader to explore this valuable framework. Howson and Urbach (1993) have written a comprehensive treatment of the logic of Bayesian approach for scientific inference which is equally valuable for its assessment of Fisherian and Neyman–Pearson approaches. The work by Box and Tiao (1973) is an often-cited classic reference that is mathematically demanding, while Pollard (1986) and Winkler (1993) are more accessible to general audiences.

## Confidence Intervals

The statistical tests in the frequentist traditions described above rest on computing the probability of a certain random deviation from a parameter of the given null population—P(data|population) (Gigerenzer & Murray, 1987). This information is typically used to make categorical yes/no decisions concerning whether the data should be considered to have come from the null distribution or not. Many times researchers are not primarily interested in rejecting the null hypothesis (typically concluding that the effect is not zero) but prefer to obtain some probabilistic assessment of what is true—a goal accomplished with confidence intervals.

Despite their common introduction in elementary statistics classes and texts (Glass & Hopkins, 1984; Moore & McCabe, 1993) confidence intervals are often misunderstood and presented simply as graphical means for conducting hypotheses tests. Confidence intervals, however, are radically different from statistical tests insofar as they are a means to estimate the range of probable population parameters rather than to test whether the population parameter has a specific value. Whereas statistical tests assess data relative to a theoretical population (P(data|population)), the confidence interval maps out a range that probably includes the population value in light of empirical data: P(population|data). A confidence interval starts with the known data and assesses what populations are consistent with those data. Statistical tests start with a hypothetical population and assess what data are consistent with that population. Stated another way, statistical tests try to show what is not true with surety, while confidence intervals try to show what is true without surety.

Confidence intervals work with a simple logical inverse of that used in the statistical test. In the statistical test, limits are set up in the sampling distribution that mark how far away from the population parameter a sample statistic can be and still be considered from that population. For example, in a large

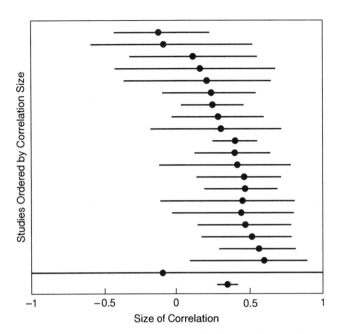

**FIGURE 30–22.** Confidence Intervals for Studies with N Greater than 10 from Data Examined by Cohen (1983).
The bottom confidence interval is obtained from the average of all the data reported above it.

sample study of mean differences, researchers may use two tails of the sampling distribution and set the cutoff points at ±1.96 SD of the sampling distribution (standard errors). This allows counting the middle 95% of the distribution as consistent with the population. The confidence interval takes this very same information and uses the logic in an inverse form: If a sample can be as far as 1.96 SD from the population parameter, then a sample statistic's population parameter can be as much as 1.96 SE away from it as well. If we start with a known sample mean, or other statistic, we can compute the range from which a population might have generated the statistic by marking the range as plus and minus 1.96 SE from the statistic. When reporting a confidence interval we tell what we know (the sample statistic) and admit our awareness that this is part of a fluctuating process whose originating population could be higher or lower than the obtained value.

For example, Cohen (1983; cited in Cooper & Hedges, 1994) reported a series of correlations between student achievement and student ratings of their instructors. These 20 correlations are plotted in the top section of Figure 30–22, along with their confidence intervals.

Typically, correlations are reported by giving their size and a $p$ value that leads to rejection of or failure to reject the null hypothesis. This informs the reader whether the correlation is consistent with the population parameter of zero. The confidence interval goes far beyond this information by informing about the entire range of parameters with which the sample correlation is consistent. For example, the second correlation reported from the top of the graph has a value of −.04, so that it is quite consistent with the null hypothesis of the population correlation equal to zero. However, the study has only a few data points (a data point represents an average student achievement and average instructor evaluation for a class), and therefore the correlation is able to fluctuate far from its population. As the confidence interval indicates, it could just as well have come from a population correlation as low as −.60 or as high as +.55. The fact that it is "nonsignificant" is dwarfed by the fact that its small size means that it could have come from either a population with a correlation of zero or a high-negative or high-positive population.

The study depicted just above the solid line crossing the bottom of the plot indicates a correlation of .68 with a confidence interval from .08 to .91. This large range also reflects the small sample size involved in this study. In this case the correlation would be considered significant because the confidence interval does not include zero and is therefore considered inconsistent with a population parameter of zero. The range of population parameters consistent with it is, nevertheless, quite wide, and the population correlation could be either quite small or quite large. This specification of the size of a sample correlation and the size of population parameters consistent with it represents description that is much more quantitative and rich than the specification of "not equal to zero" that can be gleaned from the statement of "a significant correlation." This quantifying of the size and amount of expected fluctuation of an effect is a great improvement over statistical tests that may reduce the valuable quantitative information to a mere categorization of significance. It is a very positive step toward our goal of quantitative analysis as describing relationships with quantities.

Confidence intervals also present a clear advantage when trying to determine sample size. Sample size can be chosen based on how accurate one wants the estimate of the correlation to be. In the example in Figure 30–22 the smallest interval on the top portion of the plot is in the center of the 20 correlations. This sample correlation is .4, with a confidence interval from .24 to .54 and a sample size of 121. The larger sample size has decreased the variability.

By deciding how accurate the confidence interval should be, a researcher can determine how big the sample size needs to be for that degree of accuracy. Perhaps more important, the confidence interval avoids the problem of too many subjects. In statistical testing, the $p$ value is dependent on both the effect size and the sample size. As the sample size increases, the sampling distribution becomes more narrow and the tails of the distribution are pulled in, as in Figure 30–18. With large samples, effects that are minute when examined in terms of size of the effect in the world may nevertheless be extreme enough in the sampling distribution to be statistically significant. This leads to the criticism by some reviewers that a researcher may have had too many subjects! The problem is not with too many subjects, but with making decisions based on a relative frequency of occurrence in a theoretical null distribution, which is often not the exact hypothesis intended. With the confidence interval approach, more data means a more precise estimate and a smaller interval.

Confidence intervals are typically interpreted with the frequentist's long-run definition. This implies that in the long run, 95 percent (or whatever percent matches the number of standard deviations of the sampling distribution used) of the intervals will include the true population parameter. For any individual interval, one does not know if it contains the true parameter or not. This is contrary to the common belief that a 95 percent confidence interval means that a specific obtained interval includes the population parameter 95 percent of the time. Each interval either does or does not hold the parameter—no 95 percent about it. The researcher must remember that the population parameters are fixed and the statistics fluctuate around it along with the confidence interval. Bayesian statistical approaches use a subjectivist notion of probability and go the extra step of specifying probabilities of the population parameter occurring in different parts of the confidence interval. In this framework, areas closer to the sample statistics are considered more likely to include the parameter. This is a judgment that cannot be made in the typical frequentist view since the probabilities are about the relative frequency of intervals that work, not the working of individual intervals.

## Research Synthesis

Up to this point our discussion has focused on model building, model testing, and parameter estimation in the context of individual sets of data. We have noted that because frequentist expressions of probability are only meaningful in the long run, the results of any single investigation may be either quite consistent with or somewhat deviant from a hypothesized or actual population parameter. It is only through the analysis of multiple study outcomes that one begins to obtain a picture of the actual sampling fluctuation and hence an idea of the true population parameters.

***Narrative and Vote Count Approaches.*** Prior to the advent of meta-analysis (Glass, 1976), synthesis of quantitative research generally followed either a narrative or vote count method (Glass, McGaw, & Smith, 1981). In the narrative method a number of findings from the extant literature are accumulated and major trends or themes are identified by the reviewer. Where discrepancies between results and conclusions are found in individual studies, the reviewer makes note and a comprehensive survey is provided. Jackson (1980) critically reviewed 36 published narrative reviews and made recommendations for improving reviews in the areas of selecting questions or hypotheses, sampling, representing characteristics of primary studies, analyzing the primary studies, interpreting the results, and reporting the review. Many of the recommendations centered on clarifying goals and values and on collecting and reporting data using explicit rules and precise values. Jackson reported the degree of violation of these principles in the studies he reviewed. Proper application of these methods may promote detection of patterns in method, theoretical viewpoints, or data analysis across a set of studies, and that may further understanding of a large body of studies.

The vote count method (Light & Smith, 1971) focuses on assessing study outcomes from multiple studies. This process usually entails categorizing studies according to relevant attributes, recording whether outcomes were significant or not, and looking for covariation between study characteristics and instances of statistical significance. Although this method is sometimes recommended for its simplicity, unless it is used with great sophistication, it may lead a reviewer to a wrong conclusion. The difficulty lies in using the distinct categories

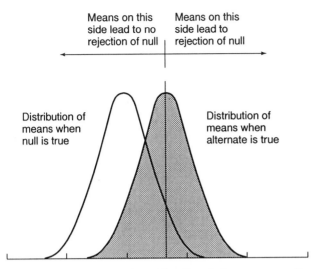

Means on this side lead to no rejection of null | Means on this side lead to rejection of null

Distribution of means when null is true

Distribution of means when alternate is true

FIGURE 30–23. Arrangement of Null and Alternate Sampling Distributions when the Effect Size is Approximately Equal to the Critical Value of a Statistic

of significant and nonsignificant as a measure of an underlying effect size. Even when the null is blatantly false, many non-null distributions have a large overlap with the null distribution. When sample means are drawn from the alternate distribution (as would occur if the null was false), some means will fall on the side of the critical value that leads to rejection and some will fall on the side that leads to failure to reject. Even if studies are replicated in all relevant detail and subjects are from exactly the same population, some studies will lead to significant results and others will not.

For example, when the alternate sampling distribution is as far from the mean of the null distribution as the cutoff for rejecting the null distribution, the results (in terms of significance) will be split 50 : 50. This scenario is illustrated in Figure 30–23, in which the mean of an alternate distribution straddles the critical value of the null distribution. Hedges and Olkin (1980) demonstrated that if the critical value is less than the power of the test, the ability of the vote count to detect a significant effect moves toward zero as the number of studies increases. In such a case, as the number of studies examined increases, the more likely the reviewer is to be misled. For cases where effect size information is not given in published reports, Hedges and Olkin (1985) present a number of techniques that can be used to convert vote-count information into effect size estimates. Because the vote count propagates the weakness of statistical testing, it is not simply a less informative approach whose simplicity recommends it, but a possibly highly misleading approach that may amplify Type II error.

*Meta-analysis.* To get beyond the confounded information of sample size, effect size, and conclusion of significance, Glass (1976) argued for the use of a standardized measure of effect size. Although effect sizes can be thought of in a number of ways (Rosenthal, 1991), Glass used J. Cohen's (1969) idea of mean differences divided by the population standard deviation—a statistic analogous to a $z$ score. According to Glass, use of the effect size would allow evaluation of practical importance

of a result, and would allow results of studies to themselves become data points in subsequent statistical analyses. Glass argued that differences in effect sizes across study conditions could be assessed using procedures such as ANOVA by using effect sizes as dependent variables and study characteristics as independent variables. In this way one could determine whether differences between effects across studies were the result of sample fluctuation or the result of different underlying populations. Because this type of analysis would constitute an analysis of analyses, it was dubbed meta-analysis.

Since that early formulation, meta-analysis has become a complete branch of data analysis. Its many important technical details are omitted here; rather, we focus on the logic of the procedure and its role in quantitative data analysis. For more detail, the interested reader is referred to Cooper and Hedges (1994), Glass et al. (1981), Hedges & Olkin (1985), Rosenthal (1991, 1993), and Wachter and Straf (1990).

For those unfamiliar with the motivation of meta-analysis, the technique may appear as overquantification of results that could be interpreted by content analysis of research reports and categorizations of significance. On the contrary, meta-analysis is a statistical technique that deals with the statistical problems inherent in using individual significance tests.

We already noted that significance tests are properly understood only in the long run. Meta-analysis addresses this limitation by examining multiple effects across multiple studies. Second, the practical implications of an effect cannot be directly determined in a significance test because the $p$ value is a function of sample size and departure from the null. This is addressed in meta-analysis by using the effect size as a common metric of study effectiveness. By using effect size as a common metric, meta-analysis moves from lists of significant and nonsignificant outcomes to reports of quantities.

A third difficulty with individual statistical tests is that trivially small effects are considered statistically significant as the sample size grows large. Meta-analysis addresses this difficulty by weighting study outcomes in proportion to their sample size and focusing on the size of study outcomes rather than on whether they are significant or not. If a meta-analysis is aimed at estimating mean population effect size, large or small sample size is not a difficulty because each study is weighted as appropriate. Summarization of significance tests (the vote count) is also a problem that meta-analysis addresses by using the size of the effect, rather than a single binary characterization. Meta-analysis even improves confidence intervals by allowing the combination of data across studies to achieve more focused estimates of population parameters.

As an integrative technique, meta-analysis is bound by the obligations of all types of research integration, including (a) justifying which studies are comparable and which are not, (b) relying on knowledge of the substantive area to identify relevant study characteristics, (c) evaluating and accounting for differences in study quality, (d) assessing possible bias due to nonpublication of significant results, (e) accounting for the case of multiple outcomes by a single experimenter or within a single study, and (f) assessing the generalizability of results from fields with very little empirical data. Each of these issues must be addressed by any good review. The good meta-analysis starts where the narrative review ends and adds the additional power of quantifying effects and their fluctuations, and quantifying the covariation between study characteristics and study outcomes. Meta-analysis is not a substitute for detailed understanding and insight, but rather a tool to aid the understanding of outcomes which by their very nature show fluctuation.

Because of the dangers inherent in the common vote count method of research integration and in the failure to observe the outcomes of multiple studies, the elementary procedures of meta-analysis should become familiar to all quantitative researchers. Researchers should be taught to conceptualize and report their findings in terms of effect sizes and confidence intervals, and the results of multiple studies should be summarized statistically when appropriate. For example, the data in Figure 30–22 have a mean (weighted) correlation of .36 with a confidence interval with lower and upper bounds of .29 and .43. This interval is depicted at the bottom of the plot. This mean confidence interval serves as a good estimate of the population parameter. As we would expect, this average is most consistent with the large sample study of 121 classrooms. Also as we would expect, other effects fluctuate randomly around this value.

As we noted above when discussing the Friedman meta-analysis of gender differences in mathematics achievement, variations within these data may further be related to differences in study attributes. For example, the studies with the three highest correlations were all conducted in general psychology classes, suggesting the possibility that the outcomes may be related to the type of course taken. As we saw in the Friedman meta-analysis, it is sometimes possible to relate the size of study outcomes to a number of study characteristics, as Glass had originally envisioned. Regression formulas such as that presented by Friedman are valuable in part because of their precise description of the way studies vary as a function of their characteristics. Procedures for testing possible relationships between outcomes and characteristics are well established and presented in Glass et al. (1981) and Hedges and Olkin (1985).

In summary, meta-analysis offers quantitative ways to synthesize quantitative research that overcome problems inherent in Fisherian significance testing (the sample size problem) and the Neyman–Pearson approach by assisting the estimation of population parameters. In addition, it can provide a framework by which studies are planned in advance to assess effect sizes in the multiple dimensions that are relevant to a research endeavor.

## Computers and Quantitative Data Analysis

Once considered a mere convenience, statistical computing is now a cornerstone of quantitative data analysis. Not only have advances in computing led to improved speed in analyzing data, they have also led to the accumulation of previously unimaginable large amounts of data, the computation of formulas that previously had only theoretical status, and the increasing accessibility of complex algorithms to practicing researchers. The sum effect of these developments has been a reevaluation of the nature of data analysis, including changing views on the role of mathematical statistics, which in some areas is being supplanted by statistical computing (Velleman & Hoaglin, 1992). As Thisted and Velleman (1992) summarized, "Computational advances have changed the face of statistical practice by transforming what we do and by challenging how we think about scientific problems" (p. 41).

As the recipients of changing ideas and products, educational psychologists face possibilities for great success or great aggravation. In this section we discuss several abilities that are important when assessing software for statistical computing.

*Capability.* As the field of data analysis grows and the number of available techniques proliferates, it will become increasingly difficult for any single software package to fill all the needs of a data analyst. To choose appropriate software, users should conduct a task analysis of their activities and compare this analysis with the range of features available on contemplated software. A researcher should be careful to consider the full range of activities that is undertaken in the data analysis process. Colorful graphics and complex multivariate analyses are enticing, yet much of a data analyst's time may be spent on the more mundane tasks of transforming irregularly formatted data into a form the software can read. Also, many data analysts perform common tasks that are not easily handled by some packages. For example, many researchers need to assess the internal reliability of a test—a task not easily handled by all packages. A package that can perform 99 percent of the needed analysis may not be appropriate if the remaining 1 percent of need occurs 99 percent of the time.

*Learnability.* A cost–benefit analysis is also necessary to determine how difficult it is to learn a new package. Packages vary in the readability of the documentation, the availability of support, and the intuitiveness of the interface. At the same time, the appropriateness of a package will largely be determined by previous packages used. As with a foreign language, a researcher may learn to construct mental models of data analyses in terms of the command structure of a package. Switching to a different package with a different set of assumptions about the nature of data analysis may require nearly starting from zero. On the other hand, switching to a different package that has the same conceptual organization for data analysis may be quite straightforward. The size and cost of documentation should also be considered.

*Reliability.* Statistical computing is a very advanced specialty in applied statistics. The algorithms used for computing such seemingly elementary estimates as the mean and standard deviation differ from those presented in general statistics textbooks. Even the so-called computational formulas that are presented were designed to simplify hand calculations and are not used in good statistical software. Accordingly, it is important to use software that is designed by experts in this specific area.

In addition, it is important not simply to rely on the market power of a program. Even widely used programs may have extensive numeric errors. As a hedge against these difficulties, potential users should read software reviews provided by statistical journals such as *American Statistician*. Reviewers in nonstatistical journals may not have the background in statistical computing to appropriately evaluate the computational nuances that are important. For example, a statistics package was once praised in a general computing magazine because it automatically handled missing values. The reviewer was unaware that the automatic conversion of missing values to zeros had no scientific justification and would, in most cases, lead to misleading summaries.

*Extendability.* Extendability concerns the degree to which a system is modifiable or can be programmed. In general, there is a trade-off between flexibility and learnability. The more flexible a system is, the more time it takes to learn the nuances. This is addressed in some programs by providing both completely menu-driven interfaces for common tasks and a programming language for additional control.

Users who are not apt to write their own programming code may benefit from the increasing availability of program segments available on the Internet. For example, the Statlib depository at Carnegie Mellon University archives contributed programs for a number of statistical packages.

*Software Connectability.* Statistical computing is often done in the same environment as word processing and related applications such as graphics production. Researchers may want to consider choosing their statistical tools in light of the program's connectability with other programs. In an integrated environment, graphics and tables produced in a statistical application can be cut and pasted, or linked, to a word processor, spreadsheet, data base, or other related applications. Such integrated environments often significantly reduce manuscript production time and aid in documenting the research program beyond a stack of printouts. For example, all the figures in this chapter were produced on a Macintosh computer and copied into a word-processing program from statistics programs that were running concurrently with the word processor.

*Goal Compatibility.* In the previous sections we argued for the usefulness of a broad range of techniques, including exploratory data analysis, confirmatory procedures, confidence intervals, and meta-analysis. Few programs do many of these things well, for the organization of software is likely to be different for different stages of data analysis.

Programs focusing on data exploration tend to emphasize interactive graphic analysis. This does not simply mean the ability to produce graphics, but rather the ability to easily produce graphics, modify existing graphics, and connect data bases and graphics. In Data Desk, for example, each plot is represented in the computer's memory. Modifying the data that are represented in a graph can lead to automatic updating of the graph. Output describing correlation coefficients and regressions and other statistical analyses are likewise linked to the underlying data. This allows the effect of changes in data, as would occur in outlier deletion, to be run through the system so that the analyses do not all have to be re-requested.

Data Desk also promotes EDA by providing context-sensitive menus with each plot. A scatterplot, for instance, includes menu items for computing a regression or correlation and adding various summary lines to the graph. Text output such as an ANOVA table likewise provides numerous options likely to be used, such as a plot of residuals. After an initial regression analysis is computed, additional variables can be added to the equation by dragging icons of the desired variables over the ANOVA summary table and releasing the mouse. The table is immediately updated with the new variable or variables. Graphics are also linked and can be acted on directly. For example,

in Figure 20–13, the point indicating Alaska was changed to an **x** using tools directly on a plot. When this occurred, the point indicating Alaska was changed on all plots automatically so that the role of Alaska in all other relationships could be seen quickly. Such a graphically oriented system with cross-plot links and updatable objects facilitates the construction of multiple tentative representations of the data and exploration of the effect of different techniques.

When working in the confirmatory mode, the user is less concerned with quick and tentative views of the data, but rather prefers the detailed results of a single preplanned analysis. Such an approach does not suffer as much from singular representations of the data and often emphasizes work in a batch mode. Batch mode occurs when a series of commands are entered and the results are computed in response to the batch of commands. Often the modifiability of output is limited in such a system. Typically the output is simply dumped to a file or graphics viewer with no internal representation that can be modified. In such a system the user may look for sets of commonly used tools packaged for easy use, and for facilities that make the results easy to export for report writing.

*Hardware Connectability.* Computer designs are changing to take advantage of the connectability of computers. One approach to software development is called client–server applications. Software designed in this way separates programs into processing and user interface aspects so that the user and the processor need not necessarily be at the same machine. For example, the Mathematica computer program has a "kernel" that performs the computation separately from the program that the user sees to enter commands. This allows users to access the computing power from inside other programs or from a remote computer. Many programs running in the Unix operating system are designed around this principle.

In addition to client–server applications, we are likely to see an increase in programs aimed at data sharing and analysis in groups. All these trends suggest that how easily a computer can connect to the local network is an important consideration in buying computing hardware.

## Conclusion: Hope for Realizing the Power of Quantitative Methods

Many treatments of quantitative methods describe the breadth of variable types and problems quantitative analysis can cover while assuming a single underlying logical perspective. Here we have discussed only a few types of data and problems while discussing a breadth of underlying logical perspectives. We have aimed to counter the cookbook emphasis found in some books with a portrait of data analysis as interactivity and flexibility guided by knowledge of a content area. We have argued that the contribution of quantitative analysis is the possibility of quantitative description of the world inherent in many aspects of EDA, the use of confidence intervals and meta-analytic procedures. On the other hand, we noted that the power of inferential statistics is limited when the quantitative size of an effect is thrown out and the result is reduced to the simple categorization of significant or nonsignificant. We value confidence intervals not only because they directly communicate the size of an effect, but because they use the probabilistic machinery of CDA to communicate our uncertainty concerning estimates and thereby make us more honest and accurate when discussing what we know and do not know. We also encouraged the use of meta-analytic techniques, not only for use in large integrative reviews, but for quantifying the effects of single studies and for conceptualizing the outcome of a study in the context of other empirical and theoretically possible outcomes.

Inherent in all of this discussion is an idea of degree of exploration that ranges from a broad openness with few or no acknowledgeable hypotheses, through stages of rough confirmation that may include statistical tests that are only sort-of tests because only a vague hypothesis is held, to specific tests of specific hypotheses. Rough confirmation can be accomplished using either descriptive techniques from the EDA tradition or the flag raising suggested by Fisherian null hypothesis testing. As argued here, in the frequentist tradition, only a specific a priori establishment of probabilistic expectations following the Neyman–Pearson tradition can even approach a test. Most statistical testing as practiced is likely to really be a form of rough confirmation. We hope that by acknowledging the importance of exploration and discovery, researchers will be allowed to clarify to themselves and their colleagues the firmness of their tests and enjoy more public exploratory data analysis.

Finally, a major theme of this section has been the plurality of traditions of logic and method in quantitative data analysis. As computers free students and researchers from the drudgery of hand computing, we hope that increased effort will be placed on understanding the logical, philosophical, and historical foundations of such approaches. Students often enter quantitative methods training by checking their critical reflection skills at the door. We must demand of our quantitative methods students the same critical reflection on theory and practice that is demanded in content areas of educational psychology. We believe that such an emphasis is the best hope for a generation of researchers who understand, value, and extend quantitative methods in educational psychology.

## QUALITATIVE DATA ANALYSIS

### What Is Qualitative Analysis?

As we turn our attention to qualitative inquiry, the independence of analysis and design sought in the quantitative section is neither possible nor desired. Qualitative data analysis cannot be extruded from the qualitative research process as a whole, with its assumptions about the nature of reality, knowledge, method, and social and educational life. This approach to research has its own traditions, aims, methods, and canons of inference. Although the forms of data are usually words and sometimes visual representations rather than numbers, what distinguishes qualitative research is its quest to understand the qualities or essences of a phenomenon by focusing on the meanings of events and phenomena and the social events that transform these meanings. According to Dabbs (1982), qualitative research examines the meanings of an event or phenomenon, whereas quantitative research assumes the meaning and examines the distribution of its occurrence.

This emphasis on processes and meanings leads qualitative inquiry to be distinguished by seven attributes. Some of these attributes may appear to be shared with quantitative methods, such as the use of large data bases. However, when considered in light of the goal of understanding participant meanings and the social processes that transform them, the similarities are seen to occur primarily at the level of surface features.

First, the qualitative researcher assumes that reality is filtered through individual interpretations and meaning perspectives. A phenomenon such as math achievement does not have a reality in the same way that a physical object has, independent of one's interpretations of it. The aim of qualitative research is not to establish universal, context-free laws about math achievement or to predict and control it. Instead, the aim of the qualitative researcher is to gain understanding of participant meaning and action within a socially bounded system. Researchers proceed inductively or abductively to the surface and identify the multiple meanings that participants hold by observing their actions and listening to their talk.

This sequence of research steps differs from the familiar, hypothetico-deductive model in which the researcher decides on the meanings of constructs in advance of data collection and that decision, through the selection of indicators and measures, persists to the end of the study. For example, the researcher might decide early on that the construct or meaning of math achievement, for the duration of the study, will be represented by the score on a particular standardized achievement test. After meaning is fixed, the researcher will proceed to collect data from that indicator, without acknowledging that the construct might hold multiple meanings, perhaps having nothing to do with an achievement test, for the participants in the study site. The qualitative researcher, in contrast, would design data collection methods to bring to the surface as many alternative meanings for math achievement as are held by the participants, and, after the data are gathered, would find clusters and patterns of meanings held that define those patterns. If on site long enough, the researcher might also be aware that meanings change over time and in relation to contextual events such as oncoming high-stakes testing.

Second, qualitative researchers assume that human action is sensitive to a variety of contexts in which it occurs. Contexts are multiple and embedded—they are material, cultural, linguistic, interactional, for example. Holistic accounts—that is, taking into account all of the contextual influences when explaining the phenomenon—are valued. The embedding of contexts makes social life complex and unpredictable, which in turn makes flexible and emergent research designs necessary. To account adequately for these contextual influences, the researcher must have familiarity with the site and the participants before deciding on the best combination of various data collection methods. A preordinate design is likely to produce distorted findings. Long-term, direct contact between the researcher and the participants is therefore required. The complexity of the design must match the complexity of the social and educational situation.

Because of the assumption of context sensitivity, qualitative researchers resist the tendency in traditional educational psychology to reduce the educational experience to simple, two-variable models or simple causal claims. The input–output design has come under particular criticism for its reductionism. For example, Erickson (1986) argued against treating the classroom as a black box, which is what happens when researchers try to explain an output (e.g., math achievement) as a simple result of difference in an input (e.g., type of math textbook used or time spent on task). Instead, it is important to study the details of everyday life in classrooms to see what interactional events occur, the meanings different participants attribute to these events, the processes by which interactions create achievement structures (e.g., variation in math achievement), and other contextual influences.

Fourth, it is accepted that the researcher is the instrument in qualitative research. She finds a social vantage point within the site, forms relationships with the participants, and collects data through the medium of the roles she assumes and relationships she forms. Thus, an interview of a participant teacher by a researcher who has been on the site for a time and has established herself as trustworthy is not the same interview that would have been conducted with the same teacher by a researcher coming in cold, even though the form of the questions might be the same in the two instances. Data collection methods are dependent on each other (what was observed in yesterday's reading groups constitutes part of tomorrow's interview agenda with the teacher). Methods are fallible, always fraught with auxiliary assumptions—for example, that the tape recorder works, the observer is close enough to the reading groups to hear what is going on, or the interview questions are understood by the participant in the way the researcher intended—which may or may not be warranted. Therefore, the researcher uses as many kinds of data collection methods as possible and looks for convergence of findings across different methods and observers (Denzin, 1978). The qualitative researcher acknowledges that perfect objectivity and replicability are neither possible nor worth pursuing as a research strategy. Rigor is more a matter of comprehensiveness of data collection, researcher self-criticism, willingness to challenge assumptions about substance and method, and willingness to subject one's work to the scrutiny of others than it is about following the correct research procedures. Qualitative researchers aim to produce coherent, credible accounts that have authenticity and verisimilitude, accounts that describe action in sufficient and significant detail so as to create in the reader a vicarious experience. The length of the data collection period, during which the researcher is in direct contact with the participants, and the degree of psychological access to participant meanings that the researcher must maintain place ethical obligations on the qualitative researcher over and above the typical human subjects' protection provisions.

Fifth, data collection and data analysis are overlapping and reflexive. Traditional hypothetico-deductive thinking separates (or seems to separate) empirical research processes from theoretical ones, on the premise that one's theory should not contaminate one's data (Hanson, 1957). There is no such pretext in qualitative research. In some approaches, the process of constructing meaning from data occurs very early in the data collection process. Early categorization and hypothesis formation guide subsequent data collection (see section on grounded theory analysis, below).

Sixth, the characteristics of qualitative research—the process of discovering participant meaning, the belief in context sensi-

tivity of human acts, the need to distribute data collection over a variety of methods, the extensive time requirements, the goal of building descriptive accounts of everyday life—result in a body of data that is vast and cumbersome. Two thousand pages of field notes, interview transcripts, and artifacts would not be an extreme example of a project data record.

The cognitive load on the researcher is thus considerable. Researchers often struggle with the task of abstracting categories, ideas, or meaning units from the textual data (that is, fractioning them), and then finding a structure for relating these ideas to an overall theory or set of propositions (integrating). The management of data—organizing, storing, locating, and retrieving instances of categories—is likewise daunting. Although several methodologists recommend systematic procedures to meet these challenges in credible ways (see, e.g., Miles & Huberman, 1984), no algorithms exist to lead the analyst to definitive conclusions. Given the complex nature of the task, there is little probability that such algorithms will be developed.

Seventh, qualitative researchers tend to focus on units of study that traditional researchers in educational psychology do not. Most psychologists place the locus of explanation in the psychological and physiological traits of individuals. For example, they search for explanations for achievement deficits in the psychological makeup of the child, in traits either inherited or ingrained at an early age through family experiences. Alternative frameworks dominate qualitative research in education. For example, organizational frameworks seek explanations in the characteristics of schools as organizations. Macrosociological frameworks seek explanations in the social and economic fabric. Interactional frameworks such as symbolic interactionism, sociolinguistics, activity theory, and the like focus researcher attention at the level of transactions between students and teachers and in the defining of the situation and the creation of labels and categories that occur at the local level. In explaining a phenomenon such as dyslexia, for example, interactional theorists would look not for neurological traits or deficits within individual children, but to the rules for determining within a school who gets classified as dyslexic, the expectations held by teachers, parents, and children about what counts as normal and abnormal reading performance, transactions between teachers and the children who are perceived to be reading abnormally, and so forth. By adopting such a conceptual framework, the qualitative researcher focuses attention on the transactions, local meanings, and expectations for reading, how decisions get made, and how it happens that some children rather than others are classified as dyslexic (Coles, 1978; Mehan, 1988). Furthermore, acknowledgment of theories, both epistemological and social, is a "hallmark of qualitative research" (Pfaffenberger, 1988).

Finally, analysis of the meaning of qualitative data rests on a foundation of description—of context, site, actors, and action. As LeCompte and Preissle (1993, p. 235) note, the "basic goal of ethnography is to create a vivid reconstruction of the culture studied."

Within the field of qualitative research, some authors argue that rich description of cases, narration, or artistic rendering of data represents the end point of the researcher's work (Barone, 1990). Wolcott (1994, p. 12) defined three modes of transforming qualitative data, beginning with description:

*Description* addresses the question, "What is going on here?" Data consists of observation made by the researcher and/or reported to the researcher by others.

*Analysis* addresses the identification of essential features and the systematic description of interrelationships among them—in short, how things work. . . .

*Interpretation* addresses procedural questions of meaning and contexts: "How does it all mean?" "What is to be made of it all?"

## Three Approaches to Qualitative Data Analysis

Because qualitative frameworks span broad philosophical and practical issues, a full accounting of them is not possible here. The following section, therefore, discusses the three approaches to qualitative research likely to be employed or encountered by members of the educational psychology community. These approaches are Erickson's analytic induction, following Erickson (1986), grounded theory (Glaser & Strauss, 1967; Strauss & Corbin, 1990), and Miles and Huberman's three-part analysis (Miles & Huberman, 1984).

*Erickson's Analytic Induction.* In the third edition of the *Handbook of Research on Teaching,* Frederick Erickson (1986) contributed a chapter titled "Qualitative Methods in Research on Teaching," probably the most complete available description and justification for an interpretivist approach to qualitative research. In that chapter, Erickson presented the theoretical justification for an idealist ontology and epistemology that acknowledges multiple realities, the primacy of the search for participant meaning and action, research validity based on coherence rather than correspondence, and frameworks for explaining social life by close examination of interactional events in the classroom. Besides this theory, the chapter offers a set of methods for data collection and analysis that a researcher operating from the interpretivist paradigm might use. The reader should be reminded that these methods are far from algorithmic. Following them carefully is not the direct path to truth, if one follows interpretivist theory.

Erickson's approach to analysis of qualitative data could be called a moderate form of analytic induction. The stiffer test was outlined by Cressey (1953), who called for an inductive process of generating assertions from data, followed by revision or deletion of an assertion when any disconfirming evidence could be found against it. Erickson also inductively derives assertions from data and conducts a rigorous search for disconfirming data. At the same time, he seems to accept as warranted an assertion that may have some disconfirming data but still a preponderance of confirming data available. There are two broad stages to Erickson's approach: finding the assertions from the data, and then establishing the warrant for those assertions. Central to this method is the idea that data analysis and data collection are not independent, sequential stages. Data analysis is founded on adequate relationships established by the researcher in the setting chosen and on a conceptual framework that is laid out at the beginning but always subject to modification as the researcher gains experience in the context. Thus, prior research, theory, and practical experience provide frameworks for the researcher as he designs the study and begins

the data collection. Although proceeding more or less inductively, the researcher is not expected to be the figurative tabula rasa and deny these sources of prior knowledge and expectations.

Issues of data analysis are foreshadowed in early stages of data collection in another way as well. The researcher needs to be assured, in advance, that sufficient data of analytic significance will have been collected by the end point. Erickson offers warnings about failing to anticipate these potential shortcomings of an analysis, which include an insufficient amount of evidence, inadequate variety in the data collection methods, "faulty interpretive status of evidence" (p. 140: "The researcher fails to have understood the key aspects of the complexity of action or of meaning perspectives held by actors in the setting"), inadequate disconfirming evidence, or discrepant case analysis (p. 140: "The researcher lacks data that might disconfirm a key assertion [or] evidence that a deliberate search was made for potentially disconfirming data while in the field setting"). To guard against these various flaws, the researcher is advised to negotiate access to as wide a field as possible within the site, develop good, collaborative relationships with participants, identify the "full range of variation in modes of formal and informal social organization (role relationships) and meaning perspectives," collect "recurrent instances of events across a wide range of event types . . . so that typicality or atypicality . . . can later be established," and look not only at the unit one is studying but at units higher and lower in the institution to try to ascertain the patterns of influence on or by the unit of interest. Although the system is usually too complex to be understood initially, the researcher's investment in long-term contact and wide sampling of events within it will enable him to develop further an analytic framework and design for subsequent data collection. A researcher who follows all of these suggestions can establish a credible trail toward a data analysis that will stand Erickson's test of warrant.

At any stage of data collection after that initial survey and preliminary understanding, the researcher's next analytic task is to examine the full corpus of available data—observation notes, videotape recordings, audio tapes and transcripts, documents, and the like—and to generate a set of assertions. These are statements that the researcher believes to be true from reading and rereading the available data as a whole. It is useful to think of this process as an intuitive grasping of the entire set of data and committing to paper the answer to the question, "What 10 (or so) things seem to be true about the phenomenon?"

Assertions may vary according to scope and level of inference. Erickson offers the example of an assertion generated from classroom observation, "There are two major groups of children in the classroom. . . .: good readers and poor readers," as broad in scope (representing many instances of data from a variety of events, generated from a variety of data collection methods) and low in level of inference (the categorization would be credible to participants, several observers, and readers and obvious from an inspection of the data). An assertion that teachers have a "regressive social relationship" with the bad readers is a broad, high-inference assertion to an abstract category related to sociological theory, and one that would be supported by "traces of evidence" throughout the data record.

The search for the warrant for the assertions is a control

against premature typification and reaction to the dramatic rare event. Erickson's analysis looks for patterns and rules of social interaction and considers rare events as probes for examining the nature and credibility of the general pattern. Warranting is an activity undertaken after the researcher has left the site, assuming that assertions can be generated at any previous step along the way. It consists of "a systematic search of the entire data corpus, looking for disconfirming and confirming evidence, keeping in mind the need to reframe the assertions as the analysis proceeds" (p. 146). Erickson illustrates this process for the assertion that the reading instruction given to good readers emphasizes comprehension, whereas bad readers receive instruction emphasizing decoding:

[T]he researcher would first search the data corpus for all instances of formal reading instruction. If the students were divided into different groups by skill level, all instances of formal reading instruction in those groups would be examined to see whether the teacher's emphasis was on higher-order or lower-order skills. Any discrepant cases, that is, higher-order skills instruction given to a low-performance reading group . . . would be identified. (p. 146)

The researcher then looks for a preponderance of evidence confirming the assertion, adding in data from interviews or other sources not directly observed in classroom life. If confirming instances do not predominate, the assertion is dropped or modified to reflect interacting conditions (e.g., by studying the field notes and samples of pupils' work for the attributes of discrepant cases, the researcher asserts instead that those pupils who are considered bad readers but are highly motivated are provided instruction in reading comprehension). Mechanically, this process involves several passes through the data notes and videotapes, marking confirming and disconfirming instances (in different-colored ink, if one is working with hard copy, or using computerized text analysis programs; see later section for examples).

Erickson refers to this process as analytic detective work, moving back and forth between data and working assertions, accounting for disconfirming evidence and discrepant cases, refining categories and restating assertions until a defensible set is achieved. He emphasizes the search for "key linkages" across data and assertions. That is, he pursues general patterns that bring together many different elements and events within the case, assertions that tie in with each other and account for most of the data. He offers as an example the discovery that the teacher's labeling of good and bad readers might reflect a more general pattern of treating pupils differently based on teacher's beliefs or mental models about individual differences. He points out that such a search for key linkages and a general explanation for the pattern discovered requires "a substantial number of analogous instances for comparison" (Erickson, 1986, p. 148).

Analysis and reporting results are reflexive. For Erickson, one part of the report is the analytic vignette, which in its finished form provides "a vivid portrayal of the conduct of an event of everyday life, in which the sights and sounds of what was being said and done are described in the natural sequence of their occurrence . . . [and] gives the reader a sense of *being there* in the scene" (pp. 149–150). The vignette also persuades the reader that the assertions are true by providing compelling

evidence of the "concrete particulars—specific actions" that instantiate the assertions. Besides the vignettes, the quotations of the participants provide further "particular description" that constitutes visible evidence for the assertions. General description provides evidence about the typicality of events portrayed in the event. Interpretive commentary links one assertion to another and displays for the reader the overall perspective of the researcher. These elements of the report allow the reader to judge the coherence and credibility of the analysis and "to function as a co-analyst" (p. 145). Although Erickson presents these elements as essential to the finished report, the acts of constructing vignettes and linking particular description to general description and interpretive commentary are themselves part of analysis.

***Grounded Theory Analysis.*** Barney Glaser and Anselm Strauss developed a coherent approach to an entire research process, encompassing design, data collection, and analysis, in their 1967 book, *The Discovery of Grounded Theory*. Since the original book, the authors have published several other books and articles (Glaser, 1978; Strauss, 1987; Strauss & Corbin, 1990) that have expanded their original notions. Their work has spawned a rich set of applications. Although some qualitative researchers have borrowed pieces from the grounded theory approach (e.g., constant-comparative methods), we will abstract the approach as a whole.

Glaser and Strauss argue that the goal of research should be to develop theories that are as complex as the nature of the social world that is to be explained. Such theories must be grounded in data from particular contexts, in which people are engaged in interaction and social process and often struggling to come to definitions of the situation. Glaser and Strauss recommend entering such a bounded setting with a general research problem rather than preconceived ideas, and allow the design of the study and the collection of data to be structured by local social processes and what is problematic for people in the case. Operating from a general conceptual orientation but not a formal theory or deductive hypothesis, a researcher might ask, for an example, "How do teachers cope with high-stakes tests?" At the early stages of the research process, therefore, the researcher operates inductively, looking for local meanings from initial data collection. Later, the researcher proceeds deductively and abductively, working back and forth between generating categories and propositions and testing them with new or reconceived data. The ability of the researcher to identify concepts from data is known as *theoretical sensitivity*. The protection against premature typification and confirmation bias lies in the researcher's design to refine the categories and explore their boundaries and contingencies. Data analysis starts early. With only a few field notes or interview transcripts, the researcher initiates *open coding,* a process not unlike brainstorming, for discovering the ideas or concepts that the data may refer to. The researcher proceeds line by line or sentence by sentence through the text and, for each instance, abstracts a possible meaning from it and attaches a code word or phrase to it. This minute fractioning of the data into meaning units that will later be reintegrated into a theory contrasts with Erickson's method of analytic induction (described earlier), which calls for the researcher to derive, from the data as a whole, a small set of themes or propositions that can then be instantiated and confirmed by referring them to data. The following illustration of the open coding process uses a small section of data from Smith and others (Smith, Edelsky, Draper, Rottenberg, Draper, & Cherland, 1989) on the role of mandated testing in elementary schools. It is a section of data from an episode of the first faculty meeting of the year in the selected case and the first opportunity to collect data for the study. The assistant principal is explaining the school's achievement test scores from the previous spring.

Opening Staff Meeting. School B. 8/26. Assistant Principal is giving the standardized testing report from last spring. He uses the library shelves to indicate levels of achievement. "Our kids started down here and made progress up to here. Other schools may have started higher than we did, but didn't make as much gains in a year as we did. In absolute terms, we started lower. We made better gains, but the others are still ahead of us. What is our goal? To get all the kids up to the national average. Fifty is the magic number. But you see that a lot of kids didn't make it. You know who they are and I know who they are. We have a large group of high ability kids, but the performance of the low ability kids brings down their scores. Our first grade average is at the 45th percentile, but if you take out those kids who are here less than 120 days, we are at the 51st percentile."

In open coding, the researcher might look at the *incident* in the last line and label it, "dis-counting," as a provisional category for analysis. What the administrator seems to be doing is massaging the test scores by removing from the school's average information on pupils who move during the year and tend to score low. But the same instance, from the point of view of grounded theory, might be coded in other ways, simultaneously or alternatively, as "rationalizing," for example. The remainder of the data from this episode and other early episodes will also be categorized, as the researcher discovers the abstract ideas to which these data refer. The *category* "dis-counting" has *properties*, or characteristics, such as who does it, when it happens, under what conditions. Some of these properties form *dimensions*, such as frequency, extent, duration, and intensity (Strauss & Corbin, 1990), that the researcher must discover during data analysis. The initial coding process, taking the categories now discovered, will shape the researcher's next efforts to collect new data that might, among other things, uncover incidents of "dis-counting."

The *method of constant comparison* requires the researcher to compare every incident that has been categorized by the same code. She must look for every incident that she has labeled "dis-counting" and compare its meaning. She might discover that the category she has been using is really two categories, "score dis-counting" and "special pleading," so she goes back and recategorizes earlier data accordingly. She also searches for additional properties of the categories. Her aim is for categories that are defined, internally consistent, fit the data from which they were abstracted, and saturated. *Saturation* is achieved when the researcher can find no more properties for a category, and new data are redundant with the old.

As Glaser (1978, p. 62) wrote,

Our concept-indicator model is based on constant comparing of (1) indicator to indicator, and then when a conceptual code is generated (2) also comparing indicators to the emerging concept. From the comparisons of indicator to indicator the analyst is forced into confronting

similarities, differences and degrees of consistency of meaning between indicators which generates an underlying uniformity which in turn results in a coded category and the beginning of properties of it. From the comparisons of further indicators to the conceptual codes, the code is sharpened to achieve its best fit while further properties are generated until the code is verified and saturated.

A vital aid in this process is the *memo*. Memo writing stimulates the researcher's thinking about the meaning of a category and its relationships with other categories and also documents the evolution of the researcher's perspective through the course of the study.

In later stages of the research study, the researcher engages in *axial coding* (Strauss & Corbin, 1990), following the "coding paradigm" (Glaser, 1978). This is a kind of theoretical coding in which the researcher elaborates and explains key categories. For example, the researcher attempts to identify the causes, contextual conditions, correlates, and consequences of the phenomenon that she has labeled "dis-counting." What are the conditions under which dis-counting occurs? (When the test is used for high-stakes purposes.) What are the consequences of dis-counting? (Teachers feel less defensive about the scores, but feel less responsible for the achievement of highly mobile pupils.) The coding paradigm also may work toward identification of the processes, sequences, or stages of a category that refers to a process or the types, degrees, clusters, or families of a category (Glaser, 1978). Axial coding is aided by more memo writing and a systematic search for data that support, disconfirm, or further contextualize the categories and propositional statements that have been identified. The researcher engages in *theoretical sampling,* which is a deliberate search for episodes and incidents that enlarge the variance of properties and thus put boundary conditions around category definitions and propositional statements and hypotheses.

The grounded theorist also engages in *selective coding* around a *core category.* Suppose that the researcher has identified "high-stakes use of test results" as the phenomenon that links most of the categories identified. This becomes the core category (Strauss & Corbin, 1990), or *basic social process* (Glaser, 1978), and the researcher goes back through all the data and codes accordingly, also looking for connections and propositions such as the following: "Teachers engage in dis-counting of test scores when they perceive that the test has high-stakes consequences for their jobs and status." This kind of analytic activity takes the fractionated data and reintegrates them into a theory. Having written memos at each stage of the analysis, the researcher looks for a structure that links together the memos into a coherent theory. Outlines and integration of topics of memos as well as diagrams and charts assist the analyst. Glaser and Strauss refer to mid-range theory as that which grounded theorists aim to achieve. The tests of quality include the fit of theory to data, the density and integration of categories, and the clarity, consistency, and credibility of the theory.

***Miles and Huberman's Three-Part Analysis.*** In *Qualitative Data Analysis: A Sourcebook of New Methods,* Miles and Huberman (1984) attempted to bring "scientific credibility" to qualitative research by offering a set of procedures and methods for analysis of data, procedures that were "practical, communicable, nonself-deluding, and teachable." They argued for a renewed concern among qualitative researchers for reliability, replicability, and validity. These procedures especially address studies that encompass multiple sites or multiple observers, where there is need for commonality. The model they propose consists of three phases: data reduction, data display, and conclusion drawing/verification. These parts are not necessarily sequential, as data collection and each part may be reflexive and recycled. They label as a grave mistake the practice of gathering all one's data and then retreating to the office to analyze them.

Data reduction refers to a fractioning of available data using an evolving set of codes:

A code is an abbreviation or symbol applied to a segment of words—most often a sentence or paragraph of transcribed field notes—in order to classify the words. Codes are categories. They usually derive from research questions, hypotheses, key concepts, or important themes. They are retrievel and organizing devices that allow the analyst to spot quickly, pull out, then cluster all the segments relating to the particular question, hypothesis, concept, or theme. (p. 56)

Codes may be purely descriptive or highly inferential, "pattern codes" (note that all codes in grounded theory are inferential in this sense). Pattern codes push the researcher away from raw data or classified data and toward a more abstract conceptual level in pursuit of patterns, explanations, and causal inferences. The researcher begins the process with a "start list" of codes and their provisional definition based on her conceptual framework or working hypotheses. These can be a kind of template for reviewing and coding the data. As the research study progresses, new codes will emerge and start-list codes will alter in definition. Some initial codes will become unimportant and drop off the list. At some point, the researcher settles on a revised list of codes, settles on a dictionary of definitions for these codes, and recodes all data with that final set. The authors recommend that sections of data be double-coded to check for reliability of the coding process. They also stress the importance of identifying a structure for organizing codes so that the conceptual links among categories can be discovered. Miles and Huberman recommend the use of memos, citing grounded theory for their rationale.

What distinguishes coding in this qualitative data analysis approach from conventional content analysis coding (see, e.g., Krippendorf, 1980) is that in the latter, coding must be exclusive and exhaustive. One data segment can be coded with one code only. In all forms of qualitative coding, by contrast, the researcher expects that a given data segment has several meanings and thus can be coded accordingly. Codes are often nested and hierarchical, with some subsuming others. The codes form the basis for an index and retrieval system, either manual or computerized. For example, all the data that are coded as "high-stakes test use" can be cut from a photocopy of the data record, and assembled in a file folder. Computerized indexing and retrieval systems are described in a later section of this chapter.

The process of data display is central to Miles and Huberman's approach. The roles played by display are two: advancing the researcher's thinking about the data and representing the data to research audiences. The usual form of display for qualitative researchers is the narrative text. But, the authors argue, this form is "weak and cumbersome . . . hard on analysts, because it

is dispersed, spread out over many pages and is hard to look at; it is sequential rather than simultaneous . . . it is only vaguely ordered" (p. 79). Data displays, in contrast, "present information . . . in spatial format . . . in a compressed, ordered form, so that the user can draw valid conclusions and take needed action" (p. 79). Types of displays are figures or summarizing tables. Data within these displays include short segments of data, titles, quotations, symbols, and the like. These data may be arrayed in matrix format, in temporal order of events, in causal chains, in checklists, cross-tabulations, typologies, scatterplots, or clusters (similar to factor and cluster analysis), to mention only a sample. The authors argue for the creation of formats suitable to each research study and against the idea that a standard rubric is appropriate. The data display that is constructed for a single site analysis then can be grouped into a cross-site display through the use of meta-matrices, according to the authors. Such a process allows the researcher to understand how different contextual constraints operate on events within a particular site and thus strengthen her analytic insights.

The last part of Miles and Huberman's analysis approach consists of drawing and verifying conclusions. They offer suggestions on "counting" instances that fall into the identified categories or that support a preliminary theme or pattern (to keep the researcher from being overly influenced by salient but rare incidents or to verify hypotheses); identifying patterns; noting plausibility (tentative assertions ripe for subsequent verification); identifying clusters (noting which categories and events tend to hang together or relate to each other); making metaphors (as a way of abstracting beyond the particular to reach a more general level of analysis and for thinking in new ways); splitting variables (as a way of making sure that a general case has clear referents in data and that the referents are internally consistent with each other); "subsuming particulars into the general . . . by asking the question, 'What is this specific thing an instance of? Does it belong to a more general class?' " p. 221); factoring (akin to factor and cluster analysis); finding intervening variables; and building temporal and causal chains. To confirm the conclusions, Miles and Huberman (1984, p. 231) recommend

checking for researcher effects . . . triangulating . . . across data sources and methods . . . weighting the evidence. . . . . Contrasts and comparisons . . . checking the meaning of outliers . . . and extreme cases. . . . Ruling out spurious relationships, replacing . . . and looking for negative evidence.

They suggest that getting feedback from informants and conducting audit trails also strengthen the inferences made.

Alone among the three approaches described here, Miles and Huberman represent qualitative analysis as a reproducible and intersubjective process, suggesting that coding and display offer the potential for control over inferences analogous to statistical procedures such as calculating correlation coefficients for the quantitative researcher. The recommendation for intercoder agreement checks also reflects their aims for systematic and impersonal analysis. Such a recommendation has brought criticism and accusations of positivism from interpretivists. The grounded theorists, in contrast (see, e.g., Strauss & Corbin, 1990), acknowledge that all the intellectual and personal baggage that a particular researcher brings to the analysis makes it unlikely that a second researcher will arrive at the same set of data, codes, or displays as the primary researcher. They invite colleagues to inspect their analysis, but not to eliminate errors and bias. Rather, other minds can promote theoretical sensitivity and critical reflection, to add to the store of concepts and challenge the researcher's formulations. Likewise, Erickson recommends the use of mechanically retrievable data and participant and co-analyst checks, but with the goal of enhancing credibility of the analysis and strengthening the claims that the assertions are warranted based on the criteria already named.

The traditional view of the reliability of ethnographic analysis is reflected in the saying, "You cannot step in the same stream twice." Accusations against the positivism of Miles and Huberman (they are perhaps more aptly labeled postpositivists or multiple-perspectivists) and denunciations against their *Handbook* may be countered with the recommendations to use their procedures, as appropriate to the research topic and context, simply to gain understanding about the data at hand, and not as a structural means to obtain validity. Use of procedures that, after the fact, are systematically described can enhance the credibility of the analysis and allow the reader to follow the researcher's logic from data to conclusions.

## Microcomputers in Qualitative Analysis

We begin this section with a word of caution: Use of software designed to help the researcher analyze qualitative data should not be seen as a structural feature to enhance the reliability and validity of inferences. Using a program such as HYPER-QUAL2, for example, does not render one's assertions more valid than using the time-honored method of cutting up field notes and putting sections in file folders. All qualitative analysis is a cognitive process, and all such programs can do is to facilitate clerical and indexing tasks so that the researcher has more time for thinking about the data and the ideas embedded in them. Further, as Pfaffenberger (1988) warned, qualitative researchers must be mindful that the use of any technology involves assumptions, preunderstandings, and values and may encourage certain types of thinking processes and discourage other, potentially fruitful processes that are incompatible with the structure of the software. For example, using a data-base program requires that data fields be specified in advance and segments of data entered into these fields. Such a structure limits the researcher's ability to modify, based on data collected later on and ideas emerging from them, the basic dimensions of the data fields. The researcher might bend her thinking to conform to this preordinate logic and miss the most important message. Pfaffenberger (1988) encouraged a critical attitude toward the use of technology. He argued that the test of a program or procedure was whether it furthered the qualitative researcher's aims and assisted in the processes of segmenting (coding) text, storing and retrieving instances of data coded according to the same category so that the researcher can readily examine the commonality of data within categories. Further, the system "must not punish" (p. 27) the researcher's renaming and redefining categories and recoding data.

Three categories of software will be covered here: word-processing, data-base, and text analysis, all appropriate to microcomputers.

*Word-Processing Programs.* A rudimentary qualitative analysis can be performed simply with word-processing software. Data in the form of expanded field notes, interview transcripts, and other text (documents gathered from the site, for example, scanned into readable form) are entered into text files. The text can be coded by attaching key words to segments, such as paragraphs or sentences (the size of the segment depends on the unit of analysis and the focus provided by the conceptual framework of the study). For example, in the episode presented in a preceding section, the excerpt, "but if you take out those kids who are here less than 120 days," can be followed by the code ⟨DISCOUNTING⟩. Key words can be entered as macros. Though differing from package to package, macros are shorthand instructions or miniprograms that allow the analyst to define a single keystroke to enter, for example, the code ⟨DISCOUNTING⟩ at each data segment that illustrates an instance of that category. Searching for all instances of a particular code involves use of the search commands typical of word-processing programs. Renaming categories can be done quickly with search-and-replace commands. Recoding, however, requires a complete iteration through the file. For analytic processes such as constant-comparison, the researcher examines each instance on-line, or can "dump" (mark and copy) an instance into another file (for example, each data segment coded as ⟨DISCOUNTING⟩ can be copied into another file with that name. In this way the researcher can examine all instances together to look for inconsistencies, commonalities, subcategories, and the like. However, important features, such as the date, location, speaker, and the sequence of action, may be lost as the instance is plucked out of its context. Further, analysis of data using word-processing software limits the researcher to a file-by-file search-and-retrieve process, according to Pfaffenberger (1988). To locate segments of text scattered across files requires a program such as ZyIndex.

*Data-Base Programs.* Programs such as Notebook II provide a prestructured form into which the researcher enters text. For example, the researcher has identified early in the research process what broad headings will be used subsequently to analyze data. These headings might refer to the characteristics of participants, settings, events, and the like. The characteristics then can be used as data fields. The data segments, such as one day's observation notes or one interview, can be entered as a data record, and the various data fields completed. For example, data fields for a multiple-case study on the role of high-stakes testing might include school identification, school level (elementary or secondary), date of data collection event, participant role (teacher, principal, pupil), whether the activity was test related or not, and so on. The researcher categorizes the data collection event according to these fields and then enters the notes. During the analysis, the researcher can search the collection of data records for all the observations that involved test-related activities to examine their patterns. Combinations of data fields can be used for more specific searches through the use of Boolean operators. The disadvantages of this approach, according to Pfaffenberger (1988), include the limited speed of search processes through large data bases and the inflexibility of design, for researchers have limited ability to include categories that emerge from the data.

*Text Analysis for DOS-Based Machines.* Although several software programs are available, we will focus on Ethnograph (Seidel, 1988) as a prototype. To use Ethnograph, the researcher must enter data using a word-processing program and then convert the text file to an ASCII file having certain prespecified character limitations. The file is designated by its context and identifying features. Within the file are contextual markers as well, for example, each time a new speaker talks during a focus group interview. From this ASCII file, Ethnograph produces a third file in which the lines of text are numbered. From a printed version of the latter file, the researcher begins the coding process. Each data segment (a line or a paragraph, for example) is given one or more category codes. A code may be embedded within a more abstract code. Line segments attached to different codes may overlap. The researcher must keep track of working category definitions. Memos are recommended for this analytic process, and memos may be coded, stored, and retrieved by Ethnograph, just as data are. When the researcher is satisfied with the coding process, she enters the codes that have been associated with designated line segments. This is done on-line. Recoding is possible at this and subsequent steps to provide flexibility and inductive thinking by the researcher. Searching for data segments by categories, either singly or in combination, is then done by the program. For example, the researcher might ask for all data segments that have been coded as ⟨DISCOUNTING⟩, and the program searches across all data files that the researcher designates and prints these segments on paper, displays them on the screen, or adds them to another file. Along with the segments themselves are printed the file context and speaker context designated earlier. This feature shows the researcher, therefore, not just the disembodied quotation or description, but which speaker stated it or in what class the activity occurred. In addition, the program identifies the categories in which the requested category was embedded, providing additional contextual information and surfacing the potential relationships among categories. From this accumulation of data segments within a category, the researcher can discover the meaning of that category by looking at the characteristics of the data associated with it. Subcategories, internal inconsistencies, and the like can also be identified. Recoding, using this more refined set of codes, can then be accomplished.

*Text Analysis for Macintosh.* The program HYPERQUAL2 (Padilla, 1993) is written in the HyperCard programming environment commonly available to Macintosh users. Unlike Ethnograph, HYPERQUAL2 allows the researcher to enter textual data directly into the program, rather than translating text from a word processor. However, material such as interviews transcribed by a word processor or archives scanned into data files can be blocked and patched into HYPERQUAL2. According to LeCompte & Preissel, 1993, pp. 290–291, "HyperCard is based on the metaphor of the card and of stacks of cards. Cards belong to a stack. The difference between a file and a card is that cards can be connected to other cards in their stack as well as to cards in other stacks." In other words, there is an associative link or series of links that runs between all parts of the data base, including memos. To code text within a card, the researcher marks portions of text that refer to a particular category and clicks a Tag Data button that will associate that incident with a new or already existing stack of similar incidents or

ideas. Search-and-retrieve processes are performed by "printing together all the cards onto which text segments with the same code have been pasted" (LeCompte & Preissle, 1993, p. 301). The researcher then performs the same kind of cognitive processes—comparing, contrasting, abstracting, particularizing, and defining—as the Ethnograph user. Even greater flexibility is possible for recoding and relinking, as the researcher gains in understanding of the data. HYPERQUAL2 allows the researcher to scan in art work or graphics (a sketch of a classroom, for example) to help facilitate the production of schematics and data displays such as those recommended by Miles and Huberman (1984). According to Padilla (1991), programs like HYPERQUAL2 can be used either inductively or deductively. In an approach such as grounded theory, the program assists the analyst in understanding a general concept or category by examining the exemplars or instances that seem to hang together. The concept modeling approach recommended by Padilla allows the researcher to specify a model in advance or to develop one inductively, and deliberately seek incidents in data that will support the model.

## A FINAL WORD ON THE TRUTHFULNESS OF DATA ANALYSIS

In the literature on qualitative methodology, there is a debate about whether quantitative and qualitative approaches are compatible or commensurable. One side argues that, whether or not one borrows from both traditions to do a study, one must still justify one's methods and results within a single paradigm. That is, standards of validity are peculiar to ontological and epistemological assumptions. One cannot claim to be an interpretivist (doing participant observation and the like) and still demand correspondence validity. In this chapter we have rejected structural notions of validity (Cook & Campbell, 1979)—the idea that the correct design and statistics produce definitive conclusions. Instead, we favor more abstract and functional (Cronbach, 1982) concepts of validity, wherein both qualitative and quantitative analysts pursue standards of coherence and credibility rather than correspondence and proof. These standards refer to reasonable and adequately disclosed decisions about methods, diversity of methods and perspectives, comprehensiveness, convergence of evidence, and theoretical and contextual understanding. Compared to traditional standards of truthfulness in research, these are both less ambitious and more appropriate for educational psychologists, regardless of the form of data they analyze. With Kvale (1989, p. 77), we agree that

[t]he quest for absolute certain knowledge is replaced by a conception of *defensible knowledge claims* [original emphasis]. . . . [A] move from correspondence with an objective reality to a social constitution of the social reality implies a change of emphasis from observation of, to a conversation and interaction with the social world, involving a communicative and pragmatic concept of validity. . . . Validation becomes investigation, continually checking, questioning, and theoretically interpreting the findings.

This is an exciting and difficult time for all data analysts. For quantitative analysts, original formulations are being reexamined in light of the computing revolution (Thisted & Velleman, 1992), historical and philosophical analyses (Gigerenzer, 1993), and experience with the problems of applied research in educational psychology. At the same time, qualitative researchers have, after a considerable wait, found forums for discussion, publication, and teaching that are much more visible and effective than could have been envisioned a short time ago. This will continue to allow a burgeoning of ideas and experiences in this community. These changes are occurring along with the rethinking of the nature of inquiry and notions of validity discussed in the previous paragraph. Because educa-tional psychologists often bridge numerous disciplines in education such as psychology, special education, personnel and program evaluation, and test construction, they have a special role in improving educational research. Educational psychologists have a responsibility to seek broad perspectives and acquire a broad range of skills for conceptualizing and conducting research. By opening and maintaining dialogues across the various subspecialties in our own field, educational psychology can continue to serve as a bridging discipline for educational methodologies and a leader in developing and enhancing valuable methods.

# References

Agresti, A. (1992). A survey of exact inference for contingency tables. *Statistical Sciences, 7,* 131–177.

Aiken, L. S., West, S. G., Sechrest, L., & Reno, R. R. (1990). Graduate training in statistics, methodology, and measurement in psychology: A survey of Ph.D. programs in North America. *American Psychologist, 45,* 721–734.

Anderson, J. R. (1987). Methodologies for studying human knowledge (with discussion). *Behavior and Brain Sciences, 10,* 467–505.

Barone, T. (1990). Using the narrative text as an occasion for conspiracy. In E. Eisner & A. Peshkin (Eds.), *Qualitative inquiry in education: The continuing debate* (pp. 305–326). New York: Teachers College Press.

Bazerman, C. (1988). *Shaping written knowledge: The genre and activity of the experimental article in science.* Madison: University of Wisconsin Press.

Beveridge, W. I. B. (1950). *The art of scientific investigation.* New York: Vintage Books.

Bode, H., Mosteller, F., Tukey, J. W., & Winsor, C. (1986). The education of the scientific generalist. In L. V. Jones (Ed.), *The collected works of John W. Tukey: Vol. III. Philosophy and principles of data analysis: 1949–1964.* Pacific Grove, CA: Wadsworth. (Original work published 1949)

Box, G. E. P., & Tiao, G. C. (1973). *Bayesian inference in statistical analysis.* Reading, MA: Addison-Wesley.

Brewer, B. (1985). Behavioral statistics textbooks: Source of myths and misconceptions? *Journal of Educational Statistics, 10,* 252–268.

Burt, C. (1961). Intelligence and social mobility. *British Journal of Statisticsl Psychology, 14,* 3–23.

Busk, P., & Marascuilo, L. (1992). Statistical analysis in single-case research: Issues, procedures, and recommendations, with applications to multiple behaviors. In D. T. Campbell, T. R. Kratochwill, & J. R. Levin (Eds.), *Single-case research design and analysis* (pp. 159–185). Hillsdale, NJ: Lawrence Erlbaum Associates.

Campbell, D. T. (1978). Qualitative knowing in action research. In M. Brenner, P. Marsh, & M. Brenner (Eds.), *The social contexts of method* (pp. 184–209). New York: St. Martin's Press.

Cleveland, W. S. (1985). *Elements of graphing data.* Monterey, CA: Wadsworth Advanced Books and Software.

Cleveland, W. S. (1993). *Visualizing Data.* Summit, NJ: Hobart Press.

Cobb, G. W. (1987). Introductory textbooks: A framework for evaluation. *Journal of the American Statistical Association, 82,* 321–339.

Cohen, J. (1969). *Statistical power analysis for the behavioral sciences.* New York: Academic Press.

Cohen, J. (1990). Things I have learned (so far). *American Psychologist, 45,* 1304–1312.

Cohen, P. A. (1983). Comment on "A selective review of the validity of student ratings of teaching." *Journal of Higher Education, 54,* 449–458.

Coles, G. S. (1978). The learning-disabilities test battery: Empirical and social issues. *Harvard Educational Review, 48,* 313–340.

Comte, A. (1974). *The essential Comte: Selected from Cours de Philosophie Positive* (S. Andreski, Ed.; M. Clarke, Trans.). New York: Barnes & Noble Books. (Original work published 1830)

Conway, J. (1959). Class differences in general intelligence: II. *British Journal of Statistical Psychology, 12,* 219–259.

Cook, T. D., & Campbell, D. T. (1979). *Quasi-experimentation: Design and analysis issues for field settings.* Chicago: Rand McNally.

Cooper, H., & Hedges, L. V. (Eds.). (1994). *The handbook of research synthesis.* New York: Russell Sage Foundation.

Cox, D. R., & Hinkley, D. V. (1974). *Theoretical statistics.* London: Chapman & Hall.

Cressey, D. R. (1953). *Other people's money: A study in the social psychology of embezzlement.* New York: Free Press.

Cronback, L. J. (1975). Beyond the two disciplines of scientific psychology. *American Psychologist, 30,* 116–127.

Cronbach, L. J. (1982). *Designing evaluations of educational and social programs.* San Francisco: Jossey-Bass.

Cronbach, L. J., Ambron, S. R., Dornbusch, S. M., Hess, R. D., Hornick, R. C., Phillips, D. C., Walker, D. F., & Weiner, S. S. (1980). *Toward reform of program evaluation.* San Francisco: Jossey-Bass.

Dabbs, J. M., Jr. (1982). Making things visible. In J. Van Maanen, J. M. Dabbs, Jr., & R. F. Faulkner (Eds.), *Varieties of qualitative research* (pp. 31–66). Beverly Hills, CA: Sage.

Danziger, K. (1990). *Constructing the subject: Historical origins of psychological research.* New York: Cambridge University Press.

Dee-Lucas, D., & Larkin, J. H. (1990). Organization and comprehensibility in scientific proofs, or, "Consider a particle p. . . ." *Journal of Educational Psychology, 82,* 701–714.

Dee-Lucas, D., & Larkin, J. H. (1991). Equations in scientific proofs: Effects on comprehension. *American Educational Research Journal, 28,* 661–682.

Denzin, N. K. (1978). *The research act: A theoretical introduction to sociological methods.* New York: McGraw-Hill.

Edgington, E. S. (1980). *Randomization tests.* New York: Marcel Dekker.

Eisner, E. W. (1991). *The enlightened eye: Qualitative inquiry and the enhancement of educational practice.* New York: Macmillan.

Emerson, J. D., & Hoaglin, D. C. (1983). Analysis of two-way tables by medians. In D. C. Hoaglin, F. Mosteller, & J. W. Tukey (Eds.), *Understanding robust and exploratory data analysis* (pp. 166–209). New York: John Wiley & Sons

Erickson, F. E. (1986). Qualitative methods in research on teaching. In M. Wittrock (Ed.), *Handbook of research on teaching* (3rd ed., pp. 119–161). New York: Macmillan.

Firestone, W. A. (1990). Accommodation: Toward a paradigm-praxis dialectic. In E. G. Guba (Ed.), *The paradigm dialog* (pp. 105–124). Newbury Park, CA: Sage.

Fisher, R. A. (1922a). On the interpretation of chi square from contingency tables, and the calculation of p. *Journal of the Royal Statistical Society, 135*(1), 87–94.

Fisher, R. A. (1922b). On the mathematical foundations of theoretical statistics. *Philosophical Transactions of the Royal Society of London, Series A, 222,* 309–368.

Fisher, R. A. (1925). Applications of "Student's" distribution. *Metron, 5,* 90–104.

Fisher, R. A. (1936). The coefficient of racial likeness and the future of craniometry. *Journal of the Royal Anthropological Institute, 66,* 57–63.

Fisher, R. A. (1949). *The design of experiments* (5th ed.). Edinburgh: Oliver & Boyd.

Fisher, R. A. (1955). Statistical methods and scientific induction. *Journal of the Royal Statistical Society B, 17,* 69–78.

Fisher, R. A. (1956). *Statistical methods and scientific inference.* New York: Hafner.

Friedman, L. (1989). Mathematics and the gender gap: A meta-analysis of recent studies on sex differences in mathematical tasks. *Review of Educational Research, 59,* 185–213.

Frigge, M., Hoaglin, D. C., & Iglewicz, B. (1989). Some implementations of the boxplot. *American Statistician, 43,* 50–54.

Gay, L. R. (1987). *Educational research: Competencies for analysis and application.* Columbus, OH: Merrill.

Gelb, S. A., & Mizokawa, D. T. (1986). Special education and social structure: The commonality of "exceptionality." *American Educational Research Journal, 23,* 543–557.

Gigerenzer, G. (1987). Probabilistic thinking and the fight against subjectivity. In L. Krüger, G. Gigerenzer, & M. S. Morgan (Eds.), *The probabilistic revolution: Vol. 2. Ideas in the sciences* (pp. 11–33). Cambridge, MA: MIT Press.

Gigerenzer, G. (1991). From tools-to-theories: A heuristic of discovery in cognitive psychology. *Psychological Review, 98,* 254–267.

Gigerenzer, G. (1993). The superego, the ego, and the id in statistical reasoning. In G. Keren & C. Lewis (Eds.), *A handbook for data anlysis in the behavioral sciences: Methodological issues* (pp. 311–339). Hillsdale, NJ: Lawrence Erlbaum Associates.

Gigerenzer, G., & Murray, D. J. (1987). *Cognition as intuitive statistics.* Hillsdale, NJ: Lawrence Erlbaum Associates.

Gigerenzer, G., Swijtink, Z., Porter, T., Daston, L. J., Beatty, J., & Krüger, L. (1989). *The empire of chance: How probability changed science and everday life.* Cambridge, England: Cambridge University Press.

Glaser, B. G. (1978). *Theoretical sensitivity.* Mill Valley, CA: Sociological Press.

Glaser, B. G., & Strauss, A. L. (1967). *The discovery of grounded theory: Strategies for qualitative research.* New York: Aldine.

Glass, G. V (1976). Primary, secondary and meta-analysis of research. *Educational Researcher, 5,* 3–8.

Glass, G. V, & Hopkins, K. D. (1984). *Statistical methods in education and psychology.* Englewood Cliffs, NJ: Prentice Hall.

Glass, G. V, McGaw, B., & Smith, M. L. (1981). *Meta-analysis in social research.* Beverly Hills, CA: Sage.

Glass, G. V, Peckham, P. D., & Sanders, J. R. (1972). Consequences of failure to meet assumptions underlying the fixed effects analysis of variance and covariance. *Review of Educational Research, 42,* 237–288.

Gould, S. J. (1981). *The mismeasure of man.* New York: Norton.

Guba, E. (1990). The alternative paradigm dialog. In E. G. Guba (Ed.), *The paradigm dialog* (pp. 17–27). Newbury Park, CA: Sage.

Hanson, N. (1957). *Patterns of discovery.* Cambridge, England: Cambridge University Press.

Hearnshaw, L. S. (1979). *Cyril Burt, psychologist.* New York: Advantage Books.

Hedges, L. V., & Olkin, I. (1980). Vote-counting methods in research synthesis. *Psychological Bulletin, 88,* 359–369.

Hedges, L. V., & Olkin, I. (1985). *Statistical methods for meta-analysis.* New York: Academic Press.

Henderson, H. V., & Velleman, P. F. (1981). Building multiple regression models interactively. *Biometrics, 37,* 391–411.

Hoaglin, D. C. (1988). Transformations in everyday experience. *Chance, 1*(4), 40–45.

Hoaglin, D. C., Mosteller, F., & Tukey, J. W. (Eds.). (1983). *Understanding robust and exploratory data analysis.* New York: Wiley.

Hoaglin, D. C., Mosteller, F., & Tukey, J. W. (Eds.). (1985). *Exploring data tables, trends, and shapes.* New York: Wiley.

Hoaglin, D. C., Mosteller, F., & Tukey, J. W. (Eds.). (1991). *Fundamentals of exploratory analysis of variance.* New York: Wiley.

Hogben, L. (1957). *Statistical theory.* New York: Norton.

Hornstein, G. A. (1988). Quantifying psychological phenomena: Debates, dilemmas, and implications. In J. G. Morawski (Ed.), *The rise of experimentation in American psychology.* New Haven, CT: Yale University Press.

Howson, C., & Urbach, P. (1993). *Scientific reasoning: The Bayesian approach.* Chicago: Open Court.

Huberty, C. J. (1987). On statistical testing. *Educational Researcher, 16*(8), 4–9.

Jackson, G. B. (1980). Methods for integrative reviews. *Review of Educational Research, 50,* 438–460.

Kant, I. (1969). *Critique of pure reason.* New York: Dutton. (Original work published 1781)

Kempthorne, O. (1955). The randomization theory of experimental inference. *Journal of the American Statistical Association, 50,* 946–967.

Kendall, M. G. (1963). Ronald Aylmer Fisher, 1890–1962. *Biometrika, 50,* 1–15.

Kraemer, H. C., & Thiemann, S. (1987). *How many subjects? Statistical power analysis in research.* Beverly Hills, CA: Sage.

Krippendorf, K. (1980). *Content analysis: An introduction to its methodology.* Beverly Hills, CA: Sage.

Kvale, S. (1983). The quantification of knowledge in education: On resistance toward qualitative evaluation and research. In B. Bain (Ed.), *The sociogenesis of language and human conduct* (pp. 433–447). New York: Plenum Press.

Kvale, S. (1989). To validate is to question. In S. Kvale (Ed.), *Issues of validity in qualitative research* (pp. 73–92). Lund, Sweden: Studentlitteratur.

LeCompte, M. D., & Preissle, J., with Tesch, R. (1993). *Ethnography and qualitative design in educational research* (2nd ed.). San Diego, CA: Academic Press.

Leinhardt, G., & Leinhardt, S. (1980). Exploratory data analysis: New tools for the analysis of empirical data. *Review of Research in Education, 8,* 85–157.

Levin, J. R. (1991). Editorial. *Journal of Educational Psychology, 83,* 5–7.

Light, R. J., & Smith, P. V. (1971). Accumulating evidence: Procedures for resolving contradictions among different research studies. *Harvard Educational Review, 41,* 429–471.

Lincoln, Y. S., & Guba, E. G. (1985). *Naturalistic inquiry.* Beverly Hills, CA: Sage.

Lind, J. C., & Zumbo, B. D. (1993). The continuity principle in psychological research: An introduction to robust statistics. *Canadian Psychology, 34,* 407–414.

Loftus, G. R. (1993). Editorial comment. *Memory & Cognition, 21,* 1–3.

Meehl, P. E. (1978). Theoretical risks and tabular asterisks: Sir Karl, Sir Ronald and the slow progress of soft psychology. *Journal of Consulting and Clinical Psychology, 46,* 806–834.

Mehan, H. (1988). Educational handicaps as a cultural meaning system. *Ethos, 16,* 73–91.

Mehta, C. R., & Patel, N. R. (1983). A network algorithm for performing Fisher's exact test in r × c contingency tables. *Journal of the American Statistical Association, 78,* 427–434.

Miles, M. B., & Huberman, A. M. (1984). *Qualitative data analysis: A sourcebook of new methods.* Beverly Hills, CA: Sage.

Miles, M. B., & Huberman, A. M. (1994). *Qualitative data analysis:*

*An expanded sourcebook.* Thousand Oaks, CA: Sage.

Moore, D. S., & McCabe, G. P. (1993). *Introduction to the practice of statistics.* New York: Freeman.

Morrison, D. E., & Henkel, R. A. (Eds.). (1970). *The significance test controversy.* Chicago: Aldine.

Mosteller, F., & Tukey, J. W. (1977). *Data analysis and regression: A second course in statistics.* Reading, MA: Addison-Wesley.

Mulaik, S. A. (1984). Empiricism and exploratory statistics. *Philosophy of Science, 52,* 410–430.

Neyman, J., & Pearson, E. S. (1928). On the use and interpretation of certain test criteria for purposes of statistical inference: Part I. *Biometrika, 20a,* 175–240.

Olkin, I. (1990). History and goals. In K. W. Wachter & M. L. Straf (Eds.), *The future of meta-analysis.* New York: Russell Sage Foundation.

Padilla, R. V. (1991). Using computers to develop concept models of social situations. *Qualitative Sociology, 14*(3), 263–274.

Padilla, R. V. (1993). *Hyperqual2.* Tempe, AZ: Arizona State University, College of Education.

Peshkin, A. (1993). The goodness of qualitative research. *Educational Researcher, 22,* 23–30.

Pfaffenberger, B. (1988). *Microcomputer Applications in Qualitative Research.* Newbury Park, CA: Sage.

Phillips, D. C. (1990). Subjectivity and objectivity: An objective inquiry. In E. W. Eisner & A. Peshkin (Eds.), *Qualitative inquiry in education: The continuing debate* (pp. 19–37). New York: Teachers College Press.

Pickering, M. (1993). *Auguste Comte: An intellectual biography* (Vol. 1). Cambridge, England: Cambridge University Press.

Pollard, W. E. (1986). *Bayesian statistics for evaluation research.* Beverly Hills, CA: Sage.

Popkewitz, T. S. (1990). Whose future? Whose past? Notes on critical theory and methodology. In E. G. Guba (Ed.), *The paradigm dialog.* Newbury Park, CA: Sage.

Resnick, L. B. (1989). Toward the thinking curriculum: An overview. In L. B. Resnick & Klopfer (Eds.), *Toward the thinking curriculum: Current cognitive research* (1989 ASCD yearbook). Association for Supervision and Curriculum Development.

Rosenthal, R. (1966). *Experimenter effects in behavioral research.* New York: Appleton-Century-Crofts.

Rosenthal, R. (1991). *Meta-analytic procedures for social research.* Newbury Park, CA: Sage.

Rosenthal, R. (1993). Cumulating evidence. In G. Keren & C. Lewis (Eds.), *A handbook for data analysis in the behavioral sciences: Methodological issues* (pp. 519–559). Hillsdale, NJ: Lawrence Erlbaum Associates.

Rosnow, R. L., & Rosenthal, R. (1989). Statistical procedures and the justification of knowledge in psychological science. *American Psychologist, 44,* 1276–1284.

Rossi, J. S. (1990). Statistical power of psychological research: What have we gained in 20 years? *Journal of Consulting and Clinical Psychology, 58,* 646–656.

Sadler, D. R. (1981). Intuitive data processing as a potential source of bias in naturalistic evaluations. *Educational Evaluation and Policy Analysis, 3*(4), 25–31.

Salsburg, D. S. (1985). The religion of statistics as practiced in medical journals. *American Statistician, 39,* 220–223.

Scott, D. W. (1992). *Multivariate density estimation: Theory, practice, and visualization.* New York: Wiley.

Searle, S. R. (1989). Statistical computing packages: Some words of caution. *American Statistician, 43,* 189–190.

Sedlmeier, P., & Gigerenzer, G. (1989). Do studies of statistical power have any effect on the power of studies? *Psychological Bulletin, 105,* 309–316.

Seidel, J. V. (1988). *The Ethnograph.* Littleton, CO: Qualis Research Associates.

Seifert, C., & Norman, D. A. (1987). Levels of research: Discussion of Anderson's methodologies for studying human knowledge. *Behavior and Brain Sciences, 10,* 490–492.

Siegler, S. R. (1987). The perils of average data over strategies: An example from children's addition. *Journal of Experimental Psychology: General, 116,* 250–264.

Signorile, V. (1989). Buridan's ass: The statistical rhetoric of science and the problem of equiprobability. In H. W. Simons (Ed.), *Rhetoric in the human sciences.* Nebur Park, CA: Sage.

Smith, M. L. (1987). Publishing qualitative research. *American Educational Research Journal, 24,* 173–184.

Smith, M. L., Edelsky, C., Draper, K., Rottenberg, C., & Cherland, M. (1989). *The role of testing in elementary schools.* Los Angeles: University of California, Los Angeles, Graduate School of Education, Center for Research on Educational Standards and Student Tests.

Stevens, J. (1990). *Intermediate statistics: A modern approach.* Hillsdale, NJ: Lawrence Erlbaum Associates.

Strauss, A. L. (1987). *Qualitative analysis for social scientists.* New York: Cambridge University Press.

Strauss, A. L., & Corbin, J. (1990). *Basics of qualitative research.* Newbury Park, CA: Sage Press.

"Student." (1908). The probable error of the mean. *Biometrika, 6,* 1–25.

Swanson, H. L., O'Conner, J. E., & Cooney, J. B. (1990). An information processing analysis of expert and novice teachers' problem solving. *American Educational Research Journal, 27,* 533–556.

Thisted, R. A., & Velleman, P. F. (1992). Computers and modern statistics. In D. C. Hoaglin & D. S. Moore (Eds.), *Perspectives on contemporary statistics,* (pp. 41–53). Washington, DC: Mathematical Association of America.

Tukey, J. W. (1977). *Exploratory data analysis.* Reading, MA: Addison-Wesley.

Tukey, J. W. (1979). Methodology, and the statistician's responsibility for BOTH accuracy AND relevance. *Journal of the American Statistical Association, 74,* 786–793.

Tukey, J. W. (1980). We need both exploratory and confirmatory. *American Statistician, 34,* 23–25.

Tukey, J. W. (1986a). Analyzing data: Sanctification or detective work? in L. V. Jones (Ed.), *The collected work of John W. Tukey: Vol. IV. Philosophy and principles of data analysis: 1965–1986* (pp. 721–739). Pacific Grove, CA: Wadsworth. (Original work published 1969)

Tukey, J. W. (1986b). *The collected works of John W. Tukey: Vol. III. Philosophy and principles of data analysis: 1949–1964.* L. V. Jones (Ed.). Pacific Grove, CA: Wadsworth.

Tukey, J. W. (1986c). *The collected works of John W. Tukey: Vol. IV: Philosophy and principles of data analysis (1965–1986)* (L. V. Jones, Ed.). Pacific Grove, CA: Wadsworth.

Tukey, J. W. (1986d). Data analysis and behavioral science, or, learning to bear the quantitative man's burden by shunning badmandments. In L. V. Jones (Ed.), *The collected works of John W. Tukey: Vol. III. Philosophy and principles of data analysis: 1949–1964.* Pacific Grove, CA: Wadsworth.

Tukey, J. W. (1988). *The collected works of John W. Tukey: Vol. V. Graphics* (W. S. Cleveland, Ed.). Pacific Grove, CA: Wadsworth.

Tukey, J. W., & Wilk, M. B. (1986). Data analysis and statistics: An expository overview. In L. V. Jones (Ed.), *The collected works of John W. Tukey: Vol. IV. Philosophy and principles of data analysis: 1965–1986* (pp. 549–578). Pacific Grove, CA: Wadsworth. (Original work published 1966)

Velleman, P. F. (1992). *Data Desk handbook.* Ithaca, NY: Data Description.

Velleman, P. F., & Hoaglin, D. C. (1992). Data analysis. In D. C. Hoaglin & D. S. Moore (Eds.), *Perspectives on contemporary statistics* (pp. 19–39). Washington, DC: Mathematical Association of America.

Velleman, P. F., & Wilkinson, L. (1993). Nominal, ordinal, interval, and ratio typologies are misleading. *American Statistician, 47,* 65–68.

von Mises, R. (1957). *Probability, statistics and truth.* New York: Dover. (Original work published 1928)

Wachter, K. W., & Straf, M. L. (Eds.). (1990). *The future of meta-analysis.* New York: Russell Sage Foundation.

Wainer, H. (1984a). An exploratory analysis of performance on the SAT. *Journal of Educational Measurement, 21,* 81–91.

Wainer, H. (1984b). How to display data badly. *American Statistician, 38,* 137–147.

Wainer, H. (1989). Graphical visions from William Playfair to John Tukey. In M. H. Gail & N. L. Johnson (Eds.), *Proceedings of the American Statistical Association: Sesquicentennial invited paper sessions* (pp. 382–390). Alexandria, VA: American Statistical Association.

Wainer, H. (1992). Understanding graphs and tables. *Educational Researcher, 21,* 14–23.

Wainer, H., & Thissen, D. (1981). Graphical data analysis. In M. R. Rosenzweig & L. W. Porter (Eds.), *Annual Review of Psychology* (pp. 191–241). Palo Alto, CA: Annual Reviews.

Winkler, R. L. (1993). Bayesian statistics: An overview. In G. Keren & C. Lewis (Eds.), *A handbook for data analysis in the behavioral sciences: Methodological issues* (pp. 201–232). Hillsdale, NJ: Lawrence Erlbaum Associates.

Wolcott, H. F. (1994). *Transforming qualitative data.* Thousand Oaks, CA: Sage.

# · 31 ·

# HISTORY OF EDUCATIONAL PSYCHOLOGY

## Ernest R. Hilgard
### STANFORD UNIVERSITY

Educational psychology has been characterized as a discipline in the "middle," as building bridges between the science of psychology and the art of education (Bagley, Bell, Seashore, & Whipple, 1910; Grinder, 1978). To the extent that that is true, its history is so bound up with both education and psychology that it is difficult to describe it as beginning with a specific event, because there were educational theories evolving, in some modern sense, over the past 200 years, while psychology was also evolving from its earlier ties with philosophy to become established as experimental psychology in the late 19th century. For an excellent single-chapter summary of the background of educational psychology, see Charles (1987). The edited volume in which this appears is devoted to various aspects of the history of educational psychology, including the subfields of education and psychology upon which educational psychology is in some respects derivative (Glover & Ronning, 1987). Another edited volume contains some historical material (Wittrock & Farley, 1989). The influence of James, Hall, Dewey and Thorndike on contemporary educational psychology is provided in Berliner (1993).

## THE BACKGROUND OF EDUCATIONAL PSYCHOLOGY

### The Continental Background in Anticipation of Educational Psychology

It is useful to have in mind some of the educational leaders in Europe during the 18th and early 19th centuries, when there was no educational psychology as such to be sharply distinguished from educational and psychological theorizing. Portions of the following discussion appeared in different form in my work, *Psychology in America* (1987, pp. 662–699).

The names of four Europeans frequently recur in the discussion of educational innovations in the late 18th and early 19th centuries: Rousseau of France, Pestalozzi of Switzerland, and Herbart and Froebel of Germany. Jean Jacques Rousseau (1712–1778) gave his proposals for education in his book *Emile* (1762/

1979). His primary message reflected his views on the natural basis for development, with an emphasis on how children discover things for themselves. The teacher should never substitute authority for reason, because the child may then no longer reason. These sensible ideas were fitted within his somewhat exaggerated developmental theory, which implied that stages in individual development represented a recapitulation of the experiences from savage to civilized life.

Johann Heinrich Pestalozzi (1746–1827) was a Swiss lawyer who had developed a model school. He, like Rousseau, had an innovative conception of education as against the formality of instruction through lessons recited in unison, answers to questions based on memorized replies, and motivation through punishment for mistakes. Many of Pestalozzi's comments on education sound very modern, even contemporary. He stressed the value of activity, the significance of industrial training combined with literary studies, education as growth rather than the acquisition of knowledge, and the desirability of a school atmosphere of love, friendliness, and understanding rather than of fear; psychology as a guide to method; and improvement of the total population through proper education (Pestalozzi, 1820/1977; Woody, 1934). There was little of formulated psychology in either Rousseau or Pestalozzi. The reforms they proposed were largely on a moral basis, with the details coming from general observations and reflections.

Johann Friedrich Herbart (1776–1841) had visited Pestalozzi's school. He was the first of these significant innovators to provide a psychological substratum to his theories, so that he figures more prominently than they in histories of psychology as well as in histories of education. He was a philosopher of sufficient distinction to have been invited to fill Kant's chair at the University of Königsberg in 1809 after Kant's immediate successor, Krug, had vacated the chair. He offered as a psychological underpinning for the educational applications of his theories an emphasis on *apperception,* namely, that all perception depends on a background in the *apperceptive mass* of ideas already in the memory. This became closely related to the role of *interest,* as later emphasized by John Dewey, because something is more interesting if readiness is aroused by features already familiar. With a sufficient store of prior experience a *many-sided* interest can develop in the learner that can be capitalized upon in education.

A scaffolding for pedagogical practices was provided in Herbart's five-step approach, stated from time to time in slightly different words, but essentially as follows (McMurry, 1892/1903):

1. Preparation
2. Presentation
3. Association and comparison
4. Generalization or abstraction
5. Practical application

The first step for any new lesson is to arouse interest through preparation by eliciting familiar ideas to which the new ones will be assimilated. The new lesson is then presented in an appropriate manner, perhaps by telling a story to young children or in a reading lesson for older ones. Some drill may be necessary to be sure that the new material has been well learned. The third step requires that the new ideas be compared with those already familiar, in preparation for arriving at some generalization. At this stage the comparison is of concrete things and experiences. What has been learned is given more abstract expression in the next step. The general idea must be expressed conceptually, without reference to its concrete embodiments. It is in the form of a general rule or principle, or perhaps a classificatory rubric. The final step is to apply what has been learned, on the basis of the conviction that knowledge, to have any value, must be in the service of life, and hence must have some useful application. The child has to be taught to use what has been learned as often and in as many cases as the narrow limits of the child's life permit.

Finally, Friedrich Froebel (1782–1852) entered the American picture as the founder of the kindergarten movement. Although his ideas were somewhat romantic, and some of the "games" he offered were overinterpreted as to their meaning for the kindergarten child, Froebel also emphasized the role of the early years in training for cooperative living, with activity the root of all education, and he assigned a role to productive and creative activity.

The first kindergarten in America was established in Waterloo, Wisconsin, by Mrs. Carl Schurz, the wife of a prominent German refugee who had left Germany when so many liberals emigrated after the failure of their revolutionary activities in 1848. As Margaretha Meyer, she had studied with Froebel and had been active in kindergarten work with her sister in Hamburg. Carl Schurz had become a friend of Abraham Lincoln, as many liberal German-Americans had, and was ambassador to Spain as well as a high officer during the Civil War. The German-English Academy in Milwaukee, and related groups in other cities, all took an interest in founding kindergartens. Private kindergartens spread rapidly, so that there were 400 kindergartens by 1880. The first public kindergarten was established by William T. Harris in St. Louis in 1873. G. Stanley Hall helped by offering the first workshop for kindergarten teachers in 1885. By 1891 the prestigious National Educational Association had passed a resolution by unanimous vote that the kindergarten should become a part of all school systems, and thereafter the public kindergarten grew rapidly.

The ideas of Rousseau, Pestalozzi, Herbart, and Froebel were representative of the kinds of thinking about desirable educational practices that came to America from the European continent in the 19th century. Rousseau's ideas influenced G. Stanley Hall, one of the founders of educational psychology, who was much impressed by Rousseau's developmental theory. Horace Mann (1796–1859) had much to do in midcentury with promoting the public school in Massachusetts, where the first compulsory attendance law on a statewide basis was passed in 1856. Mann was familiar with Pestalozzi's writings, including his beliefs on moral education. The idea of universal education became associated with the optimistic conceptions of progress toward a finer life for all.

As public schools began to flourish and normal schools for teacher training became established, some order had to be introduced into pedagogy beyond the formal traditions that had been handed down from the past. After Pestalozzi, Herbart's five formal steps came as a welcome proposal for a "scientific" approach to the methodology of instructions. Herbartianism took over with the formation of the Herbart Club at the Saratoga meeting of the National Educational Association in 1892. Many teachers had already been using Herbartian theories, and educators set about to translate more of Herbart's writings. Books on Herbart had already begun to appear prior to the formation of the Herbart Club, and between 1890 and 1893 there were available in translation a half-dozen important books by Herbart and his European followers, and at least two American books on his methods (DeGarmo, 1890; McMurry, 1892/1903). The story of Herbart and his introduction to American education was published soon thereafter by DeGarmo in a book entitled *Herbart and the Herbartians* (1895). DeGarmo was at that time president of Swarthmore College. The first yearbook of the National Herbart Society appeared in 1895. Five were published, the last in 1899, before the society changed its name to the National Society for the Study of Education and began its significant series of yearbooks in 1902.

## British Influences on American Educational Theory

Two lines of British influence on educational psychology are readily recognizable, although by contrast with the theories from the Continent they did little or nothing to foster educational innovation. One line was the association of ideas, prominent in the theory of John Locke and kept alive by Alexander Bain, who discussed this approach later in his own book on education (Bain, 1879/1902). The association of ideas was readily integrated with Herbartian psychology, so that such educational innovations as occurred, embodying these principles, owed more to Herbart than to Locke and Bain.

The second line of influence derived from the Scottish philosophers, who promoted a faculty psychology. Their views came to the attention of educators through James Sully, who published a book for teachers (Sully, 1886), although faculty psychology had taken hold in the United States much earlier through the Scottish philosophers who came to America. The main idea assimilated into educational theory was that of formal discipline. Because the mind was composed of faculties, the separate faculties had to be cultivated, just as muscles had to be strengthened by exercise. The best training for the intellectual faculties was to be found in the study of the classics. Therefore the faculty theory supported conventional practices rather than innovative ones. It should also be recalled that the faculty psychology gained some "scientific" support from another source—phrenology—in which the bumps on the head were said to correspond to the development of the faculties to which they were related. The influence of phrenology was widespread for a time and was particularly influential, even on a leader such as Horace Mann (Davies, 1955). Formal discipline remained in vogue until transfer of training displaced it.

## American Predecessors of Educational Psychology Through the 1890s

Before educational theory and teacher education became centered in the universities, most of the adaptations of education to American life were made by public school and normal school administrators, who saw their positions as opportunities for improving the schools and for achieving "the one best system" (Tyack, 1974). It is a mistake for psychologists in reviewing their history to think only of what psychologists have done, disregarding those who, more than the psychologists, produced the changes for which psychology might be glad to receive credit. One educational administrator who deserves more attention than he has received from psychologists is W. T. Harris, a superintendent of the St. Louis public schools (1868–1880), and later U.S. Commissioner of Education (1889–1906).

William Torrey Harris (1835–1909) was a remarkable man, described as "the commanding figure of his pedagogical era" (Cremin, 1961). He was a scholar in philosophy, a profound student of Hegel, and founder of the *Journal of Speculative Philosophy,* the first such journal in the English language. However, he readily assimilated the views of Pestalozzi, Herbart, and Froebel and set the pattern for others as an able administrator. He accepted the Froebel kindergarten, and his St. Louis schools were the first to make the kindergarten part of the public school system. It is worth noting that something new, like the kindergarten, permits greater freedom for the school system to use innovative methods than conventionally graded schools with a long tradition, and the same was later true for the nursery school. Parents were not worried that their children did not bring home report cards, and did not fear that they might not be promoted. This freedom doubtless appealed to Harris, while at the same time he respected orderliness as an administrator and was pleased to have Froebel's materials which the kindergarten teacher could use to put Froebel's ideas into effect.

Harris also appreciated Herbart, whose views, he felt, had gone beyond those of Pestalozzi. He referred to educational theories as following a zigzag course—a description with which moderns can agree:

At one time the schools have tended almost exclusively to memory-culture, with very little attempt at verification by original research and observation. This was the case with what is called the old education, and if we are to believe the critics, this ought to be called the prevailing system of our time.

But Pestalozzi exploded the theory on which it rests and substituted another. He laid stress on sense-perception, verification, and original research. The practice of our time may not correspond to its theory, but certainly all writers will uphold the Pestalozzian doctrine of instruction by object-lessons.

But while this reform is progressing towards its extreme, another tendency has begun within a few years, and it promises to force a new departure on our zigzag line. This is the doctrine of Herbart, which holds that it is not so much sense-perception that is wanted in education as apperception—not so much seeing and hearing and handling things, as recognizing them and understanding them. (Harris, 1893, p. 417)

Harris's innovations in educational technique may be illustrated by his introduction of a modified English alphabet for the purposes of initial instruction in reading. He was then principal of an elementary school in St. Louis, and his school was the only one in which the new method was given a tryout. The method of the transitional alphabet was similar to that known as *phonotypy*—earlier introduced in England by Sir Isaac Pitman (1813–1897), of shorthand fame—which was a method for printing English phonetically. It also anticipated the *initial teaching alphabet,* introduced a century later in England and America by his grandson, Sir James Pitman (1961). For teaching by a phonetic method, it is desirable that the letter symbol should have a recognizable sound regularly associated with it, as in other languages such as German, Russian, or Spanish. English orthography is deficient in this respect, and an improved alphabet is not too difficult to construct. Harris adopted one of the available revisions and had a first reader (Sargent's *Primer*) transliterated into the transitional alphabet. The readers for the later grades used the traditional orthography. He used the new primers in his school in 1866. The method was adopted in the remaining schools of St. Louis in the next year and was used with the universal endorsement of the teachers for some 20 years (Downing, 1967).

Harris in other ways contributed to educational theorizing and wrote one of the first texts in educational psychology (1898). However, it was his work as an administrator that left the most profound marks on American school practices. His superintendency at St. Louis began shortly after the Civil War, when the new industrialization greatly affected U.S. cities. St. Louis was a great railroad center and, on the Mississippi River, attracted factories and immigrants, who came by rail and by boat to man them. The problems of school buildings, school management, and teacher training loomed large as the heterogeneous population expanded, and Harris took seriously his efforts to provide universal education on an efficient and effective basis. He did this by adopting the graded school so that the curriculum could be planned according to the movement of the pupils through school, with careful records of attendance, of ages at leaving school, and of the progress of learning. To provide for individual differences in the rate of advance, he permitted promotion as often as quarterly, although others found this unmanageable, with many adopting semiannual promotion instead of the more easily managed annual promotion. His method meant that those who fell behind in some subject matter did not repeat everything for more than a few months, if they could then succeed in moving ahead.

Harris was undoubtedly an able and innovative administrator. The foregoing account may leave the impression that he was also progressive in his educational ideas. In fact, he stuck to his Hegelian absolutes and was essentially a conservative or traditionalist in his educational theories. He was active in the 1890s and familiar with the new generation of psychologists, but his textbook on educational psychology was still in the older tradition of Herbart, and he did not embrace experimental psychology.

Mention should be made of Colonel Francis W. Parker (1837–1902), who takes his place beside Harris as one of the significant figures in the reform of pedagogy at the time. He had made a name for himself by revolutionizing the schools of Quincy, Massachusetts, in 1873, and abandoning a set curriculum in favor of teacher-devised materials (Adams, 1879). From there he went to the Cook County Normal School in 1880. Mrs. Emmons Blaine, of the McCormick family, in 1890 gave him $1 million to set up a private teacher-training institute, which later became part of the University of Chicago under the name of the School of Education, and another million to set up a private school in line with his philosophy. That became the distinguished Francis W. Parker School in Chicago, which survived and thrives to the present time. Harris, as a traditionalist, was strongly opposed to the innovations that Parker had made at the Cook County Normal School (Harris, 1895; Parker, 1894).

As we turn now to the "new" kind of psychologist—those who founded the American Psychological Association (APA)—we meet again with G. Stanley Hall and William James as influential in promoting educational psychology. Hall, through his interest in the child study movement, had developed a professional interest in pedagogy. His professorship at Johns Hopkins in 1883 was in both psychology and pedagogy. When he became the founding president of Clark University in 1888, and started actively to build his career there the following year, his interest in educating the child and in educating teachers continued. One evidence was the naming of his new journal the *Pedagogical Seminary* when he founded it in 1891. The child study movement had a direct influence on education and educational psychology, especially in the form of what came to be called genetic psychology (Bradbury, 1937). The basic method of questionnaire studies, while perhaps overextended, still provided a research instrument that led to more careful observation of the child in school.

Courses in child study had been introduced in normal schools as early as 1863, at the normal school in Oswego, New York. The term "educational psychology" gradually entered the professional vocabulary but did not fully supplant "child study" (in this context) until early in the 20th century.

William James introduced teachers to his kind of psychology in lectures titled Talks to Teachers, delivered first in 1892 although not published in book form until a number of years later (James, 1899), having also been published that year in the *Atlantic Monthly*. The lectures had been given to elementary and secondary schoolteachers in Cambridge at the request of the Harvard Corporation, and they were well received. He had completed his *Principles* just 2 years before and his *Briefer Course* in the same year. While these were reflected in his lectures, he made it clear to James Ward in England that Ward should not presume from the popular style of the lectures that they had been dashed off; instead, he had forged it all "with *Blut und Schweiss* [blood and sweat] and groans and lamentations to heaven, and vows that I will never start to write anything again" (James to Ward, August 4, 1899, cited by Perry, 1935, Vol. 2, p. 645). Once the lectures were prepared, he delivered them again and again in the years 1895 and 1896, chiefly in summer

schools for teachers across the country, but also in the audience representing a wider constituency at Chautauqua, New York.

In the third talk to students, entitled "What Makes a Life Significant," James presented the idyllic life at the famous Assembly Grounds on the borders of Chautauqua Lake as a case study. He described how every feature of the good life was provided for, including "perpetually running soda-water fountains, and daily popular lectures by distinguished men." You have "the best fruits of what mankind has fought and bled and striven for under the name of civilization for centuries." He was spellbound by its charm when he spent a week there, but was astonished at his relief to emerge into the wicked world again. What the idyllic world lacked was "the element of precipitousness, so to call it, of strength and strenuousness, intensity and danger" (James, 1899, p. 271).

The lectures were an attempt to teach the essence of his psychology, with its emphasis on action, its biological roots, the importance of an evolutionary interpretation of the adaptive nature of consciousness, and his main teachings on associative processes, on habit, on memory (the longest chapter of all), and a final chapter on will. The strictly pedagogical advice showed his awareness of what teachers had been exposed to in the normal schools of the day. He told them not to be frightened by the child study movement and not to feel guilty if they were not passing out questionnaires and computing percentages. He showed them the good side of Herbart's doctrine of interest and helped them to overcome their fear of the term "apperception." He confined himself to processes and was uninterested in dealing with the detailed subject matter of what was taught in schools or with the administrative arrangements. He approved of the recitation method as superior to the lecture method, apparently still prominent in European schools. He was particularly happy with the introduction to concrete object teaching and of activities: keeping notebooks, making drawings, plans, and maps, taking measurements, entering the laboratory and performing experiments, consulting authorities, and writing essays. He had good things to say about the introduction of "manual training." Imitation and emulating had their places, for children admire a teacher who has skill: "Come and let me show you how."

At a somewhat more abstract level, he insisted that psychology is a science and teaching is an art. The teaching must *agree* with what psychology teaches, but diverse kinds of teaching may agree with psychological laws. Sciences never generate arts directly out of themselves. An important aspect of his lectures was his emphasis on behavior. Education was defined as "the organization of acquired habits of conduct and tendencies to behavior" (James, 1899). The final three chapters in the book include a talk identified as having been given to the graduation class of the Boston Normal School of Gymnastics (i.e., physical exercise), and two lectures with unspecified audiences. The first lecture, "The Gospel of Relaxation," treats the James–Lange theory and extends it to practical applications in the area of mental hygiene (his term, at this early date). The other two chapters are "On a Certain Blindness in Human Beings," an argument for accepting that others see things differently from the way we see them, and the final chapter, "What Makes a Life Significant," which continues the message for understanding combined with tolerance, and recognizes the good that comes from disagreement.

An appreciation of James's *Talks to Teachers* was given as part of a presidential address before the APA by Wilbert J. McKeachie of the University of Michigan (1976). He expressed his belief that the laws of learning, until recently, were mostly an extension of what James had taught.

## PSYCHOLOGY AND EDUCATION IN THE EARLY YEARS OF THE 20TH CENTURY

Three names stand out among the American psychologists who shaped educational psychology in the early years of the 20th century: John Dewey, Edward L. Thorndike, and Charles H. Judd. Of these, Dewey as a philosopher-psychologist and Thorndike as the prototype of the educational psychologist were highly visible as outstanding leaders. Judd, of the same age group, and the only one of the three with the prestige that came in that generation from having earned a doctorate under Wundt, was a distinguished psychologist and educator of high rank, but not as well known as the other two by the wider public. Judd's *Genetic Psychology for Teachers* (1903) appeared in the same year as Thorndike's first *Educational Psychology* (1903), so that they had a comparable start, although Thorndike's title was the one that was to define the new field.

Cattell at Columbia had seen the promise of both Dewey, then at the University of Chicago, and of Thorndike, who, after taking his degree with Cattell, was teaching at Western Reserve University. Cattell was instrumental in bringing them both to Columbia University and to Teachers College (the latter, established in 1887, became part of Columbia in 1893). In 1897 James Earl Russell, with a doctorate earned under Wundt from Leipzig, became dean of Teachers College and initiated its rise to eminence. Thorndike spent only a year at Western Reserve University following his Ph.D., after which, with Cattell's help, Russell was prepared to hire him, to begin in 1899. In 1905 Dewey left the University of Chicago, where he had founded his experimental school, to take up a professorship in philosophy at Columbia, also with Cattell's encouragement, and he also served at Teachers College as professor of the philosophy of education. Dewey and Thorndike had both come under William James's influence, Dewey through his writings, Thorndike by having him as a teacher. They proved to be different in every way, although their careers as active members of the faculty at Teachers College overlapped for the years 1905 to 1930, when Dewey retired. Their careers continued, for Thorndike remained influential up to his death in 1949, and Dewey, although 14 years older, survived him by 3 years.

Both accepted the logic of modern science, although differently interpreted, Dewey's pragmatism (or instrumentalism) was not as mechanical as Thorndike's positivism. Dewey was a philosopher; Thorndike was not. Dewey was interested in experimental method, but not in experimenting or in the kind of theorizing that required that he collect data that went beyond critical observation; the results of scientific methods in physical and biological science by others were enough to establish in his mind that science was the road to knowledge. Thorndike was first of all an experimenter and measurer who valued data above all else. Dewey was a progressive and a reformer in politics; Thorndike, to the extent that he was political at all, was a conservative. Dewey tried to remake the schools; Thorn-

dike, who wanted them to do better what they were already doing, was more interested in quality control than in innovation. These contrasts are not polarities along a common dimension, so that one does not find direct confrontations between Dewey and Thorndike, even though such confrontations cropped up occasionally among their followers. In other words, Thorndike's findings could be adapted for use in Dewey schools, and Thorndike had no quarrel with curricular changes that led to good, measurable outcomes. In his two mentions of Dewey in his autobiography, Thorndike (1936) is respectful toward him, although he says nothing about his views on education; Dewey (1930), in a context in which he mentions other psychologists such as Woodworth and Hunter, finds no occasion to mention Thorndike. On one of Dewey's early suggestions regarding interests, Thorndike quoted this "interest series" with approval (Thorndike, 1913b). The two could get along together, even though their disciples diverged sharply.

### John Dewey

John Dewey (1859–1952) was a philosopher-psychologist in the days when the two disciplines were close together, as they were, for example in William James, Josiah Royce, Mary Whiton Calkins, and the others who became presidents of the APA while also writing books on philosophy. One of Dewey's early essays, written at the age of 25, was titled "The New Psychology" (Dewey, 1884b); in the same year Dewey published the article "Kant and Philosophic Method" (Dewey, 1884a) in the journal that Harris had founded. His textbook on psychology (Dewey, 1886) appeared 4 years before that of William James, although he was 17 years younger than James.

Dewey's interests turned to education in the form of the Laboratory School (indicative of his "experimentalist" philosophy) at the University of Chicago (1896–1903). Just why this happened is in part speculative, despite the careful history of the school prepared later by two of its first teachers (Mayhew & Edwards, 1936). His title at the University of Chicago in 1894, when he was brought from the University of Michigan, was professor and head of the Department of Philosophy, which included psychology and pedagogy.

One influence was doubtless that of having his own children attend the practice school run by Colonel Parker in connection with his Cook County Normal School. Dewey's son Fred was a pupil there in 1894–1895, and his daughter Evelyn (later his collaborator) in 1895–1896, just before his own school opened.

In any case, Dewey liked the practices to which his children were exposed, and these influenced the practices in his laboratory school. Despite some later disagreements over merging their schools, he recognized Parker as the father of progressive education.

Dewey's emphasis on interest and effort as affecting the child's motivation and capability to solve his or her own problems represented a dynamic innovation for which psychologists were not yet ready, despite Herbart's stress on interest. James's talks to teachers had not yet been published when Dewey's school opened. Dewey's challenge was taken up by educational philosophers, such as Kilpatrick (1925), rather than by psychologists. Some of Dewey's views, as transmitted by way of James R. Angell, were prominent as functionalism within psychology, but they did not directly reflect Dewey's educational recommendations. His emphasis was on intelligent problem solving, in which each child solves the problems that are confronted by selecting appropriate materials and methods and by learning to adapt these materials and methods to his or her ends. The freedom with which the child explored available materials made the critics view Dewey's methods as "learning through play," and hence as "soft" pedagogy. Leaving initiative to the child led to such characterizations as having the child plead to the teacher, "Do I *have to do* what I *want to do* today?" Children's interests sustain their efforts as they experiment with solutions by testing them. The kinds of problems solved are social as well as individual, for education is envisaged as a preparation for life in a democracy by democratic living here and now in the school itself.

The intellectual heritage of Dewey in the traditions of the Europeans mentioned earlier is evident and was recognized in his own writings. He was impressed by Rousseau's emphasis on growth but critical of some of the "foolish things" that he said. He also valued Pestalozzi for his concept of education as social development derived from participating actively in social life (Dewey & Dewey, 1915). He gave credit to Froebel for stressing activity as the root of education (Dewey, 1900) and was profoundly influenced by Herbart, particularly by the doctrine of interest, which he apparently permitted to cover also the Herbartian concept of apperception. Dewey, along with other neo-Herbartians, was critical of Herbart even in his contribution to the first yearbook of the National Herbart Society (Dewey, 1895), the year in which be began his strictly educational publications.

Although Dewey's place as a philosopher of education became known through *The School and Society* (1899), published while he was still at Chicago, his dominance increased after he moved to Columbia in 1904, where he published a number of books that influenced educational practices, such as *Interest and Effort in Education* (1913), *Schools of Tomorrow,* written in collaboration with his daughter, Evelyn Dewey (1915), and *Democracy and Education* (1916).

## Edward L. Thorndike

Thorndike, the experimenter, had evolved his learning theory while preparing his dissertation on animal learning, one of the most cited studies in American psychology (Thorndike, 1898). An influential research paper that introduced his career as an educational psychologist was an experimental investigation with Woodworth in which together they demolished the prevailing doctrine of formal discipline by showing that the educational gains that could be expected by merely "exercising the mind" were very slight. They demonstrated how little transfer there was from one kind of learning to another unless the two kinds of learning involved very similar processes, actually called "identical elements" (Thorndike & Woodworth, 1901). Thorndike wrote a series of books for his own instructional purposes during his appointment at Teachers College, which began in 1899. These included *Educational Psychology* (1903), *Introduction to the Theory of Mental and Social Measurements* (1904), and, perhaps his most significant contribution, the three-volume *Educational Psychology* (1913a, 1913b, 1914a), along with the more accessible condensation, *Educational Psychology: Briefer Course* (1914b). This does not mean that he stopped with these;

he averaged nearly one publication a month throughout his active career.

Thorndike's empirical contributions to education can be illustrated by two of his major thrusts: the improvement of instruction in the classroom and the measurement of the learner and the products of learning. He was naturally interested in reading and arithmetic because of their importance and the amount of time devoted to them in the elementary schools. Rather than centering on the reading skill itself, such as the eye movements in reading, which were so frequently studied, he was more concerned with what was being read. After all, language is composed of words, and if the child does not understand the words, such thought processes as may be involved in reading will be nonfunctional. Therefore he sought to eliminate the useless words and to see that textbooks (the favorite American vehicle for guiding learning) would be limited to the words that were most needed because they were most frequently met. Hence he offered *The Teacher's Word Book* (1921b) with the 10,000 most common words. This eventually became *The Teacher's Word Book of 30,000 Words,* indexed by frequency of use as determined from a variety of contexts (Thorndike & Lorge, 1944). The enormous influence of these books was well recounted later (Joncich, 1968). The other aspect of his endeavors with respect to reading naturally involved measurement. Thorndike had started early on his scales for the measurement of ability in reading (Thorndike, 1914c), with a more mature series in the *Thorndike-McCall Reading Scales* (1921c).

He tackled arithmetic in the same manner, always keeping in mind his learning theory of specific connections and the identical elements principle of transfer. Hence it was important for the learner of arithmetic not to be held back by a useless vocabulary; what was needed was to have the opportunity to establish what the learner needed to know by drill on the essentials. The early *Thorndike Arithmetics* (1917) that he provided were very successful, received many statewide adoptions, such as by California and Indiana, and produced an annual income of an amount that in 1924 was said to be five times his teaching salary (Joncich, 1968, p. 400). The implication is not that Thorndike (1914d) wrote for money, but that there was a demand for what he had to say. As expected, Thorndike ventured into creating measurement scales for arithmetic as he had done for reading. In the early years at Teachers College, he developed many other scales for handwriting, English composition, spelling, and drawing, seeming to delight in measuring skills that produced obstacles to objective measurement. In the course of this work he became known for his dictum, "Whatever exists, exists in some amount. To measure it is simply to know its varying amounts" (Thorndike, 1921a, p. 379).

Through the influence of Thorndike and related events in the period following World War I, the "scientific movement" in education was well under way, just as the progressive movement was also reflecting Dewey's philosophy. The scientific movement, epitomized in Thorndike's work, meant not only use of the methods of empirical science—research employing measurement, leading to practices based on valid evidence— but an optimism that through research the aims of education could be achieved by way of efficient and uniform methods based on established truth. Dewey's progressivism, while it valued the logic of science in the sense of forming hypotheses and testing them, looked somewhat askance at measurement and uniformity and kept social considerations in the foreground. For some years the two tendencies had been able to work together with little friction, but in the late 1920s and the 1930s a tension arose between them.

The gradual polarization of the views of Dewey and Thorndike illustrates the power of ideas as they effect changes in practice. Dewey eventually had the greater influence on the conceptions of education and its aims, and his respect for the role of reflection in problem solving is more consonant with modern cognitive psychology than Thorndike's emphasis on the specific bond or connection, even though, for both, "habit" was a favorite word. Thorndike was, however, more influential on the practices in the traditional schools, which were always more numerous than the innovative ones.

## Judd

Although Judd graduated from Wesleyan University in Connecticut only a year before Thorndike, their careers separated after each graduated, with Thorndike heading for Harvard and Columbia while Judd went to Leipzig to study with Wundt. Judd was close enough to Wundt to produce authorized translations of his books, but even as a graduate student he was independent enough to take a minor in pedagogy—not so much out of interest as because it was supposed to be easy. His early brushes with pedagogy after he returned to the United States were unsuccessful, and after holding several positions he earned recognition in experimental psychology while director of the laboratory at Yale. He was elected to the presidency of the APA in 1909, the year that he became director of the Department of Education of the University of Chicago as a fitting person to revive what had declined since Dewey left. He spent the rest of his career there. His early text on genetic psychology for teachers had not been very successful, and he later thought that it had been premature. Yet it is of interest for his idea of "social inheritance," which sounded somewhat Lamarckian but instead referred to the power of tradition, often carried through words from one generation to another. He pointed out, for example, that it was the disciplinary tradition of the monks who earlier ran the schools that had continued: The discipline of the monastery was expected to be applied to today's children in the classroom. He noted misperceptions by teachers, using illusions to make the point, in spirit not unlike James's lecture on a certain blindness in human beings.

His Yale experiment that was most cited in later years was one in which he countered the famous Thorndike and Woodworth (1901) experiment on transfer of training with an experiment of his own to show where they had gone wrong (Judd, 1908). Judd selected as his experimental problem that of shooting at a target placed under water, which required the subject to overcome the visual displacement of the target because of the refraction of light. Once proficiency has been established at one depth, the problem of transfer is to find whether or not the skill will persist with water at a different depth. Judd demonstrated that if the subject had been taught the principles of diffraction, the change in depth interfered very little. If this knowledge was lacking, however, a great deal of trial and error was needed to hit the target at the new depth. There were the same objective common elements in the task in one arrangement as in the other, but these did not make them equally easy.

Judd argued that the transfer was mediated not by what they had in common but by having a generalization or principle that could be applied equally to both situations. Hence higher mental processes could be involved in transfer without invoking the old faculty psychology. In his later book, called *Psychology of High School Subjects* (1915), Judd extended his critical analysis of the Thorndike–Woodworth experiment as designed to demolish the concept of formal discipline by substituting their theory of identical elements.

As Judd moved into education and educational administration, he carried with him several conceptions from his earlier training under Wundt and his years as an experimental psychologist. During his many years at Chicago, despite the many tasks that occupied him, there were five recurrent themes that had their roots in his earlier years. The first was his interest in research on reading, which dated from his doctoral dissertation on visual space perception. At Yale, with student collaborators, he had undertaken studies of eye movements in reading (Judd, McAllister, & Steele, 1905). At Chicago, these were followed up for many years by his students and colleagues, particularly William S. Gray (1885–1960) and Guy T. Buswell (b. 1891), and in his own book, *Silent Reading* (Judd, 1927b). A second line of interest was the psychology of school subjects, already in evidence in his *Genetic Psychology for Teachers* (1903), but most clearly formulated in his *Psychology of High School Subjects* (1915) and its sequel, *Psychology of Secondary Education* (1927a). A third persistent interest was in school surveys, in which his experience had also been acquired initially while teaching at Yale and was to be extended at Chicago. Fourth was his interest in social psychology and social institutions, which manifested itself in many of his activities and also in his book, *The Psychology of Social Institutions* (1926). Fifth, and finally, all of these directions were tied together by his ruling interest in higher mental processes, culminating in his *Education as the Cultivation of Higher Mental Processes* (1936).

This eminent figure in American educational psychology left a legacy that is difficult to picture, probably because there are no labels or slogans by which to characterize him. Higher mental processes are surely desirable aspects of the mind on which to focus, but just what did he teach about thinking and problem solving that everybody can cite, in the way that they know about Dewey's progressive education or Thorndike's connectionism? He himself had an explanation for the disregard of higher mental processes during the years that he was advocating attention to them, and it had to do with the Americanization of psychology. In the early days of psychology, when he was growing up, Americans turned to Europe for their new ideas. Wundt's physiological and experimental psychology was enthusiastically endorsed in the founding of laboratories. But by the time Wundt's work on language and social psychology—most important among his writings, from Judd's point of view—appeared, James dominated American thought, then behaviorism was an American innovation, and there was no longer much interest in German sources. The *Völkerpsychologie* that colored Judd's thinking was practically disregarded.

Despite Judd's distaste for Thorndike's psychology, much of the Chicago educational psychology was viewed by the innovators and reformers as representative of the scientific movement identified so strongly with Thorndike. Judd's *Education and Social Progress* (1934) was interpreted somewhat disparagingly, as a defense of scientism as equivalent to progressivism in education (Cremin, 1961). His emphasis on improving the quality of education through research was not popular with those who had turned, as his student George S. Counts had to social analysis and criticism.

## The Scientific Movement

Psychologists, who could understand Thorndike and Judd as educational psychologists of their own stripe, felt confortable using their familiar research methods in the study of learning and of individual differences in the schools. Thorndike, the experimentalist and quantifier, was the model. In the 1930s, along with other trends in education as just described, the more familiar attempts to experiment and measure went on and became summarized in another yearbook of the National Society of Education (1938) under the chairmanship of Frank N. Freeman (1880–1961), long a professor at the University of Chicago and later dean of education at the University of California at Berkeley. The book was a summarization of the contributions of research in 37 chapters, with two final chapters on the science and philosophy implied, one written by Dewey and the other by Freeman. To a general psychologist the book reads little like the expected summaries of research because of the essay character of many of the chapters, the limited amount of quantitative data, and the few citations of the most convincing research studies. The impression is left that there was something wrong about the direction taken. The type of concrete study with which Thorndike had been identified was only tangentially represented, although many of the chapters were by his students. Judd's contribution was limited to his chapter on school surveys. Freeman, in his concluding chapter, hinted at some dissatisfaction with this approach:

"This review of the achievements of the scientific movement in education during the past generation makes an impressive showing. The ultimate significance of this movement, however, is not determined beyond question by such a review. It is possible, after examining these achievements, to view them as essentially superficial in character, as concerned with the husk rather than the kernel of the educational process. Science can, in this view, evaluate the means but not the ends; it can estimate the efficiency of the process but cannot determine or even influence its direction. It has, therefore, gone about as far as it can in improving education. (Freeman, 1938)"

## The Influence of New Viewpoints in Psychology

The conflicting psychological viewpoints among behaviorism, Thorndike's connectionism, and Dewey's functionalism did not serve to resolve psychological conflicts among educational theorists, as noted by Boyd H. Bode, an educational philosopher, in the book *Conflicting Psychologies of Learning* (1929). Bode expressed the hope that the newer Gestalt psychology might promise a way out. At the same time, psychoanalysis was bringing a searchlight to bear on the individual that strengthened those who were seeking to adapt education to the needs of the child. How did these serve in the confusion of the 1930s?

*Gestalt Psychology.* The incorporation into theories of learning of Gestalt psychology created fresh excitement. In Europe it had not been an educational psychology so much as a psychology of perception, emphasizing the wholeness properties as against analysis into components. The history of its domestication within U.S. education is one of both advance and distortion. The first of the books out of the Gestalt movement to appear in English was Koffka's *Growth of the Mind* (1924), translated by a psychologist-educator, Robert M. Ogden, dean at Cornell. Koffka's book, despite its title, was not child psychology in the sense familiar in America but was mostly an attack on Thorndike's connectionism. Ogden picked up the Gestalt alternative to Thorndike. He based his own educational psychology on it (Ogden, 1926).

Dissatisfaction with the strictures of behaviorism and the limited intellectual appeal of Thorndike's connectionism led to an enthusiasm for the Gestalt emphasis on wholeness and on organization over discreteness. Kohler's experiments brought insight and understanding back into the vocabulary, after higher mental processes had been interpreted by Thorndike as merely the exercise of habits, despite Judd's earlier efforts to offer correctives (e.g., Judd, 1912; see also Judd, 1936). Kurt Lewin brought motivation into the picture in the relevant form of level of aspiration and eventually produced an influential experiment on social climates (Lewin, Lippitt, & White, 1939).

Unfortunately for Gestalt theory, however, the theory also got into the hands of some who were overenthusiastic and did much that discredited it. Prominent among these were Raymond H. Wheeler and his young protégé, F. Theodore Perkins, who together wrote *Principles of Mental Development* (1932). This book promoted a general concept of organismic psychology, according to which all learning has to follow a few organismic laws, with prominence given to maturation. Experimentation was scarcely needed because the laws, if they were true, had to be rather obvious and of exceptionless validity. George W. Hartmann, at Teachers College, wrote a textbook on educational psychology from the Gestaltist standpoint (Hartmann, 1941) and adapted some parts of it in a yearbook chapter (Hartmann, 1942). Although not as polemical as Wheeler and Perkins, he was quite willing to use fictional examples instead of experiments to explain Gestalt psychology. One published example was a hypothetical learning curve of how we learn to swim, to demonstrate that there is always a sudden insight in an act of skill. Apparently he based the curve on the fact that he once knew a young girl who had had trouble learning to swim but caught on suddenly and swam 50 feet. This kind of evidence did not appeal to other educational psychologists, and so the doldrums in which educational psychology found itself in the 1930s was little helped by the educational representatives of Gestalt psychology. There was a worthwhile residue from Gestalt psychology, but as a rallying viewpoint for educational psychology its central position did not last (Hilgard, 1964).

*Psychoanalysis.* In the midst of the search for new light on the solution of educational problems, the question may well be asked: Did educational psychologists incorporate the new knowledge that came by way of psychoanalysis? Psychoanalysis was already becoming popularized during the 1930s, and it was finding its way into the thinking of educators, but mostly by way of the public press and literary sources rather than by way of professional sources such as the psychoanalytic literature or educational articles or books. In a careful review of the impact of psychoanalysis, Suppes and Warren (1978) made a good case for the indirect influence of psychoanalysis on elementary education, although the direct influence was meager, at least before World War II.

Despite the importance attributed to child development and the child-centered school, books on child study and child development were slow to incorporate psychoanalytic concepts, even though psychoanalytic ideas were evident in the American Orthopsychiatric Association, established in 1924, and in the conversion to psychoanalysis of William Healy, well known to education (e.g., Healy, Bronner, & Bowers, 1930). Introductions to Freud's ideas were readily accessible (e.g., Hendrick, 1934). Still, the yearbook on *Child Development and the Curriculum*, compiled under the chairmanship of Carleton Washburne (1939), gave no indication of Freud's influence. Suppes and Warren (1978) found that the books on child study and child development during the decade under review averaged less than a page of explicit references to psychoanalysis, and implicit or derived influences added four pages each. Their examination of 44 educational psychology texts gave the same picture of neglect. Explicit references to psychoanalysis averaged two pages, and implicit and derived influences added about two pages each. Only in mental hygiene texts were the explicit references to psychoanalysis more prominent. They began earlier, in the 1920s, and averaged about 20 pages in each of the decades thereafter. The implicit or derived material added four to six pages each.

Average counts of this kind have their limitations, of course, although they point to trends. Some educational psychology texts that did not themselves refer to psychoanalysis quoted abnormal psychology texts that were already becoming psychoanalytic. The point, however, is that the psychoanalytic viewpoint was not one that the educational psychologists used to restore their confidence.

The European psychoanalysts who had come to America in the late 1930s had not yet made their influences felt. In the next decades, psychoanalytic influence came from the immigrant scholars such as Bruno Bettelheim (1948), Peter Blos (1941), Erik Erikson (1950/1963), and Fritz Redl (e.g., Redl & Wattenberg, 1951), each of whom had messages for educators.

The conflicting themes in education at the end of the 1930s lacked the optimistic flavor and the heroic stances of the early years after World War I. World War II was now imminent, and new opportunities would emerge after the war, accompanied by new problems. It was no wonder that one reviewer of educational psychology later described the period before the war as the nadir of educational psychology (McDonald, 1964).

## EDUCATIONAL PSYCHOLOGY IN THE TEXTBOOKS, 1926–1956

Because nearly all teachers in preparation took a course in educational psychology, and because of the American dependence on textbooks, the books in educational psychology give some idea of what prospective teachers were taught. Two chief possibilities confronted the writers of early educational psychology textbooks. One was to write a textbook on psychology

that could be studied by teachers as a substitute for a first course in general psychology; the other was to write for those who had had an introductory course in psychology but wished to know how psychology was to be applied to the tasks faced by a prospective teacher. Arthur I. Gates (1890–1972), who was to become Thorndike's successor at Teachers College, had chosen the first approach, as indicated by the title of his first edition, *Psychology for Students of Education* (1923). He was successful in making this a first course for psychology that with little modification permitted him to write *Elementary Psychology* (1925/1929), a book used in introductory psychology at Yale when I began teaching there as an assistant in 1928. The other approach was represented by books such as those referring to subject matter in their titles, such as Edmund B. Huey's *The Psychology and Pedagogy of Reading* (1908). Huey, who had studied with Hall at Clark University and was now teaching at Johns Hopkins, was very thorough in his historical treatment of this important school subject. For secondary schools the subject-oriented type of educational psychology text was introduced by Judd (1915), and for elementary school subjects by Homer Reed (1927/1938). The nature of this approach can be appreciated by noting the content of Reed's revised book. A chapter on association had introduced the first edition; organization replaced association as a consequence of the new role of Gestalt psychology. The next chapters were on practice and motivation, followed by four chapters on reading, four on language (i.e., composition), two on spelling, one on handwriting, three on arithmetic, four on social studies, two on geography, one on elementary science, and one on health and physical education. The intent was to represent the scientific findings in relation to learning in the elementary schools:

> It is therefore the plan of this book to state the objectives of each of the usual elementary school subjects, to explain and describe the procedures by which it is most effectively learned, and to discuss the content insofar as its character facilitates the learning process and the attainment of the objectives. So far as possible our discussion will be restricted to facts which are based upon scientific investigation. (Reed, 1927/1938)

The approach represented by Reed is closer to the older meaning of instruction in pedagogy than that represented by Gates. Reed's interpretation tended to die out, except for books in special fields, but those books were often written by subject matter specialists instead of psychologists. One conspicuous exception is the field of studies of reading, in which the importance of the problem, the controversies, and the many failures by pupils kept alive the interest of those in research centers, including the educational psychologists Buswell, Gates, Gray, and Judd, and a new group of investigators later on (Carroll & Chall, 1975; Chall, 1967; Gibson & Levin, 1975).

At the beginning of the period under consideration (1926–1956), Goodwin Watson (1899–1976), then a young and popular instructor at Teachers College, published a review of widely adopted textbooks (Watson, 1926). He summarized the contents of three books, one of which was by Gates, with the result shown in Table 31–1. An absence is noted of any special emphasis on child development, personality, and mental hygiene, which became common in later books. At this time, greater attention was paid to special school subjects and the

TABLE 31-1. The Content of Educational Psychology Textbooks

| Topic | Percentage According to Pages |
|---|---|
| Tests and measurement | 14 |
| Psychology of school subjects (especially reading, writing, and arithmetic) | 14 |
| Laws of learning and general problems of teaching method | 13 |
| Physiology of sense organs, brain, and nervous system | 12 |
| Original nature, instincts, and heredity | 8 |
| General aspects of psychology, and miscellaneous | 39[a] |
| | 100 |

Note: From "What Shall Be Taught in Educational Psychology?" by G. Watson, 1926, in *Journal of Educational Psychology, 17*, 577–599.

[a] Unspecified in Watson's summary.

neurophysiological basis of learning. Gates had included dynamic psychology in his chapter, "The Dynamic Role of Instincts in Habit Formation," with an extensive treatment of the defense mechanisms, but Freud was given no credit except for his emphasis on repression (Gates, 1923).

In a later summarization of educational psychology textbooks, covering 83 texts published between 1920 and 1956 (with extensive revisions counted as new books), some interesting trends were noted (Gates et al., 1956). Gates and colleagues classified their discussion of trends under five headings, each part contributed by a different compiler under Gates's general chairmanship: general theory (Goodwin Watson) psychology of learning (Harry N. Rivlin), developmental psychology (Arthur T. Jersild), mental hygiene and personality (Edward J. Shoben, Jr.), and psychology of school subjects (Anne S. McKillop). Such quantitative data as were presented on the basis of the textbook analyses showed a clear trend toward decreased attention to the physiology of the brain, nervous system, and sense organs and increased attention to personality, mental hygiene, unconscious motivation, counseling, and psychotherapy. Although interest in learning and learning theory and in tests and measurements continued, the new topics reduced the relative emphases on the older ones, even though more pages were assigned to the older topics as the books became longer.

The important topics of development and the psychology of the school subjects were not treated quantitatively; had they been, the increasing importance of developmental psychology and the decreasing emphasis on the psychology of school subjects would have been evident (see also chapter 13, this volume). For instance, in the discussion of the psychology of school subjects it was noted that there had not been an issue of the *Review of Educational Research* assigned to that topic since 1938. It was also indicated that in reply to a question about subject matter the attitude had become: "I don't teach subjects. I teach children" (Gates et al., 1956). Another slogan, which I remember Ben Wood's using on another occasion, was: "We shouldn't *teach* children, we should *learn* them." The child-centered attitude was evident.

The authors detected that most of the changes had departed widely from Thorndike's classification of the problems of educa-

tional psychology in his three volumes as original nature, learning, and individual differences (1913–1914), and had not come from innumerable experiments on teaching school subjects. What impact of research there was came from studies conducted largely outside the fields of learning and teaching. It appeared that the contributions had come from the studies that had described psychological processes more in depth.

Although it was true that some psychological processes were better understood, it was not clear that educational psychology had finally found itself, that it was now contributing to the improvement of education in ways it was not able to before.

# INSTRUCTIONAL PSYCHOLOGY IN THE 1960s AND BEYOND

The cognitive revolution in psychology did not leave education unmoved. Piaget, standing as a symbol for cognitive growth, became an intellectual hero for education as he did for developmental psychology (e.g., Groen, 1978). His was not an educational psychology, and he sometimes had to answer requests for applications of his theory by referring to Montessori schools after a relatively quiescent period for the Montessori approach (Elkind, 1967).

There were, however, more important influences that led to an emphasis on cognitive processes. There was the shock of the Russian launching of *Sputnik* in 1957, with the fear that the United States had lost its lead in technology. This led to governmental support of education in the traditional fields of mathematics and language learning, to which schools accommodated. This, however, merely accelerated developments that were already taking place.

## The Influence of New Technologies

Among the developments affecting innovation were some adaptations of available technologies of instruction that had as their by-products new attention to the detailed processes affecting the acquisition of knowledge in the classroom setting. The new devices included audiovisual aids and, somewhat later, computers.

*Audiovisual Aids.* Projection lanterns ("magic lanterns") for projecting transparencies or opaque pictures came into use in the late 19th century, particularly when incandescent electric lights and the arc light became available. They were cumbersome and expensive and not used widely in school classrooms until the 35mm slide projectors with film strips had made their appearance. At about the same time 16mm and 8mm motion-picture projectors came into classroom use. The early phonograph had been invented by Edison, but it served mostly for music and was not convenient for recording, except in the cylinder form of the early Ediphones and dictaphones. The audio side of instructional technology became convenient with the sound motion picture and then with the electromagnetic recorder, at first the wire recorder, then the tape recorder, along with radio, television, and video recording. These changes moved rapidly, and use of the new technology in instruction was greatly accelerated by the training done in the armed forces during World War II (Glaser, 1962).

Audiovisual aids were important enough to have a yearbook devoted to them in 1949 (Corey, 1949). Dale (1954) brought instructional use of the methods to the attention of teachers. A good deal of research was done later, such as research on how to make films instructive through response instead of merely a passive experience (e.g., May & Lumsdaine, 1958). The language laboratory was another important development because the audio equipment permitted hearing the correct spoken form and allowed comparison of the student's production with that of the language model. Through the use of a monitoring control system, a teacher could provide assistance to a number of students who were moving at their own levels. Language laboratories in high schools expanded rapidly after 1945 (Haber, 1963).

The apparent advantages of these aids did not always hold up when there were careful evaluations. Hoban (1960), after reviewing 400 investigations of teaching films, concluded that people learn from films, but no strong assertions could be made in relation to success as compared with other kinds of teaching. Carroll (1963) showed a mixed record of success of language laboratories in foreign language teaching.

*The Broadcasting Media.* Radio and television added technological opportunities for instruction while at the same time causing problems through the many hours that children spent before the television screen watching commercial programs, without guidance in regard to the value of what they were watching. Psychologists and educators had to take into account the effects of television viewing because it became such a large part of the child's experience. In addition, however, it proved effective as a teaching aid, particularly in developing countries (e.g., Chu & Schramm, 1967).

*Programmed Learning: Teaching Machines and Computer-assisted Instruction.* Programmed learning gained impetus after B. F. Skinner published an article titled "The Science of Learning and the Art of Teaching" in the *Harvard Educational Review* (Skinner, 1954) and a second article, "Teaching Machines," in *Science* (Skinner, 1958). It is true that Sidney L. Pressey (1888–1980), of Ohio State University, had used a simple teaching machine as early as 1927, but Skinner's proposal was widely influential, whereas Pressey's had not been. One reason was perhaps that Pressey's teaching machine was described as related to simple drill learning, while Skinner conceived the machine as a tutor that would lead the learner along by "shaping" of behavior through reinforcement according to the learning principles that he had long espoused. The arrangements according to which particular goals could be achieved required a *program* of small steps, so that the procedure came to be called programmed learning, or programmed instruction. The details of theory and application were soon published in a number of books, of which that edited by Arthur A. Lumsdaine and Robert Glaser, *Teaching Machines and Programmed Learning* (1960), is a good example, sponsored as it was by the National Education Association to bring the original papers and subsequent developments to the attention of the educational audience.

There were many developments after Skinner's initiative, such as the replacement of teaching machines with programmed books, including those which substituted branching programs for simple linear ones (e.g., Crowder, 1959). The introduction of computer-assisted instruction added so many new dimensions that it cannot be considered a simple derivative of the teaching machine or of the kind of programmed learning that Skinner introduced (Atkinson & Wilson, 1969). Still, Skinner's programs were its immediate ancestors.

The new technology of programmed and computer-assisted instruction had at least three consequences for educational psychology: First, the new technology opened up many possibilities for individualizing instruction, for teaching diagnostically, and for obtaining accurate records of progress. Second, the usefulness of the technology was so immediate that the research was conducted in real school settings with the materials to be learned being those taught in the school, rather than artificial laboratory material. Third, the technological problems were sufficiently difficult and intriguing that a new generation of well-trained psychologists needed no persuasion to interest themselves in problems of instruction. It is quite possible that this last consequence is as important as any and reversed the belief expressed by Freeman (1938) that science had gone about as far as it could go toward improving education. With the infusion of trained scientists and their far more powerful tools, the scene had changed.

## Adapting Classroom Practices to Individual Differences

In the early years of the 20th century, when graded schools were already the rule and before intelligence tests and achievement tests were introduced, the teacher handled individual differences within the system by failing some pupils, who were then "held back" to repeat the failed grade; by promoting the typical student; and by occasionally double-promoting ("skipping") the most successful. The system worked moderately well for those who succeeded; at least for those who eventually went on to college, the younger they were at entrance to college, the better marks they made in the freshman year. Those who had to repeat grades over and over again—the "big" boys and girls found in the lower grades—must have profited little before they reached the age when they were permitted to leave school and go to work.

To correct for the disadvantages associated with these practices, socially sensitive educators introduced "social promotion" to keep age-mates together for such advantages that might accrue from those more alike in physical and social development working and playing together. However, when the promotion of slower learners became accepted, school practices had to be modified. The new intelligence tests offered the possibility of grouping children according to ability even if they were in the same grade. Because test scores were used, ability grouping (or homogeneous grouping, as it was called) resulted in many dissertations in the 1930s. Cornell (1936) summarized representative published studies, pointing out the limitations and undemocratic by-products of ability grouping. The interest in new modifications of ability grouping declined until after the criticisms of education in the *Sputnik* era that began in 1957. The desire to find ways of improving the quality of education drew fresh attention to the method, so that in a survey conducted as a project of the National Education Association in 1962, 52% of the principals responding indicated that there had been an increase in ability grouping in the previous 5 years (National Education Association, 1962). Negative findings on ability grouping predominated in the 1960s (e.g., Goldberg, Possow, & Justman, 1966). A flurry against teacher bias introduced by their expectations based on test scores was stirred up by Rosenthal and Jacobson (1968). In their study, teachers who had been given false test scores for their pupils unwittingly encouraged changes in the students' mental performances, which by the end of the term corresponded to their estimate of the brightness of the students. The report was widely acclaimed, although subject to trenchant criticisms for the statistical methods employed and the inferences from the data (Elashoff & Snow, 1971).

In any case, no one practice selected to improve the adjustment of the school to individual differences did all that was hoped for. The new technologies were welcomed because they made additional alternatives more feasible.

*Innovations in Classroom Practices in the 1960s.* The very presence of the new devices brought a fresh look to theories of instruction, as advocated by N. L. Gage (1964) and repeatedly stressed by him thereafter. Fred S. Keller, a friend and disciple of Skinner, introduced an instructional innovation in college teaching, one of the few innovations to catch on widely at that level. He called it a personalized system of instruction, or PSI (Keller, 1968; Keller & Sherman, 1974). Although based on the behavior theory embodied in programmed learning and computer-aided instruction, Keller's PSI does not use these technological devices. Instead, he assigns the teacher a modified role and gives the individual student more responsibility. The students have specified units to master at their own rates. After completing each unit students take a test, and if they do not reach the criterion they study more until they succeed, and then move to the next unit. This procedure is known as mastery learning and is not limited to PSI (e.g., Bloom, 1968). Other designs of instruction made use of essentially the same principles, under different administrative arrangements, to provide for the individualization of instruction. They all have in common an arrangement that permits the learners to make progress from the levels at which they begin; testing for general ability no longer plays a significant role in the kind of instruction the student receives.

Careful reviews began to show that educational research had in fact left some of the hoped-for permanent residues on educational practices and policies, and the newer technologies and methods were interpreted as holding genuine promise for the future (Cronbach & Suppes, 1969; Suppes, 1978; Travers, 1983).

## The Influence of Cognitive Psychology

Despite the gains that were made through the application of educational technology, there was a lingering dissatisfaction that psychology was not yet getting at the heart of its responsibility toward education. The objectives that became so carefully defined in programmed learning did not seem to carry the full meaning of the ends that education was intended to serve. When a taxonomy of education was worked out, it became recognized that a variety of different knowledge structures were appropriate to the meeting of the objectives, and even in the standard subjects, the course content required that learning be tailored specially to a variety of different cognitive demands (Bloom, 1956; Dreeben, 1968). The development of cognitive psychology produced a great change in the relationship between psychology and education. As already noted, the training psychology that developed during and after World War II had already brought more experimental psychologists into investigations on instruction via programmed learning and computer-assisted instruction. As cognitive psychology advanced, many of the same investigators, including some who had been trained in the behaviorist tradition, accepted the new theoretical stance; and their ranks were enlarged by the blossoming of a new generation of cognitive psychologists.

Under the impetus of cognitive psychology, instructional psychology began to come into its own. By 1977 a review chapter in the *Annual Review of Psychology,* which had begun reviews on instructional psychology in 1969 (Gagné & Rohwer, 1969), could now state: "A cognitive perspective implies that a behavioral analysis of instruction is often inadequate to explain the effects of instruction on learning" (Wittrock & Lumsdaine, 1977). By 1981 it was clear that cognitive psychology had taken over. "Instructional psychology, like most research on human learning and development, is now largely cognitive; it is concerned with internal mental processes and how their development can be enhanced through instruction" (Resnick, 1981).

The choice mentioned earlier—between teaching psychology to apply it to education and discovering the psychology inherent in the educational process itself—was settled by favoring the latter alternative. One way of putting it was that psychology was no longer basic psychology *applied* to education but was fundamental research *on* processes of instruction and learning. A review of the theoretical developments in cognitive psychology and how they became relevant to education was published at about the same time by Calfee (1981). He illustrated the applications to education by presenting some of the components necessary in the minds of the skilled reader, the teacher, and the principal. If there is to be an intellectual analysis of the educational process in cognitive (or information-processing) terms, what each participant is thinking becomes important (see Glaser, 1984). The impact of cognition on education was great enough to see the appearance of a new journal, *Cognition and Instruction,* with its first issue published in 1984.

Significant developments occurred in discovering what the intellectual components were as reflected in studies of reading, mathematics, science, and problem solving. The new methods, as studied by psychologists, yielded new knowledge, but it was not always ready to be put into a form for the teacher to use. This has long been a problem in relating research to instruction. It was well handled by those who were using their computers to teach reading or arithmetic in schools where the research and the instruction went on together. It was not as easy in the shift to cognitive psychology, even when studied in the school context. The difficulties became greater when larger problems were faced, such as curriculum construction. Because much of the prior basic work in cognitive psychology went on in brief presentations of materials and precise time measurements, its extension to larger educational problems of teaching and classroom management required special adaptations.

An important theoretical advance was made by Cronbach's

(1975a) insistence that experimental and differential psychology had to be combined in a theory of instruction. His own work took the direction of aptitude–treatment interactions (ATIs). The basic idea was the sensible one that what is best for one student is not necessarily best for another, a more precise formulation of the old type of belief that one child might be more eye-minded and another ear-minded, and that they ought to be taught accordingly. The results of research at first were somewhat discouraging. Although many ATIs could be found, they were neither universal nor consistent, and they were often overshadowed by general ability measures. The excitement generated by ATI theory was deserved, but the warning by Cronbach and Snow (1977) was not to be overlooked:

"We once hoped that instructional methods might be found whose outcomes correlated very little with general ability. This does not appear to be a viable hope. Outcomes from extended instruction almost always correlate with pretested ability, unless a ceiling is artificially imposed. The pervasive correlations of general ability with learning rates or outcomes in education limits the power of ATI findings to reduce individual differences." (p. 394)

A temporary setback with respect to expectations is not a reason for abandoning a good idea, and it became clear that contextual interactions, beyond those of aptitude and type of instruction, had to be brought into consideration. The work went on, in the hope that in time appropriate prescriptions for the teacher might be forthcoming (Snow, Federico, & Montague, 1980).

Cognitive psychology also intruded into aptitude testing. There had long been some uneasiness that empirical methods, including factor analysis, fell short in not being more analytical about the actual mental processes that influenced the test scores (e.g., McNemar, 1964). The tests had come under repeated public criticism (Cronbach, 1975b). The cognitive psychologists expressed their own dissatisfactions (Carroll, 1976). The purpose of aptitude tests historically had been to determine those who could profit by education, rather than to diagnose areas of weakness that could be improved by instruction. The proposed trend was to make a cognitive analysis of the abilities measured in aptitude tests, and then to determine through investigations how to modify these component processes (e.g., Curtis, 1980). There came to be a general recognition that more theory was required to assist in the construction of new measurement instruments more appropriate to the needs of education.

Hence, successes in limited areas, made possible by technological advances and behavioral methods, came under scrutiny because they did not appear to achieve the full-bodied purposes to which education was committed. The promise of cognitive psychology was being realized slowly, but it offered the kind of hope that sustains effort.

The increasing pertinence of the psychology of instruction may continue the salutary effect of causing research psychologists to conduct their investigations directly in the school settings where learning and teaching go on, where classroom management and other contextual aspects of the school experience become part of the psychologist's background information.

# References

Adams, C. F., Jr. (1879). *The new departure in the common schools of Quincy*. Boston: Estes & Lauriat.

Atkinson, R. C., & Wilson, H. A. (Eds.). (1969). *Computer-assisted instruction*. New York: Academic Press.

Bagley, W. C., Bell, J. C., Seashore, C. E., & Whipple, G. M. (1910). (Eds.) Editorial. *Journal of Educational Psychology, 1*, 1–3.

Bain, A. (1902). *Education as a science* (10th ed.). New York: Appleton. (Original work published 1879).

Berliner, D. C. (1993). The 100-year journey of educational psychology: From interest, to disdain, to respect for practice. In Thomas R. Fagin and Gary R. VandenBas (Eds.), *Exploring applied psychology: Origins and critical analyses* (pp. 39–78). Washington, DC: American Psychological Association.

Bettelheim, B. (1948). The social-studies teacher and the emotional needs of adolescents. *School Review, 56*, 585–592.

Bloom, B. S., & Krathwohl, D. (Eds.). (1956). *Taxonomy of education objectives: Handbook 1. Cognitive domain*. New York: Longman, Green.

Bloom, B. S. (1968). Learning for mastery. *Evaluation comment, 1*(2). Los Angeles: University of California, Center for the Study of Evaluation.

Blos, P. (1941). *The adolescent personality*. New York: Appleton-Century.

Bode, B. H. (1929). *Conflicting psychologies of learning*. New York: Heath.

Bradbury, D. E. (1937). The contribution of the child study movement to child psychology. *Psychological Bulletin, 34*, 21–38.

Calfee, R. C. (1981). Cognitive psychology and educational practice. *Review of Research in Education, 9*, 3–72.

Carroll, J. B. (1963). Research on teaching foreign languages. In N. L. Gage (Ed.), *Handbook of research on teaching*. Chicago: Rand McNally.

Carroll, J. B. (1976). Psychometric tests as cognitive tasks: A new "structure of intellect." In L. B. Resnick (Ed.), *The nature of intelligence*. Hillsdale, NJ: Lawrence Erlbaum Associates.

Carroll, J. B., & Chall, J. S. (Eds.) (1975). *Toward a literate society: The report of the committee on reading of the National Academy of Education*. New York: McGraw-Hill.

Chall, J. S. (1967). *Learning to read: The great debate*. New York: McGraw-Hill.

Charles, D. C. (1987). The emergence of educational psychology. In J. A. Glover & R. R. Ronning (Eds.), *Historical foundations of educational psychology*. New York: Plenum Press.

Chu, G. F., & Schramm, W. (1967). *Learning from television: What the research says*. Stanford: Institute for Communication Research.

Corey, S. M. (Chr.), N. B. Henry (Ed.) (1949). *Audio-visual materials of instruction* (48th Yearbook of the National Society for the Study of Education, Pt. 1). Chicago: University of Chicago Press.

Cornell, E. L. (1936). The effects of ability grouping determinable from published studies. In G. M. Whipple (Ed.), W. W. Coxe, Chr., *The ability grouping of students* (35th Yearbook of the National Society for the Study of Education, Pt. 1, pp. 289–304), Bloomington, IL: Public School Publ. Co.

Cremin, L. A. (1961). *The transformation of the school: Progressivism in American education, 1876–1957*. New York: Knopf.

Cronbach, L. J. (1975a). Beyond the two disciplines of scientific psychology. *American Psychologist, 30*, 116–127.

Cronbach, L. J. (1975b). Five decades of public controversy over mental testing. *American Psychology, 30,* 1–14.

Cronbach, L. J., & Snow, R. E. (1977). *Aptitudes and instructional methods.* New York: Irvington.

Cronbach, L. J., & Suppes, P. (Eds.) (1969). *Research for tomorrow's schools: Disciplined inquiry for education.* New York: Macmillan.

Crowder, N. A. (1959). Automatic tutoring by means of intrinsic programming. In E. H. Galanter (Ed.), *Automatic teaching: The state of the art.* New York: Wiley.

Curtis, M. E. (1980). Development of components of reading skill. *Journal of Educational Psychology, 72,* 656–669.

Dale, E. (1954). *Audio-visual methods in teaching.* New York: Dryden Press.

Davies, J. D. (1955). *Phrenology: Fad and science.* New Haven, CT: Yale University Press.

DeGarmo, C. (1890). *Essentials of method.* Boston: Heath.

DeGarmo, C. (1895). *Herbart and Herbartians.* New York: Scribners.

Dewey, J. (1884a). Kant and philosophic method. *Journal of Speculative Philosophy, 18,* 162–174.

Dewey, J. (1884b). The new psychology. *Andover Review, 2,* 278–289.

Dewey, J. (1886). *Psychology.* New York: Harper.

Dewey, J. (1895). Interest as related to will. In *First Yearbook of the National Herbart Society,* 2nd Suppl., pp. 5–39. Denver, CO: Charles A. McMurry.

Dewey, J. (1899). *The school and society.* Chicago: University of Chicago Press.

Dewey, J. (1900). *The elementary school record.* Chicago: University of Chicago Press.

Dewey, J. (1913). *Interest and effort in education.* New York: Houghton Mifflin.

Dewey, J. (1916). *Democracy and education: An introduction to the philosophy of education.* New York: Macmillan.

Dewey, J. (1930). Conduct and experience. In C. Murchison (Ed.), *Psychologies of 1930* (pp. 409–422). Worcester, MA: Clark University Press.

Dewey, J., & Dewey, E. (1915). *Schools of tomorrow.* New York: Dutton.

Downing, J. (1967). *Evaluating the initial teaching alphabet.* London: Cassell.

Dreeben, R. (1968). *On what is learned in school.* Reading, MA: Addison-Wesley.

Elashoff, J. D., & Snow, R. E. (1971). *Pygmalion reconsidered.* Berkeley: McCutchan.

Elkind, D. (1967). Piaget and Montessori. *Harvard Educational Review, 37,* 535–545.

Erikson, E. H. (1963). *Childhood and society* (2nd ed.). New York: Norton. (Original work published 1950).

Freeman, F. N. (Chr.) (1938). *The scientific movement in education* (37th Yearbook of the National Society for the Study of Education, Pt. 2). Bloomington, IL: Public School Publishing Co.

Gage, N. L. (1964). Theories of teaching. In E. R. Hilgard (Ed.), *Theories of learning and instruction* (63rd Yearbook of the National Society for the Study of Education, Pt. 1, pp. 268–285). Chicago: University of Chicago Press.

Gagné, R. M., & Rohwer, J. H., Jr. (1969). Instructional psychology. *Annual Review of Psychology, 20,* 381–418.

Gates, A. I. (1923). *Psychology for students of education.* New York: Macmillan.

Gates, A. I. (1929). *Elementary psychology* (2nd ed.). New York: Macmillan (Original work published 1925).

Gates, A. I., Jersild, A. T., McKillop, A. S., Rivlin, H. N., Shoben, E. J., Jr., & Watson, G. (1956). Educational psychology. *Review of Educational Research, 26,* 241–267.

Gibson, E. J., & Levin, H. (1975). *The psychology of reading.* Cambridge, MA: MIT Press.

Glaser, R. (1962). *Training research and education.* Pittsburgh: University of Pittsburgh Press.

Glaser, R. (1984). Education and thinking: The role of knowledge. *American Psychologist, 39,* 93–104.

Glover, J. A., & Ronning, R. R. (1987) (Eds.). *Historical Foundations of Educational Psychology.* New York: Plenum Press.

Goldberg, M. I., Passow, A. H., & Justman, J. (1966). *The effects of ability grouping.* New York: Teachers College Press.

Grinder, R. E. (1978). What 200 years tell us about professional priorities in educational psychology. *Educational Psychologist, 12,* 284–289.

Groen, G. J. (1978). The theoretical ideas of Piaget and educational practice. In P. Suppes (Ed.), *Impact of research on education.* (pp. 267–318). Washington, DC: National Academy of Education.

Haber, R. N. (1963). The spread of an innovation: High school language laboratories. *Journal of Experimental Education, 31,* 359–369.

Harris, W. T. (1893). Herbart and Pestalozzi compared. *Educational Review, 5,* 417–423.

Harris, W. T. (1895). The necessity of five coordinate groups in a complete course of study. *Education, 16,* 129–134.

Harris, W. T. (1898). *Psychologic foundations of education.* New York: Appleton.

Hartmann, G. W. (1941). *Educational psychology.* New York: American Book Co.

Hartmann, G. W. (1942). The field theory of learning and its educational consequences. In. T. R. McConnell (Chr.), *The psychology of learning* (41st Yearbook of the National Society for the Study of Education, Pt. 2, pp. 165–214). Bloomington, IL: Public School Publishing Co.

Healy, W., Bronner, A. F., & Bowers, A. M. (1930). *The structure and meaning of psychoanalysis.* New York: Knopf.

Hilgard, E. R. (1964). The place of Gestalt psychology and field theories in contemporary learning theory. In E. R. Hilgard (Ed.), *Theories of learning and instruction* (63rd Yearbook of the National Society for the Study of Education, Pt. 1, pp. 54–77). Chicago: University of Chicago Press.

Hilgard, E. R. (1987). *Psychology in America: A historical survey.* San Diego: Harcourt Brace Jovanovich.

Hoban, C. F. (1960). The usable residue of educational film research. In W. Schramm (Ed.), *New teaching aids for the American classroom.* Stanford, CA: Institute for Communication Research.

Huey, E. B. (1908). *The psychology and pedagogy of reading.* New York: Macmillan.

James, W. (1899). *Talks to teachers on psychology: And to students on some of life's ideals.* New York: Holt.

Joncich, G. (1968). *The sane positivist: A biography of Edward L. Thorndike.* Middleton, CT: Wesleyan University Press.

Judd, C. H. (1903). *Genetic psychology for teachers.* New York: Appleton.

Judd, C. H. (1908). The relation of special training to general intelligence. *Educational Review, 36,* 28–42.

Judd, C. H. (1912). Studies in the principles of education: 4. Initiative or the discovery of problems. *Elementary School Teacher, 13,* 146–153.

Judd, C. H. (1915). *Psychology of high school subjects.* Boston: Ginn.

Judd, C. H. (1926). *The psychology of social institutions.* New York: Macmillan.

Judd, C. H. (1927a). *Psychology of secondary education.* New York: Ginn.

Judd, C. H. & Buswell, G. T. (1927b). *Silent Reading: A study of various types.* Chicago: University of Chicago.

Judd, C. H. (1934). *Education and social progress.* New York: Harcourt, Brace.

Judd, C. H. (1936). *Education as the cultivation of higher mental processes.* New York: Macmillan.

Judd, C. H., McAllister, C. N., & Steele, W. M. (1905). Introduction to a series of studies of eye movements by means of kinetoscopic photographs. *Psychological Review Monograph Supplements, 7*(29).

Keller, F. S. (1968). Good-bye teacher! *Journal of Applied Behavioral Analysis, 1,* 79–84.

Keller, F. S., & Sherman, J. G. (1974). *The Keller Plan handbook: Essays on a personalized system of instruction.* Menlo Park, CA: Benjamin.

Kilpatrick, W. H. (1925). *Foundations of method.* New York: Macmillan.

Koffka, K. (1924). *The growth of the mind: An introduction to child psychology* (R. M. Ogden, Trans.). New York: Harcourt, Brace.

Lewin, K., Lippitt, R., & White, R. K. (1939). Patterns of aggressive behavior in experimentally created "social climates." *Journal of Social Psychology, 10,* 271–299.

Lumsdaine, A. A., & Glaser, R. (Eds.). (1960). *Teaching machines and programmed learning.* Washington, DC: National Education Association.

May, M. A., & Lumsdaine, A. A. (1958). *Learning from films.* New Haven, CT: Yale University Press.

Mayhew, K. C., & Edwards, A. C. (1936). *The Dewey School.* New York: Appleton-Century.

McDonald, F. J. (1964). The influence of learning theories on education (1900–1950). In E. R. Hilgard (Ed.), *Theories of learning and instruction* (63rd Yearbook of the National Society for the Study of Education, Pt. 1, pp. 1–26) Chicago: University of Chicago Press.

McKeachie, W. J. (1976). Psychology in America's bicentennial year. *American Psychologist, 31,* 819–833.

McMurry, C. A. (1903). *The elements of general method based on the principles of Herbart* (rev. ed.). New York: Macmillan. (Original work published 1892).

McNemar, Q. (1964). Lost: Our intelligence. Why? *American Psychologist, 19,* 871–882.

National Education Association (1962). Current curriculum studies in academic subjects. In *NEA Project on the Instructional Program in the Public Schools.* Washington, DC: National Education Association.

Ogden, R. M. 1926. *Psychology and education.* New York: Harcourt Brace.

Parker, F. W. (1894). *Talks on pedagogics.* New York: E. L. Kellogg.

Perry, R. B. (1935). *The thought and character of William James* (Vols. 1 & 2). Boston: Little, Brown.

Pestalozzi, J. H. (1977). How Gertrude teaches her children. In D. N. Robinson (Ed.), *J. H. Pestalozzi* (Significant contributions to the history of psychology, 1750–1920, Series B, Vol. 2, pp. 17–391). Washington, DC: University Publications of America. (Original work published 1820)

Pitman, I. J. (1961). Learning to read: An experiment. *Journal of the Royal Society of Arts, 109,* 149–180.

Redl, F., & Wattenberg, W. W. (1951). *Mental hygiene in teaching.* New York: Harcourt, Brace.

Reed, H. B. (1938). *Psychology of elementary school subjects.* New York: Ginn. (Original work published 1927)

Resnick, L. B. (1981). Instructional psychology. *Annual Review of Psychology, 32,* 659–704.

Rosenthal, R., & Jacobson, L. (1968). *Pygmalion in the classroom: Teacher expectation and pupils' intellectual development.* New York: Holt, Rinehart and Winston.

Rousseau, J. J. (1979). *Emile, or, On Education* (A. Bloom, Trans.). New York: Basic Books. (Original work published 1762)

Skinner, B. F. (1954). The science of learning and the art of teaching. *Harvard Educational Review, 24,* 86–97.

Skinner, B. F. (1958). Teaching machines. *Science, 128,* 969–977.

Snow, R. E., Federico, P.-A., & Montague, W. E. (Eds.) (1980). *Aptitude, learning and instruction: Cognitive process analysis.* Hillsdale, NJ: Lawrence Erlbaum Associates.

Sully, J. (1886). *Teacher's handbook of psychology.* New York: Appleton.

Suppes, P. (Ed.) (1978). *Impact of research on education: Some case studies.* Washington, DC: National Academy of Education.

Suppes, P., & Warren, H. (1978). Psychoanalysis and American elementary education. In P. Suppes (Ed.), *Impact of research on education: Some case studies* (pp. 319–396). Washington, DC: National Academy of Education.

Thorndike, E. L. (1898). Animal intelligence: An experimental study of the associative processes in animals. *Psychological Review Monograph Supplements, 2* (Serial No. 8).

Thorndike, E. L. (1903). *Educational psychology.* New York: Teachers College.

Thorndike, E. L. (1904). *Introduction to the theory of mental and social measurements.* New York: Science Press.

Thorndike, E. L. (1913a). *Educational psychology: Vol. 1. The original nature of man.* New York: Teachers College.

Thorndike, E. L. (1913b). *Educational Psychology: Vol. 2. The psychology of learning.* New York: Teachers College.

Thorndike, E. L. (1914a). *Educational Psychology: Vol. 3. Mental work and fatigue, and individual differences and their causes.* New York: Teachers College.

Thorndike, E. L. (1914b). *Educational psychology: Briefer course.* New York: Teachers College.

Thorndike, E. L. (1914c). The measurement of ability in reading: Preliminary scales and tests. *Teachers College Record, 15,* 207–277.

Thorndike, E. L. (1914d). Measurement of ability to solve arithmetical problems. *Pedagogical Seminary, 21,* 495–503.

Thorndike, E. L. (1917). *The Thorndike arithmetics* (Bks. 1–3). New York: Rand McNally.

Thorndike, E. L. (1921a). Measurement in education. *Teachers Record, 22,* 371–379.

Thorndike, E. L. (1921b). *The teacher's word book.* New York: Teachers College.

Thorndike, E. L. (1921c). *Thorndike-McCall reading scales for grades 2–12.* New York. Columbia University Press.

Thorndike, E. L. (1936). Edward Lee Thorndike. In C. Murchison (Ed.), *A history of psychology in autobiography* (Vol. 3, pp. 263–270). Worcester, MA: Clark University Press.

Thorndike, E. L., & Lorge, I. (1944). *The teacher's word book of 30,000 words.* New York: Columbia University Press.

Thorndike, E. L., & Woodworth, R. S. (1901). The influence of one mental function upon the efficiency of other functions. *Psychological Review, 8,* 247–261, 384–395, 553–564.

Travers, R. M. W. (1983). *How research has changed American schools: A history from 1840 to the present.* Kalamazoo, MI: Mythos Press.

Tyack, D. B. (1974). *The one best system: A history of American urban education.* Cambridge, MA: Harvard University Press.

Washburne, C. (Chr.) (1939). *Child development and the curriculum* (38th Yearbook of the National Society for the Study of Education, Pt. 1). Bloomington, IL: Public School Publishing Co.

Wheeler, R. H., & Perkins, F. T. (1932). *Principles of mental development: A textbook in educational psychology.* New York: Crowell.

Wittrock, M. C., & Farley, F. (Eds.). (1989). *The future of educational psychology.* Hillsdale, NJ: Lawrence Erlbaum Associates.

Wittrock, M. C., & Lumsdaine, A. A. (1977). Instructional psychology. *Annual Review of Psychology, 28,* 417–459.

Woody, T. (1934). Historical sketch of activism. In L. C. Mossman (Chr.), *The activity movement* (33rd Yearbook of the National Society for the Study of Education, Pt. 2, pp. 9–44). Bloomington, IL: Public School Publishing Co.

# PHILOSOPHICAL PERSPECTIVES

## D. C. *Phillips*
### STANFORD UNIVERSITY

Why should psychologists, and especially educational psychologists, bother to entertain—if ever so briefly—a philosophical perspective on their field? For, as the previous chapters in this handbook have illustrated, there are sufficient problems within educational psychology to fully occupy everyone's attention, without having to venture into other disciplines to seek further stimulation.

Unfortunately, the answer to this reasonable and straightforward question cannot itself be straightforward. The purpose of the following discussion is to prove, by example, that the taking of a philosophical perspective can be fruitful (or, more strongly, that it is dangerous to try to proceed without the guidance of such a perspective). A few points can be sketched at the outset.

## PHILOSOPHY AND PSYCHOLOGY IN INTERACTION

In the first place, educational psychology is not what philosophers would call a "natural kind." Nature has not arranged matters so that clear-cut and inviolable borders separate intellectual domains one from another. As John Dewey would say, "psychology" and "philosophy" are distinctions that we make, in thought, for the purposes of certain inquiries or endeavors, but they are not distinctions in reality. Dewey's general point is that a distinction useful for some purposes (e.g., for political purposes within an academic community) might not be useful for other purposes, such as inquiries into the nature of learning or motivation. But in the present context it is necessary to add that, because there is no natural boundary, we should recognize that there are two overlapping intellectual communities at work here, and each group stands to benefit from the labors of the other. Consider this example: A human learner struggles to build up a body of knowledge in some domain (a proviso is necessary because the learner is sometimes concerned with things other than knowledge, narrowly conceived); and thus the educational psychologist working on learning must grapple with the issue of what constitutes knowledge and what should count as evidence that the learner has acquired it. However, the same issues have also been the focus of attention of many philosophers; after all, epistemology, or the theory of knowledge, is a major field within philosophy. Thus, epistemology has a common border with psychology (Piaget's "genetic epistemology" makes the permeability of this border apparent). It would be intellectual imperialism of the first order for members of either community to insist that only their answers to questions of learning and knowledge are the ones that ought to be considered.

A second example is worthwhile. Often educational psychologists are concerned with rational and fairly abstract behavior: how learners come to master areas of discourse like science or mathematics and eventually are able to work creatively within them, how they come to be able to construct and criticize arguments, how they acquire the facility to give moral justifications for their actions, and so forth. But philosophers (and others) have made significant normative contributions here: They have illuminated what is to count as creativity, or as a rational argument, or as a moral reason, or as an acceptable mathematical proof, or as a piece of science. It is difficult to comprehend how an educational psychologist could proceed to do research in these fields, then, without paying some attention to the work of philosophical colleagues.

Displaying good sense, some psychologists have, indeed, been reluctant to isolate their activity into a watertight compartment that resists intrusion from outside; Piaget, Bruner, Meehl, and Cronbach, to cite only four prominent examples, have not regarded philosophy as a foreign intrusion but as integrally

Helpful comments were provided by Kenneth A. Strike, Robert H. Ennis, Harvey Siegel, and members of James Greeno's Symbolic Systems Seminar at Stanford.

related to their work. But, as Jerome Bruner writes in the preface to his recent book, *Acts of Meaning* (1990), many other psychologists *do* feel comfortable in a closed compartment; he comments, critically, that the subfields of psychology have a pronounced tendency to

seal themselves within their own rhetoric and within their own parish of authorities. This self-sealing risks making each part . . . even more remote from other inquiries dedicated to the understanding of mind and the human condition—inquiries in the humanities or in the other social sciences. (1990, pp. ix–x)

To highlight the sterility of this compartmentalization, Bruner goes on to remind his readers that Chomsky was greatly influenced by Descartes, Piaget by Kant, Vygotsky by Hegel and Marx, and the classic learning theorists by John Locke (Bruner, 1990, pp. x–xi)–Descartes, Kant, Hegel, and Locke all being philosophers.

The second preliminary point is closely related. What is true about educational psychology is also true about philosophy: The work of philosophers also should not be regarded as being cleanly separable from work in other domains. Philosophers are particularly strong in the area of raising conceptual points (that is, in detecting and discussing problems pertaining to the use of concepts in particular fields), and they are—at their best—efficient in detecting ambiguities, fallacious reasoning, and hidden and unexamined assumptions. But philosophers need concepts and theories to serve as raw materials: They need a domain to philosophize *about*; and while some choose to work with the ideas of other philosophers, many choose to become philosophers of science, philosophers of mathematics, philosophers of language, philosophers of education, or philosophers of psychology. And sometimes their conceptual or analytical work leads them to put forward substantive (rather than only clarificatory or critical) ideas in these realms—the work of Daniel Dennett and Jerry Fodor in the field of cognitive science can serve as example (see Dennett, 1978; Fodor, 1975). But it should be stressed that philosophers working in particular realms such as psychology or cognitive science (the present author recognizes that labeling these as "realms" is a convenient fiction) are not doing work that is markedly different from what reflective "native practitioners" in these realms also can do. The work of Jerome Bruner serves as an illustrative case, for in addition to doing substantive research in several areas of psychology, he has made conceptual and clarificatory contributions of the sort that philosophers also try to make.

Another example might be helpful. In a recent book, *The Embodied Mind,* the psychologist Eleanor Rosch, the philosopher Evan Thompson, and the polymath and cognitive scientist Francisco Varela discuss a problem that has surfaced in modern cognitive science—the fragmented nature of the self (Varela, Thompson, & Rosch, 1991). Their discussion offers an interesting and deep perspective on contemporary research, and they draw lucidly on ideas in Continental and Buddhist thought (together with ideas from cognitive science) to develop their own theory of cognition as embodied action. Their book is challenging, and whatever the final verdict is about the validity of their proposals, it is clear that they have produced a stimulating amalgam of ideas drawn from various intellectual traditions.

It is also clear that it would be an exercise in futility to go through the book in an attempt to categorize the different sentences as "belonging to philosophy," "belonging to psychology," and so on. Such categories are, in this context, artificial in the extreme. The book is a contribution to the discussion of an important set of problems, no matter how these problems are categorized.

Nothing that has been said so far must be taken as indicating that there are no differences at all between the work of philosophers and the work of psychologists. The point is that their interests overlap, often to a very great degree, and that a philosopher is frequently pursuing issues and using techniques that are within the domains of interest of many psychologists (and, of course, vice versa). The precise difference is difficult to pin down and is probably not worth shedding a great deal of blood over; my own predilection is to say that the philosopher usually has an overriding interest in metaquestions about the domain of psychology, an interest that psychologists also have, but to a less refined degree.

A final caveat is necessary: Although the following discussion begins with a capsule commentary on the history of philosophical writing about educational psychology, the aim of the larger discussion is not to describe the many contributions that professional philosophers and philosophers of education have made to the various branches of educational psychology. Such a task lies beyond the competence of one author and beyond the constraints of one chapter. Rather, the aim is to probe a small number of interrelated issues that, from the perspective of the present philosopher-author, seem to be of general importance for researchers across the broad field of educational psychology.

The central issue raised in this chapter is one that has received increasing attention in recent years, namely, the degree to which the work of researchers in educational psychology (in common with the work of researchers in all fields) is influenced by assumptions, analogies, metaphors, or crude models that are held at the very outset of the researchers' work. And yet many researchers consider their approaches to be pristine; they hold that their explicit models and theories have arisen during the course of their work and were directly inspired by inspection of the experimental data. Such an account often accompanies an outdated view of the nature of science and an unwillingness to entertain rival approaches or to consider broader issues. This situation, it will be argued, is serious because it tends to lock investigators into a fairly conservative position with respect to the problems that are investigated, and the methodologics that are used. Methodologies are chosen because they seem appropriate for illuminating the kinds of phenomena that are being dealt with, so that the prior decision about how to conceptualize the phenomena influences, in broad terms, the ways in which these phenomena are subsequently pursued. But new ways of conceptualizing problems are often required in science, and new methods are often needed to follow up these new research programs. Clearly, there are some complex problems here. To cite merely one that will excite attention later, can some crude models or metaphors be ruled out a priori at the very start of inquiry (for instance, on the grounds that they are not the kinds of approaches that are appropriate for a science to entertain)?

## PHILOSOPHY AND EDUCATIONAL PSYCHOLOGY: HISTORICAL BACKGROUND

The boundary or distinction between psychology and philosophy, permeable as it is, is relatively new—it was only about 120 years ago, with the establishment of the first psychological laboratories, that any distinction was made at all between the two fields. Before then, they had a joint history. A few snippets: In the ancient world, Plato held a philosophical/psychological theory of learning as remembering (see Phillips & Soltis, 1991, for a brief discussion). Closer to our own time, John Locke, who died early in the 18th century, was a major figure in the history of both philosophical empiricism and psychological associationism/atomism; he had an influential theory of learning—which he did not call by this name—and it can be argued that his work also inspired early inquiries into developmental psychology (see Phillips & Soltis, 1991; Cleverley & Phillips, 1986, chap. 2). Later, Herbart (1776–1841) was both a neo-Kantian philosopher of note and a major early figure in educational psychology (the National Society for the Study of Education was originally named The National Herbart Society). Even as late as the last decade of the 19th century, John Dewey was chairman of the Department of Philosophy, Psychology and Education at the University of Chicago—a position indicating how, in those days, the three domains were linked. His fellow pragmatist William James made notable contributions to all three of these fields; his most direct contribution to education was via *Talks to Teachers on Psychology,* a very readable little book that was reprinted almost yearly over the next few decades and is still in print.

### Some Lines of Criticism

On the whole, from the time of James onward, philosophers have not been kind during their excursions into educational psychology. Three typical critical themes are worth highlighting.

The first theme concerns the relation between research findings in educational psychology and educational practice. This can be illustrated by reference to James himself. In an oft quoted passage (James, 1958, pp. 23–24), James pointed out that psychology was a science and teaching was an art, and so there was no simple and direct link between the two because the limits of an art are not set by science—a point that Gary Fenstermacher, using a baseball analogy, echoed about seven decades later in his critique of the practical educational implications of process–product research (Fenstermacher, 1979). N. L. Gage, the father of this research paradigm, also has frankly acknowledged this point (Gage, 1978, chap. 1).

A related point was made by David Hamlyn (one-time editor of the philosophy journal *Mind*), who argued that although "psychology has much to tell us about learning," nevertheless

the best person to say how the teaching of, say, mathematics should proceed is the mathematician who has reflected adequately, and perhaps philosophically, on what is involved in his own subject. . . . (Hamlyn, 1973, p. 213)

John Dewey, a lifelong opponent of invidious "dualisms" (or distinctions), argued that a teacher needed to know *both*

psychology *and* a great deal about the subject matter, so as to be able to "psychologize" the subject matter (Dewey, 1956, p. 22). Lee Shulman has developed somewhat similar themes in his arguments for "the missing paradigm in research on teaching" (Shulman, 1986a, 1986b, 1987; and chapter 10); he has argued that experienced teachers develop bodies of "pedagogical content knowledge"—knowledge that pertains to how specific substantive ideas in a subject domain can be made accessible to students.

The point made by all these figures is similar. The scientific findings of educational psychology, by themselves, imply no particular educational practices or policies. What is also needed is some familiarity with the aims and especially with the detailed subject matter content of education.

The second critical theme is that, in educational psychology as in the parent discipline, there is conceptual confusion. Ludwig Wittgenstein, who dominated philosophy in the English-speaking world during the decades around the middle of the 20th century, wrote scathingly that

The confusion and barrenness of psychology is not to be explained by calling it a "young science"; its state is not comparable with that of physics, for instance, in its beginnings. . . . For in psychology, there are experimental methods and conceptual confusion. (Wittgenstein, 1953/1968, p. 232)

There has been no dearth of successors to Wittgenstein, although the philosophical high road has been eroded to some degree by the fact that there has been little agreement about precisely *what* the conceptual confusions are. Philosophers of education, on the whole, have been strong critics of the conceptual bases of behaviorism, yet a philosopher as noted as Gilbert Ryle, in his influential *The Concept of Mind* (1949), advocated a type of philosophical behaviorism (and key excerpts from Ryle's book were reprinted in a widely read book of readings in philosophy of education; see Scheffler, 1958). Some aspects of modern cognitive psychology and developmental psychology have been critically assessed, but from quite different points of view (Boden, 1988; Floden, 1981; Lerner, 1983; Phillips, 1983, 1987; Phillips & Kelly, 1975; Russell, 1987; van Haaften, 1990; Wright, 1986), and there has been no shortage of critics of the conceptual foundations of process–product research (Chambers, 1992, and Macmillan & Garrison, 1988, are typical; for a reply to such criticisms see Gage, 1994; Gage & Needels, 1989).

Over the years British philosophers of education have been particularly prominent in canvassing the conceptual weaknesses of educational psychology; two examples will suffice to convey the flavor of these criticisms. John Wilson argued that before we attempt to measure intelligence, we need to clarify the concept of intelligence so that we know what it is we want to measure (Wilson, 1972, chap. 6); and Paul Hirst made a similar point about research on teaching:

[W]e are clearly in need of a great deal of carefully controlled empirical research on the effectiveness of different teaching methods. But without the clearest concept of what teaching is, it is impossible to find appropriate behavioral criteria whereby to assess what goes on in the classroom. (Hirst, 1973, p. 163)

The third critical theme in philosophical writing about educational psychology overlaps with the one just discussed. Philosophers, and philosophers of education, have been concerned with deficiencies in what might be called the "images" or crude "models" or analogies that seem to underlie conceptions of the human individual and the nature of human psychological processes. As it will develop into a major focus of the remainder of the chapter, I shall introduce this third issue in a careful and leisurely manner.

## Models and Metaphors of the Person

To make this third philosophical concern clear, and to lead into the later discussion in a fruitful way, a serious terminological difficulty needs to be addressed at the outset. The word "model" is perhaps the most natural one to use in the following discussion, but in the relevant literature it is used in at least three different ways, only one of which is pertinent to the matter presently to hand; some writers prefer to use "metaphor" or even "analogy," but these terms also are far from unproblematical.

When philosophers of science talk about models and the relation of models to theories, typically they have different sets of issues in mind from the ones that are of concern to me here. For example, influenced by modern mathematics and logic, it is common for them to regard scientific theories as formal systems of uninterpreted symbols, and a model is any interpretation of any such system that makes its postulates true (see Kaplan, 1964, chap. VII; the more recent "semantic" view of theories has an even more complex conception of models, see Suppe, 1989). A second but closely related sense of the word model was particularly prevalent a few decades ago when there was lively discussion of whether or not a scientific theory must have some physical or picturable model in order for scientists to be able to work with it, such as the billiard ball model of the kinetic theory of gases (Hesse, 1963). My focus here is quite different: I am concerned with the general assumptions or analogies or "pictures" that underlie research activities, that, indeed, are present from the very start and help research get under way (that is, they are present even before any theories or models in the senses mentioned above have been constructed).

A recent volume was devoted to discussion of the role of metaphors in psychological research and theory, and this is close to what I have in mind. The editor of this volume, David Leary, stressed that "metaphor permeates all discourse, ordinary and special," and that metaphor is "particularly vital" at the "growing edges of science" (Leary, 1990, p. 357). Leary showed that over the centuries many writers have recognized that human thought expands to cover new areas and new problems by way of metaphor (Leary, 1990, chap. 1). In the same volume the distinguished neuroscientist Karl Pribram wrote that

[b]rain scientists have, in fact, repeatedly and fruitfully used metaphors, analogies, and models in their attempts to understand their data. The theme of this essay is that *only* by the proper use of analogical reasoning can current limits of understanding be transcended. (Pribram, in Leary, 1990, p. 79)

The only blemish here is that Pribram's words imply that data exist *before* a metaphor or model or analogy has been adopted.

My reservation about using the term metaphor is this: Something that starts as a metaphor can quickly become nonmeta-

phorical—an issue that only a few of the contributors to the Leary volume systematically addressed. Thus, it might have been the case that the human cognitive apparatus was once conceived as being *analogous* to a computing device, but clearly for many of today's researchers and theoreticians there is no analogy; for them, human cognition *is* computational in nature. Pribram touched on this when he said:

Analogical reasoning in science typically begins with metaphors that are only loosely coupled to the data to be organized and ends ideally by furnishing precise models of the fit of those data to the type of organization suggested by the original metaphor. (Pribram, in Leary, 1990, p. 79)

It will be noted here that Pribram used the term model in a sense different from the one I expressed a preference for in the discusson above; Pribram was suggesting that there is a progression that goes roughly like this:

Metaphor or analogy—(leads to)—precise model or theory.

Later in his essay, Pribram made this progression explicit. After considering a few historical examples, he wrote:

It seems to me that the historical episodes I have just recounted show (1) how a group of investigators can begin with a general metaphor—a broad and somewhat undefined sense of the similarities between two things (in our cases between some newly invented technological device or concept and some aspect of brain function), (2) how they can "trim" this metaphor into more and more precise shape, primarily through reasoning by analogy back and forth between the two things being compared, and (3) how, once they have gone far enough, the original metaphor is transformed into a precise scientific model, a theoretical framework. . . . (Pribram, in Leary, 1990, pp. 97–98)

As no terminology is without blemish, I will use the terms model, metaphor, or analogy interchangeably (and often together) to convey what I am getting at; and I will trust this overlong note will have forestalled any confusion. (However, there is such an expanding literature that uses the terms metaphor, model, and analogy that some confusion is bound to persist. In addition to Hesse, Kaplan, and Leary, see Boden, 1988; Lakoff & Johnson, 1980; Pepper, 1942/1970; and Sternberg, 1990.)

To pick up the main thread of the discussion: A person whose mind is a blank slate cannot do research. A researcher notices things that are of interest or that are pertinent—and interest and pertinence depend on, or are relative to, the prior beliefs or assumptions or expectations that are held by the researcher. The researcher notes these interesting and relevant things, and thinks about them—and noting and thinking require terminology, which in turn depends on the prior theory or conceptual framework or crude model or metaphor held by the researcher who is doing the thinking or noting.

Many textbooks on how to do research in the human sciences are weak in their discussions of the origins of research. An old text of which I am still fond, and portions of which I still present to students in some of my courses, states baldly that

Research begins with a hypothesis . . . this hypothesis usually concerns the statement of a relationship between two variables, one of which is considered the independent or "causal" variable, while the other is viewed as the dependent or "effect" variable. (Suchman, 1967, p. 83)

Clearly this cannot be right. Hypothesis about what? There must be some phenomenon that captured the researcher's attention—but again, why? In what theoretical terms is the hypothesis framed? And how was it decided that one "variable" was the causal one? And where did the variables come from, anyway? Lest the reader think that this is a historical aberration, books from the 1990s fare no better. One recent text (Sprinthall, Schmutte, & Sirois, 1991) depicts the scientific research process as starting from observation, without discussing how it was decided what phenomena would be observed, and without considering the issue that observations are made using some data-recording language (which presupposes the existence of either a theoretical framework or a less rigorously formulated model or analogy that can nevertheless serve to suggest a suitable vocabulary).

The position I am suggesting as a more adequate alternative is that the researcher approaching some phenomenon of interest already has certain presuppositions, or favored metaphor, or preexisting theoretical commitment, and on this basis very quickly forms a tentative account of the phenomenon that has captured his or her attention; for it seems a truism that inquiry cannot proceed unless the researcher has some basis for selecting concepts, hypotheses, variables, and so forth. Jack Douglas reminds us that it is a sound principle of research that the methods used in an inquiry should be attuned to the (supposed) nature of the object of inquiry (Douglas, 1976), which implies that the researcher has already formed a model (in my loose sense of the term) of the nature of that object.

A classic exposition of this view is also to be found in Stephen Pepper's book, *World Hypotheses*:

A man desiring to understand the world looks about for a clue to its comprehension. He pitches upon some area of commonsense fact and tries if he cannot understand other areas in terms of this one. This original area becomes then his basic analogy or root metaphor. He describes as best he can the characteristics of this area, or, if you will, discriminates its structure. A list of its structural characteristics becomes his basic concepts of explanation and description. We call them a set of categories. In terms of these categories he proceeds to study all other areas. . . . He undertakes to interpret all facts in terms of these categories. (Pepper, 1942/1970, p. 91)

To cite another classic exposition of the same general point: Abraham Kaplan, in *The Conduct of Inquiry* (1964), put it as follows:

When the poet writes, "the morn, in russet mantle clad, walks o'er the dew of yon high eastern hill," he evokes awareness of a real resemblance, and such awarenesses may be made to serve the purposes of science. When they do serve in this way, we are likely to conceptualize the situation as involving the use of *analogy*. The scientist recognizes similarities that have previously escaped us, and systematizes them. Electricity exhibits a "flow"; there is a "current" exerting a certain pressure (the voltage), having a certain volume (the amperage), and so on. Analogies, it has been held, do more than merely lead to the formulation of theories, so that afterwards they may be removed and forgotten; they are "an utterly essential part of theories. . . ." (Kaplan, 1964, p. 265)

Quotations must not be multiplied beyond necessity, but it seems appropriate to make room for words from a contemporary researcher well known to educational psychologists. In his book *Metaphors of Mind*, Robert Sternberg writes:

The root source of many of the questions asked about intelligence appears to be the model, or metaphor, that drives the theory and research. . . . one must first look at the metaphors that have motivated the theory and research and then at the questions that the metaphors have generated in the theories addressed. (Sternberg, 1990, p. 3)

Such metaphors or analogies or models of the phenomena also have something in common with what the philosopher of science Imre Lakatos has called the "hard core" of a research program (Lakatos, 1970). According to this colorful philosopher of science, broad programs or traditions of research in a field are based on certain key assumptions or ideas that, in effect, researchers treat as being unassailable and immune from revision. For example, workers in the mainstream Piagetian and Kohlbergian research programs hold, as part of their unassailable hard core, the notions that development takes place via stages that are passed through sequentially, and that there is no regression to lower stages (see Phillips, 1987, chap. 14).

## Deficient Models of Persons: The Third Critical Theme Revisited

The discussion can now return to the third line of philosophical criticism of educational psychology that was referred to earlier. Sometimes accounts of the nature of humans and of human psychological processes have arisen as consequences of lines of research that have been pursued vigorously because the researcher came to the work armed with a root metaphor or analogy or crude model that formed the initial framework and driving force; the researcher may never have backed off to gain an overall perspective or to see what view of the nature of humans was implied by his or her work. But in other cases the model or metaphor might have been chosen quite deliberately; researchers may consciously have decided to pursue a research program based on a certain conception of the nature of humans, or on a particular conception of the nature of human psychological phenomena, to see where such a program might lead. In the latter case, the model or metaphor might have won prior acceptance because of its relationship with the philosophical or metaphysical or methodological commitments of the researchers.

The main point here, which needs to be broadcast quite clearly, is that when an educational psychologist undertakes a piece of research, fairly quickly he or she develops certain views or presuppositions about the nature of the phenomena that are to be investigated—if these are not present before the work begins! Thus, whether implicitly or explicitly, a metaphorical treatment or crude model of humans and their behavior and capabilities necessarily is present. And, of course, different models will suggest different lines of subsequent research to the psychologists who hold them.

A few examples should make these matters concrete. John B. Watson, one of the founders of modern psychological behaviorism, pursued a program embodying the crude model or root metaphor or analogy that the human infant is a young animal that is equipped by nature with a set of reflex arcs that are capable of producing, by classic or stimulus-substitution conditioning, relatively complex patterns of behavior (see Watson, 1928). On the other hand, at about the same time the Gestalt psychologist Wolfgang Köhler saw even lower species of primates as capable of reflective thought; and where Watson (or, later, Skinner) was inclined to seek explanations in terms of the processes of conditioning, Köhler was inclined to seek explanations in terms of intellectual insight (Köhler, 1957). Or, to take another example, Piaget, influenced by his early studies in biology, held a model wherein the human infant was an organism equipped (via evolution) with biological capacities, which eventually Piaget identified as the capacities to assimilate, accommodate, and seek equilibrium not only in the physiological domain, but in the cognitive domain as well. Piaget's life's work was, in essence, an effort to push this approach as far as possible. These various models, then, which were not static but evolved over time and led to specific and well-formulated theories, shaped the kinds of research methods and experimental designs that were used—a matter that will be pursued in the following section, where the methodological role of models or metaphorical treatment of psychological phenomena will be pursued in more depth.

It is now possible to state precisely the third critical issue that has worried some philosophers when they have looked at the work of educational psychologists. The point has not been the methodological one, but rather it is that frequently the underlying models, when made explicit, do not do justice to human experience. In other words, the models too often depict people as being, in some ways, subhuman. The factors that are significant about human action are sometimes ignored, so that what is depicted is not a full-fledged member of the human race. Two stark but interesting examples serve to illustrate the general point. The first comes not from psychology proper, but from the related field of ethology. In his best-selling book, *The Naked Ape*, Desmond Morris provided a lengthy account of human sexual behavior in which he used terms appropriate for the description of animals. It was a marvelous parody, except that (apparently) he was offering it seriously:

Sexual behaviour in our species goes through three characteristic phases: pair formation, pre-copulatory activity, and copulation, usually but not always in that order. The pair-formation stage, usually referred to as courtship, is remarkably prolonged by animal standards, frequently lasting for weeks and even months. As with many other species it is characterized by tentative, ambivalent behaviour involving conflicts between fear, aggression and sexual attraction. The nervousness and hesitancy is slowly reduced if the mutual sexual signals are strong enough. These involve complex facial expressions, body postures and vocalisations. . . . (Morris, 1968, p. 46)

While it is clear that humans *are* animals, it is far from clear that *all there is* to human behavior is what the ethologist can discover. Morris's account ignored the influence of human culture and the concepts, ideas, values, and ideals that humans can form (and that, so far as we know, other animals cannot), and shape how we interact with each other. By reducing our behavior to the level of other animals, by neglecting what is specifically human, the model was guilty of dehumanization. (Morris's work was great "box office," of course, but it was

deficient as science, for it omitted important aspects of the phenomenon under investigation.)

The second example is one to which the discussion will revert from time to time. A little over two decades ago, B. F. Skinner attacked the use of concepts such as "attitudes," "self-respect," "initiative," "frustration," "alienation," and "loss of confidence" to explain human behavior (he had, of course, been making similar attacks for several decades):

Almost everyone who is concerned with human affairs—as political scientist, philosopher, man of letters, economist, psychologist, linguist, sociologist, educator, or psychotherapist—continues to talk about human behavior in this prescientific way. (Skinner, 1972, p. 9)

In effect, Skinner was fighting what the literature now labels as "folk psychology"; and a few philosophers have joined him in this endeavor (notably Stich, 1985; see Fodor, 1987, for an opposing view).

Now, while the issues here are complex, it is far from clear that with one bold charge of "prescientific" Skinner can do away with a mode of explanation of human behavior and an underlying model that all of us seem to use in our daily interactions with our fellows. As Jerome Bruner has pointed out, all of us are born into a culture that provides us with ways of making sense of our environment, our fellows, and ourselves—and the categories of folk psychology *are* those indispensable tools (Bruner, 1990, chap. 2). We *see* people as being alienated, or as lacking self-confidence, or as having positive and negative attitudes towards various issues, and so on; these are the terms in which we understand others, and also ourselves.

Furthermore, it is far from clear that such modes of explanation are unscientific or prescientific, as Skinner charges. In the name of science, Skinner gets rid of those human attributes—the capacity to act meaningfully in cultural contexts, and so on—that made science possible in the first place. It is difficult to resist the suggestion that he got rid of these facets of humans because his science—his underlying model or metaphor—was not able to deal with them. In addition, it can be argued that humans often act because they have reasons for so doing; and Skinner's psychology has no satisfactory place for such locutions as "reason for believing P," thus revealing his incredibly truncated and counterintuitive model of human nature (see Follesdal, 1982; Strike, 1974).

## EDUCATIONAL PSYCHOLOGY AS SCIENCE

In discussions of whether or not some branch of human inquiry is scientific (for example, psychoanalysis or astrology or folk psychology or behaviorism), the focus of attention moves quickly to the nature of the so-called scientific method and to whether or not the practitioners of the branch of inquiry under investigation adhere to it. For one recent interesting example concerning the scientific status of research on teaching, see Gage (1994). Another instance is the dispute brewing over the validity of the way in which the so-called narrative method is used (see Phillips, 1994). In such cases a great deal hinges on the analysis that is given of the "scientific method" and related matters.

However, to follow this path is to jump into the discussion in midstream, for in real life (as opposed to some cases involving doctoral students who have a stock of methodological techniques under their belts and who then search for dissertation topics where they can apply these), research programs usually do not start with a consideration of the nature of the scientific method. To revert to the point made earlier, inquiry normally starts with problems or interests or doubts about substantive matters—a topic on which Sir Karl Popper and the American pragmatists have waxed lyrical (see Phillips, 1992, chap. 6; Popper, 1972, pp. 257–258).

Indeed, consideration of the scientific method, insofar as it is the explicit object of attention at all, only enters the picture at a relatively late stage. The following sketch of the research process, which picks up some themes of my earlier discussion, is heavily indebted both to Popper's analysis and to John Dewey's (1966) discussions of "the pattern of inquiry." Typically the scientist gets interested in some problem or some striking phenomenon: Why is the high school dropout rate so high for some ethnic groups, or why is a particular teacher successful with students generally considered to be unteachable, or why do male teachers have more success with some categories of students than their female colleagues, and vice versa? Occasionally a researcher will be interested in theory testing; in this case the problem is of the form: "Does Kohlberg's theory of moral development apply to girls? Perhaps we can test this. . . ." This theory testing research is not explicitly considered in what follows, although many of the points made have bearing upon it.

After a problem has engaged the researcher's attention, a great deal of fussing around takes place, during which time the key issues are conceptualized, usually by way of browsing through any literature that might be discovered, the catch being that often the relevant literature is difficult to locate because at the outset it is not clear what key terms to use in a search. During the browsing period research designs and data analysis techniques are selected.

## The Methodological Role of Models and Metaphors

It is during the browsing stage that the underlying model of, or metaphorical approach to, the phenomenon becomes influential. An investigator who, because of training in a doctoral program or as a research assistant on a mentor's project or as a result of personal reflection, has become disposed to seeing human phenomena in terms of a cultural model of man will most likely consult the ethnographic or social-psychological literature for guidance; another who thinks in terms of subconscious motivations will consult the psychoanalytically oriented journals, and so on. These literatures will suggest key terms to use in further bibliographical searches. The journals that were most helpful, often as not, become the leading candidates for publication of any papers that might result from the research project, nicely bringing the process full circle. This is one aspect of the pervasive influence of "discourse communities" or "communities of practice."

During this stage the researcher is guided, whether or not he or she is fully aware of it, by a metaphor or by a crude model of the phenomenon under investigation. In general terms, before specific hypotheses and research designs are ac-

cepted, the researcher faced with some new and interesting phenomenon will follow a train of thought roughly along these lines: "This seems to be a case of neurotic behavior, and humans are complex organisms whose psyches are composed of both conscious and unconscious motivations [the metaphor or model], so I'll look for these," or, "This apparently is an example of learned behavior, and as such is to be explicated in terms of the learner being an information-processing device which constructs schemata and knowledge structures [the metaphor or model], so I will select an appropriate cognitive science research design, and I will use the theories of Donald Norman as my starting point."

After the problem has been conceptualized, even if only tentatively, with the help of some underlying general model or analogy or root metaphor, the researcher is in a position to proceed with more detailed planning of the research. A specific theoretical framework will be selected or slowly developed (if the researcher is not already committed to one), hypotheses will be framed, variables will be selected, research designs will be discussed, and instruments will be constructed or obtained. These matters are not pursued sequentially, but usually progress is made on all fronts at once. For clearly there is considerable overlap and interaction among choice or construction of specific theory, framing of questions, construction of a precise research design, choice of variables, and choice of instruments; researchers sometimes talk of this whole process eliptically in terms of the need for "trade-offs" during the design process. But, trade-offs or not, the point should not be lost that a degree of unity or coherence among the problems, the designs, the mode of data analysis, and the kinds of data sought is provided by the underlying model or metaphor.

It is during this trade-off period, if at all, that the investigator will consider the scientific method—although in all honesty it is likely to become the topic of explicit discussion only if the research is criticized or attacked in some way. In other words, issues concerning scientific method become of explicit importance to most investigators only in the context of justification, when they are called on to defend what they have done and the validity of their findings; the underlying model is not usually examined from this perspective. B. F. Skinner is a notable exception, as will be seen later.

## Circularity: The Dilemma of Working with Models or Metaphors

The discerning reader will have noticed some circularity in this process: The crude model or metaphor influences the specific theory, the design, and the type of data that will be collected; these then shape or constrain the nature of any results that will be found, which in turn will be published and so reinforce faith in the validity and fruitfulness of the original model or metaphor. During this process the researcher seems insulated from ideas coming from outside his or her framework. All this may seem as inevitable as a Greek tragedy, but inevitability does not reduce the circularity any more than it reduces the tragedy; and the unwary educational psychologist can easily get sucked into this self-sustaining whirlpool. The only hope of salvation is to cling to the insight that models or metaphors are not all-encompassing and that they can always be criticized or assessed.

A double-barreled example from the history of educational psychology might put flesh onto the bones of this argument. In his classic book, *The Mentality of Apes,* based on studies undertaken on chimpanzees while he was interned on the island of Tenerife during the First World War, Wolfgang Köhler criticized the experimental studies of learning carried out by E. L. Thorndike. While working on the intelligence of cats and dogs, Köhler charged, Thorndike placed them in boxes where only the ends of the built-in mechanisms that would set them free (dangling ropes and the like) were visible. The experimental setting was too difficult—Thorndike had made it impossible for the animals he was studying to display any of the intelligence that they might possess. "For," Köhler wrote, "if essential portions of the experimental apparatus cannot be seen by the animals, how can they use their intelligence faculties in tackling the situation?" (Köhler, 1957, p. 27). In terms of the language I have been using, although Thorndike did not have a specific theory at the outset of his work, he had adopted a crude model or viewpoint according to which cats and dogs are not the possessors of an inner capacity, intelligence, but rather are "mechanisms" whose behavior is explicable solely in terms of the behavior's pleasant or unpleasant consequences; Thorndike thus designed experiments and collected data based on this assumption, and he obtained results (and formulated a specific theory embodying his various laws of learning) that reinforced the general model with which he had begun.

Köhler himself was working with a different root metaphor or model. He believed that the animals he studied *were* intelligent—that, in certain respects, they were "humanlike"—and thus he set himself the task of designing situations in which the chimpanzees could display their native talents. He dangled bananas from the cage roof, with sticks and boxes clearly visible nearby, and he found that the chimpanzees fairly quickly devised simple tools out of these objects to enable them to reach the tempting snacks hanging just out of reach. In other words, his procedure was just as circular as Thorndike's: It merely was different, as he had a different model of the phenomenon of animal behavior with which to work.

The philosopher Bertrand Russell must be given the last word in this example; he was familiar with both Thorndike's and Köhler's work, and, in a book first published in the late 1920s, he summarized the issue at stake with malicious but insightful humor:

The manner in which animals learn has been much studied in recent years. . . . One may say broadly that all the animals that have been carefully observed have behaved so as to confirm the philosophy in which the observer believed before his observations began. Nay, more, they have all displayed the national characteristics of the observer. Animals studied by Americans rush about frantically, with an incredible display of hustle and pep, and at last achieve the desired result by chance. Animals observed by Germans sit still and think, and at last evolve the solution out of their inner consciousness. To the plain man, such as the present writer, this situation is discouraging. (Russell, 1927/ 1960, pp. 32–33)

Russell and Köhler not only were implicitly pointing to the phenomenon of vicious circularity, they were also demonstrating the only way that the pernicious effects of this phenomenon can be mitigated. For it is not possible to hold the view that research should proceed without being based on assumptions;

clearly, an investigator must select a design, the type of data to be gathered, and so forth, and clearly (as Jack Douglas has pointed out), such selections should be guided by some view—some model—of the nature of the phenomenon that is under investigation. But a model or root metaphor does not constitute a self-contained world from which it is impossible to break free. An effective way to offset the danger of being trapped within a circle is to have what Karl Popper would call a critical community dedicated to the giving (and to the open-minded receiving) of strong input of the very sort delivered by Russell to both Thorndike and Köhler, and by Köhler to Thorndike (Popper, 1976). So long as opposing critical voices are not stifled, and so long as inquirers do not dismiss out of hand criticism of their deepest assumptions by those who do not share them, an intellectual environment will have been established in which intelligent and relatively open-minded researchers will be forced from time to time to examine their own assumptions. Indeed, the philosopher of science Paul Feyerabend, in a paper titled "How to Be a Good Empiricist," argued that the key is to have criticism always available that comes from someone who is working within a different framework, even if the differing framework has to be invented for the sole purpose of providing a launching point for this criticism of the dominant assumptions (Feyerabend, 1968).

## Models and Metaphors: Further Clarifications

Before we leave the phenomenon of self-supporting circularity, several further points need to be made. First, the impression must not be given that simply because a researcher has a model or root metaphor, subsequent investigation thereby is bound to establish that it is viable. It was possible, for example, for Köhler to have found that his chimpanzees were unable to act sufficiently intelligently to solve the simple problems that he set. The point is, however, that research designs inspired by one model or metaphor are somewhat unlikely to turn up evidence favoring a rival model. Thorndike's model, especially as he operationalized it in his experimental studies, could not have turned up evidence that his cats and dogs were capable of reflective problem solving. More strongly, it can be asserted that although a model or metaphor enables a researcher to see a phenomenon in a certain way, the model also disables or disinclines the researcher from seeing it in a different, perhaps more fruitful light.

Second, there seems to be an obvious link with the phenomenon of compartmentalization that Bruner was so critical of. A psychologist may have no great urge to leave the intellectual compartment in which he or she is safely housed, if all seems to be going well—if the results obtained during the research appear to reinforce the view that the basic metaphorical assumptions are sound or fruitful, or both. To revert to the previous example, presumably both Thorndike and Köhler completed their research more confident of their positions (and of their models or metaphors) than they had been when they started, which only underscores the importance of obtaining an outside perspective.

Third, there is a currently popular but potentially problematic form of alternative phrasing of the points that have been made so far, namely, in terms of the Kuhnian language of "paradigms" and "normal science." Since publication of *The*

*Structure of Scientific Revolutions* (1962), it has become commonplace to view scientists as working within a framework or paradigm that only comes under challenge during a period of scientific revolution. The vast majority of scientific activity constitutes what Kuhn called "normal science." It is work that is done within the unquestioned confines of the paradigm, and its purpose is to extend the paradigm and to solve puzzles within it, but it is not intended to test or to overthrow the paradigm. From a Kuhnian perspective, then, the previous discussion could be restated roughly along these lines: "Psychologists remain firmly entrenched within their own particular paradigm, doing work that is suggested by the paradigm and which supports that paradigm when it is completed. Talk of a 'model' or 'root metaphor' is merely a way of referring to the fact that the paradigm is based on certain assumptions (think of the Newtonian paradigm, or the Copernican, each of which has distinctive ways of modeling the relevant phenomena), assumptions that are reflected in all the work that is done within that paradigm. And while the paradigm provides the overall framework, specific theories about subsets of phenomena can be formulated within the paradigm, and psychologists can even be in dispute within the paradigm about which of several alternative theories about some problem or puzzle is the best."

This is a potentially troublesome way of phrasing matters. Kuhn's work has been the subject of bitter controversy, and since his ideas were first published he has had to soften many of his claims and to refine his originally rather vague notion of paradigms. (For a guide to the relevant literature, see Kuhn, 1977; Lakatos & Musgrave, 1970; Newton-Smith, 1981.) In his earlier work Kuhn tended to depict paradigms as being completely watertight. There was a barrier of incommensurability and incomprehension between various paradigms that even the most skillful translator could not cross. Later he acknowledged that there was more permeability than that. This is good enough reason for avoiding the misleading Kuhnian terminology; but it is also the case that the argument made earlier about the importance of models and metaphors, and about circularity, can be accepted or rejected independently of the views that are held about Kuhn. The point being that there is, in the inherent logic of research design (whether or not it is held that the research takes place within the confines of a watertight paradigm), an essential role that is played by the model of the phenomenon under investigation, and that there also is a circular element about which investigators need to be sensitive.

## JUDGING AND PREJUDGING MODELS AND METAPHORS

The preceding discussion implies that educational psychologists ought to give explicit attention to the models of the phenomena that lie behind their research programs, not so that these models can be expunged but so that, like other aspects of research, they can become the objects of criticism and conscious investigation. It will be recalled that one line of criticism was outlined earlier: Models or metaphors sometimes dehumanize human beings. This need for criticism is another reason for not using Kuhnian terminology, for Kuhn suggests that paradigmatic assumptions cannot be judged by those who are within that paradigm, while criticism from outside and which necessar-

ily comes from another paradigm is regarded as irrelevant or incomprehensible.

This call for explicit attention to criticism should not be taken as a blanket charge that all psychologists have ignored this dimension of their work, for of course there have been notable cases where individuals have engaged in such criticism and discussion. Skinner is a particularly good example; his defense of the behaviorist approach and his strong attack on folk psychology were often specifically cast in terms of the respective "models of man" that were involved. In his classic *Science and Human Behavior,* first published in 1953, Skinner wrote:

Science is not concerned just with "getting the facts." . . . Science supplies its own wisdom. It leads to a new conception of a subject matter, a new way of thinking about that part of the world to which it has addressed itself. If we are to enjoy the advantages of science in the field of human affairs, we must be prepared to adopt the working model of behavior to which a science will inevitably lead. (Skinner, 1953/1965, p. 6)

Skinner was extremely negative about what he saw as the opposing model, the model of "autonomous man." Using "we" somewhat rhetorically, he wrote in a later book that

unable to understand how or why the person we see behaves as he does, we attribute his behavior to a person we cannot see. . . . The function of the inner man is to provide an explanation which will not be explained in turn. Explanation stops with him. . . Autonomous man serves to explain only the things we are not yet able to explain in other ways. (Skinner, 1972, p. 14)

Skinner's position is, in the main, that the model of autonomous man is unscientific (sometimes he says prescientific), whereas his own behavioral model is exemplary in the light of the scientific method! Now, whereas Skinner was admirable for being quite explicit about the bases of his own views, and for openly drawing the contrast with the rival model, the grounds for his criticism of the latter leave much to be desired.

Although nowadays, especially with Skinner's death, dyed-in-the-wool classic behaviorists are hard to find, some of their attitudes are alive and well. There seem to be many contemporary psychologists who, like Skinner, refuse to take rival models or metaphors seriously—when they consider them at all—because of some ill-defined suspicion that the "other kids on the block" are "unscientific" or "prescientific." The attitude evidently is this: It is better to stick with the model or metaphor that is working, that apparently is producing the research goods and that is scientifically unimpeachable, rather than to waste time considering something radical and perhaps airy-fairy. The problem is, of course, that the notion of science that is being used in so conservative a way here cannot carry such a heavy burden; most models or metaphors simply cannot be dismissed as being unscientific without consideration being given to where they lead, for most models, if not all, have the potential to be developed both in a scientific way and nonscientifically.

The discussion can make some headway by lingering for a while over B. F. Skinner; it must be stressed that he is the focus of attention here not because I regard behaviorism as a live option in the contemporary educational psychology scene, but because some central issues that are of relevance across the whole domain of psychology clearly emerge in his writings, and it is sometimes easier to make the philosophical points in the concrete rather than in the abstract. Thus, commendable as Skinner was for explicitly focusing on the underlying models or metaphors of human phenomena in rival schools of psychology, he was nonetheless guilty of oversimplifying the key issues. Often Skinner wrote as if his prime consideration was the scientific method; the model or root metaphor that he accepted was seen as following as some kind of "logical consequence":

If we are to use the methods of science in the field of human affairs, we must assume that behavior is lawful and determined. We must expect to discover that what a man does is the result of specifiable conditions. . . . (Skinner, 1953/1965, p. 6)

Skinner rejected the model of "autonomous man" using the same criterion: He did not regard it as scientific. But, as argued before, *both* models have scientific potential, and it is possible also for both to be developed in an unscientific way. Furthermore, this is another case of circularity. Skinner was not so much "discovering" that behavior had the feature he identified in this quotation as he was legislating that it should have this feature, and so he imposed conditions on inquiry that, in effect, ensured that he would not find anything else.

Apart from the circularity, and apart from a rather narrow view on the nature of science (to which the discussion will soon return), there was a further weakness in Skinner's procedure that is important to expose. This should become clear in the following satirical reworking of Skinner's words in the quotation above. In effect, he was saying something along these lines: "It is more important that a model of human behavior be compatible with the (prior) view I have accepted of the nature of science than that the model be compatible with the evidence or experience that is already available about human behavior. In other words, I am prepared to live with an inadequate—indeed, an incredible—model of behavior because I am wedded to my preexisting notion of what it is to be scientific." But, in opposition to Skinner, it could be argued that it is unscientific to accept a model or metaphorical treatment of the phenomenon of interest that grossly oversimplifies that phenomenon, or that leaves out important aspects of the phenomenon as experienced. There is thus an important choice to be made: Should the model or metaphor be adequate to the data or experience that is in hand about the phenomenon, or should the model be shaped by methodological principles that are held prior to the inquiry, even if this means that some data or experiences about the phenomenon are disregarded? Even this, of course, is overly simple, for one would have to decide whether or not the data or experiences in hand were genuine and relevant, and one would also have to weigh the validity of the prior methodological principles. On what basis can these decisions be made? Too often it is in terms of the biases that the investigator already has about the types of models that he or she is prepared to entertain!

Another example might help to make the issues clear. In this case the illustration is fictitious, although it has been suggested by some of the pioneering work of Sir Francis Galton in the 19th century. An investigator, working at a time before the science of genetics existed, has become interested in the pattern of madness that exists in one extended family. Many

fathers and mothers and sons and daughters and cousins and uncles and aunts, over several generations, are struck down by severe mental illness. Some members of the family have even migrated to distant parts of the globe, but they and their children are still struck by the malady. The investigator has an unshakable determination to stick to hypotheses that are testable, and so rejects out of hand any hereditarian model (for, at that time, he cannot see how this could be tested), and so he adopts an environmentalist model and searches for common environmental factors across all the cases (even though it seems fantastic that members of the family who were born in distant lands also get the malady). Would not a workable alternative strategy be to adopt the hereditarian model—on the grounds that it does more justice to the full set of data—and to seek ways to make this model testable? This, of course, is roughly what Galton did in his pioneering book *Hereditary Genius* (1869/1914) and in his other works; he was led to develop early forms of various statistical tests to help elucidate his data and to give scientific support to his genetic hypotheses about the heritability of great talent.

So, returning to Skinner, it is possible to argue that it is a viable alternative to his strategy to accept a nonbehaviorist model (perhaps folk psychology, or "autonomous man") according to which humans act because of reasons and motives and desires and so forth, and to seek ways to make this model testable or scientific. It boils down to a decision whether (a) to adapt your metaphor or model of behavior to your (prior) view of the nature of science, or (b) to make your view of the nature of science apply to your (prior) model of behavior. You cannot assume that the first of these alternatives is the only viable one, or assume (with Skinner) that appeals to your view of science can settle the choice in favor of the first option. For while Skinner can attempt to argue that the second alternative is, on methodological grounds, unscientific, it is also possible to argue both that it is contrary to the spirit of science to adopt a model that does not do justice to the phenomena and that an adequate nonbehaviorist model can be pursued scientifically. Jerome Bruner seems to be a supporter of alternative (b) above:

The study of the human mind is so difficult, so caught in the dilemma of being both the object and the agent of its own study, that it cannot limit its inquiries to ways of thinking that grew out of yesterday's physics. Rather, the task is so compellingly important that it deserves all the rich variety of insight that we can bring to the understanding of what man makes of his world, of his fellow beings, and of himself. (Bruner, 1990, p. xiii)

Perhaps a compromise is needed here. *Both* strategies—giving prior weight to your view of scientific method, or giving weight to your model of how humans "tick"—are up for grabs, and the decision between them is going to be complex.

## MODELS, METAPHORS, AND THE SCIENTIFIC METHOD

Skinner's specific views on the nature of science—views that enabled him to advocate a behavioral approach and to reject the categories of folk psychology are discussed next.

When Skinner wrote, in the passage cited earlier, that "[i]f we are to use the methods of science in the field of human affairs, we must assume that behavior is lawful and determined" (Skinner, 1953/1965, p. 6), he was confusing or running together several things that need to be kept separate, at least until some grounds are provided for supposing that they ought to be conjoined. The "method of science" is one thing; on the other hand, the presence of laws, and use of the principle of determinism are specific features of some sciences, but not of all, and they certainly are not identical with the former. Some sciences, notably subatomic physics or quantum mechanics, are not fully deterministic; and some sciences, like significant portions of botany and zoology and comparative anatomy, are descriptive rather than being arenas for the discovery of laws of nature (which is not to gainsay that these descriptive sciences often provide useful fuel for others who are trying to establish laws, and that they sometimes make use of the theoretical findings of other branches of inquiry).

Further, it is not the case that behavior must be seen as lawlike and determined, for not everything that humans do is similarly regarded. Consider, as a parallel case, another aspect of humans: the capacity to dream. Skinner probably did not believe that dreams were lawlike and determined; he saw them as having little scientific significance, and the fact that they were viewed in this way was no affront to his scientific aspirations. He probably regarded dreams as the by-products of neural processes that were unknown at the time he was writing. It might, then, be possible to regard behavior in a similar way—as not itself lawlike and determined in the way that physical processes are determined, but as something that could arise as the consequence of inner processes that are unknown. It should be stressed that I am not putting this forward as a rival hypothesis; I am merely using this example to highlight the point that Skinner assumed a great deal. He assumed that the phenomena that he was interested in studying are lawlike, and that the relevant laws are not at a deep level but can be discovered by observation and simple manipulation of variables that can be observed readily. And, of course, he assumed that phenomena that do not interest him are not lawlike in this sense! But it is possible that nature is so organized that Skinner's preferences carry no particular weight. How human behavior is to be explained is a matter for inquiry and debate, and we might have to push very deep, and become very sophisticated; the whole issue cannot be settled simply by legislating a solution or a methodology.

Finally, it should be stressed that Skinner went further than merely legislating that behavior is the correct focus of scientific study. As hinted at above, he legislated the *form* that scientific findings must take. He was fond of talking about a "functional analysis," an analysis in terms of observable features of behavior and the observable consequences of behavior. In this he was bold. In most branches of science, the final form that scientific understanding takes could not have been predicted, let alone legislated, at the outset of inquiry. What would have happened to chemistry and physics if the early pioneers of the atomic theory, such as Dalton and Rutherford, had legislated that only certain forms of explanatory laws and theories were to be admissible, forms that were comfortable for them, given the state of understanding of their own times? Quantum theory, modern subatomic particle physics, and relativistic physics would never have appeared. There are grounds for thinking that Skinner's

principles, applied to modern physics, would disallow quantum physics on the ground that it is prescientific or unscientific.

A large part of the problem is that Skinner's views on the nature of science, and especially on the so-called scientific method, are decidedly narrow by late 20th-century standards. His positions in these matters evidently dated from early in his academic career, when logical positivism was becoming extremely influential in the English-speaking world; classic behaviorism is merely one form of positivism (see Phillips, 1992, chap. 7). This is not the place to recount the fall of this particular philosophical position, and it will suffice to state emphatically that it has fallen.

In general, philosophy of science today is much more liberal about the nature of science than Skinner and the logical positivists were. A wider range of evidence than merely that which is directly observable is allowed; testing is conceived more widely as including logical and theoretical elements as well as purely empirical ones; we are comfortable with theorizing that takes us beyond the realms of the observable, providing the theorizing is rigorous and is supported by some kind of warrant—a matter about which we are also quite liberal nowadays. Observation is not regarded as the final court of appeal or as a theory-neutral and unshakable foundation for science. Indeed, currently there is a strong feeling that scientific beliefs are rational, in the sense that there is some warrant for them, but they are not regarded as absolutely certain or as based on any absolutely secure foundations. Scientific knowledge is tentative and fallible. (For a brief account of these issues, see Phillips, 1987, Part A.) It should be noted in passing, however, that many feminist epistemologists and post-modernists do not share this comfort with contemporary science, or with the "justificatory meta narratives"—such as the one just presented—that purport to warrant our belief in the "findings" of science (see Alcoff and Potter, 1993; Lyotard, 1984).

The educational researcher David Krathwohl and the noted sociologist Robert Merton, reflecting the new view of science, both spoke of science as "organized skepticism" (see Phillips, 1987, pp. 64–64), and the psychologist/philosopher Donald Campbell wrote, accurately, that

[n]on-laboratory social science is precariously scientific at best. But even for the strongest sciences, the theories believed to be true are radically underjustified and have, at most, the status of "better than" rather than the status of "proven." All common-sense and scientific knowledge is presumptive. In any setting in which we seem to gain new knowledge, we do so at the expense of many presumptions. . . . [S]ingle presumptions or small subsets can in turn be probed, but the total set of presumptions is not of demonstrable validity, is radically underjustified. Such are the pessimistic conclusions of the most modern developments in the philosophy of science. (Campbell, 1978, p. 185)

Campbell may find this picture to be a pessimistic one, but compared to the certainty of Skinner's view on the nature of science, it seems like a breath of fresh air.

## MODELS AND METAPHORS: A PLEA FOR TOLERANCE

As stated earlier, the aim of the preceding discussion was not to pillory B. F. Skinner; the point was to bring out, in the context of a specific case study, certain features of the present understanding of the nature of science, and also to highlight the fact that underlying metaphors or models of psychological phenomena, which guide specific investigations, cannot be rejected out of hand by an overly simple labeling of them as unscientific. A certain degree of tolerance is called for, a degree of playfulness or decompartmentalization, so that rival models or root metaphors or analogies are treated with a degree of intellectual respect. To be playful, we do not have to compromise our intelligence or our intellectual standards. The fact is, these models embody different presuppositions about the nature of the phenomenon that is the object of interest, and thus they open new perspectives and make problematic some dimensions of the phenomenon that are unanticipated from our own entrenched position. It seems to be a counsel of wisdom for all of us to consider, even if only briefly, how the phenomenon that is of interest to us, and which we are bent on seeing in one particular way, can be seen differently using a different root metaphor.

These comments are heartfelt and stem from my own indifferent success in introducing doctoral students (many of whom are planning careers in educational research) to new models of human action. In particular, I have had special problems with the interpretive or hermeneutical model or root metaphor—the model referred to earlier, according to which humans are held to act because of reasons, motives, desires, and the like—which is related quite closely to what earlier was called folk psychology. This is a model that I, too, have felt some ambivalence about in the past; but I am always surprised by the strength of the negative reaction that it engenders in a fair proportion of the students in my courses. It seems so alien to them, so based on foundations that are light-years away from anything they have met in their previous methodological or theoretical training in educational psychology and educational research. And yet the hermeneutical approach highlights aspects of human activity that are not dealt with adequately by more familiar models and that seem to be especially pertinent for those working in the field of education. The reactions of the students who are uncomfortable are interesting: Either they try to deny that the phenomena are as important as I make them out to be, or they latch on to the very real methodological vaguenesses associated with the hermeneutical model, as if these indicate that no more effort is worth expending on trying to make that approach specific enough to be a guide to detailed experimental planning. In other words, their reaction here is not unlike Skinner's way of dealing with the model of "autonomous man." It is rejected as unscientific, without enough attention being paid as to why this is the case or whether this has to be the case.

Such students have made a major mistake. Among other things, they have judged the model on the basis of its contents—in this particular case, the hermeneutical or interpretive model refers to meanings, interpretations, beliefs, understandings, social norms, and the like. The essence of the hermeneutical approach is that humans are organisms that act because they have reasons for so doing; that is, humans harbor beliefs, intentions, desires, and so on, and these things lead to human action and are therefore necessary ingredients in any attempt to understand and explain that action. In contrast, Skinner believed he could explain human action without referring to the reasons that are held, for in Skinner's view, humans are similar to the objects studied in physics, which are studied without reference to reasons, motives, beliefs, and so on. This conceptual content of hermeneutics was foreign to my students in their budding roles as social or human scientists, given their prior training (although, as argued earlier, these are concepts that they all use in everyday life as members of human society); and so the model was judged unworthy of serious inspection. It was convenient for them to categorize the model as unscientific.

But, as suggested earlier, a metaphor or model cannot be judged in this manner; it is not the content but what is done with this content that should be evaluated to see whether or not the label of "scientific" is appropriate. For *any* content, when it first becomes the object of attention, will be unfamiliar and may evoke feelings of antipathy. Consider how strange the concept of gases must have appeared at first, or of X-rays, or of magnetism and electricity. But perhaps the best example is provided by the reception given to gravitation by some of Newton's contemporaries. The model of action at a distance was for them entirely metaphysical and needed to be expunged from science; it took centuries for the entire scientific community to come to terms with it (only to have the whole issue reopened in the 20th century following Einstein's work and the development of modern particle physics). It is interesting to reflect on what would have happened to physics if everyone had washed his or her hands of Newton's theory of gravitation, instead of buckling down and devising experiments, taking measurements, and so on. Everyone washing his or her hands would have made the theory metaphysical, whereas the fact that many buckled down to nitty-gritty work helped to cement the theory as part of science. In his discussions of the demarcation between science and metaphysics, Sir Karl Popper makes the point that metaphysical ideas, which are untestable, often drive scientific work, and in the course of time ideas that are metaphysical often become scientifically testable; the boundary between science and nonscience is permeable, not impermeable (Popper, 1959; 1972).

Another, in this case psychological, example might be useful. The view that humans have extrasensory capacities is sometimes treated as metaphysical, perhaps on par with spiritualism and black magic; less pejoratively, it is commonly regarded as a nonscientific view. This is a mistake. Whether or not humans have certain capacities is an empirical matter (providing that the capacities are relatively clearly defined and require no ideological or theological commitment in order to be investigated). The real issue is this: Can this hypothesis be investigated scientifically? And the answer is "Yes, although only indirectly." (See Meehl & Scriven, 1991, for further discussion of this issue.) Parapsychologists have come up with a number of experimental designs, and although these are not able to provide absolute evidence one way or another, they can provide some relevant data (usually the designs hinge upon seeing whether people with supposed extrasensory perception can predict distant events, such as the order of cards in a shuffled deck in a distant location, at a rate significantly greater than chance). If the extrasensory hypothesis is not borne out by these data, it does not mean that the hypothesis is nonscientific—it is scientific, but incorrect. It is a common mistake to label incorrect but testable hypotheses as being nonscientific; the fact that tests were able to be conducted indicate that the hypothesis was scientific. To deny this would, in effect, be equivalent to saying that the majority of the science of the past was not science at all, for the majority of past scientific beliefs are now regarded as being incorrect.

The upshot is that it is not viable to label the hermeneutical or folk psychological model of a person as being unscientific; the real issue is whether or not it can be developed into a research program that not only yields insight into human phenomena and gives rise to precise theories, but also yields relevant data and observations that have a bearing on our reasoned acceptance or rejection of this model. Bruner, in *Acts of Meaning,* outlines the research program he favors, but this is only one among many that could be devised.

## The Hermeneutical Model

The aim of this chapter is not to defend the hermeneutical or folk psychological root metaphor or model; rather, the aim is to sensitize readers to the important role played by underlying models or analogies, and to argue for flexibility, tolerance, and caution in dismissing (in the name of science) models that rival one's own, especially when those models and metaphors embody different major assumptions about the nature of human phenomena. However, because the hermeneutical model was referred to a number of times in the preceding discussion, it is important at least to present an overview.

At the outset a major caveat needs to be registered. To this point I have referred to *the* hermeneutical model, and I have sometimes used the expression "folk psychology" as if it were a synonym. In so doing I have been guilty of gross (but deliberate) oversimplification. The general position to which I have been referring is not a unitary model or metaphor but a complex made up of a number of differing views that overlap at a number of crucial places. This is why I was able to assuage my conscience in lumping them together into one category during the preceding discussion—a course of action I took to simplify matters, for at that stage nothing much depended on being accurate about hermeneutics and its fellow travelers. (For some of these different but overlapping positions, see Dilthey, 1988; Dretske, 1991; Gadamer, 1977; Winch, 1967; also the diverse papers in Dallmayr & McCarthy, 1977.) In the overview that follows, it is the general commonalities that will be focused on, although members of the various subgroups will still, no doubt, be able to find things with which to disagree.

Most, if not all, of the authors referenced in the preceding paragraph would agree that in order to explain events occurring in the (nonhuman) physical universe—an eclipse of the moon, the splitting of a rock in frosty weather, or the behavior of a comet—the phenomenon of interest (the "explanandum") has to be tied in, in some way, to relevant natural laws and theories. The occurrence of the phenomenon has to be shown to be a consequence of the interaction between natural causal forces and the facts concerning the situation in which the phenomenon occurred. For example, the laws of tensile strength of rocks and ice, the law that freezing water expands, and the facts that the rock of interest was of such-and-such composition, it had a large crack that allowed the entry of water, and it was located in an exposed position are all required for a complete scientific explanation of the phenomenon of the rock splitting apart on

a cold night. It should be stressed that philosophers would agree only on the broad outlines of the structure of explanations in such cases, for they are engaged in a long-standing controversy over the details of the logic of scientific explanations; an overview of the issues is given in Pitt (1988).

Although the behaviorists applied this physical science model to the explanation of human behavior (their root metaphor, in other words, was that humans are like other natural objects in that their behavior can be fully explained in terms of external causal laws, forces, and the like), from other perspectives human behavior seems to be different. Certainly there are occasions on which precisely this pattern of explanation would be used, for humans are, among other things, physical and biochemical entities, and sometimes their bodies react in exactly the way other physical or biological entities react (someone freezing to death, for example, or falling out of a window). But very often it is not sufficient, in explaining the conscious and deliberate action of a person, to point to the natural laws that seem to be operating.

It should be noted here that the hermeneutical root metaphor leads to the drawing of a distinction not recognized by behaviorists. For behaviorists, humans, like all objects, merely *behave* (under the influence of laws of nature), whereas for hermeneuticists and folk psychologists, humans *act* (that is, they engage in behavior that is carried out for reasons, to achieve ends that have been selected, usually consciously and rationally). Thus, a hermeneuticist would argue, when I voluntarily walk down a corridor and open one of several doors located along its length, my behavior is not explained by referring to the fact that the law of gravitation is acting on me, that Newton's laws of motion are apposite, and that I am carrying out the biological process of respiration in order to produce the energy required to power my exertions. Neither is it necessarily the case that I have walked down that or a similar corridor before and have been positively reinforced for my trouble. The significant fact is that I opened one particular door, and to explain why I did so one either has to show that I habitually open only this door, or that I had a *reason* to open it. In countless situations in the course of a day, including a great many novel situations, I act the way I do because I have reasons or motives for doing so, and an explanation of any one of these actions will involve some reference to my reasons, desires, and so on. Furthermore, my reasons for acting in particular ways in particular situations are related to the knowledge or ideas or hypotheses or interpretations I have about those situations, and these in turn are likely to be culturally based. If, for example, I believe I am in a dangerous situation, I may act in one culturally appropriate way, whereas if I think that I am in a social situation with some friends I will act differently. Another way to put all this is that conscious, rational human behavior is *meaningful,* and an explanation of it will involve giving an account (an *interpretation*) of that meaning. The philosopher Fred Dretske put the matter this way:

I refrain from smoking, brush my teeth, avoid certain foods, look both ways before I cross a street, read the newspaper, and teach my classes for . . . reasons that have little or nothing to do with rewards received or punishments actually administered for those behaviors in the past. I have certain beliefs about the situation I am in, certain desires about the situation I would like to be (or stay) in, some ideas about how best to go from here to there. These, together with a few collateral factors (e.g., nervousness, shyness, a headache, a sprained ankle, fatigue) pretty much determine what I do and don't do. (Dretske, 1991, p. 137)

Another root metaphor of the hermeneuticists is that of a *text*: insofar as human action is meaningful, it is "textlike." To interpret a printed text, the reader has to understand the language, the symbolisms that are involved; and so it is with action. See Ricoeur, in Dallmayr & McCarthy (1977), for a classic modern statement of this metaphor that has become more than merely metaphorical.

It should be clear, then, that the root metaphors with which various hermeneuticists and folk psychologists approach the study of human behavior are quite different from the model adopted by Skinner. And, because they are different, they lead to quite different lines of research and open up different topics for further discussion. Some scholars have developed further the notion of interpretation and have argued that it is a central concept in the human sciences (see, e.g., the influential essay by Charles Taylor, reprinted in Dallmayr & McCarthy, 1977); others are interested in showing that reasons can be regarded as (or not as) *causes* of behavior; others, such as some of those

interested in situated cognition, have become interested in the social or cultural settings that determine the meanings and values that shape how humans behave; and others focus on the cognitive mechanisms that allow humans to construct meanings and to accumulte bodies of knowledge.

There is a great deal for psychologists, especially educational psychologists, to do here; the hermeneutical model is one with great scientific potential, although it is also one that is fraught with problems. And it is a model with a high degree of initial plausibility: For it might be asked why we bother to educate children—that is, expose them to theories and ideas and the great literary and scientific works of the ages, and develop their rational capacities and intellectual skills—if we do not believe that ideas and values and knowledge and meanings are efficacious in influencing their subsequent behavior? Insofar as we are researchers of educational phenomena, and not of phenomena of conditioning and the like, we must adopt a model that has prima facie adequacy in the light of the complexities of these phenomena. How we carry out truly rigorous research in the light of such a model is still an open question, but it is a question with which we should struggle, rather than continue to ignore.

## References

Alcoff, L., & Potter, E. (Eds.) (1993). *Feminist epistemologies.* New York: Routledge.

Boden, M. A. (1988). *Computer models of mind.* New York: Cambridge University Press.

Bruner, J. (1990). *Acts of meaning.* Cambridge, MA: Harvard University Press.

Campbell, D. T. (1978). Qualitative knowing and action research. In M. Brenner, P. Marsh, & M. Brenner (Eds.), *The social contexts of method.* New York: St. Martin's Press.

Chambers, J. (1992). *Empiricist research on teaching.* Dordrecht, The Netherlands: Kluwer.

Cleverley, J., & Phillips, D. C. (1986). *Visions of childhood.* New York: Teachers College Press.

Dallmayr, F., & McCarthy, T. (1977). *Understanding and social inquiry.* Notre Dame, IN: University of Notre Dame Press.

Dennett, D. (1978). *Brainstorms.* Montgomery, VT: Bradford.

Dewey, J. (1956). The child and the curriculum. In J. Dewey, *The child and the curriculum, and, The school and society.* Chicago: University of Chicago Press.

Dewey, J. (1966). *Logic: The theory of inquiry.* New York: Holt, Rinehart & Winston.

Dilthey, W. (1988). *Introduction to the human sciences* (R. Betanzos, Trans.). Detroit: Wayne State University Press.

Douglas, J. (1976). *Investigative social research* (Sage Library of Social Research No. 29). Beverly Hills, CA: Sage.

Dretske, F. (1991). *Explaining behavior.* Cambridge, MA: MIT Press.

Fenstermacher, G. (1979). A philosophical consideration of recent research on teacher effectiveness. In L. Shulman (Ed.), *Review of Research in Education* (Vol. 6, pp. 157–185.) Itasca, IL: F. E. Peacock.

Feyerabend, P. (1968). How to be a good empiricist. In P. H. Nidditch (Ed.), *The philosophy of science.* Oxford: Oxford University Press.

Floden, R. E. (1981). The logic of information-processing psychology in education. In D. Berliner (Ed.), *Review of research in education* (Vol. 9, pp. 75–109).

Fodor, J. (1975). *The language of thought.* New York: Thomas Y. Crowell.

Fodor, J. (1987). *Psychosemantics.* Cambridge, MA: MIT Press.

Follesdal, D. (1982). Intentionality and behaviorism. In L. Jonathan Cohen, *Logic, methodology and philosophy of science. VI: Proceedings of the Sixth International Congress of Logic, Methodology and Philosophy of Science, Hannover, 1979* (pp. 553–569). New York: Elsevier.

Gadamer, H-G. (1977). *Philosophical hermeneutics* (D. Linge, Trans.). Berkeley: University of California Press.

Gage, N. L. (1978). *The scientific basis of the art of teaching.* New York: Teachers College Press.

Gage, N. L. (1994). The scientific status of the behavioral sciences: The case of research on teaching. *Teaching and Teacher Education, 10,* 565–577.

Gage, N. L., & Needels, M. (1989). Process–product research on teaching: A review of criticisms. *Elementary School Journal. 89,* 253–300.

Galton, F. (1914). *Hereditary genius.* London: Macmillan. (Original work published 1869)

Hamlyn, D. (1973). The logical and psychological aspects of learning. In R. S. Peters (Ed.), *The philosophy of education* (pp. 195–213). Oxford: Oxford University Press.

Hesse, M. (1963). *Models and analogies in science.* London: Sheed & Ward.

Hirst, P. (1973). What is teaching? In R. S. Peters (Ed.), *The philosophy of education* (pp. 163–177). Oxford: Oxford University Press.

James, W. (1958). *Talks to teachers on psychology; and to students on some of life's ideals.* New York: Norton. (Original work published in 1899.)

Kaplan, A. (1964). *The conduct of inquiry.* Scranton, PA: Chandler.

Köhler, W. (1957). *The mentality of apes.* Harmondsworth, England: Penguin.

Kuhn, T. S. (1962). *The structure of scientific revolutions.* Chicago: University of Chicago Press.

Kuhn, T. S. (1977). *The essential tension.* Chicago: University of Chicago Press.

Lakatos, I. (1970). Falsification and the methodology of scientific research programs. In I. Lakatos & A. Musgrave (Eds.), *Criticism and the growth of knowledge* (pp. 91–196). Cambridge, England: Cambridge University Press.

Lakatos, I., & Musgrave, A. (Eds.) (1970). *Criticism and the growth of knowledge*. Cambridge, England: Cambridge University Press.

Lakoff, G., & Johnson, M. (1980). *Metaphors we live by*. Chicago: University of Chicago Press.

Leary, D. E. (Ed.) (1990). *Metaphors in the history of psychology*. Cambridge, England: Cambridge University Press.

Lerner, R. (1983). *Developmental psychology: Historical and philosophical perspectives*. Hillsdale, NJ: Lawrence Erlbaum Associates.

Lyotard, J.-F. (1984). *The postmodern condition: A report on knowledge*. Manchester, England: Manchester University Press.

Macmillan, C. J. B., & Garrison, J. (1988). *A logical theory of teaching*. Dordrecht, The Netherlands: Kluwer.

Meehl, P. E., & Scriven, M. (1991). Compatibility of science and ESP. In P. Meehl (Ed.), *Selected philosophical and methodological papers* (pp. 497–499). Minneapolis: University of Minnesota Press.

Morris, D. (1968). *The naked ape*. London: Corgi Books.

Newton-Smith, W. H. (1981). *The rationality of science*. London: Routledge.

Pepper, S. C. (1970). *World hypotheses*. Berkeley, CA: University of California Press. (Original work published 1942)

Phillips, D. C. (1983). On describing a student's cognitive structure. *Educational psychologist, 18*(2), 59–74.

Phillips, D. C. (1987). *Philosophy, science, and social inquiry*. Oxford: Pergamon Press.

Phillips, D. C. (1992). *The social scientist's bestiary*. Oxford: Pergamon Press.

Phillips, D. C. (1994). Telling it straight: Issues in assessing narrative research. *Educational Psychologist, 29,* 13–21.

Phillips, D. C., & Kelly, M. (1975). Hierarchical theories of development in education and psychology. *Harvard Educational Review, 45,* 351–375.

Phillips, D. C., & Soltis, J. (1991). *Perspectives on learning* (2nd ed.). New York: Teachers College Press.

Pitt, J. C. (1988). *Theories of explanation*. Oxford: Oxford University Press.

Popper, K. (1959). *The logic of scientific discovery*. London: Hutchinson.

Popper, K. (1972). *Objective knowledge*. Oxford: Oxford University Press.

Popper, K. (1976). *Unended quest*. LaSalle, IL: Open Court.

Ricoeur, P. (1977). The model of the text: Meaningful action considered as a text. In F. Dallmayr and T. McCarthy (Eds.), *Understanding and Social Inquiry* (pp. 316–334). Notre Dame: University of Notre Dame Press.

Russell, B. (1960). *An outline of philosophy*. Cleveland: Meridian Books. (Original work published 1927)

Russell, J. (1987). *Philosophical perspectives on developmental psychology*. Oxford: Basil Blackwell.

Ryle, G. (1949). *The concept of mind*. London: Hutchinson.

Scheffler, I. (1958). *Philosophy and education: Modern readings*. Boston: Allyn & Bacon.

Shulman, L. (1986a). Paradigms and research programs in the study of teaching: A contemporary perspective. In M. Wittrock (Ed.), *Handbook of research on teaching* (3rd ed., pp. 3–36). New York: Macmillan.

Shulman, L. (1986b). Those who understand: Knowledge growth in teaching. *Educational Researcher, 15,* 4–14.

Shulman, L. (1987). Knowledge and teaching: Foundations of the new reform. *Harvard Educational Review, 57*(1), 1–22.

Skinner, B. F. (1965). *Science and human behavior*. New York: Free Press. (Original work published 1953)

Skinner, B. F. (1972). *Beyond freedom and dignity*. London: Jonathan Cape.

Sprinthall, R. C., Schmutte, G., & Sirois, L. (1991). *Understanding educational research*. Englewood Cliffs, NJ: Prentice Hall.

Sternberg, R. J. (1990). *Metaphors of mind*. Cambridge, England, Cambridge University Press.

Stich, S. (1985). *From folk psychology to cognitive science*. Cambridge, MA: MIT Press.

Strike, K. A. (1974). On the expressive potential of behaviorist language. *American Educational Research Journal, 11*(2), 103–120.

Suchman, E. (1967). *Evaluative research*. New York: Russell Sage.

Suppe, F. (1989). *The semantic conception of theories and scientific realism*. Urbana: University of Illinois Press.

Taylor, C. (1977). *Interpretation and the sciences of man*. In F. Dallmayr and T. McCarthy (Eds.), *Understanding and Social Inquiry*. (pp. 101–131). Notre Dame: University of Notre Dame Press.

van Haaften, W. (1990). The justification of conceptual development claims. *Journal of Philosophy of Education, 24*(1), 51–69.

Varela, F., Thompson, E., & Rosch, E. (1991). *The embodied mind*. Cambridge, MA: MIT Press.

Watson, J. B. (1928). *Psychological care of infant and child*. London: Allen & Unwin.

Wilson, J. (1972). *Philosophy and educational research*. Windsor, England: National Foundation for Educational Research in England and Wales.

Winch, P. (1967). *The idea of a social science*. London: Routledge.

Wittgenstein, L. (1968). *Philosophical investigations*. New York: Macmillan. (Original work published 1953)

Wright, L. (1986). The concept of development and its legitimacy in the philosophy of education. *Journal of Philosophy of Education, 20*(1), 39–50.

# · 33 ·

# AFTERWORD

## David C. Berliner
ARIZONA STATE UNIVERSITY

## Robert C. Calfee
STANFORD UNIVERSITY

This *Handbook* is not a novel to be read from front to back, and so these concluding comments are less a finishing touch for the reader than a final reflection by the editors. We composed the introductory chapter at the beginning of the project before we received the thirty-one contributions that constitute the main body of the work. This brief note is our effort to summarize, not the substance of the volume, an impossible task in any event, but what we have learned from the effort, and what we think is distinctive about the *Handbook*.

The closing decades of the twentieth century have seen many challenges to the hegemony of educational psychology as the "master science." Today the production of reliable and valid knowledge emanates from many arenas of educational research: anthropology, sociology, linguistics, history and philosophy, and the various disciplines that inform the subject matters of schooling. Today's research questions are broader and more deeply contextualized than in earlier times. Other disciplines have identified attractive problems in the field of educational practice. Policy initiatives by foundations and government funding agencies have encouraged interdisciplinary approaches to the investigation of schooling.

Some observers have expressed concern about the decline in the research leadership of educational psychologists. We see a quite different picture reflected in the pages of this *Handbook*. First, it is clear that our field has been and continues to be highly productive and remarkably influential. Its findings, concepts, methods, and points of view are widely adopted by scholars in other disciplines and cross a wide range of research and evaluation activities. We are "on a roll"; the preceding chapters exhibit an astounding freshness of ideas and enthusiasm for endeavors. Psychology as a discipline is in the midst of a paradigm shift, and educational psychology, as part of this discipline, is certainly at the forefront of these developments.

Second, it is clear that the emerging influence of other disciplines has affected educational psychology. Situated cognition, contextual factors, qualitative methods, exploratory data analysis—these are only a few of the "key words" that point to the significant impact on our field of other viewpoints. Today's educational psychologist is part of a neighborhood, a member of a community. Our field has been enriched by the resulting interactions. But the field sustains a center, a focus, a point of view critically important for exploring and understanding educational issues.

Third, the size and vitality of our community remain constant. To be sure, membership in Division 15 (Educational Psychology) of the American Psychological Association dropped in the 1970s and 1980s, as did submissions to the *Journal of Educational Psychology*. These declines were among the concerns and impulses for this *Handbook*. During this same time frame, membership in the American Educational Research Association (AERA) increased to more than 20,000 members, many of them educational psychologists. Membership in Division 15 has increased in recent years, along with submissions to the *Journal of Educational Psychology*. The field is alive and growing.

And so, as we approach the close of the twentieth century, we find this a time for educational psychologists to proudly acknowledge their achievements. They have influenced the ways and means for studying education, providing evidence to demonstrate that the scientific study of education is both possible and useful. To be sure, the emergence of other disciplines as major players has established a laudatory balance in viewpoints that is important in its own right, and that has enlarged and enriched the work of educational psychologists. Meanwhile, we should celebrate the honor of serving as *the* major influence on the development of a rich and fractious research community for the scientific study of education.

Our achievements did not come easily. As a reminder, at the beginning of the twentieth century, Joseph Mayer Rice presented his empirical findings on the effectiveness of spelling instruction to a meeting of school administrators in Atlantic City, NJ. Rice was trained as a physician, but he had the spirit of an educational psychologist. He collected spelling data from students across a range of classrooms, clearly demonstrating the futility of spelling instruction as practiced at that time. His report was rudely rejected by the administrators. The Sage Foundation's Leonard Ayres (1912) described the meeting:

The presentation of these data threw that assemblage into consternation, dismay, and indignant protest. But the resulting storm of vigorously voiced opposition was directed, not against the methods and results of the investigation, but against the investigator who had pretended to measure the results of teaching spelling by testing the ability of the children to spell. In terms of scathing denunciation the educators there present, and the pedagogical experts who reported the deliberations of the meeting to the educational press, characterized as silly, dangerous, and from every viewpoint reprehensible the attempt to test the efficiency of the teacher by finding out what the pupils could do. With striking unanimity they voiced the conviction that any attempt to evaluate the teaching of spelling in terms of the ability of the pupils to spell was essentially impossible and based on a profound misconception of the function of education. (p. 300)

Rice's research was rejected by the administrators because of their convictions; it was clear to them that spelling required exercise. They believed that students should work hard and memorize spellings as a way to learn virtues like obedience, diligence, and habits of concentration. The process, not the outcomes, defined "good" teaching—a normative rather than an empirical judgment. A century ago, school leaders believed that educational issues were not to be decided by scientific methods. Judgments about what was best for children were to be made by those with religious or philosophical training, those "called" to the profession. An enormous change transpired when our field emerged as a dominant force in educational research, supplanting belief and conviction with systematic methods and replicable results. Educational psychologists prepared the way for other social scientists and empirical researchers to study education. And at the end of our first century of endeavors we remain a thriving field of scientific inquiry. This volume is a testament that reports of the death of educational psychology have been greatly exaggerated!

Where do we stand today? For one thing, it is clear that psychology has a distinctively new shape. Simple associative models of learning have moved to the sidelines and cognitive psychology has emerged as the dominant paradigm for thinking about teaching, learning, and assessment. Behavior remains an important concern, but action is seen as guided by a complex and active mind that constructs and extends meaning. Constructivist thinking runs throughout the volume, a very different portrait than would have appeared a few decades ago.

And while cognition and constructivism emerge as key words, this volume also emphasizes the interplay of these elements with other constructs: motivation, development, ability and aptitude, instruction, and assessment. In addition, coming into view are the beginnings of a situationist and contextualist perspective, a view given voice only a few years ago:

Many methods of didactic education assume a separation between knowing and doing, treating knowledge as an integral, self-sufficient substance, theoretically independent of the situations in which it is learned and used. The primary concern of schools often seems to be the transfer of this substance, which comprises abstract, decontextualized formal concepts. The activity and context in which learning takes place are thus regarded as merely ancillary to learning—pedagogically useful, of course, but fundamentally distinct and even neutral with respect to what is learned ... Recent investigations of learning, however, challenge this separating of what is learned from how it is learned and used. The activity in which knowledge is developed and deployed, it is now argued, is not separable from or ancillary to learning and cognition (Brown, Collins, & Duguid, 1989, p. 32).

The renewed interest in situated learning hails back to Dew-

ey's thinking about the place of the educational enterprise in a democracy (Dewey 1916; Bredo, 1994). Dewey was a conceptualizer more than an empiricist, but the message in this volume is that today's educational psychologist needs to master both theory and method, laboratory and schoolhouse, behavior and thought. A model appears in the "design experiments" emerging within our community (e.g. Brown, 1992). Salomon (1995) describes the trend:

Our main (though not necessarily exclusive) focus needs to change from the study of isolated and decontextualized individuals, processes, states of mind, or interventions to their study within wider psychological, disciplinary, social and cultural contexts (p. 106).

John Dewey, were he still alive, might ask . . ., "what took you so long?" It is not a great cognitive leap from a situationist to a social emphasis, to a focus on concepts like person-environment interactions and distributed intelligence. The mind seldom works alone. In today's world, thought-like activities engage individuals, groups, communities, and technologies. Similar propositions were voiced in Dewey's time, but the contemporary translations are important (cf. Salomon, 1993). Dewey's ideas were not subjected to scientific investigation, but similar proposals are being evaluated by today's researchers. Our understanding of groups and group interactions was less sophisticated then than now. We have benefitted enormously from the theoretical contributions of the Russian psychologist Lev Vygotsky, whose insights about the development of metacognitive thought by means of social-cognitive learning thread through many of the chapters in this volume. As an aside, Americans tend to be parochial, and educational psychologists are no exception. Our focus in this *Handbook* has been the U. S. scene, and although several chapters present significant contributions from abroad, the predominant perspective comes from within our shores.

Finally, today's technologies are truly remarkable. We see the potential for incredible amplification of our biological capabilities by combining societal and technological resources. These possibilities, difficult to imagine even a decade ago, have clearly influenced the writers of this *Handbook*. The research flowing from situationist perspectives, concepts of distributed cognition, the development of new technologies, and methodologies such as design experiments, should keep educational psychologists quite busy as we enter the twenty-first century.

The treatment of methodologies in this *Handbook* reflects, in microcosm, recent changes throughout the social sciences. At mid-century our field created rigorous methodologies based on the inferential statistics and factorial designs of Sir Ronald Fisher and Iowa agricultural stations. Then individuals like Jerome Bruner (1991, p. ix) diverted the agenda by raising questions about the nature of mind and its processes, questions about how children construct meanings and realities, questions about the shaping of mind by history and culture. Qualitative methodologies began to emerge, muddying our waters. All of this we knew as editors before the first methodology chapters arrived in our mailboxes. But we learned some important lessons from these contributions, even though methodology is the Maginot Line of the discipline. One new discovery was the emergence of exploratory data analysis as a significant complement to inferential and decision-making techniques. Statistical significance has dominated the field despite "significant" assaults across a half-century—there seemed no real competition. Exploratory data analysis has yet to fully secure its beachhead, but it is clearly a serious contender in the quantitative arena. A second discovery for us was the recognition of argument as a fundamentally methodological enterprise. In philosophy, the proclamation that "the warrant will not wane" has given notice that implicit and incidental claims will fall under critical scrutiny from outsiders—and that philosophers have discovered educational psychology as a fruitful hunting ground. In psychometrics, validity has changed from a technology of prediction to a rhetoric of conviction. Proving that a test means what it purports, rests not only on correlation but also on debate. Establishing the validity of an experiment depends not only on internal control, but on the tougher requirements of external generalizability and the arguments that accompany these requirements.

The extended discussions about the psychology of school subjects would not have appeared in a handbook written two decades earlier. We were delighted with the richness of these chapters and their relevance to the psychology of learning and teaching. They reveal to us three happy circumstances about this domain. First, there are some new things to say about the subject matters, an indication of the usefulness of the cognitive paradigms. Second, a pervasive optimism runs through this research. Educational psychologists writing in these areas genuinely believe that they can *do good*—that they are uncovering results useful to both the scientific establishment and the practitioner community. Finally, subject matter research has reinvigorated the emphasis on practice, a connection that had waned somewhat in educational psychology. Many educational psychologists are now deeply enmeshed in the complexities of field-based research.

These same three characteristics—freshness of ideas, optimism, and concern for practice—also appear in the chapters on the psychology of teaching. This field lacked shape until Gage's (1963) *Handbook of Research on Teaching,* where it emerged as a major subspecialty in educational psychology.

Reflecting the spirit of the 1960s, teaching was viewed in the Gage handbook from a behaviorist orientation. In the present *Handbook,* research on teaching has a predominantly cognitive flavor; to be sure, actual practice remains largely behavioral and activity-driven.

Finally, we are impressed by the way that the authors have handled the tension between complexity and control, between parsimony and reality. Simplification by isolation—a preferred strategy for experimental design only a few decades ago (Iran-Nejad, McKeachie, & Berliner, 1990)—meshed with the reductionist ideology to which many research psychologists were wedded at the time. The nonsense syllable, for example, now appears as a weak device for investigating human learning. In this volume, learning appears as a contextualized activity, connected with meaning and motivation; "Stimulus as *situated context* incorporates the entire array of circumstances that affect the individual . . ., [and] response as *performance* has become the code word for a broad examination of the individual's total reaction to a situation" (Calfee, 1995). Today's educational psychologists conceive of a complex world where teaching and learning reflect interactions among active, social, reflective, and motivated individuals operating within complex social environments. The next generation is likely to be more at ease with these complexities than were colleagues during the first two-thirds of this century.

This *Handbook* stands as a testament to the vitality of our field, and to its position at the cutting edge of research. Looking back over the preceding chapters, it is with a sense of pride and confidence in the accomplishments of our discipline that we pass the baton on to those who will confront the challenges of the next century. What we can be sure about is that they will find themselves still mulling over Schwab's commonplaces (Chapter 1)—"*Someone* teaching *something* to *someone else* in *some situation.*" We understand these commonplaces so much more deeply today than in yesteryears, and can only imagine the breakthroughs that are likely to emerge in the coming decades.

## *References*

Ayres, L. P. (1912). Measuring educational processes through educational results. *School Review, 20,* 300–309.

Bredo, E. (1994). Reconstructing educational psychology: Situated cognition and Deweyian pragmatism. *Educational Psychologist, 29,* 23–35.

Bruner, J. (1991). *Acts of meaning.* Cambridge, MA: Harvard University Press.

Brown, A. L. (1992). Design experiments: Theoretical and methodological challenges in creating complex interventions in classroom settings. *The Journal of the Learning Sciences, 2,* 141–178.

Brown, J. S., Collins, A., & Duguid, P. (1989). Situated cognition and the culture of learning. *Educational Researcher, 18,* 32–42.

Calfee, R. C. (1995). Implications of cognitive psychology for authentic assessment and instruction. In T. Oakland & R. Hambleton (Eds.), *Test use with children and youth.* (pp. 25–48). Boston MA: Kluwer Academic Publishers.

Dewey, J. (1916). *Democracy and education.* New York: Macmillan.

Gage, N. L. (Ed.). (1963). *Handbook of research on teaching.* New York: Macmillan.

Iran-Nejad, M., McKeachie, W. & Berliner, D.C. (1990). Editorial. *Review of Educational Research, 60,* 509–515.

Salomon, G. (Ed.) (1993). *Distributed cognitions.* Cambridge, England: Cambridge University Press.

Salomon, G. (1995). Reflections of the field of educational psychology by the outgoing journal editor. *Educational Psychologist, 30,* 105–108.

# NAME INDEX

Bennett, R. E., 905, 909, 939
Bennett, S., 938
Bennett, S. M., 364
Bennett, W., 431
Bentler, P. M., 192, 364
Bentley, J., 849
Bentley, J. L., 561, 576
Bentzen, F. A., 320
Benware, C. A., 104, 853
Bereiter, C., 26, 32, 35, 47, 53, 131, 245,
    252, 271, 284, 287, 349, 442, 459, 460,
    473, 477, 552, 556, 571, 575, 578,
    580–582, 659, 753, 808, 810–811, 817,
    819, 821–822, 825, 827, 854, 859, 867
Berenbaum, S. A., 362
Beretta, A., 617
Berg, C. A., 187
Berger, C. F., 824
Berger, J., 649, 859
Berger, S., 822
Berglas, S., 77
Berk, R. A., 781–782, 920–921
Berkofer, R., 431, 434
Berlin, D. F., 824
Berlin, I., 280
Berliner, D. C., 1, 6–7, 165, 226–227, 252,
    332–333, 341, 570, 590, 623, 625–626,
    629, 637, 649, 681–682, 711, 717,
    729–731, 737, 739, 741, 758–759,
    772–773, 777, 816, 900, 938, 990,
    1020, 1022
Berlyne, D. E., 25, 100–101, 245
Berman, P. W., 378
Berndt, T. J., 158, 361, 365, 380, 657
Bernieri, F., 375
Bernstein, B., 337–338, 613
Bernstein, H. T., 768, 772, 774
Bernstein, M., 187
Bernstein, S., 361
Bernzweig, J., 378, 383
Berrueta-Clement, J. R., 126
Berry, B., 341, 772
Berry, J. W., 345
Berryman, S. E., 297, 815
Bershon, B. L., 630, 644, 651, 659, 660
Berti, A. E., 423
Best, D. L., 364, 367
Bethell-Fox, C. E., 211
Betley, G., 99
Betoncourt, H., 175
Bettelheim, B., 998
Bevan, W., 331
Beveridge, W. I. B., 949
Beyerbach, B. A., 710, 712
Bhana, K., 230
Bialystok, E., 604, 607
Biber, B., 123
Bickhard, M .H., 17
Biddle, B. J., 409, 643, 710, 735–737, 776
Bielaczyc, K., 796
Bielaczyc, L., 796
Biernat, M., 364–365
Biesmans, R., 295
Bigenho, F., 824
Biggs, J. B., 282, 285
Bigler, R. S., 362, 364–365, 368–369
Bijou, S., 553
Bill, V. L., 32
Binet, A., 38, 49, 117–120, 187, 191,
    312, 317, 450, 461, 585,
    815, 927
Biological Sciences Curriculum Study, 463–
    464, 472
Birch, D., 266
Bird, T., 680, 771–772
Birman, B., 323, 614
Birman, B. F., 590
Birnbaum, A., 912, 916

Birnbaum, D. W., 375–376
Birnbaum, L., 820
Birney, R. C., 259, 266
Bisbicos, E. E., 554
Bitzer, D., 812
Bivens, J., 845–846, 867
Bixby, J., 123, 566
Bizell, R. P., 124
Björck-Åkesson, E., 263
Bjork, R. A., 813
Bjorklund, D., 151
Blachman, B. A., 583
Black, J. B., 572
Blackwell, J., 160
Blagg, N., 230
Blais, M. R., 270
Blakemore, J. E., 364–365, 368
Blanck, P. D., 97, 375
Blando, J., 807, 814, 819, 823–824
Blaney, N., 650, 848
Blashfield, R. K., 312
Bledsoe, J., 157
Bleier, R., 359
Bley-Vroman, R., 607
Bloch, M., 434
Bloch, M. N., 366
Block, J. H., 226, 264, 366–367, 372, 376–
    380, 383, 740–741
Blode, B. H., 997
Bloom, B. S., 8, 57, 91, 125, 165, 221, 226,
    246, 315, 459, 563, 627, 682, 711, 735,
    739–741, 927, 1001
Blos, P., 149, 159, 161, 998
Blume, G. W., 686, 688, 701
Blumenfeld, P., 91, 101–104, 154, 627, 630,
    632, 641, 644, 647, 650, 652, 658
Blumenfeld, P. B., 153, 156
Blumenfeld, P. C., 122, 139, 140, 272, 284,
    731–732, 810, 817–818
Blyth, D., 382
Blyth, D. A., 149–153, 156, 160–163, 165,
    381
Bobbitt, B. L., 209
Bobko, P., 88
Bock, D. R., 374
Bock, R. D., 223, 895
Bode, H., 952
Boden, M. A., 1007–1008
Boeger, A., 807, 820
Boekaerts, M., 257
Boekkooi-Timminga, E., 911
Boenig, R. W., 461, 463
Boggiano, A., 97, 99–100
Bohning, G., 568
Bohrer, A., 295
Boldizar, J. P., 379
Bolduc, D., 366
Boles, D. B., 362, 374
Boliek, C. A., 319, 324
Bollen, K. A., 192, 896
Bolles, R. C., 68
Bolt Beranek and Newman, 822, 825–827
Bolus, R., 276
Bombi, A. S., 423
Bond, G., 557, 579
Bond, L., 231, 877
Bondy, E., 131
Booch, G., 800
Book, C., 134, 580, 581, 718, 720
Boostrom, R. E., 658
Booth, M. B., 427, 434
Booth-Church, E., 551, 579
Boothby, R., 365
Borg, W. R., 878
Boring, E. G., 434
Borko, H., 673, 675, 677, 687–688, 691–
    692, 696–699, 702, 709–711, 714, 717
Borkowski, J. G., 93, 134, 151, 322

Borman, K., 175–176
Bormuth, J. R., 564, 570
Bornstein, M. H., 208
Bornstein, P., 87
Borowy, T., 374
Borthwick-Duffy, S., 323
Boruch, R. F., 929
Boruta, M. J., 821, 828
Bos, M. C., 842
Bossert, S. T., 647, 649, 850
Boston, C., 902, 905
Boston, M. B., 361
Boswell, S., 367
Botkin, M., 93
Bouchard, T. J., Jr., 209, 218, 219, 294
Bourdieu, P., 343
Bourque, M. L., 901
Bowen, C., 827, 828
Bowen-Coutler, B., 551, 579
Bower, G. H., 50, 257, 455, 469
Bowers, A. M., 998
Bowlds, M. K., 159, 166
Bowles, S., 334, 343
Bowyer, J. B., 466
Box, G. E. P., 973
Boxer, A. M., 382
Boyan, N. J., 297
Boyce, A. C., 736
Boyd, F. B., 561, 576, 849
Boyer, E., 130, 133, 644
Boyle, C. F., 19, 25, 29, 33, 34, 448, 808,
    819
Boyle, M. C., 379
Boyle, R., 821
Boyle, R. A., 155, 169, 292, 759, 760
Bozeman, W., 813
Bracht, G. H., 228, 878
Bradbard, M. R., 361, 365, 366
Bradburn, N. M., 903
Bradbury, D. E., 993
Braddock, J. H. I., 935
Bradley Commission on History in the
    Schools, 433
Bradley, J., 131, 132, 557
Bradley, R., 220
Bradley, V. N., 821
Brady, N. V., 341, 342
Brady, S., 131
Braithwaite, V. A., 289
Brand, H. J., 124
Brandon, D. P., 900
Brandsford, J. D., 817–820, 823, 826–827
Bransford, J. D., 5, 50, 58, 120, 151, 168,
    320, 554–555, 559, 565, 571, 807–811,
    813, 815–818, 820–821, 823–828, 927,
    933
Braskamp, L., 176
Brattesani, K., 93, 632–633, 645
Braun, C., 565
Braun, H. I., 249
Braves, T. D., 866
Bray, D. W., 903
Bray, J. H., 895
Bredderman, T., 468
Bredo, E., 1021
Brehm, J. W., 281
Brennan, A., 574
Brennan, R. L., 922
Brent-Palmer, C., 613
Bretherton, I., 375–376
Brett, C., 822
Brewer, B., 947, 965
Brewer, R., 566–567
Brewer, W., 458
Brewer, W. F., 571
Brickman, P., 631
Bridge, C., 574
Bridgeford, N. J., 563–564, 567

Rotter, G. S., 375
Rotter, J., 66, 70–73, 75–76, 78, 80, 88, 92, 640
Rotter, J. B., 278
Rotter, N. G., 375
Rounds, T. S., 162, 164
Rourke, B. P., 312
Rousseau, E., 737, 738
Rousseau, J. J., 118, 119, 123, 990
Rovine, M. J., 219
Rowan, B., 288, 626–628, 632
Rowe, D., 565, 624
Rowe, D. W., 820
Roy, P., 861
Royce, J. M., 230
Royce, J. R., 246
Royer, J. M., 563
Rozyeva, N. S., 126
Rubin, A., 458, 474, 586, 808, 821
Rubin, A. D., 821
Rubin, K. H., 375
Ruble, D., 97, 99, 100
Ruble, D. N., 160, 359, 360, 361, 364, 367–379
Ruble, T. L., 364
Ruddell, M. R., 550
Ruddell, R. B., 550
Rudner, L. M., 770, 772, 773, 902, 905, 918
Rueda, R., 567, 590
Ruediger, W. C., 736
Ruger, H. A., 50
Ruiz, A. I., 817
Rumbaut, R. G., 336, 341
Rumberger, R. W., 151, 152, 155, 166, 167
Rumelhart, D. E., 17, 22, 25, 214, 406, 571
Rumenik, D. K., 359
Rundquist, S. S., 684
Ruopp, R., 822
Rüsen, J., 434
Rushton, C., 272
Russell, B., 1012
Russell, G., 369
Russell, J., 820, 845, 1007
Russell, J. A., 375
Russell, S., 168
Russell, T., 720
Russell, T. L., 814
Russo, N., 933
Rutherford, F. J., 456, 467, 469, 471, 482
Rutherford, M., 26, 32, 808, 817, 818, 820, 826, 827
Rutkowski, K., 287
Rutter, M., 349, 382
Ruvolo, A. P., 277
Ryan, R., 78, 96–98, 100, 101
Ryan, R. M., 141, 154, 270, 281, 372, 631, 632, 658
Ryan, T. A., 294
Ryans, D. G., 776
Ryff, C. D., 171
Ryle, G., 1007

**S**
Saari, L., 89
Saarni, C., 376
Sabelli, N., 828
Sabers, D., 682, 717, 816
Sabers, D. S., 682, 816
Sackett, L. W., 426
Sackett, P. R., 225
Sadker, D., 373, 625
Sadker, M., 373, 625
Sadler, D. R., 948
Sadler, P. M., 448, 475
Sager, G., 365
Sahm, W. B., 364

SAIL Faculty & Administration, 581, 582
Sailor, W., 321
St. Louis Teachers Union, 772
Sajchowski, R., 134
Saklofske, D. H., 245
Salasin, S., 930
Salili, F., 98
Salinger, G. L., 449
Säljö, R., 284, 292
Sallis, R., 211
Salomon, G., 4, 48, 49, 273–275, 334, 348, 403, 415, 416, 433, 659, 759, 807, 808, 810, 813–816, 820–822, 855, 856
Salsburg, D. S., 947
Salthouse, T. A., 216
Saltzberg, J. A., 377
Salvia, J., 319
Samarapugavan, A., 807, 820
Sambursky, S., 444
Sampson, R., 375
Samuels, S., 554, 556, 583
Samuels, S. J., 53, 557, 611, 811
Sancilio, L., 821
Sanders, J. R., 930, 931, 968
Sanders, N., 565
Sanders, R., 476
Sanders, W. L., 776
Sandler, B. R., 373, 624, 625
Sandvik, E., 376
Sanford, J., 634, 694
Sanford, R. N., 262
Santrock, J., 87
Sapona, R., 87
Saranson, S. B., 332, 335
Sarason, S., 267, 702
Sardo-Brown, D., 714
Sarigiani, P. A., 377
Saslona, M., 282
Satlow, E., 122
Sattler, J. M., 318
Saul, E., 817, 820, 828
Saunders, S., 711, 712
Saunders, W., 674
Sautter, R. C., 125, 129
Savery, J. R., 810, 815, 817, 818, 826
Savin-Williams, R. C., 158
Sawin, C., 769
Saxe, G., 20
Saxe, G. B., 816, 852, 853
Saydel Education Association v. PERB, 769
Sayeki, Y., 22, 24, 30
Saylor, C., 685, 687
Scandura, J. M., 790
Scanlon, D. M., 131, 610
Scardamalia, M., 26, 32, 35, 47, 53, 131, 442, 459, 460, 473, 477, 552, 556, 571, 575, 578, 580–582, 659, 753, 808, 811, 817, 819, 821, 822, 825, 827, 854, 859, 867
Scarpati, S., 87
Scarr, S., 190, 220, 223, 294
Schachter, J., 616
Schafer, E. P. W., 208
Schafer, W. D., 567, 901
Schaie, K. W., 167, 221
Schalling, D., 150
Schank, P. K., 817
Schank, R., 214
Schank, R. C., 458, 800
Schaps, E., 861, 866
Schauble, L., 457, 475
Scheerenberger, R. C., 318
Scheffler, I., 1007
Schegloff, M. A., 20
Scheier, M. A., 154

Scheirer, M., 276
Schell, P., 212, 213
Schenck, E. A., 935
Scher, S., 173
Scherer, K. R., 376
Scheuneman, J. D., 917
Schick, C., 853
Schiefele, J., 101
Schiefele, U., 286, 289, 290
Schifter, D., 676, 685, 689, 694, 695, 698, 702, 703
Schimmel, D., 769
Schlenker, B., 276
Schlesinger, J. R., 929
Schliemann, A. D., 20, 51, 816
Schlosser, C. A., 814
Schmalt, H.-D., 268
Schmeck, R. R., 250, 281–283, 292
Schmelkin, L. P., 890
Schmid, J., 196
Schmidt, F. L., 225
Schmidt, H. G., 817
Schmidt, J., 817
Schmidt, N., 225
Schmidt, R., 609, 610
Schmidt, W., 938
Schmidt, W. H., 714
Schmitt, A. P., 269, 917
Schmitt, N., 772
Schmitz, J., 807, 820
Schmuck, P., 373, 625
Schmuck, R., 92, 649
Schmutte, G., 1008
Schneider, K., 268
Schneider, L. M., 211
Schneider, W., 151, 173, 215, 608, 811
Schneps, M. H., 448, 475
Schoefield, J. W., 810, 823
Schoenfeld, A., 58, 170
Schoenfeld, A. H., 19, 20, 26, 29, 31, 35, 36, 38, 418, 443, 448, 474, 753, 818
Schoenfeld, W. N., 811
Schofield, J. W., 159, 380
Schommer, M., 170, 558, 584
Schön, D., 711, 715, 717, 718
Schon, D. A., 677, 683, 730
School of Mathematics Study Group, 685
Schoor, L. B., 8
Schram, P., 688, 693, 694, 701, 716
Schramm, W., 469, 814, 1000
Schrauben, B., 87, 104, 155, 173, 275, 284, 290, 659, 660
Schreiter, B., 683
Schroder, H. M., 285
Schroeder, W. H., 24
Schrooten, H., 52
Schuder, T., 581, 582
Schul, Y., 853
Schulenberg, J. E., 151
Schultz, R. W., 370
Schulz, R. W., 17
Schumaker, J. B., 659
Schumann, J., 617
Schumer, H., 292
Schunk, D., 75, 87, 88, 89, 92, 93, 659
Schunk, D. H., 151, 154, 155, 173, 264, 273, 274, 276, 277, 634, 659, 734, 847
Schurz, M., 991
Schutz, R. E., 928
Schwab, J. J., 2, 10, 34, 413, 417, 676, 7171
Schwager, M. T., 138, 139, 644, 645
Schwartz, B. J., 214, 554
Schwartz, D., 807, 817–820, 823, 826, 827
Schwartz, J. L., 30
Schwartz, P., 124
Schwartz, S., 49, 214

# SUBJECT INDEX